Pocket
DICTIONARY
of
CANADIAN LAW

Fifth Edition

Daphne A. Dukelow,
B. Sc., J.D., LL.M.,
of the British Columbia Bar

CARSWELL®

ISBN 978-0-7798-3688-8

A cataloguing record for this publication is available from Library and Archives Canada.

Printed in the United States by Thomson Reuters.

Composition: Computer Composition of Canada, Inc.

 THOMSON REUTERS

CARSWELL, A DIVISION OF THOMSON REUTERS CANADA LIMITED

One Corporate Plaza
2075 Kennedy Road
Toronto, Ontario
M1T 3V4

Customer Relations
Toronto 1-416-609-3800
Elsewhere in Canada/U.S. 1-800-387-5164
Fax 1-416-298-5082
www.carswell.com
E-mail www.carswell.com/email

Preface to the Fifth Edition

It is a pleasure to prepare another edition of the Pocket Dictionary of Canadian Law. This edition contains additions and changes in the areas of administrative, commercial, securities, criminal, intellectual property, and environmental and energy law.

Thank you to O'Neil Smith and Audrey Wineberg of Carswell for making the arrangements for this edition and to Sarah Payne for editing.

Thank you to Betsy Nuse who has assisted me with the preparation of this edition.

Daphne A. Dukelow
Burnaby, B.C.
March 2011

Preface to the Fourth Edition

It is a pleasure to prepare another edition of the Pocket Dictionary of Canadian Law. This edition contains additions and changes in the areas of administrative, commercial, criminal, family, intellectual property, and international law. It also contains additions of frequently used terms and words which are used in many legal subjects.

Thank you to Steven Iseman of Carswell for making the arrangements for this edition and to Sarah Payne for editing.

Thank you to Betsy Nuse who has assisted me with the preparation of this edition.

Daphne Dukelow
Vancouver, B.C.
March 2006

Preface to the Third Edition

This edition adds new entries and new definitions from all areas of law. In particular, Intellectual Property Law terms now are included and more Administrative Law terms have been added. Both recent case law and statutes are included. Historic material is included when it is likely to be encountered by a student or reader.

I appreciate the publisher giving me the opportunity to continue to improve this work. Thank you to Steven Iseman of Carswell for making the arrangements for this edition. Thank you to the team of Patti Bayley-Thompson, editor, Lisa Middlestadt, proofreader, and Linda Rowe and staff at Computer Composition of Canada, all of whose skills have brought this project to completion.

Thank you to my friends and colleagues for their support and help during the preparation of this edition.

Daphne Dukelow
Vancouver, B.C.
June 2002

Preface to the Second Edition

The most important change in this edition of the Pocket Dictionary is the inclusion of definitions taken from Canadian case law. We have added terms and definitions relevant to the Canadian Charter of Rights and Freedoms. Again, we have emphasized terms in current use or likely to be encountered in current materials.

I wish to thank Leanne Berry and Catherine Campbell of Carswell for their assistance in preparation of this edition of the Pocket Dictionary.

Daphne A. Dukelow

Vancouver, B.C.
August, 1994

Preface

We have adapted this first edition of The Pocket Dictionary of Canadian Law from Carswell's comprehensive Dictionary of Canadian Law for a more general audience. Like its larger parent, this work was created largely from primary, Canadian sources: a term bank of definitions from federal and provincial statutes and regulations and a library of basic Canadian legal textbooks.

To create a more compact and concise reference work, we have selected more frequently encountered legal terms with the most general definitions of those terms, intending in this way to highlight the most current information with the widest appeal.

We hope that The Pocket Dictionary of Canadian Law will be useful to any group or person whose life or work touches on legal issues.

Our thanks to the editorial staff of Carswell for the opportunity to work on this project and to our good friends for their encouragement and support.

Daphne Dukelow
Betsy Nuse

Galiano, B.C.
August, 1991

How to Use This Dictionary

HEADWORD

FUNCTIONAL
LABEL

ABBUTTALS. *n.* Limits or boundaries of land.

ABC. *abbr.* Advance booking charter.

abbreviation

ABDICATE. *v.* To refuse or renounce a thing.

ABSOLUTA SENTENTIA EXPOSITORE NON INDIGET. [L.] A clean statement requires no exposition.

ETYMOLOGY

DEFINITIONS

ABSOLUTE LIABILITY. 1. Liability regardless of intention or negligence. 2. An offence for which an accused is criminally liable even though the accused acted under a reasonable mistake of fact. *R. v. Metro News Ltd.* (1986), 23 C.R.R. 77 at 89, 16 O.A.C. 319, 56 O.R. (2d) 321, 53 C.R. (3d) 289, 29 C.C.C. (3d) 35, 32 D.L.R. (4th) 321 (C.A.), the court per Martin J.A.

ABUSE OF PROCESS. 1. ". . . [I]n *R. v. D. (T.C.)* (1987), 38 C.C.C. (3d) 434 at 447 . . . (Ont. C.A.), [it was] held that the onus of establishing that an abuse of process has occurred is on the respondent who must establish, on a balance of probabilitites, that the Crown has acted in an oppressive or vexatious manner or that the prosecution is offensive to the principles of fundamental justice and fair play." *R. v. Miles of Music Ltd.* (1989), 24 C.P.R. (3d) 301 at 309, 31 O.A.C. 380, 69 C.R. (3d) 361, 48 C.C.C. (3d) 96 (C.A.), Krever J.A. 2. ". . . [T]he unreasonable multiplication of proceedings . . ." *General Foods Ltd. v. Struthers Scientific & International Corp.* (1971), 4 C.P.R. (2d) 97 at 105, [1974] S.C.R. 98, 23 D.L.R. (3d) 313, the court per Pigeon J. 3. ". . . [F]rivolous and vexatious, or if the process . . . is in fact being used for an ulterior or improper purpose, or if the process is being used in such a way as to be in itself an abuse . . ." *Canada Metal Co. v. Heap* (1975), 7 O.R. (2d) 185 at 192 (C.A.). 4. "The essence of the tort of abuse of process is the misuse or perversion of the court's process for an extraneous or ulterior purpose. There must be a purpose other than that which the process was designed to serve . . ." *D.K. Investments Ltd. v. S.W.S. Investments Ltd.*

CITATION OF AUTHORITY –

case law

(1984), 59 B.C.L.R. 333 (S.C.), Finch J., affirmed (1986), 6 B.C.L.R. (2d) 291 (C.A.).

ACCEPTANCE. *n.* 1. Signification by an offeree of willingness to enter into a contract with an offeror on the offeror's terms. G.H.L. Fridman, *The Law of Contract in Canada*, 2d ed. (Toronto: Carswell, 1986) at 41. 2. Of a bill, the signification by the drawee of assent to the drawer's order to pay the bill. F.L.G. Tyler & N.E. Palmer, eds., *Grossley Vaines' Personal Property*, 5th ed. (London: Butterworths, 1973) at 235. 3. An acceptance completed by delivery or notification. *Bills of Exchange Act*, R.S.C. 1985, c. B-4, s. 2. 4. In sale of goods, involves taking possession of the goods by the buyer. See BLANK ~; CONDITIONAL ~; LOCAL ~; NON- ~; PARTIAL ~; QUALIFIED ~.

— text

— statute

— none

ACCIDENT. *n.* A wilful and intentional act, not being the act of the employee, and a fortuitous event occasioned by a physical or natural cause. *Workers Compensation acts.* See AIRCRAFT ~; ENVIRONMENTAL ~; FATAL ~; INDUSTRIAL ~; INEVITABLE ~; NON-INDUSTRIAL ~.

CROSS REFERENCES

ACCIDENTAL DEATH INSURANCE. Insurance undertaken by an insurer as part of a contract of life insurance whereby the insurer undertakes to pay an additional amount of insurance money in the event of the death by accident of the person whose life is insured. *Insurance acts.*

CITATION OF AUTHORITY – general topical

ACCOMMODATION FACILITIES. See TRANSIENT ~.

HEADWORD USED FOR CROSS-REFERENCE ONLY

A4. Facsimile by amplitude modulation of the main carrier either directly or by frequency modulated sub-carrier. *General Radio Regulations, Part II*, C.R.C., c. 1372, s. 42.

TERM WITH A NUMERAL

AIR TIME. *var.* **AIR-TIME.** In respect of any aircraft, means the period of time commencing when the aircraft leaves the surface of the earth and terminating when the aircraft touches the surface of the earth at the next point of landing. See PRICE OF ~.

VARIANT SPELLING

ASSUMPSIT. [L. one promised] A form of action to recover damages for breach of a simple contract.

TRANSLATION INSIDE ETYMOLOGY BRACKET

BAIT. *v.* To set one animal against another which is tied or contained.

BAIT. *n.* Corn, wheat, oats or other cultivated grain or any product thereof or any manufactured product or material that may attract migratory game birds and includes plastic corn and any other imitation grain. *Migratory Birds Regulation*, C.R.C., c. 1035, s. 2.

HOMOGRAPH

BARGAINING COLLECTIVELY. 1. Negotiating in good faith with a view to the conclusion of a collective bargaining agreement, or a renewal or revision of a bargaining agreement, the embodiment in writing or writings of the terms of agreement arrived at in negotiations or required to be inserted in a collective bargaining agreement by this Act, the execution by or on behalf of the parties of such agreement, and the negotiating from time to time for the settlement of disputes and grievances of employees covered by the agreement or represented by a trade union representing the majority of employees in an appropriate unit. *The Trade Union Act*, R.S.S. 1978, c. T-17, s. 2. 2. Negotiating in good faith with a view to the conclusion of a collective bargaining agreement or a renewal or revision or a collective bargaining agreement and the embodiment in writing of the terms of agreement arrived at in negotiations or required to be inserted in a collective bargaining agreement by statute. Saskatchewan statutes.

CITATION OF AUTHORITY general geographical

Definitions in this dictionary are based largely on primary, Canadian sources: case law, a term bank of definitions from the statutes of Canada, all provinces and the Northwest Territories and Ontario and federal regulations and a library of basic Canadian legal textbooks.

In general, material is presented not historically but by frequency of use in the sources considered. Some historical terms have been included, e.g. "capital number," "non-capital murder" and any term which appeared in an earlier statute revision if this was the only definition available to us at the time.

Where definitions have been rewritten, we have attempted to remove sexual and racial bias, but material quoted verbatim has not been edited in this way.

Alphabetization

1. This dictionary is alphabetized absolutely by letter. Thus, the term "residential property" will be found after the term "resident" but before the term "resident owner".

2. Terms which include numerals are entered as though the numerals were spelled out. Thus, the term "A2" (= A- two) will be found after the term "attrition" and before the term "au besoin".

3. Abbreviations are integrated into the main work in the alphabetical order described above, rather than listed separately.

4. Homographs are ordered by function: first verbs, then nouns, adjectives, adverbs, abbreviations. Thus, the entry for "charge" used as a verb precedes the entry for "charge" used as a noun.

Elements of Each Entry

1. HEADWORD/HEADWORDS
(a) The words or phrase is presently in boldface, upper case letters.
(b) Variant spellings follow the most common spelling, in order of the frequency of their use.

2. FUNCTIONAL LABEL
(a) This identifies the grammatical part of speech or function (e.g. use as an abbreviation) of the headword/headwords. See the Table of Abbreviations Used in This Dictionary (on page xix) for the abbreviations used here.
(b) A headword entered for cross-reference purposes only is assigned a functional label only to distinguish it from any homograph.

3. ETYMOLOGY
(a) Presented in square brackets, these characters show the language of origin of a word or phrase which is or was originally in a language other than English. See the Table of Abbreviations Used in This Dictionary (on page xix) for the abbreviations used here.
(b) Where the word or phrase has adopted a more general meaning over time, a literal translation from the original language may be offered inside the brackets.

(c) A headword entered for cross-reference purposes only is assigned no etymological label.

4. DEFINITIONS

Multiple definitions are numbered. The most common or general definition is given first, less general or common definitions follow, ranked by frequency of use. In entries where case law is used, definitions are ranked from general to specific and also, where necessary, by the currency and weight of the authority.

5. CITATON OF AUTHORITY

(a) Where no authority is cited, the definition is derived from multiple sources.

(b) Specific citations of case law are complete and include pinpoint page reference from one law report. Most frequently, decisions have been quoted verbatim; such definitions are enclosed by quotation marks. Those definitions from case law which have been paraphrased or summarized do not contain quotation marks.

(c) Specific citations of legislation provide the chapter and section numbers. In most cases, legislation has been quoted verbatim, but occasionally minor editing has been done in the interest of clarity. Since this editing has been done and in some cases only the latest statute law revision has been used, those wishing to cite exactly are urged to refer to the original statutes.

(d) Specific citations of textual material provide exact page references. Since all textual material has been paraphrased or rewritten, those wishing to cite exactly are urged to refer to the original text.

(e) A general topical citation (italicized) limits a definition to a particular area of law.

(f) A general geographical citation (in ordinary type) limits a definition to a particular region or jurisdiction.

6. CROSS-REFERENCES

These refer the reader to more narrow or specific applications of the word or phrase or occasionally to related terms.

In the interest of saving space, the character "~" has been used to represent the headword/headwords in the cross-references which follow it.

Table of Abbreviations
Used in this Dictionary

abbr.	abbreviation
adj.	adjective
adv.	adverb
AS.	Anglo-Saxon
conj.	conjunction
Fr.	French
L.	Latin
n.	noun
pl.	plural
pref.	prefix
prep.	preposition
suff.	suffix
symbol	symbol
var.	variant spelling
v.	verb
[]	square brackets (enclose an etymological label; see page xvi, "How To Use This Dictionary," for explanation)
~	swung dash (see page xvii, "How To Use This Dictionary," for explanation of this character)

AAS. *abbr.* Arbitrate - Santé et services sociaux, 1983-.

AB. *abbr.* Abridgment.

ABANDON. *v.* 1. Includes (a) a wilful omission to take charge of a child by a person who is under a legal duty to do so, and (b) dealing with a child in a manner that is likely to leave that child exposed to risk without protection. *Criminal Code*, R.S.C. 1985, c. C-46, s. 214. 2. "... [A]bandon [as used in the Adoption Act, R.S.B.C. 1979, c. 4, s. 8] means: 'To desert, surrender, forsake, or cede. To relinquish or give up with intent of never again resuming one's right or interest ... to relinquish all connection with or concern in ... ' This definition illustrates that both physical and mental components are involved in the definition of abandonment." *B.C. Birth Registration No. 77-09-010612, Re* (1989), 64 D.L.R. (4th) 432 at 436 (B.C. S.C.), Melnick L.J.S.C. 3. [To abandon property requires] an intention to desert or relinquish a right permanently. There must be a sense of finality to the action. *Arndt Estate v. First Galesburg National Bank & Trust Co.*, 2001 CarswellSask 329, 2001 SKQB 234, 206 Sask. R. 261, 42 R.P.R. (3d) 66, Hunter J.

ABANDONMENT OF BARGAINING RIGHTS. The Ontario *Labour Relations Act, 1995*, S.O. 1995, c. 1 ("the Act") does not speak of abandonment of bargaining rights. The concept was developed in the Board's jurisprudence to allow termination of the bargaining rights of a union that fails to "actively promote those rights". *I.B.E.W., Local 894 v. Ellis-Don Ltd.*, 2001 CarswellOnt 99, 2001 SCC 4, 265 N.R. 2, 194 D.L.R. (4th) 385, 52 O.R. (3d) 160 (note), 2001 C.L.L.C. 220-028, 26 Admin. L.R. (3d) 171, 140 O.A.C. 201, [2001] 1 S.C.R. 221, Per Binnie J. (dissenting) (Major J. concurring).

ABATE. *v.* To break down, destroy or remove; to lower the price.

ABATEMENT. *n.* Termination, reduction, destruction. See PLEA IN ~.

ABATEMENT OF NUISANCE. Removing or putting an end to nuisance.

ABCA. Neutral citation for the Alberta Court of Appeal.

ABCP. *abbr.* Asset-backed commercial paper.

ABDICATE. *v.* To refuse or renounce a thing.

ABDICATION. *n.* Where a person in office voluntarily renounces it or gives it up.

ABDUCTION. *n.* 1. Take or cause to be taken away a person under 16 years of age from the possession of and against the will of the parent or guardian who has lawful charge of that person. *Criminal Code*, R.S.C. 1985, c. C-46, s. 280. 2. Unlawfully taking, enticing away, concealing, detaining, receiving or harbouring a person under 14 years of age with intent to deprive a parent or guardian of the possession of that person. *Criminal Code*, R.S.C. 1985, c. C-46, s. 281-283. 3. Forcibly stealing or carrying away any person. See CHILD ~.

ABET. *v.* To abet within the meaning of s. 21(1)(c) includes encouraging, instigating, promoting or procuring the crime to be committed." *R. v. Greyeyes*, [1997] 2 S.C.R. 825, at para. 26. See AID AND ABET.

ABEYANCE. *n.* 1. Lapse of an inheritance because it has no present owner. 2. In expectation.

ABIDE. *v.* "... [T]o accept without dispute or appeal any such order, and to fulfil or carry out such order if made." *Paulson v. Murray* (1922), 68 D.L.R. 643 at 644, 32 Man. R. 327, [1922] 2 W.W.R. 654 (K.B.), Dysart J.

ABILITY. *n.* Capacity to perform an act; skill. See FUNCTIONAL ~.

AB INITIO. [L.] From the beginning. See TRESPASS ~.

ABODE. *n.* Residence. *R. v. Braithwaite*, [1918] 2 K.B. 319 at 330, [1918-19] All E.R. Rep. 1145 (U.K. C.A.), Scrutton L.J.

ABOLISH. *v.* To do away with.

ABOLITION. *n.* Doing away with something; destruction of thing.

ABORIGINAL. *adj.* Relating to the Indian, Inuit or Métis peoples of Canada.

ABORIGINAL COMMUNITY. A first nation, tribal council, band, community, organization or other group with a predominantly aboriginal leadership. *Corrections and Conditional Release Act*, S.C. 1992, c. 20, s. 79.

ABORIGINAL EDUCATOR. Any of the following: (a) a first nation, as defined in the School Act, that is operating an educational institution; (b) a Community Education Authority, established by one or more participating First Nations under the First Nations Jurisdiction over Education in British Columbia Act (Canada), that is operating an educational institution; (c) a treaty first nation that is operating a school under its own laws. *Teaching Profession Act*, R.S.B.C. 1996, c. 449, s. 25.1.

ABORIGINAL FISHING RIGHTS. The spectrum of fishing rights consists of the right to fish for food, the right to exchange fish for money or other goods and the right to fish commercially.

ABORIGINAL GOVERNMENT. 1. An Indian, an Inuit or a Métis government or the "council of the band", as defined in subsection 2(1) of the Indian Act. *Federal-Provincial Fiscal Arrangements Act*, R.S.C. 1985, c. F-8, s. 2(1). 2. A governing body that is established by or under or operating under an agreement between Her Majesty in right of Canada and aboriginal people and that is empowered to enact laws respecting (a) the protection of the environment; or (b) for the purposes of Division 5 of Part 7, the registration of vehicles or engines. *Canadian Environmental Protection Act, 1999*, S.C. 1999, c. 33, s. 3(1). 3. An aboriginal organization exercising governmental functions. B.C. statutes.

ABORIGINALITY-RESIDENCE. An analogous ground of discrimination under section 15 of the Charter of Rights and Freedoms. Refers to different treatment of those living off a reserve. Recognized as an analogous ground because the decision to live on or off-reserve is a "personal characteristic essential to a band member's personal identity" which can be changed "only at great cost, if at all". *Corbiere v. Canada (Minister of Indian and Northern Affairs)*, [1999] 2 S.C.R. 203.

ABORIGINAL LAND. (a) Reserves, surrendered lands and any other lands that are set apart for the use and benefit of a band and that are subject to the Indian Act; (b) land, including any water, that is subject to a comprehensive or specific claim agreement, or a self-government agreement, between the Government of Canada and aboriginal people where title remains with Her Majesty in right of Canada; and (c) air and all layers of the atmosphere above and the subsurface below land. *Canadian Environmental Protection Act, 1999*, S.C. 1999, c. 33, s. 3(1), part.

ABORIGINAL LAW. The law relating to aboriginal people and their rights and claims.

ABORIGINAL MIDWIFERY. (a) Traditional aboriginal midwifery practices including the use and administration of traditional herbs and medicines and other cultural and spiritual practices, (b) contemporary aboriginal midwifery practices which are based on, or originate in, traditional aboriginal midwifery practices, or (c) a combination of traditional and contemporary aboriginal midwifery practices. *Health Professions Act*, R.S.B.C. 1996, c. 183, *Midwives Regulation*, B.C. Reg. 281/2008, s. 1.

ABORIGINAL ORGANIZATION. Includes an Indian band, an Indian band council, a tribal council and an organization that represents a territorially based aboriginal community. *Fisheries Act*, R.S.C. 1985, c. F-14, *Aboriginal Communal Fishing Licences Regulations*, SOR/93-332, s. 2.

ABORIGINAL PEOPLES. Persons who are Indians, Inuit or Métis. *Employment Equity Act*, S.C. 1995, c. 44, s. 3.

ABORIGINAL PERSON. A person of Indian or Inuit ancestry, including a Métis person, or a person recognized as being a member of an Indian, Inuit or Métis group by the other members of that group, who at any time ordinarily resided in the territory that is now Canada. *Cultural Property Export and Import Act*, R.S.C. 1985, c. C-51, *Canadian Cultural Property Export Control List*, C.R.C., c. 448, s. 1.

ABORIGINAL RIGHT LANDS. Those lands on which only specific aboriginal rights exist (e.g., the right to hunt for food, social and ceremonial purposes) because the occupation and use by the particular group of aboriginal people is too limited and, as a result, does not meet the criteria for the recognition, at common law, of aboriginal title. In these cases, the aboriginal rights on the land are restricted to residual portions of the aboriginal title—such as the rights to hunt, fish or trap—or to other matters not connected to land; they do not, therefore, entail the full sui generis proprietary right to occupy and use the land. Both the Canadian Parliament and provincial legislatures can enact legislation, pursuant to their respective general legislative competence, that affect native activities on aboriginal right lands. *R. v. Van der Peet*, [1996] 2 S.C.R. 507, L'Heureux-Dube (dissenting).

ABORIGINAL RIGHTS. 1. The test for identifying the aboriginal rights recognized and affirmed by s. 35(1) must be directed at identifying the crucial elements of those pre-existing distinctive societies. Identifying those traditions, customs and practices that are integral to distinctive aboriginal cultures will serve to identify the crucial elements of the distinctive aboriginal societies that occupied North America prior to the arrival of Europeans. The person or community claiming the existence of an aboriginal right protected by s. 35(1) need only show that the particular practice, custom or tradition which it is claiming to be an aboriginal right is distinctive, not that it is distinct. *R. v. Van der Peet* [1996] 2 S.C.R. 507, per Lamer, J. 2. Three factors that should guide a court's characterization of a claimed aboriginal right: (1) the nature of the action which the applicant is claiming was done pursuant to an aboriginal right; (2) the nature of the governmental legislation or action alleged to infringe the right, i.e. the conflict between the claim and the limitation; and (3) the ancestral traditions and practices relied upon to establish the right. *Mitchell v. Minister of National Revenue* [2001] 1 S.C.R. 911. See EXISTING ~.

ABORIGINAL SACRED AND CULTURALLY SENSITIVE OBJECT. Any object that: (i) has been used in an Aboriginal ceremony; (ii) reflects the spiritual power of an Aboriginal person; (iii) was left as an offering in an Aboriginal ceremony or practice; or

(iv) has ongoing historical or cultural importance to an Aboriginal community. *The Royal Saskatchewan Museum Act*, S.S. 2007, c. R-23.01, s. 2. See SACRED CEREMONIAL OBJECT.

ABORIGINAL TITLE. 1. "... [A] legal right derived from the Indians' historic occupation and possession of their tribal lands." *Calder v. Attorney General of British Columbia*, [1973] S.C.R. 313, cited in *Guerin v. R.*, [1985] 1 C.N.L.R. 120 at 132 (S.C.C.), Dickson J. 2. Aboriginal title is a right in land and, as such, is more than the right to engage in specific activities which may be themselves aboriginal rights. Rather, it confers the right to use land for a variety of activities, not all of which need be aspects of practices, customs and traditions which are integral to the distinctive cultures of aboriginal societies. Those activities do not constitute the right per se; rather, they are parasitic on the underlying title. However, that range of uses is subject to the limitation that they must not be irreconcilable with the nature of the attachment to the land which forms the basis of the particular group's aboriginal title. This inherent limit [. . .] flows from the definition of aboriginal title as a sui generis interest in land, and is one way in which aboriginal title is distinct from a fee simple. [. . .] Aboriginal title at common law is protected in its full form by s. 35(1) [of the Constitution Act, 1982]. This conclusion flows from the express language of s. 35(1) itself. . . . [Section] 35(1) did not create aboriginal rights; rather, it accorded constitutional status to those rights which were "existing" in 1982. . . . In order to make out a claim for aboriginal title, the aboriginal group asserting title must satisfy the following criteria: (i) the land must have been occupied prior to sovereignty, (ii) if present occupation is relied on as proof of occupation pre-sovereignty, there must be a continuity between present and pre-sovereignty occupation, and (iii) at sovereignty, that occupation must have been exclusive. *Delgamuukw v. British Columbia*, 153 D.L.R. (4th) 193, 220 N.R. 161, 99 B.C.A.C. 161, 162 W.A.C. 161, [1997] 3 S.C.R. 1010, [1998] 1 C.N.L.R. 14, [1999] 10 W.W.R. 34, 66 B.C.L.R. (3d) 285, Lamer C.J.C. (Cory and Major JJ. concurring) 3. [T]he aboriginal right of possession is derived from the historic occupation and use of ancestral lands by aboriginal peoples. Put another way, "aboriginal title" is based on the continued occupation and use of the land as part of the aboriginal peoples' traditional way of life. This sui generis interest is not equated with fee simple ownership; nor can it be described with reference to traditional property law concepts. . . . [T]he aboriginal right of occupancy is further characterized by two principal features. First, this sui generis interest in the land is personal in that it is generally inalienable except to the Crown. Second, in dealing with this interest, the Crown is subject to a fiduciary obligation to treat aboriginal peoples fairly. *Delgamuukw v. British Columbia*, 153 D.L.R. (4th) 193, 220 N.R. 161, 99 B.C.A.C. 161, 162 W.A.C. 161, [1997] 3 S.C.R. 1010, [1998] 1 C.N.L.R. 14, [1999] 10 W.W.R. 34, 66 B.C.L.R. (3d) 285, La Forest J. (L'Heureux-Dubé J. concurring).

ABORIGINAL TITLE LANDS. Aboriginal title lands are lands which the natives possess for occupation and use at their own discretion, subject to the Crown's ultimate title; federal and provincial legislation applies to aboriginal title lands, pursuant to the governments' respective general legislative authority. Aboriginal title of this kind is founded on the common law and strict conditions must be fulfilled for such title to be recognized. Aboriginal title can also be founded on treaties concluded between the natives and the competent government. *R. v. Van der Peet*, [1996] 9 W.W.R. 1, L'Heureux-Dube (dissenting).

ABORIGINE. *n.* The first, original or indigenous inhabitants of a country.

ABORTION. *n.* 1. Miscarriage or the premature expulsion of the fetus. F.A. Jaffe, *A Guide to Pathological Evidence for Lawyers and Police Officers*, 4th ed. (Toronto: Carswell, 1999) at 229. 2. The interruption of pregnancy before the fetus is viable. F.A. Jaffe, *A Guide to Pathological Evidence for Lawyers and Police Officers*, 4th ed. (Toronto: Carswell, 1999) at 229.

ABOUT. See ON OR ~.

ABOUT TO. On the point of.

ABOVE PAR. At a premium, at a price above face or nominal value.

ABPC. Neutral citation for the Alberta Provincial Court.

ABQB. Neutral citation for the Alberta Court of Queen's Bench.

ABR. *abbr.* Abridgment.

ABRIDGE. *v.* To shorten.

ABRIDGMENT. *n.* 1. Of law, a digest. 2. Of time, shortening. 3. The Canadian Abridgment.

ABROAD. *adv.* 1. Outside the country. 2. At large, out of doors.

ABROGATE. *v.* To annul or cancel.

ABROGATION. *n.* Annulment; repeal of a law.

ABSCOND. *v.* 1. To abscond from a trial means voluntarily absenting oneself from the trial for the purpose of impeding or frustrating it or with the intention of aborting its consequences. *R.v. Garofoli* [1990] 2 S.C.R. 1421. 2. "... One who absconds from a particular place not only leaves but leaves it with the purpose of frustrating or rendering more difficult, by his absence, the effective application of the laws current in the jurisdiction whence he absconds." *Carolus v. Minister of National Revenue*, [1976] C.T.C. 608 at 610 (Fed. T.D.), Mahoney J.

ABSCONDING DEBTOR. A debtor who hides to avoid arrest or service, or simply is not in the province. C.R.B. Dunlop, *Creditor-Debtor Law in Canada* (Toronto: Carswell, 1981) at 206.

ABSENCE. *n.* 1. Non-existence; want; lack. 2. Not being present. *R. v. Brunet* (1918), 57 S.C.R. 83 at 91, 92, 95, 30 C.C.C. 16, 42 D.L.R. 405, Anglin J. See LEAVE OF ~; TEMPORARY ~.

ABSENTEE. *n.* A person whose whereabouts is unknown.

ABSENTEEISM. *n.* 1. Absence from work. 2. When employees absent themselves from work for insufficient reasons.

ABSOLUTE. *adj.* 1. Unconditional. *R. v. Helliwell* (1914), 18 D.L.R. 550 at 552, 5 O.W.N. 936, 23 C.C.C. 146, 30 O.L.R. 594 (C.A.), the court per Meredith C.J.O. 2. Unqualified. *Bank of Montreal v. Brett* (1984), 53 B.C.L.R. 346 at 348-49 (S.C.), McLachlin J. 3. Complete. See DECREE ~; RULE ~.

ABSOLUTE ASSIGNMENT. An instrument cannot be both a security interest and an absolute assignment since an absolute assignment is complete and perfect in itself. There cannot be a residual right remaining with the debtor to recover the assets. It is simply the sale of the book debts of the company. *Alberta Treasury Branches v. Minister of National Revenue* [1996] 1 S.C.R. 963, Cory J.

ABSOLUTE CERTIFICATE OF TITLE. A certificate of title issued on the registration of an absolute fee and includes such a certificate issued before October 31, 1979. *Land Title Act,* R.S.B.C. 1996, c. 250, s. 1.

ABSOLUTE DISCHARGE. A sentence by which accused is discharged although the charge is proven or a plea of guilty entered. The effect of an absolute discharge is that the person is deemed to not be convicted of the offence.

ABSOLUTE INTEREST. Complete and full ownership.

ABSOLUTE LIABILITY. 1. Liability regardless of intention or negligence. 2. An offence for which an accused is criminally liable even though the accused acted under a reasonable mistake of fact. *R. v. Metro News Ltd.* (1986), 23 C.R.R. 77 at 89, 16 O.A.C. 319, 56 O.R. (2d) 321, 53 C.R. (3d) 289, 29 C.C.C. (3d) 35, 32 D.L.R. (4th) 321 (C.A.), the court per Martin J.A.

ABSOLUTE LIABILITY OFFENCE. Guilt follows proof of the proscribed act in such an offence.

ABSOLUTELY. *adv.* Unconditionally.

ABSOLUTE PRIVILEGE. 1. Briefly, the absolute immunity privilege with respect to defamatory communications made during judicial proceedings was developed for reasons of public policy and convenience. It reflects a balance between the right of a person to protect his or her reputation on the one hand, while on the other, the immunity is necessary to ensure that the public interest in the full disclosure of facts essential to ensure the unfettered administration of justice in its search for truth is promoted and protected. For that reason, the balance has been weighted in favour of the immunity. *Comeau v. Pole*, 2005 NBCA 113. 2. For absolute privilege to apply, the statement must "take place during, incidental to, and in the processing and furtherance of, judicial or quasi-judicial proceedings": Raymond E. Brown, The Law of Defamation in Canada, 2nd ed., looseleaf (Scarborough: Carswell, 1999) vol. 2 at para. 12.4(1). See also Patrick Milmo & W.V.H. Rogers, eds., Gatley on Libel and Slander, 9th ed. (London: Sweet & Maxwell, 1998) at para. 13.1. The purpose of the absolute privilege defence is to ensure that those involved in the administration of justice, including litigants, witnesses, advocates and judges, can speak freely without fear of an action in defamation; it is not intended to protect those who have made malicious statements: Brown at para. 12.4(2). *Liboiron v. Majola*, 2007 ABCA 18.

ABSOLUTE RESPONSIBILITY. Criminal liability regardless of fault. D. Stuart, *Canadian Criminal Law: A Treatise*, 2d ed. (Toronto: Carswell, 1987) at 157.

ABSQUE HOC. [L.] Without this.

ABSTENTION. *n.* Refusal to vote or debate.

ABSTRACT. *v.* To abridge; to remove.

ABSTRACT. *n.* Abridgment.

ABSTRACT. *adj.* Having no basis in fact. Robert J. Sharpe, ed., *Charter Litigation* (Toronto: Butterworths, 1987) at 335.

ABSTRACT BOOK. Record in which each parcel of land is assigned a separate page on which details describing the document affecting title are inscribed. B.J. Reiter, B.N. McLellan & P.M. Perell, *Real Estate Law*, 4th ed. (Toronto: Emond Montgomery, 1992) at 389.

ABSTRACT OF TITLE. History of the title to land which shows any conveyance of the land or any interest in the land in chronological order.

ABSURD. *adj.* An "absurd" interpretation of a statute is one which leads to a ridiculous or frivolous consequences or is "extremely unreasonable". *Pointe Claire v. Quebec (Labour Court)* (1997), 146 D.L.R. (4th) 1, S.C.C., L'Heureux-Dube (dissenting).

ABSURDITY. *n.* "... [I]n relation to the construction of statutes refers to disharmony between the parts of a statute or between a part and the whole, or inconsistency between the statute taken as a whole and a particular result of its application... ." *Carfrae Estates Ltd. v. Gamble* (1979), 97 D.L.R. (3d) 162 at 164, 24 O.R. (2d) 113 (Div. Ct.), Reid J. See PRESUMPTION AGAINST ~.

ABUSE. *v.* 1. To make improper or excessive use of. 2. "... [T]o cause unnecessarily substantial suffering to any animal." *R. v. Linder*, [1950] 1 W.W.R. 1035 at 1037, 10 C.R. 44, 97 C.C.C. 174 (B.C. C.A.), Bird J.A. *v.* 3. To mistreat.

ABUSE. *n.* 1. Misuse; maltreatment. 2. The deliberate mistreatment of an adult that causes the adult (a) physical, mental or emotional harm, or (b) damage to or loss of assets, and includes intimidation, humiliation, physical assault, sexual assault, overmedication, withholding needed medication, censoring mail, invasion or denial of privacy or denial of access to visitors. *Adult Guardianship Act*, R.S.B.C. 1996 (Supp.), c. 6, s. 1. 3. An act or omission by any person, where the act or omission results in (a) physical injury to the child, (b) emotional disability of a permanent nature in the child or is likely to result in such a disability, or (c) sexual exploitation of the child with or without the child's consent. *The Child and Family Services Act*, S.M. 1985-86, c. 8, s. 1. 4. Of a child by the person means that the child (a) has suffered physical harm, inflicted by the person or caused by the person's failure to supervise and protect the child adequately; (b) has been sexually abused by the person or by another person where the person, having the care of the child, knows or should know of the possibility of sexual abuse and fails to protect the child; or (c) has suffered serious emotional harm demonstrated by severe anxiety, depression, withdrawal, or self-destructive or aggressive behaviour, caused by the intentional conduct of the person. *Children and Family Services Act*, S.N.S.1990 c. 5 s. 62. See CHILD ~; DRUG ~; PHYSICAL ~.

ABUSE OF AUTHORITY. Which is oppressive conduct towards a member of the public, including, without limitation, (i) intentionally or recklessly making an arrest without good and sufficient cause, (ii) in the performance, or purported performance, of duties, intentionally or recklessly (A) using unnecessary force on any person, or (B) detaining or searching any person without good and sufficient cause, or (iii) when on duty, or off duty but in uniform, using profane, abusive or insulting language to any person including, without limitation, language that tends to demean or show disrespect to the person on the basis of that person's race, colour, ancestry, place of origin, political belief, religion, marital status, family status, physical or mental disability, sex, sexual orientation, age or economic and social status. *Police Act*, R.S.B.C. 1996, c. 367, s. 77.

ABUSE OF DISCRETION. Occurs when the possessor of power is not acting within the power as measured by the objects and purposes of that power. *R. v. Van Vliet* (1988), 38 C.R.R. 133 at 155, 45 C.C.C. (3d) 481, 10 M.V.R. (2d) 190 (B.C. C.A.), Southin J.A. See ABUSE OF POWER.

ABUSE OF POWER. "A municipality must exercise its powers in accordance with the purposes sought by the Legislature. It vitiates its acts and decisions if it abuses its discretionary power. A municipal act committed for unreasonable or reprehensible purposes, or purposes not covered by legislation is void. This illegality results not from the breach of specific provisions but from limitations imposed by the Courts on the discretionary power of government, and affects the substance of the act which must be assessed. The Court will accordingly determine whether the act is fraudulent, discriminatory, unjust or affected by bad faith, in which case it will be treated as an abuse of power." *Immeubles Port Louis Ltée c. Lafontaine (Village)* (1991), 5 M.P.L.R. (2d) 1 at 61, [1991] 1 S.C.R. 326, 78 D.L.R. (4th) 175, 121 N.R. 323, 38 Q.A.C. 253, the court per Gonthier J. See ABUSE OF DISCRETION.

ABUSE OF PROCESS. 1. Conduct on the part of government authorities that undermines the fundamental principles that underlie the community's sense of decency and fair play. *R. v. La* [1997] 8 W.W.R. 1 (S.C.C.), Sopinka J. at pp. 11-12. 2. The tort of abuse of process exists where the abuser has used the legal process for a purpose other than that which it was designed to serve, a collateral, extraneous, ulterior, improper or illicit purpose. There is no abuse where the litigant employs regular legal process to its proper conclusion even if with bad intentions. *Levi Strauss & Co. v. Roadrunner Apparel Inc.* (1997), 221 N.R. 93 (Fed. C.A.), Letourneau J.A. 3.The doctrine of abuse of process is intended to prevent the re- litigation of an issue which was determined in an earlier proceeding and which would be determinative of the later case. *Glenko Enterprises Ltd. v. Keller* 2000 MBCA 7, [2001] 1 W.W.R. 229, 5 C.L.R. (3d) 1, 150 Man. R. (2d) 1. 4. "... [I]n R. v. D. (T.C.) (1987), 38 C.C.C. (3d) 434 at 447 ... (Ont. C.A.), [it was] held that the onus of establishing that an abuse of process has occurred is on the respondent who must establish, on a balance of probabilities, that the Crown has acted in an oppressive or vexatious manner or that the prosecution is offensive to the principles of fundamental justice and fair play." *R. v. Miles of Music Ltd.* (1989), 24 C.P.R. (3d) 301 at 309, 31 O.A.C. 380, 69 C.R. (3d) 361, 48 C.C.C. (3d) 96, Krever J.A. 5. "... [T]he unreasonable multiplication of proceedings ..." *General Foods Ltd. v. Struthers Scientific & International Corp.* (1971), 4 C.P.R. (2d) 97 at 105, [1974] S.C.R. 98, 23 D.L.R. (3d) 313, the court per Pigeon J. 6. "... [F]rivolous and vexatious, or if the process ... is in fact being used for an ulterior or improper purpose, or if the process is being used in such a way as to be in itself an abuse ..." *Canada Metal Co. v. Heap* (1975), 7 O.R. (2d) 185 at 192 (C.A.). 7. "The essence of the tort of abuse of process is the misuse or perversion of the court's process for an extraneous or ulterior purpose. There must be a purpose other than that which the process was designed to serve ..." *D.K. Investments Ltd. v. S.W.S. Investments Ltd.* (1984), 59 B.C.L.R. 333 (S.C.), Finch J., affirmed (1986), 6 B.C.L.R. (2d) 291 (C.A.).

ABUSE OF STATUTORY POWERS. Abuse of process or abuse of office. Malicious prosecution is a specific tort of this category. *Starline Entertainment Centre v. Ciccarelli* (1995), 41 C.P.C. (3d) 99 (Ont. Gen. Div.).

ABUT. *v.* To border upon.

A.C. *abbr.* Law Reports, Appeal Cases, 1891.

A / C. *abbr.* Account.

ACADEMIC YEAR. The portion of the calendar year between the opening and closing dates of a school.

ACCEDE. *v.* To consent; to agree.

ACCELERATION. *n.* "The doctrine of acceleration is that all interests which fail or are undisposed of are captured by a residuary gift or go on an intestacy, but that a testator is presumed to have intended an acceleration of subsequent interests where a life interest fails in consequence of the donee being prevented by law from taking." *Kebty-Fletcher's Will Trusts, Re* (1967), (*sub nom. Public Trustee v. Swan*) [1967] 3 All E.R. 1076 at 1080 (U.K. Ch.), Stamp J.

ACCELERATION CLAUSE. 1. A clause in a credit agreement that provides that on default by the borrower or on the occurrence of another event, and whether or not at the option of the credit grantor, the whole or a part of the outstanding balance becomes immediately payable or is otherwise accelerated. *Consumer Protection and Business Practices Act*,

S.N. 2009, c. C-31.1, s. 54. 2. A clause in a mortgage or an agreement for sale of land or any agreement regarding either of them that stipulates that, if default is made in the payment of money due pursuant to the mortgage or agreement or in the observance of a covenant contained in the mortgage or agreement, the payment of other portions of the principal money is accelerated. *The Land Titles Act, 2000*, S.S. 2000, c. L-5.1, s. 124.

ACCEPTANCE. *n.* 1. Signification by an offeree of willingness to enter into a contract with an offeror on the offeror's terms. G.H.L. Fridman, *The Law of Contract in Canada*, 2d ed. (Toronto: Carswell, 1986) at 41. 2. The acceptance of a bill is the signification by the drawee of his assent to the order of the drawer. *Bills of Exchange Act*, R.S.C. 1985, c. B-4, s. 34. 3. An acceptance completed by delivery or notification. *Bills of Exchange Act*, R.S.C. 1985, c. B-4, s. 2. 4. In sale of goods, involves taking possession of the goods by the buyer. See BANKER'S ~; BLANK ~; CONDITIONAL ~; GENERAL ~; QUALIFIED ~.

ACCEPTANCE OF SERVICE. To endorse on the back of a document or a copy of it acknowledgement that the document was duly served.

ACCEPTED. See GENERALLY ~.

ACCEPTOR. *n.* The person to whom a depository bill is addressed and who signs it. *Depository Bills and Notes Act, 1998*, S. C. 1998, c. 13, s.2.

ACCESS. *n.* 1. For the purposes of Part 3, disclosure of personal information by the provision of access to personal information. *Freedom of Information and Protection of Privacy Act*, R.S.B.C. 1996, c. 165, Sched. 1, s. 1. 2. " ... [I]mplies that the custody of a child has been awarded to another person. Kay J., in Evershed v. Evershed (1882) 46 L.T. 690 at 691 (Ch.), stated at p. 691: 'The meaning of access is clear; it is that someone is to have leave to see children in custody of someone else ...'" *Glasgow v. Glasgow* (1982), 51 N.S.R. (2d) 13 at 24, 67 A.P.R. 473, 102 A.P.R. 13 (Fam. Ct.), Niedermayer Fam. Ct. J. 3. " ... '[R]ights to visit'..." *W. (E C.) . H. (P.J.J.)* 26 R.F.L. (2d) 164 at 177, [1982] 2 W.W.R. 313, 13 Man. R. (2d) 259, 131 D.L.R. (3d) 630 (C.A.), Matas J.A. (dissenting). 4. Includes visitation. *Family Relations Act*, R.S.B.C. 1996, c. 128, s. 21. 5. An exit from or an entrance to a highway. *The Highways Protection Act*, R.S.M. 1987, c. H50, s. 1. See LIMITED ~ DRUG; PUBLIC ~ TO LAW.

ACCESSION. *n.* Something belonging to one person which becomes the property of a second person because it was added to or incorporated with the second person's thing.

ACCESSION OF THE SOVEREIGN. The heir at once becomes the sovereign when a sovereign dies.

ACCESSIONS. *n.* Goods that are installed in or affixed to other goods.

ACCESS ORDER. A custody order under the Divorce Act includes an access order. An order relating to access to children by one or both of the parents.

ACCESSORY. *n.* 1. Anything joined to another; thing incident to another. 2. One who is not the chief actor in an offence but who is in some way concerned in it either before the act was committed, or at its commission, or soon after the initial and main act has been committed. *R. v. Smith* (1876), 38 U.C.Q.B. 218 at 227 (C.A.), Harrison C.J.

ACCESSORY AFTER THE FACT. To an offence, is one who, knowing that a person has been a party to the offence, receives, comforts or assists that person for the purpose of enabling that person to escape. *Criminal Code*, R.S.C. 1985, c. C-46, s. 23 as am. S.C. 2000, c. 12, s. 92.

ACCESSORY BEFORE THE FACT. At common law, one who counsels or procures another to commit an offence but who is not present or active when it is committed. *R. v. Berryman* (1990), 78 C.R. (3d) 376 at 383, 48 B.C.L.R. (2d) 105, 57 C.C.C. (3d) 375 (C.A.), the court per Wood J.A.

ACCESS RIGHT. A right, granted in an order or agreement, of access to or visitation of a child. *Family Orders and Agreements Enforcement Assistance Act*, R.S.C. 1985, c. 4 (2nd Supp.), s. 2.

ACCIDENT. *n.* 1. " ... [T]he expression 'accident' is used in the popular and ordinary sense of the word as denoting an unlooked-for mishap or an untoward event which is not expected or designed." *Fenton v. Thorley & Co. Ltd*, [1903] A.C. 443 at 448, Macnaghten L.J. 2. Includes a wilful and intentional act, not being the act of the worker, and also includes a fortuitous event occasioned by a physical or natural cause. *Workers Compensation Act*, R.S.B.C. 1996, c. 492, s. 2. 3. The word "accident" is not normally used to describe illness per se or even an unexpected but totally "natural" occurrence. There must also be some unexpected mishap or "external" factor at work. *Gibbens v. Co-operators Life Insurance Co.*, 2008 BCCA 153. See FATAL ~; INDUSTRIAL ~; INEVITABLE ~; UNAVOIDABLE ~.

ACCIDENTAL. *adj.* "... [I]ndicating an unlooked for mishap or an untoward event which is not expected or designed; or as an event which takes place out of the usual course of events without the foresight of expectation of the person injured; or as an injury happening by chance unexpectedly, or not as expected... ." *Voison v. Royal Insurance Co. of Canada* (1988), 33 C.C.L.I. 1 at 6, 66 O.R. (2d) 45, 53 D.L.R. (4th) 299, [1988] I.L.R. 1-2358, 29 O.A.C. 227 (C.A.), the court per Robins J.A.

ACCIDENTAL DEATH INSURANCE. Insurance undertaken by an insurer as part of a contract of life insurance whereby the insurer undertakes to pay an additional amount of insurance money in the event of the death by accident of the person whose life is insured. *Insurance acts*.

ACCIDENTAL MEANS. Conveys the idea that the consequences of the actions and events that produced death were unexpected. Reference to a set of consequences is therefore implicit in the word "means". "Means" refers to one or more actions or events, seen under the aspect of their causal relation to the events they bring about. *Martin v. American International Assurance Life Co.*, 2003 SCC 16.

ACCIDENT INSURANCE. Insurance by which the insurer undertakes, otherwise than incidentally to some other class of insurance defined by or under this Act, to pay insurance money in the event of accident to the person or persons insured, but does not include insurance by which the insurer undertakes to pay insurance money both in the event of death by accident and in the event of death from any other cause. *Insurance acts.*

ACCIDENT INVESTIGATION. See CANA-DIAN TRANSPORTATION ~ AND SAFETY BOARD.

ACCLAMATION. *n.* Occurs when only the number of candidates required to fill an office is nominated. The candidate(s) is (are) elected. I.M. Rogers, *The Law of Canadian Municipal Corporations*, 2d ed. (Toronto: Carswell, 1971) at 123.

ACCOMMODATE. See DUTY TO ~; DUTY TO CONSULT AND ~.

ACCOMMODATION. *n.* 1. Refers to what is required in the circumstances of employment or service provision to avoid discrimination under human rights legislation. Employers and others governed by human rights legislation are now required in all cases to accommodate the characteristics of affected groups within their standards, rather than maintaining discriminatory standards supplemented by accommodation for those who cannot meet them. Incorporating accommodation into the standard itself ensures that each person is assessed according to her or his own personal abilities, instead of being judged against presumed group characteristics. *British Columbia (Superintendent of Motor Vehicles) v. British Columbia (Council of Human Rights)*, 1999 CarswellBC 2730, [2000] 1 W.W.R. 565, 47 M.V.R. (3d) 167, 249 N.R. 45, 70 B.C.L.R. (3d) 215, 181 D.L.R. (4th) 385, 36 C.H.R.R. D / 129, [1999] 3 S.C.R. 868, 131 B.C.A.C. 280, 214 W.A.C. 280, McLachlin J. for the court. 2. The provision of lodging in hotels and motels. See HOUSING ~; LODGE ~; SANITARY ~; SEMI-PRIVATE ~.

ACCOMMODATION BILL. A bill accepted or endorsed without value to accommodate a party to the bill. The party who accommodates thus is in fact a surety for a principal debtor who may or may not be a party to the bill. I.F.G. Baxter, *The Law of Banking*, 3d ed. (Toronto: Carswell, 1981) at 116.

ACCOMMODATION PARTY. An accommodation party to a bill is a person who has signed a bill as drawer, acceptor or endorser, without receiving value therefor, and for the purpose of lending his name to some other person. *Bills of Exchange Act*, R.S.C. 1985, c. B-4, s. 54.

ACCOMPLICE. *n.* 1. "... What is necessary to become an accomplice is a participation in the crime involved, and not necessarily the actual commission of it... ." *R. v. Morris* (1979), 10 C.R. (3d) 259 at 281, [1979] 2 S.C.R. 1041, 26 N.B.R. (2d) 273, 55 A.P.R. 273, 27 N.R. 313, 47 C.C.C. (2d) 257, 99 D.L.R. (3d) 420, Spence J. (dissenting) (Laskin C.J.C., Dickson and Estey JJ. concurring). 2. "One who is concerned with another or others in committing or attempting to

commit any criminal offence... ." *R. v. Morrison* (1917), 51 N.S.R. 253 at 270, 29 C.C.C. 6, 38 D.L.R. 568 (C.A.), Chisholm J.

ACCORD. *v.* To agree.

ACCORD. *n.* Agreement by which an obligation in contract or tort is discharged. *Coulter Electronics of Canada Ltd. v. Motorways (1985) Ltd.* (1990), 42 C.P.C. (2d) 90 at 93, 65 Man. R. (2d) 45 (C.A.), O'Sullivan, Philp and Helper JJ.A.

ACCORD AND SATISFACTION. "Accord and satisfaction is the purchase of a release from an obligation whether arising under contract or tort by means of any valuable consideration, not being the actual performance of the obligation itself. The accord is the agreement by which the obligation is discharged. The satisfaction is the consideration which makes the agreement operative." *Coulter Electronics of Canada Ltd. v. Motorways (1985) Ltd.* (1990), 42 C.P.C. (2d) 90 at 93, 65 Man. R. (2d) 45 (C.A.), O'Sullivan, Philp and Helper JJ.A.

ACCOST. *v.* To solicit.

ACCOUCHEUR. *n.* [Fr.] Midwife; person presiding at birth.

ACCOUNT. *n.* 1. Settlement of debits and credits between parties. 2. Any monetary obligation not evidenced by any chattel paper, instrument or securities, whether or not it has been earned by performance. 3. An account with a bank. See ACTION OF ~; ~S; BANK ~; CAPITAL ~; CASH ~; CHARGE ~; DUTY TO ~; EXPENSE ~; FUTURES ~; INTERIM ~; PASS AN ~; RETAIL DEPOSIT ~; SECURITIES ~; TAX-FREE SAVINGS ~.

ACCOUNTABLE. *adj.* Liable; responsible.

ACCOUNTANT. See PUBLIC ~.

ACCOUNTING. *n.* "... [T]he art of recording, classifying, and summarizing, in a significant manner and in terms of money, transactions and events which are, in part at least, of a financial character and interpreting the results thereof." *Toromont Industrial Holdings Ltd. v. Thorne, Gunn, Helliwell & Christenson* (1975), 23 C.P.R. (2d) 59 at 74, 10 O.R. (2d) 65, 62 D.L.R. (3d) 225 (H.C.), Holland J. See ACCRUAL METHOD OF ~; ACTION FOR ~; GENERALLY ACCEPTED ~ PRINCIPLES.

ACCOUNTING PERIOD. Usually a year; fiscal year; period in respect of which financial statements are prepared.

ACCOUNTS. *n.* 1. The statement of profit and loss and the balance sheet. 2. Deposits in a bank are known as accounts of the depositors. See ACCOUNT; PUBLIC ~; TAKING ~.

ACCOUNTS RECEIVABLE. 1. The amounts that are owing by customers to a business for goods shipped to them or for services rendered. 2. Existing or future book debts, accounts, claims, moneys and choses in action or any class or part thereof and all contracts, securities, bills, notes, books, instruments and other documents securing, evidencing or in any way relating to the same or any of them, but shall not include uncalled share capital of the company or calls made but not paid. *Canada Corporations Act*, R.S.C. 1970, c. C-32, s. 3.

ACCOUNT STATED. "... I agree with the observation of Patterson, J.A., in Watson v. Severn, 6 A.R. 559, at p. 565 ... 'An account stated is a settlement of accounts, in which both parties or their agents agree upon the amount due from the one to the other:' Bates v. Townley, 2 Exch. 152 ..." *Robb v. Murray* (1889), 16 O.A.R. 503 at 506 (C.A.), the court per Osler J.A.

ACCRETION. *n.* 1. "... [T]he increase which land bordering on a river or on the sea undergoes through the silting up of soil, sand or other substance, or the permanent retiral of the waters. This increase must be formed by a process so slow and gradual as to be ... imperceptible, by which is meant that the addition cannot be observed in its actual progress from moment to moment or from hour to hour, although, after a certain period, it can be observed that there has been a fresh addition to the shore line. The increase must also result from the action of the water and not from some unusual or unnatural action by which a considerable quantity of soil is suddenly swept from the land of one man and deposited on, or annexed to, the land of another." *Clarke v. Edmonton (City)*, [1930] S.C.R. 137 at 144, [1949] 4 D.L.R. 1010, the court per Lamont J. 2. Something which the mortgagor adds to property to improve its value for the mortgagee's benefit. W.B. Rayner & R.H. McLaren, *Falconbridge on Mortgages*, 4th ed. (Toronto: Canada Law Book, 1977) at 19. 3. An enlargement of an existing bargaining unit.

ACCRUAL. *n.* Gradual vesting of a right in a person, without active intervention.

ACCRUAL METHOD OF ACCOUNTING. A method in which income is reported as it is earned and costs are recorded as they are incurred.

ACCRUE. *v.* 1. A right can only be said to accrue to a person at the point when the person can actually exercise the right. To say that a right accrues to a person is a passive way of saying that the person "acquires" that right. *R.v. Puskas (sub nom. R. v. Chatwell)*, (1998), 227 N.R. 1 (S.C.C.). 2. "... [T]o fall (to any one) as a natural growth, to arise as a natural growth." *Hockin v. Bank of British Columbia* (1989), 36 B.C.L.R. (2d) 220 at 226 (S.C.), Spencer J.

ACCRUED. *adj.* 1. Earned or accumulated but not yet received or receivable. 2. Vested.

ACCRUED DIVIDEND. A dividend declared but not yet paid.

ACCRUED RIGHT. "... [A] right which has come into existence... . one that may be enjoyed at a period of time that is current or past, ..." *Chafe v. Power* (1980), 117 D.L.R. (3d) 117 at 122, 125 (Nfld. T.D.), Goodridge J.

ACCRUING. *adj.* "... [N]ecessarily, or inevitably, not possibly or even probably, arising in due course... . the events giving rise to it or the condition upon which it depends for its existence, must have been so set in train or engaged as inevitably to give rise in due course to the right and its corresponding duty." *Scott v. College of Physicians & Surgeons (Saskatchewan)* (1992), 95 D.L.R. (4th) 706 at 719, [1993] 1 W.W.R. 533, 100 Sask. R. 291, 18 W.A.C. 291 (C.A.), the court per Cameron J.A.

ACCRUING RIGHT. "... [A] vested (or possibly contingent) one that may only be enjoyed at a future time." *Chafe v. Power* (1980), 117 D.L.R. (3d) 117 at 125 (Nfld. T.D.), Goodridge J.

ACCT. *abbr.* account.

ACCUMULATED DIVIDEND. A dividend due but not yet paid.

ACCUMULATED PROFITS. Profits which have not been distributed.

ACCUMULATION. *n.* 1. Adding of dividends, rents, and other incomes to capital. 2. Income from property is separated from the ownership of the property either to be an accretion to or to form the capital of any fund, or to be a restriction on and postponement of beneficial enjoyment of that property. In most jurisdictions, there is a statutory provision which limits provisions directing accumulation of income. T. Sheard, R. Hull & M.M.K. Fitzpatrick, *Canadian Forms of Wills*, 4th ed. (Toronto: Carswell, 1992) at 227-28.

ACCUMULATION TRUST. A trust requiring the trustee to accumulate specified income. D.M.W. Waters, *The Law of Trusts in Canada*, 2d ed. (Toronto: Carswell, 1984) at 491.

ACCUMULATIVE DIVIDEND. A dividend which accumulates from year to year if not paid.

ACCURACY. *n.* Accuracy [of testimony] engages consideration of the witness's ability to accurately i. observe; ii. recall; and iii. recount events in issue. *R. v. C. (H.)*, 2009 ONCA 56. SEE IN~; PRESUMPTION OF ~.

ACCUSATION. *n.* A charge that a person has committed a crime.

ACCUSE. *v.* To charge with a crime or fault. *R. v. Kempel* (1900), 31 O.R. 631 at 633 (C.A.).

ACCUSED. *n.* 1. One charged with a crime. *R. v. Kempel* (1900), 31 O.R. 631 at 633 (C.A.). 2. Includes a person to whom a peace officer has issued an appearance notice and a person arrested for a criminal offence. *Criminal Code*, R.S.C. 1985, c. C-46, s. 493. 3. Includes a defendant in summary conviction proceedings and an accused in respect of whom a verdict of not criminally responsible on account of mental disorder has been rendered. *Criminal Code*, R.S.C. 1985, c. C-46, s. 672.1.

AC ETIAM. [L.] And also.

ACID. See AMINO ~S.

ACKNOWLEDGE. *v.* 1. To admit; to accept responsibility. 2. [T]he ordinary meaning of "acknowledge" is to admit or affirm that a person is the biological father of a child. If the legislature had intended otherwise, it could have said so. *Herrington v. Green*, 1999 CarswellBC 2060, 178 D.L.R. (4th) 568 (S.C.).

ACKNOWLEDGEMENT. *n.* An admission that some claim or liability exists or that one owes a debt.

A COELO USQUE AD CENTRUM. [L.] From the heavens down to the centre of the earth.

ACQUESTS. See PARTNERSHIP OF ~.

ACQUIESCE. *v.* To agree tacitly, silently, or passively to something such as the children remaining in a jurisdiction which is not their habitual residence. Thus, acquiescence implies unstated consent. *Katsigiannis v. Kottick-Katsigiannis* (2001), 55 O.R. (3d) 456 (C.A.).

ACQUIESCED. Within the context [of the Canada Agricultural Products Act] means impliedly consented or tacitly agreed to, raised no objection to, accepted, permitted to be done. *R. v. A & A Foods Ltd.*, 1997 CarswellBC 2541, 120 C.C.C. (3d) 513 (S.C.).

ACQUIESCENCE. *n.* 1. Acquiescence has three different senses depending on the context. The first is as a synonym for estoppel where the plaintiff stands by and watches the deprivation of her rights and does nothing. The second meaning is as an aspect of laches. After the deprivation of her rights and in full knowledge of their existence, the plaintiff delays. The third usage is a confusing one related to the second branch of the laches rule in the context of an alteration of the defendant's position in reliance on the plaintiff's inaction. *M. (K.) v. M. (H.)* [1992] 3 S.C.R. 6, La Forest J. 2. In the Quebec Code of Civil Procedure, document signifying agreement to a demand. See ACTIVE~; DOCTRINE OF ~; PASSIVE~.

ACQUIRE. *v.* 1. "... [O]btaining or getting by paying or compensating therefor." *Felker v. McGuigan Construction Co.* (1909), 1 O.W.N. 946 at 948, 16 O.W.R. 417 (C.A.), Moss C.J.O. (Garrow and Meredith JJ.A. concurring). 2. "... Capable of being read as meaning, 'to get without payment or other consideration, as by way of gift', ..." *Felker v. McGuigan Construction Co.* (1909), 1 O.W.N. 946 at 948, 16 O.W.R. 417 (C.A.), Moss C.J.O. (Garrow and Meredith JJ.A. concurring).

ACQUISITION. *n.* Includes purchasing, leasing or bringing into the province for consumption or use and all derivatives of this term. *Tax Agreement Act,* S.N. 1996, c. T-0.01, s. 2.

ACQUIT. *v.* To find not guilty. 2. Originally, to free from pecuniary liability. See AUTREFOIS ~.

ACQUITTAL. *n.* A finding of "not guilty." See VERDICT OF ~.

ACQUITTANCE. *n.* A written acknowledgement that a debt was paid.

ACQUITTED. *adj.* Absolved; found free from guilt.

ACT. *v.* 1. To perform; to carry out functions. 2. To carry out a function or fill an office on a temporary basis.

ACT. *n.* 1. A statute. *R. v. Thompson,* [1931] 2 D.L.R. 282 at 285, [1931] 1 W.W.R. 26, 39 Man. R. 277, 55 C.C.C. 33 (C.A.), Dennistoun J.A. (Trueman and Robson JJ.A. concurring). 2. An act (a) of commission, or, (b) in certain particular cases, of omission, (c) by a human being, (d) that is voluntary, and, (e) has caused consequences, if consequences are included in the definition of the offence. D. Stuart, *Canadian Criminal Law: A Treatise,* 2d ed. (Toronto: Carswell, 1987) at 66. 3. An Act of a legislature, includes an ordinance of the Northwest Territories and a law of the Legislature of Yukon or of the Legislature for Nunavut. *Interpretation Act,* R.S.C. 1985, c. I-21, s. 35. See ADMINISTRATIVE ~; ANTI-COMPETITIVE ~; AUTHENTIC ~; BNA ~; BRITISH NORTH AMERICA ~, 1867; BULK SALES ~; CAMPBELL'S (LORD) ~; CANADA ~, 1982; CLARITY ~; COLONIAL LAWS VALIDITY ~, 1865; CONSOLIDATION ~; CONSTITUTION ~, 1867; CORPORATE ~; CRIMINAL ~; DELIBERATE ~; ENVIRONMENTAL ~; FEDERAL ~; JUDICIAL ~; KNOWING THAT THE ~ WAS WRONG; LEGISLATIVE ~; LOCAL ~; MARRIED WOMEN'S PROPERTY ~; MORTMAIN ~; NOTARIAL ~; OVERT ~; PIRATICAL ~S; PRELIMINARY ~; PUBLIC ~; REVENUE ~; RIOT ~; SOVEREIGN ~; SPECIAL ~; UNLAWFUL ~; WAR MEASURES ~; WRONGFUL ~.

ACT FAIRLY. "In general it means a duty to observe the rudiments of natural justice for a limited purpose in the exercise of functions that are not analytically judicial but administrative." *Nicholson v. Haldimand-Norfolk (Regional Municipality) Commissioners of Police* (1978), 88 D.L.R. (3d) 671 at 680, [1979] 1 S.C.R. 311, 78 C.L.L.C. 14,161, 23 N.R. 410, Laskin C.J.C. See DUTY TO~; FAIRNESS.

ACTING JUDICIALLY. It is well settled that the test to be applied in determining if a guilty verdict should be set aside as being unreasonable or one that cannot be supported by the evidence is whether the verdict is one that a properly instructed jury acting judicially could reasonably have rendered. ... The words "acting judicially" mean that the jury must, among other things, apply the law, adjudicate only on the basis of the record, and arrive at a conclusion that does not conflict with the bulk of judicial experience. *R. v. Liu* (2004), 190 C.C.C. (3d) 233 (Ont.C.A.).

ACTIO. [L.] Action.

ACTIO IN PERSONAM. [L.] "... [W]here the subject matter of the proceeding is the personal rights of the litigants and where the judgment affects only the immediate parties to the action... ." *Works v. Holt* (1976), 22 R.F.L. 1 at 5 (Ont. Prov. Ct.), Beaulieu Prov. J.

ACTIO IN REM. [L.] "... [W]here the subject matter touches questions of status of the person or some thing and where the judgment binds all the world... ." *Works v. Holt* (1976), 22 R.F.L. 1 at 5 (Ont. Prov. Ct.), Beaulieu Prov. J.

ACTION. *n.* 1. One party (the plaintiff) suit against another party (the defendant) for the protection or enforcement of a right, the prevention or redress of a wrong, or the punishment of an offence. 2. A civil proceeding that is not an application and includes a proceeding commenced by claim, statement of claim, notice of action, counterclaim, crossclaim, third or subsequent party claim, or divorce petition or counterpetition. *Courts of Justice Act*, R.S.O. 1990, c. C.43, s. 1. 3. Includes (i) an issue, matter, arbitration, reference, investigation or inquiry, (ii) a prosecution for an offence committed against an Act of the Legislature or in force in Alberta, or against a bylaw or regulation made under the authority of any such Act, and (iii) any other proceeding authorized or permitted to be tried, heard, had or taken by or before a court under the law of Alberta. *Alberta Evidence Act*, R.S.A. 2000, c. A-18, s. 1. See AFFIRMATIVE ~; BRING AN ~; CAUSE OF ~; CHOSE IN ~; CIVIL ~; CLASS ~; CONSOLIDATION OF ~S; CROSS- ~; DERIVATIVE ~; DISCIPLINARY ~; FORMS OF ~; INDUSTRIAL ~; LIMITATION OF ~; NOTICE OF ~; OBLIQUE ~; OPPRESSION ~; PAULIAN ~; PERSONAL ~; REAL ~; RELATOR ~; REPRESENTATIVE ~; RIGHT OF ~; SCIENTER ~; THING IN ~; VEXATIOUS ~.

ACTIONABLE. *adj.* Capable of sustaining or giving rise to an action.

ACTIONEM NON. [L.] A statement by a defendant in pleadings that a plaintiff should not have brought the action against the defendant.

ACTION EX DELICTO. An action to remedy a tort.

ACTION FOR ACCOUNTING. A cause of action which a debtor may have against a security holder who has seized and sold assets or a beneficiary may have against a trustee or other person acting in a fiduciary capacity to make known what has been done with property and to adjust and settle accounts between them.

ACTION FOR DETINUE. A claim for damages caused by the improper withholding from the plaintiff of a chattel. D.M.W. Waters, *The Law of Trusts in Canada*, 2d ed. (Toronto: Carswell, 1984) at 1035.

ACTION FOR INDEMNITY. This action was brought against M & L Leasing to indemnify the partners for the payment they made to satisfy the judgment. An action for indemnity or contribution is not the appropriate means for partners to seek indemnity; the proper remedy is an action for the taking of accounts. *Lafrentz v. M & L Leasing Ltd. Partnership* (2000), 2000 CarswellAlta 1121, 2000 ABQB 714, 8 B.L.R. (3d) 219, [2001] 1 W.W.R. 629, 85 Alta. L.R. (3d) 233, 275 A.R. 334, Perras J.

ACTION FOR MONEY HAD AND RECEIVED. An action to recover money a defendant has received and which for reasons of equity the defendant should not retain.

ACTION FOR NEGLIGENCE. The fundamental principle is that the plaintiff in an action for negligence is entitled to a sum of damages which will return the plaintiff to the position the plaintiff would have been in had the accident not occurred, insofar as money is capable of doing this. This goal was expressed in the early cases by the maxim restitutio in integrum. The plaintiff is entitled to full compensation and is not to be denied recovery of losses which he has sustained. *Cunningham v. Wheeler*, 1994 CarswellBC 121, 88 B.C.L.R. (2d) 273, [1994] 4 W.W.R. 153, 20 C.C.L.T. (2d) 1, [1994] 1 S.C.R.

359, 113 D.L.R. (4th) 1, 23 C.C.L.I. (2d) 205, 164 N.R. 81, 41 B.C.A.C. 1, 66 W.A.C. 1, 2 C.C.P.B. 217, McLachlin J. dissenting.

ACTION FOR RECOVERY OF LAND. An action brought by an owner against one unlawfully in possession of land. See EJECTMENT.

ACTION FOR REPLEVIN. An action in which a plaintiff seeks to recover possession of a chattel. D.M.W. Waters, *The Law of Trusts in Canada*, 2d ed. (Toronto: Carswell, 1984) at 1035-36.

ACTION FOR SALE. A mortgagee's action to obtain an order to require the sale of property on which he holds a mortgage when the mortgagor is in default.

ACTION FOR TORT. It may be well to state once again the principle of recovery in an action for tort. Simply, it is to compensate the injured party as completely as possible for the loss suffered as a result of the negligent action or inaction of the defendant. However, the plaintiff is not entitled to a double recovery for any loss arising from the injury. *Cunningham v. Wheeler*, 1994 CarswellBC 121, 88 B.C.L.R. (2d) 273, [1994] 4 W.W.R. 153, 20 C.C.L.T. (2d) 1, [1994] 1 S.C.R. 359, 113 D.L.R. (4th) 1, 23 C.C.L.I. (2d) 205, 164 N.R. 81, 41 B.C.A.C. 1, 66 W.A.C. 1, 2 C.C.P.B. 217, Cory J.

ACTION IN PERSONAM. An action brought against a person for recovery of damages or other relief.

ACTION IN REM. "... [A] proceeding to determine the status or condition of the thing itself, and a judgment is a decision as to the disposition of the thing." *Fry v. Botsworth* (1902), 9 B.C.R. 234 at 239 (C.A.), Irving J.A.

ACTION OF ACCOUNT. An action to settle an account between a debtor and creditor.

ACTION OF CONTRACT. An action arising on a breach of contract.

ACTION OF EJECTMENT. An action to recover possession of land. W.B. Rayner & R.H. McLaren, *Falconbridge on Mortgages*, 4th ed. (Toronto: Canada Law Book, 1977) at 411-12. See EJECTMENT.

ACTIO. NON. *abbr.* Actionem non.

ACTION ON THE CASE. 1. In the context of the Ontario Limitations Act has something of a residual character. Is a catch-all or short-hand expression to embrace personal actions for damages based upon breach of a legal duty not otherwise caught by the Act. *Perry, Farley & Onyschuk v. Outerbridge Management Ltd.* (2001), 54 O.R. (3d) 131 (C.A.). One of the common law forms of action. It is not confined to torts but includes claims such as assumpsit. 2. An action brought to recover damages for injury or loss resulting indirectly or consequentially from the act complained of. *Burd v. Macaulay* (1924), 20 Alta. L.R. 352 at 356, 358, [1924] 2 W.W.R. 393, [1924] 2 D.L.R. 815 (C.A.), the court per Stuart J.A.

ACTION TO REDEEM. An action brought by anyone who has an interest in the equity of redemption in mortgaged property or by a person who is liable for the mortgage debt. The purpose is to recover the property.

ACTIO PER QUOD CONSORTIUM AMISIT. [L.] The right of action of a husband against a defendant who has imprisoned, taken away or done physical harm to his wife so that he is deprived of her services or society. K.D. Cooper-Stephenson & I.B. Saunders, *Personal Injury Damages in Canada* (Toronto: Carswell, 1981) at 485.

ACTIO PER QUOD SERVITIUM AMISIT. [L.] "The action per quod [servitium amisit] is born of the relationship of master and servant, and though of very early origin in my opinion still persists in the common law provinces of Canada in one form or another. The action recognizes the right in the master to recover damages as against a wrongdoer who has injured his servant and thus deprived the master of his services." *R. v. Buchinsky* (1983), 24 C.C.L.T. 266 at 271, [1983] 5 W.W.R. 577, 145 D.L.R. (3d) 1, 47 N.R. 208, 22 Man. R. (2d) 121, Ritchie J. (Estey, Lamer and Wilson JJ. concurring).

ACTIVE BUSINESS CARRIED ON BY A CORPORATION. Any business carried on by the corporation other than a specified investment business or a personal services business and includes an adventure or concern in the nature of trade. *Income Tax Act*, R.S.C. 1985, c. 1 (5th Supp.), s. 125.

ACTIVE DUTY. Something which requires a trustee to carry out an activity such as making a maintenance payment, ensuring that an investment policy balances between income return and capital growth in the interest of both the one holding the remainder and the life tenant, keeping accurate accounts and retaining and instructing solicitors to the trust. D.M.W. Waters, *The Law of Trusts in Canada*, 2d ed. (Toronto: Carswell, 1984) at 28. See ACTIVE TRUST.

ACTIVE OFFER. An active offer is a greeting that informs the member of the public that they may communicate in either French or English. Its purpose ... is to ensure that an individual feels comfortable requesting a service. It is a sign of respect. An active offer can take the form of a sign, a personal greeting or a message. ... The notion of active offer was not overlooked in the OLA [Official Languages Act, R.S.N.W.T. 1988, c. O-1]. Section 34(e) provides that the Commissioner may make regulations respecting active offer. The [Government of the Northwest Territories] did not enact regulations. Rather, it developed the [Policy and Guidelines], ... which provide for active offer in specified government offices. ... s. 34(e) of the OLA suggest[s] that it was not the legislature's intention to make active offer a fundamental part of s. 11(1). ... the trial judge erred in finding that active offer was necessary in all head or central offices. Nevertheless, in those contexts where urgent or highly confidential matters are likely to arise, the person who seeks such services in French cannot easily access it or know it is available without an active offer. *Northwest Territories (Attorney General) v. Fédération Franco-Ténoise*, 2008 NWTCA 6.

ACTIVE TRUST. A trust which requires a trustee to carry out duties connected with it other than simply handing over the trust property to the beneficiary when required to do so. See ACTIVE DUTY; BARE TRUST.

ACTIVITY. *n.* Business; actions which occupy one. See INVESTOR-RELATIONS ACTIVITIES; MINING ~; TERRORIST ~; UNLAWFUL ~; WEATHER MODIFICATION ~; WILDERNESS TOURISM ~.

ACTIVITY DUTY. In occupiers' liability, a duty base on the risk entailed in an activity carried on by the occupier or someone else.

ACT OF BANKRUPTCY. An act which entitles another person to have a receiving order made against a debtor.

ACT OF GOD. "... [A]mounts to an interference in the course of nature so unexpected that any consequence arising from it is to be regarded as too remote to be foundation for successful legal action." *Tomchak v. Ste. Anne (Rural Municipality)* (1962), 39 W.W.R. 186 at 188, 33 D.L.R. (2d) 481 (Man. C.A.), Monnin J.A. (Miller C.J.M., Schultz and Guy JJ.A. concurring; Freedman J.A. concurring in the result).

ACT OF GOD CLAUSE. "... [G]enerally operates to discharge a contracting party when a supervening, sometimes supernatural, event, beyond the control of either party, makes performance impossible. The common thread is that of the unexpected, something beyond reasonable human foresight and skill." *Atlantic Paper Stock Ltd. v. St. Ann-Nackawic Pulp & Paper Co.* (1975), 10 N.B.R. (2d) 513 at 516, [1976] 1 S.C.R. 580, 4 N.R. 539, 56 D.L.R. (3d) 409, the court per Dickson J. See FORCE MAJEURE CLAUSE.

ACT OF PARLIAMENT. A statute.

ACT OF STATE. 1. "In the broad sense of the term, many lawful acts of the executive government, and many instances of the exercise of the prerogative of the Crown, might be designated 'acts of state;' ..." *Baird v. Walker* (1891), 11 C.L.T. 223 at 226 (Nfld. S.C.), the court per Pinsent J., appeal dismissed (*sub nom. Walker v. Baird*) [1892] A.C. 491, C.R. [10] A.C. 262. 2. "... [T]here is a narrower sense, and that in which the term is more technically if not exclusively employed, which related to acts done or adopted by the ruling powers of independent states, in their political and sovereign capacity, particularly 'an act injurious to the person or to the property of some person who is not at the time of that act a subject of Mer Majesty; which act is done by any representative of Her Majesty's authority, civil or military, and is either previously sanctioned or subsequently ratified by Her Majesty:' Stephen's History of the Criminal Law, p. 61." *Baird v. Walker* (1891), 11 C.L.T. 223 at 226 (Nfld. S.C.), the court per Pinsent J., appeal dismissed (*sub nom. Walker v. Baird*) [1892] A.C. 491, C.R. [10] A.C. 262.

ACT OF THE LAW. The creation, transfer or extinction of a right by operation of the law itself, in no way dependent on the consent of any concerned party.

ACTS OF CIVIL STATUS. Acts of birth, acts of marriage or civil union and acts of death. They contain only what is required by law, and are authentic. The acts of civil status are drawn up without delay from the attestations, declarations and juridical acts received by the registrar of civil status, regarding births, marriages, civil unions and deaths occurring in Québec or concerning persons domiciled in Québec. *Civil Code*, S.Q. 1991, c. 64, a. 107 and 108.

ACTUAL. *adj.* Real, in opposition to constructive, as in actual possession or actual occupation.

ACTUAL AUTHORITY. "... [A] legal relationship between principal and agent created by a consensual agreement to which they alone are parties... ." *Freeman & Lockyer v. Bockhurst Park Properties*, [1964] 2 Q.B. 480 at 502-3 (C.A.), Diplock L.J.

ACTUAL EXPRESS AUTHORITY. See EXPRESS AUTHORITY.

ACTUAL IMPLIED AUTHORITY. See IMPLIED AUTHORITY.

ACTUAL NOTICE. [A]ctual knowledge of the very fact required to be established, whereas constructive notice means knowledge of other facts which put a person on inquiry to discover the fact required to be established. The classic distinction, ...is that of Strong J. in Rose v. Peterkin (885), 13 S.C.R. 677 a 694: 'What such actual and direct notice is may well be ascertained very shortly by defining constructive notice, and then taken actual notice to be knowledge, not resume as in the case of constructive notice, but shown to be actually brought home to the party to be charged with it, either by proof of his own admission or by the evidence of witnesses who are able to establish that the very fact, of which notice is to be established, not something which would have led to the discovery of the fact if an inquiry had been pursued, was brought to his knowledge.'" *Stoimenov v. Stoimenov* (1985), 35 R.P.R. 150 at 158, 44 R.F.L. 2d 14, 7 O.A.C. 220, the court per Tarnopolsky J.A. See CONSTRUCTIVE NOTICE.

ACTUAL POSSESSION. Physical possession of goods or land.

ACTUAL PREJUDICE. The fact that a piece of evidence is missing that might or might not affect the defence will not be sufficient to establish that irreparable harm has occurred to the right to make full answer and defence. Actual prejudice occurs when the accused is unable to put forward his or her defence due to the lost evidence and not simply that the loss of the evidence makes putting forward the position more difficult. To determine whether actual prejudice has occurred, consideration of the other evidence that does exist and whether that evidence contains essentially the same information as the lost evidence is an essential consideration. *R. v. Bradford* (2001) 52 O.R. (3d) 257 (C.A.).

ACTUAL RESIDENCE. Physical presence. *Giradin v. Giradin* (1974), 15 R.F.L. 16 at 22, [1974] 2 W.W.R. 180, 42 D.L.R. (3d) 294 (Sask. Q.B.), Disbery J.

ACTUAL VALUE. 1. "... [C]ash market value ..." *Canadian National Fire Insurance Co. v. Colonsay Hotel Co.*, [1923] 3 D.L.R. 1001 at 1004, [1923] S.C.R. 688, [1923] 2 W.W.R. 1170, Idington J. 2. "... [E]xchangeable value – the price which the subject will bring when exposed to the test of competition." Lord Advocate v. Earl of Home (1881), 28 Sc. L.R. 289 at 293, Lord MacLaren, cited with approval in *Montreal Island Power Co. v. Laval-des-Rapides (Ville)*, [1935] S.C.R. 304 at 305, [1936] 1 D.L.R 621, Duff C.J.

ACTUARIAL BASIS. The assumptions and methods generally accepted and used by fellows of the Canadian Institute of Actuaries to establish, in relation to the contingencies of human life such as death, accident, sickness and disease, the costs of pension benefits, life insurance, disability insurance, health insurance and other similar benefits, including their actuarial equivalents. *Employment Standards Act, 2000*, S.O. 2000, c. 41, *Benefit Plans*, O. Reg. 286/01, s. 1.

ACTUARIAL COST. The cost of the service to be credited as determined at the date of the election and calculated with reference to the assumptions from the most recent actuarial valuation for funding purposes. *Public Service Pensions Act, 1991*, S.N. 1991, c. 12, s. 14.1.

ACTUARIAL EQUIVALENT. The equivalent in actuarial present value, calculated in accordance with demographic and economic factors that are recommended by an actuary and approved by the Minister. *Members of the Legislative Assembly Pension Plan Act*, R.S.A. 2000, c. M-12, Sched. 1, s. 1.

ACTUARIAL TABLE. Statistical data organized to show average life expectancies of persons.

ACTUARY. *n.* A Fellow of the Canadian Institute of Actuaries.

ACTUS REUS. [L.] 1. "... [T]he use of the expression 'actus reus' ... is liable to mislead, since it suggests that some positive act on the part of the accused is needed to make him guilty of a crime and that a failure or omission to act is insufficient to give rise to criminal liability unless some express provision in the statute that creates the offence so provides." *R. v. Miller*, [1983] 1 All E.R. 978 at 979 (H.L.), Diplock L.J. 2. A voluntary act of commission or of omission which caused results which constitute a criminal offence or form part of the criminal offence.

ACT WITHIN SCOPE OF EMPLOYMENT. To carry out assigned duties, functions or activities contemplated.

ACUPUNCTURE. *n.* An act of stimulation, by means of needles, of specific sites on the skin, mucous membranes or subcutaneous tissues of the human body to promote, maintain, restore or improve health, to prevent a disorder, imbalance or disease or to alleviate pain and includes the administration of manual, mechanical, thermal and electrical stimulation of acupuncture needles, the use of laser acupuncture, magnetic therapy or acupressure, and moxibustion (Jiu) and suction cup (Ba Guan). *Health Professions Act*, R.S.B.C. 1996, c. 183, *Traditional Chinese Med-*

icine Practitioners and Acupuncturists Regulation, B.C. Reg. 290/2008, s. 1.

A.C.W.S. *abbr.* All Canada Weekly Summaries, 1970-1979.

A.C.W.S. (2D). *abbr.* All Canada Weekly Summaries (Second Series), 1980-1986.

A.C.W.S. (3D). *abbr.* All Canada Weekly Summaries (Third Series), 1986-.

A.D. *abbr.* Anno Domini.

ADAPTIVE FUNCTIONING. A person's capacity to gain personal independence, based on the person's ability to learn and apply conceptual, social and practical skills in his or her everyday life. *Services and Supports to Promote the Social Inclusion of Persons with Developmental Disabilities Act, 2008*, S.O. 2008, c. 14, s. 3.

ADDED-VALUE CLAIM. Identifies a special characteristic of a product, generally a method of production or preparation, that is sought by the consumer. To qualify for an added-value claim, a product must be certified by an accredited certification body as compliant with standards defined by regulation of the Minister. *An Act respecting Reserved designations and added-value claims*, R.S.Q. c. A-20.03 s. 4 and 5.

ADDENDUM. *n.* Something added.

ADDICT. *n.* 1. Any person addicted to the improper use of cocaine, opium, or their derivatives, or any other narcotic drug which for the time being is included in the schedule to the Narcotic Control Act (Canada). *Narcotic Drug Addicts Act*, R.S.N.S. 1989, c. 307, s. 2.. 2. A person who is addicted to a substance other than alcohol. *Alcoholism and Drug Addiction Research Foundation Act*, R.S.O. 1990, c. A.16, s. 1.

ADDICTION. *n.* 1. Severe physiological and psychological dependence on drugs like narcotics or alcohol. F.A. Jaffe, *A Guide to Pathological Evidence for Lawyers and Police Officers*, 4th ed.(Toronto: Carswell, 1999) at 229. 2. Addiction to a substance other than alcohol. *Alcoholism and Drug Addiction Research Foundation* Act, R.S.O. 1990 c. A.16 s. 1.

ADDITIONAL VOLUNTARY CONTRIBU-TION. Under a pension plan means an optional contribution by a member that does not give rise to an obligation on the employer to make additional contributions. *Pension Benefits Standards Act, 1985*, R.S.C. 1985, c. 32 (2nd Supp.), s. 2.

ADDRESS. See CLOSING ~; DELIVERY ~.

ADDRESS FOR SERVICE. The address which a party gives to other parties and to the court for use in delivering documents or serving process during the course of proceedings.

ADDUCE. *v.* To present; to lead, in connection with evidence, to bring forward.

ADEMPTION. *n.* 1. "... [T]he taking away of the benefit by the act of the testator... ." *Re Tracy* (1913), 5 O.W.N. 530 at 531, 25 O.W.R. 413 (H.C.), Boyd C. 2. What occurs when a testator dies and the subject matter of a gift was converted into something else or

destroyed by the testator's act or by duly appointed authority. T. Sheard, R. Hull & M.M.K. Fitzpatrick, *Canadian Forms of Wills*, 4th ed. (Toronto: Carswell, 1982) at 168.

ADEMPTION BY ADVANCEMENT. When a testator provides in a will for a child or another person to whom that testator stands in loco parentis and after that advances to that child or person a sum of money, it is presumed that the testator did not intend to provide a double portion to that child or person at the expense of other children. T. Sheard, R. Hull & M.M.K. Fitzpatrick, *Canadian Forms of Wills*, 4th ed. (Toronto: Carswell, 1982) at 170.

ADEQUATE. *adj.* Sufficient; suitable.

ADEQUATE CONSIDERATION. Sufficient consideration; reasonable value for what is received.

ADEQUATE NOTICE. Reasonably sufficient notice.

ADEQUATE VALUABLE CONSIDERATION. A consideration of fair and reasonable money value with relation to that of the property conveyed, assigned or transferred or a consideration of fair and reasonable money value with relation to the known or reasonably to be anticipated benefits of the contract, dealing or transaction. *Bankruptcy and Insolvency Act*, R.S.C. 1985, c. B-3, s. 97(2).

ADHESION. See CONTRACT OF ~.

AD HOC. [L.] 1. For a particular purpose. 2. Appointed specially for a specified short period of time or until the occurrence of a stated event. *Public Officers Act*, R.S.C. 1985, c. P-31, *Formal Documents Regulations*, C.R.C., c. 1331, s. 2.

AD IDEM. [L. at the same point] Said when parties agree.

ADJECTIVE LAW. Law which relates to practice and procedure.

ADJOINING. *adj.* 1. Touching; coterminous. 2. "The word 'adjoining' is different from the word 'adjacent'. 'Adjoining' as its derivation implies, signifies being joint together; 'adjacent' is simply lying near." *Bowker & Richards, Re* (1905), 1 W.L.R. 194 at 196 (B.C. S.C.), Irving J. 3. "The word 'adjoining' as applied to parcels of land, does not necessarily imply that the parcels are to be in physical contact with each other; ..." *McKenzie v. Miniota School District*, [1931] 2 W.W.R. 105 at 106, [1931] 2 D.L.R. 695 (Man. K.B.), Dysart J.

ADJOURN. *v.* To postpone; to recess.

ADJOURNMENT. *n.* 1. Postponement or putting off business to another time or place. 2. Of Parliament, an interruption during the course of one and the same session. A. Fraser, W.A. Dawson & J. Holtby, eds., *Beauchesne's Rules and Forms of the House of Commons of Canada*, 6th ed. (Toronto: Carswell, 1989) at 66.

ADJUDGE. *v.* "... [T]o pronounce judicially ..." *R. v. Morris* (1979), 91 D.L.R. (3d) 161 at 182, [1979] 1 S.C.R. 405, 23 N.R. 109, 6 C.R. (3d) 36, 43 C.C.C. (2d) 129, Pratte J.

ADJUDICATE. *v.* To determine; to decide after a hearing.

ADJUDICATION. *n.* The decision or judgment of a court. See PROSPECTIVE ~.

ADJUDICATION DIVISION. A division of the Immigration and Refugee Board.

ADJUDICATIVE FACTS. 1. "... [T]wo categories of facts in constitutional litigation: 'adjudicative facts' and 'legislative facts'... . Adjudicative facts are those that concern the immediate parties: ..." *Danson v. Ontario (Attorney General)* (1990), 50 C.R.R. 59 at 69, 43 C.P.C. (2d) 165, 73 D.L.R. (4th) 686, [1990] 2 S.C.R. 1086, 41 O.A.C. 250, 74 O.R. (2d) 763n, 112 N.R. 362, the court per Sopinka J. 2. Adjudicative facts are those that concern the immediate parties and disclose who did what, where, when, how and with what motive or intent. *Public School Boards' Assn. (Alberta) v. Alberta (Attorney General)*; 2000 CarswellAlta 678, 2000 SCC 2, [2000] 1 S.C.R. 44, 182 D.L.R. (4th) 561, 251 N.R. 1, 250 A.R. 314, 213 W.A.C. 314, [2000] 10 W.W.R. 187, 82 Alta. L.R. (3d) 211, 9 C.P.C. (5th) 36, Binnie J.

ADJUDICATIVE FUNCTION. In respect of a public agency, means (i) a function assigned or authorized to be performed by the public agency under an enactment, the performance of which includes (A) the making of binding decisions in respect of applications, if the enactment authorizes the public agency to hold hearings respecting the applications, (B) the making of binding decisions in respect of disputes, other than disputes respecting applications, or (C) the hearing of reviews or appeals and the making of binding decisions in respect of those reviews or appeals, (ii) any alternative dispute resolution process that is ancillary to a function described in subclause (i), and (iii) a function specified in the regulations. *Alberta Public Agencies Governance Act*, S.A. 2009, c. A-31.5, s. 1.

ADJUDICATOR. *n.* A person who hears and determines a reference to adjudication.

ADJUNCT. *n.* Thing necessarily and actually employed in use of other thing. *McQueen v. R.* (1887), 16 S.C.R. 1.

ADJUNCT. *adj.* Additional.

ADJUST. *v.* To determine amount to be paid by insurer to insured when loss occurs.

ADJUSTER. *n.* A person who, (a) on behalf of an insurer or an insured, for compensation, directly or indirectly solicits the right to negotiate the settlement of or investigate a loss or claim under a contract or a fidelity, surety or guaranty bond issued by an insurer, or investigates, adjusts or settles any such loss or claim, (b) holds himself, herself or itself out as an adjuster, investigator, consultant or adviser with respect to the settlement of such losses or claims, but does not include, (c) a barrister or solicitor acting in the usual course of the practice of law, (d) a trustee or agent of the property insured, (e) a salaried employee of a licensed insurer while acting on behalf of such insurer in the adjustment of losses, (f) a person who is employed as an appraiser, engineer or other expert solely for the purpose of giving expert advice or evidence, or (g) a person who acts as an adjuster of marine losses only. *Insurance Act*, R.S.O. 1990, c. I.8, s. 1. See CLAIMS~.

ADJUSTMENT. *n.* 1. Settlement and ascertainment of the amount of indemnity which an insured may receive under a policy. 2. A change, usually an increase, in a salary, rate or benefit. See COST-OF-LIVING ~.

AD LIB. *abbr.* Ad libitum.

AD LIBITUM. [L.] At pleasure.

AD LITEM. [L.] For a suit; for the purposes of a suit. See ADMINISTRATOR ~; GUARDIAN ~.

ADM. CT. *abbr.* Admiralty Court.

ADMINISTER. *v.* 1. To manage; to control. 2. Includes prescribe, give, sell, furnish, distribute or deliver. *Food and Drugs Act*, R.S.C. 1985, c. F-27, *Food and Drug Regulations*, C.R.C., c. 870, c. G.04.001.

ADMINISTERING. *adj.* Acting as guardian or custodian or trustee or executor or administrator of the estate of a person or a deceased person. *Public Trustee Act*, R.S.N.S. 1989, c. 379, s. 2.

ADMINISTRATION. *n.* 1. "There is nothing in the words 'administration' and 'administrative' which excludes the proprietary or business decisions of governmental organizations. On the contrary, the words are fully broad enough to encompass all conduct engaged in by a governmental authority in furtherance of governmental policy – business or otherwise." *B.C. Developmment Corp. v. Friedmann*, [1984] 2 S.C.R. 447. 2. "... [T]he winding-up and distribution of the estate of a deceased person, ..." *Flynn v. Capital Trust Corp.* (1921), 51 O.L.R. 424 at 425, 62 D.L.R. 427 (H.C.), Middleton J. 3. Letters of administration of the property of deceased persons, whether with or without the will annexed and whether granted for general, special or limited purposes. See ANCILLARY ~; COURTS ~ SERVICE; GRANT OF ~; GRANT OF ~ WITH WILL ANNEXED; LETTERS OF ~; LETTERS OF ~ WITH WILL ANNEXED; LIMITED ~.

ADMINISTRATION AGREEMENT. An agreement between the Government of Canada and the government of a province or an aboriginal government under which (a) the Government of Canada will administer and enforce an Act of the legislature of the province, or legislation made by an aboriginal government, that imposes a tax and will make payments to the province or the aboriginal government in respect of taxes collected, in accordance with the terms and conditions of the agreement, or (b) the government of the province will administer and enforce an Act of Parliament that imposes a tax and will make payments to the Government of Canada in respect of the taxes collected, in accordance with the terms and conditions of the agreement. *Federal-Provincial Fiscal Arrangements Act*, R.S.C. 1985, c. F-8, s. 2.

ADMINISTRATION OF JUSTICE. 1. The term "administration of justice" is often used to indicate the processes by which those who break the law are investigated, charged and tried. More broadly, however, the term embraces maintaining the rule of law and upholding Charter rights in the justice system as a whole. *R. v. Grant*, 2009 SCC 32, [2009] 2 S.C.R. 353, McLachlin C.J. and Charron J. 2. (a) "[Di Iorio v. Montreal Jail (1976), 33 C.C.C. (2d) 2891 establishes that the police, criminal investigations, prosecutions, corrections, and the court system, all comprise part of the 'administration of justice' [as found in the Constitution Act, 1867 (30 & 31 Vict.), c. 3]." *MacKeigan v. Hickman* (1989), 61 D.L.R. (4th) 688 at 724, 99 N.R. 227n, 50 C.C.C. (3d) 449 (S.C.C.), McLachlin J. (L'Heureux-Dube and Gonthier JJ. concurring). (b) "Since Keable No. 1 [Quebec (Attorney General) v. Canada (Attorney General) (1978), [1979] 1 S.C.R. 218 ... and [Putnam v. Alberta (Attorney General) (1981), 37 N.R. 1], then it is clear that the boundaries of the 'administration of justice' do not include the discipline, organization and management of the R.C.M.P. In my dissent in Putnam I sought to make clear, however, that the 'administration of justice' does include the organization and management of police forces created by provincial legislation.'" *Robinson v. British Columbia* (1987) (sub nom. *O'Hara v. British Columbia*) 38 C.C.C. (3d) 233 at 243-44, [1988] 1 W.W.R. 216, 80 N.R. 127, 45 D.L.R. (4th) 527, 189 B.C.L.R. (2d) 273, [1987] 2 S.C.R. 591, Dickson C.J.C. (Beetz, McIntyre, Lamer, Wilson, Le Dain, La Forest and L'Heureux-Dube JJ. concurring). (c) " ... [I]nclude but are not limited to, the constitution, maintenance and organization of provincial Courts of civil and criminal jurisdiction and they include procedure in civil matters ..." *Di Iorio v. Montreal Jail* (1977), 73 D.L.R. (3d) 491 at 527, [1978] 1 S.C.R. 152, 35 C.R.N.S. 57, 8 N.R. 361, Dickson J. (Martland, Judson, Ritchie and Spence JJ. concurring). 3. The provision, maintenance and operation of, (a) the courts of justice of the Province of Ontario, (b) land registry offices, (c) jails, and (d) the offices of coroners and Crown Attorneys. *Administration of Justice Act*, R.S.O. 1990, c. A.6, s. 1. 4. The (a) provision, maintenance and operation of (i) courts of justice in British Columbia, (ii) court registry and land title offices, (iii) correctional centres as defined in the Correction Act, and prisons and lockups operated by (A) police forces, (B) police departments, (C) designated policing units, as defined in section 1 of the Police Act, or (D) designated law enforcement units, as defined in section 1 of the Police Act, (iv) the offices of coroner, Crown counsel, probation officers, court workers and sheriffs, and their officers, and (v) the police forces and police departments and any designated policing unit and designated law enforcement unit, as those terms are defined in section 1 of the Police Act, for the purpose of their functions, including functions given to the courts or offices, or to any official of them, under an Act, (b) prosecution of offences, and (c) provision of adequate legal services, including the operation of legal aid offices. *Justice Administration Act*, R.S.B.C. 1996, c. 243, s. 1. See BRING THE ~ INTO DISREPUTE; PROPER ~.

ADMINISTRATIVE. *adj.* 1. "... [I]t is reasonable to interpret 'administrative' as describing those func-

tions of Government which are not performed by the Legislative Assembly and the Courts. Broadly speaking, it describes that part of Government which administers the law and governmental policy." *Ontario (Ombudsman) v. Ontario (Health Disciplines Board)* (1979), 26 O.R. (2d) 105 at 148 (C.A.). 2. That which concerns ministerial or executive action, used in contradistinction to judicial, quasi-judicial or legislative.

ADMINISTRATIVE ACT. To adopt a policy, to make and issue a specific direction, and to apply a general rule to a particular case. To be contrasted with legislative and judicial acts. S.A. DeSmith, *Judicial Review of Administrative Action*, 4th ed. by J.M. Evans (London: Stevens, 1980) at 71.

ADMINISTRATIVE AUTHORITY. It is clear that the reference to "administrative" in "administrative authority" (Article 12) [of the Hague Convention on the Civil Aspects of International Child Abduction, 1980] or "administrative proceedings" (Article 7(f)) does not mean the Central Authority. Rather, the judicial or administrative authority under Article 12 means the entity charged with the responsibility of determining whether an order should be made to return the child. That entity is different in different Contracting States. In this Province, that entity is the courts. It is not the Central Authority. *M. (V.B.) v. J. (D.L.)*, 2004 NLCA 56.

ADMINISTRATIVE DISCRETION. In the work of an administrative agency, consideration not entirely susceptible of proof or disproof in relation to which the agency must make decisions.

ADMINISTRATIVE LAW. 1. Law relating to public administration. 2. The law which relates to the organization, duties and quasi-judicial and judicial powers of the executive, to proceedings before tribunals and to the making of subordinate legislation.

ADMINISTRATIVE NOTICE. The equivalent of judicial notice for an administrative tribunal. Those matters which a tribunal may accept as generally known without evidence being lead to prove the matters.

ADMINISTRATIVE PENALTY. 1. A penalty imposed for contravention of a prescribed provision of an Act or regulations, a condition of a licence, a compliance order, or an undertaking. Imposed after giving the person an opportunity to be heard. 2. [An] administrative penalty imposed is not analogous to a fine imposed in criminal proceedings where the failure to pay the fine could result in default time in prison. Enforcement of the penalty is by way of civil process. *Hogan v. British Columbia Securities Commission*, 2005 BCCA 53. 3. Administrative penalties under the Act are not punitive but are instead designed to protect the public. *Alberta Securities Commission v. Brost*, 2008 ABCA 326.

ADMINISTRATIVE TORT. Exists once it is shown that the invalid decision by a public officer is tainted by either malice or knowledge of lack of authority. *Comeau Sea Foods v. Canada (Fisheries & Oceans)* (1995), 123 D.L.R. (4th) 180 (Fed. C.A.).

ADMINISTRATIVE TRIBUNAL. A person or body before whom a matter is heard, contrasted with a court.

ADMINISTRATIVE TRIBUNAL OF QUÉBEC.
The function of the Tribunal, in the cases provided
for by law, is to make determinations in respect of
proceedings brought against an administrative authority or a decentralized authority. The Tribunal
shall consist of four divisions: the social affairs division; the immovable property division; the territory
and environment division; and the economic affairs
division. The social affairs division is charged with
making determinations in respect of the proceedings
pertaining to matters of income security or support
and social aid and allowances, of protection of persons whose mental state presents a danger to themselves or to others, of health services and social services, of pension plans, of compensation and of
immigration, which proceedings are listed in Schedule I. The immovable property division is charged
with making determinations in respect of proceedings
pertaining in particular to the accuracy, presence or
absence of an entry on the property assessment roll
or on the roll of rental values, exemptions from or
refunds of property taxes or the business tax, the
fixing of the indemnities arising from the establishment of reserves for public purposes or from the expropriation of immovables or immovable real rights
or from damage caused by public works or the value
or acquisition price of certain property, which proceedings are listed in Schedule II. The territory and
environment division is charged with making determinations in respect of proceedings pertaining in particular to decisions made or orders issued concerning
the use, subdivision or alienation of a lot, the inclusion or exclusion of a lot in or from an agricultural
zone, the removal of topsoil, the emission, deposit,
issuance or discharge of contaminants in the environment or the carrying on of an activity likely to affect
the quality of the environment, or the erection of
certain roadside advertising signs, which are listed in
Schedule III. The economic affairs division is
charged with making determinations in respect of
proceedings pertaining in particular to decisions concerning permits, licences, certificates or authorizations to carry on a trade or a professional, economic,
industrial or commercial activity, which are listed in
Schedule IV. *An Act respecting administrative justice*, R.S.Q. c. J-3.

ADMINISTRATOR. *n.* 1. The administrator of the
federal government is the Chief Justice of Canada
who acts when the Governor General is absent. The
Chief Justice of each province performs the same
function in the absence of the Lieutenant Governor.
2. " ... [T]he person to whom the property of a person
dying intestate is committed for administration and
whose duties with respect thereto correspond with
those of an executor." *Minister of National Revenue
v. Parsons* (1983), 4 Admin L.R. 64 at 79, [1983]
C.T.C. 321, 83 D.T.C. 5329 (Fed. T.D.), Cattanach
J. 3. The Governor in Council may appoint an Administrator to act as Commissioner during the Commissioner's absence or illness or other inability or
when that office is vacant. *Yukon Act, 2002*, S.C.
2002, c. 7, s. 5. See CHIEF ~; LITIGATION~.

ADMINISTRATOR AD LITEM. An administrator
of an estate appointed for the purpose of conducting

litigation. May now be referred to as a litigation administrator.

ADMINISTRATOR DE SON TORT. A person
who is neither an executor nor an administrator but
is either involved with the deceased's personal property or does other things characteristic of an executor.

ADMINISTRATOR WITH WILL ANNEXED.
An administrator appointed to administer a testator's
estate where the executors named in the will refuse
or are unable to act.

ADMINISTRATRIX. *n.* A woman appointed to administer the estate of a person who died without appointing an executor in a will or without leaving a
will.

ADMIN. L.J. *abbr.* Administrative Law Journal.

ADMIN. L.R. *abbr.* Administrative Law Reports,
1983-1992.

ADMIN L.R. (2D). *abbr.* Administrative Law Reports (Second Series), 1992-1998.

ADMIN L.R. (3D). *abbr.* Administrative Law Reports (Third Series), 1998-.

ADMIRALTY COURT. The Federal Court.

ADMIRALTY LAW. Maritime law.

ADMIRALTY PROCEEDING. The Federal
Courts Act sets out the maritime or Admiralty jurisdiction of the Federal Court. The Federal Court has
concurrent original jurisdiction, between subject and
subject as well as otherwise, in all cases in which a
claim for relief is made or a remedy is sought under
or by virtue of Canadian maritime law or any other
law of Canada relating to any matter coming within
the class of subject of navigation and shipping, except
to the extent that jurisdiction has been otherwise specially assigned. *Federal Courts Act*, R.S.C. 1985, c.
F-7, s. 22(1). See CANADIAN MARITIME LAW.

ADMISSIBILITY. See CONDITIONAL ~.

ADMISSIBLE EVIDENCE. Relevant evidence not
otherwise excluded.

ADMISSION. *n.* 1. A confession, concession or voluntary acknowledgement made by a party, or someone identified with him in legal interest, of the existence of a fact which is relevant to the cause of an
adversarial party. *Vector Energy v. Canadian Pioneer Energy Inc.* (1996) 50 C.P.C. (3d) 148 (Alta.
Q.B.). 2. Excludes confession. *R. v. Rothman* (1981),
20 C.R. (3d) 97 at 122, [1981] 1 S.C.R. 640, 59
C.C.C. (2d) 30, 121 D.L.R. (3d) 578, 35 N.R. 485,
Estey J. (dissenting) (Laskin C.J.C. concurring). 3.
Under the rules of evidence, statements made by an
accused are admissions by an opposing party and, as
such, fall into an exception to the hearsay rule. They
are admissible for the truth of their contents. When
statements are made by an accused to ordinary persons, such as friends or family members, they are
presumptively admissible without the necessity of a
voir dire. It is only where the accused makes a statement to a "person in authority", that the Crown bears
the onus of proving the voluntariness of the statement
as a prerequisite to its admission. This, of course, is

the confessions rule. *R. v. S.G.T.*, 2010 SCC 20, Charron J. 4. Facts admitted by the opposite party in civil proceeding or allegations made by the plaintiff and not disputed the defendant. 5. Silence may be taken as an admission where a denial would be the only reasonable course of action expected if that person were not responsible. *R. v. Warner* (1994), 94 C.C.C. (3d) 540 (Ont. C.A.). 6. The acknowledgment of a fact which may produce legal consequences against the person who makes it. *Civil code*, S.Q. 1991, c. 64, a. 2850. 7. In respect of a place of amusement or a seminar, an activity or an event, means a right of entry or access to, or attendance at, the place of amusement or the seminar, activity or event. *Excise Tax Act*, R.S.C. 1985, c. E-15, s. 123. 8. Call to the bar. 9. Official acceptance of a patient or resident into the hospital or facility. See FORMAL ~; JUDICIAL ~; LAWFUL ~; SOLEMN ~.

ADMISSION AGAINST INTEREST. A statement made by one of the parties to an action which amounts to a prior acknowledgement by him that one of the material facts relevant to the issues is not as he now claims it is. *Vector Energy v. Canadian Pioneer Energy Inc.* (1996) 50 C.P.C. (3d) 148 (Alta. Q.B.).

ADMISSION OF SERVICE. Acknowledgement that a true copy of the document was received.

ADOLESCENTS. *n.* Teenage children under the age of majority. *Saskatchewan School Division No. 4 v. Hall*, 2009 SKCA 118.

ADOPT. *v.* 1. To accept a contract as binding; to select; to choose. 2. To take on responsibility for a child as if the child were one's own biological child. 3. A witness may adopt a videotaped statement if he or she, whether or not presently recalling the events discussed, believes them to be true because he or she recalls giving the videotaped statement and attempting at that time to be honest and truthful. *R. v. Meddoui* [1991] 2 W.W.R. 289 (Alta. C.A.). 4. A local government adopts a bylaw where it approves or accepts the bylaw. See MATERIAL ~ED BY REFERENCE.

ADOPTION. *n.* 1. "... [I]n its popular sense it means the act by which a person adopts as his own the child of another or, in other terms, the acceptance by a person of a child of other parents to be the same as his own child." *Anderson v. Minister of National Revenue*, [1947] 4 D.L.R. 262 at 280, [1947] Ex C.R. 389, [1947] C.T.C. 223, Angers J. 2. "... '[A]doption' bears the meaning 'putting into operation' or 'passing' when used in s. 240 [of the Municipal Act, R.S.B.C. 1960, c. 255] with reference to a resolution ..." *Winter v. Surrey (District)* (1976), 72 D.L.R. (3d) 273 at 274 (B.C. S.C.), Legg J. 3. A trade-mark is deemed to have been adopted by a person when that person or his predecessor in title commenced to use it in Canada or to make it known in Canada or, if that person or his predecessor had not previously so used it or made it known, when that person or his predecessor filed an application for its registration in Canada. 4. Adoption is not another form of custody. It is the total extinguishing of the birth parents' rights and the establishment legally, retroactively and permanently, of a parent-child relationship between a child and a person who is not the biological parent of the child. *K. v. B.* (1995), 125 D.L.R. (4th) 653 (Ont. Prov. Ct.). 5. Adoption of a cheque by signing a written acknowledgement of responsibility for its face value is similar to a ratification of the cheque. *Newell v. Royal Bank of Canada* (1997), 147 D.L.R. (4th) 268 (N.S.C.A.). See HAGUE CONVENTION ON ~; INTERCOUNTRY ~.

ADOPTION BY REFERENCE. Incorporation of a separate statement, statute, by-law, etc. into the original statement, statute, by-law, etc. by referring to it.

ADOPTION LEAVE. A leave of absence allowed to an employee to care for a newly adopted child.

ADOPTION OF CONTRACT. Acceptance of a contract as binding.

ADR. *abbr.* Alternative dispute resolution.

ADS. *abbr.* [L. ad sectam] At the suit of. Used when the defendant's name is put first in the title of a proceeding.

AD SECTAM. [L. at the suit of] Used in its abbreviated form ads. or ats. when the defendant's name is put first in the title of a proceeding.

AD TESTIFICANDUM. [L.] For the purpose of testifying.

ADULT. *n.* One who is neither a young person nor a child.

ADULTERATION. *n.* Mixing into any substance intended for sale an ingredient which is either dangerous to health or which turns the substance into something other than what it is represented to be.

ADULTERY. *n.* Voluntary sexual intercourse between a spouse and any person other than his wife or her husband while the marriage exists.

ADULT INTERDEPENDENT PARTNER. A person is the adult interdependent partner of another person if (a) the person has lived with the other person in a relationship of interdependence (i) for a continuous period of not less than 3 years, or (ii) of some permanence, if there is a child of the relationship by birth or adoption, or (b) the person has entered into an adult interdependent partner agreement with the other person under section 7. *Adult Interdependent Relationships Act*, R.S.A. 2000, c. A-4.5, s. 3.

ADULT INTERDEPENDENT RELATIONSHIP. The relationship between 2 persons who are adult interdependent partners of each other. *Adult Interdependent Relationships Act*, R.S.A. 2000, c. A-4.5, s. 1.

ADULT MOTION PICTURE. Any of the following: (a) a motion picture that was submitted for review under the former Act or under section 2(1) of this Act for the purpose of exhibition in a theatre and that, following the review, (i) was not approved, (ii) was approved, but had a portion removed, or (iii) was approved, but with a condition that it may only be exhibited in theatres designated by the director; (b) a motion picture that has not been reviewed under section 5 that depicts (i) explicit sexual scenes, (ii) the coercing, through the use or threat of physical force or by other means, of a person to engage in a sexual act, if that sexual act is depicted in explicit sexual scenes or sexually suggestive scenes, (iii) incest or necrophilia, (iv) bondage in a sexual context, (v) persons who are or who appear to be under the age of 14 involved in sexually suggestive scenes, whether or not they appear nude or partially nude, (vi) persons who are or who appear to be under the age of 18 involved in explicit sexual scenes, (vii) explicit sexual scenes involving violence, (viii) scenes of brutality or torture to persons or animals, depicted in a realistic and explicit manner, or (ix) sexual conduct between a human being and an animal; (c) a motion picture that contains scenes that depict conduct or an activity that is prescribed in a regulation made under section 14(2)(d). *Motion Picture Act*, R.S.B.C. 1996, c. 314, s. 1.

ADULT SENTENCE. In the case of a young person who is found guilty of an offence, means any sentence that could be imposed on an adult who has been convicted of the same offence. *Youth Criminal Justice Act*, S.C. 2002, c. 1, s. 2.

A. DU N. *abbr.* Annales du notariat et de l'enregistrement.

ADV. *abbr.* [L.] Adversus.

AD VALOREM. [L.] According to their value, used in reference to customs or duties.

AD VALOREM DUTY. Duty is imposed in the form of a percentage on the value of the dutiable property.

ADVANCE. *v.* 1. To pay. *Foster v. Minister of National Revenue*, [1971] C.T.C. 335 at 339, 71 D.T.C. 5207 (Ex. Ct.), Jackett P. 2. Pay before due. *Bronester Ltd. v. Priddle*, [1961] 3 All E.R. 471 at 475 (C.A.), Holroyd Pearce L.J. 3. Includes lend and give.

ADVANCE. *n.* 1. Payment made before due. 2. "... [A]dvances of money either by way of loan or payment at the request of the legatee... ." *Hauck v. Schmaltz*, [1935] S.C.R. 478 at 482, [1935] 3 D.L.R. 691, the court per Lamont J. 3. Although the word could refer to something other than money the primary meaning is in relation to money. *Klaue v. Bennett* (1989), 62 D.L.R. (4th) 367 (B.C.C.A.). 4. The word "advance" is typically used in connection with payments made by a lender to a borrower. *Air Canada, Re* (2003), 66 O.R. (3d) 257 (C.A.). See FUTURE ~.

ADVANCEMENT. *n.* 1. Promotion. 2. A single outlay for a defined purpose. 3. Paying to a beneficiary part of the capital of a gift before the actual time when the capital falls into the beneficiary's hands. D.M.W. Waters, *The Law of Trusts in Canada*, 2d ed. (Toronto: Carswell, 1984) at 930. 4. The doctrine of advancement creates a presumption that where property is purchased in the name of another, or transferred to another without consideration, a resulting trust arises in favour of the person who paid the purchase price. *Chartier v. Chartier* (1999), 235 N.R. 1 (S.C.C.). See ADEMPTION BY ~; PRESUMPTION OF ~.

ADVANCEMENT OF EDUCATION. One of the four heads of charity in the classic definition of that term by Lord MacNaghten. It includes the training of the mind and the improvement of a useful branch of human knowledge and its public dissemination. See CHARITY.

ADVANCE POLLING DAY. The day preceding ordinary polling day.

ADVANTAGE. See NO MAN CAN TAKE ~ OF HIS OWN WRONG.

ADVENTURE. *n.* A hazardous enterprise. See CO-~; JOINT ~; MARINE ~.

ADVENTURE IN THE NATURE OF TRADE. 1. A transaction of the same kind carried on in the same way as a transaction of an ordinary trader or dealer in property of the same kind as the subject matter of the transaction. *Loewen v. Minister of National Revenue* (1994), 166 N.R. 266 (Fed. C.A.). 2. An adventure is in the nature of trade when it has none of the essential characteristics of an investment, but is a mere speculation if the purpose is not to earn income, but to turn to profit on prompt realization. *M.N.R. v. Sissons*, [1969] S.C.R. 507, [1969] C.T.C. 184, 69 D.T.C. 5152.

ADVERSARIAL SYSTEM. 1. A system by which disputes between opposing parties are resolved be an impartial arbiter after hearing evidence and argument presented by both parties. 2. An adversarial system, which is the norm in Canada, relies on the parties—who are entitled to disclosure of the case to meet, and to full participation in open proceedings—to produce the relevant evidence. *Charkaoui v. Canada (Citizenship and Immigration)*, 2007 SCC 9. 3. In an adversarial system of criminal trials, trial judges must, barring exceptional circumstances, defer to the tactical decisions of counsel. There is a "strong presumption" that defence counsel are competent in advancing the interests of their clients. Moreover, counsel will generally be in a better position to assess the wisdom, in light of their overall trial strategy, of a particular tactical decision than is the trial judge. By contrast, trial judges are expected to be impartial arbiters of the dispute before them; the more a trial judge second guesses or overrides the decisions of counsel, the greater is the risk that the trial judge will, in either appearance or reality, cease being a neutral arbiter and instead become an advocate for one party. For these reasons, this Court has previously held that the burden to raise evidentiary issues properly rests on the shoulders of counsel. The corollary of the preceding is that trial judges should seldom take it upon themselves, let alone be required, to second guess the tactical decisions of counsel. *R. v. S.G.T.*, 2010 SCC 20, Charron J. See ADVERSARY SYSTEM.

ADVERSARY. *n.* A party opposed to another in interest; a litigant.

ADVERSARY SYSTEM. "Procedure in our Courts is based on the adversary system, that is to say each party must present the evidence on which it seeks to rely and attempt to refute the other party's evidence by cross-examination of its witnesses or rebuttal proof... ." *Canadians for the Abolition of the Seal Hunt v. Canada (Minister of Fisheries & the Environment)* (1980), 20 C.P.C. 151 at 162, [1981] 1 F.C. 733, 10 C.E.L.R. 1, 111 D.L.R. (3d) 222 (T.D.), Walsh J. See ADVERSARIAL SYSTEM.

ADVERSE. *adj.* Opposed in interest; unfavourable; hostile.

ADVERSE CLAIM. 1. Includes a claim that a transfer was or would be unauthorized or wrongful or that a particular adverse person is the owner of or has an interest in the security. *Corporations acts.* 2. A claim that (i) the claimant has a property interest in a financial asset, and (ii) it is a violation of the rights of the claimant for another person to hold, transfer or deal with the financial asset. *Securities Transfer acts.*

ADVERSE EFFECT. 1. An unwanted effect brought about by the normal dose of a drug. F.A. Jaffe, *A Guide to Pathological Evidence for Lawyers and Police Officers*, 4th ed. (Toronto: Carswell, 1999) at 83. 2. One or more of, (a) impairment of the quality of the natural environment for any use that can be made of it, (b) injury or damage to property or to plant or animal life, (c) harm or material discomfort to any person, (d) an adverse effect on the health of any person, (e) impairment of the safety of any person, (f) rendering any property or plant or animal life unfit for human use, (g) loss of enjoyment of normal use of property, and (h) interference with the normal conduct of business. *Environmental Protection Act*, R.S.O. 1990, c. E. 19, s.1.

ADVERSE EFFECT DISCRIMINATION. 1. "... [A]rises where an employer for genuine business reasons adopts a rule or standard which is on its face neutral, and which will apply equally to all employees, but which has a discriminatory effect upon a prohibited ground on one employee or group of employees in that it imposes because of some special characteristic of the employee or group, obligations, penalties, or restrictive conditions not imposed on other members of the workforce... ." *Ontario (Human Rights Commission) v. Simpsons-Sears Ltd.* (1985), 9 C.C.E.L. 185 at 199, [1985] 2 S.C.R. 536, 52 O.R. (2d) 799, 17 Admin L.R. 89, 86 C.L.L.C. 17,002, 64 N.R. 161, 7 C.H.R.R. D / 3102, 23 D.L.R. (4th) 321, 12 O.A.C. 241, the court per McIntyre J. 2. Adverse effect discrimination occurs when a law, rule or practice is facially neutral but has a disproportionate impact on a group because of a particular characteristic of that group. *Egan v. Canada,* 1995 CarswellNat 6, 12 R.F.L. (4th) 201, 95 C.L.L.C. 210-025, C.E.B. & P.G.R. 8216, 124 D.L.R. (4th) 609, 182 N.R. 161, 29 C.R.R. (2d) 79, [1995] 2 S.C.R. 513, 96 F.T.R. 80 (note), Cory and Iacobucci JJ. (dissenting). See MEIORIN TEST.

ADVERSE INFERENCE. The "adverse inference" principle is derived from ordinary logic and experience, and is not intended to punish a party who exercises its right not to call the witness by imposing an "adverse inference" which a trial judge in possession of the explanation for the decision considers to be wholly unjustified. *R. c. Jolivet,* 2000 CarswellQue 805, 2000 SCC 29, 144 C.C.C. (3d) 97,

33 C.R. (5th) 1, 185 D.L.R. (4th) 626, [2000] 1 S.C.R. 751, 254 N.R. 1, the court per Binnie J.

ADVERSE IN INTEREST. A party is adverse in interest to another if he has a direct pecuniary or other substantial legal interest adverse to the legal interest of the other party even though they are on the same side of the record and there is no issue on the record that the court will be called upon to adjudicate between them.

ADVERSE PARTY. The opposite party.

ADVERSE POSSESSION. 1. "The essentials to be established in a case of adverse possession are that the claimant be in possession and that the true owner be out of possession... ." *Lutz v. Kawa* (1980), 15 R.P.R. 40 at 54, 112 D.L.R. (3d) 271, 23 A.R. 9 (C.A.), the court per Laycraft J.A. 2. "In order for possession to extinguish true title the adverse claimant must prove that the possession was open, notorious and continuous, to the exclusion of the owner for the full statutory period. Acts of possession which are simply equivocal, or occasional will not be enough to displace paper title." *Burke Estate v. Nova Scotia (Attorney General)* (1991), 107 N.S.R. (2d) 91 at 103, 290 A.P.R. 91 (T.D.), Saunders J.

ADVERSE WITNESS. A hostile witness, one hostile in mind to the party calling him, or a witness who gives evidence that is contrary to the prior statement of the party who calls him and who shows intention not to tell the truth. *Skender v. Barker* (1987), 18 B.C.L.R. (2d) 57 (S.C.).

ADVERSUS. [L.] Against, abbreviated "v.".

ADVERTENT NEGLIGENCE. Imports an element of intentionally driving in a manner one knows or recognizes to be dangerous or negligent. *R. v. Mason* (1990), 60 C.C.C. (3d) 338, at 340 (B.C. C.A.).

ADVERTISE. *v.* To make any representation to the public by any means, other than a label, whatever for the purpose of promoting directly or indirectly the sale of a product. *Consumer Packaging and Labelling Act*, R.S.C. 1985, c. C-38, s. 2.

ADVERTISEMENT. *n.* 1. Any representation by any means whatever for the purpose of promoting directly or indirectly the sale or disposal of any food, drug, cosmetic or device. *Food and Drugs Act*, R.S.C. 1985, c. F-27, s. 2. 2. Any of the following that refers to any election or promotes the candidacy of a particular person: (i) a visual publication, display or representation consisting of images or text; (ii) any audio publication or representation; (iii) any advertisement, hand bill, placard, poster, circular, circular letter pamphlet; (iv) any electronic or digital display; (v) any radio or television broadcast that refers to any election or promotes the candidacy of a particular person. *The Election Act, 1996,* S.S. 1996, c. E-6.01, s. 215.

ADVERTISING. See ELECTION ~.

ADVICE. *n.* 1. " ... [I]n ordinary parlance means primarily the expression of counsel or opinion, favourable or unfavourable as to action, but it may, chiefly in commercial usage, signify information or intelligence ..." *J.R. Moodie Co. v. Minister of National Revenue*, [1950] 2 D.L.R. 145 at 148, [1950]

C.T.C. 61 (S.C.C.), Rand J. (Rinfret C.J.C. concurring). 2. [I]n ordinary usage, "advice" can mean communication in the nature of a recommendation regarding a decision, as well as simply information or intelligence. "Advice" [in s. 13(1) of the Freedom of Information and Protection of Privacy Act, R.S.O. 1990, c. F.31] may be construed more broadly than "recommendation" to encompass material that permits the drawing of inferences with respect to a suggested course of action, but which does not itself make a specific recommendation. *Ontario (Ministry of Transportation) v. Cropley* (2005), 202 O.A.C. 379. See LEGAL ~.

ADVISE. *v.* To notify.

ADVISEMENT. *n.* Deliberation.

ADVISER. See MINISTERIAL ~.

ADVISORY COMMITTEE. A committee established under a statute to provide advice, usually to the government of the day.

ADVISORY OPINION. An answer to a hypothetical question put to a court.

ADVOCACY. *n.* 1. The act of pleading for, supporting a position or viewpoint. 2. Skillful advocacy involves taking information acquired as a result of the trial, the evidence, the other party's theory of the case, and various other, intangible factors, and weaving this information together with law, logic and rhetoric into a persuasive argument. *R. v. Rose* (1998), 20 C.R. (5th) 246, at 289, (S.C.C.) Cory, Iacobucci and Bastarache JJ.

ADVOCATE. *n.* 1. The supporter of a cause who assists a client with advice and pleads for the client. 2. A barrister and solicitor. 3. A member of the Bar of Quebec; a member of the Order of Advocates. See ORDER OF ~S.

ADVOCATE. *n.* The periodical, Advocate.

ADVOCATES' Q. *abbr.* The Advocates' Quarterly.

ADVOCATES' SOC. J. *abbr.* The Advocates' Society Journal.

ADVOCATE (TOR.). *abbr.* The Advocate, published by the Student Law Society, Faculty of Law, University of Toronto.

ADVOCATE (VAN.). *abbr.* The Advocate, published by the Vancouver Bar Association.

ADVOW. *v.* To maintain or justify an act.

ADWARE. *n.* Advertising placed in other software with the intent of generating revenue.

AEQUITAS EST QUASI EQUALITAS. [L.] Equity is, in a manner of speaking, equality.

AEQUITAS NUNQUAM CONTRAVENIT LEGIS. [L.] Equity never contravenes the common law.

AERODROME. *n.* Any area of land, water (including the frozen surface thereof) or other supporting surface used, designed, prepared, equipped or set apart for use either in whole or in part for the arrival, departure, movement or servicing of aircraft and includes any buildings, installations and equipment situated thereon or associated therewith. *Aeronautics Act*, R.S.C. 1985, c. A-2, s. 3.

AERONAUTICAL PRODUCT. Any aircraft, aircraft engine, aircraft propeller or aircraft appliance or part or the component parts of any of those things, including any computer system and software. *Aeronautics Act*, R.S.C. 1985, c. A-2, s. 3.

AERONAUTICS. *n.* 1. "... [A]ir transportation as a whole." *Bensol Customs Brokers v. Air Canada* (1979), 99 D.L.R. (3d) 623 at 630, [1979] 2 F.C. 575 (T.D.), Le Dain J. 2. "... [A]s used in this section [Federal Court Act, R.S.C. 1970, c. 10, s. 23], certainly includes the control and regulation of air navigation over Canada, and regulation and control of aerodromes and air stations as well as the investigation of air accidents, such as used in the Aeronautics Act, R.S.C. 1970, c. A-3." *Canadian Fur Co. v. KLM Royal Dutch Airlines* (1974), 52 D.L.R. (3d) 128 at 133, [1974] 2 F.C. 944 (T.D.), Addy J. 3. Parachuting involves aeronautics since the parachutist navigates his or her fall and controls the motion and direction of the fall. *Mercier v. Alberta (Attorney General)* (1997), 145 D.L.R. (4th) 692 (Alta. C.A.).

AFFAIRS. *n.* 1. That which concerns a person in trade or property. 2. The relationships among a body corporate, its affiliates and the shareholders, directors and officers of those bodies corporate but does not include the business carried on by those bodies corporate. 3. Professional or public business. *Law Society of Upper Canada v. Ontario (Attorney General)*, 1995 CarswellOnt 800, 31 Admin. L.R. (2d) 134, 21 O.R. (3d) 666, 121 D.L.R. (4th) 369, Borins J. 4. To be distinguished from the business of a company. A time limit for sending of proxies relates to the affairs of a company, not to its business. *Beatty v. First Exploration Fund 1987 & Co.* (1988), 25 B.C.L.R. (2d) 377 (S.C.). 5. The word "affairs" as used in s. 21(9)(c) [of Canada Business Corporations Act, R.S.C. 1985, c. C-44] relates to the relationships between the corporation, shareholders, directors and officers. Any use of the securities register that involves communication between shareholders - as shareholders, or regarding the corporation, directors and/or officers is an allowable use. *EnCana Corp. v. Douglas*, 2005 ABCA 439. See DEPARTMENT OF VETERANS ~.

AFFECT. *v.* "... '[T]o act upon or have an effect upon' ..." *Desjarlais v. Piapot Band, No. 75* (1989), [1990] 1 C.N.L.R. 39 at 41, [1989] 3 F.C. 605, 12 C.H.R.R. C / 466 (C.A.), Desjardins J.A.

AFFECTED. *adj.* [T]he ordinary and natural meaning of the phrase ["a person affected by a decision of the board" in s. 65(1) of the Assessment Act, R.S.B.C. 1996, c. 20] would include persons such as [tenants] who have an interest in the land being assessed and whose rent will be increased or decreased as a result of a change in the assessment of the property. *Morguard Investments Ltd. v. Coquitlam Assessor, Area No. 12*, 2006 BCCA 26.

AFFECTION. See INJURIOUS ~; NATURAL ~.

AFFIANT. *n.* A person who makes an affidavit.

AFFIDAVIT. *n.* 1. A written statement supported by the oath of the deponent or by a solemn affirmation, administered and attested by any person authorized by law to administer oaths. Includes a statutory declaration. 2. An affirmation when made by a person entitled to affirm. 3. Includes a solemn declaration, or statutory declaration, and an agreed statement of facts. *Judicature Act*, R.S.N. 1990, c. J-4, s. 2. See COMMISSIONER FOR TAKING ~S; CROSS-EXAMINATION ON ~.

AFFIDAVIT OF DOCUMENTS. A descriptive listing of the documents which a party to an action possesses, controls or has in their power.

AFFIDAVIT OF MERITS. An affidavit which a defendant files and which responds to a specially endorsed writ.

AFFIDAVIT OF SERVICE. An affidavit certifying that a document has been served on a party to a proceeding.

AFFILIATION. *n.* 1. The establishment of a bond between two or more organizations. 2. A process through which a child's parentage is determined. *Kirkpatrick v. Maroughan*, [1927] 3 D.L.R. 546 at 548, 60 O.L.R. 495 (C.A.), Middleton J.A.

AFFILIATION ORDER. "... There are two parts to the order; in some jurisdictions, such as Nova Scotia, there are two distinct orders. The first part of the one order or the first of two orders establishes the respondent's paternity while the second directs the payment of maintenance for the child. Maintenance can be directed if, and only if, paternity is established." *Works v. Holt* (1976), 22 R.F.L. 1 at 11 (Ont. Prov. Ct.), Beaulieu Prov. J.

AFFILIATION PROCEEDING. An application or action to determine paternity of a child.

AFFINITY. *n.* Relationship through marriage.

AFFIRM. *v.* 1. To promise in solemn form to tell the truth while giving evidence or when making an affidavit. *R. v. Jim*, 2006 BCCA 573. 2. To confirm a lower court's decision. 3. When a party who is entitled to void a contract but chooses not to avoid the contract, to carry it out or act as though bound by it, the party is said to affirm the contract.

AFFIRMANT. *n.* One who solemnly affirms.

AFFIRMATION. *n.* A solemn declaration with no oath. A person who objects to taking an oath may affirm, and the affirmation has the same effect as an oath. See OATH OR ~ OF CITIZENSHIP.

AFFIRMATIVE. *adj.* Asserting positively.

AFFIRMATIVE ACTION. "Affirmative action has been defined by Laycraft J.A. (as he then was) and adopted by the Supreme Court of Canada [in] Athabasca Tribal Council v. Amoco Can. Petroleum Co., [1981] 1 S.C.R. 699 ... : 'Terms and conditions imposed for the benefit of groups suffering from economic and social disadvantages, usually as a result of past discrimination, and designed to assist them to achieve equality with other segments of the population are referred to as "affirmative action" programs.' " *Shewchuk v. Ricard* (1986), 24 C.R.R. 45 at 52, 2

B.C.L.R. (2d) 324, [1986] 4 W.W.R. 289, 1 R.F.L. (3d) 337, 28 D.L.R. (4th) 429 (C.A.), Nemetz C.J.B.C.

AFFIRMATIVE DEFENCE. Also called confession and avoidance. The defendant confesses or admits the facts alleged but then states fresh facts or grounds which afford an answer to them. *Ryan v. Kirby* (1993), 25 C.P.C. (3d) 34 (P.E.I. T.D.).

AFFIRMATIVE EASEMENT. Confers a right on its holder to commit an act or acts upon the servient easement.

AFFIRMATIVE PREGNANT. An assertion implying a negation in favour of the adverse party.

AFFIXED. *adj.* As applied to goods, erected upon or affixed or annexed to land in a manner and under circumstances to constitute them fixtures.

AFFRAY. *n.* The act of fighting in any public street or highway, or fighting to the alarm of the public in any other place to which the public have access. *Criminal Code*, R.S.C. 1927, c. 36, s. 100.

AFFREIGHTMENT. *n.* A contract in which a shipowner agrees to carry goods in exchange for a reward.

AFFRONT. *v.* To insult; to offend especially by showing disrespect.

AFFRONT. *n.* A word or act showing intentional disrespect.

AFORESAID. *adj.* Mentioned previously.

AFORETHOUGHT. *adj.* Considered or thought of previously. See MALICE ~.

A FORTIORI. [L.] 1. By so much stronger reason. 2. Much more.

AFTER-MARKET. *n.* The market in a security once it has been sold initially by the issuer.

A.G. *abbr.* Attorney General.

AGAINST. See AS ~.

AGAINST INTEREST. Used to describe a statement or admission which is adverse to the position or interest of the person making the statement or admission.

AGE. *n.* 1. " ... [I]ndicia of maturity, reflecting a length of time which a being or thing has been in existence ..." *R. v. Panarctic Oils Ltd.* (1982), 12 C.E.L.R. 78 at 92 (N.W.T. Terr. Ct.), Bourassa Terr. Ct. J. 2. 18 years of age or older. *Alberta Human Rights Act*, R.S.A. 2000, c. A-25.5, s. 44(1). 3. Any age of 18 years or more. *Saskatchewan Human Rights Code*, S.S. 1979, c. S-24.1, s. 2. 4. An age that is 18 years or more, except in subsection 5(1) where "age" means an age that is 18 years or more. *Human Rights Code* R.S.O. 1990, c. H.19, s.10(1). 5. A person attains an age specified as a number of years at the first instant of the corresponding anniversary of his or her birth. *Legislation Act, 2006*, S.O. 2006, c. 21, Sched. F, s. 90. See FULL ~; LEGAL ~; NON-~; PENSIONABLE ~.

AGENCY. *n.* 1. A relationship existing between two persons. One, called the agent, is legally considered to represent the other, called the principal, in a way which affects the principal's legal position in relation to third parties. G.H.L. Fridman, *The Law of Agency*, 6th ed. (London: Butterworths, 1990) at 9. 2. "... [A] local place of business from which an agent acts for his principal, ...'" *Minister of National Revenue v. Panther Oil & Grease Manufacturing Co.*, [1961] C.T.C. 363 at 378, 61 D.T.C. 1222 (Ex. Ct.), Thorson P. See CANADA BORDER SERVICES ~; CANADA EMISSION REDUCTION INCENTIVES ~; CANADA REVENUE ~; CANADIAN ENVIRONMENTAL ASSESSMENT ~; CANADIAN FOOD INSPECTION ~; CANADIAN TRANSPORTATION ~; CLEARING ~; COLLECTION ~; CONSUMER REPORTING ~; CREDIT REPORTING ~; DEPOSIT PROTECTION ~; ECONOMIC DEVELOPMENT ~ OF CANADA FOR THE REGIONS OF QUEBEC; EMPLOYMENT ~; EXPRESS ~; FINANCIAL CONSUMER ~ OF CANADA; GRATUITOUS ~; INTERNATIONAL ~; LAW OF ~; MARKETING ~; PARKS CANADA ~; PERSONNEL ~; PUBLIC HEALTH ~.

AGENCY OF NECESSITY. A form of agency which arises when a person, in an emergency, acts on behalf of another despite the lack of a formal agreement between the persons to this effect.

AGENDA. *n.* A schedule or list of the business items to be considered at a meeting.

AGENT. *n.* 1. One who acts for another whether for any form of remuneration or not. 2. [A]nyone who does something for another is for that very limited purpose an "agent" *Penderville Apartments Development Partnership v. Cressey Development Corp.* (1990), 43 B.C.L.R. (2d) 57 (B.C. C.A.), Southin J.A. 3. A person who, for another or others, for compensation, gain or reward, or hope or promise thereof, either alone or through one or more officials or salesmen, trades in real estate. 4. Used to describe the position of a person who is employed by another to perform duties often of a technical or a professional nature which he discharges as that other's alter ego and not merely as a conduit pipe between the principal and the third party. *MacDonald v. Roth*, 2000 CarswellBC 2416, 2000 BCSC 1670, 83 B.C.L.R. (3d) 171.5. Includes an employee. Criminal Code, R.S.C. 1985, c. C-46, s. 426(4). See BARGAINING ~; CROWN ~; DEL CREDERE ~; ELECTRONIC ~; EXCLUSIVE ~; GENERAL ~; HAZARDOUS ~; INSURANCE ~; LITERARY~; MERCANTILE ~; OFFICIAL ~; PARLIAMENTARY ~; PATENT ~; REVISING ~; SPECIAL ~; TRADE-MARK ~; TRAVEL ~.

AGENT-GENERAL. *n.* The representative of a province in another country.

AGENT OF THE STATE. A peace officer and a person acting under the authority of, or in cooperation with, a peace officer. *Criminal Code*, R.S.C. 1985, c. C-46, s. 184.1.

AGENT PROVOCATEUR. "... [O]ne who ... provides the opportunity for a person to commit a crime that of his own volition and intent and without encouragement he intended to commit when opportu-nity presented itself, ..." *R. v. Shipley*, [1970] 2 O.R. 411 at 414 (Co. Ct.), McAndrew Co. Ct. J.

AGENT'S LIEN. The right of an agent to retain goods in her possession until the principal pays the amount owing to the agent in respect of the goods.

AGE OF CONSENT. The age at which a person may marry without parental approval.

AGE OF CRIMINAL RESPONSIBILITY. The age at which a child may be held responsible for a criminal act.

AGE OF MAJORITY. 18 or 19 years of age; traditionally was 21 years of age; the age at which a person has full rights and responsibilities in legal matters.

AGGRAVATED ASSAULT. Wounding, maiming, disfiguring or endangering the life of the complainant. *Criminal Code*, R.S.C. 1985, c. C-46, s. 268.

AGGRAVATED BY SERVICE. In respect of an injury or a disease, means an injury or a disease that has been aggravated, if the aggravation (a) was attributable to or was incurred during special duty service; or (b) arose out of or was directly connected with service in the Canadian Forces. *Canadian Forces Members and Veterans Re-establishment and Compensation Act*, S.C. 2005, c. 21, s. 2.

AGGRAVATED DAMAGES. 1. "... [A]warded to compensate for aggravated damage... . take account of intangible injuries and by definition will generally augment damages assessed under the general rules relating to the assessment of damages... ." *Vorvis v. Insurance Corp. of B.C.*, [1989] 1 S.C.R. 1085 at 1099, McIntyre J. 2. Aggravated damages may be awarded in circumstances where the defendant's conduct has been particularly high-handed or oppressive, thereby increasing the plaintiff's humiliation and anxiety arising from the libellous statement. If aggravated damages are to be awarded, there must be a finding that the defendant was motivated by actual malice, which increased the injury to the plaintiff, either by spreading further afield the damage to the reputation of the plaintiff, or by increasing the mental distress and humiliation of the plaintiff. *Hill v. Church of Scientology* [1995] 2 S.C.R. 1130. 3. Damage awards which extend beyond the class of compensatory damages have found expression in a variety of terms but the most common of these are exemplary and punitive damages. The term "exemplary" was preferred by the House of Lords, while "punitive" is the term used in many Canadian Courts. These two terms are, in effect, interchangeable. Aggravated damages are in fact a form of compensatory damages which incorporates intangible aspects of the wrong. *Carrier Lumber Ltd. v. British Columbia*, 1999 CarswellBC 1741, 47 B.L.R. (2d) 50, 30 C.E.L.R. (N.S.) 219, [1999] B.C.T.C. 192 (S.C.), Parrett J.

AGGRAVATED SEXUAL ASSAULT. Wounding, maiming, disfiguring or endangering the life of the complainant in committing a sexual assault. *Criminal Code*, R.S.C. 1985, c. C-46, s. 273.

AGGRAVATING CIRCUMSTANCE. In sentencing an individual convicted of an offence, the following are deemed to be aggravating circumstances: (i) evidence that the offence was motivated by bias, prejudice or hate based on race, national or ethnic origin, language, colour, religion, sex, age, mental or physical disability, sexual orientation, or any other similar factor, (ii) evidence that the offender, in committing the offence, abused the offender's spouse or common-law partner, (ii.1) evidence that the offender, in committing the offence, abused a person under the age of eighteen years, (iii) evidence that the offender, in committing the offence, abused a position of trust or authority in relation to the victim, (iv) evidence that the offence was committed for the benefit of, at the direction of or in association with a criminal organization, or (v) evidence that the offence was a terrorism offence. *Criminal Code*, R.S.C. 1985, c. C-46, s. 718.2 (part).

AGGRAVATION. *n.* Increasing the enormity of a wrong.

AGGREGATE. *n.* 1. Collection of people, parts or things in order to form a whole. 2. "... [I]mplies a plurality of units whose total amount it represents." *Minister of National Revenue v. Imperial Oil Ltd.*, [1960] C.T.C. 275 at 297, [1960] S.C.R. 735, 60 D.T.C. 1219, 25 D.L.R. (2d) 321, Ritchie J. (Kerwin C.J.C., Judson and Martland JJ. concurring). See CORPORATION ~.

AGGREGATION. *n.* Adding together all property passing at death in a single estate to ascertain succession.

AGGRIEVED. *adj.* 1. "... [A] party is aggrieved or may be aggrieved [under the Ombudsman Act, R.S.B.C. 1979, c. 306, s. 10] whenever he genuinely suffers, or is seriously threatened with, any form of harm prejudicial to his interests, whether or not a legal right is called into question." *British Columbia Development Corp. v. British Columbia (Ombudsman)* (1984), 11 Admin L.R. 113 at 136, [1984] 2 S.C.R. 447, [1985] 1 W.W.R. 193, 55 N.R. 298, 14 D.L.R. (4th) 129, the court per Dickson J. 2. "... [W]ronged ..." *Friends of Toronto Parkland v. Toronto (City)* (1991), 6 O.R. (3d) 196 at 205, 86 D.L.R. (4th) 669, 8 M.P.L.R. (2d) 127 (Div. Ct.), O'Driscoll, Hartt and O'Brien JJ.

AGONY OF COLLISION. The doctrine of agony of collision arises in circumstances where a party, often a motorist, is suddenly confronted by an emergency situation of someone else's making, which the party is then unable to avoid. The doctrine comes to the assistance of such a party who may happen to make a wrong decision in attempting to avoid the hazard *provided that* the party confronted by the emergency has not been negligent. *Leddicote v. Nova Scotia (Attorney General)*, 2002 NSCA 47, 203 N.S.R. (2d) 271, 635 A.P.R. 271, 28 M.V.R. (4th) 189.

AGONY OF THE MOMENT. This doctrine relieves a driver from having to exercise extraordinary skill, presence of mind, poise or self control when an emergency situation arises through no fault of their own. If the driver's instantaneous reaction was not inherently unreasonable the contract will not attract liability even though the person might otherwise be considered to be negligent in other circumstances.

AGREE. *v.* To concur; to make an agreement.

AGREED. *adj.* Settled.

AGREED STATEMENT OF FACTS. A statement of facts relating to evidence to which the parties agree and on which the case will be decided. P.K. McWilliams, *Canadian Criminal Evidence*, 3d ed. (Aurora: Canada Law Book, 1988) at 1-13.

AGREEMENT. *n.* 1. Two or more persons together express a common intention in order to alter their duties and rights. 2. A contract. 3. A collective agreement. 4. "... [I]n its more proper and correct sense, as signifying a mutual contract on consideration between two or more parties... ." *Wain v. Walters* (1804), 5 East 10 at 16-17, Lord Ellenborough C.J. 5. "... used, as synonymous to promise or undertaking, ..." *Wain v. Walters* (1804), 5 East 10 at 16-17, Lord Ellenborough C.J. 6. Conspiracy is a form of agreement which may be actual or tacit. An agreement requires the meeting of minds. Discussion, negotiation and talking alone do not constitute an agreement. See ADMINISTRATION ~; ARBITRATION ~; ASSUMPTION ~; COHABITATION ~; COLLECTIVE ~; COLLECTIVE BARGAINING ~; CONSUMER ~; CONTINGENCY ~; CREDIT ~; CUSTODY ~; DIRECT ~; ENCROACHMENT ~; ENTIRE ~ CLAUSE; EXTRADITION ~; FRAMEWORK ~; FRANCHISE ~; FUTURE PERFORMANCE ~; HIRE-PURCHASE ~; IMPACT AND BENEFIT ~; INTERNET ~; LAND CLAIMS ~; LAST CHANCE ~; LEASE ~; LEASE MODIFICATION ~; LISTING ~; LOAN ~; MARY CARTER ~; MEMORANDUM OF ~; NATIONAL MOBILITY ~; PAROL ~; PATERNITY ~; POOLING ~; PRICE MAINTENANCE ~; PROTECTION ~; RECIPROCAL TRANSFER ~; REMOTE ~; SALE ~; SALES TAX HARMONIZATION ~; SCALE ~; SECURITY ~; SELF-GOVERNMENT ~; SEPARATION ~; SOFTWOOD LUMBER ~; STANDSTILL ~; TAX COLLECTION ~; TAX TREATMENT ~; TENANCY ~; TIME SHARE ~; TITLE TRANSFER CREDIT SUPPORT ~; TRADE ~; UNANIMOUS ~; UNIT ~; WORLD TRADE ORGANIZATION ~; WTO ~.

AGREEMENT FOR SALE. A contract for the sale of an interest in land under which the purchaser agrees to pay the purchase price over a period of time, in the manner stated in the contract, and on payment of which the vendor is obliged to convey the interest in land to the purchaser.

AGREEMENT TO SELL. 1. A contract of sale under which the transfer of the property in the goods is to take place (a) at a future time, or (b) subject to a condition that is to be fulfilled after the making of the contract. *Sale of Goods Act*, R.S.N.W.T. 1988, c. S-2, s. 1. 2. A written agreement, made between a grain elevator operator and an owner of grain, for the sale of grain that is stored or to be stored. *Grains Act*, R.S.O. 1990, c. G.10, s. 1.

AGROLOGY. *n.* Using agricultural and natural sciences and agricultural and resource economics, including collecting or analyzing data or carrying out research or assessments, to design, evaluate, advise on, direct or otherwise provide professional support to (a) the cultivation, production, improvement, processing or marketing of aquatic or terrestrial plants or animals, or (b) the classification, management, use, conservation, protection, restoration, reclamation or enhancement of aquatic or terrestrial ecosystems that are affected by, sustain, or have the potential to sustain the cultivation or production of aquatic or terrestrial plants or animals. *Agrologists Act,* S.B.C. 2003, c. 13. s. 1. See PRACTICE OF ~.

AIBA. *abbr.* Aboriginal Impact and Benefit Agreement.

AID. *v.* "... [T]o assist or help." *R. v. Stevenson* (1984), 11 C.C.C. (3d) 443 at 449, 62 N.S.R. (2d) 193, 136 A.P.R. 193 (C.A.), the court per Macdonald J.A.

AID. *n.* 1. Assistance. 2. A useful device. 3. A person who provides assistance. See CERTIORARI IN ~; LEGAL ~.

AID AND ABET. 1. "Mere presence at the scene of a crime is not sufficient to ground culpability. Something more is needed: encouragement of the principal offender; an act which facilitates the commission of the offence, such as keeping watch or enticing the victim away, or an act which tends to prevent or hinder interference with accomplishment of the criminal act, such as preventing the intended victim from escaping or being ready to assist the prime culprit.... . Presence at the commission of an offence can be evidence of aiding and abetting [Criminal Code, R.S.C. 1970, c. C-34, s. 21(1)(b)] if accompanied by other factors, such as prior knowledge of the principal offender's intention to commit the offence or attendance for the purpose of encouragement." *R. v. Dunlop* (1979), 99 D.L.R. (3d) 301 at 313, 317, [1979] 2 S.C.R. 881, [1979] 4 W.W.R. 599, 47 C.C.C. (2d) 93, 8 C.R. (3d) 349, 12 C.R. (3d) 330, 27 N.R. 153, Dickson J. (Laskin C.J.C., Spence and Estey JJ. concurring). 2. "An accused who is present at the scene of an offence and who carries out no overt acts to aid or encourage the commission of the offence may none the less be convicted as a party if his purpose in failing to act was to aid in the commission of the offence.... . The authorities to which I have referred support the conclusion that where the accused had a duty to prevent the commission of an offence, or where he was in a position to have control over the acts of the offender and failed to prevent the commission of the offence, he will be guilty as an aider and abettor." *R. v. Nixon* (1990), 57 C.C.C. (3d) 97 at 109, 114, 47 B.C.L.R. (2d) 222, 78 C.R. (3d) 349, [1990] 6 W.W.R. 253 (C.A.), the court per Legg J.A.

AID TO NAVIGATION. A buoy, beacon, lighthouse, landmark, radio aid to marine navigation or any other structure or device installed, built or maintained in or on water or on land for the purpose of assisting with marine navigation. *Canada Shipping Act, 2001,* S.C. 2001, c. 26, s. 125.

AIDE. See MOBILITY ~.

AIR AMBULANCE SERVICES. Includes all services provided by an ambulance service in connection with the transportation of persons by air. *Ambulance Act,* R.S.O. 1990, c. A.19, s. 1.

AIR CARRIER. Any person who operates a commercial air service. *Aeronautics Act,* R.S.C. 1985, c. A-2, s. 3.

AIRCRAFT. *n.* 1. Any machine capable of deriving support in the atmosphere from reactions of the air. 2. Flying machines and guided missiles that derive their lift in flight chiefly from aerodynamic forces, and flying devices that are supported chiefly by their buoyancy in air, and includes any aeroplane, balloon, kite balloon, airship, glider or kite. *National Defence Act,* R.S.C. 1985, c. N-5, s. 2. See CANADIAN ~; CIVIL ~; DANGEROUS OPERATION OF ~.

AIRCRAFT INSURANCE. Insurance against (a) liability arising out of bodily injury to, or the death of, a person, or the loss of, or damage to, property, in each case caused by an aircraft or the use of an aircraft; or (b) the loss of, the loss of use of, or damage to, an aircraft. *Insurance Companies Act,* S.C. 1991, c. 47, Sched.

AIR CUSHION VEHICLE. A vehicle other than a motor vehicle, that is designed to derive support and thrust in the atmosphere primarily from reactions against the earth's surface of air expelled from the vehicle and that is commonly referred to as a "hovercraft". *The Highway Traffic Act,* S.M. 1985-86, c. 3, s. 197.

AIR OF REALITY. A judge in a criminal case must instruct a jury on any defence which has an "air of reality". The threshold test for air of reality is met when there is an evidentiary basis for the defence which, if believed, would allow a reasonable jury properly instructed to acquit. *R. v. Lemky* [1996] 1 S.C.R. 757.

AIR POLLUTION. A condition of the air, arising wholly or partly from the presence in the air of any substance, that directly or indirectly (a) endangers the health, safety or welfare of humans; (b) interferes with the normal enjoyment of life or property; (c) endangers the health of animal life; (d) causes damage to plant life or to property; or (e) degrades or alters, or forms part of a process of degradation or alteration of, an ecosystem to an extent that is detrimental to its use by humans, animals or plants. *Canadian Environmental Protection Act, 1999,* S.C. 1999, c. 33, s. 3.

AIRPORT. *n.* An aerodrome in respect of which a Canadian aviation document is in force. *Aeronautics Act,* R.S.C. 1985, c. A-2, s. 3. See AERODROME.

AIR SERVICE. A service, provided by means of an aircraft, that is publicly available for the transportation of passengers or goods, or both. *Canada Transportation Act, 1996,* S.C. 1996, c. 10, s. 55.

AIR SPACE. In relation to an air space parcel, is volumetric. *Terminal City Club Tower v. Vancouver Assessor, Area No. 09,* 2004 BCCA 466, Southin J.A.

AIR SPACE PLAN. A plan that (a) is described in the title to it as an air space plan, (b) shows on it one or more air space parcels consisting of or including air space, and (c) complies with the requirements. *Land Title Act*, R.S.B.C. 1996, c. 250, s. 138.

AIR TRAFFIC CONTROL COMMUNICA-TIONS. [Air traffic control] communications may be air-to-ground, ground-to-air and ground-to-ground communications, that is, from the air control tower to the air crew in flight or on the ground, or to vehicles on the ground. Controllers also communicate by means of interphone communication with other control towers and vehicles on the runway. *Canada (Information Commissioner) v. Canadian Transportation Accident Investigation & Safety Board*, 2006 FCA 157.

A.J.D.Q. *abbr.* Annuaire de jurisprudence et de doctrine du Québec, 1997?-.

ALARM. See FALSE ~ OF FIRE; SECURITY ~.

ALARM MONITOR. A security employee whose duties are, by his or her security employee licence, restricted to the monitoring of security alarms. *Private Investigators and Security Agencies Act*, R.S.B.C. 1996, c. 374, s. 1.

ALARM SERVICE. See SECURITY ~.

ALCOHOL. *n.* 1. A product of fermentation or distillation of grains, fruits or other agricultural products rectified once or more than once whatever may be the origin thereof, and includes synthetic ethyl alcohol. 2. Any material or substance whether in liquid or any other form containing any proportion by mass or by volume of absolute ethyl alcohol (C_2H_5OH). *Excise Act*, R.S.C. 1985, c. E-14, s. 3. 3. Ethyl alcohol, the active ingredient in alcoholic beverages, which depresses the nervous system. F.A. Jaffe, *A Guide to Pathological Evidence for Lawyers and Police Officers*, 4th ed. (Toronto: Carswell, 1999) at 239. See FETAL ~ SYNDROME.

ALCOHOL IGNITION INTERLOCK DEVICE. A device prescribed by regulation that is designed to detect, when installed in a motor vehicle, the presence of alcohol in a driver's body and, if the blood alcohol concentration level of the driver exceeds the limit prescribed by regulation, to prevent the motor vehicle from being started or from being driven. *Motor Vehicle Act*, R.S.N.B. 1973, c. M-17, s. 310.11.

ALDERMAN. *n.* A member of a council of a municipality other than the mayor.

ALDERPERSON. *n.* A member of municipal council other than the mayor.

ALEATORY CONTRACT. 1. When the extent of the obligations or of the advantages is uncertain, the contract is aleatory. *Civil Code*, S.Q. 1991, c. 64, a. 1382. 2. A contract which depends on an uncertain event or contingency. R. Colinvaux, *The Law of Insurance*, 5th ed. (London: Sweet & Maxwell, 1984) at 3.

ALIAS. *n.* A name by which a person is known.

ALIAS WRIT. A replacement for an earlier writ which has been lost or has become ineffectual.

ALIBI. *n.* 1. An alibi defence is a defence that says that the accused was elsewhere when the crime took place. *R. v. Rohde*, 246 C.C.C. (3d) 18, (Ont. C.A.).. 2. "... [N]ot confined to the situation where the accused claims to have been elsewhere when the actual offence was committed. It may refer to a separate and particular ingredient of an offence, or it may refer to a claim to have been elsewhere when any particular event is alleged to have taken place." *R. v. O'Neill* (1973), 6 N.B.R. (2d) 656 at 662, 22 C.R.N.S. 359 (C.A.), the court per Limerick J.A.

ALIEN. *v.* To transfer; to convey.

ALIEN. *n.* 1. At common law, the subject of a foreign government who was not born within the allegiance of the Crown. 2. A person who is not a Canadian citizen, Commonwealth citizen, British subject or citizen of the Republic of Ireland. *Canadian Citizenship Act*, R.S.C. 1970, c. C-19, s. 2.

ALIENABILITY. *n.* The quality of being transferable.

ALIENATE. *v.* " '... [H]as a technical legal meaning, and any transfer of real estate, short of a conveyance of the title, is not an alienation of the estate. No matter in what form the sale may be made, unless the title is conveyed to the purchaser, the estate is not alienated:' Masters v. Madison County Mututal Ins. Co. (1852), 11 Barb 624." *Meek v. Parsons* (1900), 31 O.R. 529 at 533 (Div. Ct.), Armour C.J.

ALIENATION. *n.* "... [B]ased on a voluntary transfer of the right of ownership... ." *Syndicat national des employés de la comm. scolaire régionale de l'Outaouais v. Union des employés de service, Local 298* (1988), 89 C.L.L.C. 14,045 at 12,399, 35 Admin. L.R. 153, 95 N.R. 161, 24 Q.A.C. 244, [1988] 2 S.C.R. 1048, Beetz J. See RESTRAINT ON ~.

ALIENEE. n. One to whom property is transferred.

ALIENI JURIS. [L.] Under the power of someone else, as opposed to sui juris.

ALIENOR. *n.* A person who transfers property.

ALIMENTARY. *adj.* Protective.

ALIMONY. *n.* 1. "... [O]riginally the word 'alimony' was limited to payments made by a husband to his wife up and until their marriage was dissolved and that any payments made or ordered to be paid thereafter were strictly called 'maintenance'." *Rystrom v. Rystrom* (1954), 14 W.W.R. (N.S.) 118 at 119, [1955] 2 D.L.R. 345 (Sask. C.A.), the court per Gordon J.A. 2. Includes a sum made payable for the maintenance of a wife, former wife, husband, former husband or a child pursuant to a judgment of divorce, nullity of marriage or judicial separation. *Former Maintenance Orders Enforcement acts*.

ALIQUOT. *adj.* A part of a whole obtained by dividing the whole evenly leaving no remainder. *Pinewood Aggregates Ltd. v. Ontario (Director of Titles)*, [1964] 1 O.R. 83 at 85, 41 D.L.R. (2d) 178 (H.C.), Hughes J.

ALITER. [L.] Otherwise.

ALIUNDE. [L.] From some other place or person.

ALL DUE DILIGENCE. A defence to avoid conviction for contravention of a regulatory offence. The

ALLEGATION

defendant must show that he or she exercised every precaution reasonable in the circumstances. See DUE DILIGENCE.

ALLEGATION. *n.* Assertion.

ALLEGE. *v.* To state, to assert positively. *R. v. O'Malley*, [1924] 3 D.L.R. 430 at 432, 2 W.W.R. 652 (Alta. C.A.), the court per Stuart J.A.

ALLEGIANCE. *n.* Obedience owed to the sovereign or government. See OATH OF ~.

ALL E.R. *abbr.* All England Law Reports.

ALL FOURS. A phrase to describe cases which agree in all their circumstances.

ALLOCATION. *n.* Appropriation or assignment of funds to particular purposes or people. See ENERGY SUPPLIES ~ BOARD; MANDATORY ~ PROGRAM; PATRONAGE ~.

ALLODIAL LANDS. *var.* **ALODIAL LANDS.** Lands held absolutely and not the estate of any lord or superior.

ALLONGE. *n.* Paper added to a bill of exchange to provide space for endorsements.

ALLOT. *v.* 1. To indicate that something should belong solely to a specific person. 2. To appropriate shares to those who applied for them.

ALLOTMENT. *n.* 1. "As applied to a fixed quantity of anything or a fixed number of shares, the word 'allotment' can mean nothing more than to give, to assign, to set apart, to appropriate... ." *Nelson Coke & Gas Co. v. Pellatt* (1902), 4 O.L.R. 481 at 489 (C.A.), McLellan J.A. 2. Distribution of land. 3. The portion of land distributed. 4. "... [T]he acceptance by the company of the offer to take shares." *Re Florence Land, etc. Co., Nicol's Case* (1885), 29 CH. D. 421 at 426, Chitty J.

ALLOW. *v.* 1. To permit; to admit something is valid. 2. Section 167 [of the *Criminal Code*, R.S.C. 1985, c. C-46] requires that the accused "allow" the indecent performance . . . s. 167 is a full *mens rea* offence . . . the requirement that the accused "allow" an indecent performance implies, at the very least, a requirement of concerted acquiescence or wilful blindness on the part of the accused. Indeed, I would equate "allow" in this context with "knowingly" in the context of [*R. v. Jorgensen*, [1995] 4 S.C.R. 55]. *R. v. Mara*, 1997 CarswellOnt 1983, 213 N.R. 41, 115 C.C.C. (3d) 539, 101 O.A.C. 1, 148 D.L.R. (4th) 75, 8 C.R. (5th) 1, 33 O.R. (3d) 384, 44 C.R.R. (2d) 243, [1997] 2 S.C.R. 630, the court per Sopinka J.

ALLOWANCE. *n.* 1. A limited predetermined sum of money paid to enable the recipient to provide for certain kinds of expenses; its amount is determined in advance and, once paid, it is at the complete disposition of the recipient who is not required to account for it. *The Queen v. Pascoe*, [1975] C.T.C. 58, 75 D.T.C. 5427 (Fed. C.A.). 2. An amount payable under a statutory or contractual scheme. See CAPITAL COST ~; RETIRING ~; TRADE-IN ~.

ALLOWANCE UNIT. See BC ~.

ALL RISKS. 1. An "all risks" policy of property insurance, like any other insurance policy, represents an agreed allocation between an insurer and an insured of those risks that the insurer is prepared to underwrite and those that are to be borne by the insured. Insurance policies of this type provide broad coverage for losses and damage to property. But they do not provide coverage against all conceivable perils. *Canadian National Railway v. Royal & Sun-Alliance Insurance Co. of Canada*, 222 O.A.C. 129, Rosenberg and Cronk JJ.A. 2. Coverage under an all risks policy extends to damage caused by fortuitous circumstance or causality not resulting from misconduct or fraud by the insured unless coverage is excluded by a specific provision. It does not extend to ordinary wear and tear or to depreciation.

ALL SEASONS RESORT. A resort business operated or intended to be operated for the purpose of providing (a) single-seasonal or multi-seasonal recreational activities, and (b) facilities for or related to those recreational activities, and includes a resort operated principally to provide alpine skiing and snowboarding to customers by fixed lifts, in return for user fees. *Resort Timber Administration Act*, S.B.C. 2006, c. 30, s. 1.

ALLUREMENT. *n.* An object which is likely to attract persons onto another person's property.

ALLUVION. *n.* The deposits of earth and augmentations which are gradually and imperceptibly formed on riparian lands of a watercourse. *Civil Code*, S.Q. 1991, c. 64, a. 965.

ALTA. L.R. *abbr.* Alberta Law Reports, 1908-1933.

ALTA. L.R.B.R. *abbr.* Alberta Labour Relations Board Reports, 1986-.

ALTA. L. REV. *abbr.* Alberta Law Review.

ALTA. L.R. (2D). *abbr.* Alberta Law Reports (Second Series), 1976-1992.

ALTA. L.R. (3D). *abbr.* Alberta Law Reports (Third Series), 1992-.

ALTA. P.U.B. *abbr.* Alberta Public Utilities Board Decisions, 1976-.

ALTERATION. See SUBSTANTIAL ~.

ALTER EGO. [L.] Second self.

ALTERNATIVE. *n.* One of several possibilities.

ALTERNATIVE DISPUTE RESOLUTION. 1. A term for processes such as arbitration, conciliation, mediation and settlement, designed to settle disputes without formal trials. 2. "This [nonbinding arbitration] differs from other forms of ADR [Alternative Dispute Resolution] in which the parties themselves are part of the decision-making mechanism and the neutral third party's involvement is of a facilitative nature: e.g. mediation, conciliation, neutral evaluation, non-binding opinion, non-binding arbitration. Of course, the simplest method—often overlooked—is that of non-involvement by a neutral: a negotiation between the parties. It is not unusual that ADR resolutions are conducted privately; more to the point, I suspect it would be unusual to see a public

ADR session especially where the focus is on coming to a consensual arrangement. The parties need to have the opportunity of discussion and natural give and take with brainstorming and conditional concessions giving without the concern of being under a microscope. If the parties were under constant surveillance, one could well imagine that they would be severely inhibited in the frank and open discussions with the result that settlement ratios would tend to dry up. The litigation system depends on a couple of percent of new cases only going to trial. If this were doubled to several percent the system would collapse. Therefore in my view public policy supports the non-trial resolution of disputes ...” *887574 Ontario Inc. v. Pizza Pizza Ltd.*, 1994 CarswellOnt 1214, 35 C.P.C. (3d) 323, 23 B.L.R. (2d) 239 (Ont. Gen. Div. [Commercial List]), Farley J.

ALTERNATIVE DISPUTE RESOLUTION MECHANISM. Includes mediation, conciliation, negotiation or any other means of facilitating the resolution of issues in dispute. *Statutory Powers Procedure Act*, R.S.O. 1990, c. S.22, s. 4.8. See DISPUTE RESOLUTION PROCESS.

ALTERNATIVE FORMAT. With respect to personal information, a format that allows a person with a sensory disability to read or listen to the personal information. *Personal Information Protection and Electronic Documents Act, 2000*, S.C. 2000, c. 5, s. 2.

ALTERNATIVE FUEL. Fuel that is (a) for use in motor vehicles to deliver direct propulsion, (b) less damaging to the environment than conventional fuels, and (c) prescribed by regulation, including, without limiting the generality of the foregoing, ethanol, methanol, propane gas, natural gas, hydrogen or electricity when used as a sole source of direct propulsion energy. *Alternative Fuels Act*, S.C. 1995, c. 20, s. 2(1).

ALTERNATIVE LIABILITY. “... [I]f an injured party cannot identify which of two or more defendants caused an injury, the burden of proof may shift to the defendants to show that they were not responsible for the harm... .” *Valleyview Hotel Ltd. v. Montreal Trust Co.* (1985), 33 C.C.L.T. 282 at 286, 39 Sask. R. 229 (C.A.), the court per Tallis J.A.

ALTERNATIVE MEASURES. Measures other than judicial proceedings used to deal with a young person alleged to have committed an offence under the Criminal Code or Youth Criminal Justice Act. Refers to consensual measures such as sentencing circles.

ALTERNATIVE OBLIGATION. An alternative obligation is one which has two principal prestations as its object, the performance of either of which releases the debtor for the whole. An obligation is not considered to be alternative if, when it arose, one of the prestations could not be the object of the obligation. The choice of the prestation belongs to the debtor, unless it has been expressly granted to the creditor. Where, after being put in default, the party who has the choice of the prestation fails to exercise it within the time allotted to him to do so, the choice of the prestation passes to the other party. *Civil Code*, S.Q. 1991, c. 64, a. 1545 and 1546.

AMALGAMATED COMPANY. A company that results from an amalgamation.

AMALGAMATION. *n.* The word “amalgamation” does not admit of a single meaning. Used in the corporate law context, an amalgamation may extinguish old entities and create new entities in their place, or it may blend those pre-existing entities and continue them under the auspices of the new amalgamated entity. The effect of a particular amalgamation depends on the purpose the amalgamation is intended to promote, as discerned by an examination of the agreement or statute bringing about the amalgamation. *MacPump Developments Ltd. v. Sarnia (City)*, 1994 CarswellOnt 631, 24 M.P.L.R. (2d) 1, 20 O.R. (3d) 755, 75 O.A.C. 378, 120 D.L.R. (4th) 662, 28 Admin. L.R. (2d) 127 (C.A.) Doherty J.A. See HORIZONTAL ~; VERTICAL ~.

AMBASSADOR. *n.* The head of a diplomatic mission.

AMBIGUITY. *n.* 1. Doubtfulness. 2. What, then, in law is an ambiguity? To answer, an ambiguity must be “real” The words of the provision must be “reasonably capable of more than one meaning”. For this reason, ambiguity cannot reside in the mere fact that several courts—or, for that matter, several doctrinal writers—have come to differing conclusions on the interpretation of a given provision. Just as it would be improper for one to engage in a preliminary tallying of the number of decisions supporting competing interpretations and then apply that which receives the “higher score”, it is not appropriate to take as one’s starting point the premise that differing interpretations reveal an ambiguity. It is necessary, in every case, for the court charged with interpreting a provision to undertake the contextual and purposive approach set out by Driedger [”Construction of Statutes” (3rd ed. 1994)], and *thereafter* to determine if “the words are ambiguous enough to induce two people to spend good money in backing two opposing views as to their meaning” [John Willis, “Statute Interpretation in a Nutshell” (1938), 16 Can. Bar Rev. 1, at pp. 4, 5]. *Bell ExpressVu Ltd. Partnership v. Rex* [2002] 2 S.C.R. 559. 3. Ambiguity in the meaning of criminal statues has always been resolved by choosing the meaning which is most favourable to the accused. The principle that ambiguous penal provisions must be interpreted in favour of an accused does not mean that the most restrictive possible meaning of any word used in the penal statute must always be the preferred meaning. The principle applies only where there is true ambiguity as to the meaning of a word in a penal statute . . . . The meaning of words cannot be determined by examining those words in isolation. Meaning is discerned by examining words in their context. True ambiguities in a statute exist only where the meaning remains unclear after a full contextual analysis of the statute. *R. v. Mac* (2001) 140 O.A.C. 270. See LATENT ~; PATENT ~.

AMBIGUOUS. *adj.* “[A word is ambiguous if] no meaning it reasonably has could effect the legislative intent, or if the legislative intent could not be ascertained ..." *Xerox of Canada Ltd. v. Ontario Regional Assessment Commissioner, Region No. 10* (1980), (*sub nom. Ontario Regional Assessment Commissioner, Region No. 10 v. Xerox of Canada Ltd.*) 11 O.M.B.R. 238 at 244, 30 O.R. (2d) 90, 17 R.P.R. 72, 115 D.L.R. (3d) 428 (C.A.), Jessup J.A.

AMBIT. *n.* Limit; the bounds encompassing any thing.

AMBULANCE SERVICES. See AIR ~.

AMBUSH. *v.* To take the opposite part by surprise with previously undisclosed evidence. To be taken unaware. Discovery of evidence before trial is intended to eliminate ambushes from trials.

AMELIORATING WASTE. Acts which improve an inheritance, even though they technically amount to waste. R. Megarry & H.W.R. Wade, *The Law of Real Property*, 5th ed. (London: Stevens, 1984) at 96.

AMELIORATION. *n.* We would suggest that laws designed to restrict or punish behaviour would not qualify for s. 15(2) [Charter] protection. Nor, as already discussed, should the focus be on the effect of the law. This said, the fact that a law has no plausible or predictable ameliorative effect may render suspect the state's ameliorative purpose. Governments, as discussed above, are not permitted to protect discriminatory programs on colourable pretexts. *R.v. Kapp*, 2008 SCC 41, McLachlin C.J. and Abella J. for the majority.

AMENABLE. *adj.* Capable of being led; tractable; responsible or subject to.

AMEND. *v.* 1. "... [T]o change in any way for the better. It includes removing anything that is erroneous or faulty and substituting something else in the place of what is removed ..." *Kucy v. McCallum*, [1944] 2 D.L.R. 101 at 112, 1 W.W.R. 361, 25 C.B.R. 128 (Alta. C.A.), Ewing J.A. (dissenting). 2. "[In the Judicature Act, R.S.O. 1970, c. 228, s. 114(10)] ... would include a change in form not involving a change in substance ..." *Johannes v. Johannes* (1981), 24 R.F.L. (2d) 412 at 419, 34 O.R. (2d) 548, 127 D.L.R. (3d) 88 (Div. Ct.), the court per Morden J.A. 3. "... [H]as several judicial meanings. It has been held to mean 'to annul or remove that which is faulty and substitute that which will improve.' And also, 'to substitute something in place of what is removed.' ..." *Elizabeth Shoe Co. v. Racine*, [1951] Que. K.B. 624 at 625, Barclay J.A. (Casey J.A. concurring).

AMENDING CLAUSE. Amending procedures for the Constitution absent from the B.N.A. Act but supplied by the Constitution Act, 1982.

AMENDING FORMULA. The means by which the Constitution of Canada may be amended. See DOMESTIC ~.

AMENDMENT. *n.* 1. The correction of an error. 2. The making of a change to a document. 3. "[As] contemplated by No. 1 of section 92 [Constitution Act, 1867 (30 & 31 Vict.) c. 3] ... was intended ... to alter certain details of structure or machinery deemed necessary for the efficient operation of the constitu-

tion, the essential design and purpose being preserved." *Reference re Initiative & Referendum Act (Man.)* (1916), [1917] 1 W.W.R. 1012 at 1029, 27 Man. R. 1, 32 D.L.R. 148 (C.A.), Perdue J.A. See ARTICLES OF ~.

AMENDS. *n.* Satisfaction.

AMENITY. *n.* A feature adding to enjoyment of property. See LOSS OF AMENITIES.

AMICUS CURIAE. [L.] Friend of the court. A barrister who assists the court during the course of a hearing, usually at the court's request.

AMINO ACIDS. Those L-amino acids commonly found in naturally occurring proteins and such amino acids when they have been modified. *Patent Act*, R.S.C. 1985, c. P-4, *Patent Rules*, SOR/96-423, s. 2.

AMINO ACID SEQUENCE. Has the same meaning as in the PCT sequence listing standard. *Patent Act*, R.S.C. 1985, c. P-4, *Patent Rules*, SOR/96-423, s. 2.

AMMUNITION. *n.* A cartridge containing a projectile designed to be discharged from a firearm and, without restricting the generality of the foregoing, includes a caseless cartridge and a shot shell. *Criminal Code*, R.S.C. 1985, c. C-46, s. 84(1). See CENTER FIRE ~; PROHIBITED ~.

AMNESTY. *n.* A government grant of general pardon for past offences.

AMORTIZATION. *var.* **AMORTISATION.** *n.* 1. Reduction of the amount owing under a mortgage or debt by instalment payments. 2. Of a blended payment mortgage, the period of time needed to pay all the principal and interest, assuming fixed monthly payments. D.J. Donahue & P.D. Quinn, *Real Estate Practice in Ontario*, 4th ed. (Toronto: Butterworths, 1990) at 227.

AMORTIZED VALUE. When used in relation to the value of a redeemable security at any date after purchase, means a value so determined that, if the security were purchased at that date and at that value, the yield would be the same as the yield would be with reference to the original purchase price.

AMOTION. *n.* Removal from office.

AMOUNT. *n.* 1. Money expressed in terms of the quantity of money. 2. Rights or things expressed in terms of the money value of the rights or things. 3. Money, property or a service, expressed in terms of the amount of money or the value in terms of money of the property or service. *Excise Tax Act*, R.S.C. 1985, c. E-15, s. 123. See LOAN ~.

AMOVE. *v.* To remove from a position or place.

ANALOGOUS GROUND. An analogous ground of discrimination refers to any distinction which serves to deny the essential human dignity of a person claiming rights under the Charter. It is to be contrasted with one of the enumerated grounds appearing in section 15 of the Charter. Spousal status, sexual orientation, and aboriginality-residence have been found to be analogous grounds. Once an analogous ground has been identified, it is a "constant marker of potential legislative discrimination" for all future cases.

ANALOGUE. *n.* A substance that, in relation to a controlled substance, has a substantially similar chemical structure. *Controlled Drugs and Substances Act, 1996,* S.C. 1996, c. 19, s. 2.

ANALOGY. See LIMITATION BY ~.

ANALOGY TO STATUTE. A statutory limitation period applicable to a legal claim may be applied by analogy to an equitable claim if the equitable claim and the legal claim are sufficiently similar. See LIMITATION BY ANALOGY.

ANALYSIS. See FORENSIC DNA ~; MANAGEMENT DISCUSSION AND ~; META-~L PROPORTIONALITY ~; STANDARD OF REVIEW ~.

ANCESTOR. *n.* One from whom a person is descended; progenitor.

ANCESTRY. *n.* "... [F]amily descent ... determined through the lineage of one's parents through their parents, and so on." *Cousens v. Canada (Nurses Assn.),* [1981] 2 C.H.R.R. D / 365 at D / 367 (Ont. Bd. of Inquiry), Ratushny.

ANCILLARY. *adj.* 1. "... [A]uxiliary or subordinate ..." *Whynot v. Giffin* (1984), 40 C.P.C. 344 at 350, 62 N.S.R. (2d) 112, 136 A.P.R. 112, 7 D.L.R. (4th) 68 (C.A.), the court per Macdonald J.A. 2. "... [S]omething grafted on to the primary matter... ." *Gwyn v. Mellen* (1978), 90 D.L.R. (3d) 195 at 201, 7 R.F.L. (2d) 106 (B.C. S.C.), McKenzie J. 3. "... [I]n the constitutional sense. In Re Fisheries Act, 1914; A.-G. Can. v. A.-G. B.C., [1930] 1 D.L.R. 194, [1930] A.C. 111, [1929] 3 W.W.R. 449, it was said that ancillary legislation is that which is necessarily incidental to effective legislation." *Cook v. Cook* (1981), 120 D.L.R. (3d) 216 at 228, 30 Nfld. & P.E.I.R. 42, 84 A.P.R. 42 (Nfld. T.D.), Goodridge J.

ANCILLARY ADMINISTRATION. Administration of a portion of an estate in a second jurisdiction where property of the deceased is located or where the deceased had a cause of action.

ANCILLARY RELIEF. Auxiliary relief.

ANEURYSM. See DISSECTING ~; FUSIFORM ~.

ANGINA PECTORIS. [L.] Chest pain. F.A. Jaffe, *A Guide to Pathological Evidence for Lawyers and Police Officers,* 4th ed. (Toronto: Carswell, 1999) at 53.

ANIMAL. *n.* 1. Any living being of the animal kingdom other than a human being. *Veterinary Medical Act,* S.N.S. 2001, c. 13, s. 2. 2. A member of the class Mammalia (mammals), Aves (birds), Reptilia (reptiles) or Amphibia (amphibians), but does not include a human being. *Fish and Wildlife Conservation Act, 1997,* S.O. 1997, c. 41, s. 1(1). 3. All animals except humans and includes vertebrates, invertebrates and micro-organisms whether wild, domestic, living or dead. 4. A mammal, reptile, amphibian or bird. See DOMESTIC ~; GUIDE ~.

ANIMALS DOMITAE NATURAE. [L.] "... [A]nimals which are generally tame, living in asso-

ciation with man, ... subject of absolute ownership with all the rights, duties, privileges and obligations that legal relationship entails." *Diversified Holdings Ltd. v. R.* (1982), 133 D.L.R. (3d) 712 at 716, [1982] 3 W.W.R. 516, 35 B.C.L.R. 349, 20 C.C.L.T. 202 (S.C.), Wallace J.

ANIMALS FERAE NATURAE. [L.] "... [A]nimals which under normal circumstances are usually found at liberty, ... are not the subject of absolute ownership, although a qualified property in such animals might be acquired by taking or taming them or while they are on one's estate... ." *Diversified Holdings Ltd. v. R.* (1982), 133 D.L.R. (3d) 712 at 716-17, [1982] 3 W.W.R. 516, 35 B.C.L.R. 349, 20 C.C.L.T. 202 (S.C.), Wallace J.

ANIMALS MANSUETAE NATURAE. [L.] Animals which are harmless by nature.

ANIMO. *adv.* [L.] With intention.

ANIMUS. *n.* [L.] Intent; intention. See ANTI-UNION ~.

ANIMUS CONTRAHENDI. [L.] Having an intention to enter into a contract.

ANN. AIR & SPACE L. *abbr.* Annals of Air and Space Law (Annales de droit aérien et spatial).

ANN. AIR & SP. L. *abbr.* Annals of Air and Space Law (Annales de droit aérien et spatial).

ANN. CAN. D. DE LA PERSONNE. *abbr.* Annuaire canadien des droits de la personne (Canadian Human Rights Yearbook).

ANN. CAN. D. INT. *abbr.* Annuaire canadien de droit international (Canadian Yearbook of International Law).

ANN. D. AÉRIEN & SPATIAL. *abbr.* Annales de droit aérien et spatial (Annals of Air and Space Law).

ANNEX. *v.* To add to.

ANNEXATION. *n.* 1. Adding land to a municipality or nation. 2. Incorporation of a municipality into another municipality.

ANNO DOMINI. [L.] In the year of the Lord.

ANNO REGNI. [L.] In the year of the reign.

ANNOTATION. *n.* Description; explanation; comment.

ANNOUNCE. See KNOCK AND ~ PRINCIPLE.

ANNOYANCE. See SEXUAL ~.

ANNUAL. *adj.* 1. "... [T]he word 'annual' [in s. 3 of the Income War Tax Act, R.S.C. 1927, c. 97] as applied to profit or gain or gratuity does not mean that the profit or gain or gratuity must necessarily be of a recurring nature from year to year, but rather that it is the profit or gain or gratuity of or in or during the year in respect of which the assessment is made." *Consolidated Textiles Ltd. v. Minister of National Revenue,* [1947] 2 D.L.R. 172 at 175, [1947] C.T.C. 63, [1947] Ex. C.R. 77, 3 D.T.C. 958, Thorson P. 2." ... [I]nfers the quality of being recurrent or being capable of recurrence." *Lucas v. Minister of National*

Revenue (1987), [1988] 13 F.T.R. 77 at 79, 87 D.T.C. 5277, [1987] 2 C.T.C. 23, Cullen J.

ANNUALLY. *adv.* Yearly.

ANNUITANT. *n.* A person in receipt of, or entitled to the receipt of, an annuity. *Government Annuities Act*, R.S.C. 1970, c. G-6, s. 2. 2. (a) Until such time after maturity of the plan as an individual's spouse or common-law partner becomes entitled, as a consequence of the individual's death, to receive benefits to be paid out of or under the plan, the individual referred to in paragraph (a) or (b) of the definition "retirement savings plan" in this subsection for whom, under a retirement savings plan, a retirement income is to be provided, and (b) thereafter, the spouse or common-law partner referred to in paragraph (a). *Income Tax Act*, R.S.C. 1985, c. 1 (5th Supp.), s. 146.

ANNUITY. *n.* 1. An annuity consists of an alienation of capital, a sum of money or capital asset, which is then turned into a flow of income so that the capital is used up and replaced by the flow of capital. 2. Includes an amount payable on a periodic basis whether payable at intervals longer or shorter than a year and whether payable under a contract, will or trust or otherwise. *Income Tax Act*, R.S.C. 1985, c. 1 (5th Supp.), s. 248 . 3. " ... [U]sual purpose is simply to provide, by the deposit either of a lump sum or of payments over a period of years, a sum of money sufficient, with accumulated years, to provide interest to provide an annuity to commence in one's later years, either for the life of the annuitant or for a fixed term of years. The sum repayable on death if the annuitant dies before he has reached the age when the annuity has commenced or before the stipulated number of annual payments have been made is nothing more than a refunding of moneys deposited for a defined purpose, when that purpose has wholly or partially failed owing to the death of the annuitant." *Gray v. Kerslake* (1957),11 D.L.R. (2d) 225 at 234, [1958] S.C.R. 3, Locke J. 4. " ... [S]tated sums of money payable at regular intervals ... derived from a fund or source in which the annuitant has no further property beyond the right to claim payment. Under the annuity contract, the issuer obligates himself to make those payments in return for the premium which he has extracted." *Rektor, Re* (1983), 3 P.P.S.A.C. 32 at 34, 47 C.B.R. (ICS.) 267 (Ont. S.C.), Smith J. 5. " ... [T]he annuity income—the annual amount to be paid under the annuity contract ..." *Minister of National Revenue v E.*, [1950] Ex. C.R. 509 at 514, [1950] C.T.C. 345, Cameron J. See DEFERRED ~; LIFE ~.

ANNUITY CONTRACT. A contract that provides for payment of an income for a specified period or for life and under which the sole benefit stated to be payable by reason of death does not exceed the sum of the amounts paid as consideration for the contract together with interest. *Alberta Corporate Tax Act*, R.S.A. 2000, c. A-15, s. 86.

ANNUITY METHOD. Manner of calculating the cost of an annuity to provide income and to cover medical expenses for a successful plaintiff .

ANNUL. *v.* To deprive of effectiveness or operation.

ANNULMENT. *n.* Making void; depriving of effectiveness or operation.

ANON. *abbr.* Anonymous.

ANONYMOUS. *n.* A nameless person.

ANONYMOUS. *adj.* Nameless.

ANSWER. *n.* The respondent's pleading provided in response to a petition filed to commence an action or proceeding. See FULL ~ AND DEFENCE.

ANTE. [L.] Before.

ANTECEDENT. *n.* Some time prior.

ANTECEDENT. *adj.* Prior in time.

ANTHEM. See NATIONAL ~.

ANTI-AVOIDANCE. *n.* In determining whether this Act applies to a person, entity, agreement or transaction, a court or other tribunal shall consider the real substance of the person, entity, agreement or transaction and in so doing may disregard the outward form. *Payday Loans Act*, S.P.E.I. 2009, c. 83, s. 4. See GENERAL ANTI-AVOIDANCE RULE.

ANTICIPATION. *n.* 1. Taking or doing something before the chosen time. 2. In patent law, occurs when there is an invention but it has been disclosed to the public prior to the application for the patent. 3. Requires proof of both disclosure and enablement. For anticipation, the genus patent must provide enough information so as to allow the selected invention to be performed without undue burden. *Sanofi-Synthelabo Canada Inc. v. Apotex Inc.*, 2008 SCC 61. 4. Prior knowledge, prior use, prior publication and prior sale, which are together referred to as "anticipation". The legal question is whether the prior publication, "contains sufficient information to enable a person of ordinary skill and knowledge in the field to understand 'the nature of the invention and carry it into practical use without the aid of inventive genius but purely by mechanical skill'" The touchstone test [is] set out by Hugessen J.A. in Beloit Canada Ltée/ Ltd. v. Valmet Oy (1986), 8 C.P.R. (3d) 289 (Fed. C.A.), at 297, which requires that One must, in effect, be able to look at a prior single publication and find in it all the information which, for practical purposes, is needed to produce the claimed invention without the exercise of any inventive skill. The prior publication must contain so clear a direction that a skilled person reading and following it would in every case and without the possibility of error be led to the claimed invention. Anticipation alleges that "your invention, though clever, was already known." *SmithKline Beecham Pharma Inc. v. Apotex Inc.* 2002 FCA 216, 21 C.P.R. (4th) 129, 219 D.L.R. (4th) 124, [2003] 1 F.C. 118, 226 F.T.R. 144 (note).

ANTICIPATORY BREACH. 1. Anticipatory breach occurs when a party, by express language or conduct, or as a matter of implication from what he has said or done, repudiates his contractual obligations before they fall due. The conduct of the repudiating party must be such that the other party to the contract is entitled to conclude that the repudiating party no longer intends to be bound by the provisions of the contract. For this type of breach to occur, there must be conduct amounting to a total rejection of the obligations under the contract and lack of justification for such conduct." *Armada Lines Ltd. v. Chaleur Fertilizer Ltd.* [1995] 1 F.C. 3, (Fed. C.A., per Pratte, J.A.). 2. "... [A] party is in breach from the moment that his actual breach becomes inevitable. Since the reason for the rule is that a party is allowed to anticipate an inevitable event and is not obliged to wait til it happens, it must follow that the breach which he anticipates is of just the same character as the breach which would actually have occurred if he had waited." *Universal Cargo Carriers Corporation v. Citati,* [1957] 2 Q.B. 401 at 436 (C.A.), Lord Devlin.

ANTICIPATORY CREDIT. Permitting an exporter to draw on credit prior to shipment by tender of particular documents. I.F.G. Baxter, *The Law of Banking,* 3d ed. (Toronto: Carswell, 1981) at 156.

ANTI-COMPETITIVE ACT. Without restricting the generality of the term, includes any of the following acts: (a) squeezing, by a vertically integrated supplier, of the margin available to an unintegrated customer who competes with the supplier, for the purpose of impeding or preventing the customer's entry into, or expansion in, a market; (b) acquisition by a supplier of a customer who would otherwise be available to a competitor of the supplier, or acquisition by a customer of a supplier who would otherwise be available to a competitor of the customer, for the purpose of impeding or preventing the competitor's entry into, or eliminating the competitor from, a market; (c) freight equalization on the plant of a competitor for the purpose of impeding or preventing a competitor's entry into, or eliminating the competitor from, a market; (d) use of fighting brands introduced selectively on a temporary basis to discipline or eliminate a competitor; (e) pre-emption of scarce facilities or resources required by a competitor for the operation of a business, with the object of withholding the facilities or resources from a market; (f) buying up of products to prevent the erosion of existing price levels; (g) adoption of product specifications that are incompatible with products produced by any other person and are designed to prevent his entry into, or to eliminate him from, a market; (h) requiring or inducing a supplier to sell only or primarily to certain customers, or to refrain from selling to a competitor, with the object of preventing a competitor's entry into, or expansion in, a market; and (i) selling articles at a price lower than the acquisition cost for the purpose of disciplining or eliminating a competitor. *Competition Act,* R.S.C. 1985, c. C-34, s. 78(1).

ANTIGEN. See PROSTATE SPECIFIC ~.

ANTI-HANDLING DEVICE. A device intended to protect a mine and that is part of, linked to, attached to or placed under the mine and that activates when an attempt is made to tamper with or otherwise intentionally disturb the mine. *Anti-Personnel Mines Convention Implementation Act, 1997,* S.C. 1997, c. 33, s. 2.

ANTI-PERSONNEL MINE. A mine that is designed, altered or intended to be exploded by the presence, proximity or contact of a person and that is capable of incapacitating, injuring or killing one or more persons. Mines that are designed, altered or intended to be detonated by the presence, proximity or contact of a vehicle as opposed to a person, and that are equipped with anti-handling devices, are not considered to be anti-personnel mines as a result of being so equipped. *Anti-Personnel Mines Convention Implementation Act, 1997,* S.C. 1997, c. 33, s. 2.

ANTIQUE FIREARM. Any firearm manufactured before 1898 that was not designed to discharge rimfire or centre-fire ammunition and that has not been redesigned to discharge such ammunition, or any firearm that is prescribed to be an antique firearm. *Criminal Code,* R.S.C. 1985, c. C-46, s. 84(1).

ANTITRUST LAW. A law having directly or indirectly as a purpose the preservation or enhancement of competition between business enterprises or the prevention or repression of monopolies or restrictive practices in trade or commerce.

ANTI-UNION ANIMUS. A predisposition against union activity or participation. *Calgary Flames Limited Partnership v. United Food and Commercial Workers Union, Local No. 401,* 2009 ABQB 30.

ANTON PILLER ORDER. 1. An ex parte order for seizure, inspection or preservation of property. The defendant or defendants (or at least of the main defendant or defendants) is known at the time the order is granted. There is evidence before the Court of the particular acts of copyright, trademark, or sometimes patent infringement, that it is alleged the defendants are committing. *Nike Canada Ltd. v. Jane Doe* (1999), 174 F.T.R. 131. 2. ... Permitted the appellant to enter the premises of the respondent and remove property, was an Anton Piller order, named for the English case in which it originated as an exceptional remedy. It was described by Lord Denning, M.R. in Anton Piller KG v. Manufacturing Process Ltd. (1975), [1976] 1 Ch. 55, [1976] 1 All E.R. 779 (Eng. C.A.) at 781: During the last 18 months the judges of the Chancery Division have been making orders of a kind not known before. They have some resemblance to search warrants. Under these orders the plaintiff and his solicitors are authorised to enter the defendant's premises so as to inspect papers, provided the defendant gives permission. ... In Celanese Canada Inc. v. Murray Demolition Corp., [2006] 2 S.C.R. 189, 2006 SCC 36 (S.C.C.), Binnie J. for the Supreme Court of Canada described it as a "private search warrant" (at para. 1), adding (at para. 30): It should truly be exceptional for a court to authorize the massive intrusion, without advance notice, of a privately orchestrated search on the privacy of a business competitor or other target party. Its usefulness is especially important in the modern era of heavy dependence on computer technology, where documents are easily deleted, moved or destroyed. The utility of this equitable tool in the correct circumstances should not be diminished. The party seeking the Anton Piller order has an obligation to act in good faith and to make full disclosure to the court . In addition to the requirement for full disclosure by the applicant, the order should include safeguards to protect the rights and interests of both parties . . . the court must take even greater care in considering whether to grant an order. *Solara Technologies Inc. v. Beard,* 2007

BCCA 402, Levine J.A. (Donald and Hall JJ.A. concurring). See ROLLING ~.

A.N.W.T.Y.T.R. *abbr.* Alberta, Northwest Territories & Yukon Tax Reporter, 1973-.

ANY EVENT. See COSTS IN ~ OF THE CAUSE.

ANY KIND. See NOTICE OF ~.

APART. See SEPARATE AND ~.

APARTHEID. *n.* The crime of apartheid means inhumane acts of a character similar to those referred to elsewhere in the Statute, committed in the context of an institutionalized regime of systematic oppression and domination by one racial group over any other racial group or groups and committed with the intention of maintaining that regime. *Crimes Against Humanity and War Crimes Act*, S.C. 2000, c. 24, Sched., *Rome Statute*, Article 7.

APOLOGY. *n.* 1. An expression of sympathy or regret, a statement that one is sorry or any other words or actions indicating contrition or commiseration, whether or not the words or actions admit or imply an admission of fault in connection with the matter to which the words or actions relate. *Apology Act*, S.B.C. 2006, c. 19, s. 1. 2. [In the context of a defamation suit], "any apology so offered or made must amount to a full and frank withdrawal of the charges conveyed and should be worded so that "an impartial person would consider it reasonably satisfactory in all the circumstances". [You must make and publish an apology] expressing sorrow, withdrawing the imputation, rehabilitating the plaintiff's character as well as you can; not stipulating that the plaintiff is to accept it; not making any terms but publishing it in the interest of truth, and because you are anxious to undo whatever harm which may have accrued from a wrong which you find you have been the unconscious instrument of inflicting. Quoted with approval in *Carter v. Gair* (1999) 64 B.C.L.R. (3d) 272 (C.A.).

APP. *abbr.* Appeal.

APPARATUS. See BROADCASTING RECEIVING ~; RADIO ~.

APPARENT. *adj.* Readily perceived. See HEIR ~.

APPARENT AUTHORITY. "... [A] legal relationship between the principal and the contractor created by a representation, made by the principal to the contractor, intended to be and in fact acted upon by the contractor, that the agent has authority to enter on behalf of the principal into a contract of a kind within the scope of the 'apparent' authority, so as to render the principal liable to perform any obligations imposed upon him by such contract. To the relationship so created the agent is a stranger. He need not be (although he generally is) aware of the existence of the representation but he must not purport to make the agreement as principal himself... ." *Freeman & Lockyer v. Buckhurst Park Properties (Mangal) Ltd.*, [1964] 2 Q.B. 480 at 502 (C.A.), Diplock L.J.

APPARENT CONVENIENCE. See EASEMENT OF ~.

APPARENT EASEMENT. An easement which is shown by some sign, audible or visible or otherwise perceptible upon reasonable inspection.

APPARENT SERVITUDE. A servitude is apparent if it is manifested by an external sign; otherwise it is unapparent. *Civil Code*, S.Q. 1991, c. 64, a. 1180. See UNAPPARENT ~.

APP. CAS. *abbr.* Law Reports, Appeal Cases, 1875-1890.

APPEAL. *n.* 1. A review of a decision of an inferior body by a superior court for the purpose of testing the soundness of the decision. 2. A reconsideration by a higher court of a decision of a lower court. 3. Includes any proceeding to set aside or vary any judgment of the court appealed from. *Supreme Court Act*, R.S.C. 1985, c. S-26, s. 2. 4. The distinction between "an appeal by holding a trial de novo and an appeal to the provincial Court of Appeal is that although the object of both is to determine whether the decision appealed from was right or wrong, in the latter case the question is whether it was right or wrong having regard to the evidence upon which it was based, whereas in the former the issue is to be determined without any reference, except for purposes of cross-examination, to the evidence called in the court appealed from and upon a fresh determination based upon evidence called anew and perhaps accompanied by entirely new evidence. A trial de novo envisages a new trial before a different tribunal than the one which originally decided the issue. *McKenzie v. Mason*, 1992 CarswellBC 282, 72 B.C.L.R. (2d) 53, 9 C.P.C. (3d) 1, 96 D.L.R. (4th) 558, 18 B.C.A.C. 286, 31 W.A.C. 286, Toy J.A. 5. [I]n s. 18.5 of the Federal Court Act, has as its essential nature the review of the decision of an inferior body by a superior court for the purpose of testing the soundness of the decision. An 'appeal' may include a trial de novo, an appeal to the Governor-in-Council, a stated case appeal and traditional appeals upon the record closed in the tribunal or court below. *Canada Post Corp. v. Canada (Minister of Public Works)*, 1993 CarswellNat 826, 21 Admin. L.R (2d) 152, 68 F.T.R. 235, McKeown J. See COURT OF ~; CROSS-~; FRIVOLOUS ~; NOTICE OF ~; RIGHT OF ~; VEXATIOUS ~.

APPEAL BOARD. A board established under a statute to hear appeals from administrative decisions or from decisions of first level tribunals. See VETERANS REVIEW AND ~.

APPEAL COURT. The Court of Appeal in a province or territory or the Appeal Division of the Supreme Court in a province. Also refers to the Supreme Court of Canada and Federal Court of Appeal. May refer to the Supreme Court of a province or the provincial court of a province if that court is fulfilling an appellate function under a statute. Also may refer to the Court Martial Appeal Court of Canada. See COURT MARTIAL ~.

APPEAL DE NOVO. [I]n an appeal of a decision that has been revised under subsection 84(2) of the Plan [Canada Pension Plan, R.S.C. 1985, c. C-8] the idea that the appeal to the Board must be heard de novo by the Board means something different from the traditional meaning, which is that an entirely new case is presented, independent of the original case. Here, the appeal de novo is heard on the basis of the case originally presented to the Tribunal, with the addition of the new facts that the Tribunal accepted when it revised its decision and the facts that the Board accepted as new facts. This is what I understand from the disposition by this Court in its decision in Kent v. Canada (Attorney General), 2004 FCA 420, 2004 FCA 420 in which it was held that the appeal hearing is a hearing de novo based on all the available evidence. At that hearing, the Board exercises the powers set out in subsection 83(11) of the Plan: it may take any action that might have been taken by the Tribunal under subsection 84(2). *Canada (Minister of Human Resources Development) v. Landry*, 2005 FCA 167.

APPEAL DIVISION. A division of the Immigration and Refugee Board called the Immigration Appeal Division. See IMMIGRATION ~; REFUGEE ~.

APPEAL TRIBUNAL. See TRANSPORTATION ~ OF CANADA.

APPEAR. *v.* To enter into court and submit to the court's jurisdiction. In some situations, an appearance may be entered by filing a document.

APPEARANCE. *n.* A document filed in court which indicates that a person will participate in proceedings or will defend. See CONDITIONAL ~; ENTER AN ~; VOLUNTARY ~.

APPEARANCE NOTICE. A document which requires people to appear in court to answer charges against them.

APPELLANT. *n.* The party bringing an appeal.

APPELLATE. *adj.* Appealed to.

APPELLATE COURT. In respect of an appeal from a court, means the court exercising appellate jurisdiction with respect to that appeal. See APPEAL.

APPELLATE JURISDICTION. 1. A superior court's power to review the decision of a lower court. 2. May refer to the jurisdiction of any court or tribunal to review the decision of another person or body.

APPLIANCE. See OPHTHALMIC ~S; OPTICAL ~S.

APPLICANT. *n.* 1. A person who applies or on whose behalf an application is made for assistance, a benefit, a loan or grant. 2. A person applying for a licence, registration, permit or passport. 3. One who brings an application or petition.

APPLICATION. *n.* 1. A request. 2. A motion to a judge or court. 3. The commencement of proceedings before a court of tribunal. See CORBETT ~; PATENT ~; SUMMARY ~.

APPLICATION PROGRAM. A program designed for a specific task, ordinarily chosen by the user, such as to maintain records, perform certain calculations or display graphic charts. "Application programs" are normally written in high level languages that are designed to be easily used by the unsophisticated. *Apple Computer Inc. v. Macintosh Computers Ltd.* (1985), 3 C.I.P.R 133, 3 C.P.R. (3d) 34 (Fed. T.D.), Cullen J.

APPLY. *v.* To request; to make application; to bring a motion to a court.

APPOINT. *v.* To select; designate; to assign an office or duty.

APPOINTED DAY. A day designated for a particular purpose.

APPOINTEE. *n.* A person chosen for some purpose.

APPOINTMENT. *n.* 1. Designation of a person to fill an office. 2. An appointment made in the exercise of a power to appoint property among several objects. *Power of Appointment Act*, R.S.B.C. 1996, c. 369, s. 1. 3. As used in the Public Service Employment Act, R.S.C. 1970, c. P-32, s. 2, means assignment. *Lucas v. Public Service Commission Appeal Board* (1987), 40 D.L.R. (4th) 365 at 372 (Fed. C.A.), the court per Heald J.A. 4. A scheduled meeting or consultation. See POWER OF ~.

APPOINTOR. *n.* One given a power; a person who names someone else for an office.

APPORTIONMENT. *n.* A division of a whole into proportional parts according to the claimants' rights.

APPRAISAL. *n.* Valuation. See MASS ~.

APPRAISAL REMEDY. "... [T]he statutory right granted to minority shareholders [Canada Business Corporations Act, S.C. 1974-75-76, c. 33, s. 184], even where 'oppression' as such is not in issue, to oblige either the majority or the corporation to purchase the shares of those minority shareholders who dissent from some basic change imposed by the majority. That purchase is at an appraised value effected by an independent outside instrumentality; ..." *Domglas Inc. v. Jarislowsky, Fraser & Co.* (1980), 13 B.L.R. 135 at 161, [1980] C.S. 925 (Que.), Greenberg J.

APPRAISAL RIGHT. See APPRAISAL REMEDY.

APPRAISE. *v.* To estimate or set the value of a thing.

APPRAISER. *n.* 1. "In determining whether the proceeding ... is a valuation or an arbitration, ... Generally speaking, if the person to whom a reference is made is intended to use his skill and knowledge of the particular subject without taking any evidence or hearing the parties, he is not prima facie an arbitrator, he is a valuer or appraiser." *Pfeil v. Simcoe & Erie General Insurance Co.*, [1986] 2 W.W.R. 710 at 715, 45 Sask. R. 241, 24 D.L.R. (4th) 752, [1986] I.L.R. 1-2055 (C.A.), the court per Vancise J.A. 2. A person appointed to engage in valuations. 3. A property valuator.

APPRECIATE. *v.* 1. "The verb 'know' has a positive connotation requiring a bare awareness, the act of receiving information without more. The act of appreciating, on the other hand, is a second stage in a mental process requiring the analysis of knowledge or experience in one manner or another. It is therefore clear on the plain meaning of the section [Criminal Code, R.S.C. 1970, c. C-34, s. 16] that Parliament intended that for a person to be insane within the statutory definition, he must be incapable, firstly, of appreciating in the analytical sense the nature and quality of the act or of knowing in the positive sense that his act was wrong." *R. v. Kjeldsen* (1981), 24 C.R. (3d) 289 at 295, [1981] 2 S.C.R. 617, [1982] 1 W.W.R. 577, 17 Alta. L.R. (2d) 97, 28 C.R. (3d) 81, 39 N.R. 376, 64 C.C.C. (2d) 161, 131 D.L.R. (3d) 121, 34 A.R. 576, the court per McIntyre J. 2. To increase in value.

APPRECIATION. *n.* 1. Growth in value. *Waters v. Waters* (1986), 4 R.F.L. (3d) 283 at 293, 44 Man. R. (2d) 109 (C.A.), Twaddle J.A. (Huband J.A. concurring). 2. An accused's appreciation of the nature and quality of an act or omission refers to an accused's ability to perceive the consequences, impact and results of a physical act and not to an accused's ability to appreciate that the legal consequences of an act are applicable to him or her. *R. v. Abbey*, [1982] 2 S.C.R. 24, Dickson J.

APPREHEND. *v.* "... [A]s used in s. 12 of the Act [Child Welfare Act, 1954 (Ont.), c. 8] contemplates a physical possession and custody of the child and taking him to place of safety and detaining him there until he can be brought before a Judge." *Blackmore, Re* (1958), 120 C.C.C. 19 at 23 (Ont. C.A.), Laidlaw J.A.

APPREHENSION. *n.* 1. Capturing a person on a criminal charge. 2. The act of taking a child into custody. 3. Apprehension is an interim child protection measure. Where it involves the physical removal of a child from his or her parents' care, it is also one of the most disruptive forms of intervention undertaken to protect children. *Winnipeg Child & Family Services (Central Area) v. W. (K.L.)* (2000), 2000 CarswellMan 469, 2000 SCC 48, [2001] 1 W.W.R. 1, 260 N.R. 203, 10 R.F.L. (5th) 122, 78 C.R.R. (2d) 1, [2000] 2 S.C.R. 519, 150 Man. R. (2d) 161, 230 W.A.C. 161, 191 D.L.R. (4th) 1, L'Heureux-Dubé J. (Gonthier, Major, Bastarache and Binnie JJ. concurring): See MIS~.

APPREHENSION OF BIAS. The test for finding a reasonable apprehension of bias has challenged courts in the past. It is interchangeably expressed as a "real danger of bias," a" real likelihood of bias," a "reasonable suspicion of bias" and in several other ways. The test for reasonable apprehension of bias is that set out by de Grandpré J. in *Committee for Justice & Liberty v. Canada (National Energy Board)*(1976), [1978] 1 S.C.R. 369. The apprehension of bias must be a reasonable one, held by reasonable and right-minded persons, applying themselves to the question and obtaining thereon the required information. ... [T]hat test is "what would an informed person, viewing the matter realistically and practically—and having thought the matter through—conclude. Would he think that it is more likely than not that [the decision-maker], whether consciously or unconsciously, would not decide fairly." The grounds for this apprehension must, however, be substantial and I ... [refuse] to accept the suggestion that the test be related to the "very sensitive or scrupulous conscience". See REASONABLE ~.

APPREHENSIVE. *adj.* "... [S]uspicious, or fearful of something." *Golding v. Waterhouse* (1876), 16 N.B.R. 313 at 319 (C.A.), Allen C.J. (Duff and Fisher JJ.A. concurring).

APPRENDRE. *n.* [Fr.] A profit or fee to be received or taken.

APPRENTICE. *n.* 1. An individual who has entered into a registered training agreement under which the individual is to receive workplace-based training in a trade, other occupation or skill set as part of an apprenticeship program approved by the Director. *Apprenticeship and Certification Act, 1998*, S.O. 1998, c. 22, s. 2. 2. Any person who is at least sixteen years of age and who has entered into a contract under which he is to receive, from or through his employer, training and instruction in the work of the plumbing trade under the direct and immediate supervision of a qualified plumber. *Plumbing Installation and Inspection Act*, S.N.B. 1976, c. P-9.1, s. 1.

APPROACH. See CONTEXTUAL ~; INCOME ~; LIVING TREE ~; MARKET ~; ORDER ~; PRINCIPLED ~ TO HEARSAY; PURPOSE-DRIVEN ~.

APPROPRIATE. *v.* 1. "... [T]o take it with a view to using it as one's own, to become indeed the owner in fact whatever the legality of the relationship is." *R. v. Dalzell* (1982), 3 C.C.C. (3d) 232 at 243, 54 N.S.R. (2d) 239, 111 A.P.R. 239 (Co. Ct.), O'Hearn Co. Ct. J. 2. To earmark for a purpose.

APPROPRIATE. *adj.* "... [E]mbraces a concept of suitableness, proper, and fitting to a particular situation... . Appropriate is the equivalent of 'convenable' in the sense of being the correct or suitable remedy or reparation; ..." *Kodellas v. Saskatchewan (Human Rights Commission)* (1989), 89 C.L.L.C. 17,027 at 16,303, [1989] 5 W.W.R. 1, 10 C.H.R.R. D / 6305, 60 D.L.R. (4th) 143, 77 Sask. R. 94 (C.A.), Vancise J.A.

APPROPRIATELY. *adv.* [...] The ordinary meaning of the word "appropriately" connotes the application of some degree of discretion in considering and weighing relevant factors, not the mechanical application of a narrow jurisdictional test. This is especially the case where the proceeding involves a claim for damages. *Icecorp International Cargo Express Corp. v. Nicolaus*, 2007 BCCA 97, Levine J.A. (Newbury and Saunders JJ.A. concurring).

APPROPRIATION. *n.* 1. Means by which Parliament or a legislature regulates the expenditure of public money voted to be applied to particular purposes. 2. Any authority of Parliament to pay money out of the Consolidated Revenue Fund. *Financial Administration Act*, R.S.C. 1985, c. F-11, s. 2. 3. Any authority of a legislature to pay money out of the Consolidated Fund. 4. (i) A supply vote, or (ii) a statutory appropriation. *Financial Administration Act*, R.S.A. 2000, c. F-12, s. 1. See MIS~.

APPROPRIATION BILL. A bill ordered to be brought in by the House when it concurs with the Estimates. A. Fraser, W.A. Dawson & J. Holtby, eds., *Beauchesne's Rules and Forms of the House of Commons of Canada*, 6th ed. (Toronto: Carswell, 1989) at 263.

APPROVAL. *n.* Confirmation; acceptance; ratification. See SALE ON ~.

APPROVE. *v.* To confirm, accept, ratify.

APPROVED. *adj.* Authorized, directed or ratified.

APPROXIMATE ODDS. The odds that are calculated by an association before the close of betting on a race. *Criminal Code*, R.S.C. 1985, c. C-46, *Pari-Mutuel Betting Supervision Regulations,* SOR/91-365, s. 2.

APPURTENANCE. *n.* One thing which belongs to another thing.

APPURTENANT. *adj.* 1. Belonging or pertaining to. 2. "... '[A]nnexed'... ." *Moreau Estate v. Regnier*, [1986] 4 W.W.R. 548 at 551 (Man. Q.B.), Hansen J. 3. That which an act of parties attaches to land. R. Megarry & H.W.R. Wade, *The Law of Real Property*, 5th ed. (London: Stevens, 1984) at cxxiii.

A.P.R. *abbr.* 1. Atlantic Provinces Reports, 1975-. 2. Annual percentage rate.

A PRIORI. [L.] From cause to effect.

APTITUDE. *n.* "... '[N]atural or acquired abilities for performing a task' ..." *Brossard (Town) v. Quebec (Commission des droits de la personne)* (1989), 10 C.H.R.R. D / 5515 at D / 5530, 88 C.L.L.C. 17,031, [1988] 2 S.C.R. 297, 88 N.R. 321, 18 Q.A.C. 164, 53 D.L.R. (4th) 609, Beetz J. (McIntyre, Lamer and La Forest JJ. concurring).

APT WORDS. Words which produce the intended legal effect. *Holloway v. Miner* (1916), 10 W.W.R. 995 at 999 (Man. K.B.), Curran J.

AQUACULTURE. *n.* The cultivation of aquatic plants and animals. *Bank Act*, S.C. 1991, c. 46, s. 425(1).

AQUACULTURE OPERATION. Any premises or site where aquaculture is carried out.

AQUACULTURIST. Includes the owner, occupier, landlord and tenant of an aquaculture operation. *Bank Act*, S.C. 1991, c. 46, s. 425.

AQUATIC ECOSYSTEM. The components of the earth related to, living in or located in or on water or the beds or shores of a water body, including but not limited to (a) all organic and inorganic matter, and (b) all living organisms and their habitat, and their interacting natural systems. The *Water Protection Act*, S.M. 2005, c. 26, s. 1.

A QUO. [L.] From which.

A.R. *abbr.* 1. Anno Regni. 2. Alberta Reports, 1976-.

ARABLE. *adj.* Suitable for purposes of cultivation.

ARABLE LAND. 1. Land which is suitable for cultivation. 2. "The test of arable land, in my opinion, is: Can it reasonably be cultivated, and, if so, is the soil of such a quality that it will, when cultivated, produce a reasonable crop of grain – not necessarily wheat – in an ordinary season? ..." *Mutual Life Assurance Co. v. Armstrong*, [1924] 3 W.W.R. 659 at

664, 19 Sask. L.R. 90, [1924] 4 D.L.R. 1144 (C.A.), Lamont J.A. (Haultain C.J.S. concurring).

ARB. *abbr.* Arbitrator.

ARB. BD. *abbr.* Arbitration Board.

ARBITER. *n.* Referee; arbitrator.

ARBITRABILITY. *n.* 1. The capability of matter to be determined by an arbitrator or referee. 2. The term "arbitrable" is generally used by labour lawyers as a synonym for "within jurisdiction", but this begs the question. Arbitrable [as used in s. 44(1) of the Labour Relations Act, R.S.O. 1980, c. 228] encompasses, in a restricted sense, a determination of whether the collective agreement under arbitration is in force. If the issue is arbitrable, then the arbitrator has jurisdiction, at least in the limited sense of being empowered to decide that question." *Dayco (Canada) Ltd. v. C.A.W.*, 1993 CarswellOnt 883, 14 Admin. L.R. (2d) 1, 13 O.R. (3d) 164 (note), 152 N.R. 1, 63 O.A.C. 1, (*sub nom. Dayco v. N.A.W.*) C.E.B. & P.G.R. 8141, (*sub nom. Dayco v. C.A.W.*) 93 C.L.L.C. 14,032, [1993] 2 S.C.R. 230, 102 D.L.R. (4th) 609, La Forest J.

ARBITRAGE. *n.* The act of purchasing in one place, where a thing is cheaper, and selling somewhere else simultaneously.

ARBITRAL AWARD. An award made by a board or an arbitrator appointed in respect of a dispute.

ARBITRAL TRIBUNAL. A sole arbitrator or a panel of arbitrators.

ARBITRAMENT. *n.* The award or decision of arbitrators upon a matter of dispute.

ARBITRAMENT AND AWARD. When parties had submitted a question to an arbitrator and received an award, they could successfully plead this in an action for damages as a good defence to the action.

ARBITRARILY. *adv.* Capriciously; without limits of power.

ARBITRARILY DETAINED. Detained without proper procedures having been followed.

ARBITRARILY IMPRISONED. Imprisoned without proper procedures having been followed.

ARBITRARY. *adj.* 1. A law is arbitrary when there is no real or rational connection between the purpose of the law and the means it employs to fulfill its purpose. *PHS Community Services Society v. Canada (Attorney General)*, 2010 BCCA 15, Smith J.A. (dissenting). 2. " ... A discretion if arbitrary is there are no criteria express or implied, which govern its exercise." *R. v. Hufsky* (1988), 84 N.R. 365 at 377 (S.C.C.), Le Dain J. 3... [C]apricious, despotic or unjustifiable." *R. v. Cayer* 11988 28 O.A.C. 105 at 114 6 M.V.R. (2d) 1, Howland C.J.O., Martin and Griffiths JJ.A.

ARBITRARY DETENTION. A random vehicle stop on the highway is, by definition, an arbitrary detention. The detention will only be justified under s. 1 of the Charter if the police act within the limited highway related purposes for which the powers were conferred. *R. v. Nolet*, 2010 SCC 24.

ARBITRARY PUNISHMENT. Punishment ordered at a judge's discretion.

ARBITRATION. *n.* 1. "The common law has ... developed two concepts which it regards as characteristic of arbitration: the existence of a dispute and the duty or intent of the parties, as the case may be, to submit that dispute to arbitration." *Zittrer c. Sport Masks Inc.* (1988), 38 B.L.R. 221 at 284, 83 N.R. 322, [1988] 1 S.C.R. 564, 13 Q.A.C. 241, L'Heureux-Dubé J. (Lamer, Wilson and Le Dain JJ. concurring). 2. The determination of a dispute by an arbitrator. 3. A procedure to determine an interest dispute. See BINDING ~; COMMERCIAL ~; COMPULSORY ~; FAMILY ~; GRIEVANCE ~; LABOUR ~.

ARBITRATION AGREEMENT. An agreement by the parties to submit to arbitration all or certain disputes which have arisen or which may arise between them in respect of a defined legal relationship, whether contractual or not. An arbitration agreement may be in the form of an arbitration clause in a contract or in the form of a separate agreement.

ARBITRATION BOARD. A board constituted by or pursuant to a collective agreement or by agreement between the parties of a collective agreement.

ARBITRATION CLAUSE. The clause in a contract providing for submission of disputes under contract to arbitration for resolution.

ARBITRATOR. *n.* 1. A person who decides disputes on the basis of evidence which the parties adduce. Generally disputes are referred to an arbitrator on consent by the parties to the dispute or under the terms of an agreement between the parties. 2. "... [A] person appointed under an agreement which contemplates such an appointment for the purpose of resolving a dispute between the parties to the agreement, ..." *Concord Pacific Developments Ltd. v. British Columbia Pavilion Corp.* (1991), 60 B.C.L.R. (2d) 121 at 132, 85 D.L.R. (4th) 402 (C.A.), Lambert J.A. 3. Includes umpire and referee in the nature of an arbitrator. See STATUTORY ~.

ARBROREAL EMBLEM. A tree selected to symbolize a province or territory.

ARB. SERV. REP. *abbr.* Arbitration Services Reporter, 1977-.

ARCHAEOLOGICAL SAMPLE. A sample of a substance associated with an archaeological object, and includes fauna, pollen, soil and carbon samples. *Archaeology Act*, S.P.E.I. 2006, c. 2, s. 1.

ARCHITECT. *n.* 1. Any person who is engaged for hire, gain, or hope of reward in the planning or review for others of the erection, enlargement, or alteration of buildings by persons other than himself. *The Architects Act*, R.S.M. 1987, c. A130, s. 1. 2. A person who is registered or licensed or who holds a certificate of practice or a temporary licence under the Architects Act or is registered as a member of the provincial association of architects.

ARCHITECT'S CERTIFICATE. A certificate of completion required by a building contract.

ARCHITECTURAL WORK. Any building or structure or any model of a building or structure. *Copyright Act*, R.S.C. 1985, c. C-42, s. 2.

ARCHIVES. *n.* 1. A place where old records are kept. 2. The body of documents of all kinds, regardless of date, created or received by a person or body in meeting requirements or carrying on activities, preserved for their general information value. *Archives Act*, R.S.Q. c. A-21.1, s. 2. See LIBRARY AND ~ OF CANADA; OFFICIAL ARCHIVE.

ARCHIVIST. *n.* One who maintains archives.

AREA. *n.* 1. A district designated for a particular purpose. 2. A city, town, village, county, municipal district or improvement district. 3. A polling district or districts, or a part of a polling district or districts. See COMMON ~S; COMMUNITY IMPROVEMENT PROJECT ~; COMPULSORY PILOTAGE ~; OFFSHORE ~; UNIT ~.

AREA TAX. Any tax levied on the owners of real property or immovables that is computed by applying a rate to all or part of the assessed dimension of the property and includes any tax levied on the owners of real property or immovables that is in the nature of a local improvement tax, a development tax or a redevelopment tax, but does not include a tax in respect of mineral rights. *Payments in Lieu of Taxes Act*, R.S.C. 1985, c. M-13, s. 2.

ARGUABLE CASE. A case with some merit, and some realistic chance of success. *R. v. Amin*, 2010 MBCA 15.

ARGUABLE ISSUE. On appeal, an arguable issue is one which if raised by a ground of appeal would result in the appeal being allowed if the ground of appeal were successfully demonstrated by the appellant.

ARGUENDO. [L.] While arguing.

ARGUMENT. *n.* 1. A method of establishing belief by using a course of reasoning. 2. The closing comments of counsel or the parties or their representatives in a hearing or trial. There may also be argument made by these persons on jurisdictional, procedural or evidentiary issues during the hearing or trial. See CLOSING ~; FLOODGATES ~; ORAL ~.

ARGUMENTATIVE. *adj.* 1. In describing a pleading, containing not only allegations of fact but arguments as to how those facts bear on the disputed matter. 2. In the old common law pleading, described a pleading in which a material fact was stated by inference only.

ARMCHAIR EVIDENCE. That evidence which establishes a context for the testator's words. Evidence of the testator's intention will include hearsay reports of the testator's words. The law with respect to armchair and extrinsic evidence is well developed and reasonably straight forward and may be summarized as follows: 1. Where the testamentary instrument is clear and unambiguous, no evidence beyond the document is received. Presumably because none is necessary. 2. Where the testamentary instrument is unclear as to intent or in construction, armchair evidence is receivable. 3. Where a testamentary instrument is ambiguous, extrinsic evidence of intent is receivable. In this context ambiguity does not simply mean competing possible interpretations. The interpretations must be equally plausibly intended. 4. Where there is reason to believe that the testator made a mistake and the mistake was one of fact, not law, both armchair evidence and extrinsic evidence may be received. Where the alleged mistake is established, the offending portions of the instrument are struck and what remains is then construed. *Decore v. Decore*, 2009 ABQB 440.

ARMED. *adj.* "Being 'armed' with an offensive weapon and 'using an offensive weapon' are not synonymous. A person is 'armed' with an offensive weapon if he is equipped with it; see *R. v. Sloan* (1974), 19 C.C.C. (2d) 190 at 192 (B.C. C.A.)." *R. v. Langevin (No. 1)* (1979), 10 C.R. (3d) 193 at 200, 47 C.C.C. (2d) 138 (Ont. C.A.), the court per Martin J.A.

ARMED FORCES. Includes army, naval and air forces or services, combatant or non-combatant, but does not include surgical, medical, nursing and other services that are engaged solely in humanitarian work and under the control or supervision of the Canadian Red Cross or other recognized Canadian humanitarian society. *Foreign Enlistment Act*, R.S.C. 1985, c. F-28, s. 2. See CANADIAN ~.

ARM'S LENGTH. *var.* **ARM'S-LENGTH.** 1. Arm's-length negotiation suggests negotiation between parties with opposing interests, each having an economic stake in the outcome. 2. For the purposes of this Act, (a) related persons shall be deemed not to deal with each other at arm's length; (b) a taxpayer and a personal trust (other than a trust described in any of paragraphs (a) to (e.1) of the definition "trust" in subsection 108(1)) are deemed not to deal with each other at arm's length if the taxpayer, or any person not dealing at arm's length with the taxpayer, would be beneficially interested in the trust if subsection 248(25) were read without reference to subclauses 248(25)(b)(iii)(A)(II) to (IV); and (c) where paragraph (b) does not apply, it is a question of fact whether persons not related to each other are at a particular time dealing with each other at arm's length. *Income Tax Act*, R.S.C. 1985, c. 1 (5th Supp.), s. 251, part. 3. A transaction "not at arm's length" is one in respect of which unrelated persons are, in the eyes of the law, in the same position as persons related by blood or marriage. In other words, if a transaction between unrelated persons has the same essential characteristics as one between related persons, i.e., the parties are influenced in their bargaining by something other than individual self-interest, those unrelated persons are said not to deal at arm's length. *Skalbania (Trustee of) v. Wedgewood Village Estates Ltd.* 37 B.C.L.R. (2d) 88 (C.A.), Esson J.A. 4. Where the "mind" directing the bargaining of one party to a contract is the same "mind" directing the bargaining of the other party, the parties cannot be said to be dealing at "arm's length". This principle applies whether the same person dictates the terms of the bargain on behalf of both parties, or whether several parties (either natural persons or corporations or a combination of the two) concertedly act in the same

interest, and thereby direct or dictate the conduct of another person or persons. *Minister of National Revenue v. T.R. Merritt Estate*, [1969] 2 Ex. C.R. 51, [1969] C.T.C. 207, Cattanach J.. See AT ~.

ARMY. *n.* The military force of a country intended to operate on land.

AROSE. *v.* "... [A] cause of action arises for purposes of a limitation period when the material facts on which it is based have been discovered or ought to have been discovered by the plaintiff by the exercise of reasonable diligence, ..." *Central & Eastern Trust Co. v. Rafuse* (1986), 37 C.C.L.T. 117 at 180, 42 R.P.R. 161, 34 B.L.R. 187, [1986] 2 S.C.R. 147, 31 D.L.R. (4th) 481, 75 N.S.R. (2d) 109, 186 A.P.R. 109, 69 N.R. 321, the court per Le Dain J.

ARRAIGN. *v.* To bring a prisoner to the bar of a court to answer a charge.

ARRAIGNMENT. *n.* Calling a prisoner by name, reading the indictment, demanding of the prisoner whether he or she is guilty or not guilty, and entering the prisoner's plea.

ARRANGEMENT. *n.* 1. A structure or combination of things designed to accomplish a purpose. *Pozniak Estate v. Pozniak* [1993] 7 W.W.R. 500 (Man. C.A.). 2. Includes (a) an amendment to the articles of a corporation; (b) an amalgamation of two or more corporations; (c) an amalgamation of a body corporate with a corporation that results in an amalgamated corporation subject to this Act; (d) a division of the business carried on by a corporation; (e) a transfer of all or substantially all the property of a corporation to another body corporate in exchange for property, money or securities of the body corporate; (f) an exchange of securities of a corporation for property, money or other securities of the corporation or property, money or securities of another body corporate; (f.1) a going-private transaction or a squeeze-out transaction in relation to a corporation; (g) a liquidation and dissolution of a corporation; and (h) any combination of the foregoing. *Canada Business Corporations Act*, R.S.C. 1985, c. C-44, s. 192. 3. Is broader than "compromise" and would appear to include any scheme for reorganizing the affairs of the debtor. *ATB Financial v. Metcalfe & Mansfield Alternative Investments II Corp.*, 2008 ONCA 587. See JOB-SHARING ~; TRADE-IN ~.

ARREARS. *n.* "... [S]omething which is behind in payment, or which remains unpaid, ..." *Corbett c. Taylor* (1864), 23 U.C.Q.B. 454 at 455 (C.A.), the court per Draper C.J.

ARREARS OF TAX. Tax unpaid and outstanding after the expiry of the year in which they were imposed, and includes penalties for default in payment.

ARREST. *n.* 1. "... [I]n general an arrest is effected by the compulsory restraint of a person either by actual seizure or by the touching of his body with a view to his detention. The person being arrested must be informed that he is being arrested and the reasons therefor. Until it has been made clear to the person that he is under arrest, the arrest is not complete in law: ..." *R. v. Delong* (1989), 47 C.C.C. (3d) 402 at 417 (Ont. C.A.), the court per Griffiths J.A. 2. "To constitute an arrest it is not necessary to touch the person arrested if he acquiesces in the situation by acknowledging that he is deprived of his liberty: ..." *Kozak v. Beatty* (1957), 7 D.L.R. (2d) 88 at 93, 20 W.W.R. 497, 118 C.C.C. 72 (Sask. C.A.), Martin J.A. 3. "The best expressed view of the matter that I have found is a note to Nicholl v. Darley (1828), 2 Y. & J. 399 [(U.K.)], at p. 405, (Philad. ed., 1869) viz.: 'The distinction seems to be, that if the party does not acquiesce, there must be an actual touching of his person by the officer, to constitute an arrest; and any touching of the person by the officer, in the execution of a writ, will be an arrest. But if the party submits and comes within the power of the officer, who thereupon abstains from interference with his person, this is such a conclusive confession of arrest as is equivalent in law to an arrest.' " *Higgins v. MacDonald*, [1928] 4 D.L.R. 241 at 243, [1928] 3 W.W.R. 115, 50 C.C.C. 353, 50 B.C.R. 150 (C.A.), Martin J.A. 4. An admiralty action brought against a ship. J.G. McLeod, *The Conflict of Laws* (Calgary: Carswell, 1983) at 111. 5. Seizure of property under a warrant of the Federal Court. D. Sgayias *et al.*, *Federal Court Practice 1988* (Toronto: Carswell, 1987) at 535. See DE FACTO ~; FALSE ~; INCIDENT TO ~.

ARREST WARRANT. A document issued by a judge or justice commanding peace officers to arrest the person named in the document.

ARSON. *n.* Intentionally or recklessly causing damage by fire or explosion to property, whether or not that person owns the property. With intent to defraud any other person, causing damage by fire or explosion to property. As a result of a marked departure from the standard of care that a reasonably prudent person would use to prevent or control the spread of fires or to prevent explosions, that person is a cause of a fire or explosion in that property that causes bodily harm to another person or damage to property. *Criminal Code*, R.S.C. 1985 c. C-46, s. 433-436.

ART. See TERM OF ~; WORDS OF ~.

ARTEFACT. See THERAPEUTIC ~.

ARTICLE. *v.* To serve for a period of time as an articled student or clerk.

ARTICLE. *n.* Any thing that is made by hand, tool or machine. *Industrial Design Act*, R.S.C. 1985, c. I-9, s. 2. See ~S; PATENTED ~; USEFUL ~.

ARTICLED CLERK. A student-at-law bound by contract in writing to service with a member of the Law Society, who has filed articles of clerkship in accordance with the governing legislation.

ARTICLED STUDENT. 1. Any person validly holding a certificate of admission to the training period prescribed by by-law of the General Council. *Barreau du Quebec Act*, R.S.Q. 1977, c. B-1, s. 1. 2. A person enrolled in the Bar Admission Course during the time the person is not in attendance at the teaching period thereof. *Legal Aid Services Act, 1998*, S.O. 1998, c. 26, *General*, R.R.O. 1990, Reg. 710 s. 1.

ARTICLES. *n.* 1. Clauses contained in a document. 2. The document itself. 3. The agreement between a member of a profession, the principal, and a student, the articled student, regarding the student's training from and work for the member. 4. The original or restated articles of incorporation, articles of amendment, articles of amalgamation, articles of continuance, articles of reorganization, articles of arrangement, articles of dissolution, articles of revival and includes any amendments thereto. *Canada Business Corporations Act*, R.S.C. 1985, c. C-44, s. 2. See ARTICLE.

ARTICLES OF AMENDMENT. A document which changes the capital structure or the constitution of a company and is ordinarily authorized by a special resolution of the shareholders. H. Sutherland, D.B. Horsley & J.M. Edmiston, eds., *Fraser's Handbook on Canadian Company Law*, 7th ed. (Toronto: Carswell, 1985) at 453.

ARTICLES OF ASSOCIATION. Contain the internal regulations of a corporation. One of the incorporating documents in some jurisdictions. S.M. Beck *et al.*, *Cases and Materials on Partnerships and Canadian Business Corporations* (Toronto: Carswell, 1983) at 159.

ARTICLES OF CONTINUANCE. A document which permits a body corporate incorporated in one jurisdiction to be reconstituted in another.

ARTICLES OF INCORPORATION. 1. Incorporation takes place when these articles are delivered to the appropriate Director and a certificate of incorporation is issued. H. Sutherland, D.B. Horsley & J.M. Edmiston, eds., *Fraser's Handbook on Canadian Company Law*, 7th ed. (Toronto: Carswell, 1985) at 3. 2. The original or restated articles of incorporation, articles of amalgamation, letters patent, supplementary letters patent, a special Act and any other instrument by which a corporation is incorporated, and includes any amendments thereto. 3. Correspond to memorandum of association in those jurisdictions using that method of incorporation. S.M. Beck *et al.*, *Cases and Materials on Partnerships and Canadian Business Corporations* (Toronto: Carswell, 1983) at 159.

ARTICLES OF WAR. A code of laws which regulates armed forces.

ARTICULATED VEHICLE. A vehicle which can be divided into more than one part.

ARTIFICE. *n.* Contrivance or device; used to refer to fraud or deceit.

ARTIFICIAL ISLAND. Any man-made extension of the seabed or a seabed feature, whether or not the extension breaks the surface of the superjacent waters. *Oceans Act*, S.C. 1996, c. 31, s. 2.

ARTIFICIAL PERSON. A body corporate or other body given the status of a person by law.

ARTIST. See CANADIAN ~S AND PRODUCERS PROFESSIONAL RELATIONS TRIBUNAL; CANADIAN COUNCIL ON THE STATUS OF THE ~.

ARTISTIC DEFENCE. To a charge of obscenity, test which assesses whether the exploitation of sex has a justifiable role in advancing the plot or the theme, and in considering the work as a whole, does not merely represent "dirt for dirt's sake" but has a legitimate role when measured by the internal necessities of the work itself. *R. v. Butler* [1992] 1 S.C.R. 452.

ARTISTIC MERIT. Defence to criminal charge of possession of child pornography. "the defence must be established objectively, since Parliament cannot have intended a bare assertion of artistic merit to provide a defence. ... The second meaning that can be ascribed to "artistic merit" is " possessing the quality of art", or "artistic character". On this meaning, a person who produces art of any kind is protected, however crude or immature the result of the effort in the eyes of the objective beholder. This interpretation seems more consistent with what Parliament intended. It is hard to conceive of Parliament wishing to make criminality depend on the worth of the accused's art. It would be discriminatory and irrational to permit a good artist to escape criminality, while criminalizing less fashionable, less able or less conventional artists. Such an interpretation would run counter to the need to give the defence a broad and generous meaning. I conclude that "artistic merit" should be interpreted as including any expression that may reasonably be viewed as art. *R. v. Sharpe*, 2001 CarswellBC 82, 2001 SCC 2, McLachlin C.J.C. for majority.

ARTISTIC WORK. Includes paintings, drawings, maps, charts, plans, photographs, engravings, sculptures, works of artistic craftsmanship, architectural works, and compilations of artistic works. *Copyright Act*, R.S.C. 1985, c. C-42, s. 2.

ARTISTS' ASSOCIATION. Any organization, or a branch or local thereof, that has among its objectives the management or promotion of the professional and socio-economic interests of artists who are members of the organization, and includes a federation of artists' associations. *Status of the Artist Act*, S.C. 1992, c. 33, s. 5.

A RUBRO AD NIGRUM. [L. from the red to the black] To deduce the meaning of a statute (formerly printed in black) from its title (formerly printed in red).

AS AGAINST. To contrast the positions of two people by referring to a different relationship between one of them and a third person.

AS BETWEEN. To contrast the positions of two people by referring to a different relationship between one of them and a third person.

ASCENDANT. *n.* The ancestor of a family.

ASCERTAIN. *v.* To decide upon. *Stinson v. College of Physicians & Surgeons (Ontario)* (1913), 27 O.L.R. 565 at 581, 10 D.L.R. 699 (C.A.), Riddell J.A.

ASCERTAINED GOODS. "... [D]efined by Atkin L.J. In re Waite, [1927] 1 Ch. 606 in these words: 'Ascertained' probably means identified in accordance with the agreement after the time a contract of sale is made ...' " *George Eddy Co. v. Noble Corey*

& Son (1951), 28 M.P.R. 140 at 154, [1951] 4 D.L.R. 90 (N.B. C.A.), Michaud C.J.K.B.D.

A.S.C.SUM. *abbr.* Alberta Securities Commission Summaries, 1975-.

ASIDE. See SET ~.

ASPECT. See DOUBLE ~ DOCTRINE.

ASPHYXIA. See POSITIONAL ~.

ASSASSINATION. *n.* Murder of a public figure for political motives.

ASSAULT. *n.* 1. Applying force intentionally to another person, directly or indirectly, without their consent; attempting or threatening, by an act or gesture, to apply force to another person if he has or causes the other person to believe upon reasonable grounds that he has, present ability to effect his purpose; or accosting or impeding another person or begging while openly wearing or carrying a weapon or imitation thereof. *Criminal Code*, R.S.C. 1985, c. C-46, s. 265(1). 2. In tort law, intentionally causing another person to fear imminent contact of a harmful or offensive nature. J.G. Fleming, *The Law of Torts*, 8th ed. (Sydney: Law Book, 1992) at 25. See AGGRAVATED ~; COMMON ~; INDECENT ~; SEXUAL ~.

ASSAULT AND BATTERY. The actual carrying out of the threatened harmful or offensive contact. J.G. Fleming, *The Law of Torts*, 8th ed. (Sydney: Law Book, 1992) at 25.

ASSEMBLY. *n.* 1. A meeting of persons. 2. The Legislative Assembly of a province. 3. The House of Assembly of a province. See FREEDOM OF ~; LEGISLATIVE ~; NATIONAL ~; UNLAWFUL ~.

ASSENT. *v.* 1. To agree to, concur in or recognize a matter. 2. "... [T]o be valid, must be given by a majority of eligible band members in attendance at a meeting called for the purpose of giving or withholding assent." *Cardinal v. R.*, [1982] 3 C.N.L.R. 3 at 9, [1982] 3 W.W.R. 673, 41 N.R. 300, 133 D.L.R. (3d) 513, [1982] 1 S.C.R. 508, the court per Estey J.

ASSENT. *n.* Acceptance. Concurrence. See MUTUALITY OF ~; ROYAL ~.

ASSENTED. *v.* Within the context [of the Canada Agricultural Products Act] means concurred in, agreed or consented to, approved or permitted. *R. v. A & A Foods Ltd.*, 1997 CarswellBC 2541, 120 C.C.C. (3d) 513 (S.C.), Hood J.

ASSERTION. *n.* "... [S]tatement, tale or news is an expression which, taken as a whole and understood in context, conveys an assertion of fact or facts and not merely the expression of opinion... . Expression which makes a statement susceptible of proof and disproof is an assertion of fact; ..." *R. v. Zundel* (1992), 75 C.C.C. (3d) 449 at 492, 95 D.L.R. (4th) 202, [1992] 2 S.C.R. 731, 140 N.R. 1, 56 O.A.C. 161, 16 C.R. (4th) 1, 10 C.R.R. (2d) 193, Cory and Iacobucci JJ. (dissenting) (Gonthier J. concurring). See OPINION.

ASSESS. *v.* 1. "... '[I]mpose a liability to be taxed' ..." *Ottawa (City) v. Nantel* (1921), 51 O.L.R. 269 at

274, 69 D.L.R. 727 (C.A.), Latchford J.A. 2. "As used in Section 46(1) [of the Income Tax Act, R.S.C. 1952, c. 148] ... roughly equivalent to 'ascertain and fix' and it seems to have two possible senses in one of which the mere acts of ascertaining and calculating only are included, and the other that of computing and stating the tax in the manner prescribed by the statute." *Scott v. Minister of National Revenue*, [1960] C.T.C. 402 at 415, [1961] Ex. C.R. 120, 60 D.T.C. 1273, Thurlow J. 3. "... [T]o consider and determine the whole amount necessary to be raised by rate... ." *Nova Scotia Car Works Ltd. v. Halifax (City)* (1913), 47 S.C.R. 406 at 414, 12 E.L.R. 282, 11 D.L.R. 55, Fitspatrick C.J. 4. To value property for tax purposes.

ASSESS. *abbr.* Assessment.

ASSESSED COSTS. Costs which have been assessed by an assessment officer; taxed costs.

ASSESSED DIMENSION. The frontage, area, other dimension or other attribute of real property or immovables established by an assessment authority for the purpose of computing a frontage or area tax. *Payments in Lieu of Taxes Act,* R.S.C. 1985, c. M-13, s. 2.

ASSESSED VALUE. The value established for any real property or immovable by an assessment authority for the purpose of computing a real property tax. *Payments in Lieu of Taxes Act*, R.S.C. 1985, c. M-13, s. 2.

ASSESSING AUTHORITY. A local authority or a school board or other authority that has the power to assess and levy rates, charges or taxes on land or with respect to the ownership of land. *The Condominium Property Act, 1993*, S.S. 1993, c. C-26.1, s. 2.

ASSESSMENT. *n.* 1. Valuation of property for taxation purposes. 2. The determination of an amount payable. 3. The work to be done or the payment to be made each year to entitle the owner of a mineral claim to a certificate of work. *Yukon Quartz Mining Act*, R.S.C. 1985, c. Y-4, s. 2. 4. While it is true that assessment, reassessment and confirmation refer to three specific actions by the Minister under the [Income Tax Act, R.S.C. 1985, c. 1 (5th Supp.)] in the process of determining the tax liability of a taxpayer, the word "assessment" also refers to the product of that process. That product refers to the amount of the tax owing as initially assessed or determined, and subsequently confirmed. From the perspective of the process itself, the assessment pursuant to sections 152 to 165 [of the Income Tax Act] is not completed by the Minister until, within the time allotted by the Act, the amount of the tax owing is finally determined, whether by way of reconsideration, variation, vacation or confirmation of the initial assessment .... *Canada v. Anchor Pointe Energy Ltd.*, 2007 FCA 188. 5. "In Income Tax Comm'rs for London v. Gibbs, [1942] A.C. 402 at p. 406, Viscount Simon L.C, in reference to the word 'assessment' said: 'The word "assessment" is used in our income tax code in more than one sense. Sometimes, by "assessment" is meant the fixing of the sum taken to represent the actual profit for the purpose of charging tax on it, but in another context the "assessment" may mean the ac-

tual sum in tax which the taxpayer is liable to on his profits.' That the latter meaning attached to the word 'assessment' under the [Income War Tax Act, R.S.C. 1927, c. 97] as it stood before the enactment of Part VIII ... is clear..." *Okalta Oils Ltd v. Minister of National Revenue*, [1955] 5 D.L.R. 614 at 615, [1955] S.C.R. 824, [1955] C.T.C. 271, 55 D.T.C. 1176, Fauteux J. See CERTIFICATE OF ~; COTRONI ~; ENVIRONMENTAL ~; PRACTICE OF ~; SECURITY ~.

ASSESSMENT AUTHORITY. An authority that has power by or under an Act of Parliament or the legislature of a province to establish the assessed dimension or assessed value of real property or immovables. *Payments in Lieu of Taxes Act*, R.S.C. 1985, c. M-13.

ASSESSMENT OF COSTS. Calculation of the procedural costs to which a party is entitled, formerly taxation of costs.

ASSESSMENT OFFICER. Taxing officer; officer of the court who carries out assessments of costs.

ASSESS O. *abbr.* Assessment Officer.

ASSESSOR. *n.* 1. The official who evaluates property for tax purposes. 2. A specialist who assists the court in determining a matter. D. Sgayias *et al., Federal Court Practice 1988* (Toronto: Carswell, 1987) at 494.

ASSET. *n.* 1. Any real or personal property or legal or equitable interest therein including money, accounts receivable or inventory. 2. "... [I]nclude[s] only such properties of the debtor as are available for the payment of this debt ..." *Sandberg v. Meurer* (1948), [1949] 1 D.L.R. 422 at 427, [1949] C.T.C. 35, [1949] 1 W.W.R. 117, 56 Man. R. 391 (C.A.), Adamson J.A. (MacPherson C.J.M., Richards and Coyne JJ.A. concurring). See BUSINESS ~; CAPITAL ~S; COMMON ~; CURRENT ~S; FAMILY ~; FINANCIAL ~; FIXED ~; LENDING ~; LIQUID ~S; WASTING ~.

ASSIGN. *v.* 1. To transfer property. 2. Execution and performance of every necessary or suitable deed or act for assigning, surrendering or otherwise transferring land of which that person is possessed, either for the whole estate or for any less estate. *Trustee acts*. 3. For a tenant to transfer the tenant's remaining interest in a lease or tenancy agreement.

ASSIGN. *n.* 1. A person to whom something is transferred or given. *Quaal Estate, Re*, [1920] 2 W.W.R. 271 at 272, 51 D.L.R. 720 (Sask. K.B.), Embury J. 2. "... [A]nyone to whom an assignment is made ..." *National Trust Co. v. Mead* (1990), 12 R.P.R. (2d) 165 at 177, [1990] 2 S.C.R. 410, [1990] 5 W.W.R. 459, 71 D.L.R. (4th) 488, 112 N.R. 1, 87 Sask. R. 161, Wilson J. (Lamer C.J.C., La Forest, L'Heureux-Dubé, Gonthier and Cory JJ. concurring).

ASSIGNEE. *n.* 1. The person to whom property is transferred. *Minister of National Revenue v. Parsons* (1983), 4 Admin L.R. 64 at 79, [1983] C.T.C. 321, 83 D.T.C. 5329 (Fed. T.D.), Cattanach J. 2. Includes any person in whom the right or benefit concerned has become vested, as a result of any assignment or series of assignments. *Consumer Protection acts.* 3. Includes a secured party and a receiver. *Personal Property Security acts.* 4. A contextual reading of the Copyright Act [R.S.C. 1985, c. C-42] reveals that Parliament has preserved the traditional distinction between assignees and licensees with some modification. Under the present Act, there is a distinction between "assignee", "licensee" and "exclusive licensee". An assignee possesses full ownership rights in the copyright with respect to the rights assigned. A non-exclusive licensee has no property rights in the copyright, and enjoys only contractual rights vis-à-vis the owner-licensor. As a result, it cannot sue for infringement. An exclusive licensee, on the other hand, has a limited property interest in the copyright. ... this limited property interest enables the exclusive licensee to sue third parties for infringement but precludes the exclusive licensee from suing the owner-licensor for infringement. *Kraft Canada Inc. c. Euro Excellence Inc.*, 2007 SCC 37, Rothstein J. (Binnie and Deschamps JJ. concurring).

ASSIGNMENT. *n.* 1. " ... [P]roperty is transferred to another ..." *Minister of National Revenue v. Parsons* (1983), 4 Admin L.R. 64 at 79, [1983] C.T.C. 321, 83 D.T.C. 5329 (Fed. T.D.), Cattanach J. 2. "[In s. 205(1)(b) of the Canada Shipping Act, R.S.C. 1970, c. S-9] ... a transfer of a right from one person to another..." *Makar v. "Rivtow Lion" (The) (1982)*, (*sub nom. Makar v. Rivtow Straits Ltd.*) 82 C.L.L.C. 14, 209 at 364, 43 N.R. 245, 140 D.L.R. (3d) 6 (Fed. C.A.), Thurlow C.J.A. (Verchere D.J.A. concurring). 3. Act of assigning, or the document by which a thing is assigned. 4. A transfer by a tenant of the full term remaining under the tenant's lease. W.B. Rayner & R.H. McLaren *Falconbridge on Mortgages*, 4th ed. (Toronto: Canada Law Book, 1977) at 100. 5. Includes assignment by way of security, hypothec and other charges on book debts. *Bankruptcy and Insolvency Act*, R.S.C. 1985, c. B-3, s. 98.1. 6. In bankruptcy, a voluntary act by a debtor or his legal representative for the benefit of the debtor's creditors. It transfers control over the debtor's property so that it can be distributed among his creditors. The debtor cannot continue to carry on business. 7. " ... As between mortgagors, an assignment would be an agreement between the original mortgagor and his purchaser by which the latter would assume the mortgage debt in exchange for valuable consideration ..." *National Trust Co. v. Mead* (1990), 12 R.P.R. (2d) 165 at 177, [1990] 2 S.C.R. 410, [1990] 5 W.W.R. 459, 71 D.L.R. (4th) 488, 112 N.R. 1, 87 Sask. R. 161, Wilson J. (Lamer C.J.C., La Forest, L'Heureux-Dubé, Gonthier and Cory JJ. concurring). See ABSOLUTE ~.

ASSIGNOR. *n.* 1. One who makes a transfer. 2. Any person making an assignment.

ASSISE. *var.* **ASSIZE.** *n.* The trial of a civil action before a travelling judge.

ASSISTANCE. *n.* Any amount, other than a prescribed amount, received or receivable at any time from a person or government, municipality or other public authority whether the amount is by way of a grant, subsidy, rebate, forgivable loan, deduction from royalty or tax, rebate of royalty or tax, invest-ment allowance or any other form of assistance or benefit. *Income Tax Act*, R.S.C. 1985, c. 1 (5th Supp.), s. 66. See CANADA ~ PLAN; INTERNATIONAL ~; KNOWING ~; OFFICIAL DEVELOPMENT ~; RENT-GEARED-TO-INCOME ~; SOCIAL ~; VOCATIONAL ~; WRIT OF ~.

ASSISTANT. See CLERK ~; VIRTUAL LEGAL ~.

ASSIZE. *n.* "... [A] sitting of a Judge of the Supreme Court with a jury." *Imperial Bank v. Alley*, [1926] 3 D.L.R. 86 at 90, 59 O.L.R. 1 (C.A.), the court per Orde J.A. See ASSISE.

ASSN. *abbr.* Association.

ASSOCIATE. *n.* 1. " ... [M]ay include the [partner] ... may also signify a mere companion or companionship." *Derby Development Development Corp. v. Minister of National Revenue*, [1963] C.T.C. 269 at 279 (Ex. Ct.), Kearney J. 2. With respect to a person (a) a body corporate that the person directly or indirectly controls, determined without regard to paragraph 3(1)(d), or of which they beneficially own shares or securities currently convertible into shares carrying more than 10% of the voting rights under all circumstances or by reason of the occurrence of an event that has occurred and is continuing or a currently exercisable option or right to purchase the shares or convertible securities; (b) a partner of the person acting on behalf of the partnership of which they are partners; (c) a trust or estate in which the person has a substantial beneficial interest or in respect of which they serve as a trustee or a liquidator of the succession or in a similar capacity; (d) a spouse or common-law partner of the person; (e) a child of the person or of their spouse or common-law partner; or (f) if that relative has the same residence as the person, a relative of the person or of their spouse or common-law partner. *Bank Act*, S.C. 1991, c. 46, s. 271. See FRANCHISOR'S ~.

ASSOCIATED MEANING PRINCIPLE. According to the "associated meaning" principle of statutory interpretation, "when two or more words linked by 'and' or 'or' serve an analogous grammatical and logical function within a provision, they should be interpreted with a view to their common features." *McDiarmid Lumber Ltd. v. God's Lake First Nation*, 2006 SCC 58, [2006] 2 S.C.R. 846 at para. 30, McLachlin C.J.

ASSOCIATED WORDS RULE. Rule of statutory interpretation which states that when terms are connected by "and" or "or", the terms' common feature may be "relied on to resolve ambiguity or limit the scope of the terms". Thus, when a specific term such as "medical evidence" is followed by a general term such as "other evidence", the general term is interpreted in such a way as to limit its scope in light of the preceding specific term. *R. v. Soosay* 2001 ABCA 287, 18 M.V.R. (4th) 11, 160 C.C.C. (3d) 437, 293 A.R. 292, 257 W.A.C. 292.

ASSOCIATION. *n.* 1. An employers' organization, a trade union, a professional association or a business or trade association. 2. An association of persons formed in a foreign country on the plan known as

Lloyd's, whereby each member of the association participating in a policy becomes liable for a stated, limited or proportionate part of the whole amount payable under the policy. *Insurance Companies Act*, S.C. 1991, c. 47, s. 571. 3. " ... [I]n its ordinary meaning is wide enough to include an incorporated company..." *Minister of National Revenue v. St. Catherines Flying & Training School Ltd.*, [1953] C.T.C. 362 at 369, [1953] Ex. C.R. 259, 53 D.T.C. 1232, Thorson P. See ARTICLES OF ~; ARTISTS' ~; BUSINESS OR TRADE ~; CANADIAN PAYMENTS ~; CANADIAN STANDARDS ~; CONSTITUENCY ~; COOPERATIVE ~; ELECTORAL DISTRICT ~; EMPLOYERS' ~; FREEDOM OF ~; MEMORANDUM OF ~; RIGHT OF ~; SOVEREIGNTY-~; UNINCORPORATED ~.

ASSUME. *v.* 1. To take on a debt or obligation. *Thompson v. Warwick* (1894), 21 O.A.R. 637 at 644, MacLennan J.A. 2. To take for granted. *Gillespie v. R.*, [1983] 1 W.W.R. 641 at 647, 82 D.T.C. 6334, [1982] C.T.C. 378, 45 N.R. 77, 141 D.L.R. (3d) 725 (Fed. C.A.), the court per Thurlow C.J.F.C.

ASSUMED JURISDICTION. There are two sources from which the Court of Queen's Bench in Saskatchewan acquires jurisdiction over an in personam action. The first is the common law which provides that this Court has jurisdiction where there is service of the process within the province. The second is what is frequently called "assumed jurisdiction" which is a creation of legislation. It empowers a court to assume jurisdiction over a cause of action which arose in this province despite the fact that the defendant's residence is elsewhere and the process must be served ex juris. This new jurisdiction was introduced in England by The Common Law Procedure Act, 1852, 15 & 16 Vict., c. 76. That same jurisdiction was incorporated into the law of Saskatchewan by the enactment of s. 12 of The Queen's Bench Act, R.S.S. 1978, c. Q-1. *Gray v. Dow Corning Corp.* (1996), 48 C.P.C.(3d) 50 (Sask. Q.B.), appeal to C.A. dismissed.

ASSUMPSIT. [L. one promised] A form of action to recover damages for breach of a simple contract.

ASSUMPTION AGREEMENT. An arrangement by which a purchaser in a new subdivision contracts directly with a mortgagee to make mortgage payments so that the developer in released from the covenant with the mortgage lender. D.J. Donahue & P.D. Quinn, *Real Estate Practice in Ontario*, 4th ed. (Toronto: Butterworths, 1990) at 231.

ASSUMPTION OF RISK. See VOLUNTARY ~.

ASSURANCE. *n.* 1. A transfer, deed or instrument, other than a will, by which land may be conveyed or transferred. *Limitation of Actions acts.* 2. Insurance. See INFORMATION ~.

ASSURANCE FUND. A fund established under a statute to indemnify certain persons against loss. See LAND TITLES ~.

ASSURE. *v.* To make certain; to insure.

ASSURED. *n.* One who is indemnified against particular events.

ASSURER. *n.* Indemnifier; insurer.

ASYLUM. *n.* 1. A sanctuary. 2. A place for the treatment of the mentally ill. See POLITICAL ~.

AT ARM'S LENGTH. Parties are said to be at arm's length when they are not under the control or influence of each other.

ATLANTIC PROVINCES. The provinces of Nova Scotia, New Brunswick, Prince Edward Island and Newfoundland.

AT LARGE. 1. Does not apply to livestock that is (a) tethered, (b) in the direct or continuous charge of a person, (c) confined in a structure, or (d) on enclosed land owned or occupied by the owner of the livestock. *Livestock Act*, R.S.B.C. 1996, c. 270, s. 1. 2. Not under control. *Dog Act*, R.S.P.E.I. 1988, c. D-13, s. 1(a). 3. " ... [L]eft unattended." *Thompson v. Grand Trunk Railway* (1895), 22 O.A.R. 453 at 461, the court per Osler J.A. 4. "[Refers to animals] ... which are away from home." *Hupp v. Canadian Pacific Railway* (1914), 16 D.L.R. 343 at 347, 6 W.W.R. 385, 27 W.L.R. 398, 17 C.R.C. 66, 20 B.C.R. 49 (C.A.), Galliher J.A. 5. "Damages in libel actions are 'at large' and rest upon a consideration of the injury to the plantiff, the conduct of the defendant and the plaintiff and, in some cases, the deterrent effect sought to be accomplished. Except to the extent that they are intended to be a deterrent, they are compensatory and not punitive." *Munro v. Toronto Sun Publishing Corp.* (1982), 21 C.C.L.T. 261 at 294, 39 O.R. (2d) 100 (H.C.), J. Holland J. 6. "[In Criminal Code, R.S.C. 1970, c. C-34, s. 133(1)(b)] ... has been defined, sensibly I think, in Joliffe v. Dean (1954), 54 S.R. 1V.S.W. 157 ... as free or at liberty ..." *R. v. MacCaud* (1975), 22 C.C.C. (2d) 445 at 446 (Ont. C.A.), Donohue J. See DAMAGES ~.

AT LEAST. 1. "... '[N]ot less than' ..." *R. v. Robinson* (1951), 12 C.R. 101 at 108, [1951] S.C.R. 522, 100 C.C.C. 1, Locke J. (Rand and Kellock JJ. concurring). 2. "... '[A]s much as'." *R. v. Robinson* (1951), 12 C.R. 101 at 108, [1951] S.C.R. 522, 100 C.C.C. 1, Locke J. (Rand and Kellock JJ. concurring). 3. "... [W]hen the term 'at least' is used in reference to the days between two events, that means 'clear days.' ... when the term 'at least' is used in reference to the period between two events, whether that period is expressed in years, months, weeks, hours or minutes ... the same effect must be given to those words as is given to them when the period is expressed in days. There can be no basis for anything but a consistent interpretation of such words." *R. v. Davis*, [1978] 1 W.W.R. 381 at 384, 35 C.C.C. (2d) 224 (Sask. C.A.), the court per Culliton C.J.S.

ATMOSPHERIC PRESSURE. See NORMAL ~.

AT PAR. Of stocks or bonds, sold or issued at face value.

AT PLEASURE. An employee, officer, or other appointee appointed "at pleasure" may be dismissed without cause. Where the term is used in a statute ... it is clear the legislature intended that the appointee have no security of tenure. *Martin v. Vancouver (City)*, 2008 BCCA 197.

ATS. *abbr.* At the suit of. Used when the defendant's name is put first in the title of a proceeding.

AT SIGHT. In reference to bills of exchange, payable on demand.

ATTACH. *v.* To take or apprehend; to take goods as well as persons. See ATTACHMENT.

ATTACHE. *n.* [Fr.] A person associated with an embassy.

ATTACHED. *adj.* 1. "... [P]laced ... with 'some kind of permanency' ..." *Boomars Plumbing & Heating Ltd. v. Marogna Brothers Enterprises Ltd.* (1988), 51 D.L.R. (4th) 13 at 24, 50 R.P.R. 81, 27 B.C.L.R. (2d) 305, [1988] 6 W.W.R. 289 (C.A.), the court per Esson J.A. 2. "... '[T]o lay hold of person or property by virtue of some process of law.' ..." *Barnard v. Walkem* (1880), 1 B.C.R. (Pt. 1) 120 at 127 (C.A.), Begbie C.J.

ATTACHMENT. *n.* 1. Arresting a person under an order of committal. 2. "Garnishee proceedings ... stop orders and a writ of attachment against the goods of an absconding debtor... . appointment of a receiver under judicial process, that is by order of the Court... ." *W.C. Fast Enterprises Ltd. v. All-Power Sports (1973) Ltd.* (1981), 123 D.L.R. (3d) 27 at 38, 16 Alta. L.R. (2d) 47 (C.A.), the court per McGillivray C.J.A. 3. "The security interest is said to have attached [as found in s. 12(1) of the Personal Property Security Act, R.S.O. 1980, c. 375] when all events necessary for the creation of that interest have taken place. At that time, the rights of the debtor in the collateral assets are restricted and effected by the rights of the secured party ... Attachment defines the commencement of the relationship betweeen the debtor and the secured party ..." *Royal Trust Corporation of Canada v. No. 7 Honda Sales Ltd.* (1987), 7 P.P.S.A.C. 51 at 55-6 (Ont. Dist. Ct.), Kane Dist. Ct. J. See MAJOR ~ CLAIMANT; MINOR ~ CLAIMANT.

ATTACHMENT OF DEBTS. Where judgment for the payment of money is obtained against a person to whom another person owes money, an order is made that all debts owing or accruing from that person (called the garnishee) to the judgment debtor be applied to the judgment debt.

ATTACHMENT OF WAGES. "... [A] continuous deduction or diversion of wages at source by an employer... . [which] originates by court order, ..." *Ruthven v. Ruthven* (1984), 38 R.F.L. (2d) 102 at 106 (Ont. Co. Ct.), Dandie Co. Ct. J. See GARNISHMENT.

ATTACK. *n.* [In the context of determining whether a criminal act constitutes a crime against humanity ...] An "attack" may be "a course of conduct involving the commission of acts of violence": Prosecutor v. Kunarac, Kovac and Vukovic (February 22, 2001), Doc. IT-96-23-T; IT-96-23/1-T (Int. Criminal Trib.), at para. 415. It may also be a course of conduct that is not characterized by the commission of acts of violence if it involves the imposition of a system such

as apartheid, or the exertion on the population of pressure to act in a particular manner that is orchestrated on a massive scale or in a systematic manner: Akayesu, Trial Chamber, at para. 581 [Le Procureur v. Akayesu (1998), 9 IHRR 608 (Int. Criminal Trib.)]. It is fair to say, however, that in most instances, an attack will involve the commission of acts of violence. This definition aptly conveys the idea that the existence of an attack does not presuppose armed conflict (though it does not preclude armed conflict). *Mugesera v. Canada (Minister of Citizenship and Immigration)*, 2005 SCC 40, [2005] 2 S.C.R. 100. See COLLATERAL ~; SYSTEMATIC ~; WIDESPREAD ~.

ATTACK DIRECTED AGAINST ANY CIVILIAN POPULATION. A course of conduct involving the multiple commission of acts referred to in paragraph 1 against any civilian population, pursuant to or in furtherance of a State or organizational policy to commit such attack. *Crimes Against Humanity and War Crimes Act*, S.C. 2000, c. 24, Sched., *Rome Statute*, Article 7.

ATTAINDER. *n.* Formerly, when judgment of outlawry or death was made against a person convicted of felony or treason, the principal consequences were the forfeiture and escheat of the convict's lands and the corruption of the convict's blood so that the convict was not able to hold or inherit land or transmit a title by descent to any other person.

ATTAINT. *adj.* Describing a person under attainder.

ATTEMPT. *n.* Having an intent to commit an offence, and doing or omitting to do anything for the purpose of carrying out the intention whether or not it was possible under the circumstances to commit the offence. *Criminal Code*, R.S.C. 1985, c. C-46, s. 24(1). 2. The crime of attempt consists of an intent to commit the completed offence together with some act more than merely preparatory taken in furtherance of the attempt. Section 24(1) draws no distinction between attempts to do the possible but by inadequate means, attempts to do the physically impossible, and attempts to do something that turns out to be impossible "following completion". All are varieties of attempts to do the "factually impossible" and all are crimes. Only attempts to commit imaginary crimes fall outside the scope of the provision. *United States of America v. Dynar* [1997] 2 S.C.R. 462, Cory and Iacobucci JJ. for the majority.

ATTEMPT OR THREAT TO APPLY FORCE. [T]he kicking of the bathroom door by the respondent, and his exhortations that [the complainant] come out establish beyond a reasonable doubt an attempt or threat to apply force to [the complainant] within the meaning of s. 265(1)(b) [of the Criminal Code R.S.C. 1985, c. C-46]. *HDL Investments Inc. v. Regina (City)*, 2008 SKCA 47.

ATTEND. *v.* "... '[T]o be present' or 'go regularly to' ..." *Howell v. Ontario (Minister of Community and Social Services)* (1987), 17 O.A.C. 349 at 353 (Div. Ct.), the court per Griffiths J. See ATTENDANCE.

ATTENDANCE. *n.* "... [A]ttendance in court necessarily involves making one's presence known to the presiding judge. One does not comply merely by being physically present...." *R. v. Anderson* (1983), 37 C.R. (3d) 67 at 73, 29 Alta. L.R. (2d) 66, 49 A.R. 122, 9 C.C.C. (3d) 539 (C.A.), Kerans J.A. (Moir J.A. concurring).

ATTENDANCE MONEY. 1. Conduct money. 2. Reimbursement paid to a witness for reasonable expenses incurred while going to, staying at and returning from the place where a discovery or trial is held.

ATTENDANT. *adj.* Accompanying.

ATTEST. *v.* To witness an event or act.

ATTESTATION. *n.* 1. Witnessing a written instrument and signing it as a witness. 2. "... [C]onsists, at the very least, of witnessing the execution of an instrument... ." *Cameron, Re* (1984), 63 N.S.R. (2d) 103 at 107, 141 A.P.R. 103 (S.C.), Hallett J.

ATTESTATION CLAUSE. The witness to the execution of a written instrument signs this sentence, stating that he or she has witnessed it.

ATTESTING WITNESS. A person who has seen someone else sign a written document or execute a deed.

ATTITUDINAL BIAS. Arises where a decision-maker has prejudged an issue and has not brought an open mind to the decision-making process. The rule against bias disqualifies decision-makers with attitudinal biases. *Halfway River First Nation v. British Columbia*, 1997 CarswellBC 1745 (S.C.).

ATTORN. *v.* 1. To turn over; to agree to recognize a new owner as landlord. 2. To attorn to a foreign court is to voluntarily submit to its jurisdiction. "It is a well- accepted principle of private international law that where a defendant, although he does not reside within the jurisdiction of that court, appears in a foreign court solely to preserve assets that have been seized by that court, he does not attorn to the jurisdiction of the foreign court." *Amopharm Inc. v. Harris Computer Corp.* (1992), 10 O.R. (3d) 27 (C.A.).

ATTORNEY. *n.* 1. A person appointed to act in place of or to represent another. 2. Lawyer. 3. Patent agent. 4. The donee of a power of attorney or where a power of attorney is given to two or more persons, whether jointly or severally or both, means any one or more of such persons. *Powers of Attorney Act*, R.S.O. 1990, c. P.20, s. 1. See CROWN ~; POWER OF ~; WARRANT OF ~.

ATTORNEY GENERAL. *var.* **ATTORNEY-GENERAL.** 1. The principal law officer of the Crown, a Minister of the Crown. 2. The office of Attorney General started in England as early as the thirteenth century as the King's Attorney. In essence, the Attorney General exercised on the King's behalf the prerogative to bring and terminate prosecutions. Although there are great differences between the constitution of the Canadian and English offices of Attorney General, the power to manage prosecutions of individuals for criminal acts has changed little since these early times and between these countries. In Canada, the office of the Attorney General is one with constitutional dimensions recognized in the Constitution Act, 1867. Although the specific duties con-

ventionally exercised by the Attorney General are not enumerated, s. 135 of that Act provides for the extension of the authority and duties of that office as existing prior to Confederation. A similar provision applicable to the Attorney General of Alberta is found in the Alberta Act, S.C. 1905, c. 3 (reprinted in R.S.C. 1985, App. II, No. 20), at s. 16(1). Furthermore, s. 63 of the Constitution Act, 1867 requires that the cabinets of Quebec and Ontario include in their membership the Attorneys General. Attorneys General in this country are, of course, charged with duties beyond the management of prosecutions. As in England, they serve as Law Officers to their respective legislatures, and are responsible for providing legal advice to the various government departments. Unlike England, the Attorney General is also the Minister of Justice and is generally responsible for drafting the legislation tabled by the government of the day. The numerous other duties of the provincial and federal Attorneys General are broadly outlined in the various Acts establishing the Departments of Justice in each jurisdiction. The gravity of the power to bring, manage and terminate prosecutions, which lies at the heart of the Attorney General's role, has given rise to an expectation that he or she will be in this respect fully independent from the political pressures of the government. It is a constitutional principle in this country that the Attorney General must act independently of partisan concerns when supervising prosecutorial decisions. This side of the Attorney General's independence finds further form in the principle that courts will not interfere with his exercise of executive authority, as reflected in the prosecutorial decision-making process. *Krieger v. Law Society (Alberta)* [2002] 3 S.C.R. 372. 3. '[T]he chief law officer of the provincial Crown. He is the legal representative of the province." *Lavoie v. Nova Scotia (Attorney General)* (1989), 58 D.L.R. (4th) 293 at 316, 91 N.S.R. (2d) 184, 233 A.P.R. 184 (C.A.), the court per Clarke C.J.N.S.

ATTORNEY GENERAL OF CANADA. The Attorney General of Canada (a) is entrusted with the powers and charged with the duties that belong to the office of the Attorney General of England by law or usage, in so far as those powers and duties are applicable to Canada, and also with the powers and duties that, by the laws of the several provinces, belonged to the office of attorney general of each province up to the time when the Constitution Act, 1867, came into effect, in so far as those laws under the provisions of the said Act are to be administered and carried into effect by the Government of Canada; (b) shall advise the heads of the several departments of the Government on all matters of law connected with such departments; (c) is charged with the settlement and approval of all instruments issued under the Great Seal; (d) shall have the regulation and conduct of all litigation for or against the Crown or any department, in respect of any subject within the authority or jurisdiction of Canada; and (e) shall carry out such other duties as are assigned by the Governor in Council to the Attorney General of Canada. *Department of Justice Act*, R.S.C. 1985, c. J-2, s. 5.

ATTORNMENT. *n.* Agreement to become a new owner's tenant or a mortgagee's tenant. See BAILMENT BY ~.

ATTRIBUTABLE. *adj.* That which is a natural and reasonable consequence; causally connected.

ATTRIBUTE. See ENVIRONMENTAL ~S.

ATTRIBUTION. *n.* To assign income or property to another person for certain purposes.

AUCTION. *n.* Public sale of property to the highest bidder.

AUCTIONEER. *n.* 1. "... [A] person who sells property of any kind by public auction... ." *Merritt v. Toronto (City)* (1895), 22 O.A.R. 205 at 213 (C.A.), MacLennan J.A. (Hagarty C.J.O. and Burton JJ.A. concurring). 2. An individual who conducts the bidding at a sale by auction of any property.

AUDI ALTERAM PARTEM. [L. hear the other side] 1. The Latin expression and best known name for one of the main principles of natural justice. 2. "... [P]arties must be made aware of the case being made against them and [be] given an opportunity to answer it ..." *Canadian Cable Television Assn. v. American College Sports Collective of Canada Inc.* (1991), 4 Admin L.R. (2d) 61 at 72, 81 D.L.R. (4th) 376, 36 C.P.R. (3d) 455, 129 N.R. 296, [1991] 3 F.C. 626 (C.A.), the court per MacGuigan J.A. 3. "The broad scope of the rule in Canada is demonstrated in L'Alliance des Professeurs case ... [[1953] 2 S.C.R. 140] where Rand J. said at p. 161: 'Audi alteram partem is a pervading principle of our law, and is peculiarly applicable to the interpretation of statutes which delegate judicial action in any form to inferior tribunals: in making decisions of a judicial nature they must hear both sides, and there is nothing in the statute here qualifying the application of that principle.' " *Downing v. Graydon* (1978), 9 C.C.E.L. 260 at 264, 21 O.R. (2d) 292, 78 C.L.L.C. 14,183, 92 D.L.R. (3d) 355 (C.A.), Blair J.A. 4. "... [T]he audi alteram partem rule ... is one of the basic requirements of procedural fairness. According to that rule, a party to a decision must have an opportunity to be heard and, in particular, the decision-maker cannot hear evidence in the absence of a party whose conduct is under scrutiny. (See Kane v. University of British Columbia, [1980] 1 S.C.R. 1105 ...)... ." *Ontario (Attorney General) v. Grady* (1988), 34 C.R.R. 289 at 317 (Ont. H.C.), Callaghan A.C.J.H.C.

AUDIENCE. *n.* Interview; hearing. See PRE ~; RIGHT OF ~.

AUDIOLOGY. *n.* The health profession in which a person provides, for the purposes of promoting and maintaining communicative, auditory and vestibular health, the services of assessment, treatment, rehabilitation and prevention of (a) auditory and related communication disorders and conditions, and (b) peripheral and central auditory system dysfunction and related peripheral and central vestibular system dysfunction. *Health Professions Act*, R.S.B.C. 1996, c. 183, *Speech and Hearing Health Professionals Regulation*, B.C. Reg. 413/2008, s. 1.

AUDIO RECORDING MEDIUM. 1. A recording medium, regardless of its material form, onto which a sound recording may be reproduced and that is of a kind ordinarily used by individual consumers for that purpose, excluding any prescribed kind of recording medium. *Copyright Act*, R.S.C. 1985, c. C-42, s. 79. 2. Parliament's definition of "audio recording medium" [Copyright Act, s. 79] stands in contra-distinction with a recorder or similar devices as these were known to exist at the time and whose function it is to record and play blank audio tapes. No one has ever pretended that tape recorders came within the ambit of the definition. A digital audio recorder is not a medium. *Canadian Private Copying Collective v. Canadian Storage Media Alliance*, 2004 FCA 424. See BLANK ~.

AUDIT. *n.* 1. "... [A]n examination of books of account and supporting evidence to determine the reliability of the information recorded." *Toromont Industrial Holdings Ltd. v. Thorne, Gunn, Helliwell & Christenson* (1975), 23 C.P.R. (2d) 59 at 74, 10 O.R. (2d) 65, 62 D.L.R. (3d) 225 (H.C.), Holland J. 2. (i) An independent examination of records for the purpose of expressing an opinion, or (ii) the preparation of a report or certificate or the expression of an opinion as to whether financial information is presented fairly. Alberta statutes. See ENVIRONMENTAL ~.

AUDIT COMMITTEE. A committee of the board of directors of a corporation who nominate auditors and work with them.

AUDITING STANDARDS. See GENERALLY ACCEPTED ~.

AUDITOR. *n.* 1. One who reviews and verifies accounts. 2. A person who is a member in good standing of any corporation, association or institute of professional accountants, and includes a firm every partner of which is such a person. 3. "... [A] person whose position is an independent one, whose duty it is to discover and point out the errors or mistakes of the directors if any, the gains and losses of the company, – to shew in fact, exactly the true state of the accounts; so that he stands, as it were, between the directors and the shareholders as an independent investigator of all business transactions, in which the directors, as the managers of the affairs of the company, have been engaged ..." *Ontario Forge & Bolt Co., Re* (1896), 27 O.R. 230 at 232 (H.C.), Robertson J. See PROVINCIAL ~.

AUDITOR GENERAL. 1. The federal official who examines Canada's public accounts, including those relating to public property, Crown corporations and the Consolidated Revenue Fund. 2. Some provinces use the same title to describe the person who carries out similar functions for the provincial government.

AUTHENTIC. *adj.* Original; genuine.

AUTHENTIC ACT. 1. Something executed before a notary or another duly authorized public official. 2. Is one that has been received or attested by a competent public officer according to the laws of Québec or of Canada, with the formalities required by law. Every act whose material appearance satisfies such requirements is presumed to be authentic. *Civil Code,*

AUTHENTICATION

S.Q. 1991, c. 64, a. 2813. See SEMI-AUTHENTIC ACT.

AUTHENTICATION. *n.* 1. An attestation made by an officer certifying that a record is in proper form and that the officer is the proper person to so certify. 2. A municipal corporation's signing and sealing of a by-law. I.M. Rogers, *The Law of Canadian Municipal Corporations*, 2d ed. (Toronto: Carswell, 1971-) at 446.

AUTHOR. *n.* One should always keep in mind that one of the purposes of the copyright legislation, historically, has been "to protect and reward the intellectual effort of the author (for a limited period of time) in the work" (my emphasis). The use of the word "copyright" in the English version of the Act has obscured the fact that what the Act fundamentally seeks to protect is "le droit d'auteur". While not defined in the Act, the word "author" conveys a sense of creativity and ingenuity. *Tele-Direct (Publications) Inc. v. American Business Information Inc.*, 1997 CarswellNat 2111, 221 N.R. 113, 154 D.L.R. (4th) 328, 76 C.P.R. (3d) 296, 134 F.T.R. 80 (note), [1998] 2 F.C. 22, 37 B.L.R (2d) 101 (F.C.A.), the court per Decary J.A. See WORK OF JOINT ~SHIP.

AUTHORITY. *n.* 1. Power or right to enforce obedience or to influence the conduct and actions of others. 2. A statute, case or text cited in support of a legal opinion or argument. 3. A legal power given by one person to another to do some act. 4. A person authorized to exercise a statutory power. *Administrative Procedures Act*, R.S.A. 2000, c. A-3, s. 1. 5. Body given powers by statute to oversee or carry out a government function. 6. "... '[J]urisdiction' ..." *Toronto (City) v. Morson* (1916), 37 O.L.R. 369 at 376, 28 D.L.R. 188 (C.A.), Masten J.A. See ABUSE OF ~; ACTUAL ~; ADMINISTRATIVE ~; APPARENT ~; ASSESSING ~; ASSESSMENT ~; BINDING ~; BREACH OF WARRANTY OF ~; CANADIAN INTERNET REGISTRATION ~; CERTIFICATION ~; CITATION OF AUTHORITIES; COMPETENT ~; CUSTOMARY ~; ENFORCEMENT ~; EXPRESS ~; EXPROPRIATING ~; IMPLIED ~; LICENSING ~; LIQUOR ~; LOCAL ~; OSTENSIBLE ~; PERSON IN ~; PERSUASIVE ~; PORT ~; POSITION OF ~; URBAN TRANSIT ~; USUAL OR CUSTOMARY ~.

AUTHORIZATION. *n.* Licence; certificate; registration.

AUTHORIZE. *v.* 1. To empower. 2. "Authorize" means to "sanction, approve and countenance": Muzak Corp. v. Composers, Authors & Publishers Assn. (Canada), [1953] 2 S.C.R. 182 (S.C.C.), at p. 193; de Tervagne v. Beloeil (Town), [1993] 3 F.C. 227 (Fed. T.D.). Countenance in the context of authorizing copyright infringement must be understood in its strongest dictionary meaning, namely, "give approval to, sanction, permit, favour, encourage": see The New Shorter Oxford English Dictionary (1993), vol. 1, at p. 526. Authorization is a question of fact that depends on the circumstances of each particular case and can be inferred from acts that are less than direct and positive, including a sufficient degree of indifference: C.B.S. Inc. v. Ames Records & Tapes, [1981] 2 All E.R. 812 (Eng. Ch. Div.), at pp. 823-24. However, a person does not authorize infringement by authorizing the mere use of equipment that could be used to infringe copyright. Courts should presume that a person who authorizes an activity does so only so far as it is in accordance with the law: Muzak Corp., supra. This presumption may be rebutted if it is shown that a certain relationship or degree of control existed between the alleged authorizer and the persons who committed the copyright infringement: Muzak Corp., supra; de Tervagne , supra: see also, J.S. McKeown, Fox Canadian Law of Copyright and Industrial Designs, 4th ed. (looseleaf), at p. 21-104 and P.D. Hitchcock, "Home Copying and Authorization" (1983), 67 C.P.R. (2d) 17, at pp. 29-33. *CCH Canadian Ltd. v. Law Society of Upper Canada*, 2004 SCC 13.

AUTHORIZED. *adj.* 1. Properly empowered to perform any specified duty or to do any specified act. 2. "A work is authorized by statute whether the statute is mandatory or permissive, if the work is carried out in accordance with the statute." *Tock v. St. John's (City) Metropolitan Area Board* (1989), 1 C.C.L.T. (2d) 113 at 154, 47 M.P.L.R. 113, [1989] 2 S.C.R. 1181, 64 D.L.R. (4th) 620, 104 N.R. 241, 82 Nfld. & P.E.I.R. 181, 257 A.P.R. 181, Sopinka J. 3. Within the context [of the Canada Agricultural Products Act] means empowered, enabled, sanctioned, approved or permitted. *R. v. A & A Foods Ltd.*, 1997 CarswellBC 2541, 120 C.C.C. (3d) 513 (S.C.), Hood J. See UN~.

AUTHORIZED CAPITAL. The total amount of capital which, by its incorporating documents, a company is authorized to issue.

AUTHORIZED INVESTMENT. A security in which a trust permits its trustee to invest funds.

AUTHORIZED PERSON. A person authorized by legislation to perform a specified function under it.

AUTHORIZING INSTRUMENT. (i) A law, contract or instrument that requires, permits for or permits service by mail, and (ii) if the common law requires or permits service by mail, the common law. *Judicature Act*, R.S.A. 2000, c. J-2, s. 43.

AUTOGRAPH. *n.* 1. The handwriting of a person. 2. The signature of a person.

AUTOMATIC FIREARM. A firearm that is capable of, or assembled or designed and manufactured with the capability of, discharging projectiles in rapid succession during one pressure of the trigger. *Criminal Code*, R.S.C. 1985, c. C-46, s. 84(1).

AUTOMATIC RENEWAL. Extension of an agreement from year to year or period of time to period of time when no notice of termination is given by either party.

AUTOMATISM. *n.* 1. Two forms of automatism are recognized at law: insane automatism and non-insane automatism. Involuntary action which does not stem from a disease of the mind gives rise to a claim of non-insane automatism. If successful, a claim of non-insane automatism entitles the accused to an acquittal. . . . On the other hand, involuntary action which is found, at law, to result from a disease of the mind gives rise to a claim of insane automatism. It has long been recognized that insane automatism is subsumed by the defence of mental disorder, formerly referred to as the defence of insanity. *R. v. Stone*, 1999 CarswellBC 1064, [1999] 2 S.C.R. 290, 24 C.R. (5th) 1, 239 N.R. 201, 63 C.R.R. (2d) 43, 173 D.L.R. (4th) 66, 134 C.C.C. (3d) 353, 123 B.C.A.C. 1, 201 W.A.C. 1, Bastarache J. for the majority. 2. The two concepts [of automatism and provocation] are quite distinct and their application depends on the nature of the impact on an accused of the triggering event. The key distinction between the two concepts is that automatism relates to a lack of voluntariness in the accused, an essential element of the offence, while provocation is a recognition that an accused who "voluntarily" committed all the elements of murder may nevertheless have been provoked by a wrongful act or insult that would have been sufficient, on an objective basis, to deprive an ordinary person of the power of self-control. *R. v. Stone*, 1999 CarswellBC 1064, [1999] 2 S.C.R. 290, 24 C.R. (5th) 1, 239 N.R. 201, 63 C.R.R. (2d) 43, 173 D.L.R. (4th) 66, 134 C.C.C. (3d) 353, 123 B.C.A.C. 1, 201 W.A.C. 1. 3. Refers to involuntary conduct that is the product of a mental state in which the conscious mind is disassociated from the part of the mind that controls action. A person in a state of automatism may perform acts, sometimes complicated and apparently purposeful acts, but have no control over those actions: William Wilsonm et al., "Violence, Sleepwalking and the Criminal Law: (2) The Legal Aspects" (2005) Crim. L.R. 614, at pp. 615-16. ... The automatism "defence" is not a defence in the true sense but is a denial of the commission of the actus reus of the crime. *R. v. Luedecke*, 2008 ONCA 716.

AUTOMOBILE. *n.* Any vehicle propelled by any power other than muscular force and adapted for transportation on the public highways but not on rails.

AUTOMOBILE INSURANCE. Insurance (a) against liability arising out of, (i) bodily injury to or the death of a person, or (ii) loss of or damage to property, caused by an automobile or the use or operation thereof; or (b) against loss of or damage to an automobile and the loss of use thereof, and includes insurance otherwise coming within the class of accident insurance where the accident is caused by an automobile or the use or operation thereof, whether liability exists or not, if the contract also includes insurance described in clause (a). *Insurance acts.*

AUTOPSY. *n.* The dissection of a body for the purpose of examining organs and tissues to determine changes caused by disease or violence, cause of death or manner of death. F.A. Jaffe, *A Guide to Pathological Evidence for Lawyers and Police Officers*, 4th ed. (Toronto: Carswell, 1999) at 231.

AUTRE. *adj.* [Fr.] Another.

AUTREFOIS ACQUIT. [Fr. formerly acquitted] 1. A plea which an accused may make in her own defence. 2. To make out the defence of autrefois acquit, the accused must show that the two charges laid against him are the same. In particular, he must prove that the following two conditions have been met: (1)

the matter must be the same, in whole or in part; and (2) the new count must be the same as at the first trial, or be implicitly included in that of the first trial, either in law or on account of the evidence presented if it had been legally possible at that time to make the necessary amendments. *R. v. Van Rassel* (1990), 53 C.C.C. (3d) 353 (S.C.C.), McLachlin, J. for the court. 3. An accused may not be prosecuted when he or she has been tried for and acquitted of the same offence. *R. v. Wright* (1965), 45 C.R. 38 at 39, [1965] 2 O.R. 337, [1965] 3 C.C.C. 160, 50 D.L.R. (2d) 498 (C.A.), Porter C.J.O.

AUTREFOIS CONVICT. [Fr. formerly convicted] "... [A]n absolutely effective plea in bar to the second information, if the accused has been ... convicted and it was attempted again to prosecute them for the same offence." *R. v. Ecker*, [1929] 3 D.L.R. 760 at 761, 64 O.L.R. 1, 51 C.C.C. 409 (C.A.), Latchford C.J.

AUTRE VIE. [Fr.] The life of another (period of time).

AVAILABILITY. See UN~.

AVAILABLE. *adj.* "... [D]oes not mean 'existing.' It means 'in such condition as that it can be taken advantage of.' " *Devitt v. Mutual Life Insurance Co.* (1915), 33 O.L.R. 473 at 478, 22 D.L.R. 183 (C.A.), Riddell J.A. (Falconbridge C.J.K.B. concurring). See COMMERCIALLY ~.

AVAILABLE MARKET. A particular situation of trade, area and goods in which there is enough demand that, if a purchaser defaults, the goods in question can readily be sold. G.H.L. Fridman, *Sale of Goods in Canada*, 3d ed. (Toronto: Carswell, 1986) at 359.

AVAILS. *n.* Proceeds; profits.

AVER. *v.* To allege.

AVERAGE. *n.* 1. A medium. 2. Loss or damage to goods on board a ship. See RACE ~.

AVERMENT. *n.* 1. Allegation *R. v. Bellman*, [1938] 3 D.L.R. 548 at 551, 70 C.C.C. 171, 13 M.P.R. 37 (N.B.C.A.), Baxter C.J. 2. In a pleading, affirmation of any matter.

AVERY. See SCOTT V. ~ CLAUSE.

AVIAN EMBLEM. A bird selected to symbolize a province or territory.

AVOID. *v.* To make a transaction void.

AVOIDANCE. *n.* Avoiding, setting aside or vacating. See ANTI-~; CONFESSION AND ~; TAX ~.

AVOW. *v.* To maintain or justify an act.

AVULSION. *n.* 1. Land which current orr flood tears off from property to which it originally belonged and adds to the property of another or land joined to another's property when a river changes its course. 2. Tearing away a tissue or part. F.A. Jaffe, *A Guide to Pathological Evidence for Lawyers and Police Officers*, 4th ed. (Torono: Carswell, 1999) at 13.

AWARD. *n.* 1. Judgment. 2. Instrument which embodies an arbitrator's decision. 3. A pension, compensation, an allowance or a bonus payable under this Act. *Pension Act*, R.S.C. 1985, c. P-6, s. 2. 4. The decision of an arbitrator on the dispute that was submitted to the arbitrator and includes (a) an interim award, (b) the reasons for the decision, and(c) any amendments made to the award under this Act. *Commercial Arbitration Act*, R.S.B.C. 1996, c. 55, s. 1. See ARBITRAL ~; ARBITRAMENT AND ~; SCHOLARSHIP ~.

AWAY. See CARRY ~.

A.W.L.D. *abbr.* Alberta Weekly Law Digest, 1982-.

AXIOM. *n.* A truth which is indisputable.

B

B. *abbr.* Baron.

BACHELOR. *n.* 1. The first degree in a university. 2. A never married man.

BACK. *v.* To countersign; to endorse.

BACK. See HOLD~; KICK~; LEASE~; MORTGAGE ~; RELATION ~.

BACK A WARRANT. For one justice to endorse a warrant issued by the justice of another district or jurisdiction permitting it be executed in the first justice's jurisdiction. *R. v. Solloway Mills & Co.* (1930), 65 O.L.R. 677 at 679, 54 C.C.C. 214 (C.A.), the court per Hodgins J.A.

BACK-BENCHER. *n.* A Member of Parliament or of a legislature who is a member of the government party but is not a member of Cabinet and does not hold an office in the party caucus. The name refers to where the member is likely to sit in the legislature.

BACK-BOND. *var.* **BACKBOND.** *n.* A bond of indemnity which one gives to a surety.

BACKSHEET. *n.* A page attached to the back and facing in the opposite direction to other pages of a document filed in a court proceeding; gives the title of the proceeding and other information.

BAD. *adj.* In pleadings, unsound.

BAD DEBT. A debt which is irrecoverable.

BAD FAITH. 1. To constitute bad faith the actions must be knowingly or intentionally wrong. *R. v. Smith*, 2005 BCCA 334. 2. Bad faith has been found in situations where there has been a blatant disregard for the Charter rights of an accused or where more than one Charter right has been violated. *R. v. Wise* [1992] 1 S.C.R. 527. 3. Used in municipal and administrative case law to cover a wide range of conduct in the exercise of legislatively delegated authority. Bad faith has been held to include dishonesty, fraud, bias, conflict of interest, discrimination, abuse of power, corruption, oppression, unfairness, and conduct that is unreasonable. The words have also been held to include conduct based on an improper motive, or undertaken for an improper, indirect or ulterior purpose. In all these senses, bad faith describes the exercise of delegated authority that is illegal and renders the consequential act void. And in all these senses bad faith must be proven by evidence of illegal conduct, adequate to support the finding of fact. Bad faith, however, is also used to describe the exercise of power by an administrative body that is beyond the scope or the ambit of the powers delegated to that body by the legislature. In those cases the exercise of powers is sometimes described as unauthorized, or beyond the scope, or outside the limit of the delegated power. It is an act that is ultra vires. Frequently, allegations of bad faith include both the aspect of illegality in the first sense and in the sense of ultra vires. To the extent that the allegation focuses on the way the delegated power was exercised, or on the conduct of the administrative body, there is an issue of fact. In those cases where powers are said to have been exceeded, however, there is another issue. That is the scope, or the amplitude, of the powers delegated by the legislature. That issue invariably requires an interpretation of the empowering statutes, and that raises an issue of law. *MacMillan Bloedel Ltd. v. Galiano Island Trust Committee* (1995), 10 B.C.L.R. (3d) 121 (C.A.) Finch, J.A. (leave to appeal to S.C.C. refused).

BADGE. *n.* "... [H]ad its origin in heraldry as meaning a distinctive device worn by the adherents of the lord. The badge is not comprised of the arms of the lord, which are exclusive to him, but usually it utilizes the crest. In Scotland the badge worn by a clansman is the crest of the chief within a belt and buckle with the chief's motto inscribed on the belt." *Insurance Corp. of British Columbia c. Canada (Registrar of Trade Marks)* (1978), 44 C.P.R. (2d) 1 at 7, [1980] 1 F.C. 669 (T.D.), Cattanach J.

BADGES OF FRAUD. 1. "[B]adges of fraud" vary from case to case. They are no more than typical and suspicious facts that may allow the court to make a finding of fraud absent an explanation from the debtor. *FL Receivables Trust 2002-A (Administrator of) v. Cobrand Foods Ltd.*, 2007 ONCA 425. 2. "(1) [S]ecrecy[,] (2) generality of conveyance[,] (3) continuance in possession by debtor[, and] (4) some benefit retained under the settlement to the settlor." *Re Dougmor Realty Mg. Ltd.; Fisher v. Wilgorn Invt. Ltd.*, [1967] 1 O.R. 66 (Ont. H.C.). 3. These include: the precarious financial situation of the grantor; secrecy; showing the property after the transfer as an asset of the grantor; the preservation by the grantor of an interest in the property; substantially reducing the property of the grantor that would, but for the transfer, be available to his creditors; the effect of the transfer being to delay and defeat creditors; knowledge by the grantee that the asset is worth substantially more than what he is paying for it; inadequacy of the consideration; no immediate or early change of possession following the conveyance. *Phaneuf Fertilizer Sales Ltd. v. LeBlanc*, [1999] 1 W.W.R. 659 (Sask. Q.B.).

BAD TITLE. 1. Unmarketable title. 2. One which conveys no or a very limited interest to the purchaser and a purchaser cannot be forced to accept.

BAIL. *v.* To free a person arrested or imprisoned after a particular day and place to appear are set and security is taken.

BAIL. *n.* 1. Security given by the persons into whose hands an accused is delivered. They bind themselves or become bail for the person's due appearance when required and, if they fear the person's escape, they have the legal power to deliver that person to prison. 2. "... [P]roperly the contract whereby the man is bailed (i.e. delivered) to his sureties but it is also applied to the sureties themselves... ." *R. v. Sandhu* (1984), 38 C.R. (3d) 56 at 63 (Que. S.C.), Boilard J. 3. In an admiralty proceeding, security given in order to obtain release of property under arrest. 4. In common parlance, "bail" sometimes refers to the money or other valuable security which the accused is required to deposit with the court as a condition of release. Restricting "bail" to this meaning would render s. 11(*e*) nugatory because most accused are released on less onerous terms. In order to be an effective guarantee, the meaning of "bail" in s. 11(*e*) must include all forms of judicial interim release. *R. v. Pearson* [1992] 3 S.C.R. 665, per Lamer, C.J.C. See JUSTIFY ~; REASONABLE ~.

BAIL-BOND. *n.* An instrument executed by sureties.

BAILEE. *n.* 1. A person to whom goods are entrusted for a specific purpose with no intention of transferring the ownership. 2. A person who receives possession of a thing from another or consents to receive or hold possession of a thing for another under an agreement with the other person that the person will keep and return the thing or deliver the thing or that the person will act as directed with the specific thing.

BAILIFF. *n.* 1. A sheriff's officer or person employed by a sheriff to make arrests, carry out executions, and serve writs. 2. A person who, for remuneration, acts or assists a person to act, or represents to a person that she or he is acting or is available to act, on behalf of another person in repossessing, seizing or distraining any chattel, or in evicting a person from property. 3. As used today, the word "bailiff" has two meanings. In the first meaning, it refers to a person employed in an official capacity to serve a Crown-appointed officer (such as a sheriff) or a court. In the second meaning, it refers to an agent of a private person who collects rents or manages real estate. *R. v. Burns* 2002 MBCA 161, [2003] 2 W.W.R. 638, 170 C.C.C. (3d) 288, 170 Man. R. (2d) 55, 285 W.A.C. 55.

BAILIWICK. *n.* Geographic jurisdiction of a sheriff or bailiff.

BAILMENT. *n.* "... [T]he delivery of personal chattels on trust, usually on a contract, express or implied, that the trust shall be executed and the chattels delivered in either their original or an altered form as soon as the time for which they were bailed has elapsed ... the legal relationship of bailor and bailee can exist independently of a contract. It is created by the voluntary taking into custody of good[s] which are the property of another... ." *Punch v. Savoy's Jewellers Ltd.* (1986), 33 B.L.R. 147 at 154, 54 O.R. (2d) 383, 35 C.C.L.T. 217, 14 O.A.C. 4, 26 D.L.R. (4th) 546, the court per Cory J.A. See GRATUITOUS ~.

BAILMENT BY ATTORNMENT. Occurs when, with the bailor's consent, a bailee delivers the goods to another person to hold, making that person bailee of the bailor. E.L.G. Tyler & N.E. Palmer, eds., *Crossley Vaines' Personal Property*, 5th ed. (London: Butterworths, 1973) at 84.

BAILOR. *n.* A person who entrusts something to another person for a specific purpose.

BAIT. *v.* To set one animal against another which is tied or contained.

BAIT AND SWITCH. To advertise at a bargain price a product that the person does not supply in reasonable quantities having regard to the nature of the market in which the person carries on business, the nature and size of the person's business and the nature of the advertisement. A selling practice reviewable under the Competition Act. *Competition Act*, R.S.C. 1985, c. C-34, s. 74.04.

BALANCE. *n.* The difference between the total debit entries and total credit entries in an account; the remainder.

BALANCE OF CONVENIENCE. A determination of which of the two parties will suffer the greater harm from the granting or refusal of an interlocutory injunction, pending a decision on the merits. *Metropolitan Stores (MTS) Ltd. v. Manitoba Food & Commercial Workers, Local 832* [1987] 1 S.C.R. 110, Beetz J. for the court.

BALANCE OF PROBABILITIES. 1. The words "balance of probabilities" may be expressed as "more probable than not" ... or the equivalent—more likely than not. Unless the words of a statute or the context requires otherwise, the standard of proof in civil cases is always proof on a balance of probabilities. *Li v. Canada (Minister of Citizenship & Immigration)*, 2005 FCA 1. 2. Where one thing is more probable than another; greater likelihood of one thing than another.

BALANCE OF TRADE. The difference between the value of the imports into and exports from a country.

BALANCE-SHEET. *n.* A statement showing the assets and liabilities of a business.

BALLISTICS. *n.* The study of the behaviour of projectiles. F.A. Jaffe, *A Guide to Pathological Evidence for Lawyers and Police Officers*, 4th ed. (Toronto: Carswell, 1999) at 231.

BALLOON PAYMENT. A large payment at the end of the term of a mortgage when the mortgage amount is not fully amortized over the term.

BALLOT. *n.* 1. The paper by which a voter casts the voter's vote at an election. Contains the names of candidates in the election, arranged alphabetically, taken from their nomination papers. 2. The portion of a ballot paper which has been marked by an elector, detached from the counterfoil, and deposited in the ballot box.

BALLOT PAPER. As soon as possible after the issue of the writ, the Chief Electoral Officer shall provide the returning officer with the paper on which the ballots are to be printed. The weight and opacity of the paper shall be determined by the Chief Electoral Officer. *Canada Elections Act*, S.C. 2000, c. 9, s. 115(1).

BAN. *v.* 1. To exclude. 2. To expel. 3. To prevent.

BAN. *n.* A proclamation or public notice which publicizes an intended marriage. See PUBLICATION ~.

BANC. *n.* A bench or seat of justice.

BANCO. *n.* A bench or seat of justice.

BAND. *n.* 1. A body of Indians (a) for whose use and benefit in common, lands, the legal title of which is vested in Her Majesty, have been set apart before, on or after September 4, 1951, (b) for whose use and benefit in common, moneys are held by Her Majesty, or (c) declared by the Governor in Council to be a band for the purposes of this Act. *Indian Act*, R.S.C. 1985, c. I-5, s. 2. 2. With reference to a reserve or surrendered lands, means the band for whose use and benefit the reserve or the surrendered lands were set apart. *Indian Act*, R.S.C. 1985, c. I-5, s. 2. 3. The definition of "band" does not constitute an Indian Band as a legal entity. Rather, I take it from the definition of "band", and other provisions of the Indian Act, that in relation to rights to an Indian reserve, a band is a distinct population of Indians for whose use and benefit, in common, a reserve has been set aside by the Crown. It does not follow that because an Indian band is not a legal entity, rights accruing to the band are the rights of its members or their descendants in their individual capacities. The definition of "band" uses the term "in common" in relation to the interest that the members of the band have in the reserve. The term "in common" connotes a communal, as opposed to a private, interest in the reserve, by the members of the band. In other words, an individual member of a band has an interest in association with, but not independent of, the interest of the other members of the band. *Blueberry River Indian Band v. Canada (Department of Indian Affairs & Northern Development)*, 2001 CarswellNat 963, 2001 FCA 67, 6 C.P.C. (5th) 1, 201 D.L.R. (4th) 35, 274 N.R. 304 (C.A.), the court per Rothstein J.A. See CUSTOM ~; INDIAN ~.

BAND COUNCIL. The council of the band as defined in the Indian Act (Canada).

BAND COUNCILLOR. A councillor of a band within the meaning of the Indian Act (Canada).

BANDIT. *n.* An outlaw; a person who is put under the ban by law.

BAND'S CUSTOM. Include practices for the choice of a council which are generally acceptable to members of the band, upon which there is a broad consensus. *Bigstone v. Big Eagle*, (1992), 52 F.T.R. 109 (F.C.T.D.), Strayer, J.

BANISHMENT. *n.* 1. Expulsion from a nation; loss of nationality. 2. One of the possible outcomes of a sentencing circle.

BANK. *n.* 1. A bank listed in Schedule I or II to the Bank Act. *Bank*, S.C. 1991, c. 46, s. 2. 2. An incorporated bank or savings bank carrying on business in Canada. 3. A bank to which the Bank Act or the Quebec Savings Banks Act applies. 4. Includes every member of the Canadian Payments Association established under the Canadian Payments Association Act and every local cooperative credit society, as defined in that Act, that is a member of a central, as defined in that Act, that is a member of the Canadian Payments Association. *Bills of Exchange Act*, R.S.C. 1985, c. B-4, s. 164. 5. The Bank of Canada. *Bank of Canada Act*, R.S.C. 1985, c. B-2, s. 2. 6. An organization or corporation that is set up to accept deposits of money from persons and to pay out the money according to their instructions on demand. See BUSINESS DEVELOPMENT ~; CHARTERED ~; DATA ~; HEALTH INFORMATION ~.

BANK ACCOUNT. "[Both a] ... debt, ... [and] property, ..." *Ontario (Securities Commission) v. Greymac Credit Corp.* (1986), 34 B.L.R. 29 at 45, 23 E.T.R. 81, 30 D.L.R. (4th) 1, 55 O.R. (2d) 673, 17 O.A.C. 88, the court per Morden J.A. See JOINT ~.

BANK-BOOK. *n.* 1. A record of deposits and withdrawals from a bank account. 2. "... [E]vidence of a debt... ." *Cusack v. Day*, [1925] 2 W.W.R. 715 at 722, 3 D.L.R. 1028, 36 B.C.R. 106 (C.A.), MacDonald J.A.

BANK DEPOSIT. 1. The money left with a bank by a customer. It is loaned to the bank and is to be repaid on demand by the customer. The bank pays interest while the money remains on deposit with it. 2. A bank deposit is a simple contract debt and is located by common law principles (and by legislation, see s. 461(4) of the Bank Act, S.C. 1991, c. 46, and s. 447(4) of the Trust and Loan Companies Act [S.C. 1991, c. 45]) at the branch where the account is maintained. *McDiarmid Lumber Ltd. v. God's Lake First Nation*, 2005 MBCA 22.

BANKER. *n.* 1. "... [A] person or corporation who carries on the business of banking, and to whom members of the public have access for the purpose of depositing money, opening accounts, drawing cheques, borrowing money, and a variety of other services such as are offered by banks." *655 Developments Ltd. v. Chester Dawe Ltd.* (1992), 42 C.P.R. (3d) 500 at 515, 97 Nfld. & P.E.I.R. 247, 308 A.P.R. 246 (Nfld. T.D.), Wells J. 2. "... '[A] dealer in credit.' "*Reference re Alberta Legislation*, [1938] S.C.R. 100 at 116, [1938] 2 D.L.R. 81, Duff C.J. (Davis J. concurring).

BANKER'S ACCEPTANCE. A draft drawn on and accepted by a bank used to pay for goods sold in import-export transactions and as a source of financing in trade.

BANKING. *n.* 1. From an institutional point of view, the point of view adopted by the court, involves a set of interrelated financial activities carried out by an institution that operates under the nomenclature and terms of incorporation which clearly identify it as having the distinctive institutional character of a bank. Other approaches were considered. According to the functional approach, the relation between a banker and a customer who pays money into the bank is not a fiduciary one. It is the ordinary relation of debtor and creditor, with a superadded obligation arising out of the custom of bankers to honour the customer's cheques. Possession of or property in the deposit remains with the bank, the obligation of which is a debt under a contract of mutuum, not commodatum. From the economic point of view, a view widely held in the nineteenth century, banks were considered as the main channel for the transfer of savings; the function of banking was one of financial intermediation in which the public had an interest with respect to solvency and allocation of financial resources. But under this particular economic view the list of financial intermediaries would include, as well as chartered banks, some other very different types of institutions such as life insurance companies, finance companies, mortgage companies, trust companies, etc. From a legal point of view, includes the following: (1) Receiving money on deposit from its customers, (2) Paying a customer's cheques or drafts on it to the amount on deposit by such customers, and holding Dominion Government and bank notes and coin for such purpose; (3) Paying interest by agreement on deposits; (4) Discounting commercial paper for its customers; (5) Dealing in exchange and in gold and silver coin and bullion; (6) Collecting notes and drafts deposited; (7) Arranging credits for itself with banks in other towns, cities and countries; (8) Selling its drafts or cheques on other banks and banking correspondents; (9) Issuing letters of credit; (10) Lending money to its customers (a) on the customers' notes; (b) by way of overdraft; (c) on bonds, shares and other securities. The business of a Canadian chartered bank is wider still because of the statutory rights and powers given to a bank under the provisions of The Bank Act. The business carried on by most banks includes the totality of these functions enumerated, but, of course, a banking business can be carried on without performing all of them and most corporations and individuals engaged in a financial business of any kind are required to carry on or perform some of them and it does not follow from the fact that banks perform them that every exercise of one or more of the functions is a form of banking. *Canadian Pioneer Management Ltd. v. Saskatchewan (Labour Relations Board)* [1980] 1 S.C.R. 433, Beetz J. for the majority. 2. "The legislative authority conferred by these words [s. 91.15 of the Constitution Act, 1867 (30 & 31 Vict.), s. 3] is not confined to the mere constitution of corporate bodies with the privilege of carrying on the business of bankers. It extends to the issue of paper currency... ." *Tennant v. Union Bank of Canada*, [1894] A.C. 31 at 46 (P.C.), Lord Watson.

BANKING BUSINESS. "... [I]ssuing letters of credit ... lending money; and ... accepting term deposits ... are within what, in common knowledge, would be considered the hard core of banking." *R. v. Milelli* (1989), 45 B.L.R. 209 at 215, 51 C.C.C. (3d) 165, 35 O.A.C. 241, the court per Finlayson J.A.

BANKING PRACTICES. See GENERALLY ACCEPTED ~.

BANK-NOTE. *n.* 1. Includes any negotiable instrument (a) issued by or on behalf of a person carrying on the business of banking in or out of Canada, and (b) issued under the authority of Parliament or under the lawful authority of the government of a state other than Canada, intended to be used as money or as the equivalent of money, immediately on issue or at some time subsequent thereto, and includes bank bills and bank post bills. *Criminal Code*, R.S.C. 1985, c. C-46, s. 2. 2. "... [A]n instrument which is a promissory note payable to bearer on demand." *R. v. Brown* (1854), 8 N.B.R. 13 at 15 (C.A.), the court per Carter C.J.

BANK OF CANADA. The federal body which devises and carries out monetary policy and is the fiscal agent of the government of Canada. By the Bank of Canada Act, this is the only body authorized to issue notes for circulation in Canada.

BANK OF CANADA RATE. The rate of interest set by the Bank of Canada for loans by the Bank of Canada to the chartered banks, as published by the Bank of Canada.

BANK RATE. The bank rate established by the Bank of Canada as the minimum rate at which the Bank of Canada makes short-term advances to banks listed in Schedule I to the Bank Act. *Courts of Justice Act*, R.S.O. 1990, c. C.43, s. 127(1).

BANKRUPT. *n.* A person who has made an assignment or against whom a receiving order has been made. *Bankruptcy and Insolvency Act*, R.S.C. 1985, c. B-3, s. 2.

BANKRUPT. *adj.* A person who has made an assignment or against whom a bankruptcy order has been made or the legal status of that person. [same citation but add in "and Insolvency in name of stat.] *Bankruptcy and Insolvency Act*, R.S.C. 1985, c. B-3, s. 2.

BANKRUPTCY. *n.* 1. The state of being bankrupt or the fact of becoming bankrupt. *Bankruptcy and Insolvency Act*, R.S.C. 1985, c. B-3, s. 2. 2. The debtor's property is vested in a trustee who is required to realize on the debtor's property and distribute the receipts to the debtor's creditors according to the scheme set out in the Bankruptcy and Insolvency Act. When the bankruptcy is ended, the debtor is free of debts except for certain prescribed debts for which the debtor remains liable. See ACT OF ~; CLAIM PROVABLE IN ~; TRUSTEE IN ~.

BANKRUPTCY AND INSOLVENCY. 1. A federal head of power. *Constitution Act, 1867* (U.K.), 30 & 31 Vict., c. 3, s. 91(21). 2. "... [I]t is a feature common to all the systems of bankruptcy and insolvency to which reference has been made, that the enactments are designed to secure that in the case of an insolvent person his assets shall be rateably distributed amongst his creditors whether he is willing that they shall be so distributed or not... ." *Reference re Assignments & Preferences Act (Ont.), s. 9*, [1894] A.C. 189 at 201, 70 L.T. 538, 63 L.J.P.C. 59 (Ont. P.C.), the board per Lord Chancellor.

BANNER. *v.* To carry picket signs on the picket line.

BANNS. *n.* (pl.) A proclamation or public notice which publicizes an intended marriage.

BAR. *v.* To stop; to prohibit.

BAR. *n.* 1. A barrier which separates the judge's bench and the front row of counsel's seats from the rest of the court; Queen's counsel are the only counsel allowed within the bar. 2. Obstacle; barrier. 3. Used to refer to the legal profession as a whole, usually in a geographical area. See CALL TO THE ~; OUTER ~.

BAR ADMISSION EXAMINATION. An examination in general subjects related to the practice of law including practice and procedure, ethics and the general law of a province and of Canada. The examination or set of examinations a person must take to qualify as a lawyer in a province.

BAR AND BENCH. Refers to members of the legal profession and the judiciary.

BAR CODE. A unique bar code in the symbology of the Universal Product Code (UPC), the Health Industry Business Communications Council (HIBCC) or the European Article Number (EAN), assigned to a medical device by the manufacturer. *Food and Drugs Act*, R.S.C. 1985, c. F-27, *Medical Devices Regulations*, SOR/98-282, s. 1.

BARE-BOAT CHARTER. 1. A vessel charter agreement under which the charterer has complete possession and control of the vessel, including the right to appoint its master and crew. *Canada Shipping Act, 2001*, S.C. 2001, c. 26, s. 2. 2. A charter of a ship without master or crew is commonly known as a "bareboat" charter. *North Ridge Fishing Ltd. v. "Prosperity" (The)*, 2000 CarswellBC 982, 2000 BCCA 283, 74 B.C.L.R.(3d) 383, 186 D.L.R. (4th) 374, Cumming J.A. (Prowse and Saunders JJ.A. concurring). 3. A contract of affreightment by which a lessor places an unmanned and unequipped or partly manned and partly equipped ship at the disposal of a charterer for a determinate time, and transfers to him the navigation, management, employment and agency of the ship. *Civil Code*, S.Q. 1991, c. 64, a. 2007.

BARE LAND STRATA LOT. (a) A strata lot in a bare land strata plan, and (b) in relation to land located outside British Columbia, a similar lot. *Real Estate Development Marketing Act*, S.B.C. 2004, c. 41, s. 1.

BARE LAND STRATA PLAN. A strata plan on which the boundaries of the strata lots are defined on a horizontal plane by reference to survey markers and not by reference to the floors, walls or ceilings of a building, or (b) any other strata plan defined by reg-

ulation to be a bare land strata plan. *Strata Property Act*, S.B.C. 1998, c. 43, s. 1.

BARE LICENSEE. "... [A] person merely permitted by the owner to enter without there being any obligation so to permit and with the right in the owner to revoke the permission at any time." *Musselman v. Zimmerman* (1922), 66 D.L.R. 350 at 351, [1922] 2 W.W.R. 640, 18 Alta. L.R. 104 (C.A.), Stuart J.A. (Scott C.J., Beck and Clarke JJ.A. concurring).

BARE TRUST. "[A trust under the terms of which] ... a trustee's only duty is to hold the legal estate until called upon by the beneficiary to convey... ." *Creasor v. Wall* (1982), 25 R.P.R. 1 at 16, 38 O.R. (2d) 35 (H.C.), White J. Compare ACTIVE DUTY; ACTIVE TRUST.

BARGAIN. *v.* To contract; to enter into an agreement; to negotiate an agreement. See PLEA ~; REFUSE TO ~ IN GOOD FAITH; UNDER~.

BARGAIN. *n.* Contract; agreement. See CATCHING ~.

BARGAIN AND SALE. A contract for the sale of chattels, of an estate or of any interest in land followed by payment of the price agreed.

BARGAIN COLLECTIVELY. To negotiate in good faith with a view to entering into, renewing or revising a collective agreement. See COLLECTIVE BARGAINING.

BARGAINING. *n.* "... '[N]egotiating.' " *Bloedel, Stewart & Welch Ltd. v. Stuart* (1942), 58 B.C.R. 351 at 356, [1943] 1 W.W.R. 128, [1943] 1 D.L.R. 183 (C.A.), Sloan J.A. See BLUE-SKY ~; COLLECTIVE ~.

BARGAINING AGENCY. See EMPLOYEE ~; EMPLOYER ~.

BARGAINING AGENT. (a) A trade union that has been certified by the Board as the bargaining agent for the employees in a bargaining unit and the certification of which has not been revoked, or (b) any other trade union that has entered into a collective agreement on behalf of the employees in a bargaining unit (i) the term of which has not expired, or (ii) in respect of which the trade union has, by notice given pursuant to subsection 49(1), required the employer to commence collective bargaining. *Canada Labour Code*, R.S.C. 1985, c. L-2, s. 3.

BARGAINING COLLECTIVELY. Negotiating in good faith with a view to the conclusion of a collective bargaining agreement, or a renewal or revision of a bargaining agreement, the embodiment in writing or writings of the terms of agreement arrived at in negotiations or required to be inserted in a collective bargaining agreement by this Act, the execution by or on behalf of the parties of such agreement, and the negotiating from time to time for the settlement of disputes and grievances of employees covered by the agreement or represented by a trade union representing the majority of employees in an appropriate unit. *The Trade Union Act*, R.S.S. 1978, c. T-17, s. 2. See COLLECTIVE BARGAINING.

BARGAINING POWER. See UNEQUAL ~.

BARGAINING RIGHT. "... [O]nly entitle[s] a union to be recognized as the exclusive bargaining agent for a particular group of employees... ." *Metropolitan Toronto Apartment Builders Association,* [1978] O.L.R.B. Rep. Nov. 1022 at 1034. See ABANDONMENT OF ~S; EXCLUSIVE ~.

BARGAINING UNIT. 1. A unit (a) determined by the Board to be appropriate for collective bargaining, or (b) to which a collective agreement applies. *Canada Labour Code,* R.S.C. 1985, c. L-2, s. 3. 2. " ... [F]or the purpose of s. 57 [Labour Relations Act, R.S.O. 1980, c. 228], is a unit consisting only of those of the employer's employees whom the trade union is entitled to represent." *Snow v. S.M.W., Loc. 285,* [1984] O.L.R.B. Rep. 1004 at 1010, Gray (Vice-Chair), Bell and Kobryn (Members).

BARGAINING UNIT WORK. Tasks which form part of the job description of a bargaining unit member.

BARGAINOR. *n.* The person who transfers the subject matter of a bargain and sale.

BARR. *abbr.* The Barrister (Canada).

BARRATRY. *n.* 1. Includes every wrongful act wilfully committed by the master or crew to the prejudice of the owner, or, as the case may be, the charterer. *Marine Insurance acts.* 2. The difference between champerty and barratry appears to be that while champerty is purely self-interested, barratry requires the additional intent to harm the third person: " ... if the design was not to recover his own right, but only to ruin and oppress his neighbour, that is barratry." Maintenance is further distinguished from barratry and champerty on the basis that it appears to be motivated by altruism. That is, it requires a person to "lay out money on behalf of another in suits at law to recover a just right, and this may be done in respect of the poverty of the party; but if he lends money to promote and stir up suits, then he is a barrator". In Canada, the common law criminal offences of champerty, maintenance and barratry (as well as refusing to serve in office and being a "common scold") were abolished after the 1950 Report of the Royal Commission on the Revision of the Criminal Code. There is no reference to a tort of barratry in torts texts. Nonetheless, for the purpose of this motion I will assume, but not decide, that there is such a thing as the tort of barratry. *McIntyre Estate v. Ontario (Attorney General)* (2001), 26 C.P.C. (5th) 312 (Ont. C.A.).

BARRED. Not permitted. Ended. See STATUTE ~.

BARRIER. *n.* Anything that prevents a person with a disability from fully participating in all aspects of society because of his or her disability, including a physical barrier, an architectural barrier, an information or communications barrier, an attitudinal barrier, a technological barrier, a policy or a practice. *Accessibility for Ontarians with Disabilities Act, 2005,* S.O. 2005, c. 11, s. 2. See INTERLOCK ~.

BARRIER-FREE. *adj.* That a building and its facilities can be approached, entered, and used by persons with physical or sensory disabilities. *Building Code Act, 1992,* S.O. 1992, c. 23, *Building Code,* O. Reg. 350/06, Division A.

BARRING. *conj.* or *prep.* "... '[I]n the absence of'." *Price v. Williams* (1990), 46 C.C.L.I. 161 at 164, [1990] I.L.R. 1-2681 (B.C. C.A.), the court per Hinds J.A.

BARRISTER. *n.* When used alone usually refers to a lawyer who appears as an advocate in court.

BARRISTER AND SOLICITOR. 1. The title given to a lawyer who is a member of a provincial law society in the common law provinces and territories of Canada. The legal profession is now divided into barristers and solicitors but the two words are still used, usually together to describe lawyers. When the words are used alone they tend to be used according to their original meanings. 2. "1) He is permitted to practice law in the province upon obtaining an annual certificate issued to him pursuant to the rules of the society ... 2) He is entitled to vote at an election of benchers ... 3) He is eligible to become a bencher ... 4) He is eligible to become an officer of the society ..." *Maurice v. Priel* (1987), 60 Sask. R. 241 at 245-6, [1988] 1 W.W.R. 491, 46 D.L.R. (4th) 416 (C.A.), Bayda C.J.S. (Brownridge J.A. concurring). 3. A member of the Law Society other than an honorary member or a student member thereof. *Legal Aid Act,* R.S.O. 1990, c. L.9, s. 1.

BARTER EXCHANGE NETWORK. A group of persons each member of which has agreed in writing to accept as full or partial consideration for the supply of property or services by that particular member to any other member of that group one or more credits (in this section referred to as "barter units") on an account of the particular member maintained or operated by a single administrator of all such accounts of the members, which credits can be used as full or partial consideration for supplies of property or services between members of that group. *Excise Tax Act,* R.S.C. 1985, c. E-15, s. 181.3.

BASE. *adj.* Inferior; impure.

BASE BID. A bid in which an amount of money is stated as the sum for which the bidder offers to perform the work described in the bidding document, exclusive of adjustments.

BASELINE. *n.* The low-water line along the coast or on a low-tide elevation that is situated wholly or partly at a distance not exceeding the breadth of the territorial sea of Canada from the mainland or an island. *Oceans Act,* S.C. 1996, c. 31, s. 5.

BASIC NECESSITIES. Things and services that are essential to health and well-being, including a basic living allowance, an allowance for shelter, essential health services and a funeral upon death. *Employment and Income Assistance Act,* C.C.S.M. c. E98, s. 1 and 2.

BASIC WAGE. Minimum wage.

BASIS. *n.* Foundation, main principle, starting point. See ACTUARIAL ~; CASH ~; COOPERATIVE ~.

BASIS POINT. One one-hundredth of a cent or of a percentage point.

BASKET CLAUSE. 1. Clause intended to ensure that the document covers a larger number of persons or instances than are actually specified in the document. 2. In pleadings, a request for such other relief as to this court may seem just. 3. In a wiretap authorization, a clause which would permit interception of any persons unknown to the police at the time of the application for the authorization and which would permit the police to intercept such communications at any place provided that there are reasonable and probable grounds to believe that the interception may assist. *R. v. Thompson*, [1990] 2 S.C.R. 1111.

BASTARD. *n.* A person born to unmarried parents.

BÂTONNIER. *n.* President of the Bar of Quebec. He shall have right of general supervision of the affairs of the Bar and shall preside at meetings of the General Council, sittings of the executive committee and general meetings. He shall be a member ex officio of all committees appointed by the Bar, except the disciplinary bodies, the professional inspection bodies and the committee for access to the profession. He shall prevent and reconcile disputes of a professional nature between the members of the Bar. *An Act respecting the Barreau du Québec*, R.S.Q. c. B-1, s. 11.

BATTERED CHILD SYNDROME. The collection of recent and old injuries found in children who have been repeatedly abused physically. F.A. Jaffe, *A Guide to Pathological Evidence for Lawyers and Police Officers*, 4th ed. (Toronto: Carswell, 1999) at 244.

BATTERED WOMAN. A woman who has experienced a cycle of tension-building, acute battering and loving contrition more than once. A feature of the cyclical nature of the abuse is that it begets a degree of predictability to the violence that is absent in an isolated violent encounter between two strangers. *R. v. Lavallee* [1990] 1 S.C.R. 852, Wilson J.

BATTERED WOMAN SYNDROME. Is not a legal defence in itself such that an accused woman need only establish that she is suffering from the syndrome in order to gain an acquittal. Is a psychiatric explanation of the mental state of women who have been subjected to continuous battering by their male intimate partners, which can be relevant to the legal inquiry into a battered woman's state of mind. *R. v. M. (M.A.)* [1998] 1 S.C.R. 123, L'Heureux-Dubé J. (McLachlin J. concurring).

BATTERY. *n.* 1. "... [T]he intentional infliction of unlawful force on another person." *Norberg v. Wynrib* (1992), 12 C.C.L.T. (2d) 1 at 16, [1992] 4 W.W.R. 577, 68 B.C.L.R. (2d) 29, 138 N.R. 81, 9 B.C.A.C. 1, 19 W.A.C. 1, 92 D.L.R. (4th) 449, [1992] 2 S.C.R. 226, La Forest J. (Gonthier and Cory JJ. concurring). 2. Medical procedures are battery unless consent is given. *Nagy v. Canada*, 2006 ABCA 227. See ASSAULT AND ~; NEGLIGENT ~.

BAWDY HOUSE. *var.* **BAWDY-HOUSE.** *n.* A brothel. *Singleton v. Ellison*, [1895] 1 Q.B. 607, Wills J. See COMMON ~.

B.C.A.C. *abbr.* British Columbia Appeal Cases, 1991-.

BC ALLOWANCE UNIT. A compliance unit issued under section 6 [BC Allowance Units]. *Greenhouse Gas Reduction (Cap and Trade) Act*, S.B.C. 2008, c. 32, s. 1.

BCAU. *abbr.* BC allowance unit.

B.C. BR. LECT. *abbr.* Canadian Bar Association, British Columbia Branch Lectures.

BCCA. Neutral citation for the British Columbia Court of Appeal.

BCCAT. *abbr.* British Columbia Council of Administrative Tribunals.

BCCLS. *abbr.* B.C. Courthouse Library Society.

B.C. CORPS. L.G. *abbr.* British Columbia Corporations Law Guide.

BC EMISSION REDUCTION UNIT. A compliance unit issued under section 8 [BC Emission Reduction Units]. *Greenhouse Gas Reduction (Cap and Trade) Act*, S.B.C. 2008, c. 32, s. 1.

BCERU. *abbr.* BC emission reduction unit.

B.C.H.R.C. DEC. *abbr.* British Columbia Human Rights Commission Decisions, 1975-1982.

BCHRT. Neutral citation for the British Columbia Human Rights Tribunal.

B.C.L.N. *abbr.* British Columbia Law Notes.

B.C.L.R. *abbr.* British Columbia Law Reports, 1977-1986.

B.C.L.R.B. DEC. *abbr.* British Columbia Labour Relations Board Decisions, 1979-.

B.C.L.R. (2D). *abbr.* British Columbia Law Reports (Second Series), 1986-1995.

B.C.L.R. (3D). *abbr.* British Columbia Law Reports (Third Series), 1995-.

BCPC. Neutral citation for the British Columbia Provincial Court.

B.C.R. *abbr.* 1. British Columbia Reports, 1867-1947. 2. B.C. Rail Ltd.

BCSC. Neutral citation for the British Columbia Supreme Court.

B.C.S.C.W. SUMM. *abbr.* British Columbia Securities Commission Weekly Summary, 1987-.

BCSECCOM. Neutral citation for the British Columbia Securities Commission.

B.C.T.R. *abbr.* British Columbia Tax Reports.

B.C. UTIL. COMM'N. *abbr.* British Columbia Utilities Commission Decisions, 1980-.

B.C.W.C.R. *abbr.* British Columbia Workers' Compensation Reporter, 1973-.

B.C.W.L.D. *abbr.* British Columbia Weekly Law Digest.

BD. *abbr.* Board.

B.D.M. *abbr.* Bulletin de droit municipal, 1994-.

BEAR. *n.* One who expects a fall in the price of shares.

BEARER. *n.* 1. The person in possession of a bill or note that is payable to bearer. *Bills of Exchange Act*, R.S.C. 1985, c. B-4, s. 2. 2. The person in possession of a security payable to bearer or endorsed in blank.

BEARER FORM. A security is in bearer form if it is payable to bearer according to its terms and not by reason of any endorsement.

BEAR MARKET. Name for a market when it is going down in value.

BECOME. *v.* "... [T]o come into being, ..." *R. v. Guaranty Properties Ltd.* (1990), 48 B.L.R. 197 at 209, 109 N.R. 284, 90 D.T.C. 6363, [1990] 2 C.T.C. 94, [1990] 3 F.C. 337, 37 F.T.R. 239n (C.A.), the court per MacGuigan J.A.

BED. See SEPARATION FROM ~ AND BOARD.

BEER. *n.* 1. Liquor made in whole or in part from grain, malt or other saccharine matter, whether or not the liquor is fermented or unfermented. *Excise Act*, R.S.C. 1985, c. E-14, s. 3(3). 2. A beverage that is beer for the purposes of the Liquor Licence Act, but does not include a beverage purporting to be beer that contains alcohol obtained by a means other than the fermentation of an infusion or decoction of barley, malt and hops or similar products if the alcohol so obtained increases the total alcohol content of the beverage by more than 0.5 per cent by volume. *Alcohol and Gaming Regulation and Public Protection Act, 1996*, S.O. 1996, c. 26, Sched., s. 17.

BEFORE THE COURT. In s. 5(3) [of the Family Relations Act, R.S.B.C. 1996, c. 128] may mean "physically within the court's jurisdiction" or they may mean "within the court's jurisdiction as authority has defined such jurisdiction". *Yassin v. Loubani*, 2006 BCCA 509.

BEFORE THE LAW. See EQUALITY BEFORE AND UNDER THE LAW; EQUALITY ~.

BEGGING. *n.* I am satisfied that squeegeeing, when considered in its real-life context, is an act that conveys essentially the same meaning as begging. The act of begging is communication and is evidently expression [within the meaning of s. 2(b) of the Canadian Charter of Rights and Freedoms]. ... The message "I am in need and I am requesting your help" is primary communication that seeks and invites participation in the community. *R. v. Banks* (2007), 84 O.R. (3d) 1 (C.A.).

BEGIN. *v.* To start, to commence. See RIGHT TO ~.

BEHAVIOUR. *n.* Conduct; comportment. See GOOD ~; MIS~.

BEING. *adj.* Living; existing. See HUMAN ~; IN ~.

BELIEF. *n.* "... [M]ore than acceptance, and involves knowledge, probably knowledge of consequences... ." *R. v. Budin* (1981), 20 C.R. (3d) 86 at 96, 32 O.R. (2d) 1, 58 C.C.C. (2d) 352, 120 D.L.R. (3d) 536 (C.A.), Brooke J.A. (concurring). See HONEST ~; INFORMATION AND ~.

BELIEVE. See REASONABLE GROUND TO ~.

BELONG. *v.* 1. To be the property of, to be owned. 2. "... [B]roader than legal ownership." *Agnew v. Ontario Regional Assessment Commissioner, Region No. 7* (1990), 1 M.P.L.R. (2d) 138 at 140, 74 D.L.R. (4th) 154 (Ont. Gen. Div.), Philp J.

BELOW. See COURT ~.

BELOW PAR. At a price lower than face or nominal value; at a discount.

BELT. See SAFETY ~.

BENCH. *n.* 1. The judge's seat in a court. 2. A single judge. 3. Judges collectively. See BAR AND ~; KING'S ~; QUEEN'S ~.

BENCHER. *n.* A member of the governing body of a provincial law society. May be elected by lawyers in a region of the province, in the province as a whole or may be appointed by the government to be a member of the governing body. See BACK-~; LIFE ~.

BENCH WARRANT. 1. A court-issued warrant to arrest a person. 2. Where an indictment has been preferred against a person who is at large, and that person does not appear or remain in attendance for his trial, the court before which the accused should have appeared or remained in attendance may issue a warrant for his arrest. *Criminal Code*, R.S.C. 1985, c. C-46, c. 597.

BENEFICIAL INTEREST. 1. "... [E]quitable and not a legal interest... ." *Vancouver A & W Drive-Ins Ltd. v. United Food Services Ltd.* (1980), 13 B.L.R. 89 at 102, 10 E.T.R. 34, 38 B.C.L.R. 30 (S.C.), Fulton J. 2. The interest of a beneficiary or beneficial owner. 3. An interest arising out of the beneficial ownership of securities. *Canada Business Corporations Act*, R.S.C. 1985, c. C-44, s. 2. 4. Includes ownership through a trustee, legal representative, agent or other intermediary. *Business Corporations Act*, S.N.B. 1981, c. B-9.1, s. 1.

BENEFICIAL OWNER. "... [T]he real owner of property even though it is in someone else's name." *Csak v. Aumon* (1990), 69 D.L.R. (4th) 567 at 570 (Ont. H.C.), Lane J.

BENEFICIAL OWNERSHIP. Includes ownership through a trustee, legal representative, agent or other intermediary. *Canada Business Corporations Act*, R.S.C. 1985, c. C-44, s. 2.

BENEFICIARY. *n.* 1. A person designated or appointed as one to whom or for whose benefit insurance money is to be payable. 2. A person entitled to benefit from a trust or will. 3. A person entitled to receive benefits under a statutory scheme. See IRREVOCABLE ~.

BENEFIT. *n.* 1. [S]omething that is a favourable or helpful circumstance. To provide legal representation under a contingent fee agreement to a client who is unable to pay for legal services is clearly to confer a benefit on the client. *Lee (Guardian ad litem of) v. Richmond Hospital Society*, 2005 BCCA 107. 2. A pension; a monetary amount paid under a pension or other plan. 3. A drug or other good or service that is supplied to an eligible person. 4. Compensation or an indemnity paid in money, financial assistance or services. 5. A material acquisition which confers an economic benefit on the taxpayer and does not constitute an exemption, e.g. loan or gift. (adopted by Dickson J. in *R. v. Savage* [1983] 2 S.C.R. 428nb). 6. The positive effect of one thing on another, the advantage one thing confers on another. 7. Must mean that the individual receiving it ultimately receives a net transfer of resources without expectation for repayment. *Maynard v. Maynard*, 1999 CarswellBC 333, 45 R.F.L. (4th) 395 (S.C.). See BRIDGING ~; CONTRIBUTORY ~; DEATH ~; DEFINED ~; DEFINED CONTRIBUTION ~; DETENTION ~; EMPLOYEE ~S; FRINGE ~; FUNDED ~S PLAN; IMPACT AND ~ AGREEMENT; PENSION ~; UNFUNDED ~S PLAN; UNIVERSAL CHILD CARE ~.

BENEFIT PLAN. See EMPLOYEE ~.

BENEFIT SOCIETY. See FRATERNAL ~; MUTUAL ~.

BENEVOLENT. *adj.* Charitable; conferring benefits; philanthropic.

BENEVOLENT PURPOSE. The relief of poverty, the advancement of education, the advancement of religion or any other purpose beneficial to the community. *Municipal Government Act*, R.S.A. 2000, c. M-26, *Community Organization Property Tax Exemption Regulation*, Alta. Reg. 281/98, s. 1.

BEQUEATH. *v.* To leave through a will.

BEQUEST. *n.* Personal property given by will. See RESIDUARY ~; SPECIFIC ~.

BESET. *v.* To approach, importune, assail another person. See WATCHING AND ~TING.

BEST EFFORTS. 1. "... [T]aking, in good faith, all reasonable steps to achieve the objective, carrying the process to its logical conclusion, and 'leaving no stone unturned' ..." *Bruce v. Waterloo Swim Club* (1990), 31 C.C.E.L. 321 at 336, 73 O.R. (2d) 709 (H.C.), Lane J. In summary, the principles extracted from the cases on the issue of "best efforts" are: 1. "Best efforts" imposes a higher obligation than a "reasonable effort". 2. "Best efforts" means taking, in good faith, all reasonable steps to achieve the objective, carrying the process to its logical conclusion and leaving no stone unturned. 3. "Best efforts" includes doing everything known to be usual, necessary and proper for ensuring the success of the endeavour. 4. The meaning of "best efforts" is, however, not boundless. It must be approached in the light of the particular contract, the parties to it and the contract's overall purpose as reflected in its language. 5. While "best efforts" of the defendant must be subject to such overriding obligations as honesty and fair dealing, it is not necessary for the plaintiff to prove that the defendant acted in bad faith. 6. Evidence of "inevitable failure" is relevant to the issue of causation of damage but not to the issue of liability. The onus to show that failure was inevitable regardless of whether the defendant made "best efforts" rests on the defendant. 7. Evidence that the defendant, had it acted diligently, could have satisfied the "best efforts" test is relevant evidence that the defendant did not use its best efforts. The "no stone unturned" test has been applied to contracts relating to a wide variety of subject matter. Further, courts routinely imply a term in contracts that the parties will make reasonable efforts to fulfil their respective contractual obligations. Where the parties include a "best efforts" clause in a contract, as they did in the case at bar, they must surely intend that something more than "reasonable efforts" be used. *Atmospheric Diving Systems Inc. v. International Hard Suits Inc.*, 1994 CarswellBC 158, 89 B.C.L.R. (2d) 356, [1994] 5 W.W.R. 719, 53 C.P.R. (3d) 459, 13 B.L.R. (2d) 243 (S.C.), Dorgan J.

BEST EVIDENCE RULE. Wherever possible, the original of a document must be produced. P.K. McWilliams, *Canadian Criminal Evidence*, 3d ed. (Aurora: Canada Law Book, 1988) at 6-1.

BESTIALITY. *n.* The act of a human being having sexual intercourse with an animal.

BEST INTERESTS OF THE CHILD. 1. "... [T]he physical comfort and material advantages that may be available in the home of one contender or the other. The welfare of the child must be decided on a consideration of these and all other relevant factors, including the general psychological, spiritual and emotional welfare of the child... ." *King v. Low* (1985), 16 D.L.R. (4th) 576 at 587, [1985] 1 S.C.R. 87, the court per McIntyre J. 2. The ultimate test in all cases is the best interest of the child. This is a positive test, encompassing a wide variety of factors. One of the factors which the judge seeking to determine what is in the best interests of child must have regard to is the desirability of maximizing contact between the child and each parent. But in the final analysis, decisions on access must reflect what is in the best interests of the child. *Young v. Young*, 1993 CarswellBC 264, 84 B.C.L.R. (2d) 1, [1993] 8 W.W.R. 513, 49 R.F.L. (3d) 117, 160 N.R. 1, 34 B.C.A.C. 161, 56 W.A.C. 161, 108 D.L.R. (4th) 193, [1993] 4 S.C.R. 3, 18 C.R.R. (2d) 41, [1993] R.D.F. 703, McLachlin J. 3. The general purpose of the "best interests" standard is to provide courts with a focus and perspective through which to act on behalf of those who are vulnerable. The application of an objective "best interests" standard to infants and very young children is uncontroversial. Mature adolescents, on the other hand, have strong claims to autonomy, but these claims exist in tension with a protective duty on the part of the state that is also justified. When applied to adolescents, therefore, the "best interests" standard must be interpreted in a way that reflects and addresses an adolescent's evolving capacities for autonomous decision making. It is not only an option for the court to treat the child's views as an increasingly determinative factor as his or her maturity increases, it is, by definition, in a child's best interests to respect and promote his or her autonomy to the extent that his or her maturity dictates. This approach to "best interests" finds support in the relevant provisions of the Child and Family Services Act, C.C.S.M. c. C80. The standard a judge is obliged to follow before deciding whether to authorize treatment for a child under 16 in accordance with s. 25(8) is found in s. 2(1) of the Act. That section sets out the primacy of the child's best interests and delineates a number of considerations to be included in making such a determination. The statutory factors reflect decades of careful study into children's needs and how the law can best meet them. We have come, with time, to understand the significance of so many relevant considerations which had been previously hidden behind formulaic solutions like "the tender years doctrine." With our evolving understanding has come the recognition that the quality of decision making about a child is enhanced by input from that child. The extent to which that input affects the "best interests" assessment is as variable as the child's circumstances, but one thing that can be said with certainty is that the input becomes increasingly determinative as the child matures. This is true not only when considering the child's best interests in the placement context, but also when deciding whether to accede to a child's wishes in medical treatment situations. Constitutional compliance in the context of the medical treatment decisions anticipated by ss. 25(8) and 25(9) means that the best interests standard must be interpreted in a way that is not arbitrary (to avoid violating s. 7 of the Charter); not discriminatory on the basis of age (to avoid a s. 15 violation); and not contrary to a child's right to freedom of religion protected by s. 2(a). When the "best interests" standard is applied in a way that takes into increasingly serious account the young person's views in accordance with his or her maturity in a given treatment case, the legislative scheme created by ss. 25(8) and 25(9) of the Child and Family Services Act is neither arbitrary, discriminatory, nor violative of religious freedom. *A.C. v. Manitoba (Director of Child and Family Services)*, 2009 SCC 30, [2009] 2 S.C.R. 181, Abella J. (LeBel, Deschamps and Charron JJ. concurring.).

BEST USE. See HIGHEST AND ~.

BET. *n.* 1. A bet that is placed on any contingency or event that is to take place in or out of Canada, and without restricting the generality of the foregoing, includes a bet that is placed on any contingency relating to a horse-race, fight, match or sporting event that is to take in or out of Canada. *Criminal Code,* R.S.C. 1985, c. C-46, s. 197. 2. A bet placed under the system known as pari-mutuel wagering upon a race run at a race meeting. *Race Tracks Tax Act,* R.S.O. 1990, c. R.1, s. 1. 3. Money or its equivalent representative of value that is risked on the outcome of a game of chance. *Gaming Control Act,* S.N.S. 1994-95, c. 4, *Casino Regulations,* N.S. Reg. 40/95, s. 2.

BETTER BUSINESS BUREAU. An organization which provides information to consumers regarding local businesses.

BETTER EQUITY. When one claimant should have priority over the others because of notice, priority in time or some other reason.

BETTERMENT. *n.* Increasing property value.

BETTING. *n.* A wagering contract under which financial consideration is made payable as the result of a contingency. See INTER-TRACK ~; ON-TRACK ACCOUNT ~.

BETTING HOUSE. See COMMON ~.

BETTING THEATRE. An enclosed structure that is used for theatre betting, that is affixed to the land and that contains seating for 75 per cent of the number of persons permitted by the appropriate municipal authority to occupy the structure. *Criminal Code,* R.S.C. 1985, c. C-46, *Pari-Mutuel Betting Supervision Regulations,* SOR/91-365, s. 2.

BETWEEN. See AS ~.

BEVERAGE CONTAINER. A container that (a) holds five litres or less of a beverage, and (b) is delivered sealed to (i) a retailer who sells the beverage without opening the container, or (ii) a food service. *Beverage Containers Act,* S.N.B. 1991, c. B-2.2, s. 1.

BEYOND A REASONABLE DOUBT. The standard of proof required in criminal cases. "... The burden cast upon the Crown is to prove all essential ingredients of the crime charged beyond a reasonable doubt, viz. 'outside the limit or sphere of' or 'past' a reasonable doubt... ." *R. v. Lachance* (1962), 39 C.R. 127 at 130, [1963] 2 C.C.C. 14 (Ont. C.A.), Porter C.J.O., Roach, Aylesworth, Schroeder and Kelly JJ.A.

BEYOND SEAS. "... [O]utside the jurisdiction." *Schacht v. Schacht* (1982), 30 C.P.C. 52 at 54, [1982] 5 W.W.R. 189 (B.C. C.A.), the court per Hutcheon J.A.

B.F.L.R. *abbr.* Banking & Finance Law Review.

BFOR. *abbr.* Bona fide occupational requirement.

BFR. *abbr.* Bona fide requirement.

BFRJ. *abbr.* Bona fide and reasonable justification.

BIAS. *n.* 1. Prejudice. 2. "[B]ias denotes a state of mind that is in some way predisposed to a particular result, or that is closed with regard to particular issues. *R. v. S. (R.D.)*, 1997 CarswellNS 301, 151 D.L.R. (4th) 193, 118 C.C.C. (3d) 353, 10 C.R. (5th) 1, 218 N.R. 1, 161 N.S.R. (2d) 241, 477 A.P.R. 241, [1997] 3 S.C.R. 484, 1 Admin. L.R (3d) 74, Cory J. 3. An allegation of bias is a serious charge against those who have accepted the obligations of independence and impartiality which go with judicial or quasi-judicial office, as have the members of this commission. To charge such persons with bias is not merely to say that they would be likely to decide a particular matter in a particular way, but to say that they would do so improperly. The charge implies that the quasi-judicial decision-maker would not decide the case independently, and on the basis of the evidence, but would do so under improper influence, and with a view to achieving an extraneous or otherwise improper purpose. *Bennett v. British Columbia (Superintendent of Brokers)*, 1994 CarswellBC 762, 36 C.P.C. (3d) 96, 7 C.C.L.S. 165, 30 Admin. L.R. (2d) 283, 48 B.C.A.C. 56, 78 W.A.C. 56 (C.A. [In Chambers]), Taylor J.A. 4. "... [C]overs a spectrum of disqualification ranging from partiality on one hand, to the extreme of corruption on the other... ." *Calgary General Hospital c. U.N.A., Local 1* (1983), 6 Admin. L.R. 80 at 85, 29 Alta. L.R. (2d) 3, 84 C.L.L.C. 14,032, 50 A.R. 250, 5 D.L.R. (4th) 54 (C.A.), the court per Stevenson J.A. 5. "Bias may be of two kinds.

It may arise from an interest in the proceedings... . Sometimes it is a direct pecuniary or proprietary interest in the subject-matter of the proceedings. A person possessing such an interest is disqualified from sitting as a judge thereon. Sometimes the interest is not financial but arises from a connection with the case or with the parties of such a character as to indicate a real likelihood of bias... . the second kind of bias – namely actual bias in fact." *Gooliah v. R.* (1967), (*sub nom. Gooliah, Re*) 63 D.L.R. (2d) 224 at 227-8, 59 W.W.R. 705 (Man. C.A.), Freedman J.A. [existing defs.] 6. In the context of challenges for cause, refers to an attitude that could lead jurors to discharge their function in the case at hand in a prejudicial and unfair manner. It is evident from the definition of bias that not every emotional or stereotypical attitude constitutes bias. Prejudice capable of unfairly affecting the outcome of the case is required. Bias is not determined at large, but in the context of the specific case. What must be shown is a bias that could, as a matter of logic and experience, incline a juror to a certain party or conclusion in a manner that is unfair. *R. v. Find*, 2001 CarswellOnt 1702, 2001 SCC 32, 42 C.R. (5th) 1, 154 C.C.C. (3d) 97, 199 D.L.R. (4th) 193, 269 N.R. 149, 146 O.A.C. 236, the court per McLachlin C.J.C. See APPREHENSION OF ~; ATTITUDINAL ~; INSTITUTIONAL ~.

BI-CAMERAL. *adj.* Having two chambers: in Canada, refers to the two houses of Parliament, the House of Commons and the Senate.

BID. *v.* 1. To make an offer at an auction. 2. To submit a response to a call for tenders.

BID. *n.* 1. "... [T]he submission of a tender, ..." *Ron Engineering & Construction (Eastern) Ltd. v. Ontario* (1981), 13 B.L.R. 72 at 122-23, 119 D.L.R. (3d) 267, 35 N.R. 40, [1981] 1 S.C.R. 111, Estey J. 2. "[In the Combines Investigation Act, R.S.C. 1970, c. C-23, s. 32.2(1)(b)] ... must be interpreted to be an offer which may be accepted by the offeree binding the offeror ..." *R. v. Coastal Glass & Aluminum Ltd.* (1984), 8 C.P.R. (3d) 46 at 59, 17 C.C.C. (3d) 313 (B.C. S.C.), Lander J. 3. A take over bid or an issuer bid. 4. Documentation submitted by a contractor in response to a tender for a construction contract. 5. A "Tender" is that which a General Contractor submits to an Owner. It is not to a "Bid" which is what a Subcontractor submits to a General Contractor. *Ken Toby Ltd. v. British Columbia Buildings Corp.*, 1997 CarswellBC 1087, 34 B.C.L.R. (3d) 263, [1997] 8 W.W.R. 721, 34 C.L.R. (2d) 81, 31 B.L.R. (2d) 224 (S.C.), Burnyeat J. See BASE ~; ISSUER ~; SHOPPING A ~; STALKING HORSE ~; TAKE OVER ~.

BID BOND. A bond given by a person to guarantee entry into a contract if the contract is awarded to that person.

BIDDER. *n.* At an auction, a person who makes an offer.

BIDDING. *n.* Quoting cost or price for a contract in response to a request or call for bids or tenders.

BIFURCATION. *n.* The splitting of the issues of liability and damages to be tried separately as to time

or as to trier of the issue. [The rules] permit the separate hearings of issues of liability and damages with consent of the parties. Nevertheless, the issues cannot be split between two juries. *Kovach v. Linn*, 2010 ONCA 126.

BIGAMY. *n.* Every one commits bigamy who (a) in Canada, (i) being married, goes through a form of marriage with another person, (ii) knowing that another person is married, goes through a form of marriage with that person, or (iii) on the same day or simultaneously, goes through a form of marriage with more than one person; or (b) being a Canadian citizen resident in Canada leaves Canada with intent to do anything mentioned in subparagraphs (a)(i) to (iii) and, pursuant thereto, does outside Canada anything mentioned in those subparagraphs in circumstances mentioned therein. *Criminal Code*, R.S.C. 1985, c. C-46, s. 290(1).

BILATERAL. *adj.* Involving two agreeing parties.

BILATERAL CONTRACT. A contract in which each of the two parties is bound to fulfil obligations towards the other.

BILINGUAL. *adj.* Having the ability to speak two languages. Usually refers to the ability to speak both of Canada's official languages.

BILINGUAL TRIAL. Trial before a judge and jury who speak both official languages of Canada but in which both English and French are used interchangeably as the working languages, depending upon who is speaking and in what context, and interpretation and translation are available if needed. *R. v. Sarrazin* (2005), 196 O.A.C. 224.

BILL. *n.* 1. Writing; a letter. 2. An account. 3. In parliamentary practice, the first stage in the enactment of a statute. 4. An order. 5. A bill of exchange. *Bills of Exchange Act*, R.S.C. 1985, c. B-4, s. 2. See ACCOMMODATION ~; APPROPRIATION ~; CONSUMER ~; DEPOSITORY ~; EXCHEQUER ~; FOREIGN ~; GOVERNMENT ~; MONEY ~; PRIVATE ~; PRIVATE MEMBER'S ~; PUBLIC ~; TREASURY ~; TRUE ~.

BILLING. See EXTRA-~.

BILL OF COSTS. A document setting out the claim for legal fees and disbursements in a proceeding.

BILL OF EXCHANGE. An unconditional order in writing, addressed by one person to another, signed by the person giving it, requiring the person to whom it is addressed to pay, on demand or at a fixed or determinable future time, a sum certain in money to or to the order of a specified person or to bearer. *Bills of Exchange Act*, R.S.C. 1985, c. B-4, s. 16(1). See CONSUMER BILL.

BILL OF LADING. Includes all receipts for goods, wares and merchandise accompanied by an undertaking (a) to move the goods, wares and merchandise from the place where they were received to some other place, by any means whatever, or (b) to deliver at a place other than the place where the goods, wares and merchandise were received a like quantity of goods, wares and merchandise of the same or a similar grade or kind. *Bank Act*, R.S.C. 1985, c. B-1, s. 425.

BILL OF RIGHTS. 1. The Canadian Bill of Rights. S.C. 1960, c. 44. 2. The English Statute 1688, 1 Will. & Mary, sess. 2, c. 2. 3. The first 10 amendments to the U.S. Constitution. See CANADIAN ~.

BILL OF SALE. A document in writing in conformity with this Act evidencing a sale or a mortgage, but does not include a bill of lading, a warehouse receipt, a warrant or order for the delivery of goods, or any other document used in the ordinary course of business as proof of the possession or control of goods, or authorizing or purporting to authorize the possessor of the document to transfer, either by endorsement or delivery, or receive goods represented by that means. *Bills of Sale Act*, R.S.N.W.T. 1988, c. B-1, s. 1.

BIND. *v.* To obligate; to secure payment. See FINAL AND ~ING.

BINDER. *n.* A written memorandum providing temporary insurance coverage until a policy is issued. *Kline Brothers & Co. v. Dominion Fire Insurance Co.* (1913), 47 S.C.R. 252 at 255, 9 D.L.R. 231, Fitzpatrick C.J. (Davies, Idington, Duff and Brodeur JJ. concurring).

BINDING ARBITRATION. A binding arbitration is a non-court equivalent to a court trial. In either case a neutral third party hears the case and makes his decision which (subject to appeal) is binding upon the parties. This differs from other forms of ADR [Alternative Dispute Resolution] in which the parties themselves are part of the decision-making mechanism and the neutral third party's involvement is of a facilitative nature: e.g. mediation, conciliation, neutral evaluation, non-binding opinion, non-binding arbitration. Of course, the simplest method—often overlooked—is that of non-involvement by a neutral: a negotiation between the parties. *887574 Ontario Inc. v. Pizza Pizza Ltd.*, 1994 CarswellOnt 1069, 35 C.P.C. (3d) 323, 23 B.L.R. (2d) 239 (Gen. Div. [Commercial List]), Farley J.

BINDING AUTHORITY. Compelling authority; a decision of a higher court which a lower court must follow.

BIND OVER. To enter into a bond before the court to keep the peace and be of good behaviour.

BIODIESEL. *n.* A substance that is made up of mono-alkyl esters of long chain fatty acids derived from plant or animal matter. *Carbon Tax Act*, S.B.C. 2008, c. 40, Sched. 1, s. 1. See BLENDED ~.

BIODIVERSITY. *n.* The variety of species and ecosystems in a park and the ecological processes of which they are a part. *Parks and Land Certainty Act*, R.S.Y. 2002, c. 165, s. 2.

BIOFUEL. n. Any liquid or gaseous fuel that is derived from either (i) organic material, or (ii) a metabolic byproduct of organic material. *Renewable Energy Act*, S.P.E.I. 2004, c. 16, s. 1. See BLENDED ~.

BIOLOGY. *n.* The study of life forms.

BIOMETRIC INFORMATION. 1. Information derived from an individual's unique characteristics but does not include a photographic or signature image. *Ontario Disability Support Program Act, 1997*, S.O. 1997, c. 25, Sched. B, s. 2. 2. Information derived from an individual's personal characteristics other than a representation of the individual's signature. *Electronic Transactions Act*, S.A. 2001, c. E-5.5, s. 5.

BIOMETRICS. *n.* The use of measurable human characteristics, such as fingerprints or iris images, to identify individuals.

BIOSECURITY MEASURES. Actions taken to minimize the spread of a disease or a disease-causing agent. *Animal Health Act*, S.A. 2007, c. A-40.2, s. 1.

BIOTECHNOLOGY. *n.* The application of science and engineering in the direct or indirect use of living organisms or parts or products of living organisms in their natural or modified forms.

BIPARTITE. *adj.* Having two parts.

BIRD. See MIGRATORY ~.

BIRTH. *n.* The complete expulsion or extraction from its mother, irrespective of the duration of pregnancy, of a product of conception in which, after such expulsion or extraction, there is breathing, beating of the heart, pulsation of the umbilical cord, or unmistakable movement of voluntary muscle, whether or not the umbilical cord has been cut or the placenta is attached. *Vital Statistics acts*. See LIVE ~; STILL~; WRONGFUL ~.

BIRTH NAME. The legal surname of a person as recorded in the birth registration records of the jurisdiction where that person was born. *The Change of Name Act, 1995*, S.S. 1995, c. C-6.1, s. 19;.

BLACK LIST. 1. A list of persons with whom those compiling the list advise that no one should have dealings of a certain type. 2. "... [H]istorically described the practice utilized by employers to identify and boycott unwanted employees, particularly trade-union activists and supporters." *Pacific Gillnetters Assn. v. U.F.A.W., British Columbia Provincial Council*, [1979] 1 Can. L.R.B.R. 506 at 518 (B.C.), Germaine (Vice-Chair), Fritz and Smith (Members).

BLACKMAIL. *n.* Menacing and making unwarranted demands. See EXTORTION.

BLACK MARKETING. Unauthorized dealing in or offering rationed, prohibited or restricted goods or services.

BLANK ACCEPTANCE. An acceptance written across a bill before it is filled out.

BLANK AUDIO RECORDING MEDIUM. An audio recording medium onto which no sounds have ever been fixed, and any other prescribed audio recording medium. *Copyright Act*, R.S.C. 1985, c. C-42, s. 79.

BLANK ENDORSEMENT. An endorsement written on the back of a bill of exchange before the bill is filled out.

BLANKET MORTGAGE. A second mortgage, granted when the first mortgage is small and at a low interest rate, whose principal includes the whole principal of the first mortgage even though the whole amount is not immediately advanced. The second mortgagee must make payments under the first mortgage as long as the second mortgage is valid. If the first mortgage matures, the mortgagee must pay it off and obtain a discharge so that the second mortgage becomes a first mortgage. D.J. Donahue & P.D. Quinn, *Real Estate Practice in Ontario*, 4th ed. (Toronto: Butterworths, 1990) at 226.

BLANKET RULINGS AND ORDERS. Rulings and orders issued under Canadian securities legislation in certain jurisdictions that are applicable to a class of persons, trades, intended trades, securities, exchange contracts or transactions. *Securities Act*, R.S.B.C. 1996, c. 418, *National Instrument 14-101 Definitions*, B.C. Reg. 48/97, s. 1.1.

BLASPHEMY. *n.* "... [T]he profane speaking of God or sacred things ... It may also bear the meaning of evil speaking or defamation, ..." *Ralston v. Fomich* (1992), 66 B.C.L.R. (2d) 166 at 168, [1992] 4 W.W.R. 284 (S.C.), Spencer J.

BLDG. *abbr.* Building.

BLEND. *v.* Of payment of principal and interest, to mix so that they are indistinguishable and inseparable. W.B. Rayner & R.H. McLaren, *Falconbridge on Mortgages*, 4th ed. (Toronto: Canada Law Book, 1977) at 665.

BLENDED. *adj.* 1. Describes a combined payment of principal money with interest. W.B. Rayner & R.H. McLaren, *Falconbridge on Mortgages*, 4th ed. (Toronto: Canada Law Book, 1977) at 662. 2. "... '[M]ixed so as to be inseparable and indistinguishable.' " *Kilgoran Hotels Ltd. v. Samek*, [1968] S.C.R. 3 at 5, 65 D.L.R. (2d) 534, the court per Hall J.

BLENDED BIODIESEL. A blend of biodiesel and a prescribed motive fuel or class of motive fuel. *The Biofuels Act*, S.M. 2003, c. 5, s. 1.

BLENDED BIOFUEL. Gasohol, blended biodiesel or any other blend of biofuel and one or more of the following: (a) gasoline; (b) a prescribed motive fuel or class of motive fuel. *The Biofuels Act*, S.M. 2003, c. 5, s. 1.

BLENDED FUND. A mixed fund obtained from different sources.

BLENDED PAYMENT. A periodic payment on a loan, a definite amount of which is applied first towards interest and the rest of which is applied to reducing the principal.

BLINDNESS. See WILFUL ~.

BLIND TRUST. The placing of any real or personal property in a trust where the trustee is other than a spouse or child of the settlor and where the settlor or beneficiary has no control over the trust estate during the trust, other than by way of receipt of income. *Conflict of Interest Act*, S.N.B. 1978, c. C-16.1, s. 1.

BLIND WORKER. A worker as defined in the Workers' Compensation Act, and possessing a cen-

tral visual acuity of the worker's better eye reading 6-60 or 20-200 or less, either with or without glasses. *Blind Workers' Compensation Act*, R.S.A. 2000, c. B-4, s. 1.

BLOOD. See CANADIAN ~ COMMITTEE; CORRUPTION OF ~.

BLOOD RELATIONSHIP. "... [D]escribed the relationship existing between two or more persons who stand in lawful descent from a common ancestor ..." *Army & Navy Department Store Ltd. v. Minister of National Revenues*, [1953] C.T.C. 293 at 300, [1953] 2 S.C.R. 496, [1954] 1 D.L.R. 177, 53 D.T.C. 1185, Locke J. (Taschereau and Fauteux JJ. concurring).

BLOWER. See WHISTLE ~.

B.L.R. *abbr.* Business Law Reports, 1977-1990.

B.L.R. (2D). *abbr.* Business Law Reports (Second Series), 1991-1999.

B.L.R. (3D). *abbr.* Business Law Reports (Third Series), 2000-.

BLUE CHIP. Highest quality securities.

BLUE-PENCIL SEVERANCE. 1. The blue-pencil approach is understood both as a test of the availability of severance to remedy contractual illegality and also as a technique for effecting severance. The blue-pencil approach as a test of the appropriateness of severance requires a consideration of whether an illegal contract can be rendered legal by striking out (i.e., by drawing a line through) the illegal promises in the agreement. The resulting set of legal terms should retain the core of the agreement. If the nature or core of the agreement is disturbed, then on this test the illegal clause in the contract is not a candidate for severance and the entire contract is void. The blue-pencil approach as a technique of effecting severance involves the actual excision of the provisions leading to the illegality, leaving those promises untainted by the illegality to be enforced. *Transport North American Express Inc. v. New Solutions Financial Corp.*, 2004 SCC 7, [2004] 1 S.C.R. 249, Arbour J. at para. 27. 2. Applied in limited circumstances to remove illegal features of a contract so as to render the contract in conformity with the law. effected when the part severed can be removed by running a blue pencil through it. Under the blue pencil test, severance is only possible if the judge can strike out, by drawing a line through, the portion of the contract they want to remove, leaving the portions that are not tainted by illegality, without affecting the meaning of the part remaining. *Shafron v. KRG Insurance Brokers (Western) Inc.*, 2009 SCC 6.

BLUE-SKY BARGAINING. Proposals by negotiators which are so unreasonable that there is no chance of their acceptance.

BLUE-SKY LAW. A law to protect investors from fraud in connection with sales of securities.

BN. *abbr.* Business number.

B.N.A. ACT(S). *abbr.* British North America Act(s).

BOARD. *n.* 1. A body of persons to which certain powers are delegated or assigned or who are elected for certain purposes. 2. The governing body of an institution. 3. The board of directors of a corporation. 4. "... [A] succession of meals obtained from day to day, or from week to week, or from month to month, &c... ." *R. v. McQuarrie* (1862), 22 U.C.Q.B. 600 at 601, the court per Draper C.J. See APPEAL ~; ARBITRATION ~; CANADIAN TRANSPORTATION ACCIDENT INVESTIGATION AND SAFETY ~; CANADIAN WHEAT ~; CHECKER~; COMMODITY ~; CONCILIATION ~; COPYRIGHT ~ OF CANADA; ENERGY SUPPLIES ALLOCATION ~; FEDERAL ~ COMMISSION OR OTHER TRIBUNAL; FREE ON ~; IMMIGRATION AND REFUGEE ~; LOCAL ~; MARKETING ~; MERCHANT SEAMEN COMPENSATION ~; PAROLE ~; PUBLIC SERVICE LABOUR RELATIONS ~; REVIEW ~; SEPARATION FROM BED AND ~; TREASURY ~; WILDLIFE MANAGEMENT ~.

BOARDING. *n.* Suggests that the owner of the animal makes an arrangement to leave it in the care of the boarding facility. *Woodman v. Capital (Regional District)*, 1999 CarswellBC 2193, 6 M.P.L.R. (3d) 128 (S.C.), Bauman J. See PET ~.

BOARD OF REFEREES. Consists of a chairperson and one or more members chosen from employers or representatives of employers and an equal number of members chosen from insured persons or representatives of insured persons. The first level of appeal from decisions of the employment commission. *Employment Insurance Act*, S.C. 1996, c. 23, s. 111 and 114.

BOARD OF TRADE. 1. Includes chamber of commerce, and, for the purposes of the appointment of weighers of grain under this Act, means any board of trade or chamber of commerce incorporated under any Act of Parliament, of the legislature of the former Province of Canada or of the legislature of any province. *Boards of Trade Act*, R.S.C. 1985, c. B-6, s. 2. 2. A corporation incorporated or continued pursuant to this Act as a membership corporation to carry on the activities of promoting and improving trade and commerce and as a result promoting and improving the economic, civic and social welfare of a district. *The Non-profit Corporations Act, 1995*, S.S. 1995, c. N-4.2, s. 184.

BOAT. *n.* 1. A watercraft or other artificial contrivance used or capable of being used as a means of transportation on water, whether self-propelled or not. *Parks Act*, S.N.B. 1982, c. P-2.1, s. 1. 2. "... [A]ny craft afloat, which carries goods or passengers... ." *R. v. Conrad*, [1938] 2 D.L.R. 541 at 543, 12 M.P.R. 588, 70 C.C.C. 100 (N.S. T.D.), the court per Chisholm C.J.

BODILY EVIDENCE. Evidence taken from the body of the accused, such as DNA evidence and breath samples. *R. v. Grant*, 2009 SCC 32, [2009] 2 S.C.R. 353, McLachlin C.J. and Charron J.

BODILY HARM. Any hurt or injury to a person that interferes with the health or comfort of a person and that is more than merely transient or trifling in nature. *Criminal Code*, R.S.C. 1985, c. C-46, s. 2. See GRIEVOUS ~; SERIOUS ~.

BODY. *n.* 1. The main section of any document or instrument. 2. In writs, a person. See CONCEALING ~ OF CHILD; LOCAL ~; LOCAL GOVERNMENT ~; SELF-REGULATING ~.

BODY CAVITY. The rectum or vagina. *Corrections and Conditional Release Act*, S.C. 1992, c. 20, s. 46.

BODY CAVITY SEARCH. 1. The physical probing of a body cavity, in the prescribed manner. *Corrections and Conditional Release Act*, S.C. 1992, c. 20, s. 46. 2. Involves a physical inspection of the detainee's genital or anal regions. While the mouth is a body cavity, it is not encompassed by the term "body cavity search". Searches of the mouth do not involve the same privacy concerns. *R. v. Golden*, 2001 SCC 83.

BODY CORPORATE. 1. Includes a company or other organization with legal personality wherever or however incorporated. *Canada Not-for-profit Corporations Act*, S.C. 2009, c. 23, s. 2. 2. An incorporated body wherever or however incorporated. *Bank Act*, S.C. 1991, c. 46, s. 2. 3. Any body corporate with or without share capital wherever or however incorporated. Alberta statutes. See HOLDING ~.

BODY PACKER. Somone who transports illicit drugs on their body or in body cavities. F.A. Jaffe, *A Guide to Pathological Evidence for Lawyers and Police Officers*, 4th ed. (Toronto: Carswell, 1999) at 231.

BODY POLITIC. A nation; a corporation.

BOILER AND MACHINERY INSURANCE. Insurance (a) against liability arising out of bodily injury to, or the death of, a person, or the loss of, or damage to, property, or against the loss of, or damage to, property, in each case caused by the explosion or rapture of, or accident to, pressure vessels of any kind or pipes, engines and machinery connected to or operated by those pressure vessels; or (b) against liability arising out of bodily injury to, or the death of, a person, or the loss of, or damage to, property, or against the loss of, or damage to, property, in each case caused by a breakdown of machinery. *Insurance Companies Act*, S.C. 1991, c. 47, Sched. [1].

BOILERPLATE. *n.* Standard clauses used in legal documents of a particular kind.

BOILER PLATE PROVISION. A standard clause which is inserted, by the drafter, usually *verbatim*, in instruments of the same type. *BC Tel v. Seabird Island Indian Band (Assessor of)* 2002 FCA 288, [2002] 4 C.N.L.R. 1, 216 D.L.R. (4th) 70, 292 N.R. 120, [2003] 1 F.C. 475, 231 F.T.R. 159 (note), Noël J.A. (dissenting).

BONA. *n.* [L.] Goods; property.

BONA. *adj.* [L.] Good.

BONA FIDE. [L. in good faith] "... '[H]onestly', 'genuinely' or 'in good faith': ..." *Extendicare Health Services Inc. v. Canada (Minister of National Health & Welfare)* (1987), 14 C.E.R. 282 at 286, 87 D.T.C. 5404, 15 F.T.R. 187, [1987] 3 F.C. 622, [1987] 2 C.T.C. 179, Can S.T.R. 80-127 (F.C.T.D.), Jerome A.C.J.

BONA FIDE AND REASONABLE JUSTIFI-CATION. Test used in the British Columbia Human Rights Code, R.S.B.C. 1996, c. 210, s. 8 in relation to alleged discrimination in accommodation or provision of services or facilities.

BONA FIDE OCCUPATIONAL QUALIFICA-TION. "... [M]ust be imposed honestly, in good faith, and in the sincerely held belief that such limitation is imposed in the interests of the adequate performance of the work involved with all reasonable dispatch, safety and economy, and not for ulterior or extraneous reasons ... it must be related in an objective sense to the performance of the employment concerned, in that it is reasonably necessary to assure the efficient and economical performance of the job without endangering the employee, his fellow employees and the general public." *Ontario (Human Rights Commission) v. Etobicoke (Borough)*, [1982] 1 S.C.R. 202 at 208, 40 N.R. 159, 82 C.L.L.C. 17,005, 132 D.L.R. (3d) 14, 3 C.H.R.R. D / 781, McIntyre J.

BONA FIDE OCCUPATIONAL REQUIRE-MENT. 1. Equivalent to bona fide occupational qualification. *Central Alberta Dairy Pool v. Alberta (Human Rights Commission)* (1990), 33 C.C.E.L. 1 at 14-15, 21, [1990] 2 S.C.R. 489, [1990] 6 W.W.R. 193, 72 D.L.R. (4th) 417, 76 Alta. L.R. (2d) 97, 90 C.L.L.C. 17,025, 113 N.R. 161, 12 C.H.R.R. D / 417, 111 A.R. 241, Wilson J. (Dickson C.J.C., L'Heureux-Dubé and Cory JJ. concurring). 2. The Supreme court has established a new test, the unified approach or Meiorin test: Having considered the various alternatives, I propose the following three-step test for determining whether a prima facie discriminatory standard is a BFOR. An employer may justify the impugned standard by establishing on the balance of probabilities: (1) that the employer adopted the standard for a purpose rationally connected to the performance of the job; (2) that the employer adopted the particular standard in an honest and good faith belief that it was necessary to the fulfilment of that legitimate work-related purpose; and (3) that the standard is reasonably necessary to the accomplishment of that legitimate work-related purpose. To show that the standard is reasonably necessary, it must be demonstrated that it is impossible to accommodate individual employees sharing the characteristics of the claimant without imposing undue hardship upon the employer. *British Columbia (Public Service Employee Relations Commission) v. B.C.G.E.U.*, 1999 CarswellBC 1907, 99 C.L.L.C. 230-028, [1999] 10 W.W.R. 1, 176 D.L.R. (4th) 1, 244 N.R. 145, 66 B.C.L.R. (3d) 253, 127 B.C.A.C. 161, 207 W.A.C. 161, 46 C.C.E.L. (2d) 206, 35 C.H.R.R. D / 257, 68 C.R.R. (2d) 1, [1999] 3 S.C.R. 3, the court per McLachlin J.

BONA FIDE PURCHASER. A purchaser for value in good faith and without notice of any adverse claim who takes delivery of a security in bearer form or of a security in registered form issued to the purchaser, endorsed to the purchaser or endorsed in blank. *Bank Act*, S.C. 1991, c. 46, s. 81.

BONA FIDE REQUIREMENT. Once the plaintiff establishes that the standard is prima facie discriminatory, the onus shifts to the defendant to prove on a balance of probabilities that the discriminatory standard is a BFOR or has a bona fide and reasonable justification. In order to establish this justification, the defendant must prove that: (1) it adopted the standard for a purpose or goal that is rationally connected to the function being performed; (2) it adopted the standard in good faith, in the belief that it is necessary for the fulfillment of the purpose or goal; and (3) the standard is reasonably necessary to accomplish its purpose or goal, in the sense that the defendant cannot accommodate persons with the characteristics of the claimant without incurring undue hardship. *British Columbia (Superintendent of Motor Vehicles) v. British Columbia (Council of Human Rights)*, 1999 CarswellBC 2730, [2000] 1 W.W.R. 565, 47 M.V.R. (3d) 167, 249 N.R. 45, 70 B.C.L.R. (3d) 215, 181 D.L.R. (4th) 385, 36 C.H.R.R. D / 129, [1999] 3 S.C.R. 868, 131 B.C.A.C. 280, 214 W.A.C. 280, the court per McLachlin J.

BONA FIDES. [L.] Good faith.

BONA VACANTIA. [L.] 1. Personal property without an owner, including the property of an intestate who dies without heirs, becomes the property of the Crown. 2. "... [T]he ultimate surplus of assets of the defunct company remaining after all obligations of the company are satisfied ... the residue after all obligations were discharged ... the residue only ... being the bona vacantia." *Embree v. Millar* (1917), 33 D.L.R. 331 at 334, [1917] 1 W.W.R. 1200, 11 Alta. L.R. 127 (C.A.), the court per Beck J.A. See VACANTIA BONA.

BOND. *n.* 1. "... [A] written instrument under seal whereby the person executing it makes a promise or incurs a personal liability to another." *Grimmer v. Gloucester (County)* (1902), 32 S.C.R. 305 at 310, the court per Sedgewick J. 2. A government debt obligation which is unsecured or a debt obligation of a large public corporation. 3. Includes a debenture, debenture stock or other evidences of indebtedness. *Companies' Creditors Arrangement Act*, R.S.C. 1985, c. C-36, s. 2. 4. Security of any kind, including money, given to ensure performance of an obligation arising under an enactment, a licence, a permit, a contract or another similar obligation, and includes the terms under which the security may be realized. *Bonding Act*, R.S.B.C. 1996, c. 30, s. 1. 5. An agreement in writing signed by the guarantor under which the guarantor undertakes, upon the default of another person named in the agreement in paying a debt or a debt of a class of debts specified in the agreement (i) to pay a sum of money; or (ii) to pay the debt. *The Guarantors' Liability Act*, R.S.M. 1987, c. G120, s. 1. See BACK-~; BAIL-~; BID ~; BOTTOMRY ~; CANADA DISABILITY SAVINGS ~; COMPLETION ~; CONTRACT ~; COUPON ~; MORTGAGE ~; PAYMENT ~; PEACE ~; PERFORMANCE ~; SURETY ~.

BONDED. See CUSTOMS ~ CARRIER; CUSTOMS ~ WAREHOUSE.

BONDED GOODS. Dutiable goods for which a bond was given for payment of the duty.

BONDEE. *n.* A person named in a bond upon whose default in paying a debt or a debt of a class of debts specified in the bond the guarantor undertakes to pay a sum of money or to pay the debt. *The Guarantors' Liability Act*, R.S.M. 1987, c. G120, s. 1.

BONDHOLDERS' TRUST. Assets pledged by a company which is borrowing from bondholders and held in trust.

BONDING WAREHOUSE. Any warehouse in which goods subject to excise may be stored or deposited without payment of the duty imposed by this Act. *Excise Act*, R.S.C. 1985, c. E-14, s. 2.

BONDSMAN. *n.* A surety.

BONUS. *n.* 1. Gratuity; premium. 2. " ... [M]ay be a mere gift or gratuity as a gesture of goodwill, and not enforceable. Or it may be something which an employee is entitled to on the happening of a condition precedent and is enforceable when the condition is fulfilled. But in both cases it is something in addition to or in excess of that which is ordinarily received." *Minister of National Revenue v. Great Western Garment Co.* (1947), [1948] 1 D.L.R. 225 at 233, [1947] C.T.C. 343, [1947] Ex. C.R. 458, O'Connor J. 3. Discount, premium, dues, commission, brokerage fee, finders fee or other payment made by a borrower to a mortgage lender or mortgage broker. *Mortgage Brokers Act*, R.S.N. 1990, c. M-18, s. 2. 4. The amount by which the amount secured under a mortgage exceeds the amount actually advanced. *Expropriation Act*, R.S.N.B. 1973, c. E-14, s. 42.

BONUSING. *n.* The practice of conferring benefits upon businesses in order to attract them to a municipality. *Telus Communications Inc. v. Opportunity (Municipal District) No. 17*, (1998), 235 A.R. 258 (Q.B.).

BONUS ZONING. Requirements that permit the relaxation of certain requirements if an applicant exceeds other requirements or undertakes other action, in the public interest, as specified in the requirements. *Municipal Government Act*, S.N.S. 1998, c. 18, s. 191. See INCENTIVE OR ~.

BOOK. *n.* A volume or a part or division of a volume, in printed form, but does not include (a) a pamphlet, (b) a newspaper, review, magazine or other periodical, (c) a map, chart, plan or sheet music where the map, chart, plan or sheet music is separately published, and (d) an instruction or repair manual that accompanies a product or that is supplied as an accessory to a service. *Copyright Act*, R.S.C. 1985, c. C-42, s. 2. See BANK-~; CASH ~; TEXT ~.

BOOKMAKER. *n.* " ... [A] person who engages in the occupation of taking bets (or even in negotiating bets) and the keeping of accounts, ..." *R. v. Decome* (1991), 63 C.C.C. (3d) 460 at 472, [1991] R.J.Q. 618, 40 Q.A.C. 92, Proulx J.A. (Gendreau J.A. concurring).

BOOK VALUE. 1. " ... [V]alue at which property is recorded in the financial accounts of its owner. Usually, property is recorded at historical cost less, in the case of depreciable property, the amount of accumulated depreciation ..." *Domglas Inc. v. Jarislowsky, Fraser & Co.* (1980), 13 B.L.R. 135 at 199, [1980] C.S. 925 (Qué.), Greenberg J. 2. Where used

to refer to the book value of an asset, means the original cost of that asset less all depreciation charged to that asset as shown in the books of the owner of the asset for the purposes of preparing financial statements for the shareholders of the company up to the end of the fiscal year immediately preceding the fiscal year in which the book value of the asset is material. *The Mining Tax Act*, R.S.M. 1987, c. M195, s. 1.

BORDER. See CANADA ~ SERVICES AGENCY.

BORE. See CYLINDER ~.

BORN. See STILL-~.

BORROWER. *n.* 1. A person to whom a loan has been made. 2. A person who receives credit.

BORROWING. See COST OF ~.

BOTTLE-YOUR-OWN PREMISES. Premises in which, in accordance with the laws of the province in which they are located, alcohol is supplied from a marked special container of alcohol for the purpose of being packaged by a purchaser. *Excise Act, 2001*, S.C. 2002, c. 22, s. 2.

BOTTOMRY BOND. 1. The hypothecation or mortgage of a ship in which her bottom or keel is pledged. 2. An agreement entered into by a ship's owner in which the borrower undertakes to repay money advanced for the use of the ship with interest if the ship ends her voyage successfully.

BOUNDARY. *n.* 1. Limit of territory. 2. A natural or artificial line on the surface of the earth, below the surface of the earth, in airspace or in or on any structure, the purpose of which is to indicate the extent of a legal interest in land, land under water, water, airspace or natural resources, or in a structure. *Canada Lands Surveyors Act*, S.C. 1998, c. 14, s. 2. 3. The international boundary between Canada and the United States as determined and marked by the Commission. *International Boundary Commission Act*, R.S.C. 1985, c. I-16, s. 2. 3. Patent claims are frequently analogized to "fences" and "boundaries", giving the "fields" of the monopoly a comfortable pretence of bright line demarcation. Thus, in Minerals Separation North American Corp. v. Noranda Mines Ltd., [1947] Ex. C.R. 306 (Can. Ex. Ct.), Thorson P. put the matter as follows, at p. 352: By his claims the inventor puts fences around the fields of his monopoly and warns the public against trespassing on his property. His fences must be clearly placed in order to give the necessary warning and he must not fence in any property that is not his own. The terms of a claim must be free from avoidable ambiguity or obscurity and must not be flexible; they must be clear and precise so that the public will be able to know not only where it must not trespass but also where it may safely go. In reality, the "fences" often consist of complex layers of definitions of different elements (or "components" or "features" or "integers") of differing complexity, substitutability and ingenuity. A matrix of descriptive words and phrases defines the monopoly, warns the public and ensnares the infringer. In some instances, the precise elements of the "fence" may be crucial or "essential" to the working of the invention as claimed; in others the inventor may contemplate, and the reader skilled in the art appreciate, that variants could easily be used or substituted without making any material difference to the working of the invention. The interpretative task of the court in claims construction is to separate the one from the other, to distinguish the essential from the inessential, and to give to the "field" framed by the former the legal protection to which the holder of a valid patent is entitled. *Free World Trust c. Électro Santé Inc.* 2000 CarswellQue 2728, 2000 SCC 66, 194 D.L.R. (4th) 232, 263 N.R. 150, [2000] 2 S.C.R. 1024, 9 C.P.R. (4th) 168, Binnie J. See OBLITER-ATED ~.

BOUNDARY LINE. The vertical plane or line in which the surface boundary of the tract or parcel lies. *Mines and Minerals Act*, R.S.A. 2000, c. M-17, s. 72.

BOUNDARY MONUMENT. A buoy, post, tablet, cairn or other object or structure placed, erected or maintained by the Commission to mark the boundary and includes a reference monument, triangulation station or other marker or structure placed, erected or maintained by the Commission to assist in determining the boundary. *International Boundary Commission Act*, R.S.C. 1985, c. I-16, s. 2.

BOUNDARY WATERS. The waters from main shore to main shore of the lakes and rivers and connecting waterways, or the portions thereof, along which the international boundary between the United States and Canada passes, including all bays, arms, and inlets thereof, but not including tributary waters which in their natural channels would flow into such lakes, rivers and waterways, or waters flowing from such lakes, rivers, and waterways, or the waters of rivers flowing across the boundary. *Canada Water Act*, R.S.C. 1985, c. C-11, s. 2.

BOUND OVER. See BIND OVER.

BOUNDS. See METES AND ~.

BOUNTY. *n.* Money or premium paid for the fulfilment of a particular service.

BOW. See CROSS-~.

BOYCOTT. *v.* To take part in a boycott.

BOYCOTT. *n.* An organized refusal to deal with a particular person or business.

B.R. *abbr.* 1. Cour du Banc de la Reine/du Roi. 2. Recueils de jurisprudence de la Cour de banc de la Reine (du Roi) de Québec, 1892-1941. 3. Rapports judiciaires officiels de Québec, Cour du Banc de la Reine (ou du Roi) (Quebec Official Reports, Queen's (or King's) Bench, 1942-1969.

BRANCH. *n.* 1. (a) In respect of a bank, means an agency, the head office or any other office of the bank, and (b) in respect of an authorized foreign bank, means an agency, the principal office or any other office of the authorized foreign bank in Canada at which is carried on the business in Canada of the authorized foreign bank. *Bank Act*, S.C. 1991, c. 46, s. 2. 2. "... [I]ncludes a local and subordinate office ... it also includes a component portion of an organization or system or a section, division, subdivision or department of a business." *Minister of National Rev-*

enue v. Panther Oil & Grease Manufacturing Co., [1961] C.T.C. 363 at 377, 61 D.T.C. 1222 (Ex. Ct.), Thorson P.

BRAND. *v.* See RE~.

BRAND. *n.* 1. An identification impressed or affixed on or within the body of livestock to indicate ownership. *Livestock Identification Act*, R.S.B.C. 1996, c. 271, s. 1. 2. All of the brand elements that as a whole are used by a manufacturer to identify to a consumer a tobacco product made by the manufacturer that is a cigarette. *Tobacco Act*, S.C. 1997, c. 13, *Cigarette Ignition Propensity Regulations*, SOR/2005-178, s. 1.

BRANDEIS BRIEF. A social science brief in which empirical data is appended to or included in a factum. P.W. Hogg, *Constitutional Law of Canada*, 2d ed. (Toronto: Carswell, 1985) at 182.

BRAND NAME. A name in English or French, whether or not it includes the name of a manufacturer, corporation, partnership or individual (a) that is used to distinguish the natural health product; and (b) under which a natural health product is sold or advertised. *Food and Drugs Act*, R.S.C. 1985, c. F-27; *Natural Health Products Regulations*, SOR/2003-196, s. 1.

BRAND-NAME DRUG. A prescription drug product, usually one sold by a corporation with patent rights in the product. Contrasted with generic drug. *Apotex Inc. v. Canada (Attorney General)*, (1997), 123 F.T.R. 161.

BRAWL. *v.* To create a disturbance.

BREACH. *n.* 1. Encroachment of a right. 2. Disregard of a duty. 3. Non-execution of a contract. G.H.L. Fridman, *The Law of Contract in Canada*, 2d ed. (Toronto: Carswell, 1986) at 523. See ANTICIPATORY ~; FUNDAMENTAL ~; SPENT ~ DOCTRINE.

BREACH OF CLOSE. Unjustified entry on another person's land.

BREACH OF CONFIDENCE. "... [C]onsists in establishing three elements: that the information conveyed was confidential, that it was communicated in confidence, and that it was misused by the party to whom it was communicated." *International Corona Resources Ltd. v. Lac Minerals Ltd.* (1989), 44 B.L.R. 1 at 16, [1989] 2 S.C.R. 574, 26 C.P.R. (3d) 97, 69 O.R. (2d) 287, 61 D.L.R. (4th) 14, 6 R.P.R. (2d) 1, 35 E.T.R. 1, 101 N.R. 239, 36 O.A.C. 57, La Forest J. (Wilson and Lamer JJ. concurring).

BREACH OF CONTRACT. The failure to complete a contract according to its terms. See CRIMINAL ~; INDUCING ~.

BREACH OF PRISON. Escape from a prison. See PRISON BREACH.

BREACH OF PRIVILEGE. Contempt of Parliament.

BREACH OF PROMISE TO MARRY. Conduct which permitted a common law action for damages.

BREACH OF STATUTORY DUTY. A tort involving the elements that a statutory duty is owed to the plaintiff, the injury is of the kind the statute was designed to prevent, defendant must be in breach and the breach of the duty must have caused the loss.

BREACH OF THE PEACE. 1. An act or acts which result in actual or threatened harm to someone. The act or acts may not be unlawful standing alone. *Brown v. Durham Regional Police Force* (1998), 21 C.R. (5th) 1 (Ont. C.A.). 2. Has a narrower meaning than the breach of the Queen's peace which is supposed to underlie every crime. The most flagrant instance of a breach of the peace is a riot. An unlawful assembly which has not yet become a riot is a breach of the Queen's peace. A fight between two or more persons is a breach of the peace.

BREACH OF TRUST. 1. The exercise of authority which is vested in a public official by virtue of his or her office, other than for the public benefit. Any breach of the appropriate standard of responsibility and conduct demanded of the holder of an office as a senior civil servant. *R. v. Power* (1993), 82 C.C.C. (3d) 73 (N.S.C.A.) 2. There are three ways in which a stranger to a trust can be held liable as a constructive trustee for breach of trust. First, a stranger to the trust can be liable as a trustee de son tort. Secondly, a stranger to the trust can be liable for breach of trust by knowingly assisting in a fraudulent and dishonest design on the part of the trustees ("knowing assistance"). Thirdly, liability may be imposed on a stranger to the trust who is in receipt and chargeable with trust property ("knowing receipt"). *Citadel General Assurance Co. v. Lloyds Bank Canada*, 1997 CarswellAlta 823, 152 D.L.R. (4th) 411, (*sub nom.* Citadel General Life Assurance Co. v. Lloyds Bank Canada) 206 A.R. 321, (*sub nom.* Citadel General Life Assurance Co. v. Lloyds Bank Canada) 156 W.A.C. 321, 19 E.T.R. (2d) 93, 35 B.L.R. (2d) 153, 47 C.C.L.I. (2d) 153, [1997] 3 S.C.R. 805, 219 N.R. 323, [1999] 4 W.W.R. 135. See CRIMINAL ~.

BREACH OF WARRANTY OF AUTHORITY. Breach of warranty of authority is a contractual cause of action. It focuses primarily on whether the plaintiff was induced by the specific misrepresentation (warranty) of the defendant that it had the authority of a third party. The misrepresentation in question must have induced the plaintiff to act to his or her detriment. In a breach of warranty of authority cause of action the agent's belief in the existence of his authority is immaterial so it matters not whether the warranty was given deliberately, negligently, innocently, or mistakenly. *Alvin's Auto Service Ltd. v. Clew Holdings Ltd.*, 1997 CarswellSask 433, 33 B.L.R. (2d) 11, 157 Sask. R. 278, 37 C.C.L.T. (2d) 135, [1997] 9 W.W.R. 5, 13 R.P.R. (3d) 107 (Q.B.), Baynton J.

BREAK. *v.* (a) To break any part, internal or external, or (b) to open any thing that is used or intended to be used to close or to cover an internal or external opening. *Criminal Code*, R.S.C. 1985, c. C-46, s. 321.

BREAK AND ENTER. Obtain entrance by a threat or artifice or by collusion with a person within, or enter without lawful justification or excuse by a permanent or temporary opening. *Criminal Code*, R.S.C. 1985, c. C-46, s. 350(b). See ENTER.

BREAKDOWN. *n.* 1. An event, a point in time, at which an object stops functioning correctly. *Triple Five Corp. v. Simcoe & Erie Group* (1994), 29 C.C.L.I. (2d) 219 (Alta. Q.B.). 2. Some collapse in function, mechanical, electrical or electronic malfunction. *Clark v. Waterloo Insurance Co.* (1992), 98 D.L.R. (4th) 689 (Ont. Gen. Div.).

BREAKDOWN OF MARRIAGE. A court may grant a divorce on the ground that there has been a breakdown of marriage which is established if the spouses have lived separate and apart for at least one year or the spouse against whom the divorce proceeding is brought has committed adultery or treated the other spouse with physical or mental cruelty of such kind as to render intolerable the continued cohabitation of the spouses. *Divorce Act*, R.S.C. 1985 (2d Supp.), c. 3, s. 8.

BREAKING AND ENTERING. See BREAK AND ENTER.

BREATHALYZER. *n.* An instrument to measure alcohol content in the blood by analysis of a breath sample.

B.R.E.F. *abbr.* 1. Bureau de revision de l'évaluation foncière. 2. Décisions du Bureau de révision de l'évaluation foncière, 1980-1998.

BREW. *v.* To make beer or other alcoholic beverage.

BREW. *n.* 1. A beverage made by brewing. 2. Colloquially, a beer.

BRIBE. *v.* 1. To offer a person a payment or thing in circumstances which amount to a bribe. 2. It is an offence to offer a bribe to influence an elector to vote or refrain from voting or to vote or refrain from voting for a particular candidate. It is also an offence to accept or agree to accept a bribe, during an election period, offered to vote or refrain from voting for a particular candidate. *Canada Elections Act*, S.C. 2000, c. 9, s. 481.

BRIBE. *n.* 1. A gift to any person holding a position of trust or in public or judicial office intended to induce that person to betray trust or disregard official duty for the giver's benefit. 2. "... For the purposes of the civil law a bribe means the payment of a secret commission, which only means (i) that the person making the payment makes it to the agent of the other person with whom he is dealing; (ii) that he makes it to that person knowing that that person is acting as the agent of the other person with whom he is dealing; and (iii) that he fails to disclose to the other person with whom he is dealing that he made that payment to the person whom he knows to be the other person's agent. Those three are the only elements necessary to constitute the payment of a secret commission or bribe for civil purposes." *Indust. & Gen. Mtge. Co. v. Lewis*, [1949] 2 All E.R. 573 at 575, Slade J. 3. It is an offence to offer a bribe to influence an elector to vote or refrain from voting or to vote or refrain from voting for a particular candidate. It is also an offence to accept or agree to accept a bribe, during an election period, offered to vote or refrain from voting for a particular candidate. *Canada Elections Act*, S.C. 2000, c. 9, s. 481. 4. A secret payment by one contracting party to the agent of another when it puts the agent in a position where the agent's interest is in conflict with the agent's duty to the principal. This course of dealing constitutes a "fraud" on the principal. *Ruiter Engineering & Construction Ltd. v. 430216 Ontario Ltd.* (1989), 41 B.L.R. 213 (Ont. C.A.).

BRIBERY OF JUDICIAL OFFICER. Occurs when the holder of a judicial office, or a member of Parliament or a legislature corruptly accepts or obtains, agrees to accept or attempts to obtain any money, valuable consideration, office, place or employment for himself or another person in respect of anything done or omitted or to be done or omitted by him in his official capacity or, when another person gives or offers corruptly to a person who holds a judicial office or is a member of Parliament or a legislature any money, valuable consideration, office, place or employment in respect of anything done or omitted or to be done or omitted by him in his official capacity for himself or another person. *Criminal Code*, R.S.C. 1985, c. C-46, s. 119.

BRIBERY OF OFFICERS. Occurs when (a) a justice, police commissioner, peace officer, public officer, or officer of a juvenile court, or being employed in the administration of criminal law, corruptly (i) accepts or obtains, (ii) agrees to accept, or (iii) attempts to obtain, for himself or any other person any money, valuable consideration, office, place or employment with intent (iv) to interfere with the administration of justice, (v) to procure or facilitate the commission of an offence, or (vi) to protect from detection or punishment a person who has committed or who intends to commit an offence, or (b) anyone gives or offers, corruptly, to a person mentioned in paragraph (a) any money, valuable consideration, office, place or employment with intent that the person should do anything mentioned in subparagraph (a)(iv), (v) or (vi). *Criminal Code*, R.S.C. 1985, c. C-46, s. 120.

BRIDGE. See INTERNATIONAL ~ OR TUNNEL.

BRIDGE FINANCING. Financing arranged for a short period of time, for example when one has purchased or is building a new home and is waiting to sell an existing home.

BRIDGING BENEFIT. A periodical payment provided under a pension plan to a member of the pension plan for a temporary period of time after retirement for the purpose of supplementing the members pension benefit until the member is eligible to receive benefits under the Old Age Security Act or commences to receive retirement benefits under the Canada Pension Plan or the Quebec Pension Plan. *Pension Benefits acts*.

BRIEF. *v.* To brief a case means to summarize it and its salient points.

BRIEF. *n.* A file of all pleadings, documents and memoranda which serves as the basis for argument by the lawyer in the matter in court. See BRANDEIS ~; CHAMBERS ~; SOCIAL SCIENCE ~.

BRIGHT LINE. Conceptually, a clear boundary or demarcation. For example: Section 347 of the Code invites difficulties with arbitrariness by imposing a bright line of 60 percent as demarcating legal interest from illegal interest. The legislatively mandated bright line [of 60 percent] distinguishes s. 347 [Criminal Code] cases from those involving provisions, for example, in restraint of trade, where there is no bright line. *Transport North American Express Inc. v. New Solutions Financial Corp.*, 2004 SCC 7, [2004] 1 S.C.R. 249, Arbour J. at para. 34.

BRING AN ACTION. The issuance of the writ to commence an action. Does not include serving the writ. *Kemp v. Metzner*, 2000 CarswellBC 1616, 2000 BCCA 462, 78 B.C.L.R. (3d) 187, 190 D.L.R. (4th) 388 (C.A.).

BRING THE ADMINISTRATION OF JUSTICE INTO DISREPUTE. When faced with an application for exclusion [of evidence] under s. 24(2), a court must assess and balance the effect of admitting the evidence on society's confidence in the justice system having regard to: (1) the seriousness of the Charter-infringing state conduct (admission may send the message the justice system condones serious state misconduct), (2) the impact of the breach on the Charter-protected interests of the accused (admission may send the message that individual rights count for little), and (3) society's interest in the adjudication of the case on its merits. The court's role on a s. 24(2) application is to balance the assessments under each of these lines of inquiry to determine whether, considering all the circumstances, admission of the evidence would bring the administration of justice into disrepute. *R. v. Grant*, 2009 SCC 32, [2009] 2 S.C.R. 353, McLachlin C.J. and Charron J.

BRITISH COMMONWEALTH. Has the same meaning as Commonwealth association of countries named in the schedule. *Interpretation Act*, R.S.C. 1985, c. I-21, s. 35.

BRITISH COMMONWEALTH OF NATIONS. Has the same meaning as Commonwealth association of countries named in the schedule. *Interpretation Act*, R.S.C. 1985, c. I-21, s. 35.

BRITISH NORTH AMERICA ACT, 1867. Renamed the *Constitution Act*, 1867 in 1982, this Act gave effect to the confederation scheme by uniting the provinces of Canada, Nova Scotia and New Brunswick. The Statute of the Parliament of the United Kingdom which formed the federation of Canada in 1867 from the four provinces, Lower Canada, Upper Canada, Nova Scotia and New Brunswick. Since the patriation of the constitution in 1982, it is known as the Constitution Act.

BROADCASTER. *n.* A body that, in the course of operating a broadcasting undertaking, broadcasts a communication signal in accordance with the law of the country in which the broadcasting undertaking is carried on, but excludes a body whose primary activity in relation to communication signals is their retransmission. *Copyright Act*, R.S.C. 1985, c. C-42, s. 2.

BROADCASTING. *n.* 1. Any transmission of programs, whether or not encrypted, by radio waves or other means of telecommunication for reception by the public by means of broadcasting receiving apparatus, but does not include any such transmission of programs that is made solely for performance or display in a public place. *Broadcasting Act, 1991*, S.C. 1991, c. 11, s. 2. 2. The dissemination of writing, signs, signals, pictures, sounds or intelligence of any nature intended for direct reception by, or which is available on subscription to, the general public (a) by means of a device utilizing electromagnetic waves of frequencies lower than 3 000 GHz propagated in space without artificial guide, or (b) through a community antenna television system operated by a person licensed under the Broadcasting Act (Canada) to carry on a broadcasting receiving undertaking. *Libel and Slander Act*, R.S.B.C. 1996, c. 263, s. 1. See DIRECT TO HOME ~.

BROADCASTING RECEIVING APPARATUS. A device, or combination of devices, intended for or capable of being used for the reception of broadcasting. *Broadcasting Act, 1991*, S.C. 1991, c. 11, s. 2.

BROADCASTING UNDERTAKING. Includes a distribution undertaking, a programming undertaking and a network. *Broadcasting Act, 1991*, S.C. 1991, c. 11, s. 2.

BROKEN CONCESSION. A concession any boundary of which is broken in whole or in part by a lake or river.

BROKEN LOT. An irregular lot or a regular lot whose area is diminished or increased by a natural or artificial feature shown on the original plan.

BROKER. *n.* 1. One who negotiates or makes contracts for the sale of property. 2. A person who is engaged, whether or not exclusively, in the business of buying and selling securities and who, in the transaction concerned, acts for, or buys a security from, or sells a security to a customer. *Canada Business Corporations Act*, R.S.C. 1985, c. C-44, s. 48. 3. A person who, for another or others, for compensation, gain or reward or hope or promise thereof, either alone or through one or more officials or salespersons, trades in real estate, or a person who claims to be such a person. 4. A person who, for compensation, acts or aids in any manner in negotiating contracts of insurance or placing risks or effecting insurance, or in negotiating the continuance or renewal of insurance contracts for another person. *Insurance acts.* 5. A person or company who trades in securities in the capacity of principal or agent. The *Securities Transfer Act*, S.M. 2008, c. 14, s. 1. 6. A person who, for compensation, assists a person in obtaining credit or a lease. *The Consumer Protection Act*, R.S.M. 1987, c. C200, s. 1. See CUSTOMS ~; FRANCHISOR'S ~; INSURANCE ~; MONEY ~; MORTGAGE ~; PAWN~; SECURITIES ~; STOCK~.

BROKERAGE. *n.* 1. The commission which one pays to a broker. 2. A business organization that holds a brokerage licence. *Real Estate Trading Act*, S.N.S. 1996, c. 28, s. 2. See REAL PROPERTY ~ ENTITY.

BROKERAGE FEE. The payment that a borrower makes or agrees to make to a loan broker who assists the borrower in arranging a credit agreement, and includes an amount deducted from an advance made to the borrower that is paid to the broker. *Consumer Protection Act, 2002*, S.O. 2002, c. 30, Sched. A, s. 66.

BROKERED TRANSACTION. A brokered transaction is one in which the brokerage is engaged by the issuer to solicit funds from its clients. Therefore, there is an agency agreement between the issuer and the brokerage. In a brokered transaction, the brokerage collects the subscription monies from its clients and then delivers the money by its cheque under a trust or escrow agreement until the shares are received. In a non-brokered transaction, the offer goes directly to individuals (often family or friends) and the agreement is between the issuer and the subscribing individual. *Northey-Taylor v. Casey*, 2008 ABCA 149.

BROTHEL. *n.* "... [T]he same thing as a 'bawdy-house', ... applies to a place resorted to by persons of both sexes for the purpose of prostitution... ." *Singleton v. Ellison*, [1895] 1 Q.B. 607 at 608, Wills J.

BROUGHT. *v.* 1. (Said of an action or charge or proceeding) " ... '[I]nitiate[d]' ..." *R. v. Henderson*, [1929] 2 W.W.R. 209 at 214, [1929] 4 D.L.R. 984, 52 C.C.C. 82, 41 B.C.R. 242 (C.A.), Macdonald J.A. 2. Courts in Canada have interpreted "brought" within particular legislative regimes to mean commencing a suit by filing a statement of claim. See *Kemp v. Metzner* (2000), 190 D.L.R. (4th) 388 (B.C. C.A.) and *McGrath v. Scriven* (1920), 52 D.L.R. 342 (N.S. S.C.), aff'd [1921] 1 W.W.R. 1075 at 1085 (S.C.C.). See BRING AN ACTION.

BROWNE V. DUNN. See RULE IN ~.

BRUTUM FULMEN. [L. an empty noise] An empty threat.

BUDGET. *n.* A statement of the amounts of estimated revenues and expenditures. See CASH ~.

BUGGERY. *n.* Sodomy, anal intercourse.

BUILDERS' LIEN. Provides a security or charge against real property to secure a claim for goods, services and work carried out on the property by a contractor.

BUILDING. *n.* 1. A structure consisting of foundations, walls or roof, with or without other parts. 2. A structure that is used or intended to be used for the purpose of supporting or sheltering persons or animals or storing property. See FORTIFIED ~; PUBLIC ~.

BUILDING CODE. Detailed specifications for the design and construction of buildings which ensure structural safety, fire safety and the occupants' health. D. Robertson, *Ontario Health and Safety Guide* (Toronto: De Boo, 1988) at 5-35. See NATIONAL ~.

BUILDING CONSTRUCTION CODE. A code of building construction standards. *The Buildings and Mobile Homes Act*, R.S.M. 1987, c. B93, s. 1.

BUILDING CONSTRUCTION STANDARD. A standard for (a) construction materials, or plumbing or electrical materials or installations, or equipment or appliances, or any combination thereof, to be used or installed in any building or part of a building, (a.1) the energy and water efficiency of a building or part of a building, or (b) the method to be used in the construction or demolition of any building or part of a building. *The Buildings and Mobile Homes Act*, R.S.M. 1987, c. B93, s. 1.

BUILDING CONTRACT. A contract to build anything.

BUILDING INSPECTOR. An inspector appointed by a municipality to administer and enforce the building code.

BUILDING LEASE. 1. A lease of a vacant piece of land on which the lessee covenants to erect a building or to pull down an old building and erect a new one on the site. 2. The lease of land for a rent called ground rent.

BUILDING PERMIT. A permit, issued under a building bylaw of a municipality, authorizing the construction of all or part of any structure.

BULK SALE. The sale of all or a large portion of the stock in trade of a business when that sale takes place other than in the normal course of business.

BULK SALES ACT. An Ontario statute which is intended to protect the creditors of a business when a business enters into a bulk sale. See BULK SALE.

BULL. *n.* One who buys shares expecting prices on the stock exchange to rise.

BULL. ACBD. *abbr.* Bulletin ACBD (CALL Newsletter).

BULL. AVOCATS. *abbr.* Le Bulletin des avocats (Solicitor's Journal).

BULL. CCDJ. *abbr.* Bulletin d'information juridique du CCDJ (CLIC's Legal Materials Letter).

BULL. C.V.M.Q. *abbr.* Bulletin – Commission des valeurs mobilières du Québec, 1970?-.

BULLION. *n.* Uncoined silver and gold.

BULL MARKET. Name for a market which is going up in value.

BULLOCK ORDER. 1. Named after the case of Bullock v. London General Omnibus Co., [1907] 1 K.B. 264 (C.A.). "... [O]rder under which the plaintiff paid the costs of the successful defendant and recovered them together with his own from the unsuccessful defendant ..." *Rowe v. Investors Syndicate Ltd.* (1984), 46 C.P.C. 209 at 215 (Ont. H.C.), Henry J. 2. A Bullock order directs an unsuccessful defendant to reimburse the plaintiff for the recovered costs of a successful defendant. A Sanderson order directs that the payment go directly to the successful defendant. The rationale behind both orders is the same. Where the allocation of responsibility is uncertain, usually because of interwoven facts, it is often reasonable to proceed through trial against more than one defendant. In these cases, a Bullock or Sanderson order provides a plaintiff with an appropriate form of relief. *Rooney (Litigation Guardian of) v. Graham* (2001) 53 O.R. (3d) 685 (C.A.).

BULL. O.S.C. *abbr.* Bulletin of the Ontario Securities Commission, 1981-.

BULL SPREAD. In the commodities market buying one contract and selling another in anticipation of a profit on the difference in prices at two different points in time. In a bull spread, the client is long in the nearby month and short in the later month.

BULLYING. See CYBER-~.

BUMPING. *v.* As a result of a layoff, an employee with more seniority can displace, bump, an employee with less seniority. Various rules concerning bumping may appear in the collective bargaining agreement governing the jobs in question.

BUMP UP. To receive a promotion, in effect, as a result of the bumping process.

BURDEN. *n.* The duty to perform an obligation. See EVIDENTIAL ~; EVIDENTIARY ~; MAJOR ~; OVER~; PERSUASIVE ~; PRIMARY ~.

BURDEN OF PROOF. "... [M]ay be applied to cases like this in two distinct senses: ... The first is in the sense of establishing a case. This is a matter of substantive law, ... The other sense in which the term may be applied is that of introducing evidence. This is a matter of procedure, ..." *R. v. Primak* (1930), 24 Sask. L.R. 417 at 419, [1930] 1 W.W.R. 755, [1930] 3 D.L.R. 345, 53 C.C.C. 203 (C.A.), the court per Mackenzie J.A. See LEGAL ~.

BUREAU. See BETTER BUSINESS ~; CREDIT ~.

BURGLARY. *n.* The common law offence of breaking and entering a dwelling-house at night with intent to commit a crime there.

BURIAL SITE. Land containing human remains.

BURN. *v.* To purchase a substituted or inferior illicit drug. F.A. Jaffe, *A Guide to Pathological Evidence for Lawyers and Police Officers*, 4th ed. (Toronto: Carswell, 1999) at 232.

BUS. *n.* Any vehicle adapted to carry more than six to twelve adult passengers in addition to the driver.

BUS. & L. *abbr.* Business & the Law.

BUSINESS. *n.* 1. Any business, profession, trade, calling, manufacture or undertaking of any kind carried on in Canada or elsewhere whether for profit or otherwise, including any activity or operation carried on or performed in Canada or elsewhere by any government, by any department, branch, board, commission or agency of any government, by any court or other tribunal or by any other body or authority performing a function of government. *Canada Evidence Act*, R.S.C. 1985, c. C-5, s. 30. 2. Includes a profession, calling, trade, manufacture or undertaking of any kind whatever, and includes an adventure or concern in the nature of trade but does not include an office or employment. *Canada Pension Plan*, R.S.C. 1985, c. C-8, s. 2. 3. The lawful objects and purposes for which a company is established. 4. The land and buildings used for a commercial enterprise. 5. A line must be drawn under the Act [i.e. the Income Tax Act, R.S.C. 1985, c. 1 (5th Supp.)] between a mere investment in property and an activity or activities that constitute a business. The expansive definition of the term "business" in section 248 is not exhaustive. It extends to any endeavour that occupies time, labour and attention with a view to profit. To the extent that income is derived from human activity rather than from the passive ownership of property, its source can be properly described as business. *Dansereau v. R.*, 2001 CarswellNat 2275, 2001 FCA 305, 2001 D.T.C. 5642, Noel J.A. for the court. 6. An individual who, for the purpose of gain or profit, is carrying on a commercial or industrial undertaking of any kind or providing professional, personal or other services, and a corporation, whether or not operating for the purpose of gain or profit. See ACTIVE ~ CARRIED ON BY A CORPORATION; BANKING ~; BETTER ~ BUREAU; CARRIES ON ~; CARRY ON ~; COMMON FORM ~; COURSE OF ~; FEDERAL WORK, UNDERTAKING OR ~.

BUSINESS ASSET. 1. " ... [A]ssets which have as their purpose the generation of income in an entrepreneurial sense ..." *Clarke v. Clarke* (1990), 28 R.F.L. (3d) 113 at 134, 73 D.L.R. (4th) 1, 113 N.R. 321, [1990] 2 S.C.R. 795, the court per Wilson J. 2. Property owned by one spouse and used principally in the course of a business carried on by that spouse, either alone or jointly with others, and includes shares that the spouse owns in a corporation through which he or she carries on a business. *Marital Property Act*, S.N.B. 1980, c. M-1.1, s. 1.

BUSINESS COMBINATION. An acquisition of all or substantially all of the assets of one body corporate by another, an amalgamation of two or more bodies corporate or any similar reorganization between two or more bodies corporate. *Bank Act*, S.C. 1991, c. 46, s. 265.

BUSINESS CONTACT INFORMATION. An individual's name, position name or title, business telephone number, business address, business e-mail, business fax number and other similar business information; *Personal Information Protection Act 2003*, S.A. 2003, c. P-6.5, s. 1.

BUSINESS DEVELOPMENT BANK. The bank, continued under the Business Development Bank of Canada Act, S.C. 1995, c. 28, which offers financial and management services to help businesses establish and develop themselves in Canada.

BUSINESS JUDGMENT RULE. In assessing whether directors have met their fiduciary and statutory obligations, this rule shields from court intervention decisions which have been made honestly, prudently, in good faith and on reasonable ground. *CW Shareholders v. WIC Western International* (1998), 160 D.L.R. (4th) 131 (Ont. Gen. Div.).

BUSINESS NAME. The name under which a business is carried on or is to be carried on and includes a firm name. *Partnership Act*, R.S.B.C. 1996, c. 348, s. 1.

BUSINESS NUMBER. 1. The number (other than a Social Insurance Number) used by the Minister to identify (a) a corporation or partnership, or (b) any other association or taxpayer that carries on a business or is required under this Act to deduct or withhold an amount from an amount paid or credited or deemed to be paid or credited under this Act and of which the Minister has notified the corporation, partnership, association or taxpayer. *Income Tax Act*, R.S.C. 1985, c. 1 (5th Supp.), s. 248. A federal client identification number to which businesses can register program accounts. 2. A number used by provincial officials to identify a business entity for purposes of the province.

BUSINESS OCCUPANCY. Occupancy for the transaction of business. *Professional Engineers Act*, R.S.O. 1990, c. P.28, s. 12.

BUSINESS OCCUPANCY TAX. A tax levied on occupants in respect of their use or occupation of real property or immovables for the purpose of or in connection with a business. *Payments in Lieu of Taxes Act*, R.S.C. 1985, c. H-13, s. 2.

BUSINESS OF SUPPLY. Considering estimates for interim supply, passing all stages of any bill based on them, and considering opposition motions. A. Fraser, W.A. Dawson & J. Holtby, eds., *Beauchesne's Rules and Forms of the House of Commons of Canada*, 6th ed. (Toronto: Carswell, 1989) at 255.

BUSINESS OR TRADE ASSOCIATION. An organization of persons that by an enactment, agreement or custom has power to admit, suspend, expel or direct persons in relation to any business or trade. *Human Rights acts.*

BUSINESS RECORDS. A category of records for purposes of the evidence acts and questions of admissibility. They are defined in the following terms. "... [T]hree prerequisites to their reception as admissible evidence of what they record – (1) if they are made in the usual and ordinary course of such business; (2) if it was in the usual and ordinary course of such business to make such a writing or record; (3) the record or writing was made at the time of the act, transaction, occurrence or event or a reasonable time thereafter." *Tobias v. Nolan* (1985), 71 N.S.R. (2d) 92 at 102, 171 A.P.R. 92 (T.D.), MacIntosh J.

BUSINESS TAX. "... [O]ne imposed upon, and proportioned to, either the volume of business done in, or the volume of profits derived from, some business – though the latter would perhaps be rather in the nature of an income tax... ." *Dominion Express Co. v. Brandon (City)* (1910), 20 Man. R. 304 at 306, 17 W.L.R. 71 (C.A.), Richards J.A.

BUSINESS TRANSACTION. The purchase, sale, lease, merger or amalgamation or any other type of acquisition, disposal or financing of an organization or a portion of an organization or of any of the business or assets of an organization. *Personal Information Protection Act*, S.B.C. 2003, c. 63, s. 20.

BUST. See BUY AND ~.

BUT FOR TEST. 1. The basic test for determining causation in negligence remains the "but for" test. This applies to multi-cause injuries. The plaintiff bears the burden of showing that "but for" the negligent act or omission of each defendant, the injury would not have occurred. Having done this, contributory negligence may be apportioned, as permitted by statute. This fundamental rule has never been displaced and remains the primary test for causation in negligence actions. As stated in Athey v. Leonati, [1996 CanLII 183, [1996] 3 S.C.R. 458] at para. 14, Major J., "[t]he general, but not conclusive, test for causation is the 'but for' test, which requires the plaintiff to show that the injury would not have occurred but for the negligence of the defendant". Similarly, "[t]he rules of causation consider generally whether 'but for' the defendant's acts, the plaintiff's damages would have been incurred on a balance of probabilities." The "but for" test recognizes that compensation for negligent conduct should only be made "where a substantial connection between the injury and defendant's conduct" is present. It ensures that a defendant will not be held liable for the plaintiff's injuries where they "may very well be due to factors unconnected to the defendant and not the fault of anyone". *Resurfice Corp. v. Hanke*, 2007 SCC 7, [2007] 1 S.C.R. 333. 2. Causation in negligence is established when the plaintiff proves on a balance of probabilities, that the defendant caused or contributed to the injury. The generally applicable test is the "but for" test. This test "requires the plaintiff to show that the injury would not have occurred but for the negligence of the defendant" ([Athey v. Leonati, [1996] 3 S.C.R. 458], at para.14). *Cottrelle v. Gerrard* (2003), 178 O.A.C. 142.

BUTTERFLY. *n.* . Used to describe a corporate reorganization under which the assets are distributed to some or all of the shareholders in proportion to their respective shareholdings without triggering at that time such things as the realization in taxation of any approved gain and recapture of capital cost allowance for income tax purposes in those assets. *Public Trustee v. Brown* (1993), 2 E.T.R. (2d) 181 (B.C.C.A.).

BUY. *v.* To purchase; to acquire by payment of money or equivalent.

BUY AND BUST. An undercover police operation in which police try to buy illicit drugs from individuals who appear to be inclined to sell drugs. If the officer if successful, the individuals are arrested.

BUYER. *n.* 1. A purchaser. 2. A person who buys or agrees to buy goods. *Sale of Goods Act*, R.S.A. 2000, c. S-2, s. 1. 3. A person who buys or hires goods by a conditional sale. 4. A person who (a) buys or agrees

to buy, or leases, goods under a security agreement, as defined in The Personal Property Security Act, or (b) leases goods under an agreement that (i) is not a security agreement as defined in The Personal Property Security Act, and (ii) gives the person the option of becoming the owner of the goods on compliance with the terms of the agreement. *The Limitation of Actions Act*, R.S.M. 1987, c. L150, s. 46. See PROSPECTIVE ~.

BUY IN. For the original owner or person with interest in a property to purchase it at a mortgage, tax or other forced sale.

BUY ON MARGIN. To purchase securities partly on credit extended by a broker.

BY. *adv.* At the side of, near, close. See WHERE~.

BY. *prep.* As a result of; because of; through the agency of; no later than.

BY. *prefix.* Subordinate; secondary; incidental.

BY-ELECTION. *n.* 1. An election other than a general election. Usually required to fill a vacancy in an elected position. 2. An election held in a constituency on a date on which there is no general election. 3. An election held to fill a vacancy in the office of mayor, councillor or trustee at a time other than a general election.

BY-LAW. *var.* **BYLAW.** *n.* 1. " ... [N]ot an agreement, but a law binding on all persons to whom it applies, whether they agree to be bound by it or not. All regulations made by a corporate body, and intended to bind not only themselves and their officers and servants, but members of the public who come within the sphere of their operation, may be properly called 'by-laws'." *London Association of Shipowners and Brokers v. London and Index Docks Joint Committee* (1892), 3 Ch. 242 at 252, Lindley L.J. 2. A law which a municipality makes. 3. " ... [A] local law, ..." *White v. Morely* (1899), 2 Q.B. 34 at 39, Channell J. 4. Includes a resolution on which the opinion of the electors is to be obtained. *Local Authorities Election Act*, R.S.A. 2000, c. L-21, s. 1. 5. Includes an order or resolution. *Local Government Act*, R.S.B.C. 1996, c. 323, s. 260. 6. The rules enacted by a corporation or association to govern the body's activities. See MONEY ~; ZONING ~.

C

C. *abbr.* 1. Court. 2. Chapter. 3. Chancellor.

C.A. *abbr.* 1. Court of Appeal. 2. Cour d'appel. 3. Recueils de jurisprudence de la Cour d'appel de Québec (Quebec Court of Appeals Reports), 1970-1985.

CABINET. *n.* 1. A body composed of the Prime Minister or Premier and Ministers of the Crown or a committee of Privy Council (federal) or Executive Council (provincial) which determines the direction of and makes policy decisions for the government. It is usually composed of members of the Prime Minister's or Premier's political party who have been elected as members of the House of Commons or the Legislature and is often referred to as "the government". 2. Enclosure hung on a wall or self-supporting enclosure.

CABINET DOCUMENTS. Minutes, records of Cabinet and committee meetings and recommendations made by Ministers and policy advisors to Cabinet to assist in deliberations.

CABINET GOVERNMENT. Government in which Prime Minister or Premier selects members of her or his own party elected to Parliament and perhaps others to be Ministers of the Crown. This group collectively form the Cabinet, the policy-making arm of government. The Ministers and Cabinet are responsible to Parliament for the conduct of the government. The government remains in power so long as it has the confidence of a majority of the House of Commons or the Legislature. In theory, the Privy Council or Executive Council advises the formal head of state (the Governor General or Lieutenant Governor) though, in fact, the Committee of Council, known as the Cabinet, carries out this function in most situations.

CABINET MINISTER. A member of Cabinet who is responsible for a portfolio, usually a ministry or department of government. This person acts as political head of the ministry or department and is responsible to Parliament for the affairs of that ministry or department or the conduct of that portfolio.

C.A.C. *abbr.* Canada Citizenship Appeal Court, Reasons for Judgment, 1975-1977.

C.A.C.F.P. *abbr.* Comité d'appel de la commission de la Fonction publique.

C.A.C.M. *abbr.* Recueil des arrêts de la Cour d'appel des cours martiales du Canada, 1957-.

CADASTRAL SURVEYING. Surveying in relation to (a) the identification, establishment, documentation or description of a boundary or the position of anything relative to a boundary; or (b) the generation, manipulation, adjustment, custody, storage, retrieval or display of spatial information that defines a boundary. *Canada Lands Surveyors Act*, S.C. 1998, c. 14, s. 2.

C.A.E.C. *abbr.* Commission d'appel des enregistrements commerciaux, Sommaires de décisions, 1971-?.

CAF. French neutral citation for the Federal Court of Appeal.

CAHIERS PROP. INTEL. *abbr.* Les Cahiers de propriété intellectuelle.

C.A.I. *abbr.* 1. Commission d'appel de l'immigration. 2. Décisions de la Commission d'accès à l'information, 1984-.

CALCULATE. *v.* "... [P]lan deliberately ..." *Belmont v. Millhaven Institution* (1984), 41 C.R. (3d) 91 at 95, 9 Admin. L.R. 181 (Fed. T.C.), Dubé J.

CALCULATED. *adj.* 1."... [F]itted, suited, apt ..." *R. v. Hill* (1976), 33 C.C.C. (2d) 60 at 68 (B.C. C.A.), McIntyre J.A. 2. In the context of the phrase "calculated to mislead" means 'likely' to mislead". *Bond v. Dupras*, 1995 CarswellBC 1044, 32 Admin. L.R. (2d) 161 (S.C. [In Chambers]), Spencer J. 3. Planned, intended.

CALCULATED TO DECEIVE. Of a trademark, meant to so nearly resemble another that it is likely to cause confusion about the origin of the goods or services with which it is associated or to suggest that the goods or services are from the same source as the trademark with which there is confusion.

CALDERBANK LETTER. "... [A letter written] on a 'without prejudice' basis not only setting out an offer of settlement but expressly reserving the right, if the settlement offer was not accepted, to bring this letter to the attention of the trial Judge, after judgment, on the issue of costs ..." *Goodman v. Goodman* (1992), 2 C.P.C. (3d) 316 at 319 (B.C. S.C.), Sinclair Prowse J.

CALENDAR. *n.* The order of the division of time into years, months, weeks and days.

CALENDAR MONTH. May refer to an actual month or to a period from a day in one month to the same day in the next month.

CALENDAR QUARTER. Three consecutive months. May refer to three complete months or to the period from the day in the first month until the same day in the fourth month.

CALENDAR YEAR. The year from January 1 to December 31. May refer to a period of one year commencing on any day of a year and running until the same day of the next year.

CALL. *v.* 1. To make a request or demand. 2. To demand shareholders pay amount remaining on unpaid shares.

CALL. *n.* 1. Includes instalment, assessment and any other amount paid, payable or agreed to be paid in respect of a share. H. Sutherland, D.B. Horsley & J.M. Edmiston, eds., *Fraser's Handbook on Canadian Company Law*, 7th ed. (Toronto: Carswell, 1985) at 136. 2. "... [A] contract purchased for an agreed premium entitling the holder, at his option, to buy from the vendor on or before a fixed date a specified number of shares at a pre-determined price... ." *Posluns v. Toronto Stock Exchange*, [1964] 2 O.R. 547 at 553, 46 D.L.R. (2d) 210 (H.C.), Gale J. 3. A request or command to come or assemble. 4. A demand for payment. 5. An option transferable by delivery to demand delivery of a specified number or amount of securities at a fixed price within a specified time. 6. The summons of a person to the bar of the court to be admitted to the Bar of the province. See OFFICER DOWN ~; UNKNOWN TROUBLE ~.

CALL. *abbr.* Canadian Association Of Law Librarians.

CALLABLE. *adj.* Describes an option to pay on call before maturity.

CALL-BACK CLAUSE. A provision in a collective agreement concerning the calling back of an employee to the workplace after the employee has left after his or her regular shift.

CALL-IN CLAUSE. A provision in a collective agreement concerning the calling in of an employee to the workplace from home.

CALLING. *n.* A business; occupation; profession; trade; vocation.

CALL NEWSL. *abbr.* CALL Newsletter (Bulletin ACBD).

CALL TO THE BAR. 1. Admission to the Law Society of a province or to membership in the legal profession of a province. 2. The conferral on students of the degree of barrister-at-law.

C.A.L.P. *abbr.* Décsions de la Commission d'appel en matière de lésions professionnelles, 1986-.

C.A.L.R. *abbr.* Criminal Appeals Law Reporter, 1993-.

CAM. *abbr.* Cameron's Privy Council Decisions, 1832-1929.

CA MAG. *abbr.* CA Magazine.

CAM. DIG. *abbr.* Cameron's Digest.

CAMERA. *n.* 1. A judge's chambers. 2. A room. See BI-~AL, IN ~.

CAMERA SYSTEM. See RED LIGHT ~.

CAMERON P.C. *abbr.* Cameron's Constitutional Decisions of the Privy Council, 1867-1915.

CAMERON S.C. *abbr.* Cameron's Supreme Court Cases, 1880-1900.

CAMPBELL'S (LORD) ACT. The name by which the Fatal Accidents Act, 1846, U.K. is known.

CAM. S.C. *abbr.* Reports Hitherto Unpublished, Supreme Court of Canada, Cameron, 1880-1900.

CAN. *abbr.* Canada.

CANADA. *n.* 1. The geographic unit. 2. The juristic federal unit. *Reference re Legislative Authority of Parliament of Canada* (1979), (*sub nom. Reference re Legislative Authority of Parliament to Alter or Replace Senate*) 102 D.L.R. (3d) 1 at 12, [1980] 1 S.C.R. 56, 30 N.R. 271, Laskin C.J.C., Martland, Ritchie, Pigeon, Dickson, Estey, Pratte and McIntyre JJ. 3. For greater certainty, includes the internal waters of Canada and the territorial sea of Canada. *Interpretation Act*, R.S.C. 1985, c. I-21, s. 35. See ATTORNEY GENERAL OF ~; BANK OF ~; COASTAL WATERS OF ~; CONSTITUTION OF ~; COPYRIGHT BOARD OF ~; CORRECTIONAL INVESTIGATOR OF ~; CRIME HAS BEEN COMMITTED IN ~; DANGER TO THE SECURITY OF ~; FARM CREDIT ~; FINANCIAL CONSUMER AGENCY OF ~; GOVERNOR OF ~; HEALTH ~; HUMAN RESOURCES AND SKILLS DEVELOPMENT ~; INFORMATION COMMISSIONER OF ~; INLAND WATERS OF ~; LAW OF ~; LIBRARY AND ARCHIVES OF ~; LOWER ~; MINOR WATERS OF ~; NATIONAL GALLERY OF ~; QUEEN OF ~; SEDONA ~; SOLICITOR GENERAL ~; STATUS OF WOMEN ~; SUPREME COURT OF ~; TAX COURT OF ~; TRANSPORTATION APPEAL TRIBUNAL OF ~; UNIFORM LAW CONFERENCE OF ~WORKS FOR THE GENERAL ADVANTAGE OF ~.

CANADA ACT, 1982. The statute of the Parliament of the United Kingdom which gave effect to the Constitution Act, 1982 proclaimed in force April 17, 1982. This statute patriated the Constitution and terminated the power of the U.K. Parliament to legislate for Canada.

CANADA ASSISTANCE PLAN. A group of income-support programmes and social services which began in the 1940s and 1950s. P.W. Hogg, *Constitutional Law of Canada*, 3d ed. (Toronto: Carswell, 1992) at 145.

CANADA BORDER SERVICES AGENCY. Established under the Canada Border Services Agency Act, S.C. 2005, c. 38. The Agency is responsible for providing integrated border services that support national security and public safety priorities and facilitate the free flow of persons and goods, including animals and plants, that meet all requirements under the program legislation. *Canada Border Services Agency Act*, S.C. 2005, c. 38, s. 3, 5, 12. See CANADA REVENUE AGENCY.

CANADA CORPORATION. A body corporate incorporated by or under an Act of the Parliament of Canada.

CANADA DAY. July 1, not being a Sunday, is a legal holiday and shall be kept and observed as such throughout Canada under the name of "Canada Day". When July 1 is a Sunday, July 2 is a legal holiday and shall be kept and observed as such throughout Canada under the name of "Canada Day". July 1 is the anniversary of confederation in 1867. *Holidays Act*, R.S.C. 1985, c. H-5, s. 2.

CANADA DEPOSIT INSURANCE CORPORATION. A federal body with power to insure qualified Canadian currency deposits which member institutions hold and which makes loans to those institutions and to co-operative credit societies, finance corporations and other related organizations. Established under the *Canada Deposit Insurance Corporation Act*, R.S.C. 1985, c. C-3.

CANADA DISABILITY SAVINGS BOND. The bond payable or paid under section 7. The Minister may pay a Canada Disability Savings Bond into a registered disability savings plan of a beneficiary. *Canada Disability Savings Act*, S.C. 2007, c. 35, s. 136, 2 and 7.

CANADA DISABILITY SAVINGS GRANT. The grant payable or paid under section 6. The Minister may, in respect of any contribution made to a registered disability savings plan of a beneficiary, pay a Canada Disability Savings Grant into the plan. *Canada Disability Savings Act*, S.C. 2007, c. 35, s. 136, 2 and 6.

CANADA EMISSION REDUCTION INCENTIVES AGENCY. Established by the Canada Emission Reduction Incentives Agency Act, S.C. 2005, c. 30. Section 6 of the Act provides that the object of the Agency is to provide incentives for the reduction or removal of greenhouses gases through the acquisition, on behalf of the Government of Canada, of eligible credits created as a result of the reduction or removal of those gases.

CANADA EMPLOYMENT INSURANCE COMMISSION. Governed by the Canada Employment Insurance Act, S.C. 1996, c. 23. Section 3 of the Act provides that the Commission monitors, assesses and reports on: (a) how individuals, communities and the economy are adjusting to the changes made by this Act to the insurance and employment assistance programs under the Unemployment Insurance Act; (b) whether the savings expected as a result of the changes made by this Act are being realized; and (c) the effectiveness of the benefits and other assistance provided under this Act, including (i) how the benefits and assistance are utilized by employees and employers, and (ii) the effect of the benefits and assistance on the obligation of claimants to be available for and to seek employment and on the efforts of employers to maintain a stable workforce. The Commission makes regulations under the Act. The Commission administers the employment insurance program established by the Act.

CANADA MORTGAGE AND HOUSING CORPORATION. The federal corporation which administers the National Housing Act and predecessor legislation, insures the mortgage loans which approved lenders make for new and existing homeowner and rental housing. It may undertake joint public housing projects or loan money for them. It may loan money for student housing. Established under the *Canada Mortgage and Housing Corporation Act*, R.S.C. 1985, c. C-7. See *National Housing Act*, R.S.C. 1985, c. N-11 for a list of its powers.

CANADA PENSION PLAN. A contributory federal social insurance plan which provides benefits upon retirement from employment, on disability and for survivors of beneficiaries of the plan. *Canada Pension Plan*, R.S.C. 1985, c. C-8.

CANADA POST CORPORATION. The body which gathers, sorts and delivers mail in Canada. *Canada Post Corporation Act*, R.S.C. 1985, c. C-10.

CANADA REVENUE AGENCY. Canada Customs and Revenue Agency is continued as a body corporate under the name of the Canada Revenue Agency. The Agency is responsible for (a) supporting the administration and enforcement of the program legislation; (b) implementing agreements between the Government of Canada or the Agency and the government of a Province or other public body performing a function of government in Canada to carry out an activity or administer a tax or program; (c) implementing agreements or arrangements between the Agency and departments or agencies of the Government of Canada to carry out an activity or administer a program; and (d) implementing agreements between the Government of Canada and an aboriginal government to administer a tax. *Canada Revenue Agency Act*, S.C. 1999, c. 17, s. 4 and 5. See CANADA BORDER SERVICES AGENCY.

CANADIAN. *n.* 1. A Canadian citizen. 2. A permanent resident. 3. A Canadian government, whether federal, provincial or local, or an agency thereof. 4. An entity that is Canadian-controlled. 5. A Canadian citizen or a permanent resident, within the meaning of subsection 2(1) of the Immigration Act, or a body corporate incorporated or continued under the laws of Canada or a province. *Criminal Code*, R.S.C. 1985, c. C-46, s. 83.01. See RESIDENT ~.

CANADIAN AIRCRAFT. An aircraft registered in Canada.

CANADIAN ARMED FORCES. The Canadian Forces are the armed forces of Her Majesty raised by Canada and consist of one Service called the Canadian Armed Forces. *National Defence Act*, R.S.C. 1985, c. N-5, s. 14.

CANADIAN ARTISTS AND PRODUCERS PROFESSIONAL RELATIONS TRIBUNAL. Established under the Status of the Artist Act, S.C. 1992, c. 33, s. 10. Deals with matters concerning representation of artists by associations.

C

CANADIAN BILL OF RIGHTS. This bill, enacted by 8-9 Elizabeth II, c. 44 (S.C. 1960, c. 44) (R.S.C. 1985, Appendix III), was the first attempt in Canada to give statutory recognition and protection to certain human rights, fundamental freedoms of religion, speech, assembly and association and the press and procedural rights. See BILL OF RIGHTS.

CANADIAN BLOOD COMMITTEE. An organization comprised of representatives of the federal government and of each of the provinces. It is responsible for developing and implementing policies for collecting, processing, distributing, and utilizing whole blood and blood products in Canada, and for supervising and directing programs instituted under policies formulated in that regard by the federal and provincial governments. It is responsible for providing funding annually to the Canadian Red Cross. *Endean v. Canadian Red Cross Society* (1997), 148 D.L.R. (4th) 158 (B.C. S.C.).

CANADIAN CHARTER OF RIGHTS AND FREEDOMS. Part I of the Constitution Act, 1982 which guarantees rights and freedoms. See CHARTER.

CANADIAN COMPANY. A company formed or incorporated by or under any Act of Parliament of Canada or of the Legislature of any province.

CANADIAN COUNCIL ON THE STATUS OF THE ARTIST. Established under the Statuts of the Artist Act. The mandate of the Council is (a) to provide information and advice to the Minister of Canadian Heritage in order to ensure the highest quality of decision-making in respect of artists in Canada; (b) to defend and promote the professional status of artists in Canada; (c) to maintain close contacts with associations representing artists across Canada in various disciplines of the arts in order better to assess artists' needs and propose useful responses; (d) to propose measures, based on research and studies, to improve the professional working conditions of artists; and (e) to carry out such studies as the Minister of Canadian Heritage may direct. *Status of the Artist Act*, S.C. 1992, c. 33, s. 4.

CANADIAN CULTURAL PROPERTY EXPORT REVIEW BOARD. Established under the Cultural Property Export and Import Act, R.S.C. 1985, c. C-51, s. 18. Section 20 of the Act provides that: The Review Board shall, on request, (a) pursuant to section 29, review applications for export permits; (b) pursuant to section 30, make determinations respecting fair cash offers to purchase; and (c) pursuant to section 32, make determinations for the purposes of subparagraph 39(1)(a)(i.1), paragraph 110.1(1)(c), the definition "total cultural gifts" in subsection 118.1(1) and subsection 118.1(10) of the Income Tax Act.

CANADIAN ENTITY. An entity that is incorporated or formed by or under an Act of Parliament or of the legislature of a province and that carries on business, directly or indirectly, in Canada. *Bank Act*, S.C. 1991, c. 46, s. 2.

CANADIAN ENVIRONMENTAL ASSESSMENT AGENCY. The objects of the Agency are (a) to administer the environmental assessment process and any other requirements and procedures established by this Act and the regulations; (b) to promote uniformity and harmonization in the assessment of environmental effects across Canada at all levels of government; (c) to promote or conduct research in matters of environmental assessment and to encourage the development of environmental assessment techniques and practices, including testing programs, alone or in cooperation with other agencies or organizations; (d) to promote environmental assessment in a manner that is consistent with the purposes of this Act; (e) to promote, monitor and facilitate compliance with this Act and the regulations; (f) to promote and monitor the quality of assessments conducted under this Act; (g) to ensure an opportunity for timely public participation in the environmental assessment process; and (h) to engage in consultation with aboriginal peoples on policy issues related to this Act. In carrying out its objects, the Agency shall (a) provide administrative support for mediators and review panels; (b) provide, on the request of the Minister, administrative support for any research or advisory body that the Minister may establish in the area of environmental assessment; (c) provide information or training to facilitate the conduct of environmental assessments; and (d) establish and lead a quality assurance program for assessments conducted under this Act. *Canadian Environmental Assessment Act*, S.C. 1992, c. 37, s. 61-63.

CANADIAN ENVIRONMENTAL ASSESSMENT REGISTRY. For the purpose of facilitating public access to records relating to environmental assessments and providing notice in a timely manner of the assessments, there shall be a registry called the Canadian Environmental Assessment Registry, consisting of an Internet site and project files. *Canadian Environmental Assessment Act*, S.C. 1992, c. 37, s. 55.

CANADIAN FINANCIAL INSTITUTION. 1. A financial institution that is incorporated or formed by or under an Act of Parliament or of the legislature of a province. *Bank Act*, S.C. 1991, c. 46, s. 2. 2. Any of the following that is authorized to carry on business under the laws of Canada or a province, namely, (i) a bank, (ii) an authorized foreign bank, (iii) a loan company, (iv) a trust company, (v) an insurance company to which the Insurance Companies Act applies, (vi) an insurance corporation incorporated by or under an Act of the legislature of a province, (vii) a central cooperative credit society, (viii) a cooperative credit association, or (ix) a local cooperative credit society; (b) Alberta Treasury Branches, established under the Alberta Treasury Branches Act of the Province of Alberta; or (c) the Fédération des caisses Desjardins du Québec. *Canadian Payments Act*, R.S.C. 1985, c. C-21, *Money Market Mutual Fund Conditions Regulations*, SOR/2001-475, s. 1.

CANADIAN FIREARMS REGISTRY. The registry established by the Registrar under section 83 of the Firearms Act, S.C. 1995, c. 30. Records shall be kept in the Canadian Firearms Registry of the following matters: (a) every licence, registration certificate and authorization that is issued or revoked by the

Registrar; (b) every application for a licence, registration certificate or authorization that is refused by the Registrar; (c) every transfer of a firearm of which the Registrar is informed under section 26 or 27; (d) every exportation from or importation into Canada of a firearm of which the Registrar is informed under section 42 or 50; (e) every loss, finding, theft or destruction of a firearm of which the Registrar is informed under section 88; and (f) such other matters as may be prescribed.

CANADIAN FISHERIES WATERS. All waters in the fishing zones of Canada, all waters in the territorial sea of Canada and all internal waters of Canada. *Coastal Fisheries Protection Act*, R.S.C. 1985, c. C-33, s. 2.

CANADIAN FOOD INSPECTION AGENCY. The Agency is responsible for the administration and enforcement of the Agriculture and Agri-Food Administrative Monetary Penalties Act, Canada Agricultural Products Act, Feeds Act, Fertilizers Act, Fish Inspection Act, Health of Animals Act, Meat Inspection Act, Plant Breeders' Rights Act, Plant Protection Act and Seeds Act. The Agency is responsible for the enforcement of the Consumer Packaging and Labelling Act as it relates to food, as that term is defined in section 2 of the Food and Drugs Act. The Agency is responsible for (a) the enforcement of the Food and Drugs Act as it relates to food, as defined in section 2 of that Act; and (b) the administration of the provisions of the Food and Drugs Act as they relate to food, as defined in section 2 of that Act, except those provisions that relate to public health, safety or nutrition. Established by *Canadian Food Inspection Agency Act*, S.C. 1997, c. 6, s. 3 and 11.

CANADIAN FORCES. The armed forces of Her Majesty raised by Canada. *National Defence Act*, R.S.C. 1985, c. N-5, s. 14.

CANADIAN GRAIN COMMISSION. Established under the Canada Grain Act, R.S.C. 1985, c. G-10, s. 3. The objects of the commission set out at section 10 of the Act are: Subject to this Act and any directions to the Commission issued from time to time under this Act by the Governor in Council or the Minister, the Commission shall, in the interests of the grain producers, establish and maintain standards of quality for Canadian grain and regulate grain handling in Canada, to ensure a dependable commodity for domestic and export markets.

CANADIAN HERITAGE. See DEPARTMENT OF ~.

CANADIAN HUMAN RIGHTS COMMISSION. The federal commission which administers the Canadian Human Rights Act. Established under Canadian Human Rights Act, R.S.C. 1985, c. H-6, s. 26. In addition to its duties under Part III with respect to complaints regarding discriminatory practices, the Commission is generally responsible for the administration of Parts I, II and III of the Act.

CANADIAN HUMAN RIGHTS TRIBUNAL. Conducts inquiries into complaints concerning human rights and discriminatory practices. Established

under *Canadian Human Rights Act*, R.S.C. 1985, c. H-6, s. 48.1.

CANADIAN INSTITUTES OF HEALTH RESEARCH. The Canadian Institutes of Health Research (CIHR) is the Government of Canada's agency responsible for funding health research in Canada. Established under the Canadian Institutes of Health Research Act, S.C. 2000, c. 6. The objective of the CIHR is to excel, according to internationally accepted standards of scientific excellence, in the creation of new knowledge and its translation into improved health for Canadians, more effective health services and products and a strengthened Canadian health care system. *Canadian Institutes of Health Research Act*, S.C. 2000, c. 6, s. 3-5.

CANADIAN INTERNATIONAL TRADE TRIBUNAL. The tribunal established by the federal government to: (a) conduct inquiries and report on matters referred to the Tribunal for inquiry by the Governor in Council or the Minister under this Act; (a.1) conduct mid-term reviews under section 19.02 and report on the reviews; (b) consider complaints and extension requests filed with the Tribunal by domestic producers of like or directly competitive goods under this Act and, where appropriate, conduct inquiries into the complaints and extension requests and report on them; (b.1) receive complaints, conduct inquiries and make determinations under sections 30.1 to 30.19; (c) hear, determine and deal with all appeals that, pursuant to any other Act of Parliament or regulations thereunder, may be made to the Tribunal, and all matters related thereto; and (d) exercise and perform such other duties or functions that, pursuant to any other Act of Parliament or regulations thereunder, shall or may be exercised or performed by the Tribunal. The Tribunal is a court of record. It is required to inquire into and report to the Governor in Council on any matter in relation to the economic, trade or commercial interests of Canada with respect to any goods or services or any class thereof that the Governor in Council refers to the Tribunal for inquiry. It is also required to inquire into and report to the Minister on any tariff-related matter, including any matter concerning the international rights or obligations of Canada in connection therewith, that the Minister refers to the Tribunal for inquiry. *Canadian International Trade Tribunal Act*, R.S.C. 1985, c. 47 (4th Supp.).

CANADIAN INTERNET REGISTRATION AUTHORITY. The organization which manages .CA domain registrations on the internet.

CANADIAN JUDICIAL COUNCIL. The objects of the Council are to promote efficiency and uniformity, and to improve the quality of judicial service in superior courts.

CANADIAN LEGAL INFORMATION INSTITUTE. CanLII is an initiative of the Federation of Law Societies of Canada, funded by law societies and by law foundations. It is designed as a free Canadian virtual law library to serve both the profession and the public. www.canlii.org.

CANADIAN MARITIME LAW. 1. "... [I]ncludes all that body of law which was administered in England by the High Court on its Admiralty side in 1934 as such law may, from time to time, have been amended by the federal Parliament, and as it has developed through judicial precedent to date.... a body of federal law dealing with all claims in respect of maritime and admiralty matters ... the words 'maritime' and 'admiralty' should be interpreted within the modern context of commerce and shipping. In reality, the ambit of Canadian maritime law is limited only by the constitutional division of powers in the Constitution Act 1867 (30 & 31 Vict.), c. 3.... a body of federal law encompassing the common law principles of tort, contract and bailment." *Miida Electronics Inc. v. Mitsui O.S.K. Lines Ltd.* (1986), (*sub nom. ITO – International Terminal Operators Ltd. v. Miida Electronics Inc.*) 28 D.L.R. (4th) 641 at 654, 656, 660, [1986] 1 S.C.R. 752, 68 N.R. 241, 34 B.L.R. 251, McIntyre J. (Dickson C.J.C., Estey and Wilson JJ. concurring). 2. Administered by the Exchequer Court of Canada on its Admiralty side by virtue of the Admiralty Act, chapter A-1 of the Revised Statutes of Canada, 1970, or any other statute, or that would have been so administered if that Court had had, on its Admiralty side, unlimited jurisdiction in relation to maritime and admiralty matters, as that law has been altered by this Act or any other Act of Parliament. *Federal Courts Act*, R.S.C. 1985, c. F-7, s. 2.

CANADIAN MUSEUM FOR HUMAN RIGHTS. Established under the Museums Act. The purpose of the Canadian Museum for Human Rights is to explore the subject of human rights, with special but not exclusive reference to Canada, in order to enhance the public's understanding of human rights, to promote respect for others and to encourage reflection and dialogue. *Museums Act*, S.C. 1990, c. 3, s. 15.1 and 15.2.

CANADIAN MUSEUM OF CIVILIZATION. Established under the Museums Act. The purpose of the Canadian Museum of Civilization is to increase, throughout Canada and internationally, interest in, knowledge and critical understanding of and appreciation and respect for human cultural achievements and human behavior by establishing, maintaining and developing for research and posterity a collection of objects of historical or cultural interest, with special but not exclusive reference to Canada, and by demonstrating those achievements and behaviour, the knowledge derived from them and the understanding they represent. *Museums Act*, S.C. 1990, c. 3, s. 7 and 8.

CANADIAN MUSEUM OF NATURE. Established under the Museums Act. The purpose of the Canadian Museum of Nature is to increase, throughout Canada and internationally, interest in, knowledge of and appreciation and respect for the natural world by establishing, maintaining and developing for research and posterity a collection of natural history objects, with special but not exclusive reference to Canada, and by demonstrating the natural world, the knowledge derived from it and the understanding it represents. *Museums Act*, S.C. 1990, c. 3, s. 11.

CANADIAN PATENT OFFICE RECORD. The Canadian Patent Office Record referred to in subsection 78(3) of the Act. *Patent Act*, R.S.C. 1985, c. P-4, *Patent Rules*, SOR/96-423, s. 2.

CANADIAN PAYMENTS ASSOCIATION. A corporation established by the federal government to facilitate transactions among financial institutions. The Association shall consist of the following members: (a) the Bank of Canada; (b) every bank; (c) every authorized foreign bank; (c.1) every cooperative credit association, loan company or trust company that is designated as a bridge institution under the Canada Deposit Insurance Corporation Act; and (d) any other person who is entitled under this Part to be a member and who, on application to the Association for membership in the Association, establishes entitlement to be a member. Each of the following persons is entitled to be a member of the Association if they meet the requirements set out in the regulations and the by-laws: (a) a central, a trust company, a loan company and any other person, other than a local that is a member of a central or a cooperative credit association, that accepts deposits transferable by order to a third party; (c) Her Majesty in right of a province or an agent thereof, if Her Majesty in right of the province or the agent thereof accepts deposits transferable by order to a third party; (d) a life insurance company; (e) a securities dealer; (f) a cooperative credit association; (g) the trustee of a qualified trust; and (h) a qualified corporation, on behalf of its money market mutual fund. *Canadian Payments Act*, R.S.C. 1985, c. C-21, s. 4.

CANADIAN PRIVATE COPYING COLLECTIVE. CPCC [Canadian Private Copying Collective] is the "collecting body" designated by the Board under the Act [Copyright Act, R.S.C. 1985, c. C-42] to collect and distribute the levies to rightsholders. Manufacturers and importers of blank media sold in Canada must pay the levy to the CPCC. The collecting body must distribute the levy to the collective societies that represent the above-mentioned categories of rightsholders [eligible authors, performers and makers of recorded music] in the proportion determined by the Board. The CPCC is a non-share, non-profit corporation established under Part II of the Canada Corporations Act [R.S.C. 1970, c. C-32]. Its members are collective societies that hold private copying remuneration rights on behalf of rightsholders. As noted, it is the collecting body designated by the Board under the Act. *Canadian Private Copying Collective v. Canadian Storage Media Alliance*, 2004 FCA 424.

CANADIAN PRODUCTION FUND. The Canada Television and Cable Production Fund, or its successor. *Broadcasting Act*, S.C. 1991, c. 11, *Broadcasting Distribution Regulations*, SOR/97-555, s. 1.

CANADIAN RADIO-TELEVISION AND TELECOMMUNICATIONS COMMISSION. The federal body which supervises and regulates every aspect of Canadian broadcasting (television, radio, cable and pay television and specialty services) and regulates federal telecommunications carriers. Established under the Canadian Radio-television and Telecommunications Commission Act. Its objects and powers are set out in the Broadcasting Act. It exercises powers under the Telecommunications Act as well. *Canadian Radio-television and Telecommunications Commission Act*, R.S.C. 1985, c. C-22, s. 3 and 12.

CANADIAN SECURITIES INSTITUTE. Provides courses and examinations for those seeking credentials to enter or within the securities, banking, and insurance industries.

CANADIAN SECURITIES REGULATION REGIME TRANSITION OFFICE. Established under the Canadian Securities Regulation Regime Transition Office Act, S.C. 2009, c. 2. The purpose of the Transition Office is to assist in the establishment of a Canadian securities regulation regime and a Canadian regulatory authority.

CANADIAN SECURITY INTELLIGENCE SERVICE. The Service shall collect, by investigation or otherwise, to the extent that it is strictly necessary, and analyse and retain information and intelligence respecting activities that may on reasonable grounds be suspected of constituting threats to the security of Canada and, in relation thereto, shall report to and advise the Government of Canada. The Service may provide security assessments to departments of the Government of Canada. The Service may conduct such investigations as are required for the purpose of providing security assessments. The Service may (a) advise any minister of the Crown on matters relating to the security of Canada, or (b) provide any minister of the Crown with information relating to security matters or criminal activities, that is relevant to the exercise of any power or the performance of any duty or function by that Minister under the Citizenship Act or the Immigration and Refugee Protection Act. the Service may, in relation to the defence of Canada or the conduct of the international affairs of Canada, assist the Minister of National Defence or the Minister of Foreign Affairs, within Canada, in the collection of information or intelligence relating to the capabilities, intentions or activities of (a) any foreign state or group of foreign states; or (b) any person other than (i) a Canadian citizen, (ii) a permanent resident within the meaning of subsection 2(1) of the Immigration and Refugee Protection Act, or (iii) a corporation incorporated by or under an Act of Parliament or of the legislature of a province. Established under the *Canadian Security Intelligence Service Act*, R.S.C. 1985, c. C-23., s. 3 and 12 to 16.

CANADIAN STANDARDS ASSOCIATION. A national standard-setting organization which certifies products covered by its standards. D. Robertson, *Ontario Health and Safety Guide* (Toronto: De Boo, 1988) at 5-42.

CANADIAN SUPPLIER. [. . .] The definition of Canadian supplier [in Article 518 of the Agreement on Internal Trade, Can. Gaz. 1995.1.1323] does not contain any nationality requirement in the sense of requiring any degree of ownership or control of the entity by Canadians. ... The essential element of the definition of Canadian supplier is ... a geographical requirement in respect of the business activities of the entity in question, namely, a place of business in Canada. This essential element is very similar to the concept of a "permanent establishment" as it is used in Canada's income tax legislation and treaties. That concept connotes a fixed place of business in the jurisdiction in question. To borrow that term from the income tax area, a Canadian supplier may be said to be an entity with a permanent establishment in Canada. Thus, both a Canadian incorporated corporation, which is wholly-owned by non-residents, and a Canadian situs branch operation of a non-resident corporation are within the contemplation of the definition of Canadian supplier. In both of these examples, the requirements of that definition will be met if the "permanent establishment" requirement can be established. *Northrop Grumman Overseas Services Corp. v. Canada (Department of Public Works & Government Services)*, 2008 FCA 187.

CANADIAN TRANSPORTATION ACCIDENT INVESTIGATION AND SAFETY BOARD. The body charged with the investigation of accidents involving modes of transportation within the federal sphere, particularly aviation and railways.

CANADIAN TRANSPORTATION AGENCY. Continuation of the National Transportation Agency. Exercises powers under several Acts concerning the implementation of transportation policy. Established under the *Canada Transportation Act*, S.C. 1996, c. 10, s. 7.

CANADIAN VALUES. Amongst others, values of global citizenship, equity and environmental sustainability. *Official Development Assistance Accountability Act*, S.C. 2008, c. 17, s. 3.

CANADIAN VESSEL. A vessel registered or listed under Part 2 of the Canada Shipping Act. *Canada Shipping Act, 2001*, c. 26, s. 2.

CANADIAN VIDEO TAPE. Video tape manufactured in Canada or imported into Canada and released and accounted for under the Customs Act. *Financial Administration Act*, R.S.C. 1985, c. F-11, *Exposed and Processed Film and Recorded Video Tape Remission Order*, C.R.C., c. 763, s. 2.

CANADIAN WATERS. Includes the territorial sea of Canada and all internal waters of Canada. *Interpretation Act*, R.S.C. 1985, c. I-21, s. 35.

CANADIAN WHEAT BOARD. The federal body, established under the Canadian Wheat Board Act, which supervises export sales of barley, oats and wheat produced in Western Canada and domestic sales of these grains intended for human consumption. It controls the delivery of all major grains, co-ordinating grain movement to terminal elevators. The object of the board is to market in an orderly manner, in interprovincial and export trade, grain grown in Canada. *Canadian Wheat Board Act*, R.S.C. 1985, c. C-24, s. 5.

CANADIAN WORKFORCE. All persons in Canada of working age who are willing and able to work. *Employment Equity Act*, S.C. 1995, c. 44, s. 3.

CAN-AM L.J. *abbr.* Canadian-American Law Journal.

CAN. BAR J. *abbr.* Canadian Bar Journal.

CAN. BAR REV. *abbr.* The Canadian Bar Review (La Revue du Barreau canadien).

CAN. BUS. L.J. *abbr.* Canadian Business Law Journal (Revue canadienne du droit de commerce).

CANCEL. *v.* 1. To revoke a will. *Bishop Estate v. Reesor* (1990), 39 E.T.R. 36 at 38 (Ont. H.C.), Kurisko L.J.S.C. 2. In the case of an instrument, to draw lines across it intending to indicate it is no longer in force.

CANCELLATION. *n.* "... [U]sed in relation to an insurance policy implies the bringing to an end of the policy during its term, i.e. for some reason rendering invalid what would otherwise be valid." *Bank of Nova Scotia v. Commercial Union Assurance of Canada* (1991), 104 N.S.R. (2d) 313 at 319, 283 A.P.R. 313, 6 C.C.L.I. (2d) 178 (T.D.), Tidman J.

CANCELLATION CLAUSE. A clause in an agreement that permits the parties to cancel and terminate their agreement.

CANCELLED CHEQUE. A cheque which bears the indication that it has been honoured by the bank upon which it was drawn.

CAN. C.L.G. *abbr.* Canadian Commercial Law Guide.

CAN. COMMUNIC. L. REV. *abbr.* Canadian Communications Law Review.

CAN. COMMUNITY L.J. *abbr.* Canadian Community Law Journal (Revue canadienne de droit communautaire).

CAN. COMPET. POLICY REC. *abbr.* Canadian Competition Policy Record.

CAN. COMP. POL. REC. *abbr.* Canadian Competition Policy Record.

CAN. COMPUTER L.R. *abbr.* Canadian Computer Law Reporter.

CAN. COM. R. *abbr.* Canadian Commercial Reports, 1901-1905.

CAN. COUNCIL INT. L. *abbr.* Canadian Council on International Law. Conference. Proceedings. (Conseil canadien de droit international. Congrès. Travaux).

CAN. COUNCIL INT'L L. PROC. *abbr.* Canadian Council on International Law, Proceedings.

CAN. CRIM. FORUM. *abbr.* Canadian Criminology Forum (Le Forum canadien de criminologie).

CAN. CURR. TAX. *abbr.* Canadian Current Tax.

CAN. CURRENT TAX. *abbr.* Canadian Current Tax.

C. & F. *abbr.* Cost and freight. In a sales contract, means that the price includes cost and freight and the buyer must arrange insurance.

C. & S. *abbr.* Clarke & Scully's Drainage Cases (Ontario), 1898-1903.

CANE. See WHITE ~.

CAN. ENV. L.N. *abbr.* Canadian Environmental Law News.

CAN. F.L.G. *abbr.* Canadian Family Law Guide.

CAN. H.R. ADVOC. *abbr.* Canadian Human Rights Advocate.

CAN. HUM. RTS. Y.B. *abbr.* Canadian Human Rights Yearbook (Annuaire canadien des droits de le personne).

CAN. IND. REL. ASSOC. *abbr.* Canadian Industrial Relations Association. Annual Meeting. Proceedings (Association canadienne des relations industrielles. Congrès. Travaux).

CAN. INTELL. PROP. REV. *abbr.* Canadian Intellectual Property Review.

CAN. I.T.G.R. *abbr.* Canada Income Tax Guide Report.

CAN. J. CRIM. *abbr.* Canadian Journal of Criminology (Revue canadienne de criminologie).

CAN. J. CRIM. & CORR. *abbr.* Canadian Journal of Criminology and Corrections.

CAN. J. FAM. L. *abbr.* Canadian Journal of Family Law (Revue canadienne de droit familial).

CAN. J. INS. L. *abbr.* Canadian Journal of Insurance Law.

CAN. J.L. & JURIS. *abbr.* The Canadian Journal of Law and Jurisprudence.

CAN. J.L. & SOCIETY. *abbr.* Canadian Journal of Law and Society (Revue canadienne de droit et société).

CAN. J. WOMEN & LAW. *abbr.* Canadian Journal of Women and the Law (Revue juridique "La femme et le droit").

CAN. LAW. *abbr.* Canadian Lawyer.

CAN. LAWYER. *abbr.* Canadian Lawyer.

CAN. LEGAL STUD. *abbr.* Canadian Legal Studies.

CANLII. *abbr.* Canadian Legal Information Institute. CanLII is an initiative of the Federation of Law Societies of Canada, funded by law societies and by law foundations. It is designed as a free Canadian virtual law library to serve both the profession and the public. *Home*, online: CanLII - Canadian Legal Information Institute, < http://www.canlii.org/en/index.php >. See LEGAL INFORMATION INSTITUTE; PUBLIC ACCESS TO LAW.

CAN. L.J. *abbr.* Canada Law Journal.

CAN. L.R.B.R. *abbr.* Canadian Labour Relations Board Reports, 1974-.

[] CAN. L.R.B.R. *abbr.* Canadian Labour Relations Board Reports.

CAN. L. REV. *abbr.* Canadian Law Review, 1901-1907.

CAN. L.T. (1881-1922). *abbr.* Canadian Law Times.

CAN. MUN. J. *abbr.* Canadian Municipal Journal.

CANON. *n.* 1. A rule of law. 2. A church dignitary.

CANON LAW. Church law.

CAN. PETRO. TAX J. *abbr.* Canadian Petroleum Tax Journal.

CAN. PUB. POL. *abbr.* Canadian Public Policy.

CAN. S.L.R. *abbr.* Canadian Securities Law Reports.

CAN. S.T.R. *abbr.* Canadian Sales Tax Reports.

CAN. TAX FOUND. *abbr.* Canadian Tax Foundation (Conference Report).

CAN. TAX J. *abbr.* Canadian Tax Journal (Revue fiscale canadienne).

CAN. TAX N. *abbr.* Canadian Tax News.

CAN. TAX'N: J. TAX POL'Y. *abbr.* Canadian Taxation: A Journal of Tax Policy.

CAN.-U.S. L.J. *abbr.* Canada-United States Law Journal.

CANVASS. *v.* To go door to door in sequence down a street soliciting customers or providing information and soliciting votes for a candidate at an election.

CAN. Y.B. INT. L. *abbr.* Canadian Year Book of International Law (Annuaire canadien de droit international).

CAN. Y.B. INT'L. L. *abbr.* Canadian Year Book of International Law.

CAP. *abbr.* Chapter.

CAPABLE. *adj.* Having potential to do or be; having the qualities or nature required. See IN~; MENTALLY ~.

C.A.P.A.C. *abbr.* Composers, Authors and Publishers Association of Canada Limited.

CAPACITY. *n.* The ability: (i) to understand information relevant to making a decision; and (ii) to appreciate the reasonably foreseeable consequences of making or not making a decision. *The Trustee Act, 2009*, S.S. 2009, c. T-23.01, s. 2. See CONFIDENTIAL ~; CONTRACTUAL ~; IN~; TESTAMENTARY ~.

CAPIAS. [L. that you take] The name of writs which direct the sheriff to arrest the person named in the writs.

CAPITAL. *n.* 1. The means with which a business is carried on. 2. In estates, used in contradistinction to income. "... [W]hen applied to estate problems would clearly mean the value of the assets of the estate as of the date of the testator's death." *Thomson v. Morrison* (1980), 6 E.T.R. 257 at 266, 28 O.R. (2d) 403, 111 D.L.R. (3d) 390 (H.C.), Holland J. 3. Money raised through issuing shares, certificates, bonds, debentures, long-term notes or any other long-term obligation, contributed or earned surplus and reserves. See AUTHORIZED ~; CIRCULATING ~; EQUITY ~; FIXED ~; FLOATING ~; ISSUED ~; LIQUID ~; NATIONAL ~ COMMISSION; NATIONAL ~ REGION; NOMINAL ~.

CAPITAL ACCOUNT. As applied to persons means the amount by which the assets of a person employed in the business exceed the liabilities arising from the business and all money advanced or loaned to the person by any individual, partnership, firm or company incorporated or unincorporated for capital account; but in no case shall the capital account of a person employed in the business be considered to be less than the fixed assets (less depreciation) and inventories employed in the business. *Corporations Tax Act*, R.S.N.S. 1967, c. 61, s. 1.

CAPITAL ASSETS. Things used in a business to earn the income – land, buildings, plant, machinery, motor vehicles, ships. *Canada Steamship Lines Ltd. v. M.N.R.*, [1966] C.T.C. 255, 66 D.T.C. 5305 (Exch. Ct.).

CAPITAL COST. The cost involved in acquiring, constructing, designing, equipping, adding to, replacing or altering a capital work.

CAPITAL COST ALLOWANCE. "... [A] tax term signifying the writing-off of the capital cost of an asset in an amount allowed by income tax regulations." *Canning v. C.F.M. Fuels (Ontario) Ltd.*, [1977] 2 S.C.R. 207 at 214, 12 N.R. 541, 71 D.L.R. (3d) 321, the court per Dickson J.

CAPITAL EXPENDITURE. An outlay or the incurrence of a liability for the construction or acquisition or, for the addition to, a tangible asset.

CAPITAL GAIN. The profit earned when property is sold for more than was paid for it.

CAPITAL GAIN OR LOSS. On the sale of an item of capital property, the difference between the proceeds of the disposition and the total of the adjusted cost base and the value of expenses incurred in making the disposition. A positive figure is a gain and a negative is a loss.

CAPITALISATION. *var.* **CAPITALIZATION.** *n.* 1. The total amount of shares and other securities issued by a corporation. 2. "... [U]nless the earnings as such actually or constructively pass from the company to the shareholder there is, for all purposes, capitalization.... When earnings are 'capitalized', they cease at that moment to be 'earnings'; they become part of the capital assets; ..." *Waters, Re* (*sub nom. Waters v. Toronto General Trusts Corp.*) [1956] C.T.C. 217 at 222, [1956] S.C.R. 889, 56 D.T.C. 1113, 4 D.L.R. (2d) 673, Rand J. 3. An estimate of yearly revenue in terms of the amount of capital which it is necessary to invest at a given rate of interest in order to receive that revenue.

CAPITAL LOSS. See CAPITAL GAIN OR LOSS; CARRY-OVER OF ~ES.

CAPITAL MURDER. A classification formerly used under the Criminal Code where a person personally caused or assisted in causing the death of (a) a police officer, police constable, constable, sheriff, deputy sheriff, sheriff's officer or other person employed for the preservation and maintenance of the public peace, acting in the course of that officer's duties, or (b) the warden, deputy warden, instructor, keeper, gaoler, guard or other officer or permanent employee of a prison, acting in the course of that officer's duties, or counselled or procured another person to do any act causing or assisting in causing the death. See NON-~.

CAPITAL PROPERTY. (a) Any depreciable property of the taxpayer, and (b) any property (other than depreciable property), any gain or loss from the disposition of which would if the property were disposed of, be a capital gain or a capital loss, as the case may be, of the taxpayer. *Income Tax Act*, R.S.C. 1985, c. 1 (5th Supp.), s. 54(1).

CAPITAL PUNISHMENT. Punishment by death.

CAPITAL SECURITY. Any share of any class of shares of a company or any bond, debenture, note or other obligation of a company, whether secured or unsecured. *Companies Act*, R.S.A. 2000, c. C-21, s. 95.

CAPITAL TRANSACTION. The general concept is that a transaction whereby an enduring asset or advantage is acquired for the business is a capital transaction. *Associated Investors v. M.N.R.*, [1967] C.T.C. 138, 67 D.T.C. 5096.

CAPRICIOUS. *adj.* Arbitrary. See IN A PERVERSE OR ~ MANNER OR WITHOUT REGARD TO THE MATERIAL BEFORE IT.

CAPTION. *n.* The formal heading of an affidavit, deposition, indictment, information or recognisance which states before whom it was taken, found or made.

CAPTURE. *v.* To take; arrest; seize.

C.A.Q. *abbr.* Causes en appel au Québec, 1986-1995.

CAR. See KIT ~.

CARBON DIOXIDE EQUIVALENT. The mass of carbon dioxide that would produce the same global warming impact as a given mass of another greenhouse gas, as determined in accordance with the regulations. *Greenhouse Gas Reduction (Cap and Trade) Act*, S.B.C. 2008, c. 32, s. 1.

CARBON INTENSITY. In relation to a Part 3 fuel, means the greenhouse gas emissions attributable under the regulations to the fuel proportionate to the energy provided by the fuel in its expected use for transport or another prescribed purpose, (a) expressed as grams of carbon dioxide equivalent emissions per megajoule of energy, and (b) as determined in accordance with section 6 [requirements for reduced carbon intensity]. *Greenhouse Gas Reduction (Renewable and Low Carbon Fuel Requirements) Act*, S.B.C. 2008, c. 16, s. 1.

CARBON MONOXIDE. A toxic, odorless and colourless gas produced when organic materials are burned incompletely. F.A. Jaffe, *A Guide to Pathological Evidence for Lawyers and Police Officers*, 4th ed. (Toronto: Carswell, 1999) at 232.

CARBON NEUTRAL. In relation to a public sector organization for a particular period, means that the public sector organization has complied with the obligations under section 6 [requirements for achieving carbon neutral status] to (a) pursue actions to minimize the relevant greenhouse gas emissions for that period, and (b) net those greenhouse gas emissions to zero in accordance with that section. *Greenhouse Gas Reduction Targets Act*, S.B.C. 2007, c. 42, s. 1.

CARCASS. *n.* The body of a dead animal.

CARD. See CREDIT ~; PREPAID PURCHASE ~.

CARE. *n.* 1. Safekeeping. 2. "... [I]ncludes such things as feeding, clothing, cleaning, transporting, helping and protecting another person... ." *Thornborrow v. MacKinnon* (1981), *(sub nom. Schmidt, Re)* 16 C.C.L.T. 198 at 207, 32 O.R. (2d) 740, 123 D.L.R. (3d) 124 (H.C.), Linden J. 3. "... [I]mplies at least physical possession of the motor vehicle with an element of 'control' and carries the sense of responsibility and includes a sense of charge, possession and management." *R. v. Young* (1979), 4 M.V.R. 38 at 43, 21 Nfld. & P.E.I.R. 77, 56 A.P.R. 77 (P.E.I. C.A.), M.J. McQuaid J.A. (Peake J.A. concurring). See DAY ~; DUTY OF ~; REASONABLE ~; STANDARD OF ~.

CARE AND CUSTODY. All parental rights, duties and responsibilities toward a child.

CARE FACILITY. See COMMUNITY ~.

CAREGIVER. See LIVE-IN ~.

CARELESS. *adj.* 1. "... [I]nfers an element of negligence or recklessness. It describes a state of conscious in difference [sic] or oblivion to the potential consequences of an act or a course of action." *R. v. Pawlivsky* (1981), 8 Sask. R. 356 at 359 (Div. Ct.), affirmed (1981), 10 Sask L.R. 179 (C.A.). 2. "... [N]ot caring ..." *R. v. King* (1984), 37 Sask. R. 29 at 32 (Q.B.), Hrabinsky J.

CARE OR CONTROL.. In reference to a motor vehicle, may be exercised without an intent to set the vehicle in motion when a person performs an act or series of acts involving the use of the car, its fittings or equipment and unintentionally sets the vehicle in motion. *R. v. Ford* [1982] 1 S.C.R. 231, per Ritchie, J. for the majority.

CAREY. *abbr.* Carey's Manitoba Reports, 1875.

CARGO SHIP. A commercial vessel that is engaged in international transportation of shipments of goods other than goods imported or exported as mail. *Proceeds of Crime (Money Laundering) and Terrorist Financing Act*, S.C. 2000, c. 17, *Cross-border Currency and Monetary Instruments Reporting Regulations*, SOR/2002-412, s. 1.

CARNAL KNOWLEDGE. Coitus, copulation, sexual intercourse.

CAROTID HOLD. A way to subdue someone by compressing the sides of their neck, obstructing blood flow and causing them to faint. F.A. Jaffe, *A Guide to Pathological Evidence for Lawyers and Police Officers*, 4th ed. (Toronto: Carswell 1999) at 232.

CARRIAGE. *n.* A contract of carriage generally begins when the goods are loaded aboard the carrying vessel or vehicle and continues until the goods are delivered to the final destination. May include salvage. *Bombardier Inc. v. C.P. Ltd.* (1991), 6 B.L.R. (2d) 166 (Ont. C.A.). See CONTRACT OF ~; MIS~.

CARRIER. *n.* 1. Any person engaged for hire or reward in transport of persons or commodities by railway, water, aircraft, motor vehicle undertaking or commodity pipeline. 2. An insurer. 3. A person who, without apparent symptoms of a communicable disease, harbours and may disseminate an infectious agent. *Public Health Act*, R.S.A. 2000, c. P.37, s. 1. 4. A person with whom a shipper of goods enters into a contract of carriage of the goods by water. *Canada Shipping Act, 2001*, S.C. 2001, c. 26, s. 247. See AIR; COMMON ~; CUSTOMS BONDED ~; LOCAL ~; MOTOR ~; PRIVATE ~.

CARRIES ON BUSINESS. The term "carries on business" is not defined in the Alberta Rules of Court. The term appears in many statutes and its meaning is coloured by the legislative context. It is therefore inappropriate to simply import a definition from another statute. Instead, it is necessary to look at the purpose of R. 6.1, which is to make a lawsuit more convenient and fair to all parties. See Lim v. Young, 2004 ABQB 489 (Alta. Master). This is done by requiring a significant connection between the parties and the judicial district in which the action is commenced. In order to establish whether a significant connection exists in a particular case, it is necessary to examine the particular structure of the corporation's operations, the nature of and issues in the lawsuit, and the relationship between the parties in respect of those issues. Such examinations are fact specific. *Apache Canada Ltd. v. Johnson*, 2005 ABCA 71. See CARRY ON BUSINESS.

CARRY. *v.* 1. Includes to store or have in possession. 2. In connection with insurance, to possess or hold.

CARRY AWAY. The key issue is whether the right to "carry away" a mineral includes the right to use and enjoy it. The term "carry away" is a term of art that has long been used in this context to denote wideranging rights to take possession and ownership of a mineral, often as a part of expressions such as "work, win and carry away." *Tottrup v. Clearwater (Municipal District) No. 99*, 2006 ABCA 380.

CARRYING CHARGE. A charge made by creditor in addition to interest.

CARRY ON. To perform, operate, keep, hold, occupy, deal in or use, for gain, whether as principal or as agent.

CARRY ON BUSINESS. 1. Any action for the promotion or execution of any purpose of business. 2. Transaction of business. 3. Involves continuity of time or operations as is involved in the ordinary sense of a 'business'. *Friesen v. Canada* (1995), 127 D.L.R. (4th) 193 (S.C.C.).

CARRY-OVER OF CAPITAL LOSSES. If a taxpayer does not have sufficient capital gains against which to deduct capital losses experienced in one taxation year, the taxpayer may carry the losses forward to another year.

CARSWELLALTA. Citation of case originating in Alberta in Carswell's eCarswell system.

CARSWELLBC. Citation of case originating in British Columbia in Carswell's eCarswell system.

CARSWELLMAN. Citation of case originating in Manitoba in Carswell's eCarswell system.

CARSWELLNAT. Citation of case originating in the Federal court or before a federal tribunal in Carswell's eCarswell system.

CARSWELLNB. Citation of case originating in the New Brunswick courts in Carswell's eCarswell system.

CARSWELLNFLD. Citation of case originating in Newfoundland in Carswell's eCarswell system.

CARSWELLNS. Citation of case originating in Nova Scotia in Carswell's eCarswell system.

CARSWELLNUN. Citation of case originating in Nunavut in Carswell's eCarswell system.

CARSWELLNWT. Citation of case originating in the Northwest Territories in Carswell's eCarswell system.

CARSWELLONT. Citation of case originating in Ontario in Carswell's eCarswell system.

CARSWELLPEI. citation of case originating in Prince Edward Island in Carswell's eCarswell system.

CARSWELLQUE. Citation of case originating in the province of Quebec in Carswell's eCarswell system.

CARSWELLSASK. Citation of case originating in Saskatchewan in Carswell's eCarswell system.

CARSWELLYUKON. Citation of case originating in Yukon in Carswell's eCarswell system.

CART. B.N.A. *abbr.* Cartwright's Cases on the British North America Act, 1867, 1882-1897.

CARTE BLANCHE. [Fr. white card] 1. Unlimited authority. 2. A blank card signed at the bottom which gives another person power to write anything above the signature.

CARTEL. *n.* An agreement between producers of raw materials or goods.

CARTER. See MARY ~ AGREEMENT.

CARTRIDGE MAGAZINE. A device or container from which ammunition may be fed into the firing chamber of a firearm. *Criminal Code*, R.S.C. 1985, c. C-46, s. 84(1).

C.A.S. *abbr.* 1. Children's Aid Societ(y)(ies). 2. Décisions de la Commission des affaires sociales, 1975-1997.

CASE. *v.* For a potential thief or burglar to inspect a premises.

CASE. *n.* 1. "... '[S]uit' or 'appeal' and that ... it also included 'decision, question or matter'." *Iantsis (Papatheodorou) v. Papatheodorou* (1971), 3 R.F.L. 158 at 164, [1971] 1 O.R. 245, 15 D.L.R. (3d) 53 (C.A.), the court per Schroeder J.A. 2. Instance. *Lovibond v. Grand Trunk Railway*, [1934] O.R. 729 at 743, 43 C.R.C. 38, [1935] 1 D.L.R. 179 (C.A.), Macdonnell J.A. (Fisher J.A. concurring). 3. A sealed package, carton or container. See ACTION ON THE ~; ARGUABLE ~; HARD ~; LEADING ~; MCNAGHTEN'S ~; PRIMA FACIE ~; SPECIAL ~; STATED ~; TEST ~.

CASE-BY-CASE PRIVILEGE. The communications [between the potential witness and his or her client or informant] are not privileged unless the party opposing disclosure can show they should be privileged according to the fourfold utilitarian test elaborated by Wigmore: (1)The communications must originate in a confidence that they will not be disclosed. (2)This element of confidentiality must be essential to the full and satisfactory maintenance of the relation between the parties. (3)The relation must be one which in the opinion of the community ought to be fostered sedulously. (4)The injury that would inure to the relation by the disclosure of the communications must be greater than the benefit thereby gained for the correct disposal of litigation. *A. (L.L.) v. B. (A.)*, [1995] 4 S.C.R. 536, per L'Heureux-Dube, J.

CASE CONFERENCE. See JUDICIAL ~.

CASE LAW. The decisions of judges relating to particular matters in contrast to statute law; case law is a source of law and forms legal precedents.

CASE MANAGEMENT. 1. Case management usually refers to the supervision of the progress of litigation through the court system by judges or court officers. 2. It requires that the greater share of the responsibility for managing the proceeding and moving it expeditiously to a trial, hearing, or other resolution remains with the parties; and, the nature of case management will be informed by any relevant practices, traditions, customs or judicial resource issues that apply locally in the region. Counsel bear the primary responsibility for moving a case through to a hearing. Case management does not alter that fundamental fact; case management is not a substitute for counsel managing the litigation, as they are paid to do. Judicial case management can facilitate resolving, or adjudicating, such pre-hearing disputes, thereby moving the case closer to a final hearing. Unreasonable disagreements amongst unreasonable counsel, or parties, however, do not position a proceeding well for case management. Quite the contrary. Unless counsel are prepared to co-operate, professionally and civilly, in conducting their clients' cases, effective case management stands little chance of success. Nor should case management meetings turn into forums to re-hash issues previously decided. Case management must always look forward to completing the remaining steps prior to the hearing; it is a not a forum to revisit issues already decided. *Abrams v. Abrams*, 2009 CanLII 72056 (Ont. S.C.).

CASE STATED. A written statement requesting an opinion on a question of law.

CASE SUMMARY. A summary of judicial reasons is not simply a copy of the original reasons. Even if the summary often contains the same language as the judicial reasons, the act of choosing which portions to extract and how to arrange them in the summary requires an exercise of skill and judgment. *CCH Canadian Ltd. v. Law Society of Upper Canada*, 2004 SCC 13.

CASE TO MEET. The Crown establishes a case to meet only when it adduces evidence which, if believed, would establish proof beyond a reasonable doubt. In short, "the Crown must prove its case before there can be any expectation that [the accused] will respond." *R. v. Noble*, 1997 CarswellBC 710, 210 N.R. 321, 6 C.R. (5th) 1, 89 B.C.A.C. 1, 145 W.A.C. 1, 114 C.C.C. (3d) 385, 146 D.L.R. (4th) 385, [1997] 1 S.C.R. 874, [1997] 6 W.W.R. 1, 43 C.R.R. (2d) 233, McLachlin J. (dissenting).

CASH. *v.* To convert a negotiable instrument to money.

CASH. *n.* 1. Currency. *Irving Oil Co. Assessment, Re* (1948), 22 M.P.R. 63 at 72, [1948] 2 D.L.R. 774 (N.S. C.A.), Doull J.A. (Chisholm C.J., Graham and MacQuarrie JJ.A. concurring). 2. Bank notes and coins. 3. May refer to cheques and bills of exchange as well as to bank notes and coins.

CASH ACCOUNT. 1. In bookkeeping, a record of cash transactions. 2. A brokerage firm account which is settled on a cash basis.

CASH BASIS. An accounting method which recognizes income when actually received and expenses when actually paid out.

CASH BOOK. An accounting record that combines cash receipts and disbursements.

CASH BUDGET. The estimated cash receipts and disbursements for a future period.

CASH CUSTOMER. A consumer who buys a product and who provides full payment for the product at or before the time of its receipt. *Business Practices and Consumer Protection Act*, S.B.C. 2004, c. 2, s. 57.

CASH DIVIDEND. The portion of profits and surplus paid to shareholders by a corporation in cash, in contrast to a stock dividend.

CASHIER. *v.* To dismiss from command or a position of authority.

CASHIER. *n.* A person who collects and records payments at a business.

CASH LAPPING. An illegal practice whereby employees of an armoured car company remove cash from customers' bags, use it for company operations, then replace it on the next day with cash taken from other customers' bags. *Moss v. National Armoured Ltd.* (1996), 44 C.C.L.I. (2d) 268 (Ont. Gen. Div.).

CASH-MUTUAL COMPANY. A company without share capital or with guarantee capital subject to repayment by the company, in respect of which the dividend rate is limited by its charter, which is empowered to undertake insurance on both the cash plan and the mutual plan. *Insurance Companies Act*, R.S.N. 1990, c. I-10, s. 2.

CASH-MUTUAL CORPORATION. A corporation without share capital that is empowered to undertake insurance on both the cash plan and the mutual plan. *Insurance Act*, R.S.O. 1990, c. I.8, s. 1.

CASH ON DELIVERY. A sale of goods on condition that cash be paid at the time of delivery.

CASH PLAN. See INSURANCE ON THE ~.

CASH PRICE. The price that would be charged by the seller for the goods or services to a buyer who paid cash for them at the time of purchase or hiring.

CASH SURRENDER VALUE. The amount an insurer will return to a policyholder upon cancellation of the policy.

CASH VALUE. In relation to leased goods, means (a) if the lessor or an associate of the lessor sells like goods to cash customers in the ordinary course of carrying on business, (i) a value that fairly represents the price for which the lessor or associate of the lessor sells those goods to cash customers, or (ii) if the lessor and the lessee agree on a lower cash value, that lower cash value, or (b) if the lessor or an associate of the lessor does not sell like goods to cash customers in the ordinary course of carrying on business, (i) the lessor's reasonable estimate of the price at which cash customers would buy those goods, or (ii) if the lessor and the lessee agree on a lower cash value, that lower cash value. *Business Practices and Consumer Protection Act*, S.B.C. 2004, c. 2, s. 100.

CASKET. *n.* A container intended to hold a dead human body for funeral, cremation or interment purposes.

CASS. PRAC. CAS. *abbr.* Cassels' Practice Cases (Canada).

CASS. S.C. *abbr.* Cassels' Supreme Court Decisions.

CAST. *v.* To deposit formally, as to cast a ballot.

CASTING VOTE. The deciding vote to break equality of votes, cast by the chair or presiding officer. Whether the chair has a casting vote depends on provisions of the relevant statute, by-laws, standing orders, regulations or articles.

CASUAL. *adj.* "... [T]he antonym of 'regular' and means occasional or coming at uncertain times without regularity in distinction from stated or regular... ." *R. v. C.U.P.E.* (1981), 125 D.L.R. (3d) 220 at 224 (N.B. C.A.), the court per Stratton J.A.

CASUAL EMPLOYMENT. Employment at uncertain times or at irregular intervals. Contrasted with regular employment or regular part-time employment.

CASUALTY. See PROPERTY AND ~ COMPANY.

CASUS BELLI. [L.] An incident which causes or justifies war.

CASUS OMISSUS. [L.] Something which should have been, but was not, provided for.

CATALOGUE. *n.* 1. Includes bound, stitched, sewed or stapled books or pamphlets containing a list and description of goods, wares, merchandise or services, with specific information, with or without price. *Retail Sales Tax Act*, R.S.O. 1990, c. R.31, *General*, R.R.O. 1990, Reg. 1013, s. 1. 2. A publication in printed, electronic or microfiche form that (a) is updated at least once a year; (b) lists all book titles currently in print that are available from at least one exclusive distributor; and (c) identifies the title,

the International Standard Book Number, the exclusive distributor, the author and the list price in Canada for each book listed. *Copyright Act*, R.S.C. 1985, c. C-42, *Book Importation Regulations*, SOR/99-324, s. 1.

CATCHING BARGAIN. An agreement to loan or pay money made on unfavourable terms to a person having property in reversion or expectancy.

C.A.T. (QUÉ.). *abbr.* Commission des accidents du travail (Québec).

CATTLE. *n.* Neat cattle or an animal of the bovine species by whatever technical or familiar name it is known, and includes any horse, mule, ass, pig, sheep or goat. *Criminal Code*, R.S.C. 1985, c. C-46, s. 2.

CATV. *abbr.* 1. Community Antenna Television. 2. "... [I]t provides a well-located antenna with an efficient connection to the viewer's television set... ." *Fortnightly Corp. v. United Artists Television Inc.* (1968), 392 U.S. 390 at 399, Stewart J., cited with approval in *Capital Cities Communications Inc. v. Canada (Canadian Radio-Television & Telecommunications Commission)* (1977), 36 C.P.R. (2d) 1 at 13, [1978] 2 S.C.R. 141, 81 D.L.R. (3d) 609, 18 N.R. 181, Laskin C.J. (Martland, Judson, Ritchie, Spence and Dickson JJ. concurring).

CAUCUS. *n.* The members of Parliament or a legislature who belong to the same party.

CAUSA. [L.] *n.* Cause.

CAUSA CAUSANS. [L.] The immediate cause; the last of a chain of causes.

CAUSA MORTIS. [L.] Because of death; in case of death.

CAUSA PROXIMA. [L.] The immediate cause.

CAUSA PROXIMA NON REMOTA SPECTATUR. [L.] The immediate, not the remote, cause should be considered.

CAUSA SINE QUA NON. [L.] The cause without which the event would not have occurred.

CAUSATION. *n.* 1. In determining whether a person can be held responsible for causing a particular result, in this case death, it must be determined whether the person caused that result both in fact and in law. *R. v. Nette*, 2001 SCC 78, Arbour J. (Iacobucci, Major, Binnie, LeBel JJ. concurring). 2. "... [A]n expression of the relationship that must be found to exist between the tortious act of the wrongdoer and the injury to the victim in order to justify compensation of the latter out of the pocket of the former." *Snell v. Farrell* (1990), 4 C.C.L.T. (2d) 229 at 243,110 N.R. 200, [1990] 2 S.C.R. 311, the court per Sopinka J. 3. Is established, in negligence, when the plaintiff proves on a balance of probabilities, that the defendant caused or contributed to the injury. The generally applicable test is the "but for" test. This test "requires the plaintiff to show that the injury would not have occurred but for the negligence of the defendant" ([Athey v. Leonati, [1996] 3 S.C.R. 458], at para.14). *Cottrelle v. Gerrard* (2003), 178 O.A.C. 142. See FACTUAL ~; IMPUTABLE ~; LEGAL ~.

CAUSE. *v.* "... [A] transitive verb which in its ordinary usage contemplates that someone or something brings about an effect." *Astro Tire & Rubber Co. v. Western Assurance Co.*, [1979] I.L.R. 1-1098 at 188, 24 O.R. (2d) 268, 97 D.L.R. (3d) 515 (C.A.), Blair J.A.

CAUSE. *n.* 1. A suit or action. *Hampton Lumber Mills v. Joy Logging Ltd.* (1977), 2 C.P.C. 312 at 317, [1977] 2 W.W.R. 289 (B.C. S.C.), Ruttan J. 2. That which produces an effect and includes any action, suit or other original proceeding between a plaintiff and a defendant and any criminal proceeding by the Crown. 3. In negligence cases, the defendant's fault is a cause of the damage if the damage would not have occurred but for the defendant's fault and the fault is not a cause if the damage would have happened with or without the defendant's fault. J.G. Fleming, *The Law of Torts*, 8th ed. (Sydney: Law Book, 1992) at 194. 4. "[In the context of dismissal for cause] ... relates to the acts or the omissions of the employee, not the acts or the omissions of the employer." *Alberta v. A.U.P.E.* (1987), 53 Alta. L.R. (2d) 275 at 278, 82 A.R. 19 (Q.B.), Dea J. 5. In the context of a landlord's having cause, means reason. See CHALLENGE FOR ~; CONCURRENT ~; COSTS IN ANY EVENT OF THE ~; COSTS IN THE ~; DISMISSAL FOR ~; FOR ~; GOOD ~; INTERVENING ~; JUST ~; NECESSARY ~; NO MAN SHALL BE JUDGE IN HIS OWN ~; PROBABLE ~; PROPER ~; PROXIMATE ~; ~; SHOW ~; STYLE OF ~.

CAUSE CÉLÈBRE. [Fr.] A matter of great interest or importance.

CAUSE OF ACTION. "The classic definition of a cause of action as stated by Diplock L.J. in Letang v. Cooper, [1965] 1 Q.B. 232 ... (H.L.) is as follows: 'A cause of action is simply a factual situation the existence of which entitles one person to obtain from the court a remedy against another person.' ..." *Consumers Glass Co. v. Foundation Co. of Canada/Cie fondation du Canada* (1985), 1 C.P.R. (2d) 208 at 215, 51 O.R. (2d) 385, 33 C.C.L.T. 104, 30 B.L.R. 87, 13 C.L.R. 149, 9 O.A.C. 193, 20 D.L.R. (4th) 126 (C.A.), the court per Dubin J.A. See CONTINUING ~; JOINDER OF CAUSES OF ACTION.

CAUSE OF ACTION ESTOPPEL. "... [P]recludes a person from bringing an action against another when the same cause of action has been determined in earlier proceedings by a court of competent jurisdicion ..." *Angle v. M.N.R.*, [1975] 2 S.C.R. 248 at 253-55, Dickson J.

CAUSING LOSS BY UNLAWFUL MEANS. The elements of the tort of causing loss by unlawful means are: (1) wrongful interference by the defendant with the actions of a third party in which the plaintiff has an economic interest; (2) an intention by the defendant to cause loss to the plaintiff: see [OBG Ltd. v. Allan, [2007] UKHL 21 (U.K. H.L.)] at para. 47 (Hoffman L.). Again, the intentionality of the defendant's conduct is critical: it is not enough that the loss was a foreseeable consequence of the defendant's conduct; to be actionable under this tort, the loss must have been the intended result. Furthermore, intentional conduct that causes loss but is not unlawful, is not actionable. That is considered permissible competitive commercial behaviour. *Correia v. Canac Kitchens*, 2008 ONCA 506.

CAUTION. *n.* 1. A warning. 2. A warning given to an accused concerning possibly incriminating statements. 3. "... [N]otice of adverse claim equivalent to a lis pendens and expires by lapse of time or otherwise as may be directed by the Court in an action: ..." *Ontario (Attorney General) v. Hargrave*, [1906] 11 O.L.R. 530 at 536 (H.C.), Master.

C.A.V. *abbr.* Curia advisari vult.

CAVEAT. *n.* [L. let one take heed] 1. "A caveat [under the Land Titles Act, R.S.A. 1980, c. L-5] is a warning, a notice and a prohibition. It creates no new rights, but prevents new ones arising other than subject to the claim of which it gives notice after registration. It is intended strictly to preserve the status quo ..." *Royal Bank v. Donsdale Developments Ltd.* (1986), 43 R.P.R. 59 at 75, 48 Alta. L.R. (2d) 289, [1987] 2 W.W.R. 14, 74 A.R. 161 (Q.B.), Andrekson J. 2. A document filed by an inventor before filing an application. H.G. Fox, *The Canadian Law and Practice Relating to Letters Patent for Inventions*, 4th ed. (Toronto: Carswell, 1969) at 242. 3. "[In the context of estates] ... 'a formal notice or caution given by a person interested, to a Court, Judge, or public officer, against the performance of certain judicial or ministerial acts.' A caution, or caveat, while in force, may stop probate or administration from being granted without notice to or knowledge of the person who enters it... ." *McDevitt, Re* (1913), 5 O.W.N. 333 at 335, 25 O.W.R. 309 (H.C.), Britton J.

CAVEAT ACTOR. [L.] Let the doer beware.

CAVEAT EMPTOR. [L. let the buyer beware] "The rule ... [means] that a buyer gets only what he bargains for." *Moretta v. Western Computer Investment Corp.* (1983), 26 B.L.R. 68 at 84, [1984] 2 W.W.R. 409, 29 Alta. L.R. (2d) 193 (C.A.), Kerans J.A.

CAVEAT EMPTOR; QUI IGNORARE NON DEBUIT QUOD JUS ALIENUM EMIT. [L.] A purchaser must be on guard; for the purchaser has no right to ignore the fact that what was bought belongs to someone else besides the vendor.

CAVEAT VENDITOR. [L.] Let the seller beware.

CAVITY. See BODY ~.

C.B.A. PAPERS. *abbr.* Canadian Bar Association Papers.

C.B.A. Y.B. *abbr.* Canadian Bar Year Book.

CBC. *abbr.* Canadian Broadcasting Corporation.

C.B.E.S. *abbr.* Recueils de jurisprudence du Québec - Cour du bien-être social, 1975-1985.

C.B.R. *abbr.* 1. Canadian Bankruptcy Reports, 1920-1960. 2. Copyright Board Reports, 1990-1994.

C.B.R. (4TH). *abbr.* Canadian Bankruptcy Reports (Fourth Series), 1998-.

C.B.R. (N.S.). *abbr.* Canadian Bankruptcy Reports, New Series, 1960-1990.

C.B.R. (3RD). *abbr.* Canadian Bankruptcy Reports (Third Series), 1991-1998.

C.C.A.S. *abbr.* Catholic Children's Aid Societ(y)(ies).

CCAT. *abbr.* Council of Canadian Administrative Tribunals.

C.C.C. *abbr.* Canadian Criminal Cases, 1898-1962.

[] C.C.C. *abbr.* Canadian Criminal Cases, 1963-1970.

C.C.C. (2D). *abbr.* Canadian Criminal Cases (Second Series), 1971-1983.

C.C.C. (3D). *abbr.* Canadian Criminal Cases (Third Series), 1983-.

C.C.D.P. *abbr.* Commission canadienne des droits de la personne.

C.C.E.A. *abbr.* Commission de contrôle de l'énergie atomique.

C.C.E.L. *abbr.* Canadian Cases on Employment Law, 1983-1994.

C.C.E.L. (2D). *abbr.* Canadian Cases on Employment Law (Second Series), 1994-2000.

C.C.E.L. (3D). *abbr.* Canadian Cases on Employment Law (Third Series), 2000-.

CCFTA. *abbr.* The Canada-Chile Free Trade Agreement.

C. CIRC. *abbr.* Cour de circuit.

CCL. *abbr.* Canadian Congress of Labour, which is now part of the Canadian Labour Congress.

C.C.L. *abbr.* 1. Canadian Current Law, 1948-1990. 2. Canadian Current Law: Jurisprudence – sommaires de la jurisprudence, 1991 3. Canadian Current Law: Case Law Digests / sommaires de la jurisprudence, 1992-1996. 4. Canadian Current Law: Case Digests / sommaires de la jurisprudence, 1996-.

C.C.L.I. *abbr.* Canadian Cases on the Law of Insurance, 1983-1991.

C.C.L.I. (2D). *abbr.* Canadian Cases on the Law of Insurance (Second Series), 1991-1998.

C.C.L.I. (3D). *abbr.* Canadian Cases on the Law of Insurance (Third Series), 1998-.

C.C.L. LÉGISLATION. *abbr.* Canadian Current Law: Annuaire de la législation, 1989-.

C.C.L. LEGISLATION. abbr. Canadian Current Law: Legislation Annual, 1989-.

C.C.L.R. *abbr.* 1. Canada Corporations Law Reports. 2. Canadian Computer Law Reporter, 1983-1992.

C.C.L.S. *abbr.* Canadian Cases on the Law of Securities, 1993-1998.

C.C.L.T. *abbr.* Canadian Cases of the Law of Torts, 1976-1990.

C.C.L.T. (2D). *abbr.* Canadian Cases on the Law of Torts (Second Series), 1990-2000.

C.C.L.T. (3D). *abbr.* Canadian Cases on the Law of Torts (Third Series), 2000-.

C.C.P. *abbr.* Commission canadienne des pensions.

C.C.P.B. abbr. Canadian Cases on Pensions and Benefits, 1994-.

CCRA. *abbr.* Canada Customs and Revenue Agency.

C.C.R.I. *abbr.* Conseil canadien des relations industrielles, motifs de décision, 1999-.

C.C.R.T. *abbr.* Conseil canadien des relations de travail.

C.C.R.T.D. *abbr.* Conseil canadien des relations du travail, décisions, 1999-.

C.C.R.T.D.I. *abbr.* Conseil canadien des relations du travail, décisions et informations, 1974-1998.

C.C.T.C.T.D. *abbr.* Commission canadienne des transports, comité des télécommunications – décisions, 1973-1976.

C.C.T.C.T.E.P. *abbr.* Commission canadienne des transports, comité des transports par eau – permis, 1976.

C.C.T.C.T.O. *abbr.* Commission canadienne des transports, comité des télécommunications – ordonnances, 1975-1976.

C.C.T.O. *abbr.* Commission canadienne des transports – ordonnances, 1972-1987.

C. DE D. *abbr.* Les Cahiers de droit.

C. DE L'É. *abbr.* Cour de l'Échiquier.

C. DE L'I.Q.A.J. *abbr.* Cahiers de l'institut québécois d'administration judiciaire.

CDIC. *abbr.* Canada Deposit Insurance Corporation.

C. DIST. *abbr.* Cour de district.

C. DIV. *abbr.* Cour divisionnaire.

CDN. *abbr.* Canadian.

CDRP. *abbr.* Canadian internet registration authority domain name dispute resolution policy.

CEASE. *v.* To stop; to suspend activity.

C.E.B. *abbr.* Canadian Employment Benefits and Pension Guide Reports, 1995-.

CEDE. *v.* 1. To give up or yield. 2. To transfer. 3. To surrender.

C.E.G.S.B. *abbr.* Crown Employees Grievance Settlement Board Decisions, 1876-1997.

CELEBRATION OF MARRIAGE. The formal act by which two persons become husband and wife.

C.E.L.R. *abbr.* Canadian Environmental Law Reports, 1978-1985.

C.E.L.R. (N.S.). *abbr.* Canadian Environmental Law Reports (New Series), 1986.

CEMETERY. *n.* Land set aside to be used for the interment of human remains and includes a mausoleum, columbarium or other structure intended for the interment of human remains. See COMMER-CIAL ~; PRENEED ~ OR FUNERAL SERVICES CONTRACT.

CEMETERY CARE TRUST. A trust established pursuant to an Act of a province for the care and maintenance of a cemetery. *Income Tax Act*, R.S.C. 1985, c. 1 (5th Supp.), s. 148.1.

CEMETERY GOODS. The goods supplied or to be supplied at the cemetery in conjunction with the burial of human remains including grave liners, vaults, urns, memorials and other supplies incidental to the identification or embellishment of a burial plot. *Floral Hills Memorial Gardens Administration Act*, S.P.E.I. 2006, c. 6, s. 1.

CEMETERY SERVICES. With respect to an individual means property (including interment vaults, markers, flowers, liners, urns, shrubs and wreaths) and services that relate directly to cemetery arrangements in Canada in consequence of the death of the individual including, for greater certainty, property and services to be funded out of a cemetery care trust. *Income Tax Act*, R.S.C. 1985, c. 1 (5th Supp.), s. 148.1.

CEMETERY SUPPLIES. Burial vaults, grave stones, grave markers, flowers, shrubs and artificial wreaths and other articles intended to be placed in a cemetery, monuments or bases for use in a cemetery. *Cemeteries Act*, R.S.A. 2000, c. C-3, s. 1.

CENSOR. *n.* A person who regulates or prohibits distribution, production or exhibition of films or publication of books, plays, etc.

CENSORSHIP. *n.* The prohibition or regulation of publication, distribution or production of books, plays, films.

CENSURE. *n.* An official reprimand; condemnation.

CENSUS. *n.* A count or enumeration of the people.

CENT. *n.* 1. A coin. 2. One hundredth part of a dollar.

CENTER FIRE AMMUNITION. Firearm ammunition in which the primer is located in the center of the base of the cartridge case in a well. F.A. Jaffe, *A Guide to Pathological Evidence for Lawyers and Police Officers*, 4th ed. (Toronto: Carswell, 1999) at 233.

CENTER OF OSSIFICATION. A point where bone forms. Centers can indicate the age of a fetus or young person. F.A. Jaffe, *A Guide to Pathological Evidence for Lawyers and Police Officers*, 4th ed. (Toronto: Carswell 1999) at 241.

CENTRAL COOPERATIVE CREDIT SOCIETY. A body corporate organized on cooperative principles by or under an Act of the legislature of a province, one of whose principal purposes is to receive deposits from and provide liquidity support to local cooperative credit societies, and (a) whose membership consists solely or primarily of local cooperative credit societies, or (b) whose directors are wholly or primarily persons elected or appointed by local cooperative credit societies. *Bank Act*, S.C. 1991, c. 46, s. 2.

CENTRAL COUNTER-PARTY. A corporation, association, partnership, agency or other entity in a clearing and settlement system with whom all participant's payment rights and obligations are netted to produce a single amount owing as between each participant and the central counter-party. *Payment Clearing and Settlement Act*, S.C. 1996, c. 6, Sched., s. 2.

CENTRALIST. *adj.* Describes a form of federal government in which greater power is given to the central or federal government.

CENTRE. *n.* A building or facility. See CORRECTIONAL ~; REGISTRATION ~.

CENTURY. *n.* 1. One hundred. 2. One hundred years.

C.E.P.A.R. *abbr.* Canadian Estate Planning and Administration Reporter.

C.E.P.R. *abbr.* Canadian Estate Planning and Administration Reporter.

C.E.R. *abbr.* Canadian Customs and Excise reports, 1980-1989.

CEREMONY. *n.* A formal event to mark an occasion. See CIVIL ~; CIVIL MARRIAGE ~.

CERTAIN. *adj.* 1. Definitive. 2. Free from doubt.

CERTAINTY. *n.* 1. Accuracy; absence of doubt. 2. Precision. See MORAL ~; THREE CERTAINTIES; UN~.

CERTAINTY OF INTENTION. One of the "three certainties" required of a trust. The transferor of the property to the trust must be found to have intended to create a trust. *Davis v. The Queen*, 2008 TCC 31.

CERTAINTY OF OBJECTS. One of the "three certainties" required of a trust. The intended beneficiaries of the trust must be ascertainable.

CERTAINTY OF SUBJECT MATTER. One of the "three certainties" required of a trust. The property which is subject to the trust must be identifiable.

CERTIFICATE. *n.* 1. An official assurance or representation concerning a matter within the knowledge or authority of the person making the certificate. 2. A document issued to identify those who have passed the required examinations or are members of a professional organization. 3. A document issued to show that a person has completed a course of study or training. See ARCHITECT'S ~; DIGITAL SIGNATURE ~; ESTATE ~; KIMBERLEY PROCESS ~; NOTARIAL ~; SAFETY FITNESS ~; SHARE ~.

CERTIFICATED SECURITY. A security that is represented by a certificate. *Securities Transfer acts*. See NON-~.

CERTIFICATE OF ASSESSMENT. A document given to prove that a review of the costs awarded in an action or billed by a solicitor has been completed by an assessment officer of the court.

CERTIFICATE OF COMPLETION. A certificate given by an architect under whose supervision a building contract has been carried out; contractor is generally not entitled to payment until the certificate is given.

CERTIFICATE OF CONTINUANCE. An indication that a corporation originally incorporated in one jurisdiction has transferred its governance to another jurisdiction and that the corporation's existence continues. This change must be authorized by the original jurisdiction as well as the new one.

CERTIFICATE OF CONVICTION. A certificate stating that an accused was convicted of an indictable offence, drawn up by a judge or magistrate when requested to do so by the prosecutor, the accused or a peace officer.

CERTIFICATE OF INADMISSIBILITY. The Immigration and Refugee Protection Act requires the ministers to sign a certificate declaring that a foreign national or permanent resident is inadmissible to enter or remain in Canada on grounds of security, among others. The consequences of the issuance and confirmation of a certificate of inadmissibility vary, depending on whether the person is a permanent resident of Canada or a foreign national whose right to remain in Canada has not yet been confirmed. Permanent residents who the ministers have reasonable grounds to believe are a danger to national security may be held in detention. In order to detain them, the ministers must issue a warrant stating that the person is a threat to national security or to another person, or is unlikely to appear at a proceeding or for removal. Foreign nationals, meanwhile, must be detained once a certificate is issued: under s. 82(2), the detention is automatic. *Charkaoui v. Canada (Citizenship and Immigration)*, 2007 SCC 9.

CERTIFICATE OF INCORPORATION. Documentary evidence, including letters patent, a special act or any other instrument, by which a corporation is incorporated stating that a corporation exists and was duly incorporated under the appropriate statute.

CERTIFICATE OF LIS PENDENS. A document registered against land to warn that there is litigation pending concerning an interest in the land. A former term for a certificate of pending litigation. See CERTIFICATE OF PENDING LITIGATION; LIS PENDENS.

CERTIFICATE OF PENDING LITIGATION. A document registered against land to warn that there is litigation pending concerning an interest in the land. *Courts of Justice Act*, R.S.O. 1990, c. C.43, s.103. See CERTIFICATE OF LIS PENDENS.

CERTIFICATE OF READINESS. A term for the document which a party in an action filed to indicate that the party is ready for trial. See now NOTICE OF READINESS FOR TRIAL.

CERTIFICATE OF TAXATION. A document given to prove that a review of the costs awarded in an action or billed by a solicitor has been completed by a taxation officer of the court. See also CERTIFICATE OF ASSESSMENT.

CERTIFICATE OF TITLE. A certificate of title granted pursuant to a Land Titles Act. See ABSOLUTE ~.

CERTIFICATION. *n.* 1. "... [A] mechanism whereby an association which counts among its members an absolute majority of all an employer's employees, or of a separate group of an employer's employees, is recognized as the sole representative of those employees to this employer for collective bargaining purposes... ." *Union des employés de service, local 298 v. Bibeault* (1988), 35 Admin L.R. 153 at 204, 95 N.R. 161, [1988] 2 S.C.R. 1048, the court per Beetz J. 2. "... [T]he name given to the marking of a cheque by the drawee bank to show that it is drawn by the person purporting to draw it, that it is drawn upon an existing account with the drawee, and that there are funds sufficient to meet it. Certification is demonstrated by some physical marking on the cheque, normally stamping on its face 'certified' ..." *A.E. LePage Real Estate Services Ltd. v. Rattray Publications* (1991), 84 D.L.R. (4th) 766 at 767, 5 O.R. (3d) 216 (Div. Ct.), Montgomery J. 3. A written attestation of a training organization as to the level of achievement attained by a student in an occupational training program. 4. The entry of the name of a person in the register.

CERTIFICATION AUTHORITY. A person or entity that issues digital signature certificates and that has been listed as such on the website of the Treasury Board Secretariat. *Personal Information Protection and Electronic Documents Act*, S.C. 2000, c. 5, *Secure Electronic Signature Regulations*, SOR/2005-30, s. 1.

CERTIFICATION MARK. A mark that is used for the purpose of distinguishing or so as to distinguish wares or services that are of a defined standard with respect to (a) the character or quality of the wares or services, (b) the working conditions under which the wares have been produced or the services performed, (c) the class of persons by whom the wares have been produced or the services performed, or (d) the area within which the wares have been produced or the services performed, from wares or services that are not of that defined standard. *Trade-marks Act*, R.S.C. 1985, c. T-13, s. 2.

CERTIFICATION OF LABOUR UNION. Official recognition by a labour relations board of a union as bargaining representative for employees in a particular bargaining unit.

CERTIFIED CHEQUE. A cheque which the drawer has taken to the drawer's bank and the funds are withdrawn from the drawer's account pending the cashing of the cheque. If the cheque is certified by the holder the same action occurs and the payment of the obligation is complete.

CERTIFIED COPY. A copy certified to be a true copy.

CERTIFIED UNION. A union recognized by a labour relations board as bargaining agent of a group of workers.

CERTIFY. *v.* 1. "... [H]as the connotation that the person so doing formally vouches for the statement or guarantees its certainty ..." *First Investors Corp., Re*, Doc. No. Edmonton Appeal 8803-0942-AC (Alta C.A.), the court per Laycraft J.A. 2. "... [A] word of wide import which may also refer merely to a formal or legal certificate." *R. v. Lines* (1986), 27 C.C.C. (3d) 377 at 380 (N.W.T. C.A.), the court per Laycraft C.J.N.W.T.

CERTIORARI. *n.* 1. " ... [T]he prerogative writ adopted to quash a decision based upon an error of law which is apparent from the record ..." *Minister of National Revenue v. Parsons* (1983), 4 Admin. L.R. 64 at 72, [1983] C.T.C. 321, 83 D.T.C. 5329 (Fed. T.D.), Cattanach J. 2. The word certiorari is just Latin for "to be better informed." For centuries the writ of certiorari issuing from a superior court, was virtually the only way that justices of the peace and other tribunals (other than superior courts) received any form of review or control. English substantive rights often flowed from writs and their procedure. The key feature of certiorari was a command by the monarch to the Justices of Peace or other tribunal to give up the case to, and send their entire record to, the superior court. Once thus "better informed," the superior court could either quash the decision of the tribunal, or send the record back and tell the inferior tribunal to proceed. See R. v. Titchmarsh, [R. v. Titchmarsh (1914), 22 D.L.R. 272, (Ont. C.A.)], at 277-78; de Smith, Judicial Review of Admin. Action 373-76, 388-89 (2d ed. 1968). (Recent editions of de Smith are briefer.) Where judicial review is sought to quash the decision below, Alberta Rules still order the tribunal to send up the record: Rr. 753.12 and 753.13. *Brewer v. Fraser Milner Casgrain LLP*, 2008 ABCA 160.

CERTIORARI IN AID. Certiorari ordered in connection with habeas corpus. *Perepolkin v. Superintendent of Child Welfare for British Columbia (No. 2)* (1958), 27 C.R. 95 at 97, 23 W.W.R. 592, 120 C.C.C. 67, 11 D.L.R. (2d) 417 (B.C. C.A.), Smith J.A.

CERTUM EST QUOD CERTUM REDDI POTEST. [L.] What is capable of being made certain is to be treated as certain.

C.E.S.H.G. *abbr.* Canadian Employment, Safety and Health Guide.

CESSATION OF CHARGE. An instrument which acknowledges that the claim against real property contained in a charge has been discharged.

CESTUI QUE TRUST. *pl.* **CESTUIS QUE TRUST.** A beneficiary; beneficial owner of trust property.

CESTUI QUE USE. A grantee to whom property was conveyed to use.

CESTUI QUE VIE. One for whose life someone else holds an estate or interest in property.

CETERIS PARIBUS. [L.] Other things being equal.

CF. *abbr.* Compare.

C.F. *abbr.* 1. Cour fédérale 2. In sales contract, means price included cost and freight. 3. Recueils des arrêts de la Cour fédérale du Canada, 1971-.

C.F. & I. See C.I.F.

C.F. (APPEL). *abbr.* Cour fédérale du Canada – Cour d'appel.

C.F.I. See C.I.F.

C.F.L.C. *abbr.* Canadian Family Law Cases, 1959-1977.

C.F.L.Q. *abbr.* Canadian Family Law Quarterly.

C.F.P. *abbr.* Recueil des décisions des comités d'appel de la fonction publique, 1980-1989.

CFPI. French neutral citation for the Federal Court, Trial Division.

C.F. (1RE INST.). *abbr.* Cour fédérale du Canada – Division de première instance.

CH. *abbr.* 1. Chapter. 2. Chancery.

[] CH. *abbr.* Law Reports, Chancery, 1891-.

CHAIN. See THREE ~ RESERVE.

CHAIN OF TITLE. Tracking successive transfers or other conveyances of a particular parcel of land.

CHAIRMAN. *n.* 1. A person who presides at meetings of the board of directors of a corporation. 2. A person appointed or elected head of a board, committee, commission or foundation. See IMPARTIAL ~.

CHALLENGE. *v.* 1. To object. 2. To take exception against a juror. See PEREMPTORY ~.

CHALLENGE FOR CAUSE. The suitability of a juror is objected to on basis of knowledge of the case or lack of qualifications or impartiality.

CHAMBER. *n.* The place where legislative assemblies are held; the assemblies themselves.

CHAMBER OF COMMERCE. An organization organized to promote business in a community.

CHAMBERS. *n.* 1. Judge's office. 2. A room in which motions or applications or other business not required to be carried out in court is transacted. 3. Refers to motions court, court in which interlocutory motions are heard.

CHAMBERS BRIEF. "... [A]ssist[s] in clarifying the issues and so reduce[s] the length of time for hearing a motion or trial... . it should contain the following: (a) Description of the motion. (b) Authority for the motion. (c) Statement of facts. (d) Authorities. (e) Relief asked. (f) Form of Order." *Eileen's Quality Catering Ltd. v. Depaoli* (1985), 1 C.P.C. (2d) 152 at 154, 158 (B.C. S.C.), Bouck J.

CHAMPERTOR. *n.* A person who brings suits in order to have part of the gain or proceeds.

CHAMPERTY. *n.* 1. "... [A] bargain by which A, a stranger to B, having no interest recognized by law in a given property, agrees to help B to recover such property in a Court of Justice in consideration of getting a portion of the fruits of the suit, ..." *Hopper v. Dunsmuir* (1906), 3 W.L.R. 18 at 33 (C.A.), Martin J.A. 2. "... [T]o bargain with a plaintiff to pay the expenses of a suit wholly or in part on condition that the plaintiff will divide with the party who so shares in the expenses the land or other matter sued for, if successful in such suit, is undeniably champerty." *Meloche v. Deguire* (1903), 34 S.C.R. 24 at 37, Taschereau C.J. (Sedgewick, Nesbitt and Killam JJ. concurring). 3. A form of maintenance. *Pioneer Machinery (Rentals) Ltd. v. Aggregate Machine Ltd.* (1978), 8 C.P.C. 168 at 170, 15 A.R. 588, [1978] 6 W.W.R. 484, 93 D.L.R. (3d) 726 (T.D.), Laycraft J.

CHANCE. *n.* An accident; absence of explainable causation; risk. See GAME OF ~; LOSS OF ~.

CHANCELLOR. *n.* 1. The highest official of a university. 2. The presiding judge of a court of chancery. 3. The cleric entrusted with the keeping of the archives of a diocese. *An Act Respecting Fabriques*, R.S.Q., c. F-1, s. 1. 4. The leading member of an order. See VICE ~.

CHANCERY. *n.* 1. A court which administered equity before the Judicature Acts combined this court with the common law court. 2. Originally an office where writs were issued. See COURT OF ~.

CHANGE. *v.* To alter; substitute; modify; exchange.

CHANGE. *n.* 1. Alteration, replacement, modification. *Simplex Floor Finishing Appliance Co. v. Duranceau*, [1941] 4 D.L.R. 260 at 264 (S.C.C.), Taschereau J. 2. Any change by way of alteration, substitution, modification, addition or abandonment. *Change of Name acts.* 3. Exchange of money for money of another denomination. See MATERIAL ~.

CHANGE OF NAME. Refers to alteration of an individual's name by court order or by assumption of a different name.

CHANGE OF PARTIES. Occurs where parties to litigation are added or substituted.

CHANGE OF SOLICITOR. The change of lawyer representing a client in an action effected by filing notice in court.

CHARACTER. *n.* 1. The inclination of a person to act in a particular way relating to integrity, peaceableness, lawfulness, honesty and ultimately veracity. P.K. McWilliams, *Canadian Criminal Evidence*, 3d ed. (Aurora: Canada Law Book, 1988) at 39-1. 2. Word letter or symbol. 3. Features, nature of a thing. See HERITAGE ~.

CHARGE. *v.* 1. To give instructions to a jury. 2. "... [E]xists only when a formal written complaint has been made against the accused and a prosecution initiated... ." *R. v. Chabot*, [1980] 2 S.C.R. 985 at 1005, Dickson J. 3. To lay a duty upon a person. 4. To impose a tax. 5. To purchase on credit.

CHARGE. *n.* 1. An instrument creating security against property for payment of a debt or obligation. 2. The amount required, as the price of a thing or service sold or supplied. 3. A judge's instruction to a jury. 4. A price or rate. 5. An allegation, that a crime or offence was committed or that misconduct occurred. See CARRYING ~; CESSATION OF ~; CHARGES; DEFAULT ~; DIRECT ~ CO-OPERATIVE; EQUITABLE ~; FIXED ~; FLOATING ~; PREFER A ~; RENT ~; SPECIFIC ~.

CHARGEABLE. *adj.* Capable of or subject to being charged with a duty or obligation.

CHARGE ACCOUNT. An arrangement with a store or financial institution permitting purchase of goods and services on credit under which purchaser agrees to pay within specified time or periodically.

CHARGED. *adj.* 1. "The word 'charged' or 'charge' is not one of fixed or unvarying meaning at law. It may be and is used in a variety of ways to describe a variety of events. A person is clearly charged with an offence when a charge is read out to him in court and he is called upon to plead... ." *R. v. Kalanj* (1989), 48 C.C.C. (3d) 459 at 465, 70 C.R. (3d) 260, [1989] 6 W.W.R. 577, [1989] 1 S.C.R. 1594, 96 N.R. 191, McIntyre J. (La Forest and L'Heureux-Dubé JJ. concurring). 2. "... [A] person is 'charged with an offence' within the meaning of s. 11 of the Charter when an information is sworn alleging an offence against him, or where a direct indictment is laid against him, when no information is sworn... ." *R. v. Kalanj* (1989), 48 C.C.C. (3d) 459 at 469, 70 C.R. (3d) 260, [1989] 6 W.W.R. 577, [1989] 1 S.C.R. 1594, 96 N.R. 191, McIntyre J. (La Forest and L'Heureux-Dubé JJ. concurring).

CHARGEE. A person in whose favour a charge is given.

CHARGE ON LAND. An interest, whether arising immediately or in the future, in real property given by a corporation, that secures payment or performance of an obligation. *Law of Property Act*, R.S.A. 2000, c. L-7, s. 64.

CHARGES. *n.* Expenses; costs. See CHARGE.

CHARGE THE JURY. A judge gives instructions to a jury before it deliberates with regard to the law as it applies to the case heard by them.

CHARGE TO THE JURY. The instructions which a judge gives a jury before the jury begins its deliberations at the end of a trial. See CHARGE THE JURY.

CHARGING ORDER. 1. A creditor can apply to a judge to order that shares of or in any public company stand charged with the payment of the judgment debt. 2. An order made for the benefit of a solicitor against funds in court or property realized through the endeavours of the solicitor.

CHARGOR. A person who gives a charge.

CHARITABLE. *adj.* Having purposes of a charity.

CHARITABLE CORPORATION. A body constituted exclusively for charitable purposes no part of the income of which is payable to, or is otherwise available for the personal benefit of, any proprietor, member or shareholder of the corporation. *National Housing Act*, R.S.C. 1985, c. N-11, s. 87.

CHARITABLE FOUNDATION. A corporation or trust that is constituted and operated exclusively for charitable purposes, no part of the income of which is payable to, or is otherwise available for, the personal benefit of any proprietor, member, shareholder, trustee or settlor thereof, and that is not a charitable organization. *Income Tax Act*, R.S.C. 1985, c. 1 (5th Supp.), s. 149.1.

CHARITABLE PURPOSE. "The starting point for a discussion of what may or may not constitute a good charitable purpose is the decision of the House

C

of Lords in the case of Commrs. for Special Purposes of Income Tax v. Pemsel, [1891] A.C. 531 [(U.K.)] and, in particular, the legal meaning of the word 'charity' given by Lord Macnaghten at p. 583 of the report: 'How far then, it may be asked, does the popular meaning of the word "charity" correspond with its legal meaning? "Charity" in its legal sense comprises four principal divisions: trusts for the relief of poverty; trusts for the advancement of education; trusts for the advancement of religion; and trusts for other purposes beneficial to the community, not falling under any of the preceding heads.' That definition has been applied time after time in this country and has been approved by the Supreme Court of Canada (see Guaranty Trust Co. (Towle Estate) v. M.N.R., [1967] S.C.R. 133 at p. 141) ..." *Native Communications Society of British Columbia v. Minister of National Revenue* (1986), 23 E.T.R. 210 at 218, 86 D.T.C. 6353, 67 N.R. 146, [1986] 2 C.T.C. 170, [1986] 4 C.N.L.R. 79, [1986] 3 F.C. 471 (C.A.), Stone J.A. (Heald and Mahoney JJ.A. concurring).

CHARITABLE TRUST. 1, A trust for purposes which the law treats as charitable. 2. A trust raised for benevolent, educational, cultural, charitable, religious or other similar purposes. *Public Trustee Act, 2009*, S.N. 2009, c. P-46.1, s. 2.

CHARITY. *n.* 1. An organization with a charitable purpose. 2. (a) Trusts for the relief of poverty, (b) trusts for the advancement of education, (c) trusts for the advancement of religion, (d) trusts for other purposes beneficial to the community not falling under any of the preceding heads. *Commrs. of Income Tax v. Pemsel*, [1891] A.C. 531 at 583, Lord Macnaghten. See REGISTERED ~.

CHARTER. *v.* "... [I]s not synonymous with 'hire'. It has such a meaning only when it is used in relation to a means of transportation." *Seaway Forwarding Ltd. v. Western Assurance Co.*, [1981] I.L.R. 1-1400 at 351 (Ont. H.C.), Galligan J.

CHARTER. *n.* 1. The Canadian Charter of Rights and Freedoms, Part I of the Constitution Act, 1982. 2. Includes any act, statute, or ordinance by or under which a corporation has been incorporated and any letters patent, supplementary letters patent, certificate of incorporation, memorandum of association, and any other document evidencing corporate existence. 3. An agreement to supply a vessel or aircraft for a voyage for a period of time. 4. In relation to a corporation established by an Act of Parliament or a legislature, the Act, and in relation to a corporation established by articles, the articles and in relation to a corporation established by letters patent, the letters patent. 5. The corporation's articles, notice of articles or memorandum, regulations, bylaws or agreement or deed of settlement, and every alteration to them. 6. If the corporation was incorporated, continued or converted by or under, or if the corporation resulted from an amalgamation under, an Act, statute, ordinance, letters patent, certificate, declaration or other equivalent instrument or provision of law, that record and every alteration to it applying to the corporation. See BARE-BOAT ~; CANADIAN ~ OF RIGHTS AND FREEDOMS; TIME ~; VOYAGE ~.

CHARTER BY DEMISE. A charter by demise operates as a lease of the ship itself for a period of time which puts the ship altogether out of the power and control of the owner and vests that power and control in the charterers. *North Ridge Fishing Ltd. v. "Prosperity" (The)*, 2000 CarswellBC 982, 2000 BCCA 283, 74 B.C.L.R. (3d) 383, 186 D.L.R. (4th) 374 (C.A.), the court per Cumming J.A.

CHARTER DAMAGES. [D]amages may be awarded for Charter breach under s. 24(1) where appropriate and just. The first step in the inquiry is to establish that a Charter right has been breached. The second step is to show why damages are a just and appropriate remedy, having regard to whether they would fulfill one or more of the related functions of compensation, vindication of the right, and/or deterrence of future breaches. At the third step, the state has the opportunity to demonstrate, if it can, that countervailing factors defeat the functional considerations that support a damage award and render damages inappropriate or unjust. The final step is to assess the quantum of the damages. *Vancouver (City) v. Ward*, 2010 SCC 27.

CHARTERED BANK. A bank to which the Bank Act (Canada) applies, and includes a branch agency, and office of a bank. *Interpretation Act*, R.S.N. 1990, c.I-19, s. 27.

CHARTERED SHIP. A ship hired; a ship subject to charter party.

CHARTERER. *n.* One who hires a ship or aircraft for a certain period or for a voyage.

CHARTER OF HUMAN RIGHTS AND FREEDOMS. The Quebec Statute by that name (R.S.Q. c. C-12) which contains guarantees of non-discrimination and establishes the Commission des droits de la personne et des droits de la jeunesse and the Human Rights Tribunal.

CHARTER OF THE FRENCH LANGUAGE. Appears at R.S.Q. c. C-11. Establishes French as the official language of Quebec.

CHARTER PARTY. *vars.* **CHARTERPARTY**, **CHARTER-PARTY.** An agreement to use or hire a ship or to convey goods for a specified period or on a specified voyage.

CHASE. *v.* To pursue rapidly with intent to overtake or send away.

CHASE. *n.* A pursuit with a view to catching, not a test between rivals as in a "race". *McGill v. Insurance Corp. of B.C.* (1992), 10 C.C.L.I. (2d) 65 (B.C. S.C.).

CHATTEL. *n.* 1. An item of personal property. 2. Colloquially used to refer to chattel mortgage. See CHATTELS; INCORPOREAL ~.

CHATTEL MORTGAGE. "To constitute a chattel mortgage, the contract between the parties must import a transfer of the property in the chattels from the mortgagor to the mortgagee, as security for a debt, defeasible on payment of the debt; ..." *Dealers Finance Corp. v. Masterson Motors Ltd.*, [1931] 4 D.L.R. 730 at 735, [1931] 2 W.W.R. 214 (C.A.), Martin J.A.

CHATTEL PAPER. One or more than one writing that expresses both a monetary obligation and a security interest in or lease of specific goods and accessions.

CHATTELS. *n.* 1. "... [I]nclude[s] all personal property... ." *Ontario (Attorney General) v. Royal Bank*, [1970] 2 O.R. 467 at 472, 11 D.L.R. (3d) 257 (C.A.), the court per Brooke J.A. 2. "... [T]he principles as summarized in [Stack v. Eaton Co. (1902), 4 O.L.R. 335 (C.A.) by Meredith C.J.] ... at p. 338, [are] as follows: 'I take it to be settled law: (1) That articles not otherwise attached to the land than by their own weight are not to be considered as part of the land, unless the circumstances are such as shew that they were intended to be part of the land. (2) That articles affixed to the land even slightly are to be considered part of the land unless the circumstances are such as to shew that they were intended to continue chattels. (3) That the circumstances necessary to be shewn to alter the prima facie character of the articles are circumstances which shew the degree of annexation and degree of such annexation, which are present to all to see. (4) That the intention of the person affixing the article to the soil is material only so far as it can be presumed from the degree and object of the annexation.' " *Dolan v. Bank of Montreal* (1985), 5 P.P.S.A.C. 196 at 201-2, 42 Sask. R. 202 (C.A.), Matheson J.A. 3. May refer to goods and other items capable of transfer by delivery but not chattel interests in land. See CHATTEL; TRESPASS TO ~.

CHATTELS PERSONAL. "Pure personalty", either in action or in possession. E.L.G. Tyler & N.E. Palmer, eds., *Crossley Vaines' Personal Property*, 5th ed. (London: Butterworths, 1973) at 11.

CHATTELS REAL. Leaseholds.

CHAUFFEUR. *n.* A person who drives motor vehicles as a means of livelihood.

CH. D. *abbr.* Law Reports, Chancery Division, 1875-1890.

CHECK. See STOP-~.

CHECKERBOARD. *v.* To divide land in the manner of a checkerboard so that one person owns the "red squares" and another owns the "black squares". The owners on title may be nominees or trustees for the actual landowner, or the actual landowner might retain "one set of squares" and transfer the "other set" to a nominee. B.J. Reiter, B.N. McLellan & P.M. Perell, *Real Estate Law*, 4th ed. (Toronto: Emond Montgomery, 1992) at 340.

CHECKLIST. *n.* List of items to be covered in an agreement or in a transaction.

CHEQUE. *n.* 1. A bill drawn on a bank, payable on demand. 2. Includes a bill of exchange drawn on any institution that makes it a business practice to honour bills of exchange or any particular kind thereof drawn on it by depositors. *Criminal Code*, R.S.C. 1985, c. C-46, s. 362(5) and 364(3). 3. "... [A] direction to some one, who may or may not have in his possession funds of the drawer, authorising him to pay to the payee a certain sum of money... ." *Re Bernard*, (1911), 2 O.W.N. 716 at 717, Chief Justice of Exchequer Division. See CANCELLED ~; CERTIFIED ~; CROSSED ~; POSTDATED ~; STALE ~.

CHEQUE CASHING FEE. (a) A fee, commission or other amount or consideration charged, paid or given for cashing or negotiating a government cheque; and (b) any other fee, commission, amount or consideration designated by regulation as a cheque cashing fee. *The Consumer Protection Act*, R.S.M. 1987, c. C200, s. 165.

C.H.F.L.G. *abbr.* Canadian Health Facilities Law Guide.

CHIEF. *adj.* Head, principal. See EXAMINATION-IN-~; IN ~.

CHIEF ADMINISTRATOR. Has all the powers necessary for the overall effective and efficient management and administration of all court services, including court facilities and libraries and corporate services and staffing. The Chief Administrator, in consultation with the Chief Justices of the Federal Court of Appeal, the Federal Court, the Court Martial Appeal Court and the Tax Court of Canada, shall establish and maintain the registry or registries for those courts in any organizational form or forms and prepare budgetary submissions for the requirements of those courts and for the related needs of the Service. *Courts Administration Service Act, 2002*, S.C. 2002, c. 8.

CHIEF GOVERNMENT WHIP. See CHIEF WHIP.

CHIEF JUDGE. 1. The person having authority to assign duties to the judges of a court. 2. A person having authority to assign duties to the judge. *Courts of Justice Act*, R.S.O. 1990, c. C.43, s. 123.

CHIEF JUSTICE. Of any court of which a particular judge is a member means the chief justice or other person recognized by law as having rank or status senior to all other members of, or having the supervision of, that court, but if that court is constituted with divisions, then it means the person having that rank or status in relation to all other members of the division of which the particular judge is a member. *Judges Act*, R.S.C. 1985, c. J-1, s. 41(4).

CHIEF OPPOSITION WHIP. See CHIEF WHIP.

CHIEF PUBLIC HEALTH OFFICER. The deputy head of the Public Health Agency of Canada.

CHIEF WHIP. Each party in Parliament has a person who keeps members of that party informed about the business of the House, ensures these members attend, determines pairing arrangements so that the votes of members who cannot attend divisions will be neutralized and not lost, and supplies lists of members to serve on the various House committees. A. Fraser, W.A. Dawson, & J. Holtby, eds., *Beauchesne's Rules and Forms of the House of Commons of Canada*, 6th ed. (Toronto: Carswell, 1989) at 57.

CHILD. *n.* 1. "... [H]as two primary meanings. One refers to chronological age and is the converse of the term 'adult'; the other refers to lineage and is the reciprocal of the term 'parent'. A child in the first sense was defined at common law as a person under the age of 14. This definition may be modified by statutory provision ... No statutory modification, however, fixed an age higher than the age of majority which, in Ontario, pursuant to the Age of Majority and Accountability Act, R.S.O. 1980, c. 7, s. 1(1) is 18 years. A child in the second sense was defined at common law as the legitimate offspring of a parent, but in most jurisdictions this definition has been amended by statute to constitute all offspring, whether legitimate or not, as the 'children' of their natural or adoptive parents ..." *R. v. Ogg-Moss* (1984), [1985] 11 D.L.R. (4th) 549 at 558, [1984] 2 S.C.R. 173, 54 N.R. 81, 14 C.C.C. (3d) 116, 5 O.A.C. 81, 6 C.H.R.R. D/2498, 41 C.R. (3d) 297, the court per Dickson J. 2. A person who is or, in the absence of evidence to the contrary, appears to be less than twelve years old. *Youth Criminal Justice Act*, S.C. 2002, c. 1, s. 2. See BATTERED ~ SYNDROME; BEST INTERESTS OF THE ~; CONCEALING BODY OF ~; ILLEGITIMATE ~; LURING A ~; NATURAL ~; NEWLY-BORN ~.

CHILD ABDUCTION. The kidnapping of a child by the parent not awarded custody.

CHILD ABUSE. 1. Physical, mental, sexual, emotional mistreatment of a child. 2. Corporal punishment which causes injury is child abuse. Spanking [which does not cause physical harm] is not child abuse. *Canadian Foundation for Children, Youth & the Law v. Canada (Attorney General)*, 2000 CarswellOnt 2409, 146 C.C.C. (3d) 362, 188 D.L.R. (4th) 718, 49 O.R. (3d) 662, 36 C.R. (5th) 334, 76 C.R.R. (2d) 251 (S.C.J.), McCombs J.

CHILD CARE. See UNIVERSAL ~ BENEFIT.

CHILD OF THE MARRIAGE. A child of two spouses or former spouses includes (a) any child for whom they both stand in the place of parents; and (b) any child of whom one is the parent and for whom the other stands in the place of a parent. *Divorce Act*, R.S.C, 1985, c. 3 (2nd Supp.), s. 2.

CHILD PORNOGRAPHY. (a) A photographic, film, video or other visual representation, whether or not it was made by electronic or mechanical means, (i) that shows a person who is or is depicted as being under the age of eighteen years and is engaged in or is depicted as engaged in explicit sexual activity, or (ii) the dominant characteristic of which is the depiction, for a sexual purpose, of a sexual organ or the anal region of a person under the age of eighteen years; (b) any written material, visual representation or audio recording that advocates or counsels sexual activity with a person under the age of eighteen years that would be an offence under this Act; (c) any written material whose dominant characteristic is the description, for a sexual purpose, of sexual activity with a person under the age of eighteen years that would be an offence under this Act; or (d) any audio recording that has as its dominant characteristic the description, presentation or representation, for a sexual purpose, of sexual activity with a person under the age of eighteen years that would be an offence under this Act. *Criminal Code*, R.S.C. 1985, c. C-46, s. 163.1.

CHILDREN. See CHILD; MINOR ~.

CHILDREN'S AID SOCIETY. An organized or incorporated society having among its objects the promotion of family and child welfare.

CHILD SUPPORT. Financial support, care and upbringing to which a child is entitled from his or her parent. *Nielsen v. Nielsen* (1980), 16 R.F.L. (2d) 203 at 205 (Ont. Co. Ct.), Macnab Co. Ct. J.

CHILD SUPPORT GUIDELINES. 1. The Governor in Council may establish guidelines respecting the making of orders for child support, based on the principle that spouses have a joint financial obligation to maintain the children of the marriage in accordance with their relative abilities to contribute to the performance of that obligation. *Divorce Act*, R.S.C, 1985, c. 3 (2nd Supp.), s. 26.1. 2. The "applicable guidelines" are: where both spouses or former spouses are ordinarily resident in the same province at the time an application for a child support order or a variation order in respect of a child support order is made, or the amount of a child support order is to be recalculated pursuant to section 25.1, and that province has been designated by an order made under subsection (5), the laws of the province specified in the order are for that purpose the child support guidelines, and (b) in any other case, the Federal Child Support Guidelines. *Divorce Act*, R.S.C, 1985, c. 3 (2nd Supp.), s. 2. See FEDERAL ~.

CHILD SUPPORT ORDER. An order made under subsection 15.1(1): a court of competent jurisdiction may, on application by either or both spouses, make an order requiring a spouse to pay for the support of any or all children of the marriage. *Divorce Act*, R.S.C, 1985, c. 3 (2nd Supp.), s. 2 and 15.1. See ORDER FOR CHILD SUPPORT.

CHILD WELFARE SERVICE. (a) A residential or non-residential service, including a prevention service, (b) a service provided under Part III (Child Protection), (c) a service provided under Part VII (Adoption), or (d) individual or family counselling. *Child and Family Services Act*, R.S.O. 1990, c. C.11, s. 3.

CHIMERA. *n.* An embryo into which a cell of any non-human life form has been introduced; or an embryo that consists of cells of more than one embryo, foetus or human being.

CHIMERIC PLANT GENE. One that has been molecularly engineered using multiple sources that may include plant, viral and bacterial DNA. *Monsanto Canada Inc. v. Schmeiser* 218 D.L.R. (4th) 31, 293 N.R. 340, [2003] 2 F.C. 165, 231 F.T.R. 160 (note), 21 C.P.R. (4th) 1.

CHINESE MEDICINE. See TRADITIONAL ~.

CHINESE WALL. 1. A method in which a law firm may represent more than one client in the same transaction by having the lawyer who represents one side keep everything confidential from the lawyer who represents the other. 2. "... If the attorney practices in a firm, there is a presumption that lawyers who work together share each other's confidences. Knowledge of confidential matters is therefore imputed to other members of the firm. This latter presumption can, however, in some circumstances, be rebutted. The usual methods used to rebut the presumption are the setting up of a 'Chinese Wall' ... at the time that the possibility of the unauthorized communication of confidential information arises. A 'Chinese Wall' involves effective 'screening' to prevent communication between the tainted lawyer and other members of the firm." *MacDonald Estate v. Martin* (1990), 48 C.P.C. (2d) 113 at 126, [1991] 1 W.W.R. 705, 121 N.R. 1, 77 D.L.R. (4th) 249, 70 Man. R. (2d) 241, [1990] 3 S.C.R. 1235, Sopinka J. (Dickson C.J., La Forest and Gonthier JJ. concurring). 3. "These two subsections [of the Securities Act, R.S.O. 1980, c. 466, s. 75(1) and (3)] provide for what is commonly referred to as a 'Chinese Wall' defence. That means the establishment within an organization of informational barriers to prevent the improper transmission of information within the organization concerning a material fact or material change that has not been generally disclosed. Chinese Walls are designed to insulate and to keep to a minimum persons in an organization who make investment decisions from persons in that organization who have confidential information which could affect those decisions." *R. v. Saliga* (1991), 14 O.S.C.B. 4777 at 4783 (Prov. Div.), Masse J. See CONE OF SILENCE.

CHIP. See BLUE ~.

CHIROPODY. *n.* The assessment of the foot and the treatment and prevention of diseases, disorders or dysfunctions of the foot by therapeutic, orthotic or palliative means and includes cutting into subcutaneous tissues of the foot and the administration, by injection into the foot, of a local anaesthetic agent designated in the regulations. *The Chiropodists Act*, R.S.M. 1987, c. C90, s. 1.

CHIROPRACTIC. See PRACTICE OF ~.

CHITTY'S L.J. *abbr.* Chitty's Law Journal, 1953-.

CHOICE OF LAW. "... [R]efers to the conflicts rules which have developed, through legislation or jurisprudence, in order to determine which system of substantive law the forum court will apply in respect of a legal matter having connection with other jurisdictions. There are different choice of law rules for different areas of law." *Tolofson v. Jensen* (1992), 4 C.P.C. (3d) 113 at 118, 65 B.C.L.R. (2d) 114, 9 C.C.L.T. (2d) 289, [1992] 3 W.W.R. 743, 89 D.L.R. (4th) 129, 11 B.C.A.L. 94, 22 W.A.C. 94, the court per Cumming J.A.

CHOKE HOLD. A way to subdue someone by placing a forearm or stick on the front of their throat. This presses on the windpipe and moves the larynx up. F.A. Jaffe, *A Guide to Pathological Evidence for Lawyers and Police Officers*, 4th ed. (Toronto: Carswell, 1999) at 233.

CHOREOGRAPHIC WORK. Includes any work of choreography, whether or not it has any story line. *Copyright Act*, R.S.C. 1985, c. C-42, s. 2.

CHOSE. *n.* [Fr.] A chattel personal, either in action or in possession. See CHATTEL.

CHOSE IN ACTION. 1. "In Torkington v. Magee, [1902] 2 K.B. 427 at p. 430, Channel J. said: ' "Chose in action" is a known legal expression used to describe all personal rights of property which can only be claimed or enforced by action, and not by taking physical possession'. The term covers multifarious rights, many diverse in their essential nature, such as debts, company shares, negotiable instruments and rights of action founded on tort or breach of contract." *Di Guilo v. Boland* (1958), 13 D.L.R. (2d) 510 at 513, [1958] O.R. 384 (C.A.), the court per Morden J.A. 2. "... [A]n incorporeal right to something not in one's possession and, accordingly, it is not possible for the debtor to have possession of it... ." *Ontario (Attorney General) v. Royal Bank*, [1970] 2 O.R. 467 at 472, 11 D.L.R. (3d) 257 (C.A.), the court per Brooke J.A.

CHOSE IN POSSESSION. A tangible thing which is in someone's possession.

CH. R. *abbr.* Upper Canada Chambers Reports, 1857-1872.

C.H.R.C. *abbr.* Canadian Human Rights Commission.

C.H.R.R. *abbr.* Canadian Human Rights Reporter, 1980-.

CHY. CHRS. *abbr.* Upper Canada Chancery Chambers Reports.

CICA. *abbr.* The Canadian Institute of Chartered Accountants.

CICA HANDBOOK. The handbook prepared and published by the Canadian Institute of Chartered Accountants, as amended from time to time.

C.I.C.B. *abbr.* Criminal Injuries Compensation Board Decisions, 1971-1989.

CIDA. *abbr.* Canadian International Development Agency.

CIE. *abbr.* [Fr. compagnie] Company.

C.I.F. *abbr.* Cost insurance and freight.

C.I.F. CONTRACT. A contract in which price includes cost of the goods, insurance while in transit and freight charges incurred. G.H.L. Fridman, *Sale of Goods in Canada*, 3d ed. (Toronto: Carswell, 1986) at 480.

CIFTA. *abbr.* The Canada-Israel Free Trade Agreement Implementation Act.

C.I.L.R. *abbr.* 1. Canadian Insurance Law Reports. 2. Canadian Insurance Law Review.

CINEMATOGRAPHIC WORK. Includes any work expressed by any process analogous to cinematography, whether or not accompanied by a soundtrack. *Copyright Act*, R.S.C. 1985, c. C-42, s. 2.

CIPO. *abbr.* Canadian Intellectual Property Office.

C.I.P.O.O. (M). *abbr.* Commission à l'information et à la protection de la vie privée, Ontario, Orders, M Series, 1988-1998.

C.I.P.O.O. (P). *abbr.* Commission à l'information et à la protection de la vie privée, Ontario, Orders, P Series, 1992-1998.

C.I.P.O.S. *abbr.* Commission à l'information et à la protection de la vie privée, Ontario, Sommaires, 1990-1992.

C.I.P.R.*abbr.* Canadian Intellectual Property Reports, 1984-1990.

CIRA. *abbr.* Canadian Internet Registration Authority.

C.I.R.B. *abbr.* Canada Industrial Relations Board, Reasons for Decision, 1999-.

CIRCA. [L.] About; around.

CIRC. CT. *abbr.* Circuit Court.

CIRCLE. See CONSULTATION ~; GREEN CIRCLING; SENTENCING ~.

CIRCUIT. See INTEGRATED ~ PRODUCT.

CIRCULATING CAPITAL. That part of the wealth of a taxpayer which is intended to be used, in the sense of being temporarily expended, dedicated or disposed of by circulation in the business undertaking, and which comes back to headquarters bringing a profit. Such is the case with inventory in a sales enterprise. *Johns-Manville Canada v. The Queen*, [1985] 2 S.C.R. 46, Estey, J. for the court at Para. 23.

CIRCULATION COIN. A coin composed of base metal that is listed in Part 2 of the schedule and that is put into circulation in Canada for use in day-to-day transactions. *Royal Canadian Mint Act*, R.S.C. 1985, c. R-9, s. 2. See NON-~.

CIRCUMSTANCE. *n.* 1. An attendant or auxiliary fact. 2. In the context of insurance, includes any communication made to or information received by the assured. See AGGRAVATING ~; REASONABLE IN THE ~S.

CIRCUMSTANTIAL EVIDENCE. 1. Evidence which creates an inference that a particular fact exists. 2. Evidence tending to establish the existence or non-existence of a fact that is not one of the elements of the offence charged, where the existence or non-existence of that fact reasonably leads to an inference concerning the existence or non-existence of a fact that is one of the elements of the offence charged. *National Defence Act*, R.S.C. 1985, c. N-5, *Military Rules of Evidence*, C.R.C., c. 1049, s. 2.

CIT. *abbr.* 1. Citizen. 2. Citizenship.

C.I.T. *abbr.* Canadian Import Tribunal.

CITATION. *n.* 1. Calling on a person who is not a party to a proceeding or an action to appear in court. 2. In probate matters, notice of proceedings given to anyone whose interests are or may be affected. 3. A precise reference to a case or enactment. 4. The act of referring to a case or an enactment. See CORE OF THE ~; NEUTRAL ~ STANDARD.

CITATION OF AUTHORITIES. 1. A reference to case or statute law to establish or support propositions of law advanced. 2. The act of referring to a case or an enactment.

CITATOR. *n.* A set of books which provides historical information regarding statutes, cumulates amendments to statutes since the last revision or consolidation of the statutes and traces judicial consideration of sections of statutes.

CITE. *v.* 1. To refer to legal authorities. 2. To name in citation. 3. To put a defendant on notice that he or she must show cause why he or she should not be found in contempt of court. See CITING IN CONTEMPT.

CITE. *n.* Citation of a case or enactment.

CITING IN CONTEMPT. The expression "citing in contempt", should be used not as an expression of a finding of contempt but instead, as a method of providing the accused with notice that he or she has been contemptuous and will be required to show cause why they should not be held in contempt. *R. c. Arradi*, 2003 SCC 23.

CITIZEN. *n.* 1. A Canadian citizen. *Citizenship Act*, R.S.C. 1985, c. C-29, s. 2. 2. In the *Charter*, refers to a natural person, not a corporation.

CITIZENSHIP. *n.* 1. Canadian citizenship. *Citizenship Act*, R.S.C. 1985, c. C-29, s. 2. 2. Refers to a political status conferred by a state. See DEPARTMENT OF ~ AND IMMIGRATION; OATH OR AFFIRMATION OF ~.

CITIZENSHIP JUDGE. A citizenship judge appointed under the Citizenship Act. *Citizenship Act*, R.S.C. 1985, c. C-29, s. 2.

CITIZENSHIP OFFICER. A person who is authorized by the Minister in writing to perform the duties of a citizenship officer prescribed by these Regulations. *Citizenship Act*, R.S.C. 1985, c. C-29, *Citizenship Regulations, 1993*, SOR/93-246, s. 2.

CITY. *n.* A municipal corporation incorporated as a city.

CIVIL. *adj.* 1. Of legal matters, private as opposed to criminal. 2. Used to distinguish the criminal courts and proceedings in them from military courts and proceedings. 3. Used to distinguish secular from religious. See CODE ~.

CIVIL ACTION. Any type of action except criminal proceedings.

CIVIL AIRCRAFT. All aircraft other than aircraft operated by the Canadian Forces, a police force in Canada or persons engaged in the administration or enforcement of the Customs Act the Excise Act or the Excise Act 2001. *Criminal Code*, R.S.C. 1985, c. C-46, s. 78(2).

CIVIL CEREMONY. A marriage performed by a judge or justice of the peace, distinguished from a religious ceremony.

CIVIL CLAIM. An action or proceeding in B.C. Supreme Court. *Court Rules Act*, R.S.B.C. 1996, c. 80, *Supreme Court Civil Rules*, B.C. Reg. 168/2009. See NOTICE OF ~; RESPONSE TO ~.

CIVIL CODE. The Civil Code Of Québec, S.Q., 1991, c. 64. In harmony with the Charter of human rights and freedoms and the general principles of law, governs persons, relations between persons, and property. The Civil Code comprises a body of rules which, in all matters within the letter, spirit or object of its provisions, lays down the jus commune, expressly or by implication. In these matters, the Code is the foundation of all other laws, although other laws may complement the Code or make exceptions to it.

CIVIL CONSPIRACY. 1. " ... [W]hereas the law of tort does not permit an action against an individual defendant who has caused injury to the plaintiff, the law of torts does recognize a claim against them in combination as the tort of conspiracy if: (1) whether the means used by the defendants are lawful or unlawful, the predominant purpose of the defendants' conduct is to cause injury to the plaintiff; or, (2) where the conduct is directed towards the plaintiff (alone or together with others), and the defendants should know in the circumstances that injury to the plaintiff is likely to and does result." *Canada Cement LaFarge Ltd. v. British Columbia Lightweight Aggregate Ltd.*, [1983] 1 S.C.R. 452 at 471-2, Estey J. 2. Although its origins trace to the Middle Ages, civil conspiracy is not now a well-settled tort in terms of its current utility or the scope of the remedy it affords. In Canadian law, the tort encompasses both a conspiracy to injure another person by means of lawful or unlawful acts and ... a conspiracy to commit unlawful acts where there is a constructive intent to injure. *Golden Capital Securities Ltd. v. Holmes*, 2004 BCCA 565. 3. A summary of the law relating to claims of civil conspiracy was provided by McLachlin J. (as she then was) in Nicholls v. Richmond (City) (1984), 52 B.C.L.R. 302 (S.C.), at pages 311-312: There are two categories of civil conspiracy: (1) where the predominant purpose of the defendants' conduct is to injure the plaintiff; and (2) where the defendants effect their agreed end by unlawful means knowing that the plaintiff may be injured. While only the first category is available in the United Kingdom since the decision of the House of Lords in Lonrho Ltd. v. Shell Petroleum Co. (1981), [1982] A.C. 173, [1981] 3 W.L.R. 33, [1981] 2 All E.R. 456 (H.L.), both categories are recognized in Canada: Canada Cement LaFarge Ltd. v. British Columbia Lightweight Aggregate Ltd., [1983] 6 W.W.R. 385, 21 B.L.R. 254, 24 C.C.L.T. 111, 72 C.P.R. (2d) 1, 145 D.L.R. (3d) 385, 47 N.R. 191 (S.C.C). The requirements of conspiracy to injure the plaintiff are an agreement between two or more persons whose predominant purpose is to injure the plaintiff and which when acted upon results in damage to the plaintiff. It is not a requirement that the conduct of the defendants in effecting their agreement be unlawful. The requirements of the second type of conspiracy, conspiracy by unlawful means, are an agreement between two or more persons which is effected by unlawful conduct where the defendants should know in the circumstances that damage to the plaintiff is likely to ensue and such damage does in fact ensue. Unlike the first category of conspiracy, it is not a requirement of conspiracy by unlawful means that the predominant purpose of the defendants be to cause injury to the plaintiff. Rather, a constructive intent is derived from the fact that the defendants should have known that damage to the plaintiff would result from their conduct. *923087 N.W.T. Ltd. v. Anderson Mills Ltd.*, 1997 CarswellNWT 36, 35 B.L.R. (2d) 1, 13 C.P.C. (4th) 357, [1997] N.W.T.R. 212, 40 C.C.L.T. (2d) 15 (S.C.), Vertes J.

CIVIL CONTEMPT. 1. Breach of the rules of a court, a court order or other misconduct in a private matter causing a private injury or wrong. 2. "... [T]he purpose ... is to secure compliance with the process of a tribunal including, but not limited to, the process of a court ... initiated by a party or person affected by the order sought to be enforced. In order to secure compliance in a proceeding for civil contempt, a court may impose a fine or other penalty which will be exacted in the absence of compliance. However, the object is always compliance and not punishment." *U.N.A. v. Alberta (Attorney General)* (1992), 13 C.R. (4th) 1 at 22, [1992] 3 W.W.R. 481, 89 D.L.R. (4th) 609, 71 C.C.C. (3d) 225, 135 N.R. 321, 92 C.L.L.C. 14,023, 1 Alta. L.R. (3d) 129, 125 A.R. 241, 14 W.A.C. 241, [1992] 1 S.C.R. 901, 9 C.R.R. (2d) 29, Sopinka J. (dissenting). 3. "... [A] private wrong. The intervention of the court is called upon primarily to assist the position of one of the litigants to enforce an order favourable to that party... ." *R. v. Clement* (1980), 17 R.F.L. (2d) 349 at 362, [1980] 6 W.W.R. 695, 4 Man. R. (2d) 18, 54 C.C.C. (2d) 252, 114 D.L.R. (3d) 656 (C.A.), Matas J.A. (Freedman C.J.M. concurring).

CIVIL FORFEITURE. A mechanism established under provincial legislation providing for court-ordered forfeiture of proceeds of unlawful activity, as defined in the legislation. For example, *Civil Forfeiture Act*, S.B.C. 2005, c. 29, s. 1.

CIVILIAN POPULATION. See ATTACK DIRECTED AGAINST ANY ~.

CIVILIZATION. See CANADIAN MUSEUM OF ~.

CIVIL LAW. 1. The legal system of Quebec based on the Civil Code and ultimately Roman law. 2. "... [A] body of private law, consists largely, although not exclusively, of the law enunciated in the Civil Code of Lower Canada and the Civil Code of Quebec, L.R.Q. 1977, c. C-25." *Laurentide Motels Ltd. c. Beauport (Ville)* (1989), 45 M.P.L.R. 1 at 11, 94 N.R. 1, [1989] 1 S.C.R. 705, 23 Q.A.C. 1, Beetz J. (McIntyre, Lamer, Wilson and La Forest JJ. concurring).

CIVIL LIBERTIES. Essentially that which is not a prohibited act. Include the rights protected by the Charter of Rights and Freedoms: freedom of association, assembly, religion, expression, mobility rights, voting rights, procedural and legal rights, right to equal treatment under the law, and language rights. See EGALITARIAN ~; LEGAL ~; POLITICAL ~.

CIVIL LITIGATION. Litigation involving private parties as opposed to criminal proceedings.

CIVIL MARRIAGE. Marriage, for civil purposes, is the lawful union of two persons to the exclusion of all others. For greater certainty, a marriage is not void or voidable by reason only that the spouses are of the same sex. *Civil Marriage Act*, S.C. 2005, c. 33, s. 2 and 4.

CIVIL MARRIAGE CEREMONY. A marriage performed by a judge or justice of the peace, distinguished from a religious ceremony.

CIVIL MATTER. A cause, issue or matter, other than a criminal matter, that involves or might involve a jury and includes an assessment of damages.

CIVIL ONUS. The standard of proof for the party bearing the onus is on a balance of probabilities.

CIVIL PRISON. Any prison, jail or other place in Canada in which offenders sentenced by a civil court in Canada to imprisonment for less than two years can be confined, and, if sentenced outside Canada, any prison, jail or other place in which a person, sentenced to that term of imprisonment by a civil court having jurisdiction in the place where the sentence was passed, can for the time being be confined. *National Defence Act*, R.S.C. 1985, c. N-5, s. 2.

CIVIL PROCEDURE. The law governing the process and practice of civil litigation.

CIVIL PROCEEDING. A proceeding to determine a dispute between two or more persons, one or more of whom may be a government body, the object of which is a judgment, order, decree or similar instrument that: (a) in the case of a violation of a right, requires a party to comply with a duty or pay damages; or (b) in any other case, determines the personal status or capacity of one or more of the parties. *The Enforcement of Foreign Judgments Act*, S.S. 2005, c. E-9.121, s. 2.

CIVIL RIGHTS. 1. Those rights referred to in the list of provincial powers in section 92 of the Constitution Act, 1867 are primarily proprietary, contractual or tortious rights. 2. Procedural rights of an individual. See CIVIL LIBERTIES; PROPERTY AND ~.

CIVIL RIGHTS IN THE PROVINCE. Proprietary, contractual or tortious rights referred to in section 92 of the Constitution Act, 1867.

CIVIL SERVANT. 1. A person appointed to the service of the Crown. 2. A member of the civil service. 3. A member of the staff of a department or Ministry of Government.

CIVIL SERVICE. The employees of the government.

CIVIL SOCIETY ORGANIZATION. A not-for-profit or charitable organization whose governing structure is independent of government direction, and includes, but is not limited to, registered charities, non-governmental development organizations, community groups, women's organizations, faith-based organizations, professional associations, trade unions, self-help groups, social movements, business associations, coalitions, human rights organizations and advocacy groups. *Official Development Assistance Accountability Act*, S.C. 2008, c. 17, s. 3.

CIVIL STATUS. "... [U]nder s. 10 [of the Quebec Charter of Rights and Freedoms, R.S.Q. 1977, c. C-12] includes a range of facts (and not necessarily recorded facts) relating to the three classical elements of civil status – birth, marriage, and death – to which arts. 39 et seq. C.C.L.C. refer. These facts are sometimes recorded in a person's own acts of civil status, sometimes recorded in the acts of another person, and sometimes not recorded in any act at all ... Other facts, such as interdiction or emancipation, which do not relate to birth, marriage or death but instead to legal capacity may also be included in civil status under s. 10 ... family relationships [are included in] 'civil status'. Like filiation, fraternity and sorority fall within the parameters which I have ascribed to civil status under s. 10 in this respect as well ..." *Brossard (Ville) v. Québec (Commission des droits de la personne)* (1989), 10 C.H.R.R. D/5515 at D/5520, D/5522, 88 C.L.L.C. 17,031, [1989] 2 S.C.R. 279, 88 N.R. 321, 18 Q.A.C. 164, 53 D.L.R. (4th) 609, Beetz J. (McIntyre, Lamer and La Forest JJ. concurring). See ACT OF ~.

CIVIL SUIT. A proceeding involving private parties or a private party and the government as opposed to a criminal matter. Usually refers to a claim for damages by one party against the other. See CIVIL ACTION; SUIT.

CIVIL UNION. A commitment by two persons 18 years of age or over who express their free and enlightened consent to live together and to uphold the rights and obligations that derive from that status. A civil union may only be contracted between persons who are free from any previous bond of marriage or civil union and who in relation to each other are neither an ascendant or a descendant, nor a brother or a sister. *Civil Code*, S.Q. 1991, c. 64, a. 521.1.

C.J. *abbr.* Chief Justice.

C.J.A.L.P. *abbr.* Canadian Journal of Administrative Law & Practice.

C.J.C. *abbr.* The Chief Justice of Canada. The Chief Justice of the Supreme Court of Canada.

C.J.W.L. *abbr.* Canadian Journal of Women and the Law (Revue juridique "La femme et le droit").

CLAIM. *v.* See PERIPHERAL ~ING PRINCIPLE.

CLAIM. *n.* 1. The demand or the subject matter for which any action, suit, or proceeding is brought. 2. A right, title, interest, encumbrance or demand of any kind affecting land. 3. An assertion; 4. An area granted or used for mining purposes. 5. A means of defining boundaries within which an inventor asserts his patent rights. See ADDED-VALUE ~; ADVERSE ~; CIVIL ~; COUNTER~; CROSS~; EQUITY ~; HEALTH CARE SERVICES ~; LONG TAIL ~; NOTICE OF~; QUIT ~; SMALL ~S COURT; SPECIFIC ~S TRIBUNAL; STATEMENT OF ~.

CLAIMANT. *n.* 1. One who makes a claim. 2. A person who has or is alleged to have a right to maintenance or support. 3. Any person who claims or asserts or seeks to realize a lien. 4. A person who applies or has applied for benefit or compensation. See LIEN ~; MAJOR ATTACHMENT ~; MINOR ATTACHMENT ~; STRAW ~.

CLAIM CONSTRUCTION. Claim construction is a question of law, based on the patent alone without resort to extrinsic evidence. This issue precedes other issues.

CLAIM OF RIGHT. See DEFENCE WITH ~; DEFENCE WITHOUT ~.

C

CLAIM PROVABLE. Any claim or liability provable in proceedings under this Act by a creditor. *Bankruptcy and Insolvency Act*, R.S.C. 1985, c. B-3, s. 2.

CLAIM PROVABLE IN BANKRUPTCY. Any claim or liability provable in proceedings under this Act by a creditor. *Bankruptcy and Insolvency Act*, R.S.C. 1985, c. B-3, s. 2.

CLAIMS ADJUSTER. A person who, in insurance matters, investigates a loss, assesses damage arising from it or negotiates settlement of the claim.

CLAIMS MADE AND REPORTED POLICY. Coverage under such policies applies only to claims which are both made of the insured and reported to the insurer during the policy period. *Reid Crowther & Partners Ltd. v. Simcoe & Erie General Insurance Co.*, 1993 CarswellMan 96, [1993] 2 W.W.R. 433, 6 C.L.R. (2d) 161, 147 N.R. 44, 13 C.C.L.I. (2d) 161, [1993] 1 S.C.R. 252, 99 D.L.R. (4th) 741, 83 Man. R. (2d) 81, 36 W.A.C. 81, [1993] I.L.R. 1-2914, the court per McLachlin J.

CLAIMS MADE POLICY. [T]he policy may focus on the time the claim is made by the third party on the insured. Under a "claims-made" policy, the insurer is liable to indemnify the insured for claims made during the currency of the policy, regardless of when the negligence giving rise to those claims may have occurred. Liability for negligent acts predating the policy is covered provided a claim arising from any such negligent act is made during the policy period. On the other hand, liability for negligent acts which occur within the policy period is covered only if a claim is made against the insured on their account within the policy period. *Reid Crowther & Partners Ltd. v. Simcoe & Erie General Insurance Co.*, 1993 CarswellMan 96, [1993] 2 W.W.R. 433, 6 C.L.R. (2d) 161, 147 N.R. 44, 13 C.C.L.I. (2d) 161, [1993] 1 S.C.R. 252, 99 D.L.R. (4th) 741, 83 Man. R. (2d) 81, 36 W.A.C. 81, [1993] I.L.R. 1-2914, the court per McLachlin J.

CLARITY ACT. An Act to give effect to the requirement for clarity as set out in the opinion of the Supreme Court of Canada in the Quebec Secession Reference, received Royal Assent on June 29, 2000. Its purpose was stated as: The Government of Quebec can ask Quebec voters the question of its choice. But the Government of Canada and the House of Commons, as political actors, have a duty to make their own assessment of whether the question and the majority indicate a clear support for secession before concluding that the Government of Canada is bound to enter into negotiations on the break-up of Canada.

C.L.A.S. *abbr.* Canadian Labour Arbitration Summaries, 1986-.

CLASS. *n.* 1. A group of persons or things having common attributes. 2. A group of securities with defined rights attached to it which distinguish it from another class of securities issued by the same issuer. 3. Includes any series of the class. 4. A group of positions involving duties and responsibilities so similar that the same or like qualifications may reasonably be required for, and the same schedule or range of pay can be reasonably applied to, all positions in the group. *Pay Equity Act*, R.S.P.E.I. 1988, c. P-2, s. 1. See LIMITED ~ RULE; SHARE ~.

CLASS ACTION. 1. A representative proceeding. 2. "It is necessary to consider the difference between a class action which is derivative in nature, and a representative action by persons having the same interest in the subject of the litigation. Derivative type class actions are those in which a wrong is done to the entity to which the members belong. Such an action may be brought by a member or members, but it is brought on behalf of the entity. A representative action can be brought by persons asserting a common right, and even where persons may have been wronged in their individual capacity." *Pasco v. Canadian National Railway* (1989), (*sub nom. Oregon Jack Creek Indian Band v. Canadian National Railway*) [1990] 2 C.N.L.R. 85 at 87, 34 B.C.L.R. (2d) 344, 56 D.L.R. (4th) 404 (C.A.), MacFarlane J.A.

CLASS A SHARE. In respect of a corporation, means a share of a class of shares that entitle the holders thereof to, (a) receive notice of and, subject to the legislation under which the corporation is organized, to attend and vote at all meetings of the shareholders of the corporation, (b) receive dividends at the discretion of the board of directors of the corporation, and (c) receive, on dissolution of the corporation, all the assets of the corporation that remain after payment of all amounts payable to the holders of all other classes of shares of the corporation. *Community Small Business Investment Funds Act*, S.O. 1992, c. 18, s. 1, as am.

CLASS B SHARE. In respect of a corporation, means a share of a class of shares that do not entitle the holders thereof to receive dividends but do entitle the holders thereof to, (a) receive notice of and, subject to the legislation under which the corporation is organized, to attend and vote at all meetings of the shareholders of the corporation, (b) receive, on dissolution of the corporation, an amount equal to the amount of the equity capital received by the corporation on the issue of the Class B shares, and (c) in the case of a corporation registered under Part II or III, vote as a class to elect a majority of the board of directors of the corporation. *Community Small Business Investment Funds Act*, S.O. 1992, c. 18, s. 1, as am.

CLASS COMPLAINT. A complaint in which each member of the class is said to be suffering essentially the same type of injury and is entitled, if the complaint succeeds, to the same type of remedy. *Canada Safeway Ltd. v. Saskatchewan (Human Rights Commission)*, [1998] 1 W.W.R. 155 (Sask. C.A.).

CLASS COMPOSITION. Deals with the type of student a teacher will teach. *Flin Flon Teachers' Assn. v. Flin Flon School Division No. 46* 2000 MBCA 78, [2000] 9 W.W.R. 575, 150 Man. R. (2d) 94, 230 W.A.C. 94, 9 W.W.R. 575.

CLASS GIFT. A gift to a number of persons who are united or connected by some common tie... the testator was looking to the body as a whole rather than to the members constituting the body as individuals ... if one or more of that body died in his lifetime the survivors should take the gift between them. *Kingsbury v. Walter*, [1901] A.C. 187 at 191, per Lord Macnaghten.

CLASSIFICATION. See RISK ~ SYSTEM.

CLASS OF SECURITIES. A group of securities to which certain rights, privileges or limitations are attached. Classes of securities are used in incorporating documents to provide preferential treatment of some securities.

CLASS OF SHARES. A group of shares to which certain rights, privileges or limitations are attached. Classes of shares are used in incorporating documents to provide preferential treatment of some shares. See SHARE CLASS.

CLASS SIZE. Deals with the number of students the teacher will. *Flin Flon Teachers' Assn. v. Flin Flon School Division No. 46* 2000 MBCA 78, [2000] 9 W.W.R. 575, 150 Man. R. (2d) 94, 230 W.A.C. 94, 9 W.W.R. 575.

CLAUSE. *n.* 1. A paragraph or division of a contract. 2. A sentence or part of a sentence. 3. A numbered portion of a bill called a section once the bill becomes law. A. Fraser, W.A. Dawson, & J. Holtby, eds., *Beauchesne's Rules and Forms of the House of Commons of Canada*, 6th ed. (Toronto: Carswell, 1989) at 193-4. See ACCELERATION ~; ACT OF GOD ~; AMENDING ~; ARBITRATION ~; ATTESTATION ~; BASKET ~; CALL-BACK ; CALL-IN ~; CANCELLATION ~; COLA ~; DEEMING ~; DEFEASANCE ~; DEROGATORY ~; DISCLAIMER ~; ENACTING ~; ENTIRE AGREEMENT ~; ENTRENCHMENT ~; ESCALATION ~; EXCEPTIONS ~; EXCLUSION ~; EXCLUSIVE JURISDICTION ~; EXEMPTION ~; FAINT HOPE ~; FINALITY ~; FORCE MAJEURE ~; GRANDFATHER ~; HENRY VIII ~; HIMALAYA ~; INTERPRETATION ~; NO-CERTIORARI ~; NON-DEROGATION ~; NON OBSTANTE ~; NOTWITHSTANDING ~; OBJECTS ~; PRECATORY ~; PRECLUSIVE ~; PRIVATIVE ~; PRIVILEGE ~; REMEDY ~; RESORT TO ~; SAVING ~; SCOTT V. AVERY ~; SEVERANCE ~; SHOTGUN ~; STATUS QUO ~; SUPREMACY ~; THRESHOLD ~.

CLAYTON'S CASE. See RULE IN ~.

CLEAN HANDS DOCTRINE. 1. "... [E]quity will refuse relief to any party who, in the matter of his claim, is himself tainted with fraud, misrepresentation, illegality or impropriety by reason of which his opponent has suffered a detriment of a kind rendering it unjust that the order sought should be made." *Miller v. F. Mendel Holdings Ltd.* (1984), 26 B.L.R. 85 at 100, [1984] 2 W.W.R. 683, 30 Sask. R. 298 (Q.B.), Wimmer J. 2. "... [T]he theory of the doctrine is that a shareholder cannot invoke an equitable remedy when he himself is a principal source of the conflict and controversy which threaten the future of the corporation... ." *Journet v. Superchef Food Industries Ltd.* (1984), 29 B.L.R. 206 at 224, [1984] C.S. 916 (Que.), Gomery J. See HE WHO COMES INTO EQUITY MUST COME WITH CLEAN HANDS; NO MAN CAN TAKE ADVANTAGE OF HIS OWN WRONG; NO ONE CAN BE ALLOWED TO DEROGATE FROM HIS OWN GRANT.

CLEAN SHELL COMPANY. A company which has neither assets nor liabilities.

CLEAR. *adj.* 1. Free from doubt. 2. Free from encumbrance, lien or charge. 3. Free from deductions. See FREE AND ~.

CLEARANCE. *n.* A certificate issued to indicate compliance with law or regulations.

CLEAR DAYS. Complete days in counting time for items such as notice; both first and last days are omitted.

CLEARED. *adj.* An offence is cleared when an information has been laid or when there is enough evidence to lay an information against an identified offender although such information is not in fact laid. *R. v. Slavens* (1991), 64 C.C.C. (3d) 29 (B.C.C.A.).

CLEARING. *n.* 1. In banking, making exchanges and settling balances among banks. 2. In transport, departing having complied with customs regulations. See DERIVATIVES ~; REVERSE ~.

CLEARING AGENCY. 1. (a) A person that (i) in connection with trades in securities, acts as an intermediary in paying funds, in delivering securities or in doing both of those things, and (ii) provides centralized facilities for the clearing of trades in securities, or (b) a person that provides centralized facilities as a depository in connection with trades in securities. *Securities acts.* 2. A person: (i) that carries on a business or activity as a clearing agency or clearing house within the meaning of The Securities Act, 1988 or the securities regulatory law of another province or territory in Canada; (ii) that is recognized or otherwise regulated as a clearing agency or clearing house by the Saskatchewan Financial Services Commission or by a securities regulatory authority of another province or territory in Canada; and (iii) that is a securities and derivatives clearing house for the purposes of section 13.1 of the Payment Clearing and Settlement Act (Canada) or whose clearing and settlement system is designated under Part I of that Act. *The Securities Transfer Act*, S.S. 2007, c. S-42.3, s. 1.

CLEARING AND SETTLEMENT SYSTEM. A system or arrangement for the clearing or settlement of payment obligations or payment messages in which (a) there are at least three participants, at least one of which is a bank, (b) clearing or settlement is all or partly in Canadian dollars, and (c) the payment obligations that arise from clearing within the system or arrangement are ultimately settled through adjustments to the account or accounts of one or more of the participants at the Bank and, for greater certainty, includes a system or arrangement for the clearing or settlement of securities transactions, foreign exchange transactions or other transactions where the system or arrangement also clears or settles payment obligations arising from those transactions. *Payment Clearing and Settlement Act*, S.C. 1996, c. 6, Sch., s. 2.

CLEARING HOUSE. 1. A corporation, association, partnership, agency or other entity that provides clearing or settlement services for a clearing and settlement system, but does not include a stock exchange or the Bank. *Payment Clearing and Settlement Act*, S.C. 1996, c. 6, Sch., s. 2. 2. A corporation, association, partnership, agency or other entity that carries on in Canada the business of providing its participants with the clearing and settlement of transactions in securities that are deposited with it. *Depository Bills and Notes Act*, S.C. 1998, c. 13, s. 2. 3. A body that acts as an intermediary for its clearing members in effecting securities transactions. *Bankruptcy and Insolvency Act*, R.S.C. 1985, c. B-3, s. 95. 4. An organization through which trades in options or standardized futures are cleared or settled. *Personal Property Securities acts.*

CLEARING HOUSE OPTION. An option, other than an option on futures, issued by a clearing house to its participants. *Personal Property Securities acts.*

CLEARING MEMBER. A person engaged in the business of effecting securities transactions who uses a clearing house as intermediary. *Bankruptcy and Insolvency Act*, R.S.C. 1985, c. B-3, s. 95.

CLEARING SYSTEM. A means by which transactions in securities and commodity contracts are settled between members of the system.

CLEARLY DESCRIPTIVE. In the context of trade marks, material to the composition of the goods or products and referring to an intrinsic quality or characteristic of the product.

CLEAR TITLE. 1. Good title; title free from encumbrances. 2. Title is "clear" of an encumbrance once the registrar has endorsed a note of cancellation on the registry. It may be clear when the encumbrancer has been paid off but has not delivered the discharge or when application is made to register the discharge. *Norfolk v. Aikens* (1989), 64 D.L.R. (4th) 1 (B.C.C.A.).

CLERICAL. *adj.* Relating to the office of clerk.

CLERICAL ERROR. 1. "... In Re Robert Sist Dev. Corpn. Ltd. (1977), 17 O.R. (2d) 305 ... (S.C.), Henry J. dealt with the meaning of 'clerical error' and adopted the definition given in [John Burke, ed.] Jowitt's Dictionary of English Law, 2nd ed. ([London: Sweet and Maxwell,] 1977), that a 'clerical error' is 'an error in a document which can only be explained by considering it to be a slip or mistake of the party preparing or copying it'. We believe that this furnishes an adequate definition of 'clerical error'... ." *Ovens, Re* (1979), 32 C.B.R. (N.S.) 42 at 47, 26 O.R. (2d) 468, 1 P.P.S.A.C. 131, 8 B.L.R. 186, 103 D.L.R. (3d) 352 (C.A.), the court per Houlden J.A. 2. "[In the Patent Act, R.S.C. 1970, c. P-4, s. 8] ... errors caused by a clerk or stenographer." *Novopharm Ltd. v. Upjohn Co.* (1983), (*sub nom. Upjohn Co. v. Pat. Commr.*) 74 C.P.R. (2d) 228 at 232 (Fed. T.D.), Muldoon J.

CLERK. *n.* 1. The officer of a court who accepts filings, issues process, keeps records. 2. An officer of a municipality. 3. An officer of the Legislative Assembly or House of Commons. 4. A research assistant to a judge or judges. See ARTICLED ~; COURT ~; LAW ~ AND PARLIAMENTARY COUNSEL.

CLERK ASSISTANT. A person appointed by Letters Patent under the Great Seal to assist the Clerk of the House. A. Fraser, W.A. Dawson & J. Holtby, eds., *Beauchesne's Rules and Forms of the House of Commons of Canada*, 6th ed. (Toronto: Carswell, 1989) at 60.

CLERK OF THE COURT. The officer of a court who accepts filings, issues process, keeps records.

CLERK OF THE HOUSE OF COMMONS. The chief procedural advisor to the House, its members and the Speaker, who provides procedural services, directs and controls all officers and clerks employed by the House. A. Fraser, W.A. Dawson, & J. Holtby, eds., *Beauchesne's Rules and Forms of the House of Commons of Canada*, 6th ed. (Toronto: Carswell, 1989) at 59-60.

CLERK OF THE PEACE. The person who assists justices of the peace to draw indictments, enter judgments, issue process and administer the courts.

CLERK OF THE QUEEN'S PRIVY COUNCIL. Clerk of the Privy Council and Secretary to the Cabinet. *Interpretation Act*, R.S.C. 1985, c. I-21, s. 35.

CLIC LETTER. *abbr.* CLIC's Legal Materials Letter (Bulletin d'information juridique du CCDJ).

CLIENT. *n.* 1. A person who receives services. 2. A person or body of persons on whose behalf a lawyer receives money for services. See SOLICITOR-AND—COSTS; SOLICITOR AND HIS OWN ~ COSTS; SOLICITOR-~ PRIVILEGE.

CLIMATE FUND. A phrase which may be used to refer to the Canada Emission Reduction Incentives Agency. *Canada Emission Reduction Incentives Agency Act*, S.C. 2005, c. 30, s. 4(2).

CLINIC. *n.* 1. A student organization offering free legal assistance. 2. An independent community organization structured as a corporation without share capital that provides legal aid services to the community it serves on a basis other than fee for service. *Legal Aid Services Act, 1998*, S.O. 1998, c. 26, s. 2. See LEGAL ~.

CLINIC LAW. The areas of law which particularly affect low-income individuals or disadvantaged communities, including legal matters related to, (a) housing and shelter, income maintenance, social assistance and other similar government programs, and (b) human rights, health, employment and education. *Legal Aid Services Act, 1998*, S.O. 1998, c. 26, s. 2.

CLIPPING. *n.* Impairing, diminishing or lightening a current gold or silver coin with intent that it should pass for a current gold or silver coin. *Criminal Code*, R.S.C. 1985, c. C-46, s. 455.

C.L.L. *abbr.* Canadian Current Law: Canadian Legal Literature, 1991-.

C.L.L.C. *abbr.* Canadian Labour Law Cases, 1944-.

C.L.L.R. *abbr.* Canadian Labour Law Reports, 1982-.

CLOG ON EQUITY OF REDEMPTION. 1. A provision, repugnant to either a contractual or an equitable right to redeem, which is void. W.B. Rayner & R.H. McLaren, *Falconbridge on Mortgages*, 4th ed. (Toronto: Canada Law Book, 1977) at 54. 2. A device which prevents a mortgagor from getting property back after the obligations under the mortgage are discharged. D.J. Donahue & P.D. Quinn, *Real Estate Practice in Ontario*, 4th ed. (Toronto: Butterworths, 1990) at 232-233.

CLONE. See HUMAN ~.

CLOSE. *n.* 1. Conclusion. 2. An area of land enclosed by a fence or other boundary markings. 3. An interest in land. See BREACH OF ~.

CLOSE COMPANY. A company in which shares are held by one shareholder or a very small number of shareholders.

CLOSE CORPORATION. A corporation in which shares are held by one shareholder or a very small number of shareholders.

CLOSED COMPANY. A company whose constituting documents provide for restrictions on the free transfer of shares, prohibit any distribution of securities to the public and limit the number of its shareholders to 50, exclusive of present or former employees of the company or of a subsidiary.

CLOSED MIND TEST. Because the Commission must make policy decisions and its members are expected to have experience and views on the matters to which the policies relate, the Commission is not an adjudicative body and the appropriate test for a reasonable apprehension of bias is the "closed mind" test. The question is whether it can be shown that a member of the Commission had prejudged the matter to the extent that representations to the contrary would be futile. *Doctors Hospital v. Ontario (Health Services Restructuring Commission)*, 1997 CarswellOnt 3405, 103 O.A.C. 183, 3 Admin. L.R (3d) 116 (Div. Ct.).

CLOSED SEASON. With respect to a species, the period during which hunting, trapping or fishing for that species is not permitted. *Fish and Wildlife Conservation Act, 1997*, S.O. 1997, c. 41, s. 1.

CLOSED SHOP. "... [O]ne in which membership in a particular union is a condition of employment. Its effect is not only to exclude non-union labour from jobs but also prevents the employer from hiring or retaining in his employment any one but members of a particular union." *B.S.O.I.W., Local No. 97 v. Canadian Ironworkers Union No. 1* (1970), 5 C.L.L.C. 236 at 252, 73 W.W.R. 172, 13 D.L.R. (3d) 559 (B.C. C.A.), Nemetz J.A. (dissenting).

CLOSED SHOP CONTRACT. "... [T]he effect of a 'closed shop' provision is to preclude a person from obtaining employment unless he is a member of the union certified as the bargaining agent for the bargaining unit." *Bhindi v. British Columbia Projectionists, Local 340, International Alliance of Picture Machine Operators of United States & Canada* (1986),

24 C.R.R. 302 at 321, 4 B.C.L.R. (2d) 145, [1986] 5 W.W.R. 303, 86 C.L.L.C. 14,052, 29 D.L.R. (4th) 47 (C.A.), Anderson J.A. (dissenting).

CLOSELY HELD CORPORATION. A private corporation the shares of which are not listed on a stock exchange.

CLOSE OF PLEADINGS. Pleadings end in a proceeding when the last permitted pleading is delivered and filed or the time for doing so has expired.

CLOSE SUBSTITUTE. Within the meaning of the Competition Act, said of products if buyers are willing to switch from one product to another in response to a relative change in price. *Canada (Director of Investigation & Research) v. Southam Inc.* (1995), 127 D.L.R. (4th) 263 (Fed. C.A.).

CLOSE THE DEAL. To complete a transaction by exchanging documents and funds.

CLOSING ADDRESS. A statement made by counsel at conclusion of a trial before a jury.

CLOSING ARGUMENT. A statement made by counsel at conclusion of a trial before a judge.

CLOSING A TRANSACTION. A meeting between the lawyers or agents representing the parties to complete the transaction by exchanging documents and funds.

CLOSURE. *n.* A procedure to conclude debate to force the House of Commons to decide a subject. A. Fraser, G.A. Birch & W.A. Dawson, eds., *Beauchesne's Rules and Forms of the House of Commons of Canada*, 5th ed. (Toronto: Carswell, 1978) at 117. See FORE~.

C.L.P. *abbr.* Décisions de la Commission des lésions professionelles, 1998-.

C.L.R. *abbr.* Construction Law Reports, 1983-1992.

C.L.R.B. *abbr.* Canada Labour Relations Board.

C.L.R.B.D. abbr. Canada Labour Relatons Board Reports, 1974-1982.

C.L.R.B.R. (N.S.). *abbr.* Canadian Labour Relations Board Reports (New Series), 1983-1989.

C.L.R.B.R. (2D). abbr. Canadian Labour Relations Board Reports (Second Series), 1989-.

C.L.R. (2D). *abbr.* Construction Law Reports (Second Series), 1992-2000.

C.L.R. (3D). *abbr.* Construction Law Reports (Third Series), 2000-.

C.L.S. *abbr.* Canada Labour Service.

C.L.T. *abbr.* Canadian Law Times, 1881-1922.

C.L.T. (OCC. N.). *abbr.* Canadian Law Times, Occasional Notes.

CLUB. *n.* 1. "Clubs are associations of a peculiar nature. They are societies the members of which are perpetually changing. They are not partnerships; they are not associations for gain; and the feature which distinguishes them from other societies is that no member as such becomes liable to pay to the funds of the society or to any one else any money beyond the subscriptions required by the rules of the club to be paid so long as he remains a member... ." *Taylor v. Peoples' Loan & Savings Corp.* (1928), 62 O.L.R. 564 at 568-69, [1928] 4 D.L.R. 598 (H.C.), Raney J. 2. An association of individuals for purposes of mutual entertainment and convenience. *The Liquor Control Act*, R.S.M. 1988, c. L160, s. 1, part. 3. A social, sporting, community, benevolent or fraternal order or society or any branch of it incorporated by an Act of Nunavut or under an Act of Canada, a province or another territory. *Liquor Act (Nunavut)*, R.S.N.W.T. 1988, c. L-9, s. 1. See HEALTH ~; PRICE ~; SERVICE ~.

CLUB MEMBER. A person who, whether as a charter member or admitted in accordance with the by-laws or rules of a club, approved by the commission, has become a member thereof, who maintains membership by the payment of regular periodic dues in the manner provided by the rules or by-laws, and whose name and address is entered on the list of members supplied to the commission at the time of the application for a private club licence under this Act, or if admitted thereafter, forthwith after admission. *The Liquor Control Act*, R.S.M. 1988, c. L160, s. 1.

CLUE FACT. A fact which increases the probability that a subordinate fact will be discovered and thus that an ultimate fact, and the crime, will be proved. *R. v. S. (R.J.)* (1995), 121 D.L.R. (4th) 589 (S.C.C.).

CLUSTERING. See TRIBUNAL ~.

C. MAG. *abbr.* Cour de magistrat.

C.M.A.R. *abbr.* Canadian Court Martial Appeal Reports, 1957-.

CMHC. *abbr.* 1. Canada Mortgage and Housing Corporation. 2. Central Mortgage and Housing Corporation.

C.M.M. *abbr.* Cour municipale de Montréal.

CMND. *abbr.* Command papers.

C.M.P.R. *abbr.* Canadian Mortgage Practice Reports.

C.M.Q. *abbr.* Cour municipale de Québec.

CMRRA. *abbr.* The Canadian Musical Reproduction Rights Agency.

C. MUN. *abbr.* Cour municipale.

C.N.L.C. *abbr.* 1. Canadian Native Law Cases, 1763-1978. 2. Commission nationale de libérations conditionnelles.

C.N.L.R. *abbr.* Canadian Native Law Reporter, 1979-.

CO. *abbr.* Company.

C/O. *symbol.* In care of. *McLennan, Re* [1940] 1 W.W.R. 465 at 472 (Sask. Surr. Ct.), Bryant Surr. Ct. J.

COACH. See JOB ~.

CO-ADVENTURE. *n.* A person is engaged in a co-adventure if despite the legal character of the person's association with the business, he retains a form of

interest in the business along with other persons. *Canada (Attorney General) v. Tremblay* (1986), 91 N.R. 102 (Fed. C.A.).

COAL. See LOW HEAT VALUE ~.

COAST. *n.* The edge of land bordered by a sea.

COASTAL WATERS OF CANADA. 1. Includes all of Queen Charlotte Sound, all the Strait of Georgia and the Canadian waters of the Strait of Juan de Fuca. *Criminal Code*, R.S.C. 1985, c. C-46, s. 339(6). 2. All Canadian fisheries waters not within the geographical limits of any province. *Fisheries Act*, R.S.C. 1985, c. F-14, s. 47.

COAST GUARD. Provides services for the safe, economical and efficient movement of ships in Canadian waters through the provision of (i) aids to navigation systems and services, (ii) marine communications and traffic management services, (iii) ice breaking and ice management services, and (iv) channel maintenance; provides the marine component of the federal search and rescue program; provides for marine pollution response; and provides support of departments, boards and agencies of the Government of Canada through the provision of ships, aircraft and other marine services. *Oceans Act*, S.C. 1996, c. 31, s. 41.

COC. *abbr.* The Canadian Olympic Committee, a corporation incorporated under Part II of The Companies Act, 1934, chapter 33 of the Statutes of Canada, 1934. *Olympic and Paralympic Marks Act*, S.C. 2007, c. 25, s. 2.

CO. CT. *abbr.* County Court.

C.O.D. *abbr.* See CASH ON DELIVERY.

CODE. *n.* 1. A collection or system of laws, i.e. Code Napoléon or Civil Code. 2. A consolidation of existing statute and common law, i.e. Criminal Code or Labour Code. 3. A standard or body or rules which governs the practice of a profession, i.e. Code of Ethics or Code of Practice. 4. Guidelines for a process or use of equipment to ensure safety, efficiency or a level of quality established and published by a competent authority, i.e. building code, safety code. 5. A set of letters, numbers or symbols used to identify something or someone. See BAR ~; BUILDING ~; BUILDING CONSTRUCTION ~; CIVIL ~; CRIMINAL ~; LAND ~; SOURCE ~.

CODE CIVIL. The civil law of Quebec.

CODE OF SERVICE DISCIPLINE. The provisions of part of the National Defence Act which sets out offences which may be committed by a member of the forces and the procedures involved in charging and prosecuting a member charged with an offence under the code.

CODICIL. *n.* An addition or change made to a will by a testator.

CODIFICATION. *n.* The collection of all the principles of any system or subject of law into one body of statutes or single statute.

CODIFYING STATUTE. A single statute which states all the law on a particular subject by combining pre-existing statutory provisions with common law rules relating to the subject. The prime example in Canada is the Criminal Code.

COERCION. *n.* 1. "... [I]ncludes not only such blatant forms of compulsion as direct commands to act or refrain from acting on pain of sanction, coercion includes indirect forms of control which determine or limit alternative courses of conduct available to others." *R. v. Big M Drug Mart Ltd.* (1985), 13 C.R.R. 64 at 97-8 (S.C.C.), Dickson C.J.C. 2. Compelling by force or threats. 3. A threat of serious consequences should a contract not be executed. Does not arise out of an existing state of affairs. *Permaform Plastics Ltd. v. London & Midland General Insurance Co.* [1996] 7 W.W.R. 457 (Man. C.A.). See SEXUAL ~.

COGENT. *adj.* [T]he word "cogent" is not synonymous with "admissible" or "relevant." ... "Cogency" . . . relates to "force," "power" and "incisiveness." "Cogent" evidence is desirable, but is not essential to proof. *Terracon Development Ltd. v. Winnipeg (City) Assessor*, 2002 MBCA 117, 218 D.L.R. (4th) 515, 166 Man. R. (2d) 245, 39 M.P.L.R. (3d) 67.

COGNISANCE. *n.* 1. Knowledge. 2. To take cognisance means to take judicial notice.

COGNOVIT ACTIONEM. [L. one has admitted the action] An instrument signed by a defendant in an action admitting that the plaintiff's demand is just and authorizing the signing of judgment against the defendant.

COHABIT. *v.* 1. To live together in a conjugal relationship, whether within or outside marriage. 2. To live together in a family relationship. *Child and Family Services and Family Relations Act*, S.N.B. 1980, c. F-2.2, s. 1.

COHABITATION. *n.* Dwelling or living together as spouses.

COHABITATION AGREEMENT. Two persons who are cohabiting or intend to cohabit and who are not married to each other may enter into an agreement in which they agree on their respective rights and obligations during cohabitation, or on ceasing to cohabit or on death, including, (a) ownership in or division of property; (b) support obligations; (c) the right to direct the education and moral training of their children, but not the right to custody of or access to their children; and (d) any other matter in the settlement of their affairs. *Family Law Act*, R.S.O. 1990, c. F.3, s. 53.

CO-HEIR. *n.* One of several people among whom an inheritance is divided.

CO-HEIRESS. *n.* A woman who shared an inheritance equally with another woman.

COHERENCE. See PRESUMPTION OF~.

C.O.H.S.C. *abbr.* Canadian Occupational Health and Safety Cases, 1989-1993.

COIN. *v.* To stamp pieces of metal into a set shape and size and place marks on them under the aegis of a government.

COIN. *n.* A piece of metal stamped with certain marks and put into circulation as money of a certain value by a government. See CIRCULATION ~.

CO-INSURANCE. *n.* The insured bears a portion of any loss in excess of the insurance on it. The insurer is liable only for the portion of the insured property or risk which represents the portion of the property or risk insured.

COLA. *abbr.* Cost-of-living adjustment.

COLA CLAUSE. An agreement to provide employees with an increase in wages tied to an index such as the Consumer Price Index prepared by Statistics Canada.

COLLABORATIVE FAMILY LAW PROCESS. In determining whether B. breached her duty of care, I must consider the context in which the alleged breach occurred. In this case, the parties chose to engage in the CFL process, a process where the parties commit to settlement rather than litigation. It is a process, ... where the role of the lawyers is to develop the process and the role of the parties is to take ownership of the process, gather their own information, and actively and fully participate in assessing the quality of that information. The roles of the clients and lawyers are clearly defined at the beginning of the CFL process. In the CFL process, it is the clients who have the control over the process, the cost and the outcome of the dispute. Moreover, it is the clients who are responsible for making decisions affecting the outcome. The clients are educated and empowered by the lawyers to make decisions affecting the outcome. However, the CFL lawyer still has the fundamental responsibility to provide professional legal advice to their client. CFL lawyers are to encourage the parties not to limit themselves to outcomes dictated by the law. *Webb v. Birkett*, [2009] A.J. No. 502 (Alta. Q.B.).

COLLABORATIVE LAW. The use of non-adversarial methods, mediation techniques, legal advocacy and advice, governed by the notion that cases settle. Practice of law in a manner which avoids litigation if at all possible.

COLLABORATIVE PRACTICE. A relationship among a nurse practitioner, a physician or group of physicians, an employing organization and other health professionals who are relevant to the nurse practitioner's practice, that enables the health-care providers in this relationship to work together to use their separate and shared knowledge and skills to provide optimum client-centered care in accordance with standards of practice for nurse practitioners and the guidelines for collaborative practice teams and employers of nurse practitioners approved by the College. *Registered Nurses Act*, S.N.S. 2006, c. 21, s. 2.

COLLATERAL. *n.* 1. Property used to secure the payment of a debt or performance of an obligation. 2. A blood relation who is neither a descendant nor an ancestor. R. Megarry & H.W.R. Wade, *The Law of Real Property*, 5th ed. (London: Stevens, 1984) at cxxiii.

COLLATERAL. *adj.* "... '[P]arallel' or 'additional' or 'side by side with'." *Manitoba Development Corp.*

v. Berkowits (1979), 9 R.P.R. 310 at 313, [1979] 5 W.W.R. 138, 101 D.L.R. (3d) 421 (Man. C.A.), the court per O'Sullivan J.A. See CONTRACT ~.

COLLATERAL ATTACK. An attack made in proceedings other than those whose specific object is the reversal, variation, or nullification of the order or judgment. See RULE AGAINST ~.

COLLATERAL ATTACK DOCTRINE. "... [A] court order may not be attacked collaterally – and a collateral attack may be described as an attack made in proceedings other than those whose specific object is the reversal, variation, or nullification of the order or judgment." *R. v. Wilson*, [1983] 2 S.C.R. 595 at 599, [1984] 1 W.W.R. 481, 37 C.R. (3d) 97, 26 Man. R. (2d) 194, 9 C.C.C. (3d) 97, 4 D.L.R. (4th) 577, 51 N.R. 321, McIntyre J. (Laskin C.J.C. and Estey J. concurring).

COLLATERAL BENEFITS. See DOCTRINE OF ~.

COLLATERAL CONTRACT. 1. "... [A]n oral agreement ancillary to a written agreement... ." *Ahone v. Holloway* (1988), 30 B.C.L.R. (2d) 368 at 373 (C.A.), the court per McLachlin J.A. 2. A statement, on the strength of which a person enters into a contract, may give rise to an entirely separate contract "collateral" to the main contract made between the maker of the statement and the person to whom the statement was made.

COLLATERAL ESTOPPEL. Is a subcategory of "res judicata" that has been accepted in the United States courts but not, so far, in Canada. It differs from "issue estoppel" in that the condition of identity of parties applies only to the party who is attempting to relitigate a question of fact, not to the party who is asserting the plea. *Connaught Laboratories Ltd. v. Medeva Pharma Ltd.*, 1999 CarswellNat 2809, 4 C.P.R. (4th) 508, 179 F.T.R. 200 (T.D.), Sharlow J.

COLLATERAL FACT RULE. Subject to certain exceptions, a party is not entitled to introduce extrinsic evidence to contradict the testimony of an adversary's witness unless that extrinsic evidence is relevant to some issue in the case other than merely to contradict the case. *R. v. Pargelen* (1996), 31 O.R. (3d) 504 (C.A.).

COLLATERAL QUESTION. 1. [T]he Supreme Court has repeatedly reaffirmed the essential invalidity of the old "collateral or preliminary question" doctrine. *Tyndall v. Sheeters, Deckers & Cladders Section of the Sheet Metal Workers' International Association, Local 511*, 1998 CanLII 6762 (Man. C.A.) 2. Another error which has sometimes been regarded as jurisdictional is one relating to a matter which is preliminary or collateral, but supposedly essential to the exercise of the jurisdiction as a kind of condition thereof. This however is a fleeting and vague concept against which the courts were warned by this court . . . once the initial jurisdiction of the administrative body holding the hearing has been established at the outset. *Syndicat des employés de production du Québec v. C.L.R.B.*, 1984 CanLII 26, [1984] 2 S.C.R. 412 at 421.

COLLATERAL RELATIVE. A person whose relationship to a second person is not in the direct line of descent from the second person, i.e. a brother's child.

COLLATERAL SECURITY. "... [A]ny property which is assigned or pledged to secure the performance of an obligation and as additional thereto, and which upon the performance of the obligation is to be surrendered or discharged: ..." *Royal Bank of Canada v. Slack* (1958), 11 D.L.R. (2d) 737 at 746 (Ont. C.A.), Schroeder J.A., cited in *MacLaren, Re* (1978), 88 D.L.R. (3d) 222 at 231, 30 N.S.R. (2d) 694, 49 A.P.R. 694, 4 B.L.R. 191, 28 C.B.R. (N.S.) 56 (S.C.), Cowan C.J.T.D.

COLLATERAL TERM. Outside or distinct from the terms of the main contract.

COLLATION. *n.* Comparing a copy with its original to ensure its accuracy and completeness.

COLLECT. *v.* To enforce a money judgment by execution.

COLLECTION. *n.* 1. A bank's handling of commercial and financial documents according to instructions received. 2. The process of obtaining payment of debts owing. See TAX ~ AGREEMENT.

COLLECTION AGENCY. A person, other than a collector, who carries on the business of collecting debts for other persons in consideration of the payment of a commission upon the amount collected or otherwise, whether the head office of such collection agency is within or without the Province. *Collection Agencies Act*, R.S.N.B. 1973, c. C-8, s. 1.

COLLECTION OFFICER. A person employed under The Civil Service Act and designated by the Minister of Justice to enforce payment of forfeited recognizance orders and fines. *The Garnishment Act*, R.S.M. 1987, c. G20, s. 14.4.

COLLECTIVE. See CANADIAN PRIVATE COPYING ~.

COLLECTIVE AGREEMENT. An agreement in writing between an employer or an employer's organization acting on behalf of employers, and a bargaining agent of employees acting on behalf of a unit of employees containing provisions respecting terms and conditions of employment and related matters. More than a private arrangement, it provides the foundation for labour relations and exists to provide and maintain peace in labour relations.

COLLECTIVE BARGAINING. 1. [A] process of negotiation between an employer and a labour union with the object of concluding an agreement regulating the relationship between both the employer and its employees and the employer and the union. *Health Services & Support-Facilities Subsector Bargaining Assn. v. British Columbia*, 2004 BCCA 77. 2. Negotiating with a view to the conclusion of a collective agreement or the renewal or revision thereof. The implementation of freedom of association in the workplace. See BARGAIN COLLECTIVELY; BARGAINING COLLECTIVELY.

COLLECTIVE BARGAINING AGREEMENT. 1. An agreement in writing between an employer or an employer's organization acting on behalf of an employer, on the one hand, and a bargaining agent of employees acting on behalf of the employees, on the other hand, containing terms or conditions of employment of employees. 2. An agreement between an employer and a trade union setting forth terms and conditions of employment.

COLLECTIVE BARGAINING STRIKE. A strike directed at the collective bargaining process and taking place when no agreement is in place. Aimed at the workers' employer. *Health Employers Assn. of British Columbia v. H.E.U.*, 2009 CarswellBC 192, 2009 BCCA 39.

COLLECTIVE SOCIETY. A society, association or corporation that carries on the business of collective administration of copyright or of the remuneration right conferred by the Act for the benefit of those who, by assignment, grant of licence, appointment of it as their agent or otherwise, authorize it to act on behalf in relation to that collective administration, and (a) operates a licensing scheme, applicable in relation to a repertoire of works, performer's performances, sound recordings or communication signals of more than one author, performer, sound recording maker or broadcaster, pursuant to which the society, association or corporation sets out classes of uses that it agrees to authorize under this Act, and the royalties and terms and conditions on which it agrees to authorize those classes of uses, or (b) carries on the business of collecting and distributing royalties or levies payable pursuant to this Act. *Copyright Act*, R.S.C. 1985, c. C-42, s. 2.

COLLECTIVE WORK. An encyclopaedia, dictionary, year book or similar work, a newspaper, review, magazine or similar periodical, and any work written in distinct parts by different authors, or in which works or parts of works of different authors are incorporated. *Copyright Act*, R.S.C. 1985, c. C-42, s. 2.

COLLECTOR. *n.* 1. A person authorized or required by or pursuant to a revenue act or by agreement to collect a tax. 2. Every officer of customs and excise who is appointed to collect the duties imposed by this Act in any defined district or excise division. *Excise Act*, R.S.C. 1985, c. E-14, s. 2. 3. A person employed, appointed or authorized by a collection agency to solicit business or collect debts for the agency or to deal with or trace debtors for the agency.

COLLEGE. *n.* 1. A corporation, company, or society having certain privileges, i.e., College of Physicians and Surgeons. 2. A community college. 3. A regional college. 4. A college of applied arts and technology.

COLLEGE OF PHYSICIANS AND SURGEONS. The licensing and governing body of the medical profession in a province.

COLLISION. *n.* 1. "... [I]mplies an impact, the sudden contact of a moving body with an obstruction in its line of motion. Both bodies may be in motion, or one in motion and the other stationary." *Aberdeen Paving Ltd. v. Guildhall Insurance Co.* (1966), 52 M.P.R. 349 at 362, 60 D.L.R. (2d) 45 (N.S. C.A.), Cowan J.A. 2. An action for collision includes an action for damage caused by one or more ships to another ship or ships or to property or persons on board another ship or ships as a result of carrying out or omitting to carry out a manoeuvre, or as a result of non-compliance with law, even though there has been no actual collision. *Federal Courts Act,* R.S.C. 1985, c. F-7, s. 2. See AGONY OF ~.

COLLISION COVERAGE. Coverage for loss or damage caused by the upset of a vehicle or collision of a vehicle with another object, including a person or animal. *Insurance (Vehicle) Act*, R.S.B.C. 1996, c. 231, *Insurance (Vehicle) Regulation*, B.C. Reg. 447/83, s. 147.

COLLOCATION. *n.* In the Quebec Code of Civil Procedure, the division of proceeds of execution among execution creditors.

COLLOQUIUM. *n.* In pleading in a libel or slander action, the plaintiff must show that the statement complained of was "published of and concerning the plaintiff." *S.G. v. J.C.*, (2001), 56 O.R. (3d) 215, 150 O.A.C. 305.

COLLUSION. *n.* 1. Agreement to deceive. *Edison General Electric Co. v. Vancouver & New Westminster Tramway Co.* (1896), 4 B.C.R. 460 at 483 (C.A.), Drake J.A. 2. An agreement or conspiracy to which an applicant for a divorce is either directly or indirectly a party for the purpose of subverting the administration of justice, and includes any agreement, understanding or arrangement to fabricate or suppress evidence or to deceive the court, but does not include an agreement to the extent that it provides for separation between the parties, financial support, division of property or the custody of any child of the marriage. *Divorce Act*, R.S.C. 1985 (2d Supp.), c. 3, s. 11(4). See IN ~.

COLONIAL LAW. In a colony discovered and occupied, the laws of England; in a conquered colony or one ceded to England, its own laws until England changed them.

COLONIAL LAWS VALIDITY ACT, 1865. It was a legal doctrine of the British Empire that imperial laws (that is, enactments of Westminster) applying to a colony were supreme over colonial laws. Section 2 of the Colonial Laws Validity Act 1865, 28 & 29 Vict., c. 63 provides: (2) Any Colonial Law which is or shall be in any respect repugnant to the Provisions of any Act of Parliament extending to the Colony to which such Law may relate, or repugnant to any Order or Regulation made under Authority of such Act of Parliament, or having in the Colony the Force and Effect of such Act, shall be read subject to such Act, Order, or Regulation, and shall, to the Extent of such Repugnancy, but not otherwise, be and remain absolutely void and inoperative. ... The Colonial Laws Validity Act was intended to be a liberating statute, releasing colonial legislatures from subservience to British common law (subject to Privy Council authority) and from subservience to British statute law unless such statute law applied expressly or by necessary implication to the colony. In the evolution of independence of the dominions, it came to be recognized that the United Kingdom should no longer legislate at its own instance for any dominion;

and that the latter should be free to repeal any British legislation that was or would be made applicable to it. Hence, the statement in the preamble and hence ss. 2 and 4 in their application to a dominion. *Re: Resolution to amend the Constitution*, [1981] 1 S.C.R. 753, the majority.

COLONY. *n.* 1. A place settled by people from an older city or country. 2. A number of persons who hold land or any interest therein as communal property, whether as owners, lessees or otherwise, and whether in the name of trustees or as a corporation or otherwise, and includes a number of persons who propose to acquire land to be held in such manner.

COLORE OFFICII. [L.] Colour of office. See DURESS ~.

COLOUR. *n.* Appearance, pretext or pretence, apparent or prima facie. See GANG ~S.

COLOURABILITY.*n.* A doctrine invoked when a statute is addressed to a matter outside jurisdiction though it bears the formal trappings of a matter within the jurisdiction of the enacting legislature. P.W. Hogg, *Constitutional Law of Canada*, 3d ed. (Toronto: Carswell, 1992) at 387.

COLOURABLE. *adj.* In appearance but not in substance what it claims to be.

COLOURABLE IMITATION. A trademark with such similar appearance as another mark that confusion is likely even though it is not a deliberate imitation intended to deceive.

COLOUR OF OFFICE. Pretense of authority to carry out an act for which the actor has no authority.

COLOUR OF RIGHT. 1. The essence of the defence is that the accused genuinely believes that he or she has a lawful claim to property. A belief in a moral right to property is not sufficient to ground the defence of colour of right. *R. v. Gamey* (1993), 80 C.C.C. (3d) 117 (Man. C.A.) 2. "... [G]enerally, although not exclusively, refers to a situation where there is an assertion of a proprietary or possessory right to the thing which is the subject-matter of the alleged theft... . The term ... is also used to denote an honest belief in a state of facts which, if it actually existed would at law justify or excuse the act done; ..." *R. v. DeMarco* (1973), 13 C.C.C. (2d) 369 at 372, 22 C.R.N.S. 258 (Ont. C.A.), Martin J.A. 3. A colour of right can have its basis in either a mistake of civil law . . . or in a mistake in a state of facts. The mistake in each case must give rise to either an honest belief in a proprietary or possessory right to the thing which is the subject matter of the alleged theft or an honest belief in the state of facts which if it actually existed would at law justify or excuse the act done. *R. v. Dorosh*, 2003 SKCA 134.

COLUMBARIUM. *n.* A structure designed for storing the ashes of dead human bodies or other human remains that have been cremated. *Cemeteries Act*, R.S.A. 2000, c. C-3, s. 1.

COMBINATION. *n.* An association of persons for a particular purpose. Used in reference to trade unions. See BUSINESS ~; TRADE ~.

COMBUSTIBLE LIQUID. A liquid that has a flash point at or above 37.8°C, as determined by using the methods described in the Alberta Fire Code (1997). *Occupational Health and Safety Code, 2006*, Alta. OHS Code, s. 1.

COMIC. See CRIME ~.

COMITY. *n.* 1. For my part, I much prefer the more complete formulation of the idea of comity adopted by the Supreme Court of the United States in Hilton v. Guyot, 159 U.S. 113 ... (1895) at p. 163-4 in a passage cited by Estey J. in Spencer v. R., [1985] 2 S.C.R. 278 at p. 283 ... as follows: ' "Comity" in the legal sense, is neither a matter of absolute obligation, on the one hand, nor of mere courtesy and good will, upon the other. But it is the recognition which one nation allows within its territory to the legislative, executive or judicial acts of another nation, having due regard both to international duty and convenience, and to the rights of its own citizens or of other persons who are under the protection of its laws.' " *Morguard Investments Ltd. v. De Savoye* (1990), 46 C.P.C. (2d) 1 at 17, 19, 15 R.P.R. (2d) 1, 16, 52 B.C.L.R. (2d) 160, [1991] 2 W.W.R. 217, 76 D.L.R. (4th) 256, 122 N.R. 81, [1990] 3 S.C.R. 1077, the court per La Forest J. 2. The name given to the general principle that encourages the recognition in one country of the judicial acts of another. Its basis is not simply respect for other nations, but convenience and necessity, recognizing the need to facilitate interjurisdictional transactions. The Supreme Court of Canada has said, in the context of a case involving the recognition in one province of Canada of a decision of the Courts of another province, that the content of comity must be adjusted in light of a changing world order. *Connaught Laboratories Ltd. v. Medeva Pharma Ltd.*, 1999 CarswellNat 2809, 4 C.P.R. (4th) 508, 179 F.T.R. 200 (T.D.), Sharlow J. See JUDICIAL ~.

COMITY OF NATIONS. A code of behaviour towards one another which nations observe from mutual convenience or courtesy.

COMM. *abbr.* Commission.

COMMAND. See PILOT-IN-~.

COMMANDER. See MILITARY ~.

COMMAND PAPERS. In Britain, papers presented to Parliament at the Crown's command. Include the reports of Royal Commissions.

COMMENCEMENT. *n.* 1. When used with reference to an enactment, means the time at which the enactment comes into force. 2. In the context of a limitation period, there is no substantive difference in meaning between "commencement" and "begin to run". *Howe Sound School District No. 48 v. Killick Metz Bowen Rose Architects & Planners Inc.*, 2008 BCCA 195, Mackenzie J.A. (Lowry and Bauman JJ.A. concurring).

COMMENT. See FAIR ~.

COMMERCE. *n.* Trade; exchange of goods or property. See CHAMBER OF ~; TRADE AND ~.

COMMERCIAL. *adj.* 1. Connected with trade and commerce in general. 2. Of real property, principally used for the sale of goods or services.

COMMERCIAL ARBITRATION. An adjudicative process, either voluntary or ad hoc, involving the application and interpretation of agreements. Concerning business or trade matters.

COMMERCIAL CEMETERY. A cemetery operated for the purpose of making a profit for the owner. *Cemeteries Act (Revised)*, R.S.O. 1990, c. C.4, s. 1.

COMMERCIAL DISCOVERY. A discovery of petroleum that has been demonstrated to contain reserves that justify the investment of capital and effort to bring the discovery to production. *Petroleum Resources acts.*

COMMERCIAL ENTERPRISE. A sole proprietorship, partnership, co-operative or corporation having for its object the acquisition of gain. *Agriculture Financial Services Act*, R.S.A. 2000, c. A-12, s. 1.

COMMERCIAL LAW. The law of contracts, bankruptcy, intellectual property, corporations and partnerships and any other subjects dealing with rights and relations of persons engaged in commerce or trade.

COMMERCIAL LETTER OF CREDIT. 1. The main purpose of a commercial letter of credit or letter of guarantee is to substitute the credit of a financially sound person for the unknown or doubtful credit standing of a buyer in a sales transaction or, in this case, of a borrower in a mortgage situation. At least three contracts and three parties are involved. There is the contract between the mortgagor and the mortgagee. Also, the mortgagor has contracted with the writer of the letter, the issuing bank, to substitute its credit for the mortgagor's, on stipulated terms. The bank in addition entered into a contract with the mortgagee in the letter of guarantee, stipulating that, if the mortgagee provides the funds to the mortgagor, the issuing bank will repay amounts payable, upon compliance with any conditions set out in the letter. The obligations in each of these contracts are independent of one another. Performance of one contract is not a condition precedent for the performance or enforcement of another. The issuing bank has promised to pay the lender upon compliance with the conditions and must do so, upon compliance, regardless of whether the lender is in breach of a contractual obligation to the borrower. The borrower will have promised to reimburse the issuing bank for payments made to the lender and must do so even if the borrower has claims against the lender arising from the lender's breach of contract. Payment by the borrower to the bank does not preclude a legal action against the lender for breach of the mortgage contract. The notion of autonomy or independence of the letter of credit or guarantee has long been accepted as the very basis of the letter of credit system, permitting both assurance and immediacy of payment. The principle of autonomy of the letter of credit or guarantee is not absolute. Fraud provides one exception to the rule. The fraud exception applies so long as the fraud has been brought to the knowledge of the issuing bank before the bank has paid under the letter of credit, whether or not it was brought to the knowledge of the bank before the demand for payment was made. *Bank of Nova Scotia v. Regatta Plaza Ltd.*, 1998 CanLII 13322 (NL S.C.T.D.). 2. A commercial letter of credit is one traditionally used as a payment mechanism in the international sale of goods. *Morguard Trust Co. v. Royal Bank*, (1988), 88 A.R. 351, [1988] 5 W.W.R. 415, 60 Alta. L.R. (2d) 99. 3. The whole theory of a commercial letter of credit is that when the seller parts with the documents of title to the goods he will receive in exchange some form of irrevocable commitment of the issuing bank. *Michael Doyle & Associates Ltd. v. Bank of Montreal*, (1984), 11 D.L.R. (4th) 496, 55 B.C.L.R. 196. (C.A.).

COMMERCIALLY AVAILABLE. In relation to a work or other subject-matter, (a) available on the Canadian market within a reasonable time and for a reasonable price and may be located with reasonable effort, or (b) for which a licence to reproduce, perform in public or communicate to the public by telecommunication is available from a collective society within a reasonable time and for a reasonable price and may be located with reasonable effort. *Copyright Act*, R.S.C. 1985, c. C-42, s. 2.

COMMERCIAL PAPER. A bill of exchange, cheque, promissory note, negotiable instrument, conditional sale agreement, lien note, hire purchase agreement, chattel mortgage, bill of lading, bill of sale, warehouse receipt, guarantee, instrument of assignment, things in action and, any document of title that passes ownership or possession and on which credit can be raised. *Interpretation Act*, R.S.B.C. 1996, c. 238, s. 29.

COMMERCIAL PROPERTY. All property except residential property and resource property.

COMMERCIAL REALTY. Real property owned by the Crown or any person, used for or occupied by any industry, trade, business, profession, vocation or government business. *Real Property Assessment Act*, R.S.P.E.I. 1988, c. R-4, s. 1, part.

COMMERCIAL SPEECH. "[In considering s. 2(b) of the Charter] ... whatever else may be subsumed within the rubric 'commercial speech', (a) speech which does no more than propose a commercial transaction; (b) expression related solely to the economic interests of the speaker and audience, and (c) speech which advertises a product or service for profit or a business purpose may fairly be regarded as included ..." *R. v. Smith* (1988), 44 C.C.C. (3d) 385 at 424 (Ont. H.C.), Watt J. See FREEDOM OF EXPRESSION; HATRED.

COMMERCIAL TIME. Any period of two minutes or less during which a broadcaster normally presents commercial messages, public service announcements or station or network identification. *Canada Elections Act*, S.C. 2000, c. 9, s. 344.

COMMERCIAL TREATY. An international treaty concerning financial or economic relations.

COMMERCIAL UNIT. Any building or other structure or part thereof that is used or occupied, or that is intended, arranged or designed to be used or occupied, for the manufacture, sale, resale, processing, reprocessing, displaying, storing, handling, garaging or distribution of personal property or any space, in any such building, structure or part thereof, that is used or occupied, or that is intended, arranged or designed to be used or occupied, as a separate business, professional unit or office. *The Saskatchewan Human Rights Code*, S.S. 1979, c. S-24.1, s. 2.

COMMERCIAL USE. 1. A use in connection with a trade, business, profession, manufacture or other venture for profit. 2. Any use other than for residential or agricultural purposes.

COMMERCIAL VEHICLE. 1. A motor vehicle designed or adapted for the carrying of freight, goods, wares or merchandise. 2. A motor vehicle or trailer operated on a highway for the transportation of livestock or livestock products for gain or compensation, or by or on behalf of a person dealing in livestock or livestock products.

COMMINGLE. *v.* 1. To mass together. 2. Of funds, to mix into one larger fund.

COMMISSION. *n.* 1. The authority or order to act. 2. Remuneration paid to an agent or employee based on price. 3... [I]n the section s. 207(3) of the Criminal Code R.S.C. 1927, c. 36] is not restricted to the actual instantaneous act constituting the crime but includes the preparations for same and all factors which naturally arise in connection with such crime." *R. v. Roher* (1953), 10 W.W.R. (N.S.) 309 at 312, 17 C.R. 307, 61 Man. R. 311, 107 C.C.C. 103 (C.A.), McPherson C.J.M. (Coyne J.A. concurring). 4. An authority given to a person or persons to administer a program or statute, manage a fund or a public utility, investigate a matter or perform some other public function. 5. The name of a body which carries out the functions listed in definition #4. 6. The Governor in Council may, whenever the Governor in Council deems it expedient, cause inquiry to be made into and concerning any matter connected with the good government of Canada or the conduct of any part of the public business thereof. Where an inquiry is not regulated by any special law, the Governor in Council may, by a commission, appoint persons as commissioners by whom the inquiry shall be conducted. Provincial governments have similar powers under similar legislation. *Inquiries Act*, R.S.C. 1985, c. I-11, s. 2 and 3. See CANADA EMPLOYMENT INSURANCE ~; CANADIAN GRAIN ~; CANADIAN HUMAN RIGHTS ~; CANADIAN RADIO-TELEVISION AND TELECOMMUNICATIONS ~; DEL CREDERE ~; FEDERAL BOARD, ~ OR OTHER TRIBUNAL; LAW ~; MILITARY POLICE COMPLAINTS ~; MURDER IN ~ OF OFFENCES; NATIONAL CAPITAL ~; ROGATORY ~; ROYAL CANADIAN MOUNTED POLICE PUBLIC COMPLAINTS ~; ROYAL ~; SECRET ~; STATUTE REVISION ~.

COMMISSIONER. *n.* 1. A person authorized by letters patent, statute or other lawful warrant to examine any matters or execute a public office. 2. A member of a commission. 3. A person authorized to take the evidence of another person. 4. The Commissioner of the Royal Canadian Mounted Police. *Criminal Code*, R.S.C. 1985, c. C-46, s. 2. 5. The Commissioner of Revenue appointed under section 25 of the Canada Revenue Agency Act. 6. The Commissioner of the Northwest Territories. *Northwest Territories Act*, R.S.C. 1985, c. N-27, s. 2. 7. A Commissioner of Yukon shall be appointed by order of the Governor in Council. *Yukon Act, 2002*, S.C. 2002, c. 7, s. 4. 8. The Commissioner of Nunavut. *Nunavut Act*, S.C. 1993, c. 28, s. 5. 8. The Commissioner of one of the territories is the chief executive officer of the territory. The Commissioner acts under the instructions of the Governor in Council or the Minister. *Northwest Territories Act*, R.S.C. 1985, c. N-27, s. 3 and 5; *Nunavut Act*, S.C. 1993, c. 28, s. 5 and 6; *Yukon Act, 2002*, S.C. 2002, c. 7, s. 4. See INFORMATION ~ OF CANADA; PUBLIC SECTOR INTERGRITY ~.

COMMISSIONER FOR TAKING AFFIDAVITS. One authorized to administer affirmations or oaths. A lawyer may be a commissioner for taking affidavits because of his status as a member of the provincial law society. The same may be true of certain officers of public bodies. Others have to apply to the provincial government for the appointment as a commissioner.

COMMISSIONER IN COUNCIL. The Commissioner of the Northwest Territories or Yukon acting by and with the advice and consent of the Council. The Commissioner acting by and with the advice and consent of the Council. The council consists of elected members representing the electoral districts in the territory. The Commissioner is chief executive officer of the Territory. The Commissioner administers the territory under the instructions of the Governor in Council or the Minister. The members of council are elected to represent electoral districts in the territory. In the Yukon, continued as the Legislature of Yukon, consisting of the Commissioner and the Legislative Assembly by the *Northwest Territories Act*, R.S.C. 1985, c. N-27, s. 2 and the *Yukon Act, 2002*, S.C. 2002, c. 7.

COMMISSIONER OF COMPETITION. Appointed under the Competition Act and responsible for the administration and enforcement of the Competition Act, the administration of the Consumer Packaging and Labelling Act, the enforcement of the Consumer Packaging and Labelling Act except as it relates to food, as that term is defined in section 2 of the Food and Drugs Act; and the administration and enforcement of the Precious Metals Marking Act and the Textile Labelling Act. Also has duties under the Canada Transportation Act.

COMMISSIONER OF LOBBYING. Appointed by the Governor in Council under the Lobbying Act, R.S.C. 1985, c. 44 (4th Supp.). Lobbyists are required to register with the Commissioner who maintains a registry of their returns and other documents. The Commissioner may conduct investigations. The Commissioner's duties and functions include developing and implementing educational programs to foster public awareness of the requirements of this Act, particularly on the part of lobbyists, their clients and public office holders.

COMMISSIONER OF OFFICIAL LANGUAGES. The federal official empowered to see that both Canada's official languages, French and English, have equal status, rights and privileges in federal institutions. Appointed under *Official Languages Act*, R.S.C. 1985, c. 31 (4th Supp.), s. 49.

COMMISSION EVIDENCE. A way to preserve or secure evidence when a witness is, because of (i) physical disability caused by illness, or (ii) any other good and sufficient reason, not able to attend a trial at the time it is held. The evidence is given and recorded before a commissioner appointed or recognized by the court. See COMMISSION ROGATORY; LETTERS ROGATORY; PERPETUATE TESTIMONY; ROGATORY LETTERS.

COMMISSION OF INQUIRY. An investigation into an issue or series of events. The findings of the commissioner are findings of fact and statements of opinion by the commissioner at the end of the inquiry. Neither a criminal trial nor a civil action for determination of liability. *Canada (Attorney General) v. Canada (Krever Commission)* [1997] 3 S.C.R. 440, per Cory, J.

COMMISSION OF THE PEACE. A commission by which a number of persons are appointed as justices of the peace.

COMMISSION ROGATORY. A means of collecting evidence for courts of one country through the courts of another country. The evidence is given and recorded before a commissioner in the jurisdiction where the witness is. The commissioner is appointed or recognized by the court in the jurisdiction where the matter is being heard. See COMMISSION EVIDENCE; LETTERS ROGATORY; PERPETUATE TESTIMONY; ROGATORY LETTERS.

COMMIT. *v.* 1. To complete or carry out an act or acts which constitute an offence. 2. To send to prison by reason of lawful authority. 3. To send to trial, i.e. a provincial court judge commits a person to trial before another court. 4. To refer a bill to a committee in which the bill is considered and reported. A. Fraser, W.A. Dawson & J. Holtby, eds., *Beauchesne's Rules and Forms of the House of Commons of Canada*, 6th ed. (Toronto: Carswell, 1989) at 203. 5. To direct that a person be confined in a psychiatric facility.

COMMITMENT. *n.* 1. An agreement or promise to do something. 2. Sending a person to prison. 3. Directing that a person be confined in a psychiatric facility. See LOAN ~; MORTGAGE ~.

COMMITMENT LETTER. A letter prepared by a lender, setting out the conditions and terms upon which the lender is willing to advance money to a borrower. *Cherry Tree Townhomes #2B Inc. v. Canada Life Assurance Co.*, 1991 CanLII 2322 (B.C.C.A.).

COMMITTAL. See WARRANT OF ~.

COMMITTAL ORDER. A court order for the committal of a person to a correctional facility or a federal penitentiary.

COMMITTED. *adj.* "... [An] offence is committed when the offender has completed the unlawful act or

acts ..." *R. v. MacDonald* (1989), 51 C.C.C. (3d) 191 at 192, 18 M.V.R. (2d) 276, 98 A.R. 308 (C.A.), Stevenson, Foisy and Irving JJ.A. See CRIME HAS BEEN ~ IN CANADA.

COMMITTEE. *n.* 1. A group of persons elected or appointed to whom any matter is referred by a legislative body, corporation or other institution. 2. A person appointed by the court to look after a person or the affairs of a person incapable of managing their own affairs because of a mental disorder. See ADVISORY ~; AUDIT ~; CANADIAN BLOOD ~; DISCIPLINE ~; JOINT ~; JUDICIAL ~; LEGISLATIVE ~; PARLIAMENTARY ~; REVISION ~; ROYAL CANADIAN MOUNTED POLICE EXTERNAL REVIEW ~; SELECT ~; SPECIAL ~; STANDING ~; SUB~.

COMMITTEE OF THE WHOLE HOUSE. The membership of the House when a chairman instead of the Speaker presides. This committee may deliberate any questions which, in the opinion of the House, it may more fitly discuss, including provisions of public bills. After second reading bills founded on a supply motion are referred to this committee. A. Fraser, W.A. Dawson & J. Holtby, eds., *Beauchesne's Rules and Forms of the House of Commons of Canada*, 6th ed. (Toronto: Carswell, 1989) at 249.

COMMODITY. *n.* 1. "... [A]nything that is usable for a purpose." *R. v. Robert Simpson Co.* (1964), 43 C.R. 366 at 371, [1964] O.R. 227, [1964] 3 C.C.C. 318 (H.C.), Landreville J. 2. Tangible personal property of every kind. *Ministry of Government Services Act*, R.S.O. 1990, c. M.25, s. 1. 3. (i) Any good, article, service, right or interest of which any unit is, from its nature or by mercantile custom, treated as the equivalent of any other unit; (ii) the currency of any jurisdiction; (iii) any gem, gemstone or other precious stone; (iv) any other good, article, service, right or interest, or a class of any of these, designated as a commodity pursuant to an order made under section 10. *Securities Act*, R.S.A. 2000, c. S-4, s. 1. See CONTINUOUS TRANSMISSION ~; ENERGY~.

COMMODITY BOARD. A local board under the Farm Products Marketing Act or a marketing board under the Milk Act. *Commodity Boards and Marketing Agencies Act*, R.S.O. 1990, c. C.19, s. 1.

COMMODITY CONTRACT. See FORWARD ~.

COMMODITY DERIVATIVE. A futures contract, option, exchange agreement or other derivative transaction entered into for the purpose of managing risks or maximizing benefits associated with the purchase or sale of a commodity or with any other transaction involving a commodity. *Financial Administration Act*, R.S.B.C. 1996, c. 138, s. 79.1.

COMMODITY FUTURES CONTRACT. A contract to make or take delivery of a specified quantity and quality, grade or size of a commodity during a specified future month at a price agreed upon by the parties when the contract is entered into on a commodity futures exchange pursuant to standardized terms and conditions set out in the exchange's internal regulations. *The Commodity Futures Act*, S.M. 1996, c. 73, s. 1. See OPEN ~.

COMMODITY FUTURES EXCHANGE. An organization, whether incorporated or unincorporated, operated for the purpose of providing the facilities necessary for the trading of contracts by a competitive bid and offer or by open auction or order matching process utilizing an electronic trading system. *The Commodity Futures Act*, S.M. 1996, c. 73, s. 1.

COMMODITY FUTURES OPTION. A right acquired for a consideration or an obligation incurred in exchange for a consideration received, to assume a long position or short position in a commodity futures contract at a specified strike price by buying or selling a call or a put that must be exercised within a specified period of time in accordance with the terms and conditions of the option as set out in the internal regulations of the commodity futures exchange upon which the option trades. *The Commodity Futures Act*, S.M. 1996, c. 73, s. 1.

COMMON. *n.* An interest one person can enjoy in the land of another, i.e. common of pasture is the right to pasture cattle on another person's land. See IN ~.

COMMON. *adj.* Usual, ordinary; shared.

COMMON AREAS. 1. Areas controlled by a landlord and used for access to residential premises or for the service or enjoyment of a tenant. 2. In a condominium or strata property, the areas owned by the strata corporation for the benefit of all owners of the property.

COMMON ASSAULT. "[At common law] ... any act in which one person intentionally caused another to apprehend immediate and unlawful violence... . The traditional common law definition always assumed that the absence of consent was a required element of that offence." *R. v. Jobidon* (1991), 7 C.R. (4th) 233 at 245, 66 C.C.C. (3d) 454, 128 N.R. 321, 49 O.A.C. 83, [1991] 2 S.C.R. 714, Gonthier J. (La Forest, L'Heureux-Dubé, Cory and Iacobucci JJ. concurring).

COMMON ASSET. (a) Personal property held by or on behalf of a strata corporation, and (b) land held in the name of or on behalf of a strata corporation, that is (i) not shown on the strata plan, or (ii) shown as a strata lot on the strata plan. *Strata Property Act,* S.B.C. 1998, c. 43, s. 1.

COMMON BAWDY-HOUSE. A place that is (a) kept or occupied, or (b) resorted to by one or more persons for the purpose of prostitution or the practice of acts of indecency. *Criminal Code*, R.S.C. 1985, c. C-46, c. 197.

COMMON BETTING HOUSE. A place that is opened, kept or used for the purpose of (a) enabling, encouraging or assisting persons who resort thereto to bet between themselves or with the keeper, or (b) enabling any person to receive, record, register, transmit or pay bets or to announce the results of betting. *Criminal Code*, R.S.C. 1985, c. C-46, s. 197.

COMMON CARRIER. "... [O]ne who holds himself out to the public to carry the goods of such persons as may choose to employ him." *Engel Canada Inc. v. Bingo's Transport Drivers* (1990), 23 M.V.R.

(2d) 193 at 197 (Ont. H.C.), Austin J. See TELE-COMMUNICATIONS ~.

COMMON ELEMENTS. All the property except the units. *Condominium acts.*

COMMON EXPENSES. The expenses of the performance of the objects and duties of a condominium corporation and any expenses specified as common expenses in a declaration. *Condominium acts.*

COMMON FACILITY. An improvement in the common property that is available for the use of all the owners of a condominium.

COMMON FORM BUSINESS. The business of obtaining probate or administration where there is no contention as to the right thereto, including the passing of probate and administration through court when the contest is terminated, and all business of a non-contentious nature to be taken in a surrogate court in matters of testacy and intestacy not being proceedings in a suit and also the business of lodging caveats against the grant of probate or administration. *Probate or Surrogate Court acts.*

COMMON GAMING HOUSE. A place that is (a) kept for gain to which persons resort for the purpose of playing games, or (b) kept or used for the purpose of playing games (i) in which a bank is kept by one or more but not all of the players, (ii) in which all or any portion of the bets on or proceeds from a game is paid, directly or indirectly, to the keeper of the place, (iii) in which, directly or indirectly, a fee is charged to or paid by the players for the privilege of playing or participating in a game or using gaming equipment, or (iv) in which the chances of winning are not equally favourable to all persons who play the game, including the person, if any, who conducts the game. *Criminal Code*, R.S.C. 1985, c. C-46, s. 197.

COMMON INTEREST. 1. "[In the context of a representative action refers to the fact that] ... the plaintiff and all those whom he claims to represent will gain some relief by his success, though possibly in different proportions and perhaps in different degrees." *A.E. Osler and Co. v. Solman* (1926), 59 O.L.R. 368 at 372 (H.C.), Orde J.A. 2. In condominium law, the interest in the common elements appurtenant to a unit. 3. In occupier's liability, a mutuality of interest or advantage to invitor and invitee. J.V. DiCastri, *Occupiers' Liability* (Vancouver: Burroughs/Carswell, 1980) at 35.

COMMON INTEREST PRIVILEGE. Arises in a situation where solicitor-client privilege exists with the added element that a communication of privileged material is made in confidence to a party with a common interest in the matter. *Anderson Exploration Ltd. v. Pan-Alberta Gas Ltd.* [1998] 10 W.W.R. 633 (Alta. Q.B.).

COMMON ISSUES. 1. Common but not necessarily identical issues of fact, or common but not necessarily identical issues of law that arise from common but not necessarily identical facts. *Class Proceedings acts.* 2. In the context of the [Class Proceedings Act, R.S.B.C. 1996, c. 50], "common" means that the resolution of the point in question must be applicable to all who are bound by it. *Harrington* *v. Dow Corning Corp.*, 2000 CarswellBC 2183, 2000 BCCA 605, 82 B.C.L.R. (3d) 1, [2000] 11 W.W.R. 201, 47 C.P.C. (4th) 191, 193 D.L.R. (4th) 67 (C.A.).

COMMON JAIL. Any place other than a penitentiary, in which persons charged with offences are usually kept and detained in custody. *Offence Act*, R.S.B.C. 1996, c. 338, s. 1.

COMMON KNOWLEDGE. 1. "... [K]nowledge of a general nature which has been acquired in common with other members of the general public... ." *Maslej v. Canada (Minister of Manpower & Immigration)*, [1977] 1 F.C. 194 at 198 (C.A.), the court per Urie J. 2. "... [T]he common knowledge possessed by every man on the street, of which courts of justice cannot divest themselves ..." *In re Price Bros. Etc.* (1920), 60 S.C.R. 265 at 279, Anglin J.

COMMON LAW. 1. In contrast to statute law, law which relies for its authority on the decisions of the courts and is recorded in the law reports as decisions of judges along with the reasons for their decisions. Judge-made law. Includes the interpretation of statutes and subordinate legislation by judges. 2. In contrast to canon (or ecclesiastical) and the civil (or Roman) law, the system of law in provinces other than Quebec.

COMMON LAW LIEN. A right at common law in one person to retain the property belonging to another and continuously and rightfully in his possession until the property owner satisfies the possessor's claims against the property, example a mechanic's lien, a repairperson's lien.

COMMON LAW MARRIAGE. *var.* **COMMON-LAW MARRIAGE.** "... [A] voluntary union of a man and woman during their joint lives to the exclusion of all others which, for historical reasons, was treated as being just as valid as a regular marriage." *Louis v. Esslinger* (1981), 15 C.C.L.T. 137 at 161, [1981] 3 W.W.R. 350, 22 C.P.C. 68, 29 B.C.L.R. 41, 121 D.L.R. (3d) 17 (S.C.), McEachern C.J.S.C.

COMMON-LAW PARTNER. 1. In relation to an individual, means a person who is cohabiting with the individual in a conjugal relationship, having so cohabited for a period of at least one year. Federal statutes. 2. In relation to a contributor, means a person who is cohabiting with the contributor in a conjugal relationship at the relevant time, having so cohabited with the contributor for a continuous period of at least one year. For greater certainty, in the case of a contributor's death, the "relevant time" means the time of the contributor's death. *Canada Pension Plan*, R.S.C. 1985, c. C-8, s. 2.

COMMON-LAW PARTNERSHIP. The relationship between two persons who are common-law partners of each other.

COMMON-LAW RELATIONSHIP. "... [S]ome sort of a stable relationship which involves not only sexual activity but a commitment between the parties. It would normally necessitate living together under the same roof with shared household duties and responsibilities as well as financial support ... such a couple would present themselves to society as a couple who were living together as man and wife. All or none of these elements may be necessary depending upon the intent of the parties." *Soper v. Soper* (1985), 44 R.F.L. (2d) 308 at 314, 67 N.S.R. (2d) 49, 155 A.P.R. 49 (C.A.), the court per Morrison J.A.

COMMON LAW SPOUSE. *var.* **COMMON-LAW SPOUSE.** Either (a) a person who is united to another person by a marriage that, although not a legal marriage, is valid by common law, or (b) a person who has lived and cohabited with another person in a marriage-like relationship, including a marriage-like relationship between persons of the same gender, for a period of at least 2 years immediately before the other person's death. *Estate Administration Act*, R.S.B.C. 1996, c. 122, s. 1.

COMMON MISTAKE. "Where agreement has been reached but both parties in reaching that agreement have been under a common misapprehension." *Stepps Investments Ltd. v. Security Capital Corp.* (1976), 14 O.R. (2d) 259 at 269, 73 D.L.R. (3d) 351 (H.C.), Grange J. See MISTAKE.

COMMON NUISANCE. The offence of committing a common nuisance consists of doing an unlawful act or failing to discharge a legal duty and thereby (a) endangering the lives, safety, health, property or comfort of the public, or (b) obstructing the public in the exercise or enjoyment or any right that is common to all the subjects of Her Majesty in Canada. *Criminal Code*, R.S.C. 1985, c. C-46, s. 180(2).

COMMON PERSONNEL AND WAGE POLICY. The expression "a common personnel and wage policy" connotes the existence of core objectives which are achieved by establishing the working conditions of employees, including those governed by collective agreements. This is how the Commission [Canadian Human Rights Commission] has always interpreted "establishment", an approach common sense and legislative purpose combine to endorse. *Canada (Human Rights Commission) v. Canadian Airlines International Ltd.*, 2006 SCC 1.

COMMON PROPERTY. 1. The part of the land included in a condominium plan that is not included in any unit shown in the condominium plan. This property is available for the benefit of all members of the condominium corporation. *Condominium acts.* 2. (a) That part of the land and buildings shown on a strata plan that is not part of a strata lot, and (b) pipes, wires, cables, chutes, ducts and other facilities for the passage or provision of water, sewage, drainage, gas, oil, electricity, telephone, radio, television, garbage, heating and cooling systems, or other similar services, if they are located (i) within a floor, wall or ceiling that forms a boundary (A) between a strata lot and another strata lot, (B) between a strata lot and the common property, or (C) between a strata lot or common property and another parcel of land, or (ii) wholly or partially within a strata lot, if they are capable of being and intended to be used in connection with the enjoyment of another strata lot or the common property. *Strata Property Act*, S.B.C. 1998, c. 43, s. 1. See LIMITED ~.

COMMONS. The House of Commons is referred to colloquially as the commons. See HOUSE OF ~.

COMMON SHARE. 1. A share to which no special rights or privileges attach. *The Credit Union Act, 1985*, S.S. 1984-85-86, c. C-45.1, s. 2. 2. A share the holder of which is not precluded, upon the reduction or redemption of the capital stock, from participating in the assets of the corporation beyond the amount then paid for that share plus a fixed premium and a defined rate of dividend. *Taxation Act*, R.S.Q., c. I-3, s. 1. 3. A share in a body corporate, the rights of the holders of which are equal in all respects, including equal rights to (a) receive dividends declared by the body corporate on the shares; and (b) receive the remaining property of the body corporate on dissolution. *Canada Cooperatives Act*, S.C. 1998, c. 1, s. 284.

COMMON SURPLUS. The excess of all receipts of the corporation over the expenses of the corporation. *Condominium Act, 1998*, S.O. 1998, c. 19, s. 1.

COMMON TRUST FUND. A fund maintained by a trust corporation in which money belonging to various estates and trusts in its care are combined for the purpose of facilitating investment.

COMMONWEALTH. *n.* 1. The association of countries named in the schedule. *Interpretation Act*, R.S.C. 1985, c. I-21, s. 35. 2. The social state of a country. 3. A republic. 4. The Australian federation called the Commonwealth of Australia. 5. The British government from 1649 to 1660. See BRITISH ~.

COMMONWEALTH AND DEPENDENT TER-RITORIES. The several Commonwealth countries and their colonies, possessions, dependencies, protectorates, protected states, condominiums and trust territories. *Interpretation Act*, R.S.C. 1985, c. I-21, s. 35.

COMMONWEALTH OF NATIONS. The association of countries named in the schedule to the Act. *Interpretation Act*, R.S.C. 1985, c. I-21, s. 35. The countries are former colonies or possessions of the United Kingdom and the United Kingdom itself. See BRITISH ~.

COMMORIENTES. *n.* [L.] People who die in the same accident or on the same occasion.

COMMR. *abbr.* Commissioner.

COMMUNE. *n.* A small community of people who share common interests and who own property together.

COMMUNICATE. *v.* 1. The term "communicating" found in s. 264(2)(b) [of the Criminal Code, R.S.C. 1985, c. C-46] comes from the verb to communicate, or to share or exchange information or ideas. The act of communication means the transmission of information, thought or feeling so that it is received and understood. While it may not be so in every case, generally an examination and consideration of the content of the message would be essential to the determination of whether a complainant was "harassed" by the repeated communication. *R. v. Scuby*, 2004 BCCA 28, Rowles J.A. (concurring in the result). 2. (i) Send a signed writing; or (ii) transmit information by any other means agreed to by the person transmitting the information and the person receiving the information. *The Securities Transfer Act*, S.S. 2007, c. S-42.3, s. 1. 3. To "communicate" presupposes interactions, bilateral actions between the parties. The verb "to use" [in section 4 of the Official Languages Act] does not encompass such interaction. The right is unilateral: one has the right to address the House of Commons in the official language of his choice. *Knopf v. Canada (Speaker of the House of Commons)*, 2007 FCA 308.

COMMUNICATION. *n.* 1. "... [I]nvolves the passing of thoughts, ideas, words or information from one person to another... ." *R. v. Goldman*, 108 D.L.R. (3d) 17 at 32, [1980] 1 S.C.R. 976, 30 N.R. 453, 51 C.C.C. (2d) 1, 13 C.R. (3d) 228 (Eng.), 16 C.R. (3d) 330 (Fr.), McIntyre J. (Martland, Ritchie, Pigeon, Dickson, Beetz, Estey and Pratte JJ. concurring). 2. Making available. 3. Connotes an intention to impart, convey or exchange ideas or knowledge or at least the awareness that this may be the result. *Chmara v. Nguyen*, [1993] 6 W.W.R. 286 (Man. C.A.). 4. Any form of contact, and includes oral, written or electronic communication. *Unclaimed Intangible Property Act*, R.S.O. 1990, c. U.1, s. 1. 5. The act of begging is communication and is evidently expression [within the meaning of s. 2(b) of the Canadian Charter of Rights and Freedoms]. ... The message "I am in need and I am requesting your help" is primary communication that seeks and invites participation in the community. *R. v. Banks* (2007), 84 O.R. (3d) 1 (C.A.). See AIR TRAFFIC CONTROL ~S; GRASS-ROOTS ~; PRIVATE ~; PRIVILEGED ~; RA-DIO~; RESPONSIBLE ~ ON MATTERS OF PUB-LIC INTEREST; SPOUSAL ~S PRIVILEGE.

COMMUNICATION SIGNAL. Radio waves transmitted through space without any artificial guide, for reception by the public. *Copyright Act*, R.S.C. 1985, c. C-42, s. 2.

COMMUNICATIONS SECURITY ESTAB-LISHMENT. A body within the federal public service that is charged with the following duties. (a) to acquire and use information from the global information infrastructure for the purpose of providing foreign intelligence, in accordance with Government of Canada intelligence priorities; (b) to provide advice, guidance and services to help ensure the protection of electronic information and of information infrastructures of importance to the Government of Canada; and (c) to provide technical and operational assistance to federal law enforcement and security agencies in the performance of their lawful duties. Continued under the *National Defence Act*, R.S.C. 1985, c. N-5, s. 273.62 and 273.64.

COMMUNITY. *n.* 1. "[In s. 24 of the Taxation Act, R.S.B.C. 1960, c. 376] ... must be interpreted in the sense that it means the public in general and not a community in the sense of an isolated or identifiable area or group." *Piers Island Assn. v. Saanich & Islands Area Assessor* (1976), 71 D.L.R. (3d) 270 at 275, 1 B.C.L.R. 279 (S.C.), Fulton J. 2. A city, town or village. *The Community Planning Profession Act*, R.S.S. 1978, c. C.21, s. 3. 3. A geographic region or group of persons sharing common interests within a geographic unit who provide or receive services on a collective basis. 4. A group of persons living together and observing common rules under the direction of a superior. 5. "[In the context of selecting a jury] ... a reasonably distinct, distinguishable group by language and culture. It should occupy, as well, a unique geographic area. If those conditions are met, then, it seems that those people living in that area should qualify as a community... ." *R. v. Fatt* (1986), 54 C.R. (3d) 281 at 291, [1986] N.W.T.R. 388, 30 C.C.C. (3d) 69, 24 C.R.R. 259, [1987] 1 C.N.L.R. 74 (S.C.), Marshall J. See ABORIGINAL ~; FULL ~; LAND LEASE ~; MANUFACTURED HOME ~.

COMMUNITY ANTENNA TELEVISION. A system by which television signals are received from distant stations on large antennae and transmitted by cable to individual consumers.

COMMUNITY CARE FACILITY. A premises or part of a premises (a) in which a person provides care to 3 or more persons who are not related by blood or marriage to the person and includes any other premises or part of a premises that, in the opinion of the medical health officer, is used in conjunction with the community care facility for the purpose of providing care, or (b) designated by the Lieutenant Governor in Council to be a community care facility. *Community Care and Assisted Living Act*, S.B.C. 2002, c. 75, s. 1.

COMMUNITY CORRECTIONAL SERVICE. Includes (a) service or program provided in a community that would not endanger the safety of the community, that is rehabilitative, educational, developmental, preventative, protective, monitoring or supervisory in nature and that (i) would assist or support the reformation, reconciliation and reintegration of inmates into their community, or (ii) would promote a sense of responsibility in offenders and acknowledgement of the harm done to victims, to the community and to themselves and their own families, and (b) any service or program prescribed by regulation. *Corrections Act*, R.S.N.B. 1973, c. C-26, s. 1.

COMMUNITY DEVELOPMENT SERVICES. Services designed to encourage and assist residents of a community to participate in or continue to participate in improving the social and economic conditions of the community for the purpose of preventing, lessening or removing the causes and effects of poverty, child neglect or dependence on public assistance in the community. *Social Assistance Act*, R.S.P.E.I. 1988, c. W-3, s. 1.

COMMUNITY IMPROVEMENT PROJECT AREA. A municipality or an area within a municipality, the community improvement of which in the opinion of the council is desirable because of age, dilapidation, overcrowding, faulty arrangement, unsuitability of buildings or for any other environmental, social or community economic development reason. *Planning Act*, R.S.O. 1990, c. 213, s. 28.

COMMUNITY MATRIMONIAL REGIME. Where the spouses elect for a community matrimonial regime and it is necessary to supplement the provisions of the agreement, reference shall be made to the rules respecting partnership of acquests, adapted as required. Spouses married under the former regime of legal community may invoke the rules of dissolution and liquidation of the regime of partnership of acquests where these are not inconsistent with their matrimonial regime. *Civil Code*, 1991, c. 64, a. 492.

COMMUNITY OF INTEREST DOCTRINE. An exception to the general rule against covenants in restraint of trade. Covenants restricting tenants' business in shopping centre leases may be upheld as mutually and reciprocally enforceable as between landlord and tenant and between tenants if it is clear from the respective leases that a community of interest is created.

COMMUNITY OF PROPERTY. See COMMUNITY PROPERTY REGIME; DEFERRED ~.

COMMUNITY PLAN. See OFFICIAL ~.

COMMUNITY PROPERTY REGIME. An arrangement whereby spouses share all property which one or both may own. A. Bissett-Johnson & W.M. Holland, eds, *Matrimonial Property Law in Canada* (Toronto: Carswell, 1980) at A-5.

COMMUNITY SANCTIONS. "... [R]efers to sanctions other than custody. It includes community programs or resources (e.g. supervised probation) or compensation to the community (e.g. fines or service). The sanctions are to be served or performed in the community with the community taking an active role in the rehabilitation, responsibility for, and treatment of the offender... ." *R. v. P. (J.A.)* (1991), 6 C.R. (4th) 126 at 135, [1991] N.W.T.R. 301 (Y.T. Terr. Ct.), Lilles C.J.T.C.

COMMUNITY SERVICE. "... [A]n alternative to a custodial sentence in those cases where the public interest does not demand that the offender should be imprisoned. It allows the offender to continue to live in the community with his wife and family, supporting them by his normal work. It demonstrates to the offender that society is involved in his delinquency and that he has incurred a debt which can be repaid in some measure by work or service in the community... ." *R. v. Jones* (1975), 25 C.C.C. (2d) 256 at 259 (Ont. G.S.P.), Stortini Co. Ct. J.

COMMUNITY SERVICE ORDER. An order requiring an offender to perform unpaid work in the community under supervision.

COMMUNITY STANDARD. 1. [In the context of a publisher on trial for publishing an obscenity,] "... [C]oncerned not with what Canadians would not tolerate being exposed to themselves, but what they would not tolerate other Canadians being exposed to." *R. v. Butler* (1992), 70 C.C.C. (3d) 129 at 145, [1992] 2 W.W.R. 577, [1992] 1 S.C.R. 452, 11 C.R. (4th) 137, 134 N.R. 81, 8 C.R.R. (2d) 1, 89 D.L.R. (4th) 449, 78 Man. R. (2d) 1, 16 W.A.C. 1, Sopinka J. (Lamer C.J.C., La Forest, Cory, McLachlin, Stevenson and Iacobucci JJ. concurring). 2. "... [A]re not set by those of lowest taste or interest. Nor are they set exclusively by those of rigid, austere, conservative, or puritan taste and habit of mind. Something approaching a general average of community thinking and feeling has to be discovered... . Community standards must be contemporary... ." *R. v. Dominion News & Gifts Ltd.* (1963), 40 C.R. 109 at 126, 42

W.W.R. 65, [1963] 2 C.C.C. 103 (Man. C.A.), Freed-man J.A. (dissenting).

COMMUTATION. *n.* 1. Conversion. 2. Reduction of a punishment or penalty. 3. Change to the right to receive a gross or fixed payment from the right to receive a periodic or variable payment.

COMMUTATIVE CONTRACT. Contract is commutative when, at the time it is formed, the extent of the obligations of the parties and of the advantages obtained by them in return is certain and determinate. *Civil Code*, S.Q. 1991, c. 64, a. 1382.

COMMUTED. *adj.* 1. Of a sentence or penalty, changed from greater to lesser. 2. Refers to a periodic payment which has been converted into a fixed sum payable presently. 3. Refers to the exercise of an aspect of the Crown's pardoning power with respect to a sentence imposed for the commission of a criminal offence.

COMMUTED VALUE. In relation to benefits that a person has a present or future entitlement to receive, the actuarial present value of those benefits determined, as of the time in question, (a) on the basis of actuarial assumptions and methods that are adequate and appropriate and in accordance with generally accepted actuarial practice, (b) in accordance with any prescribed conditions, and (c) in a manner acceptable to the superintendent. *Pension Benefits Standards Act*, R.S.B.C. 1996, c. 352, s. 1.

COMPANION. *n.* The title granted certain members of honorary orders.

COMPANIONSHIP. *n.* [Within the meaning of s. 61(2)(e) of the Family Law Act] is not limited to physical presence. Because companionship involves sharing interests and ideas with another person, communication of interests and ideas by email and telephone is a form of companionship. *McIntyre v. Grigg* (2006), 83 O.R. (3d) 161 (C.A.).

COMPANY. *n.* 1. An association of people formed to carry on some business or undertaking in the association's name. 2. Any body corporate. 3. A body corporate with share capital. 4. An entity distinct and separate in law from its individual shareholders or members. H. Sutherland, D.B. Horsley & J.M. Edmiston, eds., *Fraser's Handbook on Canadian Company Law*, 7th ed. (Toronto: Carswell, 1985) at 1. See AMALGAMATED ∼; CANADIAN ∼; CASH-MUTUAL ∼; CLEAN SHELL ∼; CLOSE ∼; CLOSED ∼; DOMINION ∼; EXTRA-PROVINCIAL ∼; FEDERAL ∼; GENERIC DRUG ∼; GUARANTEE ∼; HOLDING ∼; LIFE ∼; LIMITED LIABILITY ∼; MIXED ENTERPRISE ∼; PARENT ∼; PRIVATE ∼; PROPERTY AND CASUALTY ∼; PUBLIC ∼.

COMPANY-DOMINATED UNION. A union created with employer support or controlled by the employer.

COMPANY LIMITED BY GUARANTEE. A company having the liability of its members limited by the memorandum to the amount that the members may respectively thereby undertake to contribute to the assets of the company in the event of its being

wound up. *Companies Act*, R.S.A. 2000, c. C-21, s. 1.

COMPANY LIMITED BY SHARES. A company having the liability of its members limited to the amount, if any, unpaid on the shares respectively held by them. *Companies Act*, R.S.A. 2000, c. C-21, s. 1.

COMPANY UNION. 1. A union the membership of which is limited to one company. 2. A union dominated by an employer.

COMPARATOR GROUP. A person asking for equal treatment necessarily does so by reference to other people with whom he or she can legitimately invite comparison. Claims of discrimination under s. 15(1) of the Canadian Charter of Rights and Freedoms can only be evaluated "by comparison with the condition of others in the social and political setting in which the question arises": Andrews v. Law Society of British Columbia, 1989 CanLII 2, [1989] 1 S.C.R. 143, at p. 164. A s. 15(1) claim will likely fail unless it can be demonstrated that the comparison, thus invited, is to a "comparator group" with whom the claimant shares the characteristics relevant to qualification for the benefit or burden in question apart from the personal characteristic that is said to be the ground of the wrongful discrimination. The identification and function of the "comparator group" in applying s. 15(1) of the Charter was encapsulated by Iacobucci J. in Lovelace v. Ontario, 2000 SCC 37, [2000] 1 S.C.R. 950, 2000 SCC 37, at para. 62, as follows: "... there are three basic stages to establishing a breach of s. 15. Briefly, the Court must find (i) differential treatment, (ii) on the basis of an enumerated or analogous ground, (iii) which conflicts with the purpose of s. 15(1) and, thus, amounts to substantive discrimination. Each of these inquiries proceeds on the basis of a comparison with another relevant group or groups, and locating the relevant comparison groups requires an examination of the subject-matter of the law, program or activity and its effects, as well as a full appreciation of the context." It is worth repeating that the selection of the comparator group is not a threshold issue that, once decided, can be put aside. On the contrary, each step in the s. 15(1) analysis proceeds "on the basis of a comparison." Indeed in many of the decided cases, the characteristics of the "comparator group" are only developed as the analysis proceeds, especially when considering the "contextual factors" relevant at the third stage, i.e., whether discrimination, as opposed to just a "distinction", has been established. *Hodge v. Canada (Minister of Human Resources Development)*, 2004 SCC 65, [2004] 3 S.C.R. 357, Binnie J. for the court.

COMPARISON. See PHOTO-∼ TECHNOLOGY.

COMPELLABILITY. *n.* A person's being subject to testify in proceedings under legal compulsion.

COMPELLABLE. *adj.* Required by law to give evidence.

COMPELLED. *adj.* 1. "[In s. 11(c) of the Charter] ... indicates to me that the section is referring to a legal compulsion forcing an accused to give evidence in proceedings brought against him or her. The tactical obligation felt by the accused will no doubt increase with the strength of the Crown's case, but it remains a tactical and not a legal compulsion. The decision whether or not to testify remains with the accused free of any legal compulsion." *R. v. Boss* (1988), 42 C.R.R. 166 at 182, 30 O.A.C. 184, 68 C.R. (3d) 123, 46 C.C.C. (3d) 523 (C.A.), the court per Cory J.A. 2. [In interpreting the words "compelled statement"] the test for compulsion under s. 61(1) of the Motor Vehicle Act, R.S.B.C. 1979, c. 288 is whether, at the time that the accident was reported by the driver, the driver gave the report on the basis of an honest and reasonably held belief that he or she was required by law to report the accident to the person to whom the report was given. *R. v. White*, 1999 CarswellBC 1224, 63 C.R.R. (2d) 1, 240 N.R. 1, 24 C.R. (5th) 201, 135 C.C.C. (3d) 257, 174 D.L.R. (4th) 111, 42 M.V.R. (3d) 161, 123 B.C.A.C. 161, 201 W.A.C. 161, [1999] 2 S.C.R. 417.

COMPELLING PRESUMPTION. Facts sufficient to require that a given conclusion be drawn from them. J.G. Fleming, *The Law of Torts*, 8th ed. (Sydney: Law Book, 1992) at 323.

COMPENSABLE INJURY. A personal injury to a worker for which the worker is entitled to receive benefits under the workers' compensation system. A personal injury arising out of and in the course of employment.

COMPENSATION. *n.* 1. "... [A]n equitable monetary remedy which is available when the equitable remedies of restitution and account are not appropriate. By analogy with restitution, it attempts to restore to the plaintiff what has been lost as a result of the breach, ..." *Canson Enterprises Ltd. v. Boughton & Co.* (1991), 9 C.C.L.T. (2d) 1 at 41, [1991] 1 W.W.R. 245, 61 B.C.L.R. (2d) 1, 85 D.L.R. (4th) 129, 131 N.R. 321, 43 E.T.R. 201, 39 C.P.R. (3d) 449, [1991] 3 S.C.R. 534, 6 B.C.A.C. 1, 3 W.A.C. 1, McLachlin J. (Lamer C.J.C. and L'Heureux-Dubé J. concurring). 2. A rate, remuneration, reimbursement or consideration of any kind paid, payable, promised, demanded or received, directly or indirectly. 3. The total amount of money or value that is required to be paid in respect of land expropriated. 4. In expropriation proceedings, when a public body acts to acquire the property of a person, "... [T]he owner [of land taken] is made 'economically whole'... ." *British Columbia (Minister of Highways) v. Richland Estates Ltd.* (1973), 4 L.C.R. 85 at 86 (B.C. C.A.), Farris C.J.B.C. 5. "... [T]he indemnity which the statute [Exchequer Court Act, R.S.C. 1906, c. 140] provides to the owners of lands which are compulsorily taken in, or injuriously affected by, the exercise of statutory powers." *John Pigott & Son v. R.* (1916), 53 S.C.R. 626 at 627, 32 D.L.R. 461, Fitzpatrick C.J. 6. Indemnification, that which is necessary to restore an injured party to his former position, is the meaning in which [compensation] is used in these mortgage contracts. It is used in the sense of indemnification or recompense for such loss that the Credit Union may sustain by reason of the plaintiff exercising her right to prepay. I do find that the term "compensation", when used in regards to the first prepayment provision, that of three months interest on the amount prepaid, is used to

reflect a penalty charged by the defendant. *Pfeiffer v. Pacific Coast Savings Credit Union*, 2000 CarswellBC 2541, 2000 BCSC 1472, 83 B.C.L.R. (3d) 147 (S.C.), Owen-Flood J. See CRIMINAL INJURIES ~; MERCHANT SEAMEN ~ BOARD; WORKERS' ~.

COMPENSATION OF VICTIMS OF CRIME. Benefits provided by the government, on application, to victims of crime in the form of ex gratia payments.

COMPENSATION ORDER. 1. An order made by a governmental body authorized to do so providing for payment to a person for loss of a right or injury or damage to the person or his or her property. 2. A court by which a person is convicted or discharged may make an order requiring that person to pay compensation for any loss or damage to property resulting from the offence.

COMPENSATION PLAN. The provisions, however established, for the determination and administration of compensation, and includes such provisions contained in collective agreements or arbitral awards or established bilaterally between an employer and an employee, unilaterally by an employer or by or pursuant to any Act of Parliament. *Public Sector Compensation Act*, S.C. 1991, c. 30, s. 2.

COMPENSATORY DAMAGES. 1. Compensatory damages may include special damages for pecuniary loss. Compensatory damages embrace general damages and, if aggravating circumstances exist, aggravated damages. *Grassi v. WIC Radio Ltd.*, 2000 CarswellBC 209, 49 C.C.L.T. (2d) 65, [2000] 5 W.W.R. 119 (S.C.), Lysyk J. 2. In a libel case, are intended to compensate the plaintiff for the injury which he or she sustained as a result of the lessening of his or her esteem in the eyes of the community, as well as for the injury caused to the plaintiff's feelings by the defendant's defamatory statements. *Hill v. Church of Scientology* (1994), 18 O.R. (3d) 385 (C.A.).

COMPETENCE. *n.* 1. Jurisdiction. 2. Suitability and fitness. 3. The ability to integrate and apply the knowledge, skills and judgment required to practise safely and ethically in a designated role and practice setting and includes both entry-level and continuing competencies. *Registered Nurses Act*, S.N.S. 2006, c. 21, s. 2. See IN~; PRESUMPTION OF KNOWLEDGE AND ~; SUBJECT MATTER ~; TERRITORIAL ~.

COMPETENCY. *n.* Testimonial competence comprehends: (1) the capacity to observe (including interpretation); (2) the capacity to recollect; and (3) the capacity to communicate.... The judge must satisfy him- or herself that the witness possesses these capacities. Is the witness capable of observing what was happening? Is he or she capable of remembering what he or she observes? Can he or she communicate what he or she remembers? The goal is not to ensure that the evidence is credible, but only to assure that it meets the minimum threshold of being receivable. The enquiry is into capacity to perceive, recollect and communicate, not whether the witness actually perceived, recollects and can communicate about the events in question. *R. v. Marquard*, 1993

CarswellOnt 127, 25 C.R. (4th) 1, 159 N.R. 81, 66 O.A.C. 161, 85 C.C.C. (3d) 193, 108 D.L.R. (4th) 47, [1993] 4 S.C.R. 223, McLachlin J. See IN~.

COMPETENT. *adj.* 1. Legally allowed to give evidence during a trial. 2. Having adequate skill and knowledge. 3. "... '[O]f sound mind, memory and understanding' ..." *McHugh v. Dooley* (1903), 10 B.C.R. 537 at 546 (S.C.), Martin J. See IN~; MENTALLY ~.

COMPETENT AUTHORITY. A person or body authorized by statute to perform the act or carry out the function in question.

COMPETENT JURISDICTION. Having authority to hear a matter, try a case. See COURT OF ~.

COMPETITION. *n.* 1. A situation when two or more businesses seek customers in the same marketplace. 2. An event in which participants take part to demonstrate their skills or abilities in comparison to each other. See COMMISSIONER OF ~; FREE ~.

COMPETITION LAW. The law governing competition in the market place, corporate mergers, antitrust legislation, franchising, pricing.

COMPETITIVE INTELLIGENCE. The collection and analysis of information concerning competitors' business and technical plans, designs, strategies.

COMPILATION. *n.* 1. A work resulting from the selection or arrangement of literary, dramatic, musical or artistic works or of parts thereof, or a work resulting from the selection or arrangement of data. *Copyright Act,* R.S.C. 1985, c. C-42, s. 2. 2. Essentially, for a compilation of data to be original, it must be a work that was independently created by the author and which displays at least a minimal degree of skill, judgment and labour in its overall selection or arrangement. The threshold is low, but it does exist. *Tele-Direct (Publications) Inc. v. American Business Information Inc.,* 1997 CarswellNat 2111, 221 N.R. 113, 154 D.L.R. (4th) 328, 76 C.P.R. (3d) 296, 134 F.T.R. 80 (note), [1998] 2 F.C. 22, 37 B.L.R. (2d) 101, the court per Decary J.A.

COMPILATION OF QUÉBEC LAWS AND REGULATIONS. Brings together the laws and regulations in force that are of a general and permanent nature, as well as those that, although not of a general and permanent nature, are nonetheless in regular use. The compilation is updated regularly and made available to the public as an official publication. *An Act respecting the Compilation of Québec Laws and Regulations,* R.S.Q. c. R-2.2.0.0.2, s. 1.

COMPLAINANT. *n.* 1. The victim of an alleged offence. *Criminal Code,* R.S.C. 1985, c. C-46, s. 2. 2. A person who lodges or files a formal complaint.

COMPLAINT. *n.* 1. "In a rape case, ... any statement made by the alleged victim which, given circumstances of the case, will, if believed, be of some probative value in negating the adverse conclusions the trier of fact could draw as regards her credibility had she been silent." *R. v. Timm* (1981), 21 C.R. (3d) 209 at 229, [1981] 2 S.C.R. 315, 28 C.R. (3d) 133, [1981] 5 W.W.R. 577, 37 N.R. 204, 29 A.R. 509, 59 C.C.C.

(2d) 396,124 D.L.R. (3d) 582, the court per Lamer J. 2. An allegation or allegations, made orally or in writing by a member of the public, concerning misconduct of a public officer or of a contravention or violation of a statute. 3. An extra-judicial statement concerning an offence made after the alleged commission of that offence to a person other than the accused by the person in respect of whom it is alleged to have been committed. *National Defence Act,* R.S.C. 1985, c. N-5, *Military Rules of Evidence,* C.R.C., c. 1049, s. 31. 4. An extra-judicial statement concerning an offence or violation of a statute made after the alleged commission of that offence or violation of a statute to a person other than the accused or violator by the person in respect of whom the offence or violation is alleged to have been committed. 5. Includes identification of the complainant, the victim, the time during which the alleged violation took place, the location and nature of the alleged violation, the relevant section of the statute and an affirmation that the violation took place. 6. An expression of concern about the care provided or other aspects of the professional relationship which identifies a registrant of the governing body of a profession. See CLASS ~; MILITARY POLICE ~S COMMISSION; PUBLIC ~; RECENT ~.

COMPLETE. *v.* To finish.

COMPLETE. *adj.* Finished; entire.

COMPLETED. *adj.* If used with reference to a contract or subcontract in respect of an improvement, means substantially completed or performed, not necessarily totally completed or performed. *Builders Lien Act,* SBC 1997, c. 45, s.1.

COMPLETED CONTRACT METHOD. "The completed contract or substantially completed contract method [of accounting] recognizes profit only when the contract has been completed or substantially completed. The completed or substantially completed contract method has the advantage that costs are known or virtually known at the time the profit is taken." *Toromont Industrial Holdings Ltd. v. Thorne, Gunn, Helliwell & Christenson* (1975), 23 C.P.R. (2d) 59 at 77, 10 O.R. (2d) 65, 62 D.L.R. (3d) 225 (H.C.), Holland J.

COMPLETION. *n.* Full performance of a contract. *Lambton (County) v. Canadian Comstock Co.* (1959), 21 D.L.R. (2d) 689 at 695, [1960] S.C.R. 86, the court per Judson J. See CERTIFICATE OF ~; SUBSTANTIAL ~.

COMPLETION BOND. A guarantee to the owner of property that the contractor will finish the job contracted. See PERFORMANCE BOND.

COMPLETION LOAN. The advance of the whole amount, minus costs, of a mortgage loan by a lender to a borrower when construction of the borrower's new building is completed, the lender has inspected the building and is satisfied.

COMPLETION OF THE CONTRACT. Substantial performance, not necessarily total performance, of the contract. *Mechanics' Lien acts.*

COMPLEX. *n.* Several related buildings in a setting.

COMPLEX. *adj.* Having many interrelated parts, patterns or elements, difficult to understand fully.

COMPLIANCE. The distinction between the meaning of "compliance" and the meaning of "consent" is real. To consent means to actually agree and cooperate. Compliance has a more subtle meaning involving the failure to object. *R. c. Knox*, 1996 CarswellQue 1041, 202 N.R. 228, 109 C.C.C. (3d) 481, 23 M.V.R. (3d) 93, [1996] 3 S.C.R. 199, 38 C.R.R. (2d) 222, 139 D.L.R. (4th) 1, 1 C.R. (5th) 254, Lamer C.J.C. See SUBSTANTIAL ~.

COMPLIANCE ORDER. Either an order that someone take positive action, or an order that certain conduct be stopped.

COMPLIANCE UNIT. 1. A compliance unit within the meaning of the Kyoto Protocol. *Canada Emission Reduction Incentives Agency Act*, S.C. 2005, c. 30, s. 2. 2. (a) A BCAU, (b) a BCERU, or (c) an RCU. *Greenhouse Gas Reduction (Cap and Trade) Act*, S.B.C. 2008, c. 32, s. 1. See RECOGNIZED ~.

COMPLICITY. *n.* 1. Being an accomplice; being involved in crime or conspiracy. 2. The distinction between the meaning of "compliance" and the meaning of "consent" is real. To consent means to actually agree and cooperate. Compliance has a more subtle meaning involving the failure to object. *R. c. Knox*, 1996 CarswellQue 1041, 202 N.R. 228, 109 C.C.C. (3d) 481, 23 M.V.R. (3d) 93, [1996] 3 S.C.R. 199, 38 C.R.R. (2d) 222, 139 D.L.R. (4th) 1, 1 C.R. (5th) 254, Lamer C.J.C. 3. Mere membership in an organization which from time to time commits international offences is not normally sufficient to bring one into the category of an accomplice. At the same time, if the organization is principally directed to a limited, brutal purpose, such as a secret police activity, mere membership may indeed meet the requirements of personal and knowing participation. The cases also establish that mere presence at the scene of an offence, for example, as a bystander with no intrinsic connection with the persecuting group will not amount to personal involvement. Physical presence together with other factors may however qualify as a personal and knowing participation. A person who is a member of the persecuting group and who has knowledge that activities are being committed by the group and who neither takes steps to prevent them occurring (if he has the power to do so) nor disengages himself from the group at the earliest opportunity (consistent with safety for himself) but who lends his active support to the group may be an accomplice. *Penate v. Canada* [1994] 2 F.C. 79 (T.D.).

COMPLY. *v.* To conform; yield; accept.

COMPOSITION. *n.* 1. An arrangement for the payment of debts. 2. Refers to the total number of judges of a court and number of judges who must be drawn from each different region. See CLASS ~.

COMPOS MENTIS. [L.] Sound mind.

COMPOUND. *v.* 1. To compromise; to effect a composition with a creditor. 2. To combine; to unite. 3. To charge interest on interest on a loan or debt. 4. To pay interest on the interest payable on a deposit or investment.

COMPOUNDING AN INDICTABLE OFFENCE. Prohibited by s. 141 of the Criminal Code, R.S.C. 1985, c. C-46, it consists of, in return for valuable consideration, the concealment of criminal activity. It also includes the agreement to obtain or receive valuable consideration in return for compounding or concealing an indictable offence. Watt & Fuerst, *The Annotated 1995 Tremeear's Criminal Code* (Toronto: Carswell, 1994) at 230.

COMPOUND INTEREST. 1. Interest charged on interest. 2. "... [A]t periodic intervals unpaid interest is added to unpaid principal, and interest then begins to accrue on the aggregate sum ... To compound, the first overdue instalment is added to the principal, and the new amount ... commences to bear interest." *Elman v. Conto* (1978), 82 D.L.R. (3d) 742 at 747, 18 O.R. (2d) 449 (C.A.), the court per Arnup J.A.

COMPREHENSIVE COVERAGE. "... [A] form of automobile insurance that pays for loss or damage to the insured vehicle caused otherwise than by collision... ." *Turner v. Co-operative Fire & Casualty Co.* (1983), 1 C.C.L.I. 1 at 7, [1983] I.L.R. 1-1678, 147 D.L.R. (3d) 342, 58 N.S.R. (2d) 1, 123 A.P.R. 1 (C.A.), Macdonald J.A. (Morrison J.A. concurring).

COMPRISING. *v.* In a deed, made up of, consisting of, namely.

COMPROMISE. *v.* To settle differences, claims and to reach an agreement as to those differences or claims.

COMPROMISE. *n.* 1. The settlement of an action by agreement under which the plaintiff agrees not to take action and the intended defendant makes a promise in return. 2. An arrangement between a company and its shareholders and creditors. 3. An arrangement for the taxpayer to pay a lesser amount than the full amount of taxes owed and for the taxing authority to accept that lesser amount in order to settle the matter with the taxing authority. See HISTORIC ~.

COMP. TRIB. *abbr.* Competition Tribunal.

COMP. TRIB. DEC. abbr. Competition,Tribunal, decisions, 1986-?.

COMPTROLLER. *n.* 1. One who examines the accounts of collectors of public money. 2. The senior financial officer of a company or organization. See CONTROLLER.

COMPTROLLER GENERAL. Appointed by the Governor in Council under the Financial Administration Act, R.S.C. 1985, c. F-11. The Comptroller General of Canada is responsible for providing functional direction and assurance for financial management, internal audit, investment planning, procurement, project management and the management of real property and material across the federal government. *Our Mandate*, online: Treasury Board of Canada Secretariat, <http://www.tbs-sct.gc.ca/ocg-bcg/abu-ans/abu-ans-eng.asp>.

COMPULSION. *n.* 1. Duress; force. 2. The overbearing nature of statements or conduct such that the person speaking or acting is able to control the conduct of the person to whom the statements or conduct are directed.

COMPULSORY. *adj.* Forced; coerced; mandatory; required.

COMPULSORY ARBITRATION. Arbitration that is required by law.

COMPULSORY LICENCE. A licence of a patent which is mandated for production of medicine or food in certain circumstances and one which is mandated if there has been an abuse of exclusive rights.

COMPULSORY PILOTAGE. In respect of a ship, the requirement that the ship be under the conduct of a licensed pilot or the holder of a pilotage certificate. *Pilotage Act*, R.S.C. 1985, c. P-14, s. 2.

COMPULSORY PILOTAGE AREA. An area of water in which ships are subject to compulsory pilotage. *Pilotage Act*, R.S.C. 1985, c. P-14, s. 2.

COMPULSORY PURCHASE. To acquire land for public purposes.

COMPULSORY UNIONISM. Employment conditional on union membership.

COMPUTER L. *abbr.* Computer Law.

COMPUTER PASSWORD. Any data by which a computer service or computer system is capable of being obtained or used.

COMPUTER PROGRAM. 1. Data representing instructions or statements that, when executed in a computer system, causes the computer system to perform a function. *Criminal Code*, R.S.C. 1985, c. C-46, s. 342.1(2). 2. A set of instructions or statements, expressed, fixed, embodied or stored in any manner, that is to be used directly or indirectly in a computer in order to bring about a specific result. *Copyright Act*, S.C. 1989, c. 15, s. 1(3).

COMPUTER SERVICE. Includes data processing and the storage or retrieval of data. *Criminal Code*, R.S.C. 1985, c. C-46, s. 342.1(2).

COMPUTER SYSTEM. A device that, or a group of interconnected or related devices one or more of which, (a) contains computer programs or other data, and (b) pursuant to computer programs, (i) performs logic and control, and (ii) may perform any other function. *Criminal Code*, R.S.C. 1985, c. C-46, s. 342.1(2).

CON. *v.* To deceive, to trick.

CON. *adj.* Short form for confidence, as a "con game".

CON. *prep.* [L.] 1. With. 2. Against.

CON. *pref.* 1. Together. 2. Against.

CONC. BD. RPTS. *abbr.* Conciliation Board Reports, 1966-1974.

CONC. COMM'R. RPTS. *abbr.* Conciliation Commissioner Reports, 1975.

CONCEAL. *v.* To hide, cover, keep from view; to prevent discovery. See CONCEALS.

CONCEALED. *adj.* 1. "[In R. v. Lemire (1980), 18 C.R. (3d) 166 at 170 (B.C. Co. Ct.)] Melvin Co. Ct. J. (as he was then) ... reviewed the authorities and dictionary definitions of the word 'concealed' [as used in s. 87 of the Criminal Code, R.S.C. 1970, c. C-34]: 'In my view, the definition of the word "conceal" clearly demonstrates that some purpose is required in addition to the object being merely not capable of being seen. To conceal, in a sense of keeping from the knowledge or observation of others or hide, imports into this offence regarding the act of concealment a mental element on the part of the accused ... ' ... The mens rea articulated by Mr. Justice Cavanaugh [in R. v. Coughlan (1974), 27 C.R.N.S. 195 at 195 (Alta. Q.B.)] for a interpretation of the word 'concealed' was[:] 'In : 'In m view, these definitions clearly impart the idea of an intentional putting out of sight for the purpose of being out of sight.'" ' *R. v. Felawka* (1991), 9 C.R. (4th) 291 at 297, 303, 68 C.C.C. (3d) 481, 3 B.C.A.C. 241, 7 W.A.C. 241, Toy J.A. (McEachern C.J.B.C., Wallace and Proudfoot JJ.A. concurring). 2. Rendered permanently inaccessible by the structure or finish of a building.

CONCEALED DANGER. A deceptively safe appearance which hides a potential cause of injury.

CONCEALING BODY OF CHILD. It is an offence to dispose of the dead body of a child with intent to conceal the fact that its mother has been delivered of it whether it died before, during or after birth. *Criminal Code*, R.S.C. 1985, c. C-46, s. 243.

CONCEALMENT. *n.* In insurance law describes the situation when an applicant for insurance fails to inform the insurer of a material fact which is known to the applicant. See FRAUDULENT ~.

CONCEALMENT OF BIRTH. See CONCEALING BODY OF CHILD.

CONCEALS. *v.* "... [A]s used in s. 350(a)(ii) [of the Criminal Code, R.S.C. 1970, c. C-34] contemplates some positive conduct on the part of the debtor [to conceal assets] as opposed to a mere failure to disclose the existence of the property, even though under a duty to do so [under the Bankruptcy Act, R.S.C. 1970, c. B-3, ss. 129 and 132]." *R. v. Goulis* (1981), 125 D.L.R. (3d) 137 at 142, 33 O.R. (2d) 55, 20 C.R. (3d) 360, 37 C.B.R. (N.S.) 290, 60 C.C.C. (2d) 347 (C.A.), the court per Martin J.A. See CONCEAL.

CONCEPTION. *n.* The beginning of pregnancy; fertilization of the ovum by spermatozoon.

CONCERN. *v.* To relate, be of interest or importance to.

CONCERN. *n.* See GOING ~; NATIONAL ~ DOCTRINE.

CONCERNING. *adj.* Relating to; affecting.

CONCERT. *n.* 1. Agreement. 2. To act in concert is to act together to bring about a planned result.

CONCESSION. *n.* 1. A tier of township lots. *Surveys Act*, R.S.O. 1990, c. S.30, s.1. 2. A public authority grants land to a private person to establish something, i.e. an industry, a railway or to carry out a function there, such as fishing. 3. A grant by an owner of a place of amusement or business to a person permitting them to perform a service or sell articles on the premises. See BROKEN ~.

CONCILIATION. *n.* 1. The process by which a third party attempts to assist an employer and a trade union to achieve a collective agreement. 2. Facilitates dialogue between the parties and help them to identify their interests, assess their positions, negotiate and explore mutually satisfactory solutions. *An Act respecting administrative justice*, R.S.Q. c. J-3, S. 121.

CONCILIATION BOARD. A board established under labour legislation for the investigation and conciliation of a dispute.

CONCILIATION OFFICER. A person whose duties include the conciliation of disputes and who is under the control and direction of the Minister of Labour or other Minister.

CONCILIATOR. *n.* A person appointed to assist the parties to collective bargaining in reaching agreement.

CONCLUDE. *v.* To finish; to bar or estop.

CONCLUDED CONTRACT. "... [O]ne which settles everything that is necessary to be settled, and leaves nothing still to be settled by agreement between the parties. Of course, it may leave something which still has to be determined, but then that determination must be a determination which does not depend on the agreement between the parties." *May & Butcher Ltd. v. R.*, [1929] All E.R. Rep. 679 at 683-84 (U.K. H.L.), Viscount Dunedin.

CONCLUSION. *n.* 1. The finish, end, summation. 2. A rule of law or an irrefutable presumption. See RATIONAL ~.

CONCLUSION OF FACT. An inference or result drawn from evidence.

CONCLUSION OF LAW. A finding of law; a statement of law applicable to a matter.

CONCLUSIVE. *adj.* Final, decisive, clear. See FINAL AND ~.

CONCLUSIVE PRESUMPTION. 1. A presumption which cannot be overcome by evidence or argument. May be indicated by the word "deemed" in a statute. *Gray v. Kerslake* (1957), 11 D.L.R. (2d) 225 at 239, [1958] S.C.R. 3, Cartwright J.; *R. v. Johnson* (1976), 37 C.R.N.S. 370 at 373 (B.C. C.A.), McFarlane J.A. (Seaton and McIntyre JJ.A. concurring). 2. A presumption where, when one fact is proven, another fact must be taken as true and beyond dispute by a party opposing the presumption or its effect.

CONCORD. *n.* An agreement to settle or refrain from bringing an action.

CONCUR. *v.* 1. To agree, consent. 2. "... [A]s used in [s. 4 of the Trade-unions Act, R.S.B.C. 1960, c. 384] means 'to combine in action' or to 'co-operate with' ..." *Perini Pacific Ltd. v. I.U.O.E., Local 115* (1961), 36 W.W.R. 49 at 66, 28 D.L.R. (2d) 727 (B.C. S.C.), Monroe J.

CONCURRENCE. *n.* Agreement, consent.

CONCURRENT. *adj.* Contemporaneous.

CONCURRENT CAUSE. A cause acting contemporaneously with another cause and together causing injury which would not have occurred in the absence of either cause.

CONCURRENT CONDITION. Describes promises made by both parties to a contract where each party's responsibility depends on the readiness and willingness of the other to perform. The Sale of Goods acts provide that delivery of the goods and payment of the price are concurrent conditions. The buyer must be ready and willing to pay the price in exchange for the goods and the seller must be ready and willing to give possession of the goods in exchange for the price.

CONCURRENT JURISDICTION. Two or more courts or tribunals having authority to try or hear the same subject matter.

CONCURRENTLY. *adv.* At the same time, contemporaneously.

CONCURRENT NEGLIGENCE. The failure of two or more persons to fulfil their duty of care to a third person. Generally requires contribution between the tortfeasors.

CONCURRENT SENTENCE. Two or more terms of imprisonment served simultaneously.

CONCURRENT WRIT. A duplicate of an original writ. See ALIAS WRIT.

CONCURRING OPINION. The decision of a judge agreeing in the decision though not necessarily the reasons of another judge or judges.

CONDEMN. *v.* 1. To find guilty. 2. To sentence. 3. In admiralty law, to find that a vessel is a prize or that the vessel is unfit. 4. To expropriate. 5. To declare a building unfit for use or occupation.

CONDEMNATION. *n.* 1. An order that a building is unfit for use or occupation. 2. Expropriation. 3. A judgment that a prize or captured vessel has been lawfully captured or that the vessel is unfit.

CONDITION. *n.* 1. A provision in an agreement or declaration that contains an event which must occur or an action that must be taken before other provisions of the same agreement or declaration come into force or occur or are required. 2. "... [A] contractual term which the parties intended to be fundamental to its performance." *Jorian Properties Ltd. v. Zellenrath* (1984), 26 B.L.R. 276 at 285, 4 O.A.C. 107, 46 O.R. (2d) 775, 26 B.C.L.R. 276, 10 D.L.R. (4th) 458 (C.A.), Blair J.A. (dissenting). 3. "... [O]f the parties [in s. 11(1) of the Divorce Act, R.S.C. 1970, c. D-8] includes their ages; their states of health, both physical and mental; their backgrounds; their education; their attitude toward family; their motives for seeking custody; their comparative abilities to provide psycological [sic], spiritual and emotional needs of the children; their respective modes of living; and so on." *Burgmaier v. Burgmaier* (1986), 50 R.F.L. (2d) 1 at 11, 46 Sask. R. 1 (C.A.), the court per Cameron J.A. See CONCURRENT ~; EXPRESS ~; IMPLIED ~; PRECEDENT ~; TRUST ~; UNSANITARY ~S; WORKING ~S.

C

CONDITIONAL. *adj.* Dependent upon, subject to.

CONDITIONAL ACCEPTANCE. The acceptor agrees to an offer of contract only when a condition stated is fulfilled.

CONDITIONAL ADMISSIBILITY. Evidence is admitted until it is examined further. See DE BENE ESSE.

CONDITIONAL APPEARANCE. 1. "Middleton J. in Wolsely Tool & Motor Car v. Jackson Potts & Co. (1914), 6 O.W.N. 109 (H.C.), described the conditional appearance as follows: 'A conditional appearance is not intended to be a provisional appearance, as in England, but a form of appearance to be used where for some reason it is not convenient to determine the question whether the case can be brought within Rule 25 until the hearing of the action.' " *Sea Electronics Aids Inc. v. Kaytronics Ltd.* (1979), 11 C.P.C. 275 at 277, 24 O.R. (2d) 38 (H.C.), Grange J. 2. A motion filed by a defendant, with leave of the Court, to object to an irregularity in the commencement of the proceeding or the court's jurisdiction.

CONDITIONAL DEBT. A debt the payment of which is dependent upon a fact which may never happen.

CONDITIONAL DISCHARGE. 1. Disposition of a criminal matter by which a person is deemed not to be convicted after serving a period of probation. Sentence which may be imposed upon conviction for a criminal offence. 2. "... [P]uts the accused conditionally at liberty, ..." *Ahluwalia, Re* (1989), 25 F.T.R. 208 at 217, [1989] 3 F.C. 209, Muldoon J.

CONDITIONAL LICENCE. A licence authorizing an activity prior to the issue of a final licence.

CONDITIONAL OBLIGATION. An obligation is conditional where it is made to depend upon a future and uncertain event, either by suspending it until the event occurs or is certain not to occur, or by making its extinction dependent on whether or not the event occurs. *Civil Code*, S.Q. 1991, c. 64, a. 1497.

CONDITIONAL OFFER. 1. An offer which is not final until a condition is fulfilled. 2. A proposal to settle a strike with reservations.

CONDITIONAL SALE. 1. A contract for the sale of goods under which possession is to be delivered to a buyer and the property in the goods is to vest in her or him at a subsequent time on payment of the whole or part of the price or on the performance of any other condition. 2. A contract for the hiring of goods under which it is agreed that the hirer will become or have the option of becoming the owner of the goods on compliance with the terms of the contract.

CONDITIONAL SENTENCE. 1. If a person is convicted of an offence, other than a serious personal injury offence as defined in section 752, a terrorism offence or a criminal organization offence prosecuted by way of indictment for which the maximum term of imprisonment is ten years or more or an offence punishable by a minimum term of imprisonment, and the court imposes a sentence of imprisonment of less than two years and is satisfied that the service of the sentence in the community would not endanger the safety of the community and would be consistent with the fundamental purpose and principles of sentencing set out in sections 718 to 718.2, the court may, for the purpose of supervising the offender's behaviour in the community, order that the offender serve the sentence in the community, subject to the offender's compliance with the conditions imposed under section 742.3. *Criminal Code*, R.S.C. 1985, c. C-46, s. 742.1. 2. Incorporates some elements of a noncustodial sentence and some of a custodial sentence. It will generally be more effective in achieving restorative goals of sentencing than a carceral sentence because it is served in the community. It is however a punitive sanction and therefore capable of satisfying the objectives of denunciation and deterrence. It is this punitive aspect that distinguishes the conditional sentence from probation. A sentence under s. 742.1 is not just a choice between imprisonment or not. It is a community-based sentence that permits a great deal of creativity for fulfilling the objectives outlined in s. 718 to 718.2 as well as establishing consequences for a breach of the sentence... Parliament, in a typically Canadian way, has tried to blend traditional retributive goals of sentencing with concepts of restorative justice. *R. v. Laliberte*, 2000 SKCA 27, 31 C.R. (5th) 1, [2000] 4 W.W.R. 491, 143 C.C.C. (3d) 503, 189 Sask. R. 190.

CONDITIONAL WILL. A will which takes effect only in the event of the testator's death in a certain way, such as by accident, or during a certain period, such as on a trip; the will does not take effect unless the specified condition is met. *Leippi v. Potetz et al.*, 1986 CanLII 690 (Sask. Q.B.).

CONDITION OF EMPLOYMENT. 1. A qualification or circumstance required for employment. 2. All matters and circumstances that in any way affect the employment relationship of employers and employees. *Employment Standards Act*, R.S.B.C. 1996, c.113, s. 1.

CONDITION OF SALE. A term upon which an interest is to be sold by auction or tender.

CONDITION PRECEDENT. "... [A]n external condition upon which the existence of the obligation depends.... . a future uncertain event, the happening of which depends entirely upon the will of a third party ..." *Turney v. Zhilka*, [1959] S.C.R. 578 at 583, Judson J. See PRECEDENT CONDITION; TRUE ~.

CONDITION SUBSEQUENT. A term of an agreement requiring that the agreement be valid and binding unless and until a specified event or occurrence happens. A condition that will create an estate upon condition must be distinguished from a covenant to do or abstain from doing some act. The difference in effect is that the breach of a true condition may defeat an estate and give a right to re-entry, the breach of a covenant gives merely a right of action. *Roman Catholic Episcopal Corp. of Halifax v. Denson*, 1998 CanLII 4562 (N.S.S.C.).

CONDO. *abbr.* Condominium.

CONDOMINIUM. *n.* 1. A system of property ownership of multi-unit housing or commercial projects in which each unit owner is a tenant-in-common of the common elements and each unit is owned separately in fee simple. A condominium may also be a leasehold property. 2. Two or more subjects of international law jointly exercise sovereignty over one territory.

CONDOMINIUM CORPORATION. See FREEHOLD ~; LEASEHOLD ~.

CONDOMINIUM TITLE. With respect to the condominium unit for which the title has issued, means the right to: (i) an ownership share in the condominium unit; and (ii) a share in the common property. *The Land Titles Act, 2000,* S.S. 2000, c. L-5.1, s. 2.

CONDOMINIUM UNIT. A unit or additional unit in a condominium plan or a replacement plan intended to be used primarily for the residence of not more than one family but does not include a unit or additional unit that is used for a purpose other than a residence except where it is used for that other purpose by a person who resides in the unit or additional unit and that other purpose is subsidiary to the use of the unit or additional unit as a residence, and includes any structure or works used in conjunction with the unit or additional unit. *The Builders' Lien Act,* S.S. 1984-85-86, c. B-7.1, s. 38.

CONDONATION. *n.* 1. Acquiescence, forgiveness. 2. "... [T]he reinstatement in his or her former marital position of a spouse who has committed a matrimonial wrong of which all material facts are known to the other spouse, with the intention of forgiving and remitting the wrong, on condition that the spouse whose wrong is so condoned does not thenceforward commit any further matrimonial offence." *MacDougall v. MacDougall,* [1970] 3 R.F.L. 175 at 176 (Ont. C.A.). 3. "In McIntyre v. Hockin (1889), 16 O.A.R. 498 [(C.A.)], Maclennan J.A., speaking for the Court, said at pp. 501-502: 'If [the employer] retains the servant in his employment for any considerable time after discovering his fault, that is condonation, and he cannot afterwards dismiss for that fault without anything new. No doubt the employer ought to have a reasonable time to determine what to do, to consider whether he will dismiss or not, or to look for another servant. So, also, he must have knowledge of the nature and extent of the fault, for he cannot forgive or condone matters of which he is not fully informed. Further, condonation is subject to an implied condition of future good conduct, and whenever any new misconduct occurs, the old offences may be invoked and may be put on the scale against the offender as cause for dismissal.' " *Nossal v. Better Business Bureau of Metropolitan Toronto* (1985), 12 C.C.E.L. 85 at 89, 51 O.R. (2d) 279, 19 D.L.R. (4th) 547, 9 O.A.C. 184 (C.A.), the court per Zuber J.A.

CONDUCIVE. *adj.* Tending to a specific end, bringing about, leading to a particular result.

CONDUCT. *v.* 1. To manage or operate. *Saskatchewan Telecommunications v. Central Asphalt Ltd.* (1988), 70 Sask. R. 235 at 239, [1988] 6 W.W.R. 459 (Q.B.), Wright J. 2. To lead or guide. *R. v. Mackenzie*

(1982), 135 D.L.R. (3d) 374 at 379, 36 O.R. (2d) 562, 66 C.C.C. (2d) 528 (C.A.), the court per Cory J.A.

CONDUCT. *n.* 1. Any act or omission. 2. Personal behaviour. 3. "... [I]ncludes the role of the parties in the break-up of the home; their behaviour in relation to one another, the children, and the family, both before and after the break-up; such agreements, if any, as they may have arrived at; and such other conduct tending to demonstrate their characters, personalities and temperaments, and other matters bearing upon their abilities to rear the children." *Burgmaier v. Burgmaier* (1986), 50 R.F.L. (2d) 1 at 10, 46 Sask. R. 1 (C.A.), the court per Cameron J.A. See COURSE OF ~; EXCUSABLE ~; INFAMOUS ~; MIS~; NON-CULPABLE ~; POST-OFFENCE ~; RULE OF ~; UNLAWFUL ~.

CONDUCT CRIME. The conduct, the behaviour, of the accused is itself a crime. No particular result is required to constitute a conduct crime.

CONDUCT MONEY. 1. Fees payable to witnesses to defray expenses of coming to testify. 2. Attendance money.

CONDUCT UNBECOMING A LAWYER. Includes a matter, conduct or thing that is considered, in the judgment of the benchers or a panel, (a) to be contrary to the best interest of the public or of the legal profession, or (b) to harm the standing of the legal profession. *Legal Profession Act,* S.B.C. 1998, c. 9, s. 1.

CONE OF SILENCE. "... Knowledge of confidential matters is therefore imputed to other members of the firm. This latter presumption can, however, in some circumstances, be rebutted. The usual methods used to rebut the presumptions are the setting up of a ... 'cone of silence' ... at the time that the possibility of the unauthorized communication of confidential information arises ... A 'cone of silence' is achieved by means of a solemn undertaking not to disclose by the tainted solicitor." *MacDonald Estate v. Martin* (1990), 48 C.P.C. (2d) 113 at 126, [1991] 1 W.W.R. 705, 121 N.R. 1, 77 D.L.R. (4th) 249, 70 Man. R. (2d) 241, [1990] 3 S.C.R. 1235, Sopinka J. (Dickson C.J.C., La Forest and Gonthier JJ. concurring). See CHINESE WALL.

CONFABULATE. *v.* To fabricate facts or events which the person cannot recall.

CONF. COMMEM. MEREDITH. *abbr.* Conférences commémoratives Meredith (Meredith Memorial Lectures).

CONFEDERATION. *n.* 1. The joining together of the original four provinces into the Dominion of Canada on July 1, 1867. 2. Generally describes a loose association of states in which the state governments take precedence over the central government. 3. A league of nations or states.

CONFER. *v.* Grant or bestow. *Minister of National Revenue v. Pillsbury Holdings Ltd.,* [1964] C.T.C. 294 at 300, [1965] 1 Ex. C.R. 676, 64 D.T.C. 5184, Cattanach J.

CONFERENCE. *n.* 1. A meeting of persons for consideration of matters, exchange of opinions. 2. An association of organizations or businesses for a particular purpose. 3. A group of persons who are convened to give advice in accordance with section 19. A youth justice court judge, the provincial director, a police officer, a justice of the peace, a prosecutor or a youth worker may convene or cause to be convened a conference for the purpose of making a decision required to be made. The mandate of a conference may be, among other things, to give advice on appropriate extrajudicial measures, conditions for judicial interim release, sentences, including the review of sentences, and reintegration plans. *Youth Criminal Justice Act*, S.C. 2002, c. 1, s. 2, 19. See PRE-TRIAL ~; SEDONA ~; UNIFORM LAW ~ OF CANADA.

CONFESS. *v.* To admit; to concede.

CONFESSION. *n.* 1. An admission of guilt. 2. In civil procedure, a formal admission. 3. Formerly, a plea of guilty. F. Kaufman, *The Admissibility of Confessions*, 3d ed. (Toronto: Carswell, 1980) at 1. 4. "... [S]tatements made by an accused to a person in authority; ..." *R. v. Rothman* (1981), 20 C.R. (3d) 97 at 122, [1981] 1 S.C.R. 640, 59 C.C.C. (2d) 30, 121 D.L.R. (3d) 578, 35 N.R. 485, Estey J. (dissenting) (Laskin C.J.C. concurring). 5. A statement made by an accused person, whether before or after he is accused of an offence, that is completely or partially self-incriminating with respect to the offence of which he is accused. *National Defence Act*, R.S.C. 1985, c. N-5, *Military Rules of Evidence*, C.R.C., c. 1049, s. 2. See EXCULPATORY ~; INCULPATORY ~; SECONDARY ~.

CONFESSION AND AVOIDANCE. 1. A confession and avoidance admits the plaintiff's allegation of fact but introduces new facts which allegedly undermine the effect of the admission. *Patym Holdings Ltd. v. Michalakis*, 2005 BCCA 636, Smith J.A. (Saunders J.A. concurring). 2. "... [A] submission [by the defendant] that if the plaintiff's allegations are true there are facts which provide a legal justification for the defendant's conduct ..." *Royal Bank v. Rizkalla* (1984), 50 C.P.C. 292 at 295, 59 B.C.L.R. 324 (S.C.), McLachlin J.

CONFESSIONS RULE. 1. It is only where the accused makes a statement to a "person in authority", that the Crown bears the onus of proving the voluntariness of the statement as a prerequisite to its admission. This, of course, is the confessions rule. *R. v. S.G.T.*, 2010 SCC 20, Charron J. 2. In its modern formulation the confessions rule postulates that any statement by an accused to a person in authority will be disallowed as evidence on the basis of an inducement negating voluntariness if there is a reasonable doubt about whether the *quid pro quo* offer that it conveys caused the will of the accused to be overborne. *R v. Tessier* 2001 NBCA 34, 153 C.C.C. (3d) 361, 41 C.R. (5th) 242, 245 N.B.R. (2d) 1, 636 A.P.R. 1. See DERIVED ~.

CONFIDENCE. *n.* 1. Trust, reliance. 2. A communication made in reliance on another's discretion. See BREACH OF ~; DUTY TO KEEP ~.

CONFIDENCE GAME. Obtaining money or property by a trick or device.

CONFIDENTIAL. *adj.* Intended to be kept secret.

CONFIDENTIAL CAPACITY. The question under the statute is not to be determined by the test whether the employee has incidental access to this information; it is rather whether between the particular employee and the employer there exists a relation of a character that stands out from the generality of relations, and bears a special quality of confidence. Between the management and the confidential employee there is an element of personal trust which permits some degree of "thinking aloud" on special matters: it may be on matters in relation to employees, competitors or the public or on proposed action of any sort or description; but that information is of a nature out of the ordinary and is kept within a strictly limited group. In many instances it is of the essence of the confidence that the information be not disclosed to any member of any group or body of the generality of employees. *Labour Relations Board (B.C.) v. Canada Safeway Ltd.* [1953] 2 S.C.R. 46, Rand, J.

CONFIDENTIAL INFORMATION. "... 1. [T]he statement of Lord Greene in Saltman Engineering Co. v. Campbell Engineering Coy. (1948), 65 R.P.C. 203 ... at 215 ... (C.A.) is apposite: 'The information, to be confidential, must, I apprehend, apart from contract, have the necessary quality of confidence about it, namely, it must not be something which is public property and public knowledge. On the other hand, it is perfectly possible to have a confidential document, be it a formula, a plan, a sketch, or something of that kind, which is the result of work done by the maker upon materials which may be available for the use of anybody; but what makes it confidential is the fact that the maker of the document has used his brain and thus produced a result which can only be produced by somebody who goes through the same process.' " *International Corona Resources Ltd. v. Lac Minerals Ltd.* (1989), 44 B.L.R. 1 at 77, [1989] 2 S.C.R. 574, 26 C.P.R. (3d) 97, 69 O.R. (2d) 287, 61 D.L.R. (4th) 14, 6 R.P.R. (2d) 1, 35 E.T.R. 12, 101 N.R. 239, 36 O.A.C. 57, Sopinka J. (dissenting) (McIntyre and Wilson JJ. concurring in part). 2. Information obtained in the solicitor-client relationship concerning the affairs of a client. 3. [C]onfidential information does not include the general skills and knowledge acquired by the employee while working for the former employer. This is true so long as the skill and knowledge is committed to memory and not dependant on the employer's documentation. *Imperial Sheet Metal Ltd. v. Landry*, 2007 NBCA 51.

CONFIDENTIALITY. *n.* " ... There are four fundamental conditions necessary to the establishment of a privilege against the disclosure of [confidential] communications: (1) The communications must originate in a confidence that they will not be disclosed. (2) The element of confidentiality must be essential to the full and satisfactory maintenance of the relation between the parties. (3) The relation must be one which in the opinion of the community ought to be sedulously fostered. (4) The injury 'that would inure to the relation by the disclosure of the communications must be greater than the benefit thereby gained for the correct disposal of the litigation.' *Slavutych v. Baker* (1975), [1976] 1 S.C.R. 254.

CONFIDENTIAL RELATION. A relation of trust which gives rise to an expectation that communications will be held in confidence; fiduciary relation.

CONFINED. *v.* Imprisoned, shut in.

CONFINEMENT. *n.* "The essential ingredients of the offence may then be taken to be: (a) physical restraint; (b) contrary to the wishes of the person restrained; (c) to which the victim submits unwillingly; (d) depriving him of his liberty to move from one place to another." *R. v. Moore* (1989), 51 C.C.C. (3d) 566 at 572, 73 C.R. (3d) 120, 78 Nfld. & P.E.I.R. 284, 244 A.P.R. 284 (P.E.I. T.D.), McQuaid J. See FORCIBLE ~.

CONFIRM. *v.* 1. To ratify; to make firm or certain; to give approval. 2. Approve. *R. v. Briardale Investments Ltd.* (1964), 50 W.W.R. 517 at 530, 45 C.R. 358, [1965] 2 C.C.C. 273, 48 D.L.R. (2d) 315 (Man. Q.B.), Smith J. 3. "... '[R]evive' ... By confirming the will of 1909, the testator revived it and made it a new will of the date of the codicil – the last will of the testator." *Findlay v. Pae* (1916), 37 O.L.R. 318 at 325, 31 D.L.R. 281 (H.C.), Latchford J.

CONFIRMATION. *n.* 1. Formal approval. 2. Ratification; a document which validates an agreement.

CONFIRMATION ORDER. 1. A confirmation order made under the Reciprocal Enforcement of Maintenance Orders Act or under the corresponding enactment of a reciprocating state. The second state confirms the original order requiring that maintenance be paid. The order is then enforced as an order of the second court in the second jurisdiction. 2. An order of a court confirming the order of another court.

CONFISCATE. *v.* To seize property; to forfeit property.

CONFISCATION. *n.* 1. Seizure or forfeiture of property. 2. "... [T]he bringing of something into the treasury of a Government, ..." *R. v. Lane*, [1937] 1 D.L.R. 212 at 214, 67 C.C.C. 273, 11 M.P.R. 232 (N.B. C.A.), Baxter C.J. (Grimmer C.J. concurring).

CONFLICT OF INTEREST. 1. "... [T]he test must be such that the public represented by the reasonably informed person would be satisfied that no use of confidential information would occur... . Typically, these cases require two questions to be answered: (1) Did the lawyer receive confidential information attributable to a solicitor-and-client relationship relevant to the matter at hand? (2) Is there a risk that it will be used to the prejudice of the client?" *MacDonald Estate v. Martin* (1990), 48 C.P.C. (2d) 113 at 137, [1991] 1 W.W.R. 705, 121 N.R. 1, 77 D.L.R. (4th) 249, 70 Man. R. (2d) 241, [1990] 3 S.C.R. 1235, Sopinka J. (Dickson C.J.C., La Forest and Gonthier JJ. concurring). 2. "It is not part of the job description that municipal councillors be personally interested in matters that come before them beyond the interest that they have in common with the other citizens in the municipality. Where such an interest is found, both at common law and by statute, a member of council is disqualified if the interest is so related to

the exercise of public duty that a reasonably well-informed person would conclude that the interest might influence the exercise of that duty. This is commonly referred to as a conflict of interest ..." *Old St. Boniface Residents Assn. v. Winnipeg (City)* (1990), 75 D.L.R. (4th) 385 at 408, 46 Admin. L.R. 161, 2 M.P.L.R. (2d) 217, [1991] 2 W.W.R. 145, 116 N.R. 46, 69 Man. R. (2d) 134, [1990] 3 S.C.R. 1170, Sopinka J. (Wilson, Gonthier and McLachlin JJ. concurring). 3. "... [A] situation in which an employee engages in activities which are external and parallel to those he performs as part of his job, and which conflict or compete with the latter." *Canadian Imperial Bank of Commerce v. Boisvert* (1986), 13 C.C.E.L. 264 at 292, [1986] 2 F.C. 431, 68 N.R. 355 (C.A.), Marceau J.A. (Lacombe and MacGuigan JJ.A. concurring). 4. "... [P]ersonal interest sufficiently connected with his professional duties that there is a reasonable apprehension that the personal interest may influence the actual exercise of the professional responsibilities." *Cox v. College of Optometrists (Ontario)* (1988), 33 Admin. L.R. 287 at 298, 28 O.A.C. 337, 65 O.R. (2d) 461, 52 D.L.R. (4th) 298 (Div. Ct.), the court per Campbell J.

CONFLICT OF LAWS. 1. Private international law, the branch of law concerned with private relations which contain a foreign element. 2. The body of laws which each province has whether expressed in common law or in statute to govern issues concerning extraterritoriality. These issues are: (a) the provincial court's jurisdiction in cases in which facts or parties are outside the province, (b) the provincial court's recognition of judgments obtained in other jurisdictions, and (c) the choice of law in any case involving extraterritorial elements and over which the court has jurisidiction.

CONFORM. *v.* Comply. *Bourk v. Temple* (1990), 50 M.P.L.R. 125 at 132, 73 Alta. L.R. (2d) 302, 105 A.R. 61, [1990] 5 W.W.R. 87 (Q.B.), Conrad J.

CONFORMING USE. In zoning or planning, use of property which complies with restrictions of use in effect in respect of the property. See NON-~.

CONFORMITY. *n.* Correspondence in some respect; agreement.

CONFORMITY PREJUDICE. A form of juror prejudice which arises when the case is of significant interest to the community causing the juror to perceive a strong feeling in the community and an expectation in the community concerning the outcome of the case.

CONFUSING. *adj.* When applied as an adjective to a trade-mark or trade-name, means a trade-mark or trade-name the use of which would cause confusion if the use of trade-mark or trade-name would cause confusion with another trade-mark or trade-name in the manner and circumstances described in the Act. *Trade-marks Act*, R.S.C. 1985, c. T-13, s. 2 and 6, in part.

CONFUSION. *n.* To decide whether the use of a trade-mark or of a trade-name causes confusion with another trade-mark or another trade-name, the Court must ask itself whether, as a matter of first impression on the minds of an ordinary person having a vague recollection of that other mark or name, the use of both marks or names in the same area in the same manner is likely to lead to the inference that the services associated with those marks or names are performed by the same person, whether or not the services are of the same general class. *Miss Universe Inc. v. Bohna* [1995] 1 F.C. 614 (C.A.).

CON GAME. Obtaining money or property by a deceiving or tricking the owner. See CONFIDENCE GAME.

CONJECTURE. *n.* "The dividing line between conjecture and inference is often a very difficult one to draw. A conjecture may be plausible but of no legal value, for its essence is that it is a mere guess. An inference in the legal sense, on the other hand, is a deduction from the evidence, and if it is a reasonable deduction it may have the validity of legal proof. The attribution of an occurrence to a cause is, I take it, always a matter of inference... ." *Jones v. Great Western Rwy. Co.* (1930), 47 T.L.R. 39 at 45 (U.K. H.L.), Lord Macmillan.

CONJOINTS. *n.* People married to one another.

CONJUGAL. *adj.* Related to the married or marriage-like state.

CONJUGAL RIGHTS. Each spouse's right to the society, comfort and affection of the other spouse.

CONJUNCTIVE. *adj.* Joining two concepts.

CONNECTION. See RATIONAL ~.

CONNIVANCE. *n.* Culpable agreement to do wrong.

CONSANGUINITY. *n.* Relationship by descent: either collaterally, i.e. from a common ancestor or lineally, i.e. mother and daughter.

CONSCIENCE. *n.* "... [S]elf-judgement [sic] on the moral quality of one's conduct or the lack of it... ." *MacKay v. Manitoba* (1985), 23 C.R.R. 8 at 11, [1986] 2 W.W.R. 367, 24 D.L.R. (4th) 587, 39 Man. R. (2d) 274 (C.A.), Twaddle J.A. (Philp J.A. concurring). See FREEDOM OF ~ AND RELIGION.

CONSCIENTIOUS OBJECTOR. A person who, on moral or religious grounds, thinks it wrong to resist force with force and to kill.

CONSCIOUSNESS OF GUILT EVIDENCE. Evidence of after-the-fact conduct is commonly admitted to show that an accused person has acted in a manner which, based on human experience and logic, is consistent with the conduct of a guilty person and inconsistent with the conduct of an innocent person. It is introduced to show that the accused was aware of having committed the crime in question and acted for the purpose of evading detection and prosecution. That label is somewhat misleading and its use should be discouraged. "Consciousness of guilt" is simply one inference that may be drawn from the evidence of the accused's conduct; it is not a special category of evidence in itself. *R. v. White* [1998] 2 S.C.R. 72.

CONSCRIPTION. *n.* Compulsory enrolment in the military service.

CONSCRIPTIVE EVIDENCE. 1. The crucial element which distinguishes non conscriptive evidence from conscriptive evidence is not whether the evidence may be characterized as "real" or not. Rather, it is whether the accused was compelled to make a statement or provide a bodily substance in violation of the Charter. Where the accused, as a result of a breach of the Charter, is compelled or conscripted to provide a bodily substance to the state, this evidence will be of a conscriptive nature, despite the fact that it may also be "real" evidence. Therefore, it may be more accurate to describe evidence found without any participation of the accused, such as the murder weapon found at the scene of the crime, or drugs found in a dwelling house, simply as non conscriptive evidence; its status as "real" evidence, simpliciter, is irrelevant to the s. 24(2) inquiry. Evidence will be conscriptive when an accused, in violation of his Charter rights, is compelled to incriminate himself at the behest of the state by means of a statement, the use of the body or the production of bodily samples. The traditional and most frequently encountered example of this type of evidence is a self incriminating statement made by the accused following a violation of his right to counsel as guaranteed by s. 10(b) of the Charter. The other example is the compelled taking and use of the body or of bodily substances of the accused, such as blood, which lead to self incrimination. It is the compelled statements and the conscripted use of bodily substances obtained in violation of Charter rights which may render a trial unfair. ... [W]here it is established that either a non conscriptive means existed through which the evidence would have been discovered or that its discovery was inevitable, then the evidence was discoverable; it would have been discovered in the absence of the unlawful conscription of the accused. The Crown must bear the onus of establishing discoverability on a balance of probabilities. Where the evidence was "discoverable," even though it may be conscriptive, its admission will not, as a general rule, render the trial unfair. The Court should therefore proceed to consider the seriousness of the violation. *R. v. Stillman*, [1997] 1 S.C.R. 607, Cory J. for the majority. 2. Concerning unreasonable search and seizure "... refers to evidence which emanates from the accused following a violation of s. 10(b) of the [Charter] concerning unreasonable search and seizure ... ." *R. v. Wise* (1992), 11 C.R. (4th) 253 at 265, [1992] 1 S.C.R. 527, 70 C.C.C. (3d) 193, 133 N.R. 161, 8 C.R.R. (2d) 53, 51 O.A.C. 351, Cory J. (Lamer C.J.C., Gonthier, Stevenson JJ. concurring). 3. Evidence is conscriptive when an accused is compelled to incriminate himself in violation of his Charter rights by means of a statement, use of the body, or production of bodily samples. See NON-~.

CONSECUTIVE. *adj.* One after the other; following.

CONSECUTIVE INTERPRETATION. It may be useful to keep in mind the distinction between "consecutive" (after the words are spoken) and "simultaneous" (at the same time as words are spoken). Although consecutive interpretation effectively doubles the time necessary to complete the proceedings, it offers a number of advantages over simultaneous interpretation. Consecutive interpretation, on the other hand, has the advantage of allowing the accused to react at the appropriate time, such as when making objections. It also makes it easier to assess on the spot the accuracy of the interpretation, something rendered more difficult when one has to listen to the original language and its translation at the same time, as would be the case with simultaneous interpretation. *R. v. Tran*, [1994] 2 S.C.R. 951.

CONSECUTIVELY. *adv.* Following immediately upon. *R. v. Cadeddu* (1980), 19 C.R. (3d) 93 at 96, 57 C.C.C. (2d) 264 (Ont. C.A.), the court per Morden J.A.

CONSECUTIVE SENTENCES. One sentence follows another in time.

CONSEIL CAN. D. INT. *abbr.* Conseil canadien de droit international. Congrès. Travaux (Canadian Council of International Law. Conference. Proceedings).

CONSENSUS AD IDEM. [L. agreement to the same thing] The consent required for a contract to be binding.

CONSENT. *v.* To agree to something, such as the removal of children from their habitual residence. *Katsigiannis v. Kottick-Katsigiannis* (2001), 55 O.R. (3d) 456 (C.A.).

CONSENT. *n.* 1. Freely given agreement. 2. There is a difference in the concept of "consent" as it relates to the state of mind of the complainant vis-à-vis the actus reus of the offence and the state of mind of the accused in respect of the *mens rea*. For the purposes of the actus reus, "consent" means that the complainant in her mind wanted the sexual touching to take place. In the context of mens rea—specifically for the purposes of the honest but mistaken belief in consent—"consent" means that the complainant had affirmatively communicated by words or conduct her agreement to engage in sexual activity with the accused. This distinction should always be borne in mind and the two parts of the analysis kept separate. *R. v. Ewanchuk*, 1999 CarswellAlta 99, 131 C.C.C. (3d) 481, 169 D.L.R. (4th) 193, 235 N.R. 323, 22 C.R. (5th) 1, 232 A.R. 1, 195 W.A.C. 1, 68 Alta. L.R. (3d) 1, [1999] 6 W.W.R. 333, [1999] 1 S.C.R. 330, Major J. 3. The distinction between the meaning of "compliance" and the meaning of "consent" is real. To consent means to actually agree and cooperate. Compliance has a more subtle meaning involving the failure to object. *R. c. Knox*, 1996 CarswellQue 1041, 202 N.R. 228, 109 C.C.C. (3d) 481, 23 M.V.R. (3d) 93, [1996] 3 S.C.R. 199, 38 C.R.R. (2d) 222, 139 D.L.R. (4th) 1, 1 C.R. (5th) 254, Lamer C.J.C. See AGE OF ~; IMPLIED ~; INFORMED ~.

CONSENT JUDGMENT. A judgment the terms of which are agreed to by the parties.

CONSENT ORDER. An order which constitutes a bargain between the parties. *Kitchen v. Crown Coal Co. Ltd.* [1932] 1 W.W.R. 696 (C.A.).

CONSEQUENCE. See MEANINGFUL ~S.

CONSEQUENTIAL DAMAGES. The loss which occurs indirectly from the act complained of.

CONSEQUENTIAL ECONOMIC LOSS. As Earl A. Cherniak, Q.C., and Elissa How, "Policy and Predictability: Pure Economic Loss in the Supreme Court of Canada" (1999), 31 Can. Bus. L.J. 209, note (at p. 210): "... Although all economic loss cases share the common element of a plaintiff who has suffered a pure economic loss with no concurrent physical loss to the plaintiff's person or property, the claims are so varied that the Supreme Court of Canada has decided to deal with economic loss in more discrete categories. La Forest J., in Winnipeg Condominium Corp. No. 36 v. Bird Construction Co., adopted the following five categories developed by Professor Bruce Feldthusen: (1) the independent liability of statutory public authorities; (2) negligent misrepresentation; (3) negligent performance of a service; (4) negligent supply of shoddy goods or structures, and (5) relational economic loss." There is a difference between pure economic loss and "consequential" economic loss. As explained in Professor Bruce Feldthusen, Economic Negligence: The Recovery of Pure Economic Loss, 5th ed. (Scarborough: Thomson Canada Limited, 2008) (at p. 1): "... [W]hen physical damage is involved, pure economic loss must be distinguished from a consequential economic loss which, by definition, is causally consequent upon physical damage to the plaintiff or the plaintiff's property." While this distinction is important, as stated by Mr. Justice Allen M. Linden & Professor Bruce Feldthusen, Canadian Tort Law, 8th ed. (Markham: LexisNexis Canada Inc., 2006), "[c]onsequential loss is usually governed by the same principles of recovery that apply to the physical damage itself" (at p. 441). Thus, while there is a clear legal distinction between the two concepts, there will usually be little difference in practice between property damage and consequential economic loss. *Multi Pork Inc. v. A.G. Penner Farm Services Ltd.*, 2008 MBCA 119.

CONSEQUENTLY. *adv.* "... [C]an, in the one instance, import an inevitable sequence of events, one necessarily flowing from, and as a direct result of, the other ... On the other hand, it may also import something which follows by logical inference." *Campbell v. Blackett* (1978), 80 D.L.R. (3d) 252 at 257, 13 Nfld. & P.E.I.R. 64, 29 A.P.R. 64 (P.E.I. C.A.), the court per McQuaid J.A.

CONSERVATION. *n.* 1. The planning, management and implementation of an activity with the objective of protecting the essential physical, chemical and biological characteristics of the environment against degradation. *Public Lands Act*, R.S.A. 2000, c. P-40, s. 1. 2. In relation to heritage, any activity undertaken to protect, preserve or enhance the heritage value or heritage character of heritage property or an area. *Vancouver Charter*, S.B.C. 1953, c. 55, s. 2.

CONSERVATION EASEMENT. 1. A conservation easement is a voluntary agreement entered into between the grantor of the conservation easement and the holder of the conservation easement that (a)grants rights and privileges to the holder of the conservation easement respecting land that relate to the purposes for which the conservation easement is granted, and (b)may impose obligations, either positive or negative, on the holder of the conservation easement, the grantor of the conservation easement or any subsequent owner of the land respecting that land that relate to the purposes for which the conservation easement is granted. A conservation easement may exist for a fixed term or for perpetuity. A conservation easement shall be granted only for one or more of the following purposes: (a)the conservation of ecologically sensitive land; (b)the protection, enhancement or restoration of natural ecosystems; (c)the protection or restoration of wildlife habitat or wildlife; (d)the conservation of habitat of rare or endangered plant or animal species; (e)the conservation or protection of soil, air, land or water; (f)the conservation of significant biological, morphological, geological or palaeontological features; (g)the conservation of culturally important, archaeologically important or scenically important places; (h) the protection or use of land for outdoor recreation; (i)the use of land for public education; and (j)any other purpose prescribed by regulation. *Conservation Easements Act*, S.N.B. 1998, c. C-16.3, s. 2-3. 2. An interest in real property which imposes restrictions or positive obligations for (a) retaining or protecting natural, scenic, or open-space values; (b) assuring natural resources are available for recreational or open-space uses; (c) conserving or enhancing natural resources, the land in its natural state, wildlife habitat, plant habitat, or migratory routes of birds and animals; or (d) conserving or enhancing soil, air or water quality. *Environment Act*, R.S.Y. 2002, c. 76, s. 76.

CONSERVATION PROGRAMS. Includes: (i) waterfowl conservation programs, including programs related to the preservation, rehabilitation, management and development of waterfowl breeding habitat, including wetlands nesting and upland nesting habitat; (ii) programs related to the preservation, management and development of other wildlife habitat; and (iii) water conservation programs. *The Saskatchewan Watershed Authority Act*, 2005, S.S. 2005, c. S-35.03, s. 2.

CONSERVATOR. *n.* One who protects, preserves, or maintains.

CONSERVE. *v.* To keep; to save.

CONSIDER. *v.* 1. To examine, inspect; to turn one's mind to. 2. To go about deciding a case. 3. County Council was required by s. 25.4 of the Municipal Act [R.S.O. 1990, c. M.45] to do no more than "consider" the Minister's principles. In my opinion, that imposes no greater requirement on County Council than to take the principles into account when developing a restructuring proposal to be submitted to the Minister. Section 25.4 does not state how or when the principles are to be considered. Moreover, to "consider" is a somewhat conditional requirement in the sense that it does not imply that the principles must be followed in the development of a restructuring proposal. *Bruce (Township) v. Ontario (Minister of Municipal Affairs & Housing)*, 1998 CarswellOnt 3382, 112 O.A.C. 68, 164 D.L.R. (4th) 443, 48 M.P.L.R. (2d) 201, 41 O.R. (3d) 309, 8 Admin. L.R (3d) 21, Osborne J.A. for the court.

CONSIDERATION. *n.* 1. In a contract, an interest, right, profit or benefit accrues to the one party while some detriment, forebearance, loss or responsibility is suffered or undertaken by the other party. G.H.L. Fridman, *The Law of Contract in Canada*, 2d ed. (Toronto: Carswell, 1986) at 75. 2. In a contract for the sale of goods, it is called the price and must be in money. G.H.L. Fridman, *Sale of Goods in Canada*, 3d ed. (Toronto: Carswell, 1986) at 42. 3. "... [U]sed to describe that which is given or promised in order to bring a binding contract into existence. It is also used, however, to describe the performance of the promise ..." *Kiss v. Palachik* (1983), 146 D.L.R. (3d) 385 at 393, [1983] 1 S.C.R. 623, 47 N.R. 148, 22 R.F.L. (2d) 225, 15 E.T.R. 129, the court per Wilson J. 4. A promise to do something that a party to a contract is already bound to do is not consideration. *Braiden v. La-Z-Boy Canada Ltd.*, 2008 ONCA 464. See ADEQUATE ~; EXECUTED ~; EXECUTORY ~; FUTURE ~; GOOD ~; PAST ~; PRESENT ~; VALUABLE ~.

CONSIDERED. *adj.* Determined; regarded.

CONSIGN. *v.* To send goods to another to be sold to third parties.

CONSIGNEE. *n.* A person to whom the goods are sent.

CONSIGNMENT. *n.* 1. "In its simplest terms, ... the sending of goods to another. An arrangement whereby an owner sends goods to another on the understanding that such other will sell the goods to a third party and remit the proceeds to the owner after deducting his compensation for effecting the sale is an example of a consignment agreement." *Stephanian's Persian Carpets Ltd., Re* (1980), 34 C.B.R. (N.S.) 35 at 37, 1 P.P.S.A.C. 119 (Ont. S.C.), Saunders J. 2. The goods themselves. See ON ~.

CONSIGNOR. *n.* 1. A person who consigns goods. 2. A person who sends goods to another to be sold to third parties.

CONSIST. *v.* To be made up of.

CONSISTENT. *adj.* 1. Harmonious; in agreement with. 2. In contrast to the adjectives "corroborative", "confirmatory", and "supportive", which, when applied to evidence, connote the adding of strength or reinforcement from an independent source for the truth and accuracy of the complainant's evidence, the adjective "consistent" implies the absence of contradiction or conflict within the complainant's testimony itself. *R. v. Aksidan*, 2006 BCCA 258. See IN~.

CONSISTENT EXPRESSION. See PRESUMPTION OF ~.

CONSOL. *abbr.* Consolidated.

CONSOLIDATE. *v.* 1. To combine, unite. 2. In relation to statutes, to bring together several pieces of legislation into one dealing with the topic more generally. 3. In relation to statutes or regulations, to pull together all amendments to the original statute so that only provisions currently in force are contained in the consolidation made.

CONSOLIDATED FUND. The aggregate of all public money that is on hand and on deposit to the credit of a province. *Auditor General Act*, S.N.B. 1981, c. A-17.1, s. 1.

CONSOLIDATED LOAN. A loan acquired for the purpose of consolidating liabilities.

CONSOLIDATED REVENUE FUND. 1. Aggregate of all public moneys that are on deposit at the credit of the Receiver General. *Financial Administration Act*, R.S.C. 1985, c. F-11, s. 2. 2. The aggregate of all public moneys that are on deposit at the credit of the Minister of Finance or in the name of any agency of the Crown approved by the Lieutenant Governor in Council. *Financial Administration Act*, R.S.O. 1990, c. F.12, s. 1.

CONSOLIDATED STATUTE. A version of a statute prepared by drawing all amendments to the original statute together and creating a document which provides all the currently in force provisions of the statute.

CONSOLIDATING STATUTE. A statute which draws together, with only minor amendments and improvements, all statutory provisions related to a particular topic into a single act.

CONSOLIDATION. *n.* In statute law, the uniting of many acts of Parliament into one.

CONSOLIDATION ACT. An act, usually with amendments, which repeals a number of earlier acts and includes, sometimes, some rules of the common law.

CONSOLIDATION OF ACTIONS. The combination of proceedings involving the same parties or issues.

CONSORTIUM. *n.* "The term 'consortium' is not susceptible of precise or complete definition but broadly speaking, companionship, love, affection, comfort, mutual services, sexual intercourse – all belonging to the marriage state – taken together make up what we refer to as consortium." *Kungl v. Schiefer*, [1961] O.R. 1 at 7 (C.A.), Schroeder J.A.

CONSPIRACY. *n.* 1. "A conspiracy consists not merely in the intention of two or more, but in the agreement of two or more to do an unlawful act, or to do a lawful act by unlawful means. So long as such a decision rests in intention only, it is not indictable. When two agree to carry it into effect, the very plot is an act in itself, and the act of each of the parties, promise against promise, actus contra actum, capable of being enforced if lawful, punishable if for a criminal object or for the use of criminal means." *Mulcahy v. R.* (1868), L.R. 3 H.L. 306 at 317, Willes J. 2. There must be an intention to agree, the completion of an agreement, and a common design. Conspiracy is in fact a more "preliminary" crime than attempt, since the offence is considered to be complete before any acts are taken that go beyond mere preparation to put the common design into effect. The Crown is simply required to prove a meeting of the minds with regard to a common design to do something unlawful, specifically the commission of an indictable offence. See s. 465(1)(c) of the Criminal Code. A conspiracy must involve more than one person, even though all the conspirators may not either be identified, or be ca-

pable of being convicted. *United States v. Dynar*, 1997 CarswellOnt 1981, (*sub nom.* United States of America v. Dynar) 115 C.C.C. (3d) 481, 213 N.R. 321, (*sub nom.* United States of America v. Dynar) 147 D.L.R. (4th) 399, 101 O.A.C. 321, 8 C.R. (5th) 79 44 C.R.R. (2d) 189, [1997] 2 S.C.R. 462, Cory and Iacobucci JJ. 3 "... [W]hereas the law of tort does not permit an action against an individual defendant who has caused injury to the plaintiff, the law of torts does recognize a claim against them in combination as the tort of conspiracy if: (1) whether the means used by the defendants are lawful or unlawful, the predominant purpose of the defendants' conduct is to cause injury to the plaintiff; or (2) where the conduct of the defendants is unlawful, the conduct is directed toward the plaintiff ... and the defendants should know in the circumstances that injury to the plaintiff is likely to and does result. In situation (2) it is not necessary that the predominant purpose of the defendants' conduct be to cause injury to the plaintiff but, in the prevailing circumstances, it must be a constructive intent derived from the fact that the defendants should have known that injury to the plaintiff would ensue. In both situations, however, there must be actual damage suffered by the plaintiff." *Canada Cement LaFarge Ltd. v. British Columbia Lightweight Aggregate Ltd.* (1983), 21 B.L.R. 254 at 274, [1983] 1 S.C.R. 452, [1983] 6 W.W.R. 385, 24 C.C.L.T. 111, 72 C.P.R. (2d) 1, 145 D.L.R. (3d) 385, 47 N.R. 191, the court per Estey J. 4. A pleading of civil conspiracy must describe who the parties are and the relationship with each other. It should allege the agreement between the defendants to conspire, and state precisely what the purpose or what were the objects of the alleged conspiracy. The pleading must set forth with clarity and precision the overt acts which are alleged to have been done by each of the alleged conspirators in furtherance of the conspiracy. Finally, the pleading must allege the injury and damage occasioned to the plaintiff. Once these formal requirements are met, the plaintiff must show that the allegations are supported by the available evidence. To establish the tort of conspiracy, the plaintiff must show that there was an agreement to injure between the defendants, that the defendants intended to injure the plaintiff and that damages resulted and that there was no justification for the act. *Belsat Video Marketing Inc. v. Astral Communications Inc.* (1998), 81 C.P.R. (3d) 1 (Ont. Gen. Div.). See CIVIL ~; CRIMINAL ~; SEDITIOUS ~.

CONSPIRATOR. *n.* A person who takes part in a conspiracy.

CONSPIRE. *v.* "The word 'conspire' derives from two Latin words, 'con' and 'spirare', meaning 'to breathe together'. To conspire is to agree... ." *Cotroni v. R.*, [1979] 2 S.C.R. 256 at 276-77, Dickson J.

CONSTABLE. *n.* 1. "... '[T]he holder of a police office' ... exercising, so far as his police duties are concerned, an original authority ... a member of a civilian force, and I take his assimilation to a soldier ... to be an assimilation related only to whether an action per quod lies against a tortfeasor at common law for the loss of his services, and not to assimilation for other purposes, such as liability to peremptory discharge, if that be the case with a soldier." *Nicholson v. Haldimand-Norfolk (Regional Municipality) Commissioners of Police* (1978), 9 C.L.L.C. 249 at 253, [1979] 1 S.C.R. 311, 88 D.L.R. (3d) 671, 78 C.L.L.C. 14, 181, 23 N.R. 410, Laskin C.J.C. 2. Any member of a police force other than an officer.

CONSTITUENCY. *n.* 1. A place or territorial area entitled to return a member to serve in a legislative assembly or in Parliament. 2. The voters, or more generally, the people who live in the area described in definition 1. 3. The supporters of a particular person or group or the persons who share the interest of a particular person or group.

CONSTITUENCY ASSOCIATION. In an electoral district, means the association or organization endorsed by a registered party as the official association of that party in the electoral district. See REGISTERED ~.

CONSTITUENT. *n.* One entitled to vote in a constituency.

CONSTITUTION. *n.* 1. The body of law which establishes the framework of government for a nation or an organization. 2. The supreme law of Canada. *Constitution Act, 1982*, s. 52(1), being Schedule B of the *Canada Act, 1982* (U.K.), 1982, c. 11. 3. "... [I]s drafted with an eye to the future. Its function is to provide continuing framework for the legitimate exercise of governmental power and, when joined by a Bill or a Charter of Rights, for the unremitting protection of individual rights and liberties. Once enacted, its provisions cannot easily be repealed or amended. It must, therefore, be capable of growth and development over time to meet new social, political and historical realities often unimagined by its framers. *Canada (Director of Investigation & Research) v. Southam Inc.* (1984), 27 B.L.R. 297 at 307, [1984] 2 S.C.R. 145, 33 Alta. L.R. (2d) 193, 41 C.R. (3d) 97, [1984] 6 W.W.R. 577, 14 C.C.C. (3d) 97, 55 A.R. 291, 55 N.R. 241, 2 C.P.R. (3d) 1, 9 C.R.R. 355, 11 D.L.R. (4th) 641, 84 D.T.C. 6467, the court per Dickson J.

CONSTITUTION ACT, 1867. The act originally called the British North America Act (BNA Act). It became known as the Constitution Act when the constitution was patriated in 1982. *The Constitution Act, 1867* (U.K.), 30 & 31 Victoria, c. 3.

CONSTITUTIONAL CONVENTION. "We respectfully adopt the definition given by the learned Chief Justice of Manitoba, Freedman C.J.M. in the Manitoba Reference [Reference re Amendment of the Constitution of Canada (No. 3) (1981), 120 D.L.R. (3d) 385] ... : ' ... a convention occupies a position somewhere in between a usage or custom on one hand and constitutional law on the other. There is a general agreement that if one sought to fix that position with greater precision he would place convention nearer to law than to usage or custom. There is also a general agreement that "a convention is a rule which is regarded as obligatory by the officials to whom it applies": Hogg, Constitutional Law of Canada (1977), p. 9.' ... The existence of a definite convention is always unclear and a matter of debate. Furthermore conventions are flexible, somewhat imprecise and

unsuitable for judicial determination." *Reference re Questions Concerning Amendment of the Constitution of Canada as set out in O.C. 1020/80* (1981), (*sub nom. Resolution to Amend the Constitution of Canada, Re*) 1 C.R.R. 59 at 137-38, [1981] 1 S.C.R. 753, [1981] 6 W.W.R. 1, 11 Man. R. (2d) 1, 39 N.R. 1, 34 Nfld. & P.E.I.R. 1, 95 A.P.R. 1, Martland, Ritchie, Dickson, Beetz, Chouinard and Lamer JJ. See CONVENTION.

CONSTITUTIONAL EXEMPTION. A device which enables the court to uphold a law that is valid in most of its applications. The court does this by creating an exemption, declaring the law unconstitutional and invalid, in their application to specific individuals or groups.

CONSTITUTIONALISM. *n.* The constitutionalism principle bears considerable similarity to the rule of law, although they are not identical. The essence of constitutionalism in Canada is embodied in s. 52(1) of the Constitution Act, 1982 [Constitution Act, 1982, being Schedule B of the Canada Act, 1982 (U.K.), 1982, c. 11], which provides that "[t]he Constitution of Canada is the supreme law of Canada, and any law that is inconsistent with the provisions of the Constitution is, to the extent of the inconsistency, of no force or effect." Simply put, the constitutionalism principle requires that all government action comply with the Constitution. The rule of law principle requires that all government action must comply with the law, including the Constitution. *Reference re Secession of Quebec*, 1998 CarswellNat 1299, 161 D.L.R. (4th) 385, 228 N.R. 203, 55 C.R.R. (2d) 1, [1998] 2 S.C.R. 217, per curiam.

CONSTITUTIONALITY. See PRESUMPTION OF ~.

CONSTITUTIONAL LAW. The body of law which deals with the distribution or exercise of the powers of government.

CONSTITUTIONAL VALIDITY. See PRESUMPTION OF ~.

CONSTITUTION OF CANADA. 1. Includes (a) The Canada Act 1982, including this Act; (b) the Acts and orders referred to in the schedule; and (c) any amendment to any Act or order referred to in paragraph (a) or (b). *Constitution Act, 1982*, s. 52(2), being Schedule B of the *Canada Act, 1982* (U.K.), 1982, c. 11. 2. Section 52(1) of Constitution provides that the Constitution of Canada is the supreme law of Canada and any law that is inconsistent with the provisions of the Constitution is, to the extent of the inconsistency, of no force or effect. 3. "... [T]he phrases 'Constitution of Canada' and 'Canadian Constitution' do not refer to matters of interest only to the federal government or federal juristic unit. They are clearly meant in a broader sense and embrace the global system of rules and principles which govern the exercise of constitutional authority in the whole and in every part of the Canadian state." *Reference re Questions Concerning Amendment of the Constitution of Canada as set out in O.C. 1020/80* (1981), (*sub nom. Resolution to Amend the Constitution of Canada, Re*) 1 C.R.R. 59 at 131, [1981] 1 S.C.R. 753, [1981] 6 W.W.R. 1, 11 Man. R. (2d) 1, 39 N.R. 1, 34

Nfld. & P.E.I.R. 1, 95 A.P.R. 1, Martland, Ritchie, Dickson, Beetz, Chouinard and Lamer JJ. 4. "... [M]eans the constitution of the federal Government, as distinct from the provincial Governments... ." *Reference re Legislative Authority of Parliament of Canada* (1979), (*sub nom. Reference re Legislative Authority of Parliament to Alter or Replace Senate*) 102 D.L.R. (3d) 1 at 12, [1980] 1 S.C.R. 56, 30 N.R. 271, Laskin C.J.C., Martland, Ritchie, Pigeon, Dickson, Estey, Pratte and McIntyre JJ. 5. The "Constitution of Canada" certainly includes the constitutional texts enumerated in s. 52(2) of the Constitution Act, 1982. Although these texts have a primary place in determining constitutional rules, they are not exhaustive. The Constitution also "embraces unwritten, as well as written rules". Finally, the Constitution of Canada includes the global system of rules and principles which govern the exercise of constitutional authority in the whole and in every part of the Canadian state. These supporting principles and rules, which include constitutional conventions and the workings of Parliament, are a necessary part of our Constitution because problems or situations may arise which are not expressly dealt with by the text of the Constitution. In order to endure over time, a constitution must contain a comprehensive set of rules and principles which are capable of providing an exhaustive legal framework for our system of government. Such principles and rules emerge from an understanding of the constitutional text itself, the historical context, and previous judicial interpretations of constitutional meaning. *Reference re Secession of Quebec*, 1998 CarswellNat 1299, 161 D.L.R. (4th) 385, 228 N.R. 203, 55 C.R.R. (2d) 1, [1998] 2 S.C.R. 217, per curiam.

CONSTRAINT. *n.* A restriction on (a) the issue or transfer of shares of any class or series to persons who are not resident Canadians; (b) the issue or transfer of shares of any class or series to enable a corporation or any of its affiliates or associates to qualify under a law referred to in paragraph 87(1)(a) (i) to obtain a licence to carry on any business, (ii) to become a publisher of a Canadian newspaper or periodical, or (iii) to acquire shares of a financial intermediary as defined in paragraph 87(1)(b); or (c) the issue, transfer or ownership of shares of any class or series in order to assist a corporation or any of its affiliates or associates to qualify under a law referred to in subsection 87(2) to receive licences, permits, grants, payments or other benefits by reason of attaining or maintaining a specified level of Canadian ownership or control. *Canada Business Corporations Act*, R.S.C. 1985, c. C-44, *Canada Business Corporations Regulations, 2001*, SOR/2001-512, s. 73.

CONSTRUCT. *v.* To do anything in the erection, installation, extension or material alteration or repair of a building and includes the installation of a building unit fabricated or moved from elsewhere.

CONSTRUCTION. *n.* 1. "[In Chatenay v. Brazilian Submarine Telegraph Co., [1891] 1 Q.B. 79] ... Lindley L.J. at p. 85 said the following: 'The expression "construction" as applied to a document, at all events as used by English lawyers, includes two things: first,

the meaning of the words; and secondly, their legal effect, or the effect which is to be given to them. The meaning of the words I take to be a question of fact in all cases, whether we are dealing with a poem or a legal document. The effect of the words is a question of law.' " *Wald v. Greater York Developments Ltd.* (1978), 8 C.P.C. 12 at 15 (Ont. H.C.), Sandler (Master). 2. The activity of building or erecting. 3. May include demolition, alteration, repairing. See BUILDING ~ CODE; BUILDING ~ STANDARD; CLAIM ~; RE~; STRICT ~.

CONSTRUCTION LIEN. A claim secured against real property made to ensure payment for materials furnished or work performed during construction.

CONSTRUCTION LOAN. A loan to finance construction. The loan permits the borrower to take draws or advances from time to time during the course of construction.

CONSTRUCTIVE. *adj.* 1. Implied or inferred. 2. Arising out of law without reference to any party's intention.

CONSTRUCTIVE DESERTION. One spouse by misconduct forces the other spouse to leave the home.

CONSTRUCTIVE DISCHARGE. Actions by the employer which cause an employee to resign.

CONSTRUCTIVE DISCRIMINATION. A neutral "requirement, qualification or consideration" which gives rise to constructive discrimination is only allowed to operate as an exception where it is reasonable and bona fide in the circumstances. And it is only reasonable in the circumstances if accommodation cannot be accomplished without undue hardship. *Central Alberta Dairy Pool v. Alberta (Human Rights Commission)*, [1990] 2 S.C.R. 489. See ADVERSE EFFECT DISCRIMINATION.

CONSTRUCTIVE DISMISSAL. 1. Occurs when the conduct of the employer is found to repudiate the contract. *McAlpine v. Econotech Services Ltd.*, 2004 BCCA 111. 2. Occurs where an employer unilaterally makes a fundamental or substantial change to an employee's contract of employment—a change that violates the contract's terms—the employer is committing a fundamental breach of the contract that results in its termination and entitles the employee to consider himself or herself constructively dismissed. The employee can then claim damages from the employer in lieu of reasonable notice. *Farber c. Royal Trust Co.* [1997] 1 S.C.R. 846.

CONSTRUCTIVE EVICTION. Acts by the landlord which deprive a tenant of enjoyment of the property so that it is untenantable.

CONSTRUCTIVE FRAUD. 1. "... [E]quivalent of breach of fiduciary duty... ." *Proprietary Mines Ltd. v. MacKay*, [1939] 3 D.L.R. 215 at 246, [1939] O.R. 461 (C.A.), Masten J.A. (Middleton J.A. concurring). 2. An equitable principle which permits the court to set aside transactions where conduct falling below the standards demanded of equity; classified under four headings: undue influence, abuse of confidence, unconscionable bargains, and frauds on powers. *Ogilvie v. Ogilvie Estate* (1998), 106 B.C.A.C. 55. 3.

"It is a mistake to suppose that an actual intention to cheat must always be proved. A man may misconceive the extent of the obligation which a Court of Equity imposes on him. His fault is that he has violated, however innocently because of his ignorance, an obligation which he must be taken by the Court to have known, and his conduct has in that sense always been called fraudulent, even in such a case as a technical fraud on a power. It was thus that the expression 'constructive fraud' came into existence... ." *Nocton v. Lord Ashburton*, [1914] A.C. 932 at 954.

CONSTRUCTIVE KNOWLEDGE. Knowledge of circumstances which would indicate the facts to an honest person or knowledge of facts which would put an honest person on inquiry. *Air Canada v. M. & L. Travel Ltd.* [1993] 3 S.C.R. 787.

CONSTRUCTIVE LAYOFF. A significant reduction in hours in circumstances where a particular employee is singled out may amount to constructive layoff.

CONSTRUCTIVE NOTICE. 1. "... [K]nowledge of other facts [other than the very fact required to be established] which put a person on inquiry to discover the fact required to be established. The classic distinction, ... , is that of Strong J. in Rose v. Peterkin (1885), 13 S.C.R. 677 at 694: 'What such actual and direct notice is may well be ascertained very shortly by defining constructive notice, and then taking actual notice to be knowledge, not presumed as in the case of constructive notice, but shown to be actually brought home to the party to be charged with it, either by proof of his own admission or by the evidence of witnesses who are able to establish that the very fact, of which notice is to be established, not something which would have led to the discovery of the fact if an inquiry had been pursued, was brought to his knowledge.' " *Stoimenov v. Stoimenov* (1985), 35 R.P.R. 150 at 158, 44 R.F.L. (2d) 14, 7 O.A.C. 220, the court per Tarnopolsky J.A. Knowledge attributed to someone who fails to make proper inquiries into the title of property purchased, who fails to investigate a fact, brought to notice, which suggests that a claim exists, or who deliberately does not inquire in order to avoid notice. See EQUITABLE DOCTRINE OF ~.

CONSTRUCTIVE POSSESSION. 1. Is established where the accused did not have physical custody of the object in question, but did have it "in the actual possession or custody of another person" or "in any place, whether or not that place belongs to or is occupied by him, for the use or benefit of himself or of another person" (Criminal Code, s. 4(3)(a)). Constructive possession is thus complete where the accused: (1) has knowledge of the character of the object, (2) knowingly puts or keeps the object in a particular place, whether or not that place belongs to him, and (3) intends to have the object in the particular place for his "use or benefit" or that of another person. *R. v. Morelli*, 2010 SCC 8, [2010] 1 S.C.R. 253, Fish J. 2. "... The doctrine [of constructive possession] is described in Harris v. Mudie (1882), 7 O.A.R. 414 (C.A.) at p. 427, as follows: ' ... when a party having colour of title enters in good faith upon the land professed to be conveyed, he is presumed to enter ac-

cording to his title, and thereby gains a constructive possession of the whole land embraced in his deed.' ... The party must establish visible and exclusive possession of part of the property described in the deed, but occupation of a portion of the property will be extended by construction to all of the land within the boundary of the deed: Wood v. LeBlanc (1903), 36 N.B.R. 47 affirmed 34 S.C.R. 627." *Port Franks Properties Ltd. v. R.* (1979), [1981] 3 C.N.L.R. 86 at 99, 99 D.L.R. (3d) 28 (Fed. R.C.), Lieff D.J.

CONSTRUCTIVE TRUST. 1. Imposed as a "... remedy against unjust enrichment and that before unjust enrichment may ... exist, three elements must be shown – an enrichment, a corresponding deprivation and the absence of any 'juristic reason' for the enrichment (per Dickson J. in Becker v. Pettkus, [1980] 2 S.C.R. 834 ...)." *Hyette v. Pfenniger* (1991), 39 R.F.L. (3d) 30 at 41 (B.C. S.C.), Newbury J. 2. "Unjust enrichment" in equity permitted a number of remedies, depending on the circumstances. One was a payment for services rendered on the basis of quantum meruit or quantum valebat. Another equitable remedy, available traditionally where one person was possessed of legal title to property in which another had an interest, was the constructive trust. The remedy of constructive trust arises, where monetary damages are inadequate and where there is a link between the contribution that founds the action and the property in which the constructive trust is claimed. In order for a constructive trust to be found, in a family case as in other cases, monetary compensation must be inadequate and there must be a link between the services rendered and the property in which the trust is claimed. *Peter v. Beblow*, 1993 CarswellBC 44, 77 B.C.L.R. (2d) 1, [1993] 3 W.W.R. 337, 44 R.F.L. (3d) 329, 48 E.T.R. 1, 150 N.R. 1, 23 B.C.A.C. 81, 39 W.A.C. 81, 101 D.L.R. (4th) 621, [1993] 1 S.C.R. 980, [1993] R.D.F. 369, McLachlin J. See REMEDIAL ~ VALUE RECEIVED; VALUE SURVIVED.

CONSTRUCTIVE TRUSTEE. There are three ways in which a stranger to a trust can be held liable as a constructive trustee for breach of trust. First, a stranger to the trust can be liable as a trustee de son tort. Secondly, a stranger to the trust can be liable for breach of trust by knowingly assisting in a fraudulent and dishonest design on the part of the trustees ("knowing assistance"). Thirdly, liability may be imposed on a stranger to the trust who is in receipt and chargeable with trust property ("knowing receipt"). *Citadel General Assurance Co. v. Lloyds Bank Canada* 1997 CarswellAlta 823, 152 D.L.R. (4th) 411, (*sub nom. Citadel General Life Assurance Co. v. Lloyds Bank Canada*) 206 A.R. 321, (*sub nom. Citadel General Life Assurance Co. v. Lloyds Bank Canada*) 156 W.A.C. 321, 19 E.T.R. (2d) 93, 35 B.L.R. (2d) 153, 47 C.C.L.I. (2d) 153, [1997] 3 S.C.R. 805.

CONSTRUE. *v.* To interpret; to ascertain the meaning of.

CONSUL. *n.* The agent of a foreign state who assists nationals of the state and protects the state's commercial interests. J.G. McLeod, *The Conflict of Laws* (Calgary: Carswell, 1983) at 77.

CONSULAR OFFICER. See DIPLOMATIC OR ~.

CONSULATE. *n.* The residence or office of a consul.

CONSULT. See DUTY TO ~; DUTY TO ~ AND ACCOMMODATE.

CONSULTANT LOBBYIST. An individual who, for payment, undertakes to lobby on behalf of a client. *Lobbyists acts.*

CONSULTATION. See INSTITUTIONAL ~.

CONSULTATION CIRCLE. Two criteria which are absolutely essential for holding a consultation circle. First, the accused must have the firm intention to rehabilitate himself or herself. Second, the community must desire to become involved for the accused's sake. There are many other factors which should be considered, including the violence of the crime and the difficulty of the case; whether the community is affected by the crime; whether the accused has admitted his or her guilt; and the size of the community in which the accused resides. When a probation period is not applicable, there is no need to hold a circle. Where feasible the victim should participate in the consultation circle. However, the victim should not feel obliged to participate. The court should choose consultation circle members of good character and not impose on the members a duty which exceeds their capacity. *R. v. Alaku* [1994] N.W.T.R. 193.

CONSUME. *v.* 1. Includes inhale, inject into the human body, masticate and smoke. *Criminal Code,* R.S.C. 1985, c. C-46, s. 462.1. 2. In relation to liquor, includes putting liquor to any use, by drinking or otherwise. *Liquor Control and Licensing Act,* R.S.B.C. 1996, c. 267, s. 1.

CONSUMER. *n.* An individual acting for personal, family or household purposes as contrasted to a person who is acting for business purposes. See FINANCIAL ~ AGENCY OF CANADA.

CONSUMER AGREEMENT. An agreement between a supplier and a consumer in which the supplier agrees to supply goods or services for payment. *Consumer Protection Act, 2002,* S.O. 2002, c. 30, Sched. A, s. 1.

CONSUMER BILL. A bill of exchange issued in respect of a consumer purchase and on which the purchaser or any person signing to accommodate the purchaser is liable as a party, but does not include (a) a cheque that is dated the date of its issue or prior thereto, or at the time it is issued is post-dated not more than thirty days; or (b) a bill of exchange that (i) would be a cheque within the meaning of section 165 but for the fact that the party on which it is drawn is a financial institution, other than a bank, that as part of its business accepts money on deposit from members of the public and honours any such bill directed to be paid out of any such deposit to the extent of the amount of the deposit, and (ii) is dated the date of its issue or prior thereto, or at the time it is issued is post-dated not more than thirty days. *Bills of Exchange Act,* R.S.C. 1985, c. B-4, s. 189.

CONSUMER CONTRACT. A contract whose field of application is delimited by legislation respecting consumer protection whereby one of the parties, being a natural person, the consumer, acquires, leases, borrows or obtains in any other manner, for personal, family or domestic purposes, property or services from the other party, who offers such property and services as part of an enterprise which he carries on. *Civil Code,* S.Q. 1991, c. 64, a. 1384.

CONSUMER CREDIT. Loans to individuals to facilitate purchase of goods or services.

CONSUMER DEBT. Debt incurred by an individual for personal or household goods and services.

CONSUMER GOODS. Goods that are used or acquired for use primarily for personal, family or household purposes.

CONSUMER LEAFLETING. Is very different from a picket line. It seeks to persuade members of the public to take a certain course of action. It does so through informed and rational discourse which is the very essence of freedom of expression. Leafleting does not trigger the "signal" effect inherent in picket lines and it certainly does not have the same coercive component. It does not in any significant manner impede access to or egress from premises. Although the enterprise which is the subject of the leaflet may experience some loss of revenue, that may very well result from the public being informed and persuaded by the leaflets not to support the enterprise. Consequently, the leafleting activity if properly conducted is not illegal at common law. In the absence of independently tortious activity, protection from economic harm resulting from peaceful persuasion, urging a lawful course of action, has not been accepted at common law as a protected legal right. Picketing and consumer leafleting have fundamentally different effects. While the former uses coercion and obedience to a picket line to impede public access to an enterprise, the latter attempts to rationally persuade consumers to take their business elsewhere. Consumer leafleting is much more akin to a consumer boycott achieved through radio or newspaper advertisement than it is to conventional picketing. *K Mart Canada Ltd. v. U.F.C.W., Local 1518,* 1999 CarswellBC 1909, (*sub nom.* United Food & Commercial Workers, Local 1518 v. KMart Canada Ltd.) 99 C.L.L.C. 220-064, [1999] 9 W.W.R. 161, 245 N.R. 1, 176 D.L.R. (4th) 607, 66 B.C.L.R. (3d) 211, 66 C.R.R. (2d) 205, 128 B.C.A.C. 1, 208 W.A.C. 1, [1999] 2 S.C.R. 1083, Cory, J. for the court.

CONSUMER NOTE. A promissory note (a) issued in respect of a consumer purchase; and (b) on which the purchaser or any one signing to accommodate him is liable as a party. *Bills of Exchange Act,* R.S.C. 1985, c. B-4, s. 189.

CONSUMER PRICE INDEX. 1. The consumer price index for Canada as published by Statistics Canada under the authority of the Statistics Act (Canada). 2. "... [T]he phrase, 'cost of living index', is used in Canada commonly and interchangeably for the phrase, 'consumer price index', and especially for the index published by ... Statistics Canada." *Collins Cartage & Storage Co. v. McDonald* (1980), 30 O.R.

(2d) 234 at 236, 16 R.P.R. 71, 116 D.L.R. (3d) 570 (C.A.), the court per Goodman J.A. See COST OF LIVING INDEX.

CONSUMER PROTECTION LEGISLATION. Legislation regulating business practices of those dealing with consumers.

CONSUMER PURCHASE. A purchase, other than a cash purchase, of goods or services or an agreement to purchase goods or services (i) by an individual other than for resale or for use in the course of his business, profession or calling, and (ii) from a person who is engaged in the business of selling or providing those goods or services. *Bills of Exchange Act*, R.S.C. 1985, c. B-4, s. 188.

CONSUMER REPORT. A written, oral or other communication by a consumer reporting agency of credit information or personal information, or both, pertaining to a consumer for consideration in connection with a purpose set out in clause 8(1)(d). *Consumer Reporting Act*, R.S.O. 1990, c. C.33, s. 1.

CONSUMER REPORTING AGENCY. A person who, for gain or profit, or on a regular co-operative non-profit basis, furnishes consumer reports. *Consumer Reporting Act*, R.S.O. 1990, c. C.33, s. 1.

CONSUMER'S COOPERATIVE. A cooperative which purchases consumer goods for resale to its members.

CONSUMMATE. *v.* 1. To finish. 2. "A marriage is consummated once sexual intercourse has taken place... ." *Sau v. Sau* (1970), 1 R.F.L. 250 at 251 (Ont. H.C.), Parker J.

CONSUMMATE. *adj.* Completed; possessing extra skill or ability; excellent.

CONSUMMATION. *n.* Completion; act of sexual intercourse after marriage which completes the marriage.

CONTACT INFORMATION. Information to enable an individual at a place of business to be contacted and includes the name, position name or title, business telephone number, business address, business email or business fax number of the individual. *Freedom of Information and Protection of Privacy Act*, R.S.B.C. 1996, c. 165, Sched. 1, s. 1. See BUSINESS ~.

CONTAINER. *n.* 1. Transport equipment, including equipment that is carried on a chassis, is strong enough to be suitable for repeated use, and is designed to facilitate the transportation of goods without intermediate reloading, but does not include a vehicle. 2. Includes any bag, basket, bottle, box, can, carton, crate, pot or other receptacle used or suitable for use in the marketing of products. See BEVERAGE ~.

CONTAMINANT. *n.* 1. (a) Any solid, liquid, gas, micro-organism, odour, heat, cold, sound, vibration, radiation or combination of any of them, present in the environment, (i) that is foreign to or in excess of the natural constituents of the environment, (ii) that affects the natural, physical, chemical or biological quality or constitution of the environment, or (iii) that endangers the health of human, plant or animal life or the safety or comfort of a human, that causes damage to property or plant or animal life or renders them unfit for use by persons or that interferes with visibility, the normal conduct of transport or business or the normal enjoyment of life or use or enjoyment of property, (b) any pesticide or waste, or (c) anything that is designated by the Minister as a contaminant under section 7. *Clean Air Act*, S.N.B. 1997, c. C-5.2, s. 1.; 2. Any solid, liquid, gas, odour, heat, sound, vibration, radiation or combination of any of them resulting directly or indirectly from human activities that may cause an adverse effect. *Environmental Protection Act*, R.S.O. 1990, c. E-19, s. 1(1).

CONTEMPLATE. *v.* To view, consider, study, ponder.

CONTEMPLATION. *n.* 1. Consideration of a matter. 2. Contemplation of marriage refers to a time when the parties have committed themselves to marry each other.

CONTEMPORANEOUS INTERPRETATION. It may be useful to keep in mind the distinction between "consecutive" (after the words are spoken) and "simultaneous" (at the same time as words are spoken). While it is generally preferable that interpretation be consecutive rather than simultaneous, the overriding consideration is that the interpretation be contemporaneous. *R. v. Tran*, [1994] 2 S.C.R. 951.

CONTEMPT. *n.* 1. Contempt of court is the mechanism which the law provides for the protection of the authority of the court from improper interference. It is part of the court's inherent jurisdiction and is not enacted or prescribed. 2. "... [I]nterfering with the administration of the law and ... impeding and perverting the course of justice." *R. v. Kopyto* (1987), 61 C.R. (3d) 209 at 222, 24 O.A.C. 8, 62 O.R. 449, 39 C.C.C. (3d) 1, 47 D.L.R. (4th) 213 (C.A.), Dubin J.A. 3. Disobeying an order of the court. 4. "Acts which interfere with persons having duties to discharge in a Court of Justice, including parties, witnesses, jurors and officers of the Court, ..." *B.C.G.E.U., Re* (1988), 30 C.P.C. (2d) 221 at 242, [1988] 6 W.W.R. 577, 71 Nfld. & P.E.I.R. 93, 220 A.P.R. 93, 87 N.R. 241, [1988] 2 S.C.R. 214, 88 C.L.L.C. 14,047, 53 D.L.R. (4th) 1, 31 B.C.L.R. (2d) 273, 44 C.C.C. (3d) 289, the court per Dickson C.J.C. 5. A person who was required by law to attend or remain in attendance for the purpose of giving evidence, who fails, without lawful excuse, to attend or remain in attendance, is guilty of contempt of court. *Criminal Code*, R.S.C. 1985, c. C-46, s. 708(1). See CITING IN ~; CIVIL ~; CRIMINAL ~; PUBLICATION ~; SCANDALIZE THE COURT.

CONTEMPT IN PROCEDURE. Disobedience of the judgments, orders or other process of a court in circumstances which involve an injury to a private litigant.

CONTEMPT IN THE FACE OF THE COURT. "... [A]ny word spoken or act done in or in the precinct of the court which obstructs or interferes with the due administration of justice or is calculated to do so." *R. v. Kopyto* (1987), 39 C.C.C. (3d) 1 at 9, 24 O.A.C. 8, 61 C.R. (3d) 209, 62 O.R. (2d) 449, 47 D.L.R. (4th) 213 (C.A.), Cory J.A.

CONTEMPT NOT IN THE FACE OF THE COURT. "... [I]ncludes words spoken or published or acts done which are intended to interfere or are likely to interfere with the fair administration of justice." *R. v. Kopyto* (1987), 39 C.C.C. (3d) 1 at 9, 24 O.A.C. 8, 61 C.R. (3d) 209, 62 O.R. (2d) 449, 47 D.L.R. (4th) 213 (C.A.), Cory J.A.

CONTEMPT OF COURT. 1. Contempt may be dealt with by one of two procedures: the ordinary procedure, which provides the accused with the usual procedural guarantees of a criminal trial, or the summary procedure, which allows the judge to avoid the formalities of a criminal trial to convict a person of contempt of court, even *instanter* in some cases. Using the summary contempt of court procedure can be justified only in cases where it is urgent and imperative to act immediately. The summary procedure consists of citing, convicting and sentencing. *R. c. Arradi*, 2003 SCC 23. 2. Contempt of court, both civil and criminal, has existed for centuries. It is the tool used by the courts to ensure compliance with its orders and to protect its process. Is clearly aimed at punishing public acts which tend to bring the administration of justice into disrepute and interfere with the due administration of justice. *R. v. Edmonton Sun*, 2003 ABCA 3, 320 A.R. 217.

CONTEMPT OF PARLIAMENT. To obstruct the due course of proceedings in either House of Parliament.

CONTEMPT OUTSIDE THE COURT. "... [W]ords spoken or otherwise published, or acts done, outside court which are intended or likely to interfere with or obstruct the fair administration of justice... ." *R. v. Cohn* (1984), 42 C.R. (2d) 1 at 10, 48 O.R. (2d) 65, 70 C.R.R. 142, 15 C.C.C. (3d) 150, 13 D.L.R. (4th) 680, 4 O.A.C. 293 (C.A.), the court per Goodman J.A.

CONTEMPT PROCESS. A contempt process - even a civil contempt process - is criminal in nature and requires proof of the contemptuous conduct beyond a reasonable doubt. The conduct must be wilful, deliberate and of a contumacious and egregious nature. *Anthes v. Wilson Estate* (2005), 197 O.A.C. 110.

CONTEMPTUOUS DAMAGES. Small damages awarded to a plaintiff who sustained no loss, but whose legal rights were technically infringed though in the court's opinion the action should not have been brought. K.D. Cooper-Stephenson & I.B. Saunders, *Personal Injury Damages in Canada* (Toronto: Carswell, 1981) at 69.

CONTENTIOUS. *adj.* Contested. See NON-~.

CONTEST. *v.* To oppose, resist, dispute.

CONTESTATION. *n.* 1. A controversy; a disputed issue. 2. Any elector who was eligible to vote in an electoral district, and any candidate in an electoral district, may, by application to a competent court, contest the election in that electoral district on the grounds that the elected candidate was not eligible to be a candidate; or there were irregularities, fraud or corrupt or illegal practices that affected the result of the election. *Canada Elections Act*, S.C. 2000, c. 9, s. 524.

CONTESTED DIVORCE. A divorce action in which a respondent delivers an answer. That is, the respondent disputes the grounds alleged by the petitioner or the remedies sought by the petitioner.

CONTEXT. *n.* 1. Parts of text surrounding the portion under consideration. 2. For purposes of constitutional analysis includes the circumstances which led to the enactment and the mischief at which it was directed. 3. Of words in a statute, refers to the whole of the statute and other indicators of legislative meaning.

CONTEXTUAL APPROACH. 1. Refers to the method of interpretation of the Charter in which a particular right or freedom is considered in its particular context to determine the aspect of the right or freedom which is at issue. 2. Looking at the broader context of a statutory provision, such as other provisions of the same statute and parliamentary intent as an aid to interpretation of a provision.

CONTIGUOUS. *adj.* "One area is contiguous to another where both have a common boundary or even a common point of contact." *R. v. Alegria* (1992), 96 Nfld. & P.E.I.R. 128 at 140, 305 A.P.R. 128 (Nfld. C.A.), the court per Goodridge C.J.N.

CONTIGUOUS ZONE. 1. In relation to Canada, means the contiguous zone of Canada as determined under the Oceans Act, and in relation to any other state, means the contiguous zone of the other state as determined in accordance with international law and the domestic laws of that other state. *Interpretation Act*, R.S.C. 1985, c. I-21, s. 35. 2. The contiguous zone of Canada consists of an area of the sea that has as its inner limit the outer limit of the territorial sea of Canada and as its outer limit the line every point of which is at a distance of 24 nautical miles from the nearest point of the baselines of the territorial sea of Canada, but does not include an area of the sea that forms part of the territorial sea of another state or in which another state has sovereign rights. *Oceans Act*, S.C. 1996, c. 31, s. 10.

CONTINENTAL SHELF. 1. The shallow area of the ocean which adjoins each continent. 2. In relation to Canada, means the continental shelf of Canada as determined under the Oceans Act, and in relation to any other state, means the continental shelf of the other state as determined in accordance with international law and the domestic laws of that other state. *Interpretation Act*, R.S.C. 1985, c. I-21, s. 35. 3. The continental shelf of Canada is the seabed and subsoil of the submarine areas, including those of the exclusive economic zone of Canada, that extend beyond the territorial sea of Canada throughout the natural prolongation of the land territory of Canada (a) subject to paragraphs (b) and (c), to the outer edge of the continental margin, determined in the manner under international law that results in the maximum extent of the continental shelf of Canada, the outer edge of the continental margin being the submerged prolongation of the land mass of Canada consisting of the seabed and subsoil of the shelf, the slope and the rise, but not including the deep ocean floor with its oceanic ridges or its subsoil; (b) to a distance of 200 nautical miles from the baselines of the territorial sea of Canada where the outer edge of the continental margin does not extend up to that distance; or (c) in respect of a portion of the continental shelf of Canada for which geographical coordinates of points have been prescribed pursuant to subparagraph 25(a)(iii), to lines determined from the geographical coordinates of points so prescribed. Determination of the outer limit of the continental shelf of Canada. *Oceans Act*, S.C. 1996, c. 31, s. 17.

CONTINGENCY. *n.* 1. An uncertain event on which an estate, interest, liability, right or obligation depends for its existence. 2. Accident, sickness, strikes and unemployment. K.D. Cooper-Stephenson & I.B. Saunders, *Personal Injury Damages in Canada Supplement to June 30, 1987* (Toronto: Carswell, 1987) at 244. See MITIGATION ~.

CONTINGENCY AGREEMENT. An agreement which provides that the remuneration paid to a solicitor for legal services provided to or on behalf of the client is contingent, in whole or in part, on the successful disposition or completion of the matter in respect of which services are provided.

CONTINGENCY FEE. The fee paid under an agreement which provides that the remuneration paid to a solicitor for legal services provided to or on behalf of the client is contingent, in whole or in part, on the successful disposition or completion of the matter in respect of which services are provided.

CONTINGENCY INSURANCE. An agreement by an insurer to pay when an event occurs regardless of the loss suffered. Examples are life or accident insurance. To be contrasted with indemnity insurance. *Confederation Life Ins. Co. v. Causton*, [1989] 6 W.W.R. 82, 38 B.C.L.R. (2d) 69 (B.C.C.A.).

CONTINGENCY RESERVE FUND. A fund for common expenses that usually occur less often than once a year or that do not usually occur. *Strata Property Act*, S.B.C. 1998, c. 43, s. 1.

CONTINGENT. *adj.* Conditional upon the occurrence of some future uncertain event.

CONTINGENT INTEREST. A possibility conditioned on the happening of a future uncertain event.

CONTINGENT LEGACY. A legacy bequeathed payable on happening of a contingency.

CONTINGENT LIABILITY. "... [A] liability to make a payment is contingent if the terms of its creation include uncertainty in respect of any of these three things: (1) whether the payment will be made; (2) the amount payable; or (3) the time by which payment shall be made... ." *Samuel F. Investments Limited v. M.N.R.* (1988), 88 D.T.C. 1106 at 1108 (T.C.C.).

CONTINGENT REMAINDER. A remainder which depends on an uncertain condition or event that may never be performed or happen, or which may not be performed or happen until after a preceding estate is determined.

CONTINGENT RIGHT. In relation to land, means a contingent or executory interest, a possibility coupled with an interest, whether the object of the gift or limitation of the interest or possibility is or is not ascertained, also a right of entry, whether immediate or future, and whether vested or contingent. *Trustee Act*, R.S.B.C. 1996, c. 464, s. 1.

CONTINUANCE. *n.* 1. Keeping up, going on with, maintaining. 2. The ongoing existence of a company which is transferred from regulation by the jurisdiction where it was incorporated to be regulated under the control of another jurisdiction. See ARTICLES OF ~; CERTIFICATE OF ~; PRESUMPTION OF ~.

CONTINUATION. *n.* Statutes governing corporations may permit a corporation to continue its corporate existence under the law of another jurisdiction. Continuation is the method of doing so.

CONTINUE. See ORDER TO ~.

CONTINUED. *adj.* A company incorporated under one act may in certain circumstances be "continued" under the laws of some other jurisdiction so that its existence is maintained subject to the laws of the second jurisdiction.

CONTINUING. *adj.* Ongoing; enduring.

CONTINUING CAUSE OF ACTION. A cause of action which arises from a repetition of the act or omission giving rise to the cause.

CONTINUING GARNISHMENT. Refers to the taking of money coming due at intervals by garnishment proceedings.

CONTINUING GRIEVANCE. A grievance which recurs or in which the circumstances upon which the grievance are based are repeated.

CONTINUING OFFENCE. "... [N]ot simply an offence which takes or may take a long time to commit. It may be described as an offence where the conjunction of the actus reus and the mens rea, which makes the offence complete, does not, as well, terminate the offence. The conjunction of the two essential elements for the commission of the offence continues and the accused remains in what might be described as a state of criminality while the offence continues... . Conspiracy to commit murder could be a continuing offence. The actus reus and the mens rea are present when the unlawful agreement is made and continue until the killing occurs or the conspiracy is abandoned. Whatever the length of time involved, the conspirators remain in the act of commission of a truly continuing offence... ." *R. v. Bell* (1983), 8 C.C.C. (3d) 97 at 110, 36 C.R. (3d) 289, 3 D.L.R. (4th) 385, 50 N.R. 172, [1983] 2 S.C.R. 471, McIntyre J. (Beetz, Estey and Chouinard JJ. concurring).

CONTINUING REPUDIATION. Where a party to an agreement commits a fundamental breach of its terms, the agreement is repudiated. There has been what amounts to a refusal to perform. If the repudiation is not accepted, the agreement is affirmed. Where the breach is ongoing, as distinct from one instance of fundamental non-performance, there is a continuing repudiation which may, in the absence of subsequent affirmation, be accepted as long as the repudiation continues. What in my view is important is that, in order to establish the existence of a continuing repudiation, particularly when an extended period of time has elapsed following the affirmation of an agreement, it must be clear beyond question that there is a continued . . . or repeated . . . refusal to perform. The refusal may be manifest in different ways, which may include silence in response to a request for performance at the time the request is made, but the refusal must be clear for it is that refusal which is the repudiation to be accepted. *Doman Forest Products Ltd. v. GMAC Commercial Credit Corp. – Canada*, 2007 BCCA 88, Lowry J.A. (Prowse J.A. concurring).

CONTINUING SERVICES CONTRACT. A future performance contract that provides for the performance of services on a continuing basis and is designated by regulation. *Business Practices and Consumer Protection Act*, S.B.C. 2004, c. 2, s. 17.

CONTINUING TORT. One involving the continuance of the act which caused the damage.

CONTINUOUS. *adj.* Uninterrupted. *New Brunswick v. C.U.P.E.* (1981), 125 D.L.R. (3d) 220 at 224 (N.B. C.A.), the court per Stratton J.A.

CONTINUOUSLY. *adv.* Without ceasing; without break.

CONTINUOUS SERVITUDE. Such as servitudes of view or of no building, do not require the actual intervention of the holder. *Civil Code*, S.Q. 1991, c. 64, a. 1179. See DISCONTINUOUS ~.

CONTINUOUS TRANSMISSION COMMODITY. Electricity, crude oil, natural gas, or any corporeal movable property, that is transportable by means of a wire, pipeline or other conduit. *An Act respecting the Québec sales tax*, R.S.Q. c. T-0.1, s. 1.

CONTINUOUS TRIGGER THEORY. Under this theory, the property damage is effectively deemed to have occurred from the initial exposure to the time when the damage became manifest or ought to have become manifest to the plaintiffs, and if alerted, to the insured. In that case, all policies in effect over that period are called upon to respond to the loss. *Alie v. Bertrand & Frère Construction Co.* (2002), 62 O.R. (3d) 345 (C.A.).

CONTRA. [L.] Against.

CONTRABAND. *n.* 1. Goods not permitted to be exported or imported, bought or sold. 2. Anything that is in a prisoner's possession in circumstances in which possession thereof is forbidden by any act or regulation, or by an order of general or specific application within the prison or penitentiary in which the prisoner is confined. 3. (a) An intoxicant; (b) a weapon or a component thereof, ammunition for a weapon, and anything that is designed to kill, injure or disable a person or that is altered so as to be capable of killing, injuring or disabling a person, when possessed without prior authorization; (c) an explosive or a bomb or a component thereof; (d) currency over any applicable prescribed limit, when possessed without prior authorization; and, (e) any item not described in paragraphs (a) to (d) that could jeopardize the security of a penitentiary or the safety of persons, when that item is possessed without prior authorization. *Corrections and Conditional Release Act*, S.C. 1992, c. 20, s. 2.

CONTRA BONOS MORES. [L.] Contrary to good morals.

CONTRACEPTIVE DEVICE. Any instrument, apparatus, contrivance or substance other than a drug, that is manufactured, sold or represented for use in the prevention of conception. *Food and Drugs Act*, R.S.C. 1985, c. F-27, s. 2.

CONTRACT. *n.* A contract is an exchange of promises, acts, or acts and promises, as a result of which each party to the contract receives something from the other. For a contract to be binding, consideration must flow between the parties. Absent consideration, there is no contract. *Braiden v. La-Z-Boy Canada Ltd.*, 2008 ONCA 464. See ACTION OF ~; ADOPTION OF ~; ALEATORY ~; ANNUITY ~; BILATERAL ~; BREACH OF ~; BUILDING ~; C.I.F. ~; CLOSED SHOP ~; COLLATERAL ~; COMMODITY FUTURES ~; COMMUTATIVE ~; COMPLETED ~ METHOD; COMPLETION OF THE ~; CONCLUDED ~; CONSUMER ~; CONTINUING SERVICES ~; COST-PLUS ~; DESIGN-BUILD ~; DOMESTIC ~; EMPLOYMENT ~; ESSENCE OF THE ~; EXECUTED ~; EXECUTORY ~; FIXED PRICE ~; F.O.R. ~; FORMAL ~; FREEDOM OF ~; FUTURE PERFORMANCE ~; GRATUITOUS ~; ILLEGAL ~; IMMORAL ~; IMPLIED ~; INFORMAL ~; INSURANCE ~; INTERMENT RIGHT ~; LAW OF ~; MARRIAGE ~; NAKED ~; ONEROUS ~; ORAL ~; PAROL ~; PRE-INCORPORATION ~; PRIVITY OF ~; QUASI-~; SIMPLE ~; SPECIALTY ~; STIPULATED PRICE ~; SURFACE RIGHTS ~ SYNALLAGAMATIC ~ TIME SHARE ~ UNILATERAL ~ UNIT PRICE ~ WAGERING ~.

CONTRACT BOND. "... [C]ontract of suretyship and guarantee... ." *Johns-Manville Canada Inc. v. John Carlo Ltd.* (1980), (*sub nom. Canadian Johns-Manville Co. v. John Carlo Ltd.*) 12 B.L.R. 80 at 87, 29 O.R. (2d) 592, 113 D.L.R. (3d) 686 (H.C.), R.E. Holland J. See PERFORMANCE BOND.

CONTRACT COLLATERAL. 1. " ... [A]n oral agreement ancillary to a written agreement..." *Ahone v. Holloway* (1988), 30 B.C.L.R. (2d) 368 at 373 (C.A.), the court per McLachlin J.A. 2. A statement, on the strength of which a person enters into a contract, may give rise to an entirely separate contract "collateral" to the main contract made between the maker of the statement and the person to whom the statement was made.

CONTRACT DATE. The date on which a contract is signed by both parties.

CONTRACTED. *adj.* Agreed upon; effected.

CONTRACTED MURDER. Without limiting the generality of subsection (2), murder is planned and deliberate, and therefore first degree murder, when it is committed pursuant to an arrangement under which money or anything of value passes or is intended to pass from one person to another, or is promised by one person to another, as consideration for that other's causing or assisting in causing the death of anyone or counselling another person to do any act causing or assisting in causing that death. *Criminal Code*, R.S.C. 1985, c. C-46, s. 231(3).

CONTRACT EMPLOYEE. An employee engaged by means of a contract for temporary employment for a fixed term.

CONTRACT FOR SERVICES. 1. The engagement of a person as an independent contractor. 2. A contract of enterprise or for services is a contract by which a person, the contractor or the provider of services, as the case may be, undertakes to carry out physical or intellectual work for another person, the client or to provide a service, for a price which the client binds himself to pay. *Civil Code*, S.Q. 1991, c. 64, a. 2098.

CONTRACT FOR FUTURE SERVICES. An executory contract that includes a provision for services of a prescribed type or class to be rendered in the future on a continuing basis.

CONTRACT FOR SALE. A sale in which the thing sold is exchanged for a consideration in money or money's worth.

CONTRACT FOR THE RECOUNTING OF A CRIME. 1. A contract entered into before, on or after the coming into force of this Act under which: (i) a person convicted of, or charged with, a designated crime provides or agrees to provide a recounting of the designated crime, either directly or indirectly; and (ii) consideration is payable to, or at the direction of, the convicted or accused person or the person's agent. *The Profits of Criminal Notoriety Act*, S.S. 2009, c. P-28.1, s. 2. 2. A contract under which (i) any person agrees to provide a recounting of a serious crime, either directly or indirectly, and (ii) consideration is payable to, or at the direction of, the person who provides the recounting of the serious crime or an agent of that person, whether the contract was entered into before or after the coming into force of this Act. *Criminal Notoriety Act*, S.A. 2005, c. C-32.5, s. 1. See PROCEEDS OF A CONTRACT FOR RECOUNTING CRIME.

CONTRACTING IN. Involves a situation where non-bargaining unit personnel are brought into the workplace to work alongside bargaining unit employees, performing the same work as those employees, under the same supervision and utilising the same materials and equipment provided by the employer; the way in which the bargaining unit and non-bargaining unit employees work is "virtually indistinguishable." *Hydro Ottawa v. I.B.E.W., Local 636*, 2007 ONCA 292.

CONTRACTING OUT. Is said to involve a situation where "an integral function or a whole operation of the business of the employer is assigned to an independent contractor;" the work is often done off site and, where done at the same location as the bargaining unit employees, usually involves work of a different nature even though it is bargaining unit work; the independent contractor controls the work, and the employer has "effectively abdicated" the work to the outside contractor. *Hydro Ottawa v. I.B.E.W., Local 636*, 2007 ONCA 292.

CONTRACTING STATE. Any state that has ratified or adhered to a convention and whose denunciation thereof has not become effective.

CONTRACT IN RESTRAINT OF TRADE. "... Lord Hodson, [in Esso Petroleum Co. v. Harper's Garage (Stourport) Ltd., [1968] A.C. 269] at p. 317, adopted the dicta of Diplock, L.J., in Petrofina (Great Britain) Ltd. v. Martin, [1966] Ch. 146 at p. 180: 'A contract in restraint of trade is one in which a party (the covenantor) agrees with any other party (the convenantee) to restrict his liberty in the future to carry on trade with other persons not parties to the contract in such manner as he chooses.' " *Stephens v. Gulf Oil Canada Ltd.* (1975), 25 C.P.R. (2d) 64 at 77, 11 O.R. (2d) 129, 65 D.L.R. (3d) 193 (C.A.), the court per Howland J.A.

CONTRACT LAW. The branch of private law dealing with drafting, interpretation and enforcement of contracts between persons.

CONTRACT OF ADHESION. A contract in which the essential stipulations were imposed or drawn up by one of the parties, on his behalf or upon his instructions, and were not negotiable. Any contract that is not a contract of adhesion is a contract by mutual agreement. *Civil Code*, S.Q. 1991, c. 64, a. 1379.

CONTRACT OF CARRIAGE. A contract by which one person, the carrier, undertakes principally to carry a person or property from one place to another, in return for a price which another person, the passenger or the shipper or receiver of the property, undertakes to pay at the agreed time. *Civil Code*, S.Q. 1991, c. 64, a. 2030.

CONTRACT OF EMPLOYMENT. 1. A contract by which an employee agrees to provide services to an employer. 2. A contract by which a person, the employee, undertakes for a limited period to do work for remuneration, according to the instructions and under the direction or control of another person, the employer. *Civil Code*, S.Q. 1991, c. 64, a. 2085.

CONTRACT OF ENTERPRISE. A contract of enterprise or for services is a contract by which a person, the contractor or the provider of services, as the case may be, undertakes to carry out physical or intellectual work for another person, the client or to provide a service, for a price which the client binds himself to pay. *Civil Code*, S.Q. 1991, c. 64, a. 2098.

CONTRACT OF GUARANTEE. In the contract of guarantee, the guarantor agrees to repay the lender if the debtor defaults. The exact nature of the obligation owed by the guarantor to the lender depends on the construction of the contract of guarantee, but the liability of the guarantor is usually made coterminous with that of the principal debtor. Generally speaking, if the principal debt is void or unenforceable, the contract of guarantee will likewise be void or unenforceable. *Communities Economic Development Fund v. Canadian Pickles Corp.* [1991] 3 S.C.R. 388.

CONTRACT OF INDEMNITY. 1. In a contract of indemnity, the indemnifier assumes a primary obligation to repay the debt, and is liable regardless of the liability of the principal debtor. An indemnifier will accordingly be liable even if the principal debt is void or otherwise unenforceable. *Communities Economic Development Fund v. Canadian Pickles Corp.* [1991] 3 S.C.R. 388. 2. "... [A] contract by which one party agrees to make good a loss suffered by the other and includes most contracts of insurance... ." *Callaghan Contracting Ltd. v. Royal Insurance Co. of Canada* (1989), [1990] 39 C.C.L.I. 65 at 70, 97 N.B.R. (2d) 381, 245 A.P.R. 381 (C.A.), the court per Stratton C.J.N.B.

CONTRACT OF INSTANTANEOUS PERFORMANCE. Where the circumstances do not preclude the performance of the obligations of the parties at one single time, the contract is a contract of instantaneous performance. *Civil Code*, S.Q. 1991, c. 64, a. 1383.

CONTRACT OF INSURANCE. 1. "In ... Re Bendix Automotive of Can. Ltd. and U.A.W., [1971] 3 O.R. 263 ... (Ont. H.C.), [the court considered] the ... definition of contract of insurance at p. 269: 'The basic elements which are common to all of these definitions may be stated as follows; i) an undertaking of one person; ii) to indemnify another person; iii) for an agreed consideration; iv) from loss or liability in respect of an event; v) the happening of which is uncertain.' " *Arklie v. Haskell* (1986), 25 C.C.L.I. 277 at 282, 284, 33 D.L.R. (4th) 458, [1987] I.L.R. 1-2176 (B.C. C.A.), McLachlin J.A. (Hutcheon and MacFarlane JJ.A. concurring). 2. An agreement by which an insurer, for a premium, agrees to indemnify the insured against loss. 3. A policy, certificate, interim receipt, renewal receipt, or writing evidencing the contract, whether sealed or not, and a binding oral agreement.

CONTRACT OF MARINE INSURANCE. A contract under which an insurer agrees to indemnify the insured, in the way and to the extent agreed, against marine losses.

CONTRACT OF SALE. Includes an agreement to sell as well as sale. *Sale of Goods acts.*

CONTRACT OF SERVICE. 1. "In Short v. J. and W. Henderson, Ltd. (1946), 174 L.T. 416, an appeal to the House of Lords from a decision of the Court of Session, Lord Thankerton ... referred to four indicia of a contract of service which had been derived from the Lord Justice Clerk from the authorities referred to by him. They were, (a) the master's power of selection of his servant; (b) the payment of wages or other remuneration; (c) the master's right to control the method of doing work, and (d) the master's right of suspension or dismissal." *Marine Pipeline & Dredging Ltd. v. Canadian Fina Oil Ltd.* (1964), 46 D.L.R. (2d) 495 at 502 (Alta. C.A.). 2. There is a relationship of subordination between the parties. The worker, in other words, is a true employee of the employer, and not merely a contractor working for the employer pursuant to a contract of enterprise. 3. Contractor is defined variously as a person who undertakes a contract, esp. to provide materials, conduct building operations; one who contracts on predetermined terms to provide labour and materials and to be responsible for the performance of a construction job in accordance with established specifications or plans; one who contracts to provide work or labour, but not a vendor of a chattel. *Daishowa-Marubeni International Ltd. v. Toshiba International Corp.*, 2000 CarswellAlta 1518, [2001] I.L.R. I-3915, 86 Alta. L.R. (3d) 76, [2001] 5 W.W.R. 357, 12 B.L.R (3d) 297, 278 A.R. 388, 28 C.C.L.I. (3d) 309 (Q.B.), Kent J.

CONTRACT OF SUCCESSIVE PERFORMANCE. Where the circumstances absolutely require that the obligations be performed at several different times or without interruption, the contract is a contract of successive performance. *Civil Code*, S.Q. 1991, c. 64, a. 1383.

CONTRACTOR. *n.* 1. Any person who, for another, carries out construction work or causes it to be carried out or makes or submits tenders, personally or through another person, to carry out such work for personal profit. 2. A person who enters into a pre-incorporation contract in the name of or on behalf of a corporation before its incorporation. 3. One who agrees to supply work or labour. See DEPENDENT ~; GENERAL ~; INDEPENDENT ~; SUB~.

CONTRACTUAL CAPACITY. Ability in law to enter into a contract.

CONTRACTUAL ENTRANT. One who has contracted and paid for the right to enter onto premises.

CONTRACTUAL PROMISE. An undertaking or an assurance given for consideration.

CONTRACTUAL RELATIONS. See INTERFERENCE WITH ~.

CONTRACT UNDER SEAL. A contract in writing which is signed and sealed by the parties; a specialty contract.

CONTRADICT. *v.* To disprove; to prove a fact conflicting with other evidence.

CONTRADICTION IN TERMS. A group of words the parts of which are expressly inconsistent.

CONTRADICTORY EVIDENCE. Evidence disproving earlier evidence.

CONTRA PACEM. [L.] Against the peace.

CONTRA PROFERENTEM. [L. against the party putting forward] 1. "Estey J. ... wrote in McClelland & Stewart Ltd. v. Mutual Life Assurance Co. of Canada, [1981] 2 S.C.R. 6[:] 'That principle of interpretation [the contra proferentem rule] applies to contracts and other documents on the simple theory that any ambiguity in a term of a contract must be resolved against the author if the choice is between him and the other party to the contract who did not participate in the drafting.' " *McKinlay Motors Ltd. v. Honda Canada Inc.* (1989), 46 B.L.R. 62 at 77 (Nfld. T.D.), Wells J. 2. Contra proferentem operates to protect one party to a contract from deviously ambiguous or confusing drafting on the part of the other party, by interpreting any ambiguity against the drafting party. When both parties are in agreement as to the proper interpretation of the contract, however, it is not open to a third party to assert that contra proferentem should be applied to interpret the contract against both contracting parties. Indeed, a third party has no basis at all upon which to rely upon contra proferentem. *Eli Lilly & Co. v. Novopharm Ltd.*, 1998 CarswellNat 1061, 227 N.R. 201, 161 D.L.R. (4th) 1, [1998] 2 S.C.R. 129, 152 F.T.R. 160 (note), 80 C.P.R. (3d) 321, the court per Iacobucci J.

CONTRARY. *adj.* Against; opposed to.

CONTRARY TO LAW. 1. Section 18.1(4)(f) [of the Federal Courts Act] permits judicial intervention if the federal board, commission or other tribunal acted in any other way that was contrary to law. A reference to "contrary to law" necessarily includes "law" outside the Federal Courts Act including general principles of administrative law. Paragraph (f) shows, if further demonstration were necessary, that s. 18.1(4) is not intended to operate as a self-contained code, but is intended by Parliament to be interpreted and applied against the backdrop of the common law, including those elements most recently expounded in Dunsmuir [v. New Brunswick 2008 SCC 9]. *Canada (Citizenship and Immigration) v. Khosa*, 2009 SCC 12, Binnie J. 2. The reference to "acted in any other way that was contrary to law" refers, then, to legal errors that are not captured by s. 18.1(4)(c) [of the Federal Courts Act]. *Canada (Citizenship and Immigration) v. Khosa*, 2009 SCC 12, Rothstein J.

CONTRAVENE. *v.* 1. To violate, to not comply. 2. "... [T]o prevent, to obstruct the operation of and to defeat or nullify." *Collins v. Ontario (Attorney General)* (1969), 6 C.R.N.S. 82 at 88-9, [1970] 1 O.R. 207, [1970] 1 C.C.C. 305 (H.C.), Addy J.

CONTRAVENTION. *n.* 1. Failure to comply. 2. Non-compliance. 3. An offence that is created by an enactment and is designated as a contravention by regulation of the Governor in Council. *Contraventions Act*, S.C. 1992, c. 47, s. 2.

CONTRAVENTIONS COURT. In respect of a contravention alleged to have been committed in, or otherwise within the territorial jurisdiction of the courts of, a province, a court designated by order of the Governor in Council in respect of that province. *Contraventions Act*, S.C. 1992, c. 47, s. 2.

CONTRIBUTION. *n.* 1. Indemnity may arise by contract, by statute, or by the nature of the relationship itself. An obligation to indemnify means an obligation to protect against or keep free from loss, to repay for what has been lost or damaged, to compensate for a loss. Contribution, on the other hand, is only available when a co-debtor has paid more than his equal share of the debt. Contribution among co-debtors is an equitable concept, and a co-debtor, while liable to the creditor for the full amount, is only liable as among the co-debtors for his or her share. *Lafrentz v. M & L Leasing Ltd. Partnership* (2000), 2000 CarswellAlta 1121, 2000 ABQB 714, 8 B.L.R. (3d) 219, [2001] 1 W.W.R. 629, 85 Alta. L.R. (3d) 233, 275 A.R. 334, Perras J. 2. Indemnity. 3. " ... [D]escribes a situation where the wrongdoer who has paid the plaintiff's damages, or more than his share of them, is entitled to receive a portion of this amount

from the other wrongdoer ..." *Peter v. Anchor Transit Ltd.*, [1979] 4 W.W.R. 150 at 153, 100 D.L.R. (3d) 37 (B.C. C.A.), the court per Craig J.A. 4. The performance by all parties jointly liable, by contract or otherwise, of their shares of the liability. 5. Services, money or other property donated to support a political purpose. *Elections Act, 1991*, S.N. 1992, c. E-3.1, s. 269. See DEFINED ~ BENEFIT; DEFINED ~ PLAN; DEFINED ~ PROVISION; DIRECT ~; INDIRECT ~; MATERIAL ~; MONETARY ~.

CONTRIBUTION IN KIND. A contribution in a form other than cash or negotiable instruments. *Elections Act*, R.S.Y. 2002, c. 63, s. 370.

CONTRIBUTORY BENEFIT. A pension benefit or part of a pension benefit to which a member is required to make contributions under the terms of the pension plan.

CONTRIBUTORY NEGLIGENCE. "... [A] failure to take reasonable care for one's own safety in circumstances where one knows or reasonably ought to foresee danger to oneself... ." *Reekie v. Messervey* (1989), 48 C.C.L.T. 217 at 277, 36 B.C.L.R. (2d) 316, 59 D.L.R. (4th) 481, 17 M.V.R. (2d) 94 (C.A.), Southin J.A. (dissenting in part).

CONTRIBUTORY PENSION PLAN. A plan for pension of employees to which employees themselves contribute as well as employer.

CONTRIVANCE. See RECENT ~.

CONTROL. *n.* 1. Power to direct. 2. In respect of a body corporate, means (a) control in any manner that results in control in fact, whether directly through the ownership of shares, stocks, equities or securities or indirectly through a trust, a contract, the ownership of shares, stocks, equities or securities of another body corporate or otherwise, or (b) the ability to appoint, elect or cause the appointment or election of a majority of the directors of the body corporate, whether or not that ability is exercised. *Atlantic Fisheries Restructuring Act*, R.S.C. 1985, c. A-14, s. 2. See CARE OR ~; DEVELOPMENT ~; PEST ~ PRODUCT; TRANSMISSION ~ PROTOCOL.

CONTROLLED. *adj.* "It has long been decided that for the purposes of this section [s. 39(4)(a) of the Income Tax Act, R.S.C. 1952, c. 148] '... the word "controlled" contemplates the right of control that rests in ownership of such a number of shares as carries with it the right to a majority of the votes in the election of the Board of Directors' ..." *Imperial General Properties Ltd. v. R.* (1985), 85 D.T.C. 5500 at 5502, [1985] 2 S.C.R. 288, [1985] 2 C.T.C. 299, 31 B.L.R. 77, 62 N.R. 137, 21 D.L.R. (4th) 741, Estey J. (Beetz, Chouinard and La Forest JJ. concurring).

CONTROLLED SUBSIDIARY. The company so described is subordinate to a dominant company which is able, through share ownership, to exert influence or control over its affairs. *Cominco Ltd. v. Canadian Pacific Ltd.*, 1988 CarswellBC 91, 24 B.C.L.R. (2d) 124, 39 B.L.R. 172 (S.C.), Gibbs J.

CONTROLLED SUBSTANCE. A substance included in Schedule I, II, III, IV or V. Includes narcotics. *Controlled Drugs and Substances Act*, S.C. 1996, c. 19, s. 2.

CONTROLLER. *n.* 1. An official who examines and verifies the accounts of other officials. 2. The chief financial officer of a corporation or organization. See COMPTROLLER.

CONTROVERSY. *n.* A dispute between parties.

CONTUMACY. *n.* 1. Failure or refusal to obey an order or to attend court as required. 2. Being in contempt of court.

CONVENIENCE. *n.* 1. "... [R]elates to the proper conduct and management of the entire trial including, of course, the decisional process." *Wipfli v. Britten* (1981), 24 C.P.C. 164 at 170, [1982] 1 W.W.R. 709, 32 B.C.L.R. 242 (S.C.), McEachern C.J.S.C. 2. "... [A]ccording to McBride J. in MacDonald v. Leduc Utilities Ltd. (1952), 7 W.W.R. (N.S.) 603 at 608 (Alta. T.D.), relates to 'the nature of the issues raised, technical or otherwise, and not to the personal convenience of individual jurymen'." *Przybylski v. Morcos* (1986), 14 C.P.C. (2d) 126 at 130, 49 Alta. L.R. (2d) 164, 75 A.R. 233 (Q.B.), Andrekson J. See BALANCE OF ~.

CONVENTION. *n.* 1. An agreement between states which is intended to be binding in international law. P.W. Hogg, *Constitutional Law of Canada*, 3d ed. (Toronto: Carswell, 1992) at 281. 2. "We respectfully adopt the definition given by the learned Chief Justice of Manitoba, Freedman C.J.M. in the Manitoba Reference [Reference re Amendment of the Constitution of Canada (No. 3) (1981), 120 D.L.R. (3d) 385]...: '... a convention occupies a position somewhere in between a usage or custom on one hand and constitutional law on the other. There is a general agreement that if one sought to fix that position with greater precision he would place convention nearer to law than to usage or custom. There is also a general agreement that "a convention is a rule which is regarded as obligatory by the officials to whom it applies": Hogg, Constitutional Law of Canada (1977), p. 9.' ... The existence of a definite convention is always unclear and a matter of debate. Furthermore conventions are flexible, somewhat imprecise and unsuitable for judicial determination." *Reference re Questions Concerning Amendment of the Constitution of Canada as set out in O.C. 1020/80* (1981), (sub nom. *Resolution to Amend the Constitution of Canada, Re*) 1 C.R.R. 59 at 137-38, [1981] 1 S.C.R. 753, [1981] 6 W.W.R. 1, 11 Man. R. (2d) 1, 39 N.R. 1, 34 Nfld. & P.E.I.R. 1, 95 A.P.R. 1, Martland, Ritchie, Dickson, Beetz, Chouinard and Lamer JJ. 3. A meeting, assembly. See CONSTITUTIONAL ~; GENEVA ~S; HAGUE ~S; REFUGEE ~; SUB-JUDICE ~.

CONVENTION AGAINST TORTURE. The Convention Against Torture and Other Cruel, Inhuman or Degrading Treatment or Punishment, signed at New York on December 10, 1984. *Immigration and Refugee Protection Act*, S.C. 2001, c. 27, s. 2.

CONVENTIONAL. *adj.* Law not found in the usual legal sources, i.e. statutes or decided cases. Practice or usage is the usual source of this type of law.

CONVENTIONAL HYPOTHEC. May be granted only by a person having the capacity to alienate the property hypothecated. It may be granted by the debtor of the obligation secured or by a third person. *Civil Code*, S.Q. 1991, c. 64, a. 2681.

CONVENTIONAL INTERNATIONAL LAW. (a) Any convention, treaty or other international agreement (*a*) that is in force and to which Canada is a party; or (*b*) that is in force and the provisions of which Canada has agreed to accept and apply in an armed conflict in which it is involved. *Crimes Against Humanity and War Crimes Act, 2000,* S.C. 2000, c. 24, s. 2.

CONVENTIONAL SEPARATION AS TO PROPERTY. This matrimonial regime is established by a simple declaration to this effect in the marriage contract. *Civil Code*, S.Q. 1991, c. 64, a. 485.

CONVENTION FACILITY. An immovable that is acquired by way of lease, licence or similar arrangement by the sponsor or organizer of a convention for use exclusively as the site for the convention. *An Act respecting the Québec sales tax*, R.S.Q. c. T-0.1, s. 1.

CONVENTION REFUGEE. A person who, by reason of a well-founded fear of persecution for reasons of race, religion, nationality, membership in a particular social group or political opinion, (a) is outside each of their countries of nationality and is unable or, by reason of that fear, unwilling to avail themself of the protection of each of those countries; or (b) not having a country of nationality, is outside the country of their former habitual residence and is unable or, by reason of that fear, unwilling to return to that country. *Immigration and Refugee Protection Act*, S.C. 2001, c. 27, s. 96.

CONVERSATION. *n.* 1. "... [A]n interchange of a series of separate communications." *R. v. Cremascoli* (1979), (sub nom. *R. v. Goldman*) 108 D.L.R. (3d) 17 at 32, [1980] 1 S.C.R. 976, 30 N.R. 453, 51 C.C.C. (2d) 1, 13 C.R. (3d) 228, McIntyre J. (Martland, Ritchie, Pigeon, Dickson, Beetz, Estey and Pratte JJ. concurring). 2. Behaviour, conduct. See CRIMINAL ~.

CONVERSION. *n.* 1. "... [A] taking of chattels with an intent to deprive the Plaintiff of his property in them, or with an intent to destroy them or change their nature." *McLean v. Bradley* (1878), 2 S.C.R. 535 at 550, Strong J. (Taschereau and Fournier JJ. concurring). 2. "... [A]ct of wilful interference without justification with property, including money, in a manner inconsistent with the right of the owner whereby the owner is deprived of the use of possession of the property." *Austin v. Habitat Development Ltd.* (1992), 44 C.P.R. (3d) 215 at 220, 94 D.L.R. (4th) 359, 114 N.S.R. (2d) 379, 313 A.P.R. 379 (C.A.), Hallet J.A. See RE~; WRONGFUL ~.

CONVERT. *v.* To change shares into shares of another class, in the manner specified in the share provisions.

CONVERTIBLE MORTGAGE. A mortgage in which the lender has the option to purchase the property at a certain price, usually the market value of the property when the term of the mortgage began. D.J. Donahue & P.D. Quinn, *Real Estate Practice in Ontario*, 4th ed. (Toronto: Butterworths, 1990) at 232.

CONVERTIBLE SECURITY. A security of an issuer that is convertible into, or carries the right of the holder to purchase or otherwise acquire, or of the issuer to cause the purchase or acquisition of, a security of the same issuer. *Securities Act,* R.S.B.C. 1996, c. 418, *National Instrument 45-102 Resale of Securities*, B.C. Reg. 107/2004, Sched. A, s. 1.1.

CONVERTIBLE STARTER PISTOL. A device designed for signalling that, (a) discharges a blank cartridge, (b) can be adapted for use as a firearm, and (c) when so adapted can discharge a live cartridge. *Imitation Firearms Regulation Act, 2000*, S.O. 2000, c. 37, s. 1.

CONVEY. *v.* 1. To create a property right or change it between persons. 2. Applied to any person, means the execution by that person of every necessary or suitable assurance for conveying or disposing to another land of or in which the first person is seised or entitled to a contingent right, either for the first person's whole estate or for any less estate, together with the performance of all formalities required by law to validate the conveyance. *Trustee acts.* 3. To carry.

CONVEYANCE. *n.* 1. Any instrument by which a freehold or leasehold estate, or other interest in real estate, may be transferred or affected. 2. Includes transfer, assignment, delivery over, appointment, lease, settlement, other assurance and covenant to surrender, payment, gift, grant, alienation, bargain, charge, encumbrance, limitation of use or uses of, in, to or out of real property or personal property by writing or otherwise. 3. Includes ships, vessels, aircraft, trains, and motor and other vehicles. See DEED OF ~; FRAUDULENT ~; MAIL ~; RE~; VOLUNTARY ~.

CONVEYANCER. *n.* A paralegal or lawyer whose chief practice is conveyancing.

CONVEYANCING. *n.* The practice which deals with the creation and transfer of rights in real property.

CONVICT. *v.* To find guilty of offence. See AUTREFOIS ~.

CONVICT. *n.* A person against whom judgment of imprisonment has been pronounced or recorded by a court. See SERVICE ~.

CONVICTION. *n.* "... [A] word which has different meanings in different contexts. The different senses in which the word 'conviction' is used include: (i) the verdict or adjudication of guilt; (ii) the sentence; (iii) the verdict or adjudication of guilt plus the judgment of the court, that is, the sentence; (iv) the record of the conviction." *R. v. McInnis* (1973), 23 C.R.N.S. 152 at 156, 1 O.R. (2d) 1, 13 C.C.C. (2d) 471 (C.A.), the court per Martin J.A. See CERTIFICATE OF ~; SUMMARY ~ COURT; SUMMARY ~ OFFENCE.

COOLING-OFF PERIOD. *var.* **COOLING OFF PERIOD.** 1. An opportunity to resile from a contract

and cancel it within a specified time period. Many statutes directed at regulation of consumer contracts provide for such a period.. 2. The time before which a strike or lock-out may begin.

CO-OP. *abbr.* Cooperative.

COOPERATIVE. *var.* **CO-OPERATIVE.** *n.* 1. A legal person in which persons having economic and social needs in common unite for the prosecution of an enterprise according to the rules of cooperative action to meet those needs. *Cooperatives Act*, R.S.Q. c. 67.2, s. 3. 2. A building, or a portion of a building, provided for residential occupancy purposes to members of an association incorporated or continued under the Cooperative Association Act. *Homeowner Protection Act*, S.B.C. 1998, c. 31, *Homeowner Protection Act Regulation*, B.C. Reg. 29/99, s. 1. 3. A corporation carrying on an enterprise on a co-operative basis. See CONSUMER'S ~; DIRECT CHARGE ~; DISTRIBUTING ~ HOUSING ~; WORKER ~.

COOPERATIVE ASSOCIATION. *var.* **CO-OPERATIVE ASSOCIATION.** 1. An association of primary producers having for its object the marketing, under a cooperative plan, of agricultural products produced by primary producers. *Agricultural Products Cooperative Marketing Act*, R.S.C. 1985, c. A-5, s. 2. a) A corporation, as defined in the Business Corporations Act, (b) a limited liability company, as defined in the Business Corporations Act, (c) a partnership, and (d) an entity incorporated or otherwise created outside British Columbia that is similar to one described in paragraphs (a) to (c) that owns, leases or has a right to acquire land. *Real Estate Development Marketing Act*, S.B.C. 2004, c. 41, s. 1.

COOPERATIVE BASIS. *var.* **CO-OPERATIVE BASIS.** Organized, operated and administered upon the following principles and methods, (a) each member or delegate has only one vote, (b) no member or delegate may vote by proxy, (c) interest on loan capital and dividends on share capital are limited to a percentage fixed by this Act or the articles of incorporation, and (d) the enterprise of the corporation is operated as nearly as possible at cost after providing for reasonable reserves and the payment or crediting of interest on loan capital or dividends on share capital; and any surplus funds arising from the business of the organization, after providing for such reasonable reserves and interest or dividends, unless used to maintain or improve services of the organization for its members or donated for community welfare or the propagation of co-operative principles, are distributed in whole or in part among the members, (i) in accordance with the by-laws of the co-operative if the corporation is a renewable energy co-operative, or (ii) in proportion to the volume of business the members have done with or through the organization if the corporation is not a renewable energy co-operative. *Co-operative Corporations Act*, R.S.O. 1990, c. C-35, s. 1.

COOPERATIVE CORPORATION. A body corporate organized and operated on cooperative principles. *Cooperative Credit Associations Act*, S.C. 1991, c. 48, s. 2.

COOPERATIVE CREDIT SOCIETY. A cooperative corporation one of whose principal purposes is to provide financial services to its members. *Cooperative Credit Associations Act*, S.C. 1991, c. 48, s. 2. See CENTRAL ~; FEDERATION OF COOPERATIVE CREDIT SOCIETIES; LOCAL ~.

COOPERATIVE ENTITY. A body corporate that, by the law under which it is organized and operated, must be organized and operated on—and is organized and operated on—cooperative principles. *Canada Cooperatives Act*, S. C. 1998, c. 1, s. 2.

COOPERATIVE FEDERALISM. The set of relationships which has been developed among the executives of the federal and provincial governments to achieve a redistribution of powers and resources, as required, on a negotiated basis rather than resolved along legalistic lines by the courts interpreting the division of powers set out in the constitution.

COOPERATIVE INTEREST. An interest that includes both (a) a right (i) of ownership, directly or indirectly, of one or more shares in the cooperative association, or (ii) to be a partner or member, directly or indirectly, in the cooperative association, and (b) as a result of the right described in paragraph (a), a right to use or occupy a part of the land in which a cooperative association has an interest. *Real Estate Development Marketing Act*, S.B.C. 2004, c. 41, s. 1.

COOPERATIVE PLAN. An agreement or arrangement for the marketing of agricultural products that provides for (a) equal returns for primary producers for agricultural products of the like grade and quality, (b) the return to primary producers of the proceeds of the sale of all agricultural products delivered under the agreement or arrangement and produced during the year, after deduction of processing, carrying and selling costs and reserves, if any, and (c) an initial payment to primary producers of the agricultural product to which the agreement relates of an amount fixed by regulations made by the Governor in Council on the recommendation of the Minister with respect to a reasonable amount that does not exceed the amount estimated by the Minister to be the amount by which the average wholesale price according to grade and quality of the agricultural product for the year in respect of which the initial payment will be made will exceed the processing, carrying and selling costs thereof for that year. *Agricultural Products Cooperative Marketing Act*, R.S.C. 1985, c. A-5, s. 2.

CO-ORDINATED COVERAGE. The ability of an individual, through the combination of two benefit plans, to obtain reimbursement for his or her insurance claims up to the combined limit of the two plans. *British Columbia Public School Employers' Assn. v. B.C.T.F.*, 2003 BCCA 323, 15 B.C.L.R. (4th) 58.

CO-ORDINATE JURISDICTION. See CONCURRENT JURISDICTION.

CO-OWNER. *n.* The person who owns property in common or jointly with one or more other persons. See JOINT TENANT; TENANCY IN COMMON.

CO-OWNERSHIP. *n.* Ownership of the same property, jointly and at the same time, by several persons each of whom is privately vested with a share of the right of ownership. Co-ownership is called undivided where the right of ownership is not accompanied with a physical division of the property. It is called divided where the right of ownership is apportioned among the co-owners in fractions, each comprising a physically divided private portion and a share of the common portions. *Civil Code*, S.Q. 1991, c. 64, a. 1010.

COPARCENER. *n.* A person to whom an estate in common with one or more other persons has descended.

CO-PARENT. *n.* (a) In relation to a live birth, means a person other than the mother or father who is cohabiting with the mother or father of the child in a spousal relationship at the time of the child's birth and who intends to participate as a parent in the upbringing of the child; and (b) in relation to a stillbirth, means a person other than the mother or father who is cohabiting with the mother or father of the stillborn child in a spousal relationship at the time of the stillbirth and who had intended to participate as a parent in the upbringing of the child. *The Vital Statistics Act, 2007*, S.S. 2007, c. V-7.2, s. 2.

COPY. *n.* 1. A document written or taken from another document. 2. A reproduction of the original. 3. In relation to any record, includes a print, whether enlarged or not, from a photographic film of the record. *Canada Evidence Act*, R.S.C. 1985, c. C-5, s. 30(12). See CERTIFIED ~; TRUE ~.

COPYING. See CANADIAN PRIVATE ~ COLLECTIVE.

COPYRIGHT. *n.* 1. The rights described in (a) section 3, in the case of a work, (b) sections 15 and 26, in the case of a performer's performance, (c) section 18, in the case of a sound recording, or (d) section 21, in the case of a communication signal. *Copyright Act*, R.S.C. 1985, c. C-42, s. 2. 2. In relation to a work, means the sole right to produce or reproduce the work or any substantial part thereof in any material form whatever, to perform the work or any substantial part thereof in public or, if the work is unpublished, to publish the work or any substantial part thereof. *Copyright Act*, R.S.C. 1985, c. C-42, s. 3 (part). 3. The maker of a sound recording has a copyright in the sound recording, consisting of the sole right to do the following in relation to the sound recording or any substantial part thereof: (a) to publish it for the first time, (b) to reproduce it in any material form, and (c) to rent it out, and to authorize any such acts. *Copyright Act*, R.S.C. 1985, c. C-42, s. 18(part). 4. A performer has a copyright in the performer's performance, consisting of the sole right to do the following in relation to the performer's performance or any substantial part thereof: (a) if it is not fixed, (i) to communicate it to the public by telecommunication, (ii) to perform it in public, where it is communicated to the public by telecommunication otherwise than by communication signal, and (iii) to fix it in any material form, (b) if it is fixed, (i) to reproduce any fixation that was made without the performer's authorization, (ii) where the performer authorized a fixation, to reproduce any reproduction of that fixation, if the reproduction being reproduced was made for a purpose other than that for which the performer's authorization was given, and (iii) where a fixation was permitted under Part III or VIII, to reproduce any reproduction of that fixation, if the reproduction being reproduced was made for a purpose other than one permitted under Part III or VIII, and (c) to rent out a sound recording of it, and to authorize any such acts. *Copyright Act*, R.S.C. 1985, c. C-42, s. 15. 5. Where a performer's performance takes place on or after January 1, 1996 in a country that is a WTO Member, the performer has, as of the date of the performer's performance, a copyright in the performer's performance, consisting of the sole right to do the following in relation to the performer's performance or any substantial part thereof: (a) if it is not fixed, to communicate it to the public by telecommunication and to fix it in a sound recording, and (b) if it has been fixed in a sound recording without the performer's authorization, to reproduce the fixation or any substantial part thereof, and to authorize any such acts. *Copyright Act*, R.S.C. 1985, c. C-42, s. 26. 6. A broadcaster has a copyright in the communication signals that it broadcasts, consisting of the sole right to do the following in relation to the communication signal or any substantial part thereof: (a) to fix it, (b) to reproduce any fixation of it that was made without the broadcaster's consent, (c) to authorize another broadcaster to retransmit it to the public simultaneously with its broadcast, and (d) in the case of a television communication signal, to perform it in a place open to the public on payment of an entrance fee, and to authorize any act described in paragraph (a), (b) or (d). *Copyright Act*, R.S.C. 1985, c. C-42, s. 21.

COPYRIGHT BOARD OF CANADA. 1. Established under section 66 of the Copyright Act, R.S.C. 1985, c. C-42, s. 66. The Board is an economic regulatory body empowered to establish, either mandatorily or at the request of an interested party, the royalties to be paid for the use of copyrighted works, when the administration of such copyright is entrusted to a collective-administration society. The Board also has the right to supervise agreements between users and licensing bodies and issues licences when the copyright owner cannot be located. *Our Mandate*, online: Copyright Board of Canada, <http://www.cb-cda.gc.ca/about-apropos/mandate-mandat-e.html>. 2. The Board is an administrative tribunal created by the Copyright Act, R.S.C. 1985, c. C-42. Among other things, the Board is responsible for the adoption of levies and their related terms and conditions in respect of the private copying of recorded musical works, performances and sound recordings (recorded music) on blank audio recording media (blank media or medium) that are sold or otherwise disposed of in Canada. *Canadian Private Copying Collective v. Canadian Storage Media Alliance*, 2004 FCA 424.

COR. *abbr.* [L. coram] In the presence of.

CORAM JUDICE. [L.] In the presence of a judge; before an appropriate or properly constituted court.

CORAM NON JUDICE. [L.] Without jurisdiction.

CORAM PARIBUS. [L.] Before one's peers.

CORBETT APPLICATION. An application brought by an accused to exclude his or her criminal record from a jury trial because of its likely prejudicial effect on the jury. The decision on a Corbett application involves determining whether the probative value of otherwise admissible evidence (i.e. evidence of an accused person's criminal record) outweighs its potential prejudice (i.e. the likelihood that the jury will use the evidence for an improper purpose). Named after *R. v. Corbett* [1988] 1 S.C.R. 670.

CORE DOCUMENT. (a) Where used in relation to, (i) a director of a responsible issuer who is not also an officer of the responsible issuer,(ii) an influential person, other than an officer of the responsible issuer or an investment fund manager where the responsible issuer is an investment fund, or (iii) a director or officer of an influential person who is not also an officer of the responsible issuer, other than an officer of an investment fund manager, a prospectus, a take-over bid circular, an issuer bid circular, a directors' circular, a rights offering circular, management's discussion and analysis, an annual information form, an information circular, annual financial statements, and interim financial statements of the responsible issuer, (b) where used in relation to, (i) a responsible issuer or an officer of the responsible issuer, (ii) an investment fund manager where the responsible issuer is an investment fund, or (iii) an officer of an investment fund manager where the responsible issuer is an investment fund, a prospectus, a take-over bid circular, an issuer bid circular, a directors' circular, a rights offering circular, management's discussion and analysis, an annual information form, an information circular, annual financial statements, interim financial statements, and a material change report required under section 102 of the responsible issuer, and (c) such other documents as may be prescribed for the purposes of this definition. *Securities Act*, S.Y. 2007, c. 16, s. 122.

CORE OF THE CITATION. The core of the neutral citation consists of three important elements: (i) the year; (ii) the tribunal identifier; (iii) the ordinal number of the decision.

CO-RESPONDENT. *n.* A person identified in a divorce pleading as the party involved in a matrimonial offence with a spouse.

COR. JUD. *abbr.* Correspondances Judiciaires (Québec).

CORNER. See UNDISPUTED ~.

COROLLARY. *n.* A collateral or secondary consequence.

COROLLARY RELIEF. 1. Relief collateral to or secondary to the main relief granted in an action. 2. In divorce, custody or maintenance.

COROLLARY RELIEF PROCEEDING. A proceeding in a court in which either or both former spouses seek a child support order, a spousal support order or a custody order. *Divorce Act*, R.S.C. 1985, c. 3 (2nd Supp.), s. 2.

CORONER. *n.* The official who investigates the death of any person who was killed or died in suspicious circumstances, or in other circumstances in which an investigation is required. The coroner's function is to determine by means of an investigation or, as the case may be, an inquest, 1) the identity of the deceased person; 2) the date and place of death; 3) the probable causes of death, that is, the disease, pathological condition, trauma or intoxications having caused, led to or contributed to the death; 4) the circumstances of death. *An Act respecting the determination of the causes and circumstances of death*, R.S.Q. c. R-0.2, s.2.

CORP. *abbr.* Corporation.

CORP. MGMT. TAX CONF. *abbr.* Canadian Tax Foundation. Corporate Management Tax Conference. Proceedings.

CORPORAL. *adj.* Bodily; relating to the body.

CORPORAL OATH. Touching the Bible or other holy book with the hand while taking an oath.

CORPORAL PUNISHMENT. 1. Punishment of the body such as flogging, lashing or whipping. 2. Corporal punishment which causes injury is child abuse. Spanking [which does not cause physical harm] is not child abuse. *Canadian Foundation for Children, Youth & the Law v. Canada (Attorney General)*, 2000 CarswellOnt 2409, 146 C.C.C. (3d) 362, 188 D.L.R. (4th) 718, 49 O.R. (3d) 662, 36 C.R. (5th) 334, 76 C.R.R. (2d) 251 (S.C.), McCombs J.

CORPORATE. See BODY ~.

CORPORATE ACT. "... [T]he 'collective act' of ... directors as expressed by resolution... ." *Hill v. Develcon Electronics Ltd.* (1991), 37 C.C.E.L. 19 at 32, 92 Sask. R. 241 (Q.B.), Baynton J.

CORPORATE NAME. A name given to a corporation.

CORPORATE SEAL. The impression of the company's name on important documents such as share certificates, bonds and debentures. H. Sutherland, D.B. Horsley & J.M. Edmiston, eds., *Fraser's Handbook on Canadian Company Law*, 7th ed. (Toronto: Carswell, 1985) at 339.

CORPORATE VEIL. See LIFTING THE ~; PIERCE ~.

CORPORATION. *n.* 1. A legal entity distinct from its shareholders or members with liability separate from its shareholders or members vested with the capacity of continuous succession. 2. A body corporate with or without share capital. See ACTIVE BUSINESS CARRIED ON BY A ~; CANADA ~; CANADA DEPOSIT INSURANCE ~; CANADA MORTGAGE AND HOUSING ~; CANADA POST ~; CASH-MUTUAL ~; CHARITABLE ~; CLOSE ~; CLOSELY HELD ~; COOPERATIVE ~; CROWN ~; DISTRIBUTING ~; ELEEMOSYNARY ~; EXTRA-PROVINCIAL ~; FOREIGN ~; LIMITED ~; MEMBERSHIP ~; MUNICIPAL ~; MUTUAL ~; NON-PROFIT ~; NOT-FOR-PROFIT ~; OTC ~; PARENT ~; PROVINCIAL ~; STATUTORY ~; STRATA ~; SUCCESSOR ~; TRUST ~.

CORPORATION AGGREGATE. A corporation with several members, created by the Crown through Royal Prerogative or by statute. G.H.L. Fridman, *The Law of Contract in Canada*, 2d ed. (Toronto: Carswell, 1986) at 151.

CORPORATION SOLE. 1. The corporate status granted an individual natural person by the law, which is distinct from that individual's natural personality. The main example is the Crown, the sovereign. 2. "... [O]ne single person being ex officio a corporate body, ..." *Arnegard v. Barons Consolidated School District* (1917), 33 D.L.R. 735 at 739, [1917] 2 W.W.R. 303, 11 Alta. L.R. 460 (C.A.), the court per Stuart J.A.

CORPORATOR. *n.* A member of a corporation aggregate. The inhabitants and officers of a municipal corporation.

CORPOREAL. *adj.* Describes that which is capable of physical possession.

CORPOREAL HEREDITAMENT. 1. A material object in contrast to a right. It may include land, buildings, minerals, trees or fixtures. 2. Land. *Pegg v. Pegg* (1992), 38 R.F.L. (3d) 179 at 184, 21 R.P.R. (2d) 149, 1 Alta. L.R. (3d) 249, 128 A.R. 132 (Q.B.), Agrios J.

CORPOREAL PROPERTY. Property having a physical existence.

CORPSE. *n.* The dead body of a person.

CORPUS. *n.* [L.] 1. The capital of a fund in contrast to income. 2. The body, referring to a human body or the aggregation of something, such as laws. See HABEAS ~.

CORPUS DELICTI. [L. body of the offence] The ingredients of an offence: commonly, the dead body.

CORPUS JURIS. [L.] A body of law. A legal text.

CORRECTION. *n.* For s. 43 [of the Criminal Code, R.S.C. 1985, C-46] to apply, the force used on a child must be intended for correction. Punishment motivated by anger, or administered with an intent to injure the child, is not for the purpose of correction. As well, the accused must honestly and reasonably believe that the child is guilty of conduct deserving of punishment. Moreover, the child must be capable of being corrected. Therefore a parent or teacher who applies force on a child who is either too young to appreciate corrective force or mentally handicapped and clearly unable to learn from corrective force is not protected by s. 43. A consideration of what constitutes "correction" should be informed not by the particular notions of the parent or teacher, but by reference to contemporary community standards. *Canadian Foundation for Children, Youth & the Law v. Canada (Attorney General)*, 2000 CarswellOnt 2409, 146 C.C.C. (3d) 362, 188 D.L.R. (4th) 718, 49 O.R. (3d) 662, 36 C.R. (5th) 334, 76 C.R.R. (2d) 251 (S.C.), McCombs J.

CORRECTIONAL CENTRE. 1. A lawful place of confinement, jail, prison, lockup, place of imprisonment, camp, correctional institution. 2. "... [A] jail where full security is established for the confinement and rehabilitation of persons committed to it... ." *R. v. Degan* (1985), 20 C.C.C. (3d) 293 at 299, 38 Sask. R. 234 (C.A.), the court per Vancise J.A.

CORRECTIONAL FACILITY. 1. A jail, prison, correctional centre for the custody of offenders. 2. "... [I]ncludes a community-training residence, is a facility established for the confinement and rehabilitation of a person committed to it... ." *R. v. Degan* (1985), 20 C.C.C. (3d) 293 at 299, 38 Sask. R. 234 (C.A.), the court per Vancise J.A.

CORRECTIONAL INSTITUTION. Includes every reformatory, jail, lock-up, and other place approved by the Minister for the study, confinement and correction of persons committed thereto. *Corrections Act*, R.S.N.B. 1973, c. C-26, s. 1.

CORRECTIONAL INVESTIGATOR OF CANADA. It is the function of the Correctional Investigator to conduct investigations into the problems of offenders related to decisions, recommendations, acts or omissions of the Commissioner or any person under the control and management of, or performing services for or on behalf of, the Commissioner that affect offenders either individually or as a group. *Corrections and Conditional Release Act*, S.C. 1992, c. 20, s. 167.

CORRECTIONAL SERVICE. See COMMUNITY ~.

CORRECTIVE DISCIPLINE. Principle that management withholds the ultimate penalty of discharge unless it is clear that the worker is not likely to respond favourably to a lesser penalty.

CORRECTNESS. n. 1.The highest standard of judicial review of tribunals' decisions. Cases in which this standard is applied deal with issues concerning the interpretation of a provision limiting the tribunal's jurisdiction (jurisdictional error) or where there is a statutory right of appeal which allows the reviewing court to substitute its opinion for that of the tribunal and where the tribunal has no greater expertise than the court on the issue in question, for example in the area of human rights. 2. It is also without question that the standard of correctness must be maintained in respect of jurisdictional and some other questions of law. This promotes just decisions and avoids inconsistent and unauthorized application of law. When applying the correctness standard, a reviewing court will not show deference to the decision maker's reasoning process; it will rather undertake its own analysis of the question. The analysis will bring the court to decide whether it agrees with the determination of the decision maker; if not, the court will substitute its own view and provide the correct answer. From the outset, the court must ask whether the tribunal's decision was correct. Correctness review has been found to apply to constitutional questions regarding the division of powers between Parliament and the provinces in the Constitution Act, 1867: Westcoast Energy Inc. v. Canada (National Energy Board), [1998] 1 S.C.R. 322. Such questions, as well as other constitutional issues, are necessarily subject to correctness review because of the unique role of s. 96 courts as interpreters of the Constitution. Administrative bodies must also be correct in their determi-

nations of true questions of jurisdiction or vires. *Dunsmuir v. New Brunswick*, 2008 SCC 9, Bastarache and LeBel, JJ. at para. 50, 58, 59. 3. Errors of law are generally governed by a correctness standard. *Mugesera v. Canada (Minister of Citizenship and Immigration)*, 2005 SCC 40, [2005] 2 S.C.R. 100, at para. 37, for example, held that the general questions of international law and criminal law at issue in that case had to be decided on a standard of correctness. Dunsmuir (at para. 54), says that if the interpretation of the home statute or a closely related statute by an expert decision-maker is reasonable, there is no error of law justifying intervention. *Canada (Citizenship and Immigration) v. Khosa*, 2009 SCC 12, [2009] 1 S.C.R. 339, Binnie, J. for the majority, para. 44.. See PATENTLY UNREASONABLE; REASONABLE.

CORR. JUD. *abbr.* Correspondances judiciaires, 1906.

CORROBORATE. *v.* "... As Lord Diplock observed in D.P.P. v. Hester [[1972] 3 All E.R. 1056 at 1071], the ordinary sense in which the verb 'corroborate' is used in the English language is the equivalent of 'confirmed' and (at p. 1073): 'What is looked for under the common law rule is confirmation from some other source that the suspect witness is telling the truth in some part of his story which goes to show that the accused committed the offence with which he is charged.' " *R. v. Vetrovec* (1982), 136 D.L.R. (3d) 89 at 104, [1982] 1 S.C.R. 811, 41 N.R. 606, 67 C.C.C. (2d) 1, 27 C.R. (3d) 304, [1983] 1 W.W.R. 193, the court per Dickson J.

CORROBORATION. *n.* Confirmation of a witness's evidence by independent testimony.

CORROBORATIVE EVIDENCE. Must be independent of the testimony of the witness whose testimony is sought to be corroborated. It must implicate the accused, that is, connect or tend to connect the accused with the crime. It must be evidence which confirms in some material particular, not only the evidence that the crime has been committed, but also that the accused committed it. *R. v. Whynder* (1996), 149 N.S.R. (2d) 241 (C.A.).

CORRUPT. *v.* To alter morals and behaviour from good to bad.

CORRUPT. *adj.* Spoiled; debased; depraved.

CORRUPTING MORALS. (1) The offence of (a) making, printing, publishing, distributing, circulating, or having in his possession for the purpose of publication, distribution or circulation any obscene written matter, picture, model, phonograph record or other thing whatever, or (b) making, printing, publishing, distributing, selling or having in his possession for the purpose of publication, distribution or circulation, a crime comic. (2) The offence of knowingly, without lawful justification or excuse, (a) selling, exposing to public view or having in his possession for such a purpose any obscene written matter, picture, model, phonograph record or other thing whatever, (b) publicly exhibiting a disgusting object or an indecent show, (c) offering to sell, advertising, or publishing an advertisement of, or having for sale or disposal, any means, instructions, medicine, drug or article intended or represented as a method of causing abortion or miscarriage, or (d) advertising or publishing an advertisement of any means, instructions, medicine, drug or article intended or represented as a method for restoring sexual virility or curing venereal diseases or diseases of the generative organs. *Criminal Code*, R.S.C. 1985, c. C-46, s. 163.

CORRUPTION. *n.* Granting of favours inconsistent with official duties. See MUNICIPAL ~.

CORRUPTION OF BLOOD. An effect of attainder, when a person attainted was considered corrupted by the crime, so that the person could no longer hold land, inherit it or leave it to any heirs.

CORRUPT PRACTICE. 1. "... [A] phrase, a term of art, created by statute for describing or dealing with a series of widely disparate acts and omissions... . There may be corrupt practices within the meaning of the defined term where there was no debased intent and they may be corrupt practices notwithstanding that there was no element of moral turpitude." *Johansen v. Dickerson* (1980), 117 D.L.R. (3d) 176 at 180, 30 O.R. (2d) 616 (Div. Ct.), the court per Anderson J. 2. "... By the 'Common law of Parliament' it included bribery, intimidation of electors and undue influence. Statutes have added treating, which is a form of bribery, hiring vehicles to convey voters to polls, personation and some other acts... ." *Howley v. Campbell*, [1939] 1 D.L.R. 431 at 432, 71 C.C.C. 246, 13 M.P.R. 494 (N.S. C.A.), Doull J.A. (concurring in the result). 3. Any act or omission, in connection with an election, in respect of which an offence is provided under the Criminal Code (Canada) or which is a corrupt practice under this Act. *Election Act*, R.S.O. 1990, c. E.6, s. 1.

COSMETIC. *n.* Includes any substance or mixture of substances manufactured, sold or represented for use in cleansing, improving or altering the complexion, skin, hair or teeth, and includes deodorants and perfumes. *Food and Drugs Act*, R.S.C. 1985, c. F-27, s. 2.

COSMETIC. *adj.* Non-essential. *Pesticides Act*, R.S.O. 1990, c. P.11, s. 1.

COST. *n.* "[In ss. 40(1)(c) and 54 of the Income Tax Act, S.C. 1970-71-72, c. 63] ... means the price that the taxpayer gave up in order to get the asset; it does not include any expense he may have incurred in order to put himself in a position to pay that price or to keep the property afterwards." *R. v. Stirling* (1985), 85 D.T.C. 5199, [1985] 1 F.C. 342, [1985] 1 C.T.C. 275 (C.A.), the court per Pratte J. See ACTUARIAL ~; CAPITAL ~; ~S; OPPORTUNITY ~; OUTLAY ~; PAST ~ OF HEALTH CARE SERVICES; REPLACEMENT ~ INSURANCE.

COST OF BORROWING. 1. In respect of a loan made by a bank, (a) the interest or discount applicable to the loan; (b) any amount charged in connection with the loan that is payable by the borrower to the bank; and (c) any charge prescribed to be included in the cost of borrowing. *Bank Act*, S.C. 1991, c. 46, s. 449. 2. All amounts that a borrower is required to pay under or as a condition of entering into a credit agreement other than, (a) a payment or repayment of a portion of the principal under the agreement as prescribed, and (b) prescribed charges. *Consumer Protection Act, 2002*, S.O. 2002, c. 30, Sched. A, s. 66.

COST OF FUTURE CARE. Costs which a plaintiff can be expected to expend for care, particularly medical and hospital expenses, as a result of the injuries suffered and for which he is claiming damages. See FUTURE COST OF HEALTH CARE SERVICES.

COST OF LIVING. The relationship between the cost of goods to the consumer and buying power of wages.

COST-OF-LIVING ADJUSTMENT. A change in wages or pension payments designed to offset changes in cost of living.

COST OF LIVING INDEX. "... [U]sed in Canada commonly and interchangeably for the phrase, 'consumer price index,' and especially for the index published by the Dominion Bureau of Statistics. Judicial notice may be taken of the fact that this government department is now known as Statistics Canada." *Collins Cartage & Storage Co. v. McDonald* (1980), 16 R.P.R. 71 at 74, 30 O.R. (2d) 234, 116 D.L.R. (3d) 570 (C.A.), the court per Goodman J.A. See CONSUMER PRICE INDEX.

COST-PLUS CONTRACT. A contract to sell a product or perform work for the selling price or contractor's costs plus a percentage or plus a fixed fee.

COSTS. *n.* 1. An award made in favour of a successful or deserving litigant, payable by another litigant, the award of which is determined at the end of proceedings, payable by way of indemnity for allowable expenses and services relevant to the proceeding and not payable to ensure participation in the proceedings. 2. Modern costs rules accomplish various purposes in addition to the traditional objective of indemnification. An order as to costs may be designed to penalize a party who has refused a reasonable settlement offer; this policy has been codified in the rules of court of many provinces. Costs can also be used to sanction behaviour that increases the duration and expense of litigation, or is otherwise unreasonable or vexatious. In short, it has become a routine matter for courts to employ the power to order costs as a tool in the furtherance of the efficient and orderly administration of justice. *British Columbia (Minister of Forests) v. Okanagan Indian Band*, 2003 SCC 71. 3. Money expended to prosecute or defend a suit which a party is entitled to recover. 4. "... [F]or the purpose of indemnification or compensation." *Bell Canada v. Consumers' Assn. of Canada* (1986), 17 Admin L.R. 205 at 228, [1986] 1 S.C.R. 190, 9 C.P.R. (2d) 145, 65 N.R. 1, 26 D.L.R. (4th) 573, the court per Le Dain J. 5. The costs and charges after they have been ascertained, of committing and conveying to prison the person against whom costs have been awarded. *Criminal Code*, R.S.C. 1985, c. C-46, s. 809(5). 6. In National Energy Board Act (Can.) (Re), [1986] 3 F.C. 275 (C.A.), leave to appeal dismissed, (1986), 23 Admin, L.R. xxi (NEB Reference), the Federal Court of Appeal referred to the "accurate and useful discussion as to the normal legal meaning of 'costs'" of the Ontario Divisional Court in Regional Municipality of Hamilton-Wentworth and Hamilton-Wentworth Save the Valley Committee, Inc. et al. (1985), 51 O.R. (2d) 23 (Div.Ct.) (Hamilton-Wentworth), where it was determined that the word "costs" as used in the legal sense is a word having a well-defined meaning. In Hamilton-Wentworth, the court stated "[f]rom the earliest times, it has been recognized that the power to award 'costs' must be found in a statute." Describing the nature of costs, it said: The characteristics of costs, developed over many years are: (1) They are an award to be made in favour of a successful or deserving litigant, payable by the loser. (2) Of necessity, the award must await the conclusion of the proceeding, as success or entitlement cannot be determined before that time. (3) They are payable by way of indemnity for allowable expenses and services incurred relevant to the case or proceeding. (4) They are not payable for the purpose of assuring participation in the proceedings. The concept of costs in the context of administrative tribunals carries the same general connotation as legal costs ... *Canada (Attorney General) v. Mowat*, 2009 FCA 309. 7. Where costs are awarded to a party without any qualification as to their being in the cause, or in any event of the cause, as here, the award must be interpreted as meaning costs in the cause. *Miller v. Miller*, 2000 CarswellBC 350, 2000 BCSC 300, Dillon J. See ASSESSED ~; ASSESSMENT OF ~; BILL OF ~; COST; DOUBLE ~; FIXED ~; FULL ~; INCREASED ~; INTERIM ~; PARTY-AND-PARTY ~; PRE-EMPTIVE ~ ORDER; PROTECTIVE ~ ORDER; SECURITY FOR ~; SOLICITOR-AND-CLIENT ~; SOLICITOR AND HIS OWN CLIENT ~; SPECIAL ~; START-UP ~; SUBSTANTIAL INDEMNITY ~; SUNK ~; TAXATION OF ~; TAXED ~; WITH ~.

COSTS IF DEMANDED. An expression inserted in a judgment when either the successful party is a body like the Crown, presumed to be able to fund its own litigation, or the unsuccessful party faces financial ruin if required to pay costs.

COSTS IN ANY EVENT OF THE CAUSE. The issue here is whether an order that costs are payable to a party "in any event of the cause," or its shorthand version, "in any event," means the costs are payable at once or only at the conclusion of the action. The ... commonly-understood meaning of the phrase is that the costs so ordered are taxable and payable only at the conclusion of the litigation when the overall costs of the matter are dealt with. In our view that is the proper meaning of an order that costs are payable to a party in any event of the cause or in any event. *566320 Alberta Ltd. v. Lethbridge (City)*, 2005 ABCA 244.

COSTS, INSURANCE AND FREIGHT. See C.I.F.; C.I.F. CONTRACT.

COSTS IN THE ACTION. See COSTS IN THE CAUSE.

COSTS IN THE CAUSE. 1. "... [T]he costs of this motion are to be taken into account in the final taxation of the costs at the conclusion of the litigation between the parties." *Banke Electronics Ltd. v. Olvan Tool & Die Inc.* (1981), 32 O.R. (2d) 630 at 632-33 (H.C.), Cory J. 2. Where costs are awarded to a party

without any qualification as to their being in the cause, or in any event of the cause, as here, the award must be interpreted as meaning costs in the cause. *Miller v. Miller*, 2000 CarswellBC 350, 2000 BCSC 300, Dillon J.

COSTS OF AND INCIDENTAL TO. Party-and-party costs. M.M. Orkin, *The Law of Costs*, 2d ed. (Aurora: Canada Law Book, 1987) at 1-13.

COSTS OF THE DAY. Costs awarded when adjournment of the trial was caused by one party's default. M.M. Orkin, *The Law of Costs*, 2d ed. (Aurora: Canada Law Book, 1987) at 2-73.

COSTS OF THIS HEARING. Costs which include both preparation for the hearing and the hearing itself. M.M. Orkin, *The Law of Costs*, 2d ed. (Aurora: Canada Law Book, 1987) at 1-12.

COSTS OF THIS PROCEEDING. Costs for all interlocutory motions and services, not only costs at trial. M.M. Orkin, *The Law of Costs*, 2d ed. (Aurora: Canada Law Book, 1987) at 1-12.

COSTS REASONABLY INCURRED. Party-and-party costs. M.M. Orkin, *The Law of Costs*, 2d ed. (Aurora: Canada Law Book, 1987) at 1-13.

COSTS SHALL FOLLOW THE EVENT. The event referred to is the outcome of the litigation. Event is to be read distributively so that neither party gets all the costs if success is divided on the various issues. *McLeod Engines Ltd. v. Canadian Atlas Diesel Engines Co. (No. 2)* (1951), 1 W.W.R. (N.S.) 803 at 814 (B.C. C.A.), Smith J.A.

COSTS THROWN AWAY. Refers to expenses incurred in anticipation of a proceeding which did not occur through no fault of the person incurring the expenses.

COSTS TO THE SUCCESSFUL PARTY IN THE CAUSE. See COSTS IN THE CAUSE.

CO-SURETY. *n.* One who shares a surety's obligations.

COTENANCY. *n.* Includes tenancy in common and joint tenancy.

COTRONI ASSESSMENT. Before surrendering persons for extradition, the Minister of Justice must conduct what is known as a "Cotroni assessment". The assessment derives its name from the Cotroni c. Centre de Prévention de Montréal [(1989), 48 C.C.C. (3d) 193 (S.C.C.)], where the court recognized that a person's s. 6(1) rights were engaged on an extradition request and that the Minister was obligated to consider a variety of factors, including a person's rights under s. 6(1), in determining whether the Minister should surrender that person to a foreign jurisdiction. *United States v. Prudenza*, 2006 CarswellOnt 6614, 216 O.A.C. 231.

COUNCIL. *n.* 1. An assembly of people for governmental or municipal purposes. 2. The governing body of a city, village, summer village, municipal district, county or other municipality. 3. The Queen's Privy Council for Canada, committees of the Queen's Privy Council for Canada, Cabinet and committees of Cabinet. *Canada Evidence Act*, R.S.C. 1985, c. C-5, s.

C

39(3). 4. An advisory body to government. 5. Used to describe the governing body of an association, i.e. professional organizations. 6. Used in the title of administrative agencies. 7. An association of unions within an area.See BAND ~; CANADIAN ~ ON THE STATUS OF THE ARTIST; COMMISSIONER IN ~; DISTRICT ~; EXECUTIVE ~; GENERAL ~; GOVERNOR GENERAL IN ~; GOVERNOR IN ~; INTERPROFESSIONAL ~; LEGISLATIVE ~; LIEUTENANT GOVERNOR IN ~; NATIONAL FARM PRODUCTS ~; ORDER IN ~; PRIVY ~.

COUNCILLOR. *n.* A member of or a person serving on a council. See BAND ~.

COUNSEL. *v.* 1. Includes procure, solicit or incite. *Criminal Code*, R.S.C. 1985, c. C-46, s. 22(3). 2. To advise or recommend. 3. In Hamilton [R. v. Hamilton, 2005 SCC 47, 2005 SCC 47], Fish J., for the majority, summarized the elements of counselling at para. 29: In short, the actus reus for counselling is the deliberate encouragement or active inducement of the commission of a criminal offence. And the mens rea consists in nothing less than an accompanying intent or conscious disregard of the substantial and unjustified risk inherent in the counselling: that is, it must be shown that the accused either intended that the offence counselled be committed, or knowingly counselled the commission of the offence while aware of the unjustified risk that the offence counselled was in fact likely to be committed as a result of the accused's conduct.[end of quote] Nowhere is it stated that one is required to "know" a person in order to encourage or actively induce that person to commit an offence. *R. v. Comeau*, 2008 NBCA 60.

COUNSEL. *n.* 1. A barrister or solicitor, in respect of the matters or things that barristers and solicitors, respectively, are authorized by the law of a province to do or perform in relation to legal proceedings. *Criminal Code*, R.S.C. 1985, c. C-46, s. 2. Both singular and plural. 3. "... [A]n adviser whether or not he is a lawyer, ..." *Olavarria v. Canada (Minister of Manpower & Immigration)*, [1973] F.C. 1035 at 1037, 41 D.L.R. (3d) 472 (C.A.), Jackett, Thurlow and Hyde JJ.A. See CROWN ~; DUTY ~; JUNIOR ~; KING'S ~; LEGAL ~; LEGISLATIVE ~; QUEEN'S ~; RIGHT TO ~.

COUNSELLING. *n.* "... [A]cts or words ... such as to induce a person to commit the offences that one desires and passive communication does not constitute an offence even if its purpose is to have someone inflict those injuries." *R. v. Dionne* (1987), 38 C.C.C. (3d) 171 at 180, 58 C.R. (3d) 351, 79 N.B.R. (2d) 297, 201 A.P.R. 297 (C.A.), Ayles J.A.

COUNSELLOR. See FAMILY COURT ~.

COUNT. *n.* 1. A charge in an information or indictment. *Criminal Code*, R.S.C. 1985, c. C-46, s. 2. 2. The description of an offence in the formal document advising the accused of the charge against him or her. See RE~.

COUNTENANCE.*v.* 1. To encourage; to aid and abet. 2. In the context of authorizing copyright infringement must be understood in its strongest

dictionary meaning, namely, "give approval to, sanction, permit, favour, encourage": see The New Shorter Oxford English Dictionary (1993), vol. 1, at p. 526. *CCH Canadian Ltd. v. Law Society of Upper Canada*, 2004 SCC 13.

COUNTERCLAIM. *n.* "... [A]n independent action raised by a defendant, which because of the identity of the parties can conveniently be tried with the plaintiff's claim. While a counterclaim frequently (although not necessarily) arises from the same events as the plaintiff's claim, and while it may result in reduction of the plaintiff's claim, it is in principle an independent action." *Royal Bank v. Rizkalla* (1984), 50 C.P.C. 292 at 296, 59 B.C.L.R. 324 (S.C.), McLachlin J.

COUNTERFEIT. *n.* An unauthorized imitation intended to be used to defraud by passing off.

COUNTERFEIT COIN. See COUNTERFEIT MONEY.

COUNTERFEIT MONEY. Includes (a) a false coin or false paper money that resembles or is apparently intended to resemble or pass for a current coin or current paper money, (b) a forged bank-note or forged blank bank-note, whether complete or incomplete, (c) a genuine coin or genuine paper money that is prepared or altered to resemble or pass for a current coin or current paper money of a higher denomination, (d) a current coin from which the milling is removed by filing or cutting the edges and on which new milling is made to restore its appearance, (e) a coin cased with gold, silver or nickel, as the case may be, that is intended to resemble or pass for a current gold, silver or nickel coin, and (f) a coin or a piece of metal or mixed metals that is washed or coloured by any means with a wash or material capable of producing the appearance of gold, silver or nickel and that is intended to resemble or pass for a current gold, silver or nickel coin. *Criminal Code*, R.S.C. 1985, c. C-46, s. 448. See UTTERING ~.

COUNTERFEIT TOKEN OF VALUE. A counterfeit excise stamp, postage stamp or other evidence of value, by whatever technical, trivial or deceptive designation it may be described, and includes genuine coin or paper money that has no value as money. *Criminal Code*, R.S.C. 1985, c. C-46, s. 448.

COUNTERFOIL. *n.* The complementary part of a cheque or receipt used to preserve a record of the contents.

COUNTERMAND. *v.* To revoke; to recall.

COUNTER OFFER. *var.* **COUNTER-OFFER.** A statement by the offeree rejecting the offer and creating a new offer.

COUNTERPART. *n.* A part which corresponds; a duplicate.

COUNTER-PARTY. See CENTRAL ~.

COUNTERPETITION. *n.* A claim for relief against the petitioner by respondent in a divorce proceeding.

COUNTER-PROPOSAL. *n.* An opposing offer made in collective bargaining following an offer or proposal by the other party.

COUNTER-SIGN. *var.* **COUNTERSIGN.** *v.* 1. For a second person to sign a document to verify the validity of the original signature of the first person. 2. For a subordinate to sign to vouch for the authenticity of any writing by the superior.

COUNTERVAIL. *v.* To compensate; to balance.

COUNTRY. *n.* The total territory which is subject under a single sovereign to a single body of law. J.G. McLeod, *The Conflict of Laws* (Calgary: Carswell, 1983) at 5.

COUNTY. *n.* A territorial division for electoral, judicial or local government purposes.

COUNTY COURT. 1. A court with jurisdiction limited to a county by territory and limited by subject matter. 2. "... [A]n inferior statutory Court of record and its jurisdiction is to be found in its act of incorporation, namely the County Court Act, R.S.N.S. 1967, c. 64, and its antecedent enactments." *Whynot v. Giffin* (1984), 40 C.P.C. 344 at 346, 62 N.S.R. (2d) 112, 136 A.P.R. 112, 7 D.L.R. (4th) 68 (C.A.), the court per Macdonald J.A.

COUPON. *n.* Part of a commercial instrument designed to be cut off, which evidences something connected with the contract the instrument represents, usually interest.

COUPON BOND. A bond registrable as to principal only; interest is paid through coupons, payable to bearer, attached to the instrument. H. Sutherland, D.B. Horsley & J.M. Edmiston, eds., *Fraser's Handbook on Canadian Company Law*, 7th ed. (Toronto: Carswell, 1985) at 311.

COUPON DEBENTURE. A debenture registrable as to principal only; interest is paid through coupons, payable to bearer, attached to the instrument. H. Sutherland, D.B. Horsley & J.M. Edmiston, eds., *Fraser's Handbook on Canadian Company Law*, 7th ed. (Toronto: Carswell, 1985) at 311.

COURIER. *n.* An individual who, on personal account or as an employee of another person, provides to members of the public the service of carrying items of value in personal custody.

COURSE. *n.* "[As used in s. 2(f.1) of the Newfoundland Human Rights Code, R.S. Nfld. 1970, c. 262] ... imports the need for some series of events." *Aavik v. Ashbourne* (1990), 12 C.H.R.R. D/401 at D/407 (Nfld. Human Rights Comm.), Gallant (Member). See NORMAL ~; OF ~; ORDER OF ~.

COURSE OF BUSINESS. The normal activities of business. See ORDINARY ~.

COURSE OF CONDUCT. A series of actions similarly motivated; repetitive conduct.

COURSE OF EMPLOYMENT. "... [W]ork- or job-related ..." *Robichaud v. Canada (Treasury Board)*, [1987] 2 S.C.R. 84 at 92, La Forest J., cited with approval in *Janzen v. Platy Enterprises Ltd.* (1989), 47 C.R.R. 274 at 305, [1989] 1 S.C.R. 1252, 25 C.C.E.L. 1, [1989] 4 W.W.R. 39, 59 D.L.R. (4th) 352, 10 C.H.R.R. D/6205, 58 Man. R. (2d) 1, the court per Dickson C.J.C.

COURT. *n.* 1. A place where justice is administered; a body or part of the judicial system. 2. A place where a sovereign resides. 3. The court or a judge of the court. 4. "... [A]ny judicial organism whatever its importance or jurisdiction. That is the usual meaning of the [word]. As well, [it has] a narrow meaning by which ... 'court' designates more specifically a judicial organism of superior jurisdiction ..." *Québec (Commission des droites de la personne) c. Canada (Procureur général)* (1978), (*sub nom. Human Rights Commission v. Solicitor-General of Canada*) 93 D.L.R. (3d) 562 à 570 (Qué. C.A.), Mayrand J.A. (Bernier J.A. concurring). 5. Includes a judge, arbitrator, umpire, commissioner, provincial judge, justice of the peace or other office or person having by law or by the consent of the parties authority to hear, receive and examine evidence. *Evidence acts.* 6. A tribunal. See ADMIRALTY ~; APPEAL ~; APPELLATE ~; BEFORE THE ~; CIVIL CONTEMPT; CLERK OF THE ~; CONTEMPT IN THE FACE OF THE ~; CONTEMPT NOT IN THE FACE OF THE ~; CONTEMPT OF ~; CONTEMPT OUTSIDE THE ~; CONTRAVENTIONS ~; COUNTY ~; CRIMINAL CONTEMPT; DISTRICT ~; DIVIDED ~; DIVISIONAL ~; ECCLESIASTICAL ~; EXCHEQUER ~; FEDERAL ~; FOREIGN ~; FRIEND OF THE ~; FULL ~; INFERIOR ~; INTERNATIONAL ~ OF JUSTICE; MUNICIPAL ~; NAVAL ~; OPEN ~; ORIGINAL ~; PAYMENT INTO ~; POLICE ~; PRIZE ~; PROVINCIAL ~; RULES OF ~; SCANDALIZE THE ~; SMALL CLAIMS ~; STATUTORY ~; SUMMARY CONVICTION ~; SUPERIOR ~; SUPREME ~ OF CANADA; SURROGATE ~; TAX ~ OF CANADA; TERRITORIAL ~; TRIAL ~; YOUTH JUSTICE ~.

COURT BELOW. Refers to an inferior court, one from which appeals are heard.

COURT CLERK. The chief administrator of a court who issues process, enters orders and performs other duties.

COURT MARTIAL. 1. A court which tries offences against naval, military or air force discipline, or offences committed by a member of the armed forces against the ordinary law. 2. Includes a General Court Martial and a Standing Court Martial. *National Defence Act*, R.S.C. 1985, c. N-5, s. 2. See GENERAL ~; STANDING ~.

COURT MARTIAL APPEAL COURT. The court established under the National Defence Act which shall hear and determine all appeals referred to it. The judges of the Court Martial Appeal Court are not less than four judges of the Federal Court of Appeal or the Federal Court to be designated by the Governor in Council and such additional judges of a superior court of criminal jurisdiction as are appointed by the Governor in Council. *National Defence Act*, R.S.C. 1985, c. N-5, s. 234.

COURT OF APPEAL. 1. In the Province of Prince Edward Island, the Appeal Division of the Supreme Court, and in all other provinces, the Court of Appeal. *Criminal Code*, R.S.C. 1985, c. C-46, s. 2, as am. 2. The words "general court of appeal" in s. 101 [of the

Constitution Act, 1867 (U.K.), 30 & 31 Vict., c. 3] denote the status of the Court within the national court structure and should not be taken as a restrictive definition of the Court's functions. In most instances, this Court acts as the exclusive ultimate appellate court in the country, and, as such, is properly constituted as the "general court of appeal" for Canada. Moreover, it is clear that an appellate court can receive, on an exceptional basis, original jurisdiction not incompatible with its appellate jurisdiction. *Reference re Secession of Quebec*, 1998 CarswellNat 1299, 161 D.L.R. (4th) 385, 228 N.R. 203, 55 C.R.R. (2d) 1, [1998] 2 S.C.R. 217, per curiam. See APPEAL; APPEAL COURT; APPELLATE COURT; FEDERAL ~; GENERAL ~.

COURT OF CHANCERY. The main English court in which the part of law known as equity was enforced. The Lord Chancellor presided, assisted by the Master of the Rolls and judges called Vice-Chancellors.

COURT OF COMPETENT JURISDICTION. 1. One that possesses jurisdiction over the subject matter, jurisdiction over the person, and jurisdiction to grant the remedy. . . . whether a court or tribunal possesses the power to grant the remedy sought is first and foremost a matter of discerning legislative intent. The question in all cases is whether Parliament or the legislature intended to empower the court or tribunal to make rulings on Charter violations that arise incidentally to their proceedings, and to grant the remedy sought as a remedy for such violations. *R. v. Hynes* [2001] 3 S.C.R. 623. 2. May include a tribunal which has jurisdiction over the parties and subject matter of the dispute and which is empowered to make the orders sought. 3. "... [A] court is competent if it has jurisdiction, conferred by statute, over the person and the subject-matter in question and, in addition, has authority to make the order sought." *R. v. Morgentaler* (1984), 48 O.R. (2d) 519 (C.A.), Brooke J.A., cited with approval in *R. v. Mills* (1986), 29 D.L.R. (4th) 161 at 177 (S.C.C.), McIntyre J. and *Cuddy Chicks Ltd. v. Ontario (Labour Relations Board)* (1989), 39 Admin. L.R. 48 at 68, 89 C.L.L.C. 14,051, 79 O.R. (2d) 179, 62 D.L.R. (4th) 125, [1989] O.L.R.B. Rep. 989, 35 O.A.C. 94, 44 C.R.R. 75, Finlayson J.A. (dissenting).

COURT OF CRIMINAL JURISDICTION. (a) A court of general or quarter sessions of the peace, when presided over by a superior court judge, (a.1) in the Province of Quebec, the Court of Quebec, the municipal court of Montreal and the municipal court of Quebec, (b) a provincial court judge or judge acting under Part XIX, and (c) in the Province of Ontario, the Ontario Court of Justice. *Criminal Code*, R.S.C. 1985, c. C-46, s. 2.

COURT OF EQUITY. Originally separate courts heard matters of equity but reforms of the late nineteenth century combined the jurisdiction of the courts of equity with the law courts so that courts now administer both law and equity, providing equitable remedies according to equitable principles where appropriate.

COURT OF FIRST INSTANCE. A court before which an action is first brought for trial.

COURT OF KING'S BENCH. The superior court of some provinces, known by this name during the reign of a king. See QUEEN'S BENCH.

COURT OF LAST RESORT. The court from which there is no further appeal.

COURT OF PROBATE. Any court having jurisdiction in matters of probate.

COURT OF QUEEN'S BENCH. The name given to the superior court of some provinces. See QUEEN'S BENCH.

COURT OF RECORD. 1. Any court which keeps a record of its judicial acts and proceedings. 2. "... [A] Court which has power to fine and imprison ..." *R. v. Fields* (1986), 28 C.C.C. (3d) 353 at 357-58, 16 O.A.C. 286, 53 C.R. (3d) 260, 56 O.R. (2d) 213, Dubin J.A.

COURT RECORDS. 1. The records of the office of any court and documents filed therein. 2. Includes all documents, records, letters, transcripts, recordings, exhibits and papers of any kind or any thing on which information is recorded or stored by any means including graphic, electronic or mechanical means, deposited or on file with or held by a court. *Probate Act*, S.N.S. 2000, c. 31, s. 9.

COURT REPORTER. 1. A person who records proceedings of a court and the evidence given in court. 2. "... [A]n officer of the court and enjoys an official status... ." *R. v. Turner* (1981), 27 C.R. (3d) 73 at 79, [1982] 2 W.W.R. 142, 65 C.C.C. (2d) 335, 14 Sask. R. 321 (C.A.), Bayda C.J.S. (MacDonald J.A. concurring).

COURTS ADMINISTRATION SERVICE. Body established by the federal government. The purposes of this Act are to (a) facilitate coordination and cooperation among the Federal Court of Appeal, the Federal Court, the Court Martial Appeal Court and the Tax Court of Canada for the purpose of ensuring the effective and efficient provision of administrative services to those courts; (b) enhance judicial independence by placing administrative services at arm's length from the Government of Canada and by affirming the roles of chief justices and judges in the management of the courts; and (c) enhance accountability for the use of public money in support of court administration while safeguarding the independence of the judiciary. *Courts Administration Service Act, 2002*, S.C. 2002, c. 8.

COUT. DIG. *abbr.* Coutlee's Digest.

COUT. S.C. *abbr.* Notes of Unreported Cases, Supreme Court of Canada (Coutlee), 1875-1907.

COVENANT. *n.* 1. An agreement in writing signed and delivered and in the past under seal. 2. "... [R]efers to obligations of the landlord not only under any written agreement of lease between landlord and tenant, but also to any obligations imposed upon the landlord by reason of the Landlord and Tenant Act [R.S.O. 1980, c. 232]." *Kingsway v. Pooler* (1988), 4 T.L.L.R. 105 at 108 (Ont. Dist. Ct.), Davidson

D.C.J. 3. [As used in s. 248(1)(a)(iii) of the *Income Tax Act*, R.S.C. 1985, c. 1 (5th Supp.)] is a more general word, and can include any contractual promise. However, its scope is limited by the statutory context in which it is used: it must be a promise *similar* to a guarantee, security or indemnity *Citibank Canada v. R.* 2002 FCA 128, 2002 D.T.C. 6876, [2002] 2 C.T.C. 171. See CONTRACT IN RESTRAINT OF TRADE; DEED OF ~; QUIET ENJOYMENT; RESTRICTIVE ~; USUAL ~.

COVENANTEE. *n.* The party for whose benefit the covenant is made, the recipient of the covenant.

COVENANT FOR FURTHER ASSURANCE. A standard covenant which a vendor undertakes to protect the purchaser's interest in something purchased; the vendor agrees, at the purchaser's request and cost, to execute a further conveyance or other document to more perfectly assure the subject-matter conveyed.

COVENANT FOR PAYMENT. An agreement that the mortgagor will pay the mortgage money and interest.

COVENANTOR. *n.* The party who makes the covenant, who provides the covenant.

COVENANT RUNNING WITH THE LAND. See RUN WITH THE LAND; RUN WITH THE REVERSION.

COVENANT RUNNING WITH THE REVERSION. See RUN WITH THE LAND; RUN WITH THE REVERSION.

COVER. *v.* 1. To insure. 2. To buy back securities sold short.

COVERAGE. *n.* "... [C]an mean at least two things; a straight naming of the perils insured against, or on a larger view, a bundle of descriptions of the protection offered in the case of each individual peril contained in the one insurance policy. In British Columbia, I prefer the latter, more compendious understanding." *Dressew Supply Ltd. v. Laurentian Pacific Insurance Co.* (1991), [1992] 3 C.C.L.I. (2d) 286 at 310-11, 77 D.L.R. (4th) 317, 57 B.C.L.R. (2d) 198, [1991] 6 W.W.R. 174, [1991] I.L.R. 1-2755 (C.A.), the court per Locke J.A. See COLLISION ~; COMPREHENSIVE ~; CO-ORDINATED ~; DISABILITY ~; LOT ~.

COVER NOTE. A document given to an insured to indicate insurance is in effect.

COVERT. *adj.* 1. Hidden. 2. Of a woman, under the protection of her husband. See FEME ~.

COVERTURE. *n.* A woman's condition during marriage; the fact that she is married.

C.P. *abbr.* 1. Canadian Pacific. 2. Common Pleas. 3. Cour provinciale. 4. Recueils de jurisprudence du Québec: Cour provinciale, 1975-1985.

CP. *abbr.* Compare.

C.P.C. *abbr.* 1. Carswell's Practice Cases, 1976-1985. 2. Canadian Pension Commission.

CPCC. *abbr.* Canadian Private Copying Collective.

C.P.C. (5TH). *abbr.* Carswell's Practice Cases (Fifth Series), 2001-2005.

C.P.C. (4TH). *abbr.* Carswell's Practice Cases (Fourth Series), 1997-2001.

C.P.C. (OLMSTEAD). *abbr.* Canadian Constitutional Decisions of the Judicial Committee of the Privy Council (Olmstead), 1873-1954.

C.P.C. (PLAXTON). *abbr.* Canadian Constitutional Decisions of the Judicial Committee of the Privy Council (Plaxton), 1930-1939.

C.P.C. (2D). *abbr.* Carswell's Practice Cases (Second Series) 1985-1992.

C.P.C. (6TH). *abbr.* Carswell's Practice Cases (Sixth Series), 2006-.

C.P.C. (3RD). *abbr.* Carswell's Practice Cases (Third Series), 1992-1997.

C.P.D. *abbr.* Law Reports, Common Pleas Division.

C.P. DIV. CIV. *abbr.* Cour provinciale, Division civile.

C.P. DIV. CRIM. *abbr.* Cour provinciale, Division criminelle.

C.P. DIV. FAM. *abbr.* Cour provinciale, Division de la famille.

C.P. DU N. *abbr.* Cours de perfectionnement du Notariat.

CPIC. *abbr.* Canadian Police Information Centre.

C.P.R. *abbr.* Canadian Patent Reporter, 1942-1971.

C.P.R.B. *abbr.* Procurement Review Board of Canada, decisions, 1990-?.

C.P.R. (4TH). *abbr.* Canadian Patent Reporter (Fourth Series), 1999-.

C.P.R. (N.S.). *abbr.* Canadian Patent Reporter (New [Third] Series).

C. PROV. *abbr.* Cour provinciale.

C.P.R. (2D). *abbr.* Canadian Patent Reporter (Second Series), 1971-1984.

C.P.R. (3D). *abbr.* Canadian Patent Reporter (Third Series), 1985-1999.

C.R. *abbr.* Criminal Reports (Canada), 1946-1967.

C.R.A.C. *abbr.* Canadian Reports, Appeal Cases: appeals allowed or refused by the Judicial Committee of the Privy Council, 1828-1913.

CRAFT. *n.* 1. A skilled trade. 2. A small boat. 3. A guild. See PLEASURE ~.

CRAFT UNION. A union, membership in which is restricted to workers having a particular skill.

CRAFT UNIT. A collective bargaining unit consisting of employees having a particular skill.

CRASH. *n.* A time of depression after effects of a drug stimulant wear off. F.A. Jaffe, *A Guide to Pathological Evidence for Lawyers and Police Officers*, 4th ed. (Toronto: Carswell, 1999) at 234.

C.R.A.T. *abbr.* Commercial Registration Appeal Tribunal – Summaries of Decisions, 1971-1979.

C.R.C. *abbr.* Canadian Railway Cases, 1902-1939.

C.R.D. *abbr.* Charter of Rights Decisions, 1982-.

CREATE. *v.* To bring into legal existence. *Manco Home Systems Ltd., Re* (1990), 78 C.B.R. (N.S.) 109 at 113 (B.C. C.A.), Southin J.A.

CREATION. See JOB ~ PROGRAM.

CREATION OF CURRENCY. To create money which forms part of the money supply by printing more currency through the Bank of Canada.

CREATION OF LIEN. Mechanics', construction or builder's liens are created when work or services are performed or materials are placed or furnished at the direction of and on the property of another person.

CREATIVE COMMONS LICENCE. Copyright licence which reserves some rights associated with the copyright to the originator while permitting certain uses to the public or a segment of the public.

CREDIBILITY. *n.* 1. Credibility means simply worthiness of belief. *Cooper v. Cooper*, 2001 CarswellNfld 17, 2001 NFCA 4, 13 R.F.L. (5th) 29, 198 Nfld. & P.E.I.R. 1, 595 A.P.R. 1, Green J.A. (Cameron J.A. concurring). 2. "... [N]ot merely the appreciation of the witnesses' desire to be truthful but also of their opportunities of knowledge and powers of observation, judgment and memory – in a word, the trustworthiness of their testimony, ..." *Raymond v. Bosanquet (Township)* (1919), 59 S.C.R. 452 at 460, 50 D.L.R. 560, Anglin J. 3. The degree of credit the court should give to the testimony of a witness. *National Defence Act*, R.S.C. 1985, c. N-5, *Military Rules of Evidence*, C.R.C., c. 1049, s. 2. 4. Credibility and reliability are different. Credibility has to do with a witness's veracity, reliability with the accuracy of the witness's testimony. Accuracy engages consideration of the witness's ability to accurately i. observe; ii. recall; and iii. recount events in issue. Any witness whose evidence on an issue is not credible cannot give reliable evidence on the same point. Credibility, on the other hand, is not a proxy for reliability: a credible witness may give unreliable evidence. *R. v. C. (H.)*, 2009 ONCA 56.

CREDIBLE. *adj.* Believable; worthy of belief.

CREDIT. *n.* 1. Belief in a person's trustworthiness. 2. An arrangement for obtaining loans or advances. 3. The advancing of money, goods or services to or on behalf of another for repayment at a later time, whether or not there is cost of borrowing. *Consumer Protection acts.* 4. Recognition granted to a student as proof that the student has successfully completed a quantity of work. See ANTICIPATORY ~; CONSUMER ~; DOCUMENTARY ~; ELIGIBLE ~; EMISSIONS ~; FARM ~ CANADA; FIXED ~; LETTER OF ~; OPEN ~; PENSION BENEFIT ~; SALE ON ~.

CREDIT AGREEMENT. A consumer agreement under which a lender extends credit to a borrower and includes a loan of money, a supplier credit agreement and a consumer agreement under which a loan of money or supplier credit agreement may occur in the future, but does not include an agreement under which a lender extends credit on the security of a mortgage of real property or consumer agreements of a prescribed type. *Consumer Protection Act, 2002*, S.O. 2002, c. 30, Sched. A, s. 66. See SCHEDULED-PAYMENTS ~; SUPPLIER ~.

CREDIT BUREAU. An organization which collects information relating to the credit, responsibility and character of individuals and businesses for the purpose of providing the information to its members.

CREDIT CARD. 1. Any card, plate, coupon book or other device issued or otherwise distributed for the purpose of being used (a) on presentation to obtain, on credit, money, goods, services or any other thing of value, or (b) in an automated teller machine, a remote service unit or a similar automated banking device to obtain any of the services offered through the machine, unit or device. *Criminal Code*, R.S.C. 1985, c. C-46, s. 321. 2. A card or device under which a borrower can obtain advances under a credit agreement for open credit. *Consumer Protection Act, 2002*, S.O. 2002, c. 30, Sched. A, s. 1.

CREDIT INFORMATION. Information about a consumer as to name, age, occupation, place of residence, previous places of residence, marital status, spouse's name and age, number of dependants, particulars of education or professional qualifications, places of employment, previous places of employment, estimated income, paying habits, outstanding debt obligations, cost of living obligations and assets. *Consumer Reporting acts.*

CREDIT INSTITUTION. A bank, treasury branch, credit union or a trust company.

CREDIT INSURANCE. Insurance against loss to the insured through insolvency or default of a person to whom credit is given in respect of goods, wares or merchandise. *Insurance acts.*

CREDIT LINE. The amount of money a lender agrees to supply to a person.

CREDIT NOTE. A note issued by a business indicating that a customer is entitled to be credited by the issuer with a certain amount.

CREDITOR. *n.* 1. A person to whom another person owes a debt. 2. "... [A] person entitled to the fulfilment of, an obligation." *Crown Lumber Co. v. Smythe*, [1923] 3 D.L.R. 933 at 952, [1923] 2 W.W.R. 1019, 19 Alta. L.R. 558 (C.A.), Beck J.A. 3. A person having a claim provable as a claim under this Act. *Bankruptcy and Insolvency Act*, R.S.C. 1985, c. B-3, s. 2. 4. In G.T. Campbell & Associates Ltd. v. Hugh Carson Co. (1979), 99 D.L.R. (3d) 529 (Ont. C.A.), for example, the court extended the meaning of the word creditor under the Ontario Act to include any claim against a dissolved corporation whether it be in debt or for unliquidated damages. The definition of "creditor" was stretched to include a claimant who at the time the acts complained of occurred was unable to state the amount of the debt being claimed. *A E Realisations (1985) Ltd. v. Time Air Inc.*, 1994 CarswellSask 287, [1995] 3 W.W.R. 527, 17 B.L.R. (2d) 203, 127 Sask. R. 105 (Q.B.), Noble J. 5. Includes a surety or guarantor for the debt due to the creditor. *Bankruptcy and Insolvency Act*, R.S.C. 1985, c. B-3, s. 95. See JUDGMENT ~; PREFERRED ~; REGISTERED ~; SECURED ~; UNSECURED ~.

CREDITORS' INSURANCE. See GROUP ~.

CREDITORS' MEETING. The first meeting of creditors of a bankrupt.

CREDITORS' RELIEF STATUTE. A statute which forces a judgment creditor to share proportionately any proceeds of execution with other unsecured creditors who filed writs of execution or certificates with the sheriff.

CREDIT RATE. The actual annual percentage of a credit charge.

CREDIT RATING. Evaluation of the credit worthiness of a business or individual based on ability to pay and past performance in paying debt.

CREDIT RATING ORGANIZATION. Dominion Bond Rating Service Limited; Fitch, Inc.; Moody's Investors Service, Inc.; Standard & Poor's Corporation.

CREDIT REPAIR. Services or goods that are intended to improve a consumer report, credit information, file or personal information, including a credit record, credit history or credit rating. *Consumer Protection Act, 2002*, S.O. 2002, c. 30, Sched. A, s. 48.

CREDIT REPAIRER. (a) A supplier of credit repair, or (b) a person who holds themself out as a credit repairer. *Consumer Protection Act, 2002*, S.O. 2002, c. 30, Sched. A, s. 48.

CREDIT REPORT. A report of credit information or of a credit rating based on credit information, supplied by a credit reporting agency.

CREDIT REPORTING AGENCY. A person who is engaged in providing credit reports to any other person, whether for remuneration or otherwise.

CREDIT SOCIETY. See COOPERATIVE ~.

CREDIT SUPPORT AGREEMENT. See TITLE TRANSFER ~.

CREDIT UNION. A co-operative society, including caisses populaires, that provides its members with financial and other services. See FEDERAL ~.

CREED. *n.* "... [I]nvolve[s] a declaration of religious belief." *R. v. Ontario (Labour Relations Board)*, [1963] 2 O.R. 376 at 389, 39 D.L.R. (2d) 593, 63 C.L.L.C. 15,459 (H.C.), McRuer C.J.H.C.

CREMATION. *n.* Disposal of a dead body by incineration.

CREMATORIUM. *n.* A building fitted with appliances for the purpose of cremating human remains.

C. RÉV.*abbr.* Cour de révision.

C.R. (5TH). *abbr.* Criminal Reports (Fifth Series), 1997-2002.

C.R. (4TH). *abbr.* Criminal Reports (Fourth Series), 1991-1996.

CRIME. *n.* 1. "... [A]n act which the law, with appropriate penal sanctions, forbids; but as prohibitions are not enacted in a vacuum, we can properly look for some evil or injurious or undesirable effect upon the public against which the law is directed... ." *Margarine Case* (1948), [1949] 1 D.L.R. 433 at 472, [1949] S.C.R. 1, Rand J. 2. Must consist of a physical element of committing a prohibited act, creating a prohibited state of affairs or omitting to do that which is required by law and the conduct must be willed, voluntary. *R. v. Daviault* [1994] 3 S.C.R. 63. 3. A public wrong involving a violation of public rights and duties owed to the whole community in its social aggregate capacity. *Reference Re Alberta Legislation* [1938] S.C.R. 100. See COMPENSATION OF VICTIMS OF ~; CONDUCT ~; ENTERPRISE ~ OFFENCE; EXTRADITION ~; POLITICAL ~; PROCEEDS OF ~; RESULT ~; WAR ~.

CRIME AGAINST HUMANITY. 1. Murder, extermination, enslavement, deportation, imprisonment, torture, sexual violence, persecution or any other inhumane act or omission that is committed against any civilian population or any identifiable group and that, at the time and in the place of its commission, constitutes a crime against humanity according to customary international law or conventional international law or by virtue of its being criminal according to the general principles of law recognized by the community of nations, whether or not it constitutes a contravention of the law in force at the time and in the place of its commission. *Crimes Against Humanity and War Crimes Act*, S.C. 2000, c. 24, s. 4. 2. Any of the following acts when committed as part of a widespread or systematic attack directed against any civilian population, with knowledge of the attack: (a) murder; (b) extermination; (c) enslavement; (d) deportation or forcible transfer of population; (e) imprisonment or other severe deprivation of physical liberty in violation of fundamental rules of international law; (f) torture; (g) rape, sexual slavery, enforced prostitution, forced pregnancy, enforced sterilization, or any other form of sexual violence of comparable gravity; (h) persecution against any identifiable group or collectivity on political, racial, national, ethnic, cultural, religious, gender as defined in paragraph 3, or other grounds that are universally recognized as impermissible under international law, in connection with any act referred to in this paragraph or any crime within the jurisdiction of the Court; (i) enforced disappearance of persons; (j) the crime of apartheid; (k) other inhumane acts of a similar character intentionally causing great suffering, or serious injury to body or to mental or physical health. *Crimes Against Humanity and War Crimes Act*, S.C. 2000, c. 24. Sched., *Rome Statute*, Article 7.

CRIME COMIC. A magazine, periodical or book that exclusively or substantially comprises matter depicting pictorially (a) the commission of crimes, real or fictitious; or (b) events connected with the commission of crimes, real or fictitious, whether occurring before or after the commission of the crime. *Criminal Code*, R.S.C. 1985, c. C-46, s. 163(7).

CRIME HAS BEEN COMMITTED IN CANADA. The wording of [s. 18(1)(b) of the Extradition Act, R.S.C. 1985, c. E-23] requires the court to assume that "the crime has been committed in Canada." This has been interpreted to mean that the court should look to the impugned conduct and make its assessment under Canadian law on the basis of that conduct. *D'Agostino, Re*, 2000 CarswellOnt 465, 47 O.R. (3d) 257, 143 C.C.C. (3d) 158, 129 O.A.C. 166, 72 C.R.R. (2d) 198 (C.A.).

CRIMEN FALSI. [L.] Forgery; perjury; suppression of evidence.

CRIMEN FURTI. [L.] Theft.

CRIMEN INCENDII. [L.] Arson.

CRIMEN RAPTUS. [L.] Rape.

CRIMEN ROBERIAE. [L.] Robbery.

CRIME OF SPECIFIC INTENT. One which involves the performance of the actus reus couple with an intent or purpose going beyond the mere performance of the questioned act. *R. v. Bernard* [1988] 2 S.C.R. 833.

CRIMINAL. *n.* A person found guilty of an offence. See HABITUAL ~.

CRIMINAL. *adj.* Relating to crimes or to the administration of the law in respect of crimes.

CRIMINAL ACT. [I]n Canada the phrase "criminal act" [in an insurance policy] means any breach of the Criminal Code because s. 9 of the Criminal Code abolishes all common law crimes, with the exception of the common law power of judges to punish for contempt of court. *Eichmanis v. Wawanesa Mutual Insurance Co.* (2007), 84 O.R. (3d) 668 (C.A.).

CRIMINAL BREACH OF CONTRACT. Wilfully breaking a contract, knowing or having reasonable cause to believe that the probable consequences of doing so, whether alone or in combination with others, will be (a) to endanger human life, (b) to cause serious bodily injury, (c) to expose valuable property, real or personal, to destruction or serious injury, (d) to deprive the inhabitants of a city or place, or part thereof, wholly or to a great extent, of their supply of light, power, gas or water, or (e) to delay or prevent the running of any locomotive engine, tender, freight or passenger train or car, on a railway that is a common carrier, is an offence. *Criminal Code*, R.S.C. 1985, c. C-46, s. 422.

CRIMINAL BREACH OF TRUST. Every one who, being a trustee of anything for the use or benefit, whether in whole or in part, of another person, or for a public or charitable purpose, converts, with intent to defraud and in contravention of his trust, that thing or any part of it to a use that is not authorized by the trust is guilty of an indictable offence. *Criminal Code*, R.S.C. 1985, c. C-46, s. 336.

CRIMINAL CODE. The Criminal Code, R.S.C. 1985, c. C-46 as amended from time to time. The codification of the criminal law and the source of criminal law in Canada. This federal statute is frequently amended to modify the law or to add new offences.

CRIMINAL CONSPIRACY. "... [An] agreement of two or more to do an unlawful act, or to do a lawful act by unlawful means." *R. v. O'Brien*, [1954] S.C.R. 666 at 669, 672 and 674.

CRIMINAL CONTEMPT. 1. Private or public conduct which interferes with a court's process or seriously threatens the administration of justice. Dealt with by a summary process. 2. "... [W]hen the element of public defiance of the court's process in a way calculated to lessen societal respect for the courts is added to the breach [of a court order], it [the contempt] becomes criminal.... The gravamen of the offence is rather open, continuous and flagrant violation of a Court order without regard for the effect that [such actions] may have on the respect accorded to edicts of the Court.... To establish criminal contempt the Crown must prove that the accused defied or disobeyed a court order in a public way (the actus reus), with intent, knowledge or recklessness as to the fact that the public disobedience will tend to depreciate the authority of the court (the mens rea)...." *U.N.A. v. Alberta (Attorney General)* (1992), 13 C.R. (4th) 1 at 13-14, [1992] 3 W.W.R. 481, 89 D.L.R. (4th) 609, 71 C.C.C. (3d) 225, 135 N.R. 321, 92 C.L.L.C. 14,023, 1 Alta. L.R. (3d) 129, 125 A.R. 241, 14 W.A.C. 241, [1992] 1 S.C.R. 901, 9 C.R.R. (2d) 29, McLachlin J. (La Forest, Gonthier and Iacobucci JJ. concurring).

CRIMINAL CONVERSATION. A husband's claim for damages for adultery.

CRIMINAL COURT. See INTERNATIONAL ~.

CRIMINAL HARASSMENT. Conduct consisting of (a) repeatedly following from place to place the other person or anyone known to them; (b) repeatedly communicating with, either directly or indirectly, the other person or anyone known to them; (c) besetting or watching the dwelling-house, or place where the other person, or anyone known to them, resides, works, carries on business or happens to be; or (d) engaging in threatening conduct directed at the other person or any member of their family. *Criminal Code*, R.S.C. 1985, c. C-46, s. 264(2).

CRIMINAL HISTORY. The convictions which a person has received from the criminal courts during his or her lifetime.

CRIMINAL INJURIES COMPENSATION. A statutory plan to compensate victims of specified crimes, or anyone injured while attempting to arrest a person, assist a peace officer or preserve the peace. K.D. Cooper-Stephenson & I.B. Saunders, *Personal Injury Damages in Canada* (Toronto: Carswell, 1981) at 3.

CRIMINALITY. See DOUBLE ~.

CRIMINALIZATION. *n.* Rendering an act criminal and therefore punishable. See DE~.

CRIMINAL JURISDICTION. See COURT OF ~.

CRIMINAL LAW. 1. The prohibition of conduct which interferes with the proper functioning of society or which undermines the safety and security of society as a whole. *RJR-MacDonald v. Canada (Attorney General)* (1995), 127 D.L.R. (4th) 1 (S.C.C.).

2. A law which declares acts to be crimes and prescribes punishment for those crimes. 3. "... [L]egislation creating offences which have a national aspect or dimension may properly be characterized as criminal law ..." *R. v. Hoffman-La Roche Ltd.* (1981), 15 B.L.R. 217 at 265, 33 O.R. (2d) 694, 24 C.R. (3d) 193, 58 C.P.R. (2d) 1, 62 C.C.C. (2d) 118, 125 D.L.R. (3d) 607 (C.A.), the court per Martin J.A. See CRIME; CRIMINAL CODE.

CRIMINAL MATTER. A prosecution or trial for an offence triable by a judge or jury in accordance with the Criminal Code of Canada.

CRIMINAL NEGLIGENCE. 1. Every one is criminally negligent who (a) in doing anything, or (b) in omitting to do anything that it is his duty to do, shows wanton or reckless disregard for the lives or safety of other persons. *Criminal Code*, R.S.C. 1985, c. C-46, s. 219. 2. "In criminal cases, generally, the act coupled with the mental state or intent is punished. In criminal negligence, the act which exhibits the requisite degree of negligence is punished... ." *R. v. Tutton* (1989), 48 C.C.C. (3d) 129 at 140, 13 M.V.R. (2d) 161, 69 C.R. (3d) 289, 98 N.R. 19, [1989] 1 S.C.R. 1392, 35 O.A.C. 1, McIntyre J. 3. "... [T]he well-recognized tort of civil negligence: the sins of omission and commission that cause injury to one's neighbour, elevated to a crime by their magnitude of wanton and reckless disregard for the lives and safety of others." *R. v. Gingrich* (1991), 6 C.R. (4th) 197 at 209, 28 M.V.R. (2d) 161, 44 O.A.C. 290, 65 C.C.C. (3d) 188 (C.A.), Finlayson J.A. (Krever J.A. concurring).

CRIMINAL OFFENCE. 1. An activity which Parliament wishes to suppress through criminal sanction must pose a significant, grave and serious risk of harm to public health, morality, safety or security before it can fall within the purview of the criminal law power. *RJR-MacDonald v. Canada (Attorney General)* (1995), 127 D.L.R. (4th) 1 (S.C.C.). 2. "... Where the offence is criminal, the Crown must establish a mental element, namely, that the accused who committed the prohibited act did so intentionally or recklessly, with knowledge of the facts constituting the offence, or with wilful blindness toward them. Mere negligence is excluded from the concept of the mental element required for conviction. Within the context of a criminal prosecution a person who fails to make such inquiries as a reasonable and prudent person would make, or who fails to know facts he should have known, is innocent in the eyes of the law." *R. v. Sault Ste. Marie (City)* (1978), 3 C.R. (3d) 30 at 40, [1978] 2 S.C.R. 1299, 21 N.R. 295, 7 C.E.L.R. 53, 40 C.C.C. (2d) 353, 85 D.L.R. (3d) 161, the court per Dickson J. See QUASI-~.

CRIMINAL ONUS. The standard of proof, the burden of which is on the Crown or prosecutor, is that the case or issue be proved beyond a reasonable doubt.

CRIMINAL ORGANIZATION. A group, however organized, that (a) is composed of three or more persons in or outside Canada; and (b) has as one of its main purposes or main activities the facilitation or commission of one or more serious offences that, if committed, would likely result in the direct or indirect receipt of a material benefit, including a financial benefit, by the group or by any of the persons who constitute the group. It does not include a group of persons that forms randomly for the immediate commission of a single offence. *Criminal Code*, R.S.C. 1985, c. C-46, s. 467.1.

CRIMINAL ORGANIZATION OFFENCE. (a) An offence under section 467.11, 467.12 or 467.13, or a serious offence committed for the benefit of, at the direction of, or in association with, a criminal organization, or (b) a conspiracy or an attempt to commit, being an accessory after the fact in relation to, or any counselling in relation to, an offence referred to in paragraph (a). *Criminal Code,* R.S.C. 1985, c. C-46, s. 2.

CRIMINAL PROCEDURE. "... In one sense, it is concerned with proceedings in the criminal Courts and such matters as conduct within the courtroom, the competency of witnesses, oaths and affirmations, and the presentation of evidence. Some cases have defined procedure even more narrowly in finding that it embraces the three technical terms – pleading, evidence and practice. In a broad sense, it encompasses such things as the rules by which, according to the Criminal Code, police powers are exercised, the right to counsel, search warrants, interim release, procuring attendance of witnesses." *Di Iorio v. Montreal Jail* (1977), 73 D.L.R. (3d) 491 at 530, [1978] 1 S.C.R. 152, 35 C.R.N.S. 57, 8 N.R. 361, Dickson J. (Martland, Judson, Ritchie and Spence JJ. concurring).

CRIMINAL RATE. An effective annual rate of interest calculated in accordance with generally accepted actuarial practices and principles that exceeds sixty per cent on the credit advanced under an agreement or arrangement. *Criminal Code*, R.S.C. 1985, c. C-46, s. 347(2).

CRIMINAL RECORD. Refers to convictions under the Criminal Code entered in a register or data base, CPIC.

CRIMINAL RESPONSIBILITY. See AGE OF ~; VERDICT OF NOT CRIMINALLY RESPONSIBLE ON ACCOUNT OF MENTAL DISORDER.

CRIMINAL SANCTIONS. Fines, imprisonment and probation.

CRIMINATE. *v.* To implicate.

CRIMINATION. See SELF-INCRIMINATION.

CRIMINOLOGIE. *abbr.* Journal published by Presses de l'Université de Montréal.

CRIMINOLOGY. *n.* The study of the nature, causes, and treatment or punishment of criminal behaviour.

CRIM. L.Q. *abbr.* Criminal Law Quarterly.

CRIMOGENIC. *adj.* Contributing to a person's criminality.

CRITICISM. *n.* The opinion of any person about a book, play or visual image.

C.R.M.P.C. *abbr.* Commission de révision des marchés publics du Canada, décisions, 1990-?.

C.R. (N.S). *abbr.* Criminal Reports, New Series, 1967-1978.

C.R.O. *abbr.* Commission des relations ouvrières.

CROP INSURANCE PROGRAM. A program for the insurance of specified agricultural products against loss from natural causes that is established by the laws of a province and administered by the province. *Farm Insurance Protection Act*, S.C. 1991, c. 22, s. 2.

CROSS. *n.* A mark in the form of an X.

CROSS-ACTION. *n.* An action brought by a defendant against the plaintiff in the original action.

CROSS-APPEAL. *var.* **CROSS APPEAL.** 1. An appeal by the respondent to an appeal. 2. A cross-appeal is only filed by a respondent to an appeal who seeks to vary the judgment in his own favour. *Morrison v. Hicks* (1991), 82 D.L.R. (4th) 568 (B.C. C.A.).

CROSSBOW. *n.* A device with a bow and a bowstring mounted on a stock that is designed to propel an arrow, a bolt, a quarrel or any similar projectile on a trajectory guided by a barrel or groove and that is capable of causing serious bodily injury or death to a person. *Criminal Code*, R.S.C. 1985, c. C-46, s. 84(1).

CROSSCLAIM. *n.* A claim by one defendant against a co-defendant.

CROSSED CHEQUE. A cheque which is crossed generally or a cheque which is crossed specially.

CROSSED GENERALLY. Where a cheque bears across its face an addition of (a) the word "bank" between two parallel transverse lines, either with or without the words "not negotiable", or (b) two parallel transverse lines simply, either with or without the words "not negotiable", that addition constitutes a crossing, and the cheque is crossed generally. *Bills of Exchange Act*, R.S.C. 1985, c. B-4, s. 168.

CROSSED SPECIALLY. Where a cheque bears across its face an addition of the name of a bank, either with or without the words "not negotiable", that addition constitutes a crossing, and the cheque is crossed specially and to that bank. *Bills of Exchange Act*, R.S.C. 1985, c. B-4, s. 168.

CROSS-EXAMINATION. *n.* 1. A cross-examination is generally understood to include asking leading questions that cannot be asked in a direct examination. *Murao v. Blackcomb Skiing Enterprises Ltd. Partnership*, 2005 BCCA 43. 2. The examination of a witness by the party who did not call the witness and who did not examine the witness in chief. The purpose of the cross-examination is to elicit evidence in favour of the party examining the witness, to discredit the witness and to undermine the evidence given by the witness when examined in chief. In R. v. Osolin, [[1993] 4 S.C.R. 595], Cory J. reviewed the relevant authorities and, at p. 663, explained why cross-examination plays such an important role in the adversarial process, particularly, though of course not

exclusively, in the context of a criminal trial: There can be no question of the importance of cross-examination. It is of essential importance in determining whether a witness is credible. Even with the most honest witness cross-examination can provide the means to explore the frailties of the testimony. For example, it can demonstrate a witness's weakness of sight or hearing. It can establish that the existing weather conditions may have limited the ability of a witness to observe, or that medication taken by the witness would have distorted vision or hearing. Its importance cannot be denied. It is the ultimate means of demonstrating truth and of testing veracity. Cross-examination must be permitted so that an accused can make full answer and defence. The opportunity to cross-examine witnesses is fundamental to providing a fair trial to an accused. This is an old and well established principle that is closely linked to the presumption of innocence. Commensurate with its importance, the right to cross-examine is now recognized as being protected by s. 7 and 11(d) of the Canadian Charter of Rights and Freedoms. The right of cross-examination must therefore be jealously protected and broadly construed. But it must not be abused. Counsel are bound by the rules of relevancy and barred from resorting to harassment, misrepresentation, repetitiousness or, more generally, from putting questions whose prejudicial effect outweighs their probative value. Just as the right of cross-examination itself is not absolute, so too are its limitations. Trial judges enjoy, in this as in other aspects of the conduct of a trial, a broad discretion to ensure fairness and to see that justice is done - and seen to be done. In the exercise of that discretion, they may sometimes think it right to relax the rules of relevancy somewhat, or to tolerate a degree of repetition that would in other circumstances be unacceptable. *R. v. Lyttle*, 2004 SCC 5.

CROSS-EXAMINATION ON AFFIDAVIT. The opposite party's examination of an affiant on the contents of the affiant's affidavit.

CROSSING. The addition of (a) the word "bank" between two parallel transverse lines, either with or without the words "not negotiable", or (b) two parallel transverse lines simply, either with or without the words "not negotiable." *Bills of Exchange Act*, R.S.C. 1985, c. B-4, s. 168.

CROWN. *n.* 1. In Canada, the federal government and each of the provincial governments. 2. Depending on the context, Her Majesty the Queen in right of a Province, Canada or both a province and Canada. 3. Used when speaking of the rights, duties or prerogatives of the sovereign. 4. Any of the Commonwealth governments which represent the head, which is Her Majesty. 5. The Sovereign of the United Kingdom, Canada and Her other Realms and Territories, and Head of the Commonwealth. 6. "Although at one time it was correct to describe the Crown as one and indivisible, with the development of the Commonwealth this is no longer so. Although there is only one person who is the Sovereign within the British Commonwealth, it is now a truism that in matters of law and government the Queen of the United Kingdom, for example, is entirely independent and distinct from the Queen of Canada. Further, the Crown is a constitutional monarchy, and thus when one speaks today, and as was frequently done in the course of the argument on this application, of the Crown 'in right of Canada', or of some other territory within the Commonwealth, this is only a short way of referring to the Crown acting through, and on the advice of her ministers in Canada or in that other territory within the Commonwealth." *R. v. Foreign & Commonwealth Affairs (Secretary of State)* (1982), 1 C.R.R. 254 at 277, [1982] 2 All E.R. 118 (U.K. C.A.), May L.J. 7. "In Gauthier v. The King (1918), 56 S.C.R. 176 at p. 194 Mr. Justice Anglin said: ' ... a reference to the Crown in a provincial statute shall be taken to be to the Crown in right of the Province only, unless the statute in express terms or by necessary intendment makes it clear that the reference is to the Crown in some other sense... .' It has been said that the Crown is one and indivisible. That is the ideal conception of the Crown, but in this country we have under our Federal system, a distribution of powers amongst the Dominion Parliament and the Provincial Legislatures, 'the Crown in right of the Dominion,' and 'the Crown in right of the Province,' are expressions which may therefore mean different things... ." *Montreal Trust Co. v. South Shore Lumber Co.* (1924), 33 B.C.R. 280 at 284, [1924] 1 W.W.R. 657, [1924] 1 D.L.R. 1030 (C.A.), Macdonald C.J.A. See DEMISE OF THE ~; FEDERAL ~; HONOUR OF THE ~; LAW OFFICER OF THE ~; MINISTER OF THE ~; PREROGATIVE RIGHTS OF THE ~.

CROWN AGENT. The determination as to whether a particular body is an agent of the Crown depends on the "nature and degree of control" exercised over that body by the Crown. *Westeel-Rosco Ltd. v. Bd. of Gov. of South Sask. Hosp. Centre* (1976), 69 D.L.R. (3d) 334 at 342 (S.C.C.), Ritchie J.

CROWN ATTORNEY. An agent of the Attorney General; prosecutor in criminal matters on behalf of the Crown.

CROWN CORPORATION. 1. A corporation that is accountable, through a Minister, to the Legislative Assembly or Parliament for the conduct of its affairs. 2. A corporation of which not less than 90 per cent of the shares ordinarily entitled to vote in an election for directors are owned by the government of the Province or of Canada. 3. A corporation of which all the directors or members of the governing body are appointed by the Lieutenant Governor in Council or the Governor General in Council. 4. A corporation which under any Act of the Province or of Canada is designated as such.

CROWN COUN. REV. *abbr.* Crown Counsel's Review.

CROWN COUNSEL. A person entitled to practise law in the jurisdiction and who is authorized to represent the Crown before the courts in relation to the prosecution of offences.

CROWN DEBT. Any existing or future debt due or becoming due by the Crown, and any other chose in action in respect of which there is a right of recovery enforceable by action against the Crown. *Financial Administration Act*, R.S.C. 1985, c. F-11, s. 66.

CROWN GRANT. 1. A transfer of Crown lands to a private person. 2. An instrument in writing conveying Crown land in fee simple. *Land Act*, R.S.B.C. 1996, c. 245, s. 1. 3. Any of the instruments or acts referred to in section 5, a plan referred to in section 7, a notification within the meaning of the Territorial Lands Act or any other instrument or act by which federal real property may be granted or federal immovables may be conceded. *Federal Real Property and Federal Immovables Act,* S.C. 1991, c. 50, s. 2.

CROWN IMMUNITY. 1. The common law rule that the Crown is not bound by a statute, unless by express words or necessary implication. *R. v. Eldorado Nuclear Ltd.* (1983), 77 C.P.R. (2d) 1 at 8, 50 N.R. 120, 4 D.L.R. (4th) 193, 1 O.A.C. 243, 8 C.C.C. (3d) 449, [1983] 2 S.C.R. 551, 7 Admin. L.R. 195, Dickson J. (Laskin C.J.C. and Ritchie J. concurring). 2. Statutory provisions in the various Interpretation Acts to the effect that the Crown is not bound unless by express words.

CROWN LAND. Land, whether or not it is covered by water, or an interest in land, vested in the Crown.

CROWN PRIVILEGE. The rule of evidence which provides that relevant evidence which is otherwise admissible must not be admitted if to do so would injure the public interest.

CROWN'S NEWSL. *abbr.* Crown's Newsletter.

CROWN TIMBER. Includes any trees, timber and products of the forest in respect whereof the Crown is enabled to demand and receive any stumpage, royalty, revenue or money.

CROWN VESSEL. A vessel that is owned by or is in the exclusive possession of Her Majesty in right of Canada. *Canada Shipping Act, 2001,* S.C. 2001, c. 26, s. 140.

CROWN WARDSHIP ORDER. An order of a court making the Crown the legal guardian of a child in need of protection.

C.R.P. *abbr.* Conseil de révision des pensions.

C.R.R. *abbr.* Canadian Rights Reporter, 1982-1991.

C.R.R.B.D.I. *abbr.* Canada Labour Relations Board Decisions and Information, 1974-1998.

C.R.R. (2D). *abbr.* Canadian Rights Reporter, 1991-.

C.R. (6TH). *abbr.* Criminal Reports (Sixth Series), 2002-.

C.R.T. *abbr.* Canadian Radio-Television and Telecommunications decisions and policy statements, 1975-1985.

C.R.T.C. *abbr.* 1. Canadian Railway and Transport Cases, 1902-1966. 2. Canadian Radio-television and Telecommunications Commission (Conseil de la radio-diffusion et des télécommunications canadiennes).

C.R.T.F.P. *abbr.* Commission des relations de travail dans la Fonction publique.

C.R. (3D). *abbr.* Criminal Reports (Third Series), 1978-1991.

C.R.T.Q. *abbr.* Commission des relations du travail (Québec).

CRUEL AND UNUSUAL PUNISHMENT. "The general standard for determining an infringement of s. 12 [of the Charter] was set out by Lamer J. ... in R. v. Smith, [1987] 1 S.C.R. 1045 ... [at p. 1072]: 'The criterion which must be applied in order to determine whether a punishment is cruel and unusual within the meaning of s. 12 of the Charter is ... "whether the punishment prescribed is so excessive as to outrage standards of decency". In other words, though the state may impose punishment, the effect of that punishment must not be grossly disproportionate to what would have been appropriate.' " *Chiarelli v. Canada (Minister of Employment & Immigration)* (1992), 16 I.L.R. (2d) 1 at 22, 2 Admin. L.R. (2d) 125, 135 N.R. 161, 90 D.L.R. (4th) 289, 8 C.R.R. (2d) 234, 72 C.C.C. (3d) 214, [1992] 1 S.C.R. 711, the court per Sopinka J.

CRUELTY. *n.* 1. "... As used in ordinary parlance 'cruelty' signifies a disposition to inflict suffering; to delight in or exhibit indifference to the pain or misery of others; mercilessness or hard-heartedness as exhibited in action. If in the marriage relationship one spouse by his conduct causes wanton, malicious or unnecessary infliction of pain or suffering upon the body, the feelings or emotions of the other, his conduct may well constitute cruelty which will entitle a petitioner to dissolution of the marriage if, in the court's opinion, it amounts to physical or mental cruelty 'of such a kind as to render intolerable the continued cohabitation of the spouses'. That is the standard which the courts are to apply, and in the context of s. 3(d) of the [Divorce Act, S.C. 1967-68, c. 24] ... Care must be exercised in applying the standard set forth in s. 3(d) that conduct relied upon to establish cruelty is not a trivial act, but one of a 'grave and weighty' nature, and not merely conduct which can be characterized as little more than a manifestation of incompatibility of temperament between the spouses... ." *Knoll v. Knoll* (1970), 1 R.F.L. 141 at 149, 10 D.L.R. (3d) 199 (Ont. C.A.), the court per Schroeder J.A. 2. Conduct that creates a danger to life, limb or health, and includes any course of conduct that in the opinion of the Court is grossly insulting and intolerable, or is of such a character that the person seeking a separation could not reasonably be expected to be willing to live with the other after he or she has been guilty of such conduct. *Domestic Relations acts.*

CRUISE SHIP. See INTERNATIONAL ∼.

CRUMBLING SKULL RULE. A tortfeasor must take his or her victim as the tortfeasor finds the victim even though the plaintiff's losses are greater than they would be for the average person. The victim has a pre-existing condition which is inherent in the victim's condition for purposes of assessing damages.

CRYSTALLIZATION. *n.* "... [O]f a floating charge means that upon the happening of some event or events the charge that had been floating over the assets becomes fixed." *Bayhold Financial Corp. v. Clarkson Co.* (1991), (*sub nom. Barhold Financial Corp. v. Community Hotel Co. (Receiver of)*) 86 D.L.R. (4th) 127 at 149, 10 C.B.R. (3d) 159, 108 N.S.R. (3d) 198, 294 A.P.R. 198 (C.A.), the court per Hallett J.A.

CRYSTALLIZE. *v.* To convert a floating charge into a fixed charge. F. Bennett, *Receiverships* (Toronto: Carswell, 1985) at 33.

C.S. *abbr.* 1. Cour supérieure. 2. Cour supreme (provinciale). 3. Recueils de jurisprudence du Québec: Cour supérieure (Quebec Superior Court Reports), 1967-1985. 4. Rapports judiciaires officiels de Québec: Cour supérieure, 1892-1996 (Official Reports, Superior Court).

C.S.A. *abbr.* Canadian Standards Association.

CSC. French neutral citation for the Supreme Court of Canada.

C.S.C. *abbr.* Cour suprême du Canada.

C.S. CAN. *abbr.* Cour suprême du Canada.

C.S.D. *abbr.* Canadian Sentencing Digest, 1980-1994.

CSE. *abbr.* Communications Security Establishment.

CSI. *abbr.* The Canadian Securities Institute which provides courses and examinations for those seeking credentials to enter or within the securities, banking, and insurance industries.

CSIS. *abbr.* The Canadian Security Intelligence Service.

C.S.P. *abbr.* 1. Cour des Sessions de la paix. 2. Recueils de jurisprudence du Québec: Cour des Sessions de la Paix, 1975-1985.

C.S.P. QUÉ. *abbr.* Cour des sessions de la paix (Québec) (Court of Sessions of the Peace (Quebec)).

C.S. QUÉ. *abbr.* Cour supérieure (Québec).

CT. *abbr.* Court.

C.T. *abbr.* 1. Commission du tarif. 2. Jurisprudence en droit du travail: Décisions des commissaires du travail, 1969-1981.

C.T.A.B. *abbr.* Canada Tax Appeal Board Cases, 1949-1966.

C.T.A.B. (N.S.). *abbr.* Canada Tax Appeal Board Cases (New Series), 1967-1971.

C.T.B.R. *abbr.* Canada Tariff Board Reports, 1937-1988.

C.T.C. *abbr.* 1. Canadian Transport Cases, 1966-1977. 2. Canadian Transport Commission (Commission canadienne des transports). 3. Canada Tax Cases Annotated, 1917-1971.

CTC(A). *abbr.* The Air Transport Committee of the Canadian Transport Commission. Canada regulations.

C.T. CASES. *abbr.* Canadian Transport Cases, 1966-1977.

C.T.C.A.T.C. *abbr.* Canadian Transport Commission, Air Transport Committee Decisions, 1967-1987.

C.T.C.D.O. *abbr.* Canadian Transport Commission, Decisions and Orders Summary, 1970-1976.

C.T.C.M.V.T.C.D. *abbr.* Canadian Transport Commission, Motor Vehicle Transport Commission Decisions, 1973-1987.

C.T.C.M.V.T.C.O. *abbr.* Canadian Transport Commission, Motor Vehicle Transport Commission Orders, 1972-1987.

C.T.C. (N.S.). *abbr.* Canada Tax Cases, 1972-.

C.T.C.O.A. *abbr.* Canadian Transport Commission, Orders (Air), 1967-1987.

C.T.C.R. *abbr.* Canadian Transport Commission Reports, 1978-1986.

C.T.C.R.C.D. *abbr.* Canadian Transport Commission, Review Committee Decisions, 1971-1987.

C.T.C. REGULATIONS. Regulations for the Transportation of Dangerous Commodities by Rail. Canada regulations.

CT. CRIM. APP. *abbr.* Court of Criminal Appeals.

C.T.C.R.T.C. *abbr.* Canada Transport Commission, Railway Transport Committee – Judgments, Orders, Regulations, and Rulings (formerly Board of Transport Commissioners for Canada), 1967-1987.

C.T.C.T.C.D. *abbr.* Canadian Transport Commission, Telecommunication Committee Decisions, 1973-1976.

C.T.C.T.C.O. *abbr.* Canadian Transport Commission, Telecommunication Committee Orders, 1975-1976.

C.T.C.W.T.C.D. *abbr.* Canadian Transport Commission, Water Transport Committee Decisions, 1972-1987.

C.T.C.W.T.C.L. *abbr.* Canadian Transport Commission, Water Transport Committee, Licences, 1976.

C.T.C.W.T.C.O. *abbr.* Canadian Transport Commission, Water Transport Committee, Orders, 1979-1987.

CTEE. *abbr.* Committee.

C.T.M. *abbr.* Canada Tax Manual.

CT. MARTIAL APP. CT. *abbr.* Court Martial Appeal Court.

C.T.Q. *abbr.* Commission des transports du Québec.

C.T.R. *abbr.* 1. Canadian Tax Reporter, 1972-. 2. De Boo Commodity Tax Reports, 1987-1989. 3. Commission du tarif registre, 1981-1988.

C. TRANS. C. *abbr.* Canadian Transport Cases.

CT. REV. *abbr.* Court of Review.

CT. SESS. P. *abbr.* Court of Sessions of the Peace.

C.T.S.T. *abbr.* Canada Trade and Sales Tax Cases, 1989-1991.

C.T.T.T. *abbr.* Décisions du Commissaire du travail et du Tribunal du travail, 1982-1993.

C.T.T.T.C.R.A.A. *abbr.* Décisions du Commissaire du travail, du Tribunal du travail et de la Commission de reconnaissance des asiciations d'artistes, 1994-1997.

CULMINATING INCIDENT. See DOCTRINE OF ~.

CULPA. *n.* [L.] Fault; neglect; negligence.

CULPABILITY. *n.* Blameworthiness, negligence, guilt, being at fault. See MORAL ~.

CULPABLE. *adj.* That which is to be blamed. Blameworthy, negligent, guilty, criminal, faultful. See NON-~ CONDUCT.

CULPABLE HOMICIDE. 1. Murder or manslaughter or infanticide. *Criminal Code*, R.S.C. 1985, c. C-46, s. 222(4). 2. A person commits culpable homicide when he causes the death of a human being, (a) by means of an unlawful act, (b) by criminal negligence, (c) by causing that human being, by threats or fear of violence or by deception, to do anything that causes his death, or (d) by wilfully frightening that human being, in the case of a child or sick person. *Criminal Code*, R.S.C. 1985, c. C-46, s. 222(5). See NON-~.

CULPABLE NEGLIGENCE. Criminal negligence.

CULPRIT. *n.* A person accused of an offence; a person found guilty of an offence.

CULTIVATING. *n.* In the case at bar, it was the theory of the Crown that the appellant was engaged in the cultivation of cannabis (marihuana). "Cultivating" means "[t]o bestow labour and attention upon land in order to the raising of crops, to till, to improve and render fertile by husbandry" (see Bruce A. MacFarlane, Drug Offences in Canada, 3rd ed., looseleaf (Aurora, Ont.: Canada Law Book, 2005) para. 9.560, quoting the Shorter Oxford Dictionary). Acts of cultivation include any act designed to help raise plants, including the preparation and use of the soil, the removal of weeds from the vicinity of the plants and their pruning. *R. v. Mowry*, 2006 NBCA 18.

CULTURALLY SENSITIVE OBJECT. See ABORIGINAL SACRED AND ~.

CULTURAL PROPERTY. See CANADIAN ~ EXPORT REVIEW BOARD.

CUM DIV. *abbr.* Cum dividend.

CUM DIVIDEND. With dividend; when a share is sold cum div. the purchaser receives any declared and not yet paid dividend.

CUM RIGHTS. A purchaser of shares cum rights has the right to claim the rights to new shares or warrants which are about to be issued.

CUM TESTAMENTO ANNEXO. [L. with the will annexed] Administration with the will annexed is granted when a testator has not named an executor or the executor named is not willing to act.

CUMULATIVE. *adj.* Additional, to be added together, to be taken in succession.

CUMULATIVE DIVIDEND. A dividend which, if not paid in one year, continues to accumulate until paid in full. See NON~.

CUMULATIVE LEGACY. A legacy given in addition to a prior legacy in the same will.

CUMULATIVE PREFERENCE SHARE. A share the dividend of which cumulates from year to year.

CUMULATIVE REMEDY. A mode of procedure available in addition to another possible remedy; opposite to alternative remedy.

CUMULATIVE VOTING. A voting method which permits all votes attached to all a shareholder's shares to be cast for one candidate for board of directors of a corporation.

CURATIVE. *adj.* Intended to remedy.

CURATIVE SECTION. A provision that if one substantially complies with provisions, such as registration of the claim for lien, no lien will be invalidated because one failed to comply with the requirements of such a section unless the Court judges that some person was prejudiced thereby (and then the award is only to the extent of that prejudice). D.N. Macklem & D.I. Bristow, *Construction, Builders' and Mechanics' Liens in Canada*, 6th ed. (Toronto: Carswell, 1990–) at 1-9.

CURATIVE STATUTE. A statute designed to operate on past events, acts or transactions so that irregularities and errors are corrected and acts, which would otherwise be ineffective for the intended purpose, are made valid.

CURATOR. *n.* A protector of property. See PUBLIC ~.

CURB. *n.* A raised or guarded place at the edge of a roadway or a safety island, median or boulevard.

CURBSIDING. n. The sale of motor vehicles by an unlicensed dealer. *Ontario (Registrar, Motor Vehicle Dealers Act) v. Unity-A-Automotive Inc.*, 2009 CarswellOnt 7553.

CURE TITLE. To remove encumbrances or claims in order to create good or clear title.

CURFEW. *n.* A law requiring persons to remove themselves from the streets at a certain time of night.

CURIA. *n.* [L.] A court of justice.

CURIA ADVISARI VULT. [L.] The court will consider the matter.

CURIAL DEFERENCE. The degree to which a court will refrain from interfering with a decision of an administrative tribunal or a lower court. Factors such as public interest, expertise of the tribunal, the courts' treatment of a tribunal historically and the existence and type of privative clause in place are important in determining which standard of deference will be applied. See CORRECTNESS; PATENTLY UNREASONABLE; STANDARD OF REVIEW; UNREASONABLE.

CURIA REGIS. [L.] The monarch's court.

CURRENCY. *n.* 1. A period during which something is in force. 2. The medium of exchange which circulates in a country. 3. Money. See CREATION OF ~.

CURRENT. *adj.* Lawfully current in Canada or elsewhere by virtue of law, proclamation or regulation in force in Canada or elsewhere as the case may be. *Criminal Code*, R.S.C. 1985, c. C-46, s. 448.

CURRENT ASSETS. Cash, accounts receivable, inventory and assets which could be converted to cash in the near future.

CURRENT EXCHANGE RATE. The rate of exchange prevailing on the day on which a transaction takes place, as ascertained from a Canadian bank.

CURRENT LAND VALUE. The actual value of similar land held in fee simple. Thus "current land value" means the price a willing buyer would pay for fee simple title to the land. *Musqueam Indian Band v. Glass*, 2000 CarswellNat 2405, 2000 SCC 52, [2000] 11 W.W.R. 407, 36 R.P.R. (3d) 1, 192 D.L.R. (4th) 385, 82 B.C.L.R. (3d) 199, 261 N.R. 296, 186 F.T.R. 248 (note), [2000] 2 S.C.R. 633, [2001] 1 C.N.L.R. 208, McLachlin C.J.C. (dissenting on the appeal) (L'Heureux-Dubé, Iacobucci and Arbour JJ. concurring).

CURRENT LIABILITY. A debt due within a short period of time.

CURR. LEGAL PROBS. *abbr.* Current Legal Problems.

CURSE. *v.* To swear.

CURTESY. *n.* Formerly, the interest in a wife's fee simple which a husband will have after her death until his own.

CURTILAGE. *n.* The space around a dwelling house necessary, convenient and used for family purposes and carrying out domestic chores. Includes a garden. *R. v. Kelly* (1999), 132 C.C.C. (3d) 122 (N.B. C.A.).

CUSTODIA LEGIS. [L.] The custody of the law.

CUSTODIAL PORTION. With respect to a youth sentence imposed on a young person, means the period of time, or the portion of the young person's youth sentence, that must be served in custody before he or she begins to serve the remainder under supervision in the community subject to conditions or under conditional supervision. *Youth Criminal Justice Act*, S.C. 2002, c. 1, s. 2, part.

CUSTODIAN TRUSTEE. A person in whom title to trust property is vested while management of the trust is left in the hands of other trustees, the managing trustees.

CUSTODY. *n.* 1. "[As used in the Extra-Provincial Enforcement of Custody Orders Act, 1977 (Alta.), c. 20, s. 1(c)] ... is not a word that has a narrow single meaning. It may mean only the care and control of the child, or it may mean all of the rights of guardianship." *Read v. Read*, [1982] 2 W.W.R. 25 at 29, 17 Alta. L.R. (2d) 273 (C.A.), Moir, Laycraft and McClung JJ.A. 2. "... Its meaning can range from immediate effective possession and control of the person, as where a jailer has custody of his prisoner, to control by a parent of a child in the widest possible sense, that is, not only physical but also intellectual, educational, spiritual, moral and financial ... Thus the concept of custody under the Divorce Act [S.C. 1986, c. 4, s. 2] is for all practical purposes, co-extensive with guardianship of the person under the provincial Family Relations Act [R.S.B.C. 1979, c. 121, ss. 1, 25] ..." *Clarke v. Clarke* (1987), 7 R.F.L. (3d) 176 at 178, 180, 12 B.C.L.R. (2d) 290 (S.C.), Gow L.J.S.C. 3. Personal guardianship of a child and includes care, upbringing and any other incident of custody having regard to the child's age and maturity. *Children's Law Act*, S.S. 1997, c. 8.2, s. 2(1). 4. Includes care, up-bringing and any other incident of custody. *Divorce Act*, R.S.C. 1985, c. 3 (2nd Supp.), s. 2(1). 5. In the narrow sense of the word, "custody" means physical care and control or day to day care and control of a child. In the broad sense of the word, "custody" means all of the rights and obligations associated with physical, day to day care and control of a child as well as the right and obligation to nurture the child by ensuring, providing for, and making decisions in relation to, a child's physical and emotional health, education, religious or spiritual development, and all other matters that affect the welfare of the child. *Abbott v. Abbott*, 2001 CarswellBC 420, 2001 BCSC 323, 13 R.F.L. (5th) 233, 89 B.C.L.R. (3d) 68, Pitfield J. See CARE AND ~; DIVIDED ~; JOINT ~; LEGAL ~; OPEN ~; SERVICE ~; SOLE ~; YOUTH ~ FACILITY.

CUSTODY AGREEMENT. Any agreement with respect to the custody, care or control of a child.

CUSTODY ORDER. 1. The order of any court with respect to the custody, care or control of a child. 2. An order, or that part of an order, of a tribunal that grants custody of a child to any person and includes provisions, if any, granting another person a right of access or visitation to the child. *Reciprocal Enforcement of Custody Orders acts.* 3. A court of competent jurisdiction may, on application by either or both spouses or by any other person, make an order respecting the custody of or the access to, or the custody of and access to, any or all children of the marriage. *Divorce Act*, R.S.C, 1985, c. 3 (2nd Supp.), s. 16. See DEFERRED CUSTODY AND SUPERVISION ORDER.

CUSTODY PROVISION. A provision of an order or agreement awarding custody of a child.

CUSTOM. *n.* 1. An unwritten law or right, established through long use. 2. "... [I]n the sense of a rule having the force of law and existing since time immemorial is not in issue in this case. Indeed, Canadian law being largely of imported origin will rarely, if ever, evince that sort of custom. Custom in Canadian law must be given a broader definition. In any event, both courts below were not using the term in such a technical sense, as is clear from the fact that both substituted the term 'practice' as a synonym." *International Corona Resources Ltd. v. Lac Minerals Ltd.* (1989), 26 C.P.R. (3d) 97 at 121, [1989] 2 S.C.R. 574, 69 O.R. (2d) 287, 61 D.L.R. (4th) 14, 6 R.P.R. (2d) 1, 44 B.L.R. 1, 35 E.T.R. 1, 101 N.R. 239, 36 Q.A.C. 57, La Forest J. (Wilson and Lamer JJ. concurring). See BAND'S ~.

CUSTOMARY. *adj.* According to custom; usual.

CUSTOMARY AUTHORITY. An agent who is authorized to act for a principal in a particular business, market or locale has implied authority to act in accordance with the usages and customs of that business, market or locale. G.H.L. Fridman, *The Law of Agency*, 6th ed. (London: Butterworths, 1990) at 66. See USUAL OR ~.

CUSTOMARY INTERNATIONAL LAW. A national practice accepted as international law.

CUSTOM BAND. A First Nations band which devises its own election system for its band council.

CUSTOM DUTY. The fee payable when importing goods.

CUSTOMER. See CASH ~; FUTURES ~.

CUSTOM-HOUSE. *n.* The office where any duty payable or receivable upon import or export is paid or received.

CUSTOM OF THE TRADE. Any practice usually observed by people dealing in a particular product.

CUSTOMS. *n.* Duties charged when goods are imported into, or exported out of, a country. See FEDERAL ~ LAWS.

CUSTOMS BONDED CARRIER. A person who transports or causes to be transported goods in accordance with section 20 of the Customs Act. *Excise Act, 2001*, S.C. 2002, c. 22, s. 2.

CUSTOMS BONDED WAREHOUSE. A facility operated under licence from the government of Canada where goods on which duty and taxes have not been paid are stored.

CUSTOMS BROKER. A person who acts as agent to clear goods through customs.

CUSTOMS DUTY. The tax when goods are imported.

CUSTOMS OFFICER. The collector or chief officer of customs at a port.

CUSTOMS UNION. An agreement between countries for the unification of territories for purposes of customs.

CYBER-BULLYING. *n.* Using the Internet or other information or communication technologies, such as e-mail messages or text messages sent by cell phone or pager, to support deliberate, repeated and hostile behaviour by an individual or group that is intended to harm someone else. *The Public Schools Act*, C.C.S.M. c. P250, s. 47.1.

CYLINDER BORE. In a firearm without a choke, the smoothbore barrel. F.A. Jaffe, *A Guide to Pathological Evidence for Lawyers and Police Officers*, 4th ed. (Toronto: Carswell, 1999) at 234.

CY-PRES. [Fr. near to it] 1. Enables a court to apply the property of a charitable trust which would otherwise fail for impracticability or unenforceability to some other charitable purpose which resembles that of the original trust as nearly as possible. *Buchanan Estate, Re* (1997), 44 B.C.L.R. (3d) 283 (C.A.). 2.

"... [I]f the settlor or testator specifies an object but that object is or afterwards becomes impossible or impracticable of performance, the gift will not fail, but the property will be used for some similar purpose as much resembling the specified object as possible, providing the settlor has expressed, or the Court is able to gather ... from a trust instrument, the paramount instrument of charity... ." *Weatherby v. Weatherby* (1927), 53 N.B.R. 403 at 417 (S.C.), Hazen C.J.

D

DAGENAIS/MENTUCK TEST. 1. Refers to *Dagenais v. Canadian Broadcasting Corp.*, 1994 CanLII 39, [1994] 3 S.C.R. 835; *R. v. Mentuck*, 2001 SCC 76, [2001] 3 S.C.R. 442, 2001 SCC 76 and the question of publication bans in relation to criminal proceedings. 2. In Toronto Star Newspaper v. Ontario 2005 SCC 41, 2005 SCC 41, [2005] 2 S.C.R. 188, the Court held that the Dagenais/Mentuck test extends "to all discretionary court orders that limit freedom of expression and freedom of the press in relation to legal proceedings" (para. 7). It rejected the Crown's argument to the contrary based on a "generalized assertion that publicity could compromise investigative efficacy." *Shapray v. British Columbia (Securities Commission)*, 2009 BCCA 322.

DAILY DOUBLE. A type of bet on two races on a racing card to select the winning horse in the official result in each race. *Criminal Code*, R.S.C. 1985, c. C-46, *Pari-Mutuel Betting Supervision Regulations*, SOR/91-365, s. 2.

DALHOUSIE L.J. *abbr.* Dalhousie Law Journal.

DAM. *n.* A structure or work forwarding, holding back or diverting water.

DAMAGE. *n.* 1. Harm; loss. 2. "... [U]sually used to refer to a particular head of loss for which compensation is awarded. The word 'damages' is generally used to identify the amount of money that is paid by a tortfeasor for inflicting the various items of damage... . certainly includes injury but it also includes more than that. It includes all of the different heads of damage and various expenses that may be suffered as a result of tortious conduct." *Vile v. Von Wendt* (1979), 14 C.P.C. 121 at 125-6, 26 O.R. (2d) 513, 103 D.L.R. (3d) 356 (Div. Ct.), the court per Linden J. See ~ S; INEVITABLE ~; NEGATIVE ~; PROPERTY ~ INSURANCE; SPECIAL ~; STIPULATED ~; SUBSTANTIAL ~.

DAMAGES. *n.* 1. "... [A] monetary payment awarded for the invasion of a right at common law." *Canson Enterprises Ltd. v. Boughton & Co.* (1991), 9 C.C.L.T. (2d) 1 at 23, [1991] 1 W.W.R. 245, 61 B.C.L.R. (2d) 1, 85 D.L.R. (4th) 129, 131 N.R. 321, 43 E.T.R. 201, 39 C.P.R. (3d) 449, [1991] 3 S.C.R. 534, 6 B.C.A.C. 1, 3 W.A.C. 1, La Forest J. (Sopinka, Gonthier and Cory JJ. concurring). 2. In an action in contract there is a distinction between debt and damages. In an action on a debt the plaintiff claims money that is owed as money. The law of damages is concerned with the assessment of money compensation for legal wrongs—the translation, so to speak, of a legal wrong into a money sum. *Lafrentz v. M & L Leasing Ltd. Partnership*, 2000 CarswellAlta 1121, 2000 ABQB 714, 8 B.L.R. (3d) 219, [2001] 1 W.W.R. 629, 85 Alta. L.R. (3d) 233, 275 A.R. 334, Perras J. See AGGRAVATED ~; CHARTER ~; COMPENSATORY ~; CONSEQUENTIAL ~; CONTEMPTUOUS ~; DAMAGE; DERISORY ~; EXEMPLARY ~; FUTURE ~; GENERAL ~; LIQUIDATED ~; MEASURE OF ~; MITIGATION OF ~; NOMINAL ~; PUNITIVE ~; SOUND IN ~; UNLIQUIDATED ~; VINDICTIVE ~.

DAMAGES AT LARGE. "Damages other than for material loss ... These have been variously defined but appear generally to mean general damages consisting of non-economic loss and exemplary damages in appropriate cases... . Because they include compensation for loss of reputation, damages at large probably encompasses economic loss that can be foreseen but not readily quantified." *Farrell v. Canadian Broadcasting Corp.* (1987), (*sub nom. Farrell v. Canadian Broadcasting Corp. (No. 1)*) 43 D.L.R. (4th) 667 at 667, 669, 66 Nfld. & P.E.I.R. 145, 204 A.P.R. 145 (Nfld. C.A.), Goodridge C.J.N.

DAMNA. *n.* [L.] Damages.

DAMNUM. *n.* [L.] 1. Damage. 2. Harm. 3. Loss.

DAMNUM ABSQUE INJURIA. [L.] Loss without an injury. Compare INJURIA ABSQUE DAMNO.

DANCING. See LAP ~.

DANGER. *n.* Any existing or potential hazard or condition or any current or future activity that could reasonably be expected to cause injury or illness to a person exposed to it before the hazard or condition can be corrected, or the activity altered, whether or not the injury or illness occurs immediately after the exposure to the hazard, condition or activity, and includes any exposure to a hazardous substance that is likely to result in a chronic illness, in disease or in damage to the reproductive system. *Canada Labour Code*, R.S.C. 1985, c. L-2, s. 122. See CONCEALED ~; UNUSUAL ~.

DANGEROUS. *adj.* "... [L]ikely or probable to cause injury ..." *Burns v. R.* (1945), 19 M.P.R. 178 at 185 (P.E.I. C.A.), Campbell C.J.

DANGEROUS DRIVING. See DANGEROUS OPERATION OF MOTOR VEHICLES.

DANGEROUS OFFENDER. A court, acting under s. 753 of the Criminal Code, R.S.C. 1985, c. C-46, may find an offender to be a dangerous offender where the offender has been convicted of a "serious personal injury offence" and the offender constitutes a threat to the life, safety or physical or mental well-being of other persons on the basis of certain evidence defined in s. 753. Also, a person may be found to be a dangerous offender if he or she has been convicted of one of the forms of serious personal injury offence listed in s. 752 and the offender by his or her conduct in any sexual matter has shown a failure to control sexual impulses and a likelihood of causing injury, pain or other evil to other persons through failure in the future to control sexual impulses.

DANGEROUS OFFENDER PROCEEDING. A sentencing hearing that takes place after conviction for the predicate offence. *R. v. Kelly,* 2005 BCCA 373, Ryan J.A. (concurring).

DANGEROUS OPERATION OF AIRCRAFT. Operating an aircraft in a manner that is dangerous to the public, having regard to all the circumstances, including the nature and condition of that aircraft or the place or air space in or through which the aircraft is operated. *Criminal Code,* R.S.C. 1985, c. C-46, s. 249(1)(c).

DANGEROUS OPERATION OF MOTOR VE-HICLES. Operating a motor vehicle in a manner that is dangerous to the public, having regard to all the circumstances, including the nature, condition and use of the place at which the motor vehicle is being operated and the amount of traffic that at the time is or might reasonably be expected to be at that place. *Criminal Code,* R.S.C. 1985, c. C-46, s. 249(1)(a).

DANGEROUS OPERATION OF RAILWAY EQUIPMENT. Operating railway equipment in a manner that is dangerous to the public, having regard to all the circumstances, including the nature and condition of the equipment or the place in or through which the equipment is operated. *Criminal Code,* R.S.C. 1985, c. C-46, s. 249(1)(d).

DANGEROUS OPERATION OF VESSELS. Operating a vessel or any water skis, surf-board, water sled or other towed object on or over any of the internal waters of Canada or the territorial sea of Canada, in a manner that is dangerous to the public, having regard to all the circumstances, including the nature and condition of these waters or sea and the use that at the time is or might reasonably be expected to be made of these waters or sea. *Criminal Code,* R.S.C. 1985, c. C-46, s. 249(1)(b).

DANGER TO THE SECURITY OF CANADA. A person constitutes a "danger to the security of Canada" [within the meaning of s. 53(1)(b) of the Immigration Act, R.S.C. 1985, c. I-2] if he or she poses a serious threat to the security of Canada, whether direct or indirect . . . . The threat must be "serious," in the sense that it must be grounded on objectively reasonable suspicion based on evidence and in the sense that the threatened harm must be substantial rather than negligible. *Suresh v. Canada (Minister of Citizenship & Immigration)* [2002] 1 S.C.R. 3.

DATA. *n.* 1. Facts. 2. Representations of information or concepts, in any form. 3. Representations of information or of concepts that are being prepared or have been prepared in a form suitable for use in a computer system. *Criminal Code,* R.S.C. 1985, c. C-46. See MATERIAL SAFETY ~ SHEET; META~.

DATA BANK. A body of information concerning a group of people or a particular topic stored in electronic form. See DNA ~.

DATABASE. See SEX OFFENDER ~.

DATE. *n.* 1. "... [T]ime 'given' or specified, time in some way ascertained and fixed; ..." *Bement v. Trenton Locomotive Co.* (1866), 32 N.J.L. 513 at 515-6. 2. The year and the day of the month. See CONTRACT ~; EFFECTIVE ~; EXPIRY ~; FIXED ~ ELECTION; PROCLAMATION ~.

DATIVE TUTORSHIP. Tutorship conferred by the father and mother or by the court is dative. *Civil Code,* S.Q. 1991, c. 64, a. 178.

DAUGHTER. *n.* Female child.

DAY. *n.* 1. 86 400 seconds. *Weights and Measures Act,* R.S.C. 1985, c. W-6, Sched. I. 2. A calendar day. 3. "... [C]ommences at midnight and ends the following midnight: ..." *Thornbury (Town) v. Grey (County)* (1893), 15 P.R. 192 at 194 (Ont. C.A.), the court per Armour C.J. 4. The period between 6 o'clock in the forenoon and 9 o'clock in the afternoon of the same day. *Criminal Code,* R.S.C. 1985, c. C-46, s. 2. 5. Any period of 24 consecutive hours. See APPOINTED ~; CANADA ~; CLEAR ~S; COSTS OF THE ~; JURIDICAL ~; NATIONAL ~ OF REMEMBRANCE; ORDER OF THE ~; POLLING ~; REMEMBRANCE ~; SIR JOHN A. MACDONALD ~; SIR WILFRID LAURIER ~; SITTING ~; TRADING ~; VICTORIA ~; VIMY RIDGE ~; WORKERS MOURNING ~.

DAY CARE. The providing of services pertinent to a child's physical, social, emotional and intellectual development apart from the child's parents or guardian but does not include (i) organized recreational or religious activities, or (ii) services exempted by the regulations. *Day Care Act,* R.S.N.S. 1989, c. 120, s. 2.

DAY PAROLE. The authority granted to an offender by the Board or a provincial parole board to be at large during the offender's sentence in order to prepare the offender for full parole or statutory release, the conditions of which require the offender to return to a penitentiary, a community-based residential facility or a provincial correctional facility each night, unless otherwise authorized in writing. *Corrections and Conditional Release Act,* S.C. 1992, c. 20, s. 99.

DAYS OF GRACE. Time allowed to make a payment or do some other act when the time originally allowed has expired.

D.C.A. *abbr.* 1. Canada, commission de la fonction publique du Canada décisions du comité d'appel, 1979-1999. 2. Décisions de la Cour d'Appel/Queen's Bench Reports (Dorion), 1880-1886.

D.C.D.R.T. *abbr.* Décisions sur des conflits de droit dans les relations du travail, 1964-1970.

D.C.L. *abbr.* Décisions de la Commission des loyers, 1975-1981.

D.C.R.M. *abbr.* Commission de révision des marchés publics du Canada, décisions, 1990-?.

D.D.C.P. *abbr.* Décisions disciplinaires concernant les corporations professionneles, 1974-.

D.D.O.P. *abbr.* Décisions disciplinaires concernant les ordres professionnels, 1995-.

DE. *prep.* [L.] Of; from; concerning.

DEACTIVATED FIREARM. A device that, (a) was designed or adapted to discharge, (i) a shot, bullet or other projectile at a muzzle velocity exceeding 152.4 metres per second, or (ii) a shot, bullet or other projectile that is designed or adapted to attain a velocity exceeding 152.4 metres per second, and (b) has been permanently altered so that it is no longer capable of discharging any shot, bullet or other projectile. *Imitation Firearms Regulation Act, 2000*, S.O. 2000, c. 37, s. 1.

DEAL. See CLOSE THE ~.

DEALER. *n.* 1. " ... [O]ne who trades in, buys or sells goods on his own account. It does not necessarily follow he must be the owner of the goods he sells; he may be a broker ... so long as he is in the business for himself ..." *Harmon v. Russell* (1927), 21 Sask. L.R. 686 at 699, [1927] 2 W.W.R. 505, [1927] 3 D.L.R. 626 (C.A.), Mackenzie J.A. 2. Person whose business is to buy items and sell them to other persons. 3. A person or company engaging in or holding itself out as engaging in the business of (i) trading in securities or exchange contracts as principal or agent, or (ii) acting as an underwriter. *Securities Act*, R.S.A. 2000, c. S-4, s. 1. See SECURITIES ~.

DEALING. *n.* This raises a preliminary question: is it incumbent on the Law Society to adduce evidence that every patron uses the material provided for in a fair dealing manner or can the Law Society rely on its general practice to establish fair dealing? I conclude that the latter suffices. Section 29 of the Copyright Act [R.S.C. 1985, c. C-42] states that "[f]air dealing for the purpose of research or private study does not infringe copyright". The language is general. "Dealing" connotes not individual acts, but a practice or system. This comports with the purpose of the fair dealing exception, which is to ensure that users are not unduly restricted in their ability to use and disseminate copyrighted works. Persons or institutions relying on the s. 29 fair dealing exception need only prove that their own dealings with copyrighted works were for the purpose of research or private study and were fair. They may do this either by showing that their own practices and policies were research-based and fair, or by showing that all individual dealings with the materials were in fact research-based and fair. *CCH Canadian Ltd. v. Law Society of Upper Canada*, 2004 SCC 13. See DECEPTIVE~; FAIR ~; KNOWING ~.

DEATH. See ACCIDENTAL ~ INSURANCE; MOLECULAR ~.

DEATH BENEFIT. The amount received by a survivor or the deceased's estate upon or after the death of an employee in recognition of the employee's service in office or employment.

DEBASEMENT. *n.* A reduction of standard of fineness of coinage.

DEBATES. See OFFICIAL REPORT OF ~.

DE BENE ESSE. [L.] 1. To consider something well done for the moment, but when it is examined or tried more fully, it must stand or fall on its own merit. 2. "To do a thing de bene esse signifies allowing or accepting certain evidence for the present until more fully examined, valeat quantum valere potest. It is regarded as an additional examination to be utilized if necessary only in the event that witnesses cannot be examined later in the action in the regular way. This evidence therefore was taken 'for what is was worth.' ... *C.T. Gogstad & Co. v. "Camosun" (The)* (1941), 56 B.C.R. 156 at 157 (Ex. Ct.), MacDonald D.J.A.

DEBENTURE. *n.* 1. Any corporate obligation either unsecured or, frequently, secured by a floating charge. 2. "... [A] document in which a debt is acknowledged and in which the debtor covenants to repay ..." *Acmetrack Ltd. v. Bank Canadian National* (1984), 4 P.P.S.A.C. 199 at 206, 48 O.R. (2d) 49, 27 B.L.R. 319, 52 C.B.R. (N.S.) 235, 12 D.L.R. (4th) 428, 5 O.A.C. 321 (C.A.), the court per Zuber J.A. 3. Includes an instrument, secured or unsecured, issued by a corporation if that instrument is (a) in bearer form or in registered form, (b) of a kind commonly dealt in on securities exchanges or markets, or commonly recognized in any area in which it is issued or dealt in as a medium for investment, and (c) evidence of an obligation or indebtedness of the corporation, but does not include negotiable unsecured promissory notes maturing within one year after the date of issue. *Business Corporations Act*, S.B.C. 2002, c. 57, s. 1. 4. "... [I]n municipal financing [a debenture] is, ordinarily ... a promise under seal to pay the bearer a principal sum and interest at certain times, and is an instrument transferable on the markets by delivery." *Toronto (City) v. Canada Permanent Mortgage Corp.*, [1954] S.C.R. 576 at 582, [1954] 4 D.L.R. 529, Rand J. See COUPON ~; MORTGAGE ~.

DEBIT. *n.* A sum due or owing.

DEBIT NOTE. A note which states that the account of the person to whom it is sent will be debited.

DE BONIS ASPORTATIS. [L.] For goods taken away. See TRESPASS ~.

DE BONIS NON ADMINISTRATIS. [L.] A grant made when an administrator dies without having fully administered an estate or an executor dies intestate.

DEBT. *n.* 1. "... [I]ncludes any claim, legal or equitable, on contract, express or implied, or under a statute on which a certain sum of money, not being unliquidated damages, is due and payable, though an enquiry be necessary to ascertain the exact amount due." *Boldrick v. Salz*, [1952] O.W.N. 487 at 488 (C.A.), Hope J.A. 2. "... [A] sum payable in respect of a liquidated money demand recoverable by ac-

D

tion... ." *Walsh v. British Columbia (Minister of Finance)* (1979), 5 E.T.R. 179 at 191, [1979] 4 W.W.R. 161, [1979] C.T.C. 251, 13 B.C.L.R. 255 (S.C.), Anderson J. 3. The term 'debt' is a narrower term [narrower than liability] and means a specific kind of obligation for a liquidated or certain sum incurred pursuant to an agreement. The term 'loan' is even narrower and means a specific type of debt. *Royal Trust Co. v. H.A. Roberts Group Ltd.*, 1995 CarswellSask 7, 31 C.B.R. (3d) 207, [1995] 4 W.W.R. 305, 17 B.L.R. (2d) 263, 44 R.P.R. (2d) 255, 129 Sask. R. 161 (Q.B.), Baynton J. 4. In an action in contract there is a distinction between debt and damages. In an action on a debt the plaintiff claims money that is owed as money. The law of damages is concerned with the assessment of money compensation for legal wrongs—the translation, so to speak, of a legal wrong into a money sum. *Lafrentz v. M & L Leasing Ltd. Partnership*, 2000 CarswellAlta 1121, 2000 ABQB 714, 8 B.L.R. (3d) 219, [2001] 1 W.W.R. 629, 85 Alta. L.R. (3d) 233, 275 A.R. 334, Perras J. See ATTACHMENT OF ~S; BAD ~; CONDITIONAL ~; CONSUMER ~; CROWN ~; FAMILY ~; JUDGMENT ~; MUTUAL ~S; NATIONAL ~; SPECIALTY ~.

DEBT OBLIGATION. A bond, debenture, note or other evidence of indebtedness of an entity, whether secured or unsecured. *Bank Act*, S.C. 1991, c. 46, s. 2.

DEBTOR. *n.* 1. One who owes a debt. 2. A person to whom or on whose behalf money lent is advanced, and includes a surety and endorser or other person liable for the repayment of money lent or upon an agreement or collateral or other security given in respect of it. *Consumer Protection and Business Practices Act*, S.N. 2009, c. C-31.1, s. 11. 3. An insolvent person and any person who, at any time an act of bankruptcy was committed by him, resided or carried on business in Canada and, where the context requires, includes a bankrupt. *Bankruptcy and Insolvency Act*, R.S.C. 1985, c. B-3, s. 2. See ABSCONDING ~; JUDGMENT ~.

DEBT SECURITY. A right to be paid money and includes a deposit of money, but does not include a lease, licence or similar arrangement for the use of, or the right to use, property other than a financial instrument. *Excise Tax Act*, R.S.C. 1985, c. E-15, s. 123.

DÉC. B.-C. *abbr.* Décisions des Tribunaux du Bas-Canada, 1851-1867.

DECEASED. *n.* 1. A dead person. 2. A testator or a person dying intestate. *Dependants Relief acts.*

DECEIT. *n.* "... [A] false representation of fact by words or conduct ... made ... with the knowledge of its falsity; ... [and] with the intention that it be acted upon ... [and that it was in fact acted upon] in reliance upon the representation and that ... damage [was sustained in so doing]." *Bell v. Source Data Control Ltd.* (1988), 40 B.L.R. 10 at 17, 29 O.A.C. 134, 66 O.R. (2d) 78, 53 D.L.R. (4th) 580, Cory J.A. (dissenting).

DECEIVE. *v.* To induce a person to believe that something which is false is true. See CALCULATED TO ~.

DECEPTIVE DEALING. In relation to a person providing real estate services as a licensee, means any of the following: (a) an intentional misrepresentation, by word or conduct, or in any other manner, of a material fact in relation to real estate services, or in relation to a trade in real estate to which the real estate services relate, or an intentional omission to disclose such a material fact; (b) a course of conduct or business that is intended to deceive a principal about the nature of the real estate services, or about the nature of a trade in real estate to which the real estate services relate; (c) an artifice, agreement, device or scheme to obtain money, profit or property by illegal means; (d) a promise or representation about the future that is beyond reasonable expectation and not made in good faith. *Real Estate Services Act*, S.B.C. 2004, c. 42, s. 1.

DECERTIFICATION. *n.* Removal of a union's right to represent a group of employees for collective bargaining purposes.

DECISION. *n.* 1. A judgment, ruling, order, finding, or determination of a court. 2. "... [O]f a Court or Judge means the judicial opinion, oral or written, pronounced or delivered, upon which the 'judgment or order' is founded and the 'judgment or order' is the embodiment in legal procedure of the result of such decision ..." *Fermini v. McGuire* (1984), 42 C.P.C. 189 at 191, 64 N.S.R. (2d) 421, 143 A.P.R. 421 (C.A.), Macdonald J.A. 3. An order, a determination and a declaration. *Canada Labour Code*, R.S.C. 1985, c. L-2, s. 20(3). 4. A direction, decision, order, ruling or requirement made under a power or right conferred by this Act or the regulations. *Securities acts.* 5. The reasons given by the court for its judgment or other order. See FINAL ~; OPERATIONAL ~; POLICY ~; SPLIT ~ NOTICE; STATUTORY POWER OF ~.

DECISION-MAKER. See SUBSTITUTE ~.

DECLARANT. *n.* 1. One who makes a declaration. 2. The person who originally makes a hearsay statement. *National Defence Act*, R.S.C. 1985, c. N-5, *Military Rules of Evidence*, C.R.C., c. 1049, s. 2.

DECLARATION. *n.* 1. A formal statement of the opinion or decision of a court on the rights of interested parties or the construction of a will, deed or other written instrument. 2. "... [D]iffers from other judicial orders in that it declares what the law is without pronouncing any sanction against the defendant, but the issue which is determined by a declaration clearly becomes res judicata between the parties and the judgment a binding precedent." *LeBar v. Canada* (1988), 46 C.C.C. (3d) 103 at 108, 33 Admin. L.R. 107, 22 F.T.R. 160n, 90 N.R. 5 (C.A.), the court per MacGuigan J.A. See DYING ~; DYSON ~; MONTREAL ~ ON FREE ACCESS TO LAW; SOLEMN ~; STATUTORY ~; UNIVERSAL ~ OF HUMAN RIGHTS.

DECLARATION OF EMERGENCY. A proclamation issued pursuant to subsection 6(1), 17(1), 28(1) or 38(1). *Emergencies Act*, R.S.C. 1985, c. 22 (4th Supp.), s. 57.

DECLARATION OF TRUST. Creation of a trust when the trust property is already held by the intended trustee by execution of a deed declaring that the trustee holds the property in trust for the executor of the deed.

DECLARATORY JUDGMENT. Declaring the parties' rights or expressing the court's opinion on a question of law, without ordering that anything be done. Can be given without any provision for consequential relief.

DECLARATORY ORDER. A binding declaration of right whether or not any consequential relief is claimed or could be claimed.

DECLARATORY POWER. The power of the federal Parliament under s. 92(10)(C) of the Constitution Act, 1867 to bring a local work into federal jurisdiction by declaring that it is "for the general advantage of Canada." See WORKS FOR THE GENERAL ADVANTAGE OF CANADA.

DECLARATORY RELIEF. "... [A] remedy neither constrained by form nor bounded by substantive content, which avails persons sharing a legal relationship, in respect of which a 'real issue' concerning the relative interests of each has been raised and falls to be determined." *Solosky v. Canada* (1980), 105 D.L.R. (3d) 745 at 753, [1980] 1 S.C.R. 821, 30 N.R. 380, 50 C.C.C. (2d) 495, 16 C.R. (3d) 294, Dickson J. (Laskin C.J.C., Martland, Ritchie and Pigeon JJ. concurring).

DECLARATORY STATUTE. A declaration or formal statement of existing law.

DECREE. *n.* 1. Judgment. 2. In Quebec, the Government may order that a collective agreement respecting any trade, industry, commerce or occupation shall also bind all the employees and professional employers in Québec or in a stated region of Québec, within the scope determined in such decree. *An Act respecting collective agreement decrees*, R.S.Q. c. D-2, s. 2.

DECREE ABSOLUTE. 1. A final decree. 2. The final court order in a divorce action.

DECREE NISI. 1. A provisional decree which will become final or absolute unless there is reason shown not to do so. 2. A provisional court order which terminates marriage.

DECRIMINALIZATION. *n.* The removal of a matter from the Criminal Code; changing the law so that an act is no longer a crime.

DEDICATE. *v.* To make public a private road.

DEDICATED LANDS. Lands dedicated as buffer strips, environmental reserve, municipal reserve, public reserve and walkways. *The Planning and Development Act, 2007*, S.S. 2007, c. P-13.2, s. 2.

DEDICATION. *n.* The express or tacit opening of a road for public use.

DEDUCTION. *n.* 1. An amount deducted, taken away. 2. An amount withheld by an employer from an employee's wages for union dues, taxes, pension, insurance. 3. An amount permitted by tax laws to be subtracted from income before computing tax.

DEED. *n.* 1. A document signed, sealed and delivered, through which an interest, property or right passes. 2. Any instrument whereby real property is conveyed, transferred, assigned to or vested in any person. *Real Property Transfer Tax Act*, S.N.B. 1983, c. R-2.1, s. 1. 3. An instrument by which land is conveyed, transferred, assigned or vested in a person, but does not include a will, mortgage, agreement of sale or lease for a term of less than twenty-one years. *Municipal Government Act*, S.N.S. 1998, c. 18, s. 3. 4. Every deed or writing of whatsoever nature or kind relating to or affecting any interest in or title to land in the province, except a mortgage. *Evidence Act*, R.S.P.E.I. 1988, c. E-11, s. 1. See DISENTAILING ~; ESTOPPEL BY ~; EXECUTION OF ~S; PREMISES OF A ~; QUIT-CLAIM ~; REGISTRAR OF ~S; TAX ~; TRUST ~.

DEED OF CONVEYANCE. "... [A] mere transfer of title, ..." *Fraser-Reid v. Droumtskeas* (1979), 9 R.P.R. 121 at 139, [1980] 1 S.C.R. 720, 103 D.L.R. (3d) 385, Dickson J.

DEED OF COVENANT. A deed in which one party formally agrees to do certain things with another.

DEED OF GIFT. A deed which transfers property as a gift.

DEED OF GRANT. A deed which grants property.

DEED-POLL. *var.* **DEED POLL.** *n.* 1. A declaration of the act and intention of a grantor of property, so named because it was formerly polled (shaved even) at the top, whereas an indenture was indented (cut in acute angles). A sheriff who sells property seized under a writ of execution conveys the property by deed-poll. 2. A deed with one party only.

DEED TO USES. A deed purporting to grant or convey land to such uses as the grantee may appoint, regardless of the method of appointment specified in the deed, and, until appointment or in default of appointment, purporting to grant or convey the land to the use of the grantee absolutely, and includes every such deed containing words of like import, but does not include a mortgage. *Registry Act*, R.S.O. 1990, c. R. 20, s. 64(1).

DEEM. *v.* 1. "... . [W]hen used in a statute ... to bring in something which would otherwise be excluded... ." *Hillis v. Minister of National Revenue*, [1983] 6 W.W.R. 577 at 588, 15 E.T.R. 156, [1983] C.T.C. 348, 49 N.R. 1, 83 D.T.C. 5365 (Fed. C.A.), Heald J.A. (dissenting). 2. "... [T]o adjudge or decide ... to decide judicially... ." *Hunt v. College of Physicians & Surgeons (Saskatchewan)*, [1925] 4 D.L.R. 834 at 839, [1925] 3 W.W.R. 758, 45 C.C.C. 39, 20 Sask. L.R. 305 (K.B.), MacKenzie J.

DEEMED. *adj.* "... [M]ay mean 'deemed conclusively' or 'deemed until the contrary is proved'. *Gray v. Kerslake* (1957), 11 D.L.R. (2d) 225 at 239, [1958] S.C.R. 3, [1957] I.L.R. 1-279, Cartwright J.

DEEMED TRUST. A trust, created by statute, which is designed to protect certain classes of creditors or to insure the recovery of certain taxes.

DEEMING CLAUSE. "... [P]urpose of any 'deeming' clause is to impose a meaning, to cause some-

D

thing to be taken to be different from that which it might have been in the absence of the clause." *R. v. Sutherland* (1980), 113 D.L.R. (3d) 374 at 379, [1980] 2 S.C.R. 451, 35 N.R. 161, [1980] 5 W.W.R. 456, 53 C.C.C. (2d) 289, 7 Man. R. (2d) 359, [1980] 3 C.N.L.R. 71, the court per Dickson J.

DEEMING PROVISION. A statutory fiction; as a rule it implicitly admits that a thing is not what it is deemed to be but decrees that for some particular purpose it shall be taken as if it were that thing although it is not or there is doubt as to whether it is. Artificially imports into a word or an expression an additional meaning which it would not otherwise convey besides the normal meaning which it retains where it is used. *R. v. Verette* (1978), 40 C.C.C. (2d) 273 (S.C.C.), Beetz J.

DE FACTO. [L. in fact] Characterizes a state of affairs which must be accepted.

DE FACTO ARREST. May occur through the use of words that convey clearly to the accused that he or she is under arrest, in conjunction with certain conduct on the part of the arresting officers and the accused's submission to the officers' authority. A de facto arrest which is lawful cannot constitute an arbitrary detention within the meaning of the Charter. *R. v. Latimer* [1997] 1 S.C.R. 217.

DE FACTO POSSESSION. Physical control.

DEFALCATION. *n.* "... [D]oes not necessarily entail a dishonest or wrongful act. It is sufficient if there is a failure to meet an obligation by a fiduciary. A breach of trust arises whenever a trustee fails to carry out his obligations under the terms of the trust... ." *Smith v. Henderson* (1992), 64 B.C.L.R. (2d) 144 at 149, 10 C.B.R. (3d) 153, 10 B.C.A.C. 249, 16 W.A.C. 249, the court per Legg J.A.

DEFAMATION. *n.* 1. Libel or slander. *Defamation acts.* 2. The law of defamation is concerned with the protection of reputation against the publication of falsehoods that are defamatory in the sense of tending to lower reputation in the estimation of reasonable persons in the community. *Grassi v. WIC Radio Ltd.*, 2000 CarswellBC 209, 49 C.C.L.T. (2d) 65, [2000] 5 W.W.R. 119 (S.C.), Lysyk J. 3. Defamation may flow from the plain and ordinary meaning of published words or from extrinsic facts or circumstances, known to the listener or reader, which give words a defamatory meaning by way of innuendo. *Botiuk v. Toronto Free Press Publications Ltd.* (1995), 126 D.L.R. (4th) 609 (S.C.C.).

DEFAMATORY. *adj.* Tending to lower the reputation of someone in the opinion of right thinking members of society.

DEFAMATORY LIBEL. Matter published, without lawful justification or excuse, that is likely to injure the reputation of any person by exposing him to hatred, contempt or ridicule, or that is designed to insult the person of or concerning whom it is published. A defamatory libel may be expressed directly or by insinuation or irony (a) in words legibly marked on any substance, or (b) by any object signifying a defamatory libel otherwise than by words. *Criminal Code*, R.S.C. 1985, c. C-46, s. 298.

DEFAULT. *n.* 1. The failure to pay or otherwise perform the obligation secured when due or the occurrence of any event whereupon under the terms of the security agreement the security becomes enforceable. *Personal Property Security acts.* 2. The omission of something one should do; neglect. 3. Non-attendance in court. 4. A tenant's failure to pay rent in a timely fashion is "a default". *SME Holdings Ltd. v. Cappeech Coffee Corp.*, 1999 CarswellBC 1769 (S.C.), Allan J.

DEFAULT CHARGE. A charge imposed on a borrower who fails to make a payment as it comes due under a credit agreement or who fails to comply with any other obligation under a credit agreement, but does not include interest on an overdue payment. *Fair Trading Act*, R.S.A. 2000, c. F-2, s. 58.

DEFAULT JUDGMENT. The final judgment awarded to the plaintiff when the defendant fails to file an appearance or statement of defence.

DEFEASANCE. *n.* 1. A condition appended to an estate which defeats the estate when performed or a deed which defeats an estate. 2. A condition on an obligation which defeats it when performed.

DEFEASANCE CLAUSE. A proviso that a mortgage will become void on payment of the mortgage money. Thus, if one pays strictly according to the proviso, the estate without release or reconveyance becomes revested in the mortgagor or becomes vested in any other person entitled to it by subsequent mortgage or assignment from the mortgagor. W.B. Rayner & R.H. McLaren, *Falconbridge on Mortgages*, 4th ed. (Toronto: Canada Law Book, 1977) at 366.

DEFEASIBLE. *adj.* 1. Able to be abrogated or annulled. 2. "A gift that is subject to being defeated or terminated on an event such as re-marriage ..." *Dontigny v. R.*, [1974] 1 F.C. 418 at 421, [1974] C.T.C. 532, 74 D.T.C. 6437 (C.A.), Jackett and St.-Germain JJ.A.

DEFEAT. *v.* To frustrate, prevent.

DEFECT. *v.* To flee from one country to another; to give up one's relation to one country and seek asylum in another country.

DEFECT. *n.* Absence of an essential. See INHERENT ~; LATENT ~; PATENT ~.

DEFECTIVE. *adj.* Wanting in an essential ingredient.

DEFECTIVE TITLE. In respect of real property, title in respect of which there is a question as to title and not just a question as to conveyancing. To be contrasted with marketable or good title. V. Di Castri, *Law of Vendor and Purchaser* (Toronto: Carswell, 1988), para. 340.

DEFENCE. *n.* 1. (a) A statement of defence, (b) a notice of intent to defend, and (c) a notice of motion in response to an action, other than a motion challenging the court's jurisdiction. *Courts of Justice Act*, R.S.O. 1990, c. C.43, *Rules of Civil Procedure*, R.R.O. 1990, Reg. 194, s. 48.14. 2. "... [A] contention that the plaintiff's claim is not established. It adopts one or more of the following positions: (i) an objection on ground of jurisdiction; (ii) a denial of the plaintiff's allegations (traverse); (iii) a submission that if the plaintiff's allegations are true they disclose no cause of action (demurrer); and (iv) a submission that if the plaintiff's allegations are true there are facts which provide a legal justification for the defendant's conduct (confession and avoidance)." *Royal Bank v. Rizkalla* (1984), 50 C.P.C. 292 at 295, 59 B.C.L.R. 324 (S.C.), McLachlin J. 3. In criminal law, an assertion of innocence and denial of guilt. *R. v. Schwartz* (1988), 55 D.L.R. (4th) 1, [1989] 1 W.W.R. 289, 66 C.R. (3d) 251, 88 N.R. 90, [1988] 2 S.C.R. 443, 45 C.C.C. (3d) 97, 56 Man. R. (2d) 92. 4. In criminal law, generally a response to a criminal charge which would defeat the charge or an assertion which if accepted, would require an acquittal. *R. v. Chaulk* (1990), 1 C.R.R. (2d) 1 C.R. (4th) 1, 119 N.R. 161, [1991] 2 W.W.R. 385, 69 Man. R. (2d)161, 62 C.C.C. (3d)193, [1990] 3 S.C.R. 1303. 5. A guard; a justification; a protection. 6. Includes counter-claim. *Bills of Exchange Act*, R.S.C. 1985, c. B-4, s. 2. See AFFIRMATIVE ~; ARTISTIC ~; DEPARTMENT OF NATIONAL ~; EXTRANEOUS ~; FULL ANSWER AND ~; GILLETTE ~; INHERENT ~; PLEADINGS-BASED ~; SELF-~; STATEMENT OF ~.

DEFENCE OF DWELLING. Every one who is in peaceable possession of a dwelling-house, and every one lawfully assisting him or acting under his authority, is justified in using as much force as is necessary to prevent any person from forcibly breaking into or forcibly entering the dwelling-house without lawful authority. *Criminal Code*, R.S.C. 1985, c. C-46, s. 40.

DEFENCE OF EXPLANATION. An explanation of how an accident may have occurred without the defendant's negligence. *Singleton v. Morris*, 2010 BCCA 48, Finch C.J.B.C. (Prowse and Frankel JJ.A. concurring).

DEFENCE OF HOUSE OR REAL PROPERTY. Every one who is in peaceable possession of a dwelling-house and real property, and every one lawfully assisting him or acting under his authority, is justified in using force to prevent any person from trespassing on the dwelling-house or real property, or to remove a trespasser therefrom, if he uses no more force than is necessary. *Criminal Code*, R.S.C. 1985, c. C-46, s. 41(1).

DEFENCE OF PERSONAL PROPERTY. Every one who is in peaceable possession of personal property, and every one lawfully assisting him, is justified (a) in preventing a trespasser from taking it, or (b) in taking it from a trespasser who has taken it, if he does not strike or cause bodily harm to the trespasser. *Criminal Code*, R.S.C. 1985, c. C-46, s. 38(1).

DEFENCE WITH CLAIM OF RIGHT. Every one who is in peaceable possession of personal property under a claim of right, and every one acting under his authority, is protected from criminal responsibility for defending that possession, even against a person entitled by law to possession of it, if he uses no more

force than is necessary. *Criminal Code*, R.S.C. 1985, c. C-46, s. 39(1).

DEFENCE WITHOUT CLAIM OF RIGHT. Every one who is in peaceable possession of personal property, but does not claim it as of right or does not act under the authority of a person who claims it as of right, is not justified or protected from criminal responsibility for defending his possession against a person who is entitled by law to possession of it. *Criminal Code*, R.S.C. 1985, c. C-46, s. 39(2).

DEFEND. *v.* To deny. See DUTY TO ~; NOTICE OF INTENT TO ~.

DEFENDANT. *n.* 1. Includes every person served with an originating notice or other process or entitled to attend any proceeding. *Judicature Act*, R.S.N.S. 1989, c. 240, s. 2. 2. A plaintiff against whom a counter-claim is brought. *The Tortfeasors and Contributory Negligence Act*, C.C.S.M. c. T90, s. 1. 3. A person against whom a claim is asserted. *Civil Enforcement Act*, R.S.A. 2000, c. C-15, s. 16. 4. Includes a respondent to an application. *Copyright Act*, R.S.C. 1985, c. C-42, s. 2. 5. (i) A person to whom a summons is issued on the basis of an information or complaint alleging the commission by that person of an offence, or (ii) a person in respect of whom an offence notice is issued under Part 3. *Provincial Offences Procedure Act*, R.S.A. 2000, c. P-34, s. 1. 6. A person against whom a claimant has a claim, whether or not the claim has been brought. *Limitation of Actions Act*, S.N.B. 2009, c. L-8.5, s. 1.

DEFERENCE. *n.* 1. Respect. 2. The degree to which a court will refrain from interfering with a decision of an administrative tribunal or a lower court. A standard of review is established by the courts in relation to the degree of deference shown to another decision-maker, legislative, administrative or judicial. 3. Is both an attitude of the court and a requirement of the law of judicial review. It does not mean that courts are subservient to the determinations of decision makers, or that courts must show blind reverence to their interpretations, or that they may be content to pay lip service to the concept of reasonableness review while in fact imposing their own view. Rather, deference imports respect for the decision-making process of adjudicative bodies with regard to both the facts and the law. Deference in the context of the reasonableness standard therefore implies that courts will give due consideration to the determinations of decision makers. *Dunsmuir v. New Brunswick*, 2008 SCC 9, Bastarache and LeBel JJ. at paras. 48, 49. 4. The principle of appellate deference to a trial judge's fact-finding and inference-drawing applies even when the entire trial record is in writing. That is so because the principle of deference is grounded in more than a trial judge's ability to see and hear the witnesses. Deference recognizes that even on a written record, the trial judge "lives through" the trial while a court of appeal reviews the record only through the lens of appellate review. Deference also preserves the integrity of the trial process, maintains the confidence of litigants in that process, reduces the number and length of appeals and therefore, the cost of litigation, and appropriately presumes that trial judges are just as competent as appellate judges to

D

resolve disputes justly. *FL Receivables Trust 2002-A (Administrator of) v. Cobrand Foods Ltd.*, 2007 ONCA 425. See CURIAL ~; JUDICIAL ~.

DEFERRED. *adj.* 1. Of a debt, time for payment is extended. 2. Delayed.

DEFERRED ANNUITY. An annuity that becomes payable to the contributor at the time he reaches sixty years of age or another age specified by the governing statute. *Superannuation acts.*

DEFERRED COMMUNITY OF PROPERTY. Each spouse retains separate property during marriage, but when the marriage dissolves, each spouse is entitled to one-half of all property which forms the community. J.G. McLeod, *The Conflict of Laws* (Calgary: Carswell, 1983) at 372.

DEFERRED CUSTODY AND SUPERVISION ORDER. [Pursuant to s. 42(2)(p) of the Youth Criminal Justice Act, S.C. 2002, c. 1] is somewhat similar to a conditional sentence under the Criminal Code[, R.S.C. 1985, c. C-46] in that the custodial portion of the sentence is served in the community under restrictive conditions. *R. v. B.(J.)*, 2004 BCCA 487.

DEFERRED PENSION. A pension benefit, payment of which is deferred until the person entitled to the pension benefit reaches the normal retirement date under the pension plan.

DEFERRED PENSION BENEFIT. A pension benefit other than an immediate pension benefit. *Pension Benefits Standards Act*, 1985, R.S.C. 1985, c. 32 (2nd Supp.), s. 2.

DEFERRED PROFIT SHARING PLAN. A plan which allows an employer to share company profits with employees.

DEFERRED SHARING SCHEME. The sharing of matrimonial property is deferred until the happening of an event such as marriage breakdown. A. Bissett-Johnson & W.M. Holland, eds., *Matrimonial Property Law in Canada* (Toronto: Carswell, 1980) at A-5.

DEFERRED STOCK. A stock entitling holders to all the remaining net earnings after dividends have been paid to the preferred stock and ordinary stockholders.

DEFIBRILLATOR. *n.* An automated external medical heart monitor and defibrillator that is capable of, (a) recognizing the presence or absence of ventricular fibrillation or rapid ventricular tachycardia, (b) determining, without intervention by an operator, whether defibrillation should be performed, (c) automatically charging and requesting delivery of an electrical impulse to an individual's heart as medically required, and (d) satisfying any other criteria that may be prescribed by regulation. *Chase McEachern Act (Heart Defibrillator Civil Liability), 2007*, S.O. 2007, c. 10, Sched. N, s. 1.

DEFICIT. *n.* Loss; an amount by which expenditures exceed revenue.

DEFINE. *v.* To explain the meaning; to limit; to clarify.

DEFINED BENEFIT. A pension benefit other than a defined contribution benefit.

DEFINED BENEFIT PLAN. A pension plan that is not a defined contribution plan. *Pension Benefits Standards Act*, 1985, R.S.C. 1985, c. 32 (2nd Supp.), s. 2.

DEFINED BENEFIT PROVISION. A provision of a pension plan under which pension benefits for a member are determined in any way other than described in the definition "defined contribution provision". *Pension Benefits Standards Act*, 1985, R.S.C. 1985, c. 32 (2nd Supp.), s. 2.

DEFINED CONTRIBUTION BENEFIT. A pension benefit determined with reference to and provided by contributions, and the interest on the contributions, paid by or for the credit of a member and determined on an individual account basis. *Pension Benefits acts.*

DEFINED CONTRIBUTION PLAN. A pension plan that consists of defined contribution provisions and does not contain defined benefit provisions, other than (a) a defined benefit provision relating to pension benefits accrued in respect of employment before the effective date of the pension plan, or (b) a defined benefit provision that provides for a minimum pension benefit whose additional value is not significant in the Superintendent's opinion. *Pension Benefit Standards Act*, 1985, R.S.C. 1985 (2d Supp.), c. 32, s. 2.

DEFINED CONTRIBUTION PROVISION. A provision of a pension plan under which pension benefits for a member are determined solely as a function of the amount of pension benefit that can be provided by (*a*) contributions made by and on behalf of that member, and (*b*) interest earnings and other gains and losses allocated to that member. *Pension Benefits Standards Act*, 1985, R.S.C. 1985, c. 32 (2nd Supp.), s. 2.

DEFINITION SECTION. A statutory provision which states that particular words and phrases, when used in the statute, will bear certain meanings.

DEFRAUD. *v.* "... [T]wo elements are essential, 'dishonesty' and 'deprivation'... . The element of deprivation is satisfied on proof of detriment, prejudice or risk of prejudice to the economic interests of the victim... ." *R. v. Olan* (1978), 5 C.R. (3d) 1 at 7, [1978] 2 S.C.R. 1175, 86 D.L.R. (3d) 212, 41 C.C.C. (2d) 145, 21 N.R. 504, Dickson J.

DEFUNCT. *adj.* No longer in operation; no longer carrying on business.

DEGRADATION TEST. Test for obscenity which considers degrading or dehumanizing materials place women (and sometimes men) in positions of subordination, servile submission or humiliation. They run against the principles of equality and dignity of all human beings. *R. v. Butler*, [1992] 1 S.C.R. 452.

DEGREE. *n.* 1. A difference in relative importance between members of the same species. 2. One step in the line of consanguinity or descent. 3. Any recognition in writing of academic achievement which is called a degree; and includes the degrees of bachelor, master and doctor. See PROHIBITED ~.

DEHUMANIZATION TEST. Test for obscenity which considers degrading or dehumanizing materials place women (and sometimes men) in positions of subordination, servile submission or humiliation. They run against the principles of equality and dignity of all human beings. *R. v. Butler*, [1992] 1 S.C.R. 452.

DE-IDENTIFIED VITAL STATISTICS INFORMATION. Vital statistics information from which any information that may reasonably be expected to identify an individual has been removed. *The Vital Statistics Act, 2007*, S.S. 2007, c. V-7.2, s. 69.

DE JURE. [L.] By right; lawful.

DELAY. *v.* To postpone, to put off.

DELAY. *n.* Postponement. See INSTITUTIONAL ~; NEUTRAL ~; UNREASONABLE ~; WITHOUT ~.

DELAY DEFEATS EQUITIES. "[A court of equity] ... has always refused its aid to stale demands, where a party has slept upon his right and acquiesced for a great length of time. Nothing can call forth this court into activity, but conscience, good faith, and reasonable diligence; where these are wanting, the Court is passive, and does nothing." *Smith v. Clay* (1767), 3 Bro.C.C. 639n at 640n, Lord Camden L.C.

DEL CREDERE. Guarantee; warranty.

DEL CREDERE AGENT. A mercantile agent who will indemnify the principal if the third party fails to pay as contracted in respect of goods. G.H.L. Fridman, *The Law of Agency*, 6th ed. (London: Butterworths, 1990) at 38-9.

DEL CREDERE COMMISSION. An extra commission paid to a del credere agent. G.H.L. Fridman, *The Law of Agency*, 6th ed. (London: Butterworths, 1990) at 38.

D.E.L.D. *abbr.* Dismissal and Employment Law Digest, 1986-.

D.E.L.E.A. *abbr.* Digest of Environmental Law and Environmental Assessment, 1992-.

DELEGATE. *v.* The word 'delegate' is properly used to describe the disposition of one's own powers. One cannot delegate what one does not have. *Stenner v. British Columbia (Securities Commission)*, 1993 CarswellBC 1209, 23 Admin. L.R. (2d) 247 (S.C.), Spencer J.

DELEGATE. *n.* 1. A person elected to represent others. 2. The recipient of a power or authority delegated by another.

DELEGATED LEGISLATION. 1. Subordinate legislation made by authorities other than Parliament or a legislature. 2. A statutory instrument.

DELEGATION. *n.* 1. Entrusting someone else to act in one's place. 2. The assignment of a debt to someone else. See INTER-~.

DELEGATUS NON POTEST DELEGARE. [L.] 1. One who already is a delegate cannot delegate. 2. "... Unless rebutted, it stands for the proposition that there is no authority to redelegate a delegated

power... ." *Hanson v. Ontario Universities Athletic Assn.* (1975), 25 C.P.R. (2d) 239 at 248, 11 O.R. (2d) 193, 65 D.L.R. (3d) 385 (H.C.), Lieff J.

DELIBERATE. *v.* To consider.

DELIBERATE. *adj.* "... [C]onsidered, not impulsive." *R. v. Nygaard* (1989), 51 C.C.C. (3d) 417 at 432, [1989] 2 S.C.R. 1074, [1990] 1 W.W.R. 1, 70 Alta. L.R. (2d) 1, 72 C.R. (3d) 257, 101 N.R. 108, 102 A.R. 186, Cory. J.

DELIBERATE ACT. "... [O]ne proceeding from an intention and an intelligence which knows the nature and quality of the criminal act... ." *R. v. Pilon* (1965), 46 C.R. 272 at 294, [1968] 2 C.C.C. 53 (Que. C.A.), Rivard J.A.

DELIBERATIVE SECRECY. The Supreme Court of Canada in Tremblay [Québec (Commission des affaires sociales) c. Tremblay, [1992] 1 S.C.R. 952] made it clear that the doctrine of deliberative secrecy applies to administrative as well as judicial tribunals, albeit not to the same extent. Nevertheless, "secrecy remains the rule," although it can be "lifted when the litigant can present valid reasons for believing that the process followed did not comply with the rules of natural justice": Tremblay at paras. 27-28. *Apotex Inc. v. Alberta*, 2006 ABCA 133.

DELICT. *n.* A tort; a crime.

DELICTUM. *n.* [L.] A tort. See IN PARI DELICTO.

DELINQUENCY. *n.* 1. Failure; omission. 2. "... [T]wo categories of acts; the first category includes acts that are in violation of 'any provision of the Criminal Code or of any federal or provincial statute, or of any by-law or ordinance of any municipality' (Juvenile Delinquents Act, R.S.C. 1970, c. J-9, s. 2(1)), or, as Fauteux J. put it in A.G.B.C. v. Smith (S.), [1967] S.C.R. 702 at 710 ... that are 'punishable breaches of the public law, whether defined by Parliament or the Legislature'; the second category includes sexual immorality or other similar forms of vice which, while not illegal in the case of adults, should be repressed in the case of juveniles." *R. v. Morris* (1979), 6 C.R. (3d) 36 at 48, 43 C.C.C. (2d) 129, [1979] 1 S.C.R. 405, 91 D.L.R. (3d) 161, 23 N.R. 109, Pratte J. (Martland, Ritchie, Pigeon and Beetz JJ. concurring).

DELINQUENT. *n.* In respect of payments or other obligations, late or not carried out in accordance with the agreement. See DELINQUENCY; YOUNG PERSON.

DELIST. *v.* To remove a security from its trading on the stock exchange.

DELIVER. *v.* 1. With reference to a notice or other document, includes mail to or leave with a person, or deposit in a person's mail box or receptacle at the person's residence or place of business. 2. "... [T]urning over the custody of the person ..." *R. v. Dean* (1991), 5 C.R. (4th) 176 at 183 (Ont. Gen. Div.), Haley J.

DELIVERABLE STATE. Goods in such a state that the buyer would, under contract, be bound to take delivery of them. *Sale of Goods acts.*

DELIVERED. *adj.* "... [T]he party whose deed the document is expressed to be, having first sealed it, must by words or conduct expressly or impliedly acknowledge his intention to be immediately and unconditionally bound by the expressions contained therein: ..." *Metropolitan Theatres Ltd., Re* (1917), 40 O.L.R. 345 at 347 (H.C.), Rose J.

DELIVERY. *n.* 1. The voluntary transfer of possession from one person to another. *Sale of Goods acts.* 2. Transfer of possession, actual or constructive, from one person to another. *Bills of Exchange Act*, R.S.C. 1985, c. B-4, s. 2. 3. "[A] process whereby the addressee of mail is afforded access to that mail..." *R. v. Weaver* (1980), 116 D.L.R. (3d) 701 at 702, 30 O.R. (2d) 261, 55 C.C.C. (2d) 564 (C.A.), the court per Jessup J.A. 4. Includes delivery by direct electronic transmission. *Registry Act*, R.S.O. 1990, c. R.20, s. 22. 5. The natural or the lawfully, medically induced end of a pregnancy by childbirth, whether or not the child is viable. Québec statutes. 5. Transfer from one premises to another for any purpose. See CASH ON ~; MOVABLE HYPOTHEC WITH ~; NON-~; RE~; WRIT OF ~.

DELIVERY ADDRESS. For an office, the location of that office identified by an address that describes a unique and identifiable location that (a) is accessible to the public during statutory business hours for the delivery of records, and (b) except in the case of the head office of an extraprovincial company, is in British Columbia, but does not include a post office box. *Business Corporations Act*, S.B.C. 2002, c. 57, s. 1.

DEMAND. *n.* 1. A claim that a person offer something due. 2. A request that a person do something which she or he is legally bound to do once the request is made. See LIQUIDATED ~; STALE ~.

DEMANDED. See COSTS IF ~.

DEMAND LETTER. A letter requesting immediate payment of debt.

DEMAND NOTE. A promissory note payable on demand.

DEMERIT POINT. A point assessed against a driver's licence for an offence committed by a driver under highway traffic legislation.

DE MINIMIS NON CURAT LEX. [L.] The law does not bother itself about trifles.

DEMISE. *n.* 1. Includes any and every agreement or transaction whether in writing or by deed or parol whereby one person may become the tenant of another. 2. "... [C]reates an implied covenant for quiet enjoyment [pursuant to The Short Form of Leases Act, R.S.O. 1937, s. 159, Schedule B., clause 13] ..." *Bowra v. Henderson*, [1942] O.R. 734 at 739, [1943] 1 D.L.R. 672 (H.C.), Roach J. 3. "... [A]n effective word to convey an estate of freehold, and that it is of like import with and equivalent to the word 'grant.' ..." *Spears v. Miller* (1882), 32 U.C.C.P. 661 at 663 (Ont.), Armour J. See CHARTER BY ~; RE~.

DEMISE OF THE CROWN. The death, deposition or abdication of the sovereign.

DEMOCRACY. *n.* 1. Simply put, "democracy" is a political system by which the citizens of a country govern themselves (in Canada at the federal and provincial levels, not to exclude the territorial, municipal or newly emerging aboriginal levels), where their elected representatives make laws; the executive branch administers those laws and is responsible for the way it does so. *Qu v. Canada (Minister of Citizenship & Immigration)*, 2000 CarswellNat 705, 5 Imm. L.R. (3d) 129, [2000] 4 F.C. 71 (T.D.), Lemieux J. 2. Democracy is commonly understood as being a political system of majority rule. Since Confederation, efforts to extend the franchise to those unjustly excluded from participation in our political system—such as women, minorities, and aboriginal peoples—have continued, with some success, to the present day. Democracy is not simply concerned with the process of government. On the contrary democracy is fundamentally connected to substantive goals, most importantly, the promotion of self-government. Democracy accommodates cultural and group identities. The Court must be guided by the values and principles essential to a free and democratic society which embody, to name but a few, respect for the inherent dignity of the human person, commitment to social justice and equality, accommodation of a wide variety of beliefs, respect for cultural and group identity, and faith in social and political institutions which enhance the participation of individuals and groups in society. In institutional terms, democracy means that each of the provincial legislatures and the federal Parliament is elected by popular franchise. In individual terms, the right to vote in elections to the House of Commons and the provincial legislatures, and to be candidates in those elections, is guaranteed to "Every citizen of Canada" by virtue of s. 3 of the Charter. Historically, this Court has interpreted democracy to mean the process of representative and responsible government and the right of citizens to participate in the political process as voters and as candidates. In addition, the effect of s. 4 of the Charter is to oblige the House of Commons and the provincial legislatures to hold regular elections and to permit citizens to elect representatives to their political institutions. The democratic principle is affirmed with particular clarity in that section 4 is not subject to the notwithstanding power contained in s. 33. *Reference re Secession of Quebec*, 1998 CarswellNat 1299, 161 D.L.R. (4th) 385, 228 N.R. 203, 55 C.R.R. (2d) 1, [1998] 2 S.C.R. 217, per curiam. 3. Includes, but is not limited to, political and civil rights as defined by the International Covenant on Civil and Political Rights [December 16, 1966, [1976] Can T.S. No. 47, Arts. 17, 23, 24]. *Official Development Assistance Accountability Act*, S.C. 2008, c. 17, s. 3.

DEMOCRATIC. *adj.* "... [R]efer[s] to a system in which the governors are chosen by elections in which all adult citizens have the right to vote ..." *Griffin v. College of Dental Surgeons (British Columbia)* (1989), 64 D.L.R. (4th) 652 at 677, 40 B.C.L.R. (2d) 188, [1990] 1 W.W.R. 503 (C.A.), Southin J.A. See FREE AND ~ SOCIETY.

DEMOLISH. *v.* To do anything in the removal of a building or any material part thereof. *Building Code Act, 1992*, S.O. 1992, c. 23, s. 1.

DEMONSTRABLY JUSTIFIED. Determining whether it has been demonstrated that the impugned distinction is "demonstrably justified in a free and democratic society" involves two inquiries. First, the goal of the legislation is ascertained and examined to see if it is of pressing and substantial importance. Then the court must carry out a proportionality analysis to balance the interests of society with those of individuals and groups. *Miron v. Trudel* [1995] 2 S.C.R. 418, McLachlin J.

DEMONSTRATIVE EVIDENCE. Real things as opposed to testimony, i.e., weapons, models, maps, photographs.

DEMONSTRATIVE LEGACY. 1. "... [T]o be paid not out of the general assets of the testator but out of the segregated bonds." *Lasham, Re* (1924-25), 56 O.L.R. 137 at 139 (Div. Ct.), Middleton J.A. 2. A legacy, general in nature, which is supposed to be satisfied out of part of a testator's property or a specified fund. T. Sheard, R. Hull & M.M.K. Fitzpatrick, *Canadian Forms of Wills*, 4th ed. (Toronto: Carswell, 1982) at 158.

DEMUR. *v.* To object by demurrer.

DEMURRAGE. *n.* 1. A charge made by railways for the detention of a freight car beyond the free time provided for by the applicable special arrangements tariffs and is intended as an inducement to promptly release the freight car, and alternatively, to compensate partially railways, should the freight car be detained beyond the free time allowance. *Canadian Pacific Railway v. Canada (Transportation Agency)* 2003 FCA 271, 307 N.R. 378. 2. An allowance made to a shipowner for detaining a ship in port after the agreed-on sailing time.

DEMURRER. *n.* 1. The defendant pleading demurrer accepts the allegations of fact made by the plaintiff and argues that they do not as a matter of law support a cause of action against him. 2. "... [A] submission [by the defendant] that if the plaintiff's allegations are true they disclose no cause of action ..." *Royal Bank v. Rizkalla* (1984), 50 C.P.C. 292 at 295, 59 B.C.L.R. 324 (S.C.), McLachlin J. 2. "... [T]o admit all the facts that the plaintiff's pleadings alleged and to assert that these facts were not sufficient in law to sustain the plaintiff's case." *Hunt v. T & N plc.* (1990), (*sub nom. Hunt v. Carey Canada Inc.*), 74 D.L.R. (4th) 321 at 328, 4 C.C.L.T. (2d) 1, 43 C.P.C. (2d) 105, 117 N.R. 321, [1990] 6 W.W.R. 385, 49 B.C.L.R. (2d) 273, [1990] 2 S.C.R. 959, Wilson J.

DENIAL. *n.* 1. Taking issue with and disputing the facts asserted by an opposite party in pleadings in an action. 2. Refusal of a request or application. See GENERAL ~.

DENOMINATION. *n.* 1. A value or size of currency. The denominations of money in the currency of Canada are dollars and cents, the cent being one hundredth of a dollar. 2. A religious organization and members bearing a particular name. 3. The act of naming.

DE NOVO. [L.] Fresh; new. See APPEAL ~; TRIAL ~.

DE NOVO HEARING. 1. A rehearing. 2. The distinction between "an appeal by holding a trial de novo and an appeal to the provincial Court of Appeal is that although the object of both is to determine whether the decision appealed from was right or wrong, in the latter case the question is whether it was right or wrong having regard to the evidence upon which it was based, whereas in the former the issue is to be determined without any reference, except for purposes of cross-examination, to the evidence called in the court appealed from and upon a fresh determination based upon evidence called anew and perhaps accompanied by entirely new evidence. A trial de novo envisages a new trial before a different tribunal than the one which originally decided the issue. *McKenzie v. Mason*, 1992 CarswellBC 282, 72 B.C.L.R. (2d) 53, 9 C.P.C. (3d) 1, 96 D.L.R. (4th) 558, 18 B.C.A.C. 286, 31 W.A.C. 286, Toy J.A. See HEARING DE NOVO.

DE NOVO REVIEW. Strictly speaking, a de novo review is a review in which an entirely fresh record is developed and no regard at all is had to a prior decision[cases cited]. This is not what occurs in a detention review. In Canada (Minister of Citizenship & Immigration) v. Lai, [2001] 3 F.C. 326 (Fed. T.D.), at 334, Campbell J. held that, in a detention review, "all existing factors relating to custody must be taken into consideration, including the reasons for previous detention orders being made." Although Campbell J. was dealing with the former Act [Immigration Act, R.S.C. 1985, c. I-2], there is no reason why this ruling should not apply to the new Act [Immigration and Refugee Protection Act, S.C. 2001, c. 27]. Therefore, de novo review is not a precisely accurate way of describing the kind of review hearing held under ss. 57 and 58 of the new Act. *Canada (Minister of Citizenship & Immigration) v. Thanabalasingham*, 2004 FCA 4.

DENSITY RIGHTS. [D]ensity rights are concerned with the regulated uses to which land may be put by its owner. Although they are associated with the attributes of land ownership, they are not themselves property interests in land that are 'owned' by a landowner. Zoning by-laws do not create interests or rights in land per se. *2022177 Ontario Inc. v. Toronto Hanna Properties Ltd.* (2005), 203 O.A.C. 220.

DENTAL HYGIENE. The performance of dental services of a preventive and educational nature and includes the performance of dental prophylaxes, the application on teeth of topical fluorides or other anticariogenic agents, the rendering of first aid and the taking and developing of x-rays. *Dental Auxiliaries Act*, R.S.N.W.T. 1988, c. D-3, s. 1.

DENTAL TECHNOLOGY. The art or business of manufacturing or repairing any prosthetic denture, bridge, appliance or device to be used in, upon or in connection with any human tooth, jaw or associated structure or tissue, or in the treatment of any condition thereof. *Dental Technicians Act*, R.S.N.S. 1989, c. 126, s. 2.

DENTISTRY. *n.* Professional service usually performed by a dentist and includes (i) the diagnosis or treatment of, and the prescribing, treating or operating for, the prevention, alleviation or correction of disease, pain, deficiency, deformity, defect, lesion, disorder or physical condition of, in or from a human tooth, associated structure or tissue or an injury to a human tooth, associated structure or tissue, (ii) the making, producing, reproducing, constructing, fitting, furnishing, supplying, altering or repairing of or prescribing or advising the use of a prosthetic denture, bridge, appliance or thing for the purposes referred to in subparagraph (i), or to replace, improve or supplement a human tooth, or to prevent, alleviate, correct or improve a condition upon or in connection with a human tooth, associated structure or tissue, or in the treatment of a condition of a human tooth, associated structure or tissue, and (iii) the taking or making, or the giving of advice or assistance or the providing of facilities for the taking or making, of an impression, bite, cast or design preparatory to, or for the purpose of or with a view to making, producing, reproducing, constructing, fitting, furnishing, supplying, altering or repairing of a prosthetic denture, bridge, appliance or thing. *Dental Act, 2008*, S.N. 2008, c. D-6.1, s. 2.

DENTURISM. *n.* (i) The making of impressions and the determining of jaw relations for the purpose of, or with a view to, the making, producing, reproducing, constructing, furnishing, supplying, altering or repairing of any removable denture to be fitted into an edentulous or partially edentulous arch or arches, (ii) the placement of any removable denture to the edentulous or partially edentulous arch or arches, and includes the making, reproducing, constructing, furnishing, supplying, altering and repairing of any removable denture in respect of which a service is performed under subclause (i) or (ii), but does not include the adjustment or fitting of dentures in the mouth or any procedure that alters any oral tissue. *Denturists Act*, S.N.S. 2000, c. 25, s. 2. See PRACTICE OF ~.

DENUNCIATION. *n.* One of the principles of sentencing of those convicted of offences. The principle of denunciation ... is the communication of society's condemnation of an offender's conduct. *R. v. Laliberte*, 2000 SKCA 27, 31 C.R. (5th) 1, [2000] 4 W.W.R. 491, 143 C.C.C. (3d) 503, 189 Sask. R. 190. See SENTENCING.

DEP. *abbr.* Deputy.

DEPARTMENT. *n.* 1. A branch of the civil service over which a minister presides. 2. "... [I]nvolves the idea of something which forms part of a larger thing, ..." *Carlyle v. Oxford (County)* (1914), 18 D.L.R. 759 at 764, 5 O.W.N. 728, 30 O.L.R. 413 (C.A.), the court per Meredith C.J.O. 3. A department, secretariat, ministry, office or other similar agency of the executive government. 4. An academic unit administered by a head.

DEPARTMENTAL INVESTIGATION. The minister presiding over any department of the federal public administration may appoint, under the authority of the Governor in Council, a commissioner or commissioners to investigate and report on the state and management of the business, or any part of the business, of the department, either in the inside or outside service thereof, and the conduct of any person in that service, so far as the same relates to the official duties of the person. *Inquiries Act*, R.S.C. 1985, c. I-11, s. 6.

DEPARTMENT HEAD. 1. A member of the Executive Council charged with the administration of a department or agency. 2. The non-elected head of a department.

DEPARTMENT OF AGRICULTURE AND AGRI-FOOD. See AGRICULTURE AND AGRI-FOOD CANADA.

DEPARTMENT OF CANADIAN HERITAGE. The powers, duties and functions of the Minister extend to and include all matters over which Parliament has jurisdiction, not by law assigned to any other department, board or agency of the Government of Canada, relating to Canadian identity and values, cultural development and heritage. (2) The Minister's jurisdiction referred to in subsection (1) encompasses, but is not limited to, jurisdiction over (a) the promotion of a greater understanding of human rights, fundamental freedoms and related values;(b) multiculturalism;(c) the arts, including cultural aspects of the status of the artist; (d) cultural heritage and industries, including performing arts, visual and audio-visual arts, publishing, sound recording, film, video and literature; (e) national battlefields; (f) the encouragement, promotion and development of sport; (g) the advancement of the equality of status and use of English and French and the enhancement and development of the English and French linguistic minority communities in Canada; (h) state ceremonial and Canadian symbols; (i) broadcasting, except in respect of spectrum management and the technical aspects of broadcasting; (j) the formulation of cultural policy, including the formulation of cultural policy as it relates to foreign investment and copyright; (k) the conservation, exportation and importation of cultural property; and (l) national museums, archives and libraries. *Department of Canadian Heritage Act*, S.C. 1995, c. 11, s. 4.

DEPARTMENT OF CITIZENSHIP AND IMMIGRATION. The powers, duties and functions of the Minister extend to and include all matters over which Parliament has jurisdiction relating to citizenship and immigration and that are not by law assigned to any other department, board or agency of the Government of Canada. *Department of Citizenship and Immigration Act*, S.C. 1994, c. 31, s.4.

DEPARTMENT OF FINANCE. The Minister holds office during pleasure and has the management and direction of the Department, the management of the Consolidated Revenue Fund and the supervision, control and direction of all matters relating to the financial affairs of Canada not by law assigned to the Treasury Board or to any other minister. Established under the *Financial Administration Act*, R.S.C. 1985, c. F-11, s. 14 and 15.

DEPARTMENT OF FISHERIES AND OCEANS. The federal ministry which oversees coastal and inland fisheries, hydrography, marine sciences and small craft harbours.

174

DEPARTMENT OF FOREIGN AFFAIRS AND INTERNATIONAL TRADE. The powers, duties and functions of the Minister extend to and include all matters over which Parliament has jurisdiction, not by law assigned to any other department, board or agency of the Government of Canada, relating to the conduct of the external affairs of Canada, including international trade and commerce and international development. (2) In exercising his powers and carrying out his duties and functions under this Act, the Minister shall (a) conduct all diplomatic and consular relations on behalf of Canada;(b) conduct all official communication between the Government of Canada and the government of any other country and between the Government of Canada and any international organization;(c) conduct and manage international negotiations as they relate to Canada;(d) coordinate Canada's international economic relations; (e) foster the expansion of Canada's international trade and commerce; (f) have the control and supervision of the Canadian International Development Agency; (g) coordinate the direction given by the Government of Canada to the heads of Canada's diplomatic and consular missions; (h) have the management of Canada's diplomatic and consular missions; (i) administer the foreign service of Canada; (j) foster the development of international law and its application in Canada's external relations; and (k) carry out such other duties and functions as are by law assigned to him. (3) The Minister may develop and carry out programs related to the Minister's powers, duties and functions for the promotion of Canada's interests abroad including: (a) the fostering of the expansion of Canada's international trade and commerce; and (b) the provision of assistance for developing countries. *Department of Foreign Affairs and International Trade Act*, R.S.C. 1985, c. E-22, s. 10.

DEPARTMENT OF HEALTH. See HEALTH CANADA.

DEPARTMENT OF INDIAN AFFAIRS AND NORTHERN DEVELOPMENT. The Department is responsible for all matters over which Parliament has jurisdiction, not by law assigned to any other department, board or agency of the Government of Canada, relating to (a) Indian affairs; (b) Yukon, the Northwest Territories and Nunavut and their resources and affairs; and (c) Inuit affairs. *Department of Indian Affairs and Northern Development Act*, R.S.C. 1985, c. I-6, s. 4.

DEPARTMENT OF INDUSTRY. The powers, duties and functions of the Minister extend to and include all matters over which Parliament has jurisdiction, not by law assigned to any other department, board or agency of the Government of Canada, relating to (a) industry and technology in Canada;(b) trade and commerce in Canada;(c) science in Canada;(d) consumer affairs;(e) corporations and corporate securities;(f) competition and restraint of trade, including mergers and monopolies;(g) bankruptcy and insolvency;(h) patents, copyrights, trade-marks, industrial designs and integrated circuit topographies;(i) standards of identity, packaging and performance in relation to consumer products and services,

except in relation to the safety of consumer goods;(j) legal metrology;(k) telecommunications, except in relation to (i) the planning and coordination of telecommunication services for departments, boards and agencies of the Government of Canada, and(ii) broadcasting, other than in relation to spectrum management and the technical aspects of broadcasting;(l) the development and utilization generally of communication undertakings, facilities, systems and services for Canada; (m) investment;(n) small businesses; and(o) tourism.The powers, duties and functions of the Minister also extend to and include all matters over which Parliament has jurisdiction, not by law assigned to any other department, board or agency of the Government of Canada, relating to regional economic development in Ontario. *Department of Industry Act, 1995*, S.C. 1995, c. 1, s. 4.

DEPARTMENT OF JUSTICE. The Minister is ex officio Her Majesty's Attorney General of Canada, holds office during pleasure and has the management and direction of the Department. The Minister is the official legal adviser of the Governor General and the legal member of the Queen's Privy Council for Canada and shall (a) see that the administration of public affairs is in accordance with law;(b) have the superintendence of all matters connected with the administration of justice in Canada, not within the jurisdiction of the governments of the provinces; (c) advise on the legislative Acts and proceedings of each of the legislatures of the provinces, and generally advise the Crown on all matters of law referred to the Minister by the Crown; and (d) carry out such other duties as are assigned by the Governor in Council to the Minister. *Department of Justice Act*, R.S.C. 1985, c. J-2, s. 2 and 4.

DEPARTMENT OF NATIONAL DEFENCE. The Minister holds office during pleasure, has the management and direction of the Canadian Forces and of all matters relating to national defence and is responsible for (a) the construction and maintenance of all defence establishments and works for the defence of Canada; and (b) research relating to the defence of Canada and to the development of and improvements in materiel. *National Defence Act*, R.S.C. 1985, c. N-5, s. 4.

DEPARTMENT OF NATURAL RESOURCES. The powers, duties and functions of the Minister extend to and include all matters over which Parliament has jurisdiction, not by law assigned to any other department, board or agency of the Government of Canada, relating to (a) natural resources; (b) explosives; and (c) technical surveys relating to any matter other than a matter to which the powers, duties and functions of the Minister of the Environment and the Minister of Fisheries and Oceans extend by law. *Department of Natural Resources Act*, S.C. 1994, c. 41, s. 5

DEPARTMENT OF PUBLIC SAFETY AND EMERGENCY PREPAREDNESS. The powers, duties and functions of the Minister extend to and include all matters over which Parliament has jurisdiction—and that have not been assigned by law to another department, board or agency of the Government of Canada—relating to public safety and emer-

DEPT. OF PUBLIC WORKS & GOVERNMENT SERVICES

gency preparedness. The Minister is responsible for exercising leadership at the national level relating to public safety and emergency preparedness. *Department of Public Safety and Emergency Preparedness Act*, S.C. 2005, c. 10, s. 4.

DEPARTMENT OF PUBLIC WORKS AND GOVERNMENT SERVICES. The Department shall operate as a common service agency for the Government of Canada, and its activities as a common service agency shall be directed mainly toward providing the departments, boards and agencies of the Government of Canada with services in support of their programs. The powers, duties and functions of the Minister extend to and include all matters over which Parliament has jurisdiction, not by law assigned to any other department, board or agency of the Government of Canada, relating to (a) the acquisition and provision of articles, supplies, machinery, equipment and other materiel for departments; (b) the acquisition and provision of services for departments; (c) the planning and organizing of the provision of materiel and services required by departments; (d) the acquisition and provision of printing and publishing services for departments; (e) the construction, maintenance and repair of public works, federal real property and federal immovables; (f) the provision of accommodation and other facilities for departments; (g) the planning and coordination of telecommunications services for departments, boards and agencies of the Government of Canada; (h) the provision to departments of advice on or services related to architectural or engineering matters affecting any public work, federal real property or federal immovable; and (i) the provision to departments, boards and agencies of the Government of Canada of translation and related services. *Department of Public Works and Government Services Act*, S.C. 1996, c. 16, s. 5 and 6.

DEPARTMENT OF SOCIAL DEVELOPMENT. The powers, duties and functions of the Minister extend to and include all matters over which Parliament has jurisdiction relating to the social development of Canada and which are not by law assigned to any other Minister, department, board or agency of the Government of Canada. *Department of Social Development Act*, S.C. 2005, c. 35, s. 5.

DEPARTMENT OF THE ENVIRONMENT. See ENVIRONMENT CANADA.

DEPARTMENT OF TRANSPORT. See TRANSPORT CANADA.

DEPARTMENT OF VETERANS AFFAIRS. The powers, duties and functions of the Minister extend and apply to (a) the administration of such Acts of Parliament, and of such orders of the Governor in Council, as are not by law assigned to any other department of the Government of Canada or any Minister thereof, relating to (i) the care, treatment or reestablishment in civil life of any person who served in the Canadian Forces or merchant navy or in the naval, army or air forces or merchant navies of Her Majesty, of any person who has otherwise engaged in pursuits relating to war, and of any other person designated by the Governor in Council, and (ii) the care of the dependants or survivors of any person

referred to in subparagraph (i); and (b) all such other matters and such boards and other bodies, subjects, services and properties of the Crown as may be designated, or assigned to the Minister, by the Governor in Council. *Department of Veterans Affairs Act*, R.S.C. 1985, c. V-1, s. 4.

DEPARTMENT OF WESTERN ECONOMIC DIVERSIFICATION. The powers, duties and functions of the Minister extend to and include all matters over which Parliament has jurisdiction, not by law assigned to any other department, board or agency of the Government of Canada, relating to the promotion of the development and diversification of the economy of Western Canada and the advancement of the interests of Western Canada in national economic policy, program and project development and implementation. *Western Economic Diversification Act*, R.S.C. 1985, c. 11 (4th Supp.), s. 5.

DEPARTURE TAX. A capital gains tax imposed on taxpayers who cease to be residents of Canada.

DEPENDANT. *n.* 1. A person who depends upon another for maintenance. 2. A person to whom another has an obligation to provide support. See DEPENDENT.

DEPENDENT. *n.* With respect to a debtor (a) a brother, sister, parent or grandparent; (b) a child or other person who is less than 16 years of age; and (c) a person who is 16 years of age or more and who is in regular attendance at school or, because of a mental or physical disability, is unable to earn a livelihood, and who lives in the same household as the debtor or whose care in an institution is paid for by the debtor. *Judgment Enforcement Act*, S.N. 1996, c. J-1.1, s. 142. See DEPENDANT; DEPENDENTS.

DEPENDENT CHILDREN. See SURVIVOR WITH ~.

DEPENDENT CONTRACTOR. 1. (a) The owner, purchaser or lessee of a vehicle used for hauling, other than on rails or tracks, livestock, liquids, goods, merchandise or other materials, who is a party to a contract, oral or in writing, under the terms of which they are (i) required to provide the vehicle by means of which they perform the contract and to operate the vehicle in accordance with the contract, and (ii) is entitled to retain for their own use from time to time any sum of money that remains after the cost of their performance of the contract is deducted from the amount they are paid, in accordance with the contract, for that performance, (b) a fisher who, pursuant to an arrangement to which the fisher is a party, is entitled to a percentage or other part of the proceeds of a joint fishing venture in which the fisher participates with other persons, and (c) any other person who, whether or not employed under a contract of employment, performs work or services for another person on such terms and conditions that they are, in relation to that other person, in a position of economic dependence on, and under an obligation to perform duties for, that other person. *Canada Labour Code*, R.S.C. 1985, c. 2, s. 3(1). 2. An individual, whether or not he or she is employed by a contract of employment or provides his or her own tools, vehicles, equipment, machinery, material or other thing, who performs work or services for another person for compensation or reward on those terms and conditions that he or she is in a position of economic dependence upon and under an obligation to perform duties for that person more closely resembling the relationship of an employee than that of an independent contractor. *Labour Relations Act*, R.S.N. 1990, c. L-1, s. 2.

DEPENDENT RELATIVE REVOCATION. Where a will is revoked by a codicil it is a question whether it was the intention of the testator that the provisions of the will are to be effective if those contained in the codicil are declared to be invalid. *Murray v. Murray*, [1956] 1 W.L.R. 605.

DEPENDENTS. *n.* The members of the family of a worker who were wholly or partly dependent upon his earnings at the time of his death, or who but for the incapacity due to the accident would have been so dependent. *Workers' Compensation Act*, R.S.N.B. 1973, c. W-13, s. 1. See DEPENDANT.

DEPENDENT TERRITORIES. See COMMONWEALTH AND ~.

DEPONENT. *n.* 1. A person who testifies that certain facts are true. 2. One who makes an affidavit.

DEPORTATION. *n.* 1. The removal of a person from any place in Canada to the place from which the person came to Canada or to the country of the person's nationality or citizenship or to the country of the person's birth. 2. Forced displacement of the persons concerned by expulsion or other coercive acts from the area in which they are lawfully present, without grounds permitted under international law. *Crimes Against Humanity and War Crimes Act*, S.C. 2000, c. 24, Sched., *Rome Statute*, Article 7.

DEPOSE. *v.* 1. To remove from high office or a throne. 2. To affirm by making a deposition.

DEPOSIT. *v.* "... [F]iling, handing over, forwarding... ." *Sacchetti v. Lockheimer*, [1988] 1 S.C.R. 1049 at 1057, 86 N.R. 4, 49 R.P.R. 101, 15 Q.A.C. 89, the court per Lamer J.

DEPOSIT. *n.* 1. Money received that is repayable on demand or after notice or that is repayable upon the expiry of a fixed term. 2. "... [A] contract by which a customer lends money to a bank. The terms of the loan may vary as agreed upon by the banker and the customer. In the absence of such expressly agreed upon terms, the common law dictates that what is intended is a loan that is payable on demand." *Saskatchewan Co-operative Credit Society Ltd. v. Canada (Minister of Finance)* (1990), 47 B.L.R. 85 at 92, 65 D.L.R. (4th) 437, 32 F.T.R. 91, [1990] 2 F.C. 115, Collier J. See BANK ~; MARGIN ~; RETAIL ~ ACCOUNT; SECURITY ~.

DEPOSITARY AUTHORITY. See INTERNATIONAL ~.

DEPOSIT INSURANCE. See CANADA ~ CORPORATION.

DEPOSITION. *n.* Every affidavit, affirmation or statement made under oath. See VIDEO ~.

DEPOSITOR. *n.* A person whose account has been or is to be credited in respect of moneys constituting a deposit or part of a deposit or a person to whom a member institution is liable in respect of an instrument issued for moneys constituting a deposit or part of a deposit. *Canada Deposit Insurance Corporation Act*, R.S.C. 1985, c. C-3, Sch., s. 1.

DEPOSITORY BILL. An unconditional order in writing that is (a) signed by the drawer and addressed to another person, requiring the person to whom it is addressed to pay, at a fixed or determinable future time, a sum certain in money to, or to the order of, a specified person; (b) accepted unconditionally by the signature of the person to whom it is addressed; (c) marked prominently and legibly on its face and within its text, at or before the time of issue, with the words "This is a depository bill subject to the Depository Bills and Notes Act" or "Lettre de dépôt assujettie à la Loi sur les lettres et billets de dépôt"; (d) not marked with any words prohibiting negotiation, transfer or assignment of it or of an interest in it; (e) made payable, originally or by endorsement, to a clearing house; and (f) deposited with the clearing house to which it is made payable. *Depository Bills and Notes Act*, S.C. 1998, c. 13, s. 4.

DEPOSITORY NOTE. An unconditional promise in writing that is (a) signed by the maker, promising to pay, at a fixed or determinable future time, a sum certain in money to, or to the order of, a specified person; (b) marked prominently and legibly on its face and within its text, at or before the time of issue, with the words "This is a depository note subject to the Depository Bills and Notes Act" or "Billet de dépôt assujetti à la Loi sur les lettres et billets de dépôt"; (c) not marked with any words prohibiting negotiation, transfer or assignment of it or of an interest in it; (d) made payable, originally or by endorsement, to a clearing house; and (e) deposited with the clearing house to which it is made payable. *Depository Bills and Notes Act*, S.C. 1998, c. 13, s. 5.

DEPOSIT PROTECTION AGENCY. An entity established (a) to provide or administer a stabilization or mutual aid fund for local cooperative credit societies, (b) to assist in the payment of any losses incurred by the members of a local cooperative credit society in the liquidation of the society, or (c) to provide deposit insurance for members of local cooperative credit societies. *Cooperative Credit Associations Act*, S.C 1991, c. 48, s. 2.

DEPOT. See TRUCKING ~.

DEPRECIATION. *n.* "... [A]n accounting term. It signifies ... the writing-off of the cost of an asset over its useful life." *Canning v. C.F.M. Fuels (Ontario) Ltd.*, [1977] 2 S.C.R. 207 at 214, 12 N.R. 541, 71 D.L.R. (3d) 321, the court per Dickson J.

DEPRECIATION INSURANCE. Any type of coverage under which the insurance company agrees, in effect, to pay the difference between actual cash value and full replacement costs." What is insured, simply put, is depreciation. Under replacement coverage, insureds are entitled to receive the amount necessary to rebuild a structure or replace its contents in a new condition, without deducting for depreciation. Recovery is allowed, in the words of many courts, on a new-for-old basis. *Brkich & Brkich Enterprises Ltd.*

v. American Home Assurance Co. (1995), 8 B.C.L.R. (3d) 1 (C.A.) appeal to S.C.C. dismissed, reasons of Finch J.A. adopted.

DEPRIVE. *v.* To take away from; to deny; to defeat.

DEPT. *abbr.* Department.

DEPUTY. *n.* One who acts instead of another, or who exercises an office in another person's name.

DEPUTY HEAD. *var.* **DEPUTY-HEAD.** (a) In relation to a department named in Schedule I, its deputy minister; (b) in relation to any portion of the federal public administration named in Schedule IV, its chief executive officer or, if there is no chief executive officer, its statutory deputy head or, if there is neither, the person who occupies the position designated under subsection (2) in respect of that portion; (c) in relation to a separate agency, its chief executive officer or, if there is no chief executive officer, its statutory deputy head or, if there is neither, the person who occupies the position designated under subsection (2) in respect of that separate agency; and (d) in relation to any portion of the federal public administration designated for the purposes of paragraph (d) of the definition "public service", its chief executive officer or, if there is no chief executive officer, the person who occupies the position designated under subsection (2) in respect of that portion. *Financial Administration Act*, R.S.C. 1985, c. F-11, s. 11.

DEPUTY MARSHAL. In the Federal Court, each deputy sheriff is ex officio a deputy marshal. *Federal Courts Act*, R.S.C. 1985, c. F-7, s. 13.

DEPUTY MINISTER. 1. The senior civil servant in a department who advises the minister and is the senior administrator of that department. 2. (a) The deputy of a minister, (b) an officer who, by an Act, is declared to have the status of a deputy minister, or (c) a person designated as a deputy minister.

DERELICT. *n.* A ship which is voluntarily abandoned by her master and owner without intent of return or recovery.

DERELICT. *adj.* Abandoned.

DERELICTION. *n.* Abandoning something.

DERISORY DAMAGES. Small damages awarded to a plaintiff who sustained no loss, but whose legal rights were technically infringed.

DERIVATIVE. See COMMODITY ~; EXCHANGE-TRADED ~; FINANCIAL ~; STANDARDIZED ~.

DERIVATIVE ACTION. "[Arises when] ... a wrong is done to the entity to which the members belong. Such an action may be brought by a member or members, but it is brought on behalf of the entity ..." *Pasco v. Canadian National Railway* (1989), (*sub nom. Oregon Jack Creek Indian Band v. Canadian National Railway*) 34 B.C.L.R. (2d) 344 at 348, 56 D.L.R. (4th) 404, [1990] 2 C.N.L.R. 85 (C.A.), the court per MacFarlane J.A.

DERIVATIVE EVIDENCE. 1. Evidence that combines aspects of both statements and physical evidence—physical evidence discovered as a result of an unlawfully obtained statement. The cases refer to this evidence as derivative evidence. *R. v. Grant*, 2009 SCC 32, [2009] 2 S.C.R. 353, McLachlin C.J. and Charron J. 2. A subset of conscriptive evidence is "derivative evidence." This is a term frequently used to describe what is essentially conscriptive "real" evidence. It involves a Charter violation whereby the accused is conscripted against himself (usually in the form of an inculpatory statement) which then leads to the discovery of an item of real evidence. In other words, the unlawfully conscripted statement of the accused is the necessary cause of the discovery of the real evidence. *R. v. Stillman*, [1997] 1 S.C.R. 607, Cory J. for the majority. 3. "... [I]nclude all facts, events or objects whose existence is discovered as a result of a statement made to the authorities." *Thomson Newspapers Ltd. v. Canada (Director of Investigation & Research, Combines Investigation Branch)* (1990), 54 C.C.C. (3d) 417 at 528, 76 C.R. (3d) 129, 72 O.R. (2d) 415n, 67 D.L.R. (4th) 161, 29 C.P.R. (3d) 97, [1990] 1 S.C.R. 425, 39 O.A.C. 161, 106 N.R. 161, L'Heureux-Dubé J.

DERIVATIVES CLEARING. Includes all arrangements through which a clearing house, in accordance with its rules, (1) matches positions between market participants or parties to derivatives; (2) receives margin deposits or margins, and mutualizes or transfers the credit risk arising from a derivative among its members or clearing agents; (3) substitutes the credit of the clearing house for that of the parties to a derivative; and (4) nets those transactions on a multilateral basis, and settles them or, failing settlement, liquidates or cancels the relevant positions. *Derivatives Act*, R.S.Q. c. I-14.01, s. 46.

DERIVED CONFESSIONS RULE. The leading case on the derived confessions rule is R. v. I. (L.R.) and T. (E.), [1993] 4 S.C.R. 504. In brief, the derived confessions rule serves to exclude statements which, despite not appearing to be involuntary when considered alone, are sufficiently connected to an earlier involuntary confession as to be rendered involuntary and hence inadmissible. For example, in that case, a young offender was charged with second degree murder and gave an inculpatory statement to the police. The next day, after meeting with his lawyer, the accused came to the police, wishing to modify the statement that he had given the previous day. The trial judge excluded the first statement but admitted the second, and the accused was convicted by a jury. The accused appealed the conviction on the basis that the second statement should not have been admitted. His appeal was ultimately successful in this Court. *R. v. S.G.T.*, 2010 SCC 20, Charron J.

DEROGATE. *v.* To destroy; to evade; to prejudice. See NO ONE CAN BE ALLOWED TO ~ FROM HIS OWN GRANT.

DEROGATION. *n.* Evading an act passed or a rule made in the interest of the public, not for the actors' benefit. See NON-~ CLAUSE.

DEROGATORY CLAUSE. "Constitutional provisions like s. 1 [of the Charter] ... they permit some derogation from (in the sense of limitation of and not in any pejorative sense) the very human rights which are, in the words of the section, 'guaranteed' ..." *Black v. Law Society (Alberta)* (1986), 20 C.R.R. 117 at 139, [1986] 3 W.W.R. 590, 44 Alta. L.R. (2d) 1, 20 Admin. L.R. 140, 27 D.L.R. (4th) 527, 68 A.R. 259 (C.A.), Kerans J.A.

DESCENDANT. *n.* Lineal progeny; child; grand-child.

DESCENT. *n.* The title to inherit real property by reason of consanguinity, as well when the heir is an ancestor or collateral relation as where he is a child or other issue. *Probate Act*, R.S.P.E.I. 1988, c. P-21, s. 1. See LINEAL ~.

DESCRIPTION. *n.* Identification of goods or other attributes which apply to identified, defined goods. G.H.L. Fridman, *Sale of Goods in Canada*, 3d ed. (Toronto: Carswell, 1986) at 175. See JOB ~; LEGAL ~; MIS~; SALE BY ~.

DESCRIPTIVE. *adj.* Words are found to be descriptive of the wares with which they are associated when they describe something which is material to the composition of the goods. It must be material to the composition of the good or product and not in any way be descriptive of the intrinsic character or quality of the product. See CLEARLY ~.

DESERTION. *n.* 1. "... [A] forsaking and an abandonment of the conjugal relationship of husband and wife and requires the intention to desert against the wishes of the other spouse. It is not necessarily a withdrawal from a place, but from a state of things." *Reid v. Reid* (1970), 5 R.F.L. 37 at 42 (Ont. Prov. Ct.), Creighton Prov. Ct. J. 2. A person deserts who, (a) being on or having been warned for active service, duty during an emergency or other important service, is absent without authority with the intention of avoiding that service; (b) having been warned that his vessel is under sailing orders, is absent without authority with the intention of missing that vessel; (c) absents himself without authority from his place of duty with the intention of remaining absent from his place of duty; (d) is absent without authority from his place of duty and at any time during such absence forms the intention of remaining absent from his place of duty; or (e) while absent with authority from his place of duty, with the intention of remaining absent from his place of duty, does any act or omits to do anything the natural and probable consequence of which act or omission is to preclude his being at his place of duty at the time required. *National Defence Act*, R.S.C. 1985, c. N-5, s. 88. See CONSTRUCTIVE ~.

DESIGN. *n.* 1. A plan, sketch, drawing, graphic representation or specification intended to govern the construction, enlargement or alteration of a building or part of a building. *Architects Act*, R.S.O. 1990, c. A.26, s. 1. 2. "... [A] pattern or representation which the eye can see and which can be applied to a manufactured article... ." *Clatworthy & Son Ltd. v. Dale Display Fixtures Ltd.*, [1929] 3 D.L.R. 11 at 12, [1929] S.C.R. 429, the court per Lamont J. 3. Features of shape, configuration, pattern or ornament and any combination of those features that, in a finished arti-

cle, appeal to and are judged solely by the eye. *Industrial Design Act*, R.S.C. 1985, c. I-9, s. 2. See ERROR IN ~; INDUSTRIAL ~.

DESIGNATE. *n.* A person appointed.

DESIGNATED SUBSTANCE OFFENCE. 1(a) An offence under Part I, except subsection 4(1), or (b) a conspiracy or an attempt to commit , being an accessory after the fact in relation to, or any counselling in relation to, an offence referred to in paragraph (a). *Controlled Drugs and Substances Act*, S.C. 1996, c. 19, s. 2.

DESIGN-BUILD CONTRACT. The client deals with the main contractor who provides the design and the construction under one contract.

DESIGNER. See INTERIOR ~.

DESIGNER DRUG. A drug which, by a small change in molecular structure, retains the effect of a controlled or prohibited drug but is not subject to restrictive legislation. F.A. Jaffe, *A Guide to Pathological Evidence for Lawyers and Police Officers*, 4th ed. (Toronto: Carswell, 1999) at 234-235.

DESK ORDER DIVORCE. A divorce, permitted by the Rules of Court, obtained by the filing of documents without the necessity of attendance before a Judge.

DE SON TORT. [Fr.] Of his own wrong. See EXECUTOR ~.

DESPITE. *prep.* Even if; notwithstanding.

DESTITUTE. *adj.* Without means; not possessing necessaries of life.

DETAIN. *v.* To restrain; to withhold from. See DETENTION.

DETAINED. *adj.* Within the meaning of section 10 of the Charter the question whether a person has been detained invokes several criteria, including: the language used by the police office; whether the person accompanied the police officer voluntarily; whether the person left after being questioned; the point in the investigation when the person was interviewed; whether there were grounds to believe the person was in fact the guilty party; the nature of the questions asked; the subjective belief of the person. See ARBITRARILY ~.

DETAINEE. See SERVICE ~.

DETAINER. *n.* Wrongful retention. See FORCIBLE ~.

DETECTOR. See LIE ~ TEST.

DETENTION. *n.* 1. The word "detention" admits of many meanings. Read narrowly, "detention" can be seen as indicating situations where the police take explicit control over the person and command obedience. Read expansively, "detention" can be read as extending to even a fleeting interference or delay. Neither of these extremes offers an acceptable definition of "detention" as used in ss. 9 and 10 of the Charter. The first extreme was rejected by this Court in *R. v. Therens*, [1985] 1 S.C.R. 613, which held that detention for Charter purposes occurs when a state agent, by way of physical or psychological restraint, takes away an individual's choice simply to walk away. This encompasses not only explicit interference with the subject's liberty by way of physical interference or express command, but any form of "compulsory restraint". The second interpretation of "detention", reducing it to any interference, however slight, must also be rejected. In summary, we conclude as follows: 1. Detention under ss. 9 and 10 of the Charter refers to a suspension of the individual's liberty interest by a significant physical or psychological restraint. Psychological detention is established either where the individual has a legal obligation to comply with the restrictive request or demand, or a reasonable person would conclude by reason of the state conduct that he or she had no choice but to comply. 2. In cases where there is no physical restraint or legal obligation, it may not be clear whether a person has been detained. To determine whether the reasonable person in the individual's circumstances would conclude that he or she had been deprived by the state of the liberty of choice, the court may consider, inter alia, the following factors: (a) The circumstances giving rise to the encounter as they would reasonably be perceived by the individual: whether the police were providing general assistance; maintaining general order; making general inquiries regarding a particular occurrence; or, singling out the individual for focussed investigation. (b) The nature of the police conduct, including the language used; the use of physical contact; the place where the interaction occurred; the presence of others; and the duration of the encounter. (c) The particular characteristics or circumstances of the individual where relevant, including age; physical stature; minority status; level of sophistication. *R. v. Grant*, 2009 SCC 32, [2009] 2 S.C.R. 353, McLachlin C.J. and Charron J. 2. "... [M]ay be effected without the application or threat of application of physical restraint if the person concerned submits or acquiesces in the derivation of liberty and reasonably believes that the choice to do otherwise does not exist... Le Dain J.'s extension of 'detention' to instances of 'psychological' restraint or compulsion is predicated on two requirements: (1) a 'demand or direction', in response to which (2) 'the person concerned submits or acquiesces in the deprivation of liberty and reasonably believes that the choice to do otherwise does not exist'." *R. v. Elshaw*, [1991] 3 S.C.R. 24 at 52, 55, 7 C.R. (4th) 333, 59 B.C.L.R. (2d) 143, 67 C.C.C. (3d) 97, 128 N.R. 241, 6 C.R.R. (2d) 1, 3 B.C.A.C. 81, 7 W.A.C. 81, L'Heureux-Dubé J. (dissenting). See ARBITRARY ~; PREVENTIVE ~.

DETENTION BENEFIT. Paid to a member of the Canadian Forces who, while serving, is detained by a power, as defined in the Act. the period spent in detention includes the period during which the member or veteran was engaged in evading capture by, or in escaping from, any power. *Canadian Forces Members and Veterans Re-establishment and Compensation Act, S.C. 2005*, c. 21, s. 64.

DETENTION ORDER. An order that the accused be denied bail until trial.

DETERMINABLE. *adj.* Coming to an end.

DETERMINABLE FEE. A species of fee simple which terminates automatically on the happening of a specified event which may not occur.

DETERMINATE SENTENCE. A sentence of imprisonment for a limited period of time.

DETERMINATION. *n.* "... [I]mplies an ending or finality, the ending of a controversy... ." *R. v. Appleby* (1974), 18 C.P.R. (2d) 194 at 200, 10 N.B.R. (2d) 162, 21 C.C.C. (2d) 282 (C.A.), Hughes C.J.N.B. (Ryan J.A. concurring). See FINAL ~; SELF-~.

DETERMINE. *v.* 1. To decide; to come to a decision. 2. To come to an end.

DETERMINED. *adj.* Decided; fixed; delimited.

DETERRENCE. *n.* 1. "... [T]he achieving of control by fear." *R. v. McGinn* (1989), 49 C.C.C. (3d) 137 at 155, 75 Sask. R. 161 (C.A.), Vancise J.A. (dissenting). 2. One of the principles of sentencing of those convicted of offences. See GENERAL ~; SPECIFIC ~.

DETERRENT. *n.* A penalty imposed with view to preventing others from committing same act.

DETERRENT. *adj.* Preventative.

DETINUE. *n.* "... [W]here there is a wrongful taking [of goods] the victim may have the alternative of claiming in detinue, where the unsuccessful defendant must replace the goods or pay the value at the time of the trial... ." *Steiman v. Steiman* (1982), 23 C.C.L.T. 182 at 187, 18 Man. R. (2d) 203, 143 D.L.R. (3d) 396 (C.A.), O'Sullivan J.A. (Hall J.A. concurring). See ACTION FOR ~.

DEVALUATION. *n.* An official reduction in the amount of gold relating to the paper value of currency or the reduction in value of a currency in relation to a standard in use, other than gold.

DEVASTAVIT. [L.] One has wasted. Refers to loss to a deceased's estate caused by waste by the deceased's personal representative.

DEVELOPER. See OWNER-~.

DEVELOPMENT. *n.* 1. (a) The carrying out of any construction or excavation or other operations in, on, over or under land, or (b) the making of a change in the use or the intensity of use of land, buildings or premises. *City Transportation Act*, R.S.A. 2000, c. C-14, s. 9. 2. A major retail development. 3. Preparing a deposit of a prescribed mineral resource for production. *Ontario Mineral Exploration Program Act*, R.S.O. 1990, c. O.27, s. 1. See BUSINESS ~ BANK; OFFICIAL ~ ASSISTANCE; PERSONAL ~ SERVICES; SUSTAINABLE ~.

DEVELOPMENTAL DISABILITY. A condition of mental impairment present or occurring during a person's formative years, that is associated with limitations in adaptive behaviour. Ontario statutes.

DEVELOPMENT CONTROL. A type of land use control carried out by administrative means in contrast with zoning, which is accomplished through legislative means. It is used in Manitoba, Newfoundland and the Niagara Escarpment Region of Ontario. I.M.

Rogers, *The Law of Canadian Municipal Corporations*, 2d ed. (Toronto: Carswell, 1971-) at 813.

DEVELOPMENT PLAN. A development plan may contain, (a) policies for the economic, social and physical development of the area covered by the plan in respect of, (i) the distribution and density of population, (ii) the location of industry and commerce, (iii) the identification of land use areas and the provision of parks and open space and the policies in regard to the acquisition of lands, (iv) the management of land and water resources, (v) the control of all forms of pollution of the natural environment, (vi) the location and development of servicing, communication and transportation systems, (vii) the development and maintenance of educational, cultural, recreational, health and other social facilities, (viii) the adequate provision of a full range of housing, and (ix) such other matters as are, in the opinion of the Minister, advisable; (b) policies relating to the financing and programming of public development projects and capital works; (c) policies to co-ordinate planning and development among municipalities or planning boards within an area or within separate areas, as defined by the Minister; and (d) such other policies that the Minister considers advisable. *Ontario Planning and Development Act, 1994*, S.O. 1994, c. 23, Sch. A, s. 3.

DEVIATION. *n.* A major change in the method of performance agreed on in a contract.

DEVICE. *n.* Any weight, weighing machine, static measure or measuring machine and includes any equipment and accessories attached to or used in conjunction with the device that have or can have an effect on the accuracy of the device. *Weights and Measures Act*, R.S.C. 1985, c. W-6, s. 2. See ANTI-HANDLING ~; CONTRACEPTIVE ~; EXPLOSIVE OR OTHER LETHAL ~; IGNITION INTERLOCK ~; PROHIBITED ~; TOLL ~; TRACKING ~.

DEVISE. *n.* A disposition or gift by will. See EXECUTORY ~; SPECIFIC ~.

DEVISED. *adj.* Left in a will. E.L.G. Tyler & N.E. Palmer, eds., *Crossley Vaines' Personal Property*, 5th ed. (London: Butterworths, 1973) at 7.

DEVISEE. *n.* Includes the heir of a devisee and the devisee of an heir, and any person who claims right by devolution of title of a similar description. *Trustees acts.* See RESIDUARY ~.

DEVISOR. *n.* A testator.

DEVOLUTION. *n.* The transfer of an interest in property from one person to another through the operation of law, e.g., on bankruptcy or death.

DEVOLVE. *v.* To transfer property from one person to another through the operation of law, as on death, property devolves to the administrator of the deceased's estate.

D.F.Q.E. *abbr.* Droit fiscal québécois Express, 1977-.

DIAGNOSE. *v.* To identify the disease or condition from which a person or animal is suffering.

DICTA. [L.] *n.* Plural of DICTUM. See OBITER ~.

DICTUM. [L.] *n.* 1. Statement or observation. 2. "Some authorities distinguish between obiter dicta and judicial dicta. The former are mere passing remarks of the judge, whereas the latter consist of considered enunciations of the judge's opinions of the law on some point which does not arise for decision on the facts of the case before him, and so is not part of the ratio decidendi. But there is ... a third type of dictum, so far innominate. If instead of merely stating his own view of the point in question the judge supports it by stating what has been done in other cases, not reported, then his statement is one which rests not only on his own unsupported view of the law but also on the decisions of those other judges whose authority he has invoked... . Such a statement of the settled law or accustomed practice carries with it the authority not merely of the judge who makes it but also of an unseen cloud of his judicial brethren. A dictum of this type offers .... the highest authority that any dictum can bear ..." *Richard West & Partners (Inverness) Ltd. v. Dick* (1968), [1969] 1 All E.R. 289 at 292 (U.K. Ch.), Megarry J. 3. "... Sometimes they may be called almost casual expressions of opinion upon a point which has not been raised in the case, and is not really present to the judge's mind ... Some dicta however are of a different kind; they are, although not necessary for the decision of the case, deliberate expressions of opinion given after consideration upon a point clearly brought and argued before the Court ... much greater weight attaches to them than to the former class." *Slack v. Leeds Industrial Co-operative Society Ltd.*, [1923] 1 Ch. 431 at 451 (U.K. C.A.), Lord Sterndale M.R. See OBITER ~.

DIESEL. See BIO~.

DIETETICS. *n.* The assessment of nutritional needs, design, implementation and evaluation of nutritional care plans and therapeutic diets, the science of food and human nutrition, and dissemination of information about food and human nutrition to attain, maintain and promote the health of individuals, groups and the community. *Health Professions Act*, R.S.B.C. 1996, c. 83, *Dietitians Regulation*, B.C. Reg. 279/2008, s. 1.

DIETITIAN. *n.* An individual whose name appears on the Register and who is licensed to practise dietetics. *Dietitians Act*, S.N.S. 2009, c. 2, s. 2.

DIE WITHOUT ISSUE. Or any other words which import either a want or failure of issue of any person in the person's lifetime or at the time of the person's death or an indefinite failure of the person's issue shall be construed to mean a want or failure of issue in the lifetime or at the time of the death of such person and not an indefinite failure of the person's issue, unless a contrary intention appears by the will by reason of such person having a prior estate tail or of a preceding gift being, without any implication arising from such words, a limitation of an estate tail to such person or issue, or otherwise, but this Act does not extend to cases where such words so import if no issue described in a preceding gift are born or if there are no issue who live to attain the age or otherwise answer the description required for obtaining a vested estate by a preceding gift to such issue. *Wills Act*, R.S.N.S. 1989, c. 505, s. 28.

DIE WITHOUT LEAVING ISSUE. Or any other words which import either a want or failure of issue of any person in the person's lifetime or at the time of the person's death or an indefinite failure of the person's issue shall be construed to mean a want or failure of issue in the lifetime or at the time of the death of such person and not an indefinite failure of the person's issue, unless a contrary intention appears by the will by reason of such person having a prior estate tail or of a preceding gift being, without any implication arising from such words, a limitation of an estate tail to such person or issue, or otherwise, but this Act does not extend to cases where such words so import if no issue described in a preceding gift are born or if there are no issue who live to attain the age or otherwise answer the description required for obtaining a vested estate by a preceding gift to such issue. *Wills Act*, R.S.N.S. 1989, c. 505, s. 28.

DIFFERENCE. See DISTINCTION WITHOUT A ~.

DIGEST. *n.* 1. A gathering of rules of law based on particular cases, in contrast to a code. 2. An arrangement of the summarized decisions of courts made either alphabetically or systematically. 3. A private author's collection of abstract rules or principles of law.

DIGITAL MEDIA PRODUCT. See INTERACTIVE ~.

DIGITAL SIGNATURE CERTIFICATE. In respect of a person, means an electronic document that (a) identifies the certification authority that issued it and is digitally signed by that certification authority; (b) identifies, or can be used to identify, the person; and (c) contains the person's public key. *Personal Information Protection and Electronic Documents Act*, S.C. 2000, c. 5, *Secure Electronic Signature Regulations*, SOR/2005-30, s. 1.

DIGNITY. 1. Worth. 2. Serious quality. 3. The quality or state of being worthy or honourable. See HUMAN ~; PERSONAL ~.

DILATORY. *adj.* 1. Tending to cause delay in decision making. 2. Done for the purpose of causing delay.

DILATORY MOTION. A proposal that the original question be disposed of either permanently or for the time being. A. Fraser, W.A. Dawson & J. Holtby, eds., *Beauchesne's Rules and Forms of the House of Commons of Canada*, 6th ed. (Toronto: Carswell, 1989) at 173.

DILIGENCE. *n.* Care. See DUE ~.

DIMENSION. See ASSESSED ~.

DIPLOMATIC OR CONSULAR OFFICER. Includes an ambassador, envoy, minister, chargé d'affaires, counsellor, secretary, attaché, consul-general, consul, vice-consul, pro-consul, consular agent, acting consul-general, acting consul, acting vice-consul, acting consular agent, high commissioner, permanent delegate, adviser, acting high commissioner,

and acting permanent delegate. *Interpretation Act*, R.S.C. 1985, c. I-21, s. 35.

DIPLOMATIC PRIVILEGE. The privilege from prosecution for offences under domestic law afforded to diplomats residing in a country other than their own while they are on official business.

DIPLOMATIC PROTECTION. Assistance which nations grant to their citizens against other nations.

DIPPING. See DOUBLE ~.

DIR. *abbr.* Director.

DIRECT. *v.* To order; to instruct; to lead.

DIRECT. *adj.* Immediate; by the shortest route.

DIRECT AGREEMENT. A consumer agreement that is negotiated or concluded in person at a place other than, (a) at the supplier's place of business, or (b) at a market place, an auction, trade fair, agricultural fair or exhibition. *Consumer Protection Act, 2002*, S.O. 2002, c. 30, Sched. A, s. 20(1).

DIRECT CHARGE CO-OPERATIVE. A co-operative that deals with its members and prospective members only in products or services on a cost basis and that directly charges its members a fee to cover the operating expenses of the co-operative. *Co-operative Corporations Act*, R.S.O. 1990, c. C.35, s. 1(1).

DIRECT CONTRIBUTION. Financial contributions to property are examples of direct contributions. Homemaking or household management services are an example of indirect contributions. *Sanders v. Tomei*, 2000 CarswellBC 1032, 2000 BCSC 696, 9 R.F.L. (5th) 376.

DIRECT DISCOUNTING OF INCOME METHOD. Method of valuing intellectual property. Estimating the future net economic income associated with the asset and reducing the projected income for corporate income taxes on the income, research and development costs, capital expenditures, working capital, royalties for other technology required to support the income stream; and a capital charge on associated assets.

DIRECT DISCRIMINATION. Direct discrimination involves a law, rule or practice which on its face discriminates on a prohibited ground. *Egan v. Canada*, 1995 CarswellNat 6, 12 R.F.L. (4th) 201, 95 C.L.L.C. 210-025, C.E.B. & P.G.R. 8216, 124 D.L.R. (4th) 609, 182 N.R. 161, 29 C.R.R. (2d) 79, [1995] 2 S.C.R. 513, 96 F.T.R. 80 (note), [1995] 2 S.C.R. 513, Cory and Iacobucci JJ. (dissenting). See MEIORIN TEST.

DIRECTED. *v.* Advised, guided, ordered or controlled another, or something to be done.

DIRECTED VERDICT. The decision by the trial judge that there is no case to go to the jury for their deliberation. The judge directs that the accused be freed.

DIRECT EVIDENCE. 1. A witness' testimony as to what was observed through the senses. P.K. McWilliams, *Canadian Criminal Evidence*, 3d ed. (Aurora: Canada Law Book, 1988) at 1-11. 2. "... [A] necessary connection between the facts proven and the principal fact or factum probandum [exists]... ." *R. v. Mitchell* (1963), 42 C.R. 12 at 26, 45 W.W.R. 199 (B.C. C.A.), Sheppard J.A.

DIRECT EXAMINATION. Questioning of a witness by the party which called that witness.

DIRECT INDICTMENT. A procedure available to the Attorney General or Minister of Justice to prefer an indictment without a preliminary inquiry being conducted.

DIRECTION. *n.* 1. "... [A]uthoritative command ..." *R. v. Bazinet* (1986), 25 C.C.C. (3d) 273 at 284, 54 O.R. (2d) 129, 14 O.A.C. 15, 51 C.R. (3d) 139, the court per Tarnopolsky J.A. 2. The judge's instructions to the jury as to what the law is. See MIS~.

DIRECTIVE. *n.* An order; a direction.

DIRECTLY. See YOU CANNOT DO INDIRECTLY WHAT YOU CANNOT DO ~.

DIRECTOR. *n.* 1. "... [T]hose persons acting collectively to whom the duty of managing the general affairs of the company is delegated by the shareholders. Their duty is to conduct the business of the company for the greatest benefit of the shareholders... ." *Minister of National Revenue v. Parsons* (1983), 4 Admin. L.R. 64 at 79, [1983] C.T.C. 321, 83 D.T.C. 5329 (Fed. T.D.), Cattanach J. 2. A director of a corporation or an individual performing a similar function or occupying a similar position for a corporation or for any other person, *Securities acts.* 3. Includes a trustee, officer, member of an executive committee and any person occupying a similar position. *Societies acts.* 4. Includes commissioners governors and other officials of any body corporate with comparable responsibilities, whether or not they are called directors. 5. The title of the head or administrator of a government program or office. See FUNERAL ~; MANAGING ~.

DIRECTOR OF PUBLIC PROSECUTIONS. Appointed under the Director of Public Prosecutions Act, S.C. 2006, c. 9. The Director has the rank and status of a deputy head of a department. The Director, under and on behalf of the Attorney General, (a) initiates and conducts prosecutions on behalf of the Crown, except where the Attorney General has assumed conduct of a prosecution under section 15; (b) intervenes in any matter that raises a question of public interest that may affect the conduct of prosecutions or related investigations, except in proceedings in which the Attorney General has decided to intervene under section 14; (c) issues guidelines to persons acting as federal prosecutors respecting the conduct of prosecutions generally; (d) advises law enforcement agencies or investigative bodies in respect of prosecutions generally or in respect of a particular investigation that may lead to a prosecution; (e) communicates with the media and the public on all matters respecting the initiation and conduct of prosecutions; (f) exercises the authority of the Attorney General respecting private prosecutions, including to intervene and assume the conduct of—or direct the stay of—such prosecutions; and (g) exercises any other power or carries out any other duty or function assigned to the Director by the Attorney General that is compatible with the office of Director. The federal prosecutors that are necessary to enable the Director to perform any of the duties or functions of his or her office shall be appointed in accordance with the Public Service Employment Act. The Director may also for that purpose retain, on behalf of Her Majesty, the services of barristers and, in the Province of Quebec, advocates to act as federal prosecutors and, with the approval of the Treasury Board, may fix and pay their fees, expenses and other remuneration. *Director of Public Prosecutions Act*, S.C. 2006, c. 9, s. 3 and 7.

DIRECTORY. *n.* A provision from which no invalidating consequence will follow if it is disregarded, unlike a mandatory provision, which must be followed.

DIRECT SALE. 1. A sale which involves a consumer and does not take place at the seller's place of business. 2. A sale by a direct seller acting in the course of business as such. *Direct Sellers acts.*

DIRECT SELLER. (a) A supplier who enters into direct sales contracts, solicits consumers to enter into direct sales contracts, or both, or a salesperson of that supplier, and (b) a person, including an officer and a director, who performs services related to the management of the business of a supplier referred to in paragraph (a). *Business Practices and Consumer Protection Act*, S.B.C. 2004, c. 2, s. 156.

DIRECT SELLING. Selling, offering for sale or soliciting of orders for the sale of goods or services by (i) going from house to house, (ii) telephone communication, or (iii) mail.

DIRECT TAX. 1. "... [O]ne that is demanded from the very person who it is intended or desired should pay it." *Reference re Grain Futures Taxation Act (Manitoba)* (1925), (*sub nom. Manitoba (Attorney General) v. Canada (Attorney General)*) [1925] 2 D.L.R. 691 at 694, [1925] 2 W.W.R. 60, [1925] A.C. 561 (Can. P.C.), the board per Viscount Haldane. 2. "... [O]ne that is imposed on the consumer... ." *Chehalis Indian Band v. British Columbia* (1988), [1989] 1 C.N.L.R. 62 at 67, 31 B.C.L.R. (2d) 333, 53 D.L.R. (4th) 761 (C.A.), Marfarlane, Wallace and Locke JJ.A.

DIRECT TAXATION. Direct taxation refers to the method of taxation where taxes are imposed on the person intended to pay them. Income and sales tax are direct taxes.

DIRECT TO HOME BROADCASTING. DTH [direct-to-home] broadcasting makes use of satellite technology to transmit television programming signals to viewers. All DTH broadcasters own or have access to one or more satellites located in geosynchronous orbit, in a fixed position relative to the globe. The satellites are usually separated by a few degrees of Earth longitude, occupying "slots" assigned by international convention to their various countries of affiliation. The DTH broadcasters send their signals from land-based uplink stations to the satellites, which then diffuse the signals over a broad aspect of the Earth's surface, covering an area referred to as a "footprint". The broadcasting range of

D

the satellites is oblivious to international boundaries and often extends over the territory of multiple countries. Any person who is somewhere within the footprint and equipped with the proper reception devices (typically, a small satellite reception dish antenna, amplifier, and receiver) can receive the signal. *Bell ExpressVu Ltd. Partnership v. Rex* [2002] 2 S.C.R. 559.

DIRECT VISUAL SURVEILLANCE. Direct observation by a person who is physically present at the place that is under observation.

DISABILITY. *n.* 1. The absence of legal ability to do certain acts or enjoy certain benefits. 2. The incapacity of a minor or of a person who is mentally incompetent. 3. Any previous or existing mental or physical disability and includes disfigurement and previous or existing dependence on alcohol or a drug. *Canadian Human Rights Act*, R.S.C. 1985, c. H-6, s. 25. 4. The loss or lessening of the power to will and to do any normal mental or physical act. *Pension Act*, R.S.C. 1985, c. P-6, s. 3. 5. "... [P]hysical or mental incapacity, usually arising from injury or disease, although it might arise from other causes... ." *Penner v. Danbrook* (1992), 10 C.R.R. (2d) 379 at 382, [1992] 4 W.W.R. 385, 39 R.F.L. (3d) 286, 100 Sask. R. 125, 18 W.A.C. 125 (C.A.), the court per Sherstobitoff J.A. 6. The loss or lessening of the power to will and to do any normal mental or physical act. *Canadian Forces Members and Veterans Re-establishment and Compensation Act*, S.C. 2005, c. 21, s. 2. See CANADA ~ SAVINGS BOND; CANADA ~ SAVINGS GRANT; DEVELOPMENTAL ~; MENTAL ~; PARTIAL ~; PARTY UNDER ~; PERCEPTUAL ~; PERSONS WITH DISABILITIES; SENSORY ~; TOTAL ~.

DISABILITY ASSISTANCE PAYMENT. In relation to a disability savings plan of a beneficiary, means any payment made from the plan to the beneficiary or to the beneficiary's estate. *Income Tax Act*, R.S.C. 1985, c. 1 (5th Supp.), s. 146.4. See LIFE-TIME ~S.

DISABILITY BENEFIT PLAN. See LONG-TERM ~.

DISABILITY COVERAGE. [P]rovided pursuant to a contract of insurance which provides only such coverage would, on its face, come within the meaning of "accident insurance" or "sickness insurance" as these terms are used in [The Saskatchewan Insurance Act]. On the other hand, disability coverage provided pursuant to a contract providing life insurance would be considered to be "life insurance". All of this follows from the interlocking definitions of "accident insurance", "sickness insurance", "life insurance"and "disability insurance" found in s. 2 of the Act. *Saskatchewan Health-Care Assn. v. Zipchen*, 2007 SKCA 136.

DISABILITY INSURANCE. Insurance undertaken by an insurer as part of a contract of life insurance whereby the insurer undertakes to pay insurance money or to provide other benefits in the event that the person whose life is insured becomes disabled as a result of bodily injury or disease. *Insurance acts*.

DISABILITY PENSION. See OCCUPATIONAL ~.

DISABILITY PLAN. See LONG TERM ~.

DISABILITY SAVINGS PLAN. Of a beneficiary means an arrangement (a) between (i) a corporation (in this section referred to as the "issuer") (A) that is licensed or otherwise authorized under the laws of Canada or a province to carry on in Canada the business of offering to the public its services as trustee, and (B) with which the specified Minister has entered into an agreement that applies to the arrangement for the purposes of the Canada Disability Savings Act, and (ii) one or more of the following: (A) the beneficiary, (B) an entity that, at the time the arrangement is entered into, is a qualifying person in relation to the beneficiary, and (C) a legal parent of the beneficiary who, at the time the arrangement is entered into, is not a qualifying person in relation to the beneficiary but is a holder of another arrangement that is a registered disability savings plan of the beneficiary; (b) under which one or more contributions are to be made in trust to the issuer to be invested, used or otherwise applied by the issuer for the purpose of making payments from the arrangement to the beneficiary; and (c) that is entered into in a taxation year in respect of which the beneficiary is a DTC-eligible individual. *Income Tax Act*, R.S.C. 1985, c. 1 (5th Supp.), s. 146.4.

DISABLED PERSON. Persons who consider themselves disadvantaged by reason of any persistent physical, mental, psychiatric, learning or sensory impairment or who believe that a potential employer would likely consider them so disadvantaged. *Centennial Flame Research Award Act*, S.C. 1991, c. 17, s. 2.

DISADVANTAGE. *n.* Under s. 15 [Charter] connotes vulnerability, prejudice and negative social characterization. Section 15(2)'s purpose is to protect government programs targeting the conditions of a specific and identifiable disadvantaged group, as contrasted with broad societal legislation, such as social assistance programs. Not all members of the group need to be disadvantaged, as long as the group as a whole has experienced discrimination. *R. v. Kapp*, 2008 SCC 41, McLachlin C.J. and Abella J. for the majority.

DISALLOWANCE. *n.* 1. The Queen's power to annul any statute enacted by the Parliament of Canada. 2. The federal power vested in the Governor General in Council to annul provincial statutes.

DISAPPEARANCE. *n.* Enforced disappearance of persons means the arrest, detention or abduction of persons by, or with the authorization, support or acquiescence of, a State or a political organization, followed by a refusal to acknowledge that deprivation of freedom or to give information on the fate or whereabouts of those persons, with the intention of removing them from the protection of the law for a prolonged period of time. *Crimes Against Humanity and War Crimes Act*, S.C. 2000, c. 24, Sched., *Rome Statute*, Article 7.

DISASTER. See MAJOR ~; MINOR ~.

DISBAR. *v.* To expel a lawyer from membership in a law society.

DISBURSEMENT. *n.* 1. An expenditure or any other payment or transfer of public money. 2. Money expended or paid out on behalf of the client, such as a fee paid to a court officer or court reporter or witness fees, for which a lawyer is entitled to a credit when an account is submitted. 3. "... [I]ndicative of an immediate outlay or payment and signifies an expenditure... ." *R. v. McKee*, [1977] C.T.C. 491 at 494, 77 D.T.C. 5345 (Fed. T.D.), Addy J.

DISCHARGE. *v.* 1. To release a person from an obligation. *R. v. Simmons* (1984), 11 C.C.C. (3d) 193 at 214, 45 O.R. (2d) 609, 39 C.R. (3d) 223, 26 M.V.R. 168, 3 O.A.C. 1, 7 D.L.R. (4th) 719, 8 C.R.R. 333, 7 C.E.R. 159 (C.A.), Howland C.J.O. (Martin, Lacourcière and Houlden JJ.A. concurring). 2. To deprive a right or obligation of its binding force. 3. "... [T]o revoke or to rescind." *Lamontagne v. Lamontagne* (1964), 47 W.W.R. 321 at 331, 44 D.L.R. (2d) 228 (Man. C.A.), Freedman J.A. (Schultz J.A. concurring). 4. When used as a verb, includes add, deposit, leak or emit. *Environmental Protection Act*, R.S.O. 1990, c. E.19, s. 1(1).

DISCHARGE. *n.* 1. Section 662.1 of the Code gives judges discretion to release an accused after guilt is determined absolutely or on conditions a probation order prescribes. 2. An instrument by which one terminates an obligation under contract. 3. Termination of employment by an employer other than a lay-off. 4. Spilling, leaking, pumping, pouring, emitting, emptying, throwing and dumping. 5. Release of a patient. 6. In relation to oil and bunker oil, means a discharge of oil or bunker oil that directly or indirectly results in the oil or bunker oil entering the water, and includes spilling, leaking, pumping, pouring, emitting, emptying, throwing and dumping. *Marine Liability Act*, S.C. 2001, c. 6, s. 47. See ABSOLUTE ~; CONDITIONAL ~; CONSTRUCTIVE ~; WRONGFUL ~.

DISCHARGED. *adj.* 1. Relieved from further performance of the contract. 2. Of a payment, made or paid. 3. "... '[N]ot committed on the charge laid' ..." *Myers v. R.* (1991), 65 C.C.C. (3d) 135 at 140, 91 Nfld. & P.E.I.R. 37, 286 A.P.R. 37 (Nfld. C.A.), Goodridge C.J.N. (Steele J.A. concurring). 4. "... [R]ecognizance is 'discharged' (that is, the debtor is released from his or her obligations), if the conditions of the contract are fulfilled." *Purves v. Canada (Attorney General)* (1990), 54 C.C.C. (3d) 355 at 363 (B.C. C.A.), the court per Legg J.A.

DISCIPLINARY ACTION. 1. "... The reason for disciplinary action is misconduct and the purpose is to punish." *Canada v. Evans* (1983), 49 N.R. 189 at 194 (Fed. C.A.), Le Dain J.A. (Urie J.A. concurring). 2. Action which adversely affects a worker if the employer imposes discipline 3. Action which adversely affects a member of the group which imposes the discipline.

DISCIPLINARY COMMITTEE. See DISCIPLINE COMMITTEE.

DISCIPLINARY MATTER. Any matter involving an allegation of professional misconduct or fitness to practise on the part of a member, student or professional corporation.

DISCIPLINE. *n.* Correction; punishment. See CORRECTIVE ~; PROGRESSIVE ~.

DISCIPLINE COMMITTEE. A committee established under a statute regulating one of the self-governing professions. The committee usually has powers to suspend or revoke the professional's authority to practice a profession. Usually, it also has investigatory and hearing powers and duties. It also has the authority, depending on the statute, to impose fines, issue reprimands and to impose other similar types of discipline on members of the profession.

DISCLAIM. *v.* To repudiate; to refuse to recognize.

DISCLAIMER. *n.* 1. The act of renouncing generally substantiated by a deed. 2. Whenever, by any mistake, accident or inadvertence, and without any wilful intent to defraud or mislead the public, a patentee has (a) made a specification too broad, claiming more than that of which the patentee or the person through whom the patentee claims was the inventor, or (b) in the specification, claimed that the patentee or the person through whom the patentee claims was the inventor of any material or substantial part of the invention patented of which the patentee was not the inventor, and to which the patentee had no lawful right, the patentee may, on payment of a prescribed fee, make a disclaimer of such parts as the patentee does not claim to hold by virtue of the patent or the assignment thereof. *Patent Act*, R.S.C. 1985, c. P-4, s. 48. 3. The Registrar may require an applicant for registration of a trade-mark to disclaim the right to the exclusive use apart from the trade-mark of such portion of the trade-mark as is not independently registrable, but the disclaimer does not prejudice or affect the applicant's rights then existing or thereafter arising in the disclaimed matter, nor does the disclaimer prejudice or affect the applicant's right to registration on a subsequent application if the disclaimed matter has then become distinctive of the applicant's wares or services. *Trade-marks Act*, R.S.C. 1985, c. T-13, s. 35.

DISCLAIMER CLAUSE. A clause in a contract denying that guarantees or other representations have been made.

DISCLOSED PRINCIPAL. A person whose existence the agent has revealed to the third party, but whose exact identity is still unknown. G.H.L. Fridman, *The Law of Agency*, 6th ed. (London: Butterworths, 1990) at 193.

DISCLOSURE. *n.* 1. A revelation. 2. The provision of documents to a party to a proceeding. May refer to documents held by an opposing party or by an administrative body. 3. "In its simplest form, disclosure will consist of simply displaying what must be disclosed to defence counsel for examination. In its absolute form, disclosure will consist of providing copies of the materials to be disclosed where copies are available and copies of notes, copies and 'will says'." *R. v. Vokey* (1992), 10 C.R.R. (2d) 360 at 370,

D

DISCONTINUANCE

14 C.R. (4th) 311, 102 Nfld. & P.E.I.R. 275, 323 A.P.R. 275 (Nfld. C.A.), the court per Goodridge C.J.N. See INGREDIENT ~ LIST; PROTECTED ~.

DISCONTINUANCE. *n.* 1. Breaking off; interruption. 2. "Discontinuance before judgment, ... amounts to the abandoment of the exercise of a right... ." *Quebec (Expropriation Tribunal) v. Quebec (Attorney General)* (1983), 29 L.C.R. 6 at 8, [1983] R.D.J. 432 (Que. C.A.), the court per Jacques J.A.

DISCONTINUOUS SERVITUDE. Such as pedestrian or vehicular rights of way, require the actual intervention of the holder. *Civil Code*, S.Q. 1991, c. 64, a. 1179. See CONTINUOUS ~.

DISCOUNT. *v.* 1. Lessen, diminish. 2. "To discount a negotiable security is therefore to buy it at a discount; or it may mean, using another sense of the word, to lend money on the security, deducting the interest in advance ..." *Jones v. Imperial* (1876), 23 Gr. 262 at 270 (Ont. Ch.), Proudfoot V.C. See DIRECT ~ING OF INCOME METHOD.

DISCOUNT. *n.* 1. Lessening, diminishing. 2. The excess of the par or stated value of any security issued or resold over the value of the consideration received for the security. 3. "... [I]n commerce a discount on the sale of an article of trade is an abatement or deduction from the nominal value or price of that article." *Consolboard Inc. v. MacMillan Bloedel (Saskatchewan) Ltd.* (1982), 63 C.P.R. (2d) 1 at 22 (Fed. T.D.), Cattanach J.

DISCOUNT RATE. "... [T]he difference between the interest rate that can be earned on the lump sum invested and the rate of inflation ..." *McDermid v. Ontario* (1985), 5 C.P.C. (2d) 299 at 303, 53 O.R. (2d) 495 (H.C.), Rosenberg J.

DISCOVERABILITY RULE. " ... [A] cause of action arises for purposes of a limitation period when the material facts on which it is based have been discovered or ought to have been discovered by the plaintiff by the exercise of reasonable diligence, ..." *Central Trust v. Rafuse*, [1986] 2 S.C.R. 147 at 224, 37 C.C.L.T. 117, 42 R.P.R. 161, 34 B.L.R. 187, 31 D.L.R. (4th) 481, 75 N.S.R. (2d) 109, 186 A.P.R. 109, 69 N.R. 321, Le Dain J.

DISCOVERY. *n.* 1. Disclosure by the parties before trial of information and documents. 2. "... [F]ollows upon the issues having been previously defined by the pleadings and the purpose of such discovery is to prove or disprove the issues so defined, by a cross-examination on the facts relevant to such issues." *Anglo-Cdn. Timber Products Ltd. v. B.C. Electric Co.* (1960), 31 W.W.R. 604 at 605, 23 D.L.R. (2d) 656 (B.C. C.A.), Sheppard J.A. See COMMERCIAL ~; E-~; ELECTRONIC ~; EXAMINATION FOR ~; REASONABLE ~.

DISCREDIT. *v.* To throw doubt on the testimony of a witness.

DISCRETION. *n.* 1. "... [W]hen it is said that something is to be done within the discretion of the authorities ... [it] is to be done according to the rules of reason and justice, not according to private opinion ... according to law, and not humour. It is to be, not arbitrary, vague, and fanciful, but legal and regular." *Sharp v. Wakefield*, [1891] A.C. 173 at 179 Lord Halsbury, cited by Kellock J. in *Wrights Canadian Ropes Ltd. v. Minister of National Revenue*, [1946] S.C.R. 139 at 166. 2. A person's own judgment of what is best in a given situation. See ABUSE OF ~; ADMINISTRATIVE ~; EXERCISE ~; FETTERING OF ~; JUDICIAL ~. PROSECUTORIAL ~; UNFETTERED ~.

DISCRETIONARY. *adj.* At the discretion of someone; not available as of right.

DISCRETIONARY DUTY. Something required of a trustee, such as allocating trust property, choosing how much a beneficiary should have, or choosing who should have a benefit from among a class of beneficiaries, and then how much that particular beneficiary should have. D.M.W. Waters, *The Law of Trusts in Canada*, 2d ed. (Toronto: Carswell, 1984) at 28-29.

DISCRETIONARY REMEDY. Given at a court's discretion, not available as of right.

DISCRETIONARY TRUST. A trust in which trustees are given absolute discretion concerning the allocation of the capital and income of the trust fund to beneficiaries.

DISCRIMINATION. *n.* 1. "... [A] distinction, whether intentional or not but based on grounds relating to personal characteristics of the individual or group, which has the effect of imposing burdens, obligations, or disadvantages on such individual or group not imposed on others, or which withholds or limits access to opportunities, benefits, and advantages, available to other members of society... ." *Andrews v. Law Society (British Columbia)* (1989), 56 D.L.R. (4th) 1 at 18, 36 C.R.R. 193, [1989] 2 W.W.R. 289, 25 C.C.E.L. 255, 91 N.R. 255, 34 B.C.L.R. (2d) 273, 10 C.H.R.R. D/5719, [1989] 1 S.C.R. 143, McIntyre J. (Dickson C.J.C., Lamer, Wilson and L'Heureux-Dubé JJ. concurring). 2. Another definition of discrimination is provided by Justice Abella in her Royal Commission Report on Equality in Employment, (Ottawa: Minister of Supply & Services, 1984) at p. 2: Discrimination in this context means practices or attitudes that have, whether by design or impact, the effect of limiting an individual's or a group's right to the opportunities generally available because of attributed rather than actual characteristics. What is impeding the full development of the potential is not the individual's capacity but an external barrier that artificially inhibits growth. 3. Discrimination is not only about groups. It is also about individuals who are arbitrarily disadvantaged for reasons having largely to do with attributed stereotypes, regardless of their actual merit. Discrimination on the basis of marital status may be defined as practices or attitudes which have the effect of limiting the conditions of employment of, or the employment opportunities available to, employees on the basis of a characteristic relating to their marriage (or non-marriage) or family. *A. v. B.*, 2000 CarswellOnt 4203, 50 O.R. (3d) 737, 25 Admin. L.R. (3d) 1, 139 O.A.C. 13, 195 D.L.R. (4th) 405, 7 C.C.E.L. (3d) 177, 2001

C.L.L.C. 230-015. 4. Selection for or the giving of unfavourable treatment. 5. A court that is called upon to determine a discrimination claim under s. 15(1) should make the following three broad inquiries: (A) Does the impugned law (a) draw a formal distinction between the claimant and others on the basis of one or more personal characteristics, or (b) fail to take into account the claimant's already disadvantaged position within Canadian society resulting in substantively differential treatment between the claimant and others on the basis of one or more personal characteristics? (B) Is the claimant subject to differential treatment based on one or more enumerated and analogous grounds? and (C) Does the differential treatment discriminate, by imposing a burden upon or withholding a benefit from the claimant in a manner which reflects the stereotypical application of presumed group or personal characteristics, or which otherwise has the effect of perpetuating or promoting the view that the individual is less capable or worthy of recognition or value as a human being or as a member of Canadian society, equally deserving of concern, respect, and consideration? *Law v. Canada (Minister of Employment and Immigration)*, [1999] 1 S.C.R. 497. See ADVERSE EFFECT ~; CONSTRUCTIVE ~; DIRECT ~; INDIRECT ~; PRIMA FACIE ~; RACIAL ~; REVERSE ~; SEX ~; SYSTEMIC ~; WRONGFUL ~.

DISCRIMINATORY. *adj.* To be discriminatory within the meaning of section 15 of the Charter, there must be a legislative distinction, the distinction must result in a denial of one of the four equality rights on the basis of the claimant's membership in an identifiable group and the distinction must be capable of either promoting or perpetuating the view that the individual or group adversely affected by this distinction is less capable or less worthy of recognition or value as (a) human being(s) or (a) member(s) of Canadian society.

DISCUSSION. See MANAGEMENT ~ AND ANALYSIS.

DISEASE. *n.* "... [A]n ailment that disorders one or more of the vital functions or organs of the body, causing a morbid physical condition." *Tomlinson v. Prudential Insurance Co. of America*, [1954] O.R. 508 at 516, [1954] I.L.R. 1-144 (C.A.), the court per Laidlaw J.A. See INDUSTRIAL ~; OCCUPATIONAL ~; SERVICE-RELATED INJURY OR ~; SEXUALLY TRANSMITTED ~; TOBACCO-RELATED ~; VENEREAL ~.

DISEASE OF THE MIND. 1. "... Any malfunctioning of the mind or mental disorder having its source primarily in some subjective condition or weakness internal to the accused (whether fully understood or not) may be a 'disease of the mind' if it prevents the accused from knowing what he is doing, but transient disturbances of consciousness due to certain specific external factors do not fall within the concept of disease of the mind... ." *R. v. Rabey* (1977), 40 C.R.N.S. 46 at 62-63, 17 O.R. (2d) 1, 1 L. Med. Q. 280, 37 C.C.C. (2d) 461, 79 D.L.R. (3d) 414 (C.A.), Martin J.A., adopted in *R. v. Rabey* (1980), 15 C.R. (3d) 225 (Eng.), [1980] 2 S.C.R. 513, 54 C.C.C. (2d) 1, 32 N.R. 451, 20 C.R. (3d) 1 (Fr.). 2. "... [I]n a legal sense, ... embraces any illness, disorder or abnormal condition which impairs the human mind and its functioning, excluding, however, self-induced states caused by alcohol or drugs, as well as transitory mental states such as hysteria or concussion... ." *R. v. Cooper* (1979), 13 C.R. (3d) 97 at 117 (Eng.), [1980] 1 S.C.R. 1149, 18 C.R. (3d) 138 (Fr.), 51 C.C.C. (2d) 129, 31 N.R. 234, 4 Led. Med. Q. 227, 110 D.L.R. (3d) 46, Dickson J. (Laskin C.J.C., Beetz, Estey and McIntyre JJ. concurring). 3. Such a broad definition [as in R. v. Cooper] is surely large enough to encompass cases of sleepwalking that create dangers that society must address. *Canada v. Campbell*, 2000 CarswellOnt 2116, 35 C.R. (5th) 314 (S.C.J.), McCombs J. 4. Taken alone, the question of what mental conditions are included in the term disease of the mind is a question of law. However, the trial judge must also determine whether the condition the accused claims to have suffered from satisfies the legal test for disease of the mind. This involves an assessment of the particular evidence in the case rather than a general principle of law and is thus a question of mixed law and fact. *R. v. Stone*, 1999 CarswellBC 1064, [1999] 2 S.C.R. 290, [1999] 2 S.C.R. 290. See INSANITY.

DISENTAIL. *v.* To bring an entail to an end.

DISENTAILING DEED. An assurance through which a tenant in tail blocks the entail in order to convert it into a fee simple.

DISENTITLED. *adj.* Not entitled.

DISHONEST. *adj.* "... [N]ormally used to describe an act where there has been some intent to deceive or cheat... ." *Lynch & Co. v. United States Fidelity & Guaranty Co.*, [1971] 1 O.R. 28 at 37, 14 D.L.R. (3d) 294 (H.C.), Fraser J.

DISHONOUR. *v.* 1. To neglect or refuse to accept or pay a bill of exchange when it is duly presented for payment. 2. A bill is dishonoured by non-payment when (a) it is duly presented for payment and payment is refused or cannot be obtained; or (b) presentment is excused and the bill is overdue and unpaid. When a bill is dishonoured by non-payment, an immediate right of recourse against the drawer, acceptor and endorsers accrues to the holder. *Bills of Exchange Act*, R.S.C. 1985, c. B-4, s. 94. See NOTICE OF ~.

DISINHERIT. *v.* To end a right to inherit.

DISINTERMENT. *n.* The removal, for the purpose of permanent relocation, of (a) human remains, and (b) the container, or any of the remaining container, holding the human remains, from the lot in which the human remains are interred. *Cremation, Interment and Funeral Services Act*, S.B.C. 2004, c. 35, s. 1. See EXHUMATION.

DISJUNCTIVE TERM. Usually expressed by the word "or" which indicates alternative conditions or matters.

DISMISS. *v.* 1. In employment, to fire, let go, terminate. 2. In proceedings, to refuse the remedy requested.

DISMISSAL. *n.* 1. "... [O]f an employee may be effected either by words or conduct. The conduct [must] be such as to amount to a refusal by the employer to continue to be bound by the contract... ." *Gilson v. Fort Vermilion School Division No. 52* (1985), 12 C.C.E.L. 72 at 74, 61 A.R. 225 (Bd. of Reference), McFayden J. 2. "... [I]f made by a court of competent jurisdiction, a final disposition of the case against the accused sufficient to support the plea of autrefois acquit: ..." *R. v. Dubois* (1986), 25 C.C.C. (3d) 221 at 232, [1986] 1 S.C.R. 366, [1986] 3 W.W.R. 577, 26 D.L.R. (4th) 481, 66 N.R. 289, 18 Admin. L.R. 146, 51 C.R. (3d) 193, 41 Man. R. (2d) 1, the court per Estey J. See CONSTRUCTIVE ~; JUST ~; WRONGFUL ~.

DISMISSAL FOR CAUSE. "[The employer] ... is entitled to refuse to perform his future obligations because of the prior fundamental breach of the employee... ." *Carr v. Fama Holdings Ltd.* (1989), 28 C.C.E.L. 30 at 39, 41, 40 B.C.L.R. (2d) 125, 45 B.L.R. 42, [1990] 1 W.W.R. 264, 63 D.L.R. (4th) 25 (C.A.), Wallace J.A. (Hutcheon and Cumming JJ.A. concurring).

DISORDER. See MENTAL ~.

DISORDERLY HOUSE. A common bawdy-house, a common betting house or a common gaming house. *Criminal Code*, R.S.C. 1985, c. C-46, s. 197.

DISPARAGEMENT. *n.* A statement which casts doubt on ownership of property or on quality of goods.

DISPENSER. *n.* 1. A person who dispenses a drug pursuant to a prescription. *The Pharmaceutical Act*, S.M. 2006, c. 37, s. 77. 2. A person who is a member of a professional governing body and who is entitled, by virtue of their membership in that body, to manufacture or adapt a medical device in accordance with a health care professional's written directions in order to meet the specific requirements of a patient. *Food and Drugs Act*, R.S.C. 1985, c. F-27, *Medical Devices Regulations*, SOR/98-282, s. 1.

DISPOSE. *v.* 1. "... [O]f property ... to make the property over to another so that no interest therein remains ..." *Harman v. Gray-Campbell Ltd.*, [1925] 2 D.L.R. 904 at 908, [1925] 1 W.W.R. 1134, 19 Sask. L.R. 526 (C.A.), Lamont J.A. 2. To transfer by any method and includes assign, give, sell, grant, charge, convey, bequeath, devise, lease, divest, release and agree to do any of those things. *Interpretation Act*, R.S.B.C. 1996, c. 238, s. 29. 3. To destroy. *R. v. Cie Immobilière BCN*, [1979] 1 S.C.R. 865, [1979] C.T.C. 71, 79 D.T.C. 5068, 25 N.R. 361, 97 D.L.R. (3d) 238, the court per Pratte J. 4. "... '[T]o part with', 'to pass over the control of the thing to someone else' so that the person disposing no longer has the use of the property." *Victory Hotels Ltd. v. Minister of National Revenue*, [1962] C.T.C. 614 at 626, [1963] Ex. C.R. 123, 62 D.T.C. 1378, Noel J.

DISPOSING MIND. The "disposing mind and memory" essential to testamentary capacity is one able to comprehend, of its own initiative and volition, the essential elements of will-making, such as property, objects, just claims to consideration, revocation of existing dispositions and the like. *Leger v. Poirier* [1944] S.C.R. 152.

DISPOSITION. *n.* 1. Final settlement or sentencing of a criminal case. 2. "[In the context of the transfer of business from one employer to another] ... something must be relinquished from the first business and obtained by the second." *W.W. Lester (1978) Ltd. v. U.A., Local 740* (1990), 48 Admin. L.R. 1 at 23, 76 D.L.R. (4th) 389, 91 C.L.L.C. 14,002, 123 N.R. 241, 88 Nfld. & P.E.I.R. 15, 274 A.P.R. 15, [1990] 2 S.C.R. 644, McLachlin J. (Lamer C.J.C., La Forest, Sopinka and Gonthier JJ. concurring). 3. The act of disposal or an instrument by which that act is affected or evidenced, and includes a Crown grant, order in council, transfer, assurance, lease, licence, permit, contract or agreement and every other instrument whereby lands or any right, interest or estate in land may be transferred, disposed of or affected, or by which the Crown divests itself of or creates any right, interest or estate in land. 4. In the context of labour relations to accomplish a disposition something must be relinquished by the predecessor business on the one hand and obtained by the successor on the other. A transfer implies a nexus, an agreement or transaction of some sort between the predecessor and successor employers. . . There must be a mutual intent to transfer part of the business. *C.A.W., Local 222 v. Charterways Transportation Ltd.*, 2000 CarswellOnt 1253, 2000 SCC 23, 2000 C.L.L.C. 220-028, 49 C.C.E.L. (2d) 151, 47 O.R. (3d) 800 (headnote only), 185 D.L.R. (4th) 618, [2000] L.V.I. 3109-1, [2000] 1 S.C.R. 538, 253 N.R. 223, 22 Admin. L.R. (3d) 1, 133 O.A.C. 43, Bastarache J. (dissenting). 5. Includes the conferring of a power of appointment and any provision whereby an interest in property or a right, power or authority over property is disposed of, created or conferred and also includes a possibility of reverter or resulting trust, and a right of re-entry on breach of a condition subsequent. *Perpetuities Act*, R.S.A. 2000, c. P-5, s. 1. 6. Any instrument executed pursuant to this Act, the former Act, The Provincial Lands Act, R.S.A. 1942, c. 62, or the Dominion Lands Act (Canada), R.S.C. 1927, c. 113, whereby (i) any estate or interest in land of the Crown, or (ii) any other right or privilege in respect of land of the Crown that is not an estate or interest in land, is or has been granted or conveyed by the Crown to any person, but does not include a grant. *Public Lands Act*, R.S.A. 2000, c. P-40, s. 1. See FINAL ~; PRE- ~ REPORT; PROCEEDS OF ~.

DISPOSITIVE. *adj.* Capable of determining an issue.

DISPOSITIVE POWER. 1. The authority to distribute trust property, either capital or income or both, to a beneficiary or among several beneficiaries. 2. The authority of a trustee to draw on capital or income to maintain a beneficiary during incapacity, or to give capital to a beneficiary who takes an income interest under a testamentary trust.

DISPOSSESSION. *n.* Ouster; removal from possession.

DISPROOF. *n.* Proof that someone other than the accused, that is a third party committed the crime.

DISPROVE. *v.* To refute; to prove to be false.

DISPUTE. *n.* 1. A dispute arising in connection with the entering into, renewing or revising of a collective agreement, in respect of which notice may be given to the Minister under section 71. *Canada Labour Code*, R.S.C. 1985, c. L-2, s. 3. 2. A difference or apprehended difference between an employer or group of employers, and one or more of his or her or their employees or a trade union, as to matters or things affecting or relating to terms or conditions of employment or work done or to be done. *Labour Relations Code*, R.S.B.C. 1996, c. 244, s. 1. 3. Any dispute or difference or apprehended dispute or difference between an employer and one or more employees or a bargaining agent acting on behalf of the employees, as to matters or things affecting or relating to terms or conditions of employment or work done or to be done by the employee or employees or as to privileges, rights and duties of the employer or the employee or employees. *The Labour Relations Act*, R.S.M. 1987, c. L10, s. 1. See INDUSTRIAL ~; INTER-GOVERNMENTAL ~S; LABOUR ~; MATRIMONIAL ~; TRADE ~.

DISPUTE RESOLUTION PROCESS. A confidential and without prejudice process established by the tribunal to facilitate the settlement of one or more issues in dispute. *Administrative Tribunals Act*, S.B.C. 2004, c. 45, s. 1. See ALTERNATIVE DISPUTE RESOLUTION MECHANISM; JUDICIAL DISPUTE RESOLUTION.

DISQUALIFIED. *adj.* 1. Not eligible. 2. In which some condition precedent was not fulfilled.

DISREGARDS. *v.* Fails to pay attention to. See UNFAIRLY ~.

DISREPUTE. See BRING THE ADMINISTRATION OF JUSTICE INTO ~.

DISRUPT. See HORMONE ~ING SUBSTANCE.

DISS. *abbr.* Dissentiente.

DISSATISFIED. *adj.* "Dissatisfied" is much broader [than aggrieved]. I take it to mean that the result has failed to meet or fulfil the wish or desire or expectation of the person launching the appeal. *British Columbia (Mushroom Marketing Board) v. British Columbia (Marketing Board)*, 1988 CarswellBC 745, 31 Admin. L.R. 259 (S.C.), Trainor J.

DISSECTING ANEURYSM. Blood penetrating various layers of an artery's walls causing diffuse swelling. F.A. Jaffe, *A Guide to Pathological Evidence for Lawyers and Police Officers*, 4th ed. (Toronto: Carswell, 1999) at 230.

DISSENT. *n.* 1. Disagreement. 2. The decision of a judge who does not agree with the majority of the members of the court.

DISSENTIENTE. *adj.* Used in reports of judgments where one or more judges do not agree with the majority of the members of the court.

DISSENTING OFFEREE. A holder of a share who does not accept a take-over bid or a subsequent holder of the share who acquires it from the first-mentioned holder. *Bank Act*, S.C. 1991, c. 46, s. 283.

DISSENTING OPINION. The individual opinion of a judge who does not agree with the majority of the members of the court. Compare MAJORITY OPINION.

DISSOLUTION. *n.* 1. Putting an end to a legal entity or relation. 2. Of marriage, divorce. 3. Of Parliament, dissolution either by the expiration of five years or by proclamation. A. Fraser, W.A. Dawson & J. Holtby, eds., *Beauchesne's Rules and Forms of the House of Commons of Canada*, 6th ed. (Toronto: Carswell, 1989) at 66. 4. Of a corporation, ending of corporate existence. *Computerized Meetings & Hotel Systems Ltd. v. Moore* (1982), 20 B.L.R. 97, 40 O.R. (2d) 88, 141 D.L.R. (3d) 306 (Div. Ct.), Callaghan J.

DISSOLUTION OF MARRIAGE. "[Refers to] ... the decree absolute." *Pearce, Re* (1974), 18 R.F.L. 302 at 305, [1975] 2 W.W.R. 678, 52 D.L.R. (3d) 544 (B.C. S.C.), MacFarlane J.

DISSOLVE. *v.* To annul; to cancel; to put an end to.

DIST. *abbr.* District.

DISTANCE SALES CONTRACT. A contract for the supply of goods or services between a supplier and a consumer that is not entered into in person and, with respect to goods, for which the consumer does not have the opportunity to inspect the goods that are the subject of the contract before the contract is entered into, but does not include a prepaid purchase card. *Business Practices and Consumer Protection Act*, S.B.C. 2004, c. 2, s. 17.

DIST. CT. *abbr.* District Court.

DISTINCTION WITHOUT A DIFFERENCE. An expression referring to two expressions which though stated differently mean essentially the same thing. The use of the phrase "damages were sustained" rather than "cause of action arose", in the context of the *HTA*, is a distinction without a difference. *Peixeiro v. Haberman* [1997] 3 S.C.R. 549.

DISTINCTIVE. *adj.* 1. In relation to a trade-mark, means a trade-mark that actually distinguishes the wares or services in association with which it is used by its owner from the wares or services of others or is adapted so to distinguish them. *Trade-marks Act*, R.S.C. 1985, c. T-13, s. 2. 2. The characteristic of distinctive trade marks in Canada is that they actually distinguish the wares or services of the owner from the wares or services of others or are adapted to distinguish them. *Union Carbide Corp. v. W.R. Grace & Co.*, 1987 CarswellNat 657, 14 C.I.P.R. 59, (*sub nom. W.R. Grace & Co. v. Union Carbide Corp.*) 14 C.P.R. (3d) 337, 78 N.R. 124 (C.A.) Urie J.A. for the court.

DISTINGUISH. *v.* To clarify an essential difference.

DISTINGUISHING GUISE. A shaping of wares or their containers, or a mode of wrapping or packaging wares the appearance of which is used by a person for the purpose of distinguishing or so as to distinguish wares or services manufactured, sold, leased, hired or performed by him from those manufactured, sold, leased, hired or performed by others. *Trade-marks Act*, R.S.C. 1985, c. T-13, s. 2.

D

DISTRAIN. *v.* To seize goods using distress.

DISTRAINT. *n.* 1. Seizing. 2. Satisfying the wrong committed by taking a personal chattel from the wrongdoer and delivering to the party injured. Used to satisfy liens or arrears of rent.

DISTRESS. *n.* 1. Lawfully seizing chattels extrajudicially (not under a court order or writ) in order to enforce a right such as payment of arrears of rent or an outstanding lien. 2. Property which was distrained. 3. Anything done to exercise (i) a right of a landlord to distrain for unpaid rent, (ii) a right of a lessor of personal property to repossess, (iii) a right of a secured party to enforce a security interest under section 56(1)(a) or 58(1) of the Personal Property Security Act, (iv) a right to take possession of personal property under an order of the Court, (v) a right of distress under an enactment, or (vi) any other right under a law in force in Alberta to take personal property out of the possession of a person other than under the authority of a writ. *Civil Enforcement Act*, R.S.A. 2000, c. C-15, s. 1. See EXCESSIVE ~.

DISTRESS WARRANT. A written instruction to seize goods of the person named in the warrant. *Municipal Government Act*, R.S.A. 2000, c. M-26, s. 437.

DISTRIBUTE. *v.* To deliver, handle, keep for sale or sell.

DISTRIBUTING COOPERATIVE. In subsection 2(1) of the Act and subject to subsection (2), "distributing cooperative" means (a) a cooperative that is a "reporting issuer" under any legislation that is set out in column 2 of an item of Schedule 4; or (b) in the case of a cooperative that is not a "reporting issuer" referred to in paragraph (a), a cooperative (i) that has filed a prospectus or registration statement under provincial legislation or under the laws of a jurisdiction outside Canada, (ii) any of the securities of which are listed and posted for trading on a stock exchange in or outside Canada, or (iii) that is involved in, formed for, resulting from or continued after an amalgamation, a reorganization, an arrangement or a statutory procedure, if one of the participating entities is a cooperative to which subparagraph (i) or (ii) applies. *Canada Cooperatives Act*, S.C. 1998, c. 1, s. 2, *Canada Cooperatives Regulations*, SOR/99-256, s. 1.1.

DISTRIBUTING CORPORATION. 1. A corporation, any of the issued securities of which are or were part of a distribution to the public and remain outstanding and are held by more than one person.

DISTRIBUTION. *n.* Where used in relation to trading in securities, (a) a trade in a security of an issuer that has not been previously issued, (b) a trade by or on behalf of an issuer in a previously issued security of that issuer that has been redeemed or purchased by or donated to that issuer, (c) a trade in a previously issued security of an issuer from the holdings of a control person, (d) a trade by or on behalf of an underwriter in a security which was acquired by that underwriter, acting as underwriter, before the coming into force of this section, if that security continues, on the day this section comes into force, to be owned by or on behalf of that underwriter so acting, (e) a transaction or series of transactions involving further purchases and sales in the course of or incidental to a distribution. *Securities acts.* See MUTUAL FUND ~ ENTITY.

DISTRIBUTION OF POWERS. The division of legislative powers between regional authorities (provincial legislatures) and a central authority (the federal Parliament) which is the main feature of a federal constitution, binds the regional and central authorities, and cannot be altered by the unilateral action of any one of them.

DISTRIBUTION UNDERTAKING. An undertaking for the reception of broadcasting and the retransmission thereof by radio waves or other means of telecommunication to more than one permanent or temporary residence or dwelling unit or to another such undertaking. *Broadcasting Act*, S.C. 1991, c. 11, s. 2.

DISTRIBUTOR. See EXCLUSIVE ~.

DISTRICT. *n.* 1. A regional administrative unit. 2. A judicial district. 3. A local improvement district. 4. A school district. See ELECTORAL ~; IMPROVEMENT ~.

DISTRICT COUNCIL. An organization of union locals in a particular geographical area.

DISTRICT COURT. A court limited in territorial jurisdiction by subject matter and by value of property or claim at stake.

DISTURBANCE. *n.* 1. Infringement of an easement, franchise, profit à prendre or similar right. 2. Causing a tenant to leave through force, menace, persuasion or otherwise. 3. In section 175(a) of the Criminal Code, "[P]ublicly exhibited disorder ... violent noise or confusion disrupting the tranquillity of those in the area in question. *R. v. Lohnes* (1991), 10 C.R. (4th) 125 at 133, [1992] 1 S.C.R. 167, 69 C.C.C. (3d) 289, 109 N.S.R. (2d) 145, 297 A.P.R. 145, 132 N.R. 297, the court per McLachlin J. 4. Odour, dust, flies, light, smoke, noise and vibration. *Farming and Food Production Protection Act, 1998*, S.O. 1998, c. 1, s. 1.

DIV. *abbr.* Divisional.

DIV. & MATR. CAUSES CT. *abbr.* Divorce and Matrimonial Causes Court.

DIV. CT. *abbr.* Divisional Court.

DIVERS. *adj.* [Fr.] Various, sundry.

DIVERSITY. See BIO~.

DIVEST. *v.* 1. To take away; to deprive. 2. To remove an estate or interest which was already vested in a person.

DIVIDED COURT. Applied to a court consisting of more than one judge when the decision or opinion of the court is not unanimous.

DIVIDED CUSTODY. "... [T]he children to divide their time between the two homes, living in each temporarily, on some type of rotating basis... ." *Colwell v. Colwell* (1992), 38 R.F.L. (3d) 345 at 349, 128 A.R. 4 (Q.B.), Bielby J.

DIVIDEND. *n.* 1. The division of profits of a corporation or trust. 2. "A payment from profits, whether in cash, specie or the shares of another company, is in essence a dividend." *Canadian Pacific Ltd., Re* (1990), 47 B.L.R. 1 at 30, 72 O.R. (2d) 545, 68 D.L.R. (4th) 9 (H.C.), Austin J. 3. Includes bonus or any distribution to shareholders as such. *Companies Act*, R.S.A. 2000, c. C-21, s. 1. See ACCRUED ~; ACCUMULATED ~; ACCUMULATIVE ~; CASH ~; CUM ~; CUMULATIVE ~; EX ~; INTERIM ~; LIMITED-~ HOUSING COMPANY; PREFERRED ~; STOCK ~.

DIVISIBLE. *adj.* "... [T]hat may be taken apart... ." *R. v. Ciesielski* (1958), 26 W.W.R. 695 at 701, 29 C.R. 312, 122 C.C.C. 247 (Alta. C.A.), Porter J.A.

DIVISIBLE OBLIGATION. An obligation is divisible by operation of law, unless it is expressly stipulated that it is indivisible or unless the object of the obligation, owing to its nature, is not susceptible of division either materially or intellectually. *Civil Code*, S.Q. 1991, c. 64, a. 1519. See INDIVISIBLE OBLIGATION.

DIVISION. *n.* 1. In the House of Commons, a recorded vote. A. Fraser, W.A. Dawson, & J. Holtby, eds., *Beauchesne's Rules and Forms of the House of Commons of Canada*, 6th ed. (Toronto: Carswell, 1989) at 91. 2. An administrative unit. See ADJUDICATION ~; APPEAL ~; ELECTORAL ~; IMMIGRATION ~; REFUGEE PROTECTION ~; SUB~.

DIVISIONAL COURT. The Divisional Court of the Superior Court of Justice. *Legislation Act, 2006*, S.O. 2006, c. 21, Sched. F, s. 87.

DIVORCE. *n.* 1. "... [D]issolution of marriage ..." *Hurson v. Hurson* (1970), 73 W.W.R. 765 at 767, 1 R.F.L. 19, 11 D.L.R. (3d) 759 (B.C. C.A.), the court per McFarlane J.A. 2. Dissolution and annulment of marriage and includes nullity of marriage. *Vital Statistics Act*, R.S.O. 1990, c. V.4, s. 1. See CONTESTED ~; DESK ORDER ~; NO-FAULT ~; UN-CONTESTED ~.

DIVORCE PROCEEDING. A proceeding in a court in which either or both spouses seek a divorce alone or together with a child support order, a spousal support order or a custody order. *Divorce Act*, R.S.C, 1985, c. 3 (2nd Supp.), s. 2.

D.J.C. *abbr.* Canadian Current Law: Documentaton juridique au Canada, 1991-.

D.L.Q. *abbr.* Droits et libertés au Québec, 1986-1987.

D.L.R. *abbr.* Dominion Law Reports, 1912-1955.

D.L.R. (4TH). *abbr.* Dominion Law Reports (Fourth Series), 1984-.

D.L.R. (2D). *abbr.* Dominion Law Reports (Second Series), 1956-1968.

D.L.R. (3D). *abbr.* Dominion Law Reports (Third Series), 1969-1984.

DMCA. *abbr.* Digital Millennium Copyright Act, U.S.

DNA. *abbr.* 1. Deoxyribonucleic acid. *DNA Identification Act*, S.C. 1998, c. 37, s. 2. 2. A two-stranded helical molecule which bears genetic information. F.A. Jaffe, *A Guide to Pathological Evidence for Lawyers and Police Officers*, 4th ed. (Toronto: Carswell, 1999) at 235. See FORENSIC ~ ANALYSIS.

DNA DATA BANK. The national DNA data bank established by the Solicitor General of Canada under section 5 of the DNA Identification Act. *DNA Identification Act*, S.C. 1998, c. 37, *DNA Identification Regulations*, SOR/2000-300, s. 1. See NATIONAL ~.

DNA PROFILE. The results of forensic DNA analysis of a bodily substance. *DNA Identification Act*, S.C. 1998, c. 37, s. 2.

D.O.A. *abbr.* Dead on arrival. F.A. Jaffe, *A Guide to Pathological Evidence for Lawyers and Police Officers*, 4th ed. (Toronto: Carswell, 1999) at 235.

DOCK. *n.* The physical location in which a prisoner is placed during trial in a criminal court.

DOCKET. *v.* To make a list of entries; to keep track of time spent on matters.

DOCKET. *n.* 1. A record of the time and disbursements a lawyer spent on a particular matter. 2. A list of cases to be heard.

DOCTOR-PATIENT PRIVILEGE. Recognized by statute provincially. Protects the disclosure of information provided in the doctor-patient relationship.

DOCTRINE. *n.* A rule or principle of law. See CLEAN HANDS ~; COLLATERAL ATTACK ~; COMMUNITY OF INTEREST ~; DOUBLE ASPECT ~; EQUITABLE ~ OF CONSTRUCTIVE NOTICE; EXHAUSTION ~; IDENTIFICATION ~; LAST ANTECEDENT ~; LAST CLEAR CHANCE ~; NATIONAL CONCERN ~; OPEN FIELDS ~; PLAIN VIEW ~; SHAM ~; SPENT BREACH ~.

DOCTRINE OF ACQUIESCENCE. "In the first place the plaintiff must have made a mistake as to his legal rights. Secondly, the plaintiff must have expended some money or must have done some act (not necessarily upon the defendant's land) on the faith of his mistaken belief. Thirdly, the defendant, the possessor of the legal right, must know of the existence of his own right which is inconsistent with the right claimed by the plaintiff. If he does not know of it he is in the same position as the plaintiff and the doctrine of acquiesence is founded upon conduct with a knowledge of your legal rights. Fourthly, the defendant, the possessor of the legal right, must know of the plaintiff's mistaken belief of his rights. If he does not, there is nothing which calls upon him to assert his own rights. Lastly, the defendant, the possessor of the legal rights must have encouraged the plaintiff in his expenditure of money or in the other acts which he has done, either directly or by abstaining from asserting his legal right. Where all of these elements exist, there is a fraud of such a nature as will entitle the court to restrain the possessor of the legal right from exercising it, but, in my judgment, nothing short of this will do." *Wilomot v. Barber* (1880), 15 Ch. D. 96 at 105-106, Fry J. See ACQUIESCENCE.

DOCTRINE OF COLLATERAL BENEFITS. Precludes a tortfeasor from setting off monies paid to the plaintiff under an insurance contract against the damages payable to the plaintiff.

DOCTRINE OF CULMINATING INCIDENT. Where an employee has engaged in a final act of misconduct or course of conduct for which disciplinary action may be imposed, the employer properly may consider the employment record in determining the sanction that is appropriate for the final incident.

DOCTRINE OF EQUITABLE SUBORDINATION. Assuming, for the sake of argument only, that Canadian courts have the power in insolvency matters to subordinate otherwise valid claims to those of other creditors on equitable grounds relating to the conduct of these creditors inter se, this Court has been presented with insufficient grounds to justify the exercise of such a power in the case at bar. Briefly put, the reasons and limited evidence advanced by the Legal Representative before this Court disclose neither inequitable conduct on the part of the Participants nor injury to the ordinary creditors of CCB as a result of the alleged misconduct. As I understand it, in the United States there are three requirements for a successful claim of equitable subordination: (1) the claimant must have engaged in some type of inequitable conduct; (2) the misconduct must have resulted in injury to the creditors of the bankrupt or conferred an unfair advantage on the claimant; and (3) equitable subordination of the claim must not be inconsistent with the provisions of the bankruptcy statute. Even if this Court were to accept that a comparable doctrine to equitable subordination should exist in Canadian law, I do not view the facts of this case as giving rise to the "inequitable conduct" and ensuing "detriment" necessary to trigger its application. *Canada Deposit Insurance Corp. v. Canadian Commercial Bank*, 1992 CanLII 49, 97 D.L.R. (4th) 385 (S.C.C.).

DOCTRINE OF EQUIVALENTS. It has been established that a patent owner has a remedy against an alleged infringer who does not take the letter of the invention but nevertheless appropriates its substance (or "pith and marrow"). This extended protection of the patentee is recognized in Anglo-Canadian law, and also finds expression in modified form in the United States under the doctrine of equivalents, which is said to be available against the producer of a device that performs substantially the same function in substantially the same way to obtain substantially the same result. The U.S. approach is to disaggregate the invention as described in the patent claims into its constituent parts, as we do, but instead of characterizing an element as essential or non-essential, they treat all elements as "material". *Free World Trust c. Électro Santé Inc.*, 2000 CarswellQue 2728, 2000 SCC 66, 194 D.L.R. (4th) 232, 263 N.R. 150, [2000] 2 S.C.R. 1024, 9 C.P.R. (4th) 168, Binnie J.

DOCTRINE OF FEDERAL PARAMOUNTCY. See FEDERAL PARAMOUNTCY.

DOCTRINE OF FUNCTIONALITY. A thing that is primarily functional cannot be a trademark. Intended to prevent a person from obtaining a patent through the guise of a trademark. *Kirkbi AG v. Ritvik Holdings Inc. / Gestions Ritvik Inc.*, 2003 FCA 297.

DOCTRINE OF IMPLIED INVITATION. This doctrine [of implied invitation] holds that members of the public are given an implied license to pass over private property leading up to the point of access or entry (typically the front door) of a dwelling where they have a lawful reason to seek the consent from a resident to enter the dwelling. *R. v. Clarke* (2005), 196 C.C.C. (3d) 426. (Ont. C.A.).

DOCTRINE OF SHELTERING. Anyone who buys with notice from another person who bought without notice can be sheltered under the first buyer. W.B. Rayner & R.H. McLaren, *Falconbridge on Mortgages*, 4th ed. (Toronto: Canada Law Book, 1977) at 149.

DOCTRINE OF SUBROGATION. If a mortgagee or unpaid vendor insures an interest in property and receives insurance money when a loss occurs, and if that mortgagee or vendor afterwards receives the mortgage money or the purchase price with no deduction on account of the insurance, that mortgagee or vendor is liable to the insurer for a sum equal to the insurance money received, because one is not entitled to more than full indemnification. W.B. Rayner & R.H. McLaren, *Falconbridge on Mortgages*, 4th ed. (Toronto: Canada Law Book, 1977) at 792.

DOCTRINE OF THE TABULA IN NAUFRAGIO. An equitable mortgagee who takes with no notice of an earlier equitable mortgage may get in the legal estate and in some cases obtain priority over the earlier mortgagee. W.B. Rayner & R.H. McLaren, *Falconbridge on Mortgages*, 4th ed. (Toronto: Canada Law Book, 1977) at 126.

DOCUMENT. *n.* 1. "... [S]omething which gives you information... . something which makes evident what would otherwise not be evident... . the form which the so-called document takes is perfectly immaterial so long as it is information conveyed by something or other; it may be anything, upon which there is written or inscribed information." *R. v. Hill*, [1945] 1 All E.R. 414 at 417 (U.K. K.B.), Humphreys J. 2. Information inscribed on a medium constitutes a document. The information is delimited and structured, according to the medium used, by tangible or logical features and is intelligible in the form of words, sounds or images. The information may be rendered using any type of writing, including a system of symbols that may be transcribed into words, sounds or images or another system of symbols. For the purposes of this Act, a database whose structuring elements allow the creation of documents by delimiting and structuring the information contained in the database is considered to be a document. A record may comprise one or more documents. In this Act, a technology-based document is a document in any medium based on any information technology referred to in paragraph 2 of section 1. *An Act to establish a Legal framework for information technology*, R.S.Q. c. C-1.1, s. 15. See AFFIDAVIT OF ~S;

CABINET ~S; CORE ~; ELECTION ~; ELECTRONIC ~; FALSE ~; INSPECTION OF ~S; ORIGINAL ~ RULE; ORIGINATING ~; PRIVILEGED ~; PUBLIC ~; SHIPPING ~; UTTERING FORGED ~.

DOCUMENTARY CREDIT. A conditional letter of credit providing that any draft drawn under it may be negotiated only if bills of lading, invoices and insurance policies valued at least equally to the draft accompany the draft.

DOCUMENTARY EVIDENCE. A document or paper adduced to prove its contents.

DOCUMENT OF TITLE. 1. Includes any bill of lading, dock warrant, warehousekeeper's certificate and warrant or order for the delivery of goods and any other document used in the ordinary course of business as proof of the possession or control of goods, or authorizing or purporting to authorize, either by endorsement or by delivery, the possessor of the document to transfer or receive goods thereby represented. *Sale of Goods acts.* 2. A writing issued by or addressed to a bailee (a) that covers goods in the bailee's possession that are identified or are fungible portions of an identified mass, and (b) in which it is stated that the goods identified in it will be delivered to a named person, or to a transferee of the person, or bearer or to the order of a named person. Any writing that purports to be issued by or addressed to a bailee and purports to cover such goods in the bailee's possession as are identified or fungible portions of an identified mass, and that in the ordinary course of business is treated as establishing that the person in possession of it is entitled to receive, hold and dispose of the document and the goods it covers. *Personal Property Security acts.*

DOCUMENT OF TITLE TO GOODS. Includes a bought and sold note, bill of lading, warrant, certificate or order for the delivery or transfer of goods or any other valuable thing, and any other document used in the ordinary course of business as evidence of the possession or control of goods, authorizing or purporting to authorize, by endorsement or by delivery, the person in possession of the document to transfer or receive any goods thereby represented or therein mentioned or referred to. *Criminal Code*, R.S.C. 1985, c. C-46, s. 2.

DOCUMENT OF TITLE TO LANDS. Includes any writing that is or contains evidence of the title, or any part of the title, to real property or to any interest in real property, and any notarial or registrar's copy thereof and any duplicate instrument, memorial, certificate or document authorized or required by any law in force in any part of Canada with respect to registration of titles that relates to title to real property or to any interest in real property. *Criminal Code*, R.S.C. 1985, c. C-46, s. 2.

DOG. *n.* Any of the species Canis familiaris Linnaeus. See GUIDE ~; HEARING ~.

DOG GUIDE. 1. A dog trained to guide a visually handicapped person. *Act to Secure Handicapped Persons in the Exercise of Their Rights With a View to Achieving Social, School and Workplace Integration*,

S.Q. 1978, c. 7, s. 76. 2. A dog that serves as a guide or leader for a visually impaired person and has been trained for that purpose. *The Human Rights Code*, S.M. 1987-88, c. 45, s. 1. 3. A dog trained to assist a person with a disability or a disease which causes the person to require assistance. See GUIDE DOG.

DOLI CAPAX. [L.] Capable of a criminal act.

DOLI INCAPAX. [L.] Not capable of a criminal act.

DOLLAR. *n.* The monetary unit of Canada is the dollar. It is equivalent to one hundred cents.

DOM. *abbr.* Dominion.

DOMAIN. See EMINENT ~; PUBLIC ~.

DOMAIN NAME. An electronic address on the internet.

DOMESTIC AMENDING FORMULA. A procedure to amend the Constitution in Canada without the need to involve the British Parliament.

DOMESTIC ANIMAL. 1. An animal that is kept under human control or by habit or training lives in association with man. *Provincial Parks Act*, R.S.N.S. 1989, c. 367, s. 3. A horse, a dog or any other animal that is kept under human control or by habit or training lives in association with humans. 2. An animal that is tame or kept, or that has been or is being sufficiently tamed or kept, to serve some purpose for people. *Community Charter*, S.B.C. 2003, c. 26, Sched., s. 1.

DOMESTIC CONTRACT. 1. A marriage contract, separation agreement, cohabitation agreement, paternity agreement or family arbitration agreement. *Family Law Act*, R.S.O. 1990, c. F.3, s. 51. 2. A marriage contract, separation agreement, cohabitation agreement or paternity agreement. *Family Law Act*, R.S.N. 1990, c. F-2, s. 2.

DOMESTIC CREDIT. See ELIGIBLE ~.

DOMESTIC SERVICE. An air service between points in Canada, from and to the same point in Canada or between Canada and a point outside Canada that is not in the territory of another country. *Canada Transportation Act*, S.C. 1996, c. 10, s. 55.

DOMESTIC TRIBUNAL. "... [N]ot created or empowered by statute and is not part of an incorporated entity." *Rees v. U.A., Local 527* (1983), 4 Admin. L.R. 179 at 183, 43 O.R. (2d) 97, 83 C.L.L.C. 14,067, 150 D.L.R. (3d) 493 (Div. Ct.), Henry J.

DOMESTIC VIOLENCE. (i) Any intentional or reckless act or omission that causes bodily harm or damage to property; (ii) any act or threatened act that causes a reasonable fear of bodily harm or damage to property; (iii) forced confinement; or (iv) sexual abuse. *The Victims of Domestic Violence Act*, S.S. 1994, c. V-6.02, s. 2.

DOMICILE. *n.* A person's permanent home or principal establishment to which that person intends to return after every absence.

DOMINANT TENEMENT. A subject or tenement to the benefit of which an easement or servitude is constituted.

DOMINANT TIDE. 1. Refers to the following comment: The history of Canadian constitutional law has been to allow for a fair amount of interplay and indeed overlap between federal and provincial powers. It is true that doctrines like interjurisdictional and Crown immunity and concepts like "watertight compartments" qualify the extent of that interplay. But it must be recognized that these doctrines and concepts have not been the dominant tide of constitutional doctrines; rather they have been an undertow against the strong pull of pith and substance, the aspect doctrine and, in recent years, a very restrained approach to concurrency and paramountcy issues. *OPSEU v. Ontario (Attorney General)*, [1987] 2 S.C.R. 2, Dickson, C.J. 2. The "dominant tide" finds its principled underpinning in the concern that a court should favour, where possible, the ordinary operation of statutes enacted by both levels of government. In the absence of conflicting enactments of the other level of government, the Court should avoid blocking the application of measures which are taken to be enacted in furtherance of the public interest. *Canadian Western Bank v. Alberta*, [2007] 2 S.C.R. 3, 2007 SCC 22, Binnie and LeBel JJ.

DOMINION. *n.* 1. Any of the following Dominions, that is to say, the Dominion of Canada, the Commonwealth of Australia, the Dominion of New Zealand, the Union of South Africa, the Irish Free State and Newfoundland. *Statute of Westminster, 1931*, (U.K.), 22 Geo. V, c. 4, s. 1, reprinted in R.S.C. 1985, App. Doc. No. 27. 2. Dominion of Canada. *Interpretation Act*, R.S.Q., c. I-16, s. 61. 3. Includes kingdom, empire, republic, commonwealth, state, province, territory, colony, possession and protectorate and, where parts of a dominion are under both a central and a local legislature, includes all parts under the central legislature and each part under a local legislature. *Evidence acts*.

DOMINION COMPANY. A company incorporated by or under an Act of the Parliament of Canada. *The Companies Act*, R.S.S. 1978, c. C-23, s. 3.

DOMINUS LITIS. [L. master of the suit] One who has control over a judicial proceeding or an action.

DOMITAE NATURAE. See ANIMALS ~.

DONATIO. *n.* [L.] Gift.

DONATIO INTER VIVOS. [L.] A gift between persons still living.

DONATIO MORTIS CAUSA. [L.] "... [T]hree essential conditions, ... first, the gift must have been made in contemplation, though not necessarily in expectation, of death; second, there must have been delivery to the donee of the subject-matter of the gift; third, the gift must be made under such circumstances as to show that the thing is to revert to the donor in case he should recover." *Szczepkowski v. Eppler*, [1945] 4 D.L.R. 104 at 110, [1945] O.R. 540 (C.A.), the court per Roach J.A. See GIFT MORTIS CAUSA.

DONATION. *n.* 1. Includes any gift, testamentary disposition, deed, trust or other form of contribution. *Historical Resources Act*, R.S.A. 2000, c. H-9, s. 1. 2. "To constitute a valid donation there must be suf-

ficient words of gift, and an act... ." *Blain v. Terryberry* (1862), 9 Gr. 286 at 295 (Ont. H.C.), Spragge V.C.

DONATIVE INTENT. The intention of making a gift.

DONATIVE PROMISE. A promise to confer a benefit by gift.

DONE. See EQUITY LOOKS ON THAT AS ~ WHICH OUGHT TO BE ~.

DONEE. *n.* 1. Any person who receives or has received the benefit of a gift, including a gift deemed, for the purposes of this Act, to have been made. *An Act to Provide for Gift Tax*, S.N.S. 1972, c. 9, s. 1. 2. One to whom a gift is made. 3. A person to whom a power of appointment is given is sometimes called the donee of the power.

DONOR. *n.* 1. One who gives. 2. Any individual who makes or has made a gift, including a gift deemed, for the purposes of this Act, to have been made. *An Act to Provide for Gift Tax*, S.N.S. 1972, c. 9, s. 1. 3. (a) In relation to human reproductive material, the individual from whose body it was obtained, whether for consideration or not; and (b) in relation to an in vitro embryo, a donor as defined in the regulations. *Assisted Human Reproduction Act*, S.C. 2004, c. 2, s. 3.

DOSIMETRY SERVICE. A prescribed facility for the measurement and monitoring of doses of radiation. *Nuclear Safety and Control Act*, S.C. 1997, c. 9, s. 2.

DOUBLE. See DAILY ~.

DOUBLE ASPECT DOCTRINE. "... [S]ubjects which in one aspect and for one purpose fall within sect. 92 [of the Constitution Act, 1867 (30 & 31 Vict.), c.3], may in another aspect and for another purpose fall within sect. 91." *Hodge v. The Queen* (1883), 9 App. Cas. 117 at 130 (P.C.).

DOUBLE COSTS. Double the fees assessed on a party and party basis under Rule 57(2). Special costs, on the other hand, are assessed under Rule 57(3). Thus, double costs do not include double special costs, but only double party and party costs. *Insurance Corp. of British Columbia v. Eurosport Auto Co.*, 2007 BCCA 279.

DOUBLE CRIMINALITY. The test under [s. 18(1)(b) of the Extradition Act, R.S.C. 1985, c. E-23] embodies the "double criminality" rule. This rule underlies the structure of the extradition process and has its origins in the principle of reciprocity. The rule is designed to protect the fundamental rights of an individual whose extradition is being sought by ensuring that a person is not surrendered to another country for conduct not considered to be a criminal offence in the country from which extradition is sought. *D'Agostino, Re*, 2000 CarswellOnt 465, 47 O.R. (3d) 257, 143 C.C.C. (3d) 158, 129 O.A.C. 166, 72 C.R.R. (2d) 198.

DOUBLE DIPPING. Term that has come to describe the situation where, after an equal division of assets on marriage breakdown, one spouse claims continued support from the previously divided or equalized assets of the other spouse. This usually arises when a pension is involved. Describes the situation where a pension, once equalized as property between spouses, is also treated as income from which the pension-holding spouse must make spousal support payments. *Boston v. Boston*, 2001 CarswellOnt 2432, 2001 SCC 43, 201 D.L.R. (4th) 1, 17 R.F.L. (5th) 4, 271 N.R. 248, 149 O.A.C. 50, Major J. (McLachlin C.J.C., Gonthier, Iacobucci, Bastarache, Binnie and Arbour JJ. concurring).

DOUBLE ENTRY. Describing books of account kept by posting each entry as a debit and credit.

DOUBLE HEARSAY. Hearsay based upon hearsay.

DOUBLE INSURANCE. An insured is over-insured by double insurance if two or more marine policies are effected by or on behalf of the insured on the same marine adventure and interest or part thereof and the sums insured exceed the indemnity allowed by this Act. *Marine Insurance Act*, S.C. 1993, c. 22, s. 86.

DOUBLE JEOPARDY. A second prosecution for the same offence. See RULE AGAINST ~.

DOUBLE MOTHER RULE. Provided that if a child's mother and paternal grandmother did not have a right to Indian status other than by virtue of having married Indian men, the child had Indian status only up to the age of 21. *McIvor v. Canada (Registrar of Indian & Northern Affairs)*, 2009 BCCA 153, Groberman J.A. (Newbury and Tysoe JJ.A. concurring).

DOUBLE PATENTING. 1. There may only be one patent covering an invention. A challenge to patent validity based on double patenting does not require the existence of identical language in the two patent claims. Even so, the wording of the claims, however different, must claim the same invention. *Sanofi-Synthelabo Canada Inc. v. Apotex Inc.*, 2008 SCC 61. 2. The inventor is only entitled to "a" patent for each invention: Patent Act, s. 36(1). If a subsequent patent issues with identical claims, there is an improper extension of the monopoly. It is clear that the prohibition against double patenting involves a comparison of the claims rather than the disclosure, because it is the claims that define the monopoly. The question is how "identical" the claims must be in the subsequent patent to justify invalidation. *Whirlpool Corp. v. Camco Inc.*, 2000 SCC 67.

DOUBLE RECOVERY. Term that has come to describe the situation where, after an equal division of assets on marriage breakdown, one spouse claims continued support from the previously divided or equalized assets of the other spouse. This usually arises, as here, when a pension is involved. Used to describe the situation where a pension, once equalized as property, is also treated as income from which the pension-holding spouse (here the husband) must make spousal support payments. Expressed another way, upon marriage dissolution the payee spouse (here the wife) receives assets and an equalization payment that take into account the capital value of the husband's future pension income. If she later shares in the pension income as spousal support when the pension is in pay after the husband has retired, the wife can be said to be recovering twice from the pension: first at the time of the equalization of assets and again as support from the pension income. *Boston v. Boston* 2001, CarswellOnt 2432, 2001 SCC 43, 201 D.L.R. (4th) 1, 17 R.F.L. (5th) 4, 271 N.R. 248, 149 O.A.C. 50, Major J. (McLachlin C.J.C., Gonthier, Iacobucci, Bastarache, Binnie and Arbour JJ. concurring).

DOUBT. See REASONABLE ~.

DOVETAILING. *n.* The practice of merging seniority lists so that employees of both former bargaining units are credited with seniority as of their date of hire with their respective former employers.

DOWER. *n.* A life interest in one-third of any freehold estate of inheritance of which the husband died solely seised in possession either through a tenant or by himself and then brought with him into the marriage or acquired afterwards. A. Bissett-Johnson & W.M. Holland, eds., *Matrimonial Property Law in Canada* (Toronto: Carswell, 1980) at I-10.

DOWN. See READING ~; REDEEM UP, FORECLOSE ~; SET ~ FOR TRIAL.

DOWNER. *n.* A sedating or tranquilizing drug. F.A. Jaffe, *A Guide to Pathological Evidence for Lawyers and Police Officers*, 4th ed. (Toronto: Carswell, 1999) at 235.

DOWN PAYMENT. A sum of money, the value of a negotiable instrument payable on demand, or the agreed value of goods, given on account at the time of entering the contract.

D.P.P. *abbr.* Director of Public Prosecutions.

DRAFT. *n.* 1. An order drawn by one person on another for the payment of money, i.e. a bill of exchange or cheque. 2. An order for the payment of money drawn by one banker on another. See FINAL ~; OVER~.

DRAFTSMAN. *n.* Any person who drafts a legal document.

DRAIN. See LATERAL ~.

DRAINAGE WORKS. Includes a drain constructed by any means, including the improving of a natural watercourse, and includes works necessary to regulate the water table or water level within or on any lands or to regulate the level of the waters of a drain, reservoir, lake or pond, and includes a dam, embankment, wall, protective works or any combination thereof. *Drainage Act*, R.S.O. 1990, c. D.17, s. 1.

DRAMATIC WORK. Includes (a) any piece for recitation, choreographic work or mime, the scenic arrangement or acting form of which is fixed in writing or otherwise, (b) any cinematographic work, and (c) any compilation of dramatic works. *Copyright Act*, R.S.C. 1985, c. C-42, s. 2.

DRAPER. *abbr.* Draper (Ontario), 1828-1831.

DRAUGHT. *n.* 1. An order drawn by one person on another for the payment of money, i.e. a bill of exchange or cheque. 2. An order for the payment of money drawn by one banker on another.

DRAW. *v.* To write a bill of exchange and sign it.

DRAWEE. *n.* The person to whom a bill of exchange is addressed.

DRAWER. *n.* 1. The person who signs or makes a bill of exchange. 2. The person who addresses a depository bill. *Depository Bills and Notes Act*, S.C. 1998, c. 13, s. 2.

DRESSING. *n.* The physical ability of the insured, or the insured's requirement to have verbal cuing, to dress and undress himself or herself. *Automobile Accident Insurance Act*, R.S.S. 1978, c. A-35, *The Personal Injury Benefits Regulations*, R.R.S., c. A-35, Reg. 3, Appendix D, Grid A, s. 2.

DRINK. *n.* One 5 fluid ounce (142 ml) glass of wine, 12 fluid ounces (341 ml) of beer or 1 1/2 fluid ounces (42.6 ml) of 40% rum, vodka or whisky. F.A. Jaffe, *A Guide to Pathological Evidence for Lawyers and Police Officers*, 4th ed. (Toronto: Carswell, 1999) at 99.

DRIVER. *n.* 1. A person who drives or is in actual physical control of a vehicle. *Traffic Safety Act*, R.S.A. 2000, c. T-6, s. 1. 2. Includes a person who has the care or control of a motor vehicle whether it is in motion or not. 3. Includes street car operator. 4. Includes the rider of a bicycle.

DRIVER'S LICENCE. A licence which has been issued under this Act, including a licence issued to a novice driver, authorizing the person to whom it is issued to drive a motor vehicle and which has not expired or been suspended or cancelled. *Highway Traffic Act*, R.S.N. 1990, c. H-3, s. 2.

DRIVING. See NEGLIGENT ~.

D.R.L. *abbr.* Décisions de la Régie du logement (Québec), 1982-1993.

DROIT. *n.* [Fr.] Equity; justice; right.

DROP DEAD RULE. 1. A rule of court which requires a court to dismiss an action if nothing has been done to materially advance the processing of the action within a certain period of time. 2. The second rule is rule 244.1, the drop dead rule being considered in this case, which provides that an action shall be dismissed when there has been 5 or more years where no thing has been done to materially advance the action. *Sinnott v. Canadian Pacific Railway Co.*, 2009 ABQB 442.

DROWNING. See WET ~.

D.R.S. *abbr.* Dominion Report Service.

DRUG. *n.* 1. Includes any substance or mixture of substances manufactured, sold or represented for use in (a) the diagnosis, treatment, mitigation or prevention of a disease, disorder, abnormal physical state, or the symptoms thereof, in man or animal, (b) restoring, correcting or modifying organic functions in man or animal, or (c) disinfection in premises in which food is manufactured, prepared or kept. *Food and Drugs Act*, R.S.C. 1985, c. F-27, s. 2. 2. Any substance that is capable of producing a state of eu-

phoria, depression, hallucination or intoxication in a human being. 3. "... [A]ny substance or chemical agent the consumption of which will bring about impairment as contemplated by s. 234 [of the Criminal Code, R.S.C. 1970, c. C-34]." *R. v. Marionchuk* (1978), 1 M.V.R. 158 at 162, 4 C.R. (3d) 178, [1978] 6 W.W.R. 120, 42 C.C.C. (2d) 573 (Sask. C.A.), the court per Culliton C.J.S. See BRAND-NAME ~; DESIGNER ~; GENERIC ~; HALLUCINOGENIC ~; ILLICIT ~; LIMITED ACCESS ~.

DRUG ABUSE. 1. (a) Addiction to a substance other than alcohol; or (b) the use, whether habitual or not, of a substance other than alcohol that is capable of inducing euphoria, hallucinations or intoxication in a person. 2. For the purposes of this Act, a child is abusing a drug if the child is using the drug and the use caused or is likely to cause significant (a) psychological or social harm to the child, or (b) physical harm to the child or others. *Protection of Children Abusing Drugs Act*, S.A. 2005, c. P-27.5, s. 1.

DRUG COMPANY. See ORIGINATING ~.

DRUGLESS PRACTITIONER. A person who practises the treatment of any ailment, disease, defect or disability of the human body by manipulation, adjustment, manual or electro-therapy or by any similar method. *Drugless Practitioners Act*, R.S.O. 1990, c. D.18, s.1.

DRUNKENNESS. *n.* Intoxication.

D.T.C. *abbr.* Dominion Tax Cases, 1920-.

D.T.E. *abbr.* Droit du travail Express, 1982-.

DUBITANTE. *adj.* [L. doubting] Used in a law report to describe a judge's doubt that a proposition is correct without a decision that it is wrong.

DUCES TECUM. [L.] Bring with you. See SUBPOENA ~.

DUE. *adj.* 1. Payable; owing. *Mail Printing Co. v. Clarkson* (1895), 25 O.A.R. 1 (C.A.), Moss J.A. 2. "... [I]n relation to moneys in respect of which there is a legal obligation to pay them may mean either that the facts making the obligation operative have come into existence with the exception that the day of payment has not yet arrived, or it may mean that the obligation has not only been completely constituted but is also presently exigible... ." *Ontario Hydro-Electric Power Commission v. Albright* (1922), 64 S.C.R. 306 at 312, [1923] 2 D.L.R. 578, Duff J. See OVER~.

DUE COURSE. See HOLDER IN ~.

DUE DILIGENCE. 1. A defence that the accused held a reasonable belief in a mistaken set of facts or that the accused took all reasonable steps to avoid the offending event. 2. In the context of an agreement of purchase and sale, refers to the requirement for the purchaser to complete all relevant searches and investigations to satisfy herself that she should complete the transaction. 3. An organization exercises due diligence if it maintains reasonable routines for communicating significant information to the individual conducting the transaction and there is reasonable compliance with those routines. Due diligence does not require an individual acting for the organization to communicate information unless: (a) that communication is part of the individual's regular duties; or (b) the individual has reason to know of the transaction and that the transaction would be materially affected by the information. *The Securities Transfer Act*, S.S. 2007, c. S-42.3, s. 3. See ALL ~.

DUELLING. *n.* Challenging or attempting by any means to provoke another person to fight a duel, attempting to provoke a person to challenge another person to fight a duel, or accepting a challenge to fight a duel is an offence. *Criminal Code*, R.S.C. 1985, c. C-46, s. 71.

DUE PROCESS OF LAW. "... [T]he phrase 'due process of law' as used in s. 1(a) [of the Canadian Bill of Rights, R.S.C. 1970, App. III] is to be construed as meaning 'according to the legal processes recognized by Parliament and the Courts in Canada.' " *Curr v. R.*, [1972] S.C.R. 889 at 916, 18 C.R.N.S. 281, 7 C.C.C. (2d) 181, 26 D.L.R. (3d) 603, Ritchie J.

DUES. *n.* Fees, rates, charges or other moneys payable by any person to the Crown under and by virtue of a lease, licence or permit.

DULY. *adv.* In the proper manner; regularly.

DUM CASTA VIXERIT. [L.] As long as she lives chastely.

DUM SOLA. [L.] As long as she remains single or unmarried.

DUM SOLA ET CASTA. [L.] As long as she remains unmarried and lives chastely.

DUNN. See RULE IN BROWNE V. ~.

DUPLICATE. *v.* To copy.

DUPLICATE. *n.* 1. A copy. 2. A counterpart of the original instrument or document made by the registrar in the usual and ordinary course of business from the original instrument or document using any chemical, mechanical or electronic technique, including, without limitation, microphotographic reproduction and electronic recording on an optical disk, that (a) is capable of recording all significant details of the original instrument or document, and (b) does not permit additions, deletions or changes from the original instrument or document. *Land Title Act*, R.S.B.C. 1996, c. 250, s. 38.

DUPLICITY. *n.* 1. "... [I]f the information in one count charges more than one offence, it is bad for duplicity ..." *R. v. Sault Ste. Marie (City)* (1978), 7 C.E.L.R. 53 at 57, [1978] 2 S.C.R. 1299, 3 C.R. (3d) 30, 21 N.R. 295, 40 C.C.C. (2d) 353, 85 D.L.R. (3d) 161, the court per Dickson J. 2. "... [T]he practice of including more than one claim in a pleading." *Flexi-Coil Ltd. v. Rite Way Manufacturing Ltd.* (1989), 28 C.P.R. (3d) 256 at 259, 31 F.T.R. 73, [1990] 1 F.C. 108, Giles (Associate Senior Prothonotary).

DURANTE. [L.] During.

DURANTE ABSENTIA. [L.] During absence.

DURESS. *n.* 1. "... [A] threat of death or serious physical injury is necessary to constitute duress at common law: ... Mere fear does not constitute duress in the absence of a threat, either express or implied." *R. v. Mena* (1987), 34 C.C.C. (3d) 304 at 320, 322, 57 C.R. (3d) 172, 20 O.A.C. 50 (C.A.), the court per Martin J.A. 2. "... [T]hreats must be made to a person who is a party and with the intention of inducing that person to enter into the agreement sought to be avoided; ... duress makes a contract voidable at the initiative of the innocent party, but there cannot be duress unless the acts complained of constitute a coercion of the complaining party's will so as to vitiate the consent of that party: ..." *Byle v. Byle* (1990), 46 B.L.R. 292 at 304, 65 D.L.R. (4th) 641 (B.C. C.A.), the court per Macdonald J.A. 3. "Economic pressure does not amount to duress unless there is a coercion of will to the point that the payment or contract was not a voluntary act." *Century 21 Campbell Munro Ltd. v. S & G Estates Ltd.* (1992), 89 D.L.R. (4th) 413 at 417, 54 O.A.C. 315 (Div. Ct.), the court per Campbell J. 4. Can constitute a defence to a criminal charge including one of conspiracy. See ECONOMIC ~.

DURESS COLORE OFFICII. [L.] Abuse of an official or governmental position in which the official requires a person to pay in order to obtain some authority, licence, permission or power to act or proceed in a particular way.

DURESS OF PROPERTY. Wrongful seizure or detention of a plaintiff's goods.

DURESS OF THE PERSON. Actual or threatened physical violence to a person, or violence or threatened violence to the physical safety of others, such as members of a debtor's family. The concept extends to threats of criminal process which might lead to imprisonment.

DURESS PER MINAS. Duress by threat. Codified in section 17 of the Criminal Code as to principals. Parties to offences may seek to have their behaviour excused by duress by threat. *R. v. Hibbert* (1995), 99 C.C.C. (3d) 193. (S.C.C.).

DURING. *prep.* Throughout; while.

DUTIES. *n.* Any duties or taxes levied or imposed on imported goods under the Customs Tariff, the Excise Act, 2001, the Excise Tax Act, the Special Import Measures Act or any other Act of Parliament, but, for the purposes of subsection 3(1), paragraphs 59(3)(b) and 65(1)(b), sections 69 and 73 and subsections 74(1), 75(2) and 76(1), does not include taxes imposed under Part IX of the Excise Tax Act. *Customs Act*, R.S.C. 1985, c. 1 (2nd Supp.), s. 2. See CUSTOM DUTY; CUSTOMS DUTY.

DUTY. *n.* 1. A requirement which the law recognizes and which acts to avoid conduct characterized by unreasonable risk of danger to other persons. 2. A duty imposed by law. *Criminal Code*, R.S.C. 1985, c. C-46, s. 219(2). See ACTIVE ~; ACTIVITY ~; AD VALOREM ~; CUSTOM ~; CUSTOMS ~; DISCRETIONARY ~; ESTATE ~; EXCISE ~; FIDUCIARY ~; MINISTERIAL ~; NON-DELEGABLE ~ RULE; OCCUPANCY ~; PROBATE ~; SPECIAL ~ SERVICE; STATUTORY ~; SUCCESSION ~.

D

DUTY COUNSEL. A lawyer appointed to assist any person appearing in court without having retained a lawyer.

DUTY OF CARE. "... [A] device which the courts have developed to control the extent to which defendants would otherwise be liable in negligence. In its modern manifestation as a basic principle of negligence, it owes its origin to the following words of Lord Atkins in M'Alister (Donoghue) v. Stevenson, [1932] A.C. 562 ... at pp. 580-581: 'Who, then, in law is my neighbour? The answer seems to be – persons who are so closely and directly affected by my act that I ought reasonably to have them in contemplation as being so affected when I am directing my mind to the acts or omissions which are called in question.' " *Layden v. Canada (Attorney General)* (1991), (*sub nom. Brewer Brothers v. Canada (Attorney General)*) 8 C.C.L.T. (2d) 45 at 68, 129 N.R. 1, [1992] 1 F.C. 25, 45 F.T.R. 325n (C.A.), the court per Stone J.A. See NEIGHBOUR TEST; PRIMA FACIE ~.

DUTY OF FAIRNESS. See DUTY TO ACT FAIRLY.

DUTY OF LOYALTY. A lawyer has a duty to both current and former clients to keep their confidences: MacDonald Estate v. Martin, 1990 CanLII 32, [1990] 3 S.C.R. 1235. Consequently, a lawyer must not act in any matter which puts that obligation in conflict with the duties owed to current clients. To current clients, the lawyer also owes a broader duty of loyalty which goes beyond the duty to keep their confidences. This duty includes avoiding conflicting interests, providing zealous representation and being candid: R. v. Neil, 2002 SCC 70, [2002] 3 S.C.R. 631 at para. 19. *Brookville Carriers Flatbed GP Inc. v. Blackjack Transport Ltd.*, 2008 NSCA 22, Cromwell J. (Roscoe and Saunders JJ.A. concurring).

DUTY TO ACCOMMODATE. Employers and others governed by human rights legislation are now required in all cases to accommodate the characteristics of affected groups within their standards, rather than maintaining discriminatory standards supplemented by accommodation for those who cannot meet them. Incorporating accommodation into the standard itself ensures that each person is assessed according to her or his own personal abilities, instead of being judged against presumed group characteristics. *British Columbia (Superintendent of Motor Vehicles) v. British Columbia (Council of Human Rights)*, 1999 CarswellBC 2730, [2000] 1 W.W.R. 565, 47 M.V.R. (3d) 167, 249 N.R. 45, 70 B.C.L.R. (3d) 215, 181 D.L.R. (4th) 385, 36 C.H.R.R. D/129, [1999] 3 S.C.R. 868, 131 B.C.A.C. 280, 214 W.A.C. 280, the court per McLachlin J. See ACCOMODATION.

DUTY TO ACCOUNT. The duty of a trustee to have his accounts always ready, to afford all reasonable facilities for inspection and examination, and to give full information whenever required. *Sandford v. Porter* (1889), 16 O.A.R. 565 at 571.

DUTY TO ACT FAIRLY. 1. "Fairness involves compliance with only some of the principles of natural justice. Professor de Smith, Judicial Review of Administrative Action (1973), 3rd ed. p. 208, expressed lucidly the concept of a duty to act fairly: 'In general it means a duty to observe the rudiments of natural justice for a limited purpose in the exercise of functions that are not analytically judicial but administrative.' " *Martineau v. Matsqui Institution* (1979), 106 D.L.R. (3d) 385 at 411-12, [1980] 1 S.C.R. 602, 12 C.R. (3d) 1, 15 C.R. (3d) 315, 50 C.C.C. (2d) 353, 30 N.R. 119, Dickson J. 2. "... The basic objective of the duty to act fairly is to ensure that an individual is provided with a sufficient degree of participation necessary to bring to the attention of the decision-maker any fact or argument of which a fair-minded decision-maker would need to be informed in order to reach a rational conclusion." *Kindler v. Canada (Minister of Justice)* (1987), 1 Imm. L.R. (2d) 30 at 37, 8 F.T.R. 222, [1987] 2 F.C. 145, 34 C.C.C. (3d) 78, Rouleau J. See ECONOMIC DURESS; FAIRNESS.

DUTY TO CONSULT. While s. 35 of the Constitution Act does not on its face change the character of aboriginal rights, the constitutional common law has developed a "duty to consult" before some aboriginal rights can be affected. The duty to consult arises when "when the Crown has knowledge, real or constructive, of the potential existence of the Aboriginal right or title and contemplates conduct that might adversely affect it": Haida Nation v. British Columbia (Minister of Forests), 2004 SCC 73, [2004] 3 S.C.R. 511, 2004 SCC 73 at para. 35; Taku River Tlingit First Nation v. British Columbia (Project Assessment Director), 2004 SCC 74, [2004] 3 S.C.R. 550, 2004 SCC 74 at para. 25. The duty to consult is of course a duty to consult collectively; there is no duty to consult with any individual. There can however be no duty to consult prior to the passage of legislation, even where aboriginal rights will be affected: Authorson v. Canada (Attorney General), 2003 SCC 39, [2003] 2 S.C.R. 40. It cannot be suggested there are any limits on Parliament's right to amend the Indian Act. It would be an unwarranted interference with the proper functioning of the House of Commons and the Provincial Legislatures to require that they engage in any particular processes prior to the passage of legislation. The same is true of the passage of regulations and Orders in Council by the appropriate Executive Council. Enactments must stand or fall based on their compliance with the constitution, not based on the processes used to enact them. Once enactments are in place, consultation only becomes an issue if a prima facie breach of an aboriginal right is sought to be justified. Administrative tribunals often do have a duty to consult when their orders will have an impact on aboriginal rights. R. v. Lefthand, 2007 ABCA 206, Slatter J.A. See DUTY TO CONSULT AND ACCOMMODATE.

DUTY TO CONSULT AND ACCOMMODATE. The government's duty to consult with Aboriginal peoples and accommodate their interests is grounded in the honour of the Crown. The honour of the Crown is always at stake in its dealings with Aboriginal peoples: see for example R. v. Badger, 1996 CanLII 236, [1996] 1 S.C.R. 771, at para. 41; R. v. Marshall, 1999 CanLII 665, [1999] 3 S.C.R. 456. It is not a mere incantation, but rather a core precept that finds its application in concrete practices. ... The historical roots of the principle of the honour of the Crown suggest that it must be understood generously in order to reflect the underlying realities from which it stems. In all its dealings with Aboriginal peoples, from the assertion of sovereignty to the resolution of claims and the implementation of treaties, the Crown must act honourably. Nothing less is required if we are to achieve "the reconciliation of the pre-existence of aboriginal societies with the sovereignty of the Crown." The jurisprudence of this Court supports the view that the duty to consult and accommodate is part of a process of fair dealing and reconciliation that begins with the assertion of sovereignty and continues beyond formal claims resolution. Reconciliation is not a final legal remedy in the usual sense. Rather, it is a process flowing from rights guaranteed by s. 35(1) of the Constitution Act, 1982. The foundation of the duty in the Crown's honour and the goal of reconciliation suggest that the duty [to consult] arises when the Crown has knowledge, real or constructive, of the potential existence of the Aboriginal right or title and contemplates conduct that might adversely affect it. Knowledge of a credible but unproven claim suffices to trigger a duty to consult and accommodate. The content of the duty, however, varies with the circumstances. The content of the duty to consult and accommodate varies with the circumstances. Precisely what duties arise in different situations will be defined as the case law in this emerging area develops. In general terms, however, it may be asserted that the scope of the duty is proportionate to a preliminary assessment of the strength of the case supporting the existence of the right or title, and to the seriousness of the potentially adverse effect upon the right or title claimed. The duty to consult and accommodate here at issue is grounded in the assertion of Crown sovereignty which pre-dated the Union. It follows that the Province took the lands subject to this duty. It cannot therefore claim that s. 35 deprives it of powers it would otherwise have enjoyed. *Haida Nation v. British Columbia (Minister of Forests)*, [2004] 3 S.C.R. 511, 2004 SCC 73.

DUTY TO DEFEND. An insurer's duty which arises when the claim against the insured alleges a set of facts which, if proven, would fall within the coverage of the policy issued by the insurer to the insured.

DUTY TO KEEP CONFIDENCE. A lawyer has a duty to both current and former clients to keep their confidences: MacDonald Estate v. Martin, 1990 CanLII 32, [1990] 3 S.C.R. 1235. Consequently, a lawyer must not act in any matter which puts that obligation in conflict with the duties owed to current clients. To current clients, the lawyer also owes a broader duty of loyalty which goes beyond the duty to keep their confidences. This duty includes avoiding conflicting interests, providing zealous representation and being candid: R. v. Neil, 2002 SCC 70, [2002] 3 S.C.R. 631 at para. 19. *Brookville Carriers Flatbed GP Inc. v.Blackjack Transport Ltd.*, 2008 NSCA 22, Cromwell J. (Roscoe and Saunders JJ.A. concurring).

DUTY TO MITIGATE. The requirement that the plaintiff take all reasonable steps to minimize a loss which follows a breach of contract or injury.

DWELLING. *n.* 1. "... [P]lace of residence, a place in which to live, a habitation." *Read v. Read*, [1950] 2 W.W.R. 812 at 813, [1950] 4 D.L.R. 676 (B.C. C.A.), the court per Sloan C.J.B.C. 2. A premises or any part thereof occupied as living accommodation. See DEFENCE OF ~; SEASONAL ~.

DWELLING-HOUSE. *var.* **DWELLING HOUSE.** 1. Dwelling-house does not mean a separate, single-family building. It means any place a person dwells. *R. v. Kutschera*, 1999 CarswellBC 2751, 1999 BCCA 748, 141 C.C.C. (3d) 254, 131 B.C.A.C. 120, 214 W.A.C. 120, Southin J.A. (dissenting). 2. The whole or any part of a building or structure that is kept or occupied as a permanent or temporary residence and includes (a) a building within the yard of a dwelling-house that is connected to it by a doorway or by a covered and enclosed passageway, and (b) a unit that is designed to be mobile and to be used as a permanent or temporary residence and that is being used as a residence. *Anti-Personnel Mines Convention Implementation Act*, S.C. 1997, c. 33, s. 2.

DWELLING UNIT. A room or suite of rooms used or intended to be used as a domicile by one or more persons and usually containing cooking, eating, living, sleeping and sanitary facilities. *Architects Act*, R.S.O. 1990, c. A.26, s. 11.

D.W.I. *abbr.* Died without issue.

DYING DECLARATION. "... [S]tatement made under a sense of impending death ..." *R. v. Davidson* (1898), 30 N.S.R. 349 at 359 (C.A.), Henry J.A.

DYING WITHOUT ISSUE. Dying without any child being born before or after death.

DYSON DECLARATION. The name refers to Dyson v. Attorney General [1911] 1 K.B. 410 (C.A.). It is a declaratory judgment in an action in which the Attorney General, as representative of the Crown, is a party. *Cummins v. Canada* (1997), 50 B.C.L.R. (3d) 262. (S.C.).

D

E

E. & A. *abbr.* Grant's Upper Canada Error and Appeal Reports, 1846-1866.

E. & O.E. *abbr.* Errors and omissions excepted.

EARLY CHILDHOOD EDUCATION. See PRACTICE OF ~.

EARLY CHILDHOOD EDUCATOR. A member of the College of Early Childhood Educators. *Education Act*, R.S.O. 1990, c. E.2, s. 1.

EARN. *v.* 1. To acquire income or profit through effort or enterprise. 2. To acquire income on an investment. 3. Of interest, to receive.

EARNEST. *n.* That which is given by a buyer and accepted by a seller to indicate that a contract has been made.

EARNEST MONEY. Money paid as a deposit to ensure that the land sale transaction is adhered to by the purchaser. *Coal Harbour Properties Partnership v. Liu*, 2006 BCCA 385, Hall J.A. (Saunders and Lowry JJ.A. concurring).

EARNINGS. *n.* 1. The pay received or receivable by an employee for work done for an employer. 2. "[As used in the Unemployment Insurance Act, S.C. 1970-71-72, c. 48, s. 58(q)] ... in the broad sense are everything the worker derives in the form of pecuniary benefits from his work present or past, and in this sense a pension is still undoubtedly earnings, ..." *Côté v. Canada (Employment & Immigration Commission)* (1986), 13 C.C.E.L. 255 at 262, 86 C.L.L.C. 14,050, 69 N.R. 126 (Fed. C.A.), Marceau J.A. (Pratte J. concurring). See INSURABLE ~.

EASEMENT. *n.* 1. A landowner's right to use another's land for a particular purpose, for example a right of way or a right to extract a mineral. 2. "... [A] right annexed to land which permits the owner of a dominant tenement to require the owner of a servient tenement to suffer something on such land. There are four characteristics of an easement: (1) There must be a dominant and a servient tenement. (2) An easement must accommodate the dominant tenement. (3) Dominant and servient owners must be different persons. (4) A right over land cannot amount to an easement unless it is capable of forming the subject-matter of a grant." *Vannini v. Sault Ste. Marie Public Utilities Commission* (1972), [1973] 2 O.R. 11 at 16, 32 D.L.R. (3d) 661 (H.C.), Holland J. See AFFIRMA-TIVE ~; APPARENT ~; CONSERVATION ~; NEGATIVE ~; POSITIVE ~; PRESCRIPTIVE ~.

EASEMENT IN GROSS. An easement created by private grant or statute, e.g. a power line or pipeline. J.V. DiCastri, *Occupiers' Liability* (Vancouver: Burroughs/Carswell, 1980) at 212.

EASEMENT OF APPARENT CONVENIENCE. An easement which is necessary to the reasonable enjoyment of the property granted and which has been and is at the time of the grant used by the owners of the entirety for the benefit of the part granted. *Wheeldon v. Burrows* (1879), 12 Ch. D. 31.

EASEMENT OF NECESSITY. A right of way which arises by implication when access to a property is impossible without access over an adjoining property.

EBITDA. *abbr.* Earnings before interest, taxes, depreciation and amortization.

E.C.B. *abbr.* Expropriations Compensation Board.

ECCLESIASTICAL. *adj.* Set apart for or belonging to the church.

ECCLESIASTICAL COURT. A court with jurisdiction in ecclesiastical matters only.

ECCLESIASTICAL LAW. Law which relates to the government, obligations and rights of a church.

ECOLOGICAL INTEGRITY. With respect to a park, a condition that is determined to be characteristic of its natural region and likely to persist, including abiotic components and the composition and abundance of native species and biological communities, rates of change and supporting processes. *Canada National Parks Act*, S.C. 2000, c. 32, s. 2.

ECOLOGY. *n.* The study of the interrelationship of living things, including humans and plants, with their respective environments. *The Ecological Reserves Act*, R.S.M. 1987, c. E5, s. 1.

ECONOMIC DEVELOPMENT AGENCY OF CANADA FOR THE REGIONS OF QUEBEC. Established by the Economic Development Agency of Canada for the Regions of Quebec Act, S.C. 2005, c. 26, s. 2.

ECONOMIC DURESS. "... [A]s used in recent cases ... is not more than a recognition that in our modern life the individual is subject to societal pressures which can be every bit as effective, if improperly used, as those flowing from threats of physical abuse... . It must be a pressure which the law does not regard as legitimate and it must be applied to such a degree as to amount to 'a coercion of the will', ... or it must place the party to whom the pressure is directed in a position where he has no 'realistic alternative' but to submit to it, ..." *Stott v. Merit Investment Corp.* (1988), 19 C.C.E.L. 68 at 92, 25 O.A.C. 174, 63 O.R. (2d) 545, 48 D.L.R. (4th) 288 (C.A.), Finlayson J.A. (Krever J.A. concurring).

ECONOMIC EMERGENCY. A dire and exceptional situation precipitated by unusual circumstances such as the outbreak of war of pending bankruptcy. *Reference re Remuneration of Judges of the Provincial Court of Prince Edward Island)* [1997] 3 S.C.R. 3.

ECONOMIC ENTITY. See FOREIGN ~.

ECONOMIC ESPIONAGE. Every person commits an offence who, at the direction of, for the benefit of or in association with a foreign economic entity, fraudulently and without colour of right and to the detriment of Canada's economic interests, international relations or national defence or national security (a) communicates a trade secret to another person, group or organization; or (b) obtains, retains, alters or destroys a trade secret. *Security of Information Act*, R.S.C. 1985, c. O-5, s. 19.

ECONOMIC HARDSHIP. In the context of the Divorce Act and spousal support, is dependent on the circumstances of the parties, is a question of degree, is not to be equated with poverty or extreme privation, can refer to health and career disadvantages arising from the marriage breakdown. It addresses compensatory and non-compensatory factors. *Bracklow v. Brackow* [1999] 1 S.C.R. 420.

ECONOMIC INTEREST. In respect of a security, (a) a right to receive or the opportunity to participate in a reward, benefit of return from a security, or (b) an exposure to a loss or a risk of a loss in respect of a security. *Securities Act*, S.Y. 2007, c. 16, s. 1.

ECONOMIC LOSS. As a cause of action, claims concerning the recovery of economic loss are identical to any other claim in negligence in that the plaintiff must establish a duty, a breach, damage and causation. Nevertheless, as a result of the common law's historical treatment of economic loss, the threshold question of whether or not to recognize a duty of care receives added scrutiny relative to other claims in negligence. In an effort to identify and separate the types of cases that give rise to potentially compensable economic loss, La Forest J., in Norsk Pacific Steamship Co., [Canadian National Railway v. Norsk Pacific Steamship Co., [1992] S.C.R. 1021], endorsed the following categories (at p. 1049): 1. The Independent Liability of Statutory Public Authorities; 2. Negligent Misrepresentation; 3. Negligent Performance of a Service; 4. Negligent Supply of Shoddy Goods or Structures; 5. Relational Economic Loss. The allegation of negligence in the conduct of negotiations does not fall within any of these classifications. As a general proposition, no duty of care

arises in conducting negotiations. While there may well be a set of circumstances in which a duty of care may be found, it has not yet arisen. *Martel Building Ltd. v. R.*, 2000 CarswellNat 2678, 2000 SCC 60, 36 R.P.R. (3d) 175, 193 D.L.R. (4th) 1, 262 N.R. 285, 3 C.C.L.T. (3d) 1, 5 C.L.R. (3d) 161, 186 F.T.R. 231(note), [2000] 2 S.C.R. 860, the court per Iacobucci and Major JJ. See CONSEQUENTIAL ~; PURE ~; RELATIONAL ~.

ECONOMIC RELATIONS. See UNLAWFUL INTERFERENCE WITH ~.

ECONOMIC ZONE. See EXCLUSIVE ~.

ECOSYSTEM. *n.* 1. A dynamic complex of plant, animal and micro-organism communities and their non-living environment interacting as a functional unit. *Canadian Environmental Protection Act, 1999*, S.C. 1999, c. 33, s. 3. 2. A complete system composed of human beings, other animals and plants in a defined area, and with the soil and climate comprising their habitat in that area. *Ecological Reserve Act*, R.S.B.C. 1996, c. 103, s. 1. See AQUATIC ~.

E-DISCOVERY. *n.* 1. Electronic discovery. 2. Discovery of electronically stored documents.

EDUCABLE. *adj.* Capable of being educated, having a level of functioning to permit learning skills beyond the most basic ones of personal hygiene and care.

EDUC. & L.J. *abbr.* Education and Law Journal.

EDUCATION. *n.* In the context of a charitable purpose, should now be understood to connote information or training provided in a structured manner and for a genuinely educational purpose, that is, to advance the knowledge or abilities of the recipients and not solely to promote a particular point of view or political orientation. Contemplates some legitimate, targeted attempt at educating others, whether through formal or informal instruction, training, plans of self-study or otherwise. *Vancouver Society of Immigrant & Visible Minority Women v. Minister of National Revenue* (1999), 164 D.L.R. (4th) 34 (S.C.C.) 2. See ADVANCEMENT OF ~.

EDUCATIONAL ASSISTANCE PAYMENT. Any amount, other than a refund of payments, paid out of an education savings plan to or for an individual to assist the individual to further the individual's education at a post-secondary school level. *Income Tax Act*, R.S.C. 1985, c. 1 (5th Supp.), s. 146.1.

EDUCATIONAL INSTITUTION. 1. An institution of learning that offers courses at a post-secondary level. 2. A technical or vocational school, a university, college or other school of higher education in Canada, approved by the Minister for the education or instruction of students pursuant to this Act. *Children of Deceased Veterans Education Assistance Act*, R.S.C. 1985, c. C-28, s. 2. 3. (a) A non-profit institution licensed or recognized by or under an Act of Parliament or the legislature of a province to provide pre-school, elementary, secondary or post-secondary education; (b) a non-profit institution that is directed or controlled by a board of education regulated by or under an Act of the legislature of a province and that provides continuing, professional or vocational education or training; (c) a department or agency of any order of government, or any non-profit body, that controls or supervises education or training referred to in paragraph (a) or (b), or (d) any other non-profit institution prescribed by regulation. *Copyright Act*, R.S.C. 1985, c. C-42, s. 2.

EDUCATION LAW. The law relating to the administration of schools and universities and the students attending them.

EDUCATION SAVINGS PLAN. An arrangement entered into between (a) any of the following, namely, (i) an individual (other than a trust), (ii) an individual (other than a trust) and the spouse or common-law partner of the individual, and (iii) a public primary caregiver of a beneficiary, and (b) a person or organization (in this section referred to as a "promoter") under which the promoter agrees to pay or to cause to be paid educational assistance payments to or for one or more beneficiaries. *Income Tax Act*, R.S.C. 1985, c. 1 (5th Supp.), s. 146.1.

EDUCATOR. *n.* A person holding a certificate, other than an assistant. *Community Care and Assisted Living Act*, S.B.C. 2002, c. 75, *Child Care Licensing Regulation*, B.C. Reg. 332/2007, App., s. 1. See ABORIGINAL ~; EARLY CHILDHOOD ~.

EFFECT. *v.* "... '[T]o bring about an event or result' ..." *Gladstone v. Catena*, [1948] 2 D.L.R. 483 at 486-7, [1948] O.R. 182 (C.A.), Laidlaw J.A.

EFFECT. *n.* See ADVERSE ~; ENVIRONMENTAL ~; LEGAL ~; REMINISCENCE ~.

EFFECTIVE. *adj.* Suitable for its purpose; accomplishing its purpose.

EFFECTIVE DATE. The date upon which a contract or agreement or legislation comes into operation.

EFFECTIVE RATE OF INTEREST. The ratio of the amount of interest earned during the year to the amount of principle invested at the beginning of the year.

EFFECTIVITY. *n.* The principle of effectivity proclaims that an illegal act may eventually acquire legal status if, as a matter of empirical fact, it is recognized on the international plane. Our law has long recognized that through a combination of acquiescence and prescription, an illegal act may at some later point be accorded some form of legal status. In the law of property, for example, it is well-known that a squatter on land may ultimately become the owner if the true owner sleeps on his or her right to repossess the land. In this way, a change in the factual circumstances may subsequently be reflected in a change in legal status. It is, however, quite another matter to suggest that a subsequent condonation of an initially illegal act retroactively creates a legal right to engage in the act in the first place. The broader contention is not supported by the international principle of effectivity or otherwise and must be rejected. *Reference re Secession of Quebec*, 1998 CarswellNat 1299, 161 D.L.R. (4th) 385, 228 N.R. 203, 55 C.R.R. (2d) 1, [1998] 2 S.C.R. 217, per curiam.

EFFECTS MONITORING. The monitoring of environmental and socio-economic effects, or of the effectiveness of mitigative measures. *Yukon Environmental and Socio-economic Assessment Act*, S.C. 2003, c. 7, s. 2.

EFFICIENCY. See ENERGY ~ STANDARD.

EFFORT. See BEST ~S.

E-FILING. *n.* Electronic filing: the filing of documents with government offices electronically. See ELECTRONIC FILING.

EFTA. *abbr.* European Free Trade Association (Iceland, Liechtenstein, Norway, Switzerland).

EFTA STATE. A member state of the European Free Trade Association, namely: (a) the Republic of Iceland; (b) the Principality of Liechtenstein; (c) the Kingdom of Norway; or (d) the Swiss Confederation. *Canada-EFTA Free Trade Agreement Implementation Act*, S.C. 2009, c. 6, s. 2.

E.G. *abbr.* [L. exempli gratia] For instance.

EGALITARIAN CIVIL LIBERTIES. Those liberties which require equal treatment of persons under the law. These include equal access to employment, accommodation, education and benefits. The right to use either of the official languages and the rights of denominational or separate schools are included in this category of civil liberties as well.

EGALITY. *n.* Equality.

EGREGIOUS. *adj.* Extraordinarily or remarkably bad or undesirable.

EGRESS. *n.* Leaving, departing.

E-HEALTH. *n.* 1. Refers to the sharing of electronic health records (personal health information) of individuals. Databases of information are designated by order. 2. A designation order may authorize the collection and use of personal health information only for one or more of the following purposes: (a) to identify an individual who needs or is receiving health services; (b) to provide health services to, or facilitate the care of, an individual; (c) to identify a person who is providing health services; (d) to prevent or manage chronic conditions, at the individual or population level; (e) to facilitate health insurance and health service billing, including for the purposes of (i) a payment in respect of health services or prescribed drugs, devices or pharmaceutical services to be made to or by the government of British Columbia or a public body, (ii) authorizing, administering, processing, verifying or cancelling such a payment, (iii) resolving an issue regarding such a payment, or (iv) audits by a federal or Provincial government payment agency that makes reimbursement for the cost of health services or prescribed drugs, devices or pharmaceutical services; (f) to assess and address public health needs; (g) to engage in health services planning, maintenance or improvement, including (i) health service development, management, delivery, monitoring and evaluation, (ii) compiling statistical information, and (iii) public health surveillance; (h) to conduct or facilitate research into health issues; (i) to assess and address threats to public health. *E-*

Health (Personal Health Information Access and Protection of Privacy) Act, S.B.C. 2008, c. 38, s. 4.

EJECTMENT. *n.* "... [A]n action for the recovery of land; ..." *Point v. Dibblee Construction Co.*, [1934] O.R. 142 at 153, [1934] 2 D.L.R. 785 (H.C.), Armour J. See ACTION OF ~.

EJUSDEM GENERIS. [L. of the same kind] "Where there are general words following particular and specific words, the general words must be confined to things of the same kind as those specified. The principle applies only where the special words are of the same nature and can be grouped together in the same genus; where there are different genera the meaning of the general words is unaffected by their collocation with the special words and must be given their full and ordinary meaning." *Reg. v. Edmundson* (1859), 28 L.J.M.C. 213 at 215, Lord Campbell C.J.

ELDER. *n.* An Aboriginal person who is (a) a member of an Aboriginal community; and (b) is recognized by the members of the Aboriginal community as having extensive knowledge of the culture and traditional practices of that community. *Firearms Act*, S.C. 1995, c. 39, *Aboriginal Peoples of Canada Adaptations Regulations (Firearms)*, SOR/98-205, s. 1.

ELDER LAW. Law relating to mature individual clients: age discrimination, care-facility regulation, guardianship, substitute decision-makers, wills, estate planning, trust planning, powers of attorney.

ELECT. *v.* To make a choice or decision between alternatives; to choose for office.

ELECTION. *n.* 1. Making a choice. 2. Choosing a member or members to serve in the House of Commons, in a provincial legislature or on a municipal council. 3. In the context of choosing judicial review or appeal after having accepted an award, the essence of the doctrine of election is that a person is properly precluded from exercising a right that is fundamentally inconsistent with another right if he has consciously and unequivocally exercised the latter. In other words, one cannot have one's cake and eat it too, or one cannot blow hot and cold. *A.U.P.E. v. Lethbridge Community College* 2002 ABCA 125, [2002] 8 W.W.R. 299. See BY-~; ESTOPPEL BY ~; FIXED DATE ~; GENERAL ~.

ELECTION ADVERTISING. The transmission to the public by any means during an election period of an advertising message that promotes or opposes a registered party or the election of a candidate, including one that takes a position on an issue with which a registered party or candidate is associated. For greater certainty, it does not include (a) the transmission to the public of an editorial, a debate, a speech, an interview, a column, a letter, a commentary or news; (b) the distribution of a book, or the promotion of the sale of a book, for no less than its commercial value, if the book was planned to be made available to the public regardless of whether there was to be an election; (c) the transmission of a document directly by a person or a group to their members, employees or shareholders, as the case may be; or (d) the transmission by an individual, on a non-commercial basis on what is commonly known as the Internet, of his or her personal political views. *Canada Elections Act*, S.C. 2000, c. 9, s. 319.

ELECTION ADVERTISING EXPENSE. An expense incurred in relation to (a) the production of an election advertising message; and (b) the acquisition of the means of transmission to the public of an election advertising message. *Canada Elections Act*, S.C. 2000, c. 9, s. 349.

ELECTION DOCUMENT. 1. Any document or writing issued under the authority of an Act of Parliament or the legislature of a province with respect to an election held pursuant to the authority of that Act. *Criminal Code*, R.S.C. 1985, c. C-46, s. 377. 2. The following documents: (a) the writ with the return of the election endorsed on it; (b) the nomination papers filed by the candidates; (c) the reserve supply of undistributed blank ballot papers; (d) documents relating to the revision of the lists of electors; (e) the statements of the vote from which the validation of results was made; and (f) the other returns from the various polling stations enclosed in sealed envelopes, as required by Part 12, and containing (i) a packet of stubs and unused ballot papers, (ii) packets of ballot papers cast for the various candidates, (iii) a packet of spoiled ballot papers, (iv) a packet of rejected ballot papers, (v) a packet containing the list of electors used at the polling station, the written authorizations of candidates' representatives and the used transfer certificates, if any, and (vi) a packet containing the registration certificates. *Canada Elections Act*, S.C. 2000, c. 9, s. 2.

ELECTION PERIOD. 1. The period beginning with the issue of the writ and ending on polling day or, where the writ is withdrawn under subsection 59(1) or is deemed to be withdrawn under section 551, on the day that the writ is withdrawn or deemed to be withdrawn. *Canada Elections Act*, S.C. 2000, c. 9, s. 2. 2. The period starting on the day an election is called and ending on election day. *The Elections Act*, S.M. 2006, c. 15, Sched. A, s. 1.

ELECTION SURVEY. An opinion survey of how electors voted or will vote at an election or respecting an issue with which a registered party or candidate is associated. *Canada Elections Act*, S.C. 2000, c. 9, s. 319.

ELECTOR. *n.* 1. Person eligible to vote at an election. 2. A person entitled to vote at an election. 3. A person qualified to vote at an election. 4. A person who is qualified as an elector under section 3. Every person who is a Canadian citizen and is 18 years of age or older on polling day is qualified as an elector. The following persons are not entitled to vote at an election: (a) the Chief Electoral Officer; (b) the Assistant Chief Electoral Officer; and (c) every person who is imprisoned in a correctional institution serving a sentence of two years or more. *Canada Elections Act*, S.C. 2000, c. 9, s. 2 to 4. See LIST OF ~S.

ELECTORAL DISTRICT. 1. An area entitled to elect a member to serve in a legislature. 2. The area from which a school board member is to be elected.

ELECTORAL DISTRICT ASSOCIATION. Of a political party, an association of members of the political party in an electoral district.

ELECTORAL DIVISION. Any territorial division or district entitled to return a member.

ELECTORAL SYSTEM. See SINGLE TRANSFERABLE VOTE ~.

ELECTRIC VEHICLE. See HYBRID ~.

ELECTRONIC. *adj.* Includes created, recorded, transmitted or stored in digital form or in any other intangible form by electronic, magnetic or optical means or by any other means that have similar capabilities for creation, recording, transmission or storage. *Environmental Protection and Enhancement Act*, R.S.A. 2000, c. E-12, s. 1.

ELECTRONIC AGENT. A computer program, or other electronic means, used to initiate an activity or to respond to electronic information, records or activities in whole or in part without review by an individual at the time of the response or activity. *Electronic Transactions Act*, S.B.C. 2001, c. 10, s. 1.

ELECTRONIC DISCOVERY. The discovery of evidence in electronic format.

ELECTRONIC DOCUMENT. 1. Data that is recorded or stored on any medium in or by a computer system or other similar device and that can be read or perceived by a person or a computer system or other similar device. It includes a display, printout or other output of that data. *Canada Evidence Act*, R.S.C. 1985, c. C-5, s. 31. 2. Any form of representation of information or of concepts fixed in any medium in or by electronic, optical or other similar means and that can be read or perceived by a person or by any means. Federal statutes.

ELECTRONIC DOCUMENTS SYSTEM. Includes a computer system or other similar device by or in which data is recorded or stored and any procedures related to the recording or storage of electronic documents. *Canada Evidence Act*, R. S. C. 1985, c. C-5, s. 31.8.

ELECTRONIC FILING. The filing of registry or court or other government documents electronically.

ELECTRONIC FORMAT. Includes an electronic format produced by making an electronic copy, image or reproduction of a written document. *Land Registration Reform Act*, R.S.O. 1990, c. L.4, s. 17.

ELECTRONIC HEARING. A hearing held by conference telephone or some other form of electronic technology allowing persons to hear one another.

ELECTRONIC PLAN. (a) A plan that is made in relation to Crown land and that is in electronic format, and (b) any other document that is in the electronic form designated by the Surveyor General. *Land Act*, R.S.B.C. 1996, c. 245, s. 93.9.

ELECTRONIC RECORD. Data that: (a) is recorded or stored on any medium in or by a computer or other similar device; and (b) can be read or perceived by a person or a computer or other similar device; and includes a display, printout or other output of that data, other than a printout mentioned in subsection 56(2). *The Evidence Act*, S.S. 2006, c. E-11.2, s. 54.

ELECTRONIC RECORDS SYSTEM. Includes a computer system or other similar device by or in which an electronic record is recorded or stored and includes any procedures related to the recording or storing of an electronic record. *The Evidence Act*, S.S. 2006, c. E-11.2, s. 54.

ELECTRONIC SEAL. 1. A screened image of the Seal of the Trial Division which is used by software applications authorized by the Registrar that are protected by a password to which only the Registrar or persons designated by the Registrar have access. *Rules of the Supreme Court, 1986*, S.N. 1986, c. 42, Sched. D, s. 5A.01. 2. The form of identification issued by the association to any member to be used in the electronic validation of documents in computer readable form. *The Engineering and Geoscientific Professions Act*, S.M. 1998, c. 55, s. 25.

ELECTRONIC SIGNATURE. 1. Information in electronic form that a person has created or adopted in order to sign a record and that is in, attached to or associated with the record. *Electronic Transactions Act*, S.B.C. 2001, c. 10, s. 1. 2. A signature that consists of one or more letters, characters, numbers or other symbols in digital form incorporated in, attached to or associated with an electronic document. *Personal Information Protection and Electronic Documents Act*, S.C. 2000, c. 5, s. 31. See SECURE ~.

ELECTRONIC STATEMENT. A statement in electronic form on which some or all of the particulars of an event are to be entered and submitted to the director. *The Vital Statistics Act, 2007*, S.S. 2007, c. V-7.2, s. 2.

ELECTRONIC SURVEILLANCE. Wiretapping or use of other electronic means to monitor a person's conversations and whereabouts.

ELECTRONIC VERSION. A copy of a record that has been made and stored electronically pursuant to subsection 8(2) for the purpose of keeping a permanent record of the original record. *The Vital Statistics Act, 2007*, S.S. 2007, c. V-7.2, s. 2.

ELEEMOSYNARY CORPORATION. A body corporate established to perpetually distribute free alms or its founder's gift.

ELEGIT. *n.* [L. one has chosen]. A writ of execution by which a judgment creditor is awarded the debtor's land to hold until the debt is satisfied.

ELEMENT. See COMMON ~S; FLIGHT ~.

ELEVATION. See LOW-TIDE ~.

ELEVATOR RECEIPT. A document in prescribed form issued in respect of grain delivered to an elevator acknowledging receipt of the grain and, subject to any conditions contained therein or in this Act, entitling the holder of the document (a) to the delivery of grain of the same kind, grade and quantity as the grain referred to in the document, or (b) in the case of a document issued for specially binned grain, to delivery of the identical grain. *Canada Grain Act*, R.S.C. 1985, c. G-10, s. 2.

ELICIT. *v.* To draw out, to obtain.

ELIGIBILITY. *n.* Qualification.

ELIGIBLE. *adj.* Fit or proper to be chosen; deserving.

ELIGIBLE CREDIT. An eligible domestic credit or an eligible Kyoto unit. *Canada Emission Reduction Incentives Agency Act*, S.C. 2005, c. 30, s. 2.

ELIGIBLE DOMESTIC CREDIT. A tradeable unit that is of an eligible class designated by order made under paragraph 3(a). *Canada Emission Reduction Incentives Agency Act*, S.C. 2005, c. 30, s. 2.

E.L.J. *abbr.* Education & Law Journal.

E.L.L.R. *abbr.* Employment and Labour Law Reporter, 1991-.

E.L.R. *abbr.* Eastern Law Reporter, 1906-1915.

E-MAIL. *v.* Electronically mail. To transmit a message from one person's computer, through his internet service provider, over the internet, to the intended recipient's internet service provider and then to the recipient's own computer.

E-MAIL. *n.* Electronic mail. A message sent from one person's computer to another person's computer over the internet. May also refer to multiple e-mails or to the body of messages one receives.

EMANATION. *n.* That which issues or proceeds from some source. *International Railway v. Niagara Parks Commission*, [1941] 3 D.L.R. 385 at 393, [1941] A.C. 328, [1941] 2 All E.R. 456, 53 C.R.T.C. 1 (Ont. P.C.), the board per Luxmoore L.J. Use in the expression "emanation of the Crown" was disapproved.

EMANCIPATION. n. 1. Of a minor, does not put an end to minority nor does it confer all the rights resulting from majority, but it releases the minor from the obligation to be represented for the exercise of his civil rights. *Civil Code*, S.Q. 1991, c. 64, a. 170. 2. Freeing from slavery. See FULL ~.

EMBALM. *v.* To treat human remains with chemicals for the purposes of (i) reducing the presence and growth of micro-organisms, (ii) retarding decomposition, and (iii) restoring an acceptable physical appearance. *Funeral Services Act*, R.S.A. 2000, c. F-29, s. 1.

EMBALMING. *n.* 1. The preservation of a dead human body, entire or in part, by the use of chemical substances, fluids or gases ordinarily used, prepared or intended for those purposes, either by outward application of those chemical substances, fluids or gases on the body, or by the introduction of them into the body by vascular or hypodermic injection or by direct application into the organs or cavities. *Embalmers and Funeral Directors Act, 2008*, S.N. 2008, c. E-7.1, s. 2. 2. A method of preserving a body to prevent it dissolving or putrefying. F.A. Jaffe, *A Guide to Pathological Evidence for Lawyers and Police Officers*, 4th ed. (Toronto: Carswell, 1999) at 235.

EMBARRASSING. *adj.* 1. ... A plea that is "concealing or evasive" is an irregular plea under Rule 19(21) [of the Rules of Court, 1990, B.C. Reg. 221/90]: it is capable of being reformed. It is not an "embarrassing plea". An embarrassing plea amounts to an abuse of process. *Patym Holdings Ltd. v. Michalakis*, 2005 BCCA 636, Smith J.A. (Saunders J.A. concurring). 2. " ... [P]leadings framed in such a confused or ambiguous manner as to cause real and undue embarrassment or prejudice." *Rogers v. Clark* (1900), 13 Man. R. 189 at 196 (K.B.), Killam C.J. 3. " ... [B]ringing forward a defence which the defendant is not entitled to make use of: ..." *Stratford Gas Co. v. Gordon* (1892),14 P.R. 407 at 414 (Ont. H.C.), Armour C.J. 4. " ... [T]he allegations are so irrelevant that to allow them to stand would involve useless expenses and would also prejudice the trial of the action by involving the parties in a dispute that is wholly apart from the issues." *London (Mayor) v. Ho Homer* (1914), 3 L.T.R. 512 at 514 (U.K.), Pickford L.J., cited in *Meyers v. Freeholders Oil Co.* (1956), 19 W.W.R. 546 at 549 (Sask. C.A.). See IRREGULAR.

EMBASSY. *n.* 1. An ambassador's establishment. 2. The commission given by a nation to an ambassador, to deal with another nation.

EMBEDDED. *adj.* Firmly attached within a surrounding structure.

EMBEZZLEMENT. *n.* Conversion to personal use of any chattel, money or valuable security received or taken into possession by an employee for, in the name or on account of the employer.

EMBLEM. *n.* In the context of the Trade Marks Act means symbol and is not a reference to heraldry. See ARBOREAL ~; AVIAN ~; OFFICIAL ~.

EMBLEMENTS. *n.* "... [T]he growing crops of those vegetable productions of the soil which are annually produced by the labour of the cultivator. They are a species of fructus industriales, but do not exhaust the genus." *Cochlin v. The Massey-Harris Co.* (1915), 8 Alta. L.R. 392 at 396, 8 W.W.R. 286, 23 D.L.R. 397 (C.A.), Beck J.A. (dissenting).

EMBRACERY. *n.* A common law offence of attempting to instruct or influence any jury member or giving a reward to a jury member for something done by that member.

EMBRYO. *n.* 1. A human organism during the first 56 days of its development following fertilization or creation, excluding any time during which its development has been suspended, and includes any cell derived from such an organism that is used for the purpose of creating a human being. *Assisted Human Reproduction Act*, S.C. 2004, c. 2, s. 3. 2. A child developing in utero during the first three months of pregnancy. F.A. Jaffe, *A Guide to Pathological Evidence for Lawyers and Police Officers*, 4th ed. (Toronto: Carswell, 1999) at 236. See ANIMAL ~.

EMBRYOLOGY. *n.* The study of human or animal development before birth.

EMERGENCY. *n.* 1. An urgent and critical situation that (a) is caused by drought, earthquake, fire, flood, storm, act of intimidation or coercion, threat to the security of Canada, real or imminent use of force or violence, war, armed conflict, accident or other occurrence, (b) is so severe, or of such severity in its effect on life, property, the economy of Canada or a region thereof or the environment, as to constitute a matter of serious national concern, and (c) is declared by order of the Governor in Council to be an emergency for the purposes of this Act. *Spending Control Act*, S.C. 1992, c. 19, s. 2. 2. An event that requires prompt co-ordination of action or special regulation of persons or property to protect the safety, health or welfare of people or to limit damage to property. *Emergency Management Act*, R.S.A. 2000, c. E-6.8, s. 1. 3. An insurrection, riot, invasion, armed conflict or war, whether real or apprehended. *National Defence Act*, R.S.C. 1985, c. N-5, s. 2. See DECLARATION OF ~; ECONOMIC ~; ENVIRONMENTAL ~; INTERNATIONAL ~; PROVINCIAL ~; PUBLIC ORDER ~; PUBLIC WELFARE ~; WAR ~.

EMERGENCY MANAGEMENT. The prevention and mitigation of, preparedness for, response to and recovery from emergencies. *Emergency Management Act*, S.C. 2007, c. 15, s. 2.

EMERGENCY MANAGEMENT PLAN. A program, arrangement or other measure (a) for dealing with an emergency by the civil population; or (b) for dealing with a civil emergency by the Canadian Forces in accordance with the National Defence Act. *Emergency Management Act*, S.C. 2007, c. 15, s. 2.

EMERGENCY PREPAREDNESS. See DEPARTMENT OF PUBLIC SAFETY AND ~.

EMERGENCY SERVICE PROVIDER. (a) A fire department organized to serve any area of the Province, (b) an ambulance service provided in accordance with the Ambulance Services Act, (c) a search and rescue organization, (d) any member of the Canadian Forces while engaged in rendering assistance to a lawfully constituted civilian police force, or (e) such other person or service as is prescribed by regulation. *Protected Natural Areas Act*, S.N.B. 2003, c. P-19.01, s. 1.

EMERITUS. *adj.* Retired but honoured. Retaining the same or similar status as prior to retirement.

EMIGRATION. *n.* The act of moving from one country to another with no intention of returning.

EMINENT DOMAIN. A government's right to take private property for public purposes, a doctrine which is American in origin. See EXPROPRIATION.

EMISSARY. *n.* One person sent on a mission as agent of another person.

EMISSION. *n.* That which is given off as a result of combustion or another process which creates gases or fumes. See CANADA ~ REDUCTION INCENTIVES AGENCY; NATIONAL ~S MARK.

EMISSION OFFSET. An emission offset, as established, approved or recognized under the regulations for the purpose of (a) reducing greenhouse gas emissions, or (b) reducing atmospheric greenhouse gas concentrations through storage, sequestration or

other means. *Greenhouse Gas Reduction Targets Act*, S.B.C. 2007, c. 42, s. 1.

EDMISSION REDUCTION UNIT. See BC ~.

EMISSIONS CREDIT. A credit that represents (i) a verifiable reduction in the Province's greenhouse-gas emissions inventory or forecast, or (ii) a verifiable increment of atmospheric carbon dioxide removed from the atmosphere through biological, geological or hydrological storage, sequestration or other means. *Voluntary Carbon Emissions Offset Fund Act*, S.N.S. 2010, c. 10, s. 2.

EMOLUMENTS. *n.* 1. "... '[T]he profit arising from office or employment,' and not merely the gross amount of salary, fees or perquisites, but the balance remaining after deduction of the necessary expenses paid out in earning the salary, fees or perquisites." *Lawless v. Sullivan* (1879), 3 S.C.R. 117 at 146, Henry J. 2. Includes fees, percentages and other payments made or consideration given, directly or indirectly, to a director as such, and the money value of any allowance or perquisites belonging to his office. *Companies Act*, R.S.N.S. 1989, c. 81, s. 100(4).

EMPANEL. *v.* "[S]electing a new jury from the ... jurors already summoned, ..." *R. v. Gaffin* (1904), 8 C.C.C. 194 at 196 (N.S. C.A.), the court per Graham E.J. See IMPANEL; JURY.

EMPHYTEUSIS. *n.* The right which, for a certain time, grants a person the full benefit and enjoyment of an immovable owned by another provided he does not endanger its existence and undertakes to make constructions, works or plantations thereon that durably increase its value. Emphyteusis is established by contract or by will. *Civil Code*, S.Q. 1991, c. 64, a. 1195.

EMPIRICAL. *adj.* That which is based on observation, experience or experiment.

EMPLEAD. *v.* To accuse; to indict; to bring a charge against.

EMPLOY. *v.* "... [C]an be used in the sense of the common law master/servant relationship in which control is a principle factor in determining the existence of the relationship ... common, and grammatically correct, ... to use the word[s] in the sense of 'utilize'." *Pannu, Re* (1986), (*sub nom. Pannu v. Prestige Cab Ltd.*) 87 C.L.L.C. 17,003 at 16,010, 47 Alta. L.R. (2d) 56, [1986] 6 W.W.R. 617, 73 A.R. 166, 31 D.L.R. (4th) 338, 8 C.H.R.R. D/3911 (C.A.), the court per Laycraft J.A.

EMPLOY. *n.* Employment, service.

EMPLOYED. *adj.* 1. Performing the duties of an office or employment. 2. "... '[O]ccupied or engaged'." *Might v. Minister of National Revenue*, [1948] Ex. C.R. 382 at 389, [1948] C.T.C. 144, [1949] 1 D.L.R. 250, O'Connor J. See PERSON ~ IN A MANGERIAL CAPACITY.

EMPLOYEE. *n.* 1. Any person employed by an employer and includes a dependent contractor and a private constable, but does not include a person who performs management functions or is employed in a confidential capacity in matters relating to industrial relations. *Canada Labour Code*, R.S.C. 1985, c. L-2, s. 3. 2. Includes an officer. 3. Any person who is in receipt of or entitled to any compensation for labour or services performed for another. 4. Any person who performs duties and functions that entitle that person to compensation on a regular basis. 5. A person who is in receipt of or entitled to wages. See CONTRACT ~; ESSENTIAL SERVICES ~; KEY ~; NON-UNIONIZED ~.

EMPLOYEE BARGAINING AGENCY. An organization of affiliated bargaining agents that are subordinate or directly related to the same provincial, national or international trade union, and that may include the parent or related provincial, national or international trade union, formed for purposes that include the representation of affiliated bargaining agents in bargaining and which may be a single provincial, national or international trade union. *Labour Relations Act, 1995*, S.O. 1995, c. 1, Schedule A, s. 151.

EMPLOYEE BENEFIT PLAN. A system to provide increased security to workers through schemes such as group insurance and cash benefits.

EMPLOYEE BENEFITS. Includes coverage and benefits in respect of employer-sponsored pension plans and of life, income protection, health care and dental care insurance plans. *Canada Marine Act*, S.C. 1998, c. 10, s. 138.3.

EMPLOYEE INFORMATION. See PERSONAL ~.

EMPLOYEE ORGANIZATION. 1. Includes a trade union or other organization of employees or a local, the purposes of which include the negotiation of terms and conditions of employment on behalf of employees. *Canadian Human Rights Act*, R.S.C. 1985, c. H-6, s. 25. 2. Any organization of employees the purposes of which include the regulation of relations between the employer and its employees and includes, unless the context otherwise requires, a council of employee organizations. *Public Service Labour Relations Act*, S.C. 2003, c. 22, s. 2.

EMPLOYEE PERSONAL INFORMATION. Personal information about an individual that is collected, used or disclosed solely for the purposes reasonably required to establish, manage or terminate an employment relationship between the organization and that individual, but does not include personal information that is not about an individual's employment. *Personal Information Protection Act*, S.B.C. 2003, c. 63, s. 1.

EMPLOYEES' MUTUAL BENEFIT SOCIETY. *var.* **EMPLOYEES MUTUAL BENEFIT SOCIETY.** A society incorporated by the officers or officers and employees of a corporation for the purpose of providing support and pensions to such of the officers or employees as become incapacitated or as cease to be employed by the corporation or for the purpose of paying pensions, annuities or gratuities to or for dependants of such officers or employees or funeral benefits upon the death of such officers or employees. *Insurance acts.*.

EMPLOYER. *n.* 1. Any person who employs one or more employees. *Canada Labour Code*, R.S.C. 1985, c. L-2, s. 166. 2. In relation to an officer, means the person from whom the officer receives remuneration. *Excise Tax Act*, R.S.C. 1985, c. E-15, s. 123. 3. A person liable to pay salary, wages or other remuneration for services performed in employment, and in relation to an officer includes the person from whom the officer receives his remuneration. *Canada Pension Plan*, R.S.C. 1985, c. C-8, s. 2. 4. (a) Any person who employs one or more employees, and (b) in respect of a dependent contractor, such person as, in the opinion of the Board has a relationship with the dependent contractor to such extent that the arrangement that governs the performance of services by the dependent contractor for that person can be the subject of collective bargaining. *Canada Labour Code*, R.S.C. 1985, c. L-2, s. 3. 5. Includes an employers' organization. *Canada Labour Code*, R.S.C. 1985, c. L-2, s. 88. See MULTI-~ PENSION PLAN; PARTICIPATING ~.

EMPLOYER BARGAINING AGENCY. An employers' organization or group of employers' organizations formed for purposes that include the representation of employers in bargaining. *Labour Relations Act, 1995*, S.O. 1995, c. 1, Schedule A, s. 151.

EMPLOYER ORGANIZATION. An organization of employers the purposes of which include the regulation of relations between employers and employees. *Canadian Human Rights Act*, R.S.C. 1985, c. H-6, s. 25.

EMPLOYER RIGHTS. Rights, such as hiring and price fixing, which management generally argues are not proper subjects of collective bargaining.

EMPLOYERS' ASSOCIATION. A group employers having as its objects the study and safeguarding of the economic interests of its members, and particularly assistance in the negotiation and application of collective agreements. *An Act Respecting Collective Agreement Decrees*, R.S.Q., c. D-2, s. 1.

EMPLOYERS' LIABILITY INSURANCE. Insurance (not being insurance incidental to some other class of insurance defined by or under this Act) against loss to an employer through liability for accidental injury to or death of an employee arising out of or in the course of his or her employment, but does not include workers' compensation insurance. *Insurance acts.*.

EMPLOYERS' ORGANIZATION. Organization of employers formed for purposes that include the regulation of relations between employers and employees. *Canada Labour Code*, R.S.C. 1985, c. L-2, s. 3.

EMPLOYMENT. *n.* 1. The performance of services under an express or implied contract of service or apprenticeship, and includes the tenure of an office. *Canada Pension Plan*, R.S.C. 1985, c. C-8, s. 2. 2. The act of employing or the state of being employed. *Employment Insurance Act*, S.C. 1996, c. 23, s. 2. 3. Any activity for which a person receives or might reasonably be expected to receive valuable consideration. *Immigration Act* , R.S.C. 1985, c. I-2, s. 2 [repealed]. 4. The position of an individual in the service of some other person, including Her Majesty or a foreign state or sovereign. *Income Tax Act*, R.S.C. 1985, c. 1 (5th Supp.), s. 248. 5. Includes a contractual relationship with an individual for the provision of services personally by the individual. *Canadian Human Rights Act*, R.S.C. 1985, c. H-6, s. 25. 6. "... '[A]ctivity' or 'occupation'." *Canada (Attorney General) v. Skyline Cabs (1982) Ltd.* (1986), 11 C.C.E.L. 292 at 295, 45 Alta. L.R. (2d) 296, [1986] 5 W.W.R. 16, 86 C.L.L.C. 14,047, 70 N.R. 210 (Fed. C.A.), the court per MacGuigan J.A. See ACT WITHIN SCOPE OF ~; CASUAL ~; CONDITION OF ~; CONTRACT OF ~; COURSE OF ~; INSURABLE ~.

EMPLOYMENT AGENCY. Includes a person who undertakes, with or without compensation, to procure employees for employers and a person who undertakes, with or without compensation, to procure employment for persons. *Human Rights codes.*.

EMPLOYMENT CONTRACT. 1. "... [A] contract whereby a person agrees to provide sales services in consideration of payment of salary and a commission on sales, ..." *Prozak v. Bell Telephone Co. of Canada* (1984), 4 C.C.E.L. 202 at 219, 46 O.R. (2d) 385, 4 O.A.C. 12, 10 D.L.R. (4th) 382, the court per Goodman J.A. 2. Includes a collective agreement. *Employment Standards Act, 2000*, S.O. 2000, c. 41, s. 1.

EMPLOYMENT HISTORY. The ordinary meaning of "employment history" includes not only the list of positions previously held, places of employment, tasks performed and so on, but also, for example, any personal evaluations an employee might have received during his career. Such a broad definition is also consistent with the meaning generally given to that expression in the workplace. *Canada (Information Commissioner) v. Royal Canadian Mounted Police Commissioner*, 2003 SCC 8.

EMPLOYMENT INJURY. An injury or a disease arising out of or in the course of an industrial accident, or an occupational disease, including a recurrence, relapse or aggravation. *An Act respecting industrial accidents and occupational diseases*, R.S.Q. c. A-3.001, s. 2.

EMPLOYMENT INSURANCE. A contributory, federal insurance scheme for workers who are without work or unable to look for or to do work because of injury or illness. See CANADA ~ COMMISSION.

EMPLOYMENT PLAN. A written plan which identifies a person's experience, training or upgrading needs, employment barriers, career goals, employment options, appropriate employment supports and includes services offered by other agencies. *Income and Employment Support Act*, S.N. 2002, c. I-0.1, s. 2.

EMPLOYMENT PRACTICE. See FAIR ~.

EMPLOYMENT STANDARD. A requirement or prohibition that applies to an employer for the benefit of an employee. *Employment Standards Act, 2000*, S.O. 2000, c. 41, s. 1.

EMPLOYMENT SUPPORT. Services, programs and financial benefits provided by the department to assist recipients to prepare for, access and keep employment, including self-employment, and includes other specific supports for persons with disabilities. *Income and Employment Support Act*, S.N. 2002, c. I-0.1, s. 2.

EMPTOR. *n.* A buyer.

ENABLING STATUTE. A statute which gives power or authority.

ENACT. *v.* 1. To decree; to establish by law. 2. Includes to issue, make, establish or prescribe.

ENACTING CLAUSE. 1. In federal statutes, "Her Majesty, by and with the advice and consent of the Senate and House of Commons of Canada, enacts as follows:" A. Fraser, W.A. Dawson & J. Holtby, eds., *Beauchesne's Rules and Forms of the House of Commons of Canada*, 6th ed. (Toronto: Carswell, 1989) at 193. 2. The formal portion of a by-law which describes the act or thing required to be done or forbidden. I.M. Rogers, *The Law of Canadian Municipal Corporations*, 2d ed. (Toronto: Carswell, 1971) at 417.

ENACTMENT. *n.* 1. An act or a regulation or any portion of an act or regulation. *Interpretation Act*, R.S.C. 1985, c. I-21, s. 2. Any Act, regulation, order or bylaw enacted in relation to any matter over which the Legislature has legislative authority. *Provincial Offences Procedure Act*, R.S.A. 2000, c. P-34, s. 1. 3. An Act or a regulation, by-law or other instrument having the force of law made under authority of an Act. *Land Titles Act*, S.N.B. 1981, c. L-1.1, s. 3.

EN BANC. [Fr. as a bench] Used to describe the full court sitting together to hear an appeal.

ENCROACHMENT. *n.* An attempt to extend a right a person already possesses.

ENCROACHMENT AGREEMENT. An agreement under which a municipality permits the encroachment onto a road that is under the direction, control and management of the municipality of improvements made on land that is adjoining that road. *Municipal Government Act*, R.S.A. 2000, c. M-26, s. 651.2.

ENCRYPTED. *adj.* Treated electronically or otherwise for the purpose of preventing intelligible reception. See UN~.

ENCUMBER. *v.* To attach a burden, claim, lien or liability to property.

ENCUMBRANCE. *n.* 1. Any charge on land created or effected for any purpose whatever, inclusive of mortgage, mechanics' or builders' liens, when authorized by statute, and executions against land, unless expressly distinguished. *Land Titles Act*, R.S.A. 2000, c. L-4, s. 1. 2. Includes any registered claim or interest affecting land. *Land Titles Act*, S.N.B. 1981, c. L-1.1, s. 3. 3. "... [A] charge or liability to which land is subject... ." *Seltor Holdings Ltd. v. Kettles* (1983), 29 R.P.R. 214 at 221, 43 O.R. (2d) 659, 3 C.L.R. 259, 2 D.L.R. (4th) 373 (Div. Ct.), Saunders J. 4. A claim of aboriginal title constitutes an encum-

E

209

brance, an interest in land cognizable at law. *Haida Nation v. British Columbia (Minister of Forests)* (1997), 45 B.C.L.R. (3d) 80 (C.A.). See INCUMBRANCE.

ENCUMBRANCEE. *n.* The owner of an encumbrance. *Land Titles Act*, R.S.A. 2000, c. L-4, s. 1.

ENCUMBRANCER. *n.* The owner of any land or of any estate or interest in land subject to any encumbrance. *Land Titles Act*, R.S.A. 2000, c. L-4, s. 1.

ENCYCLOPEDIA. *n.* A collective work containing a series of articles by many contributors.

ENDEAVOUR. *v.* To strenuously attempt or try to achieve an objective.

ENDEAVOURS. *n.* Strenuous efforts towards an objective.

ENDORSE. *v.* 1. To place a signature on a negotiable bill of exchange. 2. Imprinting a stamp on the face of articles or other document sent to the Director. *Business Corporations Act*, R.S.O. 1990, c. B.16, s. 1. 3. To store information in the records, including information respecting a cancellation. *Land Title Act*, R.S.B.C. 1996, c. 250, s. 1.

ENDORSED. *adj.* Applies to anything written on any instrument or on any paper attached thereto by the registrar. *Land Titles Act*, R.S.Y. 2002, c. 130, s. 1.

ENDORSEMENT. *n.* 1. Applies to anything written by the registrar upon an instrument or upon a paper attached thereto. *Land Titles Act*, R.S.Y. 2002, c. 130, s. 1. 2. An endorsement completed by delivery. *Bills of Exchange Act*, R.S.C. 1985, c. B-4, s. 2. 3. Includes entry, memorandum and notation. 4. An ordinary signature. I.F.G. Baxter, *The Law of Banking*, 3d ed. (Toronto: Carswell, 1981) at 96. 5. A signature that, alone or accompanied by other words, is made on a security certificate in registered form or on a separate document for the purpose of assigning, transferring or redeeming the security or granting a power to assign, transfer or redeem the security. *Securities Transfer acts*. 6. "... [I]n its literal sense means writing one's name of the back of the bill, ..." *Gorrie Co. v. Whitfield* (1920), 58 D.L.R. 326 at 329, 19 O.W.N. 336, 48 O.L.R. 605 (C.A.), Meredith C.J.O. (Magee and Hodgins JJ.A. concurring). 7. The inscribing of additional qualifications on a certificate. 8. A judge's writing on a document. 9. In any event, in my view, an endorsement is generally not understood to be a self-contained policy. As I have noted, the title of the Endorsement describes it as a "change form." An endorsement changes or varies or amends the underlying policy. While it may be comprehensive on the subject of the particular coverage provided in the endorsement, it is built on the foundation of the policy and does not have an independent existence. In any event, the Endorsement in this case is clearly not a stand-alone policy because it specifically provides that the policy terms remain in full force and effect, unless its terms are changed by the Endorsement. *Sutherland v. Pilot Insurance Co.*, 2007 ONCA 492. See BLANK ~; INDORSEMENT; RESTRICTIVE ~.

ENDORSER. *n.* A person who, in the case of a depository bill, signs the depository bill otherwise than as drawer or acceptor, or in the case of a depository note, signs the depository note otherwise than as maker. *Depository Bills and Notes Act*, S. C. 1998, c. 13, s. 2.

ENDOWMENT. *n.* Any kind of property belonging permanently to a charity.

ENDOWMENT INSURANCE. An undertaking to pay an ascertained or ascertainable sum at a fixed future date, if the person whose life is insured is then alive, or at the person's death if she or he dies before such date. *Insurance acts.*.

ENDURING POWER OF ATTORNEY. 1. (1) A power of attorney is an enduring power of attorney if (a) the donor is an individual who is an adult at the time of executing the power of attorney, and (b) the power of attorney meets at least the following requirements: (i) it is in writing, is dated and is signed (A) by the donor in the presence of a witness, or (B) if the donor is physically unable to sign an enduring power of attorney, by another person on behalf of the donor, at the donor's direction and in the presence of both the donor and a witness; (ii) it is signed by the witness in the presence of the donor; (iii) it contains a statement indicating that it either (A) is to continue notwithstanding any mental incapacity or infirmity of the donor that occurs after the execution of the power of attorney, or (B) is to take effect on the mental incapacity or infirmity of the donor. *Powers of Attorney Act*, R.S.A. c. P-20, s. 2. 2. A power of attorney (a) in which an adult authorizes an attorney to (i) make decisions on behalf of the adult, or (ii) do certain things in relation to the adult's financial affairs, and (b) that continues to have effect while, or comes into effect when, the adult is incapable. *Power of Attorney Act*, R.S.B.C. 1996, c. 370, s. 10.

ENEMIES. See QUEEN'S ~.

ENERGY. See NUCLEAR ~; RENEWABLE ~ SOURCE.

ENERGY COMMODITY. Oil and gas and any prescribed product resulting from the processing or refining of oil or gas and, where there is a designation in respect of coal, thorium and uranium, or any of those substances, includes all those substances, or the designated substance, as the case may be, and any prescribed product resulting from the processing or refining of the designated substance or substances. *Energy Monitoring Act*, R.S.C. 1985, c. E-8, s. 2.

ENERGY EFFICIENCY STANDARD. In respect of an energy-using product, means the standard, if any, prescribed for that product or for a class of energy-using products that includes that product. *Energy Efficiency Act*, S.C. 1992, c. 36, s. 2.

ENERGY SUPPLIES ALLOCATION BOARD. Established under the Energy Supplies Emergency Act, R.S.C. 1985, c. E-9, s. 3 and 11. The Board may exercise such powers and shall perform such duties as may be conferred or imposed on it under this Act; and during any period in which the Board is not required to administer any mandatory allocation program or rationing program under this Act, it shall prepare, review and maintain contingency plans in readiness to exercise such powers and perform such duties as may be conferred or imposed on it pursuant to this Act.

ENFEOFF. *v.* To give possession of lands or tenements.

ENFEOFFMENT. *n.* 1. Investing with a dignity or possession. 2. The deed or instrument by which one invests another with possessions.

ENFORCEABLE. *adj.* 1. "Refer[s] ... to ... [a] process ... to enable measures to be taken to secure compliance ..." *U.N.A. v. Alberta (Attorney General)* (1992), 71 C.C.C. (3d) 225 at 234, [1992] 3 W.W.R. 481, 1 Alta. L.R. (3d) 129, 13 C.R. (4th) 1, 89 D.L.R. (4th) 609, 135 N.R. 321, 92 C.L.L.C. 14,023, 9 C.R.R. (2d) 29, [1992] 1 S.C.R. 901, 125 A.R. 241, 14 W.A.C. 241, Sopinka J. (dissenting). 2. Refers to providing a penalty to induce obedience. *U.N.A. v. Alberta (Attorney General)* (1992), 71 C.C.C. (3d) 225 at 234, [1992] 3 W.W.R. 481, 1 Alta. L.R. (3d) 129, 13 C.R. (4th) 1, 89 D.L.R. (4th) 609, 135 N.R. 321, 92 C.L.L.C. 14,023, 9 C.R.R. (2d) 29, [1992] 1 S.C.R. 901, 125 A.R. 241, 14 W.A.C. 241, Sopinka J. (dissenting). See UN~.

ENFORCEMENT. *n.* Seeking to prevent breaches of the law and finding and punishing those who break the law. See LAW ~; PROVINCIAL ~ SERVICE.

ENFORCEMENT AUTHORITY. In respect of a contravention, (a) any police officer or constable, including a special or auxiliary constable, (b) the minister responsible for administering the enactment creating the contravention, (c) any person, or member of a class of persons, designated by the minister responsible for administering the enactment creating the contravention, or (d) the corporation or other body that made or is responsible for administering the enactment creating the contravention. *Contraventions Act*, S.C. 1992, c. 47, s. 2.

ENFRANCHISE. *v.* 1. To bestow a liberty; to make free. 2. To give someone the liberty to vote at an election.

ENGAGEMENT. See RULES OF ~.

ENGINEERING. *n.* The science and art of designing, investigating, supervising the construction, maintenance or operation of, making specifications inventories or appraisals of, and consultations or reports on: machinery, structures, works, plants, mines, mineral deposits, processes, transportation systems, transmission systems and communication systems or any other part thereof. *Engineering Profession Act*, R.S.N.S. 1989, c. 148, s. 2. See PROFESSIONAL ~.

ENGLISH REPORTS. The reprinted reports of English cases from 1220 to 1865.

ENGRAVINGS. Includes etchings, lithographs, woodcuts, prints and other similar works, not being photographs. *Copyright Act*, R.S.C. 1985, c. C-42, s. 2.

ENGROSS. *v.* 1. To type or write an agreement, deed or like document from a draft with all amounts, dates and words set out at length, and with the formal attestation and testatum clauses, so that the document is ready to be executed. 2. Formerly, to write in a particular script derived from the courthand in which records were written in ancient times.

ENJOIN. *v.* To prohibit by court order, the effect of an injunction.

ENJOYMENT. *n.* 1. The use or application of a right. 2. "Ordinarily ... denotes the derivation of pleasure." *R. v. Phoenix* (1991), 64 C.C.C. (3d) 252 at 255 (B.C. Prov. Ct.), de Villiers Prov. J. 3. "... [A] different sense ... in reference to [real] property ... 'possession' ..." *R. v. Phoenix* (1991), 64 C.C.C. (3d) 252 at 255 (B.C. Prov. Ct.), de Villiers Prov. J. See QUIET ~.

ENLARGE. *v.* To lengthen time. To extend.

EN PASSANT. [Fr.] In passing.

ENQUIRY. See INQUIRY.

ENRG. *abbr.* Enregistré.

ENRICHMENT. *n.* A tangible benefit. See UNJUST ~.

ENROL. *v.* 1. To enter or copy a document into an official record. 2. To cause any person to become a member of the Canadian Forces. *National Defence Act*, R.S.C. 1985, c. N-5, s. 2.

ENSLAVEMENT. *n.* The exercise of any or all of the powers attaching to the right of ownership over a person and includes the exercise of such power in the course of trafficking in persons, in particular women and children. *Crimes Against Humanity and War Crimes Act*, S.C. 2000, c. 24, Sched., *Rome Statute*, Article 7.

ENSURE. *v.* To make certain.

ENTAIL. *n.* An estate or interest in land which descends only to the grantee's issue.

ENTER. *v.* 1. When any part of his body or any part of an instrument that he uses is within anything that is being entered. *Criminal Code*, R.S.C. 1985, c. C-46, s. 350(a). 2. To come onto land. 3. To note, in a record or book, a transcript of a document or a transaction. 4. To store information in the records, including information respecting a cancellation. *Land Title Act*, R.S.B.C. 1996, c. 250, s. 1. See BREAK AND ~.

ENTER AN APPEARANCE. Shall mean "deliver a Statement of Defence", "file a Statement of Defence", "defend" or as the case may be. *Saskatchewan Queen's Bench Rules*, Sask. Q.B. Rules, s. 12D.

ENTER JUDGMENT. To deliver to the Registrar an order embodying a judgment or to cause the Registrar to make a formal record of a judgment. *Rules of the Supreme Court, 1986*, S.N. 1986, c. 42, Sched. D, s. 1.03.

ENTERPRISE. See COMMERCIAL ~; CONTRACT OF ~; MIXED ~ COMPANY; PRIVATE ~ GAAP.

ENTERPRISE CRIME OFFENCE. For the purposes of the forfeiture provisions of the Code [Criminal Code, R.S.C. 1985, c. C-46], reference to a "enterprise crime offence" includes a "designated substance offence". *R. v. Marriott* 2001 NSCA 84, 42 C.R. (5th) 339, 155 C.C.C. (3d) 168, 194 N.S.R. (2d) 64.

ENTERPRISE LOBBYIST. Any person a significant part of whose job or function within a profit-seeking enterprise consists in lobbying on behalf of the enterprise. *Lobbying Transparency and Ethics Act*, R.S.Q. c. T-11.011, s. 3.

ENTERPRISE REGISTRAR. A public officer and exercises the functions provided for by law, and attends exclusively to the work and duties of the office of enterprise registrar. The enterprise registrar has investigatory and inquiry powers. *An Act respecting the enterprise registrar*, R.S.Q. c. R-17.1, s. 1.

ENTERTAINMENT LAW. The law relating to artists, actors, athletes, musicians and the film, television, music industries and sports activities.

ENTICEMENT. *n.* The deliberate inducement of a wife to leave her husband. The inducement must be made with knowledge of her marital status and with intent to interfere with the wife's duty to give consortium to her husband. J.G. Fleming, *The Law of Torts*, 8th ed. (Sydney: Law Book, 1992) at 653-54.

ENTIRE AGREEMENT CLAUSE. Indicates that the document embodies all of the terms of the agreement between the parties.

ENTIRETY. See TENANCY BY THE ~.

ENTITLE. *v.* To bestow a right.

ENTITLED. *adj.* Clearly qualified; meeting all requirements.

ENTITLEMENT. See SECURITY ~; UNIT ~.

ENTITLEMENT HOLDER. A person identified in the records of a securities intermediary as the person having a security entitlement against the securities intermediary and includes a person who acquires a security entitlement under the Act. *Securities Transfer acts.*.

ENTITLEMENT ORDER. A notice communicated to a securities intermediary directing the transfer or redemption of a financial asset to which the entitlement holder has a security entitlement. *Securities Transfer Acts.*.

ENTITY. *n.* 1. A body corporate, trust, partnership, fund, an unincorporated association or organization, Her Majesty in right of Canada or of a province, an agency of Her Majesty in either of such rights and the government of a foreign country or any political subdivision thereof and any agency thereof. *Bank Act*, S.C. 1991, c. 46, s. 2. 2. A person other than an individual. *Bankruptcy and Insolvency Act*, R.S.C. 1985, c. B-3, s. 4. 3. A body corporate, a partnership, a trust, a joint venture or an unincorporated association or organization. *Canada Business Corporations Act*, R.S.C. 1985, c. C-44, s. 2. See CANADIAN ~; COOPERATIVE ~; FOREIGN ECONOMIC ~; FOREIGN ~; MUTUAL FUND DISTRIBUTION ~; MUTUAL FUND ~; PUBLIC SECTOR ~; REAL PROPERTY BROKERAGE ~; REGULATED ~.

ENTRANT. *n.* Trespasser, licencee, invitee or one who has contracted to and paid for the right to enter premises, a contractual entrant. See CONTRACTUAL ~; RE-~.

ENTRAPMENT. *n.* 1. "[Occurs] ... when (a) the authorities provide a person with an opportunity to commit an offence without acting on a reasonable suspicion that this person is already engaged in criminal activity or pursuant to a bona fide inquiry; (b) although having such a reasonable suspicion or acting in the course of a bona fide inquiry, they go beyond providing an opportunity and induce the commission of an offence." *R. v. Mack* (1988), 37 C.R.R. 277 at 324, [1989] 1 W.W.R. 577, [1988] 2 S.C.R. 903, 67 C.R. (3d) 1, 90 N.R. 173, 44 C.C.C. (3d) 513, the court per Lamer J. 2. Entrapment is a unique area of the criminal law. In our view, it has been somewhat inappropriately referred to as an affirmative defence. In our opinion, that misdescribes it. A claim of entrapment is in reality a motion for a stay of proceedings based on the accused's allegation of an abuse of process. It does not rely on the underlying charge and does not affect the admissibility of any evidence which might influence the jury on the merits. In particular, unlike a claim of not criminally responsible on account of mental disorder, entrapment does not go to or involve mens rea or "criminal responsibility" in any way. Entrapment concerns the conduct of the police and the Crown. The question to be answered is not whether the accused is guilty, but whether his guilt was uncovered in a manner that shocks the conscience and offends the principle of decency and fair play. *R. v. Pearson*, 1998 CarswellQue 1079, 233 N.R. 367, 130 C.C.C. (3d) 293, 21 C.R. (5th) 106, [1998] 3 S.C.R. 620, Lamer C.J.C. and Major J.

ENTRENCHED. *adj.* Able to be altered solely through a constitutional amendment.

ENTRENCHMENT CLAUSE. Section 52(3) of the Constitution Act, 1982: "Amendments to the Constitution of Canada shall be made only in accordance with the authority contained in the Constitution of Canada.".

ENTRY. *n.* 1. Going onto land. 2. Setting down a record in a book. 3. Lawful permission to come into Canada as a visitor. *Immigration Act*, R.S.C. 1985, c. I-2, s. 2 [repealed]. 4. "[In the Canada Evidence Act, R.S.C. 1970, c. E-10, s. 29(1)] ... an ordinary financial or bookkeeping entry, that is, the figures and the required explanation for such figures, in a ledger, book, card system or computer card system... ." *Minister of National Revenue v. Furnasman Ltd.*, [1973] F.C. 1327 at 1333, [1973] C.T.C. 830, 73 D.T.C. 5599 (T.D.), Addy J. 5. Includes a note, a notation or a memorandum. *Registry Act*, R.S.N.B. 1973, c. R-6, s. 13.2. See DOUBLE ~; FORCIBLE ~; RE-~; RIGHT OF ~.

ENUMERATED GROUNDS. Those grounds of discrimination listed in s. 15(1) of the Charter: race, national or ethnic origin, colour, religion, sex, age, mental or physical disability.

ENUMERATION. *n.* A general residence to residence visitation to obtain or verify information respecting residence of voters and, where necessary, to obtain applications for registration for the purpose of updating or compiling new lists of voters.

ENUMERATOR. *n.* 1. A person appointed to compile or revise a list of electors. 2. A person who takes a census.

ENURE. *v.* To take effect; to operate.

EN VENTRE SA MERE. [Fr. in the mother's womb] Describes an unborn child.

ENVIRONMENT. *n.* 1. The air, land, water, plant life, animal life and ecological systems of Ontario. *Environmental Bill of Rights, 1993*, S.O. 1993, c. 28, s.1. 2. The components of the Earth, and includes (a) land, water and air, including all layers of the atmosphere, (b) all organic and inorganic matter and living organisms, and (c) the interacting natural systems that include components referred to in paragraphs (a) and (b). *Canadian Environmental Assessment Act*, S.C. 1992, c. 37, s. 2. See HOSTILE ~; NATURAL ~; POISONED WORK ~.

ENVIRONMENTAL ACT. The Antarctic Environmental Protection Act, the Canada National Marine Conservation Areas Act, the Canada National Parks Act, the Canada Water Act, the Canada Wildlife Act, the Canadian Environmental Protection Act, 1999, the International River Improvements Act, the Migratory Birds Convention Act, 1994, the Saguenay-St. Lawrence Marine Park Act or the Wild Animal and Plant Protection and Regulation of International and Interprovincial Trade Act. *Environmental Violations Administrative Monetary Penalties Act*, S.C. 2009, c. 14, s. 2.

ENVIRONMENTAL ASSESSMENT. 1. A process by which the environmental impact of an undertaking is predicted and evaluated before the undertaking has begun or occurred. *Environmental Assessment acts.* 2. In respect of a project, an assessment of the environmental effects of the project that is conducted in accordance with this Act and the regulations. *Canadian Environmental Assessment Act*, S.C. 1992, c. 37, s. 2. See CANADIAN ~ AGENCY; CANADIAN ~ REGISTRY.

ENVIRONMENTAL ATTRIBUTES. Environmental premiums or tradable credits that are recognized in Canada or elsewhere as being derived from the generation of an amount of electric energy from a renewable energy source. *Renewable Energy Act*, S.P.E.I. 2004, c. 16, s. 1.

ENVIRONMENTAL AUDIT. 1. An independent assessment of (i) a person's compliance with this Act and approvals issued under this Act, (ii) a person's environmental plans, policies, practices, controls and records, and (iii) the extent to which a person's environmental plans, policies, practices and controls have been implemented. *Environmental Protection Act*, S.N. 2002, c. E-14.2, s. 2. 2. An internal evaluation by a company or government agency verifying its compliance with legal requirements, internal policies and standards as regards environmental concerns.

ENVIRONMENTAL EFFECT. In respect of a project, (a) any change that the project may cause in the environment, including any change it may cause to a listed wildlife species, its critical habitat or the residences of individuals of that species, as those terms are defined in subsection 2(1) of the Species at Risk Act, (b) any effect of any change referred to in paragraph (a) on (i) health and socio-economic conditions, (ii) physical and cultural heritage, (iii) the current use of lands and resources for traditional purposes by aboriginal persons, or (iv) any structure, site or thing that is of historical, archaeological, paleontological or architectural significance, or (c) any change to the project that may be caused by the environment, whether any such change or effect occurs within or outside Canada. *Canadian Environmental Assessment Act*, S.C. 1992, c. 37, s. 2.

ENVIRONMENTAL EMERGENCY. An uncontrolled, unplanned or accidental release, or release in contravention of regulations made under this Part, of a substance into the environment; or the reasonable likelihood of such a release into the environment. *Canadian Environmental Protection Act, 1999*, S.C. 1999, c. 33, s. 193.

ENVIRONMENTAL IMPACT. Any change in the present or future environment that would result from an undertaking. *Environmental Assessment acts..*

ENVIRONMENTAL LAW. The law governing the environment and natural resources and the assessment of environmental impact.

ENVIRONMENTAL QUALITY. I cannot accept that the concept of environmental quality is confined to the biophysical environment alone; such an interpretation is unduly myopic and contrary to the generally held view that the "environment" is a diffuse subject matter. The point was made by the Canadian Council of Resource and Environment Ministers, following the "Brundtland Report" of the World Commission on Environment and Development, in the Report of the National Task Force on Environment and Economy, September 24, 1987, at p. 2: Our recommendations reflect the principles that we hold in common with the World Commission on Environment and Development (WCED). These include the fundamental belief that environmental and economic planning cannot proceed in separate spheres. Long-term economic growth depends on a healthy environment. It also affects the environment in many ways. Ensuring environmentally sound and sustainable economic development requires the technology and wealth that is generated by continued economic growth. Economic and environmental planning and management must therefore be integrated. Surely the potential consequences for a community's livelihood, health and other social matters from environmental change are integral to decision-making on matters affecting environmental quality, subject, of course, to the constitutional imperatives. *Friends of the Oldman River Society v. Canada (Minister of Transport)*, 1992 CarswellAlta 218, 84 Alta. L.R. (2d) 129, [1992] 1 S.C.R. 3, [1992] 2 W.W.R. 193, 7 C.E.L.R. (N.S.) 1, 132 N.R. 321, 88 D.L.R. (4th) 1, 3 Admin. L.R . (2d) 1, 48 F.T.R. 160, La Forest J. for the majority.

E

ENVOY. *n.* A diplomatic agent sent to one nation from another.

ENZYME. See RESTRICTION ~.

E.O.E. *abbr.* Errors and omissions excepted.

EQUAL INTEREST. A joint tenant has an undivided half-interest in the whole; the generic term "equal interest" is not so precise, but would include a joint tenancy. *Tavenor Estate v. Tavenor*, 2008 NLCA 2.

EQUALITY. *n.* Can refer to the condition of same treatment of all persons. Interpreted to not necessarily mean identical treatment. Different treatment may be required to promote equality in some cases. Refers to the right to be free from discrimination based on membership in a group historically disadvantaged by prejudicial assumptions. See FORMAL ~; PROCEDURAL ~; RIGHT TO ~; SUBSTANTIVE ~.

EQUALITY BEFORE AND UNDER THE LAW. "... [A] comparative concept, the condition of which may only be attained or discerned by comparison with the condition of others in the social and political setting in which the question arises. ... admittedly unattainable ideal should be that a law expressed to bind all should not because of irrelevant personal differences have a more burdensome or less beneficial impact on one than another." *Andrews v. Law Society (British Columbia)*, 56 D.L.R. (4th) 1 at 10-11, 10 C.H.R.R. D/5719, [1989] 2 W.W.R. 289, 25 C.C.E.L. 255, 91 N.R. 255, 34 B.C.L.R. (2d) 273, 36 C.R.R. 193, 56 D.L.R. (4th) 1, [1989] 1 S.C.R. 143, McIntyre J.

EQUALITY BEFORE THE LAW. "The guarantee ... is designed to advance the value that all persons be subject to the equal demands and burdens of the law and not suffer any greater disability in the substance and application of the law than others... ." *R. v. Turpin* (1989), 39 C.R.R. 306 at 333, 69 C.R. (3d) 97, 48 C.C.C. (3d) 8, 96 N.R. 115, [1989] 1 S.C.R. 1296, 34 O.A.C. 115, the court per Wilson J.

EQUALITY IS EQUITY. When there is property to be divided among persons, the persons are entitled to equal shares unless there is sufficient reason to use another basis for division. P.V. Baker & P. St. J. Langan, eds., *Snell's Equity*, 29th ed. (London: Sweet & Maxwell, 1990) at 36.

EQUALITY RIGHTS. The rights provided by section 15 of the Charter. Section 15 states: (1) Every individual is equal before and under the law and has the right to the equal protection and equal benefit of the law without discrimination and, in particular, without discrimination based on race, national or ethnic origin, colour, religion, sex, age or mental or physical disability. (2) Subsection (1) does not preclude any law, program or activity that has as its object the amelioration of conditions of disadvantaged individuals or groups including those that are disadvantaged because of race, national or ethnic origin, colour, religion, sex, age or mental or physical disability.

EQUALIZATION PAYMENT. Payment to a province to bring its share of tax rental payments up to the same per capita amount as the average per capita yield in the two provinces with the highest yield. P.W. Hogg, *Constitutional Law of Canada*, 3d ed. (Toronto: Carswell, 1992) at 138.

EQUAL PAY FOR EQUAL WORK. The same wage rate applied to jobs with no consideration of sex, race or other factors not related to ability to perform the work.

EQUIPMENT. *n.* Goods that are not inventory or consumer goods. *Personal Property Security acts.* See GAMING ~; RADIO-SENSITIVE ~; RAILWAY ~.

EQUIPMENT TRUST. A means for a company to raise funds on the security of equipment, established by setting up a certificate or indenture. D.M.W. Waters, *The Law of Trusts in Canada*, 2d ed. (Toronto: Carswell, 1984) at 452.

EQUITABLE. *adj.* Fair; according to the rules of equity.

EQUITABLE CHARGE. A security for a debt which does not provide the lender with a legal estate in the charged property.

EQUITABLE DOCTRINE OF CONSTRUCTIVE NOTICE. Any equitable claim is good against a mortgagee who should have known of it by acting prudently, i.e., if the mortgagee had made the usual title search. Mortgagees are obliged to be both honest and diligent.

EQUITABLE ESTATE. A right relating to property which another person or the equitable owner in another capacity legally owns.

EQUITABLE ESTOPPEL. "... [W]here a representation is made by one party and relied upon by another to that person's detriment, the party making the representation will be estopped from following a contrary course of action. This concept has been modified to mean a basic sense of fairness and equity. One should not be able to say one thing, have it acted upon, and then behave differently than first represented." *Marchischuk v. Dominion Industrial Supplies Ltd.* (1989), 34 C.P.C. (2d) 181 at 182, [1989] 3 W.W.R. 74, 58 Man. R. (2d) 56 (Q.B.), Kennedy J.

EQUITABLE EXECUTION. "... [T]he practice of granting an equitable substitute for execution at common law in respect of equitable property of the debtor by the appointment of a receiver... ." *Fox v. Peterson Livestock Ltd.*, [1982] 2 C.N.L.R. 58 at 60, [1982] 2 W.W.R. 204, 17 Alta. L.R. (2d) 311, 35 A.R. 471, 131 D.L.R. (3d) 716 (C.A.), the court per Belzil J.A.

EQUITABLE FRAUD. 1. The principle of "equitable fraud" is aimed at preventing a limitation period from operating "as an instrument of injustice": M. (K.) v. M. (H.), [1992] 3 S.C.R. 6 at para. 66. It has been described in many ways. Essentially, it involves some form of unconscionable conduct on the part of a wrongdoer who stands in a special relationship with another party, where the conduct conceals the existence of a claim by that party against the wrongdoer and is considered by equity to be sufficient to preclude the wrongdoer from relying on a limitation period defence. *Authorson (Litigation Guardian of) v. Canada (Attorney General)*, 2007 ONCA 501. 2. " ... [C]onduct which, having regard to some special relationship between the two parties concerned, is an unconscionable thing for the one to do towards the other." *Kitchen v. Royal Air Force Assn. et al.*, [1958] 1 W.L.R. 563 at 573 (U.K.), Lord Evershed M.R.

EQUITABLE INTEREST. A right relating to property which another person or the equitable owner in another capacity legally owns.

EQUITABLE LIEN. 1. A lien not tied to possession. 2. "... [B]ased on the principle that if a person has acquired possession of property under a contract whereby he is obligated to pay for it, he will not be allowed to retain the property unless he does pay for it. It arises by operation of law and is an incident to the contract between the vendor and purchaser... ." *Ahone v. Holloway* (1988), 30 B.C.L.R. (2d) 368 at 376 (C.A.), the court per McLachlin J.A. 3. An equitable right, such as an unpaid vendor's lien or a purchaser's lien, which the law confers on one person in the form of a charge on the real property of another person until particular claims are satisfied. W.B. Rayner & R.H. McLaren, *Falconbridge on Mortgages*, 4th ed. (Toronto: Canada Law Book, 1977) at 9-10.

EQUITABLE LIMITATIONS. Refers to rules of equity developed to govern equitable claims. Originally statutes of limitations did not govern equitable claims. Limitation by analogy, laches, and acquiescence are types of equitable limitations.

EQUITABLE MAXIM. See MAXIMS OF EQUITY.

EQUITABLE MORTGAGE. 1. The authorities cited to us make it clear that the essence of an equitable mortgage is an intention to make property security for a debt due or a present advance. ... Thus while the document need not use the formal wording of "transfer" or "mortgage" or "assign", it must in some manner show that intention to create a charge on property in equity or, put another way, to grant a property interest to the mortgagee as security for a debt. *Duncalm Resort Inc. v. Rendezvous Lodge Ltd.* 1998 CanLII 4882 (B.C. C.A.), (1998), 52 B.C.L.R. (3d) 64 (C.A.) Newbury J.A. 2. A charge or mortgage other than a statutory or registered mortgage.3. A mortgage may be equitable either (1) because the interest mortgaged is future or equitable, or (2) because the mortgagor did not execute an instrument adequate to transfer the legal estate, e.g. a mortgage of the equity of redemption. Such a mortgage may also be created by depositing title deeds in jurisdictions with a registry system as opposed to a land titles system of registration. 4. Equitable mortgages are recognized under the Torrens system of land registration in effect in Saskatchewan: Canadian Imperial Bank of Commerce v. Saskatchewan Lawyers' Insurance Association Inc. (1996), 140 Sask. R. 114 (Sask. Q.B.). An equitable mortgage is created by a written agreement for valuable consideration that provides that specified property is to stand charged as security for a specified sum: Tisdale Credit Union Ltd. v. Fettes , (1993), 117 Sask. R. 82 (Sask. Q.B.).

Toronto-Dominion Bank v. Coueslan, (2000), 198 Sask. R. 150 (Sask. Q.B.).

EQUITABLE SET-OFF. "... [I]s available where there is a claim for a money sum whether liquidated or unliquidated: ... it is available where there has been an assignment. There is no requirement of mutuality." *Telford v. Holt* (1987), 37 B.L.R. 241 at 253, 21 C.P.C. (2d) 1, 78 N.R. 321, 54 Alta. L.R. (2d) 193, [1987] 6 W.W.R. 385, [1987] 2 S.C.R. 193, 46 R.P.R. 234, 81 A.R. 385, 41 D.L.R. (4th) 385, the court per Wilson J.

EQUITABLE SUBORDINATION. See DOCTRINE OF ~.

EQUITABLY. *adv.* Fairly.

EQUITY. *n.* 1. Fairness. 2. That part of the general law which provides remedies not available at common law in many cases. Prior to the late 1800s the courts administering equity were separate from the common law courts and were known as Chancery courts. By the Judicature Acts, the courts were united so that a judge might hear cases seeking equitable or common law remedies. 3. Equity of redemption. 4. In business, the excess of assets over liabilities. 5. "... [S]uch interest as the seller has in property." *Bednarsky v. Weleschuk* (1961), 29 D.L.R. (2d) 270 at 272 (Alta. C.A.), the court per Johnson J.A. See BETTER ~; CLEAN HANDS DOCTRINE; COURT OF ~; DELAY DEFEATS EQUITIES; EQUALITY IS ~; HE WHO COMES INTO ~ MUST COME WITH CLEAN HANDS; HE WHO SEEKS ~ MUST DO ~; MAXIMS OF ~; NET ~; NO MAN CAN TAKE ADVANTAGE OF HIS OWN WRONG; PAY ~.

EQUITY ACTS IN PERSONAM. Describes the procedure in equity which is in relation to the person(s) as opposed to the object in dispute.

EQUITY AIDS THE VIGILANT AND NOT THE INDOLENT. "[A court of equity] ... has always refused its aid to stale demands, where a party has slept upon his right and acquiesced for a great length of time. Nothing can call forth this court into activity, but conscience, good faith, and reasonable diligence; where these are wanting, the Court is passive, and does nothing." *Smith v. Clay* (1767), 3 Bro. C.C. 639n at 640n, Lord Camden L.C.

EQUITY CAPITAL. Of a corporation, the amount of consideration paid in money for which the outstanding equity shares of the corporation have been issued.

EQUITY CLAIM. A claim that is in respect of an equity interest, including a claim for, among others, (a) a dividend or similar payment, (b) a return of capital, (c) a redemption or retraction obligation, (d) a monetary loss resulting from the ownership, purchase or sale of an equity interest or from the rescission, or, in Quebec, the annulment, of a purchase or sale of an equity interest, or (e) contribution or indemnity in respect of a claim referred to in any of paragraphs (a) to (d). *Bankruptcy and Insolvency Act*, R.S.C. 1985, c. B-3, s. 2.

EQUITY FOLLOWS THE LAW. Equity will interfere only in a case when an important aspect is ignored by the common law.

E

EQUITY IMPUTES AN INTENTION TO FUL-FIL AN OBLIGATION. An act other than that originally intended or required will be accepted as fulfillment of an obligation if the act is capable of being regarded as fulfillment of the obligation.

EQUITY INTEREST. (a) In the case of a corporation other than an income trust, a share in the corporation—or a warrant or option or another right to acquire a share in the corporation—other than one that is derived from a convertible debt, and (b) in the case of an income trust, a unit in the income trust—or a warrant or option or another right to acquire a unit in the income trust—other than one that is derived from a convertible debt. *Bankruptcy and Insolvency Act*, R.S.C. 1985, c. B-3, s. 2.

EQUITY LOOKS ON THAT AS DONE WHICH OUGHT TO BE DONE. A contract will be treated as completed in favour of persons who have a right to enforce that contract.

EQUITY LOOKS TO THE INTENT RATHER THAN TO THE FORM. "Courts of Equity make a distinction in all cases between that which is matter of substance and that which is matter of form; and if it find that by insisting on the form, the substance will be defeated, it holds it to be inequitable to allow a person to insist on such form, and thereby defeat the substance." *Parkin v. Thorold* (1852), 16 Beav. 59 at 466, Romilly M.R.

EQUITY OF A STATUTE. When a fact situation falls within a statute's spirit and intent, though apparently not its letter, it is within the equity of that statute.

EQUITY OF REDEMPTION. 1. A mortgagor's right to redeem a mortgage. 2. The interest remaining in a mortgagor after the execution of one or more mortgages upon any lands. 3. The amount by which a property's value exceeds the total charges, liens or mortgages against it. See CLOG ON ~.

EQUITY SECURITY. Any security of an issuer that carries a residual right to participate in the earnings of the issuer and, upon the liquidation or winding up of the issuer, in its assets. *Investors Protection Act*, S.N.S. 1990, c. 15, s. 56.

EQUITY SHARE. 1. Any share of any class of shares of a company carrying voting rights under all circumstances and any share of any class of shares carrying voting rights by reason of the occurrence of any contingency that has occurred and is continuing. *Canada Corporations Act*, R.S.C. 1970, c. C-32, s. 3. 2. A share of a class of shares of a corporation carrying voting rights under all circumstances and a share of a class of shares carrying voting rights by reason of the occurrence of a contingency that has occurred and is continuing.

EQUITY WILL NOT SUFFER A WRONG TO BE WITHOUT A REMEDY. The maxim upon which the enforcement of uses and trusts was founded by the Court of Chancery. A wrong will not go unredressed if the courts are able to remedy it.

EQUIVALENT. See ACTUARIAL ~; CARBON DIOXIDE ~; DOCTRINE OF ~S; PHARMACEUTICAL ~.

EQUIVOCAL PRIVATIVE CLAUSE. One which fits into the overall process of evaluation of the factors to determine the legislator's intended degree of deference and does not have the preclusive effect of a full privative clause.

ERGONOMICS. *n.* The study of the relationship between a person and their working environment. An ergonomic practice assessment is designed to identify ergonomic compromises in the plaintiff's practice which may be increasing the risk for development of repetitive strain injuries. *Best v. Paul Revere Life Insurance Co.* 2000 MBCA 81, [2000] 10 W.W.R. 441, 49 C.P.C. (4th) 38, 150 Man. R. (2d) 105.

ERRATA. *n.* [L.] Errors.

ERRATUM. *n.* [L.] Error.

ERRED IN LAW. "... [C]apable of several different meanings... . [for example] the trial judge offended against case authority binding on him ... the trial judge's conclusion is not in accord with the evidence." *Mallen v. Mallen* (1992), 40 R.F.L. (3d) 114 at 133, 65 B.C.L.R. (2d) 241, 11 B.C.A.C. 262, 22 W.A.C. 262, Gibbs J.A.

ERROR. *n.* 1. Incorrect information, and includes omission of information. *Vital Statistics acts.* 2. In old common law practice, a mistake in the proceeding which either the court in which it occurred or a superior court must correct. See CLERICAL ~; JURISDICTIONAL ~; OFFICIALLY INDUCED ~; PALPABLE ~; REVIEWABLE ~.

ERROR IN DESIGN. A mistake in judgment based on an incorrect belief as to the existence of matters of fact. Does not necessarily imply negligence or other blameworthiness. *B.C. Rail Ltd. v. American Home Assurance Co.* (1991), 54 B.C.L.R. (2d) 228 (C.A.).

ERROR IN PRINCIPLE. Connotes, at least, failing to take into account a relevant factor, taking into account an irrelevant factor, failing to give sufficient weight to relevant factors, overemphasizing relevant factors and, more generally, it includes an error of law. *R. v. Rezaie* (1996), 31 O.R. (3d) 713 (C.A.), Laskin J.A.

ERROR OF LAW. 1. An error of law is defined as any decision that is an erroneous interpretation or application of the law. If an error deprives the accused of a fair trial, it constitutes a miscarriage of justice. *R. c. Arradi*, 2003 SCC 23. 2. "... [A]n error committed by an administrative tribunal in good faith in interpreting or applying a provision of its enabling Act, of another Act, or of an agreement or other document which it has to interpret and apply within the limits of its jurisdiction." *C.A.W. v. Nova Scotia (Labour Relations Board)* (1988), 89 C.L.L.C. 14,003 at 12,017, 87 N.S.R. (2d) 61, 222 A.P.R. 61 (T.D.), Grant J. See MERE ~.

ERROR OF LAW ON THE FACE OF THE RECORD. The most authoritative definition of error of law on the face of the record is found in *Champsey Bhara Co. v. Jivraj Balloo Spinning and Weaving Co. Ltd.*, [1923] A.C. 480 at p. 487 (India P.C.): An error of law on the face of the record means that you can find in the award or a document actually incorporated therewith, as for instance a note appended by the arbitrator stating the reasons for judgment, some legal proposition which is the basis of the award and which you can then say is erroneous.

ERRORS AND OMISSIONS EXCEPTED. A phrase intended to excuse small mistakes or oversights in an account or document.

ERRORS AND OMISSIONS INSURANCE. Insurance which protects against defamation, invasion of privacy, violation of intellectual property rights.

ERRORS EXCEPTED. A phrase intended to excuse a small mistake or oversight in a stated account.

ESCALATION CLAUSE. 1. Clause in lease providing for increases in rent based on some factor such as tax increases. 2. Clause in wage contract or collective agreement providing for a raise in rate of pay based on a factor such as the Consumer Price Index.

ESCALATOR CLAUSE. See ESCALATION CLAUSE.

ESCAPE. *v.* Breaking prison, escaping from lawful custody or, without lawful excuse, being at large before the expiration of a term of imprisonment to which a person has been sentenced. *Criminal Code*, R.S.C. 1985, c. C-46, s. 149(2).

ESCHEAT. *n.* 1. The reversion of land or other property to the Crown when a company is dissolved or a person dies intestate without heirs. 2. "... [A]n incident of tenure by which for the failure of heirs the feud falls back into the lord's hand by a termination of the tenure, ..." *Ontario (Attorney General) v. Mercer* (1879), 5 S.C.R. 538 at 625, Ritchie C.J.

ESCROW. *n.* 1. Holding something in trust until a contingency happens or a condition is performed. 2. "... [T]he delivery of a document in escrow is to render that document inoperative pending the conditions of the escrow being met. It is common ground that a delivery in escrow is not now confined to deeds, and it is also equally well established that the delivery need not be to a stranger ..." *Draft Masonry (York) Co. v. PA Restoration Inc.* (1988), 48 R.P.R. 231 at 240, 29 C.L.R. 256 (Ont. Dist. Ct.), Hoilett D.C.J.

ESPIONAGE. *n.* 1. Spying. 2. A method of information gathering—by spying, by acting in a covert way. Its use in the analogous term "industrial espionage" conveys the essence of the matter—information gathering surreptitiously. *Qu v. Canada (Minister of Citizenship & Immigration)*, 2000 CarswellNat 705, 5 Imm. L.R. (3d) 129, [2000] 4 F.C. 71 (T.D.), Lemieux J. See ECONOMIC ~.

ESQ. *abbr.* Esquire.

ESSENCE OF THE CONTRACT. Describes a provision in a contract which both parties agreed at the time they entered into the contract was so important that performance of the contract without strict compliance with that provision would be pointless.

ESSENTIAL ELEMENTS. See NON-~.

ESSENTIAL SERVICES. 1. "... [O]ne the interruption of which would threaten serious harm to the general public or to a part of the population." *Reference re Public Service Employee Relations Act (Alberta)* (1987), (*sub nom. A.U.P.E. v. Alberta (Attorney General)*) 28 C.R.R. 305 at 348, 87 C.L.L.C. 14,021, 38 D.L.R. (4th) 161, [1987] 1 S.C.R. 313, 51 Alta. L.R. (2d) 97, [1987] 3 W.W.R. 577, 74 N.R. 99, 78 A.R. 1, [1987] D.L.Q. 225, Dickson C.J.C. (dissenting) (Wilson J. concurring). 2. A class of services designated to be maintained during strikes; employees employed in such jobs have limited or no right to strike.

ESSENTIAL SERVICES EMPLOYEE. An employee who, during a work stoppage, is required to provide essential services in accordance with an essential services agreement or a notice given under governing legislation.

ESTABLISH. *v.* 1. "... [P]lace[s] a burden on an accused to prove the ... elements delineated thereafter on a balance of probabilities ..." *R. v. Wholesale Travel Group Inc.* (1991), 67 C.C.C. (3d) 193 at 222, 4 O.R. (3d) 799n, 8 C.R. (4th) 145, 84 D.L.R. (4th) 161, 130 N.R. 1, 38 C.P.R. (3d) 451, 49 O.A.C. 161, [1991] 3 S.C.R. 154, 7 C.R.R. (2d) 36, Lamer C.J.C. (Sopinka, Gonthier, McLachlin, Stevenson and Iacobucci JJ. concurring). 2. "... '[T]o prove'... ." *R. v. Oakes* (1986), 24 C.C.C. (3d) 321 at 332, [1986] 1 S.C.R. 103, 53 O.R. (2d) 719n, 50 C.R. (3d) 1, 14 O.A.C. 335, 19 C.R.R. 308, 26 D.L.R. (4th) 200, 665 N.R. 87, Dickson C.J.C. (Chouinard, Lamer, Wilson and Le Dain JJ. concurring). 3. "... [I]n the educational statutes of Ontario ... 'set up'." *Crawford v. Ottawa (City) Board of Education*, [1971] 2 O.R. 179 at 188, 17 D.L.R. (3d) 271 (C.A.), the court per Kelly J.A.

ESTABLISHMENT. See TOURIST ~.

EST. & TR. J. *abbr.* Estates & Trusts Journal.

EST. & TR. Q. *abbr.* Estates & Trusts Quarterly.

ESTATE. *n.* 1. "... [I]n regard to its uses in conveyances, is properly defined to mean a property which one possesses, especially property in land. It is also understood as defining the nature and quantity of interests in lands, &c." *Macdonald v. Georgian Bay Lumber Co.* (1878), 2 S.C.R. 364 at 392, Henry J. 2. "... [A]s applied to interests in land has a well recognized meaning due to the fact that under our law a person is not deemed to be the absolute owner of land but only of something which has for a long time been designated as an 'estate' in it." *Coleman (Town) v. Head Syndicate* (1917), 11 Alta. L.R. 314 at 317, [1917] 1 W.W.R. 1074 (C.A.), Harvey C.J. 3. Real and personal estate of every kind, including messuages, tenements and hereditaments, corporeal and incorporeal, goods, chattels and credits of every kind and description, whatever the estate or interest in it may be, and whether legal or equitable, together with all paths, passages, ways, watercourses, water records, water rights, liberties, privileges, easements, mines, minerals, quarries, trees and timber on it, under it or appertaining to it, and mineral claims for which Crown grants have been issued. *Estate Administration Act*, R.S.B.C. 1996, c. 122, s. 33. 4. Includes both real and personal property. *Intestate Succession acts.* See EQUITABLE ~; EXECUTORY ~; EX-

PECTANT ~; FREEHOLD ~; FUTURE ~; LEASEHOLD ~; LIFE ~; PERSONAL ~; REAL ~; SETTLED ~.

ESTATE CERTIFICATE. A grant of probate, administration or testamentary guardianship by the Ontario Court (General Division) or the Surrogate Court made before January 1, 1995, but not a grant of double probate, a cessate grant or a grant of administration de bonis non administratis by either of those courts before that date, and a certificate of appointment of estate trustee issued by the Ontario Court (General Division) or the Superior Court of Justice after December 31, 1994, but not a certificate of succeeding estate trustee or a certificate of estate trustee during litigation issued by that court after that date. *Estate Administration Tax Act, 1998*, S.O. 1998, c. 34, Sched., s. 1.

ESTATE DUTY. A tax generally imposed on "property passing" when someone dies; its rate is based on the size of the estate.

ESTATE FREEZE. A transaction which replaces growth assets, i.e. common shares of an operating business corporation, with assets of limited growth potential, i.e. preferred shares, so that a ceiling approximately equal to the value at the date of the freeze is placed on the value of those assets for capital gain and succession duty purposes. Thus any future growth in the value of the assets usually benefits subsequent generations, who become common shareholders. W. Grover & F. Iacobucci, *Materials on Canadian Income Tax*, 4th ed. (Toronto: De Boo, 1980) at 793.

ESTATE PLANNING. Arranging business and property interests to pass to heirs and successors in such a way as to receive maximum benefit of laws relating to wills, income tax, estate tax, succession duty, property, insurance, securities, and so on.

ESTATE PUR AUTRE VIE. [Fr.] A grant to one person for the life of another.

ESTATE REPRESENTATIVE. Includes, with respect to the estate of a deceased person, (a) an executor or administrator of the estate, (b) a person entitled to act in the capacity of executor or administrator of the estate, (c) a person appointed as guardian of a person who is a beneficiary of the estate of the deceased person or as guardian of the beneficiary's property, (d) an estate trustee, (e) an estate trustee with a will, and (f) an estate trustee without a will. *Estate Administration Tax Act, 1998*, S.O. 1998, c. 34, Sched., s.1.

ESTATE TAIL. A devise that would have been, under the law of England, an estate tail or in quasi entail. Unless a contrary intention appears in the will, where a person to whom real property is devised for an estate tail dies in the lifetime of the testator and leaves issue who would inherit under the entail if that estate existed, if any of those issue are living at the time of the death of the testator, the devise does not lapse but takes effect as if the death of that person had happened immediately after the death of the testator. *The Wills Act, 1996*, S.S. 1996, c. W-14.1, s. 34.

ESTATE TAX. A tax levied on all a deceased person's property, irrespective of its location or who may inherit it.

ESTIMATE. *n.* 1. A representation as to the future price of a transaction. 2. An estimate of the total cost of materials and work to repair a vehicle or other thing. See ~S.

ESTIMATES. *n.* Spending estimates of the Crown transmitted to the legislature and divided into classes, each one corresponding to a separate programme and each class divided into votes, on which the House committees may make separate decisions. A. Fraser, W.A. Dawson & J. Holtby, eds., *Beauchesne's Rules and Forms of the House of Commons of Canada*, 6th ed. (Toronto: Carswell, 1989) at 259. See ESTIMATE.

ESTOPPEL. *n.* 1. An estoppel alleges a previous inconsistent act, allegation, or denial of a plaintiff which would preclude him from maintaining his action. *Patym Holdings Ltd. v. Michalakis*, 2005 BCCA 636, Smith J.A. (Saunders J.A. concurring). 2. "The essential factors giving rise to an estoppel are ... : (1) A representation or conduct amounting to a representation intended to induce a course of conduct on the part of the person to whom the representation is made. (2) An act or omission resulting from the representation, whether actual or by conduct, by the person to whom the representation is made. (3) Detriment to such person as a consequence of the act or omission." *Greenwood v. Martin's Bank Ltd.*, [1933] A.C. 51 at 57 (U.K. H.L.), Lord Tomlin. 3. "... [W]here one party has, by his words or conduct, made to the other a promise or assurance which was intended to affect the legal relations between them and to be acted on accordingly, then, once the other party has taken him at his word and acted on it, the one who gave the promise or assurance cannot afterwards be allowed to revert to the previous legal relations ... subject to the qualification which he himself has so introduced, even though it is not supported in point of law by any consideration, but only by his word." *Coombe v. Coombe*, [1951] 1 All E.R. 767 at 770 (U.K.), Denning L.J. 4. "... [A]n evidentiary rule." *Royal Bank v. McArthur* (1985), 3 C.P.C. (2d) 141 at 146, 51 O.R. (2d) 86, 10 O.A.C. 394, 19 D.L.R. (4th) 762 (Div. Ct.), the court per Montgomery J. 5. "... [H]as been sought to be limited by a series of maxims: estoppel is only a rule of evidence; estoppel cannot give rise to a cause of action; estoppel cannot do away with the need for consideration, and so forth. All these can now be seen to merge into one general principle shorn of limitations. When the parties to a transaction proceed on the basis of an underlying assumption (either of fact or law, and whether due to misrepresentation or mistake, makes no difference), on which they have conducted the dealings between them, neither of them will be allowed to go back on the assumption when it would be unfair or unjust to allow him to do so. If one of them does seek to go back on it, the courts will give the other such remedy as the equity of the case demands." *Amalgamated Investment & Property Co. Ltd. v. Texas Commerce Int'l. Bank Ltd.*, [1981] 3 All E.R. 577 at 584 (U.K. C.A.), Lord Denning M.R. See CAUSE OF ACTION ~; COLLATERAL ~; FEED-

ING THE ~; ISSUE ~; PROMISSORY ~; PROPRIETARY ~; PROSECUTION HISTORY ~; QUASI-~; TENANCY BY ~.

ESTOPPEL BY DEED. A person cannot dispute his own deed or deny the recitals contained in his own deed.

ESTOPPEL BY ELECTION. In general, election is the doctrine that if a person has a choice of one of two rights, but not both, where he chooses one, he cannot afterwards assert the other. Although an election must normally be communicated, detrimental reliance by a second party is not a necessary element. *Blueberry River Indian Band v. Canada (Department of Indian Affairs & Northern Development)*, 2001 CarswellNat 963, 2001 FCA 67, 6 C.P.C. (5th) 1, 201 D.L.R. (4th) 35, 274 N.R. 304, Rothstein J.A. for the court.

ESTOPPEL BY REPRESENTATION. The following elements must be present before the doctrine of estoppel by representation can be applied: a representation of fact made with the intention that it be acted upon or that a reasonable person would assume that it was intended to be acted upon; that the representee acted upon the representation; that the representee altered his position in reliance upon the representation and thereby suffered a prejudice. *Lidder v. Canada Lidder v. Canada (Minister of Employment & Immigration)*, [1992] 2 F.C. 621 (C.A.), at 630.

ESTOPPEL PER REM JUDICATAM. 1. "... [D]irected to the capacity of the parties to an action and, where it is properly applicable, it prevents those parties from relitigating either a cause of action or an issue that has previously been decided... ." *Masunda v. Downing* (1986), 7 R.F.L. (3d) 26 at 37, 5 B.C.L.R. (2d) 113, 27 D.L.R. (4th) 268 (S.C.), Wood J. 2. "... [A] generic term which in modern law includes two species. The first species ... 'cause of action estoppel', ... prevents a party to an action from asserting or denying, as against the other party, the existence of a particular cause of action, the non-existence or existence of which has been determined by a court of competent jurisdiction in previous litigation between the same parties... . The second species ... 'issue estoppel', ... If in litigation upon one such cause of action any of such separate issues as to whether a particular condition has been fulfilled is determined by a court of competent jurisdiction, either upon evidence or upon admission by a party to the litigation, neither party can, in subsequent litigation between one another upon any cause of action which depends upon the fulfillment of the identical condition, assert that the condition was fulfilled if the court has in the first litigation determined that it was not, or deny that it was fulfilled if the court in the first litigation determined that it was." *Thoday v. Thoday*, [1964] P. 181 at 197-8 (U.K. C.A.), Diplock L.J.

ESTRANGED. *adj.* Living separate and apart for a year or more. *Human Tissue and Organ Donation Act*, S.A. 2006, c. H-14.5, s. 1.

ESTRAY. *n.* 1. An animal that is running at large. 2. An animal found on the premises of a person other than its owner.

ESTREAT. *n.* 1. Now used only in connection with forfeitures, fines and recognizances; if the condition of a recognizance is broken, the recognizance is forfeited, and, when it is estreated, the cognisors become the Crown's debtors. 2. Formerly, a copy of a court record. A recognizance was estreated or extracted when a copy was made from the original and sent for the proper authority to enforce. *R. v. Creelman* (1893), 25 N.S.R. 404 at 418 (C.A.), Meagher J.A.

ET AL. *abbr.* 1. Et alii. 2. Et alius.

ET ALII. [L.] And others.

ET ALIUS. [L.] And another.

E.T.R. *abbr.* Estates and Trusts Reports, 1977-1994.

E.T.R. (2D). *abbr.* Estates and Trusts Reports (Second Series), 1994-.

ET SEQ. *abbr.* 1. Et sequentes. 2. Et sequentia.

ET SEQUENTES. [L.] And those following.

ET SEQUENTIA. [L.] And the following.

ET UX. *abbr.* Et uxor.

ET UXOR. [L.] And wife.

EUTHANASIA. *n.* The deliberate infliction of an intended death upon an animal.

EVADE. *v.* 1. Equates with an attempt to elude or get away from. *R. v. Kulchisky*, 2007 ABCA 110. 2. "... [I]mplies something of an underhanded or deceitful nature. In other words a deliberate attempt to escape the requirement of paying tax on income that has been earned." *R. v. Branch*, [1976] C.T.C. 193 at 196, [1976] W.W.D. 78, 76 D.T.C. 6112 (Alta. Dist. Ct.), Medhurst J. See TAX EVASION.

EVALUATION. *n.* Judgment, appraisal, rating, interpretation. See PRO RATA ~.

EVASION. *n.* The act of escaping by the use of artifice. See INCOME TAX ~; TAX ~.

EVASIVE. *adj.* Describes a pleading which answers the other party's pleading by a half-denial or a half-admission or fails to answer a substantial point.

EVENT. See COSTS IN ANY ~ OF THE CAUSE; COSTS SHALL FOLLOW THE ~; TRAUMATIC ~.

EVERY ONE. *var.* **EVERYONE.** 1. "[In s. 7 of the Charter] ... must be read in light of the rest of the section and defined to exclude corporations and other artificial entities incapable of enjoying life, liberty or security of the person, and include only human beings." *Irwin Toy Ltd. c. Québec (Procureur général)*, [1989] 1 S.C.R. 927 at 1004, 25 C.P.R. (3d) 417, 94 N.R. 167, 58 D.L.R. (4th) 577, 24 Q.A.C. 2, 39 C.R.R. 193, Dickson C.J.C., Lamer and Wilson JJ. 2. "... [I]ncludes every human being who is physically present in Canada and by virtue of such presence amenable to Canadian law." *Singh v. Canada (Minister of Employment & Immigration)* (1985), 14 C.R.R. 13 at 4, [1985] 1 S.C.R. 177, 12 Admin. L.R. 137, 17 D.L.R. (4th) 422, 58 N.R. 1, Wilson J. (Dickson C.J.C. and Lamer J. concurring). 3. "... [I]s an expression of the same kind as 'person' and there-

E

fore includes bodies corporate unless the context requires otherwise." *R. v. Union Colliery Co.* (1900), 31 S.C.R. 81 at 88, 21 C.L.T. 153, 4 C.C.C. 400, Sedgewick J. 4. Includes Her Majesty and an organization. *Criminal Code*, R.S.C. 1985, c. C-46, s. 2.

EVICTION. *n.* 1. The act of dispossessing; recovering land through legal action. 2. The recovery of possession of rented premises by the landlord. See CONSTRUCTIVE ~.

EVIDENCE. *n.* 1. The oral and written statements and information and any actual things produced in a proceeding, anything which may be used to prove a fact or support an assertion. 2. The body of law, the rules regarding the admission of information of all forms in proceedings before a court or tribunal. 3. "One of the hallmarks of the common law of evidence is that it relies on witnesses as the means by which evidence is produced in court. As a general rule, nothing can be admitted as evidence before the court unless it is vouched for viva voce by a witness. Even real evidence, which exists independently of any statement by any witness, cannot be considered by the court unless a witness identifies it and establishes its connection to the events under consideration. Unlike other legal systems, the common law does not usually provide for self-authenticating documentary evidence." *R. v. Schwartz* (1988), 55 D.L.R. (4th) 1 at 26, [1989] 1 W.W.R. 289, 66 C.R. (3d) 251, 88 N.R. 90, [1988] 2 S.C.R. 443, 45 C.C.C. (3d) 97, 56 Man. R. (2d) 92, 39 C.R.R. 260, Dickson C.J.C. (dissenting). 4. "... [P]art of the procedure which signifies those rules of law whereby, it is determined what testimony is to be admitted, and what rejected in each case, and what weight is to be given to the testimony admitted... ." *Belisle v. Moreau* (1968), 5 C.R.N.S. 68 at 70, [1968] 4 C.C.C. 229, 69 D.L.R. (2d) 530, (N.B. C.A.), the court per Hughes J.A. 5. An assertion of fact, opinion, belief or knowledge, whether material or not and whether admissible or not. *Criminal Code*, R.S.C. 1985, c. C-46, s. 118. See ADMISSIBLE ~; ARMCHAIR ~; BEST ~ RULE; BODILY ~; CIRCUMSTANTIAL ~; COMMISSION ~; CONSCIOUSNESS OF GUILT ~; CONSCRIPTIVE ~; CONTRADICTORY ~; CORROBORATIVE ~; DEMONSTRATIVE ~; DERIVATIVE ~; DIRECT ~; DOCUMENTARY ~; EXPERIMENT ~; EXPERT ~; EXTRINSIC ~; FABRICATING ~; FRESH ~; HEARSAY ~; INCRIMINATING ~; INDIRECT ~; INTRINSIC ~; MINUTES OF PROCEEDINGS AND ~; NEW ~; OBJECTIVE ~; ORAL ~; ORIGINAL ~; PAROL ~; PAROL ~ RULE; PRESUMPTIVE ~; PRIMA FACIE ~; PRIMARY ~; REAL ~; REBUTTAL ~; REPLY ~; SECONDARY ~; SIMILAR FACT ~; TESTIMONIAL ~; WEIGHT OF ~.

EVIDENCE-BASED MEDICINE. The use of the current best evidence in a conscientious, explicit and judicious manner, to make decisions about the care of individual patients.

EVIDENTIAL BURDEN. "... [T]he requirement of putting an issue into play by reference to evidence before the court ... The party with an evidential burden is not required to convince the trier of fact of anything, only to point out evidence which suggests that certain facts existed." *R. v. Schwartz* (1988), 39 C.R.R. 260 at 288, [1989] 1 W.W.R. 289, 66 C.R. (3d) 251, 88 N.R. 90, [1988] 2 S.C.R. 443, 45 C.C.C. (3d) 97, 56 Man. R. (2d) 92, 55 D.L.R. (4th) 1, Dickson C.J.C. (dissenting).

EVIDENTIARY BURDEN. Used, in contrast to persuasive burden, to describe the effect of a statutory presumption which relieves the prosecution from leading evidence to prove a material fact and used to describe the burden imposed on the defence by a mandatory rebuttable presumption that they lead evidence to avoid certain conviction. P.K. McWilliams, *Canadian Criminal Evidence*, 3d ed. (Aurora: Canada Law Book, 1988) at 25-2 and 25-3.

EX ABUNDANTI CAUTELA. [L.] Out of abundant caution.

EXACTOR. *n.* A type of bet on a race to select, in the correct order, the first two horses in the official result.

EX AEQUO ET BONO. [L. out of what is equal and good] In equity and good conscience.

EXAMINATION. *n.* 1. The questioning of a person under oath. 2. The examination of an unclothed body with or without the removal of body tissue or fluids for the purpose of toxicological examinations. *Fatality Inquiries Act*, R.S.A. 2000, c. F-9, s. 1. See BAR ADMISSION ~; CROSS-~; DIRECT ~.

EXAMINATION FOR DISCOVERY. 1. "... [E]mbraces two main elements: discovery of facts in the hands of an adversary and, the obtaining of admission for use in evidence... ." *Minute Muffler Installations Ltd. v. Alberta* (1981), 23 C.P.C. 52 at 54, 16 Alta. L.R. (2d) 35, 23 L.C.R. 128, 30 A.R. 447 (C.A.), the court per Stevenson J.A. 2. "... [A]n examination of the opposite party or an opposite party... . [and] is in the nature of a cross-examination ..." *Stoikopoulous v. Remenda* (1985), 3 C.P.C. (2d) 303 at 305, 39 Sask. R. 58 (Q.B.), Estey J.

EXAMINATION IN AID OF EXECUTION. A creditor examining the judgment debtor or other people to determine the debtor's ability to settle the judgment.

EXAMINATION-IN-CHIEF. *n.* Questioning of a witness by the counsel for the party who called that witness to adduce evidence which supports the case of that party.

EXAMINER. *n.* A person whom a court appoints to examine witnesses in an action. See OFFICIAL ~; SPECIAL ~.

EXAMINER. *abbr.* Examiner (L'Observateur) (Québec).

EXAMINER (L'OBSERVATEUR). *abbr.* Examiner (L'Observateur), 1861.

EXCELLENCY. *n.* The title of the Governor General.

EXCEPTED. See ERRORS AND OMISSIONS ~; ERRORS ~.

EXCEPTION. *n.* In a conveyance, refers to something in existence prior to the conveyance but which is not conveyed, remains in the transferor.

EXCEPTIONAL RESOLUTION. (a) A resolution passed at a general meeting under the following circumstances: (i) notice of the meeting specifying the intention to propose the resolution as an exceptional resolution is sent to all shareholders holding shares that carry the right to vote at general meetings at least the prescribed number of days before the meeting; (ii) the articles provide that, of the votes cast on the resolution by shareholders voting shares that carry the right to vote at general meetings, a specified majority must be cast in favour of the resolution before it can pass as an exceptional resolution; (iii) the majority of votes specified by the articles under subparagraph (ii) is greater than a special majority; (iv) not less than the majority of votes specified by the articles under subparagraph (ii) is cast in favour of the resolution by shareholders voting shares that carry the right to vote at general meetings, or (b) a resolution passed by being consented to in writing by all of the shareholders holding shares that carry the right to vote at general meetings. *Business Corporations Act*, S.B.C. 2002, c. 57, s. 1.

EXCEPTIONS CLAUSE. A clause in a contract which excludes liability.

EXCESSIVE. *adj.* Extreme; out of the ordinary.

EXCESSIVE DISTRESS. Refers to a situation where the rent distrained for is due but good of a higher value are distrained and to the situation where distress is made for more rent than is due and goods of a value higher than the rent due or the amount distrained for are taken.

EXCESSIVE FORCE. 1. Every one who is authorized by law to use force is criminally responsible for any excess thereof according to the nature and quality of the act that constitutes the excess. *Criminal Code*, R.S.C. 1985, c. C-46, s. 26. 2. The legal constraints on a police officer's use of force are deeply rooted in our common law tradition and are enshrined in the Criminal Code. This case engages s. 25 of the Criminal Code. Section 25(1) essentially provides that a police officer is justified in using force to effect a lawful arrest, provided that he or she acted on reasonable and probable grounds and used only as much force as was necessary in the circumstances. That is not the end of the matter. Section 25(3) also prohibits a police officer from using a greater degree of force, i.e. that which is intended or likely to cause death or grievous bodily harm, unless he or she believes that it is necessary to protect him- or herself, or another person under his or her protection, from death or grievous bodily harm. The officer's belief must be objectively reasonable. This means that the use of force under s. 25(3) is to be judged on a subjective-objective basis (Chartier v. Greaves, [2001] O.J. No. 634 (QL) (S.C.J.), at para. 59). If force of that degree is used to prevent a suspect from fleeing to avoid a lawful arrest, then it is justified under s. 25(4), subject to the limitations described above and to the requirement that the flight could not reasonably have been prevented in a less violent manner. *R. v. Nasogaluak*, 2010 SCC 6.

EXCHANGE. *n.* 1. When the consideration is giving goods to the other party, a contract of barter or exchange is formed. 2. "... [T]he act of giving or taking one thing for another ..." *Deyell v. Deyell* (1991), 90 Sask. R. 81 at 87 (C.A.), Cameron J.A. 3. A building or location where agents, merchants, brokers, bankers and others meet at certain times to trade. 4. A group of persons formed for the purpose of exchanging reciprocal contracts of indemnity or inter-insurance with each other through the same attorney. *Excise Tax Act*, R.S.C. 1985, c. E-15, s. 3. See BARTER ~ NETWORK; BILL OF ~; COMMODITY FUTURES ~; FUTURES ~; STOCK ~.

EXCHANGE RATE. At any time in respect of a currency of a country other than Canada means the rate of exchange between that currency and Canadian currency quoted by the Bank of Canada at noon on the day that includes that time or, if that day is not a business day, on the day that immediately precedes that day, or a rate of exchange acceptable to the Minister. *Income Tax Act*, R.S.C. 1985, c. 1 (5th Supp.), s. 111. See CURRENT ~.

EXCHANGE-TRADED DERIVATIVE. A derivative that is traded on an exchange that is designated under section 6, or in accordance with the rules, for the purposes of this definition. *Securities Act*, S.Y. 2007, c. 16, s. 1.

EXCHEQUER BILL. A bank-note, bond, note, debenture or security that is issued or guaranteed by Her Majesty under the authority of Parliament or the legislature of a province. *Criminal Code*, R.S.C. 1985, c. C-46, s. 321.

EXCHEQUER BILL PAPER. Paper that is used to manufacture exchequer bills. *Criminal Code*, R.S.C. 1985, c. C-46, s. 321.

EXCHEQUER COURT. The Exchequer Court of Canada, replaced by The Federal Court in 1971.

EXCISE DUTY. A tax on the distribution or manufacture of goods.

EXCISE TAXES. 1. The taxes imposed under the Excise Tax Act. 2. Taxes on the quantity of goods manufactured.

EXCISION. *n.* For greater certainty, in this section, "wounds" or "maims" includes to excise, infibulate or mutilate, in whole or in part, the labia majora, labia minora or clitoris of a person, except where (a) a surgical procedure is performed, by a person duly qualified by provincial law to practise medicine, for the benefit of the physical health of the person or for the purpose of that person having normal reproductive functions or normal sexual appearance or function; or (b) the person is at least eighteen years of age and there is no resulting bodily harm. *Criminal Code*, R.S.C. 1985, c. C-46, s. 268.

EXCLUSION. *n.* 1. Of a witness, is at the discretion of the tribunal who may, at any party's request, order that the witness stay out of the hearing room until called to give evidence 2. "... [A] term or provision of an insurance policy ..." *Ben's Ltd. v. Royal Insurance Co.*, [1985] I.L.R. 1-1969 at 7574, 7 C.C.E.L. 57, 68 N.S.R. (2d) 379, 159 A.P.R. 379 (T.D.), MacIntosh J. See IMPLIED ~ RULE.

EXCLUSIONARY RULE. A rule prohibiting the introduction of certain evidence.

EXCLUSION CLAUSE. 1. Seeks to limit or eliminate compensation for participation in a tendering process. *Tercon Contractors Ltd. v. British Columbia (Transportation and Highways)*, 2010 SCC 4, [2010] 1 S.C.R. 69, Cromwell J. 2. A clause that removes certain obligations from consideration or limits a party's liabilities for not performing or misperforming the contract. G.H.L. Fridman, *Sale of Goods in Canada*, 3d ed. (Toronto: Carswell, 1986) at 282.

EXCLUSIVE AGENT. An agent with the sole right to act on the principal's behalf in regard of a particular transaction, type of transaction or property.

EXCLUSIVE BARGAINING RIGHT. The right of the union, which is designated as bargaining representative, to bargain collectively for all employees in the unit which it represents.

EXCLUSIVE DISTRIBUTOR. In relation to a book, a person who (a) has, before or after the coming into force of this definition, been appointed in writing, by the owner or exclusive licensee of the copyright in the book in Canada, as (i) the only distributor of the book in Canada or any part of Canada, or (ii) the only distributor of the book in Canada or any part of Canada in respect of a particular sector of the market, and (b) meets the criteria established by regulations made under section 2.6, and, for greater certainty, if there are no regulations made under section 2.6, then no person qualifies under this definition as an "exclusive distributor". *Copyright Act*, R.S.C. 1985, c. C-42, s. 2.

EXCLUSIVE ECONOMIC ZONE. 1. In relation to Canada, means the exclusive economic zone of Canada as determined under the Oceans Act and includes the seabed and subsoil below that zone, and in relation to any other state, means the exclusive economic zone of the other state as determined in accordance with international law and the domestic laws of that other state. *Interpretation Act*, R.S.C. 1985, c. I-21, s. 35. 2. The exclusive economic zone of Canada consists of an area of the sea beyond and adjacent to the territorial sea of Canada that has as its inner limit the outer limit of the territorial sea of Canada and as its outer limit (a) subject to paragraph (b), the line every point of which is at a distance of 200 nautical miles from the nearest point of the baselines of the territorial sea of Canada; or (b) in respect of a portion of the exclusive economic zone of Canada for which geographical coordinates of points have been prescribed pursuant to subparagraph 25(a)(iii), lines determined from the geographical coordinates of points so prescribed. *Oceans Act, 1996*, S.C. 1996, c. 31, s. 13.

EXCLUSIVE JURISDICTION CLAUSE. A clause which states that a tribunal has exclusive and unreviewable jurisdiction to decide issues before it.

EXCLUSIVE JURISDICTION MODEL. [W]here a dispute in its essential character concerns an employment relationship and the legislature has prescribed a statutory scheme to resolve such disputes, the courts have no option but to decline jurisdiction to entertain a parallel action. Their involvement is limited to applications for judicial review of an administrative decision. This is commonly referred to as the "exclusive jurisdiction model." *Smith v. Royal Canadian Mounted Police*, 2007 NBCA 58.

EXCLUSIVE LISTING. An agreement in writing between a broker and a vendor of real estate, under which the broker has the exclusive right to negotiate a sale or lease of the real estate described therein. *The Real Estate Brokers Act*, R.S.M. 1987, c. R20, s. 1.

EXCLUSIVE POSSESSION. The right to occupy premises without any interference by another person.

EXCLUSIVITY. *n.* The constitutional doctrine which provides that each head of federal power grants power to the federal government and denies the same power to the provincial governments.

EX. C.R. *abbr.* 1. Exchequer Court of Canada Reports, 1875-1922.. 2. Canada Law Reports Exchequer Court, 1923-1970.

EX. CT. *abbr.* Exchequer Court.

EXCULPATORY. *adj.* Relieving of guilt or responsibility.

EXCULPATORY CONFESSION. A statement which relieves the person giving it of guilt or responsibility.

EXCULPATORY OPINION. An exculpatory opinion is called an "exclusion"; the suspect is excluded from the group of possible donors of the questioned sample. A difference of two base pairs or more [in mitochondrial DNA sequencing] is required by the FBI for an exclusion. *R. v. Murrin*, 1999 CarswellBC 3015, 181 D.L.R. (4th) 320, 32 C.R. (5th) 97 (S.C.), Henderson J.

EX CURIA. [L.] Out of court.

EXCUSABLE CONDUCT. Conduct which is acceptable, carries no legal consequences.

EXCUSE. *n.* "[In criminal theory] ... concedes the wrongfulness of the action but asserts that the circumstances under which it was done are such that it ought not to be attributed to the actor. The perpetrator who is incapable, owing to a disease of the mind, of appreciating the nature and consequences of his acts, the person who labours under a mistake of fact, the drunkard, the sleepwalker: these are all actors of whose 'criminal' actions we disapprove intensely, but whom, in appropriate circumstances, our law will not punish." *R. v. Perka* (1984), 13 D.L.R. (4th) 1 at 12, [1984] 2 S.C.R. 232, [1984] 6 W.W.R. 289, 42 C.R. (3d) 113, 55 N.R. 1, 14 C.C.C. (3d) 385, Dickson J. See JUSTIFICATION; LAWFUL ~.

EX. D. *abbr.* Law Reports, Exchequer Division, 1875-1890.

EX DEBITO JUSTITIAE. [L.] 1. The remedy to which an applicant is rightfully entitled. 2. "... To say in a case that the writ should issue ex debito justitiae simply means that the circumstances militate strongly in favour of the issuance of the writ rather than for refusal... ." *Harelkin v. University of Regina* (1979), 96 D.L.R. (3d) 14 at 41, [1979] 2 S.C.R. 561, 16 N.R.

364, [1979] 3 W.W.R. 676, Beetz J. (Martland, Pigeon and Pratte JJ. concurring).

EX DELICTO. See ACTION ~.

EX DIV. *abbr.* Ex dividend.

EX DIVIDEND. [L. without dividend] When selling stocks and shares on which a dividend was declared or is anticipated, ex div., the buyer may not claim the dividend.

EXECUTE. *v.* 1. To carry into effect; to complete. 2. Of a deed, to sign, seal and deliver it. 3. Of a judgment or court order, to enforce it or carry it into effect. 4. Of a writ, to obey the instructions within it. 5. Of an affidavit, to swear or affirm the truth of the affidavit's contents before a person empowered to take an affidavit.

EXECUTED. *adj.* Completed, done.

EXECUTED CONSIDERATION. Something done in exchange for a promise.

EXECUTED CONTRACT. 1. When nothing remains for either party to do, and the transaction is complete. 2. Documents amounting to a contract which have been finalized and signed and do not require any changes or signatures.

EXECUTED TRUST. A trust after the estate is conveyed to trustees for particular beneficiaries.

EXECUTION. *n.* 1. The process of enforcing or carrying out a judgment. 2. A writ of fieri facias, and every subsequent writ for giving effect to a writ of fieri facias. 3. "... [I]n some situations means 'signed' and in other situations means 'signed, sealed and delivered'... ." *Johnston, Re* (1982), 43 C.B.R. (N.S.) 39 at 40, 2 P.P.S.A.C. 150 (Ont. S.C.), Saunders J. See EQUITABLE ~; EXAMINATION IN AID OF ~; LEGAL ~; WRIT OF ~.

EXECUTION OF DEEDS. The signing, sealing, and delivery of documents.

EXECUTIVE. *n.* The Crown in its administrative role; the government. This includes government officials and departments directed by ministers of the Crown and the principal executive body, the Cabinet, headed by the Prime Minister.

EXECUTIVE COUNCIL. The premier and members of cabinet of a province.

EXECUTOR. *n.* A person appointed in a testator's will to carry out directions and requests set out there and to distribute property according to the will's provisions. See LIMITED ~.

EXECUTOR DE SON TORT. "... [A] stranger [who] takes upon himself to act as executor or administrator without any just authority (as by intermeddling with the goods of the deceased), ..." *Raiz v. Vaserbakh* (1986), 9 C.P.C. (2d) 141 at 144 (Ont. Dist. Ct.), Trotter D.C.J.

EXECUTOR'S YEAR. "... [A] year within which to gather in the estate before a legal entitlement to demand payment arises." *Cassidy, Re* (1985), 24 E.T.R. 299 at 303, 60 A.R. 92 (Surr. Ct.), Dea J.

EXECUTORY. *adj.* Still to be effected, in contrast to executed.

EXECUTORY CONSIDERATION. "... [A] promise to do or forbear from doing some act in the future." *Butt v. Humber* (1976), 6 R.P.R. 207 at 216, 17 Nfld. & P.E.I.R. 92, 46 A.P.R. 92 (Nfld. T.D.), Goodridge J.

EXECUTORY CONTRACT. A contract between a buyer and a seller for the purchase and sale of goods or services in respect of which delivery of the goods or performance of the services or payment in full of the consideration is not made at the time the contract is entered into.

EXECUTORY DEVISE. Legal limitation of a future interest in lands by a will.

EXECUTORY ESTATE. An interest dependant on some subsequent contingency or event for its enjoyment.

EXECUTORY INTEREST. A legal interest which will arise, become actual, in the future.

EXECUTORY LIMITATION. A limitation, by will or deed, of a future interest.

EXECUTORY TRUST. An imperfect trust which requires some act to perfect it.

EXECUTRIX. *n.* A woman appointed by a testator to carry out the instructions in the will.

EXEMPLARY DAMAGES. 1. "... [O]r punitive damages may be awarded where the defendant's conduct is such as to merit punishment. This may be exemplified by malice, fraud or cruelty as well as other abusive and insolent acts toward the victim. The purpose of the award is to vindicate the strength of the law and to demonstrate to the offender that the law will not tolerate conduct which wilfully disregards the rights of others." *Warner v. Arsenault* (1982), 27 C.P.C. 200 at 205, 53 N.S.R. (2d) 146, 109 A.P.R. 146 (C.A.), the court per Pace J.A. 2. Damage awards which extend beyond the class of compensatory damages have found expression in a variety of terms but the most common of these are exemplary and punitive damages. The term "exemplary" was preferred by the House of Lords, while "punitive" is the term used in many Canadian Courts. These two terms are, in effect, interchangeable. Aggravated damages are in fact a form of compensatory damages which incorporates intangible aspects of the wrong. *Carrier Lumber Ltd. v. British Columbia*, 1999 CarswellBC 1741, 47 B.L.R. (2d) 50, 30 C.E.L.R. (N.S.) 219, [1999] B.C.T.C. 192, Parrett J.

EXEMPLIFICATION. *n.* The official copy of a document made under a court's or public functionary's seal.

EXEMPLI GRATIA. [L. for example] For instance.

EXEMPTION. *n.* 1. Immunity; being free from duty or tax. "[May arise] ... by virtue of having never been made liable to a law or by having been made liable and then excluded from its application." *Crown Forest Industries Ltd. v. British Columbia* (1991), 4 M.P.L.R. (2d) 267 at 274, 55 B.C.L.R. (2d) 250 (C.A.), the court per Hollinrake J.A. 2. Freedom from, not being subject to, a requirement generally applicable. See CONSTITUTIONAL ~.

EXEMPTION CLAUSE. "... [G]enerally [has] the effect of excluding or limiting the liability of one party to a contract and ... generally, but not always, appear[s] in standard form contracts widely used in commercial matters... ." *Bauer v. Bank of Montreal* (1980), 10 B.L.R. 209 at 217, 33 C.B.R. (N.S.) 291, [1980] 2 S.C.R. 102, 110 D.L.R. (3d) 424, 32 N.R. 191, the court per McIntyre J.

EXERCISE. *v.* To use.

EXERCISE DISCRETION. To exercise discretion means to choose between two or more reasonable options. The choice must be made considering the applicable law and guiding principles and on a proper understanding of the facts. Where the facts are misapprehended and the error is an overriding factor in the exercise of the discretion such that the foundation for the option chosen no longer exists, then an injustice has been done. *Doiron v. Haché*, 2005 NBCA 75.

EX FACIE. [L.] On the face of it.

EX GRATIA. [L.] 1. Voluntary. K.D. Cooper-Stephenson & I.B. Saunders, *Personal Injury Damages in Canada* (Toronto: Carswell, 1981) at 501. 2. "... [U]sed simply to indicate ... that the party agreeing to pay does not admit any pre-existing liability on his part; but he is certainly not seeking to preclude the legal enforceability of the settlement itself by describing the contemplated payment as 'ex gratia'." *Edwards v. Skyways Ltd.*, [1964] 1 All E.R. 494 at 500, [1964] 1 W.L.R. 349 (U.K. Q.B.), Megaw J.

EXHAUSTION DOCTRINE. A doctrine which requires an applicant to exhaust all administrative remedies before resorting to the courts to challenge the validity of an order or decision made by a statutory authority.

EXHAUSTIVENESS. See PRINCIPLE OF ~.

EXHIBIT. *v.* To exhibit, (a) for direct or indirect gain, or (b) to the public. *Film Classification Act, 2005*, S.O. 2005, c. 17, s. 1.

EXHIBIT. *n.* An object admitted as evidence in court. F.A. Jaffe, *A Guide to Pathological Evidence for Lawyers and Police Officers*, 4th ed. (Toronto: Carswell, 1999) at 237. 2. A document admitted as evidence in court.

EXHUMATION. *n.* The exposure and removal of interred human remains for the purposes of viewing or examination. *Cremation, Interment and Funeral Services Act*, S.B.C. 2004, c. 35, s. 1. See DISINTERMENT.

EX HYPOTHESI. [L.] From the hypothesis.

EXIGENCY. *n.* Need; want; demand.

EXIGENT. *adj.* Requiring immediate action; demanding.

EXIGIBLE. *adj.* 1. Subject to execution. 2. Able to be demanded or required.

EXISTING ABORIGINAL RIGHTS. In section 35 of the Charter, interpreted to permit the evolution of those rights over time. May have a larger content than those rights which existed in 1982 when the Charter came into force.

EXISTING USE. The use to which land has already been put.

EX JURIS. See SERVICE ~.

EX MERO MOTU. [L.] Of one's own accord.

EX NUDO PACTO NON ORITUR ACTIO. [L.] An action does not arise from an agreement with no consideration.

EX OFFICIO. [L.] By virtue of one's office.

EXONERATION. *n.* Relief from liability when that liability is thrown on another person.

EXOR. *abbr.* Executor.

EXOTIC. *adj.* In relation to wildlife, means any wildlife of a species or type that is not indigenous to the province and that in its natural habitat is usually found wild in nature, but does not include ratite birds. *Wildlife Conservation Act*, S.P.E.I. 1998, c. 107, s. 1.

EX PARTE. [L. on behalf of] 1. "[Refers to] ... an order made at the instance of one party without the opposite party having had notice of the application." *Anderson v. Toronto-Dominion Bank* (1986), 9 C.P.C. (2d) 179 at 183, 70 B.C.L.R. (2d) 267 (C.A.), the court per Hutcheon J.A. 2. "[Used in British Columbia Supreme Court Rules, R. 52] ... in the absence of a party on the hearing of the application and not in the usual sense of an order made in the absence of service upon an interested person." *Dasmesh Holdings Ltd. v. McDonald* (1985), 49 C.P.C. 187 at 191, 60 B.C.L.R. 80 (C.A.), the court per Hutcheon J.A. 3. The Latin words ex parte, translated literally, mean from one side or party only. In a judicial sense the words ex parte refer to a proceeding granted at the instance of and for the benefit of one party only, without notice to, or contestation by, any person adversely affected. It has been held that the defining element of an ex parte proceeding is the absence of notice to the other party. *Society of Composers, Authors & Music Publishers of Canada v. 960122 Ontario Ltd.* 2003 FCA 256, 26 C.P.R. (4th) 161, 307 N.R. 390.

EXPECTANCY. *n.* Refers to an estate dependent on a contingency, a remainder or reversion. See IN ~.

EXPECTANT. *adj.* Relating to; depending on.

EXPECTANT ESTATE. An interest one will possess and enjoy at some future time, i.e. a reversion or remainder.

EXPECTANT HEIR. "... [P]hrase used in England in reference to a person who expects from a person then living and who is not allowed, under the circumstances, to encumber the future estate by improvident bargains." *Hall v. Marshall*, [1938] 3 D.L.R. 419 at 423, 13 M.P.R. 112 (N.S. S.C.), Doull J.

EXPECTATION. See LEGITIMATE ~; REASONABLE ~.

EXPECTATION OF LIFE. The number of years which someone of a certain age may, given equal chances, expect to live. See LOSS OF ~.

EXPEDITED. *adj.* Speedy, prompt.

EXPEDITION. See FISHING ~.

EXPEND. *v.* 1. To pay out. *Richer, Re* (1919), 46 O.L.R. 367 at 371, 50 D.L.R. 614, 17 O.W.N. 195 (C.A.), Meredith C.J.C.P. 2. "[Implies] ... a recurring act of consumption ..." *McFarland, Re*, [1963] 1 O.R. 273 at 275 (H.C.), Grant J.

EXPENDITURE. *n.* 1. (i) Payment authorized by a supply vote, (ii) a reimbursement, under the authority of one supply vote, of a payment charged against another supply vote, or (iii) a payment authorized by a statutory appropriation. *Financial Administration Act*, R.S.A. 2000, c. F-12, s. 1. 2. An outlay or expense or the cost or capital cost of a property. *Income Tax Act*, R.S.C. 1985, c. 1 (5th Supp.), s. 143.2. See CAPITAL ~; TAX ~.

EXPENSE. *n.* 1. Money laid out. 2. "... [W]ithin the meaning of paragraph s. 18(1)(a) of the Income Tax Act [R.S.C. 1952, c. 148 (as am. S.C. 1970-71-72, c. 63, s. 1)], is an obligation to pay a sum of money... ." *R. v. Burnco Industries Ltd.*, [1984] 2 F.C. 218 at 218, 53 N.R. 393, [1984] C.T.C. 337, 84 D.T.C. 6348 (C.A.), the court per Pratte J.A. 3. Includes, in relation to the conducting of a trial with a jury, (i) the costs of summoning a jury panel and any costs incidental to the summoning, (ii) the fees and allowances paid to jurors, (iii) costs arising from the order of a judge to view evidence ... (iv) costs for food, refreshments, accommodation and other requirements for a jury. *Jury Act*, R.S.A. 2000, c. J-3, s. 1. See ELECTION ADVERTISING ~; ~S; OPERATING ~.

EXPENSE ACCOUNT. A list of obligations incurred while working on behalf of one's employer.

EXPENSES. *n.* The [Canadian Human Rights Act, R.S.C. 1985, c. H-6] does not define "expenses" and is silent with respect to "costs". The provision in issue is a compensatory one ... In paragraph 53(2)(c), the word "expenses" is broad and non-specific. It takes its colour from the word "compensate", for only those expenses incurred as a result of the discriminatory practice qualify for compensation. The word "costs," however, is another matter. I agree with the appellant that the word "costs" is a legal term of art ... The concept of costs in the context of administrative tribunals carries the same general connotation as legal costs ... To accord different treatment to the federal legislation ? bearing in mind that the courts of Ontario, New Brunswick and Nova Scotia have determined, absent express authorization, no power to award costs exists ? flies in the face of the express interpretive direction of the Supreme Court and yields an anomalous, if not absurd, result. There are other indicia that militate against a conclusion that Parliament intended the word "expenses" to include "costs." There is no evidence of practical necessity for the exercise of the power to award costs to enable the Tribunal to attain the objects expressly prescribed by Parliament. Parliament did not intend to grant, and did not grant, to the Tribunal the power to award costs. To conclude that the Tribunal may award legal costs under the guise of "expenses incurred by the victim as a result of the discriminatory practice" would be to introduce indirectly into the Act a power which Parliament did not intend it to have. *Canada (Attorney General) v. Mowat*, 2009 FCA 309. See COMMON ~; EXPENSE; FUNERAL ~.

EXPERIMENT EVIDENCE. A combination of sworn statements and the production of things.

EXPERT. *n.* "... [G]enerally called to testify to provide information to enable the Court or a jury to understand technical and scientific issues raised in the litigation. They are also called upon to provide opinions and conclusions in areas where the Courts or jury are unable to make the necessary inferences from the technical facts presented. The role of the expert is circumscribed by his area of expertise. It is essential that the witness be shown to possess the necessary qualifications and skill in the area or field in which his opinion is sought. Those qualifications and skill can be based on or derived from academic study or practical experience." *Rieger v. Burgess* (1988), 45 C.C.L.T. 56 at 95, [1988] 4 W.W.R. 577, 66 Sask. R. 1 (C.A.), Tallis, Cameron and Vancise JJ.A.

EXPERT EVIDENCE. 1. The admissible opinion of someone whose competency to form an opinion on some subject before the court was acquired by a special course of study or experience, e.g., in engineering, foreign law or medicine. 2. The test for the admissibility of expert evidence was consolidated. Four criteria must be met by a party which seeks to introduce expert evidence: relevance, necessity, the lack of any other exclusionary rule, and a properly qualified expert. Even where these requirements are met, the evidence may be rejected if its prejudicial effect on the conduct of the trial outweighs its probative value. *R. v. D. (D.)*, 2000 CarswellOnt 3255, 2000 SCC 43, 36 C.R. (5th) 261, 148 C.C.C. (3d) 41, 191 D.L.R. (4th) 60, 259 N.R. 156, 136 O.A.C. 201, [2000] 2 S.C.R. 275. See also NECESSITY.

EXPERTISE. See RELATIVE ~.

EXPERT WITNESS. "[F]unction ... is to provide for the jury or other trier of fact an expert's opinion as to the significance of, or the inference which may be drawn from, proved facts in a field in which the expert witness possesses special knowledge and experience going beyond that of the trier of fact. The expert witness is permitted to give such opinions for the assistance of the jury... ." *R. v. Béland* (1987), 36 C.C.C. (3d) 481 at 493, 79 N.R. 263, 9 Q.A.C. 293, [1987] 2 S.C.R. 398, 60 C.R. (3d) 1, 43 D.L.R. (4th) 641, McIntyre J. (Dickson C.J.C., Beetz and Le Dain JJ. concurring).

EXPIRATION. *n.* The running out of a term or period by effluxion of time.

EXPIRY DATE. The earlier of (a) the date, expressed at minimum as a year and month, up to and including which a natural health product maintains its purity and physical characteristics and its medicinal ingredients maintain their quantity per dosage unit and their potency, and (b) the date, expressed at minimum as a year and month, after which the manufacturer recommends that the natural health product should not be used. *Food and Drugs Act*, R.S.C. 1985, c. F-27, *Natural Health Products Regulations*, SOR/2003-196, s. 1.

EXPLANATION. See DEFENCE OF ~.

EXPLANATORY NOTE. Technically not part of a bill and printed on the page across from the relevant clause. A. Fraser, W.A. Dawson & J. Holtby, eds., *Beauchesne's Rules and Forms of the House of Commons of Canada*, 6th ed. (Toronto: Carswell, 1989) at 194.

EXPLICIT KNOWLEDGE. Anything written or stored electronically in a form that is easy to reproduce and distribute, for example memoranda, books, videos.

EXPLORE. See PROSPECT AND ~.

EXPLOSIVE. *n.* Any thing that is made, manufactured or used to produce an explosion or a detonation or pyrotechnic effect, and includes any thing prescribed to be an explosive by the regulations, but does not include gases, organic peroxides or any thing prescribed not to be an explosive by the regulations. *Explosives Act*, R.S.C. 1985, c. E-17, s. 2. See PLASTIC ~.

EXPLOSIVE OR OTHER LETHAL DEVICE. An explosive or incendiary weapon or device that is designed to cause, or is capable of causing, death, serious bodily injury or substantial material damage; or a weapon or device that is designed to cause, or is capable of causing, death, serious bodily injury or substantial material damage through the release, dissemination or impact of toxic chemicals, biological agents or toxins or similar substances, or radiation or radioactive material. *Criminal Code*, R.S.C. 1985, c. C-46, s. 431.2 (1).

EXPLOSIVE SUBSTANCE. Includes anything intended to be used to make an explosive substance, anything, or any part thereof, used or intended to be used, or adapted to cause, or to aid in causing an explosion in or with an explosive substance, and an incendiary grenade, fire bomb, Molotov cocktail or other similar incendiary substance or device and a delaying mechanism or other thing intended for use in connection with such a substance or device; *Criminal Code*, R.S.C. 1985, c. C-46, s. 2.

EXPORT. *v.* 1. The transportation of goods from this to a foreign country. 2."... [I]nvolves the idea of a severance of goods from the mass of things belonging to this country with the intention of uniting them with the mass of things belonging to some foreign country. It also involves the idea of transporting the thing exported beyond the boundaries of this country with the intention of effecting that... ." *R. v. Carling Export Brewing & Malting Co.*, [1930] 2 D.L.R. 725 at 733, [1930] S.C.R. 351, Duff J. 3. Ship from Canada to any other country or from any province to any other province. *Fish Inspection Regulations*, C.R.C., c. 802, s. 2. 4. In order for there to be a sale for export, there must obviously be a person who exports. For there to be an exporter, there must be an importer. Put in a different way, a sale for export cannot exist

without a corresponding purchase to import. *Deputy Minister of National Revenue v. Mattel Canada Inc.*, 2001 CarswellNat 1032, 2001 SCC 36, 29 Admin. L.R (3d) 56, 199 D.L.R. (4th) 598, 270 N.R. 153, 12 C.P.R. (4th) 417. See CANADIAN CULTURAL PROPERTY ~ REVIEW BOARD.

EXPORT TAX. A tax on goods to be exported.

EXPOSE. *v.* 1. To exhibit, to make visible. 2. Includes (a) a wilful omission to take charge of a child by a person who is under a legal duty to do so, and (b) dealing with a child in a manner that is likely to leave that child exposed to risk without protection. *Criminal Code*, R.S.C. 1985, c. C-46, s. 214.

EX POST FACTO. [L. by something done after] Describes a statute which, after the fact, either makes an act punishable which was not punishable when it was done, or which imposes punishment for an act which is different from what would have been inflicted when the act was done.

EXPOSURE. n. Any contact with, or ingestion, inhalation or assimilation of, a tobacco product, including any smoke or other by-product of the use, consumption or combustion of a tobacco product. *The Tobacco Damages and Health Care Costs Recovery Act*, S.S. 2007, c. T-14.2, s. 2. See FOREIGN ~.

EXPOSURE RECORD. The record of a worker's exposure to harmful substances in the workplace.

EXPOSURE THEORY. On this theory, from the first exposure to the condition or conditions which ultimately cause the property damage, that damage is inevitable, a certainty. As a result, the property damage is considered to have occurred on that first exposure so that the deterioration following that exposure is merely the manifestation of the damage that has already occurred requiring repair or replacement. *Alie v. Bertrand & Frère Construction Co.* (2002), 62 O.R. (3d) 345 (C.A.).

EXPRESS. *adj.* 1. Clear; unambiguous. 2. Of some act showing intention, means done to communicate the intention directly, as opposed to by implication.

EXPRESS AGENCY. Agency deliberately created and limited by the agreement or contract governing it.

EXPRESS AUTHORITY. Actual express authority can be determined by consensual agreement and/or the contract of employment. Its scope is ascertained by applying ordinary principles of construction of contracts, including proper implications from the express words used, the usages of the trade, or the course of business between the parties. Unless the authority is restricted, the appointment of a person to an executive or director position clothes that person with the authority which a person in his or her position normally has. *D. Fogell Associates Ltd. v. Esprit de Corp (1980) Ltd. / Esprit de Corp (1980) Ltee.*, 1997 CarswellBC 1131 (S.C.), Edwards J.

EXPRESS CONDITION. A term specified in the agreement.

EXPRESSION. *n.* "All activities which convey or attempt to convey meaning prima facie fall within the scope of the guarantee [of freedom of expression in s. 2(b) of the Charter]: ..." R. v. Keegstra (1990), 61 C.C.C. (3d) 1 at 95, 1 C.R. (4th) 129, 77 Alta. L.R. (2d) 193, [1991] 2 W.W.R. 1, 117 N.R. 1, 114 A.R. 81, 3 C.R.R. (2d) 193, [1990] 3 S.C.R. 697, McLachlin J. (dissenting) (La Forest and Sopinka JJ. concurring). See *Irwin Toy Ltd. v. Québec (Procureur général)* (1989), 58 D.L.R. (4th) 577 at 607, [1989] 1 S.C.R. 927, 25 C.P.R. (3d) 417, 94 N.R. 167, 24 Q.A.C. 2, 39 C.R.R. 193, Dickson C.J.C., Lamer and Wilson JJ. See COMMERCIAL SPEECH; FREEDOM OF ~; HATRED.

EXPRESSIO UNIUS EST EXCLUSIO ALTERIUS. [L.] 1. To express one thing is to exclude another. 2. An express statutory mention of one item is presumptively exhaustive and impliedly excludes other similar items. This is the essence of the presumption known by the Latin tag, expressio unius est exclusio alterius. *Nazifpour v. Canada (Minister of Citizenship & Immigration)*, 2007 FCA 35. 3. "Often, ... invoked to compare two provisions of the same statute. If section A prohibits certain individuals from participating in a decision while section B concerns decision-making but has no parallel prohibitions, it may be concluded that the law was intentionally silent, and that the individuals referred to in section A may participate in the decision provided for in section B." *Leblanc Estate v. Bank of Montreal* (1988), [1989] 1 W.W.R. 49 at 63, 69 Sask. R. 81, 54 D.L.R. (4th) 89 (C.A.), Sherstobitoff J.A.

EXPRESSLY. *adv.* Leaving no doubt as to what is meant.

EXPRESS MALICE. "Express malice" is the term of art descriptive of ... a [dominant] motive [to injure the plaintiff]. Broadly speaking it means malice in the popular sense of a desire to injure the person who is defamed and is generally the motive which the plaintiff sets out to prove. *Teamsters, Local 987 v. U.F.C.W., Local 401*, 2005 ABCA 263.

EXPRESS TERM. A term particularly mentioned and agreed on by the parties. Its character, content and form is expressed in the agreement between them.

EXPRESS TRUST. A trust which comes into existence because the settlor has expressed the intention to accomplish that result.

EXPROPRIATE. *v.* For an expropriating authority to take land without the consent of the owner in the exercise of its statutory powers. *Expropriation acts.*.

EXPROPRIATING AUTHORITY. The Crown or an association or person empowered to acquire land by expropriation. *Expropriation acts.*.

EXPROPRIATION. *n.* 1. The acquisition of title to land without the consent of the owner. 2. Taking without the consent of the owner. 3. "... [E]xtinction of an interest in land must ... be included ..." *British Columbia v. Tener* (1985), 36 R.P.R. 291 at 301, [1985] 1 S.C.R. 533, [1985] 3 W.W.R. 673, 32 L.C.R. 340, 17 D.L.R. (4th) 1, 59 N.R. 82, 28 B.C.L.R. (2d) 241, Estey J. (Beetz, McIntyre, Chouinard and Le Dain JJ. concurring). 4. Derogation by Crown from its grant of a profit à prendre can amount to expropriation. *British Columbia v. Tener* (1985), 36 R.P.R.

291 at 319, [1985] 1 S.C.R. 533, [1985] 3 W.W.R. 673, 32 L.C.R. 340, 17 D.L.R. (4th) 1, 59 N.R. 82, 28 B.C.L.R. (2d) 241, Wilson J. (Dickson C.J.C. concurring). See PRESUMPTION AGAINST ~.

EX PROPRIO MOTU. [L.] Of one's own accord.

EX PROPRIO VIGORE. [L.] By its own strength.

EXPUNGE. *v.* To strike out all or part of a document, record, or pleading.

EX REL. *abbr.* Ex relatione.

EX RELATIONE. [L. from information or a narrative] On the information of a citizen called the relator.

EX RIGHTS. Without any right to the new issue of shares which will be made to shareholders.

EXTANT. *adj.* Existing.

EXTENDED HEALTH CARE SERVICES. The following services, as more particularly defined in the regulations, provided for residents of a province, namely, (a) nursing home intermediate care service, (b) adult residential care service, (c) home care service, and (d) ambulatory health care service. *Canada Health Act*, R.S.C. 1985, c. C-6, s. 2.

EXTENSION. *n.* 1. An indulgence by giving time to pay a debt or perform an obligation. 2. In reference to an agreement, refers to the prolonging of an agreement which already exists, not to renewal of the agreement. *Manulife Bank of Canada v. Conlin*, [1996] 3 S.C.R. 415.

EXTENT. *n.* The special writ to recover debts owed to the Crown which at one time differed from an ordinary writ of execution because a debtor's land and goods could be taken all at once in order to force payment of the debt. See WRIT OF ~.

EXTERMINATION. *n.* 1. Includes the intentional infliction of conditions of life, inter alia the deprivation of access to food and medicine, calculated to bring about the destruction of part of a population. *Crimes Against Humanity and War Crimes Act*, S.C. 2000, c. 24, Sched., *Rome Statute*, Article 7. 2. With respect to a pest, means the destruction, prevention or control of the pest by means of a pesticide. *Environmental Protection and Enhancement Act*, R.S.A. 2000, c. E-12, s. 154.

EXTERNAL REVIEW COMMITTEE. See ROYAL CANADIAN MOUNTED POLICE ~.

EXTERNAL SELF-DETERMINATION. A right to external self-determination (which in this case potentially takes the form of the assertion of a right to unilateral secession) arises in only the most extreme of cases and, even then, under carefully defined circumstances. External self-determination can be defined as in the following statement from the Declaration on Friendly Relations, supra [Declaration on Principles of International Law Concerning Friendly Relations and Co-operation Among States in Accordance with the Charter of the United Nations, GA Res. 2625 (XXV), 24 October 1970]. The establishment of a sovereign and independent State, the free association or integration with an independent State or the emergence into any other political status freely determined by a people constitute modes of implementing the right of self-determination by that people. *Reference re Secession of Quebec*, 1998 CarswellNat 1299, 161 D.L.R. (4th) 385, 228 N.R. 203, 55 C.R.R. (2d) 1, [1998] 2 S.C.R. 217, per curiam.

EXTINCTION. *n.* Hypothecs are extinguished by the loss, change of nature, exclusion from being an object of commerce or expropriation of the charged property, where such events affect the property as a whole. *Civil Code*, S.Q. 1991, c. 64, a. 2795.

EXTINGUISHED. *adj.* Of a right or obligation, no longer existing.

EXTINGUISHMENT. *n.* The termination of a right.

EXTORTION. *n.* Every one commits extortion who, without reasonable justification or excuse and with intent to obtain anything, by threats, accusation, menaces or violence induces or attempts to induce any person, whether or not he is the person threatened, accused or menaced or to whom violence is shown, to do anything or cause anything to be done. *Criminal Code*, R.S.C. 1985, c. C-46, s. 346(1).

EXTRA. See TENANT'S ~.

EXTRA-BILLING. The billing for an insured health service rendered to an insured person by a medical practitioner or a dentist in an amount in addition to any amount paid or to be paid for that service by the health care insurance plan of a province. *Canada Health Act*, R.S.C. 1985, c. C-6, s. 2.

EXTRADITION. *n.* "... [T]he surrender by one state to another, on request, of persons accused or convicted of committing a crime in the state seeking the surrender." *R. v. Schmidt* (1987), 28 C.R.R. 280 at 289, 76 N.R. 12, [1987] 1 S.C.R. 500, 58 C.R. (3d) 1, 20 O.A.C. 161, 39 D.L.R. (4th) 18, 33 C.C.C. (3d) 193, 61 O.R. (2d) 530, La Forest J. (Dickson C.J.C., Beetz, McIntyre and Le Dain JJ. concurring).

EXTRADITION AGREEMENT. An agreement that is in force, to which Canada is a party and that contains a provision respecting the extradition of persons, other than a specific agreement. *Extradition Act*, S.C. 1999, c. 18, s. 2.

EXTRADITION CRIME. An "extradition crime" is defined in s. 2 of the [Extradition Act, R.S.C. 1985, c. E-23] to mean any crime that if committed in Canada would be one of the crimes listed in the schedule to the Act or in the case of an extradition arrangement (a treaty) any crime described in such arrangement. Article 2 of the Canadian-United States Extradition Treaty no longer lists specific extradition offences. It provides that "extradition shall be granted for any offence punishable by the laws of both parties by imprisonment for a term exceeding one year or any greater punishment." It is not necessary that the Canadian offence established by the conduct be described by the same name or that it have the same legal elements as the offence charged in the requesting state. The protection afforded by the double criminality rule is ensured if the conduct that underlies the foreign charge constitutes any extradition crime

under the laws of Canada. *D'Agostino, Re*, 2000 CarswellOnt 465, 47 O.R. (3d) 257, 143 C.C.C. (3d) 158, 129 O.A.C. 166, 72 C.R.R. (2d) 198 (C.A.).

EXTRADITION PARTNER. A State or entity with which Canada is party to an extradition agreement, with which Canada has entered into a specific agreement or whose name appears in the schedule. *Extradition Act*, S.C. 1999, c. 18, s. 2.

EXTRAJUDICIAL. *var.* **EXTRA-JUDICIAL.** *adj.* Out of the usual conduct of legal procedure.

EXTRAJUDICIAL MEASURES. Measures other than judicial proceedings under this Act used to deal with a young person alleged to have committed an offence and includes extrajudicial sanctions. *Youth Criminal Justice Act*, S.C. 2002, c. 1, s. 2.

EXTRAJUDICIAL SANCTION. A sanction that is part of a program referred to in section 10. May be used to deal with a young person alleged to have committed an offence only if the young person cannot be adequately dealt with by a warning, caution or referral because of the seriousness of the offence, the nature and number of previous offences committed by the young person or any other aggravating circumstances. *Youth Criminal Justice Act*, S.C. 2002, c. 1, s. 2(1), 10(1).

EXTRANEOUS DEFENCE. In a criminal matter, a defence which raises a new issue which oversteps the Crown's case.

EXTRAORDINARY. *adj.* Exceptional; not ordinary.

EXTRAORDINARY REMEDY. A writ of mandamus, quo warranto or habeas corpus.

EXTRA PETITA. The ultra petita principle is generally understood to mean that a court will not make a ruling beyond what is requested by the parties. For instance, a judgment which grants a monetary award that goes beyond that sought by the claimant is said to be ultra petita or extra petita. The legislator is free to remove administrative tribunals from the constraints of ultra petita. This will often be the case, as administrative tribunals are generally created to advance interests that can go beyond the immediate interests of the parties who appear before them. *Canadian Private Copying Collective v. Canadian Storage Media Alliance*, 2004 FCA 424. See ULTRA PETITA PRINCIPLE.

EXTRA-PROVINCIAL. *adj.* Incorporated in another province.

EXTRA-PROVINCIAL COMPANY. *var.* **EXTRAPROVINCIAL COMPANY.** A company incorporated outside the province to which reference is made.

EXTRA-PROVINCIAL CORPORATION. 1. A corporation that was incorporated under the laws of Canada or of any province or territory other than Alberta. *Loan and Trust Corporations Act*, R.S.A. 2000, c. L-20, s. 1. 2. A company or certain class of companies incorporated in another jurisdiction which must become licensed or registered if they carry on business in a province.

EXTRA-TERRITORIAL. *adj.* Outside the territory of the jurisdiction which enacted the law in question.

EXTRATERRITORIALITY. *n.* The projection of a state's authority beyond the territory of the state.

EXTRICATE. *v.* To free oneself; release oneself.

EXTRINSIC EVIDENCE. "... [E]vidence which is not contained in the body of the document, agreement or contract which forms the, or a subject matter of the, issue under consideration and requiring determination. ..." *Saskatoon Market Mall Ltd. v. Macleod-Stedman Inc.* (1989), 78 Sask. R. 179 at 194 (Q.B.), Grotsky J.

EXTRINSIC FRAUD. Courts have drawn a distinction between "intrinsic fraud" and "extrinsic fraud" in an attempt to clarify the types of fraud that can vitiate the judgment of a foreign court. Extrinsic fraud is identified as fraud going to the jurisdiction of the issuing court or the kind of fraud that misleads the court, foreign or domestic, into believing that it has jurisdiction over the cause of action. Evidence of this kind of fraud, if accepted, will justify setting aside the judgment. The historic description of and the distinction between intrinsic and extrinsic fraud is of no apparent value and, because of its ability to both complicate and confuse, should be discontinued. *Beals v. Saldanha*, 2003 SCC 72, Major, J.

EX TURPI CAUSA NON ORITUR ACTIO. [L.] "... [R]ule means ... that the courts will not enforce a right which would otherwise be enforceable if the right arises out of an act committed by the person asserting the right (or by someone who is regarded in law as his successor) which is regarded by the court as sufficiently anti-social to justify the court's refusal to enforce that right." *Hardy v. Motor Insurers' Bureau*, [1964] 2 All E.R. 742 at 750-51 (U.K.), Lord Diplock.

EYE-WITNESS. *n.* One who testifies about facts she or he has seen.

EYRE. See RULE IN PHILLIPS V. ~.

E

F

FABRICATE. *v.* To make up or concoct; to construct or manufacture.

FABRICATING EVIDENCE. Every one who, with intent to mislead, fabricates anything with intent that it shall be used as evidence in a judicial proceeding, existing or proposed, by any means other than perjury or incitement to perjury is guilty of an indictable offence and liable to imprisonment for a term not exceeding fourteen years. *Criminal Code*, R.S.C. 1985, c. C-46, s. 137.

FABRICATION. See RECENT ~.

FACE. *n.* The text of the document, not just the first page.

FACE VALUE. The nominal value printed or written on the face of a bond, debenture, note, share certificate or other document indicating its par value.

FACIALLY NEUTRAL. Adverse effect discrimination can only emanate from a law which is facially neutral. Facially neutral means that the provision, on its face, does not confer an advantage or impose a disadvantage on any group. The classic example is height and weight restrictions set by police forces as criteria for hiring. Such restrictions are neutral in that they apply equally to all people, although their effects may be felt unequally by men and women.

FACIAS. [L. that you cause] See FIERI FACIAS.

FACILITY. See COMMON ~; CONVENTION ~; CORRECTIONAL ~; GOVERNMENT OR PUBLIC ~; INFRASTRUCTURE ~; NUCLEAR ~; OIL HANDLING ~; PORT ~; QUARANTINE ~; TELECOMMUNICATIONS ~; TRANSMISSION ~; YOUTH CUSTODY ~.

FACSIMILE. *n.* An accurate reproduction of a book, instrument, document or record and includes a print from microfilm and a printed copy generated by or produced from a computer record. *Land Titles Act*, R.S.O. 1990, c. L.5, s. 1.

FACT. *n.* "... [S]tatement, tale or news is an expression which, taken as a whole and understood in context, conveys an assertion of fact or facts and not merely the expression of opinion... . Expression which makes a statement susceptible of proof and disproof is an assertion of fact; expression which merely offers an interpretation of fact which may be embraced or rejected depending on its cogency or normative appeal, is opinion." *R. v. Zundel* (1992), 75 C.C.C. (3d) 449 at 492, 95 D.L.R. (4th) 202, [1992] 2 S.C.R. 731, 140 N.R. 1, 56 O.A.C. 161, 16 C.R. (4th) 1, 10 C.R.R. (2d) 193, Cory and Iacobucci JJ. (dissenting) (Gonthier J. concurring). See ACCESSORY AFTER THE ~; ACCESSORY BEFORE THE ~; ADJUDICATIVE ~S; CLUE ~; COLLATERAL ~ RULE; CONCLUSION OF ~; FINDING OF ~; LEGISLATIVE ~S; MATERIAL ~; MISTAKE OF ~; PRESUMPTIONS OF ~; PRIMARY ~S; QUESTION OF ~; SIMILAR ~ EVIDENCE; TRIER OF ~.

FACTA PROBANDA. [L.] Facts which must be proved; facts in issue.

FACTA PROBANTIA. [L.] Facts given in evidence to prove facta probanda; evidentiary facts.

FACT FINDER. The person or body charged with determining which evidence is believed. See FINDING OF FACT; TRIER OF FACT.

FACT IN ISSUE. A fact which the plaintiff must establish to succeed in proving his or her case and a fact which the defendant must prove in order to make out the defence.

FACTITIOUS. *adj.* Not real, genuine or natural.

FACTO. [L.] In fact.

FACTOR. *n.* 1. One who loans money on security of accounts receivable or merchandise and inventory or both, but who is in no way connected with selling them. I.F.G. Baxter, *The Law of Banking*, 3d ed. (Toronto: Carswell, 1981) at 190. 2. An agent who disposes of or sells products in the agent's control or possession. G.H.L. Fridman, *Sale of Goods in Canada*, 3d ed. (Toronto: Carswell, 1986) at 493. See NET ~; RIBIC ~S.

FACTORAGE. *n.* The commission which a factor receives.

FACTORING. *n.* A factoring of accounts receivable is based upon an absolute assignment of them. It is in effect a sale by a company of its accounts receivable at a discounted value to the factoring company for immediate consideration. Clearly a GABD does not meet the standard required for a factoring arrangement which requires an absolute transfer of the proprietary interest of the assignor in the book debts. *Pigott Project Management Ltd. v. Land-Rock Re-*

sources Ltd., 38 Alta. L.R. (3d) 1 (S.C.C.), Cory J. for majority.

FACTUAL CAUSATION. 1. Is concerned with an inquiry about how the victim came to his or her death, in a medical, mechanical, or physical sense, and with the contribution of the accused to that result. Where factual causation is established, the remaining issue is legal causation. *R. v. Nette*, 2001 SCC 78, Arbour J. (Iacobucci, Major, Binnie, LeBel JJ. concurring). 2. As stated by Arbour J. [in R. v. Nette 2001 SCC 78], factual causation is "concerned with an inquiry about how the victim came to his or her death, in a medical, mechanical, or physical sense, and with the contribution of the accused to that result" (at para. 44). Factual causation is often answered by the "but for" inquiry. *R. v. Sinclair*, 2009 MBCA 71.

FACTUAL MATRIX. In relation to a commercial agreement, the background of relevant facts that the parties must clearly have been take to have known and to have had in mind when they drafted the text of their agreement.

FACTUM. *n.* [L.] 1. A deed; an act. 2. A statement of facts and law which each party files in an application, appeal or motion.

FACULTATIVE OBLIGATION. An obligation which has only one principal prestation as its object but from which the debtor may release himself by performing another prestation. The debtor is released if the principal prestation, through no fault on his part, becomes impossible to perform. *Civil Code*, S.Q. 1991, c. 64, a. 1552.

FAILURE OF ISSUE. Death without issue.

FAINT HOPE CLAUSE. Name given to s. 745.6 of the Criminal Code which provides: (1) A person may apply, in writing, to the appropriate Chief Justice in the province in which their conviction took place for a reduction in the number of years of imprisonment without eligibility for parole if the person (a) has been convicted of murder or high treason; (b) has been sentenced to imprisonment for life without eligibility for parole until more than fifteen years of their sentence has been served; and (c) has served at least fifteen years of their sentence. (2) A person who has been convicted of more than one murder may not make an application under subsection (1), whether or not proceedings were commenced in respect of any of the murders before another murder was committed.

FAIR. *n.* A gathering of people at which shows and entertainments of various sorts are presented.

FAIR. *adj.* 1. "... [R]easonable ..." *Vanguard Coatings & Chemicals Ltd. v. R.* (1988), 30 Admin. L.R. 121 at 148, 88 D.T.C. 6374, Can. S.T.R. 80-020, [1988] 2 C.T.C. 178, 17 C.E.R. 71, 88 N.R. 241, 22 F.T.R. 80n, [1988] 3 F.C. 560, [1989] 1 T.S.T. 202.5 (C.A.), MacGuigan J.A. (Urie J.A. concurring). 2. Impartial.

FAIR COMMENT. In Cherneskey v. Armadale Publishers Ltd., 1978 CanLII 20, [1979] 1 S.C.R. 1067, Dickson J., in dissent, identified the elements of the "fair comment" defence as follows: "(a) the comment must be on a matter of public interest; (b) the comment must be based on fact; (c) the comment, though it can include inferences of fact, must be recognisable as comment; (d) the comment must satisfy the following objective test: could any man honestly express that opinion on the proved facts? (e) even though the comment satisfies the objective test the defence can be defeated if the plaintiff proves that the defendant was actuated by express malice. [Emphasis in original deleted; pp. 1099-1100.] (citing Duncan and Neill on Defamation (1978), at p. 62)." Although on that occasion a majority of the Court insisted on framing the honest belief requirement in subjective terms (the comment must express an opinion honestly held by the speaker), I believe experience has shown that Dickson J.'s "objective" formulation of the "honest belief" test better conforms to the requirements of free expression endorsed as a fundamental value of our society by s. 2(b) of the Canadian Charter of Rights and Freedoms. Of course, even if the elements of the "fair comment" defence are established, the plaintiff can still succeed by proving that the defendant was actuated by malice, i.e. for an indirect or improper motive not connected with the purpose for which the defence exists (Sun Life Assurance Co. of Canada v. Dalrymple, 1965 CanLII 9, [1965] S.C.R. 302, at p. 309). I note, parenthetically, that Duncan and Neill subsequently reformulated proposition (d) to say: "[C]ould any fair-minded man honestly express that opinion on the proved facts?"; Duncan and Neill on Defamation (2nd ed. 1983), at p. 63 ... In my respectful view, the addition of a qualitative standard such as "fair minded" should be resisted. "Fair-mindedness" often lies in the eye of the beholder. Political partisans are constantly astonished at the sheer "unfairness" of criticisms made by their opponents. Trenchant criticism which otherwise meets the "honest belief" criterion ought not to be actionable because, in the opinion of a court, it crosses some ill-defined line of "fair-mindedness." The trier of fact is not required to assess whether the comment is a reasonable and proportional response to the stated or understood facts. *WIC Radio Ltd. v. Simpson*, [2008] 2 S.C.R. 420, 2008 SCC 40, para. 1 and 28, Binnie J. for the majority.

FAIR DEALING. At the Court of Appeal [2002 CarswellNat 1000], Linden J.A. acknowledged that there was no set test for fairness, but outlined a series of factors that could be considered to help assess whether a dealing is fair. Drawing on the decision in Hubbard, supra, as well as the doctrine of fair use in the United States, he proposed that the following factors be considered in assessing whether a dealing was fair: (1) the purpose of the dealing; (2) the character of the dealing; (3) the amount of the dealing; (4) alternatives to the dealing; (5) the nature of the work; and (6) the effect of the dealing on the work. Although these considerations will not all arise in every case of fair dealing, this list of factors provides a useful analytical framework to govern determinations of fairness in future cases. *CCH Canadian Ltd. v. Law Society of Upper Canada*, 2004 SCC 13.

FAIR EMPLOYMENT PRACTICE. Practice of offering equal employment opportunities to persons regardless of race, national origin, colour, religion, age, sex, marital status, physical handicap or conviction for which a pardon has been granted.

FAIRGROUND. *n.* An outdoor open space used for fairs.

FAIR HEARING. "... [T]he tribunal which adjudicates upon his rights must act fairly, in good faith, without bias and in judicial temper, and must give to him the opportunity adequately to state his case." *Duke v. R.*, [1972] S.C.R. 917 at 923, 18 C.R.N.S. 302, 7 C.C.C. (2d) 474, 28 D.L.R. (3d) 129, the court per Fauteux C.J.C.

FAIRLY. See ACT ~; DUTY TO ACT ~.

FAIR MARKET RATE. (i) In respect of the acquisition or disposition of property, including a lease or rental of property, and subject to regulations made with respect to the valuation of property, the most probable price in terms of money that the property should bring in a competitive and open market under all conditions requisite to a fair sale or lease, assuming that the price is not affected by undue stimuli, with both the seller and the buyer acting prudently and knowledgeably, (ii) subject to subclause (iii), in respect of the acquisition or provision of services, a consideration that might reasonably be expected to be obtained or given for the services in question in an arm's length transaction in an open market between willing parties to a transaction of that nature and on terms that, having regard to open market conditions, are competitive and not unreasonable, and (iii) in respect of the provision of services that are provided generally to customers of the provincial corporation or subsidiary in question, the rate and terms that are offered in respect of those services to customers generally in the ordinary course of that corporation's or subsidiary's business. *Loan and Trust Corporations Act*, R.S.A. 2000, c. L-20, s. 1.

FAIR MARKET RENT. . [T]he use of the word "market" in this lease to define the rent to be paid for the renewal can only mean that the rent to be paid is the rent the premises would attract if exposed to the market at the time of the renewal. . . .[T]he language precludes excluding the value of the tenant's improvements in calculating the rent. If the parties had agreed that the renewal rent would be "fair rent" (i.e., fair as between them), the inquiry would have been subjective and the position might well have been different. But what they agreed was that the rent would be the fair market rent. The determination is then to be objective. I consider that the use of the word "fair" adds nothing to the meaning of market rent except that the market is to be considered a consistent market unaffected by significant transient fluctuations that may be evident at the time of renewal. *Fire Productions Ltd. v. Lauro*, 2006 BCCA 497.

FAIR MARKET VALUE. "... [T]he highest price available estimated in terms of money which a willing seller may obtain for the property in an open and unrestricted market from a willing knowledgeable purchaser acting at arm's length." *Minister of National Revenue v. Northwood Country Club* (1989), 89 D.T.C. 173 at 176, [1989] 1 C.T.C. 2230 (T.C.C.), Kempo T.C.J.

FAIRNESS. *n.* The duty of an administrator to act fairly regarding procedure. Any administrator must, minimally, let the party affected by her or his decision understand the case against that party and provide the party with a fair chance to answer it or to be heard. See ACT FAIRLY; DUTY TO ACT FAIRLY; PRINCIPLE OF ORDER AND ~; PROCEDURAL ~.

FAIRNESS LETTER. This case turns largely on a letter dated May 3, 1999 that the visa officer sent to [the applicant], care of his lawyer in Toronto. It was the standard form letter sent in medical inadmissibility cases, and is generally known as the "fairness letter" because it provides an opportunity for visa applicants to submit additional material in support of their application and to respond to the concerns of the visa officer. *Khan v. Canada (Minister of Citizenship & Immigration)* 2001 FCA 345, 208 D.L.R. (4th) 265, 283 N.R. 173, [2002] 2 F.C. 413, 213 F.T.R. 56 (note).

FAIR OPPORTUNITY. Refers to the chance for accused persons to present their cases and to know the relevant evidence.

FAIR RENT. If the parties had agreed that the renewal rent would be "fair rent" (i.e., fair as between them), the inquiry would have been subjective and the position might well have been different. But what they agreed was that the rent would be the fair market rent. The determination is then to be objective. *Fire Productions Ltd. v. Lauro*, 2006 BCCA 497.

FAIR TRIAL. "1. One that is based on the law, the outcome of which is determined by the evidence, free of bias, real or apprehended." *R. v. S. (R.D.)* [1997] 3 S.C.R. 484. 2. A trial that appears fair, both from the perspective of the accused and the perspective of the community. A fair trial must not be confused with the most advantageous trial possible from the accused's point of view. *R. v. Lyons*, [1987] 2 S.C.R. 309, at p. 362, a Forest J. Nor must it be conflated with the perfect trial; in the real world, perfection is seldom attained. A fair trial is one which satisfies the public interest in getting at the truth, while preserving basic procedural fairness to the accused. *R. v. Harrer* [1995] 3 S.C.R. 562, McLachlin, J. 3. The cornerstone of the Stillman [[1997] 1 S.C.R. 607] analysis is the court's understanding of a "fair trial." Conscriptive evidence obtained by violation of a Charter [Canadian Charter of Rights and Freedoms] right is excluded from the criminal trial because it affects the accused's right to a fair trial. However, 'fair trial' has a very special meaning in this context: it refers to the manner in which evidence was obtained, not to the way the trial itself is conducted. This notion of trial fairness is summarized in para. 73 of Cory J.'s majority reasons in Stillman : It is apparent from this passage [from R. v. Collins] that the primary aim and purpose of considering the trial fairness factor in the s. 24(2) analysis is to prevent an accused person whose Charter rights have been infringed from being forced or conscripted to provide evidence in the form of statements or bodily samples for the benefit of the state. It is because the accused is compelled as a result of a Charter breach to participate in the creation or discovery of self-incriminating evidence in the form

F

of confessions, statements or the provision of bodily samples, that the admission of that evidence would generally tend to render the trial unfair. That general rule, like all rules, may be subject to rare exceptions. This special meaning of trial fairness in the Charter context is itself rooted in the fundamental tenet of the criminal justice system that an accused is not required to assist the prosecution in making out a case against him or her and is not required to respond to the prosecution's case until the Crown has made out a case to meet without the compelled participation of the accused. *P. (D.) v. Wagg* (2004), 187 O.A.C. 26. 4. The method for determining whether a trial was fair is described by Cory J. as: The summary itself can be reduced to this short form: 1. Classify the evidence as conscriptive or non conscriptive based upon the manner in which the evidence was obtained. If the evidence is non conscriptive, its admission will not render the trial unfair and the court will proceed to consider the seriousness of the breach and the effect of exclusion on the repute of the administration of justice. 2. If the evidence is conscriptive and the Crown fails to demonstrate on a balance of probabilities that the evidence would have been discovered by alternative non conscriptive means, then its admission will render the trial unfair. The Court, as a general rule, will exclude the evidence without considering the seriousness of the breach or the effect of exclusion on the repute of the administration of justice. This must be the result since an unfair trial would necessarily bring the administration of justice into disrepute. 3. If the evidence is found to be conscriptive and the Crown demonstrates on a balance of probabilities that it would have been discovered by alternative non conscriptive means, then its admission will generally not render the trial unfair. However, the seriousness of the Charter breach and the effect of exclusion on the repute of the administration of justice will have to be considered. *R. v. Stillman*, [1997] 1 S.C.R. 607, Cory J. for the majority.

FAIR VALUE. 1. Value which is equitable and just in the circumstances; fair market value, intrinsic value or value to owner. 2. Since the provisions are an attempt to balance the different interests of minority and majority shareholders, the courts have tended to give the term "fair value" a broad and flexible meaning. Thus, most courts accept that fair value is not synonymous with fair market value and that the concept embraces some notion of equitable treatment. The need for this flexibility is especially evident where, as here, the act triggering the dissent is a squeeze out or expropriation of the shares of the minority shareholders. *Ford Motor Co. of Canada v. OMERS* (2006), 206 O.A.C. 62. 3. Can be used to arrive at a value for a right which does not have a fair market value because it cannot be transferred. Fair value is a notional concept influenced by the nature of the property and the circumstances giving rise to the transaction. While fair value includes fair market value, other values included are investment value, value to owner, and liquidation value. Fair value allows adjustments to be made to recognize internal or external financing, liquidity discounts, and the rea-

sonable expectations of the parties. *Standard Trust Ltd. (Trustee of) v. Standard Trust Co.* (1995), 26 O.R. (3d) 1(C.A.). 4. The shares are simply to be priced at "fair value." The courts have interpreted "fair value" as something more than simply "fair market value." Although "fair value" is said to be what a prudent person would pay for the property in question. *Woods Manufacturing Co. v. R.*, [1951] 2 D.L.R. 465 (S.C.C.).

FAIR WAGES. Such wages as are generally accepted as current for competent workmen in the district in which the work is being performed for the character or class of work in which those workmen are respectively engaged, but shall in all cases be such wages as are fair and reasonable and shall in no case be less than the minimum hourly rate of pay prescribed by or pursuant to Part III of the Canada Labour Code. *Fair Wages and Hours of Labour Act*, R.S.C. 1985, c. L-4, s. 2.

FAITH. See BAD ~; FULL ~ AND CREDIT; GOOD ~.

FALSE. *adj.* "... [S]hould be distinguished from the word inaccurate as the word 'false' implies an intention to mislead or deceive ..." *Kingsdale Securities Co. v. Minister of National Revenue* (1974), [1975] C.T.C. 10 at 34, [1974] 2 F.C. 760, 74 D.T.C. 6674, 6 N.R. 240 (C.A.), Bastin D.J.A. (dissenting).

FALSE ALARM OF FIRE. Every one who wilfully, without reasonable cause, by outcry, ringing bells, using a fire alarm, telephone or telegraph, or in any other manner, makes or circulates or causes to be made or circulated an alarm of fire is guilty of an offence. *Criminal Code*, R.S.C. 1985, c. C-46, s. 437.

FALSE ARREST. 1. "A necessary element of false arrest ... is that the arrest, ... is made without foundation or probable cause." *Nicely v. Waterloo Regional Police Force* (1991), 7 C.C.L.T. (2d) 61 at 69, 47 C.P.C. (2d) 105, 2 O.R. (4th) 612, 79 D.L.R. (4th) 14, 44 O.A.C. 147 (Div. Ct.), the court per Rosenberg J. 2. The detention of a person without lawful authority and without the consent of the person arrested.

FALSE DOCUMENT. 1. A document (a) the whole or a material part of which purports to be made by or on behalf of a person (i) who did not make it or authorize it to be made, or (ii) who did not in fact exist, (b) that is made by or on behalf of the person who purports to make it but is false in some material particular, (c) that is made in the name of an existing person, by him or under his authority, with a fraudulent intention that it should pass as being made by a person, real or fictitious, other than the person who makes it or under whose authority it is made. *Criminal Code*, R.S.C. 1985, c. C-46, s. 321. 2. "... [A]ny document that is false in some material particular ... a document which is false in reference to the very purpose for which the document was created ..." *R. v. Gaysek* (1971), 15 C.R.N.S. 345 at 348, 352, [1971] S.C.R. 888, 2 C.C.C. (2d) 545, 18 D.L.R. (3d) 306, Ritchie J. (Judson and Spence JJ. concurring).

FALSEHOOD. *n.* A deliberate lie. See INJURIOUS ~; MALICIOUS ~.

FALSE IMPRISONMENT. Intentional restraint of a person's liberty without lawful authority by preventing the person from leaving a place or actively confining them. J.G. Fleming, *The Law of Torts*, 8th ed. (Sydney: Law Book, 1992) at 27.

FALSE INNUENDO. In the case of "popular or false innuendo", although it need not be separately pled, the plaintiff is required to show why a reader would reasonably import to the words complained of a defamatory character, different from the ordinary meaning that the words would otherwise import. Where the words complained of are susceptible to many interpretations, the onus rests on the plaintiff to set out the meaning or meanings the plaintiff alleges the words are capable of. *Moon v. Sher*, 2003 CarswellOnt 2405 (S.C.J.).

FALSE NEWS. See SPREADING ~.

FALSE PRETENCE. A representation of a matter of fact either present or past, made by words or otherwise, that is known by the person who makes it to be false and that is made with a fraudulent intent to induce the person to whom it is made to act on it. Exaggerated commendation or depreciation of the quality of anything is not a false pretence unless it is carried to such an extent that it amounts to a fraudulent misrepresentation of fact. *Criminal Code*, R.S.C. 1985, c. C-46, s. 361.

FALSE REPRESENTATION. A statement known to be untrue or intended to be misleading concerning something. See DECEIT; FALSE PRETENCE; MISREPRESENTATION; REPRESENTATION.

FALSI CRIMEN. [L.] Fraudulently concealing or suborning in order to hide the truth, committed in words when a witness swears falsely; in writing when someone antedates a contract; or in doing something when a person sells using false weights and measures.

[] FAM. *abbr.* Law Reports, Family Division, 1972-.

FAM. CT. *abbr.* 1. Family Court. 2. Provincial Court (Family Division).

FAMILY. *n.* 1. The husband, wife, child, step-child, parent, step-parent, brother, sister, half-brother, half-sister, step-brother, step-sister, in each case whether legitimate or illegitimate, of a person. 2. Includes a man and woman living together as husband and wife, whether or not married in a permanent relationship, or the survivor of either, and includes the children of both or either, natural or adopted or to whom either stands in loco parentis, and any person lawfully related to any of the aforementioned persons. 3. The parents and any children maintained by those parents.

FAMILY ARBITRATION. An arbitration that, (a) deals with matters that could be dealt with in a marriage contract, separation agreement, cohabitation agreement or paternity agreement under this Part, and (b) is conducted exclusively in accordance with the law of Ontario or of another Canadian jurisdiction. *Family Law Act*, R.S.O. 1990, c. F.3, s. 51.

FAMILY ASSET. An asset owned by two spouses or common-law partners or either of them and used for shelter or transportation, or for household, edu-

cational, recreational, social or aesthetic purposes, including, without restricting the generality of the foregoing, (a) a family home; (b) money in a savings account, chequing account or current account with a bank, trust company, credit union or other financial institution where the account is ordinarily used for shelter or transportation or for household, educational, recreational, social or aesthetic purposes, and saving bonds and deposit receipts intended to be used for those purposes, (c) where an asset owned by a corporation, partnership or trustee would, if it were owned by a spouse or common-law partner, be a family asset, shares in the corporate or an interest in the partnership or trust owned by the spouse or common-law partner having a market value equal to the value of the benefit the spouse or common-law partner has in respect of the asset, (d) an asset over which spouse or common-law partner has, either alone or in conjunction with another person, a power of appointment exercisable in favour of the spouse or common-law partner, if the asset would be a family asset if it were owned by the spouse or common-law partner, and (e) an asset disposed of by a spouse or common-law partner but over which the spouse or common-law partner has, either alone or in conjunction with another person, a power to revoke the disposition or a power to use or dispose of the asset, if the asset would be a family asset if it were owned by the spouse or common-law partner. *The Family Property Act*, R.S.M. 1987, c. M45, s. 1.

FAMILY COURT COUNSELLOR. Mediators trained and available to assist in resolving family issues. *Court Rules Act*, R.S.B.C. 1996, c. 80, *Supreme Court Family Rules*, B.C. Reg. 169/2009, s. 1-1(1).

FAMILY DEBT. "... [A] convenient term to designate a liability of either or both of the spouses which has been incurred during the marriage for a family purpose." *Mallen v. Mallen* (1992), 40 R.F.L. (3d) 114 at 121, 65 B.C.L.R. (2d) 241, 11 B.C.A.C. 262, 22 W.A.C. 262, Wood J.A. (dissenting).

FAMILY LAW. See COLLABORATIVE ~ PROCESS.

FAMILY MEMBER. In relation to an individual, means (a) a spouse or common-law partner of the individual; (b) a child of the individual or a child of the individual's spouse or common-law partner; (c) a parent of the individual or a spouse or common-law partner of the parent; and (d) any other person who is a member of a class of persons prescribed for the purposes of this definition. *Employment Insurance Act*, S.C. 1996, c. 23, s. 23.1.

FAMILY NAME. A surname that does not contain more than one word which may occur alone as a surname. *Change of Name Act*, S.N.B. 1987, c. C-2.001, s. 1.

FAMILY ORDER. A support order, a custody order or an order granting an access right and includes an order or judgment, or any interim order or judgment, relating to family support, custody or access that is enforceable in the Province or another province. *Family Orders Information Release Act*, R.S.N.S. 1989, c. 161, s. 3.

F

FAMILY PROVISION. A support provision, a custody provision or an access right. *Family Orders and Agreements Enforcement Assistance Act*, R.S.C. 1985 c. 4 (2d Supp.), s. 2.

FAMILY STATUS. 1. Lamer C.J.C. quotes Marceau J.A. [from p. 35 [1991] 1 F.C.]: " 'Family' is not used in isolation in the Act [Canadian Human Rights Act, R.S.C. 1985, c. H-6] but rather coupled with the word 'status'. A status, to me, is primarily a legal concept which refers to the particular position of a person with respect to his or her rights and limitations as a result of his or her being a member of some legally recognized and regulated group... Even if we were to accept that two homosexual lovers can constitute 'sociologically speaking' a sort of family, it is certainly, not one which is now recognized by law as giving its members special rights and obligations." Lamer C.J. added at p. 582 that while the appeal was dismissed by the Supreme Court of Canada, "Nor should this decision be interpreted as meaning that homosexual couples cannot constitute a 'family' for the purposes of legislation other than the Canadian Human Rights Act. In this regard, each statute must be interpreted in its own context." *Canada (Attorney General) v. Mossop*, [1993] S.C.R. 554, Lamer C.J.C. affirming [1991] 1 F.C. 18, 32 C.C.E.L. 276, 71 D.L.R. (4th) 661, 90 C.L.L.C. 17,021, 12 C.H.R.R. D/355, 114 N.R. 241 (C.A.). 2. " ... [S]ufficiently broad to include couples of the same sex that were living together in a long-term relationship ..." *Canada (Attorney General) v. Mossop*, [1993] S.C.R. 554 at 648, Cory J. (dissenting). 3. The status of being in a parent and child relationship. *Human Rights acts.* 4. The status of being related to another person by blood, marriage or adoption. *Alberta Human Rights Act*, R.S.A. 2000, c. A-25.5, s. 44.

FAMILY VIOLENCE. Includes behaviour by a family or household member causing or attempting to cause physical harm to the child or another family or household member, including forced confinement or sexual abuse, or causing the child or another family or household member to reasonably fear for his or her safety or that of another person, but does not include (a) the use of force against a child as a means of correction by a guardian or person who has the care and control of the child if the force does not exceed what is reasonable under the circumstances, or (b) acts of self-protection or protection of another person. *Family Law Act*, S.A. 2003, c. F-4.5, s. 18.

FAM. L. REV. *abbr.* Family Law Review, 1978.

FAO. *abbr.* Food and Agriculture Organization of the United Nations.

FARM. *n.* Land in Canada used for the purpose of farming, which term includes livestock raising, dairying, bee-keeping, fruit growing, the growing of trees and all tillage of the soil. *Bank Act*, S.C. 1991, c. 46, s. 425.

FARM CREDIT CANADA. A corporation established under the Farm Credit Canada Act. The purpose of the Corporation is to enhance rural Canada by providing specialized and personalized business and financial services and products to farming oper-ations, including family farms, and to those businesses in rural Canada, including small and medium-sized businesses, that are businesses related to farming. The primary focus of the activities of the Corporation shall be on farming operations, including family farms. *Farm Credit Canada Act*, S.C. 1993, c. 14, s. 3 and 4.

FARMER. *n.* 1. Any individual, corporation, cooperative, partnership or other association of persons that is engaged in farming for commercial purposes. *Farm Debt Mediation Act*, S.C. 1997, c. 21, s. 2. 2. A person whose chief occupation is farming and, (a) who is living upon and tilling his or her own land, or land to the possession of which he or she is for the time being entitled, or (b) who is a settler engaged in clearing land for the purpose of bringing it to a state of cultivation. *Fish and Wildlife Conservation Act, 1997*, S.O. 1997, c. 41, s. 1. 3. A person who is in possession of a farm and whose principal occupation consists of farming that farm. 4. A producer of primary agricultural products for sale. *Pesticide Residue Compensation Act*, R.S.C. 1985, c. P-10, s. 2.

FARMING. (a) The production of field-grown crops, cultivated and uncultivated, and horticultural crops; (b) the raising of livestock, poultry and fur-bearing animals; (c) the production of eggs, milk, honey, maple syrup, tobacco, fibre, wood from wood-lots and fodder crops; and (d) the production or raising of any other prescribed thing or animal. *Farm Debt Mediation Act*, S.C. 1997, c. 21 , s. 2.

FARM PRACTICE. See NORMAL ~.

FARM PRODUCT. 1. A product of agriculture or of a forest, lake or river, and includes an article, including food or drink, that is wholly or partly derived or processed from such a product. *The Farm Products Marketing Act*, S.M. 2001, c. 16, s. 1. 2. Animals, meats, eggs, poultry, wool, dairy products, grains, seeds, fruit, fruit products, vegetables, vegetable products, maple products, honey, tobacco, wood, or any class or part of any such product, and such articles of food or drink manufactured or derived in whole or in part from any such product, and such other natural products of agriculture as are designated in the regulations, and, for the purposes of this Act, fish shall be deemed to be a farm product. *Farm Products Marketing Act*, R.S.O. 1990, c. F.9, s. 1. See NATIONAL ~S COUNCIL.

FARM PRODUCTS APP. TRIB. DEC. *abbr.* Farm Products Appeal Tribunal Decisions (Ontario), 1990-1996?.

F.A.S. *abbr.* Free alongside ship. A seller undertakes to deliver goods alongside a ship at the seller's own expense.

FAST TRACK. The procedure followed in an appeal under case management where a judge has authorized a fixed number of pages for argument to be submitted within a reduced time limit. *Criminal Code*, R.S.C. 1985, c. C-46, *Rules of the Court of Appeal of Quebec in Criminal Matters*, SI/2006-142, s. 1.

FATAL ACCIDENT. An accident causing the death of a worker under circumstances that entitle that worker's dependants, if any, to compensation under this Act. *Workers' Compensation acts.*

FATHER. See PUTATIVE ∼.

FAULT. *n.* 1. "... [I]ncludes negligence, but it is much broader than that. Fault incorporates all intentional wrongdoing, as well as other types of substandard conduct." *Bell Canada v. Cope (Sarnia) Ltd.* (1980), 11 C.C.L.T. 170 at 180 (Ont. H.C.), Linden J. 2. Wrongful act or default. *Sale of Goods acts.* 3. Blameworthiness. 4. In torts, includes negligence and intentional torts. See NO-∼ DIVORCE; NO-∼ INSURANCE.

FAULTY. *adj.* Defective, unsound, imperfect, not up to a required standard.

FAULTY WORKMANSHIP. Error in design. Unsatisfactory physical effort or poor craftmanship. May refer to negligence.

F.C. *abbr.* 1. Federal Court. 2. Canada Federal Court Reports, 1971-.

FCA. English neutral citation for the Federal Court of Appeal.

F.C.A.D. *abbr.* 1. Federal Court Appellate Division. 2. Federal Court of Appeal Decisions, 1981-1999.

FCT. English neutral citation for the Federal Court, Trial Division.

F.C.T.D. *abbr.* Federal Court Trial Division.

FEALTY. *n.* 1. A mutual bond of obligation or special oath of fidelity between a lord and a tenant. 2. The general oath of allegiance of a subject to a sovereign.

FEASANCE. *n.* Executing or doing something. See MIS∼; NON∼.

FEATURE POOL. The pool corresponding to the following types of bets, namely, a daily double, an exactor, a quinella, a triactor or any bet other than a win, place or show bet that an association is authorized to offer by its permit. *Criminal Code*, R.S.C. 1985, c. C-46, *Pari-Mutuel Betting Supervision Regulations*, SOR/91-365, s. 2.

FED. *abbr.* Federal.

FED. C.A. *abbr.* Federal Court of Canada – Appeal Division.

FEDERAL. *adj.* 1. Refers to the government or a law of Canada as opposed to that of a province. 2. . As applied to state documents, means of or pertaining to Canada. *Evidence acts.*

FEDERAL ACT. A law passed by the Parliament of Canada.

FEDERAL BOARD, COMMISSION OR OTHER TRIBUNAL. Federal board, commission or other tribunal" means any body, person or persons having, exercising or purporting to exercise jurisdiction or powers conferred by or under an Act of Parliament or by or under an order made pursuant to a prerogative of the Crown, other than the Tax Court of Canada or any of its judges, any such body constituted or established by or under a law of a province

or any such person or persons appointed under or in accordance with a law of a province or under section 96 of the Constitution Act, 1867. *Federal Court Act*, R.S.C. 1985, c. F-7, s. 2, as replaced by S.C. 2004, c. 7, s. 38.

FEDERAL CHILD SUPPORT GUIDELINES. The guidelines made under section 26.1 *Divorce Act*, R.S.C. 1985, c. 3 (2nd Supp.), s. 2. The objectives of these Guidelines are (*a*) to establish a fair standard of support for children that ensures that they continue to benefit from the financial means of both spouses after separation; (*b*) to reduce conflict and tension between spouses by making the calculation of child support orders more objective; (*c*) to improve the efficiency of the legal process by giving courts and spouses guidance in setting the levels of child support orders and encouraging settlement; and (*d*) to ensure consistent treatment of spouses and children who are in similar circumstances. *Divorce Act*, R.S.C. 1985, c. 3 (2nd Supp.), *Federal Child Support Guidelines*, SOR/97-175, s. 1. See CHILD SUPPORT GUIDELINES.

FEDERAL COMPANY. A body corporate that is incorporated under an Act of the Parliament of Canada including the Canada Business Corporations Act (Canada). *Corporations Act*, R.S.N. 1990, c. C-36, s. 431.

FEDERAL COURT. 1. The division of the Federal Court of Canada called the Federal Court—Trial Division is continued under the name "Federal Court" in English and "Cour fédérale" in French. It is continued as an additional court of law, equity and admiralty in and for Canada, for the better administration of the laws of Canada and as a superior court of record having civil and criminal jurisdiction. *Federal Courts Act*, R.S. C. 1985, c. F-7, s. 4. 2. "... [A] statutory court and its jurisdiction must be found in the Federal Court Act [R.S.C. 1970, (2d Supp.), c. 10] ..." *Piche v. Cold Lake Transmission Ltd.* (1979), [1981] 3 C.N.L.R. 78 at 85, [1980] 2 F.C. 369 (T.D.), Primrose D.J. 3. Any court, tribunal or other body that carries out adjudicative functions and is established by or pursuant to an Act of Parliament. *Official Languages Act*, R.S.C. 1985, c. 31 (4th Supp.), s. 3.

FEDERAL COURT OF APPEAL. That division of the Federal Court of Canada called the Federal Court - Appeal Division is continued as an additional court of law, equity and admiralty in and for Canada, for the better administration of the laws of Canada and as a superior court of record having civil and criminal jurisdiction. *Federal Courts Act*, R.S.C. 1985, c. F-7, s. 3.

FEDERAL CREDIT UNION. A bank that, within the meaning of section 12.1, is organized and carries on business on a cooperative basis. *Bank Act*, S.C. 1991, c. 46, s. 2.

FEDERAL CROWN. Her Majesty in right of Canada.

FEDERAL CUSTOMS LAWS. Includes (a) Acts of Parliament, (b) regulations within the meaning of the Statutory Instruments Act, and (c) rules of law applicable in connection with those Acts or regula-

F

tions, that relate to customs or excise, whether those Acts, regulations or rules come into force before or after June 30, 1983 and, for greater certainty but without restricting the generality of the foregoing, includes the following Acts, namely, the Customs Act, the Customs Tariff, the Excise Act, the Excise Act, 2001, the Excise Tax Act, the Export and Import Permits Act, the Importation of Intoxicating Liquors Act and the Special Import Measures Act. *Customs and Excise Offshore Application*, R.S.C. 1985, c. C-53, s. 2.

FEDERAL FINANCIAL INSTITUTION. (a) A bank, (b) a body corporate to which the Trust and Loan Companies Act applies, (c) an association to which the Cooperative Credit Associations Act applies or a central cooperative credit society for which an order has been made under subsection 473(1) of that Act, or (d) an insurance company or a fraternal benefit society incorporated or formed under the Insurance Companies Act. *Bank Act*, S.C. 1991, c. 46, s. 2.

FEDERAL GOVERNMENT. 1. A person or body which exercises power delegated to it by two or more independent states which have mutually agreed not to exercise certain sovereign powers but to delegate the exercise of those powers to the person or body they have chosen jointly. 2. The Governor in Council. Federal statutes.

FEDERAL IMMOVABLE. An immovable belonging to Her Majesty, and includes an immovable of which Her Majesty has the power to dispose. *Federal Real Property and Federal Immovables Act*, S.C. 1991, c. 50, s. 2.

FEDERALISM. 1. The system of government in Canada where legislative jurisdiction is divided between the provinces and the federal government under sections 91 and 92 of the Constitution Act. 2. In a federal system of government such as ours, political power is shared by two orders of government: the federal government on the one hand, and the provinces on the other. Each is assigned respective spheres of jurisdiction by the Constitution Act, 1867 [(U.K.), 30 & 31 Vict., c. 3]. It is up to the courts "to control the limits of the respective sovereignties". In interpreting our Constitution, the courts have always been concerned with the federalism principle, inherent in the structure of our constitutional arrangements, which has from the beginning been the lodestar by which the courts have been guided. This underlying principle of federalism, then, has exercised a role of considerable importance in the interpretation of the written provisions of our Constitution. There can be little doubt that the principle of federalism remains a central organizational theme of our Constitution. Less obviously, perhaps, but certainly of equal importance, federalism is a political and legal response to underlying social and political realities. The principle of federalism recognizes the diversity of the component parts of Confederation, and the autonomy of provincial governments to develop their societies within their respective spheres of jurisdiction. The federal structure of our country also facilitates democratic participation by distributing power to the government thought to be most suited to achieving the particular societal objective having regard to this diversity. The principle of federalism facilitates the pursuit of collective goals by cultural and linguistic minorities which form the majority within a particular province. *Reference re Secession of Quebec*, 1998 CarswellNat 1299, 161 D.L.R. (4th) 385, 228 N.R. 203, 55 C.R.R. (2d) 1, [1998] 2 S.C.R. 217 per curiam. See COOPERATIVE ~.

FEDERAL JURISDICTION. The legislative jurisdiction of the Parliament of Canada.

FEDERAL LAW. The whole or any portion of any Act of Parliament or any regulation, order or other instrument issued, made or established in the exercise of a power conferred by or under an Act of Parliament. *Agreement on Internal Trade Implementation Act*, S.C. 1996, c. 17, s. 9.

FEDERAL PARAMOUNTCY. The doctrine of federal paramountcy, recognizes that where laws of the federal and provincial levels come into conflict, there must be a rule to resolve the impasse. Under our system, the federal law prevails. According to the doctrine of federal paramountcy, when the operational effects of provincial legislation are incompatible with federal legislation, the federal legislation must prevail and the provincial legislation is rendered inoperative to the extent of the incompatibility. The doctrine applies not only to cases in which the provincial legislature has legislated pursuant to its ancillary power to trench on an area of federal jurisdiction, but also to situations in which the provincial legislature acts within its primary powers, and Parliament pursuant to its ancillary powers. *Canadian Western Bank v. Alberta*, [2007] 2 S.C.R. 3, 2007 SCC 22, Binnie and LeBel JJ.

FEDERAL PARLIAMENT. The parliament of Canada.

FEDERAL REAL PROPERTY. Real property belonging to Her Majesty, and includes any real property of which Her Majesty has the power to dispose. *Federal Real Property Act*, S.C. 1991, c. 50, s. 2.

FEDERAL REFERENCE. The referral of a question to the Supreme Court of Canada by the cabinet for the purpose of obtaining an advisory opinion of the court. (1) The Governor in Council may refer to the Court for hearing and consideration important questions of law or fact concerning (a) the interpretation of the Constitution Acts;(b) the constitutionality or interpretation of any federal or provincial legislation;(c) the appellate jurisdiction respecting educational matters, by the Constitution Act, 1867, or by any other Act or law vested in the Governor in Council; or (d) the powers of the Parliament of Canada, or of the legislatures of the provinces, or of the respective governments thereof, whether or not the particular power in question has been or is proposed to be exercised. Other questions (2) The Governor in Council may refer to the Court for hearing and consideration important questions of law or fact concerning any matter, whether or not in the opinion of the Court ejusdem generis with the enumerations contained in subsection (1), with reference to which the Governor in Council sees fit to submit any such question. *Supreme Court of Canada Act*, R.S.C. 1985, c. S-26, s. 53. See PROVINCIAL REFERENCE.

FEDERAL STATE. Canada is a federal state in which legislative powers are divided between the federal and provincial governments under sections 91 and 92 of the Constitution Act. Each individual is subject to the laws of a province or territory and the laws of Canada.

FEDERAL STATUTE. A law passed by the Parliament of Canada.

FEDERAL TERRITORY. By a procedure established under the Constitution Act, 1867 (U.K.), 30 & 31 Vict., c. 3, s. 146, the areas of Rupert's Land and the North-western Territory were admitted to Canada as areas under the authority of the federal Parliament. P.W. Hogg, *Constitutional Law of Canada*, 3d ed. (Toronto: Carswell, 1992) at 38-9.

FEDERAL WATERS. Other than in Yukon, waters under the exclusive legislative jurisdiction of Parliament and, in Yukon, waters in a federal conservation area within the meaning of section 2 of the Yukon Act. *Canada Water Act*, R.S.C. 1985, c. C-11, s. 2.

FEDERAL WORK, UNDERTAKING OR BUSINESS. Any work, undertaking or business that is within the legislative authority of Parliament, including, without restricting the generality of the foregoing, (a) a work, undertaking or business operated or carried on for, or in connection with, navigation and shipping, whether inland or maritime, including the operation of ships and transportation by ship anywhere in Canada, (b) a railway, canal, telegraph or other work or undertaking connecting any province with any other province, or extending beyond the limits of a province, (c) a line of ships connecting a province with any other province, or extending beyond the limits of a province, (d) a ferry between any province and any other province or between any province and any country other than Canada, (e) aerodromes, aircraft or a line of air transportation, (f) a radio broadcasting station, (g) a bank or an authorized foreign bank within the meaning of section 2 of the Bank Act, (h) a work or undertaking that, although wholly situated within a province, is before or after its execution declared by Parliament to be for the general advantage of Canada or for the advantage of two or more of the provinces, (i) a work, undertaking or business outside the exclusive legislative authority of the legislatures of the provinces, and (j) a work, undertaking or activity in respect of which federal laws within the meaning of section 2 of the Oceans Act apply pursuant to section 20 of that Act and any regulations made pursuant to paragraph 26(1)(k) of that Act. *Canada Labour Code*, R.S.C. 1985, c. L-2, s. 2.

FEDERATION. *n.* A composite state whose constitution distributes certain functions to a central authority and others to member states. See MUTUAL INSURANCE ~.

FEDERATION OF COOPERATIVE CREDIT SOCIETIES. An association under the Cooperative Credit Associations Act or a federation, league or corporation incorporated or organized by or under an Act of the legislature of a province, the membership or the shareholders of which include two or more central cooperative credit societies. *Bank Act*, S.C. 1991, c. 46, s. 2.

FED. T.D. *abbr.* Federal Court of Canada – Trial Division.

FEE. *n.* 1. "... [I]ts technical common law meaning, i.e., an estate in land unrestricted as to time and capable of descending to the heir... ." *Ameri-Cana Motel Ltd. v. Miller* (1983), 27 R.P.R. 75 at 79, [1983] S.C.R. 229, 46 N.R. 451, 143 D.L.R. (3d) 1, the court per Wilson J. 2. "... [I]n the context of s. 26 (now s. 29) of the Planning Act [R.S.O. 1970, c. 349] it was to be equated with the kind of interest in land which carries with it disposing power... ." *Ameri-Cana Motel Ltd. v. Miller* (1983), 27 R.P.R. 75 at 79, [1983] S.C.R. 229, 46 N.R. 451, 143 D.L.R. (3d) 1, the court per Wilson J. 3. Recompense or reward for services. 4. An amount to be paid when filing documents. 5. The charge made by a service provider. In the case of law firms, generally refers to charges for legal services and for required disbursements. See BROKERAGE ~; CHEQUE CASHING ~; CONTINGENCY ~; DETERMINABLE ~; ~ SIMPLE; ~ TAIL; FRANCHISE ~; MAINTENANCE ~; USER ~.

FEED. *v.* To offer additional support; to strengthen after the fact, i.e. a subsequently acquired interest feeds an estoppel.

FEED. n. Any substance or mixture of substances containing amino acids, anti-oxidants, carbohydrates, condiments, enzymes, fats, minerals, non-protein nitrogen products, proteins or vitamins, or pelletizing, colouring, foaming or flavouring agents and any other substance manufactured, sold or represented for use (a) for consumption by livestock, (b) for providing the nutritional requirements of livestock, or (c) for the purpose of preventing or correcting nutritional disorders of livestock, or any substance for use in any such substance or mixture of substances. *Feeds Act*, R.S.C. 1985, c. F-9, s. 2. See NETWORK ~.

FEEDING. *n.* Once the meal is presented in a customary manner, the physical ability of an insured, or the insured's requirement to have verbal cuing, to use utensils to feed himself or herself. *The Automobile Accident Insurance Act*, R.S.S. 1978, c. A-35, *The Personal Injury Benefits Regulations*, R.R.S., c. A-35, Reg. 3, Appendix D, Grid A, s. 2.

FEEDING THE ESTOPPEL. An interest in land is created by estoppel when the grantor has no legal estate or interest at the time of the grant. A title by estoppel is not good as against the world. It is good against the grantor who is estopped by his own deed. If the grantor later acquires legal title to the property which he has purported to grant that legal estate or interest feeds the estoppel. The original grant then takes effect as a grant in interest, not just estoppel. *Reference re Certain Titles to Land in Ontario*. [1973] 2 O.R. 613 (C.A.).

FEE SIMPLE. 1. "... [T]he largest estate in land in both time and status with a right of alienation and inheritability." *Saint John (City) v. McKenna* (1987), 45 R.P.R. 61 at 64, 78 N.B.R. (2d) 393, 198 A.P.R. 393, 37 D.L.R. (4th) 160 (C.A.), Hoyt J.A. (Ryan J.A. concurring). 2. An absolute estate in perpetuity.

FEE TAIL. An estate in land which is of smaller extent than an estate in fee simple. it is a grant to a person and his heirs. The estate is limited to the grantee's own issue.

FELON. *n.* A person who was convicted of felony.

FELONY. *n.* Originally the condition of having forfeited goods and lands to the Crown when convicted of a certain offence; later the offence which caused such forfeiture, distinguished from misdemeanour, after conviction for which forfeiture did not follow. See MISPRISION OF ~.

FEMALE PREDOMINANT. In relation to a job group or a job class, means a job group or job class, as the case may be, composed of at least 70% female employees. *Public Sector Equitable Compensation Act*, S.C. 2009, c. 2, s. 394, s. 2.

FEME. *n.* A woman; a wife.

FEME COVERT. A woman who is married.

FEME SOLE. A woman who is unmarried: spinster, widow or divorced.

FENCE. n. Patent claims are frequently analogized to "fences" and "boundaries", giving the "fields" of the monopoly a comfortable pretence of bright line demarcation. Thus, in Minerals Separation North American Corp. v. Noranda Mines Ltd., [1947] Ex. C.R. 306 (Can. Ex. Ct.), Thorson P. put the matter as follows, at p. 352: By his claims the inventor puts fences around the fields of his monopoly and warns the public against trespassing on his property. His fences must be clearly placed in order to give the necessary warning and he must not fence in any property that is not his own. The terms of a claim must be free from avoidable ambiguity or obscurity and must not be flexible; they must be clear and precise so that the public will be able to know not only where it must not trespass but also where it may safely go. In reality, the "fences" often consist of complex layers of definitions of different elements (or "components" or "features" or "integers") of differing complexity, substitutability and ingenuity. A matrix of descriptive words and phrases defines the monopoly, warns the public and ensnares the infringer. In some instances, the precise elements of the "fence" may be crucial or "essential" to the working of the invention as claimed; in others the inventor may contemplate, and the reader skilled in the art appreciate, that variants could easily be used or substituted without making any material difference to the working of the invention. The interpretative task of the court in claims construction is to separate the one from the other, to distinguish the essential from the inessential, and to give the "field" framed by the former the legal protection to which the holder of a valid patent is entitled. *Free World Trust c. Électro Santé Inc.*, 2000 CarswellQue 2728, 2000 SCC 66, 194 D.L.R. (4th) 232, 263 N.R. 150, [2000] 2 S.C.R. 1024, 9 C.P.R. (4th) 168, Binnie J.

FENERATION. *n.* 1. Usury. 2. Interest on loaned money.

FEOFFMENT. *n.* Formerly, the transfer of freehold land by livery of seisin and word of mouth.

FERAE NATURAE. [L.] Having a wild nature. See ANIMALS ~.

FERRY. *n.* 1. Any vessel (a) by which individuals or goods may be transported over water, and (b) that is part of the provincial public highway system, but does not include (c) a ferry to which the Coastal Ferry Act applies, or(d) a ferry that is part of the regional transportation system as defined in the South Coast British Columbia Transportation Authority Act. *Transportation Act*, S.B.C. 2004, c. 44, s. 1. 2. A scow, barge or boat used to carry passengers, freight, vehicles or animals across a river, stream, lake or other body of water and includes any dock, cable and appliances used in connection with it. *Highway and Transportation Act, 1997*, S.S. 1997, c. H-3.01, s. 1. 3. At common law, a toll franchise granted by the Crown.

FERTILIZER. Any substance or mixture of substances, containing nitrogen, phosphorus, potassium or other plant food, manufactured, sold or represented for use as a plant nutrient. *Fertilizers Act*, R.S.C. 1985, c. F-10, s. 2.

FETAL ALCOHOL SYNDROME. Slow prenatal growth and noticable mental and developmental deficiency in a child caused by the mother heavily consuming alcohol during pregnancy. F.A. Jaffe, *A Guide to Pathological Evidence for Lawyers and Police Officers*, 4th ed. (Toronto: Carswell, 1999) at 136.

FETTERING OF DISCRETION. The general principle of law is that a tribunal which exercises a statutory discretion may not fetter the exercise of that discretion by the adoption of an inflexible policy. In every case the Tribunal must consider the merits of the particular application. It must have regard to any policies of the Board. But a policy is only a factor for the Tribunal's consideration. In this case, the Tribunal said it was obliged to follow and was bound by the policy. This indicates that the policy was applied without regard to the merits of the applicant's case. That amounts to a fettering of discretion. *Braden-Burry Expediting Services Ltd. v. Northwest Territories (Workers' Compensation Board)*, 1998 CarswellNWT 170, 13 Admin. L.R . (3d) 232 (S.C.), Vertes J. See ON ITS MERITS; UNFETTERED DISCRETION.

FEUDAL SYSTEM. A system in which absolute or nominal ownership of land was in one feudal superior or lord while the occupation, use and benefit was in the feudal inferior or tenant who rendered the lord certain services.

FIAT. *n.* [L. let it be done] A decree; order or warrant made by a judge or public officer to allow certain processes.

FIAT JUSTITIA. [L.] Let justice be done.

FICTION. *n.* A rule of law which assumes something which is false is true, and will not allow it to be disproved. An assumption by law that something which is false is true. A statute may state that X is to be treated as Y. That a corporation is a person is sometimes said to be a legal fiction. See LEGAL ~.

FIDUCIARY. *n.* 1. "... [W]here by statute, agreement, or perhaps by unilateral undertaking, one party has an obligation to act for the benefit of another, and that obligation carries with it a discretionary power, the party thus empowered becomes a fiduciary... ." *Guerin v. R.* (1984), [1985] 1 C.N.L.R. 120 at 137, [1984] 2 S.C.R. 335, 36 R.P.R. 1, 210 E.T.R. 6, [1984] 6 W.W.R. 481, 59 B.C.L.R. 301, 13 D.L.R. (4th) 321, 55 N.R. 161, Dickson J. (Beetz, Chouinard and Lamer JJ. concurring). 2. "... [U]se[d] in at least three distinct ways... . [(a)] The focus is on the identification of relationships in which, because of their inherent purpose or their presumed factual or legal incidents, the Courts will impose a fiduciary obligation on one party to act or refrain from acting in a certain way. The obligation imposed may vary in its specific substance depending on the relationship, though compendiously it can be described as the fiduciary duty of loyalty and will most often include the avoidance of a conflict of duty and interest and a duty not to profit at the expense of the beneficiary... . [(b)] a fiduciary obligation can arise as a matter of fact out of the specific circumstances of a relationship. As such it can arise between parties in a relationship in which fiduciary obligations would not normally be expected... . [(c)] third usage of 'fiduciary' stems, it seems, from a perception of remedial inflexibility in equity. Courts have resorted to fiduciary language because of the view that certain remedies, deemed appropriate in the circumstances, would not be available unless a fiduciary relationship was present. In this sense, the label fiduciary imposes no obligations, but rather is merely instrumental or facilitative in achieving what appears to be the appropriate result." *International Corona Resources Ltd. v. LAC Minerals Ltd.* (1989), 35 E.T.R. 1 at 20, 21-2, 26 C.P.R. (3d) 97, 69 O.R. (2d) 287, 61 D.L.R. (4th) 14, [1989] 2 S.C.R. 574, 6 R.P.R. (2d) 1, 44 B.L.R. 1, 101 N.R. 239, 36 O.A.C. 57, La Forest J. (Lamer J. concurring). 3. "Relationships in which a fiduciary obligation have been imposed seem to possess three general characteristics: (1) The fiduciary has scope for the exercise of some discretion or power. (2) The fiduciary can unilaterally exercise that power or discretion so as to affect the beneficiary's legal or practical interests. (3) The beneficiary is peculiarly vulnerable to or at the mercy of the fiduciary holding the discretion or power." *Frame v. Smith* (1987), [1988] 1 C.N.L.R. 152 at 155, 78 N.R. 40, 9 R.F.L. (3d) 225, 42 C.C.L.T. 1, [1987] 2 S.C.R. 99, 23 O.A.C. 84, 42 D.L.R. (4th) 81, Wilson J. (dissenting). 4. Any person acting in a fiduciary capacity and includes a personal representative of a deceased person. *Bank Act, 1991*, S.C. 1991, c. 46, s. 2.

FIDUCIARY DUTY. 1. One that arises in the context of a trust. 2. Certain relationships give rise to this type of duty: trustee and beneficiary, guardian and ward, principal and agent. 3. A duty by which the law seeks to protect vulnerable persons in transactions with others.

FIDUCIARY OBLIGATION. Arises in a relationship in which the fiduciary has a discretion or power to exercise, the fiduciary can unilaterally exercise this discretion or power, and the beneficiary is vulnerable to or at the mercy of the fiduciary.

FIELD. *n.* 1. (a) Means a general surface area underlain or appearing to be underlain by one or more pools, and (b) includes the subsurface regions vertically beneath the general surface area referred to in paragraph (a). *Canada Oil and Gas Operations Act*, R.S.C. 1985, c. O-7, s. 2. 2. Patent claims are frequently analogized to "fences" and "boundaries", giving the "fields" of the monopoly a comfortable pretence of bright line demarcation. Thus, in Minerals Separation North American Corp. v. Noranda Mines Ltd., [1947] Ex. C.R. 306 (Can. Ex. Ct.), Thorson P. put the matter as follows, at p. 352: By his claims the inventor puts fences around the fields of his monopoly and warns the public against trespassing on his property. His fences must be clearly placed in order to give the necessary warning and he must not fence in any property that is not his own. The terms of a claim must be free from avoidable ambiguity or obscurity and must not be flexible; they must be clear and precise so that the public will be able to know not only where it must not trespass but also where it may safely go. In reality, the "fences" often consist of complex layers of definitions of different elements (or "components" or "features" or "integers") of differing complexity, substitutability and ingenuity. A matrix of descriptive words and phrases defines the monopoly, warns the public and ensnares the infringer. In some instances, the precise elements of the "fence" may be crucial or "essential" to the working of the invention as claimed; in others the inventor may contemplate, and the reader skilled in the art appreciate, that variants could easily be used or substituted without making any material difference to the working of the invention. The interpretative task of the court in claims construction is to separate the one from the other, to distinguish the essential from the inessential, and to give to the "field" framed by the former the legal protection to which the holder of a valid patent is entitled. *Free World Trust c. Électro Santé Inc.*, 2000 CarswellQue 2728, 2000 SCC 66, 194 D.L.R. (4th) 232, 263 N.R. 150, [2000] 2 S.C.R. 1024, 9 C.P.R. (4th) 168, Binnie J. See MUTUEL ~; OCCUPIED ~; OPEN ~S DOCTRINE.

FIERI FACIAS. [L. that you cause to be made] A writ of execution used to levy a judgment debt. See WRIT OF ~.

FIERI FECI. [L. I have caused to be made] A return made by the sheriff who executed a writ of execution.

FI. FA. *abbr.* Fieri facias.

FIFO METHOD OF INVENTORY VALUATION. In this method, it is assumed that the first items purchased as inventory are the first to be disposed of. The cost of inventory on hand at the end of a fiscal period is the cost of the items purchased most recently.

FIGHT. See PRIZE ~.

FILE. *v.* 1. To leave with the appropriate office for keeping. 2. Register. 3. Requires actual delivery. A

F

mailed document is not filed until received by the appropriate party.

FILIBUSTER. *n.* A tactic used to delay legislative action.

FILING. *n.* Registration; recording. See E-~; ELECTRONIC ~.

FILM. *n.* 1. Motion pictures, still photographs, photographic displays, filmstrips and such other forms of visual presentation as consist primarily of photographs or photographic reproductions. *National Film Act*, R.S.C. 1985, c. N-8, s. 2. 2. A work produced with the use of technical means resulting in a cinematographic effect, regardless of the medium, and includes a video. *An Act respecting the professional status and conditions of engagement of performing, recording and film artists*, R.S.Q., c. S-32.1, s. 1. See STANDARD ~.

FILTER. See SPAM ~.

FINAL. *v.* To put into final form. To conclude.

FINAL. *adj.* 1. Last; conclusive; terminated. 2. "... [N]ot subject to further appeal... ." *Hi-Rise Structures Inc. v. Scarborough (City)* (1992), 12 M.P.L.R. (2d) 1 at 11, 94 D.L.R. (4th) 385, 10 O.R. (3d) 299, 27 O.M.B.R. 443, 57 O.A.C. 287, the court per Carthy J.A. 3. "... [A] judgment or order is ... final ... [if] it finally disposes of the rights of the parties... ." *Kampus v. Bridgeford* (1982), 25 C.P.C. 169 at 171, 131 D.L.R. (3d) 612 (Ont. C.A.), the court per Brooke J.A. 4. Does not necessarily imply an intended restriction on judicial review. The opposite of interim. *C.J.A., Local 579 v. Bradco Construction Ltd.* [1993] 2 S.C.R. 316.

FINAL AND BINDING. 1. This phrase has limited privative effect but signals that the court should exercise some restraint on judicial review. *Trent University Faculty Assn. v. Trent University* (1997), 102 O.A.C. 346. 2. At a minimum, reflects an intention to exclude a statutory right of appeal. *Labourers International Union of North America v. Carpenters & Allied Workers* (1997), 34 O.R. (3d) 472 (C.A.). See FINAL AND CONCLUSIVE.

FINAL AND CONCLUSIVE. 1. In the judgment of Weiler J.A., concurring in the result: "The words 'final and conclusive' do not in themselves imply a binding effect on another administrative tribunal. The words 'final and conclusive' in ss. 108(1) and (2) [Labour Relations Act, R.S.O. 1990, c. L.2] mean that 'the issue as between the parties has been settled and no further steps need be taken for the decision to qualify as a determination of the rights of the parties. In other words, the ruling is not an interim one.'" *C.U.P.E., Local 1394 v. Extendicare Health Services Inc.*, 1993 CarswellOnt 887, 17 Admin. L.R . (2d) 27, 93 C.L.L.C. 14,052, 14 O.R. (3d) 65, 104 D.L.R. (4th) 8, 64 O.A.C. 126, Brooke, Doherty and Weiler JJ.A. 2. "On issues within jurisdiction, I do not attach the importance to the difference in the wording of 'final and conclusive' and 'final and binding' that Cory J. attributes to me. I do not believe that one is simply privative and the other not. The difference between these phrases is much less significant than that between either of them and the expansive privative clause in s. 108 [of the Labour Relations Act, R.S.O. 1980, c. 228] that protects decisions of the Labour Board. More importantly, this small distinction is more significant in determining whether a question is a jurisdictional one or within jurisdiction than in considering the standard of review for questions within jurisdiction. I cannot accept that courts should mechanically defer to the tribunal simply because of the presence of a 'final and binding' or 'final and conclusive' clause. These finality clauses can clearly signal deference, but they should also be considered in the context of the type of question and the nature and expertise of the tribunal." *Dayco (Canada) Ltd. v. C.A.W.*, 1993 CarswellOnt 883, 14 Admin. L.R. (2d) 1, 13 O.R. (3d) 164 (note), 152 N.R. 1, 63 O.A.C. 1, (*sub nom. Dayco v. N.A.W.*) C.E.B. & P.G.R. 8141, (*sub nom. Dayco v. C.A.W.*) 93 C.L.L.C. 14,032, [1993] 2 S.C.R. 230, 102 D.L.R. (4th) 609, La Forest J.

FINAL DECISION. [M]ust be interpreted as a decision that requires no further actions by the hearing panel to render it enforceable. A "final decision" may also be distinguishable from an interim order or a provisional order that is subject to confirmation by another level of adjudication within the tribunal's structure. In this case, an order of a mediator pending an arbitrator's confirmation of the order is not a "final decision" even though it may be enforceable pending a decision of the Board. On the other hand, a "final decision" is not restricted to decisions that have proceeded through a discretionary review process such as that found in s. 26(2) of the Petroleum and Natural Gas Act. *Vause v. Spectra Energy Midstream Corporation*, 2009 BCSC 916.

FINAL DETERMINATION. The concept of "final determination under the Assessment Act" [in s. 339(1)(q)(i) of the Local Government Act, R.S.B.C. 1996, c. 323] imports the notion that an assessment made by an assessor will be finally determined at that point in time when no objection has been made to the assessment, or if an appeal is taken and succeeds against an assessment, then that determination by a tribunal or court will be the final determination. *Norske Skog Canada Ltd. v. Courtenay Assessor, Area No. 6*, 2006 BCCA 130.

FINAL DISPOSITION. The [Manitoba Criminal Appeal Rules, SI/92-106] contemplate that an appeal may be launched only upon the final disposition of a matter. In the case of a finding of not guilty, nothing more need be done. That is the final disposition and the Crown may launch an appeal immediately upon the acquittal occurring. In the case of a finding of guilt, the matter is not finally disposed of until sentence is pronounced. Only then can the accused or the Crown launch an appeal. *R. v. Payne*, 2002 MBCA 169, 170 C.C.C. (3d) 145, 170 Man. R. (2d) 102, [2003] 5 W.W.R. 76.

FINAL DRAFT. In a publication contract, refers to a manuscript in publishable form after the completion of the editorial process.

FINALITY CLAUSE. A statement in a statute that the decisions of a tribunal are "final and conclusive" or "final and binding". See FINAL AND BINDING;

FINAL AND CONCLUSIVE; PRIVATIVE CLAUSE.

FINALITY PRINCIPLE. The doctrine of issue estoppel precludes a party from relitigating a legal or factual issue that has been conclusively resolved in a prior proceeding. The doctrine rests on the finality principle, "a compelling consideration" that ordinarily limits a litigant "to one bite at the cherry": Danyluk v. Ainsworth Technologies Inc., [2001] 2 S.C.R. 460, at paras. 18-19. Once a point has been decided, the winning litigant is entitled to rely on the result, to be assured of peace and to be able to plan the future on the basis of the court's decision. The finality principle is fundamental to a secure legal order. It avoids "duplicative litigation, potentially inconsistent results, undue costs, and inconclusive proceedings": Danyluk, at para. 18. *Smith Estate v. National Money Mart Co.*, 2008 ONCA 746.

FINAL JUDGMENT. 1. Any judgment, rule, order or decision that determines in whole or in part any substantive right of any of the parties in controversy in any judicial proceeding. *Supreme Court Act*, R.S.C. 1985, c. S-26, s. 2. 2. "... [A] judgment obtained in an action by which a previously existing liability of the defendant to the plaintiff is ascertained or established ..." *Ex Parte Chinery* (1884), 12 Q.B.D. 342 at 345 (U.K.), Cotten L.J.

FINAL ORDER. "... [F]inally disposes of the rights of the parties, ..." *Hendrickson v. Kallio*, [1932] 4 D.L.R. 580 at 585, [1932] O.R. 675 (C.A.), Middleton J.A.

FINANCE. *v.* To fund; to arrange to pay for over time, on credit.

FINANCE. *n.* The management of money. See DEPARTMENT OF ~.

FINANCIAL. *adj.* Concerning the management of money.

FINANCIAL ASSET. 1. As the context requires, either the interest itself or the means by which a person's claim to it is evidenced, including a certificated or uncertificated security, a security certificate and a security entitlement. *Securities Transfer acts.* 2. (a) A security, (b) an obligation of a person that (i) is, or is of a type, dealt in or traded on financial markets, or (ii) is recognized in any other market or area in which it is issued or dealt in as a medium for investment, (c) a share, participation or other interest in a person, or in property or an enterprise of a person, that, (i) is, or is of a type, dealt in or traded on financial markets, or (ii) is recognized in any other market or area in which it is issued or dealt in as a medium for investment, (d) any property that is held by a securities intermediary for another person in a securities account if the securities intermediary has expressly agreed with the other person that the property is to be treated as a financial asset under this Act, or (e) a credit balance in a securities account, unless the securities intermediary has expressly agreed with the person for whom the account is maintained that the credit balance is not to be treated as a financial asset under this Act. *Securities Transfer acts.*

FINANCIAL CONSUMER AGENCY OF CANADA. Established by the Financial Consumer Agency of Canada Act, S.C. 2001, c. 9. Section 3 of the Act provides: The objects of the Agency are to (a) supervise financial institutions to determine whether they are in compliance with the consumer provisions applicable to them; (b) promote the adoption by financial institutions of policies and procedures designed to implement consumer provisions applicable to them; (c) monitor the implementation of voluntary codes of conduct that are designed to protect the interests of customers of financial institutions, that have been adopted by financial institutions and that are publicly available and to monitor any public commitments made by financial institutions that are designed to protect the interests of their customers; (d) promote consumer awareness about the obligations of financial institutions under consumer provisions applicable to them; and (e) foster, in co-operation with any department, agency or agent corporation of the Government of Canada or of a province, financial institutions and consumer and other organizations, an understanding of financial services and issues relating to financial services.

FINANCIAL DERIVATIVE. A contract, instrument or security, the market price, value or payment obligations of which is derived from an underlying interest or from the relationship between certain underlying interests. *An Act respecting International financial centres*, R.S.Q. c. C-8.3, s. 4. See FOREIGN ~.

FINANCIAL INSTITUTION. See CANADIAN ~; FEDERAL ~; SUPERINTENDENT OF ~S.

FINANCIAL LEASE. A lease between a financial institution and a lessee that, after allowing for the rate of return to the financial institution agreed to by the lessee, is intended to recoup to the financial institution its entire investment in the farm implement, taking into consideration the value of any tax benefits accruing to the financial institution on account of the lease, including tax credits and capital cost allowance claims. *Farm Implement Act*, R.S.A. 2000, c. F-7, s. 1.

FINANCIAL LEASE-PURCHASE AGREEMENT. A financial lease of a farm implement under which the lessee is given the right to purchase the farm implement. *Farm Implement Act*, R.S.A. 2000, c. F-7, s. 1.

FINANCIAL MANAGEMENT BOARD. See FIRST NATIONS ~.

FINANCIAL OFFICER. (a) In relation to a regional district, the regional district officer assigned responsibility under section 199 [financial administration], and (b) in relation to the City of Vancouver, the City Treasurer under section 226 of the Vancouver Charter. *Local Government Act*, R.S.B.C. 1996, c. 323, s. 5.

FINANCIAL PACKAGING SERVICES. Providing advice or other technical assistance for project financing, including the services relating to strategic planning, term financing through private placement, the financial aspect of privatization of operations, the

F

submission of financial information to lenders, the negotiation of short-term credit contracts, the implementation of an international cash management organization and the financial aspect of business acquisitions and mergers. *An Act respecting International financial centres*, R.S.Q. c. C-8.3, s. 4.

FINANCIAL REPORTING. See INTERNATIONAL ~ STANDARDS.

FINANCIAL SECURITY. The essence of financial security is that the right to salary of a decision-maker must be established by law and there must be no way in which the Executive could interfere with that right. *Bell Canada v. C.T.E.A.*, 2000 CarswellNat 2606, 2000 C.L.L.C. 230-043, 5 C.C.E.L. (3d) 123, 194 D.L.R. (4th) 499, 26 Admin. L.R. (3d) 253, 190 F.T.R. 42, [2001] 2 F.C. 392 (T.D.), Tremblay-Lamer J.

FINANCIAL STATEMENTS. Includes (i) statements of the financial position, the results of operations and any change to the financial position, (ii) a statement of the accounting policies followed in preparing a financial statement, (iii) a comparison between the results budgeted for and the actual results, and (iv) any other statement, report, schedule, account, note, explanation and information considered necessary by the Minister of Finance to give full and proper disclosure. *Government Accountability Act*, R.S.A. 2000, c. G-7, s. 1.

FINANCIAL SUPPORT ORDER. An order or judgment for maintenance, alimony or support, including an order or judgment for arrears of payments, made pursuant to the Divorce Act, chapter D-8 of the Revised Statutes of Canada, 1970, or the Divorce Act or pursuant to the law of a province relating to family financial support or the enforcement of family financial support. *Garnishment, Attachment and Pension Diversion Act*, R.S.C. 1985, c. G-2, s. 32.

FINANCIAL YEAR. The year in respect of which the accounts of the company or of the business are made up.

FINANCING. *n.* See BRIDGE ~; RE~.

FIND. *v.* 1. To come across. 2. To make a judicial or quasi-judicial determination.

FINDER. See FACT ~.

FINDING. *n.* The conclusion drawn after an inquiry of fact. See ~S.

FINDING OF FACT. A determination that a thing exists, or that a thing has happened, or, is, or, will be happening. See FACT FINDER.

FINDING OF GUILT. The plea of guilty by a defendant to an offence or the finding that a defendant is guilty of an offence made before or by a court that makes an order directing that the defendant be discharged for the offence either absolutely or on the conditions prescribed in a probation order, where (a) the order directing the discharge is not subject to further appeal; or (b) no appeal is taken in respect of the order directing the discharge. *Evidence acts.*

FINDINGS. *n.* 1. Of a court, the result of the court's deliberations in relation to a question of fact. 2. Of a

medical practitioner, the factual information, including results of patient examination and testing, upon which the practitioner relies to make a diagnosis. See FINDING; PATTERN OF ~ OF GUILT.

FINE. *n.* 1. Includes a pecuniary penalty or other sum of money, but does not include restitution. *Criminal Code*, R.S.C. 1985, c. C-46, s. 716. 2. A sum of money ordered to be paid to the Crown by an offender, as a punishment for the offence.

FINE OPTION PROGRAM. A program in which an individual against whom a fine is imposed in respect of an offence against an enactment of Alberta or an offence referred to in section 718.1 of the Criminal Code (Canada) may discharge the fine in whole or in part by earning credits for work performed. *Corrections Act*, R.S.A. 2000, c. C-29, s. 34.

FINGERPRINT. *n.* The pattern in the skin on the finger tips, used to identify people.

FIRE. *n.* Combustion together with a visible glow or flame. C. Brown & J. Menezes, *Insurance Law in Canada*, 2d ed. (Toronto: Carswell, 1991) at 182. See FALSE ALARM OF ~.

FIREARM. *var.* **FIRE-ARM.** *n.* 1. A barrelled weapon from which any shot, bullet or other projectile can be discharged and that is capable of causing serious bodily injury or death to a person, and includes any frame or receiver of such a barrelled weapon and anything that can be adapted for use as a firearm. *Criminal Code*, R.S.C. 1985, c. C-46, s. 2. 2. Includes any gun using, as a propellant, compressed air, explosives or gas. B.C. statutes. 3. Includes an air gun, pellet gun, bow or crossbow. Ontario statutes. 4. A firearm must come within the definition of a weapon. A firearm is expressly designed to kill or wound. It operates with deadly efficiency in carrying out the object of its design. It followed that such a deadly weapon can, of course, be used for purposes of threatening and intimidating. Indeed, it is hard to imagine anything more intimidating or dangerous than a brandished firearm. A person waving a gun and calling 'hands up' can be reasonably certain that the suggestion will be obeyed. A firearm is quite different from an object such as a carving knife or an ice pick which will normally be used for legitimate purposes. A firearm, however, is always a weapon. No matter what the intention may be of the person carrying a gun, the firearm itself presents the ultimate threat of death to those in its presence." *R. v. Felawka*, 1993 CarswellBC 507, 25 C.R. (4th) 70, 159 N.R. 50, 33 B.C.A.C. 241, 54 W.A.C. 241, 85 C.C.C. (3d) 248, [1993] 4 S.C.R. 199, Cory J. See ANTIQUE ~; AUTOMATIC ~; CANADIAN ~S REGISTRY; DEACTIVATED ~; HANDGUN; IMITATION ~; PROHIBITED ~; REPLICA ~; RESTRICTED ~; REVOLVER.

FIREARMS OFFICER. (a) In respect of a province, an individual who is designated in writing as a firearms officer for the province by the provincial minister of that province, (b) in respect of a territory, an individual who is designated in writing as a firearms officer for the territory by the federal Minister, or (c) in respect of any matter for which there is no firearms officer under paragraph (a) or (b), an individual who is designated in writing as a firearms officer for the matter by the federal Minister. *Firearms Act, 1995*, S.C. 1995, c. 39, s. 2.

FIRE CODE. See NATIONAL ~.

FIREFIGHTER. *n.* A person regularly employed on a salaried basis in a fire department and assigned to fire protection services and includes technicians but does not include a volunteer firefighter. *Fire Protection and Prevention Act, 1997*, S.O. 1997, c. 4, s. 41. See VOLUNTEER ~.

FIRE INSURANCE. 1. Insurance, not being insurance incidental to some other class of insurance defined by or under this Act, against loss of or damage to property through fire, lightning or explosion due to ignition. *Insurance acts.* 2. Insurance against loss of or damage to the property insured caused by fire, lightning, smoke or explosion due to ignition, and includes sprinkler leakage insurance. *Insurance Act*, R.S.B.C. 1996, c. 226, *Insurance Classes Regulation*, B.C. Reg. 337/90, s. 2.

FIRE PROTECTION SERVICES. Includes fire suppression, fire prevention, fire safety education, communication, training of persons involved in the provision of fire protection services, rescue and emergency services and the delivery of all those services. *Fire Protection and Prevention Act, 1997*, S.O. 1997, c. 4, s. 1.

FIRM. *n.* 1. Is the collective term for persons who have entered into partnership with one another. *Partnership Act*, R.S.B.C. 1996, c. 348, s. 1. 2. A person or association of persons carrying on a business or activity employing more than 1 and fewer than 15 persons. *Jury Act, 1991*, S.N. 1991, c. 16, s. 10. 3. Includes a partnership, corporation or association of persons. *Architects Act*, S.N.W.T. 2001, c. 10, s. 1. 4. (a) A person who is the sole proprietor of a business and who uses as his business name a name other than his own or uses his own name with the addition of some other word or phrase; or (b) persons who are associated as partners in a business, and the name in which the firm carries on its business is called the firm name. *Direct Sellers' Regulation Act*, R.S.N.S. 1989, c. 129, s. 17. See LAW ~; SECURITIES ~.

FIRM NAME.. The name under which a business of a firm is carried on. *Partnership Act*, R.S.B.C. 1996, c. 348, s. 1.

FIRST DEGREE MURDER. 1. Murder when it is planned and deliberate. *Criminal Code*, R.S.C. 1985, c. C-46, s. 231. 2. Irrespective of whether it is planned and deliberate when the victim is a police officer or one of other named officials. *Criminal Code*, R.S.C. 1985, c. C-46, s. 231. 3. When death is caused while committing or attempting to commit hijacking an aircraft, sexual assault, sexual assault with a weapon, threats to a third party or causing bodily harm, aggravated sexual assault, kidnapping and forcible confinement, or hostage taking. *Criminal Code*, R.S.C. 1985, c. C-46, s. 231.

FIRST IMPRESSION. Describes a case which presents a new question of law for which there is no precedent.

FIRST INSTANCE. Refers to the court which first hears a matter. See COURT OF ~.

FIRST MINISTERS' CONFERENCE. A federal-provincial conference of the Canadian Prime Minister and the provincial Premiers.

FIRST MORTGAGE. A mortgage which has priority over all other similar mortgages against the same land.

FIRST NAME. 1. Given name. In contrast to surname or family name. 2. The name or names first in sequence as set out in the person's birth registration document. *Vital Statistics Act*, S.A. 2007, c. V-4.1, s. 8.

FIRST NATION. 1. A band within the meaning of the Indian Act. *First Nations Oil and Gas and Moneys Management Act*, S.C. 2005, c. 48, s. 2. 2. (a) A band as defined in subsection 2(1) of the Indian Act; (b) a group of persons that was, but is no longer, a band within the meaning of paragraph (a) and that has, under a land claims agreement, retained the right to bring a specific claim; and (c) a group of persons that was a band within the meaning of paragraph (a), that is no longer a band by virtue of an Act or agreement mentioned in the schedule and that has not released its right to bring a specific claim. *Specific Claims Tribunal Act*, S.C. 2008, c. 22, s. 22. 3. An aboriginal governing body, however organized and established by aboriginal people within their traditional territory in British Columbia, that has been mandated by its constituents to enter into treaty negotiations on their behalf with Her Majesty in right of Canada and Her Majesty in right of British Columbia. *British Columbia Treaty Commission Act*, S.C. 1995, c. 45, s. 2. See MEMBER OF A ~; TAXING TREATY ~.

FIRST NATION LAND. Reserve land to which a land code applies and includes all the interests in and resources of the land that are within the legislative authority of Parliament. *First Nations Land Management Act*, S.C. 1999, c. 24, s. 2.

FIRST NATION LAW. The council of a first nation has, in accordance with its land code, the power to enact laws respecting (a) interests in and licences in relation to first nation land; (b) the development, conservation, protection, management, use and possession of first nation land; and (c) any matter arising out of or ancillary to the exercise of that power. *First Nations Land Management Act*, S.C. 1999, c. 24, s. 20. See LAND CODE.

FIRST NATION MEMBER. A person whose name appears on the band list of a first nation or who is entitled to have their name appear on that list. *First Nations Oil and Gas and Moneys Management Act*, S.C. 2005, c. 48, s. 2.

FIRST NATIONS FINANCIAL MANAGEMENT BOARD. Approves financial administration laws of first nations. The purposes of the Board are to (a) assist first nations in developing the capacity to meet their financial management requirements; (b) assist first nations in their dealings with other governments respecting financial management, including matters of accountability and shared fiscal responsibility; (c) assist first nations in the

F

development, implementation and improvement of financial relationships with financial institutions, business partners and other governments, to enable the economic and social development of first nations; (d) develop and support the application of general credit rating criteria to first nations; (e) provide review and audit services respecting first nation financial management; (f) provide assessment and certification services respecting first nation financial management and financial performance; (g) provide financial monitoring services respecting first nation financial management and financial performance; (h) provide co-management and third-party management services; and (i) provide advice, policy research and review and evaluative services on the development of fiscal arrangements between first nations' governments and other governments. Established under the *First Nations Fiscal and Statistical Management Act*, S.C. 2005, c. 9, s. 38 and 49.

FIRST NATIONS STATISTICAL INSTITUTE. The purposes of the Institute are to (a) provide statistical information on, and analysis of, the fiscal, economic and social conditions of (i) Indians and other members of first nations, (ii) members of other aboriginal groups, and (iii) other persons who reside on reserve lands or lands of other aboriginal groups; (b) promote the quality, coherence and compatibility of first nations statistics and their production in accordance with generally accepted standards and practices through collaboration with first nations, federal departments and agencies, provincial departments and agencies and other organizations; (c) work with, and provide advice to, federal departments and agencies and provincial departments and agencies on first nations statistics; (d) work in cooperation with Statistics Canada to ensure that the national statistical system meets the needs of first nations and Canada; and (e) build statistical capacity within first nation governments. Established under *First Nations Fiscal and Statistical Management Act*, S.C. 2005, c. 9, s. 91 and 104.

FIRST NATIONS SUMMIT. The body that is established to represent first nations in British Columbia that agree to participate in the process provided for in the agreement to facilitate the negotiation of treaties among first nations, Her Majesty in right of Canada and Her Majesty in right of British Columbia. *Treaty Commission Act*, R.S.B.C. 1996, c. 461, s. 1 and *New Relationship Trust Act*, S.B.C. 2006, c. 6, s. 1.

FIRST NATIONS TAX COMMISSION. Approves revenue laws of first nations. The purposes of the Commission are to (a) ensure the integrity of the system of first nations real property taxation and promote a common approach to first nations real property taxation nationwide, having regard to variations in provincial real property taxation systems; (b) ensure that the real property taxation systems of first nations reconcile the interests of taxpayers with the responsibilities of chiefs and councils to govern the affairs of first nations; (c) prevent, or provide for the timely resolution of, disputes in relation to the application of local revenue laws; (d) assist first nations in

the exercise of their jurisdiction over real property taxation on reserve lands and build capacity in first nations to administer their taxation systems; (e) develop training programs for first nation real property tax administrators; (f) assist first nations to achieve sustainable economic development through the generation of stable local revenues; (g) promote a transparent first nations real property taxation regime that provides certainty to taxpayers; (h) promote understanding of the real property taxation systems of first nations; and (i) provide advice to the Minister regarding future development of the framework within which local revenue laws are made. Established under *First Nations Fiscal and Statistical Management Act*, S.C. 2005, c. 9, s. 17 and 29.

FIRST OFFENDER. One who was convicted for the first time.

FIRST READING. A purely formal stage of parliamentary deliberation decided without amendment or debate, coupled with an order to print the bill. A. Fraser, W.A. Dawson, & J. Holtby, eds., *Beauchesne's Rules and Forms of the House of Commons of Canada*, 6th ed. (Toronto: Carswell, 1989) at 195.

FISCAL. *adj.* Relating to revenue.

FISCAL PERIOD. The period for which the accounts of the business of the taxpayer have been ordinarily made up and accepted for purposes of assessment under the Income Tax Act.

FISCAL YEAR. 1. When used to mean the fiscal year of the government means the period from April 1 in one year to March 31 in the next year. 2. The period for which the business accounts of a corporation or a business of a taxpayer are made up and accepted for the purposes of the Income Tax Act.

FISH. *n.* 1. Includes (a) parts of fish, (b) shellfish, crustaceans, marine animals, and any parts of shellfish, crustaceans or marine animals and (c) the eggs, sperm, spawn, larvae, spat and juvenile stages of fish, shellfish, crustaceans and marine animals. *Fisheries Act*, R.S.C. 1986, c. F-14, s. 1. 2. Includes shellfish, crustaceans and marine animals. *Bank Act*, S.C. 1991, c. 46, s. 425.

FISHERIES. *n.* The business of catching, harvesting, raising, cultivating and handling of fish directly or indirectly by a fisherman. *Fisheries and Aquaculture Development Act*, S.N.B. 1977, c. F-15.1, s. 1. See CANADIAN ~ WATERS; FISHERY.

FISHERY. *n.* 1. "... [T]he right of catching fish in the sea, or in a particular stream of water; ... also ... used to denote the locality where such right is exercised." *R. v. Fowler* (1980), 9 C.E.L.R. 115 at 121, [1980] 2 S.C.R. 213, [1980] 5 W.W.R. 511, 113 D.L.R. (3d) 513, 53 C.C.C. (2d) 97, 32 N.R. 230, the court per Martland J. 2. Includes the area, locality, place or station in or on which a pound, seine, net, weir or other fishing appliance is used, set, placed or located, and the area, tract or stretch of water in or from which fish may be taken by the said pound, seine, net, weir or other fishing appliance, and also the pound, seine, net, weir, or other fishing appliance used in connection therewith. *Fisheries Act*, R.S.C. 1985, c. F-14, s. 2. See DEPARTMENT OF FISH-

ERIES AND OCEANS; FISHERIES; NON-QUOTA ~.

FISH HABITAT. Spawning grounds and nursery, rearing, food supply and migration areas on which fish depend directly or indirectly in order to carry out their life processes. *Fisheries Act*, R.S.C. 1985, c. F-14, s. 34.

FISHING. *n.* 1. Fishing for, catching or attempting to catch fish by any method. *Fisheries Act*, R.S.C. 1985, c. F- 4, s. 2. 2. "... [A] continuous process beginning from the time when the preliminary preparations are being made for the taking of the fish and extending down to the moment when they are finally reduced to actual and certain possession... ." *"Frederick Gerring Jr." (The) v. R.* (1897), 27 S.C.R. 271 at 280, Sedgewick J.

FISHING EXPEDITION. 1. Pejorative term to refer to the search for evidence on a speculative basis. *R. v. S. (T.)*, 2009 CarswellOnt 6785, 2009 ONCA 770. 2. Using discovery as a means to seek out a cause of action. *Lougheed Estate v. Wilson*, 2009 CarswellBC 3608, 2009 BCCA 537. 3. A challenge for cause strays into illegitimacy "if used merely, without more ... as a 'fishing expedition' in order to obtain personal information about the juror". *R. v. Sherratt*, [1991] 1 S.C.R. 509 at 533.

FISHING LICENCE. A licence granting the right to fish. It may be restricted as to time, place, species or quantity.

FISHING RIGHTS. See ABORIGINAL ~.

FISHING VESSEL. 1. Any ship or boat or any other description of vessel for use in fishing and equipment, apparatus and appliances for use in the operation thereof and forming part thereof, or any share or part interest therein. *Bank Act*, S.C. 1991, c. 46, s. 425. 2. Any vessel used, outfitted or designed for the purpose of catching, processing or transporting fish. *Fisheries Act*, R.S.C. 1985, c. F-14, s. 2.

FISLO. *abbr.* Free in stow, liner out.

FITNESS. *n.* The physical and mental condition of an individual that enables that person to function at their best in society. *The Fitness and Amateur Sport Act*, R.S.M. 1987, c. F120, s. 1. See PRESUMPTION OF ~; SAFETY ~ CERTIFICATE.

FITNESS FOR THE PURPOSE. "Section 17(2) of the [Sale of Goods Act, R.S.A. 1980, c. S-2] is primarily designed to cover the aspect of the function of specific goods from an operating point of view... . The implied condition of goods being reasonably fit for the purpose for which they are required includes not only operational fitness but also fitness to be transported and to be hoisted into position in an appropriate fashion so as to enable those goods to become operational." *Prolite Plastics Ltd. v. International Cooling Tower Inc.* (1987), 51 Alta. L.R. (2d) 299 at 306, 79 A.R. 110 (Q.B.), Gallant J.

FIT-UP. *n.* Leasehold improvements undertaken by a tenant with respect to the space it usually occupies exclusively. *Martel Building Ltd. v. R.*, 2000 CarswellNat 2678, 2000 SCC 60, 36 R.P.R. (3d) 175, 193 D.L.R. (4th) 1, 262 N.R. 285, 3 C.C.L.T. (3d) 1,

5 C.L.R. (3d) 161, 186 F.T.R. 231(note), [2000] 2 S.C.R. 860, the court per Iacobucci and Major JJ.

FIX. *v.* To determine; to ascertain.

FIXED. *adj.* Determined; ascertained.

FIXED ASSET. Property used in a business which will not be used or converted into cash during the current fiscal year.

FIXED CAPITAL. That which is in the form or shape of assets, either tangible or intangible, but identifiable as such, and which either produces income directly or can be employed to earn or produce income, for example, a machine. *Johns-Manville Canada v. The Queen*, [1985] 2 S.C.R. 46, Estey J. for the court at para. 23.

FIXED CHARGE. A security interest similar to the charge which a typical real property mortgage creates. It is a charge on specific property, contrasted to a floating charge.

FIXED COSTS. Costs set as a lump sum without being constrained by tariffs.

FIXED CREDIT. Credit under a credit agreement that is not for open credit. *Business Practices and Consumer Protection Act*, S.B.C. 2004, c. 2, s. 57.

FIXED DATE ELECTION. An election on a date determined by statute.

FIXED PLATFORM. An artificial island or a marine installation or structure that is permanently attached to the seabed for the purpose of exploration or exploitation of resources or for other economic purposes. *Criminal Code*, R.S.C. 1985, c. C-46, s. 78.1.

FIXED PRICE CONTRACT. Contract in which the price is preset regardless of actual cost. Contemplates extra work or deletions from the work, resulting in variation from the stated contract price.

FIXED TERM TENANCY. A tenancy under a residential tenancy agreement for a term that ends on a day specified in the agreement. *Residential Tenancies Act*, S.A. 2004, c. R-17.1, s. 1.

FIXTURE. *n.* 1. Tangible personal property that has been annexed to land and that is regarded in law as part of the land to which it has been annexed, but does not include building materials. *Civil Enforcement Act*, R.S.A. 2000, c. C-15, s. 1. 2. Machinery, equipment or apparatus that is (a) a fixture at common law, and (b) used directly in the manufacture, production, processing, storage, handling, packaging, display, transportation, transmission or distribution of tangible personal property or in the provision of a service. *Social Service Tax Act*, R.S.B.C. 1996, c. 431, s. 1. 3. Does not include building materials. *Personal Property Security acts*. See TENANT'S ~S; TRADE ~.

FLAG. *n.* A banner; ensign; standard. See LAW OF ~.

FLAGRANT. *adj.* 1. "... [G]laring, scandalous or conspicuously wrongful: ..." *R. v. Harris* (1987), 35 C.C.C. (3d) 1 at 25, 20 O.A.C. 26, 57 C.R. (3d) 356, the court per Martin J.A. 2. "... [C]lear or obvious ...

F

scandalous ..." *R. v. Nelson* (1987), 35 C.C.C. (3d) 347 at 350, [1987] 3 W.W.R. 144, 46 M.V.R. 145, 45 Man. R. (2d) 68, 29 C.R.R. 80 (C.A.), Huband J.A. (Hall J.A. concurring).

FLAGRANTE DELICTO. [L. while the crime is glaring] While committing the offence charged.

FLASH. *n.* The feeling of euphoria following taking a drug. F.A. Jaffe, *A Guide to Pathological Evidence for Lawyers and Police Officers*, 4th ed. (Toronto: Carswell, 1999) at 237.

FLETCHER. See RULE IN RYLANDS V. ~.

F.L.D. *abbr.* Family Law Digest, 1968-1982.

FLIGHT. *n.* 1. The act of flying or moving through the air. *Criminal Code*, R.S.C. 1985, c. C-46, s. 7(8). 2. "... '[A]ction of running away from danger,' ..." *Rowe v. R.* (1951), 100 C.C.C. 97 at 103, [1951] S.C.R. 713, 12 C.R. 148, [1951] 4 D.L.R. 238, Kellock J. 3. Every one commits an offence who, operating a motor vehicle while being pursued by a peace officer operating a motor vehicle, fails, without reasonable excuse and in order to evade the peace officer, to stop the vehicle as soon as is reasonable in the circumstances. *Criminal Code*, R.S.C. 1985, c. C-46, s. 249.1. See SPACE ~.

FLIGHT ELEMENT. A Space Station element provided by Canada or by a Partner State under the Agreement and under any memorandum of understanding or other implementing arrangement entered into to carry out the Agreement concerning the space station. *Criminal Code*, R.S.C. 1985, c. C-46, s. 7.

FLOATING CAPITAL. Capital available to meet current expenditure.

FLOATING CHARGE. 1. "... [A]n equitable charge on the assets for the time being of a going concern. It does not specifically affect any particular assets until some event occurs or some act is done on the part of the mortgagee which causes the security to crystallize into a fixed security. Until the security is crystallized the charge is an equitable one and the legal title to the goods remains in the mortgagor." *Meen v. Realty Development Co.* (1953), [1954] O.W.N. 193 at 194, [1954] 1 D.L.R. 649 (C.A.), the court per MacKay J.A. 2. "A floating security is not a future security; it is a present security, which presently affects all the assets of the company expressed to be included in it. On the other hand, it is not a specific security; the holder cannot affirm that the assets are specifically mortgaged to him. The assets are mortgaged in such a way that the mortgagor can deal with them without the concurrence of the mortgagee. A floating security is not a specific mortgage of the assets, plus a licence to the mortgagor to dispose of them in the course of his business, but a floating mortgage applying to every item comprised in the security, but not specifically affecting any item until some event occurs or some act on the part of the mortgagee is done which causes it to crystallize into a fixed security." *Evans v. Rival Granite Quarries Ltd.*, [1910] 2 K.B. 979 at 999 (U.K. C.A.), Buckley L.J. 3. A charge that secures the payment or performance of an obligation and that does not become a fixed charge on specific land until the occurrence of an event, stipulated in the instrument that created the floating charge. *Land Title Act*, R.S.B.C. 1996, c. 250, s. 203.

FLOATING HOME. A structure that is composed of a floating platform and a building designed to be occupied as a place of residence for individuals that is permanently affixed to the platform, but does not include any freestanding appliances or furniture sold with the structure or any structure that has means of, or is capable of being readily adapted for, self-propulsion. *An Act respecting the Québec sales tax*, R.S.Q. c. T-0.1, s. 1.

FLOATING HYPOTHEC. A hypothec is floating when some of the effects are suspended until, the debtor or grantor having defaulted, the creditor provokes crystallization of the hypothec by serving a notice of default and crystallization of the hypothec on the debtor or grantor. The floating character of the hypothec shall be expressly stipulated in the act. *Civil Code*, S.Q. 1991, c. 64, a. 2715.

FLOATING RATE. An interest rate that bears a specified mathematical relationship to an index rate, and includes an interest rate that (a) is subject to a minimum or maximum rate, or (b) is determined at the beginning of a period and applies throughout the period regardless of changes in the index rate during the period. *Business Practices and Consumer Protection Act*, S.B.C. 2004, c. 2, s. 57.

FLOODGATES ARGUMENT. The argument that the acceptance of the plaintiff's or applicant's claim will lead to a multitude of similar claims by others.

FLOOR. *n.* A storey; a set of rooms and spaces on the same level in a building.

FLOOR TRADER. An individual who is employed by a dealer for the purpose of entering into contracts on the floor of a commodity futures exchange on behalf of such dealer. *Commodity Futures Act*, R.S.O. 1990, c. C.20, s. 1.

FLOTSAM. *n.* Goods afloat on the surface of the sea.

FLOUT. *v.* To treat with disdain; to mock; to express contempt for.

F.L.R.A.C. *abbr.* Family Law Reform Act Cases (Ontario), 1978-1985.

F.L.R.R. *abbr.* Family Law Reform Reporter, 1978-1987.

FMCS. *abbr.* The Federal Mediation and Conciliation Service.

F.O.B. *abbr.* 1. Free on board. 2. "... [T]he seller is obliged to put the goods on the truck but thereafter the goods are at the risk of the buyer and the buyer alone is responsible for the freight and insurance ..." *George Smith Trucking Co. v. Golden Seven Enterprises Inc.* (1989), 55 D.L.R. (4th) 161 at 174, 34 B.C.L.R. (2d) 43, [1989] 3 W.W.R. 544 (C.A.), Hutcheon J.A. (dissenting).

FOETUS. *n.* 1. An unborn product of conception after the embryo stage. 2. A human organism during the period of its development beginning on the fifty-seventh day following fertilization or creation, excluding any time during which its development has been suspended, and ending at birth. *Assisted Human Reproduction Act*, S.C. 2004, c. 2, s. 3.

FOI. *abbr.* Freedom of Information.

FOI REQUEST. A request for disclosure of information held by a government body.

FOLLOW. See COSTS SHALL ~ THE EVENT.

FOOD. *n.* Any article manufactured, sold or represented for use as food or drink for human beings, chewing gum, and any ingredient that may be mixed with food for any purpose whatever. *Food and Drugs Act*, R.S.C. 1985, c. F-27, s. 2.

FOOD INSPECTION. See CANADIAN ~ AGENCY.

FOOD POISONING. [A] subset of food-borne illness, refers to illnesses caused by a toxin in food, usually created by bacteria culturing in the food. *P.G. Restaurant Ltd. v. Northern Interior Regional Health Board*, 2005 BCCA 210.

F.O.R. *abbr.* Free on rail.

FOR. *prep.* 1. "... [W]ith the intention of ..." *R. v. Chow*, [1938] 2 D.L.R. 332 at 333, [1938] 1 W.W.R. 458, 70 C.C.C. 150, 52 B.C.R. 467 (C.A.), the court per Sloan J.A. 2. "... '[W]ith the object or purpose of' ..." *Blackstock v. Insurance Corp. of British Columbia*, [1983] I.L.R. 1-1630 at 6264, [1983] 3 W.W.R. 282, 20 M.V.R. 293, 143 D.L.R. (3d) 743 (B.C. S.C.), Macdonell J. 3. In to work for, pursuant to a contractual relationship.

FORBID. *v.* "... '[P]rohibit' ..." *Krautt v. Paine* (1980), 17 R.P.R. 1 at 21, [1980] 6 W.W.R. 717, 118 D.L.R. (3d) 625, 25 A.R. 390 (C.A.), the court per Laycraft J.A.

FOR CAUSE. In relation to employee or office-holder, connotes misconduct or dishonesty, behaviour inconsistent with the employment or office.

FORCE. *n.* 1. Violence. 2. The Royal Canadian Mounted Police. 3. The members of a police department. See ATTEMPT OR THREAT TO APPLY ~; EXCESSIVE ~; ~S; IN ~; POLICE ~; REASONABLE ~; REGULAR ~; RESERVE ~; SPECIAL ~.

FORCED PREGNANCY. The unlawful confinement of a woman forcibly made pregnant, with the intent of affecting the ethnic composition of any population or carrying out other grave violations of international law. This definition shall not in any way be interpreted as affecting national laws relating to pregnancy. *Crimes Against Humanity and War Crimes Act*, S.C. 2000, c. 24, Sched., *Rome Statute*, Article 7.

FORCE MAJEURE. [Fr.] Irresistible urge.

FORCE MAJEURE CLAUSE. "... [G]enerally operates to discharge a contracting party when a supervening, sometimes supernatural, event, beyond the control of either party, makes performance impossible. The common thread is that of the unexpected, something beyond reasonable human foresight and

skill." *Atlantic Paper Stock Ltd. v. St. Anne-Nackawic Pulp & Paper Co.* (1975), 10 N.B.R. (2d) 513 at 516, [1976] 1 S.C.R. 580, 4 N.R. 539, 56 D.L.R. (3d) 409, the court per Dickson J. See ACT OF GOD CLAUSE.

FORCE OF LAW. Of a rule, must be unilateral and have binding legal effect. *Reference re Manitoba Language Rights* [1992] 1 S.C.R. 212.

FORCES. See ARMED ~; CANADIAN ~; FORCE; HER MAJESTY'S ~; MILITARY ~ OF A STATE.

FORCIBLE CONFINEMENT. Use of physical restraint, contrary to the wishes of the person restrained, but to which the victim submits unwillingly, thereby depriving the person of liberty to move from one place to another.

FORCIBLE DETAINER. 1. Refusal to restore goods to another though sufficient means were tendered. 2. A person commits forcible detainer when, being in actual possession of real property without colour of right, he detains it in a manner that is likely to cause a breach of the peace or reasonable apprehension of a breach of the peace, against a person who is entitled by law to possession of it. *Criminal Code*, R.S.C. 1985, c. C-46, s. 72(2).

FORCIBLE ENTRY. A person commits forcible entry when that person enters real property that is in the actual and peaceable possession of another in a manner that is likely to cause a breach of the peace or reasonable apprehension of a breach of the peace. *Criminal Code*, R.S.C. 1985, c. C-46, s. 72(1).

F.O.R. CONTRACT. Free on rail contract. A seller undertakes to deliver goods into railway cars at personal expense.

FORECLOSE DOWN. See REDEEM UP, FORECLOSE DOWN.

FORECLOSURE. *n.* 1. An action brought by a mortgagee when a mortgagor is in default asking that a day be fixed on which the mortgagor is to pay off the debt, and that in default of payment the mortgagor may be foreclosed of, that is deprived of her or his right to redeem, the equity of redemption. 2. A proceeding, commenced by a vendor under an agreement for sale, in which the relief claimed is an order for one or more of the following: (a) specific performance of the agreement, (b) cancellation of the agreement, or (c) determination of the agreement. *Law and Equity Act*, R.S.B.C. 1996, c. 253, s. 16. 3. A mortgagee has five principal remedies: an action on the covenant for repayment; sale; foreclosure; taking possession; and appointing a receiver ... The term "foreclosure" is often used to describe broadly this panoply of remedies ... More narrowly, an order of foreclosure transfers title to the mortgagee and terminates the mortgagor's equity of redemption: Law of Property Act, R.S.A. 2000, C. L-7, s. 48(1). *Daniels v. Mitchell*, 2005 ABCA 271.

FORECLOSURE ORDER. "... [N]ot a final order disposing of a proceeding; it merely fixes the amount due on a mortgage and forecloses the right of a mortgagor to redeem the property, unless the amount due on the mortgage plus costs is paid ..." *Golden Forest*

Holdings Ltd. v. Bank of Nova Scotia (1990), 43 C.P.C. (2d) 16 at 19, 98 N.S.R. (2d) 429, 263 A.P.R. 429 (C.A.), the court per Hallett J.A.

FOREGONE. *adj.* Gone without.

FOREIGN. *adj.* 1. Out of a certain nation's jurisdiction. 2. "... [I]n a private international law (conflicts) sense, namely, a territory which does not share precisely the same law ..." *Canadian Commercial Bank v. McLaughlan* (1990), 73 D.L.R. (4th) 678 at 685, 39 E.T.R. 54, 75 Alta. L.R. (2d) 40, 107 A.R. 232 (C.A.), Bracco and Stevenson JJ.A. and Forsyth J. (ad hoc).

FOREIGN AFFAIRS. See DEPARTMENT OF ~ AND INTERNATIONAL TRADE.

FOREIGN BILL. A bill that is neither drawn in Canada upon a person resident in Canada nor drawn and payable in Canada. I.F.G. Baxter, *The Law of Banking*, 3d ed. (Toronto: Carswell, 1981) at 117.

FOREIGN CORPORATION. 1. A corporation that (a) is not a company, (b) has issued shares, (c) is not required under the Cooperative Association Act to be registered under that Act, and (d) was (i) incorporated otherwise than by or under an Act, (ii) continued under section 308 or otherwise transferred by a similar process into a jurisdiction other than British Columbia, or (iii) the result of an amalgamation under Division 4 of Part 9 or a similar process, or of an amalgamation or similar process in a jurisdiction other than British Columbia, and includes an extraprovincial corporation within the meaning of the Financial Institutions Act. *Business Corporations Act*, S.B.C. 2002, c. 57, s. 1. 2. A body corporate that is incorporated otherwise than by or under the authority of an Act of the Legislature or of the Parliament of Canada and has gain for its purpose or object. *Corporations Registration Act*, R.S.N.S. 1989, c. 101, s. 2.

FOREIGN COURT. "In Canada, the courts of one province are, with respect to the courts of the other provinces, foreign courts." *Brand v. National Life Assurance Co.* (1918), 44 D.L.R. 412 at 420, [1918] 3 W.W.R. 858 (Man. K.B.), Mathers C.J.K.B.

FOREIGN ECONOMIC ENTITY. A foreign state or a group of foreign states, or an entity that is controlled, in law or in fact, or is substantially owned, by a foreign state or a group of foreign states. *Security of Information Act*, R.S.C. 1985, c. O-5, s. 2.

FOREIGN ENTITY. A foreign power, a group or association of foreign powers, or of one or more foreign powers and one or more terrorist groups, or a person acting at the direction of, for the benefit of or in association with a foreign power or a group or association referred to above. *Security of Information Act*, R.S.C. 1985, c. O-5, s. 2.

FOREIGN EXPOSURE. In relation to a fund, portfolio or financial product, the result of either or, as the case may be, of the total, of the following aggregates: (a) the aggregate of one or more physical securities that are qualified securities and that are not combined with a financial derivative position; and

(b) the aggregate of one or more financial derivative positions, combined or not with physical securities, the underlying interest of which, resulting from the net position, is foreign. *An Act respecting International financial centres*, R.S.Q. c. C-8.3, s. 4.

FOREIGN FINANCIAL DERIVATIVE. A financial derivative the underlying interest of which is foreign. *An Act respecting International financial centres*, R.S.Q. c. C-8.3, s. 4.

FOREIGN IMMOVABLE RULE. The courts in one jurisdiction do not have jurisdiction to adjudicate on the right and title to lands not within that jurisdiction's boundaries. Only the courts in which the land is situate may adjudicate the right and title to lands.

FOREIGN INTELLIGENCE. Information or intelligence about the capabilities, intentions or activities of a foreign individual, state, organization or terrorist group, as they relate to international affairs, defence or security. *National Defence Act*, R.S.C. 1985, c. N-5, s. 273.61.

FOREIGN JUDGMENT. "... [J]udgments from another country." *Morguard Investments Ltd. v. De Savoye* (1988), 29 C.P.C. (2d) 52 at 59, 27 B.C.L.R. (2d) 155, [1988] 5 W.W.R. 650 (C.A.), the court per Seaton J.A.

FOREIGN JURISDICTION. A province, state, country or other jurisdiction outside the province enacting the legislation.

FOREIGN LAW. The law of another jurisdiction. See FOREIGN.

FOREIGN NATIONAL. A person who is not a Canadian citizen or a permanent resident, and includes a stateless person. *Immigration and Refugee Protection Act*, S. C. 2001, c. 27, s. 2.

FOREIGN POWER. (a) The government of a foreign state, (b) an entity exercising or purporting to exercise the functions of a government in relation to a territory outside Canada regardless of whether Canada recognizes the territory as a state or the authority of that entity over the territory, or (c) a political faction or party operating within a foreign state whose stated purpose is to assume the role of government of a foreign state. *Security of Information Act*, R.S.C. 1985, c. O-5, s. 2.

FOREIGN STATE. (a) A state other than Canada, (b) a province, state or other political subdivision of a state other than Canada, or (c) a colony, dependency, possession, protectorate, condominium, trust territory or any territory falling under the jurisdiction of a state other than Canada. *Security of Information Act*, R.S.C. 1985, c. O-5, s. 2.

FOREIGN TRADE LAW. A law of a foreign jurisdiction that directly or indirectly affects or is likely to affect trade or commerce between (a) Canada, a province, a Canadian citizen or a resident of Canada, a corporation incorporated by or under a law of Canada or a province or a person carrying on business in Canada, and (b) any person or foreign state. *Foreign Extraterritorial Measures Act*, R.S.C. 1985, c. F-29, s. 2.

FOREIGN VESSEL. A vessel that is not a Canadian vessel or a pleasure craft. *Canada Shipping Act, 2001*, S.C. 2001, c. 26, s. 2.

FOREMAN. *n.* 1. The member of a jury who speaks for that body. 2. A supervisory employee.

FORENSIC. *adj.* Applied to the law; belonging to law courts.

FORENSIC DNA ANALYSIS. 1. (a) In relation to a bodily substance that is taken from a person in execution of a warrant under section 487.05, means forensic DNA analysis of the bodily substance and the comparison of the results of that analysis with the results of the analysis of the DNA in the bodily substance referred to in paragraph 487.05(1)(b), and includes any incidental tests associated with that analysis, and (b) in relation to a bodily substance that is provided voluntarily in the course of an investigation of a designated offence or is taken from a person under an order made under section 487.051 or an authorization granted under section 487.055 or 487.091, or to a bodily substance referred to in paragraph 487.05(1)(b), means forensic DNA analysis of the bodily substance. *Criminal Code*, R.S.C. 1985, c. C-46, s. 487.04. 2. In relation to a bodily substance, means forensic DNA analysis of the bodily substance. *DNA Identification Act, 1998*, S. C. 1998, c. 37, s. 2.

FORENSIC MEDICINE. 1. Legal medicine. 2. Medical skills and knowledge which may be used to solve legal problems. F.A. Jaffe, *A Guide to Pathological Evidence for Lawyers and Police Officers*, 4th ed. (Toronto: Carswell, 1999) at 237. 3. Jurisprudence of medicine.

FORESEEABILITY. *n.* A reasonable person's ability to anticipate the consequences of his or her action. See REASONABLE FORSEEABILITY.

FORESEEABLE. *adj.* In law, "foreseeable" does not mean "imaginable." The human mind is capable of imagining all sorts of fantastic and bizarre situations, but that does not make them "foreseeable" in law. The legal concept of foreseeability incorporates the idea that the event is not only imaginable, but that there is some reasonable prospect or expectation that it will arise. *Fullowka v. Royal Oak Ventures Inc.*, 2008 NWTCA 4.

FORESHORE. *n.* The area of the shore between low water mark and the highest high water mark.

FORESTRY. *n.* The conservation, cultivation, improvement, harvesting and rational utilization of timber stands and the resources contained therein and obtainable therefrom, and includes the operation of a sugar bush. *Bank Act*, S.C. 1991, c. 46, s. 425. See PRACTICE OF ~; PROFESSIONAL ~.

FOREST TENURE. The right to harvest Crown timber in an agreement referred to in section 12(1)(a), (c), (d), (e) or (g) or (2)(a) of the Forest Act. *Park Act*, R.S.B.C. 1996, c. 344, s. 11.

FORFEIT. *v.* "... '[T]o lose by some breach of condition; to lose by some offence.' ..." *R. v. Premier Cutlery Ltd.* (1980), 55 C.P.R. (2d) 134 at 154 (Ont. Prov. Ct.), Bernard Prov. J.

FORFEITURE. *n.* 1. The surrender of goods or chattels to punish someone for a crime, for failure to comply with terms of a recognizance or pay duty or fulfil some obligation and to compensate the person to whom they were forfeited for any injury. 2. Section 98 [of the Courts of Justice Act, R.S.O. 1990, c. C.43] speaks of relief from penalties and forfeitures. Each word lends meaning to the other. "Penalties" is derived from penal and connotes punishment. "Forfeiture" is a giving up of a right or property and when allied with "penalties" suggests something of the nature of goods being forfeited to customs officials. Neither penalties nor forfeitures are compensatory and both connote an added element to any money damages when associated with a breach of a contract. The failure to pay premiums on a term life insurance policy and the consequent lapse of that policy engage none of the above considerations. The premium is the payment for coverage for the next term. Subject to the grace provision, there is no coverage for that term when a payment is not made and the insurer arranges its commercial affairs accordingly. In these circumstances, the contract terminates on its own terms and not by a breach. There is no forfeiture in the sense of a loss of property. To be sure, the coverage has been lost, but it wasn't paid for in the first place. *Pluzak v. Gerling Global Life Insurance Co.*, 2001 CarswellOnt 10 (C.A.). See CIVIL ~; RELIEF AGAINST ~.

FORFEITURE ORDER. An order that property which is the proceeds of unlawful activity be forfeited to the Crown. *The Seizure of Criminal Property Act, 2009*, S.S. 2009, c. S-46.002, s. 2 and 7.

FORGERY. *n.* Making a false document, knowing it to be false, with intent (a) that it should in any way be used or acted upon as genuine, to the prejudice of any one whether within Canada or not, or (b) that some person should be induced, by the belief that it is genuine, to do or to refrain from doing anything, whether within Canada or not. *Criminal Code*, R.S.C. 1985, c. C-46, s. 366.

FORGERY OF PASSPORT. Everyone who, while in or out of Canada, (a) forges a passport, or (b) knowing that a passport is forged (i) uses, deals with or acts on it, or (ii) causes or attempts to cause any person to use, deal with, or act on it, as if the passport were genuine, is guilty of an offence. *Criminal Code*, R.S.C. 1985, c. C-46, s. 57.

FORM. *n.* 1. The contents or structure of a document distinguished from its substance. 2. A temporary structure or mould used to support concrete while it is drying. See BEARER ~; COMMON ~ BUSINESS; EQUITY LOOKS TO THE INTENT RATHER THAN TO THE ~; ORDER ~; REGISTERED ~.

FORMAL ADMISSION. A judicial admission. An admission made by a party in pleadings.

FORMAL CONTRACT. A deed; a contract under seal.

FORMAL EQUALITY. Substantive equality, as contrasted with formal equality, is grounded in the idea that: "The promotion of equality entails the promotion of a society in which all are secure in the knowledge that they are recognized at law as human beings equally deserving of concern, respect and consideration": Andrews [Andrews v. Law Society of British Columbia, 1989 CanLII 2, [1989] 1 S.C.R. 143], at p. 171, per McIntyre J., for the majority on the s. 15 issue. Pointing out that the concept of equality does not necessarily mean identical treatment and that the formal "like treatment" model of discrimination may in fact produce inequality, McIntyre J. stated (at p. 165): To approach the ideal of full equality before and under the law - and in human affairs an approach is all that can be expected - the main consideration must be the impact of the law on the individual or the group concerned. Recognizing that there will always be an infinite variety of personal characteristics, capacities, entitlements and merits among those subject to a law, there must be accorded, as nearly as may be possible, an equality of benefit and protection and no more of the restrictions, penalties or burdens imposed upon one than another. In other words, the admittedly unattainable ideal should be that a law expressed to bind all should not because of irrelevant personal differences have a more burdensome or less beneficial impact on one than another. [end of quotation]. While acknowledging that equality is an inherently comparative concept (p. 164), McIntyre J. warned against a sterile similarly situated test focussed on treating "likes" alike. An insistence on substantive equality has remained central to the Court's approach to equality claims. *R.v. Kapp*, 2008 SCC 41, McLachlin C.J. and Abella J. for the majority.

FORMA PAUPERIS. See IN ~.

FORMAT. *n.* In relation to a book, means (a) the type or quality of binding; (b) the typeface or size of print; (c) the type or quality of paper; or (d) the content, including whether the book is abridged or unabridged, or illustrated. *Copyright Act*, R.S.C. 1985, c. C-42, *Book Importation Regulations*, SOR/99-324, s. 1. See ALTERNATIVE ~; ELECTRONIC ~.

FORM OF PROXY. A written or printed form that, on completion and execution by or on behalf of a shareholder, becomes a proxy.

FORMS OF ACTION. The common law procedural devices compliance with which was necessary to seek a remedy before the courts, ex. assumpsit, trespass on the case.

FORMULA. See AMENDING ~; PARAS ~.

FORMULATION. *n.* The preparation of a bill for introduction into the legislature.

FORNICATION. *n.* Voluntary sexual intercourse between two people not married to each other.

FORTHWITH. *adv.* 1. Immediately, or as soon as possible in the circumstances. 2. Within a reasonable time, considering the circumstances and the object.

FORTIFIED BUILDING. A building protected by one or more of the following: (i) bulletproof material or material designed to be resistant to explosives on a door or window; (ii) protective metal plating on the interior or exterior of the building that is not required for the structural integrity of the building; (iii) armoured or specially reinforced doors; (iv) metal bars on exterior doors or windows; (v) any other method or material prescribed in the regulations. *The Safer Communities and Neighbourhoods Act*, S.S. 2004, c. S-0.1, s. 38.

FORTIUS CONTRA PROFERENTEM. [L.] More strongly against those using them. Refers to the construction of documents. See CONTRA PROFERENTEM.

FORUM. *n.* [L. a place] The place where legal remedies can be sought, a court. See NATURAL~; PUBLIC ~.

FORUM CAN. CRIM. *abbr.* Le Forum canadien de criminologie (Canadian Criminology Forum).

FORUM CONVENIENS. [L.] " '... [F]orum which is the more suitable for the ends of justice'." *United Oilseed Products Ltd. v. Royal Bank* (1988), 29 C.P.C. (2d) 28 at 38, 60 Alta. L.R. (2d) 73, [1988] 5 W.W.R. 181, 87 A.R. 337 (C.A.), the court per Stevenson J.A.

FORUM NON CONVENIENS. [L.] 1. A doctrine which a court may apply to decline jurisdiction in a particular case. Another forum is considered more appropriate. 2. "... [T]wo conditions must be satisfied: (a) ... (the defendant) must satisfy the court that there is another forum to whose jurisdiction he was amenable and in which justice can be done between the parties at substantially less inconvenience and expense; (b) if the first condition is met, the plaintiff may still prevent a stay being granted if he can show that a stay would deprive him of a legitimate personal or juridical advantage which would be available to him if he invoked the jurisdiction of the court where the stay is sought." *Avenue Properties Ltd. v. First City Development Corp.* (1986), 7 B.C.L.R. (2d) 45 at 51-52, [1987] 1 W.W.R. 249, 32 D.L.R. (4th) 40 (C.A.), McLachlin J.A.

FORUM REI. [L.] The court of the place where the subject thing or person is situated.

FORWARD COMMODITY CONTRACT. A financial hedge and risk management tool. Interpreting them in the context of the rest of the section requires that they share certain traits. The contracts listed in s. 11.1(1) of the Companies' Creditors Arrangement Act, [R.S.C. 1985, c. C-36] deal with units that are the equivalent of any other unit. Therefore commodities must be interchangeable, and readily identifiable as fungible commodities capable of being traded on a futures exchange or as the underlying asset of an over-the-counter derivative transaction. Commodities must trade in a volatile market, with a sufficient trading volume to ensure a competitive trading price, in order that forward commodity contracts may be "marked to market" and their value determined. This removes from the ambit of s. 11.1(1)(h) contracts for commercial merchandise and manufactured goods which neither trade on a volatile market nor are completely interchangeable for each other. *Blue Range Resource Corp., Re*, 2000 ABCA 239, 20 C.B.R. (4th) 187, 266 A.R. 98.

FORWARD-LOOKING INFORMATION. Disclosure of possible events, conditions or results of operations that is based on assumptions about future economic conditions and courses of action, and includes future-oriented financial information about the prospective results of operations, financial position or cash flows, presented either as a forecast or as a projection. *Securities Act*, S.Y. 2007, c. 16, s. 1.

FOSTER HOME. 1. A home other than the home of the parent or guardian of a child, where not more than four children who are not siblings are placed by an agency for care and supervision but not for the purposes of adoption. *The Child and Family Services Act*, S.M. 1985-86, c. 8, s. 1. 2. A private home approved by the Superintendent for the purpose of the placement of a child in the home whether or not any payment is made to the home for maintenance of the child. *Child Welfare Act*, R.S.N.W.T. 1988, c. C-6, s. 1.

F.O.T. *abbr.* Free on truck. Describing a seller's responsibility to have the goods placed on a truck.

FOUNDATION. *n.* A corporation established to receive, hold, administer and apply any property or the income from it for purposes or objects in connection with a hospital, other public or charitable purpose. See CHARITABLE ~.

FOUND GUILTY. The plea of guilty by an accused to an offence or the finding that an accused is guilty of an offence made before or by a court that makes an order directing that the accused be discharged for the offence either absolutely or on the conditions prescribed in a probation order, when (i) the order directing the discharge is not subject to further appeal, or (ii) no appeal is taken in respect of the order directing the discharge. *Evidence acts.*

FOUND IN. Present in; discovered in the premises. Refers to a person found in a bawdy house or at a gaming location.

FOURS. See ALL ~.

FOUR TRIGGER THEORIES. Four approaches have been developed in the U.S. and Canadian jurisprudence for determining the timing of property damage which is latent, or developing over time, and which does not become apparent immediately. The "Exposure Theory", the "Manifestation Theory", the "Injury in Fact Theory" and the "Continuous Trigger or Triple Trigger Theory". *Alie v. Bertrand & Frère Construction Co.*, 62 O.R. (3d) 345 (C.A.).

FOUR UNITIES. Refers to the four conditions of a joint tenancy. See UNITY OF INTEREST; UNITY OF POSSESSION; UNITY OF TIME; UNITY OF TITLE.

FOX PAT. C. *abbr.* Fox's Patent, Trade Mark, Design and Copyright Cases, 1940-1971.

FRA. *abbr.* Family Relations Act.

FRACTIONAL INTEREST IN LAND. A legal interest, an equitable interest or a beneficial interest in land that is a part, share, portion or fraction of a whole legal, equitable or beneficial interest in the land. *The Tax Administration and Miscellaneous Taxes Act*, R.S.M. 1987, c. R150, s. 111.

FRACTURE. See TRANSMITTED ~.

FRAME. *v.* To fabricate false evidence so it appears someone else committed an offence.

FRAMEWORK AGREEMENT. 1. The Framework Agreement on First Nation Land Management concluded between Her Majesty in right of Canada and the first nations on February 12, 1996, and includes any amendments to the Agreement made pursuant to its provisions. *First Nations Land Management Act*, S.C. 1999, c. 24, s. 2. 2. The Saskatchewan Treaty Land Entitlement Framework Agreement entered into on September 22, 1992, pursuant to which Canada's outstanding treaty land entitlement obligations are to be fulfilled in respect of those bands that are parties to that Agreement, certain provisions of which are set out in Schedule II. *Saskatchewan Treaty Land Entitlement Act*, S.C. 1993, c. 11, s. 2.

FRANCHISE. *n.* 1. At common law, a royal privilege. 2. An agreement whereby the right to supply electricity, natural gas or natural gas liquids to the residents of a defined area is given. 3. A method of distributing or marketing a service or product through a system. The franchisor grants the franchisee the right to carry on the business in this particular way, according to this system. 4. A right to engage in a business where the franchisee is required by contract or otherwise to make a payment or continuing payments, whether direct or indirect, or a commitment to make such payment or payments, to the franchisor, or the franchisor's associate, in the course of operating the business or as a condition of acquiring the franchise or commencing operations and, (a) in which, (i) the franchisor grants the franchisee the right to sell, offer for sale or distribute goods or services that are substantially associated with the franchisor's, or the franchisor's associate's, trade-mark, service mark, trade name, logo or advertising or other commercial symbol, and (ii) the franchisor or the franchisor's associate exercises significant control over, or offers significant assistance in, the franchisee's method of operation, including building design and furnishings, locations, business organization, marketing techniques or training, or (b) in which, (i) the franchisor, or the franchisor's associate, grants the franchisee the representational or distribution rights, whether or not a trade-mark, service mark, trade name, logo or advertising or other commercial symbol is involved, to sell, offer for sale or distribute goods or services supplied by the franchisor or a supplier designated by the franchisor, and (ii) the franchisor, or the franchisor's associate, or a third person designated by the franchisor, provides location assistance, including securing retail outlets or accounts for the goods or services to be sold, offered for sale or distributed or securing locations or sites for vending machines, display racks or other product sales displays used by the franchisee. *Arthur Wishart Act (Franchise Disclosure), 2000*, S.O. 2000, c. 3, s. 1. See MASTER ~; SUB~.

FRANCHISE AGREEMENT. Any agreement that relates to a franchise between, (a) a franchisor or franchisor's associate, and (b) a franchisee. *Arthur Wishart Act (Franchise Disclosure), 2000*, S.O. 2000, c. 3, s. 1.

F

FRANCHISEE. *n.* 1. A person to whom a franchise is granted. 2. A person to whom a franchise is granted and includes, (a) a subfranchisor with regard to that subfranchisor's relationship with a franchisor, and (b) a subfranchisee with regard to that subfranchisee's relationship with a subfranchisor. *Arthur Wishart Act (Franchise Disclosure), 2000*, S.O. 2000,c. 3, s. 1. See PROSPECTIVE ~.

FRANCHISE FEE. A direct or indirect payment to purchase a franchise or to operate a franchised business, but does not include (i) a purchase of or an agreement to purchase a reasonable amount of goods at a reasonable bona fide wholesale price, (ii) a purchase of or an agreement to purchase a reasonable amount of services at a reasonable bona fide price, or (iii) a payment of a reasonable service charge to the issuer of a credit or debit card by an establishment accepting the credit or debit card, as the case may be. *Franchises Act*, R.S.A. 2000, c. F-23, s. 1.

FRANCHISE SYSTEM. Includes, (a) the marketing, marketing plan or business plan of the franchise, (b) the use of or association with a trade-mark, service mark, trade name, logo or advertising or other commercial symbol, (c) the obligations of the franchisor and franchisee with regard to the operation of the business operated by the franchisee under the franchise agreement, and (d) the goodwill associated with the franchise. *Arthur Wishart Act (Franchise Disclosure), 2000*, S.O. 2000, c. 3, s. 1.

FRANCHISOR. *n.* 1. A person who grants a franchise. 2. One or more persons who grant or offer to grant a franchise and includes a subfranchisor with regard to that subfranchisor's relationship with a subfranchisee. *Arthur Wishart Act (Franchise Disclosure), 2000*, S.O. 2000, c. 3, s. 1.

FRANCHISOR'S ASSOCIATE. A person, (a) who, directly or indirectly, (i) controls or is controlled by the franchisor, or (ii) is controlled by another person who also controls, directly or indirectly, the franchisor, and (b) who, (i) is directly involved in the grant of the franchise, (A) by being involved in reviewing or approving the grant of the franchise, or (B) by making representations to the prospective franchisee on behalf of the franchisor for the purpose of granting the franchise, marketing the franchise or otherwise offering to grant the franchise, or (ii) exercises significant operational control over the franchisee and to whom the franchisee has a continuing financial obligation in respect of the franchise. *Arthur Wishart Act (Franchise Disclosure), 2000*, S.O. 2000, c. 3, s. 1.

FRANCHISOR'S BROKER. A person, other than the franchisor, franchisor's associate or franchisee, who grants, markets or otherwise offers to grant a franchise, or who arranges for the grant of a franchise. *Franchises Act*, S.P.E.I. 2005, c. 36, s. 1.

FRATERNAL BENEFIT SOCIETY. 1A body corporate (a) that is without share capital, (b) that has a representative form of government, and (c) that was incorporated for fraternal, benevolent or religious purposes, including the provision of insurance benefits solely to its members or the spouses, common-law partners or children of its members. *Insurance Companies Act*, S.C. 1991, c. 47, s. 2.

FRATERNAL OR SORORAL SOCIETY. A society, order or association incorporated for the purpose of making with its members only and not for profit, contracts of life, accident or sickness insurance under which benefits may be paid only to its members or their beneficiaries, in accordance with its charter and this Act. *Insurance Companies Act*, R.S.N. 1990, c. I-10, s. 2.

FRATERNAL SOCIETY. A society, order or association incorporated for the purpose of making with its members only, and not for profit, contracts of life, accident or sickness insurance in accordance with its constitution, by-laws and rules and the governing statute. *Insurance acts.*

FRAUD. *n.* 1. The essential elements of fraud are dishonesty, which can include nondisclosure of important facts, and deprivation or risk of deprivation. *R. v. Cuerrier* [1998] 2 S.C.R. 371, per Cory, J. 2. "Fraud is false representation of fact, made with a knowledge of its falsehood, or recklessly, without belief in its truth, with the intention that it should be acted upon by the complaining party, and actually inducing him to act upon it." *Parna v. G. & S. Properties Ltd.*, [1971] S.C.R. 306 at 316, 15 D.L.R. (3d) 336, the court per Spence J., adopting a quotation from Anson on Contract. 3. (1) Every one who, by deceit, falsehood or other fraudulent means, whether or not it is a false pretence within the meaning of this Act defrauds the public or any person whether ascertained or not, of any property, money or valuable security, is guilty of an offence. (2) Every one who, by deceit, falsehood or other fraudulent means, whether or not it is a false pretence within the meaning of this Act, with intent to defraud, affects the public market price of stocks, shares, merchandise or anything that is offered for sale to the public, is guilty of an offence. *Criminal Code*, R.S.C. 1985, c. C-46, s. 380 in part. 4. The elements of fraud, in the context of an application for insurance are: a representation of a material fact, in writing on the application, which judged objectively, was false at the time it was made, and upon which there was reliance to the prejudice or harm of the insurer. *35445 Alberta Ltd. v. Transamerica Life Insurance Co. of Canada* (1996), 40 Alta. L.R. (3d) 44, affirmed on appeal to Alta. C.A. 61 Alta. L.R. (3d) 215. See BADGES OF ~; CONSTRUCTIVE ~; EQUITABLE ~; EXTRINSIC ~; IDENTITY ~; INTRINSIC ~; STATUTE OF ~S.

FRAUDULENT CONCEALMENT. Fraudulent concealment has been defined to include "conduct, which, having regard to some special relationship between the two parties concerned, is an unconscionable thing for one to do towards the other." (Kitchen v. Royal Air Force Association, [1958] 2 All E.R. 241 (C.A.) per Lord Evershed M.R. at p. 249, cited with approval in M. (K.) v. M. (H.), [1992] 3 S.C.R. 6 at para. 63. See also Guerin v. The Queen, [1984] 2 S.C.R. 335). The common law doctrine of fraudulent concealment is not a rule of construction. It is an equitable principle aimed at preventing a limitation period from operating "as an instrument of injustice" (see M. (K.), supra, at para. 66). When applicable, it will "take a case out of the effect of statute of limitation" and suspend the running of the limitation clock until such time as the injured party can reasonably discover the cause of action[6] (see M. (K.) supra, at paras. 65 and 66). Its underlying rationale is grounded in the well-established principle, reiterated in Goldin (Trustee of) v. Bennett and Co. 2003 CanLII 4764 (Ont C.A.), (2003), 65 O.R. (3d) 691 at para. 35, that equity will not permit a statute to be used as an instrument of fraud. *Giroux Estate v. Trillium Health Centre*, 2005 CanLII 1488 (Ont. C.A.).

FRAUDULENT CONVEYANCE. A conveyance which defrauds, delays or hinders creditors and others. *Toronto Dominion Bank v. Miller* (1990), (*sub nom. Miller, Re*) 3 C.B.R. (3d) 285 at 288, 1 O.R. (3d) 528 (Gen. Div.), Steele J.

FRAUDULENT MEANS. See OTHER ~.

FRAUDULENT MISREPRESENTATION. "... [O]ne (1) which is untrue in fact; (2) which defendant knows to be untrue or is indifferent as to its truth; (3) which was intended or calculated to induce the plaintiff to act upon it; and (4) which the plaintiff acts upon and suffers damage... ." *Francis v. Dingman* (1983), 23 B.L.R. 234 at 253, 43 O.R. (2d) 641, 2 D.L.R. (4th) 244 (C.A.), Goodman J.A. (Zuber J.A. concurring).

FRAUDULENT PREFERENCE. "... [A]n act by which one creditor obtained an advantage over the others when two things concurred: first, that the act was voluntary on the part of the debtor; and secondly, that it was done in contemplation of bankruptcy... ." *Stephens v. McArthur* (1891), 19 S.C.R. 446 at 462, 6 Man. R. 496, Patterson J.

FREE. *adj.* 1. Without impediment. 2. Without cost. 3. Without limitation. See BARRIER-~.

FREE ACCESS TO LAW. See MONTREAL DECLARATION ON ~.

FREE ALONGSIDE SHIP. A seller undertakes to deliver goods alongside a ship at the seller's own expense.

FREE AND CLEAR.. Unencumbered.

FREE AND DEMOCRATIC SOCIETY. 1. "... [T]he values and principles essential to a free and democratic society ... embody, to name but a few, respect for the inherent dignity of the human person, commitment to social justice and equality, accommodation of a wide variety of beliefs, respect for cultural and group identity, and faith in social and political institutions which enhance the participation of individuals and groups in society... ." The underlying values and principles of a free and democratic society are the genesis of the rights and freedoms guaranteed by the Charter and the ultimate standard against which a limit on a right or freedom must be shown, despite its effects, to be reasonable and demonstrably justified. *R. v. Oakes* (1986), 19 C.R.R. 308 at 334, [1986] 1 S.C.R. 103, 50 C.R. (3d) 1, 14 O.A.C. 335, 24 C.C.C. (3d) 321, 26 D.L.R. (4th) 200, 65 N.R. 98, Dickson C.J.C. (Chouinard, Lamer, Wilson and Le Dain JJ. concurring). 2. [L]imits on ad-

vertising are contextual. Although we are not required to review the proposed standards, the Canadian Code of Advertising Standards, which is referred to in the transit authorities' advertising policies, could be used as a guide to establish reasonable limits, including limits on discriminatory content or on ads which incite or condone violence or other unlawful behaviour. Given that the transit authorities did not raise s. 1, however, the above comment is intended merely to provide guidance on what may be justified, but the determination of what is justified will depend on the facts in the particular case. *Greater Vancouver Transportation Authority v. Canadian Federation of Students—British Columbia Component*, 2009 SCC 31, [2009] 2 S.C.R. 295, Deschamps J. for the majority.

FREE COMPETITION. "... [A]s judicially understood, affirmatively may be stated, as a situation in which the freedom of any individual or firm to engage in legitimate economic activity is not restrained by (1) agreements or conspiracies between competitors, or (2) by predatory practices of a rival, contrary to The Combines Investigation Act. And 'free competition' thus understood is quite compatible with the presence of monopoly elements as understood by economists, in the economic sense of the word monopoly, for the antithesis of the economic conception of monopoly is not 'free competition', as understood by the courts, but 'pure competition'." *R. v. Canadian Coat & Apron Supply Ltd.* (1967), 2 C.R.N.S. 62 at 77 (Ex. Ct.), Gibson J.

FREEDOM. *n.* 1. "... [I]n a broad sense embraces both the absence of coercion and constraint, and the right to manifest beliefs and practices. Freedom means that, subject to such limitations as are necessary to protect public safety, order, health, or morals or the fundamental rights and freedoms of others, no one is to be forced to act in a way contrary to his beliefs or his conscience." Freedom can primarily be characterized by the absence of coercion or constraint. If a person is compelled by the state or the will of another to a course of action or inaction which he would not otherwise have chosen, he is not acting of his own volition and he cannot be said to be truly free. Coercion includes not only such blatant forms of compulsion as direct commands to act or refrain from acting on pain of sanction, coercion includes indirect forms of control which determine or limit alternative courses of conduct available to others. *R. v. Big M Drug Mart* (1985), 13 C.R.R. 64 at 97, [1985] 1 S.C.R. 295, [1985] 3 W.W.R. 481, 37 Alta. L.R. (2d) 97, 58 N.R. 81, 18 C.C.C. (3d) 385, 60 A.R. 161, 18 D.L.R. (4th) 321, 85 C.L.L.C. 14,023, Dickson C.J.C. (Beetz, McIntyre, Chouinard and Lamer JJ. concurring). 2. "... [I]s defined by determining first the area which is regulated. The freedom is then what exists in the unregulated area – a sphere of activity within which all acts are permissible. It is a residual area in which all acts are free of specific legal regulation and the individual is free to choose... ." *R. v. Zundel* (1987), 56 C.R. (3d) 1 at 23, 18 O.A.C. 161, 58 O.R. (2d) 129, 31 C.C.C. (3d) 97, 35 D.L.R. (4th) 338, 29 C.R.R. 349 (C.A.), Howland C.J.O., Brooke, Martin, Lacourcière, and Houlden JJ.A. See CANADIAN CHARTER OF RIGHTS

F

FREEDOM OF ASSEMBLY

AND ~S; CHARTER OF HUMAN RIGHTS AND ~S; FUNDAMENTAL ~; LIBERTY; OTHER RIGHTS AND ~S; RIGHT.

FREEDOM OF ASSEMBLY. The right to gather together in one another's physical presence. *Fraser v. Nova Scotia (Attorney General)* (1986), 74 N.S.R. (2d) 91 at 99, 180 A.P.R. 91, 30 D.L.R. (4th) 340, 24 C.R.R. 193 (T.D.), Grant J.

FREEDOM OF ASSOCIATION. 1. "... [T]he freedom to combine together for the pursuit of common purposes or the advancement of common causes. It is one of the fundamental freedoms guaranteed by the Charter, a sine qua non of any free and democratic society, protecting individuals from the vulnerability of isolation and ensuring the potential of effective participation in society... ." *Reference re Public Service Employee Relations Act (Alberta)* (1987), 38 D.L.R. (4th) 161 at 173, [1987] 1 S.C.R. 313, 87 C.L.L.C. 14,021, 51 Alta. L.R. (2d) 97, [1987] 3 W.W.R. 577, 74 N.R. 99, 28 C.R.R. 305, 78 A.R. 1, [1987] D.L.Q. 225, Dickson C.J.C. 2. Three elements of freedom of association are summarized, along with a crucial fourth principle, in the oft-quoted words of Sopinka J. in P.I.P.S. v. Northwest Territories (Commissioner), [1990] 2 S.C.R. 367 (S.C.C.) ("PIPSC"), at pp. 401-2: Upon considering the various judgments in the Alberta Reference, I have come to the view that four separate propositions concerning the coverage of the s. 2(d) guarantee of freedom of association emerge from the case: first, that s. 2(d) protects the freedom to establish, belong to and maintain an association; second, that s. 2(d) does not protect an activity solely on the ground that the activity is a foundational or essential purpose of an association; third, that s. 2(d) protects the exercise in association of the constitutional rights and freedoms of individuals; and fourth, that s. 2(d) protects the exercise in association of the lawful rights of individuals. In addition to the four-part formulation in PIPSC, supra, an enduring source of insight into the content of s. 2(d) is the purpose of the provision. This purpose was first articulated in the labour trilogy and has accordingly been used to define both the "positive" freedom to associate as well as the "negative" freedom not to (see Alberta Reference, supra; Lavigne v. O.P.S.E.U., [1991] 2 S.C.R. 211 (S.C.C.), at p. 318; R. c. Advance Cutting & Coring Ltd., 2001 SCC 70 (S.C.C.)). While freedom of association like most other fundamental rights has no single purpose or value, at its core rests a rather simple proposition: the attainment of individual goals, through the exercise of individual rights, is generally impossible without the aid and cooperation of others. The purpose of s. 2(d) commands a single inquiry: has the state precluded activity because of its associational nature, thereby discouraging the collective pursuit of common goals? In my view, while the four-part test for freedom of association sheds light on this concept, it does not capture the full range of activities protected by s. 2(d). In particular, there will be occasions where a given activity does not fall within the third and fourth rules, but where the state has nevertheless prohibited that activity solely because of its associational nature. These occasions will involve activities which 1) are not protected under any other constitutional freedom, and 2) cannot, for one reason or another, be understood as the lawful activities of individuals. Such activities may be collective in nature, in that they cannot be performed by individuals acting alone. The prohibition of such activities must surely, in some cases, be a violation of s. 2(d). There will, however, be occasions when no analogy involving individuals can be found for associational activity, or when a comparison between groups and individuals fails to capture the essence of a possible violation of associational rights. ... The overarching consideration remains whether a legislative enactment or administrative action interferes with the freedom of persons to join and act with others in common pursuits. The legislative purpose which will render legislation invalid is the attempt to preclude associational conduct because of its concerted or associational nature. In sum, a purposive approach to s. 2(d) demands that we "distinguish between the associational aspect of the activity and the activity itself". Such an approach begins with the existing framework which enables a claimant to show that a group activity is permitted for individuals in order to establish that its regulation targets the association per se. Where this burden cannot be met, however, it may still be open to a claimant to show, by direct evidence or inference, that the legislature has targeted associational conduct because of its concerted or associational nature. *Dunmore v. Ontario (Attorney General)* [2001] 3 S.C.R. 1016. 3. "... [I]nclude[s] freedom from forced association ..." *Lavigne v. O.P.S.E.U.* (1991), 4 C.R.R. (2d) 193 at 212, 91 C.L.L.C. 14,029, 3 O.R. (3d) 511n, 81 D.L.R. (4th) 545, 126 N.R. 161, 40 O.A.C. 241, [1991] 2 S.C.R. 211, La Forest J. (Sopinka and Gonthier JJ. concurring).

FREEDOM OF CONSCIENCE AND RELIGION. 1. "... [B]roadly construed to extend to conscientiously-held beliefs, whether grounded in religion or in a secular morality... ." *R. v. Morgentaler* (1988), 37 C.C.C. (3d) 449 at 560, 82 N.R. 1, [1988] 1 S.C.R. 30, 63 O.R. (2d) 281n, 62 C.R. (3d) 1, 26 O.A.C. 1, 44 D.L.R. (4th) 385, 31 C.R.R. 1, Wilson J. 2. "... [W]hatever else freedom of conscience and religion [in s. 2(a) of the Charter] may mean, it must at the very least mean this: government may not coerce individuals to affirm a specific religious belief or to manifest a specific religious practice for a sectarian purpose... . freedom from compulsory religious observance ..." *R. v. Big M Drug Mart* (1985), 18 C.C.C. (3d) 385 at 426-7, 85 C.L.L.C. 14,023, [1985] 1 S.C.R. 295, [1985] 3 W.W.R. 481, 37 Alta. L.R. (2d) 97, 58 N.R. 81, 13 C.R.R. 64, 60 A.R. 161, 18 D.L.R. (4th) 321, Dickson C.J.C. (Beetz, McIntyre, Chouinard and Lamer JJ. concurring).

FREEDOM OF CONTRACT. Refers to the fact that the parties to a contract are left by the court to use their own discretion and to make their own agreement.

FREEDOM OF EXPRESSION. 1. "... [P]urpose of the guarantee is to permit free expression to the end of promoting truth, political or social participation, and self-fulfilment. That purpose extends to the protection of minority beliefs which the majority regard as wrong or false: ..." *R. v. Zundel* (1992), 75 C.C.C.

(3d) 449 at 506, 95 D.L.R. (4th) 202, [1992] 2 S.C.R. 731, 140 N.R. 1, 56 O.A.C. 161, 16 C.R. (4th) 1, 10 C.R.R. (2d) 193, McLachlin J. (La Forest, L'Heureux-Dubé and Sopinka JJ. concurring). 2. "... [I]ncludes the freedom to express oneself in the language of one's choice... ." *Devine v. Quebec (Attorney General)* (1989), 10 C.H.R.R. D/5610 at D/5624, 90 N.R. 48, 19 Q.A.C. 33, [1988] 2 S.C.R. 790, 36 C.R.R. 64, 55 D.L.R. (4th) 641, Dickson C.J.C., Beetz, McIntyre, Lamer and Wilson JJ. 3. The values which underlie the protection of freedom of expression relate to the search for truth, participation in the political process, and individual self-fulfilment. *R. v. Butler*, 1992 CarswellMan 100, [1992] 2 W.W.R. 577, [1992] 1 S.C.R. 452, 11 C.R. (4th) 137, 70 C.C.C. (3d) 129, 134 N.R. 81, 8 C.R.R. (2d) 1, 89 D.L.R. (4th) 449, 78 Man. R. (2d) 1, 16 W.A.C. 1 Sopinka J. 4. Freedom of expression is fundamental to freedom. It is the foundation of any democratic society. It is the cornerstone of our democratic institutions and is essential to their functioning. *K Mart Canada Ltd. v. U.F.C.W., Local 1518, 1999 CarswellBC 1909, (sub nom. United Food & Commercial Workers, Local 1518 v. KMart Canada Ltd.)* 99 C.L.L.C. 220-064, [1999] 9 W.W.R. 161, 245 N.R. 1, 176 D.L.R. (4th) 607, 66 B.C.L.R. (3d) 211, 66 C.R.R. (2d) 205, 128 B.C.A.C. 1, 208 W.A.C. 1, [1999] 2 S.C.R. 1083, the court per Cory J.

FREEDOM OF INFORMATION. Refers to legislation governing access to government documents and records.

FREEDOM OF RELIGION. 1. "... The essence of the concept of freedom of religion is the right to entertain such religious beliefs as a person chooses, the right to declare religious beliefs openly and without fear of hindrance or reprisal, and the right to manifest religious belief by worship and practice or by teaching and dissemination. But the concept means more than that... . Freedom means that, subject to such limitations as are necessary to protect public safety, order, health, or morals or the fundamental rights and freedoms of others, no one is to be forced to act in a way contrary to his beliefs or his conscience." *R. v. Big M Drug Mart* (1985), 13 C.R.R. 64 at 97, [1985] 1 S.C.R. 295, [1985] 3 W.W.R. 481, 37 Alta. L.R. (2d) 97, 58 N.R. 81, 18 C.C.C. (3d) 385, 60 A.R. 161, 18 D.L.R. (4th) 321, 85 C.L.L.C. 14,023, Dickson C.J.C. (Beetz, McIntyre, Chouinard and Lamer JJ. concurring). 2. The performance of religious rites is a fundamental aspect of religious practice. Returning to the question before us, the Court is of the opinion that, absent unique circumstances with respect to which we will not speculate, the guarantee of religious freedom in s. 2(a) of the Charter is broad enough to protect religious officials from being compelled by the state to perform civil or religious same-sex marriages that are contrary to their religious beliefs. *Reference re Same-Sex Marriage*, 2004 SCC 79, [2004] 3 S.C.R. 698.

FREEDOM OF SPEECH. 1. Speech limited by the laws against defamation, sedition, blasphemy and other prohibited forms of speech. 2. A privilege and fundamental right of any member of Parliament on the House floor and in committee. A. Fraser, W.A.

Dawson, & J. Holtby, eds., *Beauchesne's Rules and Forms of the House of Commons of Canada*, 6th ed. (Toronto: Carswell, 1989) at 22. See FREEDOM OF EXPRESSION.

FREEDOM OF THE PRESS. 1. "... [R]efers to the dissemination of expression of thought, belief or opinion through the medium of the press." *Reference re s. 12(1) of the Juvenile Delinquents Act (Canada)* (1983), 6 C.R.R. 1 at 9, 146 D.L.R. (3d) 408, 3 C.C.C. (3d) 515, 41 O.R. (2d) 113, 33 R.F.L. (2d) 279, 34 C.R. (3d) 27 (C.A.), the court per MacKinnon A.C.J.O. 2. That the right of the public to information relating to court proceedings, and the corollary right to put forward opinions pertaining to the courts, depend on the freedom of the press " to transmit this information is fundamental to an understanding of the importance of that freedom. The full and fair discussion of public institutions, which is vital to any democracy, is the raison d'être of the s. 2(b) guarantees. Debate in the public domain is predicated on an informed public, which is in turn reliant upon a free and vigorous press. The public's entitlement to be informed imposes on the media the responsibility to inform fairly and accurately. This responsibility is especially grave given that the freedom of the press is, and must be, largely unfettered. The significance of the freedom and its attendant responsibility lead me to the second issue relating to s. 2(b). Essential to the freedom of the press to provide information to the public is the ability of the press to have access to this information. *Canadian Broadcasting Corp. v. New Brunswick (Attorney General)*, 1996 CarswellNB 462, 2 C.R. (5th) 1, 110 C.C.C. (3d) 193, [1996] 3 S.C.R. 480, 139 D.L.R. (4th) 385, 182 N.B.R. (2d) 81, 463 A.P.R. 81, 39 C.R.R. (2d) 189, 203 N.R. 169, the court per La Forest J. 3. In *Société Radio-Canada c. Lessard*, [1991] 3 S.C.R. 421, I [La Forest J.] noted that freedom of the press not only encompassed the right to transmit news and other information, but also the right to gather this information. At pp. 429-30, I stated There can be no doubt, of course, that it comprises the right to disseminate news, information and beliefs. This was the manner in which the right was originally expressed, in the first draft of s. 2(b) of the Canadian Charter of Rights and Freedoms before its expansion to its present form. However, the freedom to disseminate information would be of little value if the freedom under s. 2(b) did not also encompass the right to gather news and other information without undue governmental interference. 4. Cory J. stated in *Société Radio-Canada c. Nouveau-Brunswick (Procureur général)*, [1991] 3 S.C.R. 459, at p. 475: The media have a vitally important role to play in a democratic society. It is the media that, by gathering and disseminating news, enable members of our society to make an informed assessment of the issues which may significantly affect their lives and well-being.

FREEHOLD. *n.* 1. Free tenure. 2. An estate the maximum duration of which is unknown.

FREEHOLD CONDOMINIUM CORPORATION. A corporation in which all the units and their appurtenant common interests are held in fee simple by the owners. *Condominium Act, 1998*, S.O. 1998, c. 19, s. 1.

F

FREEHOLDER. *n.* One who possesses a freehold estate.

FREEHOLD ESTATE. An interest in land by which the freeholder is entitled to hold the land for an unfixed and uncertain period of time.

FREEHOLD LAND. Land, including land comprising a right of way, station ground, yard or terminal of a railway but not including Crown land, in respect of which (a) petroleum and natural gas is, or may be, situated, or (b) a person has the right to work, win or carry away petroleum or natural gas. *Petroleum and Natural Gas Act*, R.S.B.C. 1996, c. 361, s. 1.

FREEHOLD OIL. All oil ... : (i) produced from freehold lands; or (ii) allocated to freehold lands, or to the holder of any right thereto or interest therein, under a voluntary pooling arrangement, a pooling order, an agreement for unit operation or a unit operation order made pursuant to The Oil and Gas Conservation Act and the regulations thereunder. *The Freehold Oil and Gas Production Tax Act*, S.S. 1982-83, c. F-22.1, s. 2.

FREE ON BOARD. 1. "... [T]he seller, and not the shipper, shall pay the cost of loading the cargo on board, where it is stipulated that the price shall be for a stipulated sum f.o.b.... ." *Johnson v. Logan* (1899), 32 N.S.R. 28 at 42 (C.A.), McDonald C.J. 2. "If, upon an order for undetermined goods to be shipped f.o.b., the seller delivers to the designated common carrier, goods which answer the order, without more, the property passes forthwith to the purchaser – and this is the case also if a bill of lading is taken, and taken in the name of the purchaser. If, however, the bill of lading is taken in the name of the seller, prima facie he retains the disposing power over and property in the goods. He may, indeed, endorse it over to the purchaser forthwith, and send it forward for delivery to the purchaser; in that case the taking of the bill of lading to his own order is a mere form, and the transaction is equivalent to taking the bill of lading in the name of the purchaser. The seller may endorse in blank and send forward to his agent, bank, etc., for delivery to the purchaser upon payment for the goods, acceptance of a draft, or performance of some other condition – in that case, the goods remain in the control and are the property of the seller, at least until the condition is fulfilled or the purchaser offers to fulfil it and demands the bill of lading ..." *Vipond v. Sisco* (1913), 20 O.L.R. 200 at 203, 14 D.L.R. 129 (C.A.), Riddell J.A. (Sutherland, Leitch and Clute JJ.A. concurring).

FREE ON RAIL. Describes a contract under which the seller is responsible to have goods placed on railcars at his or her expense.

FREE ON TRUCK. Describing a seller's responsibility to have the goods which are sold placed on a truck.

FREE SOCIETY. "... [O]ne which can accommodate a wide variety of beliefs, diversity of tastes and pursuits, customs and codes of conduct. A free society is one which aims at equality with respect to the enjoyment of fundamental freedoms and I say this without any reliance upon s. 15 of the Charter. Free-dom must surely be founded in respect for the inherent dignity and the inviolable rights of the human person." *R. v. Big M Drug Mart* (1985), 13 C.R.R. 64 at 97, [1985] 1 S.C.R. 295, [1985] 3 W.W.R. 481, 37 Alta. L.R. (2d) 97, 58 N.R. 81, 18 C.C.C. (3d) 385, 60 A.R. 161, 18 D.L.R. (4th) 321, 85 C.L.L.C. 14,023, Dickson C.J.C. (Beetz, McIntyre, Chouinard and Lamer JJ. concurring).

FREE TRADE AGREEMENT. An agreement entered into by Canada and one or more other countries. See NORTH AMERICAN ~.

FREE TRADE PARTNER. A country which is a beneficiary of a free trade agreement with Canada.

FREE VOTE. A parliamentary division on a question for which party lines are ignored. A. Fraser, W.A. Dawson, & J. Holtby, eds., *Beauchesne's Rules and Forms of the House of Commons of Canada*, 6th ed. (Toronto: Carswell, 1989) at 93.

FREEZE. See ESTATE ~.

FREIGHT. *n.* 1. Includes the profit derivable by ship owners from the employment of their ships to carry their own goods or movables, as well as freight payable by a third party, but does not include passage-money. *Insurance acts.* 2. Cargo. 3. Transport from one place to another. 4. "... [T]he reward which the law entitles a person to recover for bringing goods lawfully on a lawful voyage. It is the price to be paid for the actual carriage of the goods... ." *Edmonstone v. Young* (1862), 12 U.C.C.P. 437 at 442, Draper J.

FRENCH LANGUAGE. See CHARTER OF THE ~.

FREQUENT FLYER PLAN. A contract between an airline and a member of the plan. Membership is open to individuals who benefit from the plan by acquiring points which may be redeemed, subject to rules of the plan.

FRESH EVIDENCE. The traditional test for the admission of fresh evidence on appeal was stated by this Court in R. v. Palmer (1979), [1980] 1 S.C.R. 759, at p. 775: (1) The evidence should generally not be admitted if, by due diligence, it could have been adduced at trial provided that this general principle will not be applied as strictly in a criminal case as in civil cases: see McMartin v. The Queen, [1964] S.C.R. 484. (2) The evidence must be relevant in the sense that it bears upon a decisive or potentially decisive issue in the trial. (3) The evidence must be credible in the sense that it is reasonably capable of belief, and (4) It must be such that if believed it could reasonably, when taken with the other evidence adduced at trial, be expected to have affected the result. *Public School Boards' Assn. (Alberta) v. Alberta (Attorney General)*, 2000 CarswellAlta 678, 2000 SCC 2, [2000] 1 S.C.R. 44, 182 D.L.R. (4th) 561, 251 N.R. 1, 250 A.R. 314, 213 W.A.C. 314, [2000] 10 W.W.R. 187, 82 Alta. L.R. (3d) 211, 9 C.P.C. (5th) 36, Binnie J.

FRESH PURSUIT. Used in s. 494 of the Criminal Code, R.S.C. 1985, in regard to the right to arrest without warrant. To be contrasted with a person who has lost his pursuers or was not immediately pursued at all. *R. v. Dean* (1966), 47 C.R. 311 at 321, [1966] 1 O.R. 592, [1966] 3 C.C.C. 228 (C.A.), Laskin J.A.

FRIABLE. *adj.* Easily crumbled or powdered.

FRIEND. See AMICUS CURIAE; ~ OF THE COURT; NEXT ~.

FRIENDLY SOCIETY. A society, order, association or company formed or incorporated and operated for the purpose of making with its members only, and not for profit, contracts under which (i) sickness, accident and disability benefits, or any one or more of them, not exceeding five dollars per week, or (ii) funeral benefits not exceeding one hundred and fifty dollars, or all of those benefits may be paid only to its members or their beneficiaries in accordance with its charter and this Act. *Insurance acts.*

FRIENDLY SUIT. A suit brought which parties mutually arrange to bring to obtain a decision on a point which interests both.

FRIEND OF THE COURT. Any person who, with leave of a judge or at the invitation of a presiding judge or master, and without becoming a party to the proceeding, intervenes to render assistance to the court by way of argument (Ontario, Rules of Civil Procedure, r. 13.02). G.D. Watson & C. Perkins, eds., *Holmested & Watson: Ontario Civil Procedure* (Toronto: Carswell, 1984) at 13-2.

FRINGE BENEFIT. An employment benefit such as a pension, paid holidays, health insurance. Granted by the employer at the employer's cost without affecting wage rates.

FRISK SEARCH. (a) A manual search, or a search by technical means, of the clothed body, in the prescribed manner, and (b) a search of (i) personal possessions, including clothing, that the person may be carrying, and (ii) any coat or jacket that the person has been requested to remove, in accordance with any applicable regulations made under paragraph 96(l). *Corrections and Conditional Release Act*, S.C. 1992, c. 20, s. 46.

FRIVOLOUS. *adj.* "... '[L]acking in substance' ..." *Halliday v. Gouge* (1919), 14 Alta. L.R. 296 at 303, [1919] 1 W.W.R. 359 (C.A.), Walsh J.A.

FRIVOLOUS AND VEXATIOUS. Said of a pleading which is hopeless factually and plainly cannot succeed in its purpose.

FRIVOLOUS APPEAL. A frivolous appeal is one that has no substance. For example, an appellant may assert, correctly, in a notice of appeal that the trial judge made an error, such as misstating an inconsequential date, but if that error, even if corrected, could not change the result in the case, there is no basis for proceeding with the appeal. ... Clearly, an appeal that is obviously unsustainable or without arguable merit will also be regarded as frivolous. A frivolous appeal has been described by the New Brunswick Court of Appeal in S. (B.) v. New Brunswick (Minister of Health & Community Services) (2000), 230 N.B.R. (2d) 98 (N.B. C.A.) at para. [7] as "... one in which no justiciable question has been presented and the appeal is readily recognizable as devoid of merit in that there is little prospect that it can ever succeed."

If allowed to proceed, thereby requiring the other side to engage counsel and respond to something that cannot succeed, it would also be vexatious because it would be an abuse of the court's process. *Walsh v. Johnson*, 2010 NLCA 6.

FRIVOLOUS OR VEXATIOUS ACTION. See VEXATIOUS ACTION.

FROM. *conj.* 1. In relation to geography, signifies a starting point. 2. Depending on the context, may include or exclude the date referred to in a phrase beginning with this word. *Independent Order of Foresters, Lethbridge Local 2 v. Afaganis*, [1949] 1 W.W.R. 314 at 319, [1949] 2 D.L.R. 209 (Alta. Dist. Ct.), Sissons J.

FRONTAGE. *n.* The side or limit of the lot that abuts directly on the work. *Municipalities Act*, R.S.N.B. 1973, c. M-22, s. 118. See LOT ~.

FRONTAGE TAX. Any tax levied on the owners of real property or immovables that is computed by applying a rate to all or part of the assessed dimension of the property and includes any tax levied on the owners of real property or immovables that is in the nature of a local improvement tax, a development tax or a redevelopment tax, but does not include a tax in respect of mineral rights. *Payments in Lieu of Taxes Act*, S.C. 2000, c. 8, s. 3.

FRONT YARD. That portion of private property located between the front wall of a residential building on the property and the abutting public highway. *City of Toronto Act, 2006*, S.O. 2006, c. 11, Sched. A, s. 113.2.

FROZEN. *adj.* Refers to a trust in which the trustee is required only to hold the original assets and return them to the settlor when the trust ends.

FROZEN TRUST. A trust, usually established for an office holder, in which the trustee retains the original assets and simply transfers them back to the settlor when the trust ends.

FRUCTUS INDUSTRIALES. [L.] Crops which are produced annually and industrial crops like grass and clover which are not annual.

FRUCTUS NATURALES. [L.] Natural products of the land.

FRUITS. *n.* Things spontaneously produced by property or produced by the cultivation or working of land, and the produce or increase of animals. *Civil Code*, S.Q. 1991, c. 64, a. 910.

FRUITS AND REVENUES. That which is produced by property without any alteration to its substance or that which is derived from the use of capital. They also include rights the exercise of which tends to increase the fruits and revenues of the property. *Civil Code*, S.Q. 1991, c. 64, a. 910.

FRUSTRATION. *n.* 1. The authoritative definition of frustration was stated by Lord Radcliffe in Davis Contractors Ltd. v. Fareham Urban Dist. Council, [1956] A.C. 696 at 728-29, [1956] 2 All E.R. 145 (H.L.): So perhaps it would be simpler to say at the outset that frustration occurs whenever the law recognizes that without default of either party a contrac-

259

tual obligation has become incapable of being performed because the circumstances in which performance is called for would render it a thing radically different from that which was undertaken by the contract. Non haec in foedera veni. It was not this that I promised to do. It has been adopted and applied in Canada. See Capital Quality Homes Ltd. v. Colwyn Const. Ltd. (1975), 9 O.R. (2d) 617 at 623, 61 D.L.R. (3d) 385 (C.A.). *Lockhart v. Chrysler Canada Ltd.*, (C.A.) 1984 CarswellBC 814, 7 C.C.E.L. 43, 16 D.L.R. (4th) 392 (C.A.), Taggart, Macdonald and Hutcheon JJ.A.2. "... [O]f a contract takes place when there supervenes an event (without default of either party and for which the contract makes no sufficient provision) which so significantly changes the nature (not merely the expense or onerousness) of the outstanding contractual rights and/or obligations from what the parties could reasonably have contemplated at the time of its execution that it would be unjust to hold them to the literal sense of its stipulations in the new circumstances; in such case the law declares both parties to be discharged from further performance." *National Carriers Ltd. v. Panalpina (Northern) Ltd.*, [1981] A.C. 675 at 700 (U.K. H.L.), Lord Simon. 3. In order to find that the contract at issue has been frustrated the following criteria would have to be satisfied. The event in question must have occurred after the formation of the contract and cannot be self-induced. The contract must, as a result, be totally different from what the parties had intended. This difference must take into account the distinction between complete fruitlessness and mere inconvenience. The disruption must be permanent, not temporary or transient. The change must totally affect the nature, meaning, purpose, effect and consequences of the contract so far as concerns either or both parties. Finally, the act or event that brought about such radical change must not have been foreseeable. *Folia v. Trelinski*, 1997 CarswellBC 2325, 32 R.F.L. (4th) 209, 14 R.P.R. (3d) 5, 36 B.L.R (2d) 108 (S.C.), Sigurdson J.

FTAA. *abbr.* Free Trade Agreement of the Americas.

F.T.L.R. *abbr.* Free Trade Law Reports, 1989-1991.

F.T.R. *abbr.* Federal Trial Reports, 1986-.

F.T.U. *abbr.* Free Trade Update, 1990-1996.

FUEL. *n.* Any form of matter that, in its primary use, is combusted or oxidized for the generation of energy. *Canadian Environmental Protection Act, 1999*, S.C. 1999, c. 33, s. 3. See ALTERNATIVE ~; BIO~; JET ~; NUCLEAR ~ WASTE; RENEWABLE DIESEL ~; RENEWABLE ~.

FUEL TAX. Tax imposed on the consumption of fuel.

FUGACIOUS. *adj.* Wandering, refers to substances which are not fixed in a certain place, for example, oil and gas.

FUGITIVE. *n.* A person, accused of a crime, who has left the jurisdiction.

FULL AGE. Age of majority.

FULL ANSWER AND DEFENCE. "[In the Charter] ... entitle[s] the accused to put forward all de-fences, regardless of whether they are based on a technicality or not. Indeed, the adjective 'full' permits no other conclusion. The right to make a full answer and defence cannot be diminished to the right to make non-technical answer and defence." *R. v. Garafoli* (1990), 60 C.C.C. (3d) 161 at 210, 80 C.R. (3d) 317, 116 N.R. 241, 43 O.A.C. 1, [1990] 2 S.C.R. 1421, 50 C.R.R. 206, 36 Q.A.C. 161, McLachlin J. (dissenting) (L'Heureux-Dubé J. concurring). See RIGHT TO MAKE A ~.

FULL COMMUNITY. All immovables and movables acquired during marriage over which the husband has wide powers of administration. J.G. McLeod, *The Conflict of Laws* (Calgary: Carswell, 1983) at 371.

FULL COSTS. Party-and-party costs. *Williams v. Crow* (1884), 10 O.A.R. 301 at 306 (C.A.), Hagarty C.J.O.

FULL COURT. A court with all judges present. For example, when all nine judges of the Supreme Court of Canada hear a case, the case is heard by the full court.

FULL EMANCIPATION. Of a minor, is obtained by marriage. Enables a minor to exercise his civil rights as if he were of full age. *Civil Code*, S.Q. 1991, c. 64, a. 175 and 176.

FULL FAITH AND CREDIT. Doctrine under which the courts of one province are under a constitutional obligation to recognize the decisions of the courts of another province. Constitutional rule inferred but not expressed. *Reference re Public Sector Pay Reduction Act (P.E.I.)* (1997) 151 D.L.R. (4th) 577.

FULL PAROLE. The authority granted to an offender by the Board or a provincial parole board to be at large during the offender's sentence. *Corrections and Conditional Release Act*, S.C. 1992, c. 20, s. 99.

FULLY-SECRET TRUST. Arises when a testatrix gives property to a person apparently beneficially, but has communicated to that person during his lifetime certain trusts on which the property is to be held. Arises out of a will. The trust obligation undertaken is hidden from view and revealed only by extrinsic evidence. *Jankowski v. Pelek Estate* (1995), [1996] 2 W.W.R. 457 (Man. C.A.).

FUNCTION. *n.* 1. An object, power or duty or group of them. 2. "... [T]he act of performing and is defined as the kind of action belonging to the holder of an office, hence the function is the performance of the duties of that office. By the performance of the duties of an office the holder thereof can be said to fulfil his function. Functions are therefore the powers and duties of an office." *Mudarth v. Canada (Minister of Public Works)* (1988), 27 C.C.E.L. 310 at 314-15, 22 F.T.R. 312, [1989] 3 F.C. 371 (T.D.), Addy J. 3. Includes logic, control, arithmetic, deletion, storage and retrieval and communication or telecommunication to, from or within a computer system. *Criminal Code*, R.S.C. 1985, c. C-46, s. 342.1. See ADJUDICATIVE ~; MANAGEMENT ~; UTILITARIAN ~.

FUNCTIONAL ABILITY. The ability of the insured to function alone without supervision due to a physical limitation resulting from the accident, as opposed to any cognitive limitation. *The Automobile Accident Insurance Act*, R.S.S. 1978, c. A-35, *The Personal Injury Benefits Regulations*, R.R.S., c. A-35, Reg. 3, Appendix D, Grid A, s. 2.

FUNCTIONALITY. See DOCTRINE OF ~.

FUNCTIONARY. *n.* A person who functions in a specific capacity, especially in government, an official, civil servant or bureaucrat.

FUNCTIONING. See ADAPTIVE ~.

FUNCTUS. [L.] Having pronounced judgment; having made a decision. Refers to FUNCTUS OFFICIO.

FUNCTUS OFFICIO. [L. having discharged one's duty] 1. "... [B]ased ... on the policy ground which favours finality of proceedings rather than the rule which was developed with respect to formal judgments of a Court whose decision was subject to a full appeal... . its application must be more flexible and less formalistic in respect to the decisions of administrative tribunals which are subject to appeal only on a point of law. Justice may require the reopening of administrative proceedings in order to provide relief which would otherwise be available on appeal." *Chandler v. Assn. of Architects (Alberta)* (1989), 36 C.L.R. 1 at 14, [1989] 6 W.W.R. 521, [1989] 2 S.C.R. 848, 70 Alta. L.R. (2d) 193, 40 Admin. L.R. 128, 62 D.L.R. (4th) 577, 99 N.R. 277, 101 A.R. 321, Sopinka J. (Dickson C.J.C. and Wilson J. concurring). 2. "... [A]n adjudicator, be it an arbitrator, an administrative tribunal or a court, once it has reached its decision cannot afterwards alter its award except to correct clerical mistakes or errors arising from an accidental slip or omission ..." *Chandler v. Assn. of Architects (Alberta)*, [1989] 2 S.C.R. 848 at 867, 70 Alta. L.R. (2d) 193, 40 Admin. L.R. 128, 36 C.L.R. 1, 62 D.L.R. (4th) 577, 99 N.R. 277, 101 A.R. 321, [1989] 6 W.W.R. 521, L'Heureux-Dubé J. (dissenting) (La Forest J. concurring). 3. "... [A] trial judge sitting without a jury is not functus officio until he has finally disposed of the case. Where the accused is acquitted the trial judge will have exhausted his jurisdiction when the accused is discharged and the trial judge cannot then reopen the case. Following a finding of guilt, however, the judge's duties are not spent until after a sentence is imposed... . The state of the case-law until now is as follows. [In a case heard by judge and jury, even] after discharge, a jury can be reconvened to correct an improper or incomplete transmission or registration of a verdict, but cannot reconsider a verdict or complete its deliberations with a view to handing down additional verdicts on counts or on included offences it has not finally determined prior to that discharge; nor can anyone go behind the verdict or make inquiries as regards the nature of the deliberations." *R. v. Head* (1986), 30 C.C.C. (3d) 481 at 491, 495, [1987] 1 W.W.R. 673, 70 N.R. 364, [1986] 2 S.C.R. 684, 55 C.R. (3d) 1, 53 Sask. R. 1, 35 D.L.R. (4th) 231, Lamer J.

FUND. *n.* 1, A sum of money available to pay or discharge liabilities. 2. Capital, as opposed to income or interest. See ASSURANCE ~; BLENDED ~;

CANADIAN PRODUCTION ~; CLIMATE ~; CONSOLIDATED ~; CONSOLIDATED REVENUE ~; INSURANCE ~; INTERNATIONAL ~; INVESTMENT ~; LIEN ~; MUTUAL ~; NO-LOAD ~; OPERATING ~; PENSION ~; PUBLIC ~S; RETIREMENT INCOME ~; SINKING ~; TRUST ~.

FUNDAMENTAL BREACH. "[Occurs] ... where the event resulting from the failure by one party to perform a primary obligation has the effect of depriving the other party of substantially the whole benefit which it was the intention of the parties that he should obtain from the contract." *Syncrude Canada Ltd. v. Hunter Engineering Co.* (1989), 57 D.L.R. (4th) 321 at 369, [1989] 1 S.C.R. 426, [1989] 3 W.W.R. 385, 35 B.C.L.R. (2d) 145, 92 N.R. 1, Wilson J.

FUNDAMENTAL FREEDOM. "... [T]he freedom of the individual to take action to do something, to manifest and express himself, to make what he wants of his own individual skills, talents and abilities, to seek self-realization." *Reference re Public Service Employee Relations Act (Alberta)* (1985), 85 C.L.L.C. 14,027 at 12,163, 35 Alta. L.R. (2d) 124, [1985] 2 W.W.R. 289, 16 D.L.R. (4th) 359, 57 A.R. 268 (C.A.), Belzil J.A.

FUNDAMENTAL JUSTICE. 1. Not synonymous with natural justice. *Reference re s. 94(2) of the Motor Vehicle Act (British Columbia)* (1985), 23 C.C.C. (3d) 289 at 301-3, 310, [1985] 2 S.C.R. 486, 36 M.V.R. 240, 69 B.C.L.R. 145, 48 C.R. (3d) 289, 63 N.R. 266, 24 D.L.R. (4th) 536, 18 C.R.R. 30, [1986] 1 W.W.R. 481, Lamer J. (Dickson C.J.C., Beetz, Chouinard and Le Dain JJ. concurring). 2. "... [N]ot a right, but a qualifier of the right not to be deprived of life, liberty and security of the person; its function is to set the parameters of that right. Sections 8 to 14 [of the Charter] address specific deprivations of the 'right' to life, liberty and security of the person in breach of the principles of fundamental justice, and as such, violations of s. 7. They are therefore illustrative of the meaning, in criminal or penal law, of 'principles of fundamental justice'; they represent principles which have been recognized by the common law, the international conventions and by the very fact of entrenchment in the Charter, as essential elements of a system for the administration of justice which is founded upon a belief in the dignity and worth of the human person and the rule of law. Consequently, the principles of fundamental justice are to be found in the basic tenets and principles, not only of our judicial process, but also of the other components of our legal system... . those words cannot be given any exhaustive content or simple enumerative definition, but will take on concrete meaning as the courts address alleged violations of s. 7." *Reference re s. 94(2) of the Motor Vehicle Act (British Columbia)* (1985), 23 C.C.C. (3d) 289 at 301-3, 310, [1985] 2 S.C.R. 486, 36 M.V.R. 240, 69 B.C.L.R. 145, 48 C.R. (3d) 289, 63 N.R. 266, 24 D.L.R. (4th) 536, 18 C.R.R. 30, [1986] 1 W.W.R. 481, Lamer J. (Dickson C.J.C., Beetz, Chouinard and Le Dain JJ. concurring). See PRINCIPLES OF ~.

FUNDAMENTAL MISTAKE. Occurs in a situation where both parties to an agreement make the same mistake about an underlying and fundamental fact. The error goes to the root of the contract and eliminates the subject of the contract.

FUNDAMENTAL TERM. 1. Something which must be performed, regardless of any clause in the contract which relieves a party from performing other terms or from being liable for breaching those terms. G.H.L. Fridman, *Sale of Goods in Canada*, 3d ed. (Toronto: Carswell, 1986) at 284-285. 2. "... '[S]omething which underlies the whole contract so that, if it is not complied with, the performance becomes something totally different from that which the contract contemplates' ..." *Murray v. Sperry Rand Corp.* (1979), 5 B.L.R. 284 at 295, 23 O.R. (2d) 456, 96 D.L.R. (3d) 113 (H.C.), Reid J.

FUNDED BENEFITS PLAN. A plan, including a multi-employer benefits plan, which gives protection against risk to an individual that could otherwise be obtained by taking out a contract of insurance, whether the benefits are partly insured or not, and which comes into existence when the premiums paid into a fund out of which benefits will be paid exceed amounts required for payment of benefits foreseeable and payable within thirty days after payment of the premium. *Retail Sales Tax Act*, R.S.O. 1990, c. R.31, s. 1.

FUNERAL. *n.* A rite or ceremony in connection with the death of a person where the body is present. *Funeral Directors and Establishments Act*, R.S.O. 1990, c. F.36, s. 1.

FUNERAL DIRECTOR. A person who takes charge of the body of a still-born child or a deceased person for the purpose of burial, cremation or other disposition. *Vital Statistics Act*, R.S.O. 1990, c. V.4, s. 1.

FUNERAL EXPENSES. Expenses permitted before all other debts and charges against an estate.

FUNERAL SERVICES CONTRACT. See PRE-NEED CEMETERY OR ~.

FUNGIBLE. *adj.* In respect of securities, means securities of which any unit is, by nature or usage of trade, the equivalent of any other like unit. *Bank Act*, S.C. 1991, c. 46, s. 81.

FUNGIBLE GOODS. Goods of which any unit is, from its nature or by mercantile custom, treated as the equivalent of any other unit. *Warehouse Receipts Act*, R.S.O. 1990, c. W.3, s. 1.

FURTHERANCE. *n.* Helping forward, advancement, aid.

FURTHER ASSURANCE. See COVENANT FOR ~.

FUSIFORM ANEURYSM. The entire circumference of a blood vessel distended into a spindle shape. F.A. Jaffe, *A Guide to Pathological Evidence for Lawyers and Police Officers*, 4th ed. (Toront:Carswell, 1999) at 230.

FUTILITY. *n.* State of being of no practical effect.

FUTURE. See STANDARDIZED ~.

FUTURE ADVANCE. An advance whether or not made pursuant to an obligation and includes reasonable costs incurred and expenditures made for the protection, maintenance, preservation or repair of collateral. *Personal Property Security acts.*

FUTURE CONSIDERATION. A promise to something later.

FUTURE COST OF HEALTH CARE SERVICES. The present value of the estimated total cost of all health care services that are provided, or are reasonably expected to be provided, to a beneficiary as a direct or indirect result of a personal injury described in section 2 after the date of settlement or, if there is no settlement, after the first day of trial. *Health Care Costs Recovery Act*, S.B.C. 2008, c. 27, s. 1. See COST OF FUTURE CARE.

FUTURE DAMAGES. Damages to compensate for pecuniary losses to be incurred, or expenditures to be made, after the date of the trial judgment in the proceeding. *Law and Equity Act*, R.S.B.C. 1996, c. 253, s. 56.

FUTURE ESTATE. An expectancy; a reversion; a remainder.

FUTURE GOODS. Goods to be manufactured or acquired by the seller, after the making of the contract of sale. *Sale of Goods acts.*

FUTURE INTEREST. An interest, in existing property, which will come into existence in the future upon the happening of some event. See EXPECTANCY; EXPECTANT ESTATE; FUTURE ESTATE; REMAINDER; REVERSION.

FUTURE PERFORMANCE AGREEMENT. A consumer agreement in respect of which delivery, performance or payment in full is not made when the parties enter the agreement. *Consumer Protection Act, 2002*, S.O. 2002, c. 30, Sched. A., s. 1.

FUTURE PERFORMANCE CONTRACT. A contract between a supplier and a consumer for the supply of goods or services for which the supply or payment in full of the total price payable is not made at the time the contract is made or partly executed, but does not include any of the following: (a) a contract for which the total price payable by the consumer, not including the total cost of credit, is less than a prescribed amount; (b) a contract for the supply of goods or services under a credit agreement, as defined in section 57 [definitions], if the goods or services have been supplied; (c) a time share contract; (d) a prepaid purchase card. *Business Practices and Consumer Protection Act*, S.B.C. 2004, c. 2, s. 17.

FUTURE RIGHT. "... [I]s inchoate in that while it does not now exist, it may arise in the future... ." *Elias v. Hutchison* (1981), 14 Alta. L.R. (2d) 268 at 275, 37 C.B.R. (N.S.) 149, 27 A.R. 1, 121 D.L.R. (3d) 95 (C.A.), the court per McGillivray C.J.A.

FUTURES. *n.* "... [S]peculative transactions, in which there is a nominal contract of sale for future delivery, but where in fact none is ever intended or executed... . a mere speculative contract, in which the parties speculate in the rise or fall of prices, and imply a contract in relation to the prices of the article, and not the article itself." *Betcherman v. E.A. Pierce & Co.*, [1933] 3 D.L.R. 99 at 111, [1933] O.R. 505 (C.A.), the court per Latchford C.J. See OPTION ON ~.

FUTURES ACCOUNT. An account maintained by a futures intermediary in which a futures contract is carried for a futures customer. *Personal Property Securities acts.*

FUTURES CUSTOMER. A person for which a futures intermediary carries a futures contract on its books. *Personal Property Securities acts.*

FUTURE SERVICES. See CONTRACT FOR ~.

FUTURES EXCHANGE. An association or organization operated to provide the facilities necessary for the trading of standardized futures or options on futures. *Personal Property Securities acts.*

FUTURES INTERMEDIARY. A person that (i) is registered as a dealer permitted to trade in futures contracts, whether as principal or agent, under the securities laws or commodity futures laws of a province or territory of Canada, or (ii) is a clearing house recognized or otherwise regulated by the Alberta Securities Commission or by a securities regulatory authority of another province or territory of Canada. *Personal Property Securities acts.*

F

G

GAAP. *abbr.* Generally accepted accounting principles.

GAAR. *abbr.* General anti-avoidance rule.

GAAS. *abbr.* Generally accepted auditing standards.

GABD. *abbr.* General assignment of book debts.

GAIN. *n.* "... [A] benefit, profit, or advantage, ..." *R. v. James* (1903), 6 O.L.R. 35 at 38, 7 C.C.C. 196 (C.A.), Osler J.A. See CAPITAL ~; CAPITAL ~ OR LOSS.

GALLERY. *n.* 1. Of the parliamentary chamber, consists of a press gallery, visitors galleries called the public gallery, galleries for the diplomatic corps and departmental officials and private galleries. A. Fraser, W.A. Dawson & J. Holtby, eds., *Beauchesne's Rules and Forms of the House of Commons of Canada*, 6th ed. (Toronto: Carswell, 1989) at 37. 2. The seating for visitors or the press in a legislature. See NATIONAL ~ OF CANADA.

GAMBLE. *v.* "... [A]nother form of the word 'game', ..." *R. v. Shaw* (1891), 7 Man. R. 518 at 530 (C.A.), Bain J.A.

GAMBLING. *n.* Wagering or betting. Must involve a chance of gain and risk of loss. See GAMING.

GAME. *n.* 1. A game of chance or mixed chance and skill. *Criminal Code*, R.S.C. 1985, c. C-46, s. 197. 2. Fur bearing animals, game animals and game birds, and also includes all species of animals and birds that are wild by nature. See CONFIDENCE ~; CON ~; VIDEO ~.

GAME OF CHANCE. 1. " ... [O]ne which is determined entirely, or in part, by luck, and in which judgment, practice, skill or adroitness has either no office at all, or is thwarted by chance, thus dividing games into games of chance, games of skill, and mixed games of chance and skill." *R. v. Fortier* (1903), 13 Que. K.B. 308 at 311, 7 C.C.C. 417, the court per Wurtele J. 2. "... [W]ithin the definition of the criminal law, is one in which hazard entirely predominates; ..." *R. v. Fortier* (1903), 13 Que. K.B. 308 at 313, 7 C.C.C. 417, the court per Wurtele J. 3. A lottery or other scheme under which prizes or winnings are awarded by way of chance only or by way of a mixture of chance and other factors where the result depends more on chance than on the other factors. *An*

Act respecting the Québec sales tax, R.S.Q. c. T-0.1, s. 1.

GAMING. *n.* "... [I]nvolves wagering or betting... . takes place where there is the chance not only of winning but of losing; in other words where some stake has been hazarded." *R. v. Di Pietro* (1986), 14 O.A.C. 387 at 398-9, [1986] 1 S.C.R. 250, 50 C.R. (3d) 266, 25 C.C.C. (3d) 100, 26 D.L.R. (4th) 412, 65 N.R. 245, the court per Lamer J. quoting from *Ellesmere (Earl) v. Wallace*, [1929] 2 Ch. 1 at 28 (U.K. C.A.) and *McCollom v. Wrightson*, [1968] A.C. 522 at 528 (U.K. H.L.). See INTERNET ~ SITE.

GAMING EQUIPMENT. Anything that is or may be used for the purpose of playing games or for betting. *Criminal Code*, R.S.C. 1985, c. C-46, s. 197.

GAMING HOUSE. See COMMON ~.

GAMING TERMINAL. A computer, video device or machine that is used, or could be used, to play a lottery scheme as defined in the Criminal Code (Canada) where, on insertion of money or a token or on payment of any consideration a person may receive or be entitled to receive money, either directly from the computer, video device or machine or in another manner, but does not include such a computer, video device or machine when used only for home entertainment and where there is no ability for any person to make money from its operation. *Gaming and Liquor Act*, R.S.A. 2000, c. G-1, s. 1.

GANG. *n.* A group of individuals, usually identified by a group name or designation, who associate with each other for criminal or other unlawful purposes. *Safer Communities and Neighbourhoods Act*, S.A. 2007, c. S-0.5, s. 1. See OUTLAW MOTORCYCLE ~.

GANG COLOURS. A sign, symbol, logo or other representation identifying, associated with or promoting a group of persons who conspire to engage in unlawful activities. *The Liquor Control Act*, R.S.M. 1988, c. L160, s. 120.

GAOL. *n.* 1. Prison; place to confine offenders. 2. A provincial institution where lesser offences are punished.

GARAGE. See REPAIRER'S ~.

GARNISH. *v.* 1. To attach a debt. 2. To warn.

GARNISHEE. *n.* The person who owes a judgment debtor money and against whom the court issues garnishment process.

GARNISHEE ORDER. "... [G]ives to the garnishor certain statutory rights enabling him to prevent the garnishee paying money to the original creditor and also to give a valid discharge of that original creditor's claim. It does not confer any right by way of equitable assignment or otherwise in the original debt." *MacKay & Hughes (1973) Ltd. v. Martin Potatoes Inc.* (1984), 4 P.P.S.A.C. 107 at 113, 46 O.R. (2d) 304, 51 C.B.R. (N.S.) 1, 4 O.A.C. 1, 9 D.L.R. (4th) 439 (C.A.), the court per Blair J.A.

GARNISHMENT. *n.* A way to enforce a judgment by which money owed by the garnishee to the judgment debtor is attached to pay off the judgment debtor's debt to a judgment creditor. See CONTINUING ~.

GAS. *n.* 1. Any hydrocarbon or mixture of hydrocarbons that, at a temperature of 15°C and a pressure of 101.325 kPa, is in a gaseous state. *National Energy Board Act*, R.S.C. 1985, c. N-7, s. 2. 2. Natural gas and includes all substances, other than oil, that are produced in association with natural gas. *Canada Oil and Gas Operations Act*, R.S.C. 1985, c. O-7, s. 2. See GREENHOUSE ~; REFINERY ~.

GAS LIQUIDS. A mixture of two or more of ethane, propane, butane or pentanes plus, whether in gaseous or liquid form, that (a) is obtained from the processing of natural gas or crude oil, and (b) has never been processed into separate identifiable fuels, but does not include a mixture of ethane, propane, butane or pentanes plus that is created after the ethane, propane, butane or pentanes plus have been processed into separate identifiable fuels and then remixed into a blend of one or more of the fuels. *Carbon Tax Act*, S.B.C. 2008, c. 40, Sched. 1, s. 1.

GASOHOL. *n.* A blend of gasoline and denatured ethanol.

GASOLINE. *n.* Gasoline type fuels for use in internal combustion engines other than aircraft engines. *Excise Tax Act*, R.S.C. 1985, c. E-15, s. 2. See UNLEADED ~.

GAS PROJECT. See MACKENZIE ~.

GATE-KEEPING. *n.* A "gate-keeping" function can be a decision by an impartial arbiter hearing a prosecution or dispute between two parties independent of the arbiter. The Supreme Court of Canada has very recently used the term "gate-keeping function" to refer to a British Columbia judge hearing a criminal charge of breach of the conditions of a conditional sentence order. The judge was deciding whether to act on a report of the accused's sentencing supervisor, or to require personal attendance of a witness to allow cross-examination. See R. v. McIvor, 2008 SCC 11 (para. 29). *Brewer v. Fraser Milner Casgrain LLP*, 2008 ABCA 160.

GATT. *abbr.* General Agreement on Tariffs and Trade, a multilateral international agreement concerning trade.

GAZETTE. *n.* 1. A government's official newspaper. 2. Journal published by the Law Society of Upper Canada.

GEARED-TO-INCOME. See RENT-~ ASSISTANCE; RENT-~ UNIT.

GEN. *abbr.* General.

GENE. *n.* The basic unit of heredity. A sequence of bases in a molecule of DNA. F.A. Jaffe, *A Guide to Pathological Evidence for Lawyers and Police Officers*, 4th ed. (Toronto: Carswell, 1999) at 238.. See CHIMERIC PLANT ~.

GENERAL ACCEPTANCE. A general acceptance assents without qualification to the order of the drawer. *Bills of Exchange Act*, R.S.C. 1985, c. B-4, s. 37.

GENERAL ADVANTAGE OF CANADA. See WORKS FOR THE ~.

GENERAL AGENT. 1. A person or corporation directly representing an insurance company and who can issue policies, interim receipts and give oral coverage. 2. A person acting under authority from an insurer to supervise and appoint agents, inspect risks and otherwise transact business for, or as a representative of, such insurer. *The Saskatchewan Insurance Act*, R.S.S. 1978, c. S-26, s. 2.

GENERAL ANTI-AVOIDANCE RULE. 1. Appears in section 245 of the Income Tax Act R.S.C. 1985, c. 1 (5th Supp.). Allows Canada Revenue Agency to adjust the tax benefit available to a taxpayer where the tax planning amounts to a misuse or abuse of the provisions of the act even though the taxpayer complied with all the technical provisions. 2. The determinations of "misuse" and "abuse" under s. 245(4) are not separate inquiries. Section 245(4) requires a single, unified approach to the textual, contextual and purposive interpretation of the specific provisions of the Income Tax Act that are relied upon by the taxpayer in order to determine whether there was abusive tax avoidance. The heart of the analysis under s. 245(4) lies in a contextual and purposive interpretation of the provisions of the Act that are relied on by the taxpayer, and the application of the properly interpreted provisions to the facts of a given case. The first task is to interpret the provisions giving rise to the tax benefit to determine their object, spirit and purpose. The next task is to determine whether the transaction falls within or frustrates that purpose. The overall inquiry thus involves a mixed question of fact and law. The textual, contextual and purposive interpretation of specific provisions of the Income Tax Act is essentially a question of law but the application of these provisions to the facts of a case is necessarily fact-intensive. The approach to s. 245 of the Income Tax Act may be summarized as follows. Three requirements must be established to permit application of the GAAR: (1) A tax benefit resulting from a transaction or part of a series of transactions (s. 245(1) and (2)); (2) that the transaction is an avoidance transaction in the sense that it cannot be said to have been reasonably undertaken or arranged primarily for a bona fide purpose other than to obtain a tax benefit; and (3) that there was abusive tax avoidance in the sense that it cannot be reasonably concluded that a tax benefit would be consistent with the object, spirit or purpose of the provisions relied upon by the taxpayer. The burden is on the taxpayer to refute (1) and (2), and on the Minister to establish (3). If the existence of abusive tax avoidance is unclear, the benefit of the doubt goes to the taxpayer. The courts proceed by conducting a unified textual, contextual and purposive analysis of the provisions giving rise to the tax benefit in order to determine why they were put in place and why the benefit was conferred. The goal is to arrive at a purposive interpretation that is harmonious with the provisions of the Act that confer the tax benefit, read in the context of the whole Act. Whether the transactions were motivated by any economic, commercial, family or other non-tax purpose may form part of the factual context that the courts may consider in the analysis of abusive tax avoidance allegations under s. 245(4). However, any finding in this respect would form only one part of the underlying facts of a case, and would be insufficient by itself to establish abusive tax avoidance. The central issue is the proper interpretation of the relevant provisions in light of their context and purpose. Abusive tax avoidance may be found where the relationships and transactions as expressed in the relevant documentation lack a proper basis relative to the object, spirit or purpose of the provisions that are purported to confer the tax benefit, or where they are wholly dissimilar to the relationships or transactions that are contemplated by the provisions. Where the Tax Court judge has proceeded on a proper construction of the provisions of the Income Tax Act and on findings supported by the evidence, appellate tribunals should not interfere, absent a palpable and overriding error. *Canada Trustco Mortgage Co. v. Canada*, [2005] 2 S.C.R. 601, 2005 SCC 54, McLachlin C.J. and Major J. for the Court.

GENERAL CONTRACTOR. A contractor whose principal activity consists of organizing or coordinating construction work delegated to persons under his orders or to contractors.

GENERAL COUNCIL. The governing body of the Bar of Quebec. It exercises all the rights, powers and prerogatives and assume the obligations of the board of directors within the meaning of the Professional Code (chapter C-26). *An Act respecting the Barreau du Québec*, R.S.Q. c. B-1, s. 10.

GENERAL COURT MARTIAL. May try any person who is liable to be charged, dealt with and tried on a charge of having committed a service offence. A General Court Martial is composed of a military judge and a panel of five members.

GENERAL COURT OF APPEAL. The words "general court of appeal" in s. 101 [of the Constitution Act, 1867(U.K.), 30 & 31 Vict., c. 3] denote the status of the Court within the national court structure and should not be taken as a restrictive definition of the Court's functions. In most instances, this Court acts as the exclusive ultimate appellate court in the country, and, as such, is properly constituted as the "general court of appeal" for Canada. Moreover, it is clear that an appellate court can receive, on an exceptional basis, original jurisdiction not incompatible with its

appellate jurisdiction. *Reference re Secession of Quebec*, 1998 CarswellNat 1299, 161 D.L.R. (4th) 385, 228 N.R. 203, 55 C.R.R. (2d) 1, [1998] 2 S.C.R. 217, per curiam.

GENERAL DAMAGES. 1. "... [T]hose which, upon the breach of a legal duty, the law itself presumes to arise, and they can be shown by general evidence of matters which are accepted as affected by such a breach... ." *Rowlett v. Karas*, [1944] S.C.R. 1 at 10, [1944] 1 D.L.R. 241, Rand J. (Duff C.J. concurring). 2. "... [S]uch as the law will presume to be the direct, natural, or probable consequence of the act complained of; ..." *Graham v. Saville*, [1945] 2 D.L.R. 489 at 492, [1945] O.R. 301 (C.A.), Laidlaw J.A. (dissenting in part).

GENERAL DENIAL. 1. In a pleading, a contradiction of each of the allegations of the plaintiff in the statement of claim or petition. 2. A compendious or condensed denial. *Patym Holdings Ltd. v. Michalakis*, 2005 BCCA 636, Smith J.A. (Saunders J.A. concurring).

GENERAL DETERRENCE. A sentence which will discourage others who may be inclined to commit the same or a similar offence.

GENERAL ELECTION. 1. An election in respect of which election writs are issued for all electoral districts. 2. An election that is held in respect of each constituency on the same day.

GENERALIA SPECIALIBUS NON DEROGANT. [L.] 1. The general does not detract from the specific. 2. "... [W]here there are general words in a later Act capable of reasonable and sensible application without extending them to subjects specially dealt with by earlier legislation, you are not to hold that earlier and special legislation indirectly repealed, altered or derogated from merely by force of such general words, without any indication of a particular intention to do so." *Seward v. The Vera Cruz* (1884), 10 App. Cas. 59 at 68 (U.K. H.L.), Lord Selborne.

GENERALIBUS SPECIALIA DEROGANT. [L.] The special derogates from the general.

GENERAL INTENT. "... [O]ne in which the only intent involved relates solely to the performance of the act in question with no further ulterior intent or purpose ..." *R. v. Bernard*, [1988] 2 S.C.R. 833 at 863, 67 C.R. (3d) 113, 90 N.R. 321, 45 C.C.C. (3d) 1, 32 O.A.C. 161, 38 C.R.R. 82, McIntyre J.

GENERAL INTENT OFFENCE. One in which the actor's intent is solely to perform the act in question.

GENERAL JURISDICTION. Unrestricted and unlimited authority in any matter of substantive law, criminal or civil. S.A. Cohen, *Due Process of Law* (Toronto: Carswell, 1977) at 344.

GENERAL LEGACY. Describes a legacy which does not bequeath a specified item. P.V. Baker & P. St. J. Langan, eds., *Snells' Equity*, 29th ed. (London: Sweet and Maxwell, 1990) at 360.

GENERAL LIEN. A lien on personal property for an account due or general debt to the one who claims it, which operates as a form of floating charge on any

G

of the debtor's personal property in the lien claimant's hands. D.N. Macklem & D.I. Bristow, *Construction and Mechanics' Liens in Canada*, 5th ed. (Toronto: Carswell, 1985) at 579.

GENERALLY. *adv.* On the whole, in those cases. See CROSSED ~.

GENERALLY ACCEPTED. For a practice to be generally accepted, it does not have to be a practice that everyone does or that everyone necessarily agrees with. It is simply a practice which is permissible or legitimate under the circumstances. *Lloyds Bank Canada v. Alberta Opportunity Co.*, 1989 CarswellAlta 197, 71 Alta. L.R. (2d) 257, 101 A.R. 294, [1990] 2 W.W.R. 692, 46 B.L.R. 236 (Q.B.), Power J.

GENERALLY ACCEPTED ACCOUNTING PRINCIPLES. Conventions, rules and procedures that set out accepted accounting practice, usually the principles established by the Canadian Institute of Chartered Accountants.

GENERALLY ACCEPTED AUDITING STANDARDS. (a) In the case of an audit report which references auditing standards generally accepted in Canada, the auditing standards for audits of corporations, the shares of which are publicly traded, as set out in the Assurance Handbook of the Canadian Institute of Chartered Accountants, or (b) in the case of an audit report which references generally accepted auditing standards of a jurisdiction other than Canada, the standards generally accepted in that jurisdiction. *Canadian Public Accountability Board Act (Ontario), 2006*, S.O. 2006, c. 33, Sched. D, s. 2.

GENERALLY ACCEPTED BANKING PRACTICES. Can be interpreted as meaning that anything that is permissible or legitimate as a bona fide exercise of sound banking judgment constitutes an accepted banking practice. This general definition allows the bank to carry out a number of different procedures and practices in any situation or circumstance. The failure to carry out specific practices or procedures does not mean that the plaintiff did not act in accordance with generally accepted practices. *Lloyds Bank Canada v. Alberta Opportunity Co.*, 1989 CarswellAlta 197, 71 Alta. L.R. (2d) 257, 101 A.R. 294, [1990] 2 W.W.R. 692, 46 B.L.R. 236 (Q.B.), Power J.

GENERAL MEETING. Any annual, regular, special or class meeting of the members of an organization.

GENERAL PARTNER. Person associated with one or more other persons in an enterprise and assuming personal liability. See LIMITED PARTNERSHIP.

GENERAL POWER. 1. Includes any power or authority enabling the donee or other holder thereof either alone or jointly with or, with the consent, of any other person to appoint, appropriate or dispose of property as she or he sees fit, whether exercisable by instrument inter vivos or by will, or both, but does not include (i) any power exercisable in a fiduciary capacity under a disposition not made by the donee except to the extent that having regard to the fiduciary restrictions imposed upon the donee under the dis-

position it is reasonable to regard the donee or holder of the power as capable of conferring the property or any part thereof upon herself or himself for her or his own benefit, or (ii) any power exercisable as a mortgagee, or (iii) any power exercisable jointly with, or with the consent of, any other person (A) who has a substantial interest in the property to which the power relates, and (B) whose interest in that property would be adversely affected by the exercise of the power in favour of the donee or holder. 2. The power of a donee to appoint property to anyone, including her or himself. D.M.W. Waters, *The Law of Trusts in Canada*, 2d ed. (Toronto: Carswell, 1984) at 72.

GENERAL STRIKE. Work stoppage by all union members in a geographic area.

GENERAL VERDICT. A jury's decision for either the defendant or the plaintiff generally.

GENERAL WELFARE CLAUSE. In municipalities, the source of local police power, public health, nuisances and the regulation of trades.

GENERAL WORDS. Words added to the description of a parcel of land in a conveyance or mortgage, words which describe every kind of appurtenance, easement or privilege, fixtures and produce of the land.

GENERATE. v. With respect to electricity, means to produce electricity or provide ancillary services, other than ancillary services provided by a transmitter or distributor through the operation of a transmission or distribution system. *Electricity Act, 1998*, S.O. 1998, c. 15, Sched. A, s. 2.

GENERIC. *adj.* 1. Relating to a group or class. 2. Chemical name of a drug.

GENERIC DRUG. Drug that is therapeutically equivalent to and contains the same quantities of active medicinal ingredients as a drug already marketed in Canada that is a brand-name drug. *Apotex Inc. v. Canada (Attorney General)*, (1997), 123 F.T.R. 161.

GENERIC DRUG COMPANY. A company which manufactures and sells generic drugs, drugs discovered or invented by others, under compulsory licence arrangements provided in the Patent Act.

GENETIC TESTING. The analysis of DNA, RNA or chromosomes for purposes such as the prediction of disease or vertical transmission risks, or monitoring, diagnosis or prognosis. *Food and Drugs Act*, R.S.C. 1985, c. F-27, *Medical Devices Regulations* SOR/98-282, s. 1.

GENEVA CONVENTIONS. Agreements to ameliorate the condition of wounded and sick members of the armed forces in the field, to ameliorate the condition of sick, wounded and ship-wrecked members of the armed forces at sea, to treat prisoners of war and civilian persons in time of war in particular ways.

GENOCIDE. *n.* 1. Any of the following acts committed with intent to destroy in whole or in part any identifiable group, namely, (a) killing members of the group, or (b) deliberately inflicting on the group conditions of life calculated to bring about its physical destruction. *Criminal Code*, R.S.C. 1985, c. C-46, s. 318(2). 2. Any of the following acts committed with intent to destroy, in whole or in part, a national, ethnical, racial or religious group, as such: (a) killing members of the group; (b) causing serious bodily or mental harm to members of the group; (c) deliberately inflicting on the group conditions of life calculated to bring about its physical destruction in whole or in part; (d) imposing measures intended to prevent births within the group; (e) forcibly transferring children of the group to another group. *Crimes Against Humanity and War Crimes Act*, S.C. 2000, c. 24, Sched., *Rome Statute*, Article 6. 3. An act or omission committed with intent to destroy, in whole or in part, an identifiable group of persons, as such, that, at the time and in the place of its commission, constitutes genocide according to customary international law or conventional international law or by virtue of its being criminal according to the general principles of law recognized by the community of nations, whether or not it constitutes a contravention of the law in force at the time and in the place of its commission. *Crimes Against Humanity and War Crimes Act*, S.C. 2000, c. 24, s. 4. See IDENTIFIABLE GROUP.

GENOME. *n.* The totality of the deoxyribonucleic acid sequence of a particular cell. See HUMAN ~.

GENUINE. *adj.* Free of forgery or counterfeit.

GEO-IDENTIFICATION SOFTWARE. Computer software which detects an internet user's geographic location, limiting access to users from one or more geographic areas.

GERIATRIC. *adj.* Relating to aged persons. Aged.

GERRYMANDER. *v.* To manipulate boundaries of constituencies unfairly in order to secure a disproportionate influence in an election for one party or candidate.

GET-UP. *n.* Of products, in passing-off actions, refers to their whole visible external appearance in the form in which they are likely to be seen by the public before purchase. If the goods are packaged, their get-up means the appearance of the package taken as a whole. *CIBA-Geigy Canada Ltd. v. Apotex Inc.* [1992] 3 S.C.R. 120.

GIC. *abbr.* 1. Guaranteed investment certificate. 2. (i) Evidence of indebtedness of or guaranteed by a financial institution; or (ii) a certificate or receipt issued by a financial institution for money received for guaranteed investment. *Securities Act, 1988*, S.S. 1988-89, c. S-42.2, *Securities Commission (Local Instruments) Regulations*, R.R.S., c. S-42.2, Reg. 5, s.1.

GIFT. *n.* 1. " ... [T]o constitute a 'gift', it must appear that the property transferred was transferred voluntarily and not as the result of a contractual obligation to transfer it and that no advantage of a material character was received by the transferor by way of return." *Commissioner of Taxation of the Commonwealth v. McPhail* (1967), 41 A.L.J.R. 346 at 348, Owen J., cited with approval in *R. v. McBurney*, [1985] 2 C.T.C. 214 at 218, 85 D.T.C. 5433, 20 E.T.R. 283, 62 N.R. 104 (Fed. C.A.), Heald, Urie and Stone JJ.A. 2. " ... [C]onstituted by two things—the words giving (not merely expressing a promise or

intention) and possession in the donee ..." *Standard Trust Co. v. Hill* (1922), 68 D.L.R. 722 at 723, [1922] 2 W.W.R. 1003, 18 Alta. L.R. 137 (C.A.), Beck J.A. (Stuart and Hyndman JJ.A. concurring). 3. In its usual meaning, a gift is a voluntary transfer of personal property without consideration. *Birce v. Birce* (2001), 2001 CarswellOnt 3481 (C.A.). 4. Lottery winnings are not gifts as a lottery corporation does not provide money to individuals without a winning ticket. *Souder v. Wereschuk*, 2004 ABCA 339. See CLASS ~; DEED OF ~; INTER VIVOS ~.

GIFT INTER VIVOS. A gift made by a living person to another living person. See INTER VIVOS GIFT.

GIFT MORTIS CAUSA. " ... [A] gift conditioned upon the death of the donor... ." *McIntyre v. Royal Trust Co.*, [1945] 3 D.L.R. 71 at 75, [1945] 2 W.W.R. 364, 53 Man. R. 353 (K.B.), Dysart J. See DONATIO MORTIS CAUSA.

GIFT TAX. Tax imposed on the transfer of property by gift.

GILLETTE DEFENCE. As an alternative defence, the Respondents pleaded what is known as the "Gillette Defence" arising out of the decision in Gillette Safety Razor Co. v. Anglo-American Trading Co. Ltd. (1913), 30 R.P.R. 465 (U.K. H.L.). The classic statement of the defence is as follows: The defence that "the alleged infringement is not novel at the date of the plaintiff's Letters Patent" is a good defence in law, and it would sometimes obviate the great length and expense of Patent cases if the defendant could and would put forth his case in this form and thus spare himself the trouble of demonstrating on which horn of the well-known dilemma the plaintiff had impaled himself, invalidity or non-infringement. *Gold v. Serratus Mountain Products Ltd.*, 2006 FCA 98.

GIVE. *v.* To transfer property without compensation.

GIVEN NAME. 1. " ... [A] name given at birth to distinguish it from the surname, family or ancestral name." *Wilson, Re* (1984), 51 C.B.R.(N.S.) 85 at 87, 46 O.R. (2d) 28, 8 D.L.R. (4th) 271, 4 P.P.S.A.C. 69, 26 B.L.R. 271 (S.C.), Saunders J. 2. A name other than a surname.

GLADUE PRINCIPLES. Principles enunciated in the decision of the Supreme Court of Canada in R. v. Gladue, [[1999] 1 S.C.R. 688], have application to the question of bail. However, the application judge cannot apply such principles in a vacuum. Application of the Gladue principles would involve consideration of the unique systemic or background factors which may have played a part in bringing the particular aboriginal offender before the courts. The exercise would involve consideration of the types of release plans, enforcement or control procedures and sanctions that would, because of his or her particular aboriginal heritage or connections, be appropriate in the circumstances of the offender and would satisfy the primary, secondary and tertiary grounds for release. Gladue principles, which provide a framework for interpreting s. 718.2(e) of the Criminal Code, must be considered when sentencing an aboriginal of-

G

fender who has committed an offence involving serious violence. *R. v. Robinson*, 2009 CarswellOnt 1186, 2009 ONCA 205. Gladue principles have already been extended to a variety of other contexts in the criminal justice system, including bail, parole eligibility, dangerous offender applications, and disposition hearings of the Ontario Review Board. Although Gladue was focused primarily on the serious problem of excessive imprisonment of aboriginal peoples, the case in a broader sense draws attention to the state of the justice system's engagement with Canada's First Nations. Three factors in particular were highlighted in Gladue: the estrangement of aboriginal peoples from the Canadian justice system, the impact of years of dislocation, and whether imprisonment would be meaningful to the community of which the offender is a member. The principles underlying the Gladue decision have application in the civil contempt context. *Frontenac Ventures Corp. v. Ardoch Algonquin First Nation*, 2008 ONCA 534. The law in Ontario requires that the Gladue analysis be performed in all cases involving an Aboriginal offender, regardless of the seriousness of the offence. This is also the law in Alberta: see R. v. Abraham [(2000), 261 A.R. 192 (Alta. C.A.)]. The sentencing judge has a statutory duty to consider the unique circumstances of Aboriginal offenders; the only discretion is with respect to the determination of a just and appropriate sentence (Gladue, para 82). To fulfil their duty, sentencing judges must undertake the sentencing of Aboriginal offenders individually—as with all offenders—but also differently, because the circumstances of Aboriginal people are unique and call for a special approach. Gladue establishes the framework by which a sentencing judge is to carry out his or her duty when determining a truly fit and proper sentence for Aboriginal offenders. The background considerations underlying the unique circumstances of Aboriginal offenders, which will direct the sentencing judge's analysis, are: (A) The unique systemic or background factors which may have played a part in bringing the particular aboriginal offender before the courts; and (B) The types of sentencing procedures and sanctions, which may be appropriate in the circumstances for the offender because of his or her particular aboriginal heritage or connection. (Gladue, para. 66) It is only after a thorough review of those considerations that the sentencing judge will be in a position to determine a fit and proper sentence. Unfortunately the sentencing judge in the within case did not perform this required task. Section 718.2(e) does not require, nor is there a general rule, that Aboriginal offenders must be sentenced in a way that gives the most weight to the principle of restorative justice. It may be that in certain cases the objectives of restorative justice articulated in s. 718.2(e) and Gladue will not weigh as favourably as those of separation, denunciation and deterrence. As was noted in Gladue, Aboriginal people also believe in the importance of those latter objectives. Those principles will always be relevant and may predominate for more serious offenders or where the offence is serious enough that imprisonment is necessary. *R. v. Kakekagamick*, 214 O.A.C. 127.

GLASS. See PLATE ~ INSURANCE.

GLOBAL INFORMATION INFRASTRUCTURE. Includes electromagnetic emissions, communications systems, information technology systems and networks, and any data or technical information carried on, contained in or relating to those emissions, systems or networks. *National Defence Act*, R.S.C. 1985, c. N-5, s. 273.61.

GLOBAL OFFER. An offer to settle made in respect of more than one action involving multiple parties. *C.(I.R.) v. C.(S.)*, 2006 BCCA 428.

GLOSS. *n.* Interpretation consisting of an annotation, explanation or comment on any passage in a text.

GOD. See ACT OF ~; ACT OF ~ CLAUSE.

GODSON. *abbr.* Godson, Mining Commissioner's Cases (Ontario), 1911-1917.

GOING CONCERN. A business operating in the usual and ordinary way as it was intended to operate.

GOLDEN RULE. When construing a statute, the ordinary meaning of the words and the ordinary rules of grammatical construction should be used unless that produces a result contrary to the intent of the legislators or leading to obvious repugnance or absurdity. P.St.J. Langan, ed., *Maxwell on The Interpretation of Statutes*, 12th ed. (Bombay: N.M. Tripathi, 1976) at 43.

GOOD. *adj.* 1. When describing pleading, sound or valid. 2. Satisfactory, adequate. 3. Having positive qualities.

GOOD BEHAVIOUR. The standard necessary to remain in office. Requirement of a level of integrity necessary to maintain public confidence in the institution and the process of appointment to office.

GOOD CAUSE. 1. "... [F]air and just ..." *Vernon (City) v. British Columbia Public Utilities Commission* (1953), 9 W.W.R. (N.S.) 384 at 384 (B.C. C.A.), the court per O'Halloran J.A. 2. "[In s. 73 of the County Courts Act, R.S.B.C. 1924, c. 53] ... means something that would bring the case out of the ordinary, ..." *Goldie v. Colquhoun* (1930), 42 B.C.R. 356 at 357, [1930] 1 W.W.R. 624, [1930] 2 D.L.R. 1002 (C.A.), Martin J.A. 3. "[In Saskatchewan King's Bench Rule of Court 672(3)] ... includes not only misconduct or oppression on the part of the successful party, but anything, which would make it just and reasonable, that there should be a departure from the rule that costs should follow the event. Forster v. Farquhar, [1893] 1 Q.B. 564 [(U.K.)] ..." *Dominion Fire Insurance Co. v. Thomson* (1923), 17 Sask. L.R. 527 at 531, [1923] 3 W.W.R. 1265, [1923] 4 D.L.R. 903 (C.A.), Lamont J.A. (Haultain C.J.S. and McKay J.A. concurring).

GOOD CONSIDERATION. 1. "... '[V]aluable [consideration]' ..." *China Software Corp. v. Leimbigler* (1990), 49 B.L.R. 173 at 177 (B.C. S.C.), Drake J. 2. "... [T]here must be a real and honest bargain, and not one which is so made that it is manifest that the form which it took was in reality a sham, or was intended to be and was a fraud. There may be overvaluation and yet an honest bargain. The test is honesty, and if that is present the Court will not inquire into the adequacy or inadequacy of the consideration... ." *Hood v. Caldwell* (1921), 64 D.L.R. 442 at 456, 20 O.W.N. 251, 50 O.L.R. 397 (C.A.), Hodgins J.A.

GOOD FAITH. 1. [C]onnotes an honest and reasonably held belief. If the belief is honest, but not reasonably held, it cannot be said to constitute good faith. But it does not follow that it is therefore bad faith. To constitute bad faith the actions must be knowingly or intentionally wrong. *R. v. Smith*, 2005 BCCA 334. 2. "... In the context of s. 8 of the Charter, good faith has come to mean that state of mind which relies upon express statutory authority to support the lawfulness of a search... ." *R. v. Klimchuk* (1991), 67 C.C.C. (3d) 385 at 419, 8 C.R. (4th) 327, 32 M.V.R. (2d) 202, 4 B.C.A.C. 26, 9 W.A.C. 26, 9 C.R.R. (2d) 153 (C.A.), Wood J.A. 3. Honesty in fact in the conduct of the transaction concerned. *Bank Act*, S.C. 1991, c. 46, s. 81. 4. Honestly whether done negligently or not. 5. Honesty in fact and the observance of reasonable commercial standards of fair dealing. *The Securities Transfer Act*, S.S. 2007, c. S-42.3, s. 4. 6. Good faith has been established in situations where the violation stemmed from police reliance upon a statute or from the following of a procedure which was later found to infringe the *Charter. R. v. Wise*, [1992] 1 S.C.R. 527. See IN ~; NEGOTIATE IN ~; UBERRIMAE FIDES.

GOOD GOVERNMENT. See PEACE, ORDER AND ~.

GOODS. *n.* 1. Tangible personal property other than chattel paper, a document of title, an instrument, a security certificate and money, and includes fixtures, growing crops and the unborn young of animals, but does not include trees that are crops until they are severed or minerals until they are extracted. *Civil Enforcement Act*, R.S.A. 2000, c. C-15, s. 1. 2. Anything that is the subject of trade or commerce. *Criminal Code*, R.S.C. 1985, c. C-46, s. 379. 3. Any article that is or may be the subject of trade or commerce, but does not include land or any interest therein. *Bills of Exchange Act*, R.S.C. 1985, c. B-4, s. 188. 4. "[In the Customs Act, R.S.C. 1970, c. C-40] ... must ... be taken to include all movable effects of any kind... . In the Customs Tariff ... the word 'goods' is given a general meaning to include all personal effects, and not merely to include strictly items of commerce... ." *Ladakis v. R.* (1985), 10 C.E.R. 95 at 102 (Fed. T.D.), Collier J. 5. Tangible personal property other than chattel paper, documents of title, instruments, money and securities, and includes fixtures, growing crops, the unborn young of animals, timber to be cut, and minerals and hydrocarbons to be extracted; *Personal Property Security Act*, R.S.O. 1990, c. P.10, s. 1. See ASCERTAINED ~; BONDED ~; CEMETERY ~; CONSUMER ~; DOCUMENT OF TITLE TO ~; FUNGIBLE ~; FUTURE ~; SALE OF ~; SLANDER OF ~; SPECIFIC ~; TRESPASS TO ~; UNASCERTAINED ~; UNSOLICITED ~ OR SERVICES.

GOOD SAMARITAN LAW. 1. A statute which protects those who render assistance in emergencies from liability where their assistance increases the injury to the one they seek to rescue or assist. 2. Despite the rules of common law, a person described (health care professional or person who provides first aid) in subsection (2) who voluntarily and without reasonable expectation of compensation or reward provides the services described in that subsection is not liable for damages that result from the person's negligence in acting or failing to act while providing the services, unless it is established that the damages were caused by the gross negligence of the person. *Good Samaritan Act, 2001*, S.O. 2001, c. 2, s. 2.

GOODS AND SERVICES TAX. The federal tax imposed under Part IX of the Excise Tax Act on the consumption of goods and services, including imports into Canada. Applied to the consideration paid or payable for goods or services.

GOOD TITLE. Title which an unwilling purchaser can be forced to take. It is free from pending litigation or other potentially harmful defects. It will provide peaceful possession of the property. V. DiCastri, *Law of Vendor and Purchaser* (Toronto: Carswell, 1988) at 339.

GOODWILL. *n.* In ordinary commercial use, it connotes the positive association that attracts customers towards its owner's wares or services rather than those of its competitors. *Veuve Clicquot Ponsardin v. Boutiques Cliquot Ltée*, 2006 SCC 23.

GOVERNMENT. *n.* 1. "... [I]n its generic sense – meaning the whole of the governmental apparatus of the state ..." *Dolphin Delivery Ltd. v. R.W.D.S.U., Local 580* (1986), [1987] 1 W.W.R. 577 at 597, 38 C.C.L.T. 184, 71 N.R. 83, [1986] 2 S.C.R. 573, 9 B.C.L.R. (2d) 273, 87 C.L.L.C. 14,002, 33 D.L.R. (4th) 174, 25 C.R.R. 321, [1987] D.L.Q. 69, McIntyre J. (Dickson C.J.C., Estey, Chouinard and Le Dain JJ. concurring). 2. "... [T]he executive or administrative branch of a government. This is the sense in which one generally speaks of the Government of Canada or of a province... ." *Dolphin Delivery Ltd. v. R.W.D.S.U., Local 580* (1986), [1987] 1 W.W.R. 577 at 597, 38 C.C.L.T. 184, 71 N.R. 83, [1986] 2 S.C.R. 573, 9 B.C.L.R. (2d) 273, 87 C.L.L.C. 14,002, 33 D.L.R. (4th) 174, 25 C.R.R. 321, [1987] D.L.Q. 69, McIntyre J. (Dickson C.J.C., Estey, Chouinard and Le Dain JJ. concurring). 3. In a political sense, the members of Parliament and the Senate, federally, or the legislature, provincially, who support the current Prime Minister or Premier. See ABORIGINAL ~; CABINET ~; FEDERAL ~; LOCAL ~; MUNICIPAL ~; PARLIAMENTARY ~; RESPONSIBLE ~; SELF-~ AGREEMENT.

GOVERNMENT BILL. A bill approved by cabinet and introduced into the legislature by the minister responsible.

GOVERNMENT HOUSE. Name given to house where the Lieutenant Governor resides.

GOVERNMENT HOUSE LEADER. The member of the government, responsible to the Prime Minister, who arranges government business in the House of Commons. A. Fraser, W.A. Dawson & J. Holtby, eds., *Beauchesne's Rules and Forms of the House of Commons of Canada*, 6th ed. (Toronto: Carswell, 1989) at 56.

GOVERNMENT OR PUBLIC FACILITY. A facility or conveyance, whether permanent or temporary, that is used or occupied in connection with their official duties by representatives of a state, members of a government, members of a legislature, members of the judiciary, or officials or employees of a state or of any other public authority or public entity, or by officials or employees of an intergovernmental organization. *Criminal Code*, R.S.C. 1985, c. C-46, s. 2.

GOVERNMENT SERVICES. See DEPARTMENT OF PUBLIC WORKS AND ~.

GOVERNMENT VESSEL. A vessel that is owned by and is in the service of Her Majesty in right of Canada or a province or that is in the exclusive possession of Her Majesty in that right. *Canada Shipping Act, 2001*, S.C. 2001, c. 26, s. 2.

GOVERNOR. See LIEUTENANT ~.

GOVERNOR GENERAL. *var.* **GOVERNOR-GENERAL.** The Governor General of Canada or other chief executive officer or administrator carrying on the government of Canada on behalf and in the name of the Sovereign, by whatever title that person is designated.

GOVERNOR GENERAL IN COUNCIL. *var.* **GOVERNOR-GENERAL IN COUNCIL.** The Governor General or person administrating the government of Canada, acting by and with the advice or, or by and with the advice and consent of, or in conjunction with the Queen's Privy Council for Canada.

GOVERNOR IN COUNCIL. 1. The Governor General of Canada acting by and with the advice of, or by and with the advice and consent of, or in conjunction with the Queen's Privy Council for Canada. 2. The Lieutenant Governor acting by and with the advice of the Executive Council of the Province. See LIEUTENANT ~.

GOVERNOR OF CANADA. The Governor General of Canada or other chief executive officer or administrator carrying on the Government of Canada on behalf of and in the name of the Sovereign, by whatever title that officer is designated. *Interpretation Act*, R.S.C. 1985, c. I-21, s. 35.

GOVT. *abbr.* Government.

GOWN. See SILK ~; STUFF ~.

GR. *abbr.* Upper Canada Chancery (Grant), 1849-1922.

GRACE. *n.* Dispensation; licence. See DAYS OF ~.

GRACE PERIOD. See DAYS OF GRACE.

GRAIN. See CANADIAN ~ COMMISSION.

GRAIN RECEIPT. A document in prescribed form issued in respect of grain delivered to a process elevator or grain dealer acknowledging receipt of the grain and entitling the holder of the document to payment by the operator of the elevator or the grain dealer for the grain. *Canada Grain Act*, R.S.C. 1985, c. G-10, s. 2.

GRAIN STORAGE RECEIPT. A receipt as prescribed by the regulations that is to be issued by a grain elevator operator or the operator's authorized representative to the owner of farm grain. *Grains Act*, R.S.O. 1990, c. G.10, s. 1.

GRANDFATHER CLAUSE. A provision allowing a period of time to comply with requirements of a statute or other requirements or permitting persons or situations to continue under new legislation although not technically qualified. May now be called grandparent clause. See GRANDPARENTING.

GRAND JURY. An inquisition which sits, receives indictments and hears evidence from the prosecution; any finding is only an accusation, to be tried afterwards. Compare PETIT JURY.

GRANDPARENTING. *adj.* Traditionally this has been referred to as a grandfathering. The continuation of existing rights or privileges under new legislation which would do away with them but for a grandparent(ing) provision in the legislation. See GRANDFATHER CLAUSE.

GRANT. *v.* To transfer; to sell; to dispose of. See RE-~.

GRANT. *n.* 1. " ... [T]he strongest and widest word of gift and conveyance known to the law..." *Toronto (City) Board of Education v. Doughty* (1934), [1935] 1 D.L.R. 290 at 294, [1935] O.R. 85 (H.C.), Middleton J.A. 2. [T]he distinction to be drawn between a grant and a rebate is this. The essence of a grant is the giving of a benefit, including money, from a fund. The word "rebate," on the other hand, refers to the return of a portion of money actually paid. *Fourth Generation Realty Corp. v. Ottawa (City)* (2005), 197 O.A.C. 389. 3. Any grant of Crown land, whether by letters patent under the Great Seal, a notification or any other instrument whether in fee or for years, and whether direct from Her Majesty or by or pursuant to any statute. 4. A right created or transferred by the Crown, for example the grant of a charter, franchise, patent or pension. 5. Public money devoted to a special purpose. 6. (a) A grant of probate, (b) a resealed grant of probate or administration, (c) a grant of administration, or (d) a grant of letters of guardianship of the person or estate, or both, of a minor. 7. In respect of a franchise, includes the sale or disposition of the franchise or of an interest in the franchise and, for such purposes, an interest in the franchise includes the ownership of corporation that owns the franchise. *Arthur Wishart Act (Franchise Disclosure), 2000*, S.O. 2000, c. 3, s. 1. 8. Letters patent under the Great Seal, a notification and any other instrument by which territorial lands may be granted in fee simple or for an equivalent estate. See CANADA DISABILITY SAVINGS ~; CROWN ~; DEED OF ~; IMPLIED ~; NO ONE CAN BE ALLOWED TO DEROGATE FROM HIS OWN ~; RELIEF ~.

GRANTEE. *n.* 1. A person to whom one makes a grant. 2. The person to whom real property is transferred by deed for value or otherwise. 3. Includes the bargainee, assignee, transferee, mortgagee or other person to whom a bill of sale is made.

GRANT OF ADMINISTRATION. The grant made when the proper court issues administration. See DE BONIS NON ADMINISTRATIS.

GRANT OF ADMINISTRATION WITH WILL ANNEXED. The grant made if the deceased leaves a will naming no executor or if the named executor declines to act. J.G. McLeod, *The Conflict of Laws* (Calgary: Carswell, 1983) at 400.

GRANT OF AN INTEREST. The use of the term "grant of an interest" in ss. 13(4) and 13(7) [of the Copyright Act, R.S.C. 1985, c. C-42] would seem to refer to the granting of a property right. This language stands out in comparison to s. 2.7, which suggests that an exclusive licence is not a "grant of an interest" but rather a non-proprietary "authorization" to do something that would otherwise amount to infringement. ..... [T]he exclusive licensee's property interest in the copyright is limited. An exclusive licence is not a complete assignment of copyright. The owner-licensor retains a residual ownership interest in the copyright. The owner-licensor's residual ownership interest precludes it from being liable for copyright infringement. An owner-licensor is liable to its exclusive licensee for breach of the licensing agreement but not for copyright infringement. *Kraft Canada Inc. c. Euro Excellence Inc.*, 2007 SCC 37, Rothstein J. (Binnie and Deschamps JJ. concurring).

GRANT OF PROBATE. The grant made when the proper court issues probate.

GRANTOR. *n.* A person who makes a grant.

GRASS. *n.* Slang for marijuana.

GRASS-ROOTS COMMUNICATION. Appeals to members of the public through the mass media or by direct communication that seek to persuade members of the public to communicate directly with a public office holder in an attempt to place pressure on the public office holder to endorse a particular opinion. *Lobbyists Registration Act, 1998*, S.O. 1998, c. 27, Sched., s.1.

GRATIS. *adj.* [L.] Without reward or recompense.

GRATIS DICTUM. [L.] A mere assertion; a voluntary statement.

GRATUITOUS. *adj.* Without reward or recompense.

GRATUITOUS AGENCY. The assumption of specific agency tasks, without a fee, along with the assumption of fiduciary duties associated with the trust imposed by the agency.

GRATUITOUS BAILMENT. Bailment without recompense. Three forms are: gratuitous deposit of a chattel with the bailee who is to keep the chattel for the bailor; delivery of a chattel to the bailee, who is to do something without reward for the bailee to or with the chattel; and, gratuitous loan of a chattel by the bailor to the bailee for the bailee's use.

GRATUITOUS CONTRACT. When one party obligates himself to the other for the benefit of the latter without obtaining any advantage in return, the contract is gratuitous. *Civil Code*, S.Q. 1991, c. 64, a. 1381.

GRATUITOUS PROMISE. 1. Promise made without consideration. 2. A promise to confer a benefit as a gift.

GRATUITY. *n.* A tip. *Canada (Attorney General) v. Canadian Pacific Ltd.* (1986), 86 C.L.L.C. 14,032 at 12,158, [1986] 1 S.C.R. 678, 11 C.C.E.L. 1, 66 N.R. 321, 27 D.L.R. (4th) 1, La Forest J. (Dickson C.J.C., Lamer and Le Dain JJ. concurring). 2. A reward for services rendered. *C. v. Minister of National Revenue* (1950), 2 Tax A.B.C. 6 at 10 (Can. App. Bd.), Graham (Chair) (Monet K.C. concurring).

GRAVAMEN. *n.* The essence of the complaint or grievance. The substantial complaint; the cause or matter.

GRAZING LEASE. A hybrid form of document which encompasses attributes of both a common law lease and a profit a prendre.

GREEN CIRCLING. An employee is reassigned to a lower paying position but retains the rate of pay of the old position and receives increases in pay that would have been received had the employee not been reassigned.

GREENHOUSE GAS. 1. Any gas listed in Annex A to the Kyoto Protocol. *Canada Emission Reduction Incentives Agency Act*, S.C. 2005, c. 30, s. 2. 2. Any or all of carbon dioxide, methane, nitrous oxide, hydrofluorocarbons, perfluorocarbons, sulphur hexafluoride and any other substance prescribed by regulation. *Greenhouse Gas Reduction Targets Act*, S.B.C. 2007, c. 42, s. 1.

GREEN PAPER. A paper setting out matters of concern to the government for discussion purposes. Compare WHITE PAPER.

GREEN ROOF. A roof surface that supports the growth of vegetation over a substantial portion of its area for the purpose of water conservation or energy conservation. *City of Toronto Act, 2006*, S.O. 2006, c. 11, Sched. A, s. 108.

GRIEVANCE. *n.* 1. Any disagreement between the parties to a collective bargaining agreement with respect to the meaning or application of a collective agreement or any violation of a collective bargaining agreement. *The Education Act, 1995*, S.S. 1995, c. E-0.2, s. 2. 2. A complaint in writing presented in accordance with the governing act or a collective agreement by an employee personally or on behalf of the employee and one or more other employees. See CONTINUING ~; GROUP ~; INDIVIDUAL ~; POLICY ~.

GRIEVANCE ARBITRATION. An adjudicative process by which disputes over the application or operation of a collective agreement are resolved. D.J.M. Brown & D.M. Beatty, *Canadian Labour Arbitration*, 3d ed. (Aurora: Canada Law Book, 1988) at 11.

GRIEVOR. *n.* 1. A person who has a grievance. 2. Person who has made a complaint in writing concerning dismissal from employment, working conditions or terms of employment.

GRIEVOUS BODILY HARM. The injury need not be "either permanent or dangerous, if it be such as

G

seriously to interfere with the comfort or health, it is sufficient ..." *R. v. Ashman* (1858), 175 E.R. 638, Willes J., cited with approval in *R. v. Martineau* (1990), 79 C.R. (3d) 129 at 151, [1990] 6 W.W.R. 97, 58 C.C.C. (3d) 353, 112 N.R. 83, 76 Alta. L.R. (2d) 1, [1990] 2 S.C.R. 633, 109 A.R. 321, 50 C.P.R. 110, L'Heureux-Dubé J. (dissenting).

GROOMING. *n.* The physical ability of the insured, or the insured's requirement to have verbal cuing, to wash his or her hands and face, to shave, groom hair, apply make-up and maintain his or her personal hygiene. *The Automobile Accident Insurance Act*, R.S.S. 1978, c. A-35, *The Personal Injury Benefits Regulations*, R.R.S., c. A-35, Reg. 3, Appendix D, Grid A, s. 2.

GROSS. *n.* See IN ~.

GROSS. *adj.* Entire; absolute.

GROSS INDECENCY. A marked departure from decent conduct expected of the average Canadian in the circumstances that existed. *R. v. Quesnel* (1979), 51 C.C.C. (2d) 270 (Ont. C.A.).

GROSS NEGLIGENCE. 1. "[Implies] ... conduct in which, if there is not conscious wrong doing, there is a very marked departure from the standards by which responsible and competent people in charge of motor cars habitually govern themselves... ." *McCulloch v. Murray*, [1942] 2 D.L.R. 179 at 180, [1942] S.C.R. 141, Duff C.J.C. 2. "[In the Municipal Act, R.S.O. 1914, s. 192] ... The circumstances giving rise to the duty to remove a dangerous condition, including notice, actual or imputable, of its existence, and the extent of the risk which it creates – the character and the duration of the neglect to fulfil that duty, including the comparative ease or difficulty of discharging it – these elements must vary in infinite degree; and they seem to be important, if not vital, factors in determining whether the fault (if any) attributable to the municipal corporation is so much more than merely ordinary neglect that it should be held to be very great, or gross negligence ..." *Holland v. Toronto (City)*, [1927] 1 D.L.R. 99 at 102, [1927] S.C.R. 242, 59 O.L.R. 628, the court per Anglin C.J.C. 3. "... [A] high or serious degree of negligence." *British Columbia Telephone Co. v. Quality Industries Ltd.* (1984), 49 C.P.C. 224 at 227, 59 B.C.L.R. 68 (C.A.), the court per Esson J.A. 4. Very great negligence. *Kingston (City) v. Drennan* (1897), 27 S.C.R. 46, Sedgewick J.

GROSS REVENUE INSURANCE PROGRAM. A program that combines the protection offered by a crop insurance program and the protection offered by a revenue insurance program. *Farm Income Protection Act*, S.C. 1991, c. 22, s. 2.

GROSS-UP. *n.* The practice of increasing lump sum awards for future care costs and pecuniary losses in personal injury cases (other than loss of future income) and for pecuniary losses in fatal accident cases to take into account the impact of taxation on the income generated by lump sum awards in respect of those heads of damages. It has been accepted at common law as a proper head of damages to be included

in a lump sum award at trial. *McErlean v. Sarel* (1987), 61 O.R. (2d) 396 (C.A.). See TAX ~.

GROUND. See ANALOGOUS ~; FAIR~; ~S; PLAY~; REASONABLE ~ TO BELIEVE.

GROUND LEASE. 1. Lease of bare land or land exclusive of any building on it. 2. A registered lease of land (a) granted by a leasehold landlord for the purposes of this Part, and (b) to which a model strata lot lease is attached; *Strata Property Act*, S.B.C. 1998, c. 43, s. 199.

GROUND-RENT. *n.* Rent, usually for many years, generally rent payable for land on which the lessee erects buildings under a building lease.

GROUNDS. *n.* Reasons. See ENUMERATED ~; GROUND; REASONABLE ~; SCATTERING ~.

GROUP. See COMPARATOR ~; IDENTIFIABLE ~; MUTUAL INSURANCE ~; PUBLIC INTEREST ~; RISK ~ 4; RISK ~ 3; RISK ~ 2; STAKEHOLDER ~; TERRORIST ~.

GROUP CREDITORS' INSURANCE. Form of group insurance under which a lender institution insures the collective lives of the borrowers.

GROUP GRIEVANCE. A collection of individual grievances concerning similar matters. The individual grievances are joined in one application or are determined at the same time.

GROUP INSURANCE. A policy of insurance that covers, under a master policy, the participants of a specified group or of a specified group and other persons.

GROUP PLAN. A contract for the provision of services under this Act, under which an association provides services to insure severally the well-being of a number of individuals under a single contract between the association and an employer or other person. *Prepaid Hospital and Medical Services Act*, R.S.O. 1990, c. P.21, s. 1.

GROUP TERM LIFE INSURANCE POLICY. A group life insurance policy under which the only amounts payable by the insurer are (a) amounts payable on the death or disability of individuals whose lives are insured in respect of, in the course of or because of, their office or employment or former office or employment, and (b) policy dividends or experience rating refunds. *Income Tax Act*, R.S.C. 1985, c. 1 (5th Supp.), s. 248.

GROW OPERATION. A place or premises where cannabis is grown either in soil or hydroponically.

GR. / U.C. CH. *abbr.* Grant's Upper Canada Chancery Reports, 1849-1882.

G.S.P. *abbr.* General Sessions of the Peace.

G.S.T. *abbr.* The federal Goods and Services Tax.

G.S.T.R. *abbr.* Canadian Goods and Services Tax Reporter / Reports / Monitor, 1989-.

G.T.C. *abbr.* Canadian GST and Commodity Tax Cases, 1993-.

GUARANTEE. *n.* 1. "... [A] contract between a guarantor and a lender. The subject of the guarantee is a debt owed to the lender by a debtor. In the contract of guarantee, the guarantor agrees to repay the lender if the debtor defaults. The exact nature of the obligation owed by the guarantor to the lender depends on the construction of the contract of guarantee, but the liability of the guarantor is usually made coterminous with that of the principal debtor... ." *Communities Economic Development Fund v. Canadian Pickles Corp.* (1991), 8 C.B.R. (3d) 121 at 143, [1992] 1 W.W.R. 193, 85 D.L.R. (4th) 88, 121 N.R. 81, [1991] 3 S.C.R. 388, 76 Man. R. (2d) 1, 10 W.A.C. 1, the court per Iacobucci J. 2. A written agreement under which a person agrees to answer for the default or act or omission of another person. Usually refers to payment of a debt. 3. A written agreement under which a person agrees to answer for the default or act or omission of another person. Usually refers to payment of a debt. Payment is contingent on the default of the principal debtor. See COMPANY LIMITED BY ~; CONTRACT OF ~.

GUARANTEE COMPANY. An incorporated company empowered to grant guarantee bonds or policies for the integrity and faithful accounting of public officers or other officials, servants or persons occupying positions of trust, or for other like purposes, and approved of for such purposes by the Governor in Council. *Sureties Act*, R.S.N.S. 1989, c. 451, s. 2.

GUARANTEED TRUST MONEY. Money that is received in trust for investment by a company that is a trust company pursuant to subsection 57(2) and that is subject to a guarantee by the company in respect of the payment of interest or repayment of the principal or both. *Trust and Loan Companies Act*, S.C. 1991, c. 45, s. 2.

GUARANTEE INSURANCE. The undertaking to perform an agreement or contract or to discharge a trust, duty or obligation upon default of the person liable for such performance or discharge or to pay money upon such default or in lieu of such performance or discharge, or where there is loss or damage through such default, but does not include credit insurance. *Insurance acts.*

GUARANTEE LETTER OF CREDIT. A security device and involves an obligation upon the issuing bank to pay any demand for payment by the beneficiary only upon default of the bank's customer to pay or perform its obligations owed to the beneficiary. *Morguard Trust Co. v. Royal Bank*, (1988), 88 A.R. 351, [1988] 5 W.W.R. 415, 60 Alta. L.R. (2d) 99.

GUARANTEE OF SIGNATURE. A guarantee signed by or on behalf of a person reasonably believed by the issuer to be responsible.

GUARANTOR. *n.* A surety, a person who is bound by a guarantee.

GUARANTY. *n.* A promise to pay another's debt or to perform another's obligation.

GUARD. *n.* A person employed to watch over property or persons. See COAST ~; SECURITY ~.

GUARDIAN. *n.* 1. Includes any person who has in law or in fact the custody or control of another person.

Criminal Code, R.S.C. 1985, c. C-46, s. 150. 2. Includes a person who has in law or in fact custody or control of a child. *Criminal Code*, R.S.C. 1985, c. C-46, s. 214. See LITIGATION ~; OFFICIAL ~; PUBLIC ~ AND TRUSTEE.

GUARDIAN AD LITEM. A person who sues on behalf of an infant. Formerly referred to as a "next friend". Also known as litigation guardian.

GUARDIANSHIP. *n.* 1. "... [T]he full bundle of rights and duties voluntarily assumed by an adult regarding an infant akin to those naturally arising from parenthood ... Guardianship implies the voluntary assumption of a duty to maintain, protect and educate the ward. It includes the power to correct, to grant or withhold consent to marriages and, if the guardian is also the parent, to delegate parental authority... . the full bundle of parental personal rights, including necessarily the entitlement to physical possession of the child... ." *Anson v. Anson* (1987), 10 B.C.L.R. (2d) 357 at 361-2 (Co. Ct.), Huddart Co. Ct. J. 2. The responsibilities associated with custody, other than physical or day to day care and control, are the rights and obligations embodied in the phrase "guardian of the person". *Abbott v. Abbott*, 2001 CarswellBC 420, 2001 BCSC 323, 13 R.F.L. (5th) 233, 89 B.C.L.R. (3d) 68, Pitfield J. 3. The relationship between a person and a child whereby the person has, by a written decision of the competent authority of the country where the child resides, been entrusted with the legal responsibility for the child and is authorized to act on their behalf.

GUARDIANSHIP ORDER. 1. An order which transfers the guardianship of the child, including the custody, care and control of, and all parental rights and responsibilities with respect to, the child. 2. Any order of a court appointing a person as a guardian.

GUEST. *n.* 1. A person who contracts for sleeping accommodation in a hotel and includes each member of that person's party. 2. A person permitted to stay on premises belonging to another; person to whom hospitality is extended. 3. "To be a guest one must be willingly in the vehicle ..." *King v. Hommy* (1962), 39 W.W.R. 209 at 213, 34 D.L.R. (2d) 770 (Alta. C.A.), the court per Johnson J.A.

GUEST STATUTE. A statute which imposes liability in respect of any gratuitous passenger on the driver of a car solely in a case of misconduct or gross negligence which is wanton, wilful or reckless. J.G. Fleming, *The Law of Torts*, 8th ed. (Sydney: Law Book, 1992) at 23.

GUIDANCE. See LOSS OF ~.

GUIDE. *n.* "... [O]ne who accompanies another over unfamiliar terrain being ready to point the way, being ready to give advice, ..." *R. v. Kurth* (1990), 72 Alta. L.R. (2d) 300 at 303, 103 A.R. 75 (Q.B.), Veit J. See DOG ~.

GUIDE ANIMAL. An animal used by a person with a disability to avoid hazards or to assist in compensating for the disability.

GUIDE DOG. A dog which is trained to assist a person who is disabled or has a disease which causes

G

the person to require assistance. See HEARING DOG.

GUIDELINE. *n.* 1. Form of administrative directive which cannot confer enforceable rights, but can be written to be mandatory. 2. Set of expectations for performance. See CHILD SUPPORT ~S.

GUIDELINE SENTENCE. Guideline sentences, also commonly referred to as "starting-point sentences," were introduced by appellate courts beginning in the early 1980s. By setting out starting points for sentencing purposes for certain offences, the courts were able to step past the problems under which each judge's personal view of the seriousness of a crime would drive the final sentence. Therefore, the starting point sentencing regime was - and is - a way by which appellate courts might minimize the risk of widely disparate sentences. The starting point is just that: a starting point from which the sentencing judge may move up or down in order to arrive at a fit sentence appropriate to the particular offender. *R. v. Christie*, 2004 ABCA 287.

GUILT. *n.* The state of having committed a crime or offence or being subject to punishment. See CON-SCIOUSNESS OF ~ EVIDENCE; FINDING OF ~; PATTERN OF FINDINGS OF ~.

GUILTY. *adj.* 1. Having committed a tort or crime. 2. The word used by a prisoner entering a plea and by a convicting jury. 3. "With respect to an accused who has pleaded guilty, such a plea is ordinarily regarded as an admission that the matters alleged in the information are true." *R. v. Rapien* (1954), 18 C.R. 168 at 170, 11 W.W.R. 529, 108 C.C.C. 198 (Alta. C.A.), the court per MacDonald J.A. See FOUND ~; NOT ~.

GUILTY PLEA. An admission that the accused has committed the crime charged and a consent to a conviction being entered without any trial.

GUISE. See DISTINGUISHING ~.

GUN. See HAND~.

GVWR. *abbr.* The gross vehicle weight rating specified by a manufacturer as the maximum design loaded weight of a single vehicle. *Canadian Environmental Protection Act, 1999*, S.C. 1999, c. 33, *On-Road Vehicle and Engine Emission Regulations*, SOR/2003-2, s. 1.

H

HA. *abbr.* Hectare.

HABEAS CORPUS. [L. that you have the body] 1. The writ of habeas corpus is a prerogative writ at common law, the purpose of which is to allow the timely examination of the legality of imprisonment. *Lising v. Kent Institution*, 2008 BCCA 10, Rowles J.A. (Newbury and Low JJ.A. concurring). 2. Acts as a check on the jurisdiction of the convicting court or tribunal to order the detention of the applicant. If the court or tribunal has exceeded its jurisdiction in ordering imprisonment of the accused, resort may be had to habeas corpus to secure the release of the person. Will lie to discharge a prisoner from prison when the prisoner's sentence has expired.

HABENDUM. *n.* [L. having] 1. The first word of a clause which follows a legal description of land which is being granted. 2. "[Part of a deed which] ... is intended to include the designation of the estate or interest to be conveyed in the property described in the premises of the deed such as a term of years, a term for life, a fee simple or the interest in remainder." *Wheeler v. Wheeler (No. 2)* (1979), 25 N.B.R. (2d) 376 at 378, 51 A.P.R. 376 (C.A.), Limerick, Bugold and Ryan JJ.A.

HABIT. *n.* A specific repeated response to a particular situation.

HABITAT. *n.* 1. Land, water or air where a plant, animal or other organism lives. *Endangered Species Act,* S.N.S. 1998, c. 11, s. 3. 2. In respect of aquatic species, spawning grounds and nursery, rearing, food supply, migration and any other areas on which aquatic species depend directly or indirectly in order to carry out their life processes, or areas where aquatic species formerly occurred and have the potential to be reintroduced; and in respect of other wildlife species, the area or type of site where an individual or wildlife species naturally occurs or depends on directly or indirectly in order to carry out its life processes or formerly occurred and has the potential to be reintroduced. *Species at Risk Act,* S.C. 2002, c. 29, s. 2. See FISH ~.

HABITUAL CRIMINAL. The term used for a repeat offender prior to the enactment of the current Criminal Code provisions concerning dangerous offenders. See now DANGEROUS OFFENDER.

HABITUAL RESIDENCE. "... [R]efers to the quality of residence. Duration may be a factor depending on the circumstances. It requires an animus less than that required for domicile; it is a midpoint between domicile and residence ..." *Adderson v. Adderson* (1987), 51 Alta. L.R. (2d) 193 at 198, 7 R.F.L. (3d) 185, 77 A.R. 256, 36 D.L.R. (4th) 361 (C.A.), the court per Laycraft J.A.

HAD AND RECEIVED. See MONEY ~.

HAGUE CONVENTION ON ADOPTION. The Convention on the Protection of Children and Co-operation in respect of Inter-Country Adoption that was concluded on May 29, 1993 and came into force on May 1, 1995. *Immigration and Refugee Protection Act,* S.C. 2001, c. 27, *Immigration and Refugee Protection Regulations,* SOR/2002-227, s. 2.

HAGUE CONVENTION ON SERVICE ABROAD. The Convention on the Service Abroad of Judicial and Extrajudicial Documents in Civil or Commercial Matters signed at the Hague on November 15, 1965. *Federal Courts Act,* R.S.C. 1985, c. F-7, *Federal Court Rules,* C.R.C., c. 663, s. 2.

HAGUE CONVENTIONS. Agreements on rules of international law relating to matters such as the peaceful settlement of international disputes and the conduct of war.

HAIL INSURANCE. Insurance against loss of or damage to growing crops caused by hail. *Insurance Act,* R.S.N.B. 1973, c. I-12, s. 1.

HALF-SECRET TRUST. A legatee is identified in a will as a trustee but the terms of the trust are not spelled out in the will. Extrinsic evidence is admissible to establish the missing terms of the trust.

HALFWAY HOUSE. A group home for persons having recently left a penal or psychiatric institution.

HALLUCINATION. *n.* An illusory sensory perception. F.A. Jaffe, *A Guide to Pathological Evidence for Lawyers and Police Officers,* 4th ed. (Toronto: Carswell, 1999) at 238.

HALLUCINOGENIC DRUG. A drug, such as lysergic acid diethylamide (L.S.D.) or mescaline, which produces hallucinations. F.A. Jaffe, *A Guide to Pathological Evidence for Lawyers and Police Officers,* 4th ed. (Toronto: Carswell, 1999) at 238.

HAMBURGER POLL. During an election a poll relating to the election conducted by matching goods to political candidates or parties. The sales of each item are then considered to match public sentiment concerning the candidates or parties.

HANDBOOK. See CICA ~.

HANDGUN. *n.* A firearm that is designed, altered or intended to be aimed and fired by the action of one hand, whether or not it has been redesigned or subsequently altered to be aimed and fired by the action of both hands. *Criminal Code*, R.S.C. 1985, c. C-46, s. 84(1).

HANSARD. *n.* 1. A record of speeches made in the House of Commons and verbatim answers to written questions from the Order Paper. 2. Also refers to the similar record of debates in a legislative assembly or legislature.

HARASS. *v.* 1. "... '[A]nnoy'." *R. v. Sabine* (1990), 57 C.C.C. (3d) 209 at 212, 78 C.R. (3d) 34, 107 N.B.R. (2d) 73, 267 A.P.R. 73 (Q.B.), Stevenson J. 2. Includes worry, exhaust, fatigue, annoy, plague, pester, tease or torment, but does not include the lawful hunting, trapping or capturing of wildlife. *Wildlife Act*, R.S.B.C. 1996, c. 488, s. 1. 3. To engage in a course of vexatious comment or conduct that is known or ought reasonably to be known to be unwelcome. *Human Rights Code*, R.S.N. 1990, c. H-14, s. 1. 4. Means more than to annoy, to vex. Implies being tormented, troubled, worried continually and chronically, being plagued, bedeviled and badgered. In addition, the conduct of the accused must be shown to have caused the complainant reasonably to fear for her safety or the safety of anyone known to her. *R. v. Sillipp* (1997), 55 Alta. L.R. (3d) 263 (C.A.).

HARASSMENT. *n.* 1. Engaging in a course of vexatious comment or conduct that is known or ought reasonably to be known to be unwelcome. *Human Rights Code*, R.S.O. 1990, c. H.19, s. 10(1). 2. Any inappropriate conduct, comment, display, action or gesture by a person: (i) that either: (A) is based on race, creed, religion, colour, sex, sexual orientation, marital status, family status, disability, physical size or weight, age, nationality, ancestry or place of origin; or (B) subject to subsections (3) and (4), adversely affects the worker's psychological or physical well-being and that the person knows or ought reasonably to know would cause a worker to be humiliated or intimidated; and (ii) that constitutes a threat to the health or safety of the worker. *The Occupational Health and Safety Act, 1993*, S.S. 1993, c. O-1.1, s. 2. See CRIMINAL ~; PERSONAL ~; SEXUAL ~.

HARBOUR. *v.* To give refuge to, to shelter.

HARBOUR. *n.* A place to which ships may resort for shelter or to ship or unship goods or passengers.

HARD CASE. A case in which the court feels compelled to stretch the existing law to accommodate the hardship produced by the actual fact situation on one of the litigants before them. Such decisions are said to make bad law because their logic may be unsupportable in subsequent fact situations where the element of hardship for one of the parties is missing.

HARDSHIP. *n.* Suffering or privation. See ECONOMIC ~; UNDUE ~.

HARM. *v.* To injure; to affect adversely.

HARM. *n.* 1. Connotes an adverse effect on the child's upbringing that is more than transitory. The impugned exercise by the access parent must be shown to create a substantial risk that the child's physical, psychological or moral well-being will be adversely affected. Exposure to new experiences and ideas may upset children and cause them considerable discomfort. *Young v. Young*, 1993 CarswellBC 264, 84 B.C.L.R. (2d) 1, [1993] 8 W.W.R. 513, 49 R.F.L. (3d) 117, 160 N.R. 1, 34 B.C.A.C. 161, 56 W.A.C. 161, 108 D.L.R. (4th) 193, [1993] 4 S.C.R. 3, 18 C.R.R. (2d) 41, [1993] R.D.F. 703, Sopinka J. 2. Any contamination or degradation and includes harm caused by the release of any solid, liquid, gas, odour, heat, sound, vibration or radiation. *Environmental Bill of Rights, 1993,* S.O. 1993, c. 28, s. 1. See BODILY ~; IRREPARABLE ~; PSYCHOLOGICAL ~.

HARMLESS. See HOLD ~.

HARMONIZATION. *n.* The objectives of harmonization of federal legislation with the civil law of Quebec are to ensure that federal legislation is fully consistent with the new civil law concepts and institutions, that federal legislation employs correct and precise terminology, and that amendments to federal legislation take into account French common law terminology. Let me be clear that Harmonization Act, Bill S-4 does not create substantive rights or enshrine any new individual or collective rights. *Schreiber v. Canada (Attorney General)*, [2002] 3 S.C.R. 269. See SALES TAX ~ AGREEMENT.

HARMONIZED SALES TAX. Five provinces, British Columbia, Nova Scotia, New Brunswick, Newfoundland and Labrador, and Ontario, have harmonized their provincial sales tax with GST to create Harmonized Sales Tax (HST). HST follows the same general rules as GST.

HARM PRINCIPLE. The State has no right to interfere with the personal freedom and liberty of an individual unless that individual causes harm to other persons or to society in general. The harm principle is not the constitutional standard for what conduct may or may not be the subject of the criminal law for the purposes of s. 7. The 'harm principle' is better characterized as a description of an important state interest rather than a normative 'legal' principle. There is nevertheless a state interest in the avoidance of harm to those subject to its laws which may justify parliamentary action. Avoidance of harm is a 'state interest' within the rule against arbitrary or irrational state conduct. *R. v. Malmo-Levine*, 2003 SCC 74.

HARR. & HODG. *abbr.* Harrison & Hodgins' Municipal Reports (Ontario), 1845-1851.

HAS AS ITS OBJECT. In interpreting this phrase [n section 15(2) of the Charter], two issues arise. The first is whether courts should look to the purpose or to the effect of legislation. The second is whether, in order to qualify for s. 15(2) protection, a program must have an ameliorative purpose as its sole object, or whether having such a goal as one of several objectives is sufficient. There is nothing to suggest that a test focussed on the goal of legislation must slavishly accept the government's characterization of its purpose. Courts could well examine legislation to ensure that the declared purpose is genuine. *R.v. Kapp*, 2008 SCC 41, McLachlin C.J. and Abella J. for the majority.

HASH. *n.* "... [A] colloquial term for hashish." *R. v. O'Brien* (1987), 41 C.C.C. (3d) 86 at 88, 10 Q.A.C. 135, the court per McCarthy J.A.

HASHISH. *n.* A resinous juice found in the upper leaves and the flowering tops of the plant Cannabis sativa. F.A. Jaffe, *A Guide to Pathological Evidence for Lawyers and Police Officers*, 4th ed. (Toronto: Carswell, 1999) at 238.

HATE PROPAGANDA. 1. Any writing, sign or visible representation that advocates or promotes genocide or the communication of which by any person would constitute an offence under section 319. *Criminal Code*, R.S.C. 1985, c. C-46, s. 320(8) as am. 2. "... [E]xpression intended or likely to create extreme feelings of opprobrium and enmity against a racial or religious group, ..." *R. v. Keegstra* (1990), 61 C.C.C. (3d) 1 at 18, 1 C.R. (4th) 129, 77 Alta. L.R. (2d) 193, [1991] 2 W.W.R. 1, 117 N.R. 1, 114 A.R. 81, 3 C.R.R. (2d) 193, [1990] 3 S.C.R. 697, Dickson C.J.C. (Wilson, L'Heureux-Dubé and Gonthier JJ. concurring).

HATRED. *n.* 1. "[In s. 319(2) of the Criminal Code, R.S.C. 1985, c. C-46] ... connotes emotion of an intense and extreme nature that is clearly associated with vilification and detestation... . a most extreme emotion that belies reason; an emotion, that, if exercised against members of an identifiable group, implies that those individuals are to be despised, scorned, denied respect and made subject to ill-treatment on the basis of group affiliation." *R. v. Keegstra* (1990), 3 C.R.R. (2d) 193 at 249, 1 C.R. (4th) 129, 77 Alta. L.R. (2d) 193, [1991] 2 W.W.R. 1, 61 C.C.C. (3d) 1, 117 N.R. 1, 114 A.R. 81, [1990] 3 S.C.R. 697, Dickson C.J.C. (Wilson, L'Heureux-Dubé and Gonthier JJ. concurring). 2. As referred to in human rights legislation, extreme ill-will and an emotion which allows for no redeeming qualities in the persons to whom it is directed; and unusually strong and deepfelt emotions of detestation, calumny and vilification. *Canada (Human Rights Commission) v. Taylor*, [1990] 3 S.C.R. 892, at 928, 75 D.L.R. (4th) 577, 13 C.H.R.R. D/435, 3 C.R.R. (2d) 116, 117 N.R. 191, Dickson C.J.C. See COMMERCIAL SPEECH; FREEDOM OF EXPRESSION.

HAVE. *v.* "... '[P]ossess'." *R. v. Theriault* (1951), 28 M.P.R. 412 at 417, 101 C.C.C. 233 (N.B. C.A.), Harrison J.A.

HAVE NO ISSUE. A want or failure of issue in the lifetime or at the time of death of that person, and not an indefinite failure of issue unless a contrary intention appears by the will. *Wills acts*.

HAVING. *v.* Controlling; possessing; giving birth to.

HAZARD. *n.* A danger. A risk.

HAZARDOUS AGENT. A prescribed thing that (a) may cause a risk to health if a person is contaminated with the thing, or (b) indicates the presence of a contaminant that could cause a risk to health. *Public Health Act*, S.B.C. 2008, c. 28, s. 1.

HAZARDOUS SUBSTANCE. Includes a controlled product and a chemical, biological or physical agent that, by reason of a property that the agent possesses, is hazardous to the safety or health of a person exposed to it. *Canada Labour Code*, R.S.C. 1985, c. L-2, s. 122.

HAZARD SYMBOL. Includes any design, mark, pictogram, sign, letter, word, number, abbreviation or any combination thereof that is to be displayed on a controlled product, or a container in which a controlled product is packaged, in order to show the nature of the hazard of the controlled product. *Hazardous Products Act*, R.S.C. 1985, c. H-3, s. 11.

H.C. *abbr.* 1. High Court of Justice. 2. Haute Cour.

HEAD. *n.* In respect of a government institution, means (a) in the case of a department or ministry of state, the member of the Queen's Privy Council for Canada who presides over the department or ministry, or (b) in any other case, either the person designated under subsection 3.2(2) to be the head of the institution for the purposes of this Act or, if no such person is designated, the chief executive officer of the institution, whatever their title. *Access to Information Act*, R.S.C. 1985, c. A-1, s. 3. See DEPARTMENT ~; DEPUTY ~; OVER~.

HEADING. *n.* A text prefixed to a section or group of sections in a modern statute. P.St.J. Langan, ed., *Maxwell on The Interpretation of Statutes*, 12th ed. (Bombay: N.M. Tripathi, 1976) at 11.

H

HEADNOTE. *n.* The Federal Court of Appeal [2002 CarswellNat 1000] held that "headnotes", defined as including the summary of the case, catchlines, statement of the case, case title and case information, are more than mere copies and hence "original" works in which copyright subsists. It found that the headnotes are more than simply an abridged version of the reasons; they consist of independently composed features. As Linden J.A. explained, at para. 73, the authors of the headnotes could have chosen to make the summaries "long or short, technical or simple, dull or dramatic, well written or confusing; the organization and presentation might have varied greatly"... Although headnotes are inspired in large part by the judgment which they summarize and refer to, they are clearly not an identical copy of the reasons. The authors must select specific elements of the decision and can arrange them in numerous different ways. Making these decisions requires the exercise of skill and judgment. The authors must use their knowledge about the law and developed ability to determine legal ratios to produce the headnotes. They must also use their capacity for discernment to decide which parts of the judgment warrant inclusion in the headnotes. This process is more than just a mechanical exercise. Thus the headnotes constitute "original" works in which copyright subsists. *CCH Canadian Ltd. v. Law Society of Upper Canada*, 2004 SCC 13.

HEAD OFFICE. 1. The principal office or place of business of a corporation. 2. The place where the chief executive officer of an insurer carries on business. *Insurance acts. 3.* The office required to be maintained under the governing statute. Federal statutes.

HEAD OF MISSION. (a) An ambassador, high commissioner or consul-general of Canada; (b) or any other person appointed to represent Canada in another country or a portion of another country or at an international organization or diplomatic conference and designated head of mission by the Governor in Council. *Department of Foreign Affairs and International Trade Act,* R.S.C. 1985, c. E-22, s. 13(1).

HEALTH. *n.* 1. "... [N]ot merely ... the absence of disease and infirmity, but ... a state of physical, mental and social well-being." *R. v. Morgentaler* (1988), 62 C.R. (3d) 1 at 29-30, 82 N.R. 1, [1988] 1 S.C.R. 30, 63 O.R. (2d) 281n, 26 O.A.C. 1, 44 D.L.R. (4th) 385, 31 C.R.R. 1, 37 C.C.C. (3d) 449, Dickson C.J.C. (Lamer J. concurring). 2. A state of complete physical, mental and social well-being. See E-~; NATURAL ~ PRODUCT; OCCUPATIONAL ~ AND SAFETY; PUBLIC ~ AGENCY.

HEALTH CANADA. The federal ministry which conducts ongoing consultations with Canadians to determine how to best meet their long-term health care needs, communicates information about disease prevention to protect Canadians from avoidable risks, and encourages Canadians to take an active role in their health, such as increasing their level of physical activity and eating well. *About Health Canada,* on-line: Health Canada main page, <http://www.hc-sc.gc.ca/ahc-asc/index-eng.php>.

HEALTH CARE. See PRIMARY ~.

HEALTH CARE SERVICES. See EXTENDED ~; FUTURE COST OF ~; PAST COST OF ~.

HEALTH CARE SERVICES CLAIM. In relation to personal injury suffered by a beneficiary, means a claim for the recovery of the past and future costs of health care services attributable to that personal injury. *Health Care Costs Recovery Act,* S.B.C. 2008, c. 27, s. 1.

HEALTH CLUB. A health club is generally understood to mean a facility where people sign up as members for a fee, giving them access to the facilities for a defined period of time, usually measured in months or all or part of a year. The facilities include, as a predominant feature, weight machines, exercise machines and other apparatus and facilities designed for the development of physical fitness. It is customary to have change and shower facilities on the premises. A health club could also include features such as a steam room, a sauna, a spa and perhaps even swimming facilities. Therapeutic massage would normally be considered as an appropriate component of a health club. *1423107 Ontario Inc. v. Woodstock (City),* 2001 CarswellOnt 1204, 200 D.L.R. (4th) 175, 19 M.P.L.R. (3d) 256, (S.C.J.) Heeney J.

HEALTH IMPEDIMENT. A prescribed condition, thing or activity (a) the cumulative effects of which, over a period of time, are likely to adversely affect public health, (b) that causes significant chronic disease or disability in the population, (c) that interferes with or is inconsistent with the goals of public health initiatives respecting the prevention of injury or illness in the population, including chronic disease or disability, or (d) that is associated with poor health within the population. *Public Health Act,* S.B.C. 2008, c. 28, s. 1.

HEALTH INFORMATION. See PERSONAL ~.

HEALTH INFORMATION BANK. A health information bank established or designated under section 3. *E-Health (Personal Health Information Access and Protection of Privacy) Act,* S.B.C. 2008, c. 38, s. 1.

HEALTH LAW. The law governing the healing professions and hospitals and other care-giving facilities.

HEALTH L. CAN. *abbr.* Health Law in Canada.

HEALTH RESEARCH. See CANADIAN INSTITUTES OF ~.

HEAR. See RE~.

HEARD. *v.* 1. Refers to a hearing on the merits. 2. Heard and disposed of.

HEARING. *n.* 1. "... [N]ormally ... an oral hearing. But ... a statutory board, acting in an administrative capacity, may ... [hear applications] on written evidence and arguments, ..." *Knight v. Indian Head School Division No. 19* (1990), 43 Admin. L.R. 157 at 189, 30 C.C.E.L. 237, [1990] 3 W.W.R. 289, [1990] 1 S.C.R. 653, 106 N.R. 17, 83 Sask. R. 81, 69 D.L.R. (4th) 489, 90 C.L.L.C. 14,010, L'Heureux-Dubé J. (Dickson C.J.C., La Forest and Cory JJ. concurring) quoting and agreeing with H.W.R. Wade, *Administrative Law,* 5th ed. (Oxford: Clarendon Press, 1982) at 482-3. 2. The right to be heard by the decision-maker with a full opportunity to lay before him all the pertinent facts supporting his side of the issue. 3. Generic label to describe trials, appeals, and interlocutory proceedings. 4. Need not be an auditory event. Evidence can be in written form. See COSTS OF THIS ~; DE NOVO ~; ELECTRONIC ~; FAIR ~; ORAL ~; PRELIMINARY ~; PUBLIC ~; REGISTRAR'S ~; RE-~; SENTENCING ~; TRANSFER ~; WRITTEN ~.

HEARING DE NOVO. "... [I]s ... an altogether fresh or new hearing and not limited to an inquiry to determine if the tribunal acted properly and correctly on the evidence and material before it... ." *Newterm Ltd., Re* (1988), 38 M.P.L.R. 17 at 19, 70 Nfld. & P.E.I.R. 216, 215 A.P.R. 216 (Nfld. T.D.), Steele J. See DE NOVO HEARING.

HEARING DOG. A dog trained as a guide for a deaf person.

HEARSAY. *n.* 1. Evidence of something that was said by another person. 2. Gossip. See DOUBLE ~; PRINCIPLED APPROACH TO ~.

HEARSAY EVIDENCE. 1. "Evidence of a statement made to a witness by a person who is not himself called as a witness may or may not be hearsay. It is hearsay and inadmissible when the object is to establish the truth of what is contained in the statement. It is not hearsay and is admissible when it is proposed to establish by the evidence, not the truth of the statement, but the fact it was made. The fact that the statement was made, quite apart from its truth, is frequently relevant in considering the mental state and conduct thereafter of the witness or of some other person in whose presence the statement was made." *Subramaniam v. Public Prosecutor*, [1956] 1 W.L.R. 965 at 970 (Malaya P.C.). 2. Is defined not by the nature of the evidence *per se*, but by the use to which that evidence is sought to be put: namely, to prove that what is asserted is true . ... Narrative is not considered hearsay as it is not given for the truth of its contents. *R. v. Magloir*, 2003 NSCA 74, 216 N.S.R. (2d) 257.

HEARSAY RULE. 1. Evidence of the written, oral or communicative conduct of a person who is not testifying is inadmissible as proof of the truth of the statements or as proof of the implied assertions contained in the statements. 2. A hearsay statement will be admissible for the truth of its contents if it meets the separate requirements of "necessity" and "reliability". These two requirements serve to minimize the evidentiary dangers normally associated with the evidence of an out-of-court declarant, namely the absence of an oath or affirmation, the inability of the trier of fact to assess the demeanour of the declarant, and the lack of contemporaneous cross-examination. *R. v. Hawkins*, [1996] 3 S.C.R. 1043. See RULE AGAINST HEARSAY.

HEAVY HOUSEKEEPING. The physical ability of the insured, or the insured's requirement to have verbal cuing, to carry out major household duties, including vacuuming, cleaning curtains, washing floors, walls, and windows, cleaning bathrooms and appliances. *The Automobile Accident Insurance Act*, R.S.S. 1978, c. A-35, *The Personal Injury Benefits Regulations*, R.R.S., c. A-35, Reg. 3, Appendix D, Grid A, s. 2.

HECKLING. *n.* Interruption of a speaker by any loud or audible words or noises directed at the issue upon which the speaker is speaking.

HEDGER. *n.* A person or company that carries on agricultural, mining, forestry, processing, manufacturing, importing, exporting, investment, financial or other commercial activities or services and, as a necessary part of the activities or services, becomes exposed to risks attendant upon fluctuations in (a) the price of a commodity that the person or company owns, produces, manufactures, processes, merchandises or anticipates owning, producing, manufacturing, processing or merchandising, (b) the value of liabilities that the person or company owes or anticipates incurring, or (c) the value of services that the person or company provides or purchases or anticipates providing or purchasing, and the person or company offsets the risks by trading in contracts for the commodity or related commodities and the trades are economically appropriate to the reduction of the risks incurred by the person or company in the conduct of the affairs or the operation of the business of the person or company. *The Commodity Futures Act*, S.M. 1996, c. 73, s. 1.

HEDGE TRADE. A trade in a contract by a hedger where the trade is economically appropriate to the reduction of the risks incurred or to be incurred by the hedger. *The Commodity Futures Act*, S.M. 1996, c. 73, s. 1.

HEDGING. *n.* 1. The fixing of a price for a mineral commodity before delivery by means of a forward sale or a futures contract on a recognized commodity exchange, or the purchase or sale forward of a foreign currency related directly to the proceeds of the sale of the processed product of the mineral output, but does not include speculative currency hedging except to the extent that any one of these transactions determine the final price and proceeds for the product. *Mining Tax Act*, R.S.O. 1990, c. M.15, s. 1. 2. The entering into of a derivatives transaction or a series of derivatives transactions, and the maintaining of the position or positions resulting from the transaction or series of transactions if (1) the intended effect of the transaction or series of transactions is (a) to offset or reduce the risk related to fluctuations in the value of an underlying interest or a position, or of a group of underlying interests or positions; or (b) to substitute a risk to one currency for a risk to another currency, provided the aggregate amount of currency risk to which the hedger is exposed is not increased by the substitution; (2) the transaction or series of transactions results in a high degree of negative correlation between changes in the value of the underlying interest or position or group of underlying interests or positions being hedged and changes in the value of the derivatives with which the value of the underlying interests or positions is hedged; and (3) there are reasonable grounds to believe that the transaction or series of transactions no more than offsets the effect of price changes in the underlying interest or position, or group of underlying interests or positions, being hedged. *Derivatives Act*, R.S.Q. c. I-14.01, s. 3.

HEEDLESS. *adj.* Other cases have equated "heedless" with a "complete disregard" for the consequences of one's actions. For example, in R. v. Melnyk (1985), 41 Sask. R. 10 (Sask. Q.B.), affirmed (1985), 45 Sask. R. 258 (Sask. C.A.), Scheibel J. entered a conviction on a charge of criminal negligence in the operation of a motor vehicle. He wrote (at para. 62): "The accused's conduct was heedless and indifferent and showed a complete disregard for the consequences of his actions." *R. v. Tayfel*, 2009 MBCA 124.

HEIR. *n.* 1. "... [T]he party to which by the operation of law alone or by the will of man, the estate, rights and liabilities of the deceased are transmitted." *Levesque v. Turcotte* (1931), 12 C.B.R. 290 at 297, 69 Que. S.C. 148, Lemieux J. 2. Includes a person beneficially entitled to property of an intestate. See CO- ; EXPECTANT ~; ~S; JOINT ~; ULTIMATE ~.

HEIR APPARENT. One whose right of inheritance is indisputable provided the ancestor dies first; the eldest son of the sovereign.

HEIRESS. *n.* A female heir. See CO-~.

HEIRLOOM. *n.* Originally personal chattels like evidences of title, deeds and charters which went to an heir along with the inheritance.

H

HEIR PRESUMPTIVE. A person likely to be heir if the ancestor dies immediately but who could be displaced if a nearer heir is born.

HEIRS. *n.* "... [T]he person or persons to whom the land of another person descends by operation of law, when that other person dies intestate." *Sparks v. Wolff* (1898), 25 O.A.R. 326 at 334, (C.A.), MacLennan J.A. See HEIR.

HEIRSHIP. *n.* The condition or quality of being an heir; the relation between an heir and an ancestor.

HELD. *v.* 1. Decided, as in "The court held that X owed Y a sum of money". 2. Maintained; possessed of; having title to. See HOLD.

HELD. *adj.* Decided.

HELPING. See OATH-~.

HEMP. *n.* Cannabis.

HENRY VIII CLAUSE. A clause in a statute permitting the executive to amend the statute by regulation or to make regulations inconsistent with the statute.

HEREDITAMENT. *n.* Any kind of property which may be inherited. *Tomkins v. Jones* (1889), 22 Q.B.D. 599 at 602 (U.K. C.A.), Bowen L.J. See CORPOREAL ~; INCORPOREAL ~; LANDS, TENEMENTS AND ~S.

HEREIN. *adv.* 1. Used in any section shall be understood to relate to the whole enactment, and not to that section only. *Interpretation Act*, R.S.C. 1985, c. I-21, s. 35. 2. Used in a section or part of an enactment, shall be construed as referring to the whole enactment and not to that section, provision or part only. *Interpretation Act*, R.S.A. 2000, c. I-8, s. 28.

HEREINAFTER. *prep.* Later in the same document.

HEREINBEFORE. *prep.* Earlier in the same document.

HERETOFORE. *prep.* 1. Earlier in the same document. 2. Relates to the date of coming into force of the provision in which they are used. *Legislation Act, 2006*, S.O. 2006, c. 21, Sched. F, s. 87.

HEREUNDER. *prep.* Later in the same document.

HERITAGE. See DEPARTMENT OF CANADIAN ~; MULTICULTURAL ~.

HERITAGE CHARACTER. The overall effect produced by traits or features which give property or an area a distinctive quality or appearance.

HERITAGE PROPERTY. Property that (a) in the opinion of a body or person anthorized to exercise a power under this Act or the Community Charter in relation to the property, has sufficient heritage value or heritage character to justify its conservation, or (b) is protected heritage property. *Local Government Act*, R.S.B.C. 1996, c. 323, s. 5.

HERITAGE VALUE. The historical, cultural, aesthetic, scientific or educational worth or usefulness of property or an area.

HER MAJESTY. 1. Her Majesty in right of Canada or of a province. 2. The Sovereign of the United Kingdom, Canada and Her other Realms and Territories, and Head of the Commonwealth. *Interpretation Act*, R.S.C. 1985, c. I-21, s. 35.

HER MAJESTY'S CANADIAN SHIP. Any vessel of the Canadian Forces commissioned as a vessel of war. *National Defence Act*, R.S.C. 1985, c. N-5, s. 2.

HER MAJESTY'S FORCES. The naval, army and air forces of Her Majesty wherever raised, and includes the Canadian Forces; *Criminal Code*, R.S.C. 1985, c. C-46, s. 2.

HEROIN. *n.* Diacetyl morphine, a partly-synthetic narcotic analgesic derived from morphine. F.A. Jaffe, *A Guide to Pathological Evidence for Lawyers and Police Officers*, 4th ed. (Toronto: Carswell, 1999) at 86.

HERRING. See RED ~.

HETEROSEXUALITY. *n.* The state of being sexually attracted to members of the opposite sex.

HE WHO COMES INTO EQUITY MUST COME WITH CLEAN HANDS. When a plaintiff seeks the assistance of a court of equity, that plaintiff must be prepared to act fairly and properly and must be able to show that past behaviour regarding the transaction is beyond reproach. P.V. Baker & P. St. J. Langan, eds., *Snell's Equity*, 29th ed. (London: Sweet & Maxwell, 1990) at 31-2. See CLEAN HANDS DOCTRINE.

HE WHO SEEKS EQUITY MUST DO EQUITY. "... In many instances this contains a pun on the word 'equity' and means nothing more than that, 'he who seeks the assistance of a Court of Equity must in the matter in which he so asks assistance do what is just as a term of receiving such assistance.' 'Equity' means 'Chancery' in one instance and 'right' or 'fair dealing' in the other." *Richards v. Collins* (1912), 27 O.L.R. 3909 at 398, 9 D.L.R. 249 (Div. Ct.), Riddell J. (Falconbridge C.J. and Lennox J. concurring).

HEYDON'S CASE. See RULE IN ~.

HIGHEST AND BEST USE. In expropriation law, the use which supports the highest value for the property provided it is physically possible, appropriately supported and financially feasible.

HIGH-RATIO MORTGAGE. A mortgage of real property under the security of which is advanced an amount that, when added to amounts advanced under mortgages ranking equally with or in priority to the mortgage, exceeds 75% of the value of the real property. *Business Practices and Consumer Protection Act*, S.B.C. 2004, c. 2, s. 57.

HIGH SEAS. 1. The area of the ocean beyond territorial waters. 2. Any body of water, or frozen surface thereof, that is not within the territorial waters of any state. *Aeronautics Act*, R.S.C. 1985, c. A-2, *Canadian Aviation Regulations*, SOR 96-433, s. 101.01.

HIGH-STICKING. *n.* In hockey, striking an opponent's head with an uplifted stick.

HIGH TREASON. Anyone commits high treason in Canada who kills or attempts to kill Her Majesty, or does her any bodily harm tending to death or destruction, maims or wounds her or imprisons or restrains her; levies war against Canada or does any act preparatory thereto; or assists an enemy at war with Canada, or any armed forces against whom Canadian Forces are engaged in hostilities whether or not a state of war exists between Canada and the country whose forces they are, and a Canadian citizen or person who owes allegiance to Her Majesty in right of Canada commits high treason who does any of these acts while in or out of Canada. *Criminal Code*, R.S.C. 1985, c. C-46, s. 46(1) and (3).

HIGHWAY. *n.* 1. "... [A] public road or way open equally to everyone for travel, and includes the public streets of an urban district equally with connecting roads between urban districts." *Consumers' Gas Co. v. Toronto (City)*, [1940] 4 D.L.R. 670 at 672, [1941] O.R. 175, 52 C.R.T.C. 98 (C.A.), Robertson C.J.O. 2. A road to which the public has the right of access, and includes bridges over which or tunnels through which a road passes. *Criminal Code*, R.S.C. 1985, c. C-46, s. 2. See PUBLIC ~.

HIJACKING. *n.* Unlawfully, by force or threat thereof, or by any form of intimidation, seizing or exercising control of an aircraft with intent (a) to cause any person on board the aircraft to be confined or imprisoned against his will, (b) to cause any person on board the aircraft to be transported against his will to any place other than the next scheduled place of landing of the aircraft, (c) to hold any person on board the aircraft for ransom or to service against his will, or (d) to cause the aircraft to deviate in a material respect from its flight plan. *Criminal Code*, R.S.C. 1985, c. C-46, s. 76.

HIMALAYA CLAUSE. The bill of lading expressly extended the benefit of a limitation of liability on third parties [to those it employed] such as stevedores, which is the essence of a "Himalaya clause." *London Drugs Ltd. v. Kuehne & Nagel International Ltd.* (1992), 1992 CarswellBC 315, 73 B.C.L.R. (2d) 1, [1992] 3 S.C.R. 299, (*sub nom. London Drugs Ltd. v. Brassart*) 143 N.R. 1, 18 B.C.A.C. 1, 31 W.A.C. 1, 43 C.C.E.L. 1, 13 C.C.L.T. (2d) 1, [1993] 1 W.W.R. 1, 97 D.L.R. (4th) 261, Iacobucci J.

HIRE. *n.* 1. A bailment for compensation or a reward; hiring something to use; labour and work, services and care to be bestowed or performed on the thing delivered, or the carriage of goods from one place to another. 2. Any payment, consideration, gratuity or benefit, directly or indirectly charged, demanded, received or collected by any person for the use of an aircraft. *Aeronautics Act*, R.S.C. 1985, c. A-2, s. 3.

HIRE-PURCHASE AGREEMENT. An agreement under which the hirer can, at the end of the term of the agreement, terminate the agreement or purchase the goods governed by the agreement.

HIS MAJESTY. The Sovereign of the United Kingdom, Canada and His other Realms and Territories, and Head of the Commonwealth.

HISTORIC COMPROMISE. In workers compensation law the compromise by which workers lost the right to sue their employers in return to entitlement to compensation for work-related injuries which was not dependent on the employer's fault or the employer's ability to pay.

HISTORIC TRADEOFF. In workers compensation law the compromise by which workers lost the right to sue their employers in return to entitlement to compensation for work-related injuries which was not dependent on the employer's fault or the employer's ability to pay.

HISTORY. *n.* In "history that indicates a pattern of findings of guilt" [as used in s. 39(1)(c) of Youth Criminal Justice Act] means: 1) the previous findings of guilt for which the young person has already been sentenced; 2) the finding(s) of guilt which is/are the subject of the s. 39(1)(c) consideration; and 3) other findings of guilt for which the young person has yet to be sentenced, which are also before the court for sentencing on that day and which occurred either previously or subsequently to the offence(s) which is/are the subject of the s. 39(1)(c) consideration. *R. v. M. (D.J.)*, 2007 MBCA 98. See CRIMINAL ~; EMPLOYMENT ~; LEGISLATIVE ~; MEDICAL ~; PROSECUTION ~ ESTOPPEL.

HIT AND RUN. "[A case] ... where, with the intent to escape civil or criminal liability, the driver of a motor vehicle involved in a motor vehicle accident fails to stop and give his name and address and where necessary to offer assistance." *Leggett v. Insurance Corp. of British Columbia* (1991), 50 C.C.L.I. 246 at 254 (B.C. S.C.), Harvey J.

H.L. *abbr.* House of Lords.

HODG. *abbr.* Hodgins Election Cases (Ontario), 1871-1878.

HODGES'S CASE. See RULE IN ~.

HOLD. *v.* 1. To be possessed of; to have title to; to have; to occupy. 2. Of a judge, to pronounce a legal opinion.

HOLD. *n.* See CAROTID ~; CHOKE ~; FREE~; LEASE~.

HOLDBACK. *var.* **HOLD BACK.** Amount required under a builders or construction lien act to be deducted from payments made under a contract or a sub-contract and retained for a period prescribed.

HOLDER. *n.* 1. (a) In respect of a security certificate, the person in possession of the certificate issued or endorsed to that person or to bearer or in blank, and (b) in respect of the ownership of a share, the shareholder of the share within the meaning of section 7. *Bank Act*, S.C. 1991, c. 46, s. 2. 2. The payee or endorsee of a bill or note who is in possession of it, or the bearer thereof. *Bills of Exchange Act*, R.S.C. 1985, c. B-4, s. 2. 2. The payee or endorsee of a bill or note who is in possession of it, or the bearer thereof. *Bills of Exchange Act*, R.S.C. 1985, c. B-4, s. 2. See ENTITLEMENT ~; FREE~; INTERMENT RIGHTS ~; LIEN~; POLICY~; PROXY~; SCATTERING RIGHTS ~; SHARE~; STAKE~.

HOLDER FOR VALUE. Someone who gives valuable consideration for a bill, who has a lien on it, or who claims through another holder for value. E.L.G. Tyler & N.E. Palmer, eds., *Crossley Vaines' Personal*

H

Property, 5th ed. (London: Butterworths, 1973) at 232.

HOLDER IN DUE COURSE. A holder who has taken a bill, complete and regular on the face of it, under the following conditions, namely, (a) that he became the holder of it before it was overdue and without notice that it had been previously dishonoured, if such was the fact; and (b) that he took the bill in good faith and for value, and that at the time the bill was negotiated to him he had no notice of any defect in the title of the person who negotiated it. *Bills of Exchange Act*, R.S.C. 1985, c. B-4, s. 55.

HOLD HARMLESS. To assume liability in a situation and relieve the other party of responsibility.

HOLDING. *n.* 1. Refers to property owned, usually in the form of shares or other securities. 2. Land rented to a tenant. 3. Sometimes used to refer to the decision of a court or tribunal especially on a particular issue.

HOLDING BODY CORPORATE. A body corporate is the holding body corporate of any entity that is its subsidiary. *Bank Act*, S.C. 1991, c. 46, s. 4.

HOLDING COMPANY. 1. A company the primary purpose of which is owning shares of one or more other companies. 2. In respect of an entity, a corporation that controls the entity. *Insurance Act*, R.S.O. 1990, c. I.8, s. 437.12. See INVESTMENT ~.

HOLDING OUT. 1. Representing oneself as qualified and properly authorized to practise a profession or trade. 2. Representing oneself as, lending one's credit to, a business or firm.

HOLDING TRUST. The trustee retains assets until required under an independent agreement to transfer the assets to specific persons. D.M.W. Waters, *The Law of Trusts in Canada*, 2d ed. (Toronto: Carswell, 1984) at p. 101.

HOLD OVER. For a lessee to keep possession of land after the lease has expired.

HOLDS OUT. "... [P]resents himself ..." *British Columbia (Attorney General) v. Cowen*, [1939] 1 D.L.R. 288 at 290, [1939] S.C.R. 20, Kerwin J.

HOLD-UP. *n.* A robbery.

HOLOGRAPH. *n.* A deed or writing written completely by the grantor.

HOLOGRAPH WILL. A will written entirely in the testator's own hand.

HOME. See DIRECT TO ~ BROADCASTING; FLOATING ~; FOSTER ~; LAND LEASE ~; MANUFACTURED ~; MARITAL ~; MOBILE ~.

HOME ECONOMICS. See PRACTICE OF ~.

HOME INVASION. The crime ... constitutes a home invasion because it was characterized by the invaders' forced entry into the victims' home for purposes of committing a theft or robbery, knowing that (or being reckless as to whether) the home was being occupied, and by the accompanying use or threatened use of violence with guns, together with the confine-

ment of the occupants of the home. *R. v. Wright* (2006), 83 O.R. (3d) 427 (C.A.).

HOMELESS PERSON. A person who has neither a fixed address nor a predictable safe residence to return to on a daily basis. Without endorsing that particular formulation as definitive, we find it to be a good working description of what is meant by a "homeless person" for the purposes of the order. *Victoria (City) v. Adams*, 2009 BCCA 563, 100 B.C.L.R. (4th) 28.

HOMEOWNER POLICY. See MULTI-PERIL POLICY.

HOMESTEAD. *n.* 1. (i) The house and buildings occupied by a farmer as his bona fide farm residence; and (ii) the farm land on which the house and buildings mentioned in subclause (i) are situated, not exceeding 160 acres or one quarter section, whichever is greater. *The Saskatchewan Farm Security Act*, S.S. 1988-89, c. S-17.1, s. 2. 2. A parcel of land (i) on which the dwelling house occupied by the owner of the parcel as the owner's residence is situated, and (ii) that consists of (A) not more than 4 adjoining lots in one block in a city, town or village as shown on a plan registered in the land titles office, or (B) not more than one quarter section of land other than land in a city, town or village. *Dower Act*, R.S.A. 2000, c. D-15, s. 1. 3. Land or any interest in it entitling the owner to possession of it that is registered in the records of the land title office in the name of the husband or wife and on which there is a dwelling occupied by the husband and wife as their residence, or that has been so occupied within the period of one year immediately preceding the date of the making of the application under section 2. *Land (Spouse Protection) Act*, R.S.B.C. 1996, c. 246, s. 1.

HOME-TRADE VOYAGE. A voyage, not being an inland or minor waters voyage, between places within the area following, namely, Canada, the United States other than Hawaii, St. Pierre and Miquelon, the West Indies, Mexico, Central America and the northeast coast of South America, in the course of which a ship does not go south of the sixth parallel of north latitude. *Merchant Seamen Compensation Act*, R.S.C. 1985, c. M-6, s. 2.

HOMEWORKER. *n.* An individual who performs work for compensation in premises occupied by the individual primarily as residential quarters but does not include an independent contractor. *Employment Standards Act, 2000*, S.O. 2000, c. 41, s. 1.

HOMICIDE. *n.* Directly or indirectly, by any means, causing the death of a human being. *Criminal Code*, R.S.C. 1985, c. C-46, s. 222(1). See CULPABLE ~; JUSTIFIABLE ~; MURDER; NON CULPABLE ~.

HOMOLOGATION. *n.* In civil law, a judicial confirmation of an arbitration award or appointment.

HOMOSEXUALITY. *n.* The state of being sexually attracted to members of one's own sex.

HONEST BELIEF. A belief held in good faith.

HONEST MISTAKE. Bona fide error in judgment. Connotes an action which is wrong but made without mental awareness of its being wrong on the part of the actor.

HONORARIUM. *n.* 1. "... (... [W]hich really means a gift on assuming an office, is now often used as equivalent to 'salary' by those who do not like to think they receive wages)." *Lavere v. Smith's Falls Public Hospital* (1915), 26 D.L.R. 346 at 347, 35 O.L.R. 98 (C.A.), Riddell J.A. 2. "... [A] compensation for services rendered, it is nevertheless not a payment for which the recipient, if not paid, could sue in a Court of law. It is thus in the nature of an ex gratia or gratuitous payment, unlike a salary or wage or other contracted remuneration... ." *Vladicka v. Calgary Board of Education* (1974), 45 D.L.R. (3d) 442 at 453, [1974] 4 W.W.R. 149 (Alta. T.D.), McDonald J.

HONOUR. *v.* 1. For a drawee to accept a bill of exchange. 2. For the maker of a note or the acceptor of a bill to pay it.

HONOUR. *n.* A title applied to judges and other officials.

HONOURABLE. *adj.* A title applied to judges and ministers of the Crown.

HONOUR OF THE CROWN. The historical roots of the principle of the honour of the Crown suggest that it must be understood generously in order to reflect the underlying realities from which it stems. In all its dealings with Aboriginal peoples, from the assertion of sovereignty to the resolution of claims and the implementation of treaties, the Crown must act honourably. Nothing less is required if we are to achieve "the reconciliation of the pre-existence of aboriginal societies with the sovereignty of the Crown." The honour of the Crown gives rise to different duties in different circumstances. Where the Crown has assumed discretionary control over specific Aboriginal interests, the honour of the Crown gives rise to a fiduciary duty. The honour of the Crown also infuses the processes of treaty making and treaty interpretation. In making and applying treaties, the Crown must act with honour and integrity, avoiding even the appearance of "sharp dealing." Honourable negotiation implies a duty to consult with Aboriginal claimants and conclude an honourable agreement reflecting the claimants' inherent rights. The Crown, acting honourably, cannot cavalierly run roughshod over Aboriginal interests where claims affecting these interests are being seriously pursued in the process of treaty negotiation and proof. It must respect these potential, but yet unproven, interests. The Crown is not rendered impotent. It may continue to manage the resource in question pending claims resolution. But, depending on the circumstances, discussed more fully below, the honour of the Crown may require it to consult with and reasonably accommodate Aboriginal interests pending resolution of the claim. To unilaterally exploit a claimed resource during the process of proving and resolving the Aboriginal claim to that resource, may be to deprive the Aboriginal claimants of some or all of the benefit of the resource. That is not honourable. *Haida Nation v. British Columbia (Minister of Forests)*, [2004] 3 S.C.R. 511, 2004 SCC 73.

HOPE. See FAINT ~ CLAUSE.

HORIZONTAL AMALGAMATION. An amalgamation of two or more subsidiaries of the same holding corporation.

HORMONE. *n.* A natural or synthetic biochemical compound which regulates tissues or processes of the body of a plant or animal.

HORMONE DISRUPTING SUBSTANCE. A substance having the ability to disrupt the synthesis, secretion, transport, binding, action or elimination of natural hormones in an organism, or its progeny, that are responsible for the maintenance of homeostasis, reproduction, development or behaviour of the organism. *Canadian Environmental Protection Act, 1999*, S.C. 1999, c. 33, s. 43.

HORS DE LA LOI. [Fr.] Outlawed.

HOSPITAL. *n.* Any institution, building or other premises or place established for the treatment of persons afflicted with or suffering from sickness, disease or injury, or for the treatment of convalescent or chronically ill persons.

HOSTAGE. *n.* A person held in exchange for certain behaviour.

HOSTAGE TAKING. Every one takes a person hostage who (a) confines, imprisons, forcibly seizes or detains that person, and (b) in any manner utters, conveys or causes any person to receive a threat that the death of, or bodily harm to, the hostage will be caused or that the confinement, imprisonment or detention of the hostage will be continued with intent to induce any person, other than the hostage, or any group of persons or any state or international or intergovernmental organization to commit or cause to be committed any act or omission as a condition, whether express or implied, of the release of the hostage. *Criminal Code*, R.S.C. 1985, c. C-46, s. 279.1.

HOSTEL. *n.* An institution for the temporary care of transient or homeless persons.

HOSTILE. *adj.* "... [N]ot giving her evidence fairly and with a desire to tell the truth because of a hostile animus toward the [party who called the witness] ..." *R. v. Coffin*, [1956] S.C.R. 191 at 213, 23 C.R. 1, 114 C.C.C. 1, Kellock J. (Rand and Fauteux JJ. concurring).

HOSTILE ENVIRONMENT. In the context of sexual harassment occurs when employees have to endure sexual gestures and posturing in the workplace. *Janzen v. Platy Enterprises Ltd.*, [1989] 1 S.C.R. 1252.

HOSTILE POSSESSION. See ADVERSE POSSESSION.

HOSTILE WITNESS. A witness whose demeanour, general attitude and evidence are such while under examination that the side which called that witness may, with the judge's leave, cross-examine.

HOSTILITIES. *n.* Acts of war.

HOT PURSUIT. 1. Continuous pursuit conducted with reasonable diligence so that pursuit and capture along with the commission of the offence may be

H

HOURS OF WORK

considered as forming part of a single transaction. *R. v. Macooh*, [1993] 2 S.C.R. 802. 2. A coastal state may pursue a foreign merchant ship which committed an offence against its local law within that state's territorial or national waters into the high seas.

HOURS OF WORK. See REGULAR ~; WORKING HOURS.

HOUSE. See BAWDY ~; CLEARING ~; CUSTOM-~; DEFENCE OF ~ OR REAL PROPERTY; DISORDERLY ~; DWELLING-~; GOVERNMENT ~; HALFWAY ~; LODGING ~; MANSION ~; ROOMING ~; WARE~.

HOUSEBREAKING. See BREAK AND ENTER.

HOUSEHOLD UNIT. (i) A person and that person's cohabiting partner or dependent children or both, and (ii) if a person is single and without a cohabiting partner and dependent children, that person. *Income and Employment Supports Act*, S.A. 2003, c. I-0.5, s. 1.

HOUSEKEEPING. See HEAVY ~.

HOUSE LEADER. The designated member of parliament responsible for arranging the business of the House of Commons or the legislature. See GOVERNMENT ~; OPPOSITION ~.

HOUSE OF COMMONS. The lower house of the bicameral legislature which governs Canada. The members of the House are elected from each of the federal ridings in the country. The upper house is known as the Senate. The support of the majority of members of this body, elected by universal adult suffrage, is required for a Prime Minister and cabinet to govern. See CLERK OF THE ~.

HOUSE OF LORDS. The body of lords spiritual and temporal who constitute the second branch of the British Parliament and act as a supreme court of appeal from the British Court of Appeal.

HOUSING. See CANADA MORTGAGE AND ~ CORPORATION; SPECIAL NEEDS ~.

HOUSING COMPANY. See LIMITED-DIVIDEND ~.

HOUSING COOPERATIVE. An association providing accommodation for persons the majority of whom are members of the association and are ordinarily resident in the accommodation. *Cooperative Association Act*, S.B.C. 1999, c. 28, s. 1.

HOUSING LOAN. A loan that (a) relates to a housing project; (b) is secured at least in part by security on or affecting a housing project or by an agreement relating to the use, occupancy or disposal of a housing project; (c) is made for the purpose of acquiring a financial interest in a person who, directly or indirectly, owns, leases or operates a housing project; or (d) is made for the purpose of refinancing a debt that the Corporation is of the opinion relates to a housing project or to a financial interest referred to in paragraph (c). *National Housing Act*, R.S.C. 1985, c. N-11, s. 7.

HOUSING PROJECT. See LOW-RENTAL ~; RENTAL ~.

HOWEVER. *adv.* Yet, regardless, nevertheless.

H.S.T. *abbr.* Harmonized sales tax.

HUFF. *v.* To inhale a volatile substance through a cloth. F.A. Jaffe, *A Guide to Pathological Evidence for Lawyers and Police Officers*, 4th ed. (Toronto: Carswell, 1999) at 239.

HUMAN BEING. A child becomes a human being within the meaning of this Act when it has completely proceeded, in a living state, from the body of its mother, whether or not (a) it has breathed; (b) it has an independent circulation; or (c) the navel string is severed. *Criminal Code*, R.S.C. 1985, c. C-46, s. 223.

HUMAN CLONE. An embryo that, as a result of the manipulation of human reproductive material or an in vitro embryo, contains a diploid set of chromosomes obtained from a single—living or deceased—human being, foetus or other embryo. *Assisted Human Reproduction Act*, S.C. 2004, c. 2, s. 3.

HUMAN DIGNITY. 1. The fundamental attributes of a human being, the intrinsic value which a person has. The respect to which every person is entitled simply because he or she is a human being and the respect that a person owes to himself or herself. *Québec (Curateur public) c. Syndicat national des employés de l'hôpital St-Ferdinand,* 1996 CarswellQue 916, 202 N.R. 321, (*sub nom. Quebec (Public Curator) v. Syndicat national des employés de l'hôpital St-Ferdinand*) 138 D.L.R. (4th) 577, 1 C.P.C. (4th) 183, [1996] 3 S.C.R. 211, the court per L'Heureux-Dubé J. 2. The idea of human dignity finds expression in almost every right and freedom guaranteed in the Charter. Individuals are afforded the right to choose their own religion and their own philosophy of life, the right to choose with whom they will associate and how they will express themselves, the right to choose where they will live and what occupation they will pursue. These are all examples of the basic theory underlying the Charter, namely that the state will respect choices made by individuals and, to the greatest extent possible, will avoid subordinating these choices to any one conception of the good life. *R. v. Morgentaler*, [1988] 2 S.C.R. 30, Wilson J. 3. Human dignity means that an individual or group feels self-respect and self-worth. It is concerned with physical and psychological integrity and empowerment. Human dignity is harmed by unfair treatment premised upon personal traits or circumstances which do not relate to individual needs, capacities, or merits. It is enhanced by laws which are sensitive to the needs, capacities, and merits of different individuals, taking into account the context underlying their differences. Human dignity is harmed when individuals and groups are marginalized, ignored, or devalued, and is enhanced when laws recognize the full place of all individuals and groups within Canadian society. *Law v. Canada (Minister of Employment and Immigration)*, [1999] 1 S.C.R. 497 at 530, Iacobucci J. for the court.

HUMAN GENOME. The totality of the deoxyribonucleic acid sequence of the human species. *Assisted Human Reproduction Act*, S.C. 2004, c. 2, s. 11.

HUMANITY. See CRIME AGAINST ~.

HUMAN PATHOGEN. A micro-organism, nucleic acid or protein that (a) is listed in any of Schedules 2 to 4 or in Part 2 of Schedule 5; or (b) is not listed in any of the Schedules but falls into Risk Group 2, Risk Group 3 or Risk Group 4. For the purposes of this Act, a human pathogen or toxin includes (a) a substance that contains a human pathogen or toxin; and (b) any synthetic form of the human pathogen or toxin. *Human Pathogens and Toxins Act*, S.C. 2009, c. 24, s. 3.

HUMAN REMAINS. A dead human body in any stage of decomposition but does not include cremated remains. *Funeral Services Act*, R.S.A. 2000, c. F-29, s. 1.

HUMAN REPRODUCTIVE MATERIAL. A sperm, ovum or other human cell or a human gene, and includes a part of any of them. *Assisted Human Reproduction Act*, S.C. 2004, c. 2, s. 3.

HUMAN RESOURCES AND SKILLS DEVELOPMENT CANADA. This federal ministry develops policies and programs to help enhance Canadians' participation in learning, work and their community. *About Human Resources and Skills Development Canada*, online: Human Resources and Skills Development Canada, <http://www.hrsdc.gc.ca/eng/corporate/about_us/index.shtml>.

HUMAN RIGHTS. The subject of Human Rights Codes in the provinces and federally. Refers mainly to equality rights. See CANADIAN ~ COMMISSION; CANADIAN ~ TRIBUNAL; CANADIAN MUSEUM FOR ~; CHARTER OF ~ AND FREEDOMS; INTERNATIONAL ~ STANDARDS; UNIVERSAL DECLARATION OF ~.

HUMAN SMUGGLING. Knowingly, to organize, induce, aid or abet the coming into Canada of one or more persons who are not in possession of a visa, passport or other document required by this Act. *Immigration and Refugee Protection Act*, S.C. 2001, c. 27, s. 117.

HUNG JURY. A jury unable to reach a unanimous decision in a criminal case.

HUNT. *v.* To kill, injure, seize, capture or trap, or to attempt to do so, and includes to pursue, stalk, track, search for, lie in wait for or shoot at for any of those purposes. *Canada National Parks Act*, S.C. 2000, c. 32, s. 26.

HUNT. *abbr.* Hunter's Torrens Cases (Canada).

HUNTING. *n.* Includes, (a) lying in wait for, searching for, being on the trail of, pursuing, chasing or shooting at wildlife, whether or not the wildlife is killed, injured, captured or harassed, or (b) capturing or harassing wildlife, except that "hunting" does not include, (c) trapping, or (d) lying in wait for, searching for, being on the trail of or pursuing wildlife for a purpose other than attempting to kill, injure, capture or harass it, unless the wildlife is killed, injured, captured or harassed as a result. *Fish and Wildlife Conservation Act, 1997,* S.O. 1997, c. 41, s. 1.

HYBRID ELECTRIC VEHICLE. A motor vehicle that has both an electric motor and an internal combustion engine and that (a) is designed so that (i) the vehicle's engine automatically shuts off when the vehicle is idling, braking or coasting, and (ii) the vehicle captures and stores in its battery energy generated during braking, and (b) is capable of sustained propulsion either (i) simultaneously by the motor and the engine, or (ii) solely by the motor, operating on electricity generated by the engine. *Social Service Tax Act*, R.S.B.C. 1996, c. 431, *Social Service Tax Act Regulations*, B.C. Reg. 84/58, s. 11.1.

HYBRID OFFENCE. Term applied to a criminal offence which may be tried by summary conviction procedure or by indictment at the option of the prosecutor. A hybrid offence is an indictable offence until the Crown elects to proceed by way of summary conviction.

HYBRID PLAN. A [pension] plan under which (a) some benefits, but not all of the benefits, are determined as if the plan were a defined contribution plan, and (b) some benefits, but not all of the benefits, are determined by a defined benefit formula. *Family Relations Act*, R.S.B.C. 1996, c. 128, s. 70.

HYBRID PRODUCT. An instrument, contract or security that combines elements of derivatives and securities. *Derivatives Act*, R.S.Q. c. I-14.01, s. 3.

HYBRID VEHICLE. An automobile vehicle powered by the combination of a heat engine and an electric motor. *An Act Respecting the Québec Sales Tax*, R.S.Q., c. T-0.1, s. 382.8.

HYGIENE. See DENTAL ~.

HYPERLINK. *n.* The Board was also required to consider the potential copyright infringement of "hyperlinks," particularly when the link is automatic. Automatic links employ an embedded code in the Web page that automatically instructs the browser, upon obtaining access to the first site, to download a file from a second site. The user does not need to do anything but visit the initial site before information from the second site is "pulled". A different legal issue may arise where the user must take action, such as to click the mouse button over the hyperlink, in order to obtain access to the information from the second site. *Society of Composers, Authors & Music Publishers of Canada v. Canadian Assn. of Internet Providers*, 2004 SCC 45, Binnie J.

HYPOTHEC. See CONVENTIONAL ~; FLOATING ~; IMMOVABLE ~; LEGAL ~; MOVABLE ~.

HYPOTHECATION. *n.* Pledging something as security for a demand or debt without giving up that thing.

HYPOTHETICAL. *adj.* Depending on an assumption of fact which may or may not be provable or true. R.J. Sharpe, ed., *Charter Litigation* (Toronto: Butterworths 1987) at 335.

H

I

I.A.B. *abbr.* Immigration Appeal Board.

I.A.C. *abbr.* Immigration Appeal Cases, 1970-1976.

IBA. *abbr.* Impact and Benefit Agreement.

IBID. *abbr.* Ibidem.

IBIDEM. *adv.* [L.] In the same place.

ID. *abbr.* Idem.

ID CERTUM EST QUOD CERTUM REDDI POTEST. [L.] What is certain is what can be made certain.

IDEM. [L.] The same. See AD ~.

IDENTICAL. *adj.* One and the same.

IDENTIFIABLE. *adj.* The court adopted Professor Donovan Waters' description of the distinction between "identifiable" and "traceable" property as set out in "Trusts in the Setting of Business, Commerce, and Bankruptcy" (1983), 21 Alta. Law Rev. 395. He stated at pp. 431-34 that: "identifiable" refers to the ability to point to the particular property obtained by the debtor as a result of the dealing with the collateral, while "traceable" refers to the situation where the collateral is commingled with other property so that its identity is lost. *Transamerica Commercial Finance Corp. Canada v. Royal Bank*, [1990] 4 W.W.R. 673, 79 C.B.R. (N.S.) 127, 1 P.P.S.A.C. (2d) 61, 70 D.L.R. (4th) 627, 84 Sask. R. 81 (C.A.).

IDENTIFIABLE GROUP. Any section of the public distinguished by colour, race, religion, ethnic origin or sexual orientation. *Criminal Code*, R.S.C. 1985, c. C-46, s. 318(4).

IDENTIFICATION. *n.* Showing that some person or thing is the person or thing in question.

IDENTIFICATION DOCTRINE. In criminal law, the concept that the board of directors and anyone to whom governing executive authority is delegated by the board of directors merge with the corporation for the purpose of giving it a directing mind. The conduct of any of the merged entities is attributed to the corporation.

IDENTIFICATION THEORY. In criminal law, the concept that the board of directors and anyone to whom governing executive authority is delegated by the board of directors merge with the corporation for the purpose of giving it a directing mind. The conduct

of any of the merged entities is attributed to the corporation.

IDENTITY. *n.* 1. "... [C]an be established not only by the name but also by a physical description of the person and other more sophisticated forensic methods such as fingerprints or voiceprints... ." *R. v. Khela* (1991), 68 C.C.C. (3d) 81 at 85, 9 C.R. (4th) 380 (Que. C.A.), Proulx J.A. (Tourigny J.A. concurring). 2. "... [I]nvolves all the ingredients by which a person purports to identify himself." *Francey v. Wawanesa Mutual Insurance Co.* (1990), 46 C.C.L.I. 240 at 254, 75 Alta. L.R. (2d) 257, [1990] 6 W.W.R. 329, 108 A.R. 82, 72 D.L.R. (4th) 544, [1990] I.L.R. 1-2652 (Q.B.), Fraser J. 3. "... [S]omething different from 'name and address', though name and address are sufficient to establish identity, ..." *R. v. Lloyd* (1980), 16 C.R. (3d) 221 at 240, 53 C.C.C. (2d) 121 (B.C. C.A.), Hinkson J.A. See PRESUMPTION OF ~.

IDENTITY FRAUD. Every one who fraudulently personates any person, living or dead, (a) with intent to gain advantage for themselves or another person; (b) with intent to obtain any property or an interest in any property; or (c) with intent to cause disadvantage to the person being whom he personates or another person; or (d) with intent to avoid arrest or prosecution or to obstruct, pervert or defeat the course of justice, is guilty of an indictable offence or an offence punishable on summary conviction. *Criminal Code*, R.S.C. 1985, c. C-46, s. 403.

IDENTITY INFORMATION. Any information—including biological or physiological information—of a type that is commonly used alone or in combination with other information to identify or purport to identify an individual, including a fingerprint, voice print, retina image, iris image, DNA profile, name, address, date of birth, written signature, electronic signature, digital signature, user name, credit card number, debit card number, financial institution account number, passport number, Social Insurance Number, health insurance number, driver's licence number or password. *Criminal Code*, R.S.C. 1985, c. C-46, s. 402.1. See TRAFFICKING IN ~.

IDENTITY THEFT. Knowingly obtaining or possessing another person's identity information in circumstances giving rise to a reasonable inference that the information is intended to be used to commit an indictable offence that includes fraud, deceit or falsehood as an element of the offence. *Criminal Code*, R.S.C. 1985, c. C-46, s. 402.2(1).

ID EST. [L. that is] That is to say.

IDIOPATHY. *n.* A disease or condition without a known cause.

I.E. *abbr.* Id est.

IF. *prep.* On the condition that; on the supposition that.

IFRS. *abbr.* International Financial Reporting Standards.

IGNITION INTERLOCK DEVICE. A device designed to ascertain the presence of alcohol in the driver's body and to prevent a motor vehicle from being started if the concentration of alcohol in the driver's body exceeds the prescribed limit. *Highway Traffic Act*, R.S.O. 1990, c. H.8, s. 41.2. See ALCOHOL ~.

IGNORANCE OF THE LAW. Ignorance of the law by a person who commits an offence is not an excuse for committing that offence. *Criminal Code*, R.S.C. 1985, c. C-46, s. 19.

IGNORANTIA FACTI EXCUSAT; IGNORANTIA JURIS NON EXCUSAT. [L.] Ignorance of fact is excusable; ignorance of the law is no excuse.

IGNORANTIA JURIS NEMINEM EXCUSAT. [L.] Ignorance of the law excuses no one.

IGNORANTIA JURIS NON EXCUSAT. [L.] Ignorance of the law is no excuse.

IIBA. *abbr.* Inuit Impact and Benefit Agreement.

IJC. *abbr.* International Joint Commission.

ILLEGAL. *adj.* Forbidden by law. Infringing on public policy. Infringing on the terms or object of an enactment. See UNLAWFUL.

ILLEGAL CONTRACT. 1. A contract is illegal as to formation when it is prohibited by statute. It is illegal as performed if, though lawful in its formation, it is performed by one of the parties in a manner prohibited by statute. *Still v. Minister of National Revenue* [1998] 1 F.C. 549 (C.A.). 2. An agreement to do anything forbidden either by statute or by the common law.

ILLEGALITY. *n.* 1. "... [A] generic term covering any act not in accordance with the law... ." *Immeubles Port Louis Ltée c. Lafontaine (Village)* (1991), 5 M.P.L.R. (2d) 1 at 55, [1991] 1 S.C.R. 326, 78 D.L.R. (4th) 15, 121 N.R. 323, 38 Q.A.C. 253, the court per Gonthier J. 2. A contract prohibited by statute or for an illegal purpose will be declared void even it conforms to all other requirements of a valid transaction. 3. By 'illegality' as a ground for judicial review I mean that the decision-maker must understand correctly the law that regulates his decision-making power and must give effect to it. Whether he has or not is par excellence a justiciable question to be decided, in the event of dispute, by those persons, the judges, by whom the judicial power of the state is exercisable. *Council of Civil Service Unions v. Minister for the Civil Service*, [1985] A.C. 374 at 410, 411, [1984] 3 All E.R. 935 (H.L.), Lord Diplock.

ILLEGAL OIL. Oil produced from any well in the province in violation of this Act or any regulation or order made under the authority thereof. *The Oil and Gas Conservation Act*, R.S.S. 1978, c. O-2, s. 2.

ILLEGAL OR UNLAWFUL MEANS. The case law reflects two different views of "illegal or unlawful means," one narrow, the other broad. The narrow view confines illegal or unlawful means to an act prohibited by law or by statute. The broader view, however, extends illegal or unlawful means to an act the defendant "is not at liberty to commit" - in other words, an act without legal justification. *Reach M.D. Inc. v. Pharmaceutical Manufacturers Assn. of Canada* (2002), 65 O.R. (3d) 30, 172 O.A.C. 202.

ILLEGAL PRACTICE. The practice of a regulated profession without the proper registration of licensing requirement.

ILLEGITIMATE CHILD. Obsolete expression used to refer to a child born out of wedlock, that is when the parents were not married to each other.

ILLICIT. *adj.* 1. "... '[U]nlawful' ..." *R. v. Deutsch* (1986), 18 O.A.C. 1 at 14, 52 C.R. (3d) 305, [1986] 2 S.C.R. 2, 68 N.R. 321, 27 C.C.C. (3d) 385, 30 D.L.R. (4th) 435, Le Dain J. (Beetz, McIntyre and Wilson JJ. concurring). 2. "... [R]eferring to sexual intercourse not authorized or sanctioned by lawful marriage." *R. v. Deutsch* (1986), 18 O.A.C. 1 at 14, 52 C.R. (3d) 305, [1986] 2 S.C.R. 2, 68 N.R. 321, 27 C.C.C. (3d) 385, 30 D.L.R. (4th) 435, Le Dain J. (Beetz, McIntyre and Wilson JJ. concurring).

ILLICIT DRUG. A controlled substance or precursor the import, export, production, sale or possession of which is prohibited or restricted pursuant to the Controlled Drugs and Substances Act. *Criminal Code*, R.S.C. 1985, c. C-46, s. 462.1.

ILLICIT DRUG USE. The importation, exportation, production, sale or possession of a controlled substance or precursor contrary to the Controlled Drugs and Substances Act or a regulation made under that Act. *Criminal Code*, R.S.C. 1985, c. C-46, s. 462.1. See INSTRUMENT FOR ~; LITERATURE FOR ~.

ILLNESS. *n.* Incapacitation; inability to work because of the state of one's health. See OCCUPATIONAL ~.

I.L.R. *abbr.* 1. Canadian Insurance Law Reporter, 1951-. 2. Insurance Law Reporter, 1934-1950.

I.M.A. *abbr.* Institute of Municipal Assessors of Ontario, Court Decisions, 1974-1986.

IMAGING TECHNOLOGY. See MEDICAL ~ AND RADIATION ONCOLOGY.

IMITATION. See COLOURABLE ~.

IMITATION FIREARM. 1. Any thing that imitates a firearm, and includes a replica firearm. *Criminal Code*, R.S.C. 1985, c. C-46, s. 84(1). 2. Includes any object other than a starter pistol to which section 2 applies or a deactivated firearm to which section 3 applies, if the object, (a) could reasonably be mistaken for a firearm but is not a firearm or a replica firearm as defined in section 84 of the Criminal Code (Canada), or (b) is a firearm but is not designed or adapted to discharge, (i) a shot, bullet or other projectile at a muzzle velocity exceeding 152.4 metres per second, or (ii) a shot, bullet or other projectile that is designed or adapted to attain a velocity exceeding 152.4 metres per second. *Imitation Firearms Regulation Act, 2000*, S.O. 2000, c. 37, s. 1.

IMM. A.B.D. *abbr.* Immigration Appeal Board Decisions, 1977-1988.

IMM. A.C. *abbr.* Immigration Appeal Cases, 1968-1970.

IMM. A.C (2D). *abbr.* Immigration Appeal Cases (Second Series), 1969-1977.

IMMATRICULATION. *n.* Of an immovable consists in establishing its relative position on a cadastral plan, indicating its boundaries, measurements and area and assigning a number to it. Immatriculation is completed by the identification of the owner, an indication of the mode of acquisition, the registration number of the title and, where applicable, the correspondence between the old and new cadastral numbers, or between the serial number of the file for the immovable, and the new cadastral number. *Civil Code*, S.Q. 1991, c. 64, a. 3026.

IMMEDIATE. *adj.* The word "imminent" used in the French version and the word "immediate" in the English version can be easily reconciled. Both words must mean, in the context of the subsection, that the serious danger must occur soon or within a short time. However, as to what constitutes a short time or soon in a given case must be determined on the facts of that case. *Atomic Energy of Canada Ltd. v. Chalk River Professional Employees Group*, 2002 FCA 489, 2003 C.L.L.C. 220-020, 298 N.R. 285, [2003] 3 F.C. 313.

IMMEDIATE LIFE ANNUITY. A life annuity that (a) commences periodic payments within one year after its purchase, (b) provides for equal periodic payments or periodic payments that have been varied by reference to (i) the amount of any pension payable under the Old Age Security Act, (ii) the amount of any pension payable under either the Canada Pension Plan or a provincial pension plan as defined in section 3 of the Canada Pension Plan, (iii) the Consumer Price Index for Canada as published by Statistics Canada under the authority of the Statistics Act, or (iv) the value of the assets held in a segregated fund, and (c) is issued by a person authorized to carry on a life insurance business in Canada *Pension Benefits Standards Act, 1985*, R.S.C. 1985 (2d Supp.), c. 32, *Pension Benefits Standards Regulations, 1985*, SOR/87-19, s. 2.

IMMEDIATE PENSION BENEFIT. A pension benefit that is to commence within one year after the member becomes entitled to it. *Pension Benefits Standards Act, 1985*, R.S.C. 1985, c. 32 (2nd Supp.), s. 2.

IMMEMORIAL. See TIME ~.

IMMERSION SYNDROME. Death of a person who was quickly rescued from cold water and appears not to have drowned. F.A. Jaffe, *A Guide to Pathological Evidence for Lawyers and Police Officers*, 4th. ed. (Toronto: Carswell, 1999) at 115.

IMMIGRANT. *n.* 1. A person who seeks landing. *Immigration Act*, R.S.C. 1985, c. I-2, s. 2 [repealed]. 2. A person who (a) has been granted landing within the meaning of the Immigration Act (Canada), (b) has not become a Canadian citizen, and (c) has not, under the Immigration Act (Canada), ceased to be a permanent resident within the meaning of that Act. *School Act*; R.S.B.C. 1996, c. 412, s. 1.

IMMIGRATION. *n.* Entering a country for the purpose of establishing permanent residence in it. See DEPARTMENT OF CITIZENSHIP AND ~.

IMMIGRATION AND REFUGEE BOARD. Consists of the Refugee Protection Division, the Refugee Appeal Division, the Immigration Division and the Immigration Appeal Division. *Immigration and Refugee Protection Act*, S.C. 2001, c. 27, s. 151.

IMMIGRATION APPEAL DIVISION. The competent Division of the Board with respect to appeals under this Division, which deals with immigration and permanent residency issues. It is a court of record. *Immigration and Refugee Protection Act*, S.C. 2001, c. 27, s. 67 and 174.

IMMIGRATION DIVISION. The competent Division of the Board with respect to the review of reasons for detention under this Division. *Immigration and Refugee Protection Act*, S.C. 2001, c. 27, s. 54.

IMM. L.R. *abbr.* Immigration Law Reporter, 1985-1987.

IMM. L.R. (2D). *abbr.* Immigration Law Reporter (Second Series) 1987-1999.

IMM. L.R. (3D). *abbr.* Immigration Law Reporter (Third Series) 1999-.

IMMORAL CONTRACT. A contract based on consideration contra bonos mores and considered void.

IMMOVABLE. *n.* 1. Land, and any constructions and works of a permanent nature located thereon and anything forming an integral part thereof, are immovables. Plants and minerals, as long as they are not separated or extracted from the land, are also immovables. Fruits and other products of the soil may be considered to be movables, however, when they are the object of an act of alienation. *Civil Code*, S.Q. 1991, c. 64, a. 900. 2. Includes (1) a lease pertaining to an immovable; (2) a mobile home; (3) a floating home; and (4) a leasehold or other proprietary interest in a mobile home or a floating home. *An Act respecting the Québec sales tax*, R.S.Q. c. T-0.1, s. 1. 3. " ... [C]omprises everything which could be regarded as real estate for the purposes of the taxation by-laws and resolutions ... and while it may not be so clear that such immovables as the pipes, poles, wires and transformers in question are real estate and real property, the weight of authority certainly favours that view ... the real property of English law is not entirely co-extensive with the immovables of the civil law, ..." *Montreal Light, Heat & Power Consolidated v. Westmount (Town)*, [1926] S.C.R. 515 at 523, [1926] 3 D.L.R. 466, Anglin C.J.C. (Duff, Mignault, Newcombe and Rinfret JJ. concurring). See FEDERAL ~; FOREIGN ~ RULE.

IMMOVABLE BY NATURE. "... [T]he structures ... must participate in the fixity or immobility of the land, which is the ultimate measure of whether a thing is immovable by nature. This principle is observed as long as a structure participates in the immovable nature of the land, by adhering directly to it or to another structure, which in turn adheres to the land. In either case the structure is immovable by nature because it is naturally immobile." *Cablevision (Montreal) Inc. v. Quebec*, [1978] 2 S.C.R. 64 at 73, 19 N.R. 121, the court per Beetz J.

IMMOVABLE HYPOTHEC. Is, on pain of absolute nullity, granted by notarial act en minute. An immovable hypothec is valid only so far as the constituting act specifically designates the hypothecated property. *Civil Code*, S.Q. 1991, c. 64, a. 2693 and 2694. See MOVABLE HYPOTHEC.

IMMUNITY. *n.* The state of being free or exempt. See CROWN ~; JUDICIAL ~; PUBLIC INTEREST ~; RESTRICTED ~; SOVEREIGN ~.

IMPACT. *n.* Localised force. F.A. Jaffe, *A Guide to Pathological Evidence for Lawyers and Police Officers*, 4th ed. (Toronto: Carswell, 1999) at 239. See ENVIRONMENTAL ~; VICTIM ~ STATEMENT.

IMPACT AND BENEFIT AGREEMENT. 1. These agreements are signed between mining companies and First Nation communities in Canada in order to establish formal relationships between them, to reduce the predicted impact of a mine and secure economic benefit for affected communities. IBAs are increasingly used by First Nations in Canada to influence decision making about resource exploitation in their lands. Irene Sosa and Karyn Keenan, *Impact Benefit Agreements Between Aboriginal Communities and Mining Companies: Their Use in Canada*, 2001, online: Canadian Environmental Law Association, <http://www.cela.ca/publications/impact-benefit-agreements-between-aboriginal-communities-and-mining-companies-their-use>. 2. May be implemented in relation to other industries.

IMPAIR. *v.* To make worse, to lessen the value of, to weaken.

IMPAIRED. *adj.* Ability adversely affected by drugs, alcohol, disease or condition.

IMPAIRMENT. *n.* A physical or functional abnormality or loss (including disfigurement) which results from an injury and any psychological damage arising from the abnormality or loss. *Workplace Safety and Insurance Act, 1997*, S.O. 1997, c. 16, Sched. A, s. 2. See PERMANENT ~.

IMPANEL. *v.* "... [S]ometimes means to enroll upon a panel or list for jury duty, and sometimes to draw from that panel and select a jury for a particular case."

R. v. Gaffin (1904), 8 C.C.C. 194 at 196 (N.S. S.C.), the court per Graham E.J. See EMPANEL; JURY.

IMPARTIAL. *adj.* "... [C]onnotes absence of bias, actual or perceived." *R. v. Valente (No. 2)* (1985), 23 C.C.C. (3d) 193 at 201, [1985] 2 S.C.R. 673, 52 O.R. (2d) 779, 37 M.V.R. 9, 49 C.R. (3d) 97, 24 D.L.R. (4th) 161, 64 N.R. 1, 14 O.A.C. 79, 19 C.R.R. 354, [1985] D.L.Q. 85n, the court per Le Dain J.

IMPARTIAL CHAIRMAN. The third, neutral member of a tripartite labour arbitration panel.

IMPARTIALITY. *n.* 1. [I]mpartiality can be described—perhaps somewhat inexactly—as a state of mind in which the adjudicator is disinterested in the outcome, and is open to persuasion by the evidence and submissions. *R. v. S. (R.D.)*, 1997 CarswellNS 301, 151 D.L.R. (4th) 193, 118 C.C.C. (3d) 353, 10 C.R. (5th) 1, 218 N.R. 1, 161 N.S.R. (2d) 241, 477 A.P.R. 241, [1997] 3 S.C.R. 484, 1 Admin. L.R (3d) 74, Cory J. 2. Impartiality refers first and foremost to an absence of prejudice or bias, actual or perceived, on the part of a judge in a particular case, but like independence it includes an institutional aspect. If the system is structured in such a way as to create a reasonable apprehension of bias at the institutional level, the requirement of impartiality is not met. *R. c. Lauzon*, 1998 CarswellNat 1810, 18 C.R. (5th) 288, (sub nom. *R. v. Lauzon*) 230 N.R. 272, 56 C.R.R. (2d) 30, 129 C.C.C. (3d) 399, 8 Admin. L.R. (3d) 33 (Can. Ct. Martial App. Ct.). 3. Is not the same as neutrality. Impartiality does not require that the juror's mind be a blank slate. Nor does it require jurors to jettison all opinions, beliefs, knowledge and other accumulations of life experience as they step into the jury box. Jurors are human beings, whose life experiences inform their deliberations. *R. v. Find*, 2001 CarswellOnt 1702, 2001 SCC 32, 42 C.R. (5th) 1, 154 C.C.C. (3d) 97, 199 D.L.R. (4th) 193, 269 N.R. 149, 146 O.A.C. 236, McLachlin C.J.C. See INSTITUTIONAL ~.

IMPEACH. *v.* "... [T]o call into question the veracity of evidence given by a witness by calling evidence to contradict, challenge or impugn the witness's prior testimony." *Machado v. Berlet* (1986), 15 C.P.C. (2d) 207 at 217, 57 O.R. (2d) 207, 32 D.L.R. (4th) 634 (H.C.), Ewaschuk J.

IMPEACHMENT. *n.* Attack on a patent's validity.

IMPECUNIOUS. *adj.* Lacking sufficient assets for a purpose and unable to raise the moneys required from other sources.

IMPEDIMENT. See HEALTH ~; PHYSICAL ~.

IMPERFECT OBLIGATION. A moral duty which the law cannot enforce.

IMPERFECT TRUST. An executory trust which is not sufficiently constituted or declared.

IMPERIAL. *adj.* Of or pertaining to the United Kingdom, as constituted on the coming into force of this Act, or any former kingdom which included England, whether known as the United Kingdom of Great Britain and Ireland or otherwise. *Evidence acts.*

IMPERIAL PARLIAMENT. The parliament of the United Kingdom of Great Britain and Northern Ireland, as at present constituted, or any former kingdom that included England, whether known as the United Kingdom of Great Britain and Ireland or otherwise. *Evidence acts.*

IMPERSONATION. *n.* The act of representing that one is someone else, whether dead or living, fictitious or real.

IMPLEAD. *v.* 1. "... [A]sserting jurisdiction against the opposition of the parties sought to be sued." *Canadian Commercial Bank v. McLaughlan* (1990), 73 D.L.R. (4th) 678 at 685, 39 E.T.R. 54, 75 Alta. L.R. (2d) 40 (C.A.), Bracco and Stevenson JJ.A. and Forsyth J. 2. To institute legal proceedings against a person.

IMPLICATION. *n.* An inference which is necessary or may be presumed and arises out of words or acts in evidence. See NECESSARY ~.

IMPLIED. *adj.* Used in contradistinction to express. *R. v. Clement* (1981), 23 C.R. (3d) 193 at 200, [1981] 2 S.C.R. 468, [1981] 6 W.W.R. 735, 23 R.F.L. (2d) 255, 10 Man. R. (2d) 92, 38 N.R. 302, the court per Estey J.

IMPLIED AUTHORITY. 1. A certain authority which may be read into an agent's express authority. 2. Actual implied authority is found to exist where an officer exceeds the authority usually attached to the position and does so with the knowledge and acquiescence of the corporation. *D. Fogell Associates Ltd. v. Esprit de Corp (1980) Ltd. / Esprit de Corp (1980) Ltee.*, 1997 CarswellBC 1131 (S.C.), Edwards J.

IMPLIED CONDITION. 1. The Sale of Goods Act set out implied warranties and conditions which are contained in certain contracts for sale. *The Sales of Goods Act*, R.S.O. 1990, c. S.1 provides these at sections 13 through 16. 2. In some circumstances a court has a right to conclude that everything the parties agreed is not contained in their oral statements or in the written documents which appear to constitute the contract. The additional term is said to exist in the agreement though unspecified; a statute may imply it. G.H.L. Fridman, *The Law of Contract in Canada*, 2d ed. (Toronto: Carswell, 1986) at 448.

IMPLIED CONSENT. In relation to team sports, the players are deemed to consent to forms of intentional bodily contact which are inherent in and incidental to the game.

IMPLIED CONTRACT. A contract which law concludes does exist from an act, circumstance or relationship.

IMPLIED EXCLUSION RULE. [I]n relation to the codification of the common law is referred to by Sullivan and Driedger on the Construction of Statutes, 4th Edition [citation omitted] at page 355, which in turn relies upon the Supreme Court of Canada decision in R. v. McClurg 1990 CanLII 28 (S.C.C.), (1990), 76 D.L.R. (4th) 217. This text book states at page 355: When the legislature expressly codifies only part of the law relating to a matter, the Court may rely on implied exclusion reasoning to conclude that the part of the law not expressly mentioned was meant to be excluded. ... This principle means that

specifying in section 71 the right to reopen an appeal with respect to a breach of the rules of natural justice means that Parliament intended the part of the common law not expressly mentioned was intended to be excluded. Accordingly, the right of the IAD to reopen an appeal on equitable grounds was implicitly excluded... . *Nazifpour v. Canada (Minister of Citizenship & Immigration)*, 2007 FCA 35. See PRESUMPTION OF IMPLIED EXCLUSION.

IMPLIED GRANT. An easement arises by implication under a grant where the intention to grant the easement can properly be inferred. The intention may be inferred on the basis of several different rules.

IMPLIED INVITATION. See DOCTRINE OF ~.

IMPLIED JURISDICTION. The concept of implied jurisdiction is summarized in ATCO Gas and Pipelines Ltd. v. Alberta (Energy and Utilities Board), [2006] 1 S.C.R. 140 (ATCO) at paragraph 51 as follows: ...[T]he powers conferred by an enabling statute are construed to include not only those expressly granted but also, by implication, all powers which are practically necessary for the accomplishment of the object intended to be secured by the statutory regime created by the legislature [citation omitted]. Canadian courts have in the past applied the doctrine to ensure that administrative bodies have the necessary jurisdiction to accomplish their statutory mandate. *Canada (Attorney General) v. Mowat*, 2009 FCA 309.

IMPLIED REPEAL. See PRESUMPTION AGAINST ~.

IMPLIED TERM. 1. "... [T]here may be cases where obviously some term must be implied if the intention of the parties is not to be defeated, some term of which it can be predicated that 'it goes without saying,' some term not expressed but necessary to give the transaction such business efficacy as the parties must have intended." *Luxor (Eastbourne) Ltd. v. Cooper*, [1941] A.C. 108 at 137 (U.K. H.L.), Lord Wright. 2. "... [S]ometimes ... denotes some term which does not depend on the actual intention of the parties but on a rule of law, such as the terms, warranties or conditions which, if not expressly excluded, the law imports, as for instance under the Sale of Goods Act, ..." *Luxor (Eastbourne) Ltd. v. Cooper*, [1941] A.C. 108 at 137 (U.K. H.L.), Lord Wright.

IMPLIED TRUST. A trust which comes about when an equitable interpretation is put on the conduct of the parties, for example where one person voluntarily transfers property to another person or pays for property and has that property put into another person's name.

IMPLIED UNDERTAKING. May refer to the IMPLIED UNDERTAKING RULE. May also refer to an undertaking which can be inferred in the context of a contractual or other business or governmental relationship.

IMPLIED UNDERTAKING RULE. 1. Under [this rule] evidence compelled during pre-trial discovery from a party to civil litigation can be used by the parties only for the purpose of the litigation in which it was obtained. The root of the implied undertaking is the statutory compulsion to participate fully in pre-trial oral and documentary discovery. If the opposing party seeks information that is relevant and is not protected by privilege, it must be disclosed even if it tends to self-incrimination. An application to modify or relieve against an implied undertaking requires an applicant to demonstrate to the court on a balance of probabilities the existence of a public interest of greater weight than the values the implied undertaking is designed to protect, namely privacy and the efficient conduct of civil litigation. I believe the test formulated therein (in identical terms) [in the rules of three provinces] is apt as a reflection of the common law more generally, namely: If satisfied that the interest of justice outweighs any prejudice that would result to a party who disclosed evidence, the court may order that [the implied or "deemed" undertaking] does not apply to the evidence or to information obtained from it, and may impose such terms and give such directions as are just. *Juman v. Doucette*, 2008 SCC 8, [2008] 1 S.C.R. 157. 2. The implied undertaking rule in criminal proceedings has now been codified in Great Britain in s.17 of the Criminal Procedure and Investigations Act 1996 (U.K.), 1996, c.25. To summarize, an accused who has been given a document or other object pursuant to the Crown's disclosure obligations must not use or disclose it or any information recorded in it except "in connection with the proceedings for whose purposes he was given the object or allowed to inspect it." The prohibition does not apply to any object or information to the extent that it was displayed to the public in open court. The accused may apply to a court for an order granting permission to use or disclose the object or information. *P. (D.) v. Wagg* (2004), 187 O.A.C. 26.

IMPLIED WARRANTY. 1. The Sale of Goods Act set out implied warranties and conditions which are contained in certain contracts for sale. *The Sales of Goods Act*, R.S.O. 1990, c. S.1 provides these at sections 13 through 16. 2.[T]here is no implied warranty of fitness for human habitation upon the purchase of housing property that is already completed at the time of sale. The common law doctrine of caveat emptor governs with respect to the sale of real property and the purchaser must generally seek protection either by express warranty or by independent examination of the premises. However, in the case of unfinished premises, the common law implies a warranty of construction since there is no opportunity for inspection of the finished premises at the time of sale. See Fraser-Reid v. Droumtsekas, 1979 CanLII 55, [1980] 1 S.C.R. 720. *Carleton Condominium Corporation No. 32 v. Camdev Corporation*, 124 O.A.C. 352, 1999 CanLII 2909. See IMPLIED CONDITION.

IMPORTANCE. *n.* In addition to the factors set out in s. 2(3)(a)(b) and (c) [of Rules of Court], "importance" means important to the public at large or at least to other litigation of a similar nature. Difficult issues of fact and law are to be taken into account. To find a matter of unusual difficulty, the question is whether the collection and proof of the difficult facts were uncommon, remarkable, or exceptional events.

M. (F.S.) v. Clarke, 2000 CarswellBC 878, 2000 BCSC 432 (S.C.), Dillon J. See SUFFICIENT ~.

IMPOSSIBILITY. *n.* Something either physical, legal or logical: physical when it is unnatural, legal when a rule of law makes it not possible to do and logical when it goes against the essential qualities of the transaction.

IMPOUND. *v.* To place in legal custody.

IMPRACTICABLE. *adj.* Difficult to put into practice; unmanageable.

IMPRESSION. See FIRST ~.

IMPRISONED. *adj.* Held in prison, penitentiary or lock up. See ARBITRARILY ~.

IMPRISONMENT. *n.* "... [C]arries with it a complete lack of choice. There must be an involuntary element to the confinement before it can be said to be a restraint on the personal liberty or freedom ..." *R. v. Degan* (1985), 20 C.C.C. (3d) 293 at 299, 38 Sask. R. 234 (C.A.), the court per Vancise J.A. See FALSE ~.

IMPROPER. *adj.* Not in accordance with truth, fact, reason or rule; unsuitable.

IMPROPERLY. *adv.* Incorrectly, unsuitably, in an unbecoming manner.

IMPROPER PURPOSE. In an administrative law sense, these words ['bad faith' and 'improper purpose'] are not necessarily pejorative. A purpose may be improper merely because the actor is misguided. If an extraneous purpose—no matter how laudable—enters in, it will be considered an improper one and the act will have become tainted. In this sense, the terms are judicially taken to mean 'the making of regulations for any purpose other than one authorized by the parent statute'. "'Motive' addresses that which prompts one to act in a certain way or that determines volition, and speaks to the goal or object of one's actions." 'Purpose' addresses the reason for which something exists, and speaks to the practical result, effect or advantage obtained". *Morgentaler v. Prince Edward Island (Minister of Health & Social Services)*, 1995 CarswellPEI 61, 32 Admin. L.R. (2d) 205, 126 Nfld. & P.E.I.R. 240, 393 A.P.R. 240, 122 D.L.R. (4th) 728, 122 D.L.R. (4th) 728 (T.D.), Jenkins J.

IMPROPRIETY. *n.* An irregularity; an improper action. See PROCEDURAL ~.

IMPROVEMENT. *n.* 1. "... [O]rdinary meaning ... includes buildings, structures and all things which become attached to the land, but does not include buildings, structures or fixtures which merely rested on the land and which could be removed at will without changing the character of the land itself, ..." *Beloit Sorel Walmsley Ltd. v. New Brunswick* (1976), 10 L.C.R. 373 at 376, 71 D.L.R. (3d) 240 (N.B. C.A.), the court per Limerick J.A. 2. In the leases, the word "improvement" is used to refer to things other than buildings. Clause 8(a), for example, refers to "any buildings and such other improvements, including construction of roads, water, sewer, electricity and/or gas systems". Improvements include services, and conversely "unimproved" means without services. The internal coherence of the rent review clause also supports the view that "unimproved" means unserviced. The leases were signed before any buildings were built, so the word "unimproved" would have added nothing to the phrase "unimproved lands in the same state as they were on the date of this agreement" unless it referred to the pre-existing servicing. *Musqueam Indian Band v. Glass*, 2000 CarswellNat 2405, 2000 SCC 52, [2000] 11 W.W.R. 407, 36 R.P.R. (3d) 1, 192 D.L.R. (4th) 385, 82 B.C.L.R. (3d) 199, 261 N.R. 296, 186 F.T.R. 248 (note), [2000] 2 S.C.R. 633, [2001] 1 C.N.L.R. 208, Gonthier J. (Major, Binnie and LeBel JJ. concurring). 3. In respect of property of a person, means any property or service supplied to, or property brought into Québec by, the person for the purpose of improving the property, to the extent that the consideration paid or payable by the person for the property or service or the value of the property brought in is, or would be if the person were a taxpayer within the meaning of the Taxation Act, included in determining the cost or, in the case of property that is capital property of the person, the adjusted cost base to the person of the property for the purposes of that Act. *An Act respecting the Québec sales tax*, R.S.Q. c. T-0.1, s. 1. See INTERNATIONAL RIVER ~; LOCAL ~.

IMPROVEMENT DISTRICT. 1. With respect to being allotted shares in the Corporation or borrowing from the Corporation, the Government of Alberta as represented by the Minister responsible for improvement districts. *Alberta Capital Finance Authority Act*, R.S.A. 2000, c. A-14.5, s. 1. 2. As the context requires, either the public corporate body or the tract of land incorporated under the Local Government Act and includes an improvement district constituted under a former Act. *Water Act*, R.S.B.C. 1996, c. 483, s. 1.

IMPROVEMENT PROJECT. See COMMUNITY ~ AREA.

IMPROVIDENT. *adj.* Unreasonable in the circumstances.

IMPUTABLE CAUSATION. Legal causation is also referred to as imputable causation (R. v. Nette, 2001 SCC 78 at para. 45) and is concerned with "the question of whether the accused person should be held responsible in law for the death that occurred". *R. v. Sinclair*, 2009 MBCA 71

IMPUTE. *v.* 1. To attribute responsibility to another. 2. To ascribe.

IMPUTED. *adj.* Income is said to be imputed where it was not earned but the party to whom the income is attributed had the ability to earn it. The income is imputed where necessary to permit an assessment of legal obligations, most commonly in the context of support payments in family law cases. *Strauss v. Albrico Services (1982) Ltd.*, 2008 BCCA 173.

IN. See BUY ~; CONTRACTING ~; FOUND ~; HERE~; LOCK ~ PRINCIPLE; PAID ~; READING ~; RESULT ~; WITH~.

INABILITY. *n.* The condition of being unable; lack of ability, power or means.

INACCURACY. *n.* Incorrectness.

INADMISSIBILITY. See CERTIFICATE OF ~.

INADVERTENCE. *n.* 1. "... [A]ccidental or unintentional." *Guimond v. Sornberger* (1980), 13 Alta. L.R. (2d) 228 at 242, 13 M.P.L.R. 134, 25 A.R. 18, 115 D.L.R. (3d) 321 (C.A.), Clement J.A. 2. "... [I]nvolves oversight, inattention, carelessness and the like." *Campbell v. Dowdall* (1992), 12 M.P.L.R. (2d) 27 at 37 (Ont. Gen. Div.), Rutherford J.

IN AETERNUM. [L.] For ever.

INALIENABLE. *adj.* Not able to be transferred.

IN A PERVERSE OR CAPRICIOUS MANNER OR WITHOUT REGARD FOR THE MATERIAL BEFORE IT. The words "in a perverse or capricious manner or without regard for the material before it" [in section 18 of the Federal Courts Act] are clear and unambiguous. They indicate that on questions of fact, courts are only to interfere in the most egregious cases of erroneous fact finding. *Canada (Citizenship and Immigration) v. Khosa*, 2009 SCC 12, Rothstein J.

INAUGURATION. *n.* Solemn induction into office.

IN AUTRE DROIT. [Fr.] In the right of another.

IN BANC. See BANC; IN BANCO.

IN BANCO. [L.] As a bench (of judges). Refers to the court sitting as a whole. See BANCO.

IN BANK. See BANC; BANCO; IN BANCO.

IN BEING. 1. Living or en ventre sa mere. *Perpetuities acts.* 2. Living or conceived but unborn.

INC. *abbr.* 1. Incorporated. 2. Incorporé.

IN CAMERA. [L.] "... '[W]ithout publicity, privately and, if possible, in the private office of the judge or a private room'... ." *R. v. B. (C.)* (1981), 23 C.R. (3d) 289 at 294, 62 C.C.C. (2d) 107, 38 N.R. 451, [1981] 6 W.W.R. 701, 24 R.F.L. (2d) 225, 12 Man. R. (2d) 361, [1981] 2 S.C.R. 480, 127 D.L.R. (3d) 482, the court per Chouinard J.

INCAPABLE. *adj.* Unable because of death, illness, absence from the province or otherwise. *Vital Statistics acts.*

INCAPACITY. *n.* 1. Lack of ability. 2. Referring to the capacity to form an intent to commit a crime. In criminal law, a quality attributed to people with severe mental disorders and young children and, not as widely, to those who are intoxicated. 3. The status whereby a respondent is suffering from a physical, mental or emotional condition, disorder or addiction that may endanger the health or safety of customers. Nova Scotia statutes.. See LEGAL ~; MENTAL ~.

INCARCERATE. *v.* To imprison.

INCARCERATION. *n.* Imprisonment.

INCB. *abbr.* The International Narcotics Control Board.

INCENDIARISM. *n.* Deliberate setting of fire to property. See ARSON.

INCENTIVE OR BONUS ZONING. Requirements that permit the relaxation of certain requirements if an applicant exceeds other requirements or
undertakes other action, in the public interest, as specified in the requirements. *Municipal Government Act*,
S.N.S. 1998, c. 18, s. 191.

INCENTIVE PAY. Pay that is based on productivity
rather than hours of work, including, by way of an
example, (a) a sales commission; (b) pay that is based
on piecework or a fixed amount per task; (c) a bonus
that is tied directly to the worker's performance and
is not payable at the employer's discretion. *Employment Standards Code*, S.M. 1998, c. 29, *Employment
Standards Regulation*, Man. Reg. 6/2007, s. 18.

INCERTUS. *adj.* [L.] Uncertain.

INCEST. *n.* Knowing that another person is by blood
relationship his or her parent, child, brother, sister,
grandparent or grandchild, as the case may be, having
sexual intercourse with that person. *Criminal Code*,
R.S.C. 1985, c. C-46, s. 155.

IN CHIEF. Describes the examination of a witness
by the person who called that witness.

INCHOATE. *adj.* Commenced but not finished.

INCIDENT. *n.* 1. Something which follows or ap-
pertains to another thing. 2. An event; a happening.
See OIL POLLUTION ~.

INCIDENTAL. *adj.* 1. In its simplest formulation,
the plain meaning of "incidental" is "connected with
in a meaningful way" and includes an activity that is
subordinate to a principal activity. The ordinary sense
of "incidental" does not imply or import a temporal
connection between the two related activities. *Bank
of Nova Scotia v. British Columbia (Superintendent
of Financial Institutions)* 2003 BCCA 29, 11
B.C.L.R. (4th) 206. 2. [T]he medical care that is referred to as incidental is minor in nature, casual, or
arising in a fortuitous conjunction with the spousal
relationship [which existed between the patient and
chiropractor]. *Leering v. College of Chiropractors of
Ontario*, 2010 ONCA 87, 98 O.R. (3d) 561. See
COSTS OF AND ~ TO.

INCIDENT TO ARREST. The second requirement
before a strip search incident to arrest may be performed is that the search must be incident to the arrest.
What this means is that the search must be related to
the reasons for the arrest itself. *R. v. Golden*, 2001
SCC 83.

INCITE. *v.* 1. To arouse, provoke, encourage. 2. To
incite someone to commit an offence clearly means
the alleged offender must urge or persuade the other
person to do so. *R. v. Rhynes*, 2004 PESCAD 15.

INCLOSURE. *n.* Fencing in property in order to
cultivate it.

INCLUDE. *v.* 1. "... [G]enerally used in interpretation clauses in order to enlarge the meaning of words
or phrases occurring in the body of a statute ..." *Dilworth v. New Zealand Commissioner of Stamps*,
[1899] A.C. 99 at 105 (New Zealand P.C.), Lord
Watson. 2. "... It may be equivalent to 'mean and

include', and in that case it may afford an exhaustive
explanation of the meaning ..." *Dilworth v. New Zealand Commissioner of Stamps*, [1899] A.C. 99 at 105-
6 (New Zealand P.C.), Lord Watson. 3. When used
in a definition indicates that the definition is not intended to be exhaustive. Those things listed in the
definition and, in addition, things of like import. See
~S.

INCLUDED OFFENCE. 1. A count in an indictment is divisible and where the commission of the
offence charged, as described in the enactment creating it or as charged in the count, includes the commission of another offence, whether punishable by
indictment or on summary conviction, the accused
may be convicted (a) of an offence so included that
is proved, notwithstanding that the whole offence that
is charged is not proved; or (b) of an attempt to commit an offence so included. *Criminal Code*, R.S.C.
1985, c. C-46, s. 662(1). 2. Second degree murder is
included in first degree murder; manslaughter and
infanticide are included in murder; murder includes
concealing a body of a child; manslaughter includes
dangerous operation of a vehicle, vessel, or aircraft;
breaking and entering and stealing a firearm includes
breaking and entering with intent to steal a firearm;
and, breaking and entering and committing an indictable offence includes breaking and entering with
intent to commit an indictable offence. *Criminal
Code*, R.S.C. 1985, c. C-46, s. 662(2) to (6).

INCLUDES. *v.* It is true that the word "includes" in
a definition section often suggests that the enumerated list that follows is not intended to be a comprehensive expression of the defined word or phrase.
However, in other contexts, "includes" suggests a
comprehensive description of the definition. The difference between the two possible interpretations was
well-described by Lord Watson in Dilworth v. Commissioner of Stamps, [1899] A.C. 99 (New Zealand
P.C.) at 105-06: The word "include" is very generally
used in interpretation clauses in order to enlarge the
meaning of the words or phrases occurring in the
body of a statute; and when it is so used these words
or phrases must be construed as comprehending, not
only such things as they signify according to their
natural import, but also those things which the interpretation clause declares that they shall include. But
the word "include" is susceptible of another construction, which may become imperative, if the context of
the Act is sufficient to shew that it was not merely
employed for the purpose of adding to the natural
significance of the words or expressions defined. It
may be equivalent to "mean and include," and in that
case it may afford an exhaustive explanation of the
meaning which, for the purposes of the Act, must
invariably be attached to these words or expressions.
See also R. v. Loblaw Groceterias Co. (Man.) Ltd.
(1960), [1961] S.C.R. 138. *Windsor (City) v. 564163
Ontario Ltd.* (2005), 198 O.A.C. 325. See INCLUDE.

**INCLUSIO UNIUS EST EXCLUSIO ALTER-
IUS.** [L.] To include one is to exclude another. Where
the law stipulates as to certain cases which it lists, the
law is presumed to exclude the other cases.

IN COLLUSION. In concert, by conspiratorial arrangement or by agreement for the purpose of violat-

ing a person's rights in respect of a financial asset. *Securities Transfer acts.*

INCOME. *n.* 1. The gross amount received as the product of labour, business or capital. 2. The net receipts over disbursements in the taxation year in the totality of the taxpayer's business as an ongoing concern other than capital expenditures, gifts and the like. *Premium Iron Ores Ltd. v. M.N.R.,* [1966] S.C.R. 685, [1966] C.T.C. 311, 66 D.T.C. 5280. See DIRECT DISCOUNTING OF ~ METHOD; NET ~; RETIREMENT ~ FUND.

INCOME APPROACH. In valuing a business, uses an estimation of the cash flow of the business and its profitability. The profitability is converted to value by the application of a capitalization or discount rate. Various factors are taken into account in setting the appropriate rate.

INCOME INTEREST. In a trust means a right (whether immediate or future and whether absolute or contingent) as a beneficiary under a personal trust to, or to receive, all or any part of the income of the trust and includes a right to enforce payment of an amount by the trust that arises as a consequence of any such right.

INCOME TAX. 1. Tax on net income, i.e., income after deducting expenses incurred in order to earn the income. 2. "... [A] charge upon the profits; the thing which is taxed is the profit that is made, ..." *Ashton Gas Co. v. Attorney-General* (1905), [1906] A.C. 10 at 12 (U.K. H.L.), Earl of Halsbury L.C.

INCOME TAX EVASION. Income tax evasion is a form of fraud on the public purse. *Germany (Federal Republic) v. Schreiber* (2006), 207 O.A.C. 306.

IN COMMON. The definition of "band" uses the term "in common" in relation to the interest that the members of the band have in the reserve. The term "in common" connotes a communal, as opposed to a private, interest in the reserve, by the members of the band. In other words, an individual member of a band has an interest in association with, but not independent of, the interest of the other members of the band. *Blueberry River Indian Band v. Canada (Department of Indian Affairs & Northern Development),* 2001 CarswellNat 963, 2001 FCA 67, 6 C.P.C. (5th) 1, 201 D.L.R. (4th) 35, 274 N.R. 304 (C.A.), the court per Rothstein J.A. See INTENTION ~; TENANCY ~; TENANTS ~.

INCOMPETENCE. *n.* Acts or omissions of the part of a member of a professional body, in that member's occupation, that demonstrate a lack of knowledge, skill or judgment, or disregard for the interests of the recipient of the services of such a nature and to such an extent as to render that member unfit to carry on the occupation. *Professional Regulatory acts.*

INCOMPETENCY. *n.* Absence of reasonable skill. See MENTAL ~.

INCOMPETENT. *n.* A person who lacks reasonable skill.

INCOMPETENT. *adj.* Lacking reasonable skill.

INCOMPETENT PERSON. Includes a person, not an infant, who is incapable from infirmity of mind of

managing the person's own affairs. *Incompetent Persons Act,* R.S.N.S. 1989, c. 218, s. 2.

IN CONSIMILI CASU. [L.] In a similar case.

INCONSISTENT. *adj.* 1. "[In the context of constitutional law] ... refers to a situation where two legislative enactments cannot stand together ..." *Friends of the Oldman River Society v. Canada (Minister of Transport)* (1992), 3 Admin. L.R.(2d) 1 at 37, [1992] 2 W.W.R. 193, [1992] 1 S.C.R. 3, 84 Alta. L.R. (2d) 129, 7 C.E.L.R. (N.S.), 1, 132 N.R. 321, 88 D.L.R. (4th) 1, 48 F.T.R. 160n, La Forest J. (Lamer C.J.C., L'Heureux-Dubé, Sopinka, Gonthier, Cory, McLachlin and Iacobucci JJ. concurring). 2. "Two laws are deemed to be inconsistent when 'compliance with one law involves breach of the other', see Smith v. R., [1960] S.C.R. 776 at 800 ... per Martland J., or if resort to one statute from a practical point of view precludes the other from having any application: see Multiple Access Ltd. v. McCutcheon (1978), 19 O.R. (2d) 516 ... (C.A.)... ." *James v. Lockhart* (1981), 24 R.F.L. (2d) 333 at 335-6 (Ont. Co. Ct.), Flanigan Co. Ct. J.

INCORPORATING INSTRUMENT. The special Act, letters patent, instrument of continuance or other constating instrument by which a body corporate was incorporated or continued and includes any amendment to or restatement of the constating instrument. *Insurance Companies Act,* S.C. 1991, c. 47, s. 2.

INCORPORATION. *n.* 1. The formation of a group of people into a corporation or body politic. 2. Merger of one thing with another so that the two constitute one whole. See ARTICLES OF ~; CERTIFICATE OF ~.

INCORPORATOR. *n.* 1. A person who signs articles of incorporation. 2. In relation to a company, means a person who applied for letters patent to incorporate the company.

INCORPOREAL. *adj.* Not capable of being possessed physically. R. Megarry & H.W.R. Wade, *The Law of Real Property,* 5th ed. (London: Stevens, 1984) at cxxv.

INCORPOREAL CHATTEL. An incorporeal right attached to chattels.

INCORPOREAL HEREDITAMENT. 1. "[A right] ... in land, which [includes] such things as rent charges, annuities, easements, profits à prendre, and so on." *Pegg v. Pegg* (1992), 38 R.F.L. (3d) 179 at 184, 21 R.P.R. (2d) 149, 1 Alta. L.R. (3d) 249, 128 A.R. 132 (Q.B.), Agrios J. 2. Property which is not tangible but can be inherited. See PROFIT.

INCORRIGIBLE. *adj.* Uncorrectable.

INCREASED COSTS. Increased costs will only be awarded if there is some unusual feature in the case or misconduct in addition to a significant disparity between ordinary and special costs which justifies greater indemnity than provided by ordinary costs. *Rieta v. North American Air Travel Insurance Agents Ltd.* (1998), 52 B.C.L.R. (3d) 114 (C.A.).

INCREMENT. *n.* 1. In respect of a job or position, means the difference between the compensation payable for a rate in the scale or rates applicable to the job or position and the next higher rate in that scale. 2. The monthly guaranteed annual income increment authorized to be paid under this Act, and is an amount equal to the amount by which one-twelfth of the guaranteed income limit applicable to a beneficiary exceeds the beneficiary's basic monthly income for the month for which the payment authorized under this Act is being made. *Ontario Guaranteed Annual Income Act*, R.S.O. 1990, c. O.17, s. 1.

INCRIMINATE. *v.* 1. "In this context, the word 'incriminate' need not be equated with 'tending to prove guilt of a criminal offence'. The history of the various aspects of the principle against self-incrimination shows that the word 'incriminate' was not thus limited in this context. It extended, for example, to evidence having the tendency to expose the individual to a penalty or a forfeiture ..." *R. v. Jones*, 1994 CarswellBC 580, 30 C.R. (4th) 1, 166 N.R. 321, 43 B.C.A.C. 241, 69 W.A.C. 241, 89 C.C.C. (3d) 353, [1994] 2 S.C.R. 229, 114 D.L.R. (4th) 645, 21 C.R.R. (2d) 286, Lamer C.J.C. 2. "... '[M]ay tend to bring him into the peril and possibility of being convicted as a criminal'... . [and may be extended] to any proceedings where an individual is exposed to a criminal charge, penalty or forfeiture as a result of having testified in earlier proceedings... ." *Grineage v. Coopman* (1988), 27 C.P.C. (2d) 187 at 189-90 (Ont. H.C.), O'Brien J.

INCRIMINATING EVIDENCE. Any evidence which the Crown tenders as part of its case against an accused.

INCRIMINATION. See PRINCIPLE AGAINST SELF-~; PRIVILEGE AGAINST SELF-~; SELF-~.

INCULPATORY CONFESSION. A statement which incriminates the maker.

INCULPATORY OPINION. An inculpatory opinion is to the effect that the accused, because [a mitochondrial DNA ("mtDNA")] sequence matching his was found at the crime scene, "cannot be excluded" from the group of people who could have deposited the questioned sample there. Any other person with the same mtDNA sequence could also have done so. *R. v. Murrin*, 1999 CarswellBC 3015, 181 D.L.R. (4th) 320, 32 C.R. (5th) 97 (S.C.), Henderson J.

INCUMBRANCE. *n.* 1. A charge or liability to which land is subject. 2. "By generally accepted definition ... it comprehends 'every right to or interest in land which may subsist in third persons to the diminution of the value of land, but consistent with the passing of the fee by the conveyance' ..." *Wotherspoon v. Canadian Pacific Ltd.* (1987), (*sub nom. Eaton Retirement Annuity Plan v. Canadian Pacific Ltd.*) 45 R.P.R. 138 at 192, 76 N.R. 241, 21 O.A.C. 79, [1987] 1 S.C.R. 952, 39 D.L.R. (4th) 169, the court per Estey J. See ENCUMBRANCE.

IN CURIA. [L.] In an open court.

INCURRED. *v.* 1. Rendered liable to. 2. Having become necessary. 3. Said of expenses, current or future, known with certainty.

IN CUSTODIA LEGIS. [L.] In legal custody.

INDEBTEDNESS. See SUBORDINATED ~.

INDECENCY. See GROSS ~.

INDECENT. *adj.* "... [S]uch as would shock or disgust the average member of the Canadian contemporary community." *Priape Enrg. c. Sous-Ministre du Revenu national* (1979), (*sub nom. Priape Enrg. v. Deputy Minister of National Revenue (Customs & Excise)*) 24 C.R. (3d) 66 at 71, [1980] C.S. 86, 52 C.C.C. (2d) 44, 2 C.E.R. 169 (Qué. S.C.), Hugessen A.C.J.S.C.

INDECENT ASSAULT. "... [A]n assault that is committed in circumstances of indecency, or, as sometimes described, an assault with acts of indecency... ." *R. v. Swietlinski* (1980), 18 C.R. (3d) 231 at 243, 34 N.R. 569, 55 C.C.C. (2d) 481, 117 D.L.R. (3d) 285, [1980] 2 S.C.R. 956, the court per McIntyre J.

INDEFEASIBLE. *adj.* Not able to be voided.

INDEFEASIBLE TITLE. An estate in fee simple held under a good marketable title.

INDEFINITELY. *adv.* [In the context of a prospective spousal support award] only mean[t] that no termination date [was to] be set at [that] juncture. *Cassidy v. McNeil*, 2010 ONCA 218, 99 O.R. (3d) 81.

INDEMNIFICATION. *n.* Making good.

INDEMNIFY. *v.* To make good the loss which someone suffered through another's act or default; to grant an indemnity; to agree to indemnify.

INDEMNITY. *n.* 1. Indemnity may arise by contract, by statute, or by the nature of the relationship itself. An obligation to indemnify means an obligation to protect against or keep free from loss, to repay for what has been lost or damaged, to compensate for a loss. Contribution, on the other hand, is only available when a co-debtor has paid more than his equal share of the debt. Contribution among co-debtors is an equitable concept, and a co-debtor, while liable to the creditor for the full amount, is only liable as among the co-debtors for his or her share. *Lafrentz v. M & L Leasing Ltd. Partnership*, 2000 CarswellAlta 1121, 2000 ABQB 714, 8 B.L.R. (3d) 219, [2001] 1 W.W.R. 629, 85 Alta. L.R. (3d) 233, 275 A.R. 334, Perras J. 2. "... [T]he concept of indemnity has central to it the idea of compensation, of making good, or paying moneys to a person, to reimburse them for losses sustained... ." *Arklie v. Haskell* (1986), 25 C.C.L.I. 277 at 284, 33 D.L.R. (4th) 458, [1987] I.L.R. 1-2176 (B.C. C.A.), McLachlin J.A. (Hutcheon and MacFarlane JJ.A. concurring). See ACTION FOR ~; CONTRACT OF ~; SUBSTANTIAL ~ COSTS.

INDEMNITY INSURANCE. The distinction between indemnity and non-indemnity insurance is well-recognized in the insurance industry. The following definitions, which I adopt here, were used by the 1988 Report of Inquiry into Motor Vehicle Accident Compensation in Ontario (the Osborne Commission), at p. 429: An indemnity payment is one which is intended to compensate the insured in whole or in part for a pecuniary loss ... A non-indemnity payment is a payment of a previously determined amount upon proof of a specified event, whether or not there has been pecuniary loss. Perhaps the best example of non-indemnity insurance is that of life insurance. The beneficiary under a life-insurance policy collects a set amount upon the death of the policy holder without reference to any pecuniary loss. Pensions are also considered to be non-indemnity payments. *Cunningham v. Wheeler*, 1994 CarswellBC 121, 88 B.C.L.R. (2d) 273, [1994] 4 W.W.R. 153, 20 C.C.L.I. (2d) 1, [1994] 1 S.C.R. 359, 113 D.L.R. (4th) 1, 23 C.C.L.I. (2d) 205, 164 N.R. 81, 41 B.C.A.C. 1, 66 W.A.C. 1, 20 C.C.L.T. (2d) 1, 2 C.C.P.B. 217, 23 C.C.L.I. (2d) 205, 41 B.C.A.C. 1, [1994] 1 S.C.R. 359. See NON-~

INDEMNITY PAYMENT. One which is intended to compensate the insured in whole or in part for a pecuniary loss. *Cunningham v. Wheeler,* [1994] 1 S.C.R. 359. See NON-~

INDENTURE. *n.* A deed which two or more parties made. See DEED-POLL; TRUST ~.

INDEPENDENCE. *n.* 1. The state of not being dependent on another or others. 2. Independence is based on the existence of a set of objective conditions or guarantees which ensure judges have the complete freedom to try the cases before them. It is more concerned with the status of the Court in relation to the other branches of government and bodies which can exercise pressure on the judiciary through power conferred on them by the state. *R. c. Lauzon*, 1998 CarswellNat 1810, 18 C.R. (5th) 288, (*sub nom. R. v. Lauzon*) 230 N.R. 272, 56 C.R.R. (2d) 30, (*sub nom. R. v. Lauzon*) 129 C.C.C. (3d) 399, 8 Admin. L.R . (3d) 33 (Can. Ct. Martial App. Ct.). See INSTITUTIONAL ~; JUDICIAL ~.

INDEPENDENT. *n.* An independent member of the legislature, who is a member of the legislature but not a member of one of the party caucuses represented in the legislature.

INDEPENDENT. *adj.* "[In s. 11(d) of the Charter] ... reflects or embodies the traditional constitutional value of judicial independence. As such, it connotes not merely a state of mind or attitude in the actual exercise of judicial functions, but a status or relationship to others, particularly to the Executive Branch of government, that rests on objective conditions or guarantees." *R. v. Valente (No. 2)* (1985), 23 C.C.C. (3d) 193 at 201, [1985] 2 S.C.R. 673, 52 O.R. (2d) 779, 37 M.V.R. 9, 49 C.R. (3d) 97, 24 D.L.R. (4th) 161, 64 N.R. 1, 14 O.A.C. 79, 19 C.R.R. 354, [1985] D.L.Q. 85n, the court per Le Dain J.

INDEPENDENT CONTRACTOR. 1. An individual who enters into a contract in the individual's own name to provide services as an independent contractor. *Insurance Act*, R.S.A. 2000, c. I-3, s. 451. 2. A self-employed person, including a partner in a partnership, who carries on or engages in any industry, and who does not employ any workers in connection with that industry. *The Workers' Compensation Act*, R.S.M. 1987, c. W200, s. 75.

INDEPENDENT MEMBER. A member of a legislature who does not belong to a caucus.

INDETERMINATE. *adj.* Not fixed in extent or amount; of uncertain size; indefinite.

INDETERMINATE SENTENCE. Imprisonment of undetermined length.

INDEX. *n.* 1. [L.] 1. An alphabetical list of separate subjects or items contained in a book, writing or similar thing. 2. A ratio or other number based on a series of observations and used as a standard. See CONSUMER PRICE ~; COST OF LIVING ~; TOPICAL ~.

INDIAN. *n.* 1. "... '[A]borigines.' ..." *Reference re whether the Term "Indians" in s. 91(24) of the Constitution Act 1867, includes Eskimo Inhabitants of Quebec*, [1939] S.C.R. 104 at 111, [1939] 2 D.L.R. 417, Duff C.J. 2. A person who pursuant to this Act is registered as an Indian or is entitled to be registered as an Indian. *Indian Act*, R.S.C. 1985, c. I-5, s. 2. 3. The extent of federal jurisdiction over Indians has not been definitively addressed by this Court. We have not needed to do so because the vires of federal legislation with respect to Indians, under the division of powers, has never been at issue. The cases which have come before the Court under s. 91(24) [Constitution Act, 1867 (U.K.), 30 & 31 Vict., c. 3] have implicated the question of jurisdiction over Indians from the other direction—whether provincial laws which on their face apply to Indians intrude on federal jurisdiction and are inapplicable to Indians to the extent of that intrusion. The Court has held that s. 91(24) protects a "core" of Indianness from provincial intrusion, through the doctrine of interjurisdictional immunity. It follows, at the very least, that this core falls within the scope of federal jurisdiction over Indians. That core encompasses aboriginal rights, including the rights that are recognized and affirmed by s. 35(1) [Constitution Act, 1982, being Schedule B to the Canada Act 1982 (U.K.), 1982, c. 11]. Laws which purport to extinguish those rights therefore touch the core of Indianness which lies at the heart of s. 91(24), and are beyond the legislative competence of the provinces to enact. The core of Indianness encompasses the whole range of aboriginal rights that are protected by s. 35(1). Those rights include rights in relation to land; that part of the core derives from s. 91(24)'s reference to "Lands reserved for the Indians". But those rights also encompass practices, customs and traditions which are not tied to land as well; that part of the core can be traced to federal jurisdiction over "Indians". Provincial governments are prevented from legislating in relation to both types of aboriginal rights. *Delgamuukw v. British Columbia*, 153 D.L.R. (4th) 193, 220 N.R. 161, 99 B.C.A.C. 161, 162 W.A.C. 161, [1997] 3 S.C.R. 1010, [1998] 1 C.N.L.R. 14, [1999] 10 W.W.R. 34, 66 B.C.L.R. (3d) 285, Lamer C.J.C. (Cory and Major JJ. concurring). See STATUS ~.

INDIAN AFFAIRS. See DEPARTMENT OF ~ AND NORTHERN DEVELOPMENT.

INDIAN BAND. 1. An unincorporated association of first nations persons created by statute. 2. The definition of "band" does not constitute an Indian

I

Band as a legal entity. Rather, I take it from the definition of "band", and other provisions of the Indian Act, that in relation to rights to an Indian reserve, a band is a distinct population of Indians for whose use and benefit, in common, a reserve has been set aside by the Crown. *Blueberry River Indian Band v. Canada (Department of Indian Affairs & Northern Development)* 2001 CarswellNat 963 2001 FCA 67, 6 C.P.C. (5th) 1, 201 D.L.R. (4th) 35, 274 N.R. 304, [2001] 3 C.N.L.R. 72, [2001] 4 F.C. 451, 3 C.N.L.R. 72, 2001 CarswellNat 3104, 4 F.C. 451, 203 F.T.R. 320 (note), [2001] F.C.J. No. 725.

INDIAN RESERVE. Lands conveyed or assigned to the Crown in right of Canada for the use of Indians.

INDIAN RESIDENTIAL SCHOOLS TRUTH AND RECONCILIATION COMMISSION. Its mandate is set out in Schedule "N" of the Indian Residential Schools Settlement Agreement. The Truth and Reconciliation Commission will build upon the "Statement of Reconciliation" dated January 7, 1998 and the principles developed by the Working Group on Truth and Reconciliation and of the Exploratory Dialogues (1998-1999). These principles are as follows: accessible; victim-centered; confidentiality (if required by the former student); do no harm; health and safety of participants; representative; public/transparent; accountable; open and honourable process; comprehensive; inclusive, educational, holistic, just and fair; respectful; voluntary; flexible; and forward looking in terms of rebuilding and renewing Aboriginal relationships and the relationship between Aboriginal and non-Aboriginal Canadians. The goals of the Commission shall be to: (a) Acknowledge Residential School experiences, impacts and consequences; (b) Provide a holistic, culturally appropriate and safe setting for former students, their families and communities as they come forward to the Commission; (c) Witness, support, promote and facilitate truth and reconciliation events at both the national and community levels; (d) Promote awareness and public education of Canadians about the IRS system and its impacts; (e) Identify sources and create as complete an historical record as possible of the IRS system and legacy. The record shall be preserved and made accessible to the public for future study and use; (f) Produce and submit to the Parties of the Agreement a report including recommendations to the Government of Canada concerning the IRS system and experience including: the history, purpose, operation and supervision of the IRS system, the effect and consequences of IRS (including systemic harms, intergenerational consequences and the impact on human dignity) and the ongoing legacy of the residential schools; (g) Support commemoration of former Indian Residential School students and their families in accordance with the Commemoration Policy Directive (Schedule "X" of the Agreement).

INDIANS AND LANDS RESERVED FOR INDIANS. [Since 1871, the exclusive power to legislate in relation to "Indians, and Lands reserved for Indians" has been vested with the federal government by virtue of s. 91(24) of the Constitution Act, 1867 [(U.K.) 30 & 31 Vict., c. 3]. That head of jurisdiction encompasses within it the exclusive power to extinguish aboriginal rights, including aboriginal title. *Delgamuukw v. British Columbia*, 153 D.L.R. (4th) 193, 220 N.R. 161, 99 B.C.A.C. 161, 162 W.A.C. 161, [1997] 3 S.C.R. 1010, [1998] 1 C.N.L.R. 14, [1999] 10 W.W.R. 34, 66 B.C.L.R. (3d) 285, Lamer C.J.C. (Cory and Major JJ. concurring).

INDICIA. *n.* [L.] 1. Marks; signs. 2. Facts which cause inferences to be made.

INDICTABLE OFFENCE. A criminal offence which is triable by way of indictment. The most serious criminal offences are indictable offences. Murder, for example, is an indictable offence. Some offences may be tried by indictment or by summary conviction, hybrid offences. See COMPOUNDING AN ~.

INDICTABLE ONLY OFFENCE. A criminal offence which can only be tried by way of indictment.

INDICTED. *adj.* Charged with a criminal offence in an indictment.

INDICTMENT. *n.* 1. Includes (a) information or a count therein, (b) a plea, replication or other pleading, and (c) any record. *Criminal Code*, R.S.C. 1985, c. C-46, s. 2. 2. Includes an information or charge in respect of which a person has been tried for an indictable offence under Part XIX. *Criminal Code*, R.S.C. 1985, c. C-46, s. 673. See DIRECT ~; PREFERRED ~.

INDIFFERENT. *adj.* Not having any interest which may prevent impartial judgment.

INDIGENT. *n.* 1. "... [A] person possessed of some means but such scanty means that he is needy and poor." *National Sanitarium Association v. Mattawa (Town)* (1925), 56 O.L.R. 474 at 477, [1925] 2 D.L.R. 491 (C.A.), the court per Mulock C.J.O. 2. In law, the word "indigent" does not mean a person without any means, namely a pauper, but a person possessed of some means but such scanty means that he or she is needy and poor. *Hopkins v. Hill*, 2000 CarswellBC 1021, 2000 BCSC 637, Halfyard J.

INDIGNITY. *n.* The ordinary sense of "indignity" clearly does not require any physical contact with a body. It should be noted that the French text does not include physical interference: "commet tout outrage, indécence ou indignité." This makes my claim that physical contact is not necessary even stronger. The words "whether buried or not" also reveal that physical contact is a sufficient but not a necessary element of this offence. Parliament clearly contemplated the offering of indignities taking place when the body or human remains were buried. That is, Parliament contemplated the offering of indignities to human remains separated from an accused by six feet of dirt. *R. v. Moyer*, 1994 CarswellOnt 95, 32 C.R. (4th) 232, 170 N.R. 1, 92 C.C.C. (3d) 1, [1994] 2 S.C.R. 899, 73 O.A.C. 243, the court per Lamer C.J.C.

INDIRECT CONTRIBUTION. Financial contributions to property are examples of direct contributions. Homemaking or household management services are an example of indirect contributions.

Sanders v. Tomei, 2000 CarswellBC 1032, 2000 BCSC 696, 9 R.F.L. (5th) 376, Smith J.

INDIRECT DISCRIMINATION. Occurs when the effect of a law or practice is to discriminate on one of the prohibited grounds even though that was not the intention of the law or practice. See MEIORIN TEST.

INDIRECT EVIDENCE. Proof of related circumstances from which a controversial fact, not directly proved by documents or witnesses, may be inferred. See CIRCUMSTANTIAL EVIDENCE.

INDIRECTLY. See YOU CANNOT DO ~ WHAT YOU CANNOT DO DIRECTLY.

INDIRECT TAXATION. The method of taxation where the tax is demanded from one person in the expectation that he will indemnify himself at the expense of another person. Customs and excise are indirect taxes when imposed on businesses.

INDIVIDUAL. *n.* 1. A natural person. *Rudolf Wolff & Co. v. Canada* (1990), 46 C.R.R. 263 at 269, 43 Admin. L.R. 1, 41 C.P.C. (2d) 1, [1990] 1 S.C.R. 695, 106 N.R. 1, 69 D.L.R. (4th) 392, 39 O.A.C. 1, the court per Cory J. 2. A human being as opposed to a corporation. 3. In our view, the use of the word "individual" in s. 12 relates to a sole proprietorship. If it was the intention of the Legislature to engulf citizens in their personal capacity, outside a sole proprietorship, and outside the corporate veil, in what is little short of confiscatory legislation, they must do so in clear, unambiguous language. We conclude that the Legislature did not use clear enough language to denote such personal responsibility. *550551 Ontario Ltd. v. Framingham*, 1991 CarswellOnt 184, 5 C.B.R. (3d) 204, 91 C.L.L.C. 14,031, 4 O.R. (3d) 571, 49 O.A.C. 376, 4 B.L.R. (2d) 75, (sub nom. *550551 Ontario Ltd. v. Ontario (Employment Standards Officer)*) 82 D.L.R. (4th) 731 (Div. Ct.), the court per Montgomery J. 4. A person other than a corporation. *Income Tax Act*, R.S.B.C. 1996, c. 215, s. 1. See SOURCE ~.

INDIVIDUAL GRIEVANCE. One in which the substance of the complaint directly affects the rights of an individual employee under the collective agreement.

INDIVISIBLE OBLIGATION. An indivisible obligation is not susceptible of division, either between the creditors or the debtors or between their heirs. Each of the debtors or of his heirs may separately be compelled to perform the whole obligation and, conversely, each of the creditors or of his heirs may exact the performance of the whole obligation, even though the obligation is not solidary. *Civil Code*, S.Q. 1991, c. 64, a. 1520. See DIVISIBLE OBLIGATION.

INDOLENT. See EQUITY AIDS THE VIGILANT AND NOT THE ~.

INDOOR WORKPLACE. An enclosed place, other than a vehicle, in which employees perform the duties of their employment and includes an adjacent corridor, lobby, stairwell, elevator, escalator, eating area, washroom, restroom or other enclosed area frequented by employees during the course of their employment, but does not include a private residence unless it meets the requirements of subsection (3). *Smoke-free Places Act*, S.N.B. 2004, c. S-9.5, s. 1.

INDORSEE. *n.* The individual to whom a bill of exchange, bill of lading or promissory note, for example, is assigned by indorsing it.

INDORSEMENT. *n.* Anything printed or written on the back of a document or deed. See ENDORSEMENT.

INDORSER. *n.* The person who indorses the holder or payee by writing her or his name on the back of a bill of exchange.

INDUCEMENT. *n.* Incitement, persuasion, influence.

INDUCING BREACH OF CONTRACT. The Lords defined the elements of the tort of inducing breach of contract as follows: (1) the defendant had knowledge of the contract between the plaintiff and the third party; (2) the defendant's conduct was intended to cause the third party to breach the contract; (3) the defendant's conduct caused the third party to breach the contract; (4) the plaintiff suffered damage as a result of the breach (see [OBG Ltd. v. Allan, [2007] UKHL 21 (U.K. H.L.)] at paras. 39-44 (Hoffman L.)). The Lords confined the tort to cases where the defendant actually knew that its conduct would cause the third party to breach (it is not enough that the defendant ought reasonably to have known that its conduct would cause the third party to breach); the defendant must have intended the breach (it is not enough that a breach was merely a foreseeable consequence of the defendant's conduct); and there must be an actual breach (it is not enough for the conduct to merely hinder full performance of the contract). *Correia v. Canac Kitchens*, 2008 ONCA 506. See INTENTIONAL INDUCEMENT OF BREACH OF CONTRACT.

INDUST. L.J. *abbr.* Industrial Law Journal.

INDUSTRIAL ACCIDENT. A sudden and unforeseen event, attributable to any cause, which happens to a person, arising out of or in the course of his work and resulting in an employment injury to him. *An Act Respecting industrial accidents and occupational diseases*, R.S.Q., c. A-3.001, s. 2.

INDUSTRIAL ACTION. A strike; picketing.

INDUSTRIAL DESIGN. 1. Features of shape, configuration, pattern or ornament and any combination of those features that, in a finished article, appeal to and are judged solely by the eye. *Industrial Design Act*, R.S.C. 1985, c. I-9, s. 2. 2. "... [A] design to be 'applied' to 'the ornamenting' of an article ... something that determines the appearance of an article, or some part of an article, because ornamenting relates to appearance. And it must have as its objective making the appearance of an article more attractive because that is the purpose of ornamenting... ." *Cimon Ltd. v. Bench Made Furniture Corp.* (1964), 48 C.P.R. 31 at 49, [1965] Ex. C.R. 811, 30 Fox Pat. C. 77 (Ex. Ct.), Jackett P.

INDUSTRIAL DISEASE. 1. A disease prescribed by regulation under section 90 and another disease peculiar to or characteristic of a particular industrial process, trade or occupation. *Workplace Health, Safety and Compensation Act*, R.S.N. 1990, c. W-11, s. 2. 2. Any disease in respect of which compensation is payable under the law of the province where the employee is usually employed respecting compensation for workmen and the dependants of deceased workmen. *Government Employees Compensation Act*, R.S.C. 1985, c. G-5, s. 2.

INDUSTRIAL DISPUTE. A dispute or difference or apprehended dispute or difference between an employer and one or more of his or her employees, or a bargaining agent acting on behalf of his or her employees, as to matters or things affecting or relating to terms or conditions of employment or work done or to be done by the employees or as to privileges, rights and duties of the employer or employee. *Labour Relations Act*, R.S.N. 1990, c. L-1, s. 2.

INDUSTRIAL ESPIONAGE. See ESPIONAGE.

INDUSTRIAL PROPERTY. 1. Copyright, industrial design, patent and trade mark matters. 2. Land that is constructed to be used for the assembling, processing or manufacturing of finished or partially finished products from raw materials or fabricated parts. *Commercial Concentration Tax Act*, R.S.O. 1990, c. C.16, s. 1.

INDUSTRIAL RELATIONS. The interactions among unions, management, government, employees, and employers.

INDUSTRY. See DEPARTMENT OF ~.

INERT WASTE. Solid waste that, when disposed of in a landfill or re-used, is not reasonably expected to undergo physical, chemical or biological changes to such an extent as to produce substances that may cause an adverse effect, and includes, but is not limited to, demolition debris, concrete, asphalt, glass, ceramic materials, scrap metal and dry timber or wood that has not been chemically treated. *Environmental Protection and Enhancement Act*, R.S.A. 2000, c. E-12, *Waste Control Regulation*, Alta. Reg. 192/96, s. 1.

IN ESSE. [L.] Which actually exists; in being.

INEQUITABLE. *adj.* In determining whether a transaction is inequitable, "courts should consider all the circumstances of the transaction including such factors as the risk involved, the harshness of the terms, and whether the terms are much harsher than those available to like debtors at the time the transaction was entered into". *Vencer Mortgage Investments Ltd. v. Batley*, 1984 CarswellBC 194, 54 B.C.L.R. 374, 27 B.L.R. 255 (S.C.), Lander J.

INEVITABLE. *adj.* "... Damage is said to be 'inevitable' when the body responsible for it establishes to the satisfaction of the Court that it was demonstrably impossible to avoid the damage inasmuch as it had carried out its operations with a degree of skill and care commensurate with current scientific and technical knowledge, but with due allowance for practical considerations bearing on time and expense." *Tock v. St. John's (City) Metropolitan Area Board* (1989), 47 M.P.L.R. 113 at 145, [1989] 2

S.C.R. 1181, 1 C.C.L.T. (2d) 113, 64 D.L.R. (4th) 620, 104 N.R. 241, 82 Nfld. & P.E.I.R. 181, 257 A.P.R. 181, La Forest J. (Dickson C.J.C. concurring).

INEVITABLE ACCIDENT. 1. A leading case in Ontario is McIntosh v. Bell [1932] O.R. 179 which was approved by this Court in Claxton v. Grandy [1934] 4 D.L.R. 257 at 263. At page 187 of the report of McIntosh v. Bell, Hodgins J.A. adopts the words of Lord Esher M.R. in The Schwan, [1892] P. 419 at 429 as follows:—. . .In my opinion, a person relying on inevitable accident must shew that something happened over which he had no control, and the effect of which could not have been avoided by the greatest care and skill. *Rintoul v. X-Ray and Radium Industries Ltd.*, [1956] S.C.R. 674. 2. A collision which could not possibly have been prevented by the exercise of ordinary care, caution and maritime skill on the part of the captain.

INEVITABLE DAMAGE. 1. Is often nothing but a hidden cost of running a given system. *Tock v. St. John's Metropolitan Area Board*, [1989] 2 S.C.R. 1181, LaForest J. 2. Established where the public body responsible for it shows that it was impossible to avoid the damage exercising the degree of skill and care commensurate with current scientific and technical knowledge with allowance for practical considerations of time and expense.

IN EXPECTANCY. Executory, relating to some future thing. See INTEREST ~.

IN EXTREMIS. [L.] 1. At the very last. 2. Close to death.

INFAMOUS CONDUCT. More serious than unprofessional conduct. Must be evidence of moral turpitude to constitute infamous conduct. *N v. College of Physicians and Surgeons (British Columbia)* (1997), 30 B.C.L.R. (3d) 390 (C.A.).

INFANT. *n.* 1. A person who has not attained the age of majority. 2. A person under the age of 18 years. *The Public Guardian and Trustee Act*, S.S. 1983, c. P-36.3, s. 2. 3. A child who is under 2 years of age. *Early Learning and Childcare Act*, S.N.B. 2010, c. E-0.5, s. 1. See SHAKEN ~ SYNDROME.

INFANTICIDE. *n.* 1. The murder of an infant. F.A. Jaffe, *A Guide to Pathological Evidence for Lawyers and Police Officers*, 4th ed. (Toronto: Carswell, 1999) at 239. 2. A female person commits infanticide when by a wilful act or omission she causes the death of her newly-born child, if at the time of the act or omission she is not fully recovered from the effects of giving birth to the child and by reason thereof or of the effect of lactation consequent on the birth of the child her mind is then disturbed. *Criminal Code*, R.S.C. 1985, c. C-46, s. 233.

INFECTED PERSON. A person who, or thing that, (a) is or is likely infected with, or has been or has likely been exposed to, a prescribed infectious agent, or (b) is or is likely contaminated with, or has been or has likely been exposed to, a prescribed hazardous agent regardless of whether the person or thing suffers any communicable disease or adverse effect from the infectious agent or hazardous agent, or exhibits any symptom of being ill or infected. *Public Health Act*, S.B.C. 2008, c. 28, s. 1.

INFECTED THING. A person who, or thing that, (a) is or is likely infected with, or has been or has likely been exposed to, a prescribed infectious agent, or (b) is or is likely contaminated with, or has been or has likely been exposed to, a prescribed hazardous agent regardless of whether the person or thing suffers any communicable disease or adverse effect from the infectious agent or hazardous agent, or exhibits any symptom of being ill or infected. *Public Health Act*, S.B.C. 2008, c. 28, s. 1.

INFERENCE. *n.* 1. "... [I]n the legal sense ... is a deduction from the evidence, and if it is a reasonable deduction it may have the validity of legal proof. The attribution of an occurrence to a cause is, I take it, always a matter of inference... ." *Jones v. Great Western Rwy. Co.* (1930), 47 T.L.R. 39 at 45, Lord Macmillan, cited with approval in *Gwyllt, Re*, [1944] O.W.N. 212 at 213 (C.A.), Henderson J.A. 2. Facts sufficient that a particular conclusion may be drawn from them. J.G. Fleming, *The Law of Torts*, 8th ed. (Sydney: Law Book, 1992) at 323. 3. This court, in its judgment on appeal in Willard Miller [Newfoundland (Workers' Compensation Commission) v. Miller (1998), 167 Nfld. & P.E.I.R. 115 (Nfld. T.D.)] . . . has stressed that an inference is different from speculation . . . Drawing an inference amounts to a process of reasoning by which a factual conclusion is deduced as a logical consequence from other facts established by the evidence. Speculation on the other hand is merely a guess or conjecture; there is a gap in the reasoning process that is necessary, as a matter of logic, to get from one fact to the conclusion sought to be established. Speculation, unlike an inference, requires a leap of faith. *Osmond v. Newfoundland (Workers' Compensation Commission)*, 2001 NFCA 21, 200 Nfld. & P.E.I.R. 202, 603 A.P.R. 202, 10 C.C.E.L. (3d) 56, 200 Nfld. & P.E.I.R. 202, [2001] N.J. No. 111. See ADVERSE ~; NECESSARY ~.

INFERIOR COURT. 1. A court which is subject to the control of a higher court. 2. "[A court] ... in which provincially appointed judges sat ..." *Reference re s. 6 of Family Relations Act, 1978 (British Columbia)* (1982), 26 R.F.L. (2d) 113 at 141, [1982] 1 S.C.R. 62, [1982] 3 W.W.R. 1, 36 B.C.L.R. 1, 131 D.L.R. (3d) 257, 40 N.R. 206, Estey J. 3. A court presided over by justices of the peace, magistrates or provincial court judges which has jurisdiction over minor criminal offences and small civil claims.

IN FIERI. [L.] While something was being accomplished.

INFIRMITY. *n.* "... [P]hysical weakness, debility, frailty or feebleness of body resulting from constitutional defect." *Tomlinson v. Prudential Insurance Co.*, [1954] O.R. 508 at 516, [1954] I.L.R. 1-144 (C.A.), the court per Laidlaw J.A.

IN FLAGRANTE DELICTO. [L.] In the actual act.

INFLICTED. See SELF-~.

INFLICTION. See INTENTIONAL ~ OF NERVOUS SHOCK.

INFLUENCE. *v.* To persuade.

INFLUENCE. *n.* Power, particularly power to persuade. The ability of one person to dominate the will of another. See UNDUE ~.

INFLUENTIAL PERSON. In respect of a responsible issuer, (a) a control person, (b) a promoter, (c) an insider who is not a director or officer of the responsible issuer, or (d) an investment fund manager, if the responsible issuer is an investment fund. *Securities Act*, S.N.B. 2004, c. S-5.5, s. 161.1.

INFOCRTC. *abbr.* Broadcasting decisions, public notices and policy statements / Décisions, avis publics et énoncés de politique sur la radiodiffusion (CD-ROM) (also available on the Internet / aussi disponible sur Internet), 1995-1998.

IN FORCE. 1. "... [E]ffectively enacted ..." *Lord's Day Alliance of Canada v. Manitoba (Attorney General)* (1924), [1925] 1 D.L.R. 561 at 565, [1925] 1 W.W.R. 296, [1925] A.C. 384, 43 C.C.C. 185 (Man. P.C.), the board per Lord Blanesburgh. 2. Currently valid.

INFORMAL. *adj.* Lacking proper legal form.

INFORMAL CONTRACT. A parol or simple contract.

INFORMANT. *n.* A person who lays an information. *Criminal Code*, R.S.C. 1985, c. C-46, s. 785. See JAILHOUSE ~; POLICE ~ PRIVILEGE

IN FORMA PAUPERIS. [L. in the form of a poor person] A litigant allowed to proceed in this way is not liable to pay court costs.

INFORMATION. *n.* 1. A document which alleges that an accused person has committed an offence. The laying of an information before a justice is the means to commence a criminal proceeding by way of indictment. An information is usually laid before a justice or sworn before a justice by a peace officer. However, a member of the public also can lay an information. 2. Includes (a) a count in an information, and (b) a complaint in respect of which a justice is authorized by an Act of Parliament or an enactment made thereunder to make an order. *Criminal Code*, R.S.C. 1985, c. C-46, s. 785. 3. Information respecting a consumer's identity, residence, dependents, marital status, employment, borrowing and repayment history, income, assets and liabilities, credit worthiness, education, character, reputation, health, physical or personal characteristics or mode of living. *Consumer Reporting Act*, R.S.N.S. 1989, c. 93, s. 2(1). See BIOMETRIC ~; CONFIDENTIAL ~; CONTACT ~; CREDIT ~; DE-IDENTIFIED VITAL STATISTICS ~; FORWARD-LOOKING ~; FREEDOM OF ~; GLOBAL ~ INFRASTRUCTURE; HEALTH ~ BANK; IDENTITY ~; LAYING AN ~; LEGAL ~ INSTITUTE; MATERIAL NON-PUBLIC ORDER ~; PERSONAL ~; POTENTIALLY INJURIOUS ~; SENSITIVE ~; SPECIAL OPERATIONAL ~; STATISTICAL ~.

INFORMATION ASSURANCE. The protection of information and information systems by ensuring their availability, integrity, authentication, confidentiality and non-repudiation. *Remote Sensing Space Systems Act*, S.C. 2005, c. 45, s. 2.

INFORMATION AND BELIEF. Used in relation to the contents of affidavits. "Equivalent to 'belief' simply." *Adams v. Adams* (1921), 62 D.L.R. 721 at 724, [1922] 1 W.W.R. 47 (C.A.), the court per Beck J.A.

INFORMATION COMMISSIONER OF CANADA. A federal official appointed to hear complaints of government failure to comply with the rights provided by the Access to Information Act.

INFORMATION MANAGEMENT SYSTEM. A system of software and hardware components and related technology that (a) interact and operate to integrate reception, creation, collection, recording, filing, analysis, reporting, transmission, storing, sending, reproduction and dissemination of information and data within and between policing and law enforcement jurisdictions, and (b) is approved by the minister under subsection (2). *Police Act*, R.S.B.C. 1996, c. 367, s. 68.1.

INFORMATION SYSTEM. A system used to generate, send, receive, store, or otherwise process an electronic document. Federal statutes.

INFORMED. *adj.* The requirement that an offender disqualified from driving be "informed of subsection 259(4)" [of the Criminal Code, R.S.C. 1985, c. C-46, as required by s. 260(1)(c) of the Code] means more than that offender by simply advised of its existence; "informed" means that details of significant penal exposure triggered by application of that section must be brought home to offender. Nothing less than that prerequisite is an element of the offence of driving while disqualified. *R. v. Molina*, 2008 ONCA 212.

INFORMED CONSENT. Every individual has the right to know what risks are involved in undergoing or foregoing medical treatment and the concomitant right to make meaningful decisions based on a full understanding of those risks. *Hollis v. Birch*, [1995] 4 S.C.R. 634.

INFORMER. *n.* The one who commences an action or takes some other steps to recover a penalty.

INFORMER PRIVILEGE. 1. The privilege attached to the identity of a person who provided information to police leading to an investigation. 2. A subset of public interest immunity. The value of reliable informers to the administration of justice has been recognized for a long time, so much so that it too is a class privilege. This explains why the high standard of showing that the innocence of the accused is at stake before permitting invasion of the privilege is necessary. Should the privilege be invaded, the State then generally provides for the protection of the informer through various safety programs, again illustrating the public importance of that privilege. *R. v. McLure*, [2001] 1 S.C.R. 445 3. Is an ancient and hallowed protection which plays a vital role in law enforcement. It is premised on the duty of all citizens to aid in enforcing the law. The discharge of this duty carries with it the risk of retribution from those involved in crime. The rule of informer privilege was developed to protect citizens who assist in law en-

forcement and to encourage others to do the same. Informer privilege is of such importance that once found, courts are not entitled to balance the benefit enuring from the privilege against countervailing considerations, as is the case, for example, with Crown privilege or privileges based on Wigmore's four-part test. Informer privilege prevents not only disclosure of the name of the informant, but of any information which might implicitly reveal his or her identity. *R. v. Leipert*, [1997] 1 S.C.R. 281.

INFRA. [L. under, underneath, below] In a document, reference to a later part or page of the document.

INFRASTRUCTURE. *n.* An immovable, a civil engineering work and any other equipment determined by the Government. *An Act to promote the Maintenance and renewal of public infrastructures*, R.S.Q. c. M-1.2, s. 3. See GLOBAL INFORMATION ~.

INFRASTRUCTURE FACILITY. A publicly or privately owned facility that provides or distributes services for the benefit of the public, including services relating to water, sewage, energy, fuel and communications. *Criminal Code*, R.S.C. 1985, c. C-46, s. 431.2 (1).

INFRINGEMENT. *n.* 1. The right of the owner of a registered trade-mark to its exclusive use shall be deemed to be infringed by a person not entitled to its use under the Trade-marks Act who sells, distributes or advertises wares or services in association with a confusing trade-mark or trade-name. 2. While the Patent Act, R.S. 1985, c. P-4, does not define infringement, it is established in law that an infringement is any act which interferes with the full enjoyment of a monopoly granted to its patentee. This monopoly is a statutory monopoly [Monsanto Canada Inc. v. Schmeiser, [2004] 1 S.C.R. 902 (S.C.C.) at paras. 34 and 35, as cited in R.T. Hughes and J.H. Woodley, Hughes and Woodley on Patents, 2nd ed. (Toronto: LexisNexis Canada Inc., 2005), Part I, c. D, § 38, para. 1] and is the exclusive right, privilege and liberty of making, constructing, using, vending and importing the invention [Wellcome Foundation Ltd. v. Apotex Inc., [1990] F.C.J. No. 530, [1990] 3 F.C. 528 (Fed. T.D.), as cited in Hughes and Woodley on Patents, ibid.]. *Gold v. Serratus Mountain Products Ltd.*, 2006 FCA 98. 3. Of copyright, the exercise of a right which only the owner of the copyright is entitled to exercise. 4. Of copyright in a musical work, there must be sufficient objective similarity for the infringing work to be described as a reproduction or adaptation of the copyright work and the copyright work must be the source from which the infringing work is derived, directly or indirectly. See PATENT ~.

INFRINGING. *adj.* (a) In relation to a work in which copyright subsists, any copy, including any colourable imitation, made or dealt with in contravention of this Act, (b) in relation to a performer's performance in respect of which copyright subsists, any fixation or copy of a fixation of it made or dealt with in contravention of this Act, (c) in relation to a sound recording in respect of which copyright subsists, any copy of it made or dealt with in contravention of this

Act, or (d) in relation to a communication signal in respect of which copyright subsists, any fixation or copy of a fixation of it made or dealt with in contravention of this Act. The definition includes a copy that is imported in the circumstances set out in paragraph 27(2)(e) and section 27.1 but does not otherwise include a copy made with the consent of the owner of the copyright in the country where the copy was made. *Copyright Act*, R.S.C. 1985, c. C-42, s. 2.

IN FUTURO. [L.] In future.

IN GOOD FAITH. A thing is deemed to be done "in good faith" when it is in fact done honestly whether it is done negligently or not. *Sale of Goods acts*.

INGREDIENT DISCLOSURE LIST. The Ingredient Disclosure List established by the Governor in Council pursuant to subsection 17(1). *Hazardous Products Act*, R.S.C. 1985, c. H-3, s. 11.

INGRESS. *n.* Entry.

INGROSS. *v.* To write a fair copy of an instrument or deed so that parties may formally execute it.

IN GROSS. Not appendant, appurtenant, or otherwise annexed to land. See EASEMENT ~.

INHERENT. *adj.* Intrinsic; permanently part of.

INHERENT DEFECT. An intrinsic fault or problem.

INHERENT DEFENCE. A defence such as lawful purpose, innocent intent or mistake of fact which simply denies the mens rea which must be proved by the prosecution. P.K. McWilliams, *Canadian Criminal Evidence*, 3d ed. (Aurora: Canada Law Book, 1988) at 25-8.

INHERENT JURISDICTION. 1. That which enables a court to exercise its powers by regulating the practice before the court and preventing abuse of process and punishing for contempt. 2. Operates to ensure that there will always be a court which has the power to vindicate a legal right independent of any statutory grant of jurisdiction. 3. The inherent jurisdiction of the court is traditionally invoked as an adjunct or aid to an existing common law or other right and that in such circumstances its effect is in the nature of a procedural remedy. This, in my opinion, is not its exclusive role. Its use can also be justified in novel circumstances where the failure to do so will adversely impact upon the court's ability "to administer justice according to law" (Master Jacob, at p. 52). It is in this sense that the existence of an amorphous, indefinable residual power in a superior court becomes not a weakness, but a strength. This is because it is truly impossible to define with any sense of finality (and undesirable to attempt to do so) the circumstances in which this essential reserve of judicial powers should be utilized on a principled basis in the interests of justice. *Gillespie v. Manitoba (Attorney General)*, 2000 MBCA 1, 185 D.L.R. (4th) 214, 144 C.C.C. (3d) 193, [2000] 6 W.W.R. 605, 41 C.P.C. (4th) 199, 145 Man. R. (2d) 229. 4. "... The inherent jurisdiction of a superior court is derived not from any statute or rule of law but from the very nature of the court as a superior court: ... Utilizing

this power, superior courts, to maintain their authority and to prevent their processes from being obstructed or abused, have amongst other things punished for contempt of court, stayed matters that are frivolous and vexatious and regulated their own processes... ." *R. v. Unnamed Person* (1985), 20 C.R.R. 188 at 190-91, 10 O.A.C. 305, 22 C.C.C. (3d) 284, the court per Zuber J.A. 5. The reserve or fund of powers which the Court may draw upon as necessary whenever it is just or equitable to do so. It is not an unlimited jurisdiction and, of course, it cannot be exercised in contravention of any statutory provision. Except where provided specifically to the contrary, the Court's jurisdiction is unlimited and unrestricted in substantive law in civil matters. *Zipchen v. Bainbridge*, 2008 SKCA 87.

INHERENT POWER. 1. A power vested in a court that is not derived from statutory authority. 2. Authority, possessed by a corporation, not obtained from statute or a charter, e.g. the power to own land the right of perpetual succession. I.M. Rogers, *The Law of Canadian Municipal Corporations*, 2d ed. (Toronto: Carswell, 1971-) at 361. 3. The power a judge may draw upon to assist or help him or her in the exercise of the ordinary jurisdiction of the court. It does not generally stand alone waiting to be exercised on the judge's own initiative without a suit or application or without parties. *Gillespie v. Manitoba (Attorney General)*, 2000 MBCA 1, 185 D.L.R. (4th) 214, 144 C.C.C. (3d) 193, [2000] 6 W.W.R. 605, 41 C.P.C. (4th) 199, 145 Man. R. (2d) 229.

INHERENT VICE. 1. A condition inherent in an insured property which causes it to be damaged when exposed to normal conditions. *University of Saskatchewan v. Fireman's Fund Insurance Co. of Canada* (1997), 158 Sask. R. 223 (C.A.). 2. Refers to some internal decomposition that made deterioration of the thing inevitable because of qualities inherent in the [machine]. *Canadian National Railway v. Royal & SunAlliance Insurance Co. of Canada*, 222 O.A.C. 129, Rosenberg and Cronk JJ.A.

INHERIT. *v.* 1. To acquire by descent. 2. To acquire under a will.

INHERITABLE. *adj.* Able to inherit.

INHERITANCE. *n.* What descended to the heir of the owner who died intestate, formerly a hereditament.

INHERITANCE TAX. Succession duty calculated upon the inheritance received by any beneficiary. P.W. Hogg, *Constitutional Law of Canada*, 3d ed. (Toronto: Carswell, 1992) at 746.

IN-HOUSE LOBBYIST. 1. An employee, an officer or a director of an organization (a) who receives a payment for the performance of his or her functions, and (b) whose lobbying or duty to lobby on behalf of the organization or an affiliate, either alone or together with other individuals in the organization, (i) amounts to at least 100 hours annually, or (ii) otherwise meets criteria established by the regulations. *Lobbyists Registration Act*, S.B.C. 2001, c. 42, s. 1. 2. An individual who is employed by an organization, (a) a significant part of whose duties as an employee, as determined in accordance with the regulations, is to lobby on behalf of the organization, or (b) a part of whose duties as an employee is to lobby on behalf of the organization if his or her duties to lobby together with the duties of other employees to lobby would constitute a significant part of the duties of one employee, as determined in accordance with the regulations, were those duties to lobby to be performed by only one employee. *Lobbyists Registration Act, 1998*, S.O. 1998, c. 27, Sched., s. 6.

INITIATE. *v.* To commence; to set in motion.

INITIATIVE. See WESTERM HEMISPHERE TRAVEL ~.

INITIATIVE PETITION. A petition to have a proposed law introduced into the Legislative Assembly. A legislative proposal may be made with respect to any matter within the jurisdiction of the Legislature. A registered voter may apply to the chief electoral officer for the issuance of a petition to have a legislative proposal introduced into the Legislative Assembly in accordance with this Act. If satisfied that the requirements of section 3 have been met, the chief electoral officer must (a) notify the proponent that the application has been approved in principle, (b) publish notice of the approval in principle in the Gazette and in at least one newspaper circulating in British Columbia, and (c) issue the petition 60 days after the notice is published in the Gazette. *Recall and Initiative Act*, R.S.B.C. 1996, c. 398.

IN JEOPARDY. At risk of being convicted of a criminal offence.

INJUNCTION. *n.* 1. An equitable remedy in the form of an order of a court requiring a party either to do a specific act or acts or to refrain from doing a specific act or acts. 2. Recognizes that coercive measures may be required to protect a plaintiff's entitlement to some specific right. See INTERIM ~; INTERLOCUTORY ~; MANDATORY ~; MAREVA ~; PERMANENT ~; PERPETUAL ~; PROHIBITORY ~; SPRINGBOARD ~.

INJUNCTION QUIA TIMET. The injunction which a court orders to prevent an act which is threatened or feared. See QUIA TIMET INJUNCTION.

INJURE. *v.* 1. To cause harm to. 2. To deprive one of what is in one's best interests.

INJURED. *adj.* 1. Bodily harm, and includes mental or nervous shock and pregnancy. *Criminal Injury Compensation acts.* 2. In respect of live stock or poultry means injured by wounding, worrying or pursuing. *Livestock, Poultry and Honey Bee Protection Act*, R.S.O. 1990, c. L.24, s. 1.

INJURIA. *n.* [L.] 1. Wrong. 2. An act which encroaches on some right.

INJURIA ABSQUE DAMNO. [L.] Injury or wrong without damage. Compare DAMNUM ABSQUE INJURIA.

INJURIA NON EXCUSAT INJURIUM. [L.] Wrong does not justify wrong.

INJURIA NON PRAESUMITUR. [L.] One should not presume wrongdoing.

INJURIOUS AFFECTION. 1. "The conditions required to give rise to a claim for compensation for injurious affection to a property, when no land is taken are now well established ... These conditions are: (1) the damage must result from an act rendered lawful by statutory powers of the person performing such act; (2) the damage must be such as would have been actionable under the common law, but for the statutory powers; (3) the damage must be an injury to the land itself and not a personal injury or an injury to business or trade; (4) the damage must be occasioned by the construction of the public work, not by its user." *R. v. Loiselle* (1962), 35 D.L.R. (2d) 274 at 275, [1962] S.C.R. 624, the court per Abbott J. 2. In respect of land, the permanent reduction in the appraised value of land as a result of the existence, but not the construction, erection or use, of a public work or structure for which the municipality would be liable if the existence of the public work or structure were not under the authority of an enactment. *Municipal Government Act*, R.S.A. 2000, c. M-26, s. 534. 3. (i) Where a statutory authority acquires part of the land of an owner, (A) the reduction in market value thereby caused to the remaining land of the owner by the acquisition or by the construction of the works thereon or by the use of the works thereon or any combination of them, and (B) such personal and business damages, resulting from the construction or use, or both, of the works as the statutory authority would be liable for if the construction or use were not under the authority of a statute, (ii) where the statutory authority does not acquire part of the land of an owner, (A) such reduction in the market value of the land of the owner, and (B) such personal and business damages, resulting from the construction and not the use of the works by the statutory authority, as the statutory authority would be liable for if the construction were not under the authority of a statute. *Expropriation Act*, R.S.N.S. 1989, c. 156, s. 3.

INJURIOUS FALSEHOOD. Tort of injurious falsehood consists of the publication of false statements, whether oral or written, concerning the plaintiff or his property. The statements are calculated to induce others not to deal with him.

INJURY. *n.* 1. "... The broadest acceptable sense of the word 'injury' is 'interference with a right'... ." *Guest v. Bonderove & Co.* (1988), 59 Alta. L.R. (2d) 86 at 87, 28 C.P.C. (2d) 202, 88 A.R. 277 (C.A.), the court per Kerans J.A. 2. "... [B]odily injury." *Guest v. Bonderove & Co.* (1988), 59 Alta. L.R. (2d) 86 at 88, 28 C.P.C. (2d) 202, 88 A.R. 277 (C.A.), the court per Kerans J.A. 3. Actual bodily harm and includes pregnancy and mental or nervous shock. *Criminal Injuries Compensation acts.* 4. Disrupting tissue by violence. F.A. Jaffe, *A Guide to Pathological Evidence*, 3d ed. (Toronto: Carswell, 1991) at 221. 5. [For the purposes of interpretation of s. 272(1)(a) of the Criminal Code, R.S.C. 1985, c. C-46, dealing with sexual assault with a weapon.] The expression "injury" in s. 2 is not synonymous with "bodily harm". Sexual assault causing bodily harm is the object of a separate offence, provided for by s. 272(1)(c). The expression "bodily harm", which is broadly used in the context of assaults, is defined in s. 2 to mean "any hurt or injury to a person that interferes with the health or comfort of the person and that is more than merely transient or trifling in nature" .... This in itself is sufficient to establish that the acquittal of the respondent on the charge of sexual assault causing bodily harm is not dispositive of the question of whether he used an object "in causing ... injury" so as to make that object a weapon. One cannot go as far as the appellant argues, and conclude that because all cases of sexual assault cause injury (physical or psychological), that therefore if an object is used in the course of any sexual assault, the charge of sexual assault with a weapon is automatically made out. On the other hand, if an object is used in inflicting injury, be it physical or psychological, in the commission of a sexual assault, it is not necessary that the injury amount to bodily harm to trigger the application of s. 272(1)(a). *R. v. Lamy*, [2002] 1 S.C.R. 860. See COMPENSABLE ~; CRIMINAL INJURIES COMPENSATION; EMPLOYMENT ~; NEEDLESTICK ~; PERSONAL ~; REPORTABLE ~; SERVICE-RELATED ~ OR DISEASE.

INJURY TO THE PUBLIC. Includes: (i) any unreasonable interference with the public health, safety, comfort or convenience; (ii) any unreasonable interference with the public's enjoyment of property; and (iii) any expense or increased expense incurred by the public, including any expense or increased expense incurred by the Crown in right of Saskatchewan or a municipality. *The Criminal Enterprise Suppression Act*, S.S. 2005, c. C-46.1, s. 2.

IN KIND. 1. Of the same category. 2. In the same manner. See CONTRIBUTION ~.

INLAND TRANSPORTATION INSURANCE. Insurance (other than marine insurance) against loss of or damage to property, (a) while in transit or during delay incidental to transit, or (b) where, in the opinion of the Superintendent, the risk is substantially a transit risk. *Insurance acts*.

INLAND VOYAGE. A voyage (other than a minor waters voyage) (a) on the inland waters of Canada, together with those parts of any lake or river included in the inland waters of Canada that lie within the United States; or (b) on Lake Michigan. *Excise Tax Act*, R.S.C. 1985, c. E-15, s. 68.5.

INLAND WATERS OF CANADA. All the rivers, lakes and other navigable fresh waters within Canada, and includes the St. Lawrence River as far seaward as a straight line drawn (a) from Cap des Rosiers to West Point Anticosti Island, and (b) from Anticosti Island to the north shore of the St. Lawrence River along the meridian of longitude sixty-three degrees west. *Excise Tax Act*, R.S.C. 1985, c. E-15, s. 68.5.

IN LIMINE. [L.] At the beginning; preliminary.

IN LOCO PARENTIS. [L.] 1. In the place of the parent. 2. "A person in loco parentis to a child is one who has acted so as to evidence his intention of placing himself towards the child in the situation which is ordinarily occupied by the father for the provision of the child's pecuniary wants." *Shtitz v. Canadian National Railway* (1926), [1927] 1 D.L.R. 951 at 959, [1927] 1 W.W.R. 193, 21 Sask. L.R. 345 (C.A.), Turgeon J.A.

INMATE. *n.* 1. A person who is in a penitentiary pursuant to (i) a sentence, committal or transfer to penitentiary, or (ii) a condition imposed by the National Parole Board in connection with day parole or statutory release, or a person who, having been sentenced, committed or transferred to penitentiary, (i) is temporarily outside penitentiary by reason of a temporary absence or work release authorized under this Act, or (ii) is temporarily outside penitentiary for reasons other than a temporary absence, work release, parole or statutory release, but is under the direction or supervision of a staff member or of a person authorized by the Service. *Corrections and Conditional Release Act*, S.C. 1992, c. 20. 2. A person who is sentenced to imprisonment, lawfully detained or confined for treatment, at a correctional centre, and includes a prisoner. *Correction Act*, S.B.C. 2004, c. 46, s. 1. 3. "[Of a common bawdy-house is] ... the prostitute who works on the premises with some regularity but is not responsible for any of the organizational duties involved in running the business as a business ..." *R. c. Corbeil* (1991), 64 C.C.C. (3d) 272 at 292, 5 C.R. (4th) 62, 124 N.R. 241, [1991] 1 S.C.R. 830, 40 Q.A.C. 283, L'Heureux-Dubé J. (dissenting). See PAROLED ~.

IN MEDIAS RES. [L. in the heart of the subject] Without any introduction or preface.

INNOCENCE. *n.* Lack of guilt or knowledge. See PRESUMPTION OF ~.

INNOCENT. *adj.* Not guilty; not negligent. See RIGHT TO BE PRESUMED ~.

INNOCENT MISREPRESENTATION. A misstatement which the party making it did not know was such. G.H.L. Fridman, *Sale of Goods in Canada*, 3d ed. (Toronto: Carswell, 1986) at 153.

INNUENDO. *n.* Exists when the defamatory meaning of words arises from inference or implication. See FALSE ~, LEGAL ~; POPULAR ~, TRUE ~.

IN OMNIBUS QUIDEM, MAXIME TAMEN IN JURE, AEQUITAS SPECTANDA SIT. [L.] In all things, but particularly in law, equity should be regarded.

INOPERATIVE. *adj.* Having ceased to have effect.

IN PAIS. [Fr. in the country] Describes a legal transaction which took place without legal proceedings.

IN PARI DELICTO. [L.] Equally to blame; equally at fault. G.H.L. Fridman, *Restitution*, 2d ed. (Toronto: Carswell, 1992) at 98.

IN PARI DELICTO, POTIOR EST CONDITIO DEFENDENTIS. [L.] When each party is equally at fault, the defendant's position is superior.

IN PARI DELICTO, POTIOR EST CONDITIO POSSIDENTIS. [L.] When each party is equally at fault, the one in possession has the advantage.

IN PARI MATERIA. [L.] 1. In an analogous situation. 2. Relating to the same subject matter.

IN PERPETUITY. Forever.

IN PERSONAM. [L. in person] Describes an action the only purpose of which is to affect the rights of the parties to that action inter se. See ACTIO ~; ACTION ~; EQUITY ACTS ~; JUDGMENT ~; JUS ~; TAX ~.

IN POSSE. Describes something which does not actually exist, but which may come to exist.

IN PRAESENTI. [L.] For the present time.

INQUEST. *n.* 1. An inquiry held before a coroner by a jury regarding the death of a person who was killed or died under suspicious circumstances or suddenly. Inquisatorial investigation conducted into the death of an individual and held before a coroner and jury. No lis exists and no parties rights are affected directly by the inquest. 2. A proceeding under Part 4 before a coroner, with a jury, to determine the particulars of a deceased person and the cause of that person's death. *Coroners Act*, S.B.C. 2007, c. 15, s. 1.

INQUIRE. *v.* To seek knowledge; to ask about.

INQUIRY. *n.* 1. An investigation; a hearing. 2. An inquiry under subsection 7(5). *The Fatality Inquiries Act*, S.M. 1989-90, c. 30, s. 1. 3. An inquiry conducted under Part II, Public Inquiries Act, 2006, S.N. 2006, c. P-38.1, s. 2. The Lieutenant-Governor in Council may order that there be an inquiry under this Part [Part II] into a matter that the Lieutenant-Governor in Council considers to be of public concern. (2) In an order made under subsection (1), the Lieutenant-Governor in Council shall direct how the inquiry is to be conducted, including (a) appointing one or more persons in accordance with section 21 to carry out the inquiry and submit a report; (b) specifying the mechanisms by which the inquiry is to be conducted, which may include (i) interviews and surveys, (ii) research studies, (iii) inspections and investigations, (iv) calling for written submissions, and (v) informal or formal hearings; (c) designating the minister responsible for the inquiry; and (d) specifying the nature and scope of the report to be submitted by the person or persons appointed to conduct the inquiry. *Public Inquiries Act*, 2006, S.N. 2006, c. P-38.1, s. 16. See COMMISSION OF ~; PRELIMINARY ~; PUBLIC ~.

INQUIRY REPORT. A report submitted to the chief medical examiner under subsection 7(5). *The Fatality Inquiries Act*, S.M. 1989-90, c. 30, s. 1.

IN RE. [L.] In the matter of, regarding.

IN REM. [L.] 1. Something done or directed with reference to no person in particular, and therefore with reference to or against anyone it might concern or the whole world. 2. Describes an action to determine the rights or interests of everyone with respect to a particular res, even though the action may involve only two people. J.G. McLeod, *The Conflict of Laws* (Calgary: Carswell, 1983) at 60. See ACTIO ~; ACTION ~; JUDGMENT ~; TAX ~.

IN RERUM NATURA. [L.] In the nature of things.

INSANE. *adj.* Incapable because of mental disorder of conforming conduct to the limits imposed by criminal law. A person who is insane is not legally responsible for his or her action.

INSANITY. *n.* 1. "The definition of 'legal insanity', or insanity which will preclude a criminal conviction, is found in subss. 16(2) and 16(3) of the [Criminal Code, R.S.C. 1985, c. C-46]." *R. v. Chaulk* (1990), 2 C.R. (4th) 1 at 18, 119 N.R. 116, [1991] 2 W.W.R. 385, 69 Man. R. (2d) 161, 62 C.C.C. (3d) 193, 1 C.R.R. (2d) 1, [1990] 3 S.C.R. 1303, Lamer C.J.C. (Dickson C.J.C., La Forest and Cory JJ. concurring). Criminal Code: S. 16(2) For the purposes of this section, a person is insane when the person is in a state of natural imbecility or has disease of the mind to an extent that renders the person incapable of appreciating the nature and quality of an act or omission or of knowing that an act or omission is wrong. 16(3) A person who has specific delusions, but is in other respects sane, shall not be acquitted on the ground of insanity unless the delusions caused that person to believe in the existence of a state of things that, if it existed, would have justified or excused the act or omission of that person. S. 16 now amended by S.C. 1991, c. 43, s. 2 to read in part: S. 16(1) No person is criminally responsible for an act committed or an omission made while suffering from a mental disorder that rendered the person incapable of appreciating the nature and quality of the act or omission or of knowing that it was wrong ... 2. "... Under s. 615 [of the Criminal Code, R.S.C. 1985, c. C-46], insanity includes any 'illness, disorder or abnormal condition which impairs the human mind or its functioning'." *R. v. Steele* (1991), 63 C.C.C. (3d) 149 at 181, 4 C.R. (4th) 53, 36 Q.A.C. 47, the court per Fish J.A. See DISEASE OF THE MIND.

INSCRIBE. *v.* To enter; to record.

IN SE. [L.] In and of itself. See MALA ~.

INSIDER. *n.* With respect to a corporation, (a) the corporation; (b) an affiliate of the corporation; (c) a director or an officer of the corporation or of any person described in paragraph (b), (d) or (f); (d) a person who beneficially owns, directly or indirectly, shares of the corporation or who exercises control or direction over shares of the corporation, or who has a combination of any such ownership, control and direction, carrying more than the prescribed percentage of voting rights attached to all of the outstanding shares of the corporation not including shares held by the person as underwriter while those shares are in the course of a distribution to the public; (e) a person, other than a person described in paragraph (f), employed or retained by the corporation or by a person described in paragraph (f); (f) a person who engages in or proposes to engage in any business or professional activity with or on behalf of the corporation; (g) a person who received, while they were a person described in any of paragraphs (a) to (f), material confidential information concerning the corporation; (h) a person who receives material confidential information from a person described in this subsection or in subsection (3) or (3.1), including a person described in this paragraph, and who knows or who ought reasonably to have known that the person giving the information is a person described in this subsection or in subsection (3) or (3.1), including a person described in this paragraph; and (i) a prescribed person. *Canada Business Corporations Act*, R.S.C. 1985, c. C-44, s. 131.

INSIDER TRADING. "... [T]he purchase or sale of the securities of a company by a person who, by reason of his position in the company, has access to confidential information not known to other shareholders or the general public... ." *Multiple Access Ltd. v. McCutcheon* (1982), 18 B.L.R. 138 at 142, [1982] 2 S.C.R. 161, 138 D.L.R. 93d) 1, 44 N.R. 181, Dickson J. (Laskin C.J.C., Martland, Ritchie, McIntyre and Lamer JJ. concurring).

IN SIMILI MATERIA. [L.] Dealing with similar or related subject-matter.

IN SITU. [L.] In place; in the position originally held.

INSOLVENCY. *n.* 1. "In a general sense, ... inability to meet one's debts or obligations; in a technical sense, it means the condition or standard of inability to meet debts or obligations, upon the occurrence of which the statutory law enables a creditor to intervene, with the assistance of a Court, to stop individual action by creditors and to secure administration of the debtor's assets in the general interest of creditors; the law also generally allows the debtor to apply for the same administration." *British Columbia (Attorney General) v. Canada (Attorney General)*, [1937] A.C. 391 at 402, 18 C.B.R. 217, [1937] 1 W.W.R. 320, [1937] 1 D.L.R. 695 (B.C. P.C.), the board per Lord Thankerton. 2. A broader term than bankruptcy that contemplates measures dealing with the property of debtors unable to pay their debts and other arrangements. Composition and voluntary assignment are devices which may avoid technical bankruptcy without great prejudice to creditors and hardship to the debtor. See BANKRUPTCY AND ~.

INSOLVENT. *adj.* 1. In relation to a corporation, in a situation where (i) it is unable to meet its obligations as they generally become due, (ii) it has ceased to pay its current obligations in the ordinary course of its business as they generally become due, or (iii) any other prescribed circumstances apply. *Credit Union Act*, R.S.A. 2000, c. C-32, s. 1. 2. In relation to a person, means the person has ceased to pay his or her debts in the ordinary course of business or cannot pay his or her debts as they become due. *Sale of Goods Act*, R.S.N.W.T. 1988, c. S-2, s. 1. 3. Unable to meet obligations as they come due in the ordinary course of business. *Credit Unions Act*, S.P.E.I. 1992, c. 14, s. 1.

INSOLVENT PERSON. A person who is not bankrupt and who resides, carries on business or has property in Canada, whose liabilities to creditors provable as claims under this Act amount to one thousand dollars, and (a) who is for any reason unable to meet his obligations as they generally become due, (b) who has ceased paying his current obligations in the ordinary course of business as they generally become due, or (c) the aggregate of whose property is not, at a fair valuation, sufficient, or, if disposed of at a fairly conducted sale under legal process, would not be sufficient to enable payment of all his obligations, due and accruing due. *Bankruptcy and Insolvency Act*, R.S.C. 1985, c. B-3, s. 2.

IN SPECIE. [L. in its own form] 1. In money or coin. 2. In kind.

INSPECTION. *n.* 1. Critical examination; close scrutiny. 2. An examination of real or personal property ordered by a court when an examination is necessary to determine an issue in a proceeding. See OFFICIAL ~ STATION; VEHICLE ~ SIGN.

INSPECTION OF DOCUMENTS. The disclosure of documents relevant to the issue prior to trial. See DISCOVERY.

INSPECTOR. *n.* 1. One who examines and reports. 2. A person appointed or designated under an act to carry out inspections or other duties prescribed. 3. Peace officers are inspectors for the purpose of monitoring compliance with various aspects of transportation policy, legislation and regulation. *R. v. Nolet*, 2009 SKCA 8. See BUILDING ~.

INSTALLATION. See MARINE ~ OR STRUCTURE.

INSTALMENT. *n.* 1. Part payment. 2. Episode. 3. One part of a debt.

INSTANCE. See FIRST ~.

INSTANTANEOUS PERFORMANCE. See CONTRACT OF ~.

INSTANTER. *adv.* [L.] At once, immediately.

IN STATU QUO. [L.] In its former condition.

INSTITUTE. *v.* To commence.

INSTITUTE. *n.* 1. An organization, body. 2. A treatise; a commentary. 3. In a substitution, the person who has the obligation to deliver over is called the institute and the person who is entitled to take after him is called the substitute. A substitute who takes with the obligation to deliver over becomes in turn the institute in respect of the subsequent substitute. *Civil Code*, S.Q. 1991, c. 64, a. 1219. See CANADIAN SECURITIES ~; LEGAL INFORMATION ~.

INSTITUTION. *n.* 1. A bank, credit union, trust company, treasury branch or other similar person, a public school, college, hospital, gaol, penitentiary, correctional institution. 2. "... [B]ears ... the concept of it having a public object ..." *Ontario (Attorney General) v. Tufford Rest Home* (1980), 30 O.R. (2d) 636 at 640 (Co. Ct.), Kovacs Co. Ct. J. 3. A law, rite or ceremony imposed by authority, as a permanent rule of government or conduct. See CORRECTIONAL ~; CREDIT ~; EDUCATIONAL ~; PENAL ~.

INSTITUTIONAL BIAS. The test developed by the courts for identifying this situation was: would an informed person viewing the matter realistically and practically, and having thought the matter through, have a reasonable apprehension of bias in a large number of cases arising before one particular tribunal. *Therrien c. Québec (Ministre de la justice)*, 2001 SCC 35.

INSTITUTIONAL CONSULTATION. Consultation among members of a tribunal including those not actually hearing a case. Considered appropriate to ensure consistency in decision-making within a tribunal.

I

INSTITUTIONAL DELAY. Delay in handling criminal cases expeditiously caused by lack of judges, courtrooms or adequate case management methods.

INSTITUTIONAL IMPARTIALITY. "The test for institutional impartiality is the same as the test adopted in [R. v. Valente (1985), 24 D.L.R. (4th) 161] with respect to the issue of judicial independence, that is the apprehension of an informed person, viewing the matter realistically and practically, and having thought the matter through... ." *Alex Couture Inc. c. Canada (Procureur général)* (1991), *(sub nom. Alex Couture Inc. v. Canada (Attorney General))* 38 C.P.R. (3d) 293 at 388, 83 D.L.R. (4th) 577, 41 Q.A.C. 1, [1991] R.J.Q. 2534, the court per Rousseau-Houle J.A. See IMPARTIAL.

INSTITUTIONAL INDEPENDENCE. 1. Elements are security of tenure, financial security and administrative control. Essential elements are summed as judicial control over the administrative decisions that bear directly and immediately on the exercise of the judicial function. *2747-3174 Quebec Inc. v. Quebec (Regie des permis d'alcool)*, [1996] 3 S.C.R. 919. 2. "Judicial control over ... assignment of judges, sittings of the court, and court lists ... as well as the related matters of allocation of courtrooms and direction of the administrative staff engaged in carrying out these functions, has generally been considered the essential and minimum requirement ..." *R. v. Valente (No. 2)* (1985), 19 C.R.R. 354 at 368, 372, 376, 379-80, [1985] 2 S.C.R. 673, 52 O.R. (2d) 779, 37 M.V.R. 9, 49 C.R. (3d) 97, 23 C.C.C. (3d) 193, 24 D.L.R. (4th) 161, 64 N.R. 1, 14 O.A.C. 79, [1985] D.L.Q. 85n, the court per Le Dain J.

INSTRUCT. *v.* 1. For a client to convey information to a solicitor. 2. For a client to authorize a solicitor to appear on their behalf.

INSTRUCTION. *n.* 1. Teaching. 2. Direction. 3. Imparting of knowledge. 4. A motion which gives a committee power to do something otherwise impossible, or to direct it to do something otherwise impossible. A. Fraser, W.A. Dawson & J. Holtby, eds., *Beauchesne's Rules and Forms of the House of Commons of Canada*, 6th ed. (Toronto: Carswell, 1989) at 203. 5. A notice communicated to the issuer of an uncertificated security that directs that the transfer of the security be registered or that the security be redeemed. *Securities Transfer acts.*

INSTRUMENT. *n.* 1. "... [A] word of very wide signification in our language and embraces, inter alia, such objects as implements or tools, a contrivance which produces sounds, as a musical instrument, or even a legal document." *R. v. Hayes* (1958), 29 C.R. 235 at 238, [1958] O.W.N. 449 (C.A.), the court per Schroeder J.A. 2. A formal legal document. 3. "... '[W]ritten document,' ..." *R. v. Evans* (1962), 37 W.W.R. 610 at 611, 37 C.R. 341, 132 C.C.C. 271 (B.C. C.A.), the court per Tysoe J.A. 4. (a) A writ of enforcement, or (b) a registerable instrument other than a writ of enforcement that (i) charges generally the property interest of a person, or (ii) binds in the same manner as a writ of enforcement the property interests of a person. *Land Titles Act*, R.S.A. 2000, c. L-4, s. 122. See AUTHORIZING ~; INCORPORATING ~; LAND TITLES ~; NEGOTIABLE ~; STATUTORY ~; SUBDIVIDING ~; TESTAMENTARY ~; TRUST ~.

INSTRUMENTALITY. *n.* "... An agent ..." *Medicine Hat (City) v. Canada (Attorney General)* (1985), 29 M.P.L.R. 165 at 175, 37 Alta. L.R. (2d) 208, [1985] 4 W.W.R. 367, 85 D.T.C. 5365, 18 D.L.R. (4th) 428, 59 A.R. 355 (C.A.), the court per Prowse J.A.

INSTRUMENT FOR ILLICIT DRUG USE. Anything designed primarily or intended under the circumstances for consuming or to facilitate the consumption of an illicit drug, but does not include a "device" as that term is defined in section 2 of the Food and Drugs Act. *Criminal Code*, R.S.C. 1985, c. C-46, s. 462.1.

INSTRUMENT OF UNLAWFUL ACTIVITY. Property that: (i) has been used to engage in unlawful activity that, in turn, resulted in the acquisition or production of property or in serious bodily harm to a person; or (ii) is likely to be used to engage in unlawful activity that, in turn, would be likely to or is intended to result in the acquisition or production of other property or in serious bodily harm to a person. *The Seizure of Criminal Property Act, 2009*, S.S. 2009, c. S-46.002, s. 2.

INSUBORDINATION. *n.* Failure to obey the lawful order of an employer. There must be a clear order understood by the worker and given by a person in authority and the order must be disobeyed.

INSULT. *n.* In the context of the defence of provocation, an act or the action of attacking or assailing; an open and sudden attack or assault without formal preparations; injuriously contemptuous speech or behaviour; scornful utterance or action intended to wound self-respect; an affront; indignity. Must be one which could, in light of the past history of the relationship between the accused and the deceased, deprive an ordinary person, of the same age, and sex, and sharing with the accused such other factors as would give the act or insult in question a special significance, of the power of self-control. *R. v. Thibert,* [1996] 1 S.C.R. 37.

INSURABLE EARNINGS. The total amount of the earnings, as determined in accordance with Part IV, that an insured person has from insurable employment. *Employment Insurance Act*, S.C. 1996, c. 23, s. 2.

INSURABLE EMPLOYMENT. (1) Subject to subsection (2), insurable employment is (a) employment in Canada by one or more employers, under any express or implied contract of service or apprenticeship, written or oral, whether the earnings of the employed person are received from the employer or some other person and whether the earnings are calculated by time or by the piece, or partly by time and partly by the piece, or otherwise; (b) employment in Canada as described in paragraph (a) by Her Majesty in right of Canada; (c) service in the Canadian Forces or in a police force; (d) employment included by regulations made under subsection (4) or (5); and (e) employment in Canada of an individual as the sponsor or co-ordinator of an employment benefits project. *Employment Insurance Act,* S.C. 1996, c. 23, s. 5.

INSURABLE INTEREST. 1. " ... [I]f an insured can demonstrate ... 'some relation to, or concern in the subject of the insurance, which relation or concern by the happening of the perils insured against may be so affected as to produce a damage, detriment or prejudice to the person insuring', ... To 'have moral certainty of advantage or benefit, but for those risk[s] or dangers', or 'to be so circumstanced with respect to [the subject matter of the insurance] as to have benefit from its existence, prejudice from its destruction'..." *Kosmopoulos v. Constitution Insurance Co. of Canada* (1987), (sub nom. *Constitution Insurance Co. of Canada v. Kosmopoulos*) 36 B.L.R. 233 at 255, [1987] 1 S.C.R. 2, 22 C.C.L.I. 296, [1987] I.L.R. 1-2147, 74 N.R. 360, 21 O.A.C. 4, 34 C.L.R. (4th) 208, Wilson J. (Beetz, Lamer, Le Dain and La Forest JJ. concurring). 2. A person has an insurable interest in his own life and well-being and in the life and well-being of, (a) his child or grandchild; (b) his spouse or common-law partner; (c) any person upon whom he is wholly or in part dependent for, or from whom he is receiving, support or education; (d) his employee; and (e) any person in whom he has a pecuniary interest. *The Insurance Act*, R.S.M. 1987, c. I40, c. 156.

INSURANCE. *n.* 1. The undertaking by one person to indemnify another person against loss or liability for loss in respect of a certain risk or peril to which the object of the insurance may be exposed, or to pay a sum of money or other thing of value upon the happening of a certain event. *Insurance acts.* 2. Insurance on the life or health of a borrower or buyer, or on property charged to secure payment of the indebtedness of a borrower or buyer to a lender or seller. *Consumer Protection Act*, R.S.N.S. 1989, c. 92, s. 2. See ACCIDENTAL DEATH ~; ACCIDENT ~; AIRCRAFT ~; AUTOMOBILE ~; BOILER AND MACHINERY ~; CO-~; CONTINGENCY ~; CONTRACT OF ~; CREDIT ~; CROP ~ PROGRAM; DEPRECIATION ~; DISABILITY ~; DOUBLE ~; EMPLOYMENT ~; ENDOWMENT ~; ERRORS AND OMISSIONS ~; FIRE ~; GROUP ~; GUARANTEE ~; HAIL ~; INDEMNITY ~; INLAND TRANSPORTATION ~; LIABILITY ~; LIFE ~; LOST OR NOT LOST ~; MARINE ~; MORTGAGE ~; MUTUAL ~; NO-FAULT ~; PLATE GLASS ~; PROPERTY DAMAGE ~; RE~; REPLACEMENT COST ~; REVENUE ~ PROGRAM; SPRINKLER LEAKAGE ~; THEFT ~; TITLE ~; UNDER-~; UNEMPLOYMENT~; WORKERS' COMPENSATION ~.

INSURANCE AGENT. A person who, for compensation, (i) solicits insurance on behalf of an insurer, insured or potential insured, (ii) transmits an application for insurance from an insured or potential insured to an insurer, (iii) transmits a policy of insurance from an insurer to an insured, (iv) negotiates or offers to negotiate insurance on behalf of an insurer, insured or potential insured or the continuance or renewal of insurance on behalf of an insurer or in-

sured, or (v) enrolls individuals in prescribed contracts of group insurance, but does not include an insurer. *Insurance Act*, R.S.A. 2000, c. I-3, s. 1.

INSURANCE BROKER. Any person who for any compensation, commission or other thing of value, with respect to persons or property in Ontario, deals directly with the public and, (a) acts or aids in any manner in soliciting, negotiating or procuring the making of any contract of insurance or reinsurance whether or not the person has agreements with insurers allowing the person to bind coverage and countersign insurance documents on behalf of insurers, (b) provides risk managements services including claims assistance where required, (c) provides consulting or advisory services with respect to insurance or reinsurance, (d) holds himself, herself or itself out as an insurance consultant or examines appraises, reviews or evaluates any insurance policy, plan or program or makes recommendations or gives advice with regard to any of the above. *Registered Insurance Brokers Act*, R.S.O. 1990, c. R.19, s. 1.

INSURANCE CONTRACT. Any contract under which one party, the insurer, assumes the risk of an uncertain event, which is not within its control, happening at a future time and in which event the other party, the insured, has an interest. The insurer is bound to pay money or provide its equivalent if the uncertain event occurs.

INSURANCE FUND. As applied to a fraternal society or as applied to a corporation not incorporated exclusively for the transaction of insurance, includes all money, securities for money and assets appropriated by the rules of the society or corporation to the payment of insurance liabilities or appropriated for the management of the insurance branch or department or division of the society, or otherwise legally available for insurance liabilities, but does not include funds of a trade union appropriated to or applicable for the voluntary assistance of wage earners unemployed or upon strike. *Insurance Act*, R.S.O. 1990, c. I.8, s. 1.

INSURANCE MONEY. The amount payable by an insurer under a contract, and includes all benefits, surplus, profits, dividends, bonuses and annuities payable under the contract. *Insurance acts.*

INSURANCE ON THE CASH PLAN. Any insurance that is not mutual insurance. *Insurance acts.*

INSURANCE PLAN. 1. The benefits and obligations set out in Parts III to IX. *Workplace Safety and Insurance Act, 1997*, S.O. 1997, c. 16, Sched. A, s. 2. 2. A set of insurance features for a crop under an insurance scheme. *Agricultural Insurance Act*, S.P.E.I. 1994, c. 2, s. 1.

INSURANCE POLICY. A contract under which one party, the insurer, assumes the risk of an uncertain event, which is not within its control, happening at a future time and in which event the other party, the insured, has an interest. The insurer is bound to pay money or provide its equivalent if the uncertain event occurs.

INSURANCE SALESPERSON. An individual who is employed by an insurance agent or by an insurer to solicit, obtain or take an application for general insurance, or to negotiate for or procure general insurance, or to collect or receive a premium for general insurance. *Financial Institutions Act*, R.S.B.C. 1996, c. 141, s. 168.

INSURED. *n.* 1. (a) In the case of group insurance means, in the provision of this Part relating to the designation of beneficiaries or of personal representatives as recipients of insurance money and their rights and status, the group life insured, and (b) in all other cases means the person who makes a contract with an insurer. *Insurance acts.* 2. A person insured by a contract whether named or not. *Insurance* acts. See NAMED ~.

INSURED PARTICIPANT. An insured person who requests assistance under employment benefits and, when requesting the assistance, is an unemployed person (a) for whom a benefit period is established or whose benefit period has ended within the previous 36 months; or (b) for whom a benefit period has been established in the previous 60 months and who (i) was paid special benefits under section 22 or 23 during the benefit period, (ii) subsequently withdrew from active participation in the labour force to care for one or more of their new-born children or one or more children placed with them for the purpose of adoption, and (iii) is seeking to re-enter the labour force. *Employment Insurance Act*, S.C. 1996, c. 23, s. 58.

INSURED PERSON. 1. A person who enters into a subsisting contract of insurance with an insurer and includes (a) a person insured by a contract whether named or not; and (b) a person to whom or for whose benefit all or part of the proceeds of a contract of insurance is payable; and (c) a person entitled to have insurance money applied toward satisfaction of his judgment in accordance with the Insurance Act. *Insurance acts.* 2. A person who is or has been employed in insurable employment. *Employment Insurance*, S.C. 1996, c. 23, s. 2.

INSURER. *n.* 1. A person who undertakes or agrees or offers to undertake a contract. *Insurance acts.* 2. A person who is licensed or otherwise authorized under the laws of Canada or a province to carry on in Canada an insurance business or under the laws of another jurisdiction to carry on in that other jurisdiction an insurance business. *Excise Tax Act*, R.S.C. 1985, c. E-15, s. 123.

INSURRECTION. *n.* Actions taken with an intention to overthrow the government or usurp its powers.

INTANGIBLE. *n.* Personal property other than goods, chattel paper, investment property, a document of title, an instrument and money. *Personal Property Security acts.*

INTANGIBLE PROPERTY. A right of ownership over any personal property that is not a chattel or a mortgage, and includes, without limiting the generality of the foregoing, (a) money, a cheque, a bank draft, a deposit, interest, a dividend and income, (b) a credit balance, a customer overpayment, a gift certificate, a security deposit, a refund, a credit memo, an unpaid wage and an unused airline ticket, (c) a share or any other intangible ownership interest in a business organization, (d) money deposited to redeem a share, a bond, a coupon or other security, or to make a distribution, (e) an amount due and payable by the insurer under the terms of an insurance policy, and (f) an amount distributable from a trust or custodial fund established under a plan to provide education, health, welfare, vacation, severance, retirement, death, share purchase, profit sharing, employee savings, supplemental unemployment insurance or a similar benefit. *Unclaimed Intangible Property Act*, R.S.O. 1990, c. U-1, s. 1.

INTEGRAL. *adj.* Essential to completeness; constituent.

INTEGRATED CIRCUIT PRODUCT. A product, in a final or intermediate form, that is intended to perform an electronic function and in which the elements, at least one of which is an active element, and some or all of the interconnections, are integrally formed in or on, or both in and on, a piece of material. *Integrated Circuit Topography Act*, S.C. 1990, c. 37, s. 2.

INTEGRITY. *n.* Soundness of moral principles; probity; honesty; uprightness. See ECOLOGICAL ~; PUBLIC SECTOR ~ COMMISSIONER.

INTELLECTUAL PROPERTY. Refers to property which is subject to copyright, patent, trade-mark, industrial design or integrated circuit topography legislation. See INDUSTRIAL PROPERTY; WORLD ~ ORGANIZATION.

INTELLIGENCE. *n.* [T]he retention of notes must serve a practical purpose. It follows that the meaning of the word "intelligence" in s. 12 of the CSIS Act [Canadian Security Intelligence Service Act, R.S.C. 1985, c. C-23] should not be limited to the summaries prepared by officers. The original operational notes will be a better source of information, and of evidence, when they are submitted to the ministers responsible for issuing a security certificate and to the designated judge who will determine whether the certificate is reasonable. Retention of the notes will make it easier to verify the disclosed summaries and information based on those notes. Similarly, it is important that CSIS officers retain access to their operational notes (drafts, diagrams, recordings, photographs) in order to refresh their memories should they have to testify in a proceeding to determine whether a security certificate is reasonable. *Charkaoui, Re*, 2008 SCC 38. See COMPETITIVE ~; FOREIGN ~; SECURITY ~ REVIEW COMMITTEE.

INTELLIGIBLE. *adj.* Under s. 6 of the Canada Evidence Act [R.S.C. 1985, c. C-5]: "[a] witness who is unable to speak may give his evidence in any other manner in which he can make it intelligible". Although there does not appear to be any case law on the meaning of intelligible, to render the section meaningful it must include that a witness is able to communicate to the Court in a manner which accurately and comprehensively conveys their testimony on a particular matter. To accomplish this, the manner of giving evidence must not only convey the witness's testimony to the Court, but also the questions of counsel to the witness. As long as a witness' testimony can be communicated to the Court, the fact that that witness uses a unique method of communication or language does not render the evidence inadmissible. *R. v. Carlick*, 1999 CarswellBC 1104 (S.C.), Sinclair Prowse J.

INTEND. *v.* To plan; to have in mind as a purpose or goal.

INTENSITY. See CARBON ~.

INTENT. *n.* 1. The exercise of free will to use particular means to produce a particular result. 2. In relation to legislation, refers to the state of mind of the legislators at the time of enactment. See DONATIVE ~; EQUITY LOOKS TO THE ~ RATHER THAN TO THE FORM; GENERAL ~; LETTER OF ~; MALICIOUS ~; NOTICE OF ~ TO DEFEND; SPECIFIC ~; TRANSFERRED ~.

INTENTION. *n.* Of a legislature, can only be ascertained from the express words of the enactment or by reasonable and necessary implication from them. See CERTAINTY OF ~; EQUITY IMPUTES AN ~ TO FULFIL AN OBLIGATION; SEDITIOUS ~; TESTAMENTARY ~.

INTENTIONAL. See UNLAWFUL AND ~ INTERFERENCE.

INTENTIONAL INDUCEMENT OF BREACH OF CONTRACT. Liability arises where, knowing of the contract and with intent to prevent or hinder its performance, the defendant induces one party not to perform his part of the contract or the defendant commits a wrongful act to prevent the performance of the contract. J.G. Fleming, *The Law of Torts*, 8th ed. (Sydney: Law Book, 1992) at 690. See INDUCING BREACH OF CONTRACT/

INTENTIONAL INFLICTION OF NERVOUS SHOCK. The constituent elements of the cause of action for intentional infliction of mental distress [are]: (1) flagrant or outrageous conduct on the part of the defendants; (2) which is calculated to produce harm or in circumstances where it is known that harm will ensue; and (3) actual damage to the plaintiff as a result of the conduct. In Prinzo v. Baycrest, (2002), 60 O.R. (3d) 474, at paras. 34–64, this court confirmed a) the three-pronged test to establish the tort of intentional infliction of mental distress and b) that if it is established as an actionable wrong that is separate from wrongful dismissal, then damages for the tort of intentional infliction of mental distress can be awarded in the context of a wrongful dismissal action. Therefore, a claim for intentional infliction of mental distress should not be struck or dismissed only because it is raised in a wrongful dismissal context or because the facts giving rise to the claim may overlap with those that form the basis for aggravated or punitive damages from the wrongful dismissal. *Correia v. Canac Kitchens*, 2008 ONCA 506.

INTENTIONAL TORT. A tort in which the wrongdoer either wishes to accomplish the result or believes the result will follow from his act and the result is an injury to the plaintiff.

INTENTION IN COMMON. Between a party and a principal to an offence, refers to both parties having in mind the same unlawful purpose. May also refer to a shared intention to carry out the action or purpose for the same motives.

INTER. *v.* The burial of human remains and includes the placing of human remains in a lot. *Cemeteries Act (Revised)*, R.S.O. 1990, c. C.4, s. 1.

INTERACTIVE DIGITAL MEDIA PRODUCT. A product that (a) consists of a combination of software and data files, in digital format, that are designed to be operated together, interactively by the user, to present information using sound, text and images, or any two of them; (b) is designed primarily to educate, inform or entertain the user; (c) in the case of a video game, is classified by the Entertainment Software Rating Board as anything other than "AO" (adults only); and (d) is not (i) operating system software, (ii) a product to be used primarily for interpersonal communication, (iii) a product to be used primarily for marketing or promoting of an entity, a product or an idea, (iv) a product that contains hate propaganda or child pornography as defined in the Criminal Code (Canada) or is deemed to be obscene under that Act, or any other material the publication, sale or possession of which is an offence under that Act, or (v) a product that, in the opinion of the minister, it would be contrary to public policy to support with public funds. *The Income Tax Act*, R.S.M. 1988, c. I10, s. 10.5.

INTER ALIA. [L.] Among other things.

INTERCEPT. *v.* 1. Includes listen to, record or acquire a communication or acquire the substance, meaning or purport thereof. *Criminal Code*, R.S.C. 1985, c. C-46, s. 183. 2. Includes listen to or record a function of a computer system, or acquire the substance, meaning or purport thereof. *Criminal Code*, R.S.C. 1985, c. C-46, s. 342.1(2).

INTERCHANGE. *n.* 1. A place where the line of a railway company connects the line of another railway company and where loaded or empty cars may be stored until delivered or received by that other company. *Canada Transportation Act*, S.C. 1996, c. 10, s. 111. 2. A general area where two intersecting roadways cross at different levels and includes the turning lanes between these two intersecting roadways. *The Off-Road Vehicles Act*, S.M. 1987-88, c. 64, s. 1. See THERAPEUTIC ~ PROGRAM.

INTERCHANGEABLE PRODUCT. A drug or combination of drugs in a particular dosage form and strength identified by a specific product name or manufacturer and designated as interchangeable with one or more other such products. *Interchangeability and Dispensing Fee Act*, R.S.O. 1990, c. P.23, s. 1.

INTERCOUNTRY ADOPTION. An adoption to which the Convention on Protection of Children and Co-operation in respect of Intercountry Adoption applies, or any other adoption of a child who is habitually resident outside Canada, by an Ontario resident, (i) that is intended to create a permanent parent-child relationship, and (ii) that is finalized in the child's country of origin. *Intercountry Adoption Act, 1998*, S.O. 1998, c. 29, s. 1.

INTERCOURSE. See SEXUAL ~.

INTER-DELEGATION. *n.* The delegation of provincial power to the federal level or of federal power to the provinces.

INTERDEPENDENCE. See RELATIONSHIP OF ~.

INTERESSE TERMINI. [L.] An executory interest which is a right of entry that a lessee acquires in land through a demise.

INTEREST. *n.* 1. Something which a person has in a thing when that person has advantages, duties, liabilities, losses or rights connected with it, whether ascertained or potential, present or future. 2. In the law of insurance, something which a person has in the life of a person or in property when the death of the person or destruction or damage to the property would expose that person to pecuniary liability or loss. 3. Charge or compensation for the use of or retention of money. See ABSOLUTE ~; ADMISSION AGAINST ~; ADVERSE IN ~; AGAINST ~; BENEFICIAL ~; BEST ~S OF THE CHILD; COMMON ~; COMMUNITY OF ~ DOCTRINE; COMPOUND ~; CONFLICT OF ~; CONTINGENT ~; COOPERATIVE ~; ECONOMIC ~; EQUAL ~; EQUITABLE ~; EQUITY ~; EXECUTORY ~; FRACTIONAL ~ IN LAND; FUTURE ~; GRANT OF AN ~; INCOME ~; INSURABLE ~; JOINT ~; LEGAL ~; LIFE ~; MEMBERSHIP ~; MINERAL ~; OPEN ~; POST-JUDGMENT ~; PRE-JUDGMENT ~; PROPRIETARY ~; PUBLIC ~; REAL ~ METHOD; REVERSIONARY ~; ROYALTY ~; SECURITY ~; SHARED ~ IN LAND; SPECIAL ~; TIME SHARE ~; UNDIVIDED ~; UNITY OF ~; VESTED IN ~; WORKING ~.

INTERESTED PARTY. One who has an economic, pecuniary, or proprietary interest in the subject matter of a trust.

INTEREST IN EXPECTANCY. Includes an estate or interest in remainder or reversion and any other future interest whether vested or contingent, but does not include a reversion expectant on the determination of a lease. *Succession Duties acts.*

INTEREST RATE. An annual simple interest rate that is equal to the prime lending rate of the banker to the government. *Court Order Interest Act,* R.S.B.C. 1996, c. 79, s. 7.

INTERFERE. *v.* To obstruct; to disrupt.

INTERFERENCE. *n.* Disruption; obstruction. See UNLAWFUL AND INTENTIONAL ~; UNLAWFUL ~ WITH ECONOMIC RELATIONS; UNLAWFUL ~ WITH LEGITIMATE BUSINESS EXPECTANCY.

INTERFERENCE WITH CONTRACTUAL RELATIONS. A tort in which there must be direct and deliberate interference with the performance of a contract. See UNLAWFUL ~.

INTER-GOVERNMENTAL DISPUTES. An appeal lies to the Court from a decision of the Federal Court of Appeal in the case of a controversy between Canada and a province or between two or more prov-

inces. *Supreme Court Act,* R.S.C. 1985, c. S-26, s. 35.1.

INTERIM. *adj.* 1. "... '[I]n the meantime', ... 'for the time being' ..." *Bell Canada v. Canada (Canadian Radio-Television & Telecommunications Commission)* (1987), 43 D.L.R. (4th) 30 at 46, 79 N.R. 58, [1988] 1 F.C. 296 (C.A.) Marceau J.A. 2. Not permanent or final.

INTERIM ACCOUNT. A request for money to be applied on a final account to be submitted later. *Nathanson, Schachter & Thompson v. Inmet Mining Corp.,* 2009 BCCA 385, Newbury and Smith JJ.A. (Kirkpatrick J.A. concurring).

INTERIM COSTS. Inherent jurisdiction of the courts to grant costs to a litigant, in rare and exceptional circumstances, prior to the final disposition of a case and in any event of the cause. The party seeking the order must be impecunious to the extent that, without such an order, that party would be deprived of the opportunity to proceed with the case. The claimant must establish a prima facie case of sufficient merit to warrant pursuit. And there must be special circumstances sufficient to satisfy the court that the case is within the narrow class of cases where this extraordinary exercise of its powers is appropriate. *British Columbia (Minister of Forests) v. Okanagan Indian Band,* 2003 SCC 71.

INTERIM DIVIDEND. A dividend paid during a company's financial year.

INTERIM INJUNCTION. A species of interlocutory injunction granted for a very brief period until application for an interlocutory injunction is made.

INTERIM ORDER. 1. " ... [I]nterim decisions may be reviewed and modified in a retrospective manner by a final decision. It is inherent in the nature of interim orders that their effect, as well as any discrepancy between the interim order and the final order, may be reviewed and remedied by the final order ..." *Bell Canada v. Canada (Canadian Radio-Television & Telecomunications Commission)* (1989), 38 Admin. L.R. 1 at 30, [1989] 1 S.C.R. 1722, 60 D.L.R. (4th) 682, 97 N.R. 15, the court per Gonthier J. 2. " ... [A] temporary decision that does not finally dispose of the case before the tribunal." *Bell Canada v. Canada (Canadian Radio-Television & Telecommunications Commission)* (1987), 43 D.L.R. (4th) 30 at 33, 79 N.R. 58, [1988] 1 F.C. 296 (C.A.) Pratte J.A. 3. " ... [Governs] the rights of the parties from the time it is granted until the issue is resolved finally at trial..." *Janssen v. Janssen* (1979), 11 R.F.L. (2d) 274 at 278, 25 O.R. (2d) 213, 1 F.L.R.A.C. 455 (Co. Ct.), Borins Co. Ct. J. 4. Order concerning interim custody or interim support pending confirmation. *Divorce Act,* R.S.C. 1985, c. 3 (2nd Supp.), s. 15-19.

INTERIM RECEIVER. A person appointed under The Bankruptcy Act between filing a petition and making an order judging that the debtor is bankrupt. The property does not vest in the interim receiver. The receiver's function is to preserve the assets of the business. He is not to interfere with the rights of the debtor and he is not to interfere with the debtor carrying on the business in the usual course.

INTERIM RELEASE. See JUDICIAL ~.

INTERIM RELIEF. 1. " ... [T]emporary relief which is granted pending determination of the application for final or permanent relief. An interim order terminates upon an order being made at trial." *St. Cyr v. Lechkoon* (1991), 36 R.F.L. (3d) 203 at 206 (Ont. Gen. Div.), Kozak J. 2. Interim custody, interim support and interim support pending confirmation or provisional variation. *Divorce Act,* R.S.C. 1985 (2nd Supp.), c. 3, s. 15-19.

INTERIM SUPPLY. A measure to provide a government with money to meet any obligations before its main estimates are approved. A. Fraser, W.A. Dawson & J. Holtby, eds., *Beauchesne's Rules and Forms of the House of Commons of Canada,* 6th ed. (Toronto: Carswell, 1989) at 260.

INTERIOR DESIGN. See PRACTICE OF ~.

INTERIOR DESIGNER. A member licensed to practice or a licensee of the Association of Interior Designers of Nova Scotia. *Building Code Act,* R.S.N.S. 1989, c. 46, *Nova Scotia Building Code Regulations,* N.S. Reg. 322/2009, s. 1.3.

INTERJURISDICTIONAL LAW FIRM. For the purpose of section 40, means a law firm (i) that maintains an office in the province together with an office in a foreign jurisdiction or in another Canadian jurisdiction, or both, and (ii) in which not all the partners, or in the case of a professional law corporation, not all the voting shareholders, are qualified to practise law in the province. *Law Society Act, 1999,* S.N. 1999, c. L-9.1, s. 2.

INTER-JURISDICTIONAL WATERS. Any waters, whether international, boundary or otherwise, that, whether wholly situated in a province or not, significantly affect the quantity or quality of waters outside the province. *Canada Water Act,* R.S.C. 1985, c. C-11, s. 2.

INTERLINEATION. *n.* Inserting anything into a document after it has been executed.

INTERLOCK BARRIER. With respect to a robot means a physical barrier around a work envelope that is equipped with gates and interlocks designed to stop all automatic operations of a robot and robot system when any gate within the barrier is opened. *Occupational Health and Safety Act,* R.S.A. 2000, c. O-2, *Occupational Health and Safety Code, 2006,* Alta. OHS Code, s. 1

INTERLOCUTORY. *adj.* 1. Incidental to the major intent of an action. 2. While there is a difference between the meaning of the word "interlocutory" and the word "interim," there is also a similarity in that both words carry the implication of something of a preliminary nature. An interlocutory order refers to one given in the course of a legal proceeding, as distinct from a final order. An interim order is one of a provisional or temporary nature, as distinct from a final order. *Consumers' Assn. of Canada (Manitoba) Inc. v. Manitoba (Public Utilities Board),* 2006 MBCA 156. 3. " ... [E]mployed to designate steps in an action intermediate between the initial and final proceeding, and merely leading towards the proceed-ing which finally terminates the litigation, ..." *Whiting v. Hovey* (1885), 12 O.A.R. 119 at 125, Patterson J.A. 4. Refers to an order or judgment which does not finally dispose of the rights of the parties.

INTERLOCUTORY INJUNCTION. 1. A measure intended to ensure that certain specified acts do not take place until the rights of the parties are finally determined by the court. 2. " ... [A]n extraordinary and discretionary remedy and one which will not be granted unless the court is satisfied that it is a proper case in which to exercise its discretion. A tripartite test has evolved through the jurisprudence to assist the court in making a decision: (1) has the applicant shown a prima facie/serious issue to be tried; (2) is there a danger of irreparable harm to the applicant, and; (3) does the balance of convenience lie with the applicant." *Imperial Chemical Industries PLC v. Apotex Inc.* (1989), 23 C.P.R. (3d) 1 at 15, 22 C.I.P.R. 201, [1989] 2 F.C. 608, Rouleau J.

INTERLOCUTORY ORDER. 1. "[An order which does not] ... finally dispose of the rights of the parties ..." *Hockin v. Bank of British Columbia* (1989), 35 C.P.C. (2d) 250 at 253, 37 B.C.L.R. (2d) 139 (C.A.), Wallace J.A. 2. In general, an order is interlocutory which does not dispose of the rights of the parties in the litigation but relates to matters taken for the purpose of advancing the matter towards resolution or for the purpose of enabling the conclusion of the proceedings to be enforced: see Cameron v. Bank of Nova Scotia (1981), 45 N.S.R. (2d) 303 (N.S. C.A.). *Van de Wiel v. Blaikie,* 2005 NSCA 14.

INTERMEDIARY. See FUTURES ~; SECURITIES ~.

INTERMEDIATE BALANCE. See LOWEST ~ RULE.

INTERMENT RIGHT CONTRACT. A contract that provides for a right of interment for human remains or cremated remains in a lot. *Business Practices and Consumer Protection Act,* S.B.C. 2004, c. 2, s. 17.

INTERMENT RIGHTS HOLDER. A person with interment rights with respect to a lot and includes a purchaser of interment rights. *Cemeteries Act (Revised),* R.S.O. 1990, c. C.4, s. 1, part.

INTERMENT SPACE. A lot, plot, compartment, crypt or other space for the disposition of human remains in a cemetery, mausoleum or columbarium. *Cemeteries Act,* R.S.A. 2000, c. C-3, s. 18.

INTERMITTENT SENTENCE. Where the court imposes a sentence of imprisonment of ninety days or less on an offender convicted of an offence, whether in default of payment of a fine or otherwise, the court may, having regard to the age and character of the offender, the nature of the offence and the circumstances surrounding its commission, and the availability of appropriate accommodation to ensure compliance with the sentence, order that the sentence be served intermittently at such times as are specified in the order; and that the offender comply with the conditions prescribed in a probation order when not in confinement during the period that the sentence is being served and, if the court so orders, on release from prison after completing the intermittent sentence. *Criminal Code*, R.S.C. 1985, c. C-46, s. 732.

INTERNAL CONFLICT. See PRESUMPTION AGAINST ~.

INTERNAL SELF-DETERMINATION. The recognized sources of international law establish that the right to self-determination of a people is normally fulfilled through *internal* self-determination—a people's pursuit of its political, economic, social and cultural development within the framework of an existing state. *Reference re Secession of Quebec*, 1998 CarswellNat 1299, 161 D.L.R. (4th) 385, 228 N.R. 203, 55 C.R.R. (2d) 1, [1998] 2 S.C.R. 217, per curiam.

INTERNAL WATERS. In relation to Canada, means the internal waters of Canada as determined under the Oceans Act and includes the airspace above and the bed and subsoil below those waters, and in relation to any other state, means the waters on the landward side of the baselines of the territorial sea of the other state. *Interpretation Act*, R.S.C. 1985, c. I-21, s. 35. Sections 6 and 7 of the Oceans Act, S.C. 1996, c. 31 provide that the waters on the landward side of the baselines of the territorial sea of Canada are the internal waters of Canada and that those waters and the territorial sea form part of Canada.

INTERNATIONAL AGENCY. Any organization whose objectives include global poverty reduction or international humanitarian assistance. *Official Development Assistance Accountability Act*, S.C. 2008, c. 17, s. 3.

INTERNATIONAL APPLICATION. An application filed under the Patent Cooperation Treaty. *Patent Act*, R.S.C. 1985, c. P-4, *Patent Rules*, SOR/96-423, s. 2.

INTERNATIONAL ASSISTANCE. Funding provided by government for international development, international financial institutions, global peace and security, crises overseas and international development research. *Official Development Assistance Accountability Act*, S.C. 2008, c. 17, s. 3.

INTERNATIONAL BRIDGE OR TUNNEL. A bridge or tunnel, or any part of it, that connects any place in Canada to any place outside Canada, and includes the approaches and facilities related to the bridge or tunnel. *International Bridges and Tunnels Act*, S.C. 2007, c. 1, s. 2.

INTERNATIONAL COURT OF JUSTICE. A judicial body created by the Charter of the United Nations.

INTERNATIONAL CRIMINAL COURT. The International Criminal Court established by the Rome Statute. *Crimes Against Humanity and War Crimes Act*, S.C. 2000, c. 24, s. 2..

INTERNATIONAL CRUISE SHIP. A passenger ship that is suitable for continuous ocean voyages of at least forty-eight hours duration, but does not include such a ship that is used or fitted for the primary purpose of transporting cargo or vehicles. *Criminal Code*, R.S.C. 1985, c. C-46, s. 207. 1.

INTERNATIONAL DEPOSITARY AUTHORITY. An international depositary authority within the meaning of Article 2(viii) of the Budapest Treaty. *Patent Act*, R.S.C. 1985, c. P-4, *Patent Rules*, SOR/96-423, s. 2.

INTERNATIONAL EMERGENCY. An emergency involving Canada and one or more other countries that arises from acts of intimidation or coercion or the real or imminent use of serious force or violence and that is so serious as to be a national emergency. *Emergencies Act*, R.S.C. 1985, c. 22 (4th Supp.), s. 27.

INTERNATIONAL FINANCIAL REPORTING STANDARDS. A set of reporting standards, one of the alternative methods of accounting which must be adopted by enterprises. Private enterprises must decide which of the sets of standards to adopt for years beginning on or after January 1, 2011. See PRIVATE ENTERPRISE GAAP.

INTERNATIONAL FUND. The International Oil Pollution Compensation Fund, 1992 established by Article 2 of the Fund Convention. *Marine Liability Act*, S.C. 2001, c. 6, s. 47.

INTERNATIONAL HUMAN RIGHTS STANDARDS. Standards that are based on international human rights conventions to which Canada is a party and on international customary law. *Official Development Assistance Accountability Act*, S.C. 2008, c. 17, s. 3.

INTERNATIONAL LAW. Of two kinds: public international law, a code of rules which controls the conduct of independent nations in their relations with one another and private international law, a branch of municipal law which determines before what nation's courts a certain action or suit ought to be brought and by what nation's law it should be settled. See CONVENTIONAL ~; CUSTOMARY ~; PRIVATE ~.

INTERNATIONALLY PROTECTED PERSON. A person who is (a) A head of state, including any member of a collegial body that performs the functions of a head of state under the constitution of the state concerned, a head of a government or a minister of foreign affairs, whenever that person is in a state other than the state in which he holds that position or office, (b) a member of the family of a person described in paragraph (a) who accompanies that person in a state other than the state in which that person holds that position or office, (c) a representative or an official of a state or an official or agent of an international organization of an intergovernmental character who, at the time when and at the place where an offence referred to in subsection 7(3) is committed against his person or any property referred to in section 431 that is used by him, is entitled, pursuant to international law, to special protection from any attack on his person, freedom or dignity, or (d) a member of the family of a representative, official or agent described in paragraph (c) who forms part of his household, if the representative, official or agent, at the time when and at the place where any offence referred to in subsection 7(3) is committed against the member of his family or any property referred to in section 431 that is used by that member, is entitled, pursuant to international law, to special protection from any attack on his person, freedom or dignity. *Criminal Code*, R.S.C. 1985, c. C-46, s. 2.

INTERNATIONAL ORGANIZATION. 1. An intergovernmental organization, whether or not established by treaty, of which two or more states are members, and includes an intergovernmental conference in which two or more states participate. *Foreign Missions and International Organizations Act*, S.C. 1991, c. 41, s. 2. 2. (a) Any specialized agency of which Canada is a member that is brought into relationship with the United Nations in accordance with Article 63 of the Charter of the United Nations, and (b) any international organization of which Canada is a member, the primary purpose of which is the maintenance of international peace or the economic or social well-being of a community of nations. Canada regulations.

INTERNATIONAL RIVER. Water flowing from any place in Canada to any place outside Canada. *International River Improvements Act*, R.S.C. 1985, c. I-20, s. 2.

INTERNATIONAL RIVER IMPROVEMENT. A dam, obstruction, canal, reservoir or other work the purpose or effect of which is to increase, decrease or alter the natural flow of an international river, and to interfere with, alter or affect the actual or potential use of the international river outside Canada. *International River Improvements Act*, R.S.C. 1985, c. I-20, s. 2.

INTERNATIONAL SERVICE. An air service between Canada and a point in the territory of another country. *Canada Transportation Act*, S.C. 1996, c. 10, s. 55.

INTERNATIONAL TRADE. See CANADIAN ~ TRIBUNAL; DEPARTMENT OF FOREIGN AFFAIRS AND ~.

INTERNATIONAL TRAFFIC. 1. Any transport by a ship or aircraft operated by an enterprise of a Contracting State, except when the ship or aircraft is operated solely between places within the other Contracting State. *Tax Convention acts.* 2. In respect of a non-resident person carrying on the business of transporting passengers or goods, any voyage made in the course of that business where the principal purpose of the voyage is to transport passengers or goods (a) from Canada to a place outside Canada, (b) from a place outside Canada to Canada, or (c) from a place outside Canada to another place outside Canada. *Income Tax Act*, R.S.C. 1985, c. 1 (5th Supp.), s. 248.

INTERNATIONAL VOYAGE. Any voyage (other than a voyage originating and terminating in Canada) of a vessel that is operated by a person in the course of a business of supplying passenger transportation services. *Excise Tax Act*, R.S.C. 1985, c. E-15, s. 180.1.

INTERNATIONAL WATERS. Waters of rivers that flow across the international boundary between the United States and Canada. *Canada Water Act*, R.S.C. 1985, c. C-11, s. 2.

INTERNET. *n.* The decentralized global network connecting networks of computers and similar devices to each other for the electronic exchange of information using standardized communication protocols. *Consumer Protection Act, 2002*, S.O. 2002, c. 30, Sched. A, s. 1.

INTERNET AGREEMENT. A consumer agreement formed by text-based internet communications. *Consumer Protection Act, 2002*, S.O. 2002, c. 30, Sched. A, s. 20.

INTERNET GAMING SITE. An internet site that accepts or offers to accept wagers or bets over the internet, (a) as part of the playing of or participation in any game of chance or mixed chance and skill that is to take place inside or outside of Canada, or (b) on any contingency or on any event that may or is to take place inside or outside of Canada, including, without restricting the generality of the foregoing, a casino game, card game, horse race, fight, match, sporting event or contest. *Consumer Protection Act, 2002*, S.O. 2002, c. 30, Sched. A, s. 1.

INTERNET REGISTRATION. See CANADIAN ~ AUTHORITY.

INTERNET SALES CONTRACT. A consumer transaction that is a contract in which: (i) the consideration for the goods or services exceeds the prescribed amount; and (ii) the contract is formed by text-based Internet communications. *The Consumer Protection Act*, S.S. 1996, c. C-30.1, s. 75.5.

INTERNET SERVICE PROVIDER. In Canada can play a number of roles. In addition to its function as an intermediary, it may as well act as a content provider, or create embedded links which automatically precipitate a telecommunication of copyrighted music from another source. In such cases, copyright liability may attach to the added functions. *Society of Composers, Authors & Music Publishers of Canada v. Canadian Assn. of Internet Providers*, 2004 SCC 45, Binnie J.

INTER PARES. [L.] Between or among equals.

INTER PARTES. [L.] Between or among parties.

INTERPLEADER. *n.* The process by which a person who expects to be or is sued by two or more parties with adverse claims to goods or a debt in the first person's hands, but in which the first person has no interest, obtains relief by arranging that the other parties try their rights between themselves. See STAKEHOLDER.

INTERPOLATE. *v.* To insert words in a finished document.

INTERPOLATION. *n.* The act of interpolating; the words which are inserted.

INTERPRETATION. *n.* 1. Construction of a document or statute. 2. Oral translation. 3. A basic rule of interpretation is set out in the Interpretation Acts in the following, or similar, words: Every enactment is deemed remedial, and shall be given such fair, large and liberal construction and interpretation as best ensures the attainment of its objects. 4. Primarily concerned with the spoken word as opposed to the written text. Interpretation as required by the Charter, defined by reference to a number of criteria aimed at helping to ensure that persons with language difficulties have the same opportunity to understand and be understood as if they were conversant in the language being employed in the proceedings. These criteria include, and are not necessarily limited to, continuity, precision, impartiality, competency and contemporaneousness. *R. v. Tran*, [1994] 2 S.C.R. 951. See AMBIGUITY; ASSOCIATED WORDS RULE; CONSECUTIVE ~; CONTEMPORANEOUS ~; CONTEXTUAL APPROACH; EJUSDEM GENERIS; GOLDEN RULE; LIMITED CLASS RULE; LIVING TREE APPROACH; MODERN RULE OF STATUTORY ~; PLAIN MEANING RULE; PRESUMPTION AGAINST ABSURDITY; PRESUMPTION AGAINST EXPROPRIATION; PRESUMPTION AGAINST IMPLIED REPEAL; PRESUMPTION AGAINST INTERNAL CONFLICT; PRESUMTPION AGAINST INTESTACY; PRESUMPTION AGAINST TAUTOLOGY; PRESUMPTION OF COHERENCE; PRESUMPTION OF CONSISTENT EXPRESSION; PRESUMPTION OF CONSTITUTIONAL VALIDITY; PRESUMPTION OF CONTINUANCE; PRESUMPTION OF IMPLIED EXCLUSION; PRESUMPTION OF KNOWLEDGE AND COMPETENCE; PRESUMPTION OF LEGISLATIVE COHERENCE; PRESUMPTION OF LEGITIMACY; PRESUMPTION OF LINGUISTIC COMPETENCE; PURPOSIVE ~; SHARED MEANING RULE; SIMULTANEOUS ~; STATUTORY ~.

INTERPRETATION CLAUSE. A clause which sets out the meanings of particular words used in that statute.

INTERPRETATION SECTION. A section which sets out the meanings of particular words used in that statute.

INTERPRETER. *n.* At a trial, someone sworn to interpret the evidence of someone else who speaks a language which is not that of the proceedings, a mute or a hearing impaired person.

INTERPROFESSIONAL COUNCIL. Established to advise the Minister on any matter she refers to it. It shall bring to the Minister's attention any matter which, in its opinion, requires government action. In addition to the functions conferred on it by law, the Council may, in particular, after consulting its members, (1) examine the problems of a general nature encountered by professional orders and communicate its findings to the orders concerned together with the recommendations it considers appropriate; (2) propose to the Minister objectives to be pursued, both in the short and the long term, to ensure the protection of the public by the orders, and review such objectives periodically; (3) suggest to the Minister and to the Office the measures it considers appropriate to enable the Office to perform its supervisory role; (4) at the request of the Minister or of one or more orders, provide the public with information concerning the professional system, professionals and the duties and powers of the orders; (5) make suggestions concerning amendments to be made to this Code and other Acts and in particular to the Acts constituting the professional orders, or to the regulations or by-laws made under this Code and such Acts; (6) invite groups recognized or not as professional orders, whose members are engaged in related activities, to meet to find solutions to their problems; (7) hear any group wishing to be recognized as a professional order and submit to the Government and to the Office the recommendations it considers appropriate in respect of the recognition of such group; (8) carry out studies and give its advice on any matter relating to the protection of the public that must be ensured by the orders. *Professional Code*, R.S.Q. c. C-26, s. 19.

INTERPROVINCIAL. *adj.* Between provinces.

INTERREGNUM. *n.* [L.] A time when a throne is vacant.

INTERROGATION. *n.* The conduct of an inquiry; the asking of questions particularly in an atmosphere of oppression.

INTERROGATORY. *n.* A written question addressed to one party on behalf of the other party to a cause.

IN TERROREM. [L.] By way of threat. Terrifying.

INTER SE. [L.] Between themselves.

INTERSECTION. *n.* 1. The place where 2 or more highways join or cross. *Highways Development and Protection Act*, S.A. 2004, c. H-8.5, s. 1. 2. The area embraced within the prolongation or connection of the lateral curb lines or, if none, then of the lateral boundary lines of two or more highways which join one another at an angle, whether or not one highway crosses the other. *The Off-Road Vehicles Act*, S.M. 1987-88, c. 64, s. 1. 3. Includes any portion of a highway indicated by markings on the surface of the roadway as a crossing place for pedestrians. *Highway Traffic Act*, R.S.O. 1990, c. H.8, s. 144(1).

INTERSWITCH. *v.* To transfer traffic from the lines of one railway company to the lines of another railway company in accordance with regulations. *Canada Transportation Act*, S.C. 1996, c. 10, s. 111.

INTER-TRACK BETTING. Pari-mutuel betting at one or more satellite tracks or in one or more places in one or more foreign countries on a race that is held at a host track, where the money bet on each pool at each satellite track or place is combined with the money bet on the corresponding pool at the host track to form one pool from which the pay-out price is calculated and distributed. *Criminal Code*, R.S.C. 1985, c. C-46, *Pari-Mutuel Betting Supervision Regulations*, SOR/91-365, s. 2.

INTERVENANT. *n.* 1. Someone who intervenes in a suit in which he or she was not originally involved. 2. A person or association permitted to make representations in proceedings which do not determine the person's or association's own rights.

INTERVENE. *v.* A person who is not a party to a proceeding may move for leave to intervene if the person ... claims (a) an interest in the subject matter of the proceeding; (b) that the person may be adversely affected by a judgment in the proceeding; or (c) that there exists between the person and one or more of the parties to the proceeding a question of law or fact in common with one or more of the questions in issue in the proceeding ... *Courts of Justice Act.* R.S.O. 1990, c. C.43, *Rules of Civil Procedure*, R.R.O. 1990, Reg. 194, s. 13.01).

INTERVENER. *n.* 1. A person who files an intervention or who intervenes. 2. A person or association permitted to make representations in proceedings which do not determine the person's or association's own rights. See INTERVENOR.

INTERVENING CAUSE. An act occurring after the negligence of the defendant which actively functions to produce harm. J.G. Fleming, *The Law of Torts*, 8th ed. (Sydney: Law Book, 1992) at 216. See NOVUS ACTUS INTERVENIENS.

INTERVENOR. *n.* 1. "... [D]escribe persons or associations that are permitted to participate in proceedings to promote their own views, though the proceedings will not determine their legal rights." *Canada (Attorney General) v. Aluminum Co. of Canada* (1987), 35 D.L.R. (4th) 495 at 505, 26 Admin. L.R. 18, 15 C.P.C. (2d) 289, 10 B.C.L.R. (2d) 371, [1987] 3 W.W.R. 193 (C.A.), Seaton J.A. (Hinkson J.A. concurring). 2. A newsletter of the Canadian Environmental Law Association. See INTERVENER.

INTER VIVOS. [L.] Between living people.

INTER VIVOS GIFT. A gratuitous transfer of property from the owner (donor) to another person (donee) with the intention that the transfer will take effect immediately and the title to the property will rest in the donee. See GIFT INTER VIVOS.

INTER VIVOS TRUST. A trust other than a testamentary trust. *Income Tax Act*, R.S.C. 1985, c. 1 (5th Supp.), s. 108.

INTESTACY. *n.* The condition or state of dying without a valid will. See PRESUMPTION AGAINST ~.

INTESTATE. *n.* A person owning property who dies without a will.

INTIMIDATION. *n.* 1. Wrongfully and without lawful authority, for the purpose of compelling another person to abstain from doing anything that he or she has a lawful right to do, or to do anything that he or she has a lawful right to abstain from doing, (a) uses violence or threats of violence to that person or his or her spouse or common-law partner or children, or injures his or her property; (b) intimidates or attempts to intimidate that person or a relative of that person by threats that, in Canada or elsewhere, violence or other injury will be done to or punishment inflicted on him or her or a relative of his or hers, or that the property of any of them will be damaged; (c) persistently follows that person; (d) hides any tools, clothes or other property owned or used by that person, or deprives him or her of them or hinders him or her in the use of them; (e) with one or more other persons, follows that person, in a disorderly manner, on a highway; (f) besets or watches the place where that person resides, works, carries on business or happens to be; or (g) blocks or obstructs a highway.

Criminal Code, R.S.C. 1985, c. C-46, s. 423. 2. "The essential ingredients of the tort [of intimidation] are: 1. A threat by one person to use unlawful means (such as violence, or a tort or a breach of contract) so as to compel another to obey his wishes. 2. The person so threatened must comply with the demand rather than risk the threat being carried into execution." *Roth v. Roth* (1991), 9 C.C.L.T. (2d) 141 at 152, 4 O.R. (3d) 740, 34 M.V.R. (2d) 228 (Gen. Div.), Mandel J. 3. Every person is guilty of an offence who (a) by intimidation or duress, compels a person to vote or refrain from voting or to vote or refrain from voting for a particular candidate at an election; or (b) by any pretence or contrivance, including by representing that the ballot or the manner of voting at an election is not secret, induces a person to vote or refrain from voting or to vote or refrain from voting for a particular candidate at an election. *Canada Elections Act*, S.C. 2000, c. 9, s. 482.

IN TOTO. [L.] Completely, entirely, wholly.

INTOXICANT. *n.* A substance that, if taken into the body, has the potential to impair or alter judgment, behaviour or the capacity to recognize reality or meet the ordinary demands of life, but does not include caffeine, nicotine or any authorized medication used in accordance with directions given by a staff member or a registered health care professional. *Corrections and Conditional Release Act*, S.C. 1992, c. 20, s. 2.

INTOXICATED. *adj.* The condition a person is in when their capabilities are so impaired by liquor that they are likely to cause injury to themselves or be a danger, nuisance, or disturbance to others. *Liquor Act*, R.S.Y. 2002, c. 140, s. 1.

INTOXICATING SUBSTANCE. 1. (a) Glues, adhesives, cements, cleaning solvents, thinning agents and dyes containing toluene or acetone; (b) petroleum distillates or products containing petroleum distillates, including naphtha, mineral spirits, Stoddard solvent, kerosene, gasoline, mineral seal oil and other related distillates of petroleum; (c) fingernail or other polish removers containing acetone, aliphatic acetates, or methyl ethyl ketone; (d) any substance that is required under the Hazardous Products Act (Canada) to bear the label "Vapour Harmful", "Vapour Very Harmful" or "Vapour Extremely Harmful"; (e) aerosol disinfectants and other aerosol products containing ethyl alcohol; and (f) any other product or substance that is prescribed by regulation as an intoxicating substance for the purposes of this Part. *Safer Communities and Neighbourhoods Act*, S.Y. 2006, c. 7, s. 1. 2. (i) Glues, adhesives, cements, cleaning solvents, thinning agents and dyes containing toluene or acetone; (ii) petroleum distillates or products containing petroleum distillates, including naphtha, mineral spirits, Stoddard solvent, kerosene, gasoline, mineral seal oil and other related distillates of petroleum; (iii) fingernail or other polish removers containing acetone, aliphatic acetates or methyl ethyl ketone; (iv) any substance that is required pursuant to the Hazardous Products Act (Canada) or the regulations pursuant to that Act to bear the label "Vapour Harmful", "Vapour Very Harmful" or "Vapour Extremely Harmful"; (v) aerosol disinfectants and other aerosol products containing ethyl alcohol; or (vi) any other product or substance that is prescribed in the regulations as an intoxicating substance. *The Safer Communities and Neighbourhoods Act*, S.S. 2004, c. S-0.1, s. 4.

INTOXICATION. *n.* The state of being under the influence of alcohol to the extent that physical and mental functioning is impaired. See INVOLUNTARY ~; SELF-INDUCED ~.

INTRA VIRES. [L.] 1. Within the range of authority or power. 2. Said of a law found to be valid because it was enacted under powers allocated, by the Constitution, to the legislative body which enacted it.

INTRINSIC. *adj.* Internal; inherent; essential to the nature of.

INTRINSIC EVIDENCE. In libel, relates to the libel itself and to the circumstances of its publication.

INTRINSIC FRAUD. Courts have drawn a distinction between "intrinsic fraud" and "extrinsic fraud" in an attempt to clarify the types of fraud that can vitiate the judgment of a foreign court. Intrinsic fraud is fraud which goes to the merits of the case and to the existence of a cause of action. The extent to which evidence of intrinsic fraud can act as a defence to the recognition of a judgment has not been as clear as that of extrinsic fraud. The historic description of and the distinction between intrinsic and extrinsic fraud is of no apparent value and, because of its ability to both complicate and confuse, should be discontinued. *Beals v. Saldanha*, 2003 SCC 72., Major J.

INTRINSIC VALUE. The price which a piece of property will command in the open market.

INTRODUCED. *adj.* 1. "... '[P]resented, tendered or offered'." *Maritime Construction Ltd. v. R.* (1988), [1989] 1 C.T.C. 306 at 307, 93 N.B.R. (2d) 438, 238 A.P.R. 438 (Q.B.), McLellan J. 2. Said of a bill on first reading in a legislature. 3. Said of evidence proffered in a hearing or at trial.

INTRUSIVE. See NON-~ SEARCH.

INUIT. *n.* Those persons enrolled from time to time under the terms of Article 35 of the Agreement and includes, in the case of the jointly owned lands referred to in section 0.2.8 of the Agreement, the Inuit of northern Quebec. The agreement is the land claims agreement between the Inuit of the Nunavut Settlement Area and Her Majesty the Queen in right of Canada that was ratified, given effect and declared valid by the Nunavut Land Claims Agreement Act, which came into force on July 9, 1993. *Nunavut Waters and Nunavut Surface Rights Tribunal Act,* S.C. 2002, c. 10, s. 2.

INUK. *n.* An individual member of the group of persons referred to in the definition of "Inuit."

INURE. *v.* 1. To come to the benefit of. 2. To take effect.

IN VACUO. [L.] In a vacuum.

INVALID. *adj.* 1. Void, having no effect. 2. Physically or mentally incapable of earning financial remuneration.

INVASION. See HOME ~.

INVENTION. *n.* Any new and useful art, process, machine, manufacture or composition of matter, or any new and useful improvement in any art, process, machine, manufacture or composition of matter. See SPIRIT OF THE ~.

INVENTOR. *n.* The person who applies for a patent and who invented the thing alone, not because another suggested it or because the person read about it. H.G. Fox, *The Canadian Law and Practice Relating to Letters Patent for Inventions*, 4th ed. (Toronto: Carswell, 1969) at 225.

INVENTORY. *n.* 1. Goods that are held by a person for sale or lease, or that are to be furnished or have been furnished under a contract of service, or that are raw materials, work in process or materials used or consumed in a business or profession. *Personal Property Security acts.* 2. A schedule or list which accurately describes goods and chattels. 3. A stock-taking.

INVENTORY SEARCH. 1. Itemizing visible property of apparent value. *R. v. Wint*, [2009] O.J. No. 212 (C.A.) 2. Inventory searches of vehicles after arrest are not automatically justifiable as a search incident to the arrest. This is so because inventory searches do not necessarily serve the criminal law objectives which justify the power to search as an incident of arrest. [Under the Highway Traffic Act, s. 221(1)] once the police assume control and possession of the vehicle, they had a duty to take steps to safeguard the vehicle and its contents. This included documenting the contents of the vehicle. *R. v. Nicolosi* (1998), 40 O.R. (3d) 417 (C.A.).

INVENTORY VALUATION. See FIFO METHOD OF ~; LAST-IN, FIRST-OUT METHOD OF ~.

INVEST. *v.* 1. To transfer possession. 2. To contribute money. 3. To place money in hopes of receiving an increase in the capital or income on the money.

INVESTIGATION. *n.* The action of investigating. Examining systematically; searching and inquiring. See DEPARTMENTAL ~.

INVESTIGATOR. See CORRECTIONAL ~ OF CANADA; PRIVATE ~.

INVESTITURE. *n.* 1. The free transfer of possession or seisin. 2. The formal bestowal of office or honour.

INVESTMENT. *n.* A purchase of any security or any class of securities of an issuer including loans to persons or companies, but does not include advances or loans, whether secured or unsecured, that (i) are made by a mutual fund or its management company or distribution company, and (ii) are ancillary to the main business of the mutual fund or its management company or its distribution company. *Securities Act*, R.S.A. 2000, c. S-4, s. 184. See AUTHORIZED ~; TAX SHELTER ~.

INVESTMENT BUSINESS. See SPECIFIED ~.

INVESTMENT FUND. A mutual fund or a non-redeemable investment fund. *Securities Act*, S.Y. 2007, c. 16, s. 1. See NON-REDEEMABLE ~.

INVESTMENT HOLDING COMPANY. A company incorporated under the Companies Act whose objects, as set forth in its memorandum of association, are solely as follows: (a) to hold by way of investment any real or personal property whatsoever; (b) for purposes incidental to such holding, to purchase or otherwise acquire and to sell or otherwise dispose of any such real or personal property; (c) for purposes incidental to such holding or purchase or sale, to draw, make, accept, endorse, discount, execute and issue promissory notes, bills of exchange, bills of lading, warrants and other negotiable or transferable instruments; (d) with the sanction of a special resolution, to guarantee the obligations of any shareholder and, as security for such guarantee, to mortgage, pledge, hypothecate or otherwise charge the whole or any part of its property; (e) to do all such other acts or things as are incidental or conducive to or consequential upon the attainment of the above objects. *Private Investment Holding Companies Act*; R.S.N.S. 1989, c. 357, s. 2.

INVESTMENT SHARE. A share in the capital of a cooperative that is not a membership share. *Canada Cooperatives Act*, S. C. 1998, c. 1, s. 2.

INVESTMENT TRUST. A trust which collects, retains and invests funds for multiple purposes. D.M.W. Waters, *The Law of Trusts in Canada*, 2d ed. (Toronto: Carswell, 1984) at 101.

INVESTOR. *n.* One who invests money in property or in a business venture.

INVESTOR-RELATIONS ACTIVITIES. Any activities or communications, by or on behalf of an issuer or a security holder of the issuer, that promote or could reasonably be expected to promote the purchase or sale of securities of the issuer, but does not include (a) the dissemination of records in the ordinary course of business of the issuer (i) to promote the sale of products or services of the issuer, or (ii) to raise public awareness of the issuer that cannot reasonably be considered to promote the purchase or sale of securities of the issuer, or (b) activities or communications necessary to comply with (i) Yukon securities laws, extra-provincial securities laws or foreign securities laws governing the issuer, or (ii) the requirements of an exchange or marketplace on which the issuer's securities trade. *Securities Act*, S.Y. 2007, c. 16, s. 1.

INVIOLABILITY. *n.* Section 1 of the Charter [of Human Rights and Freedoms, R.S.Q., c. C-12] guarantees the right to personal "inviolability". The common meaning of the word 'inviolability' [pursuant to s. 1 of the Charter] suggests that the interference with that right must leave some marks, some sequelae which, while not necessarily physical or permanent, exceed a certain threshold. The interference must affect the victim's physical, psychological or emotional equilibrium in something more than a fleeting manner. *Québec (Curateur public) c. Syndicat national des employés de l'hôpital St-Ferdinand,* 1996 CarswellQue 916, 202 N.R. 321, *(sub nom. Quebec (Public Curator) v. Syndicat national des employés de l'hôpital St-Ferdinand)* 138 D.L.R. (4th) 577, 1

C.P.C. (4th) 183, [1996] 3 S.C.R. 211, the court per L'Heureux-Dubé.

INVITATION FOR TENDERS. An invitation for tenders is an invitation to enter into a contract on the terms specified in the call for tenders. *Chandos Construction Ltd. v. Alberta (Minister of Infrastructure)*, 2006 ABCA 41.

INVITATION TO TREAT. A statement which indicates general commercial intent, the wish of that party to contract with another party if they can agree.

INVITEE. *n.* One who is either impliedly or expressly invited to an occupier's premises for some purpose connected indirectly or directly with the occupier's business. In law, a guest is a licensee, not an invitee.

INVITOR. *n.* A person who invites another to her or his premises for business purposes.

IN VITRO. [L. in glass] Under experimental conditions in a test tube. F.A. Jaffe, *A Guide to Pathological Evidence for Lawyers and Police Officers*, 4th ed. (Toronto: Carswell, 1999) at 239.

IN VIVO. [L.] In a living body.

INVOICE. *n.* A written account of the particulars of goods shipped or sent to a purchaser or for labour or services provided.

INVOLUNTARY INTOXICATION. Intoxication which is not self-induced.

IOTA. *n.* The smallest possible quantity.

IOU. *abbr.* I owe you. The written admission or expression of a debt.

IP. *abbr.* Intellectual property.

IPEA. *abbr.* International Preliminary Examining Authority (under PCT).

IPIC. *abbr.* Intellectual Property Institute of Canada.

I.P.J. *abbr.* Intellectual Property Journal.

IPSE DIXIT. [L. one said it oneself] A simple assertion.

IPSISSIMA VERBA. [L.] The very same words.

IPSO FACTO. [L.] By the very same act.

IPSO JURE. [L.] By the very law.

I.R.B. *abbr.* 1. Immigration and Refugee Board. 2. Industrial Relations Board.

IRP. *abbr.* The International Registration Plan, being an agreement between jurisdictions in North America, as amended from time to time, respecting commercial motor vehicle registration. *The Traffic Safety Act*, S.S. 2004, c. T-18.1, s. 2.

IRRATIONALITY. *n.* By 'irrationality' I mean what can by now be succinctly referred to as 'Wednesbury unreasonableness' *(*Associated Provincial Picture Houses Ltd. v. Wednesbury Corporation, [1948] 1 K.B. 223). It applies to a decision which is so outrageous in its defiance of logic or of accepted moral standards that no sensible person who had applied his mind to the question to be decided could have arrived at it. Whether a decision falls within this category is a question that judges by their training and experience should be well equipped to answer, or else there would be something badly wrong with our judicial system. To justify the court's exercise of this role, resort I think is today no longer needed to Viscount Radcliffe's ingenious explanation in Edwards v. Bairstow, [1956] A.C. 14 of irrationality as a ground for a court's reversal of a decision by ascribing it to an inferred though unidentifiable mistake of law by the decision-maker. 'Irrationality' by now can stand upon its own feet as an accepted ground on which a decision may be attacked by judicial review. *Council of Civil Service Unions v. Minister for the Civil Service (1984)*, [1985] A.C. 374 at 410, 411, [1984] 3 All E.R. 935 (H.L.), Lord Diplock.

IRREBUTTABLE. *adj.* Not rebuttable; not capable of disproof.

IRREFRAGABLE. *adj.* Indisputable; inviolable; undeniable.

IRREGULAR. *adj.* A plea that is "concealing or evasive" is an irregular plea under Rule 19(21) [of the Rules of Court, 1990, B.C. Reg. 221/90]: it is capable of being reformed. It is not an "embarrassing plea". An embarrassing plea amounts to an abuse of process. *Patym Holdings Ltd. v. Michalakis*, 2005 BCCA 636, Smith J.A. (Saunders J.A. concurring).

IRREGULARITY. *n.* 1. Informality, not according to form. 2. A minor defect.

IRREGULAR LOT. A township lot whose boundaries according to the original plan do not conform within one degree to the bearings shown for the corresponding boundaries of the majority of the lots in the tier in which the lot occurs. *Surveys Act*, R.S.O. 1990, c. S.30, s. 1.

IRRELEVANT. *adj.* 1. Not relevant. 2. Not related to the issue at hand.

IRREPARABLE HARM. 1. A test used in determining whether to grant interlocutory relief. "Irreparable" refers to the nature of the harm suffered rather than its magnitude. It is harm which either cannot be quantified in monetary terms or which cannot be cured, usually because one party cannot collect damages from the other. Where one party will suffer permanent market loss or irrevocable damage to its business reputation; or where a permanent loss of natural resources will be the result when a challenged activity is not enjoined. The fact that one party may be impecunious does not automatically determine the application in favour of the other party who will not ultimately be able to collect damages, although it may be a relevant consideration. The assessment of irreparable harm in interlocutory applications involving Charter rights is a task which will often be more difficult than a comparable assessment in a private law application. One reason for this is that the notion of irreparable harm is closely tied to the remedy of damages, but damages are not the primary remedy in Charter cases. *RJR-MacDonald Inc. v. Canada (Attorney General)*, [1994] 1 S.C.R. 311, at 341, Sopinka and Cory JJ. 2. "[The injury] ... must be material and one which cannot be adequately remedied by damages ..." *Spooner Oils Ltd. v. Turner Valley Gas Conservation Board*, [1932] 2 W.W.R. 641 at 646, [1932] 4 D.L.R. 681 (Alta. C.A.), McGillivary J.A.

IRREPLEVIABLE. *adj.* Unable to be replevied.

IRREPLEVISABLE. *adj.* Unable to be replevied.

IRREVOCABLE. *adj.* 1. Not able to be revoked. 2. Of a cheque, can no longer be prevented or recalled by the unilateral action of the payer.

IRREVOCABLE BENEFICIARY. A designation by an insured of a beneficiary. The designation may not be altered or revoked without the consent of the beneficiary during his or her lifetime.

ISA. *abbr.* International Searching Authority (under PCT).

ISLAND. *n.* All of the land that makes up an island, and includes surrounding land attached to and extending from an island, whether or not water flows over or under it. *Islands Trust Act*, R.S.B.C. 1996, c. 239, s. 1. See ARTIFICIAL ~.

ISP. *abbr.* Internet service provider.

ISSUE. *v.* 1. In respect of an award, means make and publish to the parties to the arbitration. 2. To release shares, securities or documents. 3. To release stamps. 4. To mail or deliver 2 or more copies of the disposition to the intended holder for execution by the intended holder. *Public Lands Act*, R.S.A. 2000, c. P-40, s. 39. 5. [T]he English word "issues" [in the Employment Insurance Act] does not mean "serves." For example, when section 88 states that the judge "may issue a warrant" permitting entry to a dwelling house, it obviously does not mean that the judge may "serve" a warrant to the person who is being authorized to enter! And when Parliament intended that a notice be served, it said so explicitly. *Canada (Attorney General) v. Savard*, 2006 FCA 327.

ISSUE. *n.* 1. A matter in dispute. 2. A proposition of law or of fact defined by the pleadings as a point on which the parties wish to have the decision of the court. *Forest Glen Wood Products Ltd. v. British Columbia (Minister of Forests)*, 2008 BCCA 480. 3. The first delivery of a bill or note, complete in form, to a person who takes it as a holder. *Bills of Exchange Act*, R.S.C. 1985, c. B-4, s. 2. 4. " ... [T]echnical meaning [is] 'descendants' ..." *Davidson, Re* (1926), 59 O.L.R. 643 at 644 (C.A.), the court per Latchford C.J. 5. One who is no longer the child of his or her biological parent can no longer be the issue. *Benefield v. Hrenko Estate*, 2001 CarswellAlta 353, 2001 ABQB 242, [2001] 7 W.W.R. 402, 38 E.T.R. (2d) 175, 92 Alta. L.R. (3d) 168, 287 A.R. 33 (Surr. Ct.), Bensler J. 6. Generally the word "issue" when used in a will is a technical term meaning "all lineal descendants" "of the remotest degree" unless the context of the will displaces this primary meaning and "makes it clear" that "issue" means "children" only. *Acreman Estate, Re*, 2001 CarswellBC 1027, 2001 BCSC 678, 38 E.T.R. (2d) 159, Edwards J. 7. The first delivery of a depository bill or note, complete in form, to the person to whom it is payable. *Depository Bills and Notes Act*, S.C. 1998, c. 13, s. 2. 8. The first release of shares or securities or postal stamps. See

ARGUABLE ~; COMMON ~S; DIE WITH-OUT ~; DIE WITHOUT LEAVING ~; DYING WITHOUT ~; FACT IN ~; FAILURE OF ~; HAVE NO ~; JOINDER OF ~; MALE ~; OVER~; POLYCENTRIC ~.

ISSUED. *adj.* Describes a court document which a registrar dates, signs and seals with the seal of the court.

ISSUED CAPITAL. The quantity of shares allotted and issued.

ISSUE ESTOPPEL. 1. [P]recludes the relitigation of the same issue between the same parties, even though the issue arises in the context of a different cause of action. *Erdos v. Canada (Minister of Citizenship & Immigration)*, 2005 FCA 419. 2. The preconditions to the operation of issue estoppel were set out by Dickson J. in Angle, [Angle v. Minister of National Revenue, [1975] 2 S.C.R. 248], at p. 254: (1) that the same question has been decided; (2) that the judicial decision which is said to create the estoppel was final; and, (3) that the parties to the judicial decision or their privies were the same persons as the parties to the proceedings in which the estoppel is raised or their privies. The rules governing issue estoppel should not be mechanically applied. The underlying purpose is to balance the public interest in the finality of litigation with the public interest in ensuring that justice is done on the facts of a particular case. (There are corresponding private interests.) The first step is to determine whether the moving party (in this case the respondent) has established the preconditions to the operation of issue estoppel set out by Dickson J. in Angle, supra. If successful, the court must still determine whether, as a matter of discretion, issue estoppel ought to be applied. Issue estoppel does not apply to investigations. *Danyluk v. Ainsworth Technologies Inc.*, [2001] 2 S.C.R. 460. 3. A subcategory of res judicata, and refers to the principle that precludes a party to litigation from seeking a judicial determination of a point of fact that has been determined with finality in another proceeding. *Connaught Laboratories Ltd. v. Medeva Pharma Ltd.* (1999), 1999 CarswellNat 2809, 4 C.P.R. (4th) 508, 179 F.T.R. 200 (T.D.). 4. " ... [P]revents [the prosecution] from raising again any of the separate issues of fact which the jury have decided, or are presumed to have decided, in reaching their verdict in the accused's favour..." *R. v. Greeno* (1983), 6 C.C.C. (3d) 325 at 328, 58 N.S.R. (2d) 261, 123 A.P.R. 261 (C.A.), the court per Macdonald J.A.

ISSUER. *n.* 1. A person or company who has outstanding, issues or proposes to issue, a security or a body corporate, (i) that is required to maintain a securities register, (ii) that directly or indirectly creates fractional interests in its rights or property and issues security certificates or uncertified securities as evidence of the fractional interests, (iii) that places or authorizes the placing of its name on a security certificate, otherwise than as an authenticating trustee, registrar or transfer agent, or that otherwise authorizes the issue of a security certificate or an uncertificated security evidencing a share, participation or other interest in its property or in an enterprise or evidencing its duty to perform an obligation, or (iv) that becomes responsible for or in place of any other person described as an issuer. 2. (i) With respect to a registration of a transfer of a security, means a person on whose behalf transfer books are maintained; (ii) with respect to an obligation on or a defence to a security, includes: (A) a person who places or authorizes the placing of the person's name on a security certificate, other than as authenticating trustee, registrar, transfer agent or the like, to evidence: (I) a share, participation or other interest in the person's property or in an enterprise; or (II) the person's duty to perform an obligation represented by the security certificate; (B) a person who creates a share, participation or other interest in the person's property or in an enterprise, or undertakes an obligation, that is an uncertificated security; (C) a person who directly or indirectly creates a fractional interest in the person's rights or property, if the fractional interest is represented by a security certificate; (D) a guarantor, to the extent of the guarantor's guarantee, whether or not the guarantor's obligation is noted on a security certificate; and (E) a person that becomes responsible for, or in place of, another person described as an issuer in this definition. *Securities Transfer acts.* 3. The person who issues a credit card. 4. An issuer of marriage licences.

ISSUER BID. A direct or indirect offer to acquire or redeem a security or a direct or indirect acquisition or redemption of a security that is (i) made by the issuer of the security, and (ii) within a prescribed class of offers, acquisitions or redemptions. *Securities acts.*

ITEM. *n.* 1. That portion of a vote used for a specific program purpose. *Financial Administration acts.* 2. "... [A]ny separate fact or statement... ." *Goddard v. Barker* (1951), 4 W.W.R. (N.S.) 433 at 437 (B.C. C.A.), O'Halloran J.A. 3. "... [A] paragraph or a short article... ." *Goddard v. Barker* (1951), 4 W.W.R. (N.S.) 433 at 437 (B.C. C.A.), O'Halloran J.A.

I

J

J. *abbr.* Justice.

J.A. *abbr.* Justice of appeal.

JAIL. *n.* A prison or gaol. See COMMON ~; GAOL.

JAILHOUSE INFORMANT. An inmate who gives evidence against a fellow inmate based on conversation with or eavesdropping on the fellow inmate.

J. BUS. L. *abbr.* Journal of Business Law.

J.C.A. *abbr.* Judgments Under the Competition Act, 1984-.

J. CAN. STUDIES. *abbr.* Journal of Canadian Studies (Revue d'études canadiennes).

J.C.A.P. *abbr.* Judgments Under the Competition Act and its Predecessors, 1904-.

JDR. *abbr.* Judicial Dispute Resolution.

J.E. *abbr.* Jurisprudence Express (Québec), 1977-.

JEOPARDY. *n.* 1. In the state of being at risk of being convicted of an offence. 2. At risk of self incrimination. See DOUBLE ~; IN ~.

JET FUEL. A substance suitable to power an aircraft that is propelled by a turbine. *Carbon Tax Act*, S.B.C. 2008, c. 40, Sched. 1, s. 1.

JETSAM. *n.* Goods thrown into the sea which sink and stay under water.

JETTISON. *v.* To throw goods overboard to lighten a vessel during a storm, to prevent capture or for other good reason.

JJ. *abbr.* Judges or Justices.

JJ. A. *abbr.* Judges or Justices of Appeal Court.

J. JUGES PROV. *abbr.* Journal des juges provinciaux (Provincial Judges Journal).

J.L. *abbr.* 1. Jurisprudence logement: Recueil trimestriel de jurisprudencce sur le bail d'habitation comprenant des décisions d la Régie du logement et des tribunaux judiciaires en matiêre de logement, 1993-. 2. Jurisprudence logement, 1982-.

J.L. & SOCIAL POL'Y. *abbr.* Journal of Law and Social Policy (Revue des lois et des politiques sociales).

J.M.V.L. *abbr.* Journal of Motor Vehicle Law.

JOB. *n.* 1. A specific assignment of work; a fulltime work position. 2. An undertaking or project for construction.

JOBBER. *n.* Someone who buys and sells goods wholesale and handles goods on commission. G.H.L. Fridman, *Sale of Goods in Canada*, 3d ed. (Toronto: Carswell, 1986) at 493.

JOB COACH. An individual who assists a newly-hired qualifying employee to attain productivity in the workplace that matches other employees by working on-site with the qualifying employee to help him or her to, (a) become oriented in the workplace, (b) learn the specific work tasks required by the position, (c) develop communication skills for interacting with supervisors and co-workers, or (d) adjust to the work environment. *Corporations Tax Act*, R.S.O. 1990, c. C.40, s. 13.3.

JOB CREATION PROGRAM. A program established to provide employment incentives to businesses, municipal governments or others by means of grants to subsidize wages and benefits paid for new jobs created. *Northern Municipalities Act*, S.S. 1983, c. N-5.1, *The Northern Revenue Sharing Capital Grants Regulations*, R.R.S., c. N-5.1, Reg. 16, s. 2.

JOB DESCRIPTION. A statement of the duties, conditions and purpose of a job.

JOB-SHARING ARRANGEMENT. An arrangement between consenting full-time employees to share the duties and responsibilities of a single position. *Civil Service Act*, R.S.N.S. 1989, c. 70, *General Civil Service Regulations*, N.S. Reg. 311/2009, s. 2.

JOHN DOE. A made-up name used in legal proceedings for an imagined or unnamed plaintiff.

JOINDER. *n.* Coupling of matters, proceeding together. See MIS~; NON-~.

JOINDER OF CAUSES OF ACTION. The coupling of several matters in one proceeding or suit.

JOINDER OF ISSUE. Occurs when, at their time to plead, a party denies one particular part or every part of the previous pleading and does not allege any new facts to support their case so that the pleadings end completely or to some extent.

JOINDER OF PARTIES. The coupling of people as plaintiffs or defendants.

JOINT. *adj.* Combined; shared between many; possessed by the same party. See WORK OF ~ AUTHORSHIP.

JOINT ADVENTURE. A species of partnership which may lack a firm name, may be limited as to time and may restrict the authority of a joint adventurer to pledge the credit of the adventure or the co-adventurers.

JOINT AND SEVERAL. Describes the obligation of two or more persons when all are liable jointly and each is liable severally.

JOINT AND SURVIVOR PENSION. A pension payable during the joint lives of the person entitled to the pension and his or her spouse and thereafter during the life of the survivor of them.

JOINT AND SURVIVOR PENSION BENEFIT. An immediate pension benefit that continues at least until the death of the member or former member or the death of the survivor of the member or former member, whichever occurs later. *Pension Benefits Standards Act, 1985*, R.S.C. 1985, c. 32 (2nd Supp.), s. 2.

JOINT BANK ACCOUNT. An account in the names of two or more persons who have equal rights to it with a right of survivorship.

JOINT COMMITTEE. 1. A group consisting of members of both houses of Parliament, usually with an investigative or administrative purpose. A. Fraser, W.A. Dawson, & J. Holtby, eds., *Beauchesne's Rules and Forms of the House of Commons of Canada*, 6th ed. (Toronto: Carswell, 1989) at 222. 2. A joint health and safety committee under Division 4 of this Part. *Workers Compensation Act*, R.S.B.C. 1996, c. 492, s. 106.

JOINT CUSTODY. A sharing of power or control over the course of a child's life, both physically and emotionally.

JOINT DEPOSIT. See JOINT BANK ACCOUNT.

JOINT HEIR. A co-heir.

JOINT INTEREST. 1. Being personally and directly interested in the result of a proceeding along with another person. 2. The admission of any one party cannot be produced in evidence against another party unless that second party has a joint interest with the party making an admission.

JOINTLY. *adv.* 1. "... '[T]ogether with' ..." *Grieve McClory Ltd. v. Dome Lumber Co.*, [1923] 2 D.L.R. 154 at 156, [1923] 1 W.W.R. 989 (S.C.C.), Davies C.J. 2. Can refer to property held by persons as tenants in common or as joint tenants.

JOINTLY AND SEVERALLY. Describes parties who are liable separately or all together.

JOINT OBLIGATION. An obligation is joint between two or more debtors where they are obligated to the creditor for the same thing but in such a way that each debtor may only be compelled to perform the obligation separately and only up to his share of the debt. An obligation is joint between two or more creditors where each creditor may only exact the performance of his share of the claim from the common debtor. *Civil Code*, S.Q. 1991, c. 64, a. 1518.

JOINT SUBMISSION. A joint submission reflects a process where both counsel advocate the same disposition for the sentencing of an offender. It takes effect, however, only upon the assent of the sentencing judge. *R. v. Christie*, 2004 ABCA 287.

JOINT TENANCY. 1. For a joint tenancy to exist there must be four unities, the unity of title, of interest, of time and of possession. 2. "... [C]reated where the same interest in real or personal property is passed by the same conveyance to two or more persons in the same right or by construction or operation of law jointly, with a right of survivorship, ie. the right of the survivor or survivors to the whole property." *R. v. Uniacke*, [1944] 4 D.L.R. 297 at 301, 3 W.W.R. 232, 82 C.C.C. 247 (Sask. C.A.), the court per Martin C.J.S.

JOINT TENANT. One who holds an undivided equal interest in the entire property; after death, the survivor acquires the deceased's interest.

JOINT TORT. 1. A breach of duty committed jointly by two or more persons. 2. "... [A] common wrongful act by several persons, in which there is but one injuria, giving rise to a joint and several liability by all, and in which each is liable for the whole damage... ." *Lambert v. Roberts Drug Stores Ltd. (No. 1)*, [1933] 4 D.L.R. 193 at 194-5, [1933] 2 W.W.R. 508, 41 Man. R. 322 (C.A.), the court per Trueman J.A.

JOINT TORTFEASOR. One who is the principal of or vicariously responsible for the other; persons who have a duty imposed jointly upon them which is not performed; when they act in concert toward a common end. To be considered joint tortfeasors the persons must combine mentally together for a purpose except in the case of nonfeasance in breach of a joint duty.

JOINT VENTURE. 1. An association of two or more person or entities, where the relationship among those associated persons or entities does not, under the laws in force in Canada, constitute a corporation, a partnership or a trust and where, in the case of an investment to which this Act applies, all the undivided ownership interests in the assets of the Canadian business or in the voting interests of the entity that is the subject of the investment are or will be owned by all the persons or entities that are so associated. *Investment Canada Act*, R.S.C. 1985, c. 28 (1st Supp.), s. 3. 2. I refer to pp. 563-5 of Williston on Contracts, 3d Ed., (N.Y., 1959), and in particular to p. 563: Besides the requirement that a joint venture must have a contractual basis, the courts have laid down certain additional requisites deemed essential for the existence of a joint venture . . . the following factors must be present: (a) A contribution by the parties of money, property, effort, knowledge, skill or other asset to a common undertaking; (b) A joint property interest in the subject matter of the venture; (c) A right of mutual control or management of the enterprise; (d) Expectation of profit, or the presence of "adventure," as it is sometimes called; (e) A right to participate in the profits; (f) Most usually, limitation of the objective to a single undertaking or ad hoc enterprise. ... I regard the foregoing when read with the 1993 supplement as a reasonable and compendious statement of the characteristics of a joint venture. *Canlan Investment Corp. v. Gettling*, 1997 CarswellBC 1380, 37 B.C.L.R. (3d) 140, 10 R.P.R. (3d) 180, 95 B.C.A.C. 16, 154 W.A.C. 16, [1998] 2 W.W.R. 431, 36 B.L.R. (2d) 117, the court per Goldie J. A.

JOINT WILL. "... [A] will made by two or more testators contained in the same document duly executed by testator and testatrix disposing either of their separate properties or their joint property. It operates on the death of each testator as his will disposing of his separate property and is in, effect, two or more wills ..." *Ohorodnyk, Re* (1979), 4 E.T.R. 233 at 244, 24 O.R. (2d) 228, 97 D.L.R. (3d) 502 (H.C.), Hollingworth J. See MUTUAL WILLS.

JOURNALISTIC-CONFIDENTIAL SOURCE PRIVILEGE. Has not previously been recognized as a class privilege by our Court (Moysa v. Alberta (Labour Relations Board), 1989 CanLII 55 (S.C.C.), [1989] 1 S.C.R. 1572), and has been rejected by courts in other common law jurisdictions with whom we have strong affinities. *R. v. National Post*, 2010 SCC 16, Binnie, J. See CASE-BY-CASE PRIVILEGE.

JOURNALS. *n.* The official and permanent record of proceedings in the House of Commons. A. Fraser, W.A. Dawson & J. Holtby, eds., *Beauchesne's Rules and Forms of the House of Commons of Canada*, 6th ed. (Toronto: Carswell, 1989) at 299.

JOURNEYPERSON. n. 1. A person who holds a certificate of qualification in a designated trade. *The Apprenticeship and Certification Act*, S.M. 2009, c. 33, s. 1. 2. A person who holds a valid and subsisting journeyperson electrician's licence issued under this Act. *The Electricians' Licence Act*, R.S.M. 1987, c. E50, s. 1.

JOYRIDE. *v.* "... [T]he unauthorized taking of a motor vehicle with the intent to drive or use it temporarily ..." *Lafrance v. R.* (1973), 23 C.R.N.S. 100 at 115, 13 C.C.C. (2d) 289, 39 D.L.R. (3d) 693, [1975] 2 S.C.R. 201, Laskin J. (dissenting) (Hall and Spence JJ. concurring).

J.P. *abbr.* Justice of the peace.

J. PLAN. & ENV. L. *abbr.* Journal of Planning and Environmental Law.

J.S.D. *abbr.* Doctor of Juristic Science; Doctor of Juridical Science.

J. SOCIAL WELFARE L. *abbr.* Journal of Social Welfare Law.

JUDGE. *n.* 1. The person authorized to determine any question or cause in a court. 2. Includes any person lawfully presiding in a court. See CHIEF ~; CITIZENSHIP ~; MILITARY ~; NO MAN SHALL BE ~ IN HIS OWN CAUSE; SUPERNUMERARY ~; SUPERVISORY ~; YOUTH JUSTICE COURT ~.

JUDGE ADVOCATE GENERAL. The Judge Advocate General, appointed by the Governor in Council, acts as legal adviser to the Governor General, the Minister, the Department and the Canadian Forces in matters relating to military law. The Judge Advocate General has the superintendence of the administration of military justice in the Canadian Forces. *National Defence Act*, R.S.C. 1985, c.N-5, s. 9, 9.1 and 9.2.

JUDGE-MADE LAW. The common law which includes the interpretation of statutes and subordinate legislation by the courts. Contrasted to statute law. See JUDICIAL LEGISLATION.

JUDGE SHOPPING. Using the Crown's scheduling privilege to get the case before a judge of its own choosing. *R. v. Regan* [2002] 1 S.C.R. 297, Binnie J. (dissenting) (Iacobucci, Major, Arbour JJ. concurring).

JUDGE'S NOTES. Notes usually taken by a judge when evidence is given viva voce.

JUDGMENT. *n.* 1. A judicial decision; the determination of a court; a court's sentence or decision on the major question in a proceeding. 2. Includes orders. *Muzak Corp. v. C.A.P.A.C.*, [1953] 2 S.C.R. 182 at 196-7, 13 Fox Pat. C. 168, 19 C.P.R. 1, Cartwright J. 3. The reasons a court gives for a decision. 4. When used with reference to the court appealed from, includes any judgment, rule, order, decision, decree, decretal order or sentence thereof, and when used with reference to the Supreme Court, includes any judgment or order of that Court. *Supreme Court Act*, R.S.C. 1985, c. S-26, s. 2. See BUSINESS ~ RULE; CONSENT ~; DECLARATORY ~; DEFAULT ~; ENTER ~; FINAL ~; FOREIGN ~; MERGER INTO ~; MONEY ~; NISI PRIUS ~; PECUNIARY ~; SUMMARY ~.

JUDGMENT CREDITOR. 1. The person by whom the judgment was obtained, and includes the executors, administrators, successors and assigns of that person. *Reciprocal Enforcement of Judgments Act*, R.S.N.B. 1973, c. R-3, s. 1. 2. The person in whose favour the judgment was given, and includes that person's executors, administrators, successors and assigns.

JUDGMENT DEBT. A sum of money or any costs, charges or expenses made payable by or under a judgment in a civil proceeding.

JUDGMENT DEBTOR. 1. Includes a party required to make a payment of money and costs, or either, under an order, and any executor, administrator or assignee of a judgment debtor. 2. The person against whom the judgment was given and includes any person against whom the judgment is enforceable under the law of the territory of origin. Federal statutes. 3. The person liable for the payment of money payable under a judgment or order. 4. A person against whom a maintenance order has been given.

JUDGMENT IN PERSONAM. One which determines the rights, liabilities and interests of the parties to the litigation only.

JUDGMENT IN REM. 1. "... [A]n adjudication pronounced upon the status of some particular subject matter by a tribunal having competent authority for that purpose. Such an adjudication being a solemn

J

declaration from the proper and accredited quarter that the status of the thing adjudicated upon is as declared, concludes all persons from saying that the status of the thing adjudicated upon was not such as declared by the adjudication." *Sleeth v. Hurlbert* (1896), 25 S.C.R. 620 at 630, 3 C.C.C. 197, Sedgewick J. (Gwynne, King and Girouard JJ. concurring). 2. Examples of these are an action in maritime law concerning the status of a ship, a divorce decree, a bankruptcy adjudication, a judgment concerning the validity of a patent, a declaration of mental incapacity, a grant of administration. Such a judgment is notice to all who deal with a person or thing on which the court has pronounced concerning the status of that person or thing.

JUDGMENT SUMMONS. An order requiring a judgment debtor to appear to be examined in front of a judge or court officer.

JUDICIAL. *adj.* 1. Relating to judges. 2. Having the quality of being judge-like. 3. "... [T]he question of whether any particular function is 'judicial' is not to be determined simply on the basis of procedural trappings. The primary issue is the nature of the question which the tribunal is called upon to decide. Where the tribunal is faced with a private dispute between parties, and is called upon to adjudicate through the application of a recognized body of rules in a manner consistent with fairness and impartiality, then, normally, it is acting in a 'judicial capacity' ... the judicial task involves questions of 'principle', that is consideration of the competing rights of individuals or groups. This can be contrasted with questions of 'policy' involving competing views of the collective good of the community as a whole ..." *Reference re Residential Tenancies Act* (1981), (*sub nom. Residential Tenancies Act of Ontario, Re*) 123 D.L.R. (3d) 554 at 571, [1981] 1 S.C.R. 714, 37 N.R. 158, Dickson J. See EXTRA~; QUASI-~.

JUDICIAL ACT. "... [A]n act done by competent authority upon consideration of acts and circumstances, and imposing liability or affecting the rights of others." *The Queen v. Corporation of Dublin* (1878), 2 L.R. Ir. 371 at 377, May C.J.

JUDICIAL ADMISSION. A formal admission. An admission made by a party in pleadings.

JUDICIAL CASE CONFERENCE. In family law matters, a meeting with the parties and judge present at which the issues that are in dispute and those that are not in dispute are identified and ways in which the issues in dispute may be resolved without recourse to trial are explored; orders to which all the parties consent may be made; any issues in dispute may be mediated; issues may be referred to private mediation on consent; parties may be referred to a family justice counsellor; and other procedural matters may be determined. *Court Rules Act*, R.S.B.C. 1996, c. 80, *Supreme Court Family Rules*, B.C. Reg. 169/2009, Rule 7-1.

JUDICIAL COMITY. The principle of judicial comity is well-recognized by the judiciary in Canada. Applied to decisions rendered by judges of the Federal Court, the principle is to the effect that a substantially similar decision rendered by a judge of this Court should be followed in the interest of advancing certainty in the law. There are a number of exceptions to the principle of judicial comity as expressed above they are: 1. The existence of a different factual matrix or evidentiary basis between the two cases; 2. Where the issue to be decided is different; 3. Where the previous condition failed to consider legislation or binding authorities that would have produced a different result, i.e., was manifestly wrong; and 4. The decision it followed would create an injustice. *Almrei v. Canada (Citizenship and Immigration)*, 2007 FC 1025, Lemieux J.

JUDICIAL COMMITTEE. A committee of the Privy Council of the United Kingdom made up of Privy Councillors who are judges. They advise the Queen how to dispose of each appeal, and their advice is considered to be a binding judgment. Historically, this was the final court of appeal for Canada. P.W. Hogg, *Constitutional Law of Canada*, 3d ed. (Toronto: Carswell, 1992) at 202-3.

JUDICIAL COMMITTEE OF THE PRIVY COUNCIL. In the days of the British empire, the final appeal court from every colonial court. It continues as a Commonwealth court for Commonwealth nations which haved retained that appeal. P.W. Hogg, *Constitutional Law of Canada*, 3d ed. (Toronto: Carswell, 1992) at 202.

JUDICIAL COUNCIL. See CANADIAN ~.

JUDICIAL DECISION. See REPORTED ~.

JUDICIAL DEFERENCE. The degree to which a court will refrain from interfering with a decision of an administrative tribunal or a lower court. Factors such as public interest, expertise of the tribunal, the courts' treatment of a tribunal historically and the existence and type of privative clause in place are important in determining which standard of deference will be applied. See CORRECTNESS; PATENTLY UNREASONABLE; STANDARD OF REVIEW; UNREASONABLE.

JUDICIAL DISCRETION. During a trial, the freedom of a judge to summarily decide certain matters which cannot afterwards be questioned.

JUDICIAL DISPUTE RESOLUTION. A term used in Alberta to refer to conferences conducted by provincial court judges under the Family Law Act. *Provincial Court Act*, R.S.A. 2000, c. P-31, *Intake and Caseflow Management Regulation*, Alta. Reg. 150/2005, s. 10.

JUDICIAL IMMUNITY. "... [A] judge of a superior court is protected when he is acting in the bona fide exercise of his office and under the belief that he has jurisdiction, though he may be mistaken in that belief and may not in truth have any jurisdiction... ." *Sirros v. Moore*, [1974] 3 All E.R. 776 at 784 (U.K.), Lord Denning M.R.

JUDICIAL INDEPENDENCE. 1. "... [T]he generally accepted core of the principle of judicial independence has been the complete liberty of individual judges to hear and decide the cases that come before them: no outsider – be it government, pressure group, individual or even another judge – should interfere in fact, or attempt to interfere, with the way in which a judge conducts his or her case and makes his or her decision." *R. v. Beauregard* (*sub nom. Beauregard v. Canada*), [1986] 2 S.C.R. 56 at 69, 73, 70 N.R. 1, 30 D.L.R. (4th) 481, 26 C.R.R. 59, Dickson C.J. (Estey J. and Laskin JJ. concurring). 2. Three conditions that are prerequisites for judicial independence. These are security of tenure, financial security and institutional independence with respect to matters of administration bearing directly on the exercise of the court's judicial function. *Lippé c. Charest* (1990), (*sub nom. R. c. Lippé*) [1991] 2 S.C.R. 114, Le Dain J. See INSTITUTIONAL INDEPENDENCE.

JUDICIAL INTERIM RELEASE. 1. Bail. 2. The judge's setting free the accused between committal for trial and the trial's completion.

JUDICIAL KNOWLEDGE. Refers to documents which the court knows or suspects exist and which the court would likely consult on its own initiative. *Eastmain Band v. Canada*, [1992] 3 F.C. 800 (C.A.).

JUDICIAL LEGISLATION. Growth or advancement of law through a judicial decision.

JUDICIALLY. *adv.* The expression most often used in the Federal Court is that a discretion must be exercised "judicially". That term is taken to mean that if a decision were made in bad faith, that is for an improper purpose or motive, in a discriminatory manner, or the decision-maker ignored a relevant factor or considered an irrelevant one, then the decision must be set aside. [Whether or not a factor is relevant may be in issue.] The same fate awaits a decision based on a mistaken principle of law or a misapprehension of the facts (as opposed to inferences drawn from accepted facts) or what is commonly referred to as a "palpable and overriding error". *Suresh v. Canada* (Minister of Citizenship & Immigration), 2000 CarswellNat 25, 183 D.L.R. (4th) 629, 5 Imm. L.R. (3d) 1, 252 N.R. 1, 18 Admin. L.R. (3d) 159, [2000] 2 F.C. 592, 180 F.T.R. 57 (note) (C.A.), the court per Robertson J.A. See ACTING ~.

JUDICALLY OBTAINED. See SEPARATION AS TO PROPERTY ~.

JUDICIAL NOTICE. 1. The acceptance of a fact without proof. It applies to two kinds of facts: facts which are so notorious as not be the subject of dispute among reasonable persons; and facts that are capable of immediate and accurate demonstration by resorting to readily accessible sources of indisputable accuracy. *R. v. Williams*, [1998] 1 S.C.R. 1128. 2. One classic statement of the content and purpose of the doctrine is outlined in Varcoe v. Lee, 181 P. 223 (Cal. S.C., 1919), at p. 226: The three requirements ... that the matter be one of common and general knowledge, that it be well established and authoritatively settled, be practically indisputable, and that this common, general, and certain knowledge exist in the particular jurisdiction—all are requirements dictated by the reason and purpose of the rule, which is to obviate the formal necessity for proof when the matter does not require proof. *Moge v. Moge* [1992] 3 S.C.R. 813, L'Heureux-Dube J.

JUDICIAL OFFICER. See BRIBERY OF ~.

JUDICIAL OR QUASI-JUDICIAL PROCEEDING. "It is possible ... to formulate several criteria for determining whether a decision or order is one required by law to be made on a judicial or quasi-judicial basis. The list is not intended to be exhaustive. (1) Is there anything in the language in which the function is conferred or in the general context in which it is exercised which suggests that a hearing is contemplated before a decision is reached? (2) Does the decision or order directly or indirectly affect the rights and obligations of persons? (3) Is the adversary process involved? (4) Is there an obligation to apply substantive rules to many individual cases rather than ... in a broad sense?" *Minister of National Revenue v. Coopers & Lybrand*, [1979] 1 S.C.R. 495 at 504, 92 D.L.R. (3d) 1, [1978] C.T.C. 829, 78 D.T.C. 6258, the court per Dickson J.

JUDICIAL PROCEEDING. 1. A proceeding (a) in or under the authority of a court of justice, (b) before the Senate or House of Commons or a committee of the Senate or House of Commons, or before a legislative council, legislative assembly or house of assembly or a committee thereof that is authorized by law to administer an oath, (c) before a court, judge, justice, provincial court judge or coroner, (d) before an arbitrator or umpire, or a person or body of persons authorized by law to make an inquiry and take evidence therein under oath, or (e) before a tribunal by which a legal right or legal liability may be established, whether or not the proceeding is invalid for want of jurisdiction or for any other reason. *Criminal Code*, R.S.C. 1985, c. C-46, s. 118. 2. Includes any action, suit, cause, matter or other proceeding in disposing of which the court appealed from has not exercised merely a regulative, administrative or executive jurisdiction. *Supreme Court Act*, R.S.C. 1985, c. S-26, s. 2.

JUDICIAL RECOUNT. A recounting, by a judge, of all used, rejected and spoiled ballots cast at an election.

JUDICIAL REVIEW. 1. As a matter of constitutional law, judicial review is intimately connected with the preservation of the rule of law. It is essentially that constitutional foundation which explains the purpose of judicial review and guides its function and operation. Judicial review seeks to address an underlying tension between the rule of law and the foundational democratic principle, which finds an expression in the initiatives of Parliament and legislatures to create various administrative bodies and endow them with broad powers. Courts, while exercising their constitutional functions of judicial review, must be sensitive not only to the need to uphold the rule of law, but also to the necessity of avoiding undue interference with the discharge of administrative functions in respect of the matters delegated to administrative bodies by Parliament and legislatures. Judicial review is the means by which the courts supervise those who exercise statutory powers, to ensure that they do not overstep their legal authority. The function of judicial review is therefore to ensure the legality, the reasonableness and the fairness of the administrative process and its outcomes.

J

Judicial review plays in upholding the rule of law, it also performs an important constitutional function in maintaining legislative supremacy. *Dunsmuir v. New Brunswick*, 2008 SCC 9, Bastarache and LeBel JJ. at para. 27, 28, 30. 2. The right of a court to investigate and question the validity of any legislation enacted by a Canadian legislative body. 3.The power of the court to review the actions and decisions of administrative decision-makers. It is not an investigation into the appropriateness of the result, but is an investigation into the propriety of the processes which brought about that result. 4. Refers to any relief that the applicant would be entitled to in any one or more of the following: Proceedings by way of application for an order in the nature of mandamus, prohibition or certiorari. Proceedings by way of an action for a declaration or for an injunction, or both, in relation to the exercise, refusal to exercise or proposed or purported exercise of a statutory power. *Judicial Review Procedure Act*, R.S.O. 1990, c. J-1, s. 2. 5. The control of the executive action by the courts.

JUDICIAL STAY. A stay of prosecution granted by a court. Amounts to an acquittal. The court effectively brings the proceedings to a final conclusion in favour of the accused. The accused has the right not to have the judicially stayed allegations raised as similar fact evidence in subsequent proceedings.

JUDICIAL SYSTEM. There are two types of judicial systems, and they ensure that the full case is placed before the judge in two different ways. In inquisitorial systems, as in Continental Europe, the judge takes charge of the gathering of evidence in an independent and impartial way. By contrast, an adversarial system, which is the norm in Canada, relies on the parties—who are entitled to disclosure of the case to meet, and to full participation in open proceedings—to produce the relevant evidence. *Charkaoui v. Canada (Citizenship and Immigration)*, 2007 SCC 9.

JUDICIARY. *n.* The bench, the judges collectively.

JUMP PRINCIPLE. The proposition that successive sentences to an offender should be increased gradually rather than by "jumps." *R. v. M. (A.)*, 30 O.R. (3d) 313 (C.A.).

JUNIOR. *adj.* Younger; of lower rank.

JUNIOR COUNSEL. Shall include a solicitor who has been admitted to the practice of law for less than 5 full years. *Legal Aid Act*, R.S.N.L. 1990, c. L-11, *Legal Aid Regulations*, C.N.R. 1010/96, s. 131.

JURAT. *n.* [L.] A clause at the bottom of an affidavit which states where, when and before whom that affidavit was sworn.

JURICERT. *n.* An online professional authentication service which creates a digital credential for each lawyer to use when carrying out electronic filing in government or court offices.

JURIDICAL. *adj.* Relating to the administration of justice.

JURIDICAL DAY. A day on which one may transact legal business. See NON-~

JURISDICTION. *n.* 1. The term jurisdiction has many meanings. In determining jurisdiction, a court may be deciding whether it has power to adjudicate over the person of the defendant or the subject matter of the claim asserted by the plaintiff in its statement of claim. Parties, by consent, waiver or any other manner, cannot confer jurisdiction over a tribunal to try a case where none exists. On the other hand, where jurisdiction to adjudicate a claim exists, as the authorities explain, it takes clear legislative language to remove jurisdiction. As well, a court may be deciding whether the tribunal has territorial jurisdiction, whether the amount claimed is within the tribunal's monetary jurisdiction, or whether the person sitting as the tribunal has jurisdiction to determine the plaintiff's claim. Jurisdiction is the power of the court to render an enforceable judgment. Therefore, for the purpose of these appeals, jurisdiction relates to whether the Ontario Superior Court has the power to adjudicate the claim, or claims pleaded in the four statements of claim. As there are not concepts such as partial, inchoate or contingent jurisdiction, either the Superior Court has jurisdiction, or it does not. *TeleZone Inc. v. Canada (Attorney General)*, 2008 ONCA 892. 2. A province or territory of Canada or a state outside Canada having sovereign power. 3. The authority of an administrative tribunal over a particular subject matter which is found in the tribunal's authorizing statute. 4. The scope of the authority of a government in terms of subject matter or territory. See APPELLATE ~; ASSUMED ~; COMPETENT ~; CONCURRENT ~; EXCLUSIVE ~ CLAUSE; EXCLUSIVE ~ MODEL; FEDERAL ~; FOREIGN ~; GENERAL ~; IMPLIED ~; INHERENT ~; LETTERS PATENT ~; ORIGINAL ~; STATUTORY ~; SUMMARY ~; TERRITORIAL ~.

JURISDICTIONAL ERROR. 1. The refusal by a body to exercise a power. 2. The purported exercise of a power which the body does not have 3. The exercise of the wrong power in the circumstances.

JURIS ET DE JURE. [L. of law and from law] Describes a presumption which is a conclusive presumption.

JURISPRUDENCE. *n.* 1. The philosophy or science of law which ascertains the principles which are the basis of legal rules. 2. A body of law. See MEDICAL ~.

JURIST. *n.* A civil lawyer; an eminent legal theorist; a civilian.

JURISTIC PERSON. See LEGAL PERSON.

JURISTIC REASON. But even if the principles of unjust enrichment are applicable, the law is clear that "a contract" can constitute a juristic reason for the enrichment. As a recent example of this, see the decision of this Court in Hill Estate v. Chevron Standard Ltd. (1992), 83 Man. R. (2d) 58 (Man. C.A.) (at p. 70): Decided cases are of little assistance in determining what is meant by "juristic reason." It simply comes down to this: if there is an explanation based upon law for the enrichment of one at the detriment of another, then the enrichment will not be considered unjust and no remedy, whether by constructive trust or otherwise, will be available. For example, there might be a contract between the parties under the terms of which an enrichment by one at the expense of the other is contemplated or justified. *Rillford Investments Ltd. v. Gravure International Capital Corp.*, 1997 CarswellMan 247, 118 Man. R. (2d) 11, 149 W.A.C. 11, 32 B.L.R (2d) 85, [1997] 7 W.W.R. 534, Scott C.J.M.

JUROR. *n.* [L.] A person who serves on a jury.

JUROR PREJUDICE. Four types of juror prejudice have been identified: interest, specific, generic and conformity. See CONFORMITY PREJUDICE.

JURORS' PRIVILEGE. Jurors are privileged against disclosing deliberations in a jury room. Section 649 of the Criminal Code, R.S.C. 1985, c. C-46 makes disclosing such information an offence. P.K. McWilliams, *Canadian Criminal Evidence*, 3d ed. (Aurora: Canada Law Book, 1988) at 35-74.

JURY. *n.* 1. A group of people sworn to deliver a verdict after considering evidence delivered to them concerning the issue. 2. The jury is a judicial organ of the criminal process. It accomplishes a large part of the function exercised by judges in non-jury criminal cases. In a jury trial, the jury is the "judge" of the facts, while the presiding judge is the "judge" of the law. They, judge and jury together, produce the judgment of the court. The jury hears all the evidence admitted at trial, receives instructions from the trial judge as to the relevant legal principles, and then retires to deliberate. It applies the law to the facts in order to arrive at a verdict. *R. v. Pan*, 2001 CarswellOnt 2261, 2001 SCC 42, 155 C.C.C. (3d) 97, 200 D.L.R. (4th) 577, 43 C.R. (5th) 203, 147 O.A.C. 1, 85 C.R.R. (2d) 1, 270 N.R. 317, the court per Arbour, J. See CHARGE THE ~; CHARGE TO THE ~; EMPANEL; GRAND ~; HUNG ~; IMPANEL; PETIT ~.

JURY PANEL. The persons who attend at court and from whom a jury may be selected for the trial of an action or issue by jury. *The Jury Act*, R.S.M. 1987, c. J30, s. 1.

JURY SECRECY. The common law rule of jury secrecy, which prohibits the court from receiving evidence of jury deliberations for the purpose of impeaching a verdict, . . . reflects a desire to preserve the secrecy of the jury deliberation process and to shield the jury from outside influences. .. A proper interpretation of the modern version of Lord Mansfield's rule is as follows: Statements made, opinions expressed, arguments advanced and votes cast by members of a jury in the course of their deliberations are inadmissible in any legal proceedings. In particular, jurors may not testify about the effect of anything on their or other jurors' minds, emotions or ultimate decision. On the other hand, the common law rule does not render inadmissible evidence of facts, statements or events extrinsic to the deliberation process, whether originating from a juror or from a third party, that may have tainted the verdict. *R. v. Pan*, 2001 CarswellOnt 2261, 2001 SCC 42, 155 C.C.C. (3d) 97, 200 D.L.R. (4th) 577, 43 C.R. (5th)

203, 147 O.A.C. 1, 85 C.R.R. (2d) 1, 270 N.R. 317, the court per Arbour J. See LORD MANSFIELD'S RULE.

JUS. *n.* [L.] Law; right; equity; rule; authority. See IGNORANTIA JURIS NON EXCUSAT.

JUS ACCRESCENDI. [L.] The right of survivorship which each joint tenant has. An essential aspect of joint tenancy.

JUS CIVILE. [L.] Local law.

JUS COMMUNE. [L.] Common law.

JUS DISPONENDI. [L.] The right to dispose.

JUS GENTIUM. [L.] Customary law.

JUS HABENDI. [L.] The right to actually possess property.

JUS HAEREDITATIS. [L.] The right to inherit.

JUS IN PERSONAM. [L.] A right which gives the one holding it power to help another person to do or not to do, to gain or give anything.

JUS IN RE. [L.] A full and complete right; a real right or a right to have something to the exclusion of everyone else.

JUS NATURALE. [L.] Natural law.

JUS POSSESSIONIS. [L.] The right to possess.

JUS PRIVATUM. [L.] The municipal or civil law.

JUS PUBLICUM. [L.] The law concerning public affairs.

JUS REGALE. [L.] A right of the King.

JUST. *adj.* 1. Conforming to law. According to the rules of law and equity. 2. "... [A] just remedy in the context of the criminal law is one which, while furthering the object of the right guaranteed by the [Charter] that has been infringed, nevertheless does that, as far as possible, in a way that does not offend the reasonable expectations of the community for the enforcement of the criminal law." *R. v. Germain* (1984), (*sub nom. Germain v. R.*) 10 C.R.R. 232 at 341, 53 A.R. 264 (Q.B.), McDonald J. See UN~.

JUST CAUSE. 1. "If an employee has been guilty of serious misconduct, habitual neglect of duty, incompetence, or conduct incompatible with his duties, or prejudicial to the employer's business, or if he has been guilty of wilful disobedience to the employer's orders in a matter of substance, the law recognizes the employer's right summarily to dismiss the delinquent employee." *Port Arthur Shipbuilding Co. v. Arthurs*, [1967] 2 O.R. 49 at 55, 62 D.L.R. (2d) 342, 67 C.L.L.C. 14,024 (C.A.), Schroeder J.A. (dissenting), approved on appeal [1969] S.C.R. 85. 2. Journal published by Canadian Legal Advocacy, Information and Research Association of the Disabled.

JUST DISMISSAL. "... [D]ismissal based on an objective, real and substantial cause, independent of caprice, convenience or purely personal disputes, entailing action taken exclusively to ensure the effective operation of the business ..." *Canadian Imperial Bank of Commerce v. Boisvert* (1986), 13 C.C.E.L. 264 at

291, [1986] 2 F.C. 431, 68 N.R. 355 (C.A.), Marceau J.A. (MacGuigan and Lacombe JJ.A. concurring).

JUS TERTII. [L.] Third party right.

JUSTICE. *n.* 1. The principle of giving every person her or his due. 2. A judge of certain courts. 3. A justice of appeal. 4. A justice of the peace. See ADMINISTRATION OF ~; CHIEF ~; DEPARTMENT OF ~; FUNDAMENTAL ~; INTERNATIONAL COURT OF ~; MISCARRIAGE OF ~; NATURAL ~; OBSTRUCTING ~; RESTORATIVE ~; YOUTH ~ COURT.

JUSTICE OF THE PEACE. A judicial officer who has authority to deal with the initiation of criminal proceedings and to try minor criminal or quasi-criminal offences.

JUSTICE REP. *abbr.* Justice Report.

JUSTICE SHOULD NOT ONLY BE DONE BUT SHOULD MANIFESTLY AND UNDOUBTEDLY BE SEEN TO BE DONE. A rule enunciated in *R. v. Sussex Justices, Ex parte McCarthy*, [1924] 1 K.B. 256 at 259 (U.K. Div. Ct.), Lord Hewart C.J.

JUSTICE SYSTEM PARTICIPANT. (a) A member of the Senate, of the House of Commons, of a legislative assembly or of a municipal council, and (b) a person who plays a role in the administration of criminal justice, including (i) the Minister of Public Safety and Emergency Preparedness and a Minister responsible for policing in a province, (ii) a prosecutor, a lawyer, a member of the Chambre des notaires du Québec and an officer of a court, (iii) a judge and a justice, (iv) a juror and a person who is summoned as a juror, (v) an informant, a prospective witness, a witness under subpoena and a witness who has testified, (vi) a peace officer within the meaning of any of paragraphs (b), (c), (d), (e) and (g) of the definition "peace officer", (vii) a civilian employee of a police force, (viii) a person employed in the administration of a court, (viii.1) a public officer within the meaning of subsection 25.1(1) and a person acting at the direction of such an officer, (ix) an employee of the Canada Revenue Agency who is involved in the investigation of an offence under an Act of Parliament, (ix.1) an employee of the Canada Border Services Agency who is involved in the investigation of an offence under an Act of Parliament, (x) an employee of a federal or provincial correctional service, a parole supervisor and any other person who is involved in the administration of a sentence under the supervision of such a correctional service and a person who conducts disciplinary hearings under the Corrections and Conditional Release Act, and (xi) an employee and a member of the National Parole Board and of a provincial parole board. *Criminal Code*, R.S.C. 1985, c. C-46, s. 2

JUSTICIABLE. *adj.* 1. Proper to be examined in a court of justice, triable. 2. The notion of justiciability is linked to the notion of appropriate judicial restraint. In exercising its discretion whether to determine a matter that is alleged to be non-justiciable, the Court's primary concern is to retain its proper role within the constitutional framework of our democratic form of government. Thus the circumstances in which the Court may decline to answer a reference question on the basis of "non-justiciability" include: (i) if to do so would take the Court beyond its own assessment of its proper role in the constitutional framework of our democratic form of government or (ii) if the Court could not give an answer that lies within its area of expertise: the interpretation of law. *Reference re Secession of Quebec*, 1998 CarswellNat 1299, 161 D.L.R. (4th) 385, 228 N.R. 203, 55 C.R.R. (2d) 1, [1998] 2 S.C.R. 217, per curiam.

JUSTIFIABLE HOMICIDE. Homicide which is not culpable, the killing of a human being when no legal guilt is incurred.

JUSTIFICATION. *n.* 1. "[In criminal theory, in contrast to excuse] ... challenges the wrongfulness of an action which technically constitutes a crime. The police officer who shoots the hostage-taker, the innocent object of an assault who uses force to defend himself against his assailant, the good Samaritan who commandeers a car and breaks the speed laws to rush an accident victim to the hospital, these are all actors whose actions we consider rightful, not wrongful... ." *R. v. Perka* (1984), 13 D.L.R. (4th) 1 at 12, [1984] 2 S.C.R. 232, [1984] 6 W.W.R. 289, 42 C.R. (3d) 113, 55 N.R. 1, 14 C.C.C. (3d) 385, Dickson J. (Ritchie J. concurring). 2. Truth, a complete defence to a defamation action. R.E. Brown, *The Law of Defamation in Canada* (Toronto: Carswell, 1987) at 361. See BONA FIDE AND REASONABLE ~.

JUSTIFIED. *adj.* Authorized. Proper. See DEMONSTRABLY ~.

JUSTIFY BAIL. To prove the sufficiency of sureties or bail.

JUV. CT. *abbr.* Juvenile Court.

JUVENILE COURT. The equivalent of Youth Court prior to the enactment of the Youth Criminal Justice Act. See YOUTH JUSTICE COURT.

JUVENILE DELINQUENT. The term used to describe a Young Offender prior to the enactment of the Youth Criminal Justice Act. See YOUNG PERSON.

JUXTA FORMAM STATUTI. [L.] According to the statute's form.

K

K.B. *abbr.* 1. King's Bench. 2. Court of King's Bench. See QUEEN'S BENCH.

K.C. *abbr.* King's Counsel. See QUEEN'S COUNSEL.

KEEP. *v.* To maintain in possession; to have available for use.

KEEP CONFIDENCE. See DUTY TO ~.

KEEPER. *n.* 1. A person who (a) is an owner or occupier of a place, (b) assists or acts on behalf of an owner or occupier of a place, (c) appears to be, or to assist or act on behalf of an owner or occupier of a place, (d) has the care or management of a place, or (e) uses a place permanently or temporarily, with or without the consent of the owner or occupier thereof. *Criminal Code*, R.S.C. 1985, c. C-46, s. 197. 2. "In terms of what it means to be a 'keeper' of a common bawdy-house, an element of participation in the wrongful use of the place is a minimum requirement: R. v. Kerim, [1963] S.C.R. 124 ..." *Reference re ss. 193 & 195.1(1)(c) of the Criminal Code (Canada)*, [1990] 4 W.W.R. 481 at 510, 77 C.R. (3d) 1, 56 C.C.C. (3d) 65, [1990] 1 S.C.R. 1123, 109 N.R. 81, 68 Man. R. (2d) 1, 48 C.R.R. 1, Lamer J.

KEEPING. See GATE-~.

KEEP THE PEACE. To prevent or avoid breaches of the peace.

KENNEL. *n.* Traditionally limited to housing dogs. One aspect of a "kennel" use is the boarding of the animal. "Boarding" suggests to me that the owner of the animal makes an arrangement to leave it in the care of the boarding facility. Includes facilities for the breeding of dogs. *Woodman v. Capital (Regional District)*, 1999 CarswellBC 2193, 6 M.P.L.R. (3d) 128 (S.C.), Bauman J.

KEY. *n.* See PRIVATE ~; PUBLIC ~.

KEY. *adj.* Main, most important.

KEY EMPLOYEE. A "key" employee is: (1) an integral and indispensable component of the management team that is responsible for guiding the business affairs of the employer; (2) necessarily involved in the decision-making process; and (3), therefore, has broad access to confidential information that if disclosed would significantly impair the competitive advantages that the former employer enjoyed. These employees fall within the categories: "top management," "senior management" or "key management." *Imperial Sheet Metal Ltd. v. Landry*, 2007 NBCA 51.

KEY PAIR. A pair of keys held by or for a person that includes a private key and a public key that are mathematically related to, but different from, each other. *Personal Information Protection and Electronic Documents Act,* S.C. 2000, c. 5, *Secure Electronic Signature Regulations*, SOR/2005-30, s. 1.

KEY SECURING SYSTEM. A system which physically prevents access to keys when locks or positive sealing devices are applied in a group lockout. *Occupational Health and Safety Act*, R.S.N.L. 1990, c. O-3, *Occupational Health and Safety Regulations, 2009*, N.L.R. 70/09, s. 127.

KICKBACK. *n.* 1. A payment for help or a favour in business matters. 2. Payment back to a seller or employer of a portion of purchase price or wages of an employee.

KIDNAP. *v.* "... The crime is complete when the person is picked up and then transported by fraud to his place of confinement... ." *R. v. Metcalfe* (1983), 10 C.C.C. (3d) 114 at 118 (B.C. C.A.), the court per Nemetz C.J.B.C.

KIENAPPLE PRINCIPLE. "Multiple convictions are only precluded under the Kienapple principle [named after Kienapple v. R., [1975] 1 S.C.R. 729] if they arise from the same 'cause', 'matter', or 'delict', and if there is sufficient proximity between the offences charged. This requirement of sufficient proximity between offences will only be satisfied if there is no additional and distinguishing element contained in the offence for which a conviction is sought to be precluded by the Kienapple principle." *R. v. Wigman* (1987), 33 C.C.C. (3d) 97 at 103, [1987] 4 W.W.R. 1, 56 C.R. (3d) 289, [1987] 1 S.C.R. 246, 75 N.R. 51, 38 D.L.R. (4th) 530, Dickson C.J.C., Beetz, McIntyre, Chouinard, Lamer, Le Dain and La Forest JJ.

KIMBERLEY PROCESS CERTIFICATE. A document, issued by a participant, that certifies that rough diamonds for export or import or in transit have been handled in a manner that meets the minimum requirements of the Kimberley Process. *Export and Import of Rough Diamonds Act*, S.C. 2002, c. 25, s. 2.

K

KIN. *n.* Relatives by blood. See NEXT OF ~.

KIND. See IN ~; NOTICE OF ANY ~.

KINDRED. *n.* Relations by blood.

KING. *n.* A male sovereign of the United Kingdom, Canada and other Realms and Territories, and Head of the Commonwealth.

KING CAN DO NO WRONG. " ... It is a general and fundamental rule that the king cannot sanction any act forbidden by law. It is in this sense that the king is under and not above the laws, and is bound by them equally with his subjects. Therefore the laws relating to contracts, as well as other laws, are binding on the sovereign... the maxim ... is further limited by the allowance of the petition of right ... giving to the subject the right to claim from the sovereign, movables, lands, debts and unliquidated damages ... This gives the subject the same right he would have by action against another subject." *R. v. McLeod* (1882), 8 S. S.C.R. 1 at 32-3, Fournier J. (dissenting).

KING'S BENCH. Title of what is now the court of Queen's Bench during the reign of a King. See COURT OF ~; QUEEN'S BENCH.

KING'S COUNSEL. Honourary title given to senior barristers, equivalent to Queen's Counsel, during the reign of a King. See QUEEN'S COUNSEL.

KING'S PRINTER. Name of a government printing office during the reign of a King. See QUEEN'S PRINTER.

KING'S PROCTOR. Name of the Queen's Proctor during the reign of a King. See QUEEN'S PROCTOR.

KINSFOLK. *n.* Relatives; members of the same family.

KINSMAN. *n.* A man of the same family or race.

KINSWOMAN. *n.* A woman of the same family or race.

KIT. *n.* A complete or substantially complete number of parts that can be assembled to construct a finished article. *Industrial Design Act*, R.S.C. 1985, c. I-9, s. 2.

KIT CAR. A motor vehicle that has been constructed using a new and complete body of a motor vehicle that is supplied without a motor, chassis or drive train. *Environmental Protection Act,* R.S.O. 1990, c. E.19, *Motor Vehicles*, O. Reg. 361/98, s. 1.

KITE. *n.* A secret letter passed from one inmate to another. *R. v. Smith*, 2007 NSCA 19.

KITING. *n.* "... [A] term used with regard to obtaining money by cheques passed through banks without value being deposited against the cheque – that is, kiting is an effort to obtain the use of money during the process of a cheque passing through one bank or through a clearing house to another, and perhaps through many more." *Corp. Agencies Ltd. v. Home Bank of Canada*, [1927] 2 D.L.R. 1 at 2, [1927] 1 W.W.R. 1004, [1927] A.C. 318 (Can. P.C.), the board per Lord Wrenbury.

KLEPTOMANIA. *n.* An uncontrollable inclination to steal.

KM. *abbr.* Knowledge management.

KNOCK AND ANNOUNCE PRINCIPLE. Except in exigent circumstances, police officers must make an announcement before forcing entry into a dwelling house. In the ordinary case, they should give: "(i) notice of presence by knocking or ringing the door bell; (ii) notice of authority, by identifying themselves as law enforcement officers and (iii) notice of purpose, by stating a lawful reason for entry. *R. v. Cornell*, 2010 SCC 31, Cromwell J.

KNOW. *v.* 1. "... [H]as a positive connotation requirng a bare awareness, the act of receiving information without more... ." *R. v. Barnier*, [1980] 1 S.C.R. 1124 at 1137, 109 D.L.R. (3d) 257, 13 C.R. (3d) 129 (Eng.), 19 C.R. (3d) 371 (Fr.), [1980] 2 W.W.R. 659, 31 N.R. 273, 51 C.C.C. (3d) 193, the court per Estey J. 2. Refers to true knowledge. One cannot say that one knows something that is not so.

KNOWING ASSISTANCE. The only basis upon which the Bank may be held liable as a constructive trustee is under the "knowing receipt" or "knowing receipt and dealing" head of liability. Under this category of constructive trusteeship it is generally recognized that there are two types of cases. First, although inapplicable to the present case, there are strangers to the trust, usually agents of the trustees, who receive trust property lawfully and not for their own benefit but then deal with the property in a manner inconsistent with the trust. These cases may be grouped under the heading "knowing dealing". Secondly, there are strangers to the trust who receive trust property for their own benefit and with knowledge that the property was transferred to them in breach of trust. In all cases it is immaterial whether the breach of trust was fraudulent. The second type of case, which is relevant to the present appeal, raises two main issues: the nature of the receipt of trust property and the degree of knowledge required of the stranger to the trust. In "knowing assistance" cases, which are concerned with the furtherance of fraud, there is a higher threshold of knowledge required of the stranger to the trust. Constructive knowledge is excluded as the basis for liability in "knowing assistance" cases. *Citadel General Assurance Co. v. Lloyds Bank Canada* (1997), 1997 CarswellAlta 823, 152 D.L.R. (4th) 411, 206 A.R. 321, 156 W.A.C. 321, 19 E.T.R. (2d) 93, 35 B.L.R. (2d) 153, 47 C.C.L.I. (2d) 153, [1997] 3 S.C.R. 805, 219 N.R. 323, [1999] 4 W.W.R. 135, 66 Alta. L.R. (3d) 241, La Forest J.

KNOWING DEALING. Under this category of constructive trusteeship it is generally recognized that there are two types of cases. First, although inapplicable to the present case, there are strangers to the trust, usually agents of the trustees, who receive trust property lawfully and not for their own benefit but then deal with the property in a manner inconsistent with the trust. These cases may be grouped under the heading "knowing dealing". *Air Canada v. M & L Travel Ltd.*, [[1993] 3 S.C.R. 787], at pp. 811-13. *Citadel General Assurance Co. v. Lloyds Bank Ca-*

nada (1997), 1997 CarswellAlta 823, 152 D.L.R. (4th) 411, 206 A.R. 321, 156 W.A.C. 321, 19 E.T.R. (2d) 93, 35 B.L.R (2d) 153, 47 C.C.L.I. (2d) 153, [1997] 3 S.C.R. 805, 219 N.R. 323, [1999] 4 W.W.R. 135, 66 Alta. L.R. (3d) 241, La Forest J.

KNOWING RECEIPT. In "knowing receipt" cases, which are concerned with the receipt of trust property or one's own benefit, there should be a lower threshold of knowledge required of the stranger to the trust. More is expected of the recipient, who, unlike the accessory, is necessarily enriched at the plaintiff's expense. Because the recipient is held to this higher standard, constructive knowledge (that is, knowledge of facts sufficient to put a reasonable person on notice or inquiry) will suffice as the basis for restitutionary liability. *Citadel General Assurance Co. v. Lloyds Bank Canada* (1997), 1997 CarswellAlta 823, 152 D.L.R. (4th) 411, 206 A.R. 321, 156 W.A.C. 321, 19 E.T.R. (2d) 93, 35 B.L.R (2d) 153, 47 C.C.L.I. (2d) 153, [1997] 3 S.C.R. 805, 219 N.R. 323, [1999] 4 W.W.R. 135, 66 Alta. L.R. (3d) 241, La Forest J. See KNOWING ASSISTANCE; KNOWING DEALING.

KNOWING THAT THE ACT WAS WRONG. [Referring to these words in s. 16 of the Criminal Code], the rule focuses not on a general capacity to understand right and wrong in some abstract sense, but on the particular capacity of the accused to understand that his or her act was wrong at the time of committing the act. The crux of the inquiry is whether the accused lacks the capacity to rationally decide whether the act is right or wrong and hence to make a rational choice about whether to do it or not. The inability to make a rational choice may result from a variety of mental dysfunctions. *R. v. Oommen*, 1994 CarswellAlta 121, 19 Alta. L.R. (3d) 305, 30 C.R. (4th) 195, [1994] 7 W.W.R. 49, 168 N.R. 200, [1994] 2 S.C.R. 507, 91 C.C.C. (3d) 8, 155 A.R. 190, 73 W.A.C. 190, the court per McLachlin J.

KNOWINGLY. *adv.* "The general principle of criminal law is that accompanying a prohibited act there must be an intent in respect of every element of the act, and that is ordinarily conveyed in statutory offences by the word 'knowingly'." *R. v. Rees* (1956), 24 C.R. 1 at 8, [1956] S.C.R. 640, 115 C.C.C. 1, 4 D.L.R. (2d) 406, Rand J. (Locke J. concurring).

KNOWLEDGE. *n.* 1. The condition of knowing something. 2. For legal purposes, is true belief. Knowledge therefore has two components—truth and belief—and of these, only belief is mental or subjective. Truth is objective, or at least consists in the correspondence of a proposition or mental state to objective reality. Accordingly, truth, which is a state of affairs in the external world that does not vary with the intention of the accused, cannot be a part of mens rea. The truth of an actor's belief that certain monies are the proceeds of crime is something different from the belief itself. That the belief be true is one of the attendant circumstances that is required if the actus reus is to be completed. In other words, the act of converting the proceeds of crime presupposes the existence of some money that is in truth the proceeds of crime. *United States v. Dynar*, [1997] 2 S.C.R. 462, Cory and Iacobucci JJ. for the majority. 3. Actual knowledge. *The Securities Transfer Act*, S.S. 2007, c. S-42.3, s. 1. See CARNAL ~; COMMON ~; CONSTRUCTIVE ~; EXPLICIT ~; JUDICIAL ~; PERSONAL ~; PRESUMPTION OF ~ AND COMPETENCE; TACIT ~.

KNOWLEDGE MANAGEMENT. The collection, organization, and dissemination of explicit and tacit knowledge of members of a legal firm for use by other members of the firm.

KNOWN. *adj.* Having actual knowledge. *The Securities Transfer Act*, S.S. 2007, c. S-42.3, s. 1.

KOREAN WAR. The military operations undertaken by the United Nations to restore peace in the Republic of Korea, and the period denoted by the term "Korean War" is the period from June 25, 1950 to July 27, 1953, inclusive.

KPA. *abbr.* Kilopascal. Measure of barometric pressure.

KYOTO PROTOCOL. The Kyoto Protocol to the United Nations Framework Convention on Climate Change done at Kyoto on December 11, 1997, and includes any decision related to the implementation of that protocol taken by the "Conference of the Parties serving as the Meeting of the Parties to the Kyoto Protocol", within the meaning of that protocol. *Canada Emission Reduction Incentives Agency Act*, S.C. 2005, c. 30, s. 2.

K

L

LABORATORY TECHNOLOGY. See MEDI-CAL ~.

LABOUR. *n.* 1. Work. 2. Physical work. See VOLUNTEER ~.

LABOUR ARBITRATION. The hearing and determination of labour disputes. Includes grievance and interest arbitration.

LABOUR DISPUTE. 1. Dispute between employers and employees, or between employees and employees, that is connected with the employment or non-employment, or the terms or conditions of employment, of any persons. *Employment Insurance Act*, S.C. 1996, c. 23, s. 2. 2. A dispute or difference concerning terms, tenure or conditions of employment or concerning the association or representation of persons in negotiating, fixing, maintaining, changing or seeking to arrange terms or conditions of employment, regardless of whether the disputants stand in the proximate relation of employer and employee. *Courts of Justice Act*, R.S.O. 1990, c. C.43, s. 102.

LABOURER. *n.* A person employed for wages in any kind of labour whether employed under a contract of service or not. *Builders' Lien Act*, R.S.A. 2000, c. B-7, s. 1.

LABOUR RELATIONS. All matters concerning the worker-employer relationship. See PUBLIC SERVICE ~ BOARD.

LABOUR UNION. Any organization of employees that has as one of its purposes the regulation of relations between employers and employees. See CERTIFICATION OF ~.

LACERATION. *n.* An injury to tissue involving a tearing or crushing.

L.A.C. *abbr.* Labour Arbitration Cases, 1948-1972.

L.A.C. (4TH). *abbr.* Labour Arbitration Cases (Fourth Series), 1989-.

LACHES. *n.* [Fr.] 1. Negligent or unreasonable delay in pursuing a remedy. 2. [I]t is important to distinguish between "laches" to indicate delay and nothing more and "laches" to describe the defence that arises when the plaintiff has delayed the prosecution of its claim and has acquiesced to the legal injury or the defendant has been prejudiced by the delay.... [T]he Supreme Court has made it clear that the defence of laches entails the notion of delay combined with either (a) evidence of conduct revealing that the plaintiff acquiesced in the alleged wrongful act in a way that leads reasonably to the inference that the plaintiff waived its right to a remedy, or (b) evidence that, in reliance on the status quo, the defendant altered its position in a way that constitutes prejudice, or evidence that through its delay, the plaintiff permitted circumstances to arise that it would be unjust to disturb. *Rivergate Properties Inc. v. West St. Paul (Rural Municipality)*, 2006 MBCA 76.

L.A.C. (2d). *abbr.* Labour Arbitration Cases (Second Series), 1973-1981.

L.A.C. (3D). *abbr.* Labour Arbitration Cases (Third Series), 1982-1989.

LACUNA. *n.* [L.] Gap.

LACUNAE. *n.* [L.] Plural of lacuna. Gaps.

LADING. *n.* Cargo. See BILL OF ~.

L.A.N. *abbr.* Labour Arbitration News.

LAND. *n.* 1. "... [I]n the great majority of cases, where the context does not require a special and technical meaning, ... it means something quite concrete and tangible, something distinguished from water as a rule, or it may be from movable property ..." *Murphy Estate, Re* (1955), 37 M.P.R. 107 at 111, [1955] 5 D.L.R. 768 (Nfld. C.A.), Winter J.A. 2. "... [I]s not, in law, the soil we touch, but the rights attached to it. Such rights include the right to work the soil, to mine beneath the surface and build in the airspace above it and the incorporeal rights to light, support and the use of water flowing across land." *Trizec Manitoba Ltd. v. Winnipeg City Assessor* (1986), 34 M.P.L.R. 9 at 12, 41 R.P.R. 176, [1986] 5 W.W.R. 97, 42 Man. R. (2d) 98 (C.A.), Twaddle J.A. (Huband J.A. concurring). 3. "... [I]n its primary meaning refers to corporeal hereditaments: ..." *Wiener v. Elgin (County)*, [1947] 2 D.L.R. 346 at 348, [1947] O.W.N. 360 (H.C.), Urquhart J. 4. Lands, messuages, tenements and hereditaments, corporeal and incorporeal, of every nature and description, and every estate or interest therein, whether the estate or interest is legal or equitable, together with all paths, passages, ways, watercourses, liberties, privileges and easements appertaining thereto and trees and timber thereon, and mines, minerals and quarrites thereon and thereunder lying or being, unless any of them are specially excepted. *Land Titles Act*, R.S.A. 2000, c. L-4, s. 1. 5. Includes (a) land covered by water, (b) quarries, and (c) sand and gravel, but does not include coal or other minerals. *Assessment Act*, R.S.B.C. 1996, c. 20, s. 1. 6.The solid part of the earth's surface and includes the foreshore and land covered by water. 7. When land is sold, "land" refers to "a right to receive a good title in fee simple" unless the agreement states otherwise. "Land" is not given a special meaning in the leases; in particular, it is *not* defined as a 99-year leasehold interest in the property under the lease. *Musqueam Indian Band v. Glass*, 2000 CarswellNat 2405, 2000 SCC 52, [2000] 11 W.W.R. 407, 36 R.P.R. (3d) 1, 192 D.L.R. (4th) 385, 82 B.C.L.R. (3d) 199, 261 N.R. 296, 186 F.T.R. 248 (note), [2000] 2 S.C.R. 633, [2001] 1 C.N.L.R. 208, Gonthier J. (Major, Binnie and LeBel JJ. concurring). See ABORIGINAL ~; ABORIGINAL RIGHT ~S; ABORIGINAL TITLE ~S; ACTION FOR RECOVERY OF ~; ALLODIAL ~S; ARABLE ~; CHARGE ON ~; CROWN ~; CURRENT ~ VALUE; DEDICATED ~S; DOCUMENT OF TITLE TO ~S; FIRST NATION ~; FRACTIONAL INTEREST IN ~; FREEHOLD ~; INDIANS AND ~S RESERVED FOR INDIANS; PARCEL OF ~; PRIVATE ~; PROVINCIAL ~; RESERVE ~S; RUN WITH THE ~; SHARED INTEREST IN ~; TERRITORIAL ~S; TRESPASS TO ~; UNIMPROVED ~; UNPATENTED ~.

L. & C. *abbr.* Lefroy & Cassels' Practice Cases (Ontario), 1881-1883.

LAND CLAIMS AGREEMENT. A land claims agreement within the meaning of section 35 of the Constitution Act, 1982. An agreement which resolves a claim to land by an aboriginal group.

LAND CODE. A first nation that wishes to establish a land management regime in accordance with the Framework Agreement and this Act shall adopt a land code applicable to all land in a reserve of the first nation, which land code must include the following matters: (a) a legal description of the land that will be subject to the land code; (b) the general rules and procedures applicable to the use and occupancy of first nation land, including use and occupancy under (i) licences and leases, and (ii) interests in first nation land held pursuant to allotments under subsection 20(1) of the Indian Act or pursuant to the custom of the first nation; (c) the procedures that apply to the transfer, by testamentary disposition or succession, of any interest in first nation land; and related matters. *First Nations Land Management Act*, S.C. 1999, c. 24, s. 6.

LANDED. *adj.* Formerly described somone having lawful permission to establish permanent residence in Canada.

LANDED IMMIGRANT. Formerly described one who lawfully has permanent resident status in Canada.

LANDFILL. *n.* A waste management facility at which waste is disposed of by placing it on or in land.

LANDING. *n.* Lawful permission to establish permanent residence in Canada. *Immigration Act*, R.S.C. 1985, c. I-2, s. 2 [repealed].

LAND LEASE COMMUNITY. The land on which one or more occupied land lease homes are situate and includes the rental units and the land, structures, services and facilities of which the landlord retains possession and that are intended for the common use and enjoyment of the tenants of the landlord. *Residential Tenancies Act, 2006*, S.O. 2006, c. 17, s. 2.

LAND LEASE HOME. A dwelling, other than a mobile home, that is a permanent structure where the owner of the dwelling leases the land used or intended for use as the site for the dwelling. *Residential Tenancies Act, 2006*, S.O. 2006, c. 17, s. 2.

LANDLORD. *n.* 1. Includes (a) the owner, or other person permitting or granting a right to occupancy of the rental unit, and his or her heirs, assigns, personal representatives and successors in title, (b) a person, other than a tenant occupying the rental unit, who is entitled to possession of the residential complex in which the rental unit is located and who attempts to enforce any of the rights of a landlord under a tenancy agreement or this Act, including the right to collect rent, and (c) a person who, in exercising rights under a mortgage or another real property encumbrance, initiates proceedings to evict a tenant from a rental unit. *The Residential Tenancies Act*, S.M. 1990-91, c. 11, s. 1. 2. Includes any holder of a leasehold interest who has subleased his interest and the holder of the fee simple estate, but does not include the holder of any estate or interest in fee simple in mines or minerals. *The Builders' Lien Act*, S.S. 1984-85-86, c. B-7.1, s. 31. 3. An owner who rents a strata lot to a tenant and a tenant who rents a strata lot to a subtenant, but does not include a leasehold landlord in a leasehold strata plan as defined in section 199. *Strata Property Act*, S.B.C. 1998, c. 43, s. 1. 4. Every lessor, owner or person giving or permitting the occupation of land and their respective successors in title. *Commercial Tenancies Act*, R.S.N.W.T. 1988, c. C-10, s. 1.

LANDMARK. *n.* An object which fixes the boundary of property or an estate.

LANDSCAPE. See MAN-MADE ~.

LANDS, TENEMENTS AND HEREDITAMENTS. A traditional description of real property, considered the most comprehensive.

LAND SURVEYING. The interpretation of boundary evidence, the spatial measurement, the demarcation and the textual and graphical definitions of either or both boundaries and points on, over or under the earth or a combination or all of those. *Land Surveyors Act, 1991*, S.N. 1991, c. 37, s. 2. See PROFESSIONAL ~.

LAND TAX. A tax that is imposed on land against the owner and assessed as a percentage of the value of the land. Generally a direct tax.

LAND TITLES. Refers to the system of registration of ownership of and interests in land. See REGISTRAR OF ~.

LAND TITLES ASSURANCE FUND. A fund available for those who suffer a loss as a result of the operation of a land titles system.

LAND TITLES INSTRUMENT. A government record that is (a) an instrument as defined in The Real Property Act; or (b) an instrument as defined in The Registry Act and includes a book. *The Archives and Recordkeeping Act*, S.M. 2001, c. 35, s. 24.

LAND TITLES REGISTRY. The Land Titles Registry established pursuant to section 4. *The Land Titles Act, 2000*, S.S. 2000, c. L-5.1, s. 2.

LAND TITLES SYSTEM. A system of registration of ownership of and interests in land. The government makes a brief, simple statement concerning the ownership of land and all outstanding interests or claims so that the purchaser need not be concerned, as in a registry system, with the history of the transactions which affected that land. B.J. Reiter, B.N. McLellan & P.M. Perell, *Real Estate Law*, 4th ed. (Toronto: Emond Montgomery, 1992) at 388.

LAND USE REGULATION. An enactment that restricts or prescribes the use to which land or premises may be put or the nature of business or activities that may be conducted on land or premises. *Farm Practices Protection (Right to Farm) Act*, R.S.B.C. 1996, c. 131, s. 1, part.

LANGUAGE. *n.* The means of communication of a person, part of the person's identity and culture and the means by which persons understand themselves and their surroundings. See MACHINE ~; OFFICIAL ~; PLAIN ~; SPEECH-~ PATHOLOGY.

LANGUAGE EDUCATION. See MINORITY ~ RIGHTS.

LAPARASCOPY. *n.* Surgery performed through an illuminated instrument inserted through a body cavity while the operative area is projected onto a screen for the surgeon to visualize the site.

LAPAROTOMY. *n.* Surgery performed through a surgical incision across the abdominal wall.

LAP DANCING. Dance by an employee which may include touching of patrons during the performance including sexual touching.

LAPPING. See CASH ~.

LAPSE. *v.* To fail, said of a bequest or devise of property which goes into residue as if the gift had not been made when the person to whom the property was bequeathed or devised dies before the testator.

LAPSE. *n.* 1. Error; failure in duty. 2. Occurs when a gift fails because the donee of the gift predeceases the donor-testator.

LARCENY. *n.* Theft.

LARGE. See AT ~.

LAST ANTECEDENT DOCTRINE. A rule of statutory interpretation which provides that a modifier will apply only to the word immediately preceding it.

LAST CHANCE AGREEMENT. An employee agrees as a condition of continued employment that he or she will abide by all company rules and policies.

LAST CHANCE SETTLEMENT. The parties to a grievance agree that certain conduct of the employee

will constitute a final incident giving the employer the right to terminate the employee.

LAST CLEAR CHANCE DOCTRINE. Assigns responsibility for a loss to a negligent party who had the "last clear chance" to avert the loss which was sustained by another party.

LAST-IN, FIRST-OUT METHOD OF INVENTORY VALUATION. A method of valuing inventory in which it is assumed that the items most recently acquired are the ones disposed of first. The inventory value at the end of the period amounts to the cost of the items which were acquired first.

LAST RESORT. Describes a court from which there is no further appeal. Generally speaking, in each of the provinces it is the court of appeal and in Canada as a whole it is the Supreme Court of Canada. See COURT OF ~.

LAST STEP. Counsel submitted that "last step" [in R. 57.20 of the Rules of the Supreme Court, 1986, S.N. 1986, c. 42, Sched. D] means a last step taken in furtherance of the appeal. I agree. In the interests of justice, the purpose of the rule is to ensure that an appellant proceeds expeditiously with the appeal. An application by a solicitor to withdraw as solicitor of record could not be said to be a step taken in furtherance of the appeal. Indeed, quite the contrary. [...] an application by a solicitor to withdraw as solicitor of record is not a step taken for purposes of rule 57.20. *Charles River Consultants Corp. v. Coombs*, 2007 NLCA 74.

LATENT. *adj.* Concealed, hidden; secret.

LATENT AMBIGUITY. A latent ambiguity differs from a patent ambiguity in that the ambiguity is not observable on the face of the document. For example, there is no apparent contradiction in its terms. The ambiguity becomes evident only when one attempts to apply the words of the lease to the facts . . . *Missilinda of Canada Ltd. v. Husky Oil Operations Ltd.*, 2007 MBCA 24, Huband J.A. (Steel J.A. concurring)..

LATENT DEFECT. 1. One not discoverable on casual inspection and not observable. A defect which a reasonably careful inspection will not reveal. 2. "... 'Not discernible by adequate inspection' ..." *Scottish Metropolitan Assurance Co. v. Canada Steamship Lines Ltd.*, [1930] S.C.R. 262 at 279, [1930] 1 D.L.R. 201, Anglin C.J.C. (Rinfret and Lamont JJ. concurring).

LATERAL. *adj.* Towards the side. F.A. Jaffe, *A Guide to Pathological Evidence for Lawyers and Police Officers*, 4th ed. (Toronto: Carswell, 1999) at 240.

LATERAL DRAIN. A drain that is designed for the drainage of one property and that begins and ends on the same property. *Drainage Act*, R.S.O. 1990, c. D.17, s. 1.

LATE SCRATCH. A horse that is withdrawn from a race after betting on that race has begun. *Criminal Code*, R.S.C. 1985, c. C-46, *Pari-Mutuel Betting Supervision Regulations*, SOR/91-365, s. 2.

L

LAUNDERING PROCEEDS OF CRIME. Every one commits an offence who uses, transfers the possession of, sends or delivers to any person or place, transports, transmits, alters, disposes of or otherwise deals with, in any manner and by any means, any property or any proceeds of any property with intent to conceal or convert that property or those proceeds, knowing or believing that all or a part of that property or of those proceeds was obtained or derived directly or indirectly as a result of (a) the commission in Canada of a designated substance offence; or (b) an act or omission anywhere that, if it had occurred in Canada, would have constituted a designated offence. *Criminal Code*, R.S.C. 1985, c. C-46, s. 462.31. See MONEY LAUNDERING.

LAW. *n.* 1. A rule to govern action. 2. An enactment. 3. In its general sense, refers to all the rules which govern society and are enforceable through the judicial or administrative systems. Law in this general sense is comprised of the written and unwritten Constitution, federal and provincial statutes and the "judge-made" common law and equity. See ABORIGINAL ~; ACT OF THE ~; ADJECTIVE ~; ADMINISTRATIVE ~; ADMIRALTY ~; ANTITRUST ~; BLUE-SKY ~; BY-~; CASE ~; CHOICE OF ~; CIVIL ~; CLINIC ~; COLLABORATIVE ~; COLONIAL ~; COMMERCIAL ~; COMMON ~; COMPETITION ~; COMPILATION OF QUÉBEC ~S AND REGULATIONS; CONCLUSION OF ~; CONFLICT OF ~S; CONSTITUTIONAL ~; CONTRACT ~; CONTRARY TO ~; CRIMINAL ~; DUE PROCESS OF ~; ECCLESIASTICAL ~; EDUCATION ~; ELDER ~; ENTERTAINMENT ~; ENVIRONMENTAL ~; EQUALITY BEFORE AND UNDER THE ~; EQUALITY BEFORE THE ~; EQUITY FOLLOWS THE ~; ERRED IN ~; ERROR OF ~; FEDERAL CUSTOMS ~S; FEDERAL ~; FIRST NATION ~; FORCE OF ~; FOREIGN ~; GOOD SAMARITAN ~; HEALTH ~; IGNORANCE OF THE ~; INTERNATIONAL ~; JUDGE-MADE ~; MARITIME ~; MARTIAL ~; MEDIA ~; MERCANTILE ~; MILITARY ~; MISTAKE OF ~; MONTREAL DECLARATION ON FREE ACCESS TO ~; MUNICIPAL ~; NATURAL ~; OIL AND GAS ~; PENAL ~; POLITICAL ~; POSITIVE ~; PRESCRIBED BY ~; PRESUMPTION OF ~; PRIVACY ~; PRIVATE ~; PROPER ~; PROPERTY ~; PUBLIC ACCESS TO ~; PUBLIC ~; QUESTION OF ~; RULE OF ~; SECURITIES ~; SHARI'A ~; SHIPPING ~; STUDENT-AT-~; SUBSTANTIVE ~; TRANSPORTATION ~; UNIFORM ~ CONFERENCE OF CANADA.

LAW CLERK AND PARLIAMENTARY COUNSEL. An official appointed by Letters Patent under the Great Seal whose principal duty is to provide comprehensive legal advice to the Speaker, officers of the House of Commons and Board of Internal Economy and who helps members of Parliament draft legislation. A. Fraser, W.A. Dawson & J. Holtby, eds., *Beauchesne's Rules and Forms of the House of Commons of Canada*, 6th ed. (Toronto: Carswell, 1989) at 61.

LAW COMMISSION. The purpose of the Commission is to study and keep under systematic review, in a manner that reflects the concepts and institutions of the common law and civil law systems, the law of Canada and its effects with a view to providing independent advice on improvements, modernization and reform that will ensure a just legal system that meets the changing needs of Canadian society and of individuals in that society, including (a) the development of new approaches to, and new concepts of, law; (b) the development of measures to make the legal system more efficient, economical and accessible; (c) the stimulation of critical debate in, and the forging of productive networks among, academic and other communities in Canada in order to ensure co-operation and coordination; and (d) the elimination of obsolete laws and anomalies in the law. *Law Commission of Canada Act*, S.C. 1996, c. 9, s. 3. Some provinces have similar bodies with similar purposes.

LAW ENFORCEMENT. (a) Policing, (b) investigations or inspections that lead or could lead to proceedings in a court or tribunal if a penalty or sanction could be imposed in those proceedings, and (c) the conduct of proceedings referred to in clause (b). *Freedom of Information and Protection of Privacy Act*, R.S.O. 1990, c. F.31, s. 2.

LAW ENFORCEMENT SERVICE. (a) The provincial police force; (b) a municipal police department; (c) any designated policing unit or designated law enforcement unit that is also designated by the minister as a law enforcement service for the purposes of this section. *Police Act*, R.S.B.C. 1996, c. 367, s. 68.1.

LAW FIRM. 1. A law corporation or a number of lawyers or a number of law corporations or any combination of lawyers and law corporations in a partnership or association for the practice of law. *Legal Profession Act*, S.B.C. 1998, c. 9, s. 64. 2. A partnership, professional law corporation or another joint arrangement carrying on, or holding out to the public its willingness to carry on, the practice of law. *Law Society Act, 1999*, S.N. 1999, c. L-9.1, s. 2. See INTERJURISDICTIONAL ~; VIRTUAL ~.

LAWFUL. *adj.* 1. Authorized by law. *R. v. Robinson* (1948), 6 C.R. 343 at 346, [1948] O.R. 857, 92 C.C.C. 223 (C.A.), Laidlaw J.A. 2. Not in contravention of any law. 3. Legal. See UN~.

LAWFUL ADMISSION. Compliance with all requirements to gain admission to Canada.

LAWFUL EXCUSE. 1. "... [N]ormally includes all of the defences which the common law considers sufficient reason to excuse a person from criminal liability. It can also include excuses specific to particular offences... ." *R. v. Holmes* (1988), 34 C.R.R. 193 at 200, 85 N.R. 21, 27 O.A.C. 321, [1988] 1 S.C.R. 914, 64 C.R. (3d) 97, 41 C.C.C. (3d) 497, Dickson C.J.C. (Lamer J. concurring). 2. "... [I]ncludes any honest and reasonable belief in a state of facts which, if they had been as the accused believed them to be, would have made his act innocent... ." *R. v. Ireco Canada II Inc.* (1988), 17 C.E.R. 245 at 258, 65 C.R. (3d) 160, 43 C.C.C. (3d) 482, 29 O.A.C. 161, Martin, Cory and Finlayson JJ.A.

LAWFUL PICKETING. The giving of information by picketers with the objective of persuading or soliciting support from third persons who can lawfully give such support.

LAWFUL PURPOSE. A search for evidence related to the offence for which an individual has been arrested constitutes a lawful purpose. *R. v. Nolet*, 2009 SKCA 8.

LAWFUL RIGHT. In the context of the Radiocommunications Act, the concept of "lawful right" refers to the person who possesses the regulatory rights through proper licensing under the Act, the authorization of the Canadian Radio-television and Telecommunications Commission as well as the contractual and copyrights necessarily pertaining to the content involved in the transmission of the encrypted subscription programming signal or encrypted network feed. *Bell ExpressVu Ltd. Partnership v. Rex* [2002] 2 S.C.R. 559.

LAW LIST. A listing of all persons who are practicing as barristers or solicitors and any other lawyers.

LAW LORDS. In England, the Lord Chancellor, the Lords of Appeal in Ordinary, former Lord Chancellors and other peers who held high judicial offices.

LAW MERCHANT. The law which governs any mercantile transaction.

LAW OF AGENCY. The law concerning the relationships between those who act for others on their behalf.

LAW OF CANADA. 1. In s. 101 of the Constitution Act, 1867 (30 & 31 Vict.), c. 3 includes federal common law. *Wewayakum Indian Band v. Canada* (1989), 3 R.P.R. (2d) 1 at 8, 13, 16, 92 N.R. 241, 25 F.T.R. 161, [1989] 3 W.W.R. 117, 35 B.C.L.R. (2d) 1, 57 D.L.R. (4th) 197, [1979] 1 S.C.R. 322, [1989] 2 C.N.L.R. 146, the court per Wilson J. 2. In Part I means an Act of the Parliament of Canada enacted before of after the coming into force of this Act, any order, rule or regulation thereunder, and any law in force in Canada or in any part of Canada at the commencement of this part that is subject to be repealed, abolished or altered by the Parliament of Canada. *Canadian Bill of Rights*, R.S.C. 1985, App. III, s. 5. 3. A law enacted by the Parliament of Canada.

LAW OF CONTRACT. The law governing agreements concerning promises to be performed.

LAW OFFICER OF THE CROWN. An Attorney-General; a Solicitor-General.

LAW OF FLAG. The law of the country the flag of which a ship is flying.

LAW OF NATIONS. Public international law.

LAW OF PRIVACY. The law relating to the storage, retrieval and manipulation of personal information.

LAW REFORM COMMISSION. See LAW COMMISSION.

LAW REPORT. 1. The published account of any legal proceeding. 2. The report of a judgment of a court on points of law, published so that it may be used as a precedent.

LAW REPR. *abbr.* The Law Reporter (Ramsay & Morin) (Québec), 1854.

LAW SCHOOL ADMISSION TEST. An aptitude test which law schools in Canada and the United States require first year applicants to take.

LAW SOCIETY. A provincial body charged, by the legislature, with governing the legal profession and regulating the conduct of members of the profession.

LAW SUIT. Litigation; an action.

LAWYER. *n.* 1. In the Province of Quebec, an advocate, lawyer or notary and, in any other province, a barrister or solicitor. 2. A person qualified to practise law. 3. A graduate of a law school. See CONDUCT UNBECOMING A ~.

LAY. *adj.* Not professional, belonging to the general population in contrast to a certain profession.

LAYING AN INFORMATION. Any person may present a statement of facts in writing and under oath upon which a criminal charge in respect of an indictable offence is to be based to a Justice. Upon hearing the evidence of the informant, and perhaps witnesses, the Justice may confirm the appearance notice, promise to appear or recognizance and endorse the information accordingly or take a variety of other possible steps.

LAY OFF. *v.* To terminate employment. To terminate work with an expectation of a return at a later date.

LAY-OFF. *var.* **LAYOFF.** *n.* 1. While in common parlance the term "layoff" is sometimes used synonymously with termination of the employment relationship, its function in the lexicon of the law is to define a cessation of employment where there is the possibility or expectation of a return to work. The expectation may or may not materialize. But because of this expectation, the employer-employee relationship is said to be suspended rather than terminated. The suspension of the employer-employee relationship contemplated by the term "layoff" arises as a result of the employer's removing work from the employee. It follows that for there to be a lay-off, there must be a cessation of work. *Canada Safeway Ltd. v. R.W.D.S.U., Local 454,* 1998 CarswellSask 298, [1998] L.V.I. 2938-1, (*sub nom. Retail, Wholesale & Department Store Union, Local 454 v. Canada Safeway Ltd.*) 98 C.L.L.C. 220-042, (*sub nom. Canada Safeway Ltd. v. Retail, Wholesale & Department Store Union, Local 454*) 226 N.R. 19, 160 D.L.R. (4th) 1, (*sub nom. Canada Safeway Ltd. v. Retail, Wholesale & Department Store Union, Local 454*) 168 Sask. R. 104, (*sub nom. Canada Safeway Ltd. v. Retail, Wholesale & Department Store Union, Local 454*) 173 W.A.C. 104, [1998] 1 S.C.R. 1079, 10 Admin. L.R. (3d) 1, [1999] 6 W.W.R. 453, Cory and McLachlin JJ. (Gonthier, Iacobucci, Major and Bastarache JJ. concurring). 2. "... [A] period during which a workman is temporarily discharged ..." *Air-Care Ltd. v. U.S.W.A.*, [1976] 1 S.C.R. 2 at 6, 3 N.R. 267, 49 D.L.R. (3d) 467, Dickson J. 2. Temporary or

L

indefinite termination of employment because of lack of work. See CONSTRUCTIVE ~.

L.C.B. *abbr.* Land Compensation Board.

L.C.J. *abbr.* Lord Chief Justice.

L.C. JUR. *abbr.* Lower Canada Jurist, 1847-1891.

L.C. JURIST. *abbr.* Lower Canada Jurist, 1848-1891.

L.C.L.J. *abbr.* Lower Canada Law Journal, 1865-1868.

L.C.R. *abbr.* 1. Land Compensation Reports, 1969-. 2. Lower Canada Reports (Québec) 1851-1867 (Décisions des Tribunaux du Bas-Canada).

L.C. REP. *abbr.* Lower Canada Reports.

LEAD. *v.* To call or adduce evidence. See MIS~.

LEADER. *n.* 1. An individual who is recognized by the members of an Aboriginal community as their representative. 2. The politician who is head of a political party. See HOUSE ~.

LEADER OF THE OPPOSITION. 1. A member of Parliament or a legislature recognized by the Speaker as the leader of Her Majesty's loyal opposition. 2. The member of the House of Commons who is presently leader of the party opposing the Government and who has certain special rights regarding the questioning of Ministers. A. Fraser, W.A. Dawson & J. Holtby, eds., *Beauchesne's Rules and Forms of the House of Commons of Canada*, 6th ed. (Toronto: Carswell, 1989) at 55-6. 3. The leader of the political party which has the second largest number of seats in the legislature, provided the leader is recognized as leader of the opposition.

LEADING CASE. A judicial precedent or decision which settled the principles in a certain branch of law.

LEADING QUESTION. A question which suggests the answer required of that witness.

LEAFLETING. See CONSUMER ~.

LEAKAGE. *n.* Escape of water under pressure through a hole or crack. See SPRINKLER ~ INSURANCE.

LEARNED INTERMEDIATE RULE. Manufacturers of drugs are required to warn physicians of propensities of drugs. The physicians, the learned intermediaries, who prescribe them are expected to bring their expertise and knowledge of their patients to bear on the process of prescribing the drugs. A rule intended to equitably distribute tort liability among manufacturer, physician, and patient.

LEASE. *n.* " ... [U]sed in various senses: it is sometimes applied to term or estate created, and sometimes to the conveyance creating the estate. To constitute a lease, however, the possession of the lessee must be exclusive ... under a lease the lessee's right to possession is exclusive until the expiration of the term agreed upon ..." *Johnston v. British Canadian Insurance Co.*, [1932] 4 D.L.R. 281 at 284, [1932] S.C.R. 680, Lamont J. 2. Every agreement in writing, and every oral agreement by which one person as landlord confers on another person as tenant the right to occupy land, and every sublease and every agreement for a sublease and every assurance by which any rent is secured by condition. *Commercial Tenancies Act*, R.S.N.W.T. 1988, c. C-10, s. 44. 3. Any agreement for the hire of goods, except an agreement for the hire of goods in connection with a residential tenancy agreement. *Fair Trading Act.* R.S.A. 2000, c. F-2, s. 58. 4. A lease granting rights to petroleum or natural gas, or both, and issued under this Act or the former Act. *Mines and Minerals Act*, R.S.A. 2000, c. M-17, s. 80. 5. A disposition other than a disposition under which the holder may become entitled to an estate in fee simple, but includes a disposition containing an option to purchase the land to the extent that its provisions do not pertain to the option. *Public Lands Act*, R.S.A. 2000, c. P-40, s. 72. 6. Includes a contract for possession and profits of tangible personal property for a consideration whether the consideration is expressed as rental, licence fee, royalty or any other consideration whatsoever. *The Retail Sales Tax Act*, R.S.M. 1987, c. R130, s. 1. 7. An instrument which expresses an intention to convey thereby a leasehold interest but does not include a standard form of lease made pursuant to the Residential Tenancies Act. *Standard Forms of Conveyances Act*, S.N.B. 1980, c. S-12.2, s. 1. 8. " ... [M]ay be a security agreement; it becomes so when it in substance is intended to have and has the effect of permitting the lessee to acquire title to the chattel leased by a series of time payments expressed as rental which will, over the term, discharge the purchase debt and give him title, or will do so on a final optional payment that is nominal and cannot reasonably be refused ..." *Corporate Leasing Inc v. William Day Construction Ltd.* (1986), 6 P.P.S.A.C. 188 at 200 (Ont. H.C.), Henry J. 9. An oil and gas lease. See BUILDING ~; FINANCIAL ~; GRATUITOUS ~; GROUND ~; LIFE ~; LONG TERM; MINERAL ~; MINING ~; NET ~; NET NET ~; OPTION ~; RESIDUAL OBLIGATION ~; REVERSIONARY ~; STRATA LOT ~; SUB~; UNDER ~.

LEASE AGREEMENT. (a) An agreement by which a leasehold estate is granted or assigned, or (b) an agreement by which an option to renew or extend the term of a lease is granted, and includes a lease modification agreement. *Property Transfer Tax Act*, R.S.B.C. 1996, c. 378, s. 1.

LEASEBACK. *var.* **LEASE BACK.** An arrangement in which land or property is sold and then leased back to the vendor. See SALE-~.

LEASEHOLD. *n.* 1. The area demised by a lease. 2. A holding or estate distinguished from a freehold because its duration is certain and both its beginning and its end are defined.

LEASEHOLD COMPLEX. See RESIDENTIAL ~.

LEASEHOLD CONDOMINIUM CORPORATION. A corporation in which all the units and their appurtenant common interests are subject to leasehold interests held by the owners. *Condominium Act, 1998*, S.O. 1998, c. 19, s. 1.

LEASEHOLD ESTATE. In contrast to a freehold estate, an estate of fixed duration. The tenant is the owner of the leasehold estate.

LEASEHOLD STRATA PLAN. A strata plan in which the land shown on the strata plan is subject to a ground lease. *Strata Property Act,* S.B.C. 1998, c. 43, s. 199.

LEASEHOLD TENANT. A person, including an owner developer, registered in the land title office as a tenant under a strata lot lease, whether entitled to it in the person's own right, in a representative capacity or otherwise, and includes a subtenant. *Strata Property Act,* S.B.C. 1998, c. 43, s. 199.

LEASEHOLD UNIT. A unit in a residential leasehold complex. *Real Estate Development Marketing Act,* S.B.C. 2004, c. 41, s. 1.

LEASE MODIFICATION AGREEMENT. An agreement between a lessor and a lessee that extends the term of the lease. *Property Transfer Tax Act,* R.S.B.C. 1996, c. 378, s. 1

LEASE OBLIGATION. Of a person includes an obligation under an agreement that authorizes the use of or the production or reproduction of property including information or any other thing. *Income Tax Act,* R.S.C. 1985, c. 1 (5th Supp.), s. 95.

LEASE-PURCHASE AGREEMENT. See FINANCIAL ~.

LEASE TERM. The period during which the lessee is entitled to retain possession of the leased goods. *Consumer Protection Act, 2002,* S.O. 2002, c. 30, s. 86.

LEAST. See AT ~.

LEAVE. *n.* 1. Permission. 2. Permission from an employer for an employee to be absent from work. 3. Period of time permitted by terms of employment during which an employee is absent from work. See ADOPTION ~; MATERNITY ~; PARENTAL ~; PREGNANCY ~; REINTEGRATION ~; SICK ~.

LEAVE AND LICENCE. A defence to a trespass action in which the defendant claims that plaintiff consented to the act complained of.

LEAVE OF ABSENCE. A period of time during which an employee is permitted to be absent from work, usually without pay.

LECTURE. *n.* Includes address, speech and sermon. *Copyright Act,* R.S.C. 1985, c. C-42, s. 2.

LEGACY. *n.* 1. The means by which personal property is disposed of by will. 2. A personal gift as opposed to a "bequest" to charity. *Smith v. Chatham (City) Home of the Friendless,* [1932] 4 D.L.R. 173 at 174, [1932] S.C.R. 713, Duff J. See CONTINGENT ~; CUMULATIVE ~; DEMONSTRATIVE ~; GENERAL ~; SPECIFIC ~; UNIVERSAL ~.

LEGACY BY GENERAL TITLE. Entitles one or several persons to take (1) the ownership of an aliquot share of the succession; (2) a dismemberment of the right of ownership of the whole or of an aliquot share of the succession; (3) the ownership or a dismemberment of the right of ownership of the whole or of an aliquot share of all the immovable or movable property, private property, property in a community or acquests, or corporeal or incorporeal property. *Civil Code,* S.Q. 1991, c. 64, a. 733.

LEGACY BY PARTICULAR TITLE. Any legacy which is neither a universal legacy nor a legacy by general title is a legacy by particular title. *Civil Code,* S.Q. 1991, c. 64, a. 734.

LEGAL. *adj.* 1. According to law, lawful. 2. Not in contravention of any law. 3. Relating to the law or lawyers. See MEDICO-~; STRICT ~ OPERATION.

LEGAL ADVICE. Not confined to merely telling the client the state of the law. It includes advice as to what should be done in the relevant legal context. It must, as a necessity, include ascertaining or investigating the facts upon which the advice will be rendered. *Gower v. Tolko Manitoba Inc.,* 2001 MBCA 11, 7 C.C.E.L. (3d) 1, 196 D.L.R. (4th) 716, 153 Man. R. (2d) 20, 238 W.A.C. 20, [2001] 4 W.W.R. 622, 2 C.P.C. (5th) 197, 4 W.W.R. 622.

LEGAL AGE. 1. The age of majority. 2. May, in a particular context, mean the age at which a person is permitted to engage in the regulated action or activity, for example, driving or consuming alcohol or tobacco.

LEGAL AID. Legal advice and services available or furnished under a legal aid act. Intended to assist those who are financially unable to retain a lawyer privately.

LEGAL BURDEN OF PROOF. The burden of establishing a case, an issue, or a fact to the standard required in the context.

LEGAL CAUSATION. 1. Legal causation, which is also referred to as imputable causation, is concerned with the question of whether the accused person should be held responsible in law for the death that occurred. It is informed by legal considerations such as the wording of the section creating the offence and principles of interpretation. These legal considerations, in turn, reflect fundamental principles of criminal justice such as the principle that the morally innocent should not be punished. *R. v. Nette,* 2001 SCC 78, Arbour J. (Iacobucci, Major, Binnie, LeBel JJ. concurring). 2. In the context of negligence claims, encompasses such concepts as novus actus interveniens, proximity, remoteness, and causa causans. All of these concepts share in the explanation of and attribution of responsibility for negligence. 3. Legal causation, which is also referred to as "imputable causation" (R. v. Nette, 2001 SCC 78 at para. 45), is concerned with "the question of whether the accused person should be held responsible in law for the death that occurred". *R. v. Sinclair,* 2009 MBCA 71.

LEGAL CIVIL LIBERTIES. These are the liberties relating to legal proceedings: freedom from unlawful search and seizure, imprisonment, arrest, cruel and unusual punishment, and unfair process.

LEGAL CLINIC. An office run by students or staff to supply legal services concerning a particular issue or issues or to provide legal services to those unable to afford or obtain advice from a lawyer in private practice. See CLINIC; CLINIC LAW.

LEGAL COUNSEL. In the Province of Quebec, an advocate or a notary and, in any other province, a barrister or solicitor.

LEGAL CUSTODY. 1. Any restraint of a person that is authorized by law. 2. Refers to the person who has been awarded custody of a child under a custody order.

LEGAL DESCRIPTION. "Normally... used to indicate the exact boundaries of a piece of land ..." *Edkar Construction Ltd. v. Thompson (City) Board of Revision*, [1992] 6 W.W.R. 563 at 568, 8 Admin. L.R. (2d) 278, 82 Man. R. (2d) 118 (Q.B.), Morse J.

LEGAL EFFECT. Refers to how legislation as a whole affects rights and liabilities of those subject to its terms. The effect is determined by the legislation itself.

LEGAL EXECUTION. Seizure of property, for purposes of satisfying a judgment, under the common law process of writ of fieri facias or equivalent process.

LEGAL FICTION. An assumption by law that something which is false is true. A statute may state that X is to be treated as Y. That a corporation is a person is sometimes said to be a legal fiction. See FICTION.

LEGAL HYPOTHEC. One of the following may give rise to a legal hypothec: (1) claims of the State for sums due under fiscal laws, and certain other claims of the State or of legal persons established in the public interest, under specific provision of law; (2) claims of persons having taken part in the construction or renovation of an immovable; (3) the claim of a syndicate of co-owners for payment of the common expenses and contributions to the contingency fund; (4) claims under a judgment. *Civil Code*, S.Q. 1991, c. 64, a. 2724.

LEGAL INCAPACITY. 1. Mental infirmity of such a nature as would, but for this Act, invalidate or terminate a power of attorney. *Powers of Attorney Act*, R.S.P.E.I. 1988, c. P.16, s. 1. 2. Mental disability of a nature (i) such that were a person to engage in an action he or she would be unable to understand its nature and effect, and (ii) that would, but for this Act, invalidate or terminate a power of attorney. *Enduring Powers of Attorney Act*, R.S.N. 1990, c. E-11, s. 2(1). See CAPACITY.

LEGAL INFORMATION. See PUBLIC ~.

LEGAL INFORMATION INSTITUTE. Institutes in various countries which promote and support free access to public legal information throughout the world, principally via the Internet; cooperate in order to achieve these goals and, in particular, to assist organizations in developing countries to achieve these goals, recognizing the reciprocal advantages that all obtain from access to each other's law; help each other and to support, within their means, other organizations that share these goals with respect to: promotion, to governments and other organizations, of public policy conducive to the accessibility of pub-

lic legal information; technical assistance, advice and training; development of open technical standards; academic exchange of research results. See CANADIAN ~.

LEGAL INNUENDO. Requires the pleading of extrinsic facts or special knowledge of the persons to whom the words were spoken so as to import to the words spoken the defamatory character alleged. *Moon v. Sher*, 2003 CarswellOnt 2405 (Sup. Ct.).

LEGAL INTEREST. An interest arising by operation of law or an interest enforceable at law.

LEGALISATION. *var.* **LEGALIZATION.** *n.* The transformation of a prima facie illegal act into a legal act. Refers to the passing of a law to legalize a formerly illegal act.

LEGALISE. *var.* **LEGALIZE.** *v.* To transform a prima facie illegal act into a legal act. Refers to passing a law to legalize a formerly illegal act.

LEGAL LIEN. Confers on a person rightfully in possession of another person's property the passive right to detain that property until the debt owing by the owner of the property is paid to the person detaining it.

LEGAL MEDICINE. The application of medical principles and knowledge to legal problems. See FORENSIC MEDICINE.

LEGAL MED. Q. *abbr.* Legal Medical Quarterly.

LEGAL MONUMENT. A device planted by a surveyor.

LEGAL MORTGAGE. Transfer of the legal estate to create a mortgage.

LEGAL N. *abbr.* Legal News, 1878-1897.

LEGAL PERSON. Any entity having juridical personality. The most obvious example of a legal person is a corporation which has the legal qualities of a person for at least some purposes.

LEGAL POSSESSION. Something more than a mere right to be on the land in question. Refers to entitlement close to an interest in land. Includes enjoying some benefit from the land.

LEGAL POWER. Enables its holder to perform tasks such as conveying an estate. D.M.W. Waters, *The Law of Trusts in Canada*, 2d ed. (Toronto: Carswell, 1984) at 71.

LEGAL PRESUMPTION. One that is specially attached by law to certain facts; it exempts the person in whose favour it exists from making any other proof. A presumption concerning presumed facts is simple and may be rebutted by proof to the contrary; a presumption concerning deemed facts is absolute and irrebuttable. *Civil Code*, S.Q. 1991, c. 64, a. 2847.

LEGAL PROCEEDING. 1. Any civil or criminal proceeding or inquiry in which evidence is or may be given, and includes an arbitration. *Evidence acts*. 2. Any civil proceeding, inquiry, proceeding before any tribunal, board or commission or arbitration, in which evidence is or may be given, and includes an action or proceeding for the imposition of punishment by fine, penalty or imprisonment for the violation of a Provincial enactment. *Evidence Act,* R.S.N.S. 1989, c. 154, s. 60.

LEGAL PROCESS. "... [D]oes not mean 'by lawful means'. It means 'by a process available through the operation of law', such as by seizure under a writ of execution... ." *Rogerson Lumber Co. v. Four Seasons Chalet Ltd.* (1980), 12 B.L.R. 93 at 102, 29 O.R. (2d) 193, 36 C.B.R. (N.S.) 141, 1 P.P.S.A.C. 160, 113 D.L.R. (3d) 671 (C.A.), Arnup J.A.

LEGAL PROFESSIONAL PRIVILEGE. 1. The ability to claim that a document should not be introduced in evidence in a proceeding because it was prepared in contemplation of litigation or for the purpose of seeking legal advice. Where legal advice has been sought communications made to the adviser in confidence by the client are at the client's instance permanently protected from disclosure by himself or his adviser unless the protection is waived. 2. "In ... Waugh v. British Railways Board, [1979] 2 All E.R. 1169 it was decided: under that authority a party need not produce a document otherwise subject to production if the dominant purpose for which the document was prepared was submission to a legal advisor for advice and use in litigation (whether in progress or as contemplated). Such documents are shielded from production by what is usually described as legal professional privilege... . the legal professional privilege should only be applied when there is a significant connection between the preparation of the document and the anticipation of litigation. This leads to the introduction of the 'dominant purpose' test." *Nova, An Alberta Corporation v. Guelph Engineering Co.* (1984), 80 C.P.R. (2d) 93 at 95, 97, [1984] 3 W.W.R. 314, 42 C.P.C. 194, 30 Alta. L.R. (2d) 183, 5 D.L.R. (4th) 755, 50 A.R. 199 (C.A.), the court per Stevenson J.A. See SOLICITOR-CLIENT PRIVILEGE.

LEGAL REPRESENTATIVE. 1. Of a person means a trustee in bankruptcy, an assignee, a liquidator, a curator, a receiver of any kind, a trustee, an heir, an administrator, an executor, a liquidator of a succession, a committee, or any other like person, administering, winding up, controlling or otherwise dealing in a representative or fiduciary capacity with any property, business, commercial activity or estate that belongs or belonged to, or that is or was held for the benefit of, the person or the person's estate. *Excise Act,* R.S.C. 1985, c. E-14, s. 111. 2. Includes heirs, executors, administrators, successors and assigns, or agents or attorneys who are thereunto duly authorized in writing. *Copyright Act,* R.S.C. 1985, c. C-42, s. 2..

LEGAL RIGHT. "[In s. 215(3) of the Criminal Code, R.S.C. 1970, c. C-34] ... a right which is sanctioned by law, for example, the right to use lawful force in self-defence, as distinct from something that a person may do without incurring any legal liability... ." *R. v. Haight* (1976), 30 C.C.C. (2d) 168 at 175 (Ont. C.A.), the court per Martin J.A.

LEGAL RIGHTS. Refers to ss. 7 to 14 of the Charter but does not have a precise meaning. Refers to the rights of persons in the criminal justice system and the limits on government powers of search, seizure, arrest, detention, trial and punishment. P.W. Hogg,

Constitutional Law of Canada, 3d ed. (Toronto: Carswell, 1992) at 1021.

LEGAL SET-OFF. 1. The netting out of a debt owed by one person to a second person against the debt owed to the first person by the second. 2. "... '[R]equires the fulfilment of two conditions. The first is that both obligations must be debts. The second is that both debts must be mutual cross obligations. Both conditions must be fulfilled at the same time': ..." *Canadian Commercial Bank (Liquidator of) v. Parlee McLaws* (1989), 72 C.B.R. (N.S.) 39 at 43, 64 Alta. L.R. (2d) 218 (Q.B.), Wachowich J.

LEGAL STANDING. A party's right to seek a remedy apart from the substantive merits of the case. There must be a serious issue, a genuine interest, and lack of any other reasonable and effective means to test the law in order for a person to have legal standing.

LEGAL TENDER. 1. A tender of payment of money is a legal tender if it is made (a) in coins that are current Under section (7) and (b) in notes issued by the Bank of Canada pursuant to the Bank of Canada Act intended for circulation in Canada. (2) A payment in coins referred to in subsection (1) is a legal tender for no more than the following amounts for the following denominations of coins: (a) forty dollars if the denomination is two dollars or greater but does not exceed ten dollars; (b) twenty-five dollars if the denomination is one dollar; (c) ten dollars if the denomination is ten cents or greater but less than one dollar; (d) five dollars if the denomination is five cents; and (e) twenty-five cents if the denomination is one cent. (2.1) In the case of coins of a denomination greater than ten dollars, a payment referred to in subsection (1) may consist of not more than one coin, and the payment is a legal tender for no more than the value of a single coin of that denomination. (3) For the purposes of subsections (2) and (2.1), where more than one amount is payable by one person to another on the same day under one or more obligations, the total of those amounts is deemed to be one amount due and payable on that day. (4) A coin that has been called in is not legal tender. *Currency Act,* R.S.C. 1985, c. C-52, s. 8.

LEGAL TERM OF ART. A legal term of art is a word or expression that, through usage by legal professionals, has acquired a distinct legal meaning. It has a technical meaning because of its conventional use by lawyers and judges: Ruth Sullivan, Sullivan on the Construction of Statutes, 5th ed. (Markham, Ont.: LexisNexis Canada, 2008) at 57 and 61. That is, it has a settled legal definition. *Canada (Attorney General) v. Mowat,* 2009 FCA 309.

LEGAL TUTORSHIP. Tutorship resulting from the law is legal. *Civil Code,* S.Q. 1991, c. 64, a. 178.

LEGATEE. *n.* 1. One to whom a legacy is left. *Smith v. Chatham (City) Home of the Friendless,* [1931] 4 D.L.R. 173 at 174, [1932] S.C.R. 713, Duff J. 2. A devisee. See RESIDUARY ~.

LEGES EXTRA TERRITORIUM NON OBLIGANT. [L.] Laws are not binding outside their own territory.

L

LEGISLATION. *n.* 1. The creation of law by passing bills into law in a legislature. 2. A collection of laws or statutory instruments or bylaws. See CONSUMER PROTECTION ~; DELEGATED ~; JUDICIAL ~; SETTLEMENT ~; SUBORDINATE ~.

LEGISLATIVE ACT. An action or decision which imposes a general rule of conduct. Contrasted with decisional or judicial act which concerns a particular case.

LEGISLATIVE ASSEMBLY. 1. The legislative assembly of a province. 2. Includes the Lieutenant Governor in Council and the Legislative Assembly of the Northwest Territories, as constituted before September 1, 1905, the Legislature of the Yukon, the Commissioner in Council of the Northwest Territories, and the Legislature for Nunavut. *Interpretation Act*, R.S.C. 1985, c. I-21, s. 35.

LEGISLATIVE ASSEMBLY OFFICE. The office of the clerk of a legislative assembly.

LEGISLATIVE COHERENCE. See PRESUMPTION OF ~.

LEGISLATIVE COMMITTEE. Appointed by the House to consider a specific bill and amendments; its existence ends when the bill is reported back to the House. A. Fraser, W.A. Dawson & J. Holtby, eds., *Beauchesne's Rules and Forms of the House of Commons of Canada*, 6th ed. (Toronto: Carswell, 1989) at 222.

LEGISLATIVE COUNCIL. Includes the Lieutenant Governor in Council and the Legislative Assembly of the Northwest Territories, as constituted before September 1, 1905, the Legislature of the Yukon, the Commissioner in Council of the Northwest Territories, and the Legislature for Nunavut. *Interpretation Act*, R.S.C. 1985, c. I-21, s. 35.

LEGISLATIVE COUNSEL. The office attached to the legislature which is responsible for the drafting of legislation in co-operation with individual ministries and agencies.

LEGISLATIVE FACTS. 1. "... [T]wo categories of facts in constitutional litigation: 'adjudicative facts' and 'legislative facts'... . Legislative facts are those that establish the purpose and background of legislation, including its social, economic and cultural context. Such facts are of a more general nature and are subject to less stringent admissibility requirements ..." *Danson v. Ontario (Attorney General)* (1990), 50 C.R.R. 59 at 69, 43 C.P.C. (2d) 165, 73 D.L.R. (4th) 686, [1990] 2 S.C.R. 1086, 41 O.A.C. 250, 74 O.R. (2d) 763n, 112 N.R. 362, the court per Sopinka J. 2. Legislative facts are traditionally directed to the validity or purpose of a legislative scheme under which relief is being sought. Such background material was originally put before the courts in United States in constitutional litigation through what became known as the Brandeis brief. Legislative facts are those that establish the purpose and background of legislation, including its social, economic and cultural context. Such facts are of a

more general nature, and are subject to less stringent admissibility requirements. The usual vehicle for reception of legislative fact is judicial notice, which requires that the "facts" be so notorious or uncontroversial that evidence of their existence is unnecessary. Legislative fact may also be adduced through witnesses. The concept of "legislative fact" does not, however, provide an excuse to put before the court controversial evidence to the prejudice of the opposing party without providing a proper opportunity for its truth to be tested. *Public School Boards' Assn. (Alberta) v. Alberta (Attorney General)*, 2000 CarswellAlta 678, 2000 SCC 2, [2000] 1 S.C.R. 44, 182 D.L.R. (4th) 561, 251 N.R. 1, 250 A.R. 314, 213 W.A.C. 314, [2000] 10 W.W.R. 187, 82 Alta. L.R. (3d) 211, 9 C.P.C. (5th) 36, Binnie J.

LEGISLATIVE HISTORY. The history of a statute from its conception through enactment.

LEGISLATIVE PRIVILEGE. In summary, it seems clear that, from an historical perspective, Canadian legislative bodies possess such inherent privileges as may be necessary to their proper functioning. These privileges are part of the fundamental law of our land, and hence are constitutional. The courts may determine if the privilege claimed is necessary to the capacity of the legislature to function, but have no power to review the rightness or wrongness of a particular decision made pursuant to the privilege. [end of quotation] If even the Charter cannot cut down the exercise of legislative privilege, and if the courts are not empowered to review decisions made pursuant to privilege, it seems that more would be required than passage of a general statute (such as the OLA [Official Languages Act, R.S.N.W.T. 1988, c. O-1]) to support the conclusion that a legislative privilege has been abrogated. In this case, the Assembly made an express decision concerning the extent to which debates would be broadcast in French and an implicit decision not to publish Hansard in French. These decisions are protected by privilege. *Northwest Territories (Attorney General) v. Fédération Franco-Ténoise*, 2008 NWTCA 6.

LEGISLATIVE UNION. The uniting of two or more states or provinces into one new state so that the original states or provinces are subjected to the power of the newly created state.

LEGISLATOR. *n.* A member of a legislature; a lawmaker.

LEGISLATURE. *n.* 1. The body exercising legislative power in a province. 2. Any legislative body or authority competent to make laws. 3. The Lieutenant Governor acting by and with the advice and consent of the legislative assembly of a province. 4. Includes the Lieutenant Governor in Council and the Legislative Assembly of the Northwest Territories, as constituted before September 1, 1905, the Legislature of the Yukon, the Commissioner in Council of the Northwest Territories, and the Legislature for Nunavut. *Interpretation Act*, R.S.C. 1985, c. I-21, s. 35. See PROVINCIAL ~.

LEGITIMACY. See PRESUMPTION OF ~.

LEGITIMATE. *adj.* Lawful; describing children who were born in wedlock.

LEGITIMATE BUSINESS EXPECTANCY. See UNLAWFUL INTERFERENCE WITH ~.

LEGITIMATE EXPECTATION. Legitimate expectations are capable of including expectations which go beyond enforceable legal rights, provided they have some reasonable basis. The justification for it is primarily that, when a public authority has promised to follow a certain procedure, it is in the interest of good administration that it should act fairly and should implement its promise, so long as implementation does not interfere with its statutory duty. The principle is also justified by the further consideration that, when the promise was made, the authority must have considered that it would be assisted in discharging its duty fairly by any representations from interested parties and as a general rule that is correct. *Attorney General of Hong Kong v. Ng Yuen Shiu*, [1983] 2 A.C. 629 at 636-638, [1983] 2 All E.R. 346 (Hong Kong P.C.), Lord Fraser of Tullybelton.

LEGITIMATION. *n.* 1. The making legal of something otherwise not. 2. The act by which one makes a person born illegitimate legitimate.

LENDER. See MONEY ~; PAYDAY ~.

LENDING ARRANGEMENT. See SECURITIES ~.

LENDING ASSET. A bond, debenture, mortgage, hypothecary claim, note, agreement of sale or any other indebtedness or a prescribed share, but does not include a prescribed property. *Income Tax Act*, R.S.C. 1985, c. 1 (5th Supp.), s. 248.

LENGTH. *n.* 1. The measure of size of a thing along the longest axis. 2. The measure of time taken by or for an event. See ARM'S ~.

LENS. *n.* The part of the eye through which light is concentrated or dispersed. 2. A glass or plastic object through which light is concentrated or dispersed.

LESS. See MORE OR ~.

LESSEE. *n.* 1. The person to whom one makes or gives a lease. 2. The holder of a lease. *Public Lands Act*, R.S.A. 2000, c. P-40, s. 72. 3. Includes an original or derivative under-lessee and the heirs, executors, administrators and assigns of a lessee and a grantee under such a grant and the grantee's heirs and assigns. *Landlord and Tenant Act*, R.S.M. 1987, c. L70, s. 18. 4. An individual who entered into, or who is negotiating to enter into, a lease if that individual, under that lease, hires or is to hire goods from another party to the agreement. *Business Practices and Consumer Protection Act*, S.B.C. 2004, c. 2, s. 57. 5. Tenant. See UNDER ~.

LESSER OFFENCE. "... [A] 'part of the offence' which is charged, and it must necessarily include some element of the 'major offence', but being lacking in some of the essentials, without which the major offence would be incomplete." *Fergusson v. R.* (1961), [1962] S.C.R. 229 at 233, 36 C.R. 271, 132 C.C.C. 112, the court per Taschereau J. For example, manslaughter is a lesser offence in relation to murder.

LESSOR. *n.* 1. The person who makes or gives anything to someone else by lease. 2. Includes an original or derivative under-lessor and the heirs, executors, administrators and assigns of a lessor and a grantor under such a grant and the grantor's heirs and assigns. *Landlord and Tenant Act*, R.S.M. 1987, c. L70, s. 18. 3. Landlord. 4. A person who entered into, or who is negotiating to enter into, a lease if that person, under that lease, leases or is to lease goods to another party to the agreement. *Business Practices and Consumer Protection Act*, S.B.C. 2004, c. 2, s. 57.

LET. *v.* 1. To lease. 2. To permit. 3. To award a contract. See SUB-~.

LETHAL DEVICE. See EXPLOSIVE OR OTHER ~.

LETTER. *n.* A statement in writing that is capable of being transmitted. See CALDERBANK ~; CLIC ~; COMMITMENT ~; DEMAND ~; FAIRNESS ~; ROGATORY ~S; UNDELIVERABLE ~.

LETTER OF CREDIT. 1. "... [A] proposal or request to the person named therein, or, in the case of an open letter, to persons generally, to advance money on the faith of it, and the advance constitutes an acceptance of the proposal, thus making a contract between the giver of the letter of credit and the person cashing or negotiating the draft, by which the former is bound to honour the draft." *Kingsway Electric Co. v. 330604 Ontario Ltd.* (1979), 9 B.L.R. 316 at 322, 27 O.R. (2d) 541, 11 R.P.R. 96, 33 C.B.R. (N.S.) 137, 107 D.L.R. (3d) 172 (H.C.), Lovekin L.J.S.C. 2. "... [I]n effect, a guarantee by the bank that upon presentation of predetermined documentation, the bank will pay the beneficiary named in the letter... ." *Canadian Pioneer Petroleums Inc. v. Federal Deposit Insurance Corp.* (1984), 25 B.L.R. 1 at 3, [1984] 2 W.W.R. 563, 30 Sask. R. 315 (Q.B.), Halvorson J. See COMMERCIAL ~; GUARANTEE ~; STAND-BY ~.

LETTER OF INTENT. 1. "... [U]sed by businessmen and contractors as an initial means of establishing a contractual relationship and at the same time, not committing themselves to legally binding commitments until details are negotiated to conclusion." *Marathon Realty Co. v. Toulon Construction Corp.* (1987), 45 R.P.R. 233 at 255, 80 N.S.R. (2d) 390, 200 A.P.R. 390 (T.D.), Davison J. 2. "[In labour law] ... documents that clarify the meaning of provisions in the main document containing the collective agreement ... documents which create obligations not contained in the main agreement... ." *Hiram Walker & Sons Ltd. v. Canadian Union of Distillery Workers, Local 1* (1976), 13 L.A.C. (2d) 417 at 421 (Ont.), Beck.

LETTERS OF ADMINISTRATION. An instrument, granted by a Surrogate Court, giving authority to an administrator to manage and distribute the estate of a person who died without making a will. Granted when there is no provable will of the deceased person whose estate the administrator will administer. See ~ WITH WILL ANNEXED; LETTERS PROBATE.

LETTERS OF ADMINISTRATION WITH WILL ANNEXED. Special letters of administration used when the executor named in the will is unwilling or unable to serve, or when no executor was named in the will.

L

LETTERS OF REQUEST. A request from one judge to another, in another jurisdiction, that the second judge cause the conduct of an examination of a witness. See LETTERS ROGATORY.

LETTERS OF VERIFICATION. Attest that the succession has opened; they certify moreover, in the case of an intestate succession, that the property has devolved to the designated persons in the proportions indicated and, in the case of a testamentary succession, that it has been proved that the will, of which a true copy is annexed, is the only will that the deceased made, or that it is the latest and that it revokes, in whole or in part, all previous wills. In addition, the letters of verification identify the person acting as the liquidator of the succession. *Code of Civil Procedure*, R.S.Q, c. C-25, a. 893.

LETTERS PATENT. 1. A document sealed with the Great Seal by which a company or person may do something or enjoy privileges not otherwise possible. The document is so called because it is open, with seal affixed, ready to be exhibited to confirm the grant. 2. A means of incorporating a corporation upon application to the responsible Minister by the applicants for incorporation, the acceptance of the application, and the granting of the letters patent under the seal of the incorporating jurisdiction. See SUPPLEMENTARY ~.

LETTERS PATENT JURISDICTION. A province in which incorporation takes place by application for and issue of letters patent. The issue of the letters patent is at the discretion of the Minister responsible.

LETTERS PROBATE. An instrument, granted by a Surrogate Court, giving authority to an executor to carry out the provisions of a person's will.

LETTERS ROGATORY. "... [S]ometimes known as letters of request. They constitute a request from one Judge to another asking for the examination of a witness by commission in the jurisdiction which is foreign to the requesting Court ..." *A-Dec Inc. v. Dentech Products Ltd.* (1988), 32 C.P.C. (2d) 290 at 294, 31 B.C.L.R. (2d) 320 (S.C.), Bouck J. See COMMISSION EVIDENCE; COMMISSION ROGATORY; PERPETUATE TESTIMONY; ROGATORY LETTERS.

LEVY. *v.* 1. "... [T]o take all the necessary steps to enforce payment, that is, such steps as under the particular circumstances of the case would be reasonable and proper." *Bayview Estates Ltd., Re* (1980), 28 Nfld. & P.E.I.R. 225 at 243, 79 A.P.R. 225 (Nfld. T.D.), Mahoney J. 2. "... [S]ignifies the execution of legislative power which charges on person or property the obligation of or liability for a tax." *Vancouver (City) v. British Columbia Telephone Co.*, [1951] S.C.R. 3 at 6, [1950] 4 D.L.R. 289, Rand J. (Rinfret C.J.C. concurring).

LEVY. *n.* 1. A payment which results directly or indirectly from a seizure under execution. C.R.B. Dunlop, *Creditor-Debtor Law in Canada* (Toronto: Carswell, 1981) at 424. 2. A tax or duty. See SEIZURE.

LEX. *n.* [L.] Law.

LEX CAUSAE. The law governing an issue according to the choice of law rules.

LEX CONVENTIONALIS. [L. conventional law] The law which the parties agree is to govern.

LEX DOMICILII. [L.] The law of the country where someone is domiciled.

LEX ET CONSUETUDO PARLIAMENTI. [L.] The law and custom of Parliament.

LEX FORI. [L. law of the forum] The law of the jurisdiction where a legal proceeding is commenced and heard. *243930 Alberta Ltd. v. Wickham* (1990), 14 R.P.R. (2d) 95 at 98, 73 D.L.R. (4th) 474, 75 O.R. (2d) 289, 40 O.A.C. 367 (C.A.), Lacourcière J.A.

LEX LOCI. [L.] The law of a place.

LEX LOCI ACTUS. [L.] The law of the jurisdiction where an act took place.

LEX LOCI CELEBRATIONIS. [L.] The law of the jurisdiction in which a marriage was celebrated. J.G. McLeod, *The Conflict of Laws* (Calgary: Carswell, 1983) at 779.

LEX LOCI CONTRACTUS. [L.] 1. The law of the jurisdiction in which the contract was made. 2. The law of the jurisdiction where the last necessary act to make a contract took place.

LEX LOCI DELICTI. [L.] The law of the place where the wrong occurred.

LEX LOCI DOMICILII. [L.] The law of the jurisdiction in which the party is domiciled.

LEX LOCI REI SITAE. [L.] The law of the jurisdiction where the thing is located.

LEX LOCI SOLUTIONIS. [L.] The law of the jurisdiction in which a debt will be paid, a contract be performed or another obligation met.

LEX PATRIAE. [L.] The law of the country to which one owes allegiance.

LEX PERSONALIS. [L. personal law] An inclusive term of which lex patriae and lex domicilii are examples.

LEX SITUS. [L.] The law of the place where land is situate.

LIABILITY. *n.* 1. The situation in which one is potentially or actually subject to some obligation. 2. The term 'liability' is a broad term and is most often used to describe an unliquidated or unspecified legal obligation which arises due to negligence, breach of contract, etc. *Royal Trust Co. v. H.A. Roberts Group Ltd.*, 1995 CarswellSask 7, 31 C.B.R. (3d) 207, [1995] 4 W.W.R. 305, 17 B.L.R. (2d) 263, 44 R.P.R. (2d) 255, 129 Sask. R. 161 (Q.B.), Baynton J. 3. In actions arising out of construction projects] can be used in different senses. It may refer simply to whether or not there was a breach of contract. But it may also refer to particular items of loss. To give a simple example, if a contractor does not install a roof according to specifications and the roof leaks, the contractor is liable, that is to say he was in breach of contract, and the damages would ordinarily be the cost of bringing the roof to specification, but the trier of fact may also have to address questions of whether the contractor is "liable" for consequential loss. For instance, is he liable for damage to the plaintiff's grand piano from the leaking if the plaintiff, although knowing the roof was leaking, failed to move the piano to a place of safety? Such an issue is characterized as one of avoidable loss or mitigation. In British Columbia, if a defendant wishes to allege that the plaintiff ought to have avoided some part of what the plaintiff says is his loss, he must so plead. [T]he issue of mitigation is one of "damages" and not "liability", at least in the narrow sense of that word. *JJM Construction Ltd. v. Sandspit Harbour Society*, 2000 CarswellBC 622, 2000 BCCA 208 (C.A.). See ABSOLUTE ~; ALTERNATIVE ~; CONTINGENT ~; CURRENT ~; LIMITED ~ COMPANY; LIMITED ~ PARTNERSHIP; LONG-TERM ~; MOTOR VEHICLE ~ POLICY; OCCUPIERS' ~; PRODUCTS ~; PUBLICLY-TRADED ~; STRICT ~; UNFUNDED ~; VICARIOUS ~.

LIABILITY INSURANCE. Insurance, other than insurance that falls within another class of insurance, (a) against liability arising out of bodily injury to, or the disability or death of, a person, including an employee; (b) against liability arising out of the loss of, or damage to, property; or (c) if the policy includes the insurance described in paragraph (a), against expenses arising out of bodily injury to a person other than the insured or a member of the insured's family, whether or not liability exists. *Insurance Companies Act*, S.C. 1991, c. 47, Sched. [1]. See EMPLOYERS' ~; PUBLIC ~.

LIABLE. *adj.* Obliged; accountable.

LIABLE. *adv.* 1. Exposed to. *R. v. Robinson* (1951), 12 C.R. 101 at 113, [1951] S.C.R. 522, Cartwright J. 2. Used to create a legal obligation. *Canada Trust Co. v. British Columbia (Attorney General)* (1980), 7 E.T.R. 93 at 113, [1980] 2 S.C.R 466, 23 B.C.L.R. 86, [1980] 5 W.W.R. 591, [1980] C.T.C. 338, 7 F.T.R. 93, 112 D.L.R. (3d) 592, 52 N.R. 326, the court per Dickson J. 3. Likely or probably. *Mermuys v. Delodder* (1990), 86 Nfld. & P.E.I.R. 326 at 330, 268 A.P.R. 326, 35 C.P.R. (3d) 146 (P.E.I. T.D.), McQuaid J.

LIBEL. *n.* 1. The making of a defamatory statement in a visible and permanent form. 2. Defamatory words in a newspaper or in a broadcast shall be deemed to be published and to constitute libel. *Libel and Slander Act*, R.S.O. 1990, c. L.12, s. 2. See DEFAMATORY ~; SEDITIOUS ~.

LIBERTY. *n.* 1. [T]he right to liberty enshrined in s. 7 of the Charter protects within its ambit the right to an irreducible sphere of personal autonomy wherein individuals may make inherently private choices free from state interference. [T]he autonomy protected by the s. 7 right to liberty encompasses only those matters that can properly be characterized as fundamentally or inherently personal such that, by their very nature, they implicate basic choices going to the core of what it means to enjoy individual dignity and independence. *Godbout c. Longueuil (Ville)*, 1997 CarswellQue 883, La Forest J. (L'Heureux-Dubé and McLachlin JJ. concurring). 2. Does not

mean unconstrained freedom and does not mean merely freedom from physical restraint. Refers to the personal autonomy to live one's own life and to make decisions that are of fundamental personal importance. 3. "... [T]he right of liberty contained in s. 7 [of the Charter] guarantees to every individual a degree of personal autonomy over important decisions intimately affecting their private lives... ." *R. v. Morgentaler* (1988), 62 C.R. (3d) 1 at 107, 82 N.R. 1, [1988] 1 S.C.R. 30, 63 O.R. (2d) 281n, 26 O.A.C. 1, 44 D.L.R. (4th) 385, 31 C.R.R. 1, 37 C.C.C. (3d) 449, Wilson J. 4. "... [N]ot confined to mere freedom from bodily restraint. It does not, however, extend to protect property or pure economic rights. It may embrace individual freedom of movement, including the right to choose one's occupation and where to pursue it, subject to the right of the state to impose, in accordance with the principles of fundamental justice, legitimate and reasonable restrictions on the activities of individuals... ." *Wilson v. British Columbia (Medical Services Commission)* (1988), 41 C.R.R. 276 at 295, 30 B.C.L.R. (2d) 1, 34 Admin. L.R. 235, [1989] 2 W.W.R. 1, 53 D.L.R. (4th) 171 (C.A.), Nemetz C.J.B.C., Carrothers, Hinkson, Macfarlane and Wallace JJ.A. 5. The most obvious engagement of the "liberty" interest is imprisonment. In Reference re s. 94(2) of the Motor Vehicle Act (British Columbia), [1985] 2 S.C.R. 486 at 515, the Supreme Court of Canada stipulated that when there is a threat of imprisonment, the "liberty" interest under s. 7 [of the Canadian Charter of Rights and Freedoms] is automatically engaged. When there is not a threat of imprisonment, courts must consider more closely whether the actions in question engage the liberty interest. The issue can be boiled down to essentially the question: is the activity of "fundamental personal importance"? *R. v. Malmo-Levine*, 2000 CarswellBC 1148, 2000 BCCA 335, 145 C.C.C. (3d) 225, 34 C.R. (5th) 91, 74 C.R.R. (2d) 189, 138 B.C.A.C. 218, 226 W.A.C. 218, Braidwood J.A. (Rowles J.A. concurring). See CIVIL LIBERTIES; FREEDOM; RESIDUAL ~; RIGHT.

LIBR. *abbr.* Lowest intermediate balance rule.

LIBRARY AND ARCHIVES OF CANADA. A branch of the federal public administration. The Librarian and Archivist of Canada has the rank of deputy minister. Replaces the National Library and the National Archives. The objects of the Library and Archives of Canada are (a) to acquire and preserve the documentary heritage; (b) to make that heritage known to Canadians and to anyone with an interest in Canada and to facilitate access to it; (c) to be the permanent repository of publications of the Government of Canada and of government and ministerial records that are of historical or archival value; (d) to facilitate the management of information by government institutions; (e) to coordinate the library services of government institutions; and (f) to support the development of the library and archival communities. *Library and Archives of Canada Act*, S.C. 2004, c. 11, s. 7.

LICENCE. var. **LICENSE.** *n.* 1. The permission given to do something which would otherwise be unlawful. 2. A permit, certificate, approval, registra-

L

tion or similar form of permission required by law. 3. An instrument issued conferring upon the holder the privilege of doing the things set forth in it, subject to the conditions, limitations and restrictions contained in it. 4. "... [U]nder a licence the licensee has no exclusive possession, and his right both to the possession and the use may be revoked at any time by the licensor, unless the licence is coupled with an interest or the circumstances raise equitable considerations to which the court will give effect." *Johnson v. British Canadian Insurance Co.*, [1932] 4 D.L.R. 281 at 284, [1932] S.C.R. 680, Lamont J. 5. Permission to occupy land and perhaps to carry out specified activities there. See COMPULSORY ~; CONDITIONAL ~; CREATIVE COMMONS ~; DRIVER'S ~; FISHING ~; LEAVE AND ~; MARRIAGE ~; SUB~.

LICENSE. *v.* The act of permitting; granting a licence. See LICENCE.

LICENSED PREMISES. The premises in respect of which a licence to sell liquor has been issued and is in force.

LICENSEE. *n.* 1. A person who holds a subsisting licence. 2. " ... [A] person who is neither a passenger, servant nor trespasser, and not standing in any contractual relation with the owner of the premises, and is permitted to come upon the premises for his own interest, convenience, or gratification." *Smiles v. Edmonton (Board of Education)* (1918), (*sub nom. Smiles v. Edmonton School District*) 43 D.L.R. 171 at 180, [1918] 3 W.W.R. 673, 14 Alta. L.R. 351 (C.A.), Hyndman J.A. 3. A contextual reading of the Copyright Act [R.S.C. 1985, c. C-42] reveals that Parliament has preserved the traditional distinction between assignees and licensees with some modification. Under the present Act, there is a distinction between "assignee", "licensee" and "exclusive licensee". An assignee possesses full ownership rights in the copyright with respect to the rights assigned. A non-exclusive licensee has no property rights in the copyright, and enjoys only contractual rights vis-à-vis the owner-licensor. As a result, it cannot sue for infringement. An exclusive licensee, on the other hand, has a limited property interest in the copyright. ... this limited property interest enables the exclusive licensee to sue third parties for infringement but precludes the exclusive licensee from suing the owner-licensor for infringement. *Kraft Canada Inc. c. Euro Excellence Inc.*, 2007 SCC 37, Rothstein J. (Binnie and Deschamps JJ. concurring). See BARE ~.

LICENSING AUTHORITY. A body which may grant or refuse to grant a licence.

LICENSING POWER. A power in municipal or local governments to enact licensing bylaws. Also known as police power. It is derived from the province's jurisdiction over property and civil rights under the Constitution.

LIE. *v.* Of an action, to be, on the facts of the case, able to be properly begun or continued. For example, "An action lies against one who has negligently harmed another".

LIE DETECTOR TEST. An analysis, examination, interrogation or test taken or performed by means of or in conjunction with a device, instrument or machine, whether mechanical, electrical, electromagnetic, electronic or otherwise, and that is taken or performed for the purpose of assessing or purporting to assess the credibility of a person.

LIEN. *n.* 1. "In law, a lien is a right to retain possession of property until a debt due to the person detaining the property is satisfied... ." *Montreal Lithographing Ltd. v. Deputy Minister of National Revenue (Customs & Excise)* (1984), 12 C.E.R. 1 at 3, [1984] 2 F.C. 22, 8 C.R.R. 299 (T.D.), Cattanach J. 2. "Originally a lien was a possessory interest, but a lien was later recognized under some circumstances in equity, notwithstanding that the holder of it had surrendered possession. Sometimes a lien was an interest in specific property, whilst at other times it was an interest in all of the debtor's property. The one characteristic which each lien had in common was that it was an interest which a person had in property belonging to another." *John Deere Ltd. v. Firdale Farms Ltd. (Receiver of)* (1987), 8 P.P.S.A.C. 52 at 82, [1988] 2 W.W.R. 406, 45 D.L.R. (4th) 641, 50 Man. R. (2d) 45 (C.A.), Twaddle J.A. (Hall J.A. concurring). 3. The right in one man to retain that which is in his possession belonging to another, till certain demands of him the person in possession are satisfied. *Hammonds v. Barclay* (1802), 2 East 227 at 235, 102 E.R. 356 at 359 (K.B.), Grose J. 4. A right which accrues to a worker or artisan who repairs, adds to, or improves a chattel for another. See AGENT'S ~; BUILDERS' ~; COMMON LAW ~; CONSTRUCTION ~; CREATION OF ~; EQUITABLE ~; GENERAL ~; LEGAL ~; MECHANICS' ~; PARTICULAR ~; POSSESSORY ~; PURCHASER'S ~; RETAINING ~; SOLICITOR'S ~; STATUTORY ~; UNPAID SELLER'S ~; VENDOR'S ~.

LIEN CLAIMANT. 1. A person having a preserved or perfected lien. 2. A person entitled to claim a lien.

LIEN FUND. The fund which is created by an owner of property upon whose property work has been performed or materials furnished by workers. The fund is the holdback of a portion of the amount otherwise owing to the contractor for the work and materials.

LIENHOLDER. *n.* Any person having a lien.

LIEUTENANT GOVERNOR. *var.* **LIEUTENANT-GOVERNOR.** The lieutenant governor or other chief executive officer or administrator carrying on the government of the province indicated by the enactment, by whatever title that officer is designated, and, in Yukon in the Northwest Territories and Nunavut means the Commissioner. *Interpretation Act*, R.S.C. 1985, c. I-21, s. 35.

LIEUTENANT GOVERNOR IN COUNCIL. *var.* **LIEUTENANT-GOVERNOR IN COUNCIL.** The lieutenant governor acting by and with the advice of, by and with the advice and consent of, or in conjunction with, the executive council of the province indicated by the enactment, and in Yukon, means the Commissioner of Yukon acting with the consent of the Executive Council of Yukon and, in the Northwest Territories and Nunavut, means the Commissioner. *Interpretation Act*, R.S.C. 1985, c. I-21, s. 35.

LIEUT. GOV. *abbr.* Lieutenant Governor.

LIFE. See EXPECTATION OF ~; NECESSARIES OF ~.

LIFE ANNUITY. A yearly payment while any particular life, or lives, continues. See IMMEDIATE ~.

LIFE BENCHER. A bencher who holds that office during his or her lifetime because of prior office-holding or other honour.

LIFE COMPANY. A company or a provincial company that is permitted to insure risks falling within the class of life insurance, other than a company or a provincial company that is also permitted to insure risks falling within any other class of insurance other than accident and sickness insurance, credit protection insurance and other approved products insurance. *Insurance Companies Act*, S.C. 1991, c. 47, s. 2(1).

LIFE ESTATE. The grant of an estate, an interest in property, for the length of the life of the person to whom the estate is granted.

LIFE INSURANCE. 1. " ... [I]n its characteristic forms involves, as its essence, a risk in a specified payment of money absolute from the moment the contract takes effect. That constitutes the security sought by the insured, the premiums for which in turn furnish the consideration to the insurer." *Gray v. Kerslake* (1957), 11 D.L.R. (2d) 225 at 227, [1957] I.L.R. 1-279, [1958] S.C.R. 3, Rand J. 2. (a) Any insurance that is payable (i) on death, (ii) on the happening of an event or contingency dependent on human life, (iii) at a fixed or determinable future time, or (iv) for a term dependent on human life; and (b) without restricting the generality of paragraph (a), includes insurance under which an insurer (i) undertakes to pay an additional sum of money in the event of the death by accident of the person whose life is insured, (ii) undertakes to pay a sum of money or to provide other benefits in the event that the person whose life is insured becomes disabled as a result of bodily injury or disease, or (iii) undertakes to provide an annuity - or what would be an annuity except that the periodic payments may be unequal in amount - for a term dependent solely or partly on the life of a person. *Insurance Companies Act*, S.C. 1991, c. 47, Sched. [1]. See GROUP TERM ~ POLICY.

LIFE INSURED. The person upon whose life insurance is placed. The person whose death will result in payment of a life policy.

LIFE INTEREST. An interest for another's life (pur autre vie) or one's own life.

LIFE LEASE. A written tenancy agreement under or in respect of which (a) an entrance fee has been paid or is payable in respect of a rental unit, and (b) the person first entitled to occupy the rental unit under the agreement is granted a right of occupancy for life or for a fixed term of not less than 50 years, if the agreement is entered into after the coming into force of this Act in respect of a rental unit in a residential complex in which no unit has been the subject of a life lease that was entered into before the coming into force of this Act, and includes any separate agreement under which the entrance fee has been paid or is payable. *The Life Leases Act*, S.M. 1998, c. 42, s. 1.

LIFE TENANT. One who beneficially holds property as long as she or he lives.

LIFETIME DISABILITY ASSISTANCE PAYMENTS. Under a disability savings plan of a beneficiary means disability assistance payments that are identified under the terms of the plan as lifetime disability assistance payments and that, after they begin to be paid, are payable at least annually until the earlier of the day on which the beneficiary dies and the day on which the plan is terminated. *Income Tax Act*, R.S.C. 1985, c. 1 (5th Supp.), s. 146.4.

LIFTING THE CORPORATE VEIL. To ignore the corporate entity to make directors liable or responsible for corporate wrongs or actions.

LIGHTING. *n.* The overall illumination of an area. The system used to provide illumination for an area.

LIGHTNING. *n.* 1. The discharge of electric energy between the earth and the atmosphere. 2. Is deemed to include other electrical currents. *Insurance acts.*

LIGHTNING RODS. The points, cables, groundings and other apparatus installed or to be installed to protect buildings and structures from damage by lightning. *Lightning Rods Act*, R.S.O. 1990, c. L.14, s. 1.

LIKELY RELEVANCE. In the context of a trial, "likely relevance" refers to a reasonable possibility that the information requested will be logically probative to an issue at trial or the competence of a witness to testify. *R. v. McNeil* (2006), 218 O.A.C. 1.

LIMIT. See REASONABLE ~S.

LIMITATION. *n.* 1. Of an interest or estate, the designation of the greatest period during which it will continue. 2. Includes any provision whereby property or any interest in property, or any right, power or authority over property, is disposed of, created or conferred. *Perpetuities Act*, R.S.O. 1990, c. P.9, s. 1. See EQUITABLE ~S; EXECUTORY ~; WORDS OF ~.

LIMITATION BY ANALOGY. A statutory limitation period applicable to a legal claim may be applied by analogy to an equitable claim if the equitable claim and the legal claim are sufficiently similar. The equitable doctrine of application by analogy cannot apply in the presence of an applicable statutory limitation period for the equitable claim. Limitation by analogy is most applicable in the case of concurrent actions in law and equity. Actions arising solely in equity will rarely be comparable to a common law analogue. Even if an analogy can be drawn, the limitation period by analogy does not necessarily apply. There is a discretion to determine this. *M.(K.) v. M. (H.)*, [1992] 3 S.C.R. 6.

LIMITATION OF ACTION. A fixed period of time within which proceedings must be begun or an action commenced. After the period of time has passed the action or proceedings cannot be commenced. The action then is said to be out of time or statute-barred. See EQUITABLE LIMITATIONS;

LIMITATION BY ANALOGY; ULTIMATE LIMITATION PERIOD; STATUTE OF ~S.

LIMITATION PROVISION. Includes a limitation period or notice provision that has the effect of a limitation period. *Limitations Act*, R.S.A. 2000, c. L-12, s. 1.

LIMITATIONS PERIOD. The time period specified by a statute and within which an action must be brought or a complaint filed. See ULTIMATE LIMITATION PERIOD.

LIMITED ACCESS DRUG. A drug that must not be sold (a) without a prescription, or (b) without the supervision or intervention of a pharmacist in accordance with the drug schedules and bylaws. *Pharmacy Operations and Drug Scheduling Act*, S.B.C. 2003, c. 77, s. 1.

LIMITED ADMINISTRATION. The temporary and special administration of a testator's or intestate's designated particular effects.

LIMITED CLASS RULE. Known as the ejusdem generis rule. In an enactment or document, where a class of things is followed by general wording, the general wording is restricted to things of the same type or genus as the listed items.

LIMITED COMMON PROPERTY. Common property designated for the exclusive use of the owners of one or more strata lots. *Strata Property Act*, S.B.C. 1998, c. 43, s. 1.

LIMITED CORPORATION. A corporation whose shareholders are not, as shareholders, liable for any liability, act or default of the corporation except under section 38(4), 146(7) or 227(4). *Business Corporations Act*, R.S.A. 2000, c. B-9, s. 15.1.

LIMITED-DIVIDEND HOUSING COMPANY. A company incorporated to construct, hold and manage a low-rental housing project, whose dividends payable are limited by the terms of its charter or instrument of incorporation to 5 per cent per annum or less. *National Housing Act*, R.S.C. 1985, c. N-11, s. 2.

LIMITED EXECUTOR. An executor with an appointment which is limited in time or place or subject-matter.

LIMITED LIABILITY COMPANY. A business entity that (a) was organized in a jurisdiction other than British Columbia, (b) is recognized as a legal entity in the jurisdiction in which it was organized, (c) is not a corporation, and (d) is not a partnership or a limited partnership. *Business Corporations Act*, S.B.C. 2002, c. 57, s. 1.

LIMITED LIABILITY PARTNERSHIP. A partner in a limited liability partnership is not liable, by means of indemnification, contribution, assessment or otherwise, for debts, obligations and liabilities of the partnership or any partner arising from negligent acts or wrongful acts or omissions that another partner or an employee, agent or representative of the partnership commits in the course of the partnership business while the partnership is a limited liability partnership. A partner is not liable for other debts incurred while the partnership is a limited liability one. This does not affect the liability of a partner in a limited liability partnership for the partner's own negligence or the negligence of a person under the partner's direct supervision or control or acts of omissions involving crime or fraud. A limited liability partnership may carry on business in Ontario only for the purpose of practising a profession governed by an Act and only if, (a) that Act expressly permits a limited liability partnership to practise the profession; (b) the governing body of the profession requires the partnership to maintain a minimum amount of liability insurance; and (c) the partnership complies with section 44.3 if it is not an extra-provincial limited liability partnership or section 44.4 if it is an extra-provincial limited liability partnership. *Partnerships Act*, R.S.O. 1990, c. P-5, s. 10 and 44.2, part.

LIMITED OWNER. A tenant for life, by the curtesy or in tail, or any person who does not have a fee simple absolutely.

LIMITED PARTNERSHIP. Partnership in which the liability of some partners is limited to their capital contribution and in which these limited partners do not exercise management functions with respect to the business of the partnership. *Limited Partnership acts*. See PARTNERSHIP.

LINE. *n.* 1. An ordered series of relatives. 2. A boundary. See BASE~; BOUNDARY ~; BRIGHT ~; CREDIT ~; GUIDE~; LOT ~; PICKET ~; PIPE~; POVERTY ~; PROOF ~.

LINEAGE. *n.* A family, progeny or race in either ascending or descending order.

LINEAL DESCENT. The proper bequest of an estate from an ancestor to an heir.

LINEAR PROPERTY. Gas pipelines are both "linear property" and "improvements" for purposes of municipal taxation under the MGA [Municipal Government Act, 1994, S.A. 1994, c. M-26.1]. As such, they are assessable for tax purposes. *Alliance Pipeline Ltd. v. Alberta (Minister of Municipal Affairs)*, 2006 ABCA 9.

LINE-UP. *n.* The presentation of a group of persons including a suspect for identification by a witness.

LINGUISTIC COMPETENCE. See PRESUMPTION OF ~.

LIQUID. See COMBUSTIBLE ~; GAS ~S.

LIQUID ASSETS. Cash or property which can be easily realized.

LIQUIDATE. *v.* To change assets into cash.

LIQUIDATED. *adj.* Ascertained, fixed. See UN~.

LIQUIDATED DAMAGES. 1. "The essence of liquidated damages is a genuine covenanted pre-estimate of damage ..." *Canadian General Electric Co. v. Canadian Rubber Co.* (1915), 27 D.L.R. 294 at 295, 52 S.C.R. 349, Fitzpatrick C.J. 2. In Dunlop Pneumatic Tyre Co. v. New Garage & Motor Co., [1915] A.C. 79, Lord Dunedin is quoted at 86 as follows: The essence of a penalty is a payment of money stipulated as in terrorem of the offending party; the essence of liquidated damages is a genuine covenanted pre-estimate of damage. More recently, in H.F. Clarke Ltd. v. Thermidaire Corp. (1974), 54 D.L.R. (3d) 385, Chief Justice Laskin suggested at p. 397 that a sum would be held to be a penalty if it is "extravagant and unconscionable in amount in comparison with the greatest loss that could conceivably be proved to have followed from the breach." An emphasis on the need to show oppression is apparent. *32262 B.C. Ltd. v. See-Rite Optical Ltd.*, 1998 CarswellAlta 239, 216 A.R. 33, 175 W.A.C. 33, 60 Alta. L.R. (3d) 223, [1998] 9 W.W.R. 442, 39 B.L.R (2d) 102, Hunt J.A.

LIQUIDATED DEMAND. 1. "[A demand] ... the amount of which had been ascertained or settled by agreement of the parties... ." *Logistique & Transport Internationaux Ltée v. Armada Lines Ltd.* (1991), 50 F.T.R. 21 at 23, Dubé J. 2. The operative test as to what constitutes a liquidated demand is expressed in Standard Oil Co. of B.C. Ltd. v. Wood (1964), 47 W.W.R. 494 at p. 497 (B.C. Co Ct.): A liquidated demand in the nature of a debt, i.e., a specific sum of money due and payable under or by virtue of a contract. Its amount must either be already ascertained or capable of being ascertained as a mere matter of arithmetic. If the ascertainment of a sum of money, even though it be specified or named as a definite figure, requires investigation, beyond mere calculation, then the sum is not a 'debt or liquidated demand,' but constitutes 'damages.' This claim can otherwise be a liquidated demand only if it is a "specific sum" which is either "already ascertained or capable of being ascertained as a mere matter of arithmetic". *Busnex Business Exchange Ltd. v. Canadian Medical Legacy Corp.*, 1999 CarswellBC 218, 119 B.C.A.C. 78, 194 W.A.C. 78.

LIQUIDATING TRADE. Effecting settlement of a commodity futures contract, (a) in relation to a long position, by assuming an offsetting short position in relation to a contract entered into on the same commodity futures exchange for a like quantity and quality, grade or size of the same commodity deliverable during the same designated future month, (b) in relation to a short position, by assuming an offsetting long position in relation to a contract entered into on the same commodity futures exchange for a like quantity and quality, grade or size of the same commodity deliverable during the same designated future month. *Commodity Futures Act*, R.S.O. 1990, c. C.20, s. 1.

LIQUIDATION. *n.* "... [A] winding up of the affairs of the company by getting in all its assets and distributing the proceeds to those entitled... ." *Linder v. Rutland Moving & Storage Ltd.*, [1991] 4 W.W.R. 355 at 362, 54 B.C.L.R. (2d) 98, 78 D.L.R. (4th) 755, [1991] 1 C.T.C. 517 (C.A.), the court per Hollinrake J.A.

LIQUIDATOR. *n.* 1. "... [A] person appointed to carry out the winding up of a company whose duty is to get in and realize the property of the company, to pay its debts and to distribute the surplus (if any) among the shareholders." *Minister of National Rev-* *enue v. Parsons* (1983), 4 Admin. L.R. 64 at 79, [1983] C.T.C. 321, 83 D.T.C. 5329 (Fed. T.D.), Cattanach J. 2. On his appointment, shall take into his custody or under his control all the property, effects and choses in action to which the company is or appears to be entitled, and shall perform such duties with reference to winding-up the business of the company as are imposed by the court or by this Act. A court may appoint, at any time when found advisable, one or more inspectors, whose duty it is to assist and advise a liquidator in the liquidation of a company. *Winding-up and Restructuring Act*, R.S.C. 1985, c. W-11.

LIQUID CAPITAL. The amount by which active assets exceed the sum of total liabilities.

LIQUOR. *n.* 1. " ... [A]lcoholic spiritous liquids if distilled or fermented, ... peculiarly applicable to distilled drink as distinguished from a fermented beverage; ..." *R. v. Foxton* (1920), 48 O.L.R. 207 at 208, 34 C.C.C. 9 (H.C.), Middleton J. 2. (a) fermented, spirituous and malt liquors, (b) combinations of liquors, and (c) drinks and drinkable liquids that are intoxicating, and includes beer, or a substance that, by being dissolved or diluted, is capable of being made a drinkable liquid that is intoxicating and which substance is declared by order of the Lieutenant Governor in Council to be liquor. *Liquor Distribution Act*, R.S.B.C. 1996, c. 268, s. 1.

LIQUOR AUTHORITY. A government board, commission or agency that is authorized by the laws of a province to sell intoxicating liquor. *Excise Act, 2001*, S.C. 2002, c. 22, s. 2.

LIS. *n.* [L.] An action or suit; a controversy or dispute.

LIS ALIBI PENDENS. [L. a suit pending somewhere else] 1. A plea that an action in one forum should be postponed until litigation begun elsewhere is concluded. C.R.B. Dunlop, *Creditor-Debtor Law in Canada* (Toronto: Carswell, 1981) at 484. 2. "... [U]sed to describe a situation in which the defendant may have instituted his own action against the plaintiffs in a foreign jurisdiction ... the applicant must establish that the foreign jurisdiction is the more appropriate natural forum to try the actions in the sense that the foreign jurisdiction has the most real and substantial connection with the lawsuit." *Galatco Redlaw Castings Corp. v. Brunswick Industrial Supply Co.* (1989), 69 O.R. (2d) 478 at 482, 36 C.P.C. (2d) 225 (H.C.), Gray J.

LIS MOTA. [L.] Anticipated or existing litigation.

LIS PENDENS. [L. a pending suit] To register a lis pendens is to give intending mortgagees or purchasers notice of the litigation. Gives notice that the pending litigation affects an interest in the land against which the lis pendens is registered. See CERTIFICATE OF ~.

LIST. *n.* 1. A calendar of cases to be heard in a particular court on a particular day or during a particular session. 2. A list of persons made for a particular purpose such as voting or employment. See BLACK ~; CHECK~; INGREDIENT DISCLOSURE ~; LAW ~; ~ OF ELECTORS; VOTERS ~.

L

LISTED. *adj.* 1. Offered for sale. 2. On a specified list. 3. Listed on the list of Wildlife Species at Risk. *Species at Risk Act*, S.C. 2002, c. 29, s. 2.

LISTED STOCK. A security admitted for trading on a stock exchange.

LISTING. *n.* An agreement between an agent or broker and a vendor for the agent or broker to offer the vendor's property for sale upon terms agreed. See EXCLUSIVE ~; MULTIPLE ~; OPEN ~.

LISTING AGREEMENT. An agreement between an agent or broker and a vendor for the agent or broker to offer the vendor's property for sale upon terms agreed. During the term of the agreement, the vendor is required to pay the agent or broker the commission for any sale or transfer of the property.

LIST OF ELECTORS. The list showing the surname, given names, civic address and mailing address of every elector in a polling division and the identifier that is assigned to the elector by the Chief Electoral Officer. *Canada Elections Act*, S.C. 2000, c. 9, s. 2.

LITERAL PROOF. Evidence in writing.

LITERARY AGENT. A person who acts on behalf of an author to place a manuscript for publication and to negotiate the terms of the publishing contract.

LITERARY WORK. 1. Includes tables, computer programs, and compilations of literary works. *Copyright Act*, R.S.C. 1985, c.C-42, s. 2. 2. The computer programme in its source code form (i.e., as written by the programmer in a programming language readable by other people) met the test set out in the jurisprudence regarding the meaning of "literary work". The computer programme in such form was an expression of thought in an original form. A literary work need not be "literature". If the idea expressed by the computer programme was capable of various modes of expression, then the programme was copyrightable. *International Business Machines Corp. v. Ordinateurs Spirales Inc./Spirales Computers Inc.*, 1984 CarswellNat 15, 27 B.L.R. 190, 80 C.P.R. (2d) 187, 2 C.I.P.R. 56, 12 D.L.R. (4th) 351 (T.D.), Reed J.

LITERATURE. *n.* The creation and the translation of original literary works such as novels, stories, short stories, dramatic works, poetry, essays or any other written works of the same nature. *An Act respecting the professional status of artists in the visual arts, arts and crafts and literature, and their contracts with promoters*, R.S.Q., c. S-32.01, s. 2.

LITERATURE FOR ILLICIT DRUG USE. Any printed matter or video describing or depicting, and designed primarily or intended under the circumstances to promote, encourage or advocate, the production, preparation or consumption of illicit drugs. *Criminal Code*, R.S.C. 1985, c. C-46, s. 462.1.

LITIGANT. *n.* 1. A person who engages in a lawsuit. 2. Refers to a lawyer, a barrister, whose main work is representing clients in proceedings in the courts or before tribunals.

LITIGATION. *n.* 1. A lawsuit and all the related proceedings. 2. May refer to any proceeding before a court or tribunal. See CIVIL ~.

LITIGATION ADMINISTRATOR. An administrator appointed for the purposes of conducting litigation on behalf of an estate of a deceased person. Formerly known as an administrator ad litem.

LITIGATION GUARDIAN. A person who acts on behalf of a child or person incapable of acting on their own behalf during the course of litigation. Known as a next friend or guardian ad litem in some jurisdictions and in some circumstances.

LITIGATION PRIVILEGE. Attaches to correspondence and other material prepared in anticipation of litigation. It provides the right to claim privilege over these documents, that is to refuse to produce the documents during proceedings.

LITIGATION REPRESENTATIVE. A person who is appointed by the court to represent, in an action or other legal proceeding, the estate of a deceased party for whom no other legal personal representative exists. *Public Guardian and Trustee Act*, R.S.B.C. 1996 (Supp.), c. 383, s. 6.1.

LITIGIOUS. *adj.* 1. Said of a person who frequently commences law suits. 2. Said of a matter which is subject to an action or other proceeding.

LIVE BIRTH. 1. The complete expulsion or extraction from the mother, irrespective of the duration of the pregnancy, of a product of conception in which, after the expulsion or extraction, there is breathing, beating of the heart, pulsation of the umbilical cord or unmistakable movement of voluntary muscle, whether or not the umbilical cord is cut or the placenta is attached. *The Vital Statistics Act, 2009*, S.S. 2009, c. V-7.21, s. 2. 2. The complete expulsion or extraction from the mother, irrespective of the duration of the pregnancy, of a product of conception in which, after the expulsion or extraction, there is breathing, beating of the heart, pulsation of the umbilical cord or unmistakable movement of voluntary muscle, whether or not the umbilical cord is cut or the placenta is attached. *The Vital Statistics Act, 2007*, S.S. 2007, c. V-7.2, s. 2.

LIVE-IN CAREGIVER. An individual who, (a) provides child care, senior home support care or care of the disabled in a private household where the person being cared for resides, and (b) resides in that household. *Employment Protection for Foreign Nationals Act (Live-in Caregivers and Others), 2009*, S.O. 2009, c. 32, s. 1.

LIVELIHOOD. *n.* 1. In our view, taking into account the purposes of s. 6, any attempt by residents of an origin province to create wealth, whether by production, marketing, or performance in a destination province constitutes "the gaining of a livelihood *in* any province" (emphasis added) and satisfies the requirement of mobility implied by the title of the section. *Canadian Egg Marketing Agency v. Richardson*, 1998 CarswellNWT 118, 231 N.R. 201, 166 D.L.R. (4th) 1, 57 C.R.R. (2d) 1, 223 A.R. 201, 183 W.A.C. 201, [1998] 3 S.C.R. 157, Bastarache and Iacobucci JJ. 2. Means of support or subsistence.

LIVERY. *n.* 1. Delivery; giving possession or seisin. 2. A motor vehicle with the capacity to carry several people which operates on a regular schedule.

LIVESTOCK SECURITY INTEREST. A security interest registered under the Personal Property Security Act or under the Bank Act (Canada), and (i) taken or reserved in livestock to secure payment of all or part of the purchase price of the livestock, (ii) taken in livestock by a person who gave value for the purpose of enabling the owner of the livestock to acquire rights in the livestock, to the extent that the value was applied to acquire rights in the livestock, or (iii) taken in livestock and other property by a person who gave value for the purpose of enabling the owner of the livestock to acquire rights in the livestock, to the extent that the value was applied to acquire rights in the livestock. *Livestock Identification and Commerce Act*, S.A. 2006, c. L-16.2, s. 1.

LIVING. See COST OF ~.

LIVING TREE APPROACH. Approach to constitutional interpretation was developed in *Edwards v. Canada (Attorney General)*. "The British North America Act planted in Canada a living tree capable of growth and expansion within its natural limits". Edwards v. A.G. Can., [1930] A.C. 124 (P.C.), per Lord Sankey at p. 136. This approach eschews narrow technical interpretation. The past plays a critical but not exclusive role in determining interpretation but the approach must be capable of growth to meet the future.

L.J. *abbr.* 1. Law Journal Reports. 2. Lord Justice of Appeal.

LL.B. *abbr.* Bachelor of Laws.

LL.D. *abbr.* Doctor of Laws.

L. LIB. *abbr.* Law Librarian.

LL.M. *abbr.* Master of Laws.

LLP. *var.* **L.L.P.** *abbr.* Limited liability partnership.

L.N. *abbr.* Legal News, 1878-1897?.

LOAD. See OVER~.

LOAN. *n.* 1. Anything given or lent to someone on condition that it be repayed or returned. 2. "... [T]he lending of money with the expectation that the money will be repaid... ." *Canada Deposit Insurance Corp. v. Canadian Commercial Bank* (1990), 73 Alta. L.R. (2d) 230 at 244, [1990] 4 W.W.R. 445, 105 A.R. 368 (Q.B.), Wachowich J. 3. The term 'debt' is a narrower term and means a specific kind of obligation for a liquidated or certain sum incurred pursuant to an agreement. The term 'loan' is even narrower and means a specific type of debt. *Royal Trust Co. v. H.A. Roberts Group Ltd.*, 1995 CarswellSask 7, 31 C.B.R. (3d) 207, [1995] 4 W.W.R. 305, 17 B.L.R. (2d) 263, 44 R.P.R. (2d) 255, 129 Sask. R. 161 (Q.B.), Baynton J. See COMPLETION ~; CONSOLIDATED ~; CONSTRUCTION ~; HOUSING ~; MEMBER ~; PAYDAY ~; SYNDICATED ~

LOAN AGREEMENT. A document or memorandum in writing (a) evidencing a loan, (b) made or given as security for a loan, or (c) made or given as security for a past indebtedness. *Consumer Protection Act*, R.S.N.W.T. 1988, c. C-17, s. 1

LOAN AMOUNT. The amount lent. The principal amount of a loan.

LOAN BROKER. A person who: (i) carries on the business of providing services or products to a consumer to assist the consumer in obtaining or attempting to obtain a loan of money from another person, whether or not the person actually obtains the loan for the consumer; (ii) holds himself, herself or itself out to be in the business described in subclause (i); or (iii) requests, requires or accepts any direct or indirect payment or any security for a payment from a consumer respecting a loan of money. *The Trust and Loan Corporations Act, 1997*, S.S. 1997, c. T-22.2, s. 44.

LOAN COMMITMENT. A document setting out the undertaking to loan money and the conditions under which a lender agrees to loan money to a borrower.

LOBBY. *v.* To communicate with a public-office holder in an attempt to influence (i) the development of any legislative proposal by the Government of the Province or by a member of the House of Assembly, (ii) the introduction of any bill or resolution in the House of Assembly or the passage, defeat or amendment of any bill or resolution that is before the House of Assembly, (iii) the making or amendment of any regulation as defined in the Regulations Act, (iv) the development or amendment of any policy or program of the Government of the Province or the termination of any program of the Government of the Province, (v) a decision by the Executive Council to transfer from the Crown for consideration all or part of, or any interest in or asset of, any business, enterprise or institution that provides goods or services to the Crown or to the public, (vi) a decision by the Executive Council, a committee of the Executive Council or a minister of the Crown to have the private sector instead of the Crown provide goods or services to the Crown, or (vii) the awarding of any grant, contribution or other financial benefit by or on behalf of the Crown, and, in relation to a consultant lobbyist referred to in Section 5, (viii) to communicate with a public-office holder in an attempt to influence the awarding of any contract by or on behalf of the Crown, or (ix) to arrange a meeting between a public-office holder and any other person. *Lobbyists' Registration Act*, S.N.S. 2001, c. 34, s. 2.

LOBBYING. See COMMISSIONER OF ~.

LOBBYIST. *n.* 1. A person engaged to represent the interests of a certain group in dealings with the government. 2. A consultant lobbyist or an in-house lobbyist. *Lobbyists Registration Act*; S.B.C. 2001, c. 42, s. 1. See CONSULTANT ~; ENTERPRISE ~; IN-HOUSE ~; ORGANIZATION ~.

LOC. *abbr.* Local.

LOCAL ACT. An act which deals with a matter relating to a particular area, usually a municipality. See LOCAL STATUTE.

LOCAL AUTHORITY. 1. Any public organization created by an act of a legislature and exercising jurisdiction or powers of a local nature. 2. The council of a municipality.

LOCAL BOARD. A municipal service board, transportation commission, public library board, board of health, police services board, planning board, or any other board, commission, committee, body or local authority established or exercising any power under any Act with respect to the affairs or purposes of one or more municipalities, excluding a school board and a conservation authority. *Municipal Act, 2001*, S.O. 2001, c. 25, s. 1.

LOCAL BODY. (i) A board of school trustees established pursuant to the Education Act, (ii) a school board as defined by the Education Act, (iii) a regional library board to which the Libraries Act applies, (iv) the Metropolitan Authority continued by the Metropolitan Authority Act, (v) a service commission as defined by the Municipal Affairs Act, (vi) a district planning commission established pursuant to or within the meaning of the Planning Act, (vii) a regional transit authority incorporated pursuant to the Regional Transit Authority Act, (viii) fire protection commissioners incorporated pursuant to the Rural Fire District Act or to whom the Rural Fire District Act applies, (ix) village commissioners incorporated pursuant to the Village Service Act or to whom the Village Service Act applies. *Municipal Fiscal Year Act*, S.N.S. 1990, c. 19, s. 2.

LOCAL CARRIER. A railway company that moves traffic to or from an interchange on a continuous route from the point of origin or to the point of destination that is served exclusively by the railway company. *Canada Transportation Act*, S.C. 1996, c. 10, s. 111.

LOCAL COOPERATIVE CREDIT SOCIETY. A cooperative credit society incorporated by or under an Act of the legislature of a province (a) whose members consist substantially of individuals, and (b) whose principal purpose is to receive deposits from, and make loans to, its members. *Canadian Payments Association Act*, R.S.C. 1985, c. C-21, s. 2.

LOCAL CTS. & MUN. GAZ. *abbr.* Local Courts' and Municipal Gazette, 1865-1872.

LOCAL GOVERNMENT. 1. A system of government by which administration of local affairs is entrusted to local authority. 2. A municipal government at any level. 3. (a) In relation to land within a municipality, the municipal council, (b) in relation to land within an electoral area but not within a local trust area, the board of the regional district, and (c) in relation to land within a local trust area under the Islands Trust Act, the local trust committee or the executive committee acting as a local trust committee for that area. *Agricultural Land Commission Act*, S.B.C. 2002, c. 36, s. 1.

LOCAL GOVERNMENT BODY. (a) A municipality, (b) a board of trustees of a school division or school district, (c) a local government district, (d) a council of a community under The Northern Affairs Act, or (e) any unincorporated board, commission or body created by a municipality for the purposes of carrying out any of the duties or functions of a municipality on behalf of the municipality. *The Health and Post-Secondary Education Tax Levy Act*, R.S.M. 1987, c. H24, s. 1.

LOCAL IMPROVEMENT. A project (a) that the council considers to be of greater benefit to an area

of the municipality than to the whole municipality, and (b) that is to be paid for in whole or in part by a tax imposed under this Division. *Municipal Government Act*, R.S.A. 2000, c. M-26, s. 391.

LOCAL STATUTE. A statute which deals with a matter relating to a particular area, usually a municipality. See LOCAL ACT.

LOCATION. See VOTING ~.

LOC. CIT. *abbr.* [L.] Loco citato. At the quoted passage.

LOC. CT. GAZ. *abbr.* Local Courts and Municipal Gazette (Ontario), 1865-1872.

LOCKED-IN REGISTERED RETIREMENT SAVINGS PLAN. A registered retirement savings plan, as defined in subsection 146(1) of the Income Tax Act, that meets the requirements set out in section 20. *Pension Benefits Standards Act, 1985*, R.S.C. 1985, c. 32 (2nd Supp.), *Pension Benefits Standards Regulations, 1985*, SOR/87-19, s. 2(1).

LOCK IN PRINCIPLE. The facts relevant to determining whether a visa applicant meets the selection criteria are "locked in" at the date of the visa application; subsequent changes to those facts do not disqualify an applicant from being issued a visa. The "lock in" principle is designed to protect visa applicants from the vagaries of the application process. In particular, the fate of an application should not depend on the fortuitous length of time between its receipt and determination, a period which varies from time to time and from place to place, and is outside applicants' control. *Hamid v. Canada (Minister of Citizenship and Immigration)*, 2006 FCA 217.

LOCK-OUT. *n.* Includes the closing of a place of employment, a suspension of work, a substantial alteration in the normal pattern of operation in a place of employment, or a refusal by an employer to continue to employ a number of his employees, done with a view to compel or induce his employees, or to aid another employer to compel or induce his employees, to refrain from exercising any rights or privileges under this Act or to agree to provisions or changes in provisions respecting terms or conditions of employment or the rights, privileges or duties of the employer, the employers' organization, the trade union, the council of trade unions or the employees. *Industrial Relations Act*, R.S.N.B. 1973, c. I-4, s. 1.

LOCK-UP. *n.* A jail. Usually refers to holding cells for brief stays by prisoners.

LOCO CITATO. [L.] At the quoted passage.

LOCO PARENTIS. See IN LOCO PARENTIS.

LOCUM TENENS. [L.] A person who lawfully executes another person's office, a deputy.

LOCUS. [L.] Place.

LOCUS IN QUO. [L. a place in which] A place where.

LOCUS SIGILLI. [L. the place of the seal] The place at the bottom of a document which requires a seal.

LOCUS STANDI. [L. a place to stand] The right to be heard or appear during a proceeding.

LODGER. *n.* A person who occupies rooms in a house.

LODGING HOUSE. Any house or other building or portion of it in which persons are lodged for hire, but does not include a hotel, hospital, long-term care home, home for the young or institution if it is licensed, approved or supervised under any other Act. *Municipal Act, 2001,* S.O. 2001, c. 25, s. 11.1.

LOGICALLY PROBATIVE. Tending to make the existence of a fact in issue more or less probable.

LOIR. *abbr.* Lost opportunity for an interdependent relationship. Head of pecuniary loss in personal injury law.

LOITER. *v.* 1. "... '[H]anging around' ..." *R. v. Andsten* (1960), 32 W.W.R. 329 at 331, 33 C.R. 213 (B.C. C.A.), the court per Davey J.A. 2. In s. 179(1)(b) [of the Criminal Code, R.S.C. 1985, c. C-46] should be given its ordinary meaning, namely to stand idly around, hang around, linger, tarry, saunter, delay, dawdle, etc. This is consistent with the meaning given to the word as used elsewhere in the Code, and with the context and purpose of s. 179(1)(b). *R. v. Heywood,* 1994 CarswellBC 592, 34 C.R. (4th) 133, 174 N.R. 81, 50 B.C.A.C. 161, 82 W.A.C. 161, [1994] 3 S.C.R. 761, 94 C.C.C. (3d) 481, 24 C.R.R. (2d) 189, 120 D.L.R. (4th) 348, Cory J.

LOITERER. *n.* "... [A]n individual who is wandering about, apparently without precise destination, who does not have, in his manner of moving, a purpose or reason to do so other than to pass the time, who is not looking for anything identifiable and who often is merely motivated by the whim of the moment... ." *R. v. Cloutier* (1991), 66 C.C.C. (3d) 149 at 154, 51 Q.A.C. 143, the court per Chevalier J.A.

L.O.M.J. *abbr.* Law Office Management Journal.

LONG POSITION. Where used in relation to a commodity futures contract, means to be under an obligation to take delivery. *Commodity Futures Act,* R.S.O. 1990, c. C.20, s. 1.

LONG TAIL CLAIM. In Canada, Cavell primarily reinsured insurers writing casualty policies covering claims such as those arising from pollution, asbestos, sexual abuse, tobacco and tainted blood. These types of claims are sometimes referred to as "long tail" claims because they may come to light many years after the policies are written, and may take many more years for coverage and quantum issues to be resolved. *Cavell Insurance Co., Re* (2006), 80 O.R. (3d) 500 (C.A.).

LONG-TERM DISABILITY BENEFIT PLAN. A disability benefit plan under which the payments or benefits to an employee are payable for a period of not less than 52 weeks or until recovery, retirement or death, whichever period is shorter. *Employment Standards Act, 2000,* S.O. 2000, c. 41, *Benefit Plans,* O. Reg. 286/01, s. 1.

LONG TERM DISABILITY PLAN. Insurance to provide benefits to employees who are unable to work

because of illness or injury. The pre-condition to receipt of benefits may be total disability.

LONG TERM LEASE. 1. In respect of land, means a lease, licence or similar arrangement under which continuous possession of the land is provided for a period of at least twenty years or a lease, licence or similar arrangement that contains an option to purchase the land. *Excise Tax Act,* R.S.C. 1985, c. E-15, s. 254.1. 2. A lease to the same person for a set term of 3 years or more. *Strata Property Act,* S.B.C. 1998, c. 43, s. 148.

LONG-TERM LIABILITY. A debt which is due over a long period of time, over a year.

LONG TERM OFFENDER. The court may, on application made following the filing of an assessment report, find an offender to be a long-term offender if it is satisfied that (a) it would be appropriate to impose a sentence of imprisonment of two years or more for the offence for which the offender has been convicted; (b) there is a substantial risk that the offender will reoffend; and (c) there is a reasonable possibility of eventual control of the risk in the community. *Criminal Code,* R.S.C. 1985, c. C-46, s. 753.1.

LONG-TERM SUPERVISION. Long-term supervision ordered under provisions of the Criminal Code, dealing with long term offenders. The offender is subject to supervision after completing any sentence. *Corrections and Conditional Release Act,* S.C. 1992, c. 20, s. 2.

LONG TITLE. A description which sets out the purposes of a bill or statute in general terms. A. Fraser, W.A. Dawson & J. Holtby, eds., *Beauchesne's Rules and Forms of the House of Commons of Canada,* 6th ed. (Toronto: Carswell, 1989) at 192. Contrast with the short title which is the name by which the statute is known and cited.

LONG VACATION. The months July and August when the courts traditionally did not sit. D. Sgayias *et al., Federal Court Practice 1988* (Toronto: Carswell, 1987) at 253.

LORD. *n.* 1. Title given to a Supreme Court Judge. 2. Traditionally, in relation to real property, the person whose land another holds as tenant. See HOUSE OF ~S; LAND~; LAW ~S; MESNE ~.

LORD MANSFIELD'S RULE. The common law rule of jury secrecy, which prohibits the court from receiving evidence of jury deliberations for the purpose of impeaching a verdict, similarly reflects a desire to preserve the secrecy of the jury deliberation process and to shield the jury from outside influences. The common law rule, also referred to as Lord Mansfield's rule, can be traced back to the case of Vaise v. Delaval (1785), 1 Term Rep. 11, 99 E.R. 944 (Eng. K.B.), in which Lord Mansfield ruled that the court could not receive affidavits from jurors attesting to their own misconduct in reaching a verdict by lot. The rule was explicitly adopted by this Court in Danis v. Saumure, [1956] S.C.R. 403 (S.C.C.), in the context of a civil jury trial. *R. v. Pan,* 2001 CarswellOnt 2261, 2001 SCC 42, 155 C.C.C. (3d) 97, 200 D.L.R. (4th) 577, 43 C.R. (5th) 203, 147 O.A.C. 1, 85 C.R.R.

L

(2d) 1, 270 N.R. 317, Arbour J. for the court. See JURY SECRECY.

LOSS. *n.* 1. Includes the happening of an event or contingency by reason of which a person becomes entitled to a payment under a contract of insurance of money other than a refund of unearned premiums. *Insurance acts.* 2. "... [T]he inverse of profit ..." *Mountain Park Coals Ltd. v. Minister of National Revenue*, [1952] Ex. C.R. 560 at 568, [1952] C.T.C. 392, [1952] D.T.C. 1221, Thorson P. 3. "Injury" refers to the initial physical or mental impairment of the plaintiff's person as a result of the sexual assault, while "loss" refers to the pecuniary or non-pecuniary consequences of that impairment. *Blackwater v. Plint*, 2001 CarswellBC 1468, 2001 BCSC 997, 93 B.C.L.R. (3d) 228 (S.C.), Brenner C.J.S.C. See CAPITAL GAIN OR ~; CAUSING ~ BY UNLAWFUL MEANS; ECONOMIC ~; PARTIAL ~; PECUNIARY ~; TOTAL ~.

LOSS OF AMENITIES. A loss for which the victim may be compensated by damages. In expropriation, refers to substantially diminished enjoyment.

LOSS OF CHANCE. "... [T]he damage which results from the loss of an opportunity either to realize a benefit or to avoid an injury... . the damage is future or hypothetical and clearly not certain. It is distinguished by the fact that it is contingent, or dependent on an element of chance which must be evaluated in terms of probabilities. This contingent or probabilistic aspect provides the potential for ascertainment of damages in the present... ." *Laferrière v. Lawson* (1991), 6 C.C.L.T. (2d) 119 at 196, 123 N.R. 325, 38 Q.A.C. 161, [1991] R.R.A. 320, [1991] 1 S.C.R. 541, 78 D.L.R. (4th) 609, Gonthier J. (Lamer, L'Heureux-Dubé, Sopinka, Cory and McLachlin JJ. concurring).

LOSS OF EXPECTATION OF LIFE. Shortening of the length of the victim's life. K.D. Cooper-Stephenson & I.B. Saunders, *Personal Injury Damages in Canada* (Toronto: Carswell, 1981) at 358. A loss for which the victim may be compensated by damages.

LOSS OF GUIDANCE. A loss for which the victim may be compensated by damages. Refers to loss of a parent or person standing in the place of a parent.

LOSS OF SERVICES. A claim by a husband against a person who injured his wife wrongfully or a claim by a parent for loss occasioned by the wrongful injury of his or her child or a claim by a master in respect of an injury to her or his servant. J.G. Fleming, *The Law of Torts*, 8th ed. (Sydney: Law Book, 1992) at 658, 660, 684.

LOST. *adj.* "... [T]he location of the person or thing is unknown or uncertain. In other usages, 'lost' may mean mislaid and not found after reasonably diligent search." *Gagnon v. Northwest Territories (Registrar of Vehicles)*, [1983] N.W.T.R. 289 at 292 (C.A.), the court per Laycraft J.A.

LOST OPPORTUNITY FOR AN INTERDEPENDENT RELATIONSHIP. Head of pecuniary loss in personal injury law.

LOST OR NOT LOST INSURANCE. Normally, in order to recover under a contract for a loss, the insured must have an insurable interest in the subject-matter insured at the time of the loss, but need not have such an interest when the contract is concluded. However, where the subject-matter is insured "lost or not lost" the insured may recover in respect of an insurable interest in the subject-matter acquired after a loss unless, at the time the contract was concluded, the insured was aware of the loss and the insurer was not. *Marine Insurance Act*, S.C. 1993, c. 22, s. 7.

LOT. *n.* 1. (i) A quarter section, (ii) a river lot shown on an official plan, as defined in the Surveys Act, that is filed or lodged in a land titles office, (iii) a settlement lot shown on an official plan, as defined in the Surveys Act, that is filed or lodged in a land titles office, (iv) a part of a parcel of land described in a certificate of title if the boundaries of the part are described in the certificate of title other than by reference to a legal subdivision, or (v) a part of a parcel of land described in a certificate of title if the boundaries of the part are described in a certificate of title by reference to a plan of subdivision. *Municipal Government Act*, R.S.A. 2000, c. M-26, s. 616. 2. The method of determining the successful candidate by placing the names of the candidates on equal size pieces of paper placed in a box and one name being drawn by a person chosen by the clerk. *Municipal Elections Act*, R.S.N.S. 1989, c. 300, s. 138. 3. A space that is (a) in a place of interment, and (b) used or intended to be used for the interment of human remains or cremated remains under a right of interment and includes a grave, crypt, niche or plot. *Cremation, Interment and Funeral Services Act*, S.B.C. 2004, c. 35, s. 1. 4. An amount, of a thing, which is sold or traded. See BROKEN ~; IRREGULAR ~; REGULAR ~; STRATA ~; UNBROKEN ~.

LOT COVERAGE. The portion of the lot area covered by the ground floor area of all buildings and structures on a lot, and expressed as a percentage of the lot area. *Planning Act*, R.S.O. 1990, c. P.13, *Zoning Area*, O. Reg. 154/03, s. 1.

LOT FRONTAGE. (a) The horizontal distance between parallel side lot lines of a lot, or (b) the distance between not parallel side lot lines of a lot measured on a line parallel to and 7.5 metres distant from the front lot line. *Planning Act*, R.S.O. 1990, c. P.13, *Zoning Area*, O. Reg. 154/03, s. 1.

LOT LINE. The line dividing one parcel of land from another.

LOT NUMBER. Any combination of letters, figures, or both, by which a natural health product can be traced in manufacture and identified in distribution. *Food and Drugs Act*, R.S.C. 1985, c. F-27, *Natural Health Products Regulations*, SOR/2003-196, s. 1(1).

LOTTERY. *n.* A game of chance; a division and sharing of prizes by chance or lot. See VIDEO ~ TERMINAL.

LOW. CAN. R. *abbr.* Lower Canada Reports, 1851-1867.

LOWER CANADA. That part of Canada which heretofore constituted the Province of Lower Canada, and means now the province of Québec. *Interpretation Act*, R.S.Q., c. I-16, s. 61.

LOWER TIER MUNICIPALITY. A municipality that forms part of an upper-tier municipality for municipal purposes. *Municipal Act, 2001*, S.O. 2001, c. 25, s. 1.

LOWEST INTERMEDIATE BALANCE RULE. The "lowest intermediate balance rule" states that a claimant to a mixed fund cannot assert a proprietary interest in that fund in excess of the smallest balance in the fund during the interval between the original contribution and the time when a claim with respect to that contribution is being made against the fund. Descendant of the Rule in Clayton's case. Originally articulated by Sargant J. in James Roscoe (Bolton) Ltd. v. Winder, [1915] 1 Ch. 62 (Eng. Ch. Div.). *Law Society of Upper Canada v. Toronto Dominion Bank*, (1998) 42 O.R. (3d) 257 (C.A.).

LOW HEAT VALUE COAL. Sub-bituminous coal and any other coal with a heating value up to and including 27 000 kJ per kg. *Carbon Tax Act*, S.B.C. 2008, c. 40, Sched. 1, s. 1.

LOW-RENTAL HOUSING PROJECT. A housing project undertaken to provide decent, safe and sanitary housing accommodation, complying with standards approved by the Corporation, to be leased to families of low income or to such other persons as the Corporation, (*a*) in its discretion, in the case of a housing project owned by it, or (*b*) under agreement with the owner, in the case of a housing project not owned by it, designates, having regard to the existence of a condition of shortage, overcrowding or congestion of housing. *National Housing Act*, R.S.C. 1985, c. N-11, s. 2.

LOW-TIDE ELEVATION. A naturally formed area of land that is surrounded by and above water at low tide but submerged at high tide. *Oceans Act*, S.C. 1996, c. 31, s. 5.

LOYALTY. See DUTY OF ~.

L.Q. REV. *abbr.* Law Quarterly Review.

L.R. *abbr.* Law Reports.

L.R.B. *abbr.* Labour Relations Board.

L.R. 1 A. & E. *abbr.* Law Reports, Admiralty and Ecclesiastical Cases, 1865-1875.

L.R. 1 C.C.R. *abbr.* Law Reports, Crown Cases Reserved, 1865-1875.

L.R. 1 CH. *abbr.* Law Reports, Chancery Appeals, 1865-1875.

L.R. 1 C.P. *abbr.* Law Reports, Common Pleas, 1865-1875.

L.R. 1 EQ. *abbr.* Law Reports, Equity Cases, 1865-1875.

L.R. 1 EX. *abbr.* Law Reports, Exchequer, 1865-1875.

L.R. 1 H.L. *abbr.* Law Reports, House of Lords Cases, 1865-1875.

L.R. 1 P. & D. *abbr.* Law Reports, Probate and Divorce, 1865-1875.

L.R. 1 P.C. *abbr.* Law Reports, Privy Council Cases, 1865-1875.

L.R. 1 Q.B. *abbr.* Law Reports, Queen's Bench, 1865-1875.

L.R. 1 SC. & DIV. *abbr.* Law Reports, Scottish and Divorce.

L.R.P.C. *abbr.* Law Reports Privy Council Appeals.

L.S. *abbr.* [L.] Locus sigilli. The place for the seal.

LSAT. *abbr.* Law School Admission Test.

L. SOC. GAZ. *abbr.* Law Society Gazette (Law Society of Upper Canada).

L.S.U.C. *abbr.* Law Society of Upper Canada.

L.T. *abbr.* Law Times Reports.

LTO. *abbr.* Land Titles Office.

LUMBER. See SOFTWOOD ~ AGREEMENT.

LURING A CHILD. Using the internet to attract a child or children for the purposes of committing certain offences.

L.V.A.C. *abbr.* Land Value Appraisal Commission.

L

M

MACE. *n.* 1. The symbol of authority of the House of Commons or a legislature. 2. An agent used to control crowds. F.A. Jaffe, *A Guide to Pathological Evidence for Lawyers and Police Officers*, 4th ed. (Toronto: Carswell, 1999) at 240.

MACHINE. See PINBALL ~; SLOT ~.

MACHINE LANGUAGE. Since the computer only responds to machine language, a computer programme written in another language must be translated. The language in which the programme is written is called the source code and the language into which it is translated is called the object code. Object code in many instances, and in the jurisprudence, I notice, is used as synonymous with machine language and I will adopt that usage. *International Business Machines Corp. v. Ordinateurs Spirales Inc./Spirales Computers Inc.*, 27 B.L.R. 190, 80 C.P.R. (2d) 187, 2 C.I.P.R 56, 12 D.L.R. (4th) 351 (T.D.), Reed J.

MACHINERY. See BOILER AND ~ INSURANCE.

MACKENZIE GAS PROJECT. The project proposed by a consortium led by Imperial Oil Resources Ventures Limited that includes the development of the natural gas fields of Niglintgak, Taglu and Parsons Lake, and the construction and operation of (a) a gathering system related to those fields; (b) a natural gas liquids pipeline; (c) the natural gas pipeline that is the subject of the application GH-12004 made to the National Energy Board on October 7, 2004; and (d) facilities related to the fields, the gathering system or the pipelines. *Mackenzie Gas Project Impacts Act*, S.C. 2006, c. 4, s. 208, s. 2.

MACNAUGHTON'S CASE. See MCNAGH-TEN'S CASE.

MADE. *adj.* 1. [In relation to an order,] "... [R]efers to pronouncement, not entry: ..." *Levesque v. Levesque* (1992), 41 R.F.L. (3d) 96 at 98, 3 Alta. L.R. (3d) 193, 131 A.R. 106, 25 W.A.C. 106 (C.A.), Côté J.A. 2. "... [P]ronouncement [or] ... signed or entered in court ..." *Harvey v. Harvey* (1989), 23 R.F.L. (3d) 53 at 55, 60 Man. R. (2d) 302 (C.A.), Helper J.A. 3. Of an application, the date when the application is heard by the court. 4. Of a claim under an insurance policy, the time when the person asserting the claim brings it to the attention of or notifies the person against whom it is asserted. 5. Of an arbitral award, to have done everything necessary to perfect it.

MAG. *abbr.* Magistrate(s).

MAGAZINE. See CARTRIDGE ~.

MAGAZINES. *n.* Printed and bound publications in a magazine format (a) that are issued at regular intervals each year by professional bodies, trade or industrial organizations, commercial publishing firms or non-profit corporations, and (b) where at least 10% of the content, determined in accordance with the regulations and in accordance with section 72(2), is composed of technical, literary, editorial or pictorial content, other than advertising and promotional content, but does not include a prescribed type of publication. *Social Service Tax Act*, R.S.B.C. 1996, c. 431, s. 1.

MAG. CT. *abbr.* Magistrate's Court.

MAGISTER LITIS. [L.] The master of the action.

MAGISTRATE. *n.* A provincial judge authorized to accept informations to commence criminal proceedings and to hear and determine regulatory and lesser criminal offences.

MAGNA CARTA. A charter or collection of statutes based largely on Saxon common law granted by the British King John in 1215 to confirm certain liberties.

MAHR. *n.* In Islamic law, an obligatory gift or contribution made by the husband-to-be to his wife-to-be for her exclusive property.

MAIL. *v.* Refers to the deposit of the matter to which the context applies in the Canada Post Office at any place in Canada, postage prepaid, for transmission by post, and includes delivery *Interpretation Act*, R.S.B.C. 1996 c. 238, s. 29. See E-~; POST.

MAIL. *n.* Mailable matter from the time it is posted to the time it is delivered to the addressee thereof. *Canada Post Corporation Act*, R.S.C. 1985, c. C-10, s. 2. See BLACK~; E-~.

MAILABLE MATTER. Any message, information, funds or goods that may be transmitted by post. *Canada Post Corporation Act*, R.S.C. 1985, c. C-10, s. 2.

MAIL CONVEYANCE. Any physical, electronic, optical or other means used to transmit mail. *Canada Post Corporation Act*, R.S.C. 1985, c. C-10, s. 2.

M

MAINTAIN. *v.* 1. "[To provide] ... financial or other material support ..." *Desjarlais v. Macdonell Estate* (1988), 31 E.T.R. 18 at 24, [1988] 3 W.W.R. 534, 23 B.C.L.R. (2d) 195 (C.A.), Anderson J.A. (Esson and McLachlin JJ.A. concurring). 2. "... [M]ay mean either to bring or institute an action or proceeding or to continue or further prosecute an action already commenced... ." *Komnick System Sandstone Brick Machinery Co. v. B.C. Pressed Brick Co.* (1918), 56 S.C.R. 539 at 549, 41 D.L.R. 423, [1918] 2 W.W.R. 564, Anglin J. 3. "... [T]o keep in being, to keep up and to repair... ." *Red Lake (Township) v. Drawson*, [1964] 1 O.R. 324 at 328, 42 D.L.R. (2d) 121 (H.C.), Ferguson J.

MAINTENANCE. *n.* 1. "... [I]n the ordinary sense, mean[s] 'keep in repair'; ..." *Canadian Pacific Railway v. Grand Trunk Railway* (1914), 20 D.L.R. 56 at 63, 49 S.C.R. 525, 17 C.R.C. 300, Brodeur J. 2. Maintenance, support or alimony and includes (i) an amount payable periodically, whether annually or otherwise and whether for an indefinite or limited period or until the happening of a specified event, (ii) a lump sum, (iii) expenses in respect of prenatal care and the birth of a child, (iv) an amount payable under a Queen's Bench protection order under the Protection Against Family Violence Act, (v) a charge on property or otherwise as security for the payment of maintenance, or (vi) interest or the payment of legal fees or other expenses arising in relation to maintenance. *Maintenance Enforcement Act*, R.S.A. 2000, c. M-1, s. 1. 3. "The law of maintenance as I understand it upon the modern constructions, is confined to cases where a man improperly and for the purpose of stirring up litigation and strife, encourages others either to bring actions or to make defences which they have no right to make." *Findon (Finden) v. Parker* (1843), 152 E.R. 976 at 979 (U.K. Ex.), Lord Abinger C.B. See PRICE ~ AGREEMENT.

MAINTENANCE FEE. A patentee of a patent issued by the Patent Office under this Act after the coming into force of this section shall, to maintain the rights accorded by the patent, pay to the Commissioner such fees, in respect of such periods, as may be prescribed. *Patent Act*, R.S.C. 1985, c. P-4, s. 46.

MAINTENANCE ORDER. 1. An order or interim order of a court in Alberta, a Queen's Bench protection order under the Protection Against Family Violence Act or an order, other than a provisional order that has not been confirmed, registered under the Reciprocal Enforcement of Maintenance Orders Act or the Interjurisdictional Support Orders Act that has a provision requiring the payment of maintenance. *Maintenance Enforcement Act*, R.S.A. 2000, c. M-1, s. 1. 2. A provision for the payment of maintenance in an order or judgment that is enforceable in British Columbia and includes (a) an interim order made under Part 8 of the Family Relations Act, (b) an order made under section 21, (c) an agreement deemed to be a maintenance order under subsection (2), and (d) an order that is a support order under the Interjurisdictional Support Orders Act, but does not include a provisional order or a provisional variation order, as defined in section 1(1) of the Interjurisdictional Support Orders Act. *Family Maintenance Enforcement Act*, R.S.B.C. 1996, c. 127, s. 1.

MAJOR ATTACHMENT CLAIMANT. A claimant who qualifies to receive benefits and has 600 or more hours of insurable employment in their qualifying period. *Employment Insurance Act, 1996*, S.C. 1996, c. 23, s. 6.

MAJOR BURDEN. "... [T]he burden of establishing a case ..." *R. v. Schwartz* (1988), 45 C.C.C. (3d) 97 at 115, [1989] 1 W.W.R. 289, 66 C.R. (3d) 251, 88 N.R. 90, [1988] 2 S.C.R. 443, 56 Man. R. (2d) 92, 55 D.L.R. (4th) 1, Dickson C.J.C. (dissenting).

MAJOR DISASTER. An event caused by a natural phenomenon, a technological failure or an accident, whether or not resulting from human intervention, that causes serious harm to persons or substantial damage to property and requires unusual action on the part of the affected community, such as a flood, earthquake, ground movement, explosion, toxic emission or pandemic. *Civil Protection Act*, R.S.Q. c. S-2.3, s. 2.

MAJORITY. *n.* 1. Age of maturity. 2. The largest number. See AGE OF ~.

MAJORITY OPINION. 1. The opinion agreed upon by the greater number of the members of a hearing panel or court consisting of three or more members or judges. 2. The opinion of the greater number of a group. Compare DISSENTING OPINION.

MAJOR SEXUAL ASSAULT. 1. An assault in which the perpetrator by violence or threat of violence forces an adult victim to submit to sexual activity of a sort that a reasonable person would know that the victim likely would suffer a lasting emotional or psychological injury whether or not there was a physical injury. 2. The injury might come from the sexual aspect of the situation or from the violence used or from any combination of the two. This category, which we would describe as major sexual assault, includes not only what we suspect will continue to be called rape, but obviously also many cases of attempted rape, fellatio, cunnilingus, and buggery where the foreseeable major harm which we later describe more fully is present. *R. v. Sandercock* (1985), 62 A.R. 382, [1986] 1 W.W.R. 291, 22 C.C.C. (3d) 79, 48 C.R. (3d) 154, 40 Alta. L.R. (2d) 265.

MAKER. *n.* 1. The person who signs the promise in a promissory note. 2. The person who makes a depository note. *Depository Bills and Notes Act*, S.C. 1998, c. 13, s. 2. 3. In relation to a cinematographic work, the person by whom the arrangements necessary for the making of the work are undertaken, or in relation to a sound recording, the person by whom the arrangements necessary for the first fixation of the sounds are undertaken. *Copyright Act*, R.S.C. 1985, c. C-42, s. 2. See BOOK~; RAIN~.

MAL. *pref.* Wrong; bad; fraudulent.

MALA FIDE. [L.] In bad faith.

MALA FIDES. [L.] Bad faith, contrasted to bona fides, good faith.

MALA IN SE. [L.] "[At] common law ... truly criminal conduct ... [was designated] mala in se ... today [such] prohibited acts are ... classified as ... crimes ..." *R. v. Wholesale Travel Group Inc.* (1991), 8 C.R. (4th) 145 at 159, 67 C.C.C. (3d) 193, 4 O.R. (3d) 799n, 84 D.L.R. (4th) 161, 130 N.R. 1, 38 C.P.R. (3d) 451, 49 O.A.C. 161, [1991] 3 S.C.R. 154, 7 C.R.R. (2d) 36, Cory J. (L'Heureux-Dubé J. concurring).

MALA MENS. [L.] An malevolent mind.

MALA PROHIBITA. [L.] "[At] common law ... conduct, otherwise lawful, which is prohibited in the public interest ... today ... [such] prohibited acts are ... classified as ... regulatory offences." *R. v. Wholesale Travel Group Inc.* (1991), 8 C.R. (4th) 145 at 159, 67 C.C.C. (3d) 193, 4 O.R. (3d) 799n, 84 D.L.R. (4th) 161, 130 N.R. 1, 38 C.P.R. (3d) 451, 49 O.A.C. 161, [1991] 3 S.C.R. 154, 7 C.R.R. (2d) 36, Cory J. (L'Heureux-Dubé J. concurring).

MALE ISSUE. Descendants in the male line. T. Sheard, R. Hull & M.M.K. Fitzpatrick, *Canadian Forms of Wills*, 4th ed. (Toronto: Carswell, 1982) at 191.

MALEVOLENT. *adj.* Desirous of evil to others; disposed to ill will; actuated by ill will.

MALFEASANCE. *n.* The commission of an unlawful act. See MISFEASANCE.

MALFUNCTION. *n.* Faulty function.

MALICE. *n.* 1. "Malice has been described as 'improper purpose.' Lamer J. in Nelles [Nelles v. Ontario, (1989), 41 Admin. L.R . 1], supra, at p. 22, referred to John G. Fleming, The Law of Torts, 5th ed. (Sydney: Law Book Company, 1977), at p. 609, where Fleming stated that malice has a 'wider meaning than spite, ill-will or a spirit of vengeance, and includes any other improper purpose, such as to gain a private collateral advantage." *Falloncrest Financial Corp. v. Ontario*, 1995 CarswellOnt 1064, 33 Admin. L.R. (2d) 87 (Gen. Div.), Ground J. 2."[In defamation] ... not limited to spite or ill will, although these are its most obvious instances. Malice includes any indirect motive or ulterior purpose, and will be established if the plaintiff can prove that the defendant was not acting honestly when he published the comment... ." *Cherneskey v. Armadale Publishers Ltd.*, [1979] 1 S.C.R. 1067 at 1099, 24 N.R. 271, [1978] 6 W.W.R. 618, 7 C.C.L.T. 69, 90 D.L.R. (3d) 321, Dickson J. (dissenting) (Spence and Estey JJ. concurring). 3. Malice is commonly understood, in the popular sense, as spite or ill-will. However, it also includes, as Dickson J. pointed out in dissent in Cherneskey, supra, at p. 1099, "any indirect motive or ulterior purpose" that conflicts with the sense of duty or the mutual interest which the occasion created. See also Taylor v. Despard, [1956] O.R. 963 (C.A.). Malice may also be established by showing that the defendant spoke dishonestly, or in knowing or reckless disregard for the truth. *Hill v. Church of Scientology of Toronto* [1995] 2 S.C.R. 1130. 4. [In the tort of malicious prosecution] the core meaning of malice is the use of the criminal justice system for an improper purpose, the proper use of it being to bring before the court a person whom the prosecutor has reasonable and probable cause to believe has committed a criminal offence. As the authorities indicate, malice has a "wider meaning than spite, ill-will or a spirit of vengeance, and includes any other improper purpose". *Oniel v. Metropolitan Toronto (Municipality) Police Force*, (2001) 141 O.A.C. 201, Borins J.A. (Sharp J.A. concurring). See EXPRESS ~.

MALICE AFORETHOUGHT. 1. "... [W]as ... adopted to distinguish murder from manslaughter, which denoted all culpable homicides other than murder... . was not limited to its natural and obvious sense of premeditation, but would be implied whenever the killing was intentional or reckless. In these instances, the malice was present and it is the premeditation which was implied by law." *R. v. Vaillancourt* (1987), 60 C.R. (3d) 289 at 321, 81 N.R. 115, [1987] 2 S.C.R. 636, 68 Nfld. & P.E.I.R. 281, 209 A.P.R. 281, 10 Q.A.C. 161, 39 C.C.C. (3d) 118, 47 D.L.R. (4th) 399, 32 C.R.R. 18, Lamer J. (Dickson C.J.C. and Wilson J. concurring). 2. "... [A]t least in modern usage, is misleading, but it has come to be a comprehensive term to describe the various forms of mens rea or the various mental elements which must be present to justify a conviction for murder ... has been greatly broadened in modern times... ." *R. v. Switelinski* (1980), 18 C.R. (3d) 231 at 246, 248, 34 N.R. 569, 55 C.C.C. (2d) 481, 117 D.L.R. (3d) 285, [1980] 2 S.C.R. 956, the court per McIntyre J.

MALICIOUS. *adj.* With an intent to cause harm or while being reckless about whether that harm will occur. *Reliable Distributors Ltd. v. Royal Insurance Co. of Canada*, 1986 CanLII 959 (B.C. C.A.)

MALICIOUS FALSEHOOD. A tort designed to provide a remedy for a falsehood which causes monetary harm.

MALICIOUS INTENT. Demonstrates bad faith. *Hanbidge v. Saskatchewan*, 2006 SKCA 33.

MALICIOUS PROSECUTION. "... [F]our necessary elements which must be proved for a plaintiff to succeed in an action for malicious prosecution: (a) the proceedings must have been initiated by the defendant; (b) the proceedings must have terminated in favour of the plaintiff; (c) the absence of reasonable and probable cause; (d) malice, or a primary purpose other than that of carrying the law into effect." *Nelles v. Ontario* (1989), 37 C.P.C. (2d) 1 at 21, 49 C.C.L.T. 217, [1989] 2 S.C.R. 170, 71 C.R. (3d) 358, 60 D.L.R. (4th) 609, 98 N.R. 321, 69 O.R.(2d) 448n, 35 O.A.C. 161, 42 C.R.R. 1, 41 Admin. L.R. 1, Lamer J. (Dickson C.J.C. and Wilson J. concurring).

MALPRACTICE. *n.* 1. "... [B]ad or unskilful practice by a physician or surgeon, whereby the health of the patient is injured... ." *Town v. Archer* (1902), 4 O.L.R. 383 at 387, 1 O.W.R. 391 (H.C.), Falconbridge C.J. 2. The negligent or careless act of a professional.

MALUM IN SE. [L.] See MALA IN SE.

MALUM PROHIBITUM. [L.] See MALA PROHIBITA.

MALUS ANIMUS. [L.] Malevolent intent.

M

MANAGEMENT. See CASE ~; EMERGENCY ~; INFORMATION ~ SYSTEM; KNOWLEDGE ~; STRATA ~ SERVICES; WATER QUALITY ~; WATER RESOURCE ~; WILDLIFE ~ BOARD..

MANAGEMENT FUNCTION. Actions such as the preparation of a budget, decisions as to organization of the enterprise and staffing levels, representation of the employer in collective bargaining or in contract administration, formulation of corporate policy, hiring, firing, promoting, and disciplining of employees, and authorizing leave.

MANAGEMENT RIGHTS. Rights which an employer retains such as hiring, contracting and price fixing.

MANAGEMENT'S DISCUSSION AND ANAL-YSIS. The section of an annual information form, annual report or other document that contains management's discussion and analysis of the financial condition and results of operations of a responsible issuer as required under New Brunswick securities law. *Securities Act*, S.N.B. 2004, c. S-5.5, s. 161.1.

MANAGER. *n.* 1. A person who has significant administrative responsibilities and exercises powers of independent action, autonomy, and discretion. 2. Chief officer. See PORTFOLIO ~; RECEIVER AND ~.

MANAGERIAL CAPACITY. See PERSON EMPLOYED IN A ~.

MANAGING DIRECTOR. 1. "... [A] director having the management of affairs." *Claudet v. Golden Giant Mines Ltd.* (1910), 13 W.L.R. 348 at 350, 15 B.C.R. 13 (C.A.), Galliher J.A. (Macdonald C.J.A. concurring). 2. "... [A]n ordinary director entrusted with some special powers: ..." *Standard Construction Co. v. Crabb* (1914), 7 W.W.R. 719 at 721, 30 W.L.R. 151, 7 Sask. L.R. 365 (C.A.), the court per Lamont J.A.

MAN. & SASK. TAX R. *abbr.* Manitoba & Saskatchewan Tax Reports.

MAN. BAR N. *abbr.* Manitoba Bar News.

MANDAMUS. *n.* [L. we command] 1. An order issued in the name of the court to compel performance of a public legal duty. It has long been the means by which private litigants have required governmental authorities to discharge their obligations. However, that said, mandamus remains a discretionary remedy and one which is available only in specific circumstances. *Dolan v. Moose Jaw (City)*, 2008 SKCA 170. 2. "[An extraordinary remedy which] ... lies to secure the performance of a public duty in the performance of which the applicant has sufficient legal interest. The applicant must show that he demanded the performance of the duty and that performance of it has been refused by the authority obliged to discharge it ... Another principle is that a mandamus will not be issued to order a body as to how to exercise its jurisdiction or discretion." *Turmel v. Canada (Canadian Radio-Television & Telecommunications Commission)* (1980), 60 C.P.R. (2d) 37 at 38, 117 D.L.R. (3d) 697, [1981] 2 F.C. 411 (T.D.), Walsh J.

MANDATE. *n.* 1. A request; a directive. 2. A bailment of goods, without recompense, to have something done in connection with them or to be transported from one place to another. 3. A contract by which a person, the mandator, empowers another person, the mandatary, to represent him in the performance of a juridical act with a third person, and the mandatary, by his acceptance, binds himself to exercise the power. The power and, where applicable, the writing evidencing it are called the power of attorney. *Civil Code*, S.Q. 1991, c. 64, a. 2130.

MANDATARY. *n.* Person who empowers another person, the mandatary, to represent him in the performance of a juridical act with a third person. *Civil Code*, S.Q. 1991, c. 64, a. 2130.

MANDATORY. *adj.* 1. Imperative. 2. Refers to a provision which must be followed. If not complied with, the action performed or completed will be invalid.

MANDATORY ALLOCATION PROGRAM. A program established to control the allocation of supplies of an energy product at the level of the suppliers and wholesale customers thereof. When the Governor in Council is of the opinion that a national emergency exists by reason of actual or anticipated shortages of petroleum or disturbances in the petroleum markets that affect or will affect the national security and welfare and the economic stability of Canada, and that it is necessary in the national interest to conserve the supplies of petroleum products within Canada, the Governor in Council may, by order, so declare and by that order authorize the establishment of a program for the mandatory allocation of petroleum products within Canada in accordance with this Act. *Energy Supplies Emergency Act*, R.S.C. 1985, c. E-9.

MANDATORY INJUNCTION. An injunction to restrain the continuance of some wrongful omission, that is, requiring action.

MANDATORY ORDER. Includes equitable remedies resulting from imperative or peremptory orders such as an order for specific performance. Includes orders such as mandamus.

MANDATORY PRESUMPTION. 1. "... [R]equires that the inference which flows from the facts be made." *R. v. Oakes* (1986), 24 C.C.C. (3d) 321 at 330, [1986] 1 S.C.R. 103, 53 O.R. (2d) 719, 50 C.R. (3d) 1, 14 O.A.C. 335, 19 C.R.R. 308, 26 D.L.R. (4th) 200, 65 N.R. 87, Dickson C.J.C. (Chouinard, Wilson and Le Dain JJ. concurring). 2. "... [R]equires the trier of fact to find the presumed fact upon proof of the fact giving rise to the presumption, in the absence of some countering evidence." *R. v. Oakes* (1983), 3 C.R.R. 289 at 308, 40 O.R. (2d) 660, 2 C.C.C. (3d) 339, 32 C.R. (3d) 193, 145 D.L.R. (3d) 123 (C.A.), the court per Martin J.A.

MANIFEST. *v.* To become apparent; to become evident.

MANIFEST. *n.* 1. The document designed to identify the quantity, composition, origin and destination of things during transportation and the persons consigned, transporting and accepting those things. 2. Of a merchant ship, a list of the goods which comprise her cargo.

MANIFESTATION THEORY. On this theory, damage only occurs when it becomes known (on one formulation, to the insured, and on another, to the third party whose property is affected). Therefore, coverage is triggered when the insured or third party first becomes or could have become aware of the damage. *Alie v. Bertrand & Frère Construction Co.* (2002), 62 O.R. (3d) 345 (C.A.).

MANIFESTLY UNLAWFUL. An overt violation of the law; a certain and obvious unlawfulness.

MANIFEST UNFAIRNESS. There must be a rational connection between the deprivation of life, liberty or security of the person and the purpose of the law [being challenged under s. 7 of the Canadian Charter of Rights and Freedoms]. In [Rodriguez v. British Columbia (Attorney General), [1993] 3 S.C.R. 519] ... , Sopinka J. stated at p. 596 that if the deprivation of the right "does little or nothing to enhance the State's purpose, then the deprivation is not in accordance with the principles of fundamental justice." Courts have often used the term "manifest unfairness" to describe such situations. *R. v. Malmo-Levine*, 2000 CarswellBC 1148, 2000 BCCA 335, 145 C.C.C. (3d) 225, 34 C.R. (5th) 91, 74 C.R.R. (2d) 189, 138 B.C.A.C. 218, 226 W.A.C. 218, Braidwood J.A. (Rowles J.A. concurring).

MAN. L.J. *abbr.* Manitoba Law Journal.

MAN. L.R. *abbr.* Manitoba Law Reports (Queen's Bench)), 1884-1890.

MAN-MADE LANDSCAPE. An area established to protect the biodiversity of an inhabited area of water or land whose landscape and natural features have been shaped over time by human activities in harmony with nature and present outstanding intrinsic qualities the conservation of which depends to a large extent on the continuation of the practices that originally shaped them. *Natural Heritage Conservation Act,* R.S.Q., c. C-61.01, s. 2.

MAN. M.T.B.D. *abbr.* Manitoba Motor Transport Board Decisions, 1985-.

MANNER. *n.* The mode or method in which something is done or happens or one acts. See IN A PERVERSE OR CAPRICIOUS ~ OR WITHOUT REGARD FOR THE MATERIAL BEFORE IT.

MANSFIELD. See LORD ~'S RULE.

MANSION HOUSE. Means a dwelling house. Dwelling-house does not mean a separate, single-family building. It means any place a person dwells. *R. v. Kutschera,* 1999 CarswellBC 2751, 1999 BCCA 748, 141 C.C.C. (3d) 254, 131 B.C.A.C. 120, 214 W.A.C. 120, Southin J.A. (dissenting).

MANSLAUGHTER. *n.* 1. Culpable homicide that is not murder or infanticide. *Criminal Code,* R.S.C. 1985, c. C-46, s. 234. 2. Culpable homicide that otherwise would be murder may be reduced to manslaughter if the person who committed it did so in the heat of passion caused by sudden provocation. *Criminal Code,* R.S.C. 1985, c. C-46, s. 232(1). 3. "... [A]n

unlawful killing without proof of the existence of the required specific intent has always been characterized as manslaughter." *R. v. Switelinski* (1980), 18 C.R. (3d) 231 at 248, 34 N.R. 569, 55 C.C.C. (2d) 481, 117 D.L.R. (3d) 285, [1980] 2 S.C.R. 950, the court per McIntyre J. 4. The offence of manslaughter is committed when a person causes the death of another person by means of an unlawful act without the necessary intent to commit murder. Thus the difference between murder and manslaughter is this; while murder requires a specific intent, the element of intent is not necessary to constitute the offence of manslaughter as long as there is a voluntary unlawful act. *R. v. Mercier,* 2004 BCCA 663.

MANSUETAE NATURAE. [L.] Harmless animals. Of a tame disposition. See ANIMALS ~.

MANUFACTURE. *v.* To manufacture is to fabricate. It is the act or process of making articles for use. It is the operation of making goods or wares of any kind. It is the production of articles produced from raw or prepared material by giving to these materials new forms, qualities and properties or combinations whether by hand or machine. *Minister of National Revenue v. Dominion Shuttle Co.* (1933), 72 C.S. 15 (Que. S.C.). See RE~D.

MANUFACTURE. *n.* 1. This word does not include higher forms of life. As a result a mouse was not patentable. Commonly understood to denote a non-living mechanistic product or process. *Harvard College v. Canada (Commissioner of Patents),* 2002 SCC 76, Bastarache, J. for the majority. 2. However, the tradition of patent jurisprudence has been expansive, not restrictive. By 1851 the learned text Godson on Patents (2nd ed.) noted that the word "manufactures" had received from the English courts "very extended signification. It has not, as yet, been accurately defined; for the objects which may possibly come within the spirit and meaning of that act, are almost infinite" (p. 35). We should not encourage the Commissioner to try to circle each of the five definitional words with tight language that creates arbitrary gaps between, for example, "manufacture" and "composition of matter" through which useful inventions can fall out of the realm of patentability. To do so would conflict with this Court's earlier expression of a "judicial anxiety to support a really useful invention". The definition of invention should be read as a whole and expansively with a view to giving protection to what is novel and useful and unobvious. *Harvard College v. Canada (Commissioner of Patents),* [2002] 4 S.C.R. 45, Binnie J. (dissenting) (McLachlin C.J.C., Major and Arbour JJ. concurring).

MANUFACTURED HOME. 1. Any structure, whether ordinarily equipped with wheels or not, that is designed, constructed or manufactured to provide residential accommodation and to be moved from one place to another by being towed or carried. *Manufactured Home Act,* S.B.C. 2003, c. 75, s. 1. 2. Any structure, whether ordinarily equipped with wheels or not, that is manufactured to meet or exceed the Canadian Standards Association standard CSA Z240 and that is used as a residence or for any other purpose. *Municipal Government Act,* R.S.A. 2000, c. M-26, s. 284.

M

MANUFACTURED HOME COMMUNITY. A parcel of land that (i) is designated in the land use bylaw of a municipality as a manufactured home community, and (ii) includes at least 3 designated manufactured home sites that are rented or available for rent. *Municipal Government Act*, R.S.A. 2000, c. M-26, s. 284.

MANUFACTURED HOME PARK. Land used or occupied by a person for the purpose of providing space for the accommodation of 3 or more manufactured homes and for imposing a charge or rental for the use of that space. *Manufactured Home Act*, S.B.C. 2003, c. 75, s. 23.

MANUFACTURED HOME SITE. A site in a manufactured home park, which site is rented or intended to be rented to a tenant for the purpose of being occupied by a manufactured home. *Manufactured Home Park Tenancy Act*, S.B.C. 2002, c. 77, s. 1.

MAREVA INJUNCTION. 1. In a series of decisions between 1975 and 1980, the English Court of Appeal established the principle that: . . . If it appears that the debt is due and owing, and there is a danger that the debtor may dispose of his assets so as to defeat it before judgment, the court has jurisdiction in a proper case to grant an interlocutory judgment so as to prevent him disposing of those assets. Mareva Compania Naviera SA v. International Bulkcarriers SA, [1980] 1 All E.R. 213 at 215 (C.A.). *Clark et al. v. Nucare PLC*, 2006 MBCA 101. 2. "What therefore sprung out of the fertile ground of jurisprudence in the mid-1970's in the courts of the United Kingdom as a limited interlocutory injunctive remedy for plaintiffs who were in pursuit of ubiquitous charterers of shipping, has matured into a sub-principle or exception to a general rule of long standing. .... There must be assets of the defendant within the jurisdiction susceptible to execution. The defendant need not be outside the jurisdiction. There must be a real risk that the remaining significant assets of the defendant within the jurisdiction are about to be removed or so disposed of by the defendant as to render nugatory any judgment to be obtained after trial. Mareva injunctions are therefore available not just to prevent the removal of assets from the jurisdiction, but also disposal within the jurisdiction. . . .The gist of the Mareva action is the right to freeze exigible assets when found within the jurisdiction, wherever the defendant may reside, providing, of course, there is a cause between the plaintiff and the defendant which is justiciable in the Courts of England. However, unless there is a genuine risk of disappearance of assets, either inside or outside the jurisdiction, the injunction will not issue. This generally summarizes the position in this country ... " *Aetna Financial Services Ltd. v. Feigelman* (1985), 29 B.L.R. 5 at 25, [1985] 1 S.C.R. 2, [1985] 2 W.W.R. 97, 55 C.B.R. (N.S.) 1, 56 N.R. 241, 15 D.L.R. (4th) 161, 4 C.P.R. (3d) 145, 32 Man. R (2d) 241, the court per Estey J.

MARGIN. *n.* The difference between the cost and selling price of a commodity. See BUY ON ~.

MARGINAL NOTE. Something printed beside the section of an act which summarizes the effect of that section.

MARGIN DEPOSIT. A payment, deposit or transfer to a clearing house under the rules of the clearing house to assure the performance of the obligations of a clearing member in connection with security transactions, including, without limiting the generality of the foregoing, transactions respecting futures, options or other derivatives or to fulfil any of those obligations. *Bankruptcy and Insolvency Act*, R.S.C. 1985, c. B-3, s. 95.

MARINE ADVENTURE. Any situation where insurable property is exposed to maritime perils, and includes any situation where (a) the earning or acquisition of any freight, commission, profit or other pecuniary benefit, or the security for any advance, loan or disbursement, is endangered by the exposure of insurable property to maritime perils, and (b) any liability to a third party may be incurred by the owner of, or other person interested in or responsible for, insurable property, by reason of maritime perils. *Marine Insurance Act*, S.C. 1993, c. 22, s. 2.

MARINE INSTALLATION OR STRUCTURE. Includes any ship and any anchor, anchor cable or rig pad used in connection therewith, any offshore drilling unit, production platform, subsea installation, pumping station, living accommodation, storage structure, loading or landing platform, dredge, floating crane, pipelaying or other barge or pipeline and any anchor, anchor cable or rig pad used in connection therewith, and any other work or work within a class of works prescribed. *Oceans Act*, S.C. 1996, c. 31, s. 2.

MARINE INSURANCE. A contract of marine insurance is a contract whereby the insurer undertakes to indemnify the insured, in the manner and to the extent agreed in the contract, against (a) losses that are incidental to a marine adventure or an adventure analogous to a marine adventure, including losses arising from a land or air peril incidental to such an adventure if they are provided for in the contract or by usage of the trade; or (b) losses that are incidental to the building, repair or launch of a ship. Subject to the Act, any lawful marine adventure may be the subject of a contract. *Marine Insurance Act*, S.C. 1993, c. 22, s. 6.. See CONTRACT OF ~.

MARINE PLANT. Includes all benthic and detached algae, marine flowering plants, brown algae, red algae, green algae and phytoplankton. *Fisheries Act*, R.S.C. 1985, c. F-14, s. 47.

MARINE POLLUTION. The introduction by humans, directly or indirectly, of substances or energy into the sea that results, or is likely to result, in (a) hazards to human health; (b) harm to living resources or marine ecosystems; (c) damage to amenities; or (d) interference with other legitimate uses of the sea. *Canadian Environmental Protection Act, 1999*, S.C. 1999, c. 33, s. 120.

MARITAL. *adj.* Pertaining to the state of marriage; relating to a husband.

MARITAL HOME. Property in which one or both spouses have an interest and that is or has been occupied as their family residence, and where property that includes a marital home is used for a purpose in addition to a family residence, that marital home is that portion of the property that may reasonably be regarded as necessary to the use and enjoyment of the family residence. *Child and Family Services and Family Relations Act*, S.N.B. 1980, c. C-2.1, s. 111.

MARITAL PROPERTY. (a) Family assets; (b) property owned by one spouse or by both spouses that is not a family asset and that was acquired while the spouses cohabited, or in contemplation of marriage, except (i) a business asset, (ii) property that was a gift from one spouse to the other, including income from that property, (iii) property that was a gift, devise, or bequest from any other person to one spouse only, including income from that property, (iv) property that represents the proceeds of disposition of property that was not a family asset and was not acquired while the spouses cohabited or in contemplation of marriage, or that was acquired in exchange for or was purchased with the proceeds of disposition of such property or that represents insurance proceeds with respect to loss of or damage to such property; and (v) property that represents the proceeds of disposition of property referred to in subparagraphs (ii) and (iii) or that was acquired in exchange for or was purchased with the proceeds of disposition of such property or that represents insurance proceeds with respect to loss of or damage to such property; and (c) property that was acquired by one spouse after the cessation of cohabitation and that was acquired through the disposition of property that would have been marital property had the disposition not occurred; but does not include property that the spouses have agreed by a domestic contract is not to be included in marital property. *Marital Property Act*, S.N.B. 1980, c. M-1.1, s. 1.

MARITAL REGIME. Refers to the laws, of a particular territory, which govern spousal and family relationships, divorce, and ownership of property.

MARITAL STATUS. 1. The status of being single, engaged to be married, married, separated, divorced, widowed or a man and woman living in the same household as if they were married. *Human Rights Act*, R.S.N.S. 1989, c. 214, s. 3. 2. "... [I]n the Canadian Human Rights Act, S.C. 1976-77, c. 33 does not mean the status of a married person but, rather, the status of a person in relation to marriage, namely, whether that person is single, married, divorced or widowed." *Schaap v. Canada (Canadian Armed Forces)* (1988), 27 C.C.E.L. 1 at 8, 56 D.L.R. (4th) 105 (Fed. C.A.), Pratte J.A. (concurring). 3. The status of being married, single, widowed, divorced or separated and includes the status of living with a person in a conjugal relationship outside marriage. *Human Rights Code,* R.S.O. 1990, c. H.19, s. 10.

MARITIME LAW. The law relating to ships, harbours and mariners. See CANADIAN ~.

MARITIME PERILS. The perils consequent on or incidental to the navigation of the sea, that is to say, perils of the seas, fire, war perils, pirates, rovers, thieves, captures, seizures, restraints, and detainments of princes and peoples, jettisons, barratry, and any other perils, either of the like kind or which may be designated by the policy. *Insurance acts.*

MARITIME TORT. A tort committed on water as opposed to one committed on land.

MARK. *n.* A mark, brand, seal, wrapper or design used by or on behalf of (a) the government of Canada or a province, (b) the government of a state other than Canada, or (c) any department, board, commission or agent established by a government mentioned in paragraph (a) or (b) in connection with the service or business of that government. *Criminal Code*, R.S.C. 1985, c. C-46, s. 376. See CERTIFICATION ~; LAND~; NATIONAL EMISSIONS ~; OFFICIAL ~; PROHIBITED ~; QUALITY ~; SAFETY ~; TRADE- ~.

MARKER. *n.* A plaque or monument of metal, concrete, stone or other material installed or to be installed in a cemetery, columbarium or mausoleum in memory of a deceased person.

MARKET. *n.* 1. An area of rivalry between suppliers of goods and services who vie with each other for the patronage of consumers of the goods and services. 2. "... [T]he action or business of buying and selling commodities." *Schecter v. Bluestein* (1981), 23 C.R. (3d) 39 at 45, [1981] C.S. 477, 121 D.L.R. (3d) 345, 58 C.C.C. (2d) 208 (Que. S.C.), Malouf J. 3. "... [D]efined by a certain number of properties which establish equivalence of price, of goods and of availability. It is often in relation to a geographic place which may be local, regional, national or international, depending upon the clientele. Often, and more and more frequently, a market will depend on a network such as in the case of currency or electronics ..." *Alex Couture Inc. c. Canada (Procureur général)* (1990), (*sub nom. Alex Couture Inc. v. Canada (Attorney General)*) 30 C.P.R. (3d) 486 at 514, 69 D.L.R. (4th) 635 (Qué. C.S.), Philippon J. See AFTER-~; AVAILABLE ~; BEAR ~; BULL ~; MONEY ~ MUTUAL FUND; OPEN ~; ORGANIZED ~.

MARKETABLE TITLE. See GOOD TITLE.

MARKET APPROACH. In relation to the valuation of a business, involves looking at the value of comparable properties which have sold on the open market and then making adjustments to take into account the special features of the business being evaluated.

MARKETING. *n.* 1. Buying, selling, shipping for sale or offering for sale. 2. The preparation and advertisement of agricultural products and includes the conveyance, purchase and sale of agricultural products and any other act necessary to make agricultural products available for consumption or use. *Canada Agricultural Products Act*, R.S.C. 1985, c. 20 (4th Supp.), s. 2. 3. Includes bartering, advertising, packing, processing, storing, shipping, and transporting, for the purposes of sale or in anticipation of sale. See BLACK ~; TELE~.

MARKETING AGENCY. (a) An association of producers whose object is the marketing, under a cooperative plan, of agricultural products produced by the producers; (b) a person engaged in the processing of agricultural products for marketing under a cooperative plan; (c) a person authorized by one or more associations or persons mentioned in paragraphs (a) and (b) to market agricultural products

M

under a single cooperative plan; or (d) the Board. *Agricultural Marketing Programs Act*, S.C. 1997, c. 20, s. 2.

MARKETING BOARD. A body which promotes, develops, regulates and controls the production, marketing or production and marketing of an agricultural product or agricultural products through a plan funded by a levy that is not refundable to producers. *The Agri-Food Act, 2004*, S.S. 2004, c. A-15.21, s. 2, part.

MARKET ORDER. A direction by a client to sell or buy a security immediately at the best possible price.

MARKET OVERT. An open, public, and legally constituted market.

MARKET PARTICIPANT. A dealer, adviser or representative, an accredited counterparty with direct access to trading on a published market, a subscriber of an alternative trading system, or any other person designated as such by regulation. *Derivatives Act*, R.S.Q. c. I-14.01, s. 3.

MARKET PRICE. 1. In its ordinary sense the market price means the actual price at which a commodity is commonly sold at the place of the contract. *Kidston v. Stirling & Pitcairn Ltd.*, [1921] 1 W.W.R. 162, 61 S.C.R. 193, 55 D.L.R. 366, Brodeur J. (dissenting) at 205. 2. The weighted average market price of the securities as determined Kidston v. Sterling and Pitcairn, Ltd., (1920), 61 S.C.R. 193 with respect to the first 20 trading days for that security following the general disclosure of the material fact or material change. *Securities Act*, R.S.A. 2000, c. S-4, s. 195. See MARKET VALUE.

MARKET RATE. See FAIR ~.

MARKET RENTAL VALUE. A rental amount which the current rental market would bear assuming willing participants.

MARKET VALUATION STANDARD. The standard achieved when the assessed value of property: (i) is prepared using mass appraisal; (ii) is an estimate of the market value of the estate in fee simple in the property; (iii) reflects typical market conditions for similar properties; and (iv) meets quality assurance standards established by order of the Saskatchewan Assessment Management agency. *The Municipalities Act*, S.S. 2005, c. M-36.1, s. 193.

MARKET VALUE. 1. "... '[R]ealizable money value'... ." *R. v. Thomas Lawson & Sons Ltd.*, [1948] Ex. C.R. 44 at 82, [1948] 3 D.L.R. 334, 62 C.R.T.C. 277, Thorson P. 2. The amount in terms of cash that would probably be realized for property in an arm's length sale in an open market under conditions requisite to a fair sale, the buyer and seller each acting knowledgeably and willingly. *Loan and Trust Companies acts.* 3. In respect of an estate or interest in land, is the amount that the estate or interest might be expected to realize if sold in the open market by a willing seller to a willing buyer. *Alberta Land Stewardship Act*, S.A. 2009, c. A-26.8, s. 39. See FAIR ~.

MARKMAN ORDER. Named after 1996 U.S. case. Noel, J. in *Realsearch Inc. v. Valon Kone Brunette* 2003 FCT 669 has given first one in Canada. The order requires the parties to proceed with a separate determination of claim construction prior to trial for patent infringement.

MARKSMAN. *n.* A person who can only sign a document with an X.

MARK-UP. *n.* A margin of profit that the retailer adds to the value of a commodity sold.

MARRIAGE. *n.* 1. Marriage, for civil purposes, is the lawful union of two persons to the exclusion of all others. For greater certainty, a marriage is not void or voidable by reason only that the spouses are of the same sex. *Civil Marriage Act*, S.C. 2005, c. 33, s. 2 and 4. 2. The common law definition of marriage is inconsistent with the Charter to the extent that it excludes same-sex couples. The remedy that best corrects the inconsistency is to declare invalid the existing definition of marriage to the extent that it refers to "one man and one woman", and to reformulate the definition of marriage as "the voluntary union for life of two persons to the exclusion of all others". This remedy achieves the equality required by s. 15(1) of the Charter but ensures that the legal status of marriage is not left in a state of uncertainty. *Halpern v. Canada (Attorney general)*, (2003-06-10) ONCA C39172; C39174. 3. "... [T]he classic definition of marriage is provided by Lord Penzance in Hyde v. Hyde (1866), L.R. 1 P. & D. 130, as [at p. 133]: 'the voluntary union for life of one man and one woman, to the exclusion of all others.' " *Keddie v. Currie* (1991), 44 E.T.R. 61 at 76 (B.C. C.A.), Cumming J.A. (Legg J.A,. concurring). See BREAKDOWN OF ~; CELEBRATION OF ~; CHILD OF THE ~; CIVIL ~; COMMON LAW ~; DISSOLUTION OF ~; NULLITY OF ~; RESTRAINT OF ~; SOLEMNIZATION OF ~.

MARRIAGE CONTRACT. 1. An agreement between a man and a woman entered into before their marriage, or during their marriage while cohabiting, in which they agree on their respective rights and obligations under the marriage or on the breakdown of their marriage, including (a) ownership in or division of property, (b) support obligations, and (c) any other matter in the settlement of their affairs. *Family Property and Support Act*, R.S.Y. 2002, c. 83, s. 1. 2. Two persons who are married to each other or intend to marry may enter into an agreement in which they agree on their respective rights and obligations under the marriage or on separation, on the annulment or dissolution of the marriage or on death, including, (a) ownership in or division of property; (b) support obligations; (c) the right to direct the education and moral training of their children, but not the right to custody of or access to their children; and (d) any other matter in the settlement of their affairs. *Family Law Act*, R.S.O. 1990, c. F-3, s. 52.

MARRIAGE LICENCE. Required by a provincial government prior to entering into a marriage.

MARRIAGE SETTLEMENT. Any indenture, contract, agreement, covenant or settlement entered into in consideration of marriage whereby one of the parties agrees to pay a sum or sums of money to or for the benefit of self or the other party or any other person or the issue of the marriage, and whereby that party settles, grants, conveys, transfers, mortgages, or charges, or agrees to settle, grant, convey, transfer, mortgage or charge, real or personal property of any description upon or to or in favour of any person for the benefit of self or the other party or any other person or the issue of the marriage. *The Marriage Settlement Act*, R.S.S. 1978, c. M-5, s. 2.

MARRIED WOMEN'S PROPERTY ACT. An act most provinces passed to give a wife the right to acquire and hold property in her own name.

MARRY. See BREACH OF PROMISE TO ~.

MARSHAL. *v.* 1. Marshalling is an equitable remedy that may arise when you have two creditors of the same debtor, with one creditor, sometimes referred to as the senior creditor, having the right to resort to two funds of the debtor for payment of the debt, and the other creditor, the junior creditor, has the right to resort to one fund only. The court can "marshal" or arrange the funds so that both creditors are paid to the greatest possible extent. Equity will be invoked to protect the junior creditor, make the senior creditor realize on assets in such a way that the senior creditor will not wipe out assets that would only be available to the junior creditor. The junior creditor will be subrogated and will have a charge on the second or subsequent funds. *Bockhold v. Lawson Lundell Lawson & McIntosh*, 1999 CarswellBC 989, 10 C.B.R. (4th) 90 (S.C.), Morrison J. 2. "The doctrine of marshalling, in its application to mortgages or charges upon two estates or funds, may be stated as follows: If the owner of two estates mortgages them both to one person, and then one of them to another, either with or without notice, the second mortgagee may insist that the debt of the first mortgagee shall be satisfied out of the estate not mortgaged to the second, so far as that will extend. This right is always subject to two important qualifications: first, that nothing will be done to interfere with the paramount right of the first mortgagee to pursue his remedy against either of the two estates; and, second, that the doctrine will not be applied to the prejudice of third parties: ..." *Ernst Brothers Co. v. Canada Permanent Mortgage Corp.* (1920), 47 O.L.R. 362 at 367 (H.C.), Orde J.

MARSHAL. *n.* An ex officio court officer; every sheriff of the Federal Court. *Federal Courts Act*, R.S.C. 1985, c. F-7, s. 13. See DEPUTY ~.

MARTIAL LAW. 1. Military law. 2. The replacement of ordinary law and the temporary government of a nation or area by a military council if this is done following a government proclamation or notice by military authorities.

MARY CARTER AGREEMENT. Named after Booth v. Mary Carter Paint Co. 202 So. (2d) 8 (Fla. Dist. Ct. App.). An agreement with the following characteristics: the plaintiff and one of multiple defendants agree; the contracting defendant guarantees the plaintiff a certain amount and the exposure of the defendant is "capped" at a certain amount; the contracting defendant remains a party to the action; the

contracting defendant's liability is decreased in direct proportion to the increase in the non-contracting defendant's liability; the agreement is kept secret.

MASSAGE THERAPY. 1. The kneading, rubbing or massaging of the human body, whether with or without steam baths, vapour baths, fume baths, electric light baths or other appliances, and hydrotherapy or any similar method taught in schools of massage approved under the former Physiotherapists Act, but does not include any form of medical electricity. B.C. Regulations. 2. The practice of massage therapy is the assessment of the soft tissue and joints of the body and the treatment and prevention of physical dysfunction and pain of the soft tissues and joints by manipulation to develop, maintain, rehabilitate or augment physical function, or relieve pain. *Massage Therapy Act, 1991*, S.O. 1991, c. 27, s. 3.

MASS APPRAISAL. The process of preparing assessments for a group of properties as of the base date using standard appraisal methods, employing common data and allowing for statistical testing. *The Municipalities Act*, S.S. 2005, c. M-36.1, s. 193.

MASTER. *n.* 1. A judicial officer of the Supreme Court who may decide certain matters before or after trial. 2. The person in command and charge of a vessel. It does not include a licensed pilot, within the meaning of section 1.1 of the Pilotage Act, while the pilot is performing pilotage duties under that Act. *Canada Shipping Act, 2001*, S.C. 2001, c. 26, s. 2. 3. A person who has completed an apprenticeship and worked as a journeyman for a period of time.

MASTER AND SERVANT. "... [T]he relationship imports the existence of power in the employer not only to direct what work the servant is to do, but also the manner in which it is to be done ..." *Atlas Industries Ltd. v. Goertz* (1985), 4 C.P.C. (2d) 187 at 193, [1985] 4 W.W.R. 598, 38 Sask. R. 294 (Q.B.), Grotsky J.

MASTER FRANCHISE. A franchise which is a right granted by a franchisor to a subfranchisor to grant or offer to grant franchises for the subfranchisor's own account. *Arthur Wishart Act (Franchise Disclosure), 2000*, S.O. 2000, c. 3, s. 1.

MASTER OF THE MINT. The Master of the Mint and such other persons as constitute the Board of Directors of the Mint are hereby incorporated as a body corporate under the name of the Royal Canadian Mint. The objects of the Mint are to mint coins in anticipation of profit and to carry out other related activities. *Royal Canadian Mint Act*, R.S.C. 1985, c. R-9, s. 3.

MATERIA. *n.* [L.] Subject matter. See IN PARI ~.

MATERIAL. *n.* Every kind of movable property. *Repairers Lien Act*, R.S.B.C. 1996, c. 404, s. 1. See IN A PERVERSE OR CAPRICIOUS MANNER OR WITHOUT REGARD TO THE ~ BEFORE IT; ~S; MUSEUM ~; NUCLEAR ~; ORGANIC ~.

MATERIAL. *adj.* 1. Important; essential. 2. "... [T]hat which goes to the foundation of the decision or which goes to the crux of a central issue before the court... ." *International Corona Resources Ltd. v. Lac*

369

Minerals Ltd. (1988), 54 D.L.R. (4th) 647 at 658, 66 O.R. (2d) 610 (H.C.), Osborne J.

MATERIAL ADOPTED BY REFERENCE. (a) A code of, or standard set by, a provincial, national, international or any other code or standard making body, or (b) a map, plan, geological survey, illustration, diagram, photograph, graph or table or any other similar record or thing, that will reasonably be available to persons likely to be affected by it and is adopted or incorporated by reference into a regulation but is not attached to or accompanying the regulation. *Regulations Act*, R.S.B.C. 1996, c. 402, s. 1.

MATERIAL CHANGE. 1. In relation to spousal support payments means one that had it been known earlier would likely have resulted in different terms. 2. (a) If used in relation to an issuer other than an investment fund, (i) a change in the business, operations or capital of the issuer that would reasonably be expected to have a significant effect on the market price or value of a security of the issuer, or (ii) a decision to implement a change referred to in subparagraph (i) made by (A) the directors of the issuer, or (B) senior management of the issuer who believe that confirmation of the decision by the directors is probable, and (b) if used in relation to an investment fund, (i) a change in the business, operations or affairs of the investment fund that would be considered important by a reasonable investor in determining whether to purchase or continue to hold a security of the investment fund, or (ii) a decision to implement a change referred to in subparagraph (i) made (A) by the directors of the investment fund or the directors of the investment fund manager, (B) by senior management of the investment fund who believe that confirmation of the decision by the directors is probable, or (C) by senior management of the investment fund manager who believe that confirmation of the decision by the directors of the manager is probable. *Securities acts.*

MATERIAL CONTRIBUTION. Beyond de minimis. Material contribution [to damage], as that phrase was used in Athey v. Leonati [[1997] 1 W.W.R. 97 (S.C.C.)], is synonymous with "substantial connection", as that phrase was used by McLachlin C.J.C. . . . in Hanke v. Resurfice Corp. [(2007), 69 Alta. L.R. (4th) 1 (S.C.C.)]. This causal yardstick should not be confused with the "material contribution test". *Sam v. Wilson*, 2007 BCCA 622, Smith J.A. (Ryan J.A. concurring).

MATERIAL CONTRIBUTION TEST. It is a rule of law based on policy. It applies as an exception to the "but for" test of causation when it is impossible for the plaintiff to prove that the defendant's negligent conduct caused the plaintiff's injury using the "but for" test, where it is clear that the defendant breached a duty of care owed the plaintiff thereby exposing the plaintiff to an unreasonable risk of injury, and where the plaintiff's injury falls within the ambit of the risk. The purpose of the exception is to provide a cause of action against a defendant who has materially increased the risk that the claimant will suffer damage and may have caused that damage, but cannot be proved to have done so because it is impossible to show, on a balance of probability, that some other

exposure to the same risk may not have caused it instead. *Sam v. Wilson*, 2007 BCCA 622, Smith J.A. (Ryan J.A. concurring).

MATERIAL FACT. 1. One that is necessary to formulate a complete cause of action. 2. In tort, the damage sustained by the plaintiff and the damage resulting from the injury and the conduct of the defendant which caused the injury. 3. In the context of ex parte family law proceedings, the facts that there is a dispute concerning the relief claimed, and that the other party has communicated that he or she intends to file a statement of defence, are material. *Walker v. Schober*, 2008 BCCA 19. 4. Where used in relation to securities issued or proposed to be issued, a fact that significantly affects, or would reasonably be expected to have a significant effect on the market price or value of those securities. *Securities acts.*

MATERIAL NON-PUBLIC ORDER INFORMATION. Information respecting the imminent execution of trades in contracts, or in commodities that are the subject matter of contracts, by a person or company. *The Commodity Futures Act,* S.M. 1996, c. 73, s. 59.

MATERIALS. *n.* 1. Goods that are used in the processing of other goods, and includes parts or ingredients. *Customs Tariff*, S.C. 1997, c. 36, s. 95. 2. Includes books, periodicals, pamphlets, newspapers, photographic reproductions, paintings, films, filmscripts, sheet music and sound recordings. *Libraries Act*, R.S.N.B. 1973, c. L-5, s. 1. See MATERIAL.

MATERIAL SAFETY DATA SHEET. 1. A document providing certain required information concerning the nature of, effects of and remedies for exposure to hazardous products. 2. A document on which words, figures or symbols disclosing the information referred to in subparagraphs 13(a)(i) to (v) may be written, printed or otherwise expressed. *Hazardous Products Act*, R.S.C. 1985, c. H-3, s. 11.

MATERIAL WITNESS. A person whose evidence is important in the prosecution or defence of a case.

MATERIEL. *n.* All public property, other than real property, immovables and money, provided for the Canadian Forces or for any other purpose under this Act, and includes any vessel, vehicle, aircraft, animal, missile, arms, ammunition, clothing, stores, provisions or equipment so provided. *National Defence Act*, R.S.C. 1985, c. N-5, s. 2.

MATERNITY. *n.* The state of motherhood.

MATERNITY LEAVE. A leave of absence allowed to a worker who is pregnant or who has given birth.

MATRIMONIAL. *adj.* Relating to the act of marrying or to the state of being married.

MATRIMONIAL DISPUTE. There is no statutory definition of the term "matrimonial dispute" and the question is whether "matrimonial" was intended to encompass only matters arising out of legal marriages or can be interpreted to include marriage-like common-law relationships. In the case at bar, the petitioner co-habited with the proposed defendant for over twenty years, and she used his surname, but they were not legally married. I conclude that the petitioner's contingent fee agreement is not in respect of a matrimonial dispute. *Legal Profession Act (British Columbia), Re*, 2000 CarswellBC 971, 2000 BCSC 690, 74 B.C.L.R. (3d) 302, 187 D.L.R. (4th) 167 (S.C.), Meiklem J.

MATRIMONIAL REGIME. Spouses who, before the solemnization of their marriage, have not fixed their matrimonial regime in a marriage contract, are subject to the regime of partnership of acquests. *Civil Code*, S.Q. 1991, c. 64, a. 432. See COMMUNITY ~; CONVENTIONAL SEPARATION AS TO PROPERTY; PARTNERSHIP OF ACQUESTS; SEPARATION AS TO PROPERTY JUDICIALLY OBTAINED; SEPARATION FROM BED AND BOARD.

MATRIX. See FACTUAL ~.

MATTER. *n.* 1. Includes every proceeding in the Supreme Court not in a cause. *Judicature Act*, R.S.N.W.T. 1988, c. J-1, s. 1. 2. Includes every proceeding in the court not in an action. *Judicature Act*, R.S.P.E.I. 1974, c. J-3, s. 1. 3. "The content or subject matter" of the law. *Reference re Anti-Inflation Act, 1975 (Canada)*, [1976] 2 S.C.R. 373 at 450, 9 N.R. 541, 68 D.L.R. (3d) 452, Beetz J. 4. Of a law, its leading feature or true character, its pith and substance, its dominant or most important characteristic. 5. [A] matter," in the sense those words are used in s. 5(1) [of the Municipal Council Conflict of Interest Act, R.S.M. 1987, c. M255], means an issue upon which there can be some meaningful discussion or debate and the prospect of some decision being made. *Lovatt v. Glenwood (Rural Municipality)*, 2004 MBCA 18. See CIVIL ~; CRIMINAL ~; DISCIPLINARY ~; MAILABLE ~; RESPONSIBLE COMMUNICATION ON ~S OF PUBLIC INTEREST.

MATTER OF FACT. See QUESTION OF FACT.

MATTER OF LAW. See QUESTION OF LAW.

MATURITY. *n.* The date on which a note, loan or obligation becomes due.

MAUSOLEUM. *n.* A building or structure, other than a columbarium, used as a place for the interment of the human remains in sealed crypts or compartments.

MAXIM. *n.* A general principle; an axiom.

MAXIMS OF EQUITY. These include: equity will not allow a wrong to exist without a remedy; equity looks to intent rather than to form; equity considers what ought to be done as having been done; an equitable remedy is discretionary; delay defeats equity; one who comes to equity must come with clean hands; one who seeks equity must do equity; equity never lacks a trustee. These are not rigid rules but principles to be applied in particular situations. See CLEAN HANDS DOCTRINE; DELAY DEFEATS EQUITIES; EQUALITY IS EQUITY; EQUITY ACTS IN PERSONAM; EQUITY AIDS THE VIGILANT AND NOT THE INDOLENT; EQUITY FOLLOWS THE LAW; EQUITY IMPUTES AN INTENTION TO FULFIL AN OBLIGATION; EQUITY LOOKS ON THAT AS DONE WHICH OUGHT TO BE DONE; EQUITY LOOKS TO THE INTENT RATHER THAN TO THE FORM; EQUITY WILL NOT SUFFER A WRONG TO BE WITHOUT A REMEDY; HE WHO COMES INTO EQUITY MUST COME WITH CLEAN HANDS; HE WHO SEEKS EQUITY MUST DO EQUITY; NO MAN CAN TAKE ADVANTAGE OF HIS OWN WRONG; NO ONE CAN BE ALLOWED TO DEROGATE FROM HIS OWN GRANT.

MAY. v. 1. "... [C]ommonly used to denote a discretion ..." R. c. Potvin, [1989] 1 S.C.R. 525 at 547, 93 N.R. 42, 68 C.R. (3d) 193, 47 C.C.C. (3d) 289, 21 Q.A.C. 258, La Forest J. and Dickson C.J. 2. "... [P]ermissive and empowering and confers an 'area of discretion'." *Charles v. Insurance Corp. of British Columbia* (1989), 34 B.C.L.R. (2d) 331 at 337 (C.A.), the court per Lambert J.A. 3. "... [S]hould not be construed as imperative unless the intention that it should be so construed is clear from the context... ." *Heare v. Insurance Corp. of British Columbia* (1989), 34 B.C.L.R. (2d) 324 at 327 (C.A.), the court per Lambert J.A. 4. It is clear from past decisions of various courts that the word "may" can have a mandatory meaning, just as the word "shall" can have a permissive meaning, depending on context. See reference to Johnsons Tyne Foundry Pty. Ltd. v. Maffra Corp., [1949] A.L.R. 89 (Australia H.C.), referred to in Words and Phrases Legally Defined, 3d ed. (London: Butterworth & Co. (Publishers) Ltd., 1989) vol. 3: K-Q at 116. *R. v. Neves*, 2005 MBCA 112. 5. In Ruby v. Canada (Solicitor General), [2000] 3 F.C. 589 (Fed. C.A.), at pp. 623 to 626, Létourneau J.A. reminded us that the use of the word "may" is often a signal that a margin of discretion is given to an administrative decision maker. It can sometimes be read in context as "must" or "shall," thereby rebutting the presumptive rule in section 11 of the Interpretation Act (R.S.C. 1985, c. I-21) that "may" is permissive. It can also be read as no more than a signal from the legislator that an official is being empowered to do something. Even when "may" is read as granting discretion, all grants of discretion are not created equal: depending on the purpose and object of the legislation, there may be considerable discretion, or there may be little. *Cha v. Canada (Minister of Citizenship and Immigration)*, 2006 FCA 126.

MAYOR. *n.* The chief elected officer of a municipality.

MBCA. Neutral citation for the Manitoba Court of Appeal.

MBPC. Neutral citation for the Manitoba Provincial Court.

MBQB. Neutral citation for the Manitoba Court of Queen's Bench.

M.C. *abbr.* Master's Chambers.

M.C.C. *abbr.* Mining Commissioner's Cases, 1906-1979?.

MCGILL L.J. *abbr.* McGill Law Journal (Revue de droit de McGill).

M

MCNAGHTEN'S CASE. R. v. McNaghten or M'Naghten or Macnaughton (1843) 4 St.Tr. (N.S.) 847, a British case which established the law relating to insanity with special reference to criminal responsibility.

M.C.R. *abbr.* Montreal Condensed Reports / Précis des décisions des tribunaux du district de Montréal (Québec),, 1853-1854.

MDP. *abbr.* Multi-disciplinary practice.

MEAL PREPARATION. The physical ability of the insured, or the insured's requirement to have verbal cuing, to prepare three meals per day. *The Automobile Accident Insurance Act*, R.S.S. 1978, c. A-35, *The Personal Injury Benefits Regulations*, R.R.S., c. A-35, Reg. 3, Appendix D, Grid A, s. 2.

MEAN. *v.* 1. Where a definition uses the word "means" and not "includes" "... the definition is to be construed as being exhaustive." *Yellow Cab Ltd. v. Alberta (Industrial Relations Board)*, [1980] 2 S.C.R. 761 at 768, 14 Alta. L.R. (2d) 39, 24 A.R. 275, 80 C.L.L.C. 14,066, 33 N.R. 585, 114 D.L.R. (3d) 427, the court per Ritchie J. 2. "... [N]ormally construed as comprehending that which is specifically described or defined ..." *R. v. Hauser* (1979), 98 D.L.R. (3d) 193 at 213, [1979] 1 S.C.R. 984, 26 N.R. 541, [1979] 5 W.W.R. 1, 46 C.C.C. (2d) 481, 16 A.R. 91, 8 C.R. (3d) 89 (Eng.), 8 C.R. (3d) 281 (Fr.), Dickson J. (dissenting) (Pratte J. concurring). See ~S.

MEANING. See ASSOCIATED ~ PRINCIPLE; ORDINARY ~; ORDINARY ~ RULE; PLAIN ~ RULE; SHARED ~ RULE.

MEANINGFUL CONSEQUENCES. While the term "meaningful consequences" is notionally similar to the concept of specific deterrence, there is a distinction between these two concepts. "Meaningful consequences" seemingly requires that a sentence be based on the young person's past conduct, while specific deterrence is intended to discourage future conduct considered to be inappropriate. Although there may only be a thin line between imposing a "meaningful consequence" and creating a deterrent effect, a sentence will be appropriate so long as it is intended to ensure the long-term protection of the public by focussing on the rehabilitation of the young person, without regard to any consequential deterrent effect such a penalty may have. *R. v. M. (M.L.)*, 2008 ABCA 212.

MEANS. *v.* When used in a definition, the definition is construed as being comprehensive and including that which is specifically described or listed. To be contrasted with "includes." See MEAN.

MEANS. *n.* 1. "... [T]he historical interpretation of the term as including all pecuniary resources, capital assets, income from employment or earning capacity, and other sources from which the person receives gains or benefits." *Strang v. Strang* (1992), 3 Alta. L.R. (3d) 1 at 7, 137 N.R. 203, 39 R.F.L. (3d) 233, 125 A.R. 331, 14 W.A.C. 331, 92 D.L.R. (4th) 762, [1992] 2 S.C.R. 112, the court per Cory J. 2. In my view, the phrase "accidental means" conveys the idea that the consequences of the actions and events that produced death were unexpected. Reference to a set of consequences is therefore implicit in the word "means". "Means" refers to one or more actions or events, seen under the aspect of their causal relation to the events they bring about. *Martin v. American International Assurance Life Co.*, 2003 SCC 16. See ACCIDENTAL ~; ILLEGAL OR UNLAWFUL ~; THE ~; UNLAWFUL ~; WAYS AND ~ MOTION.

MEASURE OF DAMAGES. A test to determine the amount of damages which should be given.

MEASURES. See BIOSECURITY ~; EXTRAJUDICIAL ~.

MECHANICS' LIEN. 1. A lien which favours a mechanic or other person who conferred skill, money and materials on a chattel. 2. A right in the nature of a lien on any money paid by the owner of land to a contractor given to a worker or supplier of materials.

MECHANISM. See ALTERNATIVE DISPUTE RESOLUTION ~.

MEDIA LAW. The law concerning the press and broadcast media. Deals with telecommunications law, regulation of the media, intellectual property issues, defamation, journalistic sources and the like.

MEDIATION. *n.* The reconciliation of a dispute by a third party.

MEDIATOR. *n.* 1. One who resolves disputes by mediation. 2. "The status of a mediator allows its holder to decide on the basis of equity, without being bound by substantive or procedural rules of law, except of course for rules of public order such as those of natural justice which provide for impartiality, opportunity for the parties to be heard, reasons to be given for the award, and so on. Mediation is not, as such, a legal concept distinct from that of arbitration. Rather, the mediator is an arbitrator who is exempted from compliance with the rules of law as provided in art. 948 [of the Code of Civil Procedure, R.S.Q. 1977, c. C-25] ... The mediator is in fact only the 'bon père de famille' of the Civil Code transposed to arbitration matters. Mediation is a departure from the law of arbitration. Like any exception it must, if it is not expressly provided for, at least result from a clear and unambiguous intent ..." *Zittrer c. Sport Maska Inc.* (1988), 38 B.L.R. 221 at 310, 83 N.R. 322, [1988] 1 S.C.R. 564, 13 Q.A.C. 241, L'Heureux-Dubé J. (Lamer, Wilson and Le Dain JJ. concurring).

MEDICAL HISTORY. The history of illness, treatment, and surgeries which an individual has had during their life.

MEDICAL IMAGING TECHNOLOGY AND RADIATION ONCOLOGY. The practice of medical imaging technology and radiation oncology consists in using ionizing radiation, radioelements and other forms of energy for treatment or to produce images or data for diagnostic or therapeutic purposes. The following activities in the practice of medical imaging technology and radiation oncology are reserved to medical imaging technologists and radiation oncology technologists: (1) administering prescribed medications or other prescribed substances; (2) using ionizing radiation, radioelements or other forms of energy, according to a prescription; (3) monitoring reactions to medications and other substances; (4) introducing an instrument, according to a prescription, in and beyond the pharynx or beyond the urinary meatus, labia majora or anal margin or into a peripheral vein or artificial opening; and (5) mixing substances to complete the preparation of a medication, according to a prescription. *Act respecting medical imaging technologists and radiation oncology technologists*, R.S.Q. c. T-5, s. 7.

MEDICAL JURISPRUDENCE. The part of the law related to the practice of medicine.

MEDICAL LABORATORY TECHNOLOGY. The collection and handling of laboratory specimens, analysis of specimens and the interpretation of quality-control data to verify the accuracy and precision of test results for use by health-care practitioners in diagnosis, treatment and prevention of disease. *Medical Laboratory Technology Act*, S.N.S. 2000, c. 8, s. 2.

MEDICAL RADIATION TECHNOLOGIST. A person who practises medical radiation technology as a radiographic technologist, a radiation therapy technologist or a nuclear medicine technologist. *Medical Radiation Technologists Act*, R.S.N.S. 1989, c. 280, s. 2.

MEDICAL RADIATION TECHNOLOGY. The act, process, science or art of carrying out on humans for medical purposes the technical aspects of radiation-diagnosis or radiation-therapeutics. *Medical Radiation Technologists Act*, R.S.N.S. 1989, c. 280, s. 2.

MEDICAL REHABILITATION. Includes any physical or psychological treatment whose object is to stabilize and restore the basic physical and psychological functions of a person. *Canadian Forces Members and Veterans Re-establishment and Compensation Act*, S.C. 2005, c. 21, s. 2.

MEDICARE. *n.* A medical care programme which makes hospital and physician services universally available.

MEDICINE. *n.* The practice of medicine is the assessment of the physical or mental condition of an individual and the diagnosis, treatment and prevention of any disease, disorder or dysfunction. *Medicine Act, 1991*, S.O. 1991, c. 30, s. 3. See EVIDENCE-BASED ~; FORENSIC ~; LEGAL ~; NATURO-PATHIC ~; PATENT ~S; TRADITIONAL CHINESE ~; VETERINARY ~.

MEDICO-LEGAL. *adj.* Concerning the law relating to medical issues.

MEET. See CASE TO ~.

MEETING. *n.* A gathering of people to decide, by proper voting procedure, whether something should be done. See PUBLIC ~.

MEGATRIAL. *n.* A criminal trial involving multiple accused and multiple charges lasting for a lengthy period.

MEIORIN TEST. 1. The Meiorin test was developed in the employment context, it applies to all claims for discrimination under the B.C. Human Rights Code. Meiorin announced a unified approach to adjudicating discrimination claims under human rights legislation. The distinction between direct and indirect discrimination has been erased. *British Columbia (Superintendent of Motor Vehicles) v. British Columbia (Council of Human Rights)* (1999), 1999 CarswellBC 2730, [2000] 1 W.W.R. 565, 47 M.V.R. (3d) 167, 249 N.R. 45, 70 B.C.L.R. (3d) 215, 181 D.L.R. (4th) 385, 36 C.H.R.R. D/129, [1999] 3 S.C.R. 868, 131 B.C.A.C. 280, 214 W.A.C. 280, the court per McLachlin J. 2. The Supreme Court established the Meiorin test to determine whether a prima facie discriminatory standard is a bona fide occupational requirement. It consists of the following three factors: 1. that the employer adopted the standard for a purpose rationally connected to the performance of the job; 2. that the employer adopted the particular standard in an honest and good faith belief that it was necessary to the fulfilment of that legitimate work-related purpose; and 3. that the standard is reasonably necessary to the accomplishment of that legitimate work-related purpose. To show that the standard is reasonably necessary, it must be demonstrated that it is impossible to accommodate individual employees sharing the characteristics of the claimant without imposing undue hardship upon the employer. *Wikwemikong Tribal Police Services Board v. Corbiere*, 2007 FCA 97. See BONA FIDE OCCUPATIONAL REQUIREMENT.

MEMBER. *n.* 1. A subscriber of the memorandum of a company, and includes every other person who agrees to become a member of a company and whose name is entered in its register of members or a branch register of members. 2. In relation to a pension plan, means a person who has become a member of the pension plan and has neither ceased membership in the plan nor retired. *Pension Benefits Standards Act 1985*, R.S.C. 1985, c. 32 (2nd Supp.), s. 2. 3. A member of the House of Commons. 4. A member of the Legislative Assembly. See CLEARING ~; CLUB ~; FAMILY ~; FIRST NATION ~; INDEPENDENT ~; NON-COMMISSIONED ~; PRIVATE ~'S BILL; PUBLIC ~; SIDE-~; WTO ~.

MEMBER LOAN. A loan required by the cooperative from its members as a condition of membership or to continue membership in the cooperative. *Canada Cooperatives Act*, S. C. 1998, c. 1, s. 2.

MEMBER OF A FIRST NATION. (a) When used in respect of a First Nation that has a final agreement, a person enrolled or eligible to be enrolled under the final agreement; and (b) when used in respect of a First Nation that is a band under the provisions of the Indian Act (Canada), a person who is a member of the band under that Act. *Child and Family Services Act*, S.Y. 2008, c. 1, s. 1.

MEMBER OF AN ORDER. Any person who holds a permit issued by an order and who is entered on the roll of the latter. *Professional Code,* R.S.Q., C-26, s. 1.

MEMBERSHIP. *n.* 1. A state of being one of a group of individuals composing a group. 2. Includes a share of a credit union. 3. Includes a share of a corporation.

M

MEMBERSHIP CORPORATION. A corporation incorporated or continued to carry on activities that are primarily for the benefit of its members.

MEMBERSHIP INTEREST. The rights, privileges, restrictions and conditions conferred or imposed on a member or each class of members of a corporation in accordance with the provisions of its articles or bylaws. *Non-profit Corporations Act, 1995*, SS. 1995, c. N-4.2, s. 2(1).

MEMBERSHIP SHARE. A cooperative with membership shares must have one class of membership shares, designated as such in the articles. Membership shares may be issued only to members, each of whom must hold the minimum number of membership shares prescribed by the by-laws. Subject to Parts 20 and 21, the membership shares of a cooperative confer on their holders equal rights, including equal rights to (a) receive dividends declared on membership shares; and (b) subject to the articles, receive the remaining property of the cooperative on dissolution. *Canada Cooperatives Act*, S. C. 1998, c. 1, ss. 117, 118.

MEMBERS OF VISIBLE MINORITIES. Persons, other than aboriginal peoples, who are non-Caucasian in race or non-white in colour. *Employment Equity Act*, S.C. 1995, c. 44, s. 3.

MEMORANDUM. *n.* 1. The memorandum of association of a company, as originally framed or as altered. 2. The memorandum of association for incorporation of a society incorporated under this Act. *Societies Act*, R.S.N.S. 1989, c. 435, s. 2. 3. The endorsement on the certificate of title and on the duplicate copy thereof of the particulars of any instrument presented for registration. *Land Titles acts.* 4. A document summarizing the state of the law on a particular issue.

MEMORANDUM OF AGREEMENT. 1. A document evidencing the terms of an agreement between or among the parties to the agreement. 2. A written, ratified and signed document which frequently precedes a formal collective agreement. Usually when the collective agreement is executed, the memorandum is merged. D.J.M. Brown & D.M. Beatty, *Canadian Labour Arbitration*, 3d ed. (Aurora: Canada Law Book, 1988-) at 4-2.

MEMORANDUM OF ASSOCIATION. An incorporating document in some jurisdictions for some types of organizations. It contains the name, objects, and subscribers of the society, co-operative or credit union and share structure, if any.

MEMORIAL. *n.* 1. A tombstone; a marker on a grave. 2. Whatever contains the details of a deed. 3. A record of a judgment signed by the Registrar or clerk, as the case may be, containing the names of the parties, the sum recovered, or the amount ordered to be paid as alimony or otherwise, as the case may be, and the date of signing the judgment or of the decree, as the case may be, and verified by affidavit. 4. A document issued by the Federal Court evidencing a certificate registered under subsection (2) in respect of a debtor and includes a writ of that Court issued pursuant to the certificate or any notification of the document or writ. *Customs Act*, R.S.C. 1985, c. 1 (2nd Supp.), s. 97.24.

MENIAL. *adj.* Domestic.

MENSA ET THORO. [L.] From bed and board.

MENS REA. [L.] 1. A mental state, the subjective element of a crime. The intent to commit the offence in question. Does not encompass the objective truth of a proposition which the accused believes. Knowledge, for legal purposes, is true belief. Knowledge therefore has two components—truth and belief—and of these, only belief is mental or subjective. Truth is objective, or at least consists in the correspondence of a proposition or mental state to objective reality. Accordingly, truth, which is a state of affairs in the external world that does not vary with the intention of the accused, cannot be a part of mens rea. *United States v. Dynar* [1997] 2 S.C.R. 462. 2. "... [A] basis for the imposition of liability. Mens rea focuses on the mental state of the accused and requires proof of a positive state of mind such as intent, recklessness or wilful blindness." *R. v. Wholesale Travel Group Inc.* (1991), 8 C.R. (4th) 145 at 176, 67 C.C.C. (3d) 193, 4 O.R. (3d) 799n, 84 D.L.R. (4th) 161, 130 N.R. 1, 38 C.P.R. (3d) 451, 49 O.A.C. 161, [1991] 3 S.C.R. 154, 7 C.R.R. (2d) 36, Cory J. (L'Heureux-Dubé J. concurring). 3. "... [A] complex concept having different meanings in different contexts, but is most frequently used to describe the minimum necessary mental element required for criminal liability where a particular mental element is not expressly made a constituent element of the offence. The minimum mental element required for criminal liability for most crimes is knowledge of the circumstances which make up the actus reus of the crime and foresight or intention with respect to any consequence required to constitute the actus reus of the crime. *R. v. Metro News Ltd.* (1986), 23 C.R.R. 77 at 95, 16 O.A.C. 319, 56 O.R. (2d) 321, 53 C.R. (3d) 289, 29 C.C.C. (3d) 35, 32 D.L.R. (4th) 321, the court per Martin J.A. See SUBJECTIVE ~.

MENTAL DISABILITY. 1. Any mental disorder, developmental disorder or learning disorder, regardless of the cause or duration of the disorder. *Alberta Human Rights Act*, Enforcement; R.S.A. 2000, c. H-14, s. 44. 2. (i) An intellectual disability or impairment; or (ii) a mental disorder. *The Limitations Act*, S.S. 2004, c. L-16.1, s. 2.

MENTAL DISORDER. 1. A disease of the mind. *Criminal Code*, R.S.C. 1985, c. C-46, s. 2. A substantial disorder of thought, mood, perception, orientation or memory, any of which grossly impairs judgment, behaviour, capacity to recognize reality or ability to meet the ordinary demands of life. *Mental Health Act*, R.S.A. 2000, c. M-13, s. 1. 3. No person is criminally responsible for an act committed or an omission made while suffering from a mental disorder that rendered the person incapable of appreciating the nature and quality of the act or omission or of knowing that it was wrong. *Criminal Code*, R.S.C. 1985, c. C-46, s. 16. See VERDICT OF NOT CRIMINALLY RESPONSIBLE ON ACCOUNT OF ~.

MENTAL INCAPACITY. Unless otherwise specified in a power of attorney, means the inability of a person, due to infirmity or impaired judgment, whether arising from disease, disability, age, addiction or other cause (a) to understand information that is relevant to making a decision concerning his or her property or financial interests, or (b) to appreciate the reasonably foreseeable consequences of a decision concerning his or her property or financial interests or the lack of such a decision. *Powers of Attorney Act*, S.Nu. 2005, c. 9, s. 1.

MENTAL INCOMPETENCY. The condition of mind or physical incapacity of a mentally incompetent person. *Infirm Persons Act*, R.S.N.B. 1973, c. I-8, s. 1.

MENTALLY CAPABLE. Able to understand the information that is relevant to making a decision concerning the subject-matter and able to appreciate the reasonably foreseeable consequences of a decision or lack of decision. *Long-Term Care Act, 1994*, S.O. 1994, c. 26, s. 2.

MENTALLY COMPETENT. Having the ability to understand the subject matter in respect of which consent is requested and the ability to appreciate the consequences of giving or withholding consent. *Mental Health Act (Nunavut)*, R.S.N.W.T. 1988, c. M-10, s. 1.

MENTALLY DISORDERED PERSON. A person with a mental disorder as defined in section 1 of the Mental Health Act. *Interpretation Act*, R.S.B.C. 1996, c. 238, s. 29.

MENTALLY INCOMPETENT PERSON. A person with a mental disorder as defined in section 1 of the Mental Health Act. *Interpretation Act*, R.S.B.C. 1996, c. 238, s. 29.

MENTIO UNIUS EXCLUSIO ALTERIUS. [L.] To mention one thing excludes another.

MENTUCK. See DAGENAIS/~ TEST.

MERCANTILE. *adj.* Relating to manufacturing; merchants or their trade; commercial.

MERCANTILE AGENT. A person having, in the customary course of business as an agent, authority either to sell goods or to consign goods for the purpose of sale, or to buy goods or to raise money on the security of goods. *Factors acts.*

MERCANTILE LAW. The law concerning matters like bills of exchange, marine insurance and contracts of affreightment.

MERCHANT. See LAW ~.

MERCHANTABLE. *adj.* "... [W]hatever else merchantable may mean, it does mean that the article sold, if only meant for one particular use in ordinary course, is fit for that use; ..." *Grant v. Australian Knitting Mills Ltd.* (1935), [1936] A.C. 85 at 99, [1936] 1 W.W.R. 145, 105 L.J.P.C. 6, [1932] All E.R. 209 (Australia P.C.), the board per Lord Wright.

MERCHANTABLE QUALITY. Of a quality and in a condition that a reasonable person would, after a full examination, accept it under the circumstances in performance of the person's offer to buy it, whether the person is buying it for the person's own use or for resale.

MERCHANT NAVY. The ships, service on which qualified for the 1939-45 Star, being the service medal awarded in respect of service at sea in the merchant navy, the creation of which was approved by His Majesty King George VI under conditions of award set out in Command Papers 6463 of 1943, 6633 of 1945 and 6837 of 1946. *Volunteer War Service Medal Act, 1993*, S.N. 1993, c. V-7.1, s. 2.

MERCHANT SEAMEN COMPENSATION BOARD. Established under the Merchant Seamen Compensation Act, R.S.C. 1985, c. M-6. Provides for compensation to seamen injured at work but not covered by provincial workers' compensation or by the Government Employees Compensation Act, R.S.C. 1985, c. G-5.

MERCY. *n.* Compassion or forbearance. See PARDON.

MEREDITH MEM. LECT. *abbr.* Meredith Memorial Lectures (Conférences commémoratives Meredith).

MERE ERROR OF LAW. "... [A]n error committed by an administrative tribunal in good faith in interpreting or applying a provision of its enabling Act, of another Act, or of an agreement or other document which it has to interpret and apply within the limits of its jurisdiction. A mere error of law is to be distinguished from one resulting from a patently unreasonable interpretation of a provision which an administrative tribunal is required to apply within the limits of its jurisidiction.... A mere error of law should also be distinguished from a jurisdictional error." *Syndicat des employés de production du Québec et de l'Acadie v. Canada (Labour Relations Board)*, [1984] 2 S.C.R. 412 at 420, 14 Admin. L.R. 72, 84 C.L.L.C. 14,069, 55 N.R. 321, 14 D.L.R. (4th) 457, Beetz J.

MERGE. *v.* 1. Of original cause of action, to include in the judgment of a domestic court of record if the plaintiff succeeds. J.G. McLeod, *The Conflict of Laws* (Calgary: Carswell, 1983) at 606. 2. When the ownership of a mortgage and the land to which it is subject is in one person, title can merge in the person. *Standard Trust Co. v. Panstar Developments Inc.*, 1993 CanLII 1391 (B.C.S.C.). 3. Sentences for criminal charges may merge. *R. v. Pauls*, 2008 BCCA 322. 4. May refer to the joining together of businesses into one entity. *Grand Trunk Railway Co. v. County of Halton*, 21 S.C.R. 716.

MERGED. *adj.* 1. Of the rights and duties created by a contract for the sale of land, subsumed by a deed and discharged when the deed of conveyance is delivered and accepted. 2. Of original remedies for a debt subsumed in a higher security, when that security is taken or obtained for the debt.

MERGER. *n.* 1. "... [I]n real estate law merger occurs when two estates coalesce through a vesting in the same person at the same time in the same right... ." *Fraser-Reid v. Droumtsekas* (1979), 9 R.P.R. 121 at 139, [1980] 1 S.C.R. 720, 103 D.L.R. (3d) 385, 29 N.R. 424, Dickson J. (Martland, Estey and McIntyre JJ. concurring). 2. The acquisition or establishment, direct or indirect, by one or more persons, whether

M

by purchase or lease of shares or assets, by amalgamation or by combination or otherwise, of control over or significant interest in the whole or a part of the business of a competitor, supplier, customer or other person. *Competition Act*, R.S.C. 1985, c. C-34, s. 91. 3. "... [T]hat branch of res judicata which is known as merger: [is described as follows] all claims which the plaintiff might have had against the defendants ... have merged in the judgment ... and the maxim nemo debet bis vexari pro una et eadem causa applies." *Thornton v. Tittley* (1985), 4 C.P.C. (2d) 13 at 19, 51 O.R. (2d) 315 (H.C.), Scott L.J.S.C.

MERGER INTO JUDGMENT. A theory that once a creditor begins an action against a debtor which is carried to judgment, the original obligation is transformed into a judgment debt.

MERIT. See ARTISTIC ~; MERITS.

MERIT PRINCIPLE. When there is an opportunity for promotion, the most meritorious person should be promoted.

MERITS. *n.* 1. Used to describe a good cause of action or defence when it is based, not on technical grounds, but on the real issues in question. *R. v. Cronin* (1875), 36 U.C.Q.B. 342 at 345 (C.A.), the court per Richards C.J. 2. Of a cause of action or defence, the substance, elements or grounds. See AFFIDAVIT OF ~; MERIT; ON ITS ~.

MERO MOTU. [L.] Of one's own motion. See EX ~.

MESNE. *adj.* Intermediate. E.L.G. Tyler & N.E. Palmer, eds., *Crossley Vaines' Personal Property*, 5th ed. (London: Butterworths, 1973) at 4.

MESNE LORD. A lord who holds something on behalf of a higher lord, and on whose behalf an inferior lord or tenant holds something.

MESNE PROCESS. 1. Pre-judgment process. C.R.B. Dunlop, *Creditor-Debtor Law in Canada* (Toronto: Carswell, 1981) at 198. 2. In an action or suit, writs which come between the beginning and end.

MESNE PROFIT. An action for damages suffered when possession of land has been withheld improperly. *Mortimer v. Shaw* (1922), 66 D.L.R. 311 at 312, [1922] 2 W.W.R. 562, 15 Sask. L.R. 476 (C.A.), Lamont J.A. (McKay J.A. concurring).

MESSUAGE. *n.* A dwelling-house including any out-buildings, adjacent land and curtilage assigned to its use.

META-ANALYSIS. *n.* A medical or scientific study which manipulates and considers the data from all available studies of a particular issue. The combination of the data from various studies may be considered more reliable than the data from individual studies.

METADATA. *n.* Data about data. Information about the history, tracking, or management of an electronic document. Some more obvious metadata, such as file dates and sizes, can easily be seen by users while other metadata can be hidden or embedded within a file.

METAL. See PRECIOUS ~.

METERING. See NET-~ SYSTEM.

METES AND BOUNDS. The description of land's boundaries beginning at a fixed point and then outlining the borders in north, south, west and east directions and in degrees, minutes and seconds.

METHOD. *n.* The system or procedure followed. See ANNUITY ~; COMPLETED CONTRACT ~; DIRECT DISCOUNTING OF INCOME ~; FIFO ~ OF INVENTORY VALUATION; QUANTITY SURVEY ~; REAL INTEREST ~; RETIREMENT ~; ROYALTY-RELIEF ~; SCIENTIFIC ~; TERMINATION ~.

METIS. *n.* 1. A person of aboriginal ancestry who identifies with Metis history and culture. *Metis Settlements Act*, RSA 2000, c. M-14, s. 1. 2. A person of mixed Aboriginal and European heredity.

METRIC SYSTEM. All units of measurement used in Canada shall be determined on the basis of the International System of Units established by the General Conference of Weights and Measures. *Weights and Measures Act*, R.S.C. 1985, c. W-6, s. 4.

M.H.R.C. DEC. *abbr.* Manitoba Human Rights Commission Decisions, 1971-1982.

MID-CONTRACT STRIKE. A strike taking place during the term of a collective agreement. *Health Employers Assn. of British Columbia v. H.E.U.*, 2009 CarswellBC 192, 2009 BCCA 39.

MIDWIFERY. *n.* The practice of midwifery is the assessment and monitoring of women during pregnancy, labour and the post-partum period and of their newborn babies, the provision of care during normal pregnancy, labour and post-partum period and the conducting of spontaneous normal vaginal deliveries. *Midwifery Act, 1991*, S.O. 1991, c. 31, s. 3. See ABORIGINAL ~; PRACTICE OF ~.

MIGRATORY BIRD. Migratory game birds, migratory insectivorous birds and migratory non-game birds as defined in the Act, and includes any such birds raised in captivity that cannot readily be distinguished from wild migratory birds by their size, shape or colour, and any part or parts of such birds. *Migratory Birds Convention Act, 1994*, S.C. 1994, c. 22, *Migratory Birds Regulations*, C.R.C., c. 1025, s. 2.

MILITARY. *adj.* 1. Relating to all or any part of the Canadian Forces. Federal statutes. 2. Relating to any warlike force. *Cultural Property Export and Import Act*, R.S.C. 1985, c. C-51, *Canadian Cultural Property Export Control List*, C.R.C., c. 448, s. 1.

MILITARY COMMANDER. Includes a person effectively acting as a military commander and a person who commands police with a degree of authority and control comparable to a military commander. *Crimes Against Humanity and War Crimes Act*, S.C. 2000, c. 24, s. 5.

MILITARY FORCES OF A STATE. The armed forces that a state organizes, trains and equips in accordance with the law of the state for the primary purpose of national defence or national security, and every person acting in support of those armed forces who is under their formal command, control and responsibility. *Explosives Act*, R.S.C. 1985, c. E-17, s. 2.

MILITARY JUDGE. Military judges preside at courts martial and perform other judicial duties under this Act that are required to be performed by military judges. The Governor in Council may designate a military judge to be the Chief Military Judge. The Chief Military Judge assigns military judges to preside at courts martial and to perform other judicial duties. *National Defence Act*, R.S.C. 1985, c. N-5, s. 165.23 to 165.25.

MILITARY LAW. 1. "[In s. 11(f) of the Charter means] ... a system of law administered by the military itself and the most important institution of which has always been the General Court Martial." *R. v. Genereux* (1990), 60 C.C.C. (3d) 536 at 543, 70 D.L.R. (4th) 207, 114 N.R. 321, 4 C.R.R.(2d) 307, (Can. Ct. Martial Appeal Ct.), Pratte J. 2. Includes all laws, regulations or orders relating to the Canadian Forces. *Criminal Code*, R.S.C. 1985, c. C-46, s. 2.

MILITARY OFFENCE. An offence recognized by a military court, e.g. insubordination.

MILITARY OPERATION. Any operation undertaken to protect national security, support humanitarian relief efforts, participate in multilateral military or peace-keeping activities under the auspices of international organizations or defend a member state of the North Atlantic Treaty Organization. *Canadian Environmental Protection Act, 1999*, S.C. 1999, c. 33, *Volatile Organic Compound (VOC) Concentration Limits for Automotive Refinishing Products Regulations*, SOR/2009-197, s. 2.

MILITARY POLICE. The officers and non-commissioned members appointed under regulations for the purposes of section 156. Officers and non-commissioned members who are appointed as military police under regulations for the purposes of this section may (a) detain or arrest without a warrant any person who is subject to the Code of Service Discipline, regardless of the person's rank or status, who has committed, is found committing, is believed on reasonable grounds to be about to commit or to have committed a service offence or who is charged with having committed a service offence; and (b) exercise such other powers for carrying out the Code of Service Discipline as are prescribed in regulations made by the Governor in Council. *National Defence Act*, R.S.C. 1985, c. N-5, s. 156 and 250.

MILITARY POLICE COMPLAINTS COMMISSION. Established under the National Defence Act to hear and dispose of reviews about conduct complaints and to deal with conduct and interference complaints relating to the military police. Any person, including any officer or non-commissioned member, may make a complaint under this Division about the conduct of a member of the military police in the performance of any of the policing duties or functions that are prescribed for the purposes of this section in regulations made by the Governor in Council. Any member of the military police who conducts or supervises a military police investigation, or who has done so, and who believes on reasonable grounds

that any officer or non-commissioned member or any senior official of the Department has improperly interfered with the investigation may make a complaint about that person under this Division. *National Defence Act*, R.S.C. 1985, c. N-5, s. 250.1, 250.18, 250.19, and 250.31.

MILITARY SERVICE. Service as a member of the armed forces. *Pension Act*, R.S.C. 1985, c. P-6, s. 3.

MILITARY VEHICLE. A vehicle that is designed to be used in combat or in a combat support role. *Canadian Environmental Protection Act, 1999*, S.C. 1999, c. 33, *Federal Halocarbon Regulations, 2003*, SOR/2003-289, s. 1.

MILL RATE. The applicable figure, expressed in parts per thousand, established to calculate municipal property taxes.

MIN. *abbr.* 1. Minister. 2. Ministry. 3. Minute.

MIND. *n.* The mental faculties of reason, memory, and understanding. See CLOSED ~ TEST; DISEASE OF THE ~; DISPOSING ~; INSANITY; OPERATING ~; UNSOUND ~.

MINE. *n.* 1. A munition designed, altered or intended to be placed under, on or near the ground or other surface area and to be exploded by the presence, proximity or contact of a person or a vehicle. *Anti-Personnel Mines Convention Implementation Act*, S.C. 1997, c. 33, s. 2. 2. Any opening in, excavation in or working of the surface or subsurface for the purpose of working, recovering, opening up or proving coal, a coal bearing substance, oil sands or an oil sands bearing substance, and includes any associated infrastructure. *Environmental Protection and Enhancement Act*, R.S.A. 2000, c. E-12, s. 1. 3. A (a) mineral deposit, (b) site, or (c) separate economic unit designated by the commissioner in British Columbia from which a mineral will be or has been obtained, together with (d) the works or undertaking, and (e) the chattels, whether located inside or outside British Columbia, that are used to obtain, transport and produce mineral product from the mineral deposit, site or designated separate economic unit. *Mineral Tax Act*, R.S.B.C. 1996, c. 291, s. 1.. See ANTI-PERSONNEL ~.

MINE PROPERTY. A property from which an operator has a right to win minerals. *Mineral Tax Act*, R.S.B.C. 1996, c. 291, s. 1.

MINERAL. *n.* 1. Any natural, solid, inorganic or fossilized organic substance. 2. Any nonliving substance formed by the processes of nature which occurs in, on or under land, of any chemical or physical state, but does not include oil, earth, surface water and ground water. 3. "... [M]ineral substances and ... petroleum and natural gas ..." *Crows Nest Pass Coal Co. v. R.*, [1961] S.C.R. 750 at 761, 36 W.W.R. 513, 82 C.R.T.C. 10, 30 D.L.R. (2d) 93, the court per Locke J. 4. "... '[M]ining rights' ..." *Tisdale (Township) v. Cavana*, [1942] 4 D.L.R. 65 at 68, [1942] S.C.R. 384, the court per Kerwin J. See ~S.

MINERAL INTEREST. A legal or equitable interest in minerals or mineral rights under a mineral dis-

M

position or a lease. *The Mines and Minerals Act*, S.M. 1991-92, c. 9, s. 1.

MINERAL LEASE. A lease granted under subsection 14(6) in respect of Crown minerals or a mineral lease granted under subsection 103(1), but does not include a quarry lease granted under subsection 139(2). *The Mines and Minerals Act*, S.M. 1991-92, c. 9, s. 1.

MINERAL RIGHT. An estate in fee simple in a mineral located in a tract. *Freehold Mineral Rights Tax Act*, R.S.A. 2000, c. F-26, s. 1.

MINERAL RIGHTS. The right to enter upon or use lands for the sole purpose of exploring, drilling for, winning, taking, removing or raising the minerals situate therein and includes such easements, rights of way or other similar rights of access as are incidental to winning, taking, removing or raising the minerals situate therein. *Land Transfer Tax Act*, R.S.O. 1990, c. L.6, *Taxation of Mineral Lands*, R.R.O. 1990, Reg. 703, s. 1.

MINERALS. *n.* 1. Includes base and precious metals, coal, salt and every other substance that is an article of commerce obtained from the earth by any method of extraction, but does not include hydrocarbons or any animal or vegetable substance other than coal. *Bank Act*, S.C. 1991, c. 46, s. 425. 2. Any non-viable substance formed by the processes of nature, irrespective of chemical or physical state, and includes such substances both before and after extraction, or any interest in the same, and further includes any interest or improvement in the nature of a mine but does not include any surface or ground water, agricultural soil, sand or gravel. *Saskatchewan Treaty Land Entitlement Act*, S.C. 1993, c. 11, Sched. II, Art. 1, s. 1.01. See MINERAL.

MINERAL SUBSTANCE. Any natural mineral substance, whether solid, gaseous or liquid, except water, and includes a fossilized organic substance or mine tailings, but does not include a mineral substance the well head value of which is subject to the royalty referred to in section 204 of the Mining Act (chapter M-13.1). *Mining Duties Act*, R.S.Q., c. D-15, s. 1.

MINERAL TITLE. A claim or a lease. *Mineral Tenure Act*, R.S.B.C. 1996, c. 292, s. 1.

MINIMUM WAGE. The lowest compensation established by statute.

MINING ACTIVITY. Any activity related to (a) the search for a mineral or placer mineral, (b) the exploration and development of a mineral or placer mineral, or (c) the production of a mineral or placer mineral, and includes the reclamation of a previously mined area and the monitoring and long term protection, control and treatment of a previously mined area. *Mineral Tenure Act*, R.S.B.C. 1996, c. 292, s. 1.

MINING LEASE. A lease, grant or licence for mining purposes, including the searching for, working, getting, making merchantable, smelting or otherwise converting or working for the purposes of any manufacture, carrying away or disposing of mines or minerals, and substances in, on or under the land, obtainable by underground or by surface working or purposes connected therewith. *Commercial Tenancies Act*, R.S.N.W.T. 1988, c. C-10, s. 44.

MINING OPERATIONS. 1. The extraction or production, within the province, of minerals up to and including primary crushing, and includes the transportation, handling, storing, distribution and sale of those minerals, mine rehabilitation and decommissioning, but does not include processing. *Revenue Administration Act*, S.N. 2009, c. R-15.01, s. 2. 2. The extraction or production of mineral ore from or in any mine or its transportation to, or any part of the distance to the point of egress from the mine including any processing thereof prior to or in the course of such transportation and the sale or exchange of the output of the mine but not including any processing thereof after removal from the mine. *Metallic Minerals Tax Act*, R.S.N.B. 1973, c. M-11.01, s. 1.

MINING PROPERTY. A right, licence or privilege to prospect, explore, drill or mine for minerals in a mineral resource in Canada; or, real property in Canada (other than depreciable property) the principal value of which depends on its mineral resource content. *Income Tax Act*, R.S.C. 1985 c.1 (5th Supp) s. 35(2).

MINING RIGHT. A mining or mineral claim, a mining licence or lease.

MINING RIGHTS. 1. " ... '[M]inerals' ..." *Banner Coal Co. v. Gervais (No. 1)* (1922), 18 Alta. L.R. 535 at 541, 70 D.L.R. 206, [1922] 3 W.W.R. 564 (C.A.), the court per Beck J.A. 2. Unless the contrary appears to be the intent of the instrument, where in a conveyance the "mining rights" in respect of any land are granted or reserved, the grant or reservation shall be construed to convey or reserve the ores, mines and minerals on or under the land, together with such right of access for the purpose of winning the ores, mines and minerals as is incidental to a grant of ores, mines and minerals. *Conveyancing and Law of Property Act*, R.S.O. 1990, c. C.34, s. 16.

MINISTER. *n.* 1. A member of the Cabinet. 2. A member of the Queen's Privy Council for Canada as is designated by the Governor in Council. 3. A member of the Executive Council appointed as a Minister who is responsible for the enactment or its subject matter or the department to which its context refers. See CABINET ~; DEPUTY ~; FIRST ~S' CONFERENCE; PRIME ~; TERRITORIAL ~.

MINISTERIAL. *adj.* Describes the discharge of a duty without discretion or independent judgment or the issue of a formal instruction determined beforehand. S.A. DeSmith, *Judicial Review of Administrative Action*, 4th ed. by J.M. Evans (London: Stevens, 1980) at 70.

MINISTERIAL ADVISER. A person, other than a public servant, who occupies a position in the office of a minister of the Crown or a minister of state and who provides policy, program or financial advice to that person on issues relating to his or her powers, duties and functions as a minister of the Crown or a minister of state, whether or not the advice is provided on a full-time or part-time basis and whether or not the person is entitled to any remuneration or other compensation for the advice. *Conflict of Interest Act*, S.C. 2006, c. 9, s. 2, s. 2.

MINISTERIAL DUTY. A duty involved in operating a trust, i.e., keeping of accounts or hiring an agent like a solicitor or valuer. D.M.W. Waters, *The Law of Trusts in Canada*, 2d ed. (Toronto: Carswell, 1984) at 28.

MINISTERIAL RESPONSIBILITY. The traditional responsibility of a minister of government for all the activities of his department.

MINISTERIAL STAFF. Those persons, other than public servants, who work on behalf of a minister of the Crown or a minister of state. *Conflict of Interest Act*, S.C. 2006, c. 9, s. 2, s. 2.

MINISTER OF THE CROWN. A member of the Queen's Privy Council for Canada in that member's capacity of managing and directing or having responsibility for a department. *Payments in Lieu of Taxes Act*, R.S.C. 1985, c. M-13, s. 2.

MINISTER WITHOUT PORTFOLIO. A member of the cabinet not in charge of a department.

MINISTRY. *n.* A department of government.

MINISTRY OF STATE. Where it appears to the Governor in Council that the requirements for formulating and developing new and comprehensive policies in relation to any matter or matters coming within the responsibility of the Government of Canada warrant the establishment of a special portion of the federal public administrationpresided over by a minister charged with responsibility for the formulation and development of such policies, the Governor in Council may, by proclamation, establish a ministry of State for that purpose. *Ministries and Ministers of State Act*, R.S.C. 1985, c. M-8, s. 2.

MINOR. *n.* 1. A person who has not attained the age of majority. 2. A person under the age of eighteen years. Alberta statutes. 3. Has the same meaning as in the applicable provincial law and in the absence of any such law has the same meaning as the word "child" in the United Nations Convention on the Rights of the Child adopted in the United Nations General Assembly on November 20, 1989. *Bank Act*, S.C. 1991, c. 46, s. 2. 4. A person under the age of 19. Nunavut, Saskatchewan and Northwest Territories statutes.

MINOR ATTACHMENT CLAIMANT. A claimant who qualifies to receive benefits and has fewer than 600 hours of insurable employment in their qualifying period *Employment Insurance Act, 1996*, S.C. 1996, c. 23, s. 6.

MINOR CHILDREN. Includes adolescents under the age of majority. *Saskatchewan School Division No. 4 v. Hall*, 2009 SKCA 118.

MINOR DISASTER. An exceptional event of a nature similar to a major disaster, but which only affects the safety of one or of a few persons. *Civil Protection Act*, R.S.Q. c. S-2.3, s. 2

MINORITY. *n.* 1. The situation of being under the age of majority. 2. The smaller part or smaller number. See PROTECTION OF MINORITIES.

MINORITY LANGUAGE EDUCATION RIGHTS. The rights, set out and limited by section 23 of the Canadian Charter of Human Rights and Freedoms, of persons to receive education in French or English when they are part of the French or English linguistic minority in the province in which they reside.

MINORITY OPINION. The decision and reasons of the minority of three or more judges who heard and decided a case.

MINOR VARIANCE. 1. " ... The term is a relative one and should be flexibly applied: ... No hard and fast criteria can be laid down, the question whether a variance is minor must in each case be determined in the light of the particular facts and circumstances of the case..." *McNamara Corp. v. Colekin Investments Ltd.* (1977), 2 M.P.L.R. 61 at 64, 15 O.R. (2d) 718, 76 D.L.R. (3d) 609 (Div. Ct.), the court per Robins J. 2. An authorization granted by a chief inspector to vary from a minor requirement in this Act, the regulations or a standard or permission for the use of a regulated product in a manner other than the standard use that is not specifically prohibited under this Act. *Technical Safety Act*, S.N.S. 2008, c. 10, s. 3.

MINOR WATERS OF CANADA. All inland waters of Canada other than Lakes Ontario, Erie, Huron, including Georgian Bay, and Superior and the St. Lawrence River east of a line drawn from Father Point to Point Orient, and includes all bays, inlets and harbours of or on those lakes and Georgian Bay and such sheltered waters on the sea-coasts of Canada as the Minister of Transport may specify. *Merchant Seamen Compensation Act*; R.S.C. 1985, c. M-6.

MINOR WATERS VOYAGE. A voyage within the following limits, namely, the minor waters of Canada together with the part of any lake or river forming part of the minor waters of Canada that lie within the United States. *Merchant Seamen Compensation Act*; R.S.C. 1985, c. M-6, s. 2.

MINT. *n.* 1. A place where money is coined. 2. The Royal Canadian Mint established by this Act to mint coins in anticipation of profit and to carry out other related activities. *Royal Canadian Mint Act*, R.S.C. 1985, c. R-9. s. 3. See MASTER OF THE ~; ROYAL CANADIAN ~.

MINT. *adj.* New; in fine condition.

MINUTE. *n.* A record or note of a transaction.

MINUTES OF PROCEEDINGS AND EVIDENCE. Of legislative and standing committees, a record of the proceedings of a committee prepared and signed by the clerk of that committee. A. Fraser, W.A. Dawson & J. Holtby, eds., *Beauchesne's Rules and Forms of the House of Commons of Canada*, 6th ed. (Toronto: Carswell, 1989) at 233.

MINUTES OF SETTLEMENT. A document filed with a court which sets out terms by which the parties have agreed to settle the dispute. May also refer to

M

the document which sets out the terms agreed to settle an arbitration.

MIRANDA WARNING. Named after Miranda v. Arizona, 384 U.S. 436 (1966)]. and given in the following terms: You have the right to remain silent. Anything you say can and will be used against you in a court of law. You have the right to talk to a lawyer before you are questioned and to have him present with you while you're being questioned. If you cannot afford to hire a lawyer, one will be appointed to represent you before questioning if you wish one. You can decide at any time to exercise these rights, not to answer any questions or make any statements. Okay, do you understand each of the rights I've read to you? *R. v. Terry*, [1996] 2 S.C.R. 207.

MISAPPREHENSION. *n.* Misapprehension of the evidence must go to the substance rather than to the detail; it must be material to the reasoning of the judge and not peripheral; and the errors must play an essential part not only in the narrative of the judgment but in the reasoning process itself. *R. v. Peters*, 2008 BCCA 446.

MISAPPROPRIATION. *n.* 1. "... [Dishonest or fraudulent appropriation of] money or other property entrusted to or received by [a person] whether to his own use or to the use of a third party." *Poy v. Law Society (British Columbia)* (1987), 36 D.L.R. (4th) 313 at 318, [1987] 3 W.W.R. 659, 11 B.C.L.R. (2d) 246 (C.A.), the court per Hinkson J.A. 2. In its ordinary sense connotes some element of wrongdoing, improper conduct or improper accounting. *Valastiak v. Valastiak*, 2010 BCCA 71.

MISAPPROPRIATION OF PERSONALITY. The common law tort of misappropriation of personality was first articulated by Estey J.A. in the Court of Appeal in Krouse v. Chrysler Canada Ltd. (1974), 40 D.L.R. (3d) 15 (Ont. C.A.). While no formal definition of the tort was offered, he stated at pp. 30-1: there may well be circumstances in which the Courts would be justified in holding a defendant liable in damages for appropriation of a plaintiff's personality, amounting to an invasion of his right to exploit his personality by the use of his image, voice, or otherwise with damage to the plaintiff. *Gould Estate v. Stoddart Publishing Co.* 30 O.R. (3d) 520 (Gen Div.).

MISBEHAVIOUR. *n.* "[In relation to an office] ... improper exercise of the functions appertaining to the office, or non-attendance or neglect of or refusal to perform the duties of the office." *Chesley v. Lunenburg (Town)* (1916), 28 D.L.R. 571 at 572, 50 N.S.R. 85 (C.A.), Harris J.A. (Graham C.J. concurring).

MISC. *abbr.* Miscellaneous.

MISCARRIAGE. *n.* 1. "... [S]uch departure from the rules which permeate all judicial procedure as to make that which happened not in the proper use of the word judicial procedure at all." *Robins v. National Trust Co.*, [1927] 1 W.W.R. 692 at 695, [1927] A.C. 515, [1927] 2 D.L.R. 97, [1927] All E.R. Rep. 73 (Ont. P.C.), Viscount Dunedin. 2. "... Proof of actual prejudice resulting from an error of law is not requisite to a finding that a 'miscarriage of justice' has occurred. It may be enough that an appearance of

unfairness exists: ..." *R. v. Duke* (1985), 39 Alta. L.R. (2d) 313 at 319, [1985] 6 W.W.R. 386, 62 A.R. 204, 22 C.C.C. (3d) 217 (C.A.), the court per McClung J.A. 3. The expulsion of a fetus, usually in the second third of a pregnancy. F.A. Jaffe, *A Guide to Pathological Evidence for Lawyers and Police Officers*, 4th ed. (Toronto: Carswell, 1999) at 240.

MISCARRIAGE OF JUSTICE. An error of law is defined as any decision that is an erroneous interpretation or application of the law. If an error deprives the accused of a fair trial, it constitutes a miscarriage of justice within the meaning of s. 686(1)(a)(iii) of the Criminal Code. *R. c. Arradi*, 2003 SCC 23.

MISCHIEF. *n.* 1. Wilfully destroying or damaging property; rendering property dangerous, useless, inoperative or ineffective; obstructing, interrupting or interfering with the lawful use, enjoyment or operation of property; or obstructing, interrupting or interfering with any person in the lawful use, enjoyment or operation of property. *Criminal Code*, R.S.C. 1985, c. C-46, s. 430(1). 2. Wilfully destroying or altering data, rendering data meaningless, useless or ineffective, obstructing, interrupting or interfering with the lawful use of data; or obstructing, interrupting or interfering with any person in the lawful use of data or denying access to data to any person who is entitled to access thereto. *Criminal Code*, R.S.C. 1985, c. C-46, s. 430(1.1). 3. "... [R]efers to the misuse of confidential information by a lawyer against a former client." *MacDonald Estate v. Martin* (1990), 48 C.P.C. (2d) 113 at 125, [1991] 1 W.W.R. 705, 121 N.R. 1, 77 D.L.R. (4th) 249, 70 Man. R. (2d) 241, [1990] 3 S.C.R. 1235, Sopinka J. (Dickson C.J.C., La Forest and Gonthier JJ. concurring). See PUBLIC ~.

MISCHIEF RULE. 1. It is the duty of every judge to always construe a situation to suppress mischief and advance the remedy. *Heydon's Case* (1584), 3 Co. Rep. 7a at 7b, 76 E.R. 637 (U.K.). 2. A test of the purpose or object of a statute. "... [R]equires the court to consider the evil or defect the law was meant to remedy and to see that the decision reached reinforces the remedy and does not compound the mischief." *Vijendren v. Hopkins* (1987), 11 R.F.L. (3d) 132 at 135 (Ont. Prov. Ct.), Campbell Prov. J.

MISCONDUCT. *n.* 1. Wilful disobedience. 2. Serious digression from recognized or established standards or rules of conduct in a profession. 3. Failure to perform a duty. 4. The commission of an offence by a member of the forces. 5. "[A servant] ... not being able to perform, in a due manner, his duties [to his master], or ... not being able to perform his duty in a faithful manner ..." *Pearce v. Foster* (1885), 17 Q.B. 536 at 539 (U.K. C.A.), Lord Esher M.R. See PROFESSIONAL ~.

MISDEMEANOUR. *n.* A lesser offence than a felony.

MISDESCRIPTION. *n.* An incorrect description.

MISDIRECTION. *n.* 1. An error in law made when a judge charges a jury or when a judge sitting alone puts the wrong questions forward to answer. 2. May include making an error as to the facts of the case, taking into consideration irrelevant factors or failing to take into account relevant factors, all of which would amount to an error in principle. *Elsom v. Elsom*, [1989] 1 S.C.R. 1367 at 1377. 3. Failure to refer to a specific piece of evidence will amount to misdirection by a judge requiring a new trial only where that item is the foundation of the defence. *R. v. Demeter* (1975), 22 C.C.C. (2d) 417 (Ont. C.A.) aff'd. on other grounds (1977), 34 C.C.C. (2d) 137 (S.C.C.).

MISFEASANCE. *n.* The improper execution of a lawful act, e.g. to be guilty of negligence in fulfilling a contract.

MISFEASANCE IN PUBLIC OFFICE. What then are the essential ingredients of the tort, at least insofar as it is necessary to determine the issues that arise on the pleadings in this case? In Three Rivers [Three Rivers District Council v. Bank of England (No. 3), [2000] 2 W.L.R. 1220], the House of Lords held that the tort of misfeasance in a public office can arise in one of two ways, what I shall call Category A and Category B. Category A involves conduct that is specifically intended to injure a person or class of persons. Category B involves a public officer who acts with knowledge both that she or he has no power to do the act complained of and that the act is likely to injure the plaintiff. This understanding of the tort has been endorsed by a number of Canadian courts [cases cited]. It is important, however, to recall that the two categories merely represent two different ways in which a public officer can commit the tort; in each instance, the plaintiff must prove each of the tort's constituent elements. It is thus necessary to consider the elements that are common to each form of the tort. In my view, there are two such elements. First, the public officer must have engaged in deliberate and unlawful conduct in his or her capacity as a public officer. Second, the public officer must have been aware both that his or her conduct was unlawful and that it was likely to harm the plaintiff. What distinguishes one form of misfeasance in a public office from the other is the manner in which the plaintiff proves each ingredient of the tort. In Category B, the plaintiff must prove the two ingredients of the tort independently of one another. In Category A, the fact that the public officer has acted for the express purpose of harming the plaintiff is sufficient to satisfy each ingredient of the tort, owing to the fact that a public officer does not have the authority to exercise his or her powers for an improper purpose, such as deliberately harming a member of the public. In each instance, the tort involves deliberate disregard of official duty coupled with knowledge that the misconduct is likely to injure the plaintiff. *Odhavji Estate v. Woodhouse*, [2003] 3 S.C.R. 263, 2003 SCC 69, Iacobucci J. for the court, para. 22.

MISJOINDER. *n.* The erroneous involvement of someone as a plaintiff or defendant in an action.

MISLEAD. *v.* "To withhold truthful, relevant and pertinent information may very well have the effect of 'misleading' just as much as to provide, positively, incorrect information." *Hilario v. Canada (Minister*

of Manpower & Immigration) (1978), 18 N.R. 529 at 530, [1978] 1 F.C. 697 (C.A.), the court per Heald J.A.

MISNOMER. *n.* Naming wrongly.

MISPLEADING. *n.* Omission of anything essential to a defence or action.

MISPRISION. *n.* 1. Negligence; neglect; oversight. 2. Used to describe an offence which is not given a specific name.

MISPRISION OF FELONY. For someone who knows that another person committed a felony to conceal or bring about the concealment of that knowledge.

MISREPRESENT. *v.* "... [A]lways connotes a positive act. One cannot misrepresent without positively representing, either by words or conduct, a material circumstance, which circumstance does not truly accord with the representation... ." *Taylor v. London Assurance Corp.*, [1934] O.R. 273 at 279, [1934] O.W.N. 199, [1934] 2 D.L.R. 657 (C.A.), Masten J.A. (dissenting).

MISREPRESENTATION. *n.* 1. "... [M]ay consist just as well in the concealment of that which should be disclosed as in the statement of that which is false for misrepresentation unquestionably may be made by concealment. If the non-disclosure of a material fact which the representor is bound to communicate is deliberate the misrepresentation is a fraudulent one; if it is unintentional it is none the less a misrepresentation though an innocent one." *Stearns v. Stearns* (1921), 56 D.L.R. 700 at 708, [1921] 1 W.W.R. 40 (Alta. T.D.), Walsh J. 2. "... [M]ay be made by silence when either the representee or a third person in his presence, or to his knowledge, states something false which indicates to the representor that the representee either is being, or will be, misled unless the necessary correction is made. Silence under the circumstances is either a tacit adoption by the party of another's misrepresentation as his own or a tacit confirmation of another's error as true." *Toronto Dominion Bank v. Leigh Instruments Ltd. (Trustee of)* (1991), 40 C.C.E.L. 262 at 289, 51 D.A.C. 321, 4 B.L.R. (2d) 220 (Div. Ct.), the court per Rosenberg J. 3. "... [A]s used in the relevant sections [of the Income Tax Act (Canada)] must be construed to mean any representation which was false in substance and in fact at the material date and it includes both innocent and fraudulent representations." *Hawrish v. Minister of National Revenue*, [1975] C.T.C. 446 at 453, 75 D.T.C. 5314 (Fed. T.D.), Heald J. 4. (a) An untrue statement of a material fact, or (b) an omission to state a material fact that is (i) required to be stated, or (ii) necessary to prevent a statement that is made from being false or misleading in the circumstances in which it was made. *Securities acts*. See FRAUDULENT ~; INNOCENT ~; NEGLIGENT ~.

MISSION. See HEAD OF ~.

MISTAKE. *n.* 1. Misunderstanding about the existence of something which arises either from a false belief or ignorance. 2. "... [A] written instrument does not accord with the true intention of the party who prepared it... ." *Farbwerke Hoechst A.G. Vormals*

M

Meister Lucius & Bruning v. Canada (Commissioner of Patents) (1966), 33 Fox Pat. C. 99 at 108, [1966] S.C.R. 604, 50 C.P.R. 220, the court per Martland J. See COMMON ~; FUNDAMENTAL ~; HONEST ~; MUTUAL ~; NON EST FACTUM; UNILATERAL ~.

MISTAKE OF FACT. 1. "... [A] defence, ... where it prevents an accused from having the mens rea which the law requires for the very crime with which he is charged. Mistake of fact is more accurately seen as a negation of guilty intention than as the affirmation of a positive defence. It avails an accused who acts innocently, pursuant to a flawed perception of the facts, ..." *R. v. Pappajohn (sub nom. Pappajohn v. R.)* (1980), 52 C.C.C. (2d) 481 at 494, [1980] 2 S.C.R. 120, 14 C.R. (3d) 243, 19 C.R. (3d) 97, [1980] 4 W.W.R. 387, 111 D.L.R. (3d) 1, 32 N.R. 104, Dickson J. 2. That a bank has a right to recover from a recipient a payment made under a mistake of fact was made clear in a restatement of the law by Goff J. (as he then was) in Barclays Bank Ltd. v. W. J. Simms Son & Cooke (Southern) Ltd., [1979] 3 All E.R. 522 (Q.B.), at p. 541. The test laid down in Simms for recovering money paid under a mistake of fact (at p. 535) is straightforward: 1. If a person pays money to another under a mistake of fact which causes him to make the payment, he is prima facie entitled to recover it as money paid under a mistake of fact. 2. His claim may however fail if: (a) the payer intends that the payee shall have the money at all events, whether the fact be true or false, or is deemed in law so to intend; (b) the payment is made for good consideration, in particular if the money is paid to discharge, and does discharge, a debt owed to the payee (or a principal on whose behalf he is authorised to receive the payment) by the payer or by a third party by whom he is authorised to discharge the debt; (c) the payee has changed his position in good faith, or is deemed in law to have done so. *B.M.P. Global Distribution Inc. v. Bank of Nova Scotia*, 2009 SCC 15, [2009] 1 S.C.R. 504. 3. A misunderstanding about the existence of some fact or about the existence of a right which depends on questions of mixed fact and law.

MISTAKE OF LAW. 1. An error, not in the actual facts, but relating as to their legal consequence, relevance or significance. D. Stuart, *Canadian Criminal Law: A Treatise*, 2d ed. (Toronto: Carswell, 1987) at 299. 2. An error regarding some general rule of law. 3. Examples of mistakes of law which a statutory decision maker may make include "... addressing his or her mind to the wrong question, applying the wrong principle, failing to apply a principle he or she should have applied, or incorrectly applying a legal principle." *Fraser v. Canada (Treasury Board, Department of National Revenue)* (1985), (*sub nom. Fraser v. Public Service Staff Relations Board*) 9 C.C.E.L. 233 at 242, [1985] 2 S.C.R. 455, 18 Admin. L.R. 72, 86 C.L.L.C. 14,003, 63 N.R. 161, 23 D.L.R. (4th) 122, 19 C.R.R. 152, [1986] D.L.Q. 84n, the court per Dickson C.J.C. 4. This Court has abandoned the distinction between mistake of fact and mistake of law as it applies to the law of unjust enrichment. There can be no doubt that the ordinary principles of unjust enrichment now apply in cases of payments made pursuant to mutual mistake of law. *Kingstreet*

Investments Ltd. v. New Brunswick (Finance), 2007 SCC 1, [2007] 1 S.C.R. 3.

MISTAKE OF TITLE. "... '[T]he belief that the land is his own.' If the land turns out not to be the property of the person occupying it, and that belief is bona fide, then that is a mistake of title." *Robertson v. Saunders* (1977), 75 D.L.R. (3d) 507 at 512 (Man. Q.B.), Hamilton J.

MISTRIAL. *n.* An incorrect trial. The trial is of no effect and reaches no conclusion.

MITIGATE. *v.* To lessen the effect of. See DUTY TO ~.

MITIGATION. *n.* 1. Reduction. 2. A duty or requirement that one who has suffered a loss seek to reduce the damages suffered as a result of the loss. 3. [T]he issue of mitigation is . . . one of "damages" and not "liability", at least in the narrow sense of that word. *JJM Construction Ltd. v. Sandspit Harbour Society*, 2000 CarswellBC 622, 2000 BCCA 208.

MITIGATION CONTINGENCY. In relation to claims for damages for death of a family member, an event which will reduce the size of loss experienced because of the family member's death. The two most common events are remarriage and adoption.

MITIGATION OF DAMAGES. "... [T]he defendant cannot be called upon to pay for avoidable losses which would result in an increase in the quantum of damages payable to the plaintiff... . the extent of those losses [a plaintiff may recover] depend on whether he has taken reasonable steps to avoid their unreasonable accumulation." *Michaels v. Red Deer College*, [1976] 2 S.C.R. 324 at 330-1, [1975] 5 W.W.R. 575, 5 N.R. 99, 75 C.L.L.C. 14,280, 57 D.L.R. (3d) 386, Laskin C.J.C.

MIXED ENTERPRISE COMPANY. A municipal entity may found a mixed enterprise company. The company may exercise any of the powers that are within the jurisdiction of a municipal entity, except the powers that relate to the supply of drinking water, water treatment, police matters and fire prevention and safety or any power the exercise of which was delegated temporarily to the municipal entity otherwise than under an agreement entered into with the Government pursuant to a pilot project. *An Act respecting mixed enterprise companies in the municipal sector*, R.S.Q. c. S-25.01, s. 2.

MIXED PROPERTY. A combination of personalty and realty.

MIXED QUESTION. A question which arises when foreign and domestic laws conflict. See ~ OF LAW AND FACT.

MIXED QUESTION OF LAW AND FACT. A case in which a jury finds the particular facts, and the court must decide on the legal quality of those facts using established rules of law, without general inferences or conclusions drawn by the jury.

M.L.B. DEC. *abbr.* Manitoba Labour Board Decisions, 1985-.

M.L. DIG. & R. *abbr.* Monthly Law Digest and Reporter (Québec), 1892-1893.

M.L.R. (K.B.). *abbr.* Montreal Law Reports, King's Bench (Québec), 1885-1891.

M.L.R. (Q.B.). *abbr.* Montreal Law Reports, Queen's Bench (Québec), 1885-1891.

M.L.R. (S.C.). *abbr.* Montreal Law Reports, Superior Court (Québec), 1885-1891.

M.M.C. *abbr.* Martin's Mining Cases (B.C.), 1853-1908.

M'NAGHTEN'S CASE. See MCNAGHTEN'S CASE.

M'NAUGHTEN'S CASE. See MCNAGHTEN'S CASE.

M.N.R. *abbr.* Minister of National Revenue.

MOBILE HOME. A building, the manufacture and assembly of which is completed or substantially completed, that is equipped with complete plumbing, electrical and heating facilities and that is designed to be moved to a site for installation on a foundation and connection to service facilities and to be occupied as a place of residence, but does not include any travel trailer, motor home, camping trailer or other vehicle or trailer designed for recreational use. *Excise Tax Act*, R.S.C. 1985, c. E-15, s. 123. 2.

MOBILE HOME PARK. The land on which one or more occupied mobile homes are located and includes the rental units and the land, structures, services and facilities of which the landlord retains possession and that are intended for the common use and enjoyment of the tenants of the landlord. *Residential Tenancies Act, 2006*, S.O. 2006, c. 17, s. 2.

MOBILITY. *n.* The physical ability of the insured to transfer himself or herself into or out of a vehicle or a wheelchair. *The Automobile Accident Insurance Act*, R.S.S. 1978, c. A-35, *The Personal Injury Benefits Regulations*, R.R.S., c. A-35, Reg. 3, Appendix D, Grid A, s. 2. See NATIONAL ~ AGREEMENT.

MOBILITY AIDE. The words "mobility aides" were not intended to be closely defined. It is obvious [in the context] that those words exceed the concept of "wheelchairs and accessories,". The ordinary meaning of the words "mobility aides" suggests that they could be anything which help or assist the individual to be more mobile or to retain his or her mobility. . . . . it serves no useful purpose, and indeed would be legally improper, to define the words "mobility aides" by a process of exclusion; by declaring that an ATV is not a mobility aide. *Dean v. Manitoba Public Insurance Corp.*, 2006 MBCA 97.

MOBILITY RIGHTS. 1. "[In s. 6 of the Charter] ... [R]ights of the person to move about, within and outside the national boundaries." *Skapinker v. Law Society of Upper Canada*, [1984] 1 S.C.R. 357 at 377, 9 D.L.R. (4th) 161, 8 C.R.R. 193, 53 N.R. 169, 3 O.A.C. 321, 11 C.C.C. (3d) 481, 20 Admin. L.R. 1, the court per Estey J. 2. "... Section 6(2) [of the Charter] touches only (a) the right to move freely from one province to another; (b) the right to take up residence in the province of one's choice; and (c) the right to work in any province, whether resident there or not." *Reference re Lands Protection Act (Prince Edward Island)* (1987), 48 R.P.R. 92 at 110, 64 Nfld. & P.E.I.R. 249, 197 A.P.R. 249, 40 D.L.R. (4th) 1 (P.E.I. C.A.), McQuaid J.A. (Carruthers C.J.P.E.I. concurring).

MODEL. See EXCLUSIVE JURISDICTION ~.

MODERN RULE OF STATUTORY INTERPRETATION. 1. Although much has been written about the interpretation of legislation (see, e.g., Ruth Sullivan, Statutory Interpretation (1997); Ruth Sullivan, Driedger on the Construction of Statutes (3rd ed. 1994) (hereinafter "Construction of Statutes"); Pierre-André Côté, The Interpretation of Legislation in Canada (2nd ed. 1991)), Elmer Driedger in Construction of Statutes (2nd ed. 1983) best encapsulates the approach upon which I prefer to rely. He recognizes that statutory interpretation cannot be founded on the wording of the legislation alone. At p. 87 he states: Today there is only one principle or approach, namely, the words of an Act are to be read in their entire context and in their grammatical and ordinary sense harmoniously with the scheme of the Act, the object of the Act, and the intention of Parliament. [end of quotation] Recent cases which have cited the above passage with approval include: R. v. Hydro-Québec, 1997 CanLII 318, [1997] 3 S.C.R. 213; Royal Bank of Canada v. Sparrow Electric Corp., 1997 CanLII 377, [1997] 1 S.C.R. 411; Verdun v. Toronto-Dominion Bank, 1996 CanLII 186, [1996] 3 S.C.R. 550; Friesen v. Canada, 1995 CanLII 62, [1995] 3 S.C.R. 103. *Rizzo & Rizzo Shoes Ltd. (Re)*, [1998] 1 S.C.R. 27, Iacobucci J. for the court. 2. Rizzo [cited above] postulates that the interpretation of legislation is a holistic exercise in the sense that its outcome is fashioned by a wide array of contextual considerations. Beyond the word or words at issue, the court must consider the other words used in the provision, any related provisions including definitional sections, the object of both the provision and the statute as a whole, the scheme that the legislation seeks to put in place and, where available, the descriptions of legislative intention provided in the course of ministerial interventions preceding passage in the assembly. Ultimately, courts may properly decline to give effect to legislative intention only where that intention has been incompetently expressed. *R. v. Joncas*, 2007 NBCA 28.

MODERN RULES AGAINST PERPETUITIES. Includes the operation of the rule with regard to remoteness of vesting and perpetual duration and with regard to testamentary executory interests in personalty. *The Trustee Act, 2009*, S.S. 2009, c. T-23.01, s. 57. See RULE AGAINST PERPETUITIES.

MODIFICATION. See LEASE ~ AGREEMENT; WEATHER ~ ACTIVITY.

MODIFY. *v.* To enlarge, extend, decrease, change.

MOD. L. REV. *abbr.* Modern Law Review.

MODUS. *n.* [L.] Manner; method.

MODUS OPERANDI. [L.] Method of operating.

MODUS PROCEDENDI. [L.] Method of proceeding.

MODUS TENENDI. [L.] Manner of holding.

M

MODUS TRANSFERRENDI. [L.] Manner of transferring.

MODUS VACANDI. [L.] Manner of vacating.

MODUS VIVENDI. [L.] Way of living.

MOIETY. *n.* A half; any fraction.

MOLECULAR DEATH. Cells permanently lose their functional integrity. F.A. Jaffe, *A Guide to pathological Evidence for Lawyers and Police Officers*, 4th ed. (Toronto: Carswell, 1999) at 234.

MOMENT. See AGONY OF THE ~.

MONARCHY. *n.* A government in which a single person holds supreme power.

MONETARY. *adj.* [T]he use of the adjective 'monetary' narrows the meaning of the word 'consideration.' The Oxford English Dictionary (2d ed., Oxford: Oxford University Press, 1998) defines 'monetary' as "of or relating to coinage or currency, especially that of a particular country; relating to money in the form of coins, notes or other units of account." Clearly, cash, cheques, credit card and debit transactions and pre-paid gift certificates easily come within that definition but the value of points redeemed for tobacco products in these narrow circumstances is not the equivalent of 'monetary consideration' as required to satisfy paragraph 29(b) of the [Tobacco Act, S.C. 1997, c. 13]. *Falls Management Co. v. Canada (Minister of Health)*, 2006 FCA 69.

MONETARY CONTRIBUTION. An amount of money provided that is not repayable.

MONEY. *n.* 1. "... [A]s commonly understood is not necessarily legal tender. Any medium which by practice fulfils the function of money and which everybody will accept in payment of a debt is money in the ordinary sense of the words even though it may not be legal tender ..." *Reference re Alberta Legislation*, [1938] 2 D.L.R. 81 at 92, [1938] S.C.R. 100, Duff C.J.C. (Davis J. concurring). 2. "... [W]hen used in a will means money in its strict sense unless there is a context which is sufficient to show that the testator used it in a more extended sense ..." *Lubeck, Re*, [1927] 1 W.W.R. 980 at 981 (Alta. C.A.), Clarke J.A. 3. "... [I]n the strict sense includes cash in hand and in the bank and any money for which at the time of his death the testator might have claimed immediate payment: ..." *Couperthwaite v. Couperthwaite*, [1950] 2 W.W.R. 58 at 63, [1950] 3 D.L.R. 229 (Sask. C.A.), the court per Martin C.J.S. 4. Includes any currency, cheque, promissory note, letter of credit, draft, traveller's cheque, bill of exchange, postal note, money order, postal remittance and other similar instrument, whether Canadian or foreign, but does not include currency the fair market value of which exceeds its stated value as legal tender in the country of issuance or currency that is supplied or held for its numismatic value. *Excise Tax Act*, R.S.C. 1985, c. E-15, s. 123. 5. Includes negotiable instruments. *Financial Administration Act*, R.S.C. 1985, c. F-11, s. 2. 6. A medium of exchange authorized by the Parliament of Canada or authorized or adopted by a foreign government as part of its currency. *Personal Property Security Act*, R.S.A. 2000, c. P-7, s. 1. 7. "[In the Jury

Act, S.A. 1982, c. J-2.1, s. 17(1)] ... should be interpreted to mean money or money's worth." *Sayers v. Shell Canada Resources Ltd.* (1984), 64 A.R. 319 at 320 (C.A.), the court per Kerans J.A. See ATTENDANCE ~; CONDUCT ~; COUNTERFEIT ~; EARNEST ~; GUARANTEED TRUST ~; INSURANCE ~; MORTGAGE ~; PUBLIC ~.

MONEY BILL. A bill to impose, repeal, remit, alter or regulate taxation, to impose charges on a consolidated fund to pay debt or for other financial purposes or to supply government requirements.

MONEY BROKER. A person who raises or lends money for or to other people.

MONEY BY-LAW. A by-law for contracting a debt or obligation or for borrowing money.

MONEY HAD AND RECEIVED. Money a defendant has received and which for reasons of equity the defendant should not retain. See ACTION FOR ~.

MONEY JUDGMENT. A judgment requiring a person to pay money or that part of a judgment that requires a person to pay money. *Civil Enforcement Act*, R.S.A. 2000, c. C-15, s. 1.

MONEY LAUNDERING. Occurs when money produced through criminal activity is converted into "clean money", the criminal origins of which are obscured. See LAUNDERING PROCEEDS OF CRIME.

MONEY LAUNDERING OFFENCE. An offence under subsection 462.31(1) of the Criminal Code. *Proceeds of Crime (Money Laundering) and Terrorist Financing Act*, S.C. 2000, c. 17, s. 2.

MONEY LENDER. A person who carries on the business of money lending or advertises or claims in any way to carry on that business, but does not include a registered pawn broker. *Consumer Protection Act*, R.S.N.W.T. 1988, c. C-17, s. 1.

MONEY MARKET MUTUAL FUND. A fund (a) the assets of which are fully or principally invested in short-term and highly liquid debt securities, and (b) that satisfies conditions prescribed by regulation. *Canadian Payments Act*, R.S.C. 1985, c. C-21, s. 2.

MONEY ORDER. An order to pay money which may be purchased at a bank or post office.

MONITOR. See EFFECTS ~ING.

MONITORING WELL. A well that (a) is used or intended to be used for the purpose of ongoing monitoring, observing, testing, measuring or assessing (i) the level, quantity or quality of ground water, or (ii) subsurface conditions, including geophysical conditions, and (b) is not used or intended to be used for the purpose of (i) exploring for or extracting ground water for use, or (ii) injecting water or any other substance into ground water on an ongoing basis. *Water Act*, R.S.B.C. 1996, c. 483, s. 1.

MONOGAMY. *n.* The marriage of one wife to one husband.

MONOPOLY. *n.* A situation where one or more persons either substantially or completely control throughout Canada or any area thereof the class or species of business in which they are engaged and have operated that business or are likely to operate it to the detriment or against the interest of the public, whether consumers, producers or others, but a situation shall not be deemed a monopoly within the meaning of this definition by reason only of the exercise of any right or enjoyment of any interest derived under the Patent Act or any other Act of Parliament. *Competition Act*, R.S.C. 1985, c. C-34, s. 2 [repealed].

MONTH. *n.* 1. A calendar month. *Bills of Exchange Act*, R.S.C. 1985, c. B-4, s. 45. 2. A period calculated from a day in one month to a day numerically corresponding to that day in the following month. 3. A period beginning on a particular day in a calendar month and ending on (a) the day immediately before the day in the next calendar month that has the same calendar number as the particular day; or (b) if the next calendar month does not have a day that has the same calendar number as the particular day, the last day of that next calendar month. *Air Travellers Security Charge Act*, S.C. 2002, c. 9, s. 5, s. 2. See CALENDAR ~.

MONTREAL DECLARATION ON FREE ACCESS TO LAW. Legal information institutes of the world, meeting in Montreal, declare that: Public legal information from all countries and international institutions is part of the common heritage of humanity. Maximizing access to this information promotes justice and the rule of law; Public legal information is digital common property and should be accessible to all on a non-profit basis and free of charge. Organizations such as legal information institutions have the right to publish public legal information and the government bodies that create or control that information should provide access to it so that it can be published by other parties. This declaration was made by legal information institutes meeting in Montreal in 2002, as amended at meetings in Sydney (2003), Paris (2004) and Montreal (2007). *Declaration on Free Access to Law*, online: World Legal Information Institute, <http://www.worldlii.org/worldlii/declaration/>. See CANADIAN LEGAL INFORMATION INSTITUTE; LEGAL INFORMATION INSTITUTE.

MONUMENT. *n.* An iron post, wooden post, mound, pit or trench, or anything else used to mark a boundary corner or line by a qualified surveyor. See BOUNDARY ~; LEGAL ~.

MOO. P.C. *abbr.* Moore, Privy Council.

MOO. P.C. (N.S.). *abbr.* Moore (N.S.) Privy Council.

MOOT. *n.* An exercise in which students plead and argue doubtful questions and cases.

MOOT. *adj.* A case is moot when something occurs after proceedings are commenced which eliminates the issue between the parties.

MOOTNESS. *n.* 1. "... [A]n aspect of a general policy or practice that a court may decline to decide a case which raises merely a hypothetical or abstract question. The general principle applies when the decision of the court will not have the effect of resolving some controversy which affects or may affect the rights of the parties. If the decision of the court will have no practical effect on such rights, the court will decline to decide the case. This essential ingredient must be present not only when the action or proceeding is commenced but at the time when the court is called upon to reach a decision. Accordingly if, subsequent to the initiation of the action or the proceeding, events occur which affect the relationship of the parties so that no present live controversy exists which affects the rights of the parties, the case is said to be moot." *Borowski v. Canada (Attorney General)* (1989), 38 C.R.R. 232 at 239, [1989] 3 W.W.R. 97, 33 C.P.C. (2d) 105, 47 C.C.C. (3d) 1, 57 D.L.R. (4th) 231, 92 N.R. 110, [1989] 1 S.C.R. 342, 75 Sask. R. 82, the court per Sopinka J. 2. The criteria for courts to consider in exercising discretion to hear a moot case (at pp. 358-63) are: (1) the presence of an adversarial context; (2) the concern for judicial economy; and (3) the need for the Court to be sensitive to its role as the adjudicative branch in our political framework. Sopinka, J. in *Borowski v. Canada*, cited above.

MORAL CERTAINTY. Has been interpreted as equivalent to reasonable doubt. The Ontario Court of Appeal first expressly embraced the language of moral certainty in R. v. Sears (1947), 90 C.C.C. 159 (Ont. C.A.), as follows: Moral certainty does not mean absolute certainty. Absolute, that is demonstrable, certainty is generally impossible and juries might well be told that in discharging their serious responsibility their consciences need not be racked and tortured because of the fact that absolute certainty is impossible. They do their full duty when they bring to bear upon all the evidence presented to them all the mental faculties with which Divine Providence has endowed them. No more is expected and if, after applying themselves to the best of their ability, they are, in a criminal trial, morally certain of the guilt of the accused, then it is their duty to return a verdict of guilty. It might even turn out later that they were wrong but they need not be mentally tormented by that possibility provided that they presently use their best judgment and are presently morally certain of the prisoner's guilt. *R. v. Jenkins*, (1996) 29 O.R. (3d) 30; 90 O.A.C. 263.

MORAL CULPABILITY. 1. In sentencing, examination of the intentional risks taken by the offender, the harm caused, and the degree of deviation from acceptable standards of behaviour the conduct constitutes. 2. The assessment of moral culpability is a question of mixed fact and law subject to deference in the absence of palpable and overriding error or an extricable error of principle. *R. v. Ferguson*, 2006 ABCA 261 at para. 63, cited in *R. v. McLeod*, 2008 ABCA 31.

MORALITY. *n.* Section 76(2) of the School Act clearly distinguishes between "the highest morality" and religious dogmas or creeds. That morality, while it may originate in religious reflection, must stand independently of its origins to maintain the allegiance of the whole of society including the plurality of religious adherents and those who are not religious. In this context, the highest morality is public virtue

M

in a truly free society. Public virtue upholds the dignity of the individual, the first principle which underlies the Charter and informs all of public life in a truly free society. That highest morality includes non-discrimination on grounds of sexual orientation. *Chamberlain v. Surrey School District No. 36*, 2000 CarswellBC 2009, 80 B.C.L.R. (3d) 181, [2000] 10 W.W.R. 393, 191 D.L.R. (4th) 128, 143 B.C.A.C. 162, 235 W.A.C. 162, 26 Admin. L.R. (3d) 297, Esson, Mackenzie and Proudfoot JJ.A.

MORAL OBLIGATION. "[Considering oneself] ... compelled to [do something] by what [one] thought was the right thing to do." *Norman v. Norman* (1972), 11 R.F.L. 105 at 106, 32 D.L.R. (3d) 262 (N.S. T.D.), Bissett J.

MORAL PREJUDICE. Moral prejudice has been defined as including loss of enjoyment of life, esthetic prejudice, physical and psychological pain and suffering, inconvenience, loss of amenities, and sexual prejudice. *Québec (Curateur public) c. Syndicat national des employés de l'hôpital St-Ferdinand*, 1996 CarswellQue 916, 202 N.R. 321, (*sub nom. Quebec (Public Curator) v. Syndicat national des employés de l'hôpital St-Ferdinand*) 138 D.L.R. (4th) 577, 1 C.P.C. (4th) 183, [1996] 3 S.C.R. 211, the court per L'Heureux-Dubé J.

MORAL RIGHTS. The author of a work has, subject to the Copyright Act, to the right to the integrity of the work and, in connection with an act mentioned in section 3 [right of copyright holder], the right, where reasonable in the circumstances, to be associated with the work as its author by name or under a pseudonym and the right to remain anonymous. *Copyright Act*, R.S.C. 1985, c. C-42, s. 14.1(1).

MORALS. See CORRUPTING ~.

MORAL TURPITUDE. Baseness or depravity in private or social duties, contrary to the customary rules of behaviour among persons.

MORATORIUM. *n.* The authorized delay in paying a debt.

MORE OR LESS. 1. A phrase used to compensate for slight inaccuracies in description in a contract for the sale of land or conveyance. 2. "... '[A]bout' ... words of general import and the excess or deficiency, as the case may be, which they cover bears a very small proportion to the amount named... ." *Canada Law Book Co. v. Boston Book Co.* (1922), 64 S.C.R. 182 at 200-201, 66 D.L.R. 209, Anglin J. (Mignault J. concurring).

MORTGAGE. *v.* To convey as security for a debt.

MORTGAGE. *n.* 1. The conveyance of land as a security for the discharge of an obligation or the payment of a debt, a security which may be redeemed when the obligation or debt is discharged or paid. B.J. Reiter, B.N. McLellan & P.M. Perell, *Real Estate Law*, 4th ed. (Toronto: Emond Montgomery, 1992) at 813. 2. A mortgage is a contract pursuant to which a borrower (mortgagor) pledges his land as security for the repayment of money he has borrowed from a lender (mortgagee). *Daniels v. Mitchell*, 2005 ABCA

271. 3. A charge on land created merely for securing a debt or loan. *Land Titles Act*, R.S.A. 2000, c. L-4, s. 1. See BLANKET ~; CANADA ~ AND HOUSING CORPORATION; CHATTEL ~; CONVERTIBLE ~; EQUITABLE ~; FIRST ~; HIGH-RATIO ~; LEGAL ~; PURCHASE-MONEY ~; SECOND ~; SUB~; VENDOR TAKE-BACK ~; WRAP-AROUND ~.

MORTGAGE BACK. The vendor receives a mortgage on property in exchange for loaning part of the purchase price.

MORTGAGE BOND. A type of corporate debt security in which the indenture is a mortgage on property of the corporation and the indenture trustee is mortgagee on behalf of the bondholders.

MORTGAGE BROKER. (i) A person who on behalf of another person for consideration or other compensation (A) solicits a person to borrow or lend money to be secured by a mortgage, (B) negotiates a mortgage transaction, (C) collects mortgage payments and otherwise administers mortgages, or (D) buys, sells or exchanges mortgages or offers to do so, or (ii) a person who holds out that the person is a person referred to in subclause (i). *Real Estate Act*, R.S.A. 2000, c. R-5, s. 1.

MORTGAGE COMMITMENT. A document issued by a lender to a borrower when, based on a credit report and property appraisal, the lender decides to go ahead with the loan.

MORTGAGE DEBENTURE. "... [F]orm of security, a debenture which is both an obligation for the payment of the money which is payable by the terms of it, and a mortgage on the property of the company by which it is issued, or some part of it, or secured by such a mortgage, ..." *Farmers' Loan & Savings Co., Re* (1898), 20 O.R. 337 at 354 (C.A.), Meredith J.A.

MORTGAGEE. *n.* 1. The owner of a mortgage. 2. The person who assumes a mortgage to secure a loan.

MORTGAGE INSURANCE. Insurance against loss caused by default on the part of a borrower under a loan secured by a mortgage upon real property, a hypothec upon immovable property or an interest in real or immovable property. *Insurance Act*, R.S.B.C. 1996, c. 226, *Insurance Classes Regulation*, B.C. Reg. 337/90, s. 2.

MORTGAGE MONEY. Money or money's worth secured by a mortgage. *Casson v. Westmorland Investment Ltd.* (1961), 27 D.L.R. (2d) 674 at 677, 33 W.W.R. 28 (B.C. C.A.), the court per Tysoe J.A.

MORTGAGE TRUST. A trustee holds mortgaged assets on behalf of multiple lenders on the same mortgage security. D.M.W. Waters, *The Law of Trusts in Canada*, 2d ed. (Toronto: Carswell, 1984) at 450.

MORTGAGOR. *n.* 1. One who borrows. 2. A person who gives a mortgage to secure a loan. 3. The owner or transferee of land or of any estate or interest in land pledged as security for a debt or loan. 4. Includes chargor.

MORTIS CAUSA. See DONATIO ~; GIFT ~.

MORTIS CAUSA DONATIO. See DONATIO MORTIS CAUSA.

MORTMAIN. *n.* [Fr. dead hand] 1. The state of possession of land which makes it inalienable. 2. Refers to a corporation's owning of real property. R. Megarry & H.W.R. Wade, *The Law of Real Property*, 5th ed. (London: Stevens, 1984) at cxxvi.

MORTMAIN ACT. An act which forbade the conveyance of land into the "dead hand" of the church or another corporation because a lord might thus be deprived of the benefits of tenure which arose in the lord's favour when the tenant died, because such conveyance prevented free alienation. Under these acts, the Crown always had the power to regulate the holding of land and there were significant statutory exceptions to these rules. E.L.G. Tyler & N.E. Palmer, eds., *Crossley Vaines' Personal Property*, 5th ed. (London: Butterworths, 1973) at 16.

MOTHER. See DOUBLE ~ RULE; SURROGATE ~.

MOTION. *n.* An oral or written application that the court rule or make an order before, during or after a trial. See DILATORY ~; NON-SUIT ~; NOTICE OF ~; WAYS AND MEANS ~.

MOTION PICTURE. See ADULT ~.

MOTIVE. *n.* 1. "... [T]hat which precedes and induces the exercise of the will... . in criminal law sense [means] 'ulterior intention' ..." *R. v. Lewis* (1979), 98 D.L.R. (3d) 111 at 120-1, [1979] 2 S.C.R. 821, 27 N.R. 451, 10 C.R. (3d) 299 (Eng.), 12 C.R. (3d) 315 (Fr.), 47 C.C.C. (2d) 24, the court per Dickson J. 2. "... [R]efers to an emotion or inner feeling such as hate or greed which is likely to lead to the doing of an act. The word 'motive' is also used, however, to refer to external events, for example, a previous quarrel, which is likely to excite the relevant feeling." *R. v. Malone* (1984), 11 C.C.C. (3d) 34 at 43, 2 O.A.C. 321 (C.A.), Martin J.A. (Lacourcière and Goodman JJ.A. concurring).

MOTOR CARRIER. A person operating a motor vehicle with or without trailer attached, as a public passenger vehicle, a public service vehicle, or as a freight vehicle.

MOTORIST. *n.* One who uses or operates a motor vehicle.

MOTOR VEHICLE. 1. "... [A] vehicle which is capable of being and is ordinarily self propelled by power generated within itself, as distinct, for example, from a horse drawn vehicle, or from one that is propelled by the application of externally generated power." *R. v. Thornton* (1950), 25 M.P.R. 140 at 148, 96 C.C.C. 323 (N.S. C.A.), Parker J.A. (Hall, MacQuarrie and Ilsley JJ.A. concurring). 2. A vehicle that uses or incorporates a motor as a source of power. *Environmental Protection Act*, R.S.O. 1990, c. E.19, s. 21. See DANGEROUS OPERATION OF ~S; REGISTRAR OF ~S.

MOTOR VEHICLE LIABILITY POLICY. A policy or part of a policy evidencing a contract insuring, (a) the owner or driver of an automobile, or (b) a person who is not the owner or driver thereof where the automobile is being used or operated by that person's employee or agent or any other person on that person's behalf, against liability arising out of bodily injury to or the death of a person or loss or damage to property caused by an automobile or the use or operation of an automobile. *Insurance Act*, R.S.O. 1990, c. I.8, s. 1.

MOURNING. See WORKERS ~ DAY.

MOVABLE HYPOTHEC. One made without delivery shall, on pain of absolute nullity, be granted in writing. A sufficient description of the hypothecated property shall be contained in the act constituting a movable hypothec or, in the case of a universality of movables, an indication of the nature of that universality. *Civil Code*, S.Q. 1991, c. 64, a. 2696 and 2697.

MOVABLE HYPOTHEC WITH DELIVERY. Is granted by physical delivery of the property or title to the creditor or, if the property is already in his hands, by his continuing to physically hold it, with the grantor's consent, to secure his claim. *Civil Code*, S.Q. 1991, c. 64, a. 2702.

MOVABLES. *n.* Any movable tangible property, other than the ship, and includes money, valuable securities, and other documents. *Insurance acts*.

MOVE. *v.* To bring a motion or an application before a court or tribunal.

M.P.L.R. *abbr.* Municipal and Planning Law Reports, 1976-1990.

M.P.L.R (2D). *abbr.* Municipal and Planning Law Reports (Second Series), 1991-.

M.P.R. *abbr.* Maritime Provinces Reports, 1929-1968.

M.R. *abbr.* Master of the Rolls.

M.R.N. *abbr.* Ministre du Revenu national.

MSDS. *abbr.* Material safety data sheet.

M.T.R. *abbr.* Maritime Tax Reports.

MULE. *n.* One who transports contraband. F.A. Jaffe, *A Guide to Pathological Evidence for Lawyers and Police Officers*, 4th ed. (Toronto: Carswell, 1999) at 241.

MULTICULTURAL HERITAGE. Section 27 of the Charter recognizes the multi-cultural heritage of Canadians in the following terms: This Charter shall be interpreted in a manner consistent with the preservation and enhancement of the multicultural heritage of Canadians.

MULTICULTURALISM POLICY. *n.* It is the policy of the Government of Saskatchewan to: (a) support the continued development and expression of all cultures within the framework of democratic principles and the laws of Canada; (b) preserve, strengthen and promote Aboriginal cultures and acknowledge their historical and continued contribution to the development of Saskatchewan; (c) preserve, strengthen and promote all cultures and acknowledge the role of ethnic communities in building Saskatchewan and shaping its future; (d) promote the full, free and equal participation of all individuals in Saskatchewan so-

M

ciety; (e) act in partnership with community groups and organizations to encourage and enhance co-operation and understanding among cultures. *Multiculturalism Act*, S.S. 1997, c. M-23.01, s. 4.

MULTI-DISCIPLINARY PARTNERSHIP. Lawyers may enter into partnership with non-lawyers, provided the partnership can comply with the Rules of the governing body and rules of professional conduct governing such practices. The lawyers involved in the partnership must have effective control over the legal services the partnership provides, but non-lawyer partners will not be able to provide services to the public unless they support or supplement the practice of law by the MDP. May occur with patent agents or realtors, for example. *B.C. Law Society Rules*, online: The Law Society of B.C., <http://www.lawsociety.bc.ca/publications_forms/rules/rules_toc.html>, Rules 2-23.1 to 2-23.12.

MULTI-EMPLOYER PENSION PLAN. A pension plan organized and administered for employees of two or more employers who contribute to the plan pursuant to an agreement, by-law or statute, where the pension plan provides pension benefits that are determined by periods of employment with any or all of the participating employers, but does not include a pension plan where more than ninety-five per cent of the plan members are employed by participating employers who are incorporated and are affiliates within the meaning of the Canada Business Corporations Act. *Pension Benefits Standards Act*, 1985, R.S.C. 1985, c. 32 (2nd Supp.), s. 2.

MULTILATERAL. *adj.* Concerning more than two nations.

MULTIPARTITE. *adj.* Divided into many parts.

MULTI-PERIL POLICY. A policy of insurance which insures against loss from several causes. A typical homeowner policy is a multi-peril policy.

MULTIPLE LISTING. 1. An agreement between a vendor and one broker authorizing other brokers to sell the property for a portion of the commission agreed. 2. Property listed through a real estate board's multiple listing service.

MULTIPLE SUFFICIENT CAUSATION. Two legally relevant causes, each alone sufficient to cause an injury or loss and each required (in a but for sense) if the other were absent, combine to originate an injury or loss. K.D. Cooper-Stephenson & I.B. Saunders, *Personal Injury Damages in Canada* (Toronto: Carswell, 1981) at 653.

MULTIPLICITY. *n.* Excessive division or fracture of one cause or suit.

MUN. *abbr.* 1. Municipal. 2. Municipality.

MUNCHAUSEN BY PROXY SYNDROME. Reporting a fictional illness or injuring a child so that the child can be admitted to hospital. F.A. Jaffe, *A Guide to Pathological Evidence for Lawyers and Police Officers*, 4th ed. (Toronto: Carswell, 1999) at 136.

MUNCHAUSEN SYNDROME. Reporting a fictional illness so one can get medical attention. F.A.

Jaffe, *A Guide to Pathological Evidence for Lawyers and Police Officers*, 4th ed. (Toronto: Carswell, 1999) at 245.

MUN. CT. *abbr.* Municipal Court.

MUNICIPAL. *adj.* Related to a municipal corporation.

MUNICIPAL CORPORATION. 1. The legal entity established under legislation which is distinct from residents, ratepayers or members of municipal council and which transacts the business of a municipality. 2. "... [A] public corporation created by the government for political purposes and having subordinate and local powers of legislation. It can exercise its corporate powers only within its defined limits. It does not own its defined territorial area, but is limited thereto as to its jurisdiction." *Hatch v. Rathwell* (1909), 12 W.L.R. 376 at 377, 19 Man. R. 465 (C.A.), the court per Cameron J.A. 3. The corporation of a locality the inhabitants of which are incorporated. *Power Corporation Act*, R.S.O. 1990, c. P.18, s. 1.

MUNICIPAL CORRUPTION. Every one who offers or agrees to give or offer to a municipal official or to anyone for the benefit of a municipal official—or, being a municipal official, directly or indirectly demands, accepts or offers or agrees to accept from any person for themselves or another person—a loan, reward, advantage or benefit of any kind as consideration for the official (a) to abstain from voting at a meeting of the municipal council or a committee of the council; (b) to vote in favour of or against a measure, motion or resolution; (c) to aid in procuring or preventing the adoption of a measure, motion or resolution; or (d) to perform or fail to perform an official act is guilty of an indictable offence. Every one is guilty of an indictable offence who influences or attempts to influence a municipal official to do anything mentioned in paragraphs (1)(a) to (d) by (a) suppression of the truth, in the case of a person who is under a duty to disclose the truth; (b) threats or deceit; or (c) any unlawful means. *Criminal Code*, R.S.C. 1985, c. C-46, s. 123.

MUNICIPAL COURT. One or more municipalities may establish a municipal court. A municipal court is a court of original jurisdiction in the matters devolved upon it by law; it is a court of record. In civil matters, a municipal court has jurisdiction to dispose of (1) any action brought under a municipal by-law, resolution or order for the recovery of any sum of money due to the municipality in respect of a tax, licence, tariff, water rate, fee, compensation or permit or otherwise; (2) any action for the recovery of school taxes which the municipality collects on behalf of a school board; (3) any action in which the amount claimed is under $30,000, brought by the municipality as the lessor of movable or immovable property situated in its territory other than an immovable for housing purposes, or any action of the same nature instituted by the lessee of such property against the municipality. In penal matters, a municipal court has jurisdiction to dispose of penal proceedings for the prosecution of an offence under any provision of (1) the charter of the municipality or a municipal by-law, resolution or order; (2) the Act governing the municipality. *An Act respecting municipal courts*, R.S.Q. c. C-72.01, various.

MUNICIPAL GOVERNMENT. A body subordinate to national authority with legislative power over a local territory.

MUNICIPALITY. *n.* 1. A locality the inhabitants of which are incorporated. 2. Includes the corporation of a city, town, village, county, township, parish or other territorial or local division of a province, the inhabitants of which are incorporated or are entitled to hold property collectively for a public purpose. *Criminal Code*, R.S.C. 1985, c. C-46, s. 2. 3. An incorporated city, metropolitan authority, town, village, township, district or rural municipality or other incorporated municipal body however designated. *Excise Act, 2001*, S.C. 2002, c. 22, s. 211. 4. An area under the jurisdiction of a municipal council. See LOWER TIER ~.

MUNICIPAL LAW. 1. Law relating to municipal corporations and their government. 2. Law relating exclusively to the citizens and inhabitants of a country, differing thus from the law of nations and political law.

MUNICIPAL OFFICIAL. A member of a municipal council or a person who holds an office under a municipal government. *Criminal Code*, R.S.C. 1985, c. C-46, s. 123.

MUNICIPAL PURPOSES. Are determined by reference to not only those that are expressly stated but those that are compatible with the purpose and objects of the enabling statute. *Shell Canada Products Ltd. v. Vancouver (City)*, 1994 CarswellBC 115, 88 B.C.L.R. (2d) 145, [1994] 3 W.W.R. 609, 20 M.P.L.R. (2d) 1, 110 D.L.R. (4th) 1, 163 N.R. 81, [1994] 1 S.C.R. 231, 41 B.C.A.C. 81, 66 W.A.C. 81, 20 Admin. L.R. (2d) 202, Sopinka J.

MUNICIPAL QUESTION. One which deals with municipal governance or the structure of the municipal government, a question which may be submitted to the electorate by plebiscite.

MUNICIPAL TAX. "... [T]axes imposed by the governing body of a municipality for the purposes of the municipality... ." *Canadian Pacific Railway v. Winnipeg (City)* (1900), 30 S.C.R. 558 at 564, the court per Sedgewick J.

MUNICIPAL TAX RATE. The tax rate imposed on property by way of municipal property value taxes. *Ports Property Tax Act*, S.B.C. 2004, c. 7, s. 1.

MUNIMENT. *n.* A record; defence; a written document upon which one establishes a right or claim and depends; evidence.

MUNITIONS OF WAR. Arms, ammunition, implements or munitions of war, military stores or any articles deemed capable of being converted there into or made useful in the production thereof. *Security of Information Act*, R.S.C. 1985, c. O-5, s. 2.

M.U.R.B. *abbr.* Multi-unit residential building.

MURDER. *n.* 1. "The classic definition of murder is that of Sir Edward (Chief Justice) Coke ... 'Murder is when a man ... unlawfully killeth ... any reasonable creature in rerum natura under the king's peace, with malice aforethought, either expressed by the party, or implied by law, so as the party wounded, or hurt, etc., die of the wound, or hurt, etc. within a year and a day after the same.' ... Murder requires, positively, the mental element traditionally known as 'malice aforethought', and, negatively, the absence of certain mitigating circumstances that would turn the case into one of manslaughter... . the law has consistently required that murder be an offence of specific intent. The specific intents have generally been clearly described in Canada in statutory form, and an unlawful killing without proof of the existence of the required specific intent has always been characterized as manslaughter. On all the authorities, the mental element – the 'malice aforethought' of ancient usage – must always be demonstrated in order to procure a conviction of murder." *R. v. Swietlinski* (1980), 18 C.R. (3d) 231 at 247-9, 34 N.R. 569, 55 C.C.C. (2d) 481, 117 D.L.R. (3d) 285, [1980] 2 S.C.R. 956, the court per McIntyre J. 2. Culpable homicide is murder (a) where the person who causes the death of a human being (i) means to cause his death, or (ii) means to cause him bodily harm that he knows is likely to cause his death, and is reckless whether death ensues or not; (b) where a person, meaning to cause death to a human being or meaning to cause him bodily harm that he knows is likely to cause his death, and being reckless whether death ensues or not, by accident or mistake causes death to another human being, notwithstanding that he does not mean to cause death or bodily harm to that human being; or (c) where a person, for an unlawful object, does anything that he knows or ought to know is likely to cause death, and thereby causes death to a human being, notwithstanding that he desires to effect his object without causing death or bodily harm to any human being. *Criminal Code*, R.S.C. 1985, c. C-46, s. 229. 3. Culpable homicide is murder when committed while committing or attempting to commit certain offences if certain conditions are met. *Criminal Code*, R.S.C. 1985, c. C-46, s. 230. See CAPITAL ~; CONTRACTED ~; FIRST DEGREE ~; NON-CAPITAL ~; SECOND DEGREE ~.

MURDER IN COMMISSION OF OFFENCES. Culpable homicide is murder where a person causes the death of a human being while committing or attempting to commit high treason or treason or sabotage, piracy, hijacking an aircraft, escape or rescue from prison or lawful custody, assaulting a peace officer, resisting lawful arrest, sexual assault, kidnapping, forcible confinement, hostage taking, breaking and entering, robbery, or arson whether or not the person means to cause death to any human being and whether or not he knows that death is likely to be caused to any human being, if (a) he means to cause bodily harm for the purpose of (i) facilitating the commission of the offence, or (ii) facilitating his flight after committing or attempting to commit the offence, and the death ensues from the bodily harm; (b) he administers a stupefying or overpowering thing for a purpose mentioned in paragraph (a), and the death ensues therefrom; (c) he wilfully stops, by any means, the breath of a human being for a purpose

M

mentioned in paragraph (a), and the death ensues therefrom. *Criminal Code*, R.S.C. 1985, c. C-46, s. 230.

MUSEUM. See CANADIAN ~ FOR HUMAN RIGHTS; CANADIAN ~ OF CIVILIZATION; CANADIAN ~ OF NATURE; NATIONAL ~ OF SCIENCE AND TECHNOLOGY.

MUSEUM MATERIAL. Objects and documentary material, regardless of medium or form, of a type normally kept by a museum for reference or exhibition purposes. *Museums Act*, S.C. 1990, c. 3, s. 2

MUSICAL WORK. Any work of music or musical composition, with or without words, and includes any compilation thereof. *Copyright Act*, R.S.C. 1985, c. C-42, s. 2.

MUST. *v.* 1. Shall. 2. An imperative, expresses command, obligation, duty.

MUTATIS MUTANDIS. [L.] With needed changes in the details. *R. v. Century 21 Ramos Realty Inc.* (1987), 56 C.R. (3d) 150 at 181-2, 87 D.T.C. 5158, 19 O.A.C. 25, 32 C.C.C. (3d) 353, 37 D.L.R. (4th) 649, 29 C.R.R. 320, [1987] 1 C.T.C. 340, 58 O.R. (2d) 737, Martin, Houlden and Tarnopolsky JJ.A.

MUTILATION. *n.* Depriving of any necessary part or limb.

MUTINY. *n.* Collective insubordination or a combination of two or more persons in the resistance of lawful authority in any of Her Majesty's Forces or in any forces cooperating therewith. *National Defence Act*, R.S.C. 1985, c. N-5, s. 2.

MUTUAL. See CASH-~ COMPANY.

MUTUAL BENEFIT SOCIETY. A body corporate formed for the purpose of providing sick, disability or funeral benefits for its members. *Insurance Act*, R.S.A. 2000, c. I-3, s. 13. See EMPLOYEES' ~.

MUTUAL CORPORATION. A corporation without share capital that is empowered to undertake mutual insurance exclusively. *Insurance Act*, R.S.O. 1990, c. I.8, s. 1. See CASH-~.

MUTUAL DEBTS. Cross obligations.

MUTUAL FUND. (i) An issuer whose primary purpose is to invest money provided by its security holders and whose securities entitle the holder to receive on demand, or within a specified period after demand, an amount computed by reference to the value of a proportionate interest in the whole or in part of the net assets, including a separate fund or trust account, of the issuer, or (ii) an issuer that is designated as a mutual fund under section 10 or in accordance with the regulations, but does not include an issuer, or class of issuers, that is designated under section 10 not to be a mutual fund. *Securities Act*, R.S.A. 2000, c. S-4, s. 1. See MONEY MARKET ~.

MUTUAL FUND CORPORATION. A company that offers public participation in an investment portfolio through the issue of one or more classes of mutual fund shares.

MUTUAL FUND DISTRIBUTION ENTITY. An entity whose principal activity is acting as a selling agent of units, shares or other interests in a mutual fund and acting as a collecting agent in the collection of payments for any such interests if (a) the proceeds of the sales of any such interests, less any sales commissions and service fees, are paid to the mutual fund; and (b) the existence of a sales commission and service fee in respect of the sale of any such interest is disclosed to the purchaser of the interest before the purchase of the interest. *Bank Act*, S.C. 1991, c. 46, s. 464.

MUTUAL FUND ENTITY. An entity (a) whose activities are limited to the investing of the funds of the entity so as to provide investment diversification and professional investment management to the holders of its securities; and (b) whose securities entitle their holders to receive, on demand, or within a specified period after demand, an amount computed by reference to the value of a proportionate interest in the whole or in a part of its net assets, including a separate fund or trust account of the entity. *Bank Act*, S.C. 1991, c. 46, s. 464.

MUTUAL FUND SECURITY. A share, unit or similar equity interest issued by an open-end mutual fund, but does not include an insurance policy, endowment policy or annuity contract issued by an insurance company. *Securities Transfer Act*, S.B.C. 2007, c. 10, s. 11.

MUTUAL FUND SHARE. A share having conditions attached thereto that include conditions requiring the company issuing the share to accept, at the demand of the holder thereof and at prices determined and payable in accordance with the conditions, the surrender of the share, or fractions or parts thereof, that are fully paid. *Companies Act*, R.S.A. 2000, c. C-21, s. 84.

MUTUAL INSURANCE. A contract of insurance in which the consideration is not fixed or certain at the time the contract is made and is to be determined at the termination of the contract or at fixed periods during the term of the contract according to the experience of the insurer in respect of all similar contracts, whether or not the maximum amount of such consideration is predetermined. *Insurance Act*, R.S.O. 1990, c. I.8, s. 1.

MUTUAL INSURANCE FEDERATION. A corporation each member of which is a mutual insurance corporation that is required, under an Act of the legislature of a province, to be a member of the corporation, but does not include a corporation the main purpose of which is (a) related to automobile insurance, (b) to provide compensation to insurance policy holders of, or claimants on, insolvent insurers, or (c) to establish and manage a guarantee fund, cash reserve fund, mutual aid fund or similar fund for the benefit of its members and to provide financial assistance with regard to losses sustained on the winding-up or dissolution of its members. *Excise Tax Act*, R.S.C. 1985, c. E-15, s. 123.

MUTUAL INSURANCE GROUP. A group that consists of (a) a mutual insurance federation and its members, (b) where the members of the mutual insurance federation are the sole investors in an investment fund, that fund, and (c) where there exists a mutual reinsurance corporation each member of which is a member of the mutual insurance federation and is not entitled to obtain reinsurance from any other reinsurance corporation, that mutual reinsurance corporation. *Excise Tax Act*, R.S.C. 1985, c. E-15, s. 123.

MUTUALITY OF ASSENT. Regarding the main or necessary part of any agreement, for each party to intend the same thing and to know what the other will do.

MUTUALITY OF OBLIGATION. For each party to an agreement to be bound to do something.

MUTUALITY OF REMEDY. For each party to an agreement to be able to enforce that agreement against the other.

MUTUAL MISTAKE. Mistake which is suffered by both parties to an agreement. Each party is mistaken as to the intention of the other party, but neither party realizes that their respective promises have been misunderstood. *Stepps Investments Ltd. v. Security Capital Corp.* (1976), 14 O.R. (2d) 259 at 269, 73 D.L.R. (3d) 351 (H.C.), Grange J.

MUTUAL PROMISES. Simultaneous considerations which support each other.

MUTUAL WILLS. "... [T]hey confer mutual benefits upon two or more testators and there must be something in the nature of a contract, that is one contracting party agrees to confer certain benefits by will, the other contracting party will confer reciprocal benefits by his will. The situation should be one in which one party would not make his will unless the other one also made a will conferring similar benefits... ." *Ohorodnyk, Re* (1979), 4 E.T.R. 233 at 244, 97 D.L.R. (3d) 502, 24 O.R. (2d) 228 (H.C.), Hollingworth J.

MUTUEL FIELD. Two or more horses in a race that, for the purpose of making a bet, are treated as one horse because the number of horses in the race exceeds the number that can be dealt with individually by the pari-mutuel system. *Criminal Code*, R.S.C. 1985, c. C-46, *Pari-Mutuel Betting Supervision Regulations*, SOR/91-365, s. 2.

M.V.R. *abbr.* Motor Vehicle Reports, 1979-1988.

M.V.R. (4TH). *abbr.* Motor Vehicle Reports (Fourth Series), 2000-.

M.V.R. (2D). *abbr.* Motor Vehicle Reports (Second Series), 1988-1994.

M.V.R. (3D). *abbr.* Motor Vehicle Reports (Third Series), 1994-2000.

MYTH. See TWIN ~S.

M

N

NAFTA. *abbr.* The North American Free Trade Agreement.

NAKED CONTRACT. A contract which lacks consideration.

NAKED TRUST. See BARE TRUST.

NAME. *n.* A given name and surname. See BIRTH ~; BRAND ~; BUSINESS ~; CHANGE OF ~; CORPORATE ~; DOMAIN ~; FAMILY ~; FIRM ~; FIRST ~; GIVEN ~; SUR~; TRADE-~.

NAMED INSURED. A person specified in a contract of insurance as the one protected by the contract.

NAMED PRINCIPAL. The party for whom an agent acts and whose name was revealed by the agent to the third party(ies).

NARCOTIC. *n.* A drug which controls pain, induces sleep and stupor. F.A. Jaffe, *A Guide to Pathological Evidence for Lawyers and Police Officers*, 4th ed. (Toronto: Carswell, 1999) at 241. Formerly controlled under the Narcotics Control Act and more recently under the *Controlled Drugs and Substances Act, 1996*, S.C. 1996, c. 19.

NAT. BANKING L. REV. *abbr.* National Banking Law Review.

NAT. CREDITOR/DEBTOR REV. *abbr.* National Creditor/Debtor Review.

NAT. INSOLVENCY REV. *abbr.* National Insolvency Review.

NATION. *n.* People distinct from other people, usually because of language or government. See COMITY OF ~S; COMMONWEALTH OF ~S; FIRST ~; INTERNATIONAL LAW; LAW OF ~S.

NATIONAL. *n.* 1. An individual possessing the nationality of a state. 2. Any legal person, partnership and association deriving its status as such from the law in force in a state. See FOREIGN ~.

NATIONAL ANTHEM. The words and music of the song "O Canada" are designated as the national anthem of Canada.

NATIONAL ASSEMBLY. The legislative assembly of the province of Quebec. The National Assembly is composed of the Members elected for each of the electoral divisions established in accordance with the Election Act (chapter E-3.3) and whose names have been transmitted to the Secretary General by the chief electoral officer in accordance with section 380 of the said Act. *An Act respecting the National Assembly*, R.S.Q. c. A-23.1, s. 1.

NATIONAL BUILDING CODE. The National Building Code of Canada 1995, issued by the Canadian Commission on Building and Fire Codes, National Research Council of Canada, dated 1995, as amended from time to time. *Canada Labour Code*, R.S.C. 1985, c. L-2, *Canada Occupational Health and Safety Regulations*, SOR/86-304, s. 1.2.

NATIONAL CAPITAL COMMISSION. A corporation, called the National Capital Commission, consisting of a Chairperson, a Chief Executive Officer and thirteen other members. The objects and purposes of the Commission are to (a) prepare plans for and assist in the development, conservation and improvement of the National Capital Region in order that the nature and character of the seat of the Government of Canada may be in accordance with its national significance; and (b) organize, sponsor or promote such public activities and events in the National Capital Region as will enrich the cultural and social fabric of Canada, taking into account the federal character of Canada, the equality of status of the official languages of Canada and the heritage of the people of Canada. The Commission shall, in accordance with general plans prepared under the National Capital Act, coordinate the development of public lands in the National Capital Region. *National Capital Act*, R.S.C. 1985, c. N-4, s. 3, 11, and 12.

NATIONAL CAPITAL REGION. The seat of the Government of Canada and its surrounding area, more particularly described in the schedule. *National Capital Act*, R.S.C. 1985, c. N-4, s. 2.

NATIONAL CONCERN DOCTRINE. Features of the doctrine are: 1.The national concern doctrine is separate and distinct from the national emergency doctrine of the peace, order and good government power, which is chiefly distinguishable by the fact that it provides a constitutional basis for what is necessarily legislation of a temporary nature. 2. The national concern doctrine applies to both new matters which did not exist at Confederation and to matters which, although originally matters of a local or private nature in a province, have since, in the absence of national emergency, become matters of national concern. 3. For a matter to qualify as a matter of national concern in either sense it must have a singleness, distinctiveness and indivisibility that clearly distinguishes it from matters of provincial concern and a scale of impact on provincial jurisdiction that is reconcilable with the fundamental distribution of legislative power under the Constitution. 4. In determining whether a matter has attained the required degree of singleness, distinctiveness and indivisibility that clearly distinguishes it from matters of provincial concern it is relevant to consider what would be the effect on extra-provincial interests of a provincial failure to deal effectively with the control or regulation of the intra-provincial aspects of the matter. *R. v. Crown Zellerbach Canada Ltd.*, [1988] 1 S.C.R. 401, Le Dain, J.

NATIONAL DAY OF REMEMBRANCE. On December 6, 1989, fourteen women died as a result of a massacre at the University of Montreal. Throughout Canada, in each and every year, 6th day of December shall be known under the name of "National Day of Remembrance and Action on Violence Against Women." *National Day of Remembrance Act*, S.C. 1991, c. 36.

NATIONAL DEBT. Money which a national government owes and on which interest is paid.

NATIONAL DEFENCE. See DEPARTMENT OF ~.

NATIONAL DNA DATA BANK. The Minister of Public Safety and Emergency Preparedness shall, for criminal identification purposes, establish a national DNA data bank, consisting of a crime scene index and a convicted offenders index, to be maintained by the Commissioner. *DNA Identification Act*, S.C. 1998, c. 37, s. 5.

NATIONAL EMISSIONS MARK. A mark established by regulation for use in respect of emissions from vehicles, engines or equipment and which may be applied by a company authorized to do so. *Canadian Environmental Protection Act, 1999*, S.C. 1999, c. 33, s. 149, 151.

NATIONAL FARM PRODUCTS COUNCIL. Established by the Farm Products Agencies Act, R.S.C. 1985, c. F-4. Section 6 provides that the duties of the Council are: (a) to advise the Minister on all matters relating to the establishment and operation of agencies under this Act with a view to maintaining and promoting an efficient and competitive agriculture industry; (b) to review the operations of agencies with a view to ensuring that they carry on their operations in accordance with their objects set out in section 21 or 41, as the case may be; and (c) to work with agencies in promoting more effective marketing of farm products in interprovincial and export trade and, in the case of a promotion-research agency, in promoting such marketing in import trade and in connection with research and promotion activities relating to farm products. The agencies referenced are farm products marketing agencies.

NATIONAL FIRE CODE. The National Fire Code of Canada 1995, issued by the Canadian Commission on Building and Fire Codes, National Research Council of Canada, dated 1995, as amended from time to time. *Canada Labour Code*, R.S.C. 1985, c. L-2, *Canada Occupational Health and Safety Regulations*, SOR/86-304, s. 1.2.

NATIONAL GALLERY OF CANADA. Shall include the Canadian Museum of Contemporary Photography and such other affiliated museums as the Board of the National Gallery of Canada may, by by-law, establish with the approval of the Governor in Council. *Museums Act*, S.C. 1990, c. 3, s. 4.

NATIONALITY. *n.* The character or quality which originates in a person belonging to a particular nation and which determines that individual's political status.

NATIONALIZATION. *n.* The acquisition of a business by government.

NATIONAL MOBILITY AGREEMENT. An agreement among law societies to permit members of one society to practise in another jurisdiction on a temporary basis.

NATIONAL MUSEUM OF SCIENCE AND TECHNOLOGY. Established under the Museums Act. The purpose of the National Museum of Science and Technology is to foster scientific and technological literacy throughout Canada by establishing, maintaining and developing a collection of scientific and technological objects, with special but not exclusive reference to Canada, and by demonstrating the products and processes of science and technology and their economic, social and cultural relationships in society. *Museums Act*, S.C. 1990, c. 3, s. 13 and 14.

NATIONAL OCCUPATIONAL CLASSIFICATION. The National Occupational Classification published by the Department of Human Resources Development, as amended from time to time.

NATIONAL PAROLE BOARD. A federal body with exclusive authority and final discretion to grant an unescorted temporary absence or parole to terminate or revoke day parole for inmates in federal institutions and inmates in provincial institutions in the Atlantic and Prairie provinces. *Corrections and Conditional Release Act*, S.C. 1992, c. 20, s. 103.

NATIONAL SAFETY MARK. The expression "Canada Motor Vehicle Safety Standard" or "Norme de sécurité des véhicules automobiles du Canada," the abbreviation "CMVSS" or "NSVAC." *Motor Vehicle Safety Act*, S.C. 1993, c. 16, s. 2.

NATIONAL STANDARD. A standard recognized by the National Standards System of the Standards Council of Canada. *Hazardous Products Act*, R.S.C. 1985, c. H-3, *Consumer Chemicals and Containers Regulations, 2001*, SOR/2001-269, s. 1.

NATIONAL STANDARDS SYSTEM. The system for voluntary standards development, promotion and implementation in Canada. *Standards Council of Canada Act*, R.S.C. 1985, c. S-16, s. 4.

NAT. LABOUR REV. *abbr.* National Labour Review.

NAT'L BANKING L. REV. *abbr.* National Banking Law Review.

NAT'L INSOLV. REV. *abbr.* National Insolvency Review.

NAT. PROPERTY REV. *abbr.* National Property Review.

NATURAL AFFECTION. The love which someone has for kin, held to be not a valuable but a good consideration in certain circumstances.

NATURAL CHILD. A child of one's body; a child in fact.

NATURAL ENVIRONMENT. Any part or combination of the air, land and water. *Environmental acts.* See ENVIRONMENT.

NATURAL FORUM. 1. The forum where a matter "ought" to be tried. 2. The place where the tort occurred or operates, the usual or significant residence of the parties, convenience in relation to the availability of evidence required by the parties are considerations in determining the natural forum for a dispute.

NATURAL HEALTH PRODUCT. A substance set out in Schedule 1 or a combination of substances in which all the medicinal ingredients are substances set out in Schedule 1, a homeopathic medicine or a traditional medicine, that is manufactured, sold or represented for use in (a) the diagnosis, treatment, mitigation or prevention of a disease, disorder or abnormal physical state or its symptoms in humans; (b) restoring or correcting organic functions in humans; or (c) modifying organic functions in humans, such as modifying those functions in a manner that maintains or promotes health. However, a natural health product does not include a substance set out in Schedule 2, any combination of substances that includes a substance set out in Schedule 2 or a homeopathic medicine or a traditional medicine that is or includes a substance set out in Schedule 2. *Food and Drugs Act*, R.S.C. 1985, c. F-27, *Natural Health Products Regulations*, SOR/2003-196, s. 1.

NATURALIZATION. *var.* **NATURALISATION.** *n.* 1. The act of becoming the subject of a nation. 2. "... [S]eems prima facie to include the power of enacting what shall be the consequences of naturalization, or, in other words, what shall be the rights and privileges pertaining to residents in Canada after they have been naturalized... ." *Union Colliery Co. of British Columbia v. Bryden*, [1899] A.C. 580 at 586, 15 T.L.R. 598, 1 M.M.C. 337 (B.C. P.C.), the board per Lord Watson.

NATURAL JUSTICE. 1. "... [T]wo main components, the right to be heard and the right to a hearing from an unbiased tribunal, ..." *Wark v. Green* (1985), *(sub nom. Wark v. C.U.P.E.)* 66 N.B.R. (2d) 77 at 83, 169 A.P.R. 77, 86 C.L.L.C. 14,020, 23 D.L.R. (4th) 594 (C.A.), Hoyt J.A. 2. "The concept of natural justice is an elastic one, that can and should defy precise definition. The application of the principle must vary with the circumstances. How much or how little is encompassed by the term will depend on many factors; to name a few, the nature of the hearing, the nature of the tribunal presiding, the scope and effect of the ruling made." *Tandy Electronics Ltd. v. U.S.W.A.* (1979), 79 C.L.L.C. 14,216 at 170, 26 O.R.

(2d) 68, 102 D.L.R. (3d) 126 (Div. Ct.), the court per Cory J. See RULES OF ~.

NATURAL LAW. The code of rules which originates with the divine, nature or reason in contrast to laws people make.

NATURAL OBLIGATION. A duty with a definite purpose which is not necessarily governed by legal obligation.

NATURAL PERSON. A human being.

NATURAL RESOURCES. See DEPARTMENT OF ~.

NATURAL WATER. Includes water that has been treated for the control of impurities in the interest of public health, but does not include water that is sold in bottles and other containers each containing one litre or less. *Retail Sales Tax Act*, R.S.O. 1990, c. R.31, *General*, R.R.O. 1990, c. 1013, s. 1.

NATURE. *n.* The "nature" of the injury, loss or damage [under s. 5(1)(a)(iv) of the Limitations Act, 2002, S.O. 2002, c. 24, Sched. B] is important in assessing whether the claimant should know a proceeding is appropriate. The "nature" of an injury, loss or damage requires consideration of matters beyond the mere fact that such exists. "Nature" is a general word. It would seem to include the character as well as the extent of the injury, loss or damage. *Hare v. Hare* (2006), 218 O.A.C. 164, Juriansz J.A. (dissenting). See CANADIAN MUSEUM OF ~; IMMOVABLE BY ~; SEXUAL ~.

NATURE RESERVE. Land under private ownership recognized as a nature reserve because it has significant biological, ecological, wildlife, floristic, geological, geomorphic or landscape features that warrant preservation. *Natural Heritage Conservation Act*, R.S.Q. c. C-61.01, s. 2.

NATUROPATHIC MEDICINE. The health profession in which a person provides the services of prevention, assessment and treatment of an individual's diseases, disorders and conditions using education and naturopathic techniques, therapies or therapeutics to stimulate or support healing processes and promote, maintain or restore the overall health of the individual. *Health Professions Act*, R.S.B.C. 1996, c. 183, *Naturopathic Physicians Regulation*, B.C. Reg. 282/2008, s. 1.

NAVAL COURT. Any officer who commands a ship belonging to Her Majesty on any foreign station or any consular officer may hold such a court when a complaint which requires immediate investigation arises, when the owner's interest in any Canadian ship or cargo seems to require it or when a Canadian ship is abandoned, wrecked or lost. R.M. Fernandes & C. Burke, *The Annotated Canada Shipping Act* (Toronto: Butterworths, 1988) at 213.

NAVIGATION. *n.* The direction of movement of vessels on navigable waters. See AID TO ~.

NAVIGATION AND SHIPPING. Head of power in section 91(1) of the Constitution Act refers to traffic on navigable waters and the use to which such waters are put. Includes the commercial shipping and pleasure craft.

NAVY. See MERCHANT ~.

N.B. *abbr.* 1. New Brunswick. 2. Nota bene.

NBCA. Neutral citation for New Brunswick Court of Appeal.

N.B. EQ. *abbr.* New Brunswick Equity Reports (Trueman), 1894-1911.

N.B. EQ. CAS. *abbr.* New Brunswick Equity Cases (Trueman), 1876-1893.

N.B.E.S.T.D. *abbr.* New Brunswick Employment Standards Tribunal Decisions, 1986-.

N.B.L.L.C. *abbr.* New Brunswick Labour Law Cases, 1965-1979.

NBPC. Neutral citation for New Brunswick Provincial Court.

N.B.R. *abbr.* New Brunswick Reports, 1825-1928.

N.B.R. (2D). *abbr.* New Brunswick Reports (Second Series), 1969-.

NBQB. Neutral citation for the New Brunswick Court of Queen's Bench.

NCR. *abbr.* Not criminally responsible on account of mental disorder, verdict in a criminal trial.

NEAR RELATIVE. A grandfather, grandmother, father, mother, son, daughter, husband, wife, brother, sister, half brother or half sister, friend, caregiver or companion designated by patient and includes the legal guardian of a minor and a representative under an agreement made under the Representation Agreement Act and a committee having custody of the person of a patient under the Patients Property Act. *Mental Health Act*, R.S.B.C. 1996, c. 288, s. 1.

N.E.B. *abbr.* National Energy Board.

N.E.B.D. *abbr.* National Energy Board – Reasons for Decision, 1970-.

NECESSARIES OF LIFE. "... In order to establish that the articles are necessaries, it must be shown that they are necessary to maintain the person in the station in life in which he finds himself." *Consumers Gas Co. v. Stewart* (1980), 31 O.R. (2d) 559 at 561, 36 C.B.R. (N.S.) 136, 119 D.L.R. (3d) 286 (Div. Ct.), Southey J.

NECESSARY. *adj.* 1. Useful; probative of an issue. 2. Hearsay evidence is considered necessary and admissible when the declarant is unavailable to testify at trial and the party presenting the evidence is unable to obtain it from another source of similar quality. See UN~.

NECESSARY CAUSE. A cause without which the loss or injury would not have happened.

NECESSARY IMPLICATION. The Crown may be bound by a statute by its express terms or by necessary implication. Necessary implication exists where it is manifest from the terms of the statute that the legislature intended the Crown to be bound or where it is apparent from the terms of the statute when it was passed and received royal assent that its beneficial purpose would be wholly frustrated if the Crown were not bound.

NECESSARY INFERENCE. The only possible deduction which can be made from a proposition.

NECESSARY PARTY. A party whose participation in an action is required in order to satisfactorily resolve the issues before the court.

NECESSITY. *n.* 1. "The [defence of necessity] doctrine exists as an excusing defence, operating in very limited circumstances, when conduct that would otherwise be illegal and sanctionable is excused and made unsanctionable because it is properly seen as the result of a 'morally involuntary' decision ..." *R. v. Goltz*, [1991] 3 S.C.R. 485 at 519, 8 C.R. (4th) 82, 31 M.V.R. (2d) 137, 61 B.C.L.R. (2d) 145, 67 C.C.C. (3d) 481, 131 N.R. 1, 7 C.R.R. (2d) 1, 5 B.C.A.C. 161, 11 W.A.C. 161, Gonthier J. (La Forest, L'Heureux-Dubé, Sopinka, Cory and Iacobucci JJ. concurring). 2. "... [R]efers to the necessity of the hearsay evidence to prove a fact in issue... . the criterion of necessity must be given a flexible definition, capable of encompassing diverse situations. What these situations will have in common is that the relevant direct evidence is not, for a variety of reasons, available." *R. v. Smith* (1992), 75 C.C.C. (3d) 257 at 271, 15 C.R. (4th) 133, 139 N.R. 323, 94 D.L.R. (4th) 590, 55 O.A.C. 321, [1992] 2 S.C.R. 915, the court per Lamer C.J.C. 3. [In the context of admissibility of expert evidence] The second requirement of the analysis exists to ensure that the dangers associated with expert evidence are not lightly tolerated. Mere relevance or "helpfulness" is not enough. The evidence must also be necessary. I agree with the Chief Justice that some degree of deference is owed to the trial judge's discretionary determination of whether the requirements have been met on the facts of a particular case, but that discretion cannot be used erroneously to dilute the requirement of necessity. Mere helpfulness is too low a standard to warrant accepting the dangers inherent in the admission of expert evidence. A fortiori, a finding that some aspects of the evidence "might reasonably have assisted the jury" is not enough. As stated by Sopinka et al., expert evidence must be necessary in order to allow the fact finder: (1) to appreciate the facts due to their technical nature, or; (2) to form a correct judgment on a matter if ordinary persons are unlikely to do so without the assistance of persons with special knowledge. (J. Sopinka, S. N. Lederman and A. W. Bryant, The Law of Evidence in Canada (2nd ed. 1999), at p. 620.) *R. v. D. (D.)*, 2000 CarswellOnt 3255, 2000 SCC 43, 36 C.R. (5th) 261, 148 C.C.C. (3d) 41, 191 D.L.R. (4th) 60, 259 N.R. 156, 136 O.A.C. 201, [2000] 2 S.C.R. 275, Major J. 4 When it comes to necessity, the question is whether the expert will provide information which is likely to be outside the ordinary experience and knowledge of the trier of fact: B. (R.H.), supra; Mohan, supra; R. v. Lavallee, [1990] 1 S.C.R. 852; R. v. Abbey, [1982] 2 S.C.R. 24; Kelliher (Village) v. Smith, [1931] S.C.R. 672. "Necessity" means that the evidence must be more than merely "helpful", but necessity need not be judged "by too strict a standard": Mohan, supra, at p. 23. Absolute necessity is not required. *R. v. D. (D.)*, 2000 CarswellOnt 3255, 2000 SCC 43, 36 C.R. (5th) 261, 148 C.C.C. (3d) 41, 191 D.L.R. (4th) 60, 259 N.R. 156, 136 O.A.C. 201, [2000] 2 S.C.R. 275, Mc-

Lachlin J. for minority. 5. In terms of admissibility of hearsay evidence, hearsay evidence will be necessary in circumstances where the declarant is unavailable to testify at trial and where the party is unable to obtain evidence of a similar quality from another source. Consistent with a flexible definition of the necessity criterion, there is no reason why the unavailability of the declarant should be limited to closed, enumerated list of causes. *R. v. Hawkins*, [1996] 3 S.C.R. 1043. 6. If all members of a tribunal competent to determine a matter are subject to disqualification they may be authorized to hear and determine a matter by virtue of necessity. See AGENCY OF ~; BASIC NECESSITIES; EASEMENT OF ~; WAY OF ~.

NEED. See PERSONAL ~S; SPECIAL ~S HOUSING; URGENT ~ OF PROTECTION.

NEEDLE. See SAFETY-ENGINEERED ~.

NEEDLESTICK INJURY. An injury caused by a hollow-bore or intravenous needle puncturing a person's skin or mucous membrane. *The Workplace Safety and Health Act*, R.S.M. 1987, c. W210, s. 45.1.

NEGATIVE. *v.* To deny or contradict.

NEGATIVE. *n.* Denial.

NEGATIVE. *adj.* Describes that which denies or contradicts.

NEGATIVE DAMAGE. The removal of desirable things: amenities, earnings, enjoyment and expectation of life. K.D. Cooper-Stephenson & I.B. Saunders, *Personal Injury Damages in Canada* (Toronto: Carswell, 1981) at 52.

NEGATIVE EASEMENT. One which involves a right to prohibit the commission of certain acts on the servient tenement, acts which the servient owner otherwise would be entitled to commit.

NEGATIVE PREGNANT. In pleading, an evasive answer to something alleged, a literal answer but not an answer to substance.

NEGLECT. *n.* 1. A lack or failure to provide necessary care, aid, guidance or attention which causes or is reasonably likely to cause the victim severe physical or psychological harm or significant material loss to his estate. *Adult Protection Act*, R.S.P.E.I. 1988, c. A-5, s. 1(k). 2. Any failure to provide necessary care, assistance, guidance or attention to an adult that causes, or is reasonably likely to cause within a short period of time, the adult serious physical, mental or emotional harm or substantial damage to or loss of assets, and includes self neglect. *Adult Guardianship Act*, R.S.B.C. 1996 (Supp.), c. 6, s. 1. See SELF-~.

NEGLIGENCE. *n.* 1. An independent tort which consists of breach of a legal duty to take care which results in damage, undesired by the defendant, to the plaintiff. 2. "... [C]onduct which falls below the standard required in particular circumstances in order to protect others against unreasonable risk of harm, as opposed to some risk of harm." *Funk v. Clapp* (1986), 68 D.L.R. (4th) 229 at 244, 35 B.C.L.R. 266 (C.A.),

Craig J.A. (dissenting). 3. "... [M]easures the conduct of the accused on the basis of an objective standard, irrespective of the accused's subjective mental state. Where negligence is the basis of liability, the question is not what the accused intended, but rather whether the accused exercised reasonable care." *R. v. Wholesale Travel Group Inc.* (1991), 8 C.R. (4th) 145 at 176, 67 C.C.C. (3d) 193, 4 O.R. (3d) 799n, 84 D.L.R. (4th) 161, 130 N.R. 1, 38 C.P.R. (3d) 451, 49 O.A.C. 161, [1991] 3 S.C.R. 154, 7 C.R.R. (2d) 36, Cory J. (L'Heureux-Dubé J. concurring). 4. The concept of fault in the Negligence Act [R.S.O. 1990, c. N.1, s. 1] includes negligence, but is much broader than negligence. It incorporates all intentional wrongdoing as well as other types of substandard conduct. *Alpha Tire Corp. v. South China Industries (Canada) Inc.*, 2000 CarswellOnt 178 (S.C.J.), J. Macdonald J. See ACTION FOR ~; ADVERTENT ~; CONCURRENT ~; CONTRIBUTORY ~; CRIMINAL ~; CULPABLE ~; GROSS ~; PENAL ~; SYSTEMIC ~; ULTIMATE ~.

NEGLIGENT BATTERY. Concerned with the physical consequences of one's actions. Accordingly, negligent battery will only be properly pleaded when it is alleged that the defendant negligently harmed the plaintiff by disregarding a foreseeable risk of physical contact. *S. (J.A.) v. Gross*, 2002 ABCA 36, [2002] 5 W.W.R. 54, 100 Alta. L.R. (3d) 310.

NEGLIGENT DRIVING. A continuum from momentary lack of attention giving rise to civil responsibility to dangerous driving under the Criminal Code.

NEGLIGENT MISREPRESENTATION. Five general requirements to establish the cause of action are: (1) there must be a duty of care based on a "special relationship" between the representor and the representee; (2) the representation in question must be untrue, inaccurate, or misleading; (3) the representor must have acted negligently in making said misrepresentation; (4) the representee must have relied, in a reasonable manner, on said negligent misrepresentation; and (5) the reliance must have been detrimental to the representee in the sense that damages resulted. *Queen v. Cognos*, [1993] 1 S.C.R. 87, Iacobucci J.

NEGOTIABILITY. *n.* Capable of being exchanged for currency, money.

NEGOTIABLE INSTRUMENT. 1. Something which: (i) if payable to bearer, is transferable by delivery alone, or if payable to order, by delivery together with endorsement; (ii) presumes the giving of consideration; (iii) permits a transferee to take in good faith and for value to acquire good title despite lack of or defects in the transferor's title. E.L.G. Tyler & N.E. Palmer, eds., *Crossley Vaines' Personal Property*, 5th ed. (London: Butterworths, 1973) at 208. 2. Includes any cheque, draft, traveller's cheque, bill of exchange, postal note, money order, postal remittance and any other similar instrument.

NEGOTIABLE RECEIPT. A receipt in which it is stated that the goods therein specified will be delivered to bearer or to the order of a named person. *Warehouse Receipts acts*. See NON-~.

NEGOTIATE. *v.* 1. To transfer for value, by indorsement or delivery, a bill of exchange or other negotiable instrument. 2. To bargain in good faith with a view to the conclusion of an agreement or the revision or the renewal of an existing agreement.

NEGOTIATE IN GOOD FAITH. A party may commence negotiations by presenting an extreme position but in a series of meetings gradually withdraws to a more reasonable position.

NEGOTIATION. *n.* 1. Transference of a bill from one person to another so that the transferee becomes the holder of the bill. E.L.G. Tyler & N.E. Palmer, eds., *Crossley Vaines' Personal Property*, 5th ed. (London: Butterworths, 1973) at 222. 2. Deliberation and discussion upon the terms of a proposed agreement, and includes conciliation and arbitration. See PLEA ~.

NEIGHBOURING RIGHTS. Musical performers' and record manufacturers' entitlement to compensation whenever qualifying sound recordings in which they hold rights are performed in public.

NEIGHBOUR TEST. The test of proximity between defendant and plaintiff in a negligence suit per Lord Atkin in *Donoghue v. Stevenson*, [1932] A.C. 562, 580: "You must take reasonable care to avoid acts or omissions which you can reasonably foresee would be likely to injure your neighbour. Who, then, in law is my neighbour? The answer seems to be – persons who are so closely and directly affected by my act that I ought reasonably to have them in contemplation as being so affected when I am directing my mind to the acts or omissions which are called in question."

NEM. CON. *abbr.* [L. nemine contradicente] Without anyone saying otherwise.

NEM. DIS. *abbr.* [L. nemine dissentiente] Without dissent.

NEMO DAT QUOD NON HABET. [L.] No one gives what one does not possess.

NEMO DEBET BIS PUNIRE PRO UNO DE-LICTO. [L.] An accused cannot be convicted twice for precisely the same offence arising out of the same act. Once an accused is found guilty of the principle offence, this is a bar against further convictions being entered for included offences in the same proceeding or in a subsequent one where the accused can plead autrefois acquit.

NEMO DEBET BIS VEXARI, SI CONSTAT CU-RIAE QUOD SIT PRO UNA ET EADEM CAUSA. [L.] Non one should be harassed twice, if the court agrees that it is for one and the same cause.

NEMO DEBET ESSE JUDEX IN PROPRIA CAUSA. [L.] No one should judge one's own cause.

NEMO EST HAERES VIVENTIS. [L.] No one is the heir of a living person.

NEMO EST SUPRA LEGIS. [L.] No one is above the law.

NEMO JUDEX IN CAUSA SUA DEBET ESSE. [L.] "... [N]o one ought to be a Judge in his own cause... ." *Barry v. Alberta Securities Commission* (1989), 35 Admin. L.R. 1 at 10, 93 N.R. 1, 65 Alta. L.R. (2d) 97, [1989] 3 W.W.R. 456, 57 D.L.R. (4th) 458, [1989] 1 S.C.R. 301, 96 A.R. 241, the court per L'Heureux-Dubé J.

NEMO PLUS JURIS TRANSFERE POTEST QUAM SE IPSE HABET. [L.] No one can confer a greater right on another than he or she has.

NEMO POTEST ESSE SIMUL ACTOR ET JUDEX. [L.] No one can be suitor and judge at the same time.

NEMO POTEST EXUERE PATRIAM. [L.] No one can shed their homeland.

NEMO REUS EST NISI MENS SIT REA. [L.] No one is guilty unless they have a guilty mind.

NEMO SIBI CAUSAM POSSESSIONIS MU-TARE POTEST. [L.] No one can change the reason of his or her possession for himself or herself.

NEMO TENETUR SEIPSUM ACCUSARE. [L.] No one is bound to accuse herself. "... [T]he privilege of a witness not to answer a question which may incriminate him. That is all that is meant by the Latin maxim, nemo tenetur seipsum accusare, often incorrectly advanced in support of a much broader proposition... ." *Marcoux v. R.* (1975), 60 D.L.R. (3d) 119 at 122, [1976] 1 S.C.R. 763, 29 C.R.N.S. 211, 4 N.R. 64, 24 C.C.C. (2d) 1, Dickson J. See PRIVILEGE AGAINST SELF-INCRIMINATION.

NERVOUS SHOCK. 1. "... [T]he claimant [must] show through the application of the relevant principles of negligence law that the negligent conduct of the defendant caused injuries to others whose suffering was seen and heard by the plaintiff, who was shocked by the experience and, as a result, developed a recognizable psychiatric or emotional illness. The plaintiff must show he suffers from some medically recognizable psychiatric or emotional illness, but damages will only be awarded if he shows the negligent conduct of the defendant caused the illness." *Beecham v. Hughes* (1988), 45 C.C.L.T. 1 at 18-19, 27 B.C.L.R. (2d) 1, [1988] 6 W.W.R. 33, 52 D.L.R. (4th) 635 (C.A.), Taggart J.A. (Carrothers J.A. concurring). 2. A legal label for types of mental or psychological injury which courts have recognized as worthy of an award of damages. Grief and sorrow are not included. See INTENTIONAL INFLICTION OF ~.

NET. *n.* In accounting, an amount of money after all specified expenditures or deductions are deducted.

NET. *adj.* Obtained after adjustments and deductions have been made.

NET EQUITY. Net proceeds less sales commission, legal fees and any penalties.

NET FACTOR. The difference between one and the sum of the legal percentages that an association deducts from the value of each bet made on a pool, expressed as a fraction. *Criminal Code*, R.S.C. 1985, c. C-46, *Pari-Mutuel Betting Supervision Regulations*, SOR/91-365, s. 2.

NET INCOME. Income less expenses and an amount for anticipated income tax.

NET LEASE. "... [T]ype of lease, wherein the lessor undertakes to pay certain expenses ..." *Boots Drug Stores (Canada) Ltd. v. Ritt* (1980), 12 R.P.R. 114 at 116 (Ont. H.C.), Callaghan J.

NET-METERING SYSTEM. A system that operates in parallel with the electrical distribution facilities of a public utility and that measures, by means of one or more meters, the amount of electric energy that is supplied (i) by the public utility to a small capacity renewable energy generator, and (ii) by the small capacity renewable energy generator to the public utility. *Renewable Energy Act*, S.P.E.I. 2004, c. 16, s. 1.

NET NET LEASE. "... [L]ease under which a tenant pays all such costs and the landlord rents the premises in an 'as is' state without covenanting to pay any costs attendant upon the maintenance or operation of the leasehold premises... ." *Boots Drug Stores (Canada) Ltd. v. Ritt* (1980), 12 R.P.R. 114 at 116 (Ont. H.C.), Callaghan J.

NET PROCEEDS. The amount remaining from a sale of property after deduction of expenses of the sale.

NET PROFIT. Clear profit after every deduction.

NET SALE PROCEEDS. The amount remaining after payment of commission and taxes.

NET VALUE. The value of the property of a deceased person after payment of the charges on it and the debts, funeral expenses and expenses of administration, including succession duty. *Intestate Succession acts.*

NETWORK. *n.* Includes any operation where control over all or any part of the programs or program schedules of one or more broadcasting undertakings is delegated to another undertaking or person. *Broadcasting Act*, S.C. 1991, c. 11, s. 2. See BARTER EXCHANGE ~.

NETWORK FEED. Any radiocommunication that is transmitted (a) by a network operation to its affiliates, (b) to a network operation for retransmission by it to its affiliates, or (c) by a lawful distributor to a programming undertaking. *Radiocommunication Act*, R.S.C. 1985, c. R-2, s. 2.

NETWORK OPERATOR. Any person to whom permission has been granted by the Canadian Radio-television and Telecommunications Commission to form and operate a network. *Canada Elections Act, 2000*, S.C. 2000, c. 9, s. 319.

NEUTRAL. See CARBON ~; FACIALLY ~.

NEUTRAL CITATION STANDARD. The neutral citation consists of three (3) principal elements : (1) style of cause ; (2) core of the citation ; (3) optional elements. The core of the citation is constituted of three important elements : (i) the year ; (ii) the tribunal identifier ; (iii) the ordinal number of the decision.

NEUTRAL DELAY. Refers to delay that is not attributable to the Crown or the accused and is not systemic or inherent. *R. v. Port Chevrolet Oldsmobile Ltd.*, 2009 BCCA 357.

NEUTRALISATION. *n.* By treaty, exclusion of some territory from a region at war so that the territory has neutral status.

NEUTRALITY. *n.* A situation in which a territory is allied to neither side of a war.

NEVERTHELESS. *prep. or conj.* In spite of; notwithstanding. Creates an exclusion from or a diminution of the ambit of immediately preceding words.

NEW. *adj.* Not previously existing.

NEW EVIDENCE. Evidence which did not previously exist. Can also mean evidence not available previously even though a diligent search was carried out for it. See FRESH EVIDENCE.

NEWLY-BORN CHILD. A person under the age of one year. *Criminal Code*, R.S.C. 1985, c. C-46, s. 2.

NEWSPAPER. *n.* Any paper, magazine or periodical containing public news, intelligence or reports of events, or any remarks or observations thereon, printed for sale and published periodically or in parts or numbers, at intervals not exceeding thirty-one days between the publication of any two such papers, parts or numbers, and any paper, magazine or periodical printed in order to be dispersed and made public, weekly or more often, or at intervals not exceeding thirty-one days, that contains advertisements, exclusively or principally. *Criminal Code*, R.S.C. 1985, c. C-46, s. 297.

NEW TRIAL. Application to the court for this is the only remedy when there is any defect in judgment through entirely extrinsic causes or something outside the record.

NEXT FRIEND. The person who intervenes to bring an action on behalf of an infant. See LITIGATION GUARDIAN.

NEXT OF KIN. *var.* **NEXT-OF-KIN.** The mother, father, children, brothers, sisters, spouse and common law spouse of a deceased person, or any of them.

NEXUS. *n.* Refers to a causative relationship. Bond, connection, chain.

NFCA. Neutral citation for the Newfoundland Court of Appeal.

NFLD. & P.E.I.R. *abbr.* Newfoundland and Prince Edward Island Reports, 1971-.

NFLD. L.R. *abbr.* Newfoundland Law Reports, 1817-1949.

NFLD. R. *abbr.* Newfoundland Reports, 1817-1949.

NFLD. SEL. CAS. *abbr.* Tucker's Select Cases (Newfoundland), 1817-1828.

NI 45-106. National Instrument 45-106 Prospectus and Registration Exemptions. *Securities Act*, R.S.B.C. 1996, c. 418, *National Instrument 45-102 Resale of Securities*, B.C. Reg. 107/2004, Sched. A, s. 1.1.

NIGHT. *n.* 1. The period between nine o'clock in the afternoon and six o'clock in the forenoon of the following day. *Criminal Code*, R.S.C. 1985, c. C-46, s. 2. 2. The period from one-half hour after sunset to one-half hour before sunrise. 3. The period commencing one half-hour after sunset and ending one half-hour before sunrise. *The Traffic Safety Act*, S.S. 2004, c. T-12.1, s. 157.

NIHIL. [L.] Nothing.

NIHIL AD REM. [L.] Not to the point.

NIHIL DAT QUI NON HABET. [L.] One who has nothing gives nothing.

NIHIL PROBETUR NISI ALLEGATUM. [L.] Nothing is to be proved unless it is alleged.

NIL. *n.* [L.] Nothing.

NIL DEBET. [L.] One owes nothing.

NIL FACET ERROR NOMINIS CUM DE CORPORE VEL PERSONA CONSTAT. [L.] An error in a name is of no effect as long as there is certainty as to the identity of the person.

1908. See TREATY OF ~.

NIOSH. *abbr.* The National Institute for Occupational Safety and Health in the United States. *Canada Labour Code*, R.S.C. 1985, c. L-2, *Maritime Occupational Health and Safety Regulations*, SOR/2010-120, s. 1

NISI. [L.] Describes an order effective only when the affected party fails to respond to it by a certain time. See DECREE ~; RULE ~.

NISI PRIUS. [L.] Unless before.

NISI PRIUS JUDGMENT. Judgment given in circumstances where the exigencies require an immediate decision without the opportunity to fully consider the authorities.

N.L. *abbr.* [L.] Non liquet. It is not evident.

NLSCTD. Neutral citation for the Newfoundland Supreme Court Trial Division.

NO. *abbr.* Number.

NOBIS DICERE NON DARE. [L.] It is for judges (us) to state the law not to give it (make it).

NOC. *abbr.* 1. Notice of compliance. 2. National Occupational Classification.

NO-CERTIORARI CLAUSE. A clause in a statute governing an administrative tribunal which provides that certiorari and any similar remedy is not available to judicially review a decision of the tribunal.

NO-FAULT DIVORCE. Divorce based on grounds other than a matrimonial offence i.e. adultery or cruelty.

NO-FAULT INSURANCE. No-fault means that the respondent's liability to pay benefits occurs when injury arises out of the ownership, use or operation of a vehicle, regardless of the presence or absence of fault. The injury must still arise out of the ownership, use or operation. *Amos v. Insurance Corp. of British Columbia*, 1995 CarswellBC 424, 10 B.C.L.R. (3d)

1, [1995] 9 W.W.R. 305, 13 M.V.R. (3d) 302, [1995] I.L.R. 1-3232, 31 C.C.L.I. (2d) 1, 186 N.R. 150, 127 D.L.R. (4th) 618, 63 B.C.A.C. 1, 104 W.A.C. 1, [1995] 3 S.C.R. 405, 127 D.L.R. (4th) 618, the court per Major J.

NOISE. *n.* Loud, unpleasant or unwanted sound.

NOLLE PROSEQUI. [L.] 1. To be not willing to prosecute. 2. A stay of proceedings.

NO-LOAD FUND. A mutual fund which charges little or no fee in the sale of its shares.

NO MAN CAN TAKE ADVANTAGE OF HIS OWN WRONG. "... [M]axim ... recognized by Courts of law and of equity, ..." *Houghton v. May* (1910), 22 O.L.R. 434 at 439 (H.C.), Clute J. See CLEAN HANDS DOCTRINE.

NO MAN SHALL BE JUDGE IN HIS OWN CAUSE. See *House Repair & Service Co. v. Miller* (1921), 49 O.L.R. 205 at 212-13, 64 D.L.R. 115 (C.A.), the court per Hodgins J.A.

NOM DE PLUME. [Fr.] Pen name.

NOMINAL CAPITAL. The quantity of shares or the aggregate par value of shares which a company is authorized to issue asfixed in the company's memorandum or articles of incorporation or letters patent.

NOMINAL DAMAGES. "... [A] technical phrase which means that you have negatived anything like real damage, but that you are affirming by your nominal damages that there is an infraction of a legal right which, though it gives you no right to any real damages at all, yet gives you a right to the verdict or judgment because your legal right has been infringed ..." *Mediana (The)*, [1900] A.C. 113 at 116 (U.K. H.L.), Lord Halsbury L.C.

NOMINAL PARTNER. A person who does not have any actual interest in a business, trade or its profits but appears to have an interest because her or his name is used in the trade or business.

NOMINAL PLAINTIFF. 1. "... [O]ne who merely represents others ..." *U.F.C.W. Local 1252, Fishermen's Union v. Cashin* (1987), 6 Nfld. & P.E.I.R. 181 at 185, 204 A.P.R. 181 (Nfld. T.D.), Cameron J. 2. "... [A] plaintiff is only a nominal plaintiff within the meaning of [Ontario Rules of Practice] R. 373(f) if he has no interest whatever in the result of the action." *Lincoln Terrace Restaurant Ltd. v. Bray* (1980), 19 C.P.C. 290 at 292 (Ont. Master), Garfield (Master).

NOMINATION. *n.* A mention by name.

NOMINEE. *n.* One who is designated to act as representative of an other. May refer to an agent or trustee. See SENATE ~.

NOMOGENIC. *adj.* Of subjective symptoms, an absence of organic causes, not genuine, motivated by desire for pecuniary gain.

NON AD IDEM. [L.] Not in agreement.

NON-AGE. *n.* The state of being a minor.

NON ASSUMPSIT. [L.] One did not promise.

NON-CAPITAL MURDER. All murder other than capital murder. *Criminal Code*, R.S.C. 1970, c. C-34, s. 214. See now SECOND DEGREE MURDER.

NON-CERTIFICATED SECURITY. Includes a security for which no certificate is issued and a certificated security held within a security clearing and settlement system in the custody of a custodian or nominee. *Financial Administration Act*, R.S.C. 1985, c. F–11 s. 2.

NON-CIRCULATION COIN. A coin composed of base metal, precious metal or any combination of those metals that is not intended for circulation. *Royal Canadian Mint Act*, R.S.C. 1985, c. R-9, s. 2.

NON-COMMISSIONED MEMBER. Any person, other than an officer, who is enrolled in, or who pursuant to law is attached or seconded otherwise than as an officer to, the Canadian Forces. *National Defence Act*, R.S.C. 1985, c. N-5, s. 2.

NON COMPOS MENTIS. [L.] Not sound in mind.

NON-CONFORMING SITE. A site, consisting of one or more contiguous parcels, that, on the date a zoning bylaw or any amendment to a zoning bylaw becomes effective, contains a use that conforms to the bylaw, but the site area or site dimensions do not conform to the standards of the bylaw for that use. *The Planning and Development Act, 2007*, S.S. 2007, c. P-13.2, s. 2.

NON-CONFORMING USE. 1. Use of land or buildings in a manner or for a purpose "lawful when it commenced and lawful prior to a change in a government land use by-law... ." *Mehta v. Truro (Town)* (1991), 5 M.P.L.R. (2d) 216 at 218, 104 N.S.R. (2d) 440, 283 A.P.R. 440 (C.A.), Hallett J.A. 2. A lawful specific use: (i) being made of land or a building or intended to be made of land or of a building lawfully under construction, or with respect to which all required permits have been issued, at the date a zoning bylaw or any amendment to a zoning bylaw affecting the land or building becomes effective; and (ii) that on the date a zoning bylaw or any amendment to a zoning bylaw becomes effective does not, or in the case of a building under construction or with respect to which all required permits have been issued will not, comply with the zoning bylaw. *The Planning and Development Act, 2007*, S.S. 2007, c. P-13.2, 2.

NON-CONSCRIPTIVE EVIDENCE. The crucial element which distinguishes non conscriptive evidence from conscriptive evidence is not whether the evidence may be characterized as "real" or not. Rather, it is whether the accused was compelled to make a statement or provide a bodily substance in violation of the Charter. Where the accused, as a result of a breach of the Charter, is compelled or conscripted to provide a bodily substance to the state, this evidence will be of a conscriptive nature, despite the fact that it may also be "real" evidence. Therefore, it may be more accurate to describe evidence found without any participation of the accused, such as the murder weapon found at the scene of the crime, or drugs found in a dwelling house, simply as non conscriptive evidence; its status as "real" evidence, simpliciter, is irrelevant to the s. 24(2) inquiry. *R. v. Stillman*, [1997] 1 S.C.R. 607, Cory J. for the majority.

NON CONSTAT. [L.] It does not follow; it is not clear.

NON-CONTENTIOUS. *adj.* Not disputed.

NON-CULPABLE CONDUCT. Conduct which an employee cannot change such as incompetence or inability to perform duties of the employee's employment.

NON CULPABLE HOMICIDE. Homicide that is not culpable is not an offence. *Criminal Code*, R.S.C. 1985, c. C-46, s. 222(3).

NONCUMULATIVE DIVIDEND. A dividend which need not be paid in a subsequent year if it was not paid in an earlier year.

NON DAT QUI NON HABET. [L.] One who does not have cannot give.

NON-DELEGABLE DUTY RULE. A person cannot escape liability for the negligence by delegating the performance of the duty to a contractor.

NON-DELIVERY. *n.* Neglect or failure to deliver goods on the part of a bailee, carrier, or other expected to deliver.

NON-DEROGATION CLAUSE. A clause in a statute which provides that nothing in the statute abrogates or derogates from aboriginal or treaty rights.

NON-ESSENTIAL ELEMENTS. Thus the elements of the invention are identified as either essential elements (where substitution of another element or omission takes the device outside the monopoly), or non-essential elements (where substitution or omission is not necessarily fatal to an allegation of infringement). For an element to be considered non-essential and thus substitutable, it must be shown either (i) that on a purposive construction of the words of the claim it was clearly not intended to be essential, or (ii) that at the date of publication of the patent, the skilled addressees would have appreciated that a particular element could be substituted without affecting the working of the invention, i.e., had the skilled worker at that time been told of both the element specified in the claim and the variant and "asked whether the variant would obviously work in the same way", the answer would be yes: Improver Corp. v. Remmington, [[1990] F.S.R. 181], at p. 192. In this context, I think "work in the same way" should be taken for our purposes as meaning that the variant (or component) would perform substantially the same function in substantially the same way to obtain substantially the same result. *Free World Trust c. Électro Santé Inc.*, 2000 CarswellQue 2728, 2000 SCC 66, 194 D.L.R. (4th) 232, 263 N.R. 150, [2000] 2 S.C.R. 1024, 9 C.P.R. (4th) 168, Binnie J.

NON EST FACTUM. [L.] 1. It is not that person's deed. 2. "... [A] form of mistake, where the mistake goes to the very nature of the document which is being signed. Where such a mistake is established, it is invariably a fundamental mistake causing the contract to be void." *Granville Savings & Mortgage*

Corp. v. Slevin (1992), 12 C.C.L.T. (2d) 275 at 297, [1992] 5 W.W.R. 1, 24 R.P.R. (2d) 185, 93 D.L.R. (4th) 268, 6 B.L.R. (2d) 192, 78 Man. R. (2d) 241, 16 W.A.C. 241 (C.A.), O'Sullivan J.A. (dissenting in part). 3. Where a document was executed as a result of a misrepresentation as to its nature and character and not merely its contents the defendant was entitled to raise the plea of non est factum on the basis that his mind at the time of the execution of the document did not follow his hand. In such a circumstance the document was void ab initio. Any person who fails to exercise reasonable care in signing a document is precluded from relying on the plea of non est factum as against a person who relies upon that document in good faith and for value. *Marvco Color Research Ltd. v. Harris*, 1982 CarswellOnt 142, 20 B.L.R. 143, [1982] 2 S.C.R. 774, 26 R.P.R. 48, 45 N.R. 302, 141 D.L.R. (3d) 577, Estey J.

NONFEASANCE. *n.* The failure or neglect to do something which a person ought to do.

NON-INDEMNITY INSURANCE. The distinction between indemnity and non-indemnity insurance is well-recognized in the insurance industry. The following definitions, which I adopt here, were used by the 1988 Report of Inquiry into Motor Vehicle Accident Compensation in Ontario (the Osborne Commission), at p. 429: An indemnity payment is one which is intended to compensate the insured in whole or in part for a pecuniary loss. A non-indemnity payment is a payment of a previously determined amount upon proof of a specified event, whether or not there has been pecuniary loss. Perhaps the best example of non-indemnity insurance is that of life insurance. The beneficiary under a life-insurance policy collects a set amount upon the death of the policy holder without reference to any pecuniary loss. Pensions are also considered to be non-indemnity payments: *Cunningham v. Wheeler*, 1994 CarswellBC 121, 88 B.C.L.R. (2d) 273, [1994] 4 W.W.R. 153, 20 C.C.L.I. (2d) 1, [1994] 1 S.C.R. 359, 113 D.L.R. (4th) 1, 23 C.C.L.I. (2d) 205, 164 N.R. 81, 41 B.C.A.C. 1, 66 W.A.C. 1, 20 C.C.L.T. (2d) 1, 2 C.C.P.B. 217, 23 C.C.L.I. (2d) 205, 41 B.C.A.C. 1, [1994] 1 S.C.R. 359, McLachlin J. (dissenting).

NON-INDEMNITY PAYMENT. A payment of a previously determined amount upon proof of a specified event, whether or not there has been pecuniary loss. *Cunningham v. Wheeler*, [1994] 1 S.C.R. 359, McLachlin J. (dissenting). Life insurance and fixed sum accident benefits are examples.

NON-INTRUSIVE SEARCH. (a) A search of a non-intrusive nature of the clothed body by technical means, in the prescribed manner, and (b) a search of (i) personal possessions, including clothing, that the person may be carrying, and (ii) any coat or jacket that the person has been requested to remove, in accordance with any applicable regulations made under paragraph 96(l). *Corrections and Conditional Release Act*, S.C. 1992, c. 20, s. 46.

NON-JOINDER. *n.* The omission of someone from an action who should be made party.

NON JURIDICAL DAY. A day on which no business is normally done in the civil courts.

NON LIQUET. [L.] It is not evident.

NON-NEGOTIABLE RECEIPT. A receipt in which it is stated that the goods therein specified in it will be delivered to the holder of it. *Warehouse Receipts Act*, R.S.O. 1990, c. W.3, s. 1.

NON NISI JURATUS IN LITE CREDITUR. [L.] No person is believed at trial unless that person is sworn.

NON OBSTANTE. [L.] Notwithstanding.

NON OBSTANTE CLAUSE. In reference to the Charter, refers to a provision in federal or provincial legislation permitted by section 33 which states: (1) Parliament or the legislature of a province may expressly declare in an Act of Parliament or of the legislature, as the case may be, that the Act or a provision thereof shall operate notwithstanding a provision included in section 2 or sections 7 to 15 of this Charter. (2) An Act or a provision of an Act in respect of which a declaration made under this section is in effect shall have such operation as it would have but for the provision of this Charter referred to in the declaration. (3) A declaration made under subsection (1) shall cease to have effect five years after it comes into force or on such earlier date as may be specified in the declaration. (4) Parliament or the legislature of a province may re-enact a declaration made under subsection (1). (5) Subsection (3) applies in respect of a re-enactment made under subsection (4).

NON OBSTANTE VEREDICTO. [L.] The verdict notwithstanding.

NON-PECUNIARY DAMAGES. Compensation for past, present and future pain and suffering, but the future aspect of such an award does not involve a future sum to be invested and managed as is the case in awards for future care or income loss. [. . .] Non-pecuniary awards are a form of solatium that the law provides for injury to a person. The sad fact is that often no amount of money would suffice to compensate for the injury suffered. Such an award is not designed to support a person in future or replace a lost capacity to earn. There is no sensible rationale for treating such a head of damages in the same fashion as future care and future loss awards and I reject the argument of the respondent that such sums should be treated as ones susceptible to a management fee award. *Bystedt (Guardian ad litem of) v. Bagdan*, 2007 BCCA 84, Hall J.A. (Ryan and Newbury JJ.A. concurring).

NON-PECUNIARY LOSS. 1. Compensation for suffering and pain, for loss of enjoyment of life and amenities, and for shortened expectation of life. *Reekie v. Messervey* (1989), 48 C.C.L.T. 217 at 235, 36 B.C.L.R. (2d) 316, 59 D.L.R. (4th) 481, 17 M.V.R. (2d) 94 (C.A.), Lambert J.A. 2. Includes loss of care and guidance from a parent or loss generally of guidance, care and companionship.

NON-PERFORMANCE. *n.* The failure to complete a contract.

NON-PROFIT. *adj.* Having a purpose to promote a specific goal rather than to generate profit.

NON-PROFIT CORPORATION. A corporation, no part of the income of which is payable to or is otherwise available for the personal benefit of any proprietor, member or shareholder thereof. *National Housing Act*, R.S.C. 1985, c. N-11, s. 2.

NON-PROFIT ORGANIZATION. A person (other than an individual, an estate, a trust, a charity, a public institution, a municipality or a government) that was organized and is operated solely for a purpose other than profit, no part of the income of which is payable to, or otherwise available for the personal benefit of, any proprietor, member or shareholder thereof unless the proprietor, member or shareholder is a club, a society or an association the primary purpose and function of which is the promotion of amateur athletics in Canada. *Excise Tax Act*, R.S.C. 1985, c. E-15, s. 123.

NON PROS. *abbr.* Non prosequitur.

NON PROSEQUITUR. [L.] One does not follow up.

NON-QUOTA FISHERY. The parties were involved in a non-quota fishery in the Spiller Channel. In such a fishery, fishing vessels travel to the opening's location to await word from the Department of Fisheries and Oceans ("DFO") that the fishery has opened. These vessels compete for a school of fish, often within very close confines. A non-quota fishery can last for as little as several minutes before the DFO closes it down. By contrast, a quota fishery can last for several days or weeks, thus eliminating the need for fishing vessels to compete within close confines. *North Ridge Fishing Ltd. v. "Prosperity" (The)*, 2000 CarswellBC 982, 2000 BCCA 283, 74 B.C.L.R. (3d) 383, 186 D.L.R. (4th) 374, Cumming J.A. (Prowse and Saunders JJ.A. concurring).

NON-PUBLIC ORDER. See MATERIAL ~ INFORMATION.

NON-REDEEMABLE INVESTMENT FUND. (a) An issuer (i) whose primary purpose is to invest money provided by its security holders, (ii) that does not invest (A) for the purpose of exercising or seeking to exercise control of an issuer, other than an issuer that is a mutual fund or a non-redeemable investment fund, or (B) for the purpose of being actively involved in the management of any issuer in which it invests, other than an issuer that is a mutual fund or a non-redeemable investment fund, and (iii) that is not a mutual fund, or (b) an issuer that is designated under section 6, or in accordance with the rules, to be a non-redeemable investment fund, but does not include an issuer, or class of issuers, that is designated under section 6, or in accordance with the rules, not to be a non-redeemable investment fund. *Securities Act*, S.Y. 2007, c. 16, s. 1.

NON-REGENERATIVE TISSUE. Tissue other than regenerative tissue. *Human Tissue Gift acts.*

NON-RESIDENT. *var.* **NON RESIDENT.** *var.* **NONRESIDENT.** *n.* A person not resident in Canada.

NON-RESIDENT PERSON. At any time, with respect to a taxpayer, includes a person that the taxpayer, based on reasonable inquiries, believes at that time to be a person not resident in Canada. *Income Tax Act*, R.S.C. 1985, c. 1 (5th Supp.), s. 33.1

NON-SECTARIAN. *adj.* 1. The dual requirements that education be "secular" and "non-sectarian" refer to keeping the schools free from inculcation or indoctrination in the precepts of any religion and do not prevent persons with religiously based moral positions on matters of public policy from participating in deliberations concerning moral education in public schools. *Chamberlain v. Surrey School District No. 36*, [2002] 4 S.C.R. 710. 2. Must now be extended to include other religious traditions as well as those who do not adhere to any religious faith or tradition. The section precludes the teaching of religious doctrine associated with any particular faith or tradition (except in a context which is intended to educate students generally about the various religious traditions for the purpose of advancing religious tolerance and understanding and does not advance any particular doctrinal position over others). *Chamberlain v. Surrey School District No. 36*, 2000 CarswellBC 2009, 80 B.C.L.R. (3d) 181, [2000] 10 W.W.R. 393, 191 D.L.R. (4th) 128, 143 B.C.A.C. 162, 235 W.A.C. 162, 26 Admin. L.R. (3d) 297 (C.A.), Esson, Mackenzie, Proudfoot JJ.A.

NON SEQUITUR. [L.] It does not follow.

NON-STRUCTURAL. *adj.* Refers to interior elements or components of a structure that are not load-bearing and do not require design computations for a building structure and includes ceiling and partition systems that employ normal and typical bracing conventions and are not part of the structural integrity of a building but does not include the structural frame systems supporting a building. *Interior Designers Act*, S.N.S. 2003, c. 6, s. 2.

NON SUI JURIS. [L.] Not able to manage one's own affairs; with no legal capacity.

NON-SUIT. *n.* The term "non-suit" refers to a motion brought by the defendant at the close of the plaintiff's evidence to dismiss the action on the ground that the plaintiff has failed to make out a case for the defendant to answer. Neither the Courts of Justice Act, R.S.O. 1990, c. C.43, nor the Rules of Civil Procedure [R.R.O. 1990, Reg. 194] specifically provides for non-suit motions, but judges continue to have a recognized jurisdiction to entertain these motions. *FL Receivables Trust 2002-A (Administrator of) v. Cobrand Foods Ltd.*, 2007 ONCA 425.

NON-SUIT MOTION. A motion that there is no evidence or no evidence upon an essential element of the plaintiff's case or a motion to weigh the evidence that there is and determine that it is not of sufficient strength to establish a prima facie case.

NON SUNT PROBANDA NISI SECUNDUM ALLEGATA. [L.] Facts should not be proven unless they have been alleged.

NON-TOXIC SHOT. Bismuth shot, steel shot, tin shot, tungsten-bronze-iron shot, tungsten-iron shot, tungsten-iron-nickel-copper shot, tungsten-matrix shot, tungsten-nickel-iron shot or tungsten-polymer shot. *Migratory Birds Convention Act, 1994*, S.C.

1994, c. 22, *Migratory Birds Regulations*, C.R.C., c. 1035, s. 2.

NON-UNIONIZED EMPLOYEE. An employee who is not a member of a bargaining unit that is represented by a bargaining agent. *Public Sector Equitable Compensation Act*, S.C. 2009, c. 2, s. 394, s. 2.

NO ONE CAN BE ALLOWED TO DEROGATE FROM HIS OWN GRANT. See *Keewatin Power Co. v. Keewatin Flour Mills Ltd.*, [1928] 1 D.L.R. 32 at 53, 61 O.L.R. 363 (H.C.), Grant J. See CLEAN HANDS DOCTRINE.

NORMAL ATMOSPHERIC PRESSURE. An absolute pressure of 101.324 kPa at 20°C.

NORMAL COURSE. In relation to a trade mark, evidence of a single transaction is not evidence of the normal course of trade. Normal course refers to a functioning business.

NORMAL FARM PRACTICE. A practice that, (a) is conducted in a manner consistent with proper and acceptable customs and standards as established and followed by similar agricultural operations under similar circumstances, or (b) makes use of innovative technology in a manner consistent with proper advanced farm management practices. *Farming and Food Production Protection Act, 1998*, S.O. 1998, c. 1, s. 1.

NORMALLY. *adv.* Regularly; usually.

NORTH AMERICAN FREE TRADE AGREEMENT. Commonly referred to as NAFTA. The North American Free Trade Agreement entered into between the Government of Canada, the Government of the United Mexican States and the Government of the United States of America and signed on December 17, 1992, and includes any rectifications thereto made prior to its ratification by Canada.

NORTHERN DEVELOPMENT. See DEPARMENT OF INDIAN AFFAIRS AND ~.

NOSCITUR A SOCIIS. [L.] 1. One is known by one's associates. The meaning of a particular word or expression may be determined by its association with other words. 2. "... [W]here general words are closely associated with preceding specific words the meaning of the general words must be limited by reference to the specific words." *Insurance Corp. of British Columbia v. Canada (Registrar of Trade Marks)* (1978), 44 C.P.R. (2d) 1 at 11, [1980] 1 F.C. 669 (T.D.), Cattanach J.

NOSCITUR EX SOCIO, QUI NON COGNOSCITUR EX SE. [L.] One who cannot be known from the self is known from an associate.

NOSCUNTUR A SOCIIS. [L.] They are known by their companions (refers to words). When one joins words which could have analogous meaning, one is using them in their cognate sense. P. St. J. Langan, ed., *Maxwell on The Interpretation of Statutes*, 12th ed. (Bombay: N.M. Tripathi, 1976) at 289. See NOSCITUR A SOCIIS.

NOTA BENE. [L.] Note well.

NOTARIAL ACT. 1. A notary's written authentication or certification, under official seal or signature, of any entry or document. 2. Any attestation, certificate or instrument which a notary executes.

NOTARIAL CERTIFICATE. An instrument which certifies the authenticity of the document to which it is attached.

NOTARY. *n.* 1. One who attests a deed or document to make it authentic in another jurisdiction. 2. In Quebec, a notary is a public officer and takes part in the administration of justice. A notary is also a legal adviser. The mission of a notary, in his or her capacity as a public officer, is to execute acts which the parties wish or are required to endow with the authenticity attaching to acts of public authority, to provide such acts with a fixed date, and to keep all acts executed en minute in his or her notarial records and issue copies of or extracts from them. *Notaries Act*, R.S.Q. c. N-3, s. 10.

NOTARY PUBLIC. One who attests a deed or document to make it authentic in another jurisdiction and is empowered to take affidavits and declarations and to perform various other acts relating to legal matters.

NOTE. *v.* 1. Of a dishonoured foreign bill, for a notary public to record her or his initials, the day, month, year and reason, if given, for non-payment. 2. To note up a case is to find references to it in later cases.

NOTE. *n.* 1. A promissory note. *Bills of Exchange Act*, R.S.C. 1985, c. B-4, s. 2. 2. Any corporate obligation, unsecured or secured. H. Sutherland, D.B. Horsley & J.M. Edmiston, eds., *Fraser's Handbook on Canadian Company Law*, 7th ed. (Toronto: Carswell, 1985) at 310. See BANK-~; CONSUMER ~; COVER ~; CREDIT ~; DEBIT ~; DEMAND ~; DEPOSITORY ~; EXPLANATORY ~; HEAD~; JUDGE'S ~S; MARGINAL ~; PREMIUM ~; PROMISSORY ~; SIDE~; TREASURY ~.

NOT-FOR-PROFIT CORPORATION. A corporation without share capital incorporated or continued under the Canada Not-for-profit Corporations Act, S.C. 2009, c. 23. Applied generally to corporations without share capital.

NOT GUILTY. The plea appropriate to an indictment when the accused chooses to raise a general issue, *i.e.*, to deny everything and let the prosecution prove whatever they can.

NOTICE. *n.* 1. Cognisance; knowledge. 2. Judicial notice. 3. To give someone notice of a fact is to bring that fact to the person's attention. 4. A document which informs or advises someone that that person's interests are involved in a proceeding or which informs the person of something which that person has a right to know. 5. "... [S]omething which is in a form calculated to attract attention." *Montreal Trust v. Canadian Pacific Airlines Ltd.*, [1977] 2 S.C.R. 793 at 802, 12 N.R. 408, 72 D.L.R. (3d) 257, Ritchie J. (Laskin C.J.C., Spence and Dickson JJ. concurring). See ACTUAL ~; ADEQUATE ~; ADMINISTRATIVE ~; APPEARANCE ~; CONSTRUCTIVE ~; JUDICIAL ~; OFFICIAL ~; PURCHASER FOR VALUE WITHOUT ~; SPLIT DECISION ~.

NOTICE OF ACTION. A document containing a short statement about the nature of the claim which may commence any action other than a divorce action when there is not enough time to prepare a full statement of claim. *Courts of Justice Act*, R.S.O. 1990, c. C.43, *Rules of Civil Procedure*, R.R.O. 1990, Reg. 194, r. 14.03(2).

NOTICE OF ANY KIND. Includes a recital or reference made in any registered instrument. *Land Transfer Tax Act*, R.S.O. 1990, c. L.6, s. 1.

NOTICE OF APPEAL. A document by which an appeal is commenced.

NOTICE OF CIVIL CLAIM. The document which initiates a an action or civil proceeding. *Court Rules Act*, R.S.B.C. 1996, c. 80, *Supreme Court Civil Rules*, B.C. Reg. 168/2009.

NOTICE OF CLAIM. In insurance law, informs the insurer of the possibility of a future action, allows the insurer time to investigate the merits and to negotiate a settlement.

NOTICE OF DISHONOUR. Subject to this Act, when a bill has been dishonoured by non-acceptance or by non-payment, notice of dishonour must be given to the drawer and each endorser, and any drawer or endorser to whom the notice is not given is discharged. *Bills of Exchange Act*, R.S.C. 1985, c. B-4, s. 95.

NOTICE OF INTENT TO DEFEND. In Ontario practice, the document which a defendant who intends to defend an action delivers and which gives that defendant 10 more days to file a statement of defence.

NOTICE OF MOTION. In Ontario practice, the document which initiates a motion and notifies other parties of the motion, used unless the circumstances or the nature of the motion make it unnecessary.

NOTICE OF READINESS FOR TRIAL. In Ontario practice, the document, formerly called a certificate of readiness, which the party who is ready for trial and who wishes to set the action down for trial serves on every other party to the action.

NOTICE PAPER. A document by which members of Parliament give notice that they intend to introduce bills, seek answers to written questions or move a motion as Private Members' business. A. Fraser, W.A. Dawson & J. Holtby, eds., *Beauchesne's Rules and Forms of the House of Commons of Canada*, 6th ed. (Toronto: Carswell, 1989) at 300.

NOTICE TO QUIT. The notice required for either a landlord or a tenant to terminate a tenancy without the other's consent when that tenancy runs from year to year or for some other indefinite period.

NOTIFY. *v.* "... [M]eans, in its everyday sense, 'to inform expressly', and in law: ... 'to make known, to give notice, to inform'." *Brière v. Canada (Employment & Immigration Commission)* (1988), 89 C.L.L.C. 14,025 at 12,203, 93 N.R. 115, 25 F.T.R. 80n, 57 D.L.R. (4th) 402 (C.A.), Lacombe J.A.

NOTING. *n.* A notary's record on a bill at the time it is dishonoured. I.F.G. Baxter, *The Law of Banking*, 3d ed. (Toronto: Carswell, 1981) at 117.

NOTIONAL SEVERANCE. Applied in limited circumstances to remove illegal features of a contract so as to render the contract in conformity with the law. involves reading down an illegal provision in a contract that would be unenforceable in order to make it legal and enforceable. *Shafron v. KRG Insurance Brokers (Western) Inc.*, 2009 SCC 6.

NOT LOST. See LOST OR ~ INSURANCE.

NOTORIOUS. *adj.* In evidence, describes a matter which need not be proved.

NOTWITHSTANDING. *conj.* Although.

NOTWITHSTANDING. *prep.* Despite.

NOTWITHSTANDING CLAUSE. In reference to the Charter, refers to a provision in federal or provincial legislation permitted by section 33 which states: (1) Parliament or the legislature of a province may expressly declare in an Act of Parliament or of the legislature, as the case may be, that the Act or a provision thereof shall operate notwithstanding a provision included in section 2 or sections 7 to 15 of this Charter. (2) An Act or a provision of an Act in respect of which a declaration made under this section is in effect shall have such operation as it would have but for the provision of this Charter referred to in the declaration. (3) A declaration made under subsection (1) shall cease to have effect five years after it comes into force or on such earlier date as may be specified in the declaration. (4) Parliament or the legislature of a province may re-enact a declaration made under subsection (1). (5) Subsection (3) applies in respect of a re-enactment made under subsection (4).

N.O.V. *abbr.* Non obstante veredicto.

NOVA CAUSA INTERVENIENS. [L.] A new cause intervenes. *Emerson v. Skinner* (1906), 12 B.C.R. 154 at 155, 4 W.L.R. 255 (C.A.), Hunter C.J.A.

NOVATION. *n.* "... [A] trilateral agreement by which an existing contract is extinguished and a new contract brought into being in its place. Indeed, for an agreement to effect a valid novation the appropriate consideration is the discharge of the original debt in return for a promise to discharge some new obligation. The assent of the beneficiary (the creditor or mortgagee) of those obligations to the discharge and substitution is crucial. The Courts have established a three part test for determining if novation has occurred. It is set out in Polson v. Wulffsohn (1890), 2 B.C.R. 39 at 43 (S.C.) as follows: ' ... first, the new debtor must assume the complete liability; second, the creditor must accept the new debtor as a principal debtor, and not merely as an agent or guarantor; and third, the creditor must accept the new contract in full satisfaction and substitution for the old contract ...' " *National Trust Co. v. Mead* (1990), 12 R.P.R. (2d) 165 at 180, [1990] 2 S.C.R. 410, [1990] 5 W.W.R. 459, 71 D.L.R. (4th) 488, 112 N.R. 1, Wilson J. (Lamer C.J.C., La Forest, L'Heureux-Dubé, Gonthier and Cory JJ. concurring).

NOVELTY. *n.* 1. In the context of constitutional law refers to legislation which responds to new societal interest and approach concerning the subject matter of the legislation, legislation based on principles of law distinct from similar legislation and legislation where there is an identifiable social policy different from the policy goals of analogous legislation. *Reference re Residential Tenancies Act (Nova Scotia)*, [1996] 1 S.C.R. 186. 2. In the context of patent law, something completely new. A lack of novelty is a ground for an attack on a patent.

NOVUS ACTUS INTERVENIENS. [L.] 1. A new act intervenes. 2. "... [A] ' ... conscious act of human origin intervening between a negligent act or omission of a defendant and the occurrence by which the plaintiff suffers damage ... ' ... The important element in the defence 'novus actus interveniens' is that the intervening act must be one which the party defending could not reasonably [sic] forsee... ." *Mercantile Bank of Canada v. Carl B. Potter Ltd.* (1979), 7 B.L.R. 54 at 77-8, 31 N.S.R. (2d) 402, 52 A.P.R. 402 (C.A.), Coffin J.A. 3. "... One such case is where, although an act of the accused constitutes a cause sine qua non of (or necessary condition for) the death of the victim, nevertheless the intervention of a third person may be regarded as the sole cause of the victim's death, thereby relieving the accused of criminal responsibility. Such intervention, if it has such an effect, has often been described by lawyers as a novus actus interveniens." *R. v. Pagett* (1983), 76 Cr. App. R. 279 at 288 (U.K. C.A.), the court per Lord Goff.

N.P.B. *abbr.* National Parole Board.

N.R. *abbr.* National Reporter, 1974-.

NRCC. *abbr.* Neighbouring Rights Collective of Canada.

NSCA. Neutral citation for the Nova Scotia Court of Appeal.

N.S.C.G.A. DEC. *abbr.* Nova Scotia Compendium of Grievance Arbitration Decisions, 1978-.

N.S.F. *abbr.* Not sufficient funds.

N.S. L. NEWS. *abbr.* Nova Scotia Law News.

NSPC. Neutral citation for Nova Scotia Provincial Court.

N.S.R. *abbr.* Nova Scotia Reports, 1834-1929.

N.S.R. (2D). *abbr.* Nova Scotia Reports (Second Series), 1969-.

N.S.R.U.D. *abbr.* Nova Scotia Reported and Unreported Decisions, 1979-1984.

NSSC. The neutral citation for the Nova Scotia Supreme Court.

NSSF. Neutral citation for Supreme Court of Nova Scotia, Family Division.

N.T.A.D. (AIR). *abbr.* National Transportation Agency Decisions (Air), 1988-1992.

N.T.A.D. (RWY). *abbr.* National Transportation Agency Decisions (Railway), 1988-1991.

N.T.A.O. (AIR). *abbr.* National Transportation Agency Orders (Air), 1988-1992.

N.T.A.R. *abbr.* National Transportation Agency of Canada Reports, 1988-1995.

NUCA. Neutral citation for Nunavut Court of Appeal.

NUCJ. The neutral citation for the Nunavut Court of Justice.

NUCLEAR ENERGY. Any form of energy released in the course of nuclear fission or nuclear fusion or of any other nuclear transmutation. *Nuclear Safety and Control Act*, S.C. 1997, c. 9, s. 2.

NUCLEAR ENERGY WORKER. A person who is required, in the course of the person's business or occupation in connection with a nuclear substance or nuclear facility, to perform duties in such circumstances that there is a reasonable probability that the person may receive a dose of radiation that is greater than the prescribed limit for the general public. *Nuclear Safety and Control Act*, S.C. 1997, c. 9, s. 2.

NUCLEAR FACILITY. Any of the following facilities, namely, a nuclear fission or fusion reactor or subcritical nuclear assembly, a particle accelerator, a uranium or thorium mine or mill, a plant for the processing, reprocessing or separation of an isotope of uranium, thorium or plutonium, a plant for the manufacture of a product from uranium, thorium or plutonium, a plant for the processing or use, in a quantity greater than 10 [to the power of 15] Bq per calendar year, of nuclear substances other than uranium, thorium or plutonium, a facility for the disposal of a nuclear substance generated at another nuclear facility, a vehicle that is equipped with a nuclear reactor, and any other facility that is prescribed for the development, production or use of nuclear energy or the production, possession or use of a nuclear substance, prescribed equipment or prescribed information, and includes, where applicable, the land on which the facility is located, a building that forms part of, or equipment used in conjunction with, the facility and any system for the management, storage or disposal of a nuclear substance. *Nuclear Safety and Control Act*, S.C. 1997, c. 9, s. 2.

NUCLEAR FUEL WASTE. Irradiated fuel bundles removed from a commercial or research nuclear fission reactor. *Nuclear Fuel Waste Act*, S.C. 2002, c. 23.

NUCLEAR MATERIAL. (a) Plutonium, except plutonium with an isotopic concentration of plutonium-238 exceeding eighty per cent, (b) uranium-233, (c) uranium containing uranium-233 or uranium-235 or both in such an amount that the abundance ratio of the sum of those isotopes to the isotope uranium-238 is greater than 0.72 per cent, (d) uranium with an isotopic concentration equal to that occurring in nature, and (e) any substance containing anything described in paragraphs (a) to (d), but does not include uranium in the form of ore or ore-residue. *Criminal Code*, R.S.C. 1985, c. C-46, s. 7.

NUCLEAR SUBSTANCE. (a) Deuterium, thorium, uranium or an element with an atomic number greater than 92; (b) a derivative or compound of deuterium, thorium, uranium or of an element with an atomic number greater than 92; (c) a radioactive nuclide; (d) a substance that is prescribed as being capable of releasing nuclear energy or as being required for the production or use of nuclear energy; (e) a radioactive by-product of the development, production or use of nuclear energy; and (f) a radioactive substance or radioactive thing that was used for the development or production, or in connection with the use, of nuclear energy. *Nuclear Safety and Control Act*, S.C. 1997, c. 9, s. 2.

NUDA PACTIO OBLIGATIONEM NON PARIT. [L.] A simple promise does not create an obligation.

NUDUM PACTUM. [L. a bare agreement] An agreement made with no consideration.

NUISANCE. *n.* 1. At common law, nuisance is a field of liability that focuses on the harm suffered rather than on prohibited conduct (A. M. Linden and B. Feldthusen, Canadian Tort Law (8th ed. 2006), at p. 559; L. N. Klar, Tort Law (2nd ed. 1996), at p. 535). Nuisance is defined as unreasonable interference with the use of land (Linden and Feldthusen, at p. 559; Klar, at p. 535). Whether the interference results from intentional, negligent or non faulty conduct is of no consequence provided that the harm can be characterized as a nuisance (Linden and Feldthusen, at p. 559). The interference must be intolerable to an ordinary person (p. 568). This is assessed by considering factors such as the nature, severity and duration of the interference, the character of the neighbourhood, the sensitivity of the plaintiff's use and the utility of the activity (p. 569). The interference must be substantial, which means that compensation will not be awarded for trivial annoyances (Linden and Feldthusen, at p. 569; Klar, at p. 536). *St. Lawrence Cement Inc. v. Barrette*, 2008 SCC 64 at para. 77. 2. An animal, bird, insect, plant or disease declared to be a nuisance under section 2. *Agricultural Pests Act*, R.S.A. 2000, c. A-8, s. 1. See ABATEMENT OF ~; COMMON ~; PRIVATE ~; PUBLIC ~.

NULLA BONA. [L. no goods] The proper return of a writ when the judgment debtor has no goods in the sheriff's bailiwick or there are no proceeds from a sale or seizure of the debtor's property available to satisfy the writ.

NULLA CRIMEN SINE LEGE, NULLA POENA SINE LEGE. [L.] There can be no crime or punishment unless it is in accordance with law that is certain, unambiguous and not retroactive.

NULLA EST INJURIA QUAE IN VOLENTEM FIT. [L.] No wrongdoing is done to a willing person.

NULLA POENA SINE LEGE. [L.] 1. There can be no punishment unless it is in accordance with law that is certain, unambiguous and not retroactive. 2. An accused's silence in the face of a police accusation can be considered a particular example of the liberty to do that which is not prohibited as expressed in this maxim.

NULLIS EXCEPTIS. [L.] There were no exceptions made.

NULLITY. *n.* 1. Something which has no legal effect. 2. A charge may be quashed as a nullity if it refers to an offence not known to law or it is so badly drawn not to give the accused notice of the charge.

NULLITY OF MARRIAGE. The total invalidity of an attempted, pretended or supposed marriage which was void from the beginning because the parties lacked consent or capacity to marry or which was voidable or liable to annulment later because one spouse was unable to consummate the marriage.

NULLUM CRIMEN SINE LEGE. [L.] There should be no crime except according to predetermined, fixed law. D. Stuart, *Canadian Criminal Law: A Treatise*, 2d ed. (Toronto: Carswell, 1987) at 15.

NUMBER. See BUSINESS ~; LOT ~.

NUMBER RECORDER. Any device that can be used to record or identify the telephone number or location of the telephone from which a telephone call originates, or at which it is received or is intended to be received. *Criminal Code*, R.S.C. 1985, c. C-46, s. 492.1.

NUNAVUT. *n.* A territory of Canada consisting of (a) all that part of Canada north of the sixtieth parallel of north latitude and east of the boundary described in Schedule I that is not within Quebec or Newfoundland; and (b) the islands in Hudson Bay, James Bay and Ungava Bay that are not within Manitoba, Ontario or Quebec. A Legislature for Nunavut consisting of the Commissioner and the Legislative Assembly of Nunavut is established. There is established a Legislative Assembly of Nunavut, each member of which is elected to represent an electoral district in Nunavut. *Nunavut Act*, S.C. 1993, c. 28, s. 3, 12, 13.

NUNC PRO TUNC. [L. now for then] 1. The order of a court that a proceeding be dated with an earlier date than the date it actually took place, or that the same effect be produced as if the proceeding had happened at an earlier date. 2. "... [U]sed to refer to the common law power of the Court to permit that to be done now which ought to have been done before... ." *Krueger v. Raccah* (1981), 24 C.P.C. 14 at 17, 12 Sask. R. 130, 128 D.L.R. (3d) 177 (Q.B.), Cameron J.

NUNCUPATIVE WILL. "... [A] will made by a soldier under circumstances in which it is presumed he would not be able to have a proper will drawn and properly witnessed." *Smith v. Hubbard*, [1917] 1 W.W.R. 1237 at 1238 (B.C. S.C.), Macdonald J.

NURSE PRACTITIONER. A nurse with special training to permit him or her to work in a remote area without the presence of a physician. See PRACTICE OF A ~.

NURSING. *n.* The practice of nursing is the promotion of health and the assessment of, the provision of care for and the treatment of health conditions by supportive, preventive, therapeutic, palliative and rehabilitative means in order to attain or maintain optimal function.

NUTRIENT. *n.* 1. Any substance or combination of substances that, if released in any waters, provides nourishment that promotes the growth of aquatic vegetation. *Canadian Environmental Protection Act*, S.C. 1999, c. 33, s. 116. 2. Any material, including fertilizer, manure, compost, sewage biosolids and pulp and paper biosolids, that can be applied to land for the purpose of improving the growing of agricultural crops or for the purpose of a prescribed use, but does not include any material that the regulations specify does not come within the definition of "nutrient". *Nutrient Management Act, 2002*, S.O. 2002, c. 4, s. 2.

N.W.T. *abbr.* 1. Northwest Territories. 2. North West Territories Reports, 1887-1898.

NWTCA. Neutral citation for the Northwest Territories Court of Appeal.

N.W.T.R. *abbr.* Northwest Territories Reports, 1983-1998.

NWTSC. Neutral citation for the Northwest Territories Supreme Court.

N.W.T.S.C.R. *abbr.* Northwest Territories Supreme Court Reports, 1889-1900.

NWTTC. Neutral citation for the Northwest Territories Territorial Court.

O

O.A.C. *abbr.* Ontario Appeal Cases, 1984-.

OAKES TEST. The test applied to determine whether a restriction of rights under the Charter is salvaged by s. 1 of the Charter involves the application of the decision of the Supreme Court of Canada in R. v. Oakes, [1986] 1 S.C.R. 103, 50 C.R. (3d) 1, 26 D.L.R. (4th) 200, 24 C.C.C. (3d) 321, 14 O.A.C. 335, 19 C.R.R. 308. *R. v. Penno* (1990), 29 M.V.R. (2d) 161 at 176, [1990] 2 S.C.R. 865, 80 C.R. (3d) 97, 59 C.C.C. (3d) 344, 49 C.R.R. 50, 115 N.R. 249, 42 O.A.C. 271, Lamer C.J.C. See PROPORTIONALITY TEST; REASONABLE LIMITS.

O.A.R. *abbr.* Ontario Appeal Reports, 1876-1900.

OATH. *n.* 1. "... [A]n appeal to a Supreme Being in whose existence the person taking the oath believes to be a rewarder of truth and an avenger of falsehood: ... The purpose of the oath is to bind the conscience of the witness ..." *R. v. Defillipi*, [1932] 1 W.W.R. 545 at 546, 57 C.C.C. 401, 26 Alta. L.R. 134 (C.A.), the court per McGillivray J.A. 2. "... . Canada's emerging multi-cultural society requires an acknowledgement in the courts that the Judaic-Christian form of oath is not necessarily the only form of religious oath to be administered, and that persons of other religious persuasions should not automatically be given affirmation as the only alternative." *R. v. Kalevar* (1991), 4 C.R. (4th) 114 at 117 (Ont. Gen. Div.), Haley J. 3. Includes a solemn affirmation or declaration when the context applies to any person by whom and to any case in which a solemn affirmation or declaration may be made instead of an oath, and in the same cases the expression "sworn" includes the expression "affirmed" or "declared". *Interpretation Act*, R.S.C. 1985, c. I-21, s. 35. See CORPORAL ~.

OATH-HELPING. *n.* 1. Evidence is precluded as oath-helping if its purpose is to prove a witness to be truthful, as contrasted with evidence called for the purpose of showing the witness's statements to be true. *R. v. Mallory* (2007), 220 O.A.C. 239. 2. Evidence adduced to prove that a witness is truthful. It is not admissible. 3. The actual credibility of a particular witness is not generally the proper subject of opinion evidence. This is known as the rule against oath-helping. *R. v. D. (D.)*, 2000 CarswellOnt 3255, 2000 SCC 43, 36 C.R. (5th) 261, 148 C.C.C. (3d) 41, 191 D.L.R. (4th) 60, 259 N.R. 156, 136 O.A.C. 201, [2000] 2 S.C.R. 275, McLachlin C.J.C. (dissenting) (L'Heureux-Dubé and Gonthier JJ. concurring).

OATH OF ALLEGIANCE. The words of the oath are: I, _____, do swear that I will be faithful and bear true allegiance to Her Majesty Queen Elizabeth the Second, Queen of Canada, Her Heirs and Successors. So help me God. *Oaths of Allegiance Act*, R.S.C. 1985, c. O-1, s. 2(1).

OATH OR AFFIRMATION OF CITIZENSHIP. The words of the oath are: I swear (or affirm) that I will be faithful and bear true allegiance to Her Majesty Queen Elizabeth the Second, Queen of Canada, Her Heirs and Successors, and that I will faithfully observe the laws of Canada and fulfill my duties as a Canadian citizen. *Citizenship Act*, R.S.C. 1985, c. C-29, Schedule.

OBITER DICTA. [L.] 1. "... [M]ere passing remarks of the judge, ..." *Richard West & Partners (Inverness) Ltd. v. Dick* (1968), [1969] 1 All E.R. 289 at 292 (U.K. Ch.), Megarry J. 2. As Green J.A. observed in para. 34 of his judgment in R. v. Hynes (1999), 177 Nfld. & P.E.I.R. 232 (Nfld. C.A.), a reading of Sellars [[1980] 1 S.C.R. 527] and authorities from which it drew indicates the Sellars' direction should be interpreted as saying: obiter statements of legal principle in majority judgments of the Supreme Court of Canada will be regarded as declaratory of the law, and binding on lower courts, where from a reading of the judgment, it appears that: (i) the Court considered it desirable to express its opinion on the matter; (ii) the matter was fully argued; and (iii) accordingly, the comments are the fully-considered opinion of the Court. Although Green J.A. wrote these words in dissent, no exception is taken with this passage as an accurate synopsis of the criteria for attributing binding effect to obiter pronounced in the Supreme Court of Canada. One important rider must be attached to the endorsement of the foregoing passage from Green J.A.'s judgment in Hynes as representative of the law regarding the authoritative effect of Supreme Court obiter, however. This is that it will be very much the exception, rather than the rule, that it will be possible to demonstrate the criterion of "fully-considered opinion" requisite for authoritative obiter was not fulfilled. In other words, very rare will be the instances where the circumstances will afford latitude for lower courts to treat obiter emanating from the Supreme Court of Canada as other than binding legal principle. *Newfoundland Assn. of Provincial Court Judges v. Newfoundland*, 2000 CarswellNfld 266, 2000 NFCA 46, 191 D.L.R. (4th) 225, 50 C.P.C. (4th) 1, 27 Admin. L.R (3d) 1 (C.A.), Marshall J.A. (dissenting).

OBITER DICTUM. [L. a remark in passing] 1. An opinion not required in a judgment and so not a binding precedent. 2. "... [T]he time is past ... when the language of a conclusion is minutely scrutinized regardless of the underlying reasons and the conclusions sought in the action, and everything not echoed in the conclusion [is] necessarily regarded as an obiter dictum." *Celliers du Monde Inc. c. Dumont Vins & Spiriteux Inc.* (1992), 42 C.P.R. (3d) 197 at 204, 139 N.R. 357, [1992] 2 F.C. 634 (C.A.), the court per Decary J.A.

OBJECT. *v.* To take issue with.

OBJECT. *n.* 1. Goal or purpose. 2. A tangible item. See ABORIGINAL SACRED AND CULTURALLY SENSITIVE ~; HAS AS ITS ~; SACRED CEREMONIAL ~.

OBJECT CODE. See MACHINE LANGUAGE.

OBJECTIVE. *n.* Aim, intended end.

OBJECTIVE. *adj.* Reasoned; impersonal; observed.

OBJECTIVE EVIDENCE. Information that can be proved true, based on facts obtained through observation, measurement, testing or other means, as set out in the definition "objective evidence" in section 2.19 of International Organization for Standardization standard ISO 8402:1994, Quality management and quality assurance—Vocabulary, as amended from time to time. *Food and Drugs Act*, R.S.C. 1985, c. F-27, *Medical Devices Regulations*, SOR/98-282, s. 1.

OBJECTIVELY. *adv.* Having an evidentiary base.

OBJECT OF A POWER. A person in whose favour one may exercise a power of appointment.

OBJECTOR. See CONSCIENTIOUS ~.

OBJECTS. *n.* The purposes of a corporation. The purposes of a trust. See CERTAINTY OF ~.

OBJECTS CLAUSE. The clause in an incorporating document which sets out the purposes for which the corporation is established.

OBLIGATION. *n.* 1. "... [R]efers to something in the nature of a contract, such as a covenant, bond or agreement... ." *Stokes v. Leavens* (1918), 40 D.L.R. 23 at 24, [1918] 2 W.W.R. 188, 28 Man. R. 479 (C.A.), Perdue J.A. 2. "[Not restricted] to a duty arising out of contract [but] ... also includes a duty or liability arising from an actionable tort." *Smith v. Canadian Broadcasting Corp.*, [1953] O.W.N. 212 at 214, [1953] 1 D.L.R. 510 (H.C.), Judson J. 3. "... [T]hat which constitutes legal duty and which renders one liable to coercion for neglecting it – an act which binds a person to some performance." *Ging, Re* (1890), 20 O.R. 1 at 5 (H.C.), Robertson J. 4. "[In the definition of property in the Bankruptcy Act, R.S.C. 1970, c. B-3, s. 2] ... an asset owing to the bankrupt as an obligee ..." *Targa Holdings Ltd. v. Whyte*

(1974), 21 C.B.R. (N.S.) 54 at 71, [1974] 3 W.W.R. 632, 44 D.L.R. (3d) 208 (Alta. C.A.), Clement J.A. See ALTERNATIVE ~; CONDITIONAL ~; DEBT ~; DIVISIBLE ~; EQUITY IMPUTES AN INTENTION TO FULFIL AN ~; FACULTATIVE ~; FIDUCIARY ~; IMPERFECT ~; INDIVISIBLE ~; JOINT ~; LEASE ~; MORAL ~; MUTUALITY OF ~; NATURAL ~; RESIDUAL ~ LEASE; SOLIDARY ~.

OBLIGATION IN SOLIDUM. The purpose of the concept is to organize the manner in which more than one debt relating to a single object may coexist. Reiterates the fundamental elements of the institution of joint and several liability. When two debts relate to the same object, it allows the creditor to look to any one of the debtors for payment. The debtor who has paid is then subrogated in the rights of the creditor against its co-debtor. *Perras c. Immeubles Les Castels de Greenfield Park Inc.*, [2001] 3 S.C.R. 882.

OBLIQUE ACTION. A creditor whose claim is certain, liquid and exigible may exercise the rights and actions belonging to the debtor, in the debtor's name, where the debtor refuses or neglects to exercise them to the prejudice of the creditor. However, he may not exercise rights and actions which are strictly personal to the debtor. *Civil Code*, S.Q. 1991, c. 64, a. 1627.

OBLITERATED BOUNDARY. A boundary established during an original survey or during a survey of a plan of subdivision registered under the Land Titles Act or the Registry Act where the original posts or blazed trees no longer exist and which cannot be re-established from the field notes of either of such surveys or by evidence under oath. *Surveys Act*, R.S.O. 1990, c. S.30, s. 1.

OBSCENE. *adj.* 1. Any publication whose dominant characteristic is the undue exploitation of sex, or of sex and any one or more of the following subjects, namely: crime, horror, cruelty and violence, shall be deemed to be obscene. *Criminal Code*, R.S.C. 1985, c. C-46, s. 163(8). 2. In determining whether the exploitation of sex is "undue," three tests are considered: the "community standards test" is concerned not with what Canadians would not tolerate being exposed to themselves, but what they would not tolerate other Canadians being exposed to; the "degradation or dehumanization test" considers degrading or dehumanizing materials place women (and sometimes men) in positions of subordination, servile submission or humiliation. They run against the principles of equality and dignity of all human beings; the "internal necessities test" assesses whether the exploitation of sex has a justifiable role in advancing the plot or the theme, and in considering the work as a whole, does not merely represent "dirt for dirt's sake" but has a legitimate role when measured by the internal necessities of the work itself. *R. v. Butler*, [1992] 1 S.C.R. 452.

OBSOLETE. *adj.* 1. Invalid because it was discontinued. 2. Discarded; no longer used.

OBSTACLE. *n.* The term "obstacle" has to be read in context. In its immediate legislative context, it is associated with "mobility" (in French, "possibilités de déplacement"). "Obstacle," "mobility," "déplacement," in their primary and ordinary meaning, refer to obstacles of a physical nature. *VIA Rail Canada Inc. v. Canadian Transportation Agency*, 2006 FCA 45.

OBSTRUCT. *v.* To do any act which makes it more difficult for a peace officer or other official to carry out their duties.

OBSTRUCTING JUSTICE. 1. Every one who wilfully attempts in any manner to obstruct, pervert or defeat the course of justice in a judicial proceeding, (a) by indemnifying or agreeing to indemnify a surety, in any way and either in whole or in part; or (b) where he is a surety, by accepting or agreeing to accept a fee or any form of indemnity whether in whole or in part from or in respect of a person who is released or is to be released from custody is guilty of an offence. *Criminal Code*, R.S.C. 1985, c. C-46, s. 139(1). 2. Every one shall be deemed wilfully to attempt to obstruct, pervert or defeat the course of justice who in a judicial proceeding, existing or proposed, (a) dissuades or attempts to dissuade a person by threats, bribes or other corrupt means from giving evidence; (b) influences or attempts to influence by threats, bribes or other corrupt means a person in his conduct as a juror; or (c) accepts or obtains, agrees to accept or attempts to obtain a bribe or other corrupt consideration to abstain from giving evidence, or to do or to refrain from doing anything as a juror. *Criminal Code*, R.S.C. 1985, c. C-46, s. 139(3).

OBSTRUCTION. *n.* 1. " ... [A]ny act, not necessarily an unlawful act, including a concealment, which frustrates or makes more difficult the execution of a peace officer's duty..." *R. v. Moore* (1977), 40 C.R.N.S. 93 at 105, [1977] 5 W.W.R. 241, 36 C.C.C. (2d) 481 (B.C. C.A.), Carrothers J.A. 2. Any slide, dam or other obstruction impeding the free passage of fish. *Fisheries Act*, R.S.C. 1985, c. F-14, s. 2. 3. Every person is guilty of an offence who, with the intention of delaying or obstructing the electoral process. *Canada Elections Act*, S.C. 2000, c. 9, s. 480(1). Every person is guilty of an offence who, at any time between the issue of a writ and the day after polling day at the election, acts, incites others to act or conspires to act in a disorderly manner with the intention of preventing the transaction of the business of a public meeting called for the purposes of the election. *Canada Elections Act*, S.C. 2000, c. 9, s. 480(2).

OBTAIN. *v.* To acquire, procure, get, have granted to.

OBVIATE. *v.* To do away with.

OBVIOUS. *adj.* 1. Apparent. 2. In the law of patents, something is obvious when it would occur directly to an ordinary person skilled in the relevant art or subject searching for something normal without serious thought, research or experiment.

OBVIOUSNESS. *n.* An attack on a patent based on its lack of inventiveness. Obviousness alleges that "any fool could have done that", while anticipation alleges that "your invention, though clever, was already known." *SmithKline Beecham Pharma Inc. v. Apotex Inc.*, 2002 FCA 216, 21 C.P.R. (4th) 129, 219

D.L.R. (4th) 124, [2003] 1 F.C. 118, 226 F.T.R. 144 (note).

O.C. *abbr.* Order in Council.

OCCASION. *v.* Cause. *Jackson Brothers Grain* Co. *v. United States Fidelity & Guaranty Co.* (1934), 42 Man. R. 469 at 471, [1934] 3 W.W.R. 485 (K.B.), Adamson J.

OCCASION. *n.* An event; occurrence. See PRIVILEGED ~.

OCCASIONAL. *adj.* Limited to specific occasions.

OCCUPANCY. *n.* The use or intended use of a building or part thereof for the shelter or support of persons, animals or property. *Local Government Act*, R.S.B.C. 1996, c. 323, *Vancouver Olympic and Paralympic Facilities Regulation*, B.C. Reg. 430/2008, s. 1. See BUSINESS ~; PARAMOUNT ~.

OCCUPANCY DUTY. In occupiers' liability, a duty based on occupancy.

OCCUPANCY PERMIT. A permit, certificate or other document issued by a municipality or an official thereof in respect of a building indicating that the building or a part thereof may be occupied.

OCCUPANT. *n.* 1. The owner, lessee, or other person having possession of or control over lands. 2. "To be an 'occupant' of premises, as that word is understood in law, a person must have control of them." *Stinson v. Middleton (Township)*, [1949] O.R. 237 at 252, [1949] 2 D.L.R. 328 (C.A.), Robertson C.J.O. 3. " ... [I]n a wide sense means 'one who occupies, resides in or is at the time in a place'." *Stinson v. Middleton (Township)*, [1949] 2 D.L.R. 328 at 333, [1949] O.R. 237 (C.A.), Laidlaw J.A. 4. Includes the person in charge of a house, building or premises or under whose care they are, and a person apparently in charge thereof or exercising control or authority thereover. 5. Includes the resident occupier of and or, if there is no resident occupier, the person entitled to the possession thereof, a leaseholder and a person having or enjoying in any way for any purpose the use of land otherwise than as owner, whether or not the land or part thereof is in an unsurveyed area, and also includes a squatter. 6. A person who occupies an immoveable otherwise than as owner or, in the case of a business establishment, the person who carries on therein an activity giving rise to the imposition of the business tax or the payment of a sum in lieu thereof. *An Act respecting municipal taxation*, R.S.Q., c. F-2.1, s. 1. 7. Under an automobile insurance policy, a person driving, being carried in or upon or entering or getting onto or alighting from an automobile.

OCCUPATION. *n.* 1. An employment, business, calling, pursuit, trade, vocation or profession. 2. The act of possessing. 3. " ... [T]hat which engages the time and attention... ." *Northern Trusts Co. v. Eckert*, [1942] 3 D.L.R. 121 at 124, 23 C.B.R. 387, [1942] 2 W.W.R. 382 (Alta. C.A.), Ewing J.A. (Hawsen J.A. concurring). See PERMISSIVE ~; USE AND ~.

OCCUPATIONAL CLASSIFICATION. See NATIONAL ~.

O

411

OCCUPATIONAL DISABILITY PENSION. A private pension plan which provides benefits in the event that a participant becomes disabled from employment.

OCCUPATIONAL DISEASE. 1. A disease or ill health arising out of and directly related to an occupation. *Occupational Health and Safety Act*, R.S.A. 2000, c. O-2, s. 1. 2. A disease arising out of and in the course of employment and resulting from causes and conditions (a) peculiar to or characteristic of a particular trade or occupation; or (b) peculiar to the particular employment; but does not include (c) an ordinary disease of life; and (d) stress, other than an acute reaction to a traumatic event. *The Workers' Compensation Act*, R.S.M. 1987, c. W200, s. 1. 3. Includes, (a) a disease resulting from exposure to a substance relating to a particular process, trade or occupation in an industry, (b) a disease peculiar to or characteristic of a particular industrial process, trade or occupation, (c) a medical condition that in the opinion of the Board requires a worker to be removed either temporarily or permanently from exposure to a substance because the condition may be a precursor to an occupational disease, (d) a disease mentioned in Schedule 3 or 4, or (e) a disease prescribed under clause 15.1(8)(d). *Workplace Safety and Insurance Act, 1997*, S.O. 1997, c. 16, Sched. A, s. 2(1).

OCCUPATIONAL HEALTH AND SAFETY. (i) The promotion and maintenance of the highest degree of physical, mental and social well-being of workers; (ii) the prevention among workers of ill health caused by their working conditions; (iii) the protection of workers in their employment from factors adverse to their health; (iv) the placing and maintenance of workers in working environments that are adapted to their individual physiological and psychological conditions; and (v) the promotion and maintenance of a working environment that is free of harassment. *The Occupational Health and Safety Act, 1993*, S.S. 1993, c. O-1.1, s. 2.

OCCUPATIONAL HEALTH AND SAFETY SERVICE. A service organized in or near a place of employment for the purposes of: (i) protecting workers against any health or safety hazard that may arise out of their work or the conditions under which it is carried on; (ii) contributing to the workers' physical and mental adjustment in their employment and their assignment to jobs for which they are suited; and (iii) contributing to the establishment and maintenance of a high degree of physical and mental well-being in the workers. *The Occupational Health and Safety Act, 1993*, S.S. 1993, c. O-1.1, s. 2.

OCCUPATIONAL ILLNESS. A condition that results from exposure in a workplace to a physical, chemical or biological agent to the extent that the normal physiological mechanisms are affected and the health of the worker is impaired thereby and includes an occupational disease for which a worker is entitled to benefits under the Workplace Safety and Insurance Act, 1997. *Occupational Health and Safety Act*, R.S.O. 1990, c. 0.1, s. 1(1).

OCCUPATIONAL QUALIFICATION. See BONA FIDE ~; REASONABLE ~.

OCCUPATIONAL REQUIREMENT. 1. The Supreme court has established a new test, the unified approach or Meiorin test: Having considered the various alternatives, I propose the following three-step test for determining whether a prima facie discriminatory standard is a BFOR. An employer may justify the impugned standard by establishing on the balance of probabilities: (1) that the employer adopted the standard for a purpose rationally connected to the performance of the job; (2) that the employer adopted the particular standard in an honest and good faith belief that it was necessary to the fulfilment of that legitimate work-related purpose; and (3) that the standard is reasonably necessary to the accomplishment of that legitimate work-related purpose. To show that the standard is reasonably necessary, it must be demonstrated that it is impossible to accommodate individual employees sharing the characteristics of the claimant without imposing undue hardship upon the employer. *British Columbia (Public Service Employee Relations Commission) v. B.C.G.E.U.*, 1999 CarswellBC 1907, 99 C.L.L.C. 230-028, [1999] 10 W.W.R. 1, 176 D.L.R. (4th) 1, 244 N.R. 145, 66 B.C.L.R. (3d) 253, 127 B.C.A.C. 161, 207 W.A.C. 161, 46 C.C.E.L. (2d) 206, 35 C.H.R.R. D/257, 68 C.R.R. (2d) 1, [1999] 3 S.C.R. 3, the court per McLachlin J. 2. "... [A] requirement for the occupation, not a requirement limited to an individual. It must apply to all members of the employee group concerned because it is a requirement of general application concerning the safety of employees. The employee must meet the requirement in order to hold the employment. It is, by its nature, not susceptible to individual application." *Bhinder v. Canadian National Railway*, [1985] 2 S.C.R. 561 at 558-9, 9 C.C.E.L. 135, 17 Admin. L.R. 111, 86 C.L.L.C. 17,003, 7 C.H.R.R. D/3093, 23 D.L.R. (4th) 481, 63 N.R. 185, McIntyre J. See BONA FIDE ~.

OCCUPATIONAL THERAPY. The performance of professional services requiring substantial specialized knowledge of occupational therapy theory in order to promote, develop, restore, improve or maintain optimal occupational functioning in the area of self-care, productivity and leisure and includes, but is not limited to, (i) the application and interpretation of procedures designed to evaluate occupational functioning, (ii) the planning, administration and evaluation of developmental, restorative, maintenance, preventative and educational programs, (iii) providing education, health promotion, consultation, management, research or other such services that implement and advance the practice of occupational therapy. *Occupational Therapists Act*, S.N.S. 1998, c. 21, s. 2.

OCCUPIED FIELD. Refers to the notion that if Parliament has enacted constitutionally valid legislation and it conflicts with provincial legislation, Parliament's legislation prevails since it is considered to have occupied the field.

OCCUPIER. *n.* 1. The person occupying any dwelling, and includes the person having the management or charge of any public or private institution where persons are cared for or confined and the proprietor, manager, keeper or other person in charge of a hotel, inn, apartment, lodging house or other dwelling or accommodation. *Vital Statistics acts.* 2. A person having a sufficient degree of control over premises that he ought to realize that any failure to take care may result in injury to a person coming lawfully onto the premises.

OCCUPIERS' LIABILITY. An area of the law of negligence concerning the duty owed by a person having control over premises such that he should realize that any failure to take care may result in injury to a person coming lawfully onto the premises. See ACTIVITY DUTY; OCCUPANCY DUTY.

OCCUR. *v.* To happen.

OCCURRENCE. *n.* A happening; an event.

OCCURRENCE POLICY. Every insurance policy must provide a mechanism for determining the claims for which the insurer is liable in a temporal sense. The traditional way has been to focus on the occurrence giving rise to the claim. For example, most automobile insurance liability policies provide coverage for accidents caused by the insured's negligence during the policy period. Provided that the negligent act occurred in the policy period, the insurer is required to indemnify the insured for all loss arising from it, regardless of when a claim is made against the insured for that loss. This type of insurance policy is called an "occurrence" policy. *Reid Crowther & Partners Ltd. v. Simcoe & Erie General Insurance Co.*, 1993 CarswellMan 96, [1993] 2 W.W.R. 433, 6 C.L.R. (2d) 161, 147 N.R. 44, 13 C.C.L.I. (2d) 161, [1993] 1 S.C.R. 252, 99 D.L.R. (4th) 741, 83 Man. R. (2d) 81, 36 W.A.C. 81, (*sub nom. Simcoe & Erie General Insurance Co. v. Reid Crowther & Partners Ltd.*) [1993] I.L.R. 1-2914, the court per McLachlin J.

OCEAN. See DEPARTMENT OF FISHERIES AND ~S.

O.C.M. *abbr.* Ontario Corporation Manual.

ODDS. *n.* The probable pay-out price in the win pool or the ratio that represents that pay-out price. *Criminal Code*, R.S.C. 1985, c. C-46, *Pari-Mutuel Betting Supervision Regulations*, SOR/91-365, s. 2. See APPROXIMATE ~.

O.E.L.D. *abbr.* Ontario Environmental Law Digest, 1996-.

OF. *prep.* From; through; under.

OF COURSE. Describes a step in a proceeding or action which a court or its officers may not refuse provided that the proper formalities were observed.

OFF. See LAY-~; PASSING ; PASS ~; SET ~.

OFFENCE. *n.* 1. "... The rights guaranteed by s. 11 of the Charter are available to persons prosecuted by the state for public offences involving punitive sanctions, i.e., criminal, quasi-criminal and regulatory offences, either federally or provincially enacted... . a true penal consequence which would attract the application of s. 11 is imprisonment or a fine which by its magnitude would appear to be imposed for the purpose of redressing the wrong done to society at large rather than to the maintenance of internal discipline within the limited sphere of activity." *R. v. Wigglesworth* (1987), 37 C.C.C. (3d) 385 at 397, 401, [1988] 1 W.W.R. 193, 61 Sask. R. 105, 60 C.R. (3d) 193, 81 N.R. 161, 28 Admin. L.R. 294, [1987] 2 S.C.R. 541, 24 O.A.C. 321, 45 D.L.R. (4th) 235, 32 C.R.R. 219, Wilson J. (Dickson C.J.C., Beetz, McIntyre, Lamer and La Forest JJ. concurring). 2. "... [T]hree categories of offences ... 1. Offences in which mens rea, consisting of some positive state of mind such as intent, knowledge, or recklessness, must be proved by the prosecution either as an inference from the nature of the act committed, or by additional evidence. 2. Offences in which there is no necessity for the prosecution to prove the existence of mens rea; the doing of the prohibited act prima facie imports the offence, leaving it open to the accused to avoid liability by proving that he took all reasonable care. This involves consideration of what a reasonable man would have done in the circumstances. The defence will be available if the accused reasonably believed in a mistaken set of facts which, if true, would render the act or omission innocent, or if he took all reasonable steps to avoid the particular event. These offences may properly be called offences of strict liability. 3. Offences of absolute liability where it is not open to the accused to exculpate himself by showing that he was free of fault. Offences which are criminal in the true sense fall in the first category. Public welfare offences would prima facie be in the second category. They are not subject to the presumption of full mens rea. An offence of this type would fall in the first category only if such words as 'wilfully', 'with intent', 'knowingly' or 'intentionally' are contained in the statutory provision creating the offence. On the other hand, the principle that punishment should in general not be inflicted on those without fault applies. Offences of absolute liability would be those in respect of which the Legislature had made it clear that guilt would follow proof merely of the proscribed act. The overall regulatory pattern adopted by the Legislature, the subject matter of the legislation, the importance of the penalty, and the precision of the language used will be primary considerations in determining whether the offence falls into the third category. *R. v. Sault Ste. Marie (City)* (1978), 7 C.E.L.R. 53 at 70, [1978] 2 S.C.R. 1299, 3 C.R. (3d) 30, 21 N.R. 295, 40 C.C.C. (2d) 353, 85 D.L.R. (3d) 161, the court per Dickson J. 3. An offence created by an act or by any regulation or by-law made under an act or a municipal by-law. 4. The contravention of an enactment. See ABSOLUTE LIABILITY ~; CONTINUING ~; CRIMINAL ~; CRIMINAL ORGANIZATION ~; DESIGNATED SUBSTANCE ~; ENTERPRISE CRIME ~; GENERAL INTENT ~; HYBRID ~; INCLUDED ~; INDICTABLE ~; INDICTABLE ONLY ~; LESSER ~; MILITARY ~; MONEY LAUNDERING ~; MURDER IN COMMISSION OF ~S; PARTIES TO AN ~; PRESUMPTIVE ~; PUBLIC WELFARE ~; REGULATORY ~; SERIOUS PERSONAL INJURY ~; SERVICE ~; SEX ~; SPECIFIC INTENT ~; STRICT LIABILITY ~; SUMMARY CONVICTION ~; TERRORISM ~; VIOLENT ~.

OFFENCE-RELATED PROPERTY. Any property, within or outside Canada, (a) by means or in respect of which an indictable offence under this Act or the Corruption of Foreign Public Officials Act is committed, (b) that is used in any manner in connection with the commission of such an offence, or (c) that is intended to be used for committing such an offence. *Criminal Code*, R.S.C. 1985, c. C-46, s. 2.

OFFENDER. *n.* A person who has been determined by a court to be guilty of an offence, whether on acceptance of a plea of guilty or on a finding of guilt. *Criminal Code*, R.S.C. 1985, c. C-46, s. 2. See DANGEROUS ~; FIRST ~; LONG TERM ~; SEX ~.

OFFENSIVE WEAPON. Has the same meaning as "weapon." *Criminal Code*, R.S.C. 1985, c. C-46, s. 2.

OFFER. *n.* 1. The indication by one person that the person is willing to enter into an agreement with another person. 2. "... [A]n offer to sell or deliver a narcotic is complete once the offer is put forward by the accused in a serious manner intending to induce [the offeree] to act upon it and accept it as an offer." *R. v. Sherman*, [1977] 5 W.W.R. 283 at 283, 39 C.R.N.S. 255, 36 C.C.C. (2d) 207 (B.C. C.A.), the court per McFarlane J.A. 3. Includes an invitation to make an offer. 4. An invitation to treat. *Saskatchewan Human Rights Code*, S.S. 1979, c. S-24.1, s. 2. See ACTIVE ~; CONDITIONAL ~; COUNTER ~; GLOBAL ~.

OFFEREE. *n.* 1. A person to whom an offer is made. Acceptance will result in the formation of a contract. 2. A person to whom a take-over bid is made. See DISSENTING ~.

OFFERING. *n.* 1. Putting up for sale. 2. Presenting.

OFFEROR. *n.* 1. A person, other than an agent, who makes a take-over bid, and includes two or more persons who, directly or indirectly, (a) make take-over bids jointly or in concert; or (b) intend to exercise jointly or in concert voting rights attached to shares for which a take-over bid is made. *Bank Act*, S.C. 1991, c. 46, s. 283. 2. A person who makes an offer to acquire or an issuer bid.

OFFER TO SETTLE. In the context of litigation, an admission of limited liability and an offer to pay a certain amount or a denial of liability and an offer to pay something to end the dispute.

OFFICE. *n.* 1. "... [A] position of duty, trust or authority in the public service or is a service under constituted authority... ." *R. v. Sheets* (1971), 15 C.R.N.S. 232 at 236, [1971] S.C.R. 614, [1971] 1 W.W.R. 672, 1 C.C.C. (2d) 508, 16 D.L.R. (3d) 221, the court per Fauteux C.J.C. 2. A room, building or other place where business is conducted. See COLOUR OF ~; HEAD ~; LEGISLATIVE ASSEMBLY ~; PATENT ~; POST ~; PURCHASING ~; REGISTERED ~; SELLING ~.

OFFICE HOLDER. See PUBLIC ~.

OFFICER. *n.* 1. A person holding the position entitling that person to a fixed or ascertainable stipend or remuneration and includes a judicial office, the office of a minister of the Crown, the office of a lieutenant governor, the office of a member of the Senate or House of Commons, a member of a legislative assembly or a member of a legislative or executive council and any other office the incumbent of which is elected by popular vote or is elected or appointed in a representative capacity, and also includes the position of a corporation director. 2. In relation to the Crown, includes a minister of the Crown and any servant of the Crown. 3. Includes a trustee, director, manager, treasurer, secretary or member of the board or committee of management of an insurer and a person appointed by the insurer to sue and be sued in its behalf. 4. A person employed in connection with the administration and management of a department. 5. The chairman and any vice-chairman of the board of directors, the president, any vice-president, the secretary, any assistant secretary, the treasurer, any assistant treasurer, the general manager and any other person designated an officer by by-law or by resolution of the directors, and any other individual who performs functions for a company similar to those normally performed by an individual occupying any of those offices. *Companies acts.* 6. A person who holds Her Majesty's commission in the Canadian Forces, a person who holds the rank of officer cadet in the Canadian Forces, and any person who pursuant to law is attached or seconded as an officer to the Canadian Forces. *National Defence Act*, R.S.C. 1985, c. N-5, s. 2(1). 7. The chairperson of the board of directors, the president, a vice-president, the secretary, the treasurer, the comptroller, the general counsel, the general manager, a managing director, of an entity, or any other individual who performs functions for an entity similar to those normally performed by an individual occupying any of those offices. *Canada Business Corporations Act*, R.S.C. 1985, c. C-44, s. 126. 8. A commissioned officer of the R.C.M.P. Force. 9. A peace officer or public officer. *Criminal Code*, R.S.C. 1985, c. C-46, s. 488.1(1). See ASSESSMENT ~; BRIBERY OF ~S; CITIZENSHIP ~; COLLECTION ~; CONCILIATION ~; CUSTOMS ~; DIPLOMATIC OR CONSULAR ~; FINANCIAL ~; FIREARMS ~; LAW ~ OF THE CROWN; PEACE ~; PROBATION ~; PUBLIC ~; REGISTRATION ~; RETURNING ~; SENIOR ~S; SUPERIOR ~; TAXING ~.

OFFICER DOWN CALL. An emergency call by police indicating that an officer is in difficulty and requires assistance.

OFFICER OF A PUBLIC INSTITUTION. The meaning of the phrase "officer of a public institution" as used in the Privacy Act [R.S.C. 1985, c. P-21] should be determined from the contextual factors within the Privacy Act itself (including its legislative history), and other statutes that are related or deal with the same subject matter, such as the Access to Information Act [R.S.C. 1985, c. A-1]. ... if Parliament had intended the Prime Minister to be treated as an "officer" of the PCO for the purposes of the Privacy Act, it would have said so expressly. ... it would be inconsistent with the intention of Parliament to interpret the Privacy Act in a way that would include the Prime Minister within the scope of the phrase "officer of a government institution" as used in paragraph (j) of the definition of "personal information" in section 3 of the Privacy Act. *Canada (In-*

formation Commissioner) v. Canada (Minister of National Defence), 2009 FCA 181.

OFFICIAL. *n.* 1. Includes president, vice-president, secretary, treasurer, managing director, general manager, department manager, branch office manager and every person acting in a similar capacity whether so designated or not. 2. Any person employed in, or occupying a position of responsibility in, the service of Her Majesty and includes any person formerly so employed or formerly occupying such a position. See MUNICIPAL ~.

OFFICIAL. *adj.* Authorized; formal.

OFFICIAL AGENT. The official agent of a candidate is responsible for administering the candidate's financial transactions for his or her electoral campaign and for reporting on those transactions in accordance with the provisions of this Act. *Canada Elections Act*, S.C. 2000, c. 9, s. 436.

OFFICIAL ARCHIVE. The Library and Archives of Canada or any archive established under the law of a province for the preservation of the official archives of the province. *Copyright Act*, R.S.C. 1985, c. C-42, s. 30.8(7).

OFFICIAL COMMUNITY PLAN. A master plan of community development and land utilization prepared by a local planning authority and legally adopted by or on behalf of a municipality. *National Housing Act*, R.S.C. 1985, c. N-11, s. 2.

OFFICIAL DEVELOPMENT ASSISTANCE. International assistance (a) that is administered with the principal objective of promoting the economic development and welfare of developing countries, that is concessional in character, that conveys a grant element of at least 25%, and that meets the requirements set out in section 4; or (b) that is provided for the purpose of alleviating the effects of a natural or artificial disaster or other emergency occurring outside Canada. *Official Development Assistance Accountability Act*, S.C. 2008, c. 17, s. 3.

OFFICIAL EMBLEM. Any bird, tree, mineral, flag, flower or other item designated as an official emblem of a jurisdiction. An emblem used in connection with the official business of the jurisdiction.

OFFICIAL EXAMINER. The officer of a court who presides over examinations for discovery, cross-examinations on affidavits and other examinations.

OFFICIAL GUARDIAN. The provincial official who is charged with acting on behalf of minors or persons incapable of managing their own affairs. May manage the estates of such persons.

OFFICIAL INSPECTION STATION. A place of business registered to provide inspection services in connection with motor vehicle legislation.

OFFICIAL LANGUAGE. The English language or the French language. Section 16 of the Charter provides: English and French are the official languages of Canada and have equality of status and equal rights and privileges as to their use in all institutions of the Parliament and government of Canada. See COMMISSIONER OF ~S.

OFFICIALLY INDUCED ERROR. 1. "The defence of 'officially induced error', exists where the accused, having adverted to the possibility of illegality, is led to believe, by the erroneous advice of an official, that he is not acting illegally." *R. v. Cancoil Thermal Corp.* (1986), 23 C.R.R. 257 at 265, 11 C.C.E.L. 219, 14 O.A.C. 225, 52 C.R. (3d) 188, 27 C.C.C. (3d) 295, the court per Lacourcière J.A. 2. Occurs when an accused is led to believe by erroneous advice of an official responsible for enforcement of a regulatory statute that he is not acting illegally.

OFFICIAL MARK. A mark adopted and used by a public authority and protected under the Trade-marks Act from use by other persons.

OFFICIAL NOTICE. The power of a tribunal to take notice of publicly available information which amounts to general knowledge. Equivalent of judicial notice.

OFFICIAL OPPOSITION. The largest minority political party which is prepared, in the event the government resigns, to assume office. Known as Her Majesty's Loyal Opposition. A. Fraser, W.A. Dawson & J. Holtby, eds., *Beauchesne's Rules and Forms of the House of Commons of Canada*, 6th ed. (Toronto: Carswell, 1989) at 55.

OFFICIAL PLAN. Sets out the goals, objectives and policies established to manage and direct physical change and its effects on the social, economic and natural environment of a municipality or part of it, or an area that is without municipal organization. See OFFICAL COMMUNITY PLAN.

OFFICIAL RECEIVER. A person delegated by the Superintendent to accept debtors' assignments in bankruptcy and generally supervise trustees' administration of bankrupt estates. F. Bennett, *Receiverships* (Toronto: Carswell, 1985) at 3.

OFFICIAL REPORT. The publication of reports of cases directed by statute or a court itself.

OFFICIAL REPORT OF DEBATES. Hansard, a record of speeches made in the House of Commons and verbatim answers to written questions from the Order Paper. A. Fraser, W.A. Dawson & J. Holtby, eds., *Beauchesne's Rules and Forms of the House of Commons of Canada*, 6th ed. (Toronto: Carswell, 1989) at 300.

OFFICIAL RESULT. The order of finish of the horses in a race as declared by the stewards or judges, as the case may be. *Criminal Code*, R.S.C. 1985, c. C-46, *Pari-Mutuel Betting Supervision Regulations*, SOR/91-365, s. 2.

OFFICIAL TRUSTEE. The title for the public trustee in some provinces.

OFFICIO. See EX ~.

OFFSET. *v.* Offset is a business or an accounting term. I do not agree that offset means the same as the legal term set-off, which normally refers to an amount claimed by a defendant as a counter-claim or cross claim against a plaintiff arising out of the same subject matter. *Belliveau v. Royal Bank*, 2000 CarswellNB 74, 14 C.B.R. (4th) 17, 23 C.C.P.B. 113,

3 B.L.R. (3d) 43, 224 N.B.R. (2d) 354, 574 A.P.R. 354 (C.A.), the court per Turnbull J.A.

OFFSET. *n.* See EMISSION ~.

OFFSHORE AREA. Sable Island or any area of land not within a province that belongs to Her Majesty in right of Canada or in respect of which Her Majesty in right of Canada has the right to dispose of or exploit the natural resources and that is situated in submarine areas in the internal waters of Canada, the territorial sea of Canada or the continental shelf of Canada. *Energy Administration Act*, R.S.C. 1985, c. E-6, s. 20.

O.F.L.R. *abbr.* Ontario Family Law Reporter, 1987-.

O.H.R.C.B.I. *abbr.* Ontario Human Rights Commission - Board of Inquiry, 1963-1996.

O.H.R.C. DEC. *abbr.* Ontario Human Rights Commission Decisions, 1956-1995?.

O.I.C. ARB. *abbr.* Ontario Insurance Commission – Arbitration Cases, 1995-.

OIL. *n.* Crude petroleum regardless of gravity produced at a well-head in liquid form, and any other hydrocarbons, except coal and gas, including hydrocarbons that may be extracted or recovered from surface or subsurface deposits, including deposits of oil sand, bitumen, bituminous sand, oil shale and other types of deposits. See FREEHOLD ~; ILLEGAL ~.

OIL AND GAS LAW. Specialized area of law developed as a result of the unique and fleeting nature of the subject matter. Hydrocarbon molecules change phases and migrate to other tracts of land as no other substances do. *Alberta Energy Co. v. Goodwell Petroleum Corp.*, 2003 ABCA 277.

OIL AND GAS RIGHTS. In respect of a parcel of land, rights to search for and produce oil and gas found in or under the land. *The Oil and Gas Act*, S.M. 1993, c. 4, s. 1.

OIL HANDLING FACILITY. A facility, including an oil terminal, that is used in the loading or unloading of petroleum in any form, including crude oil, fuel oil, sludge, oil refuse and refined products, to or from vessels. *Canada Shipping Act, 2001*, S.C. 2001, c. 26, s. 2.

OIL POLLUTION INCIDENT. An occurrence, or a series of occurrences having the same origin, that results or is likely to result in a discharge of oil. *Canada Shipping Act, 2001*, S.C. 2001, c. 26, s. 185.

OLMSTED P.C. *abbr.* Olmsted's Privy Council Decisions, 1867-1954.

O.L.R. *abbr.* Ontario Law Reports, 1900-1931.

O.L.R.B. *abbr.* Ontario Labour Relations Board.

O.L.R.B. REP. *abbr.* Ontario Labour Relations Board Reports, 1944-.

O.M.B. *abbr.* Ontario Municipal Board.

O.M.B. DEC. *abbr.* Ontario Municipal Board Decisions, 1953-1994.

O.M.B.E.A.B. *abbr.* Joint Board of Ontario Municipal Board and the Environmental Assessment Board Decisions, 1984-.

O.M.B. INDEX. *abbr.* Ontario Municipal Board Index to Applications Disposed of, 1969-1992.

O.M.B.R. *abbr.* Ontario Municipal Board Reports, 1973-.

OMBUDSMAN. *n.* A person appointed to consider and investigate complaints of members of the public concerning the administration of the government.

OMISSION. *n.* 1. "... [M]eans the failure to do something which it is one's duty to do, or which a reasonable man would do." *Greenlaw v. Canadian Northern Railway* (1913), 12 D.L.R. 402 at 405, [1913] 4 W.W.R. 847, 15 C.R.C. 329, 23 Man. R. 410, 24 W.L.R. 509 (C.A.), Perdue J.A. (Howell C.J.M., Cameron and Haggart JJ.A. concurring). 2. Includes a deliberate choice to leave something out. See ERRORS AND ~S EXCEPTED.

OMNIA PRAESUMUNTUR IN ODIUM SPOLIATORIS. [L.] All is presumed against the person who destroyed evidence. A rebuttable presumption is raised that the person who destroyed a document is adversely affected by the document or the document is not favourable to the person.

OMNIA PRAESUMUNTUR RITE ACTA ESSE. [L.] "... [W]here acts are of an official nature or require the concurrence of official persons a presumption arises in favour of their due execution." *Kane v. University of British Columbia* (1980), 31 N.R. 214 at 229, [1980] 2 S.C.R. 1105, 18 B.C.L.R. 124, [1980] 3 W.W.R. 125, 110 D.L.R. (3d) 311, Ritchie J. (dissenting).

OMNIA PRAESUMUNTUR RITE ET SOLEMNITER ESSE ACTA. [L.] All things are presumed to be done correctly and solemnly. See *Davidson v. Garrett* (1899), 30 O.R. 653 at 660, 5 C.C.C. 200 (C.A.), Rose J.A.

OMNIA PRAESUMUNTUR RITE ET SOLEMNITER ESSE DONEC PROBETUR IN CONTRARIUM. [L.] "[The] ... presumption of the proper and due performance of administrative acts, until the contrary is proved ..." *Ettershank v. Owen* (1981), 26 C.P.C. 228 at 233 (Ont. Prov. Ct.), Vogelsang Prov. J.

ON. *prep.* Situated over or supported by another. See CARRY ~.

ON CONSIGNMENT. For payment by the consignee after sale by him or her.

ONE. See EVERY ~.

O.N.E. *abbr.* Office national de l'énergie.

O.N.E.D. *abbr.* Office national de l'énergie, décisions, 1970-.

ONEROUS CONTRACT. Contract is onerous when each party obtains an advantage in return for his obligation. When one party obligates himself to the other for the benefit of the latter without obtaining any advantage in return, the contract is gratuitous. *Civil Code*, S.Q. 1991, c. 64, a. 1381.

ON ITS MERITS. The general principle of law is that a tribunal which exercises a statutory discretion may not fetter the exercise of that discretion by the adoption of an inflexible policy. What is essential is that each case be considered individually on its own merits. The legislation clearly intends that the Tribunal make independent decisions. Its only obligation is to apply, where applicable, Board policies. But, it must surely also enjoy the power to decide when a policy should not apply. That is what is meant by deciding a case on its merits. *Braden-Burry Expediting Services Ltd. v. Northwest Territories (Workers' Compensation Board)*, 1998 CarswellNWT 170, 13 Admin. L.R. (3d) 232 (S.C.), Vertes J.

ON OR ABOUT. 1. Within some period of time. 2. On but not inside a person.

ON POINT. Cases which decide a point of law, not cases in which the facts resemble the case before the court.

ON-ROAD VEHICLE. Any self-propelled vehicle that is designed to be driven on roads. *Canadian Environmental Protection Act, 1999*, S.C. 1999, c. 33, *Gasoline and Gasoline Blend Dispensing Flow Rate Regulations*, SOR/2000-43, s. 1.

ONT. BUILDING CODE COMM'N RULINGS. *abbr.* Ontario Building Code Commission Rulings, 1980-?.

ONT. CASE LAW DIG. *abbr.* Ontario Case Law Digest.

ONT. C.I.P.O.M. *abbr.* Commissaire à l'information et à la protection de la vie privée de l'Ontario, ordonnances, série M, 1988-1998.

ONT. C.I.P.O.P. *abbr.* Commissaire à l'information et à la protection de la vie privée de l'Ontario, ordonnances, série P, 1989-1998.

ONT. C.I.P. SOMM. APP. *abbr.* Commissaire à l'information et à la protection de la vie privée de l'Ontario, sommaires des appels, 1990-1992.

ONT. CORPS. LAW GUIDE. *abbr.* Ontario Corporations Law Guide.

O.N.T.D. (AÉRIAN). *abbr.* Office national des transports du Canada décisions (transport aérien), 1988-1992.

O.N.T.D. (CHEMIN DE FER). *abbr.* Office national des transports du Canada décisions (transport chemin de fer), 1988-1991.

ONT. D. CRIM. *abbr.* Ontario Decisions – Criminal, 1997-1999.

ONT. D. CRIM. CONV. *abbr.* Ontario Decisions – Criminal Convictions Cases, 1980-1996.

ONT. D. CRIM. SENT. *abbr.* Ontario Decisions – Criminal Sentence Cases, 1984-1996.

ONT. DIV. CT. *abbr.* Supreme Court of Ontario, High Court of Justice (Divisional Court).

ONT. ELEC. *abbr.* Ontario Election Cases, 1884-1900.

ONT. EN. BD. DEC. *abbr.* Ontario Energy Board Decisions, 1961-.

ONT. ENVTL. ASSESSMENT BD. DEC. *abbr.* Ontario Environmental Assessment Board Decisions, 1980-.

ONT. H.C. *abbr.* Supreme Court of Ontario, High Court of Justice (including Family Law Division).

ONT. HEALTH DISCIPLINES BD. DEC. *abbr.* Ontario Health Disciplines Board Decisions, 1980-.

ONT. I.P.C.O.M. *abbr.* Ontario Information and Privacy Commissioner, Orders, M Series, 1988-1998.

ONT. I.P.C.O.P. *abbr.* Ontario Information and Privacy Commissioner, Orders, P Series, 1989-1998.

ONT. I.P.C. SUM. APP. *abbr.* Ontario Information and Privacy Commissioner, Summary of Apeals, 1990-1992.

O.N.T.O. (AÉRIAN). *abbr.* Office national des transports du Canada arrêtés (transport aérien), 1988-1992.

ONT. POL. R. *abbr.* Ontario Police Reports, 1980-.

ONT. PROV. CT. (CIV. DIV.). *abbr.* Ontario Provincial Court, Civil Division.

ON-TRACK ACCOUNT BETTING. Pari-mutuel betting conducted at a race-course or in a betting theatre of an association otherwise than by buying a ticket, and in accordance with sections 84.1 to 84.9. *Criminal Code*, R.S.C. 1985, c. C-46, *Pari-Mutuel Betting Supervision Regulations*, SOR/91-365, s. 2.

ONT. R.E.L.G. *abbr.* Ontario Real Estate Law Guide.

ONT. S.C. *abbr.* Formerly the Supreme Court of Ontario (in Bankruptcy).

ONT. TAX R. *abbr.* Ontario Tax Reports.

ONUS. *n.* [L.] Burden. See CIVIL ~; CRIMINAL ~.

ONUS OF PROOF. "... [S]hould be restricted to the persuasive burden, since an issue can be put into play without being proven." *R. v. Schwartz* (1988), 45 C.C.C. (3d) 97 at 115, [1989] 1 W.W.R. 289, 66 C.R. (3d) 251, 99 N.R. 90, [1988] 2 S.C.R. 443, 56 Man. R. (2d) 92, 55 D.L.R. (4th) 1, Dickson C.J.C.

ONUS PROBANDI. [L. the burden of proving] "The strict meaning of the term onus probandi is this, that if no evidence is given by the party on whom the burden is cast, the issue must be found against him." *Barry v. Butlin* (1838), 2 Moo. P.C. 480 at 484, Parke B.

ONWSIAT. Neutral citation for the Ontario Workplace Safety and Insurance Appeals Tribunal.

OP. CIT. *abbr.* [L.] Opere citato.

OPEN COMMODITY FUTURES CONTRACT. An outstanding obligation under a commodity futures contract for which settlement has not been effected by the tender and receipt of the commodity or of an instrument evidencing title or the right to such commodity or by a liquidating trade. *Commodity Futures Act*, R.S.O. 1990, c. C-20, s. 1.

OPEN COURT. "... [T]he Court must be open to any who may present themselves for admission. The remoteness of the possibility of any public attendance must never by judicial action be reduced to the certainty that there will be none." *McPherson v. McPherson*, [1936] 1 D.L.R. 321 at 327 (Alta. P.C.), Lord Blanesborough.

OPEN CREDIT. Credit under a credit agreement if the credit agreement (a) anticipates multiple advances that are to be made when requested by the borrower in accordance with the agreement, and (b) does not establish the total amount to be advanced to the borrower under the agreement, although it may impose a credit limit. *Consumer Protection acts.*

OPEN CUSTODY. (a) The level of custody with the least degree of restraint of the young person, in the case of a youth custody facility designated under subsection 85(2) of the federal Act, or (b) custody in a youth custody facility designated under subsection 28(1.1) of the former Act. *Youth Justice Act*, S.N.W.T. 2003, c. 31, s. 1.

OPENED. *adj.* Not closed; uncovered; unconfined.

OPEN FIELDS DOCTRINE. In American constitutional law, there is no constitutionally protected right of privacy in open spaces.

OPENING. *n.* Gap, aperture.

OPEN INTEREST. Where used in relation to commodity futures contracts, means the total outstanding long positions or the total outstanding short positions, for each delivery month and in aggregate, in commodity futures contracts relating to a particular commodity entered into on a commodity futures exchange. *Commodity Futures Act*, R.S.O. 1990, c. C.20, s. 1(1).

OPEN LISTING. Authority, given to a single or multiple agents, which usually implies or states that a commission will be paid only when a sale is consummated and in which the vendor usually retains a right to sell the property without reference to any agent. B.J. Reiter, R.C.B. Risk & B.N. McLellan, *Real Estate Law*, 3d ed. (Toronto: Emond Montgomery, 1986) at 74 and 75.

OPEN MARKET. A market of willing sellers and willing buyers.

OPEN TO THE PUBLIC. 1. In my view, there is nothing in this record that in any way offends s. 135(1) of the Courts of Justice Act, R.S.O. 1990, c. C-43, which provides: "[s]ubject to subsection 2 and the rules of court, all court hearings shall be open to the public." There is also nothing in the record which suggests anyone was excluded from the judge's chambers. No one requested that the appellants personally be permitted to attend on the motion judge with their counsel. In short, the agreed statement of fact provides: "[n]either counsel objected at the time to dealing with the motion in this way." In my view, counsel had an obligation to object when before the motion judge. It is inappropriate to raise this procedural objection now for the first time on appeal. If they wanted their motion heard in the courtroom, as opposed to chambers, they had the obligation to tell the judge so at the time. Simply because a matter is dealt with in a judge's chambers does not mean the hearing was not open to the public. Moreover, in my view, courtrooms, and by courtrooms I mean anywhere where judicial business is conducted, are presumed to be open to the public. It is for this reason that whenever a party wishes to have specific persons, or indeed the public, excluded from a courtroom, an application must be made to the presiding judge or an order to that effect. *Palkowski v. Ivancic*, 2009 ONCA 705, MacFarland J.A. (Watt, J.A., concurring). 2. [T]he phrase "open to the public" when interpreted to foster its enormously important purposes must be taken to mean a forum where the public understands it is free to enter without specifically requesting admission. *Palkowski v. Ivancic*, 2009 ONCA 705, Juriansz J.A. (dissenting).

OPERATE. *v.* 1. " ... '[U]se' ..." *Hudson v. Insurance Corp. of British Columbia* (1991), 2 C.C.L.I. (2d) 157 at 163, 57 B.C.L.R. (2d) 183, 83 D.L.R. (4th) 377, [1992] I.L.R. 1-2792, 8 B.C.A.C. 13, 17 W.A.C. 13, the court per Locke J.A. 2. " ... [T]o superintend, or conduct, or manage, or direct." *O'Reilly v. Canada Accident & Fire Assurance Co.*, [1928] 4 D.L.R. 415 at 417, 62 O.L.R. 654 (H.C.), Kelly J. 3. To have the management and control. 4. To carry on the activity permitted by a licence. *Health Facilities Special Orders Act*, R.S.O. 1990, c. H.5, s. 1. 5. (a) Means, in respect of a motor vehicle, to drive the vehicle; (b) means, in respect of railway equipment, to participate in the direct control of its motion, whether (i) as a member of the crew of the equipment, (ii) as a person who, by remote control, acts in lieu of such crew, or (iii) as other than a member or person described in subparagraphs (i) and (ii), and (c) includes in respect of a vessel or an aircraft, to navigate the vessel or aircraft. *Criminal Code*, R.S.C. 1985, c. C-46, s. 214. 6. Having physical control of a vehicle.

OPERATING. *adj.* Maintaining; functioning; carrying on; repairing; keeping going.

OPERATING AGREEMENT. See UNIT ~

OPERATING EXPENSE. An expenditure for administration or management.

OPERATING FUND. A fund for common expenses that usually occur either once a year or more often than once a year. *Strata Property Act*, S.B.C. 1998, c. 43, s. 1.

OPERATING MIND. In relation to confessions, a test requiring an accused to possess a limited degree of cognitive ability to understand what she is saying and to comprehend that the evidence may be used against her. *R. v. Whittle*, [1994] 2 S.C.R. 914.

OPERATING SYSTEM PROGRAM. Designed primarily to facilitate the operation of "application programs" and perform tasks common to any "application program", such as reading and writing data to a disk. Without them, each "application program" would need to duplicate its functions. *Apple Computer Inc. v. Macintosh Computers Ltd. (1985)*, 3 C.I.P.R 133, 3 C.P.R. (3d) 34, (Fed. T.D.) Cullen J.

OPERATION. *n.* 1. Is broad enough to include almost any activity whatsoever carried out on an owner's property. *Vancouver (City) v. Reid*, 2006 BCCA 251. 2. "... [M]ay be given two distinct meanings – a wider meaning when used figuratively (as where a person 'operates' a fleet of vehicles by organizing a system of activity, without necessarily driving any of the vehicles himself), and a more narrow meaning restricted to the physical acts or omissions of the operator of a vehicle while it is being driven." *R. v. Twoyoungmen* (1979), 48 C.C.C. (2d) 550 at 559, 16 A.R. 413, [1979] 5 W.W.R. 712, 3 M.V.R. 186, 101 D.L.R. (3d) 598 (C.A.), the court per Prowse J.A. See AQUACULTURE ~; DANGEROUS ~ OF AIRCRAFT; DANGEROUS ~ OF MOTOR VEHICLES; DANGEROUS ~ OF RAILWAY EQUIPMENT; DANGEROUS ~ OF VESSELS; GROW ~; MILITARY ~; MINING ~S; STRICT LEGAL ~; UNITED NATIONS ~; UNIT ~.

OPERATIONAL. *adj.* Describes a "... function of government [which] ... involves the use of governmental powers for the purpose of implementing, giving effect to or enforcing compliance with the general or specific goals of a policy decision." *Just v. British Columbia* (1985), 33 C.C.L.T. 49 at 52, 34 M.V.R. 124, 64 B.C.L.R. 349, [1985] 5 W.W.R. 570 (S.C.), McLachlin J. See SPECIAL ~ INFORMATION.

OPERATIONAL DECISION. The operational area is concerned with the practical implementation of the formulated policies, it mainly covers the performance or carrying out of a policy. Operational decisions will usually be made on the basis of administrative direction, expert or professional opinion, technical standards or general standards of reasonableness. *Brown v. British Columbia (Minister of Transportation & Highways)*, [1994] 1 S.C.R. 420.

OPERATION OF LAW. See SURRENDER BY ~.

OPERATIVE PART. In a mortgage, lease, conveyance or other formal instrument, the part which expresses the main object of that instrument.

OPERATIVE WORD. A word which contributes to the origin or transfer of an estate.

OPERATOR. *n.* 1. In relation to any work, undertaking or business, means the person having the charge, management or control of the work, undertaking or business, whether on that person's own account or as the agent of any other person. 2. A person who drives a motor vehicle on a public highway. 3. In respect of an aircraft, the person who has possession of the aircraft as owner, lessee or otherwise. *Aeronautics Act*, R.S.C. 1985, c. A-2, *Canadian Aviation Regulations*, SOR/96-433, s. 101.01(1). See NETWORK ~; OWNER-~; UNIT ~.

OPERE CITATO. [L.] In the work just cited.

OPHTHALMIC APPLIANCES. Lenses, spectacles, eyeglasses, frames, contact lenses, artificial eyes or other specified devices, for the relief, prevention or correction of visual or other anomalies of the eyes. *Opticians Act*, R.S.A. 2000, c. O-9, s. 1.

OPIATE. *n.* A drug derived from opium. F.A. Jaffe, *A Guide to Pathological Evidence for Lawyers and Police Officers*, 4th ed. (Toronto: Carswell, 1999) at 241.

OPINION. *n.* 1. The advice a counsel gives on the facts of a case. 2. A statement which may be admissible as evidence. The opinion of an expert witness is called expert evidence. 3. Any inference from observed fact. 4. "... [S]tatement, tale or news is an expression which, taken as a whole and understood in context, conveys an assertion of fact or facts and not merely the expression of opinion... . Expression which makes a statement susceptible of proof and disproof is an assertion of fact; expression which merely offers an interpretation of fact which may be embraced or rejected depending on its cogency or normative appeal, is opinion." *R. v. Zundel* (1992), 75 C.C.C. (3d) 449 at 492, 95 D.L.R. (4th) 202, [1992] 2 S.C.R. 731, 140 N.R. 1, 56 O.A.C. 161, 16 C.R. (4th) 1, 10 C.R.R. (2d) 193, Cory and Iacobucci JJ. (dissenting) (Gonthier J. concurring). 5. "In section 742 [of the Criminal Code, S.C. 1892, c. 29] the word 'opinion' must be construed as meaning the decision or judgment of the court ..." *R. v. Viau* (1898), 2 C.C.C. 540 at 544, 29 S.C.R. 90, the court per Strong C.J. See ADVISORY ~; CONCURRING ~; DICTUM; DISSENTING ~; EXCULPATORY ~; EXPERT EVIDENCE; INCULPATORY ~; MAJORITY ~; MINORITY ~; OBITER DICTUM.

OPINION SURVEY. A poll.

OPIOID. *n.* A synthetic drug with effects similar to opiates. F.A. Jaffe, *A Guide to Pathological Evidence for Lawyers and Police Officers*, 4th ed. (Toronto: Carswell, 1999) at 241.

OPPORTUNITY. *n.* 1. A possibility of doing something; a chance to do something. 2. A requirement for the finding of guilt in relation to commission of a crime. The accused must have been capable of being at the scene of the crime at the relevant time. See FAIR ~; LOST ~ FOR AN INTERDEPENDENT RELATIONSHIP.

OPPORTUNITY COST. A form of overhead which accounts for the fact that but for the disruption people would be able to do other things valuable to their contractual interests if they did not have to deal with the effects of the disruption.

OPPOSITE. *adj.* Placed or lying on the other or farther side; across from.

OPPOSITE PARTY. "... [A] party on the other side of the record to the applicant, or a party on the same side between whom and the applicant there is some right to be adjusted in the action... ." *Rose & Laflamme Ltd. v. Campbell, Wilson & Strathdee Ltd.*, [1923] 2 W.W.R. 1067 at 1068-9, [1923] 4 D.L.R. 92, 17 Sask. L.R. 332 (C.A.), the court per Lamont J.A.

OPPOSITION. *n.* 1. In a legislature, the members who are not members of the government caucus. 2.

An objection to the registration of a trademark. See LEADER OF THE ~; OFFICIAL ~.

OPPOSITION HOUSE LEADER. A member of the Official Opposition designated by its Leader to discuss with the Government House Leader business arrangements for the House and to reach compromise on the length of debate on each item. A. Fraser, W.A. Dawson & J. Holtby, eds., *Beauchesne's Rules and Forms of the House of Commons of Canada*, 6th ed. (Toronto: Carswell, 1989) at 56.

OPPOSTION PARTY. A party other than the governing party in the legislature.

OPPRESSION. *n.* 1. No case has laid down a comprehensive definition of oppression. I use the term "oppression" to include conduct that is "oppressive or unfairly prejudicial to or that unfairly disregards" the interests of, in this case, the minority shareholders of the affiliate. *Ford Motor Co. of Canada v. OMERS* (2006), 206 O.A.C. 62. 2. The state from which a minority shareholder may claim relief. A majority exercises "... [I]ts authority in a manner 'burdensome, harsh, wrongful' ..." *Scottish Co-operative Wholesale Society v. Meyer*, [1959] A.C. 324 at 342, [1958] 3 All E.R. 66 (U.K. H.L.), Viscount Simonds. Suggests "... [A] lack of probity and fair dealing in the affairs of a company to the prejudice of some portion of its members." *Scottish Co-operative Wholesale Society v. Meyer*, [1959] A.C. 324 at 364, [1958] 3 All E.R. 66 (U.K. H.L.), Lord Keith. 3. The broad outlines of the legal concept of "oppression", as it relates to the confessions rule, are sketched in the following excerpt from Justice Iacobucci's opinion in [R. v. Oickle, [2000] 2 S.C.R. 3], at paras. 58-62: Oppression clearly has the potential to produce false confessions. If the police create conditions distasteful enough, it should be no surprise that the suspect would make a stress-compliant confession to escape those conditions. Alternately, oppressive circumstances could overbear the suspect's will to the point that he or she comes to doubt his or her own memory, believes the relentless accusations made by the police, and gives an induced confession. Without trying to indicate all the factors that can create an atmosphere of oppression, such factors include depriving the suspect of food, clothing, water, sleep, or medical attention; denying access to counsel; and excessively aggressive, intimidating questioning for a prolonged period of time. A final possible source of oppressive conditions is the police use of non-existent evidence. ... The use of false evidence is often crucial in convincing the suspect that protestations of innocence, even if true, are futile. *R v. Tessier*, 2001 NBCA 34, 153 C.C.C. (3d) 361, 41 C.R. (5th) 242, 245 N.B.R. (2d) 1, 636 A.P.R. 1.

OPPRESSION ACTION. A remedy for minority shareholders to protect them from unfairly prejudicial activity by the corporaton. See OPPRESSION REMEDY.

OPPRESSION REMEDY. The oppression remedy is designed to afford a remedy when a corporation acts in an oppressive, unfair or prejudicial manner towards a minority shareholder or creditor or in a manner that unfairly disregards their interests. Important underpinnings of the oppression remedy are the expectations, intentions and understandings of the minority shareholder and creditor. Against these are to be balanced the extent to which the acts complained of were unforeseeable or the extent to which the creditor and minority shareholder could reasonably have protected itself from the acts about which complaint is now made. *Bank Leu AG v. Gaming Lottery Corp.* (2003), 175 O.A.C. 143, 37 B.L.R. (3d) 1, 231 D.L.R. (4th) 251.

OPPRESSIVE. *adj.* 1. "... [B]urdensome, harsh and wrongful ..." *Scottish Co-operative Wholesale Society v. Meyer*, [1959] A.C. 324 at 342, [1958] 3 All E.R. 66 (U.K. H.L.), Viscount Simonds. 2. The word oppressive has been legally defined as usually referring to deliberate acts of moral, although not necessarily legal, delinquency such as an unfair abuse of power by the stronger party in order that a weaker party may be put in difficulties in obtaining his just rights. *Whitehead v. Taber*, 1983 CarswellAlta 379, 46 A.R. 14 (Q.B.), Crossley J. 3. In the context of extradition, that the decision to surrender was made in disregard of the merits of the case, was clearly unreasonable or that the Minister exercised his statutory power arbitrarily, or in a way that overwhelmed the applicant's efforts to resist surrender. *United States v. Taylor*, 2005 BCCA 440, Finch C.J.B.C. (concurring).

O.P.R. *abbr.* Ontario Practice Reports, 1848-1901.

OPTICAL APPLIANCES. Lenses, spectacles, eye glasses, contact lenses or parts connected or attached to these for the relief or correction of a visual or muscular error or defect of the eyes. *Dispensing Opticians Act, 2005*, S.N. 2005, c. D-25.1, s. 2.

OPTICAL PRESCRIPTION. A written record of the refractive error of the eye, including, if appropriate, reading add, prisms and back vertex distance. *Health Professions Act*, R.S.A. 2000, c. H-7, Sched. 17, s. 5.

OPTICIANRY. See PRACTICE OF ~.

OPTING OUT. This occurs when the legislative assembly of a province passes, by constitutional formula, a resolution dissenting from an amendment to the constitution so that the amendment has no effect in that province. P.W. Hogg, *Constitutional Law of Canada*, 3d ed. (Toronto: Carswell, 1992) at 75.

OPTION. *n.* 1. "... [A] right acquired by contract to accept or reject a present offer within a limited, or, it may be, a reasonable time in the future." *Paterson v. Houghton* (1909), 19 Man. R. 168 at 175 (C.A.), Cameron J.A. 2. A privilege, acquired by consideration, to call or to make delivery or both, within a certain time, of some specified article or stock at a certain price. 3. An agreement that provides the holder with the right, but not the obligation, to do one or more of the following on terms or at a price established by or determinable by reference to the agreement at or by a time established by the agreement: (i) receive an amount of cash determinable by reference to a specified quantity of the underlying interest of the option; (ii) purchase a specified quantity of the underlying interest of the option; (iii) sell a specified quantity of the underlying interest of the option. *Personal Property Securities Acts*. 4. An option does not create a security interest. An option is a right; it is not a payment or an obligation. *Kaak v. Bank of Montreal* 2003 CarswellOnt 3490 (C.A.). See CLEARING HOUSE ~; COMMODITY FUTURES ~; FINE ~ PROGRAM; STOCK ~.

OPTION LEASE. A lease that gives the lessee the right to acquire title to or retain permanent possession of the leased goods by making a payment in addition to the payments required under the lease or by satisfying other specified conditions. *Business Practices and Consumer Protection Act*, S.B.C. 2004, c. 2, s. 100.

OPTION ON FUTURES. An option the underlying interest of which is a standardized future. *Personal Property Securities Acts.*

OPTION PRICE. The amount of the additional payment that the lessee must make in order to exercise the option under an option lease. *Business Practices and Consumer Protection Act*, S.B.C. 2004, c. 2, s. 100.

OPTION TO PURCHASE. An option gives to the optionee, at the time it is granted, a right, which he may exercise in the future, to compel the optionor to convey to him the optioned property. The essence of an option to purchase is that, forthwith upon the granting of the option, the optionee upon the occurrence of certain events solely within his control can compel a conveyance of the property to him. *Canadian Long Island Petroleums Ltd. v. Irving Wire Products*, [1975] 2 S.C.R. 715, Martland J. at 731-732.

OPTOMETRY. *n.* (a) The examination of the human eye and its related structures and the human vision system in order to measure, assess, diagnose, or refer for consultation or treatment, any conditions of the human eye or its related structures or the human vision system, (b) the treatment of conditions of the human eye and its related structures and the human vision system through the prescribing and dispensing of ophthalmic appliances, therapeutic pharmaceutical agents as authorized by the regulations, or other aids, and the prescribing and provision of orthoptics or perceptual training and the offering of advice, consultation, or counselling, (c) the provision of other vision care services as authorized by the regulations. *Optometrists Act*, R.S.Y. 2002, c. 164, s. 1.

OR. *conj.* [T]he word "or" in s. 490.014 [of the Criminal Code, R.S.C. 1985, c. C-46], while unarguably disjunctive, is intended to be inclusive, and not exclusive. *R. v. Mullins*, 2005 NBCA 111.

O.R. *abbr.* Ontario Reports, 1882-1900.

[] O.R. *abbr.* Ontario Reports, 1931-1973.

ORAL. *adj.* Conveyed by mouth; not in writing.

ORAL ARGUMENT. The presentation of an argument before a court.

ORAL CONTRACT. A contract whose terms are not written down.

ORAL EVIDENCE. Evidence given by a witness by spoken word.

ORAL HEARING. A hearing at which the parties or their counsel or agents attend before the court or tribunal in person.

ORAL QUESTION. A question put to the government by a member of the legislature during question period in the legislature. Used to deal with urgent business.

ORDER. *n.* 1. The direction of a court or judge which commands a party to do or not to do something in particular. 2. "... [A] proposal in the nature of an offer which invites, without more, some form of acceptance intended to lead to an obligation; that acceptance, according to the nature of the order, may be by promise or by some act as, say, the delivery of goods to a carrier." *Canadian Atlas Diesel Engines Co. v. McLeod Engines Co.*, [1952] 2 S.C.R. 122 at 129, [1952] 3 D.L.R. 513, Rand J. (dissenting) (Cartwright J. concurring). 3. "... [A] proper term for describing an act of the Governor-in-council by which he exercises a law-making power, whether the power exist as part of the prerogative or devolve upon him by statute." *Gray, Re* (1918), 57 S.C.R. 150 at 167, [1918] 3 W.W.R. 111, 42 D.L.R. 1, Duff J. 4. "... [A] ruling which a tribunal is specifically authorized to make by statute and which takes immediate effect to force the doing or not doing of something by somebody... ." *Canadian Pacific Air Lines Ltd. v. C.A.L.P.A.* (1988), 30 Admin. L.R. 277 at 281, 84 N.R. 81 (Fed. C.A.), the court per Hugessen J.A. 5. Any professional order listed in Schedule I to this Code or constituted in accordance with this Code. *Professional Code*, R.S.Q., c. C-26, s. 1. See ACCESS ~; AFFILIATION ~; ANTON PILLER ~; BLANKET RULINGS AND ~S; BULLOCK ~; CHARGING ~; CHILD SUPPORT ~; COMMITTAL ~; COMMUNITY SERVICE ~; COMPENSATION ~; COMPLIANCE ~; CONFIRMATION ~; CONSENT ~; CUSTODY ~; DECLARATORY ~; DETENTION ~; ENTITLEMENT ~; FAMILY ~; FINAL ~; FORECLOSURE ~; FORFEITURE ~; GARNISHEE ~; GUARDIANSHIP ~; HOLD ~; INTERIM ~; INTERLOCUTORY ~; MAINTENANCE ~; MANDATORY ~; MARKET ~; MARKMAN ~; MEMBER OF AN ~; MONEY ~; PAYABLE TO ~; PEACE, ~ AND GOOD GOVERNMENT; PRE-EMPTIVE COSTS ~; PREROGATIVE ~; PRINCIPLE OF ~ AND FAIRNESS; PROBATION ~; PROFESSIONAL ~; PROHIBITION ~; PROTECTION ~; PROTECTIVE COSTS ~; PROVISIONAL ~; QUIETING ~; RECEIVING ~; REGISTERED ~; REMOVAL ~; RESTITUTION ~; RESTRAINING ~; SANDERSON ~; SHOW CAUSE ~; STANDING ~; STANDING, SESSIONAL AND SPECIAL ~S; STOP ~; SUPPORT ~; VARIATION ~; VESTING ~; WARDSHIP ~; WINDING-UP ~.

ORDER APPROACH. 1. Under this approach, an order is final and, therefore, appealable as of right, only if it disposes of all of the rights of the parties to the litigation. If matters remain outstanding in the litigation after the making of the order sought to be appealed, then that order is interlocutory. *Yaremy v.*

Insurance Corp. of British Columbia, 2008 BCCA 235. 2. The classic formulation of the order approach refers to disposition of all the rights of the parties. It should now be understood to include partial dispositions whereby the order determines a substantive issue in the litigation. *Forest Glen Wood Products Ltd. v. British Columbia (Minister of Forests)*, 2008 BCCA 480.

ORDER FOR CHILD SUPPORT. (3) In subsection (1), ... means (a) an order or interim order made under section 15.1; (b) a variation order in respect of a child support order; or (c) an order or an interim order made under section 19. *Divorce Act*, R.S.C. 1985, c. 3 (2nd supp.) s. 26.1. See CHILD SUPPORT ORDER.

ORDER FORM. A security is in order form where the security is not a share and, by its terms, it is payable to the order or assigns of any person therein specified with reasonable certainty or to the person or the person's order. *Bank Act*, S.C. 1991, c. 46, s. 83.

ORDER FOR THE RECOVERY OF PERSONAL PROPERTY. See REPLEVIN.

ORDER IN COUNCIL. *var.* **ORDER-IN-COUNCIL.** An order made by the Lieutenant Governor or Governor General by and with the advice of the Executive or Privy Council, sometimes under statutory authority or sometimes by virtue of royal prerogative.

ORDER OF ADVOCATES. The professional body composed of all the members of the Bar. *An Act respecting the Barreau du Québec*, R.S.Q. c. B-1, s. 1.

ORDER OF COURSE. An order, made on an ex parte application, which a party is rightfully entitled to on that party's own statement and at that party's own risk.

ORDER OF THE DAY. A proceeding which may be considered only as the result of a previous order made in the House itself, except for a measure requiring immediate consideration such as the successive stages of a bill. A. Fraser, W.A. Dawson & J. Holtby, eds., *Beauchesne's Rules and Forms of the House of Commons of Canada*, 6th ed. (Toronto: Carswell, 1989) at 110-11.

ORDER PAPER. The official agenda which lists every item which may be brought forward during that day's sitting. A. Fraser, W.A. Dawson & J. Holtby, eds., *Beauchesne's Rules and Forms of the House of Commons of Canada*, 6th ed. (Toronto: Carswell, 1989) at 300.

ORDER TO CONTINUE. An order obtained by someone entitled to carry on the proceedings or someone not already a party on whom the interest devolved, e.g., the personal representative of a plaintiff who is deceased. G.D. Watson & C. Perkins, eds., *Holmested & Watson: Ontario Civil Procedure* (Toronto: Carswell, 1984) at 11-15.

ORDINANCE. *n.* 1. Includes an ordinance of the Territories passed before, on or after April 1, 1955. *Northwest Territories Act*, R.S.C. 1985, c. N-27, s. 2. 2. Includes an ordinance of the Territory passed be-

fore, on or after April 1, 1955. *Yukon Act*, R.S.C. 1985, c. Y-2, s. 2 [repealed]. 3. An ordinance of the Yukon enacted pursuant to the Yukon Act. *Interpretation Act*, R.S.Y. 2002, c. 125, s. 21.

ORDINARY COURSE OF BUSINESS. The regular transactions in which people in that business engage.

ORDINARY MEANING. The meaning understood, in the context, by a competent user of the language. Can refer to the meaning in the vernacular of a particular special community.

ORDINARY MEANING RULE. The ordinary meaning of an enactment prevails in the absence of a reason to reject it. Even if the meaning appears clear, the court must consider the purpose and scheme of the enactment and the consequences of adopting the proposed meaning. After considering these other factors, the court may adopt a modified meaning which must be plausible and one which the words are reasonably capable of bearing.

ORDINARY PERSON. In relation to the provocation defence, must be a person of the same age and sex and share with the accused such other factors as would give the act or insult in question a special significance and have experienced the same series of acts or insults as those experienced by the accused. *R. v. Thibert*, [1996] 1 S.C.R. 37.

ORDINARY RESOLUTION. A resolution passed by a majority of the votes cast by or on behalf of the shareholders who voted in respect of that resolution.

ORGAN. *n.* A means of action; an instrument; a person or body of persons by which some purpose is carried out or function performed.

ORGANIC MATERIAL. Organic material from recently living plants or animals that is harvested, collected or used for the purpose of producing energy, and includes (i) biofuel, (ii) effluent, and (iii) organic material obtained from municipal waste or garbage. *Renewable Energy Act*, S.P.E.I. 2004, c. 16, s. 1.

ORGANIZATION. *n.* (a) A public body, body corporate, society, company, firm, partnership, trade union or municipality, or (b) an association of persons that (i) is created for a common purpose, (ii) has an operational structure, and (iii) holds itself out to the public as an association of persons. *Criminal Code*, R.S.C. 1985, c. 46, s. 2. See ABORIGINAL ~; CIVIL SOCIETY ~; CREDIT RATING ~; CRIMINAL ~; EMPLOYEE ~; EMPLOYER ~; EMPLOYERS' ~; INTERNATIONAL ~; NON-PROFIT ~; RE~; WORLD INTELLECTUAL PROPERTY ~; WORLD TRADE ~.

ORGANIZATION LOBBYIST. Any person a significant part of whose job or function consists in lobbying on behalf of an association or other non-profit group. *Lobbying Transparency and Ethics Act*, R.S.Q. c. T-11.011, s. 3.

ORGANIZED MARKET. A recognized exchange for a class of securities or a market that regularly publishes the price of that class of securities in a publication that is generally available to the public.

ORIENTATION. See SEXUAL ~.

ORIGIN. *n.* 1. Of a grievance, the point at which the union became aware of the company's position in relation to the type of grievance presented. 2. The place from which a thing comes.

ORIGINAL. *n.* The document actually prepared, not a copy.

ORIGINAL. *adj.* 1. For a compilation of data to be original, it must be a work that was independently created by the author and which displays at least a minimal degree of skill, judgment and labour in its overall selection or arrangement. *Tele-Direct (Publications) Inc. v. American Business Information Inc.*, [1998] 2 F.C. 22 (C.A.). 2. For a work to be "original" within the meaning of the Copyright Act [R.S.C. 1985, c. C-42], it must be more than a mere copy of another work. At the same time, it need not be creative, in the sense of being novel or unique. What is required to attract copyright protection in the expression of an idea is an exercise of skill and judgment. By skill, I mean the use of one's knowledge, developed aptitude or practised ability in producing the work. By judgment, I mean the use of one's capacity for discernment or ability to form an opinion or evaluation by comparing different possible options in producing the work. This exercise of skill and judgment will necessarily involve intellectual effort. The exercise of skill and judgment required to produce the work must not be so trivial that it could be characterized as a purely mechanical exercise. For example, any skill and judgment that might be involved in simply changing the font of a work to produce "another" work would be too trivial to merit copyright protection as an "original" work. *CCH Canadian Ltd. v. Law Society of Upper Canada*, 2004 SCC 13.

ORIGINAL COURT. In relation to any judgment means the court by which the judgment was given.

ORIGINAL DOCUMENT RULE. The original of a document is preferred, as evidence, to a copy. Wherever possible, the original should be produced as evidence. See BEST EVIDENCE RULE.

ORIGINAL EVIDENCE. Evidence offered to prove that a statement was made, either in a document or orally, not that the statement is true. P.K. McWilliams, *Canadian Criminal Evidence*, 3d ed. (Aurora: Canada Law Book, 1988) at 1-13.

ORIGINALITY. *n.* The characteristic of distinctive trade marks in Canada is that they actually distinguish the wares or services of the owner from the wares or services of others or are adapted to distinguish them. *Union Carbide Corp. v. W.R. Grace & Co.*, 1987 CarswellNat 657, 14 C.I.P.R. 59, (*sub nom. W.R. Grace & Co. v. Union Carbide Corp.*) 14 C.P.R. (3d) 337, 78 N.R. 124 (Fed. C.A.), the court per Urie J.A.

ORIGINAL JURISDICTION. Conferred on or inherent in a court and enabling it to proceed at first instance.

ORIGINAL POST. Any object that defines a point and that was placed, planted or marked during the original survey or during a survey of a plan of subdivision registered under the Land Titles Act or the Registry Act. *Surveys Act*, R.S.O. 1990, c. S.30, s. 1.

ORIGINAL WORK. Under the Copyright Act is one that originates from an author and is not copied from another work. That alone, however, is not sufficient to find that something is original. In addition, an original work must be the product of an author's exercise of skill and judgment. The exercise of skill and judgment required to produce the work must not be so trivial that it could be characterized as a purely mechanical exercise. While creative works will by definition be "original" and covered by copyright, creativity is not required to make a work "original." *CCH Canadian Ltd. v. Law Society of Upper Canada*, 2004 SCC 13.

ORIGINATING DOCUMENT. A writ of summons, counter-claim, petition for divorce, counter-petition for divorce or originating notice that initiates an application, an originating application or a statement of claim that commences a proceeding.

ORIGINATING DRUG COMPANY. A company which engages in original research, development and marketing of pharmaceutical products.

ORIGINATING PATENT. [Is] based on an originating invention, namely, the discovery of a new reaction or a new compound. *Sanofi-Synthelabo Canada Inc. v. Apotex Inc.*, 2008 SCC 61.

ORIGINATING PLEADING. A notice of civil claim, counterclaim, third party notice or any document, other than a petition, that starts a proceeding. *Court Rules Act*, R.S.B.C. 1996, c. 80, *Supreme Court Civil Rules*, B.C. Reg. 168/2009, Rule 1-1.

ORIGINATING PROCESS. The document by which a proceeding is commenced. A writ of summons, a petition, and a notice of application are examples.

O.R. (2D). *abbr.* Ontario Reports (Second Series), 1974-1990.

O.R. (3D). *abbr.* Ontario Reports (Third Series), 1991-.

O.S. *abbr.* 1. Old Series. 2. Upper Canada, Queen's Bench Old Series, 1831-1844.

O.S.C. BULL. *abbr.* Ontario Securities Commission Bulletin, 1949-.

OSGOODE HALL L.J. *abbr.* Osgoode Hall Law Journal.

OSSIFICATION. See CENTER OF ~.

OSTENSIBLE. *adj.* Apparent; professed.

OSTENSIBLE AUTHORITY. "... 1. [A] legal relationship between the principal and the contractor created by a representation, made by the principal to the contractor, intended to be and in fact acted upon by the contractor, that the agent has authority to enter on behalf of the principal into a contract of a kind within the scope of the 'apparent' authority, so as to render the principal liable to perform any obligations imposed upon him by such contract. To the relationship so created the agent is a stranger. He need not be (although he generally is) aware of the existence of the representation but he must not purport to make the agreement as principal himself." *Freeman & Lockyer v. Buckhurst Park Properties (Magnal) Ltd.*, [1964] 2 Q.B. 480 at 503 (U.K. C.A.), Diplock L.J. 2. Ostensible authority is the authority of an agent as it appears to others. Ostensible authority is concerned with what the outsider thinks while negotiating with the agent. *D. Fogell Associates Ltd. v. Esprit de Corp (1980) Ltd. / Esprit de Corp (1980) Ltee.*, 1997 CarswellBC 1131 (S.C.), Edwards J.

O.T.C. *abbr.* Over the counter.

OTC CORPORATION. The Canadian Dealing Network Inc. *Toronto Stock Exchange Act*, R.S.O. 1990, c. T.15, s. 1.

OTC QUOTATION AND TRADE REPORTING SYSTEM. The quotation and trade reporting system operated by the OTC Corporation. *Toronto Stock Exchange Act*, R.S.O. 1990, c. T.15, s. 1.

OTHER FRAUDULENT MEANS. In the context of fraud under section 380(1) of the Criminal Code, has been used to support convictions in a number of situations where deceit or falsehood cannot be shown. These situations include, to date, the use of corporate funds for personal purposes, non-disclosure of important facts, exploiting the weakness of another, unauthorized diversion of funds, and unauthorized arrogation of funds or property. Fraud by "other fraudulent means" does not require that the accused subjectively appreciate the dishonesty of his or her acts. The accused must knowingly, i.e. subjectively, undertake the conduct which constitutes the dishonest act, and must subjectively appreciate that the consequences of such conduct could be deprivation, in the sense of causing another to lose his or her pecuniary interest in certain property or in placing that interest at risk. *R. v. Zlatic*, [1993] 2 S.C.R. 29.

OTHER PROCEEDINGS. In the context of section 13 of the Charter which guarantees a witness protection from the use of incriminating evidence in other proceedings, a retrial of the same offence would be an example of another proceeding.

OTHER RIGHTS AND FREEDOMS. [In the context of the phrase "other rights or freedoms that pertain to the aboriginal people of Canada], can be determined by considering the ordinary meaning of the words in the context of s. 25 and the Constitution as a whole. The Concise Oxford English Dictionary, 11th ed. [Dictionary], defines "pertain" as "be appropriate, related, or applicable to". The Dictionary defines the word "peoples" as "a particular nation, community, or ethnic group: the native peoples of Canada" [emphasis in original]. Therefore, "aboriginal peoples" may be described as a particular aboriginal nation, community or ethnic group, meaning that group rights or freedoms rather than individual rights or freedoms are protected by s. 25. *R. v. Kapp*, 2006 BCCA 277.

OTTAWA L. REV. *abbr.* Ottawa Law Review (Revue de droit d'Ottawa).

OUGHT. *v.* The use of the word "ought" encompasses all those cases in which joining the person is a necessity and may even be broader ... to include situations in which joining the person may be more than mere convenience but less than a necessity. *Kitimat (District) v. British Columbia (Minister of Energy & Mines)*, 2006 BCCA 562.

OUST. *v.* To put out of possession.

OUSTER. *n.* Wrongfully being put out of possession.

OUT. See CONTRACTING ~; HOLDING ~; HOLDS ~; LOCK-~; OPTING ~; STRIKE ~; WALK~.

OUTER BAR. The area outside the bar where junior barristers plead in contrast to Queen's Counsel, who plead within the bar.

OUTLAW MOTORCYCLE GANG. Term now commonly used to describe motorcycle clubs around the world which have adopted a fairly stereotyped lifestyle which the members themselves consider that of a 'righteous outlaw'. The term 'outlaw' is intended to differentiate such bikers from those who are law-abiding. *Brown v. Durham Regional Police Force* (1996), 19 M.V.R. (3d) 207 (Ont. Gen. Div.).

OUTLAY. *n.* The expending of a sum of money.

OUTLAY COST. A cash disbursement.

OUTLET. See SUFFICIENT ~.

OUTLINE. *n.* A summary; a precis; a drawing showing the exterior limit.

OUT-PATIENT. *n.* A person who is received in a hospital for examination or treatment or both, but who is not admitted as a patient.

OUTPUT. *n.* 1. The act or fact of turning out; production. 2. Product, of a mine, for example.

OUTSIZED VEHICLE. (a) A road vehicle or a combination of road vehicles the axle load, the total loaded mass, or one dimension of which does not conform to the standards established by regulation; or (b) a combination of road vehicles made up of more than four motorized road vehicles or chassis of motor vehicles, or of more than three vehicles, a detachable axle supporting a semi-trailer not being considered when calculating the number of vehicles making up the combination. *Highway Safety Code*, R.S.Q., c. C-24.2, s. 462.

OUTSTANDING. *adj.* Not yet paid; not yet claimed.

OUTSTANDING TICKET. A winning ticket that has not been cashed before the end of the racing day for which it was issued. *Criminal Code*, R.S.C. 1985, c. C-46, *Pari-Mutuel Betting Supervision Regulations*, SOR/91-365, s. 2.

OVER. See BIND ~; CARRY-~ OF CAPITAL LOSSES; HOLD ~; PLEAD ~.

OVERBREADTH. *n.* Overbreadth and vagueness are different concepts, but are sometimes related in particular cases. [T]he meaning of a law may be unambiguous and thus the law will not be vague; however, it may still be overly broad. Where a law is vague, it may also be overly broad, to the extent that the ambit of its application is difficult to define. Overbreadth and vagueness are related in that both are the result of a lack of sufficient precision by a legislature in the means used to accomplish an objective. In the case of vagueness, the means are not clearly defined. In the case of overbreadth the means are too sweeping in relation to the objective. Overbreadth analysis looks at the means chosen by the state in relation to its purpose. In considering whether a legislative provision is over broad, a court must ask the question: are those means necessary to achieve the State objective? If the State, in pursuing a legitimate objective, uses means which are broader than is necessary to accomplish that objective, the principles of fundamental justice will be violated because the individual's rights will have been limited for no reason. The effect of overbreadth is that in some applications the law is arbitrary or disproportionate. Reviewing legislation for overbreadth as a principle of fundamental justice is simply an example of the balancing of the State interest against that of the individual. *R. v. Heywood*, 1994 CarswellBC 592, 34 C.R. (4th) 133, 174 N.R. 81, 50 B.C.A.C. 161, 82 W.A.C. 161, [1994] 3 S.C.R. 761, 94 C.C.C. (3d) 481, 24 C.R.R. (2d) 189, 120 D.L.R. (4th) 348, Cory J.

OVERBURDEN. *n.* All material which overlies an ore body and which must be removed before ore can be extracted.

OVERDRAFT. *n.* "... [A]ny adverse balance in the customer's general account, whether this balance was created by charging up cheques of the customer or debiting past due bills and notes to that account. The resulting debit balance against the customer would be an 'overdraft,' ..." *Cox v. Canadian Bank of Commerce* (1911), 18 W.L.R. 568 at 574, 21 Man. R. 1 (C.A.), Perdue J.A.

OVERDUE. *adj.* Past the time a payment should be made.

OVERHEAD. *n.* The costs of operating an enterprise, costs which cannot be assigned to a particular business activity, such as rent, electricity, heating.

OVERHOLDING TENANT. A person who was a tenant of premises and who does not vacate the premises after the tenancy has expired or been terminated. *Residential Tenancies Act*, S.A. 2004, c. R-17.1, s. 1.

OVER-ISSUE. *n.* The issue of securities in excess of any maximum number of securities that the issuer is authorized to issue.

OVERLAYING. *v.* Accidentally smothering a small child in a bed by a sleeping adult. F.A. Jaffe, *A Guide to Pathological Evidence for Lawyers and Police Officers*, 4th ed. (Toronto: Carswell, 1999) at 241.

OVERLOAD. *n.* The larger of the following: (a) the number of kilograms derived by subtracting from the gross vehicle weight of a commercial vehicle the licensed gross vehicle weight; (b) the number of kilograms derived by subtracting from the weight on any one axle or combination of axles of a commercial vehicle the weight authorized by regulation to be carried on the axle or combination of axles. *Commercial Transport Act*, R.S.B.C. 1996, c. 58, s. 1.

OVERRIDE. *v.* 1. Under section 33, for Parliament or a legislature to disregard a provision of the Charter

included in section 2 or sections 7 to 15. This is accomplished by having the statute expressly declare that this statute will operate notwithstanding that provision. P.W. Hogg, *Constitutional Law of Canada*, 3d ed. (Toronto: Carswell, 1992) at 304-5. 2. In reference to the Charter, refers to a provision in federal or provincial legislation permitted by section 33 which states: (1) Parliament or the legislature of a province may expressly declare in an Act of Parliament or of the legislature, as the case may be, that the Act or a provision thereof shall operate notwithstanding a provision included in section 2 or sections 7 to 15 of this Charter. (2) An Act or a provision of an Act in respect of which a declaration made under this section is in effect shall have such operation as it would have but for the provision of this Charter referred to in the declaration. (3) A declaration made under subsection (1) shall cease to have effect five years after it comes into force or on such earlier date as may be specified in the declaration. (4) Parliament or the legislature of a province may re-enact a declaration made under subsection (1). (5) Subsection (3) applies in respect of a re-enactment made under subsection (4).

OVERRULE. *v.* To set aside an earlier decision's authority.

OVERT. *adj.* Open. See MARKET ~.

OVERT ACT. An act done in the open.

OVER-THE-COUNTER DERIVATIVE. Any derivative other than a standardized derivative. *Derivatives Act*, R.S.Q. c. I-14.01, s. 3.

OWE. *v.* Of a sum of money, to be under the obligation to pay it.

OWING. *adj.* 1. Due. *Smith v. McIntosh* (1893), 3 B.C.R. 26 at 28 (S.C.), Crease J. 2. Required to be paid.

O.W.N. *abbr.* Ontario Weekly Notes, 1909-1962.

OWNED. *adj.* 1. Having an interest in. 2. Beneficially owned.

OWNER. *n.* 1. "... [H]as no definite meaning. It may refer to owners having either the whole or partial interests. It is not a legal term but must be understood from its ordinary use. It may be taken to mean any parties who have any interest... ." *Royal Bank v. Port Royal Pulp & Paper Co.*, [1937] 4 D.L.R. 254 at 257, 12 M.P.R. 219 (N.B. C.A.), the court per Baxter C.J. 2. "Ordinarily the word 'owner' of land means the person who holds it in fee simple, though it may be used to include one who is not the actual owner or who has an interest less than a fee simple. In the latter cases the subject matter dealt with, and the context in connection with which it is used, extend its ordinary meaning to cover other situations in particular instances; but it does not (unless possibly in special connection) mean a person without any interest in the land who is neither occupant nor in possession." *Springhill (Town) v. McLeod* (1929), 60 N.S.R. 272 at 277, [1929] 1 D.L.R. 882 (C.A.), Graham J.A. (Harris C.J., Chisholm, Jenks and Paton JJ.A. concurring). See BENEFICIAL ~; CO-~; LIMITED ~; PART-~; REGISTERED ~; ROYALTY ~.

OWNER DEVELOPER. (a) A person (i) who, on the date that application is made to the registrar for deposit of the strata plan, is registered in the land title office as (A) the owner of the freehold estate in the land shown on the strata plan, or (B) in the case of a leasehold strata plan as defined in section 199, the lessee of the ground lease of the land, or (ii) who acquires all the strata lots in a strata plan from the person referred to in subparagraph (i), and (b) a person who acquires all of the interest of a person who is an owner developer under paragraph (a) in more than 50% of the strata lots in a strata plan. *Strata Property Act*, S.B.C. 1998, c. 43, s. 1.

OWNER-OPERATOR. *n.* 1. A person who has an ownership interest in a business he or she operates. 2. A commercial driver who has an ownership interest in the vehicle that he or she drives.

OWNERSHIP. *n.* 1. The most far-ranging right in rem the law allows to a person: to deal with something to the exclusion of everyone else or of everyone except one or more designated people. 2. A patentee who makes a patented article has his monopoly as patent owner and also has ownership of the thing, the right to possess and use it, the right to destroy it, and to alienate or encumber it. See BENEFICIAL ~; CO-~; TIME SHARE ~ PLAN.

OWNER'S POLICY. A motor vehicle liability policy insuring a person in respect of the ownership, use or operation of an automobile owned by that person and within the description or definition thereof in the policy and, if the contract so provides, in respect of the use or operation of any other automobile. *Insurance Act*, R.S.O. 1990, c. I.8, s.1.

O.W.R. *abbr.* Ontario Weekly Reporter, 1902-1916.

OYER. [Fr.] To hear.

OYER AND TERMINER. [Fr.] To hear and decide.

OYEZ. [Fr. hear ye] Pay attention.

P

P. *abbr.* President, chief judge or chief justice of a court (Exchequer Court in Canada).

[] P. *abbr.* Law Reports, Probate, 1891-1971.

PACKAGE. *n.* Includes any container or holder ordinarily associated with wares at the time of the transfer of the property in or possession of the wares in the course of trade. *Trade-marks Act*, R.S.C. 1985, c. T-13, s. 2. See TOUR ~.

PACKAGING. *n.* Any receptacle or enveloping material used to contain or protect goods. See FINANCIAL ~ SERVICES.

PACKER. See BODY ~.

PACT. *n.* Bargain; contract; covenant.

PACTA SUNT SERVANDA. [L.] Contracts should be kept.

PACTUM. See NUDUM ~.

PACTUM DE CONTRAHENDO. [L.] An agreement to negotiate or complete a contract.

PAEDOPHILIA. *var.* **PEDOPHILIA.** *n.* The sexual desire or fantasies of an adult for a child; sexual behaviour of an adult with a child.

PAID. See UN~.

PAID IN. When applied to the capital stock of an insurer or to any shares thereof, means the amount paid to the insurer on its shares not including the premium, if any, paid thereon, whether such shares are or are not fully paid. *Insurance Act*, R.S.N.B. 1973, c. I-12, s. 1.

PAID UP. *var.* **PAID-UP.** When applied to the capital stock of an insurer or to any shares thereof, means capital stock or shares on which there remains no liability, actual or contingent, to the issuing insurer. *Insurance Act*, R.S.N.B. 1973, c. I-12, s. 1.

PAIN AND SUFFERING. Non-pecuniary general damages for every kind of emotional distress which a victim feels and which was caused by a personal injury.

PAIR. See KEY ~.

PALPABLE ERROR. An error which can be plainly seen. *Housen v. Nikolaisen*, [2002] 2 S.C.R. 235.

PANEL. *n.* 1. A page or schedule which contains the names of jurors called to serve. 2. A list of consultants or authoritative people from whom one might seek a decision or advice. 3. The members of a tribunal who are charged with conducting a hearing or giving a decision. See JURY ~.

PAPER. *n.* A form or document. See BALLOT ~; CHATTEL ~; COMMAND ~S; COMMERCIAL ~; EXCHEQUER BILL ~; GREEN ~; NEWS~; NOTICE ~; ORDER ~; REVENUE ~; WHITE ~.

PAPERBACK. *n.* Any printed matter other than a periodical that is published for general distribution to the public and that is not bound in a hard cover, and includes paperback books. *Paperback and Periodical Distributors Act*, R.S.O. 1990, c. P.1, s. 1.

PAR. *n.* State of equality; equal value. See ABOVE ~; AT ~; BELOW ~.

PARAGRAPH. *n.* 1. A section or part of an affidavit, contract, pleading, statute or will. 2. In a statute, part of a subsection.

PARALEGAL. *n.* A non-lawyer who, under a lawyer's supervision, performs tasks essential to the provision of legal services to clients. Usually specialized in one area of practice. Conveyancers, law clerks, litigation clerks and secretaries may be referred to as paralegals.

PARAMEDIC. *n.* A practising member of the College of Paramedics who provides an emergency treatment or administers a medication must do so in accordance with any protocols respecting the provision of emergency treatment or administration of medication by a paramedic, an emergency medical technician or an emergency medical responder that are approved by the College of Physicians and Surgeons of Saskatchewan. *The Paramedics Act*, S.S. 2007, c. P-0.1, s. 23.

PARAMOUNT. *adj.* Superior; of the highest jurisdiction.

PARAMOUNTCY. *n.* "There can be a domain in which provincial and Dominion legislation may overlap in which case neither legislation will be ultra vires if the field is clear, but if the field is not clear and the two legislations meet the Dominion legislation must prevail ..." *Reference re Fisheries Act, 1914 (Ca-*

nada), *(sub nom. Canada (Attorney General) v. British Columbia (Attorney General))* [1930] A.C. 111 at 118, [1929] 3 W.W.R. 449, [1930] 1 D.L.R. 194 (P.C.), Lord Tomlin. See FEDERAL ~.

PARAMOUNT OCCUPANCY. The principle of paramount occupancy holds that when two persons occupy or use the same land at the same time assessability depends on who has the paramount occupancy or use of the land for its business. The court must determine which of the two competing occupants had the greater business interest in using the land. Three main considerations bear on this determination: first, an occupant's physical presence on the land, second, any controls imposed by one occupant on the other occupant's use of the land and the purpose and effect of those controls and third, the relative significance of the activities carried out on the land to the primary business of each of the competing occupants. *Gottardo Properties (Dome) Inc. v. Toronto (City)* (1998), 111 O.A.C. 272.

PARAPHILIA. *n.* A condition in which the individual experiences sexual arousal and satisfaction in relation to an object that is inappropriate, either by virtue of age or in terms of the nature of the object. *R. v. Saddlemire* (2007), 219 O.A.C. 259.

PARAS FORMULA. General objectives of child support had previously been examined in detail by Kelly J.A. of the Ontario Court of Appeal in Paras v. Paras (1970), [1971] 1 O.R. 130. The ratio of this decision, which has become known as the "Paras formula," suggests that a court calculate the appropriate quantum of child support by, firstly, arriving at a sum which would be adequate to care for, support, and educate the children, and, secondly, dividing this sum in proportion to the respective incomes and resources of the parents. This formula has subsequently been used as a guideline for the determination of the amount of child support payable by a spouse after separation or divorce. *Willick v. Willick*, [1994] 3 S.C.R. 670, L'Heureux-Dube J.

PARCEL. *n.* Any lot, block or other area in which land is held or into which land is divided or subdivided.

PARCEL OF LAND. 1. A lot or block within a registered plan of subdivision. 2. A quarter section of land or any smaller area owned by one person. 3. Area owned by one person, or by more persons than one as tenants in common or as joint tenants.

PARCEL TIE. An electronic code imposed by the Registrar to link two or more parcels together so as to prevent those parcels from being individually dealt with in the land titles registry or abstract directory. *The Planning and Development Act, 2007*, S.S. 2007, c. P-13.2, s. 2.

PARCENER. *n.* A person who, with one or more others, equally shares an estate inherited from a common ancestor. See CO~.

PARDON. *v.* For the Crown to release a person from the punishment that person incurred for some offence.

PARDON. *n.* A pardon granted by the National Parole Board. The Board may grant a pardon for serious personal injury offences after ten years; for offences prosecuted by indictment or certain service offences if the Board is satisfied that the applicant, during the period of five years, (a) has been of good conduct; and (b) has not been convicted of an offence under an Act of Parliament or a regulation made under an Act of Parliament. A pardon for certain offences punishable on summary conviction or for certain service offences may be issued if the offender has not been convicted of an offence under an Act of Parliament or a regulation made under an Act of Parliament during the period of three years. *Criminal Records Act*, R.S.C. 1985, c. C-47, ss. 2, 4 and 4.1. A free pardon also may be granted under Her Majesty's prerogative of mercy.

PARENS PATRIAE. [L.] The parens patriae doctrine means different things in different contexts. Historically, it referred to a broad and virtually undefined authority of the Crown over the property and person of children and the mentally incompetent. These powers of the Crown came to be exercised by the courts so that it is now recognized that the superior courts have certain powers to step into the shoes of the parent and make orders in the best interests of the child: E. (Mrs.) v. Eve, [1986] 2 S.C.R. 388. It has also sometimes been said that the Attorney General's standing to act in the public interest, such as in pursuing civil claims in public nuisance, is attributable to the Crown's role as parens patriae: British Columbia v. Canadian Forest Products Ltd., 2004 SCC 38, [2004] 2 S.C.R. 74, at para. 67. The parens patriae power of the courts, as I understand it, is conceived of as a protective jurisdiction which confers the power to act. It is commonly exercised by a superior court on a case by-case basis as a matter of judicial discretion; it is not generally thought of as a power of the executive branch of government. While it is sometimes spoken of as a duty on the part of the Crown (as, for example, in King v. Low, [1985] 1 S.C.R. 87, at p. 94, and Re B.C. Family Relations Act, [1982] 1 S.C.R. 62, at p. 107), no authority has been presented for the proposition that the parens patriae doctrine imposes a positive duty to seek out and address cases of potential child abuse. *Reference re Broome v. Prince Edward Island*, 2010 SCC 11.

PARENT. *n.* 1. The father or mother of a child and includes an adoptive parent. 2. Includes, in respect of another person, any person who is under a legal duty to provide for that other person or any person who has, in law or in fact, the custody or control of that other person. 3. A person who has demonstrated a settled intention to treat a child as a member of his or her family whether or not that person is the natural parent of the child. 4. Includes a person with whom a child resides and who stands in place of the child's father or mother. 5. Includes a father, mother, grandfather, grandmother, stepfather, stepmother, a person who adopted a child, and a person who stood in loco parentis to a deceased person. 6. " ... [T]he word 'parent' has no precise meaning in the law of companies. One can readily understand if one company is a wholly owned subsidiary of another company that the latter could be said to be the parent company.

But that does not necessarily mean that the parent company controls the activities of the subsidiary... Before the parent is liable in law for the acts and omissions of the subsidiary, one must show that control existed and was exercised." *Hunt v. T & N plc* (1989), 38 C.P.C. (2d) 1 at 3-4, 41 B.C.L.R. (2d) 269 (C.A.), the court per Hutcheon J.A. See CHILD; CO-~.

PARENTAL LEAVE. A leave of absence allowed to an employee to care for a child or children.

PARENT COMPANY. A company is deemed to be another's parent company if, but only if, that other is its subsidiary.

PARENT CORPORATION. A corporation that controls another corporation.

PARENTING. See GRAND~.

PARENTIS. See IN LOCO ~.

PARI DELICTO. See IN ~.

PARI-MUTUEL SYSTEM. 1. A pari-mutuel system of betting through the agency of which bets may be placed and recorded and tickets or other documents showing the amount of money bet by a bettor issued to the bettor. *Pari-Mutuel Levy Act*, S.M. 1996, c. 44, s. 1. 2. The manual, electro-mechanical or computerized system and all software, including the totalizator, the telephone account betting system, the on-track account betting system and the inter-track betting equipment, that are used to record bets and to transmit betting data. *Criminal Code*, R.S.C. 1985, c. C-46, *Pari-Mutuel Betting Supervision Regulations*, SOR/91-365, s. 2.

PARI PASSU. [L.] Equally; with no preference.

PARK. See MANUFACTURED HOME ~; MOBILE HOME ~.

PARKS CANADA AGENCY. Established by the Parks Canada Agency Act, S.C. 1998, c. 31. Under section 5, the Agency may exercise the powers and shall perform the duties and functions that relate to national parks, national historic sites, national marine conservation areas, other protected heritage areas and heritage protection programs that are conferred on, or delegated, assigned or transferred to, the Minister under any Act or regulation. Under section 6, The Agency is responsible for the implementation of policies of the Government of Canada that relate to national parks, national historic sites, national marine conservation areas, other protected heritage areas and heritage protection programs.

PARK WARDEN. A person designated by the Minister under the Parks Canada Agency Act, whose duties include the enforcement of the Canada National Parks Act, to be park wardens for the enforcement of this Act and the regulations in any part of Canada and for the preservation and maintenance of the public peace in parks, and for those purposes park wardens are peace officers within the meaning of the Criminal Code. *Canada National Parks Act*, S.C. 2000, c. 32, s. 18.

PARLIAMENT. *n.* 1. The Queen, the House of Commons and the Senate. *Constitution Act, 1867* (U.K.), 30 & 31 Vict., c. 3, s. 17. 2. The Parliament of Canada. *Interpretation Act*, R.S.C. 1985, c. I-21, s. 35. 3. This title, generally, is limited to the federal parliament but may be applied to a provincial legislature as well, see Parliament of Quebec. 4. A period between the Governor General's summons after a general election and dissolution by the Crown before a general election which does not exceed 5 years. A. Fraser, W.A. Dawson & J. Holtby, eds., *Beauchesne's Rules and Forms of the House of Commons of Canada*, 6th ed. (Toronto: Carswell, 1989) at 65. See ACT OF ~; CONTEMPT OF ~; FEDERAL ~; IMPERIAL ~.

PARLIAMENTARY AGENT. A person who promotes private bills and conducts proceedings upon petitions against such bills. A. Fraser, W.A. Dawson & J. Holtby, eds., *Beauchesne's Rules and Forms of the House of Commons of Canada*, 6th ed. (Toronto: Carswell, 1989) at 296.

PARLIAMENTARY COMMITTEE. A committee of the whole House, a standing or joint committee.

PARLIAMENTARY COUNSEL. See LAW CLERK AND ~.

PARLIAMENTARY GOVERNMENT. Government in which Prime Minister or Premier selects members of her or his own party elected to Parliament and perhaps others to be Ministers of the Crown. This group collectively form the Cabinet, the policy-making arm of government. The Ministers and Cabinet are responsible to Parliament for the conduct of the government. The government remains in power so long as it has the confidence of a majority of the House of Commons or the Legislature. In theory, the Privy Council or Executive Council advises the formal head of state (the Governor General or Lieutenant Governor) though, in fact, the Committee of Council, known as the Cabinet, carries out this function in most situations.

PARLIAMENTARY PRIVILEGE. A necessary immunity provided to members of Parliament and the legislatures in order to permit those legislators to do their work. Ensures that members and the bodies themselves are free from outside interference which might prohibit them from carrying out their functions. Also provided to persons taking part in proceedings in Parliament or a legislature. The authority and power of both Houses of Parliament and of the legislatures to enforce the immunity.

PARLIAMENT OF QUÉBEC. The National Assembly and the Lieutenant-Governor form the Parliament of Québec. The Parliament of Québec assumes all the powers conferred on the Legislature of Québec. The National Assembly is composed of the Members elected for each of the electoral divisions established in accordance with the Quebec Election Act. *An Act respecting the National Assembly*, R.S.Q., chapter A-23.1.

PARODY. *n.* A new literary, musical, or artistic work which mimics and mocks the style and ideas of an original.

PAROL. *adj.* Verbal, oral.

PAROL AGREEMENT. An oral agreement.

PAROL CONTRACT. An oral contract.

PAROLE. *n.* 1. System to allow release of prisoners before the expiration of their full sentence on a part-time or full-time basis. Federal and provincial parole boards make the decisions regarding granting of parole. 2. Full parole or day parole. *Corrections and Conditional Release Act*, S.C. 1992, c. 20, s. 2. See DAY ~; FULL ~.

PAROLE. *adj.* [Fr.] Oral.

PAROLE BOARD. See NATIONAL ~; PROVINCIAL ~.

PAROLED INMATE. A person to whom parole has been granted.

PAROLEE. *n.* An inmate who has been granted parole.

PAROL EVIDENCE. Oral testimony by a witness.

PAROL EVIDENCE RULE. "... [I]f there be contract which has been reduced into writing, verbal evidence is not allowed to be given of what passed between the parties, either before the written instrument was made, or during the time that it was in the state of preparation, so as to add to or subtract from, or in any manner to vary or qualify the written contract; but after the agreement has been reduced into writing, it is competent to the parties, at any time before breach of it, by a new contract not in writing, either altogether to waive, dissolve, or annul the former agreements, or in any manner to add to, or subtract from, or vary or qualify the terms of it, and thus to make a new contract; which is to be proved, partly by the written agreement, and partly by the subsequent verbal terms engrafted upon what will be thus left of the written agreement... ." *Goss v. Lord Nugent* (1833), 5 B. & Ad. 58 at 64-5, 110 E.R. 713 at 716 (U.K.), Denman C.J.

PART. *n.* 1. A portion of a whole. 2. A class into which parties to a formal instrument are divided according to their interests or estates in the subject-matter. See COUNTER~; OPERATIVE ~.

PARTIAL DISABILITY. Unable to perform all of one's duties as those duties existed prior to injury or disease.

PARTIALITY. *n.* 1. Section 638(1)(b) of the [Criminal Code, R.S.C. 1985, c. C-46] permits a party to challenge for cause on the ground that "a juror is not indifferent between the Queen and the accused". Lack of indifference may be translated as "partiality". Both terms describe a predisposed state of mind inclining a juror prejudicially and unfairly toward a certain party or conclusion. *R. v. Find*, 2001 CarswellOnt 1702, 2001 SCC 32, 42 C.R. (5th) 1, 154 C.C.C. (3d) 97, 199 D.L.R. (4th) 193, 269 N.R. 149, 146 O.A.C. 236, the court per McLachlin C.J.C. 2. Has both an attitudinal and a behavioural component, referring to one who has biases and who will allow those biases to affect his or her verdict.

PARTIAL LOSS. "... [O]ne in which the insurers are liable to pay an amount less than that insured for damage happening to the subject, or expense incurred and occasioned by the perils insured against." *Mowat v. Boston Marine Insurance Co.* (1895), 33 N.B.R. 108 at 121 (C.A.), Tuck J.A.

PARTIAL PRIVATIVE CLAUSE. One which fits into the overall process of evaluation of the factors to determine the legislator's intended degree of deference and does not have the preclusive effect of a full privative clause.

PARTICEPS CRIMINIS. [L.] "... [O]ne who shares or co-operates in a criminal offence... ." *R. v. Morris*, (1979) 10 C.R. (3d) 259 at 281, [1979] 2 S.C.R. 1041, 26 N.B.R. (2d) 273, 55 A.P.R. 273, 27 N.R. 313, 47 C.C.C. (2d) 257, 99 D.L.R. (3d) 420, Spence J. (dissenting) (Laskin C.J.C., Dickson and Estey JJ. concurring).

PARTICIPANT. See INSURED ~; JUSTICE SYSTEM ~; MARKET ~.

PARTICIPATE. *v.* "... [T]o take part or share ..." *Graham, Re*, [1945] 3 W.W.R. 713 at 717, [1946] 1 D.L.R. 357 (Alta.C.A.), the court per Harvey C.J.A.

PARTICIPATED. *v.* Within the context [of the Canada Agricultural Products Act] means took part in or was privy to. *R. v. A & A Foods Ltd.*, 1997 CarswellBC 2541, 120 C.C.C. (3d) 513 (S.C.), Hood J.

PARTICIPATING EMPLOYER. In relation to a multi-employer pension plan, means an employer who is required to contribute to that plan. *Pension Benefits Standards Act, 1985*, R.S.C. 1985, c. 32 (2nd Supp.), s. 2.

PARTICIPATING POLICY. A policy issued by a company that entitles its holder to participate in the profits of the company. *Insurance Companies Act*, S.C. 1991, c. 47, s. 2.

PARTICIPATION. See TRACT ~.

PARTICULAR LIEN. A right to retain the chattels upon which materials and labour have been expended until all charges incurred are paid.

PARTICULAR PURPOSE. What constitutes a particular purpose is a "question of fact and degree". A "particular purpose" does not exclude the possibility of more than one purpose or an aesthetic purpose. *Pusch v. Freshair Enterprises Ltd.*, 2007 SKCA 60.

PARTICULARS. *n.* 1. In a pleading, the details of an allegation which are ordered (1) to define any issues; (2) to prevent surprise; (3) to enable the parties to get ready for trial and (4) to facilitate a hearing. *Fairbairn v. Sage* (1925), 56 O.L.R. 462 at 470 (C.A.), Ferguson J.A. 2. "The function of particulars in a criminal trial is twofold. Primarily their function is to give such exact and reasonable information to the accused respecting the charge against him as will enable him to establish fully his defence. The second purpose is to facilitate the administration of justice: ..." *R. v. Canadian General Electric Co.* (1974), 16 C.P.R. (2d) 175 at 184, 17 C.C.C. (2d) 433 (Ont. H.C.), Pennell J. 3. "... [G]iven to supplement paragraphs of a statement of claim or a defense as the case may be and should stand by themselves in connection with the paragraphs which they particularize without any reference to the evidence supporting them." *Cercast Inc. v. Shellcast Foundaries Inc. (No. 3)* (1973), 9 C.P.R. (2d) 18 at 29, [1973] F.C. 28 (T.D.), Walsh J.

PARTIES. *n.* 1. In any act or deed, the people concerned; litigants. 2. (a) In relation to collective bargaining or arbitration of a dispute, the employer and a bargaining agent, and (b) in relation to a grievance, the employer and the employee who presented the grievance. 3. (a) In relation to the entering into, renewing or revising of a collective agreement and in relation to a dispute, the employer and the bargaining agent that acts on behalf of the employer's employees; (b) in relation to a difference relating to the interpretation, application, administration or alleged contravention of a collective agreement, the employer and the bargaining agent; and (c) in relation to a complaint to the Board under this Part, the complainant and any person or organization against whom or which a complaint is made. *Canada Labour Code*, R.S.C. 1985, c. L-2, s. 3. See CHANGE OF ~; JOINDER OF ~; PARTY.

PARTIES TO AN OFFENCE. 1. Every one is a party to an offence who actually commits it, does or omits to do anything for the purpose of aiding any person to commit it, or abets any person in committing it. *Criminal Code*, R.S.C. 1985, c. C-46, s. 21. 2. Where two or more persons form an intention in common to carry out an unlawful purpose and to assist each other therein and any one of them, in carrying out the common purpose, commits an offence, each of them who knew or ought to have known that the commission of the offence would be a probable consequence of carrying out the common purpose is a party to that offence. *Criminal Code*, R.S.C. 1985, c. C-46, s. 21(2).

PARTITION. *n.* 1. Division. 2. A proceeding involving dividing real property, previously owned by tenants in common or joint tenants, into different parts. 3. A wall that does not support a vertical load of a structure other than its own weight and does not extend further than from the floor of an interior area to the structure above. *Interior Designers Act*, S.N.S. 2003, c. 6, s. 2.

PARTITION OR SALE. The name of a proceeding concerning division of land.

PARTNER. *n.* A member of a partnership. See ADULT INTERDEPENDENT ~; COMMON LAW ~; EXTRADITION ~; FREE TRADE ~; GENERAL ~; NOMINAL ~; SILENT ~.

PARTNERSHIP. *n.* 1. A contractual relationship, an agreement, between two or among more persons to run a business together in order to make a profit. Only persons who intend to or by their conduct can be seen to have intended to can become partners. 2. "... [T]here should be some common profit or gain to be derived from it. Whether or not the element of division or distribution of the common profit or gain among the members is an essential, need not be discussed; but there must be ... a community of interest in the benefits accruing from the joint activity of the partners. If that community of interest is lacking, there is no partnership... ." *Ottawa Lumbermen's Credit Bureau v. Swan*, [1923] 4 D.L.R. 1157 at 1163, 53 O.L.R. 135 (C.A.), Orde J.A. See COMMONLAW ~; LIMITED LIABILITY ~; LIMITED ~; MULTI-DISCIPLINARY ~.

PARTNERSHIP OF ACQUESTS. The property that the spouses possess individually when the regime comes into effect or that they subsequently acquire constitutes acquests or private property according to the rules that follow in the Code. *Civil Code*, S.Q. 1991, c. 64, a. 448.

PART-OWNER. *n.* A person entitled to property in common, jointly or in coparcenary.

PART PAYMENT. "... [P]ayment ... made on account of a greater debt, ..." *Stark v. Sommerville* (1918), 41 D.L.R. 496 at 496, 41 O.L.R. 591 (C.A.), the court per Meredith C.J.C.P.

PART PERFORMANCE. In relation to a contract, partial completion.

PART-TIME. *adj.* 1. In relation to an employee, means engaged to work on other than a full-time basis. 2. Employed for irregular hours of duty or for specific intermittent periods or both. 3. Employed to work less than the full number of regular working hours or less than the full number of regular working days per week.

PARTY. *n.* 1. A person by or against whom a legal suit is brought. 2. A political party registered under an Election Act. 3. A person whose rights will be varied or affected by the exercise of a statutory power or by an act or thing done pursuant to that power. 4. A person bound by a collective agreement, or involved in a dispute. See ACCOMMODATION ~; ADVERSE ~; CHARTER ~; INTERESTED ~; NECESSARY ~; OPPOSITE ~; OPPOSITION ~; PARTIES; POLITICAL ~; RESPONDING ~. SECURED ~; THIRD ~.

PARTY-AND-PARTY COSTS. *var.* **PARTY AND PARTY COSTS.** 1. "The fundamental principle of party and party costs has always been that they are given as an indemnity to the party entitled to them." *Kendall v. Hunt (No. 2)* (1979), 12 C.P.C. 264 at 267, 16 B.C.L.R. 295, 106 D.L.R. (3d) 277 (C.A.), Craig J.A. 2. These represent only a partial indemnity, calculated from a prescribed tariff designed to strike the proper balance between the burden of costs which must be borne by a successful litigant, and the risk of putting litigation beyond the reach of a potential loser. *Holloway v. Holloway*, 2001 NFCA 17, 199 Nfld. & P.E.I.R. 1, 600 A.P.R. 1, 6 C.P.C. (5th) 34, 199 Nfld. & P.E.I.R. 1.

PARTY UNDER DISABILITY. A general term which includes those legally incapable of managing their affairs such as minors and those declared by a court as incapable of managing their affairs such as absentees and mentally disabled persons.

PARTY WALL. 1. "... [M]ay ... be used in four different senses. First, a wall of which the two adjoining owners are tenants in common ... that is the most common and the primary meaning of the term. [Secondly,] a wall divided longitudinally into two strips, one belonging to each of the neighbouring owners ... thirdly, ... a wall which belongs entirely to one of the adjoining owners, but is subject to an easement or right in the other to have it maintained as a dividing wall between the two tenements; [and fourthly,] a wall divided longitudinally into two moieties, each moiety being subject to a cross easement in favour of the owner of the other moiety." *Watson v. Gray* (1880), 14 Ch. D. 192 at 195 (U.K.), Fry J. 2. A wall jointly owned and jointly used by 2 parties under easement agreement or by right in law, and erected at or upon a line separating 2 parcels of land each of which is, or is capable of being, a separate real-estate entity. *Building Code Act*, 1992, S.O. 1992, c. 23, *Building Code Act*, O. Reg. 403/97, s. 1.1.3.2.

PAR VALUE. 1. The face value of a share or security, as opposed to its market or selling price. 2. An arbitrary value placed on a share at the time of issue.

PASS. *v.* 1. To transfer or to be transferred. 2. To change hands. *Wagstaff, Re*, [1941] O.R. 71 at 77, [1941] D.L.R. 108 (H.C.), Roach J. 3. For a legislature to give final approval to an act. 4. To bring into court an account for approval. 5. Of a by-law, to deliberate on the merits of a proposal framed as a draft by-law and finally to adopt it as the law of the municipal corporation. A by-law is considered passed when the enacting is finished and the presiding officer announces that the motion for final reading has been carried. I.M. Rogers, *The Law of Canadian Municipal Corporations*, 2d ed. (Toronto: Carswell, 1971-) at 458.

PASSAGE. *n.* 1. "... [C]oming into operation... ." *Winnipeg (City) v. Brock* (1911), 20 Man. R. 669 at 683, 18 W.L.R. 28 (C.A.), Perdue J.A. (Cameron J.A. concurring). 2. The easement to pass over a body of water.

PASS AN ACCOUNT. For a court to approve an account.

PASSENGER. *n.* 1. A person carried on a vessel by the owner or operator, other than the crew. 2. The word "passenger", [in s. 224(1) of the Insurance Act, R.S.O. 1990, c. I.8] like the word "driver" identifies a status rather than a physical activity. . . . It does not follow that the person is *only* to be considered a passenger while he or she is actually being conveyed. *McIntyre Estate v. Scott* (2003), 178 O.A.C. 44.

PASSENGER SERVICE. See PUBLIC ~ PROVIDER.

PASSING OFF. Every one commits an offence who, with intent to deceive or defraud the public or any person, whether ascertained or not, (a) passes off other wares or services as and for those ordered or required; or (b) makes use, in association with wares or services, of any description that is false in a material respect regarding (i) the kind, quality, quantity or composition, (ii) the geographical origin, or (iii) the mode of the manufacture, production or performance of those wares or services. *Criminal Code*, R.S.C. 1985, c. C-46, s. 408.

PASS OFF. 1. "... [T]he gist of the action of 'passing off' is that the defendant is attempting to sell its wares, services or business under a description which would mislead customers of the plaintiff into thinking that they were buying the plaintiff's wares or doing business with the plaintiff." *Westfair Foods Ltd. v. Jim Pattison Industries Ltd.* (1990), 30 C.P.R. (3d) 174 at 179, 45 B.C.L.R. (2d) 253, 68 D.L.R. (4th) 481, [1990] 5 W.W.R. 484 (C.A.), the court per Wallace J.A. 2. "To succeed in a passing-off action, the plaintiff must first establish that there is a distinguishing feature to his goods and that his goods are known and have acquired a reputation by reason of that distinguishing feature. Secondly, the plaintiff must show that the defendant passed off his goods for those of the plaintiff: ..." *Ayerst, McKenna & Harrison Inc. v. Apotex Inc.* (1983), 72 C.P.R. (2d) 57 at 66, 41 O.R. (2d) 366, 146 D.L.R. (3d) 93 (C.A.), the court per Cory J.A. 3. Where goodwill or reputation is attached to the plaintiff's wares or services and identifies the plaintiff's name with the wares or services, to misrepresent the facts in a manner that leads or is likely to lead the public to believe that the wares or services are those of the plaintiff or the plaintiff's authorized representative and to cause damage to the plaintiff or create a situation which is likely to cause damage to the plaintiff.

PASSPORT. *n.* A document issued by or under the authority of the Minister of Foreign Affairs for the purpose of identifying the holder thereof. *Criminal Code*, R.S.C. 1985, c. C-46. See FORGERY OF ~; UTTERING FORGED ~.

PASSWORD. See COMPUTER ~.

PAST CONSIDERATION. Consideration for services already performed which do not support a promise or create a contract which may be enforced. G.H.L. Fridman, *The Law of Contract in Canada*, 2d ed. (Toronto: Carswell, 1986) at 96.

PAST COST OF HEALTH CARE SERVICES. The total cost of all health care services provided to a beneficiary as a direct or indirect result of a personal injury described in section 2, including those services provided up to and including the date of settlement or, if there is no settlement, the first day of trial. *Health Care Costs Recovery Act*, S.B.C. 2008, c. 27, s. 1.

PAT. APP. BD. *abbr.* Patent Appeal Board.

PAT. COMMR. *abbr.* Commissioner of Patents.

PAT DOWN SEARCH. The patting down of outside clothing, examining of pocket contents, lasting briefly, to determine if the person has a weapon or contraband on their person.

PATENT. *v.* See DOUBLE ~ING.

PATENT. *n.* 1. A method by which inventive solutions to practical problems are coaxed into the public domain by the promise of a limited monopoly for a limited time. *Apotex Inc. v. Wellcome Foundation Ltd.*, [2002] 4 S.C.R. 153. 2. Letters patent for an invention. Every patent granted under this Act shall contain the title or name of the invention, with a reference to the specification, and shall, subject to this Act, grant to the patentee and the patentee's legal representatives for the term of the patent, from the granting of the patent, the exclusive right, privilege and liberty of making, constructing and using the invention and selling it to others to be used, subject to adjudication in respect thereof before any court of competent jurisdiction. *Patent Act*, R.S.C. 1985, c. P-4, ss. 2 and 42. 3. A grant from the Crown in fee simple or for a less estate under the Great Seal. See LETTERS ~; ORIGINATING ~; SELECTION ~.

PATENT AGENT. 1. A register of patent agents shall be kept in the Patent Office on which shall be entered the names of all persons and firms entitled to represent applicants in the presentation and prosecution of applications for patents or in other business before the Patent Office. *Patent Act*, R.S.C. 1985, c. P-4, s. 15. 2. A person knowledgeable in the technology of the patents they draft and in legal issues relating thereto. 3. Any person or firm whose name is entered on the register of patent agents pursuant to section 15. *Patent Act*, R.S.C. 1985, c. P-4, *Patent Rules*, SOR/96-423, s. 2.

PATENT AMBIGUITY. Something clearly doubtful in the text of an instrument.

PATENT APPLICATION. The Commissioner shall grant a patent for an invention to the inventor or the inventor's legal representative if an application for the patent in Canada is filed in accordance with this Act and all other requirements for the issuance of a patent under this Act are met. The prescribed application fee must be paid and the application must be filed in accordance with the regulations by the inventor or the inventor's legal representative and the application must contain a petition and a specification of the invention. *Patent Act*, R.S.C. 1985, c. P-4, s. 27.

PATENT DEFECT. A defect which a purchaser is likely to discover if she inspects the subject property with ordinary care.

PATENTED ARTICLE. Includes articles made by a patented process. *Patent Act*, R.S.C. 1985, c. P-4, s. 65(5).

PATENTEE. *n.* 1. The person for the time being entitled to the benefit of a patent. *Patent Act*, R.S.C. 1985, c. P-4, s. 26. 2. Grantee.

PATENT INFRINGEMENT. 1. The correct test is: whether persons with practical knowledge and experience of the kind of work in which the invention was intended to be used would understand that strict compliance with a particular descriptive word or phrase appearing in a claim was intended by the patentee to be an essential requirement of the invention so that any variant would fall outside the monopoly claimed, even though it could have no material effect upon the way the invention worked. (formulated by Lord Diplock in Catnic Components Ltd. v. Hill & Smith Ltd., [1982] R.P.C. 183 (U.K. H.L.); *Bourgault Industries Ltd. v. Flexi-Coil Ltd.* (1998), 141 F.T.R. 268, 80 C.P.R. (3d) 1. 2. Any act that "interferes with the full enjoyment of the monopoly granted": Lishman v. Eron Roche Inc. (1996), 68 C.P.R. (3d) 72 (F.C.T.D.) ... [T]he definition of infringement as stated in Lishman is intended to reflect the idea that what constitutes infringement in a particular case is a function of the scope of the statutory monopoly, so that any act that impairs the statutory monopoly is by definition "infringement"... Thus, to determine whether a certain act amounts to an infringement, the scope of the statutory monopoly must be determined by construing the claims of the patent. *Monsanto Canada Inc. v. Schmeiser* (2002), 218 D.L.R. (4th) 31, 293 N.R. 340, [2003] 2 F.C. 165, 231 F.T.R. 160 (note), 21 C.P.R. (4th) 1.

PATENTLY UNREASONABLE. 1. [A] patently unreasonable defect, once identified, can be explained simply and easily, leaving no real possibility of doubting that the decision is defective. A patently unreasonable decision has been described as "clearly irrational" or "evidently not in accordance with reason" .... A decision that is patently unreasonable is so flawed that no amount of curial deference can justify letting it stand. A decision may be unreasonable without being patently unreasonable when the defect in the decision is less obvious and might only be discovered after "significant searching or testing". Explaining the defect may require a detailed exposition to show that there are no lines of reasoning supporting the decision which could reasonably lead that tribunal to reach the decision it did. *Law Society of New Brunswick v. Ryan*, [2003] 1 S.C.R. 247, 2003 SCC 20, Iacobucci, J. for the court, at para. 52, 53. 2. Generally speaking, most if not all judicial review statutes are drafted against the background of the common law of judicial review. Even the more comprehensive among them, such as the British Columbia Administrative Tribunals Act, S.B.C. 2004, c. 45, can only sensibly be interpreted in the common law context because, for example, it provides in s. 58(2)(a) that "a finding of fact or law or an exercise of discretion by the tribunal in respect of a matter over which it has exclusive jurisdiction under a privative clause must not be interfered with unless it is patently unreasonable". The expression "patently unreasonable" did not spring unassisted from the mind of the legislator. It was obviously intended to be understood in the context of the common law jurisprudence, although a number of indicia of patent unreasonableness are given in s. 58(3). Despite Dunsmuir, "patent unreasonableness" will live on in British Columbia, but the content of the expression, and the precise degree of deference it commands in the diverse circumstances of a large provincial administration, will necessarily continue to be calibrated according to general principles of administrative law. That said, of course, the legislature in s. 58 was and is directing the B.C. courts to afford administrators a high degree of deference on issues of fact, and effect must be given to this clearly expressed legislative intention. *Canada (Citizenship and Immigration) v. Khosa*, 2009 SCC 12, [2009] 1 S.C.R. 339, Binnie J. for the majority, para. 19. 3. A discretionary decision is patently unreasonable if the discretion (a) is exercised arbitrarily or in bad faith, (b) is exercised for an improper purpose, (c) is based entirely or predominantly on irrelevant factors, or (d) fails to take statutory requirements into account. *Administrative Tribunals Act*, S.B.C. 2004, c. 45, s. 58(3) and 59(4).

PATENT MEDICINES. Drugs and medicines commonly known as household medical aids that are sold for the purpose of treating, mitigating or preventing a disease or ailment in humans. *Social Service Tax Act*, R.S.B.C. 1996, c. 431, *Social Service Tax Act Regulations*, B.C. Reg. 84/58, s. 3.21, part.

PATENT OFFICE. The Patent Office established by section 3 of the Act. *Patent Act*, R.S.C. 1985, c. P-4, *Patent Rules*, SOR/96-423, s. 2. See CANADIAN ~ RECORD.

PATERNITY. *n.* The relationship of a father.

PATERNITY AGREEMENT. If a man and a woman who are not spouses enter into an agreement for, (a) the payment of the expenses of a child's prenatal care and birth; (b) support of a child; or (c) funeral expenses of the child or mother, on the application of a party, or a children's aid society, to the Ontario Court of Justice or the Family Court of the Superior Court of Justice, the court may incorporate the agreement in an order, and Part III (Support Obligations) applies to the order in the same manner as if it were an order made under that Part. *Family Law Act*, R.S.O. 1990, c. F.3, s. 59.

PATHOGEN. See HUMAN ~.

PATHOLOGY. See SPEECH-LANGUAGE ~.

PATIENT. See OUT-~; PHYSICIAN-~ RELATIONSHIP.

PATR. ELEC. CAS. *abbr.* Patrick's Election Cases (Upper Canada / Canada West), 1824-1849.

PATRIATION. *n.* The bringing of the Constitution to Canada. The ending of the United Kingdom's control over Canada's consitution. See RE~.

PATRICIDE. *n.* 1. Killing a father. 2. One who kills a father.

PATRON. *n.* 1. A person who uses the services provided by a business or service-provider. 2. A supporter.

PATRONAGE. *n.* 1. The right to make appointments to an office. 2. Doing business with.

PATRONAGE ALLOCATION. An amount that an association allocates among and credits or pays to its members or to its member and non-member patrons based on the business done by them with or through the association, and includes (a) a patronage refund, and (b) an allocation in proportion to borrowing. *Co-operative Credit Associations Act*, S.C. 1991, c. 48, s. 2.

PATRONAGE RETURN. An amount that the co-operative allocates among and credits or pays to its members or to its member and non-member patrons based on the business done by them with or through the cooperative. *Canada Cooperatives Act*, S. C. 1998, c. 1, s. 2.

PATTERN OF FINDINGS OF GUILT. I agree with the analysis of the Alberta Court of Appeal on this issue in R. v. C.D.J., 2005 ABCA 293, [2005] A.J. No. 1190; 205 C.C.C. (3d) 56. On the meaning of "pattern of findings of guilt" the court said: The section [s. 39(1)(c)] refers to the plural, "findings of guilt," clearly indicating that there must be at least two, and likely more, findings of guilt before a pattern can be found. This is supported by the phrase used in

the French version of the section, "plusieurs déclarations de culpabilité," which translates as "several findings of guilt," indicating there must be three or more findings of guilt in order to make out a pattern. Further, the history referred to is of "findings of guilt," not sentences or dispositions, leading us to conclude that both prior findings of guilt and the current findings of guilt for which the young person is being sentenced may be considered. ... We conclude that there must be some recognizable regularity, consistency or similarity to the offences in order to demonstrate a pattern of findings of guilt. If it were sufficient to show merely that the young person had a prior history of findings of guilt, there would have been no need to include the word "pattern" in s. 39(1)(c). *R. v. S.A.C.*, 2007 NSCA 55.

PAULIAN ACTION. A creditor who suffers prejudice through a juridical act made by his debtor in fraud of his rights, in particular an act by which he renders or seeks to render himself insolvent, or by which, being insolvent, he grants preference to another creditor may obtain a declaration that the act may not be set up against him. *Civil Code*, S.Q. 1991, c. 64, a. 1631.

PAWN. *n.* A pledge, a kind of bailment, in which a debtor delivers goods to the creditor for the creditor to keep until the debt is discharged.

PAWNBROKER. *n.* A person whose business is taking any article as a pawn or pledge for the repayment of money lent against that article.

PAWNER. *n.* A person who delivers an article for pawn to a pawnbroker.

PAY. *v.* "... [M]eans primarily to discharge a debt by money." *McIntosh, Re*, [1923] 2 W.W.R. 605 at 607 (Man. K.B.), Dysart J. See YIELDING AND ~ING.

PAY. *n.* 1. Remuneration in any form. 2. Wages due or paid to an employee and compensation paid or due to an employee but does not include deductions from wage that may lawfully be made by an employer. See EQUAL ~ FOR EQUAL WORK; INCENTIVE ~; SEVERANCE ~; SICK ~; TAKE-HOME ~; TERMINATION ~.

PAYABLE. *adj.* 1. Requiring to be paid; due. 2. Describes a sum of money when someone is obliged to pay it.

PAYABLE TO ORDER. Describes a cheque or bill of exchange payable to the person named on it or in any way directed by an endorsement.

PAYDAY LENDER. A person that offers or provides a payday loan, and includes any person that arranges a payday loan or that facilitates, enables or acts as a conduit for another person that offers or provides a payday loan. *The Payday Loans Act*, S.S. 2007, c. P-4.3, s. 2.

PAYDAY LOAN. Any advancement of money that is: (i) in an amount of $1,500 or less; (ii) for a term of 62 days or less; and (iii) in exchange for a post-dated cheque, a pre-authorized debit or a future payment of a similar nature but not for any guarantee, suretyship, overdraft protection or security on property and not through a margin loan, pawnbroking, a line of credit or a credit card. *The Payday Loans Act*, S.S. 2007, c. P-4.3, s. 2.

PAY EQUITY. A compensation practice which is based primarily on the relative value of the work performed, irrespective of the gender of employees, and includes the requirement that no employer shall establish or maintain a difference between the wages paid to male and female employees, employed by that employer, who are performing work of equal or comparable value.

PAY IN LIEU. A term used to mean the damages paid in compensation for the breach of the employment contract where the employer has failed to give reasonable notice. . . . To limit entitlement to benefits where there has been "payment in lieu", would be tantamount to giving the company the power to circumscribe benefits during the notice period where notice is provided. In the absence of such a power having been expressly reserved in the termination policy itself, it follows that the phrase "or similar employment benefits" should be construed broadly so as to equate "payment in lieu" as closely as possible with the "notice" alternative. *Gilchrist v. Western Star Trucks Inc.*, 2000 CarswellBC 2136, 2000 BCSC 1523, 82 B.C.L.R. (3d) 99, 25 C.C.P.B. 22 (S.C.), Stromberg-Stein J.

PAYMENT. *n.* 1. Remuneration in any form. 2. "... [A] sum expressly applicable in reduction of the particular demand on which it is made; that demand is therefore reduced by the extent of the payment... ." *Miron v. McCabe* (1867), 4 P.R. 171 at 174 (H.C.), Wilson J. 3. Includes the set-off of any amount against indebtedness incurred. 4. Delivery to another person, voluntarily or otherwise, of a sum of money or thing. 5. Not restricted to money. *Nelson v. Rentown Enterprises Inc.*, 1992 CarswellAlta 145, 5 Alta. L.R. (3d) 149, 96 D.L.R. (4th) 586, [1993] 2 W.W.R. 71, 7 B.L.R. (2d) 319, 134 A.R. 257 (Q.B.), Hunt J. 6. Delivery to another person, voluntarily or otherwise, of a sum of money or thing. See BALLOON ~; CANADIAN ~S ASSOCIATION; COVENANT FOR ~; DISABILITY ASSISTANCE ~; DOWN ~; EDUCATIONAL ASSISTANCE ~; EQUALIZATION ~; INDEMNITY ~; LIFETIME DISABILITY ASSISTANCE ~S; PART ~.

PAYMENT BOND. A bond held by the Crown as security for the payment of certain classes of persons who perform labour or services or supply material in connection with a contract.

PAYMENT INTO COURT. The deposit of money with a court official in connection with proceedings commenced in that court.

PAY-OUT PRICE. In respect of a pool, means the amount of money that is payable to the holder of a winning ticket or to an account holder who has made a winning bet, for each dollar bet by the holder or account holder, as the case may be, calculated in accordance with Part IV. *Criminal Code*, R.S.C. 1985, c. C-46, *Pari-Mutuel Betting Supervision Regulations*, SOR/91-365, s. 2.

P.C. *abbr.* 1. Privy Council. 2. Privy Councillor. 3. Police constable.

PCT. *abbr.* Patent Cooperation Treaty.

P.D. *abbr.* Law Reports, Probate, Divorce and Admiralty Division, 1875-1890.

PEACE. *n.* 1. Quiet behaviour towards the sovereign and the sovereign's subjects. 2. The condition of international relations in which a nation does not bring military force against another. See BREACH OF THE ~; CLERK OF THE ~; COMMISSION OF THE ~; JUSTICE OF THE ~; KEEP THE ~; QUEEN'S ~.

PEACE BOND. A written promise made to a court to keep the peace.

PEACE OFFICER. Includes (a) a mayor, warden, reeve, sheriff, deputy sheriff, sheriff's officer and justice of the peace, (b) a member of the Correctional Service of Canada who is designated as a peace officer pursuant to Part I of the Corrections and Conditional Release Act, and a warden, deputy warden, instructor, keeper, jailer, guard and any other officer or permanent employee of a prison other than a penitentiary as defined in Part I of the Corrections and Conditional Release Act, (c) a police officer, police constable, bailiff, constable, or other person employed for the preservation and maintenance of the public peace or for the service or execution of civil process, (d) an officer within the meaning of the Customs Act, the Excise Act or the Excise Act, 2001, or a person having the powers of such an officer, when performing any duty in the administration of any of those Acts, (d.1) an officer authorized under subsection 138(1) of the Immigration and Refugee Protection Act, (e) a person designated as a fishery guardian under the Fisheries Act when performing any duties or functions under that Act and a person designated as a fishery officer under the Fisheries Act when performing any duties or functions under that Act or the Coastal Fisheries Protection Act, (f) the pilot in command of an aircraft (i) registered in Canada under regulations made under the Aeronautics Act, or (ii) leased without crew and operated by a person who is qualified under regulations made under the Aeronautics Act to be registered as owner of an aircraft registered in Canada under those regulations, while the aircraft is in flight, and (g) officers and non-commissioned members of the Canadian Forces who are (i) appointed for the purposes of section 156 of the National Defence Act, or (ii) employed on duties that the Governor in Council, in regulations made under the National Defence Act for the purposes of this paragraph, has prescribed to be of such a kind as to necessitate that the officers and non-commissioned members performing them have the powers of peace officers. *Criminal Code*, R.S.C. 1985, c. C-46, s. 2.

PEACE, ORDER AND GOOD GOVERNMENT. 1. "[Under s. 91 of the Constitution Act, 1867 (30 & 31 Vict.), c. 3 includes] ... federal competence [based] on the existence of a national emergency; ... federal competence [may arise] because the subject-matter did not exist at the time of Confederation and clearly cannot be put into the class of matters of merely local or private nature; [or] ... Where the subject-matter 'goes beyond local or provincial concern or interests and must, from its inherent nature be the concern of the Dominion as a whole' ..." *Labatt Breweries of Canada Ltd. v. Canada (Attorney General)* (1979), 9 B.L.R. 181 at 208, [1980] 1 S.C.R. 914, 30 N.R. 496, Estey J. (Martland, Dickson, Beetz and Pratte JJ. concurring). 2. "... [T]he true test must be found in the real subject matter of the legislation; if it is such that it goes beyond local or provincial concern or interests and must from its inherent nature be the concern of the Dominion as a whole ... then it will fall within the competence of the Dominion Parliament as a matter affecting the peace, order and good government of Canada [contained in s. 91 of the Constitution Act, 1867 (30 & 31 Vict.), c. 3], though it may in another aspect touch on matters specially reserved to the provincial legislature." *Reference re Canada Temperance Act*, [1946] A.C. 193 at 205, 1 C.R. 229, [1946] 2 W.W.R. 1, 85 C.C.C. 225, [1946] 2 D.L.R. 1 (Ont. P.C.), the board per Viscount Simon. See RESIDUARY POWER.

PECUNIARY. *adj.* Concerning money.

PECUNIARY DAMAGES. See NON-~

PECUNIARY JUDGMENT. A judgment which can be enforced by a writ of seizure and sale—the modern equivalent of a writ of fi. fa. *S.G. & S. Investments (1972) Ltd. v. Golden Boy Foods Inc.*, 1991 CarswellBC 261, 60 B.C.L.R. (2d) 305, 84 D.L.R. (4th) 751, 3 B.L.R. (2d) 80 at 93, (*sub nom. S.G. & S. Investments (1972) Ltd. v. Golden Boy Foods Inc. (No. 2)*) 4 B.C.A.C. 105, 9 W.A.C. 105, 3 B.L.R. (2d) 80 at 93 (C.A.), Southin J.A.

PECUNIARY LOSS. 1. Consists of the support, services, and contributions which the claimant might reasonably have expected to receive. 2. "... As applied to a dependent's loss from death the term has been interpreted to mean 'the reasonable expectation of pecuniary benefit from the continued life of the deceased' ... In a later decision, Mason v. Peters (1982), 139 D.L.R. (3d) 104 ... Robins J.A. ... said at p. 109: 'Pecuniary loss may consist of the support, services or contributions which the claimant might reasonably have expected to receive from the deceased had he not been killed.' Thus, the courts have recognized that the child of a deceased mother may recover, as pecuniary loss, an amount to compensate for the loss of a mother's care and moral training ..." *Harris Estate v. Roy's Midway Transport Ltd.* (1989), 60 D.L.R. (4th) 99 at 103, 50 C.C.L.T. 67 (N.B. C.A.), the court per Stratton C.J.N.B. 3. Does not include loss arising from pain and suffering, physical inconvenience and discomfort, social discredit, injury to reputation, mental suffering, injury to feelings, loss of amenities and of expectation of life or loss of society of spouse or child. See NON-~

PEDDLE. *v.* 1. To carry alcohol, spirits, cider, wine or beer on one's person or to transport it with one, or with the aid of another person, with intent to sell it outside any establishment where the sale thereof is allowed. 2. To carry any goods with intent to sell them.

PEDESTRIAN. *n.* 1. A person afoot. 2. A person afoot, or a person in a wheelchair or a child's carriage or physically handicapped person operating a motorized mobility-aid. *The Highway Traffic Act*, S.M.

1985-86, c. 3, s. 1. 3. A person on foot, an invalid in a wheelchair or a child in a carriage or sleigh. 4. [T]he ordinary and grammatical meaning of the word "pedestrian" is broad enough to encompass persons travelling on skateboards or similar devices. *R. v. Atchison*, 2006 ABCA 258.

PEDIGREE. *n.* In relation to an animal, means genealogical information showing the ancestral line of descent of the animal. *Animal Pedigree Act*, R.S.C. 1985, c. 8 (4th Supp.), s. 2.

PEDOPHILIA. *n.* The sexual desire or fantasies of an adult for a child; sexual behaviour of an adult with a child.

PEER. *n.* 1. An equal, a person of the same rank. 2. In England, a member of the House of Lords.

PEER REVIEW. The process of submitting one's hypothesis, methods and conclusions to the scrutiny of other, independent experts in the field. Publication in a refereed journal of wide circulation in the field is a major, although not the only, method of inviting peer review. When a scientific conclusion has been published and a reasonable time has elapsed without any meritorious criticism of it, the publication and peer review process provides a circumstantial guarantee of trustworthiness. *R. v. Murrin*, 1999 CarswellBC 3015, 181 D.L.R. (4th) 320, 32 C.R. (5th) 97 (S.C.), Henderson J.

PE GAAP. *abbr.* Private enterprise generally accepted accounting principles.

P.E.I. *abbr.* 1. Prince Edward Island. 2. Prince Edward Island Supreme Court Reports, 1850-1882.

PELT. *n.* The untanned skin of a furbearing mammal, whether or not the skin is on a carcass.

PENAL. *adj.* 1. "... [A]n accurate and convenient way of describing provincial 'criminal' proceedings." *Trumbley v. Metropolitan Toronto Police Force* (*sub nom. Trumbley v. Fleming*) (1986), 21 Admin. L.R. 232 at 254, 55 O.R. (2d) 570, 29 D.L.R. (4th) 557, 24 C.R.R. 333, 15 O.A.C. 279, the court per Morden J.A. 2. Inflicting punishment.

PENAL INSTITUTION. Includes jail, prison, lockup, or adult custodial institution.

PENAL LAW. Laws in favour of the state for the recovery of pecuniary penalties for violation of statutes for the protection of revenue and other statutes.

PENAL NEGLIGENCE. Negligence in a criminal setting which unlike negligence under civil law, which is concerned with the apportionment of loss, is concerned with the punishment of moral blameworthiness. Incorporates the particular frailties of the accused, if any, because he or she could not have acted other than they did in the circumstances. Does not involve the fault element of criminal negligence. *R. v. Gosset*, [1993] 3 S.C.R. 76.

PENAL STATUTE. A law which imposes a penalty or punishment for the offence committed.

PENALTY. *n.* 1. " ... [A] sum of money the purpose of which is not to compensate, but to discourage certain conduct." *Bank of Nova Scotia v. Dunphy*

Leasing Enterprises Ltd. (1987), 51 Alta. L.R. (2d) 324 at 328, 77 A.R. 181, 38 D.L.R. (4th) 575 (C.A.), Prowse J.A. 2. The essence of a penalty is a payment of money stipulated in terrorem of the party in default rather than a genuine pre-estimate of the damage suffered. *Reliant Capital Ltd. v. Silverdale Development Corp.*, 2006 BCCA 226. 3. (a) A fine; or (b) a term of imprisonment including a term of imprisonment in default of payment or satisfaction of a fine. 4. Includes any forfeiture or pecuniary penalty imposed or authorized to be imposed by any Act of Parliament for any contravention of the laws relating to the collection of the revenue, or to the management of any public work producing tolls or revenue, notwithstanding that part of such forfeiture or penalty is payable to the informer or prosecutor, or to any other person. 5. Includes any forfeiture or pecuniary penalty imposed or authorized to be imposed by any Act of Parliament for any contravention of the laws relating to the collection of the revenue, or to the management of any public work producing tolls or revenue, notwithstanding that part of such forfeiture or penalty is payable to the informer or prosecutor, or to any other person. *Financial Administration Act*, R.S.C. 1985, c. F-11, s. 23. 6. Section 98 [of the Courts of Justice Act, R.S.O. 1990, c. C.43] speaks of relief from penalties and forfeitures. Each word lends meaning to the other. "Penalties" is derived from penal and connotes punishment. "Forfeiture" is a giving up of a right or property and when allied with "penalties" suggests something of the nature of goods being forfeited to customs officials. Neither penalties nor forfeitures are compensatory and both connote an added element to any money damages when associated with a breach of a contract. The failure to pay premiums on a term life insurance policy and the consequent lapse of that policy engage none of the above considerations. The premium is the payment for coverage for the next term. Subject to the grace provision, there is no coverage for that term when a payment is not made and the insurer arranges its commercial affairs accordingly. In these circumstances, the contract terminates on its own terms and not by a breach. There is no forfeiture in the sense of a loss of property. To be sure, the coverage has been lost, but it wasn't paid for in the first place. *Pluzak v. Gerling Global Life Insurance Co.* (2001), 2001 CarswellOnt 10 (C.A.). 7. G.H.L. Fridman in The Law of Contract in Canada, 5th ed. (Toronto: Carswell, 2006) at 774 explains that a penalty is a sum that is fixed in advance as being subject to forfeiture or payment in the event of non-performance or misperformance of a contract. The author distinguishes between payment of a sum in the event of non-performance of a contractual obligation and payment of a sum on the happening of an event. In the latter scenario, no question of a penalty arises and courts will refuse relief. The author emphasizes that the "doctrine is not designed to relieve a party from the consequences of what might in the event prove to be an onerous or even commercially imprudent bargain" (at 774). Accordingly, the law regarding penalties has narrow scope. *Doman Forest Products Ltd. v. GMAC Commercial Credit Corp. – Canada*, 2007 BCCA 88, Lowry J.A. (Prowse J.A. concurring). See ADMINISTRATIVE ~.

PENDENS. See LIS ALIBI ~; LIS ~.

PENDENTE LITE. [L.] During litigation.

PENDING. *adj.* During; commenced but not completed.

PENDING LITIGATION. See CERTIFICATE OF ~.

PENITENTIARY. *n.* A facility of any description, including all lands connected therewith, that is operated, permanently or temporarily, by the Correctional Service for the care and custody of inmates, and any place declared to be a penitentiary. *Corrections and Conditional Release Act*, S.C. 1992, c. 20, s. 2.

PENOLOGY. *n.* The study of prison management and rehabilitation of inmates.

PENSION. *n.* 1. A pension right arises as an *asset* or a contingent bundle of rights to a future *income* stream. After retirement, when the pension produces an income, the pension asset is, in a sense, being liquidated. This has caused debate about whether a pension is property (a capital asset) or income (a maintenance asset), or a combination of both. *Boston v. Boston*, 2001 CarswellOnt 2432, 2001 SCC 43, 201 D.L.R. (4th) 1, 17 R.F.L. (5th) 4, 271 N.R. 248, 149 O.A.C. 50, Major J. 2. "... [A] pension is the fruit, through insurance, of all the money which was set aside in the past in respect of his past work." *Parry v. Cleaver*, [1970] A.C. 1 at 16 (U.K. H.L.), Lord Reid. 3. "... [I]ncludes periodic money payments payable on involuntary retirement due to disability occasioned by illness or injury as well as retirement due to age... ." *Webb v. Webb* (1985), 49 R.F.L. (2d) 279 at 285, 70 B.C.L.R. 15 (S.C.), Lysyk J. 4. An annual allowance made to a person, usually in consideration of past services. 5. A series of payments that continues for the life of a former member of a pension plan, whether or not it is thereafter continued to any other person. See DEFERRED ~; JOINT AND SURVIVOR ~; RETIREMENT ~; VESTED ~.

PENSIONABLE AGE. In relation to a member, means the earliest age (taking into account the period of employment with the employer or the period of membership in the pension plan, if applicable) at which a pension benefit, other than a benefit in respect of a disability (as defined in the regulations), is payable to the member under the terms of the pension plan without the consent of the administrator and without reduction by reason of early retirement. *Pension Benefits Standards Act, 1985*, R.S.C. 1985, c. 32 (2nd Supp.), s. 2.

PENSION BENEFIT. A periodic amount to which, under the terms of a pension plan, a member or former member, or the spouse, common-law partner, survivor or other beneficiary or estate or succession of a member or former member, is or may become entitled. *Pension Benefits Standards Act, 1985*, R.S.C. 1985, c. 32 (2nd Supp.), s. 2. See DEFERRED ~; IMMEDIATE ~; JOINT AND SURVIVOR ~.

PENSION BENEFIT CREDIT. In relation to any person, means the aggregate value at a particular time of that person's pension benefit and other benefits provided under a pension plan, calculated in prescribed manner. *Pension Benefits Standards Act, 1985*, R.S.C. 1985, c. 32 (2nd Supp.), s. 2.

PENSION FUND. The fund maintained to provide benefits under or related to a pension plan.

PENSION PLAN. A superannuation or other plan organized and administered to provide pension benefits to employees employed in included employment (and former employees) and to which the employer is required under or in accordance with the plan to contribute, whether or not provision is also made for other benefits or for benefits to other persons, and includes a supplemental pension plan, whether or not the employer is required to make contributions under or in accordance with the supplemental pension plan, but does not include (a) an employees' profit sharing plan or a deferred profit sharing plan as defined in sections 144 and 147, respectively, of the Income Tax Act; (b) an arrangement to provide a "retiring allowance" as defined in subsection 248(1) of the Income Tax Act; or (c) any other prescribed arrangement. *Pension Benefits Standards Act, 1985*, R.S.C. 1985, c. 32 (2nd Supp.), s. 4. See CANADA ~; CONTRIBUTORY ~; MULTI-EMPLOYER ~; REGISTERED ~.

PEOPLES. *n.* International law grants the right to self-determination to "peoples." Accordingly, access to the right requires the threshold step of characterizing as a people the group seeking self-determination. However, as the right to self-determination has developed by virtue of a combination of international agreements and conventions, coupled with state practice, with little formal elaboration of the definition of "peoples," the result has been that the precise meaning of the term "people" remains somewhat uncertain. It is clear that "a people" may include only a portion of the population of an existing state. The right to self-determination has developed largely as a human right, and is generally used in documents that simultaneously contain references to "nation" and "state." The juxtaposition of these terms is indicative that the reference to "people" does not necessarily mean the entirety of a state's population. *Reference re Secession of Quebec*, 1998 CarswellNat 1299, 161 D.L.R. (4th) 385, 228 N.R. 203, 55 C.R.R. (2d) 1, [1998] 2 S.C.R. 217, per curiam. See ABORIGINAL ~; PERSON.

PEPPERCORN RENT. A rent far below actual value.

P.E.R. *abbr.* Pay Equity Reports (Ontario), 1990-.

PER. *prep.* For each; for every.

PER ANNUM. [L.] By year.

PER AUTRE VIE. [Fr.] For the length of someone else's life.

PER CAPITA. [L. by heads] In equal shares. See PER STIRPES.

PER CENT. *abbr.* [L.] Per centum. By one hundred.

PER CENTUM. [L.] By one hundred.

PERCEPTUAL DISABILITY. A disability that prevents or inhibits a person from reading or hearing a literary, musical, dramatic or artistic work in its original format, and includes such a disability resulting from (a) severe or total impairment of sight or hearing or the inability to focus or move one's eyes, (b) the inability to hold or manipulate a book, or (c) an impairment relating to comprehension. *Copyright Act*, R.S.C. 1985, c. C-42, s. 2.

PER CUR. *abbr.* [L.] Per curiam. By a court.

PER CURIAM. [L.] By a court.

PER DIEM. [L.] By day.

PEREMPTORY. *adj.* Determinate, final and, concerning statutes, obligatory in contrast to permissive.

PEREMPTORY CHALLENGE. "... [A]llows a party to dismiss a person from serving on [a] jury without providing a reason... ." *R. v. Bain* (1992), 10 C.R. (4th) 257 at 274, [1992] 1 S.C.R. 91, 69 C.C.C. (3d) 481, 87 D.L.R. (4th) 449, 133 N.R. 1, 51 O.A.C. 161, 7 C.R.R. (2d) 193, Stevenson J.

PERFECT. *v.* To register or to attach.

PERFECTED SECURITY INTEREST. "... [A]n interest the protection of which against third parties has been accomplished by the doing of whatever was necessary to achieve such in the jurisdiction from which the debtor has moved." *Juckes (Trustee of) v. Holiday Chevrolet Oldsmobile (1983) Ltd.* (1990), 82 Sask. R. 303 at 307, 68 D.L.R. (4th) 142, 79 C.B.R. (N.S.) 143 (Q.B.), Armstrong J.

PERFECTION. *n.* "... [O]f a security interest deals with those steps legally required to give the secured party an interest in the property against the grantor's creditors. An instrument such as a debenture or mortgage is said to become perfected when it is recorded or registered in the appropriate registry as a matter of record, and that recording or registration renewed and kept current and subsisting so that notice to the grantor's debtors does not lapse." *First City Capital Ltd. v. Ampex Canada Inc.* (1989), 75 C.B.R. (N.S.) 109 at 140, 97 A.R. 256 (Q.B.), Yanosik J.

PERFORM. *v.* To carry out an action; to achieve; to execute an action.

PERFORMANCE. *n.* 1. "... [T]he equitable doctrine of performance [is] expressed in the maxim 'equity imputes an intention to fulfil an obligation'. According to this doctrine a man under an obligation, who does an act which is suitable to be the means of performing the obligation, will be presumed in equity to have done the act with that intention... . The difference between performance and satisfaction is that whereas the former does not, the latter does, depend upon intention." *Northern Trust Co. v. Coldwell* (1914), 18 D.L.R. 512 at 514, 516, 6 W.W.R. 1165, 25 Man. R. 120, 28 W.L.R. 625 (K.B.), Mathers C.J. 2. Any acoustic or visual representation of a work, performer's performance, sound recording or communication signal, including a representation made by means of any mechanical instrument, radio receiving set or television receiving set. *Copyright Act*, R.S.C. 1985, c. C-42, s. 2. See CONTRACT OF INSTANTANEOUS ~; CONTRACT OF SUCCESSIVE ~; FUTURE ~ AGREEMENT; FUTURE ~

CONTRACT; NON-~; PART ~; PERFORMER'S ~; SPECIFIC ~; SUBSTANTIAL ~.

PERFORMANCE BOND. 1. A bond that is conditioned upon the completion by the principal of a contract in accordance with its terms. 2. "... [G]uarantee to the owner that the contractor will perform the terms of the contract." *Johns-Manville Canada Inc. v. John Carlo Ltd.* (1980), (*sub nom. Canadian Johns-Manville Co. v. John Carlo Ltd.*) 12 B.L.R. 80 at 87, 29 O.R. (2d) 592, 113 D.L.R. (3d) 686 (H.C.), R.E. Holland J. See CONTRACT BOND.

PERFORMER'S PERFORMANCE. Any of the following when done by a performer: (a) a performance of an artistic work, dramatic work or musical work, whether or not the work was previously fixed in any material form, and whether or not the work's term of copyright protection under this Act has expired, (b) a recitation or reading of a literary work, whether or not the work's term of copyright protection under this Act has expired, or (c) an improvisation of a dramatic work, musical work or literary work, whether or not the improvised work is based on a pre-existing work. *Copyright Act*, R.S.C. 1985, c. C-42, s. 2.

PERIL. *n.* 1. A risk of unavoidable misfortune. 2. Danger arising from failure to be duly circumspect. See MARITIME ~S.

PERILS OF THE SEAS. 1. "Where there is an accidental incursion of seawater into a vessel at a part of the vessel and in a manner where seawater is not expected to enter in the ordinary course of things and there is consequent damage to the thing insured, there is prima facie a loss by perils of the sea... . It is the fortuitous entry of the seawater which is the peril of the sea in such cases... ." *Canada Rice Mills v. Union Marine & General Insurance Co.* (1940), [1941] 1 D.L.R. 1 at 9, [1941] A.C. 55, [1941] 3 W.W.R. 401, [1940] 4 All E.R. 169, 8 I.L.R. 1 (P.C.), Lord Wright for their Lordships. 2. Refers only to fortuitous accidents or casualties of the seas. It does not include the ordinary action of the winds and waves. *Marine Insurance acts.*

PERI MORTEM. [L. around death] Shortly after or shortly before death. F.A. Jaffe, *A Guide to Pathological Evidence for Lawyers and Police Officers*, 4th ed. (Toronto: Carswell, 1999) at 241.

PER INCURIAM. [L.] Through inadvertence or by overlooking an applicable principle.

PERIOD. *n.* 1. An interval of time. 2. A space of time. 3. Any length of time. See ACCOUNTING ~; COOLING-OFF ~; ELECTION ~; FISCAL ~; LIMITATIONS ~; PROBATIONARY ~; RENTAL ~; TRAINING ~; TRIAL ~.

PERIODICAL. *n.* Any printed matter that is published for general distribution to the public and that purports to be a copy of one publication in a series of publications at regular intervals, and that is not bound in a hard cover but does not include a periodic publication that is devoted primarily to conveying current news. *Paperback and Periodical Distributors Act*, R.S.O. 1990, c. P.1, s. 1.

PERIODIC TENANCY. 1. Tenancy from week to week, month to month or year to year. 2. (i) A tenancy under a tenancy agreement that is renewed or continued without notice, and (ii) with respect to a fixed term tenancy that contains a provision allowing for renewal or continuation of the tenancy without notice, that part of the tenancy that arises after the end of the fixed term tenancy. *Mobile Home Sites Tenancies Act*, R.S.A. 2000, c. M-20, s. 1.

PERIOD OF PROBATION. A period during which a person convicted of an offence was directed by the court that convicted him (a) to be released on his own recognizance to keep the peace and be of good behaviour, or (b) to be released on or comply with the conditions prescribed in a probation order. *Criminal Records Act*, R.S.C. 1985, c. C-47, s. 2.

PERIPHERAL CLAIMING PRINCIPLE. The Patent Act [R.S.C. 1985, c. P-4] requires the letters patent granting a patent monopoly to include a specification which sets out a correct and full "disclosure" of the invention, i.e., "correctly and fully describes the invention and its operation or use as contemplated by the inventor" (s. 34(1)(a)). The disclosure is followed by "a claim or claims stating distinctly and in explicit terms the things or combinations that the applicant regards as new and in which he claims an exclusive property or privilege" (s. 34(2)). It is the invention thus claimed to which the patentee receives the "exclusive right, privilege and liberty" of exploitation (s. 44). These provisions, and similar provisions in other jurisdictions, have given rise to two schools of thought. One school holds that the claim embodies a technical idea and claims construction ought to look to substance rather than form to protect the inventive idea underlying the claim language. This is sometimes called the "central claims drafting principle" and is associated with the German and Japanese patent systems [. . .] . The other school of thought supporting what is sometimes called the "peripheral claiming principle" emphasizes the language of the claims as defining not the underlying technical idea but the legal boundary of the state-conferred monopoly. Traditionally, for reasons of fairness and predictability, Canadian courts have preferred the latter approach. *Free World Trust c. Électro Santé Inc.*, 2000 CarswellQue 2728, 2000 SCC 66, 194 D.L.R. (4th) 232, 263 N.R. 150, [2000] 2 S.C.R. 1024, 9 C.P.R. (4th) 168, Binnie J.

PERJURY. *n.* With intent to mislead, making before a person who is authorized by law to permit it to be made before him a false statement under oath or solemn affirmation, by affidavit, solemn declaration or deposition or orally, knowing that the statement is false. *Criminal Code*, R.S.C. 1985, c. C-46, s. 131(1).

PERMANENT. *adj.* 1. Intended to remain in place while useful. 2. Not occasional. 3. Prolonged.

PERMANENT IMPAIRMENT. Impairment that continues to exist after an injured worker reaches maximum medical recovery. *Workplace Safety and Insurance Act, 1997*, S.O. 1997, c. 16, Sched. A, s. 2.

PERMANENT INJUNCTION. An injunction to finally settle and enforce the rights of disputing parties.

P

PERMANENT RESIDENT. A person who has acquired permanent resident status and has not subsequently lost that status under section 46. *Immigration and Refugee Protection Act*, S. C. 2001, c. 27, s 2.

PERMISSIVE OCCUPATION. A situation in which the occupier has a mere permission or licence from the person who is otherwise entitled to occupy the property.

PERMISSIVE PRESUMPTION. "[Leaves] ... it optional as to whether the inference of the presumed fact is drawn following proof of the basic fact." *R. v. Oakes* (1986), 24 C.C.C. (3d) 321 at 330, [1986] 1 S.C.R. 103, 50 C.R. (3d) 1, 14 O.A.C. 335, 19 C.R.R. 308, 26 D.L.R. (4th) 200, 65 N.R. 87, Dickson C.J.C. (Chouinard, Lamer, Wilson and Le Dain JJ. concurring).

PERMISSIVE WASTE. 1. "... [W]aste is either voluntary or permissive ... Permissive waste involves the failure or omission to take some precaution which results in damage to the property." *Prior v. Hanna* (1987), 55 Alta. L.R. (2d) 276 at 282, 82 A.R. 3, 43 D.L.R. (4th) 612 (Q.B.), Miller A.C.J.Q.B. 2. Neglect to make needed repairs.

PERMIT. *v.* 1. To allow. To authorize. 2. [In the context of a regulation, stating: The licence holder shall not permit drunkenness ... to occur on the premises,] permitting drunkenness on the premises requires proof that the licensee knew or ought to have known of the drunkenness on the premises. *1213963 Ontario Ltd. v. Ontario (Registrar of Alcohol & Gaming Commission)*, 2009 ONCA 323.

PERMIT. *n.* 1. An authorization, a written authority. 2. A permit issued under this Code and the Charter of the French language which allows the exclusive practice of the profession mentioned therein and the use of a title reserved to the professionals practising such profession or only allows the use of a title reserved to the members of the order issuing the permit, subject to entry of the holder of such permit on the roll of that order. *Professional Code*, R.S.Q., c. C-26, s. 1. See BUILDING ~; OCCUPANCY ~; STUDY ~; WORK ~.

PERPETUAL DURATION. See RULE AGAINST ~.

PERPETUAL INJUNCTION. An injunction to finally settle and enforce the rights of disputing parties.

PERPETUAL SUSTAINED YIELD. Continuous management of a resource to maintain a steady yield or harvest by keeping annual growth or increase at least as high as annual yield or harvest.

PERPETUATE TESTIMONY. To preserve and perpetuate evidence which is likely to be lost because the witness is old, infirm or going away before the matter it relates to can be investigated judicially so that justice does not fail. See COMMISSION EVIDENCE; COMMISSION ROGATORY; LETTERS ROGATORY; ROGATORY LETTERS.

PERPETUITY. *n.* 1. Time without limit. 2. The term "perpetuity" literally means something that lasts forever, but as used in [the] context [of the rule against perpetuities] it is generally used to refer to limitations of contingent future interests which may or will not vest beyond the period prescribed by the rule. In this context a perpetuity is a limitation upon the common law right of every person to dispose of his land to any other person at his or her discretion. *Taylor v. Scurry-Rainbow Oil (Sask) Ltd.*, 2001 SKCA 85, 203 D.L.R. (4th) 38, 207 Sask. R. 266, 247 W.A.C. 266, [2001] 11 W.W.R. 25. See IN ~.

PERPETUITY RULE. Limits the time during which a grantor may withdraw property granted from commerce or effectively control the use of property by future generations, by making the property subject to a series of successive interests. D.M.W. Waters, *The Law of Trusts in Canada*, 2d ed. (Toronto: Carswell, 1984) at 282. See MODERN RULES AGAINST PERPETUITIES; RULE AGAINST PERPETUITIES; RULES AGAINST PERPETUITIES.

PERQUISITE. *n.* An emolument, privilege or incidental profit resulting from one's position or employment in addition to regular salary.

PER QUOD. [L.] Whereby; sometimes used to refer to an action per quod servitium amisit.

PER QUOD CONSORTIUM AMISIT. [L.] Whereby one lost the benefit of the other's society.

PER QUOD SERVITIUM AMISIT. [L.] Whereby one lost the benefit of the other's service. An action founded on an employer's right to recover damages against a wrongdoer who injured the servant and deprived the employer of the servant's services.

PER SE. [L. by itself] Alone.

PERSECUTION. *n.* 1. The intentional and severe deprivation of fundamental rights contrary to international law by reason of the identity of the group or collectivity. *Crimes Against Humanity and War Crimes Act*, S.C. 2000, c. 24, Sched., *Rome Statute*, Article 7. 2. Harassing or afflicting with repeated acts of cruelty or annoyance.

PERSON. *n.* 1. "The scope of 'person' as set out in s. 2 of the [Criminal Code, R.S.C. 1985, c. C-46] extends somewhat beyond the individual, covering additionally public bodies, corporations, societies and companies, but groups having common characteristics such as race, religion, colour and ethnic origin are not included in the definition." *R. v. Keegstra* (1990), 61 C.C.C. (3d) 1 at 19, 1 C.R. (4th) 129, 77 Alta. L.R. (2d) 193, [1991] 2 W.W.R. 1, 117 N.R. 1, 114 A.R. 81, 3 C.R.R. (2d) 193, [1990] 3 S.C.R. 697, Dickson C.J.C. (Wilson, L'Heureux-Dubé and Gonthier JJ. concurring). 2. "... [T]he term, as used in s. 203 of the Criminal Code, R.S.C. 1970, c. C-34 is synonymous with the term 'human being' [as used in s. 206]." *R. v. Sullivan* (1991), 3 C.R. (4th) 277 at 288, 122 N.R. 166, 63 C.C.C. (3d) 97, 55 B.C.L.R. (2d) 1, [1991] 1 S.C.R. 489, Lamer C.J.C. (Wilson, La Forest, Sopinka, Gonthier, Cory, McLachlin and Stevenson JJ. concurring). 3. "... [I]n the context of s. 11(b) of the Charter includes corporations." *R. v. C.I.P. Inc.* (1992), 12 C.R. (4th) 237 at 250, 71 C.C.C. (3d) 129, 135 N.R. 90, 52 O.A.C. 366, [1992] 1 S.C.R. 843, 9 C.R.R. (2d) 62, 7 C.O.H.S.C. 1, the court per Stevenson J. 4. "... [A]ny being that is capable of having rights and duties, and is confined to that. Persons are of two classes only – natural persons and legal persons. A natural person is a human being that has the capacity for rights or duties. A legal person is anything to which the law gives a legal or fictional existence or personality, with capacity for rights and duties. The only legal person known to our law is the corporation – the body corporate." *Hague v. Cancer Relief & Research Institute*, [1939] 4 D.L.R. 191 at 193, [1939] 3 W.W.R. 160, 47 Man. R. 325 (K.B.), Dysart J. See ABORIGINAL ~; ALDER~; ARTIFICIAL ~; AUTHORIZED ~; DISABLED ~; DURESS OF THE ~; HOMELESS ~; INCOMPETENT ~; INFECTED ~; INFLUENTIAL ~; INSOLVENT ~; INSURED ~; JOURNEY~; LEGAL ~; MENTALLY DISORDERED ~; MENTALLY INCOMPETENT ~; NATURAL ~; NON-RESIDENT ~; ORDINARY ~; PEOPLES; PROTECTED ~; REASONABLE ~; SECURITY OF THE ~; SELF-EMPLOYED ~; STATUTORY ~; TRAFFICKING IN ~S; TRESPASS TO THE ~; VULNERABLE ~S; YOUNG ~.

PERSONA DESIGNATA. 1. Someone described or designated as an individual, in contrast to someone who is a member of a class or represents a particular characteristic. 2. The concept came from the courts and it can be modified or abolished by the courts. This court should declare that whenever a statutory power is conferred upon a judge or officer of a court, the power should be deemed exercisable in official capacity as representing the court unless there is express provision to the contrary. *Herman v. Canada (Deputy Attorney General)*, [1979] 1 S.C.R. 729, Laskin C.J.C.

PERSONA GRATA. [L.] An acceptable person.

PERSONAL. *adj.* Referring to an individual's person. See CHATTELS ~.

PERSONAL ACTION. "The general, indeed the invariable, rule is: that a personal action is one brought for the specific recovery of goods and chattels, or for damages or other redress for breach of contract, or other injuries, of whatever description, the specific recovery of lands, tenements, and hereditament only excepted ..." *McConnell v. McGee* (1917), 39 O.L.R. 460 at 463, 37 D.L.R. 486 (C.A.), Meredith C.J.C.P. (Lennox J.A. concurring).

PERSONAL DEVELOPMENT SERVICES. (a) Services provided for, (i) health, fitness, diet or matters of a similar nature, (ii) modelling and talent, including photo shoots relating to modelling and talent, or matters of a similar nature, (iii) martial arts, sports, dance or similar activities, and (iv) other matters as may be prescribed, and (b) facilities provided for or instruction on the services referred to in clause (a) and any goods that are incidentally provided in addition to the provision of the services. *Consumer Protection Act, 2002*, S.O. 2002, c. 30, Sched. A, s. 20.

PERSONAL DIGNITY. The fundamental entitlement of every human being to be respected as a human being by others and to respect himself or herself.

PERSONAL EMPLOYEE INFORMATION. In respect of an individual who is an employee or a potential employee, personal information reasonably required by an organization that is collected, used or disclosed solely for the purposes of establishing, managing or terminating (i) an employment relationship, or (ii) a volunteer work relationship between the organization and the individual but does not include personal information about the individual that is unrelated to that relationship. *Personal Information Protection Act*, S.A. 2003, c. P-6.5, s. 1.

PERSONAL ESTATE. Includes leasehold estates and other chattels real, and also money, shares of government and other funds, securities for money (not being real estate), debts, choses in action, rights, credits, goods, and all other property, except real estate, which by law devolves upon the executor or administrator, and any share or interest therein. *The Trustee Act*, R.S.M. 1987, c. T160, s. 1.

PERSONAL HARASSMENT. Objectionable comments or conduct directed toward a specific person or persons which serves no legitimate work purpose and which creates an intimidating, humiliating, hostile or offensive workplace.

PERSONAL HEALTH INFORMATION. With respect to an individual, whether living or deceased, means (a) information concerning the physical or mental health of the individual; (b) information concerning any health service provided to the individual; (c) information concerning the donation by the individual of any body part or any bodily substance of the individual or information derived from the testing or examination of a body part or bodily substance of the individual; (d) information that is collected in the course of providing health services to the individual; or (e) information that is collected incidentally to the provision of health services to the individual. *Personal Information Protection and Electronic Documents Act*, S. C. 2000, c. 5, s. 2.

PERSONAL INFORMATION. 1. Information about an identifiable individual. 2. Information other than credit information about a consumer's character, reputation, health, physical or personal characteristics or mode of living or about any other matter concerning the consumer. See EMPLOYEE ~.

PERSONAL INJURY. 1. Bodily or physical injury. K.D. Cooper-Stephenson & I.B. Saunders, *Personal Injury Damages in Canada* (Toronto: Carswell, 1981) at 5. 2. [T]he civil law concepts of "préjudice corporel - bodily injury," despite their flexibility, incorporate an inner limitation to the potential ambit of s. 6(a) of the Act, requiring some form of interference with physical integrity. Although the terms "death" or "personal injury" found in the English version allow the possibility of non-physical injury to be captured within the s. 6(a) exception, the civil law concept of "dommages corporels" found in the French version of s. 6(a) does not. ... It signals the presence of a legislative intent to create an exception to state immunity which would be restricted to a class of claims arising out of a physical breach of personal integrity, consistent with the Quebec civil law term "préjudice corporel." This type of breach could conceivably cover an overlapping area between physical harm and mental injury, such as nervous stress; however, the mere deprivation of freedom and the normal consequences of lawful imprisonment, as framed by the claim, do not allow the appellant to claim an exception to the State Immunity Act. *Schreiber v. Canada (Attorney General)* [2002] 3 S.C.R. 269. See SERIOUS ~ OFFENCE.

PERSONALITY. See MISAPPROPRIATION OF ~.

PERSONAL KNOWLEDGE. Actual knowledge or knowledge of the affairs of a business based on perusal of the business' records.

PERSONAL NEEDS. Refers to items such as grooming supplies, toiletries, tobacco.

PERSONAL POSSESSION. The requirement of knowledge, section 4(3) of the Criminal Code comprises two elements: the accused must be aware that he or she has physical custody of the thing in question, and must be aware as well of what that thing is. Both elements must co-exist with an act of control (outside of public duty). *Beaver v. The Queen*, [1957] S.C.R. 531, at 541-42.

PERSONAL PROPERTY. 1. "... [G]oods, wares, merchandise, or effects [but not land] ..." *Merritt v. Toronto (City)* (1895), 22 O.A.R. 205 at 213, MacLennan J.A. (Hagarty C.J.O. and Burton J.A. concurring). 2. Chattel paper, documents of title, goods, instruments, intangibles, money and securities and includes fixtures but does not include building materials that have been affixed to real property. *Personal Property Security Act*, R.S.O. 1990, c. P.10, s. 1. See DEFENCE OF ~; TANGIBLE ~.

PERSONAL REPRESENTATIVE. A person who stands in place of and represents another person and, without limiting the generality of the foregoing, includes, as the circumstances require, a trustee, an executor, an administrator, a committee, a guardian, a tutor, a curator, an assignee, a receiver, an agent or an attorney of any person.

PERSONAL SERVICE. "... Hogg J.A. stated in Re Avery, [1952] 2 D.L.R. 413 at p. 415 ... (C.A.): 'Personal service has been said to be service made by delivering the process into the defendant's hands or by seeing him and bringing the process to his notice.' Modern cases stress that the question of whether the purpose of giving notice to the person being served has been achieved is the relevant question [in satisfying the requirement of being 'served personally' within the meaning of the Federal Court Rules, C.R.C. 1978, c. 663, s. 355(4)]. In Re Consiglio, [1971] 3 O.R. 798 (Master's Ch.) ... the court held that personal service was satisfied if it appeared that the document came to the knowledge or into possession of the person to be served either directly or indirectly from a third party. Then, in Rupertsland Mortgage Investment Ltd. v. City of Winnipeg (1981), 25 Man. R. (2d) 29 ... (Co. Ct.) ... It was held that ... personal service will be effected if it can be shown that the person to be served actually received the document and was apprised of the contents whether directly or through an intermediary." *Polo*

Ralph Lauren Corp. v. Ashby (1990), 31 C.P.R. (3d) 129 at 137, 36 F.T.R. 81, [1990] F.C. 541, Reed J.

PERSONAL SERVICES BUSINESS. Carried on by a corporation in a taxation year means a business of providing services where (a) an individual who performs services on behalf of the corporation (in this definition and paragraph 18(1)(p) referred to as an "incorporated employee"), or (b) any person related to the incorporated employee is a specified shareholder of the corporation and the incorporated employee would reasonably be regarded as an officer or employee of the person or partnership to whom or to which the services were provided but for the existence of the corporation, unless (c) the corporation employs in the business throughout the year more than five full-time employees, or (d) the amount paid or payable to the corporation in the year for the services is received or receivable by it from a corporation with which it was associated in the year. *Income Tax Act*, R.S.C. 1985, c. 1 (5th Supp.), s. 125.

PERSONAL TRUST. (1) A testamentary trust, or (2) an inter vivos trust that is a personal trust, within the meaning of section 1 of the Taxation Act, all the beneficiaries, other than contingent beneficiaries, of which are individuals and all the contingent beneficiaries, if any, of which are individuals, charities or public institutions. *An Act respecting the Québec sales tax*, R.S.Q. c. T-0.1, s. 1.

PERSONALTY. *n.* Personal property.

PERSONATING POLICE OFFICER. Falsely representing oneself to be a peace officer or public officer, or using a badge or article of uniform or equipment in a manner that is likely to cause persons to believe that one is a peace officer or a public officer. *Criminal Code*, R.S.C. 1985, c. C-46, s. 130.

PERSONATION. *n.* 1. The act of representing that one is someone else, whether dead or living, fictitious or real. 2. Every one who fraudulently personates any person, living or dead, (a) with intent to gain advantage for themselves or another person; (b) with intent to obtain any property or an interest in any property; or (c) with intent to cause disadvantage to the person being personates or another person; or (d) with intent to avoid arrest or prosecution or to obstruct, pervert or defeat the course of justice, is guilty of an indictable offence or an offence punishable on summary conviction. *Criminal Code*, R.S.C. 1985, c. C-46, s. 403.

PERSON EMPLOYED IN A MANAGERIAL CAPACITY. (a) Any person who regularly participates to a significant degree in the formulation and determination of government policies and proposals, (b) any person who is directly involved on behalf of the employer in the processes provided for in this Act, (c) any person who is appointed in a managerial or confidential capacity, and (d) does not include a principal or vice-principal appointed under the Education Act. *Education Labour Relations Act*, R.S.Y. 2002, c. 62, s. 1.

PERSON IN AUTHORITY. The "person in authority" requirement is an integral component of the confessions rule and reviewed in considerable detail the law on persons in authority, including the trial judge's obligation to hold a voir dire. A person in authority is typically a person who is "formally engaged in the arrest, detention, examination or prosecution of the accused": Hodgson, at para. 32. Importantly, there is no category of persons who are automatically considered persons in authority solely by virtue of their status. The question as to who should be considered as a person in authority is determined according to the viewpoint of the accused. To be considered a person in authority, the accused must believe that the recipient of the statement can control or influence the proceedings against him or her, and that belief must be reasonable. Because the evidence necessary to establish whether or not an individual is a person in authority lies primarily with the accused, the person in authority requirement places an evidential burden on the accused. While the Crown bears the burden of proving the voluntariness of a confession beyond a reasonable doubt, the accused must provide an evidential basis for claiming that the receiver of a statement is a person in authority. *R. v. S.G.T.*, 2010 SCC 20, Charron J.

PERSON IN NEED OF PROTECTION. A person in Canada whose removal to their country or countries of nationality or, if they do not have a country of nationality, their country of former habitual residence, would subject them personally (a) to a danger, believed on substantial grounds to exist, of torture within the meaning of Article 1 of the Convention Against Torture; or (b) to a risk to their life or to a risk of cruel and unusual treatment or punishment if (i) the person is unable or, because of that risk, unwilling to avail themself of the protection of that country, (ii) the risk would be faced by the person in every part of that country and is not faced generally by other individuals in or from that country, (iii) the risk is not inherent or incidental to lawful sanctions, unless imposed in disregard of accepted international standards, and (iv) the risk is not caused by the inability of that country to provide adequate health or medical care. A person in Canada who is a member of a class of persons prescribed by the regulations as being in need of protection is also a person in need of protection. *Immigration and Refugee Protection Act*, S.C. 2001, c. 27, s. 97.

PERSONNEL. *n.* Workers; employees. See COMMON ~ AND WAGE POLICY; STRATEGIC ~; UNITED NATIONS ~.

PERSONNEL AGENCY. An intermediary in the labour market who supplies businesses with the services of employees. A three-party relationship results among the agency, the employee, and the person contracting with the agency for services.

PERSONS WITH DISABILITIES. Persons who have a long-term or recurring physical, mental, sensory, psychiatric or learning impairment and who (a) consider themselves to be disadvantaged in employment by reason of that impairment, or (b) believe that an employer or potential employer is likely to consider them to be disadvantaged in employment by reason of that impairment, and includes persons whose functional limitations owing to their impairment have been accommodated in their current job or workplace. *Employment Equity Act*, S.C. 1995, c. 44, s. 3.

PER STIRPES. [L. according to stocks] "... [M]eans 'by roots' or 'by stocks.' When used in the context of a gift to issue, it indicates that the gift will be divided among a certain number of 'stirpes' on the date that the gift vests, and will be distributed within each stirpe according to generation. Children never take concurrently with their parents in a stirpital distribution. Instead, all generations of descendants represent their ancestors and take the share to which those ancestors have been entitled had they survived until the distribution date." *Fraser Estate, Re* (1986), 23 E.T.R. 57 at 66 (Ont. H.C.), White J. See PER CAPITA.

PERSUASIVE AUTHORITY. A judgment or other origin of law whose intrinsic value takes strength from something other than its being binding in character.

PERSUASIVE BURDEN. "[Refers] ... to the requirement of proving a case or disproving defences, ... The party who has the persuasive burden is required to persuade the trier of fact, to convince the trier of fact that a certain set of facts existed. Failure to persuade means that the party loses... ." *R. v. Schwartz* (1988), 55 D.L.R. (4th) 1 at 19, [1989] 1 W.W.R. 289, 66 C.R. (3d) 251, 88 N.R. 90, [1988] 2 S.C.R. 443, 45 C.C.C. (3d) 97, 56 Man.R. (2d) 92, Dickson C.J.C. (dissenting).

PER TOTAM CURIAM. [L.] By the whole court; a unanimous decision.

PERVERSE. *adj.* Contrary to the weight of evidence. See IN A ~ OR CAPRICIOUS MANNER OR WITHOUT REGARD FOR THE MATERIAL BEFORE IT.

PERVERSE VERDICT. 1. A verdict in which a jury refuses to follow the judge's direction on a point of law. 2. "... [O]ne, for instance, in which it appears that the jury have not confined themselves to the terms of the issue and to the evidence legitimately brought before them, but have allowed extraneous topics to be introduced into the jury box." *Evenden v. Merchants Casualty Insurance Co.*, [1935] 2 W.W.R. 484 at 490, 2 I.L.R. 288 (Sask. C.A.), Turgeon J.A. 3. One which is wholly contrary to the evidence.

PESCAD. Neutral citation for the Prince Edward Island Supreme Court, Appeal Division.

PESCTD. Neutral citation for the Prince Edward Island Supreme Court, Trial Division.

PEST. *n.* 1. Any injurious, noxious or troublesome plant or animal life and includes any injurious, noxious or troublesome organic function of a plant or animal. *Environmental Protection and Enhancement Act*, R.S.A. 2000, c. E-12, s. 1. 2. An animal, a plant or other organism that is injurious, noxious or troublesome, whether directly or indirectly, and an injurious, noxious or troublesome condition or organic function of an animal, a plant or other organism. *Pest Control Products Act*, S.C. 2002, c. 28, s. 2.

PEST CONTROL PRODUCT. (a) A product, an organism or a substance, including a product, an organism or a substance derived through biotechnology, that consists of its active ingredient, formulants and contaminants, and that is manufactured, represented, distributed or used as a means for directly or indirectly controlling, destroying, attracting or repelling a pest or for mitigating or preventing its injurious, noxious or troublesome effects; (b) an active ingredient that is used to manufacture anything described in paragraph (a); or (c) any other thing that is prescribed to be a pest control product. *Pest Control Products Act*, S.C. 2002, c. 28, s. 2.

PESTICIDE. *n.* Any organism, substance or thing that is manufactured, represented, sold or used as a means of directly or indirectly controlling, preventing, destroying, mitigating, attracting or repelling any pest or of altering the growth, development or characteristics of any plant life that is not a pest and includes any organism, substance or thing registered under the Pest Control Products Act (Canada). *Pesticides Act*, R.S.O. 1990, c. P.11, s. 1.

PET BOARDING. A "pet boarding facility" covers one aspect of a "kennel" use - that is the boarding of the animal. "Boarding" suggests to me that the owner of the animal makes an arrangement to leave it in the care of the boarding facility. A "pet boarding facility" extends to include all domesticated animals, whereas a "kennel" seems to be traditionally limited to housing dogs. *Woodman v. Capital (Regional District)*, 1999 CarswellBC 2193, 6 M.P.L.R. (3d) 128 (S.C.), Bauman J.

PETERS. *abbr.* Peters' Prince Edward Island Reports, 1850-1872.

PETITION. *n.* 1. The process which originates a divorce action. 2. An inferior's supplication to a superior who has jurisdiction to grant redress. 3. A written document by which an ordinary citizen asks the Crown and Parliament for redress, presented through a member following conditions laid down in the Standing Orders of the House. A. Fraser, W.A. Dawson, & J. Holtby, eds., *Beauchesne's Rules and Forms of the House of Commons of Canada*, 6th ed. (Toronto: Carswell , 1989) at 277. 4. A pleading by which a petitioner commences his action. *Court of Queen's Bench Act*, R.S.A. 2000, c. C-31, *Alberta Rules of Court*, Alta. Reg. 390/68, s. 5. See COUNTER~; INITIATIVE ~; PRAYER; RECALL ~.

PETITIONER. *n.* 1. One who brings a petition. 2. Any person applying to court no matter what the formal document used to make the application is called.

PETITION OF RIGHT. A common law method to obtain possession or restitution of real or personal property from the Crown or damages to compensate for breach of a contract. Such a petition could proceed to hearing only if the monarch consented by endorsing it "fiat justitiae" (let right be done). P.W. Hogg, *Constitutional Law of Canada*, 3d ed. (Toronto: Carswell, 1992) at 263.

PETITION PROCEEDING. A proceeding started by a petition. *Court Rules Act*, R.S.B.C. 1996, c. 80, *Supreme Court Civil Rules*, B.C. Reg. 168/2009, s. 1-1(1).

PETITION RESPONDENT. A person who files a response to petition under subrule (4). *Court Rules Act*, R.S.B.C. 1996, c. 80, *Supreme Court Civil Rules*, B.C. Reg. 168/2009, s. 16-1(1).

PETIT JURY. The jury which tries cases with a judge. Contrasted with the grand jury, which had an investigatory role. Consists of various numbers of jurors, from six to twelve, depending on the type of case tried and the jurisdiction.

PETROLEUM. *n.* Oil or gas.

P.G. *abbr.* Procureur général.

PGO. *abbr.* Permanent guardianship order.

PHARMACEUTICAL EQUIVALENT. A new drug that, in comparison with another drug, contains identical amounts of the identical medicinal ingredients, in comparable dosage forms, but that does not necessarily contain the same non-medicinal ingredients. *Food and Drugs Act*, R.S.C. 1985, c. F-27, *Food and Drug Regulations*, C.R.C., c. 870, Pt. C, Div. 8, C.08.001.1.

PHARMACEUTICAL PREPARATION. Includes (a) any substance or mixture of substances manufactured, sold or represented for use in (i) the diagnosis, treatment, mitigation or prevention of a disease, disorder or abnormal physical state, or the symptoms thereof, in humans or animals, or (ii) restoring, correcting or modifying organic functions in humans or animals, and (b) any substance to be used in the preparation or production of any substance or mixture of substances described in paragraph (a), but does not include any such substance or mixture of substances that is the same or substantially the same as a substance or mixture of substances that is a proprietary medicine within the meaning from time to time assigned to that expression by regulations made pursuant to the Food and Drugs Act. *Trade-marks Act*, R.S.C. 1985, c. T-13, s. 51.

PHARMACY. *n.* The custody, compounding and dispensing of drugs, the provision of non-prescription drugs, health care aids and devices and the provision of information related to drug use.

PHILANTHROP. *abbr.* The Philanthropist (Le Philanthrope).

PHILANTHROPIC. *adj.* "... '[B]enevolent' ..." *Brewer v. McCauley*, [1954] S.C.R. 645 at 647, [1955] 1 D.L.R. 415, Rand J.

PHILLIPS V. EYRE. See RULE IN ~.

PHOBIA. *n.* An irrational fear.

PHOTO-COMPARISON TECHNOLOGY. A software application that measures the characteristics of a person's face in a photograph and compares the results of that measurement with those of other photographs. *Photo Card Act*, S.O. 2008, c. 17, s. 7.

PHOTOGRAPH. *n.* 1. Includes photo-lithograph and any work expressed by any process analogous to photography. *Copyright Act*, R.S.C. 1985, c. C-42, s. 2. 2. A photograph taken digitally or by the use of photographic film and includes: (a) a print, including an enlargement or a reduction, prepared from a digital photograph or from a film negative; (b) a photographic plate or film; (c) a microphotographic film; (d) a photocopy, including an enlargement or a reduction; (e) an image created by the electronic scanning of a document; and (f) a print, including an enlargement or a reduction, prepared from an image created by the electronic scanning of a document. *The Evidence Act*, S.S. 2006, c. E-11.2, s. 49.

PHYSICAL ABUSE. Improper use of the body of another person. Maltreatment.

PHYSICAL IMPEDIMENT. A material hindrance, obstruction or obstacle.

PHYSICIAN. See COLLEGE OF ~S AND SURGEONS.

PHYSICIAN-PATIENT RELATIONSHIP. A fiduciary relationship giving rise to a duty of care, the breach of which constitutes negligence. Includes a duty not to touch the patient without consent, breach of which constitutes battery.

PHYSIOTHERAPY. *n.* The application of professional physical therapy in the assessment and treatment of the human body in order to obtain, regain or maintain optimal function by the use of suitable therapeutic methods, including mobilization, manipulation and the use of physical agents. *Physiotherapy Act, 2006*, S.N. 2006, c. P-13.1, s. 2.

PICKET. *n.* A barrier. A person on a picket line.

PICKETING. *n.* Attending at or near a person's place of business, operations or employment for the purpose of persuading or attempting to persuade anyone not to (a) enter that place of business, operations or employment, (b) deal in or handle that person's products, or (c) do business with that person, and a similar act at such a place that has an equivalent purpose. *Labour Relations Code*, R.S.B.C. 1996, c. 244, s. 1. See LAWFUL ~; SECONDARY ~.

PICKET LINE. An area in which picketing is carried on.

PIECE. See SATISFACTION ~.

PIERCE CORPORATE VEIL. To find corporate officers or directors liable or responsible for acts where the existence of the corporation would ordinarily shield them from liability or responsibility.

PIERRINGER SETTLEMENT. A Pierringer agreement arises from the 1963 decision of the Wisconsin Supreme Court in Pierringer v. Hoger 124 N.W.2d 106 (U.S. S.C. 1963). Like a Mary Carter agreement, a Pierringer settlement is an agreement between the plaintiff and one of several joint tortfeasors. However, the contracting tortfeasor does not remain a party to the action. The key aspects of a Pierringer settlement are therefore: (a) segregation of the contracting defendant's liability; (b) satisfaction of the contracting defendant's liability to the credit of all parties to the litigation; (c) the plaintiff's ability to continue with the action against the remaining de-

fendants; (d) the plaintiff's agreement that it will indemnify the contracting defendant for any contribution it pays to the other defendants and covenants to satisfy any judgment against the contracting defendant. *Hudson Bay Mining & Smelting Co. v. Fluor Daniel Wright* (1997), 120 Man. R. (2d) 214 (Q.B.).

PILLER. See ANTON ~ ORDER.

PILOT. *n.* I . Any person not belonging to a ship who has the conduct thereof. *Pilotage Act*, R.S.C. 1985, c. P-14, s. 1. 2. " ... [A] person who operates the controls of an aircraft in motion." *Holmes v. Sun Life Assurance Co. of Canada*, [1977] I.L.R. 1-904 at 770, 6 A.R. 171 (T.D.), Moore J.

PILOTAGE. See COMPULSORY ~.

PILOT-IN-COMMAND. In relation to an aircraft, the pilot having responsibility and authority for the operation and safety of the aircraft during flight time. *Aeronautics Act*, R.S.C. 1985, c. A-2, s. 3.

PINBALL MACHINE. A mechanical or electronic device in which a ball propelled by a plunger scores points as it rolls down a slanting surface among pins and targets.

PIPEDA. *abbr.* Personal Information Protection and Electronic Documents Act, 2000, S.C. 2000, c. 5.

PIPELINE. *var.* **PIPE LINE.** 1. (i) A pipe for the transmission of any substance, and installations in connection with that pipe; or (ii) a sewer or sewage system and installations in connection with that sewer or sewage system. 2. A flow line, gas line, oil line, mineral line, secondary line, distribution line or private line.

PIRACY. *n.* 1. Acts of violence and robbery at sea. 2. Every one commits piracy who does any act that, by the law of nations, is piracy. *Criminal Code*, R.S.C. 1985, c. C-46, s. 74(1). See PIRATICAL ACTS.

PIRATES. *n.* Passengers on the insured ship who mutiny and persons who attack the ship from land. *Marine Insurance Act*, S.C. 1993, c. 22, Sched., s. 1.

PIRATICAL ACTS. (a) Stealing a Canadian ship; (b) stealing or without lawful authority throwing overboard, damaging or destroying anything that is part of the cargo, supplies or fittings in a Canadian ship; (c) doing or attempting to do a mutinous act on a Canadian ship or (d) counselling a person to do anything mentioned in paragraph (a), (b) or (c). *Criminal Code*, R.S.C. 1985, c. C-46, s. 75.

PITH AND SUBSTANCE. 1. Though pith and substance may be described in different ways, the expressions "dominant purpose" or "true character" used in R. v. Morgentaler, [1993] 3 S.C.R. 463, at pp. 481-82, or "the dominant or most important characteristic of the challenged law" used in Whitbread v. Walley, [1990] 3 S.C.R. 1273, at p. 1286, and in Oldman River, supra, at p. 62, appropriately convey the meaning to be attached to the term. *Canada (Procureure générale) c. Hydro-Québec*, 1997 CarswellQue 3705, (sub nom. *R. v. Hydro-Québec*) 118 C.C.C. (3d) 97, 151 D.L.R. (4th) 32, 9 C.R. (5th) 157, 217 N.R. 241, [1997] 3 S.C.R. 213, 24 C.E.L.R.

(N.S.) 167, La Forest J. 2. Variously described as the matter, a name for the content or subject matter, leading feature or true nature and character of a law. P.W. Hogg, *Constitutional Law of Canada*, 3d ed. (Toronto: Carswell, 1992) at 377. 3. "In determining the 'pith and substance' of the legislation, 'it is necessary to identify the dominant or most important characteristic of the challenged law': see Hogg, Constitutional Law of Canada, 2nd ed., p. 313 ..." *R. v. Swain* (1991), 63 C.C.C. (3d) 481 at 525, 5 C.R. (4th) 253, 125 N.R. 1, 3 C.R.R. (2d) 1, 47 O.A.C. 81, [1991] 1 S.C.R. 933, Lamer C.J.C. (Sopinka and Cory JJ. concurring).

PL. *abbr.* [L.] Placitum. Any point decided in a judgment summarized by the reporter.

PLACE. *v.* To transfer a child from the care and control of one person or agency to another person or agency.

PLACE. *n.* 1. "[In s. 10(1)(a) of the Narcotic Control Act, R.S.C. 1970, c. N-1] ... includes places of fixed location such as offices or ships or gardens as well as vehicles, vessels and aircraft. It does not, however, include public streets, or other public places: ... when found in a statute is usually associated with other words which control its meaning... ." *R. v. Rao* (1984), 12 C.C.C. (3d) 97 at 125, 46 O.R. (2d) 80, 40 C.R. (3d) 1, 4 O.A.C. 162, 9 D.L.R. (4th) 542, 10 C.R.R. 275 (C.A.), the court per Martin J.A. 2. A type of bet on a race to select a horse to finish first or second in the official result. *Criminal Code*, R.S.C. 1985, c. C-46, *Pari-Mutuel Betting Supervision Regulations*, SOR/91-365, s. 2. See PUBLIC ~.

PLACEBO. *n.* An inert substance used for comparison purposes in a controlled study of an active substance, that is, a drug.

PLACED. *adj.* The key factor in determining whether machines or structures have been so "placed" as to render them assessable as "improvements", although not in law "fixtures", is simply whether they have been given "some permanency of position." *British Columbia Assessment Commissioner v. Woodwards Stores Ltd.*, 1982 CarswellBC 180, 38 B.C.L.R. 152, [1982] 4 W.W.R. 686 (S.C.), Taylor J.

PLACE OF PUBLIC USE. Those parts of land, a building, street, waterway or other location that are accessible or open to members of the public, whether on a continuous, periodic or occasional basis, and includes any commercial, business, cultural, historical, educational, religious, governmental, entertainment, recreational or other place that is accessible or open to the public on such a basis. *Criminal Code*, R.S.C. 1985, c. C-46, s. 431.2 (1).

PLACITUM. *n.* [L.] Any point decided in a judgment summarized by the reporter.

PLAGIARISM. *n.* The act of publishing the thought or writing of someone else as one's own.

PLAGIARIST. *n.* One who publishes the thought or writing of someone else as one's own.

PLAIN LANGUAGE. Refers to the use of ordinary, not technical, words and writing style in legal documents.

PLAIN MEANING RULE. If the words of a statute are ambiguous on their face then one may go beyond them to ascertain their meaning but if they precise words used are plain and unambiguous, they are to be construed in their ordinary sense according to the intent of Parliament. This rule originated in a passage from the judgment of Lord Tindal in the Sussex Peerage case [(1844), 11 Cl. & Fin. 85 at 143, 8 E.R. 1034 at 1057]. He wrote: "If the words of the statute are in themselves precise and unambiguous, then no more can be necessary than to expound those words in their natural and ordinary sense. The words themselves alone do, in such case, best declare the intention of the lawgiver. But if any doubt arises from the terms employed by the legislature, it has always been held a safe means of collecting the intention, to call in aid the ground and cause of making the statute, and to have recourse to the preamble... and "the mischiefs which [the makers of the Act] intended to redress."" *Sun-Rype Products Ltd. v. Archer Daniels Midland Co.*, 2008 BCCA 278.

PLAINTIFF. *n.* 1. A person who commences an action. 2. A person at whose instance a summons is issued. See NOMINAL ~.

PLAIN VIEW DOCTRINE. Officers may seize evidence which is in plain view even though the evidence is not specified in the search warrant.

PLAN. *n.* 1. The map of a piece of real property divided into lots and parcels. 2. "... [D]esign is the concept of the project when finally completed. A plan is a description of that design set out graphically... ." *Bird Construction Co. v. United States Fire Insurance Co.* (1985), 45 Sask. R. 96 at 99, 18 C.L.R. 115, [1987] I.L.R. 1-2047, 24 D.L.R. (4th) 104, 18 C.C.L.I. 92 (Sask. C.A.), Vancise J.A. 3. A plan to provide for the control and regulation of the producing or marketing or both of a farm product. See AIR SPACE ~; CANADA ASSISTANCE ~; COMPENSATION ~; COOPERATIVE ~; DEFINED BENEFIT ~; DEFINED CONTRIBUTION ~; DEVELOPMENT ~; ELECTRONIC ~; EMERGENCY MANAGEMENT ~; EMPLOYMENT ~; FREQUENT FLYER ~; FUNDED BENEFITS ~; GROUP ~; HYBRID ~; INSURANCE ~; OFFICIAL ~; PENSION ~; SCHOLARSHIP ~; STRATA ~; TIME SHARE OWNERSHIP ~; TIME SHARE ~; TIME SHARE USE ~; TREATMENT ~; UNFUNDED BENEFITS ~.

PLANNING. *n.* "... . [E]ssential to orderly development of a municipality. Generally, a plan is developed for the municipality, and zoning by-laws implement the plan... ." *Zive Estate v. Lynch* (1989), 47 M.P.L.R. 310 at 314, 7 R.P.R. (2d) 180, 94 N.S.R. (2d) 401, 247 A.P.R. 401 (C.A.), the court per Macdonald J.A. See ESTATE ~; URBAN ~.

PLANNING SCHEME. A statement of policy with respect to the use and development of land and the use, erection, construction, relocation and enlargement of buildings within a defined area.

PLAN OF SUBDIVISION. A plan by which the owner of land divides the land into areas designated on the plan.

PLANT. See MARINE ~; RENDERING ~.

PLASTIC EXPLOSIVE. An explosive that (a) is formulated with one or more high explosives that in their pure form have a vapour pressure less than 10 [to the power of minus 4] Pa at a temperature of 25 degrees C, (b) is formulated with a binder material, and (c) is, when mixed, malleable or flexible at normal room temperature. *Explosives Act*, R.S.C. 1985, c. E-17, s. 2. See UNMARKED ~.

PLATE. *n.* Includes (a) any stereotype or other plate, stone, block, mould, matrix, transfer or negative used or intended to be used for printing or reproducing copies of any work, and (b) any matrix or other appliance used or intended to be used for making or reproducing sound recordings, performer's performances or communication signals. *Copyright Act*, R.S.C. 1985, c. C-42, s. 2.

PLATE GLASS INSURANCE. Insurance (not being insurance incidental to some other class of insurance defined by or under this Act) against loss of or damage to plate, sheet or window glass, whether in place or in transit. *Insurance acts*.

PLATFORM. See FIXED ~.

PLAYGROUND. *n.* Referring to an outdoor area the purpose of which is to accommodate play by children. *R. v. Lachapelle*, 2009 BCCA 406.

PLEA. *v.* 1. To make a statement as to guilt. 2. To make submissions.

PLEA. *n.* 1. An action or suit. 2. A way to put forward a defence in certain proceedings. 3. A defendant's factual answer to a plaintiff's declaration. 4. The answer of a defendant in a criminal proceeding as to guilt in relation to an offence charged. See GUILTY ~; ROLLED UP ~; UNTENABLE ~; VOLUNTARY ~.

PLEA BARGAIN. For an accused person to agree to plead guilty, or to give material information or testimony in exchange for an apparent advantage which the prosecutor offers, acting within the scope of a prosecutor's seeming authority. The advantage for which the accused bargains is conviction on a lesser offence than the greater one with which the accused was charged originally or a shorter or lesser sentence.

PLEAD. *v.* 1. To allege something in a cause. 2. To argue a case in court. 3. To answer to an offence charged in criminal court.

PLEADING. *n.* 1. The process in which parties to an action alternately present written statements of their contentions, each one responding to the preceding statement, and each statement attempting to better define the controversial areas. 2. "... [A] statement in writing, in summary form, of material facts on which a party to a dispute relies in support of a claim or defence... ." *Zavitz Technology Inc. v. 146732 Canada Inc.* (1991), 49 C.P.C. (2d) 26 at 38 (Ont. Gen. Div.), Isaac J. See CLOSE OF ~S; MIS~; ORIGI-NATING ~; PRIMARY ~; RESPONDING ~; RULES OF ~.

PLEADINGS-BASED DEFENCE. [O]ne that has nothing to do with the merits of the allegation or any legitimate fairness concerns. *London (City) v. Young*, 2008 ONCA 429, Doherty J.A. (dissenting).

PLEAD OVER. To reply to an opponent's pleading but to overlook a defect to which one might have taken exception.

PLEA IN ABATEMENT. Such a plea must point out the plaintiff's error and show how it may be corrected and furnish material for avoiding the same mistake in another action in regard to the same subject matter.

PLEA NEGOTIATION. For an accused person to agree to plead guilty, or to give material information or testimony in exchange for an apparent advantage which the prosecutor offers, acting within the scope of a prosecutor's seeming authority. S.A. Cohen, *Due Process of Law* (Toronto: Carswell, 1977) at 179.

PLEASURE. See AT ~.

PLEASURE CRAFT. A vessel that is used for pleasure and does not carry passengers. *Canada Shipping Act, 2001*, S.C. 2001, c. 26, s. 2.

PLEBISCITE. *n.* 1. The referral of an issue to the population to decide by vote. 2. Is advisory and non-binding in nature and is a means to secure an expression of the public's opinion on a particular issue. *Municipal Act*, R.S.Y. 2002, c. 154, s. 1.

PLEDGE. *n.* 1. An article pawned with a pawnbroker. 2. "Delivery is necessary to constitute a pledge, and the pledgee's right or special property is to hold the goods as security for the debt, and on default to sell the goods as pledged... ." *N.M. Patterson & Co. v. Carnduff*, [1931] 2 W.W.R.221 at 227 (Sask. C.A.), Martin J.A. 3. A promise to contribute money to a charity. 4. A movable hypothec with delivery, which is commonly called a "pledge" (see art. 2665, para. 2 [of the Civil Code of Quebec, S.Q. 1991, c. 64], enables a creditor and a debtor to grant a hypothec on a property without the hypothec having to be registered in the registry in order for it to be set up against third persons. The hypothec is granted by handing over the property to the creditor, and the holding of the property by the creditor is sufficient to publish the hypothec. *Re Blouin*, 2003 SCC 31, Gonthier J. (Iacobucci, Bastarache, Arbour JJ. concurring). See PAWN.

PLENARY. *adj.* 1. Complete, full. 2. Describes a proceeding with formal steps and gradations, in contrast to summary.

PLENE ADMINISTRAVIT. [L. one has fully administered] An executor's or administrator's defence that that person fully administered all the assets which that person received.

PLOTTAGE. *n.* In expropriation, the advantage of a large holding in organizing an assembly for development.

P.L.T.C. *abbr.* Professional Legal Training Course, the bar admission course administered by the Law

Society and the Continuing Legal Education Society of B.C.

PLUMBING. *n.* A drainage system, a venting system and a water system or parts thereof.

PLURAL. *adj.* Referring to more than one.

PLURALITY. *n.* A greater number.

P.M. *abbr.* 1. Prime Minister. 2. "... Police Magistrate... ." *R. v. Linder*, [1924] 3 D.L.R. 505 at 507, [1924] 2 W.W.R. 646, 42 C.C.C. 289, 20 Alta. L.R. 415 (C.A.), the court per Becker J.A.

P.O. *abbr.* Post office.

P.O.G.G. *abbr.* Peace, order and good government. See RESIDUARY POWER.

POINT. See BASIS ~; DEMERIT ~; ON ~.

POISONED WORK ENVIRONMENT. One which exhibits an atmosphere of prejudice which makes work difficult or impossible for the worker.

POISONING. See FOOD ~.

POLICE. *n.* A force of people charged with maintenance of public order, detection, and prevention of crime. See MILITARY ~; ROYAL CANADIAN MOUNTED ~.

POLICE COURT. The court of a magistrate.

POLICE FORCE. "... [A] body of police... ." *R. v. Gendron* (1985), 22 C.C.C. (3d) 312 at 321, 10 O.A.C. 122 (C.A.), Grange J.A. (dissenting).

POLICE INFORMANT PRIVILEGE. Protects from disclosure the identity of an informer whose assistance to the police is important in the investigation and detection of crime.

POLICE OFFICER. See PERSONATING ~.

POLICE POWER. The authority municipalities have to govern, control and regulate licensed trades or businesses and those engaged in them.

POLICY. *n.* 1. The instrument evidencing a contract. *Insurance acts.* 2. A government commitment to the public to follow an action or course of action in pursuit of approved objectives. *Public Service Act*, R.S.N.W.T. 1988, c. P-16, s. 34(1). 3. "... [D]ecisions concerning budgetary allotments for departments or government agencies will be classified as policy decisions." *Just v. British Columbia* (1989), 1 C.C.L.T. (2d) 1 at 18, [1989] 2 S.C.R. 1228, 18 M.V.R. (2d) 1, [1990] 1 W.W.R. 385, 41 B.C.L.R. (2d) 350, 103 N.R. 1, 64 D.L.R. (4th) 689, 41 Admin. L.R. 161, [1990] R.R.A. 140n, Cory J. (Dickson C.J.C., Wilson, La Forest, L'Heureux-Dubé and Gonthier JJ. concurring). 4. "... [R]efers to a decision of a public body at the planning level involving the allocation of scarce resources or balancing such factors as efficiency and thrift ... One hallmark of a policy, as opposed to an operational, decision is that it involves planning... . A second characteristic of a policy decision as opposed to an operational function is that a policy decision involves allocating resources and balancing factors such as efficiency or thrift ... A third criterion is found in the suggestion that the greater the discretion conferred on the decision-making

body, the more likely the resultant decision is to be a matter of policy rather than operational ... Fourthly, it has been suggested that where there are standards against which conduct can be evaluated, a decision may move into the operational area and immunity should not be granted: ... The setting of a standard is a policy function; its implementation is an operational function... . the fact the person or body making the decision is working in the field does not prevent it from being a policy decision ..." *Just v. British Columbia* (1985), 33 C.C.L.T. 49 at 52-4, 34 M.V.R. 124, 64 B.C.L.R. 349, [1985] 5 W.W.R. 570 (S.C.), McLachlin J. 5. Any written contract of insurance or reinsurance whether contained in one or more documents and, in the case of insurance in a fraternal benefit society, any contract of insurance whether evidenced by a written document or not and any certificate of membership relating in any way to insurance, and includes any annuity contract and any endowment insurance contract. *Insurance Companies Act*, S.C. 1991, c. 47, s. 2. See CLAIMS MADE AND REPORTED ~; CLAIMS MADE ~; COMMON PERSONNEL AND WAGE ~; INSURANCE ~; MOTOR VEHICLE LIABILITY ~; MULTICULTURALISM ~; MULTI-PERIL ~; OCCURRENCE ~; OWNER'S ~; PARTICIPATING ~; PUBLIC ~; TIME ~; UMBRELLA ~; UNVALUED ~; VALUED ~; VOYAGE ~.

POLICY DECISION. Generally made by a person at a high level of authority and is identified by its nature. Decisions concerning budget allotment are policy decisions.

POLICY GRIEVANCE. The subject matter of the grievance is of general interest and individual employees may not be affected at the time the grievance is filed.

POLICYHOLDER. *n.* A person who owns an insurance policy.

POLITIC. See BODY ~.

POLITICAL ASYLUM. The granting of falls within the Crown's prerogative. To be contrasted with a political refugee whose status is determined by the Immigration and Refugee Board.

POLITICAL CIVIL LIBERTIES. Include freedom of assembly, association, religion and speech, the right to be a candidate for elected office and vote, the freedom to leave and enter Canada and move between provinces. P.W. Hogg, *Constitutional Law of Canada*, 3d ed. (Toronto: Carswell, 1992) at 765.

POLITICAL CRIME. Determination of what is a political crime involves the proportionality to a legitimate political objective.

POLITICAL LAW. The interdisciplinary study of the interaction among law, public policy and administration, and politics, and with the influence of law on the other types of instruments of democratic governance. It incorporates elements of constitutional and administrative law with public administration and political science. It deals specifically with topics such as: the factors motivating the choice of instruments for governing, the balance of law and politics in the legislative process, the precedence of law and its accommodation with other types of instruments in government management, the legal value to be ascribed to political and campaign promises, as well as with the relative weight of legal, administrative and political influences in the adjudication of political disputes on issues of public governance. The Quebec Secession reference was the most fundamental and the most comprehensive political law judgment to arise from the Canadian judiciary since Confederation. Gregory Tardi, "The Latest Phase in the Sovereignty Debate: A Feud of Statutes." *Ontario Bar Association Constitutional, Civil Liberties and Human Rights Section newsletter* (Vol.6, No. 1 – November 2002), pp 8-14.

POLITICAL PARTY. 1. An association, organization or affiliation of voters comprising a political organization whose prime purpose is the nomination and support of candidates at elections. 2. A group of individuals comprising a political organization whose primary purpose is to field candidates for election as members. *The Election Act, 1996*, S.S. 1996, c. E-6.01, s. 2.

POLITICAL SUBDIVISION. Any province, state, territory, dependency or any other similar subdivision of a state. *Foreign Missions and International Organizations Act*, S.C. 1991, c. 41, s. 2.

POLL. *v.* 1. At an election, to give a vote or to receive a vote. 2. To take the votes of everyone entitled to vote.

POLL. *n.* See DEED-~; HAMBURGER ~.

POLLING DAY. In relation to an election, means the date fixed for voting at the election. See ADVANCE ~.

POLLING STATION. A place established for electors to cast their votes.

POLL-TAX. *n.* A tax on every person.

POLLUTANT. *n.* (a) A substance that, if added to any waters, would degrade or alter or form part of a process of degradation or alteration of the quality of the waters to an extent that is detrimental to their use by humans or by an animal or a plant that is useful to humans; and (b) any water that contains a substance in such a quantity or concentration, or that has been so treated, processed or changed, by heat or other means, from a natural state, that it would, if added to any waters, degrade or alter or form part of a process of degradation or alteration of the quality of the waters to an extent that is detrimental to their use by humans or by an animal or a plant that is useful to humans. It includes oil and any substance or class of substances that is prescribed to be a pollutant. *Canada Shipping Act, 2001*, S.C. 2001, c. 26, s. 165.

POLLUTION. *n.* 1. The presence in the environment of substances or contaminants that substantially alter or impair the usefulness of the environment. *Environmental Management Act*, S.B.C. 2003, c. 53, s. 1(1). 2. Alteration of the physical, chemical, biological or aesthetic properties of the environment including the addition or removal of any contaminant that will render the environment harmful to the public health, that is unsafe or harmful for domestic, munic-

ipal, industrial, agricultural, recreational or other lawful uses or that is harmful to wild animals, birds or aquatic life. See AIR ~; MARINE ~; OIL ~ INCIDENT.

POLYANDRY. *n.* Polygamy in which one woman has several husbands.

POLYCENTRIC ISSUE. An issue which deals with a number of interwoven and interacting interests and considerations.

POLYCENTRICITY. *n.* The broad principle of "polycentricity" well known to academic commentators who suggest that it provides the best rationale for judicial deference to non-judicial agencies. A "polycentric issue is one which involves a large number of interlocking and interacting interests and considerations" (P. Cane, An Introduction to Administrative Law (3rd ed. 1996), at p. 35). While judicial procedure is premised on a bipolar opposition of parties, interests, and factual discovery, some problems require the consideration of numerous interests simultaneously, and the promulgation of solutions which concurrently balance benefits and costs for many different parties. Where an administrative structure more closely resembles this model, courts will exercise restraint. The polycentricity principle is a helpful way of understanding the variety of criteria developed under the rubric of the "statutory purpose". The purpose of the Convention [Convention Relating to the Status of Refugees, [1969] C.T.S. 6] and particularly that of the exclusions contained in Article 1F is clearly not the management of flows of people, but rather the conferral of minimum human rights' protection. The context in which the adjudicative function takes place is not a "polycentric" one of give-and-take between different groups, but rather the vindication of a set of relatively static human rights, and ensuring that those who fall within the prescribed categories are protected. *Pushpanathan v. Canada (Minister of Employment & Immigration)*, 1998 CarswellNat 830, 226 N.R. 201, (*sub nom. Pushpanathan v. Canada (Minister of Citizenship & Immigration)*) 160 D.L.R. (4th) 193, [1998] S.C.J. No. 46, (*sub nom. Pushpanathan v. Canada (Minister of Citizenship & Immigration)*) [1998] 1 S.C.R. 982, 43 Imm. L.R. (2d) 117, 11 Admin. L.R. (3d) 1, Bastarache J.

POLYGAMY. *n.* 1. The state of having many wives or husbands. 2. It is an offence (a) to practise or enter into or in any manner agree or consent to practise or enter into (i) any form of polygamy, or (ii) any kind of conjugal union with more than one person at the same time, whether or not it is by law recognized as a binding form of marriage; or (b) to celebrate, assist or be a party to a rite, ceremony, contract or consent that purports to sanction a relationship mentioned in subparagraph (a)(i) or (ii). *Criminal Code*, R.S.C. 1985, c. C-46, s. 293(1).

POLYGRAPH. *n.* A lie detector; an apparatus which records physiological changes in the body.

POOL. *n.* 1. An aggregation of interest or property or throwing of revenue or property into one common fund or a sharing of interest in that fund by all on an equal or previously agreed basis. 2. A source of employees. 3. A natural underground reservoir containing or appearing to contain an accumulation of oil or gas or both oil and gas and being separated or appearing to be separated from any other such accumulation. *Oil and Gas acts.* 4. In respect of each type of bet that may be made on a race, means the total amount of money bet on the race. *Criminal Code*, R.S.C. 1985, c. C-46, *Pari-Mutuel Betting Supervision Regulations*, SOR/91-365, s. 2. See FEATURE ~.

POOLED SPACING UNIT. The area that is subject to a pooling agreement or a pooling order. *Canada Oil and Gas Operations Act*, R.S.C. 1985, c. O-7, s. 29.

POOLED TRACT. The portion of a pooled spacing unit defined as a tract in a pooling agreement or a pooling order. *Canada Oil and Gas Operations Act*, R.S.C. 1985, c. O-7, s. 29.

POOLING AGREEMENT. An agreement to pool the interests of owners in a spacing unit and to provide for the operation or the drilling and operation of a well thereon. *Canada Oil and Gas Operations Act*, R.S.C. 1985, c. O-7, s. 29.

POPPING. See SKIN ~.

POPULAR INNUENDO. In the case of "popular or false innuendo", although it need not be separately pled, the plaintiff is required to show why a reader would reasonably import to the words complained of a defamatory character, different from the ordinary meaning that the words would otherwise import. Where the words complained of are susceptible to many interpretations, the onus rests on the plaintiff to set out the meaning or meanings the plaintiff alleges the words are capable of. *Moon v. Sher* (2003), 2003 CarswellOnt 2405 (S.C.J.).

PORNOGRAPHY. *n.* "... [C]an be usefully divided into three categories: (1) explicit sex with violence; (2) explicit sex without violence but which subjects people to treatment that is degrading or dehumanizing, and (3) explicit sex without violence that is neither degrading nor dehumanizing. Violence in this context includes both actual physical violence and threats of physical violence... ." *R. v. Butler* (1992), 11 C.R. (4th) 137 at 163, [1992] 2 W.W.R. 577, [1992] 1 S.C.R. 452, 70 C.C.C. (3d) 129, 134 N.R. 81, 8 C.R.R. (2d) 1, 89 D.L.R. (4th) 449, 78 Man. R. (2d) 1, 16 W.A.C. 1, Sopinka J. (Lamer C.J.C., La Forest, Cory, McLachlin, Stevenson and Iacobucci JJ. concurring). See CHILD ~.

PORT. *n.* 1. A place where vessels or vehicles may discharge or load cargo. 2. The navigable waters under the jurisdiction of a port authority and the real property that the port authority manages, holds or occupies as set out in the letters patent. *Canada Marine Act*, S. C. 1998, c. 10, s. 5.

PORTABILITY. *n.* Of a mortgage, refers to the carrying of a mortgage's terms, such as penalties and rate, to a new mortgage on the same property or to a new mortgage on another property.

PORT AUTHORITY. A port authority established under the Canada Marine Act. The Minister may issue letters patent of incorporation for a port authority without share capital for the purpose of operating a particular port in Canada if the Minister is satisfied that the port (a) is, and is likely to remain, financially self-sufficient; (b) is of strategic significance to Canada's trade; (c) is linked to a major rail line or a major highway infrastructure; and (d) has diversified traffic. *Canada Marine Act*, S. C. 1998, c. 10, s. 2 and 8.

PORT FACILITY. A wharf, pier, breakwater, terminal, warehouse or other building or work located in, on or adjacent to navigable waters used in connection with navigation or shipping and includes all land incidental to their use. *Canada Marine Act*, S. C. 1998, c. 10, s. 2.

PORTFOLIO. See MINISTER WITHOUT ~.

PORTFOLIO MANAGER. An adviser registered for the purpose of managing the investment portfolio of clients through discretionary authority granted by the clients.

PORTFOLIO SALE. A sale in which the parties agree to buy and sell several properties for a single sale price in one agreement. *HDL Investments Inc. v. Regina (City)*, 2008 SKCA 47.

PORTFOLIO SECURITY. A security held or proposed to be purchased by the mutual fund.

PORTION. See CUSTODIAL ~.

POSITION. See SHORT ~.

POSITIONAL ASPHYXIA. Restraining the body, unconsciousness or immobility causing breath to breathe. F.A. Jaffe, *A Guide to Pathological Evidence for Lawyers and Police Officers*, 4th ed. (Toronto: Carswell, 1999) at 230.

POSITION OF AUTHORITY. In relation to the consent defence to a charge of sexual touching, does not necessarily entail just the exercise of a legal right over the young person, but also a lawful or unlawful power to command which the adult may acquire in the circumstances. *R. v. Audet*, [1996] 2 S.C.R. 171.

POSITION OF TRUST. In relation to the consent defence to a charge of sexual touching, where the nature of the relationship between an adult and a young person is such that it creates an opportunity for all of the persuasive and influencing factors which adults hold over children and young persons to come into play, and the child or young person is particularly vulnerable to the sway of these factors, the adult is in a position where those concepts of reliability and truth and strength are put to the test. Taken together, all of these factors combine to create a 'position of trust' towards the young person. *R. v. Audet*, [1996] 2 S.C.R. 171.

POSITIVE EASEMENT. Confers a right on its holder to commit an act or acts upon the servient easement.

POSITIVE LAW. Rules of conduct set down and enforced with the sanction of authority.

POSSE. *n.* [L.] A possibility. Something in posse is something which possibly may be; something in esse is something which actually is. See IN ~.

POSSE COMITATUS. [L.] The sheriff of a county traditionally could summon it to defend that county against enemies of the Crown, to pursue felons, to keep the peace or to enforce a royal writ.

POSSESSION. *n.* 1. In relation to land, primarily connotes physical control. Used to refer to present use and enjoyment as opposed to future or contingent interests. 2. For the purposes of this Act, (a) a person has anything in possession when he has it in his personal possession or knowingly (i) has it in the actual possession or custody of another person, or (ii) has it in any place, whether or not that place belongs to or is occupied by him, for the use or benefit of himself or of another person; and (b) where one of two or more persons, with the knowledge and consent of the rest, has anything in his custody or possession, it shall be deemed to be in the custody and possession of each and all of them. *Criminal Code*, R.S.C. 1985, c. C-46, s. 4(3). 3. The right of control or disposal of any article, irrespective of the actual possession or location of such article. 4. In relation to stolen property, [p]ersonal possession is established where an accused person exercises physical control over a prohibited object with full knowledge of its character, however brief the physical contact may be, and where there is some evidence to show the accused person took custody of the object willingly with intent to deal with it in some prohibited manner. *R. v. York*, 2005 BCCA 74. 5. To be in possession of child pornography, it is not necessary for the individual to have viewed the material. ... It is the element of control, including deciding what will be done with the material, that is essential to possession. *R. v. Daniels*, 2004 NLCA 73. 6. When applied to persons claiming title to land, includes the reception of the rents and profits thereof. 7. In the context of section 283(1) of the Criminal Code does not refer solely to the physical control of a child exercised by the deprived parent at the time of taking but extends to the ability of the deprived parent to exercise control over the child. *R. v. Dawson*, [1996] 3 S.C.R. 783. See ACTUAL ~; ADVERSE ~; CHOSE IN ~; CONSTRUCTIVE ~; DE FACTO ~; DIS~; EXCLUSIVE ~; LEGAL ~; PERSONAL ~; RECENT ~; UNITY OF ~; VACANT ~; VESTED IN ~; WRIT OF ~.

POSSESSORY. *adj.* Describes something arising out of or concerned with possession.

POSSESSORY LIEN. A common law lien which arises from an express or implied agreement and which can be extinguished when the amount due is tendered and can be lost by an express or implied waiver. It continues only as long as one retains actual possession.

POSSESSORY TITLE. The claimant must have actual possession, the intention to exclude the true owner from possession and to have effectively excluded the true owner from possession.

POSSIBILITY. *n.* 1. A future event, which may or may not happen. 2. In real property, an interest in land which depends on such an event happening.

POSSIBILITY OF REVERTER. A future interest dependent on a conditional or determinable fee simple, the possibility of acquiring an interest in land some time in the future. A limitation on the grant in fee simple.

POSSIBLE. *adj.* "... [C]ould in some circumstances be coloured by context to mean more likely than not. But in the case at bar it is coupled with words indicating that the prognosis is 'uncertain'." *Bola v. Canada (Minister of Employment & Immigration)* (1990), 107 N.R. 311 at 316 (Fed. C.A.), MacGuigan J.A.

POST. *v.* To leave in a post office or with a person authorized by the Corporation to receive mailable matter. *Canada Post Corporation Act*, R.S.C. 1985, c. C-10, s. 2.

POST. *n.* See ORIGINAL ~; TRANSMIT BY ~.

POST. *adv.* [L.] After.

POSTAGE. *n.* The charge or surcharge payable for the collection, transmission and delivery by the Corporation of messages, information, funds or goods and for insurance or other special services provided by the Corporation in relation thereto. *Canada Post Corporation Act*, R.S.C. 1985, c. C-10, s. 2.

POSTAGE STAMP. Any stamp, postage impression or postage meter impression authorized by Canada Post Corporation for the purpose of paying postage. *Canada Post Corporation Act*, R.S.C. 1985, c. C-10, s. 2.

POSTAL REMITTANCE. Any instrument authorized by Canada Post Corporation for the remittance of funds. *Canada Post Corporation Act*, R.S.C. 1985, c. C-10, s. 2.

POSTDATE. *v.* To give a bill, note or cheque a date after its date of issue in order to delay the payment date.

POSTDATED CHEQUE. One which is dated after its date of issue in order to delay payment.

POST-JUDGMENT INTEREST. Interest payable on the amount awarded under a judgment including costs calculated from the date of the order calculated at the postjudgment interest rate.

POST MORTEM. [L.] *adj.* Occuring after or present at death. F.A. Jaffe, *A Guide to Pathological Evidence for Lawyers and Police Officers*, 4th ed. (Toronto, Carswell, 1999) at 242.

POST-OFFENCE CONDUCT. Is not a special category of evidence; rather, it is circumstantial evidence to be considered with other relevant evidence. *R. v. Gagnon*, 2006 MBCA 125.

POST OFFICE. Includes any place, receptacle, device or mail conveyance authorized by the Corporation for the posting, receipt, sorting, handling, transmission or delivery of mail. *Canada Post Corporation Act*, R.S.C. 1985, c. C-10, s. 2.

POSTPONEMENT. *n.* 1. A document which subordinates a separate document to another separate document. 2. Putting off; adjournment.

POST TIME. The time that is set for the start of a race. *Criminal Code*, R.S.C. 1985, c. C-46, *Pari-*

Mutuel Betting Supervision Regulations, SOR/91-365, s. 2.

POTENTIALLY INJURIOUS INFORMATION. Information of a type that, if it were disclosed to the public, could injure international relations or national defence or national security. *Canada Evidence Act*, R.S.C. 1985, c. C-5, s. 38.

POUND. *n.* 1. Premises where stray animals are confined. 2. An enclosure, building or piece of land where a distrainor places goods which have been seized as distress.

POVERTY. *n.* The condition of a human being who is deprived of the resources, means, choices and power necessary to acquire and maintain economic self-sufficiency or to facilitate integration and participation in society. *An Act to combat poverty and social exclusion*, R.S.Q. c. L-7, s. 2.

POVERTY LINE. There is no official measure which is equated to the poverty line. Several agencies publish income measurements which are referred to as the poverty line, the line between poor persons and others.

POWER. *n.* 1. A right or privilege. 2. Jurisdiction. 3. "... [T]he description of an authority in respect to property or an interest in property which does not itself belong to the person holding the power. Even when a power to dispose of property is wide enough to enable the holder of the power to exercise it in favour of himself the power itself, in the absence of any exercise of it is not regarded as equivalent to ownership of the property... ." *Montreal Trust Co. v. Minister of National Revenue* (1960), 60 D.T.C. 1183 at 1185, [1960] C.T.C. 308, [1960] Ex. C.R. 543, Thurlow J. 4. Rule 212(1) [of the Saskatchewan Queen's Bench Rules] requires disclosure of documents in the "possession" or "power" of the litigant. ... If the litigant has the right to direct the third party to produce the document, it would follow that the document is in his power. *Spencer v. Canada (Attorney General)*, 2000 SKCA 96, 199 Sask. R. 127, 232 W.A.C. 127, [2001] 7 W.W.R. 476, 7 C.P.C. (5th) 280, 7 W.W.R. 476. 5. Includes hydraulic, electrical, steam or other power and also includes energy. 6. Includes energy, light and heat however developed or produced, and includes electricity and natural, manufactured or mixed gas, or liquified petroleum gas. 7. (a) An enemy or an opposing force of Canada; (b) a person or a group that has as one of its purposes or activities the facilitating or carrying out of a terrorist activity; and (c) any prescribed entity. *Canadian Forces Members and Veterans Re-establishment and Compensation Act, S.C. 2005*, c. 21, s. 64. See ABUSE OF ~; DECLARATORY ~; DISPOSITIVE ~; DISTRIBUTION OF ~S; FOREIGN ~; GENERAL ~; INHERENT ~; LEGAL ~; LICENSING ~; OBJECT OF A ~; POLICE ~; RESIDUARY ~; SEPARATION OF ~S; SPENDING ~; STATUTORY ~; TRUST ~; VISITATORIAL ~S.

POWER OF APPOINTMENT. The power of a donee or appointor to appoint by will the people who will succeed to property after the person to whom the power is given dies. This power is given by a donor using an instrument such as a trust inter vivos, marriage settlement or will. J.G. McLeod, *The Conflict of Laws* (Calgary: Carswell, 1983) at 428.

POWER OF ATTORNEY. Authority for a donee or donees to do on behalf on a donor or principal anything which that donor can lawfully do through an attorney. G.H.L. Fridman, *The Law of Agency*, 6th ed. (London: Butterworths, 1990) at 55-6. See ENDURING ~.

POWER OF SALE. The power of a mortgagee to sell the property subject to his mortgage in order to realize on the mortgage debt.

POWLEY TEST. 1. Set out in *R. v. Powley*, 2003 2 SCR, 207. Modification of the *R. v. Van der Peet*, 1996 CanLII 216, [1996] 2 S.C.R. 507 factors to be considered in determining entitlement to a Charter section 35 exemption from the application of a general law in the case of Metis. 2. The Powley test has been adopted in New Brunswick in order to determine aboriginal status for non-status Indians. *Hopper v. R.*, 2008 NBCA 42.

PPSA. *abbr.* Personal Property Security Act.

P.P.S.A.C. *abbr.* Personal Property Security Act Cases, 1977-1990.

P.P.S.A.C. (2D). *abbr.* Personal Property Security Act Cases (Second Series), 1991-2000.

P.P.S.A.C. (3D). *abbr.* Personal Property Security Act Cases (Third Series), 2001-.

PPSC. *abbr.* Public Prosecution Service of Canada.

P.R. *abbr.* Practice Reports (Ontario), 1848-1900.

PRACTICABLE. *adj.* "... [W]hen it is capable of being done, having regard to all the circumstances 'feasible'." *R. v. Cambrin* (1982), 1 C.C.C. (3d) 59 at 61, [1983] 2 W.W.R. 250, 18 M.V.R. 160 (B.C. C.A.), Craig J.A.

PRACTICAL. *adj.* "... [C]apable of being done usefully or at not too great a cost ..." *Crédit foncier franco-canadien v. McGuire* (1979), 12 C.P.C. 103 at 105, 14 B.C.L.R. 281 (S.C.), van der Hoop L.J.S.C.

PRACTICAL NURSING. See PRACTICE OF ~.

PRACTICE. *n.* 1. "... [T]hose legal rules which direct the course of proceedings to bring parties into court, and the course of the court after they are brought in ..." *Delisle v. Moreau* (1968), 5 C.R.N.S. 68 at 70, [1968] 4 C.C.C. 229, 69 D.L.R. (2d) 530, (N.B. C.A.), the court per Hughes J.A. 2. "... [I]n its larger sense,' says Lord Justice Lush in Payser v. Minors, (1881); 7 Q.B.D. 329 at 333 (C.A.), 'denotes the mode of proceeding by which a legal right is enforced as distinguished from the law which gives or defines the right.' Where used in its ordinary and common sense, it denotes the rules that make or guide the cursus curiae and regulate procedure within the walls or limits of the Court itself: Attorney-General v. Sillem, 33 L.J. Ex. 209." *Morris Provincial Election, Re* (1907), 6 W.L.R. 742 at 748 (Man. K.B.), Mathers J. 3. "... [T]he exercise of [a] profession or calling frequently, customarily or habitually:..." *R. v. Mills* (1963), [1964] 1 O.R. 74 at 76 (C.A.), the court per McLennan J.A. 4. "... [T]he accepted 'way of doing things'; [the parties' in collective bargaining] uniform and constant response to a recurring set of circumstances: ..." *Dominion-Consolidated Truck Lines Ltd. v. I.T.B., Local 141* (1980), 28 L.A.C. (2d) 45 at 49 (Ont.), Adams, McRae and Fosbery. 5. For a fee or remuneration, performing or directing works, services or undertakings which, because of their scope and implications, require specialized knowledge, training and experience. See COLLABORATIVE ~; CORRUPT ~; ILLEGAL ~; MAL~; STANDARDS OF ~.

PRACTICE OF AGROLOGY. The development, acquisition or application of or advising on scientific principles and practices relating to the cultivation, production, utilization and improvement of plants and animals and the management of associated resources and includes (i) the certification of compliance with Acts, regulations, directives, standards and guidelines related to agrology, (ii) the conducting of economic, statistical, financial, sociological and other studies related to agrology, (iii) the production, processing, marketing and protection of agricultural and related products and supplies, (iv) the analysis, classification and evaluation of land and water systems, (v) the undertaking of agricultural design and advising on the use of buildings, structures, machinery and equipment, (vi) the conservation, decommissioning, reclamation, remediation and improvement of soils, land and water systems, and (vii) the development, management and use of waste treatment and ecological systems. *Agrology Profession Act*, S.A. 2005, c. A-13.5, s. 1.

PRACTICE OF A NURSE PRACTITIONER. The application of advanced nursing knowledge, skills and judgment in addition to the practice of nursing in which a nurse practitioner in collaborative practice may, in accordance with standards for nurse practitioners, do one or more of the following: (i) make a diagnosis identifying a disease, disorder or condition, (ii) communicate the diagnosis to the client and health care professionals as appropriate, (iii) perform procedures, (iv) initiate, order or prescribe consultations, referrals and other acts, (v) order and interpret screening and diagnostic tests, and recommend, prescribe or reorder drugs, blood, blood products and related paraphernalia, and also includes research, education, consultation, management, administration, regulation, policy or system development relevant to subclauses (i) to (v). *Registered Nurses Act*, S.N.S. 2006, c. 21, s. 2.

PRACTICE OF ASSESSMENT. Specialized consulting services in real property appraisal, assessment administration and tax policy and, without limitation, includes the following: (i) preparing property and business assessment using legislative mass appraisal and single property appraisal standards, policies and procedures; (ii) communicating or explaining assessments to property owners and the administration of public relations programs related to understanding the assessment process and the role of the property tax in funding government services; (iii) the formulation, advocacy and development of assessment legislation, policy and standards; (iv) providing expert testimony, evidence, argument and case management services in the administration of assessment tribunals and other courts of law in their review of assessments; (v) providing services as a member of an assessment tribunal member; (vi) the design, development and delivery of assessment training, education, workplace learning and professional development courses and seminars; (vii) the management and administration of assessment service operations, and the internal and external auditing of those operations; (viii) the analysis of assessment data elements, development of data standards and the collection of assessment data; (ix) computer assisted system designs and implementation in mass appraisal systems and related geographic information systems or information management systems; (x) the development of appraisal software and construction cost and valuation manuals; (xi) the administration and implementation of discretionary property tax exemption programs. *Professional and Occupational Associations Registration Act*, R.S.A. 2000, c. P-26, *Municipal Assessor Regulation*, Alta. Reg. 347/2009, s. 1.

PRACTICE OF CHIROPRACTIC. (a) Any professional service usually performed by a chiropractor, including the examination and treatment, principally by hand and without use of drugs or surgery, of the spinal column, pelvis and extremities and associated soft tissues; and (b) such other services as may be approved by the regulations. *The Chiropractic Act*, R.S.M. 1987, c. C100, s. 1.

PRACTICE OF DENTURISM. Includes (i) the making of impressions and the determining of jaw relations for the purpose of making, producing, reproducing, constructing, supplying, altering or repairing of a removable denture to be fitted into the edentulous or partially edentulous arch of a person's mouth, (ii) determining the placement of a removable denture in respect of the edentulous or partially edentulous arch of a person's mouth, (iii) the making, reproducing, constructing, supplying, altering and repairing of a removable complete or partial denture or fabrication of a removable complete or partial denture where the service is performed further to subclause (i) or (ii), but does not include any procedure that alters oral tissue of a person. *Denturists Act*, S.P.E.I. 2003, c. 2, s. 1.

PRACTICE OF EARLY CHILDHOOD EDUCATION. The practice of early childhood education is the planning and delivery of inclusive play-based learning and care programs for children in order to promote the well-being and holistic development of children, and includes, (a) the delivery of programs to pre-school children and school aged children, including children with special needs; (b) the assessment of the programs and the progress of children in the programs; (c) communication with the parents or persons with legal custody of the children in the programs in order to improve the development of the children; and (d) such other services or activities as may be prescribed by the regulations. *Early Childhood Educators Act, 2007*, S.O. 2007, c. 7, Sched. 8, s. 2.

PRACTICE OF FORESTRY. The development, acquisition or application of scientific principles and practices relating to forestry, products of forested land and integrated management of forested land and includes, without limitation, (i) the inventory, classification, appraisal and evaluation of forests and forested land, (ii) the development and implementation of programs for harvesting and renewal of forests and forested land, (iii) the conservation, reclamation, improvement or protection of forests, forested land or forest soils for forestry purposes, (iv) the preparation of forest resource management plans, (v) the development of integrated resource management plans and administration of forested land, (vi) the teaching of forestry at a college, technical institute or university, and (vii) the conducting of research activities related to forestry. *Regulated Forestry Profession Act*, R.S.A. 2000, c. R-13, s. 1. See PROFESSIONAL ~.

PRACTICE OF HOME ECONOMICS. Includes every act with or without reward which has as its objective the discovery, integration and application of physical and social science principles for the purpose of enhancing the quality of people's daily lives and, without restricting the generality of the foregoing, includes the act of advising individuals, families, organizations and businesses, disseminating information, planning, conducting and evaluating educational programs and conducting research related to (a) knowledge and skills required for satisfying basic needs for food, clothing, shelter and human relationships, (b) consumer goods and services, (c) management of individual and family resources, and (d) public and private sector policies and programs affecting the well-being of individuals and families. *The Professional Home Economists Act*, S.M. 1989-90, c. 92, s. 1.

PRACTICE OF INTERIOR DESIGN. Providing or offering to provide, for a fee, commission or hope of reward, design services in relation to the non-structural construction of and non-structural alterations to the interior area of a structure designed for human habitation and includes (i) analyzing the intended use of the interior area of a structure, the life-safety requirements and applicable codes, (ii) developing preliminary and final designs for the alteration or construction of an interior area of a structure, (iii) preparing and filing with the authority having jurisdiction for the purpose of obtaining a building permit, technical submissions for non-structural interior construction, materials, finishes, space planning, reflected ceiling plans, furnishings, fixtures and equipment, (iv) consulting and collaborating with licensed design professionals, (v) preparing and administering bids and contract documents, and (vi) reviewing and evaluating the implementation of projects while in progress and upon completion. *Interior Designers Act*, S.N.S. 2003, c. 6, s. 2.

PRACTICE OF MIDWIFERY. (i) The assessment and monitoring of the health of a mother and her baby during pregnancy, labour and the post-partum period, (ii) the provision of care in the normal course of pregnancy, labour and the post-partum period, (iii) the management of vaginal deliveries, (iv) the ordering and interpreting of screening and diagnostic tests and the recommending, prescribing or re-ordering of

drugs restricted to actual delivery and care, blood products and related paraphernalia respecting the provision of care in the normal course of pregnancy, labour and the post-partum period, and (v) invasive procedures restricted to actual delivery and care, as prescribed by regulation, either within or outside of a hospital setting and research, education, consultation, management, administration, regulation, policy or system development relating to subclauses (i) to (v). *Midwifery Act*, S.N.S. 2006, c. 18, s. 2.

PRACTICE OF OPTICIANRY. (i) The supplying, preparing or dispensing of ophthalmic appliances, (ii) the interpretation of prescriptions from ophthalmologists or optometrists in respect of ophthalmic appliances, or (iii) the fitting, adjusting or adapting of ophthalmic appliances to the needs of the intended wearer in accordance with a prescription from an ophthalmologist or optometrist, or without a prescription when lenses are duplicated with no change in their refractive value, whether for hire, gain or reward or not, but does not include the measurement of ocular refractive error of an individual through refraction, providing a prescription or diagnosing a condition. *Opticians Act*, R.S.A. 2000, c. O-9, s. 1.

PRACTICE OF PRACTICAL NURSING. The provision of nursing services (i) independently, for clients considered stable with predictable outcomes, and (ii) under the guidance or direction of a registered nurse, medical practitioner or other health care professional authorized to provide such consultation, guidance or direction, for clients considered unstable with unpredictable outcomes. *Licensed Practical Nurses Act*, S.N.S. 2006, c. 17, s. 2.

PRACTICE OF PROFESSIONAL GEOSCIENCE. 1. Reporting, advising, acquiring, processing, evaluating, interpreting, surveying, sampling or examining related to any activity that (a) is directed towards the discovery or development of oil, natural gas, coal, metallic or non-metallic minerals, precious stones, other natural resources or water, or the investigation of surface or sub-surface geological conditions, and (b) requires the professional application of the principles of geology, geophysics or geochemistry. *Engineers and Geoscientists Act*, R.S.B.C. 1996, c. 116, s. 1. 2. Any act of documenting, analysing, evaluating, interpreting or reporting on the earth's materials or on resources, forms or processes, or managing any of the foregoing, that requires the application of the principles of geology, geophysics or geochemistry and that concerns the safeguarding of life, health, property, economic interests, the public interest or the environment. *The Engineering and Geoscientific Professions Act*, S.M. 1998, c. 55, s. 1.

PRACTICE OF PROFESSIONAL PLANNING. Any act of planning including, without restricting the generality of the foregoing, (i) investigating, designing, commissioning, composing, evaluating, advising, reporting, directing or supervising, or managing any of the foregoing, that requires or involves the application of principles of planning and that concerns the safeguarding of life, health, property, economic interests, public welfare or the environment, (ii) the preparation and implementation of plans, studies or strategies involving the application of the principles of planning including, without restricting the generality of the foregoing, regional or municipal plans or strategies, urban or rural plans, land development plans or strategies, land-use by-laws, site plans, subdivision plans, economic plans, environmental plans or studies, social plans, recreation plans, conservation plans, organizational plans, heritage plans, lifestyle plans, conceptual plans and strategic plans, (iii) the application of skills or techniques for the purpose of planning including, without restricting the generality of the foregoing, computer analysis and data queries, environmental analysis, geological studies, morphology studies, air-photo analysis, cartography or mapping, cost-benefit analysis, physical sciences, social sciences, statistical analysis, demographic research, environmental design and planning, project planning and implementation, research and communication, (iv) any tasks necessary to implement the planning legislation of the Province involving the use or application of the principles of planning, (v) project management where the principles of planning are involved, and (vi) any other tasks that involve the principles of planning. *Professional Planners Act*, S.N.S. 2005, c. 45, s. 3.

PRACTICE OF PROFESSIONAL SURVEYING. The determination or analysis of spatial attributes of natural and artificial features on, above or below the surface of the earth, whether or not the surface of the earth is situated below water, and the storage and representation of such features on a chart, map, plan or graphic representation, and includes the practice of cadastral surveying. *Surveyors Act*, R.S.O. 1990, c. S.29, s. 1.

PRACTICE OF PUBLIC ACCOUNTING. Providing or offering to provide one or more of the following services to the public: (i) performing an assurance engagement as defined in the CICA Handbook, (ii) performing a specified auditing procedures engagement as defined in the CICA Handbook, (iii) performing a compilation engagement as defined in the CICA Handbook, (iv) providing an accounting service insofar as it involves summarization, analysis, advice, counsel or interpretation, but excluding an accounting service which is part of, but incidental to, the provider's primary occupation which is not accounting, (v) providing a forensic accounting, financial investigation or financial litigation support service, (vi) providing advice, counsel or interpretation with respect to taxation matters when such advice, counsel or interpretation is in connection with a practice offering or providing a service described in clauses (i) to (v), (vii) preparing a tax return or other statutory information filing when such preparation is inc onnection with a practice offering or providing a service described in clauses (i) to (v). *Public Accounting and Auditing Act*, S.P.E.I. 2004, c. 13, s. 1.

PRACTICE OF REAL ESTATE APPRAISAL. Includes the analysis and evaluation of real estate, or any interest therein, for the purpose of giving an opinion, estimate or recommendation on the value of such interest, and providing advice and counselling with respect to value. *Real Estate Appraisers Act*, S.N.S. 1998, c. 25, s. 2

PRACTICE OF RESPIRATORY THERAPY. The application of professional respiratory therapy knowledge, skills and judgement in the provision of diagnostic, assessment, and therapeutic modalities to assist in the management of cardio-respiratory and related disorders, in collaboration with physicians and other health care professionals, to achieve optimal respiratory health, wellness and functional performance and includes, but is not limited to, (i) conducting patient cardio-respiratory assessment, (ii) performing basic respiratory care therapy modalities, (iii) performing airway management techniques, (iv) optimizing pulmonary ventilation, (v) applying medical gas therapy, (vi) providing cardio-pulmonary resuscitation and stability, (vii) administering and monitoring prescribed pharmaceutical substances, (viii) procuring blood samples from various sites, (ix) performing pulmonary diagnostic testing, (x) performing cardiac diagnostic testing, (xi) performing hemodynamic monitoring, (xii) performing hyperbaric medicine therapy, (xiii) performing anaesthesia assistance within the scope of practice of the profession, (xiv) such delegated medical functions as are approved in accordance with the Medical Act, (xv) educating patients, families, colleagues and health care professionals concerning respiratory care, (xvi) such other aspects of respiratory therapy as may be prescribed in regulations approved by the Governor in Council, and research, administration and education relevant to subclauses (i) to (xvi). *Respiratory Therapists Act*, S.N.S. 2007, c. 13, s. 2.

PRACTISING. *v.* Carrying on a practice. It means the ongoing activity customarily and usually employed in the treatment of patients. It does not include the acquisition of a practice. One cannot be "practising" before one has a practice. *Sandilands v. Powell*, 2003 ABCA 162, 34 C.P.C. (5th) 81.

PRACTITIONER. See DRUGLESS ~; NURSE ~.

PRAECIPE. *n.* [L.] 1. A requisition. 2. "... [I]nstructions to the Registrar to issue the writ. In old times it was the name given to the writ itself; now it is nothing more than instructions to the officer... ." *Kimpton v. McKay* (1895), 4 B.C.R. 196 at 211 (C.A.), Drake J.A. (Walkem J.A. concurring). 3. A piece of paper on which one party to a proceeding specifies what document that party wishes to have prepared or issued and the particulars of the document.

PRAIRIE PROVINCES. The provinces of Manitoba, Saskatchewan and Alberta.

PRAYER. *n.* The conclusion of a petition to Parliament which expresses the petitioners' particular object. A. Fraser, W.A. Dawson & J. Holtby, eds., *Beauchesne's Rules and Forms of the House of Commons of Canada*, 6th ed. (Toronto: Carswell, 1989) at 278. See PETITION.

PRAYER FOR RELIEF. The portion of a statement of claim requesting damages or an order of the court. That portion of a statement of claim or petition or other procedure-initiating pleading which sets out the remedy or remedies the plaintiff or applicant is seeking.

P.R.B. *abbr.* Pension Review Board.

P.R.B.C. *abbr.* Procurement Review Board of Canada Decisions, 1990-?.

P.R.B.R. *abbr.* Pension Review Board Reports, 1972-1986.

PREAMBLE. *n.* A preface which states the reasons for and intended effects of legislation. A. Fraser, W.A. Dawson & J. Holtby, eds., *Beauchesne's Rules and Forms of the House of Commons of Canada*, 6th ed. (Toronto: Carswell, 1989) at 193.

PREAUDIENCE. *n.* The right of being heard before another. The usual order in court is the Attorney General, Queen's counsel, junior barristers in order of the year in which they were called.

PRECATORY CLAUSE. In a will, expresses the testator's hope or wish that another party will do something.

PRECATORY TRUST. Created when a gift or bequest to a charitable corporation is combined with a moral obligation to use the property in a certain way. The moral obligation is expressed in words of expectation, desire, or purpose.

PRECATORY WORDS. An expression in a will which indicates a wish, desire or request that something be done.

PRECEDENCE. *n.* The state or act of going first.

PRECEDENT. *n.* 1. A decision or judgment of a court of law which is cited as the authority for deciding a similar situation in the same manner, on the same principle or by analogy. 2. Decisions of the courts in the common law system are governed by precedent, the prior decisions of equal or higher courts. 3. Standard contracts or other agreements or documents used as examples for later documents. Law offices develop their own sets of precedents for various types of agreements or documents. Also available commercially. See STARE DECISIS.

PRECEDENT CONDITION. Something which must be performed or happen before an interest can vest or grow or an obligation be performed. See CONDITION PRECEDENT.

PRECEDING. *adj.* Coming before in time; happening or existing before.

PRECEPT. *n.* Direction, order.

PRECINCT. *n.* 1. The immediate environs of a court. 2. The district of a constable.

PRECIOUS METAL. Gold, palladium, platinum and silver and an alloy of any of those metals and any other metal and an alloy thereof that is designated by the regulations as a precious metal for the purposes of this Act. *Precious Metals Marking Act*, R.S.C. 1985, c. P-19, s. 2.

PRECIPE. See PRAECIPE.

PRECLUSIVE CLAUSE. 1. In the context of administrative law, a privative clause. 2. The existence of a privative or preclusive clause gives rise to a strong indication of review pursuant to the reasonableness standard. This conclusion is appropriate because a privative clause is evidence of Parliament or a legislature's intent that an administrative decision maker be given greater deference and that interference by reviewing courts be minimized. This does not mean, however, that the presence of a privative clause is determinative.... Judicial review is necessary to ensure that the privative clause is read in its appropriate statutory context and that administrative bodies do not exceed their jurisdiction. *Dunsmuir v. New Brunswick*, 2008 SCC 9, Bastarache and LeBel JJ. at para. 52.

PREDECESSOR. *n.* One person who preceded another.

PREDECESSOR IN TITLE. Refers to a person separate from and going before the applicant for a trade-mark.

PREDICTABLE. *adj.* The extent to which one can identify in advance a client's response on the basis of observation, experience or scientific reason. *Registered Nurses Act*, S.N.S. 2006, c. 21, s. 2.

PREDICTION. See SOUND ~.

PRE-DISPOSITION REPORT. *var.* **PREDISPOSITION REPORT.** A report on the personal and family history and present environment of a young person.

PREDOMINANT. See FEMALE ~.

PREDOMINATE. *adj.* Main.

PRE-EMPTIVE COSTS ORDER. In public interest cases, there is more reason for a court to avoid penalizing the pro bono litigant. It may even be appropriate for the court to grant costs, or at least disbursements, to an unsuccessful pro bono party. In England, for example, there is a limited practice of granting "pre-emptive costs orders" or "protective costs orders" ("PCO"s) in public interest cases where the applicant has no private interest in the case. In R. (on the application of Corner House Research) v. Secretary of State for Trade & Industry, [2005] 4 All E.R. 1 (Eng. C.A.), the English Court of Appeal explained these orders as follows at para. 6: The general purpose of a PCO is to allow a claimant of limited means access to the court in order to advance his case without the fear of an order for substantial costs being made against him, a fear which would inhibit him from continuing with the case at all. *1465778 Ontario Inc. v. 1122077 Ontario Ltd.* (2006), 82 O.R. (3d) 757 (C.A.).

PREEMPTIVE RIGHT. The right to purchase shares or other securities to be issued or subjected to rights or options to purchase, as such right is defined in this section. *Loan and Trust Companies Act*, S.N.B. 1987, c. L-11.2, s. 74.

PREFER. *v.* 1. To move for, to apply. 2. To place before the court for consideration and action. 3. " ... [T]o bear or carry before, or to give the object of the preference a place before some other... . conveys the idea of giving one creditor a position more advanced than the others, or precedence in relation to the payment of his debt... ." *Stephens v. McArthur* (1891), 19 S.C.R. 446 at 464-5, 6 Man. R. 496, Patterson J.

PREFER A CHARGE. 1. "... [D]one by reading to him, as it appears from the information and complaint laid against him upon which he was committed for trial (as well as such additional charges as may by leave of the Judge be preferred by the prosecuting officer under sec. 834 [of the Criminal Code, S.C. 1892, c. 29]), and when this is done the preferring of the charge is complete and constitutes the first part of the arraignment ..." *R. v. Goon* (1916), 25 C.C.C. 415 at 421, 28 D.L.R. 374, 10 W.W.R. 24, 22 B.C.R. 381 (C.A.), Martin J.A. (McPhillips J.A. concurring). 2. A charge is preferred when the charge sheet in respect of the charge is signed by the Director of Military Prosecutions, or an officer authorized by the Director of Military Prosecutions to do so, and referred to the Court Martial Administrator. *National Defence Act*, R.S.C. 1985, c. N-5, s. 165(2).

PREFERENCE. *n.* "... [O]f one creditor over another ... consists ... in the voluntary disposition by an insolvent of some portion of his property so as to confer greater benefit upon one or more of his creditors than upon others, when unable to pay all in full. To constitute a preference it must have been given by the insolvent of his own mere motion, and as a favour or bounty proceeding voluntarily from himself." *Molsons Bank v. Halter* (1890), 18 S.C.R. 88 at 102, Gwynne J. See FRAUDULENT ~; SEXUAL ~.

PREFERENCE SHARE. "... [S]hares which carry a preference may properly be denominated preference shares, though in certain respects they may be shorn of rights which belong to common shares ..." *Rubas v. Parkinson* (1929), 64 O.L.R. 87 at 93, 56 O.W.N. 133, [1929] 3 D.L.R. 558 (C.A.), Masten J.A. (Latchford C.J., Orde, Fisher and Riddell JJ.A. concurring). See CUMULATIVE ~.

PREFERRED. *adj.* 1. "... [A]n indictment based upon a committal for trial without the intervention of a grand jury is not 'preferred' against an accused until it is lodged with the trial court at the opening of the accused's trial, with a court ready to proceed with the trial." *R. v. Chabot* (1980), 18 C.R. (3d) 258 at 271, [1980] 2 S.C.R. 985, 22 C.R. (3d) 350, 34 N.R. 361, 55 C.C.C. (2d) 385, 117 D.L.R. (3d) 527, the court per Dickson J. 2. Having an advantage over another.

PREFERRED CREDITOR. A creditor whom the common law or legislation gives some advantage over other claimants. C.R.B. Dunlop, *Creditor-Debtor Law in Canada* (Toronto: Carswell, 1981) at 434.

PREFERRED DIVIDEND. A dividend attached to a class of shares other than common shares. A preferred dividend must be paid in full before dividends may be distributed to common or other classes of shares.

PREFERRED INDICTMENT. "... [L]odged by the Attorney-General against an accused ..." *R. v. Biernacki* (1962), 37 C.R. 226 at 235 (Que. S.P.), Trottier J.S.P. See PREFERRED.

PREFERRED SHARE. A share other than a common share. See PREFERENCE SHARE.

PREGNANCY. *n.* The state of having a child in utero. See FORCED ~; WRONGFUL ~.

PREGNANCY LEAVE. A leave of absence, from employment, beginning some time before delivery of a child and ending sometime after the delivery.

PREGNANT. See AFFIRMATIVE ~; NEGATIVE ~.

PRE-INCORPORATION CONTRACT. *var.* **PREINCORPORATION CONTRACT.** A contract entered into by a contractor in the name of or on behalf of a corporation before its incorporation.

PRE-JUDGMENT INTEREST. An award which compensates the plaintiff for the loss and use of the value of a monetary award until it is paid.

PREJUDICE. *n.* 1. An injury. 2. Being denied the right to which one is entitled. 3. Unjustly made to suffer. 4. Based on stereotypes formed with incomplete and inaccurate information. 5. [T]he words, "to the prejudice of the corporation" in s. 136(b) of the Regulations [Revised Regulations (1984) under the Insurance (Motor Vehicle) Act, B.C. Reg. 447/83], means "to the detriment of the legal interests of the corporation". *Thornber v. Insurance Corp. of British Columbia*, 2005 BCCA 45. See ACTUAL ~; CONFORMITY ~; JUROR ~; MORAL ~; WITHOUT ~.

PREJUDICED. *adj.* 1. "[In Mechanics' Lien Act, S.A. 1906, s. 21, s. 14] ... I think must be taken to mean 'unjustly made to suffer' ..." *Rendall, MacKay, Michie Ltd. v. Warren & Dyett* (1915), 8 W.W.R. 113 at 118, 21 D.L.R. 801 (Alta. T.D.), Beck J. 2. "... [S]uffered a pecuniary loss or damage ..." *Gray-Campbell v. Jamieson*, [1923] 3 D.L.R. 845 at 847, [1923] 3 W.W.R. 478, 17 Sask. L.R. 405 (K.B.), Maclean J.

PREJUDICIAL. *adj.* Causing harm. See UNFAIRLY ~.

PRELIMINARY ACT. A statement of particulars, accompanying a notice of civil claim, response to civil claim or counterclaim, in a sealed envelope, and bearing the style of proceeding that lists: (a) the names of the ships that came into collision and the names of their masters; (b) the time of the collision; (c) the place of the collision; (d) the direction and force of the wind; (e) the state of the weather; (f) the state and force of the tide or, if the collision occurred in non-tidal waters, of the current; (g) the course being steered and the speed through the water of the ship when the other ship was first seen or immediately before any measures were taken with reference to her presence, whichever was the earlier, and all subsequent alterations to the course or speed of the ship up to the time of the collision; (h) the lights, if any, carried by the ship; (i) the distance and bearing of the other ship if and when her echo was first observed by radar; (j) the distance, bearing and approximate heading of the other ship when it was first seen; (k) the lights, if any, of the other ship that were first seen; (l) the lights, if any, of the other ship other than those first seen that came into view before the collision; (m) the measures that were taken to avoid the collision and when they were taken; (n) the parts of each ship that first came into contact and the approximate angle, as illustrated by an appropriate sketch annexed, between the two ships at the moment of contact; (o) the sound signals that were given, if any, and when they were given; (p) the fault or default, if any, attributed to the other ship; (q) the sound signals, if any, that were heard from the other ship and when they were heard. A preliminary act must not be opened unless all parties consent or the court, on application of one of the parties, orders it to be opened. After a preliminary act has been opened, it forms part of the appropriate pleadings of the party. *Court Rules Act*, R.S.B.C. 1996, c. 80, *Supreme Court Civil Rules*, B.C. Reg. 168/2009, Rule 21-1.

PRELIMINARY HEARING. The hearing, held in accordance with procedure set out in Part XVIII of the Criminal Code, in which a justice determines whether there is sufficient evidence to commit an accused for trial.

PRELIMINARY INQUIRY. 1. The procedure conducted by a provincial court or equivalent judge to determine whether the Crown has sufficient evidence to warrant a full trial of the accused. The Crown's evidence against the accused is heard in part or in its entirety at the hearing. 2. There is substantial body of jurisprudence to the effect that the sole purpose of the preliminary inquiry provisions of the Criminal Code [R.S.C. 1985, c. C- 46] is to establish a charge screening device. The proceedings are oriented towards the determination of whether there is sufficient evidence to force the accused to stand trial . . . In this sense, the purpose of the preliminary inquiry is directed squarely at the accused who is subject of the proceedings. While the [accused] is a compellable witness to give evidence at a preliminary inquiry, it is unfair to use that process for the predominate purpose of compelling the [accused] to incriminate himself for the purpose of creating new evidence against him from another witness. *R. v. Z.(L.)* (2001), 54 O.R. (3d) 97 (C.A.). See PRELIMINARY HEARING.

PRELIMINARY QUESTION. 1. A question collateral to the merits or the heart of an inquiry but which is not the major question to be decided. S.A. DeSmith, *Judicial Review of Administrative Action*, 4th ed. by J.M. Evans (London: Stevens, 1980) at 114. 2. "The current tendency is ... to limit the concept of a 'preliminary question' as far as possible. Even those who favour retaining this concept limit it to questions concerning jurisdiction in the strict sense, of the initial power to proceed with an inquiry ... These questions are identified by the fact that they fall outside the limits of the enabling legislation itself, and are not usually within the area of expertise of the administrative tribunal ..." *Blanchard c. Control Data Canada Ltée* (1984), 14 Admin. L.R. 133 at 170, [1984] 2 S.C.R. 476, 84 C.L.L.C. 14,070, 55 N.R. 194, 14 D.L.R. (4th) 289, Lamer J. (McIntyre J. concurring).

PREMATURE. *adj.* In relation to an application to court, anticipated circumstances have not materialized or there are existing reasons to defer the application.

PREMIER. *n.* 1. A minister of the Crown holding the recognized position of first Minister. 2. The Prime Minister.

PREMISES. *n.* 1. "... . [A]lthough in popular language it is applied to buildings, in legal language means 'a subject or thing previously expressed'; ..." *Beacon Life Assurance & Fire Co. v. Gibb* (1862), 7 L.C. Jur. 57 at 61, 15 E.R. 630, 1 Moo. P.C. (N.S.) 73, 8 R.U.R.Q. 476, 13 Low. Can. R. 81 (P.C.), their Lordships per Lord Chelmsford. 2. "... [I]n the ordinary acceptation of the term, means the grounds immediately surrounding a house." *Martin v. Martin* (1904), 8 O.L.R. 462 at 466 (C.A.), Falconbridge C.J. See BOTTLE-YOUR-OWN ~; LICENSED ~.

PREMISES OF A DEED. 1. "It is customary to include in the premises [of a deed] the effectual date of the transfer; the names of the parties to the transfer of title as grantor and grantees, the recitals, the words of grant and the description of the property transferred." *Wheeler v. Wheeler (No. 2)* (1979), 25 N.B.R. (2d) 376 at 378 (C.A.), Limerick, Bugold and Ryan JJ.A. 2. "... [A]ll the foreparts of a deed before the habendum, and the office of this part of the deed is rightly to name the grantor and grantee, and to comprehend the certainty of the thing granted, and herein is sometimes (though improperly) set down, the estate ..." *Jamieson v. London & Canadian Loan & Agency Co.* (1896), 23 O.A.R. 602 at 619, Burton J.A.

PREMIUM. *n.* A single or periodical payment.

PREMIUM NOTE. An instrument given as consideration for insurance whereby the maker undertakes to pay such sum or sums as may be legally demanded by the insurer, but the aggregate of which sums does not exceed an amount specified in the instrument. *Insurance Act*, R.S.O. 1990, c. I.8, s.1.

PRENEED CEMETERY OR FUNERAL SERVICES CONTRACT. A future performance contract that provides for cemetery or funeral services for one or more persons who are alive at the time the contract is entered into. *Cremation, Interment and Funeral Services Act*, S.B.C. 2004, c. 35, s. 1.

PREPAID PURCHASE CARD. A card, written certificate or other voucher or device with a monetary value that is issued or sold to a person in exchange for the future supply of goods or services to a consumer, and includes a gift card and gift certificate, but does not include a cash card as defined in Part 6.1 [Payday Loans]. *Business Practices and Consumer Protection Act*, S.B.C. 2004, c. 2, s. 56.1.

PREPARATION. See MEAL ~; PHARMACEUTICAL ~; TRIAL ~.

PREPONDERANCE. *n.* "... [T]he most weight... ." *Snider v. Harper* (1922), 66 D.L.R. 149 at 158, [1922] 2 W.W.R. 417, 18 Alta. L.R. 82 (C.A.), Hyndman J.A. (Beck J.A. concurring).

PREREQUISITE. *n.* [T]here are two possible meanings to be given to the word "prerequisite". On the one hand, that word can be taken to mean that the payments must be made as a temporal condition precedent to the registration of the Plan of Subdivision.

On the other hand, the term "prerequisite" can be taken to mean that the obligation to make the payments must be undertaken by the respondent prior to registration of the Plan of Subdivision. *Juol Sands Inc. v. Grand Sheppard Building & Development Corp.*, 2009 ONCA 469.

PREROGATIVE. *n.* An exceptional power, privilege or pre-eminence which the law grants to the Crown. See ROYAL ~.

PREROGATIVE ORDER. An act by which a superior court prevents a subordinate tribunal from exceeding jurisdiction, from making errors of law on the face of its judgments and from denying natural justice. Examples are writs of habeas corpus or prohibition. Refers to some forms of the order resulting from the judicial review of a decision.

PREROGATIVE RIGHTS OF THE CROWN. The body of special common law rules which apply to Her Majesty.

PREROGATIVE WRIT. A writ of certiorari, habeas corpus, mandamus, prohibition or quo warranto. These writs are the precursors to current judicial review remedies which may be said to take these forms.

PRESCRIBE. *v.* 1. In a modern act of Parliament, to regulate the details after the general nature of the proceedings is indicated. This is done by regulations made pursuant to the Statutory Instruments Act, R.S.C. 1985, c. S-22. In the provinces this is done by regulation or equivalent. 2. Concerning a levy, includes the power to fix the amount payable and to impose the legal obligation to pay that amount. 3. To issue a prescription for a dental appliance, drug, vaccine, vision appliance or wearable hearing instrument. *The Regulated Health Professions Act*, S.M. 2009, c. 15, s. 3.

PRESCRIBED BY LAW. 1. In its decisions on the "prescribed by law" requirement in s. 1 [of the Charter], the Court has distinguished between challenges to government acts and challenges to "laws." This case raises the latter type of claim: the policies are being challenged, not the decision made by the transit authorities pursuant to the policies. In assessing whether the impugned policies satisfy the "prescribed by law" requirement, it must first be determined whether the policies come within the meaning of the word "law" in s. 1 of the Charter. To do this, it must be asked whether the government entity was authorized to enact the impugned policies and whether the policies are binding rules of general application. If so, the policies can be "law" for the purposes of s. 1. At the second stage of the enquiry, to find that the limit is "prescribed" by law, it must be determined whether the policies are sufficiently precise and accessible. ... [T]he Court does not require that the limit be prescribed by a "law" in the narrow sense of the term; it may be prescribed by a regulation or by the common law. Moreover, it is sufficient that the limit simply result by necessary implication from either the terms or the operating requirements of the "law." The Court has also implicitly recognized other forms of limits that were not originally identified in Therens as being prescribed by law, including limits contained in municipal by laws, provisions of a collective agree-ment involving a government entity and rules of a regulatory body. Such limits satisfy the "prescribed by law" requirement because, much like those resulting from regulations and other delegated legislation, their adoption is authorized by statute, they are binding rules of general application, and they are sufficiently accessible and precise to those to whom they apply. In these regards, they satisfy the concerns that underlie the "prescribed by law" requirement insofar as they preclude arbitrary state action and provide individuals and government entities with sufficient information on how they should conduct themselves. Where a policy is not administrative in nature, it may be "law" provided that it meets certain requirements. In order to be legislative in nature, the policy must establish a norm or standard of general application that has been enacted by a government entity pursuant to a rule-making authority. A rule making authority will exist if Parliament or a provincial legislature has delegated power to the government entity for the specific purpose of enacting binding rules of general application which establish the rights and obligations of the individuals to whom they apply. For the purposes of s. 1 of the Charter, these rules need not take the form of statutory instruments. So long as the enabling legislation allows the entity to adopt binding rules, and so long as the rules establish rights and obligations of general rather than specific application and are sufficiently accessible and precise, they will qualify as "law" which prescribes a limit on a Charter right. Thus, where a government policy is authorized by statute and sets out a general norm or standard that is meant to be binding and is sufficiently accessible and precise, the policy is legislative in nature and constitutes a limit that is "prescribed by law." *Greater Vancouver Transportation Authority v. Canadian Federation of Students—British Columbia Component*, 2009 SCC 31, [2009] 2 S.C.R. 295, Deschamps J. for the majority. 2. "The limit will be prescribed by law within the meaning of s. 1 [of the Charter] if it is expressly provided for by statute or regulation, or results by necessary implication from the terms of a statute or regulation or from its operating requirements. The limit may also result from the application of a common law rule." The requirement that the limit be prescribed by law is chiefly concerned with the distinction between a limit imposed by law and one that is arbitrary. The limit will be prescribed by law within the meaning of s. 1 if it is expressly provided for by statute or regulation, or results by necessary implication from the terms of a statute or regulation or from its operating requirements. *R. v. Therens*, [1985] 1 S.C.R. 613 at 645, [1985] 4 W.W.R. 286, 32 M.V.R. 153, 45 C.R. (3d) 97, 38 Alta. L.R. (2d) 99, 18 C.C.C. (3d) 481, 13 C.R.R. 193, 40 Sask. R. 122, 18 D.L.R. (4th) 655, 59 N.R. 122, Le Dain J.

PRESCRIPTION. *n.* 1. A common law doctrine extended by statute whereby profits and easements can be acquired over others' land. It is fundamentally a rule of evidence which presumes that the owner granted the land so that title is derived from her or him. R. Megarry & H.W.R. Wade, *The Law of Real Property*, 5th ed. (London: Stevens, 1984) at 1030. 2. A means of acquiring or of being released by the lapse of time and according to the conditions fixed by law: prescription is called acquisitive in the first case and extinctive in the second. *Civil Code*, S.Q. 1991, c. 64, a. 2875. 3. A direction from a person authorized to prescribe drugs within the scope of his or her practice of a health discipline directing the dispensing of a drug or mixture of drugs for a specified person. *Drug Interchangeability and Dispensing Fee Act*, R.S.O. 1990, c. P.23, s. 1. 4. The direction of a medical practitioner directing a physiotherapist to treat a named person. 5. A written and dated authorization signed by a dentist or a qualified medical practitioner, directing that a service be performed that a dental laboratory technician may be licensed to perform. 6. In respect of a controlled drug, an authorization given by a practitioner that a stated amount of the controlled drug be dispensed for the person named therein. *Food and Drugs Act*, R.S.C. 1985, c. F-27, s. 38. 7. In respect of a narcotic, an authorization given by a practitioner that a stated amount of the narcotic be dispensed for the person named therein. *Narcotic Control Act*, R.S.C. 1985, c. N-1, s. 2. 8. " ... [D]elegated legislation containing rules that, along with the rules in the statute, must be applied in the computation of 'value for duty' [in s. 47(1)(a) of the Customs Act, R.S.C. 1970, c. C-40] or 'normal value' [in s. 11 of the Anti-Dumping Act, R.S.C. 1970, c. A-15]." *Canada (Tariff Board) v. Danmour Shoe Co.* (1974), (*sub nom. Danmour Shoes Co., Re*) 1 F.C. 22 at 24-5, 1 N.R. 422 (C.A.), Jackett, Pratte and Hyde JJ.A. 9. The prohibition of something. See OPTICAL ~.

PRESCRIPTIVE EASEMENT. To establish the easement the claimant must demonstrate a use and enjoyment of the right of way under a continuous, uninterrupted, open and peaceful claim of right for the prescribed period of time immediately prior to the commencement of the action making claim to the easement.

PRESENT. *v.* To offer; to tender.

PRESENT CONSIDERATION. A consideration exchanged at time of contract formation.

PRE-SENTENCE REPORT. 1. A report prepared before sentencing containing information concerning the offender's history to be used in assisting the court in passing sentence. 2. A report on the personal and family history and present environment of a young person. *Youth Criminal Justice Act*, S.C. 2002, c. 1, s. 2.

PRESENTMENT. *n.* 1. Subject to this Act, a bill must be duly presented for payment. If a bill is not duly presented for payment, the drawer and endorsers are discharged. Where the holder of a bill presents it for payment, he shall exhibit the bill to the person from whom he demands payment. *Bills of Exchange Act*, R.S.C. 1985, c. B-4, s. 84. 2. A species of report given by a jury. 3. "The public return of the bill [of indictment] in open court was termed the 'presentment' of the indictment." *R. v. Chabot* (1980), 18 C.R. (3d) 258 at 265, [1980] 2 S.C.R. 985, 22 C.R. (3d) 350, 34 N.R. 361, 55 C.C.C. (2d) 385, 117 D.L.R. (3d) 527, the court per Dickson J.

PRESENTS. *n.* In a deed, the term which refers to the deed itself.

PRESERVATION. *n.* The duty of a secured party to hold and preserve property that has been pledged. In the case of intangible property, the secured party must preserve the rights against parties liable secondarily on the instrument.

PRESIDENT. *n.* 1. A person placed in authority over other people; a person in charge of others. 2. One who exercises chief executive functions. 3. A Chief Justice or Chief Judge.

PRESS. See FREEDOM OF THE ~.

PRESSURE TACTIC. Includes (a) a cessation of work or a refusal to work or to continue to work by artists or artists' associations in combination, in concert or in accordance with a common understanding, and a slowdown of work or other concerted activity by artists or artists' associations respecting the provision of their services, done to compel a producer to agree to terms or conditions of engagement, or (b) the closing of a place of work, a suspension of production or a refusal to continue the engagement of one or more artists by a producer, done to compel artists, or to assist another producer to compel artists, to agree to terms or conditions of engagement. *Status of the Artist Act*, S.C. 1992, c. 33, s. 5.

PRESUME. *v.* To assume to be true; to take for granted.

PRESUMPTION. *n.* 1. An inference established by law or the court from a known fact to an unknown fact. *Civil Code*, S.Q. 1991, c. 64, a. 2846. 2. Presumptions can be classified into two general categories: presumptions without basic facts and presumptions with basic facts. A presumption without a basic fact is simply a conclusion which is to be drawn until the contrary is proved. A presumption with a basic fact entails a conclusion to be drawn upon proof of the basic fact. Basic fact presumptions can be further categorized into permissive and mandatory presumptions. A permissive presumption leaves it optional as to whether the inference of the presumed fact is drawn following proof of the basic fact. A mandatory presumption requires that the inference be made. Presumptions may also be either rebuttable or irrebuttable. If a presumption is rebuttable, there are three potential ways the presumed fact can be rebutted. First, the accused may be required merely to raise a reasonable doubt as to its existence. Secondly, the accused may have an evidentiary burden to adduce sufficient evidence to bring into question the truth of the presumed fact. Thirdly, the accused may have a legal or persuasive burden to prove on a balance of probabilities the non-existence of the presumed fact. Finally, presumptions are often referred to as either presumptions of law or presumptions of fact. The latter entail "frequently recurring examples of circumstantial evidence", while the former involve actual legal rules. *R. v. Oakes*, [1986] 1 S.C.R. 103. 3. " ... [A]n evidentiary technique by which the elements of a cause of action may be established; it cannot itself stand as an element of a cause of action." *Machtinger v. HOJ Industries* (1992), 40 C.C.E.L. 1 at 20, 7 O.R. (3d) 480n, 92 C.L.L.C. 14,022, 91 D.L.R. (4th)

491, [1992] 1 S.C.R. 986, 136 N.R. 40, 53 O.A.C. 200, McLachlin J. 4. " ... [E[]ffect is to impose a duty on the party against whom they operate to adduce some evidence ..." *Powell v. Cockburn* (1976), 22 R.F.L. 155 at 161, [1977] 2 S.C.R. 218, 8 N.R. 215, 68 D.L.R. (3d) 700, Dickson J. (Laskin C.J., Spence and Beetz JJ. concurring). See COMPELLING ~; CONCLUSIVE ~; LEGAL ~; MANDATORY ~; PERMISSIVE ~.

PRESUMPTION AGAINST ABSURDITY. The interpretation which leads to an unreasonable or absurd result should be rejected where there are two possible interpretations of a provision.

PRESUMPTION AGAINST EXPROPRIA-TION. The legislature or Parliament is presumed not to intend to take away private property rights unless the intention is clearly indicated.

PRESUMPTION AGAINST IMPLIED RE-PEAL. There is a presumption against the implied repeal of one statute by another. An interpretation which reconciles the two provisions is preferred.

PRESUMPTION AGAINST INTERNAL CON-FLICT. The court presumes that legislative provisions in a statute are intended to work together as a whole.

PRESUMTPION AGAINST INTESTACY. The court prefers an interpretation of a will which will avoid intestacy.

PRESUMPTION AGAINST TAUTOLOGY. It is presumed that the legislature avoids superfluous or meaningless words.

PRESUMPTION OF ACCURACY. The presumption of accuracy permits the Crown to prove the accused's blood alcohol level at the time the breathalyzer test was administered without calling a qualified breathalyzer technician. According to this presumption, the lowest result of the analyzed samples reported in the certificate provided by the qualified breathalyzer technician is presumed to accurately reflect the blood alcohol level of the accused at the time the test was administered, absent evidence to the contrary. This presumption is the product of s. 258(1)(g) of the [Criminal Code, R.S.C. 1985, c. C-46] which makes the certificate admissible and s. 25(1) of the Interpretation Act, [R.S.C. 1985, c. I-21] which makes the certificate presumptive proof of those facts absent evidence to the contrary. *R. v. Suttie* (2004), 189 O.A.C. 148.

PRESUMPTION OF ADVANCEMENT. An exception to ordinary equitable rules relating to resulting trusts, in which property paid for by a husband and conveyed into the name of his wife or child is presumed to be a gift by the husband. A. Bissett-Johnson & W.M. Holland, eds., *Matrimonial Property Law in Canada* (Toronto: Carswell, 1980) at I-13.

PRESUMPTION OF COHERENCE. 1. A presumption against internal conflict within a statute. 2. In determining the legislator's intention there is a presumption of coherence between related statutes.

Provisions are only deemed inconsistent where they cannot stand together. The co-existence of a short limitation period and a rule for its postponement is not an absurd result. *Murphy v. Welsh*, 1993 CarswellOnt 428, 18 C.P.C. (3d) 137, 47 M.V.R. (2d) 1, 156 N.R. 263, 65 O.A.C. 103, [1993] 2 S.C.R. 1069, 106 D.L.R. (4th) 404, 18 C.C.L.T. (2d) 101, Major J. for the court. See PRESUMPTION OF LEG-ISLATIVE COHERENCE.

PRESUMPTION OF CONSISTENT EXPRES-SION. Words within the same statute have the same meaning and different words have different meanings.

PRESUMPTION OF CONSTITUTIONALITY. An impugned statute should be construed, if possible, in a way which makes it conform to the Constitution.

PRESUMPTION OF CONSTITUTIONAL VA-LIDITY. 1. An impugned statute should be construed, if possible, in a way which makes it conform to the Constitution. 2. The onus on establishing that legislation contravenes the Charter is on the person who challenges the statute.

PRESUMPTION OF CONTINUANCE. An evidentiary inference that when an issue exists, evidence of action by a particular person at a previous time is some evidence of action by that same person at a later time.

PRESUMPTION OF FITNESS. An accused is presumed fit to stand trial unless the court is satisfied on the balance of probabilities that the accused is unfit to stand trial. *Criminal Code*, R.S.C. 1985, c. C-46, s. 672.22.

PRESUMPTION OF IDENTITY. Section 258(1)(c)(ii) [of the Criminal Code, R.S.C. 1985, c. C-46] provides that where the breath samples were taken "as soon as practicable after the time when the offence was alleged to have been committed and, in the case of the first sample, not later than two hours after that time, with an interval of at least fifteen minutes between the times when the samples were taken" then, provided certain other conditions are fulfilled, the prosecution may rely upon the presumption of identity. This presumption simply deems the results of the breath tests to be proof of the accused's blood alcohol level at the time of the offence in the absence of evidence to the contrary. *R. v. Vander-bruggen* (2006), 208 O.A.C. 379.

PRESUMPTION OF IMPLIED EXCLUSION. When legislation expresses one thing, it excludes another. Failure to mention something indicates an intention to exclude it. See IMPLIED EXCLUSION RULE.

PRESUMPTION OF INNOCENCE. The provision in section 11(d) of the Charter of Rights that any person charged with an offence has the right to be presumed innocent until proven guilty according to law in a fair and public hearing by an independent and impartial tribunal. P.W. Hogg, *Constitutional Law of Canada*, 3d ed. (Toronto: Carswell, 1992) at 1100. See RIGHT TO BE PRESUMED INNO-CENT.

PRESUMPTION OF KNOWLEDGE AND COMPETENCE. The legislature is presumed to know the existing statutory and common law and to understand the functioning of the courts and tribunals.

PRESUMPTION OF LAW. 1. "[Their] ... influence on the resolution of the issue is limited to the burden of proof. Text writers and courts are divided on whether presumptions of law affect only the evidential burden or both the evidential and the legal burden. This Court, in Circle Film Enterprises Inc. v. Canadian Broadcasting Corp., [1959] S.C.R. 602 ... adopted the former or evidentiary burden view ..." *Goodman Estate v. Geffen* (1991), 42 E.T.R. 97 at 136, [1991] 5 W.W.R. 389, 80 Alta. L.R. (2d) 293, 125 A.R. 81, 14 W.A.C. 81, 81 D.L.R. (4th) 211, [1991] 2 S.C.R. 353, Sopinka J. 2. "... [I]nvolves actual legal rules." *R. v. Oakes* (1986), 24 C.C.C. (3d) 321 at 331, [1986] 1 S.C.R. 103, 53 O.R. (2d) 719n, 50 C.R. (3d) 1, 14 O.A.C. 335, 19 C.R.R. 308, 26 D.L.R. (4th) 200, 65 N.R. 87, Dickson C.J.C. (Chouinard, Lamer, Wilson and Le Dain JJ. concurring). See REBUTTABLE ~.

PRESUMPTION OF LEGISLATIVE COHERENCE. 1. When a legislature enacts two statutes and the provisions are in conflict in that compliance with one necessitates violation of the other, the courts will attempt to interpret the statutes to resolve this conflict. 2. A presumption against internal conflict within a statute.

PRESUMPTION OF LEGITIMACY. A child borne of a married woman is presumed to be a child of that marriage.

PRESUMPTION OF LINGUISTIC COMPETENCE. There is a presumption that the legislature knew what it intended and knew the language of enactment and expressed its meaning accurately.

PRESUMPTION OF REGULARITY. The presumption of regularity is a reflection of the Latin maxim: omnia praesumuntur rite et solemniter esse acta donec probetur in contrarium (everything is presumed to be rightly and duly performed until the contrary is shown). As Watt J. noted in R. v. Kapoor reflex, (1989), 52 C.C.C. (3d) 41 at 68 (Ont. H.C.), it "has especial application in the case of persons who discharge a public or statutory duty." Various authorities have drawn on the treatise of the great American authority on evidence, Professor John Henry Wigmore, in dealing with the underpinnings of the doctrine. In Wigmore A Treatise on the Anglo-American System of Evidence in Trials at Common Law on Evidence, 3rd ed. (1940), vol. IX, p. 488, that learned author proposes several conditions for the application of the omnia praesumuntur rule: . . . first, that the matter is more or less in the past, and incapable of easily procured evidence; secondly, that it involves a mere formality, or detail of required procedure, in the routine of a litigation or of a public officer's action; next, that it involves to some extent the security of apparently vested rights, so that the presumption will serve to prevent an unwholesome uncertainty; and finally, that the circumstances of the particular case add some element of probability. ...

This Court approved that statement in R. v. McNamara, (1982), 66 C.C.C. (2d) 24 at 28-29, leave to appeal to S.C.C. refused, (1982) 66 C.C.C. (2d) 24n. It also approved the following additional admonition by Prowse J.A. in Scott at 114: I am in respectful agreement with the observation of Parker L.C.J. in Scott v. Baker (1968), 52 Cr. App. R. 566 at p. 571, that very great care must be taken in applying the presumption of regularity in criminal proceedings. To purport to establish the guilt of an accused solely or largely by reliance on such a presumption would amount to a fundamental contradiction of the principles upon which our system of criminal law is based. That is not to say, however, that the presumption has no application. *R. v. Molina*, 2008 ONCA 212.

PRESUMPTION OF RESULTING TRUST. "... [A] presumption of a (resulting) trust arises 'where a person transfers his property into another's name gratuitously', but that presumption is rebuttable by the transferee: Goodfriend v. Goodfriend, [1972] S.C.R. 640." *Fediuk v. Gluck* (1990), 26 R.F.L. (3d) 454 at 459 (Man. Q.B.), Wright J.

PRESUMPTION OF SURVIVORSHIP. Where two or more people die in the same accident it is presumed that the younger survived.

PRESUMPTIONS OF FACT. "... A natural inference which has become standardized and which may be drawn by the tribunal of fact, although it is not obliged to draw the inference." *R. v. Boyle* (1983), 5 C.C.C. (3d) 193 at 205, 41 O.R. (2d) 713, 35 C.R. (3d) 34, 148 D.L.R. (3d) 449, 5 C.R.R. 218 (C.A.), the court per Martin J.A.

PRESUMPTIVE. See HEIR ~.

PRESUMPTIVE EVIDENCE. Evidence which implies the large probability if not the certainty that the facts and the inference are related. P.K. McWilliams, *Canadian Criminal Evidence*, 3rd ed. (Aurora: Canada Law Book, 1988) at 1-12 and 1-13. See now CIRCUMSTANTIAL EVIDENCE.

PRESUMPTIVE OFFENCE. (a) An offence committed, or alleged to have been committed, by a young person who has attained the age of fourteen years, or, in a province where the lieutenant governor in council has fixed an age greater than fourteen years under section 61, the age so fixed, under one of the following provisions of the Criminal Code: (i) section 231 or 235 (first degree murder or second degree murder within the meaning of section 231), (ii) section 239 (attempt to commit murder), (iii) section 232, 234 or 236 (manslaughter), or (iv) section 273 (aggravated sexual assault); or (b) a serious violent offence for which an adult is liable to imprisonment for a term of more than two years committed, or alleged to have been committed, by a young person after the coming into force of section 62 (adult sentence) and after the young person has attained the age of fourteen years, or, in a province where the lieutenant governor in council has fixed an age greater than fourteen years under section 61, the age so fixed, if at the time of the commission or alleged commission of the offence at least two judicial determinations have been made under subsection 42(9), at different proceedings, that the young person has committed a serious violent offence. *Youth Criminal Justice Act*, S.C. 2002, c. 1, s. 2.

PRETENCE. *n.* Pretext; excuse; show of intention. See FALSE ~.

PRE-TRIAL CONFERENCE. A meeting to consider possibly settling any or all of the issues in a proceeding, simplifying the issues, possibly obtaining admissions which would facilitate the hearing, liability or any other matter that might assist in a just, efficient and inexpensive disposition of that proceeding.

PREVENTIVE DETENTION. Detention in a penitentiary for an indeterminate period. *Criminal Code*, R.S.C. 1970, c. C-34, s. 687.

PRICE. *n.* 1. Consideration in the form of money. 2. Includes rate or charge for any service. See CASH ~; CONSUMER ~ INDEX; FIXED ~ CONTRACT; MARKET ~; OPTION ~; PAY-OUT ~; PURCHASE ~; SALE ~; SETTLEMENT ~; STIPULATED ~ CONTRACT; STRIKING ~; SUBSCRIPTION ~; UNIT ~ CONTRACT.

PRICE. *abbr.* Price's Mining Commissioner's Cases (Ontario), 1906-1910.

PRICE CLUB. A large open warehouse offering its customers, who are members paying a membership fee, a wide variety of products at retail and at wholesale.

PRICE MAINTENANCE AGREEMENT. An agreement between a manufacturer and a retailer in which the retailer contracts not to sell the manufacturer's goods at less than a specified price.

PRIMA FACIE. [L.] At first glance; on the surface.

PRIMA FACIE CASE. "... [I]n this context [adverse effect discrimination] is one which covers the allegations made and which, if they are believed, is complete and sufficient to justify a verdict in the complainant's favour in the absence of an answer from the respondent-employer." *Ontario (Human Rights Commission) v. Simpsons-Sears Ltd.* (1985), 7 C.R.H.H. D/3102 at D/3108, 9 C.C.E.L. 185, 17 Admin. L.R. 89, 86 C.L.L.C. 17,002, 64 N.R. 161, 23 D.L.R. (4th) 321, 12 O.A.C. 241, [1985] 2 S.C.R. 536, the court per McIntyre J.

PRIMA FACIE DISCRIMINATION. [In relation to family status,] [i]n the usual case where there is no bad faith on the part of the employer and no governing provision in the applicable collective agreement or employment contract, it seems to me that a prima facie case of discrimination is made out when a change in a term or condition of employment imposed by an employer results in a serious interference with a substantial parental or other family duty or obligation of the employee. *Campbell River & North Island Transition Society v. H.S.A.B.*, 2004 BCCA 260.

PRIMA FACIE DUTY OF CARE. A duty of care arises, prima facie, when a loss is caused as a foreseeable consequence of a defendant's act or omission. This is subject to restrictions or exclusions based on considerations of policy, fairness, or reasonableness in the circumstances of the case.

PRIMA FACIE EVIDENCE. "... [H]as two meanings as described by authors such as Dean Wigmore and Sir Rupert Cross, namely: 1. Where the Crown evidence is so strong that no reasonable man would fail to convict. (This is the mandatory sense in which the term is used and compels conviction if there is no evidence to displace the prima facie case). 2. Where the Crown evidence is sufficiently strong to entitle a reasonable man to find the accused guilty although as a matter of common sense he is not obliged to do so. (This is the permissive and usual sense in which the term is used)... ." *R. v. Pye* (1984), 11 C.C.C. (3d) 64 at 68, 38 C.R. (3d) 375, 62 N.S.R. (2d) 10, 136 A.P.R. 10, 7 D.L.R. (4th) 275 (C.A.), the court per Macdonald J.A.

PRIMARY. *adj.* 1. Original or foundational. 2. Major importance.

PRIMARY BURDEN. "The burden of establishing a case ..." *R. v. Schwartz* (1988), 45 C.C.C. (3d) 97 at 115, [1989] 1 W.W.R. 289, 66 C.R. (3d) 251, 88 N.R. 90, [1988] 2 S.C.R. 443, 56 Man. R. (2d) 92, 55 D.L.R. (4th) 1, Dickson C.J.C. (dissenting).

PRIMARY EVIDENCE. The best evidence, in contrast to secondary evidence. For example the original of a document is preferred to a copy. The witness' own recollection is preferred to another's evidence about what he told the other person he remembered.

PRIMARY FACTS. "... [F]acts which are observed by witnesses and proved by oral testimony or facts proved by the production of a thing itself, such as original documents. Their determination is essentially a question of fact for the tribunal of fact, and the only question of law that can arise on them is whether there was any evidence to support the finding." *British Launderers' Research Association v. Hendon Rating Authority*, [1949] 1 K.B. 462 at 471 (U.K. C.A.), Denning L.J.

PRIMARY HEALTH CARE. The first level of a client's care in the health system requiring a strong foundation of community based services that enables clients to maintain and strengthen their health based on a population health model, and includes health promotion and disease prevention, education, acute episodic care, advocacy, support and treatment for illness and injury, continuing care of chronic conditions, rehabilitation and palliation. *Registered Nurses Act*; S.N.S. 2006, c. 21, s. 2.

PRIMARY PLEADING. The initial pleading in a civil proceeding. *B.C. Supreme Court Rules*.

PRIMARY PROCESSING. The production of softwood lumber products from softwood sawlogs. *Softwood Lumber Products Export Charge Act, 2006*, S.C. 2006, c. 13, s. 2.

PRIME MINISTER. The minister with power to select, promote, demote or dismiss other ministers, who is personally responsible for advising the Governor General about when Parliament should be dissolved for an election and when the elected parliament should be called into session and who enjoys special authority because she or he was selected as the leader of a political party which was victorious in the previous election. See PREMIER.

PRIME RATE. The lowest rate of interest quoted by a bank to its most credit-worthy borrowers for prime business loans.

PRIME TIME. In the case of a radio station, means the time between the hours of 6 a.m. and 9 a.m., noon and 2 p.m. and 4 p.m. and 7 p.m., and, in the case of a television station, means the hours between 6 p.m. and midnight. *Canada Elections Act*, S.C. 2000, c. 9, s. 319.

PRIMOGENITURE. *n.* 1. Seniority; the status of being born first. 2. A rule of inheritance by which the oldest of two or more males of the same degree succeeds to an ancestor's land, excluding all the others.

PRINCIPAL. *n.* 1. A chief; a head. 2. A capital amount of money loaned at interest. 3. The lawyer to whom a law student is articled. See DISCLOSED ~; NAMED ~; UNDISCLOSED ~.

PRINCIPALLY. *adv.* Chiefly, for the most part.

PRINCIPAL RESIDENCE. Residential premises that constitute a person's normal or permanent place of residence and to which, when that person is absent, that person has the intention of returning.

PRINCIPLE. *n.* Something which, unlike a rule, does not set out legal consequences which follow automatically if certain conditions are met. S.A. Cohen, *Due Process of Law* (Toronto: Carswell, 1977) at 203. See ASSOCIATED MEANING ~; ERROR IN ~; FINALITY ~; GENERALLY ACCEPTED ACCOUNTING ~S; GLADUE ~S; HARM ~; JUMP ~; KIENAPPLE ~; KNOCK AND ANNOUNCE ~; MERIT ~; PERIPHERAL CLAIMING ~; REALIZATION ~; SEDONA CANADA ~S; TOTALITY ~; ULTRA PETITA ~; WAGG ~S AND PROCEDURE.

PRINCIPLE AGAINST SELF-INCRIMINATION. 1. It is now well-established that there exists, in Canadian law, a principle against self-incrimination that is a principle of fundamental justice under s. 7 of the [Canadian Charter of Rights and Freedoms]. The principle against self-incrimination is that an accused is not required to respond to an allegation of wrongdoing made by the state until the state has succeeded in making out a prima facie case against him or her. *R. v. White*, 1999 CarswellBC 1224, 63 C.R.R. (2d) 1, 240 N.R. 1, 24 C.R. (5th) 201, 135 C.C.C. (3d) 257, 174 D.L.R. (4th) 111, 42 M.V.R. (3d) 161, 123 B.C.A.C. 161, 201 W.A.C. 161, [1999] 2 S.C.R. 417, [1999] 2 S.C.R. 417. 2. "It should therefore be made clear here that I distinguish between the principle against self-incrimination and the privilege against self-incrimination ... The privilege is the narrow traditional common law rule relating only to testimonial evidence at trial. Much of the confusion around such issues as silence, non-compellability, and self-incrimination has, I believe, arisen as a result of the failure to distinguish between these two levels of protection against self-incrimination. The principle is a general organizing principle of criminal law from which particular rules can be derived (for example, rules about non-compellability of the accused and admissibility of confessions). The

privilege is merely one rule that has been derived from the principle. When the protection against self-incrimination is limited to the privilege against self-incrimination, then the underlying rationale for the various common law rules protecting against self-incrimination is lost and principled decisions about particular cases as they arise become impossible." (2) "The principle against self-incrimination, in its broadest form, can be expressed in the following manner: the individual is sovereign and proper rules of battle between government and individual require that the individual not be conscripted by his opponent to defeat himself. Or, put another way, nemo tenetur seipsum accusare and nemo tenetur seipsum prodere and nemo tenetur armare adversarium contra se—no one shall be required to accuse or betray or arm his enemy against himself." *R. v. Jones*, 1994 CarswellBC 580, 30 C.R. (4th) 1, 166 N.R. 321, 43 B.C.A.C. 241, 69 W.A.C. 241, 89 C.C.C. (3d) 353, [1994] 2 S.C.R. 229, 114 D.L.R. (4th) 645, 21 C.R.R. (2d) 286, Lamer C.J.C.

PRINCIPLED APPROACH TO HEARSAY. The Supreme Court of Canada in R. v. Starr [(2000), 147 C.C.C. (3d) 449 (S.C.C.)] confirmed the process it had begun in R. v. Khan, [[1990] 2 S.C.R. 531] and R. v. Smith [(1992), 75 C.C.C. (3d) 257 (S.C.C.)]. Described as the principled approach to hearsay, the Supreme Court of Canada identified the twin requirements of necessity and reliability as the touchstones for the admission of hearsay evidence. Any evidence which is not the best evidence but which is necessary is potentially admissible if it is reliable. Necessity in this context means the proposed evidence will advance the inquiry and there is no better existing source for the evidence. Reliability, in relation to admissibility, means that the evidence has trustworthiness. Additionally, where there exists a traditional exception to the rule against the admission of hearsay evidence, the evidence will be presumptively admissible unless it fails to meet the required necessity or lacks sufficient threshold reliability. The Supreme Court of Canada refined the principled approach in R. v. Khelawon, [[2006] S.C.J. No. 57]. In determining threshold reliability, it is now appropriate to look at the circumstances surrounding the hearsay event. *Decore v. Decore*, 2009 ABQB 440.

PRINCIPLE OF EXHAUSTIVENESS. The principle of exhaustiveness, an essential characteristic of the federal distribution of powers, ensures that the whole of legislative power, whether exercised or merely potential, is distributed as between Parliament and the legislatures: Attorney-General for Ontario v. Attorney-General for Canada, [1912] A.C. 571 (P.C.) at p. 581; and Attorney-General for Canada v. Attorney-General for Ontario, [1937] A.C. 326 (P.C.). In essence, there is no topic that cannot be legislated upon, though the particulars of such legislation may be limited by, for instance, the Charter. A jurisdictional challenge in respect of any law is therefore limited to determining to which head of power the law relates. Legislative competence over same-sex marriage must be vested in either Parliament or the legislatures. Neither s. 92(12) nor s. 92(13) can accommodate this matter. Given that a legislative void is precluded, s. 91(26) most aptly subsumes it. *Ref-*

erence re Same-Sex Marriage, 2004 SCC 79, [2004] 3 S.C.R. 698.

PRINCIPLE OF ORDER AND FAIRNESS. The principle of order and fairness relates to the analysis involved in exercising jurisdiction over an action. The purpose of the principle is to ensure that the court is not arbitrarily taking jurisdiction over a matter to which there is no real and substantial connection. *British Columbia v. Imperial Tobacco Canada Ltd.*, 2006 BCCA 398, Rowles J.A. (Hall and Smith JJ.A. concurring).

PRINCIPLES OF FUNDAMENTAL JUSTICE. 1. A "principle of fundamental justice" must fulfill three criteria: R. v. Malmo-Levine, [2003] 3 S.C.R. 571, 2003 SCC 74, at para. 113. First, it must be a legal principle. This serves two purposes. First, it "provides meaningful content for the s. 7 guarantee"; second, it avoids the "adjudication of policy matters": Re B.C. Motor Vehicle Act, [1985] 2 S.C.R. 486, at p. 503. Second, there must be sufficient consensus that the alleged principle is "vital or fundamental to our societal notion of justice": Rodriguez v. British Columbia (Attorney General), [1993] 3 S.C.R. 519, at p. 590. The principles of fundamental justice are the shared assumptions upon which our system of justice is grounded. They find their meaning in the cases and traditions that have long detailed the basic norms for how the state deals with its citizens. Society views them as essential to the administration of justice. Third, the alleged principle must be capable of being identified with precision and applied to situations in a manner that yields predictable results. Examples of principles of fundamental justice that meet all three requirements include the need for a guilty mind and for reasonably clear laws. *Canadian Foundation for Children, Youth and the Law v. Canada (Attorney General)*, 2004 SCC 4, [2004] 1 S.C.R. 76, para. 8., McLachlin C.J. for the majority. 2. "... [R]eflect the fundamental tenets on which our legal system is based. Those tenets include, but are not limited to, the rules of natural justice and the duty to act fairly that have been developed over the years in the administrative law context... . included in these fundamental principles is the concept of a procedurally fair hearing before an impartial decision-maker... ." *Pearlman v. Law Society (Manitoba)* (1991), 6 C.R.R. (2d) 259 at 268, [1991] 6 W.W.R. 289, 2 Admin. L.R. (2d) 185, 84 D.L.R. (4th) 105, 130 N.R. 121, 75 Man. R. (2d) 81, 6 W.A.C. 81, [1991] 2 S.C.R. 869, the court per Iacobucci J. 3. Include the right to make full answer in defence, procedural fairness, right to a fair trial, accused's right to an interpreter in a trial, right of defence to control his own defence in a criminal trial, and the privilege against self incrimination. 4. "... [P]rinciples that govern the justice system. They determine the means by which one may be brought before or within the justice system, and govern how one may be brought within the system and, thereafter, the conduct of judges and other actors once the individual is brought within it. Therefore, the restrictions on liberty and security of the person that s. 7 [of the Charter] is concerned with are those that occur as a result of an individual's interaction with the justice system, and its administration... ." *Reference re ss. 193 and 195(1)(c) of the*

Criminal Code (Canada) (1990), 56 C.C.C. (3d) 65 at 102, 77 C.R. (3d) 1, [1990] 1 S.C.R. 1123, [1990] 4 W.W.R. 481, 109 N.R. 81, 68 Man. R. (2d) 1, 48 C.R.R. 1 , Lamer J. 5. " ... Have both a substantive and a procedural component ..." *R. v. Morgentaler* (1988), 37 C.C.C. (3d) 449 at 471, 82 N.R. 1, [1988] 1 S.C.R. 30, 63 O.R. (2d) 281n, 62 C.R. (3d) 1, 26 O.A.C. 1, 44 D.L.R. (4th) 385, 31 C.R.R. 1, Dickson C.J.C. (Lamer J. concurring). See PRINCIPLE AGAINST SELF INCRIMINATION.

PRINCIPLES OF SENTENCING. 1. The fundamental purpose of sentencing is to contribute, along with crime prevention initiatives, to respect for the law and the maintenance of a just, peaceful and safe society by imposing just sanctions that have one or more of the following objectives: (a) to denounce unlawful conduct; (b) to deter the offender and other persons from committing offences; (c) to separate offenders from society, where necessary; (d) to assist in rehabilitating offenders; (e) to provide reparations for harm done to victims or to the community; and (f) to promote a sense of responsibility in offenders, and acknowledgment of the harm done to victims and to the community. *Criminal Code*, R.S.C. 1985, c. C-46, s. 718. Proportionality is another principle of sentencing which must be applied by the Court. A sentence must be proportionate to the gravity of the offence and the degree of responsibility of the offender. In addition the following principles are applied in sentencing: (a) a sentence should be increased or reduced to account for any relevant aggravating or mitigating circumstances relating to the offence or the offender, and, without limiting the generality of the foregoing, (i) evidence that the offence was motivated by bias, prejudice or hate based on race, national or ethnic origin, language, colour, religion, sex, age, mental or physical disability, sexual orientation, or any other similar factor, (ii) evidence that the offender, in committing the offence, abused the offender's spouse or common-law partner or child, (ii.1) evidence that the offender, in committing the offence, abused a person under the age of eighteen years, (iii) evidence that the offender, in committing the offence, abused a position of trust or authority in relation to the victim, or (iv) evidence that the offence was committed for the benefit of, at the direction of or in association with a criminal organization shall be deemed to be aggravating circumstances; (b) a sentence should be similar to sentences imposed on similar offenders for similar offences committed in similar circumstances; (c) where consecutive sentences are imposed, the combined sentence should not be unduly long or harsh; (d) an offender should not be deprived of liberty, if less restrictive sanctions may be appropriate in the circumstances; and (e) all available sanctions other than imprisonment that are reasonable in the circumstances should be considered for all offenders, with particular attention to the circumstances of aboriginal offenders. *Criminal Code*, R.S.C. 1985, c. C-46, s. 718 and 718.1. 2. Balancing of these goals is required to fashion a sentence that is just and appropriate and that reflects the culpability of the offender and the circumstances of the offence. See GENERAL DETERRENCE; PROPORTION-

ALITY; RETRIBUTION; SENTENCING; SPE-CIFIC DETERRENCE; TOTALITY PRINCIPLE.

PRINTER. See KING'S ~; QUEEN'S ~.

PRIORITY. *n.* When two or more competing claims which arose at different times against the same parcel of land are asserted, the one who is entitled to exercise rights to the exclusion of the others is said to have priority. B.J. Reiter, B.N. McLellan & P.M. Perell, *Real Estate Law*, 4th ed. (Toronto: Emond Montgomery, 1992) at 403.

PRISON. *n.* 1. Includes a penitentiary, common jail, public or reformatory prison, lock-up, guard-room or other place in which persons who are charged with or convicted of offences are usually kept in custody. *Criminal Code*, R.S.C. 1985, c. C-46, s. 2. 2. A place of confinement other than a penitentiary. See CIVIL ~.

PRISON BREACH. Every one who (a) by force or violence breaks a prison with intent to set at liberty himself or any person confined therein; or (b) with intent to escape forcibly breaks out of, or makes any breach in, a cell or other place within a prison in which he is confined. *Criminal Code*, R.S.C. 1985, c. C-46, s. 144. SEE BREACH OF PRISON.

PRISONER. *n.* A person under arrest, remand or sentence who is confined in a correctional centre according to law. See REMAND ~; SERVICE ~.

PRIVACY. *n.* 1. This Court has most often characterized the values engaged by privacy in terms of liberty, or the right to be left alone by the state. For example, in R. v. Dyment, [1988] 2 S.C.R. 417 at 427, La Forest J. commented that "privacy is at the heart of liberty in a modern state". In R. v. Edwards, [1996] 1 S.C.R. 128 at para. 50, per Cory J., privacy was characterized as including "[t]he right to be free from intrusion or interference". This interest in being left alone by the state includes the ability to control the dissemination of confidential information. As La Forest J. stated in R. v. Sanelli, [1990] 1 S.C.R. 30 at 53-54: ... it has long been recognized that this freedom not to be compelled to share our confidences with others is the very hallmark of a free society. Yates J., in Millar v. Taylor (1769), 4 Burr. 2303, 98 E.R. 201, states, at p. 2379 and p. 242: It is certain every man has a right to keep his own sentiments, if he pleases: he has certainly a right to judge whether he will make them public, or commit them only to the sight of his friends. These privacy concerns are at their strongest where aspects of one's individual identity are at stake, such as in the context of information "about one's lifestyle, intimate relations or political or religious opinions": Thomson Newspapers, supra, at pp. 517-18, per La Forest J., cited with approval in Baron, supra, at pp. 444-45. The significance of these privacy concerns should not be understated. Many commentators have noted that privacy is also necessarily related to many fundamental human relations. *R. v. Mills*, 1999 CarswellAlta 1055, 139 C.C.C. (3d) 321, 248 N.R. 101, 28 C.R. (5th) 207, [2000] 2 W.W.R. 180, 244 A.R. 201, 209 W.A.C. 201, 75 Alta. L.R. (3d) 1, 180 D.L.R. (4th) 1, 69 C.R.R. (2d) 1, [1999] 3 S.C.R. 668, the court per McLachlin and Iacobucci JJ. 2. "... [M]ay be defined as the right of the individual to determine for himself when, how, and to what extent he will release personal information about himself, ..." *R. v. Sanelli* (1990), (*sub nom. R. v. Duarte*) 45 C.R.R. 278 at 290, 74 C.R. (3d) 281, 103 N.R. 86, 37 O.A.C. 322, [1990] 1 S.C.R. 30, 53 C.C.C. (3d) 1, 65 D.L.R. (4th) 240, 71 O.R. (2d) 575, La Forest J. (Dickson C.J.C., L'Heureux-Dubé, Sopinka, Gonthier and McLachlin JJ. concurring). 3. Privacy ... connotes concepts of intimacy, identity, dignity and integrity of the individual. *Canada (Information Commissioner) v. Canadian Transportation Accident Investigation & Safety Board*, 2006 FCA 157. See LAW OF ~.

PRIVACY LAW. The law regarding the collection and storage of and access to personal information.

PRIVATE BILL. 1. A bill relating to matters of particular interest or benefit to an individual or group. A. Fraser, W.A. Dawson & J. Holtby, eds., *Beauchesne's Rules and Forms of the House of Commons of Canada*, 6th ed. (Toronto: Carswell, 1989) at 192. 2. A bill relating to a particular person, institution or locality which is often introduced by a private member and enacted by a different and simpler procedure, not requiring government sponsorship. P.W. Hogg, *Constitutional Law of Canada*, 3d ed. (Toronto: Carswell, 1992) at 244.

PRIVATE CARRIER. "... [O]ne who undertakes to carry goods in a particular case, but is not engaged in the business of so carrying as a public employment and does not undertake to carry goods for persons generally." *Tri-City Drilling Co. Ltd. v. Velie* (1960), 30 W.W.R. 61 at 64, 82 C.R.T.C. 69 (Alta. T.D.), Riley J.

PRIVATE COMMUNICATION. Any oral communication, or any telecommunication, that is made by an originator who is in Canada or is intended by the originator to be received by a person who is in Canada and that is made under circumstances in which it is reasonable for the originator to expect that it will not be intercepted by any person other than the person intended by the originator to receive it, and includes any radio-based telephone communication that is treated electronically or otherwise for the purpose of preventing intelligible reception by any person other than the person intended by the originator to receive it. *Criminal Code*, R.S.C. 1985, c. C-46, s. 183.

PRIVATE COMPANY. A company that by its memorandum or articles, special act, letters patent or other incorporating document: (i) restricts the right to transfer its shares; (ii) limits the number of its members to 50 or less, the number so limited being, unless the memorandum or articles otherwise provide, exclusive of persons who are in the employment of the company and of persons who are members while in the employment of the company and continue to be members after the termination of the employment, but where two or more persons hold one or more shares in the company jointly they shall be counted as a single member; and (iii) prohibits any invitation to the public to subscribe for shares or debentures of the company. *Companies acts.*

PRIVATE COPYING. See CANADIAN ~ COLLECTIVE.

PRIVATE ENTERPRISE GAAP. This set of simplified standards is one of the choices Canadian businesses may choose to adopt. Private enterprises must decide which of the sets of standards to adopt for years beginning on or after January 1, 2011. See INTERNATIONAL FINANCIAL REPORTING STANDARDS.

PRIVATE INTERNATIONAL LAW. Or conflict of laws, the part of a country's law that is concerned with resolving legal disputes which involve one or more foreign elements.

PRIVATE INVESTIGATOR. A person who, for hire or reward, investigates and provides information, and includes a person who (i) searches for and provides information as to the personal character or actions of a person, or the character or kind of business or occupation of a person, (ii) searches for offenders against the law, (iii) searches for missing persons or property, (iv) performs shopping or other services in civilian or plain clothes for a client for the purpose of reporting to the client upon the conduct, integrity or trustworthiness of his or her employees, or (v) provides services in civilian or plain clothes for the prevention or detection of shoplifting. *Private Investigation and Security Services Act*, R.S.N. 1990, c. P-24, s. 2.

PRIVATE KEY. A string of data that (a) is used in asymmetric cryptography to encrypt data contained in an electronic document; and (b) is unique to the person who is identified in, or can be identified through, a digital signature certificate and corresponds only to the public key in that certificate. *Personal Information Protection and Electronic Documents Act*, S.C. 2000, c. 5, *Secure Electronic Signature Regulations*, SOR/2005-30, s. 1.

PRIVATE LAND. Land other than land vested in the Crown.

PRIVATE LAW. All law relating to persons; used in distinction to public law.

PRIVATE MEMBER'S BILL. A bill, either public or private, introduced by a private member as opposed to a government member.

PRIVATE NUISANCE. Substantial and unreasonable interference which damages the enjoyment by its occupier of land. *Pugliese v. Canada (National Capital Commission)* (1979), 8 C.E.L.R. 68 at 74, [1979] 2 S.C.R. 104, 8 C.C.L.T. 69, 25 N.R. 498, 97 D.L.R. (3d) 631, the court per Pigeon J.

PRIVATE PROSECUTION. A prosecution commenced by a member of the public, as opposed to a peace officer, laying an information.

PRIVATE RECEIVER. A receiver appointed by a letter or similar instrument by one who holds security over a debtor's assets according to the powers specified in the security instrument. F. Bennett, *Receiverships* (Toronto: Carswell, 1985) at 2.

PRIVATE RECORD. Any record, held by a third party, in respect of which a reasonable expectation of privacy exists.

PRIVATE RIGHT. A right at common law or created by statute the infringement of which gives rise to a cause of action for tort, breach of contract or trust or other cause. *Finlay v. Canada (Minister of Finance)* (1986), 17 C.P.C. (2d) 289 at 301, [1986] 1 W.W.R. 603, [1986] 2 S.C.R. 607, 71 N.R. 338, 23 Admin. L.R. 197, 33 D.L.R. (4th) 321, 8 C.H.R.R. D/3789, the court per Le Dain J.

PRIVATE WRITING. A writing setting forth a juridical act and bearing the signature of the parties; it is not subject to any other formality. *Civil Code*, S.Q. 1991, c. 64, a. 2826.

PRIVATIVE CLAUSE. Provisions in the tribunal's enabling Act that give the tribunal exclusive and final jurisdiction to inquire into, hear and decide certain matters and questions and provide that a decision of the tribunal in respect of the matters within its jurisdiction is final and binding and not open to review in any court. *Administrative Tribunals Act*, S.B.C. 2004, c. 45, s. 1. See EQUIVOCAL ~; FINALITY CLAUSE; PARTIAL ~.

PRIVILEGE. *n.* 1. An exceptional advantage or right; an exemption to which certain people are entitled from an attendance, burden or duty. 2. "... [A]n exclusionary rule of evidence which is appropriately asserted in court... ." *Thomson Newspapers Ltd. v. Canada (Director of Investigation & Research)* (1990), 47 C.R.R. 1 at 94, 76 C.R. (3d) 129, 72 O.R. (2d) 415n, 54 C.C.C. (3d) 417, 67 D.L.R. (4th) 161, 29 C.P.R. (3d) 97, [1990] 1 S.C.R. 425, 39 O.A.C. 161, 106 N.R. 161, Sopinka J. (dissenting in part). 3. Acts as an exception to the truth finding process of trials. All relevant evidence is presumed admissible but some probative and trustworthy evidence is excluded in order to serve other overriding social interests. Similarly, some communications arising out of defined relationships are exempt from disclosure in judicial proceedings. See ABSOLUTE ~; BREACH OF ~; CASE-BY-CASE ~; COMMON INTEREST; CROWN ~; DIPLOMATIC ~; DOCTOR-PATIENT ~; INFORMER ~; JOURNALISTIC-CONFIDENTIAL SOURCE ~; JURORS' ~; LEGISLATIVE ~; LITIGATION ~; PARLIAMENTARY ~; POLICE INFORMANT ~; QUALIFIED ~; RELIGIOUS COMMUNICATIONS ~; SOLICITOR-CLIENT ~; SPOUSAL COMMUNICATIONS ~.

PRIVILEGE AGAINST SELF-INCRIMINATION. 1. "... [O]ften used as a general term embracing aspects of the right to remain silent ... in modern usage, the privilege against self-incrimination is limited to the right of an individual to resist testimony as a witness in a legal proceeding. A privilege is an exclusionary rule of evidence which is appropriately asserted in court. A modern statement of the privilege emphasizing its application in juridicial proceedings is contained in the judgment of Goddard L.J. in Blunt v. Park Lane Hotel Ltd. ... [1942] 2 K.B. 253 [(U.K. C.A.)]. He stated, at p. 257: ' ... the rule is that no one is bound to answer any question if the answer thereto would, in the opinion of the judge, have a tendency to expose the deponent to any criminal charge, penalty or [in a criminal case] forfeiture which the judge regards as reasonably likely to be preferred or sued for.' " *Thomson Newspapers Ltd. v. Canada (Director of Investigation & Research)* (1990), 47 C.R.R. 1 at 94, 76 C.R. (3d) 129, 72 O.R. (2d) 415n, 54 C.C.C. (3d) 417, 67 D.L.R. (4th) 161, 29 C.P.R. (3d) 97, [1990] 1 S.C.R. 425, 39 O.A.C. 161, 106 N.R. 161, Sopinka J. (dissenting in part). 2. "... [T]he privilege of a witness not to answer a question which may incriminate him. That is all that is meant by the Latin maxim, nemo tenetur seipsum accusare, often incorrectly advanced in support of a much broader proposition.... . As applied to witnesses generally, the privilege must be expressly claimed by the witness when the question is put to him in the witness box, Canada Evidence Act, R.S.O. 1970, c. E-10, s. 5. As applied to an accused the privilege is the right to stand mute. An accused cannot be asked, much less compelled, to enter the wintess-box or to answer incriminating questions. If he chooses to testify, the protective shield, of course, disappears. In short, the privilege extends to the accused qua witness and not qua accused, it is concerned with testimonial compulsion specifically and not with compulsion generally ..." *Marcoux v. R.* (1975), 60 D.L.R. (3d) 119 at 112-3, [1976] 1 S.C.R. 763, 29 C.R.N.S. 211, 4 N.R. 64, 24 C.C.C. (2d) 1, Dickson J. 3. "It should therefore be made clear here that I distinguish between the principle against self-incrimination and the privilege against self-incrimination ... The privilege is the narrow traditional common law rule relating only to testimonial evidence at trial. Much of the confusion around such issues as silence, non-compellability, and self-incrimination has, I believe, arisen as a result of the failure to distinguish between these two levels of protection against self-incrimination. The principle is a general organizing principle of criminal law from which particular rules can be derived (for example, rules about non-compellability of the accused and admissibility of confessions). The privilege is merely one rule that has been derived from the principle. When the protection against self-incrimination is limited to the privilege against self-incrimination, then the underlying rationale for the various common law rules protecting against self-incrimination is lost and principled decisions about particular cases as they arise become impossible." *R. v. Jones*, 1994 CarswellBC 580, 30 C.R. (4th) 1, 166 N.R. 321, 43 B.C.A.C. 241, 69 W.A.C. 241, 89 C.C.C. (3d) 353, [1994] 2 S.C.R. 229, 114 D.L.R. (4th) 645, 21 C.R.R. (2d) 286, Lamer C.J.C. See PRINCIPLE AGAINST SELF INCRIMINATION.

PRIVILEGE CLAUSE. 1. Reserves a privilege to the person requesting tenders. 2. The privilege clause provided that the lowest or any tender would not necessarily be accepted, and the issue was whether this barred a claim based on breach of an implied term that the owner would accept only compliant bids. *Tercon Contractors Ltd. v. British Columbia (Transportation and Highways)*, 2010 SCC 4, [2010] 1 S.C.R. 69, Cromwell J.

PRIVILEGED COMMUNICATION. 1. A communication which one cannot compel a witness to divulge. 2. "In slander or libel the term 'privileged communication' comprehends all cases of communications made bona fide in pursuance of a duty, or with a fair and reasonable purpose of protecting the interest of the party uttering the defamatory matter: ... Privileged communications are of four kinds, viz.: (1). When the publisher of the alleged slander acted in good faith in the discharge of a public or private duty, legal or moral, or in prosecution of his own rights or interests. (2). Anything said or written by a master concerning the character of a servant who has been in his employment. (3). Words used in the course of a legal or judicial proceeding. (4). Publications duly made in the ordinary mode of parliament: Clarke v. Molyneux (1877), 3 Q.B.D. 237." *Trafton v. Deschene* (1917), 36 D.L.R. 433 at 435, 44 N.B.R. 552 (C.A.), Grimmer J.A.

PRIVILEGED DOCUMENT. "A document which was produced or brought into existence with either the dominant purpose of its author, or of the person or authority under whose direction, whether particular or general, it was produced or brought into existence, of using it or its contents in order to obtain legal advice or to conduct or aid in the conduct of litigation, at the time of its production in reasonable prospect, should both be privileged and excluded for inspection." Voth Brothers Construction (1974) Ltd. v. North Vancouver School District No. 44, [1981] 5 W.W.R. 91 at 94, 29 B.C.L.R. 114 (C.A.), Nemetz J.A. adopting the test of Barwick C.J. Aust. in *Grant v. Downs* (1976), 135 C.L.R. 674 at 677 (H.C.).

PRIVILEGED OCCASION. An occasion when the person who makes a communication has an interest or a legal, social, or moral duty to make it to the person to whom it is made and the person to whom it is made has a corresponding interest or duty to receive it.

PRIVILEGED WILL. A will executed by a member of the military or a seaman or mariner and not meeting the general formality requirements.

PRIVITY. *n.* 1. The doctrine of privity of contract has been stated by many different authorities sometimes with varying effect. Broadly speaking, it stands for the proposition that a contract cannot, as a general rule, confer rights or impose obligations arising under it on any person except the parties to it. *London Drugs Ltd. v. Kuehne & Nagel International Ltd.*, 1992 CarswellBC 315, 73 B.C.L.R. (2d) 1, [1992] 3 S.C.R. 299, (*sub nom. London Drugs Ltd. v. Brassart*) 143 N.R. 1, 18 B.C.A.C. 1, 31 W.A.C. 1, 43 C.C.E.L. 1, 13 C.C.L.T. (2d) 1, [1993] 1 W.W.R. 1, 97 D.L.R. (4th) 261, Iacobucci J. 2. Being a participant in or a party to a contract. G.H.L. Fridman, *The Law of Contract in Canada*, 2d ed. (Toronto: Carswell, 1986) at 161. 3. The direct connection between the one to pay the money being sought in an action for recovery and the one to receive such money. G.H.L. Fridman, *Restitution*, 2d ed. (Toronto: Carswell, 1992) at 65.

PRIVITY OF CONTRACT. The doctrine of privity of contract has been stated by many different authorities sometimes with varying effect. Broadly speaking, it stands for the proposition that a contract cannot, as a general rule, confer rights or impose obligations arising under it on any person except the parties to it. *London Drugs Ltd. v. Kuehne & Nagel International Ltd.*, [1992] 3 S.C.R. 299, (*sub nom. London Drugs Ltd. v. Brassart*), Iacobucci J. for the majority.

PRIVY. *n.* 1. Someone who partakes or has an interest in some action or thing. 2. Someone related to another person.

PRIVY. *adj.* Participating in some act.

PRIVY COUNCIL. 1. In Canada, the Queen's Privy Council for Canada including cabinet ministers and other people as well. P.W. Hogg, *Constitutional Law of Canada*, 3d ed. (Toronto: Carswell, 1992) at 234. 2. In the United Kingdom, a large body which now exercises formal functions only. The Queen, on the advice of the Prime Minister, appoints its members. P.W. Hogg, *Constitutional Law of Canada*, 3d ed. (Toronto: Carswell, 1992) at 202. See JUDICIAL COMMITTEE OF THE ~; QUEEN'S ~ FOR CANADA.

PRIZE COURT. The Federal Court of Canada has and shall exercise, subject to the Canada Prize Act, jurisdiction in all matters of prize in Canada. The Court shall, subject to this section, take cognizance of and judicially proceed upon all, and all manner of, captures, seizures, prizes and reprisals made under the authority of Her Majesty in right of Canada of all ships, aircraft or goods, and shall hear and determine the same and, according to the Course of Admiralty and the Law of Nations, adjudge and condemn all such ships, aircraft or goods as belong to any enemy country or the citizens or subjects thereof or any other persons inhabiting any of the countries, territories or dominions of any enemy country or that are otherwise condemnable as prize. *Canada Prize Act*, R.S.C. 1970, c. P-24.

PRIZE FIGHT. An encounter or fight with fists or hands between two persons who have met for that purpose by previous arrangement made by or for them, but a boxing contest between amateur sportsmen, where the contestants wear boxing gloves of not less than one hundred and forty grams each in mass, or any boxing contest held with the permission or under the authority of an athletic board or commission or similar body established by or under the authority of the legislature of a province for the control of sport within the province, shall be deemed not to be a prize fight. *Criminal Code*, R.S.C. 1985, c. C-46, s. 83(2).

PRO. *prep.* [L.] For, in respect of.

PROBABILITIES. See BALANCE OF ~.

PROBABLE CAUSE. 1. In R. v. Debot, 30 C.C.C. (3d) 207 (Ont. C.A.) affirmed 1989 CanLII 13, [1989] 2 S.C.R. 1140, the Supreme Court of Canada approved of the standard described by Martin J.A. in the Ontario Court of Appeal where he stated: The standard of 'reasonable ground to believe' or 'probable cause' is not to be equated with proof beyond a reasonable doubt or a prima facie case. The standard to be met is one of reasonable probability. *R. v. Graham*, 2008 PESCAD 7. 2. Grounds which are reasonable. *Archibald v. McLaren* (1892), 21 S.C.R. 588 at 594, Strong J. (Fournier J. concurring). See REASONABLE AND ~.

PROBABLE GROUNDS. See REASONABLE AND ~.

PROBATE. *n.* A process to prove the originality and validity of a will. See COURT OF ~; GRANT OF ~; LETTERS ~.

PROBATE DUTY. A tax on the gross value of a deceased testator's personal property.

PROBATION. *n.* 1. The disposition of a court authorizing a person to be at large subject to the conditions of a probation order or community service order. 2. Temporarily appointing a person to an office until that person has, by conduct, proved to be fit to fill it. See PERIOD OF ~.

PROBATIONARY PERIOD. The period of time at the beginning of employment with a new employer during which the employer has an opportunity to determine the suitability of the employee.

PROBATIONER. *n.* A convicted person who is placed on probation by a court or a person who is discharged conditionally by a probation order of a court.

PROBATION OFFICER. The person who supervises another person placed on probation.

PROBATION ORDER. An order made in respect of a particular individual and so long as it remains in force, it attaches to that individual wherever he or she may go. Orders of disposition and probation orders are not identical. All dispositions under s. 20(1) of the [Young Offenders Act, R.S.C. 1985, c. Y-1], including custodial or probation dispositions, are subject to the requirements of s. 20(6). In contrast, s. 23 is specific to probation orders. It identifies the required and optional contents of a probation order and provides statutory rules designed to ensure that the conditions of a probation order are read to, and understood by, the affected young person and, further, are brought to the attention of the parent of the young person, if the parent is in attendance at the proceedings against the young person. Accordingly, the scope of s. 20(6) is wider than that of s. 23. *R. v. H. (J.)*, 161 C.C.C. (3d) 392, 155 O.A.C. 146, [2002] O.J. No. 268.

PROBATIVE. See LOGICALLY ~.

PROBATIVE VALUE. "To have probative value the evidence must be susceptible of an inference relevant to the issues in the case other than the inference that the accused committed the offence because he or she has a disposition to the type of conduct charged ... As in the case of relevance, evidence can be logically probative but not legally probative. When the term 'probative value' is employed in the cases, reference is made to legally probative value." *R. v. B. (C.R.)* (1990), 55 C.C.C. (3d) 1 at 7, [1990] 3 W.W.R. 385, 73 Alta. L.R. (2d) 1, [1990] 1 S.C.R. 717, 107 N.R. 241, 109 A.R. 81, Sopinka J.

PROB. CT. *abbr.* Probate Court.

PROBE. *n.* Single-stranded DNA in short segments which complements a specific portion of single-stranded DNA and is labelled with fluorescent or radioactive material. F.A. Jaffe, *A Guide to Pathological Evidence for Lawyers and Police Officers*, 4th ed. (Toronto: Carswell, 1999) at 242.

PRO BONO PUBLICO

PRO BONO PUBLICO. [L.] For the public good. Often shortened to "pro bono". See PRO BONO SERVICES.

PRO BONO SERVICES. Legal services donated to individuals or to groups.

PROCEDURAL EQUALITY. Equality of application of the law without necessarily treating persons equally.

PROCEDURAL FAIRNESS. Procedural fairness is a cornerstone of modern Canadian administrative law. Public decision makers are required to act fairly in coming to decisions that affect the rights, privileges or interests of an individual. Thus stated the principle is easy to grasp. It is not, however, always easy to apply. As has been noted many times, "the concept of procedural fairness is eminently variable and its content is to be decided in the specific context of each case". In Canada, the modern concept of procedural fairness in administrative law was inspired by the House of Lords' landmark decision in Ridge v. Baldwin, [1963] 2 All E.R. 66, a case which involved the summary dismissal of the chief constable of Brighton. The House of Lords declared the chief constable's dismissal a nullity on the grounds that the administrative body which had dismissed him had failed to provide the reasons for his dismissal or to accord him an opportunity to be heard in violation of the rules of natural justice. Central to the reasoning in the case was Lord Reid's distinction between (i) master servant relationships (i.e. contractual employment), (ii) offices held "at pleasure", and (iii) offices where there must be cause for dismissal, which included the chief constable's position. According to Lord Reid, only the last category of persons was entitled to procedural fairness in relation to their dismissal since both contractual employees and office holders employed "at pleasure" could be dismissed without reason (p. 72). The principles established by Ridge v. Baldwin were followed by this Court in Nicholson v. Haldimand Norfolk Regional Board of Commissioners of Police, [1979] 1 S.C.R. 311. Its overarching purpose is not difficult to discern: administrative decision makers, in the exercise of public powers, should act fairly in coming to decisions that affect the interests of individuals. In other words, "[t]he observance of fair procedures is central to the notion of the 'just' exercise of power". *Dunsmuir v. New Brunswick*, 2008 SCC 9, Bastarache and LeBel JJ. at para. 79, 85, 86, 90.

PROCEDURAL IMPROPRIETY. I have described the third head as 'procedural impropriety' rather than failure to observe basic rules of natural justice or failure to act with procedural fairness towards the person who will be affected by the decision. This is because susceptibility to judicial review under this head covers also failure by an administrative tribunal to observe procedural rules that are expressly laid down in the legislative instrument by which its jurisdiction is conferred, even where such failure does not involve any denial of natural justice. But the instant case is not concerned with the proceedings of an administrative tribunal at all. *Council of Civil Service Unions v. Minister for the Civil Service*, [1985] A.C. 374 at 410, 411, [1984] 3 All E.R. 935 (H.L.), Lord Diplock.

PROCEDURE. *n.* 1. "The concept of procedure, too, is ... a comprehensive one, including process and evidence, methods of execution, rules of limitation affecting the remedy and the course of the Court with regard to the kind of relief that can be granted to a suitor... ." *Livesley v. E. Clemens Horst Co.* (1924), [1925] 1 D.L.R. 159 at 161, [1924] S.C.R. 605, the court per Duff J. 2. "... [P]roperly means neither the machinery nor the product, but rather the rules set forth by the managers of the machine, showing not who have the right to use it, but how those who have the right are to behave. If the machine exists for you, if there is a Court of Appeal in criminal matters, these shall be the rules by which you shall approach the machine to obtain your result... ." *R. v. Johnson* (1892), 2 B.C.R. 87 at 88 (C.A.), Begbie C.J.A. (Drake J.A. concurring). 3. "... [W]hen used in a statute such as the Bankruptcy Act [R.S.C. 1970, c. B-3] refers to the mode or method by which a litigant secures his rights... ." *Eisler, Re* (1984), 54 C.B.R. (N.S.) 235 at 239 (B.C. S.C.), Murray J. 4. " ... [P]leading, evidence and practice... ." *Delisle v. Moreau* (1968), 5 C.R.N.S. 68 at 70, [1968] 4 C.C.C. 229, 69 D.L.R. (2d) 530, (N.B. C.A.), the court per Hughes J.A. See CIVIL ~; CONTEMPT IN ~; CRIMINAL ~; WAGG PRINCIPLES AND ~.

PROCEEDING. *n.* 1. "... [O]ne of those words of very wide import that must be interpreted according to the context in which it is used... ." *I.W.A., Local 1-324 v. Wescana Inn Ltd.* (1978), 27 C.B.R. (N.S.) 201 at 206, [1978] 1 W.W.R. 679, 82 D.L.R. (3d) 368 (Man. C.A.), O'Sullivan J.A. (Freedman C.J.M. concurring). 2. "... [C]apable of including every species of activity in matters legal, from an interlocutory application in Chambers to an appeal in a Court of last resort." *Ontario (Attorney General) v. Palmer* (1979), 108 D.L.R. (3d) 349 at 358-9, 28 O.R. (2d) 35, 15 C.P.C. 125, [1980] I.L.R. 1-1196 (C.A.), Anderson J.A. (dissenting). 3. "... [R]efers to the whole event, from the commencement of action by the issuance of a writ to the conclusion of the trial, no matter how many causes of action are raised by way of pleadings in either the statement of claim or in the counterclaim." *Hughes v. O'Sullivan* (1986), 12 C.P.C. (2d) 62 at 66 (B.C. S.C.), Toy J. 4. A matter, cause or action, whether civil or criminal, before the court. 5. "' ... [A] step in an action.' " *Hannah v. Flagstaff*, [1926] 4 D.L.R. 470 at 473, [1926] 3 W.W.R. 301 (Alta. T.D.), Simmons C.J. 6. The [Companies' Creditors Arrangement Act, R.S.C. 1985, c. C-36] has consistently been read as authorizing a stay of proceedings beyond the narrowly judicial. The word "proceeding" includes "...judicial or extra-judicial conduct against the debtor company the effect of which is, or would be, seriously to impair the ability of the debtor company to continue in business during the compromise or arrangement negotiating period." Quintette Coal Ltd. v. Nippon Steel Corp. (1990), 51 B.C.L.R. (2d) 105 at 113.... Unlike the United States Code, which specifically exempts governmental regulatory enforcement proceedings from the stay (11 USC para. 362(b)(4)), the [Companies' Creditors Arrangement Act, R.S.C. 1985, c. C-36] does not so limit the powers of the Court. *Toronto Stock Exchange Inc. v. United Keno Hill Mines Ltd.*, 2000 CarswellOnt 1770, 48 O.R. (3d) 746, 7 B.L.R. (3d) 86, 19 C.B.R. (4th) 299 (S.C.J.) [Commercial List], Lane J. See ADMIRALTY ~; AFFILIATION ~; CIVIL ~; COROLLARY RELIEF ~; COSTS OF THIS ~; DANGEROUS OFFENDER ~; DIVORCE ~; JUDICIAL OR QUASI-JUDICIAL ~; JUDICIAL ~; LEGAL ~; MINUTES OF ~S AND EVIDENCE ~; OTHER ~S; PETITION ~; RECORD OF ~S; STAY OF ~S; STYLE OF ~; THIRD PARTY ~; TITLE OF ~; VARIATION ~; VEXATIOUS ~; VOTES AND ~S.

PROCEEDS. *n.* 1. The amount, sum or value of any land goods or investments sold or converted into cash. 2. Identifiable or traceable personal property in any form derived directly or indirectly from any dealing with collateral or the proceeds therefrom, and includes (a) any payment representing indemnity or compensation for loss of or damage to the collateral or proceeds therefrom, (b) any payment made in total or partial discharge or redemption of an intangible, chattel paper, an instrument or investment property, and (c) rights arising out of, or property collected on, or distributed on account of, collateral that is investment property. *Personal Property Security Act*, R.S.O. 1990, c. P.10, s. 1.1(1). 3. "[P]roceeds of the lottery scheme" within the meaning of s. 207(1)(b) [of Criminal Code] means proceeds net of reasonable and incidental expenses, including taxes. I see nothing in s. 207(1)(b) which suggests that Parliament intended to restrict in any way the right of the Province to tax lottery proceeds, even assuming that Parliament had such a power. Nor am I persuaded that because s. 207(1)(a) clearly permits the provinces to participate in the lottery business, they cannot exact a benefit under s. 207(1)(b) by way of taxes. The language of that section simply does not give rise to such a restrictive interpretation. *Nanaimo Immigrant Settlement Society v. British Columbia*, 2004 BCCA 410. 4. When the plain meaning of the word is applied, the word "proceeds" appears to mean something which has been derived as a result of converting an article or item into something else. It is something which can be identifiable, traceable or linked to the original item. *P.E.I. Lending Agency v. McCain Produce Inc.*, 2010 PECA 4. See NET ~; NET SALE ~.

PROCEEDS OF A CONTRACT FOR RECOUNTING CRIME. (a) money or other consideration paid under a contract for recounting crime to a person convicted of or charged with a designated crime or the agent of a person convicted of or charged with a designated crime, whether the money or other consideration is paid before or after this Act came into force, or (b) property acquired, directly or indirectly, in whole or in part, from money or other consideration referred to in clause (a), whether the property was acquired before or after this Act came into force. *Prohibiting Profiting from Recounting Crimes Act, 2002*, S.O. 2002, c. 2, s. 2. See CONTRACT FOR THE RECOUNTING OF A CRIME.

PROCEEDS OF CRIME. Any property, benefit or advantage, within or outside Canada, obtained or derived directly or indirectly as a result of (a) the commission in Canada of an enterprise crime offence or a designated substance offence, or (b) an act or omission anywhere that, if it had occurred in Canada, would have constituted an enterprise crime offence or a designated substance offence. *Criminal Code*, R.S.C. 1985, c. C-46, s. 462.3. See LAUNDERING ~.

PROCEEDS OF DISPOSITION. Of property includes (a) the sale price of property that has been sold, (b) compensation for property unlawfully taken, (c) compensation for property destroyed and any amount payable under a policy of insurance in respect of loss or destruction of property, (d) compensation for property taken under statutory authority or the sale price of property sold to a person by whom notice of an intention to take it under statutory authority was given, (e) compensation for property injuriously affected, whether lawfully or unlawfully or under statutory authority or otherwise, (f) compensation for property damaged and any amount payable under a policy of insurance in respect of damage to property, except to the extent that the compensation or amount, as the case may be, has within a reasonable time after the damage been expended on repairing the damage, (g) an amount by which the liability of a taxpayer to a mortgagee or hypothecary creditor is reduced as a result of the sale of mortgaged or hypothecated property under a provision of the mortgage or hypothec, plus any amount received by the taxpayer out of the proceeds of the sale, and (h) any amount included because of section 79 in computing a taxpayer's proceeds of disposition of the property. *Income Tax Act*, R.S.C. 1985, c. 1 (5th Supp.), s. 13.

PROCEEDS OF UNLAWFUL ACTIVITY. 1. (i) Property acquired directly or indirectly, in whole or in part, as a result of unlawful activity, whether the property was acquired before or after the coming into force of this Act; and (ii) an increase in the value of property, or a decrease in a debt obligation secured against property, if the increase or decrease resulted directly or indirectly from unlawful activity. *The Seizure of Criminal Property Act, 2009*, S.S. 2009, c. S-46.002, s. 2. 2. Property acquired, directly or indirectly, in whole or in part, as a result to unlawful activity, whether the property was acquired before or after this Act came into force, but does not include proceeds of a contract for recounting crime within the meaning of the Prohibiting Profiting from Recounting Crimes Act, 2002. *Civil Remedies Act, 2001*, S.O. 2001, c. 28, s. 2.

PROCESS. *n.* 1. Includes, with respect to goods, the adjustment, alteration, assembly, manufacture, modification, production or repair of the goods. *Customs Tariff*, S.C. 1997, c. 36, s. 80. 2. "... [A]s a legal term is a word of comprehensive signification. In its broadest sense it is equivalent to 'proceedings' or 'procedure' and may be said to embrace all the steps and proceedings in a case from its commencement to its conclusion. 'Process' may signify the means whereby a Court compels a compliance with its demands. Every writ is of course, a process, and in its narrowest sense the term 'process' is limited to writs or writings issued from or out of a Court under the seal of the Court and returnable to the Court... ." *Selkirk, Re* (1961), 27 D.L.R. (2d) 615 at 621, [1961] O.R. 391 (C.A.), Schroeder J.A. (McGillivray J.A. concurring). 3. "... [A] writ or other judicial order: ..." *R. v. Landry* (1986), 50 C.R. (3d) 55 at 72, [1986] 1 S.C.R. 145, 54 O.R. (2d) 512n, 65 N.R. 161, 25 C.C.C. (3d) 1, 14 O.A.C. 241, 26 D.L.R. (4th) 368, La Forest J. (dissenting). See ABUSE OF ~; COLLABORATIVE FAMILY LAW ~; CONTEMPT ~; DISPUTE RESOLUTION ~; DUE ~ OF LAW; KIMBERLEY ~ CERTIFICATE; LEGAL ~; MESNE ~; ORIGINATING ~; SERVICE OF ~.

PROCESSING. See PRIMARY ~.

PROCLAMATION. *n.* 1. Authorized publication. 2. A proclamation under the Great Seal.

PROCLAMATION DATE. The date on which a statute is proclaimed in force when the statute provides that it will come into force when proclaimed.

PROCTOR. See KING'S ~; QUEEN'S ~.

PROCURE. *v.* "... [I]n the context in which is used is s. 422 [of the Criminal Code, R.S.C. 1970, c. C-34] means to instigate, persuade or solicit." *R. v. Gonzague* (1983), 4 C.C.C. (3d) 505 at 508, 34 C.R. (3d) 169 (Ont. C.A.), the court per Martin J.A.

PRODUCER. See CANADIAN ARTISTS AND ~S PROFESSIONAL RELATIONS TRIBUNAL

PRODUCT. See AERONAUTICAL ~; FARM ~; HYBRID ~; INTEGRATED CIRCUIT ~; INTERACTIVE DIGITAL MEDIA ~; INTERCHANGEABLE ~; NATURAL HEALTH ~; PEST CONTROL ~; REGULATED ~.

PRODUCTION. *n.* In court, the exhibition of a document. See CANADIAN ~ FUND.

PRODUCTS LIABILITY. Liability of manufacturers and sellers to buyers and others for damages suffered because of defects in the goods manufactured or sold.

PROFESSIONAL. *n.* Any person who holds a permit issued by an order and who is entered on the roll of the latter. *Professional Code*, R.S.Q., c. C-26, s. 1.

PROFESSIONAL. *adj.* Relating to an occupation requiring special training in the liberal arts and sciences. Involving mutual or intellectual labour or skill rather than physical or manual labour and skill.

PROFESSIONAL ENGINEERING. Any act of planning, designing, composing, measuring, evaluating, inspecting, advising, reporting, directing or supervising, or managing any of those acts, that requires the application of engineering principles. *Engineering and Geoscience Professions Act*, S.N.W.T. 2006, c. 16, s. 1.

PROFESSIONAL FORESTRY. The practice of professional forestry is the provision of services in relation to the development, management, conservation and sustainability of forests and urban forests.

PROFESSIONAL GEOSCIENCE. See PRACTICE OF ~.

PROFESSIONAL LAND SURVEYING. The advising on, the reporting on, the supervising of and the conducting of surveys to determine the horizontal and vertical position of any point and the direction and length of any line required to control, establish, locate, define or describe the extent or limitations of title. *Land Surveyors Act*, R.S.N.S. 1989, c. 249, s. 2.

PROFESSIONAL MISCONDUCT. 1. "... [C]onduct which would be reasonably regarded as disgraceful, dishonourable, or unbecoming of a member of the profession by his well respected brethren in the group – persons of integrity and good reputation amongst the membership." *Law Society (Manitoba) v. Savino* (1983), 6 C.R.R. 336 at 343, [1983] 6 W.W.R. 538, 23 Man. R. (2d) 293, 1 D.L.R. (4th) 285 (C.A.), Monnin C.J.M. 2. "... [S]omething improper, disgraceful, or professionally inappropriate." *Forster v. Saskatchewan Teachers' Federation* (1992), 89 D.L.R. (4th) 283 at 286, [1992] 2 W.W.R. 651, 97 Sask. R. 98, 12 W.A.C. 98 (C.A.), the court per Gerwing J.A. 3. On the part of a solicitor, conduct involving a failure to fulfill his duty to the court or to realize his duty to aid in promoting the cause of justice in his own sphere. A failure to observe the duty owed by the members of the profession to the public at large and to the state. 4. Includes such conduct or acts relevant to the practice of optical dispensing that, having regard to all of the circumstances, would reasonably be regarded as disgraceful, dishonourable or unprofessional which, without limiting the generality of the foregoing, may include (i) failing to maintain standards of practice, (ii) failing to uphold any code of ethics adopted by the College, (iii) violating this Act, the regulations or the by-laws, (iv) abusing a person verbally, physically, emotionally or sexually, (v) misappropriating personal property or other property belonging to a customer or an employer, (vi) allowing a person who is not licensed by the College to practise optical dispensing, unless the person is a student optician or a specialty student optician or is otherwise authorized to practise optical dispensing pursuant to this Act, (vii) the committing of an indictable offence, (viii) falsifying records, (ix) publishing, or causing to be published, any advertisement that is false, fraudulent, deceptive or misleading, (x) engaging or assisting in fraud, misrepresentation, deception or concealment of a material fact when applying for or securing registration or a licence, or the taking of any examinations provided for in this Act or the regulations, including using fraudulently procured credentials. *Dispensing Opticians Act*, S.N.S. 2005, c. 39, s. 21.

PROFESSIONAL ORDER. Any professional order listed in Schedule I to this Code or constituted in accordance with this Code. *Professional Code*, R.S.Q., c. C-26, s. 1.

PROFESSIONAL PLANNING. See PRACTICE OF ~.

PROFESSIONAL PRACTICE OF FORESTRY. The provision of services in relation to the development, management, conservation and sustainability of forests, forested land and forest resources where those services require knowledge, training and experience equivalent to that required to become a member pursuant to this Act, and includes all or any of the following: (i) the planning, classification, inventory, mapping, measurement, certification, appraisal and evaluation of forests and forested land; (ii) the development, implementation, examination or auditing of programs for harvesting and renewal of forests and forested land; (iii) the conservation, reclamation, improvement or protection of forests, forested land or forest soils for forestry purposes; (iv) the preparation, review or approval of forest management and operating plans; (v) the development of integrated forest land use plans; (vi) the administration, inspection or monitoring of forested land; (vii) the teaching of forestry at a college, technical institute or university; (viii) the conducting of research activities related to forestry. *The Forestry Professions Act*, S.S. 2006, c. F-19.2, s. 2.

PROFESSIONAL PRIVILEGE. See LEGAL ~.

PROFESSIONAL RELATIONS. See CANADIAN ARTISTS AND PRODUCERS ~ TRIBUNAL

PROFESSIONAL SURVEYING. See PRACTICE OF ~.

PROFESSIONAL SYNDICATE. Fifteen persons or more, Canadian citizens, engaged in the same profession, the same employment or in similar trades, or doing correlated work having for object the establishing of a determined product, may make and sign a memorandum setting forth their intention of forming an association or professional syndicate. *Professional Syndicates Act*, R.S.Q., c. S-40, s. 1.

PROFILE. See DNA ~.

PROFILING. See RACIAL ~.

PROFIT. *n.* 1. "... [T]he profit of a trade or business is the surplus by which the receipts from the trade or business exceed the expenditure necessary for the purpose of earning those receipts." *Russell v. Town & Country Bank* (1888), 13 App. Cas. 418 at 424 (U.K.), Lord Herschell. 2. The difference between the receipts of a trade or business and the expenditures made to earn those receipts. 3. It seems to me that in its ordinary sense, the word "profit" connotes a "net" concept—the excess of returns over outlay. *Tran v. Aujla*, 2008 BCCA 115. See ACCUMULATED ~S; NET ~; NON-~; SECRET ~.

PROFIT À PRENDRE. [Fr.] 1. "... [A] right to take something off the land of another person... . more fully defined as a right to enter on the land of another person and take some profit of the soil such as minerals, oil, stones, trees, turf, fish or game, for the use of the owner of the right. It is an incorporeal hereditament, and unlike an easement it is not necessarily appurtenant to a dominant tenement but may be held as a right in gross, and as such may be assigned and dealt with as a valuable interest according to the ordinary rules of property." *Cherry v. Petch*, [1948] O.W.N. 378 at 380 (H.C.), Wells J. 2. "... [I]t is the right of severance which results in the holder of the profit à prendre acquiring title to the thing severed. The holder of the profit does not own the minerals in situ. They form part of the fee. What he owns are mineral claims and the right to exploit them ..." *Brit-*

ish Columbia v. Tener (1985), 36 R.P.R. 291 at 309, [1985] 1 S.C.R. 533, [1985] 3 W.W.R. 673, 32 L.C.R. 340, 17 D.L.R. (4th) 1, 59 N.R. 82, 28 B.C.L.R. (2d) 241, Wilson J. (dissenting) (Dickson C.J. concurring).

PROFIT A PRENDRE IN ALIENO SOLO. [Fr. and L.] The right to take something from the soil of another.

PROFIT SHARING PLAN. See DEFERRED ~.

PRO FORMA. [L.] In order to observe proper form.

PROGRAM. *n.* 1. A plan for the provision of services. 2. A series or group of courses leading to a statement of standing. 3. Sounds or visual images, or a combination of sounds and visual images, that are intended to inform, enlighten or entertain, but does not include visual images, whether or not combined with sounds, that consist predominantly of alphanumeric text. *Broadcasting Act*, S.C. 1991, c. 11, s. 2(1). See APPLICATION ~; COMPUTER ~; CONSERVATION ~S; FINE OPTION ~; JOB CREATION ~; OPERATING SYSTEM ~; RATIONING ~; REVENUE INSURANCE ~; SOCIAL ~S; THERAPEUTIC INTERCHANGE ~; WITNESS PROTECTION ~.

PROGRAMMING SIGNAL. See SUBSCRIPTION ~.

PROGRAMMING UNDERTAKING. An undertaking for the transmission of programs, either directly by radio waves or other means of telecommunication or indirectly through a distribution undertaking, for reception by the public by means of broadcasting receiving apparatus. *Broadcasting Act*, S.C. 1991, c. 11, s. 2.

PROGRAM TIME. Any period longer than two minutes during which a broadcaster does not normally present commercial messages, public service announcements or station or network identification. *Canada Elections Act*, S.C. 2000, c. 9, s. 344.

PROGRESS. See WORK IN ~.

PROGRESSIVE DISCIPLINE. Discipline in the workplace for violations. Describes proceeding by first warning, orally or in writing, then giving increasingly long suspensions and resorting last to termination to punish violations.

PROHIBIT. *v.* "... '[F]orbid' ..." *Krautt v. Paine* (1980), 17 R.P.R. 1 at 21, [1980] 6 W.W.R. 717, 118 D.L.R. (3d) 625, 25 A.R. 390 (C.A.), the court per Laycraft J.A.

PROHIBITED AMMUNITION. Ammunition, or a projectile of any kind, that is prescribed to be prohibited ammunition. *Criminal Code*, R.S.C. 1985, c. C-46, s. 84(1).

PROHIBITED DEGREE. The prohibited degrees of marriage. Subject to the exceptions listed, persons related by consanguinity, affinity or adoption are not prohibited from marrying each other by reason only of their relationship. No person shall marry another person if they are related lineally, or, as brother or sister or half-brother or half-sister, including by adop-

P

tion. *Marriage (Prohibited Degrees) Act*, S.C. 1990, c. 46 s. 2.

PROHIBITED DEVICE. (a) Any component or part of a weapon, or any accessory for use with a weapon, that is prescribed to be a prohibited device, (b) a handgun barrel that is equal to or less than 105 mm in length, but does not include any such handgun barrel that is prescribed, where the handgun barrel is for use in international sporting competitions governed by the rules of the International Shooting Union, (c) a device or contrivance designed or intended to muffle or stop the sound or report of a firearm, (d) a cartridge magazine that is prescribed to be a prohibited device, or (e) a replica firearm. *Criminal Code*, R.S.C. 1985, c. C-46, s. 84(1).

PROHIBITED FIREARM. (a) A handgun that (i) has a barrel equal to or less than 105 mm in length, or (ii) is designed or adapted to discharge a 25 or 32 calibre cartridge, but does not include any such handgun that is prescribed, where the handgun is for use in international sporting competitions governed by the rules of the International Shooting Union, (b) a firearm that is adapted from a rifle or shotgun, whether by sawing, cutting or any other alteration, and that, as so adapted, (i) is less than 660 mm in length, or (ii) is 660 mm or greater in length and has a barrel less than 457 mm in length, (c) an automatic firearm, whether or not it has been altered to discharge only one projectile with one pressure of the trigger, or (d) any firearm that is prescribed to be a prohibited firearm. *Criminal Code*, R.S.C. 1985, c. C-46, s. 84(1).

PROHIBITED MARK. A mark adopted and used by a public authority and protected under the Trademarks Act from use by other persons.

PROHIBITED WEAPON. *(a)* A knife that has a blade that opens automatically by gravity or centrifugal force or by hand pressure applied to a button, spring or other device in or attached to the handle of the knife, or *(b)* any weapon, other than a firearm, that is prescribed to be a prohibited weapon. *Criminal Code*, R.S.C. 1985, c. C-46, s. 84(1).

PROHIBITION. *n.* 1. An order of the court which lies to prevent a tribunal from acting or continuing to act in excess of its jurisdiction or contrary to the rules of natural justice. 2. An order to prevent a person from driving a motor vehicle.

PROHIBITION ORDER. An order made under this Act or any other Act of Parliament prohibiting a person from possessing any firearm, cross-bow, prohibited weapon, restricted weapon, prohibited device, ammunition, prohibited ammunition or explosive substance, or all such things. *Criminal Code*, R.S.C. 1985, c. C-46, s. 84(1).

PROHIBITORY INJUNCTION. An injunction restraining the doing or continuance of a wrongful act.

PROLIXITY. *n.* "... [A]pplied to pleadings ... taken to imply length and wordiness; diffuseness, discussion at great length; tediousness... ." *Maclean v. Kingdon Printing Co.* (1908), 9 W.L.R. 370 at 371, Cameron J.

PROMISE. *n.* An undertaking as to future conduct; agreeing to act or refrain from acting in a certain way in order to benefit another person. See BREACH OF ~ TO MARRY; CONTRACTUAL ~; DONATIVE ~; GRATUITOUS ~; MUTUAL ~S.

PROMISEE. *n.* One to whom one makes a promise.

PROMISOR. *n.* One who makes a promise.

PROMISSORY ESTOPPEL. "... The party relying on the doctrine must establish that the other party has, by words or conduct, made a promise or assurance which was intended to affect their legal relationship and to be acted on. Furthermore, the representee must establish that, in reliance on the representation, he acted on it or in some way changed his position... ." *Maracle v. Travellers Indemnity Co. of Canada* (1991), 50 C.P.C. (2d) 213 at 220, I.L.R. 1-2728, 125 N.R. 294, 3 O.R. (3d) 510n, 80 D.L.R. (4th) 652, 3 C.C.L.I. (2d) 186, 47 O.A.C. 333, [1991] 2 S.C.R. 50, the court per Sopinka J. See PUBLIC ~.

PROMISSORY NOTE. An unconditional promise in writing made by one person to another person, signed by the maker, engaging to pay, on demand or at a fixed or determinable future time, a sum certain in money to, or to the order of, a specified person or to bearer. *Bills of Exchange Act*, R.S.C. 1985, c. B-4, s. 176. See CONSUMER NOTE.

PROMOTER. *n.* 1. When used in relation to an issuer, a person who (a) acting alone or in concert with one or more other persons, directly or indirectly, takes the initiative in founding, organizing or substantially reorganizing the business of the issuer; or (b) in connection with the founding, organization or substantial reorganization of the business of the issuer, directly or indirectly receives, in consideration of services or property or both, 10% or more of a class of the issuer's own securities or 10% or more of the proceeds from the sale of a class of the issuer's own securities of a particular issue but does not include a person who (c) receives securities or proceeds referred to in paragraph (b) solely (i) as underwriting commissions; or (ii) in consideration for property; and (d) does not otherwise take part in founding, organizing or substantially reorganizing the business. *Securities acts.* 2. A person named in the application or petition for incorporation. 3. An individual who enters into a contract on behalf of a company not yet, but about to be, incorporated.

PROMULGATION. *n.* The act of publishing.

PRONOUNCEMENT. *n.* The pronouncement of judgment is a judicial act. It is complete when the judge has signed the reasons for judgment and delivered them to the registry in their final form with instructions, express or implied, to communicate them to the parties. At that point, the judicial function is complete. *CIBC Mortgage Corp. v. British Columbia Insurance Co.*, 2005 BCCA 137, Smith J.A. (Mackenzie J.A. concurring).

PROOF. *n.* 1. Testimony; evidence. 2. Of a will, obtaining probate of it. See BURDEN OF ~; DIS~; LITERAL ~; ONUS OF ~; STANDARD OF ~.

PROOF LINE. A line surveyed across one or more concessions in the original survey of a single front township or of a double front township to govern the course of a side line of a lot. *Surveys Act*, R.S.O. 1990, c. S.30, s. 1.

PROOF OF SERVICE. Proof provided by the affidavit of the person who served it, by a certificate of service or by a solicitor's written admission or acceptance of the service or in accordance with rules regarding document exchanges..

PROPAGANDA. *n.* Information used to support a doctrine or interest. See HATE ~.

PROP. COMP. BD. *abbr.* Property Compensation Board.

PROPER. *adj.* Correct, fit, suitable.

PROPER ADMINISTRATION OF JUSTICE. Includes ensuring that (a) the interests of witnesses under the age of eighteen years are safeguarded in all proceedings; and (b) justice system participants who are involved in the proceedings are protected. *Criminal Code*, R.S.C. 1985, c. C-46, s. 486.

PROPER CAUSE. A nexus or reasonable relationship between an employee's misconduct and the employer's response by way of discipline or termination of the employee.

PROPER LAW. 1. The system of law which the parties intend to govern the contract, or, if their intention is not expressed or inferred from their circumstances, the system of law with which the transaction is most closely and really connected. G.H.L. Fridman, *Sale of Goods in Canada*, 3d ed. (Toronto: Carswell, 1986) at 473. 2. What determines the lex causae by referring to every fact in the individual case. J.G. McLeod, *The Conflict of Laws* (Calgary: Carswell, 1983) at 195.

PROPER QUESTION. 1. In relation to a cross-examination on an affidavit, a question which is relevant to the issue in relation to which the affidavit was given or to the credibility of the witness, is fair, and is asked with the intention that it be directed at the issue in the case or the credibility of the witness. 2. Relevant to the issues raised and allegations made in the pleadings.

PROPERTY. *n.* 1. "The plain and ordinary meaning of 'property' is legal title and not a contingent future equitable right to reacquire property which one does not presently hold." *Canada Trustco Mortgage Corp. v. Port O'Call Hotel Inc.*, 1996 CarswellAlta 366, (sub nom. *Pigott Project Management Ltd. v. Land-Rock Resources Ltd.*) 38 Alta. L.R. (3d) 1, 11 P.P.S.A.C. (2d) 1, [1996] 1 C.T.C. 395, (sub nom. *Minister of National Revenue v. Alberta (Treasury Branches)*) 196 N.R. 105, 184 A.R. 1, 122 W.A.C. 1, 133 D.L.R. (4th) 609, (sub nom. *Alberta (Treasury Branches) v. Minister of National Revenue*) [1996] 1 S.C.R. 963, (sub nom. *R. v. Alberta Treasury Branches*) 96 D.T.C. 6245, 39 C.B.R. (3d) 157, 27 B.L.R (2d) 147, [1996] 5 W.W.R. 153, [1996] G.S.T.C. 17, (sub nom. *R. v. Province of Alberta Treasury Branches*) 4 G.T.C. 6103, Major J. (dissenting) (Iacobucci J. concurring). 2. "... [I]n its ordinary sense may include both personalty and realty. But in any particular case its meaning must be gath-

ered from the whole of the instrument." *London Guarantee & Accident Co. v. George* (1906), 3 W.L.R. 236 at 238, 16 Man. R. 132 (K.B.), Richards J. 3. "... [E]ven in its widest sense, is limited to things which are capable of ownership and which are transferable or assignable. It does not include purely personal rights such as the right to personal safety ... the right to privacy or the right to be free from physical restraint. None of these are considered subject to ownership in the ordinary sense... ." *Marr v. Marr Estate* (1989), 71 Alta. L.R. (2d) 168 at 176, 63 D.L.R. (4th) 500, 101 A.R. 43, [1990] 2 W.W.R. 638 (Q.B.), O'Leary J. 4. "... [A] broad term which embraces choses in action... ." *Herchuk v. Herchuk* (1983), 35 R.F.L. (2d) 327 at 336, [1983] 6 W.W.R. 474 (Alta. C.A.), the court per Stevenson J.A. 5. "... [I]mports the right to exclude others from the enjoyment of, interference with or appropriation of a specific legal right... ." *National Trust Co. v. Bouckhuyt* (1987), 38 B.L.R. 77 at 86, 46 R.P.R. 221, 21 C.P.C. (2d) 226, 7 P.P.S.A.C. 273, 23 O.A.C. 40, 61 O.R. (2d) 640, 43 D.L.R. (4th) 543, the court per Cory J.A. 6. "... [A] word of wide signification and certainly includes money." *R. v. Ruggles* (1973), 21 C.R.N.S. 359 at 360, 12 C.C.C. (2d) 65 (Ont. C.A.), the court per Schroeder J.A. See CAPITAL ~; COMMERCIAL ~; COMMON ~; COMMUNITY ~ REGIME; CONVENTIONAL SEPARATION AS TO ~; CORPOREAL ~; DURESS OF ~; HERITAGE ~; INDUSTRIAL ~; INTANGIBLE ~; INTELLECTUAL ~; LINEAR ~; MARITAL ~; MARRIED WOMEN'S ~ ACT; MINE ~; MINING ~; MIXED ~; OFFENCE-RELATED ~; PERSONAL ~; PUBLIC ~; QUALIFIED ~; REAL ~; SEPARATION AS TO ~ JUDICIALLY OBTAINED; SPECIAL ~; TANGIBLE ~; TAXABLE ~.

PROPERTY AND CASUALTY COMPANY. A company or a provincial company that is not a life company or a marine company. *Insurance Companies Act*, S.C. 1991, c. 47, s. 2.

PROPERTY AND CIVIL RIGHTS. An area in relation to which provincial legislatures have power to make laws under section 92(13) of the Constitution Act, 1867.

PROPERTY DAMAGE INSURANCE. Insurance against loss of or damage to property that is not included in or incidental to some other class of insurance defined by or under this Act. *Insurance acts*.

PROPERTY LAW. Law which deals with ownership, rights and interests in property.

PROPERTY MANAGEMENT. See RENTAL ~ SERVICES.

PROPERTY TAX. Tax levied on property. *Petrofina Canada Ltd. v. Markland Developments Ltd.* (1977), 3 R.P.R. 33 at 37, 29 N.S.R. (2d) 158, 45 A.P.R. 158 (T.D.), Hallett J.

PROPORTIONALITY. *n.* 1. Principle of sentencing expressed in the Criminal Code as follows: A sentence must be proportionate to the gravity of the offence and the degree of responsibility of the offender. *Criminal Code*, R.S.C. 1985, c. C-46, s. 718.1. 2. The Sedona Canada Principles also recognize that when considering disclosure requests and standards for disclosure, the court should balance a variety of factors. Principle 2 advances a rule of proportionality. It states: "In any proceeding, the parties should ensure that steps taken in the discovery process are proportionate, taking into account (i) the nature and scope of the litigation, including the importance and complexity of the issues, interest and amounts at stake; (ii) the relevance of the available electronically stored information; (iii) its importance to the court's adjudication in a given case; and (iv) the costs, burden and delay that may be imposed on the parties to deal with electronically stored information." *Vector Transportation Services Inc. v. Traffic Tech Inc.*, 2008 CanLII 11050 (Ont. S.C.)

PROPORTIONALITY ANALYSIS. Used in assessing whether discriminatory legislation is demonstrably justified in a free and democratic society. The proportionality analysis comprises three branches. First, the connection between the goal and the discriminatory distinction is examined to ascertain if it is rational. Second, the law must impair the right no more than is reasonably necessary to accomplish the objective. Finally, if these two conditions are met, the court must weigh whether the effect of the discrimination is proportionate to the benefit thereby achieved. *Miron v. Trudel*, [1995] 2 S.C.R. 418.

PROPORTIONALITY TEST. "There are ... three important components of a proportionality test. First, the measures adopted ... must be rationally connected to the objective. Second, the means, even if rationally connected to the objective in this first sense, should impair 'as little as possible' the right or freedom in question ... Third, there must be a proportionality between the effects of the measures which are responsible for limiting the Charter right or freedom, and the objective which has been identified as of 'sufficient importance'." *R. v. Oakes*, [1986] 1 S.C.R. 103 at 139, 50 C.R. (3d) 1, 14 O.A.C. 335, 19 C.R.R. 308, 24 C.C.C. (3d) 321, 26 D.L.R. (4th) 200, 65 N.R. 87, Dickson C.J.C. (Chouinard, Lamer, Wilson and Le Dain JJ. concurring). See OAKES TEST; REASONABLE LIMITS.

PROPORTIONALLY. *adv.* In due proportion; corresponding in degree or amount.

PROPOSAL. *n.* A contract between an insolvent debtor and his or her creditors giving the debtor some degree of freedom over his or her property as agreed. See COUNTER-~.

PROPOSED TRADE-MARK. A mark that is proposed to be used by a person for the purpose of distinguishing or so as to distinguish wares or services manufactured, sold, leased, hired or performed by him from those manufactured, sold, leased, hired or performed by others. *Trade-marks Act*, R.S.C. 1985, c. T-13, s. 2.

PROPOSITUS. *n.* [L. the one proposed] The person from whom one traces descent.

PROPOUND. *v.* With respect to a will, to offer as authentic.

PROPRIETARY. *adj.* Owned by a private organization or an individual and operated for profit.

PROPRIETARY ESTOPPEL. Estoppel by encouragement or acquiescence. Arises where one party knowingly encourages another to act or acquiesces in the other's actions to the first party's detriment, infringing rights. The party who encouraged or acquiesced cannot later complain about the infringement or detriment suffered.

PROPRIETARY INTEREST. An interest as an owner. *Cooney v. Sheppard* (1895), 23 O.A.R. 4 at 6 (C.A.), Osler J.A.

PROPRIETOR. *n.* 1. The owner, lessee or other person in lawful possession of any property. 2. (i) An individual who owns and operates a business (A) the general business activity of which usually involves performing work for more than one person concurrently, and (B) in connection with which the individual does not employ any workers, and (ii) any other individual or class of individuals deemed by a direction or order of the Board to be proprietors. *Workers' Compensation Act*, R.S.A. 2000, c. W-15, s. 1.

PROPRIETORSHIP. *n.* One who carries on business under a name other than one's own. See SOLE ~.

PRO RATA. [L.] In proportion, according to a certain percentage or rate.

PRO RATA EVALUATION. In marriage breakdown, a method to divide a spouse's pension based on the ratio of number of years of cohabitation to the number of years of service accumulated in the pension plan.

PRORATED. *adj.* Proportional.

PROROGATION. *n.* 1. Prolongation or postponement until another day. 2. The termination of a session of Parliament. A. Fraser, W.A. Dawson & J. Holtby, eds., *Beauchesne's Rules and Forms of the House of Commons of Canada*, 6th ed. (Toronto: Carswell, 1989) at 66.

PROROGUE. *v.* To terminate a session of Parliament.

PRO SE. [L.] For oneself.

PROSECUTE. *v.* To commence proceedings and to carry the proceedings through to their ultimate conclusion including pursuing any available appeal rights.

PROSECUTION. *n.* 1. "... [I]mplies 'suit', but that is only one meaning of the word in its legal sense because it is just as much attributable to a pressing of claims without suit... ." *Taylor v. Mackintosh*, [1924] 3 D.L.R. 926 at 932, [1924] 3 W.W.R. 97, 42 C.C.C. 327, 34 B.C.R. 56 (C.A.), Martin J.A. 2. The putting of an offender on trial. See DIRECTOR OF PUBLIC ~S; MALICIOUS ~; PRIVATE ~; WANT OF ~.

PROSECUTION HISTORY ESTOPPEL. In the United States, representations to the Patent Office were historically noted on the file cover or "wrapper", and the doctrine is thus known in that country as "file wrapper estoppel" or "prosecution history estoppel." In its recent decision in Warner-Jenkinson Co., [Warner-Jenkinson Co. v. Hilton Davis Chemical Co., 520 U.S. 17 (1997)], the United States Supreme Court

P

affirmed that a patent owner is precluded from claiming the benefit of the doctrine of equivalents to recapture ground conceded by limiting argument or amendment during negotiations with the Patent Office. The availability of file wrapper estoppel was affirmed, but it was narrowed in the interest of placing "reasonable limits on the doctrine of equivalents", per Thomas J., at p. 34. While prosecution history estoppel is still tied to amendments made to avoid the prior art, or otherwise to address a specific concern—such as obviousness—that arguably would have rendered the claimed subject matter unpatentable, the court placed the burden on the patentee to establish the reason for an amendment required during patent prosecution. Where no innocent explanation is established, the court will now presume that the Patent Office had a substantial reason related to patentability for including the limiting element added by amendment. In those circumstances, prosecution history estoppel bars the application of the doctrine of equivalents as to that element. The use of file wrapper estoppel in Canada was emphatically rejected by Thorson P. in Lovell Manufacturing Co. v. Beatty Brothers Ltd. (1962), 41 C.P.R. 18 (Can. Ex. Ct.), and our Federal Court has in general confirmed over the years the exclusion of file wrapper materials tendered for the purpose of construing the claims: see, e.g., P.L.G. Research Ltd. v. Jannock Steel Fabricating Co. (1991), 35 C.P.R. (3d) 346 (Fed. T.D.), at p. 349. No distinction is drawn in this regard between cases involving allegations of literal infringement and those involving substantive infringement. *Free World Trust c. Électro Santé Inc.*, 2000 CarswellQue 2728, 2000 SCC 66, 194 D.L.R. (4th) 232, 263 N.R. 150, [2000] 2 S.C.R. 1024, 9 C.P.R. (4th) 168, Binnie J.

PROSECUTOR. *n.* 1. The Attorney General or, where the Attorney General does not intervene, means the person who institutes proceedings to which this Act applies, and includes counsel acting on behalf of either of them. *Criminal Code*, R.S.C. 1985, c. C-46, s. 2. 2. The Attorney General or, where the Attorney General does not intervene, the informant, and includes counsel or an agent acting on behalf of either of them. *Criminal Code*, R.S.C. 1985, c. C-46, s. 785.

PROSECUTORIAL DISCRETION. Without being exhaustive, we believe the core elements of prosecutorial discretion encompass the following: (a) the discretion whether to bring the prosecution of a charge laid by police; (b) the discretion to enter a stay of proceedings in either a private or public prosecution, as codified in the Criminal Code, R.S.C. 1985, c. C-46, ss. 579 and 579.1; (c) the discretion to accept a guilty plea to a lesser charge; (d) the discretion to withdraw from criminal proceedings altogether: R. v. Osborne (1975), 25 C.C.C. (2d) 405 (N.B. C.A.); and (e) the discretion to take control of a private prosecution: Osiowy v. Linn (1989), 50 C.C.C. (3d) 189 (Sask. C.A.). While there are other discretionary decisions, these are the core of the delegated sovereign authority peculiar to the office of the Attorney General. Significantly, what is common to the various elements of prosecutorial discretion is that they involve the ultimate decisions as to whether a prosecution should be brought, continued or ceased, and what the prosecution ought to be for. Put differently, prosecutorial discretion refers to decisions regarding the nature and extent of the prosecution and the Attorney General's participation in it. Decisions that do not go to the nature and extent of the prosecution, i.e., the decisions that govern a Crown prosecutor's tactics or conduct before the court, do not fall within the scope of prosecutorial discretion. Rather, such decisions are governed by the inherent jurisdiction of the court to control its own processes once the Attorney General has elected to enter into that forum. It is a constitutional principle in this country that the Attorney General must act independently of partisan concerns when supervising prosecutorial decisions. This side of the Attorney General's independence finds further form in the principle that courts will not interfere with his exercise of executive authority, as reflected in the prosecutorial decision-making process. *Krieger v. Law Society (Alberta)*, [2002] 3 S.C.R. 372.

PROSPECT AND EXPLORE. To carry out work preliminary to mining operations, with the purpose of discovering an ore deposit or an underground reservoir and demonstrating the existence thereof.

PROSPECTING. *n.* The investigating of, or searching for, minerals. *Mining* Act, R.S.O. 1990, c. M.14, s. 1.

PROSPECTIVE. *adj.* Governing the future and affecting vested rights.

PROSPECTIVE ADJUDICATION. A challenge to the employer's formulation of a rule or policy without an incident having occurred to trigger the operation of the rule or policy.

PROSPECTIVE BUYER. A prospective buyer is someone who has a prospect or expectation of buying something in the future. *Rosling Real Estate (Nelson) Ltd. v. Robertson Hilliard Cattell Realty Co.*, 1999 CarswellBC 1554 (S.C.), Smith J.

PROSPECTIVE FRANCHISEE. A person who has indicated, directly or indirectly, to a franchisor or a franchisor's associate or broker an interest in entering into a franchise agreement, and a person whom a franchisor or a franchisor's associate or broker, directly or indirectly, invites to enter into a franchise agreement. *Franchises Act*, S.P.E.I. 2005, c. 36, s. 1.

PROSPECTUS. *n.* A document published by a corporation or persons acting on its behalf describing the nature and objects of an issue of shares or other securities of the company and inviting persons to subscribe for those shares or securities.

PROSTATE SPECIFIC ANTIGEN. A protein which originates in human prostate glands and blood group substances. F.A. Jaffe, *A Guide to Pathological Evidence for Lawyers and Police Officers*, 4th ed. (Toronto: Carswell, 1999) at 169.

PROSTITUTE. *n.* A person of either sex who engages in prostitution.

PROSTITUTION. *n.* "... [T]he exchange of sexual services of one person in return for payment by another." *Reference re ss. 193 & 195.1(1)(c) of the Criminal Code (Canada)* (1990), 48 C.R.R. 1 at 30,

77 C.R. (3d) 1, 56 C.C.C. (3d) 65, [1990] 4 W.W.R. 481, [1990] 1 S.C.R. 1123, 109 N.R. 81, 68 Man. R. (2d) 1, Lamer J.

PRO TANTO. [L. for so much] To such an extent.

PROTECTED DISCLOSURE. A disclosure that is made in good faith and that is made by a public servant (a) in accordance with this Act; (b) in the course of a parliamentary proceeding; (c) in the course of a procedure established under any other Act of Parliament; or (d) when lawfully required to do so. *Public Servants Disclosure Protection Act*, S.C. 2005, c. 46, s. 2.

PROTECTED PERSON. 1. A person on whom refugee protection is conferred under subsection (1), and whose claim or application has not subsequently been deemed to be rejected under subsection 108(3), 109(3) or 114(4). *Immigration and Refugee Protection Act*, S.C. 2001, c. 27, s. 95(2). 2. (i) A witness who is a party to a protection agreement; or (ii) an associated person at risk who is a party to a protection agreement. *The Witness Protection Act*, S.S. 2009, c. W-14.2, s. 2. See INTERNATIONALLY ~.

PROTECTED PURCHASER. 1. A purchaser of a certificated or uncertificated security, who (i) gives value, (ii) does not have notice of any adverse claim to the security, and (iii) obtains control of the security. *Securities Transfer acts.* 2. A purchaser of a certificated or uncertificated security, or of an interest in the security, who: (i) gives value; (ii) does not have notice of any adverse claim to the security; and (iii) obtains control of the security. *The Securities Transfer Act*, S.S. 2007, c. S-42.3, s. 1.

PROTECTION. *n.* In respect of a protectee, may include relocation, accommodation and change of identity as well as counselling and financial support for those or any other purposes in order to ensure the security of the protectee or to facilitate the protectee's re-establishment or becoming self-sufficient. *Witness Protection Program Act*, S.C. 1996, c. 15, s. 2. See CONSUMER ~ LEGISLATION; DEPOSIT ~ AGENCY; DIPLOMATIC ~; PERSON IN NEED OF ~; REFUGEE ~; URGENT NEED OF ~; WHISTLE BLOWER ~; WITNESS ~ PROGRAM.

PROTECTION AGREEMENT. An agreement between the director and a protected person that meets the requirements of section 12. *The Witness Protection Act*, S.S. 2009, c. W-14.2, s. 2.

PROTECTION OF MINORITIES. The fourth underlying constitutional principle we address here concerns the protection of minorities. There are a number of specific constitutional provisions protecting minority language, religion and education rights. Some of those provisions are, as we have recognized on a number of occasions, the product of historical compromises. However, we highlight that even though those provisions were the product of negotiation and political compromise, that does not render them unprincipled. Rather, such a concern reflects a broader principle related to the protection of minority rights. We emphasize that the protection of minority rights is itself an independent principle underlying our con-

stitutional order. *Reference re Secession of Quebec*, 1998 CarswellNat 1299, 161 D.L.R. (4th) 385, 228 N.R. 203, 55 C.R.R. (2d) 1, [1998] 2 S.C.R. 217, per curiam.

PROTECTION ORDER. Order made under the Act which protects the interests in property held by persons who hold prior secured interests or interests acquired without knowledge of that the property was the proceeds of unlawful activity. The order may sever or partition any interest in the property, order that the Crown takes the property subject to an interest of a person, or direct proceeds of sale of the property to be applied to any debt or other measures which are necessary to reasonably protect any interest in the property. *The Seizure of Criminal Property Act, 2009*, S.S. 2009, c. S-46.002, s. 2 and 8.

PROTECTION SERVICE. A service intended to protect or assist in protecting a person's safety or security and, without limiting the generality of the foregoing, includes the provision of: (i) transportation to and from a safe location; (ii) accommodation; (iii) transportation and storage of personal possessions; (iv) reasonable financial support; (v) security services and equipment; (vi) counselling;(vii) any other service that may be prescribed. *The Witness Protection Act*, S.S. 2009, c. W-14.2, s. 2. See FIRE ~S.

PROTECTIVE COSTS ORDER. In public interest cases, there is more reason for a court to avoid penalizing the pro bono litigant. It may even be appropriate for the court to grant costs, or at least disbursements, to an unsuccessful pro bono party. In England, for example, there is a limited practice of granting "pre-emptive costs orders" or "protective costs orders" ("PCO"s) in public interest cases where the applicant has no private interest in the case. In R. (on the application of Corner House Research) v. Secretary of State for Trade & Industry, [2005] 4 All E.R. 1 (Eng. C.A.), the English Court of Appeal explained these orders as follows at para. 6: The general purpose of a PCO is to allow a claimant of limited means access to the court in order to advance his case without the fear of an order for substantial costs being made against him, a fear which would inhibit him from continuing with the case at all. *1465778 Ontario Inc. v. 1122077 Ontario Ltd.* (2006), 82 O.R. (3d) 757 (C.A.).

PROTECTOR. See PUBLIC ~.

PRO TEM. *abbr.* Pro tempore.

PRO TEMPORE. [L. for the time being] Temporarily.

PROTEST. *n.* 1. The solemn declaration that a bill is dishonoured. I.F.G. Baxter, *The Law of Banking*, 3d ed. (Toronto: Carswell, 1981) at 117. 2. A serious declaration of opinion, usually dissent. 3. The express declaration by someone doing something that the act does not imply what it might. See SUPRA ~.

PROTEST STRIKE. A strike directed at government action, including legislation. *Health Employers Assn. of British Columbia v. H.E.U.*, 2009 CarswellBC 192, 2009 BCCA 39.

PROTHONOTARY. *n.* Of the Federal Court, a barrister or advocate from any province who is needed for the Court to work efficiently and whose powers are set out in the rules.

PROTOCOL. *n.* 1. The rules concerning ceremony observed in the official relations between nations and their representatives. 2. The minutes of a deliberative gathering of representatives of different countries. 3. The original drafts or copy of any document. 4. Guidelines for the design, operation and maintenance of complex equipment or processes. 5. The Internet operates by means of a series of protocols that enable higher level applications such as the World Wide Web to operate. Transmission control protocol ("TCP") is the most common protocol and it controls most of the applications used on the Internet. The TCP resides in both host server and end user computers and it controls the sending and receipt of packets transmitted over the Internet. However, routers and other intermediate points on the Internet have no involvement in TCP operation. *Society of Composers, Authors & Music Publishers of Canada v. Canadian Assn. of Internet Providers,* 2004 SCC 45, Binnie J. See KYOTO ~; RECONCILIATION ~; TRANSMISSION CONTROL ~; VOICE OVER INTERNET ~ SERVICE.

PROV. *abbr.* 1. Provincial. 2. Province.

PROVABLE. See CLAIM ~.

PROV. CT. *abbr.* 1. Provincial Court. 2. Provincial Court (Criminal Division).

PROV. CT. CIV. DIV. *abbr.* Provincial Court Civil Division.

PROV. CT. CRIM. DIV. *abbr.* Provincial Court Criminal Division.

PROV. CT. FAM. DIV. *abbr.* Provincial Court Family Division.

PROVE. *v.* 1. To establish. *R. v. Whyte* (1988), 35 C.R.R. 1 at 9, 6 M.V.R. (2d) 138, [1988] 45 W.W.R. 26, 86 N.R. 328, 64 C.R. (3d) 123, 42 C.C.C. (3d) 97, [1988] 2 S.C.R. 8, 29 B.C.L.R. (2d) 273, 51 D.L.R. (4th) 481, the court per Dickson C.J.C. 2. "... [I]n criminal law [requires] ... convincing proof, at least on the balance of probabilities." *R. v. Whyte* (1988), 35 C.R.R. 1 at 9, 6 M.V.R. (2d) 138, [1988] 45 W.W.R. 26, 86 N.R. 328, 64 C.R. (3d) 123, 42 C.C.C. (3d) 97, [1988] 2 S.C.R. 8, 29 B.C.L.R. (2d) 273, 51 D.L.R. (4th) 481, the court per Dickson C.J.C. 3. With respect to a will, to obtain probate. See DIS ~.

PROVINCE. *n.* 1. A province of Canada. 2. A field of duty. 3. Her Majesty the Queen in right of the Province. 4. A province of Canada, and includes Yukon, the Northwest Territories and Nunavut. *Interpretation Act,* R.S.C. 1985, c. I-21, s. 35. See ATLANTIC ~ S; CIVIL RIGHTS IN THE ~; PRAIRIE ~ S.

PROVINCIAL. See EXTRA- ~.

PROVINCIAL AUDITOR. The officer charged by law with the audit of the accounts of the government of a province.

PROVINCIAL CORPORATION. A corporation that is incorporated by or under the act of a legislature.

PROVINCIAL COURT. 1. Under section 92(14) of the Constitution Act, 1867 the body which a provincial legislature constitutes, maintains, and organizes to administer justice in the province. P.W. Hogg, *Constitutional Law of Canada,* 3d ed. (Toronto: Carswell, 1992) at 660. 2. "... [C]ourts which, as to their jurisdiction are primarily subjects of provincial legislation and whose process in civil matters, save in certain exceptional cases which will be adverted to, does not run beyond the limits of the province." *Reference re Privy Council Appeals (1940),* (*sub nom. Reference re Supreme Court Act Amendment*) [1940] S.C.R. 49 at 56, [1940] 1 D.L.R. 289, Duff C.J.

PROVINCIAL EMERGENCY. An emergency occurring in a province if the province or a local authority in the province has the primary responsibility for dealing with the emergency. *Emergency Management Act,* S.C. 2007, c. 15, s. 2.

PROVINCIAL ENFORCEMENT SERVICE. Any service, agency or body designated in an agreement with a province that is entitled under the laws of the province to enforce family provisions. *Family Orders and Agreements Enforcement Assistance Act,* R.S.C. 1985, c. 4 (2nd Supp.), s. 2.

PROVINCIAL LAND. Land vested in the Crown in right of a province.

PROVINCIAL LEGISLATURE. Any legislative body other than the Parliament of Canada.

PROVINCIAL PAROLE BOARD. The Ontario Board of Parole, la Commission québécoise des libérations conditionnelles, the Board of Parole for the Province of British Columbia or any other parole board established by the legislature or the lieutenant governor in council of a province. A provincial parole board for a province shall exercise jurisdiction in accordance with this Part in respect of the parole of offenders serving sentences in provincial correctional facilities in that province, other than (a) offenders sentenced to life imprisonment as a minimum punishment; (b) offenders whose sentence has been commuted to life imprisonment; or (c) offenders sentenced to detention for an indeterminate period. A provincial parole board may, but is not required to, exercise its jurisdiction under this section in relation to day parole. *Corrections and Conditional Release Act,* S.C. 1992, c. 20, s. 99 and 112.

PROVINCIAL PUBLIC UNDERTAKING. Any improvement or other work of public utility that relates to transportation, including, without limitation, (a) ferries, (b) provincial public highways, (c) hydraulic powers created by the construction of highways or works of public utility, and (d) canals, ditches, drains, drainage, irrigation works and earthworks required for the planning, design, acquisition, holding, construction, use, operation, upgrading, alteration, expansion, extension, maintenance, repair, rehabilitation, protection, removal, discontinuance, closure and disposal of highways and public works. *Transportation Act,* S.B.C. 2004, c. 44, s. 1.

PROVINCIAL REFERENCE. Each province has enacted legislation which permits the provincial government to send a reference, a question or questions, to its court of appeal.

PROVINCIAL SUPERIOR COURT. 1. "... They are descendants of the Royal Courts of Justice as Courts of general jurisdiction. They cross the dividing line, as it were, in the federal-provincial scheme of division of jurisdiction, being organized by the provinces under s. 92(15) of the [Constitution Act, 1867 (30 & 31 Vict.), c. 3] and are presided over by Judges appointed and paid by the federal government (s. 96 and 100 of the Constitution Act, 1867)... ." *Canada (Attorney General) v. Law Society (British Columbia)* (1982), 19 B.L.R. 234 at 257, [1982] 2 S.C.R. 307, 37 B.C.L.R. 145, [1982] 5 W.W.R. 289, 43 N.R. 451, 137 D.L.R. (3d) 1, 66 C.P.R. (2d) 1, the court per Estey J. 2. "They are not mere local courts for the administration of the local laws passed by the Local Legislatures of the Provinces in which they are organized. They are the courts which were established courts of the respective Provinces before Confederation ... They are the Queen's Courts, bound to take cognizance of and execute all laws, whether enacted by the Dominion Parliament or the Local Legislatures." *Valin v. Langlois* (1879), 3 S.C.R. 1 at 19-20, Ritchie C.J.C.

PROVING A WILL IN SOLEMN FORM. Proving the will in open Court upon notice to all interested parties.

PROVISION. *n.* 1. In a legal document, a clause. 2. The act of providing, supplying. See BOILER PLATE ~; CUSTODY ~; DEEMING ~; DEFINED BENEFIT ~; DEFINED CONTRIBUTION ~; FAMILY ~; LIMITATION ~; SUNSET ~; SUPPORT ~.

PROVISIONALLY. *adv.* Conditionally.

PROVISIONAL ORDER. 1. An order that has no effect until it is confirmed by another court. 2. An order made by a court which does not have personal jurisdiction over the person against whom the order is made.

PROVISO. *n.* [L.] 1. A clause in a document which sets a condition, limits, qualifies or covenants, as the case may be. 2. "[Something] ... which, according to the ordinary rules of construction, the effect must be to except out of the earlier part of the section something which, but for the proviso, would be within it." *Duncan v. Dixon* (1890), 38 W.R. 700 at 701 (U.K. Ch. D.), Kekewich J.

PROV. JUDGES J. *abbr.* Provincial Judges Journal (Journal des juges provinciaux).

PROVOCATEUR. See AGENT ~.

PROVOCATION. *n.* 1. A wrongful act or insult that is of such a nature as to be sufficient to deprive an ordinary person of the power of self-control is provocation for the purposes of this section if the accused acted upon it on the sudden and before there was time for his passion to cool. *Criminal Code*, R.S.C. 1985, c. C-46, s. 232(2). 2. Includes, for the purposes of

sections 34 and 35, provocation by blows, words or gestures. *Criminal Code*, R.S.C. 1985, c. C-46, s. 36. 3. "... [T]wo key elements to a defence of provocation reducing what would otherwise be culpable murder to manslaughter [under s. 215 of the Criminal Code, R.S.C. 1970, c. C-34]. The person causing death must have done so (i) in the 'heat of passion', caused by (ii) 'sudden provocation'. Whether the accused was provoked to lose his self-control is a question of fact for the jury." *R. v. Faid* (1983), 33 C.R. (3d) 1 at 12, [1983] 1 S.C.R. 265, [1983] 3 W.W.R. 673, 25 Alta. L.R. (2d) 1, 2 C.C.C. (3d) 513, 145 D.L.R. (3d) 67, 46 N.R. 461, 42 A.R. 308, the court per Dickson J. 4. The two concepts [of automatism and provocation] are quite distinct and their application depends on the nature of the impact on an accused of the triggering event. The key distinction between the two concepts is that automatism relates to a lack of voluntariness in the accused, an essential element of the offence, while provocation is a recognition that an accused who "voluntarily" committed all the elements of murder may nevertheless have been provoked by a wrongful act or insult that would have been sufficient, on an objective basis, to deprive an ordinary person of the power of self-control. Provocation simply operates, where applicable, to reduce murder to manslaughter. Thus, while evidence relating to the events preceding the commission of an offence may raise questions about both automatism and provocation, very different proof of facts must be made before either one of these issues can be left with the jury. *R. v. Stone*, 1999 CarswellBC 1064, [1999] 2 S.C.R. 290. See SUDDEN ~.

PROXIMATE CAUSE. 1. "... [A]n expression referring to the efficiency as an operating factor upon the result. Where various factors or causes are concurrent, and one has to be selected, the matter is determined as one of fact, and the choice falls upon the one to which may be variously ascribed the qualities of reality, predominance, efficiency. The true efficient cause never loses its hold. The result is produced, a result attributable in common language to the casualty as a cause, and this result, proximate as well as continuous in its efficiency, properly meets, whether under contract or under the statute, the language of the expression 'proximately caused.' " *Leyland Shipping Co., Ltd. v. Norwich Union Fire Ins. Society, Ltd.*, [1918] A.C. 350 at 370-71 (U.K. H.L.), Lord Shaw of Dunfermline. 2. "... [E]ffective cause ..." *Boulay v. Rousselle* (1984), 30 C.C.L.T. 149 at 164, 57 N.B.R. (2d) 235, 148 A.P.R. 235 (Q.B.), Meldrum J. See CAUSA CAUSANS.

PROXIMITY. *n.* "... [B]efore the law will impose liability there must be a connection between the defendant's conduct and [the] plaintiff's loss which makes it just for the defendant to indemnify the plaintiff ... In tort, [this] notion is proximity. Proximity may consist of various forms of closeness – physical, circumstantial, causal or assumed – which serve to identify the categories of cases in which liability lies... . Proximity is the controlling factor which avoids the spectre of unlimited liability." *Canadian National Railway v. Norsk Pacific Steamship Co.* (1992), 11 C.C.L.T. (2d) 1 at 26, 137 N.R. 241, 91 D.L.R. (4th) 289, [1992] 1 S.C.R. 1021, 53 F.T.R.

79n, McLachlin J. (L'Heureux-Dubé and Cory JJ. concurring). See SUFFICIENT ~.

PROXY. *n.* 1. "... [U]sed in two senses. It may be used to designate the person appointed by a shareholder (or a limited partner) to vote his shares in the company (or his interest in a limited partnership). It may also be used to designate the instrument by which a person is appointed to vote the shares (or interest) of another." *Beatty v. First Exploration Fund (1987) & Co.* (1988), 40 B.L.R. 90 at 95, 25 B.C.L.R. (2d) 377 (S.C.), Hinds J. 2. A completed and executed form of proxy by means of which a security holder or policyholder has nominated a person or company to attend and act on her or his behalf at a meeting of security holders or policyholders. See FORM OF ~; MUNCHAUSEN BY ~ SYNDROME.

PROXYHOLDER. *n.* The person appointed by proxy to attend and act on behalf of a shareholder at a meeting of shareholders.

P.S. *abbr.* Post script.

PSA. *abbr.* Prostate specific antigen.

P.S.A.B. *abbr.* Public Service Adjudication Board.

P.S.C.A.B. *abbr.* Public Service Commission Appeal Board.

PSEUDONYM. *n.* A nom de plume.

P.S.L.R. ADJUD. *abbr.* Public Service Labour Relations Act Adjudicator.

P.S.L.R.B. *abbr.* Public Service Labour Relations Board.

P.S.S.R.B. *abbr.* Public Service Staff Relations Board.

PSYCHOLOGICAL HARM. A psychological condition that (a) interferes with the health or comfort of a person, and (b) is more than merely transient or trifling in nature. *Crime Victim Assistance Act*, S.B.C. 2001, c. 38, s. 1.

PSYCHOLOGY. *n.* The practice of psychology is the assessment of behavioral and mental conditions, the diagnosis of neuropsychological disorders and dysfunctions and psychotic, neurotic and personality disorders and dysfunctions and the prevention and treatment of behavioral and mental disorders and dysfunctions and the maintenance and enhancement of physical, intellectual, emotional, social and interpersonal functioning. *Psychology Act, 1991*, S.O. 1991, c. 38, s. 3.

PSYCHO-SOCIAL REHABILITATION. Includes any psychological or social intervention whose object is to restore a person to a state of independent functioning and to facilitate their social adjustment. *Canadian Forces Members and Veterans Re-establishment and Compensation Act*, S.C. 2005, c. 21, s. 2.

PUBLIC. See INJURY TO THE ~; NOTARY ~; OPEN TO THE ~.

PUBLIC ACCESS TO LAW. Legal information institutes of the world, meeting in Montreal, declare that: Public legal information from all countries and international institutions is part of the common heritage of humanity. Maximizing access to this information promotes justice and the rule of law; Public legal information is digital common property and should be accessible to all on a non-profit basis and, where possible, free of charge; Independent non-profit organizations have the right to publish public legal information and the government bodies that create or control that information should provide access to it so that it can be published.

PUBLIC ACCOUNTANT. A person who either alone or in partnership engages in the practice of public accounting.

PUBLIC ACCOUNTING. See PRACTICE OF ~.

PUBLIC ACCOUNTS. The accounts of a country's or province's expenditures.

PUBLIC ACT. See ACT OF PARLIAMENT.

PUBLICATION. *n.* 1. "... [A]ny act of communication from one to another: ..." *Peel Board of Education v. B. (W.)* (1987), 36 M.P.L.R. 95 at 103, 24 Admin. L.R. 164, 59 O.R. (2d) 654, 38 D.L.R. (4th) 566 (H.C.), Reid J. 2. (a) In relation to works, (i) making copies of a work available to the public, (ii) the construction of an architectural work, and (iii) the incorporation of an artistic work into an architectural work, and (b) in relation to sound recordings, making copies of a sound recording available to the public, but does not include (c) the performance in public, or the communication to the public by telecommunication, of a literary, dramatic, musical or artistic work or a sound recording, or (d) the exhibition in public of an artistic work. *Copyright Act*, R.S.C. 1985, c.C-42, s. 2.2. 3. Includes any words legibly marked upon any substance or any object signifying the matter otherwise than by words, exhibited in public or caused to be seen or shown or circulated or delivered with a view to its being seen by any person. *Defamation Act*, R.S.M. 1987, c. C20, s. 19. 4. Includes a newspaper or a broadcast. *Defamation Act*, R.S.N. 1990, c. D-3, s. 2. 5. For a document to qualify as a "publication", it must: (1) have become generally available, without restriction, to members of the public, (2) the person or persons receiving the document, to be categorized as members of the public, must have no special relationship to the author of the so-called publication. *Xerox of Can. Ltd. v. IBM Can. Ltd.* (1977), 33 C.P.R. (2d) 24 at 85 (Fed. T.D.), Collier J. See SINGLE ~ RULE.

PUBLICATION BAN. In assessing whether to issue common law publication bans, therefore, in my opinion, a better way of stating the proper analytical approach for cases of the kind involved herein would be: A publication ban should only be ordered when: (a) such an order is necessary in order to prevent a serious risk to the proper administration of justice because reasonably alternative measures will not prevent the risk; and (b) the salutary effects of the publication ban outweigh the deleterious effects on the rights and interests of the parties and the public, including the effects on the right to free expression, the right of the accused to a fair and public trial, and the efficacy of the administration of justice. This reformulation of the Dagenais test aims not to disturb the essence of that test, but to restate it in terms that more plainly recognize, as Lamer C.J. himself did in that case, that publication bans may invoke more interests and rights than the rights to trial fairness and freedom of expression. This version encompasses the analysis conducted in Dagenais, and Lamer C.J.'s discussion of the relative merits of publication bans remains relevant. *R. v. Mentuck*, [2001] 3 S.C.R. 442.

PUBLICATION CONTEMPT. Canadian courts have consistently applied a definition [of publication contempt] which finds its origins in Lord Russell's commentary [in R. v. Gray, in [1900] 2 Q.B. (Eng. Q.B.)]. "The gravamen of the matter [is] the interference with the administration of justice by publishing articles that [pose] a real risk of prejudice to the accused". The current test requires that the court be satisfied beyond a reasonable doubt that the publication of the material constituted a real and substantial risk of prejudice to the administration of justice. The definition of criminal contempt of court by publication cannot be re-written so as to eliminate all restrictions to freedom of the press and freedom of expression without risking the elimination of the contempt of court power. *R. v. Edmonton Sun*, 2003 ABCA 3, 320 A.R. 217.

PUBLICATION OF RIGHTS. Concerning an immovable is made in the land register, in the land book for the registration division in which the immovable is situated. Rights concerning a movable and any other rights are published by registration in the register of personal and movable real rights; if the movable real right also pertains to an immovable, registration shall also be made in the land register in accordance with the standards applicable to that register and determined by this Book or by the regulations under this Book. *Civil Code*, S.Q. 1991, c. 64, a. 2970.

PUBLIC BILL. A bill relating to public policy matters. A. Fraser, W.A. Dawson & J. Holtby, eds., *Beauchesne's Rules and Forms of the House of Commons of Canada*, 6th ed. (Toronto: Carswell, 1989) at 192.

PUBLIC BUILDING. 1. Any building to which the public has a right of access. 2. A place of public resort or amusement.

PUBLIC COMPANY. 1. A company that is not a private company. 2. A company that (a) is a reporting issuer, (b) is a reporting issuer equivalent, (c) has registered its securities under the Securities Exchange Act of 1934 of the United States of America, (d) has any of its securities, within the meaning of the Securities Act, traded on or through the facilities of a securities exchange, or (e) has any of its securities, within the meaning of the Securities Act, reported through the facilities of a quotation and trade reporting system. *Business Corporations Act*, S.B.C. 2002, c. 57, s. 1.

PUBLIC COMPLAINT. A complaint having a public aspect, that is, made by a member of the public, initiated by a public official or resulting in a public hearing. See ROYAL CANADIAN MOUNTED POLICE ~S COMMISSION.

PUBLIC CURATOR. Has the powers conferred on him by the Civil Code, this Act or any other Act. The Public Curator is responsible, in particular, for (1) supervision of the administration of tutorships and curatorships to persons of full age, of certain tutorships to minors and of tutorships to absentees; (2) tutorships, curatorships or other duties related to the administration of the property of others, where such duties are assigned to him by a court; (3) tutorship to property of minors and tutorship or curatorship to persons of full age under protective supervision who are not already provided with a tutor or a curator. *Public Curator Act*, R.S.Q. c. C-81, s. 12.

PUBLIC DOCUMENT. Includes certificates under the Great Seal of a province, legal documents, vouchers, cheques, accounting records, correspondence, maps, photographs and all other documents created in the administration of public affairs. Must have a public purpose or objective, be retained and be open for inspection by interested parties, prepared pursuant to a public duty, and may be required to determine the truth of the facts recorded in the document.

PUBLIC DOMAIN. The sphere in which the public operates. Something is in the public domain if it is generally known to the public.

PUBLIC FACILITY. See GOVERNMENT OR ~.

PUBLIC FORUM. A place which constitutes a favourable platform for the public to exercise its right of freedom of expression.

PUBLIC FUNDS. 1. Money from the treasury of the federal, provincial or municipal government. *Les Soeurs de la Visitation d'Ottawa v. Ottawa*, [1952] O.R. 61 at 71, 72. 2. The case law is clear that the term "public funds" in sub-paragraph 12(iii) of s. 3(1) of the Assessment Act [R.S.O. 1990, c. A.31] means funds received from a government source, not from members of the public. *Causeway Foundation v. Ontario Property Assessment Corp., Region No. 3* (2004), 181 O.A.C. 218.

PUBLIC GUARDIAN AND TRUSTEE. Public official who attends to matters relating to persons who are incapable of managing their own affairs whether because of mental incapacity or minority. The official may also act as administrator of certain estates.

PUBLIC HEALTH AGENCY. Established by the Public Health Agency of Canada Act, S.C. 2006, c. 5, headed by the Minister of Health and to which the Minister may delegate functions. To take public health measures, including measures relating to health protection and promotion, population health assessment, health surveillance, disease and injury prevention, and public health emergency preparedness and response; to foster collaboration within the field of public health and to coordinate federal policies and programs in the area of public health; to promote cooperation and consultation in the field of public health with provincial and territorial governments; to foster cooperation in that field with foreign governments and international organizations, as well as other interested persons or organizations.

PUBLIC HEALTH OFFICER. See CHIEF ~.

PUBLIC HEARING. 1. "... [O]ne in open court which the public including representatives of the media are entitled to attend." *Canadian Newspapers Co. v. Canada (Attorney General)* (1985), 14 C.R.R. 276 at 302, 49 O.R. (2d) 557, 17 C.C.C. (3d) 385, 16 D.L.R. (4th) 642, 44 C.R. (3d) 97, 7 O.A.C. 161, the court per Howland C.J.O. 2. A hearing of which public notice is given, which is open to the public, and at which any person who has an interest in a matter may be heard.

PUBLIC HIGHWAY. Any part of a bridge, road, street, place, square or other ground open to public vehicular traffic.

PUBLIC INQUIRY. The Governor in Council may, whenever the Governor in Council deems it expedient, cause inquiry to be made into and concerning any matter connected with the good government of Canada or the conduct of any part of the public business thereof. Where an inquiry is not regulated by any special law, the Governor in Council may, by a commission, appoint persons as commissioners by whom the inquiry shall be conducted. A Lieutenant Governor in Council has similar powers to establish an inquiry.

PUBLIC INSTITUTION. See OFFICER OF A ~.

PUBLIC INTEREST. 1. "In R. v. Collins, [(1987), 33 C.C.C. (3d) 1 (S.C.C.)], ... at p. 18 ... Lamer J. (now C.J.C.) writing for the Supreme Court of Canada, set out one of the criteria that a judge must take into consideration when dealing with public interest: 'It serves as a reminder to each individual judge that his discretion is grounded in community values and in particular long term community values.' " *R. v. Shah* (1991), 7 C.R. (4th) 102 at 115 (Ont. Gen. Div.), Caswell J. 2. Includes matters broader than the mere protection of the public and includes the public's perception of and confidence in the administration of justice. 3. The term 'public interest' in s. 25(1)(b) [of the Freedom of Information and Protection of Privacy Act, S.B.C. 1992, c. 61] cannot be so broad as to encompass anything that the public may be interested in learning. The term is not defined by the various levels of public curiosity. The public is, however, truly 'interested' in matters that may affect the health or safety of children." *Clubb v. Saanich (District)*, 1996 CarswellBC 231, 46 C.R. (4th) 253, 35 Admin. L.R. (2d) 309, 35 C.R.R. (2d) 325 (S.C.), Melvin J. 4. Includes concerns of society generally and the particular interests of identifiable groups in the context of weighing the balance of convenience on an application for an interlocutory injunction. See RESPONSIBLE COMMUNICATION ON MATTERS OF ~.

PUBLIC INTEREST GROUP. An organization without personal, proprietary or pecuniary interest in the outcome of proceedings which has as its object the taking of public initiative, including litigation, to affect policy in relation to matters of interest to the group and to enforce constitutional, statutory and common law rights in relation to these matters.

PUBLIC INTEREST IMMUNITY. Rule of evidence which permits the Crown to exclude evidence, records of Cabinet discussions and planning documents, in order to ensure the proper functioning of the executive branch of government.

PUBLIC INTERNATIONAL LAW. See INTERNATIONAL LAW.

PUBLIC KEY. A string of data contained in a digital signature certificate that (a) is used in asymmetric cryptography to decrypt data contained in an electronic document that was encrypted through the application of the private key in the key pair; and (b) corresponds only to the private key in the key pair. *Personal Information Protection and Electronic Documents Act*, S.C. 2000, c. 5, *Secure Electronic Signature Regulations*, SOR/2005-30, s. 1.

PUBLIC LAW. All law dealing with relations between an individual and the state or between states and the organization of government, i.e., criminal, administrative, constitutional and international law.

PUBLIC LEGAL INFORMATION. Legal information produced by public bodies that have a duty to produce law and make it public. It includes primary sources of law, such as legislation, case law and treaties, as well as various secondary (interpretative) public sources, such as law reform reports, and reports from boards of inquiry.

PUBLIC LIABILITY INSURANCE. Insurance against loss or damage to the person or property of others that is not included in or incidental to some other class of insurance defined by or under this Act. *Insurance acts.*

PUBLICLY-TRADED LIABILITY. Of an entity, means a liability that is a security of the entity, that is not equity of the entity and that is listed or traded on a stock exchange or other public market. *Income Tax Act*, R.S.C. 1985, c. 1 (5th Supp.), s. 122.1. See UNAFFILIATED ~.

PUBLIC MEETING. 1. A meeting bona fide and lawfully held for a lawful purpose and for the furtherance or discussion of any matter of public concern, whether admission thereto is general or restricted. *Defamation acts.* 2. In examining these submissions it is helpful to recognize that section 4 of the British Columbia Libel and Slander Act [R.S.B.C. 1996, c. 263] is substantially similar to section 7 of the English Defamation Act, 1952 [15 & 16 Geo. 6 & 1 Eliz. S.c.66]. In its structure, however, the British Columbia legislation sets out within section 4 the types of meetings and reports entitled to the statutory privilege where the English legislation describes those matters in schedules to the legislation. Gatley on Libel and Slander, 8th ed. (London: Sweet & Maxwell, 1981) reviews the legislative history of this statutory privilege. In describing the nature of a "public meeting" covered by the privilege the author states at p. 281: It is submitted that the mere fact that admission to a meeting is restricted to those members of the public who purchase a ticket does not prevent it from being a public meeting within the meaning of the Act, unless the price of the ticket is so exorbitant as to exclude the general public. But if admission to a meeting can only be obtained by virtue of some personal qualification, it is not a "public meeting."

P

Cassidy v. Abbotsford (City) Police Department, 1999 CarswellBC 2887 (S.C. [In Chambers]), Ralph J.

PUBLIC MEMBER. A person representing the public, the state, on an arbitration panel or board as opposed to a member representing a particular interest.

PUBLIC MISCHIEF. With intent to mislead, causes a peace officer to enter on or continue an investigation by (a) making a false statement that accuses some other person of having committed an offence; (b) doing anything that is intended to cause some other person to be suspected of having committed an offence that the person has not committed, or to divert suspicion from himself; or (c) reporting that an offence has been committed when it has not been committed; or (d) reporting or in any other way making it known or causing it to be made known that he or some other person has died when he or that other person has not died. *Criminal Code,* R.S.C. 1985, c. C-46, s. 140.

PUBLIC MONEY. 1. All money belonging to Canada received or collected by the Receiver General or any other public officer in his official capacity or any person authorized to receive or collect such money, and includes (a) duties and revenues of Canada; (b) money borrowed by Canada or received through the issue or sale of securities; (c) money received or collected for or on behalf of Canada; and (d) all money that is paid to or received or collected by a public officer under or pursuant to any Act, trust, treaty, undertaking or contract, and is to be disbursed for a purpose specified in or pursuant to that Act, trust, treaty, undertaking or contract. All public money shall be deposited to the credit of the Receiver General. The Receiver General may establish, in the name of the Receiver General, accounts for the deposit of public money. *Financial Administration Act,* R.S.C. 1985, c. F-11 ss. 2 and 17. 2. All money belonging to the province received or collected by a minister or any public officer in an official capacity or any person authorized to receive or collect such money, and includes (i) revenues of a province; (ii) money borrowed by the province or received through the sale of securities; (iii) money received or collected for or on behalf of the province; and (iv) money paid to the province for a special purpose.

PUBLIC NUISANCE. 1. Activity which unreasonably interferes with the interest, of the public or a class of the public, in health, safety, morality, comfort, or convenience. 2. "... [O]ne which affects citizens generally as opposed to a private nuisance which only affects particular individuals, but a normal and legitimate way of proving a public nuisance is to prove a sufficiently large collection of similar private nuisances ..." *British Columbia (Attorney General) v. Couillard* (1984), 31 C.C.L.T. 26 at 32, 42 C.R. (3d) 273, 59 B.C.L.R. 102, 11 D.L.R. (4th) 567, 14 C.C.C. (3d) 169 (S.C.), McEachern C.J.

PUBLIC OFFICE. See MISFEASANCE IN ~.

PUBLIC OFFICE HOLDER. (a) A minister of the Crown, a minister of state or a parliamentary secretary; (b) a member of ministerial staff; (c) a ministe-rial adviser; (d) a Governor in Council appointee, other than the following persons, namely, (i) a lieutenant governor, (ii) officers and staff of the Senate, House of Commons and Library of Parliament, (iii) a person appointed or employed under the Public Service Employment Act who is a head of mission within the meaning of subsection 13(1) of the Department of Foreign Affairs and International Trade Act, (iv) a judge who receives a salary under the Judges Act, (v) a military judge within the meaning of subsection 2(1) of the National Defence Act, and (vi) an officer of the Royal Canadian Mounted Police, not including the Commissioner; (d.1) a ministerial appointee whose appointment is approved by the Governor in Council; and (e) a full-time ministerial appointee designated by the appropriate minister of the Crown as a public office holder. *Conflict of Interest Act,* S.C. 2006, c. 9, s. 2, s. 2. See REPORTING ~.

PUBLIC OFFICER. 1. "... [E]very one who is appointed to discharge a public duty, and receives a compensation in whatever shape, whether from the crown or otherwise, is constituted a public officer ..." *Henly v. Mayor and Burgesses of Lyme* (1828), 5 Bing. 91 at 107, 130 E.R. 995 at 1001, Best C.J. 2. Includes any person in the public service (i) who is authorized by or under an enactment to do or enforce the doing of an act or thing or to exercise a power; or (ii) upon whom a duty is imposed by or under an enactment. 3. Includes a minister of the Crown and any person employed in the public service. 4. Includes (a) an officer of customs and excise; (b) an officer of the Canadian Forces; (c) an officer of the Royal Canadian Mounted Police; and (d) any officer while the officer is engaged in enforcing the laws of Canada relating to revenue, customs, excise, trade or navigation. *Criminal Code,* R.S.C. 1985, c. C-46, s. 2.

PUBLIC ORDER EMERGENCY. An emergency that arises from threats to the security of Canada and that is so serious as to be a national emergency. *Emergencies Act,* R.S.C., 1985, c. 22 (4th Supp.), s. 16.

PUBLIC PASSENGER SERVICE PROVIDER. VIA Rail Canada Inc., a passenger rail service provider designated by the Minister or an urban transit authority. *Canada Transportation Act,* S.C. 1996, c. 10, s. 87.

PUBLIC PLACE. 1. Includes any place to which the public have access as of right or by invitation, express or implied. *Criminal Code,* R.S.C. 1985, c. C-46, s. 150. 2. A place to which ordinary members of the public have access by right or otherwise.

PUBLIC POLICY. 1. A highly indefinite moral value, usually resorted to as a principle of judicial legislation or interpretation based on the perceived needs of the community. It is not usually dependent on evidence, but on judicial impression of what is or is not in the public interest. *Simpson v. Chiropractors' Assn. (Saskatchewan),* 2001 CarswellSask 92, 2001 SKCA 21, 31 Admin. L.R. (3d) 87 (C.A.), the court per Cameron J.A. 2. The notion that no person can lawfully do what tends to injure the public or go against the public good. G.H.L. Fridman, *The Law of*

Contract in Canada, 2d ed. (Toronto: Carswell, 1986) at 350. 3. "... [A]n action [will be barred] on the ground of public policy only if we could say it was contrary to 'essential public or moral interest' or 'contrary to our conceptions of essential justice and morality.' " *Block Brothers Realty Ltd. v. Mollard* (1981), 122 D.L.R. (3d) 323 at 330, [1981] 4 W.W.R. 65, 27 B.C.L.R. 17 (C.A.), the court per Craig J.A. 4. "... [F]ederal and provincial statutes and public law may be resorted to as a guide to public policy ..." *Seneca College of Applied Arts & Technology v. Bhadauria* (1979), 9 B.L.R. 117 at 125, 27 O.R. (2d) 142, 11 C.C.L.T. 121, 105 D.L.R. (3d) 707, 80 C.L.L.C. 14,003 (C.A.), the court per Wilson J.A. 5. The use of the defence of public policy to challenge the enforcement of a foreign judgment involves impeachment of that judgment by condemning the foreign law on which the judgment is based. It is not a remedy to be used lightly. The expansion of this defence to include perceived injustices that do not offend our sense of morality is unwarranted. The defence of public policy should continue to have a narrow application. *Beals v. Saldanha*, 2003 SCC 72, Major J.

PUBLIC PROMISSORY ESTOPPEL. The requirements of public law promissory estoppel are the same as private law promissory estoppel except that legislative intent will be considered. *St Anthony Seafoods Limited Partnership v. Newfoundland and Labrador (Minister of Fisheries and Aquaculture)* (2003), 227 Nfld. & P.E.I.R. 310.

PUBLIC PROPERTY. Property, immovable or movable, real or personal, belonging to Her Majesty in right of a province or in right of Canada and includes property belonging to an agency of government.

PUBLIC PROTECTOR. 1. Shall intervene, subject to sections 18 to 19.1, whenever he has reasonable cause to believe that a person or group of persons has suffered or may very likely suffer prejudice as the result of an act or omission of a public body, its chief executive officer, its members or a person holding an office, employment or position accountable to the chief executive officer. *Public Protector Act*, R.S.Q. c. P-32, s. 13. 2. The official required to transmit to the Commission des droits de la personne et des droits de la jeunesse every complaint received that is within the sphere of investigation of the commission, unless the complainant objects thereto. *Charter of human rights and freedoms*, R.S.Q. c. C-12, s. 75.

PUBLIC SAFETY. See DEPARTMENT OF ~ AND EMERGENCY PREPAREDNESS.

PUBLIC SALE. A sale either by public auction or public tender.

PUBLIC SECTOR ENTITY. A department or agency of the Government of Canada, a Crown corporation established by or under an Act of Parliament or any other entity to which the Governor in Council may appoint a person, but does not include the Senate or the House of Commons. *Conflict of Interest Act*, S.C. 2006, c. 9, s. 2, s. 2.

PUBLIC SECTOR INTEGRITY COMMISSIONER. Appointed under the Public Servants Disclosure Protection Act, S.C. 2005, c. 46. Section 13 of the Act provides that a public servant may disclose to the Commissioner any information that the public servant believes could show that a wrongdoing has been committed or is about to be committed, or that could show that the public servant has been asked to commit a wrongdoing. Section 14 of the Act provides: A disclosure that a public servant is entitled to make under section 13 that concerns the Office of the Public Sector Integrity Commissioner may be made to the Auditor General of Canada who has, in relation to that disclosure, the powers, duties and protections of the Commissioner under this Act. Section 19 of the Act provides: A public servant or a former public servant who has reasonable grounds for believing that a reprisal has been taken against him or her may file with the Commissioner a complaint in a form acceptable to the Commissioner.

PUBLIC SERVANT. 1. Has the meaning assigned by subsection 2(1) of the Public Servants Disclosure Protection Act, but includes officers and non-commissioned members of the Canadian Forces and employees of the Canadian Security Intelligence Service or the Communications Security Establishment. *Conflict of Interest Act*, S.C. 2006, c. 9, s. 2, s. 2. 2. Every person employed in the public sector, every member of the Royal Canadian Mounted Police and every chief executive. *Public Servants Disclosure Protection Act*, S.C. 2005, c. 46, s. 2. 3. Any person employed in a department, and includes a member of the Canadian Forces or the Royal Canadian Mounted Police. *Public Servants Inventions Act*, R.S.C. 1985, c. P-32, s. 2. 4. A person appointed under this Act to the service of the Crown by the Lieutenant Governor in Council, by the Commission or by a minister. *Public Service Act*, R.S.O. 1990, c. P.47, s. 1. 5. In my opinion, however, the balance of the evidence favours the conclusion that, as ordinarily understood, the term "public servants" does not include judges but approximates to "civil servants" or "government employees", not independent office holders. It does not include members of the judicial branch of government, which performs its work independently of the executive and legislative branches. *Crowe v. R.*, 2003 FCA 191, 2003 D.T.C. 5288, [2003] 3 C.T.C. 271, 303 N.R. 305.

PUBLIC SERVICE. 1. Except in Part 3, means the several positions in or under (a) the departments named in Schedule I to the Financial Administration Act; (b) the other portions of the federal public administration named in Schedule IV to that Act; and (c) the separate agencies named in Schedule V to that Act.. *Public Service Labour Relations Act*, S.C. 2003, c. 22, s. 2. 2. All ministries or any part thereof.

PUBLIC SERVICE LABOUR RELATIONS BOARD. Established under the Public Service Labour Relations Act, S.C. 2003, c. 22. The Board administers the Act. The Board hears certification applications, determines appropriate bargaining units, and other functions generally associated with a Labour Relations Board. Section 14 provides: the adjudication services to be provided by the Board consist of the hearing of applications and complaints made under this Part, the referral of grievances to adjudication in accordance with Part 2 and the hearing of matters brought before the Board under Part 3. Section 15 provides: the mediation services to be provided by the Board consist of (a) assisting parties in the negotiation of collective agreements and their renewal; (b) assisting parties in the management of the relations resulting from the implementation of collective agreements; (c) mediating in relation to grievances; and (d) assisting the Chairperson in discharging his or her responsibilities under this Act. Section 16 provides. The compensation analysis and research services to be provided by the Board include conducting compensation surveys, compiling information relating to compensation, analyzing that information and making it, and the analysis, available to the parties and to the public, and conducting any research relating to compensation that the Chairperson may direct.

PUBLIC SERVICE STAFFING TRIBUNAL. Continued under the Public Service Employment Act. The mandate of the tribunal is to consider and dispose of complaints made under subsection 65(1) and sections 74, 77 and 83 which concern lay-offs, appointments and revocation of appointments to the public service.

PUBLIC'S RIGHT TO KNOW. The right of members of the public to be informed about the operations of government and public officials.

PUBLIC STORES. Includes any personal property that is under the care, supervision, administration or control of a public department or of any person in the service of a public department. *Criminal Code*, R.S.C. 1985, c. C-46, s. 2.

PUBLIC SWITCHED TELEPHONE NETWORK. A telecommunication facility the primary purpose of which is to provide a land line-based telephone service to the public for compensation. *Criminal Code*, R.S.C. 1985, c. C-46, s. 183.

PUBLIC TRANSPORTATION SYSTEM. A publicly or privately owned facility, conveyance or other thing that is used in connection with publicly available services for the transportation of persons or cargo. *Criminal Code*, R.S.C. 1985, c. C-46, s. 431.2 (1).

PUBLIC TRUST. A trust established to benefit the public or a section of it.

PUBLIC TRUSTEE. Public official who attends to matters relating to persons who are incapable of managing their own affairs whether because of mental incapacity or minority. The official may also act as administrator of certain estates.

PUBLIC UNDERTAKING. See PROVINCIAL ~.

PUBLIC USE. The phrase "public use" in s. 914(2) [Local Government Act, R.S.B.C. 1996, c. 323] is used in contradistinction to "private use" . . . the words "public use" mean that the lands may be freely used by the public at large subject only to restrictions imposed by one of the three levels of government or are used by a public institution owned by one of the three levels of government. To have privately owned property restricted to a public use, the general public would have to be given a right to use the property for a particular purpose and the owner of the property would have to be compelled by statute or bylaw to permit such use by the public. The words "public use" are [not] sufficiently broad to include any use which involves the public being given general access to the lands. For example, a restriction of the use of property to the use of a department store would not amount to a restriction to a public use. Although the public has general access to a department store, the owner of the store has the right to control access to the public and the purpose of operating the store is to make a profit for the benefit of a private institution. Similarly with a railway, the owner of the railway has the right to control access to the public and is entitled to generate a profit by imposing charges on persons who wish to use the railway. *535534 British Columbia Ltd. v. White Rock (City)*, 2001 CarswellBC 2159, 2001 BCSC 1381, Tysoe J. See PLACE OF ~.

PUBLIC UTILITY. 1. Any person or association of persons that owns, operates or manages an undertaking (a) for the supply of petroleum or petroleum products by pipeline; (b) for the supply, transmission or distribution of gas, electricity, steam or water; (c) for the collection and disposal of garbage or sewage or for the control of pollution; (d) for the transmission, emission, reception or conveyance of information by any telecommunication system; or (e) for the provision of postal services. *Statistics Act*, R.S.C. 1985, c. S-19, s. 17(3). 2. "[In s. 2(j), Public Utilities Board Act, R.S.A. 1970, c. 302] ... a concept embracing physical plant and nonphysical service elements." *Atco Ltd. v. Calgary Power Ltd.* (1982), 20 B.L.R. 227 at 232, [1982] 2 S.C.R. 557, [1983] 1 W.W.R. 385, 23 Alta. L.R. (2d) 1, 41 A.R. 1, 45 N.R. 1, 140 D.L.R. (3d) 193, Estey J. (Beetz, Chouinard and Lamer JJ. concurring).

PUBLIC WATER SUPPLY SYSTEM. A water supply system that is owned or operated by a municipality, a rural community or the Crown in right of the Province and includes such other water supply systems owned or operated by other persons as are prescribed by the regulations. *Public Health Act*, S.N.B. 1998, c. P-22.4, s. 1.

PUBLIC WELFARE EMERGENCY. An emergency that is caused by a real or imminent (a) fire, flood, drought, storm, earthquake or other natural phenomenon, (b) disease in human beings, animals or plants, or (c) accident or pollution and that results or may result in a danger to life or property, social disruption or a breakdown in the flow of essential goods, services or resources, so serious as to be a national emergency. *Emergencies Act*, R.S.C. 1985, c. 22 (4th Supp.), s. 5.

PUBLIC WELFARE OFFENCE. A form of offence, the legislative object of which is to regulate some activities in the interests of the public as a whole.

PUBLIC WORKS. See DEPARTMENT OF ~ AND GOVERNMENT SERVICES.

PUBLISH. *v.* With respect to a libel, when he (a) exhibits it in public; (b) causes it to be read or seen; or (c) shows or delivers it, or causes it to be shown or delivered, with intent that it should be read or seen by the person whom it defames or by any other person. *Criminal Code*, R.S.C. 1985, c. C-46, s. 299.

PUBLISHED. *adj.* 1. Released for public distribution or sale. 2. Communicated to someone else besides the plaintiff. R.E. Brown, *The Law of Defamation in Canada* (Toronto: Carswell, 1987) at 247.

PUFF. *n.* A statement which praises a seller's goods but which an ordinary, reasonable buyer does not usually regard as important. G.H.L. Fridman, *Sale of Goods in Canada*, 3d ed. (Toronto: Carswell, 1986) at 149-150.

PUFFER. *n.* A person appointed to bid on the part of the seller. *Conveyancing and Law of Property Act*, R.S.O. 1990, c. C.34, s. 1(1).

PUFFERY. *n.* Exaggeration or embellishment of the qualities of goods by the seller.

PUISNE. *adj.* [Fr.] Junior, of lower rank. Used to describe a judge or justice other than the chief judge or justice of a court.

PUNISHABLE. *adj.* Subject to punishment.

PUNISHMENT. *n.* 1. A penalty for breaking the law. *R. v. Johnson* (1972), 17 C.R.N.S. 254 at 256, [1972] 3 W.W.R. 145, 6 C.C.C. (2d) 380 (B.C. C.A.), the court per Bull J.A. 2. A deprivation of property or right. 3. In [Rodriguez v. British Columbia (Attorney General), [1993] 3 S.C.R. 519, 85 C.C.C. (3d) 15], the Supreme Court considered the applicability of s. 12 [of the Canadian Charter of Rights and Freedoms] in the context of a Criminal Code provision that had the effect of imposing cruel and unusual punishment on someone other than an accused person. Sopinka J., for the majority of the Court, held that the negative effects of a Criminal Code provision upon a person not facing a criminal charge could not amount to being subjected by the state to any form of punishment within the meaning of s. 12. *Canadian Foundation for Children, Youth & the Law v. Canada (Attorney General)*, 2000 CarswellOnt 2409, 146 C.C.C. (3d) 362, 188 D.L.R. (4th) 718, 49 O.R. (3d) 662, 36 C.R. (5th) 334, 76 C.R.R. (2d) 251 (S.C.), McCombs J. See ARBITRARY ~; CAPITAL ~; CORPORAL ~; CRUEL AND UNUSUAL ~.

PUNITIVE DAMAGES. 1. "... [A]warded to punish the defendant and to make an example of him or her in order to deter others from committing the same tort: ..." *Norberg v. Wynrib* (1992), 12 C.C.L.T. (2d) 1 at 29, [1992] 4 W.W.R. 577, 68 B.C.L.R. (2d) 29, 138 N.R. 81, 8 B.C.A.C. 1, 19 W.A.C. 1, 92 D.L.R. (4th) 449, [1992] 2 S.C.R. 226, La Forest J. (Gonthier and Cory JJ. concurring). 2. "... [M]ay only be employed in circumstances where the conduct giving the cause for complaint is of such nature that it merits punishment... . may only be awarded in respect of conduct which is of such nature as to be deserving of punishment because of its harsh, vindictive, reprehensible and malicious nature ... in any case where such an award is made the conduct must be extreme in its nature and such that by any reasonable standard it is deserving of full condemnation and punishment ..." *Vorvis v. Insurance Corp. of British Columbia* (1989), 58 D.L.R. (4th) 193 at 201-2, 205-9, [1989]

1 S.C.R. 1085, [1989] 4 W.W.R. 193, 25 C.C.E.L. 81, 90 C.L.L.C. 14,035, 36 B.C.L.R. (2d) 273, 94 N.R. 321, 42 B.L.R. 111, McIntyre J. (Beetz and Lamer JJ. concurring). 3. Punitive damages may be awarded in situations where the defendant's misconduct is so malicious, oppressive, and high-handed that it offends the court's sense of decency. Punitive damages bear no relation to what the plaintiff should receive by way of compensation. Their aim is not to compensate the plaintiff, but rather to punish the defendant. It is the means by which the jury or judge expresses its outrage at the egregious conduct of the defendant. They are in the nature of a fine, which is meant to act as a deterrent to the defendant and to others from acting in this manner. *Hill v. Church of Scientology*, [1995] 2 S.C.R. 1130.

PUR AUTRE VIE. [Fr.] For or during the life of another. R. Megarry & H.W.R. Wade, *The Law of Real Property*, 5th ed. (London: Stevens, 1984) at cxxvii. See ESTATE ~.

PURCHASE. *v.* 1. Includes to take as mortgagee or as pledgee. *Warehouse Receipt acts.* 2. A taking by sale, discount, negotiation, mortgage, hypothec, pledge, security interest, issue or reissue, gift or any other voluntary transaction that creates an interest in property. *Securities Transfer acts.* See HIRE-~ AGREEMENT; OPTION TO ~.

PURCHASE. *n.* 1. Contract, conveyance or assignment under or by which any beneficial interest in any kind of property may be acquired. 2. Includes taking by sale, lease, negotiation, mortgage, pledge, lien, gift or any other consensual transaction creating an interest in personal property. *Personal Property Security acts.* See COMPULSORY ~; CONSUMER ~; PREPAID ~ CARD.

PURCHASE-MONEY MORTGAGE. A mortgage given by a purchaser of land to the vendor of the land or the vendor's nominee as security for the payment of all or part of the consideration for the sale.

PURCHASE-MONEY SECURITY INTEREST. (a) A security interest taken or reserved in collateral, other than investment property, to secure payment of all or part of its price, (b) a security interest taken in collateral, other than investment property, by a person who gives value for the purpose of enabling the debtor to acquire rights in or to the collateral, to the extent that the value is applied to acquire the rights, or (c) the interest of a lessor of goods under a lease for a term of more than one year. *Personal Property Security Act*, R.S.O. 1990, c. P.10, s. 1.

PURCHASE PRICE. "[In a contract for commission means] ... the actual price or sum at which the property was sold ..." *George v. Howard* (1913), 16 D.L.R. 468 at 469, 5 W.W.R. 1152, 49 S.C.R. 75, 27 W.L.R. 425, Davies J.

PURCHASER. *n.* 1. A person who buys or agrees to buy goods or services. 2. 2. A person who takes by purchase. *The Securities Transfer Act*, S.S. 2007, c. S-42.3, s. 1. 3. A person who takes by sale, mortgage, hypothec, pledge, issue, reissue, gift or any other voluntary transaction creating an interest in a

P

security. 4. Includes a lessee, a mortgagee and an intending purchaser, lessee or mortgagee, or other person, who, for valuable consideration, takes or deals for any property. *Conveyancing acts*. See BONA FIDE ~; PROTECTED ~; SPECIAL ~.

PURCHASER FOR VALUE WITHOUT NO-TICE. One who purchased property bona fide for a valuable, even if inadequate, consideration without notice of any prior title or right that, if upheld, would restrict or limit the title which the purchaser supposedly acquired.

PURCHASER'S LIEN. A lien which protects the deposit and any other money that a person who agreed to purchase land paid on account of the purchase price, as well as costs and interest. B.J. Reiter, B.N. McLellan & P.M. Perell, *Real Estate Law*, 4th ed. (Toronto: Emond Montgomery, 1992) at 777.

PURCHASING OFFICE. Every one who purports to purchase or gives a reward or profit for the purported purchase of any such appointment, resignation or consent, or agrees or promises to do so, is guilty of an indictable. *Criminal Code*, R.S.C. 1985, c. C-46, s. 124.

PURE ECONOMIC LOSS. 1. "[Usually refers to] ... a diminution of worth incurred without any physical injury to any asset of the plaintiff ..." *Ontario (Attorney General) v. Fatehi* (1984), 31 M.V.R. 301 at 307, [1984] 2 S.C.R. 536, 31 C.C.L.T. 1, 56 N.R. 62, 6 O.A.C. 270, 15 D.L.R. (4th) 132, the court per Estey J. 2. Five different categories of negligence claims for which a duty of care has been found with respect to pure economic losses [are recognized]: 1. The Independent Liability of Statutory Public Authorities; 2. Negligent Misrepresentation; 3. Negligent Performance of a Service; 4. Negligent Supply of Shoddy Goods or Structures; 5. Relational Economic Loss. *Canadian National Railway Co. v. Norsk Pacific Steamship Co.*, [1992] 1 S.C.R. 1021.

PURGE. *v.* With respect to contempt, to make amends for or clear oneself of contempt of court.

PURPORT. *n.* The substance of an instrument as it appears on the instrument's face.

PURPOSE. *n.* 1. The word "purpose" in s. 258(1)(a) [of the Criminal Code, R.S.C. 1985, c. C-46] refers to intent and not ability. *R. v. MacAulay*, 2002 PES-CAD 24, 169 C.C.C. (3d) 321, 218 Nfld. & P.E.I.R. 312, 8 C.R. (6th) 109, 30 M.V.R. (4th) 263, 653 A.P.R. 312. 2. Object. 3. Reason for which something exists. 4. The mens rea requirement reflected in the word "purpose" under s. 21(1)(b) has two components: intent and knowledge. For the intent component, it was settled in R. v. Hibbert, [1995] 2 S.C.R. 973, that "purpose" in s. 21(1)(b) should be understood as essentially synonymous with "intention." The Crown must prove that the accused intended to assist the principal in the commission of the offence. The Court emphasized that "purpose" should not be interpreted as incorporating the notion of "desire" into the fault requirement for party liability. It is therefore not required that the accused desired that the offence be successfully committed (Hibbert, at para. 35). Even in respect of murder, there is no "additional

requirement that an aider or abettor subjectively approve of or desire the victim's death" (Hibbert, at para. 37 (emphasis deleted)). *R.v. B.*, 2010 SCC 13, para. 16. See BASE ~; BENEVOLENT ~; CHARITABLE ~; FITNESS FOR THE ~; IMPROPER ~; LAWFUL ~; MUNICIPAL ~S; PARTICULAR ~; SENTENCING ~.

PURPOSE-DRIVEN APPROACH. The purpose-driven approach [to determining whether a law is discriminatory in violation of section 15 of the Charter] also reflects the language of the provision itself, which focusses on the "object" of the program, law or activity rather than its impact. Moreover, the effects of a program in its fledgling stages cannot always be easily ascertained. The law or program may be experimental. If the sincere purpose is to promote equality by ameliorating the conditions of a disadvantaged group, the government should be given some leeway to adopt innovative programs, even though some may ultimately prove to be unsuccessful. The government may learn from such failures and revise equality-enhancing programs to make them more effective. ... we believe the "purpose"-based approach is more appropriate than the "effect"-based approach: where a law, program or activity creates a distinction based on an enumerated or analogous ground, was the government's goal in creating that distinction to improve the conditions of a group that is disadvantaged? In examining purpose, courts may therefore find it necessary to consider not only statements made by the drafters of the program but also whether the legislature chose means rationally related to that ameliorative purpose, in the sense that it appears at least plausible that the program may indeed advance the stated goal of combatting disadvantage. *R.v. Kapp*, 2008 SCC 41, McLachlin C.J. and Abella J. for the majority.

PURPOSIVE INTERPRETATION. Remedies provisions must be interpreted in a way that provides "a full, effective and meaningful remedy for Charter violations" since "a right, no matter how expansive in theory, is only as meaningful as the remedy provided for its breach." A purposive approach to remedies in a Charter context gives modern vitality to the ancient maxim ubi jus, ibi remedium: where there is a right, there must be a remedy. More specifically, a purposive approach to remedies requires at least two things. First, the purpose of the right being protected must be promoted: courts must craft responsive remedies. Second, the purpose of the remedies provision must be promoted: courts must craft effective remedies. *Doucet-Boudreau v. Nova Scotia (Department of Education)*, 2003 SCC 62, Iacobucci and Arbour JJ.

PURSUANT. *adv.* 1. "... '[W]ithin the limits of' or 'as circumscribed by' ..." *R. v. Melford Developments Inc.*, [1981] 2 F.C. 627 at 634, 36 N.R. 9, [1981] C.T.C. 30, 81 D.T.C. 5020 (C.A.), Urie J.A. (Thurlow C.J. concurring). 2. "... '[B]y reason of' ..." *Canada (Minister of National Revenue) v. Armstrong*, [1954] C.T.C. 236 at 240, [1954] Ex. C.R. 529, 54 D.T.C. 1104, Potter J.

PURSUANT TO. Following upon; consequent upon; in consequence of.

PURSUE. *v.* Of an authority or warrant, to execute or carry it out.

PURSUIT. See FRESH ~; HOT ~.

PURVIEW. *n.* The policy or scope of a statute.

PUT. *v.* With respect to a question, to read a motion or amendment from the Chair, seeking the House's pleasure. A. Fraser, W.A. Dawson & J. Holtby, eds., *Beauchesne's Rules and Forms of the House of Commons of Canada*, 6th ed. (Toronto: Carswell, 1989) at 93.

PUT. *n.* An option transferable by delivery to deliver a specified number or amount of securities at a fixed price within a specified time.

PUTATIVE. *adj.* Supposed, reputed.

PUTATIVE FATHER. A person alleged to have caused the pregnancy whereby a woman has become a mother.

PYKE. *abbr.* Pyke's Reports (Québec), 1809-1810.

PYRAMIDING. *n.* The provision of two or more employment benefits for the same period of time.

PYRAMID SELLING. See SCHEME OF ~.

P

Q

Q.A.C. *abbr.* Quebec Appeal Cases, 1986-1995.

Q.B. *abbr.* 1. Queen's Bench. 2. Court of Queen's Bench. 3. Supreme Court, Queen's Bench Division.

[] Q.B. *abbr.* Law Reports, Queen's Bench, 1891-.

Q.B.D. *abbr.* 1. Queen's Bench Division. 2. Law Reports, Queen's Bench Division, 1875-1890.

Q.C. *abbr.* Queen's Counsel.

QC. COMM. D.P. DÉC. *abbr.* Québec Commission des droits de la personne, décisions des tribunaux, 1977-1981.

QCTP. Neutral citation for the Tribunal des professions du Quebec.

Q.L.R. *abbr.* Quebec Law Reports, 1875-1891.

Q.P.R. *abbr.* Québec Practice Reports, 1896-1944.

QUA. *adv.* [L.] As, in the aspect of.

QUAERE. [L.] Inquire. Used to indicate that the proposition which follows is not settled law.

QUAINTANCE ESTATE TEST. In Quaintance Estate, Re, [2006 ABCA 47 (Alta. C.A.)], an adult child (not a beneficiary under the will) was granted standing to apply for proof in solemn form. The appropriate legal test to determine if formal proof of a will is required is whether there is a genuine issue to be tried. *Anderson Estate, Re*, 2009 CarswellAlta 803, 2009 ABQB 285.

QUALIFICATION. *n.* 1. An ability, quality or attribute that fits a person to perform a particular task or function. 2. Limitation; diminishing. 3. Of an expert witness, ability to be an expert established after hearing evidence for and against, and after cross-examination. P.K. McWilliams, *Canadian Criminal Evidence*, 3d ed. (Aurora: Canada Law Book, 1988) at 9-10. See BONA FIDE OCCUPATIONAL ~.

QUALIFIED. *adj.* 1. Suggests that certain conditions must be met as a precondition. 2. Limited, modified, restricted in some aspect. 3. Possessed of capacity or ability to perform a job or task.

QUALIFIED ACCEPTANCE. 1. An acceptance with some change in the effect of the bill as originally drawn. 2. In express terms varies the effect of the bill as drawn and, in particular, an acceptance is qualified

that is (a) conditional, that is to say, that makes payment by the acceptor dependent on the fulfilment of a condition therein stated; (b) partial, that is to say, an acceptance to pay part only of the amount for which the bill is drawn; (c) qualified as to time; or (d) the acceptance of one or more of the drawees, but not of all. *Bills of Exchange Act*, R.S.C. 1985, c. B-4, s. 37.

QUALIFIED PRIVILEGE. 1. The legal effect of the defence of qualified privilege is to rebut the inference, which normally arises from the publication of defamatory words, that they were spoken with malice. Where the occasion is shown to be privileged, the bona fides of the defendant is presumed and the defendant is free to publish, with impunity, remarks which may be defamatory and untrue about the plaintiff. However, the privilege is not absolute and can be defeated if the dominant motive for publishing the statement is actual or express malice. *Hill v. Church of Scientology of Toronto*, [1995] 2 S.C.R. 1130. 2. Attaches to the occasion upon which the communication is made, and not to the communication itself. It was explained in this way by Lord Atkinson in Adam v. Ward (1916), [1917] A.C. 309 (H.L.), at p. 334: ... a privileged occasion is ... an occasion where the person who makes a communication has an interest or a duty, legal, social or moral, to make it to the person to whom it is made, and the person to whom it is so made has a corresponding interest or duty to receive it. This reciprocity is essential. *Botiuk v. Toronto Free Press Publications Ltd.*, [1995] 3 S.C.R. 3.

QUALIFIED PROPERTY. Limited and special ownership.

QUALIFIED TITLE. A registered title which is subject to an excepted estate, interest or right arising under a particular instrument or before a particular date, or otherwise specifically described in the register.

QUALIFY. *v.* To become legally entitled.

QUALITY. *n.* In relation to evidence, weight. See ENVIRONMENTAL ~; MERCHANTABLE ~; WATER ~ MANAGEMENT.

QUALITY MARK. A mark indicating or purporting to indicate the quality, quantity, fineness, weight, thickness, proportion or kind of precious metal in an article. *Precious Metals Marking Act*, R.S.C. 1985, c. P-19, s. 2.

QUANTITY SURVEY METHOD. A valuation of a building, inclusive of permanent fixtures, using replacement or intrinsic value without allowing for depreciation.

QUANTUM. *n.* [L.] An amount.

QUANTUM MERUIT. [L. as much as one earned] 1. [I]s a quasi-contractual remedy. It allows a court to order payment of the reasonable value of services to a service provider when the contract under which the services were provided does not state a price for those services or when that contract cannot be enforced. *Tri Level Claims Consultant Ltd. v. Koliniotis* (2005), 201 O.A.C. 282. 2. "The remedy of quantum meruit exists in two distinct settings. In a contractual setting, remuneration is said to be paid on a quantum meruit basis when, although a valid contract is found to exist in fact and law, there is no clause spelling out in express terms the consideration for the contract. In such circumstances, the Courts award reasonable remuneration to the person who has rendered the services. In an unjust enrichment setting, an action for quantum meruit is based, in general, upon the rendering of services by one person to another who has requested such services be rendered or freely accepted them with the knowledge that they are not rendered gratuitously." *Gill v. Grant* (1988), 30 E.T.R. 255 at 271 (B.C. S.C.), Rowles J.

QUANTUM VALEAT. [L.] As much as it is worth.

QUANTUM VALEBANT. [L. as much as they were worth] A claim for the value of goods sold or disposed of improperly.

QUARANTINE. *n.* (a) In respect of a person or animals, the limitation of freedom of movement and contact with other persons or animals; and (b) in respect of premises, the prohibition against or the limitation on entering or leaving the premises, during the incubation period of the communicable disease in respect of which the quarantine is imposed. *Public Health Act*, R.S.A. 2000, c. P-37, s. 1.

QUARANTINE FACILITY. Any place that is used for the detention of a traveller. *Quarantine Act*, S.C. 2005, c. 20, s. 2.

QUARANTINE STATION. Any place that is used for the administration and enforcement of this Act. *Quarantine Act*, S.C. 2005, c. 20, s. 2.

QUARE. [L.] Inquire. Used to introduce a statement which is not a settled proposition of law. See QUAERE.

QUARE CLAUSUM FREGIT. [L. why one broke the close] Trespass on the plaintiff's lands.

QUARREL. *n.* A contest; a dispute.

QUARTER. See CALENDAR ~.

QUASH. *v.* 1. "[In s. 39 of the Supreme Court Act, R.S.C. 1906, s. 139] ... 'annul' or 'make void.' " *Shawinigan Hydro Electric Co. v. Shawinigan Water & Power Co.* (1910), 43 S.C.R. 650 at 653, Fitzpatrick C.J.C. 2. "... [A] discharging or setting aside [of

a by-law] and any remedy would be the simple act of quashing in itself... ." *Gray v. Ottawa (City)*, [1971] 3 O.R. 112 at 115, 19 D.L.R. (3d) 524 (H.C.), Henderson J. 3. Said of the act of setting aside a decision of an administrative tribunal on judicial review.

QUASI. *adv.* [L.] As if; as it were.

QUASI. *pref.* [L.] Similar but not the same as.

QUASI-CONTRACT. *n.* 1. "A contract is in some cases said to be implied by law, which really is an obligation imposed by law independently of any actual agreement between the parties, and may even be imposed notwithstanding an expressed intention by one of the parties to the contrary; it is an obligation of the class known in the civil law as quasi-contracts." *Dominion Distillery Products Co. v. R.*, [1938] 1 D.L.R. 597 at 613, [1937] Ex. C.R. 145, Maclean J. 2. A liability which cannot be attributed to any other legal principle and which requires someone to pay money to another person because non-payment would confer an unjust benefit on the proposed payor. 3. A notional or fictional contract implied in law and not based upon the intention of the parties where no contract exists. *Canada (Attorney General) v. Becker* (1998), 64 Alta. L.R. (3d) 292 (C.A.). See RESTITUTION; UNJUST ENRICHMENT.

QUASI-CRIMINAL OFFENCE. An offence created by provincial law which carries a penalty similar to that for a crime.

QUASI-ESTOPPEL. *n.* Once one party makes a representation about a present or past fact and the other party relies on it detrimentally, the representor cannot repudiate the representation and put forward the true facts. G.H.L. Fridman, *The Law of Contract in Canada*, 2d ed. (Toronto: Carswell, 1986) at 110.

QUASI-JUDICIAL. *adj.* Describes functions which are judicial in nature but performed by a tribunal. The hearing of a dispute, investigation, inquiry into a matter, determining facts, and the exercising of discretion in a judicial manner are examples of this type of function. See JUDICIAL OR ~ PROCEEDING.

QUÉBEC. See COMPILATION OF ~ LAWS AND REGULATIONS; ECONOMIC DEVELOPMENT AGENCY OF CANADA FOR THE REGIONS OF ~; PARLIAMENT OF ~; SERVICES ~.

[] QUE. C.A. *abbr.* Quebec Official Reports (Court of Appeal), 1970-.

QUEEN. *n.* 1. A woman who is the monarch of a kingdom. 2. The Sovereign of the United Kingdom, Canada and Her other Realms and Territories, and Head of the Commonwealth. 3. The Queen is Head of State. She is Queen of Canada. See ROYAL STYLE AND TITLES.

QUEEN OF CANADA. The head of state, represented in most capacities within the federal sphere by the Governor General.

QUEEN'S BENCH. 1. In some provinces, the name given to the superior court. 2. In England, a superior court of common law. See COURT OF ~.

QUEEN'S COUNSEL. A barrister appointed counsel to the Crown who wears a silk gown, sits within the bar and in court takes precedence over ordinary barristers.

QUEEN'S ENEMIES. Refers to war and rebellion, not to riots and civil commotions.

QUEEN'S L.J. *abbr.* Queen's Law Journal.

QUEEN'S PEACE. The peace and security of life and property guaranteed by the Crown. All criminal acts defined in the Criminal Code are disturbances of the Queen's Peace.

QUEEN'S PRINTER. Government printer or other official printer.

QUEEN'S PRIVY COUNCIL FOR CANADA. The federal cabinet and additional members appointed by the Governor General or ex officio members. See CLERK OF THE QUEEN'S PRIVY COUNCIL; PRIVY COUNCIL.

QUEEN'S PROCTOR. A representative of the Crown who may intervene in a divorce proceeding.

QUE. K.B. *abbr.* Quebec Official Reports (King's Bench), 1892-1941.

[] QUE. K.B. *abbr.* Quebec Official Reports (King's Bench), 1942-1969.

QUE. LAB. CT. *abbr.* Quebec Labour Court (Tribunal du travail)

QUE. L.R.B. *abbr.* Quebec Labour Relations Board (Commission des relations de travail du Québec).

QUE. P.R. *abbr.* Quebec Practice Reports, 1897-1944 (Rapports de Pratique du Québec).

[] QUE. P.R. *abbr.* Quebec Practice Reports, 1945- (Rapports de Pratique du Québec).

QUE. Q.B. *abbr.* 1. Quebec Court of Queen's (King's) Bench Reports. 2. Quebec Official Reports (Queen's Bench), 1892-1941.

[] QUE. Q.B. *abbr.* Quebec Official Reports (Queen's Bench), 1942-1969.

QUE. S.C. *abbr.* Quebec Official Reports (Superior Court), 1892-1941 (Rapports Judiciaires du Québec, Cour Supérieure).

[] QUE. S.C. *abbr.* Quebec Official Reports (Superior Court), 1942- (Recueils de jurisprudence du Québec, Cour Supérieure).

QUESTION. *n.* 1. An interrogation. 2. "... '[I]ssue'." *Blackburn v. Kochs Trucking Inc.* (1988), 25 C.P.C. (2d) 113 at 121, 58 Alta. L.R. (2d) 358, [1988] 34 W.W.R. 272, 86 A.R. 321 (Q.B.), McDonald J. 3. "[In s. 42(1) of the Marital Property Act, 1980, S.N.B. 1980, c. M-1.1] ... means a point on which the parties are not agreed, that is, it means 'dispute' and does not simply mean an interrogatory." *George v. George* (1987), 37 D.L.R. (4th) 466 at 467, 8 R.F.L. (3d) 368, 80 N.B.R. (2d) 357, 202 A.P.R. 357 (Q.B.), Montgomery J. See COLLATERAL ~; LEADING ~; MIXED ~; MUNICIPAL ~; ORAL ~; PRELIMINARY ~; PROPER ~; SERIOUS ~.

QUESTION OF FACT. 1. "... Where the term is simple and ordinary, and, as it were, can be reduced no further in simplicity or definition, and which to define would require words that themselves need definition, the question is one of fact. The terms 'resident' and 'insulting' are good examples. Where the term gives rise to some complexity, or has acquired a special or technical meaning, the question is likely, but not always, one of law." *Peters v. University Hospital* (1983), 1 Admin. L.R. 221 at 234, [1983] 5 W.W.R. 193, 4 C.H.R.R. D/1464, 147 D.L.R. (3d) 385, 23 Sask. R. 123 (C.A.), Bayda C.J.S. 2. "The construction of a statutory enactment is a question of law, while the question of whether the particular matter or thing is of such a nature or kind as to fall within the legal definition of its term is a question of fact." *Hollinger Consolidated Gold Mines Ltd. v. Tisdale (Township)*, [1933] 3 D.L.R. 15 at 16, [1933] S.C.R. 321, the court per Cannon J. 3. Questions of law are questions about what the correct legal test is; questions of fact are questions about what actually took place between the parties; and questions of mixed law and fact are questions about whether the facts satisfy the legal tests. A simple example will illustrate these concepts. In the law of tort, the question what "negligence" means is a question of law. The question whether the defendant did this or that is a question of fact. And, once it has been decided that the applicable standard is one of negligence, the question whether the defendant satisfied the appropriate standard of care is a question of mixed law and fact. *Canada (Director of Investigation and Research) v. Southam Inc.*, [1997] 1 S.C.R. 748 (at paragraph 35).

QUESTION OF LAW. 1. "... [I]n construing a will, deed, contract, prospectus or other commercial document, the legal effect to be given to the language employed, is a question of law ..." *R. v. Alberta Giftwares Ltd.* (1973), 11 C.P.R. (2d) 233 at 237, [1974] S.C.R. 584, [1973] 5 W.W.R. 458, 11 C.C.C. (2d) 513, 36 D.L.R. (3d) 321, the court per Ritchie J. 2. "... [W]ould include (without attempting anything like an exhaustive definition which would be impossible) questions touching the scope, effect or application of a rule of law which the Courts apply in determining the rights of parties; and by long usage, the term 'question of law' has come to be applied to questions which, when arising at a trial by a Judge and jury, would fall exclusively to the Judge for determination; for example, questions touching the construction of documents and a great variety of others including questions whether, in respect of a particular issue of fact, there is any evidence upon which a jury could find the issue in favour of the party on whom rests the burden of proof... ." *Canadian National Railway v. Bell Telephone Co.*, [1939] 3 D.L.R. 8 at 15, [1939] S.C.R. 308, 50 C.R.C.10, the court per Duff C.J.C. 3. "The construction of a statutory enactment is a question of law, while the question of whether the particular matter or thing is of such a nature or kind as to fall within the legal definition of its term is a question of fact." *Hollinger Consolidated Gold Mines Ltd. v. Tisdale (Township)*, [1933] 3 D.L.R. 15 at 16, [1933] S.C.R. 321, the court per Cannon J. 4. "...[W]hether a person's constitutional right has been infringed is a question of law." *R. v. Dunnett* (1990), 26 M.V.R. (2d) 194 at 200, 62 C.C.C. (3d) 14, 111 N.B.R. (2d) 67, 277 A.P.R. 67 (C.A.), Hoyt J.A. (Ayles J.A. concurring). 5. Questions of law are questions about what the correct legal test is; questions of fact are questions about what actually took place between the parties; and questions of mixed law and fact are questions about whether the facts satisfy the legal tests. A simple example will illustrate these concepts. In the law of tort, the question what "negligence" means is a question of law. The question whether the defendant did this or that is a question of fact. And, once it has been decided that the applicable standard is one of negligence, the question whether the defendant satisfied the appropriate standard of care is a question of mixed law and fact. *Canada (Director of Investigation and Research) v. Southam Inc.*, [1997] 1 S.C.R. 748 (at paragraph 35).

QUESTION OF MIXED LAW AND FACT. Questions of law are questions about what the correct legal test is; questions of fact are questions about what actually took place between the parties; and questions of mixed law and fact are questions about whether the facts satisfy the legal tests. A simple example will illustrate these concepts. In the law of tort, the question what "negligence" means is a question of law. The question whether the defendant did this or that is a question of fact. And, once it has been decided that the applicable standard is one of negligence, the question whether the defendant satisfied the appropriate standard of care is a question of mixed law and fact. *Canada (Director of Investigation and Research) v. Southam Inc.*, [1997] 1 S.C.R. 748 (at paragraph 35). See MIXED QUESTION OF LAW AND FACT.

QUE. TAX R. *abbr.* Quebec Tax Reports.

QUIA EMPTORES. See STATUTE OF ~.

QUIA TIMET. [L.] Because one fears.

QUIA TIMET INJUNCTION. [L. because one fears] 1. "... [A]n interim injunction to protect against feared future harm." *Bradley Resources Corp. v. Kelvin Energy Ltd.* (1985), 18 D.L.R. (4th) 468 at 471, [1985] 5 W.W.R. 763, 39 Alta.L.R. (2d) 193, 61 A.R. 169 (C.A.), the court per Kerans J.A. 2. It is not necessary to wait for actual damage to occur. Used when there is an apprehension that property will be removed from the jurisdiction. See INJUNCTION QUIA TIMET.

QUICQUID PLANTATUR SOLO, SOLO CEDIT. [L.] Whatever is affixed to the soil goes with the soil. *Canadian Imperial Bank of Commerce v. Alberta (Assessment Appeal Board)* (1990), 73 D.L.R. (4th) 271 at 277, 75 Alta. L.R. (2d) 362, [1990] 6 W.W.R. 425, 109 A.R. 203 (Q.B.), Andrekson J. and *Collis v. Carew Lumber Co.*, [1930] 4 D.L.R. 996 at 999, 65 O.L.R. 520, 38 O.W.N. 237 (C.A.), Middleton J.A.

QUID PRO QUO. [L. something for something] A consideration.

QUID PRO QUO SEXUAL HARASSMENT. Sexual harassment of this type involves situations in which tangible employment-related benefits are made contingent upon an employee's participation in sexual activity. *Janzen v. Platy Enterprises Ltd.*, [1989] 1 S.C.R. 1252.

QUIET. *v.* To settle; to render unassailable.

QUIET. *adj.* Unmolested, free from interference.

QUIET ENJOYMENT. 1. A covenant that a lessor or anyone claiming through or under the lessor may not enter. 2. "... [N]o act of a lessor will constitute an actionable breach of a convenant for quiet enjoyment unless it involves some physical or direct interference with the enjoyment of demised premises." *Owen v. Gadd*, [1956] 2 All E.R. 28 at 32 (U.K. C.A.), Romer L.J.

QUIETING ORDER. An order establishing the legal existence or corporate status of a municipality, or establishing its proper area and boundaries or any of its boundaries, in order to quiet doubts affecting the same. *Municipal Corporations Quieting Orders Act*, R.S.O. 1990, c. M.51, s. 1.

QUIETING TITLE. The judicial investigation of title and the ascertainment and declaration of the validity of title to real property.

QUINELLA. *n.* A type of bet on a race to select, in any order, the first two horses in the official result. *Criminal Code*, R.S.C. 1985, c. C-46, *Pari-Mutuel Betting Supervision Regulations*, SOR/91-365, s. 2.

QUISTCLOSE TRUST. Has been referred to as a purpose trust. The trust that arises is a resulting trust in favour of the supplier of the funds if the funds are not applied for the stated purpose. The name is derived from *Barlcay's Bank Ltd. v. Quistclose Investments Ltd.*, [1968] 3 All E.R. 651 (H.L.).

QUIT. *v.* 1. With respect to a job, to resign. 2. With respect to leased premises, to surrender possession. See NOTICE TO ~.

QUIT CLAIM. 1. To relinquish or release any claim to real property. 2. Where a debtor transfers property which is subject to a security interest to a secured party, and the secured party agrees to "settle the claim" it has against the debtor, the resulting agreement must be considered a quitclaim of the debtor's interest in the secured property. *Travel West (1987) Inc. v. Langdon Towers Apartment Ltd.*, 2002 SKCA 51, 217 Sask. R. 233, 265 W.A.C. 233, [2002] 9 W.W.R. 449.

QUIT-CLAIM DEED. The conveyance without promises or warranties only of an interest, if any, which the grantor has in the land. It is often used to release an interest in land, e.g. the purchaser's interest, under an agreement of purchase and sale, which was registered against the title. B.J. Reiter, B.N. McLellan & P.M. Perell, *Real Estate Law*, 4th ed. (Toronto: Emond Montgomery, 1992) at 805.

QUIT RENT. A rent by which a tenant quits and is free of any other service.

QUITTANCE. *n.* An acquittal, a release.

QUOD VIDE. [L.] See this.

QUORUM. *n.* [L. of whom] 1. The minimum number of members who must be present for that body to exercise its powers validly. 2. The required number of participants who must participate in the collective decision by assenting to the decision or by dissenting to it.

QUOTA. *n.* 1. The quantity of a product authorized to be produced, marketed or delivered from a particular person or property. 2. The number of a species of game which may be taken during a particular period of time. See NON-~ FISHERY.

QUOTATION AND TRADE REPORTING SYSTEM. A person who operates facilities that permit the dissemination of price quotations for the purchase and sale of securities and reports of completed transactions in securities for the exclusive use of registered dealers, but does not include an exchange or a registered dealer. *Securities Act*, S.N.B. 2004, c. S-5.5, s. 1. See OTC ~.

QUO WARRANTO. [L. by what authority] 1. "... [C]ivil proceedings. They are instituted by the Attorney-General, or through the intervention of the Attorney-General, ..." *R. v. Quesnel* (1909), (*sub nom. Tuttle v. Quesnel*) 11 W.L.R. 96 at 98 (Man. C.A.), the court per Howell C.J.A. 2. "... [L]ies against persons who claim any office, franchise, or privilege of a public nature, and not merely ministerial and held at the will and pleasure of others ..." *R. v. Roberts* (1912), 26 O.L.R. 263 at 271, 22 O.W.R. 50, 4 D.L.R. 278 (H.C.), Riddell J.

Q.V. *abbr.* [L. quod vide]. See this.

Q

R

R. *abbr.* 1. [L. regina] Queen. 2. [Fr. reine] Queen. 3. [L. rex] King. 4. [Fr. roi] King. 5. Rule.

R.A.C. *abbr.* Ramsay's Appeal Cases (Québec), 1873-1886.

RACE. *n.* 1. A test between rivals. *McGill v. Insurance Corp. of B.C.* (1992), 10 C.C.L.I. (2d) 65 (B.C.S.C.). 2. In a list of prohibited grounds of discrimination, refers to a group of inheritable, physical attributes.

RACIAL DISCRIMINATION. "... [C]learly involves something more than merely burdening a particular individual or group under the law; it involves the imposition of some such burden in a manner which creates or involves some stigma, as where there is 'a denial of the essential worth and dignity of the class against whom the law is directed' or 'a denial based upon unwarranted stereotypes about the capacities and roles of members of that class.' " *R. v. Punch* (1985), [1986] 2 C.N.L.R. 114 at 124, [1985] N.W.T.R. 373, [1986] 1 W.W.R. 592, 48 C.R. (3d) 374, 22 C.C.C. (3d) 289, 18 C.R.R. 74 (S.C.), de Weerdt J.

RACIAL PROFILING. There is no dispute about what racial profiling means. . . . "Racial profiling involves the targeting of individual members of a particular racial group, on the basis of the supposed criminal propensity of the entire group." Racial profiling provides its own motivation - a belief by a police officer that a person's colour, combined with other circumstances, makes him or her more likely to be involved in criminal activity. *R. v. Brown* (2003), 173 C.C.C. (3d) 23 (Ont. C.A.).

RACING. See STREET ~.

RACISM. *n.* Intolerance by members of one race characterized by stereotyping, prejudice, and discrimination towards members of another race.

RACK-RENT. *n.* Rent which is not less than 2/3 of the full annual net value of the property out of which the rent arises and the full net annual value shall be taken to be the rent at which the property might reasonably be expected to be let from year to year. *City of St. John's Act*, R.S.N. 1990, c. C-17, s. 2.

RADIATION. *n.* 1. Energy in the form of electromagnetic waves or acoustical waves. *Radiation Emit-* *ting Devices Act*, R.S.C. 1985, c. R-1, s. 2. 2. The emission by a nuclear substance, the production using a nuclear substance, or the production at a nuclear facility of, an atomic or subatomic particle or electromagnetic wave with sufficient energy for ionization. *Nuclear Safety and Control Act*, S.C. 1997, c. 9, s. 2. See MEDICAL IMAGING TECHNOLOGY AND ~ ONCOLOGY; MEDICAL ~ TECHNOLOGIST; MEDICAL ~ TECHNOLOGY.

RADIO. *n.* Any transmission, emission or reception of signs, signals, writing, images, sounds or intelligence of any nature by means of electromagnetic waves of frequencies lower than 3 000 GHz propagated in space without artificial guide. *Interpretation Act*, R.S.C. 1985, c. I-21, s. 35.

RADIO APPARATUS. A device or combination of devices intended for, or capable of being used for, radiocommunication. *Radiocommunication Act*, R.S.C. 1985, c. R-2, s. 2.

RADIO-BASED TELEPHONE COMMUNICATION. Any radiocommunication within the meaning of the Radiocommunication Act that is made over apparatus that is used primarily for connection to a public switched telephone network. *Criminal Code*, R.S.C. 1985, c. C-46, s. 183.

RADIOCOMMUNICATION. *n.* Any transmission, emission or reception of signs, signals, writing, images, sounds or intelligence of any nature by means of electromagnetic waves of frequencies lower than 3 000 GHz propagated in space without artificial guide. *Interpretation Act*, R.S.C. 1985, c. I-21, s. 35.

RADIO-SENSITIVE EQUIPMENT. Any device, machinery or equipment, other than radio apparatus, the use or functioning of which is or can be adversely affected by radiocommunication emissions. *Radiocommunication Act*, R.S.C. 1985, c. R-2, s. 2.

RADIO STATION. A place in which radio apparatus is located.

RADIO-TELEGRAPH. *n.* " ... '[W]ireless system for conveying electric signals or messages'." *R. v. Gignac*, [1934] O.R. 195 at 203, 61 C.C.C. 371, [1934] 2 D.L.R. 113 (H.C.), Armour J.

RADIO-TELEPHONE. *n.* " ... [W]ireless telephone[s]." *R. v. Gignac*, [1934] 2 D.L.R. 113 at 121, [1934] O.R. 195, 61 C.C.C. 371 (H.C.), Armour J.

RADIO-TELEVISION. See CANADIAN ~ AND TELECOMMUNICATIONS COMMISSION.

RADIO WAVES. Electromagnetic waves of frequencies lower than 3 000 GHz that are propagated in space without artificial guide. *Broadcasting Act*, S.C. 1991, c. 11, s. 2.

RAGE. See ROAD ~.

RAIL. See FREE ON ~.

RAILWAY. *n.* A way on which a train passes by means of tracks.

RAILWAY EQUIPMENT. (a) A machine that is constructed for movement exclusively on lines of railway, whether or not the machine is capable of independent motion, or (b) a vehicle that is constructed for movement both on and off lines of railway while the adaptations of that vehicle for movement on lines of railway are in use. *Railway Safety Act*, R.S.C. 1985, c. 32, (4th Supp.) s. 4. See DANGEROUS OPERATION OF ~.

RAINMAKER. *n.* A lawyer who is adept at attracting and maintaining clients.

RAM. & MOR. *abbr.* Ramsay & Morin, The Law Reporter (Journal de jurisprudence).

RANDOM VEHICLE STOP. A random vehicle stop on the highway is, by definition, an arbitrary detention. The detention will only be justified under s. 1 of the Charter if the police act within the limited highway related purposes for which the powers were conferred. Random roadside stops must be limited to their intended purposes. *R. v. Nolet*, 2010 SCC 24. See ROVING RANDOM STOP.

RANDOM VIRTUE TESTING. Arises when a police officer presents a person with the opportunity to commit an offence without a reasonable suspicion that: (a) the person is already engaged in the particular criminal activity, or (b) the physical location with which the person is associated is a place where the particular criminal activity is likely occurring. *R. v. Barnes*, [1991] 1 S.C.R. 449.

RAPE. *n.* "... [N]on-consensual sexual intercourse... ." *R. v. McCraw* (1991), 7 C.R. (4th) 314 at 325, 66 C.C.C. (3d) 517, 128 N.R. 299, 49 O.A.C. 47, [1991] 3 S.C.R. 72, the court per Cory J. See AGGRAVATED SEXUAL ASSAULT; SEXUAL ASSAULT.

R.A.T. *abbr.* Recueil d'arrêts sur les transports, 1966-1977.

RATE. *n.* 1. Includes a general, individual or joint rate, fare, toll, charge, rental or other compensation of a public utility, a rule, regulation, practice, measurement, classification or contract of a public utility or corporation relating to a rate and a schedule or tariff respecting a rate. 2. An amount payable under a contract of insurance for an identified risk whether expressed in dollar terms or in some other manner and includes commissions, surcharges, fees, discounts, rebates and dividends. 3. The method of calculating wages. 4. A fixed percentage of value applied equally to all properties within a jurisdiction. See BANK OF CANADA ~; BANK ~; CREDIT ~; CRIMINAL ~; DISCOUNT ~; EXCHANGE ~; FLOATING ~; INTEREST ~; MILL ~; MUNICIPAL TAX ~; PRIME ~; ~S.

RATEABLE. *adj.* 1. Subject to taxation. 2. Proportionate.

RATE OF INTEREST. See EFFECTIVE ~.

RATEPAYER. *n.* Taxpayer.

RATES. *n.* The charges set or made for the supply of a public utility. See RATE.

RATIFICATION. *n.* 1. The act of confirming. 2. "In order to find the parties, in whose name and behalf an unauthorized person has assumed to enter into a contract, by subsequent recognition and adoption it must be shown that either expressly, or impliedly by conduct, the parties whom it is sought to bind have, with a full knowledge of all the terms of the agreement come to by the person who assumed to bind them, assented to the same terms and agreed to abide by and be bound by the contract undertaken on their behalf." *Cameron v. Paxton, Tate & Co.* (1888), 15 S.C.R. 622 at 633, Strong J. 3. Agency is created by ratification when an agent does something on behalf of a principal when they are not yet in the relation of principal and agent. Later, however, the principal accepts and adopts the agent's act as if there had been prior authorisation to do what was done. G.H.L. Fridman, *The Law of Agency*, 6th ed. (London: Butterworths, 1990) at 74. 4. Formal approval given to terms negotiated in collective bargaining. 5. "... [I]n respect of treaties, the formal adoption by the high contracting party of a previous assent conveyed by the signature of so-called plenipotentiaries." *Canada (Attorney General) v. Ontario (Attorney General)*, [1937] 1 D.L.R. 673 at 677, [1937] A.C. 326, [1937] 1 W.W.R. 299, [1937] W.N. 53 (Can. P.C.), the court per Lord Atkin.

RATING. *n.* The process by which tax rates are fixed and imposed by local authorities. See CREDIT ~.

RATIO. *n.* [L. a reason] The grounds or reason for deciding.

RATIO DECIDENDI. [L.] The grounds or reason for deciding.

RATIO LEGIS EST ANIMA LEGIS. [L.] The reason for the law is the essence of the law.

RATIONAL CONCLUSION. A conclusion based on and supported by the evidence.

RATIONAL CONNECTION. Between legislative objectives and the means employed to attain them, means showing that the legitimate and important goals of the legislature are logically furthered by the means government chose to adopt. *Lavigne v. O.P.S.E.U.*, [1991] 2 S.C.R. 211.

RATIONING PROGRAM. A mandatory allocation program extended to include additional measures. Where the Governor in Council considers that the available supplies of a controlled product, energy-related, are or are likely to be in such short supply as to cause the mandatory allocation program to fail unless additional measures are taken, the purchase and sale of the controlled product at any or all levels, including the level of the final consumer or user, be made in such quantities, by such persons and for such uses as may be authorized on documentary evidence. *Energy Supplies Emergency Act*, R.S.C. 1985, c. E-8, ss. 2 and 29.

R.C.C.T. *abbr.* Recueil des décisions de la Commission canadianne des transports, 1978-1986.

R.C.D.A. *abbr.* 1. Recueil de jurisprudence canadiennce en droit des assurances, 1983-1991. 2. Recueil des décisions de la Commission du droit d'auteur, 1990-1994.

R.C.D.A. (2E). *abbr.* Recueil de jurisprudence canadiennce en droit des assurances (deuxième série), 1991-1998.

R.C.D.A. (3E). *abbr.* Recueil de jurisprudence canadiennce en droit des assurances (troisième série), 1998-.

R.C.D.E. *abbr.* Recueil de jurisprudence canadienne en droit de l'environnement, 1978-1985.

R.C. DE L'É. *abbr.* 1. Rapports judiciaires du Canada: Cour de l'Échiquier, 1923-1970. 2. Recueils des arrêts de la Cour de l'Echiquier, 1875-1922.

R.C.D.E. (N.S.). *abbr.* Recueil de jurisprudence canadienne en droit de l'environnement nouvelle série), 1986-.

R.C.D.F. *abbr.* Recueil de jurisprudence canadienne en droit de la faillie, 1920-1960.

R.C.D.F. (2E). *abbr.* Recueil de jurisprudence canadienne en droit de la faillie (deuxième série), 1920-1960.

R.C.D.F. (4E). *abbr.* Recueil de jurisprudence canadienne en droit de la faillie (quatrième série), 1920-1960.

R.C.D.F. (3E). *abbr.* Recueil de jurisprudence canadienne en droit de la faillie (troisième série), 1920-1960.

R.C.D.S.S.T. *abbr.* Recueil de jurisprudence canadienne en droit de la santé et de sécurité au travail, 1989-1993.

R.C.D.T. *abbr.* Recueil de jurisprudence canadienne en droit du travail, 1983-1994.

R.C.D.T. (2E). *abbr.* Recueil de jurisprudence canadienne en droit du travail (deuxième série), 1994-2000.

R.C.D.T. (3E). *abbr.* Recueil de jurisprudence canadienne en droit du travail (troisième série), 2000-.

R.C.D.V.M. *abbr.* Recueil de jurisprudence canadienne en droit des valeurs mobilières, 1993-1998.

R.C.L.J. *abbr.* Revue critique de législation et de jurisprudence du Canada.

RCMP. *abbr.* Royal Canadian Mounted Police.

R.C.P.I. *abbr.* Revue canadienne de propriété intellectuelle.

R.C.R.A.S. *abbr.* Recueil de jurisprudence canadienne en matière de retraite et d'avantages sociaux, 1994-.

R.C.R.C. *abbr.* Recueil de jurisprudence canadienne en responsabilité civile, 1976-1990.

R.C.R.C. (2E). *abbr.* Recueil de jurisprudence canadienne en responsabilité civile (deuxième série), 1990-2000.

R.C.R.C. (3E). *abbr.* Recueil de jurisprudence canadienne en responsabilité civile (troisième série), 2000-.

R.C.R.P. *abbr.* Recueil des arrêts du Conseil de révision des pensions, 1972-1986.

R.C.S. *abbr.* 1. Rapports judiciaires du Canada, Cour Suprême, 1923-1969. 2. Recueils des arrêts de la Cour Suprême du Canada, 1877-1922.

R.C.T.C. *abbr.* Rapports de la Commission de Tarif, 1937-1988.

RCU. *abbr.* Recognized compliance unit.

R.D.C.F.Q. *abbr.* Recueil des décisions, Commission de la fonction publique et Comité d'appel de la fonction publique, 1990-.

R. DE J. *abbr.* Revue de jurisprudence.

R. DE L. *abbr.* Revue de Législation, 1845-1848.

R.D.F. *abbr.* Recueil de droit de la famille, 1986-.

R.D.F.Q. *abbr.* Recueil de droit fiscal Québécois, 1977-.

R.D.I. *abbr.* Recueil de droit immobilier (Québec), 1986-.

R.D.J. *abbr.* Revue de droit judiciaire (Québec), 1983-1996.

R.D.J.C. *abbr.* Recueil de droit judiciaire de Carswell, 1976-1985.

R.D.J.C. (5E). *abbr.* Recueil de droit judiciaire de Carswell (cinquième série), 2001-.

R.D.J.C. (2E). *abbr.* Recueil de droit judiciaire de Carswell (deuxième série), 1985-1992.

R.D.J.C. (4E). *abbr.* Recueil de droit judiciaire de Carswell, (quatrième série), 1997-2001.

R.D.J.C. (3E). *abbr.* Recueil de droit judiciaire de Carswell (troisième série), 1992-1997.

R.D. MCGILL. *abbr.* Revue de droit de McGill (McGill Law Journal).

R.D.P. *abbr.* Revue de droit pénal (Québec), 1978-1983.

R.D.R.T.Q. *abbr.* Recueil des décisions, Régie des télécommunication du Québec, 1990-.

R.D.T. *abbr.* Revue de droit de travail (Québec), 1963-1976.

R. DU B. *abbr.* La Revue du Barreau.

R. DU B. CAN. *abbr.* La Revue du Barreau canadien (The Canadian Bar Review).

R. DU D. *abbr.* Revue du droit, 1922-1939.

R. DU N. *abbr.* La Revue du Notariat.

R.D. U.N.-B. *abbr.* Revue de droit de l'Université du Nouveau-Brunswick (University of New Brunswick Law Review).

R.D.U.S. *abbr.* Revue de droit, Université de Sherbrooke.

RE. *prep.* [L.] Concerning, in the matter of.

READ. *v.* To vote on a bill in a legislature. A bill must be read three times to become law.

READER. See TOLL ~.

READINESS. See CERTIFICATE OF ~; NOTICE OF ~ FOR TRIAL.

READING. *n.* The vote on a bill in a legislature. A bill must undergo three readings to become law. See FIRST ~; SECOND ~; THIRD ~.

READING DOWN. 1. A canon of construction of legislation. Whenever possible a statue is interpreted as having been enacted within the power of the legislature. The doctrine is applied to valid provincial legislation of general application which limits or prohibits some activity which in turn impacts negatively on the functioning of a federal power. General language in a statute which is apt to extend beyond the power of the enacting legislature is construed narrowly to keep it within the permitted scope of power. 2. [In the context of the pith and substance analysis] is a technique of statutory interpretation that is used to narrow the meaning of the general words of an enactment, which may appear to extend beyond the enacting body's mandate, in order to contain the effect of the legislation to within the limits of its constitutional mandate. *PHS Community Services Society v. Canada (Attorney General)*, 2010 BCCA 15, Smith J.A. (dissenting).

READING IN. Where an inconsistency exists in a statute because of something wrongly excluded from it, the result of declaring that provision inoperative is to "read in" the excluded group or circumstance. The statute is extended by reading in.

REAL. *abbr.* 1. Relating to land as opposed to chattels. 2. Tangible. See CHATTELS ~.

REAL ACTION. The common law proceeding by which a freeholder was able to recover land.

REAL AND SUBSTANTIAL CONNECTION. 1. By tendering his products in the market place directly or through normal distributive channels, a manufacturer ought to assume the burden of defending those products wherever they cause harm as long as the forum into which the manufacturer is taken is one that he reasonably ought to have had in his contemplation when he so tendered his goods. This is particularly true of dangerously defective goods placed in the interprovincial flow of commerce. The approach of permitting suit where there is a real and substantial connection with the action provides a reasonable balance between the rights of the parties. It affords some protection against being pursued in jurisdictions having little or no connection with the transaction or the parties. The above rationale is not limited to torts. *Morguard Investments Ltd. v. De Savoye*, [1990] 3 S.C.R. 1077. 2. The "real and substantial connection" test, which is applied to interprovincial judgments, should apply equally to the recognition of foreign judgments. The "real and substantial connection" test requires that a significant connection exist between the cause of action and the foreign court. Furthermore, a defendant can reasonably be brought within the embrace of a foreign jurisdiction's law where he or she has participated in something of significance or was actively involved in that foreign jurisdiction. A fleeting or relatively unimportant connection will not be enough to give a foreign court jurisdiction. The connection to the foreign jurisdiction must be a substantial one. *Beals v. Saldanha*, 2003 SCC 72, Major J.

REAL ESTATE. 1. "... [A]ll hereditaments... ." *Montreal Light, Heat & Power Consolidated v. Westmount (Town)*, [1926] S.C.R. 515 at 523, [1926] 3 D.L.R. 466, Anglin C.J.C. (Duff, Mignault, Newcombe and Rinfret JJ. concurring). 2. Includes messuages, lands, tenements and hereditaments, whether freehold or of any other tenure, and whether corporeal or incorporeal, and any undivided share thereof, and any estate, right or interest therein.

REAL ESTATE APPRAISAL. See PRACTICE OF ~.

REAL ESTATE SERVICES. (a) Rental property management services, (b) strata management services, or (c) trading services. *Real Estate Services Act*, S.B.C. 2004, c. 42, s. 1.

REAL EVIDENCE. 1. "Evidence has been found to be 'real' when it referred to tangible items... ." *R. v. Wise* (1992), 11 C.R. (4th) 253 at 265, [1992] 1 S.C.R. 527, 70 C.C.C. (3d) 193, 133 N.R. 161, 8 C.R.R. (2d) 53, 51 O.A.C 351, Cory J. (Lamer C.J.C., Gonthier and Stevenson JJ. concurring). 2. "... [E]xists independently of any statement by any witness, ..." *R. v. Schwartz* (1988), 55 D.L.R. (4th) 1 at 26, [1989] 1 W.W.R. 289, 66 C.R. (3d) 251, 88 N.R. 90, [1988] 2 S.C.R. 443, 45 C.C.C. (3d) 97, 56 Man. R. (2d) 92, 39 C.R.R. 260, Dickson C.J.C. (dissenting). 3. All evidence supplied by material objects when they are offered for direct perception by the court. *National Defence Act*, R.S.C. 1985, c. N-5, *Military Rules of Evidence*, C.R.C., c. 1049, s. 2.

REAL INTEREST METHOD. A method of determining the value of a person's interest in a group pension for the purposes of dividing property in a marriage breakdown. The value of the future income stream is calculated assuming the member will continue to be employed until retirement. Likely future earnings are assumed.

REALITY. See AIR OF ~.

REALIZATION PRINCIPLE. In Income Tax, an amount may have the quality of income even though it is not actually received by the taxpayer, but only "realized" in accordance with the accrual method of accounting. The ultimate effect of this principle is clear: amounts received or realized by a taxpayer, free of conditions or restrictions upon their use, are taxable in the year realized, subject to any contrary provision of the Act or other rule of law. *Ikea Ltd. v. Canada*, [1998] 1 S.C.R. 196.

REALIZE. *v.* "... [T]o sell, to convert into money, ..." *Bayne, Re,* [1946] 3 D.L.R. 49 at 50 (N.S. S.C.), Chisholm C.J. (Hall J. concurring).

REAL LIKELIHOOD OF BIAS. See REASONABLE APPREHENSION OF BIAS.

REALM. *n.* A country; a territory subject to a sovereign.

REAL PROPERTY. 1. "... [C]orporeal and incorporeal hereditaments ... land [and]... . rights in land, ..." *Pegg v. Pegg* (1992), 38 R.F.L. (3d) 179 at 184, 21 R.P.R. (2d) 149, 1 Alta. L.R. (3d) 249, 128 A.R. 132 (Q.B.), Agrios J. 2. Land and improvements on the land and includes (a) an interest held in land or an improvement, (b) air, surface or subsurface rights and interests in respect of land, and does not include mines or minerals. *The Municipal Assessment Act,* S.M. 1989-90, c. 24, s. 1. 3. The ground or soil and everything annexed to it, and includes land covered by water, all quarries and substances in or under land other than mines or minerals and all buildings, fixtures, machinery, structures and things erected on or under or affixed to land. 4. Includes any estate, interest or right to or in land, but does not include a mortgage secured by real property. See DEFENCE OF HOUSE OR ~; FEDERAL ~.

REAL PROPERTY BROKERAGE ENTITY. An entity that is primarily engaged in(a) acting as an agent for vendors, purchasers, mortgagors, mortgagees, lessors or lessees of real property; and (b) the provision of consulting or appraisal services in respect of real property. *Bank Act,* S.C. 1991, c. 46, s. 464.

REAL PROPERTY TAX. A tax of general application to real property or immovables or any class of them that is (a) levied by a taxing authority on owners of real property or immovables or, if the owner is exempt from the tax, on lessees or occupiers of real property or immovables, other than those lessees or occupiers exempt by law, and (b) computed by applying a rate to all or part of the assessed value of taxable property. *Payments in Lieu of Taxes Act,* R.S.C. 1985, c. M-13, s. 2.

REAL RISK. A risk which a reasonable person would not ignore as far-fetched or fanciful. The standard of care is based on what a reasonably prudent person would perceive as a real risk of harm to another person.

REALTOR. *n.* A person who belongs to a professional group of real estate dealers who describe themselves as realtors.

REALTY. See COMMERCIAL ~.

REASON. See JURISTIC ~; ~S.

REASONABLE. *adj.* 1. Refers to a rational inference from evidence or established truths. 2. "... [I]mplies a reason related to the purpose of the regulation, a rational connection between purpose and action and, in my view, it also implies a qualification on the nature of the action taken, that it be reasonable in the circumstances... ." *Jackson v. Joyceville Penitentiary* (1990), 55 C.C.C. (3d) 50 at 80, 75 C.R. (3d) 174, 32 F.T.R. 96, 1 C.R.R. (2d) 327 (T.D.), Mackay

J. 3. "A search will be reasonable if it is authorized by law, if the law itself is reasonable and if the manner in which the search was carried out is reasonable." *R. v. Collins,* [1987] 3 W.W.R. 699 at 712, 56 C.R. (3d) 193, 74 N.R. 276, 13 B.C.L.R. (2d) 1, [1987] 1 S.C.R. 265, 33 C.C.C. (3d) 1, 28 D.L.R. (4th) 508, 28 C.R.R. 122, Lamer J. 4. "... [T]he term 'reasonable' when used in the context of an interpretation of a provision in a collective agreement means an interpretation that is not absurd, one that is not ridiculous, outrageous, patently unjustifiable, extreme or excessive, but one that is a product of a sensible analysis, which may or may not be flawed, and one that may generally be described as within the bounds of reason. The interpretation does not have to be correct to be reasonable... ." *University Hospital v. S.E.I.U., Local 333 U.H.* (1986), 26 D.L.R. (4th) 248 at 250, 46 Sask. R. 19, 86 C.L.L.C. 14,064 (C.A.), Bayda C.J.S. (dissenting). 5. "... [A]s used in the law of nuisance must be distinguished from its use elsewhere in the law of tort and especially as it is used in negligence actions... . [In nuisance] 'reasonable' means something more than merely 'taking proper care'. It signifies what is legally right between the parties, taking into account all the circumstances of the case, ..." *Russell Transport Ltd. v. Ontario Malleable Iron Co.,* [1952] O.R. 621 at 629, [1952] 4 D.L.R. 719 (H.C.), McRuer C.J.H.C. 6. In negligence, to take reasonable care means to take proper care. *Russell Transport Ltd. v. Ontario Malleable Iron Co.,* [1952] O.R. 621 at 629, [1952] 4 D.L.R. 719 (H.C.), McRuer C.J.H.C. See BONA FIDE AND ~ JUSTIFICATION; UN~.

REASONABLE AND PROBABLE CAUSE. "Reasonable and probable cause has been defined as (Hicks v. Faulkner (1878), 8 Q.B.D. 167, at p. 171, per Hawkins J.): '... an honest belief in the guilt of the accused based upon a full conviction, founded on reasonable grounds, of the existence of a state of circumstances which, assuming them to be true, would reasonably lead any ordinary prudent and cautious man, placed in the position of the accuser, to the conclusion that the person charged was probably guilty of the crime imputed.' This test contains both a subjective and objective element. There must be both actual belief on the part of the prosecutor and that belief must be reasonable in the circumstances. The existence of reasonable and probable cause is a matter for the judge to decide as opposed to the jury." *Nelles v. Ontario* (1989), 42 C.R.R. 1 at 20, 49 C.C.L.T. 217, [1989] 2 S.C.R. 170, 37 C.P.C. (2d) 1, 71 C.R. (3d) 358, 60 D.L.R. (4th) 609, 98 N.R. 321, 69 O.R. (2d) 448n, 35 O.A.C. 161, 41 Admin. L.R. 1, Lamer J. (Dickson C.J.C. and Wilson J. concurring).

REASONABLE AND PROBABLE GROUNDS. Requires that the police officer subjectively have an honest belief that the suspect has committed the offence and objectively there must exist reasonable grounds for this belief. Per Sopinka J. Credibly-based probability. Reasonable probability. Reasonable belief. The context in which the phrase is used and the values underlying it are most important in interpretation of the meaning of the phrase. *R. v. Bernshaw,* [1995] 1 S.C.R. 254, L'Heureux-Dubé J..

REASONABLE APPREHENSION OF BIAS. "The proper test to be applied in a matter of this type was correctly expressed by the Court of Appeal ... the apprehension of bias must be a reasonable one, held by reasonable and right minded persons, applying themselves to the question and obtaining thereon the required information. In the words of the Court of Appeal, that test is 'what would an informed person, viewing the matter realistically and practically—and having thought the matter through—conclude' ... I can see no real difference between the expressions found in the decided cases, be they 'reasonable apprehension of bias', 'reasonable suspicion of bias' or 'real likelihood of bias'... ." *Committee for Justice & Liberty v. Canada (National Energy Board)*, [1978] 1 S.C.R. 369 at 394-5, 9 N.R. 115, 68 D.L.R. (3d) 716, de Grandpré J. (dissenting).

REASONABLE BAIL. In section 11 of the Charter, refers to the terms of bail. Thus the quantum of bail and the restrictions imposed on the accused's liberty while on bail must be "reasonable". "Just cause" refers to the right to obtain bail. *R. v. Pearson*, [1992] 3 S.C.R. 665, Lamer C.J.C.

REASONABLE CARE. A level of care determined by what a reasonable person with the level of knowledge possessed by the person in question would exercise.

REASONABLE DISCOVERY. [In relation to limitation of actions] the reasonable discovery rule which prevents the injustice of a claim's being statute barred before the plaintiff becomes aware of its existence. *Murphy v. Welsh*, 1993 CarswellOnt 987, 18 C.P.C. (3d) 137, 47 M.V.R. (2d) 1, 156 N.R. 263, 14 O.R. (3d) 799, 65 O.A.C. 103, 156 N.R. 263, [1993] 2 S.C.R. 1069, 106 D.L.R. (4th) 404, 66 O.A.C. 240, 18 C.C.L.T. (3d) 101, the court per Major J.

REASONABLE DOUBT. The following explanation for use in a charge to a jury is given: Not an imaginary or frivolous doubt. It must not be based upon sympathy or prejudice. Rather, it is based on reason and common sense. It is logically derived from the evidence or absence of evidence. Even if you believe the accused is probably guilty or likely guilty, that is not sufficient. In those circumstances you must give the benefit of the doubt to the accused and acquit because the Crown has failed to satisfy you of the guilt of the accused beyond a reasonable doubt. On the other hand you must remember that it is virtually impossible to prove anything to an absolute certainty and the Crown is not required to do so. Such a standard of proof is impossibly high. In short if, based upon the evidence or lack of evidence you are sure that the accused committed the offence you should convict since this demonstrates that you are satisfied of his guilt beyond a reasonable doubt. *R.v. Lifchus*, [1997] 3 S.C.R. 320. See BEYOND A ~.

REASONABLE EXPECTATION. Doctrine which applies to resolve ambiguity to achieve a result which might reasonably have been expected by the parties when they entered into the contract. It is up to the insurer to establish that his words clearly and aptly describe the contingency that has arisen and this cannot be done in this case. The court is supposed to avoid an interpretation under the doctrine of "reasonable expectations" which would either give the insurer or the insured a windfall in the form of unanticipated saving or payment. In this case recovery would be for a loss which the plaintiff clearly thought was covered by the insurance policy. The doctrine of reasonable expectations applies to resolve ambiguity to achieve a result which might reasonably be expected by the parties. *Goderich Elevators Ltd. v. Royal Insurance Co.* (1997), 34 O.R. (3d) 768 (Gen. Div.), affirmed on appeal at (1999), 42 O.R. (3d) 577 (C.A.).

REASONABLE FORCE. Every one is justified in using as much force as is reasonably necessary (a) to prevent the commission of an offence (i) for which, if it were committed, the person who committed it might be arrested without warrant, and (ii) that would be likely to cause immediate and serious injury to the person or property of anyone; or (b) to prevent anything being done that, on reasonable grounds, he believes would, if it were done, be an offence mentioned in paragraph (a). *Criminal Code*, R.S.C. 1985, c. C-46, s. 27.

REASONABLE FORESEEABILITY. [T]he test for the existence of a duty of care - and, therefore, for liability - in cases of psychiatric harm is whether it is reasonably foreseeable that a person of normal fortitude or sensibility is likely to suffer some type of psychiatric harm as a consequence of the defendant's careless conduct. That is what reasonable foreseeability means. *Mustapha v. Culligan of Canada Ltd.* (2006), 84 O.R. (3d) 457 (C.A.).

REASONABLE GROUNDS. Reasonable probability.

REASONABLE GROUND TO BELIEVE. In R. v. Debot, 30 C.C.C. (3d) 207 (Ont.C.A.) affirmed 1989 CanLII 13, [1989] 2 S.C.R. 1140, the Supreme Court of Canada approved of the standard described by Martin J.A. in the Ontario Court of Appeal where he stated: The standard of 'reasonable ground to believe' or 'probable cause' is not to be equated with proof beyond a reasonable doubt or a prima facie case. The standard to be met is one of reasonable probability. *R. v. Graham*, 2008 PESCAD 7.

REASONABLE IN THE CIRCUMSTANCES. Although interpretation of the meaning of the phrase "reasonable in the circumstances" [in s. 43 of the Criminal Code, R.S.C. 1985, C-46] is not without difficulty, the phrase clearly provides an intelligible standard for legal debate. The [R. v. Dupperon (1984), 16 C.C.C. (3d) 453 (Sask. C.A.)] test requires a court to determine the reasonableness of the force in the circumstances of each case. This approach involves examining the entire context within which the punishment took place, and holds that the test should be objective, applying the standards of the community as a reference point. *Canadian Foundation for Children, Youth & the Law v.Canada (Attorney General)*, 2000 CarswellOnt 2409, 146 C.C.C. (3d) 362, 188 D.L.R. (4th) 718, 49 O.R. (3d) 662, 36 C.R. (5th) 334, 76 C.R.R. (2d) 251 (S.C.J.), McCombs J.

REASONABLE LIMITS. 1. In section 1 of the Charter, rights are subject to such legal limitation as one can demonstrate is justified in a free and democratic society. 2. "... [O]ne which having regard to the principles enunciated in [R. v. Oakes (1986), 26 D.L.R. (4th) 200 (S.C.C.)], it was reasonable for the Legislature to impose... ." *R. v. Videoflicks Ltd.* (1986), (*sub nom. Edwards Books & Art Ltd. v. R.*) 35 D.L.R. (4th) 1 at 51, 87 C.L.L.C. 14,001, 28 C.R.R. 1, 55 C.R. (3d) 193, 19 O.A.C. 239, 71 N.R. 161, [1986] 2 S.C.R. 713, 30 C.C.C. (3d) 385, 58 O.R. (2d) 442n, Dickson C.J.C. (Chouinard and Le Dain JJ. concurring). 3. A limitation to a constitutional guarantee will be sustained once two conditions are met. First, the objective of the legislation must be pressing and substantial. Second, the means chosen to attain this legislative end must be reasonable and demonstrably justifiable in a free and democratic society. In order to satisfy the second requirement, three criteria must be satisfied: (1) the rights violation must be rationally connected to the aim of the legislation; (2) the impugned provision must minimally impair the Charter guarantee; and (3) there must be a proportionality between the effect of the measure and its objective so that the attainment of the legislative goal is not outweighed by the abridgement of the right. In all s. 1 cases the burden of proof is with the government to show on a balance of probabilities that the violation is justifiable. *Egan v. Canada*, [1995] 2 S.C.R. 513, Iacobucci J.

REASONABLENESS. *n.* 1. Reasonableness is a deferential standard animated by the principle that underlies the development of the two previous standards of reasonableness: certain questions that come before administrative tribunals do not lend themselves to one specific, particular result. Instead, they may give rise to a number of possible, reasonable conclusions. Tribunals have a margin of appreciation within the range of acceptable and rational solutions. A court conducting a review for reasonableness inquires into the qualities that make a decision reasonable, referring both to the process of articulating the reasons and to outcomes. In judicial review, reasonableness is concerned mostly with the existence of justification, transparency and intelligibility within the decision-making process. But it is also concerned with whether the decision falls within a range of possible, acceptable outcomes which are defensible in respect of the facts and law. *Dunsmuir v. New Brunswick*, 2008 SCC 9, Bastarache and LeBel, JJ. at para. 47. 2. "Reasonableness" is a big tent that will have to accommodate a lot of variables that inform and limit a court's review of the outcome of administrative decision making. A single "reasonableness" standard will now necessarily incorporate both the degree of deference formerly reflected in the distinction between patent unreasonableness and reasonableness simpliciter, and an assessment of the range of options reasonably open to the decision maker in the circumstances, in light of the reasons given for the decision. Any reappraisal of our approach to judicial review should, I think, explicitly recognize these different dimensions to the "reasonableness" standard. *Dunsmuir v. New Brunswick*, 2008 SCC 9, Binnie, J. para. 144 and 149. 3. Reasonableness is a single standard that takes its colour from the context. One of the objectives of Dunsmuir was to liberate judicial re-

view courts from what came to be seen as undue complexity and formalism. Where the reasonableness standard applies, it requires deference. Reviewing courts cannot substitute their own appreciation of the appropriate solution, but must rather determine if the outcome falls within "a range of possible, acceptable outcomes which are defensible in respect of the facts and law" (Dunsmuir, at para. 47). There might be more than one reasonable outcome. However, as long as the process and the outcome fit comfortably with the principles of justification, transparency and intelligibility, it is not open to a reviewing court to substitute its own view of a preferable outcome. *Canada (Citizenship and Immigration) v. Khosa*, 2009 SCC 12, [2009] 1 S.C.R. 339, Binnie J. for the majority, para. 59. See UN~.

REASONABLE OCCUPATIONAL QUALIFICATION. Equivalent to bona fide occupational requirement and qualification.

REASONABLE PERSON. 1. "[In the context of provocation in criminal law] ... the ordinary or reasonable person has a normal temperament and level of self-control. It follows that the ordinary person is not exceptionally excitable, pugnacious or in a state of drunkenness... . particular characteristics that are not peculiar or idiosyncratic can be ascribed to an ordinary person wihout subverting the logic of the objective test of provocation." *R. v. Hill* (1985), 51 C.R. (3d) 97 at 114, [1986] 1 S.C.R. 313, 27 D.L.R. (4th) 187, 68 N.R. 161, 25 C.C.C. (3d) 322, 17 O.A.C. 33, Dickson C.J.C. (Beetz, Chouinard and La Forest JJ. concurring). 2. "[In the context of determining the existence of bias] ... it obviously is neither the 'anti-establishment or complaisant' person (Tremblay v. Quebec (Commission des Affaires Sociales) [(1989), 25 Q.A.C. 169 (Que. C.A.)] ... or even someone who is narrow-minded. Nor a functionary in the justice system or a person who knows all the intricacies of the justice system. Rather, it is the average person in society who must serve as the model." *Lippé c. Charest* (1990), (*sub nom. R. v. Lippé*) 60 C.C.C. (3d) 34 at 71, 80 C.R. (3d) 1, [1990] R.J.Q. 2200, 31 Q.A.C. 161, Proulx J.A. 3. The 'reasonable person' of negligence law was described by Laidlaw J.A. in this way in Arland v. Taylor, [1955] O.R. 131 (C.A.), at p. 142: "He is not an extraordinary or unusual creatre; he is not superhuman; he is not required to display the highest skill of which anyone is capable; he is not a genius who can perform uncommon feats, nor is he possessed of unusual powers of foresight. He is a person of normal intelligence who makes prudence a guide to his conduct. He does nothing that a prudent man would not do and does not omit to do anything a prudent man would do. He acts in accord with general and approved practice. His conduct is guided by considerations which ordinarily regulate the conduct of human affairs. His conduct is the standard 'adopted in the community by persons of ordinary intelligence and prudence.' " *Stewart v. Pettie*, 1995 CarswellAlta 1, 25 Alta. L.R. (3d) 297, 23 C.C.L.T. (2d) 89, 8 M.V.R. (3d) 1, [1995] 3 W.W.R. 1, 177 N.R. 297, [1995] 1 S.C.R. 131, 121 D.L.R. (4th) 222, 162 A.R. 241, 83 W.A.C. 241, the court per Major J. 4. [In the context of a claim for professional negligence] . . . the "reasonable person" who sets the standard for the objective test must be taken to possess the patient's reasonable beliefs, fears, desires and expectations and further that the patient's expectations and concerns will usually be revealed by the questions posed. *De Vos v. Robertson*, 2000 CarswellOnt 44, 48 C.C.L.T. (2d) 172 (S.C.J.), Lofchik J.

REASONABLE SEARCH. 1. "A search will be reasonable if it is authorized by law, if the law itself is reasonable and if the manner in which the search was carried out is reasonable." *R. v. Collins* (1987), 28 C.R.R. 122 at 132, [1987] 3 W.W.R. 699, 56 C.R. (3d) 193, 74 N.R. 276, 13 B.C.L.R. (2d) 1, [1987] 1 S.C.R. 265, 33 C.C.C. (3d) 1, 28 D.L.R. (4th) 508, Lamer J. 2. The criteria which must be met in order that a search be "reasonable" are: (a) a system of prior authorization, by an entirely neutral and impartial arbiter who is capable of acting judicially in balancing the interests of the State against those of the individual; (b) a requirement that the impartial arbiter must satisfy himself that the person seeking the authorization has reasonable grounds, established under oath, to believe that an offence has been committed; (c) a requirement that the impartial arbiter must satisfy himself that the person seeking the authorization has reasonable grounds to believe that something which will afford evidence of the particular offence under investigation will be recovered; and (d) a requirement that the only documents which are authorized to be seized are those which are strictly relevant to the offence under investigation. *Thomson Newspapers Ltd. v. Canada (Director of Investigation and Research, Restrictive Trade Practices Commission)* (1990), 67 D.L.R. (4th) 161. (S.C.C.).

REASONABLE SUSPICION OF BIAS. See REASONABLE APPREHENSION OF BIAS.

REASONABLY INCURRED. See COSTS ~.

REASONS. *n.* 1. Constitute the primary form of accountability of the decision-maker to the applicant, to the public and to a reviewing court. *Canada (Citizenship and Immigration) v. Khosa*, 2009 SCC 12, [2009] 1 S.C.R. 339, Binnie J. for the majority, at para. 63. 2. More than a recital of matters which the decision-maker was required to consider and a statement of conclusions drawn from those matters. Must also enable the person concerned to assess whether he has grounds of appeal. Must be proper, adequate, and intelligible.

REBRAND. *v.* (i) To reclassify a type of fuel, (ii) to change a fuel to another type of fuel or to a non-taxable product, or (iii) to change a non-taxable product that was originally a fuel back to a fuel. *Fuel Tax Act*, S.A. 2006, c. F-28.1, s. 1.

REBUT. *v.* To contradict; to reply.

REBUTTABLE PRESUMPTION OF LAW. "... [T]hree categories of rebuttable presumptions (s. 241(1)(c) [of the Criminal Code, R.S.C. 1970, c. C-34] ... First, a permissive presumption may tactically require an accused merely to raise a reasonable doubt once the Crown establishes a proved fact giving rise to the presumed fact, failing which the trier of fact may infer the presumed fact. Second, a mandatory presumption legally requires an accused to raise reasonable doubt as to the presumed fact, failing which the trier of fact must infer the presumed fact. Third, a mandatory presumption legally requires an accused to disprove the presumed fact on a balance of probabilities, failing which the trier of fact must infer the presumed fact." *R. v. Hummel* (1987), 36 C.C.C. (3d) 8 at 13, 1 M.V.R. (2d) 4, 60 O.R. (2d) 545, 60 C.R. (3d) 78 (H.C.), Ewaschuk J.

REBUTTAL EVIDENCE. Evidence which rebuts or contradicts evidence which the defendant or respondent adduced in the case.

REBUTTER. *n.* In pleadings, the defendant's response to the surrejoinder.

RECALL. *v.* For voters to end prematurely the term of an elected official.

RECALL PETITION. A petition issued by the chief electoral officer for the recall of a Member. *Recall And Initiative Act*, R.S.B.C. 1996, c. 398, s. 1(1).

REC. ANN. WINDSOR ACCÈS JUSTICE. *abbr.* Recueil annuel de Windsor d'accès à la justice (Windsor Yearbook of Access to Justice).

RECEIPT. *n.* An acknowledgment in writing that one received money or property. See ELEVATOR ~; GRAIN ~; KNOWING ~; NEGOTIABLE ~; WAREHOUSE ~.

RECEIVABLE. *adj.* "... '[T]o be received' ..." *Wilson & Wilson Ltd. v. Minister of National Revenue*, [1960] C.T.C. 1 at 10, [1960] Ex. C.R. 205, 60 D.T.C. 1018, Cameron J. See ACCOUNTS ~.

RECEIVED. *v.* Actual physical receipt; to be put in possession of a thing. See VALUE ~.

RECEIVER. *n.* 1. A person who was appointed to take possession of property which belongs to a third party. 2. A person appointed by a court to receive the rent and profit of real estate or to collect personal goods. When the appointment is by way of equitable execution, the receiver has the power to sell the personalty and to distribute the rents, proceeds and profits of the real estate to any judgment creditors. C.R.B. Dunlop, *Creditor-Debtor Law in Canada* (Toronto: Carswell, 1981) at 281. 3. "... [C]an encompass a receiver-manager... ." *Cook's Ferry Band v. Cook's Ferry Band Council* (1989), (*sub nom. Minnabarriet v. Cook's Ferry Band Council*) 75 C.B.R. (N.S.) 228 at 232, [1989] 4 C.N.L.R. 105 (Fed. T.D.), Reed J. See INTERIM ~; OFFICIAL ~; PRIVATE ~.

RECEIVER AND MANAGER. A person appointed to carry on or superintend a trade, business or undertaking in addition to receiving rents and profits, or to get in outstanding property.

RECEIVERSHIP. *n.* A legal or equitable proceeding in which a receiver is appointed to take over the property of an insolvent company or individual. The receivership operates with respect to all of the assets of the insolvent party.

RECEIVING ORDER. An order which declares a debtor to be bankrupt and which results in the trustee of the bankrupt estate being appointed rather than a receiver.

RECENT COMPLAINT. A common law doctrine which allowed the complainant in a rape case to bring evidence of a complaint made shortly after the incident to show that the complainant's conduct was consistent with the complaint.

RECENT CONTRIVANCE. Demonstrated by evidence that the witness did not speak of the matter earlier at a time when it would have been natural to speak. The earlier silence is argued as evidence of inconsistency with current statements.

RECENT FABRICATION. An allegation of recent fabrication is no more than an allegation that the complainant has made up a false story to meet the exigencies of the case. The word "recent" means that the complainant's evidence has been invented or fabricated after the events in question and thus is a "recent" invention or fabrication. *R. v. O'Connor* (1995), 25 O.R. (3d) 19 (C.A.).

RECENT POSSESSION. 1. "... [T]he presumption ... resulting from the mere circumstances of recent possession of stolen goods, is that the initial possession was gained with the knowledge that the goods were stolen." *R. v. Suchard*, [1956] S.C.R. 425 at 427, 23 C.R. 207, 114 C.C.C. 257, 2 D.L.R. (2d) 609, Fauteux J. (Taschereau J. concurring). 2. The unexplained recent possession of stolen goods, standing alone, will permit the inference that the possessor stole the goods. The inference is not mandatory; it may but need not be drawn. Further, where an explanation is offered for such possession which could reasonably be true, no inference of guilt on the basis of recent possession alone may be drawn, even where the trier of fact is not satisfied of the truth of the explanation. The burden of proof of guilt remains upon the Crown. *R. v. Kowlyk*, [1988] 2 S.C.R. 59.

RECESS. *n.* 1. The period between Parliament being prorogated and reassembling for a new session. A. Fraser, W.A. Dawson & J. Holtby, eds., *Beauchesne's Rules and Forms of the House of Commons of Canada*, 6th ed. (Toronto: Carswell, 1989) at 66. 2. A short pause in a sitting of a court.

RECIDIVIST. *n.* A person who repeatedly commits crimes.

RECIPROCAL TRANSFER AGREEMENT. An agreement related to two or more pension plans that provides for the transfer of money or credits for employment or both in respect of individual members. *Pension Benefits acts.*

RECIPROCITY. *n.* Refers to agreements to recognize orders or judgments of another state. Usually accomplished by the enactment of similar legislation in both states. See, for example, Reciprocal Enforcement of Maintenance acts and Reciprocal Enforcement of Judgments acts.

RECISSION. *n.* Commonly, the ending of a contract because a contract term classified as a condition was breached or a party repudiated or absolutely refused to perform its contractual obligations. B.J. Reiter, B.N. McLellan & P.M. Perell, *Real Estate Law*, 4th ed. (Toronto: Emond Montgomery, 1992) at 681. 2. Technically, an equitable remedy that restores parties to their position before the contract. B.J. Reiter, B.N.

McLellan & P.M. Perell, *Real Estate Law*, 4th ed. (Toronto: Emond Montgomery, 1992) at 681.

RECITAL. *n.* A statement in an agreement, deed or other formal document intended to lead up to or explain the operative part of the document.

R.E.C.J. *abbr.* Records of the Early Courts of Justice of Upper Canada (Ontario), 1789-1984.

RECKLESS. *adj.* 1. Refers to the attitude of a person who is aware that the danger exists that his conduct may cause a result prohibited by criminal law but who persists in the conduct. *R. v. Cooper* (1993), 78 C.C.C. (3d) 289 (S.C.C.) . 2. "... [H]eedless of consequences, headlong or irresponsible... ." *R. v. Barron* (1984), 39 C.R. (3d) 379 at 391 (Ont. H.C.), Ewaschuk J. 3. "[In s. 202 of the Criminal Code, R.S.C. 1970, c. C-34] ... reckless means a person shows carelessness for the consequence of his act so far as the lives or safety of other persons are concerned... ." *R. v. Canadian Liquid Air Ltd.* (1972), 20 C.R.N.S. 208 at 210 (B.C. S.C.), McKay J. See WANTON AND ~.

RECKLESSLY. *adv.* "... [I]ntention will be attributed or imputed to an accused where he acts recklessly in the circumstances. In such a situation, 'The term "recklessly" is ... used to denote the subjective state of mind of a person who foresees that his conduct may cause the prohibited result but, nevertheless, takes a deliberate and unjustifiable risk of bringing it about ...": see R. v. Buzzanga (1979), 25 O.R. (2d) 705 ... (C.A.). Depending on the definitional elements of and terms employed in the crime, the accused may be sufficiently reckless to have imputed to him the necessary guilty intention where his foresight indicates to him that the unjustified risk will probably result in the prohibited harm, will be highly probable or, for certain crimes, substantially certain to occur ..." *R. v. Barron* (1984), 39 C.R. (3d) 379 at 390 (Ont. H.C.), Ewaschuk J.

RECLAMATION. *n.* Bringing of land formerly covered by water into a state fit for cultivation.

RECOGNIZANCE. *n.* 1. A performance bond: an acknowledgement by the person from whom it is taken that he is indebted to the Crown in the amount fixed therein, provided always, that if he fulfills the condition of the undertaking and appears as required the debt ceases ..." *McMillan v. Bassett* (1983), [1984] 1 W.W.R. 150 at 154, 29 Sask. R. 272, 9 C.C.C. (3d) 45 (C.A.), the court per Cameron J.A. 2. A person's own promise to appear.

RECOGNIZED COMPLIANCE UNIT. A Recognized Compliance Unit under section 11 [Recognized Compliance Units]. *Greenhouse Gas Reduction (Cap and Trade) Act*, S.B.C. 2008, c. 32, s. 1.

RECOMMEND. *v.* To advise; may encompass a duty to act fairly in making a recommendation.

RECOMMENDATION. *n.* 1. " ... [O]rdinarily means the offering of advice and should not be taken to mean a binding decision..." *Thomson v. Canada (Department of Agriculture)* (1992), 3 Admin. L.R. (2d) 242 at 255, 133 N.R. 345, 89 D.L.R. (4th) 218, [1992] 1 S.C.R. 385, 51 F.T.R. 267n, Cory J. (La

Forest, Sopinka, Gonthier, McLachlin and Stevenson JJ. concurring). 2. A "recommendation" [in s. 13(1) of the Freedom of Information and Protection of Privacy Act, R.S.O. 1990, c. F.31] may be understood to "relate to a suggested course of action" more explicitly and pointedly than "advice." *Ontario (Ministry of Transportation) v. Cropley (2005)*, 202 O.A.C. 379.

RECONCILIATION. *n.* 1. The settlement of differences after an estrangement. 2. "... [D]oes not take place unless and until mutual trust and confidence are restored. It is not to be expected that the parties can ever recapture the mutual devotion which existed when they were first married, but their relationship must be restored, by mutual consent, to a settled rhythm in which the past offences, if not forgotten, at least no longer rankle and embitter their daily lives. Then, and not till then, are the offences condoned. Reconciliation being the test of condonation, nothing short of it will suffice." *Mackrell v. Mackrell*, [1948] 2 All E.R. 858 at 860-61 (U.K. C.A.), Denning L.J. 3. The jurisprudence of this Court supports the view that the duty to consult and accommodate is part of a process of fair dealing and reconciliation that begins with the assertion of sovereignty and continues beyond formal claims resolution. Reconciliation is not a final legal remedy in the usual sense. Rather, it is a process flowing from rights guaranteed by s. 35(1) of the Constitution Act, 1982. This process of reconciliation flows from the Crown's duty of honourable dealing toward Aboriginal peoples, which arises in turn from the Crown's assertion of sovereignty over an Aboriginal people and de facto control of land and resources that were formerly in the control of that people. To limit reconciliation to the post-proof sphere risks treating reconciliation as a distant legalistic goal, devoid of the "meaningful content" mandated by the "solemn commitment" made by the Crown in recognizing and affirming Aboriginal rights and title: Sparrow, supra, at p. 1108. It also risks unfortunate consequences. When the distant goal of proof is finally reached, the Aboriginal peoples may find their land and resources changed and denuded. This is not reconciliation. Nor is it honourable. *Haida Nation v. British Columbia (Minister of Forests)*, [2004] 3 S.C.R. 511, 2004 SCC 73.

RECONCILIATION PROTOCOL. The Kunst'aa guu - Kunst'aayah Reconciliation Protocol between the Haida Nation and British Columbia, dated for reference December 11, 2009, and includes an amendment under section 8 of this Act at the time (a) that the amendment is published under subsection (2) (b) of this section, if the amendment can be implemented without an Act of the Legislature, and (b) that implementing legislation has been enacted by the Legislature and the amendment is published under subsection (2) (b) of this section, if the amendment requires an Act of the Legislature to be implemented. *Haida Gwaii Reconciliation Act*, S.B.C. 2010, c. 17, s. 1.

RECONSTRUCTION. *n.* 1. Renewal, alteration, remodelling of a substantial part of premises. 2. Transferring the assets, or a major part of them, of one company to a new company formed for just that purpose in exchange for shares of the new company to be distributed among the old company's shareholders. H. Sutherland, D.B. Horsley & J.M. Edmiston, eds., *Fraser's Handbook on Canadian Company Law*, 7th ed. (Toronto: Carswell, 1985) at 349. See REORGANIZATION.

RECONVERSION. *n.* An imaginary process in which an earlier constructive conversion is annulled and the converted property is restored to its original condition in contemplation of law.

RECONVEYANCE. *n.* Conveying mortgaged property again, free from the mortgage debt, to the mortgagor or the mortgagor's representatives after the mortgage debt is paid off.

RECORD. *n.* 1. Includes any correspondence, memorandum, book, plan, map, drawing, diagram, pictorial or graphic work, photograph, film, microform, sound recording, videotape, machine-readable record and any other documentary material, regardless of physical form or characteristics, and any copy of any of those things. *Personal Information Protection and Electronic Documents Act*, S.C. 2000, c. 5, s. 2. 2. [In the sense of the record of proceedings before a tribunal], "... [M]ust contain at least the document which initiates the proceedings, the pleadings, if any, and the adjudication, but not the evidence, nor the reasons, unless the tribunal chooses to incorporate them." *R. v. Northumberland Comp. App. Trib.; Ex parte Shaw*, [1952] 1 All E.R. 122 at 131 (U.K. C.A.), Denning L.J. 3. The record consisted only of the initiating document, the pleadings, if any, and the adjudication (including the reasons if incorporated in the decision) but not the evidence or the supporting documents referred to in the adjudication... ." *Woodward Stores (Westmount) Ltd. v. Alberta (Assessment Appeal Board, Division No. 1)*, [1976] 5 W.W.R. 496 at 511, 69 D.L.R. (3d) 450 (Alta. T.D.), McDonald J. 4. The history of a person's convictions. See BUSINESS ~S; CANADIAN PATENT OFFICE ~; COURT OF ~; COURT ~S; CRIMINAL ~; ELECTRONIC ~; ERROR OF LAW ON THE FACE OF THE ~; EXPOSURE ~; PRIVATE ~; SOLICITOR OF ~.

RECORDER. See NUMBER ~.

RECORDING. See AUDIO ~ MEDIUM; SOUND ~.

RECORD OF PROCEEDINGS. In that event, the appellants seek to rely on ss. 18(3) [of the Radiocommunication Act, R.S.C. 1985, c. R-2] so that the record of proceedings in the criminal proceedings becomes evidence in this case. [...] Subsection 18(3) contains two evidentiary rules. The first is that the record of proceedings before the court which convicted a person of an offence under paragraph 9(1)(c), (d) or (e) or 10(1)(b) is proof that the defendant engaged in the conduct which constitutes the offence, unless there is evidence to the contrary. In other words proof of the conviction is, in the absence of evidence to the contrary, proof of the facts in respect of which a conviction was entered. The conviction could be proved by means of a transcript of the proceedings, or the minutes of the proceedings, in those jurisdictions in which the clerk takes minutes of the proceedings. Or, a party could rely on ss. 12(2) of the Canada Evidence Act which provides for proof of conviction by means of a certificate of conviction and proof of identity. The second evidentiary rule found in ss. 18(3) is that any evidence given in the criminal trial as to the effect of the conduct of the defendant on the rights holders is evidence "thereof" in the civil action. In other words, evidence of damages in the criminal trial can be used as evidence of damages in the civil trial. Once again, this would require either a transcript or some other record of the evidence such as the minutes of the proceedings if they exist and if they disclose the particulars of the evidence. It is clear from this that the Crown Brief, which is simply the information in the Crown's hands as to the facts disclosed by the police investigation, is not the record of proceedings since it does not relate to the proceedings but to the investigation. Consequently, the appellants were not entitled to rely upon ss. 18(3). *Columbia Pictures Industries Inc. v. Gaudreault*, 2006 FCA 29.

RECOUNT. See JUDICIAL ~.

RECOUNTING. *n.* 1. Includes the recollection and retelling of circumstances relating to a designated crime, an expression of thoughts or feelings about a designated crime and a re-enactment of a designated crime. *The Profits of Criminal Notoriety Act*, S.S. 2009, c. P-28.1, s. 2. 2. Includes the recollection and retelling of circumstances relating to a serious crime, an expression of thoughts or feelings about a serious crime and a re-enactment of a serious crime. *Criminal Notoriety Act*, S.A. 2005, c. C-32.5, s. 1. See CONTRACT FOR THE ~ OF A CRIME; PROCEEDS OF A CONTRACT FOR ~ CRIME.

RECOUPMENT. *n.* Complete repayment in that the whole sum of money spent effectively discharges the debt for which, though both parties are liable, the defendant is largely liable. G.H.L. Fridman, *Restitution*, 2d ed. (Toronto: Carswell, 1992) at 242.

RECOURSE. *n.* 1. The right to recover against a party secondarily liable. 2. When a bill is dishonoured by non-payment, an immediate right of recourse against the drawer, acceptor and endorsers accrues to the holder. *Bills of Exchange Act*, R.S.C. 1985, c. B-4, s. 94(2). See WITHOUT ~ TO ME.

RECOVER. *v.* 1. "... The usual meaning in the context of the judicial process is that of 'gaining through a judgment or order'... ." *Centrac Industries Ltd. v. Vollan Enterprises Ltd.* (1989), 70 Alta. L.R. (2d) 396 at 398, 100 A.R. 301, 39 C.P.C. (2d) 136 (C.A.), Lieberman, Stevenson and Irving JJ.A. 2. "... [T]he taking of possession of some form of property ..." *Prism Petroleum Ltd. v. Omega Hydrocarbons Ltd.* (1992), 4 Alta. L.R. (3d) 332 at 348, [1993] 1 W.W.R. 204, 130 A.R. 114 (Q.B.), Egbert J.

RECOVERY. *n.* 1. Obtaining something which was wrongfully taken or withheld from someone, or to which that person is otherwise entitled. 2. That a person who is, or was, a patient is no longer disabled or infectious. See ACTION FOR ~ OF LAND; DOUBLE ~.

RECTIFICATION. *n.* 1. A equitable remedy which enables the court to make a contract conform with the true intentions of the contracting parties. 2. "... [O]perates in a proper case to reform the instruments in order to ensure that they express the agreement actually reached by the parties... ." *Soni v. Malik* (1985), 1 C.P.C. (2d) 53 at 57, 61 B.C.L.R. 36 (S.C.), McEachern C.J.S.C. 3. The correction of an error in a judgment or order.

RECTIFY. *v.* To make a contract conform to the true intentions of the contracting parties, using the equitable remedy of rectification.

RECUSATION. *n.* The removal of a judge or tribunal member from hearing a particular matter due to an appearance of possible bias or conflict of interest.

RECUSE. *v.* For a judge or tribunal member to remove himself or herself from hearing a particular matter due to an appearance of possible bias or conflict of interest.

RECYCLE. *v.* To do anything that results in providing a use for a thing that otherwise would be disposed of or dealt with as waste, including collecting, transporting, handling, storing, sorting, separating and processing the thing, but does not include the application of waste to land or the use of a thermal destruction process. *Environmental Protection and Enhancement Act*, R.S.A. 2000, c. E-12, s. 1.

RECYCLER. *n.* A person who carries on the business, or holds himself or herself out as carrying on the business, of (a) buying motor vehicles or parts of motor vehicles (i) to destroy them for scrap or dismantle them for parts, or (ii) to resell to another for the purpose of destroying them for scrap or dismantling them for parts; or (b) buying and selling used motor vehicle parts. *The Drivers and Vehicles Act*, S.M. 2005, c. 37, Sched. A, s. 1.

R.E.D. *abbr.* 1. Russell's Equity Decisions (N.S.), 1873-1882. 2. Ritchie's Equity Decisions (Can.) 3. Ritchie's Equity Decisions, by Russell (N.S.). 4. Ritchie's Equity Reports, by Russell (N.S.).

REDDENDUM. *n.* [L. that which is to be paid or rendered] The clause in a lease, usually using the words "yielding and paying", which states the amount of the rent and the time at which it should be paid.

REDEEM. *v.* To buy back. See ACTION TO ~.

REDEEMABLE. *adj.* That may be repurchased by the issuer. See NON-~ INVESTMENT FUND.

REDEEMABLE SECURITY. A security which exists for a fixed term and is redeemable at the end of that term at a specified value.

REDEEMABLE SHARE. A share issued by a corporation (a) that the corporation may purchase or redeem on the demand of the corporation; or (b) that the corporation is required by its articles to purchase or redeem at a specified time or on the demand of a shareholder.

REDEEM UP, FORECLOSE DOWN. Expression which refers to the mortgagor's right to redeem the interest of all mortgagees and the right of a mortgagee to redeem the interest of all mortgagees prior to (above) him in title. A third mortgagee may redeem the interest of a first mortgagee. However, a second mortgagee may only foreclose the interest of subsequent (lower) mortgagees or encumbrancers and cannot foreclose the interest of the first mortgagee.

REDELIVERY. *n.* Yielding and delivering something back.

REDEMISE. *n.* Re-granting land.

REDEMPTION. *n.* 1. The payment of the amount owing under a mortgage to, in effect, buy back the title to the property. An equitable right of the mortgagor or those who claim under him. 2. The buying back of securities by the issuer. 3. The right to have property freed from a secured charge. See EQUITY OF ~.

RED HERRING. An issue or fact which seems important but in fact is of no or little importance.

RED LIGHT CAMERA SYSTEM. A device that is installed at an intersection with a traffic control signal and that is capable of photographing a vehicle or part of a vehicle and recording data related to the vehicle and the traffic control signal. *The Traffic Safety Act*, S.S. 2004, c. T-18.1, s. 2.

REDRESS. *v.* To give satisfaction or compensation for a wrong or loss sustained.

REDRESS. *n.* Relief in the form of damages or equitable relief.

REDUCTIO AD ABSURDUM. [L.] The way to disprove an argument by demonstrating that it leads to an unreasonable conclusion.

REDUNDANCY. *n.* Unneeded or extraneous material inserted in a pleading.

RE-ENTRANT. *n.* A person who, having been unemployed, begins to seek employment once again.

RE-ENTRY. *n.* In a lease, a proviso which empowers the lessor to re-enter the leased premises if the rent has not been paid for a certain period.

REF. *abbr.* Reference.

REFER. *v.* 1. With respect to a question, to have it decided by someone nominated for that purpose. 2. To direct a person to someone or something for information or assistance.

REFEREE. *n.* A person to whom a court refers a pending cause so that that person may take testimony, hear the parties, and report back. See BOARD OF ~S.

REFERENCE. *n.* 1. Sending a whole proceeding or a particular issue to the referring judge, a registrar or other court officer, or another person the parties agree on. 2. A question which a government presents to a court for an opinion concerning the constitutionality of an enactment although there is no real dispute. 3. In the context of a reference, the Court, rather than acting in its traditional adjudicative function, is acting in an advisory capacity. The very fact that the Court may be asked hypothetical questions in a reference,

such as the constitutionality of proposed legislation, engages the Court in an exercise it would never entertain in the context of litigation. No matter how closely the procedure on a reference may mirror the litigation process, a reference does not engage the Court in a disposition of rights. *Reference re Secession of Quebec*, 1998 CarswellNat 1299, 161 D.L.R. (4th) 385, 228 N.R. 203, 55 C.R.R. (2d) 1, [1998], 2 S.C.R. 217, per curiam. 4. The lieutenant governor in council may refer a question for opinion to the court of appeal in the province. See ADOPTION BY ~; FEDERAL ~; MATERIAL ADOPTED BY ~; PROVINCIAL ~.

REFERENDUM. *n.* 1. The direct vote of electors concerning a particular by-law or question affecting the municipality. 2. Where the Governor in Council considers that it is in the public interest to obtain by means of a referendum the opinion of electors on any question relating to the Constitution of Canada, the Governor in Council may, by proclamation, direct that the opinion of electors be obtained by putting the question to the electors of Canada or of one or more provinces specified in the proclamation at a referendum called for that purpose. 3. If the Lieutenant Governor in Council considers that an expression of public opinion is desirable on any matter of public interest or concern, the Lieutenant Governor in Council may, by regulation, order that a referendum be conducted in the manner provided for in this Act. *Referendum Act*, R.S.B.C. 1996, c. 400, s. 1(1).

REFINANCING. *n.* [As used in defining the obligation of a partner under a partnership agreement] contemplates renewing or replacing a mortgage, either because of expiry of the term of the mortgage or because of default and acceleration, not paying the full amount of the debt owing on maturity. The concept of servicing a mortgage debt clearly implies making periodic payments of principal and interest, not retiring the entire debt. *Western Delta Lands Partnership v. 3557537 Canada Inc.*, 2000 CarswellBC 1483, 2000 BCSC 1096 (S.C. [In Chambers]), Allan J.

REFINERY GAS. Gas for use in an oil refinery that is produced as a result of distillation, cracking, reforming or other oil refining processes. *Carbon Tax Act*, S.B.C. 2008, c. 40, Sched. 1, s. 1.

REFORM. *v.* With respect to an instrument, to rectify it.

REFORMATORY. *n.* An institution where offenders are sent to be reformed.

REFRESH. *v.* With respect to a witness' memory, to refer to a document which may not itself be admissible as evidence.

REFUGEE. *n.* A person who, by reason of a well-founded fear of persecution for reasons of race, religion, nationality, political opinion or membership in a particular social group, seeks admission to Canada or seeks to remain in Canada. See CONVENTION ~; IMMIGRATION AND ~ BOARD.

REFUGEE APPEAL DIVISION. A person or the Minister may appeal, in accordance with the rules of the Board, on a question of law, of fact or of mixed law and fact, to the Refugee Appeal Division against a decision of the Refugee Protection Division to allow or reject the person's claim for refugee protection, or a decision of the Refugee Protection Division rejecting an application by the Minister for a determination that refugee protection has ceased or an application by the Minister to vacate a decision to allow a claim for refugee protection. *Immigration and Refugee Protection Act*, S.C. 2001, c. 27, s. 110.

REFUGEE CONVENTION. The United Nations Convention Relating to the Status of Refugees, signed at Geneva on July 28, 1951, and the Protocol to that Convention, signed at New York on January 31, 1967. *Immigration and Refugee Protection Act*, S.C. 2001, c. 27, s. 2.

REFUGEE PROTECTION. Conferred on a person when (a) the person has been determined to be a Convention refugee or a person in similar circumstances under a visa application and becomes a permanent resident under the visa or a temporary resident under a temporary resident permit for protection reasons; (b) the Board determines the person to be a Convention refugee or a person in need of protection; or (c) except in the case of a person described in subsection 112(3), the Minister allows an application for protection. *Immigration and Refugee Protection Act*, S.C. 2001, c. , 27, s. 95(1).

REFUGEE PROTECTION DIVISION. Inquires into claims for refugee protection. It shall accept a claim for refugee protection if it determines that the claimant is a Convention refugee or person in need of protection, and shall otherwise reject the claim. If the Refugee Protection Division is of the opinion, in rejecting a claim, that there was no credible or trustworthy evidence on which it could have made a favourable decision, it shall state in its reasons for the decision that there is no credible basis for the claim. *Immigration and Refugee Protection Act*, S.C. 2001, c. 27, s. 107.

REFUND. *n.* The restitution or return of a sum received or taken; reimbursement. Generally involves return of money from one party to another.

REFUSE. *v.* Wilfully failing to comply with an order; imports some guilty knowledge that the actor is not complying with the order.

REFUSE TO BARGAIN IN GOOD FAITH. Where one party remains fixed in its bargaining position and refuses to move from the position adopted initially.

REG. *abbr.* 1. [L. regina] Queen. 2. Regulation. 3. Registrar.

REGARD. See IN A PERVERSE OR CAPRICIOUS MANNER OR WITHOUT ~ FOR THE MATERIAL BEFORE IT.

REGENERATIVE TISSUE. Tissue that, after injury within or removal from the body of a living person, is replaced in the person's body by natural processes. *Human Tissue Gift acts.* See NON-~

REGIME. See COMMUNITY PROPERTY ~; MARITAL ~; MATRIMONIAL ~.

REGION. See NATIONAL CAPITAL ~

REGISTER. *v.* To file or deposit.

REGISTER. *n.* 1. That part of the records where information respecting registered titles is stored. 2. The register of members and students of a professional body. 3. The register of Trade-marks. See SECURITIES ~.

REGISTERED. *adj.* Filed, listed or holder of a particular status in accordance with an act.

REGISTERED CHARITY. At any time means (a) a charitable organization, private foundation or public foundation, within the meanings assigned by subsection 149.1(1), that is resident in Canada and was either created or established in Canada, or (b) a branch, section, parish, congregation or other division of an organization or foundation described in paragraph 248(1) "registered charity" (a), that is resident in Canada and was either created or established in Canada and that receives donations on its own behalf, that has applied to the Minister in prescribed form for registration and that is at that time registered as a charitable organization, private foundation or public foundation. *Income Tax Act*, R.S.C. 1985, c. 1 (5th Supp.), s. 248.

REGISTERED CONSTITUENCY ASSOCIATION. A registered constituency association under the Election Finances and Contributions Disclosure Act. *Alberta Corporate Tax Act*, R.S.A. 2000, c. A-15, s. 24.

REGISTERED CREDITOR. A creditor who is named in a consolidation order. *Bankruptcy and Insolvency Act*, R.S.C. 1985, c. B-3, s. 217.

REGISTERED FORM. 1. A security is in registered form if (a) it specifies a person entitled to the security or to the rights it evidences, and its transfer is capable of being recorded in a securities register; or (b) it bears a statement that it is in registered form. *Bank Act*, S.C. 1991, c. 46, s. 83. 2. In respect of a certificated security, a form in which (i) the security certificate specifies a person entitled to the security, and (ii) a transfer of the security may be registered on books maintained for that purpose by or on behalf of the issuer, or the security certificate states that it may be so registered. *Securities Transfer acts*.

REGISTERED OFFICE. A head office or chief place of business the address of which is provided to the provincial or federal authority governing the company and where notices and process may be served on the company and certain documents and books must be kept.

REGISTERED OWNER. 1. An owner of land whose interest in the land is defined and whose name is specified in an instrument in the registry office. 2. The person registered in a land titles office as owner of the fee simple in land unless it appears from the records of the land titles office that another person has purchased the land under an agreement for sale in which case it means that other person. 3. A person in whose name a vehicle is registered.

REGISTERED PENSION PLAN. 1. A pension plan that is registered and in respect of which a certificate of registration has been issued by the Superintendent under this Act. *Pension Benefits Standards Act, 1985*, R.S.C. 1985, c. 32 (2nd Supp.), s. 2. 2. A pension plan that has been registered by the Minister for the purposes of this Act, which registration has not been revoked. *Income Tax Act*, R.S.C. 1985, c. 1 (5th Supp.), s. 248.

REGISTERED RETIREMENT SAVINGS PLAN. A retirement savings plan accepted by the Minister for registration for the purposes of this Act as complying with the requirements of this section. *Income Tax Act*, R.S.C. 1985, c. 1 (5th Supp.), s. 146. See LOCKED-IN ~.

REGISTERED TRADE-MARK. A trade-mark that is on the register. *Trade-marks Act*, R.S.C. 1985, c. T-13, s. 2.

REGISTERING. *n.* The filing or depositing of an instrument in the appropriate government office.

REGISTRAR. *n.* 1. The person responsible for the operation and management of a registration system. 2. With respect to a court, the administrative officer who is responsible for filing and issuing particular documents, retaining court files and occasionally for assessing costs. 3. The registrar or master of deeds or land titles or other officer with whom a title to land is registered or recorded. See ENTERPRISE ~.

REGISTRAR GENERAL. 1. The provincial officer who registers any birth, death and marriage. 2. The Registrar General as defined in the Vital Statistics Act.

REGISTRAR OF DEEDS. Includes the registrar of land titles or other officer with whom a title to the land is registered. *National Energy Board Act*, R.S.C. 1985, c. N-7, s. 2.

REGISTRAR OF LAND TITLES. A registrar of land titles appointed under a Land Titles Act.

REGISTRAR OF MOTOR VEHICLES. The person who from time to time performs the duties of superintending the registration of motor vehicles in a province. *Criminal Code*, R.S.C. 1985, c. C-46, s. 260, part.

REGISTRAR'S HEARING. An inquiry, an assessment, an accounting, a review of a bill, an examination of an agreement or an assessment of a bill of costs. *Court Rules Act*, R.S.B.C. 1996, c. 80, *Supreme Court Civil Rules*, B.C. Reg. 168/2009, Rule 1-1.

REGISTRATION. *n.* 1. (a) Bringing lands under this Act; (b) entering upon the certificate of title a memorandum authorized by this Act, of any document. *Land Titles acts.* 2. A valid and subsisting registration permit. 3. The admission of an individual to membership in a professional association and enrolment of that person's name in a register. 4. The entry of the name of a person in a register.

REGISTRATION CENTRE. A place that is designated as a registration centre under the Act or under the National Defence Act. *Sex Offender Information Registration Act*, S.C. 2004, c. 10, s. 3.

REGISTRATION OFFICER. The returning officer shall appoint, for each registration desk, a regis-

tration officer to receive, on polling day, the applications for registration of electors whose names are not on the list of electors. *Canada Elections Act*, S.C. 2000, c. 9, s. 39.

REGISTRY. *n.* The office of the Registrar. See CANADIAN ENVIRONMENTAL ASSESSMENT ~; CANADIAN FIREARMS ~; LAND TITLES ~; SEX OFFENDER ~.

REGISTRY ACT SYSTEM. 1. A person acquiring an interest in land registered in this system must examine the title as it is recorded in the Registry Office, and a vendor usually must show that she or he is lawfully entitled to own the land through a chain of title extending back for a period of years. W.B. Rayner & R.H. McLaren, *Falconbridge on Mortgages*, 4th ed. (Toronto: Canada Law Book, 1977) at 127. 2. Under such a system, anyone who acquires interest in land may register a copy of the document which transfers that interest. The registered documents are organized so that any person may, for a small fee, examine those which affect a particular piece of land. In most cases, a claim which is not registered does not affect a later mortgagee or purchaser who acquired an interest for value and without actually being notified of the unregistered claim, but simple registration of a document does not assure its effectiveness. B.J. Reiter, B.N. McLellan & P.M. Perell, *Real Estate Law*, 4th ed. (Toronto: Emond Montgomery, 1992) at 388.

REGNAL YEAR. A year calculated from a sovereign's accession to the throne, thus 7 Eliz. 2 means the seventh year after the accession of Elizabeth II on February 6, 1952 (February 6, 1958, to February 5, 1959).

RE-GRANT. *v.* For a grantor to grant again granted property which came back.

REGULAR FORCE. 1. The component of the Canadian Forces, that consists of officers and non-commissioned members who are enrolled for continuing, full-time military service. The maximum numbers of officers and non-commissioned members is authorized by the Governor in Council. The regular force includes units and other elements. *National Defence Act*, R.S.C. 1985, c. N-5, ss. 2, 15. 2. The component of the Canadian Forces that is referred to in the National Defence Act as the regular force. *Interpretation Act*, R.S.C. 1985, c. I-21, s. 35.

REGULAR HOURS OF WORK. The hours of work, not exceeding standard hours of work, during which an employee is required by an employer to be present for or engaged in work. *The Employment Standards Code*, S.M. 1998, c. 29, s. 1.

REGULARITY. *n.* The doctrine of regularity derives from the maxim "omnia praesumuntur rite esse act[a]" [all things are presumed to be done properly] and may be stated in essentially the same terms. It was described by Lindley L.J. in Harris v. Knight (1890), 15 P.D. 170 (C.A.) at p. 179 as follows: The maxim, 'Omnia praesumuntur rite esse acta,' is an expression, in a short form, of a reasonable probability, and of the propriety in point of law of acting on such probability. The maxim expresses an inference which may reasonably be drawn when an intention to do some formal act is established; when the evidence is consistent with that intention having been carried into effect in a proper way; but when the actual observance of all due formalities can only be inferred as a matter of probability. The maxim is not wanted where such observance is proved, nor had it any place where such observance is disproved. The maxim only comes into operation where there is no proof one way or the other; but where it is more probable that what was intended to be done was done as it ought to have been done to render it valid; rather than that it was done in some other manner which would defeat the intention proved to exist, and would render what is proved to have been done of no effect. *R. v. Larsen* (1992), 97 Sask. R. 310, (C.A.). See PRESUMPTION OF ~.

REGULAR LOT. A township lot whose boundaries according to the original plan conform within one degree to the bearings shown for the corresponding boundaries of the majority of the lots in the tier in which the lot occurs. *Surveys Act*, R.S.O. 1990, c. S.30, s. 1.

REGULARLY. *adv.* Opposite of casual or intermittent. Denotes a fixed pattern.

REGULATE. *v.* "... [T]he regulation and governance of a trade may involve the imposition of restrictions on its exercise both as to time and to a certain extent as to place where such restrictions are in the opinion of the public authority necessary to prevent a nuisance or for the maintenance of order. But ... there is a marked distinction to be drawn between the prohibition or prevention of a trade and the regulation or governance of it, indeed a power to regulate [as described in the Municipal Act, ...] and govern seems to imply the continued existence of that which is to be regulated or governed ... when the Legislature intended to give power to prevent or prohibit it did so by express words... . a municipal power of regulation ... without express words of prohibition, does not authorize the making it unlawful to carry on a lawful trade in a lawful manner." *Toronto (City) v. Virgo*, [1896] A.C. 88 at 93 (Can. P.C.), the board per Lord Davey. See SELF-REGULATING BODY.

REGULATED ENTITY. An exchange, an alternative trading system not registered as a dealer, or another published market, a clearing house, an information processor, a self-regulatory organization or any person the Authority, where it considers it necessary for the proper operation of the market, designates as a regulated entity in accordance with the rules prescribed by regulation. *Derivatives Act*, R.S.Q. c. I-14.01, s. 3.

REGULATED PRODUCT. A natural product that is regulated by a commodity board or a marketing agency.

REGULATION. *n.* 1. A rule of conduct, enacted by a regulation-making authority pursuant to an Act of Parliament, which has the force of law for an undetermined number of persons. *Reference re Manitoba Language Rights*, [1992] 1 S.C.R. 212. 2. Includes an order, regulation, rule, rule of court, form, tariff of costs or fees, letters patent, commission, warrant,

proclamation, by-law, resolution or other instrument issued, made or established (a) in the execution of a power conferred by or under the authority of an Act; or (b) by or under the authority of the Governor in Council. *Interpretation Act*, R.S.C. 1985, c. I-21, s. 2. 3. A statutory instrument (a) made in the exercise of a legislative power conferred by or under an Act of Parliament, or (b) for the contravention of which a penalty, fine or imprisonment is prescribed by or under an Act of Parliament, and includes a rule, order or regulation governing the practice or procedure in any proceedings before a judicial or quasi-judicial body established by or under an Act of Parliament, and any instrument described as a regulation in any other Act of Parliament; *Statutory Instruments Act*, R.S.C. 1985, c. S-22, s. 2. See COMPILATION OF QUÉBEC LAWS AND ~S; C.T.C. ~S; LAND USE ~.

REGULATORY AUTHORITY. See SECURITIES ~.

REGULATORY OFFENCE. "... '[A] wide category of offences created by statutes enacted for the regulation of individual conduct in the interests of health, convenience, safety and general welfare of the public' which are not subject to the common law presumption of mens rea as an essential element to be proven by the Crown." *R. v. Wholesale Travel Group Inc.* (1991), 8 C.R. (4th) 145 at 160, 67 C.C.C. (3d) 193, 4 O.R. (3d) 799n, 84 D.L.R. (4th) 161, 130 N.R. 1, 38 C.P.R. (3d) 451, 49 O.A.C. 161, [1991] 3 S.C.R. 154, 7 C.R.R. (2d) 36, Cory J. (L'Heureux-Dubé J. concurring).

REHABILITATE. *v.* 1. To restore to former rank, right or privilege. 2. To qualify again. 3. To restore a lost right.

REHABILITATION. *n.* 1. The establishment or the restoration of a disabled person to a state of economic and social sufficiency. 2. One of the principles applied in sentencing individuals convicted of offences. The goal is to rehabilitate the offender. See MEDICAL ~; PSYCHO-SOCIAL ~; SENTENCING; VOCATIONAL ~.

REHEAR. *v.* Section 71 [Immigration and Refugee Protection Act, S.C. 2001, c. 27] speaks of the power to "reopen" (« la réouverture ») an appeal. This verb is generally used in the context of the reconsideration of a decision in the light of new evidence, while "rehearing" is more usual when a matter is heard afresh and decided again after a breach of natural justice has vitiated the first decision. ... The legal principles governing the jurisdiction of administrative tribunals at large to reopen or rehear a matter already decided were restated in Chandler v. Alberta Association of Architects, 1989 CanLII 41 (S.C.C.), [1989] 2 S.C.R. 848. Writing for the majority, Sopinka J. made the following three points which are relevant to the broader legal context of the present appeal. First, an important reason for the application of the functus officio rule to administrative tribunals is the public interest in the finality of their proceedings (at page 861). Second, the rule should not be applied as rigidly to administrative tribunals from which there is a right of appeal only on questions of law as it is to courts from which there is an unrestricted right of appeal. Sopinka J. regarded Grillas as a case where the functus principle was not strictly applied because of indications in the legislation that a power to reopen was consistent with the Board's mandate to determine appeals on an "equitable" basis (at page 862). Third, a tribunal may always rehear a matter anew if its original decision was vitiated by an error rendering it a nullity, including a breach of the principles of natural justice which taints the whole proceeding (at pages 862-864). In other words, a tribunal does not have to wait for a court order setting aside a fatally flawed decision before it rehears the matter afresh and decides it again. *Nazifpour v. Canada (Minister of Citizenship & Immigration)*, 2007 FCA 35.

RE-HEARING. *n.* 1. Presentation of evidence and argument and the pronunciation of a second judgment in a cause or matter which is already decided. 2. It is perfectly true that an appeal is by way of rehearing; but it must not be forgotten that the Court of Appeal does not rehear the witnesses. It only reads the evidence and rehears the counsel. Neither is it a reseeing court. There are different meanings to be attached to the word 'rehearing'. *Powell and Wife v. Streatham Manor Nursing Home*, [1935] A.C. 243 at 249 (H.L.), Viscount Sankey L.C.

REIMBURSEMENT. *n.* Indemnification through repayment to someone of an expense or loss incurred; repayment; refund. Generally involves the intervention of a third person.

REINSTATE. *v.* In an insurance policy, to restore buildings or chattels which have been damaged.

REINSTATEMENT. *n.* A remedy available from a labour board when a former employee proves a claim of unfair dismissal against an employer. It requires that the employer act as though the employee had never been dismissed.

REINSURANCE. *n.* 1. An agreement whereby contracts made by a licensed insurer or any class or group thereof are undertaken or reinsured by another insurer either by novation, transfer, assignment or as a result of amalgamation of the insurers. *Insurance acts.* 2. New insurance under a new policy upon the same risk, which may be in wider or narrower form and which was insured before, that indemnifies the insurer from previous liability. R. Colinvaux, *The Law of Insurance*, 5th ed. (London: Sweet & Maxwell, 1984) at 186.

REINTEGRATION LEAVE. Leave granted from a youth custody facility for medical, humanitarian, rehabilitative or reintegrative purposes.

REJECT. *v.* To refuse to accept (a statement).

REJOINDER. *n.* The defendant's answer to the plaintiff's reply. See SUR~.

RELATE. *v.* To stand in relation to; to pertain to; to refer to; to concern.

RELATED RETAINER. In my view, putting aside issues of informed consent, lawyers have a duty not to act against a former client in a related matter whether or not confidential information is at risk. A matter is "related" for this purpose if the new retainer involves the lawyer taking an adversarial position against the former client with respect to the legal work which the lawyer performed for the former client or a matter central to the earlier retainer. *Brookville Carriers Flatbed GP Inc. v.Blackjack Transport Ltd.*, 2008 NSCA 22, Cromwell J. (Roscoe and Saunders JJ.A. concurring).

RELATION. *n.* 1. Next-of-kin of any degree. 2. A doctrine by which an act produces the same effect as it would have if it had happened at an earlier time. See CONFIDENTIAL ~; INDUSTRIAL ~S; LABOUR ~S; TRESPASS BY ~.

RELATIONAL ECONOMIC LOSS. One of five recognized categories of pure economic loss. A situation in which "the defendant negligently causes personal injury or property damage to a third party. The plaintiff suffers pure economic loss by virtue of some relationship, usually contractual, it enjoys with the injured third party or the damaged property." *Design Services Ltd. v. R.*, 2008 SCC 22.

RELATION BACK. A doctrine by which an act produces the same effect as it would have if it had happened at an earlier time.

RELATIONSHIP. See ADULT INTERDEPENDENT ~; BLOOD ~; COMMON-LAW ~; VOLUNTEER WORK ~.

RELATIONSHIP OF INTERDEPENDENCE. A relationship outside marriage in which any 2 persons (i) share one another's lives, (ii) are emotionally committed to one another, and (iii) function as an economic and domestic unit. *Adult Interdependent Relationships Act*, R.S.A. 2000, c. A-4.5, s. 1.

RELATIVE. *n.* 1. "... [C]ommonly understood to refer to a relation of consanguinity, close or distant, and to a legally recognized affinity created, for instance, by marriage or adoption." *Leroux v. Co-operators General Insurance Co.* (1990), 44 C.C.L.I. 253 at 259, [1990] I.L.R. 1-2566, 65 D.L.R. (4th) 702, 71 O.R. (2d) 641 (H.C.), Arbour J. 2. A person related to another by marriage, common-law partnership, birth, adoption or affinity. See COLLATERAL ~; DEPENDENT ~ REVOCATION; NEAR ~.

RELATIVE EXPERTISE. Of an administrative tribunal, recognizes that legislatures will sometimes remit an issue to a decision-making body that has particular topical expertise or is adept in the determination of particular issues. Where this is so, courts will seek to respect this legislative choice when conducting judicial review. *Q. v. College of Physicians & Surgeons (British Columbia)*, [2003] 1 S.C.R. 226.

RELATOR ACTION. An action in which a relator tries by injunction to prevent any interfering with or infringing of a public right, to stop a public nuisance or to force a public duty to be performed or observed. The relator brings this action in the Attorney-General's name after obtaining leave to do so.

RELEASE. *v.* 1. To surrender or relinquish a claim or interest in property. *Donnell, Re*, [1930] 4 D.L.R. 1037 at 1037 (Ont. Surr. Ct.), Widdifield Surr. Ct. J.

2. To communicate, disclose or make available information, a document, recording or statement. 3. In respect of goods, means to authorize the removal of the goods from a customs office, sufferance warehouse, bonded warehouse or duty free shop for use in Canada. *Customs Act*, R.S.C. 1985, c. 1 (2nd Supp.), s. 2, part.

RELEASE. *n.* 1. The document by which a claim or interest in property is surrendered or relinquished. 2. The termination of the service of an officer or non-commissioned member in any manner. *National Defence Act*, R.S.C. 1985, c. N-5, s. 2. 3. A document issued by the Court which releases property arrested by warrant. See STATUTORY ~; WORK ~.

RELEVANCE. *n.* 1. In its narrow sense, relevance means that the evidence is so related to a fact in issue that it tends to establish it. The evidence proffered here is circumstantial evidence tending to establish identity and is clearly relevant in the narrow sense. The broader meaning given to relevance in [R. v. Mohan, 89 C.C.C. (3d) 402, [1994] 2 S.C.R. 9, 114 D.L.R. (4th) 419 (S.C.C.)] requires what the court described as a "cost benefit analysis". Logically relevant evidence may be excluded if its probative value is overborne by its prejudicial effect. The evidence may prove to be misleading, in the sense that its effect on the jury will be out of proportion to its reliability. *R. v. Murrin*, 1999 CarswellBC 3015, 181 D.L.R. (4th) 320, 32 C.R. (5th) 97 (S.C.). 2. In the context of Crown disclosure obligations in a criminal case, information ought not to be withheld if there is a reasonable possibility that the withholding of information will impair the right of the accused to make full answer and defence, unless the non-disclosure is justified by the law of privilege. *R. v. Chaplin*, [1995] 1 S.C.R. 727. See LIKELY ~.

RELEVANT. *adj.* The basic rule is that all relevant evidence is admissible. Relevance depends on the facts in issue in any particular case. The facts in issue are in turn determined by the charge in the indictment and the defence, if any, raised by the accused. To be logically relevant, an item of evidence does not have to firmly establish, on any standard, the truth or falsity of a fact in issue. The evidence must simply tend to "increase or diminish the probability of the existence of a fact in issue." *R. v. Arp*, [1998] 3 S.C.R. 339.

RELIABILITY. *n.* 1. The requirement of reliability for admissibility of hearsay evidence will be satisfied where the hearsay statement was made in circumstances which provide sufficient guarantees of its trustworthiness. In particular, the circumstances must counteract the traditional evidentiary dangers associated with hearsay. *R. v. Hawkins*, [1996] 3 S.C.R. 1043. 2. Credibility and reliability are different. Credibility has to do with a witness's veracity, reliability with the accuracy of the witness's testimony. Accuracy engages consideration of the witness's ability to accurately i. observe; ii. recall; and iii. recount events in issue. Any witness whose evidence on an issue is not credible cannot give reliable evidence on the same point. Credibility, on the other hand, is not a proxy for reliability: a credible witness may give unreliable evidence. *R. v. C. (H.)*, 2009 ONCA 56.

RELICTION. *n.* The sudden receding of sea from the land.

RELIEF. *n.* 1. Remedy. 2. The end result of civil litigation. 3. Includes every species of relief, whether by way of damages, payment of money, injunction, declaration, restitution of an incorporeal right, return of land or chattels or otherwise. 4. Alleviation of the consequences of default. See ANCILLARY ~; COROLLARY ~; CREDITORS' ~ STATUTE; DECLARATORY ~; INTERIM ~; PRAYER FOR ~; ROYALTY-~ METHOD.

RELIEF AGAINST FORFEITURE. In an appropriate and limited case a court of equity will grant this relief for breach of a condition or covenant when the main object of the deal was to secure a certain result and provision for forfeiture was added to secure that result. F. Bennett, *Receiverships* (Toronto: Carswell, 1985) at 355.

RELIEF GRANT. Payment generally made under unusual or anomalous situations and connotes assistance freely given to the destitute.

RELIGION. See FREEDOM OF CONSCIENCE AND ~; FREEDOM OF ~.

RELIGIOUS COMMUNICATIONS PRIVILEGE. A privilege attached to communications between a confessor and her priest or to other adherents to a religion and their religious adviser.

RELY. *v.* To be influenced by.

REM. *abbr.* Remanet.

REMAINDER. *n.* That part of a grantor's interest in an estate which is disposed of, but which is postponed to some estate in possession created at the same time. R. Megarry and H.W.R. Wade, *The Law of Real Property*, 5th ed. (London: Stevens, 1984) at 236 and cxxvii. See CONTINGENT ~; VESTED ~.

REMAINDERMAN. *n.* A person who is entitled to the remainder of an estate after some part of that estate has expired or has been extracted. For example, the person who inherits after a life estate is ended.

REMAINS. See HUMAN ~..REMAIN SILENT. See RIGHT TO ~.

REMAND. *v.* To adjourn a hearing to a future date, ordering the defendant, unless permitted bail, to be kept in the meantime in custody.

REMAND PRISONER. A prisoner (i) remanded in custody by a judge or court; and (ii) awaiting trial, or the resumption or conclusion of a trial, for contravention of an Act of the Parliament of Canada or a legislature or of any regulations or order made pursuant to any such act.

REMAND TIME. Pre-sentence custody or remand time is deemed to be part of the sentence. *R. v. Chiasson*, 2005 NBCA 78.

REMANET. *n.* [L.] 1. Whatever remains. 2. An action, scheduled for trial in a certain session, which does not come on so that it stands over to the next session.

REMANUFACTURED. *adj.* Means, in relation to a softwood lumber product, that the softwood lumber product, in order to produce a semi-finished or finished softwood lumber product, has been subjected to changes including changes in thickness, width, length, profile, texture, moisture or grading, has been joined together by finger jointing or has been turned. *Softwood Lumber Products Export Charge Act, 2006*, S.C. 2006, c. 13, s. 13.

REMEDIAL CONSTRUCTIVE TRUST. "... [T]he acts of the parties are such that a wrong is done by one of them to another so that, while no substantive trust relationship is then and there brought into being by those acts, nonetheless a remedy is required in relation to property and the court grants that remedy in the form of a declaration which, when the order is made, creates a constructive trust by one of the parties in favour of another party... . A remedial constructive trust is a trust imposed by Court order as a remedy for a wrong ... the trust itself [is created] by the order of the Court." *Atlas Cabinets & Furniture Ltd. v. National Trust Co.* (1990), 37 E.T.R. 16 at 27, 38 C.L.R. 106, 45 B.C.L.R. (2d) 99, 68 D.L.R. (4th) 161 (C.A.), Lambert J.A. (Hinkson, Toy and Cumming JJ.A. concurring).

REMEDIAL STATUTE. A statute drafted to remedy a defect in the law.

REMEDIATION. *n.* Action to eliminate, limit, correct, counteract, mitigate or remove any contaminant or the adverse effects on the environment or human health of any contaminant. *Environmental Management Act*, S.B.C. 2003, c. 53, s. 1, part.

REMEDY. *n.* 1. The means by which one prevents, redresses or compensates the violation of a right. 2. Cure for a default. 3. Any order, judgment, damages, compensation or other relief provided for in this Act. *Residential Tenancies Act*, S.A. 2004, c. R-17.1, s. 54.1. See APPRAISAL ~; CUMULATIVE ~; DISCRETIONARY ~; EQUITY WILL NOT SUFFER A WRONG TO BE WITHOUT A ~; EXTRAORDINARY ~; MUTUALITY OF ~; OPPRESSION ~; STRUCTURAL ~.

REMEDY CLAUSE. Section 24(1) of the Charter, which allows a remedy to be granted to enforce the rights or freedoms the Charter guarantees. P.W. Hogg, *Constitutional Law of Canada*, 3d ed. (Toronto: Carswell, 1992) at 915.

REMEMBRANCE. See NATIONAL DAY OF ~.

REMEMBRANCE DAY. November 11, being the day in the year 1918 on which the Great War was triumphantly concluded by an armistice, is a holiday and shall be kept and observed as such throughout Canada. *Holidays Act*, R.S.C. 1985, c. H-5, s. 3.

REMINISCENCE EFFECT. [A forensic psychologist's] testimony included evidence of the reminiscence effect by which recall of a person may increase with time as a person reflects on the memory. *R. v. N. (E.A.)*, 2000 CarswellBC 274, 2000 BCCA 61, 135 B.C.A.C. 154, 221 W.A.C. 154.

REMISSION. *n.* 1. A release; a pardon. 2. A decrease in the length of imprisonment. 3. Every prisoner serving a sentence, other than a sentence on conviction for criminal or civil contempt of court where the sentence includes a requirement that the prisoner return to that court, shall be credited with fifteen days of remission of the sentence in respect of each month and with a number of days calculated on a pro rata basis in respect of each incomplete month during which the prisoner has earned that remission by obeying prison rules and conditions governing temporary absence and by actively participating in programs, other than full parole, designed to promote prisoners' rehabilitation and reintegration. *Prisons and Reformatories Act*, R.S.C. 1985, c. P-20, s. 6.

REMIT. *v.* To send back.

REMITMENT. *n.* The act of sending back into custody.

REMITTANCE. *n.* Money which one person sends to another. See POSTAL ~.

REMITTEE. *n.* The person to whom one sends a remittance.

REM JUDICATAM. See ESTOPPEL PER ~.

REMORSE. *n.* Feeling of deep regret for wrong done. Can be a justification for leniency in sentencing.

REMOTE AGREEMENT. A consumer agreement entered into when the consumer and supplier are not present together. *Consumer Protection Act, 2002*, S.O. 2002, c. 30, Sched. A, s. 20.

REMOTENESS. *n.* 1. Lack of close relation between a wrong and damages. 2. "In Koufos v. C. Czarnikow (The Heron II), [1969] 1 A.C. 350 ... [(U.K.H.L.)] ... it was determined that the proper test for remoteness [for recovery of damages for breach of contract] was not the 'reasonable forseeability' of the head of damages claimed as in an action in tort, but whether the probability of the occurrence of the damage in the event of breach should have been within the reasonable contemplation of the contracting parties at the time of the entry into the contract. (Vide Brown & Root Ltd. v. Chimo Shipping Ltd., [1967] S.C.R. 642 per Ritchie J. at p. 648 ..." *Baud Corp., N.V., v. Brook* (1978), *(sub nom. Asamera Oil Corp. v. Sea Oil & General Corp.)* 5 B.L.R. 225 at 237, [1979] 1 S.C.R 633, [19878] 6 W.W.R. 301, 23 N.R. 181, 12 A.R. 271, 89 D.L.R. (3d) 1, the court per Estey J.

REMOVAL ORDER. If the judge [reviewing a ministerial certificate of inadmissibility finds the certificate to be reasonable, it becomes a removal order. The removal order cannot be appealed and may be immediately enforced, thus eliminating the requirement of holding or continuing an examination or an admissibility hearing. *Charkaoui v. Canada (Citizenship and Immigration)*, 2007 SCC 9..

REMOVER. *n.* The transfer of a cause or suit from one court to another.

REMUNERATION. *n.* Payment for services provided. *Sheridan v. Minister of National Revenue* (1985), 57 N.R. 69 at 74, 85 C.L.L.C. 14,048 (Fed. C.A.), the court per Heald J.A.

RENDERING PLANT. A place (a) where animal by-products are prepared or treated for use in, or converted into, fertilizers, animal food, fats or oils, other than fats or oils used for human consumption, (b) where a substance resulting from a process mentioned in paragraph (*a*) is stored, packed or marked, or (c) from which a substance resulting from a process mentioned in paragraph (a) is shipped. *Health of Animals Act, 1990*, S.C. 1990, c. 21, s. 2.

RENEWABLE DIESEL FUEL. (a) Biodiesel fuel, or (b) hydrogenated-derived renewable diesel fuel. *Carbon Tax Act*, S.B.C. 2008, c. 40, Sched. 1, s. 1.

RENEWABLE ENERGY SOURCE. 1. Any source of renewable energy from which electric energy may be generated and includes (i) the sun, (ii) the wind, (iii) flowing water, (iv) organic material, and (v) such other sources as are prescribed by the regulations. *Renewable Energy Act*, S.P.E.I. 2004, c. 16, s. 1. 2. An energy source that is renewed by natural processes and includes wind, water, biomass, biogas, biofuel, solar energy, geothermal energy, tidal forces and such other energy sources as may be prescribed by the regulations, but only if the energy source satisfies such criteria as may be prescribed by the regulations for that energy source. *Green Energy Act, 2009*, S.O. 2009, c. 12, Sched. A, s. 1.

RENEWABLE FUEL. (a) In relation to gasoline class fuel, (i) ethanol produced from biomass, or (ii) another substance prescribed by regulation as a renewable fuel in relation to gasoline class fuel, and (b) in relation to diesel class fuel, (i) biodiesel, or (ii) another substance prescribed by regulation as a renewable fuel in relation to diesel class fuel. *Greenhouse Gas Reduction (Renewable and Low Carbon Fuel Requirements) Act*, S.B.C. 2008, c. 16, s. 1.

RENEWAL. *n.* 1. Refers to the revival of an agreement which has expired, not to extension of an existing agreement. *Manulife Bank of Canada v. Conlin*, [1996] 3 S.C.R. 415. 2. "... [T]he more 'standard' meaning is the one that assumes the continued existence of the matter 'renewed'. If it is not in existence then the process is really one of re-creation rather than renewal. Further, in a general legal context concerned with the renewal of rights, privileges and other interests, conferred under instruments such as leases, contracts and licences, it is, I think, a general understanding that renewal involves the temporal extension of something that is in existence and not the revival of something that has ceased to exist." *R. v. Pleich* (1980), 55 C.C.C. (2d) 13 at 28, 16 C.R. (3d) 194 (Ont. C.A.), the court per Morden J.A. ....3. Two separate meanings can be ascribed to a "renewal" of an insurance policy. The first meaning results from a continuous policy. Such policies provide for further extensions to the term of an existing contract, subject to the rights of either of the parties to terminate the contract. In a single continuous policy, questions of formation are answered by reference to the original offer and acceptance that initiated the coverage. By contrast, the other meaning of a "renewal" of an insurance policy involves the situation where a separate and distinct contract comes into existence at each renewal. Automobile insurance renewals fall into the latter category, in that each renewal represents a new contract with its own offer and acceptance. *Patterson v. Gallant*, [1994] 3 S.C.R. 1080. See AUTOMATIC ~.

RENOUNCE. *v.* 1. Of a right, to give up. 2. Of probate, for an executor to decline to take probate of a will.

RENOVATION. See SUBSTANTIAL ~.

RENT. *v.* To let. *Daugherty v. Armaly* (1921), 58 D.L.R. 380 at 382, 49 O.L.R. 310, 19 O.W.N. 573 (C.A.), the court per Meredith C.J.O.

RENT. *n.* 1. "... [T]he compensation which a tenant of the land or other corporeal hereditament makes to the owner for the use thereof. It is frequently treated as a profit arising out of the demised land... ." *Johnson v. British Canadian Insurance Co.*, [1932] S.C.R. 680 at 684, [1932] 4 D.L.R. 281, Lamont J. 2. Includes the amount of any consideration paid or given or required to be paid or given by or on behalf of a tenant to a landlord or the landlord's agent for the right to occupy a rental unit and for any services and facilities and any privilege, accommodation or thing that the landlord provides for the tenant in respect of the occupancy of the rental unit, whether or not a separate charge is made for services and facilities or for the privilege, accommodation or thing. *Residential Tenancies Act, 2006*, S.O. 2006, c. 17, s. 2, part. See FAIR MARKET ~; FAIR ~; GROUND-~; PEPPERCORN ~; QUIT ~; RACK-~.

RENTAL HOUSING PROJECT. A housing project occupied or intended to be occupied primarily by a person other than the owner.

RENTAL PERIOD. The interval for which rent is paid or is payable.

RENTAL PROPERTY MANAGEMENT SERVICES. Any of the following services provided to or on behalf of an owner of rental real estate: (a) trading services in relation to the rental of the real estate; (b) collecting rents or security deposits for the use of the real estate; (c) managing the real estate on behalf of the owner by (i) making payments to third parties, (ii) negotiating or entering into contracts, (iii) supervising employees or contractors hired or engaged by the owner, or (iv) managing landlord and tenant matters but does not include an activity excluded by regulation. *Real Estate Services Act*, S.B.C. 2004, c. 42, s. 1.

RENTAL UNIT. Any living accommodation used or intended for use as rented residential premises.

RENTAL VALUE. See MARKET ~.

RENT CHARGE. A right to receive a periodic sum from land together with the right to use distress to remedy non-payment.

RENT-GEARED-TO-INCOME ASSISTANCE. Financial assistance provided in respect of a household under a housing program to reduce the amount the household must otherwise pay to occupy a unit in a housing project.

RENT-GEARED-TO-INCOME UNIT. A unit in a housing project that either is occupied by a household receiving rent-geared-to-income assistance or is

R

available for occupancy by a household eligible for rent-geared-to-income assistance.

RENUNCIATION. *n.* "... [O]f a contract may be express or implied. A party to a contract may state before the time of performance that he will not, or cannot, perform his obligations. This is tantamount to an express renunciation. On the other hand, a renunciation will be implied if the conduct of a party is such as to lead a reasonable person to the conclusion that he will not perform, or will not be able to perform, when the time for performance arises." *McCallum v. Zivojinovic* (1977), 16 O.R. (2d) 721 at 723, 2 R.P.R. 164, 26 Chitty's L.J. 169, 79 D.L.R. (3d) 133 (C.A.), the court per Howland J.A.

RENVOI. *n.* When one determines, by the appropriate choice of law rule, that the questionable issue may be decided according to "the law" of a certain country, the court must decide whether the term "the law" refers to the internal domestic law of that country or to its conflict of laws rules as well. This concept is not firmly entrenched in Canadian law. J.G. McLeod, *The Conflict of Laws* (Calgary: Carswell, 1983) at 198 and 201.

REOPEN. *v.* Section 71 [Immigration and Refugee Protection Act, S.C. 2001, c. 27] speaks of the power to "reopen" (« la réouverture ») an appeal. This verb is generally used in the context of the reconsideration of a decision in the light of new evidence, while "rehearing" is more usual when a matter is heard afresh and decided again after a breach of natural justice has vitiated the first decision. ... The legal principles governing the jurisdiction of administrative tribunals at large to reopen or rehear a matter already decided were restated in Chandler v. Alberta Association of Architects, 1989 CanLII 41, [1989] 2 S.C.R. 848. Writing for the majority, Sopinka J. made the following three points which are relevant to the broader legal context of the present appeal. First, an important reason for the application of the functus officio rule to administrative tribunals is the public interest in the finality of their proceedings (at page 861). Second, the rule should not be applied as rigidly to administrative tribunals from which there is a right of appeal only on questions of law as it is to courts from which there is an unrestricted right of appeal. Sopinka J. regarded Grillas as a case where the functus principle was not strictly applied because of indications in the legislation that a power to reopen was consistent with the Board's mandate to determine appeals on an "equitable" basis (at page 862). Third, a tribunal may always rehear a matter anew if its original decision was vitiated by an error rendering it a nullity, including a breach of the principles of natural justice which taints the whole proceeding (at pages 862-864). In other words, a tribunal does not have to wait for a court order setting aside a fatally flawed decision before it rehears the matter afresh and decides it again. *Nazifpour v. Canada (Minister of Citizenship & Immigration)*, 2007 FCA 35.

REORGANIZATION. *n.* 1. A court order made under (a) a Corporations Act; (b) the Bankruptcy and Insolvency Act approving a proposal; or (c) any other act that affects the rights among the corporation, its shareholders and creditors. *Corporations acts.* 2. Changes within a company in the way in which different parts of the company relate to one another and changes in the size and objects of the company.

REPAIR. *v.* 1. "[R]estoration to a previously designed or constructed state... ." *Fry v. Henry* (1985), 64 A.R. 304 at 305 (C.A.), the court per Laycraft C.J.A. 2. To bring a dwelling or non-residential building into compliance with building code or by-law standards.

REPAIR. *n.* See CREDIT ~

REPAIRER. See CREDIT ~.

REPAIRER'S GARAGE. A place of business primarily designed or used for the purpose of repairing motor vehicles or trailers, but does not include a place of business from which motive fuel, lubricating oil, antifreeze or other similar products, and services incidental to them, are sold or provided except in relation to repairs. *Motor Vehicle Act*, R.S.B.C. 1996, c. 318, s. 44.

REPARATION. *n.* 1. Restitution. 2. "[In s. 663(2)(e) of the Criminal Code, R.S.C. 1970, c. C-34] ... would have the additional meaning [to the meaning of restitution which refers to property only] of compensating a victim for loss or damage—both to property and person... ." *R. v. Groves* (1977), 39 C.R.N.S. 366 at 380, 17 O.R. (2d) 65, 37 C.C.C. (2d) 429, 79 D.L.R. (3d) 561 (H.C.), O'Driscoll J. 3. Reparation for harm done to the victim or to the community is one of the principles applied in sentencing individuals convicted of offences.

REPATRIATION. *n.* 1. Recovering possession of the nationality which a person lost or abandoned. 2. Sometimes used in reference to the patriation of the Canadian constitution. 3. The transfer to a First Nation by the Crown of the Crown's title to a sacred ceremonial object, and the acceptance by the First Nation of that transfer. *First Nations Sacred Ceremonial Objects Repatriation Act*, R.S.A. 2000, c. F-14, s. 1. See PATRIATION.

REPEAL. *v.* To strike out, revoke, cancel or rescind.

REPEATEDLY. *adv.* Many times over. More than once or twice.

REPLACE. *v.* 1. To take away and substitute another. 2. In insurance, to restore buildings or chattels which have been destroyed. R. Colinvaux, *The Law of Insurance*, 5th ed. (London: Sweet & Maxwell, 1984) at 181.

REPLACEMENT. *n.* In an insurance policy, to put back the insured property in the same position as before the loss.

REPLACEMENT COST INSURANCE. "... [A]ny type of coverage under which the insurance company agrees, in effect, to pay the difference between actual cash value and full replacement costs." What is insured, simply put, is depreciation. Under replacement coverage, insureds are entitled to receive the amount necessary to rebuild a structure or replace its contents in a new condition, without deducting for depreciation. Recovery is allowed, in the words of many courts, on a new-for-old basis. *Brkich & Brkich*

Enterprises Ltd. v. American Home Assurance Co. (1995), 8 B.C.L.R. (3d) 1 (C.A.) appeal to S.C.C. dismissed, reasons of Finch J.A. adopted.

REPLACEMENT WORKER. One hired to replace a worker who is on strike. A strike-breaker.

REPLEVIN. *n.* "... [N]ow called an order for the recovery of possession of personal property, has remained what its new name suggests: a means of getting back the possession which an applicant for the remedy has lost." *Manitoba Agricultural Credit Corp. v. Heaman* (1990), 70 D.L.R. (4th) 518 at 523, [1990] 4 W.W.R. 269, 65 Man. R. (2d) 269 (C.A.), the court per Twaddle J.A. See ACTION FOR ~.

REPLEVY. *v.* To redeliver goods which were unlawfully taken or detained to their owner.

REPLICA FIREARM. Any device that is designed or intended to exactly resemble, or to resemble with near precision, a firearm, and that itself is not a firearm, but does not include any such device that is designed or intended to exactly resemble, or to resemble with near precision, an antique firearm. *Criminal Code*, R.S.C. 1985, c. C-46, s. 84(1).

REPLY. *n.* The pleading of a petitioner, plaintiff or party, who institutes a proceeding, in answer to the defendant.

REPLY EVIDENCE. Rebuttal evidence which a plaintiff may present at the end of the defendant's case to contradict or qualify new facts or issues which the defendant raised in the course of presenting her or his case.

REPORT. *n.* 1. " ... [A]n account of an event. It can be either oral or written. Even an act or gesture that conveys information without words could amount to a report..." *Peel (Board of Education) v. B.(W.)* (1987), 36 M.P.L.R. 95 at 103, 24 Admin. L.R. 164, 59 O.R. (2d) 654, 38 D.L.R. (4th) 566 (H.C.), Reid J. 2. An assertion of fact, opinion, belief or knowledge, whether material or not and whether admissible or not. *Criminal Code*, R.S.C. 1985, c. C-46, s. 107. 3. Accommodates an interpretation which requires the [professional ethics committee] to provide an explanation of its decision. In this regard, the fact that s. 37(c) [Teachers' Federation Act, R.S.S. 1978, c. T-7] refers to a report of "findings" tends to suggest that the meaning of "report" involves more than just the statement of a conclusion. *Casavant v. S.T.F.*, 2005 SKCA 52. See CONSUMER ~; CREDIT ~; ENGLISH ~S; INQUIRY ~; LAW ~; OFFICIAL ~; OFFICIAL ~ OF DEBATES; PRE-DISPOSITION ~; PRE-SENTENCE ~.

REPORTABLE INJURY. Any of the following: (a) an injury caused by discharge of a firearm; (b) an injury requiring emergency care by a medical practitioner or nurse practitioner and transfer to a hospital; (c) an injury described by regulation under section 184(2)(c). *Police Act*, R.S.B.C. 1996, c. 367, s. 76.

REPORTED. See CLAIMS MADE AND ~ POLICY.

REPORTED JUDICIAL DECISION. The reported judicial decisions, when properly understood as a compilation of the headnote and the accompanying edited judicial reasons, are "original" works covered by copyright. Copyright protects originality of form or expression. A compilation takes existing material and casts it in a different form. The arranger does not have copyright in the individual components. However, the arranger may have copyright in the form represented by the compilation. "It is not the several components that are the subject of copyright, but the over-all arrangement of them which the plaintiff through his industry has produced": Slumber-Magic Adjustable Bed Co. v. Sleep-King Adjustable Bed Co. (1984), 3 C.P.R. (3d) 81 (B.C. S.C.), at p. 84; see also Ladbroke (Football) Ltd. v. William Hill (Football) Ltd., [1964] 1 All E.R. 465 (U.K. H.L.), at p. 469 ... The reported judicial decisions here at issue meet the test for originality. The authors have arranged the case summary, catchlines, case title, case information (the headnotes) and the judicial reasons in a specific manner. The arrangement of these different components requires the exercise of skill and judgment. The compilation, viewed globally, attracts copyright protection ... This said, the judicial reasons in and of themselves, without the headnotes, are not original works in which the publishers could claim copyright. *CCH Canadian Ltd. v. Law Society of Upper Canada*, 2004 SCC 13.

REPORTER. See COURT ~.

REPORTING PUBLIC OFFICE HOLDER. A public office holder who is (a) a minister of the Crown, minister of state or parliamentary secretary; (b) a member of ministerial staff who works on average 15 hours or more a week; (c) a ministerial adviser; (d) a Governor in Council appointee, or a ministerial appointee whose appointment is approved by the Governor in Council, who exercises his or her official duties and functions on a part-time basis but receives an annual salary and benefits; (e) a Governor in Council appointee, or a ministerial appointee whose appointment is approved by the Governor in Council, who exercises his or her official duties and functions on a full-time basis; or (f) a full-time ministerial appointee designated by the appropriate minister of the Crown as a reporting public office holder. *Conflict of Interest Act*, S.C. 2006, c. 9, s. 2, s. 2.

REPORTING SYSTEM. See QUOTATION AND TRADE ~.

REPREHENSIBLE. *adj.* Scandalous, outrageous, deserving of reproof or rebuke.

REPRESENT. *v.* To act for a client as his or her solicitor or attorney. See MIS~.

REPRESENTATION. *n.* 1. A statement of fact, implied or expressed, made by a party to a transaction or tending to facilitate the conclusion of the transaction. 2. Standing in someone else's place for a certain purpose. 3. "... The element of representation in s. 163 of the [Criminal Code, R.S.C. 1985, c. C-46] is therefore a suggestion, a depiction to the public... ." *R. v. Butler* (1992), 11 C.R. (4th) 137 at 184, [1992] 2 W.W.R. 577, [1992] 1 S.C.R. 452, 70 C.C.C. (3d) 129, 134 N.R. 81, 8 C.R.R. (2d) 1, 89 D.L.R. (4th) 449, 78 Man. R. (2d) 1, 16 W.A.C. 1, Gonthier J. (L'Heureux-Dubé J. concurring). 4. Making a statement of facts, reasons or argument on matters that affect the party; the statement made, itself. See ESTOPPEL BY ~; FALSE ~; MIS~.

REPRESENTATIVE. *n.* 1. The person who takes the place of or represents another person. A deceased person's executor or administrator is called a personal representative. 2. Any person who acts on behalf of another. See ESTATE ~; LEGAL ~; LITIGATION ~; PERSONAL ~.

REPRESENTATIVE ACTION. 1. "... [F]or a proper representative action there must be a 'common interest' of the plaintiff with those he claims to represent, the exertion of a 'common right' or a 'common grievance', normally arising from a 'common origin', but once the alleged rights of the class are denied or ignored it is immaterial that the individuals have been wronged in their individual capacity, provided, of course, that their claims were not for personal damages. It appears to me that the many passages uttered by Judges of high authority over the years really boil down to a simple proposition that a class action is appropriate where if the plaintiff wins the other persons he purports to represent win too, and if he, because of that success, becomes entitled to relief whether or not in a fund or property, the others also become likewise entitled to that relief, having regard, always, for different quantitative participations." *Shaw v. Vancouver Real Estate Board* (1973), 36 D.L.R. (3d) 250 at 253-4, [1973] 4 W.W.R. 391 (B.C. C.A.), Bull J.A. 2. "... [C]an be brought by persons asserting a common right, and even where persons may have been wronged in their individual capacity." *Pasco v. Canadian National Railway* (1989), 34 B.C.L.R. (2d) 344 at 348, [1990] 2 C.N.L.R. 85, 56 D.L.R. (4th) 404 (C.A.), the court per Macfarlane J.A. 3. "An action by members of a corporation challenging allegedly ultra vires acts thus should normally be taken in representative form so that all members or shareholders of the company will be bound by judgment and the company not harassed by a multiplicity of actions... ." *Gordon v. N.S.T.U.* (1983), 36 C.P.C. 150 at 156, 59 N.S.R. (2d) 124, 125 A.P.R. 124, 1 D.L.R. (4th) 676 (C.A.), the court per MacKeigan C.J.N.S.

REPRIEVE. *n.* The temporary withdrawal of a sentence so that its execution is suspended.

REPRIMAND. *n.* The giving of an official or pointed rebuke. A reproach.

REPRISAL. *n.* 1. Recaption; taking one thing in place of another. 2. Any of the following measures taken against a public servant because the public servant has made a protected disclosure or has, in good faith, cooperated in an investigation into a disclosure or an investigation commenced under section 33: (a) a disciplinary measure; (b) the demotion of the public servant; (c) the termination of employment of the public servant, including, in the case of a member of the Royal Canadian Mounted Police, a discharge or dismissal; (d) any measure that adversely affects the employment or working conditions of the public servant; and (e) a threat to take any of the measures referred to in any of paragraphs (a) to (d). *Public Servants Disclosure Protection Act*, S.C. 2005, c. 46, s. 2.

REPRODUCTION. *n.* In relation to copyright infringement, involves the entire work or a substantial part of it and a causal connection between the copyrighted work and the infringing work. The copyrighted work must be the source of the infringing work. Includes making copies of a work.

REPRODUCTION RIGHTS. Compensation to which copyright holders are entitled when broadcasters make recordings of musical works in another format.

REPRODUCTIVE MATERIAL. See HUMAN ~.

REPUBLICATION. *n.* Of a codicil or will, execution again by the testator.

REPUDIATION. *n.* 1. "... [O]rdinarily means a refusal to carry out all one's obligations under a contract." *Park v. Parsons Brown & Co.* (1989), 27 C.C.E.L. 224 at 242, 39 B.C.L.R. (2d) 107, 62 D.L.R. (4th) 108 (B.C. C.A.), Southin J.A. 2. To find a repudiation there must be conduct which amounts to total rejection of the obligations of the contract; there must be lack of justification for that conduct; and the repudiation must be accepted by the innocent party who treats the contract as ended. *Norfolk v. Aikens* (1989), [1990] 2 W.W.R. 401 (B.C. C.A.) at 417-418. See CONTINUING ~.

REPUGNANCY. *n.* "... [W]here one clear clause contradicts another clause equally clear. In a deed where there is a repugnancy the rule is the first shall prevail, but in a will the second: ..." *Westholme Lumber Co. v. St. James Ltd.* (1915), 21 D.L.R. 549 at 555, 8 W.W.R. 122, 21 B.C.R. 100, 30 W.L.R. 781 (C.A.), Irving J.A. (Macdonald C.J.A. concurring).

REPUGNANT. *adj.* Inconsistent with; contrary to.

REPUTATION. *n.* 1. "... [M]erely hearsay, simply what the public says about a person, ..." *R. v. Sands* (1915), 25 C.C.C. 120 at 123, 28 D.L.R. 375, 9 W.W.R. 496, 25 Man. R. 690 (C.A.), the court per Howell C.J.M. 2. Immediately before a defamatory publication, the long-range composite view which the general public had of the plaintiff's character, credit, honour or good name. R.E. Brown, *The Law of Defamation in Canada* (Toronto: Carswell, 1987) at 1030.

REQUEST. *v.* An active or positive proposal or solicitation.

REQUEST. *n.* See FOI ~; LETTERS OF ~.

REQUIRE. *v.* 1. To need. 2. To demand, as of right. 3. Mandate. 4. Compel.

REQUIREMENT. See BONA FIDE ~; OCCUPATIONAL ~; SECURITY ~.

REQUISITION. *n.* 1. A praecipe. 2. A written instruction which requires a court registrar to do something.

REQUISITION ON TITLE. A written inquiry to the solicitor for a vendor of real estate requesting that defects and clouds in the title be removed.

RES. *n.* [L.] Any physical thing in which someone may claim a right.

RESALE. *n.* 1. A right reserved by the vendor if the purchaser defaults in paying the purchase price. 2. A sale by a producer of a volume of natural gas after that volume has been acquired by the minister under section 2 and sold back to the producer under section 4(1). *Natural Gas Price Act*, R.S.B.C. 1996, c. 329, s. 1.

RESCIND. *v.* 1. With respect to a contract, for one or more parties to end it. 2. "... [D]ischarging [an order] or setting it aside... ." *Stewart v. Braun*, [1924] 3 D.L.R. 941 at 942, [1924] 2 W.W.R. 1103 (Man. K.B.), Mathers C.J.K.B.

RESCISSION. *n.* 1. "... [W]ill only occur where the changes go to the very root of the original agreement such that there is patent the intention to completely extinguish the first contract, nor merely to alter it, however extensively, in terms which leave the original subsisting ..." *Niagara Air Bus Inc. v. Camerman* (1989), 37 C.P.C. (2d) 267 at 285, 69 O.R. (2d) 717 (H.C.), Watt J. 2. Exercise of an option which ends the necessity to perform. B.J. Reiter, B.N. McLellan & P.M. Perell, *Real Estate Law*, 4th ed. (Toronto: Emond Montgomery, 1992) at 681.

RESCUE. *v.* To knowingly and forcibly free someone from an imprisonment or arrest.

RESCUER. *n.* A person who, having reasonable cause to believe another person to be in danger of his life or of bodily harm, benevolently comes to his assistance. *An act to promote good citizenship*, R.S.Q. c. C-20, s. 1.

RESEALING. *n.* Validation of a grant of representation originally issued by a court in a jurisdiction with similar laws and allegiance to the same sovereign, i.e. in the United Kingdom, any territory or province of Canada, the Commonwealth or any British possession. This has the same effect as if the validating court had made the original grant. J.G. McLeod, *The Conflict of Laws* (Calgary: Carswell, 1983) at 404 and 405.

RESERVATION. *n.* 1. A clause in a deed by which a donor, grantor or lessor claims or reserves something new out of whatever was granted by the same deed earlier. 2. Power of the Lieutenant-Governor with regard to a bill passed by the Legislature. It is subject "... to the restriction that the discretion of the Lieutenant-Governor shall be exercised subject to the Governor General's Instructions." *Reference re Power of Disallowance & Power of Reservation (Canada)*, [1938] S.C.R. 71 at 79, [1938] 2 D.L.R. 81, Duff C.J. (Davis J. concurring).

RESERVE. *v.* For the Governor General to withhold the royal assent from a bill which both Houses of Parliament passed "for the signification of the Queen's Pleasure" or, similarly, for a Lieutenant Governor to withhold assent from a provincial bill for the Governor General's pleasure.

RESERVE. *n.* 1. A tract of land, the legal title to which is vested in Her Majesty, that has been set apart by Her Majesty for the use and benefit of a band. *Indian Act*, R.S.C. 1985, c. I-5, s. 2, part. 2. A parcel of land reserved for use as a park, recreation area or a school site. 3. "... [S]omething set aside that can be

relied upon for future use; ..." *Crane Ltd. v. Minister of National Revenue*, [1960] C.T.C. 371 at 378, [1961] Ex. C.R. 147, 60 D.T.C. 1248, Kearney J. See INDIAN ~; NATURE ~; ~S; THREE CHAIN ~.

RESERVE FORCE. The component of the Canadian Forces that consists of officers and non-commissioned members who are enrolled for other than continuing, full-time military service when not on active service. The maximum numbers of officers and non-commissioned members in the reserve force is authorized by the Governor in Council, and the reserve force includes units and other elements. *National Defence Act*, R.S.C. 1985, c. N-5, s. 15.

RESERVE FUND. See CONTINGENCY ~.

RESERVE LANDS. Those lands set aside by the Federal government for the exclusive use of Indian people. These lands are regulated under the *Indian Act*, R.S.C. 1985, c. I-5.

RESERVES. *n.* In respect of a financial institution for a taxation year, means the amount at the end of the year of all of the institution's reserves, provisions and allowances (other than allowances in respect of depreciation or depletion) and, for greater certainty, includes any provision in respect of deferred taxes. *Taxation acts.* See RESERVE.

RES GESTAE. [L. things done] 1. "One of the earliest definitions of res gestae was given by Cockburn C.J. in his commentary on R. v. Bedingfield (1879), 14 Cox C.C. 341... . 'Whatever acts or series of acts constitute or in point of time immediately accompany and terminate in the principal act charged as an offence against the accused from its inception to its consummation or final completion, or its prevention or abandonment, whether on the part of the agent or wrongdoer in order to its performance, or on that of the patient or party wronged in order to its prevention, and whatever may be said by either of the parties during the continuance of the transaction with reference to it ... form part of the principal transaction, and may be given in evidence as part of the res gestae or particulars of it ..." *R. v. Klippenstein* (1981), 19 C.R. (3d) 56 at 63, [1981] 3 W.W.R. 111, 57 C.C.C. (2d) 393, 26 A.R. 568 (C.A.), the court per Laycraft J.A. 2. A phrase used in the law of evidence to explain the admissibility of words used by a person that shed light upon the quality of the act they accompany. The words are considered to be so interrelated to a fact in issue that they become a part of the fact itself. To qualify, the words must introduce the fact in issue, explain its nature, or form in connection with it one continuous transaction. *R. v. F. (J.E.)* (1993), 16 O.R. (3d) 1 (C.A.).

RESIDE. *v.* ["Resident" refers] to having one's home in a particular place "for a considerable length of time", and . . . "residential" [is defined as] "occupied mainly by private houses." No hard and fast line in terms only of length of stay can be drawn as a matter of law. A traveller or tourist may stay in a hotel for a few weeks without being said to "reside" there, just as a person may "reside" in his or her own house for a short period and then find it necessary for some reason to stay elsewhere for an extended period. . . . many factors, in addition to the length of stay, are involved in determining "residence"—whether one lives out of a suitcase or brings all one's possessions to the unit; whether one establishes roots and connections in the local community or remains only a sojourner; whether one is accompanied by family and is employed permanently or semi-permanently in the area; location of bank accounts and other records. *Kamloops (City) v. Northland Properties Ltd.*, 2000 CarswellBC 1172, 2000 BCCA 344, 76 B.C.L.R. (3d) 63, 11 M.P.L.R. (3d) 10, 139 B.C.A.C. 275, 227 W.A.C. 275.

RESIDENCE. *n.* 1. ".... [C]hiefly a matter of the degree to which a person in mind and fact settles into or maintains or centralizes his ordinary mode of living with its accessories in social relations, interests and conveniences at or in the place in question. It may be limited in time from the outset, or it may be indefinite, or so far as it is thought of, unlimited... ." *Thomson v. Minister of National Revenue*, [1946] S.C.R. 209 at 225, [1946] C.T.C. 51, [1946] 1 D.L.R. 689, Rand J. 2. The chief or habitual place of abode of a person. 3. "... [T]he head office or other place designated in the incorporating instrument as being the chief place of business of the corporation." *Canada Life Assurance Co. v. Canadian Imperial Bank of Commerce* (1979), 8 B.L.R. 55 at 63, 27 N.R. 227, [1979] 2 S.C.R. 669, 98 D.L.R. (3d) 670, the court per Estey J. 4. A dwelling-place, such as a den, nest or other similar area or place, that is occupied or habitually occupied by one or more individuals during all or part of their life cycles, including breeding, rearing, staging, wintering, feeding or hibernating. *Species at Risk Act*, S.C. 2002, c. 29, s. 2. See ABORIGINALITY-~; ACTUAL ~; HABITUAL ~; PRINCIPAL ~.

RESIDENT. *n.* 1. [For income tax purposes] a person is resident in the country where he or she, in the settled routine of life, regularly, normally or customarily lives, as opposed to the place where the person unusually, casually or intermittently stays. *Canada v. Laurin*, 2008 FCA 58. 2. ["Resident" refers] to having one's home in a particular place "for a considerable length of time", *Kamloops (City) v. Northland Properties Ltd.*, 2000 CarswellBC 1172, 2000 BCCA 344, 76 B.C.L.R. (3d) 63, 11 M.P.L.R. (3d) 10, 139 B.C.A.C. 275, 227 W.A.C. 275. See NON-~; PERMANENT ~; WTO MEMBER ~.

RESIDENT CANADIAN. A natural person who is (a) a Canadian citizen ordinarily resident in Canada, (b) a Canadian citizen not ordinarily resident in Canada who is a member of a prescribed class of persons, or (c) a permanent resident within the meaning of subsection 2(1) of the Immigration and Refugee Protection Act and ordinarily resident in Canada, except a permanent resident who has been ordinarily resident in Canada for more than one year after the time at which the individual first became eligible to apply for Canadian citizenship. Federal statutes.

RESIDENTIAL. *adj.* Connected with or related to a residence or residences.

RESIDENTIAL LEASEHOLD COMPLEX. A complex containing one or more buildings capable of being used, in whole or in part, for leasehold residential purposes, other than buildings comprised of strata lots, cooperative interests or shared interests in land. *Real Estate Development Marketing Act*, S.B.C. 2004, c. 41, s. 1.

RESIDENTIAL SCHOOLS. See INDIAN ~ TRUTH AND RECONCILIATION COMMISSION.

RESIDENTIAL UNIT. Any living accommodation used or intended for use as residential premises. *Residential Tenancies Act, 2006*, S.O. 2006, c. 17, s. 2, part..

RESIDING. *adj.* Staying for an extended time or permanently.

RESIDUAL LIBERTY. The liberty which remains to a prisoner, the liberty which is permitted to a prison population generally.

RESIDUAL OBLIGATION LEASE. A lease under which the lessor may require the lessee at the end of the lease term to pay the lessor an amount based in whole or in part on the difference, if any, between, (a) the estimated wholesale value of the leased goods at the end of the lease term, and (b) the realizable value of the leased goods at the end of the lease term. *Consumer Protection Act, 2002*, S.O. 2002, c. 30, Sched. A, s. 86.

RESIDUARY. *adj.* Relating to the part which remains.

RESIDUARY BEQUEST. A gift of any of the testator's personal property which the will does not otherwise give. T. Sheard, R. Hull & M.M.K. Fitzpatrick, *Canadian Forms of Wills*, 4th ed. (Toronto: Carswell, 1982) at 178.

RESIDUARY DEVISEE. The person designated in a will to take the real property which remains after the other devises.

RESIDUARY LEGATEE. The person to whom a testator leaves what remains of a personal estate after all debts and specific legacies are discharged.

RESIDUARY POWER. 1. With respect to the federal parliament, the power conferred by section 91 of the Constitution Act, 1867 to make laws for the "peace, order, and good government of Canada" which is residuary in relation to provincial governments because it is specifically limited to matters not assigned to the provincial legislatures. P.W. Hogg, *Constitutional Law of Canada*, 3d ed. (Toronto: Carswell, 1992) at 435-6. 2. With respect to a provincial parliament, the power conferred by section 92(16) over "all matters of a merely local or private nature in the province." P.W. Hogg, *Constitutional Law of Canada*, 3d ed. (Toronto: Carswell, 1992) at 540.

RESIDUE. *n.* 1. "[What remained of an estate] ... after payment of debts, funeral and testamentary expenses." *Prout, Re*, [1943] 2 D.L.R. 125 at 128, [1943] O.W.N. 156 (C.A.), Robertson C.J.O., Fisher and Kellock JJ.A. 2. "... [T]he testator meant by the word 'residue' ... that part of his estate which might remain after the death of his wife... . the run of this language shows that his mind was directed to what remained of his estate at the death of his wife, and not what remained at his own death." *Wilson v. Wilson*, [1944] 2 D.L.R. 729 at 732, [1944] 2 W.W.R. 412, 60 B.C.R. 287 (C.A.), Smith J.A. (O'Halloran and Roberson JJ.A. concurring).

RESIGNATION. *n.* Requires an employee's subjective intention to quit and some objective confirmation by conduct.

RESILE. *v.* To draw back, to return to prior position.

RES IPSA LOQUITUR. [L. the thing speaks for itself] 1. For res ipsa loquitur to arise, the circumstances of the occurrence must permit an inference of negligence attributable to the defendant. The strength or weakness of that inference will depend on the factual circumstances of the case. Whatever value res ipsa loquitur may have once provided is gone. Various attempts to apply the so-called doctrine have been more confusing than helpful. Its use has been restricted to cases where the facts permitted an inference of negligence and there was no other reasonable explanation for the accident. Given its limited use it is somewhat meaningless to refer to that use as a doctrine of law. It would appear that the law would be better served if the maxim was treated as expired and no longer used as a separate component in negligence actions. After all, it was nothing more than an attempt to deal with circumstantial evidence. That evidence is more sensibly dealt with by the trier of fact, who should weigh the circumstantial evidence with the direct evidence, if any, to determine whether the plaintiff has established on a balance of probabilities a prima facie case of negligence against the defendant. *Fontaine v. British Columbia (Official Administrator)*, [1998] 1 S.C.R. 424. 2. [In the context of a claim for negligence] "... [U]sed in connection with ... class of cases where, by force of a specific rule of law, if certain facts are established then the defendant is liable unless he proves that the occurrence out of which the damage has arisen falls within the category of inevitable accident." *Hutson v. United Motor Service Ltd.*, [1937] 1 D.L.R. 737 at 739, [1937] S.C.R. 294, 4 I.L.R. 91, Duff C.J.C. 3. "... [D]escribes the situation where the happening of the accident is sufficient in the absence of an explanation to justify the inference that most probably the defendant was negligent and that his negligence caused the injury even though the plaintiff may not be able to establish the precise cause of the accident... ." *Schanilec Estate v. Harris* (1987), (*sub nom. Rocha v. Harris*) 39 C.C.L.T. 279 at 291, 11 B.C.L.R. (2d) 233, 36 D.L.R. (4th) 410 (C.A.), the court per Craig J.A.

RES JUDICATA. [L.] 1. A final judicial decision. 2. A plea in defence to an action. 3. "Three requirements for a finding of res judicata are confirmed by the Manitoba Court of Appeal in Solomon v. Smith, [1988] 1 W.W.R. 410 ... They are: 1. That the same question has previously been decided. 2. That the judicial decision which is said to create the estoppel was final; and 3. It is necessary at this point to distinguish between issue estoppel and res judicata as the terms have been used more or less interchangeably in this appeal. Res judicata, the doctrine which holds that a matter can only be litigated once, includes cause of action estoppel and issue estoppel. Cause of action estoppel prevents the relitigation of the same cause of action between the same parties. Issue estoppel precludes the relitigation of the same issue between the same parties, even though the issue arises in the context of a different cause of action. *Erdos v. Canada (Minister of Citizenship & Immigration)*, 2005 FCA 419. 4. That the parties to the judicial decision or their privies were the same persons as the parties to the proceedings in which the estoppel is raised or their privies." *Newman v. Newman* (1990), 26 R.F.L. (3d) 313 at 318, 65 Man. R. (2d) 294 (Q.B.), Davidson J. See COLLATERAL ESTOPPEL; ESTOPPEL PER REM JUDICATAM; ISSUE ESTOPPEL.

RESOLUTION. *n.* 1. A solemn decision or judgment. 2. A meeting's expression of intention or opinion. 3. The revocation of a contract. 4. Declares the intention of a municipal council regarding a matter of a temporary nature without prescribing a permanent rule. See DISPUTE ~ PROCESS; EXCEPTIONAL ~; ORDINARY ~; SPECIAL ~.

RESOLVED. *v.* Indicates unanimity of sentiment or intention.

RESORT. *n.* A tourist establishment that operates through all or part of the year and that has facilities for serving meals and furnishes equipment, supplies or services to persons in connection with angling, hunting, camping or recreational purposes. See ALL SEASONS ~; LAST ~.

RESORT TO CLAUSE. In a wiretap authorization, permits authorities to intercept phone calls in places to which the subjects of the wiretap are believed to resort.

RESOURCE. See HUMAN ~S AND SKILLS DEVELOPMENT CANADA; WATER ~ MANAGEMENT.

RESPECT. *n.* Relation to.

RESPIRATORY THERAPY. The practice of respiratory therapy is the providing of oxygen therapy, cardio-respiratory equipment monitoring and the assessment and treatment of cardio-respiratory and associated disorders to maintain or restore ventilation. See PRACTICE OF ~.

RESPITE. *n.* An interruption, reprieve or suspension of sentence.

RESPONDEAT SUPERIOR. [L. let the principal answer] 1. Over the years courts have constricted the once accepted simple proposition captured under the maxim, respondeat superior, that an employer who has enabled an employee to cause a person to suffer a loss will be required to compensate the victim. Moreover, the test developed to set limits on an employer's liability for employee wrongdoing has become the test for establishing liability. *B. (P.A.) v. Curry* (1997), 30 B.C.L.R. (3d) 1 (C.A.). 2. In certain circumstances when a servant acted in the course of employment, the master is liable for the servant's wrongful acts. *Lavere v. Smith's Falls Public Hospital* (1915), 26 D.L.R. 346 at 363, 35 O.L.R. 98 (C.A.), Latchford J. See VICARIOUS LIABILITY.

RESPONDENT. *n.* 1. A person against whom one presents a petition, issues a summons or brings an appeal. 2. A person or a department in respect of whom or which or in respect of whose activities any report or information is sought or provided. *Statistics acts.* See CO-~; PETITION ~.

RESPONDENTIA. *n.* [L.] The hypothecation of the goods or cargo on a ship to secure repayment of a loan.

RESPONDING PARTY. A person against whom a motion is made.

RESPONDING PLEADING. A response to civil claim, a response to counterclaim, a response to third party notice, a reply or any other document filed in response to an originating pleading. *Court Rules Act,* R.S.B.C. 1996, c. 80, *Supreme Court Civil Rules,* B.C. Reg. 168/2009, Rule 1-1.

RESPONSE. *n.* Resulting action; reply.

RESPONSE TO CIVIL CLAIM. The initial document filed by the respondent to a civil claim. *Court Rules Act,* R.S.B.C. 1996, c. 80, *Supreme Court Civil Rules,* B.C. Reg. 168/2009.

RESPONSIBILITY. See ABSOLUTE ~; MINISTERIAL ~; VICARIOUS ~.

RESPONSIBLE. *adj.* Liable, accountable legally, answerable.

RESPONSIBLE COMMUNICATION ON MATTERS OF PUBLIC INTEREST. A new defence to defamation action. Distinct from qualified privilege. ... would formulate the test as follows. First, the publication must be on a matter of public interest. Second, the defendant must show that publication was responsible, in that he or she was diligent in trying to verify the allegation(s), having regard to all the relevant circumstances. *Grant v. Torstar Corp.,* 2009 SCC 61, McLachlin C.J. for the majority.

RESPONSIBLE GOVERNMENT. The formal head of state (monarch, Governor General or Lieutenant Governor) must always act under the direction of ministers who are members of the majority elected to the legislative branch. P.W. Hogg, *Constitutional Law of Canada,* 3d ed. (Toronto: Carswell, 1992) at 229.

RESTITUTIO IN INTEGRUM. [L.] 1. The fundamental principle is that the plaintiff in an action for negligence is entitled to a sum of damages which will return the plaintiff to the position the plaintiff would have been in had the accident not occurred, insofar as money is capable of doing this. This goal was expressed in the early cases by the maxim restitutio in integrum. *Cooper v. Miller,* [1994] 1 S.C.R. 359, McLachlin J. 2. In a case in which someone according to strict law lost a right and a court decision restores the original position on equitable principles. 3. Equitable relief given when a contract is rescinded because of fraud or in a similar case in which each party can be restored to its original position.

RESTITUTION. *n.* 1. "... [T]he function of the law of restitution 'is to ensure that where a plaintiff has been deprived of wealth that is either in his possession or would have accrued to his benefit, it is restored to him.' Restitution is a distinct body of law governed by its own developing system of rules. Breaches of

fiduciary duties and breaches of confidence are both wrongs for which restitutionary relief is often appropriate." *International Corona Resources Ltd. v. Lac Minerals Ltd.* (1989), 44 B.L.R. 1 at 45, [1989] 2 S.C.R. 574, 26 C.P.R. (3d) 97, 69 O.R. (2d) 287, 61 D.L.R. (4th) 14, 6 R.P.R. (2d) 1, 35 E.T.R. 1, 101 N.R. 239, 26 O.A.C. 57, La Forest J. (Wilson and Lamer JJ. concurring in part). 2. The law which relates to any claim, whether quasi-contractual in nature or not, which is based on unjust enrichment. 3. "An examination of the language of these sections [ss. 653 and 654 of the Criminal Code, R.S.C. 1970, c. C-34] indicates that Parliament viewed the term 'restitution' as dealing with the return of identical property obtained as a result of the commission of an offence to its owner, ... a restoration of property." *R. v. Groves* (1977), 39 C.R.N.S. 366 at 380, 17 O.R. (2d) 65, 37 C.C.C. (2d) 429, 79 D.L.R. (3d) 561 (H.C.), O'Driscoll J.

RESTITUTION ORDER. An order imposed as part of a sentence upon conviction for a criminal offence requiring the offender to restore property to its rightful owner.

RESTORATION. *n.* 1. The restoring of a deteriorated monument. *The Land Surveys Act,* S.S. 2000, c. L-4, s. 2. 2. The reinstatement of a corporation which has been dissolved or the reinstatement of registration of a foreign company in the province.

RESTORATIVE JUSTICE. The creation of a positive environment for change, healing and reconciliation for offenders, victims and communities. It is a condemnation of criminal actions rather than perpetrators and an integration of offenders into the community rather than a stigmatization or marginalization of them. *R. v. Laliberte,* 2000 SKCA 27, 31 C.R. (5th) 1, [2000] 4 W.W.R. 491, 143 C.C.C. (3d) 503, 189 Sask. R. 190.

RESTORE. *v.* 1. In insurance, to reinstate or replace buildings or chattels which have been damaged or destroyed. R. Colinvaux, *The Law of Insurance,* 5th ed. (London: Sweet & Maxwell, 1984) at 181. 2. To reinstate a corporation which was dissolved or to reinstate registration of a foreign company in the province.

RESTRAINING ORDER. 1. Refers to an order forbidding a person from being in the presence of another as a term of a recognizance or probation or otherwise. 2. In some provinces, the order of a court to prevent disposal or waste of family property. C.R.B. Dunlop, *Creditor-Debtor Law in Canada,* Second Cumulative Supplement (Toronto: Carswell, 1986) at 211. 3. "... [A] restrictive injunction ..." *Peterson v. MacPherson* (1991), 32 R.F.L. (3d) 333 at 338, [1991] N.W.T.R. 178 (S.C.), de Weerdt J.

RESTRAINT OF MARRIAGE. In general, any contract designed to prevent someone from marrying is void.

RESTRAINT OF TRADE. Refers to a contract otherwise freely entered into, that restricts a party's future use of skill, time and expertise. G.H.L. Fridman, *The Law of Contract in Canada,* 2d ed. (Toronto: Carswell, 1986) at 368. See CONTRACT IN ~.

RESTRAINT ON ALIENATION. A condition which restrains alienation of absolute interest in either real or personal property is generally considered void because it is repugnant.

RESTRAINT SYSTEM. A removable device designed to be installed in a vehicle for use in the restraint of an infant, a child or a mobility-impaired occupant but does not include booster cushions or vehicle seat belts. *Motor Vehicle Safety Act*, S.C. 1993, c. 16, *Motor Vehicle Restraint Systems and Booster Cushions Safety Regulations*, SOR/98-159, s. 1 [repealed].

RESTRICTED FIREARM. (a) A handgun that is not a prohibited firearm, (b) a firearm that (i) is not a prohibited firearm, (ii) has a barrel less than 470 mm in length, and (iii) is capable of discharging centre-fire ammunition in a semi-automatic manner, (c) a firearm that is designed or adapted to be fired when reduced to a length of less than 660 mm by folding, telescoping or otherwise, or (d) a firearm of any other kind that is prescribed to be a restricted firearm. *Criminal Code*, R.S.C. 1985, c. C-46, s. 84(1).

RESTRICTED IMMUNITY. Recognizes that when states enter into commercial or other private transactions with individuals, those individuals must be permitted to bring their disputes before the courts. *Athabasca Chipewyan First Nation v. Canada (Minister of Indian Affairs & Northern Development)*, 2001 ABCA 112, 281 A.R. 38.

RESTRICTED WEAPON. Any weapon, other than a firearm, that is prescribed to be a restricted weapon. *Criminal Code*, R.S.C. 1985, c. C-46, s. 84(1).

RESTRICTION. See WEIGHT ~.

RESTRICTION ENZYME. An enzyme capable of severing a long DNA molecule into shorter fragments. F.A. Jaffe, *A Guide to Pathological Evidence for Lawyers and Police Officers*, 4th ed. (Toronto: Carswell, 1999) at 236.

RESTRICTION FRAGMENT LENGTHS POLYMORPHISM. A method of DNA profiling. F.A. Jaffe, *A Guide to Pathological Evidence for Lawyers and Police Officers*, 4th ed. (Toronto: Carswell, 1999) at 208-209.

RESTRICTIVE COVENANT. 1. A restrictive covenant in a contract is what the common law refers to as a restraint of trade. Restrictive covenants are frequently found in agreements for the purchase and sale of a business and in employment contracts. A restrictive covenant precludes the vendor in the sale of a business from competing with the purchaser and, in an employment contract, the restrictive covenant precludes the employee, upon leaving employment, from competing with the former employer. [Although severance may be permitted in limited circumstances] the general rule must be that a restrictive covenant in an employment contract found to be ambiguous or unreasonable in its terms will be void and unenforceable. *Shafron v. KRG Insurance Brokers (Western) Inc.*, 2009 SCC 6, [2009] 1 S.C.R. 157. 2. "... [S]omething in the nature of a negative easement, requiring for its creation and continuance a dominant and a servient tenement ..." *Hunt v. Bell* (1915), 34

O.L.R. 256 at 262, 24 D.L.R. 590 (C.A.), Garrow J.A. (Meredith C.J.O., MacLaren and Magee JJ.A. concurring).

RESTRICTIVE ENDORSEMENT. A notation which prohibits any further negotiation of a promissory note or bill of exchange.

RESTRUCTURING. *n.* Includes the reorganization, refinancing, modernization, rationalization of an enterprise to improve its economic performance. Can include the injection of capital.

RESULT. See OFFICIAL ~.

RESULT CRIME. One the actus reus of which consists of conduct personal to the defendant, and the causation of substantive harm by this conduct. Penalizes the actual infliction of this harm, and in so doing deters its infliction. *R. v. Hinchey*, [1996] 3 S.C.R. 1128, L'Heureux-Dubé J.

RESULT IN. Leading to; refers to something which is reasonably forseeable; weaker than "to cause".

RESULTING. *adj.* Describes the return of property to the grantor or the remaining in him of property as a result of the implication of law or equity. R. Megarry & H.W.R. Wade, *The Law of Real Property*, 5th ed. (London: Stevens, 1984) at cxxvii.

RESULTING TRUST. 1. "... [W]ill be presumed in favour of a person who is proved to have paid the purchase-money for real property in the character of purchaser if the real property is conveyed to another." *Rathwell v. Rathwell* (1978), 1 R.F.L. (2d) 1 at 10, [1978] 2 S.C.R. 436, [1978] 2 W.W.R. 101, 19 N.R. 91, 1 E.T.R. 307, 83 D.L.R. (3d) 289, Dickson J. (Laskin C.J.C. and Spence J. concurring). 2. "... [A]rises when a court of equity presumes from the nature of the transaction, the relations of the parties and the requirement of good faith that a trust was intended." *Gerry v. Metz* (1979), 12 R.F.L. (2d) 346 at 351 (Sask. C.A.), the court per Hall J.A. See PRESUMPTION OF ~.

RESULTING USE. A use which is implied.

RETAIL DEPOSIT ACCOUNT. A personal deposit account that is opened with a deposit of less than $150,000 or any greater amount that may be prescribed. Federal statutes.

RETAIL SALES TAX. A general retail sales tax imposed under an Act of the legislature of a province at a percentage rate on all goods other than those specifically enumerated in that Act. *Excise Tax Act*, R.S.C. 1985, c. E-15, s. 348.

RETAIN. *v.* For a client to engage a solicitor or counsel to defend or take proceedings, to advise or act on one's behalf.

RETAINER. *n.* 1. A contract and the parties are bound by its terms. These may be expressly agreed, implied by law, or imposed by statute. In the case of a retainer to conduct an action, it is an implied term that the solicitor will take all steps necessary to bring the action to an end. In other words, such a retainer is an "entire contract." *Nathanson, Schachter & Thompson v. Inmet Mining Corp.*, 2009 BCCA 385, Newbury and Smith JJ.A. (Kirkpatrick J.A. concurring). 2. "... [T]he act of employing a solicitor or counsel, or ... the document by which such employment is evidenced [or] ... a preliminary fee given to secure the services of the solicitor and induce him to act for the client... ." *Solicitor, Re* (1910), 22 O.L.R. 30 at 31 (C.A.), the court per Riddell J.A. See RELATED ~.

RETAINING LIEN. A solicitor's right to retain property already in his or her possession until payment of fees due to the solicitor in his or her professional capacity are paid.

RETIRE. *v.* 1. To withdraw to consider a decision or verdict. 2. To cease employment.

RETIREMENT. *n.* "... [A] cessation of or withdrawal from work because of an age stipulation or because of some other condition agreed between employer and employee." *Specht v. R.*, [1975] C.T.C. 126 at 133, [1975] F.C. 150, 75 D.T.C. 5069 (T.D.), Collier J.

RETIREMENT INCOME FUND. An arrangement between a carrier and an annuitant under which, in consideration for the transfer to the carrier of property, the carrier undertakes to pay to the annuitant and, where the annuitant so elects, to the annuitant's spouse or common-law partner after the annuitant's death, in each year that begins not later than the first calendar year after the year in which the arrangement was entered into one or more amounts the total of which is not less than the minimum amount under the arrangement for the year, but the amount of any such payment shall not exceed the value of the property held in connection with the arrangement immediately before the time of the payment. *Income Tax Act*, R.S.C. 1985, c. 1 (5th Supp.), s. 146.3(1).

RETIREMENT METHOD. A method of determining the value of a person's interest in a group pension for the purposes of dividing property in a marriage breakdown. The value of the future income stream is calculated assuming the member will continue to be employed until retirement. Likely future earnings are assumed. See SPECULATIVE ~.

RETIREMENT PENSION. Periodic payments for life intended to replace wages or salary. Intended to guarantee a level of income to a person no longer employed.

RETIRING ALLOWANCE. An amount (other than a superannuation or pension benefit, an amount received as a consequence of the death of an employee or a benefit described in subparagraph 6(1)(a)(iv)) received (a) on or after retirement of a taxpayer from an office or employment in recognition of the taxpayer's long service, or (b) in respect of a loss of an office or employment of a taxpayer, whether or not received as, on account or in lieu of payment of, damages or pursuant to an order or judgment of a competent tribunal, by the taxpayer or, after the taxpayer's death, by a dependant or a relation of the taxpayer or by the legal representative of the taxpayer. *Income Tax Act*, R.S.C. 1985, c. 1 (5th Supp.), s. 248.

RETRACTATION. *n.* In probate practice, withdrawal of renunciation.

RETRIAL. *n.* A rehearing of a matter.

RETRIBUTION. *n.* 1. Something given or demanded in payment; punishment based on the notion that every crime demands payment in the form of punishment. 2. Retribution, as an objective of sentencing, represents nothing less than the hallowed principle that criminal punishment, in addition to advancing utilitarian considerations related to deterrence and rehabilitation, should also be imposed to sanction the moral culpability of the offender. Retribution is integrally woven into the existing principles of sentencing in Canadian law through the fundamental requirement that a sentence imposed be "just and appropriate" under the circumstances. Indeed, retribution represents an important unifying principle of our penal law by offering an essential conceptual link between the attribution of criminal liability and the imposition of criminal sanctions. The legitimacy of retribution as a principle of sentencing has often been questioned as a result of its unfortunate association with "vengeance" in common parlance. But it should be clear from my foregoing discussion that retribution bears little relation to vengeance, and I attribute much of the criticism of retribution as a principle to this confusion. As both academic and judicial commentators have noted, vengeance has no role to play in a civilized system of sentencing. *R. v. M. (C.A.)*, 1996 CarswellBC 1000, 46 C.R. (4th) 269, 194 N.R. 321, 105 C.C.C. (3d) 327, 73 B.C.A.C. 81, 120 W.A.C. 81, [1996] 1 S.C.R. 500, Lamer C.J.C.

RETROACTIVE STATUTE. 1. "... [O]ne that operates backwards, i.e., that is operative as of a time prior to its enactment, either by being deemed to have come into force at a time prior to its enactment (e.g., budgetary measures) or by being expressed to be operative with respect to past transactions as of a past time (e.g., acts of indemnity)... ." *Royal Canadian Mounted Police Act (Canada), Re*, [1991] 1 F.C. 529 at 548 (C.A.), MacGuigan J.A. 2. "... [O]perates forward in time, starting from a point further back in time than the date of its enactment; so it changes the legal consequences of past events as if the law had been different than it really was at the time those events occurred." *Hornby Island Trust Commmittee v. Stormwell* (1988), 53 D.L.R. (4th) 435 at 441, 39 M.P.L.R. 300, 30 B.C.L.R. (2d) 383 (C.A.), Lambert J.A. (Hutcheon J.A. concurring).

RETROFIT. *n.* A renovation of the common areas of a building generally undertaken by the landlord. *Martel Building Ltd. v. R.*, 2000 CarswellNat 2678, 2000 SCC 60, 36 R.P.R. (3d) 175, 193 D.L.R. (4th) 1, 262 N.R. 285, 3 C.C.L.T. (3d) 1, 5 C.L.R. (3d) 161, 186 F.T.R. 231(note), [2000] 2 S.C.R. 860, the court per Iacobucci and Major JJ.

RETROSPECTIVE STATUTE. 1. "... [C]hanges the law only for the future but looks backward by attaching new consequences to completed transactions. It thus opens up closed transactions ..." *Royal Canadian Mounted Police Act (Canada), Re*, [1991] 1 F.C. 529 at 548 (C.A.), MacGuigan J.A. 2. "... [O]perates forward in time, starting only from the date of its enactment, but from that time forward it changes the legal consequences of past events." *Hornby Island Trust Commmittee v. Stormwell*

(1988), 39 M.P.L.R. 300 at 307-8, 53 D.L.R. (4th) 435, 30 B.C.L.R. (2d) 383 (C.A.), Lambert J.A. (Hutcheon J.A. concurring).

RETURN. *n.* 1. The report of an officer of a court, e.g. a sheriff, which shows how a duty imposed on that officer was performed. 2. The record of any report or information provided by a respondent. *Statistics acts.* 3. A return prescribed pursuant to any revenue act. 4. The returning officer shall declare elected the candidate who obtained the largest number of votes by completing the return of the writ in the prescribed form on the back of the writ. *Canada Elections Act,* S.C. 2000, c. 9, s. 313(1), part. See PATRONAGE ~.

RETURNING OFFICER. 1. A person responsible for conducting a municipal or parliamentary election. 2. Appointed for each electoral district and is responsible, under the general direction of the Chief Electoral Officer, for the preparation for and conduct of an election in his or her electoral district. After the issue of the writ, a returning officer appoints the other election officers. *Canada Elections Act,* S.C. 2000, c. 9.

REV. CAN. CRIM. *abbr.* Revue canadienne de criminologie (Canadian Journal of Criminology).

REV. CAN. D.A. *abbr.* Revue canadienne du droit d'auteur.

REV. CAN. D. COMM. *abbr.* Revue canadienne du droit de commerce (Canadian Business Law Journal).

REV. CAN. D. COMMUNAUTAIRE. *abbr.* Revue canadienne du droit communautaire (Canadian Community Law Journal).

REV. CAN. D. & SOCIÉTÉ. *abbr.* Revue canadienne de droit et société (Canadian Journal of Law and Society).

REV. CAN. D. FAM. *abbr.* Revue canadienne de droit familial (Canadian Journal of Family Law).

REV. CRIT. *abbr.* Revue critique, 1870-1875.

REV. D. OTTAWA. Revue de droit d'Ottawa (Ottawa Law Review).

REVENUE. *n.* 1. Annual profit; income. 2. All public money collected or due. See CANADA ~ AGENCY; CONSOLIDATED ~ FUND; ~S.

REVENUE ACT. A statute imposing a tax or fee.

REVENUE INSURANCE PROGRAM. A program that is designed to insure a portion of the value of an eligible agricultural product produced or marketed by a producer participating in the program. *Farm Income Protection Act,* S.C. 1991, c. 22, s. 2. See GROSS ~.

REVENUE PAPER. Paper that is used to make stamps, licences or permits or for any purpose connected with the public revenue. *Criminal Code,* R.S.C. 1985, c. C-46, s. 321.

REVENUES. *n.* Sums of money yielded by property, such as rents, interest and dividends, except those representing the distribution of capital of a legal person; they also comprise sums received by reason of the resiliation or renewal of a lease or of prepayment, or sums allotted or collected in similar circumstances. *Civil Code,* S.Q. 1991, c. 64, a. 910. See FRUITS AND ~; REVENUE.

REVERSAL. *n.* Making a judgment void because of error.

REVERSE. *v.* To make void, repeal or undo. A judgment is reversed when a court of appeal sets it aside.

REVERSE CLEARING. A mechanism established by member banks of the Canadian Payment Association. Cheques must be "forged" or "unauthorized" as a pre-condition to reverse clearing. Section 49(1) Bills of Exchange Act gives a person on whose behalf a bill is paid containing "a forged or an unauthorized endorsement" the "right to recover" the amount paid from the person to whom it was paid, in this case the Kovals or BACC, or from any endorser who has endorsed the bill subsequent to the forged or unauthorized endorsement, in this case, RBC. Thus, an endorsement must be "forged" or "unauthorized" as a necessary precondition to a drawer ("the person ... on whose behalf the payment is made") having a right to recover the amount of the bill from a collecting bank ("any endorser who has endorsed the bill subsequent to the forged or unauthorized endorsement"). *Aronowicz v. EMTWO Properties Inc.,* 2010 CarswellOnt 598, 2010 ONCA 96 and *Royal Bank v. Société Générale (Canada),* (2006), 31 B.L.R. (4th) 63 (Ont. C.A.).

REVERSE DISCRIMINATION. 1. When an "affirmative action" program is in place a member of the general population may argue that she is subject to reverse discrimination. Subsection 15(1) of the Charter prohibits discrimination on enumerated and analogous grounds, while s. 15(2) permits the adoption of affirmative action programs to ameliorate past discrimination thereby foreclosing the argument of reverse discrimination. 2. "... [D]iscriminates against [persons not belonging to one race, for example] because whenever there is a finite number of persons seeking some advantage (in this case employment), to prefer one because of his race is to the disadvantage of another because of the race of the first person." *Athabasca Tribal Council v. Amoco Canada Petroleum Co.,* [1981] 1 C.N.L.R. 35 at 48, [1980] 5 W.W.R. 165, 22 A.R. 541, 112 D.L.R. (3d) 200, 1 C.H.R.R. D/174 (C.A.), Laycraft J.A. (McGillivray C.J.A. concurring).

REVERSE STING. In sting operations, undercover police officers pose as purchasers of narcotics. . . . In a reverse sting, police undercover officers offer to sell large quantities of drugs to the target. If the negotiations are successful, the police operatives produce the drugs, give them to the target upon receiving payment and the target is arrested shortly afterwards. *R. v. Jageshur,* (2002), 165 O.A.C. 230.

REVERSION. *n.* "... [A]n undisposed of estate in property, left in a grantor after he has parted with some particular interest less than the fee simple therein. In the second place, it is an estate which returns to the grantor after the determination of such particular estate ..." *Ferguson v. MacLean,* [1931] 1

R

D.L.R. 61 at 67, [1930] S.C.R. 630, Anglin C.J.C. (Rinfret J. concurring). See RUN WITH THE ~.

REVERSIONARY INTEREST. "... [F]uture interests in real as well as personal property which are not by operation of law or otherwise interests reserved to the grantor or donor; but are merely interests which take effect at the expiration of a preceding estate or interest, or ... interests which simply take effect in the future... ." *Ferguson v. MacLean*, [1931] 1 D.L.R. 61 at 79, [1930] S.C.R. 630, Duff J.

REVERSIONARY LEASE. A lease which takes effect in the future; a second lease which becomes effective after the first lease expires.

REVERSIONARY VALUE. "... [S]ome value to the landowner which will accrue to him once the 'taking' has served its use." *Dome Petroleum Ltd. v. Grekul* (1983), 28 Alta. L.R. (2d) 260 at 268, [1988] 1 W.W.R. 447, 29 C.L.R. 111, 5 Admin. L.R. 252, 49 A.R. 256 (Q.B.), Miller J.

REVERT. *v.* 1. To return; e.g., when the owner of land grants a small estate to another person and when that estate terminates, the land reverts to the grantor. 2. "[T]o ... 'fall back into' his estate." *Carter v. Goldstein* (1921), 66 D.L.R. 34 at 35, 63 S.C.R. 207, Davies C.J.

REVERTER. *n.* Reversion. See POSSIBILITY OF ~.

REV. ÉTUDES CAN. *abbr.* Revue d'études canadiennes (Journal of Canadian Studies).

REV. FISCALE CAN. *abbr.* Revue fiscale canadienne (Canadian Tax Journal).

REVIEW. *n.* "... [I]s occasionally taken in popular use as meaning more than a first instance 'looking over' or 'examination'. In its legal sense ... it usually means more than that, as implying a formal, second instance 're-examination' or 'reconsideration' with a view to revision or re-determination if something be found wrong or lacking." *Saskatoon (City) v. Plaxton* (1989), 33 C.P.C. (2d) 238 at 250, [1989] 2 W.W.R. 577, 78 Sask. R. 215 (C.A.), Cameron J.A. (Gerwing J.A. concurring). See DE NOVO ~; JUDICIAL ~; PEER ~; STANDARD OF ~; SYSTEMATIC ~.

REVIEWABLE ERROR. "... [A]n arbitrator in construing a statutory provision in the course of an arbitration proceeding commits reviewable error if his or her construction is wrong... ." *Cape Breton Development Corp. v. U.M.W., District No. 26, Local 4522* (1985), 85 C.L.L.C. 14,041 at 12,222, 68 N.S.R. (2d) 181, 159 A.P.R. 181 (T.D.), MacIntosh J.

REVIEWABLE TRANSACTION. In bankruptcy matters, a transaction which was not at arm's length or was made by people who are "related."

REVIEW BOARD. 1. The Review Board established or designated for a province under subsection 672.38(1). *Criminal Code*, R.S.C. 1985, c. C-46. 2. A board established to review certain orders. *Youth Criminal Justice Act*, S.C. 2002, c. 1, s. 2. See CANADIAN CULTURAL PROPERTY EXPORT ~; VETERANS REVIEW AND APPEAL BOARD.

REVIEW COMMITTEE. See ROYAL CANADIAN MOUNTED POLICE EXTERNAL ~; SECURITY INTELLIGENCE ~.

REVISED STATUTES. 1. A consolidation and declaration of the law as contained in the acts which they replace; they do not come into force as new or independent statutes. 2. The latest revised and consolidated statutes of a province or the federal government.

REVISING AGENT. A returning officer shall appoint revising agents to work in pairs and each pair shall consist, as far as possible, of persons recommended by different registered parties. *Canada Elections Act*, S.C. 2000, c. 9, s. 33(3).

REVISION. *n.* The arrangement, revision and consolidation of the public general statutes of Canada and the regulations authorized under the *Legislation Revision and Consolidation Act*, R.S.C. 1985, c. S-20. See STATUTE ~.

REVISION COMMITTEE. Revision committee established consists of officials of government who prepare a revision of all or any public enactments. In preparing a revision, the revisionc ommittee may do all or any of the following: (a) consolidate in the revision all amendments made to a public enactment since the date of its enactment or last revision, as the case may be; (b) combine or divide public enactments and, if a public enactment is divided, incorporate common provisions necessary to the resulting revised public enactments; (c) change the numbering and the arrangement of public enactments; (d) add, change or omit any title of or heading within a public enactment; (e) revise and alter language to achieve a gender-neutral style; (f) revise and alter language: (i) to give a better expression to the meaning of the law; or (ii) in the case of a public enactment that has been enacted in English and French, to make the form of expression in one of the languages more compatible with the expression in the other language; (g) make any alterations in language, spelling and punctuation that are desirable to obtain a uniform mode of expression; (h) change any outdated reference to an organization, person or other entity or to a statute, regulation or other document to make the reference current and accurate; (i) make minor amendments: (i) to clarify the intent of the Legislature; (ii) to reconcile inconsistent provisions; or (iii) to correct clerical, grammatical or typographical errors; (j) omit public enactments that are obsolete, are spent or have no legal effect; (k) omit any public enactments that do not apply throughout Saskatchewan; (l) omit, without repealing, any portion of a public enactment that: (i) provides for the retroactive effect of that public enactment; or (ii) is of a limited duration or transitional in nature; (m) include in the revision as a supplement those public enactments that, although enacted, have not yet come into force and indicate how they are to come into force; (n) make minor consequential changes to other public enactments not being revised that are required to reconcile them with a revised public enactment; (o) identify in schedules to the revision those public enactments that have beena dded, omitted, moved or combined by the revision; (p) with respect to the public enactments being replaced by revised public enactments, identify in a schedule to the revision the public enactments to be repealed. (2) No change may be made pursuant to subsection (1) that has the effect of changing the intent of any public enactment. *The Statutes and Regulations Revision Act*, S.S. 2008, c. S-59.01, s. 2 to 5.

REVIVAL. *n.* 1. Re-execution of a will by a testator after it was revoked; execution of a will or codicil which shows the intention to revive it. 2. The reinstatement and recreation of a corporation which has been dissolved for failure to file returns or for some other act. 3. "[A corporation through] revival ... acquires all the rights and privileges and is liable for all the obligations that it would have had if it had not been dissolved ..." *Computerized Meetings & Hotel Systems Ltd. v. Moore* (1982), 20 B.L.R. 97 at 106, 40 O.R. (2d) 88, 141 D.L.R. (3d) 306 (Div. Ct.), Callaghan J.

REVIVOR. *n.* A motion needed to continue proceedings when the suit abated before final consummation because of death or some other reason.

REV. JUR. FEMME & D. *abbr.* Revue juridique "La Femme et le droit" (Canadian Journal of Women and the Law).

REV. LOIS & POL. SOCIALES. *abbr.* Revue des lois et des politiques sociales (Journal of Law and Social Policy).

REVOCATION. *n.* 1. Undoing something granted; destroying or voiding a deed which existed until revocation made it void; revoking. 2. Cancellation. *Motor Vehicle Act*, R.S.N.B. 1973, c. M-17, s. 2. 3. "... [C]ancellation ..." *R. v. Whynacht*, [1942] 1 D.L.R. 238 at 240, 16 M.P.R. 267, 77 C.C.C. 1 (N.S. C.A.), Chisholm C.J. 4. With respect to a will, for a testator to render it inoperative or annul it by a later act. 5. The setting aside of a judgment of conviction given in default. See DEPENDENT RELATIVE ~.

REVOKE. *v.* To annul, cancel, repeal, rescind.

REVOLVER. *n.* A rifled handgun in which a cylinder revolves, removing fired rounds and placing new rounds into position in a firing chamber. F.A. Jaffe, *A Guide to Pathological Evidence for Lawyers and Police Officers*, 4th ed. (Toronto: Carswell, 1999) at 242.

REV. SERV. ARB. *abbr.* Revue des services d'arbitrage, 1977-.

REWARD. *n.* 1. Something tangible and pecuniary, that is payment or profit. 2. Payment of financial consideration to a person who helped apprehend another charged with an offence.

REX. *n.* [L. king] Monarch.

R.F.L. *abbr.* Reports of Family Law, 1971-1978.

RFLP. *abbr.* Restriction Fragment Lengths Polymorphism.

R.F.L. (5TH). *abbr.* Reports of Family Law (Fifth Series), 2000-.

R.F.L. (4TH). *abbr.* Reports of Family Law (Fourth Series), 1994-2000.

R.F.L. REP. *abbr.* Reports of Family Law, Reprint Series.

R.F.L. (2D). *abbr.* Reports of Family Law (Second Series), 1978-1986.

R.F.L. (3D). *abbr.* Reports of Family Law (Third Series), 1986-1994.

RFP. *abbr.* Request for proposals.

R.G.D. *abbr.* Revue générale de droit (Section de droit civil, Faculté de droit, Université d'Ottawa).

RIBIC FACTORS. The majority of the IAD [Immigration Appeal Division] recognized (at para. 12) that its discretionary jurisdiction to grant "special relief" on humanitarian and compassionate grounds under s. 67(1)(c) of the IRPA [Immigration and Refugee Protection Act] should be exercised in light of the following factors: (1) the seriousness of the offence leading to the removal order; (2) the possibility of rehabilitation; (3) the length of time spent, and the degree to which the individual facing removal is established, in Canada; (4) the family and community support available to the individual facing removal; (5) the family in Canada and the dislocation to the family that removal would cause; and (6) the degree of hardship that would be caused to the individual facing removal to his country of nationality. *Ribic v. Canada (Minister of Employment and Immigration)*, [1985] I.A.B.D. No. 4 (QL). These were endorsed by *Chieu v. Canada (Minister of Citizenship and Immigration)*, 2002 SCC 3, [2002] 1 S.C.R. 84, at paras. 40, 41 and 90.

R.I.B.L. *abbr.* Review of International Business Law.

RIDE. See JOY~; OVER~.

RIDER. *n.* A clause inserted later.

RIDICULE. *v.* To make fun of someone or something. Making someone or something the object of contemptuous amusement.

RIF. *abbr.* Retirement Income Fund.

RIG. *v.* To manipulate a bid in an underhanded or fraudulent way.

RIGHT. *n.* 1. " ... [I]s defined positively as what one can do." *R. v. Zundel* (1987), 29 C.R.R. 349 at 365, 18 O.A.C. 161, 58 O.R. (2d) 129, 31 C.C.C. (3d) 97, 56 C.R. (3d) 1, 35 D.L.R. (4th) 338, Howland C.J.O., Brooke, Martin, Lacourcière and Houlden JJ.A. 2. " ... [S]pecific, detailed and imposes a duty; ..." *R.W.D.S.U., Locals 496, 544, 635, 955 v. Saskatchewan* (1985), 85 C.L.L.C. 14,054 at 12,277, [1985] 5 W.W.R. 97, 39 Sask. R. 193, 21 C.R.R. 286 (C.A.), Bayda C.J.S. 3. Includes power, authority, privilege and licence. *Interpretation Act*, R.S.B.C. 1996, c. 238, s. 29. 4. Includes power, authority, benefit, privilege and remedy. *Water Act*, R.S.B.C. 1996, c. 483, s. 1. See ABORIGINAL ~ LANDS; ACCESS ~; ACCRUED ~; ACCRUING ~; BARGAINING ~; COLOUR OF ~; CONTINGENT ~; DEFENCE WITH CLAIM OF ~; DEFENCE WITHOUT CLAIM OF ~; FREEDOM; FUTURE ~; INTERMENT ~ CONTRACT; LAWFUL ~; LEGAL ~; LIBERTY; MINERAL ~; MINING ~; PETITION

R

OF ~; PREEMPTIVE ~; PRIVATE ~; ~S; SUB-STANTIVE ~; USER AS OF ~; VESTED ~.

RIGHT OF ACTION. 1. "... [T]he right to institute civil proceedings in court for the determination of a right or claim." *Reference re Sections 32 & 34 of the Workers' Compensation Act, 1983 (Newfoundland)* (1987), 36 C.R.R. 112 at 145, 67 Nfld. & P.E.I.R. 16, 206 A.P.R. 16, 44 D.L.R. (4th) 501 (Nfld. C.A.), Morgan J.A. 2. "... A bare 'right of action' is not a right in the ordinary use of the term. It is rather a mere claim to a right, and it only becomes an actual right when it has ripened into a judgment." *McGregor v. Campbell* (1909), 11 W.L.R. 153 at 161, 19 Man. R. 38 (C.A.), Richards J.A.

RIGHT OF APPEAL. "... [T]he right of appeal is a statutory right, and there is no such right unless it is expressly given." *Dale v. Commercial Union Assurance Co. of Canada* (1981), 22 C.P.C. 29 at 31, 32 O.R. (2d) 238, [1981] I.L.R. 1-1342, 121 D.L.R. (3d) 503 (C.A.), the court per Brooke J.A.

RIGHT OF ASSOCIATION. The right of workers to form unions or other trade associations.

RIGHT OF AUDIENCE. A superior court's inherent right to permit a non-lawyer to appear before it as a representative or advocate for another person.

RIGHT OF ENTRY. The right to take or resume possession of land by entering it peacefully.

RIGHT OF SURVIVORSHIP. The right of a surviving joint tenant to take the property of the other, deceased joint tenant.

RIGHT OF WAY. *var.* **RIGHT-OF-WAY.** 1. In its traditional sense, a "right of way" is a type of easement, and at common law the acquisition of a right of way does not give the holder a fee simple interest or the right to exclusive possession: E. C. E. Todd, The Law of Expropriation and Compensation in Canada (2nd ed. 1992). However . . . in modern usage the term right of way does not always correspond to the common law concept and in some circumstances may refer to a right to the exclusive use and occupation of a corridor of land. *Osoyoos Indian Band v. Oliver (Town)*, [2001] 3 S.C.R. 746, Iacobucci J. (McLachlin C.J.C., Binnie, Arbour and LeBel JJ. concurring). 2. "... [A] generally understood meaning as the land reserved for placement of a physical improvement such as a railway, transmission line or pipeline... ." *British Columbia Assessment Commissioner v. Canadian National Railway Co.* (1989), 42 M.P.L.R. 71 at 79 (B.C. S.C.), McLachlin C.J.S.C. 3. The privilege of the immediate use of the highway. *Motor Vehicle Act*, R.S.N.S. 1989, c. 293, s. 2. 4. The right of an expropriating authority to carry its pipes, wires, conductors or transmission lines on, over or under land and that is registrable under the Land Titles Act. *Expropriation Act*, R.S.A. 2000, c. E-13, s. 1.

RIGHTS. *n.* Are general and universal and represent the means by which the inherent dignity of each individual in society is respected. See ABORIGINAL ~; BILL OF ~; CANADIAN CHARTER OF ~ AND FREEDOMS; CIVIL ~; CONJUGAL ~; CUM ~; DENSITY ~; EMPLOYER ~; EQUAL-ITY ~; HUMAN ~; INTERMENT ~ HOLDER; LEGAL ~; MANAGEMENT ~; MINERAL ~; MINING ~; MINORITY LANGUAGE EDUCATION ~; MOBILITY ~; MORAL ~; NEIGHBOURING ~; OIL AND GAS ~; OTHER ~ AND FREEDOMS; PREROGATIVE ~ OF THE CROWN; PROPERTY AND CIVIL ~; PUBLICATION OF ~; REPRODUCTION ~; RIGHT; RIPARIAN ~; SCATTERING ~; SOLE ~; SURFACE ~ CONTRACT; UNION ~.

RIGHT TO BEGIN. The right to be first to address a court or jury.

RIGHT TO BE PRESUMED INNOCENT. "... [I]s, in popular terms, a way of expressing the fact that the Crown has the ultimate burden of establishing guilt; if there is any reasonable doubt at the conclusion of the case on any element of the offence charged, an accused person must be acquitted. In a more refined sense, the presumption of innocence gives an accused the initial benefit of a right of silence and the ultimate benefit (after the Crown's evidence is in and as well as any evidence tendered on behalf of the accused) of any reasonable doubt: ..." *R. v. Appleby*, [1972] S.C.R. 303 at 317, 16 C.R.N.S. 35, [1971] 4 W.W.R. 601, 3 C.C.C. (2d) 354, 21 D.L.R. (3d) 325, Laskin J. See PRESUMPTION OF INNOCENCE.

RIGHT TO COUNSEL. 1. Everyone has the right on arrest or detention to retain and instruct counsel without delay and to be informed of that right. *Canadian Charter of Rights and Freedoms*, Part I of the *Constitution Act, 1982*, being Schedule B of the *Canada Act, 1982* (U.K.), 1982, c. 11, s. 10(b). 2. "... [T]he right to retain and instruct counsel [in s. 10(b) of the Charter], in modern Canadian society, has come to mean more than the right to retain a lawyer privately. It now also means the right to have access to counsel free of charge where the accused meets certain financial criteria set up by the provincial legal aid plan, and the right to have access to immediate, although temporary, advice from duty counsel irrespective of financial status... ." *R. v. Brydges* (1990), 46 C.R.R. 236 at 256, [1990] 2 W.W.R. 220, [1990] 1 S.C.R. 190, 71 Alta. L.R. (2d) 145, 103 N.R. 282, 74 C.R. (3d) 129, 53 C.C.C. (3d) 330, 104 A.R. 124, Lamer J. (Wilson, Gonthier and Cory JJ. concurring). 3. The purpose of the right to counsel guaranteed by s. 10(b) of the Charter is to provide detainees with an opportunity to be informed of their rights and obligations under the law and, most importantly, to obtain advice on how to exercise those rights and fulfil those obligations. This opportunity is made available because, when an individual is detained by state authorities, he or she is put in a position of disadvantage relative to the state. Not only has this person suffered a deprivation of liberty, but also this person may be at risk of incriminating him- or herself. Accordingly, a person who is "detained" within the meaning of s. 10 of the Charter is in immediate need of legal advice in order to protect his or her right against self-incrimination and to assist him or her in regaining his or her liberty. Under s. 10(b), a detainee is entitled as of right to seek such legal advice "without delay" and upon request. The right to counsel protected by s.

10(b) is designed to ensure that persons who are arrested or detained are treated fairly in the criminal process. This court has said on numerous previous occasions that s. 10(b) of the Charter imposes the following duties on state authorities who arrest or detain a person: (1) to inform the detainee of his or her right to retain and instruct counsel without delay and of the existence and availability of legal aid and duty counsel; (2) if a detainee has indicated a desire to exercise this right, to provide the detainee with a reasonable opportunity to exercise the right (except in urgent and dangerous circumstances); and (3) to refrain from eliciting evidence from the detainee until he or she has had that reasonable opportunity (again, except in cases of urgency or danger). *R. v. Bartle*, 1994 CarswellOnt 100, 33 C.R. (4th) 1, 6 M.V.R. (3d) 1, 19 O.R. (3d) 802 (note), 172 N.R. 1, 92 C.C.C. (3d) 289, 74 O.A.C. 161, 118 D.L.R. (4th) 83, [1994] 3 S.C.R. 173, 23 C.R.R. (2d) 193, Lamer C.J.C.

RIGHT TO EQUALITY. The right to equality is not a right to be treated as well as one particular comparator group. Rather, it is, prima facie, a right to be treated as well as the members of all appropriate comparator groups. *McIvor v. Canada (Registrar of Indian & Northern Affairs)*, 2009 BCCA 153, Groberman J.A. (Newbury and Tysoe JJ.A. concurring.)

RIGHT TO KNOW. See PUBLIC'S ~.

RIGHT TO MAKE A FULL ANSWER AND DEFENCE. The right of an accused to cross-examine prosecution witnesses without significant and unwarranted constraint is an essential component of the right to make a full answer and defence. The right of the innocent not to be convicted is dependent on the right to present full answer and defence. This, in turn, depends on being able to call the evidence necessary to establish a defence and to challenge the evidence called by the prosecution. In short, the denial of the right to call and challenge evidence is tantamount to the denial of the right to rely on a defence to which the law says one is entitled. *R. v. Lyttle*, 2004 SCC 5. See FULL ANSWER AND DEFENCE.

RIGHT TO REMAIN SILENT. "... [T]he basis for the non-compellability of the accused as a witness at trial but it extends beyond the witness box. In R. v. Esposito (1985), 20 C.R.R. 102, at p. 108, Martin J.A. outlined its scope: 'The right of a suspect or an accused to remain silent ... operates both at the investigative stage of the criminal process and at the trial stage." ... it is a right not to be compelled to answer questions or otherwise communicate with police officers or others whose function it is to investigate the commission of criminal offences. As with the privilege against self-incrimination, the right to remain silent protects the individual against the affront to dignity and privacy which results if crime enforcement agencies are allowed to conscript the suspect against himself or herself... ." *Thomson Newspapers Ltd. v. Canada (Director of Investigation & Research)* (1990), 47 C.R.R. 1 at 94, 97, 76 C.R. (3d) 129, 72 O.R. (2d) 415n, 54 C.C.C. (3d) 417, 67 D.L.R. (4th) 161, 29 C.P.R. (3d) 98, [1990] 1 S.C.R. 425, 39 O.A.C. 161, 106 N.R. 161, Sopinka J. (dissenting in part).

RIGHT TO SILENCE. "In R. v. Hebert [1990] 2 S.C.R. 151, this Court found that s. 7 of the Charter includes a right to silence which includes the right to choose whether or not to make a statement to the authorities. In Hebert, Justice McLachlin described the right as follows, at p. 186: 'The essence of the right to silence is that the suspect be given a choice; the right is quite simply the freedom to choose—the freedom to speak to the authorities on the one hand, and the right to refuse to make a statement to them on the other.' " *R. v. Broyles*, [1991] 3 S.C.R. 595 at 605, 9 C.R. (4th) 1, [1992] 1 W.W.R. 289, 68 C.C.C. (3d) 308, 84 Alta. L.R. (2d) 1, 131 N.R. 118, 120 A.R. 189, 8 W.A.C. 189, 8 C.R.R. (2d) 274, the court per Iacobucci J.

RIGHT TO VOTE. "[In s. 3 of the Charter] ... should be defined as guaranteeing the right to effective representation. The concept of absolute voter parity does not accord with the development of the right to vote in the Canadian context and does not permit of sufficient flexibility to meet the practical difficulties inherent in representative government in a country such as Canada." *Reference re Provincial Electoral Boundaries*, [1991] 2 S.C.R. 158 at 188, [1991] 5 W.W.R. 1, 127 N.R. 1, 81 D.L.R. (4th) 16, McLachlin J. (La Forest, Gonthier, Stevenson and Iacobucci JJ. concurring).

RIGHT TO WORK. 1. The right of an employee to keep a job without being a union member. 2. "[Used to describe] ... the right not to be regulated. It had little to do with the important personal right of otherwise qualified professional people to have an opportunity to attempt to build a practice in their province and in their chosen communities. One may be deprived of such a right in accordance with the principles of fundamental justice: ..." *Wilson v. British Columbia (Medical Services Commission)* (1988), 34 Admin. L.R. 235 at 262, 30 B.C.L.R. (2d) 1, [1989] 2 W.W.R. 1, 53 D.L.R. (4th) 17 (C.A.), Nemetz C.J.B.C., Carrothers, Hinkson, Macfarlane and Wallace JJ.A.

RIGOR MORTIS. [L.] The stiffening and contracting of the voluntary and involuntary muscles in the body after death. F.A. Jaffe, *A Guide to Pathological Evidence for Lawyers and Police Officers*, 4th ed. (Toronto: Carswell, 1999) at 243.

RIOT. *n.* An unlawful assembly that has begun to disturb the peace tumultuously. *Criminal Code*, R.S.C. 1985, c. C-46, s. 64.

RIOT ACT. The name commonly given to the proclamation set out in section 67 of the Criminal Code, R.S.C. 1985, c. C-46 which is read at the time of a riot.

RIPARIAN. *adj.* "... [A]pplies to a river and flowing water... ." *Rickey v. Toronto (City)* (1914), 30 O.L.R. 523 at 524, 19 D.L.R. 146 (H.C.), Boyd C.

RIPARIAN RIGHTS. 1. "... [D]o not carry exclusive possession; they exist as incorporeal rights arising from ownership, in the nature of servitudes, among other things, over foreshore." *Canada (Attorney General) v. Higbie, (sub nom. Canada (Attorney General) v. Western Higbie)* [1945] 3 D.L.R. 1 at 44,

[1945] S.C.R. 385, Rand J. 2. "The rights enjoyed by a riparian owner are classified as follows in [G.V. LaForest, Water Law in Canada: The Atlantic Provinces] ([Ottawa: Information Canada,] 1973), at p. 201: '(1) the right of access to water; (2) the right of drainage; (3) rights relating to the flow of water; (4) rights relating to the quality of water (pollution); (5) rights relating to the use of water; and (6) the right of accretion.' " *Welsh v. Marantette* (1983), 27 C.C.L.T. 113 at 125-6, 44 O.R. (2d) 137, 30 R.P.R. 111, 3 D.L.R. (4th) 401 (H.C.), Maloney J.

RISK. *n.* 1. "... [I]n insurance contracts refer to the very object of the contract of insurance, the happening of which—the 'loss'—triggers the obligation of the insurer to indemnify the insured or his beneficiary." *Metropolitan Life Insurance Co. v. Frenette*, [1992] I.L.R. 1-2823 at 1784, 89 D.L.R. (4th) 653, [1992] 1 S.C.R. 647, 46 Q.A.C. 161, [1992] R.R.A. 466, L'Heureux-Dubé J. 2. A probability statement about the extent of danger in an ordinary orderly environment. 3. The peril insured against in the policy defines the risk which is the hazard or chance of misfortune or loss at some time in the future. *University of Saskatchewan v. Fireman's Fund Insurance Co.* (1997), 158 Sask. R. 223 (C.A.). See ALL ~S; REAL ~; SPECIES AT ~; SYSTEMIC ~; VOLUNTARY ASSUMPTION OF ~.

RISK CLASSIFICATION SYSTEM. In relation to automobile insurance, means the elements used for the purpose of classifying risks in the determination of rates for a coverage or category of automobile insurance, including the variables, criteria, rules and procedures used for that purpose. *Insurance Act*, R.S.O. 1990, c. I-8, s.1.

RISK GROUP 4. A category of human pathogens that pose a high risk to the health of individuals and a high risk to public health and includes the human pathogens listed in Schedule 4. They are likely to cause serious disease in a human. Effective treatment and preventive measures are not usually available and the risk of spread of disease caused by those pathogens is high. *Human Pathogens and Toxins Act*, S.C. 2009, c. 24, s. 3.

RISK GROUP 3. A category of human pathogens that pose a high risk to the health of individuals and a low risk to public health and includes the human pathogens listed in Schedule 3. They are likely to cause serious disease in a human. Effective treatment and preventive measures are usually available and the risk of spread of disease caused by those pathogens is low. *Human Pathogens and Toxins Act*, S.C. 2009, c. 24, s. 3.

RISK GROUP 2. A category of human pathogens that pose a moderate risk to the health of individuals and a low risk to public health and includes the human pathogens listed in Schedule 2. They are able to cause serious disease in a human but are unlikely to do so. Effective treatment and preventive measures are available and the risk of spread of disease caused by those pathogens is low. *Human Pathogens and Toxins Act*, S.C. 2009, c. 24, s. 3.

RIVER. See INTERNATIONAL ~.

R.J.C. *abbr.* Recueil de jurisprudence en droit criminel, 1946-1967.

R.J.C. (5E). *abbr.* Recueil de jurisprudence en droit criminel (cinquième série), 1997-2002.

R.J.C. (N.S.) *abbr.* Recueil de jurisprudence en droit criminel (nouvelle série), 1967-1986.

R.J.C. (4E). *abbr.* Recueil de jurisprudence en droit criminel (quatrième série), 1991-1996.

R.J.C. (6E). *abbr.* Recueil de jurisprudence en droit criminel (sixième série), 2002-.

R.J.C. (3E). *abbr.* Recueil de jurisprudence en droit criminel (troisième série), 1978-1991.

R.J.D.A. *abbr.* Recueil de jurisprudence en droit des affiares, 1977-1990.

R.J.D.A. (2E). *abbr.* Recueil de jurisprudence en droit des affiares (deuxième série), 1991-1999.

R.J.D.A. (3E). *abbr.* Recueil de jurisprudence en droit des affiares (troisième série), 2000-.

R.J.D.C. *abbr.* Recueil de jurisprudence en droit de la construction, 1983-1992.

R.J.D.C. (2E). *abbr.* Recueil de jurisprudence en droit de la construction (deuxième série), 1992-2000.

R.J.D.C. (3E). *abbr.* Recueil de jurisprudence en droit de la construction (troisième série), 2000-.

R.J.D.I. *abbr.* Recueil de jurisprudence en droit immobilier, 1977-1989.

R.J.D.I. (2E). *abbr.* Recueil de jurisprudence en droit immobilier (deuxième série), 1989-1996.

R.J.D.I. (3E). *abbr.* Recueil de jurisprudence en droit immobilier (troisième série), 1996-.

R.J.D.M. *abbr.* Recueil de jurisprudence en droit municipal, 1976-1990.

R.J.D.M. (2E). *abbr.* Recueil de jurisprudence en droit municipal (deuxième série), 1990-.

R.J.D.T. *abbr.* Recueil de jurisprudence en droit du travail (Québec), 1998-.

R.J.E.L. *abbr.* Revue juridique des étudiants de l'Université Laval.

R.J.F. *abbr.* Recueil de jurisprudence en droit de la famille, 1971-1978.

R.J.F. (5E). *abbr.* Recueil de jurisprudence en droit de la famille (cinquième série), 2000-.

R.J.F.D. *abbr.* Revue juridique "La Femme et le droit" (Canadian Journal of Women and the Law).

R.J.F. (2E). *abbr.* Recueil de jurisprudence en droit de la famille (deuxième série), 1978-1986.

R.J.F. (4E). *abbr.* Recueil de jurisprudence en droit de la famille (quatrième série), 1994-2000.

R.J.F. (3E). *abbr.* Recueil de jurisprudence en droit de la famille (troisième série), 1986-1994.

R.J. IMM. *abbr.* Recueil de jurisprudence en droit de l'immigration, 1985-1987.

R.J. IMM. (2E). *abbr.* Recueil de jurisprudence en droit de l'immigration (deuxième série), 1987-1999.

R.J. IMM. (3E). *abbr.* Recueil de jurisprudence en droit de l'immigration (troisième série), 2000-.

R.J.O. (3E). *abbr.* Recueil de jurisprudence de l'Ontario (troisième série), 1991-.

R.J.Q. *abbr.* Recueil de jurisprudence du Québec, 1875-1891, 1975-.

R.J.R.Q. *abbr.* Rapports judiciaires revisés de la province de Québec (Mathieu), 1726-1891 (Quebec Revised Reports).

R.J.T. *abbr.* La Revue juridique Thémis.

R.L. *abbr.* Revue légale (Québec), 1869-1892, 1943 -.

R.L. (N.S.). *abbr.* Revue légale (nouvelle série) (Québec), 1895-1943.

R.L.N.S. *abbr.* La Revue Légale (N.S.) (Québec), 1895-1942.

R.L.O.S. *abbr.* La Revue Légale (Québec), 1869-1891.

R.N.B. (2D). *abbr.* Recueil des arrêts du Nouveau Brunswick (deuxième série), 1969-.

ROAD. *n.* Land used or intended for use for the passage of motor vehicles.

ROAD RAGE. Misconduct arising when a person reacts in an unreasonable and extreme way in response to the conduct of others using the road or highway.

ROADWAY. *n.* 1. That part of a public highway ordinarily used for vehicular traffic. *Highways Development and Protection Act*, S.A. 2004, c. H-8.5, s. 1. 2. The continuous strip of land owned or occupied by a person as a right of way for trains, leading from place to place in Alberta, but not including (i) land that is outside the right of way and owned or occupied by the corporation for station grounds or extra right of way for sidings, spur tracks, wyes or other trackage for trains, or (ii) land within the right of way that is used by the corporation for purposes other than the operation of trains. *Municipal Government Act*, R.S.A. 2000, c. M-26, s. 284. 3. With reference to "roadway" as defined in the Motor Vehicle Act, it relates to a portion of a highway that is improved, designed or ordinarily used for vehicular traffic, but does not include the shoulder. For a surface to be a "roadway" it should be currently designed and improved or used for the passage of vehicles. *Busch Estate v. Lewers*, 1999 CarswellBC 1730 (S.C.), Melvin J.

ROB. & JOS. DIG. *abbr.* Robinson & Joseph's Digest.

ROBBERY. *n.* (a) Stealing; and for the purpose of extorting whatever is stolen or to prevent or overcome resistance to the stealing, using violence or threats of violence to a person or property; (b) stealing from any person and, at the time he steals or immediately before or immediately thereafter, wounding, beating, striking or using any personal violence to that person; (c) assaulting any person with intent to steal from him; or (d) stealing from any person while armed with an offensive weapon or imitation thereof. *Criminal Code*, R.S.C. 1985, c. C-46, s. 343.

ROCKET. *n.* A projectile that contains its own propellant and that depends for its flight on a reaction set up by the release of a continuous jet of rapidly expanding gases. *Aeronautics Act*, R.S.C. 1985, c. A-2, *Canadian Aviation Regulations* SOR 96-433, s. 101.01.

ROD. See LIGHTNING ~S.

ROGATORY. See COMMISSION EVIDENCE; COMMISSION ~; LETTERS ~; PERPETUATE TESTIMONY; ~ LETTERS.

ROGATORY COMMISSION. A commissioner may be appointed to receive the deposition of a witness who is unable to attend to testify because of his state of health or who is outside Québec despite the efforts made to procure his attendance. The judge shall not make such an appointment unless the testimony is essential to the determination of the case. *Code of Penal Procedure*, R.S.Q., c. C-25.1, a. 54.

ROGATORY LETTERS. A commission in which one judge requests another to examine a witness. See COMMISSION EVIDENCE; COMMISSION ROGATORY; LETTERS ROGATORY; PERPETUATE TESTIMONY.

ROLL. *n.* 1. The list of the members in good standing of a professional body. 2. A real estate assessment roll. 3. The list of the members in good standing of an order, prepared under this Code. *Professional Code*, R.S.Q., c. C-26, s. 1. See STRIKE OFF THE ~.

ROLLED UP PLEA. "... [S]tates that the allegations of fact in the libel are true, that they are of public interest, and that the comments upon them contained in the libel were fair. The allegation of truth is confined to the facts averred, and the averment as to the comments is not that they are true but only that they were made in good faith, and that they are fair and do not exceed the proper standard of comment upon such matters." *Sutherland v. Stopes*, [1925] A.C. 47 at 62-3 (U.K. C.A.), Viscount Finlay.

ROLLING ANTON PILLER ORDER. An order granted when the identity of the defendant or defendants is not known. The proceeding is commenced against John and Jane Doe. Particulars of the alleged infringing activity of the as yet to be identified defendants are not known. A general statement is made in the affidavit filed to support the issuance of the Anton Piller order that the plaintiff is suffering irreparable harm because of the manufacture and sale of counterfeit merchandise, that is, merchandise that infringes the plaintiff's copyright, trademark or other intellectual property rights. Once granted, an Anton Piller order of the rolling type typically lasts for approximately a year, and is executed during that time against numerous individuals and corporate entities identified by the plaintiff's agents. *Nike Canada Ltd. v. Jane Doe* (1999), 174 F.T.R. 131.

ROLLING STOCK. Includes a locomotive, engine, motor car, tender, snow-plough, flanger and any car or railway equipment that is designed for movement on its wheels on the rails of a railway. *Canada Transportation Act*, S.C. 1996, c. 10, s. 6.

R.O.N.T.C. *abbr.* Recueil des décisions de l'Office national des transports du Canada, 1988-.

ROOF. See GREEN ~.

ROOMING HOUSE. A place where persons live in separate rooms but share kitchen and bathroom with others.

ROME STATUTE. The Rome Statute of the International Criminal Court adopted by the United Nations Diplomatic Conference of Plenipotentiaries on the Establishment of an International Criminal Court on July 17, 1998, as corrected by the procès-verbaux of November 10, 1998, July 12, 1999, November 30, 1999 and May 8, 2000, portions of which are set out in the schedule. *Crimes Against Humanity and War Crimes Act*, S.C. 2000, c. 24, s. 2.

ROOT OF TITLE. One traces ownership of property from the document which forms the root of title. R. Megarry & H.W.R. Wade, *The Law of Real Property*, 5th ed. (London: Stevens, 1984) at cxxvii.

ROVING RANDOM STOP. A stop which is not motivated on the part of the police officer who orders it by a belief based on reasonable grounds that the driver has committed, or is committing, an offence of any sort, whether it be under the Criminal Code, the Motor Vehicle Act or the regulations promulgated under the Motor Vehicle Act, and which is not ordered as part of any organized program of traffic safety. *R. v. Wilson* (1993), 86 B.C.L.R. (2d) 103 (C.A.).

ROY. *n.* [Fr. king] Monarch.

ROYAL ASSENT. Royal assent to a bill passed by the Houses of Parliament may be signified, during the session in which both Houses pass the bill, (a) in Parliament assembled; or (b) by written declaration. *Royal Assent Act*, S.C. 2002, c. 15. In a province, the Lieutenant Governor gives royal assent to a bill in order to make it a law. Unless the bill contains a clause setting another date, a bill comes into force on the day on which it receives royal assent.

ROYAL CANADIAN MINT. The Master of the Mint and such other persons as constitute the Board of Directors of the Mint are incorporated as a body corporate under the name of the Royal Canadian Mint. The objects of the Mint are to mint coins in anticipation of profit and to carry out other related activities.

ROYAL CANADIAN MOUNTED POLICE. A police force for Canada. It is the duty of members who are peace officers, subject to the orders of the Commissioner, (a) to perform all duties that are assigned to peace officers in relation to the preservation of the peace, the prevention of crime and of offences against the laws of Canada and the laws in force in any province in which they may be employed, and the apprehension of criminals and offenders and others who may be lawfully taken into custody; (b) to execute all warrants, and perform all duties and services in relation thereto, that may, under this Act or the laws of Canada or the laws in force in any province, be lawfully executed and performed by peace officers; (c) to perform all duties that may be lawfully performed by peace officers in relation to the escort and conveyance of convicts and other persons in custody to or from any courts, places of punishment or confinement, asylums or other places; and (d) to perform such other duties and functions as are prescribed by the Governor in Council or the Commissioner. The Minister may, with the approval of the Governor in Council, enter into an arrangement with the government of any province for the use or employment of the Force, or any portion thereof, in aiding the administration of justice in the province and in carrying into effect the laws in force therein. Arrangements with municipalities. The Minister may, with the approval of the Governor in Council and the lieutenant governor in council of any province, enter into an arrangement with any municipality in the province for the use or employment of the Force, or any portion thereof, in aiding the administration of justice in the municipality and in carrying into effect the laws in force therein. *Royal Canadian Mounted Police Act*, R.S.C. 1985, c. R-10, s. 3, 18 and 20..

ROYAL CANADIAN MOUNTED POLICE EXTERNAL REVIEW COMMITTEE. The Commissioner of the RCMP may refer certain grievances and appeals by members to the committee for review. Established under the *Royal Canadian Mounted Police Act*, R.S.C. 1985, c. R-10, s. 25.

ROYAL CANADIAN MOUNTED POLICE PUBLIC COMPLAINTS COMMISSION. Established under the Royal Canadian Mounted Police Act, R.S.C. 1985, c. R-10, s. 45.29. Under section 45.37, where the Commission Chairman is satisfied that there are reasonable grounds to investigate the conduct, in the performance of any duty or function under this Act, of any member or other person appointed or employed under the authority of this Act, the Commission Chairman may initiate a complaint in relation thereto. Under section 45.41, a complainant who is not satisfied with the disposition of the complaint by the Force may refer the complaint to the Commission for review.

ROYAL COMMISSION. A person or body appointed to inquire into and report on a matter of general public interest.

ROYAL PREROGATIVE. 1. Generally speaking, in my view, the royal prerogative means "the powers and privileges accorded by the common law to the Crown" (see P. W. Hogg, Constitutional Law of Canada (loose-leaf ed.), vol. 1, at p. 1:14). The royal prerogative is confined to executive governmental powers, whether federal or provincial. The extent of its authority can be abolished or limited by statute: "once a statute [has] occupied the ground formerly occupied by the prerogative, the Crown [has to] comply with the terms of the statute". (See P. W. Hogg and P. J. Monahan, Liability of the Crown (3rd ed. 2000), at p. 17; also, Hogg, supra, at pp. 1:15-1:16; P. Lordon, Crown Law (1991), at pp. 66- 67.) In summary, then, as statute law expands and encroaches upon the purview of the royal prerogative, to that extent the royal prerogative contracts. However, this displacement occurs only to the extent that the statute does so explicitly or by necessary implication. *Ross River Dena Council Band v. Canada* [2002] 2 S.C.R. 816, LeBel J. (Arbour, Binnie, Gonthier, Iacobucci, Major JJ. concurring). 2. 2. "... [W]hat has been left to the King from the wide discretionary powers he enjoyed at the time he governed as an absolute monarch ..." *Operation Dismantle Inc. v. R.* (1983), 39 C.P.C. 120 at 156, [1983] 1 F.C. 429 (C.A.), Marceau J.A.

ROYAL STYLE AND TITLES. ELIZABETH THE SECOND, by the Grace of God of the United Kingdom, Canada and Her other Realms and Territories QUEEN, Head of the Commonwealth, Defender of the Faith. *Royal Style and Titles Act*, R.S.C. 1985, c. R-12, s. 2.

ROYALTIES. *n.* 1. "[In s. 3(1)(f) of the Income War Tax Act, R.S.C. 1927, c. 97] ... does not bear the original meaning ascribed to it as rights belonging to the Crown jure coronae ... it has a special sense when used in mining grants or licences signifying that part of the reddendum which is variable and depends upon the quantity of minerals gotten. It is a well-known term in connection with patents and copyrights." *Minister of National Revenue v. Wain-Town Gas & Oil Co.*, [1952] 2 S.C.R. 377 at 382, 13 Fox Pat. C. 5, [1952] C.T.C. 147, 16 C.P.R. 73, [1952] 4 D.L.R. 81, 52 D.T.C. 1138, Kerwin J. (Rinfret C.J.C. and Taschereau J. concurring). 2. "... [B]ona vacantia falls within the term 'royalties' ..." *R. v. British Columbia (Attorney General)* (1922), 68 D.L.R. 106 at 115, 63 S.C.R. 622, [1922] 3 W.W.R. 269, Anglin J. 3. "Assuming then, though without deciding, that the term 'royalties' as used in s. 109 of the Constitution Act, 1867 (30 & 31 Vict.), c. 3 is apt to include fines imposed for infraction of the criminal law, ..." *Toronto (City) v. R.*, [1932] 1 D.L.R. 161 at 165, 56 C.C.C. 273 (Ont. P.C.), the court per Lord Macmillan. See ROYALTY.

ROYALTY. *n.* 1. A financial consideration paid for the right to use a copyright or patent or to exercise a similar incorporeal right; payment made from the production from a property which the grantor still owns. 2. The amount payable to the Crown for timber harvested on Crown Lands. 3. A payment made for the right or privilege to explore for, bring into production, take or dispose of oil or gas. In its original sense refers to Crown prerogatives or Crown rights . . . The word "royalty" is still used in Canada to describe a payment that is required by a provincial statute to be paid to the province as a share of the production of a resource. Typically, in the case of a resource that the province owns, there is a provincial statute that authorizes the granting of a lease subject to the payment of royalties . . . However, there is no authority that suggests that the word "royalty" must be limited to amounts paid pursuant to such an arrangement. In the context of payments to a province, the word "royalty" may describe any share of resource production that is paid to the province in connection with its interest in the resource. *Mobil Oil*

Canada Ltd. v. R., 2001 FCA 333, 2001 D.T.C. 5668, [2002] 1 C.T.C. 55, 281 N.R. 367, 215 F.T.R. 32 (note) See ROYALTIES; TIMBER ~.

ROYALTY INTEREST. Any interest in, or the right to receive a portion of, any oil or gas produced and saved from a field or pool or part of a field or pool or the proceeds from the sale thereof, but does not include a working interest or the interest of any person whose sole interest is as a purchaser of oil or gas from the pool or part thereof. *Canada Oil and Gas Operations Act*, R.S.C. 1985, c. O-7, s. 29.

ROYALTY OWNER. A person, including Her Majesty in right of Canada, who owns a royalty interest. *Canada Oil and Gas Operations Act*, R.S.C. 1985, c. O-7, s. 29.

ROYALTY-RELIEF METHOD. Method of valuing intellectual property. Estimation of income stream expected to accrue from the intellectual property asset compared to the cost to rent the asset through a third party licensing arrangement for the economic life of the asset.

R.P. *abbr.* Rapports de Pratique du Québec, 1898-1944 (Quebec Practice Reports).

[] R.P. *abbr.* Rapports de Pratique du Québec, 1945-1982 (Quebec Practice Reports).

R.P.C. *abbr.* Reports of Patent Cases.

R.P.F.S. *abbr.* Revue de planification fiscale et successorale.

R.P.Q. *abbr.* Rapports de pratique de Québec, 1897-1982.

R.P.R. *abbr.* Real Property Reports, 1977-1989.

R.P.R. (2D). *abbr.* Real Property Reports (Second Series), 1989-1996.

R.P.R. (3D). *abbr.* Real Property Reports (Third Series), 1996-.

R.P.T.A. *abbr.* Recueil en matière de protection du territoire agricole (Québec), 1990-.

R.Q.D.I. *abbr.* Revue québécoise de droit international.

R.R.A. *abbr.* Recueil en responsabilité et assurance (Québec), 1986-..

RRSP. *abbr.* A registered retirement savings plan within the meaning of the tax act that is registererd under that act. *Employment Pension Plan Act*, R.S.A. 2000, c. E-8, s. 1.

R.S. *abbr.* Revised Statutes.

R.S.A. *abbr.* Recueil de sentences arbitrales (Québec), 1981-1983.

R.S.C. *abbr.* 1. Revised Statutes of Canada. 2. Rules of the Supreme Court.

R.S.E. *abbr.* Recueil des sentences de l'éducation (Québec), 1974-.

R.S.F. *abbr.* Recueil de jurisprudence en droit des successions et des fiducies, 1977-1994.

R

R.S.F. (2E). *abbr.* Recueil de jurisprudence en droit des successions et des fiducies (deuxième série), 1994-.

R.S.P. *abbr.* Recueil des ordonnances de la Régie des services publics (Québec), 1973-1978.

R.T.C. *abbr.* Décisions et énoncés de politique sur la radiodiffusion et les télécommunications canadiennes, 1975-1985.

R.T.P. COMM. *abbr.* Restrictive Trade Practices Commission.

RUBRIC. *n.* 1. Heading or category. 2. With respect to a statute, its title, which was formerly written in red.

RULE. *n.* A law which an administrative agency or court enacts to regulate its procedure. See ASSOCIATED WORDS ~; BEST EVIDENCE ~; BUSINESS JUDGMENT ~; COLLATERAL FACT ~; CONFESSIONS ~; CRUMBLING SKULL ~; DERIVED CONFESSIONS ~; DISCOVERABILITY ~; DOUBLE MOTHER ~; DROP DEAD ~; EXCLUSIONARY ~; FOREIGN IMMOVABLE ~; GENERAL ANTI-AVOIDANCE ~; GOLDEN ~; HEARSAY ~; IMPLIED EXCLUSION ~; IMPLIED UNDERTAKING ~; LEARNED INTERMEDIATE ~; LIMITED CLASS ~; LORD MANSFIELD'S ~; LOWEST INTERMEDIATE BALANCE ~; MISCHIEF ~; MODERN ~ OF STATUTORY INTERPRETATION; NON-DELEGABLE DUTY ~; ORDINARY MEANING ~; ORIGINAL DOCUMENT ~; PAROL EVIDENCE ~; PERPETUITY ~; PLAIN MEANING ~; SHARED MEANING ~; SIMILAR FACT EVIDENCE ~; SINGLE PUBLICATION ~; SLIP ~; THIN SKULL ~; WORK TO ~.

RULE ABSOLUTE. "... [O]ne that is operative forthwith and constitutes an adjudication upon some point at some stage in an action or a proceeding ..." *R. v. U.F.A.W.* (1967), [1968] 1 C.C.C. 194 at 197, 60 W.W.R. 370, 63 D.L.R. (2d) 356 (B.C. C.A.), Davey C.J.B.C. (Branca J.A. concurring).

RULE AGAINST COLLATERAL ATTACK. A court order, made by a court having jurisdiction to make it, stands and is binding and conclusive unless it is set aside on appeal or lawfully quashed. It is also well settled in the authorities that such an order may not be attacked collaterally. *R. v. Wilson*, [1983] 2 S.C.R. 594, at p. 599.

RULE AGAINST DOUBLE JEOPARDY. After an accused is tried for an offence and finally convicted or acquitted, that person may not be placed in jeopardy a second time, i.e. be tried again, for the same offence. See AUTREFOIS ACQUIT; AUTREFOIS CONVICT.

RULE AGAINST HEARSAY. Requires that evidence of a witness be restricted to what she or he perceived herself or himself (primary evidence) and excludes anything she or he gathered from other sources. A rule to which there are many exceptions.

RULE AGAINST PERPETUAL DURATION. A rule with the same object as the rule against perpetuities, but which is applied to any trust with non-charitable purposes. D.M.W. Waters, *The Law of Trusts in Canada*, 2d ed. (Toronto: Carswell, 1984) at 282.

RULE AGAINST PERPETUITIES. For an interest in property to be good it must vest no later than 21 years after some life in being when the interest was created. T. Sheard, R. Hull & M.M.K. Fitzpatrick, *Canadian Forms of Wills*, 4th ed. (Toronto: Carswell, 1982) at 231. See MODERN RULES AGAINST PERPETUITIES; PERPETUITY RULE.

RULE IN BROWNE V. DUNN. The rule in Browne v. Dunn [[1893] 6 R. 67 (U.K. H.L)] requires defence counsel to put to the plaintiff in cross examination the evidence that the defendant will be calling during the defendant's case. The reason for the rule is based on fairness. The rule stands for the proposition that if counsel is going to challenge the credibility of a witness by calling contradictory evidence, the witness must be given the chance to address the contradictory evidence in cross-examination while he or she is in the witness-box. If the defendant is making an allegation against the interests of the plaintiff, it is only fair to put the evidence in support of that allegation to the plaintiff, so that the plaintiff can respond to it while the plaintiff is on the witness stand. It is not necessary for the defendant to put every detail of the defendant's evidence to the plaintiff, but it is necessary for the plaintiff to be presented with sufficient detail to allow the plaintiff to understand the nature of the defendant's evidence against her. *Hanna v. Royal & SunAlliance Insurance Co. of Canada* (2007), 2007 CarswellOnt 3017 (Ont. S.C.J.). Browne v. Dunn is a rule of fairness that prevents the "ambush" of a witness by not giving him an opportunity to state his position with respect to later evidence which contradicts him on an essential matter. It is not, however, an absolute rule and counsel must not feel obliged to slog through a witness's evidence-in-chief, putting him on notice of every detail that the defence does not accept. *R. v. McNeill* (2000), 33 C.R. (5th) 390 (Ont. C.A.).

RULE IN CLAYTON'S CASE. What is known as the rule in Clayton's Case derives from the decision of the English Court of Appeal in Devaynes v. Noble (1816), 1 Mer. 572, 35 E.R. 781 (Eng. Ch. Div.) . The so-called rule—which is really a statement of evidentiary principle—presumes that in the state of accounts as between a bank and its customer the sums first paid in are the sums first drawn out, absent evidence of an agreement or any presumed intent to the contrary: see Clayton's Case, per Sir William Grant, at pp. 608 - 609, Mer. As Morden J.A. remarked in Greymac, (p. 677) "the short form statement of the rule ... is 'first in, first out'". In the result, where there are competing claims against a shortfall, the shortfall is applied first to the first deposits made, and later contributors to the fund take the benefit of what remains.11 The role of the rule in Clayton's Case in competing beneficiary cases, and its history, were examined thoroughly by this Court in Greymac . The application of the rule was rejected as being "unfair and arbitrary" and "based on a fiction" (p. 686). The Court concluded that it was not bound to apply the rule in Clayton's Case, and it did not do so. *Law So-*

ciety of Upper Canada v. Toronto Dominion Bank (1998), 42 O.R. (3d) 257(C.A.).

RULE IN HEYDON'S CASE. The Rule in Heydon's Case [(1584), 76 E.R. 637 (Eng. K.B.)] is alive and well now. What is that Rule? When interpreting legislation, the court must look to what was the mischief in the old law which the new legislation was aimed at. Then the court must see what solution the new legislation was intended to adopt. *Bowes v. Edmonton (City)*, 2007 ABCA 347, Côté J.A.

RULE IN HODGES'S CASE. "... [I]n a criminal case, where proof of any issue of fact essential to the case of the Crown consists of circumstantial evidence it is the duty of the judge to instruct the jury that before they can find the accused guilty they must be satisfied not only that the circumstances are consistent with an affirmative finding on the issue so sought to be proved but that the circumstances are inconsistent with any other rational conclusion ... the rule is not one merely of prudent practice but of positive law." *R. v. Mitchell* (1964), 43 C.R. 391 at 401, [1964] S.C.R. 471, 47 W.W.R. 591, 46 D.L.R. (2d) 384, [1965] 1 C.C.C. 155, Cartwright J.

RULE IN PHILLIPS V. EYRE. "As a general rule, in order to found a suit in England for a wrong alleged to have been committed abroad, two conditions must be fulfilled. First, the wrong must be of such a character that it would have been actionable if committed in England ... Secondly, the act must not have been justifiable by the law of the place where it was done." *Phillips v. Eyre* (1870), L.R. 6 Q.B. 1 at 28-9 (U.K. Ex. Ct.), Willes J.

RULE IN RYLANDS V. FLETCHER. The case, reported at (1868) L.R. 3 H.L. 330, which stands for the following proposition: anyone who, for their own reasons, brings on their land, collects and keeps there anything which may do harm if it escapes, must keep it in at their own peril. If they do not do so, they are prima facie answerable for any damages which result from its escape

RULE IN SAUNDERS V. VAUTIER. Narrowly it states that a court will not enforce a trust for accumulation, in which no one but the legatee has any interest when an absolute vested gift is made payable at a future event, with direction in the meantime to accumulate any income and pay it with the principal. More broadly it states that, if beneficiaries agree and they are not under a disability, the specific performance of a trust may be arrested, and they may extinguish or modify the trust without referring to the wishes of either the settlor or the trustees. D.M.W. Waters, *The Law of Trusts in Canada*, 2d ed. (Toronto: Carswell, 1984) at 963.

RULE IN SHELLEY'S CASE. If one vests land in trustees in fee simple in trust for some person for life, placing the remainder in trust for that person's heirs or the heirs of that person's body, that person takes an estate tail or equitable fee simple. D.M.W. Waters, *The Law of Trusts in Canada*, 2d ed. (Toronto: Carswell, 1984) at 22.

RULE NISI. "... [I]ndicates that the Court is satisfied that a prima facie case has been made out to justify

calling upon the other side to make answer at the time and place indicated to the contention upon which the rule was founded." *R. v. U.F.A.W.* (1967), [1968] 1 C.C.C. 194 at 197, 60 W.W.R. 370, 63 D.L.R. (2d) 356 (B.C. C.A.), Davey C.J.B.C. (Branca J.A. concurring).

RULE OF CONDUCT. A rule which sets norms or standards of conduct, which determine the manner in which rights are exercised and responsibilities are fulfilled. *Reference re Manitoba Language Rights*, [1992] 1 S.C.R. 212.

RULE OF LAW. 1. The principles of constitutionalism and the rule of law lie at the root of our system of government. The rule of law, is "a fundamental postulate of our constitutional structure." At its most basic level, the rule of law vouchsafes to the citizens and residents of the country a stable, predictable and ordered society in which to conduct their affairs. It provides a shield for individuals from arbitrary state action. First, the rule of law provides that the law is supreme over the acts of both government and private persons. There is, in short, one law for all. Second "the rule of law requires the creation and maintenance of an actual order of positive laws which preserves and embodies the more general principle of normative order". A third aspect of the rule of law is, "the exercise of all public power must find its ultimate source in a legal rule". Put another way, the relationship between the state and the individual must be regulated by law. Taken together, these three considerations make up a principle of profound constitutional and political significance. *Reference re Secession of Quebec*, 1998 CarswellNat 1299, 161 D.L.R. (4th) 385, 228 N.R. 203, 55 C.R.R. (2d) 1, [1998] 2 S.C.R. 217 Per curiam. 2. "... [A] highly textured expression, importing many things ... but conveying, for example, a sense of orderliness, of subjection to known legal rules and of executive accountability to legal authority." *Reference re Questions Concerning Amendment of the Constitution of Canada as set out in O.C. 1020/80* (1981), (*sub nom. Resolution to Amend the Constitution of Canada, Re*) 1 C.R.R. 59 at 99, [1981] 1 S.C.R. 753, [1981] 6 W.W.R. 1, 11 Man. R. (2d) 1, 39 N.R. 1, 34 Nfld. & P.E.I.R. 1, 95 A.P.R. 1, Laskin C.J.C., Dickson, Beetz, Estey, McIntyre, Chouinard and Lamer JJ.

RULES AGAINST PERPETUITIES. Includes: (i) the modern rules against perpetuities; and (ii) the rule in Whitby v. Mitchell [(1889) 42 Ch.D. 494, (1890) 44 Ch. D. 85]. *The Trustee Act, 2009*, S.S. 2009, c. T-23.01, s. 57. See MODERN ~; PERPETUITY RULE.

RULES OF COURT. Rules made by the authority having for the time being power to make rules or orders regulating the practice and procedure of that court.

RULES OF ENGAGEMENT. The rules governing the use of force in armed combat including issues relating to self defence, proportional use of force, levels of force, definitions of "hostile act" and "hostile intent."

RULES OF NATURAL JUSTICE. The fundamental rules of procedure which must be observed by all

R

who are required to make quasi-judicial decisions. See NATURAL JUSTICE; PROCEDURAL FAIRNESS.

RULES OF PLEADING. Rules governing the form that pleadings take which have three basic requirements: (a) to plead the material facts; (b) to deny material facts and (c) to plead an affirmative defence. One might add the right of a party to request, and the court to order, particulars. G.D. Watson & C. Perkins, eds., *Holmested & Watson: Ontario Civil Procedure* (Toronto: Carswell, 1984) at 25-13 and 14.

RULING. *n.* 1. Determination obtained by a motion to the court of the propriety of a question in an examination to which one objected without receiving an answer (Ontario, Rules of Civil Procedure, r. 34.12(3)). G.D. Watson & C. Perkins, eds., *Holmested & Watson: Ontario Civil Procedure* (Toronto: Carswell, 1984) at 34-7. 2. "... [A] disposition of a motion for non-suit made during the course of a trial is not an order ... . [I]t is instead, in my judgment, what [is] more properly described as a ruling, or a ruling on evidence which is part of the trial process, and it is not appealable until after the trial has been completed." *Rahmatian v. HFH Video Biz, Inc.* (1991), 46 C.P.C. (2d) 312 at 315 (B.C. C.A.), MacEachern C.J.B.C. See BLANKET ~S AND ORDERS.

RUN. *v.* To take effect at a certain place or time. See HIT AND ~.

RUN WITH THE LAND. Said of a covenant with land conveyed in fee when either the right to take advantage of it or the liability to perform it, passes to the person to whom that land is assigned.

RUN WITH THE REVERSION. Said of a covenant with leased land when either the right to take advantage of it or the liability to perform it, passes to the person to whom that reversion is assigned.

RUSS. E.R. *abbr.* Russell's Election Reports (N.S.), 1874.

RYLANDS V. FLETCHER. See RULE IN ~.

S

S. *abbr.* Section.

S.A. *abbr.* Société Anonyme.

SABOTAGE. *n.* 1. Doing a prohibited act for a purpose prejudicial to (a) the safety, security or defence of Canada; or (b) the safety or security of the naval, army or air forces of any state other than Canada that are lawfully present in Canada. *Criminal Code*, R.S.C. 1985, c. C-46, s. 52. 2. Malicious damaging or destruction of an employer's property by the deliberate conduct of workers.

SACRED CEREMONIAL OBJECT. An object, the title to which is vested in the Crown, that (i) was used by a First Nation in the practice of sacred ceremonial traditions, (ii) is in the possession and care of the Provincial Museum of Alberta or the Glenbow-Alberta Institute or on loan from one of those institutions to a First Nation, or is otherwise in the possession and care of the Crown, and (iii) is vital to the practice of the First Nation's sacred ceremonial traditions. *First Nations Sacred Ceremonial Objects Repatriation Act*, R.S.A. 2000, c. F-14, s. 1. See ABORIGINAL SACRED AND CULTURALLY SENSITIVE OBJECT.

SADISM. See SEXUAL ~.

SAFETY. *n.* 1. Protection from danger and hazards arising out of, linked with or occurring in the course of employment. 2. In the context of the stalking provisions of the Criminal Code, freedom from physical harm and includes freedom from the apprehension of mental, emotional or psychological harm. *Canada Labour Code*, R.S.C. 1985, c. L-2, s. 122. See CANADIAN TRANSPORTATION ACCIDENT INVESTIGATION AND ~ BOARD; MATERIAL ~ DATA SHEET; OCCUPATIONAL HEALTH AND ~.

SAFETY BELT. 1. A body support device consisting of a strap with a means for securing it about the waist and attaching it to other components. *Workers Compensation Act*, R.S.B.C. 1996, c. 492, *Occupational Health and Safety Regulation*; B.C. Reg. 296/97, s. 11.1. 2. A personal restraint system consisting of either a lap strap or a lap strap combined with a shoulder harness. *Aeronautics Act*, R.S.C. 1985, c. A-2, *Canadian Aviation Regulations* SOR 96-433, s. 101.01.

SAFETY CONVENTION VESSEL. A vessel in respect of which the International Convention for the Safety of Life at Sea, listed in Schedule 1, applies. *Canada Shipping Act, 2001*, S.C. 2001, c. 26, s. 2.

SAFETY-ENGINEERED NEEDLE. Includes a shielded needle device, a retractable needle system and a needleless device. *The Workplace Safety and Health Act*, R.S.M. 1987, c. W210, s. 45.1.

SAFETY FITNESS CERTIFICATE. A safety fitness certificate issued pursuant to a provincial highway or traffic safety act.

SAFETY MARK. 1. Includes a design, symbol, device, sign, label, placard, letter, word, number, abbreviation or any combination of these that is to be displayed on dangerous goods or containers, packaging, road vehicles or rail vehicles used in the handling or transportation of dangerous goods. *Transport of Dangerous Goods Act*, R.S.B.C. 1996, c. 458, s. 1. 2. A dangerous goods mark or a compliance mark. *Transportation of Dangerous Goods Act, 1992*, S.C. 1992, c. 34, s. 2. See NATIONAL ~.

SAFETY SERVICES. Inspections, evaluations, repairs and other services provided by persons licensed under this Act to carry out inspections of commercial vehicles. *Traffic Safety Act*, R.S.A. 2000, c. T-6, s. 139.

S.A.F.P. *abbr.* Sentences arbitrales de la fonction publique (Québec), 1983-.

S.A.G. *abbr.* Sentences arbitrales de griefs (Québec), 1970-1981.

SAID. *adj.* "... [G]rammatically applies to the last antecedent ..." *Toronto General Trusts Co. v. Irwin* (1896), 27 O.R. 491 at 495 (H.C.), Meredith C.J.

SALARY. *n.* Compensation paid to an employee for labour or services.

SALE. *n.* 1. "... [T]he primary meaning of sale was the transfer of property to another for a price... ." *Leading Investments Ltd. v. New Forest Investments Ltd.* (1986), 38 R.P.R. 201 at 213, [1986] 1 S.C.R. 70, 65 N.R. 209, 14 O.A.C. 159, 25 D.L.R. (4th) 161, La Forest J. (Dickson C.J.C. and Lamer J. concurring). 2. "... [M]ay be interpreted to mean either a binding agreement for sale or a completed sale... ." *Leading Investments Ltd. v. New Forest Investments Ltd.* (1986), 38 R.P.R. 201 at 223, [1986] 1 S.C.R.

70, 65 N.R. 209, 14 O.A.C. 159, 25 D.L.R. (4th) 161, Estey J. (McIntyre and Chouinard JJ. concurring). 3. In the context of labour relations to accomplish a sale something must be relinquished by the predecessor business on the one hand and obtained by the successor on the other. A sale implies a nexus, an agreement or transaction of some sort between the predecessor and successor employers. There must be a mutual intent to transfer part of the business. *C.A.W., Local 222 v. Charterways Transportation Ltd.*, 2000 CarswellOnt 1253, 2000 SCC 23, 2000 C.L.L.C. 220-028, 49 C.C.E.L. (2d) 151, 47 O.R. (3d) 800 (headnote only), 185 D.L.R. (4th) 618, [2000] L.V.I. 3109-1, [2000] 1 S.C.R. 538, 253 N.R. 223, 22 Admin. L.R. (3d) 1, 133 O.A.C. 43, Bastarache J. (dissenting). See ACTION FOR ~; AGREEMENT FOR ~; BARGAIN AND ~; BILL OF ~; BULK ~; CONDITIONAL ~; CONDITION OF ~; CONTRACT FOR ~; CONTRACT OF ~; DIRECT ~; NET ~ PROCEEDS; PARTITION OR ~; PORTFOLIO ~; POWER OF ~; PUBLIC ~; RE~; TIME ~; TRUST FOR ~.

SALE AGREEMENT. An agreement to purchase.

SALE BY DESCRIPTION. "... [T]here is a sale by description even though the buyer is buying something displayed before him on the counter: a thing is sold by description, though it is specific, so long as it is sold not merely as the specific thing but as a thing corresponding to a description ..." *Grant v. Australian Knitting Mills Ltd.*, [1936] S.C. 85 at 100 (Australia P.C.), Lord Wright for their Lordships.

SALE BY SAMPLE. "To constitute a sale by sample, in the legal sense of that term, it must, ... appear that the parties contracted with reference to a sample, and with a mutual understanding that the sample furnished a description (in this case) of the quality of the oats and that the bulk must conform with the sample." *Wawryk v. McKenzie Co.* (1921), 61 D.L.R. 25 at 26, [1921] 2 W.W.R. 951 (Sask. C.A.), the court per Lamont J.A.

SALE-LEASEBACK. *n.* A way to raise money on land by which a vendor receives from the purchaser the full market value of the property and becomes a tenant of the purchaser under a long term lease of the property.

SALE OF GOODS. 1. A contract by which a seller agrees to transfer or transfers property in goods to a buyer for financial consideration called the price. 2. Includes any transaction in which goods are sold, whether separately or together with services. *Consumer Protection acts.*

SALE ON APPROVAL. The sale of goods with the right of the purchaser to return the goods if the purchaser is not satisfied with them within a specified time.

SALE ON CREDIT. A sale in which payment of the whole price is delayed, or the price is paid in instalments over a period of time along with interest on the outstanding balance of the purchase price.

SALE PRICE. 1. Actual value of thing exchanged. 2. Amount paid for a thing purchased. 3. The phrase "sale price" is not apt to describe an offered price. In this context, sale price means a price agreed upon between the seller and a buyer who was obtained with the assistance of the co-operating agent. *Rosling Real Estate (Nelson) Ltd. v. Robertson Hilliard Cattell Realty Co.*, 1999 CarswellBC 1554 (S.C.), Smith J.

SALES CONTRACT. See DISTANCE ~; INTERNET ~.

SALESPERSON. See INSURANCE ~.

SALES TAX. 1. The tax imposed under Part IX of the Excise Tax Act and taxes levied under Acts of the legislature of a province in respect of supplies of property or services. 2. Consumption tax. 3. Any tax of general application payable on a value, price or quantity basis by a person in respect of the sale, rental, supply, consumption or use of a property or service. *First Nations Sales Tax*, S.C. 2003, c. 15, s. 67, s. 17. See HARMONIZED ~; RETAIL ~.

SALES TAX HARMONIZATION AGREEMENT. An agreement or arrangement entered into by the Minister on behalf of the Government of Canada and authorized, or ratified and confirmed, under Part III.1 including any amendments or variations to the agreement or arrangement that are authorized, or ratified and confirmed, under that Part. *Federal-Provincial Fiscal Arrangements Act*, R.S.C. 1985, c. F-8, s. 2.

SALVAGE. *v.* 1. "... [R]escue from threatened loss or injury... ." *Canadian Pacific Navigation Co. v. "C.F. Sargent" (The)* (1893), 3 B.C.R. 5 at 7 (Ex. Ct.), Begbie L.J.A. 2. "... [T]o rescue or save from wreckage, ..." *R. v. Greenspoon Brothers Ltd.*, [1965] 2 O.R. 528 at 529, [1965] 4 C.C.C. 53 (C.A.), the court per Roach J.A.

SALVAGE. *n.* 1. A reward, not for services attempted without result, but for benefits conferred. A salvor must show that, when the services were rendered, the cargo or ship was in danger of being destroyed. G.H.L. Fridman, *Restitution*, 2d ed. (Toronto: Carswell, 1992) at 281. 2. "... [T]hat which is ... rescued or saved [from wreckage]... ." *R. v. Greenspoon Brothers Ltd.*, [1965] 2 O.R. 528 at 529, [1965] 4 C.C.C. 53 (C.A.), the court per Roach J.A. 3. Includes second-hand, used, discarded or surplus metals, bottles or goods, unserviceable, discarded or junked motor vehicles, bodies, engines or other component parts of a motor vehicle, and articles of every description.

SAMARITAN. See GOOD ~ LAW.

SAMPLE. *n.* A small amount of a commodity displayed as a specimen at a private or public sale. See ARCHAEOLOGICAL ~; SALE BY ~.

SANCTION. *n.* 1. A punishment or penalty used to enforce obedience to law. 2. A sanction imposed under the Criminal Code must have one or more of the following objectives: (a) to denounce unlawful conduct; (b) to deter the offender and other persons from committing offences; (c) to separate offenders from society, where necessary; (d) to assist in rehabilitating offenders; (e) to provide reparations for harm done to victims or to the community; and (f) to promote a sense of responsibility in offenders, and acknowledgment of the harm done to victims and to the community. *Criminal Code*, R.S.C. 1985, c. C-46, s. 718. See COMMUNITY ~S; CRIMINAL ~S; EXTRA-JUDICIAL ~.

SANCTUARY. *n.* A place where criminal and civil process cannot be executed.

SANDERSON ORDER. 1. A simpler form of a Bullock order by which the unsuccessful defendant must pay the successful defendant's costs directly. The name comes from *Sanderson v. Blyth Theatre Co.*, [1903] 2 K.B. 644. 2. A Bullock order directs an unsuccessful defendant to reimburse the plaintiff for the recovered costs of a successful defendant. A Sanderson order directs that the payment go directly to the successful defendant. The rational behind both orders is the same. Where the allocation of responsibility is uncertain, usually because of interwoven facts, it is often reasonable to proceed through trial against more than one defendant. In these cases, a Bullock or Sanderson order provides a plaintiff with an appropriate form of relief. *Rooney (Litigation Guardian of) v. Graham* (2001), 53 O.R. (3d) 685 (C.A.).

SANITARY. *adj.* Free from or designed to prevent influences deleterious to health.

SANITARY SEWER. A sewer for the collection and transmission of residential, commercial, institutional or industrial sewage, or any combination thereof. *Ontario Water Resources Act*, R.S.O. 1990, c. O.40, *Approval Exemptions*, O. Reg. 525/98, s. 1.

S.A.R.B. DEC. *abbr.* Social Asssistance Review Board Selected Decisions (Ontario), 1975-1986.

S.A.R.B. SUM. *abbr.* Social Asssistance Review Board Summaries of Decisions (Ontario), 1988-1994.

SASK. BAR REV. *abbr.* Saskatchewan Bar Review.

SASK. C. COMP. B. *abbr.* Saskatchewan Crimes Compensation Board, Awards, 1968-1992.

SASK. HUMAN RIGHTS COMM'N DEC. *abbr.* Saskatchewan Human Rights Commission Decisions, 1973-1981.

SASK. L.R. *abbr.* Saskatchewan Law Reports, 1907-1931.

SASK. L.R.B.D. *abbr.* Saskatchewan Labour Relations Board Decisions, 1945-1977.

SASK. L.R.B.D.C. *abbr.* Saskatchewan Labour Relations Board, Decisions and Court Cases, 1945-1964.

SASK. L.R.B.R. *abbr.* Saskatchewan Labour Relations Board, Report of Meetings, 1967-1973.

SASK. L. REV. *abbr.* Saskatchewan Law Review.

SASK. R. *abbr.* Saskatchewan Reports, 1980-.

SASK. S.C. BULL. *abbr.* Saskatchewan Securities Commission Monthly Bulletin, 1984-.

SATISFACTION. *n.* 1. Compensation under law. 2. Payment for an injury or of money owed. 3. Completion of an obligation by performance or something equivalent to performance. See ACCORD AND ~.

SATISFACTION PIECE. 1. "... [A] specialized form of receipt ..." *Heitman Financial Services Ltd. v. Towncliff Properties Ltd.* (1981), 24 C.P.C. 116 at 120, 35 O.R. (2d) 189 (H.C.), Callaghan J. 2. A judgment creditor's formal written acknowledgment, filed in court, that the judgment debtor has fully paid.

SATISFIED. *adj.* 1. Freed from doubt, anxiety, or uncertainty; having one's mind at rest. 2. Having been paid.

SATISFY. *v.* 1. To free from uncertainty or doubt. 2. To pay completely.

SAUNDERS V. VAUTIER. See RULE IN ~.

SAVING CLAUSE. A provision in a contract stating that if any term is found invalid the rest of the contract will not be affected.

SAVINGS PLAN. See DISABILITY ~; EDUCATION ~; REGISTERED RETIREMENT ~.

SAY. See WILL-~

S.C. *abbr.* 1. Supreme Court. 2. Supreme Court (provincial) [of Judicature]. 3. Superior Court. 4. Same case. 5. Sessions Cases.

SC. *abbr.* [L.] Scilicet. That is to say.

S.C.A.D. *abbr.* Supreme Court (provincial) [of Judicature] Appellate Division.

SCALE AGREEMENT. An agreement in writing between a producer and an artists' association respecting minimum terms and conditions for the provision of artists' services and other related matters. *Status of the Artist Act*, S.C. 1992, c. 33, s. 4.

SCANDALIZE THE COURT. "... [T]raditionally encompasses two forms of conduct: (a) scurrilous abuse of a court, or of a judge not in his personal capacity but as a judge: ... and (b) attacks upon the integrity or impartiality of a judge or court: ... there may be a third form, namely, 'publications that are thought to lower the repute of a judge or court.' " *R. v. Kopyto* (1987), 39 C.C.C. (3d) 1 at 36, 24 O.A.C. 8, 61 C.R. (3d) 209, 62 O.R. (2d) 449, 47 D.L.R. (4th) 213, Houlden J.A. See CONTEMPT.

SCANDALOUS. *adj.* Indecent or offensive and made for the purpose of abusing or prejudicing the opposite party. Unbecoming for the court to hear. Unnecessary allegations bearing cruelly on the moral character of a person.

SCAN TEAM. A Suspected Child Abuse or Neglect team from a pediatric institution. F.A. Jaffe, *A Guide to Pathological Evidence for Lawyers and Police Officers*, 4th ed. (Toronto: Carswell, 1999) at 137.

SCATTERING GROUND. The land within a cemetery that is set aside to be used for the scattering of cremated human remains. *Funeral, Burial and Cremation Services Act, 2002*, S.O. 2002, c. 33, s. 1.

SCATTERING RIGHTS. Includes the right to require or direct the scattering of cremated human remains on the scattering grounds of a cemetery. *Fu-*

S

neral, Burial and Cremation Services Act, 2002, S.O. 2002, c. 33, s. 1.

SCATTERING RIGHTS HOLDER. The person who holds the scattering rights with respect to a scattering ground whether the person be the purchaser of the rights, the person named in the certificate of scattering or such other person to whom the scattering rights have been assigned. *Funeral, Burial and Cremation Services Act, 2002*, S.O. 2002, c. 33, s. 1.

SCC. English neutral citation for the Supreme Court of Canada.

S.C.C. *abbr.* Supreme Court of Canada.

S.C.C.B. *abbr.* Supreme Court of Canada Bulletin of Proceedings, 1970-.

S.C.C. CAM. *abbr.* Canada Supreme Court Cases (Cameron) (published in 1918), 1887-1890.

S.C.C. CAM. (2D). *abbr.* Canada Supreme Court Cases (Cameron) (published in 1925), 1876-1922.

S.C.C. COULT. *abbr.* Canada Supreme Court Cases (Coutlée), 1875-1907.

S.C.C.D. *abbr.* Supreme Court of Canada Decisions, 1978-.

S.C.C.R. *abbr.* Supreme Court of Canada Reports Service, 1971-.

SCHED. *abbr.* Schedule.

SCHEDULE. *n.* 1. An inventory. 2. Additional or appendant writing. 3. Detailed information attached to a statute or regulation.

SCHEDULED-PAYMENTS CREDIT AGREE-MENT. A credit agreement for fixed credit under which the amount advanced is to be repaid in accordance with a specified schedule of payments, which schedule of payments may be subject to adjustment to accommodate contingencies, including changes in the interest rate. *Business Practices and Consumer Protection Act*, S.B.C. 2004, c. 2, s. 81.

SCHEME. *n.* 1. A plan for marketing or regulating any natural product. 2. A plan for distributing property among people with conflicting claims. 3. "... [I]n the commercial sense of that word, that is a plan, design, formula or programme of action devised in order to attain some end, usually unilaterally described or stated ..." *Canadian Allied Property Investment Ltd., Re* (1979), (*sub nom. Gregory v. Canadian Allied Property Investment Ltd.*) 98 D.L.R. (3d) 358 at 364, [1979] 3 W.W.R. 609, 11 B.C.L.R. 253 (C.A.), the court per Carrothers J.A. See DEFERRED SHARING ~; PLANNING ~.

SCHEME OF PYRAMID SELLING. A multi-level marketing plan whereby (a) a participant in the plan gives consideration for the right to receive compensation by reason of the recruitment into the plan of another participant in the plan who gives consideration for the same right; (b) a participant in the plan gives consideration, as a condition of participating in the plan, for a specified amount of the product, other than a specified amount of the product that is bought at the seller's cost price for the purpose only of facilitating sales; (c) a person knowingly supplies the product to a participant in the plan in an amount that is commercially unreasonable; or (d) a participant in the plan who is supplied with the product (i) does not have a buy-back guarantee that is exercisable on reasonable commercial terms or a right to return the product in saleable condition on reasonable commercial terms, or (ii) is not informed of the existence of the guarantee or right and the manner in which it can be exercised. *Competition Act*, R.S.C. 1985, c. C-34, s. 55.1(1).

SCHOLARSHIP AWARD. Any amount, other than a refund of contributions, that is paid or payable directly or indirectly to further the education of a beneficiary designated under an education savings plan. *Securities Act*, R.S.Q., c. V-1.1, *Regulation 81-106 respecting investment fund continuous disclosure*, Que. Reg. 2005, G.O. 2, 1602, s. 1.1.

SCHOLARSHIP PLAN. An arrangement under which contributions to education savings plans are pooled to provide scholarship awards to designated beneficiaries. *Securities Act*, R.S.Q., c. V-1.1, *Regulation 81-106 respecting investment fund continuous disclosure*, Que. Reg. 2005, G.O. 2, 1602, s. 1.1.

SCHOOL. See SEPARATE ~.

SCIENCE. See NATIONAL MUSEUM OF ~ AND TECHNOLOGY; SOCIAL ~ BRIEF.

SCIENS. *adj.* [L.] "... '[K]nowing' ..." *Waldick v. Malcolm* (1991), 8 C.C.L.T. (2d) 1 at 17, 3 O.R. (3d) 471n, 125 N.R. 372, 47 O.A.C. 241, 83 D.L.R. (4th) 114, [1991] 2 S.C.R. 456, the court per Iacobucci J.

SCIENTER. *adv.* [L.] Knowingly.

SCIENTER ACTION. "At common law the principle of scienter governed the owner's liability for damage caused by his animals. For example, if a dog bit a person liability depended upon proof that the owner of the dog knew or ought to have known of the animal's dangerous character.... . The common law also recognized that certain animals were, by their nature, so dangerous to man that the keeper of them could not be heard to say that he did not know of their character. Scienter, in such a case, was to be conclusively presumed. 'Strict liability' was imposed in such cases, with certain defences permitted... ." *Brewer v. Saunders* (1986), 37 C.C.L.T. 237 at 242 (N.S. C.A.), the court per Matthews J.A.

SCIENTIA. *n.* [L.] Knowledge.

SCIENTIFIC METHOD. Scientific method involves the generation of hypotheses and the testing of them to see if they can be falsified or refuted. An hypothesis which is inherently incapable of falsification is also incapable of scientific verification. *R. v. Murrin*, 1999 CarswellBC 3015, 181 D.L.R. (4th) 320, 32 C.R. (5th) 97 (S.C.), Henderson J.

SCIENTI NON FIT INJURIA. [L.] No harm is done to one who knows the risk that's run.

SCILICET. [L.] That is to say.

SCINTILLA JURIS. [L.] A fragment or spark of right.

SCOPE OF EMPLOYMENT. See ACT WITHIN ~.

SCOTT v. AVERY CLAUSE. A clause making arbitration a condition precedent to the bringing of an action. Named after Scott v. Avery (1856), 25 L.J. Exch. 308, 5 H.L.C. 811. *Burns & Roe of Canada Ltd. v. Deuterium of Canada Ltd.*, [1975] 2 S.C.R. 124.

S.C.R. *abbr.* 1. Canada Law Reports, Supreme Court of Canada, 1923-1969 (Rapports judiciaires du Canada, Cour Suprême du Canada). 2. Canada Supreme Court Reports, 1977-1922, 1970-.

SCRATCH. *n.* Injury to the skin's surface caused by a pointed object. F.A. Jaffe, *A Guide to Pathological Evidence for Lawyers and Police Officers*, 4th ed. (Toronto: Carswell, 1999) at 13. See LATE ~.

SCRATCHED. *adj.* In respect of a horse, means a horse that does not start or compete in a race because it is (a) declared a late scratch, (b) determined not to have had a fair start, pursuant to the applicable rules of racing, (c) declared to be a non-contestant, pursuant to the applicable rules of racing, (d) added to the race after betting has begun, in contravention of subsection 52(3), or (e) a horse in relation to which an officer has ordered that betting be closed under subsection 52(4). *Criminal Code*, R.S.C. 1985, c. C-46, *Pari-Mutuel Betting Supervision Regulations*, SOR/ 91-365, s. 2.

S.C.R.R. *abbr.* Securities and Corporate Regulation Review.

S.C.T.D. *abbr.* Supreme Court (provincial) [of Judicature] Trial Division.

SCULPTURE. *n.* 1. An artistic representation or work in three dimensions that is carved, modeled or constructed and includes such a representation that has subsequentially been cast in plaster, metal or other substance that will take on a rigid form. *Cultural Property Export and Import Act*, R.S.C. 1985, c. C-51, *Canadian Cultural Property Export Control List*, C.R.C., c. 448, Group V, s. 1. 2. Includes a cast or model. *Copyright Act*, R.S.C. 1985, c. C-42, s. 2.

SEA. See BEYOND ~S; HIGH ~S; PERILS OF THE ~S; TERRITORIAL ~.

SEA-GOING. *adj.* Implies something more than travel in salt water and that the term implies the ability to travel upon the open sea and actual travel on the sea outside of protected coastal waters. *Courtenay Assessor Area No. 6 v. Quinsam Coal Corp.*, 2002 BCCA 68, 164 B.C.A.C. 67.

SEAL. *v.* 1. "[One seals] ... a contract by placing paper seals opposite the signatures to it ..." *R. v. Crane* (1985), 55 Nfld. & P.E.I.R. 340 at 342, 162 A.P.R. 340 (Nfld. Dist. Ct.), Barry D.C.J. 2. To perform a formal act by placing a waxed impression, gummed wafer or impression by metal stamp. See RE~ING.

SEAL. *n.* 1. A wafer or wax marked with an impression. 2. A gummed wafer or impression made with metal stamp. 3. The portion of a licence that is required to be detached from the licence and cancelled immediately after the wildlife is killed, or a tag that may be supplied with a wildlife licence. *Wildlife Act*, S.S. 1998, c. W-13.12, s. 2. See CORPORATE ~; ELECTRONIC ~; UNDER ~.

SEAMEN. See MERCHANT ~ COMPENSATION BOARD.

SEARCH. *v.* 1. Of title to property, to search in public offices to be sure that the vendor can convey the property free of all competing claims. 2. To look for or seek out evidence.

SEARCH. *n.* 1. The exploration of a place with a view to seizing therein an animate or inanimate thing (1) which may be used as evidence of the commission of an offence; (2) the possession of which constitutes an offence; (3) which was obtained, directly or indirectly, by the commission of an offence. *Code of Penal Procedure*, R.S.Q., c. C-25.1, a. 95. 2. "In determining whether the beeper monitoring ... constitutes a search [within the meaning of Charter, s. 8], the initial question is whether there is a reasonable expectation of privacy in respect of the monitored activity. If the police activity invades a reasonable expectation of privacy, then the activity is a search." *R. v. Wise* (1992), 8 C.R.R. (2d) 53 at 57, 11 C.R. (4th) 253, [1992] 1 S.C.R. 527, 70 C.C.C. (3d) 193, 133 N.R. 161, 51 O.A.C. 351, Cory J. (Lamer C.J.C., Gonthier and Stevenson JJ. concurring). 3. "... [I]mplies an effort to find what is concealed, to get past the shield surrounding privacy, to defeat the efforts of an individual to keep hidden certain elements pertaining to his life or personality... ." *Weatherall v. Canada (Attorney General)* (1990), 78 C.R. (3d) 257 at 265, 58 C.C.C. (3d) 424, 73 D.L.R. (4th) 57, 49 C.R.R. 347, [1991] 1 F.C. 85, 112 N.R. 379, 37 F.T.R. 80n (C.A.), Marceau J.A. (dissenting in part). 4. Examination of original documents, official books and records while investigating a title to land. See BODY CAVITY ~; FRISK ~; INVENTORY ~; NON-INTRUSIVE ~; PAT DOWN ~; REASONABLE ~; STRIP ~; UNREASONABLE ~; WARRANT-LESS ~.

SEARCH OR SEIZURE. 1. "... [I]mply an intrusion into the citizen's home or place of business by a third person who looks for and removes documents or things. Searches and seizures are normally effected under a warrant or writ which is addressed to the officer conducting the search or seizure and permits him to enter the premises for those purposes... ." *Ziegler v. Canada (Director of Investigation & Research, Combines Investigation Branch)* (1983), (*sub nom. Ziegler v. Hunter*) 39 C.P.C. 234 at 259, 8 D.L.R. (4th) 648, [1984] 2 F.C. 608, 51 N.R.1, 8 C.R.R. 47 (C.A.), Hugessen J.A. 2. "... [E]lectronic surveillance constitutes a 'search or seizure' within the meaning of s. 8 of the [Charter] ..." *R. v. Thompson* (1990), 59 C.C.C. (3d) 225 at 267, [1990] 6 W.W.R. 481, 49 B.C.L.R. (2d) 321, 80 C.R. (3d) 129, 73 D.L.R. (4th) 596, 114 N.R. 1, 50 C.R.R. 1, [1990] 2 S.C.R. 1111, Sopinka J. (Dickson C.J.C., Lamer C.J.C. and L'Heureux-Dubé J. concurring).

SEARCH WARRANT. "... [A]n order issued by a Justice under statutory powers, authorizing a named person to enter a specified place to search for and seize specified property which will afford evidence of the actual or intended commission of a crime." *MacIntyre v. Nova Scotia (Attorney General)* (1982), 132 D.L.R. (3d) 385 at 397, [1982] S.C.R. 175, 26 C.R. (3d) 193, 40 N.R. 181, 49 N.S.R. (2d) 609, 96

A.P.R. 609, 65 C.C.C. (2d) 129, Dickson J. (Laskin C.J.C., McIntyre, Chouinard and Lamer JJ. concurring).

SEASON. See CLOSED ~.

SEASONAL DWELLING. A residence not occupied full time.

SEAT BELT. Any strap, webbing, or similar device designed to secure the driver or a passenger in a motor vehicle.

SEA TIME. For the purpose of advancement of naval ratings includes time served in (a) a sea-going ship, (b) a defensively-equipped merchant ship, or (c) any ship employed in harbour, other than a boom defence scow, gate vessel, depot ship or harbour craft, as well as time served in combined operations organizations, but does not include time served on any ship prior to its commissioning. *War Veterans Allowance Act*, R.S.C. 1985, c. W-3, s. 37(8.1).

SEAWAY. *n.* The deep waterway between the port of Montreal and the Great Lakes that is constructed and maintained pursuant to the Agreement between Canada and the United States providing for the development of navigation and power in the Great Lakes-St. Lawrence Basin, dated March 19, 1941, including the locks, canals and facilities between the port of Montreal and Lake Erie and generally known as the St. Lawrence Seaway. *Canada Marine Act*, S.C. 1998, c. 10, s. 2.

SECESSION. *n.* Secession is the effort of a group or section of a state to withdraw itself from the political and constitutional authority of that state, with a view to achieving statehood for a new territorial unit on the international plane. In a federal state, secession typically takes the form of a territorial unit seeking to withdraw from the federation. Secession is a legal act as much as a political one. *Reference re Secession of Quebec*, 1998 CarswellNat 1299, 161 D.L.R. (4th) 385, 228 N.R. 203, 55 C.R.R. (2d) 1, [1998] 2 S.C.R. 217, per curiam.

SECK. *adj.* Barren; dry.

SECONDARY CONFESSION. A statement made to a person in authority that are sufficiently connected to a previous involuntary confession to be deemed also involuntary. *R. v. S.G.T.*, 2010 SCC 20, Charron J.

SECONDARY EVIDENCE. Proof admitted when primary evidence is lost. For example a copy instead of the lost original of a document is secondary evidence.

SECONDARY PICKETING. Picketing of a third party not involved in the dispute giving rise to the picketing.

SECONDARY STRIKE. A strike against one employer with a view to influencing another employer.

SECOND DEGREE MURDER. 1. All murder which is not first degree murder. *Criminal Code*, R.S.C. 1985, c. C-46, s. 231. 2. Murder other than planned or deliberate murder and other than murder of the types specified as first degree murder in s. 231 of the Criminal Code.

SECOND-HAND SMOKE. A mixture of smoke from an ignited tobacco product and smoke exhaled by the smoker. *Smoke-free Places Act*, S.P.E.I. 2002, c. 25 (4th Sess.), s. 1.

SECOND MORTGAGE. A charge or mortgage which ranks after a prior charge or mortgage.

SECOND READING. Parliamentary consideration of the principle of a measure at which time one may consider other methods of reaching its proposed objective. At this stage, the order is made to commit the bill. A. Fraser, W.A. Dawson & J. Holtby, eds., *Beauchesne's Rules and Forms of the House of Commons of Canada*, 6th ed. (Toronto: Carswell, 1989) at 195.

SECRECY. See DELIBERATIVE ~; JURY ~.

SECRET. See FULLY-~ TRUST; TRADE ~.

SECRETARY. *n.* 1. The head of a government department. 2. The officer of an association, club or company. 3. The corporate officer who takes minutes of meetings of directors and shareholders, sends out notices of meetings and is in charge of the minute books and other books of the company. H. Sutherland, D.B. Horsley & J.M. Edmiston, eds., *Fraser's Handbook on Canadian Company Law*, 7th ed. (Toronto: Carswell, 1985) at 253.

SECRETARY OF STATE. 1. A title applied to some members of cabinet or heads of departments. 2. The federal ministry empowered to support multiculturalism and youth and to encourage the use of both official languages.

SECRET BALLOT. See VOTE BY ~.

SECRET COMMISSION. A gift or compensation received by an agent without the knowledge of the principal and for which the agent must account to the principal.

SECRETED. *adj.* Concealed or hidden inside or outside of person's body. *R. v. Monney*, 1999 CarswellOnt 935, 237 N.R. 157, 133 C.C.C. (3d) 129, 171 D.L.R. (4th) 1, 24 C.R. (5th) 97, 119 O.A.C. 272, [1999] 1 S.C.R. 652, 61 C.R.R. (2d) 244.

SECRET PROFIT. A financial advantage, including a bribe, which an agent receives over and above what the agent is entitled to receive from the principal as remuneration. G.H.L. Fridman, *The Law of Agency*, 6th ed. (London: Butterworths, 1990) at 162.

SECRET TRUST. "... [T]he three necessary requirements to establish a secret trust are an intention on the part of the deceased to create a trust, notwithstanding the apparent benefit to a named legatee; communication of the intention to the intended recipient of the property; and acceptance of the trust by the intended recipient of the property." *Riffel Estate, Re* (1987), 28 E.T.R. 1 at 4, 64 Sask. R. 190 (Q.B.), Matheson J.

SECTARIAN. See NON-~

SECTION. *n.* 1. A numbered paragraph in a statute. 2. A division of land equalling one square mile or 640 acres. See CURATIVE ~; DEFINITION ~; INTERPRETATION ~.

SECULAR. *adj.* 1. The dual requirements that education be "secular" and "non-sectarian" refer to keeping the schools free from inculcation or indoctrination in the precepts of any religion and do not prevent persons with religiously based moral positions on matters of public policy from participating in deliberations concerning moral education in public schools. *Chamberlain v. Surrey School District No. 36*, [2002] 4 S.C.R. 710. 2. "Strictly secular" in the School Act can only mean pluralist in the sense that moral positions are to be accorded standing in the public square irrespective of whether the position flows out of a conscience that is religiously informed or not. The meaning of strictly secular is thus pluralist or inclusive in its widest sense. *Chamberlain v. Surrey School District No. 36*, 2000 CarswellBC 2009, 80 B.C.L.R. (3d) 181, [2000] 10 W.W.R. 393, 191 D.L.R. (4th) 128, 143 B.C.A.C. 162, 235 W.A.C. 162, 26 Admin. L.R. (3d) 297 (C.A.), Esson, Mackenzie and Proudfoot JJ.A.

SECULARISM. *n.* What secularism does rule out, however, is any attempt to use the religious views of one part of the community to exclude from consideration the values of other members of the community. A requirement of secularism implies that, although the Board is indeed free to address the religious concerns of parents, it must be sure to do so in a manner that gives equal recognition and respect to other members of the community. Religious views that deny equal recognition and respect to the members of a minority group cannot be used to exclude the concerns of the minority group. *Chamberlain v. Surrey School District No. 36*, [2002] 4 S.C.R. 710.

SECURE. *v.* To assure. To guarantee. See KEY SECURING SYSTEM.

SECURED CREDITOR. A person holding a mortgage, hypothec, pledge, charge, lien or privilege on or against the property of the debtor or any part of that property as security for a debt due or accruing due to that person from the debtor. A person whose claim is based on, or secured by, a negotiable instrument held as collateral security and on which the debtor is only indirectly or secondarily liable. *Bankruptcy and Insolvency Act*, R.S.C. 1985, c. B-3, s. 2 (part).

SECURED PARTY. A person who has a security interest.

SECURED TRANSACTION. A transaction with two main elements: that consideration flows from the creditor and creates a debt and that an interest in the debtor's property secures payment of the debt. F. Bennett, *Receiverships* (Toronto: Carswell, 1985) at 27.

SECURE ELECTRONIC SIGNATURE. 1. An electronic signature that results from the application of a technology or process prescribed by regulations. The Governor in Council may prescribe a technology or process only if the Governor in Council is satisfied that it can be proved that (a) the electronic signature resulting from the use by a person of the technology or process is unique to the person; (b) the use of the technology or process by a person to incorporate, attach or associate the person's electronic signature to an electronic document is under the sole control of the person; (c) the technology or process can be used to identify the person using the technology or process; and (d) the electronic signature can be linked with an electronic document in such a way that it can be used to determine whether the electronic document has been changed since the electronic signature was incorporated in, attached to or associated with the electronic document. *Personal Information Protection and Electronic Documents Act*, S.C. 2000, c. 5, s. 31 and 48. 2. An electronic signature that is applied to a prescribed electronic record (a) by a prescribed person, and (b) in accordance with any prescribed terms, conditions or restrictions. *Evidence Act*, R.S.B.C. 1996, c. 124, s. 41.3.

SECURITIES. *n.* (a) Bonds, debentures and obligations of or guaranteed by governments, corporations or unincorporated bodies, whether such corporations and unincorporated bodies are governmental, municipal, school, ecclesiastical, commercial or other, secured on real or personal property or unsecured, and rights in respect of such bonds, debentures and obligations; (b) shares of capital stock of corporations and rights in respect of such shares; (c) equipment trust certificates or obligations; (d) all documents, instruments and writings commonly known as securities; and (e) mortgages and hypothecs. See CANADIAN ~ INSTITUTE; CLASS OF ~; SECURITY.

SECURITIES ACCOUNT. An account to which a financial asset is or may be credited in accordance with an agreement under which the person maintaining the account undertakes to treat the person for whom the account is maintained as entitled to exercise the rights that constitute the financial asset. *Securities Transfer Acts*.

SECURITIES BROKER. A person who is engaged for all or part of the person's time in the business of buying and selling securities and who, in the transaction concerned, acts for, or buys a security from, or sells a security to, a customer. *Bank Act*, S.C. 1991, c. 46, s. 81.

SECURITIES DEALER. A body corporate that is registered or licensed under the laws of a province to trade in securities, as agent or for its own behalf. *Canadian Payments Act*, R.S.C. 1985, c. C-21, s. 2.

SECURITIES FIRM. A person who carries on the business of buying and selling securities from, to or for a customer, whether or not as a member of an exchange, as principal, or agent or mandatary, and includes any person required to be registered to enter into securities transactions with the public, but does not include a corporate entity that is not a corporation within the meaning of section 2. *Bankruptcy and Insolvency Act*, R.S.C. 1985, c. B-3, s. 253.

SECURITIES INTERMEDIARY. A clearing agency, or (b) a person, including a broker, bank or trust company, who, in the ordinary course of the person's business, maintains securities accounts for others and is acting in that capacity; *Securities Transfer Acts*.

S

SECURITIES LAW. The law relating to the regulation of the issuance and distribution of shares and debt securities by corporations and governments.

SECURITIES LENDING ARRANGEMENT. An arrangement under which (a) a person (in this section referred to as the "lender") transfers or lends at any particular time a qualified security to another person (in this section referred to as the "borrower") with whom the lender deals at arm's length, (b) it may reasonably be expected, at the particular time, that the borrower will transfer or return after the particular time to the lender a security (in this section referred to as an "identical security") that is identical to the security so transferred or lent, (c) where the qualified security is a share of the capital stock of a corporation, the borrower is obligated to pay to the lender amounts equal to and as compensation for all dividends, if any, paid on the security that would have been received by the borrower if the borrower had held the security throughout the period beginning after the particular time and ending at the time an identical security is transferred or returned to the lender, and (d) the lender's risk of loss or opportunity for gain or profit with respect to the security is not changed in any material respect, but does not include an arrangement one of the main purposes of which may reasonably be considered to be avoid or defer the inclusion in income of any gain or profit with respect to the security. *Income Tax Act*, R.S.C. 1985, c. 1 (5th Supp.), s. 260.

SECURITIES REGISTER. A record of securities which a company issues.

SECURITIES REGULATION REGIME. See CANADIAN ~ TRANSITION OFFICE.

SECURITIES REGULATORY AUTHORITY. (a) An extra-provincial securities commission referred to in subsection (3) and includes any member, officer, employee, appointee or agent of that commission, (b) any person referred to in paragraph (3)(b), or (c) any exchange, self-regulatory organization or quotation and trade reporting system referred to in paragraph (3)(c). *Securities Act*, S.N.B. 2004, c. S-5.5, s. 195.6.

SECURITIES UNDERWRITER. A person who, as principal, agrees to purchase securities with a view to the distribution of the securities or who, as agent for a body corporate or other person, offers for sale or sells securities in connection with a distribution of the securities, and includes a person who participates, directly or indirectly, in a distribution of securities, other than a person whose interest in the distribution of securities is limited to receiving a distributor's or seller's commission payable by a securities underwriter. *Bank Act*, S.C. 1991, c. 46, s. 2.

SECURITIZATION. *n.* A financing mechanism that provides lower cost access to the financial marketplace for corporations seeking to raise capital. In essence, it involves the transformation of a corporation's income-producing assets into negotiable securities that are issued to the public. *Metropolitan Toronto Police Widows & Orphans Fund v. Telus Communications Inc.* (2005), 75 O.R. (3d) 784 (C.A.).

SECURITY. *n.* 1. A thing which makes the enforcement or enjoyment of a right more certain or secure. 2. "Security for a debt, in the ordinary meaning of the term, carries with it the idea of something or somebody to which, or to whom, the creditor can resort in order to aid him in realizing or recovering the debt, in case the debtor fails to pay; the word implies something in addition to the mere obligation of the debtor... ." *Child & Gower Piano Co. v. Gambrel*, [1933] 2 W.W.R. 273 at 281 (Sask. C.A.), Martin J.A. (MacKenzie J.A. concurring). 3. An obligation of an issuer or a share, participation or other interest in an issuer or in property or an enterprise of an issuer (a) that is represented by a security certificate in bearer form or registered form, or the transfer of which may be registered on books maintained for that purpose by or on behalf of the issuer, (b) that is one of a class or series, or by its terms is divisible into a class or series, of shares, participations, interests or obligations, and (c) that (i) is, or is of a type, dealt in or traded on securities exchanges or securities markets, or (ii) is a medium for investment and by its terms expressly provides that it is a security for the purposes of this Act. *Securities Transfer acts.* 4. Something which is given to ensure the repayment of a loan. See CAPITAL ~; CERTIFICATED ~; COLLATERAL ~; CONVERTIBLE ~; DANGER TO THE ~ OF CANADA; DEBT ~; EQUITY ~; FINANCIAL ~; MUTUAL FUND ~; PORTFOLIO ~; REDEEMABLE ~; SECURITIES; TRANSPORTATION ~; UNION ~; VALID ~; VOTING ~.

SECURITY AGREEMENT. 1. An agreement that creates or provides for a security interest, and, if the context permits, includes (i) an agreement that creates or provides for a prior security interest, and (ii) a writing that evidences a security agreement. *Personal Property Securities acts.* 2. An agreement that creates or provides for a security interest.

SECURITY ALARM. Any assembly of electronic equipment and devices intended to protect property, other than motor vehicles, from vandalism, intrusion, trespass or theft, and includes (a) any system of security alarms and the interconnecting parts of the system, and (b) any prescribed electronic equipment or electronic device or system. *Security Services Act*, S.B.C. 2007, c. 30, s. 1.

SECURITY ALARM SERVICE. A person who (a) sells, supplies, provides advice on, services or installs a security alarm or offers to do any of these things, unless the person does so without attending at the premises where the security alarm has been or will be installed, or (b) repairs, maintains, monitors or responds to security alarms installed on the property of another person. *Security Services Act*, S.B.C. 2007, c. 30, s. 1.

SECURITY ASSESSMENT. An appraisal of the loyalty to Canada, and so far as it relates thereto, the reliability of an individual. *Canadian Security Intelligence Service Act*, R.S.C. 1985, c. C-23, s. 2.

SECURITY DEPOSIT. Any money, property or right paid or given by a tenant of residential premises to a landlord or to anyone on the landlord's behalf to be held by or for the landlord as security for the performance of an obligation or the payment of a liability by the tenant or to be returned to the tenant on the happening of a condition. *Residential Tenancies Act*, S.A. 2004, c. R-17.1, s. 1.

SECURITY ENTITLEMENT. The rights and property interest of an entitlement holder with respect to a financial asset that are specified in the Act. *Securities Transfer acts*.

SECURITY ESTABLISHMENT. See COMMUNICATIONS ~.

SECURITY FOR COSTS. Security which a plaintiff may be required to provide in a proceeding to ensure that the plaintiff will be able to pay any costs which may be awarded to the defendant.

SECURITY GUARD. A person who, for hire or reward, guards or patrols for the purpose of protecting persons or property. *The Private Investigators and Security Guards Act, 1997*, S.S. 1997, c. P-26.01, s. 2.

SECURITY INTELLIGENCE. See CANADIAN ~ SERVICE.

SECURITY INTELLIGENCE REVIEW COMMITTEE. The Security Intelligence Review Committee (SIRC) is an independent review body that monitors the activities of the Canadian Security Intelligence Service (CSIS). Established in 1984 under the Canadian Security Intelligence Service Act, S.C. 1984, c. 21 (now R.S.C. 1985, c. C-23), [. . .] Empowered to develop its own investigative procedures, SIRC established a formal adversarial process, with "a court-like hearing room" and "procedures that mirrored judicial proceedings as much as possible". The process also included an independent panel of lawyers with security clearances to act as counsel to SIRC ... . *Charkaoui v. Canada (Citizenship and Immigration)*, 2007 SCC 9.

SECURITY INTEREST. 1. An interest in collateral that secures payment or performance of an obligation. 2. An interest in or charge upon the property of a body corporate by way of mortgage, hypothec, pledge or otherwise, to secure payment of a debt or performance of any other obligation of the body corporate. 3. A right to or an interest in a deposit in a financial institution that secures payment or performance of an obligation to the financial institution. See LIVESTOCK ~; PERFECTED ~; PURCHASE-MONEY ~.

SECURITY OF TENURE. 1. A tenant's right to remain in leased premises unless the tenancy is terminated by the landlord for a cause specified in the governing legislation. 2. An ingredient of judicial independence. Fixed tenure secure against interference by the executive or appointing authority in a discretionary or arbitrary manner. Removal from office may be for cause only and after an independent review is completed at which the judge has an opportunity to be heard.

SECURITY OF THE PERSON. 1. "... [T]he right to 'security of the person' under s. 7 of the Charter protects both the physical and psychological integrity of the individual ..." *R. v. Morgentaler* (1988), 31 C.R.R. 1 at 87, 82 N.R. 1, [1988] 1 S.C.R. 30, 63 O.R. (2d) 281n, 63 C.R. (3d) 1, 26 O.A.C. 1, 44 D.L.R. (4th) 385, 37 C.C.C. (3d) 449, Wilson J. 2. "... The case law leads me to the conclusion that state interference with bodily integrity and serious state-imposed psychological stress at least in the Criminal law context constitute a breach of security of the person." *R. v. Morgentaler* (1988), 31 C.R.R. 1 at 20, 82 N.R. 1, [1988] 1 S.C.R. 30, 63 O.R. (2d) 281n, 63 C.R. (3d) 1, 26 O.A.C. 1, 44 D.L.R. (4th) 385, 37 C.C.C. (3d) 449, Dickson C.J.C. (Lamer J. concurring). 3. Right to bodily integrity and personal autonomy are included in this interest protected by the Charter.

SECURITY REQUIREMENT. A requirement for persons engaged in importing, offering for transport, handling or transporting dangerous goods established under regulations made under section 27.1. *Transportation of Dangerous Goods Act, 1992*, S.C. 1992, c. 34, s. 2.

SEDITION. *n.* Advocating a change of government through the use of force. See SEDITIOUS CONSPIRACY; SEDITIOUS INTENTION; SEDITIOUS WORDS.

SEDITIOUS CONSPIRACY. An agreement between two or more persons to carry out a seditious intention. *Criminal Code*, R.S.C. 1985, c. C-46, s. 59(3).

SEDITIOUS INTENTION. Everyone who teaches or advocates, or publishes or circulates any writing that advocates the use, without authority of law, of force as a means of accomplishing a governmental change within Canada is presumed to have a seditious intention. *Criminal Code*, R.S.C. 1985, c. C-46, s. 59(4) in part.

SEDITIOUS LIBEL. A libel that expresses a seditious intention. *Criminal Code*, R.S.C. 1985, c. C-46, s. 59(2).

SEDITIOUS WORDS. Words that express a seditious intention. *Criminal Code*, R.S.C. 1985, c. C-46, s. 59(1).

SEDONA CANADA. The mission of Working Group 7 (of the Sedona Conference) - Sedona Canada - is to create forward-looking principles and best practice recommendations for lawyers, courts, businesses, and others who regularly confront e-discovery issues in Canada. The Sedona Canada Principles was released in early 2008 (in both English and French) and was immediately recognized by federal and provincial courts as an authoritative source of guidance for Canadian practitioners. It was explicitly referenced in the Ontario court rules and practice directives that went into effect in January 2010. Working Group 7 provides materials and speakers for Sedona Conference Institute program and bar association conferences across the country. *Working Group Series*, online: The Sedona Group, <http://www.thesedonaconference.org/wgs>.

SEDONA CANADA PRINCIPLES. The Sedona Canada principles recognize that when considering disclosure requests and standards for disclosure the

S

courts must balance a number of factors. The courts apply the principle of proportionality to ensure that the costs of discovery do not unduly interfere with a just, speedy and inexpensive resolution of a dispute. *Borst v. Zilli*, 2009 CanLII 55302 (Ont. S.C.).

SEDONA CONFERENCE. The Sedona Conference®, a legal think tank. *The Sedona Conference*, online: < http://www.thesedonaconference.org/>.

SEDUCTION. *n.* Inducing a person to have unlawful intercourse.

SEEN TO BE DONE. See JUSTICE SHOULD NOT ONLY BE DONE BUT SHOULD MANIFESTLY AND UNDOUBTEDLY BE ~.

SEGREGATION. *n.* 1. The act of setting apart, isolating, or secluding a person or body of persons from the general body of persons. 2. [S]egregation, whether administrative as in Cardinal or punitive as in this appeal, is a form of incarceration more restrictive than the incarceration experienced by the general prison population. It results in a deprivation of that residual liberty interest possessed by prisoners within our penitentiaries. This deprivation represents a further confinement of the appellant in a prison within a prison. *Winters v. Legal Services Society (British Columbia)*, 1999 CarswellBC 1969, [1999] 9 W.W.R. 327, 137 C.C.C. (3d) 371, 244 N.R. 203, 177 D.L.R. (4th) 94, 27 C.R. (5th) 1, 66 C.R.R. (2d) 241, 128 B.C.A.C. 161, 208 W.A.C. 161, [1999] 3 S.C.R. 160, 73 B.C.L.R. (3d) 193, Cory J. (dissenting).

SEIGN. QUESTIONS. *abbr.* Lower Canada Reports, Seignorial Questions, vols. A & B (Décisions des Tribunaux du Bas-Canada).

SEIGN. REP. *abbr.* Seignorial Reports (Québec).

SEISED. *adj.* 1. Is applicable to any vested estate for life or of a greater description, and shall extend to estates at law and in equity, in possession or in futurity, in land. *Trustee acts.* 2. Taken in execution of a judgment or order or under statutory authority.

SEISIN. *n.* A freeholder's holding of land. R. Megarry & H.W.R. Wade, *The Law of Real Property*, 5th ed. (London: Stevens, 1984) at cxxvii. See UNITY OF ~.

SEIZED. *adj.* 1. Is applicable to any vested interest for life, or of a greater description, and extends to estates, legal and equitable, in possession, or in futurity, in any land. *Trustee acts.* 2. Taken in execution of a judgment or order or under statutory authority. See SEISED.

SEIZURE. *n.* 1. "... [T]he essence of seizure under s. 8 [of the Charter] is the taking of a thing from a person by a public authority without that person's consent... . If I were to draw the line between a seizure and a mere finding of evidence, I would draw it logically and purposefully at the point at which it can reasonably be said that the individual had ceased to have a privacy interest in the subject-matter allegedly seized." *R. v. Dyment* (1988), 38 C.R.R. 301 at 312, 316, 10 M.V.R. (2d) 1, 66 C.R. (3d) 348, 89 N.R. 249, [1988] 2 S.C.R. 417, 45 C.C.C. (3d) 244, 73 Nfld. & P.E.I.R. 13, 229 A.P.R. 13, 55 D.L.R. (4th)

503, La Forest J. (Dickson C.J.C. concurring). 2. A species of execution in which a sheriff executes a writ of fi. fa. by taking possession of the chattels of the debtor. 3. What takes place when goods are confiscated as a punishment for smuggling. See SEARCH OR ~.

SEIZURE AND SALE. See WRIT OF ~.

SELECT COMMITTEE. A committee of Parliament or a legislature set up to investigate a particular matter.

SELECTION PATENT. [A] selection patent is one whose subject matter (compounds) is a fraction of a larger known class of compounds which was the subject matter of a prior originating patent. A selection patent that claims a compound that is patentably distinct from the genus patent will not be invalid for obviousness double patenting. *Sanofi-Synthelabo Canada Inc. v. Apotex Inc.*, 2008 SCC 61.

SELF-CRIMINATION. See SELF-INCRIMINATION.

SELF-DEFENCE. *n.* 1. Defence of one's person or property directly against another exerting unlawful force. D. Stuart, *Canadian Criminal Law: A Treatise*, 2d ed. (Toronto: Carswell, 1987) at 405. 2. [I]s a justification based on the necessity of self-preservation. *R. v. Pilon*, 2009 ONCA 248, Doherty J.A. (Simmons and Gillese JJ.A. concurring). 3. " ... [A] man who is attacked may defend himself. It is both good law and good sense that he may do, but only do, what is reasonably necessary..." *Palmer v. R.*, [1971] 1 All E.R. 1077 at 1088, [1971] A.C. 814, 55 Cr. App. R. 223 (Jamaica P.C.), the board per Lord Morris of Borth-Y-Gest. 4. The basic version of the defence of self-defence is set out in the Criminal Code: every one who is unlawfully assaulted without having provoked the assault is justified in repelling force by force if the force he uses is not intended to cause death or grievous bodily harm and is no more than is necessary to enable him to defend himself. *Criminal Code*, R.S.C. 1985, c. C-46, s. 34(1). Other variations of the defence exist where there is an apprehension of death or grievous bodily harm or where the aggressor is himself attacked. 5. A justification for otherwise criminal conduct. *R. v. Teskey*, 2008 BCCA 288, Smith J.A. (Newbury, Levine JJ.A. concurring).

SELF-DETERMINATION. A right to external self-determination (which in this case potentially takes the form of the assertion of a right to unilateral secession) arises in only the most extreme of cases and, even then, under carefully defined circumstances. External self-determination can be defined as in the following statement from the Declaration on Friendly Relations, supra [Declaration on Principles of International Law Concerning Friendly Relations and Co-operation Among States in Accordance with the Charter of the United Nations, GA Res. 2625 (XXV), 24 October 1970], as the establishment of a sovereign and independent State, the free association or integration with an independent State or the emergence into any other political status freely determined by a people constitute modes of implementing the right of self-determination by that people. The recognized sources of international law establish that the right to self-determination of a people is normally fulfilled through internal self-determination—a people's pursuit of its political, economic, social and cultural development within the framework of an existing state. *Reference re Secession of Quebec*, 1998 CarswellNat 1299, 161 D.L.R. (4th) 385, 228 N.R. 203, 55 C.R.R. (2d) 1, [1998] 2 S.C.R. 217, per curiam. See EXTERNAL ~; INTERNAL ~.

SELF-EMPLOYED PERSON. A person who is engaged in an occupation on his or her own behalf.

SELF-GOVERNING. *adj.* Refers to a profession which has been given authority by the legislature to govern itself and to regulate membership in and the conduct of members of the profession.

SELF-GOVERNMENT AGREEMENT. An agreement concluded by a first nation with Her Majesty the Queen in right of Canada and the Yukon Government respecting government by and for the first nation. *Yukon First Nations Self-Government Act*, S.C. 1994, c. 35, s. 2.

SELF-HELP. *n.* An action in which an injured party seeks redress without resorting to a court.

SELF-INCRIMINATION. *n.* 1. Behaviour indicating one's guilt. 2. The principle against self-incrimination was described by Lamer as "a general organizing principle of criminal law". The principle is that an accused is not required to respond to an allegation of wrongdoing made by the state until the state has succeeded in making out a prima facie case against him or her. It is a basic tenet of our system of justice that the Crown must establish a "case to meet" before there can be any expectation that the accused should respond. The jurisprudence of this Court is clear that the principle against self-incrimination is an overarching principle within our criminal justice system, from which a number of specific common law and Charter rules emanate, such as the confessions rule, and the right to silence, among many others. The principle can also be the source of new rules in appropriate circumstances. *R. v. White*, 1999 CarswellBC 1224, 63 C.R.R. (2d) 1, 240 N.R. 1, 24 C.R. (5th) 201, 135 C.C.C. (3d) 257, 174 D.L.R. (4th) 111, 42 M.V.R. (3d) 161, 123 B.C.A.C. 161, 201 W.A.C. 161, [1999] 2 S.C.R. 417, [1999] 2 S.C.R. 417, Iacobucci J. See PRINCIPLE AGAINST ~; PRIVILEGE AGAINST ~.

SELF-INDUCED INTOXICATION. It is not a defence to an offence, which includes assault or interference or threat of interference with the bodily integrity of another, that the accused, by reason of self-induced intoxication, lacked the general intent or the voluntariness required to commit the offence, where the accused departed markedly from the standard of care as described in subsection (2) (being unaware or incapable of consciously controlling certain behaviours). *Criminal Code*, R.S.C. 1985, c. C-46, s. 33.1.

SELF-INFLICTED. *adj.* Self-caused or self-imposed. *Booth v. British Columbia Life & Casualty Co.*, 2004 BCCA 133.

SELF-NEGLECT. *n.* Any failure of an adult to take care of himself or herself that causes, or is reasonably likely to cause within a short period of time, serious physical or mental harm or substantial damage to or loss of assets, and includes (a) living in grossly unsanitary conditions, (b) suffering from an untreated illness, disease or injury, (c) suffering from malnutrition to such an extent that, without intervention, the adult's physical or mental health is likely to be severely impaired, (d) creating a hazardous situation that will likely cause serious physical harm to the adult or others or cause substantial damage to or loss of assets, and (e) suffering from an illness, disease or injury that results in the adult dealing with his or her assets in a manner that is likely to cause substantial damage to or loss of the assets. *Adult Guardianship Act*, R.S.B.C. 1996, c. 6, s. 1.

SELF-REGULATING BODY. Organization recognized by a government body as one which regulates its own members. The professions are governed by self-regulating bodies.

SELF-SERVING STATEMENT. An exculpatory statement.

SELL. *v.* 1. Includes (a) to agree to sell, to offer, keep, expose, transmit, send, convey or deliver for sale; (b) to exchange or agree to exchange; and (c) to dispose of, or agree to dispose of, to any person in any manner for a consideration. 2. Includes offer for sale, expose for sale, have in possession for sale and distribute, whether or not the distribution is made for consideration. See AGREEMENT TO ~; DIRECT ~ING.

SELLING OFFICE. Every one who purports to sell or agrees to sell an appointment to or a resignation from an office, or a consent to any such appointment or resignation, or receives or agrees to receive a reward or profit from the purported sale thereof, is guilty of an indictable offence. *Criminal Code*, R.S.C. 1985, c. C-46, s. 124.

SELLING SHORT. Selling a stock position one does not own, in the expectation that by the time one is required to deliver the shares to the buyer the share price will have come down. See SHORT SELLING.

SEMBLE. *v.* [Fr. appears] A word used to introduce a legal proposition which one does not intend to state definitely.

SEMI-AUTHENTIC ACT. An act purporting to be issued by a competent foreign public officer makes proof of its content against all persons and neither the quality nor the signature of the officer need be proved. Similarly, a copy of a document in the custody of the foreign public officer makes proof of its conformity to the original against all persons, and replaces the original if it purports to be issued by the officer. *Civil Code*, S.Q. 1991, c. 64, a. 2822. See AUTHENTIC ACT.

SENATE. *n.* The second federal legislative body whose members are appointed by the Governor General, which means, in fact, by the cabinet. The upper house of the legislature. Appointments are made to represent the regions and the diversity of Canada. Referred to as the chamber of sober second thought. In order to become law a bill must pass through the senate as well as the House of Commons.

SENATE NOMINEE. A person declared elected under this Act. The Government of Alberta shall submit the names of the Senate nominees to the Queen's Privy Council for Canada as persons who may be summoned to the Senate of Canada for the purpose of filling vacancies relating to Alberta. A person remains as a Senate nominee until (a) the person is appointed to the Senate of Canada, (b) the person resigns as a Senate nominee by submitting a resignation in writing to the Minister determined under section 16 of the Government Organization Act as the Minister responsible for this Act, (c) the person's term as a Senate nominee expires, (d) the person takes an oath or makes a declaration or acknowledgment of allegiance, obedience, or adherence to a foreign power, or does an act whereby the person becomes a subject or citizen, or entitled to the rights or privileges of a subject or citizen, of a foreign power, (e) the person is adjudged bankrupt or insolvent, or applies for the benefit of any law relating to insolvent debtors, or becomes a public defaulter, (f) the person is convicted of treason or convicted of a felony or of any infamous crime, or (g) the person ceases to be eligible to be nominated as a candidate under section 8, whichever occurs first. *Senatorial Selection Act*, R.S.A. 2000, c. S-5, s. 1 and 3.

SENATOR. *n.* A person who is a member of a senate.

SENIOR OFFICERS. Officers at the management level. *Canada Labour Code*, R.S.C. 1985, c. L-2, *Maritime Occupational Health and Safety Regulations*, SOR/2010-120, s. 28.

SENSITIVE INFORMATION. Information relating to international relations or national defence or national security that is in the possession of the Government of Canada, whether originating from inside or outside Canada, and is of a type that the Government of Canada is taking measures to safeguard. *Canada Evidence Act*, R.S.C. 1985, c. C-5, s. 38.

SENSORY DISABILITY. A disability that relates to sight or hearing. *Access to Information Act*, R.S.C. 1985, c. A-1, s. 3.

SENTENCE. *n.* "... [U]sed in reference to the determination or pronouncement of punishment or like action following a finding of guilt; ... utilized to define the fate or punishment of a person who has been adjudged guilty, ..." *Morris v. R.* (1979), 91 D.L.R. (3d) 161 at 177, [1979] 1 S.C.R. 405, 23 N.R. 109, 6 C.R. (3d) 36, 43 C.C.C. (2d) 129, Pratte J. (Martland, Ritchie, Pigeon and Beetz JJ. concurring). See ADULT ~; CONCURRENT ~; CONDITIONAL ~; CONSECUTIVE ~S; DETERMINATE ~; GUIDELINE ~; INDETERMINATE ~; INTERMITTENT ~; PRE-~ REPORT; STARTING-POINT ~; SUSPENDED ~; THRESHOLD ~; YOUTH ~.

SENTENCING. *n.* The fundamental purpose of sentencing is to contribute, along with crime prevention initiatives, to respect for the law and the maintenance of a just, peaceful and safe society by imposing just sanctions that have one or more of the following objectives: (a) to denounce unlawful conduct; (b) to deter the offender and other persons from committing offences; (c) to separate offenders from society, where necessary; (d) to assist in rehabilitating offenders; (e) to provide reparations for harm done to victims or to the community; and (f) to promote a sense of responsibility in offenders, and acknowledgment of the harm done to victims and to the community. *Criminal Code*, R.S.C. 1985, c. C-46, s. 718. Proportionality is another principle of sentencing which must be applied by the Court. In addition the following principles are applied in sentencing: (a) a sentence should be increased or reduced to account for any relevant aggravating or mitigating circumstances relating to the offence or the offender, and, without limiting the generality of the foregoing, (i) evidence that the offence was motivated by bias, prejudice or hate based on race, national or ethnic origin, language, colour, religion, sex, age, mental or physical disability, sexual orientation, or any other similar factor, (ii) evidence that the offender, in committing the offence, abused the offender's spouse or common-law partner or child, (ii.1) evidence that the offender, in committing the offence, abused a person under the age of eighteen years, (iii) evidence that the offender, in committing the offence, abused a position of trust or authority in relation to the victim, or (iv) evidence that the offence was committed for the benefit of, at the direction of or in association with a criminal organization, or (v) evidence that the offence was a terrorism offence shall be deemed to be aggravating circumstances; (b) a sentence should be similar to sentences imposed on similar offenders for similar offences committed in similar circumstances; (c) where consecutive sentences are imposed, the combined sentence should not be unduly long or harsh; (d) an offender should not be deprived of liberty, if less restrictive sanctions may be appropriate in the circumstances; and (e) all available sanctions other than imprisonment that are reasonable in the circumstances should be considered for all offenders, with particular attention to the circumstances of aboriginal offenders. *Criminal Code*, R.S.C. 1985, c. C-46, s. 718. See GENERAL DETERRENCE; PRINCIPLES OF ~; PROPORTIONALITY; RETRIBUTION; SPECIFIC DETERRENCE; TOTALITY PRINCIPLE.

SENTENCING CIRCLE. An alternative to sentencing by a judge used in aboriginal communities. A sentencing circle is more than a fact-finding exercise with an aboriginal twist. While it assists the judge in fashioning a fit sentence, it is conducted at a quintessentially human level and represents a stock-taking or accountability exercise on the part of the offender and the community that produced the offender. Healing is at the centre of the circle's restorative approach. The validity of the circle here was saved by the attitude, conduct and thinking of the circle participants. *R. v. Taylor*, 1997 CarswellSask 720, 122 C.C.C. (3d) 376, 163 Sask. R. 29, 165 W.A.C. 29, 15 C.R. (5th) 48, [1998] 7 W.W.R. 704, (*sub nom.* R. v. W.B.T.) [1998] 2 C.N.L.R. 140. The judge, the accused, and representatives of the community must participate.

SENTENCING HEARING. Follows a finding of guilt and forms part of the trial procedure.

SENTENCING PURPOSE. The fundamental purpose of sentencing is to contribute, along with crime prevention initiatives, to respect for the law and the maintenance of a just, peaceful and safe society by imposing just sanctions that have one or more of the following objectives: (a) to denounce unlawful conduct; (b) to deter the offender and other persons from committing offences; (c) to separate offenders from society, where necessary; (d) to assist in rehabilitating offenders; (e) to provide reparations for harm done to victims or to the community; and (f) to promote a sense of responsibility in offenders, and acknowledgment of the harm done to victims and to the community. *Criminal Code*, R.S.C. 1985, c. C-46, s. 718.

SEPARATE AND APART. These words are interpreted as disjunctive. There must be a withdrawal from the matrimonial obligation with the intent of destroying the matrimonial consortium as well as physical separation.

SEPARATE SCHOOL. Provides a program of education which has a denominational nature by way of formal religious education or by promotion and preservation of Roman Catholic beliefs and values by other means.

SEPARATION. *n.* 1. The decision by spouses to live apart. 2. The termination of employment.

SEPARATION AGREEMENT. 1. An agreement in writing between spouses who are living or intend to live separate and apart. 2. Two persons who cohabited and are living separate and apart may enter into an agreement in which they agree on their respective rights and obligations, including, (a) ownership in or division of property; (b) support obligations; (c) the right to direct the education and moral training of their children; (d) the right to custody of and access to their children; and (e) any other matter in the settlement of their affairs. *Family Law Act*, R.S.O. 1990, c. F.3, s. 54. 3. Includes an agreement by which a person agrees to make payments on a periodic basis for the maintenance of a former spouse or common-law partner, children of the marriage or common-law partnership or both the former spouse or common-law partner and children of the marriage or common-law partnership, after the marriage or common-law partnership has been dissolved, whether the agreement was made before or after the marriage or common-law partnership was dissolved. *Income Tax Act*, R.S.C. 1985, c. 1 (5th Supp.), s. 248. See CONVENTIONAL ~ AS TO PROPERTY.

SEPARATION AS TO PROPERTY JUDICIALLY OBTAINED. Either spouse may obtain separation as to property when the application of the rules of the matrimonial regime appears to be contrary to the interests of that spouse or of the family. Separation as to property judicially obtained entails dissolution of the matrimonial regime and puts the spouses in the situation of those who are conventionally separate as to property. Between spouses, the effects of the separation are retroactive to the day of the application unless the court makes them retroactive to the date on which the spouses ceased to live together. *Civil Code*, S.Q. 1991, c. 64, a. 488 and 489.

SEPARATION FROM BED AND BOARD. Is granted when the will to live together is gravely undermined. *Civil Code*, S.Q. 1991, c. 64, a. 493.

SEPARATION OF POWERS. A defining feature of the Canadian Constitution. Refers to the separation of the powers of the executive, legislative and judicial branches of government. The judiciary interprets and applies the law. The legislature decides upon and enunciates policy. The executive administers and implements policy.

SEPTICEMIA. *n.* Blood poisoning. F.A. Jaffe, *A Guide to Pathological Evidence for Lawyers and Police Officers*, 4th ed. (Toronto: Carswell, 1999) at 54. See WATERHOUSE-FRIDERICHSEN SYNDROME.

SEPULTURE. *n.* A lot, plot, compartment or other space in a cemetery, columbarium, mausoleum or any other place used for the same purposes. *An Act respecting Prearranged funeral services and sepultures*, R.S.Q. c. A-23.001, s. 2.

SEQUENCE. See AMINO ACID ~.

SEQUESTER. *v.* 1. To place the members of a jury in a private room for their deliberations so that they have no contact with members of the public generally. 2. To prevent the owners from using by setting aside.

SEQUESTRATION. *n.* 1. Property is temporarily placed by some judicial or quasi-judicial process in the hands of persons called sequestrators, who manage it and receive the rents and profits. 2. The deposit by which persons place property over which they are in dispute in the hands of another person chosen by them, who binds himself to restore it, once the issue is decided, to the person who will then be entitled to it. *Civil Code*, S.Q. 1991, c. 64, a. 2305. See WRIT OF ~.

SERIATIM. *adv.* [L.] Separately and in order.

SERIES. *n.* 1. In relation to shares, means a division of a class of shares. 2. A numerical, spatial, or temporal sequence of things which are logically or factually related.

SERIOUS BODILY HARM. "... [F]or the purposes of the section [s. 264.1 of the Criminal Code, R.S.C. 1985, c. C-46] is any hurt or injury, whether physical or psychological, that interferes in a substantial way with the physical or psychological integrity, health or well-being of the complainant." *R. v. McCraw* (1991), 66 C.C.C. (3d) 517 at 523, 7 C.R. (4th) 314, 128 N.R. 299, 49 O.A.C. 47, [1991] 3 S.C.R. 72, the court per Cory J.

SERIOUS PERSONAL INJURY OFFENCE. (a) An indictable offence, other than high treason, treason, first degree murder or second degree murder, involving (i) the use or attempted use of violence against another person; or (ii) conduct endangering or likely to endanger the life or safety of another person or inflicting or likely to inflict severe psychological damage on another person, and for which the offender may be sentenced to imprisonment for 10 years or more; or (b) an offence or attempt to commit an offence mentioned in section 271 (sexual assault), 272 (sexual assault with a weapon, threats to a third party or causing bodily harm) or 273 (aggravated sexual assault). *Criminal Code*, R.S.C. 1985, c. C-46, s. 752.

SERIOUS QUESTION. In the context of the granting of an interlocutory injunction, Nadon, J. accepted the following definition: 'Serious question' has been considered synonymous with 'chance of success', not 'frivolous or vexatious': 'real prospect of succeeding', and 'probability that plaintiff is entitled to relief'. Without attempting to precisely and conclusively redefine the phrase 'serious question', we can say that it implies a burden of proof of less than the balance of probability, less than fifty-one per cent ... but more than a 'speculative' risk or a 'mere possibility' from Patricia Carlson, "Granting An Interlocutory Injunction: What is the Test?" (1982) 12 Man. L.J. 109, at 116. *Quebec Trotting & Pacing Assn. v. Canada (Department of Agriculture)*, 1993 CarswellNat 840, 24 Admin. L.R. (2d) 268, 76 F.T.R. 81 (T.D.), Nadon J.

SERIOUS VIOLENT OFFENCE. 1. An offence in the commission of which a young person causes or attempts to cause serious bodily harm. *Youth Criminal Justice Act*, S.C. 2002, c. 1, s. 2. 2. [T]he determination that an offence was a serious violent offence [pursuant to s. 2(1) of Youth Criminal Justice Act, S.C. 2002, c. 1] must be made if facts properly proven or agreed to convince the youth justice court judge beyond a reasonable doubt that, in the commission of the offence, the young person caused physical or psychological injury or hurt and such injury or hurt interfered in a substantial way with the physical or psychological integrity, health or well-being of a victim; or, in the commission of the offence, the young person attempted to cause physical or psychological injury or hurt that, if caused, would reasonably be expected to have interfered in a substantial way with the physical or psychological integrity, health or well-being of a victim. *R. v. B. (K.G.)*, 2005 NBCA 96. 3. The loss of an eye and serious facial injuries obviously meet the definition [in section 2 of the Young Offenders Act [R.S.C. 1985, c. Y-1]. *R. v. G. (D.)*, 2005 BCCA 417.

SERVANT. *n.* 1. "... [A] person subject to the command of his master as to the manner in which he shall do his work ..." *Tully v. Genbey*, [1939] 1 D.L.R. 559 at 565, [1939] 1 W.W.R. 161, 46 Man. R. 439 (C.A.), Trueman J.A. 2. "... '[E]mployee' ..." *Atherton v. Boycott* (1989), 36 C.P.C. (2d) 250 at 255 (Ont. H.C.), Cusinato L.J.S.C. 3. Includes agent, but does not include any person appointed or employed by or under the authority of an ordinance of the Northwest Territories or a law of the Legislature of Yukon or of the Legislature for Nunavut. *Crown Liability and Proceedings Act*, R.S.C. 1985, c. C-50, s. 2. See CIVIL ~; MASTER AND ~; PUBLIC ~.

SERVE. *v.* Of a copy of a legal document, to deliver it to parties interested in a legal proceeding so that they know about the proceeding.

SERVED. *adj.* 1. Served personally. 2. Served personally on a person or on an adult residing at the residence of the person who is at the residence at the time of service, or sent by registered mail to the person at his or her latest known address.

SERVICE. *n.* 1. Service as a member of the armed forces. 2. With respect to a document, the act of serving it. 3. "... [D]oes not necessarily means 'personal service' ... means bringing it to the attention of the person to be served." *Canada Trust Co. v. Kakar Properties Ltd.* (1983), 32 C.P.C. 280 at 289, 26 R.P.R. 202 (Ont. Master), Peppiatt (Master). 4. Employment. See ACCEPTANCE OF ~; ADDRESS FOR ~; ADMISSION OF ~; AFFIDAVIT OF ~; AGGRAVATED BY ~; AIR ~; CANADIAN SECURITY INTELLIGENCE ~; CHILD WELFARE ~; CIVIL ~; COMMUNITY ~; COMPUTER ~; CONTRACT OF ~; DOMESTIC ~; DOSIMETRY ~; LAW ENFORCEMENT ~; COURTS ADMINISTRATION ~; INTERNATIONAL ~; MILITARY ~; OCCUPATIONAL HEALTH AND SAFETY ~; PERSONAL ~; PROOF OF ~; PROTECTION ~; PROVINCIAL ENFORCEMENT ~; PUBLIC ~; ~S; SPECIAL DUTY ~; SUBSCRIPTION ~; SUBSTITUTED ~; TELECOMMUNICATIONS ~; TRAVEL ~; VOICE OVER INTERNET PROTOCOL ~

SERVICE ABROAD. See HAGUE CONVENTION ON ~.

SERVICE CLUB. An association of business and professional people whose objectives are to make contributions of various sorts to the community in which the club exists.

SERVICE CONVICT. A person who is under a sentence that includes a punishment of imprisonment for life or for two years or more imposed on that person pursuant to the Code of Service Discipline. *National Defence Act*, R.S.C. 1985, c. N-5, s. 2.

SERVICE CUSTODY. The holding under arrest or in confinement of a person by the Canadian Forces, and includes confinement in a service prison or detention barrack. *National Defence Act*, R.S.C. 1985, c. N-5, s. 2.

SERVICE DETAINEE. A person who is under a sentence that includes a punishment of detention imposed on that person pursuant to the Code of Service Discipline. *National Defence Act*, R.S.C. 1985, c. N-5, s. 2.

SERVICE DISCIPLINE. See CODE OF ~.

SERVICE EX JURIS. Service of process of the court on a person who is outside the territory of the issuing court.

SERVICE OFFENCE. An offence under this Act, the Criminal Code or any other Act of Parliament, committed by a person while subject to the Code of Service Discipline. *National Defence Act*, R.S.C. 1985, c. N-5, s. 2.

SERVICE OF PROCESS. Bringing the effect or contents of a document to the attention of a person affected.

SERVICE PRISONER. A person who is under a sentence that includes a punishment of imprisonment for less than two years imposed on that person pursuant to the Code of Service Discipline. *National Defence Act*, R.S.C. 1985, c. N-5, s. 2.

SERVICE PROVIDER. See EMERGENCY ~; INTERNET ~.

SERVICE-RELATED INJURY OR DISEASE.
An injury or a disease that (a) was attributable to or was incurred during special duty service; or (b) arose out of or was directly connected with service in the Canadian Forces. *Canadian Forces Members and Veterans Re-establishment and Compensation Act, S.C. 2005, c. 21, s. 2.*

SERVICES. *n.* 1. "... [T]he product of the work supplying it." *Xerox of Canada Ltd. v. Ontario Regional Assessment Commissioner, Region No. 10* (1981), 13 O.M.B.R. 41 at 42, [1981] 2 S.C.R. 137, 127 D.L.R. (3d) 511, Martland, Dickson, Beetz, McIntyre and Chouinard JJ. 2. "... '[H]elp' or 'benefit' or 'advantage' conferred... ." *R. v. Laphkas* (1942), 77 C.C.C. 142 at 145, [1942] S.C.R. 84, [1942] 2 D.L.R. 47, Taschereau J. 3. "[In s. 20 of the Charter] ... means, generally, the administration of public affairs as the same applies to the individual... ." *Jenkins v. Prince Edward Island (Workers' Compensation Board)* (1986), 15 C.C.E.L. 55 at 65-6, 21 C.C.L.I. 149, 31 D.L.R. (4th) 536, 61 Nfld. & P.E.I.R. 206, 185 A.P.R. 206, 9 C.H.R.R. D/5145 (P.E.I. C.A.), the court per McQuaid J.A. 4. The expression "services provided to land or improvements" by its plain meaning includes electrical services provided to apartments. [The definition of "service" applies] equally to the supply of electricity as to the supply of water or gas. It applies to the apparatus of supply, such as wires and meters, as well as to the supply itself. *B.C. Apartment Owners & Managers Assn. v. New Westminster (City)*, 2001 CarswellBC 1075, 2001 BCSC 684, 19 M.P.L.R. (3d) 249, Shaw J. See CEMETERY ~; COMMUNITY DEVELOPMENT ~; CONTINUING ~ CONTRACT; CONTRACT FOR ~; ESSENTIAL ~; FINANCIAL PACKAGING ~; LOSS OF ~; PERSONAL DEVELOPMENT ~; PERSONAL ~ BUSINESS; REAL ESTATE ~; RENTAL PROPERTY MANAGEMENT ~; SAFETY ~; SERVICE; STRATA MANGEMENT ~; TRADING ~; UNSOLICITED GOODS OR ~; WELFARE ~.

SERVICES QUÉBEC. A mandatary of Quebec. The mission of Services Québec is to offer citizens and businesses throughout Québec a single window for simplified access to public services. *An Act respecting Services Québec*, R.S.Q. c. S-6.3, s. 2 and 4.

SERVICE TRIBUNAL. A court martial or a person presiding at a summary trial. *National Defence Act*, R.S.C. 1985, c. N-5, s. 2.

SERVIENT TENEMENT. The land over which one exercises an easement.

SERVITUDE. *n.* A charge imposed on an immovable, the servient land, in favour of another immovable, the dominant land, belonging to a different owner. Under the charge the owner of the servient land is required to tolerate certain acts of use by the owner of the dominant land or himself abstain from exercising certain rights inherent in ownership. A servitude extends to all that is necessary for its exercise. *Civil Code*, S.Q. 1991, c. 64, a. 1177. See APPARENT ~; CONTINUOUS ~; DISCONTINU-

OUS ~; PENAL ~; PRAEDIAL ~; UNAPPARENT ~.

SESSION. *n.* 1. The period of time between the first meeting of Parliament and a prorogation. One Parliament usually includes several sessions. A. Fraser, W.A. Dawson & J. Holtby, eds., *Beauchesne's Rules and Forms of the House of Commons of Canada*, 6th ed. (Toronto: Carswell, 1989) at 65. 2. "... [T]he period of time during which members of the Legislature are called together for the despatch of public business." *Sessional Allowances under the Ontario Legislative Assembly Act, Re*, [1945] 2 D.L.R. 631 at 636, [1945] O.R. 336 (C.A.), McRuer J.A. 3. The sitting of a court. 4. "The word 'term' would be more accurate than 'session' to describe the time prescribed by law for holding court, as a session of the Court is the time of its actual sitting and terminates each day with its rising. The distinction is not always observed, however, and the words are often used interchangeably." *MacDonald v. Dawson* (1955), 20 C.R. 357 at 358, 36 M.P.R. 34, 112 C.C.C. 44 (Nfld. C.A.), the court per Walsh C.J.

SESSIONAL. See STANDING, ~ AND SPECIAL ORDERS.

SET. *n.* A number of articles of the same general character ordinarily on sale together or intended to be used together, to each of which the same design or variants thereof are applied. *Industrial Design Act*, R.S.C. 1985, c. I-9, s. 2.

SET ASIDE. To nullify the decision or order of another decision-maker. A court may set aside the decision or order of an administrative tribunal on judicial review. On appeal, a higher court may set aside the judgment or order of a lower court.

SET DOWN FOR TRIAL. Any step in civil proceedings which indicates that the matter is ready to proceed to trial.

SET OFF. *var.* **SET-OFF.** 1. "A statutory set-off was available, before the fusion of law and equity, either in equity or at law. It is still available. It requires the fulfilment of two conditions. The first is that both obligations must be debts. The second is that both debts must be mutual cross obligations. Both conditions must be fulfilled at the same time: ..." *Canadian Imperial Bank of Commerce v. Tucker Industries Inc.* (1988), 48 C.B.R. (N.S.) 1 at 3, [1983] 5 W.W.R. 602, 46 B.C.L.R. 7, 149 D.L.R. (3d) 172 (C.A.), the court per Lambert J.A. 2. Offset is a business or an accounting term. I do not agree with the Royal Bank that offset means the same as the legal term set-off, which normally refers to an amount claimed by a defendant as a counter-claim or cross claim against a plaintiff arising out of the same subject matter. *Belliveau v. Royal Bank*, 2000 CarswellNB 74, 14 C.B.R. (4th) 17, 23 C.C.P.B. 113, 3 B.L.R. (3d) 43, 224 N.B.R. (2d) 354, 574 A.P.R. 354 (C.A.), the court per Turnbull J.A. 3. "Equitable set-off is available where there is a claim for a money sum whether liquidated or unliquidated: Abacus Cities Ltd. v. Aboussafy [1981] 4 W.W.R. 660 ... (Alta. C.A.) at p. 666 ... it is available where there has been an assignment. There is no requirement of mutuality... . The party relying on a set-off must show some equitable ground for

S

being protected against his adversary's demands: ... The equitable ground must go to the very root of the plaintiff's claim before a set-off will be allowed: ... A cross-claim must be so clearly connected with the demand of the Plaintiff that it would be manifestly unjust to allow the plaintiff to enforce payment without taking into consideration the cross-claim: ... The plaintiff's claim and the cross-claim need not arise out of the same contract: ... Unliquidated claims are on the same footing as liquidated claims: ..." *Telford v. Holt* (1987), 21 C.P.C. (2d) 1 at 13, 18, 78 N.R. 321, 54 Alta. L.R. (2d) 193, [1987] 6 W.W.R. 385, [1987] 2 S.C.R. 193, 46 R.P.R. 234, 81 A.R. 385, 41 D.L.R. (4th) 385, 37 B.L.R. 241, the court per Wilson J. 4. "... [S]omething in the way of a defence: where claim and cross-claim are merged and the lesser is thereby extinguished. True set-off must be distinguished from procedural set-off, where two unrelated claims are balanced up and a net judgment given: ..." *Abacus Cities Ltd. v. Aboussafy* (1981), (sub nom. *Aboussafy v. Abacus Cities Ltd.*) 39 C.B.R. (N.S.) 1 at 10, [1981] 4 W.W.R. 660, 124 D.L.R. (3d) 150, 29 A.R. 607 (C.A.), the court per Kerans J.A. 5. "Where a customer has two accounts with the same bank and one is in credit and the other in debit the bank may set off one against the other and combine the two accounts: ..." *Bank of Montreal v. R & R Entertainment Ltd.* (1984), 27 B.L.R. 159 at 166, 56 N.B.R. (2d) 154, 146 A.P.R. 154, 13 D.L.R. (4th) 726 (C.A.), the court per Hughes C.J.N.B. See EQUITABLE ~; LEGAL ~; STATUTORY ~.

SETTLE. *v.* 1. "... [T]o bring a dispute to an end by arrangement of the parties as opposed to by judgment of a court on the merits [and does not necessarily require a compromise]." *Data General (Canada) Ltd. v. Molnar Systems Group Inc.* (1991), 3 C.P.C. (3d) 180 at 187, 85 D.L.R. (4th) 392, 6 O.R. (3d) 409, 52 O.A.C. 212 (C.A.), the court per Morden J.A. 2. With respect to property, to limit it, or the income from it, to several people in succession, so that any person who possesses or enjoys it does not have power to deprive another of the right to enjoy it in future. 3. With respect to a document, to make it right in substance and in form. See OFFER TO ~.

SETTLED ESTATE. Land and all estates or interests in land that are the subject of a settlement.

SETTLEMENT. *n.* 1. An agreement by parties in dispute. 2. An unincorporated community of persons. 3. "... [A] disposition of property to be held, either in original form or in such form that it can be traced, for the enjoyment of some other person ..." *Geraci, Re*, [1970] 3 O.R. 49 at 51, 14 C.B.R. (N.S.) 253, [1970] I.L.R. 1-343, 12 D.L.R. (3d) 314 (C.A.), the court per Jessup J.A. 4. A statute, deed, agreement, will or other instrument, or any number of such instruments, under or by virtue of which land or any estate or interest in land stands limited to or in trust for any persons by way of succession, including any such instruments affecting the estates of any one or more of such persons exclusively. *Settled Estates Act*, R.S.O. 1990, c. S.7, s. 1. See CLEARING AND ~ SYSTEM; LAST CHANCE ~; MARRIAGE ~; MINUTES OF ~; PIERRINGER ~; STRUCTURED ~; VIATICAL ~.

SETTLEMENT LEGISLATION. The Acts of Parliament and the Acts of the Legislature of British Columbia that give effect to the Nisga'a Final Agreement, including this Act and the Nisga'a Final Agreement Act (British Columbia). *Nisga'a Final Agreement Act*, S.C. 2000, c. 7, s. 2.

SETTLEMENT PRICE. Where used in relation to a commodity futures contract, means the price which is used by a commodity futures exchange or its clearing house to determine, daily, the net gains or losses in the value of open commodity futures contracts; *Commodity Futures Act*, R.S.O. 1990, c. C.20, s. 1.

SETTLOR. *n.* 1. A person who creates a trust. 2. A party to a marriage settlement who agrees or is liable to pay any sum or sums of money thereunder, or who settles, grants, conveys, transfers, mortgages, or charges, or agrees to settle, grant, convey, transfer, mortgage, or charge, any real or personal property upon or to any person. *Marriage Settlement Act*, R.S.S. 1978, c. M-5, s. 2, .

SEVER. *v.* To divide.

SEVERABLE. *adj.* Able to be divided.

SEVERAL. *adj.* 1. Individual, separate. The opposite of "joint." 2. A number of things or persons, more than two. See JOINT AND ~.

SEVERALLY. *adv.* Individually, separately. See JOINTLY AND ~.

SEVERAL TENANCY. A tenancy which is separate and not held jointly with another person.

SEVERAL TORTFEASORS. Those whose acts occur in the same sequence of events causing the damage but who have not acted in common. They are responsible for the same damage, but not for the same tort. J.G. Fleming, *The Law of Torts*, 8th ed. (Sydney: Law Book, 1992) at 255.

SEVERALTY. *n.* 1. Property belongs to people "in severalty" when each person's share can be distinguished in contrast to joint ownership, coparcency or ownership in common in which owners hold undivided shares. 2. "[W]hen one considers the provisions of the Indian Act [R.S.C. 1985, c. I-5] concerning enfranchisement, one is driven to the conclusion that, at least on the part of the commissioners, they had in mind that the persons who chose land in severalty would be obtaining private enclosed property as opposed to property held in common with other members of the tribe. *Chingee v. British Columbia (Attorney General)*, 2005 BCCA 446.

SEVERANCE. *n.* 1. Separation; severing. 2. A court order for the separate trials of two or more people jointly indicted, done in the interests of justice. S.A. Cohen, *Due Process of Law* (Toronto: Carswell, 1977) at 273. 3. Division of one statute into an invalid and a valid part regarding them as two laws concerning two different "matters" because one assumes that the legislature would have enacted the valid part even if it understood that it could not enact the other. P.W. Hogg, *Constitutional Law of Canada*, 3d ed. (Toronto: Carswell, 1992) at 391. 4. [Of a term of a contract], when permitted, appears to take two forms. "Notional" severance involves reading down a contractual provision so as to make it legal and enforceable. "Blue-pencil" severance consists of removing part of a contractual provision. *Shafron v. KRG Insurance Brokers (Western) Inc.*, 2009 SCC 6, [2009] 1 S.C.R. 157. 5. "... [T]o put an end to the joint ownership relationship of property." *Laprise (Crow) v. Crow* (1991), 32 R.F.L. (3d) 82 at 93, 101 N.S.R. (2d) 194, 275 A.P.R. 194 (C.A.), the court per Hallett J.A. 6. "... [A] complete separation of the employment relationship... ." *Max Factor Canada v. U.S.W.A., Local 9050* (1988), 33 L.A.C. (3d) 274 at 276 (Ont.), Simmons. 7. "... Severance at law of a joint tenancy, therefore, occurs when one or more of the four unities (title, interest, possession and time) is destroyed, either as a result of the actions of one of the joint tenants or as a consequence of the common intention of the joint tenants." *Walker v. Dubord* (1991), 41 E.T.R. 307 at 313-14 (B.C. S.C.), Callaghan J. See BLUE-PENCIL ~; NOTIONAL ~.

SEVERANCE CLAUSE. The section of a statute which provides that, if any part of that statute is judged to be unconstitutional, the rest will continue to be effective. P.W. Hogg, *Constitutional Law of Canada*, 3d ed. (Toronto: Carswell, 1992) at 392.

SEVERANCE PAY. "... [T]he nature and purpose of severance pay is similar to the nature and purpose of common law damages for failure to give reasonable notice of termination of employment. The triggering event is the same, namely, termination of employment. Severance pay cushions economic hardship and provides some compensation for loss of employment ... this payment is made whether or not the employee gets another job ..." *Mattocks v. Smith & Stone (1982) Inc.* (1990), 34 C.C.E.L. 273 at 279 (Ont. Gen. Div.), Corbett J.

SEWER. See SANITARY ~.

SEX. *n.* "Gender, ..." *Janzen v. Platy Enterprises Ltd.* (1986), 8 C.H.R.R. D/3831 at D/3845, [1987] 1 W.W.R. 385, 33 D.L.R. (4th) 32, 87 C.L.L.C. 17,014, 43 Man. R. (2d) 293 (C.A.), Twaddle J.A.

SEX DISCRIMINATION. 1. "... [P]ractices or attitudes which have the effect of limiting the conditions of employment of, or the employment opportunities available to, employees on the basis of a characteristic related to gender." *Janzen v. Platy Enterprises Ltd.* (1989), 47 C.R.R. 274 at 295, [1989] 1 S.C.R. 1252, 25 C.C.E.L. 1, [1989] 4 W.W.R. 39, 59 D.L.R. (4th) 352, 10 C.H.R.R. D/6205, 58 Man. R. (2d) 1, 89 C.L.L.C. 17,011, 95 N.R. 81, the court per Dickson C.J.C. 2. "... Discrimination on the basis of pregnancy is a form of sex discrimination because of the basic biological fact that only women have the capacity to become pregnant... ." *Brooks v. Canada Safeway Ltd.* (1989), 10 C.H.R.R. D/6183 at D/6193, 26 C.C.E.L. 1, [1989] 4 W.W.R. 193, 89 C.L.L.C. 17,012, 94 N.R. 373, [1989] 1 S.C.R. 1219, 59 D.L.R. (4th) 321, 58 Man. R. (2d) 161, 45 C.R.R. 115, Dickson C.J.C. (Beetz, McIntyre, Wilson, La Forest and L'Heureux-Dubé JJ. concurring).

SEX OFFENCE. An offence under section 151 (sexual interference), 152 (invitation to sexual touching), subsection 153 (1) (sexual exploitation), 155 (1) (incest), 160 (1), (2) or (3) (bestiality), 163.1 (2), (3) or

(4) (child pornography), section 170 (parent or guardian procuring sexual activity), subsection 173 (2) (exposure), section 271 (sexual assault), subsection 272 (1) (sexual assault with a weapon, threats to a third party or causing bodily harm) or section 273 (aggravated sexual assault) of the Criminal Code (Canada), an offence under a predecessor or successor to a provision set out above or an offence under a provision of the Criminal Code (Canada) that is prescribed. *Christopher's Law (Sex Offender Registry), 2000*, S.O. 2000, c. 1, s. 1.

SEX OFFENDER. A person who is subject to one or more orders or to an obligation under section 490.019 of the Criminal Code or section 227.06 of the National Defence Act. *Sex Offender Information Registration Act*, S.C. 2004, c. 10, s. 3.

SEX OFFENDER DATABASE. The database maintained under the Sex Offender Information Registration Act, S.C. 2004, c. 10.

SEX OFFENDER REGISTRY. The ministry shall establish and maintain a registry containing the names, dates of birth and addresses of offenders, the sex offences for which, on or after the day section 3 comes into force, they are serving or have served a sentence or of which they have been convicted or found not criminally responsible on account of mental disorder and such additional information as may be prescribed. *Christopher's Law (Sex Offender Registry), 2000*, S.O. 2000, c. 1, s. 2.

SEXUAL ANNOYANCE. One category of sexual harassment. Sexually-related conduct which is hostile, intimidating or offensive but without any direct link to a tangible job benefit or detriment. Creates an offensive work environment for an employee.

SEXUAL ASSAULT. 1. "... [A]n assault within any one of the definitions of that concept in s. 244(1) of the Criminal Code ... which is committed in circumstances of a sexual nature, such that the sexual integrity of the victim is violated. The test to be applied in determining whether the impugned conduct has the requisite sexual nature is an objective one: 'Viewed in the light of all the circumstances, is the sexual or carnal context of the assault visible to a reasonable observer?' (R. v. Taylor (1985), 19 C.C.C. (3d) 156 ... Laycraft C.J.A., at 162 (C.C.C.)). The part of the body touched, the nature of the contact, the situation in which it occurred, the words and gestures accompanying the act, and all other circumstances surrounding the conduct, including threats which may or may not be accompanied by force, will be relevant: ... The intent or purpose of the person committing the act, to the extent that this may appear from the evidence, may also be a factor in considering whether the conduct is sexual... ." *R. v. Chase* (1987), 37 C.C.C. (3d) 97 at 103, 59 C.R. (3d) 193, [1987] 2 S.C.R. 293, 80 N.R. 247, 82 N.B.R. (2d) 229, 208 A.P.R. 245 D.L.R. (4th) 98, the court per McIntyre J. 2. The true substance of the offence is the violation of the sexual integrity of the victim, and the test to be applied in determining whether there has been such a violation is an objective one. . . . Some assaults are so obviously, objectively sexual that nothing more need to be known than that the acts took place. For example, forced intercourse is so obviously a sexual assault that one cannot imagine any circumstances that would deprive them of their sexual character. *R. v. Muchikekwanape*, 2002 MBCA 78, 166 C.C.C. (3d) 144, 166 Man. R. (2d) 81, 278 W.A.C. 81. See AGGRAVATED ~; MAJOR ~.

SEXUAL COERCION. One category of sexual harassment. Sexually-related conduct which results in some direct consequence, beneficial or detrimental, to the worker's employment status.

SEXUAL HARASSMENT. 1. Any conduct, comment, gesture or contact of a sexual nature (a) that is likely to cause offence or humiliation to any employee; or (b) that might, on reasonable grounds, be perceived by that employee as placing a condition of a sexual nature on employment or on any opportunity for training or promotion. *Canada Labour Code*, R.S.C. 1985, c. L-2, s. 247.1. 2. "... [I]n the workplace may be broadly defined as unwelcome conduct of a sexual nature that detrimentally affects the work environment or leads to adverse job-related consequences for the victims of the harassment. It is ... an abuse of power." *Janzen v. Platy Enterprises Ltd.* (1989), 89 C.L.L.C. 17,011 at 16,072, 47 C.R.R. 274, [1989] 1 S.C.R. 1252, 25 C.C.E.L. 1, [1989] 4 W.W.R. 39, 59 D.L.R. (4th) 352, 10 C.H.R.R. D/6205, 58 Man. R. (2d) 1, 95 N.R. 81, the court per Dickson C.J.C. See QUID PRO QUO ~.

SEXUAL INTERCOURSE. For the purposes of the Criminal Code, sexual intercourse is complete on penetration to even the slightest degree, notwithstanding that seed is not emitted. *Criminal Code*, R.S.C. 1985, c. C-46, s. 4(5).

SEXUALLY TRANSMITTED DISEASE. A disease caused by an infectious agent usually transmitted during sexual contact. *Health Protection and Promotion Act*, R.S.O. 1990, c. H.7, s. 1(1).

SEXUAL NATURE. A crime is of a sexual nature if it consists of one or more acts that (a) are either sexual in nature or committed with the intent to commit an act or acts that are sexual in nature; and (b) constitute an offence. *Sex Offender Information Registration Act*, S.C. 2004, c. 10, s. 3.

SEXUAL ORIENTATION. "[Denotes] ... an individual's orientation or preference in terms of sexual relationship to others, whether homosexual or heterosexual or perhaps both ..." *Leshner v. Ontario* (1992), (*sub nom. Leshner v. Ontario (No. 2)*) 16 C.H.R.R. D/184 at D/196, 92 C.L.L.C. 17,035, C.E.B. & P.R.G. 8133 (Ont. Bd. of Inquiry), Cumming, Dawson and Plaut (Members).

SEXUAL PREFERENCE. An individual's preference for sexual relationship with others, either of opposite sex or of the same sex.

SEXUAL SADISM. A condition in which the individual experiences sexual arousal and satisfaction through the infliction of pain upon a sexual object, and through the infliction of humiliating or denigrating behaviours in respect of the object. *R. v. Saddlemire* (2007), 219 O.A.C. 259.

SHAKEN INFANT SYNDROME. Injuries to the brain, subdural or eye hemorrhages caused when someone vigorously shakes a small child or infant. F.A. Jaffe, *A Guide to Pathological Evidence for Lawyers and Police Officers*, 4th ed. (Toronto: Carswell, 1999) at 245.

SHALL. *v.* 1. Must. 2. Is to be construed as imperative. 3. "... Parliament when it used the word 'shall' in s. 23 of the Manitoba Act, 1870, and s. 133 of the Constitution Act, 1867 [(30 & 31 Vict.), c. 3] intended that those sections be construed as mandatory or imperative, in the sense that they must be obeyed, unless such an interpretation of the word 'shall' would be utterly inconsistent with the context in which it has been used and would render the sections irrational or meaningless... ." *Reference re Language Rights Under s. 23 of Manitoba Act, 1870 and s. 133 of Constitution Act, 1867*, [1985] 1 S.C.R. 721 at 737, [1985] 4 W.W.R. 385, 35 Man. R. (2d) 83, 59 N.R. 321, 19 D.L.R. (4th) 1, Dickson C.J., Beetz, Estey, McIntyre, Lamer, Wilson and Le Dain JJ. 4. It is clear from past decisions of various courts that the word "may" can have a mandatory meaning, just as the word "shall" can have a permissive meaning, depending on context. See reference to Johnsons Tyne Foundry Pty. Ltd. v. Maffra Corp., [1949] A.L.R. 89 (Australia H.C.), referred to in Words and Phrases Legally Defined, 3d ed. (London: Butterworth & Co. (Publishers) Ltd., 1989) vol. 3: K-Q at 116. *R. v. Neves*, 2005 MBCA 112.

SHAM. *n.* "... [A] transaction purporting to create apparent legal rights and obligations which are at variance with the legal relationships which in fact characterize the arrangement... ." *Jodrey v. Nova Scotia* (1980), (*sub nom. Covert v. Nova Scotia (Minister of Finance)*) 8 E.T.R. 69 at 118, [1980] 2 S.C.R. 774, 41 N.S.R.(2d) 181, 76 A.P.R. 181, [1980] C.T.C. 437, 32 N.R. 275, Dickson J. (dissenting) (Ritchie and McIntyre JJ. concurring).

SHAM DOCTRINE. The "sham doctrine" applies where an individual deceitfully misleads the government away from his or her true taxable income through the creation of arrangements that, while facially valid, are in reality devoid of substance. *Germany (Federal Republic) v. Schreiber* (2006), 207 O.A.C. 306.

SHAM TRANSACTION. "... [A] transaction conducted with an element of deceit so as to create an illusion calculated to lead the tax collector away from the taxpayer or the true nature of the transaction; or, simple deception whereby the taxpayer creates a facade of reality quite different from the disguised reality." *Stubart Investments Ltd. v. R.*, [1984] 1 S.C.R. 536 at 545, 53 N.R. 241, [1984] C.T.C. 294, 84 D.T.C. 6305, 10 D.L.R. (4th) 1, Estey J. (Beetz and McIntyre JJ. concurring).

SHARE. *n.* 1. An integral, separate part of a company's authorized capital. H. Sutherland, D.B. Horsley & J.M. Edmiston, eds., *Fraser's Handbook on Canadian Company Law*, 7th ed. (Toronto: Carswell, 1985) at 107. 2. "... [I]s not an isolated piece of property. It is rather, in the well-known phrase, a 'bundle' of interrelated rights and liabilities. A share is not an entity independent of the statutory provisions that govern its possession and exchange. Those provisions make up its constituent elements. They define the very rights and liabilities that constitute the share's existence. The Canada Business Corporations Act [S.C. 1974-75-76, c. 33] defines and governs the right to vote at shareholders' meetings, to receive dividends, to inspect the books and records of the company, and to receive a portion of the corporation's capital upon a winding up of the company, among many others. A 'share' and thus a 'shareholder' are concepts inseparable from the comprehensive bundle of rights and liabilities created by the Act." *Sparling v. Québec (Caisse de dépôt & de placement)* (1988), 41 B.L.R. 1 at 11, 55 D.L.R. (4th) 63, [1988] 2 S.C.R. 1015, 89 N.R. 120, 20 Q.A.C. 174, the court per La Forest J. 3. "... [I]ntangible, incorporeal property rights represented or evidenced by share certificates. They are not in themselves capable of individual identification and isolation from all other shares of the corporation of the same class." *Baud Corp., N.V. v. Brook* (1978), (*sub nom. Asamera Oil Corp. v. Sea Oil & General Corp.*) 5 B.L.R. 225 at 235, [1979] 1 S.C.R. 633, [1978] 6 W.W.R. 301, 23 N.R. 181, 12 A.R. 271, 89 D.L.R. (3d) 1, the court per Estey J. See CLASS A ~; CLASS B ~; CLASS OF ~S; COMMON ~; COMPANY LIMITED BY ~S; EQUITY ~; INVESTMENT ~; MEMBERSHIP ~; MUTUAL FUND ~; PREFERENCE ~; PREFERRED ~; REDEEMABLE ~; VOTING ~.

SHARE CERTIFICATE. 1. An instrument certifying that the person named in it (the shareholder) is entitled to a certain number of shares of the corporation. 2. "... [I]s not in itself a share or shares of the corporation but only evidence thereof, ..." *Baud Corp., N.V. v. Brook* (1978), (*sub nom. Asamera Oil Corp. v. Sea Oil & General Corp.*) 5 B.L.R. 225 at 235, [1979] 1 S.C.R. 633, [1978] 6 W.W.R. 301, 23 N.R. 181, 12 A.R. 271, 89 D.L.R. (3d) 1, the court per Estey J. 3. "... [I]s in no sense a contractual document and even though it is required to be issued under the corporate seal it is not a deed. The holder's legal right depends not on the certificate but upon entry in the share register. A share certificate is not a negotiable instrument whereas a share warrant or a share purchase warrant is." *Henderson v. Minister of National Revenue*, [1973] C.T.C. 636 at 660, 73 D.T.C. 5471 (Fed. T.D.), Cattanach J.

SHARE CLASS. "The concept of share 'classes' is not technical in nature, but rather is simply the accepted means by which differential treatment of shares is recognized in the articles of incorporation of a company. As Professor Welling ... succinctly explains, 'a class is simply a sub-group of shares with rights and conditions in common which distinguish them from other shares' ..." *McClung v. Canada (Minister of National Revenue)* (1990), 50 B.L.R. 161 at 187, [1991] 1 C.T.C. 169, 119 N.R. 101, 91 D.T.C. 5001, [1991] 2 W.W.R. 244, 76 D.L.R. (4th) 217, 49 F.T.R. 80n, [1990] 3 S.C.R. 1020, Dickson C.J.C. (Sopinka, Gonthier and Cory JJ. concurring). See CLASS OF SHARES.

SHARED INTEREST IN LAND. A person's interest in one or more parcels of land if (a) the parcel or parcels are owned or leased, directly or indirectly, by the person and at least one other person, and (b) as part of any arrangement relating to the acquisition of the person's interest, that person's right of use or occupation of the land is limited to a part of the land. *Real Estate Development Marketing Act*, S.B.C. 2004, c. 41, s. 1.

SHARED MEANING RULE. Where two versions of a bilingual statute appear to express different things, the shared meaning rule for the interpretation of bilingual statutes requires that the meaning that is shared by both versions ought to be adopted. The rule is not absolute, however, and can be rejected if the meaning shared between the two statutory versions is contrary to Parliament's intention or the purpose or objects of the enactment. *Canada 3000 Inc., Re*, 2004 CarswellOnt 149 (C.A.).

SHAREHOLDER. *n.* 1. Someone who holds shares in a company. 2. A subscriber to or holder of stock in a company. 3. A shareholder of a corporation and includes a member of a corporation or other person entitled to receive payment of a dividend or to a share in a distribution on the winding-up of the corporation. 4. "... [O]ne who has a proportionate interest in its [a corporation's] assets and is entitled to take part in its control and receive its dividends." *Kootenay Valley Fruit Lands Co., Re* (1911), 18 W.L.R. 145 at 147 (Man. K.B.), MacDonald J. See UNANIMOUS ~ AGREEMENT.

SHARE WARRANT. A document under a corporate seal which certifies that its bearer is entitled to shares specified in the document. H. Sutherland, D.B. Horsley & J.M. Edmiston, eds., *Fraser's Handbook on Canadian Company Law*, 7th ed. (Toronto: Carswell, 1985) at 103.

SHARI'A LAW. Muslim or Islamic law; a code of living which may be adopted by Muslims.

SHARING. See DEFERRED ~ SCHEME; JOB-~ ARRANGEMENT; WORK ~.

SHEET. See BACK~; BALANCE-~; MATERIAL SAFETY DATA ~.

SHELF. See CONTINENTAL ~.

SHELLEY'S CASE. See RULE IN ~.

SHELTER. See DOCTRINE OF ~ING; TAX ~.

SHERIFF. *n.* 1. An officer charged with the execution of a writ or other process. 2. A sheriff enforces any order of a court arising out of a civil proceeding which is enforceable in Ontario, unless an act provides otherwise (Courts of Justice Act, R.S.O. 1990, c. C.43, s. 141(1)). G.D. Watson & C. Perkins, eds., *Holmested & Watson: Ontario Civil Procedure* (Toronto: Carswell, 1984-) at CJA-249.

SHIFTING USE. An executory or secondary use, which, when executed, derogates from a preceding estate, e.g. land is conveyed to the use of one person provided that when a second person pays a designated sum of money, the estate will go to a third person.

SHIP. *v.* The act of any person leading to the movement, by common carrier or other means of public conveyance, of any livestock or livestock product from or to a point outside the province in which that person carries on business. See NAVIGATION AND ~ PING.

SHIP. *n.* 1. Every description of vessel, boat or craft designed, used or capable of being used solely or partly for marine navigation, whether self-propelled or not and without regard to the method of propulsion, and includes a sea-plane and a raft or boom of logs or lumber. *Canada Marine Act*, S. C. 1998, c. 10, s. 2. 2. Includes any description of vessel, boat or craft designed, used or capable of being used solely or partly for marine navigation without regard to method or lack of propulsion. *Oceans Act*, S.C. 1996, c. 31, s. 2. See CARGO ~; CHARTERED ~; FREE ALONGSIDE ~; HER MAJESTY'S CANADIAN ~.

SHIPPER. *n.* A person who sends or receives goods by means of a carrier or intends to do so.

SHIPPING DOCUMENT. Any document that accompanies dangerous goods being transported and that describes or contains information relating to the goods and includes a bill of lading, cargo manifest, shipping order or way-bill.

SHIPPING LAW. The law relating to the shipment of goods and people.

SHOCK. See NERVOUS ~.

SHOP. See CLOSED ~.

SHOPLIFTING. *var.* **SHOP-LIFTING.** *n.* Theft of merchandise.

SHOPPING. See JUDGE ~.

SHOPPING A BID. Soliciting a bid from a contractor with whom one does not intend to deal and then disclosing that bid or using it to reduce the prices bid by other contractors with whom there is an intention to deal.

SHOP STEWARD. An officer of a union elected to represent union members. A main function is to hear a worker's complaint or grievance and to assist the worker in processing the complaint or grievance through the procedures provided.

SHORED EXIT WOUND. An exit wound supported by something firm. F.A. Jaffe, *A Guide to Pathological Evidence for Lawyers and Police Officers*, 4th ed. (Toronto: Carswell, 1999) at 185.

SHORT POSITION. Where used in relation to a commodity futures contract, means to be under an obligation to make delivery. *Commodity Futures Act*, R.S.O. 1990, c. C.20, s. 1

SHORT SELLING. [S]elling shares before they are acquired. Shares are sold in a falling market and then bought at a lower price to cover the sale. The difference in the selling and buying prices is pocketed as profit. *Golden Capital Securities Ltd. v. Holmes*, 2004 BCCA 565. See SELLING SHORT.

SHORT TITLE. The brief name by which a statute is known and cited.

SHOT. See NON-TOXIC ~.

SHOTGUN CLAUSE. A provision in a shareholders' agreement under which one shareholder may require another to sell his shares at a particular price or to purchase the other shareholder's shares at the same price. *Aronowicz v. EMTWO Properties Inc.*, 2010 CarswellOnt 598, 2010 ONCA 96.

SHOULDER. *n.* Usually it is that portion of the roadbed that extends beyond the improved or asphalt surface of the roadway. There is no limit as to the width of a shoulder. *Busch Estate v. Lewers*, 1999 CarswellBC 1730 (S.C.), Melvin J.

SHOW. *n.* A type of bet on a race to select a horse to finish first, second or third in the official result. *Criminal Code*, R.S.C. 1985, c. C-46, *Pari-Mutuel Betting Supervision Regulations*, SOR/91-365, s. 2.

SHOW CAUSE. 1. The presentation to a court of reasons why a certain order should not take effect. 2. "In s. 457.5(7)(e) of the Criminal Code [R.S.C. 1970, c. C-34] 'To show cause' means not merely to show that the justice made some error, but to show that the detention is wrong." *R. v. English* (1983), 8 C.C.C. (3d) 487 at 491 (Ont. Co. Ct.), Zaler Co. Ct. J.

SHOW CAUSE ORDER. "... [I]s simply the document which initiates the hearing under R. 355(4) [of the Federal Court Rules]. The show cause order is analogous to a summons ... It is at the subsequent hearing, not in the application for the show cause order, that the contempt ultimately must be proved." *Cutter (Canada) Ltd. v. Baxter Travenol Laboratories of Canada Ltd.* (1984), 3 C.I.P.R. 143 at 152, 1 C.P.R. (3d) 289, 56 N.R. 282 (Fed. C.A.), the court per Urie J.A., quoting Dickson C.J.C. for the Court in *Baxter Travenol Laboratories of Canada Ltd. v. Cutter (Canada) Ltd. (sub nom. Baxter Laboratories of Canada Ltd. v. Cutter (Can.) Ltd.)* (1983), 1 C.I.P.R. 46 at 66, [1983] 2 S.C.R. 388, 36 C.P.C. 305, 75 C.P.R. (2d) 1, [1983] R.D.J. 481, 2 D.L.R. (4th) 621, 50 N.R. 1.

SHOW CAUSE SUMMONS. A document which requires a debtor or other person to appear again in court and show why the debtor or other person should not be jailed for contempt of an order.

S.I. *abbr.* Statutory instrument.

SIBLING. *n.* A person who has the same biological mother or biological father as another person.

SIC. *adv.* [L. so, thus] This word is put in brackets in a quoted passage to show that any mistakes or apparent omissions in the quotation appear also in the original source.

SICK LEAVE. Time off from work allowed for illness or disability.

SICK PAY. An earned benefit which compensates employees who otherwise would lose pay by reason of illness.

SIC UTERE TUO UT ALIENUM NON LAEDAS. [L. use your own property so as not to injure your neighbour's] "... [T]he defendant [landowner] can protect himself in any way he pleases as long as in so doing he does not injure his neighbour who is no party to the nuisance." *Canadian Pacific Railway* *v. McBryan* (1896), 5 B.C.R. 187 at 208 (C.A.), Drake J.A.

SIDE-MEMBER. One of the members of a tribunal who is not the chair of the panel conducting a hearing. Also referred to as winger.

SIDENOTE. *n.* A marginal note.

SIFT TRUST. A specified investment flow-through trust, for a taxation year means a trust (other than an excluded subsidiary entity, or a real estate investment trust, for the taxation year) that meets the following conditions at any time during the taxation year: (a) the trust is resident in Canada; (b) investments in the trust are listed or traded on a stock exchange or other public market; and (c) the trust holds one or more non-portfolio properties. *Income Tax Act*, R.S.C. 1985, c. 1 (5th Supp.), s. 122.1(1).

SIGHT. See AT ~.

SIGIL. *n.* [L.] A signature; a seal.

SIGN. See COUNTER-~; VEHICLE INSPECTION ~; YIELD ~.

SIGNAL. See COMMUNICATION ~.

SIGNATURE. *n.* 1. "... [T]he name or special mark of a person written with his or her own hand as an authentication of some document or writing ... It is not essential that a signature be in any particular form, as for example, that it include all the given names as well as the surname of the signatory, or that it be legible. Indeed, in some cases, it may amount to no more than a mark." *R. v. Kapoor* (1989), 52 C.C.C. (3d) 41 at 65, 19 M.V.R. (3d) 41 (Ont. H.C.), Watt J. 2. "... [S]tamped impressions have been recognized as valid in connection with certain legal documents. Today's business could not be conducted if stamped signatures were not recognized as legally binding. The affixing of a stamp conveys the intention to be bound by the document so executed just as effectively as the manual writing of a signature by hand ..." *United Canso Oil & Gas Ltd., Re* (1980), 12 B.L.R. 130 at 136, 41 N.S.R. (2d) 282, 76 A.P.R. 282 (T.D.), Hallett J. 3. A mark or sign impressed on something. 4. The name which one writes oneself. 5. A device whereby the "signer" can confirm to the intended recipient that he or she is advising as to the choice selected. That this is accomplished by the use of electronic passwords does not detract from that advice, but rather enhances it. *Newbridge Networks Corp., Re*, 2000 CarswellOnt 1401, 48 O.R. (3d) 47, 186 D.L.R. (4th) 188, 7 B.L.R. (3d) 136 (S.C.J. [Commercial List]), Farley J. See DIGITAL ~ CERTIFICATE; ELECTRONIC ~; GUARANTEE OF ~.

SILENCE. See CONE OF ~; RIGHT TO ~.

SILENT. See RIGHT TO REMAIN ~.

SILENT PARTNER. A partner who puts money into a partnership without taking an active part in management.

SILICOSIS. *n.* A fibrotic condition of the lungs caused by the inhalation of silica dust.

SILK GOWN. The gown worn by Queen's Counsel; thus "to take silk" means to become a Queen's Counsel.

SILOIZATION. *n.* Restriction of information to one's own department within an organization.

SIMILAR. *adj.* 1. Same. 2. Resemble partially. 3. Obviously, "similar" does not mean "identical." Benefits may be similar in kind while differing in quantum. "Similar" does not refer to the system of law in which the benefits originate, the overall regime under which they are administered or the legal process by which they are claimed. To my mind, the legislature's use of the word "similar" in this context was intended to convey the principle that the benefits in question must be of the same general nature or character as the benefits described in Part 6 of the British Columbia Insurance Act [R.S.B.C. 1996, c. 231]. *Gurniak v. Nordquist* 2003 SCC 59.

SIMILAR FACT EVIDENCE. Evidence which tends to show propensity, which shows past discreditable conduct. In considering the admissibility of similar fact evidence, the basic rule is that the trial judge must first determine whether the probative value of the evidence outweighs its prejudicial effect. In most cases where similar fact evidence is adduced to prove identity it might be helpful for the trial judge to consider the following suggestions in deciding whether to admit the evidence: (1) Generally where similar fact evidence is adduced to prove identity a high degree of similarity between the acts is required in order to ensure that the similar fact evidence has the requisite probative value of outweighing its prejudicial effect to be admissible. The similarity between the acts may consist of a unique trademark or signature on a series of significant similarities. (2) In assessing the similarity of the acts, the trial judge should only consider the manner in which the acts were committed and not the evidence as to the accused's involvement in each act. (3) There may well be exceptions but as a general rule if there is such a degree of similarity between the acts that it is likely that they were committed by the same person then the similar fact evidence will ordinarily have sufficient probative force to outweigh its prejudicial effect and may be admitted. (4) The jury will then be able to consider all the evidence related to the alleged similar acts in determining the accused's guilt for any one act. Once again these are put forward not as rigid rules but simply as suggestions that may assist trial judges in their approach to similar fact evidence. The test for admissibility of similar fact evidence adduced to prove identity is the same whether the alleged similar acts are definitively attributed to the accused, or are the subject of a multi-count indictment against the accused. *R. v. Arp*, [1998] 3 S.C.R. 339.

SIMILAR FACT EVIDENCE RULE. Evidence of discreditable conduct of the accused which the prosecution tries to introduce is inadmissible except when its probative value outweighs its prejudicial effect.

SIMPLE. See FEE ~.

SIMPLE CONTRACT. A contract not under seal.

SIMPLE TRUST. A trust in which one person holds property in trust for another and, because the trust is not qualified by the settlor, the law determines its parameters. P.V. Baker & P. St. J. Langan, eds.,

Snell's Equity, 29th ed. (London: Sweet & Maxwell, 1990) at 103. See BARE TRUST.

SIMULATION. *n.* Exists where the parties agree to express their true intent, not in an apparent contract, but in a secret contract, also called a counter letter. Between the parties, a counter letter prevails over an apparent contract. *Civil Code*, S.Q. 1991, c. 64, a. 1451.

SINE DIE. [L. without a day being fixed] Indefinitely.

SINE QUA NON. [L. without which not] An indispensible condition or necessity.

SINGLE PUBLICATION RULE. Stated simply, the single publication rule is an American rule of law (adopted in many but not all states) under which several communications to a third party of a defamatory statement are held to be only one publication and the limitation period begins to run from the date of the first such communication: Firth v. State, 775 N.E.2d 463 (U.S. N.Y. Ct. App. 2002). *Carter v. B.C. Federation of Foster Parents Assn.*, 2005 BCCA 398.

SINGLE TRANSFERABLE VOTE ELECTORAL SYSTEM. The model for electing members of the Legislative Assembly that was proposed by the Citizens' Assembly on Electoral Reform in its report issued December 10, 2004. *Electoral Reform Referendum 2009 Act*, S.B.C. 2008, c. 9, s. 1.

SINKING FUND. 1. An amount which is set aside annually with interest which if capitalized annually will be great enough at maturity to retire the principal with interest. I.M. Rogers, *The Law of Canadian Municipal Corporations*, 2d ed. (Toronto: Carswell, 1971-) at 654. 2. A special account to which is credited annually an actuarially determined amount for the purpose of providing a fund for future payments.

SIR JOHN A. MACDONALD DAY. January 11.

SIR WILFRID LAURIER DAY. November 20.

SITE. See BURIAL ~; INTERNET GAMING ~; MANUFACTURED HOME ~; NON-CONFORMING ~.

SITTING. *n.* "Generally speaking, a sitting of a court [as used in the Criminal Code, R.S.C. 1970, c. C-34, s. 645(4)(c)] is said to refer to time during which judicial business is transacted before the court; in that sense, it could mean a day or, again, different days within a given timespan for transacting that court's business." *R. v. Paul* (1982), 27 C.R. (3d) 193 at 203, [1982] 1 S.C.R. 621, 67 C.C.C. (2d) 97, 138 D.L.R. (3d) 455, 41 N.R. 1, the court per Lamer J.

SITTING DAY. A day on which either House of Parliament is sitting.

SITTINGS. *n.* A term or session of court: the part of the year in which one transacts judicial business.

SITUS. *n.* [L.] A location; a situation.

SIZE. See CLASS ~.

SKCA. Neutral citation for the Saskatchewan Court of Appeal.

SKILLS DEVELOPMENT. See HUMAN RESOURCES AND ~ CANADA.

SKIN POPPING. Drug injection under the skin. F.A. Jaffe, *A Guide to Pathological Evidence for Lawyers and Police Officers*, 4th ed. (Toronto: Carswell, 1999) at 244.

SKQB. Neutral citation for the Saskatchewan Court of Queen's Bench.

SKULL. See CRUMBLING ~ RULE; THIN ~ RULE.

SLANDER. *n.* Making a defamatory statement orally or in a more transitory form. R.E. Brown, *The Law of Defamation in Canada* (Toronto: Carswell, 1987) at 9.

SLANDER OF GOODS. "... [A]n action for slander of goods will lie whenever one maliciously publishes a false statement in disparagement of the goods of another and, thereby, causes the other special damage. The false statement may be in writing or by word of mouth... ." *Rust Check Canada Inc. v. Young* (1988), 22 C.P.R. (3d) 512 at 529, 530 (Ont. H.C.), Watt J.

SLANDER OF TITLE. Writing, speaking or publishing words which impeach a plaintiff's title to any property, real or personal, which that plaintiff owns. I.H. Jacob, ed., *Bullen and Leake and Jacob's Precedents of Pleadings*, 12th ed. (London: Sweet and Maxwell, 1975) at 544.

SLIP RULE. "... [M]inor corrections to an order can be made. There is no doubt that a court can correct clerical or mathematical errors and other minor slips or omissions in an order so long as the alterations are confined to expounding its manifest intent ... and it is equally clear that a similar rule applies to orders of administrative bodies, ..." *Lodger's International Ltd. v. O'Brien* (1983), 4 C.H.R.R. D/1349 at D/1352, 45 N.B.R. (2d) 342, 118 A.P.R. 243, 83 C.L.L.C. 17,014, 145 D.L.R. (3d) 293 (C.A.), the court per La Forest J.A.

SLOT MACHINE. Any automatic machine or slot machine (a) that is used or intended to be used for any purpose other than vending merchandise or services, or (b) that is used or intended to be used for the purpose of vending merchandise or services if (i) the result of one of any number of operations of the machine is a matter of chance or uncertainty to the operator, (ii) as a result of a given number of successive operations by the operator the machine produces different results, or (iii) on any operation of the machine it discharges or emits a slug or token, but does not include an automatic machine or slot machine that dispenses as prizes only one or more free games on that machine. *Criminal Code*, R.S.C. 1985, c. C-46, s. 198.

S.L.R *abbr.* Statute Law Revision Act of England.

SMALL CLAIMS COURT. An inferior court with a limited jurisdiction over civil matters limited as to monetary jurisdiction and as to subject matter.

SM. & S. *abbr.* Smith & Sager's Drainage Cases (Ontario), 1901-1913.

SMOKE. *v.* To consume, hold or otherwise have control over an ignited tobacco product.

SMOKE. *n.* See SECOND-HAND ~.

SMUGGLING. *n.* The offence of exporting or importing forbidden or restricted goods, or of exporting or importing goods without paying any duties imposed on them. See HUMAN ~.

SNARE. *n.* A device for the capturing of animals by a noose.

SNEAKWARE. *n.* Software embedded within other software and used by advertisers to monitor an internet user's surfing habits for marketing or demographic research purposes.

SNIFF. *v.* To inhale a substance through the nose. F.A. Jaffe, *A Guide to Pathological Evidence for Lawyers and Police Officers*, 4th ed. (Toronto: Carswell, 1999) at 244.

SNORT. *v.* To inhale a substance through the nose. F.A. Jaffe, *A Guide to Pathological Evidence for Lawyers and Police Officers*, 4th ed. (Toronto: Carswell, 1999) at 244.

SOAR. *abbr.* Society of Ontario Adjudicators and Regulators.

SOC. *abbr.* Society.

SOCAGE. *n.* A kind of tenure with certain temporal services which originally were agricultural. Common free socage is equivalent to freehold tenure.

SOCAN. *abbr.* The Society of Composers, Authors and Music Publishers of Canada.

SOCIAL ASSISTANCE. 1. Aid in any form to or in respect of a person in need. 2. Any benefit in the form of money, goods or services provided to or on behalf of a person by a province under a program of social assistance, including a program of social assistance designated by a province to provide for basic requirements including food, shelter, clothing, fuel, utilities, household supplies, personal requirements and health care not provided by public health care, including dental care and eye care.

SOCIAL DEVELOPMENT. See DEPARTMENT OF ~.

SOCIAL PROGRAMS. Includes programs in respect of health, post-secondary education, social assistance and social services, including early childhood development.

SOCIAL SCIENCE BRIEF. A document by which empirical data is appended to or included in the factum.

SOCIETY. *n.* 1. Includes a society or club that is incorporated by an act of a legislature and that has for its object the provision of facilities for the social intercourse and recreation of its members. 2. A religious society, organization or order or a charitable or philanthropic organization. 3. In British Columbia, a society may be incorporated for any lawful purpose or purposes such as national, patriotic, religious, philanthropic, charitable, provident, scientific, fraternal, benevolent, artistic, educational, social, professional, agricultural, sporting or other useful purposes. Carrying on a business, trade, industry or profession as an incident to the purposes of a society is not prohibited by this section, but a society must not distribute any gain, profit or dividend or otherwise dispose of its assets to a member of the society without receiving full and valuable consideration except during winding up or on dissolution and then only as permitted. *Society Act*, R.S.B.C. 1996, c. 433. See CHILDREN'S AID ~; CIVIL ~ ORGANIZATION; COLLECTIVE ~; FRATERNAL OR SORORAL ~; FRATERNAL ~; FREE AND DEMOCRATIC ~; FREE ~; FRIENDLY ~; LAW ~.

SODOMY. *n.* Anal intercourse.

SODRAC. *abbr.* Society for Reproduction Rights of Authors, Composers and Publishers in Canada.

SOFTWARE. *n.* The computer programs which give specific instructions to a computer and permit a user to perform a specific set of tasks or activities. See GEO-IDENTIFICATION ~.

SOFTWOOD LUMBER AGREEMENT. The Softwood Lumber Agreement between the Government of Canada and the Government of the United States of America signed on September 12, 2006 and amended on October 12, 2006, and includes any rectifications made to it before its ratification by Canada. *Export and Import Permits Act*, R.S.C. 1985, c. E-17, s. 2.

SOLATIUM DOLORIS. [L.] A type of moral prejudice that is compensable in Quebec civil law. Compensation for the grief and distress felt when someone close to us dies. *Augustus v. Gosset*, [1996] 3 S.C.R. 268.

SOLE. *adj.* Single; alone; not married. See CORPORATION ~; FEME ~.

SOLE CUSTODY. Custody of a child by one parent only under an agreement or order.

SOLELY. *adv.* One and only; exclusively.

SOLEMN ADMISSION. A plea of guilty when one is arraigned in court. P.K. McWilliams, *Canadian Criminal Evidence*, 3d ed. (Aurora: Canada Law Book, 1988) at 14-7.

SOLEMN DECLARATION. A solemn declaration in the form and manner from time to time provided by the provincial evidence acts or by the Canada Evidence Act. A declaration made knowing that it has the same force and effect as if made under oath or affirmation.

SOLEMN FORM. See PROVING A WILL IN ~.

SOLEMNIZATION. *n.* Entering into marriage publicly before witnesses.

SOLEMNIZATION OF MARRIAGE. "... [N]ot confined to the ceremony itself. It legitimately includes the various steps or preliminaries leading to it." *Albert (Attorney General) v. Underwood*, [1934] S.C.R. 635 at 639, [1934] 4 D.L.R. 167, the court per Rinfret J.

SOLE PROPRIETORSHIP. An unincorporated business organization having one owner who must

S

and does make all major decisions concerning the business.

SOLE RIGHTS. Intellectual property rights to produce or reproduce a work or a substantial part in any way.

SOLICIT. *v.* 1. "... [T]o endeavour to obtain by asking... ." *Burns v. Chiropractic Assn. (Alberta)* (1981), 31 A.R. 176 at 177, 16 Alta. L.R. (2d) 128, 125 D.L.R. (3d) 475 (C.A.), the court per Clement J.A. 2. In [s. 195.1 of the Criminal Code, R.S.C. 1970, c. C-34] includes an element of persistence or pressure. It was decided that the mere demonstration by a woman of her willingness and availability for prostitution would not suffice to ground a conviction. In addition, the Crown would be required to prove that her approach to a prospective customer was accompanied by pressure or persistent conduct... ." *Hutt v. R.* (1978), 38 C.C.C. (2d) 418 at 422-3, [1978] 2 S.C.R. 476, 1 C.R. (3d) 164, [1978] 2 W.W.R. 247, 19 N.R. 330, 82 D.L.R. (3d) 95, Spence J. (Laskin C.J., Dickson, Martland and Estey JJ. concurring). 3. To communicate, in person, using the spoken, written or printed word, a gesture or another means, for the purpose of receiving money or another thing of value, regardless of whether consideration is offered or provided in return. *Safe Streets Act*, S.B.C. 2004, c. 75, s. 1. See SOLICITATION.

SOLICITATION. *n.* (a) A request for a proxy whether or not it is accompanied by or included in a form of proxy; (b) a request to execute or not to execute a form of proxy or to revoke a proxy; (c) the sending of a form of proxy or other communication to a shareholder under circumstances reasonably calculated to result in the procurement, withholding or revocation of a proxy; or (d) the sending of a form of proxy to a shareholder, but does not include (e) the sending of a form of proxy to a security holder in response to an unsolicited request made by the security holder or on that person's behalf; or (f) the performance by any person of administrative acts or professional services on behalf of a person soliciting a proxy. *Bank Act*, S.C. 1991, c. 46, s. 156.01, part.

SOLICITOR. *n.* 1. In the Province of Quebec, an advocate or a notary and, in any other province, a barrister or solicitor. *Criminal Code*, R.S.C. 1985, c. C-46, s. 183. 2. When used alone, refers to one who does not appear in court regularly but does any of the other work of being a lawyer. 3. "In some jurisdictions there is a distinction between a barrister or counsel and a solicitor. The kind of work which may be undertaken or performed by each is clearly defined. The business of a barrister is advocacy, drafting pleadings and advising on questions of law, while the solicitor interviews clients, takes instructions and prepares the necessary material in the litigation, which is submitted to counsel who will appear at the trial. In those jurisdictions where the distinction exists solicitors do not appear in court." *Griffen v. Spanier*, [1947] 1 W.W.R. 489 at 491 (Sask. C.A.), McNiven J.A. See BARRISTER AND ~; CHANGE OF ~.

SOLICITOR-AND-CLIENT COSTS. These represent all disbursements, charges and fees, taxable by the solicitor against his client as necessary for the proper presentation of the proceeding in respect of which the costs are awarded, but limited to the four corners of that proceeding. Holloway v. Holloway, 2001 NFCA 17, 199 Nfld. & P.E.I.R. 1, 600 A.P.R. 1, 6 C.P.C. (5th) 34, 199 Nfld. & P.E.I.R. 1, [2001] N.J. No. 61. "The underlying purpose of an award of costs on the basis of those between solicitor and client is to provide complete indemnification for all costs, including fees and disbursements, reasonably incurred in the course of defending or prosecuting the action but excluding the costs for extra services not reasonably necessary." *Scott Paper Co. v. Minnesota Mining & Manufacturing Co.* (1982), 70 C.P.R. (2d) 68 at 79 (Fed. T.D.), Cattanach J.

SOLICITOR AND OWN CLIENT COSTS. 1. "[Allowing the costs which would] ... provide complete indemnity to her [the client] as to the costs essential to, and ... 'arising within, the four corners of litigation.' " *Seitz, Re* (1974), 6 O.R. (2d) 460 at 465, 53 D.L.R. (3d) 223 (H.C.), Lerner J. 2. These will usually be the same as solicitor and client costs, but where circumstances justify, there will be added any further disbursements, charges or fees that may arise out of the equities as between the solicitor and the client, except such as would result from unreasonableness on the part of the solicitor. *Holloway v. Holloway*, 2001 NFCA 17, 199 Nfld. & P.E.I.R. 1, 600 A.P.R. 1, 6 C.P.C. (5th) 34, 199 Nfld. & P.E.I.R. 1, [2001] N.J. No. 61.

SOLICITOR-CLIENT PRIVILEGE. 1. [I]s fundamental to the Canadian legal system and is more than a rule of evidence. It has evolved into a fundamental and substantive rule of law which commands a unique status within the legal system, integral to the workings of the legal system itself (see R. v. McClure, 2001 SCC 14 (CanLII), [2001] 1 S.C.R. 445 at paragraphs 24, 31-32). As such, this privilege "must be as close to absolute as possible to ensure public confidence and retain relevance" (see McClure at paragraph 35) and it is to be "jealously guarded and should only be set aside in the most unusual circumstances" (see Pritchard v. Ontario (Human Rights Commission), 2004 SCC 31, [2004] 1 S.C.R. 809 at paragraph 17). The substantive rule of solicitor-client privilege, as formulated in Descôteaux v. Mierzwinski, 1982 CanLII 22, [1982] 1 S.C.R. 860 and referred to by the Applications Judge, has been consistently applied by the Supreme Court of Canada (see Lavallee, Rackel & Heintz v. Canada (Attorney General), 2002 SCC 61, [2002] 3 S.C.R. 209 at paragraph 18). This substantive rule was set out by Lamer J. (as he then was) in Descôteaux at 875 as follows: 1. The confidentiality of communications between solicitor and client may be raised in any circumstances where such communications are likely to be disclosed without the client's consent. 2. Unless the law provides otherwise, when and to the extent that the legitimate exercise of a right would interfere with another person's right to have his communications with his lawyer kept confidential, the resulting conflict should be resolved in favour of protecting the confidentiality. 3. When the law gives someone the authority to do something which, in the circumstances of the case, might interfere with that confidentiality, the decision to do so and the choice of means of exercising that authority should be determined with a view to not interfering with it except to the extent absolutely necessary in order to achieve the ends sought by the enabling legislation. 4. Acts providing otherwise in situations under paragraph 2 and enabling legislation referred to in paragraph 3 must be interpreted restrictively. *Canada (Attorney General) v. Canada (Information Commissioner)*, 2005 FCA 199. 5. "... [T]he privilege belongs to the client alone. One consequence of this is that confidential communications between solicitor and client can only be divulged in certain circumscribed situations. The client may ... herself choose to disclose the contents of her communications with her legal representative and thereby waive the privilege. Or, the client may authorize the solicitor to reveal those communications for her. So important is the privilege that the courts have also stipulated that the confidentiality of communications between solicitor and client survives the death of the client and enures to his or her next of kin, heirs or successors in title." *Goodman Estate v. Geffen* (1991), 42 E.T.R. 97 at 125-6, [1991] 5 W.W.R. 389, 80 Alta. L.R. (2d) 293, 125 A.R. 81, 14 W.A.C. 81, 81 D.L.R. (4th) 211, [1991] 2 S.C.R. 353, Wilson J. (Cory J. concurring). See LEGAL PROFESSIONAL PRIVILEGE.

SOLICITOR GENERAL CANADA. The federal ministry which controls penitentiaries, paroles and remissions and law enforcement and supervises the National Parole Board, the Correctional Service and the RCMP.

SOLICITOR OF RECORD. The lawyer who is shown on pleadings or other documents filed in a court proceeding as being the lawyer who is acting for a particular party.

SOLICITOR'S J. *abbr.* Solicitor's Journal (Le Bulletin des avocats).

SOLICITOR'S LIEN. The lien to which a solicitor is entitled in respect to his or her fees. The lien may entitle a solicitor to retain papers or other property of the client which are in his or her possession. In other cases, it may entitle the solicitor to an order charging the proceeds, in court, of a successful action (otherwise belonging to the client) with the lien.

SOLIDARY OBLIGATION. An obligation is solidary between the debtors where they are obligated to the creditor for the same thing in such a way that each of them may be compelled separately to perform the whole obligation and where performance by a single debtor releases the others towards the creditor. *Civil Code*, S.Q. 1991, c. 64, a. 1523.

S.O.L.R. *abbr.* Sexual Offences Law Reporter, 1994-.

SORORAL SOCIETY. See FRATERNAL OR ~

SOUND IN DAMAGES. To have the basic quality of damages, said of actions brought to recover damages.

SOUND PREDICTION. [S]ound prediction and obviousness are considerations with different perspectives. Sound prediction is relied upon by an inventor to justify patent claims whose utility is not actually demonstrated but can be soundly predicted from information and expertise that is available. Obviousness is relied upon by a potential competitor of the patentee, who argues that what is claimed in a patent is something that a skilled technician keeping up with the state of the art and common general knowledge would be able to come to directly and without difficulty in the absence of the solution taught by the patent. These are different concepts and they are not to be conflated. The doctrine of sound prediction has no application to the doctrine of obviousness. *Genpharm Inc. v. Procter & Gamble Pharmaceuticals Canada Inc.*, 2004 FCA 393

SOUND RECORDING. A recording, fixed in any material form, consisting of sounds, whether or not of a performance of a work, but excludes any soundtrack of a cinematographic work where it accompanies the cinematographic work. *Copyright Act*, R.S.C. 1985, c. C-42, s. 2.

SOURCE. See JOURNALISTIC-CONFIDENTIAL ~ PRIVILEGE.

SOURCE CODE. Source code consists of algorithms and looks like lines of text. Source code can be defined as the exact sequence of commands used to instruct a microprocessor on how to execute an algorithm. The source code is in a format that can be read by a computer programmer and consists of names and logical operations represented utilizing the symbols entered on standard, compatible computer keyboard. *Teklogix Inc. v. Zaino* (1997), 79 C.P.R. (3d) 1 (Ont. Gen. Div.).

SOURCE INDIVIDUAL. An individual from whom a sample of a bodily substance is sought for the purposes of testing. *Mandatory Testing and Disclosure Act*, S.A. 2006, c. M-3.5, s. 1.

SOVEREIGN. *n.* 1. Any supreme or chief person. 2. The Sovereign of the United Kingdom, Canada and Her or His other realms and territories and head of the Commonwealth. See ACCESSION OF THE ~.

SOVEREIGN ACT. A sovereign act is an act done by a sovereign body acting in accordance with its sovereign privileges. *Miller c. R.*, 2001 CarswellQue 181, 2001 SCC 12, 196 D.L.R. (4th) 385, 266 N.R. 201, [2001] 1 S.C.R. 407, 10 C.C.E.L. (3d) 173, the court per Bastarache J.

SOVEREIGN IMMUNITY. 1. Canadian courts will not exercise jurisdiction over the property or person of an independent foreign state or sovereign without consent. Any such proceedings may be stayed if the state or sovereign moves to set the proceedings aside or remains passive. A foreign state includes any state which the forum recognizes, de facto or de jure. J.G. McLeod, *The Conflict of Laws* (Calgary: Carswell, 1983) at 68. 2. "... [T]he doctrine of absolute sovereign immunity ... . [was] stated by Lord Denning M.R., in Trendtex Trading Corp. v. Central Bank of Nigeria [1977] 1 Q.B. 529 (C.A.) at page 559. Lord Denning said: 'The doctrine grants immunity to a foreign government or its department of state, or any body which can be regarded as an "alter ego or organ" of the government.' " *Ferranti-*

S

Packard Ltd. v. Cushman Rentals Ltd. (1980), 19 C.P.C. 132 at 133, 30 O.R. (2d) 194, 115 D.L.R. (3d) 691 (Div. Ct.), the court per Reid J.

SOVEREIGNTY. *n.* The supreme authority within a state.

SOVEREIGNTY-ASSOCIATION. *n.* A compromise proposed in Quebec between outright separation and continuance as a province of Canada. Although it involved the secession of Quebec (sovereignty), it also involved economic association between Quebec and the rest of Canada (association). P.W. Hogg, *Constitutional Law of Canada*, 3d ed. (Toronto: Carswell, 1992) at 125.

S.P. *abbr.* Sessions of the Peace.

SPACE. See AIR ~; INTERMENT ~; STRATA ~.

SPACE FLIGHT. The period that begins with the launching of a crew member of the Space Station, continues during their stay in orbit and ends with their landing on earth. *Criminal Code*, R.S.C. 1985, c. C-46, s. 7.

SPACE STATION. The civil international Space Station that is a multi-use facility in low-earth orbit, with flight elements and dedicated ground elements provided by, or on behalf of, the Partner States. *Criminal Code*, R.S.C. 1985, c. C-46, s. 7.

SPACING UNIT. The area allocated to a well for the purpose of drilling for or producing oil or gas. See POOLED ~.

SPAM. *n.* E-mail messages soliciting purchases of products or services received by persons who have not expressed interest in or solicited information concerning the products or services offered.

SPAM FILTER. An electronic automated process that is established by an Internet service provider to analyze incoming messages and that maintains the confidentiality of, and does not reveal to the provider or any person, the content of any message, and rates every incoming message to determine whether it is likely to be spam.

SPANKING. *n.* All social science witnesses accepted a definition of spanking as "the administering of one or two mild to moderate 'smacks' with an open hand, on the buttocks or extremities which does not cause physical harm." Spanking [as defined here] is not child abuse. *Canadian Foundation for Children, Youth & the Law v. Canada (Attorney General)*, 2000 CarswellOnt 2409, 146 C.C.C. (3d) 362, 188 D.L.R. (4th) 718, 49 O.R. (3d) 662, 36 C.R. (5th) 334, 76 C.R.R. (2d) 251 (S.C.J.), McCombs J.

SPEAK. *v.* The verb "to speak" refers to more than the faculty of speech. The Canadian Oxford Dictionary, 2nd ed., also defines it as: ... 2 transitive a utter (words). b make known or communicate (one's opinion, the truth, etc.) in this way (never speaks sense). 3 intransitive a ... hold a conversation (spoke to him for an hour, spoke with them about their work). b ... mention in writing etc. (speaks of it in his novel). c ... articulate the feelings of (another person etc.) in speech or writing (speak for our generation). 4 intransitive a ... address; converse with (a person etc.)

... . *Knopf v. Canada (Speaker of the House of Commons)*, 2007 FCA 308.

SPEAKER. *n.* 1. With respect to the House of Commons, the representative of the House itself in power, proceedings and dignity; the representative of the House in relation to the Crown, the Senate and other people and authorities outside Parliament; the person who presides over debates and enforces observance of any rule for preserving order. This person is elected by the House itself and, on behalf of the House, controls the accommodation and services in the part of the Parliament Buildings and its precincts which the House of Commons occupies. A. Fraser, W.A. Dawson & J. Holtby, eds., *Beauchesne's Rules and Forms of the House of Commons of Canada*, 6th ed. (Toronto: Carswell, 1989) at 33 and 47. 2. The person who fulfills the same role in a provincial legislature.

SPECIAL. *adj.* 1. Usually means of a peculiar, not general kind. *Wood v. Wood*, 2001 SKCA 2, 13 R.F.L. (5th) 216, 203 Sask. R. 82, 240 W.A.C. 82. 2. Unusual, uncommon, exceptional. See STANDING, SESSIONAL AND ~ ORDERS.

SPECIAL ACT. A local, personal or private act; an act which applies to a certain kind of person or thing only.

SPECIAL AGENT. One authorized to transact only a particular business for the principal, as opposed to a general agent. Contrast GENERAL AGENT.

SPECIAL CASE. The statement of a question of law for the opinion of the court by all parties to a proceeding, and which any party moves that the judge determine. *Courts of Justice Act*, R.S.O. 1990, c. C.43, *Rules of Civil Procedure*, r. 22.01 (1).

SPECIAL COMMITTEE. A body the House appoints to inquire into a specified subject. When its final report is presented, it ceases to exist. A. Fraser, W.A. Dawson & J. Holtby, eds., *Beauchesne's Rules and Forms of the House of Commons of Canada*, 6th ed. (Toronto: Carswell, 1989) at 222.

SPECIAL CONCERN. See SPECIES OF ~.

SPECIAL COSTS. 1. "... [M]ore or less the old solicitor-and-client costs as described in the 1989 Rules [British Columbia Rules of Court]: ..." *Bradshaw Construction Ltd v. Bank of Nova Scotia* (1991), 48 C.P.C. (2d) 74 at 89, 54 B.C.L.R. (2d) 309 (S.C.), Bouck J. 2. The purpose of special costs is to punish a litigant or counsel for misconduct during litigation and deter further misconduct. It is well established that special costs may be ordered for reprehensible conduct falling short of scandal or outrage. Misconduct deserving of reproof or rebuke is "reprehensible". *Chances Housing Cooperative v. Progressive Homes Ltd.*, 2000 CarswellBC 744, 2000 BCSC 596, 46 C.P.C. (4th) 334 (S.C. [In Chambers]), Allan J. 3. Special costs are an offshoot of solicitor-and-client costs. ... [S]pecial costs do not comprise all legal costs actually incurred. Rather, special costs must be objectively reasonable. *Campbell River Woodworkers' & Builders' Supply (1966) Ltd. v. British Columbia (Minister of Transportation & Highways)*, 2004 BCCA 27.

SPECIAL DAMAGE. 1. Pecuniary loss before the trial. K.D. Cooper-Stephenson & I.B. Saunders, *Personal Injury Damages in Canada* (Toronto: Carswell, 1981) at 29 and 43. 2. Loss of earnings or profits before a trial and pre-trial expenses. K.D. Cooper-Stephenson & I.B. Saunders, *Personal Injury Damages in Canada* (Toronto: Carswell, 1981) at 51. 3. " ... A private person can bring an action for an alleged or anticipated breach of the law only where that breach would constitute a breach of his private rights or would inflict 'special' or 'peculiar' damage upon him: ... The common thread which runs through the authorities is that private citizens cannot maintain actions for public nuisance where the suffering and inconvenience complained of is shared by the public or a recognizable class of the public. The ultimate question is simple: is the damage suffered by the plaintiff different from that suffered by other members of the community?" *Stein v. Gonzales* (1984), 31 C.C.L.T. 19 at 22, 58 B.C.L.R. 110, [1984] 6 W.W.R. 428, 14 D.L.R. (4th) 283 (S.C.), McLachlin J.

SPECIAL DUTY SERVICE. Service as a member in a special duty area designated under section 69, or as a member as part of a special duty operation designated under section 70, during the period in which the designation is in effect. It includes any of the following that occurred during that period but not earlier than September 11, 2001: (a) periods of training for the express purpose of service in that area or as part of that operation, wherever that training takes place; (b) travel to and from the area, the operation or the location of training referred to in paragraph (a); and (c) authorized leave of absence with pay during that service, wherever that leave is taken. *Canadian Forces Members and Veterans Re-establishment and Compensation Act, S.C. 2005, c. 21, s. 2.*

SPECIAL EXAMINER. An official examiner.

SPECIAL FORCE. Such component of the Canadian Forces as may be established. In an emergency, or if considered desirable in consequence of any action undertaken by Canada under the United Nations Charter or the North Atlantic Treaty, the North American Aerospace Defence Command Agreement or any other similar instrument to which Canada is a party, the Governor in Council may establish and authorize the maintenance of a component of the Canadian Forces, called the special force, consisting of (a) officers and non-commissioned members of the regular force who are placed in the special force under conditions prescribed in regulations; (b) officers and non-commissioned members of the reserve force who, being on active service or having applied and been accepted for continuing, full-time military service, are placed in the special force under conditions prescribed in regulations; and (c) officers and non-commissioned members not of the regular force or the reserve force who are enrolled in the special force for continuing, full-time military service. The maximum numbers of officers and non-commissioned members in the special force shall be as authorized by the Governor in Council, and the special force shall include such units and other elements as are embodied therein. *National Defence Act*, R.S.C. 1985, c. N-5, s. 2, 16.

SPECIALIA GENERALIBUS DEROGANT. [L.] Special words restrict general ones.

SPECIAL INTEREST. A pecuniary or proprietary interest including physical injury or the risk of injury.

SPECIALLY. See CROSSED ~.

SPECIAL NEEDS HOUSING. A unit that is occupied by or is made available for occupancy by a household having one or more individuals who require accessibility modifications or provincially-funded support services in order to live independently in the community. *Social Housing Reform Act*, S.O. 2000, c. 27, s. 2.

SPECIAL OPERATIONAL INFORMATION. Information that the Government of Canada is taking measures to safeguard that reveals, or from which may be inferred, (a) the identity of a person, agency, group, body or entity that is or is intended to be, has been approached to be, or has offered or agreed to be, a confidential source of information, intelligence or assistance to the Government of Canada; (b) the nature or content of plans of the Government of Canada for military operations in respect of a potential, imminent or present armed conflict; (c) the means that the Government of Canada used uses or intends to use, or is capable of using, to covertly collect or obtain, or to decipher, assess, analyse, process, handle, report, communicate or otherwise deal with information or intelligence, including any vulnerabilities or limitations of those means; (d) whether a place, person, agency, group, body or entity was, is or is intended to be the object of a covert investigation, or a covert collection of information or intelligence, by the Government of Canada; (e) the identity of any person who is, has been or is intended to be covertly engaged in an information- or intelligence-collection activity or program of the Government of Canada that is covert in nature; (f) the means that the Government of Canada used, uses or intends to use, or is capable of using, to protect or exploit any information or intelligence referred to in any of paragraphs (a) to (e), including, but not limited to, encryption and cryptographic systems, and any vulnerabilities or limitations of those means; or (g) information or intelligence similar in nature to information or intelligence referred to in any of paragraphs (a) to (f) that is in relation to, or received from, a foreign entity or terrorist group. *Security of Information Act* (was *Official Secrets Act*), R.S.C. 1985, c. O-5, s. 8.

SPECIAL PROPERTY. Limited or qualified property.

SPECIAL PURCHASER. A person willing to pay more than the fair market value for a given asset because the asset has some special value to that person.

SPECIAL RESOLUTION. A resolution passed by a majority of not less than two-thirds or three-quarters, or other percentage specified by governing legislation, of the votes cast by the shareholders or members who voted in respect of that resolution.

S

SPECIALTY. *n.* A bond, an obligation created by statute, a contract under seal.

SPECIALTY CONTRACT. A contract under seal.

SPECIALTY DEBT. 1. A bond, mortgage or debt which one secures by writing under seal. 2. "... [S]ometimes used to denote any contract under seal, but it is more often used in the sense of meaning a specialty debt, that is, an obligation under seal securing a debt or a debt due from the Crown or under statute... ." *Williams v. R.*, [1942] 3 D.L.R. 1 at 1, [1942] 2 W.W.R. 321, [1942] A.C. 541, [1942] 2 All E.R. 951 (P.C.), the court per Viscount Maugham.

SPECIE. *n.* 1. Metallic money. 2. Something in its own true form, not a substitute, equivalent or compensation.

SPECIES. *n.* Any taxonomic classification of non-human life. *Assisted Human Reproduction Act*, S.C. 2004, c. 2, s. 11. See THREATENED ~; WILD-LIFE ~.

SPECIES AT RISK. An extirpated, endangered or threatened species or a species of special concern. *Species at Risk Act*, S.C. 2002, c. 29, s. 2.

SPECIES OF SPECIAL CONCERN. A wildlife species that may become a threatened or an endangered species because of a combination of biological characteristics and identified threats. *Species at Risk Act*, S.C. 2002, c. 29, s. 2.

SPECIFICATION. *n.* 1. "[Details] ... the kind and type of material to be used to construct a project, ..." *Bird Construction Co. v. United States Fire Insurance Co.* (1985), 45 Sask. R. 96 at 100, 18 C.L.R. 115, [1986] I.L.R. 1-2047, 24 D.L.R. (4th) 104, 18 C.C.L.I. 92 (C.A.), the court per Vancise J.A. 2. A specification of an invention in accordance with subsections 27(3) and (4) of the Act. *Patent Act*, R.S.C. 1985, c. P-4, *Patent Rules*, SOR/96-423, s. 2. 3. The specification of an invention must (a) correctly and fully describe the invention and its operation or use as contemplated by the inventor; (b) set out clearly the various steps in a process, or the method of constructing, making, compounding or using a machine, manufacture or composition of matter, in such full, clear, concise and exact terms as to enable any person skilled in the art or science to which it pertains, or with which it is most closely connected, to make, construct, compound or use it; (c) in the case of a machine, explain the principle of the machine and the best mode in which the inventor has contemplated the application of that principle; and (d) in the case of a process, explain the necessary sequence, if any, of the various steps, so as to distinguish the invention from other inventions. The specification must end with a claim or claims defining distinctly and in explicit terms the subject-matter of the invention for which an exclusive privilege or property is claimed. *Patent Act*, R.S.C. 1985, c. P-4, s. 27(3), (4).

SPECIFIC BEQUEST. The gift of a certain item of personal estate in a will.

SPECIFIC CHARGE. "One that, without more, fastens on ascertained and definite property, or property capable of being ascertained and defined." *Illing-*worth v. Houldsworth*, [1904] A.C. 355 at 358, Lord Macnaghten.

SPECIFIC CLAIMS TRIBUNAL. The Governor in Council shall establish a roster of 6 to 18 superior court judges to act as members of the Tribunal. The Tribunal is responsible for holding hearings to decide the validity of specific claims and any compensation arising from those claims. Subject to certain exceptions, a First Nation may file with the Tribunal a claim based on any of the following grounds, for compensation for its losses arising from those grounds: (a) a failure to fulfil a legal obligation of the Crown to provide lands or other assets under a treaty or another agreement between the First Nation and the Crown; (b) a breach of a legal obligation of the Crown under the Indian Act or any other legislation—pertaining to Indians or lands reserved for Indians—of Canada or of a colony of Great Britain of which at least some portion now forms part of Canada; (c) a breach of a legal obligation arising from the Crown's provision or non-provision of reserve lands, including unilateral undertakings that give rise to a fiduciary obligation at law, or its administration of reserve lands, Indian moneys or other assets of the First Nation; (d) an illegal lease or disposition by the Crown of reserve lands; (e) a failure to provide adequate compensation for reserve lands taken or damaged by the Crown or any of its agencies under legal authority; or (f) fraud by employees or agents of the Crown in connection with the acquisition, leasing or disposition of reserve lands. *Specific Claims Tribunal Act*, S.C. 2008, c. 22, s. 6 and 14.

SPECIFIC DETERRENCE. 1. Refers to a sentence intended to discourage the accused from committing the same offence again. 2. While the term "meaningful consequences" is notionally similar to the concept of specific deterrence, there is a distinction between these two concepts. "Meaningful consequences" seemingly requires that a sentence be based on the young person's past conduct, while specific deterrence is intended to discourage future conduct considered to be inappropriate. Although there may only be a thin line between imposing a "meaningful consequence" and creating a deterrent effect, a sentence will be appropriate so long as it is intended to ensure the long-term protection of the public by focussing on the rehabilitation of the young person, without regard to any consequential deterrent effect such a penalty may have. *R. v. M. (M.L.)*, 2008 ABCA 212.

SPECIFIC DEVISE. The gift of a certain item of real property in a will.

SPECIFIC GOODS. 1. Goods identified and agreed upon at the time a contract of sale is made. *Sale of Goods acts.* 2. Goods identified and agreed on at the time a security agreement in respect of those goods is made. *Personal Property Security acts.*

SPECIFIC INTENT. "[A degree of intent required for some criminal offences. In committing an offence] ... which involves the performance of the actus reus, coupled with an intention or purpose going beyond the mere performance of the questioned act. Striking a blow or administering poison with intent to kill, or assault with intent to maim or wound, are examples of such offences." *R. v. Bernard* (1988), 38 C.R.R. 82 at 90, 67 C.R. (3d) 113, 90 N.R. 321, 45 C.C.C. (3d) 1, [1988] 2 S.C.R. 833, 32 O.A.C. 161, McIntyre J. (Beetz J. concurring). See CRIME OF ~.

SPECIFIC INTENT OFFENCE. An offence requiring a specific intent. See SPECIFIC INTENT.

SPECIFIC LEGACY. A gift by will of a particular thing.

SPECIFIC PERFORMANCE. 1. A special remedy available where a person seeks to enforce a contract to purchase a unique property. *Basi v. Levert*, 2008 BCCA 156. 2. A court order which compels a person to do something previously promised according to a contractual obligation.

SPECIFIED INVESTMENT BUSINESS. 1. Carried on by a corporation in a taxation year means a business (other than a business carried on by a credit union or a business of leasing property other than real property) the principal purpose of which is to derive income (including interest, dividends, rents and royalties) from property but, except where the corporation was a prescribed labour-sponsored venture capital corporation at any time in the year, does not include a business carried on by the corporation in the year where (a) the corporation employs in the business throughout the year more than 5 full-time employees, or (b) any other corporation associated with the corporation provides, in the course of carrying on an active business, managerial, administrative, financial, maintenance or other similar services to the corporation in the year and the corporation could reasonably be expected to require more than 5 full-time employees if those services had not been provided. *Income Tax Act*, R.S.C. 1985, c. 1 (5th Supp.), s. 125. 2. The definition of "specified investment business" does not ask about the general nature of the business of a corporation, or the degree of activity or passivity actually required by that business. Rather, it asks about the legal character of the income that the business is intended principally to earn. If on the relevant date the legal character of that income is rent, for example, then the business meets the definition unless once of the statutory exceptions applies (none of those exceptions is relevant in this case). *Weaver v. Canada*, 2008 FCA 238.

SPEC. LECT. L.S.U.C. *abbr.* Special Lectures of the Law Society of Upper Canada.

SPECULATION. *n.* This court, in its judgment on appeal in Willard Miller [Newfoundland (Workers' Compensation Commission) v. Miller (1998), 167 Nfld. & P.E.I.R. 115 (Nfld. T.D.)] . . . has stressed that an inference is different from speculation . . . Drawing an inference amounts to a process of reasoning by which a factual conclusion is deduced as a logical consequence from other facts established by the evidence. Speculation on the other hand is merely a guess or conjecture; there is a gap in the reasoning process that is necessary, as a matter of logic, to get from one fact to the conclusion sought to be established. Speculation, unlike an inference, requires a leap of faith. *Osmond v. Newfoundland (Workers' Compensation Commission)*, 2001 NFCA 21, 200

Nfld. & P.E.I.R. 202, 603 A.P.R. 202, 10 C.C.E.L. (3d) 56, 200 Nfld. & P.E.I.R. 202, [2001] N.J. No. 111.

SPECULATIVE RETIREMENT METHOD. A method of determining the value of a person's interest in a group pension for the purposes of dividing property in a marriage breakdown. The value of the future income stream is calculated assuming the member will continue to be employed until retirement. Likely future earnings are assumed.

SPEECH. *n.* ". . . [A]udible oral communication." *Tadman v. Seaboard Life Insurance Co.* (1989), 64 Alta. L.R. (2d) 285 at 288, 93 A.R. 83, [1989] I.L.R. 1-2441, 36 C.C.L.I. 215 (C.A.), Belzil, Bracco and Foisy JJ.A. See COMMERCIAL ~; FREEDOM OF ~.

SPEECH FROM THE THRONE. 1. The Governor General's speech which opens a session of Parliament and outlines the legislative programme for that session as planned by cabinet. This speech is written by the Prime Minister. P.W. Hogg, *Constitutional Law of Canada*, 3d ed. (Toronto: Carswell, 1992) at 244. 2. The similar speech given by a Lieutenant Governor in the legislature of a province.

SPEECH-LANGUAGE PATHOLOGY. The assessment of speech and language functions and the treatment and prevention of speech and language dysfunctions or disorders to develop, maintain, rehabilitate or augment oral motor or communicative functions.

SPENDING POWER. A power, though not explicitly mentioned in the Constitution Act, 1867, which is inferred from the powers to legislate in relation to "public property" (section 91(1A)), to levy taxes (section 91(3)), and to appropriate federal funds (section 106). P.W. Hogg, *Constitutional Law of Canada*, 3d ed. (Toronto: Carswell, 1992) at 150.

SPENT BREACH DOCTRINE. The person seeking to exercise an option to purchase is allowed to exercise it notwithstanding past breaches or deficiently performed conditions precedent provided these breaches have been cured or the conditions remedied, that is, spent, by the time the option is to be exercised.

SPES SUCCESSIONIS. [L.] Hope of succession, in contrast to a vested right.

SPIRIT OF THE INVENTION. The "spirit of the invention" school in this country relies on Dominion Manufacturers Ltd. v. Electrolier Manufacturing Co., [1934] S.C.R. 436. In that case, which involved a method to pivot handles for coffins, Rinfret J. spoke of "the spirit of the invention" but did so in a direct quote from the patent itself, at p. 443: What the appellant did—and in that his infringement truly consists—was to take the idea which formed the real subject-matter of the invention. It does not matter whether he also adopted the substitution of the two holes for the bar in the pivoting means. The precise form of these means was immaterial. In the language of the patent, they could be changed "without departing from the spirit of the invention". The patent owner, competitors, potential infringers and the public generally are thus entitled to clear and definite rules as to the extent of the monopoly conferred. This in turn requires that the subjective or discretionary element of claims interpretation (e.g., the elusive quest for "the spirit of the invention") be kept to the minimum, consistent with giving "the inventor protection for that which he has actually in good faith invented" (Western Electric Co. v. Baldwin International Radio of Canada Ltd., [1934] S.C.R. 570 (S.C.C.), at p. 574). Predictability is achieved by tying the patentee to its claims; fairness is achieved by interpreting those claims in an informed and purposive way. *Free World Trust c. Électro Santé Inc.*, 2000 CarswellQue 2728, 2000 SCC 66, 194 D.L.R. (4th) 232, 263 N.R. 150, [2000] 2 S.C.R. 1024, 9 C.P.R. (4th) 168, Binnie J.

SPIRITS. *n.* 1. Any beverage containing alcohol obtained by distillation. 2. Any material or substance containing more than 0.5 [per cent] absolute ethyl alcohol by volume other than (a) wine; (b) beer; (c) vinegar; (d) denatured alcohol; (e) specially denatured alcohol; (f) fusel oil or other refuse produced as a result of the distillation process; (g) an approved formulation; or (h) any product containing or manufactured from a material or substance referred to in paragraphs (b) to (g) that is not consumable as a beverage. *Excise Act, 2001*, S.C. 2002, c. 22, s. 2.

SPLIT. *v.* With respect to a cause of action, to sue for only a part of a demand or claim, with intent to sue for the rest in another action.

SPLIT DECISION NOTICE. Allows the offeree under a shotgun clause to divide all of the assets into two packages for division between the two shareholders. *Aronowicz v. EMTWO Properties Inc.*, 2010 CarswellOnt 598, 2010 ONCA 96.

SPLIT TRIALS. A form of trial that occur when a judge decides that the issues can properly be divided. One or more issues of fact or law are decided before the others. *Yaremy v. Insurance Corp. of British Columbia*, 2008 BCCA 235.

SPOLIATION. *n.* In conclusion, therefore, I would summarize the Canadian law of spoliation in the following way: 1. Spoliation currently refers to the intentional destruction of relevant evidence when litigation is existing or pending. 2. The principal remedy for spoliation is the imposition of a rebuttable presumption of fact that the lost or destroyed evidence would not assist the spoliator. The presumption can be rebutted by evidence showing the spoliator did not intend, by destroying the evidence, to affect the litigation, or by other evidence to prove or repel the case. 3. Outside this general framework other remedies may be available – even where evidence has been unintentionally destroyed. Remedial authority for these remedies is found in the court's rules of procedure and its inherent ability to prevent abuse of process, and remedies may include such relief as the exclusion of expert reports and the denial of costs. 4. The courts have not yet found that the intentional destruction of evidence gives rise to an intentional tort, nor that there is a duty to preserve evidence for purposes of the law of negligence, although these issues, in most jurisdictions, remain open. 5. Generally, the issues of whether spoliation has occurred, and what remedy should be given if it has, are matters best left for trial where the trial judge can consider all of the facts and fashion the most appropriate response. 6. Pre-trial relief may be available in the exceptional case where a party is particularly disadvantaged by the destruction of evidence. But generally this is accomplished through the applicable rules of court, or the court's general discretion with respect to costs and the control of abuse of process. *McDougall v. Black & Decker Canada Inc.*, 2008 ABCA 353, Conrad J.A. for the court.

SPONTANEOUS. *adj.* Arising from natural impulse without any external prompting or constraint.

SPOUSAL COMMUNICATIONS PRIVILEGE. Communications between spouses is privileged in criminal law and generally in civil proceedings.

SPOUSAL SUPPORT ORDER. A court of competent jurisdiction may, on application by either or both spouses, make an order requiring a spouse to secure or pay, or to secure and pay, such lump sum or periodic sums, or such lump sum and periodic sums, as the court thinks reasonable for the support of the other spouse. *Divorce Act*, R.S.C., 1985, c. 3 (2nd Supp.), s. 15.2.

SPOUSE. *n.* 1. Section 29 [of the Family Law Act, R.S.O. 1990, c. F.3] defines "spouse" as "either of a man and a woman" who meet the other requirements of the section. It follows that the definition could not have been meant to define a couple. Rather it explicitly refers to the individual members of the couple. Same-sex couples are necessarily excluded from this definition, thereby giving rise to the charge that the legislation is underinclusive. *M v. H*, 1999 CarswellOnt 1348, (sub nom. *M. v. H.*) 171 D.L.R. (4th) 577, (sub nom. *M. v. H.*) 238 N.R. 179, (sub nom. *M. v. H.*) 43 O.R. (3d) 254 (headnote only), (sub nom. *M. v. H.*) 62 C.R.R. (2d) 1, (sub nom. *M. v. H.*) 121 O.A.C. 1, 46 R.F.L. (4th) 32, (sub nom. *Attorney General for Ontario v. M. & H.*) C.E.B. & P.G.R. 8354 (headnote only), (sub nom. *M. v. H.*) [1999] 2 S.C.R. 3, Cory J. (Lamer C.J.C., L'Heureux-Dubé, McLachlin, Iacobucci and Binnie JJ. concurring). 2. Either of two persons who are married to each other. *Divorce Act*, R.S.C, 1985, c. 3 (2nd Supp.), s. 2. 3. A person of the opposite sex to whom the person is married or with whom the person is living in a conjugal relationship outside marriage. Ontario statutes. 4. A person who (a) is married to another person, or (b) is living and cohabiting with another person in a marriage-like relationship, including a marriage-like relationship between persons of the same gender. B.C. statutes. 5. " ... [A] man married to a woman, or a woman married to a man... A person is a spouse only while married..." *British Columbia (Public Trustee) v. Price* (1990), 25 R.F.L. (3d) 113 at 118, 43 B.C.L.R. (2d) 368, [1990] 4 W.W.R. 52, 67 D.L.R. (4th) 481 (C.A.), the court per Lambert J.A. 6. " ... [A]pplicable to persons living in a common law relationship..." *Novick Estate v. Lachuk Estate* (1987), (*sub nom. Novick (Novick Estate) v. Miller (Lachuk Estate)*) 6 R.F.L. (3d) 187 at 199, 55 Sask. R. 216 (Q.B.), Grotsky J. 7. A person of the opposite sex to whom the person is married or with whom the person is living in a conjugal relationship outside marriage. 8. Does not include a person from whom a public office holder is separated if all support obligations and family property or patrimony have been dealt with by a separation agreement or a court order. *Conflict of Interest Act*, S.C. 2006, c. 9, s. 2, s. 2. See COMMON LAW ~ WIFE.

SPREAD. See BULL ~.

SPREADING FALSE NEWS. A person who wilfully publishes a statement, tale or news that he knows is false and that causes or is likely to cause injury or mischief to a public interest is guilty of an offence. *Criminal Code*, R.S.C. 1985, c. C-46, s. 181.

SPRINGBOARD INJUNCTION. One which is issued to prevent the misuse of confidential information. A person who has obtained information in confidence is not allowed to use it as a springboard for activities detrimental to the party who made the confidential communication.

SPRINGING USE. A use like an executory interest which directs property to vest at a future time which need not coincide with the common law termination of a legal estate.

SPRINKLER LEAKAGE INSURANCE. Insurance against loss of or damage to property through the breakage or leakage of sprinkler equipment or other fire protection system, or of pumps, water pipes or plumbing and its fixtures. *Insurance acts*.

SPYWARE. *n.* Software embedded within other software and used by advertisers to monitor internet users' surfing habits for marketing or demographic research purposes.

SQUATTER. *n.* Someone who occupies land without consent or licence.

SQUATTER'S TITLE. Title acquired by someone who has occupied land without paying rent or in any other way acknowledging superior title for so long that that person acquires indefeasible title.

SQUEEZE-OUT TRANSACTION. A transaction by a corporation that is not a distributing corporation that would require an amendment to its articles and would, directly or indirectly, result in the interest of a holder of shares of a class of the corporation being terminated without the consent of the holder, and without substituting an interest of equivalent value in shares issued by the corporation, which shares have equal or greater rights and privileges than the shares of the affected class.

S.R. *abbr.* Saskatchewan Reports, 1979-.

S.R. & O. *abbr.* Statutory rules and orders in England.

STABLE. *adj.* Situations in which the client's health status can be anticipated with predictable outcomes. *Registered Nurses Act*, S.N.S. 2006, c. 21, s. 2.

STAFF. See MINISTERIAL ~.

STAFFING. See PUBLIC SERVICE ~ TRIBUNAL.

STAGING. *n.* Refers to a deliberate alteration of the crime scene by the perpetrator of the crime to mislead the police as to the identity of the perpetrator. *R. v. Klymchuk* (2005), 205 O.A.C. 57.

STAKE. *n.* A deposit made in hopes a particular event takes place.

STAKEHOLDER. *n.* 1. A person who holds money pending the outcome of a wager or bet. 2. A person who holds property or money which rival claimants claim, but who claims no personal interest in that property or money. 3. A person or group having an interest in particular issues facing government. See INTERPLEADER.

STAKEHOLDER GROUP. A group of members of a multi-stakeholder co-operative, (a) with a common interest, or (b) residing within a defined geographical area. *Co-operative Corporations Act*, R.S.O. 1990, c. C.35, s. 1.

STALE CHEQUE. A cheque which a bank may dishonour after a certain period, without breaching the banker-customer contract. I.F.G. Baxter, *The Law of Banking*, 3d ed. (Toronto: Carswell, 1981) at 85.

STALE DEMAND. A claim made so long ago that it is presumed that it was waived.

STALKING HORSE BID. In disposing of the assets or business of an insolvent company, a binding commitment to purchase the business or assets if a higher offer is not obtained at auction or other sale process. If a higher offer is accepted, the bidder may be compensated for its expenses or may receive a fee.

STAMP. *n.* An impressed or adhesive stamp used for the purpose of revenue by the government of Canada or a Canadian province or by the government of a foreign state. *Criminal Code*, R.S.C. 1985, c. C-46, s. 376(3). See POSTAGE ~.

STANDARD. *n.* Something which has authority and tests other things of the same kind. See BUILDING CONSTRUCTION ~; CANADIAN ~S ASSOCIATION; COMMUNITY ~; EMPLOYMENT ~; ENERGY EFFICIENCY ~; INTERNATIONAL FINANCIAL REPORTING ~S; INTERNATIONAL HUMAN RIGHTS ~S; MARKET VALUATION ~; NATIONAL ~; NEUTRAL CITATION ~.

STANDARD FILM. Cinematographic film of 35 millimetres or more in width. *Theatres Act*, R.S.O. 1990, c. T-6, s. 1. [repealed].

STANDARD DERIVATIVE. A derivative that is traded on a published market, whose intrinsic characteristics are determined by that market and whose trade is cleared and settled by a clearing house. *Derivatives Act*, R.S.Q. c. I-14.01, s. 3.

STANDARDIZED FUTURE. An agreement traded on a futures exchange pursuant to standardized conditions contained in the bylaws, rules or regulations of the futures exchange, and cleared and settled by a clearing house, to do one or more of the following at a price established by or determinable by reference to the agreement and at or by a time established by or determinable by reference to the agreement: (i) make or take delivery of the underlying interest of the agreement; (ii) settle the obligation in cash instead of delivery of the underlying interest. *Personal Property Security Acts*.

S

STANDARD OF CARE. The standard of care is the measure by which the discharge of the duty owed by one person to another is determined in the law of negligence. *Murao v. Blackcomb Skiing Enterprises Ltd. Partnership*, 2005 BCCA 43.

STANDARD OF PROOF. A standard which sets the degree of probability which the evidence must create in order to entitle the party who bears the burden of proof to succeed in proving her or his case or an issue in the case. J. Sopinka and S.N. Lederman, *The Law of Evidence in Civil Cases* (Toronto: Butterworths, 1974) at 384-85. See also BALANCE OF PROBABILITIES; CIVIL ONUS; CRIMINAL ONUS; BEYOND A REASONABLE DOUBT.

STANDARD OF REVIEW. [In review of decisions of administrative tribunals], [t]here ought to be two standards of review—correctness and reasonableness. The two variants of reasonableness review [patent unreasonableness and reasonableness simpliciter] should be collapsed into a single form of "reasonableness" review. *Dunsmuir v. New Brunswick*, 2008 SCC 9, Bastarache and LeBel JJ. at para. 34, 45. See CORRECTNESS; CURIAL DEFERENCE; DEFERENCE; JUDICIAL DEFERENCE; PATENTLY UNREASONABLE; POLYCENTRICITY; UNREASONABLE.

STANDARD OF REVIEW ANALYSIS. The existing approach to determining the appropriate standard of review has commonly been referred to as "pragmatic and functional". That name is unimportant. Reviewing courts must not get fixated on the label at the expense of a proper understanding of what the inquiry actually entails. Because the phrase "pragmatic and functional approach" may have misguided courts in the past, we prefer simply to the "standard of review analysis" in the future. The analysis must be contextual. As mentioned above, it is dependent on the application of a number of relevant factors, including: (1) the presence or absence of a privative clause; (2) the purpose of the tribunal as determined by interpretation of enabling legislation; (3) the nature of the question at issue, and; (4) the expertise of the tribunal. In many cases, it will not be necessary to consider all of the factors, as some of them may be determinative in the application of the reasonableness standard in a specific case. *Dunsmuir v. New Brunswick*, 2008 SCC 9, Bastarache and LeBel JJ. at para. 63 and 64.

STANDARDS OF PRACTICE. The methods and practices, approved by a governing body of a profession, which regulate the practice of the profession by the body's members.

STANDARD TRACK. The procedure followed when an appeal proceeds with factums, within the time limits provided for in these Rules and without case management. *Canada Federal Rules, Rules of the Court of Appeal of Quebec in Criminal Matters*, SI/2006-142, s. 1.

STAND-BY LETTER OF CREDIT. A security device and involves an obligation upon the issuing bank to pay any demand for payment by the beneficiary only upon default of the bank's customer to pay or perform its obligations owed to the beneficiary. It is also referred to as a guarantee letter of credit. *Morguard Trust Co. v. Royal Bank*, (1988), 88 A.R. 351, [1988] 5 W.W.R. 415, 60 Alta. L.R. (2d) 99.

STANDING. *n.* 1. "... [T]o establish status as a plaintiff in a suit seeking a declaration that legislation is invalid, if there is a serious issue as to its invalidity, a person need only to show that he is affected by it directly or that he has a genuine interest as a citizen in the validity of the legislation and that there is no other reasonable and effective manner in which the issue may be brought before the Court." *Borowski v. Canada (Minister of Justice), (sub nom. Canada (Minister of Justice) v. Borowski* [1981] 2 S.C.R. 575 at 598, [1982] 1 W.W.R. 97, 24 C.P.C. 62, 24 C.R. (3d) 352, 12 Sask. R. 420, 64 C.C.C. (2d) 97, 130 D.L.R. (3d) 588, 39 N.R. 331, Martland J. (Ritchie, Dickson, Beetz, Estey, McIntyre and Chouinard JJ. concurring). 2. "... [I]n order to obtain standing as a person 'interested' in litigation between other parties, the applicant must have an interest in the actual lis between those parties." *Schofield v. Ontario (Minister of Consumer & Commercial Relations)* (1980), 19 C.P.C. 245 at 251, 28 O.R. (2d) 764, 112 D.L.R. (3d) 132 (C.A.), Wilson J.A. See LEGAL ~; LOCUS STANDI.

STANDING COMMITTEE. A body appointed under a standing order to consider and report on estimates, to examine and report on government agencies and departments and, to conduct any investigation or inquiry which the House requires. Since 1985, they have been given permanent general orders of reference. A. Fraser, W.A. Dawson & J. Holtby, eds., *Beauchesne's Rules and Forms of the House of Commons of Canada*, 6th ed. (Toronto: Carswell, 1989) at 221-2.

STANDING COURT MARTIAL. May try any officer or non-commissioned member who is liable to be charged, dealt with and tried on a charge of having committed a service offence. Every military judge is authorized to preside at a Standing Court Martial, and a military judge who does so constitutes the Standing Court Martial. *National Defence Act*, R.S.C. 1985, c. N-5, ss. 173, 174.

STANDING, SESSIONAL AND SPECIAL ORDERS. The rules and regulations which the House of Commons uses to govern its proceedings. A. Fraser, W.A. Dawson & J. Holtby, eds., *Beauchesne's Rules and Forms of the House of Commons of Canada*, 6th ed. (Toronto: Carswell, 1989) at 5.

STANDSTILL AGREEMENT. 1. An agreement between parties to litigation not to take any further steps in the action pending negotiation of a settlement. 2. A standstill agreement existed whereby the respondent undertook to withhold taking formal steps to advance the claim in consideration of the continuing settlement negotiations and the appellant's implied waiver of the right to rely on expiry of the limitation period. *Brar v. Roy*, 2005 ABCA 269. 3. The leading case is Bugg v. Beau Canada Exploration Ltd. 2006 ABCA 201. In that case the counsel for the two parties had entered into correspondence about the timing of the filing of a statement of defence and some extensions had been requested. A letter confirmed the Defendant Bugg's undertaking to file a statement of defence. Having undertaken to do something that would materially advance the action and restart the five year clock, the court held that Bugg was contractually bound not to do something inconsistent; he was precluded from bringing an application under R. 244.1 to dismiss the action for want of prosecution based on the passage of time. The court held that this arrangement was an express standstill agreement. [The court] said that it is preferable that the agreement state precisely what steps in the litigation process are waived or suspended pending the exploration of settlement. *Sinnott v. Canadian Pacific Railway Co.*, 2009 ABQB 442. 4. Can be written, oral, or partly written and partly oral, as long as it is express and not based on intent or inference. *Bugg v. Beau Canada Exploration Ltd.*, 2006 ABCA 201.

STARE DECISIS. [L.] 1. The principle by which a precedent or decision of one court binds courts lower in the judicial hierarchy. P.W. Hogg, *Constitutional Law of Canada*, 3d ed. (Toronto: Carswell, 1992) at 219. 2. "... [D]ecided cases which lay down a rule of law are authoritative and must be followed. The general statement is, of course, subject to qualifications, ... The decisions of our own Supreme Court of Canada until reversed are binding on all Canadian Courts, and the Supreme Court is bound by its own previous decisions ..." *Reference re Canada Temperance Act*, [1939] 4 D.L.R. 14 at 33, 72 C.C.C. 145, [1939] O.R. 570 (C.A.), McTague J.A. 3. Each panel of an appeal court is bound by the decisions of other panels on questions of law. 4. One trial judge will not except in extraordinary circumstances refuse to follow the decision of another judge of the same court.

STARTER PISTOL. See CONVERTIBLE ~.

STARTING-POINT SENTENCE. Guideline sentences, also commonly referred to as "starting-point sentences," were introduced by appellate courts beginning in the early 1980's. By setting out starting points for sentencing purposes for certain offences, the courts were able to step past the problems under which each judge's personal view of the seriousness of a crime would drive the final sentence. Therefore, the starting point sentencing regime was - and is - a way by which appellate courts might minimize the risk of widely disparate sentences. The starting point is just that: a starting point from which the sentencing judge may move up or down in order to arrive at a fit sentence appropriate to the particular offender. *R. v. Christie*, 2004 ABCA 287.

START-UP COSTS. One time costs associated with a new business or a significant change to an existing business.

STATE. *n.* 1. A group of people who occupy a certain territory and have an executive and legislative organization under their own, exclusive control. 2. Part of a larger state, i.e. the separate organizations which collectively make up Australia. 3. Includes a political subdivision of a state and an official agency of a state. 4. "... [T]he definition of the word 'state' [in s. 2 of the Reciprocal Enforcement of Maintenance Orders Act, R.S.N.B. 1973, c. R-4] is sufficiently broad to include the concept of 'law district' and in Canada it has long been recognized that each province is a separate and distinct law district, ..." *Brewer (Mousseau) v. Brewer* (1981), 35 N.B.R. (2d) 329 at 340, 88 A.P.R. 329, 22 C.P.C. 143 (C.A.), the court per Richard J.A. 5. Any state or territory of the United States of America and includes the District of Columbia. See ACT OF ~; AGENT OF THE ~; CONTRACTING ~; DELIVERABLE ~; EFTA ~; FEDERAL ~; FOREIGN ~; MILITARY FORCES OF A ~; MINISTRY OF ~; SECRETARY OF ~; UNITARY ~.

STATED. See ACCOUNT ~; CASE ~.

STATED CASE. A case tried on the basis of a statement of facts agreed on by the parties.

STATEMENT. *n.* 1. "... [A] written or oral communication. I have no doubt that a nod of the head to indicate yes or a shaking of the head to indicate no would also be considered a 'statement' within the meaning of s. 56 [of the Young Offenders Act, S.C. 1980-81-82-83, c. 110]... ." *R. v. J. (J.T.)* (1988), 40 C.C.C. (3d) 97 at 123, [1988] 2 W.W.R. 509, 50 Man. R.(2d) 300 (C.A.), Huband J.A. 2. "[In s. 9(1) of the Evidence Act, R.S.C. 1970, c. E-10] ... there is a mention only of 'a statement'. That 'statement' has been held to include an oral statement: ..." *R. v. Carpenter* (1982), 1 C.C.C. (3d) 149 at 154, 31 C.R. (3d) 261, 142 D.L.R. (3d) 237 (Ont. C.A.), the court per Grange J.A. 3. An assertion of fact, opinion, belief or knowledge, whether material or not and whether admissible or not. *Criminal Code*, R.S.C. 1985, c. C-46, s. 118. 4. The originating process which commences an action (Ontario, Rules of Civil Procedure, r. 14.03(1)). G.D. Watson & C. Perkins, eds., *Holmested & Watson: Ontario Civil Procedure* (Toronto: Carswell, 1984) at 14-3. 5. Any representation of fact whether made in words or otherwise. See ELECTRONIC ~; FINANCIAL ~S; SELF-SERVING ~; VICTIM IMPACT ~; VOLUNTARY ~.

STATEMENT OF CLAIM. 1. "[The function of a statement of claim] is not to cast the plaintiff's right of action into formal legal shape but to state the constitutive facts giving rise to the right upon which he relies and to formulate the relief he demands ..." *Smith v. Upper Canada College* (1920), 57 D.L.R. 648 at 661, 61 S.C.R. 413, [1921] 1 W.W.R. 1154, Duff J. 2. A printed or written statement by the plaintiff in an action which shows the facts relied on to support any claim against the defendant and the remedy or relief sought.

STATEMENT OF DEFENCE. A brief written statement by a defendant to respond to each allegation in a statement of claim: (a) by admission; (b) by denial; (c) by a statement that the defendant does not know; or (d) by a statement of the defendant's own version of the facts.

STATEMENT OF FACTS. See AGREED ~.

STATION. See OFFICIAL INSPECTION ~; POLLING ~; QUARANTINE ~; RADIO ~; SPACE ~.

STATISTICAL INFORMATION. Information relative to the economic, financial, industrial, com-

S

mercial, social and general activities and condition of persons, whether such information is collected by means of sampling or any other statistical method.

STATISTICAL INSTITUTE. See FIRST NATIONS ~.

STATISTICS. See VITAL ~.

STATU QUO. See IN ~.

STATUS. *n.* 1. The legal capacity or incapacity of an individual in relation to that person's community. 2. "[In s. 9(1)(c)(ii) of the Canadian Human Rights Act, S.C. 1976-77, c. 33] ... a legal concept which refers to the particular position of a person with respect to his or her rights and limitations as a result of his or her being a member of some legally recognized and regulated group." *Canada (Attorney General) v. Mossop* (1990), 32 C.C.E.L. 276 at 291, 12 C.H.R.R. D/355, 114 N.R. 241, [1991] 1 F.C. 18 (C.A.), Marceau J.A. See CIVIL ~; FAMILY ~; MARITAL ~.

STATUS INDIAN. A person registered as an Indian under the Indian Act or entitled to be registered under that Act.

STATUS OF WOMEN CANADA. A federal government organization that promotes the full participation of women in the economic, social and democratic life of Canada. SWC works to advance equality for women and to remove the barriers to women's participation in society, putting particular emphasis on increasing women's economic security and eliminating violence against women. *Welcome*, online: Status of Women Canada home, <http://www.swc-cfc.gc.ca/index-eng.html>.

STATUS QUO. [L.] The state in which something is or was.

STATUS QUO CLAUSE. A provision in a collective agreement that the conditions which existed prior to an action or circumstance giving rise to a grievance will be maintained until the grievance is settled.

STATUTE. *n.* A law or act which expresses the will of a legislature or Parliament. See ANALOGY TO ~; CODIFYING ~; CONSOLIDATED ~; CONSOLIDATING ~; CREDITORS' RELIEF ~; CURATIVE ~; DECLARATORY ~; ENABLING ~; EQUITY OF A ~; FEDERAL ~; GUEST ~; LOCAL ~; PENAL ~; REMEDIAL ~; RETROACTIVE ~; RETROSPECTIVE ~; REVISED ~S; ROME ~.

STATUTE BARRED. Said of a cause of action for which proceedings cannot be brought because the limitation period has expired.

STATUTE OF FRAUDS. The Statute of Frauds requires that certain contracts are in writing or are evidenced by an appropriate memorandum. If one fails to conform to the statutory provisions, the contract is unenforceable. Refers to rules now incorporated in the law in other statutes.

STATUTE OF LIMITATIONS. 1. A statute which prescribes the specified period of time within which criminal charges must be laid or legal actions must be taken. 2. This Court recently described the purpose of limitations legislation in M.(K.) v. M.(H.), [1992]

3 S.C.R. 6. M.(K.) v. M.(H.) was a claim for damages for incest brought well after the expiration of the limitation period, even allowing for the plaintiff to reach majority. La Forest J. stated at pp. 29-30: In order to determine the time of accrual of the cause of action in a manner consistent with the purposes of the Limitations Act, it is helpful to examine its underlying rationales. There are three, and they may be described as the certainty, evidentiary, and diligence rationales. Statutes of limitations have long been said to be statutes of repose. The reasoning is straightforward enough. There comes a time, it is said, when a potential defendant should be secure in his reasonable expectation that he will not be held to account for ancient obligations. The second rationale is evidentiary and concerns the desire to foreclose claims based on stale evidence. Once the limitation period has lapsed, the potential defendant should no longer be concerned about the preservation of evidence relevant to the claim. Finally, plaintiffs are expected to act diligently and not "sleep on their rights". Statutes of limitation are an incentive for plaintiffs to bring suit in a timely fashion. While these rationales benefit the potential defendant, the Court also recognized that there must be fairness to the plaintiff as well. Hence, the reasonable discovery rule which prevents the injustice of a claim's being statute barred before the plaintiff becomes aware of its existence. A limitations scheme must attempt to balance the interests of both sides. *Murphy v. Welsh*, 1993 CarswellOnt 428, 18 C.P.C. (3d) 137, 47 M.V.R. (2d) 1, 156 N.R. 263, 14 O.R. (3d) 799, 65 O.A.C. 103, 157 N.R. 372, [1993] 2 S.C.R. 1069, 106 D.L.R. (4th) 404, 66 O.A.C. 240, 18 C.C.L.T. (3d) 101, the court per Major J.

STATUTE OF QUIA EMPTORES. "The primary purpose of [the Statute of Quia Emptores 1290, 18 Edw. 1, St. 1] was to prevent the practice of the day of subinfeudation which resulted in the feudal landlords losing control of their property. As an incident of the abolition of subinfeudation, the right of unrestricted alienation of fee simple estates was pronounced without loss to the feudal landlords." *Laurin v. Iron Ore Co.* (1977), 7 R.P.R. 137 at 154, 19 Nfld. & P.E.I.R. 111, 50 A.P.R. 111, 82 D.L.R. (3d) 634 (Nfld. T.D.), Goodridge J.

STATUTE OF WESTMINSTER. The 1931 British statute which repealed the Colonial Laws Validity Act as it applied to the dominions. By section 2(2) it granted each dominion power to amend or repeal imperial statutes which were part of the law of that dominion and it stated that no dominion statute would be void on grounds of repugnancy to an existing or future imperial statute. Section 7(2) clarified that section 2 applied to Canada's provincial Legislatures in addition to Canada's federal Parliament, but that the Parliament and each legislature could only enact laws within their own jurisdiction under the B.N.A. Act. The power to amend or repeal extended to both future and existing imperial statutes. P.W. Hogg, *Constitutional Law of Canada*, 3d ed. (Toronto: Carswell, 1992) at 50.

STATUTE REVISION. A continuing revision and consolidation of the statutes and regulations of Canada or a province.

STATUTE REVISION COMMISSION. Established by the Legislation Revision and Consolidation Act, R.S.C. 1985, c. S-20, s. 3. The commission revises the statutes and regulations of Canada from time to time. The commission maintains the consolidation of the statutes and regulations.

STATUTORY. *adj.* Governed or introduced by statute law.

STATUTORY ARBITRATOR. A person to whom parties are required by statute to resort.

STATUTORY CORPORATION. A corporation the business of which is confined to the powers conferred in the statute which created the corporation.

STATUTORY COURT. A court which derives its existence and powers from statute, e.g., The Federal Court of Canada.

STATUTORY DECLARATION. A solemn declaration in the form and manner from time to time provided by the provincial evidence acts or by the Canada Evidence Act. A declaration made knowing that it has the same force and effect as if made under oath or affirmation.

STATUTORY DUTY. A duty imposed, by statute, on a person or body. See BREACH OF ~.

STATUTORY INSTRUMENT. (a) Any rule, order, regulation, ordinance, direction, form, tariff of costs or fees, letters patent, commission, warrant, proclamation, by-law, resolution or other instrument issued, made or established (i) in the execution of a power conferred by or under an Act of Parliament, by or under which that instrument is expressly authorized to be issued, made or established otherwise than by the conferring on any person or body of powers or functions in relation to a matter to which that instrument relates, or (ii) by or under the authority of the Governor in Council, otherwise than in the execution of a power conferred by or under an Act of Parliament, but (b) does not include (i) any instrument referred to in paragraph (a) and issued, made or established by a corporation incorporated by or under an Act of Parliament unless (A) the instrument is a regulation and the corporation by which it is made is one that is ultimately accountable, through a Minister, to Parliament for the conduct of its affairs, or (B) the instrument is one for the contravention of which a penalty, fine or imprisonment is prescribed by or under an Act of Parliament, (ii) any instrument referred to in paragraph (a) and issued, made or established by a judicial or quasi-judicial body, unless the instrument is a rule, order or regulation governing the practice or procedure in proceedings before a judicial or quasi-judicial body established by or under an Act of Parliament, (iii) any instrument referred to in paragraph (a) and in respect of which, or in respect of the production or other disclosure of which, any privilege exists by law or whose contents are limited to advice or information intended only for use or assistance in the making of a decision or the determination of policy, or in the ascertainment of any matter necessarily incidental thereto, or (iv) an ordinance of the Northwest Territories, a law made by the Legislature of Yukon or the Legislature for Nunavut, a rule made by the Legislative Assembly of Yukon under section 16 of the Yukon Act or by the Legislative Assembly of Nunavut under section 21 of the Nunavut Act or any instrument issued, made or established under any such ordinance, law or rule. *Statutory Instruments Act*, R.S.C. 1985, c. S-22, s. 2.

STATUTORY INTERPRETATION. The process of applying certain principles to determine the meaning of an enactment. See CONSECUTIVE INTERPRETATION; CONTEXTUAL APPROACH; GOLDEN RULE; INTERPRETATION; MODERN RULE OF ~; PRESUMPTION OF COHERENCE; PURPOSIVE INTERPRETATION; STRICTLY.

STATUTORY JURISDICTION. Jurisdiction the source of which is a statute which defines the limits within which the jurisdiction must be exercised.

STATUTORY LIEN. A lien on property which arises purely by statute; the lienholder's rights depend on the relevant statutory provisions.

STATUTORY PERSON. A non-living entity which is recognized by law as possessing a legal personality separate and apart from any constituent members. Corporations, societies, the Crown in right of Canada, the Crown in right of a province, foreign sovereigns and foreign states.

STATUTORY POWER. A power or right conferred by or under a statute, (i) to make any regulation, rule, by-law or order, or to give any other direction having force as subordinate legislation; (ii) to exercise a statutory power of decision; (iii) to require any person or party to do or to refrain from doing any act or thing that, but for such requirement, such person or party would not be required by law to do or to refrain from doing; (iv) to do any act or thing that would, but for such power or right, be a breach of the legal rights of any person or party. See ABUSE OF ~S.

STATUTORY POWER OF DECISION. A power or right conferred by or under a statute to make a decision deciding or prescribing, (i) the legal rights, powers, privileges, immunities, duties or liabilities of any person or party; or (ii) the eligibility of any person or party to receive, or to the continuation of, a benefit or licence, whether that person or party is legally entitled thereto or not, and includes the powers of an inferior court.

STATUTORY RELEASE. Release from imprisonment subject to supervision before the expiration of an offender's sentence, to which an offender is entitled under the provision of the Act dealing with remission. *Corrections and Conditional Release Act*, S.C. 1992, c. 20, s. 99.

STATUTORY SET-OFF. [To net out a debt owed by one person against another owed to that person] "... [R]equires the fulfilment of two conditions. The first is that both obligations must be debts. The second is that both debts must be mutual cross obligations." *Telford v. Holt* (1987), 37 B.L.R. 241 at 251, 21 C.P.C. (2d) 1, 78 N.R. 321, 54 Alta. L.R. (2d) 193,

S

[1987] 6 W.W.R. 385, [1987] 2 S.C.R. 193, 46 R.P.R. 234, 81 A.R. 385, 41 D.L.R. (4th) 385, the court per Wilson J.

STAY. *n.* With respect to proceedings, an action to suspend them. See JUDICIAL ~.

STAY OF PROCEEDINGS. 1. A prospective rather than a retroactive remedy. A stay of proceedings does not merely redress a past wrong. It aims to prevent the perpetuation of a wrong that, if left alone, will continue to trouble the parties and the community as a whole, in the future. *R. v. Regan*, [2002] 1 S.C.R. 297, LeBel J. (McLachlin C.J.C., L'Heureux-Dubé, Gonthier, Bastarache JJ. concurring). 2. "... [A] stopping or arresting of a judicial proceedings by the direction or order of a court... . A stay may imply that the proceedings are suspended to await some action required to be taken by one of the parties, as, for example, when a non-resident has been ordered to give security for costs. In certain circumstances, however, a stay may mean the total discontinuance or permanent suspension of the proceedings." *R. v. Jewitt* (1985), 47 C.R. (3d) 193 at 203, [1985] 2 S.C.R. 128, [1985] 6 W.W.R. 127, 61 N.R. 159, 21 C.C.C. (3d) 7, 20 D.L.R. (4th) 651, the court per Dickson C.J.C.

STEAL. *v.* To commit theft. *Criminal Code*, R.S.C. 1985, c. C-46, s. 2.

STEP. *n.* A matter or development in an action which advances the action toward trial. See LAST ~.

STEPHENS' DIG. *abbr.* Stephens' Quebec Digest.

STEREOTYPE. *n.* A generalization by which a person or group of people is unfairly portrayed as possessing undesirable traits.

STET. [L.] Let it stand.

STEVEDORING. *n.* The loading or unloading of vessels or railway cars.

STEVENS' DIG. *abbr.* Stevens' New Brunswick Digest.

STEWARD. See SHOP ~.

STEWART. *abbr.* Stewart's Vice-Admiralty Reports (N.S.), 1803-1813.

STICKING. See HIGH ~.

STILLBIRTH. *var.* **STILL-BIRTH.** *n.* 1. The complete expulsion or extraction from the mother after at least 20 weeks' pregnancy, or after attaining a weight of at least 500 grams, of a product of conception in which, after the expulsion or extraction, there is no breathing, beating of the heart, pulsation of the umbilical cord or unmistakable movement of voluntary muscle. *The Vital Statistics Act, 2009*, S.S. 2009, c. V-7.21, s. 2. 2. A dead infant born at term or in the last trimester of pregnancy. F.A. Jaffe, *A Guide to Pathological Evidence for Lawyers and Police Officers*, 4th ed. (Toronto: Carswell, 1999) at 244.

STILL-BORN. *n.* The body of a child born as a result of a still-birth. *Vital Statistics Act*, R.S.O. 1990, c. V.4, *General*, R.R.O. 1990, Reg. 1094, s. 0.1.

STILL-BORN. *adj.* 1. Born as a result of a still-birth. *Vital Statistics Act*, R.S.O. 1990, c. V.4, *General*, R.R.O. 1990, Reg. 1094, s. 0.1. 2. Showing no signs of life when completely outside the mother. F.A. Jaffe, *A Guide to Pathological Evidence for Lawyers and Police Officers*, 4th ed. (Toronto: Carswell, 1999) at 244.

STING. *n.* 1. Occurs when a police agent offers to buy controlled drugs or other contraband from a suspected dealer who is arrested when the purchase is made. 2. The term "sting" in relation to defamation refers to the injurious imputation that a publication conveys. *P.G. Restaurant Ltd. v. Northern Interior Regional Health Board*, 2005 BCCA 210. See REVERSE ~.

STIPEND. *n.* Salary.

STIPULATED DAMAGE. Liquidated damages.

STIPULATED PRICE CONTRACT. One in which the parties have agreed the contract is to be performed for the amount stated in the tender document.

STIPULATION. *n.* 1. A bargain. 2. In an agreement, a material term.

STIRPES. See PER ~.

ST.-M.S.D. *abbr.* Saint-Maurice's Speakers' Decisions (Québec), 1868-.

STOCK. *n.* 1. Any horse, cattle, sheep or poultry or any fur-bearing animal. 2. Includes a share, stock, fund, annuity or security transferable in books kept by a company or society established or to be established, or transferable by deed alone or by deed accompanied by other formalities, and a share or interest in it. See DEFERRED ~; LISTED ~; ROLLING ~.

STOCKBROKER. *n.* ... [O]ne who buys and sells stock as an agent for others. The relationship between client and broker is that of principal and agent, fiduciary in its nature and one of the governing principles of law demands the fullest disclosure by agent to principal... ." *R. v. Solloway*, [1930] 2 W.W.R. 516 at 519, 54 C.C.C. 129 (Alta. T.D.), Ives J.

STOCK DIVIDEND. 1. "... [S]tock distributed to those already holding stock, by way of dividend upon their holdings. It is not a new investment in any sense; it is a mode of distributing accumulated profits in the shape of new stock, which, pro tanto, reduces the value of the stock held." *Fulford, Re* (1913), 14 D.L.R. 844 at 846-7, 5 O.W.N. 125, 29 O.L.R. 375 (H.C.), Middleton J. 2. Includes any dividend paid by a corporation to the extent that it is paid by the issuance of shares of any class of its capital stock.

STOCK EXCHANGE. "The four essential elements appearing in each definition [of 'stock exchange', Criminal Code, R.S.C. 1970, c. C-34, s. 340(c)] are, namely, a reunion of persons, a particular place, buying and selling, and, finally buying and selling of a particular class of things, namely, securities." *Schecter c. Bluestein* (1981), (*sub nom. Bluestein c. Schecter*) 121 D.L.R. (3d) 345 at 349, 23 C.R. (3d) 39, [1981] C.S. 477, 58 C.C.C. (2d) 208 (C.S. Qué.), Malouf J.

STOCK IN TRADE. "... [G]oods which a merchant has in his possession, for sale or hire... ." *R. v. North American Van Lines (Alberta) Ltd.* (1986), 2 M.V.R. (2d) 176 at 187, 16 O.A.C. 230, the court per Blair J.A.

STOCK OPTION. "[Takes] ... the form of negotiable bearer contracts [which] are simply bought and sold like any other commodity for the trading of which there is no exchange. There are six types of stock options: a call; a put; a straddle; a strap; a strip; and a spread... ." *Posluns v. Toronto Stock Exchange*, [1964] 2 O.R. 547 at 553, 46 D.L.R. (2d) 210 (H.C.), Gale J.

STOCKTON. *abbr.* Stockton's Vice-Admiralty Reports (N.B.), 1879-1891.

STOP. *n.* When prohibited, means the halting of a vehicle, even momentarily, whether occupied or not, except when necessary to avoid conflict with other traffic or in compliance with the directions of a police officer or of a traffic control sign or signal. *Highway Traffic Act*, R.S.O. 1990, c. H.8, s. 1(1). See RANDOM VEHICLE ~; ROVING RANDOM ~.

STOP-CHECK. *n.* Check of vehicle made by police to check for improper registration and deficiencies in vehicles.

STOP ORDER. 1. An order issued on application to the court by someone who claims to be entitled to securities or money held or to be held by the accountant for the benefit of someone else which directs that the securities or money shall not be handled without notifying the applicant or moving party. 2. Order the person to whom it is directed to immediately stop or cause the source of contaminant to stop adding to, emitting or discharging into the natural environment any contaminant either permanently or for a specific period of time. 3. An order by a client to stop selling a commodity or stock if its price goes down or up to a price set by the client.

STOPPAGE. *n.* A cessation of work as a result of a lockout or strike.

STOPPAGE IN TRANSITU. The right of an unpaid seller to take back the possession of goods sold on credit and to retain them until the buyer, who became insolvent before possessing the goods, tenders the price.

STORAGE RECEIPT. See GRAIN ~.

STORE. See PUBLIC ~S.

STORER. *n.* A person who receives goods for storage or reward.

S.T.R. abbr. Canadian Sales Tax Reporter, 1968-1989.

STRADDLE TREE. Trees whose trunks straddle the common boundary between adjoining properties at ground level. Included therein are three sub-categories: the first includes only those trees planted along a common boundary with the consent of the adjoining owners, or their predecessors in title ("Consensual Trees"). The second encompasses those trees planted on one property but whose trunks have expanded over a common boundary onto the adjoining property ("Straying Trees"). The third includes trees whose origins are unknown ("Voluntary Trees"). *Koenig v. Goebel* (1998), 162 Sask. R. 81.

STRATA CORPORATION. A strata corporation established by the deposit of a strata plan in a land title office. The owners of the strata lots are members of the strata corporation.

STRATA LOT. A lot shown on a strata plan. *Strata Property Act*, S.B.C. 1998, c. 43, s. 1. See BARE LAND ~.

STRATA LOT LEASE. A lease of a strata lot arising from the conversion of a ground lease under section 203 (1), and includes an assignment or transmission of a strata lot lease. *Strata Property Act*, S.B.C. 1998, c. 43, s. 199.

STRATA MANAGEMENT SERVICES. Any of the following services provided to or on behalf of a strata corporation: (a) collecting or holding strata fees, contributions, levies or other amounts levied by, or due to, the strata corporation under the Strata Property Act; (b) exercising delegated powers and duties of a strata corporation or strata council, including (i) making payments to third parties on behalf of the strata corporation, (ii) negotiating or entering into contracts on behalf of the strata corporation, or (iii) supervising employees or contractors hired or engaged by the strata corporation but does not include an activity excluded by regulation. *Real Estate Services Act*, S.B.C. 2004, c. 42, s. 1.

STRATA PLAN. The plan which describes the strata lots and which establishes the strata corporation. See BARE LAND ~; LEASEHOLD ~.

STRATA SPACE. Volumetric space, whether it is (a) located below or above or below and above the surface of the land, or (b) occupied in whole or in part by any structure, and that is shown as strata space on a strata space plan. *Land Titles Act*, R.S.A. 2000, c. L-4, s. 86.

STRATEGIC PERSONNEL. Of a business of a corporation or partnership means the personnel of the corporation or partnership who is assigned to the direction and design of the back office activities carried on by the corporation or partnership in the course of the operations of the business or who has specific expertise in the field of back office activities and is assigned to client solicitation activities in relation to the back office activities carried on by the corporation or partnership in the course of those operations. *An Act respecting International financial centres*, R.S.Q. c. C-8.3, s. 4.

STRAW CLAIMANT. A corporate shell which has no assets and exists solely for the purpose of commencing or continuing a lawsuit.

STRAYING TREE. A tree planted on one property but whose trunks have expanded over a common boundary onto the adjoining property. *Koenig v. Goebel* (1998), 162 Sask. R. 81.

STREET RACING. Operating a motor vehicle in a race with at least one other motor vehicle on a street, road, highway or other public place. *Criminal Code*, R.S.C. 1985, c. C-46, s. 2.

STRICT CONSTRUCTION. Interpretation of a tax or penal statute strictly against the body imposing the tax or penalty where there is any ambiguity.

STRICTI JURIS. [L.] The letter of the law.

STRICTISSIMI JURIS. [L.] Of the strictest law. *Dragun v. Dragun* (1984), 47 C.P.C. 106 at 108, [1984] 6 W.W.R. 171, 30 Man. R. (2d) 126 (Q.B.), Helper J. Calls for the court's most careful attention to ensure adherence to all necessary safeguards of the liberty of the person and the perception that justice is done.

STRICT LEGAL OPERATION. Refers to how legislation as a whole affects rights and liabilities of those subject to its terms. The effect is determined by the legislation itself.

STRICT LIABILITY. 1. Criminal liability based on simple negligence. 2. Imposed in tort law when a lawful activity exposes others to extraordinary risks even though no fault is involved on the part of the "wrongdoer."

STRICT LIABILITY OFFENCE. "Offences in which there is no necessity for the prosecution to prove the existence of mens rea; the doing of the prohibited act prima facie imports the offence, leaving it open to the accused to avoid liability by proving that he took all reasonable care. This involves consideration of what a reasonable man would have done in the circumstances. The defence will be available if the accused reasonably believed in a mistaken set of facts which, if true, would render the act or omission innocent, or if he took all reasonable steps to avoid the particular event. These offences may be properly called offences of strict liability." *R. v. Sault Ste. Marie (City)*, [1978] 2 S.C.R. 1299 at 1326, 3 C.R. (3d) 30, 21 N.R. 295, 7 C.E.L.R. 53, 40 C.C.C. (2d) 353, 85 D.L.R. (3d) 161, the court per Dickson J.

STRICTLY. *adv.* In construing a penal statute, the conduct which gave rise to the charge against the accused or the conduct of anyone for whom the accused may be held answerable must be such as can clearly and unmistakably be demonstrated to fall within the range of conduct which is prohibited by the statute.

STRIKE. *v.* To cease work, or to refuse to work or to continue to work, in combination or in concert or in accordance with a common understanding.

STRIKE. *n.* 1. Includes a cessation of work or a refusal to work by employees, in combination, in concert or in accordance with a common understanding, and a slowdown of work or other concerted activity on the part of employees in relation to their work that is designed to restrict or limit output. 2. [As used in a "force majeure" clause of a contract for the supply of electricity] is not necessarily limited to labour disturbances affecting one's own workforce. [I]f the "officious bystander" were asked about the natural and ordinary meaning of "strike" in subclause 18(d) he or she would say a strike at the pulp mills who accounted for 90 per cent of [the plaintiff's business] was surely caught. [T]here is an answer in this case to the rhetorical questions regarding where to draw the line between strikes besetting customers and

those besetting suppliers of customers, suppliers of suppliers of customers, etc. The line surely becomes clear where the plant of one of the contracting parties has had to shut down due to a strike and has virtually no need for electricity. The effect on the customer is exactly the same as if its own workforce had been on strike. *Tenneco Canada Inc. v. British Columbia Hydro & Power Authority*, 1999 CarswellBC 1455, 126 B.C.A.C. 9, 206 W.A.C. 9 (C.A.). See COLLECTIVE BARGAINING ~; GENERAL~; MID-CONTRACT ~; PROTEST ~; SECONDARY ~; WILDCAT ~.

STRIKE OFF THE ROLL. To remove the name of a solicitor from the rolls of a court and thereby disentitle that person to practise.

STRIKE OUT. To expunge part or all of a document or pleading, with or without leave to amend. *Courts of Justice Act*, R.S.O. 1990, c. C.43, Rules of Civil Procedure, R.R.O. 1990, Reg. 194, r. 25.11.

STRIKING PRICE. Where used in relation to a commodity futures option, means the price at which the purchaser of the option has the right to assume a long or short position in relation to the commodity futures contract that is the subject of the option. *Commodity Futures Act*, R.S.O. 1990, c. C.20, s. 1.

STRIP SEARCH. 1. (a) A visual inspection of the naked body, in the prescribed manner, and (b) a search, in accordance with any applicable regulations made under paragraph 96(l), of all clothing, things in the clothing, and other personal possessions that the person may be carrying. *Corrections and Conditional Release Act*, S.C. 1992, c. 20, s. 46. 2. The removal or rearrangement of some or all of the clothing of a person so as to permit a visual inspection of a person's private areas, namely genitals, buttocks, breasts (in the case of a female), or undergarments. This definition in essence reflects the definition of a strip search that has been adopted in various statutory materials and policy manuals in Canada and other jurisdictions . . . . This definition distinguishes strip searches from less intrusive "frisk" or "pat down" searches, which do not involve the removal of clothing, and from more intrusive body cavity searches, which involve a physical inspection of the detainee's genital or anal regions. *R. v. Golden*, 2001 SCC 83.

STRUCTURAL. See NON-~

STRUCTURAL REMEDY. Declaratory relief identifies a constitutional or quasi-constitutional breach and may direct that the breach be remedied. A structural remedy not only identifies the breach(es) and directs government to provide a remedy, but also details how government is to proceed in doing so. *Northwest Territories (Attorney General) v. Fédération Franco-Ténoise*, 2008 NWTCA 6.

STRUCTURE. See MARINE INSTALLATION OR ~.

STRUCTURED SETTLEMENT. 1. "... [A]n agreement to pay the plaintiff, as compensation for the damages suffered by him, a sum of money by periodic payments, rather than a lump sum payment." *Fuchs v. Brears* (1986), 44 Sask. R. 112 at 115, [1986] 3 W.W.R. 409 (Q.B.), Vancise J. 2. The periodic payment of damages by means of an annuity; the annuity is purchased by the defendant's casualty insurer from a life insurer. Annuity payments flow to the injured plaintiff as tax-free damages. The annuity contract is owned by the casualty insurer, which guarantees payment to the injured person. The increasing popularity of structured settlements is largely attributable to the cost of gross-up. Because periodic payments flowing to the injured party are non- taxable, gross-up is not an issue. *Wilson v. Martinello* (1995), 23 O.R. (3d) 417 (C.A.).

STU. ADM. *abbr.* Stuart's Vice-Admiralty Reports (Lower Canada) (Québec), 1836-1874.

STUD. CANON. *abbr.* Studia Canonica.

STUDENT. *n.* 1. A person enrolled or registered in a school. 2. A person enrolled in a course of studies at an educational institution. 3. A person who is pursuing formal education as a full-time or part-time student and is employed by an employer for the purposes of the employer's industry, although not as a learner or an apprentice. *Workplace Safety and Insurance Act, 1997*, S.O. 1997, c. 16, Sched. A, s. 2. See ARTICLED ~.

STUDENT-AT-LAW. *n.* A person serving articles of clerkship.

STUDY PERMIT. A written authorization to engage in studies in Canada issued by an officer to a foreign national. *Immigration and Refugee Protection Act*, S.C. 2001, c. 27, *Immigration and Refugee Protection Regulations*, SOR/2001-475, s. 1.

STUFF GOWN. The court robe worn by lawyers who are not Queen's Counsel.

STU. K.B. *abbr.* Stuart's Reports (Lower Canada) (Québec), 1810-1835.

STYLE. *v.* To name, call or entitle someone.

STYLE. *n.* A title; an appellation. See ROYAL ~ AND TITLES.

STYLE OF CAUSE. The name or title of a proceeding which sets out the names of all the parties and their capacity, if other than a personal capacity.

STYLE OF PROCEEDING. In relation to a document that is or is to be filed in a proceeding, that portion of the document that (a) sets out the registry number attributed to the proceeding and the court and registry in which the proceeding is being or is to be conducted, and (b) identifies the parties to the proceeding or, if there is no person named as a defendant, the subject matter of the proceeding. *Court Rules Act*, R.S.B.C. 1996, c. 80, *Supreme Court Civil Rules*, B.C. Reg. 168/2009, Rule 1-1.

SUBCOMMITTEE. *n.* A committee which is formed from and acts under a main committee.

SUBCONTRACTOR. *var.* **SUB-CONTRACTOR.** *n.* 1. A person who has contracted with a prime contractor or with another subcontractor to perform a contract. 2. A person not contracting with or employed directly by an owner or the owner's agent for the doing of any work, rendering of any services or the furnishing of any material but contracting with or

employed by a contractor or under the contractor by another subcontractor, but does not include a labourer. *Mechanics' Lien Act*, R.S.N.B. 1973, c. M-6, s. 1.

SUBDIVIDE. *v.* To divide a parcel of land into two or more parcels.

SUBDIVIDING INSTRUMENT. An interest that is less than title based on an agreement for sale, easement, lease or mortgage, or any other document or group of documents that: (i) affects or encumbers only part of a parcel; (ii) creates or declares any right, interest or estate in only part of a parcel; or (iii) otherwise has the effect of subdividing land. *The Planning and Development Act, 2007*, S.S. 2007, c. P-13.2, s. 120.

SUBDIVISION. *var.* **SUB-DIVISION.** *n.* 1. "... [O]ccurs not only where lots or parcels are divided one from the other, but where interests in such lots or parcels are divided for the purpose of sale... ." *J.C.D. Holdings Ltd. v. Buie* (1985), 61 B.C.L.R. 119 at 125, 17 D.L.R. (4th) 373 (S.C.), McLachlin J. 2. A division of a parcel by means of a plan of subdivision, plan of survey, agreement or any instrument, including a caveat, transferring or creating an estate or interest in part of the parcel. See PLAN OF ~; POLITICAL ~.

SUBFRANCHISE. *n.* A franchise granted by a subfranchisor to a subfranchisee. *Arthur Wishart Act (Franchise Disclosure)*, 2000, S.O. 2000, c. 3, s. 1.

SUBINFEUDATION. *n.* Division of land first granted to tenants in chief among their followers. E.L.G. Tyler & N.E. Palmer, eds., *Crossley Vaines' Personal Property*, 5th ed. (London: Butterworths, 1973) at 4.

SUBJECTIVE MENS REA. The accused intended the consequences of his or her acts or knowing of the likely consequences acted recklessly in the face of the risk.

SUBJECT MATTER. See CERTAINTY OF ~.

SUBJECT MATTER COMPETENCE. The aspects of a court's jurisdiction that depend on factors other than those pertaining to the court's territorial competence.

SUBJECT TO. 1. "In a contract, 'subject to' a stipulated condition, ... means that the dominant but conditional obligation of the contract, namely, to purchase, is to become operative and effective only on fulfilment of the condition or occurrence of the event stipulated in the condition; unless there is such fulfilment or occurrence the conditional contract never becomes unconditional, operative or binding and the parties are in the same position as if no contract had been entered into... ." *Kiernicki v. Jaworski* (1956), 18 W.W.R. 289 at 293 (Man. C.A.), Coyne J.A. 2. "The meaning of the expression 'subject to' in statutes was, in my opinion, correctly stated by the late Professor Elmer A. Driedger in The Composition of Legislation: Legislative Forms and Precedents, 2d ed. (Ottawa: Canadian Government Publishing Centre, Supply & Services Canada, 1976) at pp. 139-40 as follows: 'Subject to – Used to assign a subordinate position to an enactment, or to pave the way for qualifications. Where two sections conflict, and one is not merely an exception to the other, the subordinate one should be preceded by subject to; this reconciles the conflict and serves as a warning that there is more to come.' " *Murphy v. Welsh* (1991), 4 C.P.C. (3d) 301 at 309-10, 30 M.V.R. (2d) 163, 3 O.R. (3d) 182, 81 D.L.R. (4th) 475, 50 O.A.C. 246, the court per Blair J.A. 3. The introductory words of s. 2(2) [Limitations Act] "Subject to sections 11 and 13," also suggest that this section was not intended to be interpreted in isolation; rather, the "subject to" words indicate that the individual provisions of the Act operate together to create a coherent limitations regime. *N. (J.) v. Kozens*, 2004 ABCA 394.

SUB JUDICE. [L.] 1. In the course of a trial. 2. Under consideration by the court.

SUB-JUDICE CONVENTION. The expectation that members of Parliament will not discuss matters that are before tribunals or the courts which are courts of record. A. Fraser, W.A. Dawson & J. Holtby, eds., *Beauchesne's Rules and Forms of the House of Commons of Canada*, 6th ed. (Toronto: Carswell, 1989) at 153.

SUBLEASE. *var.* **SUB-LEASE.** *n.* 1. A tenant's grant of interest in the leased premises which is less than that tenant's own. 2. Includes an agreement for a sublease where the sublessee has become entitled to have his sublease granted. *Landlord and Tenant acts.*

SUB-LET. *v.* For a tenant to lease the whole or part of the premises during a portion of the unexpired balance of the lease's term.

SUBLICENSE. *n.* In patent law, a grant by a licensee of certain licensed rights to a third party, the sublicensee.

SUBMISSION. *n.* 1. Statements and rhetoric urging the trier of fact to make particular findings of fact and apply the law in the manner proposed by the person making the submissions. Made on behalf of a party before a tribunal or court. 2. Acquisition of jurisdiction which it would not otherwise possess by a court because the defendant, by conduct, cannot object to the jurisdiction. This may occur either impliedly or expressly, provided the person submitting is capable of doing so. C.R.B. Dunlop, *Creditor-Debtor Law in Canada* (Toronto: Carswell, 1981) at 470. 3. Definition of an arbitrator's jurisdiction over a particular case, i.e. a written grievance or a separate document. D.J.M. Brown & D.M. Beatty, *Canadian Labour Arbitration*, 3d ed. (Aurora: Canada Law Book, 1988-) at 2-14. 4. A written agreement to submit present or future differences to arbitration whether an arbitrator is named therein or not. 5. An argument made to a tribunal on behalf of a party. See JOINT ~.

SUBMIT. *v.* 1. To offer, as an advocate, a proposition to a court. 2. To bring under a person's consideration or notice. 3. Deliver.

SUB MODO. [L.] Under restriction or condition.

SUBMORTGAGE. *n.* A mortgage of a mortgage. R. Megarry & H.W.R. Wade, *The Law of Real Property*, 5th ed. (London: Stevens, 1984) at cxxvii.

SUB NOM. *abbr.* Sub nomine.

SUB NOMINE. [L.] Under a name.

SUBORDINATED INDEBTEDNESS. An instrument evidencing an indebtedness of a company that by its terms provides that the indebtedness will, in the event of the insolvency or winding-up of the company, be subordinate in right of payment to all deposit liabilities of the company and all other liabilities of the company except those that, by their terms, rank equally with or are subordinate to such indebtedness. Federal statutes.

SUBORDINATE LEGISLATION. 1. Legislation of a subordinate body, i.e. one other than a legislature or Parliament, such as a statutory instrument, regulation or by-law. 2. Any regulation, proclamation, rule, order, by-law or instrument that is of a legislative nature and made or approved under the authority of an Act.

SUBORNATION. *n.* The crime of getting someone else to do something unlawful.

SUBPOENA. *n.* A document requiring a person to attend as a witness, to produce documents or other articles or to testify before a court or tribunal.

SUBPOENA AD TESTIFICANDUM. [L.] Under threat of penalty you are required to come to testify.

SUBPOENA DUCES TECUM. [L. subpoena you shall bring with you] 1. A document requiring a witness to give evidence in court or tribunal, or before an examiner and also to bring along documents specified in the subpoena. 2. ... [A]n order in the nature of a subpoena duces tecum ... would compel not the production of documents but rather would require the attendance before the inquiry of [a witness] with [her or his] relevant documents." *Canada Deposit Insurance Corp. v. Code* (1988), 49 D.L.R. (4th) 57 at 60 (Alta. C.A.), the court per Kerans J.A.

SUBROGATE. *v.* "... [T]o put one in the place of, or to substitute one for, another in respect of a right or a claim." *Big Wheels Transport & Leasing Ltd. v. Richard* (1987), 46 D.L.R. (4th) 108 at 110, 27 C.C.L.I. 243, 70 Nfld. & P.E.I.R. 104, 215 A.P.R. 104 (P.E.I. C.A.), the court per McQuaid J.A.

SUBROGATED. *adj.* Describes the rights acquired by a singly secured creditor in property in which she or he had no rights when a doubly secured creditor realized a claim out of the parcel on which the singly secured creditor had her or his security making it unavailable to the singly secured creditor. W.B. Rayner & R.H. McLaren, *Falconbridge on Mortgages*, 4th ed. (Toronto: Canada Law Book, 1977) at 314.

SUBROGATION. *n.* 1. The principle of subrogation is a device which gives effect to the contract of insurance, protecting the insurer by permitting it to pursue claims against a third party in the name of the insured in respect of losses which have been indemnified. *Pacific Forest Products Ltd. v. AXA Pacific Insurance Co.*, 2003 BCCA 241, 12 B.C.L.R. (4th) 293. 2. "... [W]hen one person has been bound to indemnify another against a loss, he is entitled to any benefit in respect of the indemnified loss received by that person over and above the full amount of the loss.

From this it follows that the right of subrogation does not arise until there has been recovery in full by the person suffering the loss ..." *Bigl v. Alberta* (1989), 37 C.C.L.I. 40 at 45, 67 Alta. L.R. (2d) 349, 60 D.L.R. (4th) 438 (C.A.), the court per Laycraft J.A. 3. "The most common [way of avoiding double recovery] is subrogation. Indemnity insurance is subject to the insurer's right to claim back payments to the extent the plaintiff recovers damages. Many statutory benefits, such as worker's compensation, are subject to legislative indemnity provisions." *Ratych v. Bloomer* (1990), 3 C.C.L.T. (2d) 1 at 23, 30 C.C.E.L. 161, 69 D.L.R. (4th) 25, [1990] 1 S.C.R. 940, 107 N.R. 335, 73 O.R. (2d) 448n, 39 O.A.C. 103, [1990] R.R.A. 651n, McLachlin J. (Lamer, La Forest, L'Heureux-Dubé and Sopinka JJ. concurring). 4. "To subrogate is to substitute. An insurer to recover a loss by way of subrogation must be able to place itself in the position of the insured. It follows, then, that the insurer is only entitled to make such claims, in the name of the insured, as could have been made by the insured... ." *Bow Helicopters Ltd. v. Bell Helicopter Textron* (1981), 14 B.L.R. 133 at 142, 16 Alta. L.R. (2d) 149, 31 A.R. 49, 125 D.L.R. (3d) 386, [1981] I.L.R. 1-1415 (C.A.), the court per Haddad J.A. See DOCTRINE OF ~.

SUBSCRIBE. *v.* 1. To write under. 2. To sign.

SUBSCRIPTION PRICE. 1. For an interest in a limited partnership, the consideration payable for the interest as set out in the offering memorandum. *Excise Tax Act*, R.S.C. 1985, c. E-15, s. 336. 2. The price per security at which the securities issuable on the exercise of rights may be subscribed for under a rights offering. *Securities Act*, R.S.B.C. 1996, c. 418, *National Instrument 45-101 Rights Offerings*, B.C. Reg. 165/2001, s. 1.1.

SUBSCRIPTION PROGRAMMING SIGNAL. Radiocommunication that is intended for reception either directly or indirectly by the public in Canada or elsewhere on payment of a subscription fee or other charge. *Radiocommunication Act*, R.S.C. 1985, c. R-2, s. 2.

SUBSCRIPTION SERVICE. The provision to the subscriber of amended or new documents published during the year.

SUBSEQUENT. See CONDITION ~.

SUBSIDIARY. *n.* A corporation is a subsidiary of another corporation if (a) it is controlled by (i) that other corporation, (ii) that other corporation and one or more corporations controlled by that other corporation, or (iii) 2 or more corporations controlled by that other corporation, or (b) it is a subsidiary of a subsidiary of that other corporation. *Business Corporations Act*, S.B.C. 2002, c. 57, s. 2. See CONTROLLED ~.

SUB SILENTIO. [L.] Silently.

SUBSTANCE. See CONTROLLED ~; DESIGNATED ~ OFFENCE; EXPLOSIVE ~; HAZARDOUS ~; HORMONE DISRUPTING ~; INTOXICATING ~; MINERAL ~; NUCLEAR ~; PITH AND ~.

SUBSTANTIAL. *adj.* Significant; important; essential.

SUBSTANTIAL ALTERATION. Any change to a structure, premises or property that increases or decreases the floor area of an occupancy or that affects any of the following: (a) a major occupancy classification, (b) an exit or entrance in or of a structure, premises or property, including means of egress, and travel distance to an exit, (c) a fire alarm system, (d) a system for the prevention or suppression of fire. *Fire Prevention Act*, R.S.N.W.T. 1988, c. F-6, s. 1.

SUBSTANTIAL COMPLETION. For a sub-contractor the point in time when the sub-contractor is able to sue for his contract price in full, the point when he has performed all he contracted to do.

SUBSTANTIAL COMPLIANCE. "When a statute requires substantial compliance ... it requires the doing of those things which are of real importance, of substance, having regard to the object and scheme of the Act ... I would therefore interpret 'substantial' as importing a measure of compliance – has the claimant made a reasonable effort to provide the information that the Act requires for its effective operation... ." *Ed Miller Sales & Rental Ltd. v. Canadian Imperial Bank of Commerce* (1987), 51 Alta. L.R. (2d) 54 at 57, 37 D.L.R. (4th) 179, 7 P.P.S.A.C. 87, 79 A.R. 161 (C.A.), the court per Stevenson J.A.

SUBSTANTIAL CONNECTION. See REAL AND ~

SUBSTANTIAL DAMAGE. Damage to a building for which the cost of repairs would equal at least 25% of the value of the building immediately prior to the damage occurring, or a greater percentage if specified in the declaration. *Condominium Property Act*, S.N.B. 2009, c. C-16.05, s. 49.

SUBSTANTIAL INDEMNITY COSTS. 1. [W]hile [the judge, in awarding substantial indemnity costs,] indicated he was not awarding solicitor-and-client costs, there is not a sufficient distinction between substantial indemnity costs and solicitor-and-client costs. An award approaching solicitor-and-client costs is still a punitive order and, as there is no authority for the awarding of substantial indemnity costs, relies upon the same jurisprudential base as solicitor-and-client costs. *ICR Commercial Real Estate (Regina) Ltd. v. Bricore Land Group Ltd.*, 2007 SKCA 72. 2. Costs awarded in an amount that is 1.5 times what would otherwise be awarded in accordance with Part I of Tariff A. *Courts of Justice Act*, R.S.O. 1990, c. C.43, *Rules of Civil Procedure*, R.R.O. 1990, Reg. 194, s. 1.03.

SUBSTANTIAL PERFORMANCE. Exists where a contract has been carried out in all its essentials and only technical or unimportant omissions or defects have occurred.

SUBSTANTIAL RENOVATION. Of a residential complex means the renovation or alteration of a building to such an extent that all or substantially all of the building that existed immediately before the renovation or alteration was begun, other than the foundation, external walls, interior supporting walls, floors, roof and staircases, has been removed or re-

S

placed where, after completion of the renovation or alteration, the building is, or forms part of, a residential complex. *Excise Tax Act*, R.S.C. 1985, c. E-15, s. 123.

SUBSTANTIVE EQUALITY. 1. Substantive equality, as contrasted with formal equality, is grounded in the idea that: "The promotion of equality entails the promotion of a society in which all are secure in the knowledge that they are recognized at law as human beings equally deserving of concern, respect and consideration": Andrews [Andrews v. Law Society of British Columbia, 1989 CanLII 2, [1989] 1 S.C.R. 143] , at p. 171, per McIntyre J., for the majority on the s. 15 issue. Pointing out that the concept of equality does not necessarily mean identical treatment and that the formal "like treatment" model of discrimination may in fact produce inequality, McIntyre J. stated (at p. 165): "To approach the ideal of full equality before and under the law - and in human affairs an approach is all that can be expected - the main consideration must be the impact of the law on the individual or the group concerned. Recognizing that there will always be an infinite variety of personal characteristics, capacities, entitlements and merits among those subject to a law, there must be accorded, as nearly as may be possible, an equality of benefit and protection and no more of the restrictions, penalties or burdens imposed upon one than another. In other words, the admittedly unattainable ideal should be that a law expressed to bind all should not because of irrelevant personal differences have a more burdensome or less beneficial impact on one than another." While acknowledging that equality is an inherently comparative concept (p. 164), McIntyre J. warned against a sterile similarly situated test focussed on treating "likes" alike. An insistence on substantive equality has remained central to the Court's approach to equality claims. Sections 15(1) and 15(2) work together to promote the vision of substantive equality that underlies s. 15 as a whole. Section 15(1) is aimed at preventing discriminatory distinctions that impact adversely on members of groups identified by the grounds enumerated in s. 15 and analogous grounds. This is one way of combatting discrimination. However, governments may also wish to combat discrimination by developing programs aimed at helping disadvantaged groups improve their situation. Through s. 15(2), the Charter preserves the right of governments to implement such programs, without fear of challenge under s. 15(1). This is made apparent by the existence of s. 15(2). Thus s. 15(1) and s. 15(2) work together to confirm s. 15's purpose of furthering substantive equality. *R. v. Kapp*, 2008 SCC 41, McLachlin C.J. and Abella J. for the majority. 2. In the context of institutional bilingualism in the courts, substantive equality is "equal access to services of equal quality for members of both official language communities": Beaulac [R. v. Beaulac (1999), [1999] 1 S.C.R. 768] at para. 22. *Northwest Territories (Attorney General) v. Fédération Franco-Ténoise*, 2008 NWTCA 6.

SUBSTANTIVE LAW. ".... [C]reates rights and obligations and is concerned with the ends which the administration of justice seeks to attain, ... substantive law determines [the parties'] conduct and relations in respect of the matters litigated." *Sutt v. Sutt*, [1969] 1 O.R. 169 at 175, 2 D.L.R. (3d) 33 (C.A.), Schroeder J.A. (McGillivray J.A. concurring).

SUBSTANTIVE RIGHT. 1. Contrasted to a procedural right. 2. Section 482 [Criminal Code] authorizes appellate courts to enact rules dealing primarily with criminal procedure. Notably, the section does not authorize appellate courts to enact rules that create substantive rights. A right of appeal from a single appeal judge to the court is a substantive right that does not fall within any of the categories set out in s. 482. *R. v. Harness*, 2005 ABCA 245.

SUBSTITUTE. See CLOSE ~.

SUBSTITUTE DECISION-MAKER. In relation to a person to whom a record, information or an approved agency's decision relates, means, (a) any person who is a substitute decision-maker within the meaning of the Personal Health Information Protection Act, 2004, or (b) any other person who is lawfully authorized to make a decision concerning a community service on behalf of the person to whom the record, information or approved agency's decision relates. *Long-Term Care Act, 1994*, S.O. 1994, c. 26, s. 2.

SUBSTITUTED SERVICE. Service of a document on a person representing the party to be served, instead of on the party personally or by some means not involving personal service.

SUBSTITUTION. *n.* Exists where a person receives property by a liberality with the obligation of delivering it over to a third person after a certain period. Substitution is established by gift or by will; it shall be evidenced in writing and published in the registry office. *Civil Code*, S.Q. 1991, c. 64, a. 1218.

SUBTENANCY. *n.* A tenancy created by sublease.

SUBTENANT. *var.* **SUB-TENANT.** *n.* 1. A person entering into a lease with a head tenant who reserves at least one day of her or his original term of tenancy. 2. Includes any person deriving title under a sublease.

SUBVERSION. *n.* Connotes accomplishing change by illicit means or for improper purposes related to an organisation. *Qu v. Canada (Minister of Citizenship & Immigration)*, 2000 CarswellNat 705, 5 Imm. L.R. (3d) 129, [2000] 4 F.C. 71 (T.D.), Lemieux J.

SUB VOCE. [L.] Under title.

SUCCESSION. *n.* As the case requires, (i) the property of the deceased to which a successor becomes beneficially entitled; or (ii) the acquisition by a successor of any property of the deceased by reason of the death of the deceased or a successor's becoming beneficially entitled to property of a deceased by reason of the death of the deceased. *Succession Duties Act*, S.N.S. 1972, c. 17, s. 1.

SUCCESSION DUTY. 1. Inheritance tax levied against each beneficiary on an inheritance. 2. Tax on the gratuitous acquisition of property. 3. Tax paid by the person who inherits as a result of an intestacy, a will or an inter vivos gift when the gift arises because of death.

SUCCESSIVE PERFORMANCE. See CONTRACT OF ~.

SUCCESSOR. *n.* 1. One who takes another's place. 2. An heir, executor or administrator. *Land Registration Reform Act*, R.S.O. 1990, c. L.4, s. 1. 3. "When used in reference to corporations, ... generally denotes another corporation which, through merger, amalgamation or some other type of legal succession, assumes the burdens and becomes vested with the rights of the first corporation... ." *National Trust Co. v. Mead* (1991), 12 R.P.R. (2d) 165 at 177, [1990] 2 S.C.R. 410, [1990] 5 W.W.R. 459, 71 D.L.R. (4th) 488, 112 N.R. 1, Wilson J. (Lamer C.J.C., La Forest, L'Heureux-Dubé, Gonthier and Cory JJ. concurring).

SUCCESSOR CORPORATION. In relation to an unlimited liability company, means any corporation that results from the company, or any of its successor corporations, transforming. *Business Corporations Act*, S.B.C. 2002, c. 57, s. 51.3.

SUCH. *adj.* Associates the word or words it modifies with earlier word or words in a document.

SUCH AS. Has the same meaning as "includes". Words which follow the phrase are examples of or demonstrative of the words or phrases which precede it.

SUDDEN. *adj.* Unexpected; unforeseen.

SUDDEN PROVOCATION. The wrongful act or insult must strike a mind unprepared for it, that it must make an unexpected impact that takes the understanding by surprise and sets the passions aflame. *R. v. Tripodi*, [1955] S.C.R. 438.

SUE. *v.* To bring a civil action against a person.

SUFFER. *v.* To permit; to allow.

SUFFERANCE. See TENANT AT ~.

SUFFERING. See PAIN AND ~.

SUFFICIENT CAUSATION. See MULTIPLE ~.

SUFFICIENT IMPORTANCE. Leave to appeal should be granted only where there is "a question of law of sufficient importance."... A question of law is one of sufficient importance if there is something novel or unsettled about the question. A decision having wide ranging implications is one of sufficient importance. *R. v. Terroco Industries Ltd.*, 2004 ABCA 159, Wittmann J.A.

SUFFICIENT OUTLET. The safe discharge of water at a point where it will do no injury to land or roads.

SUFFICIENT PROXIMITY. The question of whether there is sufficient proximity is concerned with whether the relationship between the plaintiff and defendant is sufficiently close and direct to give rise to a legal duty of care, considering such factors as physical closeness, expectations, representations, reliance and the property or other interests involved. *Hill v. Hamilton-Wentworth Regional Police Services Board*, 2007 SCC 41, [2007] 3 S.C.R. 129, at paras. 23- 24 and 29.

SUFFRAGE. *n.* Vote; electoral franchise.

SUGGESTIVE. *adj.* Providing evidence of; disclosing.

SUICIDE. *n.* Killing oneself. The intentional act of a party who knows the probable consequences.

SUI GENERIS. [L.] Of one's own class or kind.

SUI JURIS. [L.] Of one's own right, without disability. R. Megarry & H.W.R. Wade, *The Law of Real Property*, 5th ed. (London: Stevens, 1984) at cxxvii.

SUIT. *n.* "... [W]as authoritatively defined by the Supreme Court of Canada in Lenoir v. Ritchie (1879), 3 S.C.R. 575. Fournier, J. said, at p. 601, 'The term (suit) is certainly a very comprehensive one, and is understood to apply to any proceeding in a Court of justice, by which an individual pursues that remedy in a Court of justice, which the law affords him. The modes of proceeding may be various, but if a right is litigated between parties in a Court of justice, the proceeding by which the decision of the Court is sought, is a suit.' This definition has been adopted by this court ..." *Canadian Workers' Union v. Frankel Structural Steel Ltd.*, (1976), 76 C.L.L.C. 14,010 at 51, 12 O.R. (2d) 560 (Div. Ct.), Reid J. See CIVIL ~; FRIENDLY ~; LAW ~; NON~.

SUITABLE WORK. Work which the worker has the necessary skills to perform, is medically able to perform and which does not pose a health or safety hazard to the worker or any co-workers. *Workers' Compensation Act*, S.N.S. 1994-95, c. 10, s. 89.

SUM. *n.* Quantity or amount of money.

SUMMARY. *n.* An abridgment. See CASE ~.

SUMMARY APPLICATION. A request to a judge or court without a full and formal proceeding.

SUMMARY CONVICTION COURT. A person who has jurisdiction in the territorial division where the subject-matter of the proceedings is alleged to have arisen and who (a) is given jurisdiction over the proceedings by the enactment under which the proceedings are taken; (b) is a justice or provincial court judge, where the enactment under which the proceedings are taken does not expressly give jurisdiction to any person or class of persons; or (c) is a provincial court judge, where the enactment under which the proceedings are taken gives jurisdiction in respect thereof to two or more justices. *Criminal Code*, R.S.C. 1985, c. C-46, s. 785.

SUMMARY CONVICTION OFFENCE. An offence which is tried summarily. This type of offence is less serious. Theft under $5000 is a summary conviction offence. Some offences may be tried by indictment or by summary conviction procedure. See HYBRID OFFENCE.

SUMMARY JUDGMENT. Once the defendant has served a notice of motion or delivered a statement of defence, a plaintiff may apply for summary judgment in respect of part or all of the claim set out in the statement of claim. The proper test for summary judgment - as articulated by Morden A.C.J.O. in Irving Ungerman Ltd. v. Galanis [(1991), 4 O.R. (3d) 545 (Ont. C.A.), at pp. 550-551] - is whether there is a genuine issue of material fact that requires a trial for its resolution. the essential purpose of summary judgment is to isolate, and then terminate, claims and defences that are factually unsupported. A defendant who seeks to dismiss an action on a summary judgment motion bears the burden of proving that there is no genuine issue of a material fact requiring a trial. On a summary judgment motion, the Court is not to assess credibility, weigh evidence or draw factual inferences. On the other hand, the Court is entitled to assume that the record contains all of the evidence which the parties will present if there is a trial. *Aronowicz v. EMTWO Properties Inc.*, 2010 CarswellOnt 598, 2010 ONCA 96.

SUMMARY JURISDICTION. The ability of a court to make an order or give a judgment on its own initiative at once.

SUMMARY TRIAL. A trial conducted by or under the authority of a commanding officer pursuant to section 163 and a trial by a superior commander pursuant to section 164. *National Defence Act*, R.S.C. 1985, c. N-5, s. 2.

SUMMIT. *n.* The body that is established to represent first nations in British Columbia that agree to participate in the process provided for in the agreement to facilitate the negotiation of treaties among first nations, Her Majesty in right of Canada and Her Majesty in right of British Columbia. *Treaty Commission Act*, R.S.B.C. 1996, c. 461, s. 1. See FIRST NATIONS ~.

SUMMONS. *n.* 1. A citation; a warning to appear in court. 2. Document issued by a court, an agency, board or commission, or another person authorized to issue summonses, requiring a person to attend as a witness at a trial, hearing or examination, to produce documents or other things or to testify before the issuing body or person. See JUDGMENT ~; SHOW CAUSE ~; WRIT OF ~.

SUMMONS TO WITNESS. Used instead of a subpoena, this document directs a witness to appear in court at a given time and place or to bring certain documents or things along.

SUM UP. For a judge to recapitulate evidence or parts of it for a jury, directing what form of verdict they should give. Each counsel has the right to sum up evidence adduced and the judge sums up everything.

SUNK COSTS. The part of an investment required for entry into a particular market which cannot be recovered in the event that the attempt fails.

SUNSET PROVISION. A provision in a statute stating that the act or a portion of it is repealed on a date in the future. May also provide for a review of the statute or provision before the date in the future.

SUP. CT. *abbr.* Superior Court.

SUP. CT. L. REV. *abbr.* The Supreme Court Law Review.

SUPERANNUATION. *n.* The allowance or pension granted to one who is discharged from employment because of age.

SUPERFICIARY. *n.* One who owns by superficies.

SUPERFICIES. *n.* Ownership of the constructions, works or plantations situated on an immovable belonging to another person, the owner of the subsoil. *Civil Code*, S.Q. 1991, c. 64, a. 1011. Superficies results from division of the object of the right of ownership of an immovable, transfer of the right of accession or renunciation of the benefit of accession. *Civil Code*, S.Q. 1991, c. 64, a. 1110.

SUPERINTENDENT OF FINANCIAL INSTITUTIONS. The person appointed pursuant to the Office of the Superintendent of Financial Institutions Act. The Superintendent has the powers, duties and functions assigned to the Superintendent by the Acts referred to in the schedule to this Part and shall examine into and report to the Minister from time to time on all matters connected with the administration of the provisions of those Acts except those that are consumer provisions as defined in section 2 of the Financial Consumer Agency of Canada Act. Financial institutions are (a) a bank within the meaning of section 2 of the Bank Act, (a.1) an authorized foreign bank within the meaning of section 2 of the Bank Act, (b) a company to which the Trust and Loan Companies Act applies, (c) an association to which the Cooperative Credit Associations Act applies or a central cooperative credit society for which an order has been made under subsection 473(1) of that Act, (d) a company, society, foreign company or provincial company to which the Insurance Companies Act applies, and (e) Green Shield Canada. *Office of the Superintendent of Financial Institutions Act*, R.S.C. 1985, c. 18 (3rd Supp.), s. 3 and 6.

SUPERIOR. *n.* A person in authority, other than a military commander. *Crimes Against Humanity and War Crimes Act*, S.C. 2000, c. 24, s. 5.

SUPERIOR COURT. 1. The Supreme Court of a province or territory including the Courts of Appeal in the various provinces. The trial division is known as the Court of Queen's Bench in some provinces. The Federal Court and the Supreme Court Of Canada are superior courts. 2. A court not under the control of any other court except by appeal. 3. "... [D]escribed in s. 96 [of the Constitution Act, 1867 (30 & 31 Vict.), c. 3] were referred to as 'superior courts' ..." *Reference re s.6 of the Family Relations Act (British Columbia)* (1982), 26 R.F.L. (2d) 113 at 131, [1982] 1 S.C.R. 62, [1982] 3 W.W.R. 1, 36 B.C.L.R. 1, 131 D.L.R. (3d) 257, 40 N.R. 206, Estey J. 4. A court with jurisdiction throughout a province, not limited to any subject matter. P.W. Hogg, *Constitutional Law of Canada*, 3d ed. (Toronto: Carswell, 1992) at 162. See PROVINCIAL ~.

SUPERIOR OFFICER. Any officer or non-commissioned member who, in relation to any other officer or non-commissioned member, is by this Act, or by regulations or custom of the service, authorized to give a lawful command to that other officer or non-commissioned member. *National Defence Act*, R.S.C. 1985, c. N-5, s. 2.

SUPERNUMERARY JUDGE. A judge who has elected to give up regular judicial duties and hold office only as a supernumerary judge. May refer to one who has been appointed for a further term after reaching the mandatory retirement age.

SUPERSEDE. *v.* 1. "... [A] meaning that connotes superiority, priority or preference; ..." *National Trust Co. v. Massey Combines Corp.* (1988), 39 B.L.R. 245 at 249, 69 C.B.R. (N.S.) 171 (Ont. H.C.), Saunders J. 2. "... [A] meaning that connotes removal, setting aside, annulment or alteration, followed by a replacement." *National Trust Co. v. Massey Combines Corp.* (1988), 39 B.L.R. 245 at 249, 69 C.B.R. (N.S.) 171 (Ont. H.C.), Saunders J. 3. Rescind.

SUPERSEDEAS. *n.* A writ which ordered, when good cause was shown, the stay of an ordinary proceeding which should otherwise proceed.

SUPERVISE. *v.* To oversee or direct; to monitor.

SUPERVISION. *n.* 1. The provision of counselling services by a probation officer. 2. The caring for, assisting, guiding, protecting, or overseeing of persons. See LONG-TERM ~.

SUPERVISION ORDER. See DEFERRED CUSTODY AND ~.

SUPERVISORY JUDGE. (i) In respect of a judge, the Chief Judge, the Deputy Chief Judge or an Assistant Chief Judge of the Provincial Court of Alberta; (ii) in respect of a justice of the peace, the Chief Judge of the Provincial Court of Alberta or another judge to whom a delegation is made under section 9(b) of the Justice of the Peace Act. *Judicature Act*, R.S.A. 2000, c. J-2, s. 41.1,

SUPPLEMENTARY LETTERS PATENT. Any letters patent granted to the company subsequent to the letters patent incorporating the company.

SUPPLIER. See CANADIAN ~;

SUPPLIER CREDIT AGREEMENT. A consumer agreement, other than a consumer agreement involving leases to which Part VIII applies, under which a supplier or an associate of the supplier, extends fixed credit to a consumer to assist the consumer in obtaining goods or services, other than credit, from the supplier. *Consumer Protection Act, 2002*, S.O. 2002, c. 30, Sched. A, s. 66.

SUPPLY. *n.* Reservation; capacity to provide. See BUSINESS OF ~; CEMETERY SUPPLIES; INTERIM ~.

SUPPLY VOTE. The authority contained in an Act and identified as a vote in that Act to spend the amount of money in the General Revenue Fund indicated in the vote.

SUPPORT. *n.* 1. "[In Succession Law Reform Act, R.S.O. 1980, c. 488] ... financial assistance to permit a dependant to provide for the necessities and amenities of life." *Mannion v. R.* (1982), 140 D.L.R. (3d) 189 at 190, 39 O.R. (2d) 609, 13 E.T.R. 49, 31 R.F.L. (2d) 133 (Div. Ct.), the court per Saunders J. 2. Includes maintenance or alimony. *Reciprocal Enforcement of Support Orders Act*, R.S.N. 1990, c. R-5, s. 2. See CHILD ~; EMPLOYMENT ~.

SUPPORT ORDER. 1. A child support order or a spousal support order. *Divorce Act*, R.S.C. 1985, c.

3 (2nd Supp.), s. 2. 2. An order or judgment or interim order or judgment for family financial support. *Bank Act*, S.C. 1991, c. 46, s. 462. See FINANCIAL ~; SPOUSAL ~.

SUPPORT PROVISION. 1. A provision of an order or agreement relating to maintenance, alimony or family financial support. 2. A provision in an agreement relating to the payment of maintenance or family financial support that is enforceable by a garnishee summons under provincial garnishment law.

SUPRA. *prep.* [L.] Above.

SUPRA PROTEST. After protesting.

SUPREMACY CLAUSE. Section 52(1) of the Constitution Act, 1982 which gives the Charter power to override other provisions.

SUPREME COURT OF CANADA. The court of law and equity in and for Canada now existing under the name of the Supreme Court of Canada is hereby continued under that name, as a general court of appeal for Canada, and as an additional court for the better administration of the laws of Canada, and shall continue to be a court of record. The Court shall have and exercise an appellate, civil and criminal jurisdiction within and throughout Canada. An appeal lies to the Court from a decision of the Federal Court of Appeal in the case of a controversy between Canada and a province or between two or more provinces. An appeal lies to the Court from an opinion pronounced by the highest court of final resort in a province on any matter referred to it for hearing and consideration by the lieutenant governor in council of that province whenever it has been by the statutes of that province declared that such opinion is to be deemed a judgment of the highest court of final resort and that an appeal lies therefrom as from a judgment in an action. The Governor in Council may refer to the Court for hearing and consideration important questions of law or fact concerning (a) the interpretation of the Constitution Acts; (b) the constitutionality or interpretation of any federal or provincial legislation; (c) the appellate jurisdiction respecting educational matters, by the Constitution Act, 1867, or by any other Act or law vested in the Governor in Council; or (d) the powers of the Parliament of Canada, or of the legislatures of the provinces, or of the respective governments thereof, whether or not the particular power in question has been or is proposed to be exercised.The Governor in Council may refer to the Court for hearing and consideration important questions of law or fact concerning any matter, whether or not in the opinion of the Court ejusdem generis with those enumerated above, with reference to which the Governor in Council sees fit to submit any such question. *Supreme Court Act*, R.S.C. 1985, c. S-26, ss. 3, 35, 35.1, 36 and 53.

SUPT. *abbr.* Superintendent.

SURETY. *n.* "... [I]s one who contracts with a creditor that he will be answerable for the debt, default, or miscarriage of another who is the principal debtor and primarily liable." *Schmidt v. Gavriloff*, [1923] 2 W.W.R. 173 at 174, 17 Sask. L.R. 218 (C.A.), Lamont J.A. See CO-~.

SURETY BOND. 1. A written promise under seal committing the issuer, the surety, to pay a named beneficiary, the obligee, a sum up to a stipulated amount. Subject to the obligation ceasing if certain specified conditions are met. 2. A guarantee of the performance of an expressed obligation. *Insurance Adjusters, Agents and Brokers Act*, R.S.N. 1990, c. I-9, s. 2.

SURFACE RIGHTS CONTRACT. A right-of-way, a surface lease or an exploratory licence. *Indian Oil and Gas Act*, R.S.C. 1985, c. I-7, *Indian Oil and Gas Regulations, 1995*, SOR/94-753, s. 2.

SURGEON. See COLLEGE OF PHYSICIANS AND ~S.

SURNAME. *n.* Family name. Patronymic.

SURPLUS. *n.* The amount by which assets exceed liabilities. See COMMON ~.

SURPRISE. *n.* Any event which causes a party to litigation to be put at a disadvantage. This may involve the introduction of evidence, a witness or an issue previously unknown to the party opposite.

SURR. CT. *abbr.* Surrogate Court.

SURREBUTTAL. *n.* 1. The calling of evidence by the defence to meet the Crown's rebuttal evidence. P.K. McWilliams, *Canadian Criminal Evidence*, 3d ed. (Aurora: Canada Law Book, 1988) at 31-12. 2. A response to a plaintiff's or appellant's rebuttal of a defendant or respondent's evidence.

SURREBUTTER. *n.* In pleadings, the plaintiff's response to the rebutter.

SURREJOINDER. *n.* In pleadings, the plaintiff's response to the rejoinder.

SURRENDER. *n.* 1. The giving up by a tenant of premises. 2. An unequivocal, irrevocable and unconditional act to give up a security over property of a debtor. 3. Relinquishment. See CASH ~ VALUE.

SURRENDER BY OPERATION OF LAW. Occurs when the parties to a lease participate in a course of action inconsistent with the continued existence of the lease. Both parties are estopped from denying that a surrender has occurred.

SURROGATE. *n.* One who is appointed or substituted for another.

SURROGATE COURT. A court which deals with matters of probate and the administration of estates.

SURROGATE MOTHER. A female person who carries an embryo or foetus derived from the genes of a donor or donors with the intention of surrendering the child at birth to a donor or another person.

SURTAX. *n.* Tax payable in addition to tax at the standard rate.

SURVEILLANCE. *n.* 1. Location of a person suspected of engaging in criminal activity, following that person, observing their activities and overhearing their conversations with other people. 2. Watching, monitoring of employees by an employer for purposes of the employer. See DIRECT VISUAL ~; ELECTRONIC ~.

SURVEY. *v.* To determine the boundaries of a lot with reference to monuments set by previous surveyors; to determine the form and extent and location of a tract of land by linear and angular measurements so that a plan or detailed description can be drawn or given.

SURVEY. *n.* See ELECTION ~; OPINION~; QUANTITY ~ METHOD.

SURVEYING. *n.* The determination of the form of the earth or the position of natural or artificial things, boundaries or points on, above or under the surface of the earth or the collection, storage, management, integration, analysis or representation of spatial and spatially related information pertaining to the earth or the interpreting of or reporting or advising on that information. *Canada Lands Surveyors Act*, S.C. 1998, c. 14, s. 2. See CADASTRAL ~; LAND ~.

SURVIVE. See VALUE ~D.

SURVIVOR. *n.* 1. A person who outlives another, who is alive at the death of the other. 2. In relation to a deceased individual, means their surviving spouse or common-law partner. See JOINT AND ~ PENSION; JOINT AND ~ PENSION BENEFIT.

SURVIVORSHIP. *n.* 1. The living of one of several people after the death of one or all of the group. 2. The right of the joint tenant who outlives the other(s) to the whole of the jointly held estate. See PRESUMPTION OF ~; RIGHT OF ~.

SURVIVOR WITH DEPENDENT CHILDREN. A survivor of a contributor who wholly or substantially maintains one or more dependent children of the contributor. *Canada Pension Plan*, R.S.C. 1985, c. C-8, s. 42.

SUSPECT. *n.* "... In ordinary parlance, whether someone is a 'suspect' refers to the existence of grounds to believe that the individual has engaged in forbidden activities." *Thomson Newspapers Ltd. v. Canada (Director of Investigation & Research)* (1990), 47 C.R.R. 1 at 67, 76 C.R. (3d) 129, 72 O.R. (2d) 415n, 54 C.C.C. (3d) 417, 67 D.L.R. (4th) 161, 29 C.P.R. (3d) 97, [1990] 1 S.C.R. 425, 39 O.A.C. 161, 106 N.R. 161, L'Heureux-Dubé J.

SUSPEND. *v.* Of a licence, to debar the holder for a period of time from exercising the function or enjoying the privilege authorized or given by the licence.

SUSPENDED SENTENCE. 1. Involves the release of the convicted person on certain conditions contained in a probation order. 2. "... [S]uspension of the imposition of a sentence ..." *R. v. Cruickshanks*, [1946] 3 W.W.R. 225 at 226, 63 B.C.R. 102, 2 C.R. 323, 86 C.C.C. 257, [1946] 4 D.L.R. 645 (C.A.), O'Halloran J.A. 3. "... [S]uspending the passing of the sentence." *R. v. Switzki*, [1930] 2 W.W.R. 479 at 480, 54 C.C.C. 332, 24 Sask. L.R. 587 (C.A.), the court per Haultain C.J.S.

SUSTAINABLE DEVELOPMENT. Development that meets the needs of the present without compromising the ability of future generations to meet their own needs. *Federal Sustainable Development Act*, S.C. 2008, c. 33, s. 2.

SUSTAINABILITY. *n.* The capacity of a thing, action, activity, or process to be maintained indefinitely. *Federal Sustainable Development Act*, S.C. 2008, c. 33, s. 2.

SUSTAINED. *adj.* 1. Endured. 2. Undergone. See PERPETUAL ~ YIELD.

S.V. *abbr.* Sub voce.

SWARMING. *n.* An unprovoked attack on a person in public by a group of persons.

SWC. *abbr.* Status of Women Canada.

SWEAR. *v.* 1. To put under oath, to administer an oath to. 2. In the case of persons for the time being allowed by law to affirm or declare instead of swearing, includes affirm and declare.

SWEARING. *n.* 1. Declaration under oath. 2. "The essence of swearing [as found is s. 160(a) of the Criminal Code, S.C. 1953-54, c. 51] appears to be a reference to God and in the form of an oath. Often used in legal proceedings and in legal documents as an appeal to the truth by invoking the deity the word also includes the use of language which is contemptuous or irreverent of God or the deity." *R. v. Enns* (1968), 66 W.W.R. 318 at 320, 5 C.R.N.S. 115 (Sask. Dist. Ct.), Maher D.C.J.

SWITCH. See BAIT AND ~; INTER~.

SWITCHED TELEPHONE NETWORK. See PUBLIC ~.

SYMBOL. *n.* A shorthand way of visually communicating a message or instruction. See HAZARD ~.

SYNALLAGMATIC. *adj.* 1. Involving reciprocal and mutual duties and obligations. 2. Describing a situation in which one party undertakes to another party to do or not to do something, and, if that party fails to perform the undertaking, the law provides a remedy to the other party. G.H.L. Fridman, *The Law of Contract in Canada*, 2d ed. (Toronto: Carswell, 1986) at 10.

SYNALLAGAMATIC CONTRACT. A contract is synallagmatic, or bilateral, when the parties obligate themselves reciprocally, each to the other, so that the obligation of one party is correlative to the obligation of the other. When one party obligates himself to the other without any obligation on the part of the latter, the contract is unilateral. *Civil Code*, S.Q. 1991, c. 64, a. 1380.

SYNDICATE. See PROFESSIONAL ~.

SYNDICATED LOAN. 1. A syndicated loan is a loan including any related credit facilities made under a syndicated loan agreement by a credit union, a league, Central 1 Credit Union, La Fédération des caisses Desjardins du Québec, La Caisse centrale Desjardins du Québec or Credit Union Central of Canada acting as the syndicating credit union where: 1. The parties to the syndicated loan agreement are the borrower, the syndicating credit union and one or more of the following: i. Another credit union or its subsidiary or affiliate. ii. A league, Central 1 Credit Union, La Fédération des caisses Desjardins du Québec, La Caisse centrale Desjardins du Québec or

Credit Union Central of Canada. iii. A financial institution other than a securities dealer. 2. Each of the parties to the syndicated loan agreement, other than the borrower, agrees to contribute a specified portion of the loan and to be bound by the terms and conditions of the syndicated loan agreement. 3. The syndicating credit union contributes at least 10 per cent of the loans, including any related credit facilities, and underwrites, disburses and administers them on behalf of the parties to the syndicated loan agreement. *Credit Unions and Caisses Populaires Act, 1994*, S.O. 1994, c. 11, *General*, O. Reg. 237/09, s. 56. 2. Eron acted as a mortgage broker for large syndicated loans. It arranged for numerous lenders (or investors) to pool their funds for the purpose of making a single loan to a borrower, which was typically a developer of commercial real estate. The syndicated loans were made in the name of Eron or one of its related companies, which held the security in trust for the investors. *Cooper v. Hobart*, 2001 SCC 79, [2001] 3 S.C.R. 537.

SYNDROME. See BATTERED CHILD ~; BATTERED WOMAN ~; FETAL ALCOHOL ~; IMMERSION ~; MUNCHAUSEN ~; SHAKEN INFANT ~; WATERHOUSE-FRIDERICHSEN ~.

SYNOPSIS. *n.* A brief or condensed statement presenting a combined or general view of something.

SYSTEM. 1. " ... [A] practice..." *Creveling v. Canadian Bridge Co.* (1915), 21 D.L.R. 662 at 667, 8 W.W.R. 619, 51 S.C.R. 216, Duff J. (Brodeur J. concurring). 2. " ... [P]lan ..." *Mako v. Kelowna (City)* (1988), 40 M.P.L.R. 213 at 215, 53 D.L.R. (4th) 604 (B.C. C.A.), the court per Southin J.A. 3. " ... [R]efers to the physical aspect of the utility ... *Charles A. Pender Ltd, Re*, [1940] 3 D.L.R. 39 at 41, 15 M.P.R. 159, 51 C.R.T.C. 230 (N.S. C.A.), the court per Archibald J.A. 4. The connection between actions about which one seeks evidence and the act of which the prisoner is accused, i.e. a prisoner has in mind a scheme to obtain money by fraud; the act of which the prisoner is accused is part of a planned fraud; and one seeks evidence that the plan existed, and, therefore, that the prisoner has a guilty mind. P.K. McWilliams, *Canadian Criminal Evidence*, 3d ed. (Aurora: Canada Law Book, 1988) at 11-11. See ADVERSARIAL ~; ADVERSARY ~; CLEARING AND SETTLEMENT ~; CLEARING ~; COMPUTER ~; ECO~; ELECTRONIC DOCUMENTS ~; ELECTRONIC RECORDS ~; FEUDAL ~; FRANCHISE ~; INFORMATION MANAGEMENT ~; INFORMATION ~; JUDICIAL ~; KEY SECURING ~; LAND TITLES ~; METRIC ~; NATIONAL STANDARDS ~; NET-METERING ~; OPERATING ~ PROGRAM; PARI-MUTUEL ~; REGISTRY ACT ~; RESTRAINT ~; RISK CLASSIFICATION ~; TRANSIT ~; TRANSMISSION ~.

SYSTEMATIC ATTACK. A systematic attack is one that is "thoroughly organised and follow[s] a regular pattern on the basis of a common policy involving substantial public or private resources" and is "carried out pursuant to a ... policy or plan", although the policy need not be an official state policy and the number of victims affected is not determinative: Akayesu, Trial Chamber, at para. 580; and Kayishema, at para. 123. As noted by the ICTY's Trial Chamber II in Kunarac, at para. 429: "The adjective 'systematic' signifies the organised nature of the acts of violence and the improbability of their random occurrence. Patterns of crimes—that is the non-accidental repetition of similar criminal conduct on a regular basis—are a common expression of such systematic occurrence." *Mugesera v. Canada (Minister of Citizenship and Immigration)*, 2005 SCC 40, [2005] 2 S.C.R. 100.

SYSTEMATIC REVIEW. A medical or scientific study which evaluates the strengths and weaknesses of all relevant reported research over a particular period of time. It attempts to allocate a measure of reliability to the strength of the evidence in support of a given proposition.

SYSTEMIC DISCRIMINATION. Systemic discrimination arises from the existence of a particular policy which creates the discriminatory effect. The effect is usually obvious (e.g. height and weight restrictions). Systemic discrimination arises out of long-standing stereotypes and value assumptions which create the discriminatory effect. Systemic discrimination is quite often the result of unintentional behaviour. There is no desire to exclude certain people or classes of people but, as the result of stereotypes, mind-sets and attitudes which have been acquired over a long period of time, the effect is discriminatory. *Ayangma v. Prince Edward Island*, 2001 CarswellPEI 103, 2001 PESCAD 22 (C.A.).

SYSTEMIC NEGLIGENCE. Negligence not specific to any one victim but rather to the class of victims as a group. *Rumley v. British Columbia*, 2001 CarswellBC 2166, 2001 SCC 69, the court per McLachlin C.J.C.

SYSTEMIC RISK. The risk that the inability of a participant to meet its obligations in a clearing and settlement system as they become due or a disruption to a clearing and settlement system could, through the transmittal of financial problems through the system, cause (a) other participants in the clearing and settlement system to be unable to meet their obligations as they become due, (b) financial institutions in other parts of the Canadian financial system to be unable to meet their obligations as they become due, or (c) the clearing and settlement system's clearing house or the clearing house of another clearing and settlement system within the Canadian financial system to be unable to meet its obligations as they become due. *Payment Clearing and Settlement Act*, S.C. 1996, c. 6, Sch., s. 2.

T

T.A. *abbr.* Décisions du Tribunal d'arbitrage (Québec), 1982-1997.

T.A.A.T. *abbr.* Tribunal d'appel des accidents du travail (Ontario), 1985-1997.

T.A.B. *abbr.* Tax Appeal Board.

TABLE. *v.* To set aside a matter; to put off; to delay; to postpone.

TABLE. *n.* See ACTUARIAL ~.

TABULA IN NAUFRAGIO. See DOCTRINE OF THE ~.

TACIT. *adj.* Inferred or understood, but not openly expressed.

TACIT KNOWLEDGE. Knowledge acquired by individuals by experience and not committed to an easily reproducible form as explicit knowledge.

TACKING. *n.* 1. Extending a mortgagee's security to cover a subsequent loan. R. Megarry & H.W.R. Wade, *The Law of Real Property*, 5th ed. (London: Stevens, 1984) at cxxviii. 2. A doctrine concerning priorities between competing mortgages on the same property. If a third mortgage is taken without notice of a second and the third mortgagee purchases the first mortgage, the third mortgagee may "tack" the third mortgage to the first mortgage and so obtain priority. W.B. Rayner & R.H. McLaren, *Falconbridge on Mortgages*, 4th ed. (Toronto: Canada Law Book, 1977) at 195. 3. A doctrine by which a mortgagor's devisees or heirs may not redeem the mortgage without also paying a judgment debt or bond owing by the mortgagor because any equity of redemption in the hands of the devisees or heirs are assets for the payment of that debt. W.B. Rayner & R.H. McLaren, *Falconbridge on Mortgages*, 4th ed. (Toronto: Canada Law Book, 1977) at 196-197. 4. "A first or prior mortgagee may claim priority, up to the face amount of the mortgage, for moneys advanced under the first or prior mortgage subsequent to the registration and advancement of funds under a second or subsequent mortgage provided that such first or prior mortgagee did not have 'notice' of the second or subsequent mortgage at the time such subsequent advances were made. The 'notice' previously referred to is actual notice, not constructive notice." *I.W.A. Credit Union v. Johnson* (1978), 6 B.C.L.R.

271 at 280, 4 R.P.R. 181 (S.C.), Hinds L.J.S.C. See TIME-~.

TACTIC. See PRESSURE ~.

TAIL. See ESTATE ~; FEE ~; LONG ~ CLAIM.

TAKE. *v.* 1. The word "take" in relation to land does not necessarily refer to the acquisition of full title. Rather, The Dictionary of Canadian Law (2nd ed. 1995) defines "take lands" as including to "enter upon, take possession of, use and take lands for a limited time or otherwise or for a limited estate or interest". Similarly, several courts including this one have acknowledged that a "taking" of land includes the acquisition of possession and other interests less than full title. *Osoyoos Indian Band v. Oliver (Town)*, [2001] 3 S.C.R. 746, Iacobucci J. (McLachlin C.J.C., Binnie, Arbour and LeBel JJ. concurring). 2. To cause a person to come or go with. 3. To physically get something into one's hand or hold. See HOSTAGE TAKING.

TAKE-BACK. See VENDOR ~ MORTGAGE.

TAKE-HOME PAY. Net pay after withholding tax and other deductions.

TAKEN. *adj.* 1. "... [L]and is taken under the [Municipal Act, R.S.B.C. 1911, c. 170] when the notice to treat is served. *Hanna v. Victoria (City)* (1915), 22 B.C.R. 555 at 560, 10 W.W.R. 457, 34 W.L.R. 307, 27 D.L.R. 213 (C.A.), Galliher J.A. 2. "... [T]he word 'taken' ... in [Criminal Code, R.S.C. 1970, c. C-34, s. 454(1)] must be held to encompass situations in which the accused surrenders or voluntarily appears." *Alberta (Attorney General) v. Kennedy*, [1983]1 W.W.R. 406 at 410 (Alta. C.A.), the court per Harradence J.A. 3. "... '[A]pprehended' ..." *R. v. Hughes* (1895), 2 C.C.C. 332 at 334 (Ont. H.C.), Rose J. (Meredith C.J.C.P. concurring).

TAKE OVER BID. *var.* **TAKE-OVER BID.** 1. An offer made by an offeror to shareholders of a distributing corporation at approximately the same time to acquire all of the shares of a class of issued shares, and includes an offer made by a distributing corporation to repurchase all of the shares of a class of its shares. 2. A direct or indirect offer to acquire a security, that is (a) made by a person or company other than the issuer of the security, and (b) within a class of offers to acquire prescribed by the regulations. *Securities acts*.

TAKING ACCOUNTS. This action was brought against M & L Leasing to indemnify the partners for the payment they made to satisfy the judgment. An action for indemnity or contribution is *not* the appropriate means for partners to seek indemnity; the proper remedy is an action for the taking of accounts. *Lafrentz v. M & L Leasing Ltd. Partnership*, 2000 CarswellAlta 1121, 2000 ABQB 714, 8 B.L.R. (3d) 219, [2001] 1 W.W.R. 629, 85 Alta. L.R. (3d) 233, 275 A.R. 334 (Q.B.), Perras J.

TANGIBLE PERSONAL PROPERTY. Personal property that can be seen, weighed, measured, felt or touched or that is in any way perceptible to the senses.

TANGIBLE PROPERTY. Property having a physical existence.

T.A.Q. *abbr.* Décisions du Tribunal administratif du Québec, 1998-.

TARIFF. *n.* 1. "[In the National Energy Board Act, R.S.C. 1970, c. N-6] ... a list of tolls or rates... . It has been sometimes defined as 'a schedule of rates together with rules and regulations.' " *Saskatchewan Power Corp. v. Trans-Canada Pipelines Ltd.* (1981), 130 D.L.R. (3d) 1 at 11, 39 N.R. 595, [1982] 1 W.W.R. 289, 14 Sask. R. 271, [1982] 2 S.C.R. 688, the court per Laskin C.J.C. 2. The schedule of fees to be charged for various legal services. 3. A schedule of fares, rates, charges and terms and conditions of carriage applicable to the provision of a transportation service.

TAUTOLOGY. See PRESUMPTION AGAINST ~.

TAX. *n.* 1. "... [T]he ... levies ... are taxes... . Compulsion is an essential feature of taxation ... the committee is a public authority, and ... the imposition of these levies is for the public purposes... ." *British Columbia (Lower Mainland Dairy Products Sales Adjustment Committee) v. Crystal Dairy Ltd.*, [1933] 1 D.L.R. 82 at 85, [1933] 3 W.W.R. 639, [1933] A.C. 168 (P.C.), Lord Thankerton. 2. "Tax is a term of general import, including almost every species of imposition on persons or property for supplying the public treasury, as tolls, tributes, subsidies, excise, imposts, or customs ..." *Lovitt v. Nova Scotia (Attorney General)* (1903), 33 S.C.R. 350 at 360, Mills J. 3. "... [E]very contribution to a public purpose imposed by superior authority is a 'tax' and nothing less." *Monette v. LeFebvre* (1889), 16 S.C.R. 387 at 403, Strong J. (Patterson J. concurring). 4. Includes any tax, impost, duty or toll payable to Her Majesty, imposed or authorized to be imposed by any Act of Parliament. *Financial Administration Act*, R.S.C. 1985, c. F-11, s. 23. See AREA ~; ARREARS OF ~; BUSINESS OCCUPANCY ~; BUSINESS ~; DEPARTURE ~; DIRECT ~; ESTATE ~; EXCISE ~ES; EXPORT ~; FRONTAGE ~; FUEL ~; GIFT ~; GOODS AND SERVICES ~; INCOME ~; INHERITANCE ~; LAND ~; MUNICIPAL ~; POLL-~; PROPERTY ~; REAL PROPERTY ~; SALES ~; SUR~.

TAX A.B.C. *abbr.* Tax Appeal Board Cases, 1949-1966.

TAX A.B.C. (N.S.). *abbr.* Tax Appeal Board Cases (New Series), 1967-1972.

TAXABLE PROPERTY. 1. Real property and immovables in respect of which a person may be required by a taxing authority to pay a real property tax or a frontage or area tax; *Payments in Lieu of Taxes Act*, R.S.C. 1985, c. M-13, s. 2. 2. Assessed property that is liable to taxation. *Property Assessment and Taxation Act*, R.S.N.W.T. 1988, c. P-10, s. 1.

TAXATION. *n.* 1. The scheme of imposing charges on persons, income and property for the purpose of raising revenue for the purposes of the legislative authority. 2. Direct taxation refers to taxes imposed on the person intended to pay them. Income and sales tax are direct taxes. Indirect taxation refers to a tax demanded from one person in the expectation that he will indemnify himself at the expense of another person. Customs and excise are indirect taxes when imposed on businesses. 3. The process by which costs awarded to parties at a trial or in relation to work which a solicitor has performed for a client are referred, examined and certified by an officer of the court. See CERTIFICATE OF ~; DIRECT ~; INDIRECT ~.

TAXATION OF COSTS. The review of a lawyer's bill for services by an official of the court. See ASSESSMENT OF COSTS.

TAXATION YEAR. 1. The fiscal year in relation to which the amount of tax is being computed. 2. In the case of a corporation, a fiscal period and in the case of an individual, a calendar year.

TAX AVOIDANCE. Attempts by a taxpayer to minimize or eliminate a tax obligation either by deliberately arranging income earning affairs to benefit from provisions of income tax legislation or by relying on reasonable and different interpretations of that legislation. W. Grover & F. Iacobucci, *Materials on Canadian Income Tax*, 4th ed. (Toronto: De Boo, 1980) at 993.

TAX COLLECTION AGREEMENT. An agreement between the Government of Canada and the government of a province pursuant to which the Government of Canada will collect, on behalf of the province, taxes that the province imposes on the incomes of individuals or corporations, or both, and will make payments to the province in respect of the taxes so collected in accordance with the terms and conditions of the agreement. *Federal-Provincial Fiscal Arrangements Act*, R.S.C. 1985, c. F-8, s. 2.

TAX COMMISSION. See FIRST NATIONS ~.

TAX COURT OF CANADA. The Tax Review Board, established by the Tax Review Board Act, chapter 11 of the Statutes of Canada, 1970-71-72, was continued under the name of the Tax Court of Canada as a court of record. The Court has exclusive original jurisdiction to hear and determine references and appeals to the Court on matters arising under the Air Travellers Security Charge Act, the Canada Pension Plan, the Cultural Property Export and Import Act, Part V.1 of the Customs Act, the Employment Insurance Act, the Excise Act, 2001, Part IX of the Excise Tax Act, the Income Tax Act, the Old Age

Security Act, the Petroleum and Gas Revenue Tax Act and the Softwood Lumber Products Export Charge Act, 2006, where references or appeals to the Court are provided for in those Acts. The Court has exclusive original jurisdiction to hear and determine appeals on matters arising under the War Veterans Allowance Act and the Civilian War-related Benefits Act and referred to in section 33 of the Veterans Review and Appeal Board Act. The Court also has exclusive original jurisdiction to hear and determine questions referred to it under section 51 or 52 of the Air Travellers Security Charge Act, section 97.58 of the Customs Act, section 204 or 205 of the Excise Act, 2001, section 310 or 311 of the Excise Tax Act, section 173 or 174 of the Income Tax Act or section 62 or 63 of the Softwood Lumber Products Export Charge Act, 2006. The Court has exclusive original jurisdiction to hear and determine applications for extensions of time under section 45 or 47 of the Air Travellers Security Charge Act, subsection 28(1) of the Canada Pension Plan, section 33.2 of the Cultural Property Export and Import Act, section 97.51 or 97.52 of the Customs Act, subsection 103(1) of the Employment Insurance Act, section 197 or 199 of the Excise Act, 2001, section 304 or 305 of the Excise Tax Act, or section 166.2 or 167 of the Income Tax Act. The Court has exclusive original jurisdiction to hear and determine applications referred to in subsection 188.2(4) of the Income Tax Act by a registered charity for a postponement of a period of suspension of the authority of the charity to issue official receipts referred to in Part XXXV of the Income Tax Regulations. *Tax Court of Canada Act*, R.S.C. 1985, c. T-2.

TAX DEED. A deed conveying property which has been sold for arrears of taxes to a purchaser.

TAXED COSTS. Costs fixed by the court officer assigned the duty of reviewing and setting the costs of litigation to which a party is entitled.

TAX EVASION. In a case where the law clearly obliges one to report income and pay tax, a wilful attempt by the taxpayer not to disclose or to suppress income and thus not to pay tax on it. W. Grover & F. Iacobucci, *Materials on Canadian Income Tax*, 4th ed. (Toronto: De Boo, 1980) at 991. See INCOME ~.

TAX EXPENDITURE. A feature of the income tax system such as an exemption, exclusion, or deduction which is in fact a method of providing financial assistance and is not required for purposes of administering the income tax itself. W. Grover & F. Iacobucci, *Materials on Canadian Income Tax*, 4th ed. (Toronto: De Boo, 1980) at 163.

TAX-FREE SAVINGS ACCOUNT. An account set up under the conditions set out in section 146.2 of the *Income Tax Act*, R.S.C. 1985, c. 1 (5th Supp.).

TAX GROSS-UP. *n.* The practice of increasing lump sum awards for future care costs and pecuniary losses in personal injury cases (other than loss of future income) and for pecuniary losses in fatal accident cases to take into account the impact of taxation on the income generated by lump sum awards in respect of those heads of damages. It has been accepted at common law as a proper head of damages to be included in a lump sum award at trial. *McErlean v. Sarel* (1987), 61 O.R. (2d) 396 (C.A.).

TAXING OFFICER. 1. The registrar or other officer appointed for the taxation or fixing of costs or the passing of accounts. 2. An assessment officer.

TAXING TREATY FIRST NATION. For a taxation year, means a treaty first nation that (a) is a party to a Real Property Tax Co-ordination Agreement under which the treaty first nation is authorized to impose on persons who are not its treaty first nation members taxes in relation to those persons' ownership or occupation of its treaty lands, and (b) has complied with section 2(1) or (2) in a previous taxation year. *Treaty First Nation Taxation Act*, S.B.C. 2007, c. 38, s. 1.

TAX IN PERSONAM. A tax which is imposed on a person rather than on property.

TAX IN REM. A tax on property rather than on an individual person.

TAXPAYER. *n.* A person required by a revenue Act to pay a tax.

TAX SHELTER. (a) A gifting arrangement described by paragraph (b) of the definition "gifting arrangement"; and (b) a gifting arrangement described by paragraph (a) of the definition "gifting arrangement", or a property (including any right to income) other than a flow-through share or a prescribed property, in respect of which it can reasonably be considered, having regard to statements or representations made or proposed to be made in connection with the gifting arrangement or the property, that, if a person were to enter into the gifting arrangement or acquire an interest in the property, at the end of a particular taxation year that ends within four years after the day on which the gifting arrangement is entered into or the interest is acquired, (i) the total of all amounts each of which is (A) an amount, or a loss in the case of a partnership interest, represented to be deductible in computing the person's income for the particular year or any preceding taxation year in respect of the gifting arrangement or the interest in the property (including, if the property is a right to income, an amount or loss in respect of that right that is stated or represented to be so deductible), or (B) any other amount stated or represented to be deemed under this Act to be paid on account of the person's tax payable, or to be deductible in computing the person's income, taxable income or tax payable under this Act, for the particular year or any preceding taxation year in respect of the gifting arrangement or the interest in the property, other than an amount so stated or represented that is included in computing a loss described in clause (A), would equal or exceed (ii) the amount, if any, by which (A) the cost to the person of the property acquired under the gifting arrangement, or of the interest in the property at the end of the particular year, determined without reference to section 143.2, would exceed (B) the total of all amounts each of which is the amount of any prescribed benefit that is expected to be received or enjoyed, directly or indirectly, in respect of the property acquired under the gifting arrangement, or of the interest in the property, by the person or another person with whom the person does not deal at arm's length. *Income Tax Act*, R.S.C. 1985, c. 1 (5th Supp.), s. 237.1.

TAX SHELTER INVESTMENT. (a) A property that is a tax shelter for the purpose of subsection 37.1(1); or (b) a taxpayer's interest in a partnership where (i) an interest in the taxpayer (A) is a tax shelter investment, and (B) the taxpayer's partnership interest would be a tax shelter investment if (I) this Act were read without reference to this paragraph and to the words "having regard to statements or representations made or proposed to be made in connection with the property" in the definition "tax shelter" in subsection 237.1(1), (II) the references in that definition to "represented" were read as references to "that can reasonably be expected", and (III) the reference in that definition to "is represented" were read as a reference to "can reasonably be expected", (ii) another interest in the partnership is a tax shelter investment, or (iii) the taxpayer's interest in the partnership entitles the taxpayer, directly or indirectly, to a share of the income or loss of a particular partnership where (A) another taxpayer holding a partnership interest is entitled, directly or indirectly, to a share of the income or loss of the particular partnership, and (B) that other taxpayer's partnership interest is a tax shelter investment. *Income Tax Act*, R.S.C. 1985, c. 1 (5th Supp.), s. 143.2.

TAX TREATMENT AGREEMENT. An agreement among a treaty first nation, British Columbia and Canada that (a) under the chapter of the treaty first nation's final agreement that sets out the agreement of the parties in relation to taxation, is required to come into effect on the date the final agreement comes into effect, and (b) is tabled in the Legislative Assembly on or before the date settlement legislation in relation to the final agreement receives Third Reading, and, for greater certainty, does not include amendments to the agreement made after the date the settlement legislation receives Third Reading. *Treaty First Nation Taxation Act*, S.B.C. 2007, c. 38, s. 1.

TAYLOR. *abbr.* Taylor's King's Bench Reports (Ontario), 1823-1827.

T.B. *abbr.* Tariff Board.

TBA. *abbr.* To be agreed.

T. BD. *abbr.* Transport Board.

T.B.R. *abbr.* Tariff Board Reports, 1937-1988.

T.C.C. *abbr.* Tax Court of Canada.

T.C.D. *abbr.* Tribunal de la Concurrence, décisions, 1986-.

T.C.I. *abbr.* Tribunal canadien des importations.

T.C.J. *abbr.* Tax Court Judge.

TCP. *abbr.* Transmission control protocol.

T.C.T. *abbr.* Canadian Trade and Commodity Tax Cases, 1989-1992.

T.D. *abbr.* Supreme Court, Trial Division.

T.E. *abbr.* Recueils de jurisprudence du Tribunal de l'expropriation (Québec), 1972-1986.

TEAM. See SCAN ~.

TEAR. See WEAR AND ~.

TECHNOLOGY. *n.* 1. Includes technical data, technical assistance and information necessary for the development, production or use of an article. *Export and Import Permits Act*, R.S.C. 1985, c. E-19, s. 2. 2. A software application which is capable of carrying out a particular function. 3. Computer systems (both hardware and software) and related data files. See BIO~; DENTAL ~; NATIONAL MUSEUM OF SCIENCE AND ~; PHOTO-COMPARISON ~.

TELECOMMUNICATION. *n.* Any transmission, emission or reception of signs, signals, writing, images or sounds or intelligence of any nature by wire, radio, visual, or other electro-magnetic system. *Criminal Code*, R.S.C. 1985, c. C-46, s. 326(2). See CANADIAN RADIO-TELEVISION AND ~S COMMISSION.

TELECOMMUNICATIONS COMMON CARRIER. A person who owns or operates a transmission facility used by that person or another person to provide telecommunications services to the public for compensation. *Telecommunications Act*, S.C. 1993, c. 38, s. 2.

TELECOMMUNICATIONS FACILITY. Any facility, apparatus or other thing that is used or is capable of being used for telecommunications or for any operation directly connected with telecommunications, and includes a transmission facility. *Telecommunications Act*, S.C. 1993, c. 38, s. 2.

TELECOMMUNICATIONS SERVICE. A service provided by means of telecommunications facilities and includes the provision in whole or in part of telecommunications facilities and any related equipment, whether by sale, lease or otherwise. *Telecommunications Act*, S.C. 1993, c. 38, s. 2.

TELEGRAPH. See RADIO-~.

TELEMARKETING. *n.* The practice of using interactive telephone communications for the purpose of promoting, directly or indirectly, the supply or use of a product or for the purpose of promoting, directly or indirectly, any business interest. *Competition Act*, R.S.C. 1985, c. C-34, s. 52.1.

TELEPHONE. See RADIO-~

TELEPHONE COMMUNICATION. See RADIO-BASED ~

TELEVISION. See COMMUNITY ANTENNA ~.

TELEWARRANT. *n.* An application for a search telewarrant must be supported by an oral statement submitted by telephone or other means of telecommunication and is deemed to be made under oath. *Code of Penal Procedure*, R.S.Q., c. C-25.1, a. 99.

TEMPORARY ABSENCE. Permission for an inmate to leave the institution in which he is imprisoned for a period of time during the time he is serving his sentence. The purpose of a temporary absence program is to contribute to the maintenance of a just, peaceful and safe society by facilitating, through decisions on the timing and conditions of absence, the rehabilitation of prisoners and their reintegration into the community as law-abiding citizens. See UNESCORTED ~.

TENANCY. *n.* 1. The exclusive right to occupy residential premises granted to a tenant by a landlord, for which the tenant agrees to pay or provide rent for a term that may be terminated by the landlord or tenant. 2. The condition of being a tenant. 3. The relation of a tenant to the property the tenant holds. See CO~; FIXED TERM ~; JOINT ~; PERIODIC ~; SEVERAL ~; TERM OF ~.

TENANCY AGREEMENT. 1. An agreement between a landlord and a tenant for possession or occupation of residential premises, whether written, oral or implied. 2. A written, oral or implied agreement between a tenant and a landlord for occupancy of a rental unit and includes a licence to occupy a rental unit. *Residential Tenancy Act, 2006*, S.O. 2006, c. 17, s. 2.

TENANCY AT WILL. An interest which permits a grantee to enter into possession of land at the pleasure of the grantor and her or himself.

TENANCY BY ESTOPPEL. Created when a person without title or interest in land or having only an equitable interest in the land, lets a tenant into possession and receives rent from the tenant. The tenant is estopped from disputing the title of the lessor while the tenant remains in possession.

TENANCY BY THE ENTIRETY. A condition like a joint tenancy, which cannot be severed, created through a conveyance to a husband and wife with no words of severance. A. Bissett-Johnson & W.M. Holland, eds., *Matrimonial Property Law in Canada* (Toronto: Carswell, 1980) at I-11.

TENANCY IN COMMON. A condition in which two or more people are required to have a unity of possession, only, in property. Each tenant may dispose of her property by will or deed. There is no right of survivorship as in a joint tenancy.

TENANCY WEEK. The period on which a weekly periodic tenancy is based whether or not it is a calendar week, and the week begins on the day rent is payable unless another date is specified in the residential tenancy agreement. *Residential Tenancies Act*, S.A. 2004, c. R-17.1, s. 1.

TENANT. *n.* 1. "... [T]he person who, by reason of his possession of occupancy or his rights thereto, whether by privity of contract or estate, for the time being holds the premises under title immediately or mediately from the landlord or his predecessor in title, and by reason of his so holding is the person liable for the time being to pay the rent... ." *Calgary Brewing & Malting Co., Re* (1915), 9 W.W.R. 563 at 565, 25 D.L.R. 859 (Alta. T.D.), Beck J. 2. "... [O]ne of a class of persons ... who have a right to use the premises, not by license or invitation as occasion arises, but by a contract which gives a right to such use continuously during the currency of the contract without licence or invitation." *Watt v. Adams Brothers Harness Manufacturing Co.* (1927), 23 Alta. L.R. 94 at 97, [1927] 3 W.W.R. 580, [1928] 1 D.L.R. 59 (C.A.), Beck J.A. 3. Includes a person who pays rent in return for the right to occupy a rental unit and includes the tenant's heirs, assigns and personal representatives, but tenant does not include a person who has the right to occupy a rental unit by virtue of being, (a) a co-owner of the residential complex in which the rental unit is located, or (b) a shareholder of a corporation that owns the residential complex; *Residential Tenancies Act, 2006*, S.O. 2006, c. 17, s. 2. See JOINT ~; LEASEHOLD ~; LIFE ~; OVERHOLDING ~; SUB~; UN~ABLE.

TENANT AT SUFFERANCE. One who overstays the term of a tenancy.

TENANT AT WILL. One who holds possession, without a fixed term, of premises by permission of the owner.

TENANT'S EXTRA. An alteration or improvement that is agreed to by the landlord and the tenant before the rental unit is first occupied by the tenant under a life lease, and (a) in the case of an initial tenant, means an alteration or improvement to the landlord's standard specifications respecting the tenant's rental unit, and (b) in the case of a tenant other than an initial tenant, means an alteration or improvement to the tenant's rental unit. *The Life Leases Act*, S.M. 1998, c. 42, s. 1.

TENANT'S FIXTURES. Fixtures which the tenant installed into the premises for the purposes of a trade. These fixtures do not become part of the structure itself.

TENANTS IN COMMON. Two or more people who are required to have a unity of possession, only, in property. Each tenant may dispose of their interest by will or deed. There is no right of survivorship as in a joint tenancy.

TENDER. *n.* 1. A payment of the precise amount that is due. To offer a larger amount without asking for change is acceptable, but to offer less is not. If it was agreed that the debt to be paid on a certain day, payment after or before that date is not proper, and for the payment to be proper it must be unconditional. C.R.B. Dunlop, *Creditor-Debtor Law in Canada* (Toronto: Carswell, 1981) at 21 and 22. 2. Legal currency. 3. A call for tender by written public advertisement. 4. A "Tender" is that which a General Contractor submits to an Owner. It is not to a "Bid" which is what a Subcontractor submits to a General Contractor. *Ken Toby Ltd. v. British Columbia Buildings Corp.*, 1997 CarswellBC 1087, 34 B.C.L.R. (3d) 263, [1997] 8 W.W.R. 721, 34 C.L.R. (2d) 81, 31 B.L.R. (2d) 224 (S.C.), Burnyeat J. 5. An offer to carry out work specified on and subject to the terms and conditions stated at the price quoted. Once a tender is accepted there is a binding contract. See INVITATION FOR ~S; LEGAL ~.

TENEMENT. *n.* Something which may be held; something which is subject to tenure. See DOMINANT ~; LANDS, ~S AND HEREDITAMENTS; SERVIENT ~.

TENURE. *n.* 1. A way to hold or occupy. 2. The mode in which all land is theoretically owned and occupied. See FORESTRY ~; SECURITY OF ~.

T

T.E. (QUÉ.). *abbr.* Tribunal de l'expropriation (Québec).

TERM. *n.* 1. A contract provision which explains an obligation or group of obligations imposed on one or more of the parties. G.H.L. Fridman, *The Law of Contract in Canada*, 2d ed. (Toronto: Carswell, 1986) at 427. 2. "[Used] ... to designate the length of time for which a person is elected to serve in political office or for which a person is incarcerated as a penalty for the commission of a crime." *R. v. Laycock* (1989), 51 C.C.C. (3d) 65 at 68, 17 M.V.R. (2d) 1 (Ont. C.A.), the court per Goodman J.A. 3. "The word 'term' would be more accurate than 'session' to describe the time prescribed by law for holding court, as a session of the Court is the time of its actual sitting and terminates each day with its rising. The distinction is not always observed, however, and the words are often used interchangeably." *MacDonald v. Dawson* (1955), 20 C.R. 357 at 358, 36 M.P.R. 34, 112 C.C.C. 44 (Nfld. C.A.), the court per Walsh C.J. 4. Of a lease agreement, its limit in time. In the law of real property, the estate granted to a lessor, an estate in years. See COLLATERAL ~; CONTRADICTION IN ~S; DISJUNCTIVE ~; EXPRESS ~; FIXED ~ TENANCY; FUNDAMENTAL ~; GROUP ~ LIFE INSURANCE POLICY; IMPLIED ~; LEASE ~.

TERMINAL. See GAMING ~; VIDEO LOTTERY ~.

TERMINATE. *v.* To remove from the employer's payroll and from the employer's workplace.

TERMINATION. *n.* 1. "... [W]hen in the context of a breach of contract one speaks of 'termination' what is meant is no more than that the innocent party or, in some cases, both parties are excused from further performance." *Photo Production Ltd. v. Securicor Transport Ltd.*, [1980] 1 All E.R. 556 at 562 (U.K. H.L.), Lord Wilberforce. 2. "[Includes] ... an ending of the contract [of insurance] by time lapse." *Bank of Nova Scotia v. Commercial Union Assurance of Canada* (1991), 104 N.S.R. (2d) 313 at 319, 283 A.P.R. 313, 6 C.C.L.I. (2d) 178 (T.D.), Tidman J. 3. The severance of a relationship between employer and employee. *Goguen v. Metro Oil Co.*, 1989 CarswellNB 7, 42 B.L.R. 30, 95 N.B.R. (2d) 295, 241 A.P.R. 295 (C.A.), the court per Angers J.A. 4. In relation to employment, includes retirement and death. *Pension Benefits Act*, R.S.O. 1990, c. P.8, s. 1. See VOLUNTARY ~.

TERMINATION METHOD. In marriage breakdown, a method of establishing the value of an accrued pension. The value of the accrued pension is determined assuming that the member terminated employment as at the date of the marriage breakdown. The value of the pension is crystallized as of the date of separation.

TERMINATION PAY. The pay given to an employee instead of a termination notice. *Employment Standards Code*, R.S.A. 2000, c. E-9, s. 1.

TERM OF ART. "Some expressions in common use in documents dealing with legal rights or obligations acquire in a legal context a special meaning different from, or more precise than, their meaning in common speech—they become 'terms of art'." *Prestcold (Central) Ltd. v. Minister of Labour*, [1969] 1 All E.R. 69 at 75, [1969] 1 W.L.R. 89 (U.K. C.A.), Lord Diplock. See LEGAL ~.

TERM OF TENANCY. The length of time during which a tenancy agreement is to run.

TERRA NULLIUS. [L.] Land of no one. Land without an owner.

TERR. CT. *abbr.* Territorial Court.

TERR. CT. J. *abbr.* Territorial Court Judge.

TERRITORIAL. See EXTRA-~.

TERRITORIAL COMPETENCE. The aspects of a court's jurisdiction that depend on a connection between the territory or legal system of the state in which the court is established, and a party to a proceeding in the court or the facts on which the proceeding is based.

TERRITORIAL COURT. A court which continued the Magistrate's Court in two federal territories, the Northwest Territories and the Yukon Territory.

TERRITORIAL JURISDICTION. 1. The territory where the court is given jurisdiction. 2. [I]n s. 504 of the Criminal Code [R.S.C. 1985, c. C-46] refers to the entire province of Ontario. *R. v. Ellis*, 2009 ONCA 483.

TERRITORIAL LANDS. Lands, or any interest in lands, in the Northwest Territories or Nunavut that are vested in the Crown or of which the Government of Canada has power to dispose. *Territorial Lands Act*, R.S.C. 1985, c. T-7, s. 2.

TERRITORIAL MINISTER. Any minister of the government of a territory.

TERRITORIAL SEA. 1. "... [A]s defined by international law, i.e., the waters and submerged lands to a width of three miles seaward of the coast of the mainland but when the mainland coast is deeply indented or has a fringe of islands in its immediate vicinity, seaward from baselines enclosing these features." *Canada (Attorney General) v. British Columbia (Attorney General)*, [1984] 4 W.W.R. 289 at 299, [1984] 1 S.C.R. 388, 8 D.L.R. (4th) 161, 52 N.R. 335, 54 B.C.L.R. 97, Dickson J. (Beetz, Estey and Chouinard JJ. concurring). 2. In relation to Canada, means the territorial sea of Canada as determined under the Oceans Act and includes the airspace above and the seabed and subsoil below that sea, and in relation to any other state, means the territorial sea of the other state as determined in accordance with international law and the domestic laws of that other state. *Interpretation Act*, R.S.C. 1985, c. I-21, s. 35. 3. The territorial sea of Canada consists of a belt of sea that has as its inner limit the baselines described in the Act and as its outer limit the line every point of which is at a distance of 12 nautical miles from the nearest point of the baselines or where geographical coordinates of points have been prescribed, lines determined from the geographical coordinates of points so prescribed. *Oceans Act*, S.C. 1996, c. 31.

TERRITORY. *n.* 1. Yukon, the Northwest Territories and Nunavut. *Interpretation Act*, R.S.C. 1985, c. I-21, s. 35. 2. With respect to Canada, the territory to which its customs laws apply, including any areas beyond the territorial seas of Canada within which, in accordance with international law and its domestic law, Canada may exercise rights with respect to its sea bed and subsoil and their natural resources. *Free Trade Agreement acts.* 3. " ... [O]f the Dominion ... is all those lands and lands covered with water which form part of or are under the Parliamentary control of the Dominion." *Canadian Pacific Railway v. James Bay Railway* (1905), 36 S.C.R. 42 at 71, Girouard J. See FEDERAL ∼.

TERR. L.R. *abbr.* Territories Law Reports (N.W.T.), 1885-1907.

TERRORISM. *n.* 1. [In light of the International Convention for the Suppression of the Financing of Terrorism, 1999] "terrorism" in s. 19 of the [Immigration Act, R.S.C. 1985, c. I-2] includes any "act intended to cause death or serious bodily injury to a civilian, or to any other person not taking an active part in the hostilities in a situation of armed conflict, when the purpose of such act, by its nature or context, is to intimidate a population, or to compel a government or an international organization to do or to abstain from doing any act." *Suresh v. Canada (Minister of Citizenship & Immigration)*, [2002] 1 S.C.R. 3. 2. "[N]ations may be unable to reach a consensus as to an exact definition of terrorism. But this cannot be taken to mean that there is no common ground with respect to certain types of conduct. At the very least, I cannot conceive of anyone seriously challenging the belief that the killing of innocent civilians, that is crimes against humanity, does constitute terrorism. As stated earlier, it is one matter for an organization to pursue political goals such as self-determination and quite another to pursue those goals through the use of violence directed at the civilian population. International human rights codes might not condemn deaths resulting from a civil war, that is to say as between two armed factions. But I know of no authority, international or otherwise, which condones the indiscriminate maiming and killing of innocent civilians." *Suresh v. Canada (Minister of Citizenship & Immigration)*, 2000 CarswellNat 25, 183 D.L.R. (4th) 629, 5 Imm. L.R. (3d) 1, 252 N.R. 1, 18 Admin. L.R. (3d) 159, [2000] 2 F.C. 592, 180 F.T.R. 57 (note) (C.A.), the court per Robertson J.A.

TERRORISM OFFENCE. An offence under any of sections 83.02 to 83.04 or 83.18 to 83.23, an indictable offence under this or any other Act of Parliament committed for the benefit of, at the direction of or in association with a terrorist group, an indictable offence under this or any other Act of Parliament where the act or omission constituting the offence also constitutes a terrorist activity, or a conspiracy or an attempt to commit, or being an accessory after the fact in relation to, or any counselling in relation to, an offence referred to in this definition. *Criminal Code*, R.S.C. 1985, c. C-46, s. 2.

TERRORIST ACTIVITY. (a) An act or omission that is committed in or outside Canada and that, if committed in Canada, is one of the following offences: (i) the offences referred to in subsection 7(2) that implement the Convention for the Suppression of Unlawful Seizure of Aircraft, signed at The Hague on December 16, 1970, (ii) the offences referred to in subsection 7(2) that implement the Convention for the Suppression of Unlawful Acts against the Safety of Civil Aviation, signed at Montreal on September 23, 1971, (iii) the offences referred to in subsection 7(3) that implement the Convention on the Prevention and Punishment of Crimes against Internationally Protected Persons, including Diplomatic Agents, adopted by the General Assembly of the United Nations on December 14, 1973, (iv) the offences referred to in subsection 7(3.1) that implement the International Convention against the Taking of Hostages, adopted by the General Assembly of the United Nations on December 17, 1979, (v) the offences referred to in subsection 7(3.4) or (3.6) that implement the Convention on the Physical Protection of Nuclear Material, done at Vienna and New York on March 3, 1980, (vi) the offences referred to in subsection 7(2) that implement the Protocol for the Suppression of Unlawful Acts of Violence at Airports Serving International Civil Aviation, supplementary to the Convention for the Suppression of Unlawful Acts against the Safety of Civil Aviation, signed at Montreal on February 24, 1988, (vii) the offences referred to in subsection 7(2.1) that implement the Convention for the Suppression of Unlawful Acts against the Safety of Maritime Navigation, done at Rome on March 10, 1988, (viii) the offences referred to in subsection 7(2.1) or (2.2) that implement the Protocol for the Suppression of Unlawful Acts against the Safety of Fixed Platforms Located on the Continental Shelf, done at Rome on March 10, 1988, (ix) the offences referred to in subsection 7(3.72) that implement the International Convention for the Suppression of Terrorist Bombings, adopted by the General Assembly of the United Nations on December 15, 1997, and (x) the offences referred to in subsection 7(3.73) that implement the International Convention for the Suppression of the Financing of Terrorism, adopted by the General Assembly of the United Nations on December 9, 1999, or (b) an act or omission, in or outside Canada, (i) that is committed (A) in whole or in part for a political, religious or ideological purpose, objective or cause, and (B) in whole or in part with the intention of intimidating the public, or a segment of the public, with regard to its security, including its economic security, or compelling a person, a government or a domestic or an international organization to do or to refrain from doing any act, whether the public or the person, government or organization is inside or outside Canada, and (ii) that intentionally (A) causes death or serious bodily harm to a person by the use of violence, (B) endangers a person's life, (C) causes a serious risk to the health or safety of the public or any segment of the public, (D) causes substantial property damage, whether to public or private property, if causing such damage is likely to result in the conduct or harm referred to in any of clauses (A) to (C), or (E) causes serious interference with or serious disruption of an essential service, facility or system, whether public or private, other than as a result of advocacy, protest, dissent or stoppage of work that is not intended to result in the conduct or

T

harm referred to in any of clauses (A) to (C), and includes a conspiracy, attempt or threat to commit any such act or omission, or being an accessory after the fact or counselling in relation to any such act or omission, but, for greater certainty, does not include an act or omission that is committed during an armed conflict and that, at the time and in the place of its commission, is in accordance with customary international law or conventional international law applicable to the conflict, or the activities undertaken by military forces of a state in the exercise of their official duties to the extent that those activities are governed by other rules of international law. *Criminal Code*, R.S.C. 1985, c. C-46, s. 83.01.

TERRORIST GROUP. An entity that has as one of its purposes or activities facilitating or carrying out any terrorist activity, or a listed entity, and includes an association of such entities. *Criminal Code*, R.S.C. 1985, c. C-46, s. 83.01.

TEST. *v.* 1. To determine veracity. 2. "... [T]o try out, experiment with, check out." *Murray v. Insurance Corp. of British Columbia* (1992), 10 C.C.L.I. (2d) 47 at 56 (B.C. S.C.), Gow J. See GENETIC ~ING.

TEST. *n.* 1. A standard by which one judges. 2. Of evidence, the determination of veracity. See BUT FOR ~; CLOSED MIND ~; DAGENAIS/MENTUCK ~; DEGRADATION ~; DEHUMANIZATION ~; LAW SCHOOL ADMISSION ~; LIE DETECTOR ~; MATERIAL CONTRIBUTION ~; MEIORIN ~; NEIGHBOUR ~; OAKES ~; POWLEY ~; PROPORTIONALITY ~; QUAINTANCE ESTATE ~; VAN DER PEET ~; WIGMORE ~.

TESTAMENT. *n.* 1. A bequest of personal property. 2. A will.

TESTAMENTARY. *adj.* With respect to a document or gift, made to take effect only after the person making it dies. *Cock v. Cooke* (1866), L.R. 1 P. & P. 241 at 243, Wilde J.

TESTAMENTARY CAPACITY. Ability to make a valid will. Having a disposing mind and memory, able to comprehend on one's own initiative and volition the essential elements of will-making—property, object, just claims, and revocation of existing dispositions.

TESTAMENTARY INSTRUMENT. Includes any will, codicil or other testamentary writing or appointment, during the life of the testator whose testamentary disposition it purports to be and after his death, whether it relates to real or personal property or to both. *Criminal Code*, R.S.C. 1985, c. C-46, s. 2.

TESTAMENTARY INTENTION. A deliberate fixed and final expression of an intention as to the disposal of property on one's death.

TESTAMENTARY TRUST. A trust that arises upon and in consequence of the death of an individual.

TESTATE. *adj.* Having executed a will.

TESTATOR. *n.* 1. The person making a will, whether the person be male or female. 2. A person who has died leaving a will.

TESTATRIX. *n.* A woman who has made a will.

TESTATUM. *n.* A part of an indenture, known as the witnessing clause, which begins with the words "now this indenture witnesseth".

TEST CASE. 1. An action whose result determines liability in other actions. 2. "[A case in which there is a] ... factual or legal relationship between [the case] ... and ... other actions depending on its result... ." *Asbjorn Horgard A/S v. Gibbs/Nortac Industries Ltd.* (1987), 81 N.R. 1 at 2 (Fed. C.A.), Urie J.A. 3. One chosen from a number of cases pending for the purpose of settling issues of law and fact for all. *Rosling Real Estate (Nelson) Ltd. v. Robertson Hilliard Cattell Realty Co.*, 2000 CarswellBC 23, 2000 BCSC 3, Smith J.

TESTE. *n.* The final part of a writ which gives the date and place it was issued.

TESTIFY. *v.* "... [T]he giving of evidence by means of oral communication in a proceeding... ." *Thomson Newspapers Ltd. v. Canada (Director of Investigation & Research, Combines Investigation Branch)* (1990), (*sub nom. Thomson Newspapers v. Canada (Director of Investigation & Research, Restrictive Trade Practices Commission)*) 29 C.P.R. (3d) 97 at 218, 76 C.R. (3d) 129, 72 O.R. (2d) 415n, 54 C.C.C. (3d) 417, 67 D.L.R. (4th) 161, [1990] 1 S.C.R. 425, 39 O.A.C. 161, 106 N.R. 161, L'Heureux-Dubé J.

TESTIMONIAL EVIDENCE. In a broad sense, any evidence about which a competent witness testifies, even to simply identify an object. P.K. McWilliams, *Canadian Criminal Evidence*, 3d ed. (Aurora: Canada Law Book, 1988) at 1-11.

TESTIMONIUM. *n.* Of a deed, the concluding part which reads "In witness whereof ..." and contains the signatures of the parties and witnesses.

TESTIMONY. *n.* 1. The evidence which a witness gives viva voce in a court or tribunal. 2. A statement whereby a person relates facts of which he has personal knowledge or whereby an expert gives his opinion. To make proof, testimony shall be given by deposition in a judicial proceeding unless otherwise agreed by the parties or provided by law. *Civil Code*, S.Q. 1991, c. 64, a. 2843. 3. "[In s. 43 of the Canada Evidence Act, R.S.C. 1970, c. E-10] ... includes both oral evidence and documentary evidence (Radio Corp. of Amer. v. Rauland Corp., [1956] 1 Q.B. 618 [(U.K.)] and Radio Corp. of Amer. v. Rauland Corp., (Can.) [[1956] O.R. 630 (H.C.)]." *United States District Court, Middle District of Florida v. Royal American Shows Inc.*, [1981] 4 W.W.R. 148 at 152, 58 C.C.C. (2d) 274, 120 D.L.R. (3d) 732, 26 A.R. 136 (C.A.), Lieberman J.A. See PERPETUATE ~.

TEXT BOOK. *var.* **TEXTBOOK.** A treatise which collects decisions or explains principles concerning some branch of the law.

TFSA. *abbr.* Tax-free savings account. *Income Tax Act*, R.S.C. 1985, c. 1 (5th Supp.), s. 248.

TGO. *abbr.* Temporary guardianship order.

THE. *Definite article.* Indicates that the noun following it is someone or something previously mentioned or understood from the context.

THEATRE. *n.* Includes any place that is open to the public where entertainments are given, whether or not any charge is made for admission. *Criminal Code*, R.S.C. 1985, c. C-46, s. 150. See BETTING ~.

THEFT. *n.* 1. Fraudulently and without colour of right taking, or fraudulently and without colour of right converting to his use or to the use of another person, anything whether animate or inanimate, with intent, (a) to deprive, temporarily or absolutely, the owner of it or a person who has a special property or interest in it; (b) to pledge it or deposit it as security; (c) to part with it under a condition with respect to its return that the person who parts with it may be unable to perform; or (d) to deal with it in such a manner that it cannot be restored in the condition in which it was at the time it was taken or converted. *Criminal Code*, R.S.C. 1985, c. C-46, s. 322(1). 2. "Steal" is defined in s. 2 of the Criminal Code, [R.S.C. 1985, c. C-46] as: "means to commit theft." "Theft" is defined generally in s. 322. Also relevant in this case is s. 588 which concerns the ownership of property, here the financial institution's money. From these definitions and the jurisprudence which has considered them, one sees that in simplistic terms the difference between "robbery" and "theft" is that robbery is committed by confronting and intimidating the person whose property is taken, whereas theft is committed without violence or threats of violence, and often occurs secretly, such that the victim is left unaware of being relieved of their property. *R. v. Bourassa*, 2004 NSCA 127. See IDENTITY ~.

THEFT INSURANCE. Insurance against loss or damage through theft, wrongful conversion, burglary, house-breaking, robbery or forgery.

THE MEANS. Section 2.4(1)(b) [of the Copyright Act, R.S.C. 1985, c. C-42] shields from liability the activities associated with providing the means for another to communicate by telecommunication. "The means", as the Board found, "... are not limited to routers and other hardware. They include all software connection equipment, connectivity services, hosting and other facilities and services without which such communications would not occur" (at p. 452). I agree. So long as an Internet intermediary does not itself engage in acts that relate to the content of the communication, i.e. whose participation is content neutral, but confines itself to providing "a conduit" for information communicated by others, then it will fall within s. 2.4(1)(b). *Society of Composers, Authors & Music Publishers of Canada v. Canadian Assn. of Internet Providers*, 2004 SCC 45, Binnie J.

THEORY. See CONTINUOUS TRIGGER ~; EXPOSURE ~; FOUR TRIGGER THEORIES; IDENTIFICATION ~; MANIFESTATION ~.

THERAPEUTIC ARTEFACT. An alteration to the body left by surgical or medical treatment. F.A. Jaffe, *A Guide to Pathological Evidence for Lawyers and Police Officers*, 4th ed. (Toronto: Carswell, 1999) at 17.

THERAPEUTIC INTERCHANGE PROGRAM. A program or protocol under which alternate drugs are dispensed in place of prescribed drugs where the alternate drugs have different chemical compositions but essentially the same therapeutic objectives as the prescribed drugs for which they are substituted. *Pharmacy Operations and Drug Scheduling Act*, S.B.C. 2003, c. 77, s. 1.

THERAPIST. *n.* A person registered or licensed to provide healing services or carry out procedures in relation to another person.

THERAPY. *n.* The provision of healing services by a registered or licensed practitioner. See MASSAGE ~; OCCUPATIONAL ~; PHYSIO~; RESPIRATORY ~.

THEREUPON. *adv.* Thereafter.

THING. *n.* 1. A subject of dominion or property. 2. Includes (a) tangible things, and (b) organisms, other than humans. *Public Health Act*, S.B.C. 2008, c. 28, s. 1. See INFECTED ~.

THING IN ACTION. "... [A]n anglicization of the more usual and well-known common law expression '[chose] in action'... ." *Deloitte, Haskins & Sells Ltd. v. Graham* (1983), 47 C.B.R. (N.S.) 172 at 177, [1983] 3 W.W.R. 687, 32 R.F.L. (2d) 356, 25 Alta. L.R. (2d) 84, 144 D.L.R. (3d) 539, 42 A.R. 76 (Q.B.), D.C. MacDonald J. See CHOSE IN ACTION.

THIN SKULL RULE. One who injures another must take the victim as found. Makes a tortfeasor liable for a person's injuries even though the injuries are unexpectedly severe because of a pre-existing condition.

THIRD PARTY. 1. A person who is not a party to an action but from whom a defendant claims relief. The party is not a party at the commencement of the original action, but the defendant claims relief from the party and the defendant adds the party to the action. 2. The second largest party sitting in the legislature or Parliament in opposition to the government.

THIRD PARTY PROCEEDING. Serves to enforce duties which a third party owes to the defendant who commences the third party proceeding.

THIRD READING. Parliamentary review of a bill in its final form. A. Fraser, W.A. Dawson & J. Holtby, eds., *Beauchesne's Rules and Forms of the House of Commons of Canada*, 6th ed. (Toronto: Carswell, 1989) at 195.

THREAT. *n.* 1. "... [A] 'tool of intimidation which is designed to instil a sense of fear in its recipient': R. v. McCraw ... [(1991), 66 C.C.C. (3d) 517 (S.C.C.)]... . may be express or implicit and made by means of words, writings or actions... ." *R. v. Pelletier* (1992), 71 C.C.C. (3d) 438 at 441 (Que. C.A.), the court per Proulx J.A. 2. Under the section the threat must be of death or serious bodily harm. It is impossible to think that anyone threatening death or serious bodily harm in a manner that was meant to be taken seriously would not intend to intimidate or cause fear. That is to say, a serious threat to kill or cause serious bodily harm must have been uttered with the intent to intimidate or instill fear. Conversely, a threat uttered with the intent to intimidate or cause fear must have been uttered with the intent that it be taken seriously. Both of these formulations of the mens rea constitute an intention to threaten and comply with the aim of the section. Section 264.1(1)(a) is directed at words which cause fear or intimidation. Its purpose is to protect the exercise of freedom of choice by preventing intimidation. The section makes it a crime to issue threats without any further action being taken beyond the threat itself. Thus, it is the meaning conveyed by the words that is important. Yet it cannot be that words spoken in jest were meant to be caught by the section. *R. v. Clemente*, 1994 CarswellMan 152, [1994] 8 W.W.R. 1, 31 C.R. (4th) 28, 168 N.R. 310, 91 C.C.C. (3d) 1, [1994] 2 S.C.R. 758, 95 Man. R. (2d) 161, 70 W.A.C. 161, the court per Cory J. 3. The threat [to the safety of the public in s. 672.54(a) of the Criminal Code, R.S.C. 1985, c. C-46] must be more than speculation. It must be supported by the evidence and it must be a real risk of physical or psychological harm to members in the community and the potential harm must be serious. A slight risk of grave harm or a high risk of slight harm will not suffice. The conduct leading to the harm must be criminal in nature. *R. v. Campagna*, 1999 CarswellBC 1961 (S.C.), Singh J. See ATTEMPT OR ~ TO APPLY FORCE; UTTERING ~.

THREATENED SPECIES. A wildlife species that is likely to become an endangered species if nothing is done to reverse the factors leading to its extirpation or extinction. *Species at Risk Act*, S.C. 2002, c. 29, s. 2.

THREE CERTAINTIES. The three essential characteristics required to create a trust: (a) certain intention; (b) certain subject-matter; (c) certain objects. D.M.W. Waters, *The Law of Trusts in Canada*, 2d ed. (Toronto: Carswell, 1984) at 107.

THREE CHAIN RESERVE. In Quebec a reserve of at least three chains in depth reserved to the Crown along banks of rivers and lakes. A chain is 66 feet in length. Chain refers to a surveyor's chain.

THRESHOLD CLAUSE. Requires an employer to appoint the most senior capable applicant even though there are junior applicants who are more capable.

THRESHOLD SENTENCE. A sentence customarily imposed in the same jurisdiction for the same or similar crimes. A guide to judges to help in reducing disparity in sentencing.

THRONE. See SPEECH FROM THE ~.

THROUGHOUT. *prep.* During the whole of.

THROWN AWAY. See COSTS ~.

THUS. *conj.* In accordance with; consequently; therefore.

TICKET. See OUTSTANDING ~; WEIGH ~.

TIDE. See DOMINANT ~.

TIE. See PARCEL ~.

TIMBER. *n.* 1. "... [G]enerally treated as connoting growing trees which are a part of the realty and pass with a conveyance of land unless expressly reserved... ." *Highway Sawmills Ltd. v. Minister of National Revenue*, [1966] C.T.C. 150 at 160 (S.C.C.),

Ritchie J. (dissenting). 2. Trees standing or fallen, logs and bolts, cants, boards and lumber, and any other sawn or shaped product of trees. See CROWN ~.

TIMBER ROYALTY. Includes any consideration for a right under or pursuant to which a right to cut or take timber from a timber limit in Canada is obtained or derived, to the extent that such consideration is dependent upon, and computed by reference to, the amount of timber cut or taken. *Corporations Tax Act*, R.S.O. 1990, c. C.40, s. 1.

TIME. See COMMERCIAL ~; PART-~; POST ~; PRIME ~; PROGRAM ~; REMAND ~; SEA ~; UNITY OF ~.

TIME CHARTER. 1. A charterparty for a certain time. 2. A contract of affreightment by which a lessor places a fully-equipped and manned ship at the disposal of a charterer for a fixed time and under which he retains the navigation and management of the ship but transfers its employment and agency to the charterer. *Civil Code*, S.Q. 1991, c. 64, a. 2014.

TIME IMMEMORIAL. For purposes of the period of legal memory is defined as the year 1189, the beginning of the reign of King Richard I. *Kaminskas v. Storm*, 2009 ONCA 318.

TIME POLICY. A marine policy is a time policy if the contract insures the subject-matter for a definite period. *Marine Insurance acts*.

TIME SALE. (a) Any retail sale of goods or of goods and services under which possession of the goods is to be delivered to the buyer, but the transfer of the property in the goods is to take place after the delivery, on payment by the buyer of all or part of the price and cost of borrowing, if any, whether or not the transfer is also subject to the fulfillment of some other condition, (b) any retail hire-purchase of goods, and (c) for the purpose of sections 46 to 56, any retail sale of goods or of goods and services in which the seller takes back a chattel mortgage on those goods to secure payment of all or part of the price. *Consumers Protection Act*, R.S.Y. 2002, c. 40, s. 1.

TIME SHARE AGREEMENT. A consumer agreement by which a consumer, (*a*) acquires the right to use property as part of a plan that provides for the use of the property to circulate periodically among persons participating in the plan, whether or not the property is located in Ontario, or (*b*) is provided with access to discounts or benefits for the future provision of transportation, accommodation or other goods or services related to travel. *Consumer Protection Act, 2002*, S.O. 2002, c. 30, Sched. A, s. 20.

TIME SHARE CONTRACT. A contract by which the consumer acquires the right to use property, whether or not the property is located in British Columbia, (a) for a period of time each year or other interval, and (b) as part of a plan that provides for the use of the property to circulate, in any year or other interval, among persons participating in the plan, but does not include a time share plan as defined in the Real Estate Development Marketing Act. *Business Practices and Consumer Protection Act*, S.B.C. 2004, c. 2, s. 1.

TIME SHARE INTEREST. The interest of a person in a time share plan.

TIME SHARE OWNERSHIP PLAN. Any plan by which a person participating in the plan acquires an ownership interest in real property and the right to use or occupy all or part of that property, including accommodations or facilities situated on all or part of that property, for specific or determinable periods of time. *Real Estate Trading Act*, R.S.P.E.I. 1988, c. R-2, s. 1.

TIME SHARE PLAN. Any time share ownership plan or time share use plan, whether in respect of land situated inside or outside a province, that provides for the use, occupation or possession of real property to circulate in any year among persons participating in the plan. *Real Estate Trading Act*, R.S.P.E.I. 1988, c. R-2, s. 1.

TIME SHARE USE PLAN. Any plan by which a person participating in the plan acquires a right to use or occupy real property, including accommodations or facilities situated on that property, for specific or determinable periods of time but does not acquire an ownership interest in that property. *Real Estate Trading Act*, R.S.P.E.I. 1988, c. R-2, s. 1.

TIME-TACKING. *n.* In the context of a standstill agreement and the drop dead rule, [a]n agreement which has a time-tacking term means that the time during which time is suspended is added on to the five-year period. *Sinnott v. Canadian Pacific Railway Company*, 2010 ABQB 185.

TIPPING. *n.* In the context of securities legislation, giving insider information or information not generally disclosed to another person.

TIRE. See WINTER ~.

TISSUE. A part of a living or dead human body and includes an organ but, unless otherwise prescribed by the Lieutenant Governor in Council, does not include bone marrow, spermatozoa, an ovum, an embryo, a foetus, blood or blood constituents. *Trillium Gift of Life Network Act*, R.S.O. 1990, c. H.20, s. 1. See REGENERATIVE ~.

TITLE. *n.* 1. The way in which a property owner justly possesses property. 2. "... [A] vested right or title, something to which the right is already acquired, though the enjoyment may be postponed." *O'Dell v. Gregory* (1895), 24 S.C.R. 661 at 663, the court per Strong C.J. 3. "... [M]ay simply describe the right (or entitlement) to an interest in property... ." *Canadian Imperial Bank of Commerce v. 64576 Man. Ltd.* (1990), 1 P.P.S.A.C. (2d) 1 at 7 (Man. Q.B.), Jewers J. 4. A general heading which includes particulars, i.e. of a book. 5. An appellation of dignity or honour. See ABORIGINAL ~; ABSTRACT OF ~; BAD ~; CERTIFICATE OF ~; CHAIN OF ~; CLEAR ~; CONDOMINIUM ~; CURE ~; DEFECTIVE ~; DOCUMENT OF ~; GOOD ~; INDEFEASIBLE ~; LAND ~S; LEGACY BY GENERAL ~; LEGAL BY PARTICULAR ~; LONG ~; MINERAL ~; MISTAKE OF ~; POSSESSORY ~; PREDECESSOR IN ~; QUALIFIED ~; QUIETING ~; REQUISITION ON ~; ROOT OF ~; ROYAL STYLE AND ~S; SHORT ~; SLANDER OF ~; SQUATTER'S ~; UNITY OF ~.

TITLE INSURANCE. 1. Insurance against loss or liability for loss due to the invalidity of the title to any property or of any instrument, or to any defect in such title or instrument. 2. Insurance against loss or damage caused by (a) the existence of a mortgage, charge, lien, encumbrance, servitude or any other restriction on real property; (b) the existence of a mortgage, charge, lien, pledge, encumbrance or any other restriction on personal property; (c) a defect in any document that evidences the creation of any restriction referred to in paragraph (a) or (b); (d) a defect in the title to property; or (e) any other matter affecting the title to property or affecting the right to the use and enjoyment of property. *Insurance Companies Act*, S.C. 1991, c. 47, Sched.

TITLE OF PROCEEDING. The name which sets out the names of all the parties and their capacity, if other than a personal capacity *Courts of Justice Act*, R.S.O. 1990, c. C.43, *Rules of Civil Procedure*, R.R.O. 1990, Reg. 194, r. 14.06 (1)).

TITLE TRANSFER CREDIT SUPPORT AGREEMENT. An agreement under which a debtor company has provided title to property for the purpose of securing the payment or performance of an obligation of the debtor company in respect of an eligible financial contract. *Companies' Creditors Arrangement Act*, R.S.C. 1985, c. C-36, s. 2.

T.J. *abbr.* Recueils de Jurisprudence du Québec, Tribunal de la Jeunesse, 1975-1985.

T.J. (QUÉ.). *abbr.* Tribunal de la jeunesse (Québec).

T.L.L.R. *abbr.* Tenant and Landlord Law Reports (Ontario), 1983-1988.

T.L.R. *abbr.* Times Law Reports.

T.M. *abbr.* Trade Marks.

T.O. *abbr.* 1. Taxing Officer. 2. Taxing Office.

TOBACCO-RELATED DISEASE. Disease caused or contributed to by exposure to a tobacco product. *The Tobacco Damages and Health Care Costs Recovery Act*, S.S. 2007, c. T-14.2, s. 2.

TOBACCO-RELATED WRONG. (i) A tort committed in Saskatchewan by a manufacturer which causes or contributes to tobacco-related disease; or (ii) in an action under subsection 3(1), a breach of a common law, equitable or statutory duty or obligation owed by a manufacturer to persons in Saskatchewan who have been exposed or might become exposed to a tobacco product. *The Tobacco Damages and Health Care Costs Recovery Act*, S.S. 2007, c. T-14.2, s. 2.

TOILETING. *n.* The physical ability of the insured to transfer to the toilet or use a bedpan or urinal and to maintain perineal hygiene. *The Automobile Accident Insurance Act*, R.S.S. 1978, c. A-35, *The Personal Injury Benefits Regulations*, R.R.S., c. A-35, Reg. 3, Appendix D, Grid A, s. 2.

TOKEN OF VALUE. See COUNTERFEIT ~.

TOLERATE. *v.* To allow; permit.

TOLERATION. *n.* In the context of allegedly obscene materials, the permitting by Canadians of viewing by other Canadians.

TOLL. *n.* 1. Any fee or rate charged, levied or collected by any person for the carriage of passengers or goods by a public vehicle. 2. Any rate, charge or allowance charged or made for the shipment, transportation, transmission, care, handling or delivery of hydrocarbons or of another commodity that is transmitted through a pipeline, or for storage or demurrage or the like, for the provision of a pipeline when the pipeline is available and ready to provide for the transmission of oil or gas, and in respect of the purchase and sale of gas that is the property of a company and that is transmitted by the company through its pipeline, excluding the cost to the company of the gas at the point where it enters the pipeline. *National Energy Board Act*, R.S.C. 1985, c. N-7, s. 2. 3. A charge for the use of some or all of a concession highway by a vehicle. *Transportation Investment Act*, S.B.C. 2002, c. 65, s. 1.

TOLL DEVICE. A device that (a) may be installed or carried in or on, or attached to, a vehicle, and (b) allows electronic identification of the person who is to pay the toll, or the account from which the toll is paid, arising from the vehicle's use of a concession highway. *Transportation Investment Act*, S.B.C. 2002, c. 65, s. 1.

TOLL READER. Equipment that detects toll devices. *Transportation Investment Act*, S.B.C. 2002, c. 65, s. 1.

TOPICAL INDEX. Provides a listing of cases with short headings to indicate the main topics covered by the decision and very brief summaries of the decisions. *CCH Canadian Ltd. v. Law Society of Upper Canada*, 2004 SCC 13.

TOPOGRAPHY. *n.* The design, however expressed, of the disposition of (a) the interconnections, if any, and the elements for the making of an integrated circuit product, or (b) the elements, if any, and the interconnections for the making of a customization layer or layers to be added to an integrated circuit product in an intermediate form. *Integrated Circuit Topography Act, 1990*, S.C. 1990, c. 37, s. 2.

TOPPING UP. The practice, when an employee is off work because of a compensable injury, is paid full salary during the compensation period in exchange for endorsing his benefits over to the employer.

TORT. *n.* 1. Wrong. 2. Provides a means by which compensation, usually in the form of damages, is paid for injuries suffered by a party as a result of wrongful conduct by another. 3. "... [I]ntended to restore the injured person to the position he enjoyed prior to the injury, rather than to punish the tortfeasor whose only wrong may have been a moment of inadvertence... ." *Ratych v. Bloomer* (1990), 30 C.C.E.L. 161 at 171, 39 O.A.C. 103, [1990] 1 S.C.R. 940, 69 D.L.R. (4th) 25, 107 N.R. 335, 3 C.C.L.T. (2d) 1, McLachlin J. (Lamer, La Forest, L'Heureux-Dubé and Sopinka JJ. concurring). 4. "A fundamental proposition underlies the law of tort: that a person who by his or her fault causes damage to another may be held responsible."

Canadian National Railway v. Norsk Pacific Steamship Co. (1992), 11 C.C.L.T. (2d) 1 at 16, 137 N.R. 241, 91 D.L.R. (4th) 289, [1992] 1 S.C.R. 1021, 53 F.T.R. 79n, McLachlin J. (L'Heureux-Dubé and Cory JJ. concurring). See ACTION FOR ~; ADMINISTRATIVE ~; ADMINISTRATOR DE SON ~; CONTINUING; INTENTIONAL ~; JOINT ~; MARITIME ~; WAIVER OF ~.

TORTFEASOR. *var.* **TORT-FEASOR.** *n.* 1. A wrongdoer. 2. A party who commits a tort. See JOINT ~; SEVERAL ~S.

TORTIOUS. *adj.* Wrongful.

TORTURE. *n.* 1. Any act or omission by which severe pain or suffering, whether physical or mental, is intentionally inflicted on a person (a) for a purpose including (i) obtaining from the person or from a third person information or a statement, (ii) punishing the person for an act which that person or a third person has committed or is suspected of having committed, and (iii) intimidating or coercing the person or a third person, or (b) for any reason based on discrimination of any kind, but does not include an act or omission arising only from, inherent in or incidental to lawful sanctions. *Criminal Code*, R.S.C. 1985, c. C-46 s. 269.1. 2. Any act or omission by which severe pain or severe suffering, whether physical or mental, is intentionally inflicted on a person (a) for a purpose including (i) obtaining from the person or from a third person information or a statement, (ii) punishing the person for an act that the person or a third person has committed or is suspected of having committed, or (iii) intimidating or coercing the person or a third person, or (b) for any reason based on discrimination of any kind, but does not include any act or omission arising from, inherent in, or incidental to lawful sanctions. *Torture Prohibition Act*, R.S.Y. 2002, c. 220, s. 5. See CONVENTION AGAINST ~.

TOTAL DISABILITY. A disability which prevents an insured from performing a remunerative occupation. Includes the situation where a person must refrain from engaging in his occupation in order to recover from an injury or illness.

TOTALITY PRINCIPLE. Requires a sentencing judge who orders an offender to serve consecutive sentences for several offences to ensure that the cumulative sentence does not exceed the overall culpability of the offender.

TOTAL LOSS. 1. "... [I]n the case of a ship the subject of insurance must be either such an entire wreck as to be reduced, as it is said, to a mere 'congeries of planks', or if it still subsists in specie it must, as a result of perils insured against, be placed in such a situation that it is totally out of the power of the owner or the underwriter at any labor, and by means of any expenditure, to get it afloat and used again as a ship." *McGhee v. Phoenix Insurance Co.* (1890), 18 S.C.R. 61 at 70, Strong J. 2. With respect to a vehicle, a vehicle that has been damaged by collision, impact, fire or flood, or has been stolen and dismantled, such that the estimated cost of repairing it exceeds the difference between the fair market value of the vehicle immediately before it was damaged or stolen and its salvage value.

Highway Traffic Act, R.S.O. 1990, c. H.8, *Classification Of Vehicles As Irreparable, Salvage and Rebuilt*, O. Reg. 376/02, s. 1.

TOURISM. See WILDERNESS ~.

TOURIST ESTABLISHMENT. (a) Any premises or boat that provides sleeping accommodation; (b) any campsite equipped for the supplying of water or electricity or the disposal of garbage or sewage; or (c) any picnic area, bathing area or recreation area for the travelling public or persons engaging in outdoor recreational activities, but does not include a private cottage or residence. *Travel and Tourism Act*, R.S.N.W.T. 1988, c. T-9, s. 1.

TOUR PACKAGE. A combination of two or more services, or of property and services, that includes transportation services, accommodation, a right to use a campground or trailer park, or guide or interpreter services, where the property and services are supplied together for an all-inclusive price. *Excise Tax Act*, R.S.C. 1985, c. E-15, s. 163.

TO WIT. Namely.

TRACEABLE. *adj.* Describes property which is commingled with other property so that its individual identity is lost.

TRACING. *n.* Tracing at common law and equity is a proprietary remedy. It involves following an item of property either as it is transformed into other forms of property, or as it passes into other hands, so that the rights of a person in the original property may extend to the new property. In establishing that one piece of property may be traced into another, it is necessary to establish a close and substantial connection between the two pieces of property, so that it is appropriate to allow the rights in the original property to flow through to the new property. The question has most often arisen in the context of a trust, when the trustee has improperly disposed of the trust assets. *Agricultural Credit Corp. of Saskatchewan v. Pettyjohn*, [1991] 3 W.W.R. 689 at 702-3, 1 P.P.S.A.C. (2d) 273, 79 D.L.R. (4th) 22, 90 Sask. R. 206 (C.A.), Sherstobitoff J.A.

TRACK. See FAST ~; STANDARD ~.

TRACKING DEVICE. 1. Any device that, when installed in or on any thing, may be used to help ascertain, by electronic or other means, the location of any thing or person. *Criminal Code*, R.S.C. 1985, c. C-46, s. 492.1. 2. A substance or tracking device that, when placed or installed in or on any place, land or thing, may be used to help ascertain, by electronic or other means, the origin, identity or location of any thing. *Toxics Reduction Act, 2009*, S.O. 2009, c. 19, s. 26.1 [not yet in force].

TRACKING WARRANT. A justice who is satisfied by information on oath in writing that there are reasonable grounds to suspect that an offence under this or any other Act of Parliament has been or will be committed and that information that is relevant to the commission of the offence, including the whereabouts of any person, can be obtained through the use of a tracking device, may at any time issue a warrant authorizing a peace officer or a public officer who has been appointed or designated to administer or enforce a federal or provincial law and whose duties include the enforcement of this Act or any other Act of Parliament and who is named in the warrant (a) to install, maintain and remove a tracking device in or on any thing, including a thing carried, used or worn by any person; and (b) to monitor, or to have monitored, a tracking device installed in or on any thing. A warrant is valid for the period, not exceeding sixty days, mentioned in it. A justice may issue further warrants under this section. *Criminal Code*, R.S.C. 1985, c. C-46, s. 492.1.

TRACT. See POOLED ~; UNIT ~.

TRACT PARTICIPATION. The share of production from a unitized zone that is allocated to a unit tract under a unit agreement or unitization order or the share of production from a pooled spacing unit that is allocated to a pooled tract under a pooling agreement or pooling order. *Canada Oil and Gas Operations Act*, R.S.C. 1985, c. O-7, s. 29.

TRADE. *v.* 1. Buying and selling property as a business. 2. Includes, entering into contracts, whether as principal or agent, acting as a floor trader, any receipt by a registrant of an order to effect a transaction in a contract, any assignment or other disposition of rights under a contract except a disposition arising from the death of an individual enjoying rights under a contract, and any act, advertisement, solicitation, conduct or negotiation directly or indirectly in furtherance of the foregoing. *Commodity Futures Act*, R.S.O. 1990, c. C.20, s. 1, as am.

TRADE. *n.* 1. Occupation. 2. The knowledge requisite to carry out the activities involved in an occupation. See ADVENTURE IN THE NATURE OF ~; BALANCE OF ~; BOARD OF ~; BUSINESS OR ~ ASSOCIATION; CUSTOM OF THE ~; HEDGE ~; LIQUIDATING ~; QUOTATION AND ~ REPORTING SYSTEM; RESTRAINT OF ~; STOCK IN ~; WORLD ~ ORGANIZATION.

TRADE AGREEMENT. An agreement or arrangement relating to international trade to which the Government of Canada is a party. *Customs Tariff Act*, S.C. 1997, c. 36, s. 53. See FREE ~.

TRADE AND COMMERCE. 1. A power of the federal Parliament under section 91(2) of the Constitution Act, 1867. P.W. Hogg, *Constitutional Law of Canada*, 3d ed. (Toronto: Carswell, 1992) at 521. 2. "... [T]he power to regulate international and interprovincial trade and ... 'the general regulation of trade affecting the whole of Canada' ..." *Alex Couture Inc. c. Canada (Procureur général)* (1991), 38 C.P.R. (3d) 293 at 308, 83 D.L.R. (4th) 577, 41 Q.A.C. 1, [1991] R.J.Q. 2534, the court per Rousseau-Houle J.A.

TRADE COMBINATION. Any combination between masters or workmen or other persons for the purpose of regulating or altering the relations between masters or workmen, or the conduct of a master or workman in or in respect of his business, employment or contract of employment or service. *Criminal Code*, R.S.C. 1985, c. C-46, s. 467(2).

TRADE DISPUTE. A dispute between employers and workers or between groups of workers, connected with the employment of a person, the terms or conditions of employment or related matters.

TRADE FIXTURE. A chattel which is annexed to leased property by a tenant during the term of his or her tenancy and which may be severed by the tenant at the end of his or her tenancy when it resumes its character as a chattel rather than a fixture.

TRADE-IN ALLOWANCE. The greater of, (a) the price or value of the consumer's goods or services as set out in a trade-in arrangement, and (b) the market value of the consumer's goods or services when taken in trade under a trade-in arrangement. *Consumer Protection Act, 2002*, S.O. 2002, c. 30, Sched. A, s. 13(9).

TRADE-IN ARRANGEMENT. An arrangement under which a consumer agrees to sell his or her own goods or services to the supplier and the supplier accepts the goods or services as all or part of the consideration for supplying goods or services. *Consumer Protection Act, 2002*, S.O. 2002, c. 30, Sched. A, s. 13(9).

TRADE LAW. See FOREIGN ~.

TRADE L. TOPICS. *abbr.* Trade Law Topics.

TRADE-MARK. *var.* **TRADE MARK.** (a) A mark that is used by a person for the purpose of distinguishing or so as to distinguish wares or services manufactured, sold, leased, hired or performed by him from those manufactured, sold, leased, hired or performed by others; (b) a certification mark; (c) a distinguishing guise; or (d) a proposed trade-mark. *Trade-marks Act*, R.S.C. 1985, c. T-13, s. 2. See PROPOSED ~; REGISTERED ~.

TRADE-MARK AGENT. 1. A person knowledgeable in legal issues relating to trademarks. 2. A person whose name is entered on the list of trade-mark agents. *Trade-marks Act*, R.S.C. 1985, c. T-13, *Trade-marks Regulations*, SOR/96-195, s. 2.

TRADE-NAME. *var.* **TRADE NAME.** The name under which any business is carried on, whether or not it is the name of a corporation, a partnership or an individual. *Trade-marks Act*, R.S.C. 1985, c. T-13, s. 2.

TRADEOFF. See HISTORIC ~.

TRADER. See FLOOR ~.

TRADE SECRET. 1. Must be something, probably of a technical nature, which is guarded very closely and is of such peculiar value to the owner of the trade secret that harm to him would be presumed by its mere disclosure. *Société Gamma Inc. v. Canada (Secretary of State)*, 1994 CarswellNat 1301, 17 B.L.R. (2d) 13, 79 F.T.R. 42, (*sub nom. Société Gamma Inc. v. Canada (Department of the Secretary of State)*) 56 C.P.R. (3d) 58, 27 Admin. L.R. (2d) 102, 56 C.P.R. (3d) 58 (T.D.) Strayer J. 2. Information, including a formula, pattern, compilation, program, device, product, method, technique or process (i) that is used, or may be used, in business or for any commercial purpose, (ii) that derives independent economic value, actual or potential, from not being generally known to anyone who can obtain economic value from its disclosure or use, (iii) that is the subject of reasonable efforts to prevent it from becoming generally known, and (iv) the disclosure of which would result in significant harm or undue financial loss or gain. *Freedom of Information and Protection of Privacy Act*, R.S.A. 2000, c. F-25, s. 1.

TRADE UNION. *var.* **TRADE-UNION.** 1. Any organization of employees formed for purposes that include the regulation of relations between employers and employees. 2. A combination, whether temporary or permanent, having among its objects the regulating of relations between employees and employers or between employees and employees or between employers and employers. *Rights of Labour Act*, R.S.O. 1990, c. R.33, s.1. 3. Such combination, whether temporary or permanent, for regulating the relations between workmen and masters, or for imposing restrictive conditions on the conduct of any trade or business, as would, but for this Act, have been deemed to be an unlawful combination by reason of some one or more of its purposes being in restraint of trade. *Trade Unions Act*, R.S.C. 1985, c. T-14, s. 2.

TRADING. *n.* Includes a disposition or acquisition of or transaction in real estate by sale, purchase, agreement for sale, exchange, option, lease, rental or otherwise and any offer or attempt to list real estate for the purpose of such a disposition or transaction, and any act, advertisement, conduct or negotiation, directly or indirectly, in furtherance of any disposition, acquisition, transaction, offer or attempt, but does not include a listing service operated by or for an organized real estate board in any community. *Real Estate Agents Act*, R.S.N.B. 1973, c. R-1, s. 1. See INSIDER ~.

TRADING DAY. A day during which the principal market, as defined in the regulations, for the security is open for trading. *Securities acts.*

TRADING SERVICES. Any of the following services provided to or on behalf of a party to a trade in real estate: (a) advising on the appropriate price for the real estate; (b) making representations about the real estate; (c) finding the real estate for a party to acquire; (d) finding a party to acquire the real estate; (e) showing the real estate; (f) negotiating the price of the real estate or the terms of the trade in real estate; (g) presenting offers to dispose of or acquire the real estate; (h) receiving deposit money paid in respect of the real estate but does not include an activity excluded by regulation. *Real Estate Services Act*, S.B.C. 2004, c. 42, s. 1.

TRADITIONAL CHINESE MEDICINE. The promotion, maintenance and restoration of health and prevention of a disorder, imbalance or disease based on traditional Chinese medicine theory by utilization of the primary therapies of (a) Chinese acupuncture (Zhen), moxibustion (Jiu) and suction cup (Ba Guan), (b) Chinese manipulative therapy (Tui Na), (c) Chinese energy control therapy (Qi Gong), (d) Chinese rehabilitation exercises such as Chinese shadow boxing (Tai Ji Quan), and (e) prescribing, compounding or dispensing Chinese herbal formulae (Zhong Yao

Chu Fang) and Chinese food cure recipes (Shi Liao). *Health Professions Act*, R.S.B.C. 1996, c. 183, *Traditional Chinese Medicine Practitioners and Acupuncturists Regulation*, B.C. Reg. 290/2008, s. 1.

TRAFFIC. See INTERNATIONAL ~.

TRAFFICKING. *n.* Manufacturing, buying, selling, dealing in. See WEAPONS ~.

TRAFFICKING IN IDENTITY INFORMATION. Transmitting, making available, distributing, selling or offering for sale another person's identity information, or having it in one's possession for any of those purposes, knowing that or being reckless as to whether the information will be used to commit an indictable offence that includes fraud, deceit or falsehood as an element of the offence. *Criminal Code*, R.S.C. 1985, c. C-46, s. 402.2(2).

TRAFFICKING IN PERSONS. Knowingly, to organize the coming into Canada of one or more persons by means of abduction, fraud, deception or use or threat of force or coercion. *Immigration and Refugee Protection Act*, S.C. 2001, c. 27, s. 118.

TRAIN. *v.* To give information and explanation to a worker with respect to a particular subject-matter and require a practical demonstration that the worker has acquired knowledge or skill related to the subject-matter. *The Occupational Health and Safety Act, 1993*, S.S. 1993, c. O-1.1, *The Occupational Health and Safety Regulations*, R.R.S., c. O-1.1, Reg. 1, s. 2.

TRAINING PERIOD. A period during which an employee is not expected to be able to do the job for which he or she was hired but during which he or she is enabled to do it.

TRANSACTION. See BROKERED ~; BUSINESS ~; CAPITAL ~; CLOSING A ~; REVIEWABLE ~; SECURED ~; SHAM ~; SQUEEZE-OUT ~.

TRANSCRIPT. *n.* 1. Something copied from an original. 2. In a court, an official copy of proceedings. 3. "... [A] direct, written copy of words used in a conversation... ." *R. v. Ouellet* (1976), 33 C.C.C. (2d) 417 at 422, [1977] 2 W.W.R. 295 (B.C. Prov. Ct.), Paradis J.

TRANSFER. *v.* 1. " ... [T]o give or hand over property from one person to another." *Murphy v. R.* (1980), 8 E.T.R. 120 at 131 (Fed. T.D.), Cattanach J. 2. " ... [N]ot a term of art and has not a technical meaning ... All that is required is that [party A] should so deal with the property as to divest himself of it and vest it in [party B], that is to say, pass the property from [A] to [B]. The means by which he accomplishes this result, whether direct or circuitous, may properly be called a transfer." *Fasken v. Canada (Minister of National Revenue)* (1948), [1949] 1 D.L.R. 810 at 822, [1948] C.T.C. 265, [1948] Ex. C.R. 580, Thorson P. 3. To convey a title pursuant to this Act, whether voluntarily or otherwise and whether for value or otherwise, and includes a Crown grant unless the context requires otherwise. *The Land Titles Act, 2000*, S.S. 2000, c. L-5.1, s. 2. 4. [T]o move from one

job to another..." *Metropolitan Authority of Halifax, Dartmouth & Halifax County v. Correction Officers Assn. (Nova Scotia)* (1983), 10 L.A.C. (3d) 265 at 273 (N.S.), Outhouse and McDougall. 5. In relation to firearms, sell, provide, barter, give, lend, rent, send, transport, ship, distribute or deliver. *Criminal Code*, R.S.C. 1985, c. C-46, s. 84. 6. The definition of "transfer" is given in s. 84 [of the Criminal Code] as "sell, provide, barter, give, lend, rent, send, transport, ship, distribute or deliver." Of these words, only "transport" can plausibly be said to include moving a thing from place to place without the thing actually changing hands. The common element is the notion of a transaction. This suggests a more restrictive meaning than indicated by the dictionary definition of "transport". the inclusion of the phrase "whether or not for consideration" in s. 100(1)(a) suggests that Parliament did not intend to criminalize simple movement of firearms by this provision, but rather transport for purposes that implicate another person. Further, the criminalization of an "offer" to transfer a firearm under s. 100(1)(b) suggests that a "transfer" is transactional in nature. *R. v. Grant*, 2009 SCC 32, [2009] 2 S.C.R. 353, McLachlin C.J. and Charron J.

TRANSFER. *n.* 1. The passing of any estate or interest in land, whether for valuable consideration or otherwise. 2. In relation to stock, includes the performance and execution of every deed, power of attorney, act, and thing on the part of the transferor to effect and complete the title in the transferee. *Trustee acts.* 3. Includes transmission by operation of law. *Corporations acts.* 4. Includes gift, conveyance, assignment, delivery over, or payment of property. *Assignments and Preferences Act*, R.S.N.S. 1989, c. 25, s. 2. 5. In the context of labour relations to accomplish a transfer something must be relinquished by the predecessor business on the one hand and obtained by the successor on the other. A transfer implies a nexus, an agreement or transaction of some sort between the predecessor and successor employers. .... There must be a mutual intent to transfer part of the business. *C.A.W., Local 222 v. Charterways Transportation Ltd.*, 2000 CarswellOnt 1253, 2000 SCC 23, 2000 C.L.L.C. 220-028, 49 C.C.E.L. (2d) 151, 47 O.R. (3d) 800 (headnote only), 185 D.L.R. (4th) 618, [2000] L.V.I. 3109-1, [2000] 1 S.C.R. 538, 253 N.R. 223, 22 Admin. L.R. (3d) 1, 133 O.A.C. 43, Bastarache J. (dissenting). 6. A change in ownership of a patent, of an application or of an interest in an invention and includes an assignment. *Patent Act*, R.S.C. 1985, c. P-4, *Patent Rules*, SOR/96-423, s. 2. See RECIPROCAL ~ AGREEMENT; TITLE ~ CREDIT SUPPORT AGREEMENT.

TRANSFERABLE. *adj.* Capable of being transferred.

TRANSFER AT UNDERVALUE. A disposition of property or provision of services for which no consideration is received by the debtor or for which the consideration received by the debtor is conspicuously less than the fair market value of the consideration given by the debtor. *Bankruptcy and Insolvency Act*, R.S.C. 1985, c. B-3, s. 2.

TRANSFEREE. *n.* 1. A person in whose favour a transfer is given. 2. The person to whom any interest or estate in land is transferred whether for value or otherwise. *Land Titles acts.*

TRANSFER HEARING. A hearing to determine whether a young offender will be tried as an adult offender in adult court.

TRANSFEROR. *n.* 1. The person by whom any interest or estate in land is transferred, whether for valuable consideration or otherwise. *Land Titles acts.* 2. A person who gives a transfer. 3. The person by whom title is transferred. *The Land Titles Act*, 2000, S.S. 2000, c. L-5.1, s. 2.

TRANSFERRED INTENT. "The literature on transferred intent distinguishes between two kinds of situations in which the 'wrong victim' suffers harm at the hands of the accused. The first, sometimes called error in objecto involves a mistake by the perpetrator as to the identity of the victim ... It is the second 'wrong victim' situation, sometimes called aberratio ictus, or more poetically, 'a mistake of the bullet' that has led to the controversy surrounding the doctrine of transferred intent. In this second situation the perpetrator aims at X but by chance or lack of skill hits Y." *R. v. Droste* (1984), 10 C.C.C. (3d) 404 at 410, [1984] 1 S.C.R. 208, 39 C.R. (3d) 26, 6 D.L.R. (4th) 607, 52 N.R. 176, 3 O.A.C. 179, Dickson J. (Ritchie, Estey, McIntyre, Chouinard and Lamer JJ. concurring).

TRANSGENICS. *n.* No person shall, except in accordance with the regulations and a licence, combine any part or any proportion of the human genome specified in the regulations with any part of the genome of a species specified in the regulations. *Assisted Human Reproduction Act*, S.C. 2004, c. 2, s. 11.

TRANSIT. *n.* The portion of an international transboundary movement of material through the territory of a country that is neither the country of origin nor the country of destination of the movement. Federal statutes. See URBAN ~ AUTHORITY.

TRANSITION OFFICE. See CANADIAN SECURITIES REGULATION REGIME ~.

TRANSIT SYSTEM. A system for the transportation of passengers and parcel express. See URBAN RAIL ~.

TRANSMISSION. *n.* 1. "... [I]n the ordinary sense of the language, connotes the delivery from an origination point to a reception point. It does not connote a conceptual transfer of something with neither sender nor receiver. ..." *R. v. McLaughlin* (1980), 18 C.R. (3d) 339 at 348, [1980] 2 S.C.R. 331, [1981] 1 W.W.R. 298, 32 N.R. 350, 23 A.R. 530, 53 C.C.C. (2d) 417, 113 D.L.R. (3d) 386, Estey J. (concurring). 2. . The passing of title to land, mortgages, encumbrances, or leases, in any manner other than by transfer from the owner. *The Real Property Act*, R.S.M. 1988, c. R30, s. 1. 3. "[With regard to shares] ... used to express the legal result which follows on death, but not to express the actual step which is necessary to invest the new holder. That is done by transfer, and that transfer in such a case is effectuated by a change in the register where the shares are registered, ..." *Brassard v. Smith* (1924), [1925] 1 D.L.R. 528 at 531, [1925] A.C. 371, [1925] 1 W.W.R. 311, 38 Que. K.B. 208 (Que. P.C.), the board per Lord Dunedin. 4. Includes storage. *Gas Utilities acts.* 5. A change of ownership (a) effected by the operation of an Act or law, (b) under an order of a court, or(c) consequent on any change in the office of a personal representative or trustee, but does not include (d) an amalgamation of 2 or more corporations, however effected, whether or not the amalgamation is in respect of a beneficial or a trust estate or interest in land, or (e) an amalgamation under the Strata Property Act. *Land Title Act*, R.S.B.C. 1996, c. 250, s. 1.

TRANSMISSION CONTROL PROTOCOL. Transmission control protocol ("TCP") is the most common protocol and it controls most of the applications used on the Internet. The TCP resides in both host server and end user computers and it controls the sending and receipt of packets transmitted over the Internet. However, routers and other intermediate points on the Internet have no involvement in TCP operation. *Society of Composers, Authors & Music Publishers of Canada v. Canadian Assn. of Internet Providers*, 2004 SCC 45, Binnie J.

TRANSMISSION FACILITY. 1. Any wire, cable, radio, optical or other electromagnetic system, or any similar technical system, for the transmission of intelligence between network termination points, but does not include any exempt transmission apparatus. *Telecommunications Act*, S.C. 1993, c. 38, s. 2. 2. A transmission facility is a facility for the transmission of "intelligence". The phrase "transmission facility" does not, of course, occur in s. 43(5). Yet, the Utilities submit that the term "transmission" in s. 43(5) must be read harmoniously with the definition of "transmission facility" so that in both provisions the thing being transmitted is "intelligence." The Utilities' power poles do not serve to transmit intelligence. They serve to transmit electricity. I agree with the Utilities that a harmonious interpretation of these two provisions is to be preferred. While I do not consider this point to be conclusive, it is another factor suggesting that s. 43(5) does not encompass the Utilities' power poles. *Barrie Public Utilities v. Canadian Cable Television Assn.*, 2003 SCC 28 [Per Gonthier J. (McLachlin C.J.C., Major, Arbour, LeBel, Deschamps JJ. concurring).

TRANSMISSION SYSTEM. A system for transmitting electricity, and includes any structures, equipment or other things used for that purpose.

TRANSMIT. *v.* 1. To send or convey from one place to another place by any physical, electronic, optical or other means; *Canada Post Corporation Act*, R.S.C. 1985, c. C-10, s. 2. 2. With respect to electricity, means to convey electricity at voltages of more than 50 kilovolts. *Electricity Act, 1998*, S.O. 1998, c. 15, Sched. A, s. 2.

TRANSMIT BY POST. To transmit through or by means of Canada Post Corporation; *Canada Post Corporation Act*, R.S.C. 1985, c. C-10, s. 2.

TRANSMITTED FRACTURE. Fracture, caused by transmitted stress, to a bone distant from impact.

F.A. Jaffe, *A Guide to Pathological Evidence for Lawyers and Police Officers*, 4th ed. (Toronto: Carswell, 1999) at 238.

TRANSMITTER. *n.* 1. A person who supplies a hydrocarbon by pipeline to a distributor. *Technical Standards and Safety Act, 2000*, S.O. 2000, c. 16, *Oil and Gas Pipeline Systems*, O. Reg. 210/01, s. 1. 2. A person who owns or operates a transmission system. *Electricity Act, 1998*, S.O. 1998, c. 15, Sched. A, s. 2. 3. A facility or instrument by which a purchaser of a telecommunication service may send or receive the telecommunications that may be sent or received under that service. *The Retail Sales Tax Act*, R.S.M. 1987, c. R130, s. 4.

TRANSPLANT. *n.* The removal of tissue from a human body, whether living or dead, and its implantation in a living human body. *Human Tissue Gift Acts.*

TRANSPLANTATION. *n.* The operation of transferring tissue or an organ from a human donor to a human recipient. *Human Tissue and Organ Donation Act*, S.A. 2006, c. H-14.5, s. 1.

TRANSPORTATION. See INLAND ~ INSURANCE.

TRANSPORTATION APPEAL TRIBUNAL OF CANADA. Established by subsection 2(1) of the Transportation Appeal Tribunal of Canada Act, the Tribunal has jurisdiction in respect of reviews and appeals as expressly provided for under the Aeronautics Act, the Canada Shipping Act, 2001, the Marine Transportation Security Act, the Railway Safety Act and any other federal Act regarding transportation. The Tribunal also has jurisdiction in respect of reviews and appeals in connection with administrative monetary penalties provided for under sections 177 to 181 of the Canada Transportation Act, sections 43 to 55 of the International Bridges and Tunnels Act and sections 129.01 to 129.19 of the Canada Marine Act.

TRANSPORTATION LAW. The law governing the carriage of goods and people.

TRANSPORTATION SECURITY. The protection of any means of transportation or of any transportation infrastructure, including related equipment, from any actual or attempted action that could cause, or result in, (a) loss of life or personal injury; (b) substantial damage to or destruction of a means of transportation or any transportation infrastructure; or (c) interference with any means of transportation or with any transportation infrastructure that is likely to result in loss of life or personal injury, or substantial damage to or destruction of any means of transportation or any transportation infrastructure. *Aeronautics Act*, R.S.C. 1985, c. A-2, s. 4.81.

TRANSPORTATION SYSTEM. See PUBLIC ~.

TRAP. *v.* 1. To conceal and surprise under circumstances which appear safe but mask real danger. 2. To catch or to attempt to catch game or fur bearing animals by means of a trap.

TRAP. *n.* 1. "... [A]n intrinsically dangerous situation. The danger should not be apparent but hidden:

... generally includes some connotation of abnormality and surprise, in view of the circumstances; ..." *Rubis v. Gray Rocks Inn Ltd.*, [1982] 1 S.C.R. 452 at 466, 41 N.R. 108, 21 C.C.L.T. 64, Beetz J. (Chouinard and Lamer JJ. concurring). 2. A device for catching game.

TRAUMATIC EVENT. The words "traumatic event" are equally consistent with an objective or a more subjective interpretation. As the Tribunal points out, the word "trauma" has at least two senses. One is that a trauma is a "deeply distressing experience" and the other, the medical sense, is that a trauma is a "physical injury." Similarly, the word "traumatic" may be used synonymously with "distressing" or "emotionally disturbing" or in reference to "wounds": K. Barber, The Canadian Oxford Dictionary (1998) at 1554. Thus, it seems that a traumatic event may be defined by its emotional impact on the observer ("distressing" or "emotionally disturbing") which is a more subjective view, or by its results more objectively determined such as, for example, in reference to an injury or a wound. The ordinary grammatical sense, in my view, does not exclude either an objective or a subjective approach. *Logan v. Nova Scotia (Workers' Compensation Appeals Tribunal)*, 2006 NSCA 88.

TRAVEL. See WESTERN HEMISPHERE ~ INITIATIVE.

TRAVEL AGENT. A person who sells travel services supplied by another person.

TRAVEL SERVICE. Transportation, sleeping accommodation or other service for the use of a traveller, tourist or sightseer.

TRAVEL WHOLESALER. A person who acquires rights to a travel service for the purpose of resale to a travel agent or who carries on the business of dealing with travel agents or travel wholesalers for the sale of travel services provided by another person. *Travel Industry Act, 2002*, S.O. 2002, c. 30, Sched. D, s. 1.

TRAVERSE. *n.* 1. "... [A] denial [by the defendant] of the plaintiff's allegations ..." *Royal Bank v. Rizkalla* (1984), 50 C.P.C. 292 at 295, 59 B.C.L.R. 324 (S.C.), McLachlin J. 2. A traverse is a denial or a refusal to admit. *Patym Holdings Ltd. v. Michalakis*, 2005 BCCA 636, Smith J.A. (Saunders J.A. concurring).

T.R.B. *abbr.* Tax Review Board.

TREASON. *n.* (a) Using force or violence for the purpose of overthrowing the government of Canada or a province; (b) without lawful authority, communicating or making available to an agent of a state other than Canada, military or scientific information or any sketch, plan, model, article, note or document of a military or scientific character that he knows or ought to know may be used by that state for a purpose prejudicial to the safety or defence of Canada; (c) conspiring with any person to commit high treason or to do anything mentioned in paragraph (a); (d) forming an intention to do anything that is high treason or that is mentioned in paragraph (a) and manifesting that intention by an overt act; or (e) conspiring with any person to do anything mentioned in paragraph (b) or forming an intention to do anything mentioned in paragraph (b) and manifesting that intention by an overt act. *Criminal Code*, R.S.C. 1985, c. C-46, s. 46(2). See HIGH ~.

TREASURE TROVE. Any coin, money, gold, silver, bullion or plate buried or hidden in a private place; because its owner is unknown it belongs to the Crown.

TREASURY BILL. A bill in certificated form, or a non-certificated security, issued by or on behalf of Her Majesty for the payment of a principal sum specified in the bill to a named recipient or to a bearer at a date not later than twelve months after the date of issue of the bill. *Financial Administration Act*, R.S.C. 1985, c. F-11, s. 2.

TREASURY BOARD. 1. A committee of the Queen's Privy Council for Canada over which the President of the Treasury Board appointed by Commission under the Great Seal presides. The Treasury Board shall, in addition to the President of the Treasury Board, consist of the Minister and four other members of the Queen's Privy Council for Canada to be nominated from time to time by the Governor in Council. The Treasury Board may act for the Queen's Privy Council for Canada on all matters relating to general administrative policy in the public service of Canada; the organization of the public service of Canada or any portion thereof, and the determination and control of establishments therein; financial management, including estimates, expenditures, financial commitments, accounts, fees or charges for the provision of services or the use of facilities, rentals, licences, leases, revenues from the disposition of property, and procedures by which departments manage, record and account for revenues received or receivable from any source whatever, etc. *Financial Administration Act*, R.S.C. 1985, c. F-11. 2. The equivalent body for a provincial government.

TREASURY NOTE. A note in certificated form, or a non-certificated security, issued by or on behalf of Her Majesty for the payment of a principal sum specified in the note to a named recipient or to a bearer at a date not later than twelve months after the date of issue of the note. *Financial Administration Act*, R.S.C. 1985, c. F-11, s. 2.

TREAT. See INVITATION TO ~.

TREATMENT. *n.* 1. "[In s. 12 of the Charter] ... connotes any conduct, action or behaviour towards another person. It is a word of more expansive or comprehensive import than is its disjunctive partner 'punishment', in that it extends, or potentially so, to all forms of disability or disadvantage and not merely to those imposed as a penalty to ensure the application and enforcement of a rule of law ..." *R. v. Blakeman* (1988), 48 C.R.R. 222 at 239 (Ont. H.C.), Watt J. 2. [Within the meaning of s. 12 of the Canadian Charter of Rights and Freedoms] has a broader scope than punishment. In [Rodriguez v. British Columbia (Attorney General), [1993] 3 S.C.R. 519, 85 C.C.C. (3d) 15 (S.C.C.)], Sopinka J. . . . found that, in the realm of state action, there was a necessary distinction between merely prohibiting certain behaviour and ac-

tually subjecting individuals to "treatment". He held that there must be an active state process in operation involving an exercise of state control over the individual, in order for the action, prohibition, or inaction to be considered treatment: p. 611-12. Section 43 [of the Criminal Code, R.S.C. 1985, c. C-46] does not involve "treatment" of children in the sense contemplated by s. 12 of the Charter. *Canadian Foundation for Children, Youth & the Law v. Canada (Attorney General)*, 2000 CarswellOnt 2409, 146 C.C.C. (3d) 362, 188 D.L.R. (4th) 718, 49 O.R. (3d) 662, 36 C.R. (5th) 334, 76 C.R.R. (2d) 251 (S.C.J.), McCombs J. See TAX ~ AGREEMENT.

TREATMENT PLAN. A plan that is developed by a health care provider for the provision of health care to or the withholding or withdrawal of health care from an adult with respect to a disease, illness, ailment or health condition that the adult has or may have in the future. *Adult Guardianship and Trusteeship Act*, S.A. 2008, c. A-4.2, s. 1.

TREATY. *n.* 1. An agreement between states, political in nature, even though it may contain provisions of a legislative character which may pass into law, produces binding effects between the parties to it. 2. A treaty within the meaning of section 35 of the *Constitution Act, 1982*. 3. "... [A] treaty with the Indians is unique, ... it is an agreement sui generis which is neither created nor terminated according to the rules of international law... . it is clear that what characterizes a treaty is the intention to create obligations, the presence of mutually binding obligations and a certain measure of solemnity... ." *Sioui v. Quebec (Attorney General)* (1990), (*sub nom. R. v. Sioui*) 56 C.C.C. (3d) 225 at 239, [1990] 1 S.C.R. 1025, 109 N.R. 22, 70 D.L.R. (4th) 427, [1990] 3 C.N.L.R. 127, 30 O.A.C. 280, the court per Lamer J. 3. "[In s. 88 of the Indian Act, R.S.C. 1970, c. I-6] ... is not a word of art and ... it embraces all such engagements made by persons in authority as may be brought within the term 'the word of the white man' the sanctity of which was, at the time of British exploration and settlement, the most important means of obtaining the goodwill and co-operation of the native tribes ... On such assurance the Indians relied." *R. v. White* (1964), 50 D.L.R. (2d) 613 at 648-9, 52 W.W.R. 193 (B.C. C.A.), Norris J.A. See COMMERCIAL ~; TAXING ~ FIRST NATION.

TREATY OF 1908. The treaty between His Majesty King Edward VII and the United States respecting the demarcation of the international boundary between the United States and Canada signed at Washington on April 11, 1908. *International Boundary Commission Act*, R.S.C. 1985, c. I-16, s. 2.

TREE. *n.* Includes, a growing tree or shrub planted or left growing on either side of a highway for the purpose of shade or ornament. *Municipal Act*, R.S.O. 1990, c. M.45, s. 312. See STRADDLE ~; STRAYING ~; VOLUNTARY ~.

TRESPASS. *n.* 1. "... [U]njustified invasion of another's possession... ." *Harrison v. Carswell* (1975), 75 C.L.L.C. 14,286 at 614, [1976] 2 S.C.R. 200, [1975] 6 W.W.R. 673, 5 N.R. 523, 25 C.C.C. (2d) 186, 62 D.L.R. (3d) 68, the court per Dickson J. 2.

All forcible, direct and immediate injury to the plaintiff's person, land or goods. May be committed by propelling a person or object onto the land or by refusing to leave land after a licence to enter has terminated. J.G. Fleming, *The Law of Torts*, 8th ed. (Sydney: Law Book, 1992) at 16, 41-2. 3. "... [A]n action for the wrong committed in respect of the plaintiff's land by entry on the same without lawful authority." *Point v. Dibblee Construction Co.* [1934] O.R. 142 at 153, [1934] 2 D.L.R. 785 (H.C.), Armour J.

TRESPASS AB INITIO. A person who lawfully entered another's land lost immunity from action for trespass if that person abused the privilege by committing a tort against the possessor or the possessor's property. J.G. Fleming, *The Law of Torts*, 6th ed. (Sydney: Law Book, 1983) at 95.

TRESPASS BY RELATION. A person who has a right to immediate possession of land may, upon entry, sue for any trespass committed after that right to entry accrued. J.G. Fleming, *The Law of Torts*, 8th ed. (Sydney: Law Book, 1992) at 44.

TRESPASS DE BONIS ASPORTATIS. A writ used as a remedy in a case in which something was totally carried away or destroyed. J.G. Fleming, *The Law of Torts*, 8th ed. (Sydney: Law Book, 1992) at 52.

TRESPASSER. *n.* Someone who goes on another's land without any lawful authority, right or express or implied licence or invitation, and whose presence is either unknown to the occupier or is objected to if known.

TRESPASS TO CHATTELS. Unlawfully disturbing possession of goods by seizing them or removing them or by damaging them.

TRESPASS TO GOODS. Intentional interference or use of a chattel in such a way as to violate the plaintiff's possessory rights.

TRESPASS TO LAND. The act of entering on land which is in the possession of another person or placing, throwing, or erecting something on that land without any legal right to do so.

TRESPASS TO THE PERSON. Conventionally, the term "cause of action" means the fact or set of facts which give a right to bring an action, which in the case of trespass to the person is complete without resulting harm, meaning such cause of action arises on the commission itself of the wrongful act or, at the instance of a child, when the child reaches adulthood. In the case of negligence, the cause of action is not complete without resulting harm and so the cause of action is traditionally taken to arise on the combination of a wrongful act and resulting harm, subject in the case of an infant to the infant reaching the age of majority. *L. (H.) v. Canada (Attorney General)*, 2002 SKCA 131, 227 Sask. R. 165, [2003] 5 W.W.R. 421, 287 W.A.C. 165.

TRIACTOR. *n.* A type of bet on a race to select, in the correct order, the first three horses in the official result. *Criminal Code*, R.S.C. 1985, c. C-46, *Pari-*

Mutuel Betting Supervision Regulations, SOR/91-365, s. 2.

TRIAL. *n.* 1. The hearing of a civil or criminal matter by a court. 2. "... In its popular and general sense a trial by jury consists of arraignment and plea, calling and swearing the jury, the opening address of Crown counsel, the examination and cross-examination of witnesses for the Crown and for the defence, the closing addresses of counsel, the judge's charge and, last, the jury's verdict. The cases have, by and large, tended to give a rather more restricted meaning to the word 'trial'... ." *R. v. Basarabas* (1982), 31 C.R. (3d) 193 at 197, [1982] 2 S.C.R. 730, [1983] 4 W.W.R. 289, 144 D.L.R. (3d) 115, 2 C.C.C. (3d) 257, 46 N.R. 69, the court per Dickson J. 3. "[In the case of a trial by jury] ... the trial proper does not start until the accused is given in charge to the jury which stage is, of course, not reached until after the plea has been taken and the adoption of this more restricted meaning of the word 'trial' has been widely accepted in our own courts for many years." *R. v. Dennis* (1960), 30 W.W.R. 545 at 550, [1960] S.C.R. 286, 32 C.R. 210, 125 C.C.C. 321, the court per Ritchie J. 4. "... [T]he investigation and determination of a matter in issue between parties before a competent tribunal, advancing through progressive stages from its submission to the court or jury to the pronouncement of judgment." *Catherwood v. Thompson*, [1958] O.R. 326 at 331, 13 D.L.R. (2d) 238 (C.A.), the court per Schroeder J.A. 5. In determining when an accused is required to be present during a trial, three types of actions which courts have found form part of the trial: (1) hearing motions on the admissibility of evidence, (2) communications between the presiding judge, or the Crown, and the jury, and (3) taking the court to view a person, place or thing. *R. v. Tran*, [1994] 2 S.C.R. 951 See BILINGUAL ~; FAIR ~; MEGA~; MIS~; NEW ~; NOTICE OF READINESS FOR ~; PRE-~ CONFERENCE; SET DOWN FOR ~; SPLIT ~S; SUMMARY ~; ~ WITHIN A ~; UNFIT TO STAND ~.

TRIAL COURT. 1. The court by which an accused was tried and includes a judge or a provincial court judge acting under Part XIX. *Criminal Code*, R.S.C. 1985, c. C-46, s. 673. 2. The court which conducts the initial proceedings in civil litigation.

TRIAL DE NOVO. 1. A form of appeal in which the case is retried. 2. The distinction between "an appeal by holding a trial de novo and an appeal to the provincial Court of Appeal is that although the object of both is to determine whether the decision appealed from was right or wrong, in the latter case the question is whether it was right or wrong having regard to the evidence upon which it was based, whereas in the former the issue is to be determined without any reference, except for purposes of cross-examination, to the evidence called in the court appealed from and upon a fresh determination based upon evidence called anew and perhaps accompanied by entirely new evidence. *R. v. Dennis*, [1960] S.C.R. 286, 30 W.W.R. 545 at 548, 32 C.R. 210, 125 C.C.C. 321, Ritchie J. 3. A trial de novo envisages a new trial before a different tribunal than the one which originally decided the issue. *McKenzie v. Mason*, 1992

CarswellBC 282, 72 B.C.L.R. (2d) 53, 9 C.P.C. (3d) 1, 96 D.L.R. (4th) 558, 18 B.C.A.C. 286, 31 W.A.C. 286, Toy J.A.

TRIAL PERIOD. A period of time during which an employee is given a chance to demonstrate his or her abilities.

TRIAL PREPARATION. The work done at a time reasonably close in time to the trial. May include organization of documents for trial and preparation of exhibit books.

TRIAL WITHIN A TRIAL. An enquiry held by a judge to determine whether a statement or confession is admissible in evidence or to determine other questions of admissibility of evidence or of law which are for the judge alone to determine. The proceeding is held in the absence of the jury. See VOIR DIRE.

TRIB. *abbr.* Tribunal.

TRIB. CONC. *abbr.* Tribunal de la concurrence.

TRIB. CONC. DEC. *abbr.* Tribunal de concurrence, décisions, 1986-?.

TRIBUNAL. *n.* 1. "... [A] generic word which includes courts in its scope. Thus, in this generic sense, all courts are tribunals, but all tribunals are not courts... ." *Russell v. Radley* (1984), 11 C.C.C. (3d) 289 at 305, [1984] 1 F.C. 543, 5 Admin. L.R. 39 (T.D.), Muldoon J. 2. The first significant difference between courts and tribunals relates to the difference in the manner in which decisions are rendered by each type of adjudicating body. Courts must decide cases according to the law and are bound by stare decisis. By contrast, tribunals are not so constrained. When acting within their jurisdiction, they may solve the conflict before them in the way judged to be most appropriate. . . . A second difference lies in the institutional organization and functioning of tribunals, as opposed to that of courts. Tribunals are intended to provide adjudicating bodies with specialized knowledge the courts are unable to offer. They are also designed structurally to provide decisions in a shorter amount of time and with less expense than the courts. *Weber v. Ontario Hydro*, 1995 CarswellOnt 240, 24 C.C.L.T. (2d) 217, 95 C.L.L.C. 210-027, 12 C.C.E.L. (2d) 1, 30 Admin. L.R (2d) 1, 24 O.R. (3d) 358 (note), 125 D.L.R. (4th) 583, 183 N.R. 241, 30 C.R.R. (2d) 1, 82 O.A.C. 321, [1995] 2 S.C.R. 929, [1995] L.V.I. 2687-1, Iacobucci J. (dissenting in part) (La Forest and Sopinka JJ. concurring). 3. [S]tatutory tribunals created by Parliament or the Legislatures may be courts of competent jurisdiction to grant Charter remedies, provided they have jurisdiction over the parties and the subject matter of the dispute and are empowered to make the orders sought. *Weber v. Ontario Hydro*, 1995 CarswellOnt 240, 24 C.C.L.T. (2d) 217, 95 C.L.L.C. 210-027, 12 C.C.E.L. (2d) 1, 30 Admin. L.R (2d) 1, 24 O.R. (3d) 358 (note), 125 D.L.R. (4th) 583, 183 N.R. 241, 30 C.R.R. (2d) 1, 82 O.A.C. 321, [1995] 2 S.C.R. 929, [1995] L.V.I. 2687-1 . McLachlin J. (L'Heureux-Dubé, Gonthier and Major JJ. concurring). 4. A court of justice. 5. A body or person which exercises a judicial or quasi-judicial function outside the regular court system. 6. One or more persons, whether or not incorporated and however described, on whom a statutory power of decision is conferred. See ADMINISTRATIVE ~; ADMINISTRATIVE ~ OF QUÉBEC; ARBITRAL ~; CANADIAN ARTISTS AND PRODUCERS PROFESSIONAL RELATIONS ~; CANADIAN HUMAN RIGHTS ~; CANADIAN INTERNATIONAL TRADE ~; DOMESTIC ~; FEDERAL BOARD, COMMISSION OR OTHER ~; PUBLIC SERVICE STAFFING ~; SERVICE ~; SPECIFIC CLAIMS ~.

TRIBUNAL CLUSTERING. The Lieutenant Governor in Council may by regulation designate two or more adjudicative tribunals as a cluster if, in the opinion of the Lieutenant Governor in Council, the matters that the tribunals deal with are such that they can operate more effectively and efficiently as part of a cluster than alone. *Adjudicative Tribunals Accountability, Governance and Appointments Act, 2009*, S.O. 2009, c. 33, Sched. 5, s. 15.

TRIER OF FACT. The person or group who must make findings of fact in a hearing before a tribunal or court. The jury is the trier of fact in a jury trial. In a trial without a jury, the judge is the trier of fact as well as the decision maker with regard to matters of law.

TRIGGER. See CONTINUOUS ~ THEORY; FOUR ~ THEORIES.

TRIPARTITE. *adj.* 1. Consisting of three parts. 2. Refers to a panel of adjudicators or arbitrators consisting of one member chosen by each party and a third neutral member who is usually the chair.

TROUBLE. See UNKNOWN ~ CALL.

TROVE. See TREASURE ~.

TROVER. *n.* An action on the case, the remedy for a plaintiff who is deprived, by wrongful taking, detention or disposal, of goods.

TRU. *abbr.* Trueman's Equity Cases (N.B.), 1876-1903.

TRUCK. See FREE ON ~.

TRUCKING DEPOT. Land where commercial vehicles are stationed and from which they are dispatched.

TRUE BILL. An indorsement made by a grand jury on a bill of indictment when after hearing the evidence they are satisfied that the accusation is probably true. *R. v. Chabot* (1980), 18 C.R. (3d) 258 at 264, [1980] 2 S.C.R. 985, 34 N.R. 361, 55 C.C.C. (2d) 385, 117 D.L.R. (3d) 527, the court per Dickson J.

TRUE CONDITION PRECEDENT. A future uncertain event upon which the obligations of both parties to the contract are dependent. The happening of the uncertain event is dependent upon the will of a third party.

TRUE COPY. 1. "It has been said (per Kay J., Sharp v. McHenry, (1887) 38 Ch. D. 427), that a copy is true if it is true in all essential particulars, so that no one can be misled as to the effect of the instrument, but that if the true effect is mis-stated it is immaterial whether it is mis-stated in favour of one party or of the other." *Commercial Credit Co. v. Fulton Brothers*, [1923] 3 D.L.R. 611 at 618, [1923] A.C. 798 (Can. P.C.), the board per Lord Sumner. 2. (a) In relation to a paper document, an exact copy of the document, and (b) in relation to an electronic return, a legible paper copy of the electronic return containing every material provision and particular contained in the original. *Property Transfer Tax Act*, R.S.B.C. 1996, c. 378, s. 1.

TRUE INNUENDO. One in which the defamatory meaning of words depends upon extrinsic circumstances. The words are not per se defamatory in their natural and ordinary meaning.

TRUST. *n.* 1. A confidence or reliance which rests expressly or impliedly in a person (the trustee) for the benefit of another (the beneficiary or the cestui que trust). The simplest form of trust requires the trustee to hold property for the beneficiary's benefit. Must possess three essential attributes: certainty of intention, certainty of subject matter, and certainty of objects. 2. "... A trust arises ... whenever a person is compelled in equity to hold property over which he has control for the benefit of others (the beneficiaries) in such a way that the benefit of the property accrues not to the trustee, but to the beneficiaries." *Guerin v. R.* (1984), [1985] 1 C.N.L.R. 120 at 155, [1984] 2 S.C.R. 335, 36 R.P.R. 1, 20 E.T.R. 6, [1984] 6 W.W.R. 481, 59 B.C.L.R. 301, 13 D.L.R. (4th) 321, 55 N.R. 161, Dickson J. (Beetz, Chouinard and Lamer JJ. concurring). See ACCUMULATION ~; ACTIVE ~; BARE ~; BLIND ~; BOND-HOLDER'S ~; BREACH OF ~; CEMETERY CARE ~; CESTUI QUE ~; CHARITABLE ~; CONSTRUCTIVE ~; DECLARATION OF ~; DEEMED ~; DISCRETIONARY ~; EQUIPMENT ~; EXECUTED ~; EXECUTORY ~; EXPRESS ~; FROZEN ~; FULLY-SECRET ~; GUARANTEED ~ MONEY; HALF-SECRET ~; HOLDING ~; IMPERFECT ~; IMPLIED ~; INTER VIVOS ~; INVESTMENT ~; MORTGAGE ~; PERSONAL ~; POSITION OF ~; PRECATORY ~; PUBLIC ~; QUITCLOSE ~; RESULTING ~; SECRET ~; SIFT ~; SIMPLE ~; TESTAMENTARY ~; UNIT ~; VARIATION OF ~; VOTING ~.

TRUST CONDITION. In a contract for purchase and sale of real property, denotes an obligation imposed by one lawyer on the other lawyer concerning the mechanics of closing the transaction.

TRUST CORPORATION. A body corporate incorporated or operated, (a) for the purpose of offering its services to the public to act as trustee, bailee, agent, executor, administrator, receiver, liquidator, assignee, guardian of property or attorney under a power of attorney for property, and (b) for the purpose of receiving deposits from the public and of lending or investing such deposits. *Loan and Trust Corporations Act*, R.S.O. 1990, c. L.25, s. 1.

TRUST DEED. 1. A separate document in favour of a trust company as trustee for the holders of the instruments which evidences an obligation, the usual way to issue a corporate obligation sold to the public,

which may contain a specific charge or mortgage or a floating charge or both. 2. Any deed, indenture or document, however designated, including any supplement or amendment thereto, by the terms of which a person issues or guarantees, or provides for the issue or guarantee of, debt obligations and in which a person is appointed as trustee for the holder of the debt obligations issued, guaranteed or provided for thereunder and secured by a security interest. *Personal Property Security Act*, R.S.Y. 2002, c. 169, s. 1.

TRUSTEE. *n.* 1. Someone who holds property in trust. 2. Includes a liquidator, receiver, receiver-manager, trustee in bankruptcy, assignee, executor, administrator, sequestrator or any other person performing a function similar to that performed by any such person. 3. A person who is declared by any Act to be a trustee or is, by the law of a province, a trustee, and, without restricting the generality of the foregoing, includes a trustee on an express trust created by deed, will or instrument in writing, or by parol. *Criminal Code*, R.S.C. 1985, c. C-46, s. 2. See CONSTRUCTIVE ~; CUSTODIAN ~; OFFICIAL ~; PUBLIC GUARDIAN AND ~; PUBLIC ~.

TRUSTEE DE SON TORT. To be liable as trustees de son tort, strangers to the trust must commit a breach of trust while acting as trustees. Such persons are not appointed trustees but "take on themselves to act as such and to possess and administer trust property". *Citadel General Assurance Co. v. Lloyds Bank Canada*, [1997] 3 S.C.R. 805.

TRUSTEE IN BANKRUPTCY. The person in whom a bankrupt's property is vested in trust for creditors.

TRUST FOR SALE. Imposes an obligation on the trustee to sell when the testator or settlor transfers property to the trustee on trust to convert the assets into money, and to distribute or invest these proceeds as directed.

TRUST FUND. 1. Money or property held in trust. 2. Money paid to a contractor by an owner or to a subcontractor by a contractor for the benefit of workers and people who supplied material for a contract. D.N. Macklem & D.I. Bristow, *Construction, Builders' and Mechanics' Liens in Canada*, 6th ed. (Toronto: Carswell, 1990-) at 1-3. See COMMON ~.

TRUST INDENTURE. Any deed, indenture, security agreement, or other instrument, including any supplement or amendment thereto, made by a body corporate under which the body corporate issues or guarantees debt obligations and in which a person is appointed as trustee for the holders of the debt obligations issued or guaranteed thereunder. *Bank Act*, S.C. 1991, c. 46, s. 294.

TRUST INSTRUMENT. A will, deed, declaration or other instrument in writing by which a person creates a trust. *Minors' Property Act*, S.A. 2004, c. M-18.1, s. 1.

TRUST POWER. Imposes an obligation on the donee to exercise the power.

TRUTH AND RECONCILIATION COMMISSION. See INDIAN RESIDENTIAL SCHOOLS ~.

T

T.S.P.A.A.T. *abbr.* Tribunal d'appel de la sécurité professionnelle et de l'assurance contre les accidents du travail (Ontario), 1998-.

T.T. *abbr.* Tribunal du Travail (Jurisprudence en droit du travail).

T.T.C. *abbr.* Hunter's Torrens Title Cases, 1865-1893.

T.T.J. *abbr.* Jurisprudence en droit du travail: Tribunal du travail (Québec), 1970-1981.

T.T. (QUÉ.). *abbr.* Tribunal du travail (Québec).

T.T.R. abbr. Trade and Tariff Reports, 1990-1996.

T.T.R. (2D). *abbr.* Trade and Tariff Reports (Second Series), 1996-.

TUNNEL. See INTERNATIONAL BRIDGE OR ~.

TURPIS CAUSA. [L.] A consideration so vile that no action can be founded on it. See EX TURPI CAUSA NON ORITUR ACTIO.

TURPITUDE. See MORAL ~.

TUTORSHIP. *n.* Is established in the interest of the minor; it is intended to ensure the protection of his person, the administration of his patrimony and, generally, to secure the exercise of his civil rights. *Civil Code*, R.S.Q., a. 177. See DATIVE ~; LEGAL ~.

TWIN MYTHS. 1. The notions that an "unchaste woman" is likely to have consented to sexual activity and that she is less worthy of belief. 2. Section 276(1) [of the Criminal Code, R.S.C. 1985, c. C-46] addresses the "twin myths". The section provides that evidence of the complainant's sexual activity with the accused or anyone else is not admissible to support an inference that, by reason of the sexual activity, the complainant is more likely to have consented to the sexual activity that forms the subject-matter of the charge; or is less worthy of belief. Section 276(2) operates to exclude evidence of the complainant's sexual activity if its admission would serve only to foster such twin-myth reasoning. Because of the danger twin-myth reasoning poses to the fairness of a trial, evidence of prior sexual conduct of the complainant probative of a relevant issue must be scrutinized under s. 276(2) before it may be admitted to ensure that its probative value is not outweighed by its prejudicial effect. The twin myths relate to "unchaste women". They have nothing to do with pre-pubescent children. *R. v. S. (L.H.)*, 1999 CarswellBC 1018 (C.A.).

TWISTING. *n.* A practice by which an insurance policy holder is improperly induced by an agent to replace an existing policy with a new policy of less value to the policy holder.

TWP. *abbr.* Township.

U

U.B.C. L. REV. *abbr.* University of British Columbia Law Review.

UBERRIMA FIDES. [L.] "... [A] longstanding tenet of insurance law which holds parties to an insurance contract to a standard of utmost good faith in their dealing. It places a heavy burden on those seeking insurance coverage to make full and complete disclosure of all relevant information when applying for a policy." *Coronation Insurance Co. v. Taku Air Transport Ltd.*, [1991] 3 S.C.R. 622 at 636, [1992] 1 W.W.R. 217, 61 B.C.L.R. (2d) 41, 4 C.C.L.I. (2d) 115, 85 D.L.R. (4th) 609, [1992] I.L.R. 1-2797, 131 N.R. 241, 6 B.C.A.C. 161, 13 W.A.C. 161, Cory J.

U.C. *abbr.* Upper Canada.

U.C. CHAMB. *abbr.* Upper Canada Chambers Reports, 1846-1852.

U.C. CH. REP. *abbr.* Grant, Upper Canada Chambers Reports (Ontario), 1846-1852.

U.C.C.P. *abbr.* Upper Canada Common Pleas Reports (Ontario), 1850-1882.

U.C.E. & A. *abbr.* Upper Canada Error & Appeal Reports (Grant), 1846-1866.

U.C. JUR. *abbr.* Upper Canada Jurist, 1844.

U.C. JURIST. *abbr.* Upper Canada Jurist, 1844-1848.

U.C.K.B. *abbr.* Upper Canada, King's Bench Reports (Old Series) (Ontario), 1831-1844.

U.C.L.J. *abbr.* Upper Canada Law Journal, 1855-1864.

U.C.O.S. *abbr.* Upper Canada, King's Bench Reports (Old Series), 1831-1844.

U.C.Q.B. *abbr.* Upper Canada, Queen's Bench Reports (New Series) (Ontario), 1842-1882.

U.C.Q.B. (O.S.). *abbr.* Upper Canada Queen's Bench Reports (Old Series) (Ontario), 1831-1838.

UDRP. *abbr.* Uniform Domain Name Dispute Resolution Policy.

U.F.C. *abbr.* Unified Family Court.

U.I.C. DEC. UMP. *abbr.* Unemployment Insurance Commission – Decisions of the Umpire, 1943-.

U.K. *abbr.* United Kingdom.

ULTIMATE HEIR. The person entitled to take by descent or distribution the property of whatsoever nature of an intestate in the event of failure of heirs or next of kin entitled to take that property by the law in force before July 1, 1929. The Crown in right of Alberta is the ultimate heir (a) of any person dying intestate in fact with regard to any property situated in Alberta, and (b) of any person domiciled in Alberta and dying intestate with regard to any movable property or chose in action wherever situated. *Ultimate Heir Act*, R.S.A. 2000, c. U-1, s. 1 [repealed].

ULTIMATE LIMITATION PERIOD. A limitation period beyond which no extension, postponement or suspension of time for any reason, such as incapacity or discoverability, can be obtained. The period of 30 years is commonly used.

ULTIMATE NEGLIGENCE. The last clear chance or last opportunity doctrine.

ULTRA. *prep.* [L.] Beyond.

ULTRA PETITA PRINCIPLE. The ultra petita principle is generally understood to mean that a court will not make a ruling beyond what is requested by the parties. For instance, a judgment which grants a monetary award that goes beyond that sought by the claimant is said to be ultra petita or extra petita. The legislator is free to remove administrative tribunals from the constraints of ultra petita. This will often be the case, as administrative tribunals are generally created to advance interests that can go beyond the immediate interests of the parties who appear before them. *Canadian Private Copying Collective v. Canadian Storage Media Alliance*, 2004 FCA 424.

ULTRA VIRES. [L. beyond the powers] 1. Describes a statute judicially determined to be outside the powers conferred by the Constitution on the legislative body that enacted the statute; it is therefore invalid. 2. That a particular transaction is outside the capacity or power of a corporation. 3. "... [I]s not a principle of the English common law and does not rest upon any theory as to the nature of corporations or as to the legal relationship subsisting between a corporation and its governing body ... It is a rule resting upon the interpretation of the legislative enactments through which the companies to which it applies derive their corporate existence and capacity." *Prevost v. Bedard* (1915), 24 D.L.R. 153 at 154, 51 S.C.R. 149, Duff J. 4. Describes an invalid enactment, order or decision made outside the jurisdiction of the body purporting to make it. 5. A bylaw is ultra vires if it prohibits a condition or activity for which a conviction could be sustained under the criminal law, if it is repugnant to the general law, if it does not conform to the specific power as to subject matter or if the same subject-matter is dealt with in a statute of general application to the whole province. *Ontario (Attorney General) v. Mississauga (City)* (1981), 15 M.P.L.R. 212 at 222-4 (C.A.), Weatherston J.A.

UMBRELLA POLICY. [Insurer's] policy expressly and correctly identifies itself as an umbrella policy. An umbrella policy generally provides two types of coverage: standard form excess coverage; and broader coverage than that provided by the underlying insurance including a duty to defend lawsuits not covered by the underlying coverage. An umbrella policy is in effect a hybrid policy that combines aspects of both a primary policy and an excess policy. *Trenton Cold Storage v. St. Paul Fire & Marine* (2001) 146 O.A.C. 348.

UMPIRE. *n.* The Governor in Council appoints from among the judges of the Federal Court such number of umpires as the Governor in Council considers necessary for the purposes of this Employment Insurance Act. Umpires hear appeals from board of referees under the Act.

U.N. *abbr.* United Nations.

UNABLE. *adj.* Cannot because of physical inability.

UNANIMOUS AGREEMENT. A written agreement to which all the members and shareholders, if any, of a cooperative are or are deemed to be parties. *Cooperatives acts.*

UNANIMOUS SHAREHOLDER AGREEMENT. A written agreement to which all the shareholders of a corporation are or are deemed to be parties, whether or not any other person is also a party, or a written declaration by a person who is the beneficial owner of all the issued shares of a corporation. *Business Corporations acts.*

UNAPPARENT SERVITUDE. A servitude is apparent if it is manifested by an external sign; otherwise it is unapparent. *Civil Code*, S.Q. 1991, c. 64, a. 1180. See APPARENT ~.

UNASCERTAINED GOODS. 1. Goods defined by referring to a genus. G.H.L. Fridman, *Sale of Goods in Canada*, 3d ed. (Toronto: Carswell, 1986) at 57. 2. Goods identified only by description. G.H.L. Fridman, *Sale of Goods in Canada*, 3d ed. (Toronto: Carswell, 1986) at 89.

UNAUTHORIZED. *adj.* Done or made without authority, implied, actual or apparent.

UNAVAILABILITY. *n.* In the context of determining the necessity of admitting hearsay evidence, the unavailability of a witness is determined as follow. Without restricting the precise content of "unavailability", the categories of absence recognized under s. 715 [of the Criminal Code], specifically death, illness, and insanity, offer a helpful guide to the types of circumstances under which it will be sufficiently necessary to consider the admission of the witness's

former testimony. *R. v. Hawkins* [1996] 3 S.C.R. 104.3

UNAVOIDABLE ACCIDENT. A defence to a negligence action. An occurrence which was not intended and which under the circumstances could not be foreseen or prevented by the exercise of reasonable precautions.

U.N.B.L.J. *abbr.* University of New Brunswick Law Journal.

U.N.B. L. REV. *abbr.* University of New Brunswick Law Journal (Revue de droit de l'Université du Nouveau-Brunswick).

UNBROKEN LOT. A regular lot whose area is not diminished or increased by a natural or artificial feature shown on the original plan. *Surveys Act*, R.S.O. 1990, c. S.30, s. 1.

UNCERTAINTY. *n.* In interpreting a will, a general reason to consider some gift or provision void because it is impossible to ascertain what the testator's intention was.

UNCONSCIONABILITY. *n.* 1. "... [E]quity will grant relief where there is inequality combined with substantial unfairness, and that in its modern application poverty and ignorance combined with lack of independent advice on the part of the party seeking relief (plus, presumably, some evidence of unfairness) places an onus on the other party to show that the bargain was in fact fair... ." *Smyth v. Szep* (1992), 8 C.C.L.I. (2d) 81 at 90, 63 B.C.L.R. (2d) 52, [1992] 2 W.W.R. 673, 10 B.C.A.C. 108, 21 W.A.C. 108 (C.A.), Taylor J.A. (Wood J.A. concurring). 2. "The test for setting aside an agreement on grounds of unconscionability was set out by McIntyre J.A. in Harry v. Kreutziger (1978), 9 B.C.L.R. 166 ... (C.A.) [at p. 173]: 'Where a claim is made that a bargain is unconscionable, it must be shown ... that there was inequality in the position of the parties due to the ignorance, need or distress of the weaker, which would leave him in the power of the stronger, coupled with proof of substantial unfairness in the bargain.' The essential idea of unconscionability is therefore that of fraud." *Ahone v. Holloway* (1988), 30 B.C.L.R. (2d) 368 at 374 (C.A.), the court per McLachlin J.A. 3. Refers to a false, misleading or deceptive consumer representation.

UNCONSCIONABLE. *adj.* The allegation that a contract is unconscionable is of course a serious one, carrying as it does the implication of unfair use of power amounting to fraud. . . . The term ["unconscionable"] was developed by courts of Equity to refer to bargains that were "contrary to good conscience," against which Equity would grant relief in the form of rescission. *Gindis v. Brisbourne*, 2000 CarswellBC 174, 2000 BCCA 73, 72 B.C.L.R. (3d) 19, [2000] 3 W.W.R. 656, 48 C.C.L.T. (2d) 117, 183 D.L.R. (4th) 431, 133 B.C.A.C. 66, 217 W.A.C. 66 (C.A.), Newbury J.A.

UNCONSCIOUSNESS. *n.* Is used in the sense that the accused, like the sleepwalker, is shown "not to have known what he was doing". . . . This excludes the person who is provoked and says, "I couldn't help myself", or who simply professes to be at a loss to explain uncharacteristic conduct. *R. v. Stone*, 1999 CarswellBC 1064, [1999] 2 S.C.R. 290, [1999] 2 S.C.R. 290.

UNCONTESTED DIVORCE. A divorce proceeding in which a respondent does not file a counter-petition or answer.

UNDELIVERABLE LETTER. Any letter that for any reason cannot be delivered to the addressee thereof and includes any letter the delivery of which is prohibited by law or is refused by the addressee or on which postage due is not paid by the sender on demand. *Canada Post Corporation Act*, R.S.C. 1985, c. C-10, s. 2.

UNDER. *prep.* 1. Arising out of, i.e. with reference to or arising out of an agreement. 2. With authority from, i.e. a claim is made under a statute when the statute is the source of the right to make the claim. See HERE~.

UNDERBARGAIN. *v.* To enter into a collective agreement which explicitly or by implication does not cover all employees which a plain reading of the certificate authorizing the union as bargaining agent would suggest should be included in the bargaining unit.

UNDEREMPLOYED WORKER. A person who is able and available to work full-time but is unable to find full-time employment.

UNDER-INSURANCE. 1. Where an insured is insured for a sum that is less than the insurable value of the subject-matter insured, in the case of an unvalued policy, or less than the value of the subject-matter insured specified by the policy, in the case of a valued policy, the insured is deemed to be self-insured in respect of the uninsured difference. *Marine Insurance Act*, S.C. 1993, c. 22, s. 88. 2. If the assured is insured for an amount less than the insurable value or, in the case of a valued policy, for an amount less than the policy valuation, the assured is deemed to be the assured's own insurer in respect of the uninsured balance. *Marine Insurance acts*.

UNDER LEASE. *var.* **UNDER-LEASE.** A lessee's grant to someone else (the under-lessee, under-tenant, sub-lessee or sub-tenant) of part of the whole interest under the original lease which reserves a reversion to the lessee.

UNDER LESSEE. *var.* **UNDER-LESSEE.** Includes any person deriving title under or from a lessee or an under lessee. *Landlord and Tenant acts*.

UNDER SEAL. Some form mark amounting to a seal has been affixed to the parties' signatures to the contract. See CONTRACT ~.

UNDERTAKING. *n.* 1. An assurance. 2. Every kind of business that an association or company is authorized to carry on. 3. An enterprise or activity, or a proposal, plan or program in respect of an enterprise or activity. 4. An undertaking in Form 11.1 or Form 12. *Criminal Code*, R.S.C. 1985, c. C-46, s. 493, as am. S.C. 2002, c. 7, s 143. 5. An undertaking is a promise given by one party to another party to the lawsuit in exchange for obtaining something from that party. *Kitchenham v. AXA Insurance (Canada)*,

2008 ONCA 877. 6. "... [I]s not a physical thing, but is an arrangement under which ... physical things are used." *Regulation & Control of Radio Communication in Canada, Re*, [1932] A.C. 304 at 315, [1932] 1 W.W.R. 563, 39 C.R.C. 49, [1932] 2 D.L.R. 81 (P.C.), Viscount Dunedin for their Lordships. 7. Refers to the whole of the enterprise within which a work or works is or are situated. See BROADCASTING ~; DISTRIBUTION ~; FEDERAL WORK, ~ OR BUSINESS; IMPLIED ~; PROGRAMMING ~.

UNDER THE LAW. See EQUALITY BEFORE AND ~.

UNDERVALUE. See TRANSFER AT ~.

UNDERWRITER. *n.* A person or company that, (i) as principal, agrees to purchase securities with a view to distribution, or (ii) as agent, offers for sale or sells securities in connection with a distribution, and includes a person or company that has a direct or indirect participation in the distribution, but does not include, (iii) a person or company whose interest in the transaction is limited to receiving the usual and customary distributor's or seller's commission payable by an underwriter or issuer, (iv) a mutual fund that, under the laws of the jurisdiction to which it is subject, accepts its shares or units for surrender and resells them, (v) a company that, under the laws of the jurisdiction to which it is subject, purchases its shares and resells them, or (vi) a bank listed in Schedule I, II or III of the Bank Act (Canada) with respect to the securities described in the regulations and to those banking transactions designated by the regulations. *Securities Act*, R.S.A. 2000, c. S-4, s. 1. See SECURITIES ~.

UNDERWRITING. *n.* With respect to a security, means the primary or secondary distribution of the security, in respect of which distribution (a) a prospectus is required to be filed, accepted or otherwise approved under or pursuant to a law enacted in Canada or in a jurisdiction outside Canada for the supervision or regulation of trade in securities; or (b) a prospectus would be required to be filed, accepted or otherwise approved but for an express exemption contained in or given pursuant to a law mentioned in paragraph (a). *Competition Act*, R.S.C. 1985, c. C-34, s. 5(2).

UNDISCLOSED PRINCIPAL. Any person upon whose behalf something is done but whose identity and even the fact of their existence remains unknown to the other party or parties.

UNDISPUTED CORNER. A corner of a parcel of land at which the original post exists, or a corner established under this Act or any predecessor of this Act. *Surveys Act*, R.S.O. 1990, c. S.30, s. 1.

UNDIVIDED INTEREST. Refers to the interest of a tenant in common in property. The percentage share of a tenant in common in property. The share is not divided from the shares of the other tenants in common. The interest is fixed for all time and is not affected by the death of one of the tenants in common, as is the case with the interest of a joint tenant in property. R. Megarry & M.P. Thompson, *Megarry's*

Manual of Real Property, 7th ed. (London: Sweet & Maxwell, 1993) at 284.

UNDUE. *adj.* While "undue" is a word of common usage which does not have a precise technical meaning the Supreme Court has variously defined "undue" to mean "improper, inordinate, excessive or oppressive" or to express "a notion of seriousness or significance." To this list of synonyms, the Concise Oxford Dictionary adds "disproportionate." What is clear from all of these terms is that "undue-ness" is a relative concept. The proper approach to determining if something is "undue", then, is a contextual one. Undue-ness must be defined in light of the aim of the relevant enactment. It can be useful to assess the consequences or effect if the undue thing is allowed to remain in place. *VIA Rail Canada Inc. v. Canada (National Transportation Agency)*, 2000 CarswellNat 2531, 261 N.R. 184, 193 D.L.R. (4th) 357, 26 Admin. L.R (3d) 1, [2001] 2 F.C. 25 (C.A.).

UNDUE HARDSHIP. The type of hardship contemplated by Section 10 of the Guidelines [Federal Child Support Guidelines, SOR/97-175] was "undue", meaning "exceptional", "excessive", or "disproportionate". *Gillespie v. Gormley* 2003 NBCA 72, 43 R.F.L. (5th) 331.

UNDUE INFLUENCE. 1. "... '[U]nconscientious use by one person of power possessed by him over another in order to induce the other to' do something." *Berdette v. Berdette* (1991), 33 R.F.L. (3d) 113 at 125, 41 E.T.R. 126, 3 O.R. (3d) 513, 81 D.L.R. (4th) 194, 47 O.A.C. 345 (C.A.), the court per Galligan J.A. 2. "... [T]he ability of one person to dominate the will of another, whether through manipulation, coercion, or outright but subtle abuse of power ... To dominate the will of another simply means to exercise a persuasive influence over him or her. The ability to exercise such influence may arise from a relationship of trust or confidence, but it may arise from other relationships as well. The point is that there is nothing per se reprehensible about persons in a relationship of trust or confidence exerting influence, even undue influence, over their beneficiaries. It depends on their motivation and the objective they seek to achieve thereby." *Goodman Estate v. Geffen* (1991), 42 E.T.R. 97 at 119, [1991] 5 W.W.R. 389, 80 Alta. L.R. (2d) 293, 125 A.R. 81, 14 W.A.C. 81, 81 D.L.R. (4th) 211, [1991] 2 S.C.R. 353, Wilson J. (Cory J. concurring). 3. Influence which overbears the will of the person influenced so that in truth what she does is not his or her own act. *Longmuir v. Holland*, 2000 CarswellBC 1951, 2000 BCCA 538, 81 B.C.L.R. (3d) 99, 192 D.L.R. (4th) 62, 35 E.T.R. (2d) 29 (C.A.), Southin J.A. (dissenting in part).

UNEMPLOYMENT INSURANCE. A contributory, federal social insurance program to provide earnings-related benefits to anyone who is off work or unable to accept or look for work because of injury or other cause. Now known as Employment Insurance.

UNENCRYPTED. *adj.* Refers to an electronic message which has not been processed by a program which encodes it.

UNENFORCEABLE. *adj.* Describes a contract which, although it is valid, cannot be sued upon, for example because the Statute of Frauds requires written evidence.

UNEQUAL BARGAINING POWER. Some parties are in no position to negotiate more favourable conditions and they are at times forced to accept unfavourable contractual conditions dictated by their more powerful counterparts, conditions which expose them to unduly harsh penalties in case of default. *Garcia Transport Ltée v. Royal Trust Co.*, [1992] 2 S.C.R. 499.

U.N.E.S.C.O. *abbr.* United Nations Educational, Scientific and Cultural Organisation.

UNESCORTED TEMPORARY ABSENCE. An unescorted temporary absence from penitentiary authorized by the Board taking into account risk of re-offence and other factors. *Corrections and Conditional Release Act*, S.C. 1992, c. 20, s. 99.

UNEXECUTED. *adj.* Of a contract, one of the parties has not completed that party's part of the bargain.

UNFAIRLY DISREGARDS. To unjustly or without cause pay no attention to, ignore or treat as of no importance the interests of security holders. See *Stech v. Davies*, [1987] 5 W.W.R. 563 (Alta. Q.B.), Egbert J.

UNFAIRLY PREJUDICIAL. Acts that are unjustly or inequitably detrimental. *Diligenti v. RWMD Operations Kelowna Ltd.* (1976), 1 B.C.L.R. 36 (S.C.).

UNFAIRNESS. See MANIFEST ~.

UNFETTERED DISCRETION. The law does not recognize the concept of "unfettered discretion". All discretionary powers must be exercised "according to law" and, therefore, their exercise by administrative officers are subject to certain implied limitations. Those implied limitations are in addition to those which involve procedural deficiencies amounting to breaches of the fairness rules. The expression most often used in the Federal Court is that a discretion must be exercised "judicially". That term is taken to mean that if a decision were made in bad faith, that is for an improper purpose or motive, in a discriminatory manner, or the decision-maker ignored a relevant factor or considered an irrelevant one, then the decision must be set aside. [Whether or not a factor is relevant may be in issue.] The same fate awaits a decision based on a mistaken principle of law or a misapprehension of the facts (as opposed to inferences drawn from accepted facts) or what is commonly referred to as a "palpable and overriding error". More recently, the Supreme Court held that where a tribunal is vested with a "broad discretion" a reviewing court should not disturb the exercise of that discretion unless that tribunal has "made some error in principle in exercising its discretion or has exercised its discretion in a capricious or vexatious manner"; per Iacobucci J. in Pezim v. British Columbia (Superintendent of Brokers), supra, at 607 [1994] 2 S.C.R. 577]. (Quaere: could this limitation be equated with the "patent unreasonableness" standard of review.) The common law limitations placed on the exercise of an administrative discretion exercised by executive members of government reflect the understanding that all powers granted by Parliament to the executive are fettered only to the extent necessary to ensure that basic tenets of the law are observed. But assuming that the decision-maker has acted "judicially" the question remains whether the discretionary decision may be set aside on other grounds. *Suresh v. Canada (Minister of Citizenship & Immigration)*, 2000 CarswellNat 25, 183 D.L.R. (4th) 629, 5 Imm. L.R. (3d) 1, 252 N.R. 1, 18 Admin. L.R. (3d) 159, [2000] 2 F.C. 592, 180 F.T.R. 57 (note)(C.A.), Robertson J.A. for the court. See FETTERING OF DISCRETION.

UNFIT. *adj.* A sentence is "unfit," and will be varied, where: (a) the sentence is clearly unreasonable; (b) the trial judge applied wrong principles; (c) the trial judge ignored or overstressed proper factors; or, (d) the sentence imposed is outside the acceptable range of sentence normally imposed for that type of offence: see R. v. Shropshire, [1995] 4 S.C.R. 227 (S.C.C.), at 249-251. However, it is not enough that there be the application of a wrong principle or a misinterpretation of the facts. Such errors will only lead to a finding of unfitness if they result in the sentence being clearly inadequate or excessive (that is to say, clearly unreasonable). Unfitness, rather than disagreement, is the basis for appellate interference. *Canada v. Domtar Specialty Fine Papers*, 2001 CarswellOnt 1572, 39 C.E.L.R. (N.S.) 56 (C.A.), J.W. Quinn J.

UNFIT TO STAND TRIAL. Unable on account of mental disorder to conduct a defence at any stage of the proceedings before a verdict is rendered or to instruct counsel to do so, and, in particular, unable on account of mental disorder to (a) understand the nature or object of the proceedings, (b) understand the possible consequences of the proceedings, or (c) communicate with counsel. *Criminal Code*, R.S.C. 1995, c. C-46, s. 2.

UNFUNDED BENEFITS PLAN. A plan which gives protection against risk to an individual that could otherwise be obtained by taking out a contract of insurance, whether the benefits are partly insured or not, and where payments are made by the planholder directly to or on behalf of the member of the plan or to the vendor upon the occurrence of the risk. *Retail Sales Tax Act*, R.S.O. 1990, c. R.31, s. 1.

UNFUNDED LIABILITY. Exists when the calculated liabilities of a pension fund exceed the calculated assets of the fund.

UNIF. FAM. CT. *abbr.* Unified Family Court.

UNIF. L. CONF. PROC. *abbr.* Uniform Law Conference of Canada, Proceedings.

UNIFORM. *n.* Distinctive clothing worn by an employee, service member, police constable or officer while on duty.

UNIFORM. *adj.* Essentially identical.

UNIFORM LAW CONFERENCE OF CANADA. Founded in 1918 to harmonize the laws of the provinces and territories of Canada, and where appropriate the federal laws. Makes recommendations for changes to federal criminal legislation based on identified deficiencies, defects or gaps in the existing law, or based on problems created by judicial interpretation of existing law.

UNILATERAL. *adj.* Having one side.

UNILATERAL CONTRACT. 1. One in which a party makes a promise in return for the performance or forbearance of an act. No counter-promise is made to perform the act or forbearance. Only one party undertakes a promise. 2. An agreement between someone who auctions goods with no reserve and the highest bidder. G.H.L. Fridman, *Sale of Goods in Canada*, 3d ed. (Toronto: Carswell, 1986) at 460. 3. In dealing with unilateral contracts, it is clear that the offeree (in this case the plaintiff) can accept the contract so as to make it binding by simply performing and that it is not necessary for the plaintiff to give notice of the acceptance of the contract to the offeror (the defendant). *Ken Toby Ltd. v. British Columbia Buildings Corp.*, 1997 CarswellBC 1087, 34 B.C.L.R. (3d) 263, [1997] 8 W.W.R. 721, 34 C.L.R. (2d) 81, 31 B.L.R. (2d) 224 (S.C.), Burnyeat J.

UNILATERAL MISTAKE. "To succeed on a plea of unilateral mistake the defendant must establish: (1) that a mistake occurred; (2) that there was fraud or the equivalent of fraud on the plantiff's part in that she knew or must be taken to have known when the agreement was executed that the defendant misunderstood its significance and that she did nothing to enlighten the defendant ..." *Alampi v. Swartz*, [1964] 1 O.R. 488 at 494, 43 D.L.R. (2d) 11 (C.A.), the court per McGillivray J.A.

UNILINGUAL. *adj.* 1. Knowing and using one language only. 2. Fluent in only one of the two official languages of Canada.

UNIMPROVED LAND. "Unserviced" lands, not just lands without buildings. . . . In [Planet Parking Ltd. v. Metropolitan Toronto Assessment Commissioner, [1970] 3 O.R. 657 (Ont. H.C.)], the court found that the word "unimproved" in the context of the Assessment Act [R.S.O. 1970 c. 32] related to the "ordinary and natural" meaning of "improvement" as in "making . . . better" . . . . The court rejected "the contention that unimproved land as distinguished from improved land means land without buildings erected thereupon" . . . . In the . . . leases, the word "improvement" is used to refer to things other than buildings. Clause 8(a), for example, refers to "any buildings . . . and . . . such other improvements, including construction of roads, water, sewer, electricity and/or gas systems". . . . Improvements include services, and conversely "unimproved" means without services. The internal coherence of the rent review clause also supports the view that "unimproved" means unserviced. The leases were signed before any buildings were built, so the word "unimproved" would have added nothing to the phrase "unimproved lands in the same state as they were on the date of this agreement" unless it referred to the pre-existing servicing. *Musqueam Indian Band v. Glass*, 2000 CarswellNat 2405, 2000 SCC 52, [2000] 11 W.W.R. 407, 36 R.P.R. (3d) 1, 192 D.L.R. (4th) 385, 82 B.C.L.R. (3d) 199, 261 N.R. 296, 186 F.T.R. 248

U

(note), [2000] 2 S.C.R. 633, [2001] 1 C.N.L.R. 208, Gonthier J. (Major, Binnie and LeBel JJ. concurring).

UNINCORPORATED ASSOCIATION. "... [H]as no legal existence, apart from its members, and is not a legal entity capable of suing or being sued." *Tel-Ad Advisors Ontario Ltd. v. Tele-Direct (Publications) Inc.* (1986), 8 C.P.C. (2d) 217 at 218 (Ont. H.C.), Griffiths J.

UNION. *n.* 1. A trade union. 2. "... [A]n unincorporated group or association of workmen who have banded together to promote certain objectives for their mutual benefit and advantage ..." *Astgen v. Smith*, [1970] 1 O.R. 129 at 134, 7 D.L.R. (3d) 657 (C.A.), Evans J.A. 3. Any organization of employees, or any branch or local thereof, the purposes of which include the regulation of relations between employers and employees. See CERTIFIED ~; CIVIL ~; COMPANY-DOMINATED ~; COMPANY ~; CRAFT ~; CREDIT ~; CUSTOMS ~; LABOUR ~; LEGISLATIVE ~; TRADE ~.

UNIONISM. See COMPULSORY ~.

UNION RIGHTS. Specific provisions which a union frequently attempts to include in the terms of an agreement and which benefit the union itself, its officers or officials. The overriding purpose of such clauses is usually to insure that the union may fully discharge its statutory and contractual function to supervise the terms of the agreement. D.J.M. Brown & D.M. Beatty, *Canadian Labour Arbitration*, 3d ed. (Aurora: Canada Law Book, 1988-) at 9-1.

UNION SECURITY. Provisions like voluntary check-off of union dues, union and closed shops which insure that any employees who are the beneficiaries of the agreement share any costs associated with the union's activities. D.J.M. Brown & D.M. Beatty, *Canadian Labour Arbitration*, 3d ed. (Aurora: Canada Law Book, 1988-) at 9-2.

UNIT. *n.* 1. A part of the property designated as a unit by the description and includes the space enclosed by its boundaries and all of the land, structures and fixtures within this space in accordance with the declaration and description. *Condominium Act, 1998,* S.O. 1998, c. 19, s. 1. 2. An individual body of the Canadian Forces that is organized as such with the personnel and material thereof. *National Defence Act,* R.S.C. 1985, c. N-5, s. 2. See BARGAINING ~; BC ALLOWANCE ~; BC EMISSION REDUCTION ~; COMMERCIAL ~; COMPLIANCE ~; CONDOMINIUM ~; CRAFT ~; DWELLING ~; HOUSEHOLD ~; LEASEHOLD ~; RENTAL ~; RENT-GEARED-TO-INCOME ~; RESIDENTIAL ~; SPACING ~.

UNIT AGREEMENT. An agreement to unitize the interests of owners in a pool or a part of a pool exceeding in area a spacing unit, or such an agreement as varied by a unitization order. *Canada Oil and Gas Operations Act,* R.S.C. 1985, c. O-7, s. 29.

UNIT AREA. The area that is subject to a unit agreement. *Canada Oil and Gas Operations Act,* R.S.C. 1985, c. O-7, s. 29.

UNITARY STATE. A nation in which supreme authority is in one centre.

UNITED NATIONS OPERATION. An operation that is established by the competent organ of the United Nations in accordance with the Charter of the United Nations and is conducted under United Nations authority and control, if the operation is for the purpose of maintaining or restoring international peace and security or if the Security Council or the General Assembly of the United Nations has declared, for the purposes of the Convention on the Safety of United Nations and Associated Personnel, that there exists an exceptional risk to the safety of the personnel participating in the operation. It does not include an operation authorized by the Security Council as an enforcement action under Chapter VII of the Charter of the United Nations in which any of the personnel are engaged as combatants against organized armed forces and to which the law of international armed conflict applies. *Criminal Code,* R.S.C. 1985, c. C-46, s. 2.

UNITED NATIONS PERSONNEL. Persons who are engaged or deployed by the Secretary-General of the United Nations as members of the military, police or civilian components of a United Nations operation, or any other officials or experts who are on mission of the United Nations or one of its specialized agencies or the International Atomic Energy Agency and who are present in an official capacity in the area where a United Nations operation is conducted. *Criminal Code,* R.S.C. 1985, c. C-46, s. 2.

UNIT ENTITLEMENT. Of a strata lot means the number indicated in the Schedule of Unit Entitlement established under section 246, that is used in calculations to determine the strata lot's share of (*a*) the common property and common assets, and (*b*) the common expenses and liabilities of the strata corporation. *Strata Property Act,* S.B.C. 1998, c. 43, s. 1.

UNITIZED ZONE. A geological formation that is within a unit area and subject to a unit agreement. *Canada Oil and Gas Operations Act,* R.S.C. 1985, c. O-7, s. 29.

UNIT OPERATING AGREEMENT. An agreement, providing for the management and operation of a unit area and a unitized zone, that is entered into by working interest owners who are parties to a unit agreement with respect to that unit area and unitized zone, and includes a unit operating agreement as varied by a unitization order. *Canada Oil and Gas Operations Act,* R.S.C. 1985, c. O-7, s. 29.

UNIT OPERATION. Those operations conducted pursuant to a unit agreement or a unitization order. *Canada Oil and Gas Operations Act,* R.S.C. 1985, c. O-7, s. 29.

UNIT OPERATOR. A person designated as a unit operator under a unit operating agreement. *Canada Oil and Gas Operations Act,* R.S.C. 1985, c. O-7, s. 29.

UNIT PRICE CONTRACT. A contract in which it is agreed to measure the work by a convenient unit of measure so that the contractor is paid a fixed price per unit.

UNIT TRACT. The portion of a unit area that is defined as a tract in a unit agreement. *Canada Oil and Gas Operations Act*, R.S.C. 1985, c. O-7, s. 29.

UNIT TRUST. A trust under which the interest of each beneficiary is described by reference to units of the trust.

UNITY. See FOUR UNITIES.

UNITY OF INTEREST. Said of a joint tenant who has no greater interest in a property than any other joint tenant.

UNITY OF POSSESSION. Said of joint tenants who have undivided possession.

UNITY OF SEISIN. A situation in which someone seised of land which is subject to a profit à prendre, easement or similar right also becomes seised of the land to which that profit or right is annexed.

UNITY OF TIME. Said of joint tenants whose interests must arise at the same time.

UNITY OF TITLE. Said of joint tenants who hold their property by one and the same title.

UNIVERSAL CHILD CARE BENEFIT. Purpose is to assist families by supporting their child care choices through direct financial support to a maximum of $1,200 per year in respect of each of their children who has not attained the age of six years. *Universal Child Care Benefit Act*, S.C. 2006, c. 4, s. 168, s. 3.

UNIVERSAL DECLARATION OF HUMAN RIGHTS. The 1948 declaration, adopted by the United Nations General Assembly, of persons' entitlement to legal equality, other fundamental rights and which recognizes the inherent dignity and the equal and inalienable rights of all persons.

UNIVERSALITY. *n.* A principle contrasted with territoriality. Permits the exercise of jurisdiction by a state in respect of criminal acts committed by non-nationals against non- nationals wherever they take place. Jurisdiction is based upon the accused's attack upon the international order as a whole and is of common concern to all mankind as a sort of international public policy. Historically, the universality principle has been employed to prosecute piracy and, more recently, hijacking. Under the principle of universality the criminal act is a violation of national law. International law merely gives states a liberty to punish but it does not itself declare the act illegal. By contrast, some acts are crimes under international law. They may be punished by any state which has custody of the accused. *R. v. Finta*, [1994] 1 S.C.R. 701.

UNIVERSAL LEGACY. Entitles one or several persons to take the entire succession. *Civil Code*, S.Q. 1991, c. 64, a. 732.

UNJUST. *adj.* In the context of extradition, undeserved, unfounded, or disproportionate in all the circumstances. *United States v. Taylor*, 2005 BCCA 440, Finch C.J.B.C. (concurring).

UNJUST ENRICHMENT. 1. "The determination that the enrichment is 'unjust' does not refer to abstract notions of morality and justice, but flows directly from the finding that there was a breach of a legally recognized duty for which the Courts will grant relief." *International Corona Resources Ltd. v. Lac Minerals Ltd.* (1989), 44 B.L.R. 1 at 45, [1989] 2 S.C.R. 574, 26 C.P.R. (3d) 97, 69 O.R. (2d) 287, 61 D.L.R. (4th) 14, 6 R.P.R. (2d) 1, 25 E.T.R. 1, 101 N.R. 239, 36 O.A.C. 57, La Forest J. (Wilson and Lamer JJ. concurring). 2. An action for unjust enrichment arises when three elements are satisfied: (1) an enrichment; (2) a corresponding deprivation; and (3) the absence of a juristic reason for the enrichment. These proven, the action is established and the right to claim relief made out. At this point, a second doctrinal concern arises: the nature of the remedy. "Unjust enrichment" in equity permitted a number of remedies, depending on the circumstances. One was a payment for services rendered on the basis of quantum meruit or quantum valebat. Another equitable remedy, available traditionally where one person was possessed of legal title to property in which another had an interest, was the constructive trust. ... the remedy of constructive trust arises, where monetary damages are inadequate and where there is a link between the contribution that founds the action and the property in which the constructive trust is claimed. ... in order for a constructive trust to be found, in a family case as in other cases, monetary compensation must be inadequate and there must be a link between the services rendered and the property in which the trust is claimed. *Peter v. Beblow*, 1993 CarswellBC 44, 77 B.C.L.R. (2d) 1, [1993] 3 W.W.R. 337, 44 R.F.L. (3d) 329, 48 E.T.R. 1, 150 N.R. 1, 23 B.C.A.C. 81, 39 W.A.C. 81, 101 D.L.R. (4th) 621, [1993] 1 S.C.R. 980, [1993] R.D.F. 369, McLachlin J.

UNKNOWN TROUBLE CALL. A call to police or emergency services where the phone is disconnected before the caller says anything. Treated as a call for help and given priority to all but calls for assistance to an officer in distress.

UNLAWFUL. *adj.* 1. Illegal. 2. "... There appear to be three categories of actions or events which are contrary to the law and which sometimes fall into the description 'unlawful' or 'illegal'. These are: (a) offences against statutes prohibiting defined conduct; (b) actions which are without legal consequence in the sense of creating enforceable rights, such as gaming contracts; and (c) actions taken by statutory bodies outside the limits of authority granted or established in the statute... ." *Nepean Hydro-Electric Commission v. Ontario Hydro*, [1982] 1 S.C.R. 347 at 406-7, 18 B.L.R. 215, 132 D.L.R. (3d) 193, 41 N.R. 1, Estey J. (Martland and Lamer JJ. concurring). See ILLEGAL; MANIFESTLY ~.

UNLAWFUL ACT. "... [T]he concept of an unlawful act as it is used in that section [s. 269 of the Criminal Code, R.S.C. 1985, c. C-46] includes only federal and provincial offences. Excluded from this general category of offences are any offences which are based on absolute liabilty and which have constitutionally insufficient mental elements on their own. Additionally, the term 'unlawfully' ... requires an act which is at least objectively dangerous." *R. v. De-*

Sousa (1992), 15 C.R. (4th) 66 at 81, 142 N.R. 1, 9 O.R. (3d) 544n, 76 C.C.C.(3d) 124, 95 D.L.R. (4th) 595, 56 O.A.C. 109, [1992] 2 S.C.R. 944, 11 C.R.R. (2d) 193, the court per Sopinka J.

UNLAWFUL ACTIVITY. An act or omission that is an offence pursuant to: (i) an Act, an Act of any province or territory of Canada or an Act of the Parliament of Canada; or (ii) an Act of a jurisdiction outside Canada, if a similar act or omission would be an offence pursuant to an Act or an Act of the Parliament of Canada if it were committed in Saskatchewan. *The Seizure of Criminal Property Act, 2009*, S.S. 2009, c. S-46.002, s. 2. See INSTRUMENT OF ~; PROCEEDS OF ~.

UNLAWFUL AND INTENTIONAL INTERFERENCE. To find that there has been unlawful interference, it must be shown that a right protected by the Charter was infringed and that the infringement resulted from wrongful conduct. A person's conduct will be characterized as wrongful if, in engaging therein, he or she violated a standard of conduct considered reasonable in the circumstances under the general law or, in the case of certain protected rights, a standard set out in the Charter itself. . . . . . There will be unlawful and intentional interference within the meaning of the second paragraph of s. 49 of the [Charter of Human Rights and Freedoms, R.S.Q., c. C-12] when the person who commits the unlawful interference has a state of mind that implies a desire or intent to cause the consequences of his or her wrongful conduct, or when that person acts with full knowledge of the immediate and natural or at least extremely probable consequences that his or her conduct will cause. This test is not as strict as specific intent, but it does go beyond simple negligence. Thus, an individual's recklessness, however wild and foolhardy, as to the consequences of his or her wrongful acts will not in itself satisfy this test. *Québec (Curateur public) c. Syndicat national des employés de l'hôpital St-Ferdinand*, 1996 CarswellQue 916, 202 N.R. 321, (*sub nom. Quebec (Public Curator) v. Syndicat national des employés de l'hôpital St-Ferdinand*) 138 D.L.R. (4th) 577, 1 C.P.C. (4th) 183, [1996] 3 S.C.R. 211, the court per L'Heureux-Dubé J.

UNLAWFUL ASSEMBLY. An assembly of three or more persons who, with intent to carry out any common purpose, assemble in such a manner or so conduct themselves when they are assembled as to cause persons in the neighbourhood of the assembly to fear, on reasonable grounds that they (a) will disturb the peace tumultuously; or (b) will by that assembly needlessly and without reasonable cause provoke other persons to disturb the peace tumultuously. *Criminal Code*, R.S.C. 1985, c. C-46, s. 63(1).

UNLAWFUL CONDUCT. Includes crime, tort, breach of contract and breach of statute and breach of a fiduciary obligation.

UNLAWFUL INTERFERENCE WITH CONTRACTUAL RELATIONS. "The tort of unlawful interference with contractual relations is established where the defendant, with knowledge of a contract and with intent to prevent or hinder its performance,

(1) persuades, induces or procures a party to the contract not to perform its obligations, or (2) commits some act, wrongful, in itself, to prevent performance of the contract ..." *Niedner Ltd. v. Lloyds Bank of Canada* (1990), 72 D.L.R. (4th) 147 at 153, 77 O.R. (2d) 574, 38 E.T.R. 306 (Ont. H.C.), Ewaschuk J.

UNLAWFUL INTERFERENCE WITH ECONOMIC RELATIONS. 1. A tort, referring to someone intentionally employing unlawful means to interfere with a business relationship or expectancy. 2. Although there remains some uncertainty about how broadly the expression "unlawful interference" should be interpreted, it is accepted that the commission of an intentional tort constitutes unlawful means. This requirement could be satisfied if, for example, Drouillard had established that Cogeco's actions and interference were defamatory. It has also been held by this court in Reach M.D. Inc. v. Pharmaceutical Manufacturers Association of Canada 2003 CanLII 27828, (2003), 65 O.R. (3d) 30 at paras. 50-52 (C.A.), that unlawful means also includes acts which the tortfeasor "is not at liberty to commit." In that decision, the court adopted the view of Lord Denning as expressed in Torquay Hotel Co. Ltd. v. Cousins, [1969] 1 All E.R. 522 at 530 (C.A.), where he stated: I must say a word about unlawful means, because that brings in another principle. I have always understood that if one person deliberately interferes with the trade or business of another, and does so by unlawful means, that is, by an act which he is not at liberty to commit, then he is acting unlawfully, even though he does not procure or induce any actual breach of contract. If the means are unlawful, that is enough. *Drouillard v. Cogeco Cable Inc.*, 2007 ONCA 322. See CAUSING LOSS BY UNLAWFUL MEANS.

UNLAWFUL INTERFERENCE WITH LEGITIMATE BUSINESS EXPECTANCY. The elements of this tort are the existence of a valid business relationship or expectancy, knowledge by the defendant of the relationship or expectancy, intentional interference inducing or causing termination of the relationship or expectancy by unfair or unlawful means, proximate cause and resultant damages.

UNLAWFULLY. *adv.* 1. "... [W]ithout legal authority or justification... ." *R. v. Kapij* (1905), 1 W.L.R. 130 at 136, 15 Man. R. 110, 9 C.C.C. 186 (C.A.), the court per Perdue J.A. 2. As it is used in s. 281 [of the Criminal Code] does not require the commission of an additional unlawful act. Rather, it represents verbal surplusage that enunciates no more than the general defences, justifications, and excuses already available under the Code. It is appropriate to interpret the expression "unlawfully" as meaning "without lawful justification, authority or excuse", as that term is used in s. 281 of the Criminal Code; this interpretation is in accord with the purpose of the section which is to prevent and punish strangers intending to deprive a parent (guardian, etc.) of his or her child (the child for whom they act as guardian, etc.). To require that an additional unlawful act occur beyond the physical act of taking the child is at cross-purposes with the mischief Parliament wanted to cure; such an interpretation would not adequately achieve the goal of prevention, and the rights of the parents could not be vindicated. *R. v. Chartrand*, 1994 CarswellOnt 83, 31 C.R. (4th) 1, 91 C.C.C. (3d) 396, [1994] 2 S.C.R. 864, 116 D.L.R. (4th) 207, 170 N.R. 161, 74 O.A.C. 257, the court per L'Heureux-Dubé J.

UNLAWFUL MEANS. The question of what amounts to "unlawful means" [in the context of the tort of causing loss by unlawful means] is the one that has caused the most difficulty for judges and scholars. The majority of the Lords [in OBG Ltd. v. Allan, Douglas v. Hello! Ltd., and Mainstream Properties Ltd. v. Young, [2007] UKHL 21] agreed with the following definition found at para. 51 of Lord Hoffman's reasons: Unlawful means therefore consists of acts intended to cause loss to the claimant by interfering with the freedom of a third party in a way which is unlawful as against that third party and which is intended to cause loss to the claimant. It does not in my opinion include acts which may be unlawful against a third party but which do not affect his freedom to deal with the claimant. Lord Hoffman summarized his definition of unlawful means as acts against a third party that are actionable by that third party, or would have been actionable if the third party had suffered a loss. This excludes criminal conduct that is not directed at the third party and is not otherwise actionable by that party. In contrast, Lord Nicholls of Birkenhead views the breadth of conduct under the rubric of "unlawful means" as encompassing any conduct that is deliberately intended to harm the plaintiff and in breach of a legal or equitable obligation under either civil or criminal law. He views the true rationale of the tort as providing a remedy for intentional economic harm "caused by unacceptable means," which includes all means that would violate an obligation under the law: para. 153. Lord Nicholls' approach may be viewed as similar to the one espoused by the decision of this court in Reach M.D. Inc. v. Pharmaceutical Manufacturers Association of Canada 2003 CanLII 27828, (2003), 65 O.R. (3d) 30 (Ont. C.A.), which adopted Lord Denning's characterization of unlawful [citation omitted], as acts which the tortfeasor "is not at liberty to commit." In Reach M.D., the defendant association made a ruling that was beyond its powers against one of its members, which the court found to constitute "unlawful means." However, Rouleau J.A. in Drouillard [Drouillard v. Cogeco Cable Inc., 2007 ONCA 322], at paras. 19–25, distinguished Reach M.D. and limited its scope, when he concluded that Cogeco's conduct in not following its internal corporate policy or acting in bad faith did not amount to unlawful means and that the tort of intentional interference with economic relations was therefore not made out in that case. *Correia v. Canac Kitchens*, 2008 ONCA 506. See CAUSING LOSS BY ~; ILLEGAL OR ~.

UNLEADED GASOLINE. Gasoline to which lead has not been added during the production process.

UNLIQUIDATED. *adj.* Not ascertained.

UNLIQUIDATED DAMAGES. Damages whose amount depends on circumstances, and on the parties' conduct or is fixed by an estimate or opinion.

UNMARKED PLASTIC EXPLOSIVE. A plastic explosive that does not contain a detection agent, or at the time of manufacture, does not contain the required minimum concentration level of a detection agent as required by the Convention. *Explosives Act*, R.S.C. 1985, c. E-17, s. 2.

UNNECESSARY. *adj.* Of a pleading, one that alleges immaterial facts.

UNPAID. *adj.* When the payor has defaulted in its obligation to pay. *Canadian-Automatic Data Processing Services Ltd. v. Syntecor Ltd.*, 2004 BCCA 408.

UNPAID SELLER'S LIEN. A possessory lien which entitles the creditor to keep the debtor's goods until the debt is paid.

UNPATENTED LAND. (i) Land for which no letters patent have issued from the Crown; (ii) land for which no Crown grant has been issued; (iii) land that has not otherwise been conveyed from the Crown; or (iv) land expropriated by the Crown in right of Canada that was at one time: (A) land for which letters patent had issued from the Crown in right of Canada or Saskatchewan; (B) land for which a grant from the Crown in right of Canada or Saskatchewan had been issued; (C) land that had been otherwise conveyed from the Crown in right of Canada or Saskatchewan. *The Land Titles Act, 2000*, S.S. 2000, c. L-5.1, s. 69.

UNREASONABLE. *adj.* 1. The Supreme Court of Canada has introduced a third standard of review in cases where there is a statutory right of appeal. The statutory right of appeal obviates the need to find a jurisdictional error. Because the standard of patent unreasonableness is principally a test for determining whether a tribunal has exceeded its jurisdiction, it will rarely be the appropriate standard of review in statutory appeals. However, because tribunals typically enjoy more expertise and deal with problems of a difficult and complex nature, a standard more differential than correctness was found to be needed. This third standard has been defined as the standard of "unreasonableness". *Canada (Director of Investigation & Research) v. Southam Inc.*, [1997] 1 S.C.R. 748 . 2. In [R. v. Shropshire, [1995] 4 S.C.R. 227], the Court concluded . . . that unreasonableness in the sentencing context refers to an order falling outside the "acceptable range" of sentences under similar circumstances. In an adversarial system, it seems logical to assume that if no appeal against sentence is taken, neither of the parties found anything "clearly" unreasonable in it. *R. v. W. (G.)*, 1999 CarswellNfld 253, 138 C.C.C. (3d) 23, 178 D.L.R. (4th) 76, 27 C.R. (5th) 203, 247 N.R. 135, 181 Nfld. & P.E.I.R. 139, 550 A.P.R. 139, [1999] 3 S.C.R. 597, Lamer C.J.C. See PATENTLY ~; REASONABLE.

UNREASONABLE DELAY. Delay which is excessive in the circumstances.

UNREASONABLENESS. *n.* The test of unreasonableness is whether the verdict is one that a properly instructed jury, acting judicially, could reasonably have rendered. *R. v. Mah*, 2002 NSCA 99, 207 N.S.R. (2d) 262.

UNREASONABLE SEARCH. Unlawful search, one conducted pursuant to an invalid order. See REASONABLE SEARCH.

U

UNREASONABLE VERDICT. A verdict is unreasonable verdict if materially undermined by an error (such as speculation or logical inconsistency) on a significant issue or the conclusion simply cannot be supported by the evidence as seen through the lens of judicial experience. *R. v. Enright*, 2009 ABCA 236.

UNSANITARY CONDITIONS. Conditions or circumstances as might contaminate with dirt or filth, or render injurious to health, a food, drug or cosmetic. *Food and Drugs Act*, R.S.C. 1985, c. F-27, s. 2.

UNSAVOURY. *adj.* A witness is considered unsavoury where it is suspected that his or her evidence is proffered for an ulterior motive—for example, to divert suspicion or blame from himself or herself, or to gain advantage such as immunity from prosecution for the current offence or concessions in relation to another offence, or for monetary reward. *R. v. Campbell*, 2002 NSCA 35, 202 N.S.R. (2d) 170, 632 A.P.R. 170, 163 C.C.C. (3d) 485, 1 C.R. (6th) 343.

UNSECURED CREDITOR. Any creditor of a company who is not a secured creditor.

UNSEEMLY. *adj.* Competition becomes "unseemly" or unprofessional when it is misleading, contravenes good taste, makes unfavourable reflections on the competence or integrity of another member, or includes subjective claims of superiority that cannot be substantiated. *Assie v. Institute of Chartered Accountants (Saskatchewan)*, 2001 CarswellSask 545, 2001 SKQB 396 (Q.B.), Smith J.

UNSOLICITED GOODS OR SERVICES. (a) Goods that are supplied to a consumer who did not request them but does not include, (i) goods that the recipient knows or ought to know are intended for another person, (ii) a change to periodically supplied goods, if the change in goods is not a material change, or (iii) goods supplied under a written future performance agreement that provides for the periodic supply of goods to the recipient without further solicitation, or (b) services that are supplied to a consumer who did not request them but does not include, (i) services that were intended for another person from the time the recipient knew or ought to have known that they were so intended, (ii) a change to ongoing or periodic services that are being supplied, if the change in the services is not a material change, or (iii) services supplied under a written future performance agreement that provides for the ongoing or periodic supply of services to the recipient without further solicitation. *Consumer Protection Act, 2002*, S.O. 2002, c. 30, Sched. A, s. 13(9).

UNSOUND MIND. 1. As provided in s. 47 [of the Limitations Act, R.S.O. 1990, c. L.15], means in context lack of mental capacity from whatever source to perform the requisite steps called for by the Limitations Act or the Municipal Act, R.S.O. 1990, c. M.45. *Bannon v. Thunder Bay (City)*, [2002] 1 S.C.R. 716. 2. In the context of the Limitations Act, a person is of unsound mind when he or she, by reason of mental illness, is incapable of managing his or her affairs as a reasonable person would do in relation to the inci-dent, or event, which entitles the person to bring an action. *Bisoukis v. Brampton (City)* (1999), 46 O.R. (3d) 417 (C.A.).

UNSUITABILITY. *n.* A standard applied to probationary employees. Lower standard than "just cause", includes qualities such as having a bad attitude, being unable to get along with colleagues or customers in a reasonable manner.

UNTENABLE PLEA. One that is clearly impossible of success at law.

UNTENANTABLE. *adj.* Refers to the actual physical state of property being unsuitable for occupation by tenants.

UNTIL. *prep.* To.

UNUSUAL. *adj.* Not usual; out of the ordinary. See CRUEL AND ~ PUNISHMENT.

UNUSUAL DANGER. In occupier's liability, used in an objective sense, danger which is not usually found in carrying out the task or fulfilling the function which the invitee is expected to carry out or fulfil. What is unusual varies with the purpose for which the invitee enters the premises. *London Graving Dock Co. v. Horton*, [1951] A.C. 737.

UNVALUED POLICY. A marine policy is an unvalued policy if it does not specify the value of the subject-matter insured and, subject to the limit of the sum insured, leaves the value to be determined in accordance with the Act. *Marine Insurance Act*, S.C. 1993, c. 22, s. 30.

UP. See FIT-~; GET-~; GROSS-~; HOLD-~; LINE-~; LOCK-~; MARK-~; PAID ~; REDEEM ~, FORECLOSE DOWN; SUM ~; TOPPING ~; WINDING ~

UPC. *abbr.* Universal Product Code.

UPON. *prep.* Immediately, on the occasion of. Before the act done to which it relates or simultaneously with the act done or after the act is done according to the context.

UPPER. *n.* A drug which produces excitement and alertness. F.A. Jaffe, *A Guide to Pathological Evidence for Lawyers and Police Officers*, 4th ed. (Toronto: Carswell, 1999) at 246.

URBAN PLANNING. The guiding and shaping of development, growth, and change in urban centres with the aim of harmonizing as many aspects of the life of the inhabitants and visitors as possible.

URBAN RAIL TRANSIT SYSTEM. A street railway, tramway, light rail transit railway or similar undertaking the purpose of which is to transport the general public within an urban or inter-urban area. *Highways Development and Protection Act*, S.A. 2004, c. H-8.5, s. 1.

URBAN TRANSIT AUTHORITY. An entity owned or controlled by the federal government or a provincial, municipal or district government that provides commuter services. *Canada Transportation Act*, S.C. 1996, c. 10, s. 87.

URGENT. *adj.* Passage of time will threaten serious irreparable harm.

URGENT NEED OF PROTECTION. In respect of a member of the Convention refugee abroad, the country of asylum or the source country class, that their life, liberty or physical safety is under immediate threat and, if not protected, the person is likely to be (a) killed; (b) subjected to violence, torture, sexual assault or arbitrary imprisonment; or (c) returned to their country of nationality or of their former habitual residence. *Immigration and Refugee Protection Act*, S.C. 2001, c. 27, R.S.C. 1985, c. F-11, *Immigration and Refugee Protection Regulations*, SOR/2002-227, s. 138.

URINALYSIS. *n.* A prescribed procedure by which a person provides a urine sample, by the normal excretory process, for analysis. *Corrections and Conditional Release Act*, S.C. 1992, c. 20, s. 46.

USAGE. *n.* 1. "... [A] course of conduct which is recognized as being normal in various types of occupations and contractual relationships... ." *Gainers Ltd. v. United Packinghouse, Food & Allied Workers, Local 319* (1964), 47 W.W.R. 544 at 552, 64 C.L.L.C. 14,030 (Alta. T.D.), Riley J. 2. A practice which a government ordinarily follows, though it is not obligatory. Such a practice may become a convention. P.W. Hogg, *Constitutional Law of Canada*, 3d ed. (Toronto: Carswell, 1992) at 21. See CONVENTION.

USE. *v.* 1. "... [U]tilization or employment of, with some aim or purpose... ." *Andison Estate, Re* (1986), 44 Man. R. (2d) 135 at 137 (Q.B.), Kennedy J. 2. "... [C]onnotation of the actual carrying into action, operation or effect ..." *R. v. Chang* (1989), 50 C.C.C. (3d) 413 at 422 (B.C. C.A.), Carrothers J.A. 3. "... '[U]se' of property involves control or personal possession of the property by the insured and/or the insured putting the property to his own service... ." *Kenting Drilling Ltd. v. General Accident Assurance Co. of Canada* (1979), [1980] I.L.R. 1-1168 at 542, [1979] 5 W.W.R. 68, 26 A.R. 90, 102 D.L.R. (3d) 99 (T.D.), Moshansky J. 4. "... [T]he working, manipulation, operation, handling or employment of the vehicle, not just merely making use of it by riding in it... ." *Watts v. Centennial Insurance Co.* (1967), 62 W.W.R. 175 at 177, [1969] I.L.R. 1-220, 65 D.L.R. (2d) 529 (B.C. S.C.), Wilson C.J.S.C. 5. To "communicate" presupposes interactions, bilateral actions between the parties. The verb "to use" [in section 4 of the Official Languages Act] does not encompass such interaction. The right is unilateral: one has the right to address the House of Commons in the official language of his choice. *Knopf v. Canada (Speaker of the House of Commons)*, 2007 FCA 308. 6. [In the context of the Patent Act, R.S.C. 1985, c. P-4] "Use" or "exploiter", in their ordinary dictionary meaning, denote utilization with a view to production or advantage. *Monsanto Canada Inc. v. Schmeiser*, 2004 SCC 34, McLachlin C.J.

USE. *n.* 1. Habitual practice. 2. The employment of a thing to achieve a purpose. 3. The purpose for which land is intended or may be put. 4. Legal interpretation of meaning of the word is context-specific. See CESTUI QUE ~; COMMERCIAL ~; CONFORMING ~; DEED TO ~S; EXISTING ~; HIGHEST AND BEST ~; ILLICIT DRUG ~; PUBLIC ~; RESULT-ING ~; SHIFTING ~; SPRINGING ~; TIME SHARE ~ PLAN.

USE AND OCCUPATION. A person may claim for use and occupation of his land by a person who occupies it without a lease, leasing agreement or a set rent.

USEFUL ARTICLE. An article that has a utilitarian function and includes a model of any such article. *Industrial Design Act*, R.S.C. 1985, c. I-9, s. 2.

USER. *n.* 1. A person who uses a thing. 2. Enjoyment or use, not the person who uses.

USER AS OF RIGHT. The use has been uninterrupted, open, peaceful and without permission for the relevant period of time. *Kaminskas v. Storm*, 2009 ONCA 318.

USER FEE. A fee, charge or levy for a product, regulatory process, authorization, permit or license, facility, or for a service that is provided only by a regulating authority, that is fixed pursuant to the authority of an Act of Parliament and which results in a direct benefit or advantage to the person paying the fee. *User Fees Act*, S.C. 2004, c. 6, s. 2.

USQUE AD COELUM ET AD INFEROS. [L.] Up to the sky and down to the depths.

USQUE AD SOLUM. [L.] As far as the soil.

USUAL COVENANT. One of the covenants ordinarily inserted in a deed.

USUAL OR CUSTOMARY AUTHORITY. The authority which an agent in that particular business, trade, profession or place would customarily or normally possess unless the principal expressly said something to contradict it. G.H.L. Fridman, *The Law of Agency*, 6th ed. (London: Butterworths, 1990) at 55.

USUFRUCT. *n.* The right of use and enjoyment, for a certain time, of property owned by another as one's own, subject to the obligation of preserving its substance. *Civil Code*, S.Q. 1991, c. 64, a. 1120..

USUFRUCTUARY. *n.* The person who enjoys a usufruct.

USURY. *n.* "In ancient times the lending of money at interest was described as the practice of usury. Today, usury is generally thought of as lending money at an excessive rate of interest." *Pioneer Envelopes Ltd. v. British Columbia (Minister of Finance)* (1980), 18 C.P.C. 119 at 121, 21 B.C.L.R. 175 (S.C.), Bouck J.

UTC. *abbr.* Coordinated Universal Time.

U.T. FAC. L. REV. *abbr.* University of Toronto Faculty of Law Review.

UTILITARIAN FUNCTION. In respect of an article, means a function other than merely serving as a substrate or carrier for artistic or literary matter. *Industrial Design Act*, R.S.C. 1985, c. I-9, s. 2.

UTILITY. *n.* Of an invention, depends on whether it will be put into practice by a competent person, do what it assumes to do, and be practical and useful at

U

the time when the patent was granted for the purposes indicated by the patentee. See PUBLIC ~.

U.T.L.J. *abbr.* University of Toronto Law Journal.

U. TORONTO FACULTY L. REV. *abbr.* University of Toronto Faculty of Law Review.

U. TORONTO L.J. *abbr.* University of Toronto Law Journal.

UT SUPRA. [L.] As above.

UTTER. *v.* 1. Includes sell, pay, tender and put off. *Criminal Code*, R.S.C. 1985, c. C-46, s. 448. 2. Publish, deliver, put into circulation.

UTTERING COUNTERFEIT MONEY. Every one who, without lawful justification or excuse, the proof of which lies on him, (a) utters or offers to utter counterfeit money or uses counterfeit money as if it were genuine, or (b) exports, sends or takes counterfeit money out of Canada, is guilty of an indictable offence and liable to imprisonment for a term not exceeding fourteen years. *Criminal Code*, R.S.C. 1985, c. C-46, s. 452.

UTTERING FORGED DOCUMENT. Every one who, knowing that a document is forged, (a) uses, deals with or acts on it, or (b) causes or attempts to cause any person to use, deal with or act on it, as if the document were genuine. *Criminal Code*, R.S.C. 1985, c. C-46, s. 368.

UTTERING FORGED PASSPORT. While in or out of Canada, (a) forges a passport; or (b) knowing that a passport is forged (i) uses, deals with or acts upon it; or (ii) causes or attempts to cause any person to use, deal with, or act upon it, as if the passport were genuine. *Criminal Code*, R.S.C. 1985, c. C-46, s. 57(1).

UTTERING THREAT. Every one commits an offence who, in any manner, knowingly utters, conveys or causes any person to receive a threat (a) to cause death or bodily harm to any person; (b) to burn, destroy or damage real or personal property; or (c) to kill, poison or injure an animal or bird that is the property of any person. *Criminal Code*, R.S.C. 1985, c. C-46, s. 264.1.

U.W.O. L. REV. *abbr.* University of Western Ontario Law Review.

V

V. *abbr.* 1. Versus. 2. Volume. 3. Victoria.

VACANT. *adj.* 1. "... [A]pplies to the absence of inanimate objects in a premises ..." *Mohammed v. Canadian Northern Shield Insurance Co.* (1992), 10 C.C.L.I. (2d) 118 at 124, [1992] B.C.W.L.D. 1776 (S.C.), Lamperson J. 2. "[In a fire insurance policy applies to] ... inanimate objects ..." *Miller v. Portage la Prairie Mutual Insurance Co.*, [1936] 2 D.L.R. 787 at 791, [1936] 2 W.W.R. 104, 3 I.L.R. 377 (Sask. C.A.), the court per Gordon J.A.

VACANTIA BONA. Things found which have no apparent owner. See BONA VACANTIA.

VACANT POSSESSION. 1. "... [A] house free of household furniture and effects as well as animate occupancy." *Burke v. Campbell* (1978), 87 D.L.R. (3d) 427 at 432, 20 O.R. (2d) 300, [1979] I.L.R. 1-1148 (H.C.), Craig J. 2. Usual term of an agreement of purchase and sale of residential property. The vendor is required to give vacant possession to the purchaser upon closing.

VACATE. *v.* 1. To cancel; to make ineffective. 2. "[Used in Criminal Code, R.S.C. 1970, c. C-34] ... to indicate what has occurred is terminated but without impairing what has previously occurred." *Purves v. Canada (Attorney General)* (1990), 54 C.C.C. (3d) 355 at 364 (B.C. C.A.), the court per Legg J.A. 3. To leave, to move out, to empty.

VACATION. *n.* As Chief Justice Macdonald stated in Andler v. Duke (1931), 44 B.C.R. 201 (B.C. S.C.) at 202, "vacation" is when the Court of Appeal is not "in session", i.e., a division of the Court is not sitting. *Whitehorse (City) v. Darragh*, 2008 YKCA 19. See LONG ~.

VAGRANCY. *n.* Every one commits vagrancy who (a) supports himself in whole or in part by gaming or crime and has no lawful profession or calling by which to maintain himself; or (b) having at any time been convicted of an offence under section 151, 152 or 153, subsection 160(3) or 173(2) or section 271, 272 or 273 or of an offence under a provision referred to in paragraph (b) of the definition "serious personal injury offence" in section 687 of the Criminal Code, chapter C-34 of the Revised Statutes of Canada, 1970, as it read before January 4, 1983, is found loitering or wandering in or near a school ground, playground, public park or bathing area. *Criminal Code*, R.S.C. 1985, c. C-46, s. 179(1).

VAGUENESS. *n.* "... [A] law will be found unconstitutionally vague if it so lacks in precision as not to give sufficient guidance for legal debate. This statement of the doctrine best conforms to the dictates of the rule of law in the modern state, and it reflects the prevailing argumentative, adversarial framework for the administration of justice." *R. v. Pharmaceutical Society (Nova Scotia)* (1992), (*sub nom. R. v. Nova Scotia Pharmaceutical Society*) 43 C.P.R. (3d) 1 at 26, 15 C.R. (4th) 1, 93 D.L.R. (4th) 36, 74 C.C.C. (3d) 289, 10 C.R.R. (2d) 34, [1992] 2 S.C.R. 606, 139 N.R. 241, 114 N.S.R. (2d) 91, 313 A.P.R. 91, the court per Gonthier J.

VALID. *adj.* 1. Having force legally. 2. Issued in accordance with the applicable law and the articles of the issuer or validated. *Business Corporations acts.* 3. In respect of a licence, registration, or certificate of authority, not under suspension and not having been cancelled or revoked. See IN~.

VALIDATE. *v.* 1. To render in force for a prescribed period of time. Ontario statutes. 2. To render in force.

VALIDITY. See COLONIAL LAWS ~ ACT, 1865.

VALID SECURITY. A security is valid if it is issued in accordance with the applicable law described in subsection 44(1) and the constating provisions governing the issuer. *The Securities Transfer Act*, S.S. 2007, c. S-42.3, s. 2.

VALUABLE CONSIDERATION. 1. " ...There is a distinction between what is sufficient consideration as between two parties to a contract to permit enforcement of it, and valuable consideration required to oust the title of a person who has paid valuable consideration for a property but not recorded his deed. The $1.00 consideration paid might be determined to be sufficient in a dispute to require performance of the bargain between the purchaser and seller, but the issue here is whether, as between the purchaser and a third party, the purchaser is a purchaser for valuable consideration. He is not. *Glenelg v. Wile*, 2005 NSCA 4. 2. [M]ay consist either in some right, interest, profit, or benefit accruing to the one party, or some forbearance, detriment, loss, or responsibility, given, suffered, or undertaken by the other ..." *Currie v. Misa* (1875), L.R. 10 Ex. 153 at 162 (U.K.), the court

per Lusk J. See ADEQUATE ~; GOOD CONSIDERATION.

VALUATION. *n.* 1. "... [A]n expression of an opinion as to value." *Sanwa Bank California v. Quebec, North Shore & Labrador Railway* (1988), 48 D.L.R. (4th) 360 at 364, 69 Nfld. & P.E.I.R. 220, 211 A.P.R. 220 (Nfld. T.D.), Russell J. 2. The determination of the value of property for taxation purposes. See MARKET ~ STANDARD.

VALUE. *n.* 1. "... [I]n the case of Montreal Island Power Co. v. Laval des Rapides, [1936] 1 D.L.R. 621, [1935] S.C.R. 304. At pp. 621-2 D.L.R., p. 305 S.C.R. [Duff C.J.C.] quotes from a judgment of Lord MacLaren in Lord Advocate v. Earl of Home (1891), 28 Sc. L.R. 289 at p. 293: ' ... [W]hen it occurs in a contract ... means exchangeable value—the price which the subject will bring when exposed to the test of competition.' " Continuing, Duff C.J.C. says: 'When used for the purpose of defining the valuation of property for taxation purposes, the Courts have, in this country, and, generally speaking, on this continent, accepted this view of the term "value".' *Withycombe Estate, Re,* [1945] 2 D.L.R. 274 at 286, (*sub nom. A.G. of Alta. v. Royal Trust Co.*) [1945] S.C.R. 267, Hudson J. (Taschereau J. concurring). 2. In real estate law generally means the fair market value of the land, which is based on what a seller and buyer, "each knowledgeable and willing," would pay for it on the open market. . . . . .Market value generally is the exchange value of land, rather than its use value to the lessee. *Musqueam Indian Band v. Glass,* 2000 CarswellNat 2405, 2000 SCC 52, [2000] 11 W.W.R. 407, 36 R.P.R. (3d) 1, 192 D.L.R. (4th) 385, 82 B.C.L.R. (3d) 199, 261 N.R. 296, 186 F.T.R. 248 (note), [2000] 2 S.C.R. 633, [2001] 1 C.N.L.R. 208, Gonthier J. (Major, Binnie and LeBel JJ. concurring). 3. Any consideration sufficient to support a simple contract. *Personal Property Security acts.* 4. Valuable consideration. *Bills of Exchange Act,* R.S.C. 1985, c. B-4, s. 2. See ACTUAL ~; ADDED-~ CLAIM; AMORTIZED ~; ASSESSED ~; BOOK ~; CANADIAN ~S; CASH SURRENDER ~; CASH ~; COMMUTED ~; CURRENT LAND ~; FACE ~; FAIR ~; HERITAGE ~; HOLDER FOR ~; INTRINSIC ~; MARKET ~; NET ~; PAR ~; PROBATIVE ~; PURCHASER FOR ~ WITHOUT NOTICE; REVERSIONARY ~.

VALUED POLICY. 1. The policy of insurance is based on an agreement as to the value of the item insured. In the event of total loss, the insured can recover the total value and in the event of partial loss, a proportion of the agreed value. 2. A marine policy is a valued policy if it specifies the agreed value of the subject-matter insured. *Marine Insurance Act,* S.C. 1993, c. 22, s. 30.

VALUE RECEIVED. Method of calculating value of constructive trust. The value of the services which the claimant has received. For a monetary award, the "value received" approach is appropriate; the value conferred on the property is irrelevant. *Peter v. Beblow,* 1993 CarswellBC 44, 77 B.C.L.R. (2d) 1, [1993] 3 W.W.R. 337, 44 R.F.L. (3d) 329, 48 E.T.R.

1, 150 N.R. 1, 23 B.C.A.C. 81, 39 W.A.C. 81, 101 D.L.R. (4th) 621, [1993] 1 S.C.R. 980, [1993] R.D.F. 369, McLachlin J.

VALUE SURVIVED. Method of calculating value of constructive trust. Where the claim is for an interest in the property one must of necessity, it seems to me, determine what portion of the value of the property claimed is attributable to the claimant's services. The value of that trust is to be determined on the basis of the actual value of the matrimonial property. It reflects the court's best estimate of what is fair having regard to the contribution which the claimant's services have made to the value surviving, bearing in mind the practical difficulty of calculating with mathematical precision the value of particular contributions to the family property. How is the contribution to the property to be determined? One starts, of necessity, by defining the property. One goes on to determine what portion of that property is attributable to the claimant's efforts. *Peter v. Beblow,* 1993 CarswellBC 44, 77 B.C.L.R. (2d) 1, [1993] 3 W.W.R. 337, 44 R.F.L. (3d) 329, 48 E.T.R. 1, 150 N.R. 1, 23 B.C.A.C. 81, 39 W.A.C. 81, 101 D.L.R. (4th) 621, [1993] 1 S.C.R. 980, [1993] R.D.F. 369, McLachlin J.

VANDALISM. *n.* "... There must be a wrongful intention accompanying the destruction of property to warrant the term 'vandalism'... ." *Reliable Distributors Ltd. v. Royal Insurance Co. of Canada* (1986), 5 B.C.L.R. (2d) 367 at 370, [1986] 6 W.W.R. 1, 18 C.C.L.I. 267, 30 D.L.R. (4th) 426, [1987] I.L.R. 1-2123 (C.A.), Seaton J.A.

VAN DER PEET TEST. 1. Refers to R. v. Van der Peet, 1996 CanLII 216, [1996] 2 S.C.R. 507. The core question in Van der Peet was: "How should the aboriginal rights recognized and affirmed by s. 35(1) of the Constitution Act, 1982 be defined?" (para. 15, per Lamer C.J.). Lamer C.J. wrote for the majority, at para. 31: [W]hat s. 35(1) does is provide the constitutional framework through which the fact that aboriginals lived on the land in distinctive societies, with their own practices, traditions and cultures, is acknowledged and reconciled with the sovereignty of the Crown. The substantive rights which fall within the provision must be defined in light of this purpose; the aboriginal rights recognized and affirmed by s. 35(1) must be directed towards the reconciliation of the pre-existence of aboriginal societies with the sovereignty of the Crown. *R. v. Powley,* [2003] 2 S.C.R. 207, 2003 SCC 43. 2. In determining whether there is an aboriginal right using the Van der Peet test, the first step is to characterize the right claimed. The right must be characterized in context and with sufficient specificity to allow the court "to identify a practice that helps to define the way of life or distinctiveness of the particular aboriginal community": R. v. Sappier, R. v. Gray, 2006 SCC 54 (CanLII), [2006] 2 S.C.R. 686 [Sappier] at paras. 22, 24. The right claimed should not be framed in excessively general terms or artificially broadened or narrowed or otherwise distorted to fit the desired result: Mitchell v. M.N.R., 2001 SCC 33 (CanLII), [2001] 1 S.C.R. 911 [Mitchell] at paras. 15, 20; Pamajewon at para. 27; Delgamuukw v. British Columbia, 1997 CanLII 302,

[1997] 3 S.C.R. 1010 [Delgamuukw] at para. 170. Three factors shape the characterization of the right claimed: (i) the nature of the action that is claimed to have been carried out pursuant to an aboriginal right; (ii) the nature of the government regulation, statute or action being impugned; and (iii) the practice, custom or tradition relied upon to establish the right: Van der Peet at para 53. Once the claimed right is characterized, it is for the claimant to establish that an aboriginal right exists. The following elements must be proved: (i) the existence of an aboriginal practice, custom or tradition that supports the right; (ii) that this practice, custom or tradition was integral to the distinctive culture of the claimant group's pre-contact society; and (iii) reasonable continuity between the pre-contact practice, custom or tradition and the contemporary claim: Van der Peet at paras. 53-59, 64-65; Mitchell at para. 12. *Mississaugas of Scugog Island First Nation v. National Automobile, Aerospace, Transportation and General Workers Union of Canada*, 2007 ONCA 814.

VARIANCE. *n.* 1. Permission to contravene a by-law to permit development of certain land which does not meet criteria prescribed in the by-law. 2. A document without precedential value issued, for an individual circumstance on a single occasion, by a safety officer or safety manager allowing (a) a deviation from the application of an enactment, or (b) a use, other than the standard use, of a regulated product if the proposed use is not specifically prohibited. *Safety Standards Act*, S.B.C. 2003, c. 39, s. 1. See MINOR ~.

VARIANTS. *n.* Designs applied to the same article or set and not differing substantially from one another. *Industrial Design Act*, R.S.C. 1985, c. I-9, s. 2.

VARIATION. *n.* An express or implied agreement by which parties agree on a new contract or a new contract term which is mutually convenient and beneficial.

VARIATION OF TRUST. The power of the court to change the terms of a trust or the powers of the trustees on behalf of a person entitled or who may become entitled to an interest under the trust. See, for example, *Variation of Trusts Act*, R.S.O. 1990, c. V.1.

VARIATION ORDER. An order making changes to a custody or support order made under the Divorce Act.

VARIATION PROCEEDING. A proceeding in a court in which either or both former spouses seek a variation order. *Divorce Act*, R.S.C. 1985 (2d Supp.), c. 3, s. 2.

VARIOUS. *adj.* 1. Different, diverse. 2. Separate, several.

VARY. *v.* To change; to substitute; to alter.

VAUTIER. See RULE IN SAUNDERS V. ~.

V.C. *abbr.* Vice-chancellor.

VECTOR. *n.* 1. An insect or animal capable of transmitting a communicable disease. *Quarantine Act*, S.C. 2005, c. 20, s. 2. 2. An animal that has the potential to transmit a disease, directly or indirectly, from one animal or its excreta to another animal.

VEHICLE. *n.* 1. "... [I]n its original sense conveys the meaning of a structure on wheels for carrying persons or goods. We have generally distinguished carriage from haulage, and mechanical units whose chief function is to haul other units, to do other kinds of work than carrying, are not usually looked upon as vehicles. But that meaning has ... been weakened by the multiplied forms in which wheeled bodies have appeared with the common features of self-propulsion by motor ..." *Bennett & White (Calgary) Ltd. v. Sugar City (Municipality)*, [1950] S.C.R. 450 at 463, [1950] C.T.C. 410, [1950] 3 D.L.R. 81, Rand J. (Taschereau, Estey and Locke JJ. concurring). 2. Any conveyance that may be used for transportation by sea, land or air. See AIR CUSHION~; ARTICULATED ~; COMMERCIAL ~; HYBRID ELECTRIC ~; HYBRID ~; MILITARY ~; MOTOR ~; ON-ROAD ~; OUTSIZED ~; RANDOM ~ STOP.

VEHICLE INSPECTION SIGN. A traffic control device that is designed to indicate to the driver of a commercial vehicle that the driver of the vehicle is required to report to a vehicle inspection station. *Traffic Safety Act*, R.S.A. 2000, c. T-6, s. 130.

VENDEE. *n.* The person to whom one sells something.

VENDING. *n.* "... [S]elling ..." *Domco Industries Ltd. v. Mannington Mills Inc.* (1990), 29 C.P.R. (3d) 481 at 490, 107 N.R. 198 (Fed. C.A.), the court per Iacobucci C.J.

VENDITIONI EXPONAS. See WRIT OF ~.

VENDOR. *n.* A person who sells something.

VENDOR'S LIEN. 1. When a vendor sells property on credit, the vendor may be entitled to a lien on it to secure an obligation from the purchaser. B.J. Reiter, B.N. McLellan & P.M. Perell, *Real Estate Law*, 4th ed. (Toronto: Emond Montgomery, 1992) at 781. 2. "... [C]an only arise on the sale of land, or of an equitable interest in land, and the lien may exist in favour of an equitable owner... ." *Horn v. Sanford*, [1929] 3 D.L.R. 130 at 133, [1929] 2 W.W.R. 33, 23 Sask. L.R. 509 (C.A.), the court per Haultain C.J.S.

VENDOR TAKE-BACK MORTGAGE. A vendor lends the purchaser part of the purchase price in exchange for a mortgage on the property.

VENEREAL DISEASE. Includes syphilis, gonorrhea, chancroid, granuloma inguinale and lymphogranuloma venereum.

VENGEANCE. *n.* An act of harm, motivated by emotion and anger, as a reprisal for harm inflicted by that person.

VENTILATION. *n.* 1. The removal of gas, vapour, dust, mist, fumes or smoke from the air by mechanical means. 2. The forced movement of fresh air into and foul air out of a structure.

VENTURE. *n.* 1. Commercial speculation attended with risk. 2. A business. See JOINT ~.

VENUE. *n.* 1. "... [T]he place where the charges are laid and the place where the trial takes place: ..." *R. v. Gagne* (1990), 59 C.C.C. (3d) 282 at 286, [1990] R.J.Q. 2165 (C.A.), Bernier J.A. 2. "... [T]he place

V

where the crime is charged to have been committed... ." *Smitheman, Ex parte* (1904), 35 S.C.R. 490 at 493, 9 C.C.C. 17, the court per Killam J. 3. "... [O]riginally indicated the locality of the crime only, has come to indicate with equal propriety, and is more often used to signify, the locality of the trial: as when we speak of the change of venue, which cannot possibly mean a change of the locality of the crime." *R. v. Malott* (1886), 1 B.C.R. (Pt. II) 212 at 215 (C.A.), Begbie C.J.A.

VERDICT. *n.* 1. "... [T]he finding of a jury ..." *R. v. Murray* (1912), 8 D.L.R. 208 at 210, 27 O.L.R. 382, 4 O.W.N. 368, 23 O.W.R. 492, 20 C.C.C. 197 (C.A.), Maclaren J.A. (Garrow, Meredith and Magee JJ.A. and Lennox J. concurring). 2. Includes the finding of a jury and the decision of a judge in an action. 3. In the case of an action being tried by a judge without a jury includes judgment. 4. (a) The findings of fact made by a jury, (b) the recommendations made by a jury, and (c) any comments in respect of an inquest made by the coroner who presided over the inquest. *Coroners Act*, S.B.C. 2007, c. 15, s. 1. See DIRECTED ~; GENERAL ~; PERVERSE ~; UNREASONABLE ~.

VERDICT OF ACQUITTAL. Includes a verdict of not criminally responsible on account of mental disorder.

VERDICT OF NOT CRIMINALLY RESPONSIBLE ON ACCOUNT OF MENTAL DISORDER. A verdict that the accused committed the act or made the omission that formed the basis of the offence with which the accused is charged but is not criminally responsible on account of mental disorder. *Criminal Code*, R.S.C. 1985, c. C-46, s. 672.1.

VERIFICATION. See LETTERS OF ~.

VERIFY. *v.* "To verify" may well mean something more than "to give notice" i.e., to adduce proof that the fact is true. However, I do not think to verify something to another could mean anything less than giving notice. *Dallas Park Shopping Centre Ltd. v. Buy-Low Foods Ltd.*, 2002 BCCA 585, 6 B.C.L.R. (4th) 302.

VERSION. See ELECTRONIC ~.

VERSUS. *prep.* [L.] Against.

VERTICAL AMALGAMATION. An amalgamation of a holding corporation and one or more of its subsidiary corporations.

VESSEL. *n.* 1. A boat, ship or craft designed, used or capable of being used solely or partly for navigation in, on, through or immediately above water, without regard to method or lack of propulsion, and includes such a vessel that is under construction. It does not include a floating object of a prescribed class. *Canada Shipping Act, 2001*, S.C. 2001, c. 26, s. 2. 2. Includes a machine designed to derive support in the atmosphere primarily from reactions against the earth's surface of air expelled from the machine. *Criminal Code*, R.S.C. 1985, c. C-46, s. 214. See CANADIAN ~; CROWN ~; DANGEROUS OPERATION OF ~S; FISHING ~; FOREIGN ~; GOVERNMENT ~; SAFETY-CONVENTION ~.

VEST. *v.* 1. With respect to a right or estate, to rest in some person. 2. Of a pension, to obtain or become entitled to an unalterable right to either transfer or withdraw that lump sum to another pension plan or R.R.S.P. or to receive, in the future, a deferred life annuity. A. Bissett-Johnson & W.M. Holland, eds., *Matrimonial Property Law in Canada* (Toronto: Carswell, 1980) at V-91. 3. In the context of the contract as a whole, when the parties in [a schedule to the employment contract] used the phrase "will vest in" they simply meant "will be paid to". *Urton v. SRI Homes Inc.*, 2007 BCCA 372.

VESTED. *adj.* 1. Fixed, accrued, settled, not capable of being defeated by a condition precedent. 2. "... [A] future estate or interest is vested when there is a person who has an immediate right to that interest upon the cessation of the present or previous interest... ." *Re Legh's Resettlement Trusts; Pub. Trustee v. Legh*, [1938] Ch. 39 at 52 (U.K. C.A.), MacKinnon L.J.

VESTED IN INTEREST. With respect to an existing fixed right of future enjoyment.

VESTED IN POSSESSION. With respect to a right of present enjoyment which actually exists.

VESTED PENSION. An individual's pension is vested when the individual has rights to all the benefits purchased by the individual and the employer even if the person is no longer employed by the employer.

VESTED REMAINDER. An expectant interest which is limited or transmitted to the one who is able to receive it.

VESTED RIGHT. 1. "... [O]ne which exists and produces effects. That does not include a right which could have been exercised but was not, and which is no longer available under the law... ." *Quebec (Expropriation Tribunal) v. Quebec (Attorney General)* (1986), 35 L.C.R. 1 at 8, [1986] 1 S.C.R. 732, 66 N.R. 380, the court per Chouinard J. 2. A right which is not contingent or may not be defeated by a condition precedent.

VESTING. *adj.* "... [I]n relation to the rule against perpetuities has a special meaning as three conditions must be satisfied before an interest can be said to be vested: (1) the beneficiaries must be ascertained; (2) the interests they take must be determined; and (3) any conditions attached to the interests must be satisfied... ." *Ogilvy, Re*, [1966] 2 O.R. 755 at 763, 58 D.L.R. (2d) 385 (H.C.), Lieff J.

VESTING ORDER. A court order to give a person an interest in real or personal property which the court has authority to dispose of, encumber or convey.

VETERANS AFFAIRS. See DEPARTMENT OF ~.

VETERANS REVIEW AND APPEAL BOARD. The Board has full and exclusive jurisdiction to hear, determine and deal with all applications for review that may be made to the Board under the Pension Act or the Canadian Forces Members and Veterans Re-establishment and Compensation Act, and all matters related to those applications. The Board has full and exclusive jurisdiction to hear, determine and deal with all appeals that may be made to the Board under section 25 or under the War Veterans Allowance Act or any other Act of Parliament, and all matters related to those appeals. A person who has been refused an award under the Pension Act, or a disability award, a death benefit, a clothing allowance or a detention benefit under Part 3 of the Canadian Forces Members and Veterans Re-establishment and Compensation Act, and who has exhausted all procedures for review and appeal under this Act may apply to the Board for a compassionate award. *Veterans Review and Appeal Board Act*, S.C. 1995, c. 18, ss. 4, 18, 26 and 34.

VETERINARY MEDICINE. The practice of veterinary medicine includes the practice of dentistry, obstetrics including ova and embryo transfer, and surgery, in relation to an animal other than a human being; *Veterinarians Act*, R.S.O. 1990, c. V.3, s. 1.

VETO. *n.* 1. A prohibition; the right to forbid. 2. "... '[D]isallowance' ... [refers] to the provisions of secs. 55 and 56 [of the Constitution Act 1867] as applied to a province." *Reference re Initiative & Referendum Act (Manitoba)* (1916), 32 D.L.R. 148 at 170, 1 W.W.R. 1012, 27 Man. R. 1, (C.A.), Perdue J.A.

VETROVEC WARNING. The term is derived from the case of: R. v. Vetrovec, [1982] 1 S.C.R. 811]. The central purpose of a Vetrovec warning is to alert the jury to the danger of relying on the unsupported evidence of unsavoury witnesses and to explain the reasons for special scrutiny of their testimony. In appropriate cases, the trial judge should also draw the attention of the jurors to evidence capable of confirming or supporting the material parts of the otherwise untrustworthy evidence. The crafting of a caution appropriate to the circumstances of the case is best left to the judge who has conducted the trial. No particular set of words is mandatory. In evaluating its adequacy, appellate courts will focus on the content of the instruction and not on its form. Intervention on appeal will not be warranted unless a cautionary instruction should have been given but was not, or the cautionary instruction that was given failed to serve its intended purpose. The proposed framework is composed of four main foundation elements: (1) drawing the attention of the jury to the testimonial evidence requiring special scrutiny; (2) explaining why this evidence is subject to special scrutiny; (3) cautioning the jury that it is dangerous to convict on unconfirmed evidence of this sort, though the jury is entitled to do so if satisfied that the evidence is true; and (4) that the jury, in determining the veracity of the suspect evidence, should look for evidence from another source tending to show that the untrustworthy witness is telling the truth as to the guilt of the accused. *R. v. Khela*, 2009 SCC 4.

VEXATIOUS. *adj.* Annoying, distressing; multiplicitous; the bringing of one or more actions to determine an issue which has already been determined; the bringing of actions which cannot succeed or lead to any possible positive outcome. See FRIVOLOUS AND ~.

VEXATIOUS ACTION. 1. "An action may be vexatious if it is obvious that it cannot succeed: ... or if no reasonable person can possibly expect to obtain relief in it: ... or if the Court has no power to grant the relief sought: ... or if the applicant has no status to pursue the remedy, or no proper authority to do so: ... or if the same relief might be sought in a subsisting action: ... or if the same purpose might have been effected in a previous action: ... In some cases the Courts have considered the lack of bona fides in classifying an action as vexatious, as where the plaintiff had no cause of action at all: ... A legal proceeding may be vexatious even though there were reasonable grounds for its institution if, for instance, the plaintiff is asking for relief in a way which necessarily involves injustice." *Foy v. Foy (No. 2)* (1979), 12 C.P.C. 188 at 197, 26 O.R. (2d) 220, 102 D.L.R. (3d) 342 (C.A.), Howland C.J.O. (Brooke J.A. concurring). 2. Vexatious was said to involve overtones of an irresponsible pursuit of litigation by someone who either knows he has no proper cause of action or is mentally incapable of forming a rational opinion on the topic. *Whitehead v. Taber*, 1983 CarswellAlta 379, 46 A.R. 14 (Q.B.), Crossley J.

VEXATIOUS APPEAL. A vexatious appeal is one that is brought for an improper purpose such as to harass, annoy or embarrass a party and not for the legitimate purpose of seeking the vindication of legal rights. *Walsh v. Johnson*, 2010 NLCA 6.

VEXATIOUS PROCEEDING. A proceeding in which the party bringing it wishes only to embarrass or annoy the other party.

VIABLE. *adj.* Workable; sustainable.

VIATICAL SETTLEMENT. The sale of a life insurance policy to a third party. The policy owner receives payment and the purchaser assumes responsibility for premium payment and acquires the right to collect on the policy on maturity.

VICARIOUS LIABILITY. 1. Liability imposed on one person for the acts of another based on the relationship between the two persons. Liability imposed on an employer for the acts of the employees. 2. In determining whether an employer is vicariously liable for an employee's unauthorized, intentional wrong in cases where precedent is inconclusive, courts should be guided by the following principles: (1) They should openly confront the question of whether liability should lie against the employer, rather than obscuring the decision beneath semantic discussions of "scope of employment" and "mode of conduct." (2) The fundamental question is whether the wrongful act is sufficiently related to conduct authorized by the employer to justify the imposition of vicarious liability. Vicarious liability is generally appropriate where there is a significant connection between the creation or enhancement of a risk and the wrong that accrues therefrom, even if unrelated to the employer's desires. Where this is so, vicarious liability will serve the policy considerations of provision of an adequate and just remedy and deterrence. Incidental connections to the employment enterprise, like time and place (without more), will not suffice. Once engaged in a particular business, it is fair that an employer be made to pay the generally foreseeable costs of that business. In contrast, to impose liability

V

for costs unrelated to the risk would effectively make the employer an involuntary insurer. (3) In determining the sufficiency of the connection between the employer's creation or enhancement of the risk and the wrong complained of, subsidiary factors may be considered. These may vary with the nature of the case. When related to intentional torts, the relevant factors may include, but are not limited to, the following: (a) the opportunity that the enterprise afforded the employee to abuse his or her power; (b) the extent to which the wrongful act may have furthered the employer's aims (and hence be more likely to have been committed by the employee); (c) the extent to which the wrongful act was related to friction, confrontation or intimacy inherent in the employer's enterprise; (d) the extent of power conferred on the employee in relation to the victim; (e) the vulnerability of potential victims to wrongful exercise of the employee's power. *B. (P.A.) v. Curry*, [1999] 2 S.C.R. 534, McLachlin J. 3. "In the criminal law, a natural person is responsible only for those crimes in which he is the primary actor either actually or by express or implied authorization. There is no vicarious liability in the pure sense in the case of the natural person. That is to say that the doctrine of respondeat superior is unknown in the criminal law where the defendant is an individual... . where the defendant is corporate the common law has become pragmatic, as we have seen, and a modified and limited 'vicarious liability' through the identification doctrine has emerged... ." *R. v. McNamara (No. 1)*, *(sub nom. R. v. Canadian Dredge & Dock Co.)* [1985] 1 S.C.R. 662 at 692, 45 C.R. (3d) 289, 9 O.A.C. 321, 19 C.C.C. (3d) 1, 19 D.L.R. (4th) 314, 59 N.R. 241, the court per Estey J.

VICARIOUS RESPONSIBILITY. The automatic responsibility of one person for another's wrongdoing through prior relationship only, irrespective of the first person's fault or deed. It is clear common law doctrine in the law of torts that a master can be vicariously liable for a tort committed by a "servant" who acts in the course and scope of employment. D. Stuart, *Canadian Criminal Law: A Treatise*, 2d ed. (Toronto: Carswell, 1987) at 522.

VICE. See INHERENT ~.

VICE CHANCELLOR. *n.* The deputy chief judge of a court of chancery.

VICE VERSA. Conversely.

VICINAGE. *n.* Neighbourhood; places next to one another.

VICTIM. *n.* 1. A person to whom harm was done or who suffered physical or emotional damage as a result of the commission of an offence, and where the person is dead, ill or otherwise incapacitated, the person's spouse, an individual who is cohabiting, or was cohabiting at the time of the person's death, with the person in a conjugal relationship, having so cohabited for a period of at least one year, any relative or dependant of the person, or anyone who has in law or fact custody or is responsible for the care or support of the person. Federal statutes. 2. A person who, as a result of the commission of a crime by another, suffers emotional or physical harm, loss of or damage to property or economic harm and, if the commission

of the crime results in the death of the person, includes, a child or parent of the person, and a dependant, spouse of the person, but does not include a child, parent, dependant, spouse who is charged with or has been convicted of committing the crime. See COMPENSATION OF ~S OF CRIME.

VICTIM IMPACT STATEMENT. In determining sentence or possible discharge of an offender under the Criminal Code, the court shall consider a statement of a victim of the offence describing the harm done to, or loss suffered by, the victim arising from the commission of the offence. *Criminal Code*, R.S.C. 1985, c. C-46, s. 722.

VICTORIA DAY. The first Monday immediately preceding May 25 is a legal holiday and is kept and observed as such throughout Canada under the name of "Victoria Day" in honour of Queen Victoria.

VIDE. *v.* [L.] See.

VIDE ANTE. [L.] See an earlier passage in the text.

VIDE INFRA. [L.] See a later passage in the text.

VIDELICET. *adv.* [L.] Namely; that is to say.

VIDEO DEPOSITION. A videorecording made outside of the courtroom in the presence of counsel and the defendant when children are unavailable to give evidence at trial.

VIDEO GAME. An object or device that stores recorded data or instructions, receives data or instructions generated by a person who uses it, and by processing the data or instructions, creates an interactive game capable of being played, viewed or experienced on or through a computer, gaming system, console or other technology.

VIDEO LOTTERY TERMINAL. The video lottery terminal has a video monitor built into the machine. It is operated by touching the video monitor and it can be asked to play a number of different games, one of which is usually a game like the traditional game of the pull-arm slot machine where three spinning wheels come to a stop and a win or a loss depends on the representations on the three wheels and on their alignment. *Great Canadian Casino Co. v. Surrey (City)*, 1999 CarswellBC 2420, 130 B.C.A.C. 189, 211 W.A.C. 189, 7 M.P.L.R. (3d) 33, 71 B.C.L.R. (3d) 199, [2000] 3 W.W.R. 681.

VIDEO TAPE. See CANADIAN ~.

VIDE POST. [L.] See a later passage in the text.

VIDE SUPRA. [L.] See an earlier passage in the text.

VI ET ARMIS. [L.] By force and arms.

VIEW. *n.* 1. A jury's inspection of any controversial thing, place where a crime was committed or person which a judge may order in the interest of justice at any time between when the jury is sworn and when they give their verdict. 2. A visit to a site relevant to the issue at hand by a judge or the hearing panel of an administrative tribunal. See PLAIN ~ DOCTRINE.

VIGILANT. See EQUITY AIDS THE ~ AND NOT THE INDOLENT.

VIMY RIDGE DAY. April 9, commemorates World War I battle.

VIN. *abbr.* Vehicle Identification Number.

VINDICTIVE DAMAGES. Damages based on punishing the defendant, beyond compensating the plaintiff.

VINTNERS QUALITY ALLIANCE WINE. (VQA wine). Wine, (a) that is produced in Ontario from grapes that have been grown in Ontario or from grape juice or grape must produced from such grapes, and (b) that meets the standards of the wine authority. *Vintners Quality Alliance Act, 1999*, S.O. 1999, c. 3, s. 2.

VIOLENCE. *n.* 1. "... [C]onnotes actual or threatened physical interference with the activities of others." *R. v. Keegstra* (1990), 1 C.R. (4th) 129 at 236, 77 Alta. L.R. (2d) 193, [1991] 2 W.W.R. 1, 61 C.C.C. (3d) 1, 117 N.R. 1, 114 A.R. 81, 3 C.R.R. (2d) 193, [1990] 3 S.C.R. 697, McLachlin J. (dissenting) (Sopinka J. concurring). 2. [T]he meaning of "violence" in this definition [of serious personal injury offence in section 752 of the Criminal Code] must be informed by the entirety of the definition of a serious personal injury offence. A serious personal injury offence is defined, in part, either as an offence involving the use or attempted use of violence against another person, or "conduct endangering or likely to endanger the life or safety of another person or inflicting or likely to inflict severe psychological damage upon another person." Taken together, and especially taking into account the far-reaching meaning of the word "safety," these two clauses point to the legislature's intention to cover a very expansive range of dangerous behaviour with the term "serious personal injury offence." A finding that violence was used remains a matter of factual determination for the trial judge. Whether the criminal conduct amounted to the use or attempted use of violence is a matter relating to the circumstances under which the crime was committed. This is not tantamount to an objective assessment of the seriousness of the violence; rather it is a question of determining whether the evidence proves that violence was actually used. *R. v. Lebar*, 2010 ONCA 220. See DOMESTIC ~; FAMILY ~.

VIOLENT OFFENCE. Definitions for the term "violent offence" may be divided into two categories: those force-based definitions that identify violence where force is exerted, and those harm-based definitions that identify violence where harm is suffered. Below, I first explain why a harm-based definition of "violent offence" for purposes of the YCJA [Youth Criminal Justice Act] is to be preferred. Then, examining what the scope of this harm-based definition should be, I conclude that a "violent offence" is an offence in the commission of which a young person causes, attempts to cause or threatens to cause bodily harm. Accordingly, for the three reasons discussed above, I am of the view that the definition of "violent offence" should not be extended to capture those offences where bodily harm is merely reasonably foreseeable. Although I do not favour extending the definition of "violent offence" to those offences where bodily harm is merely reasonably foreseeable, in gen-

eral, I still support extending this definition beyond those offences in which bodily harm is caused or attempted, in order to make the definition of "violent offence" something more than simply a replica of the definition of "serious violent offence" with the word "serious" omitted. Specifically, as indicated above, I support extending the definition to capture those offences in which bodily harm is threatened. This would make the definition of "violent offence" an offence in the commission of which a young person causes, attempts to cause or threatens to cause bodily harm. I am of the view that, for purposes of s. 39(1)(a) of the YCJA, the term "violent offence" must be defined as an offence in the commission of which a young person causes, attempts to cause or threatens to cause bodily harm. *R. v. C.D.*; *R. v. C.D.K.*, 2005 SCC 78, [2005] 3 S.C.R. 668, Bastarache J. for the majority. See SERIOUS ~.

VIRTUAL LAW FIRM. A firm which practices law using electronic media and works without a physical office. Legal reference material, client files, practice management tools, and conference "rooms" are electronically based.

VIRTUAL LEGAL ASSISTANT. Refers to a legal assistant who works online rather than in a physical office.

VIRTUE TESTING. See RANDOM ~.

VIRUS. *n.* 1. A subcellular parasite dependent on its cellular host to provide material for production of more viruses. 2. A computer program which attacks a host computer.

VISA. *n.* A document issued by one country which permits a resident of another to visit the first country.

VISIBLE MINORITIES. See MEMBERS OF ~.

VISITATORIAL POWERS. An incident of an eleemosynary corporation. Some educational institutions are eleemosynary corporations. The visitor has general jurisdiction over all matters relating to the statute establishing the corporation and the internal affairs of the corporation.

VISITOR. *n.* 1. (i) An entrant as of right; (ii) a person who is lawfully present on premises by virtue of an express or implied term of a contract; (iii) any other person whose presence on premises is lawful; or (iv) a person whose presence on premises becomes unlawful after his entry on those premises and who is taking reasonable steps to leave those premises. *Occupiers' Liability Act*, R.S.A. 2000, c. O-4, s. 1. 2. An inspector for an eleemosynary, ecclesiastical or other corporation or institution such as a university. Has general jurisdiction over all matters relating to the statute establishing the corporation and the internal affairs of an eleemosynary corporation. Under the *Religious Corporations Act*, R.S.Q., c.-71, s. 9, when the letters patent of a religious corporation provide for a visitor, he shall exercise the powers conferred upon any general or special meeting of the members by the Companies Act. A visitor may, as such, visit the corporation and take cognizance of everything relating to the administration and management of its affairs; he may, subject to the by-laws of the corporation but without prejudice to the rights of third

V

parties, compel it to do whatever he considers useful or necessary for the management, administration and improvement of its works and to cease doing whatever he considers inappropriate or unnecessary for such purposes. 3. "The unique position of a Judge is reflected by s. 7 of the Legal Profession Act [R.S.S. 1987, c. L-10] which designates Judges as visitors of the Society. The title is a hollow and anachronistic one: there is no role or function assigned to a visitor. Nor does a visitor hold an office, or derive any rights from or owe any responsibilities to the Law Society. Whatever it may be, a visitor is not a barrister or solicitor." *Maurice v. Priel* (1989), 36 Admin. L.R. 169 at 178, [1989] 3 W.W.R. 673, 96 N.R. 178, [1989] 1 S.C.R. 1023, 58 D.L.R. (4th) 736, 77 Sask. R. 22, Cory J. (Lamer, Wilson, L'Heureux-Dubé, Sopinka and Gonthier JJ. concurring).

VIS MAJOR. The operation of natural forces and the malicious acts of strangers. J.G. Fleming, *The Law of Torts*, 8th ed. (Sydney: Law Book, 1992) at 345. See ACT OF GOD.

VISUAL SURVEILLANCE. See DIRECT ~.

VITAL STATISTICS. The registration of births, deaths and marriages. See DE-IDENTIFIED ~ INFORMATION.

VITIATE. *v.* To render void.

VIVA VOCE. [L.] When describing the examination of witnesses, means orally.

VIZ. *abbr.* Videlicet.

VLA. *abbr.* Virtual legal assisant.

VLF. *abbr.* Virtual law firm.

VLT. *abbr.* Video lottery terminal.

VOCATIONAL ASSISTANCE. Includes employability assessments, career counselling, training, job-search assistance and job-finding assistance, whose object is to help a person to find appropriate employment. *Canadian Forces Members and Veterans Re-establishment and Compensation Act,* S.C. 2005, c. 21, s. 2.

VOCATIONAL REHABILITATION. 1. Any process of restoration, training and employment placement, including related services whose object is to enable a person to pursue regularly a gainful occupation. 2. Includes any process designed to identify and achieve an appropriate occupational goal for a person with a physical or a mental health problem, given their state of health and the extent of their education, skills and experience. *Canadian Forces Members and Veterans Re-establishment and Compensation Act,* S.C. 2005, c. 21, s. 2.

VOICE OVER INTERNET PROTOCOL (VOIP) SERVICE. A Voice over Internet Protocol (VoIP) service that transfers emergency calls to a public safety answering point. *Emergency 911 Act,* S.P.E.I. 1999, c. 23, s. 1.

VOID. *adj.* "... [L]acking validity and so without legal force." *British Columbia (Minister of Finance) v. Woodward Estate,* [1971] D.T.C. 341 at 348, [1971] 3 W.W.R. 645, 21 D.L.R. (3d) 681 (B.C. C.A.), Tysoe J.A.

VOIDABLE. *adj.* "... [D]oes not necessarily mean 'valid until rescinded.' It is sometimes used to mean 'invalid until validated'; ..." *American-Abell Engine & Thresher Co. v. McMillan* (1909), 42 S.C.R. 377 at 396, Duff J.

VOIDANCE. *n.* Avoidance.

VOIP. *abbr.* Voice over Internet Protocol. *Emergency 911 Act,* S.P.E.I. 1999, c. 23, s. 1.

VOIR DIRE. [Fr.] 1. An initial examination to determine the competency of a juror or witness. 2. "... [A] 'trial within a trial'. It is merely a descriptive phrase to describe a procedure which takes place, namely. a procedure to determine the admissibility of certain evidence." *R. v. Brydon* (1983), 6 C.C.C. (3d) 68 at 70 (B.C. C.A.), Craig J.A.

VOLENTI NON FIT INJURIA. [L.] 1. Wrong is not done to someone who is willing. 2. "... [V]olenti will arise only where the circumstances are such that it is clear that the plaintiff, knowing of the virtually certain risk of harm, in essence bargained away his right to sue for injuries incurred as a result of any negligence on the defendant's part. The acceptance of risk may be express or may arise by necessary implication from the conduct of the parties, but it will arise, in cases such as the present, only where there can truly be said to be an understanding on the part of both parties that the defendant assumed no responsibility to take due care for the safety of the plaintiff, and that the plaintiff did not expect him to." *Dubé v. Labar* (1986), 36 C.C.L.T. 105 at 114-5, 2 B.C.L.R. (2d) 273, 27 D.L.R. (4th) 653, [1986] 3 W.W.R. 750, [1986] 1 S.C.R. 649, Estey J. (McIntyre, Chouinard and Le Dain JJ. concurring). 3. "... [I]nvolves not only knowledge of the risk, but also a consent to the legal risk, or, in other words, a waiver of legal rights that may arise from the harm or loss that is being risked... ." *Waldick v. Malcolm*, 8 C.C.L.T. (2d) 1 at 17, 3 O.R. (3d) 471n, 125 N.R. 372, 47 O.A.C. 241, 83 D.L.R. (4th) 114, [1991] 2 S.C.R. 456, the court per Iacobucci J. See VOLUNTARY ASSUMPTION OF RISK.

VOLUNTARY. *adj.* 1. In criminal law, made without fear of prejudice or hope of advantage. 2. "... '[W]ithout compulsion' ..." *R. v. British Columbia (Workmen's Compensation Board)*, [1942] 2 W.W.R. 129 at 133, 57 B.C.R. 412, [1942] 2 D.L.R. 665 (C.A.), McDonald C.J.B.C. (dissenting) (McQuarrie, Sloan, O'Halloran and Fisher JJ.A. concurring).

VOLUNTARY APPEARANCE. Appearing before a foreign court on one's own volition.

VOLUNTARY ASSUMPTION OF RISK. [In a negligence claim] "[t]he defence of voluntary assumption of risk is based on the moral supposition that no wrong is done to one who consents. By agreeing to assume the risk the plaintiff absolves the defendant of all responsibility for it ... Since the volenti defence is a complete bar to recovery and therefore anomalous in an age of apportionment, the Courts have tightly circumscribed its scope. It only applies in situations where the plaintiff has assumed both the physical and the legal risk involved in the activity ..."

Crocker v. Sundance Northwest Resorts Ltd. (1988), 44 C.C.L.T. 225 at 239, 86 N.R. 241, 64 O.R. (2d) 64n, [1988] 1 S.C.R. 1186, 29 O.A.C. 1, 51 D.L.R. (4th) 321, [1988] R.R.A. 444, the court per Wilson J. See VOLENTI NON FIT INJURIA.

VOLUNTARY CONTRIBUTION. See ADDITIONAL ~.

VOLUNTARY CONVEYANCE. A conveyance by something like a gift with no valuable consideration.

VOLUNTARY OVERTIME. Overtime work which an employee is not required to perform under a collective agreement and which the employee may refuse to do if requested.

VOLUNTARY PLEA. Conscious decision of choice by an accused to plead guilty for reasons which the accused considers appropriate.

VOLUNTARY STATEMENT. No statement by an accused is admissible in evidence against him unless it is shown by the prosecution to have been obtained without fear of prejudice or hope of advantage. *Ibrahim v. R.*, [1914] A.C. 599 at 609-610 (Hong Kong P.C.), Lord Sumner for their Lordships.

VOLUNTARY TERMINATION. An act of quitting a job which indicates a subjective intention to quit combined with an objective confirming action.

VOLUNTARY TREE. A tree whose origin is unknown. *Koenig v. Goebel* (1998), 162 Sask. R. 81.

VOLUNTARY WASTE. "... [W]aste is either voluntary or permissive ... voluntary waste involves an act that is either wilful or negligent. Hence, damage to rented premises caused by a fire started by the negligence of the tenant constitutes voluntary waste and the tenant can be held liable: ..." *Prior v. Hanna* (1987), 55 Alta. L.R. (2d) 276 at 282, 82 A.R. 3, 43 D.L.R. (4th) 612 (Q.B.), Miller A.C.J.Q.B.

VOLUNTEER FIREFIGHTER. A firefighter who provides fire protection services either voluntarily or for a nominal consideration, honorarium, training or activity allowance.

VOLUNTEER LABOUR. Any service provided free of charge by a person outside of that person's working hours, but does not include a service provided by a person who is self-employed if the service is one that is normally sold or otherwise charged for by that person. *Elections acts.*

VOLUNTEER WORKER. A voluntary member of a fire or ambulance service or local emergency response control group established by a community, or any other volunteer performing duties authorized by a community.

VOLUNTEER WORK RELATIONSHIP. A relationship between an organization and an individual under which a service is provided for or in relation to or is undertaken in connection with the organization by an individual who is acting as a volunteer or is otherwise unpaid with respect to that service and includes any similar relationship involving an organization and an individual where, in respect of that relationship, the individual is a participant or a student. *Personal Information Protection Act*, S.A. 2003, c. P-6.5, s. 1.

VOTE. *v.* 1. To cast a ballot at an election. 2. To signify agreement or dissent when a question is called at a meeting. See RIGHT TO ~.

VOTE. *n.* 1. A ballot paper which has been detached from the counterfoil, and has been furnished to a voter, and has been marked and deposited as a vote by the voter. 2. Suffrage. See CASTING ~; FREE ~; SINGLE TRANSFERABLE ~ ELECTORAL SYSTEM; SUPPLY ~.

VOTE BY SECRET BALLOT. A vote by ballots cast in such a manner that a person expressing a choice cannot be identified with the choice expressed.

VOTER. *n.* 1. Any person entitled to vote. 2. Any person who votes at an election.

VOTERS LIST. *var.* **VOTERS' LIST.** 1. Includes any list made and revised of persons entitled to vote at an election. 2. A list of electors required to be prepared.

VOTES AND PROCEEDINGS. 1. A record of proceedings of the House of Commons. 2. The similar record of the business of a legislative assembly.

VOTING. See CUMULATIVE ~.

VOTING LOCATION. When these provisions [of the Samson Cree Nation Election Law] are considered together, it becomes apparent that the terms "voting location," "polling booth," "poll" and "ballot box" have different meanings. In my view, while a "polling booth" and a "poll" can be found within a "voting location," they are not the same thing as a "voting location." *Bruno v. Samson Cree Nation*, 2006 FCA 249.

VOTING SECURITY. Any security other than a debt security of an issuer carrying a voting right either under all circumstances or under some circumstances that have occurred and are continuing.

VOTING SHARE. Any share that carries voting rights under all circumstances or by reason of an event that has occurred and is continuing.

VOTING TRUST. The rights to vote some or all shares of a corporation are settled upon trustees who under the terms of the trust have authority, with or without restriction, to exercise the voting rights.

VOUCH. *v.* To call on; to rely on; to quote authoritatively.

VOUCHER. *n.* 1. A document which is evidence of a transaction, i.e. a receipt for money paid. 2. Any document that purports to give the holder of the document the right to obtain goods or a service or the right to obtain goods or a service at a discounted or reduced price. *Fair Trading Act*, R.S.A. 2000, c. F-2, s. 1. 3. A cheque or other instrument issued under this Act or the regulations that authorizes the supplying of specified goods and the rendering of specified services to the person named in the cheque or other instrument. *Family Income Security Act*, S.N.B. 1994, c. F-2.01, s. 1.

V

VOYAGE. See HOME-TRADE ~; INLAND ~; INTERNATIONAL ~; MINOR WATERS ~.

VOYAGE CHARTER. A contract of affreightment by which a lessor places all or part of a fully-equipped and manned ship at the disposal of a charterer for the carriage of cargo on one or more specified voyages and under which he retains the navigation, management, employment and agency of the ship. The contract specifies the nature and quantity of the cargo as well as the place of loading and discharge and the time allowed for those operations. *Civil Code*, S.Q. 1991, c. 64, a. 2021.

VOYAGE POLICY. A marine policy may be a voyage policy or a time policy. A marine policy is a voyage policy if the contract insures the subject-matter "at and from", or "from", one place to another place or other places. *Marine Insurance Act*, S.C. 1993, c. 22, s. 29(1)-(2).

VQA WINE. Wine, (a) that is produced in Ontario from grapes that have been grown in Ontario or from grape juice or grape must produced from such grapes, and (b) that meets the standards of the wine authority. *Vintners Quality Alliance Act, 1999*, S.O. 1999, c. 3, s. 2.

VS. *abbr.* Versus.

V.S.A. *abbr.* Vital signs absent. F.A. Jaffe, *A Guide to Pathological Evidence for Lawyers and Police Officers*, 4th ed. (Toronto: Carswell, 1999) at 246.

VULNERABLE. *adj.* 1. " ... [S]usceptible to harm, or open to injury ..." *International Corona Resources Ltd. v. LAC Minerals Ltd.* (1989), 35 E.T.R. 1 at 34, 26 C.P.R. (3d) 97, [1989] 2 S.C.R. 574, 69 O.R. (2d) 287, 61 D.L.R. (4th) 14, 6 R.P.R. (2d) 1, 44 B.L.R. 1, 101 N.R. 239, 36 O.A.C. 57, La Forest J. (Lamer J. concurring). 2. In respect of a Convention refugee or a person in similar circumstances, that the person has a greater need of protection than other applicants for protection abroad because of the person's particular circumstances that give rise to a heightened risk to their physical safety. *Immigration and Refugee Protection Act*, S.C. 2001, c. 27, *Immigration and Refugee Protection Regulations*, SOR/2002-227, s. 138.

VULNERABLE PERSONS. Persons who, because of their age, a disability or other circumstances, whether temporary or permanent, (a) are in a position of dependence on others; or (b) are otherwise at a greater risk than the general population of being harmed by persons in a position of authority or trust relative to them. *Criminal Records Act*, R.S.C. 1985, c. C-47, s. 6.3.

W

W.A.C. *abbr.* Western Appeal Cases, 1991-.

WAFER. *n.* A small circle of red paper used to seal a deed instead of sealing wax.

WAGE. *n.* 1. Any compensation measured by time, piece or otherwise. 2. Salary, pay, commission or remuneration for work. See BASIC ~; COMMON PERSONNEL AND ~ POLICY; MINIMUM ~; ~S.

WAGER. *n.* "[A contract by which] ... two persons, professing to hold opposite views touching the issue of a future uncertain event, mutually agree that dependent upon the determination of that event one shall win from the other, and that the other shall pay or hand over to him a sum of money or other stake, neither of the contracting parties having any other interest in that contract than the sum or stake he will win or lose, there being no other real consideration for the making of such a contract by either of the parties. It is essential to a wagering contract that each party may under it either win or lose ..." *Carlill v. Carbolic Smoke Ball Co.*, [1892] 2 Q.B. 484 at 490-91 (U.K.), Hawkins J.

WAGERING CONTRACT. A mutual promise by which each party gains or loses by the outcome of an uncertain event. Each party's promise is her or his only interest in the transaction. G.H.L. Fridman, *The Law of Contract in Canada*, 2d ed. (Toronto: Carswell, 1986) at 334.

WAGES. *n.* 1. "... [A]ny compensation for labour or services." *Davenport, Re* (1930), (*sub nom. Davenport v. McNiven*) [1930] 4 D.L.R. 386 at 387, [1930] 2 W.W.R. 263, 42 B.C.R. 468 (C.A.), Macdonald C.J.B.C. 2. Amount paid in respect of employment whether payable by time or by the job or piece or otherwise. See ATTACHMENT OF ~; FAIR ~; WAGE.

WAGG PRINCIPLES AND PROCEDURE. Refers to the case: D.P. v. Wagg, (2002), 61 O.R. (3d) 746 (Div. Ct.) ("Wagg"), aff'd in part (2004), 71 O.R. (3d) 229 (C.A.) ("Wagg, C.A."). The Wagg procedure accordingly requires notice to be given to the Attorney General and the relevant police authorities in any civil case where a party seeks production of a Crown brief. Production may then occur with the consent of the Attorney General and the parties to the litigation (which would not require a court order), or in the event of disagreement, on application to the Superior Court, whose function is to weigh the interests and to determine the scope of permitted disclosure of the Crown brief in the civil action. *College of Physicians and Surgeons of Ontario v. Peel Regional Police*, 2009 CanLII 55315 (Ont. S.C.D.C.).

WAIVE. *v.* To surrender or renounce a right, privilege or claim.

WAIVER. *n.* 1. Waiver involves the test enunciated in Western Canada Investment Co. v. McDiarmid (1922), 15 Sask. L.R. 142 (Sask. C.A.), at 146, where Lamont, J.A. said: "To constitute waiver, two essential prerequisites are in general necessary. There must be knowledge of the existence of the right or privilege relinquished and of the possessor's right to enjoy it, and there must be a clear intention of foregoing the exercise of such right." *Ericsson Inc. v. Novatel Inc.*, 2001 ABCA 199, 286 A.R. 190, 253 W.A.C. 190, 12 C.P.C. (5th) 212. 2. "[To forego] ... reliance upon some known right or defect. It is important that the right or defect, as the case may be, be known, since one should not be able to waive rights of which he was not fully aware or apprised.... In determining whether waiver applies, the defendant must take steps in the proceedings knowingly and to its prejudice, which amount to foregoing a reliance upon some right or defect. In order to waive a right it must be a known right... ." *Marchischuk v. Dominion Industrial Supplies Ltd.* (1991), 3 C.C.L.I. (2d) 173 at 176-7, 30 M.V.R. (2d) 102, [1991] 4 W.W.R. 673, [1991] I.L.R. 1-2729, 125 N.R. 306, 80 D.L.R. (4th) 670, 50 C.P.C. (2d) 231, [1991] 2 S.C.R. 61, 73 Man. R. (2d) 271, 3 W.A.C. 271, the court per Sopinka J. adopting the reasons of the trial judge. 3. "... [W]aiver does not confer rights, it repudiates them. If you waive your right to A, it does not mean that you are entitled to B. It means only that you are no longer entitled to A." *R. v. Turpin* (1989), 39 C.R.R. 306 at 329, 69 C.R. (3d) 97, 48 C.C.C. (3d) 8, 96 N.R. 115, [1989] 1 S.C.R. 1296, 34 O.A.C. 115, the court per Wilson J. 4. Surrender of an advantage or right intending not to exercise the advantage or right.

WAIVER OF TORT. An uncertain area of the law. A restitutionary remedy. There is considerable controversy over whether it exists as an independent cause of action at all or whether it is "parasitic" in the sense that it requires proof of an underlying tort and - since a tort requires damage -proof of harm to the plaintiff. By invoking waiver of tort, a plaintiff gives up the right to sue in tort but seeks to recover on the basis of restitution, claiming the benefits the wrongdoer has derived from the wrongful conduct regardless of whether the plaintiff has suffered damages or not. *Aronowicz v. EMTWO Properties Inc.*, 2010 CarswellOnt 598, 2010 ONCA 96.

WALKOUT. *n.* The withdrawal of employees from their place of employment.

WALL. See CHINESE ~; PARTY ~.

WANT OF PROSECUTION. In relation to dismissal of an action, inordinate delay, inexcusable delay, and serious prejudice to the defendants by the delay.

WANTON AND RECKLESS. In R. v. L. (J.) (2006), 204 C.C.C. (3d) 324 (Ont. C.A.), Weiler J.A. addressed the meaning of wanton and reckless by citing, with approval, the following comments of Hill J. in R. v. Menezes (2002), 50 C.R. (5th) 343 (Ont. S.C.J.) (at para. 72): .... The term wanton means "heedlessly" (R. v. Waite (1986), 28 C.C.C. (3d) 326 (Ont. C.A.) at 341, Cory J.A. (as he then was)) or "ungoverned" and "undisciplined" (as approved in R. v. Sharp (1984), 12 C.C.C. (3d) 428 (Ont. C.A.) at 430, Morden J.A.)) or an "unrestrained disregard for the consequences" (R. v. Pinske (1988), 6 M.V.R. (2d) 19 (B.C. C.A.) at 33, Craig J.A. (affirmed on a different basis R. v. Pinske, [1989] 2 S.C.R. 979, Lamer J. (as he then was)). The word "reckless" means "heedless of consequences, headlong, irresponsible": R. v. Sharp, supra, at [430]. In R. v. Waite (1986), 28 C.C.C. (3d) 326 (Ont. C.A.), referred to above, the actual quote by Cory J.A., as he then was, reads (at p. 341): .... The word "wanton" means "heedlessly." "Wanton" coupled as it is with the word "reckless", must mean heedless of the consequences or without regard for the consequences. .... *R. v. Tayfel*, 2009 MBCA 124.

WANTONNESS. *n.* "[In Criminal Code, R.S.C. 1970, c. C-34, s. 202(1)] . . perhaps a subclass of recklessness. It is a wild, mad or arrogant kind of recklessness and thus closely related to 'wilfulness'." *R. v. Walker* (1974), 26 C.R.N.S. 268 at 273, 18 C.C.C. (2d) 179 (N.S. C.A.), MacKeigan C.J.N.S.

WAR. *n.* Armed conflict. See ARTICLES OF ~; KOREAN ~; MUNITIONS OF ~; WORLD ~ I; WORLD ~ II.

WAR CRIME. An act or omission committed during an armed conflict that, at the time and in the place of its commission, constitutes a war crime according to customary international law or conventional international law applicable to armed conflicts, whether or not it constitutes a contravention of the law in force at the time and in the place of its commission. *Crimes Against Humanity and War Crimes Act*, S.C. 2000, c. 24, s. 4.

WARD. *n.* 1. An electoral division. 2. A child committed to the care and custody of the Director or a Society. *Child Welfare acts.*

WARDEN. See PARK ~.

WARDSHIP. *n.* Guardianship.

WARDSHIP ORDER. An order of the court making a child a ward of the Crown or of the Court or a society or person. See CROWN ~.

WAREHOUSE. *n.* Land that is used as a repository, storehouse or shed for the storage of goods and includes any building or structure from which goods are distributed for sale off the premises, but does not include a building or structure, the primary purpose of which is the sale of goods to the public. *Commercial Concentration Tax Act*, R.S.O. 1990, c. C.16, s. 1. See BONDING ~; CUSTOMS BONDED ~.

WAREHOUSE RECEIPT. 1. A receipt given by any person for any goods in the person's actual, visible and continued possession as bailee thereof in good faith and not as of the person's own property. 2. An acknowledgment in writing by a storer of the receipt for storage of another's goods.

WAR EMERGENCY. War or other armed conflict, real or imminent, involving Canada or any of its allies that is so serious as to be a national emergency. *Emergencies Act*, R.S.C. 1985, c. 22 (4th Supp.), s. 37.

WAR MEASURES ACT. The now repealed federal statute gave the federal cabinet extraordinary powers when the cabinet declared that a war or insurrection was apprehended or existing. This statute gained notoriety in 1970 when then Prime Minister Trudeau and his Cabinet invoked the Act in peace time for the first time. By doing so they gave authorities extraordinary powers for a period of time. More specific powers are now set out in the *Emergencies Act*, R.S.C. 1985, c. 22 (4th Supp.).

WARNING. *n.* 1. Putting on notice; making aware. 2. No magic combination of words need be resorted to in order to constitute a warning to an employee that their future employment may be at risk due to their conduct. The question in all the circumstances should be whether or not there was such communication to the employee in such a way that the employee should conclude that he stood in danger of being terminated. *Thomas v. Canex Foods Ltd.*, 2000 CarswellBC 1013, 2000 BCSC 748, Melvin J. See MIRANDA ~; VETROVEC ~.

WARRANT. *v.* To justify.

WARRANT. *n.* 1. The order of a judicial authority that a ministerial officer arrest, seize, search or execute some judicial sentence. 2. An option; an agreement by a corporation to sell to the holder a certain number of shares at a price specified in the agreement. S.M. Beck *et al.*, *Cases and Materials on Partnerships and Canadian Business Corporations* (Toronto: Carswell, 1983) at 788. 3. A right to subscribe for a share of a corporation. 4. Any record issued by a company as evidence of conversion or exchange privileges or options or rights to acquire shares of the company. *Business Corporations Act, 2002*, S.B.C. 2002, c. 57, s. 1. See ARREST ~; BACK A ~; BENCH ~; DISTRESS ~; SEARCH ~; SHARE ~; TELE~; TRACKING ~.

WARRANTEE. *n.* A person to whom one makes a warranty.

WARRANTLESS SEARCH. A warrantless search is presumptively unreasonable and contrary to s. 8 of the Charter, which guarantees to everyone "the right to be secure against unreasonable search or seizure." In the absence of a warrant, the Crown must establish on a balance of probabilities that the search was authorized by law, that the law itself is reasonable, and that the manner in which the search was carried out was reasonable. *R. v. Nolet*, 2010 SCC 24.

WARRANT OF ATTORNEY. An instrument given before an action is commenced by which a debtor names an attorney and empowers the attorney to confess judgment in an action.

WARRANT OF COMMITTAL. An order directing that a person sentenced or committed to prison be taken there and that the keeper of the prison receive the person into custody and imprison the person.

WARRANTOR. *n.* A party who warrants.

WARRANTY. *n.* 1. "... [A] term in contract which does not go to the root of the agreement between the parties but simply expresses some lesser obligation, the failure to perform which can give rise to an action for damages but never to the right to rescind or repudiate the contract: ..." *Fraser-Reid v. Droumtsekas* (1980), 103 D.L.R. (3d) 385 at 392, [1980] 1 S.C.R. 720, 29 N.R. 424, 9 R.P.R. 121, Dickson J. (Martland, Estey and McIntyre JJ. concurring). 2. An agreement with reference to goods which are the subject of a contract of sale, but collateral to the main purpose of such contract, the breach of which gives rise to a claim for damages, but not a right to reject the goods and treat the contract as repudiated. *Sale of Goods acts.* See BREACH OF ~ OF AUTHORITY; IMPLIED ~.

WASTE. *n.* 1. "Waste in law is destruction of a part of the inheritance by a limited owner, such as a tenant for life or years." *"Freiya" (The) v. "R.S." (The)* (1922), 65 D.L.R. 218 at 222, [1922] 1 W.W.R. 409, 21 Ex. C.R. 232, Audette J. 2. "... [W]aste is either voluntary or permissive ... voluntary waste involves an act that is either wilful or negligent. Hence, damage to rented premises caused by a fire started by the negligence of the tenant constitutes voluntary waste and the tenant can be held liable: ... Permissive waste involves the failure or omission to take some precaution which results in damage to the property." *Prior v. Hanna* (1987), 55 Alta. L.R. (2d) 276 at 282, 82 A.R. 3, 43 D.L.R. (4th) 612 (Q.B.), Miller A.C.J.Q.B. 3. Any substance that, if added to any water, would degrade or alter or form part of a process of degradation or alteration of the quality of that water to an extent that is detrimental to their use by man or by any animal, fish or plant that is useful to man, and any water that contains a substance in such a quantity or concentration, or that has been so treated, processed or changed, by heat or other means, from a natural state that it would, if added to any other water, degrade or alter or form part of a process of degradation or alteration of the quality of that water to the extent described. *Canada Water Act*, R.S.C. 1985, c. C-11, s. 2. See AMELIORATING ~; INERT ~; NUCLEAR FUEL ~; PERMISSIVE ~; VOLUNTARY ~.

WASTING ASSET. Property which exists under restriction, such as a natural resource or leasehold.

WATCHING. *v.* Continuously observing for a purpose.

WATCHING AND BESETTING. Watching is passive and besetting is active. Observing and assailing.

WATER. *n.* Natural surface and ground water in liquid, gaseous or solid state, but does not include water packaged as a beverage or in tanks. *Trade Agreement Acts.* See BOUNDARY ~S; CANADIAN FISHERIES ~S; CANADIAN ~S; COASTAL ~S OF CANADA; FEDERAL ~S; INLAND ~S OF CANADA; INTER-JURISDICTIONAL ~S; INTERNAL ~S; INTERNATIONAL ~S; MINOR ~S OF CANADA; MINOR ~S VOYAGE; NATURAL ~.

WATERHOUSE-FRIDERICHSEN SYNDROME. Sudden and unexpected death caused by meningococcal septicemia. F.A. Jaffe, *A Guide to Pathological Evidence for Lawyers and Police Officers*, 4th ed. (Toronto: Carswell, 1999) at 54.

WATER QUALITY MANAGEMENT. Any aspect of water resource management that relates to restoring, maintaining or improving the quality of water.

WATER RESOURCE MANAGEMENT. *n.* The conservation, development and utilization of water resources and includes, with respect thereto, research, data collection and the maintaining of inventories, planning and the implementation of plans, and the control and regulation of water quantity and quality. *Canada Water Act*, R.S.C. 1985, c. C-11, s. 2.

WATERSHED. *n.* An area drained by a river and its tributaries.

WATER SUPPLY SYSTEM. See PUBLIC ~.

WAVES. See RADIO ~.

WAY OF NECESSITY. 1. A right of way implied in favour of a grantee of land over the land of the grantor when there is no other way by which the grantee can get to the land granted to him. 2. A right of way over land retained by the grantee when land kept by the grantor is landlocked.

WAYS AND MEANS MOTION. The first step needed before Parliament imposes a new tax, continues an expiring tax, increases the rate of an existing tax or extends a tax to include people not already paying. A. Fraser, W.A. Dawson, & J. Holtby, eds., *Beauchesne's Rules and Forms of the House of Commons of Canada*, 6th ed. (Toronto: Carswell, 1989) at 265.

W.C.A.T. DEC. *abbr.* Workers' Compensation Appeal Tribunal Decisions (Newfoundland), 1987-.

W.C.A.T.R. *abbr.* Workers' Compensation Appeals Tribunal Reporter (Ontario), 1986-1997.

W.C.B. *abbr.* 1. Workers' Compensation Board. 2. Workmen's Compensation Board. 3. Weekly Criminal Bulletin, 1976-1986.

W.C.B. (2D). *abbr.* Weekly Criminal Bulletin (Second Series), 1986-.

W.D.C.P. *abbr.* Weekly Digest of Civil Procedure, 1985-1989.

W.D.C.P. (2D). *abbr.* Weekly Digest of Civil Procedure (Second Series), 1990-1994.

W.D.C.P. (3D). *abbr.* Weekly Digest of Civil Procedure (Third Series), 1994-.

W.D.F.L. *abbr.* Weekly Digest of Family Law, 1982-.

WEAPON. *n.* 1. Any thing used, designed to be used or intended for use (a) in causing death or injury to any person, or (b) for the purpose of threatening or intimidating any person and, without restricting the generality of the foregoing, includes a firearm. *Criminal Code*, R.S.C. 1985, c. C-46, s. 2. 2. A firearm must come within the definition of a weapon. A firearm is expressly designed to kill or wound. It operates with deadly efficiency in carrying out the object of its design. It followed that such a deadly weapon can, of course, be used for purposes of threatening and intimidating. Indeed, it is hard to imagine anything more intimidating or dangerous than a brandished firearm. A person waving a gun and calling 'hands up' can be reasonably certain that the suggestion will be obeyed. A firearm is quite different from an object such as a carving knife or an ice pick which will normally be used for legitimate purposes. A firearm, however, is always a weapon. No matter what the intention may be of the person carrying a gun, the firearm itself presents the ultimate threat of death to those in its presence. *R. v. Felawka*, 1993 CarswellBC 507, 25 C.R. (4th) 70, 159 N.R. 50, 33 B.C.A.C. 241, 54 W.A.C. 241, 85 C.C.C. (3d) 248, [1993] 4 S.C.R. 199, Cory J. 3. [In s. 2 of the Criminal Code , R.S.C. 1985, c. C-46, for the purposes of interpretation of s. 272(1)(a) of the Code, dealing with sexual assault with a weapon.] [The] French version of the definition of "weapon" ("arme ") in s. 2, taken literally, could suggest that for an object to become a weapon, it must be designed, used, or intended to be used for the purpose of causing injury. The English version provides a clarification that is consistent with a sound interpretation of the intent required for an object to become a weapon in all the different sets of circumstances contemplated by the provision. In contrast to the design, the use or the intended use of an object to threaten or intimidate, when an object is actually used in causing death or injury, the English text does not import a requirement that the object be used "for the purpose" of killing or injuring, but merely "in causing" death or injury. *R. v. Lamy*, [2002] 1 S.C.R. 860. See OFFENSIVE ~; PROHIBITED ~; RESTRICTED ~.

WEAPONS TRAFFICKING. Every person commits an offence who (a) manufactures or transfers, whether or not for consideration, or (b) offers to do anything referred to in paragraph (a) in respect of a firearm, a prohibited weapon, a restricted weapon, a prohibited device, any ammunition or any prohibited ammunition knowing that the person is not authorized to do so under the Firearms Act or any other Act of Parliament or any regulations made under any Act of Parliament. *Criminal Code*, R.S.C. 1985, c. C-46, s. 99.

WEAR AND TEAR. The waste of any material by ordinary use.

WEATHER MODIFICATION ACTIVITY. Includes any action designed or intended to produce, by physical or chemical means, changes in the composition or dynamics of the atmosphere for the purpose of increasing, decreasing or redistributing precipitation, decreasing or suppressing hail or lightning or dissipating fog or cloud. *Weather Modification Information Act*, R.S.C. 1985, c. W-5, s. 2.

WEBCASTING. *n.* Broadcasting an event electronically over the internet.

WEEK. See TENANCY ~.

WEIGH. *v.* In relation to evidence, to measure, to ponder, to examine the force of.

WEIGH TICKET. A receipt that is issued by a grain elevator operator or the operator's employee to the owner of grain or the owner's agent.

WEIGHT OF EVIDENCE. 1. For the evidence of one side to be so far superior to the other's that the verdict should go to the first. 2. The amount of importance attached to any particular piece of evidence.

WEIGHT RESTRICTION. With reference to a highway or bridge, any maximum restriction imposed.

WELFARE. *n.* Commonly used to refer to public assistance provided by the province or municipality to persons with minimal financial means. See PUBLIC ~ EMERGENCY; PUBLIC ~ OFFENCE.

WELFARE CLAUSE. See GENERAL ~.

WELFARE SERVICES. Services, such as case work, homemaker, and day-care, intended to lessen, remove or prevent the causes of poverty, child neglect and dependence on public assistance. See CHILD WELFARE SERVICE.

WELL. *n.* 1. An artificial opening in the ground from which water is or is intended to be obtained. 2. Any opening in the ground, not being a seismic shot hole, that is made, to be made or is in the process of being made, by drilling, boring or other method, (a) for the production of oil or gas, (b) for the purpose of searching for or obtaining oil or gas, (c) for the purpose of obtaining water to inject into an underground formation, (d) for the purpose of injecting gas, air, water or other substance into an underground formation, or (e) for any purpose, if made through sedimentary rocks to a depth of at least one hundred and fifty metres. *Canada Oil and Gas Operations Act*, R.S.C. 1985, c. O-7, s. 2. See MONITORING ~.

WESTERN ECONOMIC DIVERSIFICATION. See DEPARTMENT OF ~.

WESTERN HEMISPHERE TRAVEL INITIATIVE. The Western Hemisphere Travel Initiative established under the Intelligence Reform and Terrorism Prevention Act of 2004 (United States of America). *The Drivers and Vehicles Act*, S.M. 2005, c. 37, Sched. A, s. 1.

WEST. L. REV. *abbr.* Western Law Review, 1961-1966.

WESTMINSTER. See STATUTE OF ~.

WEST. ONT. L. REV. *abbr.* Western Ontario Law Review, 1967-1976.

WEST'S ALASKA. *abbr.* West's Alaska Digest (Alberta), 1987-.

WET DROWNING. Death from breathing in large quantities of fluid. F.A. Jaffe, *A Guide to Pathological Evidence for Lawyers and Police Officers*, 4th ed. (Toronto: Carswell, 1999) at 235.

WHEAT. See CANADIAN ~ BOARD.

WHERE. *adv.* At the same time or at some time after or before.

WHEREBY. *adv.* By or through which.

WHIP. See CHIEF ~.

WHISTLE BLOWER. A person, including an employee, who reports or gives evidence of a violation of a statute or regulation or refuses to work under conditions in violation of legislation.

WHISTLE BLOWER PROTECTION. Protection from, eviction, discharge, discipline, intimidation, coercion, penalty afforded to persons who point out violations by their employer or others of legislation. Protection may be afforded by legislation or by terms of a collective agreement.

WHITE CANE. A cane or walking-stick the major portion of which is white and which is intended for use by a person with impaired vision.

WHITE PAPER. An official government memorandum which sets out a problem and the issues related to it with the policy the government recommends.

WHMIS. *abbr.* Workplace hazardous materials information system.

WHOLE HOUSE. See COMMITTEE OF THE ~.

WHOLESALER. *n.* 1. Person who sells to persons other than the end-user or consumer. 2. "... [T]o be one, the sale must not only be in large quantities but it must be to a person other than the end-user... ." *Buchman & Son Lumber Co. v. Ontario Regional Assessment Commissioner, Region No., 9* (1982), 141 D.L.R. (3d) 95 at 97, 20 M.P.L.R. 78, 14 O.M.B.R. 166 (Div. Ct.), Steele J. (O'Leary J. concurring). See TRAVEL ~.

WHOLLY. *adv.* Exclusively; entirely.

WIDESPREAD. *adj.* The . . . concept, "widespread", relates to the prevalence or incidence of the bias in question. Generally speaking, the alleged bias must be established as sufficiently pervasive in the community to raise the possibility that it may be harboured by one or more members of a representative jury pool . . . . *R. v. Find*, 2001 CarswellOnt 1702, 2001 SCC 32, 42 C.R. (5th) 1, 154 C.C.C. (3d) 97, 199 D.L.R. (4th) 193, 269 N.R. 149, 146 O.A.C. 236, the court per McLachlin C.J.C.

WIDESPREAD ATTACK. A widespread attack "may be defined as massive, frequent, large scale action, carried out collectively with considerable seriousness and directed against a multiplicity of victims"—it need not be carried out pursuant to a specific strategy, policy or plan: Akayesu, Trial Chamber, at para. 580; and Prosecutor v. Kayishema (May 21, 1999), Doc. ICTR-95-1-T (Int. Criminal Trib.), at para. 123. It may consist of a number of acts or of one act of great magnitude: Mettraux, at p. 260 [G. Mettraux, "Crimes Against Humanity in the Jurisprudence of the International Criminal Tribunals for the Former Yugoslavia and for Rwanda" (2002), 43 Harv. Intn'l L.J. 237]. *Mugesera v. Canada (Minister of Citizenship and Immigration)*, 2005 SCC 40, [2005] 2 S.C.R. 100.

WIDOW. *n.* A female person whose spouse has died.

WIDOWER. *n.* A male person whose spouse has died.

WIFE. *n.* A woman who has entered into a marriage.

WIGMORE TEST. [O]bjections to the disclosure of communications that are sourced in claims of non-generic privilege stand to be determined on the basis of the principles derived from John Henry Wigmore, Evidence in Trials at Common Law, vol. VIII (Revised by John T. McNaughton) (Boston: Little, Brown and Company 1961) at para. 2285. For such an objection to prevail, four conditions must be met: (1) the communication must originate in a confidence; (2) the confidence must be essential to the relationship in which the communication arises; (3) the relationship must be one which should be "sedulously fostered" in the public good; and (4) the interests served by protecting the communication from disclosure outweigh the interest in getting at the truth and disposing correctly of the litigation. *Clements v. Fougère*, 2007 NBCA 4.

WILDCAT STRIKE. A strike commenced without the authorization of a union or in violation of a no-strike clause in a collective agreement.

WILDERNESS. *n.* Any area of the Yukon in a largely natural condition in which ecosystem processes are generally unaltered by human activity, and may include areas of visible human activity that does not detract from wilderness tourism. *Wilderness Tourism Licensing Act*, R.S.Y. 2002, c. 228, s. 2.

WILDERNESS TOURISM. A sector of the tourism industry where an operator, for gain, reward, or for material or financial benefit received, provides a wilderness based activity. *Wilderness Tourism Licensing Act*, R.S.Y. 2002, c. 228, s. 2.

WILDERNESS TOURISM ACTIVITY. Any type of commercially guided tourism activity occurring in the wilderness, including, without limiting the generality of the foregoing, canoeing, cross country skiing, dog mushing, heli-hiking, heli-skiing, hiking and backpacking, horseback riding, kayaking, motorized boat tours, mountain biking, mountaineering, photographic safaris, river rafting, rock climbing, snowmobiling, sport fishing, and First Nation cultural interpretive tours. An activity which takes place partly in a wilderness area and partly in a non wilderness area is deemed to be a wilderness tourism activity.

Wilderness Tourism Licensing Act, R.S.Y. 2002, c. 228, s. 2.

WILDLIFE. *n.* An animal that belongs to a species that is wild by nature and not dependent on people to provide it with food, water or shelter.

WILDLIFE MANAGEMENT BOARD. Any board or other body established under a land claims agreement that is authorized by the agreement to perform functions in respect of wildlife species. *Species at Risk Act*, S.C. 2002, c. 29, s. 2.

WILDLIFE SPECIES. A species, subspecies, variety or geographically or genetically distinct population of animal, plant or other organism, other than a bacterium or virus, that is wild by nature and (a) is native to Canada; or (b) has extended its range into Canada without human intervention and has been present in Canada for at least 50 years. *Species at Risk Act*, S.C. 2002, c. 29, s. 2.

WILFUL. *adj.* [W]hile the word "wilful" has not been uniformly interpreted, it may reasonably be thought to refer to intentional but not reckless behaviour. ... [A]s I have shown, there is a long-standing and well-recognized distinction between intentional and reckless conduct and that it is also well-recognized that "wilful" may be used to mean only "intentional." In light of this, it was not unreasonable, in the context of interpreting the major offence penalty provision [willful disobedience] in a collective agreement, for the arbitrator to have equated "wilful" with "intentional" and to have distinguished it from "reckless." The arbitrator said, in effect, that the employees knew they should be at work and should have gone to work, but they did not intend to defy the authority of management. In my view, neither the distinction he drew between "wilful" and "reckless," nor the inferences he drew concerning the grievors' states of mind was unreasonable. *Halifax Shipyard v. Industrial Union of Marine & Shipbuilding Workers of Canada, Local 1*, 2005 NSCA 111, Cromwell J.A., (Saunders J.A. concurring).

WILFUL BLINDNESS. Does not define the mens rea required for particular offences. Rather, it can substitute for actual knowledge whenever knowledge is a component of the mens rea. The doctrine of wilful blindness imputes knowledge to an accused whose suspicion is aroused to the point where he or she sees the need for further inquiries, but deliberately chooses not to make those inquiries. [A] finding of wilful blindness involves an affirmative answer to the question: Did the accused shut his eyes because he knew or strongly suspected that looking would fix him with knowledge? Courts and commentators have consistently emphasized that wilful blindness is distinct from recklessness. Professor Don Stuart makes the useful observation that the expression "deliberate ignorance" seems more descriptive than "wilful blindness", as it connotes "an actual process of suppressing a suspicion". Properly understood in this way, "the concept of wilful blindness is of narrow scope and involves no departure from the subjective focus on the workings of the accused's mind" (Canadian Criminal Law: A Treatise (5th ed. 2007), at p. 241). While

a failure to inquire may be evidence of recklessness or criminal negligence, as for example, where a failure to inquire is a marked departure from the conduct expected of a reasonable person, wilful blindness is not simply a failure to inquire but, to repeat Professor Stuart's words, "deliberate ignorance." *R. v. B.*, 2010 SCC 13.

WILFULLY. *adv.* 1. "... [D]eliberately and purposefully ..." *R. v. Hafey* (1985), (*sub nom. R. v. Stoke-Graaham*) 44 C.R. (3d) 289 at 298, [1985] 1 S.C.R. 106, 67 N.S.R. (2d) 181, 155 A.P.R. 181, 17 C.C.C. (3d) 289, 16 D.L.R. (4th) 321, 57 N.R. 321, Dickson J. 2. "... [H]as not been uniformly interpreted and its meaning to some extent depends upon the context in which it is used. Its primary meaning is 'intentionally', but it is also used to mean 'recklessly' ... The word 'wilfully' has, however, also been held to mean no more than that the accused's act is done intentionally and not accidentally." *R. v. Buzzanga* (1979), 101 D.L.R. (3d) 488 at 498, 500, 25 O.R. (2d) 705, 49 C.C.C. (2d) 369 (C.A.), Martin J.A.

WILFULNESS. *n.* "... [M]ust imply both deliberation and knowledge ..." *R. v. Hafey* (1985), (*sub nom. R. v. Stoke-Graaham*) 44 C.R. (3d) 289 at 307, [1985] 1 S.C.R. 106, 67 N.S.R. (2d) 181, 155 A.P.R. 181, 17 C.C.C. (3d) 289, 16 D.L.R. (4th) 321, 57 N.R. 321, Wilson J.

WILL. *n.* The written statement by which a person instructs how her or his estate should be distributed after death. See ADMINISTRATOR WITH ~ ANNEXED; CONDITIONAL ~; GOOD~; GRANT OF ADMINISTRATION WITH ~ ANNEXED; HOLOGRAPH ~; JOINT ~; LETTERS OF ADMINISTRATION WITH ~ ANNEXED; MUTUAL ~S; NUNCUPATIVE ~; PRIVILEGED ~; PROVING A ~ IN SOLEMN FORM; TENANCY AT ~; TENANT AT ~ .

WILL-SAY. *n.* An indication of the expected testimony of a witness. Designed as a procedural tool to ensure fairness, efficiency, preparedness, and to prevent ambush at trial.

WIN. *n.* A type of bet on a race to select a horse to finish first in the official result. *Criminal Code*, R.S.C. 1985, c. C-46, *Pari-Mutuel Betting Supervision Regulations*, SOR/91-365, s. 2.

WINDFALL. *n.* 1. Receipt of capital. 2. Refers to timber blown down on a tenant's land was required to be sold and the proceeds invested as capital.

WINDING UP. *var.* **WINDING-UP.** 1. The process of ending the business of a corporation or partnership by settling accounts and liquidating assets. 2. In relation to a pension plan that has been terminated, the process of distributing the assets of the plan.

WINDING-UP ORDER. An order granted by a court under this Act to wind up the business of a company, and includes any order granted by the court to bring under this Act any company in liquidation or in process of being wound up. *Winding-up and Restructuring Act*, R.S.C. 1985, c. W-11, s. 2.

WINDSOR Y.B. ACCESS JUST. *abbr.* The Windsor Yearbook of Access to Justice.

WINDSOR Y.B. ACCESS JUSTICE. *abbr.* The Windsor Yearbook of Access to Justice (Recueil annuel de Windsor d'accès à la justice).

WINE. *n.* Any beverage containing alcohol obtained by the fermentation of the natural sugar contents of fruits, including grapes, apples and other agricultural products containing sugar, and including honey and milk. See VINTERS QUALITY ALLIANCE ~; VQA ~.

WINERY. A person licensed as a manufacturer of wine for the purpose of sale.

WINGER. *n.* Expression used to refer to two side-members of a tribunal hearing a case; the members of the tribunal, other than the chair.

WINTER TIRE. A tire that is (a) advertised or represented by its manufacturer or a person in the business of selling tires to be a tire intended principally for winter use, and that provides, or is designed to provide, adequate traction in snow or mud; and (b) in the condition respecting tread wear and other particulars the regulations prescribe. *Motor Vehicle Act,* R.S.B.C. 1996, c. 318, s. 208.

WIPO. *abbr.* World Intellectual Property Organization.

WIT. See TO ~.

WITCHCRAFT. *n.* Fraudulently pretending to use any kind of witchcraft, sorcery, enchantment or conjuration. *Criminal Code,* R.S.C. 1985, c. C-46, s. 365.

WITH COSTS. In the expression "motion dismissed with costs", means that costs will be assessed and paid only when the trial is over.

WITHDRAWAL. *n.* 1. Unlike a stay of proceedings which has statutory basis in Canadian law, withdrawal of a charge is based on English common law, in force through section 8(2) of the Criminal Code. 2. "... When a charge has been withdrawn, there is no charge on record, and in order to continue the prosecution a new charge would have to be laid. Withdrawing a charge has the effect of ending the proceedings." *R. v. Leonard* (1962), (*sub nom. Crown Practice Rules, Re*) 38 W.W.R. 300 at 303, 37 C.R. 374, 133 C.C.C. 230 (Alta. T.D.), Kirby J. 3. For a defendant to retract a defence by filing and serving written notice. Formerly also meant discontinuance by a plaintiff of part, not the whole, action.

WITHIN. *prep.* 1. In relation to time, before the expiration of, at or before, not beyond, not exceeding, not later than. 2. A geographic limitation.

WITHOUT DELAY. To allow for a delay between the outset of a detention and the engagement of the police duties under s. 10(b) [of the Charter] creates an ill defined and unworkable test of the application of the s. 10(b) right. The right to counsel requires a stable and predictable definition. What constitutes a permissible delay is abstract and difficult to quantify, whereas the concept of immediacy leaves little room for misunderstanding. An ill defined threshold for the application of the right to counsel must be avoided, particularly as it relates to a right that imposes specific obligations on the police. In our view, the words "without delay" mean "immediately" for the purposes of s. 10(b). Subject to concerns for officer or public safety, and such limitations as prescribed by law and justified under s. 1 of the Charter, the police have a duty to inform a detainee of his or her right to retain and instruct counsel, and a duty to facilitate that right immediately upon detention. *R.v. Suberu,* 2009 SCC 33.

WITHOUT PREJUDICE. 1. "The use of this expression ['without prejudice'] is commonly understood to mean that if there is no settlement, the party making the offer is free to assert all its rights, unaffected by anything stated or done in the negotiations." *Maracle v. Travellers Indemnity Co. of Canada* (1991), 50 C.P.C. (2d) 213 at 222, [1991] I.L.R. 1-2728, 125 N.R. 294, 3 O.R. (3d) 510n, 80 D.L.R. (4th) 652, 3 C.C.L.I. (2d) 186, 47 O.A.C. 333, [1991] 2 S.C.R. 50, the court per Sopinka J. 2. "... [A] party to a correspondence within the 'without prejudice' privilege is, generally speaking, protected from being required to disclose it on discovery or at trial in proceedings by or against a third party." *I. Waxman & Sons Ltd. v. Texaco Canada Ltd.,* [1968] 2 O.R. 452 at 453, 69 D.L.R. (2d) 543 (C.A.), the court per Aylesworth J.A. quoting the trial judge. 3. "... [T]he words 'without prejudice' [endorsing an order] do not operate to freeze time limitations or suspend any other application of the law, but simply prevent the respondent from raising the defence of res judicata and that the endorsement should be given its plain meaning ..." *Ternoey v. Goulding* (1982), 25 R.F.L. (2d) 113 at 120, 35 O.R. (2d) 29, 132 D.L.R. (3d) 44 (C.A.), Houlden J.A. (Howland C.J.O. concurring).

WITHOUT RECOURSE TO ME. A phrase used to protect the indorser of a note or bill from liability.

WITNESS. *n.* 1. "... [O]ne who, in the course of judicial processes, attests to matters of fact; ..." *Bell v. Klein (No. 1),* [1955] S.C.R. 309 at 317, [1955] 2 D.L.R. 513, Rand J. 2. A person who gives evidence orally under oath or by affidavit in a judicial proceeding, whether or not he is competent to be a witness, and includes a child of tender years who gives evidence but does not give it under oath, because, in the opinion of the person presiding, the child does not understand the nature of the oath. *Criminal Code,* R.S.C. 1985, c. C-46, s. 118. 3. Any person, whether a party or not, to be examined under this Act. *Supreme Court Act,* R.S.C. 1985, c. S-26, s. 2. 4. (a) A person who has given or has agreed to give information or evidence, or participates or has agreed to participate in a matter, relating to an inquiry or the investigation or prosecution of an offence and who may require protection because of risk to the security of the person arising in relation to the inquiry, investigation or prosecution, or (b) a person who, because of their relationship to or association with a person referred to in paragraph (a), may also require protection for the reasons referred to in that paragraph. *Witness Protection Program Act,* S.C. 1996, c. 15, s. 2. See ADVERSE ~; ATTESTING ~; EXPERT ~; EYE-~; HOSTILE ~; MATERIAL ~; SUMMONS TO ~.

WITNESS PROTECTION PROGRAM. The purpose of the program is to promote law enforcement by facilitating the protection of persons who are involved directly or indirectly in providing assistance in law enforcement matters in relation to activities conducted by the R.C.M.P. or activities conducted by any law enforcement agency or international criminal court or tribunal in respect of which an agreement or arrangement has been entered into under the Act. The program is administered by the Commissioner of the R.C.M.P. *Witness Protection Program Act*, S.C. 1996, c. 15, s. 3.

WKRS. *abbr.* Workers(').

W.L.A.C. *abbr.* Western Labour Arbitration Cases, 1966-1985.

W.L.R. *abbr.* Western Law Reporter, 1905-1917.

[] W.L.R. *abbr.* Weekly Law Reports.

W.L.T. *abbr.* Western Law Times, 1890-1895.

WOMAN. See BATTERED ~; BATTERED ~ SYNDROME; STATUS OF WOMEN CANADA.

WORDS. *n.* 1. Includes figures, punctuation marks and typographical, monetary and mathematical symbols. 2. Includes pictures, visual images, gestures or other methods of signifying meaning. *Defamation Act*, R.S.N.S. 1989, c. 122, s. 2. See APT ~; ASSOCIATED ~ RULE; GENERAL ~; OPERATIVE WORD; PRECATORY ~; SEDITIOUS ~.

WORDS OF ART. Words employed in a technical sense.

WORDS OF LIMITATION. Words which effectively restrict the continuation of an estate.

WORK. *n.* 1. "... [M]ay mean action or exertion put forth to accomplish some end or it may mean the product of or the result of action or exertion." *Ruthenian Sisters of the Immaculate Conception v. Saskatoon (City)*, [1937] 2 W.W.R. 625 at 628 (Sask. C.A.), Martin J.A. (Mackenzie J.A. concurring). 2. Includes the title thereof when such title is original and distinctive. *Copyright Act*, R.S.C. 1985, c. C-42, s. 2. 3. A computer program is a "work" within the meaning of the Copyright Act. Copyright may reside in either a language, or form of language, where it is an original creation of an author: Anderson (D.P.) & Co. Ltd. v. Lieber Code Co., [1917] 2 K.B. 469 (telegraph code system); Pitman v. Hine (1884), 1 T.L.R. 39 (shorthand system), or, more traditionally, in the particular form of expression of an idea or concept. In my opinion, a program such as this is either a novel language or an expression of thought, albeit in numeric form. In either case it is a work within the meaning of the Copyright Act. *Canavest House Ltd. v. Lett* (1984), 4 C.I.P.R 103, 2 C.P.R. (3d) 386 (H.C.). See ARCHITECTURAL ~; ARTISTIC ~; BARGAINING UNIT ~; CHOREOGRAPHIC ~; CINEMATOGRAPHIC ~; COLLECTIVE ~; DRAMATIC ~; EQUAL PAY FOR EQUAL ~; LITERARY ~; FEDERAL ~, UNDERTAKING OR BUSINESS; MUSICAL ~; ORIGINAL ~; POISONED ~ ENVIRONMENT; RIGHT TO ~; SUITABLE ~; VOLUNTEER ~ RELATIONSHIP; ~S; YARD ~.

WORKER. *n.* 1. An employee. 2. A person who has entered into or works under a contract of service or apprenticeship, written or oral, express or implied, whether by way of manual labour or otherwise and includes a learner. 3. "The word 'worker' includes: (1) a person who enters into a contract of service, and (2) a person who works under a contract of service... ." *British Airways Board v. British Columbia (Workers' Compensation Board)* (1985), 61 B.C.L.R. 1 at 16, 13 Admin. L.R. 78, 17 D.L.R. (4th) 36 (C.A.), Macfarlane J.A. (Seaton J.A. concurring). 4. "The definition of 'worker' [in s. 1 of the Occupational Health and Safety Act, R.S.O. 1980, c. 32] applies equally to employment or independent contractor relationships. It does not, for example, restrict the applicability of the statute to contracts of employment as it might have done if the word 'employee' and not the work 'worker' had been used as the correlative to the word 'employer'." *R. v. Wyssen* (1992), 10 O.R. (3d) 193 at 197, 58 O.A.C. 67 (C.A.), Blair J.A. (Dubin C.J.O. concurring). See BLIND ~; HOME~; NUCLEAR ENERGY ~; REPLACEMENT ~; UNDEREMPLOYED ~; VOLUNTEER ~; YOUTH ~

WORKER CO-OPERATIVE. A co-operative, the articles of which provide that the co-operative's primary object is to provide employment to its members, and the articles of which provide that it is a condition of membership that, except in circumstances prescribed by the regulations, a member must be employed by the co-operative.

WORKERS' COMPENSATION. 1. A program to provide financial, rehabilitation and medical assistance to any worker who is partially or totally disabled by an accident which arose "out of and in the course of employment" or by an occupational disease due to the worker's employment. 2. "... [I]s paid to partially replace lost wages due to injury on the job. It is not ... insurance, nor is it damages, nor is it a settlement." *Dixon v. Dixon* (1981), 25 R.F.L. (2d) 266 at 269, 14 Man. R. (2d) 40 (Co. Ct.), Ferg Co. Ct. J. 3. "The primary object of the legislation, broadly speaking, is to provide a mechanism whereby workmen, who fall within the ambit of the Act and who are injured in the workplace, receive compensation, presumably commensurate with their degree of injury, regardless of fault, and, with respect to any such workman who is killed in the workplace, that their dependants receive such compensation as the Act provides. The latter also applies regardless of where fault may lie. The Legislature has also provided that, in return for such benefits as are guaranteed to the workman, or his dependant, any right of action which might otherwise arise out of the incident which occasioned injury or death is forfeited. This is not a government or funded scheme, but rather it is funded by industrial levy. It is not available to all who find employment in the workplace, but only to those who are employed in industry subject to levy." *Jenkins v. Prince Edward Island (Workers' Compensation Board)* (1986), 21 C.C.L.I. 149 at 154, 31 D.L.R. (4th) 536, 61 Nfld. & P.E.I.R. 206, 185 A.P.R. 206, 15 C.C.E.L. 55, 9 C.H.R.R. D/5145 (P.E.I. S.C.), the court per McQuaid J.

WORKERS' COMPENSATION INSURANCE. Insurance of an employer against the cost of compensation prescribed by statute for bodily injury, disability or death of a worker through accident or disease arising out of or in the course of employment.

WORKERS MOURNING DAY. Throughout Canada, in each and every year, the 28th day of April shall be known under the name of "Day of Mourning for Persons Killed or Injured in the Workplace".

WORKFORCE. See CANADIAN ~.

WORKING CONDITIONS. "... [C]onditions under which a worker or workers, individually or collectively, provide their services, in accordance with the rights and obligations included in the contract of employment by the consent of the parties or by operation of law, and under which the employer receives those services... . a worker's obligation to provide his or her services and the employer's obligation to pay his or her wages... . the right to refuse to work, the continuation of the right to wages and other benefits, availability, assignment to other duties and the right to return to employment at the end of the assignment or cessation or work ..." *Québec (Commission de la Santé & de la Sécurité du travail) v. Bell Canada*, [1988] 1 S.C.R. 749 at 798, 801-2, 51 D.L.R. (4th) 161, 21 C.C.E.L. 1, 85 N.R. 295, 15 Q.A.C. 217, the court per Beetz J.

WORKING HOURS. The hours during which an employee works or performs labour or service for the employer.

WORKING INTEREST. 1. A right, in whole or in part, to produce and dispose of oil or gas from a pool or part of a pool, whether that right is held as an incident of ownership of an estate in fee simple in the oil or gas or under a lease, agreement or other instrument, if the right is chargeable with and the holder thereof is obligated to pay or bear, either in cash or out of production, all or a portion of the costs in connection with the drilling for, recovery and disposal of oil or gas from the pool or part thereof. *Canada Oil and Gas Operations Act*, R.S.C. 1985, c. O-7, s. 29. 2. Typically, the owner of minerals in situ will lease to a potential producer the right to extract such minerals [oil and gas]. This right is known as a working interest. *Bank of Montreal v. Dynex Petroleum Ltd.*, [2002] 1 S.C.R. 146.

WORK IN PROGRESS. An inventory of partly-finished services the value of which is equal to the amount that can be expected to become receivable after the year end.

WORKMANSHIP. See FAULTY ~.

WORK OF JOINT AUTHORSHIP. A work produced by the collaboration of two or more authors in which the contribution of one author is not distinct from the contribution of the other author or authors. *Copyright Act*, R.S.C. 1985, c. C-42, s. 2.

WORK PERMIT. A written authorization to work in Canada issued by an officer to a foreign national. *Immigration and Refugee Protection Act*, S.C. 2001, c. 27, *Immigration and Refugee Protection Regulations*, SOR/2001-475, s. 2.

WORKPLACE. See INDOOR ~.

WORK RELEASE. The privilege of doing work in the community while serving a sentence in a correctional institution.

WORKS. *n.* "... '[P]hysical things, not services'." *Shur Gain Division, Canada Packers Inc., Re* (1991), 85 D.L.R. (4th) 317 at 336, 91 C.L.L.C. 14,046, [1992] 2 F.C. 3, 135 N.R. 6 (C.A.), Desjardins J.A. See DRAINAGE ~; WORK.

WORKS FOR THE GENERAL ADVANTAGE OF CANADA. By virtue of section 92(10)(c) and section 91(29) of the Constitution Act, the federal Parliament has power to make laws relating to: "(c) Such works as, although wholly situate within the province, are before or after their execution declared by the Parliament of Canada to be for the general advantage of Canada or for the advantage of two or more of the provinces." P.W. Hogg, *Constitutional Law of Canada*, 3d ed. (Toronto: Carswell, 1992) at 579. See DECLARATORY POWER.

WORK SHARING. The distribution of available work among employees to avoid layoffs.

WORK TO RULE. 1. A slowdown in production brought about by employees obeying all rules pertaining to their work. 2. Refusing to carry out duties not explicitly included in a job description.

WORLD INTELLECTUAL PROPERTY ORGANIZATION. Provider of international domain name dispute resolution.

WORLD TRADE ORGANIZATION. The organization established by the World Trade Organization agreement.

WORLD TRADE ORGANIZATION AGREEMENT. The Agreement Establishing the World Trade Organization, including (a) the agreements set out in Annexes 1A, 1B, 1C, 2 and 3 to that Agreement, and (b) the agreements set out in Annex 4 to that Agreement that have been accepted by Canada, all forming an integral part of the Final Act Embodying The Results Of The Uruguay Round Of Multilateral Trade Negotiations, signed at Marrakesh on April 15, 1994. *World Trade Organization Agreement Implementation Act*, S.C. 1994, c. 47, s. 2.

WORLD WAR I. The war waged by the German Emperor and His Allies against His Majesty and His Majesty's Allies, and the period denoted by the term "World War I" is the period between August 4, 1914 and August 31, 1921, both dates inclusive. *Pension Act*, R.S.C. 1985, P-6, s. 3.

WORLD WAR II. The war waged by His Majesty and His Majesty's Allies against Germany and Germany's Allies, and the period denoted by the term "World War II" is the period between September 1, 1939 and April 1, 1947, both dates inclusive. *Pension Act*, R.S.C. 1985, P-6, s. 3.

WORSHIP. *n.* The title of a magistrate or mayor.

WOUND. *n.* 1. "... [A] breaking of the skin, ..." *R. v. Hostetter* (1902), 7 C.C.C. 221 at 222 (N.W.T. C.A.), the court per Prendergast J.A. 2. The disrupting of tissue caused by violence. F.A. Jaffe, *A Guide to Pathological Evidence for Lawyers and Police Offi-*

cers, 4th ed. (Toronto: Carswell, 1999) at 247. 3. "... [A]n appropriate description of assault causing bodily harm... ." *R. v. Lucas* (1987), 34 C.C.C. (3d) 28 at 33, 10 Q.A.C. 47, [1987] R.L. 212 (C.A.), the court per L'Heureux-Dubé J.A. See SHORED EXIT ~.

WRAP-AROUND MORTGAGE. A second mortgage, granted when the first mortgage is small and at a low interest rate, whose principal includes the whole principal of the first mortgage even though the whole amount is not immediately advanced. The second mortgagee must make payments under the first mortgage as long as the second mortgage is valid. If the first mortgage matures, the mortgagee must pay it off and obtain a discharge so that the second mortgage becomes a first mortgage. D.J. Donahue & P.D. Quinn, *Real Estate Practice in Ontario*, 4th ed. (Toronto: Butterworths, 1990) at 226.

WRECK. *n.* 1. Jetsam, flotsam, lagan and derelict and any other thing that was part of or was on a vessel wrecked, stranded or in distress; and aircraft wrecked in waters and anything that was part of or was on an aircraft wrecked, stranded or in distress in waters. *Canada Shipping Act, 2001*, S.C. 2001, c. 26, s. 153. 2. Includes the cargo, stores and tackle of a vessel and all parts of a vessel separated from the vessel, and the property of persons who belong to, are on board or have quitted a vessel that is wrecked, stranded or in distress at any place in Canada. *Criminal Code*, R.S.C. 1985, c. C-46, s. 2.

WRIT. *n.* 1. The formal order or command of a court which directs or enjoins a person or persons to do or refrain from doing something in particular. 2. A document which originates certain legal proceedings. 3. "... [T]he initial process issuing out of the Court." *Fleishman v. T.A. Allan & Sons* (1932), 45 B.C.R. 553 at 560 (C.A.), Macdonald C.J.B.C. 4. The document addressed by the Chief Electoral Officer to a returning officer requiring an election to be held. The Governor in Council or the Lieutenant Governor in Council issues a proclamation directing the Chief Electoral Officer to issue the writ to the returning officer for the electoral district in which the election is to be held. The proclamation fixes the date of the writ and the date of the election. See ALIAS ~; CONCURRENT ~; PREROGATIVE ~.

WRITING. *n.* 1. Any term of like import, includes words printed, typewritten, painted, engraved, lithographed, photographed or represented or reproduced by any mode of representing or reproducing words in visible form. *Interpretation Act*, R.S.C. 1985, c. I-21, s. 35. 2. Includes a document of any kind and any mode in which, and any material on which, words or figures, whether at length or abridged, are written, printed or otherwise expressed, or a map or plan is inscribed. *Criminal Code*, R.S.C. 1985, c. C- 46, s. 2. See PRIVATE ~.

WRIT OF ASSISTANCE. 1. A writ which operates like a search warrant with respect to a crime under the Narcotic Control Act, the Food and Drugs Act, the Customs Act or the Excise Act. It is a general warrant, unlimited in time or place. S.A. Cohen, *Due Process of Law* (Toronto: Carswell, 1977) at 94. 2. "... [A] document issued out of the Federal Court which identifies the holder as a person entitled to exercise without a warrant the statutory powers of search and seizure under the relevant statute. It is like an identification card signifying that the holder is entitled to conduct warrantless searches and seizures pursuant to the search and seizure powers conferred by the relevant statute. Consequently, searches under a writ of assistance are warrantless searches by designated persons pursuant to statutory powers." *R. v. Noble* (1984), 16 C.C.C. (3d) 146 at 156, 48 O.R. (2d) 643, 42 C.R. (3d) 209, 6 O.A.C. 11, 14 D.L.R. (4th) 216, 12 C.R.R. 138 (C.A.), the court per Martin J.A.

WRIT OF DELIVERY. A writ of execution directing that goods be delivered by the defendant to the plaintiff.

WRIT OF EXECUTION. 1. Includes, (a) a writ of seizure and sale, (b) a writ of seizure and sale of land, (c) a writ of seizure and sale of personal property, (d) a writ of sequestration, (e) a subsequent writ that may issue for giving effect to a writ listed in any of clauses (a) to (d), (f) an order for seizure and sale of personal property, real property or both real property and personal property, (g) any other process of execution issued out of the Superior Court of Justice or the Ontario Court of Justice having jurisdiction to grant and issue warrants or processes of execution. *Execution Act*, R.S.O. 1990, c. E.24, s. 1. 2. The narrower interpretation, refers to the writ of fieri facias (fi.fa.) or its contemporary equivalent, writ of seizure and sale or writ of execution. 3. "... [C]ommands the sheriff to levy of the goods and lands of the debtor the amount of the judgment debt. Its authority is not limited to property of which the debtor is then presently the owner. It is a warrant to the sheriff to seize and sell any property of the debtor which is not exempt from seizure which he may at any time during its currency be able to find in his bailiwick." *Lee v. Armstrong* (1917), 37 D.L.R. 738 at 749, [1917] 3 W.W.R. 889, 13 A.L.R. 160 (C.A.), Walsh J.A.

WRIT OF EXTENT. A writ by which a sheriff may seize the lands, goods and body of a debtor without having to choose between execution against the person and execution against property. C.R.B. Dunlop, *Creditor-Debtor Law in Canada* (Toronto: Carswell, 1981) at 449.

WRIT OF FIERI FACIAS. An order that someone, out of a party's real property and goods and chattels, collect the sum recovered by the judgment along with any interest on that sum.

WRIT OF FI. FA. See WRIT OF FIERI FACIAS.

WRIT OF POSSESSION. A writ to recover the possession of land.

WRIT OF SEIZURE AND SALE. The equivalent of a writ of fieri facias.

WRIT OF SEQUESTRATION. Where a person who is required by an order to perform an act within a specified time refuses or neglects to do so within that time, or where a person disobeys an order to abstain from doing an act, the order may, with the leave of the Court, be enforced by (a) a writ of sequestration against the property of the person; (b) where the person is a corporation, a writ of sequestration against the property of any director or officer of the corporation; and (c) subject to subsection (2), in respect of an order other than for payment of money, an order of committal against the person or, where the person is a body corporate, against any director or officer of the corporation. *Federal Courts Act*, R.S.C. 1985, c. F-7, *Federal Courts Rules*, SOR/ 98-106, rule 429.

WRIT OF SUMMONS. The writ by which an action is commenced.

WRIT OF VENDITIONI EXPONAS. An order that a sheriff sell goods for the best possible price. C.R.B. Dunlop, *Creditor-Debtor Law in Canada* (Toronto: Carswell, 1981) at 400.

WRITTEN HEARING. A hearing held by means of the exchange of documents, whether in written form or by electronic means. *Statutory Powers Procedure Act*, R.S.O. 1990, c. S.22, s. 1.

WRONG. *n.* 1. Deprivation of a right; an injury. 2. The consequence of the violation or infringement of a right. 3. "[In s. 16(2) of the Criminal Code, R.S.C. 1985, c. C-46] ... '[M]orally wrong' ..." *R. v. Ratti* (1991), 2 C.R. (4th) 293 at 301, 120 N.R. 91, 62 C.C.C. (3d) 105, 44 O.A.C. 161, [1991] 1 S.C.R. 68, Lamer C.J.C. (La Forest and Cory JJ. concurring). See EQUITY WILL NOT SUFFER A ~ TO BE WITHOUT A REMEDY; KING CAN DO NO ~; NO MAN CAN TAKE ADVANTAGE OF HIS OWN ~; TOBACCO-RELATED ~.

WRONG. *adj.* See KNOWING THAT THE ACT WAS ~.

WRONGFUL ACT. A failure to exercise reasonable skill or care toward the deceased which causes or contributes to the death of the deceased. *Fatal Accidents Act*, R.S.P.E.I. 1988, c. F-5, s. 1(n).

WRONGFUL BIRTH. An action instituted by parents of a child who was born with birth defects as a result of a planned pregnancy. The tortfeasor has interfered with the mother's right to terminate the pregnancy if an informed option had been available to her.

WRONGFUL CONVERSION. Need not connote a criminal act. Pecuniary loss suffered by reason of dishonest or fraudulent conversion of property.

WRONGFUL DISCHARGE. The phrase need not be interpreted narrowly. It must be interpreted broadly to include all of those actions taken by the employer against the employee . . . for her whistleblower activities, and which culminated in her termination and formed part of her wrongful discharge. *R. v. I.A.B.S.O.I., Local 771*, 2007 SKCA 6.

WRONGFUL DISCRIMINATION. In relation to a bylaw, the bylaw must discriminate in fact and it must do so for an improper motive of favouring or hurting one individual and without regard for the public interest.

WRONGFUL DISMISSAL. 1. The unjustified dismissal of an employee from employment by the employer. 2. "In wrongful dismissal cases, the wrong suffered by the employee is the breach by the employer of the implied contractual term to give reasonable notice before terminating the contract of employment. Damages are awarded to place the employee in the same position as he/she would have been had reasonable notice been given." *Piazza v. Airport Taxi Cab (Malton) Assn.* (1989), 26 C.C.E.L. 191 at 194, 69 O.R. (2d) 281, 60 D.L.R. (4th) 759, 234 O.A.C. 349, 10 C.H.R.R. D/6347, Zuber J.A.

WRONGFUL PREGNANCY. An action brought by a person who becomes pregnant through some act or omission of the defendant.

W.S.I.A.T.R. *abbr.* Workplace Safety and Insurance Appeals Tribunal Reporter (Ontario), 1998-.

WTO AGREEMENT. World Trade Organization Agreement.

WTO MEMBER. A Member of the World Trade Organization established by Article I of the WTO Agreement.

WTO MEMBER RESIDENT. (a) A natural person who is ordinarily resident in a country or territory that is a WTO Member, as defined in subsection 2(1) of the World Trade Organization Agreement Implementation Act, other than Canada; (b) a body corporate, association, partnership or other organization that is incorporated, formed or otherwise organized in a country or territory that is a WTO Member, as defined in subsection 2(1) of the World Trade Organization Agreement Implementation Act, other than Canada, and that is controlled (i) directly or indirectly, by one or more persons referred to in paragraph (a), or (ii) by a government of a WTO Member, whether federal, state or local, or an agency of one of those governments; (c) a trust established by one or more persons referred to in paragraph (a) or (b) or a trust in which one or more of those persons have more than 50 per cent of the beneficial interest; or (d) a body corporate, association, partnership or other organization that is controlled, directly or indirectly, by a trust referred to in paragraph (c). *Bank Act*, S.C. 1991, c. 46, s. 11.1.

W.W.D. *abbr.* Western Weekly Digests, 1975-1976.

W.W.R. *abbr.* Western Weekly Reports, 1911-1950, 1971-.

W.W.R. (N.S.). *abbr.* Western Weekly Reports (New Series), 1951-1970.

Y

Y.A.D. *abbr.* Young's Admiralty Decisions (N.S.), 1864-1880.

YARD. See FRONT ~.

YARD WORK. The physical ability of the insured, or the insured's requirement to have verbal cuing, to complete the following tasks: (i) planting, maintaining and harvesting a garden; (ii) maintaining and caring for a lawn and trees or shrubs; (iii) shovelling snow. *Automobile Accident Insurance Act*, R.S.S. 1978, c. A-35, *The Personal Injury Benefits Regulations*, R.R.S., c. A-35, Reg. 3, Appendix D, Grid A, s. 2.

YCJA. *abbr.* Youth Criminal Justice Act, S.C. 2002, c. 1.

YEAR. *n.* 1. A calendar year. 2. Any period of 12 consecutive months. 3. Any period of 12 consecutive months, except that a reference (a) to a "calendar year" means a period of 12 consecutive months commencing on January 1; (b) to a "financial year" or "fiscal year" means, in relation to money provided by Parliament, or the Consolidated Revenue Fund, or the accounts, taxes or finances of Canada, the period beginning on April 1 in one calendar year and ending on March 31 in the next calendar year; and (c) by number to a Dominical year means the period of 12 consecutive months commencing on January 1 of that Dominical year. *Interpretation Act*, R.S.C. 1985, c. I-21, s. 37. 4. Three hundred and sixty-five days. See ACADEMIC ~; CALENDAR ~; EXECUTOR'S ~; FISCAL ~; REGNAL ~; TAXATION ~.

YIELD. *v.* 1. To give way; 2. To earn; to pay.

YIELD. *n.* When used in relation to a redeemable security, means the effective rate of interest that will be returned on the purchase price if the payments of interest specified in the security are made up to and including the redemption date and the security is then redeemed at the specified value. See PERPETUAL SUSTAINED ~.

YIELDING AND PAYING. In a lease, the first words used in a reddendum clause.

YIELD SIGN. A sign requiring the driver of a vehicle facing the sign to give the right of way to oncoming traffic on the intersecting or connecting roadway.

YKCA. Neutral citation for the Yukon Territory Court of Appeal.

YKSC. Neutral citation for the Yukon Territory Supreme Court.

Y.O.A. *abbr.* Young Offenders Act.

YOU CANNOT DO INDIRECTLY WHAT YOU CANNOT DO DIRECTLY. "The maxim 'you cannot do indirectly what you cannot do directly" is a much abused one. It was used to invalidate legislation ... It is a pithy way of describing colourable legislation: ... However, it does not preclude a limited legislature from achieving directly under one head of legislative power what it could not do directly under another head." *Reference re Questions Concerning Amendment to the Constitution of Canada as set out in O.C. 1020/80* (1981), (*sub nom. Resolution to Amend the Constitution of Canada, Re*) 1 C.R.R. 59 at 94, [1981] 1 S.C.R. 753, [1981] 6 W.W.R. 1, 11 Man. R. (2d) 1, 39 N.R. 1, 34 Nfld. & P.E.I.R. 1, 95 A.P.R. 1, Laskin C.J.C., Dickson, Beetz, Estey, McIntyre, Chouinard and Lamer JJ.

YOUNG ADM. *abbr.* Young's Admiralty Decisions (N.S.) , 1864-1880.

YOUNG PERSON. 1. A person who is or, in the absence of evidence to the contrary, appears to be twelve years old or older, but less than eighteen years old and, if the context requires, includes any person who is charged under this Act with having committed an offence while he or she was a young person or who is found guilty of an offence under this Act. *Youth Criminal Justice Act*, S.C. 2002, c. 1, s. 2. 2. A person 16 years of age or more but under the age of eighteen years. *Criminal Code*, R.S.C. 1985, c. C-46, s. 153.

YOUTH CUSTODY FACILITY. A facility designated for the placement of young persons and, if so designated, includes a facility for the secure restraint of young persons, a community residential centre, a group home, a child care institution and a forest or wilderness camp. *Youth Criminal Justice Act*, S.C. 2002, c. 1, s. 2.

YOUTH JUSTICE COURT. A youth justice court referred to in section 13. A youth justice court is any court that may be established or designated by or under an Act of the legislature of a province, or designated by the Governor in Council or the lieutenant

Y

governor in council of a province, as a youth justice court for the purposes of this Act. A youth justice court is a court of record. Certain courts are deemed to be youth justice courts. *Youth Criminal Justice Act,* S.C. 2002, c. 1, s. 2 and 13.

YOUTH JUSTICE COURT JUDGE. A youth justice court judge referred to in section 13. A youth justice court judge is a person who may be appointed or designated as a judge of the youth justice court or a judge sitting in a court established or designated as a youth justice court. Certain judges are deemed to be youth justice court judges. *Youth Criminal Justice Act,* S.C. 2002, c. 1, s. 2 and 13.

YOUTH SENTENCE. A sentence imposed under section 42, 51 or 59 or any of sections 94 to 96 and includes a confirmation or a variation of that sentence. *Youth Criminal Justice Act,* S.C. 2002, c. 1, s. 2.

YOUTH WORKER. 1. Any person appointed or designated, whether by title of youth worker or probation officer or by any other title, by or under an Act of the legislature of a province or by the lieutenant governor in council of a province or his or her delegate to perform in that province, either generally or in a specific case, any of the duties or functions of a youth worker under this Act. *Youth Criminal Justice Act,* S.C. 2002, c. 1, s. 2. 2. The duties and functions of a youth worker in respect of a young person whose case has been assigned to him by the provincial director include supervising the young person in complying with the conditions of a probation order or in carrying out any other disposition made together with it, supervising the young person in complying with the conditions under conditional supervision, giving assistance to a young person found guilty up until the young person is discharged or the disposition of his case terminates, and other duties as required. 3. A probation officer.

Y.R. *abbr.* Yukon Reports, 1986-1989.

Z

ZONE. See CONTIGUOUS ~; UNITIZED ~.

ZONING. *n.* 1. The control of the use of land. 2. "The objectives of modern zoning legislation are described in [I.M.] Rogers's Canadian Law of Planning and Zoning (Toronto: Carswell, 1973 (looseleaf)) at 115 where the author states: 'Zoning is a form of regulation of property by local governments. It is the division of a municipality into zones or areas and in each area either prohibiting certain uses and allowing all the others or permitting the uses which may be carried on to the exclusion of all others... . Zoning is the deprivation for the public good of certain uses by owners of property to which the property might otherwise be put. Underlying planning statutes is the principle that the interest of landowners in securing the maximum value of their land must be controlled by the community... . The objective of zoning must be considered from the standpoint of the public welfare and of all the property within any particular use district.' " *Zive Estate v. Lynch* (1989), 47 M.P.L.R. 310 at 314, 7 R.P.R. (2d) 180, 94 N.S.R. (2d) 401, 247 A.P.R. 401 (C.A.), the court per Macdonald J.A. See BONUS ~; DEVELOPMENT CONTROL.

ZONING BYLAW. "... [R]emedial in character in that one of their objectives is to preserve existing property from depreciation. They are designed not only to protect residential neighbourhoods against intrusion of buildings to be used for commercial and manufacturing or trade purposes, but to confine commercial and industrial purposes to specific parts of the municipality to the exclusion of residential construction: ..." *Zive Estate v. Lynch* (1989), 47 M.P.L.R. 310 at 315, 7 R.P.R. (2d) 180, 94 N.S.R. (2d) 401, 247 A.P.R. 401 (C.A.), the court per Macdonald J.A.